Instructor's Solutions Manual with CD-ROM

ENGINEERING MECHANICS STATICS

NINTH EDITION

R. C. HIBBELER

Instructor's Solutions Manual
with CD-ROM

ENGINEERING MECHANICS
STATICS

NINTH EDITION

R. C. HIBBELER

Prentice Hall

Upper Saddle River, NJ 07458

Assistant Managing Editor: John Matthews
Production Editor: Barbara A. Till
Supplement Cover Manager: Paul Gourhan
Supplement Cover Designer: PM Workshop Inc.
Manufacturing Buyer: Lisa McDowell
Cover photo: Paul Sounders/Stone USA, Maryland, Chesapeake Bay Bridge and Tanker, Elevated View (Detail)

Published by Prentice Hall
Upper Saddle River, NJ 07458

Printed in the United States of America

10 9 8 7 6 5 4 3 2 1

ISBN 0-13-028215-4

Prentice-Hall International (UK) Limited, London
Prentice-Hall of Australia Pty. Limited, Sydney
Prentice-Hall Canada, Inc., Toronto
Prentice-Hall Hispanoamericana, S.A., Mexico City
Prentice-Hall of India Private Limited, New Delhi
Pearson Education Asia Pte. Ltd., Singapore
Prentice-Hall of Japan, Inc., Tokyo
Editora Prentice-Hall do Brazil, Ltda., Rio de Janeiro

Contents

To the Instructor

This manual contains the solutions to all the problems in *Engineering Mechanics: Statics, Ninth Edition.* As stated in the preface of the text, the problems in every section are arranged in an approximate order of increasing difficulty. Be aware that answers to all but every fourth problem, which is indicated by an asterisk (*), are listed in the back of the book. Also, those problems indicated by a square ( ) will require additional numerical work. The solutions may be readily determined using a numerical analysis method as outlined in Appendix B.

You may wish to use one of the lists of homework problems given on the following pages. Here you will find three lists for which the answers are in the back of the book, a fourth list for problems without answers, and a fifth sheet which can be used to develop your own personal syllabus. The prepared lists generally represent assigments with an easy, a moderate, and sometimes a more challenging problem.

If you have any questions regarding the solutions in this manual, or any problems with the textbook, I would greatly appreciate hearing from you.

R. C. Hibbeler

hibbeler@bell south.net

*Section	Topic	Assignment List 1
1.1-1.6	Introduction, Units	1.1, 1.5, 1.10
2.1-2.3	Parallelogram Law	2.6, 2.19, 2.27
2.4	Addition of Rectangular Components	2.32, 2.35, 2.49
2.5-2.6	Cartesian Vectors	2.61, 2.65, 2.71
2.7-2.8	Position and Force Vectors	2.83, 2.90, 2.95
2.9	Dot Product	2.110, 2.114, 2.119
3.1-3.3	2-D Equilibrium	3.2, 3.11, 3.19
3.4	3-D Equilibrium	3.42, 3.47, 3.53
4.1	Moment of a Force 2D	4.5, 4.10, 4.19, 4.21
4.2-4-4	Moment of a Force 3D	4.34, 4.41, 4.50
4.5	Moment of a Force-Specified Axis	4.51, 4.55, 4.57
4.6	Moment of a Couple	4.70, 4.74, 4.81
4.7-4.8	Simplification of a Force System	4.99, 4.109, 4.110
4.9	Further Simp. of a Force System	4.114, 4.118, 4.123, 4.133
4.10	Simple Distributed Loadings	4.139, 4.149, 4.155
5.1-5.2	Free-Body Diagrams	5.1, 5.3, 5.6, 5.10
5.3-5.4	2-D Equilibrium	5.19, 5.23, 5.27
		5.29, 5.33, 5.42
5.5-5.7	3-D Equilibrium	5.63, 5.69, 5.75
6.1-6.3	Method of Joints	6.2, 6.7, 6.11
6.4	Method of Sections	6.31, 6.41, 6.47
*6.5	Space Trusses	6.55,6.59
6.6	Frames and Machines	6.67, 6.77, 6.94
		6.101, 6.105, 6.110
7.1	Internal Forces in Members	7.3, 7.7, 7.15
*7.2	Shear and Bending Moment Diagrams	7.43, 7.49, 7.58
*7.3	Relations between Shear and Moment	7.73, 7.75, 7.81
*7.4	Cables-Conc. Loads	7.89, 7.94
*7.4	Cables Dist. Loads and Weight	7.98, 7.105, 7.111
8.1-8.2	Friction	8.2, 8.21, 8.29
		8.31, 8.37, 8.46
8.3	Wedges	8.62, 8.67, 8.70
*8.4	Screws	8.75, 8.78, 8.82
*8.5	Flat Belts	8.86, 8.89, 8.91
*8.6-*8.7	Collar and Journal Bearings	8.107, 8.111, 8.118, 8.122
*8.8	Rolling Resistance	8.129, 8.133
9.1-9.2	Centroids, Cent. of Grav. Integration	9.2, 9.9, 9.35
9.3	Composite Bodies	9.45, 9.53, 9.73
*9.4	Theorems of Pappus and Guldinus	9.85, 9.90, 9.95
*9.5-*9.6	Gen. Dist. Loads, Hydrostatics	9.107, 9.113, 9.117
10.1-10.4	Area Moment of Inertia-Integration	10.2, 10.7, 10.17
10.5	Composite Bodies	10.26, 10.29, 10.37
*10.6	Product of Inertia	10.54, 10.59, 10.67
*10.7-*10.8	Inclined Axes and Mohr's Circle	10.74, 10.77, 10.87
10.9	Mass Moment of Inertia	10.91, 10.94, 10.98, 10.101
11.1-11.3	Virtual Work	11.2, 11.7, 11.21
*11.4-*11.7	Potential Energy	11.27, 11.33, 11.41

Section	Topic	Assignment List 2
1.1-1.6	Introduction, Units	1.2, 1.7, 1.18
2.1-2.3	Parallelogram Law	2.5, 2.11, 2.25
2.4	Addition of Rectangular Components	2.31, 2.38, 2.50
2.5-2.6	Cartesian Vectors	2.59, 2.67, 2.79
2.7-2.8	Position and Force Vectors	2.87, 2.93, 2.98
2.9	Dot Product	2.111, 2.118, 2.125
3.1-3.3	2-D Equilibrium	3.1, 3.15, 3.21
3.4	3-D Equilibrium	3.41, 3.51, 3.63
4.1	Moment of a Force 2D	4.6, 4.17, 4.25, 4.31
4.2-4-4	Moment of a Force 3D	4.35, 4.42, 4.45
4.5	Moment of a Force-Specified Axis	4.53, 4.58, 4.63
4.6	Moment of a Couple	4.71, 4.79, 4.93
4.7-4.8	Simplification of a Force System	4.101, 4.113, 4.117, 130
4.9	Further Simp. of a Force System	4.115, 4.121, 4.133
4.10	Simple Distributed Loadings	4.141, 4.147, 4.158
5.1-5.2	Free-Body Diagrams	5.2, 5.5, 5.9, 5.10
5.3-5.4	2-D Equilibrium	5.21, 5.30, 5.34
		5.41, 5.46, 5.55
5.5-5.7	3-D Equilibrium	5.66, 5.73, 5.87
6.1-6.3	Method of Joints	6.1, 6.13, 6.25
6.4	Method of Sections	6.33, 6.43, 6.50
*6.5	Space Trusses	6.58,6.62
6.6	Frames and Machines	6.66, 6.74, 6.82
		6.95, 6.103, 6.113
7.1	Internal Forces in Members	7.1, 7.11, 7.19
*7.2	Shear and Bending Moment Diagrams	7.42, 7.50, 7.57
*7.3	Relations between Shear and Moment	7.74, 7.79, 7.82
*7.4	Cables-Conc. Loads	7.90, 7.93
*7.4	Cables Dist. Loads and Weight	7.101, 7.109, 7.115
8.1-8.2	Friction	8.3, 8.10, 8.23
		8.33, 8.43, 8.53
8.3	Wedges	8.63, 8.65, 8.69
*8.4	Screws	8.73, 8.77, 8.81
*8.5	Flat Belts	8.85, 8.87, 8.97, 8.103
*8.6-*8.7	Collar and Journal Bearings	8.109, 8.113, 8.121, 8.124
*8.8	Rolling Resistance	8.131, 8.134
9.1-9.2	Centroids, Cent. of Grav. Integration	9.11, 9.23, 9.37
9.3	Composite Bodies	9.47, 9.55, 9.63, 9.75
*9.4	Theorems of Pappus and Guldinus	9.86, 9.91, 9.97
*9.5-*9.6	Gen. Dist. Loads, Hydrostatics	9.109, 9.114, 9.122
10.1-10.4	Area Moment of Inertia-Integration	10.5, 10.10, 10.13
10.5	Composite Bodies	10.25, 10.33, 10.42
*10.6	Product of Inertia	10.55, 10.61, 10.69
*10.7-*10.8	Inclined Axes and Mohr's Circle	10.74, 10.78, 10.85
10.9	Mass Moment of Inertia	10.93, 10.98, 10.105
11.1-11.3	Virtual Work	11.1, 11.9, 11.14
*11.4-*11.7	Potential Energy	11.29, 11.35, 11.45

Section	Topic	Assignment List 3
1.1-1.6	Introduction, Units	1.3, 1.13, 1.19
2.1-2.3	Parallelogram Law	2.7, 2.14, 2.21
2.4	Addition of Rectangular Components	2.33, 2.46, 2.55
2.5-2.6	Cartesian Vectors	2.62, 2.70, 2.77
2.7-2.8	Position and Force Vectors	2.89, 2.94, 2.105
2.9	Dot Product	2.115, 2.121, 2.129
3.1-3.3	2-D Equilibrium	3.6, 3.17, 3.27
3.4	3-D Equilibrium	3.45, 3.54, 3.65
4.1	Moment of a Force 2D	4.9, 4.18, 4.30, 4.33
4.2-4-4	Moment of a Force 3D	4.39, 4.43, 4.47
4.5	Moment of a Force-Specified Axis	4.54, 4.59, 4.61
4.6	Moment of a Couple	4.73, 4.82, 4.87
4.7-4.8	Simplification of a Force System	4.103, 4.107, 4.110,4.129
4.9	Further Simp. of a Force System	4.119, 4.122, 4.137
4.10	Simple Distributed Loadings	4.142, 4.153, 4.162
5.1-5.2	Free-Body Diagrams	5.1, 5.7, 5.6, 5.10
5.3-5.4	2-D Equilibrium	5.25, 5.35, 5.39
		5.43, 5.49, 5.58
5.5-5.7	3-D Equilibrium	5.65, 5.83, 5.86
6.1-6.3	Method of Joints	6.6, 6.10, 6.23
6.4	Method of Sections	6.34, 6.45, 6.51
*6.5	Space Trusses	6.61,6.63
6.6	Frames and Machines	6.69, 6.75, 6.85
		6.98, 6.102, 6.114
7.1	Internal Forces in Members	7.6, 7.14, 7.26
*7.2	Shear and Bending Moment Diagrams	7.47, 7.54, 7.61
*7.3	Relations between Shear and Moment	7.78, 7.85, 7.87
*7.4	Cables-Conc. Loads	7.91, 7.95
*7.4	Cables Dist. Loads and Weight	7.103, 7.110, 7.114
8.1-8.2	Friction	8.6, 8.17, 8.26
		8.34, 8.47, 8.57
8.3	Wedges	8.61, 8.63, 8.66
*8.4	Screws	8.74, 8.79, 8.83
*8.5	Flat Belts	8.87, 8.93, 8.105
*8.6-*8.7	Collar and Journal Bearings	8.101, 8.115, 8.123,8.125
*8.8	Rolling Resistance	8.130, 8.133
9.1-9.2	Centroids, Cent. of Grav. Integration	9.5, 9.14, 9.26, 9.38
9.3	Composite Bodies	9.51, 9.58, 9.65, 9.77
*9.4	Theorems of Pappus and Guldinus	9.87, 9.93, 9.101
*9.5-*9.6	Gen. Dist. Loads, Hydrostatics	9.106, 9.111, 9.115
10.1-10.4	Area Moment of Inertia-Integration	10.6, 10.11, 10.19
10.5	Composite Bodies	10.22, 10.33, 10.45
*10.6	Product of Inertia	10.58, 10.63, 10.71
*10.7-*10.8	Inclined Axes and Mohr's Circle	10.75, 10.81, 10.89
10.9	Mass Moment of Inertia	10.95, 10.99, 10.110
11.1-11.3	Virtual Work	11.6, 11.13, 11.18
*11.4-*11.5	Potential Energy	11.31, 11.38, 11.43

Section	Topic	Assignment Without Answers in Book
1.1-1.6	Introduction, Units	1.4, 1.12, 1.16
2.1-2.3	Parallelogram Law	2.4, 2.16, 2.28
2.4	Addition of Rectangular Components	2.36, 2.44, 2.52
2.5-2.6	Cartesian Vectors	2.66, 2.72, 2.80
2.7-2.8	Position and Force Vectors	2.84, 2.92, 2.100
2.9	Dot Product	2.112, 2.120, 2.128
3.1-3.3	2-D Equilibrium	3.4, 3.16, 3.28
3.4	3-D Equilibrium	3.48, 3.52, 3.60
4.1	Moment of a Force 2D	4.4, 4.12, 4.20, 4.32
4.2-4-4	Moment of a Force 3D	4.36, 4.44, 4.48
4.5	Moment of a Force-Specified Axis	4.52, 4.56, 4.64
4.6	Moment of a Couple	4.76, 4.84, 4.96
4.7-4.8	Simplification of a Force System	4.100, 4.108, 4.112
4.9	Further Simp. of a Force System	4.116, 4.120, 4.132
4.10	Simple Distributed Loadings	4.140, 4.156, 4.160
5.1-5.2	Free-Body Diagrams	5.4, 5.8
5.3-5.4	2-D Equilibrium	5.20, 5.28, 5.36 5.40, 5.52, 5.60
5.5-5.7	3-D Equilibrium	5.64, 5.76, 5.84
6.1-6.3	Method of Joints	6.4, 6.12, 6.24
6.4	Method of Sections	6.32, 6.40, 6.52
*6.5	Space Trusses	6.56,6.60
6.6	Frames and Machines	6.72, 6.80, 6.92 6.100, 6.116, 6.120
7.1	Internal Forces in Members	7.4, 7.16, 7.28
*7.2	Shear and Bending Moment Diagrams	7.44, 7.52, 7.60
*7.3	Relations between Shear and Moment	7.66, 7.80, 7.84
*7.4	Cables-Conc. Loads	7.92, 7.96
*7.4	Cables Dist. Loads and Weight	7.100, 7.108, 7.112
8.1-8.2	Friction	8.4, 8.8, 8.24 8.32, 8.36, 8.44
8.3	Wedges	8.64, 8.68
*8.4	Screws	8.72, 8.76, 8.80
*8.5	Flat Belts	8.88, 8.96, 8.100
*8.6-*8.7	Collar and Journal Bearings	8.108, 8.116, 8.120, 8.124
*8.8	Rolling Resistance	8.132
9.1-9.2	Centroids, Cent. of Grav. Integration	9.4, 9.16, 9.36
9.3	Composite Bodies	9.48, 9.52, 9.68, 9.76
*9.4	Theorems of Pappus and Guldinus	9.84, 9.98, 9.104
*9.5-9.6	Gen. Dist. Loads, Hydrostatics	9.108, 9.116, 9.120
10.1-10.4	Area Moment of Inertia-Integration	10.4, 10.16, 10.20
10.5	Composite Bodies	10.28, 10.32, 10.44
*10.6	Product of Inertia	10.56, 10.64, 10.68
*10.7-*10.8	Inclined Axes and Mohr's Circle	10.76, 10.80, 10.88
10.9	Mass Moment of Inertia	10.92, 10.96, 10.104
11.1-11.3	Virtual Work	11.8, 11.12, 11.20
*11.4-*11.5	Potential Energy	11.28, 11.40, 11.52

Section	Topic	Assignment
1.1-1.6	Introduction, Units	
2.1-2.3	Parallelogram Law	
2.4	Addition of Rectangular Components	
2.5-2.6	Cartesian Vectors	
2.7-2.8	Position and Force Vectors	
2.9	Dot Product	
3.1-3.3	2-D Equilibrium	
3.4	3-D Equilibrium	
4.1	Moment of a Force 2D	
4.2-4-4	Moment of a Force 3D	
4.5	Moment of a Force-Specified Axis	
4.6	Moment of a Couple	
4.7-4.8	Simplification of a Force System	
4.9	Further Simp. of a Force System	
4.10	Simple Distributed Loadings	
5.1-5.2	Free-Body Diagrams	
5.3-5.4	2-D Equilibrium	
5.5-5.7	3-D Equilibrium	
6.1-6.3	Method of Joints	
6.4	Method of Sections	
*6.5	Space Trusses	
6.6	Frames and Machines	
7.1	Internal Forces in Members	
*7.2	Shear and Bending Moment Diagrams	
*7.3	Relations between Shear and Moment	
*7.4	Cables-Conc. Loads	
*7.4	Cables Dist. Loads and Weight	
8.1-8.2	Friction	
8.3	Wedges	
*8.4	Screws	
*8.5	Flat Belts	
*8.6-*8.7	Collar and Journal Bearings	
*8.8	Rolling Resistance	
9.1-9.2	Centroids, Cent. of Grav. Integration	
9.3	Composite Bodies	
*9.4	Theorems of Pappus and Guldinus	
*9.5-*9.6	Gen. Dist. Loads, Hydrostatics	
10.1-10.4	Area Moment of Inertia-Integration	
10.5	Composite Bodies	
*10.6	Product of Inertia	
*10.7-*10.8	Inclined Axes and Mohr's Circle	
10.9	Mass Moment of Inertia	
11.1-11.3	Virtual Work	
*11.4-*11.5	Potential Energy	

1-1. Round off the following numbers to three significant figures: (a) 4.65735 m, (b) 55.578 s, (c) 4555 N, (d) 2768 kg.

a) 4.66 m b) 55.6 s c) 4.56 kN d) 2.77 Mg **Ans**

1-2. Represent each of the following combinations of units in the correct SI form: (a) μMN, (b) N/μm, (c) MN/ks^2, (d) kN/ms.

(a) $\mu\text{MN} = 10^{-6}(10^6)\text{ N} = \text{N}$ **Ans**

(b) $\dfrac{\text{N}}{\mu\text{m}} = \dfrac{\text{N}}{10^{-6}\text{ m}} = 10^6\text{ N/m} = \text{MN/m}$ **Ans**

(c) $\dfrac{\text{MN}}{\text{ks}^2} = \dfrac{10^6\text{ N}}{(10^3)^2\text{ s}^2} = \text{N/s}^2$ **Ans**

(d) $\dfrac{\text{kN}}{\text{ms}} = \dfrac{10^3\text{ N}}{10^{-3}\text{ s}} = 10^6\dfrac{\text{N}}{\text{s}} = \text{MN/s}$ **Ans**

1-3. Represent each of the following quantities in the correct SI form using an appropriate prefix: (a) 0.000431 kg, (b) 35.3(10^3) N, (c) 0.00532 km.

a) $0.000431\text{ kg} = 0.000431(10^3)\text{ g} = 0.431\text{ g}$ **Ans**

b) $35.3(10^3)\text{ N} = 35.3\text{ kN}$ **Ans**

c) $0.00532\text{ km} = 0.00532(10^3)\text{ m} = 5.32\text{ m}$ **Ans**

***1-4.** Represent each of the following combinations of units in the correct SI form: (a) Mg/ms, (b) N/mm, (c) mN/(kg$\cdot\mu$s).

(a) $\dfrac{\text{Mg}}{\text{ms}} = \dfrac{10^3\text{ kg}}{10^{-3}\text{ s}} = 10^6\text{ kg/s} = \text{Gg/s}$ **Ans**

(b) $\dfrac{\text{N}}{\text{mm}} = \dfrac{1\text{ N}}{10^{-3}\text{ m}} = 10^3\text{ N/m} = \text{kN/m}$ **Ans**

(c) $\dfrac{\text{mN}}{(\text{kg}\cdot\mu\text{s})} = \dfrac{10^{-3}\text{ N}}{10^{-6}\text{ kg}\cdot\text{s}} = \text{kN/(kg}\cdot\text{s)}$ **Ans**

1-5. Represent each of the following combinations of units in the correct SI form using an appropriate prefix: (a) kN/μs, (b) Mg/mN, and (c) MN/(kg$\cdot$ms).

a) $\text{kN}/\mu\text{s} = \dfrac{(10^3)\text{ N}}{(10^{-6})\text{ s}} = \dfrac{(10^9)\text{ N}}{\text{s}} = \text{GN/s}$ **Ans**

b) $\text{Mg/mN} = \dfrac{(10^6)\text{ g}}{(10^{-3})\text{ N}} = \dfrac{(10^9)\text{ g}}{\text{N}} = \text{Gg/N}$ **Ans**

c) $\text{MN/(kg}\cdot\text{ms)} = \dfrac{(10^6)\text{ N}}{\text{kg}\cdot(10^{-3})\text{ s}} = \dfrac{(10^9)\text{ N}}{\text{kg}\cdot\text{s}} = \text{GN/(kg}\cdot\text{s)}$ **Ans**

1-6. Represent each of the following to three significant figures and express each answer in SI units using an appropriate prefix: (a) 45 320 kN, (b) 568(10^5) mm, and (c) 0.005 63 mg.

(a) $45\,320\text{ kN} = 45.3(10^6)\text{N} = 45.3\text{ MN}$ **Ans**

(b) $568\,(10^5)\text{ mm} = 56.8(10^6)(10^{-3})\text{m} = 56.8\text{ km}$ **Ans**

(c) $0.005\,63\text{ mg} = 5.63(10^{-6})\text{g} = 5.63\ \mu\text{g}$ **Ans**

1-7. A rocket has a mass of $250(10^3)$ slugs on earth. Specify (a) its mass in SI units, and (b) its weight in SI units. If the rocket is on the moon, where the acceleration due to gravity is $g_m = 5.30\ \text{ft/s}^2$, determine to three significant figures (c) its weight in SI units, and (d) its mass in SI units.

Using Table 1-2 and applying Eq. 1-3, we have

$$\text{a) } 250(10^3)\text{ slugs} = [250(10^3)\text{ slugs}]\left(\frac{14.5938\text{ kg}}{1\text{ slugs}}\right)$$
$$= 3.64845(10^6)\text{ kg}$$
$$= 3.65\text{ Gg} \qquad \textbf{Ans}$$

$$\text{b) } W_e = mg = [3.64845(10^6)\text{ kg}](9.81\text{ m/s}^2)$$
$$= 35.791(10^6)\text{ kg}\cdot\text{m/s}^2$$
$$= 35.8\text{ MN} \qquad \textbf{Ans}$$

$$\text{c) } W_m = mg_m = [250(10^3)\text{ slugs}](5.30\text{ ft/s}^2)$$
$$= [1.325(10^6)\text{ lb}]\left(\frac{4.4482\text{ N}}{1\text{ lb}}\right)$$
$$= 5.894(10^6)\text{ N} = 5.89\text{ MN} \qquad \textbf{Ans}$$

Or

$$W_m = W_e\left(\frac{g_m}{g}\right) = (35.791\text{ MN})\left(\frac{5.30\text{ ft/s}^2}{32.2\text{ ft/s}^2}\right) = 5.89\text{ MN}$$

d) Since the mass is independent of its location, then

$$m_m = m_e = 3.65(10^6)\text{ kg} = 3.65\text{ Gg} \qquad \textbf{Ans}$$

***1-8.** If a car is traveling at 55 mi/h, determine its speed in kilometers per hour and meters per second.

$$55\text{ mi/h} = \left(\frac{55\text{ mi}}{1\text{ h}}\right)\left(\frac{5280\text{ ft}}{1\text{ mi}}\right)\left(\frac{0.3048\text{ m}}{1\text{ ft}}\right)\left(\frac{1\text{ km}}{1000\text{ m}}\right)$$
$$= 88.5\text{ km/h} \qquad \textbf{Ans}$$

$$88.5\text{ km/h} = \left(\frac{88.5\text{ km}}{1\text{ h}}\right)\left(\frac{1000\text{ m}}{1\text{ km}}\right)\left(\frac{1\text{ h}}{3600\text{ s}}\right) = 24.6\text{ m/s} \qquad \textbf{Ans}$$

1-9. The *pascal* (Pa) is actually a very small unit of pressure. To show this, convert $1\ \text{Pa} = 1\ \text{N/m}^2$ to lb/ft^2. Atmospheric pressure at sea level is $14.7\ \text{lb/in}^2$. How many pascals is this?

Using Table 1-2, we have

$$1\text{ Pa} = \frac{1\text{ N}}{\text{m}^2}\left(\frac{1\text{ lb}}{4.4482\text{ N}}\right)\left(\frac{0.3048^2\text{ m}^2}{1\text{ ft}^2}\right) = 20.9(10^{-3})\text{ lb/ft}^2 \qquad \textbf{Ans}$$

$$1\text{ ATM} = \frac{14.7\text{ lb}}{\text{in}^2}\left(\frac{4.4482\text{ N}}{1\text{ lb}}\right)\left(\frac{144\text{ in}^2}{1\text{ ft}^2}\right)\left(\frac{1\text{ ft}^2}{0.3048^2\text{ m}^2}\right)$$
$$= 101.3(10^3)\text{ N/m}^2$$
$$= 101\text{ kPa} \qquad \textbf{Ans}$$

1-10. What is the weight in newtons of an object that has a mass of: (a) 10 kg, (b) 0.5 g, (c) 4.50 Mg? Express the result to three significant figures. Use an appropriate prefix.

(a) $W = (9.81\text{ m/s}^2)(10\text{ kg}) = 98.1\text{ N}$ **Ans**

(b) $W = (9.81\text{ m/s}^2)(0.5\text{ g})(10^{-3}\text{ kg/g}) = 4.90\text{ mN}$ **Ans**

(c) $W = (9.81\text{ m/s}^2)(4.5\text{ Mg})(10^3\text{ kg/Mg}) = 44.1\text{ kN}$ **Ans**

1-11. Evaluate each of the following to three significant figures and express each answer in SI units using an appropriate prefix: (a) 354 mg(45 km)/(0.035 6 kN), (b) (.004 53 Mg)(201 ms), (c) 435 MN/23.2 mm.

a) $(354\text{ mg})(45\text{ km})/0.0356\text{ kN} = \dfrac{[354(10^{-3})\text{ g}][45(10^{3})\text{ m}]}{0.0356(10^{3})\text{ N}}$

$= \dfrac{0.447(10^{3})\text{ g}\cdot\text{m}}{\text{N}}$

$= 0.447\text{ kg}\cdot\text{m/N}$ **Ans**

b) $(0.00453\text{ Mg})(201\text{ ms}) = [4.53(10^{-3})(10^{3})\text{ kg}][201(10^{-3})\text{ s}]$

$= 0.911\text{ kg}\cdot\text{s}$ **Ans**

c) $435\text{ MN}/23.2\text{ mm} = \dfrac{435(10^{6})\text{ N}}{23.2(10^{-3})\text{ m}} = \dfrac{18.75(10^{9})\text{ N}}{\text{m}} = 18.8\text{ GN/m}$ **Ans**

***1-12.** The specific weight (wt./vol.) of brass is 520 lb/ft³. Determine its density (mass/vol.) in SI units. Use an appropriate prefix.

$520\text{ lb/ft}^3 = \left(\dfrac{520\text{ lb}}{\text{ft}^3}\right)\left(\dfrac{\text{ft}}{0.3048\text{ m}}\right)^3\left(\dfrac{4.4482\text{ N}}{1\text{ lb}}\right)\left(\dfrac{1\text{ kg}}{9.81\text{ N}}\right)$

$= 8.33\text{ Mg/m}^3$ **Ans**

1-13. Convert each of the following to three significant figures. (a) 20 lb · ft to N · m, (b) 450 lb/ft³ to kN/m³, and (c) 15 ft/h to mm/s.

Using Table 1-2, we have

a) $20\text{ lb}\cdot\text{ft} = (20\text{ lb}\cdot\text{ft})\left(\dfrac{4.4482\text{ N}}{1\text{ lb}}\right)\left(\dfrac{0.3048\text{ m}}{1\text{ ft}}\right)$

$= 27.1\text{ N}\cdot\text{m}$ **Ans**

b) $450\text{ lb/ft}^3 = \left(\dfrac{450\text{ lb}}{\text{ft}^3}\right)\left(\dfrac{4.4482\text{ N}}{1\text{ lb}}\right)\left(\dfrac{1\text{ kN}}{1000\text{ N}}\right)\left(\dfrac{1\text{ ft}^3}{0.3048^3\text{ m}^3}\right)$

$= 70.7\text{ kN/m}^3$ **Ans**

c) $15\text{ ft/h} = \left(\dfrac{15\text{ ft}}{\text{h}}\right)\left(\dfrac{304.8\text{ mm}}{1\text{ ft}}\right)\left(\dfrac{1\text{ h}}{3600\text{ s}}\right) = 1.27\text{ mm/s}$ **Ans**

1-14. The density (mass/volume) of aluminum is 5.26 slug/ft³. Determine its density in SI units. Use an appropriate prefix.

$5.26\text{ slug/ft}^3 = \left(\dfrac{5.26\text{ slug}}{\text{ft}^3}\right)\left(\dfrac{\text{ft}}{0.3048\text{ m}}\right)^3\left(\dfrac{14.5938\text{ kg}}{1\text{ slug}}\right)$

$= 2.71\text{ Mg/m}^3$ **Ans**

1-15. Water has a density of 1.94 slug/ft³. What is the density expressed in SI units? Express the answer to three significant figures.

Using Table 1-2, we have

$\rho_w = \left(\dfrac{1.94\text{ slug}}{\text{ft}^3}\right)\left(\dfrac{14.5938\text{ kg}}{1\text{ slug}}\right)\left(\dfrac{1\text{ ft}^3}{0.3048^3\text{ m}^3}\right)$

$= 999.8\text{ kg/m}^3 = 1.00\text{ Mg/m}^3$ **Ans**

***1-16.** Two particles have a mass of 8 kg and 12 kg, respectively. If they are 800 mm apart, determine the force of gravity acting between them. Compare this result with the weight of each particle.

$$F = G\frac{m_1 m_2}{r^2}$$

Where $G = 66.73(10^{-12})\ \text{m}^3/(\text{kg}\cdot \text{s}^2)$

$$F = 66.73(10^{-12})\left[\frac{8(12)}{(0.8)^2}\right] = 10.0(10^{-9})\ \text{N} = 10.0\ \text{nN}$$ **Ans**

$$W_1 = 8(9.81) = 78.5\ \text{N}$$ **Ans**

$$W_2 = 12(9.81) = 118\ \text{N}$$ **Ans**

1-17. Determine the mass in kilograms of an object that has a weight of (a) 20 mN, (b) 150 kN, (c) 60 MN. Express the answer to three significant figures.

Applying Eq. 1 – 3, we have

a) $m = \frac{W}{g} = \frac{20(10^{-3})\ \text{kg}\cdot\text{m/s}^2}{9.81\ \text{m/s}^2} = 2.04\ \text{g}$ **Ans**

b) $m = \frac{W}{g} = \frac{150(10^{3})\ \text{kg}\cdot\text{m/s}^2}{9.81\ \text{m/s}^2} = 15.3\ \text{Mg}$ **Ans**

c) $m = \frac{W}{g} = \frac{60(10^{6})\ \text{kg}\cdot\text{m/s}^2}{9.81\ \text{m/s}^2} = 6.12\ \text{Gg}$ **Ans**

1-18. Evaluate each of the following to three significant figures and express each answer in SI units using an appropriate prefix: (a) $(200\text{kN})^2$, (b) $(0.005\ \text{mm})^2$, (c) $(400\ \text{m})^3$.

(a) $(200\ \text{kN})^2 = 40\,000(10^6)\ \text{N}^2 = 0.04(10^{12})\ \text{N}^2 = 0.04\ \text{MN}^2$ **Ans**

(b) $(0.005\ \text{mm})^2 = 25(10^{-12})\ \text{m}^2 = 25\ \mu\text{m}^2$ **Ans**

(c) $(400\ \text{m})^3 = 0.064(10^9)\ \text{m}^3 = 0.064\ \text{km}^3$ **Ans**

1-19. Using the base units of the SI system, show that Eq. 1-2 is a dimensionally homogeneous equation which gives F in newtons. Determine to three significant figures the gravitational force acting between two spheres that are touching each other. The mass of each sphere is 200 kg and the radius is 300 mm.

Using Eq. 1 – 2.

$$F = G\frac{m_1 m_2}{r^2}$$

$$\text{N} = \left(\frac{\text{m}^3}{\text{kg}\cdot\text{s}^2}\right)\left(\frac{\text{kg}\cdot\text{kg}}{\text{m}^2}\right) = \frac{\text{kg}\cdot\text{m}}{\text{s}^2} \qquad (Q.E.D.)$$

$$F = G\frac{m_1 m_2}{r^2}$$

$$= 66.73(10^{-12})\left[\frac{200(200)}{0.6^2}\right]$$

$$= 7.41(10^{-6})\ \text{N} = 7.41\ \mu\text{N}$$ **Ans**

***1-20.** Evaluate each of the following to three significant figures and express each answer in SI units using an appropriate prefix: (a) $(0.631\ \text{Mm})/(8.60\ \text{kg})^2$, (b) $(35\ \text{mm})^2(48\ \text{kg})^3$.

(a) $0.631\ \text{Mm}/(8.60\ \text{kg})^2 = \left(\frac{0.631(10^6)\ \text{m}}{(8.60)^2\ \text{kg}^2}\right) = \frac{8532\ \text{m}}{\text{kg}^2}$

$$= 8.53(10^3)\text{m/kg}^2 = 8.53\ \text{km/kg}^2$$ **Ans**

(b) $(35\ \text{mm})^2(48\ \text{kg})^3 = \left[35(10^{-3})\ \text{m}\right]^2(48\ \text{kg})^3 = 135\ \text{m}^2\text{kg}^3$ **Ans**

2-1. Determine the magnitude of the resultant force and its direction measured clockwise from the positive x axis.

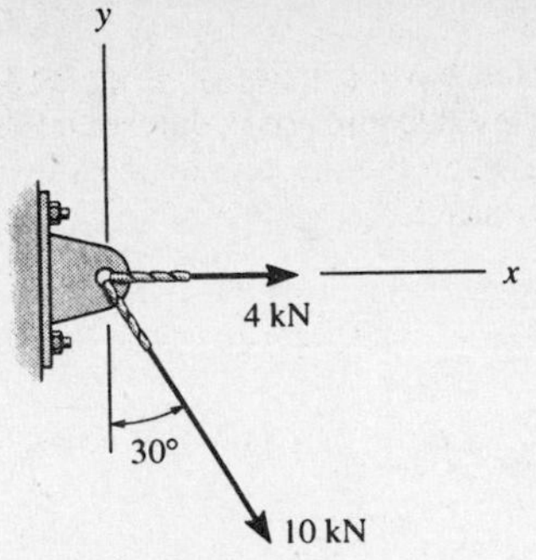

$F_R = \sqrt{(4)^2 + (10)^2 - 2(4)(10)\cos 120^\circ} = 12.49 = 12.5 \text{ kN}$ **Ans**

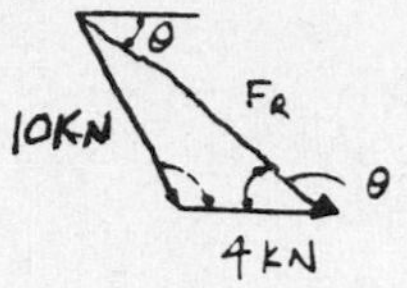

$\frac{\sin\theta}{10} = \frac{\sin 120^\circ}{12.49}$; $\theta = 43.9^\circ$ **Ans**

2-2. Determine the magnitude of the resultant force if: (a) $\mathbf{F}_R = \mathbf{F}_1 + \mathbf{F}_2$; (b) $\mathbf{F}_R = \mathbf{F}_1 - \mathbf{F}_2$.

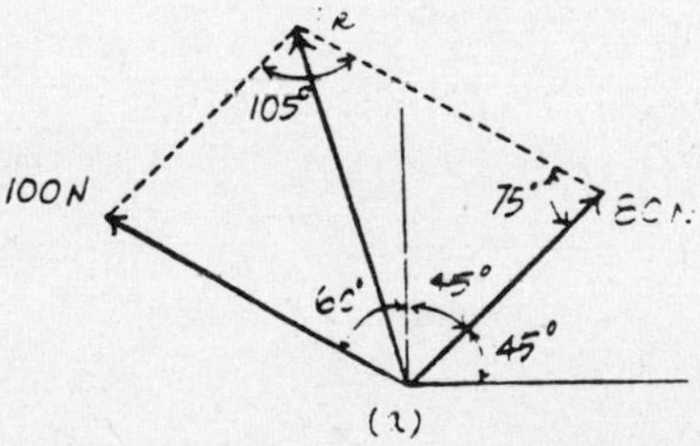

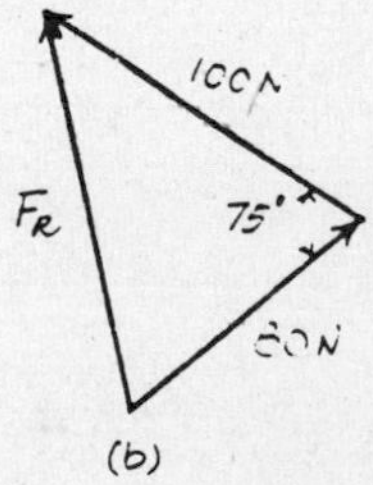

Parallelogram Law : The parallelogram law of addition is shown in Fig. (a) and (c).

Trigonometry : Using law of cosines [Fig. (b) and (d)], we have

a) $F_R = \sqrt{100^2 + 80^2 - 2(100)(80)\cos 75^\circ}$
$= 111 \text{ N}$ **Ans**

b) $F_R' = \sqrt{100^2 + 80^2 - 2(100)(80)\cos 105^\circ}$
$= 143 \text{ N}$ **Ans**

2-3. Resolve the 200-N force into components acting along the x and y' axes and determine the magnitudes of the components.

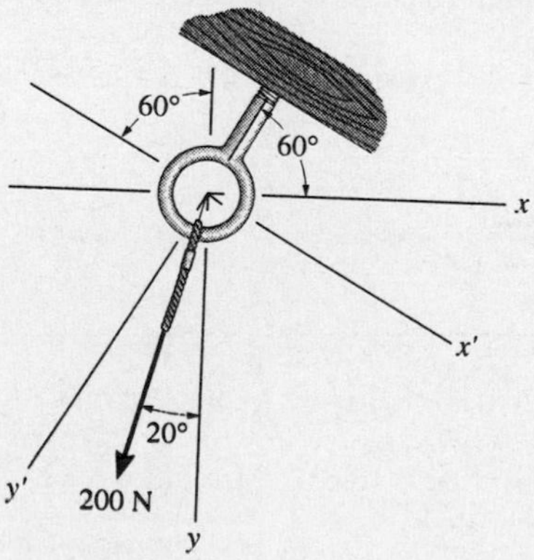

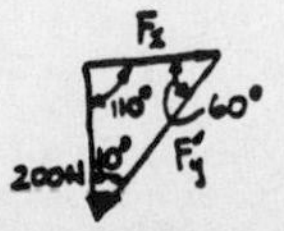

$\frac{F_{y'}}{\sin 110^\circ} = \frac{200}{\sin 60^\circ}$; $F_{y'} = 217 \text{ N}$ **Ans**

$\frac{F_x}{\sin 10^\circ} = \frac{200}{\sin 60^\circ}$; $F_x = 40.1 \text{ N}$ **Ans**

***2-4.** Determine the magnitude of the resultant force $\mathbf{F}_R = \mathbf{F}_1 + \mathbf{F}_2$ and its direction measured clockwise from the positive u axis.

$$F_R = \sqrt{(200)^2 + (300)^2 - 2(200)(300)\cos 100^\circ} = 388.378 = 388\text{ N} \quad \textbf{Ans}$$

$$\frac{\sin\theta'}{200} = \frac{\sin 100^\circ}{388.378}; \quad \theta' = 30.473^\circ$$

$$\theta = 50^\circ - 30.473^\circ = 19.5^\circ \quad \textbf{Ans}$$

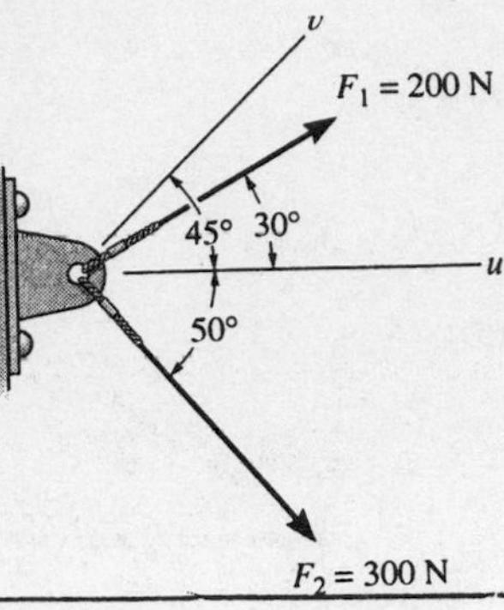

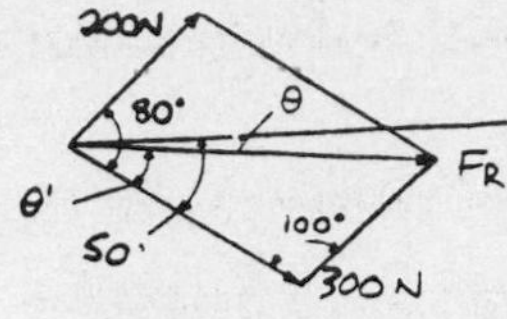

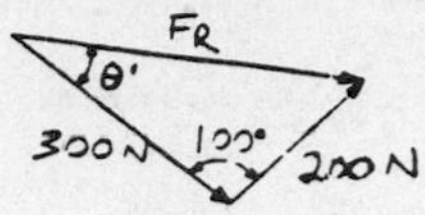

2-5. Resolve the force $\mathbf{F}_1$ into components acting along the u and v axes and determine the magnitudes of the components.

$$\frac{F_u}{\sin 15^\circ} = \frac{200}{\sin 135^\circ}; \quad F_u = 73.2\text{ N} \quad \textbf{Ans}$$

$$\frac{F_v}{\sin 30^\circ} = \frac{200}{\sin 135^\circ}; \quad F_v = 141\text{ N} \quad \textbf{Ans}$$

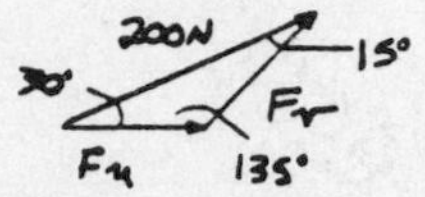

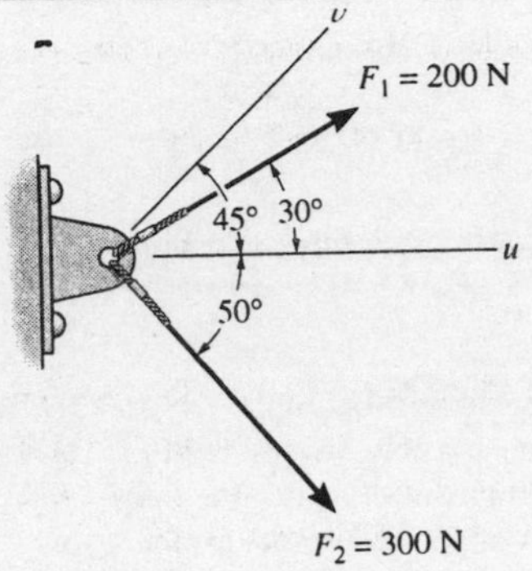

2-6. Resolve the force $\mathbf{F}_2$ into components acting along the u and v axes and determine the components.

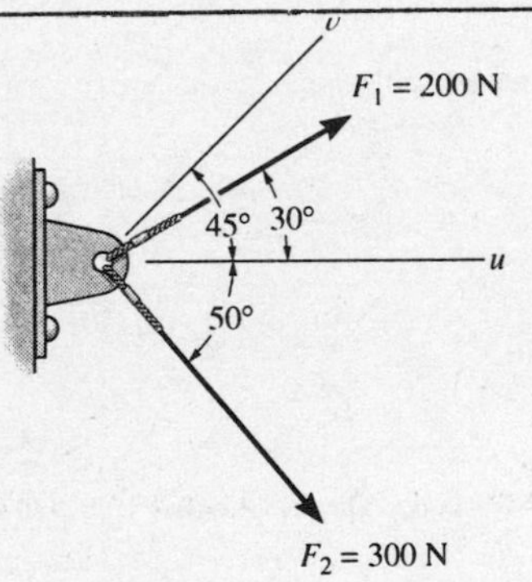

$$\frac{F_u}{\sin 85^\circ} = \frac{300}{\sin 45^\circ}; \quad F_u = 423\text{ N} \quad \textbf{Ans}$$

$$\frac{-F_v}{\sin 50^\circ} = \frac{300}{\sin 45^\circ}; \quad F_v = -325\text{ N} \quad \textbf{Ans}$$

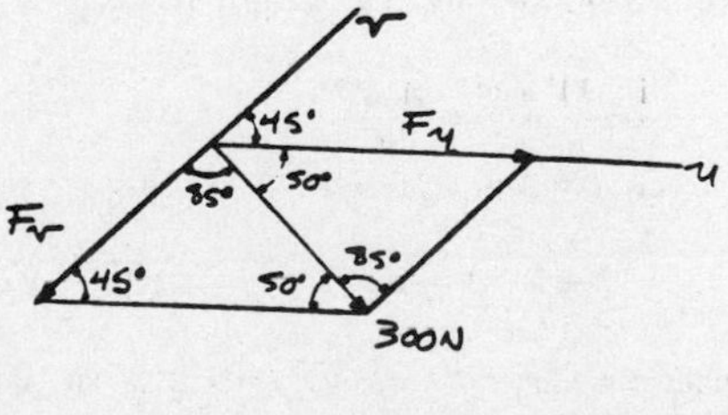

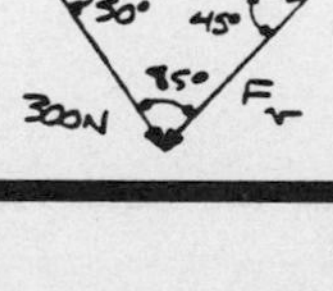

2-7. The plate is subjected to the two forces at A and B as shown. If $\theta = 60°$, determine the magnitude of the resultant of these two forces and its direction measured from the horizontal.

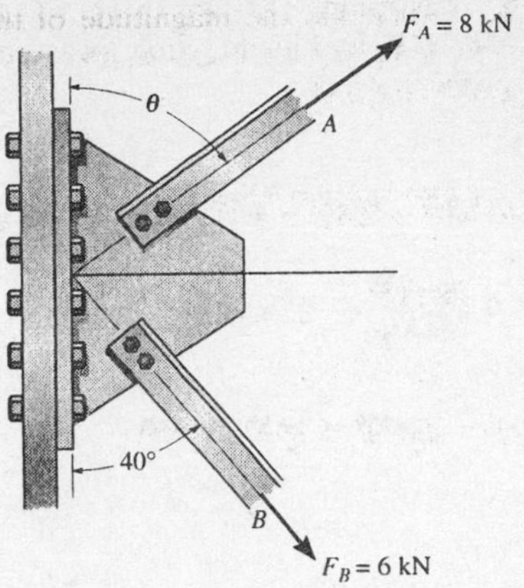

Parallelogram Law : The parallelogram law of addition is shown in Fig. (a).

Trigonometry : Using law of cosines [Fig. (b)], we have

$$F_R = \sqrt{8^2 + 6^2 - 2(8)(6)\cos 100°}$$
$$= 10.80 \text{ kN} = 10.8 \text{ kN} \qquad \textbf{Ans}$$

The angle θ can be determined using law of sines [Fig. (b)].

$$\frac{\sin\theta}{6} = \frac{\sin 100°}{10.80}$$
$$\sin\theta = 0.5470$$
$$\theta = 33.16°$$

Thus, the direction ϕ of $\mathbf{F}_R$ measured from the x axis is

$$\phi = 33.16° - 30° = 3.16° \qquad \textbf{Ans}$$

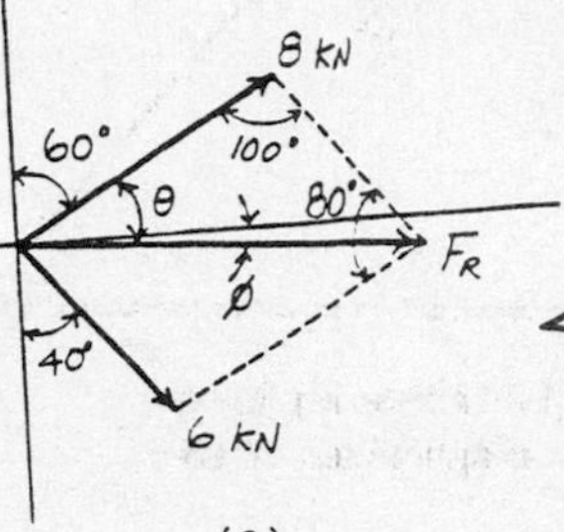

(a)

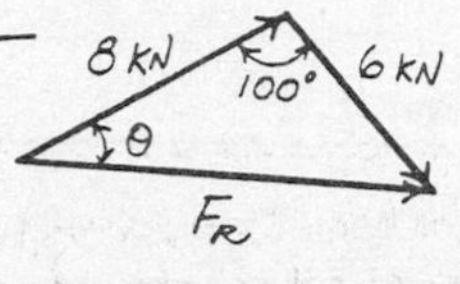

(b)

***2-8.** Determine the angle θ for connecting member A to the plate so that the resultant force of F_A and F_B is directed horizontally to the right. Also, what is the magnitude of the resultant force.

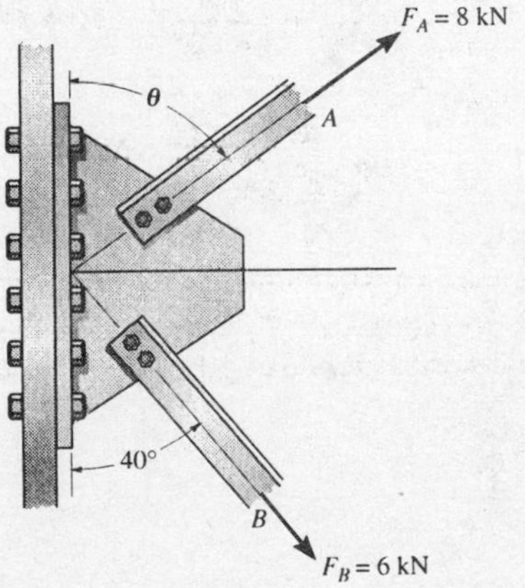

Parallelogram Law : The parallelogram law of addition is shown in Fig. (a).

Trigonometry : Using law of sines [Fig. (b)], we have

$$\frac{\sin(90° - \theta)}{6} = \frac{\sin 50°}{8}$$
$$\sin(90° - \theta) = 0.5745$$

$$\theta = 54.93° = 54.9° \qquad \textbf{Ans}$$

From the triangle, $\phi = 180° - (90° - 54.93°) - 50° = 94.93°$. Thus, using law of cosines, the magnitude of $\mathbf{F}_R$ is

$$F_R = \sqrt{8^2 + 6^2 - 2(8)(6)\cos 94.93°}$$
$$= 10.4 \text{ kN} \qquad \textbf{Ans}$$

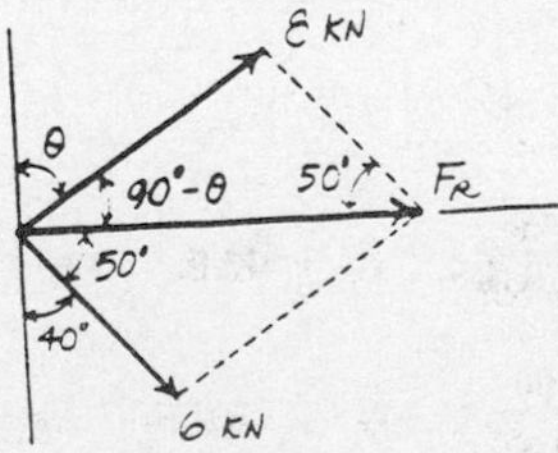

(a)

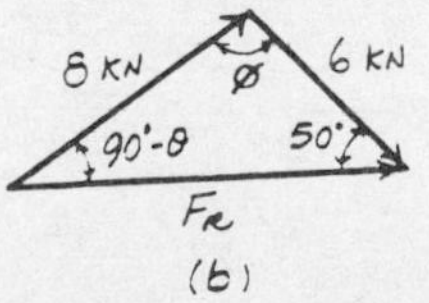

(b)

2-9. The vertical force **F** acts downward at A on the two-membered frame. Determine the magnitudes of the two components of **F** directed along the axes of AB and AC. Set $F = 500$ N.

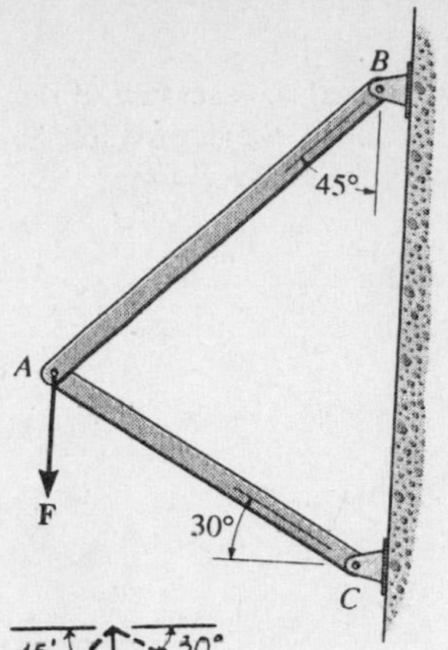

Parallelogram Law : The parallelogram law of addition is shown in Fig. (a).

Trigonometry : Using law of sines [Fig. (b)], we have

$$\frac{F_{AB}}{\sin 60^\circ} = \frac{500}{\sin 75^\circ}$$

$F_{AB} = 448$ N **Ans**

$$\frac{F_{AC}}{\sin 45^\circ} = \frac{500}{\sin 75^\circ}$$

$F_{AC} = 366$ N **Ans**

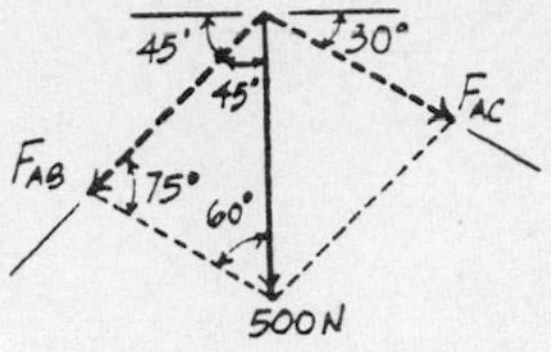

(a)

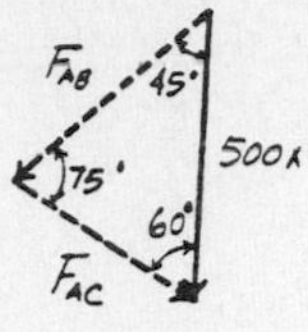

(b)

2-10. Solve Prob. 2-10 with $F = 350$ lb.

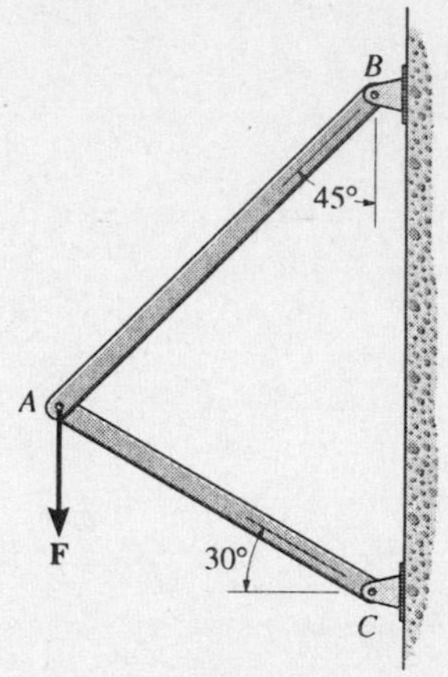

Parallelogram Law : The parallelogram law of addition is shown in Fig. (b).

Trigonometry : Using law of sines [Fig. (c)], we have

$$\frac{F_{AB}}{\sin 60^\circ} = \frac{350}{\sin 75^\circ}$$

$F_{AB} = 314$ lb **Ans**

$$\frac{F_{AC}}{\sin 45^\circ} = \frac{350}{\sin 75^\circ}$$

$F_{AC} = 256$ lb **Ans**

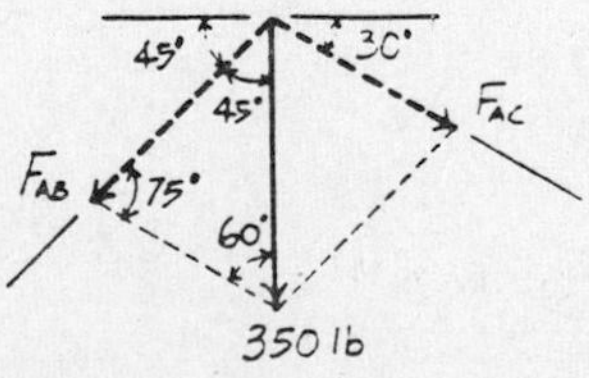

(a)

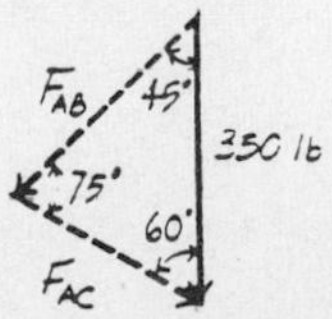

(b)

2-11. The device is used for surgical replacement of the knee joint. If the force acting along the leg is 360 N, determine its components along the x and y' axes.

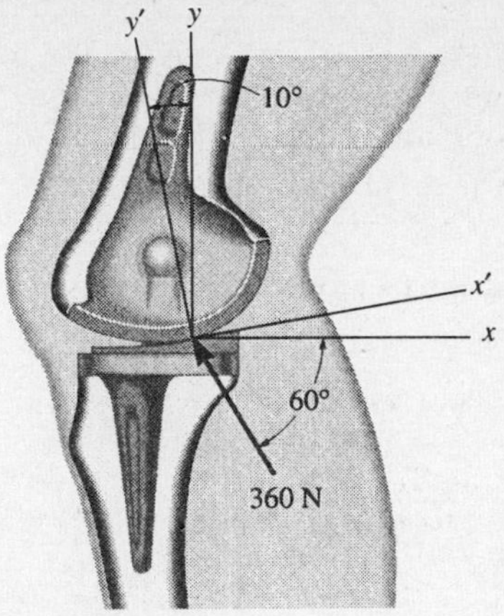

$$\frac{-F_x}{\sin 20^\circ} = \frac{360}{\sin 100^\circ}; \quad F_x = -125 \text{ N} \quad \textbf{Ans}$$

$$\frac{F_{y'}}{\sin 60^\circ} = \frac{360}{\sin 100^\circ}; \quad F_{y'} = 317 \text{ N} \quad \textbf{Ans}$$

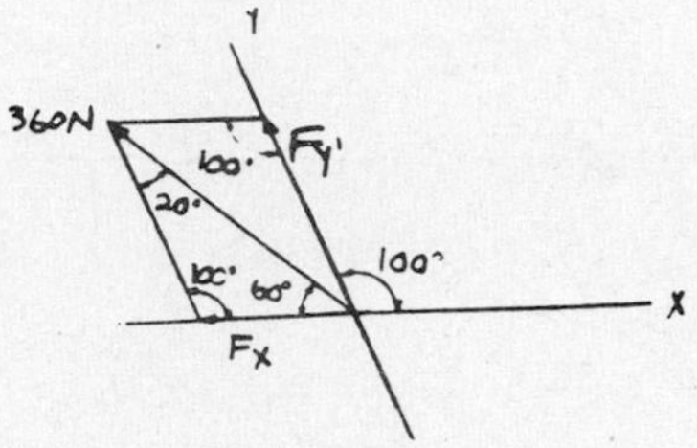

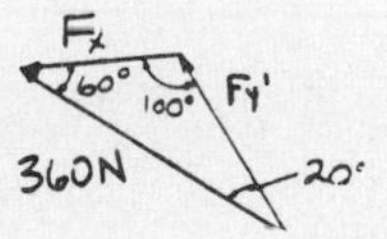

***2-12.** The device is used for surgical replacement of the knee joint. If the force acting along the leg is 360 N, determine its components along the x' and y axes.

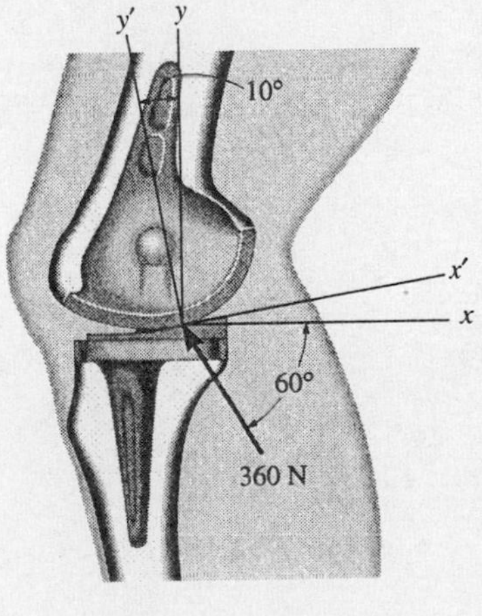

$$\frac{-F_{x'}}{\sin 30^\circ} = \frac{360}{\sin 80^\circ}; \quad F_{x'} = -183 \text{ N} \quad \textbf{Ans}$$

$$\frac{F_y}{\sin 70^\circ} = \frac{360}{\sin 80^\circ}; \quad F_y = 344 \text{ N} \quad \textbf{Ans}$$

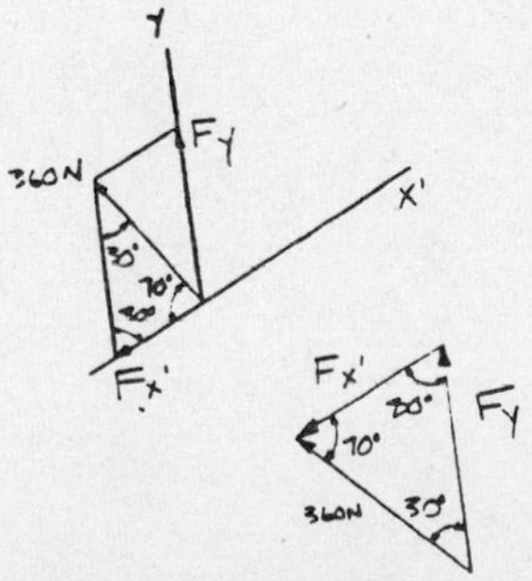

2-13. The 500-lb force acting on the frame is to be resolved into two components acting along the axis of the struts AB and AC. If the component of force along AC is required to be 300 lb, directed from A to C, determine the magnitude of force acting along AB and the angle θ of the 500-lb force.

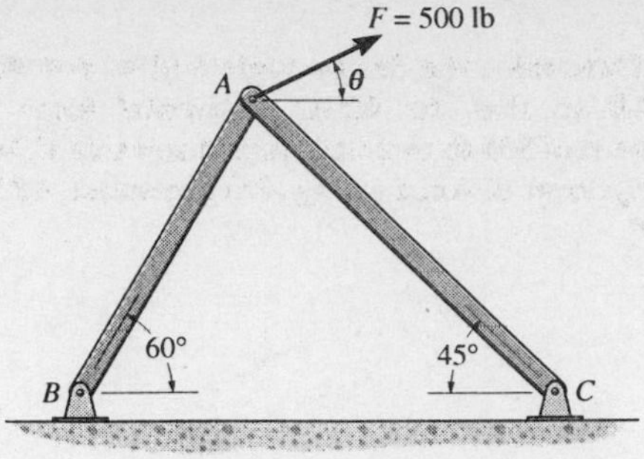

Parallelogram Law : The parallelogram law of addition is shown in Fig. (a).

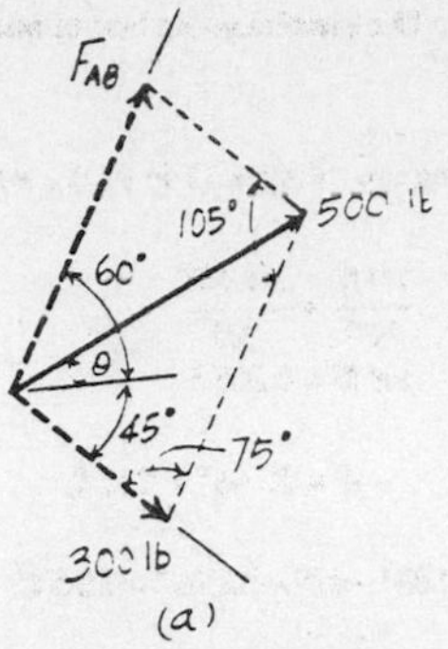

Trigonometry : Using law of sines [Fig. (b)], we have

$$\frac{\sin\phi}{300} = \frac{\sin 75°}{500}$$
$$\sin\phi = 0.5796$$

$$\phi = 35.42°$$

Thus, $$45° + \theta + 75° + 35.42° = 180°$$

$$\theta = 24.58° = 24.6°$$

$$\frac{F_{AB}}{\sin(45° + 24.58°)} = \frac{500}{\sin 75°}$$

$$F_{AB} = 485 \text{ lb}$$ **Ans**

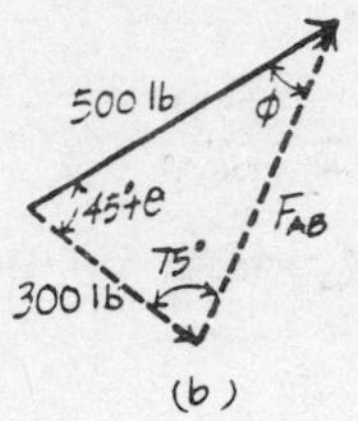

2-14. Determine the magnitudes of the two components of the 600-N force, one directed along cable AC and the other along the axis of strut AB.

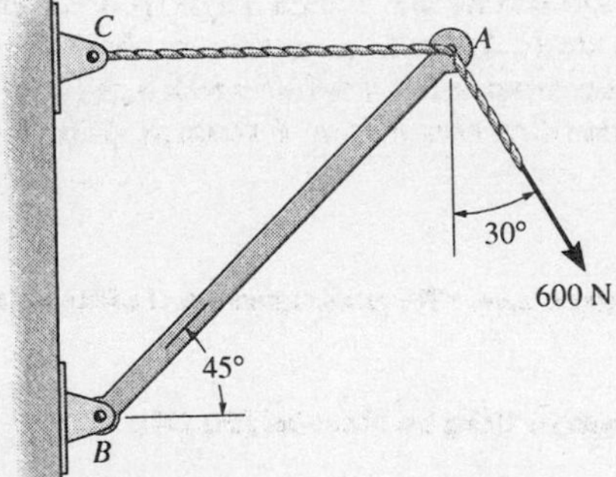

$$\frac{F_{AB}}{\sin 60°} = \frac{600}{\sin 45°}; \quad F_{AB} = 735 \text{ N}$$ **Ans**

$$\frac{F_{AC}}{\sin 75°} = \frac{600}{\sin 45°}; \quad F_{AC} = 820 \text{ N}$$ **Ans**

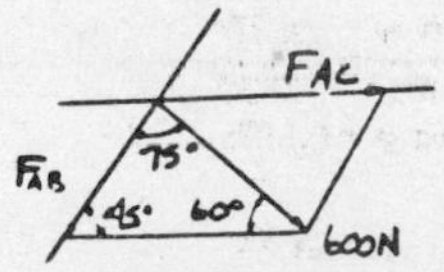

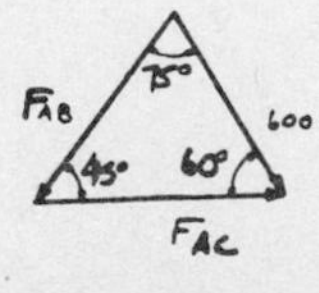

2-15. Determine the design angle θ ($0° \le \theta \le 90°$) for strut AB so that the 400-lb horizontal force has a component of 500-lb directed from A towards C. What is the component of force acting along member AB? Take $\phi = 40°$.

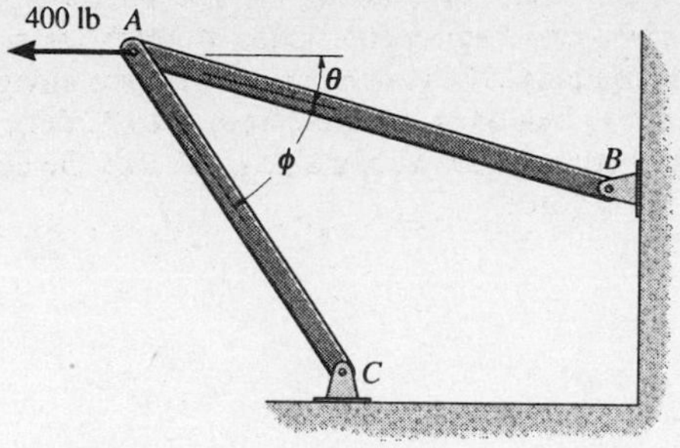

Parallelogram Law : The parallelogram law of addition is shown in Fig. (a).

Trigonometry : Using law of sines [Fig. (b)], we have

$$\frac{\sin\theta}{500} = \frac{\sin 40°}{400}$$

$$\sin\theta = 0.8035$$

$$\theta = 53.46° = 53.5° \qquad \textbf{Ans}$$

Thus, $\phi = 180° - 40° - 53.46° = 86.54°$

Using law of sines [Fig. (b)]

$$\frac{F_{AB}}{\sin 86.54°} = \frac{400}{\sin 40°}$$

$$F_{AB} = 621 \text{ lb} \qquad \textbf{Ans}$$

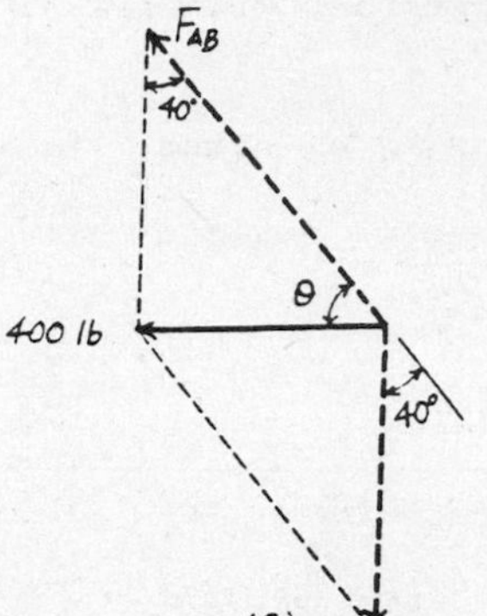

(a)

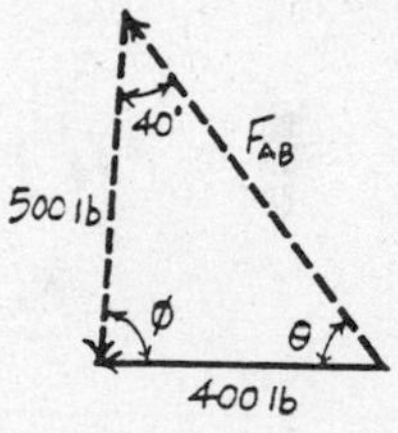

(b)

***2-16.** Determine the design angle ϕ ($0° \le \phi \le 90°$) between struts AB and AC so that the 400-lb horizontal force has a component of 600-lb which acts up to the left, in the same direction as from B towards A. Take $\theta = 30°$.

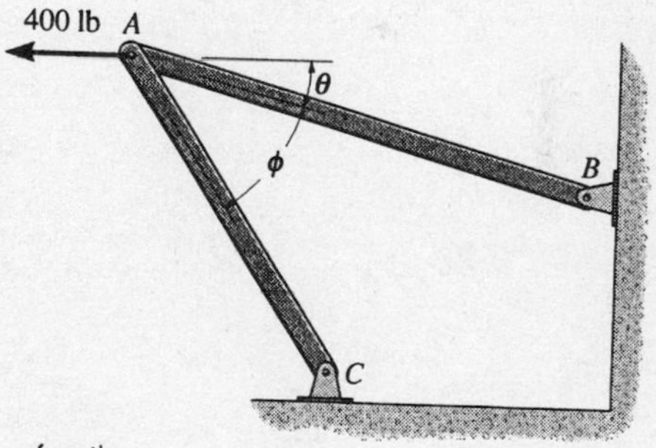

Parallelogram Law : The parallelogram law of addition is shown in Fig. (a).

Trigonometry : Using law of cosines [Fig. (b)], we have

$$F_{AC} = \sqrt{400^2 + 600^2 - 2(400)(600)\cos 30°} = 322.97 \text{ lb}$$

The angle ϕ can be determined using law of sines [Fig. (b)].

$$\frac{\sin\phi}{400} = \frac{\sin 30°}{322.97}$$

$$\sin\phi = 0.6193$$

$$\phi = 38.3° \qquad \textbf{Ans}$$

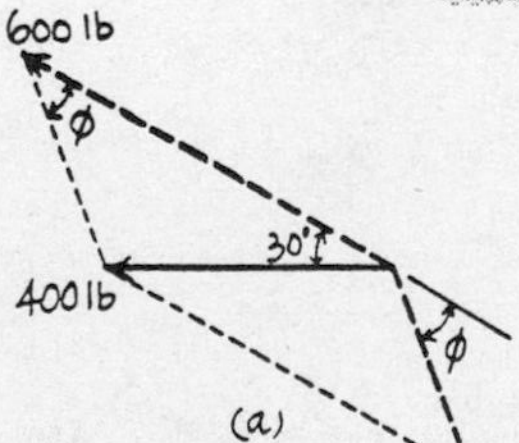

(a)

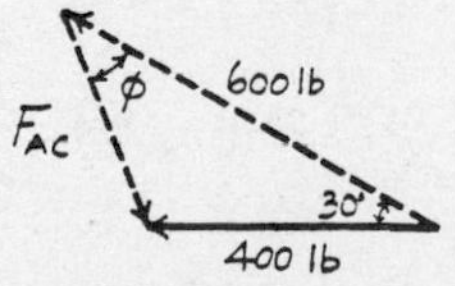

(b)

2-17. Determine the magnitude and direction of the resultant force $\mathbf{F}_R$. Express the result in terms of the magnitudes of the components $\mathbf{F}_1$ and $\mathbf{F}_2$ and the angle ϕ.

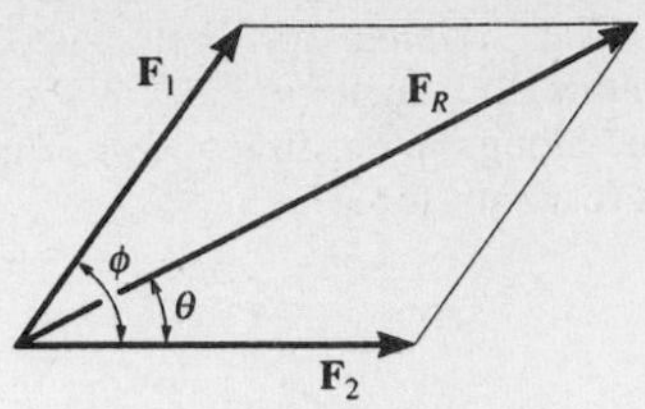

$$F_R^2 = F_1^2 + F_2^2 - 2F_1F_2\cos(180^\circ - \phi)$$

Since $\cos(180^\circ - \phi) = -\cos\phi$,

$$F_R = \sqrt{F_1^2 + F_2^2 + 2F_1F_2\cos\phi} \qquad \textbf{Ans}$$

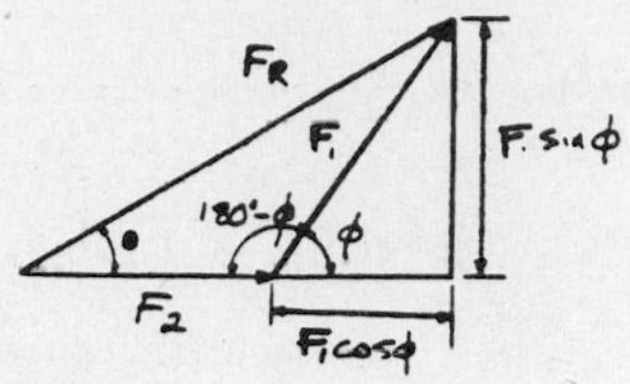

From the figure,

$$\tan\theta = \frac{F_1\sin\phi}{F_2 + F_1\cos\phi} \qquad \textbf{Ans}$$

2-18. Two forces are applied at the end of a screw eye in order to remove the post. Determine the angle θ ($0^\circ \leq \theta \leq 90^\circ$) and the magnitude of force **F** so that the resultant force acting on the post is directed vertically upward and has a magnitude of 750 N.

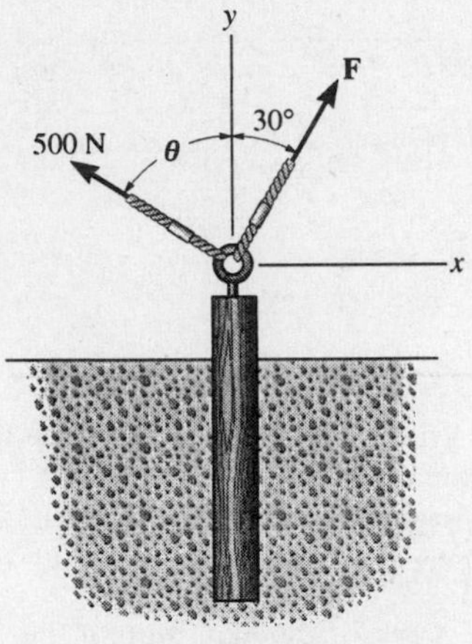

Parallelogram Law **:** The parallelogram law of addition is shown in Fig. (a).

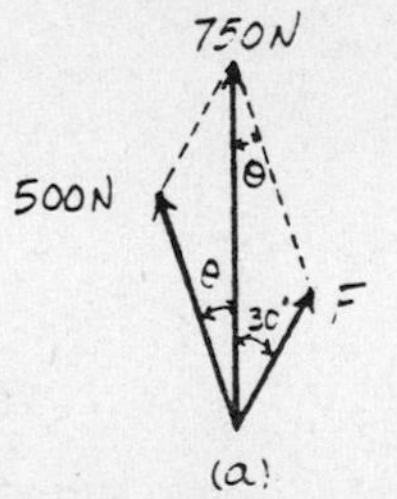

Trigonometry **:** Using law of sines [Fig. (b)], we have

$$\frac{\sin\phi}{750} = \frac{\sin 30^\circ}{500}$$
$$\sin\phi = 0.750$$
$$\phi = 131.41^\circ \text{ (By observation, } \phi > 80^\circ)$$

Thus, $\theta = 180^\circ - 30^\circ - 131.41^\circ = 18.59^\circ = 18.6^\circ$ **Ans**

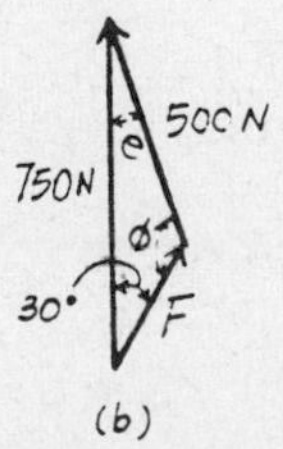

$$\frac{F}{\sin 18.59^\circ} = \frac{500}{\sin 30^\circ}$$

$$F = 319\text{ N} \qquad \textbf{Ans}$$

2-19. The riveted bracket supports two forces. Determine the angle θ so that the resultant force is directed along the negative x axis. What is the magnitude of this resultant force?

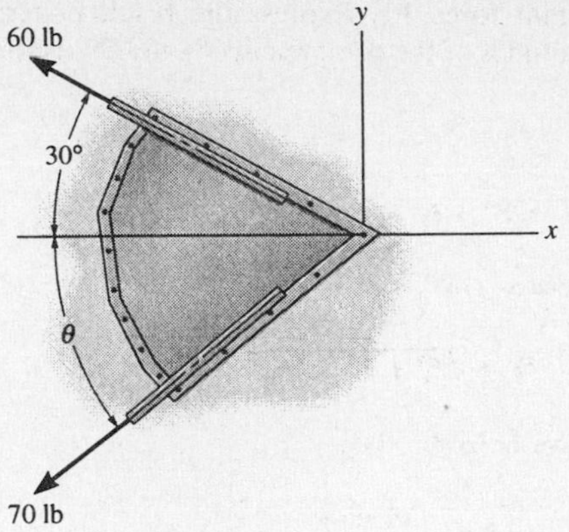

$$\frac{\sin\theta}{60} = \frac{\sin 30^\circ}{70}; \quad \theta = 25.38^\circ = 25.4^\circ \quad \textbf{Ans}$$

$$\phi = 180^\circ - 25.38^\circ - 30^\circ = 124.62^\circ$$

$$R = \sqrt{(60)^2 + (70)^2 - 2(60)(70)\cos 124.62^\circ} = 115\ \text{lb} \quad \textbf{Ans}$$

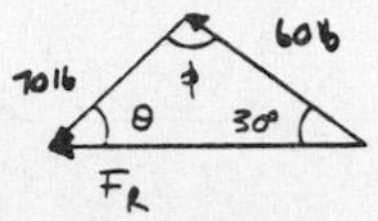

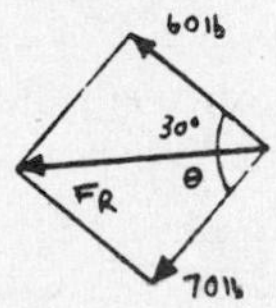

***2-20.** The truck is to be towed using two ropes. Determine the magnitude of forces $\mathbf{F}_A$ and $\mathbf{F}_B$ acting on each rope in order to develop a resultant force of 950 N directed along the positive x axis. Set $\theta = 50^\circ$.

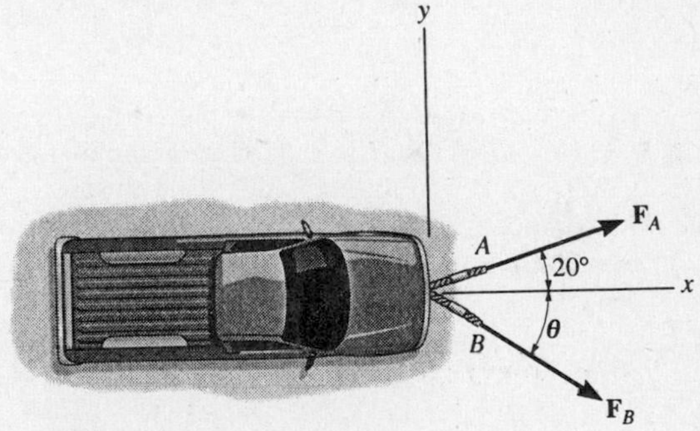

Parallelogram Law **:** The parallelogram law of addition is shown in Fig. (a).

Trigonometry **:** Using law of sines [Fig. (b)], we have

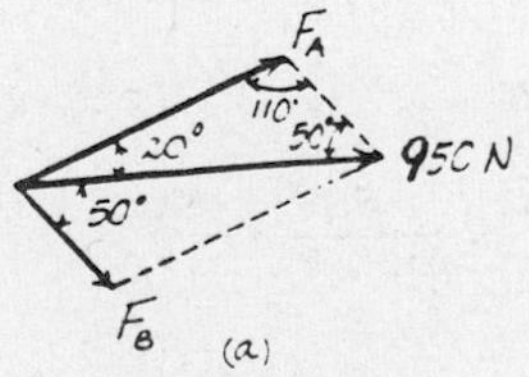

$$\frac{F_A}{\sin 50^\circ} = \frac{950}{\sin 110^\circ}$$

$$F_A = 774\ \text{N} \qquad \textbf{Ans}$$

$$\frac{F_B}{\sin 20^\circ} = \frac{950}{\sin 110^\circ}$$

$$F_B = 346\ \text{N} \qquad \textbf{Ans}$$

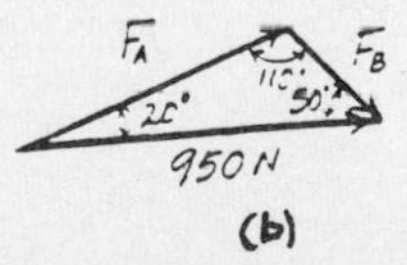

2-21. The truck is to be towed using two ropes. If the resultant force is to be 950 N, directed along the positive x axis, determine the magnitudes of forces $\mathbf{F}_A$ and $\mathbf{F}_B$ acting on each rope and the angle of θ of $\mathbf{F}_B$ so that the magnitude of $\mathbf{F}_B$ is a *minimum*. $\mathbf{F}_A$ acts at 20° from the x axis as shown.

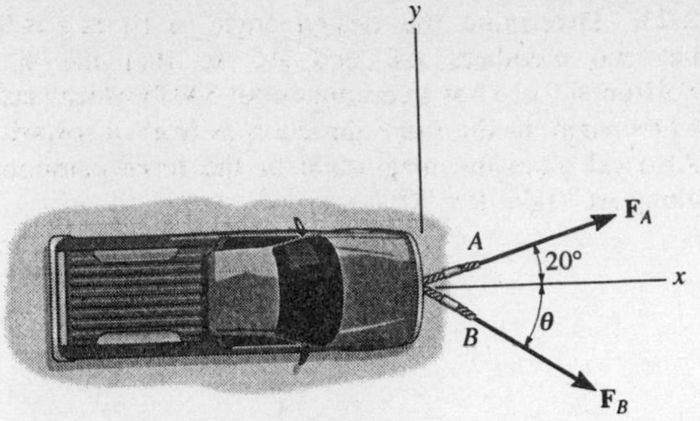

Parallelogram Law : In order to produce a ***minimum*** force F_B, F_B has to act perpendicular to F_A. The parallelogram law of addition is shown in Fig. (a).

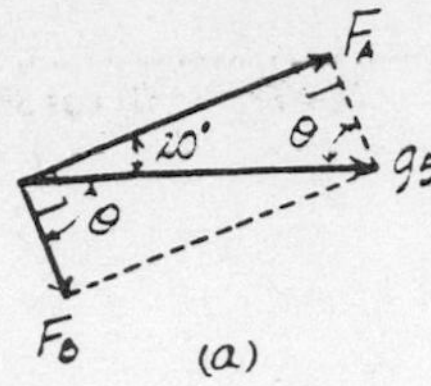

(a)

Trigonometry : Fig. (b).

$$F_B = 950 \sin 20° = 325 \text{ N} \qquad \textbf{Ans}$$

$$F_A = 950 \cos 20° = 893 \text{ N} \qquad \textbf{Ans}$$

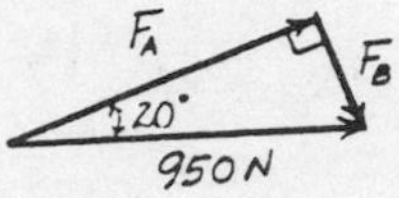

(b)

The angle θ is

$$\theta = 90° - 20° = 70.0° \qquad \textbf{Ans}$$

2-22. Determine the design angle θ ($0° \leq \theta \leq 90°$) for member AB so that the 400-lb horizontal force has a component of 500 lb directed from A toward C. What is the component of force acting along member AB? Take $\phi = 40°$.

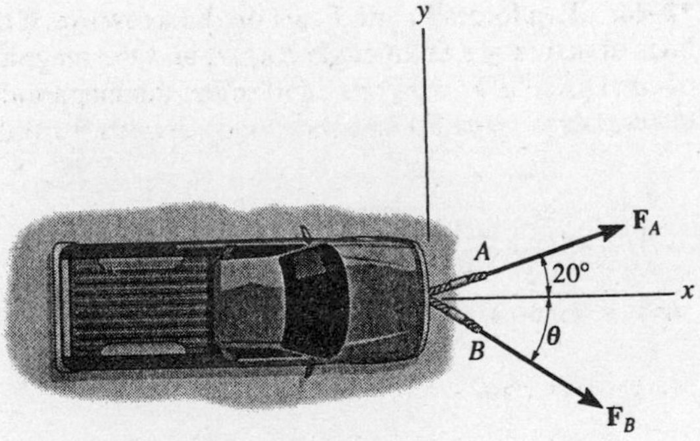

Sine law :

$$\frac{\sin\theta}{500} = \frac{\sin 40°}{400} \qquad \theta = 53.5° \qquad \textbf{Ans}$$

$$\frac{F_{AB}}{\sin(180° - 40° - 53.5°)} = \frac{400}{\sin 40°} \qquad F_{AB} = 621 \text{ lb} \qquad \textbf{Ans}$$

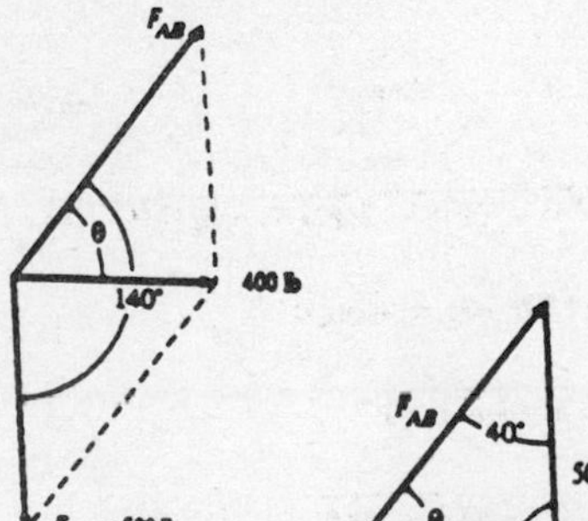

2-23. Determine the design angle ϕ ($0° \le \phi \le 90°$) between members AB and AC so that the 400-lb horizontal force has a component of 600 lb which acts up to the right, in the same direction as from B toward A. Also calculate the magnitude of the force component along AC. Take $\theta = 30°$.

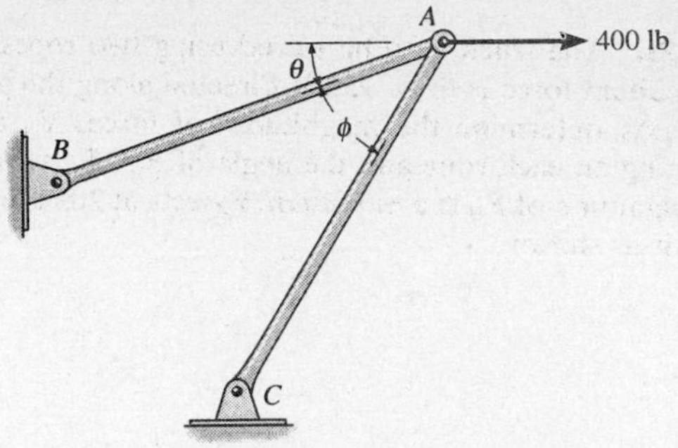

Cosine law :

$$F_{AC} = \sqrt{400^2 + 600^2 - 2(400)(600)\cos 30°} = 323 \text{ lb} \qquad \textbf{Ans}$$

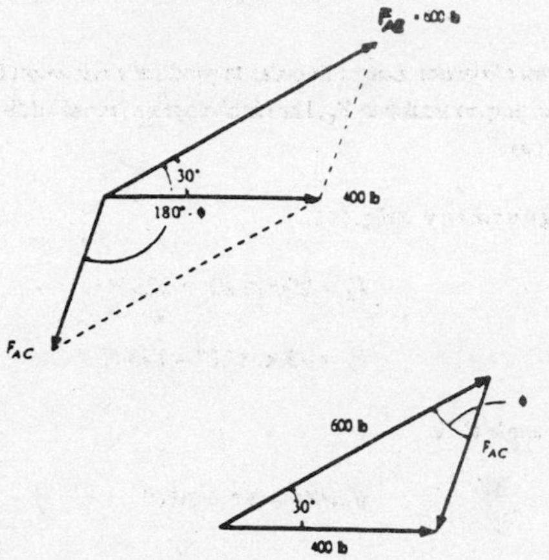

Sine law :

$$\frac{\sin 30°}{323} = \frac{\sin\phi}{400} \qquad \phi = 38.3° \qquad \textbf{Ans}$$

***2-24.** Two forces $\mathbf{F}_1$ and $\mathbf{F}_2$ act on the screw eye. If their lines of action are at an angle θ apart and the magnitude of each force is $F_1 = F_2 = F$, determine the magnitude of the resultant force $\mathbf{F}_R$ and the angle between $\mathbf{F}_R$ and $\mathbf{F}_1$.

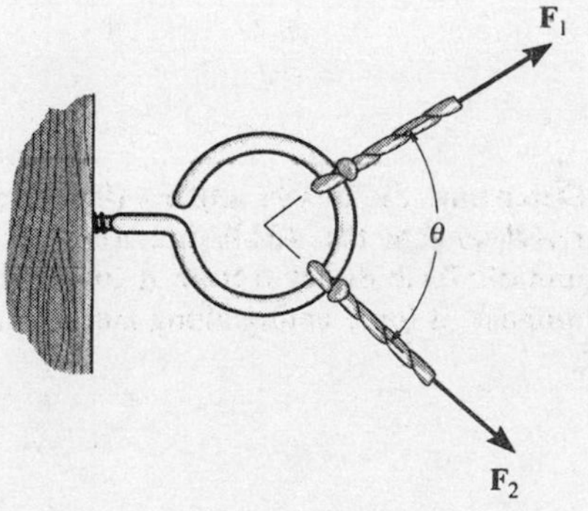

$$\frac{F}{\sin\phi} = \frac{F}{\sin(\theta - \phi)}$$

$$\sin(\theta - \phi) = \sin\phi$$

$$\theta - \phi = \phi$$

$$\phi = \frac{\theta}{2} \qquad \textbf{Ans}$$

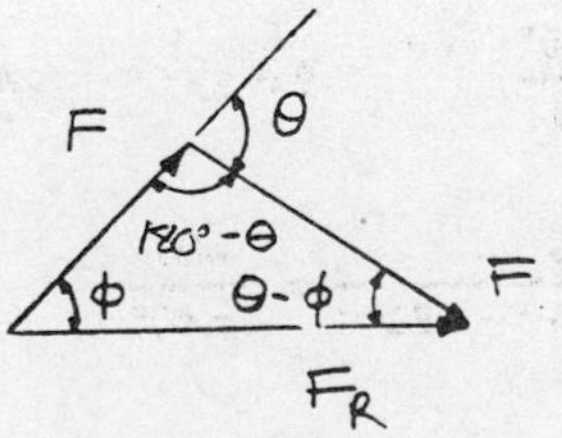

$$F_R = \sqrt{(F)^2 + (F)^2 - 2(F)(F)\cos(180° - \theta)}$$

Since $\cos(180° - \theta) = -\cos\theta$

$$F_R = F(\sqrt{2})\sqrt{1 + \cos\theta}$$

Since $\cos(\frac{\theta}{2}) = \sqrt{\frac{1 + \cos\theta}{2}}$

Then

$$F_R = 2F\cos(\frac{\theta}{2}) \qquad \textbf{Ans}$$

2-25. The log is being towed by two tractors A and B. Determine the magnitude of the two towing forces $\mathbf{F}_A$ and $\mathbf{F}_B$ if it is required that the resultant force have a magnitude $F_R = 10$ kN and be directed along the x axis. Set $\theta = 15°$.

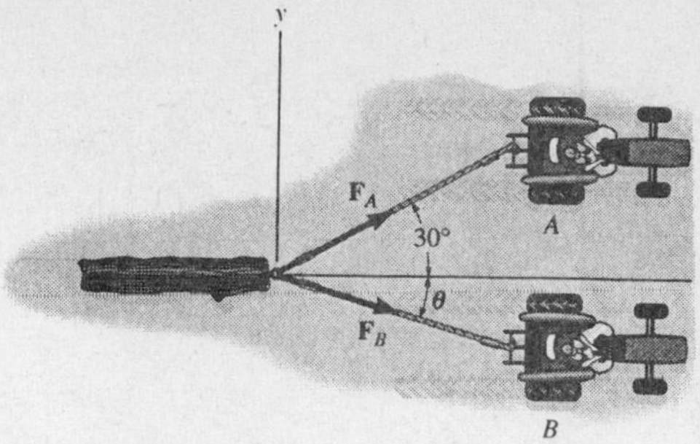

Parallelogram Law *:* The parallelogram law of addition is shown in Fig. (a).

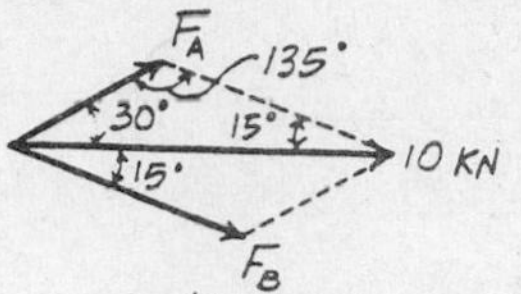

(a)

Trigonometry *:* Using law of sines [Fig. (b)], we have

$$\frac{F_A}{\sin 15°} = \frac{10}{\sin 135°}$$

$$F_A = 3.66 \text{ kN} \qquad \textbf{Ans}$$

$$\frac{F_B}{\sin 30°} = \frac{10}{\sin 135°}$$

$$F_B = 7.07 \text{ kN} \qquad \textbf{Ans}$$

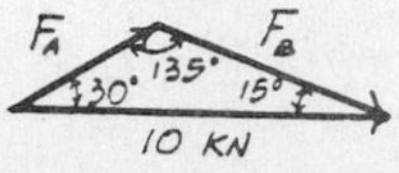

(b)

2-26. If the resultant $\mathbf{F}_R$ of the two forces acting on the log is to be directed along the positive x axis and have a magnitude of 10 kN, determine the angle θ of the cable, attached to B such that the force $\mathbf{F}_B$ in this cable is minimum. What is the magnitude of the force in each cable for this situation?

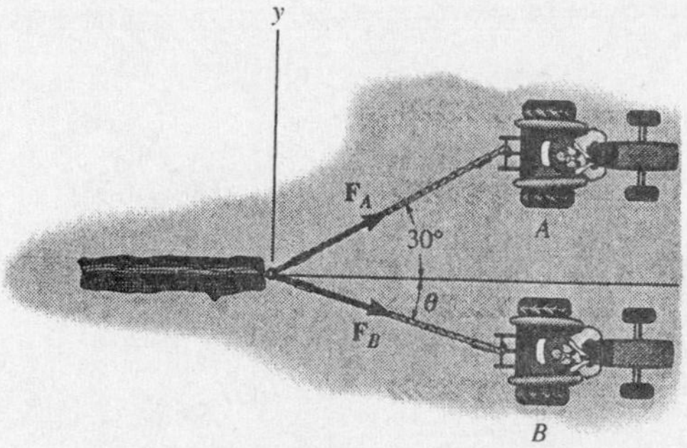

Parallelogram Law *:* In order to produce a *minimum* force $\mathbf{F}_B$, $\mathbf{F}_B$ has to act perpendicular to $\mathbf{F}_A$. The parallelogram law of addition is shown in Fig. (a).

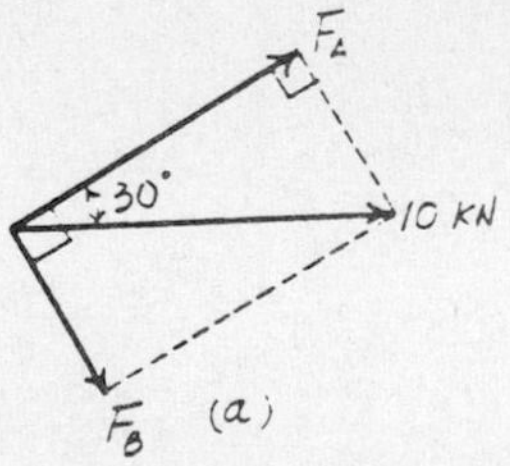

(a)

Trigonometry *:* Fig. (b).

$$F_R = 10\sin 30° = 5.00 \text{ kN} \qquad \textbf{Ans}$$

$$F_A = 10\cos 30° = 8.66 \text{ kN} \qquad \textbf{Ans}$$

The angle θ is

$$\theta = 90° - 30° = 60.0° \qquad \textbf{Ans}$$

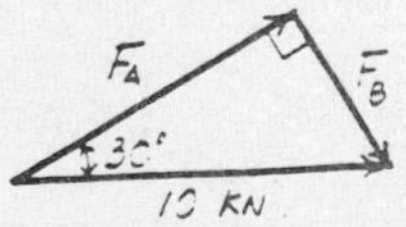

(b)

2-27. The beam is to be hoisted using two chains. Determine the magnitudes of forces $\mathbf{F}_A$ and $\mathbf{F}_B$ acting on each chain in order to develop a resultant force of 600 N directed along the positive y axis. Set $\theta = 45°$.

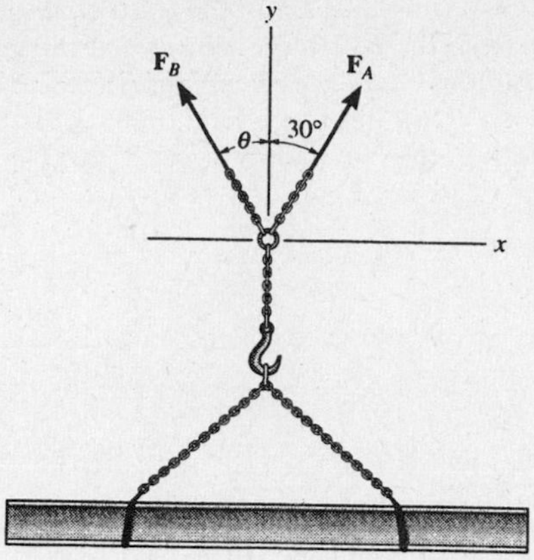

$$\frac{F_A}{\sin 45°} = \frac{600}{\sin 105°}; \quad F_A = 439 \text{ N} \quad \text{Ans}$$

$$\frac{F_B}{\sin 30°} = \frac{600}{\sin 105°}; \quad F_B = 311 \text{ N} \quad \text{Ans}$$

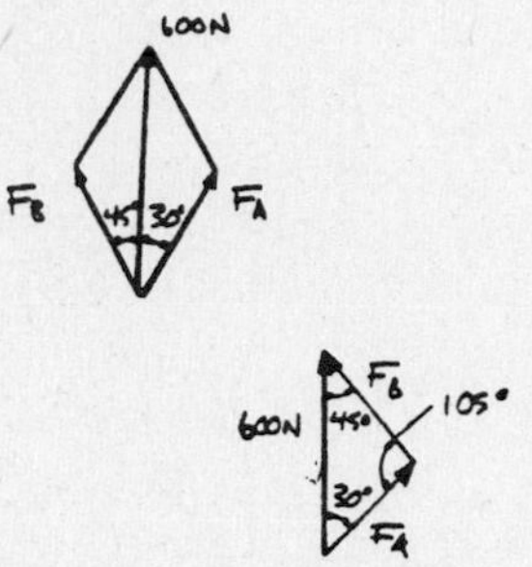

***2-28.** The beam is to be hoisted using two chains. If the resultant force is to be 600 N, directed along the positive y axis, determine the magnitudes of forces $\mathbf{F}_A$ and $\mathbf{F}_B$ acting on each chain and the orientation θ of $\mathbf{F}_B$ so that the magnitude of $\mathbf{F}_B$ is a *minimum*. $\mathbf{F}_A$ acts at 30° from the y axis as shown.

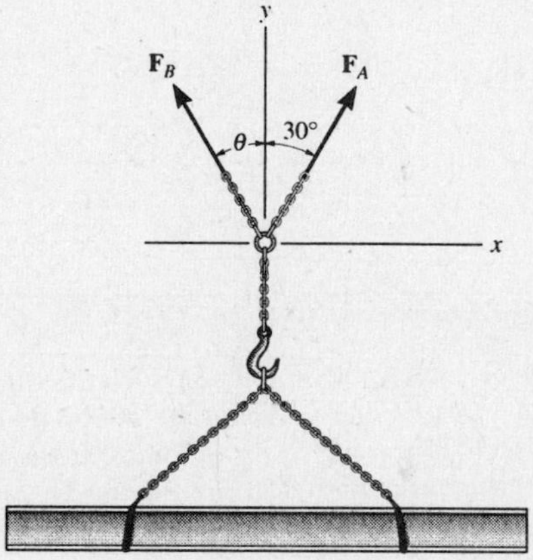

For minimum F_B, require

$\theta = 60°$ Ans

$F_A = 600 \cos 30° = 520$ N Ans

$F_B = 600 \sin 30° = 300$ N Ans

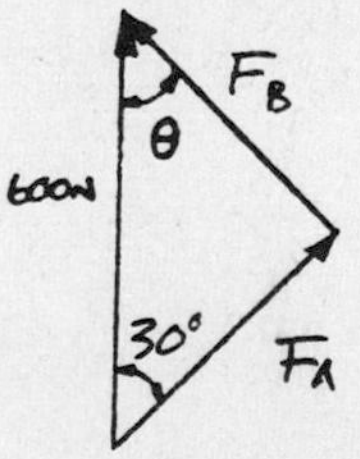

2-29. Three chains act on the bracket such that they create a resultant force having a magnitude of 500 lb. If two of the chains are subjected to known forces, as shown, determine the orientation θ of the third chain, measured clockwise from the positive x axis, so that the magnitude of force **F** in this chain is a *minimum*. All forces lie in the x–y plane. What is the magnitude of **F**? *Hint:* First find the resultant of the two known forces. Force **F** acts in this direction.

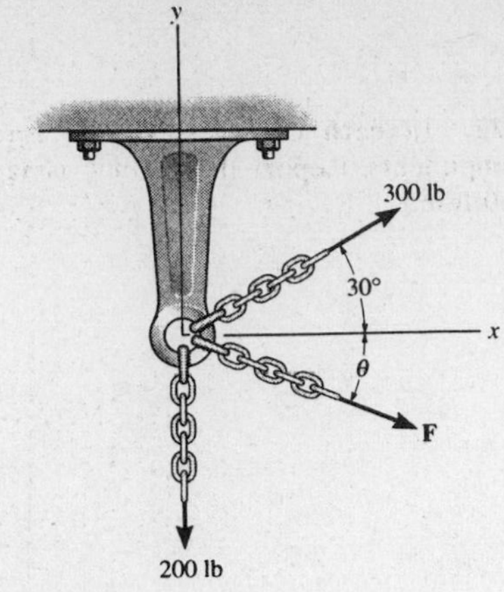

Cosine law :

$$F_{R1} = \sqrt{300^2 + 200^2 - 2(300)(200)\cos 60^\circ} = 264.6 \text{ lb}$$

Sine law :

$$\frac{\sin(30^\circ + \theta)}{200} = \frac{\sin 60^\circ}{264.6} \qquad \theta = 10.9^\circ \qquad \textbf{Ans}$$

When **F** is directed along $\mathbf{F}_{R1}$, F will be minimum to create the resultant force.

$$F_R = F_{R1} + F$$

$$500 = 264.6 + F_{min}$$

$$F_{min} = 235 \text{ lb} \qquad \textbf{Ans}$$

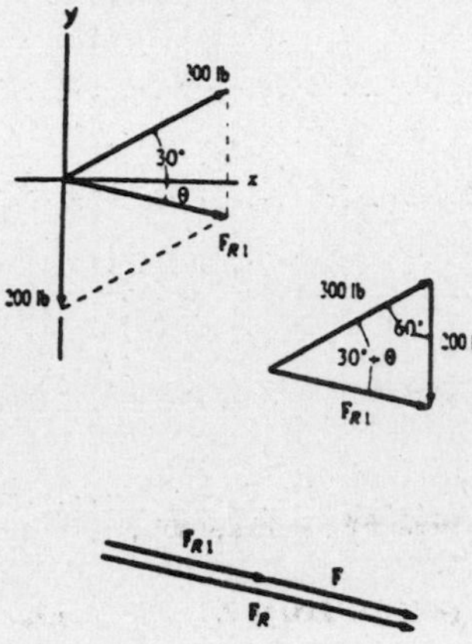

2-30. Three cables pull on the pipe such that they create a resultant force having a magnitude of 900 lb. If two of the cables are subjected to known forces, as shown in the figure, determine the direction θ of the third cable so that the magnitude of force **F** in this cable is a *minimum*. All forces lie in the x–y plane. What is the magnitude of **F**? *Hint:* First find the resultant of the two known forces.

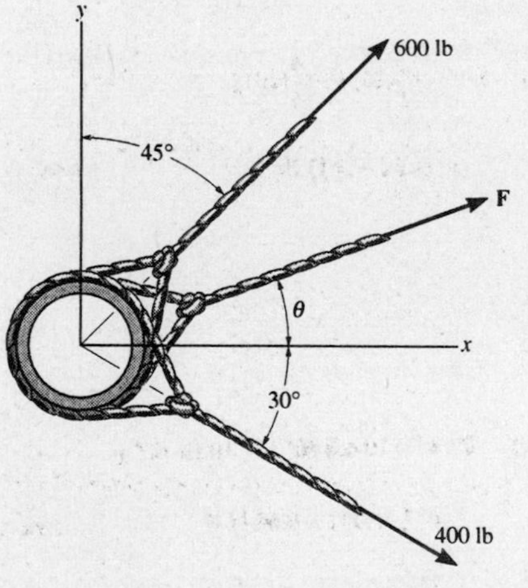

$$F' = \sqrt{(600)^2 + (400)^2 - 2(600)(400)\cos 105^\circ} = 802.64 \text{ lb}$$

$$F = 900 - 802.64 = 97.4 \text{ lb} \qquad \textbf{Ans}$$

$$\frac{\sin\phi}{600} = \frac{\sin 105^\circ}{802.64}; \quad \phi = 46.22^\circ$$

$$\theta = 46.22^\circ - 30^\circ = 16.2^\circ \qquad \textbf{Ans}$$

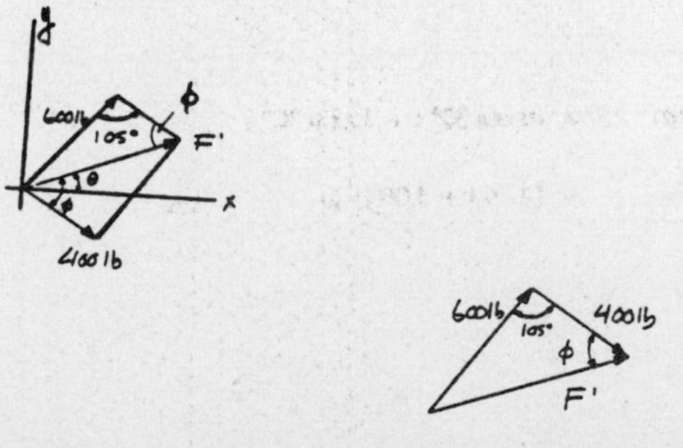

2-31. In each case resolve the force into x and y components. Report the results using Cartesian vector notation.

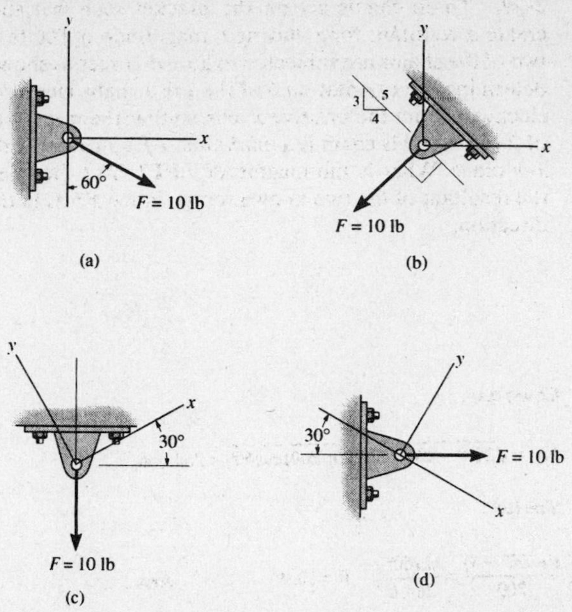

(a) $\mathbf{F} = 10 \sin 60° \, \mathbf{i} - 10 \cos 60° \, \mathbf{j}$

$= \{8.66 \, \mathbf{i} - 5.00 \, \mathbf{j}\}$ lb **Ans**

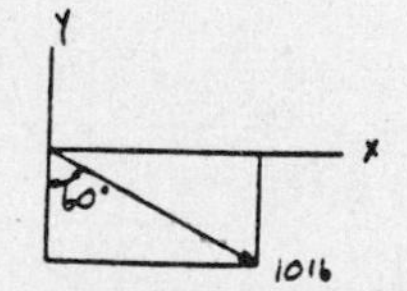

(b) $\mathbf{F} = -\frac{3}{5}(10)\,\mathbf{i} - \frac{4}{5}(10)\,\mathbf{j}$

$= \{-6\,\mathbf{i} - 8\,\mathbf{j}\}$ lb **Ans**

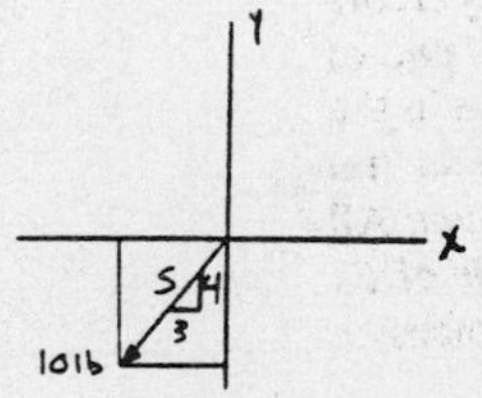

(c) $\mathbf{F} = -10 \cos 60° \, \mathbf{i} - 10 \sin 60° \, \mathbf{j}$

$= \{-5.00\,\mathbf{i} - 8.66\,\mathbf{j}\}$ lb **Ans**

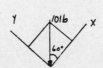

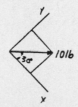

(d) $\mathbf{F} = 10 \cos 30° \, \mathbf{i} + 10 \sin 30° \, \mathbf{j}$

$= \{8.66\,\mathbf{i} + 5.00\,\mathbf{j}\}$ lb **Ans**

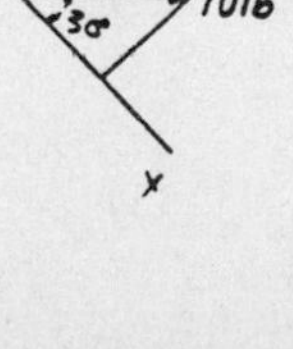

*2-32. In each case resolve the force into x and y components. Report the results using Cartesian vector notation.

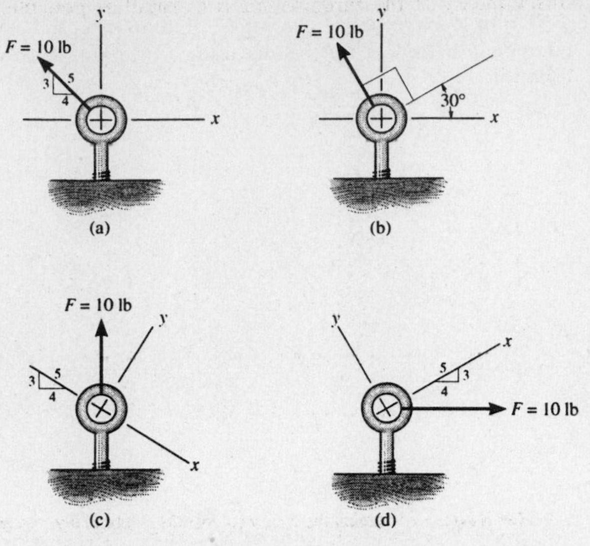

2-32

(a) $\mathbf{F} = -10\left(\frac{4}{5}\right)\mathbf{i} + 10\left(\frac{3}{5}\right)\mathbf{j}$

$= \{-8\,\mathbf{i} + 6\,\mathbf{j}\}$ lb **Ans**

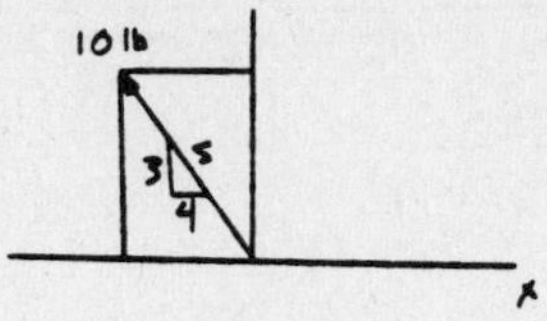

(b) $\mathbf{F} = -10 \sin 30°\,\mathbf{i} + 10 \cos 30°\,\mathbf{j}$

$= \{-5.00\,\mathbf{i} + 8.66\,\mathbf{j}\}$ lb **Ans**

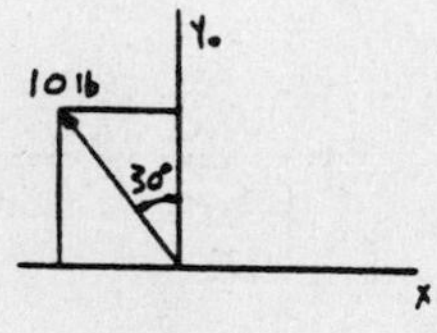

(c) $\mathbf{F} = -\frac{3}{5}(10)\,\mathbf{i} + \frac{4}{5}(10)\,\mathbf{j}$

$= \{-6\,\mathbf{i} + 8\,\mathbf{j}\}$ lb **Ans**

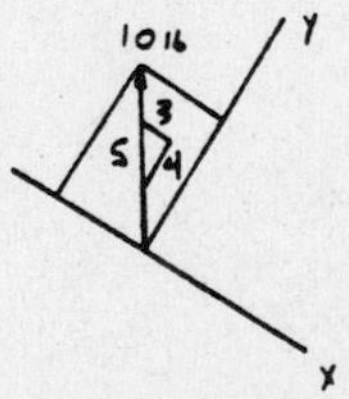

(d) $\mathbf{F} = \frac{4}{5}(10)\,\mathbf{i} - \frac{3}{5}(10)\,\mathbf{j}$

$= \{8\,\mathbf{i} - 6\,\mathbf{j}\}$ lb **Ans**

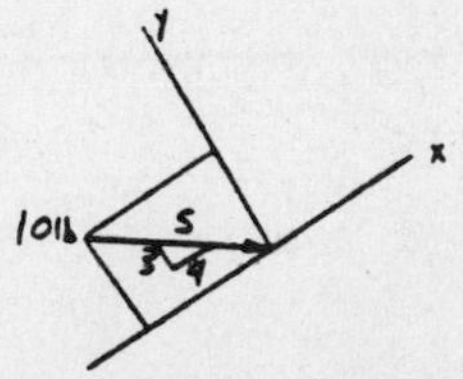

2-33. Determine the magnitude of force **F** so that the resultant $\mathbf{F}_R$ of the three forces is as small as possible.

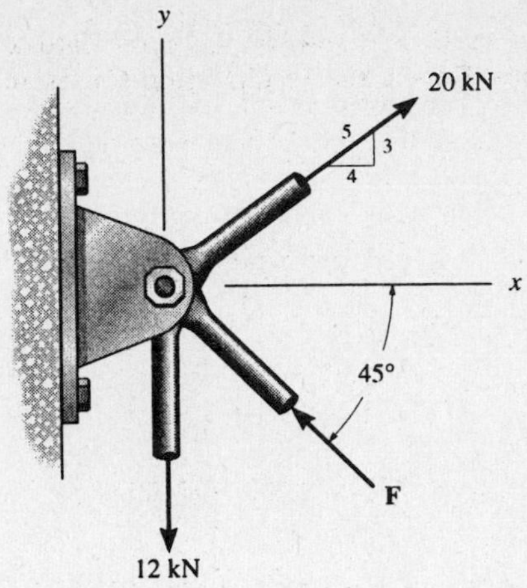

Scalar Notation : Suming the force components algebraically, we have

$$\xrightarrow{+} F_{R_x} = \Sigma F_x; \quad F_{R_x} = 20\left(\frac{4}{5}\right) - F\cos 45^\circ$$
$$= 16.0 - 0.7071F \rightarrow$$

$$+\uparrow F_{R_y} = \Sigma F_y; \quad F_{R_y} = 20\left(\frac{3}{5}\right) - 12 + F\sin 45^\circ$$
$$= 0.7071F \uparrow$$

The magnitude of the resultant force $\mathbf{F}_R$ is

$$F_R = \sqrt{F_{R_x}^2 + F_{R_y}^2}$$
$$= \sqrt{(16.0 - 0.7071F)^2 + (0.7071F)^2}$$
$$= \sqrt{F^2 - 22.63F + 256} \qquad [1]$$

$$F_R^2 = F^2 - 22.63F + 256$$
$$2F_R\frac{dF_R}{dF} = 2F - 22.63 \qquad [2]$$
$$\left(F_R\frac{d^2F_R}{dF^2} + \frac{dF_R}{dF} \times \frac{dF_R}{dF}\right) = 1 \qquad [3]$$

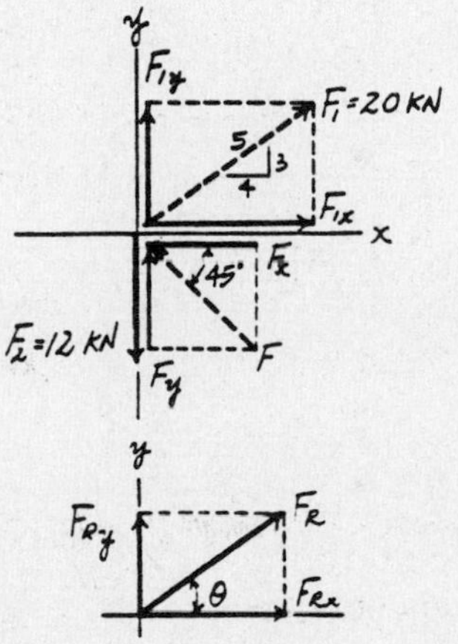

In order to obtain the *minimum* resultant force $\mathbf{F}_R$, $\frac{dF_R}{dF} = 0$. From Eq.[2]

$$2F_R\frac{dF_R}{dF} = 2F - 22.63 = 0$$

$$F = 11.31 \text{ kN} = 11.3 \text{ kN} \qquad \textbf{Ans}$$

Substitute $F = 11.31$ kN into Eq.[1], we have

$$F_R = \sqrt{11.31^2 - 22.63(11.31) + 256} = \sqrt{128} \text{ kN}$$

Substitute $F_R = \sqrt{128}$ kN with $\frac{dF_R}{dF} = 0$ into Eq.[3], we have

$$\left(\sqrt{128}\frac{d^2F_R}{dF^2} + 0\right) = 1$$
$$\frac{d^2F_R}{dF^2} = 0.0884 > 0$$

Hence, $F = 11.3$ kN is indeed producing a minimum resultant force.

2-34. The contact point between the femur and tibia bones of the leg is at A. If a vertical force of 175 lb is applied at this point, determine the components along the x and y axes. Note that the y component represents the normal force on the load-bearing region of the bones. Both the x and y components represent the force that causes synovial fluid to be squeezed out of the bearing space.

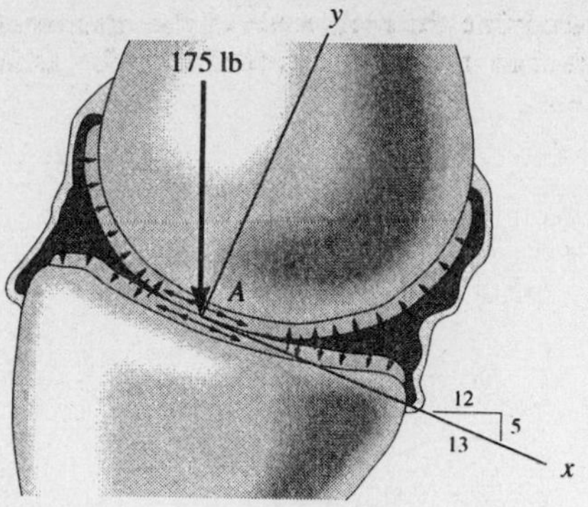

$$F_x = 175\left(\frac{5}{13}\right) = 67.3 \text{ lb} \qquad \textbf{Ans}$$

$$F_y = -175\left(\frac{12}{13}\right) = -162 \text{ lb} \qquad \textbf{Ans}$$

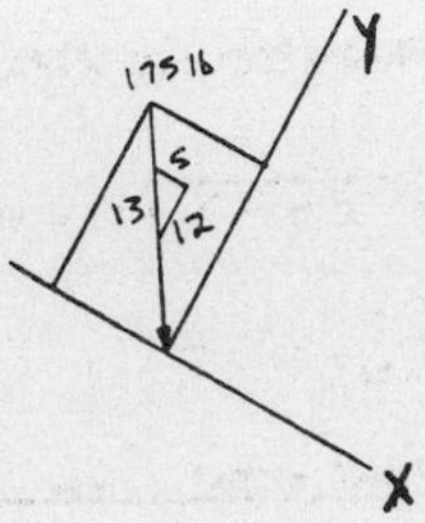

2-35. Express $\mathbf{F}_1$, $\mathbf{F}_2$, and $\mathbf{F}_3$ as Cartesian vectors.

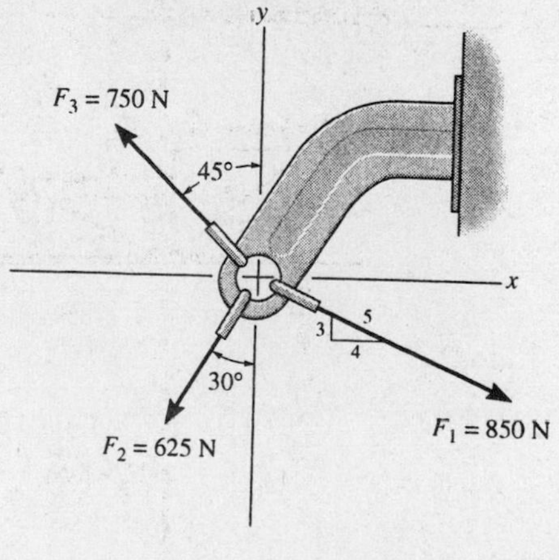

$$\mathbf{F}_1 = \frac{4}{5}(850)\,\mathbf{i} - \frac{3}{5}(850)\,\mathbf{j}$$

$$= \{680\,\mathbf{i} - 510\,\mathbf{j}\} \text{ N} \qquad \textbf{Ans}$$

$$\mathbf{F}_2 = -625 \sin 30^\circ\,\mathbf{i} - 625 \cos 30^\circ\,\mathbf{j}$$

$$= \{-312\,\mathbf{i} - 541\,\mathbf{j}\} \text{ N} \qquad \textbf{Ans}$$

$$\mathbf{F}_3 = -750 \sin 45^\circ\,\mathbf{i} + 750 \cos 45^\circ\,\mathbf{j}$$

$$= \{-530\,\mathbf{i} + 530\,\mathbf{j}\} \text{ N} \qquad \textbf{Ans}$$

***2-36.** Determine the magnitude of the resultant force and its direction measured counterclockwise from the positive x axis.

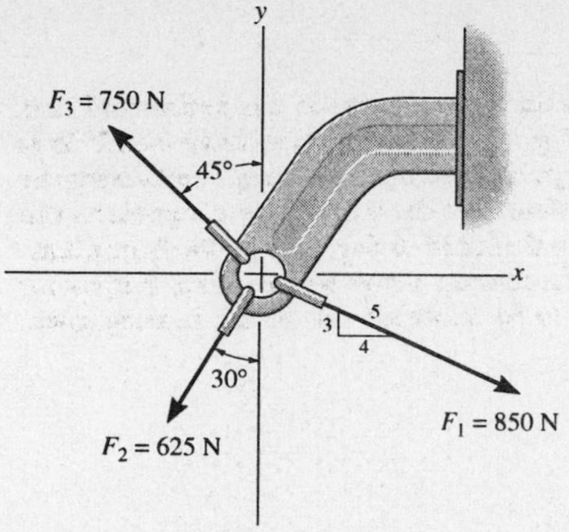

$\xrightarrow{+} F_{Rx} = \Sigma F_x;\quad F_{Rx} = \frac{4}{5}(850) - 625\sin 30° - 750\sin 45° = -162.83\text{ N}$

$+\uparrow F_{Ry} = \Sigma F_y;\quad F_{Ry} = -\frac{3}{5}(850) - 625\cos 30° + 750\cos 45° = -520.94\text{ N}$

$F_R = \sqrt{(-162.83)^2 + (-520.94)^2} = 546\text{ N}$ **Ans**

$\phi = \tan^{-1}\left(\frac{520.94}{162.83}\right) = 72.64°$

$\theta = 180° + 72.64° = 253°$ **Ans**

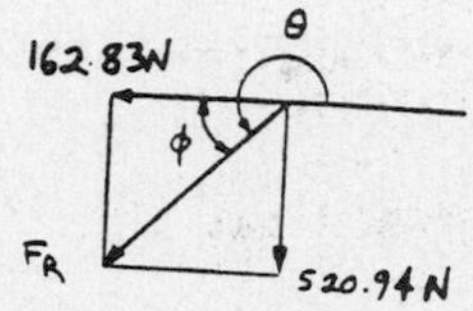

2-37. Determine the magnitude and direction θ of $\mathbf{F}_1$ so that the resultant force is directed vertically upward and has a magnitude of 800 N.

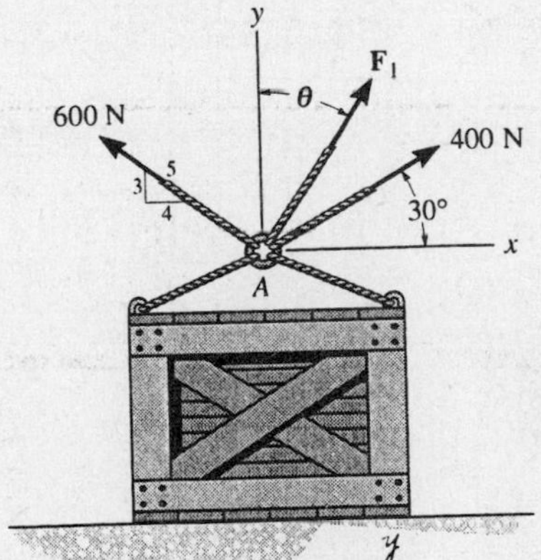

Scalar Notation : Suming the force components algebraically, we have

$\xrightarrow{+} F_{R_x} = \Sigma F_x;\quad F_{R_x} = 0 = F_1\sin\theta + 400\cos 30° - 600\left(\frac{4}{5}\right)$

$F_1 \sin\theta = 133.6 \quad [1]$

$+\uparrow F_{R_y} = \Sigma F_y;\quad F_{R_y} = 800 = F_1\cos\theta + 400\sin 30° + 600\left(\frac{3}{5}\right)$

$F_1\cos\theta = 240 \quad [2]$

Solving Eq.[1] and [2] yields

$\theta = 29.1°$ $\quad F_1 = 275\text{ N}$ **Ans**

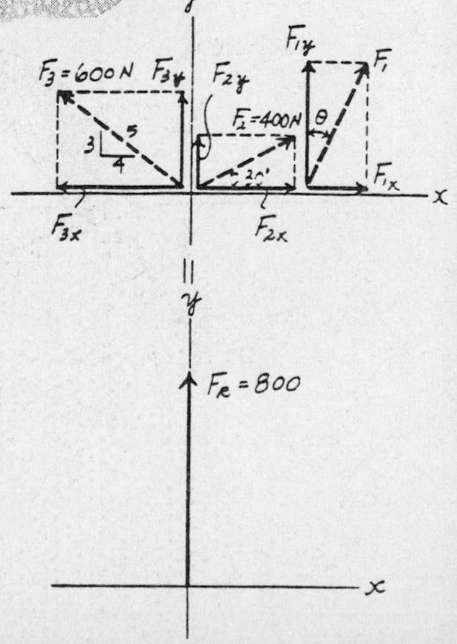

2-38. Determine the magnitude and direction measured counterclockwise from the positive x axis of the resultant force of the three forces acting on the ring A. Take $F_1 = 500$ N and $\theta = 20°$.

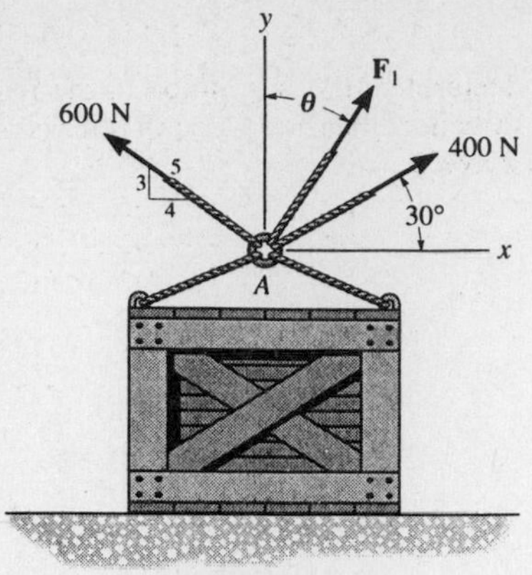

Scalar Notation : Suming the force components algebraically, we have

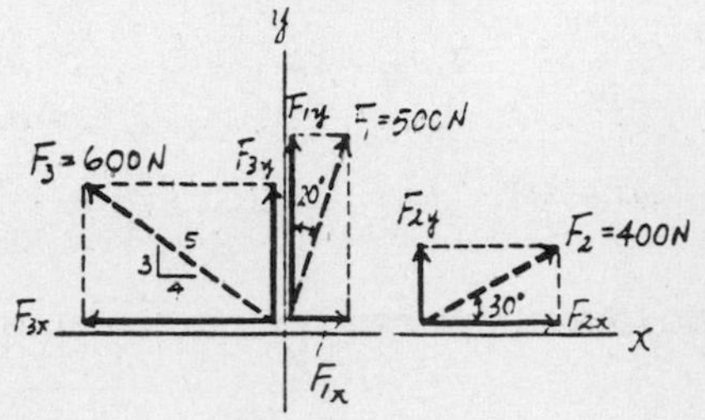

$$\xrightarrow{+} F_{R_x} = \Sigma F_x; \quad F_{R_x} = 500\sin 20° + 400\cos 30° - 600\left(\frac{4}{5}\right)$$
$$= 37.42 \text{ N} \rightarrow$$

$$+\uparrow F_{R_y} = \Sigma F_y; \quad F_{R_y} = 500\cos 20° + 400\sin 30° + 600\left(\frac{3}{5}\right)$$
$$= 1029.8 \text{ N} \uparrow$$

The magnitude of the resultant force $\mathbf{F}_R$ is

$$F_R = \sqrt{F_{R_x}^2 + F_{R_y}^2} = \sqrt{37.42^2 + 1029.8^2} = 1030.5 \text{ N} = 1.03 \text{ kN} \qquad \textbf{Ans}$$

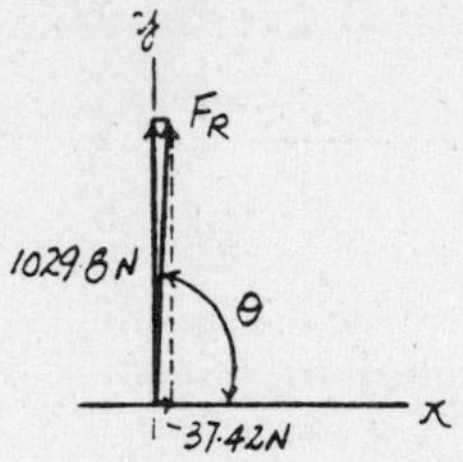

The directional angle θ measured counterclockwise from positive x axis is

$$\theta = \tan^{-1}\frac{F_{R_y}}{F_{R_x}} = \tan^{-1}\left(\frac{1029.8}{37.42}\right) = 87.9° \qquad \textbf{Ans}$$

2-39. Express $\mathbf{F}_1$ and $\mathbf{F}_2$ as Cartesian vectors.

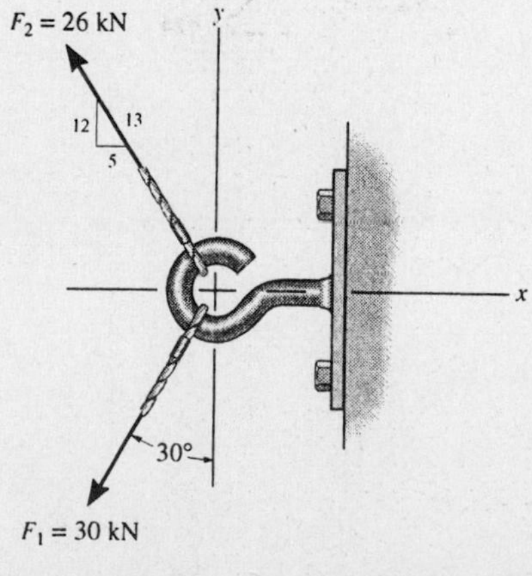

$$\mathbf{F}_1 = -30\sin 30°\,\mathbf{i} - 30\cos 30°\,\mathbf{j}$$
$$= \{-15.0\,\mathbf{i} - 26.0\,\mathbf{j}\} \text{ kN} \qquad \textbf{Ans}$$

$$\mathbf{F}_2 = -\frac{5}{13}(26)\,\mathbf{i} + \frac{12}{13}(26)\,\mathbf{j}$$
$$= \{-10.0\,\mathbf{i} + 24.0\,\mathbf{j}\} \text{ kN} \qquad \textbf{Ans}$$

***2-40.** Determine the magnitude of the resultant force and its direction measured counterclockwise from the positive x axis.

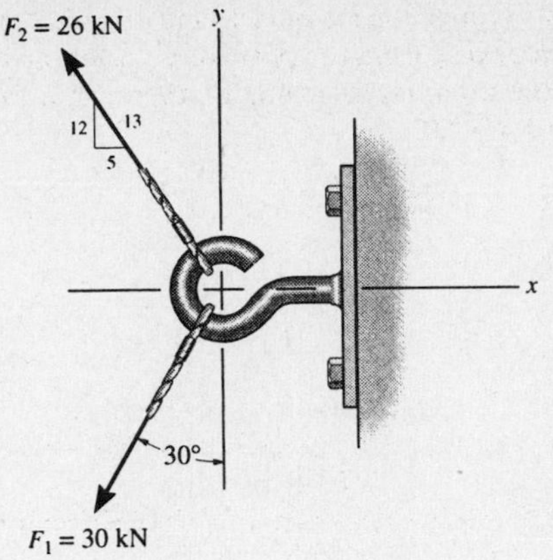

$\xrightarrow{+} F_{Rx} = \Sigma F_x;\quad F_{Rx} = -30\sin 30° - \frac{5}{13}(26) = -25$ kN

$+\uparrow F_{Ry} = \Sigma F_y;\quad F_{Ry} = -30\cos 30° + \frac{12}{13}(26) = -1.981$ kN

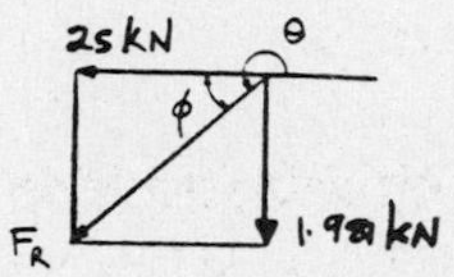

$F_R = \sqrt{(-25)^2 + (-1.981)^2} = 25.1$ kN **Ans**

$\phi = \tan^{-1}\left(\frac{1.981}{25}\right) = 4.53°$

$\theta = 180° + 4.53° = 185°$ **Ans**

2-41. Solve Prob. 2-1 by summing the rectangular or x, y components of the forces to obtain the resultant force.

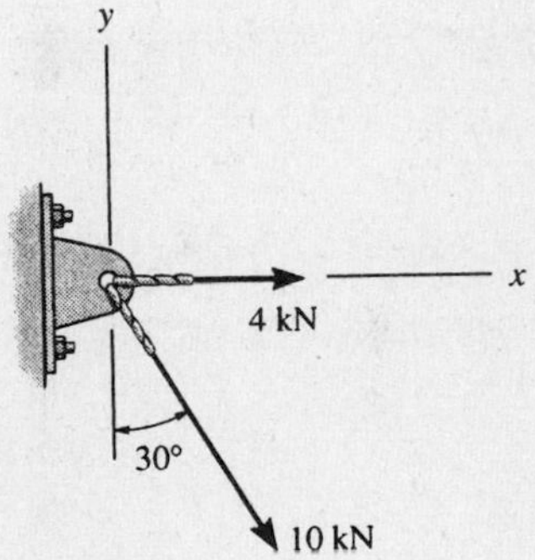

$\xrightarrow{+} F_{Rx} = \Sigma F_x;\quad F_{Rx} = 4 + 10\sin 30° = 9$ kN

$+\uparrow F_{Ry} = \Sigma F_y;\quad F_{Ry} = -10\cos 30° = -8.660$ kN

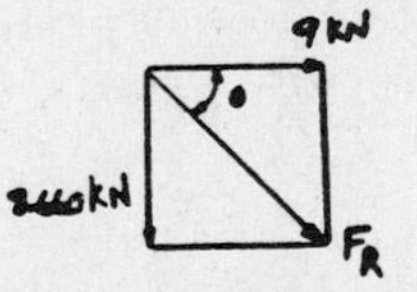

$F_R = \sqrt{(9)^2 + (-8.660)^2} = 12.5$ kN **Ans**

$\theta = \tan^{-1}\left(\frac{8.660}{9}\right) = 43.9°$ **Ans**

2-42. Solve Prob. 2-4 by summing the rectangular or x, y components of the forces to obtain the resultant force.

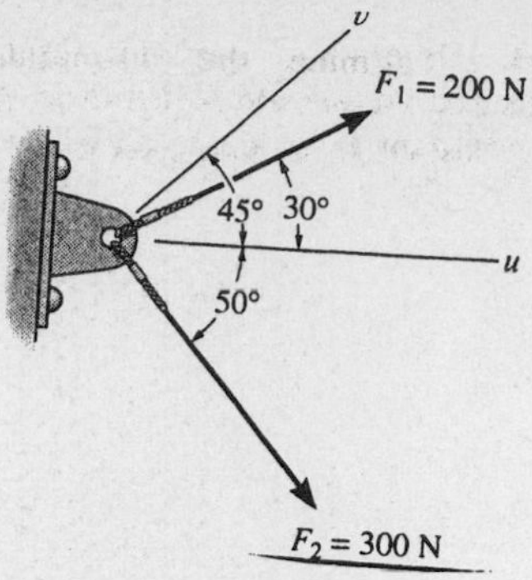

$\xrightarrow{+} F_{Rx} = \Sigma F_x;\quad F_{Rx} = 60 - 80 \sin 30° = 20$ lb

$+\uparrow F_{Ry} = \Sigma F_y;\quad F_{Ry} = 80 \cos 30° = 69.28$ lb

$F_R = \sqrt{(20)^2 + (69.28)^2} = 72.1$ lb **Ans**

$\theta = \tan^{-1}\left(\frac{69.28}{20}\right) = 73.9°$ **Ans**

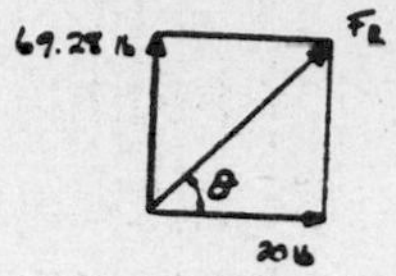

2-43. Determine the magnitude and orientation θ of $\mathbf{F}_B$ so that the resultant force is directed along the positive y axis and has a magnitude of 1500 N.

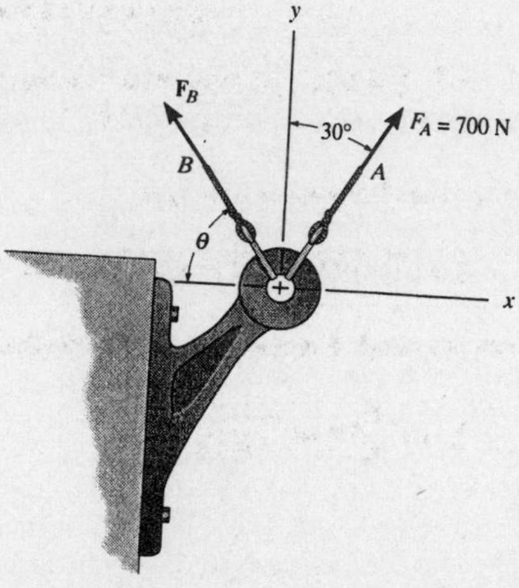

Scalar Notation : Suming the force components algebraically, we have

$\xrightarrow{+} F_{R_x} = \Sigma F_x;\quad 0 = 700 \sin 30° - F_B \cos \theta$

$F_B \cos \theta = 350$ [1]

$+\uparrow F_{R_y} = \Sigma F_y;\quad 1500 = 700 \cos 30° + F_B \sin \theta$

$F_B \sin \theta = 893.8$ [2]

Solving Eq. [1] and [2] yields

$\theta = 68.6°\quad F_B = 960$ N **Ans**

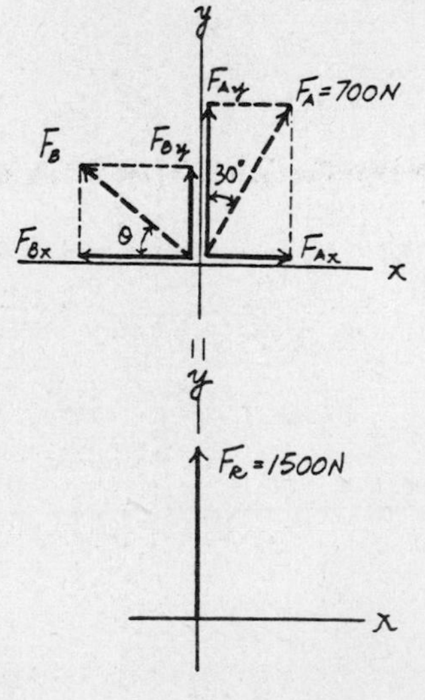

2-44. Determine the magnitude and orientation, measured counterclockwise from the positive y axis, of the resultant force acting on the bracket, if $F_B = 600$ N and $\theta = 20°$.

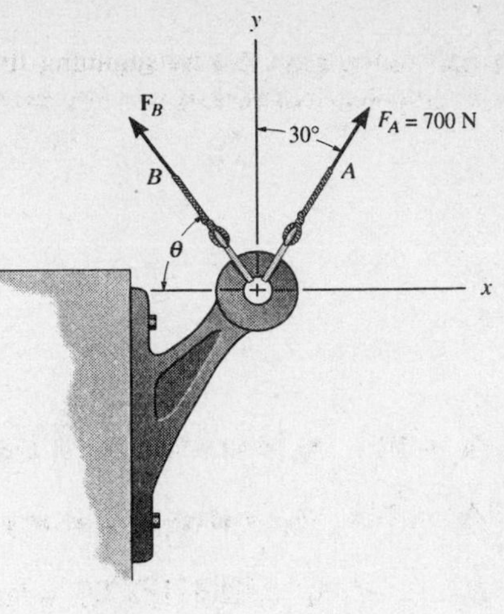

Scalar Notation **:** Suming the force components algebraically, we have

$$\xrightarrow{+} F_{R_x} = \Sigma F_x; \quad F_{R_x} = 700\sin 30° - 600\cos 20°$$
$$= -213.8 \text{ N} = 213.8 \text{ N} \leftarrow$$

$$+\uparrow F_{R_y} = \Sigma F_y; \quad F_{R_y} = 700\cos 30° + 600\sin 20°$$
$$= 811.4 \text{ N} \uparrow$$

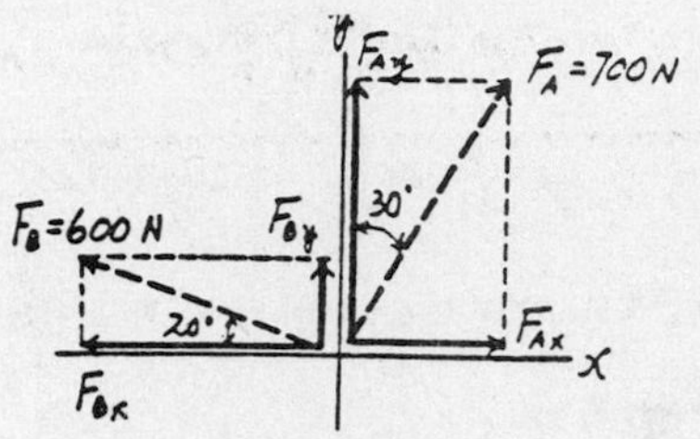

The magnitude of the resultant force $\mathbf{F}_R$ is

$$F_R = \sqrt{F_{R_x}^2 + F_{R_y}^2} = \sqrt{213.8^2 + 811.4^2} = 839 \text{ N} \qquad \textbf{Ans}$$

The directional angle θ measured counterclockwise from positive y axis is

$$\theta = \tan^{-1}\frac{F_{R_x}}{F_{R_y}} = \tan^{-1}\left(\frac{213.8}{811.4}\right) = 14.8° \qquad \textbf{Ans}$$

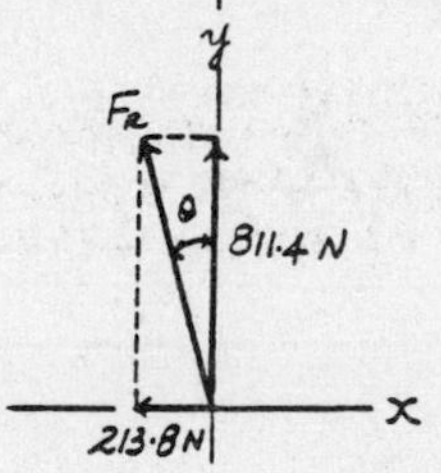

2-45. Express $\mathbf{F}_1$, $\mathbf{F}_2$, and $\mathbf{F}_3$ as Cartesian vectors.

$$\mathbf{F}_1 = \{15 \sin 40° \,\mathbf{i} + 15 \cos 40° \,\mathbf{j}\} \text{ kN} = \{9.64\mathbf{i} + 11.5\mathbf{j}\} \text{ kN} \qquad \textbf{Ans}$$

$$\mathbf{F}_2 = \left\{-\frac{12}{13}(26)\,\mathbf{i} + \frac{5}{13}(26)\,\mathbf{j}\right\} \text{kN} = \{-24\mathbf{i} + 10\mathbf{j}\} \text{ kN} \qquad \textbf{Ans}$$

$$\mathbf{F}_3 = \{36 \cos 30° \,\mathbf{i} - 36 \sin 30° \mathbf{j}\} \text{ kN} = \{31.2\mathbf{i} - 18\mathbf{j}\} \text{ kN} \qquad \textbf{Ans}$$

2-46. Determine the magnitude of the resultant force and its orientation measured counterclockwise from the positive x axis.

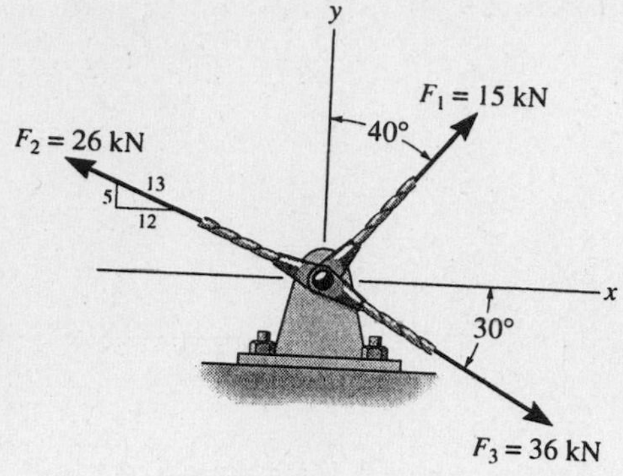

$\xrightarrow{+} F_{Rx} = \Sigma F_x;\quad F_{Rx} = 15 \sin 40° - \frac{12}{13}(26) + 36 \cos 30° = 16.82\text{ kN}$

$+\uparrow F_{Ry} = \Sigma F_y;\quad F_{Ry} = 15 \cos 40° + \frac{5}{13}(26) - 36 \sin 30° = 3.491\text{ kN}$

$F_R = \sqrt{(16.82)^2 + (3.491)^2} = 17.2\text{ kN}$ **Ans**

$\theta = \tan^{-1}\left(\frac{3.491}{16.82}\right) = 11.7°$ **Ans**

Also,

$\mathbf{F}_1 = \{15 \sin 40°\ \mathbf{i} + 15 \cos 40°\ \mathbf{j}\}\text{ kN} = \{9.64\mathbf{i} + 11.5\mathbf{j}\}\text{ kN}$

$\mathbf{F}_2 = \left\{-\frac{12}{13}(26)\mathbf{i} + \frac{5}{13}(26)\mathbf{j}\right\}\text{kN} = \{-24\mathbf{i} + 10\mathbf{j}\}\text{ kN}$

$\mathbf{F}_3 = \{36 \cos 30°\mathbf{i} - 36 \sin 30°\mathbf{j}\}\text{ kN} = \{31.2\mathbf{i} - 18\mathbf{j}\}\text{ kN}$

$\mathbf{F}_R = \mathbf{F}_1 + \mathbf{F}_2 + \mathbf{F}_3$

$= \{9.64\mathbf{i} + 11.5\mathbf{j}\} + \{-24\mathbf{i} + 10\mathbf{j}\} + \{31.2\mathbf{i} - 18\mathbf{j}\}$

$= \{16.8\mathbf{i} + 3.49\mathbf{j}\}\text{ kN}$

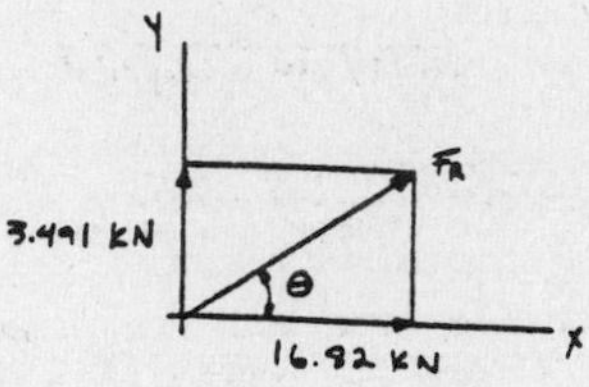

2-47. Express $\mathbf{F}_1$, $\mathbf{F}_2$, and $\mathbf{F}_3$ as Cartesian vectors.

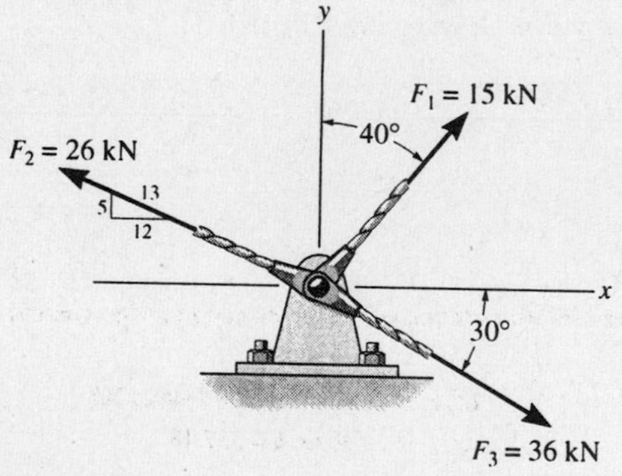

$\mathbf{F}_1 = \{-200\ \mathbf{i}\}\text{ lb}$ **Ans**

$\mathbf{F}_2 = -250 \sin 30°\ \mathbf{i} + 250 \cos 30°\ \mathbf{j}$

$= \{-125\ \mathbf{i} + 217\ \mathbf{j}\}\text{ lb}$ **Ans**

$\mathbf{F}_3 = 225 \cos 30°\ \mathbf{i} + 225 \sin 30°\ \mathbf{j}$

$= \{195\ \mathbf{i} + 112\ \mathbf{j}\}\text{ lb}$ **Ans**

***2-48.** Determine the magnitude of the resultant force and its direction measured counterclockwise from the positive x axis.

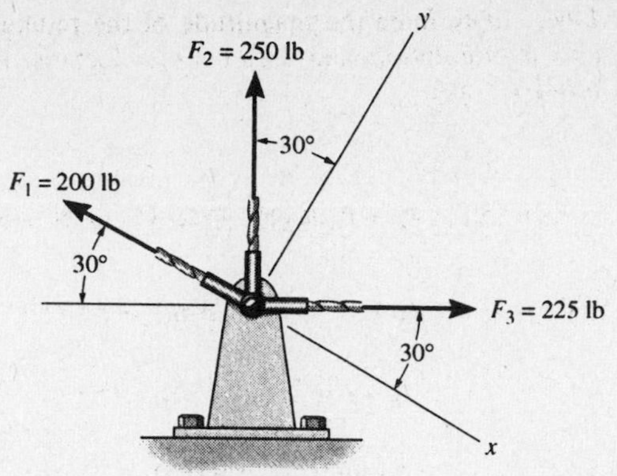

$\searrow^{+} F_{Rx} = \Sigma F_x;\quad F_{Rx} = -200 - 250\sin 30° + 225\cos 30° = -130.14$ lb

$+\nearrow F_{Ry} = \Sigma F_y;\quad F_{Ry} = 250\cos 30° + 225\sin 30° = 329.01$ lb

$F_R = \sqrt{(-130.14)^2 + (329.01)^2} = 354$ lb **Ans**

$\phi = \tan^{-1}\left(\frac{329.01}{130.14}\right) = 68.4°$

$\theta = 180° - 68.4° = 112°$ **Ans**

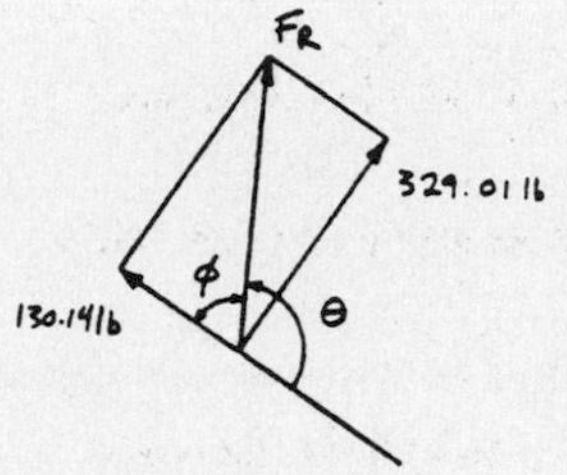

2-49. Determine the magnitude and direction θ of $\mathbf{F}_A$ so that the resultant force is directed along the positive x axis and has a magnitude of 1250 N.

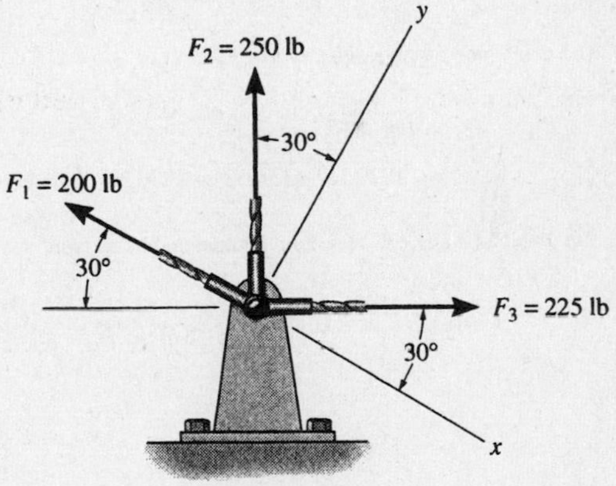

Scalar Notation : Suming the force components algebraically, we have

$\xrightarrow{+} F_{R_x} = \Sigma F_x;\quad 1250 = F_A \sin\theta + 800\cos 30°$

$F_A \sin\theta = 557.18$ [1]

$+\uparrow F_{R_y} = \Sigma F_y;\quad 0 = F_A\cos\theta - 800\sin 30°$

$F_A\cos\theta = 400$ [2]

Solving Eq. [1] and [2] yields

$\theta = 54.3°\quad F_A = 686$ N **Ans**

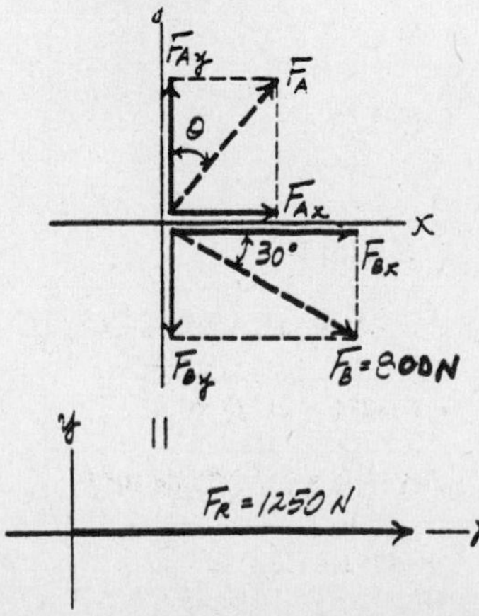

2-50. Determine the magnitude and direction, measured counterclockwise from the positive x axis, of the resultant force acting on the ring at O, if $F_A = 750$ N and $\theta = 45°$.

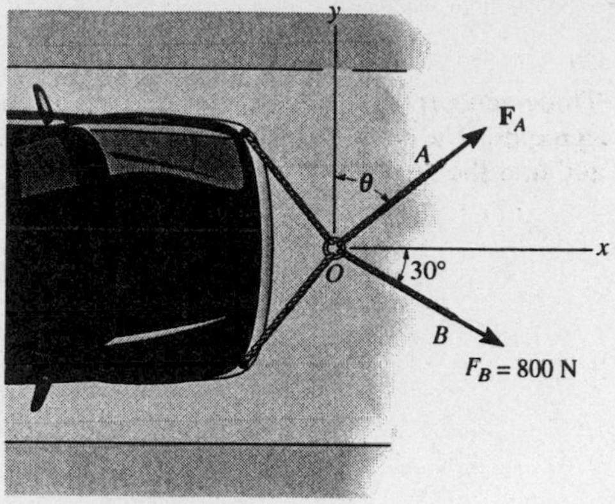

Scalar Notation : Suming the force components algebraically, we have

$$\overset{+}{\rightarrow} F_{R_x} = \Sigma F_x; \quad F_{R_x} = 750\sin 45° + 800\cos 30° = 1223.15 \text{ N} \rightarrow$$

$$+\uparrow F_{R_y} = \Sigma F_y; \quad F_{R_y} = 750\cos 45° - 800\sin 30° = 130.33 \text{ N} \uparrow$$

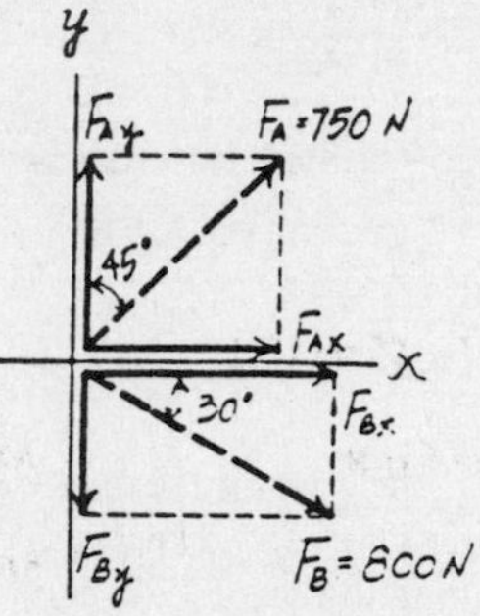

The magnitude of the resultant force $\mathbf{F}_R$ is

$$F_R = \sqrt{F_{R_x}^2 + F_{R_y}^2} = \sqrt{1223.15^2 + 130.33^2} = 1230 \text{ N} = 1.23 \text{ kN} \qquad \textbf{Ans}$$

The directional angle θ measured counterclockwise from positive x axis is

$$\theta = \tan^{-1}\frac{F_{R_y}}{F_{R_x}} = \tan^{-1}\left(\frac{130.33}{1223.15}\right) = 6.08° \qquad \textbf{Ans}$$

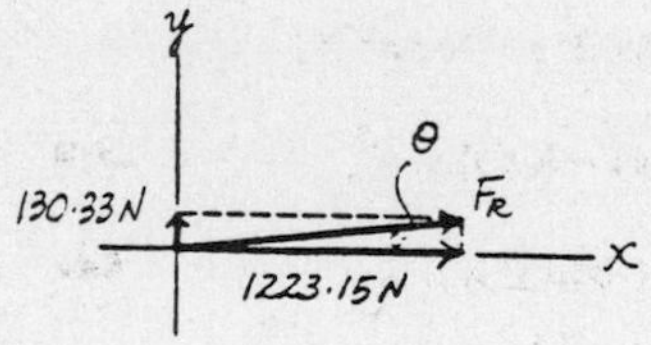

2-51. Three concurrent forces act on the ring. If each has a magnitude of 80 N, express each force as a Cartesian vector and find the resultant force.

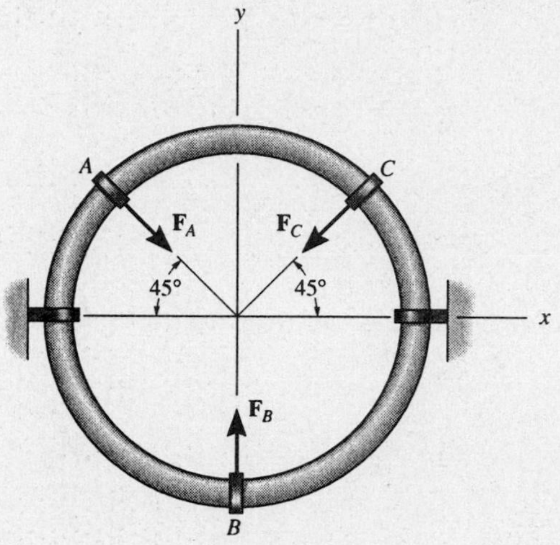

$F_A = 80 \cos 45° \, \mathbf{i} - 80 \sin 45° \, \mathbf{j}$

$= \{56.6 \, \mathbf{i} - 56.6 \, \mathbf{j}\}$ N **Ans**

$F_B = \{80 \, \mathbf{j}\}$ N **Ans**

$F_C = -80 \cos 45° \, \mathbf{i} - 80 \sin 45° \, \mathbf{j}$

$= \{-56.6 \, \mathbf{i} - 56.6 \, \mathbf{j}\}$ N **Ans**

$\Sigma F = F_R = \{-33.1 \, \mathbf{j}\}$ N **Ans**

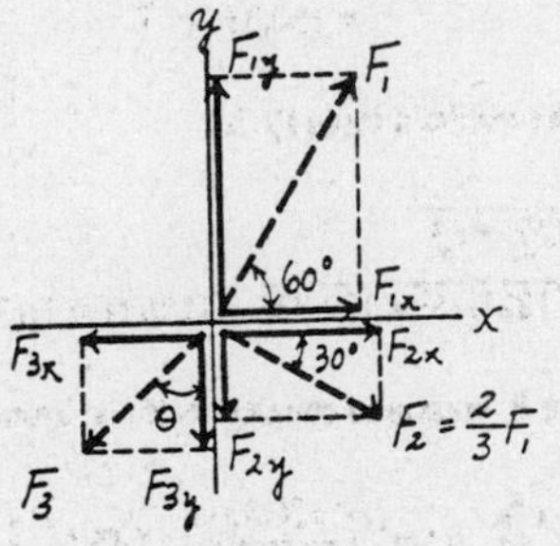

***2-52.** The three concurrent forces acting on the screw eye produce a resultant force $\mathbf{F}_R = 0$. If $F_2 = \frac{2}{3}F_1$ and $\mathbf{F}_1$ is to be 90° from $\mathbf{F}_2$ as shown, determine the required magnitude of $\mathbf{F}_3$ expressed in terms of F_1 and the angle θ.

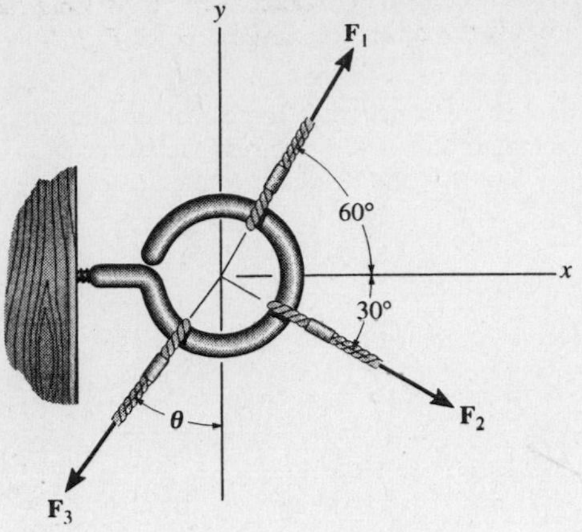

Cartesian Vector Notation :

$$\mathbf{F}_1 = F_1 \cos 60°\mathbf{i} + F_1 \sin 60°\mathbf{j}$$
$$= 0.50F_1\mathbf{i} + 0.8660F_1\mathbf{j}$$

$$\mathbf{F}_2 = \frac{2}{3}F_1 \cos 30°\mathbf{i} - \frac{2}{3}F_1 \sin 30°\mathbf{j}$$
$$= 0.5774F_1\mathbf{i} - 0.3333F_1\mathbf{j}$$

$$\mathbf{F}_3 = -F_3 \sin \theta\mathbf{i} - F_3 \cos \theta\mathbf{j}$$

Resultant Force :

$$\mathbf{F}_R = \mathbf{0} = \mathbf{F}_1 + \mathbf{F}_2 + \mathbf{F}_3$$
$$\mathbf{0} = (0.50F_1 + 0.5774F_1 - F_3 \sin \theta)\mathbf{i} + (0.8660F_1 - 0.3333F_1 - F_3 \cos \theta)\mathbf{j}$$

Equating **i** and **j** components, we have

$$0.50F_1 + 0.5774F_1 - F_3 \sin \theta = 0 \qquad [1]$$

$$0.8660F_1 - 0.3333F_1 - F_3 \cos \theta = 0 \qquad [2]$$

Solving Eq. [1] and [2] yields

$$\theta = 63.7° \qquad F_3 = 1.20F_1 \qquad \textbf{Ans}$$

2-53. Determine the magnitude of force **F** so that the resultant $\mathbf{F}_R$ of the three forces is as small as possible. What is the minimum magnitude of $\mathbf{F}_R$?

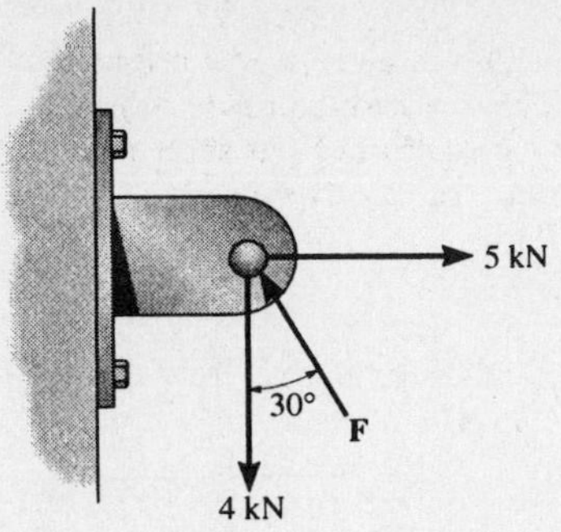

Scalar Notation : Suming the force components algebraically, we have

$$\xrightarrow{+} F_{R_x} = \Sigma F_x; \quad F_{R_x} = 5 - F\sin 30^\circ$$
$$= 5 - 0.50F \rightarrow$$

$$+\uparrow F_{R_y} = \Sigma F_y; \quad F_{R_y} = F\cos 30^\circ - 4$$
$$= 0.8660F - 4 \uparrow$$

The magnitude of the resultant force $\mathbf{F}_R$ is

$$F_R = \sqrt{F_{R_x}^2 + F_{R_y}^2}$$
$$= \sqrt{(5-0.50F)^2 + (0.8660F-4)^2}$$
$$= \sqrt{F^2 - 11.93F + 41} \qquad [1]$$

$$F_R^2 = F^2 - 11.93F + 41$$
$$2F_R\frac{dF_R}{dF} = 2F - 11.93 \qquad [2]$$
$$\left(F_R\frac{d^2F_R}{dF^2} + \frac{dF_R}{dF}\times\frac{dF_R}{dF}\right) = 1 \qquad [3]$$

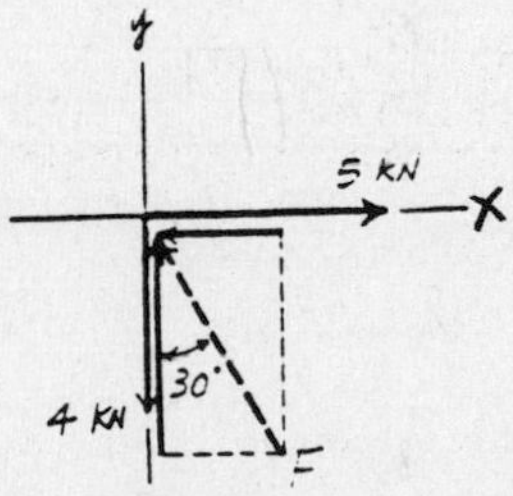

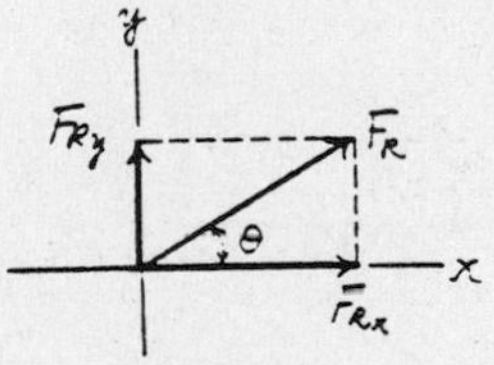

In order to obtain the *minimum* resultant force $\mathbf{F}_R$, $\frac{dF_R}{dF} = 0$. From Eq.[2]

$$2F_R\frac{dF_R}{dF} = 2F - 11.93 = 0$$

$$F = 5.964 \text{ kN} = 5.96 \text{ kN} \qquad \textbf{Ans}$$

Substituting $F = 5.964$ kN into Eq.[1], we have

$$F_R = \sqrt{5.964^2 - 11.93(5.964) + 41}$$
$$= 2.330 \text{ kN} = 2.33 \text{ kN} \qquad \textbf{Ans}$$

Substituting $F_R = 2.330$ kN with $\frac{dF_R}{dF} = 0$ into Eq.[3], we have

$$\left[(2.330)\frac{d^2F_R}{dF^2} + 0\right] = 1$$
$$\frac{d^2F_R}{dF^2} = 0.429 > 0$$

Hence, $F = 5.96$ kN is indeed producing a minimum resultant force.

2-54. The three cable forces act on the eyebolt. Determine two possible magnitudes for **P** so that the resultant force has a magnitude of 800 lb.

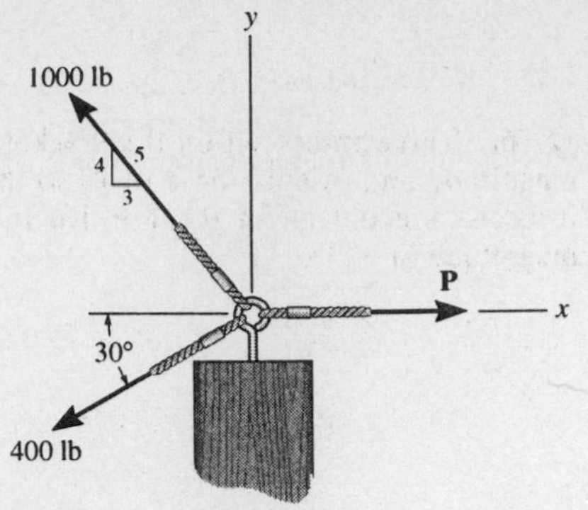

$\xrightarrow{+} F_{Rx} = \Sigma F_x;\quad F_{Rx} = P - 400\cos 30° - 1000\left(\frac{3}{5}\right) = P - 946.41$

$+\uparrow F_{Ry} = \Sigma F_y;\quad F_{Ry} = 1000\left(\frac{4}{5}\right) - 400\sin 30° = 600$

$$F_R = \sqrt{(P - 946.41)^2 + (600)^2} = 800$$

$$(P - 946.41)^2 + (600)^2 = (800)^2$$

$$(P - 946.41)^2 = 280\,000$$

$$P - 946.41 = \pm 529.15$$

$P - 946.41 = 529.15;\quad P = 1475.6 \text{ lb} = 1.48 \text{ kip}$ **Ans**

$P - 946.41 = -529.15;\quad P = 417 \text{ lb}$ **Ans**

2-55. The three forces are applied to the bracket. Determine the range of values for the magnitude of force **P** so that the resultant of the three forces does not exceed 2400 N.

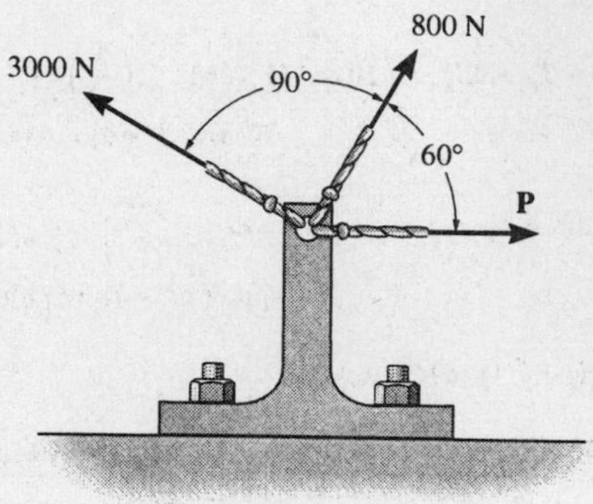

$\rightarrow F_{Rx} = \Sigma F_x;\quad F_{Rx} = P + 800\cos 60° - 3000\cos 30° = P - 2198.08$

$+\uparrow F_{Ry} = \Sigma F_y;\quad F_{Ry} = 800\sin 60° + 3000\sin 30° = 2192.82$

$$F_R = \sqrt{(P - 2198.08)^2 + (2192.82)^2} \le 2400$$

$$(P - 2198.08)^2 + (2192.82)^2 \le (2400)^2$$

$$|(P - 2198.08)| \le 975.47$$

$$-975.47 \le P - 2198.08 \le 975.47$$

$$1222.6 \text{ N} \le P \le 3173.5 \text{ N}$$

$1.22 \text{ kN} \le P \le 3.17 \text{ kN}$ **Ans**

***2-56.** Three forces act on the bracket. Determine the magnitude and orientation θ of $\mathbf{F}_2$ so that the resultant force is directed along the positive u axis and has a magnitude of 50 lb.

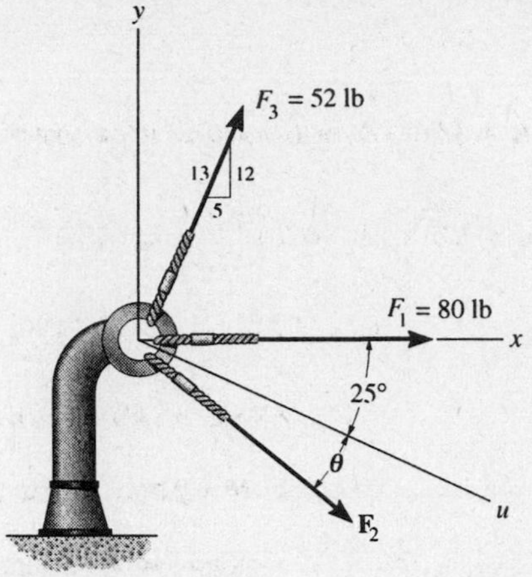

Scalar Notation : Suming the force components algebraically, we have

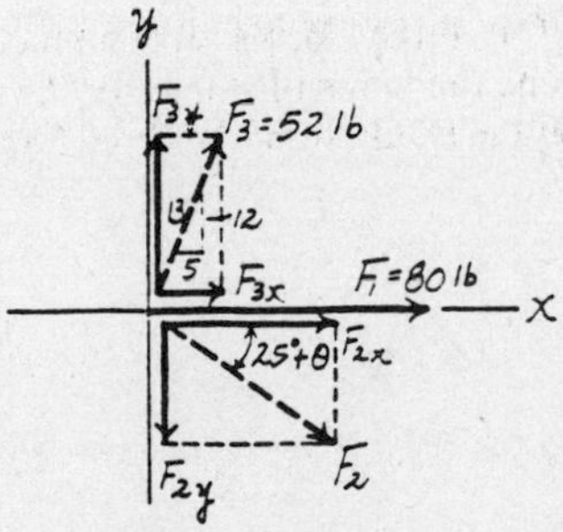

$$\xrightarrow{+} F_{R_x} = \Sigma F_x; \quad 50\cos 25° = 80 + 52\left(\frac{5}{13}\right) + F_2\cos(25° + \theta)$$

$$F_2\cos(25° + \theta) = -54.684 \qquad [1]$$

$$+\uparrow F_{R_y} = \Sigma F_y; \quad -50\sin 25° = 52\left(\frac{12}{13}\right) - F_2\sin(25° + \theta)$$

$$F_2\sin(25° + \theta) = 69.131 \qquad [2]$$

Solving Eq. [1] and [2] yields

$25° + \theta = 128.35°$ $\quad\theta = 103°$ $\quad$ **Ans**

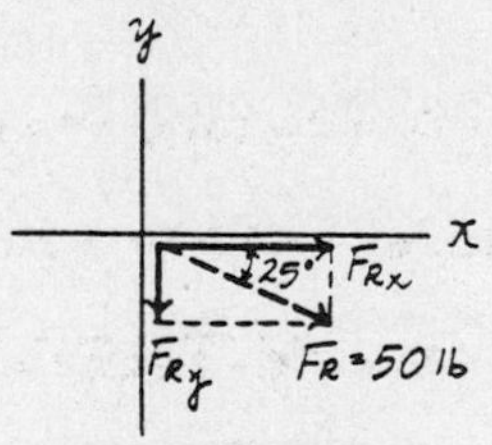

$F_2 = 88.1$ lb $\quad$ **Ans**

***2-57.** If $F_2 = 150$ lb and $\theta = 55°$, determine the magnitude and orientation, measured clockwise from the positive x axis, of the resultant force of the three forces acting on the bracket.

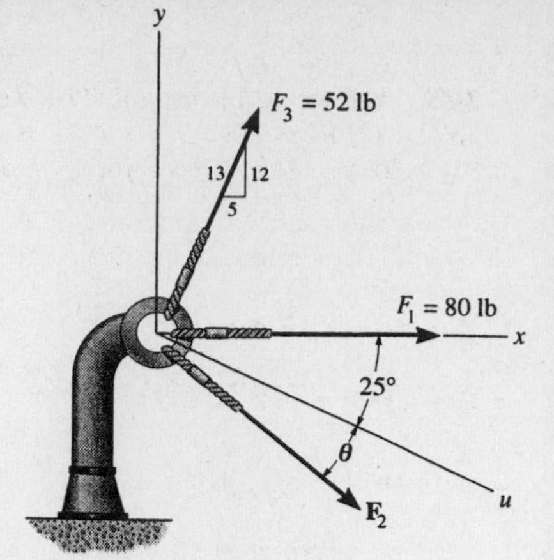

Scalar Notation : Suming the force components algebraically, we have

$$\xrightarrow{+} F_{R_x} = \Sigma F_x; \quad F_{R_x} = 80 + 52\left(\frac{5}{13}\right) + 150\cos 80°$$
$$= 126.05 \text{ lb} \rightarrow$$

$$+\uparrow F_{R_y} = \Sigma F_y; \quad F_{R_y} = 52\left(\frac{12}{13}\right) - 150\sin 80°$$
$$= -99.72 \text{ lb} = 99.72 \text{ lb} \downarrow$$

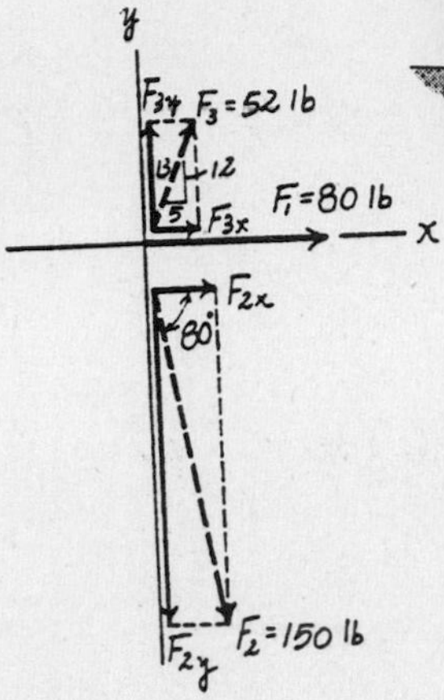

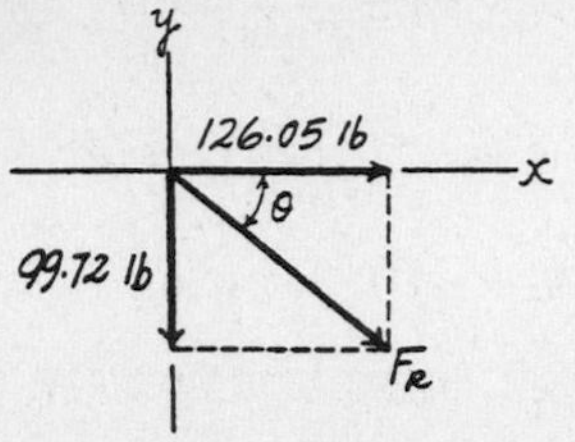

The magnitude of the resultant force $\mathbf{F}_R$ is

$$F_R = \sqrt{F_{R_x}^2 + F_{R_y}^2} = \sqrt{126.05^2 + 99.72^2} = 161 \text{ lb} \qquad \textbf{Ans}$$

The directional angle θ measured clockwise from positive x axis is

$$\theta = \tan^{-1}\frac{F_{R_y}}{F_{R_x}} = \tan^{-1}\left(\frac{99.72}{126.05}\right) = 38.3° \qquad \textbf{Ans}$$

2-58. Determine the magnitude of force **F** so that the resultant force of the three forces is as small as possible. What is the magnitude of the resultant force?

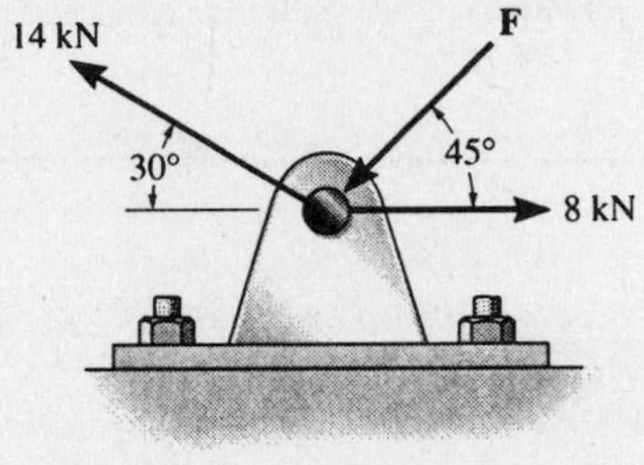

$$\xrightarrow{+} F_{Rx} = \Sigma F_x; \quad F_{Rx} = 8 - F\cos 45° - 14\cos 30°$$
$$= -4.1244 - F\cos 45°$$

$$+\uparrow F_{Ry} = \Sigma F_y; \quad F_{Ry} = -F\sin 45° + 14\sin 30°$$
$$= 7 - F\sin 45°$$

$$F_R^2 = (-4.1244 - F\cos 45°)^2 + (7 - F\sin 45°)^2 \qquad (1)$$

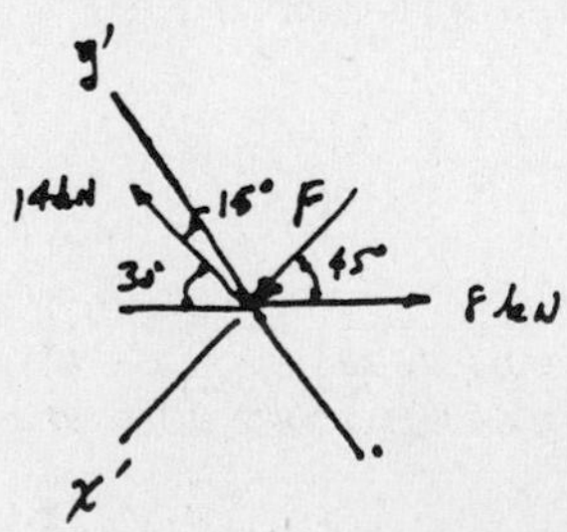

$$2F_R\frac{dF_R}{dF} = 2(-4.1244 - F\cos 45°)(-\cos 45°) + 2(7 - F\sin 45°)(-\sin 45°) = 0$$

$$F = 2.03 \text{ kN} \qquad \textbf{Ans}$$

From Eq. (1); $\quad F_R = 7.87$ kN $\quad$ **Ans**

Also, from the figure require

$$(F_R)_{x'} = 0 = \Sigma F_{x'}; \quad F + 14\sin 15° - 8\cos 45° = 0$$

$$F = 2.03 \text{ kN} \qquad \textbf{Ans}$$

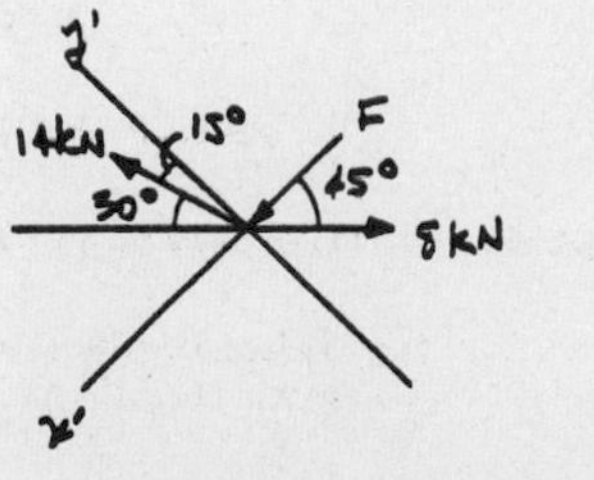

$$(F_R)_{y'} = \Sigma F_{y'}; \quad F_R = 14\cos 15° - 8\sin 45°$$

$$F_R = 7.87 \text{ kN} \qquad \textbf{Ans}$$

2-59. Determine the magnitude and coordinate direction angles of $\mathbf{F}_1 = \{60\mathbf{i} - 50\mathbf{j} + 40\mathbf{k}\}$ N and $\mathbf{F}_2 = \{-40\mathbf{i} - 85\mathbf{j} + 30\mathbf{k}\}$ N. Sketch each force on an x, y, z reference.

$$\mathbf{F}_1 = 60\mathbf{i} - 50\mathbf{j} + 40\mathbf{k}$$

$$F_1 = \sqrt{(60)^2 + (-50)^2 + (40)^2} = 87.750 = 87.7 \text{ N} \quad \textbf{Ans}$$

$$\alpha_1 = \cos^{-1}\left(\frac{60}{87.750}\right) = 46.9° \quad \textbf{Ans}$$

$$\beta_1 = \cos^{-1}\left(\frac{-50}{87.750}\right) = 125° \quad \textbf{Ans}$$

$$\gamma_1 = \cos^{-1}\left(\frac{40}{87.750}\right) = 62.9° \quad \textbf{Ans}$$

$$\mathbf{F}_2 = -40\mathbf{i} - 85\mathbf{j} + 30\mathbf{k}$$

$$F_2 = \sqrt{(-40)^2 + (-85)^2 + (30)^2} = 98.615 = 98.6 \text{ N} \quad \textbf{Ans}$$

$$\alpha_2 = \cos^{-1}\left(\frac{-40}{98.615}\right) = 114° \quad \textbf{Ans}$$

$$\beta_2 = \cos^{-1}\left(\frac{-85}{98.615}\right) = 150° \quad \textbf{Ans}$$

$$\gamma_2 = \cos^{-1}\left(\frac{30}{98.615}\right) = 72.3° \quad \textbf{Ans}$$

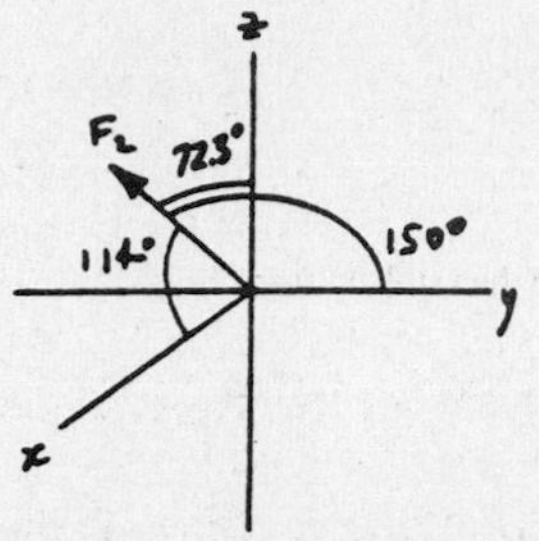

***2-60.** The cable at the end of the crane boom exerts a force of 250 lb on the boom as shown. Express **F** as a Cartesian vector.

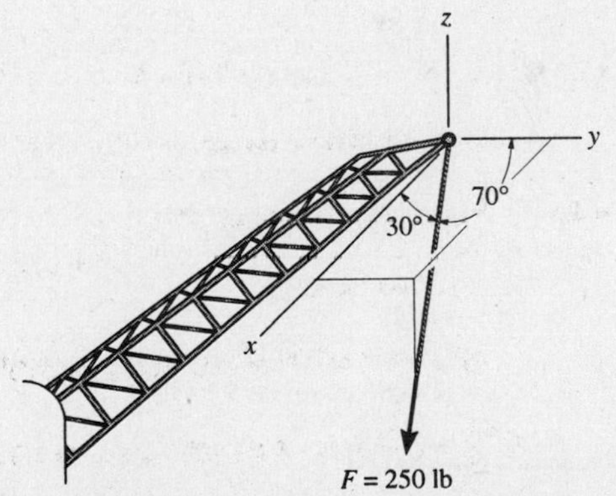

Cartesian Vector Notation : With $\alpha = 30°$ and $\beta = 70°$, the third coordinate direction angle γ can be determined using Eq. 2 – 10.

$$\cos^2\alpha + \cos^2\beta + \cos^2\gamma = 1$$
$$\cos^2 30° + \cos^2 70° + \cos^2\gamma = 1$$
$$\cos\gamma = \pm 0.3647$$

$$\gamma = 68.61° \text{ or } 111.39°$$

By inspection, $\gamma = 111.39°$ since the force **F** is directed in negative octant.

$$\mathbf{F} = 250\{\cos 30°\mathbf{i} + \cos 70°\mathbf{j} + \cos 111.39°\} \text{ lb}$$
$$= \{217\mathbf{i} + 85.5\mathbf{j} - 91.2\mathbf{k}\} \text{ lb} \quad \textbf{Ans}$$

2-61. Express each force in Cartesian vector form.

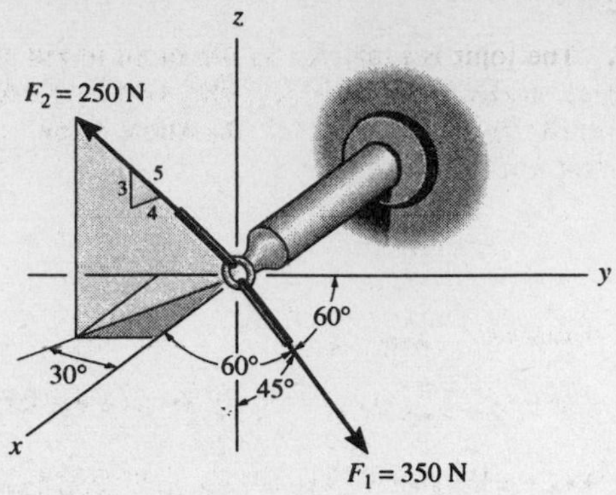

$$\mathbf{F}_1 = 350\cos 60°\,\mathbf{i} + 350\cos 60°\,\mathbf{j} + 350\cos 135°\,\mathbf{k}$$

$$= \{175\,\mathbf{i} + 175\,\mathbf{j} - 247\,\mathbf{k}\}\text{ N} \qquad \textbf{Ans}$$

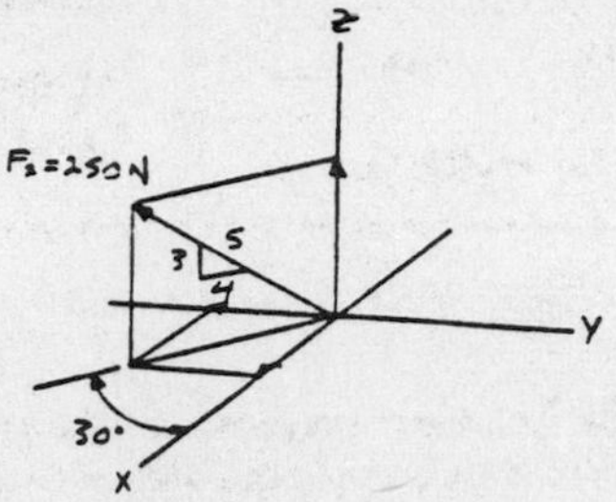

$$\mathbf{F}_2 = 250\left(\frac{4}{5}\right)\cos 30°\,\mathbf{i} - 250\left(\frac{4}{5}\right)\sin 30°\,\mathbf{j} + 250\left(\frac{3}{5}\right)\mathbf{k}$$

$$= \{173\,\mathbf{i} - 100\,\mathbf{j} + 150\,\mathbf{k}\}\text{ N} \qquad \textbf{Ans}$$

2-62. Determine the magnitude and the coordinate direction angles of the resultant force.

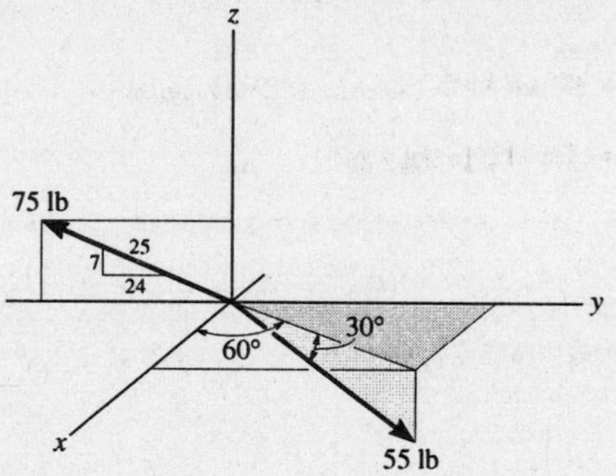

Cartesian Vector Notation :

$$\mathbf{F}_1 = 75\left\{-\frac{24}{25}\mathbf{j} + \frac{7}{25}\mathbf{k}\right\}\text{ lb} = \{-72.0\mathbf{j} + 21.0\mathbf{k}\}\text{ lb}$$

$$\mathbf{F}_2 = 55\{\cos 30°\cos 60°\mathbf{i} + \cos 30°\sin 60°\mathbf{j} - \sin 30°\mathbf{k}\}\text{ lb}$$
$$= \{23.82\mathbf{i} + 41.25\mathbf{j} - 27.5\mathbf{k}\}\text{ lb}$$

Resultant Force :

$$\mathbf{F}_R = \mathbf{F}_1 + \mathbf{F}_2$$
$$= \{23.82\mathbf{i} + (-72.0 + 41.25)\mathbf{j} + (21.0 - 27.5)\mathbf{k}\}\text{ lb}$$
$$= \{23.82\mathbf{i} - 30.75\mathbf{j} - 6.50\mathbf{k}\}\text{ lb}$$

The magnitude of the resultant force is

$$F_R = \sqrt{F_{R_x}^2 + F_{R_y}^2 + F_{R_z}^2}$$
$$= \sqrt{23.82^2 + (-30.75)^2 + (-6.50)^2}$$
$$= 39.43\text{ lb} = 39.4\text{ lb} \qquad \textbf{Ans}$$

The coordinate direction angles are

$$\cos\alpha = \frac{F_{R_x}}{F_R} = \frac{23.82}{39.43} \qquad \alpha = 52.8° \qquad \textbf{Ans}$$

$$\cos\beta = \frac{F_{R_y}}{F_R} = \frac{-30.75}{39.43} \qquad \beta = 141° \qquad \textbf{Ans}$$

$$\cos\gamma = \frac{F_{R_z}}{F_R} = \frac{-6.50}{39.43} \qquad \gamma = 99.5° \qquad \textbf{Ans}$$

2-63. The joint is subjected to the three forces shown. Express each force in Cartesian vector form and determine the magnitude and direction angles of the resultant force.

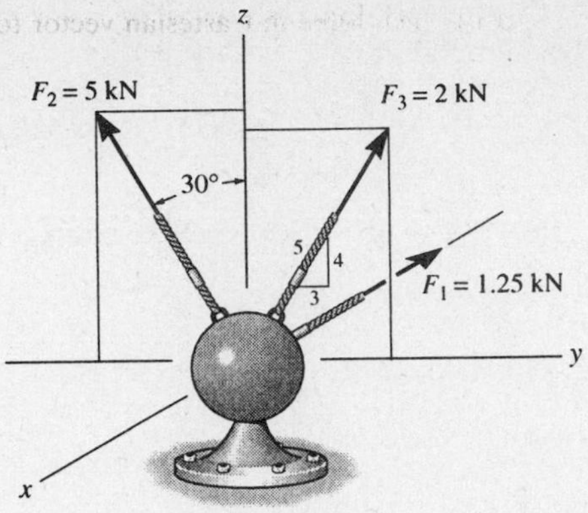

$\mathbf{F}_1 = \{-1.25\,\mathbf{i}\}$ kN **Ans**

$\mathbf{F}_2 = -5\sin 30°\,\mathbf{j} + 5\cos 30°\,\mathbf{k}$

$= \{-2.5\,\mathbf{j} + 4.33\,\mathbf{k}\}$ kN **Ans**

$\mathbf{F}_3 = \frac{3}{5}(2)\,\mathbf{j} + \frac{4}{5}(2)\,\mathbf{k}$

$\mathbf{F}_3 = \{1.2\mathbf{j} + 1.6\mathbf{k}\}$ kN **Ans**

$\mathbf{F}_R = \Sigma\mathbf{F} = \{-1.25\mathbf{i} - 1.3\mathbf{j} + 5.930\mathbf{k}\}$ kN

$F_R = 6.198 = 6.20$ kN **Ans**

$\alpha = \cos^{-1}\left(\frac{-1.25}{6.198}\right) = 102°$ **Ans**

$\beta = \cos^{-1}\left(\frac{-1.3}{6.198}\right) = 102°$ **Ans**

$\gamma = \cos^{-1}\left(\frac{5.930}{6.198}\right) = 16.9°$ **Ans**

***2-64.** The spur gears are subjected to the two forces, caused by contact with other gears. Express each force as a Cartesian vector.

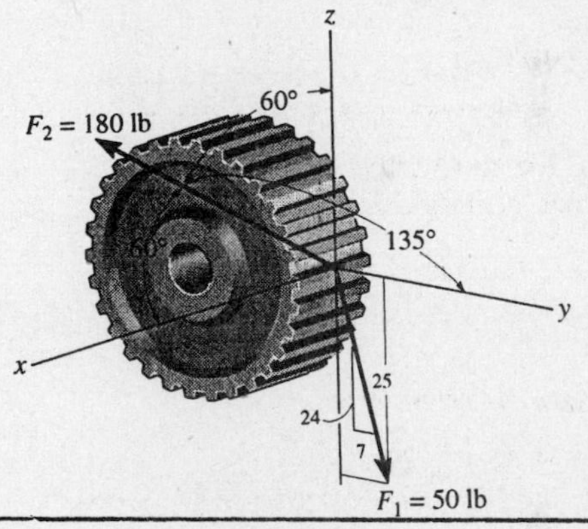

$\mathbf{F}_1 = \frac{7}{25}(50)\mathbf{j} - \frac{24}{25}(50)\mathbf{k} = \{14.0\,\mathbf{j} - 48.0\mathbf{k}\}$ lb **Ans**

$\mathbf{F}_2 = 180\cos 60°\mathbf{i} + 180\cos 135°\mathbf{j} + 180\cos 60°\mathbf{k}$

$= \{90\mathbf{i} - 127\mathbf{j} + 90\mathbf{k}\}$ lb **Ans**

2-65. The spur gears are subjected to the two forces, caused by contact with other gears. Determine the resultant of the two forces and express the result as a Cartesian vector.

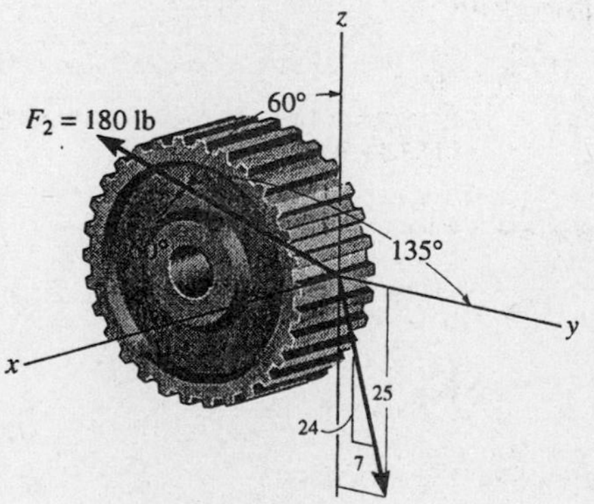

$F_{Rx} = 180\cos 60° = 90$

$F_{Ry} = \frac{7}{25}(50) + 180\cos 135° = -113$

$F_{Rz} = -\frac{24}{25}(50) + 180\cos 60° = 42$

$\mathbf{F}_R = \{90\mathbf{i} - 113\mathbf{j} + 42\mathbf{k}\}$ lb **Ans**

2-66. The screw eye is subjected to the two forces shown. Express each force in Cartesian vector form and then determine the resultant force. Find the magnitude and coordinate direction angles of the resultant force.

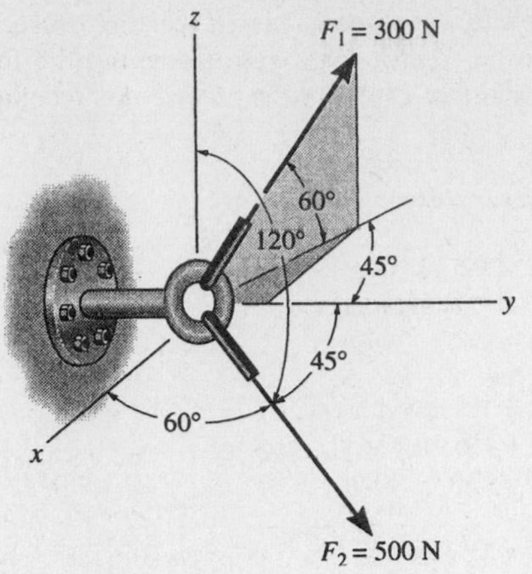

$$\mathbf{F}_1 = 300(-\cos 60°\sin 45°\,\mathbf{i} + \cos 60°\cos 45°\,\mathbf{j} + \sin 60°\,\mathbf{k})$$

$$= \{-106.07\,\mathbf{i} + 106.07\,\mathbf{j} + 259.81\,\mathbf{k}\}\text{N}$$

$$= \{-106\,\mathbf{i} + 106\,\mathbf{j} + 260\,\mathbf{k}\}\text{N} \quad \textbf{Ans}$$

$$\mathbf{F}_2 = 500(\cos 60°\,\mathbf{i} + \cos 45°\,\mathbf{j} + \cos 120°\,\mathbf{k})$$

$$= \{250.0\,\mathbf{i} + 353.55\,\mathbf{j} - 250.0\,\mathbf{k}\}\text{ N}$$

$$= \{250\,\mathbf{i} + 354\,\mathbf{j} - 250\,\mathbf{k}\}\text{ N} \quad \textbf{Ans}$$

$$\mathbf{F}_R = \mathbf{F}_1 + \mathbf{F}_2$$

$$= -106.07\,\mathbf{i} + 106.07\,\mathbf{j} + 259.81\,\mathbf{k} + 250.0\,\mathbf{i} + 353.55\,\mathbf{j} - 250.0\,\mathbf{k}$$

$$= 143.93\,\mathbf{i} + 459.62\,\mathbf{j} + 9.81\mathbf{k}$$

$$= \{144\,\mathbf{i} + 460\,\mathbf{j} + 9.81\,\mathbf{k}\}\text{ N} \quad \textbf{Ans}$$

$$F_R = \sqrt{143.93^2 + 459.62^2 + 9.81^2} = 481.73\text{ N} = 482\text{ N} \quad \textbf{Ans}$$

$$\mathbf{u}_{F_R} = \frac{\mathbf{F}_R}{F_R} = \frac{143.93\mathbf{i} + 459.62\mathbf{j} + 9.81\mathbf{k}}{481.73} = 0.2988\mathbf{i} + 0.9541\mathbf{j} + 0.02036\mathbf{k}$$

$\cos\alpha = 0.2988$ $\quad\alpha = 72.6°$ **Ans**

$\cos\beta = 0.9541$ $\quad\beta = 17.4°$ **Ans**

$\cos\gamma = 0.02036$ $\quad\gamma = 88.8°$ **Ans**

2-67. Determine the coordinate direction angles of $\mathbf{F}_1$.

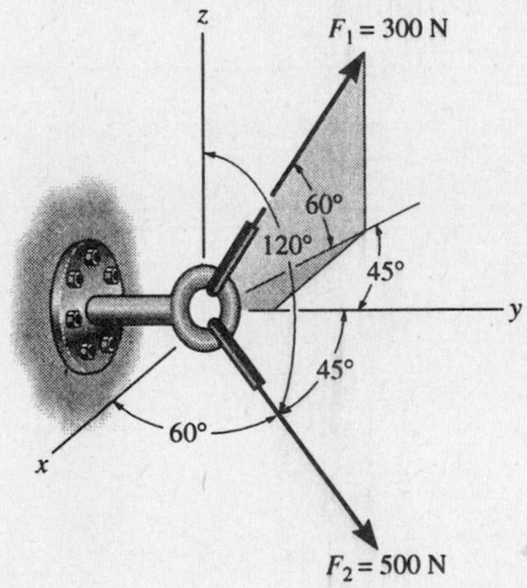

$$\mathbf{F}_1 = 300(-\cos 60°\sin 45°\,\mathbf{i} + \cos 60°\cos 45°\,\mathbf{j} + \sin 60°\,\mathbf{k})$$

$$= \{-106.07\,\mathbf{i} + 106.07\,\mathbf{j} + 259.81\,\mathbf{k}\}\text{ N}$$

$$= \{-106\,\mathbf{i} + 106\,\mathbf{j} + 260\,\mathbf{k}\}\text{ N}$$

$$\mathbf{u}_1 = \frac{\mathbf{F}_1}{300} = -0.3536\,\mathbf{i} + 0.3536\,\mathbf{j} + 0.8660\,\mathbf{k}$$

$\alpha_1 = \cos^{-1}(-0.3536) = 111°$ **Ans**

$\beta_1 = \cos^{-1}(0.3536) = 69.3°$ **Ans**

$\gamma_1 = \cos^{-1}(0.8660) = 30.0°$ **Ans**

***2-68.** The cables attached to the screw eye are subjected to the three forces shown. Express each force in Cartesian vector form and determine the magnitude and coordinate direction angles of the resultant force.

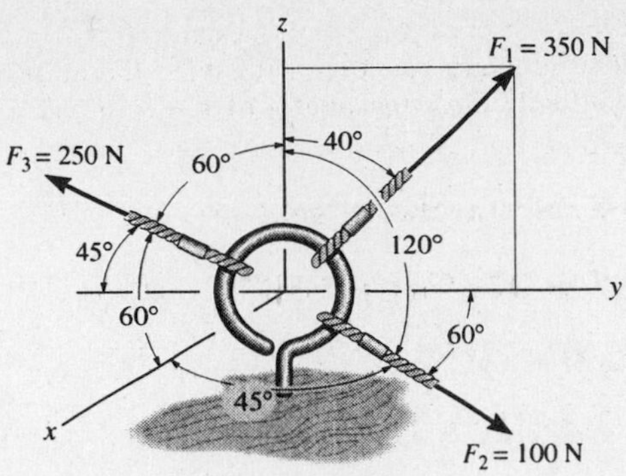

Cartesian Vector Notation :

$$\mathbf{F}_1 = 350\{\sin 40°\mathbf{j} + \cos 40°\mathbf{k}\}\ \text{N}$$
$$= \{224.98\mathbf{j} + 268.12\mathbf{k}\}\ \text{N}$$
$$= \{225\mathbf{j} + 268\mathbf{k}\}\ \text{N}$$ **Ans**

$$\mathbf{F}_2 = 100\{\cos 45°\mathbf{i} + \cos 60°\mathbf{j} + \cos 120°\mathbf{k}\}\ \text{N}$$
$$= \{70.71\mathbf{i} + 50.0\mathbf{j} - 50.0\mathbf{k}\}\ \text{N}$$
$$= \{70.7\mathbf{i} + 50.0\mathbf{j} - 50.0\mathbf{k}\}\ \text{N}$$ **Ans**

$$\mathbf{F}_3 = 250\{\cos 60°\mathbf{i} + \cos 135°\mathbf{j} + \cos 60°\mathbf{k}\}\ \text{N}$$
$$= \{125.0\mathbf{i} - 176.78\mathbf{j} + 125.0\mathbf{k}\}\ \text{N}$$
$$= \{125\mathbf{i} - 177\mathbf{j} + 125\mathbf{k}\}\ \text{N}$$ **Ans**

Resultant Force :

$$\mathbf{F}_R = \mathbf{F}_1 + \mathbf{F}_2 + \mathbf{F}_3$$
$$= \{(70.71 + 125.0)\mathbf{i} + (224.98 + 50.0 - 176.78)\mathbf{j} + (268.12 - 50.0 + 125.0)\mathbf{k}\}\ \text{N}$$
$$= \{195.71\mathbf{i} + 98.20\mathbf{j} + 343.12\mathbf{k}\}\ \text{N}$$

The magnitude of the resultant force is

$$F_R = \sqrt{F_{R_x}^2 + F_{R_y}^2 + F_{R_z}^2}$$
$$= \sqrt{195.71^2 + 98.20^2 + 343.12^2}$$
$$= 407.03\ \text{N} = 407\ \text{N}$$ **Ans**

The coordinate direction angles are

$$\cos\alpha = \frac{F_{R_x}}{F_R} = \frac{195.71}{407.03} \qquad \alpha = 61.3°$$ **Ans**

$$\cos\beta = \frac{F_{R_y}}{F_R} = \frac{98.20}{407.03} \qquad \beta = 76.0°$$ **Ans**

$$\cos\gamma = \frac{F_{R_z}}{F_R} = \frac{343.12}{407.03} \qquad \gamma = 32.5°$$ **Ans**

2-69. The force **F** has a magnitude of 80 lb and acts within the octant shown. Determine the magnitudes of the *x*, *y*, *z* components of **F**.

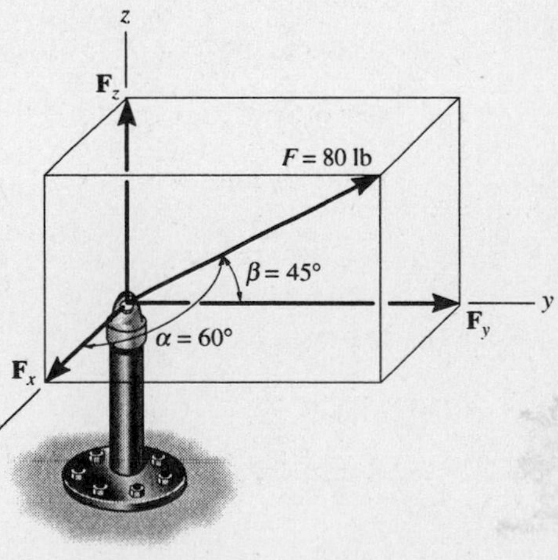

$$1 = \cos^2 60° + \cos^2 45° + \cos^2\gamma$$

Solving for the positive root, $\gamma = 60°$

$F_x = 80\cos 60° = 40.0$ lb **Ans**

$F_y = 80\cos 45° = 56.6$ lb **Ans**

$F_z = 80\cos 60° = 40.0$ lb **Ans**

2-70. The man pulls on the rope with a force of 60 lb. If **F** acts within the octant shown, determine the x, y, z components of **F**.

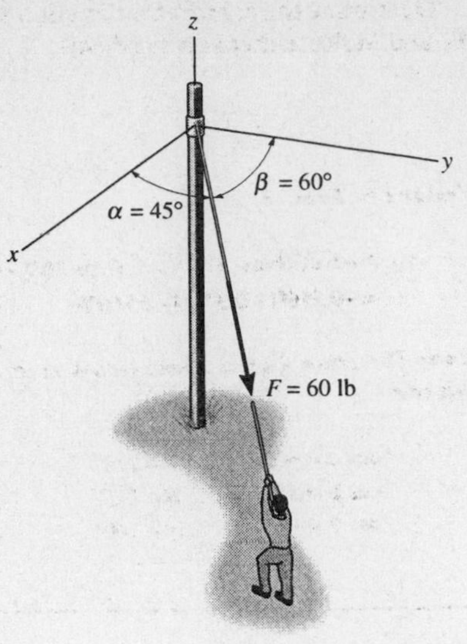

$$1 = \cos^2 45° + \cos^2 60° + \cos^2 \gamma$$

Solving for the root > 90°, $\gamma = 120°$

$F_x = 60 \cos 45° = 42.4 \text{ lb}$ **Ans**

$F_y = 60 \cos 60° = 30 \text{ lb}$ **Ans**

$F_z = 60 \cos 120° = -30 \text{ lb}$ **Ans**

2-71. The two forces $\mathbf{F}_1$ and $\mathbf{F}_2$ acting at A have a resultant force of $\mathbf{F}_R = \{-100\mathbf{k}\}$ lb. Determine the magnitude and coordinate direction angles of $\mathbf{F}_2$.

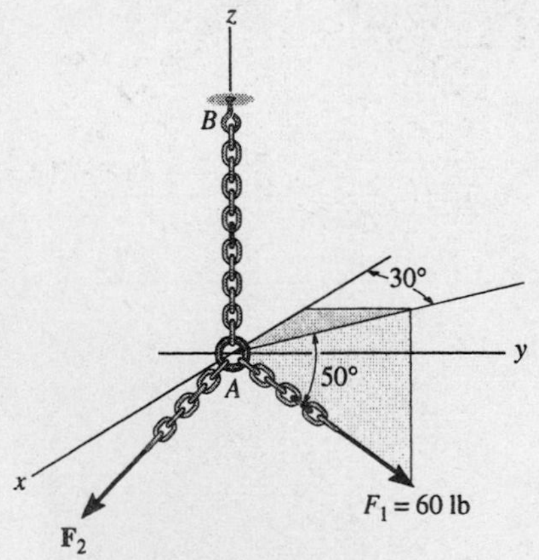

Cartesian Vector Notation :

$$\mathbf{F}_R = \{-100\mathbf{k}\} \text{ lb}$$

$$\mathbf{F}_1 = 60\{-\cos 50° \cos 30° \mathbf{i} + \cos 50° \sin 30° \mathbf{j} - \sin 50° \mathbf{k}\} \text{ lb}$$
$$= \{-33.40\mathbf{i} + 19.28\mathbf{j} - 45.96\mathbf{k}\} \text{ lb}$$

$$\mathbf{F}_2 = \{F_{2_x}\mathbf{i} + F_{2_y}\mathbf{j} + F_{2_z}\mathbf{k}\} \text{ lb}$$

Resultant Force :

$$\mathbf{F}_R = \mathbf{F}_1 + \mathbf{F}_2$$
$$-100\mathbf{k} = \{(F_{2_x} - 33.40)\mathbf{i} + (F_{2_y} + 19.28)\mathbf{j} + (F_{2_z} - 45.96)\mathbf{k}\}$$

Equating **i**, **j** and **k** components, we have

$$F_{2_x} - 33.40 = 0 \qquad F_{2_x} = 33.40 \text{ lb}$$
$$F_{2_y} + 19.28 = 0 \qquad F_{2_y} = -19.28 \text{ lb}$$
$$F_{2_z} - 45.96 = -100 \qquad F_{2_z} = -54.04 \text{ lb}$$

The magnitude of force $\mathbf{F}_2$ is

$$F_2 = \sqrt{F_{2_x}^2 + F_{2_y}^2 + F_{2_z}^2}$$
$$= \sqrt{33.40^2 + (-19.28)^2 + (-54.04)^2}$$
$$= 66.39 \text{ lb} = 66.4 \text{ lb}$$ **Ans**

The coordinate direction angles for $\mathbf{F}_2$ are

$\cos\alpha = \frac{F_{2_x}}{F_2} = \frac{33.40}{66.39}$ $\quad \alpha = 59.8°$ **Ans**

$\cos\beta = \frac{F_{2_y}}{F_2} = \frac{-19.28}{66.39}$ $\quad \beta = 107°$ **Ans**

$\cos\gamma = \frac{F_{2_z}}{F_2} = \frac{-54.04}{66.39}$ $\quad \gamma = 144°$ **Ans**

***2-72.** Determine the coordinate direction angles of the force $\mathbf{F}_1$ and indicate them on the figure.

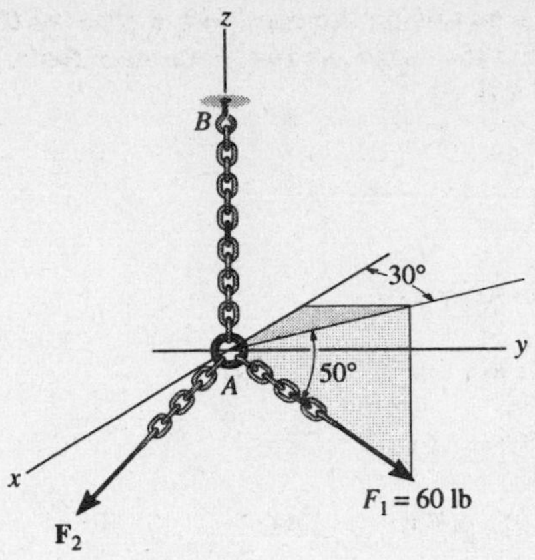

Unit Vector For Foce $\mathbf{F}_1$ **:**

$$\mathbf{u}_{F_1} = -\cos 50°\cos 30°\mathbf{i} + \cos 50°\sin 30°\mathbf{j} - \sin 50°\mathbf{k}$$
$$= -0.5567\mathbf{i} + 0.3214\mathbf{j} - 0.7660\mathbf{k}$$

Coordinate Direction Angles : From the unit vector obtained above, we have

$\cos\alpha = -0.5567$ $\quad \alpha = 124°$ **Ans**

$\cos\beta = 0.3214$ $\quad \beta = 71.3°$ **Ans**

$\cos\gamma = -0.7660$ $\quad \gamma = 140°$ **Ans**

2-73. The bracket is subjected to the two forces shown. Express each force in Cartesian vector form and then determine the resultant force $\mathbf{F}_R$. Find the magnitude and coordinate direction angles of the resultant force.

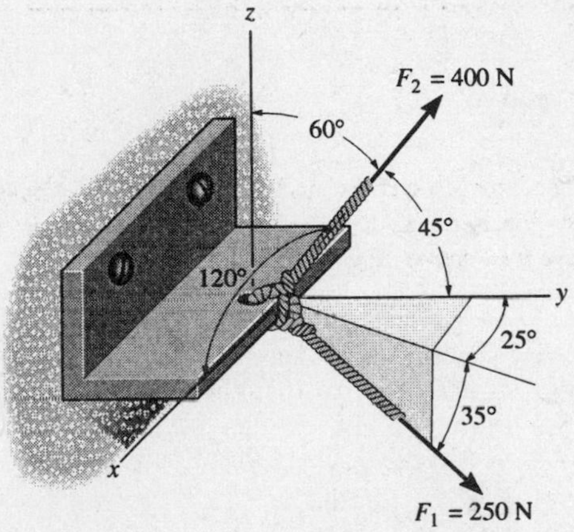

Cartesian Vector Notation :

$$\mathbf{F}_1 = 250\{\cos 35°\sin 25°\mathbf{i} + \cos 35°\cos 25°\mathbf{j} - \sin 35°\mathbf{k}\}\ \text{N}$$
$$= \{86.55\mathbf{i} + 185.60\mathbf{j} - 143.39\mathbf{k}\}\ \text{N}$$
$$= \{86.5\mathbf{i} + 186\mathbf{j} - 143\mathbf{k}\}\ \text{N} \qquad \textbf{Ans}$$

$$\mathbf{F}_2 = 400\{\cos 120°\mathbf{i} + \cos 45°\mathbf{j} + \cos 60°\mathbf{k}\}\ \text{N}$$
$$= \{-200.0\mathbf{i} + 282.84\mathbf{j} + 200.0\mathbf{k}\}\ \text{N}$$
$$= \{-200\mathbf{i} + 283\mathbf{j} + 200\mathbf{k}\}\ \text{N} \qquad \textbf{Ans}$$

Resultant Force :

$$\mathbf{F}_R = \mathbf{F}_1 + \mathbf{F}_2$$
$$= \{(86.55 - 200.0)\mathbf{i} + (185.60 + 282.84)\mathbf{j} + (-143.39 + 200.0)\mathbf{k}\}$$
$$= \{-113.45\mathbf{i} + 468.44\mathbf{j} + 56.61\mathbf{k}\}\ \text{N}$$
$$= \{-113\mathbf{i} + 468\mathbf{j} + 56.6\mathbf{k}\}\ \text{N} \qquad \textbf{Ans}$$

The magnitude of the resultant force is

$$F_R = \sqrt{F_{R_x}^2 + F_{R_y}^2 + F_{R_z}^2}$$
$$= \sqrt{(-113.45)^2 + 468.44^2 + 56.61^2}$$
$$= 485.30\ \text{N} = 485\ \text{N} \qquad \textbf{Ans}$$

The coordinate direction angles are

$$\cos\alpha = \frac{F_{R_x}}{F_R} = \frac{-113.45}{485.30} \qquad \alpha = 104° \qquad \textbf{Ans}$$

$$\cos\beta = \frac{F_{R_y}}{F_R} = \frac{468.44}{485.30} \qquad \beta = 15.1° \qquad \textbf{Ans}$$

$$\cos\gamma = \frac{F_{R_z}}{F_R} = \frac{56.61}{485.30} \qquad \gamma = 83.3° \qquad \textbf{Ans}$$

2-74. Determine the magnitude and coordinate direction angles of $\mathbf{F}_2$ so that the resultant of the two forces acts along the positive x axis and has a magnitude of 500 N.

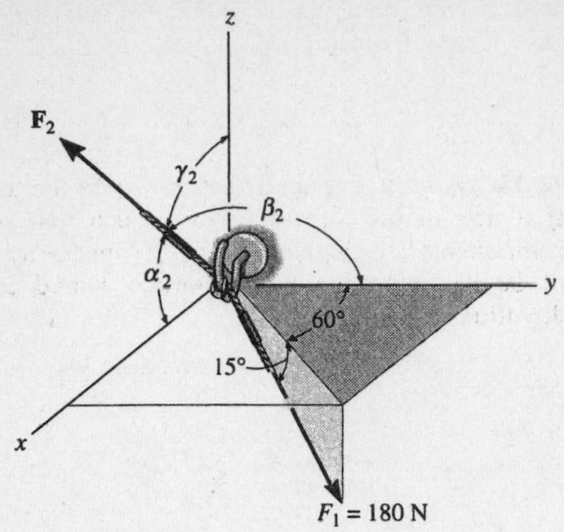

$\mathbf{F}_1 = (180 \cos 15°) \sin 60°\ \mathbf{i} + (180 \cos 15°) \cos 60°\ \mathbf{j} - 180 \sin 15°\ \mathbf{k}$

$= 150.57\ \mathbf{i} + 86.93\ \mathbf{j} - 46.59\ \mathbf{k}$

$\mathbf{F}_2 = F_2 \cos \alpha_2\ \mathbf{i} + F_2 \cos \beta_2\ \mathbf{j} + F_2 \cos \gamma_2\ \mathbf{k}$

$\mathbf{F}_R = \{500\ \mathbf{i}\}$ N

$\mathbf{F}_R = \mathbf{F}_1 + \mathbf{F}_2$

i components :

$500 = 150.57 + F_2 \cos \alpha_2$

$F_{2x} = F_2 \cos \alpha_2 = 349.43$

j components :

$0 = 86.93 + F_2 \cos \beta_2$

$F_{2y} = F_2 \cos \beta_2 = -86.93$

k components :

$0 = -46.59 + F_2 \cos \gamma_2$

$F_{2z} = F_2 \cos \gamma_2 = 46.59$

Thus,

$F_2 = \sqrt{F_{2x}^2 + F_{2y}^2 + F_{2z}^2} = \sqrt{(349.43)^2 + (-86.93)^2 + (46.59)^2}$

$F_2 = 363$ N **Ans**

$\alpha_2 = 15.8°$ **Ans**

$\beta_2 = 104°$ **Ans**

$\gamma_2 = 82.6°$ **Ans**

2-75. Determine the magnitude and coordinate direction angles of $\mathbf{F}_2$ so that the resultant of the two forces is zero.

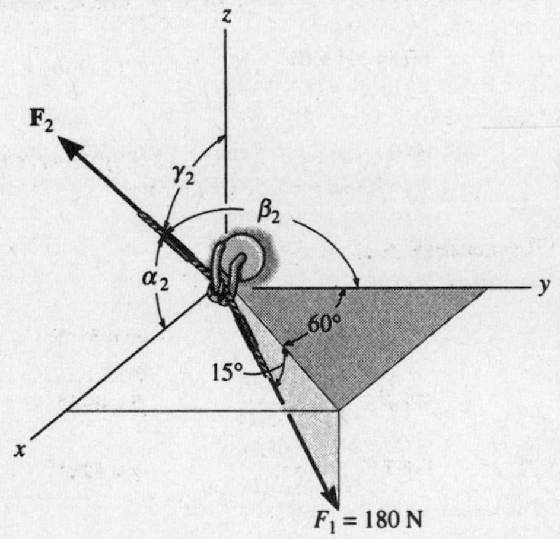

$\mathbf{F}_1 = (180 \cos 15°) \sin 60°\ \mathbf{i} + (180 \cos 15°) \cos 60°\ \mathbf{j} - 180 \sin 15°\ \mathbf{k}$

$= 150.57\ \mathbf{i} + 86.93\ \mathbf{j} - 46.59\ \mathbf{k}$

$\mathbf{F}_2 = F_2 \cos \alpha_2\ \mathbf{i} + F_2 \cos \beta_2\ \mathbf{j} + F_2 \cos \gamma_2\ \mathbf{k}$

$\mathbf{F}_R = \mathbf{0}$

i components :

$0 = 150.57 + F_2 \cos \alpha_2$

$F_2 \cos\alpha_2 = -150.57$

j components :

$0 = 86.93 + F_2 \cos \beta_2$

$F_2 \cos \beta_2 = -86.93$

k components :

$0 = -46.59 + F_2 \cos \gamma_2$

$F_2 \cos \gamma_2 = 46.59$

$F_2 = \sqrt{(-150.57)^2 + (-86.93)^2 + (46.59)^2}$

Solving,

$F_2 = 180$ N **Ans**

$\alpha_2 = 147°$ **Ans**

$\beta_2 = 119°$ **Ans**

$\gamma_2 = 75.0°$ **Ans**

***2-76.** A force **F** is applied at the top of the tower at A. If it acts in the direction shown such that one of its components lying in the shaded y-z plane has a magnitude of 80 lb, determine its magnitude F and coordinate direction angles α, β, γ.

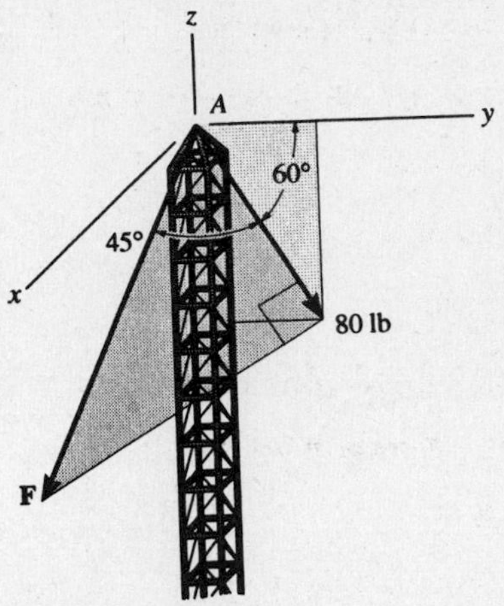

Cartesian Vector Notation : The magnitude of force **F** is

$$F\cos 45° = 80 \qquad F = 113.14 \text{ lb} = 113 \text{ lb} \qquad \textbf{Ans}$$

Thus,

$$\mathbf{F} = \{113.14\sin 45°\mathbf{i} + 80\cos 60°\mathbf{j} - 80\sin 60°\mathbf{k}\} \text{ lb}$$
$$= \{80.0\mathbf{i} + 40.0\mathbf{j} - 69.28\mathbf{k}\} \text{ lb}$$

The coordinate direction angles are

$$\cos\alpha = \frac{F_x}{F} = \frac{80.0}{113.14} \qquad \alpha = 45.0° \qquad \textbf{Ans}$$

$$\cos\beta = \frac{F_y}{F} = \frac{40.0}{113.14} \qquad \beta = 69.3° \qquad \textbf{Ans}$$

$$\cos\gamma = \frac{F_z}{F} = \frac{-69.28}{113.14} \qquad \gamma = 128° \qquad \textbf{Ans}$$

2-77. Three forces act on the hook. If the resultant force $\mathbf{F}_R$ has a magnitude and direction as shown, determine the magnitude and the coordinate direction angles of force $\mathbf{F}_3$.

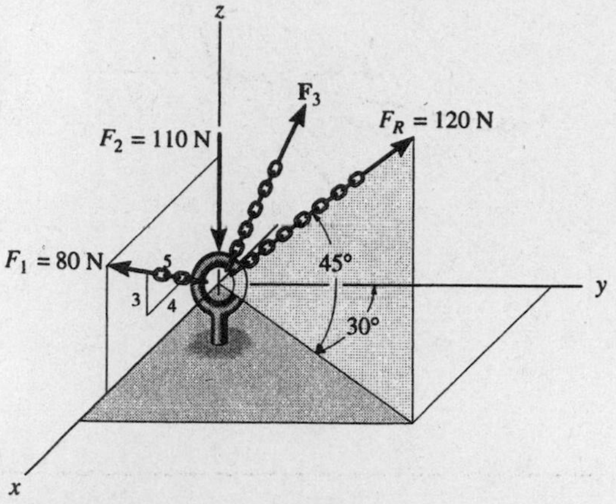

Cartesian Vector Notation :

$$\mathbf{F}_R = 120\{\cos 45°\sin 30°\mathbf{i} + \cos 45°\cos 30°\mathbf{j} + \sin 45°\mathbf{k}\}\text{ N}$$
$$= \{42.43\mathbf{i} + 73.48\mathbf{j} + 84.85\mathbf{k}\}\text{ N}$$

$$\mathbf{F}_1 = 80\left\{\frac{4}{5}\mathbf{i} + \frac{3}{5}\mathbf{k}\right\}\text{N} = \{64.0\mathbf{i} + 48.0\mathbf{k}\}\text{ N}$$

$$\mathbf{F}_2 = \{-110\mathbf{k}\}\text{ N}$$

$$\mathbf{F}_3 = \{F_{3_x}\mathbf{i} + F_{3_y}\mathbf{j} + F_{3_z}\mathbf{k}\}\text{ N}$$

Resultant Force :

$$\mathbf{F}_R = \mathbf{F}_1 + \mathbf{F}_2 + \mathbf{F}_3$$
$$\{42.43\mathbf{i} + 73.48\mathbf{j} + 84.85\mathbf{k}\} = \{(64.0 + F_{3_x})\mathbf{i} + F_{3_y}\mathbf{j} + (48.0 - 110 + F_{3_z})\mathbf{k}\}$$

Equating **i**, **j** and **k** components, we have

$$64.0 + F_{3_x} = 42.43 \qquad F_{3_x} = -21.57\text{ N}$$
$$F_{3_y} = 73.48\text{ N}$$
$$48.0 - 110 + F_{3_z} = 84.85 \qquad F_{3_z} = 146.85\text{ N}$$

The magnitude of force $\mathbf{F}_3$ is

$$F_3 = \sqrt{F_{3_x}^2 + F_{3_y}^2 + F_{3_z}^2}$$
$$= \sqrt{(-21.57)^2 + 73.48^2 + 146.85^2}$$
$$= 165.62\text{ N} = 166\text{ N} \qquad \textbf{Ans}$$

The coordinate direction angles for $\mathbf{F}_3$ are

$$\cos\alpha = \frac{F_{3_x}}{F_3} = \frac{-21.57}{165.62} \qquad \alpha = 97.5° \qquad \textbf{Ans}$$
$$\cos\beta = \frac{F_{3_y}}{F_3} = \frac{73.48}{165.62} \qquad \beta = 63.7° \qquad \textbf{Ans}$$
$$\cos\gamma = \frac{F_{3_z}}{F_3} = \frac{146.85}{165.62} \qquad \gamma = 27.5° \qquad \textbf{Ans}$$

2-78. Determine the coordinate direction angles of $\mathbf{F}_1$ and $\mathbf{F}_R$.

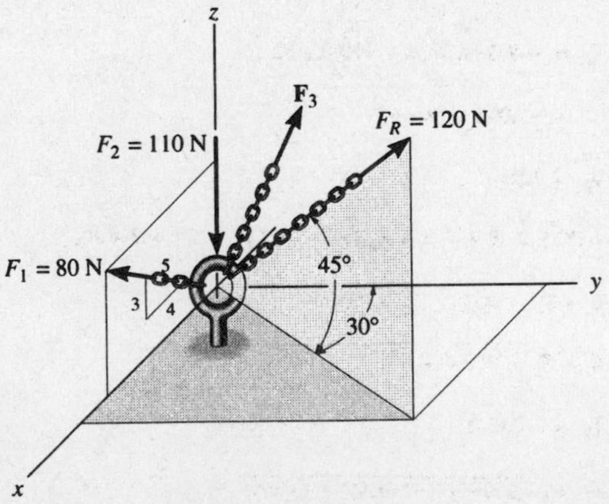

Unit Vector of $\mathbf{F}_1$ and $\mathbf{F}_R$:

$$\mathbf{u}_{F_1} = \frac{4}{5}\mathbf{i} + \frac{3}{5}\mathbf{k} = 0.8\mathbf{i} + 0.6\mathbf{k}$$

$$\mathbf{u}_R = \cos 45°\sin 30°\mathbf{i} + \cos 45°\cos 30°\mathbf{j} + \sin 45°\mathbf{k}$$
$$= 0.3536\mathbf{i} + 0.6124\mathbf{j} + 0.7071\mathbf{k}$$

Thus, the coordinate direction angles $\mathbf{F}_1$ and $\mathbf{F}_R$ are

$$\cos\alpha_{F_1} = 0.8 \qquad \alpha_{F_1} = 36.9° \qquad \textbf{Ans}$$
$$\cos\beta_{F_1} = 0 \qquad \beta_{F_1} = 90.0° \qquad \textbf{Ans}$$
$$\cos\gamma_{F_1} = 0.6 \qquad \gamma_{F_1} = 53.1° \qquad \textbf{Ans}$$

$$\cos\alpha_R = 0.3536 \qquad \alpha_R = 69.3° \qquad \textbf{Ans}$$
$$\cos\beta_R = 0.6124 \qquad \beta_R = 52.2° \qquad \textbf{Ans}$$
$$\cos\gamma_R = 0.7071 \qquad \gamma_R = 45.0° \qquad \textbf{Ans}$$

2-79. The pith ball is subjected to an electrostatic repulsive force **F** which has measured components of $F_x = 40$ mN and $F_z = 20$ mN. If the angle $\beta = 135°$, determine the magnitudes of **F** and $\mathbf{F}_y$.

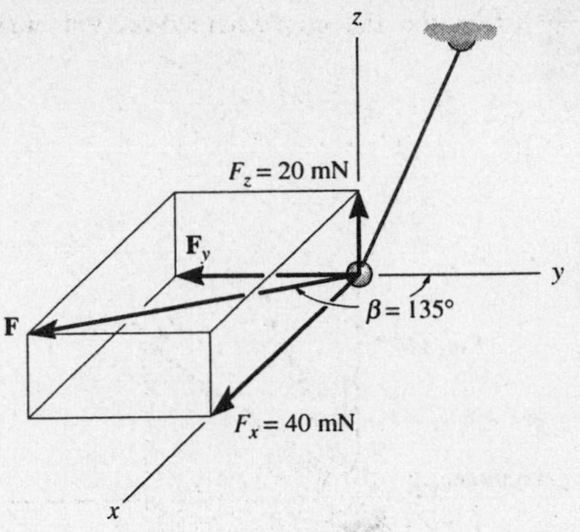

$F^2 = (40)^2 + (F\cos 135°)^2 + (20)^2$

$F = 63.2$ mN **Ans**

$F_y = 63.2\cos 135° = -44.7$ mN

Thus

$|F_y| = 44.7$ mN **Ans**

***2-80.** Specify the magnitude and coordinate direction angles α_1, β_1, γ_1 of $\mathbf{F}_1$ so that the resultant of the three forces acting on the bracket is $\mathbf{F}_R = \{-350\mathbf{k}\}$ lb. Note that $\mathbf{F}_3$ lies in the x–y plane.

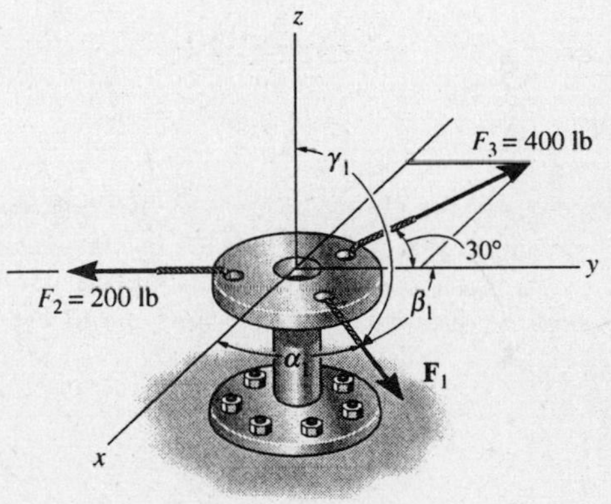

$\mathbf{F}_1 = F_x\,\mathbf{i} + F_y\,\mathbf{j} + F_z\,\mathbf{k}$

$\mathbf{F}_2 = -200\,\mathbf{j}$

$\mathbf{F}_3 = -400\sin 30°\,\mathbf{i} + 400\cos 30°\,\mathbf{j}$

$= -200\,\mathbf{i} + 346.4\,\mathbf{j}$

$\mathbf{F}_R = \Sigma\mathbf{F}$

$-350\,\mathbf{k} = F_x\,\mathbf{i} + F_y\,\mathbf{j} + F_z\,\mathbf{k} - 200\,\mathbf{j} - 200\,\mathbf{i} + 346.4\,\mathbf{j}$

$0 = F_x - 200;\quad F_x = 200$ lb

$0 = F_y - 200 + 346.4;\quad F_y = -146.4$ lb

$F_z = -350$ lb

$F_1 = \sqrt{(200)^2 + (-146.4)^2 + (-350)^2}$

$F_1 = 428.9$ lb $= 429$ lb **Ans**

$\alpha_1 = \cos^{-1}\left(\frac{200}{428.9}\right) = 62.2°$ **Ans**

$\beta_1 = \cos^{-1}\left(\frac{-146.4}{428.9}\right) = 110°$ **Ans**

$\gamma_1 = \cos^{-1}\left(\frac{-350}{428.9}\right) = 145°$ **Ans**

2-81. If $\mathbf{r}_1 = \{3\mathbf{i} - 4\mathbf{j} + 3\mathbf{k}\}$ m, $\mathbf{r}_2 = \{4\mathbf{i} - 5\mathbf{k}\}$ m, $\mathbf{r}_3 = \{3\mathbf{i} - 2\mathbf{j} + 5\mathbf{k}\}$ m, determine the magnitude and direction of $\mathbf{r} = 2\mathbf{r}_1 - \mathbf{r}_2 + 3\mathbf{r}_3$.

$$\mathbf{r} = 2\mathbf{r}_1 - \mathbf{r}_2 + 3\mathbf{r}_3$$

$$= 6\mathbf{i} - 8\mathbf{j} + 6\mathbf{k} - 4\mathbf{i} + 5\mathbf{k} + 9\mathbf{i} - 6\mathbf{j} + 15\mathbf{k}$$

$$= 11\mathbf{i} - 14\mathbf{j} + 26\mathbf{k}$$

$$r = \sqrt{(11)^2 + (-14)^2 + (26)^2} = 31.51 \text{ m} = 31.5 \text{ m} \quad \textbf{Ans}$$

$$\mathbf{u}_r = \frac{11}{31.51}\mathbf{i} - \frac{14}{31.51}\mathbf{j} + \frac{26}{31.51}\mathbf{k}$$

$$\alpha = \cos^{-1}\left(\frac{11}{31.51}\right) = 69.6^\circ \quad \textbf{Ans}$$

$$\beta = \cos^{-1}\left(\frac{-14}{31.51}\right) = 116^\circ \quad \textbf{Ans}$$

$$\gamma = \cos^{-1}\left(\frac{26}{31.51}\right) = 34.4^\circ \quad \textbf{Ans}$$

2-82. Represent the position vector **r** acting from point $A(3\text{ m}, 5\text{ m}, 6\text{ m})$ to point $B(5\text{ m}, -2\text{ m}, 1\text{ m})$ in Cartesian vector form. Determine its coordinate direction angles and find the distance between points A and B.

Position Vector *:* This can be established from the coordinates of two points.

$$\mathbf{r}_{AB} = \{(5-3)\mathbf{i} + (-2-5)\mathbf{j} + (1-6)\mathbf{k}\} \text{ ft}$$
$$= \{2\mathbf{i} - 7\mathbf{j} - 5\mathbf{k}\} \text{ ft} \quad \textbf{Ans}$$

The distance between point A and B is

$$r_{AB} = \sqrt{2^2 + (-7)^2 + (-5)^2} = \sqrt{78} \text{ ft} = 8.83 \text{ ft} \quad \textbf{Ans}$$

The coordinate direction angles are

$$\cos\alpha = \frac{2}{\sqrt{78}} \qquad \alpha = 76.9^\circ \quad \textbf{Ans}$$

$$\cos\beta = \frac{-7}{\sqrt{78}} \qquad \beta = 142^\circ \quad \textbf{Ans}$$

$$\cos\gamma = \frac{-5}{\sqrt{78}} \qquad \gamma = 124^\circ \quad \textbf{Ans}$$

2-83. A position vector extends from the origin to point A (2 m, 3 m, 6 m). Determine the angles α, β, γ which the tail of the vector makes with the x, y, z axes, respectively.

Position Vector : This can be established from the coordinates of two points.

$$\mathbf{r}_{AB} = \{(5-3)\mathbf{i} + (-2-5)\mathbf{j} + (1-6)\mathbf{k}\} \text{ ft}$$
$$= \{2\mathbf{i} - 7\mathbf{j} - 5\mathbf{k}\} \text{ ft} \qquad \textbf{Ans}$$

The distance between point A and B is

$$r_{AB} = \sqrt{2^2 + (-7)^2 + (-5)^2} = \sqrt{78} \text{ ft} = 8.83 \text{ ft} \qquad \textbf{Ans}$$

The coordinate direction angles are

$$\cos\alpha = \frac{2}{\sqrt{78}} \qquad \alpha = 76.9^\circ \qquad \textbf{Ans}$$
$$\cos\beta = \frac{-7}{\sqrt{78}} \qquad \beta = 142^\circ \qquad \textbf{Ans}$$
$$\cos\gamma = \frac{-5}{\sqrt{78}} \qquad \gamma = 124^\circ \qquad \textbf{Ans}$$

***2-84.** Express the position vector **r** in Cartesian vector form; then determine its magnitude and coordinate direction angles.

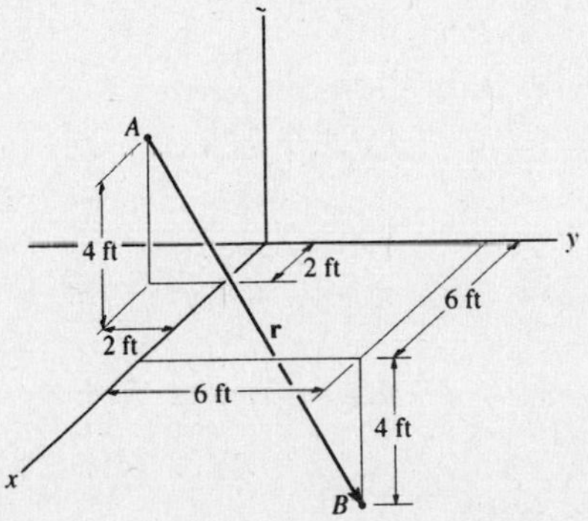

Position Vector :

$$\mathbf{r} = \{(6-2)\mathbf{i} + [6-(-2)]\mathbf{j} + (-4-4)\mathbf{k}\} \text{ ft}$$
$$= \{4\mathbf{i} + 8\mathbf{j} - 8\mathbf{k}\} \text{ ft} \qquad \textbf{Ans}$$

The magnitude of **r** is

$$r = \sqrt{4^2 + 8^2 + (-8)^2} = 12.0 \text{ ft} \qquad \textbf{Ans}$$

The coordinate direction angles are

$$\cos\alpha = \frac{4}{12.0} \qquad \alpha = 70.5^\circ \qquad \textbf{Ans}$$
$$\cos\beta = \frac{8}{12.0} \qquad \beta = 48.2^\circ \qquad \textbf{Ans}$$
$$\cos\gamma = \frac{-8}{12.0} \qquad \gamma = 132^\circ \qquad \textbf{Ans}$$

2-85. Express the position vector **r** in Cartesian vector form; then determine its magnitude and coordinate direction angles.

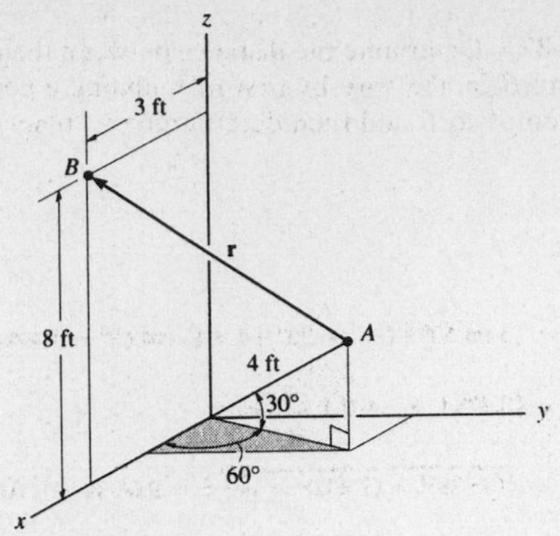

$$\mathbf{r} = (3 - 4\cos 30^\circ \cos 60^\circ)\,\mathbf{i} + (-4\cos 30^\circ \sin 60^\circ)\,\mathbf{j} + (8 - 4\sin 30^\circ)\,\mathbf{k}$$

$$= \{1.268\,\mathbf{i} - 3\,\mathbf{j} + 6\,\mathbf{k}\}\ \text{ft}$$

$$r = \sqrt{(1.268)^2 + (-3)^2 + (6)^2} = 6.827 = 6.83\ \text{ft} \qquad \textbf{Ans}$$

$$\alpha = \cos^{-1}\left(\frac{1.268}{6.827}\right) = 79.3^\circ \qquad \textbf{Ans}$$

$$\beta = \cos^{-1}\left(\frac{-3}{6.827}\right) = 116^\circ \qquad \textbf{Ans}$$

$$\gamma = \cos^{-1}\left(\frac{6}{6.827}\right) = 28.5^\circ \qquad \textbf{Ans}$$

2-86. Express force **F** as a Cartesian vector; then determine its coordinate direction angles.

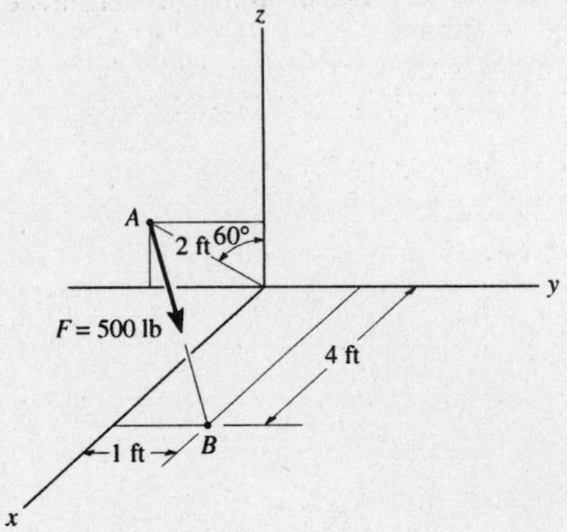

Unit Vector :

$$\mathbf{r}_{AB} = \{(4-0)\,\mathbf{i} + [1-(-2\sin 60^\circ)]\,\mathbf{j} + (0 - 2\cos 60^\circ)\,\mathbf{k}\}\ \text{ft}$$
$$= \{4.00\mathbf{i} + 2.732\mathbf{j} - 1.00\mathbf{k}\}\ \text{ft}$$
$$r_{AB} = \sqrt{4.00^2 + 2.732^2 + (-1.00)^2} = 4.946\ \text{ft}$$

$$\mathbf{u}_{AB} = \frac{\mathbf{r}_{AB}}{r_{AB}} = \frac{4.00\mathbf{i} + 2.732\mathbf{j} - 1.00\mathbf{k}}{4.946}$$
$$= 0.8087\mathbf{i} + 0.5524\mathbf{j} - 0.2022\mathbf{k}$$

Force Vector :

$$\mathbf{F} = F\mathbf{u}_{AB} = 500\{0.8087\mathbf{i} + 0.5524\mathbf{j} - 0.2022\mathbf{k}\}\ \text{lb}$$
$$= \{404\mathbf{i} + 276\mathbf{j} - 101\mathbf{k}\}\ \text{lb} \qquad \textbf{Ans}$$

Coordinate Direction Angles : From the unit vector $\mathbf{u}_{AB}$ obtained above, we have

$\cos\alpha = 0.8087$	$\alpha = 36.0^\circ$	**Ans**
$\cos\beta = 0.5524$	$\beta = 56.5^\circ$	**Ans**
$\cos\gamma = -0.2022$	$\gamma = 102^\circ$	**Ans**

2-87. Determine the distance between the end points A and B on the wire by first formulating a position vector from A to B and then determining its magnitude.

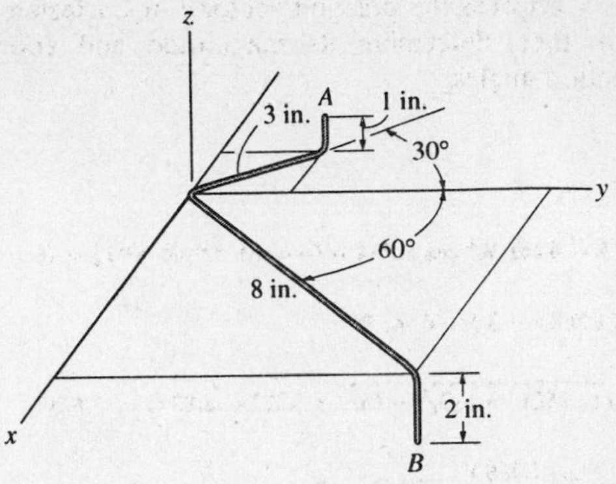

$$\mathbf{r}_{AB} = (8\sin 60° - (-3\sin 30°))\,\mathbf{i} + (8\cos 60° - 3\cos 30°)\,\mathbf{j} + (-2 - 1)\,\mathbf{k}$$

$$\mathbf{r}_{AB} = \{8.428\,\mathbf{i} + 1.402\,\mathbf{j} - 3\,\mathbf{k}\}\text{ in.}$$

$$r_{AB} = \sqrt{(8.428)^2 + (1.402)^2 + (-3)^2} = 9.06\text{ in.} \qquad \textbf{Ans}$$

***2-88.** At a given instant, the position of a plane at A and a train at B are measured relative to a radar antenna at O. Determine the distance d between A and B at this instant. To solve the problem, formulate a position vector, directed from A to B, and then determine its magnitude.

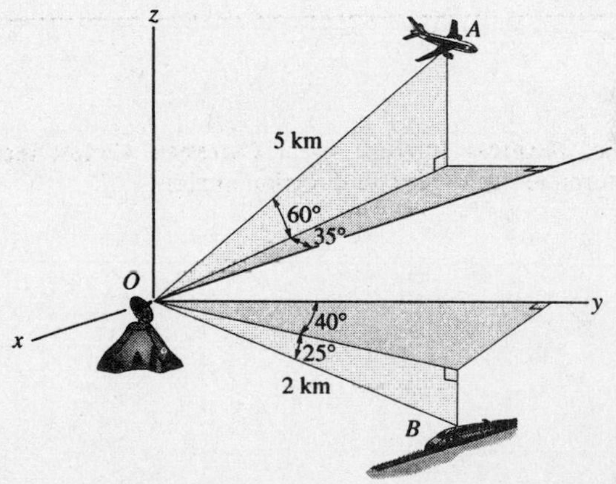

Position Vector : The coordinates of points A and B are

$$A(-5\cos 60°\cos 35°,\ -5\cos 60°\sin 35°,\ 5\sin 60°)\text{ km}$$
$$= A(-2.048,\ -1.434,\ 4.330)\text{ km}$$

$$B(2\cos 25°\sin 40°,\ 2\cos 25°\cos 40°,\ -2\sin 25°)\text{ km}$$
$$= B(1.165,\ 1.389,\ -0.845)\text{ km}$$

The position vector $\mathbf{r}_{AB}$ can be established from the coordinates of points A and B.

$$\mathbf{r}_{AB} = \{[1.165-(-2.048)]\mathbf{i} + [1.389-(-1.434)]\mathbf{j} + (-0.845-4.330)\mathbf{k}\}\text{ km}$$
$$= \{3.213\mathbf{i} + 2.822\mathbf{j} - 5.175\mathbf{k}\}\text{ km}$$

The distance between points A and B is

$$d = r_{AB} = \sqrt{3.213^2 + 2.822^2 + (-5.175)^2} = 6.71\text{ km} \qquad \textbf{Ans}$$

2-89. The hinged plate is supported by the cord AB. If the force in the cord is $F = 340$ lb, express this force, directed from A toward B, as a Cartesian vector. What is the length of the cord?

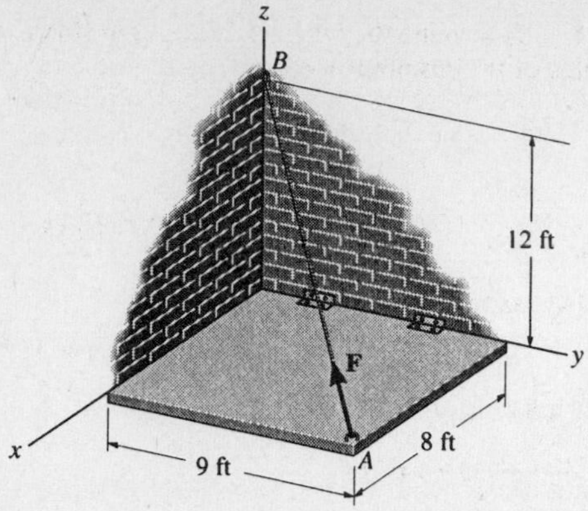

Unit Vector :

$$\mathbf{r}_{AB} = \{(0-8)\mathbf{i}+(0-9)\mathbf{j}+(12-0)\mathbf{k}\}\text{ ft}$$
$$= \{-8\mathbf{i}-9\mathbf{j}+12\mathbf{k}\}\text{ ft}$$

$$r_{AB} = \sqrt{(-8)^2+(-9)^2+12^2} = 17.0\text{ ft} \qquad \textbf{Ans}$$

$$\mathbf{u}_{AB} = \frac{\mathbf{r}_{AB}}{r_{AB}} = \frac{-8\mathbf{i}-9\mathbf{j}+12\mathbf{k}}{17} = -\frac{8}{17}\mathbf{i}-\frac{9}{17}\mathbf{j}+\frac{12}{17}\mathbf{k}$$

Force Vector :

$$\mathbf{F} = F\mathbf{u}_{AB} = 340\left\{-\frac{8}{17}\mathbf{i}-\frac{9}{17}\mathbf{j}+\frac{12}{17}\mathbf{k}\right\}\text{ lb}$$
$$= \{-160\mathbf{i}-180\mathbf{j}+240\mathbf{k}\}\text{ lb} \qquad \textbf{Ans}$$

2-90. Determine the magnitude and coordinate direction angles of the resultant force.

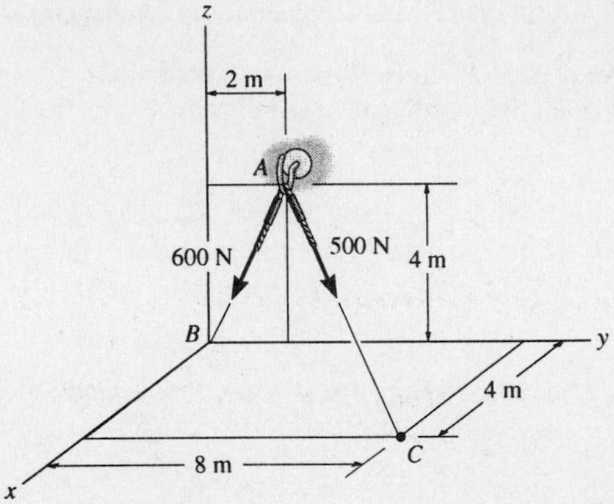

$\mathbf{r}_{AB} = \{-2\mathbf{j}-4\mathbf{k}\}$m; $\quad r_{AB} = 4.472$ m

$$\mathbf{u}_{AB} = \left(\frac{\mathbf{r}_{AB}}{r_{AB}}\right) = -0.447\mathbf{j} - 0.894\mathbf{k}$$

$$\mathbf{F}_{AB} = 600\,\mathbf{u}_{AB} = \{-268.33\mathbf{j} - 536.66\mathbf{k}\}\text{N}$$

$\mathbf{r}_{AC} = \{4\mathbf{i} + 6\mathbf{j} - 4\mathbf{k}\}$m; $\quad r_{AC} = 8.246$ m

$$\mathbf{u}_{AC} = \left(\frac{\mathbf{r}_{AC}}{r_{AC}}\right) = 0.485\mathbf{i} + 0.728\mathbf{j} - 0.485\mathbf{k}$$

$$\mathbf{F}_{AC} = 500\,\mathbf{u}_{AC} = \{242.54\mathbf{i} + 363.80\mathbf{j} - 242.54\mathbf{k}\}\text{N}$$

$$\mathbf{F}_R = \mathbf{F}_{AB} + \mathbf{F}_{AC}$$

$$\mathbf{F}_R = \{242.54\mathbf{i} + 95.47\mathbf{j} - 779.20\mathbf{k}\}$$

$$F_R = \sqrt{(242.54)^2 + (95.47)^2 + (-779.20)^2} = 821.64 = 822\text{ N} \qquad \textbf{Ans}$$

$$\alpha = \cos^{-1}\left(\frac{242.54}{821.64}\right) = 72.8° \qquad \textbf{Ans}$$

$$\beta = \cos^{-1}\left(\frac{95.47}{821.64}\right) = 83.3° \qquad \textbf{Ans}$$

$$\gamma = \cos^{-1}\left(\frac{-779.20}{821.64}\right) = 162° \qquad \textbf{Ans}$$

2-91. Determine the magnitude and coordinate direction angles of the resultant force.

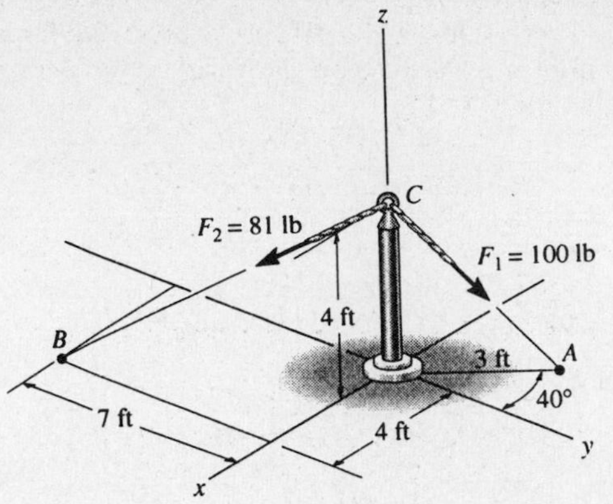

$$\mathbf{F}_1 = -100\left(\frac{3}{5}\right)\sin 40°\,\mathbf{i} + 100\left(\frac{3}{5}\right)\cos 40°\,\mathbf{j} - 100\left(\frac{4}{5}\right)\mathbf{k}$$

$$= \{-38.567\,\mathbf{i} + 45.963\,\mathbf{j} - 80\,\mathbf{k}\}\text{ lb}$$

$$\mathbf{F}_2 = 81\text{ lb}\left(\frac{4}{9}\,\mathbf{i} - \frac{7}{9}\,\mathbf{j} - \frac{4}{9}\,\mathbf{k}\right)$$

$$= \{36\,\mathbf{i} - 63\,\mathbf{j} - 36\,\mathbf{k}\}\text{ lb}$$

$$\mathbf{F}_R = \mathbf{F}_1 + \mathbf{F}_2 = \{-2.567\,\mathbf{i} - 17.04\,\mathbf{j} - 116.0\,\mathbf{k}\}\text{ lb}$$

$$F_R = \sqrt{(-2.567)^2 + (-17.04)^2 + (-116.0)^2} = 117.27\text{ lb} = 117\text{ lb} \quad \textbf{Ans}$$

$$\alpha = \cos^{-1}\left(\frac{-2.567}{117.27}\right) = 91.3° \quad \textbf{Ans}$$

$$\beta = \cos^{-1}\left(\frac{-17.04}{117.27}\right) = 98.4° \quad \textbf{Ans}$$

$$\gamma = \cos^{-1}\left(\frac{-116.0}{117.27}\right) = 172° \quad \textbf{Ans}$$

***2-92.** Express force **F** as a Cartesian vector; then determine its coordinate direction angles.

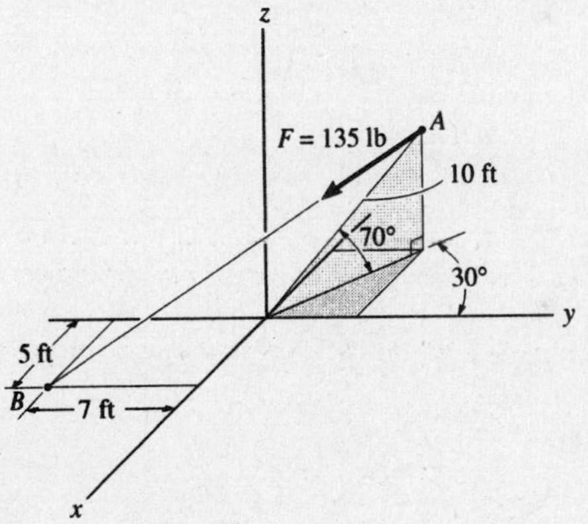

Unit Vector : The coordinates of point A are

$$A(-10\cos 70°\sin 30°,\ 10\cos 70°\cos 30°,\ 10\sin 70°)\text{ ft}$$
$$= A(-1.710,\ 2.962,\ 9.397)\text{ ft}$$

Then

$$\mathbf{r}_{AB} = \{[5-(-1.710)]\mathbf{i} + (-7-2.962)\mathbf{j} + (0-9.397)\mathbf{k}\}\text{ ft}$$
$$= \{6.710\mathbf{i} - 9.962\mathbf{j} - 9.397\mathbf{k}\}\text{ ft}$$
$$r_{AB} = \sqrt{6.710^2 + (-9.962)^2 + (-9.397)^2} = 15.250\text{ ft}$$

$$\mathbf{u}_{AB} = \frac{\mathbf{r}_{AB}}{r_{AB}} = \frac{6.710\mathbf{i} - 9.962\mathbf{j} - 9.397\mathbf{k}}{15.250}$$
$$= 0.4400\mathbf{i} - 0.6532\mathbf{j} - 0.6162\mathbf{k}$$

Force Vector :

$$\mathbf{F} = F\mathbf{u}_{AB} = 135\{0.4400\mathbf{i} - 0.6532\mathbf{j} - 0.6162\mathbf{k}\}\text{ lb}$$
$$= \{59.4\mathbf{i} - 88.2\mathbf{j} - 83.2\mathbf{k}\}\text{ lb} \quad \textbf{Ans}$$

Coordinate Direction Angles : From the unit vector $\mathbf{u}_{AB}$ obtained above, we have

$\cos\alpha = 0.4400$ $\qquad \alpha = 63.9°$ **Ans**
$\cos\beta = -0.6532$ $\qquad \beta = 131°$ **Ans**
$\cos\gamma = -0.6162$ $\qquad \gamma = 128°$ **Ans**

2-93. Express each of the forces in Cartesian vector form and determine the magnitude and coordinate direction angles of the resultant force.

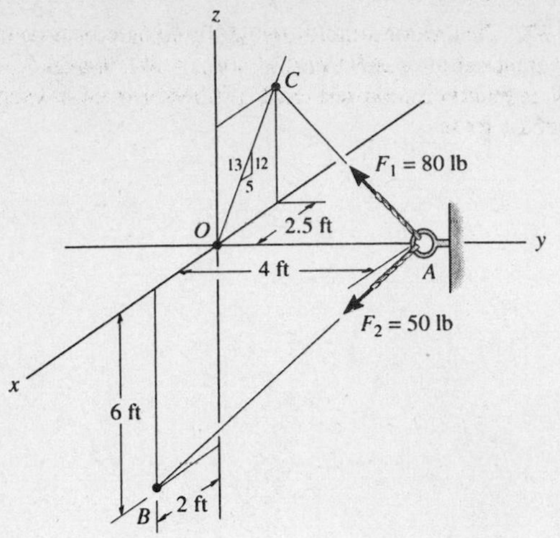

$$\mathbf{r}_{AC} = \left\{-2.5\,\mathbf{i} - 4\,\mathbf{j} + \frac{12}{5}(2.5)\,\mathbf{k}\right\} \text{ ft}$$

$$\mathbf{F}_1 = 80 \text{ lb}\left(\frac{\mathbf{r}_{AC}}{r_{AC}}\right) = -26.20\,\mathbf{i} - 41.93\,\mathbf{j} + 62.89\,\mathbf{k}$$

$$= \{-26.2\,\mathbf{i} - 41.9\,\mathbf{j} + 62.9\,\mathbf{k}\} \text{ lb} \qquad \textbf{Ans}$$

$$\mathbf{r}_{AB} = \{2\,\mathbf{i} - 4\,\mathbf{j} - 6\,\mathbf{k}\}\text{ft}$$

$$\mathbf{F}_2 = 50 \text{ lb}\left(\frac{\mathbf{r}_{AB}}{r_{AB}}\right) = 13.36\,\mathbf{i} - 26.73\,\mathbf{j} - 40.09\,\mathbf{k}$$

$$= \{13.4\,\mathbf{i} - 26.7\,\mathbf{j} - 40.1\,\mathbf{k}\} \text{ lb} \qquad \textbf{Ans}$$

$$\mathbf{F}_R = \mathbf{F}_1 + \mathbf{F}_2$$

$$= -12.84\,\mathbf{i} - 68.65\,\mathbf{j} + 22.80\,\mathbf{k}$$

$$= \{-12.8\,\mathbf{i} - 68.7\,\mathbf{j} + 22.8\,\mathbf{k}\}\text{lb}$$

$$F_R = \sqrt{(-12.84)^2\,(-68.65)^2 + (22.80)^2} = 73.47 = 73.5 \text{ lb} \qquad \textbf{Ans}$$

$$\alpha = \cos^{-1}\left(\frac{-12.84}{73.47}\right) = 100° \qquad \textbf{Ans}$$

$$\beta = \cos^{-1}\left(\frac{-68.65}{73.47}\right) = 159° \qquad \textbf{Ans}$$

$$\gamma = \cos^{-1}\left(\frac{22.80}{73.47}\right) = 71.9° \qquad \textbf{Ans}$$

2-94. The crate, supported by the shear-leg derrick, creates a force of $F_B = 600$ N along strut AB and $F_C = 900$ N along cable AC. Represent each force as a Cartesian vector.

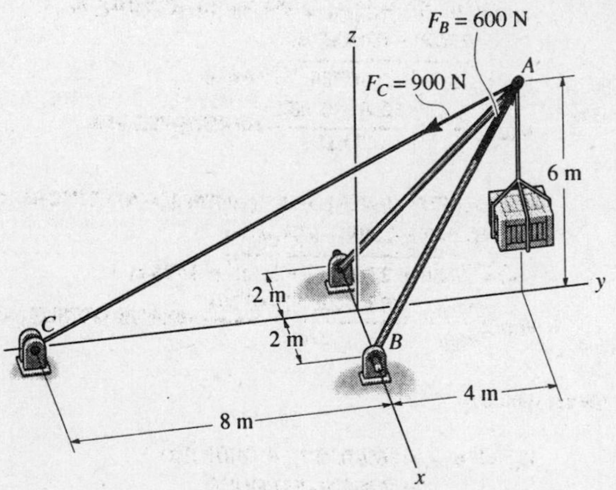

$$\mathbf{r}_{AB} = \{2\,\mathbf{i} - 4\,\mathbf{j} - 6\,\mathbf{k}\}\text{m}$$

$$r_{AB} = \sqrt{(2)^2 + (-4)^2 + (-6)^2} = 7.483 \text{ m}$$

$$\mathbf{u}_{AB} = \left(\frac{\mathbf{r}_{AB}}{r_{AB}}\right) = 0.267\,\mathbf{i} - 0.534\,\mathbf{j} - 0.802\,\mathbf{k}$$

$$\mathbf{F}_B = 600\,\mathbf{u}_{AB} = \{160\,\mathbf{i} - 321\,\mathbf{j} - 481\,\mathbf{k}\}\text{ N} \qquad \textbf{Ans}$$

$$\mathbf{r}_{AC} = \{-12\,\mathbf{j} - 6\,\mathbf{k}\}\text{m}$$

$$r_{AC} = \sqrt{(-12)^2 + (-6)^2} = 13.42 \text{ m}$$

$$\mathbf{u}_{AC} = \left(\frac{\mathbf{r}_{AC}}{r_{AC}}\right) = -0.894\,\mathbf{j} - 0.447\,\mathbf{k}$$

$$\mathbf{F}_C = 900\,\mathbf{u}_{AC} = \{-805\,\mathbf{j} - 402\,\mathbf{k}\}\text{ N} \qquad \textbf{Ans}$$

2-95. The door is held opened by means of two chains. If the tension in AB and CD is $F_A = 300$ N and $F_C = 250$ N, respectively, express each of these forces in Cartesian vector form.

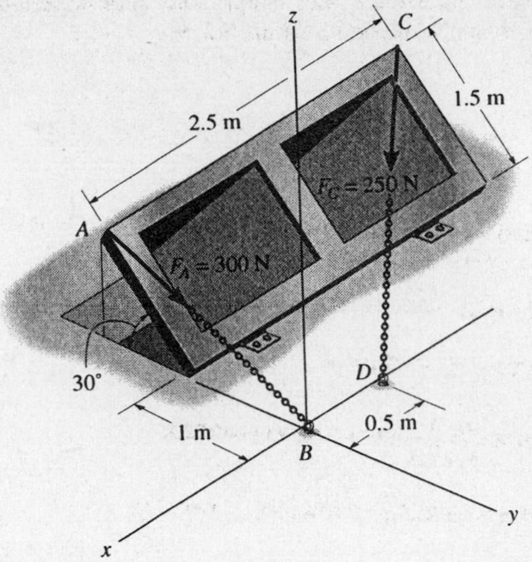

Unit Vector : First determine the position vector $\mathbf{r}_{AB}$ and $\mathbf{r}_{CD}$. The coordinates of points A and C are

$$A[0,\ -(1+1.5\cos 30°),\ 1.5\sin 300°]\ \text{m} = A(0,\ -2.299,\ 0.750)\ \text{m}$$
$$C[-2.50,\ -(1+1.5\cos 30°),\ 1.5\sin 300°]\ \text{m} = C(-2.50,\ -2.299,\ 0.750)\ \text{m}$$

Then

$$\mathbf{r}_{AB} = \{(0-0)\mathbf{i} + [0-(-2.299)]\mathbf{j} + (0-0.750)\mathbf{k}\}\ \text{m}$$
$$= \{2.299\mathbf{j} - 0.750\mathbf{k}\}\ \text{m}$$
$$r_{AB} = \sqrt{2.299^2 + (-0.750)^2} = 2.418\ \text{m}$$
$$\mathbf{u}_{AB} = \frac{\mathbf{r}_{AB}}{r_{AB}} = \frac{2.299\mathbf{j} - 0.750\mathbf{k}}{2.418} = 0.9507\mathbf{j} - 0.3101\mathbf{k}$$

$$\mathbf{r}_{CD} = \{[-0.5-(-2.5)]\mathbf{i} + [0-(-2.299)]\mathbf{j} + (0-0.750)\mathbf{k}\}\ \text{m}$$
$$= \{2.00\mathbf{i} + 2.299\mathbf{j} - 0.750\mathbf{k}\}\ \text{m}$$
$$r_{CD} = \sqrt{2.00^2 + 2.299^2 + (-0.750)^2} = 3.138\ \text{m}$$
$$\mathbf{u}_{CD} = \frac{\mathbf{r}_{CD}}{r_{CD}} = \frac{2.00\mathbf{i} + 2.299\mathbf{j} - 0.750\mathbf{k}}{3.138} = 0.6373\mathbf{i} + 0.7326\mathbf{j} - 0.2390\mathbf{k}$$

Force Vector :

$$\mathbf{F}_A = F_A\mathbf{u}_{AB} = 300\{0.9507\mathbf{j} - 0.3101\mathbf{k}\}\ \text{N}$$
$$= \{285.21\mathbf{j} - 93.04\mathbf{k}\}\ \text{N}$$
$$= \{285\mathbf{j} - 93.0\mathbf{k}\}\ \text{N} \qquad \textbf{Ans}$$

$$\mathbf{F}_C = F_C\mathbf{u}_{CD} = 250\{0.6373\mathbf{i} + 0.7326\mathbf{j} - 0.2390\mathbf{k}\}\ \text{N}$$
$$= \{159.33\mathbf{i} + 183.15\mathbf{j} - 59.75\mathbf{k}\}\ \text{N}$$
$$= \{159\mathbf{i} + 183\mathbf{j} - 59.7\mathbf{k}\}\ \text{N} \qquad \textbf{Ans}$$

***2-96.** The two mooring cables exert forces on the stern of a ship as shown. Represent each force as as Cartesian vector and determine the magnitude and direction of the resultant.

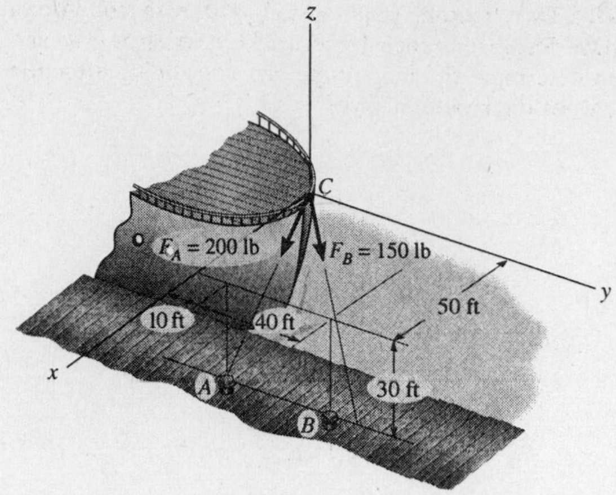

Unit Vector :

$$\mathbf{r}_{CA} = \{(50-0)\mathbf{i}+(10-0)\mathbf{j}+(-30-0)\mathbf{k}\}\text{ ft} = \{50\mathbf{i}+10\mathbf{j}-30\mathbf{k}\}\text{ ft}$$

$$r_{CA} = \sqrt{50^2+10^2+(-30)^2} = 59.16\text{ ft}$$

$$\mathbf{u}_{CA} = \frac{\mathbf{r}_{CA}}{r_{CA}} = \frac{50\mathbf{i}+10\mathbf{j}-30\mathbf{k}}{59.16} = 0.8452\mathbf{i}+0.1690\mathbf{j}-0.5071\mathbf{k}$$

$$\mathbf{r}_{CB} = \{(50-0)\mathbf{i}+(50-0)\mathbf{j}+(-30-0)\mathbf{k}\}\text{ ft} = \{50\mathbf{i}+50\mathbf{j}-30\mathbf{k}\}\text{ ft}$$

$$r_{CB} = \sqrt{50^2+50^2+(-30)^2} = 76.81\text{ ft}$$

$$\mathbf{u}_{CB} = \frac{\mathbf{r}_{CA}}{r_{CA}} = \frac{50\mathbf{i}+50\mathbf{j}-30\mathbf{k}}{76.81} = 0.6509\mathbf{i}+0.6509\mathbf{j}-0.3906\mathbf{k}$$

Force Vector :

$$\begin{aligned}\mathbf{F}_A = F_A\mathbf{u}_{CA} &= 200\{0.8452\mathbf{i}+0.1690\mathbf{j}-0.5071\mathbf{k}\}\text{ lb}\\ &= \{169.03\mathbf{i}+33.81\mathbf{j}-101.42\mathbf{k}\}\text{ lb}\\ &= \{169\mathbf{i}+33.8\mathbf{j}-101\mathbf{k}\}\text{ lb} \qquad \textbf{Ans}\end{aligned}$$

$$\begin{aligned}\mathbf{F}_B = F_B\mathbf{u}_{CB} &= 150\{0.6509\mathbf{i}+0.6509\mathbf{j}-0.3906\mathbf{k}\}\text{ lb}\\ &= \{97.64\mathbf{i}+97.64\mathbf{j}-58.59\mathbf{k}\}\text{ lb}\\ &= \{97.6\mathbf{i}+97.6\mathbf{j}-58.6\mathbf{k}\}\text{ lb} \qquad \textbf{Ans}\end{aligned}$$

Resultant Force :

$$\begin{aligned}\mathbf{F}_R &= \mathbf{F}_A+\mathbf{F}_B\\ &= \{(169.03+97.64)\mathbf{i}+(33.81+97.64)\mathbf{j}+(-101.42-58.59)\mathbf{k}\}\text{ lb}\\ &= \{266.67\mathbf{i}+131.45\mathbf{j}-160.00\mathbf{k}\}\text{ lb}\end{aligned}$$

The magnitude of $\mathbf{F}_R$ is

$$\begin{aligned}F_R &= \sqrt{266.67^2+131.45^2+(-160.00)^2}\\ &= 337.63\text{ lb} = 338\text{ lb} \qquad \textbf{Ans}\end{aligned}$$

The coordinate direction angles of $\mathbf{F}_R$ are

$$\cos\alpha = \frac{266.67}{337.63} \qquad \alpha = 37.8° \qquad \textbf{Ans}$$

$$\cos\beta = \frac{131.45}{337.63} \qquad \beta = 67.1° \qquad \textbf{Ans}$$

$$\cos\gamma = -\frac{160.00}{337.63} \qquad \gamma = 118° \qquad \textbf{Ans}$$

2-97. Two tractors pull on the tree with the forces shown. Represent each force as a Cartesian vector and then determine the magnitude and coordinate direction angles of the resultant force.

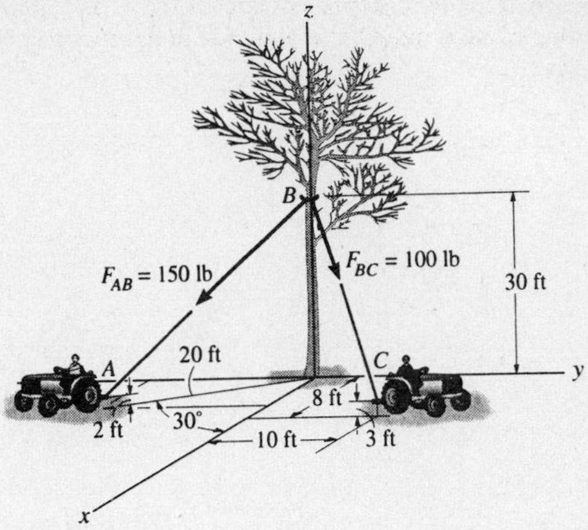

$$\mathbf{r}_{BA} = \{(20\cos 30° - 0)\mathbf{i} + (-20\sin 30° - 0)\mathbf{j} + (2 - 30)\mathbf{k}\}\text{ ft}$$
$$= \{17.32\mathbf{i} - 10.0\mathbf{j} - 28.0\mathbf{k}\}\text{ ft}$$
$$r_{BA} = \sqrt{17.32^2 + (-10.0)^2 + (-28.0)^2} = 34.41\text{ ft}$$
$$\mathbf{u}_{BA} = \frac{\mathbf{r}_{BA}}{r_{BA}} = \frac{17.32\mathbf{i} - 10.0\mathbf{j} - 28.0\mathbf{k}}{34.41} = 0.5034\mathbf{i} - 0.2906\mathbf{j} - 0.8137\mathbf{k}$$

$$\mathbf{r}_{BC} = \{(8-0)\mathbf{i} + (10-0)\mathbf{j} + (3-30)\mathbf{k}\}\text{ ft} = \{8\mathbf{i} + 10\mathbf{j} - 27\mathbf{k}\}\text{ ft}$$
$$r_{BC} = \sqrt{8^2 + 10^2 + (-27)^2} = 29.88\text{ ft}$$
$$\mathbf{u}_{BC} = \frac{\mathbf{r}_{BC}}{r_{BC}} = \frac{8\mathbf{i} + 10\mathbf{j} - 27\mathbf{k}}{29.88} = 0.2677\mathbf{i} + 0.3346\mathbf{j} - 0.9035\mathbf{k}$$

Force Vector:

$$\mathbf{F}_{AB} = F_{AB}\mathbf{u}_{BA} = 150\{0.5034\mathbf{i} - 0.2906\mathbf{j} - 0.8137\mathbf{k}\}\text{ lb}$$
$$= \{75.51\mathbf{i} - 43.59\mathbf{j} - 122.06\mathbf{k}\}\text{ lb}$$
$$= \{75.5\mathbf{i} - 43.6\mathbf{j} - 122\mathbf{k}\}\text{ lb}$$ **Ans**

$$\mathbf{F}_{BC} = F_{BC}\mathbf{u}_{BC} = 100\{0.2677\mathbf{i} + 0.3346\mathbf{j} - 0.9035\mathbf{k}\}\text{ lb}$$
$$= \{26.77\mathbf{i} + 33.46\mathbf{j} - 90.35\mathbf{k}\}\text{ lb}$$
$$= \{26.8\mathbf{i} + 33.5\mathbf{j} - 90.4\mathbf{k}\}\text{ lb}$$ **Ans**

Resultant Force:

$$\mathbf{F}_R = \mathbf{F}_{AB} + \mathbf{F}_{BC}$$
$$= \{(75.51 + 26.77)\mathbf{i} + (-43.59 + 33.46)\mathbf{j} + (-122.06 - 90.35)\mathbf{k}\}\text{ lb}$$
$$= \{102.28\mathbf{i} - 10.13\mathbf{j} - 212.41\mathbf{k}\}\text{ lb}$$

The magnitude of $\mathbf{F}_R$ is

$$F_R = \sqrt{102.28^2 + (-10.13)^2 + (-212.41)^2}$$
$$= 235.97\text{ lb} = 236\text{ lb}$$ **Ans**

The coordinate direction angles of $\mathbf{F}_R$ are

$\cos\alpha = \dfrac{102.28}{235.97}$ $\qquad \alpha = 64.3°$ **Ans**

$\cos\beta = -\dfrac{10.13}{235.97}$ $\qquad \beta = 92.5°$ **Ans**

$\cos\gamma = -\dfrac{212.41}{235.97}$ $\qquad \gamma = 154°$ **Ans**

2-98. The guy wires are used to support the telephone pole. Represent the force in each wire in Cartesian vector form.

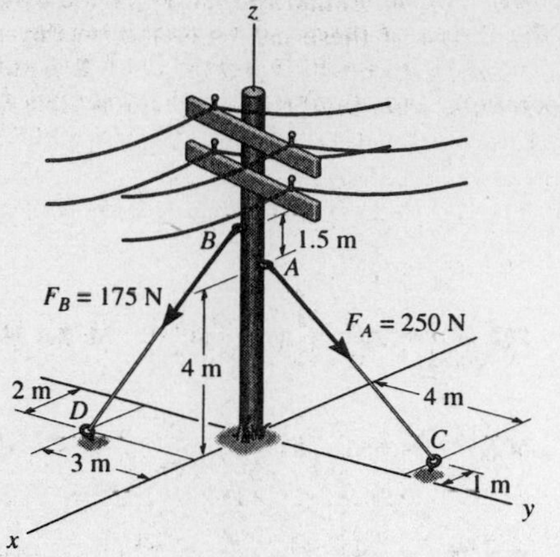

Unit Vector:

$$\mathbf{r}_{AC} = \{(-1-0)\mathbf{i}+(4-0)\mathbf{j}+(0-4)\mathbf{k}\}\text{ m} = \{-1\mathbf{i}+4\mathbf{j}-4\mathbf{k}\}\text{ m}$$

$$r_{AC} = \sqrt{(-1)^2+4^2+(-4)^2} = 5.745\text{ m}$$

$$\mathbf{u}_{AC} = \frac{\mathbf{r}_{AC}}{r_{AC}} = \frac{-1\mathbf{i}+4\mathbf{j}-4\mathbf{k}}{5.745} = -0.1741\mathbf{i}+0.6963\mathbf{j}-0.6963\mathbf{k}$$

$$\mathbf{r}_{BD} = \{(2-0)\mathbf{i}+(-3-0)\mathbf{j}+(0-5.5)\mathbf{k}\}\text{ m} = \{2\mathbf{i}-3\mathbf{j}-5.5\mathbf{k}\}\text{ m}$$

$$r_{BD} = \sqrt{2^2+(-3)^2+(-5.5)^2} = 6.576\text{ m}$$

$$\mathbf{u}_{BD} = \frac{\mathbf{r}_{BD}}{r_{BD}} = \frac{2\mathbf{i}-3\mathbf{j}-5.5\mathbf{k}}{6.576} = 0.3041\mathbf{i}-0.4562\mathbf{j}-0.8363\mathbf{k}$$

Force Vector:

$$\mathbf{F}_A = F_A\mathbf{u}_{AC} = 250\{-0.1741\mathbf{i}+0.6963\mathbf{j}-0.6963\mathbf{k}\}\text{ N}$$
$$= \{-43.52\mathbf{i}+174.08\mathbf{j}-174.08\mathbf{k}\}\text{ N}$$
$$= \{-43.5\mathbf{i}+174\mathbf{j}-174\mathbf{k}\}\text{ N}$$ **Ans**

$$\mathbf{F}_B = F_B\mathbf{u}_{BD} = 175\{0.3041\mathbf{i}-0.4562\mathbf{j}-0.8363\mathbf{k}\}\text{ N}$$
$$= \{53.22\mathbf{i}-79.83\mathbf{j}-146.36\mathbf{k}\}\text{ N}$$
$$= \{53.2\mathbf{i}-79.8\mathbf{j}-146\mathbf{k}\}\text{ N}$$ **Ans**

2-99. The cable AO exerts a force on the top of the pole of $\mathbf{F} = \{-120\mathbf{i} - 90\mathbf{j} - 80\mathbf{k}\}$ lb. If the cable has a length of 34 ft, determine the height z of the pole and the location (x, y) of its base.

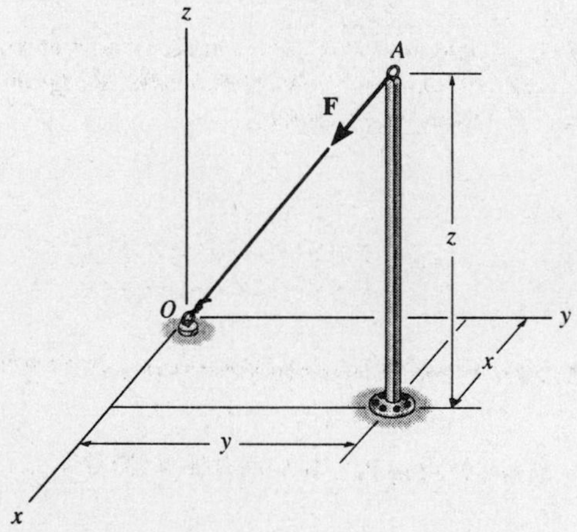

$$F = \sqrt{(-120)^2+(-90)^2+(-80)^2} = 170\text{ lb}$$

$$\mathbf{u} = \frac{\mathbf{F}}{F} = -\frac{120}{170}\mathbf{i} - \frac{90}{170}\mathbf{j} - \frac{80}{170}\mathbf{k}$$

$$\mathbf{r} = 34\,\mathbf{u} = \{-24\mathbf{i} - 18\mathbf{j} - 16\mathbf{k}\}\text{ ft}$$

Thus,

$x = 24$ ft **Ans**

$y = 18$ ft **Ans**

$z = 16$ ft **Ans**

*2-100. The antenna tower is supported by three cables. If the forces of these cables acting on the antenna are $F_B = 520$ N, $F_C = 680$ N, and $F_D = 560$ N, determine the magnitude and direction of the resultant force acting at A.

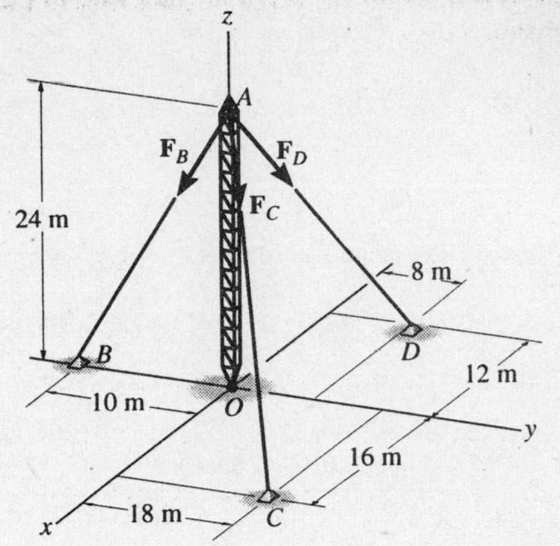

$$F_B = 520\left(\frac{\mathbf{r}_{AB}}{r_{AB}}\right) = 520\left(-\frac{10}{26}\mathbf{j} - \frac{24}{26}\mathbf{k}\right) = -200\mathbf{j} - 480\mathbf{k}$$

$$F_C = 680\left(\frac{\mathbf{r}_{AC}}{r_{AC}}\right) = 680\left(\frac{16}{34}\mathbf{i} + \frac{18}{34}\mathbf{j} - \frac{24}{34}\mathbf{k}\right) = 320\mathbf{i} + 360\mathbf{j} - 480\mathbf{k}$$

$$F_D = 560\left(\frac{\mathbf{r}_{AD}}{r_{AD}}\right) = 560\left(-\frac{12}{28}\mathbf{i} + \frac{8}{28}\mathbf{j} - \frac{24}{28}\mathbf{k}\right) = -240\mathbf{i} + 160\mathbf{j} - 480\mathbf{k}$$

$$\mathbf{F}_R = \Sigma\mathbf{F} = \{80\mathbf{i} + 320\mathbf{j} - 1440\mathbf{k}\}\text{ N}$$

$$F_R = \sqrt{(80)^2 + (320)^2 + (-1440)^2} = 1477.3 = 1.48\text{ kN} \quad \textbf{Ans}$$

$$\alpha = \cos^{-1}\left(\frac{80}{1477.3}\right) = 86.9° \quad \textbf{Ans}$$

$$\beta = \cos^{-1}\left(\frac{320}{1477.3}\right) = 77.5° \quad \textbf{Ans}$$

$$\gamma = \cos^{-1}\left(\frac{-1440}{1477.3}\right) = 167° \quad \textbf{Ans}$$

2-101. The load at A creates a force of 60 lb in wire AB. Express this force as a Cartesian vector acting on A and directed toward B as shown.

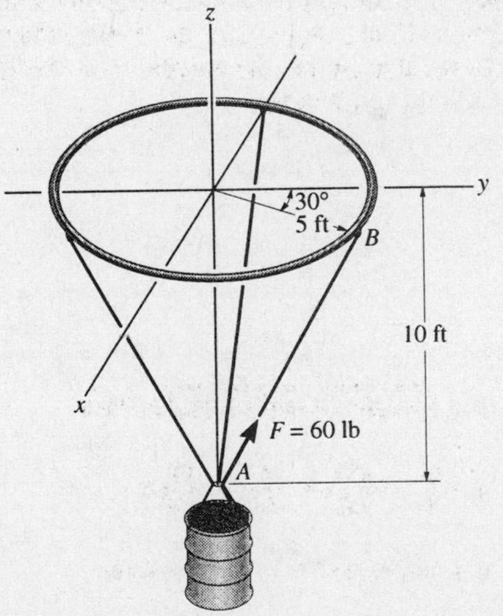

Unit Vector: First determine the position vector $\mathbf{r}_{AB}$. The coordinates of point B are

$$B(5\sin 30°, 5\cos 30°, 0)\text{ ft} = B(2.50, 4.330, 0)\text{ ft}$$

Then

$$\mathbf{r}_{AB} = \{(2.50-0)\mathbf{i} + (4.330-0)\mathbf{j} + [0-(-10)]\mathbf{k}\}\text{ ft}$$
$$= \{2.50\mathbf{i} + 4.330\mathbf{j} + 10.0\mathbf{k}\}\text{ ft}$$
$$r_{AB} = \sqrt{2.50^2 + 4.330^2 + 10.0^2} = 11.180\text{ ft}$$

$$\mathbf{u}_{AB} = \frac{\mathbf{r}_{AB}}{r_{AB}} = \frac{2.50\mathbf{i} + 4.330\mathbf{j} + 10.0\mathbf{k}}{11.180}$$
$$= 0.2236\mathbf{i} + 0.3873\mathbf{j} + 0.8944\mathbf{k}$$

Force Vector:

$$\mathbf{F} = F\mathbf{u}_{AB} = 60\{0.2236\mathbf{i} + 0.3873\mathbf{j} + 0.8944\mathbf{k}\}\text{ lb}$$
$$= \{13.4\mathbf{i} + 23.2\mathbf{j} + 53.7\mathbf{k}\}\text{ lb} \quad \textbf{Ans}$$

2-102. The pipe is supported at its ends by a cord AB. If the cord exerts a force of $F = 12$ lb on the pipe at A, express this force as a Cartesian vector.

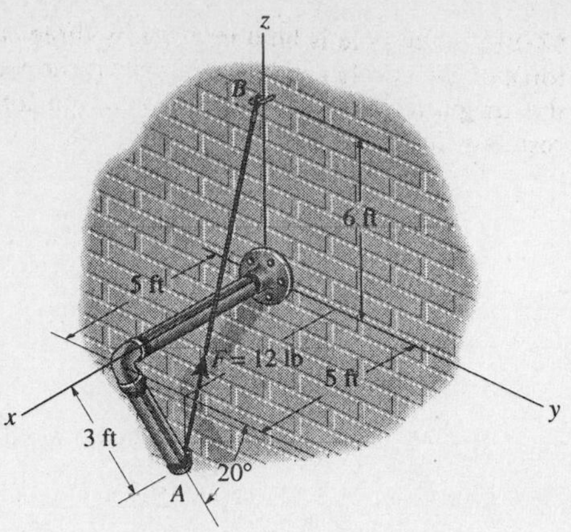

Unit Vector: The coordinates of point A are

$$A(5,\ 3\cos 20^\circ,\ -3\sin 20^\circ)\ \text{ft} = A(5.00,\ 2.819,\ -1.026)\ \text{ft}$$

Then

$$\mathbf{r}_{AB} = \{(0-5.00)\mathbf{i} + (0-2.819)\mathbf{j} + [6-(-1.026)]\mathbf{k}\}\ \text{ft}$$
$$= \{-5.00\mathbf{i} - 2.819\mathbf{j} + 7.026\mathbf{k}\}\ \text{ft}$$
$$r_{AB} = \sqrt{(-5.00)^2 + (-2.819)^2 + 7.026^2} = 9.073\ \text{ft}$$

$$\mathbf{u}_{AB} = \frac{\mathbf{r}_{AB}}{r_{AB}} = \frac{-5.00\mathbf{i} - 2.819\mathbf{j} + 7.026\mathbf{k}}{9.073}$$
$$= -0.5511\mathbf{i} - 0.3107\mathbf{j} + 0.7744\mathbf{k}$$

Force Vector:

$$\mathbf{F} = F\mathbf{u}_{AB} = 12\{-0.5511\mathbf{i} - 0.3107\mathbf{j} + 0.7744\mathbf{k}\}\ \text{lb}$$
$$= \{-6.61\mathbf{i} - 3.73\mathbf{j} + 9.29\mathbf{k}\}\ \text{lb}$$ **Ans**

2-103. The pole is held in place by three cables. If the force of each cable acting on the pole is shown, determine the position $(x,\ 0,\ z)$ for fixing cable DA so that the resultant force exerted on the pole is directed along its axis, from D towards O.

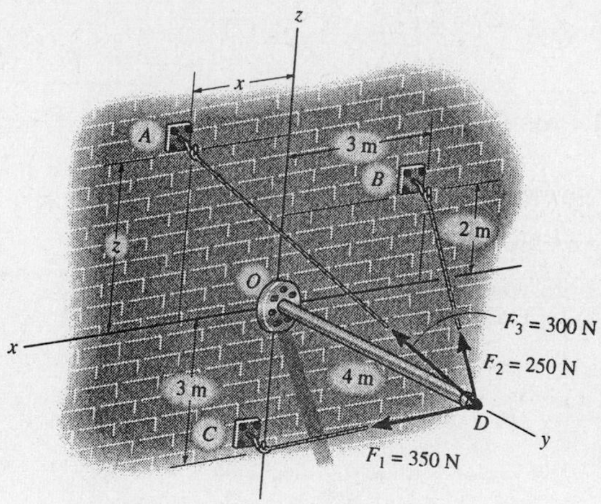

$$\Sigma F_x = F_{Rx};\qquad 300\frac{x}{\sqrt{x^2+4^2+z^2}} - 250\frac{3}{\sqrt{(-3)^2+(-4)^2+(2)^2}} = 0$$

$$\frac{x}{\sqrt{x^2+4^2+z^2}} = 0.464 \qquad (1)$$

$$\Sigma F_z = F_{Rz};\qquad 300\frac{z}{\sqrt{x^2+4^2+z^2}} + 250\frac{2}{\sqrt{(-3)^2+(-4)^2+(2)^2}} - 350\left(\frac{3}{5}\right) = 0$$

$$\frac{z}{\sqrt{x^2+4^2+z^2}} = 0.391 \qquad (2)$$

$$\cos^2\alpha + \cos^2\beta + \cos^2\gamma = 1$$

$$(0.464)^2 + \left(\frac{-4}{\sqrt{x^2+4^2+z^2}}\right)^2 + (0.391)^2 = 1$$

$$\sqrt{x^2+4^2+z^2} = 5.032 \qquad (3)$$

Substitute Eq. (3) into Eqs. (1) and (2). Solving:

$x = 2.34$ m **Ans**

$z = 1.96$ m **Ans**

***2-104.** The pole is held in place by three cables. If the force of each cable acting on the pole is shown, determine the magnitude and coordinate direction angles of the resultant force. Set $x = 3.50$ m, $z = 3$ m.

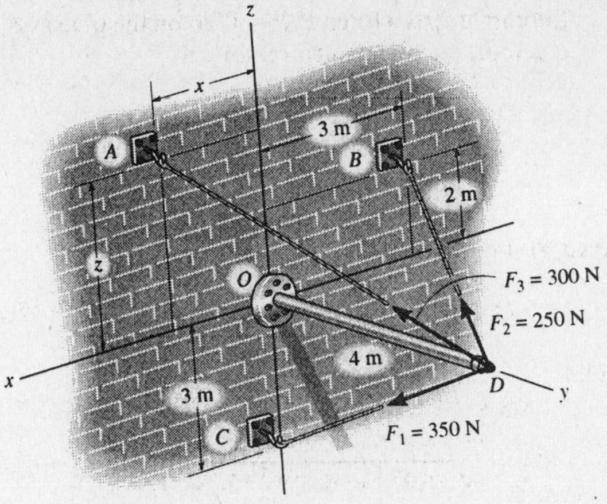

$$F_{Rx} = 300\frac{3.50}{\sqrt{(3.50)^2 + (4)^2 + (3)^2}} - 250\frac{3}{\sqrt{(-3)^2 + (-4)^2 + (2)^2}} = 32.77 \text{ N}$$

$$F_{Ry} = -350\left(\frac{4}{5}\right) - 300\frac{4}{\sqrt{(3.50)^2 + 4^2 + 3^2}} - 250\frac{4}{\sqrt{(-3)^2 + (-4)^2 + (2)^2}} = -662.3 \text{ N}$$

$$F_{Rz} = -350\left(\frac{3}{5}\right) + 300\frac{3}{\sqrt{(3.50)^2 + 4^2 + 3^2}} + 250\frac{2}{\sqrt{(-3)^2 + (-4)^2 + (2)^2}} = 30.31 \text{ N}$$

$$F_R = \sqrt{(32.77)^2 + (-662.3)^2 + (30.31)^2} = 663.8 = 664 \text{ N} \quad \textbf{Ans}$$

$$\alpha = \cos^{-1}\left(\frac{32.77}{663.8}\right) = 87.2^\circ \quad \textbf{Ans}$$

$$\beta = \cos^{-1}\left(\frac{-662.3}{663.8}\right) = 176^\circ \quad \textbf{Ans}$$

$$\gamma = \cos^{-1}\left(\frac{30.31}{663.8}\right) = 87.4^\circ \quad \textbf{Ans}$$

2-105. The load at A creates a force of 200 N in wire AB. Express this force as a Cartesian vector, acting on A and directed towards B.

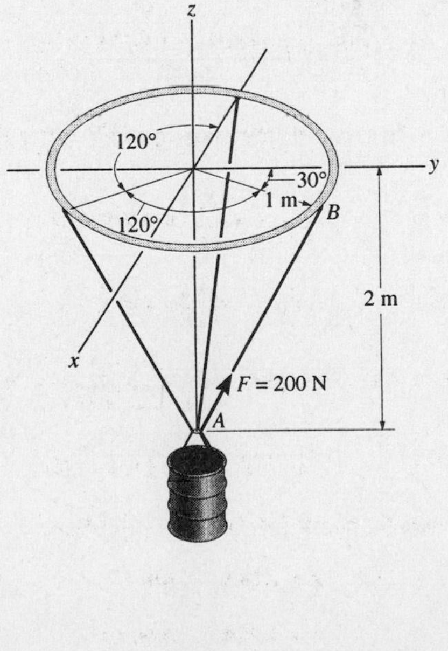

$$\mathbf{r}_{AB} = (1\sin 30^\circ - 0)\mathbf{i} + (1\cos 30^\circ - 0)\mathbf{j} + (2 - 0)\mathbf{k}$$

$$= \{0.5\,\mathbf{i} + 0.866\,\mathbf{j} + 2\mathbf{k}\}\text{m}$$

$$r_{AB} = \sqrt{(0.5)^2 + (0.866)^2 + (2)^2} = 2.236 \text{ m}$$

$$\mathbf{u}_{AB} = \left(\frac{\mathbf{r}_{AB}}{r_{AB}}\right) = 0.2236\mathbf{i} + 0.3873\,\mathbf{j} + 0.8944\,\mathbf{k}$$

$$\mathbf{F} = 200\,\mathbf{u}_{AB} = \{44.7\,\mathbf{i} + 77.5\,\mathbf{j} + 179\,\mathbf{k}\}\text{ N} \quad \textbf{A}$$

2-106. The cylindrical plate is subjected to the three cable forces which are concurrent at point D. Express each force which the cables exert on the plate as a Cartesian vector, and determine the magnitude and coordinate direction angles of the resultant force.

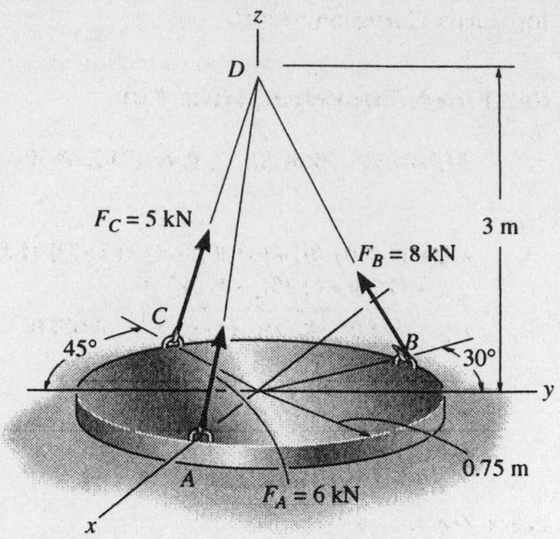

$$\mathbf{r}_A = (0-0.75)\mathbf{i} + (0-0)\mathbf{j} + (3-0)\mathbf{k} = \{-0.75\,\mathbf{i} + 0\,\mathbf{j} + 3\,\mathbf{k}\}\text{ m}$$

$$r_A = \sqrt{(-0.75)^2 + 0^2 + 3^2} = 3.0923\text{ m}$$

$$\mathbf{F}_A = F_A\left(\frac{\mathbf{r}_A}{r_A}\right) = 6\left(\frac{-0.75\,\mathbf{i} + 3\,\mathbf{k}}{3.0923}\right)$$

$$= \{-1.4552\,\mathbf{i} + 5.8209\,\mathbf{k}\}\text{ kN}$$

$$= \{-1.46\,\mathbf{i} + 5.82\,\mathbf{k}\}\text{ kN} \qquad \textbf{Ans}$$

$$\mathbf{r}_C = [0-(-0.75\sin 45°)]\mathbf{i} + [0-(-0.75\cos 45°)]\mathbf{j} + (3-0)\mathbf{k}$$

$$= \{0.5303\,\mathbf{i} + 0.5303\,\mathbf{j} + 3\,\mathbf{k}\}\text{ m}$$

$$r_C = \sqrt{(0.5303)^2 + (0.5303)^2 + 3^2} = 3.0923\text{ m}$$

$$\mathbf{F}_C = F_C\left(\frac{\mathbf{r}_C}{r_C}\right) = 5\left(\frac{0.5303\,\mathbf{i} + 0.5303\,\mathbf{j} + 3\,\mathbf{k}}{3.0923}\right)$$

$$= \{0.8575\,\mathbf{i} + 0.8575\,\mathbf{j} + 4.8507\,\mathbf{k}\}\text{ kN}$$

$$= \{0.857\,\mathbf{i} + 0.857\,\mathbf{j} + 4.85\,\mathbf{k}\}\text{ kN} \qquad \textbf{Ans}$$

$$\mathbf{r}_B = [0-(-0.75\sin 30°)]\mathbf{i} + (0-0.75\cos 30°)\mathbf{j} + (3-0)\mathbf{k}$$

$$= \{0.375\,\mathbf{i} - 0.6495\,\mathbf{j} + 3\,\mathbf{k}\}\text{ m}$$

$$r_B = \sqrt{(0.375)^2 + (-0.6495)^2 + 3^2} = 3.0923\text{ m}$$

$$\mathbf{F}_B = F_B\left(\frac{\mathbf{r}_B}{r_B}\right) = 8\left(\frac{0.375\,\mathbf{i} - 0.6495\,\mathbf{j} + 3\,\mathbf{k}}{3.0923}\right)$$

$$= \{0.9701\mathbf{i} - 1.6803\mathbf{j} + 7.7611\mathbf{k}\}\text{ kN}$$

$$= \{0.970\mathbf{i} - 1.68\mathbf{j} + 7.76\mathbf{k}\}\text{ kN} \qquad \textbf{Ans}$$

$$\mathbf{F}_R = \mathbf{F}_A + \mathbf{F}_B + \mathbf{F}_C$$

$$= \{-1.4552\,\mathbf{i} + 5.8209\,\mathbf{k}\} + \{0.9701\,\mathbf{i} - 1.6803\,\mathbf{j} + 7.7611\,\mathbf{k}\}$$

$$+ \{0.8575\,\mathbf{i} + 0.8575\,\mathbf{j} + 4.8507\,\mathbf{k}\}$$

$$= \{0.3724\,\mathbf{i} - 0.8228\,\mathbf{j} + 18.4327\,\mathbf{k}\}\text{ kN}$$

$$F_R = \sqrt{(0.3724)^2 + (-0.8228)^2 + (18.4327)^2}$$

$$= 18.4548\text{ kN} = 18.5\text{ kN} \qquad \textbf{Ans}$$

$$\mathbf{u}_R = \frac{\mathbf{F}_R}{F_R} = \frac{0.3724\mathbf{i} - 0.8228\mathbf{j} + 18.4327\mathbf{k}}{18.4548}$$

$$= 0.02018\mathbf{i} - 0.04459\mathbf{j} + 0.9988\mathbf{k}$$

$\cos\alpha = 0.02018$ $\qquad \alpha = 88.8°$ $\qquad$ **Ans**

$\cos\beta = -0.04458$ $\qquad \beta = 92.6°$ $\qquad$ **Ans**

$\cos\gamma = 0.9988$ $\qquad \gamma = 2.81°$ $\qquad$ **Ans**

2-107. The cable, attached to the shear-leg derrick, exerts a force on the derrick of $F = 350$ lb. Express this force as a Cartesian vector.

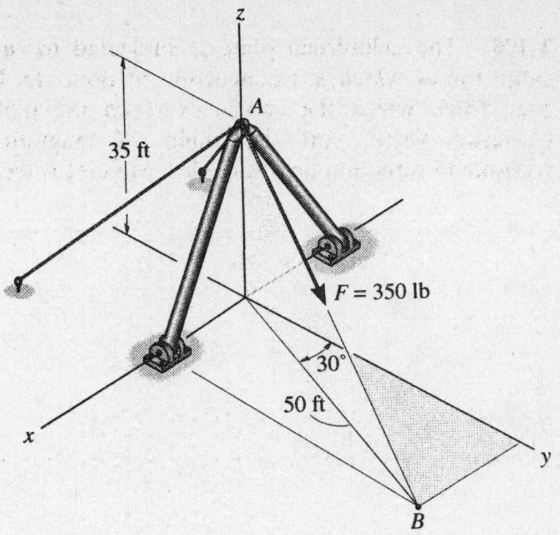

Unit Vector : The coordinates of point *B* are

$$B(50\sin 30°,\ 50\cos 30°,\ 0)\ \text{ft} = B(25.0,\ 43.301,\ 0)\ \text{ft}$$

Then

$$\mathbf{r}_{AB} = \{(25.0-0)\mathbf{i}+(43.301-0)\mathbf{j}+(0-35)\mathbf{k}\}\ \text{ft}$$
$$= \{25.0\mathbf{i}+43.301\mathbf{j}-35.0\mathbf{k}\}\ \text{ft}$$
$$r_{AB} = \sqrt{25.0^2+43.301^2+(-35.0)^2} = 61.033\ \text{ft}$$

$$\mathbf{u}_{AB} = \frac{\mathbf{r}_{AB}}{r_{AB}} = \frac{25.0\mathbf{i}+43.301\mathbf{j}-35.0\mathbf{k}}{61.033}$$
$$= 0.4096\mathbf{i}+0.7094\mathbf{j}-0.5735\mathbf{k}$$

Force Vector :

$$\mathbf{F} = F\mathbf{u}_{AB} = 350\{0.4096\mathbf{i}+0.7094\mathbf{j}-0.5735\mathbf{k}\}\ \text{lb}$$
$$= \{143\mathbf{i}+248\mathbf{j}-201\mathbf{k}\}\ \text{lb} \qquad \textbf{Ans}$$

***2-108.** The window is held open by chain *AB*. Determine the length of the chain, and express the 50-lb force acting at *A* along the chain as a Cartesian vector and determine its coordinate direction angles.

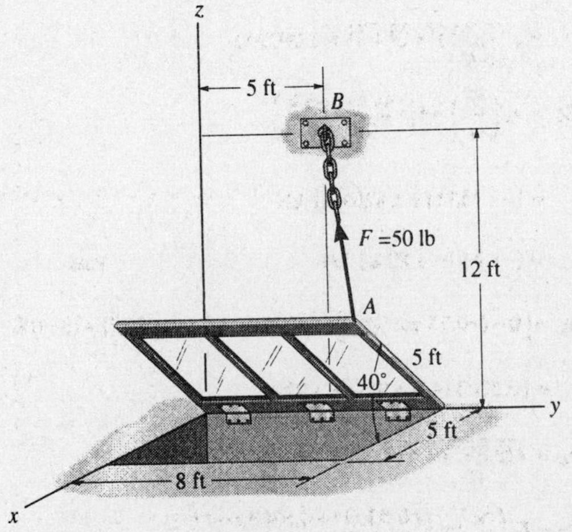

Unit Vector : The coordinates of point *A* are

$$A(5\cos 40°,\ 8,\ 5\sin 40°)\ \text{ft} = A(3.830,\ 8.00,\ 3.214)\ \text{ft}$$

Then

$$\mathbf{r}_{AB} = \{(0-3.830)\mathbf{i}+(5-8.00)\mathbf{j}+(12-3.214)\mathbf{k}\}\ \text{ft}$$
$$= \{-3.830\mathbf{i}-3.00\mathbf{j}+8.786\mathbf{k}\}\ \text{ft}$$
$$r_{AB} = \sqrt{(-3.830)^2+(-3.00)^2+8.786^2} = 10.043\ \text{ft} = 10.0\ \text{ft} \qquad \textbf{Ans}$$

$$\mathbf{u}_{AB} = \frac{\mathbf{r}_{AB}}{r_{AB}} = \frac{-3.830\mathbf{i}-3.00\mathbf{j}+8.786\mathbf{k}}{10.043}$$
$$= -0.3814\mathbf{i}-0.2987\mathbf{j}+0.8748\mathbf{k}$$

Force Vector :

$$\mathbf{F} = F\mathbf{u}_{AB} = 50\{-0.3814\mathbf{i}-0.2987\mathbf{j}+0.8748\mathbf{k}\}\ \text{lb}$$
$$= \{-19.1\mathbf{i}-14.9\mathbf{j}+43.7\mathbf{k}\}\ \text{lb} \qquad \textbf{Ans}$$

Coordinate Direction Angles : From the unit vector $\mathbf{u}_{AB}$ obtained above, we have

$$\cos\alpha = -0.3814 \qquad \alpha = 112° \qquad \textbf{Ans}$$
$$\cos\beta = -0.2987 \qquad \beta = 107° \qquad \textbf{Ans}$$
$$\cos\gamma = 0.8748 \qquad \gamma = 29.0° \qquad \textbf{Ans}$$

2-109. Given the three vectors **A, B,** and **D,** show that $\mathbf{A}\cdot(\mathbf{B}+\mathbf{D}) = (\mathbf{A}\cdot\mathbf{B}) + (\mathbf{A}\cdot\mathbf{D})$.

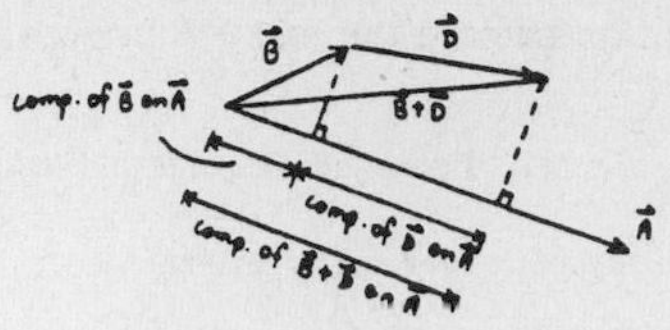

Since the component of $(\mathbf{B}+\mathbf{D})$ is equal to the sum of the components of $\mathbf{B}$ and $\mathbf{D}$, then

$$\mathbf{A}\cdot(\mathbf{B}+\mathbf{D}) = \mathbf{A}\cdot\mathbf{B} + \mathbf{A}\cdot\mathbf{D} \qquad \text{(QED)}$$

Also,

$$\mathbf{A}\cdot(\mathbf{B}+\mathbf{D}) = (A_x\mathbf{i} + A_y\mathbf{j} + A_z\mathbf{k})\cdot[(B_x + D_x)\mathbf{i} + (B_y + D_y)\mathbf{j} + (B_z + D_z)\mathbf{k}]$$

$$= A_x(B_x + D_x) + A_y(B_y + D_y) + A_z(B_z + D_z)$$

$$= (A_xB_x + A_yB_y + A_zB_z) + (A_xD_x + A_yD_y + A_zD_z)$$

$$= (\mathbf{A}\cdot\mathbf{B}) + (\mathbf{A}\cdot\mathbf{D}) \qquad \text{(QED)}$$

2-110. Determine the angle θ between the tails of the two vectors.

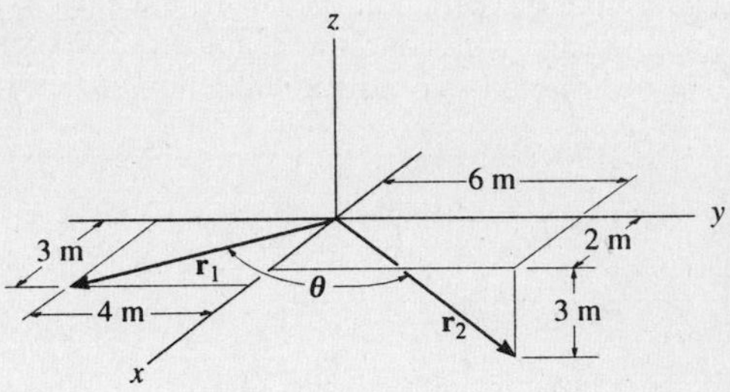

Position Vectors :

$$\mathbf{r}_1 = \{(3-0)\mathbf{i} + (-4-0)\mathbf{j} + (0-0)\mathbf{k}\}\ \text{m}$$
$$= \{3\mathbf{i} - 4\mathbf{j}\}\ \text{m}$$

$$\mathbf{r}_2 = \{(2-0)\mathbf{i} + (6-0)\mathbf{j} + (-3-0)\mathbf{k}\}\ \text{m}$$
$$= \{2\mathbf{i} + 6\mathbf{j} - 3\mathbf{k}\}\ \text{m}$$

The magnitude of postion vectors are

$$r_1 = \sqrt{3^2 + (-4)^2} = 5.00\ \text{m} \qquad r_2 = \sqrt{2^2 + 6^2 + (-3)^2} = 7.00\ \text{m}$$

Angle Between Two Vectors θ:

$$\mathbf{r}_1\cdot\mathbf{r}_2 = (3\mathbf{i} - 4\mathbf{j})\cdot(2\mathbf{i} + 6\mathbf{j} - 3\mathbf{k})$$
$$= 3(2) + (-4)(6) + 0(-3)$$
$$= -18.0\ \text{m}^2$$

Then,

$$\theta = \cos^{-1}\left(\frac{\mathbf{r}_1\cdot\mathbf{r}_2}{r_1 r_2}\right) = \cos^{-1}\left[\frac{-18.0}{5.00(7.00)}\right] = 121° \qquad \textbf{Ans}$$

2-111. Determine the angle θ between the two cables.

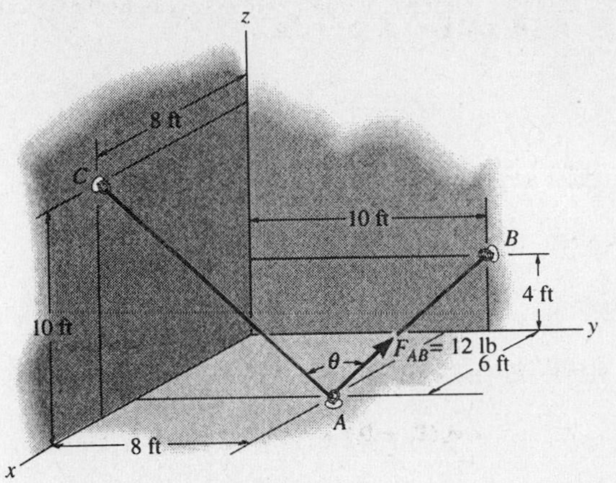

$$\theta = \cos^{-1}\left(\frac{\mathbf{r}_{AC}\cdot\mathbf{r}_{AB}}{r_{AC}\,r_{AB}}\right)$$

$$= \cos^{-1}\left[\frac{(2\mathbf{i} - 8\mathbf{j} + 10\mathbf{k})\cdot(-6\mathbf{i} + 2\mathbf{j} + 4\mathbf{k})}{\sqrt{2^2 + (-8)^2 + 10^2}\,\sqrt{(-6)^2 + 2^2 + 4^2}}\right]$$

$$= \cos^{-1}\left(\frac{12}{96.99}\right)$$

$\theta = 82.9°$ **Ans**

***2-112.** Determine the projected component of the force $F = 12$ lb acting in the direction of cable AC. Express the result as a Cartesian vector.

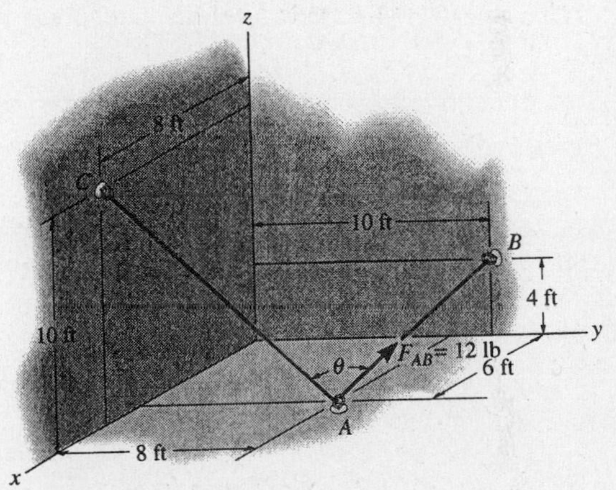

$\mathbf{r}_{AC} = \{2\mathbf{i} - 8\mathbf{j} + 10\mathbf{k}\}$ ft

$\mathbf{r}_{AB} = \{-6\mathbf{i} + 2\mathbf{j} + 4\mathbf{k}\}$ft

$$\mathbf{F}_{AB} = 12\left(\frac{\mathbf{r}_{AB}}{r_{AB}}\right) = 12\left(-\frac{6}{7.483}\mathbf{i} + \frac{2}{7.483}\mathbf{j} + \frac{4}{7.483}\mathbf{k}\right)$$

$\mathbf{F}_{AB} = \{-9.621\mathbf{i} + 3.207\mathbf{j} + 6.414\mathbf{k}\}$ lb

$$\mathbf{u}_{AC} = \frac{2}{12.961}\mathbf{i} - \frac{8}{12.961}\mathbf{j} + \frac{10}{12.961}\mathbf{k}$$

$$\text{Proj}F_{AB} = \mathbf{F}_{AB}\cdot\mathbf{u}_{AC} = -9.621\left(\frac{2}{12.961}\right) + 3.207\left(-\frac{8}{12.961}\right) + 6.414\left(\frac{10}{12.961}\right)$$

$= 1.4846$

$\text{Proj}\mathbf{F}_{AB} = F_{AB}\,\mathbf{u}_{AC}$

$$\text{Proj}\mathbf{F}_{AB} = (1.4846)\left[\frac{2}{12.962}\mathbf{i} - \frac{8}{12.962}\mathbf{j} + \frac{10}{12.962}\mathbf{k}\right]$$

$\text{Proj}\mathbf{F}_{AB} = \{0.229\mathbf{i} - 0.916\mathbf{j} + 1.15\mathbf{k}\}$ lb **Ans**

2-113. Determine the angle θ between the y axis of the pole and the wire AB.

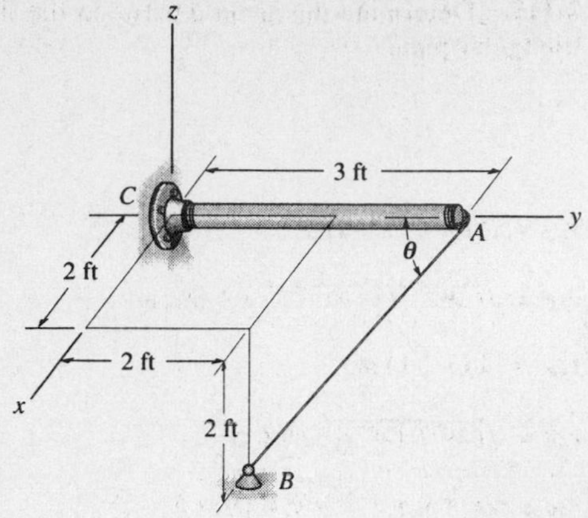

Position Vector :

$$\mathbf{r}_{AO} = \{-3\mathbf{j}\}\ \text{ft}$$

$$\mathbf{r}_{AB} = \{(2-0)\mathbf{i} + (2-3)\mathbf{j} + (-2-0)\mathbf{k}\}\ \text{ft}$$
$$= \{2\mathbf{i} - 1\mathbf{j} - 2\mathbf{k}\}\ \text{ft}$$

The magnitudes of the postion vectors are

$$r_{AO} = 3.00\ \text{ft} \qquad r_{AB} = \sqrt{2^2 + (-1)^2 + (-2)^2} = 3.00\ \text{ft}$$

The Angles Between Two Vectors $\boldsymbol{\theta}$ **:** The dot product of two vectors must be determined first.

$$\mathbf{r}_{AO} \cdot \mathbf{r}_{AB} = (-3\mathbf{j}) \cdot (2\mathbf{i} - 1\mathbf{j} - 2\mathbf{k})$$
$$= 0(2) + (-3)(-1) + 0(-2)$$
$$= 3$$

Then,

$$\theta = \cos^{-1}\left(\frac{\mathbf{r}_{AO} \cdot \mathbf{r}_{AB}}{r_{AO} r_{AB}}\right) = \cos^{-1}\left[\frac{3}{3.00(3.00)}\right] = 70.5^\circ \qquad \textbf{Ans}$$

2-114. The force $\mathbf{F} = \{25\mathbf{i} - 50\mathbf{j} + 10\mathbf{k}\}$ N acts at the end A of the pipe assembly. Determine the magnitude of the components $\mathbf{F}_1$ and $\mathbf{F}_2$ which act along the axis of AB and perpendicular to it.

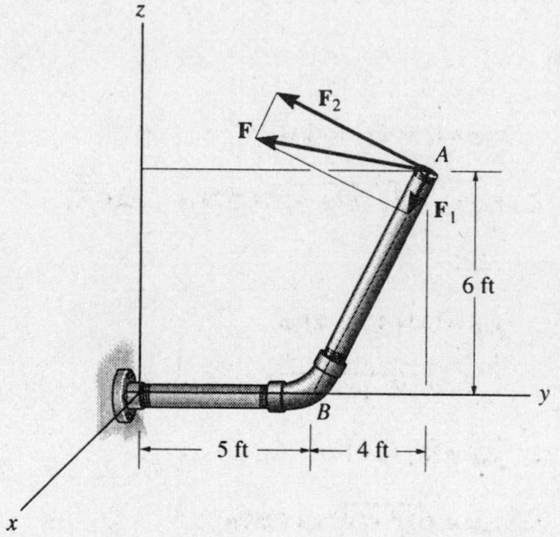

Unit Vector : The unit vector along Aa axis is

$$\mathbf{u}_{AB} = \frac{(0-0)\mathbf{i} + (5-9)\mathbf{j} + (0-6)\mathbf{k}}{\sqrt{(0-0)^2 + (5-9)^2 + (0-6)^2}} = -0.5547\mathbf{j} - 0.8321\mathbf{k}$$

Projected Component of* F *Along AB Axis :

$$F_1 = \mathbf{F} \cdot \mathbf{u}_{AB} = (25\mathbf{i} - 50\mathbf{j} + 10\mathbf{k}) \cdot (-0.5547\mathbf{j} - 0.8321\mathbf{k})$$
$$= (25)(0) + (-50)(-0.5547) + (10)(-0.8321)$$
$$= 19.414\ \text{N} = 19.4\ \text{N} \qquad \textbf{Ans}$$

Component of* F *Perpendicular to AB Axis : The magnitude of force **F** is $F = \sqrt{25^2 + (-50)^2 + 10^2} = 56.789$ N.

$$F_2 = \sqrt{F^2 - F_1^2} = \sqrt{56.789^2 - 19.414^2} = 53.4\ \text{N} \qquad \textbf{Ans}$$

2-115. Determine the angle θ between the sides of the triangular plate.

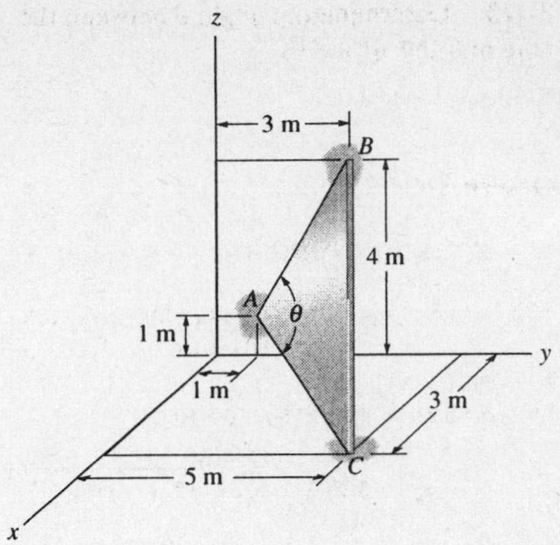

$\mathbf{r}_{AC} = \{3\mathbf{i} + 4\mathbf{j} - 1\mathbf{k}\}$ m

$r_{AC} = \sqrt{(3)^2 + (4)^2 + (-1)^2} = 5.0990$ m

$\mathbf{r}_{AB} = \{2\mathbf{j} + 3\mathbf{k}\}$ m

$r_{AB} = \sqrt{(2)^2 + (3)^2} = 3.6056$ m

$\mathbf{r}_{AC} \cdot \mathbf{r}_{AB} = 0 + 4(2) + (-1)(3) = 5$

$$\theta = \cos^{-1}\left(\frac{\mathbf{r}_{AC} \cdot \mathbf{r}_{AB}}{r_{AC}\, r_{AB}}\right) = \cos^{-1}\frac{5}{(5.0990)(3.6056)}$$

$\theta = 74.219° = 74.2°$ **Ans**

***2-116.** Determine the length of side BC of the triangular plate. Solve the problem by finding the magnitude of $\mathbf{r}_{BC}$; then check the result by first finding θ, r_{AB}, and r_{AC} and then use the cosine law.

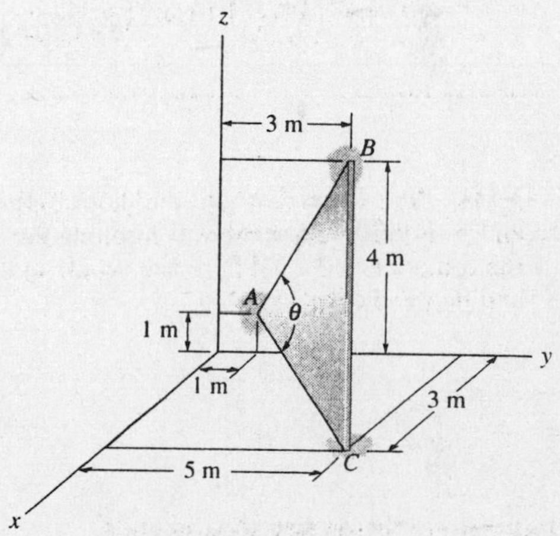

$\mathbf{r}_{BC} = \{3\mathbf{i} + 2\mathbf{j} - 4\mathbf{k}\}$ m

$r_{BC} = \sqrt{(3)^2 + (2)^2 + (-4)^2} = 5.39$ m **Ans**

Also,

$\mathbf{r}_{AC} = \{3\mathbf{i} + 4\mathbf{j} - 1\mathbf{k}\}$ m

$r_{AC} = \sqrt{(3)^2 + (4)^2 + (-1)^2} = 5.0990$ m

$\mathbf{r}_{AB} = \{2\mathbf{j} + 3\mathbf{k}\}$ m

$r_{AB} = \sqrt{(2)^2 + (3)^2} = 3.6056$ m

$\mathbf{r}_{AC} \cdot \mathbf{r}_{AB} = 0 + 4(2) + (-1)(3) = 5$

$$\theta = \cos^{-1}\left(\frac{\mathbf{r}_{AC} \cdot \mathbf{r}_{AB}}{r_{AC}\, r_{AB}}\right) = \cos^{-1}\frac{5}{(5.0990)(3.6056)}$$

$\theta = 74.219°$

$r_{BC} = \sqrt{(5.0990)^2 + (3.6056)^2 - 2(5.0990)(3.6056)\cos 74.219°}$

$r_{BC} = 5.39$ m **Ans**

2-117. Two forces act on the hook. Determine the angle θ between them. Also, what are the projections of $\mathbf{F}_1$ and $\mathbf{F}_2$ along the y axis?

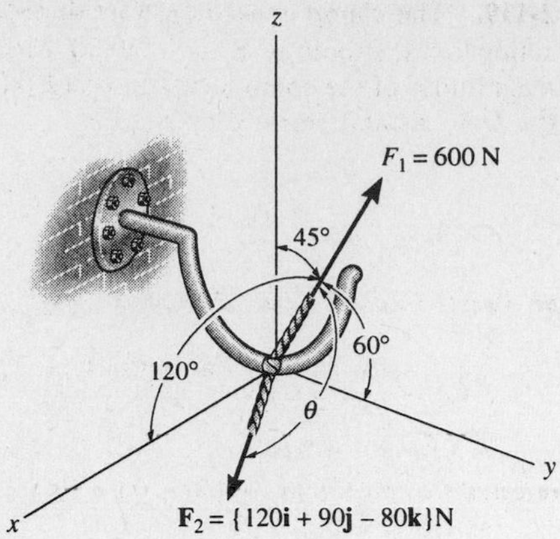

$$\mathbf{F}_1 = 600\cos 120°\,\mathbf{i} + 600\cos 60°\,\mathbf{j} + 600\cos 45°\,\mathbf{k}$$

$$= -300\,\mathbf{i} + 300\,\mathbf{j} + 424.3\,\mathbf{k}\,; \quad F_1 = 600\text{ N}$$

$$\mathbf{F}_2 = 120\,\mathbf{i} + 90\,\mathbf{j} - 80\,\mathbf{k}\,; \quad F_2 = 170\text{ N}$$

$$\mathbf{F}_1 \cdot \mathbf{F}_2 = (-300)(120) + (300)(90) + (424.3)(-80) = -42\,944$$

$$\theta = \cos^{-1}\left(\frac{-42\,944}{(170)(600)}\right) = 115° \qquad \textbf{Ans}$$

$$\mathbf{u} = \mathbf{j}$$

So,

$$F_{1y} = \mathbf{F}_1 \cdot \mathbf{j} = (300)(1) = 300\text{ N} \qquad \textbf{Ans}$$

$$F_{2y} = \mathbf{F}_2 \cdot \mathbf{j} = (90)(1) = 90\text{ N} \qquad \textbf{Ans}$$

2-118. Two forces act on the hook. Determine the magnitude of the projection of $\mathbf{F}_2$ along $\mathbf{F}_1$.

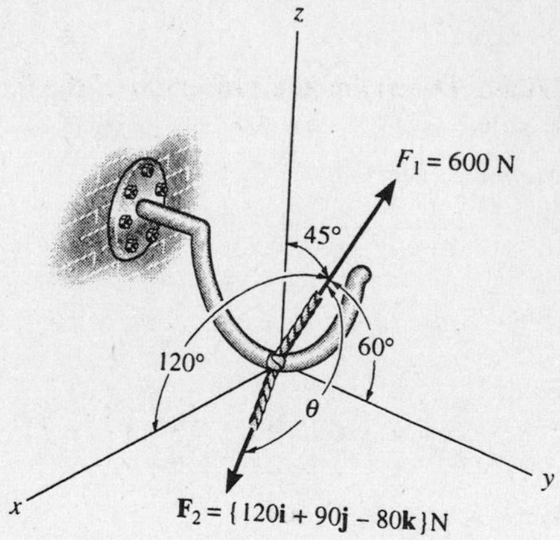

$$\mathbf{u}_1 = \cos 120°\,\mathbf{i} + \cos 60°\,\mathbf{j} + \cos 45°\,\mathbf{k}$$

$$\text{Proj } F_2 = \mathbf{F}_2 \cdot \mathbf{u}_1 = (120)(\cos 120°) + (90)(\cos 60°) + (-80)(\cos 45°)$$

$$|\text{Proj } F_2| = 71.6\text{ N} \qquad \textbf{Ans}$$

2-119. The clamp is used on a jig. If the vertical force acting on the bolt is $\mathbf{F} = \{-500\mathbf{k}\}$ N, determine the magnitudes of the components $\mathbf{F}_1$ and $\mathbf{F}_2$ which act along the OA axis and perpendicular to it.

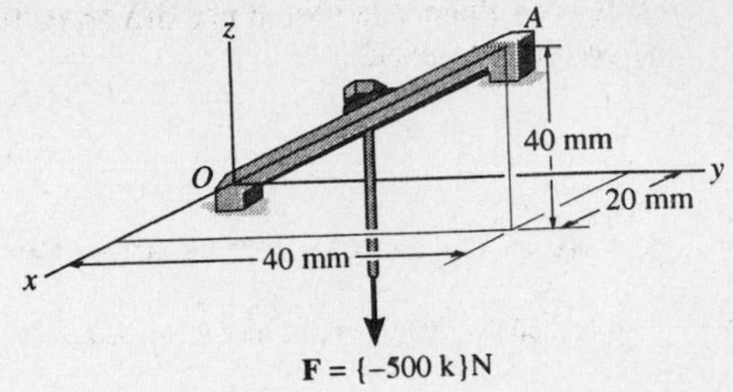

Unit Vector : The unit vector along OA axis is

$$\mathbf{u}_{AO} = \frac{(0-20)\mathbf{i}+(0-40)\mathbf{j}+(0-40)\mathbf{k}}{\sqrt{(0-20)^2+(0-40)^2+(0-40)^2}} = -\frac{1}{3}\mathbf{i}-\frac{2}{3}\mathbf{j}-\frac{2}{3}\mathbf{k}$$

Projected Component of* F *Along OA Axis :

$$F_1 = \mathbf{F}\cdot\mathbf{u}_{AO} = (-500\mathbf{k})\cdot\left(-\frac{1}{3}\mathbf{i}-\frac{2}{3}\mathbf{j}-\frac{2}{3}\mathbf{k}\right)$$

$$= (0)\left(-\frac{1}{3}\right)+(0)\left(-\frac{2}{3}\right)+(-500)\left(-\frac{2}{3}\right)$$

$$= 333.33 \text{ N} = 333 \text{ N}$$ **Ans**

Component of* F *Perpendicular to OA Axis : Since the magnitude of force **F** is $F = 500$ N so that

$$F_2 = \sqrt{F^2 - F_1^2} = \sqrt{500^2 - 333.33^2} = 373 \text{ N}$$ **Ans**

***2-120.** Determine the projection of the force **F** along the pole.

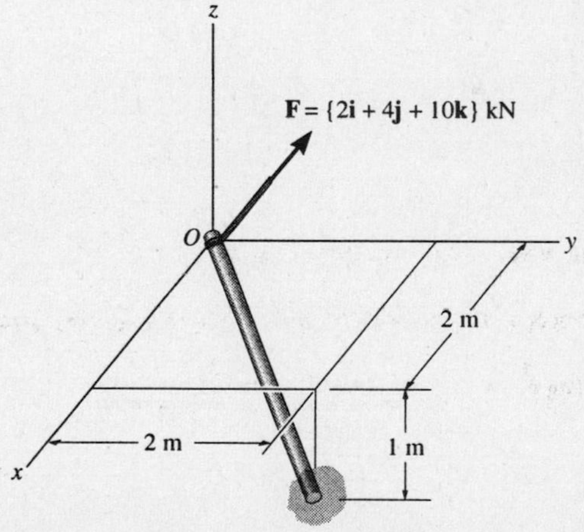

$$\text{Proj } F = \mathbf{F}\cdot\mathbf{u}_a = (2\mathbf{i}+4\mathbf{j}+10\mathbf{k})\cdot\left(\frac{2}{3}\mathbf{i}+\frac{2}{3}\mathbf{j}-\frac{1}{3}\mathbf{k}\right)$$

Proj F = 0.667 kN **Ans**

2-121. Determine the magnitude of the projected component of force **F** along the pole.

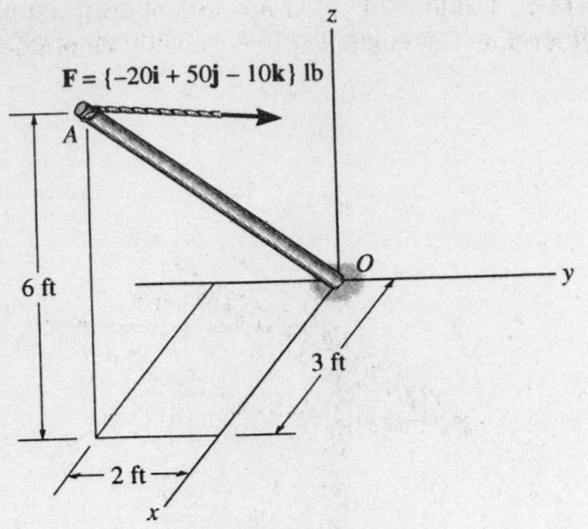

$\mathbf{r}_{OA} = \{3\mathbf{i} - 2\mathbf{j} + 6\mathbf{k}\}$ ft

$$\text{Proj } F = \mathbf{F} \cdot \mathbf{u}_{OA} = (-20\mathbf{i} + 50\mathbf{j} - 10\mathbf{k}) \cdot \frac{(3\mathbf{i} - 2\mathbf{j} + 6\mathbf{k})}{\sqrt{(3)^2 + (-2)^2 + (6)^2}}$$

$\text{Proj } F = -31.4$ lb

$|\text{Proj } F| = 31.4$ lb **Ans**

2-122. Cable OA is used to support column OB. Determine the angle θ it makes with beam OC.

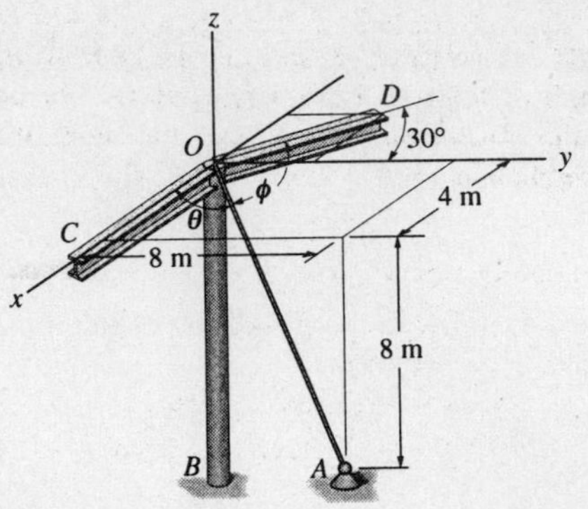

Unit Vector:

$$\mathbf{u}_{OC} = 1\mathbf{i}$$

$$\mathbf{u}_{OA} = \frac{(4-0)\mathbf{i} + (8-0)\mathbf{j} + (-8-0)\mathbf{k}}{\sqrt{(4-0)^2 + (8-0)^2 + (-8-0)^2}}$$

$$= \frac{1}{3}\mathbf{i} + \frac{2}{3}\mathbf{j} - \frac{2}{3}\mathbf{k}$$

The Angles Between Two Vectors θ:

$$\mathbf{u}_{OC} \cdot \mathbf{u}_{OA} = (1\mathbf{i}) \cdot \left(\frac{1}{3}\mathbf{i} + \frac{2}{3}\mathbf{j} - \frac{2}{3}\right) = 1\left(\frac{1}{3}\right) + (0)\left(\frac{2}{3}\right) + 0\left(-\frac{2}{3}\right) = \frac{1}{3}$$

Then,

$$\theta = \cos^{-1}(\mathbf{u}_{OC} \cdot \mathbf{u}_{OA}) = \cos^{-1}\frac{1}{3} = 70.5^\circ$$ **Ans**

2-123. Cable OA is used to support column OB. Determine the angle ϕ it makes with beam OD.

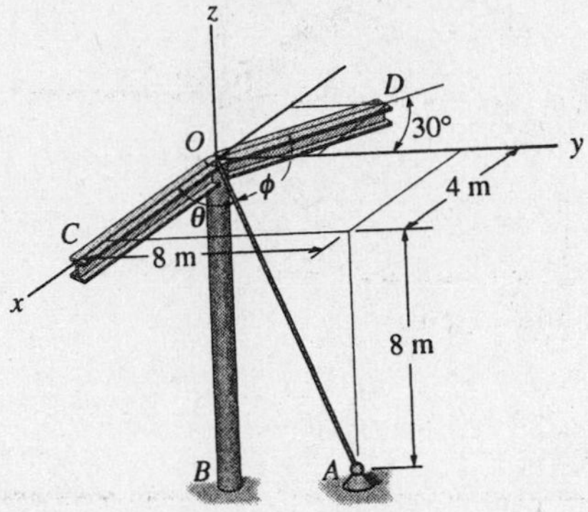

Unit Vector :

$$\mathbf{u}_{OD} = -\sin 30°\mathbf{i} + \cos 30°\mathbf{j} = -0.5\mathbf{i} + 0.8660\mathbf{j}$$

$$\mathbf{u}_{OA} = \frac{(4-0)\mathbf{i}+(8-0)\mathbf{j}+(-8-0)\mathbf{k}}{\sqrt{(4-0)^2+(8-0)^2+(-8-0)^2}} = \frac{1}{3}\mathbf{i}+\frac{2}{3}\mathbf{j}-\frac{2}{3}\mathbf{k}$$

The Angles Between Two Vectors ϕ :

$$\mathbf{u}_{OD}\cdot\mathbf{u}_{OA} = (-0.5\mathbf{i}+0.8660\mathbf{j})\cdot\left(\frac{1}{3}\mathbf{i}+\frac{2}{3}\mathbf{j}-\frac{2}{3}\right)$$
$$= (-0.5)\left(\frac{1}{3}\right)+(0.8660)\left(\frac{2}{3}\right)+0\left(-\frac{2}{3}\right)$$
$$= 0.4107$$

Then,

$$\phi = \cos^{-1}(\mathbf{u}_{OD}\cdot\mathbf{u}_{OA}) = \cos^{-1}0.4107 = 65.8° \qquad \textbf{Ans}$$

***2-124.** The force **F** acts at the end A of the pipe assembly. Determine the magnitudes of the components $\mathbf{F}_1$ and $\mathbf{F}_2$ which act along the axis of AB and perpendicular to it.

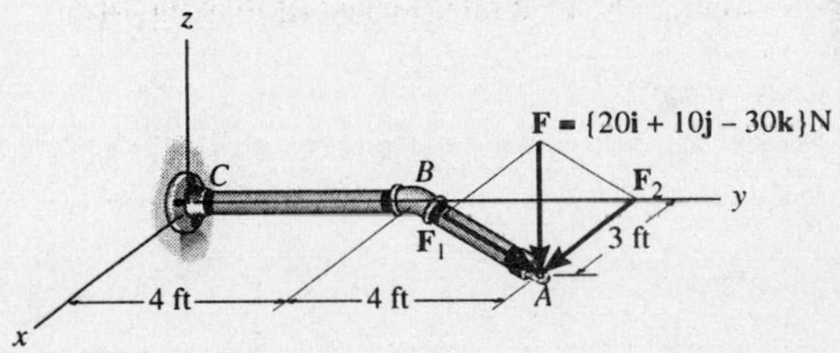

Unit Vector : The unit vector along AB axis is

$$\mathbf{u}_{BA} = \frac{(3-0)\mathbf{i}+(8-4)\mathbf{j}+(0-0)\mathbf{k}}{\sqrt{(3-0)^2+(8-4)^2+(0-0)^2}} = \frac{3}{5}\mathbf{i}+\frac{4}{5}\mathbf{j}$$

Projected Component of F Along AB Axis :

$$F_1 = \mathbf{F}\cdot\mathbf{u}_{BA} = (20\mathbf{i}+10\mathbf{j}-30\mathbf{k})\cdot\left(\frac{3}{5}\mathbf{i}+\frac{4}{5}\mathbf{j}\right)$$
$$= (20)\left(\frac{3}{5}\right)+(10)\left(\frac{4}{5}\right)+(-30)(0)$$
$$= 20.0\text{ N} \qquad \textbf{Ans}$$

Component of F Perpendicular to AB Axis : The magnitude of force **F** is $F = \sqrt{20^2+10^2+(-30)^2} = 37.417$ N.

$$F_2 = \sqrt{F^2-F_1^2} = \sqrt{37.417^2-20.0^2} = 31.6\text{ N} \qquad \textbf{Ans}$$

2-125. Two cables exert forces on the pipe. Determine the magnitude of the projected component of $\mathbf{F}_1$ along the line of action of $\mathbf{F}_2$.

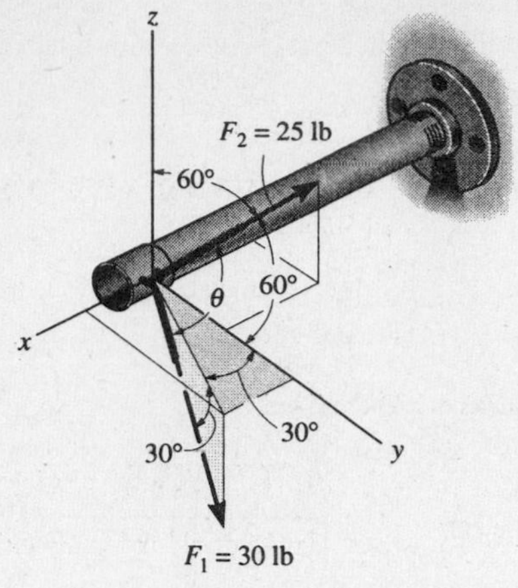

Force Vector:

$$\mathbf{u}_{F_1} = \cos 30° \sin 30° \mathbf{i} + \cos 30° \cos 30° \mathbf{j} - \sin 30° \mathbf{k}$$
$$= 0.4330\mathbf{i} + 0.75\mathbf{j} - 0.5\mathbf{k}$$

$$\mathbf{F}_1 = F_1 \mathbf{u}_{F_1} = 30(0.4330\mathbf{i} + 0.75\mathbf{j} - 0.5\mathbf{k}) \text{ lb}$$
$$= \{12.990\mathbf{i} + 22.5\mathbf{j} - 15.0\mathbf{k}\} \text{ lb}$$

Unit Vector: One can obtain the angle $\alpha = 135°$ for $\mathbf{F}_2$ using Eq. 2 – 10, $\cos^2\alpha + \cos^2\beta + \cos^2\gamma = 1$, with $\beta = 60°$ and $\gamma = 60°$. The unit vector along the line of action of $\mathbf{F}_2$ is

$$\mathbf{u}_{F_2} = \cos 135° \mathbf{i} + \cos 60° \mathbf{j} + \cos 60° \mathbf{k} = -0.7071\mathbf{i} + 0.5\mathbf{j} + 0.5\mathbf{k}$$

Projected Component of $\mathbf{F}_1$ Along the Line of Action of $\mathbf{F}_2$:

$$(F_1)_{F_2} = \mathbf{F}_1 \cdot \mathbf{u}_{F_2} = (12.990\mathbf{i} + 22.5\mathbf{j} - 15.0\mathbf{k}) \cdot (-0.7071\mathbf{i} + 0.5\mathbf{j} + 0.5\mathbf{k})$$
$$= (12.990)(-0.7071) + (22.5)(0.5) + (-15.0)(0.5)$$
$$= -5.44 \text{ lb}$$

Negative sign indicates that the projected component $(\mathbf{F}_1)_{F_2}$ acts in the opposite sense of direction to that of $\mathbf{u}_{F_2}$.

The magnitude is $(\mathbf{F}_1)_{F_2} = 5.44$ lb. **Ans**

2-126. Determine the angle θ between the two cables attached to the pipe.

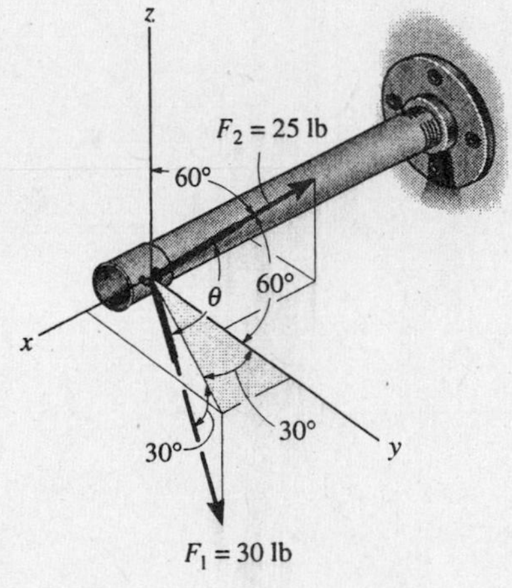

Unit Vector:

$$\mathbf{u}_{F_1} = \cos 30° \sin 30° \mathbf{i} + \cos 30° \cos 30° \mathbf{j} - \sin 30° \mathbf{k}$$
$$= 0.4330\mathbf{i} + 0.75\mathbf{j} - 0.5\mathbf{k}$$

$$\mathbf{u}_{F_2} = \cos 135° \mathbf{i} + \cos 60° \mathbf{j} + \cos 60° \mathbf{k}$$
$$= -0.7071\mathbf{i} + 0.5\mathbf{j} + 0.5\mathbf{k}$$

The Angles Between Two Vectors θ:

$$\mathbf{u}_{F_1} \cdot \mathbf{u}_{F_2} = (0.4330\mathbf{i} + 0.75\mathbf{j} - 0.5\mathbf{k}) \cdot (-0.7071\mathbf{i} + 0.5\mathbf{j} + 0.5\mathbf{k})$$
$$= 0.4330(-0.7071) + 0.75(0.5) + (-0.5)(0.5)$$
$$= -0.1812$$

Then,

$$\theta = \cos^{-1}(\mathbf{u}_{F_1} \cdot \mathbf{u}_{F_2}) = \cos^{-1}(-0.1812) = 100°$$ **Ans**

2-127. Determine the angle θ between cables AB and AC.

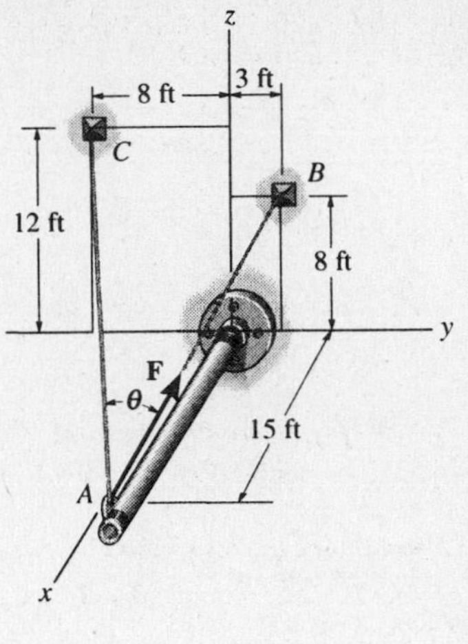

Position Vector :

$$\mathbf{r}_{AB} = \{(0-15)\mathbf{i} + (3-0)\mathbf{j} + (8-0)\mathbf{k}\} \text{ ft} = \{-15\mathbf{i} + 3\mathbf{j} + 8\mathbf{k}\} \text{ ft}$$

$$\mathbf{r}_{AC} = \{(0-15)\mathbf{i} + (-8-0)\mathbf{j} + (12-0)\mathbf{k}\} \text{ ft} = \{-15\mathbf{i} - 8\mathbf{j} + 12\mathbf{k}\} \text{ ft}$$

The magnitudes of the postion vectors are

$$r_{AB} = \sqrt{(-15)^2 + 3^2 + 8^2} = 17.263 \text{ ft}$$
$$r_{AC} = \sqrt{(-15)^2 + (-8)^2 + 12^2} = 20.809 \text{ ft}$$

The Angles Between Two Vectors θ:

$$\mathbf{r}_{AB} \cdot \mathbf{r}_{AC} = (-15\mathbf{i} + 3\mathbf{j} + 8\mathbf{k}) \cdot (-15\mathbf{i} - 8\mathbf{j} + 12\mathbf{k}) = (-15)(-15) + (3)(-8) + 8(12) = 297 \text{ ft}^2$$

Then,

$$\theta = \cos^{-1}\left(\frac{\mathbf{r}_{AB} \cdot \mathbf{r}_{AC}}{r_{AB} r_{AC}}\right) = \cos^{-1}\left[\frac{297}{17.263(20.809)}\right] = 34.2^\circ \quad \textbf{Ans}$$

2-128. If **F** has a magnitude of 55 lb, determine the magnitude of its projected component acting along the x axis and along cable AC.

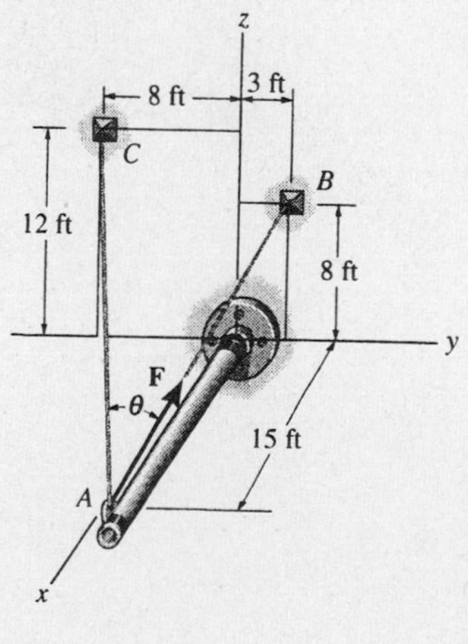

Force Vector :

$$\mathbf{u}_{AB} = \frac{(0-15)\mathbf{i} + (3-0)\mathbf{j} + (8-0)\mathbf{k}}{\sqrt{(0-15)^2 + (3-0)^2 + (8-0)^2}} = -0.8689\mathbf{i} + 0.1738\mathbf{j} + 0.4634\mathbf{k}$$

$$\mathbf{F} = F\mathbf{u}_{AB} = 55(-0.8689\mathbf{i} + 0.1738\mathbf{j} + 0.4634\mathbf{k}) \text{ lb} = \{-47.791\mathbf{i} + 9.558\mathbf{j} + 25.489\mathbf{k}\} \text{ lb}$$

Unit Vector : The unit vector along negative x axis and AC are

$$\mathbf{u}_x = -1\mathbf{i}$$

$$\mathbf{u}_{AC} = \frac{(0-15)\mathbf{i} + (-8-0)\mathbf{j} + (12-0)\mathbf{k}}{\sqrt{(0-15)^2 + (-8-0)^2 + (12-0)^2}} = -0.7209\mathbf{i} - 0.3845\mathbf{j} + 0.5767\mathbf{k}$$

Projected Component of F :

$$F_x = \mathbf{F} \cdot \mathbf{u}_x = (-47.791\mathbf{i} + 9.558\mathbf{j} + 25.489\mathbf{k}) \cdot (-1\mathbf{i}) = (-47.791)(-1) + 9.558(0) + 25.489(0) = 47.8 \text{ lb} \quad \textbf{Ans}$$

$$F_{AC} = \mathbf{F} \cdot \mathbf{u}_{AC} = (-47.791\mathbf{i} + 9.558\mathbf{j} + 25.489\mathbf{k}) \cdot (-0.7209\mathbf{i} - 0.3845\mathbf{j} + 0.5767\mathbf{k}) = (-47.791)(-0.7209) + (9.558)(-0.3845) + (25.489)(0.5767) = 45.5 \text{ lb} \quad \textbf{Ans}$$

The projected component acts along cable AC, F_{AC}, can also be determined using $F_{AC} = F\cos\theta$. From the solution of Prob. 2 – 137, $\theta = 34.2^\circ$. Then

$$F_{AC} = 55\cos 34.2^\circ = 45.5 \text{ lb}$$

2-129. A force of $\mathbf{F} = \{500\mathbf{k}\}$ N acts at point A. Determine the magnitudes of the components $\mathbf{F}_1$ and $\mathbf{F}_2$ which act along the OA axis and perpendicular to it.

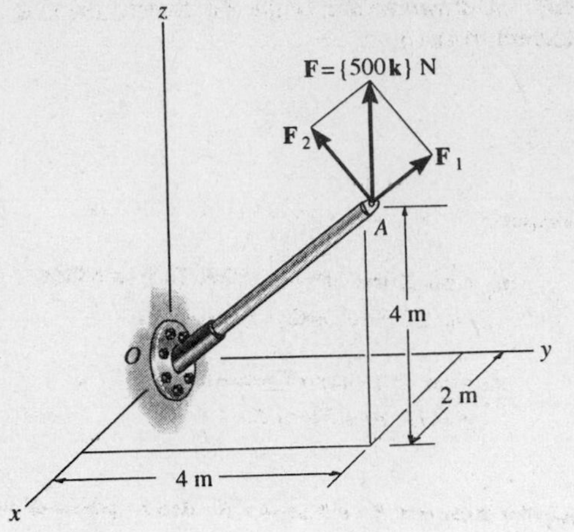

$$\mathbf{r}_{OA} = \{2\mathbf{i} + 4\mathbf{j} + 4\mathbf{k}\}\ \text{m}$$

$$F_1 = \mathbf{F} \cdot \frac{\mathbf{r}_{OA}}{r_{OA}}$$

$$= (500\,\mathbf{k}) \cdot \frac{(2\mathbf{i} + 4\mathbf{j} + 4\mathbf{k})}{\sqrt{2^2 + 4^2 + 4^2}}$$

$$F_1 = 500\left(\frac{4}{\sqrt{2^2 + 4^2 + 4^2}}\right) = 333\ \text{N} \qquad \textbf{Ans}$$

$$F_2 = \sqrt{(500)^2 - (333)^2} = 373\ \text{N} \qquad \textbf{Ans}$$

2-130. The cables each exert a force of 400 N on the post. Determine the magnitude of the projected component of $\mathbf{F}_1$ along the line of action of $\mathbf{F}_2$.

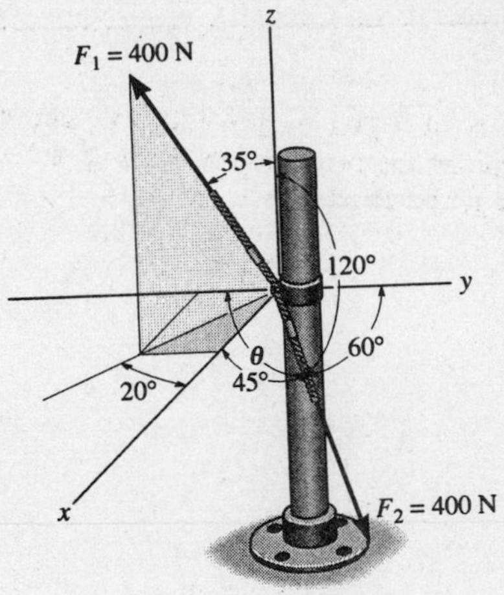

Force Vector:

$$\mathbf{u}_{F_1} = \sin 35°\cos 20°\mathbf{i} - \sin 35°\sin 20°\mathbf{j} + \cos 35°\mathbf{k}$$
$$= 0.5390\mathbf{i} - 0.1962\mathbf{j} + 0.8192\mathbf{k}$$

$$\mathbf{F}_1 = F_1\mathbf{u}_{F_1} = 400(0.5390\mathbf{i} - 0.1962\mathbf{j} + 0.8192\mathbf{k})\ \text{N}$$
$$= \{215.59\mathbf{i} - 78.47\mathbf{j} + 327.66\mathbf{k}\}\ \text{N}$$

Unit Vector: The unit vector along the line of action of $\mathbf{F}_2$ is

$$\mathbf{u}_{F_2} = \cos 45°\mathbf{i} + \cos 60°\mathbf{j} + \cos 120°\mathbf{k}$$
$$= 0.7071\mathbf{i} + 0.5\mathbf{j} - 0.5\mathbf{k}$$

Projected Component of $\mathbf{F}_1$ Along Line of Action of $\mathbf{F}_2$:

$$(F_1)_{F_2} = \mathbf{F}_1 \cdot \mathbf{u}_{F_2} = (215.59\mathbf{i} - 78.47\mathbf{j} + 327.66\mathbf{k}) \cdot (0.7071\mathbf{i} + 0.5\mathbf{j} - 0.5\mathbf{k})$$
$$= (215.59)(0.7071) + (-78.47)(0.5) + (327.66)(-0.5)$$
$$= -50.6\ \text{N}$$

Negative sign indicates that the force component $(\mathbf{F}_1)_{F_2}$ acts in the opposite sense of direction to that of $\mathbf{u}_{F_2}$.

thus the magnitude is $(\mathbf{F}_1)_{F_2} = 50.6$ N **Ans**

2-131. Determine the angle θ between the two cables attached to the post.

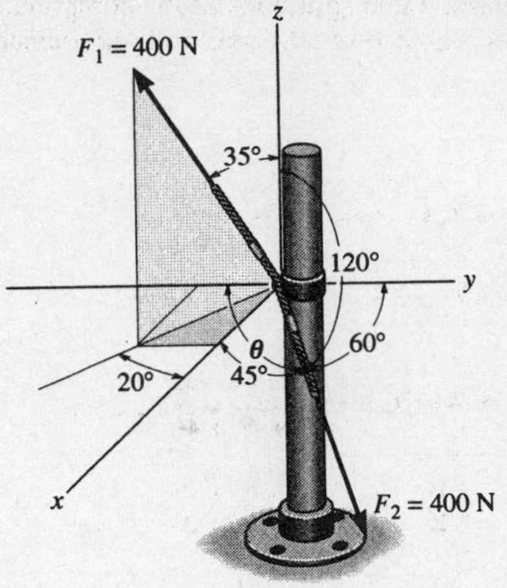

Unit Vector :

$$\mathbf{u}_{F_1} = \sin 35°\cos 20°\mathbf{i} - \sin 35°\sin 20°\mathbf{j} + \cos 35°\mathbf{k}$$
$$= 0.5390\mathbf{i} - 0.1962\mathbf{j} + 0.8192\mathbf{k}$$

$$\mathbf{u}_{F_2} = \cos 45°\mathbf{i} + \cos 60°\mathbf{j} + \cos 120°\mathbf{k}$$
$$= 0.7071\mathbf{i} + 0.5\mathbf{j} - 0.5\mathbf{k}$$

The Angles Between Two Vectors θ **:** The dot product of two unit vectors must be determined first.

$$\mathbf{u}_{F_1} \cdot \mathbf{u}_{F_2} = (0.5390\mathbf{i} - 0.1962\mathbf{j} + 0.8192\mathbf{k}) \cdot (0.7071\mathbf{i} + 0.5\mathbf{j} - 0.5\mathbf{k})$$
$$= 0.5390(0.7071) + (-0.1962)(0.5) + 0.8192(-0.5)$$
$$= -0.1265$$

Then,

$$\theta = \cos^{-1}\left(\mathbf{u}_{F_1} \cdot \mathbf{u}_{F_2}\right) = \cos^{-1}(-0.1265) = 97.3° \qquad \textbf{Ans}$$

***2-132.** If $\mathbf{F} = \{16\mathbf{i} + 10\mathbf{j} - 14\mathbf{k}\}$ N, determine the magnitude of the projection of **F** along the axis of the pole and perpendicular to it.

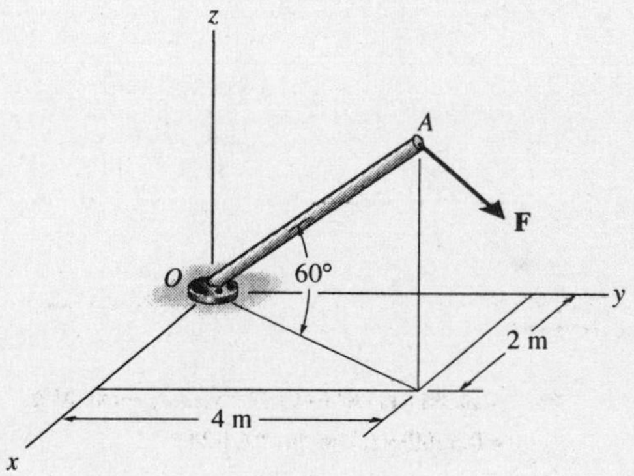

$$\mathbf{r}_{OA} = 2\,\mathbf{i} + 4\,\mathbf{j} + \left(\sqrt{(4)^2 + (2)^2}\ \tan 60°\right)\mathbf{k}$$

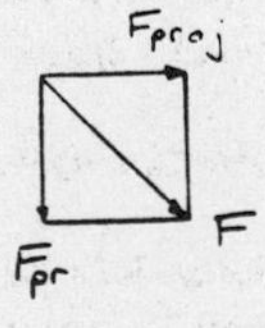

$$\mathbf{u}_{OA} = \left(\frac{\mathbf{r}_{OA}}{r_{OA}}\right) = 0.2236\,\mathbf{i} + 0.4472\,\mathbf{j} + 0.8660\,\mathbf{k}$$

$$\text{Proj}F = \mathbf{F}\mathbf{u}_{OA} = (16)(0.2236) + (10)(0.4472) + (-14)(0.8660)$$

$$|\text{Proj}F| = |-4.0745\ \text{N}| = 4.07\ \text{N} \qquad \textbf{Ans}$$

$$F = \sqrt{(16)^2 + (10)^2 + (-14)^2} = 23.49\ \text{N}$$

$$F_\perp = \sqrt{(23.49)^2 - (4.0745)^2} = 23.1\ \text{N} \qquad \textbf{Ans}$$

2-133. If the force $F = 100$ N lies in the plane $DBEC$, which is parallel to the x–z plane, and makes an angle of 10° with the extended line DB as shown, determine the angle that **F** makes with the diagonal AB of the crate.

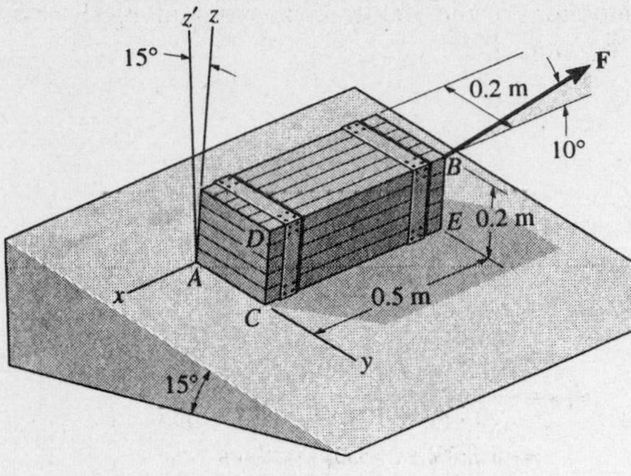

Use the x, y, z axes.

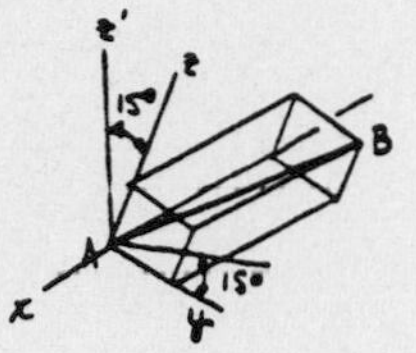

$$\mathbf{u}_{AB} = \left(\frac{-0.5\,\mathbf{i} + 0.2\,\mathbf{j} + 0.2\,\mathbf{k}}{0.57446}\right)$$

$$= -0.8704\,\mathbf{i} + 0.3482\,\mathbf{j} + 0.3482\,\mathbf{k}$$

$$\mathbf{F} = -100\cos 10^\circ\,\mathbf{i} + 100\sin 10^\circ\,\mathbf{k}$$

$$\theta = \cos^{-1}\left(\frac{\mathbf{F}\cdot\mathbf{u}_{AB}}{F\,u_{AB}}\right)$$

$$= \cos^{-1}\left(\frac{-100\,(\cos 10^\circ)\,(-0.8704) + 0 + 100\sin 10^\circ\,(0.3482)}{100(1)}\right)$$

$$= \cos^{-1}(0.9176) = 23.4^\circ \qquad \textbf{Ans}$$

2-134. Determine the x and y components of the 700-lb force.

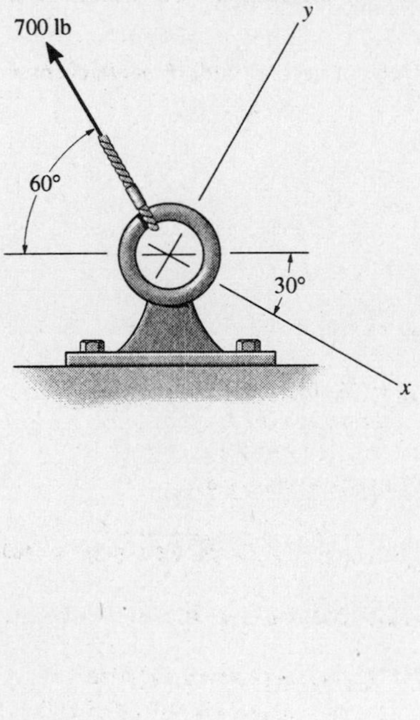

$$F_x = -700\cos 30^\circ = -606 \text{ lb} \qquad \textbf{Ans}$$

$$F_y = 700\sin 30^\circ = 350 \text{ lb} \qquad \textbf{Ans}$$

2-135. Determine the magnitude of the projected component of the 100-lb force acting along the axis BC of the pipe.

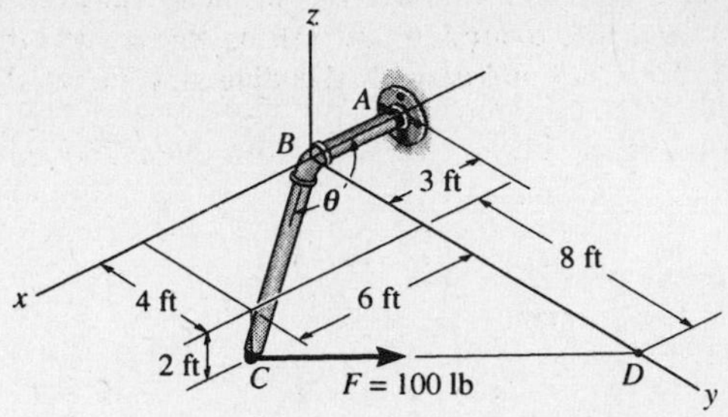

Force Vector :

$$\mathbf{u}_{CD} = \frac{(0-6)\mathbf{i}+(12-4)\mathbf{j}+[0-(-2)]\mathbf{k}}{\sqrt{(0-6)^2+(12-4)^2+[0-(-2)]^2}} = -0.5883\mathbf{i}+0.7845\mathbf{j}+0.1961\mathbf{k}$$

$$\mathbf{F} = F\mathbf{u}_{CD} = 100(-0.5883\mathbf{i}+0.7845\mathbf{j}+0.1961\mathbf{k}) = \{-58.835\mathbf{i}+78.446\mathbf{j}+19.612\mathbf{k}\}\text{ lb}$$

Unit Vector : The unit vector along CB is

$$\mathbf{u}_{CB} = \frac{(0-6)\mathbf{i}+(0-4)\mathbf{j}+[0-(-2)]\mathbf{k}}{\sqrt{(0-6)^2+(0-4)^2+[0-(-2)]^2}} = -0.8018\mathbf{i}-0.5345\mathbf{j}+0.2673\mathbf{k}$$

Projected Component of F Along CB :

$$F_{CB} = \mathbf{F}\cdot\mathbf{u}_{CB} = (-58.835\mathbf{i}+78.446\mathbf{j}+19.612\mathbf{k})\cdot(-0.8018\mathbf{i}-0.5345\mathbf{j}+0.2673\mathbf{k})$$
$$= (-58.835)(-0.8018)+(78.446)(-0.5345)+(19.612)(0.2673)$$
$$= 10.5\text{ lb}$$
Ans

***2-136.** Determine the angle θ between pipe segments BA and BC.

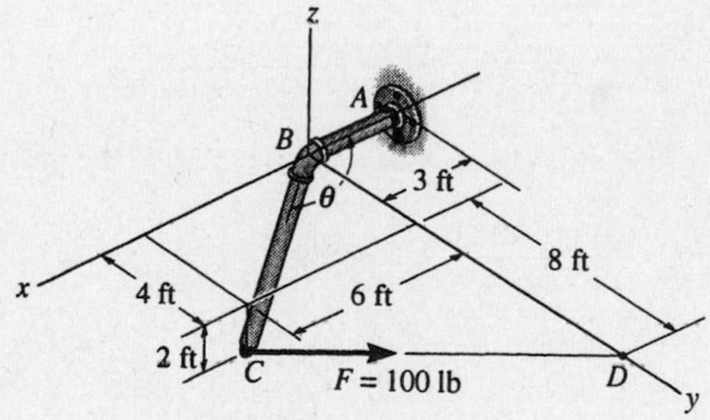

Position Vector :

$$\mathbf{r}_{BA} = \{-3\mathbf{i}\}\text{ ft}$$

$$\mathbf{r}_{BC} = \{(6-0)\mathbf{i}+(4-0)\mathbf{j}+(-2-0)\mathbf{k}\}\text{ ft} = \{6\mathbf{i}+4\mathbf{j}-2\mathbf{k}\}\text{ ft}$$

The magnitudes of the postion vectors are

$$r_{BA} = 3.00\text{ ft} \qquad r_{BC} = \sqrt{6^2+4^2+(-2)^2} = 7.483\text{ ft}$$

The Angles Between Two Vectors θ :

$$\mathbf{r}_{BA}\cdot\mathbf{r}_{BC} = (-3\mathbf{i})\cdot(6\mathbf{i}+4\mathbf{j}-2\mathbf{k}) = (-3)(6)+(0)(4)+0(-2) = -18.0\text{ ft}^2$$

Then,

$$\theta = \cos^{-1}\left(\frac{\mathbf{r}_{BA}\cdot\mathbf{r}_{BC}}{r_{BA}r_{BC}}\right) = \cos^{-1}\left[\frac{-18.0}{3.00(7.483)}\right] = 143°$$ **Ans**

2-137. Determine the magnitude and direction of the resultant $\mathbf{F}_R = \mathbf{F}_1 + \mathbf{F}_2 + \mathbf{F}_3$ of the three forces by first finding the resultant $\mathbf{F}' = \mathbf{F}_1 + \mathbf{F}_3$ and then forming $\mathbf{F}_R = \mathbf{F}' + \mathbf{F}_2$. Specify its direction measured counterclockwise from the positive x axis.

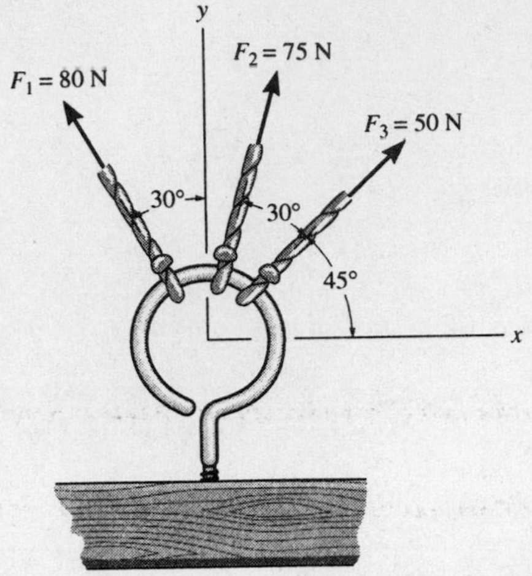

$$F' = \sqrt{(80)^2 + (50)^2 - 2(80)(50)\cos 105^\circ} = 104.7\ \text{N}$$

$$\frac{\sin\phi}{80} = \frac{\sin 105^\circ}{104.7}; \quad \phi = 47.54^\circ$$

$$F_R = \sqrt{(104.7)^2 + (75)^2 - 2(104.7)(75)\cos 162.46^\circ}$$

$$F_R = 177.7 = 178\ \text{N} \qquad \textbf{Ans}$$

$$\frac{\sin\beta}{104.7} = \frac{\sin 162.46^\circ}{177.7}; \quad \beta = 10.23^\circ$$

$$\theta = 75^\circ + 10.23^\circ = 85.2^\circ \qquad \textbf{Ans}$$

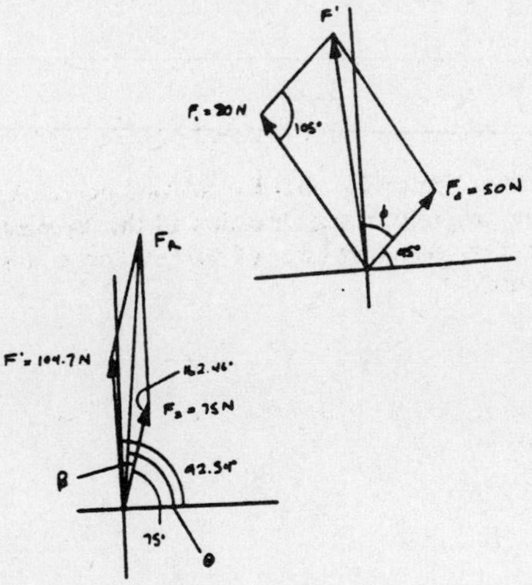

2-138. Determine the design angle θ ($\theta < 90°$) between the two struts so that the 500-lb horizontal force has a component of 600-lb directed from A toward C. What is the component of force acting along member BA?

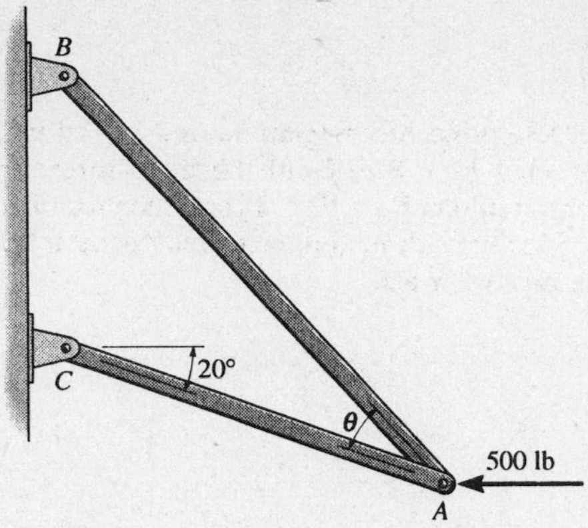

Parallelogram Law : The parallelogram law of addition is shown in Fig. (a).

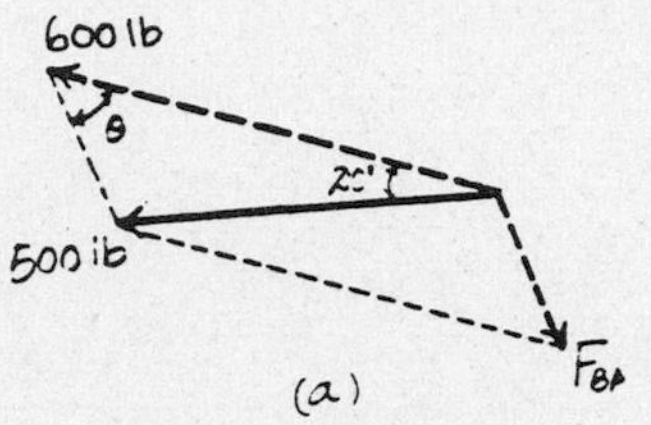

The Force Components : Using law of sines [Fig. (b)], we have

$$\frac{F_{AB}}{\sin 60°} = \frac{600}{\sin 45°}$$

$$F_{AB} = 735 \text{ N} \qquad \textbf{Ans}$$

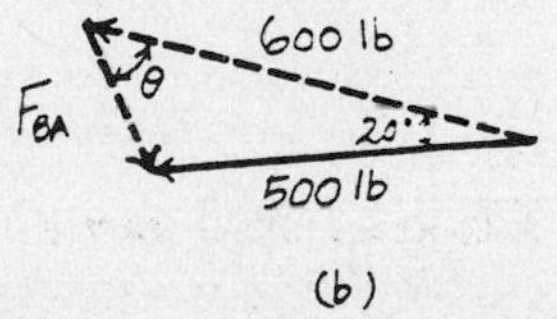

$$\frac{F_{AC}}{\sin 75°} = \frac{600}{\sin 45°}$$

$$F_{AC} = 820 \text{ N} \qquad \textbf{Ans}$$

2-139. The two forces $\mathbf{F}_1$ and $\mathbf{F}_2$ act on the hook. Determine the magnitude and direction of the *smallest* force $\mathbf{F}_3$ so that the resultant force of all three forces has a magnitude of 20 lb.

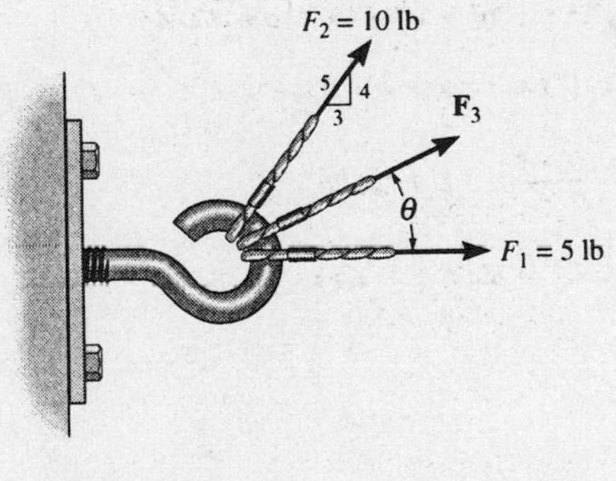

F_3 is minimum :

$F_3 = 20 - |\mathbf{F}_1 + \mathbf{F}_2|$

$$\mathbf{F}_1 + \mathbf{F}_2 = \left(5 + 10\left(\frac{3}{5}\right)\right)\mathbf{i} + \left(10\left(\frac{4}{5}\right)\right)\mathbf{j} = 11\,\mathbf{i} + 8\,\mathbf{j}$$

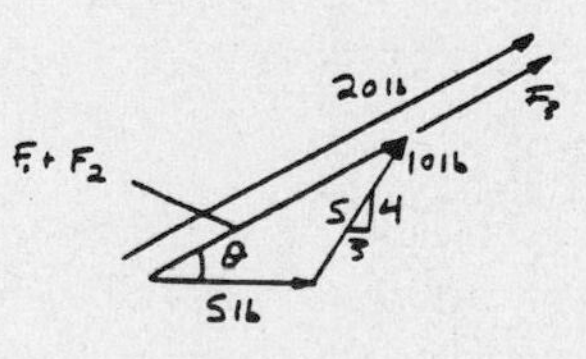

$$|\mathbf{F}_1 + \mathbf{F}_2| = \sqrt{11^2 + 8^2} = 13.601 \text{ lb}$$

$$\theta = \tan^{-1}\left(\frac{8}{11}\right) = 36.0° \qquad \textbf{Ans}$$

Thus

$$(F_3)_{min} = 20 - 13.601 = 6.40 \text{ lb} \qquad \textbf{Ans}$$

*2-140. Resolve the 250-N force into components acting along the u and v axes and determine the magnitudes of the components.

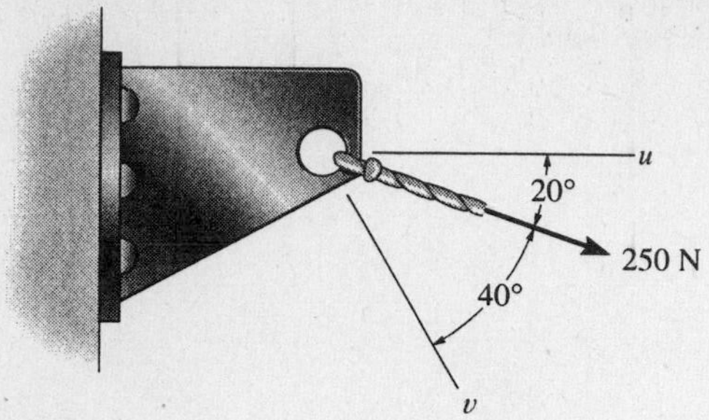

$$\frac{250}{\sin 120°} = \frac{F_u}{\sin 40°}; \quad F_u = 186 \text{ N} \quad \textbf{Ans}$$

$$\frac{250}{\sin 120°} = \frac{F_v}{\sin 20°}; \quad F_v = 98.7 \text{ N} \quad \textbf{Ans}$$

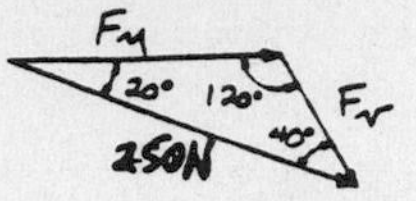

2-141. Cable AB exerts a force of 80 N on the end of the 3-m long boom OA. Determine the magnitude of the projection of this force along the boom.

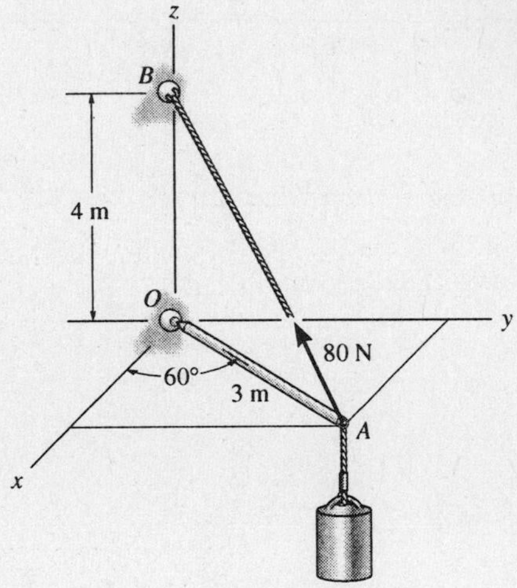

Vector Analysis :

$$\mathbf{F} = 80\left(\frac{\mathbf{r}_{AB}}{r_{AB}}\right) = 80\left(-\frac{3\cos 60°}{5}\mathbf{i} - \frac{3\sin 60°}{5}\mathbf{j} + \frac{4}{5}\mathbf{k}\right)$$

$$= -24\mathbf{i} - 41.57\mathbf{j} + 64\mathbf{k}$$

$$\mathbf{u}_{AO} = -\cos 60°\,\mathbf{i} - \sin 60°\,\mathbf{j} = -0.5\mathbf{i} - 0.866\mathbf{j}$$

$$\text{Proj } F = \mathbf{F} \cdot \mathbf{u}_{AO} = (-24)(-0.5) + (-41.57)(-0.866) + (64)0 = 48.0 \text{ N} \quad \textbf{Ans}$$

Scalar Anaysis :

$$\text{Angle } OAB = \tan^{-1}\left(\frac{4}{3}\right) = 53.13°$$

$$\text{Proj } F = 80\cos 53.13° = 48.0 \text{ N} \quad \textbf{Ans}$$

2-142. Express each force in Cartesian vector form.

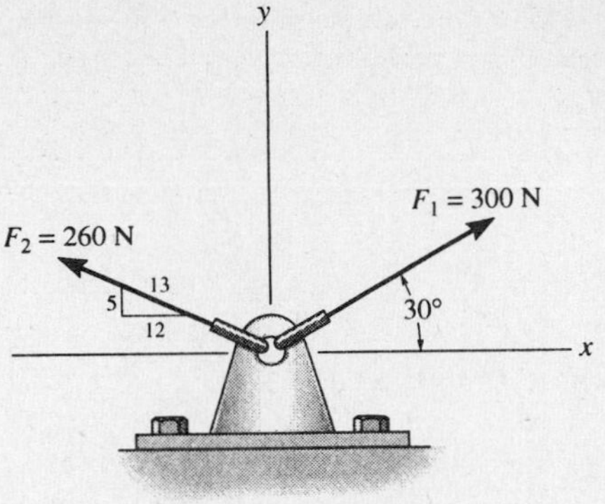

$$\mathbf{F}_1 = 300\cos 30°\,\mathbf{i} + 300\sin 30°\,\mathbf{j}$$

$$= \{260\,\mathbf{i} + 150\,\mathbf{j}\}\text{ N} \qquad \textbf{Ans}$$

$$\mathbf{F}_2 = -260\left(\frac{12}{13}\right)\mathbf{i} + 260\left(\frac{5}{13}\right)\mathbf{j}$$

$$= \{-240\,\mathbf{i} + 100\,\mathbf{j}\}\text{ N} \qquad \textbf{Ans}$$

2-143. The three supporting cables exert the forces shown on the sign. Represent each force as a Cartesian vector.

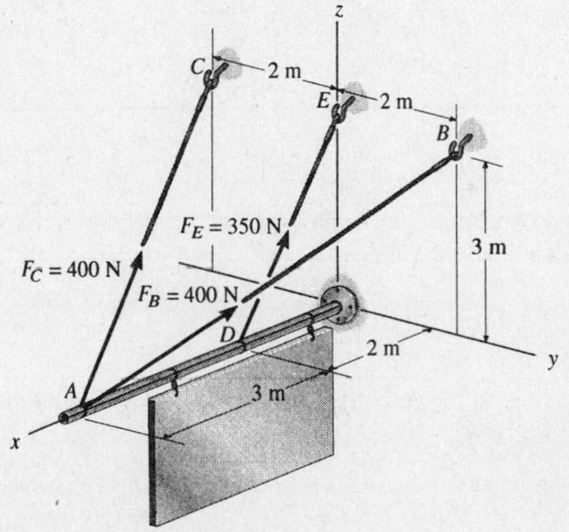

Unit Vector:

$$\mathbf{r}_{AB} = \{(0-5)\mathbf{i} + (2-0)\mathbf{j} + (3-0)\mathbf{k}\}\text{ m} = \{-5\mathbf{i} + 2\mathbf{j} + 3\mathbf{k}\}\text{ m}$$

$$r_{AB} = \sqrt{(-5)^2 + 2^2 + 3^2} = 6.164\text{ m}$$

$$\mathbf{u}_{AB} = \frac{\mathbf{r}_{AB}}{r_{AB}} = \frac{-5\mathbf{i} + 2\mathbf{j} + 3\mathbf{k}}{6.164} = -0.8111\mathbf{i} + 0.3244\mathbf{j} + 0.4867\mathbf{k}$$

$$\mathbf{r}_{AC} = \{(0-5)\mathbf{i} + (-2-0)\mathbf{j} + (3-0)\mathbf{k}\}\text{ m} = \{-5\mathbf{i} - 2\mathbf{j} + 3\mathbf{k}\}\text{ m}$$

$$r_{AC} = \sqrt{(-5)^2 + (-2)^2 + 3^2} = 6.164\text{ m}$$

$$\mathbf{u}_{AC} = \frac{\mathbf{r}_{AC}}{r_{AC}} = \frac{-5\mathbf{i} - 2\mathbf{j} + 3\mathbf{k}}{6.164} = -0.8111\mathbf{i} - 0.3244\mathbf{j} + 0.4867\mathbf{k}$$

$$\mathbf{r}_{DE} = \{(0-2)\mathbf{i} + (0-0)\mathbf{j} + (3-0)\mathbf{k}\}\text{ m} = \{-2\mathbf{i} + 3\mathbf{k}\}\text{ m}$$

$$r_{DE} = \sqrt{(-2)^2 + 3^2} = 3.605\text{ m}$$

$$\mathbf{u}_{DE} = \frac{\mathbf{r}_{DE}}{r_{DE}} = \frac{-2\mathbf{i} + 3\mathbf{k}}{3.605} = -0.5547\mathbf{i} + 0.8321\mathbf{k}$$

Force Vector:

$$\mathbf{F}_B = F_B\mathbf{u}_{AB} = 400\{-0.8111\mathbf{i} + 0.3244\mathbf{j} + 0.4867\mathbf{k}\}\text{ N}$$
$$= \{-324.44\mathbf{i} + 129.78\mathbf{j} + 194.67\mathbf{k}\}\text{ N}$$
$$= \{-324\mathbf{i} + 130\mathbf{j} + 195\mathbf{k}\}\text{ N} \qquad \textbf{Ans}$$

$$\mathbf{F}_C = F_C\mathbf{u}_{AB} = 400\{-0.8111\mathbf{i} - 0.3244\mathbf{j} + 0.4867\mathbf{k}\}\text{ N}$$
$$= \{-324.44\mathbf{i} - 129.78\mathbf{j} + 194.67\mathbf{k}\}\text{ N}$$
$$= \{-324\mathbf{i} - 130\mathbf{j} + 195\mathbf{k}\}\text{ N} \qquad \textbf{Ans}$$

$$\mathbf{F}_E = F_E\mathbf{u}_{DE} = 350\{-0.5547\mathbf{i} + 0.8321\mathbf{k}\}\text{ N}$$
$$= \{-194.15\mathbf{i} + 291.22\mathbf{k}\}\text{ N}$$
$$= \{-194\mathbf{i} + 291\mathbf{k}\}\text{ N} \qquad \textbf{Ans}$$

3-1. Determine the magnitudes of $\mathbf{F}_1$ and $\mathbf{F}_2$ so that particle P is in equilibrium.

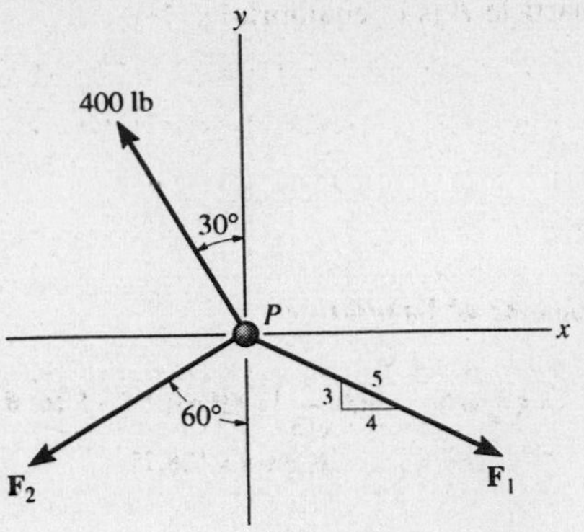

Equations of Equilibrium :

$\xrightarrow{+} \Sigma F_x = 0;\quad F_1\left(\frac{4}{5}\right) - 400 \sin 30° - F_2 \sin 60° = 0$

$0.8F_1 - 0.8660F_2 = 200.0$ [1]

$+\uparrow \Sigma F_y = 0;\quad 400\cos 30° - F_1\left(\frac{3}{5}\right) - F_2 \cos 60° = 0$

$0.6F_1 + 0.5F_2 = 346.41$ [2]

Solving Eqs.[1] and [2] yields

$F_1 = 435$ lb $\quad F_2 = 171$ lb **Ans**

3-2. Determine the magnitudes of $\mathbf{F}_1$ and $\mathbf{F}_2$ so that the particle is in equilibrium.

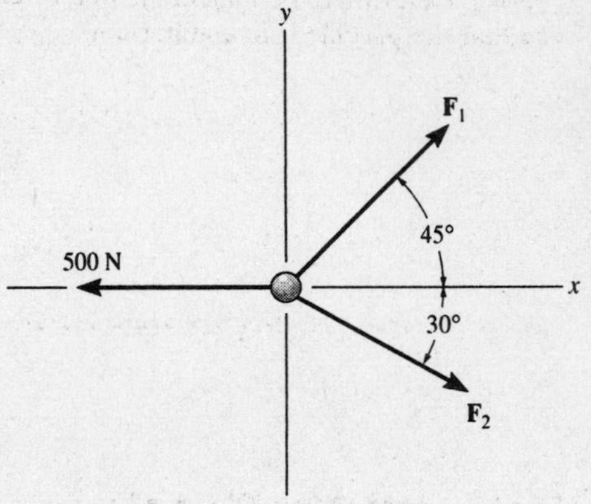

$+\uparrow \Sigma F_y = 0;\quad F_1 \sin 45° - F_2 \sin 30° = 0$

$F_2 = 1.414F_1$

$\xrightarrow{+} \Sigma F_x = 0;\quad F_1 \cos 45° + F_2 \cos 30° - 500 = 0$

Solving:

$F_1 = 259$ N **Ans** $\quad F_2 = 366$ N **Ans**

3-3. Determine the magnitude and angle θ of $\mathbf{F}_1$ so that particle P is in equilibrium.

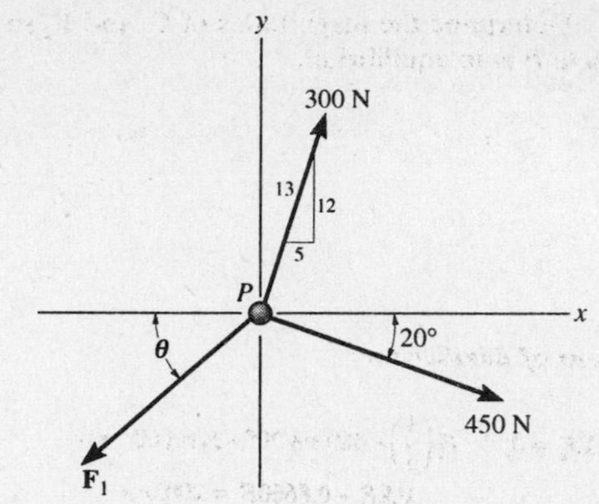

Equations of Equilibrium :

$\xrightarrow{+} \Sigma F_x = 0;\quad 300\left(\frac{5}{13}\right) + 450\cos 20° - F_1 \cos\theta = 0$

$F_1 \cos\theta = 538.25 \qquad [1]$

$+\uparrow \Sigma F_y = 0;\quad 300\left(\frac{12}{13}\right) - 450\sin 20° - F_1 \sin\theta = 0$

$F_1 \sin\theta = 538.25 \qquad [2]$

Solving Eqs. [1] and [2] yields

$\theta = 12.9° \qquad F_1 = 552\text{ N}$ **Ans**

***3-4.** Determine the magnitude and orientation θ of $\mathbf{F}$ so that the particle is in equilibrium.

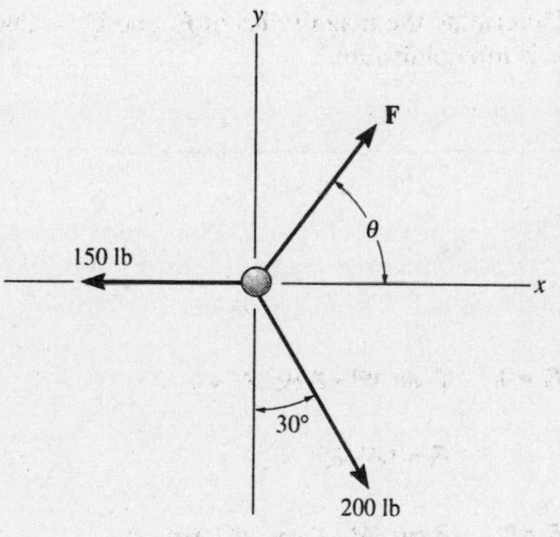

$\xrightarrow{+} \Sigma F_x = 0;\quad F\cos\theta + 200\sin 30° - 150 = 0$

$+\uparrow \Sigma F_y = 0;\quad F\sin\theta - 200\cos 30° = 0$

Solving:

$\theta = 73.9°$ **Ans** $\qquad F = 180\text{ lb}$ **Ans**

3-5. The members of a truss are pin-connected at joint O. Determine the magnitudes of $\mathbf{F}_1$ and $\mathbf{F}_2$ for equilibrium. Set $\theta = 60°$.

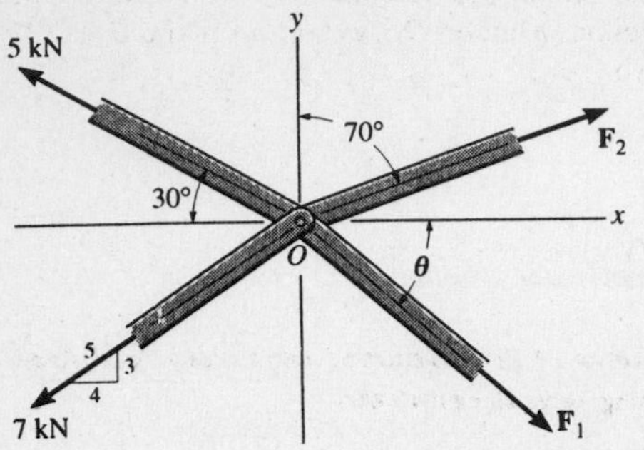

Equations of Equilibrium :

$$\xrightarrow{+} \Sigma F_x = 0; \quad F_1 \cos 60° + F_2 \sin 70° - 5\cos 30° - 7\left(\frac{4}{5}\right) = 0$$

$$0.5F_1 + 0.9397F_2 = 9.9301 \qquad [1]$$

$$+\uparrow \Sigma F_y = 0; \quad F_2 \cos 70° - F_1 \sin 60° + 5\sin 30° - 7\left(\frac{3}{5}\right) = 0$$

$$0.3420F_2 - 0.8660F_1 = 1.70 \qquad [2]$$

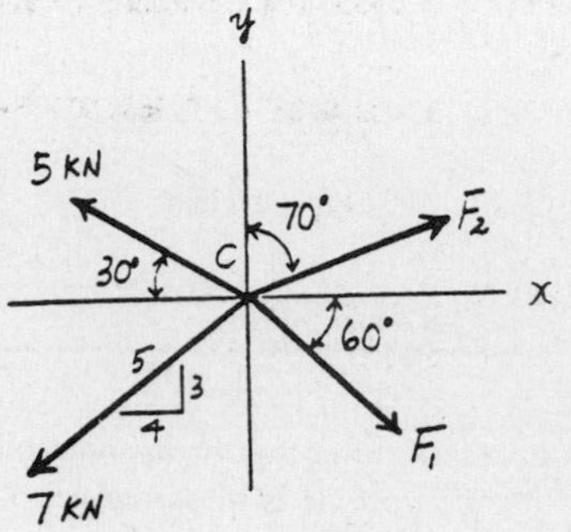

Solving Eqs. [1] and [2] yields

$F_1 = 1.83$ kN $\quad F_2 = 9.60$ kN **Ans**

3-6. The members of a truss are pin-connected at joint O. Determine the magnitude of $\mathbf{F}_1$ and its angle θ for equilibrium. Set $F_2 = 6$ kN.

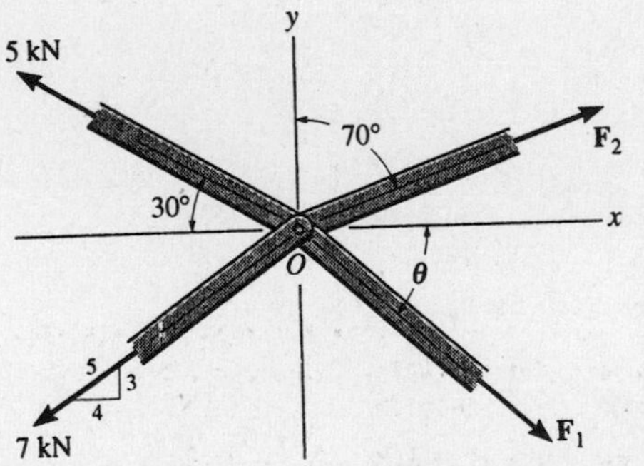

Equations of Equilibrium :

$$\xrightarrow{+} \Sigma F_x = 0; \quad F_1 \cos \theta + 6 \sin 70° - 5\cos 30° - 7\left(\frac{4}{5}\right) = 0$$

$$F_1 \cos \theta = 4.2920 \qquad [1]$$

$$+\uparrow \Sigma F_y = 0; \quad 6\cos 70° - F_1 \sin \theta + 5\sin 30° - 7\left(\frac{3}{5}\right) = 0$$

$$F_1 \sin \theta = 0.3521 \qquad [2]$$

Solving Eqs. [1] and [2] yields

$\theta = 4.69°$ $\quad F_1 = 4.31$ kN **Ans**

3-7. The device shown is used to straighten the frames of wrecked autos. Determine the tension of each segment of the chain, i.e., AB and BC, if the force which the hydraulic cylinder DB exerts on point B is 3.50 kN, as shown.

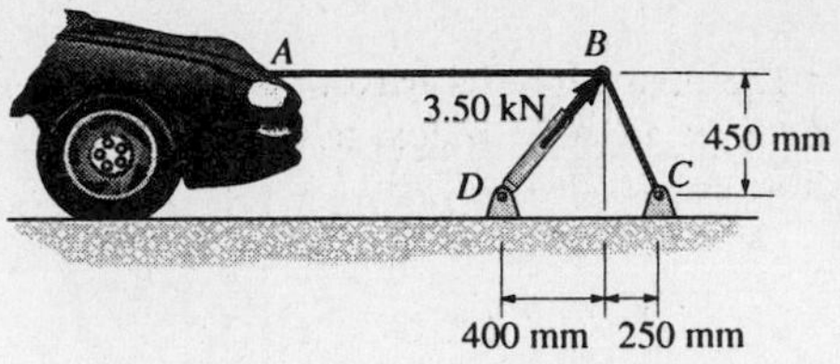

Equations of Equilibrium : A direct solution for F_{BC} can be obtained by summing forces along the y axis.

$$+\uparrow \Sigma F_y = 0; \quad 3.5\sin 48.37^\circ - F_{BC}\sin 60.95^\circ = 0$$

$$F_{BC} = 2.993 \text{ kN} = 2.99 \text{ kN} \qquad \textbf{Ans}$$

Using the result $F_{BC} = 2.993$ kN and summing forces along x axis, we have

$$\overset{+}{\rightarrow} \Sigma F_x = 0; \quad 3.5\cos 48.38^\circ + 2.993\cos 60.95^\circ - F_{AB} = 0$$

$$F_{AB} = 3.78 \text{ kN} \qquad \textbf{Ans}$$

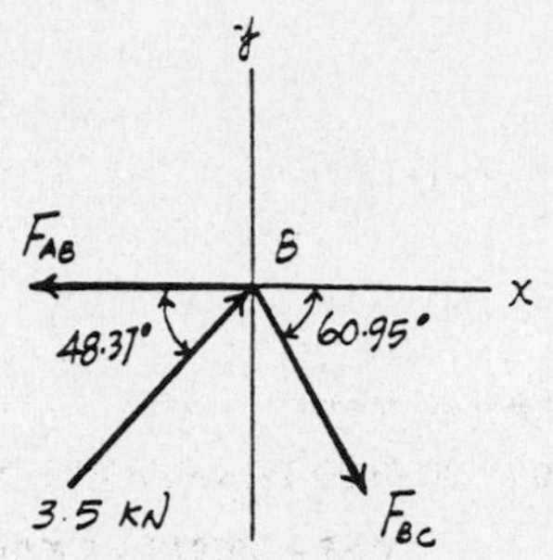

***3-8.** Determine the force in cables AB and AC necessary to support the 12-kg traffic light.

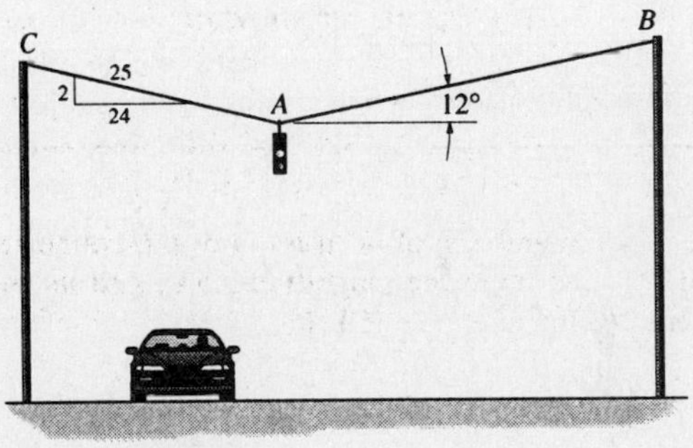

Equations of Equilibrium :

$$\overset{+}{\rightarrow} \Sigma F_x = 0; \quad F_{AB}\cos 12^\circ - F_{AC}\left(\frac{24}{25}\right) = 0$$

$$F_{AB} = 0.9814F_{AC} \qquad [1]$$

$$+\uparrow \Sigma F_y = 0; \quad F_{AB}\sin 12^\circ + F_{AC}\left(\frac{7}{25}\right) - 117.72 = 0$$

$$0.2079F_{AB} + 0.28F_{AC} = 117.72 \qquad [2]$$

Solving Eqs. [1] and [2] yields

$$F_{AB} = 239 \text{ N} \quad F_{AC} = 243 \text{ N} \qquad \textbf{Ans}$$

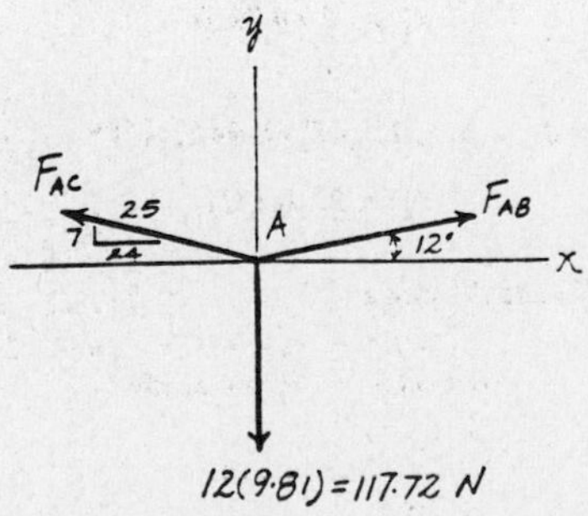

3-9. The towing pendant AB is subjected to the force of 50 kN which is developed from a tugboat. Determine the force that is in each of the bridles, BC and BD, if the ship is moving forward with constant velocity.

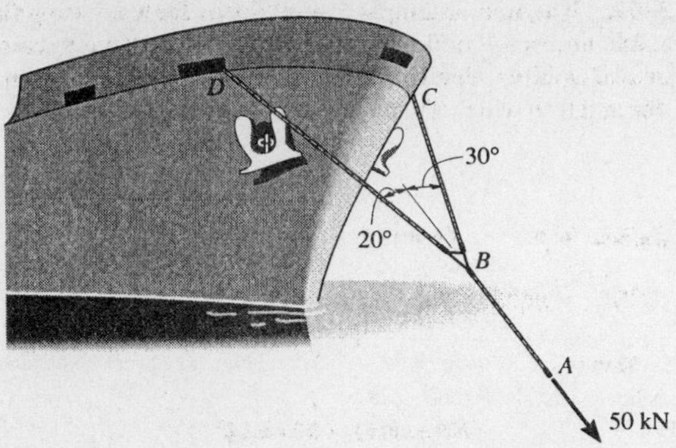

$\xrightarrow{+} \Sigma F_x = 0;\quad T_{BC} \sin 30° - T_{BD} \sin 20° = 0$

$+\uparrow \Sigma F_y = 0;\quad T_{BC} \cos 30° + T_{BD} \cos 20° - 50 = 0$

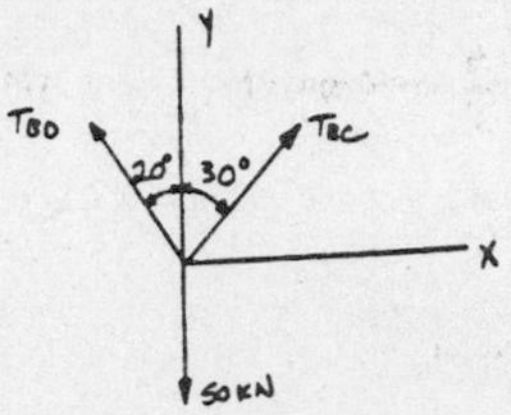

Solving,

$T_{BC} = 22.3 \text{ kN}$ **Ans**

$T_{BD} = 32.6 \text{ kN}$ **Ans**

3-10. The bearing consists of rollers, symmetrically confined within the housing. The bottom one is subjected to a 125-N force at its contact A due to the load on the shaft. Determine the normal reactions N_B and N_C on the bearing at its contact points B and C for equilibrium.

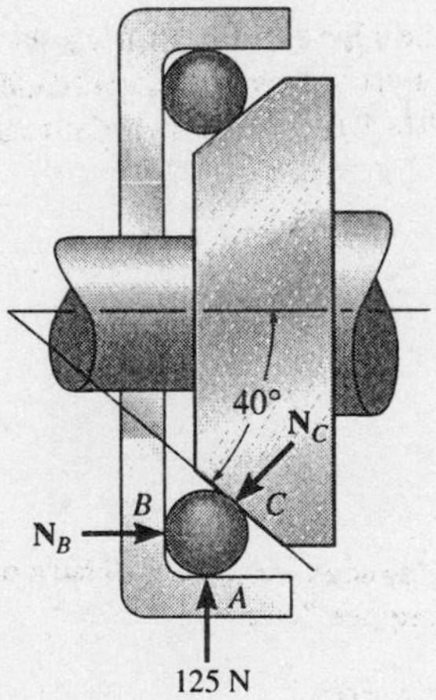

$+\uparrow \Sigma F_y = 0;\quad 125 - N_C \cos 40° = 0$

$N_C = 163.176 = 163 \text{ N}$ **Ans**

$\xrightarrow{+} \Sigma F_x = 0;\quad N_B - 163.176 \sin 40° = 0$

$N_B = 105 \text{ N}$ **Ans**

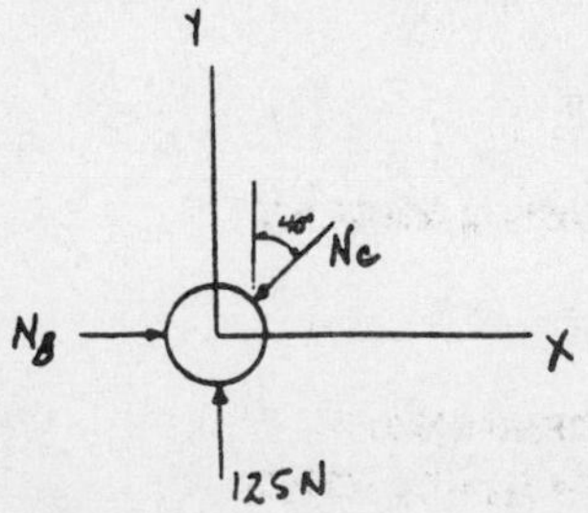

3-11. The man attempts to pull down the tree using the cable and *small* pulley arrangement shown. If the tension in AB is 60 lb, determine the tension in cable CAD and the angle θ which the cable makes at the pulley.

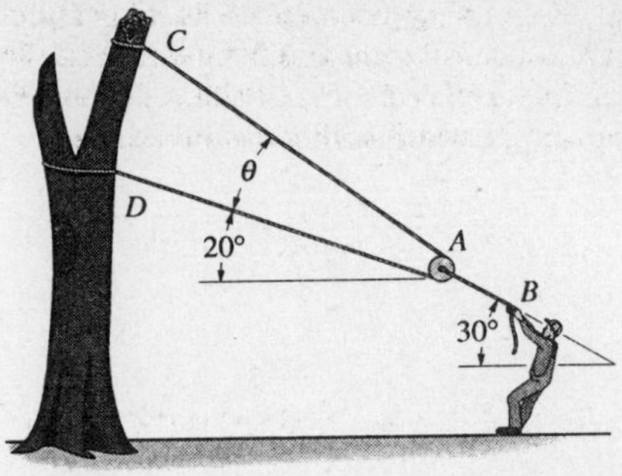

$\nwarrow^{+} \Sigma F_{x'} = 0;$ $\quad 60 \cos 10° - T - T\cos\theta = 0$

$\nearrow^{+} \Sigma F_{y'} = 0;$ $\quad T\sin\theta - 60 \sin 10° = 0$

Thus,

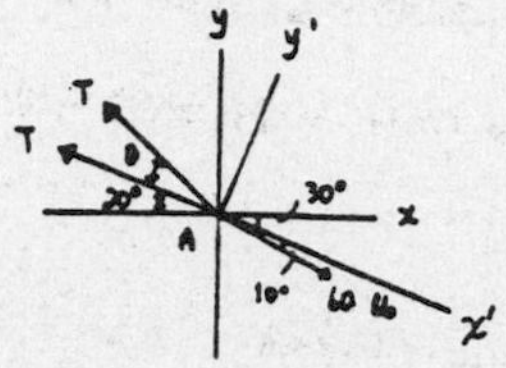

$$T(1+\cos\theta) = 60 \cos 10°$$

$$T(2\cos^2\frac{\theta}{2}) = 60 \cos 10° \qquad (1)$$

$$2T\sin\frac{\theta}{2}\cos\frac{\theta}{2} = 60 \sin 10° \qquad (2)$$

Divide Eq.(2) by Eq.(1)

$$\tan\frac{\theta}{2} = \tan 10°$$

$\theta = 20°$ **Ans**

$T = 30.5$ lb **Ans**

***3-12.** The concrete pipe elbow has a weight of 400 lb and the center of gravity is located at point G. Determine the force in the cables AB and CD needed to support it.

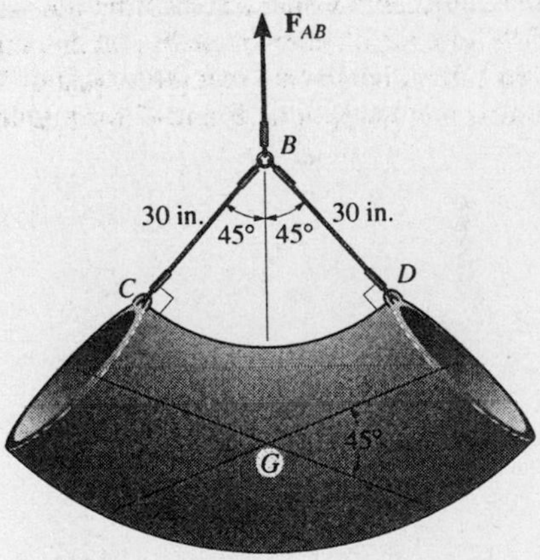

Free Body Diagram : By observation, cable AB has to support the entire weight of the concrete pipe. Thus,

$F_{AB} = 400$ lb **Ans**

The tension force in cable CD is the same throughout the cable, that is $F_{BC} = F_{BD}$.

Equations of Equilibrium :

$\xrightarrow{+} \Sigma F_x = 0;$ $\quad F_{BD} \sin 45° - F_{BC} \sin 45° = 0$

$F_{BC} = F_{Bc} = F$

$+\uparrow \Sigma F_y = 0;$ $\quad 400 - 2F\cos 45° = 0$

$F = F_{BD} = F_{CB} = 283$ lb **Ans**

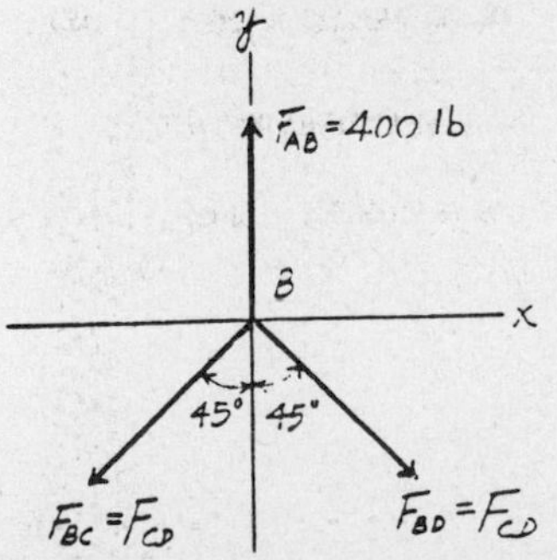

3-13. The members of a truss are connected to the gusset plate. If the forces are concurrent at point O, determine the magnitudes of **F** and **T** for equilibrium. Take $\theta = 90°$.

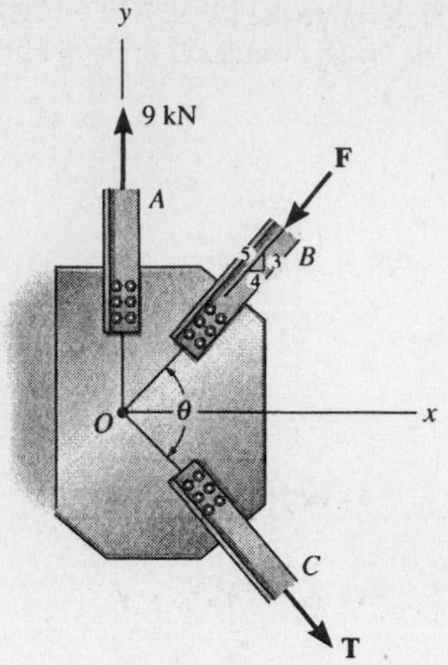

$\phi = 90° - \tan^{-1}\left(\frac{3}{4}\right) = 53.13°$

$\xrightarrow{+} \Sigma F_x = 0; \quad T\cos 53.13° - F\left(\frac{4}{5}\right) = 0$

$+\uparrow \Sigma F_y = 0; \quad 9 - T\sin 53.13° - F\left(\frac{3}{5}\right) = 0$

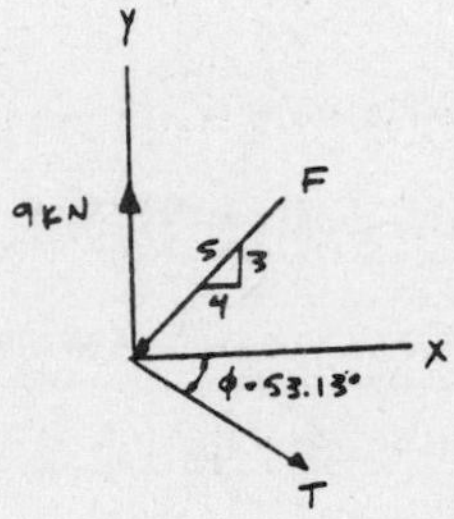

Solving,

$T = 7.20\ \text{kN}$ **Ans**

$F = 5.40\ \text{kN}$ **Ans**

3-14. The gusset plate is subjected to the forces of three members. Determine the tension force in member C and its proper orientation θ for equilibrium. The forces are concurrent at point O. Take $F = 8$ kN.

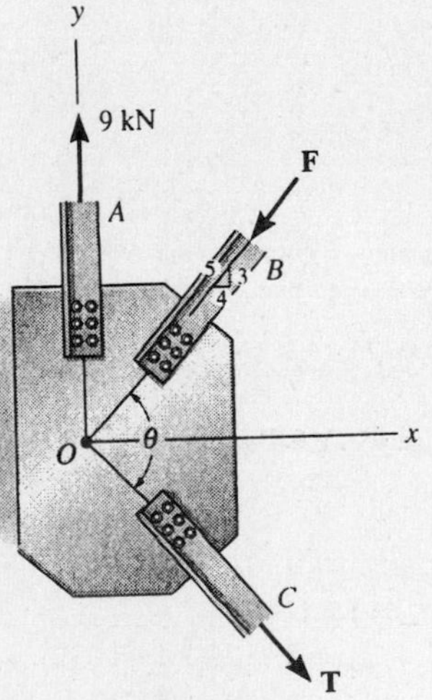

$\xrightarrow{+} \Sigma F_x = 0; \quad T\cos\phi - 8\left(\frac{4}{5}\right) = 0 \quad (1)$

$+\uparrow \Sigma F_y = 0; \quad 9 - 8\left(\frac{3}{5}\right) - T\sin\phi = 0 \quad (2)$

Rearrange then divide Eq. (1) into Eq. (2):

$\tan\phi = 0.656, \quad \phi = 33.27°$

$T = 7.66\ \text{kN}$ **Ans**

$\theta = \phi + \tan^{-1}\left(\frac{3}{4}\right) = 70.1°$ **Ans**

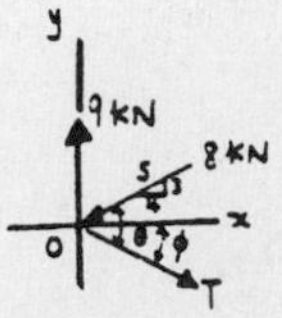

3-15. Determine the forces in cables AC and AB needed to hold the 20-kg cylinder D in equilibrium. Set $F = 300$ N and $d = 1$ m.

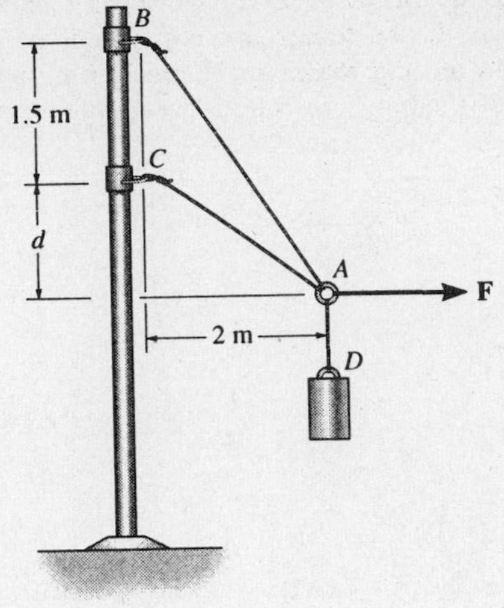

$$\phi = \tan^{-1}\left(\frac{2}{2.5}\right) = 38.660°$$

$$\theta = \tan^{-1}\left(\frac{1}{2}\right) = 26.565°$$

$\xrightarrow{+} \Sigma F_x = 0;$ $\quad -F_{AB}\sin 38.660° - F_{AC}\cos 26.565° + 300 = 0$

$$0.6247F_{AB} + 0.8944F_{AC} = 300$$

$+\uparrow \Sigma F_y = 0;$ $\quad F_{AC}\sin 26.565° + F_{AB}\cos 38.660° - 20(9.81) = 0$

$$0.7809F_{AB} + 0.4472F_{AC} = 196.2$$

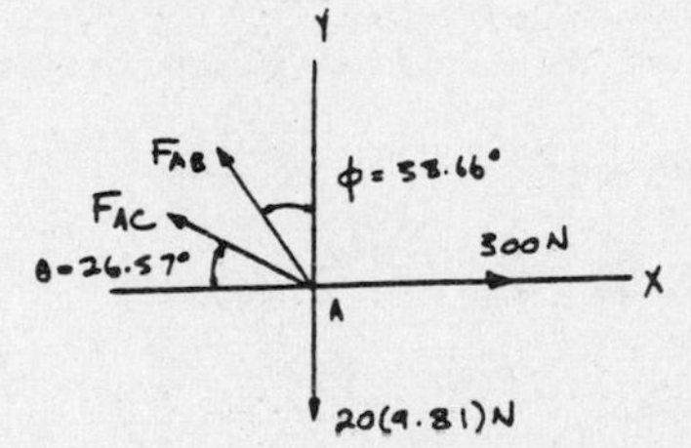

Solving :

$F_{AC} = 267$ N **Ans** $\quad F_{AB} = 98.6$ N **Ans**

***3-16.** The cylinder D has a mass of 20 kg. If a force of $F = 100$ N is applied horizontally to the ring at A, determine the largest dimension d so that the force in cable AC is zero.

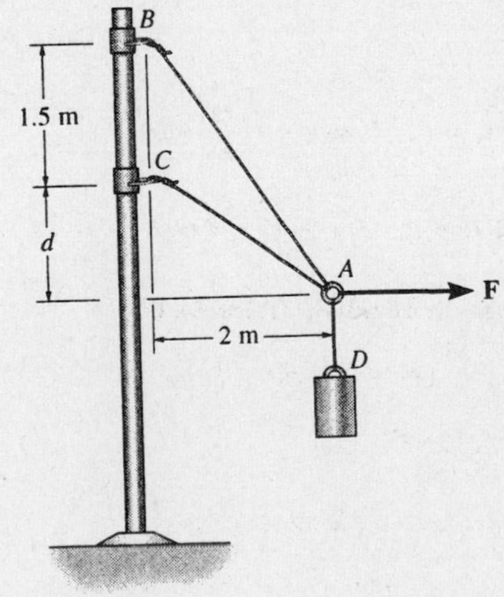

$\xrightarrow{+} \Sigma F_x = 0;$ $\quad -F_{AB}\cos\theta + 100 = 0$

$+\uparrow \Sigma F_y = 0;$ $\quad F_{AB}\sin\theta - 20(9.81) = 0$

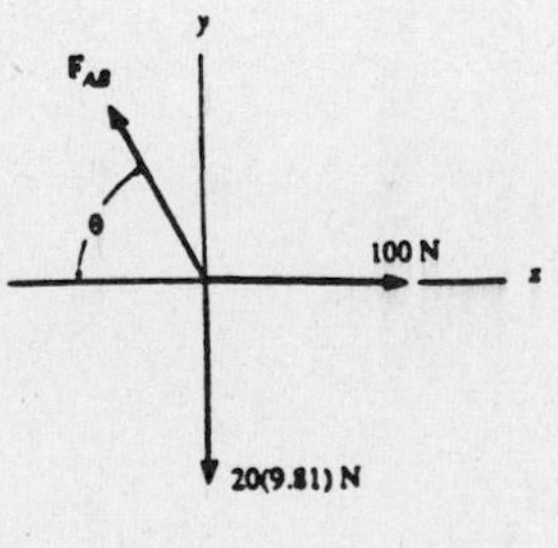

Solving :

$\theta = 62.99°$ $\quad F_{AB} = 220.2$ N

From geometry :

$\tan\theta = \dfrac{1.5 + d}{2}$ $\quad \tan 62.99° = \dfrac{1.5 + d}{2}$ $\quad d = 2.42$ m **Ans**

3-17. Determine the maximum weight of the flowerpot that can be supported without exceeding a cable tension of 50 lb in either cable AB or AC.

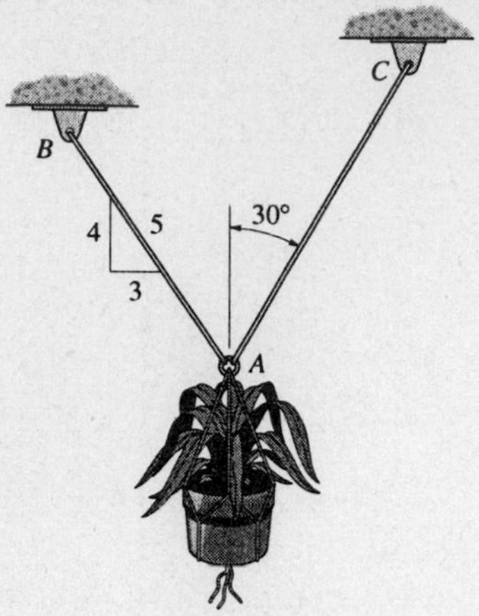

Free Body Diagram : The tension force is the same throughout the cord.

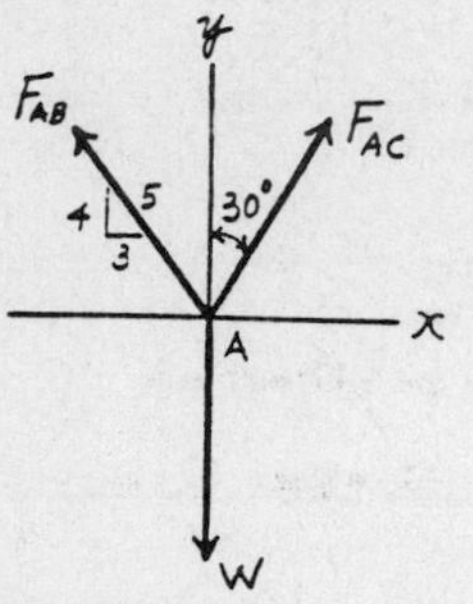

Equations of Equilibrium :

$\xrightarrow{+} \Sigma F_x = 0;$ $\quad F\sin\theta - F\sin\theta = 0 \quad$ ***(Satisfied!)***

$+\uparrow \Sigma F_y = 0;$ $\quad 2F\cos\theta - 147.15 = 0$

$F = \{73.6\sec\theta\}$ N **Ans**

3-18. The 30-kg pipe is supported at A by a system of five cords. Determine the force in each cord for equilibrium.

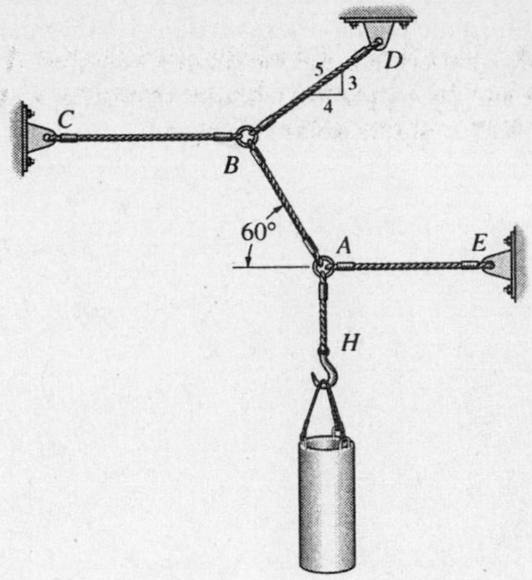

At H:

$+\uparrow \Sigma F_y = 0;\quad T_{HA} - 30(9.81) = 0$

$T_{HA} = 294 \text{ N}$ **Ans**

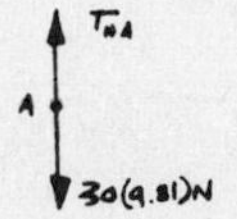

At A:

$+\uparrow \Sigma F_y = 0;\quad T_{AB}\sin 60^\circ - 30(9.81) = 0$

$T_{AB} = 339.83 = 340 \text{ N}$ **Ans**

$\xrightarrow{+} \Sigma F_x = 0;\quad T_{AE} - 339.83\cos 60^\circ = 0$

$T_{AE} = 170 \text{ N}$ **Ans**

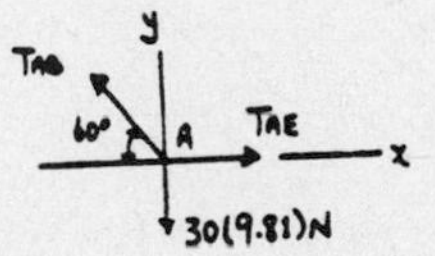

At B:

$+\uparrow \Sigma F_y = 0;\quad T_{BD}\left(\frac{3}{5}\right) - 339.83\sin 60^\circ = 0$

$T_{BD} = 490.50 = 490 \text{ N}$ **Ans**

$\xrightarrow{+} \Sigma F_x = 0;\quad 490.50\left(\frac{4}{5}\right) + 339.83\cos 60^\circ - T_{BC} = 0$

$T_{BC} = 562 \text{ N}$ **Ans**

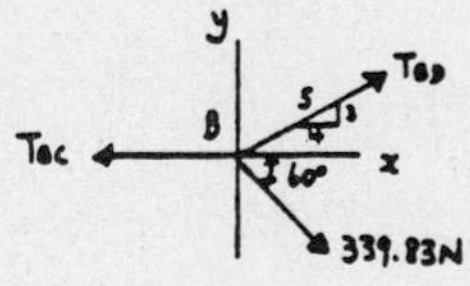

3-19. Each cord can sustain a maximum tension of 500 N. Determine the largest mass of pipe that can be supported.

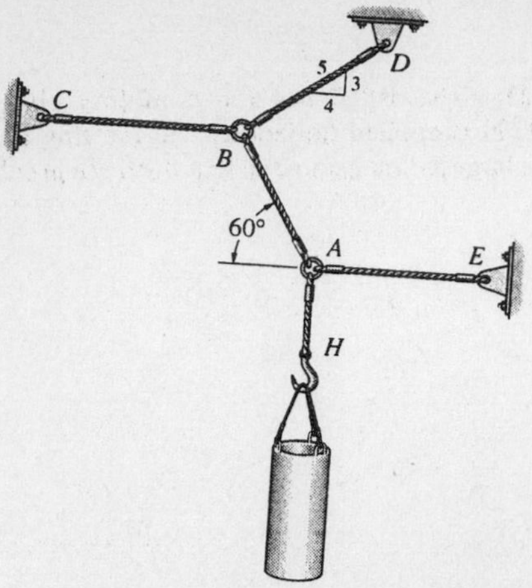

At H:

$+\uparrow \Sigma F_y = 0; \quad F_{HA} = W$

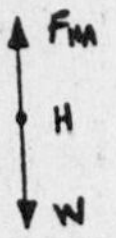

At A:

$+\uparrow \Sigma F_y = 0; \quad F_{AB} \sin 60° - W = 0$

$F_{AB} = 1.1547\, W$

$\xrightarrow{+} \Sigma F_x = 0; \quad F_{AE} - (1.1547\, W) \cos 60° = 0$

$F_{AE} = 0.5774\, W$

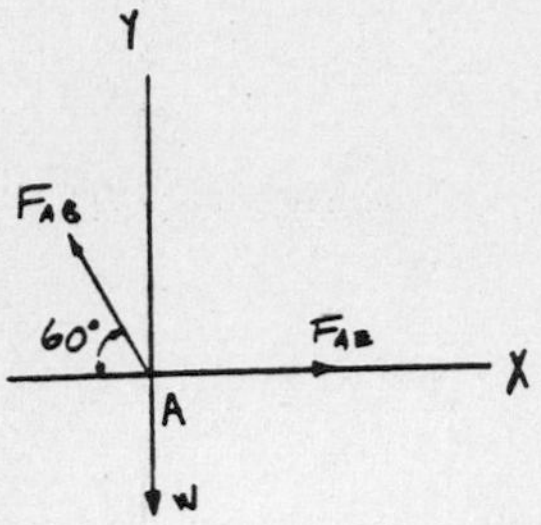

At B:

$+\uparrow \Sigma F_y = 0; \quad F_{BD}\left(\frac{3}{5}\right) - (1.1547 \cos 30°)\, W = 0$

$F_{BD} = 1.667\, W$

$\xrightarrow{+} \Sigma F_x = 0; \quad -F_{BC} + 1.667\, W\left(\frac{4}{5}\right) + 1.1547 \sin 30° = 0$

$F_{BC} = 1.9107\, W$

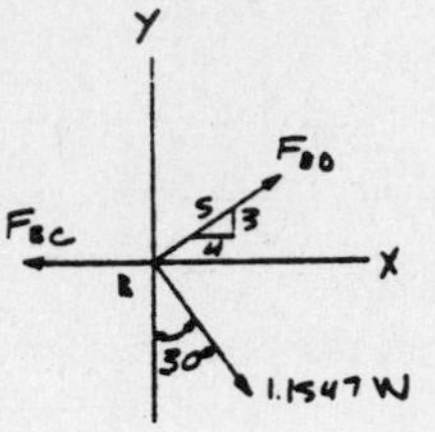

By comparison, cord BC carries the largest load. Thus

$500 = 1.9107\, W$

$W = 261.69$ N

$m = \frac{261.69}{9.81} = 26.7$ kg **Ans**

***3-20.** Determine the forces in cables AC and AB needed to hold the 20-kg ball D in equilibrium. Take $F = 300$ N and $d = 1$ m.

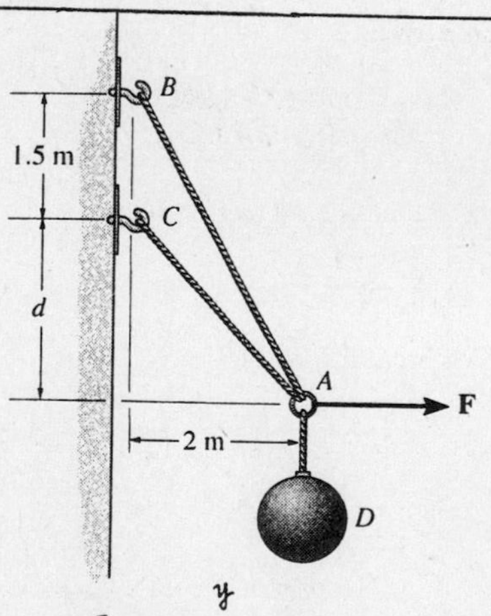

Equations of Equilibrium :

$\xrightarrow{+} \Sigma F_x = 0; \quad 300 - F_{AB}\left(\frac{4}{\sqrt{41}}\right) - F_{AC}\left(\frac{2}{\sqrt{5}}\right) = 0$

$06247 F_{AB} + 0.8944 F_{AC} = 300 \quad [1]$

$+\uparrow \Sigma F_y = 0; \quad F_{AB}\left(\frac{5}{\sqrt{41}}\right) + F_{AC}\left(\frac{1}{\sqrt{5}}\right) - 196.2 = 0$

$0.7809 F_{AB} + 0.4472 F_{AC} = 196.2 \quad [2]$

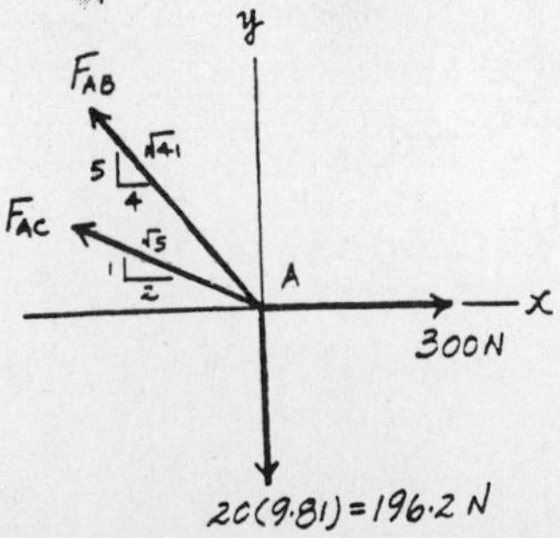

Solving Eqs. [1] and [2] yields

$F_{AB} = 98.6$ N $\quad F_{AC} = 267$ N **Ans**

3-21. The ball D has a mass of 20 kg. If a force of $F = 100$ N is applied horizontally to the ring at A, determine the largest dimension d so that the force in cable AC is zero.

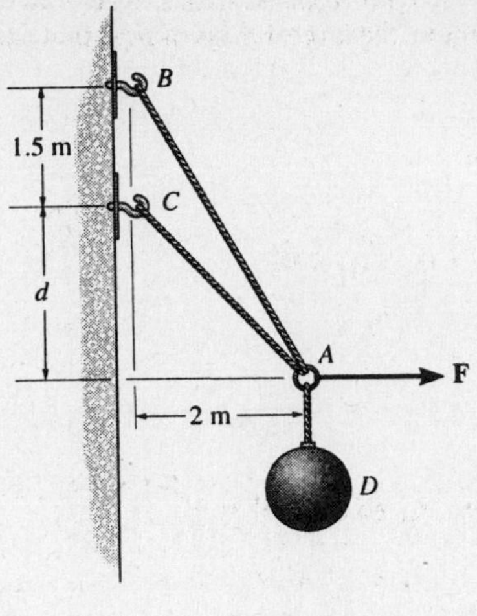

Equations of Equilibrium :

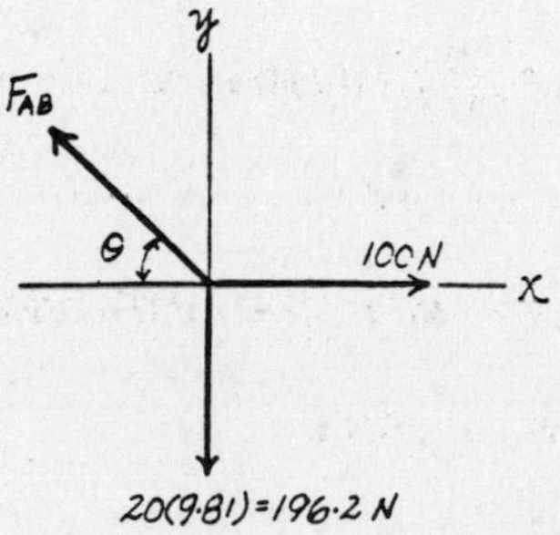

$\xrightarrow{+} \Sigma F_x = 0;\quad 100 - F_{AB}\cos\theta = 0 \qquad F_{AB}\cos\theta = 100 \qquad [1]$

$+\uparrow \Sigma F_y = 0;\quad F_{AB}\sin\theta - 196.2 = 0 \qquad F_{AB}\sin\theta = 196.2 \qquad [2]$

Solving Eqs. [1] and [2] yields

$$\theta = 62.99^\circ \qquad F_{AB} = 220.21 \text{ N}$$

From the geometry,

$$d + 1.5 = 2\tan 62.99^\circ$$
$$d = 2.42 \text{ m} \qquad \textbf{Ans}$$

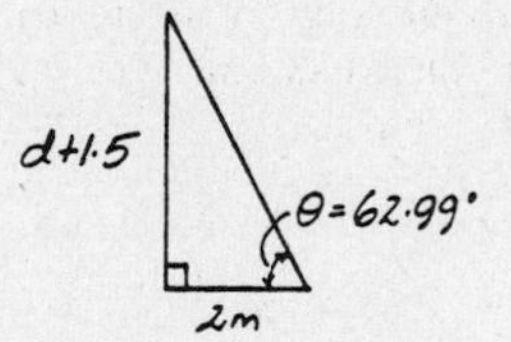

3-22. The springs on the rope assembly are originally unstretched when $\theta = 0°$. Determine the tension in each rope when $F = 90$ lb. Neglect the size of the pulleys at B and D.

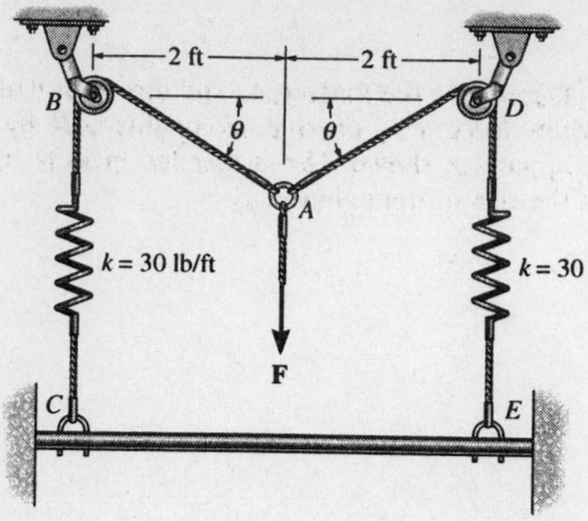

$$l = \frac{2}{\cos\theta}$$

$$T = kx = k(l - l_0) = 30\left(\frac{2}{\cos\theta} - 2\right) = 60\left(\frac{1}{\cos\theta} - 1\right) \qquad (1)$$

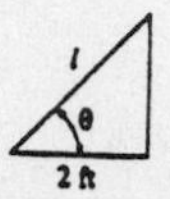

$+\uparrow \Sigma F_y = 0; \qquad 2T\sin\theta - 90 = 0 \qquad (2)$

Substituting Eq. (1) into (2) yields:

$$120(\tan\theta - \sin\theta) - 90 = 0$$

$$\tan\theta - \sin\theta = 0.75$$

By trial and error:

$$\theta = 57.957°$$

From Eq. (1),

$$T = 60\left(\frac{1}{\cos 57.957°} - 1\right) = 53.1 \text{ lb} \qquad \textbf{Ans}$$

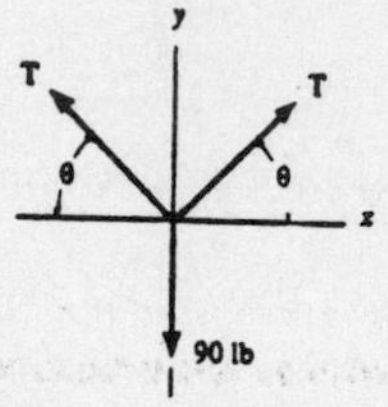

3-23. The springs on the rope assembly are originally stretched 1 ft when $\theta = 0°$. Determine the vertical force **F** that must be applied so that $\theta = 30°$.

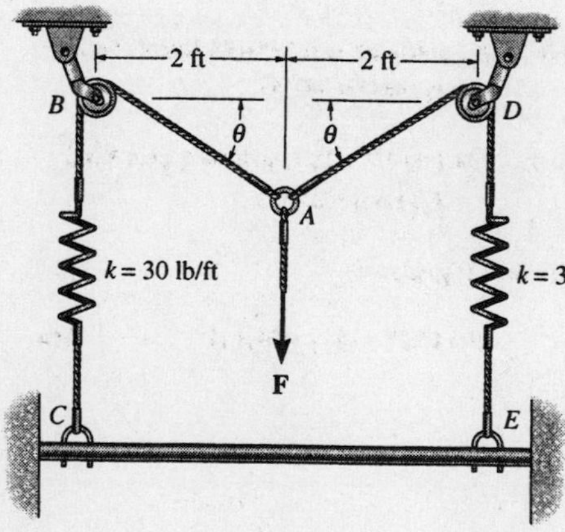

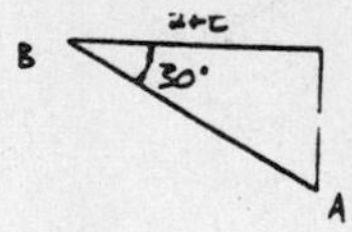

$$BA = \frac{2}{\cos 30°} = 2.3094 \text{ ft}$$

When $\theta = 30°$, the springs are stretched 1 ft + (2.3094 − 2) ft = 1.3094 ft

$F_s = kx = 30\,(1.3094) = 39.28$ lb

$+\uparrow \Sigma F_y = 0; \qquad 2\,(39.28)\sin 30° - F = 0$

$F = 39.3$ lb **Ans**

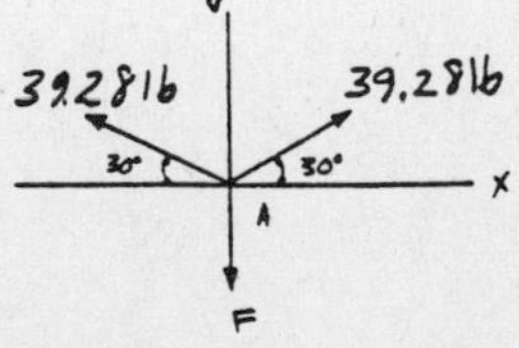

***3-24.** Determine the magnitude and direction θ of the equilibrium force F_{AB} exerted along link AB by the tractive apparatus shown. The suspended mass is 10 kg. Neglect the size of the pulley at A.

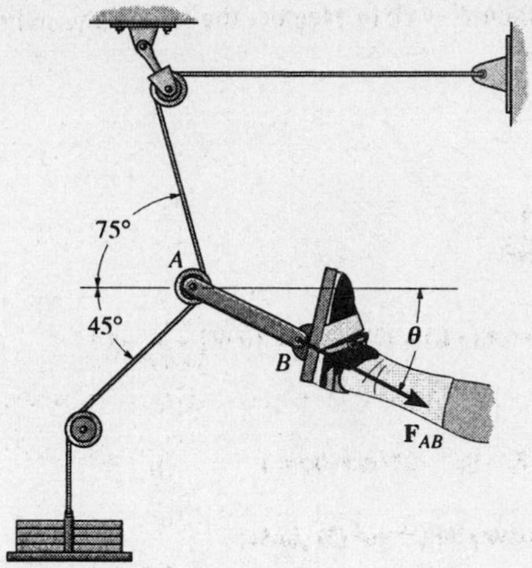

Free Body Diagram : The tension in the cord is the same throughout the cord, that is $10(9.81) = 9.81$ N.

Equations of Equilibrium :

$$\overset{+}{\rightarrow} \Sigma F_x = 0; \quad F_{AB}\cos\theta - 98.1\cos 75° - 98.1\cos 45° = 0$$
$$F_{AB}\cos\theta = 94.757 \qquad [1]$$

$$+\uparrow \Sigma F_y = 0; \quad 98.1\sin 75° - 98.1\sin 45° - F_{AB}\sin\theta = 0$$
$$F_{AB}\sin\theta = 25.390 \qquad [2]$$

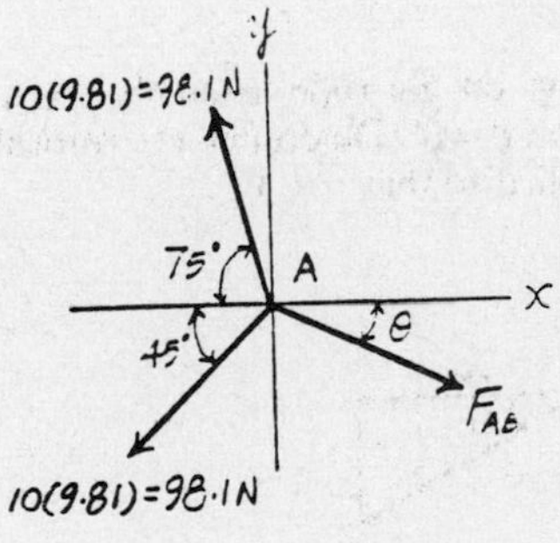

Solving Eqs. [1] and [2] yields

$\theta = 15.0°$ $\quad F_{AB} = 98.1$ N **Ans**

3-25. The wire forms a loop and passes over the small pulleys at A, B, C, and D. If its end is subjected to a force of $P = 50$ N, determine the force in the wire and the magnitude of the resultant force that the wire exerts on each of the pulleys.

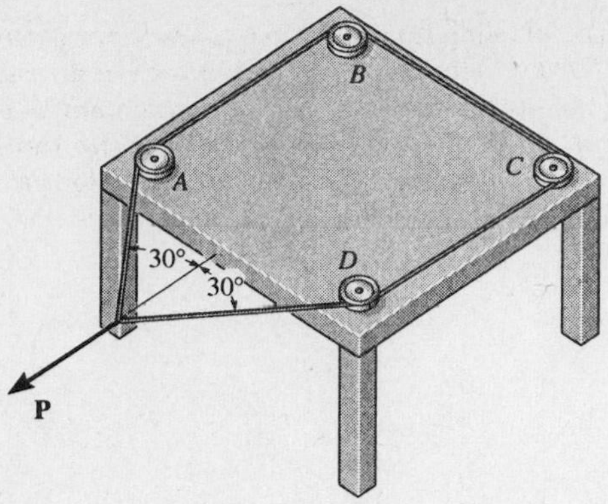

$+\uparrow \Sigma F_y = 0; \quad 2\,(T \cos 30^\circ) - 50 = 0$

$T = 28.868 = 28.9 \text{ N}$ **Ans**

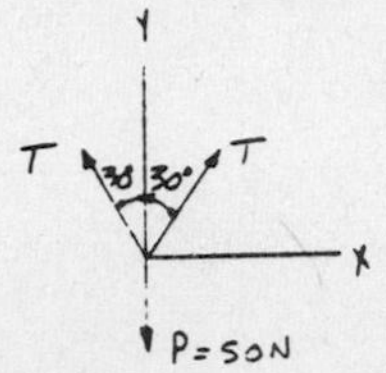

For A and D:

$F_{Rx} = \Sigma F_x; \quad F_{Rx} = 28.868 \sin 30^\circ = 14.43 \text{ N}$

$F_{Rx} = \Sigma F_y; \quad F_{Ry} = 28.868 - 28.868 \cos 30^\circ = 3.868 \text{ N}$

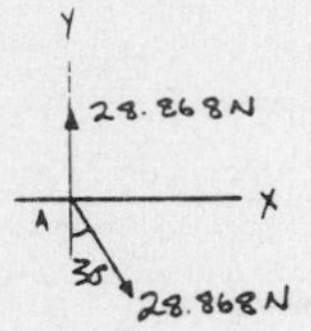

$F_R = \sqrt{(14.43)^2 + (3.868)^2} = 14.9 \text{ N}$ (A and D) **Ans**

For B and C:

$F_R = \sqrt{(28.868)^2 + (28.868)^2} = 40.8 \text{ N}$ (B and C) **Ans**

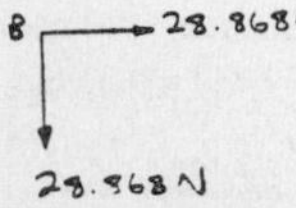

3-26. The wire forms a loop and passes over the small pulleys at A, B, C, and D. If the maximum *resultant force* that the wire can exert on each pulley is 120 N, determine the greatest force P that can be applied to the wire as shown.

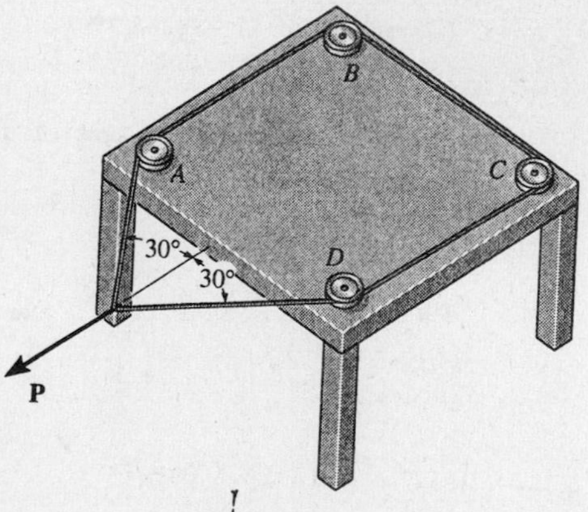

$+\uparrow \Sigma F_y = 0; \quad 2\,T \cos 30^\circ - P = 0; \quad T = 0.57735\,P$

Maximum resultant force is resisted by pulleys B and C.

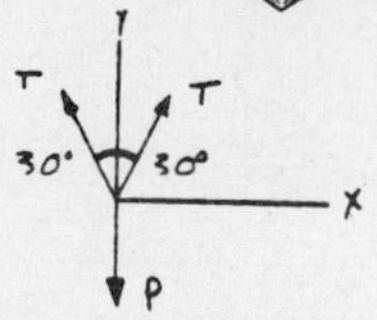

$F_R = \sqrt{(0.57735\,P)^2 + (0.57735\,P)^2}$

$F_R = 0.8165\,P = 120$

$P = 147 \text{ N}$ **Ans**

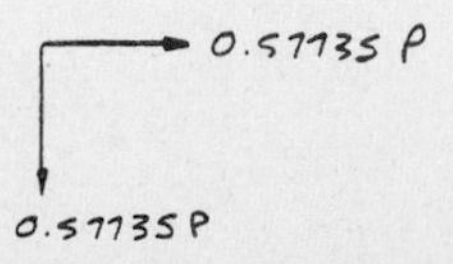

3-27. The lift sling is used to hoist a container having a mass of 500 kg. Determine the force in each of the cables AB and AC as a function of θ. If the maximum tension allowed in each cable is 5 kN, determine the shortest lengths of cables AB and AC that can be used for the lift. The center of gravity of the container is located at G.

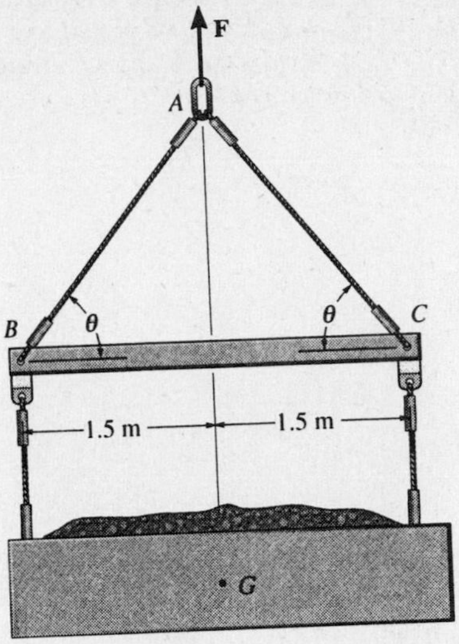

Free Body Diagram : By observation, the force $\mathbf{F}_1$ has to support the entire weight of the container. Thus, $F_1 = 500(9.81) = 4905$ N.

Equations of Equilibrium :

$\xrightarrow{+} \Sigma F_x = 0;\quad F_{AC}\cos\theta - F_{AB}\cos\theta = 0 \quad F_{AC} = F_{AB} = F$

$+\uparrow \Sigma F_y = 0;\quad 4905 - 2F\sin\theta = 0 \quad F = \{2452.5\csc\theta\}$ N

Thus, $\quad F_{AC} = F_{AB} = F = \{2.45\csc\theta\}$ kN **Ans**

If the maximum allowable tension in the cable is 5 kN, then

$$2452.5\csc\theta = 5000$$
$$\theta = 29.37^\circ$$

From the geometry, $l = \dfrac{1.5}{\cos\theta}$ and $\theta = 29.37^\circ$. Therefore

$$l = \frac{1.5}{\cos 29.37^\circ} = 1.72 \text{ m}$$ **Ans**

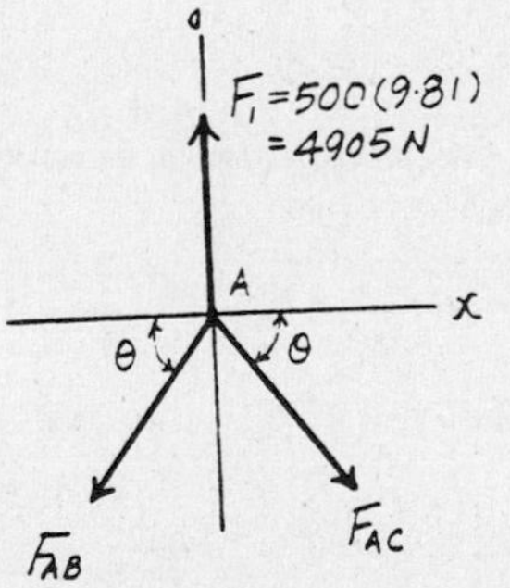

*3-28. The load has a mass of 15 kg and is lifted by the pulley system shown. Determine the force **F** in the cord as a function of the angle θ. Plot the function of force F versus the angle θ for $0 \le \theta \le 90°$.

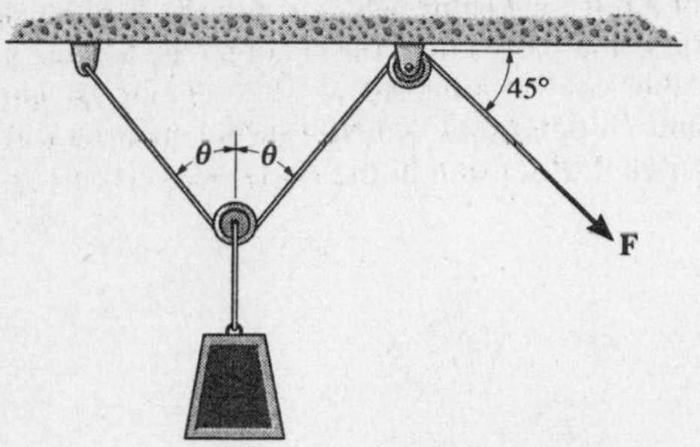

Free Body Diagram : The tension force is the same throughout the cord.

Equations of Equilibrium :

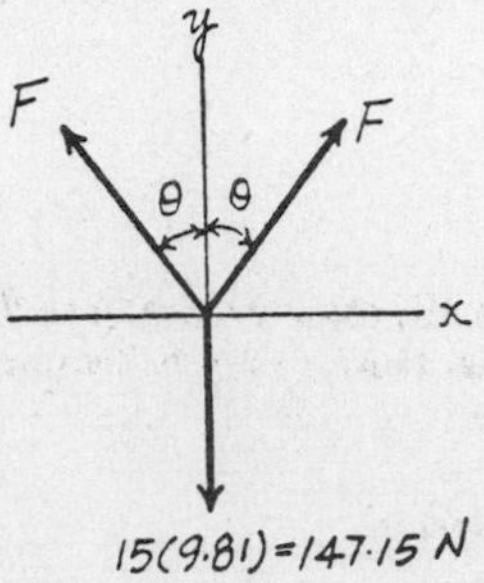

$\overset{+}{\rightarrow} \Sigma F_x = 0; \quad F\sin\theta - F\sin\theta = 0 \quad$ *(Satisfied!)*

$+\uparrow \Sigma F_y = 0; \quad 2F\cos\theta - 147.15 = 0$

$F = \{73.6\sec\theta\}$ N **Ans**

3-29. The picture has a weight of 10 lb and is to be hung over the smooth pin B. If a string is attached to the frame at points A and C, and the maximum force the string can support is 15 lb, determine the shortest string that can be safely used.

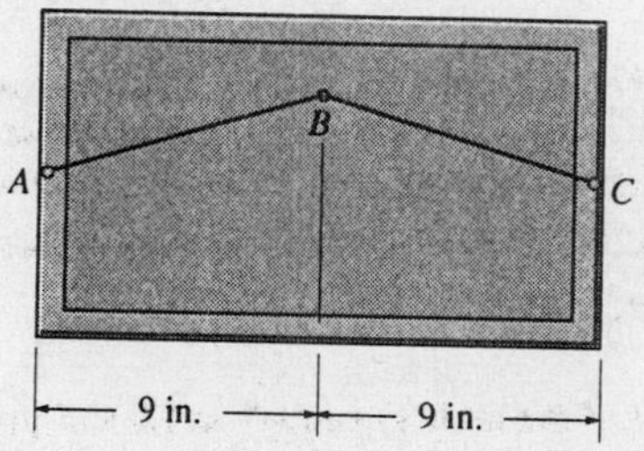

Free Body Diagram : Since the pin is smooth, the tension force in the cord is the same throughout the cord.

Equations of Equilibrium :

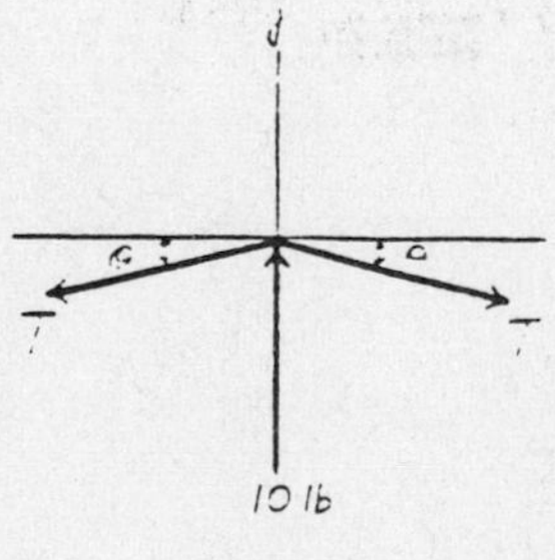

$\overset{+}{\rightarrow} \Sigma F_x = 0; \quad T\cos\theta - T\cos\theta = 0 \quad$ *(Satisfied!)*

$+\uparrow \Sigma F_y = 0; \quad 10 - 2T\sin\theta = 0 \quad T = \dfrac{5}{\sin\theta}$

If tension in the cord cannot exceed 15 lb, then

$$\frac{5}{\sin\theta} = 15$$
$$\theta = 19.47°$$

From the geometry, $\dfrac{l}{2} = \dfrac{9}{\cos\theta}$ and $\theta = 19.47°$. Therefore

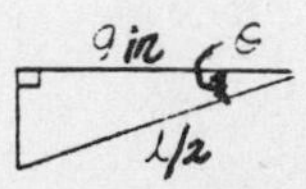

$$l = \frac{18}{\cos 19.47°} = 19.1 \text{ in.}$$ **Ans**

3-30. The 200-lb uniform tank is suspended by means of a 6-ft-long cable, which is attached to the sides of the tank and passes over the small pulley located at O. If the cable can be attached at either points A and B, or C and D, determine which attachment produces the least amount of tension in the cable. What is this tension?

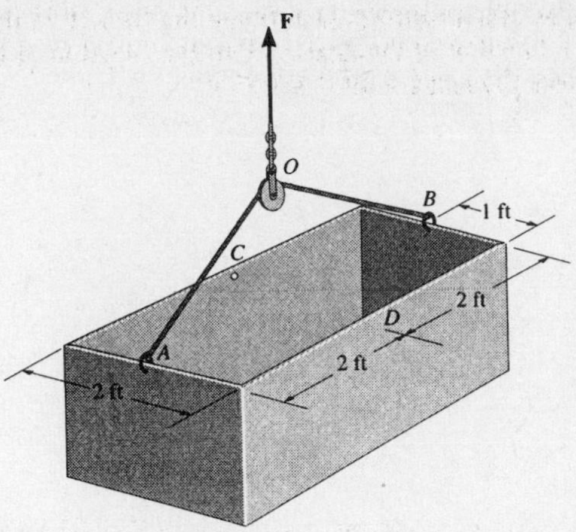

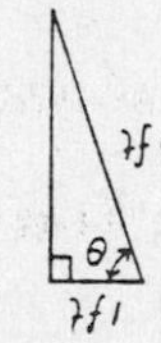

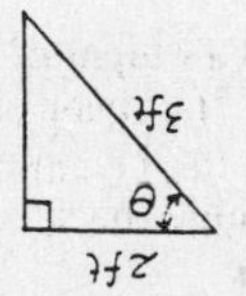

Free Body Diagram **:** By observation, the force **F** has to support the entire weight of the tank. Thus, $F = 200$ lb. The tension in cable is the same throughout the cable.

Equations of Equilibrium **:**

$\xrightarrow{+} \Sigma F_x = 0;\quad T\cos\theta - T\cos\theta = 0$ ***(Satisfied!)***

$+\uparrow \Sigma F_y = 0;\quad 200 - 2T\sin\theta = 0 \quad T = \dfrac{100}{\sin\theta}$ [1]

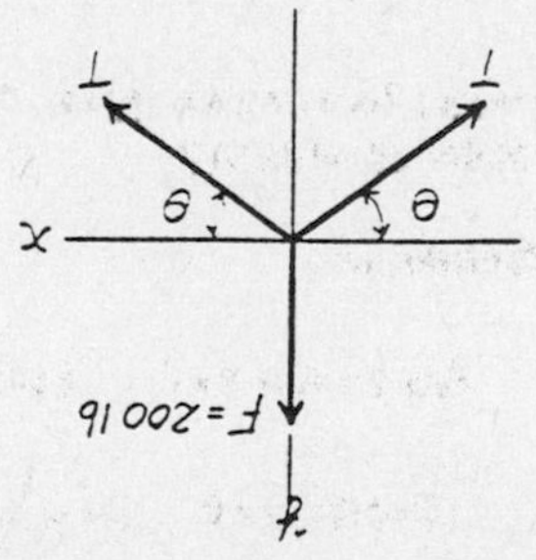

From the function obtained above, one realizes that in order to produce the least amount of tension in the cable, $\sin\theta$ hence θ must be as great as possible. Since the attachment of the cable to point C and D produces a greater θ $\left(\theta = \cos^{-1}\frac{1}{3} = 70.53^\circ\right)$ as compared to the attachment of the cable to points A and B $\left(\theta = \cos^{-1}\frac{2}{3} = 48.19^\circ\right)$,

The attachment of the cable to point C and D will produce the least amount of tension in the cable. **Ans**

Thus,

$$T = \frac{100}{\sin 70.53^\circ} = 106 \text{ lb}$$ **Ans**

■3-31. The 10-lb weight is supported by the cord AC and roller and by the spring that has a stiffness of $k = 10$ lb/in. and an unstretched length of 12 in. Determine the distance d to where the weight is located when it is in equilibrium.

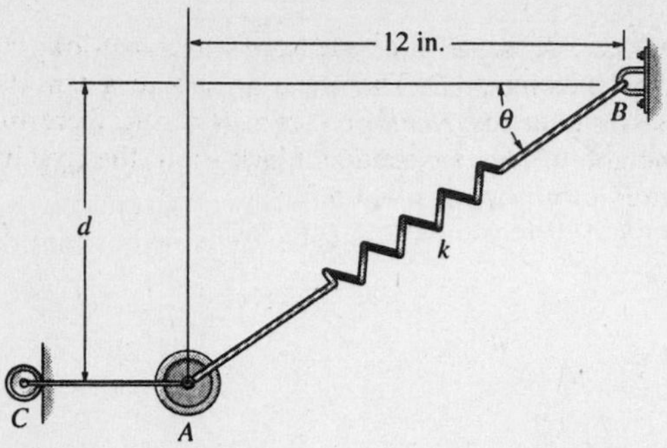

$\xrightarrow{+} \Sigma F_x = 0; \quad -T_{AC} + F_s \cos\theta = 0$

$+\uparrow \Sigma F_y = 0; \quad F_s \sin\theta - 10 = 0$

$F_s = kx; \quad F_s = 10\left(\frac{12}{\cos\theta} - 12\right)$

$= 120(\sec\theta - 1)$

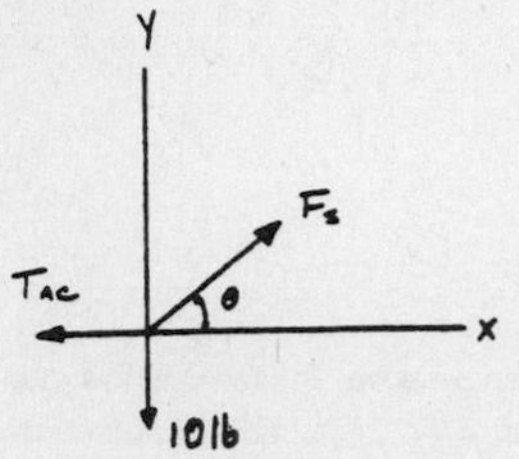

Thus,

$$120(\sec\theta - 1)\sin\theta = 10$$

$$(\tan\theta - \sin\theta) = \frac{1}{12}$$

Solving,

$$\theta = 30.71°$$

$$d = 12 \tan 30.71° = 7.13 \text{ in.}$$ **Ans**

***3-32.** The 10-lb weight is supported by the cord AC and roller and by a spring. If the spring has an unstretched length of 8 in., and the weight is in equilibrium when $d = 4$ in., determine the stiffness k of the spring.

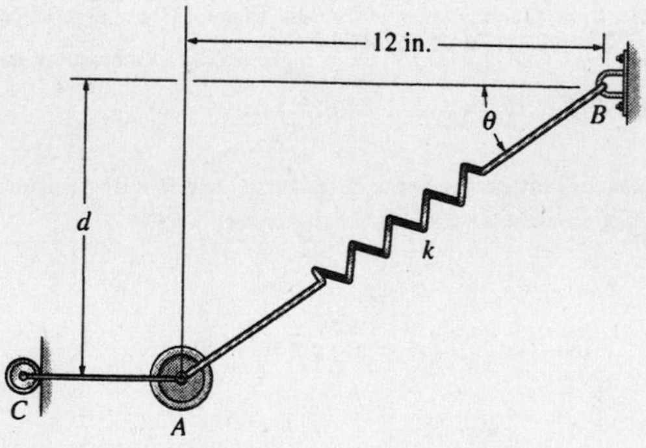

$+\uparrow \Sigma F_y = 0; \quad F_s \sin\theta - 10 = 0$

$F_s = kx; \quad F_s = k\left(\frac{12}{\cos\theta} - 8\right)$

$\tan\theta = \frac{4}{12}; \quad \theta = 18.435°$

Thus,

$$k\left(\frac{12}{\cos 18.435°} - 8\right)\sin 18.435° = 10$$

$k = 6.80$ lb/in. **Ans**

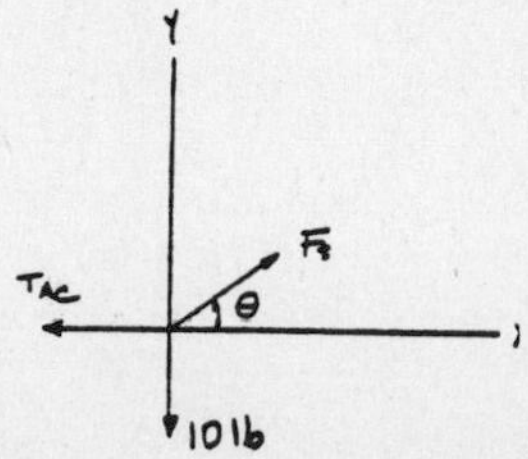

■3-33. A "scale" is constructed with a 4-ft-long cord and the 10-lb block D. The cord is fixed to a pin at A and passes over two *small* pulleys at B and C. Determine the weight of the suspended block E if the system is in equilibrium when s = 1.5 ft.

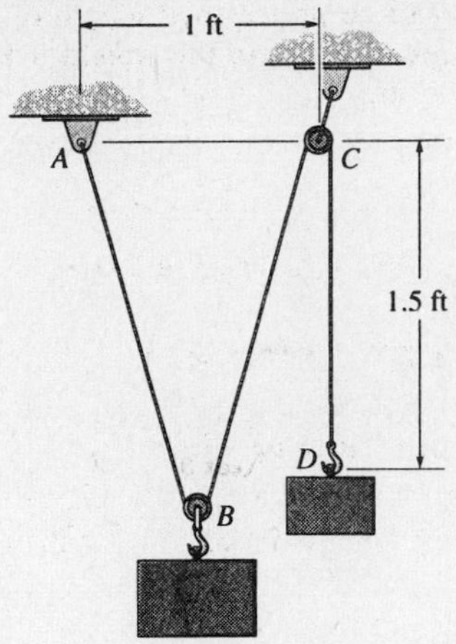

Free Body Diagram : The tension force in the cord is the same throughout the cord, that is 10 lb. From the geometry,

$$\theta = \sin^{-1}\left(\frac{0.5}{1.25}\right) = 23.58°.$$

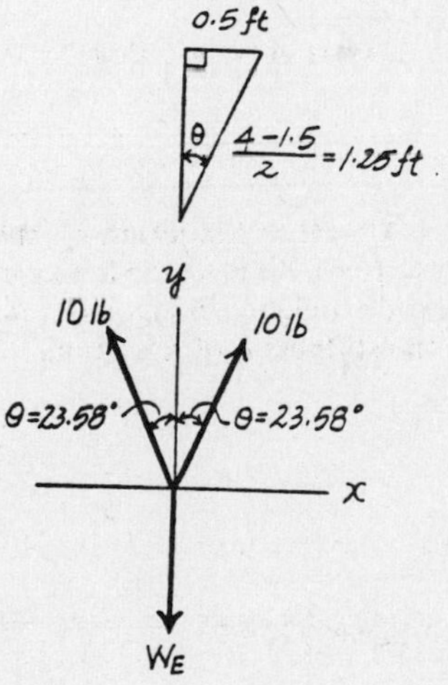

Equations of Equilibrium :

$\xrightarrow{+} \Sigma F_x = 0;$ $10\sin 23.58° - 10\sin 23.58° = 0$ ***(Satisfied!)***

$+\uparrow \Sigma F_y = 0;$ $2(10)\cos 23.58° - W_E = 0$

$W_E = 18.3$ lb **Ans**

3-34. The man attempts to pull the log at C by using the three ropes. Determine the direction θ in which he should pull on his rope with a force of 80 lb, so that he exerts a maximum force on the log. What is the force on the log for this case? Also, determine the direction in which he should pull in order to maximize the force in the rope attached to B. What is this maximum force?

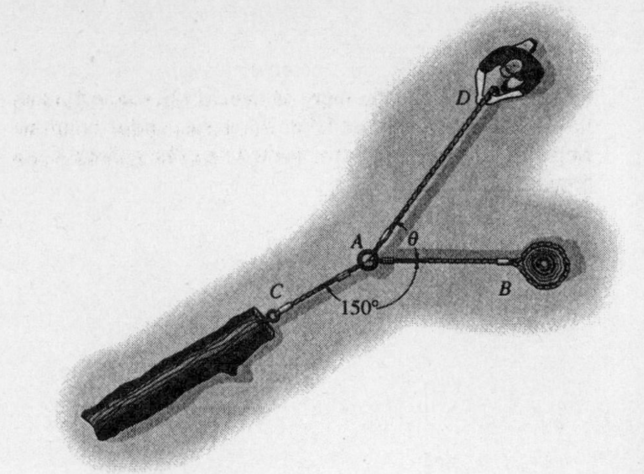

$\xrightarrow{+}\Sigma F_x = 0;\quad F_{AB} + 80\cos\theta - F_{AC}\sin 60° = 0 \qquad (1)$

$+\uparrow\Sigma F_y = 0;\quad 80\sin\theta - F_{AC}\cos 60° = 0 \qquad (2)$

$F_{AC} = 160\sin\theta$

$\frac{dF_{AC}}{d\theta} = 160\cos\theta = 0$

$\theta = 90°$ **Ans**

$F_{AC} = 160\text{lb}$ **Ans**

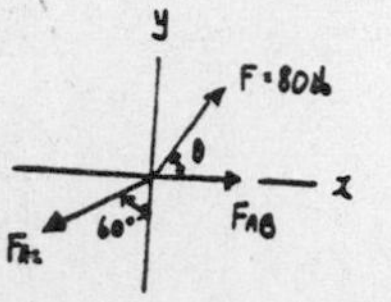

From Eq. (1),

$F_{AC}\sin 60° = F_{AB} + 80\cos\theta$

Substitute into Eq. (2),

$80\sin\theta\sin 60° = (F_{AB} + 80\cos\theta)\cos 60°$

$F_{AB} = 138.6\sin\theta - 80\cos\theta$

$\frac{dF_{AB}}{d\theta} = 138.6\cos\theta + 80\sin\theta = 0$

$\theta = \tan^{-1}\left[\frac{138.6}{-80}\right] = 120°$ **Ans**

$F_{AB} = 138.6\sin 120° - 80\cos 120° = 160\text{ lb}$ **Ans**

■*3-35. The spring has a stiffness of $k = 800$ N/m and an unstretched length of 200 mm. Determine the force in cables BC and BD when the spring is held in the position shown.

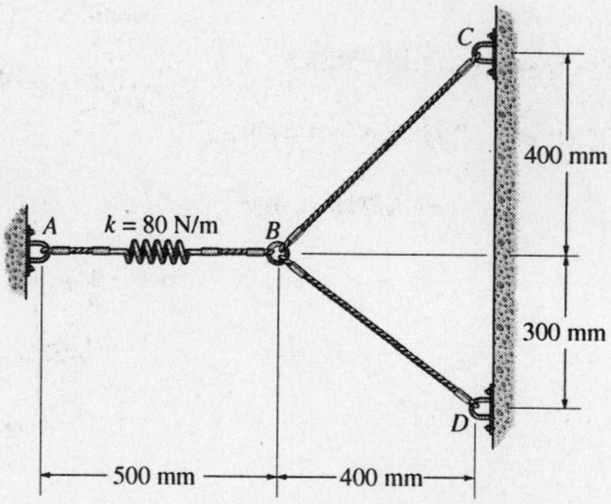

The Force in The Spring : The spring stretches $s = l - l_0 = 0.5 - 0.2 = 0.3$ m. Applying Eq. 3 – 2, we have

$$F_{sp} = ks = 800(0.3) = 240\text{ N}$$

Equations of Equilibrium :

$\xrightarrow{+}\Sigma F_x = 0;\quad F_{BC}\cos 45° + F_{BD}\left(\frac{4}{5}\right) - 240 = 0$

$0.7071F_{BC} + 0.8F_{BD} = 240 \qquad [1]$

$+\uparrow\Sigma F_y = 0;\quad F_{BC}\sin 45° - F_{BD}\left(\frac{3}{5}\right) = 0$

$F_{BC} = 0.8485F_{BD} \qquad [2]$

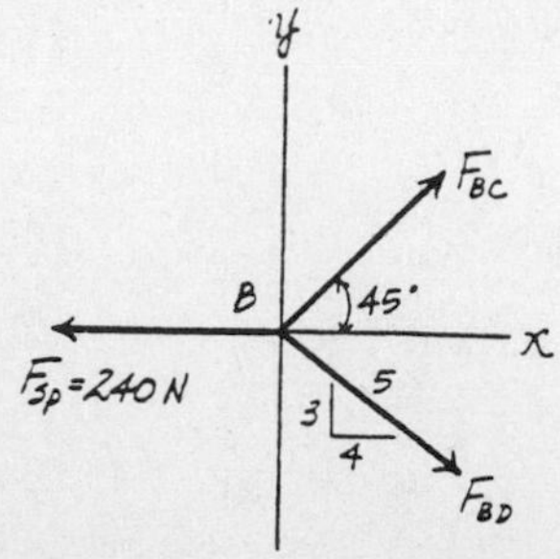

Solving Eqs. [1] and [2] yields,

$F_{BD} = 171\text{ N} \quad . F_{BC} = 145\text{ N}$ **Ans**

*3-36. Determine the mass of each of the two cylinders if they cause a sag of $s = 0.5$ m when suspended from the rings at A and B. Note that $s = 0$ when the cylinders are removed.

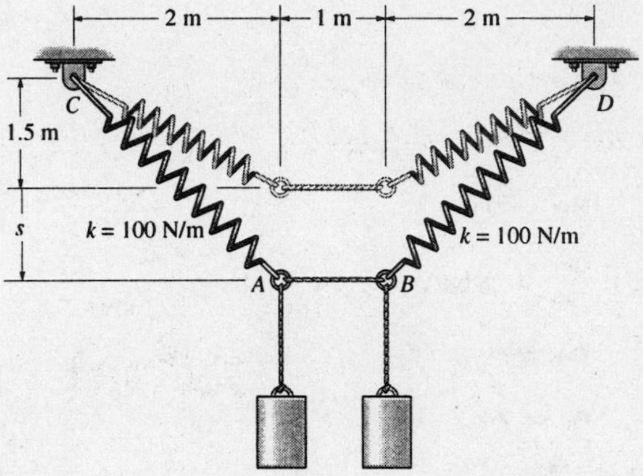

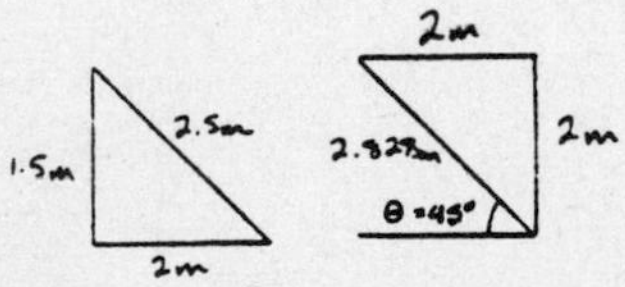

$F_{AC} = 100 \text{ N/m}(2.828 - 2.5) = 32.84 \text{ N}$

$+\uparrow \Sigma F_y = 0;\quad 32.84 \sin 45° - m(9.81) = 0$

$m = 2.37 \text{ kg}$ **Ans**

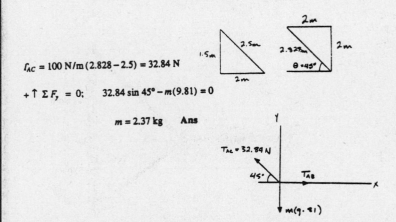

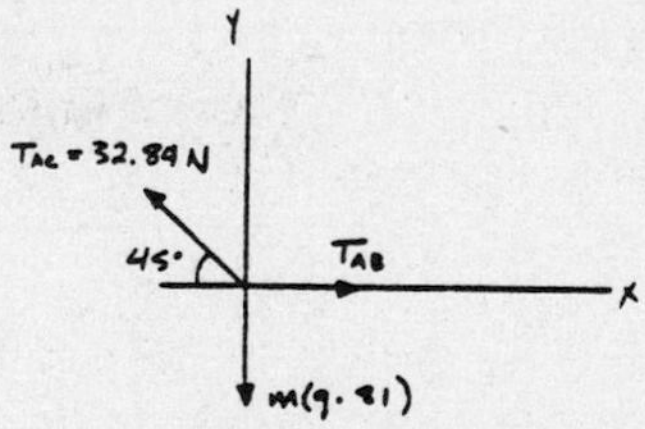

■3-37. The ring of negligible size is subjected to a vertical force of 200 lb. Determine the required length l of cord AC such that the tension acting in AC is 160 lb. Also, what is the force in cord AB? *Hint:* Use the equilibrium condition to determine the required angle θ for attachment, then determine l using trigonometry applied to triangle ABC.

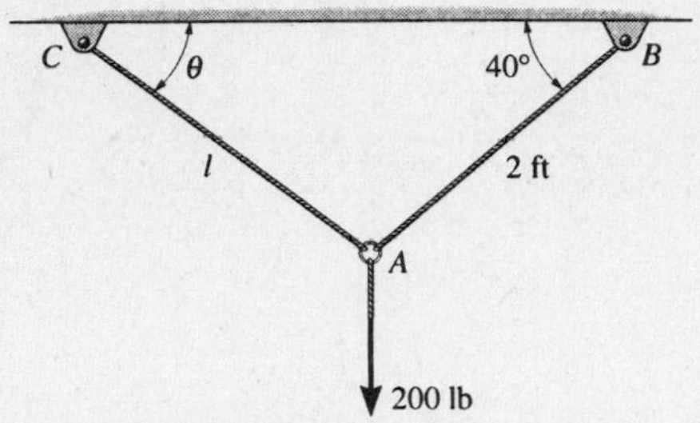

$\xrightarrow{+} \Sigma F_x = 0;$ $\quad F_{AB}\cos 40° - 160\cos\theta = 0$

$+\uparrow \Sigma F_y = 0;$ $\quad 160\sin\theta + F_{AB}\sin 40° - 200 = 0$

Thus,

$$\sin\theta + 0.8391\cos\theta = 1.25$$

Solving by trial and error,

$\theta = 33.25°$

$F_{AB} = 175 \text{ lb}$ **Ans**

$$\frac{2}{\sin 33.25°} = \frac{l}{\sin 40°}$$

$l = 2.34 \text{ ft}$ **Ans**

Also,

$\theta = 66.75°$

$F_{AB} = 82.4 \text{ lb}$ **Ans**

$$\frac{2}{\sin 66.75°} = \frac{l}{\sin 40°}$$

$l = 1.40 \text{ ft}$ **Ans**

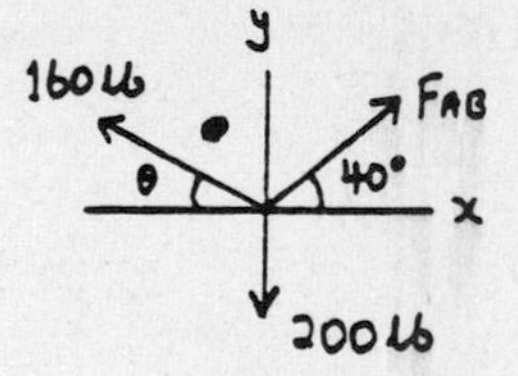

■3-38. The pail and its contents have a mass of 60 kg. If the cable is 15 m long, determine the distance y of the pulley for equilibrium. Neglect the size of the pulley at A.

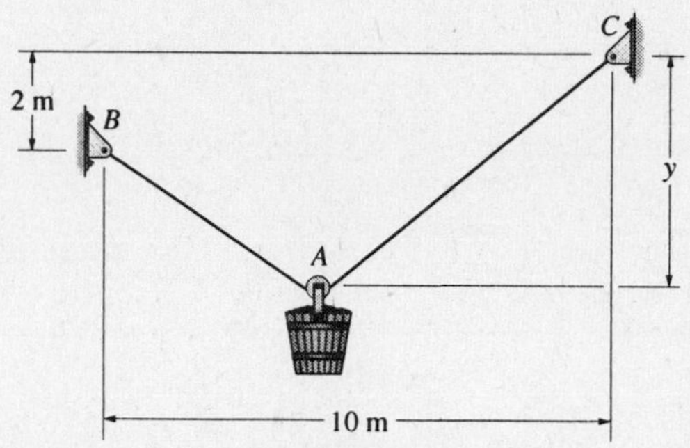

Free Body Diagram : Since the pulley is smooth, the tension in the cable is the same throughout the cable.

Equations of Equilibrium :

$$\xrightarrow{+} \Sigma F_x = 0; \quad T\sin\theta - T\sin\phi = 0 \quad \theta = \phi$$

Geometry :

$$l_1 = \sqrt{(10-x)^2 + (y-2)^2} \quad l_2 = \sqrt{x^2+y^2}$$

Since $\theta = \phi$, two triangles are similar.

$$\frac{10-x}{x} = \frac{y-2}{y} = \frac{\sqrt{(10-x)^2+(y-2)^2}}{\sqrt{x^2+y^2}} \quad [1]$$

Also,

$$l_1 + l_2 = 15$$

$$\sqrt{(10-x)^2+(y-2)^2} + \sqrt{x^2+y^2} = 15$$

$$\left(\frac{\sqrt{x^2+y^2}}{\sqrt{x^2+y^2}}\right)\sqrt{(10-x)^2+(y-2)^2} + \sqrt{x^2+y^2} = 15 \quad [2]$$

However, from Eq. [1] $\dfrac{\sqrt{(10-x)^2+(y-2)^2}}{\sqrt{x^2+y^2}} = \dfrac{10-x}{x}$, Eq. [2] becomes

$$\sqrt{x^2+y^2}\left(\frac{10-x}{x}\right) + \sqrt{x^2+y^2} = 15 \quad [3]$$

Dividing both sides of Eq. [3] by $\sqrt{x^2+y^2}$ yields

$$\frac{10}{x} = \frac{15}{\sqrt{x^2+y^2}} \qquad x = \sqrt{0.8y} \quad [4]$$

From Eq. [1] $\dfrac{10-x}{x} = \dfrac{y-2}{y} \qquad x = \dfrac{5y}{y-1} \quad [5]$

Equating Eq. [1] and [5] yields

$$\sqrt{0.8y} = \frac{5y}{y-1}$$

$$y = 6.59 \text{ m} \qquad \textbf{Ans}$$

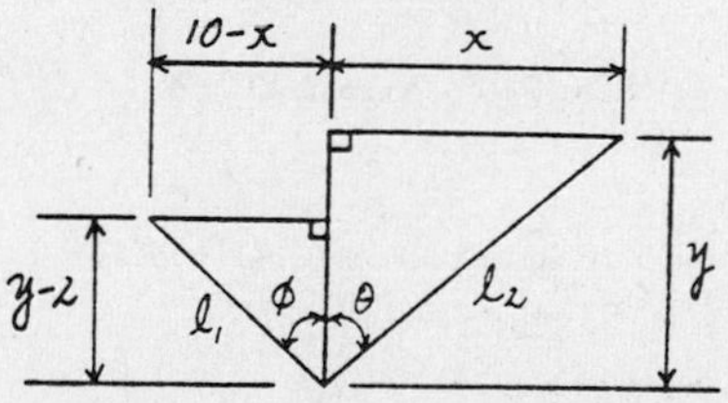

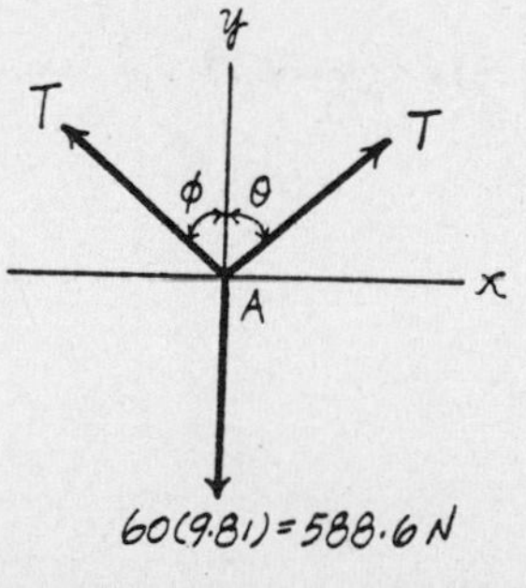

3-39. A 4-kg sphere rests on the smooth parabolic surface. Determine the normal force it exerts on the surface and the mass m_B of block B needed to hold it in the equilibrium position shown.

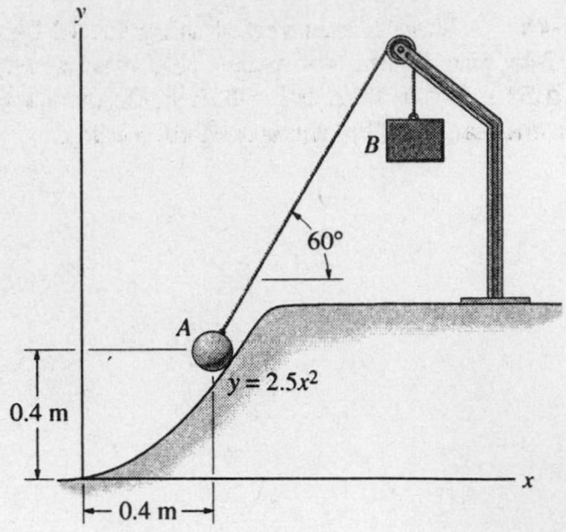

Geometry **:** The angle θ which the surface make with the horizontal is to be determined first.

$$\tan\theta\Big|_{x=0.4\text{m}} = \frac{dy}{dx}\Big|_{x=0.4\text{m}} = 5.0x\Big|_{x=0.4\text{m}} = 2.00$$

$$\theta = 63.43^\circ$$

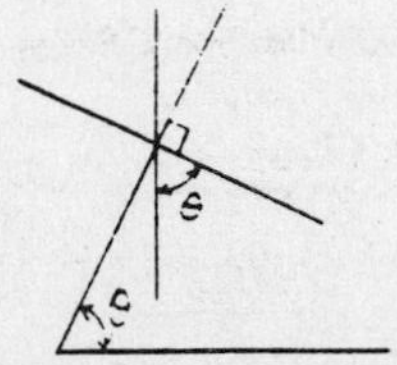

Free Body Diagram **:** The tension in the cord is the same throughout the cord and is equal to the weight of block B, $W_B = m_B\,(9.81)$.

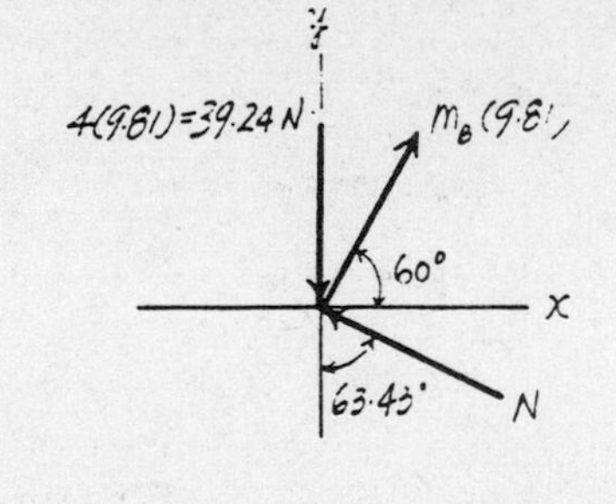

Equations of Equilibrium **:**

$\xrightarrow{+} \Sigma F_x = 0;\quad m_B\,(9.81)\cos 60^\circ - N\sin 63.43^\circ = 0$

$$N = 5.4840 m_B \qquad [1]$$

$+\uparrow \Sigma F_y = 0;\quad m_B\,(9.81)\sin 60^\circ + N\cos 63.43^\circ - 39.24 = 0$

$$8.4957 m_B + 0.4472N = 39.24 \qquad [2]$$

Solving Eqs. [1] and [2] yields

$$m_B = 3.58 \text{ kg} \qquad N = 19.7 \text{ N} \qquad \textbf{Ans}$$

■*3-40. A scale is constructed using the 10-kg mass A, the 2-kg pan P, and the pulley and cord arrangement. Cord BCA is 2-m long. If $s = 0.75$ m, determine the mass D in the pan. Neglect the size of the pulley.

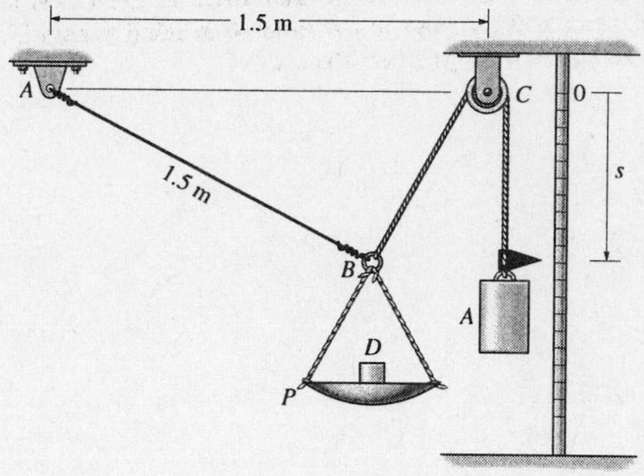

$\xrightarrow{+} \Sigma F_x = 0;\quad 98.1\cos\theta - T_{AB}\cos\phi = 0 \quad (1)$

$+\uparrow \Sigma F_y = 0;\quad T_{AB}\sin\phi + 98.1\sin\theta - m(9.81) = 0 \quad (2)$

$$(1.5)^2 = x^2 + y^2$$

$$(1.25)^2 = (1.5 - x)^2 + y^2$$

$$(1.25)^2 = (1.5 - x)^2 + (1.5)^2 - x^2$$

$$-3x + 2.9375 = 0$$

$$x = 0.9792 \text{ m}$$

$$y = 1.1363 \text{ m}$$

Thus,

$$\phi = \sin^{-1}\left(\frac{1.1363}{1.5}\right) = 49.25^\circ$$

$$\theta = \sin^{-1}\left(\frac{1.1363}{1.25}\right) = 65.38^\circ$$

Solving Eq. (1) and (2),

$$T_{AB} = 62.62 \text{ N}$$

$$m = 13.9 \text{ kg}$$

Therefore,

$$m_D = 13.9 \text{ kg} - 2 \text{ kg} = 11.9 \text{ kg} \quad \textbf{Ans}$$

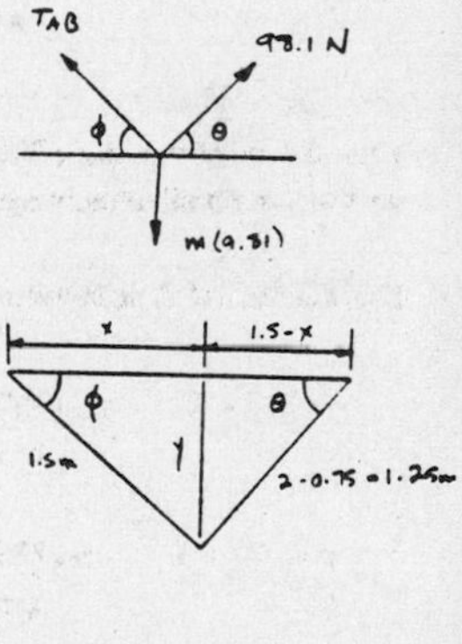

3-41. Determine the magnitude and direction of $\mathbf{F}_1$ required to keep the concurrent force system in equilibrium.

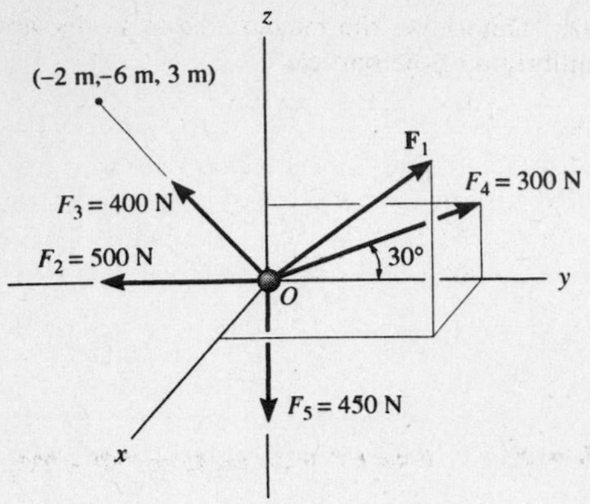

Cartesian Vector Notation :

$$\mathbf{F}_1 = F_{1_x}\mathbf{i} + F_{1_y}\mathbf{j} + F_{1_z}\mathbf{k}$$

$$\mathbf{F}_2 = \{-500\mathbf{j}\}\ \text{N}$$

$$\mathbf{F}_3 = 400\left(\frac{-2\mathbf{i} - 6\mathbf{j} + 3\mathbf{k}}{\sqrt{(-2)^2 + (-6)^2 + 3^2}}\right) = \{-114.29\mathbf{i} - 342.86\mathbf{j} + 171.43\mathbf{k}\}\ \text{N}$$

$$\mathbf{F}_4 = 300\{\cos 30°\mathbf{j} + \sin 30°\mathbf{k}\}\ \text{N} = \{259.81\mathbf{j} + 150.0\mathbf{k}\}\ \text{N}$$

$$\mathbf{F}_5 = \{-450\mathbf{k}\}\ \text{N}$$

Equations of Equilibrium :

$$\Sigma\mathbf{F} = 0; \quad \mathbf{F}_1 + \mathbf{F}_2 + \mathbf{F}_3 + \mathbf{F}_4 + \mathbf{F}_5 = \mathbf{0}$$

$$\left(F_{1_x} - 114.29\right)\mathbf{i} + \left(F_{1_y} - 500 - 342.86 + 259.81\right)\mathbf{j} + \left(F_{1_z} + 171.43 + 150.0 - 450\right)\mathbf{k} = \mathbf{0}$$

Equating **i**, **j** and **k** components, we have

$$F_{1_x} - 114.29 = 0 \qquad F_{1_x} = 114.29\ \text{N}$$

$$F_{1_y} - 500 - 342.86 + 259.81 = 0 \qquad F_{1_y} = 583.05\ \text{N}$$

$$F_{1_z} + 171.43 + 150.0 - 450 = 0 \qquad F_{1_z} = 128.57\ \text{N}$$

The magnitude of $\mathbf{F}_1$ is

$$F_1 = \sqrt{F_{1_x}^2 + F_{1_y}^2 + F_{1_z}^2} = \sqrt{114.29^2 + 583.05^2 + 128.57^2} = 607.89\ \text{N} = 608\ \text{N} \qquad \textbf{Ans}$$

The coordinate direction angles are

$$\alpha = \cos^{-1}\left(\frac{F_{1_x}}{F_1}\right) = \cos^{-1}\left(\frac{114.29}{607.89}\right) = 79.2° \qquad \textbf{Ans}$$

$$\beta = \cos^{-1}\left(\frac{F_{1_y}}{F_1}\right) = \cos^{-1}\left(\frac{583.05}{607.89}\right) = 16.4° \qquad \textbf{Ans}$$

$$\gamma = \cos^{-1}\left(\frac{F_{1_z}}{F_1}\right) = \cos^{-1}\left(\frac{128.57}{607.89}\right) = 77.8° \qquad \textbf{Ans}$$

3-42. Determine the magnitudes of $\mathbf{F}_1$, $\mathbf{F}_2$, and $\mathbf{F}_3$ for equilibrium of the particle.

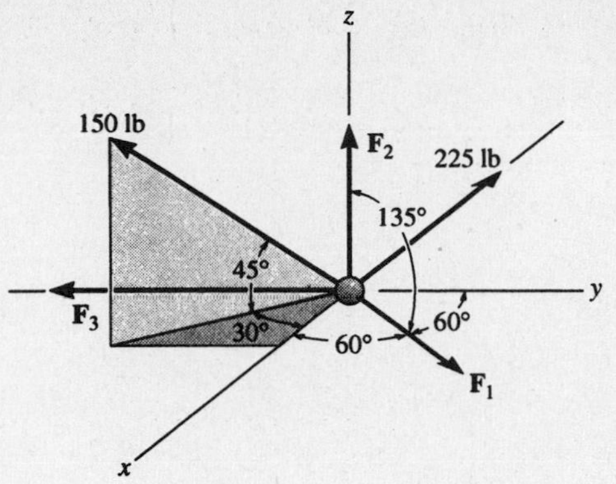

$\Sigma F_x = 0;\quad F_1 \cos 60° + 150 \cos 45° \cos 30° - 225 = 0$

$F_1 = 266.29 = 266 \text{ lb}$ **Ans**

$\Sigma F_y = 0;\quad -F_3 - 150 \cos 45° \sin 30° + 266.29 \cos 60° = 0$

$F_3 = 80.1 \text{ lb}$ **Ans**

$\Sigma F_z = 0;\quad F_2 + 150 \sin 45° + 266.29 \cos 135° = 0$

$F_2 = 82.2 \text{ lb}$ **Ans**

3-43. Determine the magnitudes of $\mathbf{F}_1$, $\mathbf{F}_2$, and $\mathbf{F}_3$ for equilibrium of the particle.

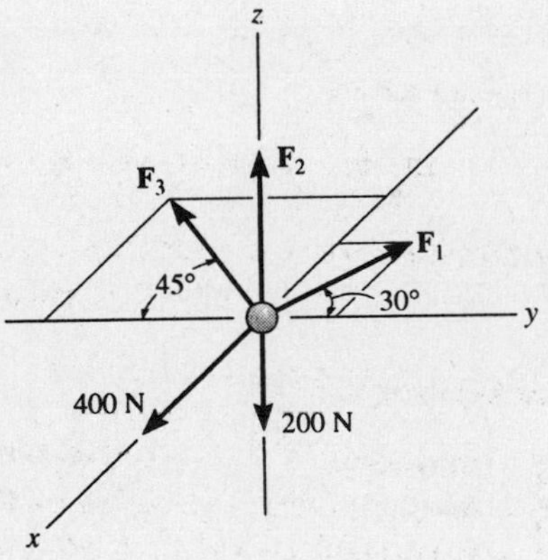

$\Sigma F_x = 0;\quad 400 - F_1 \sin 30° - F_3 \sin 45° = 0$

$\Sigma F_y = 0;\quad F_1 \cos 30° - F_3 \cos 45° = 0$

$\Sigma F_z = 0;\quad F_2 - 200 = 0$

$F_1 = 293 \text{ N}$ **Ans**

$F_2 = 200 \text{ N}$ **Ans**

$F_3 = 359 \text{ N}$ **Ans**

*3-44. Determine the magnitude and direction of the force **P** required to keep the concurrent force system in equilibrium.

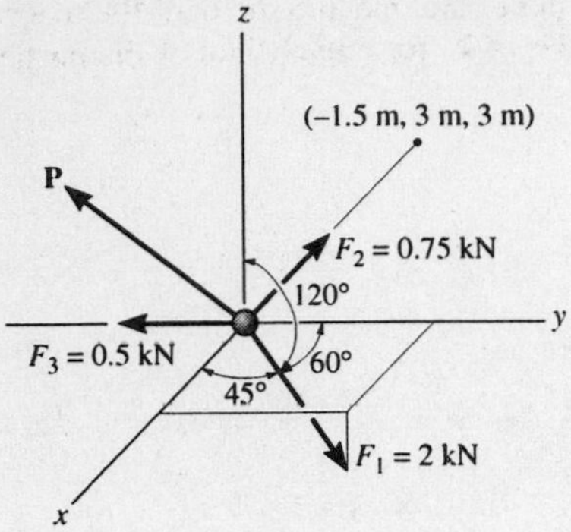

Cartesian Vector Notation :

$$\mathbf{F}_1 = 2\{\cos 45°\mathbf{i} + \cos 60°\mathbf{j} + \cos 120°\mathbf{k}\}\ \text{kN} = \{1.414\mathbf{i} + 1.00\mathbf{j} - 1.00\mathbf{k}\}\ \text{kN}$$

$$\mathbf{F}_2 = 0.75\left(\frac{-1.5\mathbf{i} + 3\mathbf{j} + 3\mathbf{k}}{\sqrt{(-1.5)^2 + 3^2 + 3^2}}\right) = \{-0.250\mathbf{i} + 0.50\mathbf{j} + 0.50\mathbf{k}\}\ \text{kN}$$

$$\mathbf{F}_3 = \{-0.50\mathbf{j}\}\ \text{kN}$$

$$\mathbf{P} = P_x\mathbf{i} + P_y\mathbf{j} + P_z\mathbf{k}$$

Equations of Equilibrium :

$$\Sigma\mathbf{F} = 0; \qquad \mathbf{F}_1 + \mathbf{F}_2 + \mathbf{F}_3 + \mathbf{P} = 0$$

$$(P_x + 1.414 - 0.250)\mathbf{i} + (P_y + 1.00 + 0.50 - 0.50)\mathbf{j} + (P_z - 1.00 + 0.50)\mathbf{k} = 0$$

Equating **i**, **j** and **k** components, we have

$$P_x + 1.414 - 0.250 = 0 \qquad P_x = -1.164\ \text{kN}$$
$$P_y + 1.00 + 0.50 - 0.50 = 0 \qquad P_y = -1.00\ \text{kN}$$
$$P_z - 1.00 + 0.50 = 0 \qquad P_z = 0.500\ \text{kN}$$

The magnitude of $\mathbf{F}_1$ is

$$P = \sqrt{P_x^2 + P_y^2 + P_z^2}$$
$$= \sqrt{(-1.164)^2 + (-1.00)^2 + (0.500)^2}$$
$$= 1.614\ \text{kN} = 1.61\ \text{kN} \qquad \textbf{Ans}$$

The coordinate direction angles are

$$\alpha = \cos^{-1}\left(\frac{P_x}{P}\right) = \cos^{-1}\left(\frac{-1.164}{1.614}\right) = 136° \qquad \textbf{Ans}$$

$$\beta = \cos^{-1}\left(\frac{P_y}{P}\right) = \cos^{-1}\left(\frac{-1.00}{1.614}\right) = 128° \qquad \textbf{Ans}$$

$$\gamma = \cos^{-1}\left(\frac{P_z}{P}\right) = \cos^{-1}\left(\frac{0.500}{1.614}\right) = 72.0° \qquad \textbf{Ans}$$

3-45. Determine the magnitude and the coordinate direction angles of $\mathbf{F}_4$ for equilibrium of the particle.

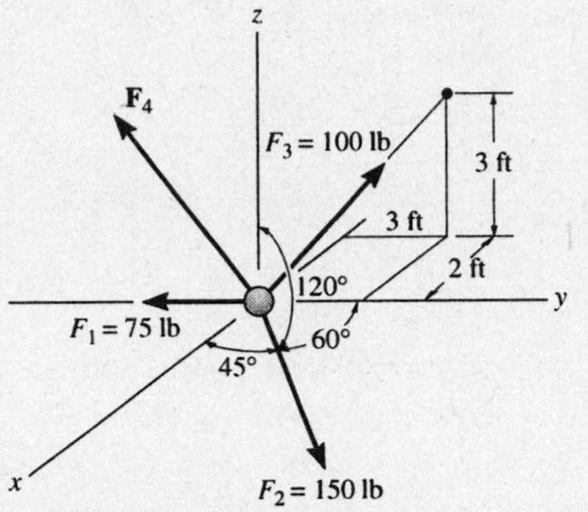

$\mathbf{F}_1 = -75\,\mathbf{j}$

$\mathbf{F}_2 = 150\cos 45°\,\mathbf{i} + 150\cos 60°\,\mathbf{j} + 150\cos 120°\,\mathbf{k}$

$= 106.07\,\mathbf{i} + 75\,\mathbf{j} - 75\,\mathbf{k}$

$\mathbf{F}_3 = 100\left(\frac{-2}{\sqrt{22}}\right)\mathbf{i} + 100\left(\frac{3}{\sqrt{22}}\right)\mathbf{j} + 100\left(\frac{3}{\sqrt{22}}\right)\mathbf{k}$

$= -42.64\,\mathbf{i} + 63.96\,\mathbf{j} + 63.96\,\mathbf{k}$

$\mathbf{F}_4 = F_x\,\mathbf{i} + F_y\,\mathbf{j} + F_z\,\mathbf{k}$

$\Sigma F_x = 0;\quad 106.07 - 42.64 + F_x = 0$

$F_x = -63.43\text{ lb}$

$\Sigma F_y = 0;\quad -75 + 75 + 63.96 + F_y = 0$

$F_y = -63.96\text{ lb}$

$\Sigma F_z = 0;\quad -75 + 63.96 + F_z = 0$

$F_z = 11.04\text{ lb}$

$F_4 = \sqrt{(-63.43)^2 + (-63.96)^2 + (11.04)^2} = 90.75 = 90.8\text{ lb}$ **Ans**

$\alpha_4 = \cos^{-1}\left(\frac{-63.43}{90.75}\right) = 134°$ **Ans**

$\beta_4 = \cos^{-1}\left(\frac{-63.96}{90.75}\right) = 135°$ **Ans**

$\gamma_4 = \cos^{-1}\left(\frac{11.04}{90.75}\right) = 83.0°$ **Ans**

3-46. If cable AB is subjected to a tension of 700 N, determine the tension in cables AC and AD and the magnitude of the vertical force $\mathbf{F}$.

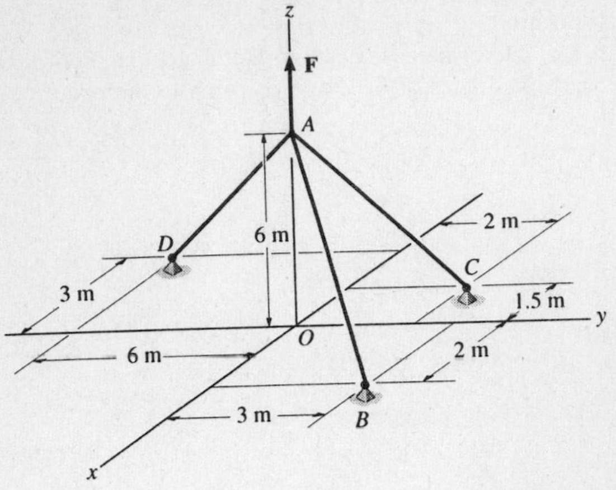

Cartesian Vector Notation :

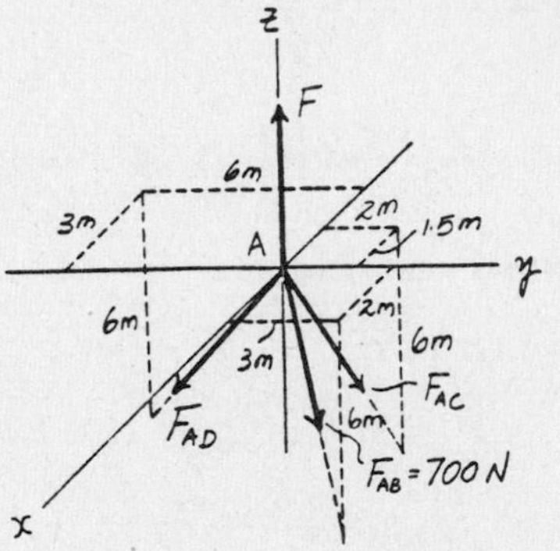

$$\mathbf{F}_{AB} = 700\left(\frac{2\mathbf{i}+3\mathbf{j}-6\mathbf{k}}{\sqrt{2^2+3^2+(-6)^2}}\right) = \{200\mathbf{i}+300\mathbf{j}-600\mathbf{k}\}\ \text{N}$$

$$\mathbf{F}_{AC} = F_{AC}\left(\frac{-1.5\mathbf{i}+2\mathbf{j}-6\mathbf{k}}{\sqrt{(-1.5)^2+2^2+(-6)^2}}\right) = -0.2308F_{AC}\mathbf{i}+0.3077F_{AC}\mathbf{j}-0.9231F_{AC}\mathbf{k}$$

$$\mathbf{F}_{AD} = F_{AD}\left(\frac{-3\mathbf{i}-6\mathbf{j}-6\mathbf{k}}{\sqrt{(-3)^2+(-6)^2+(-6)^2}}\right) = -0.3333F_{AD}\mathbf{i}-0.6667F_{AD}\mathbf{j}-0.6667F_{AD}\mathbf{k}$$

$$\mathbf{F} = F\mathbf{k}$$

Equations of Equilibrium :

$$\Sigma\mathbf{F} = 0; \quad \mathbf{F}_{AB}+\mathbf{F}_{AC}+\mathbf{F}_{AD}+\mathbf{F} = \mathbf{0}$$

$$(200-0.2308F_{AC}-0.3333F_{AD})\mathbf{i}+(300+0.3077F_{AC}-0.6667F_{AD})\mathbf{j}$$
$$+(-600-0.9231F_{AC}-0.6667F_{AD}+F)\mathbf{k} = \mathbf{0}$$

Equating **i**, **j** and **k** components, we have

$$200-0.2308F_{AC}-0.3333F_{AD} = 0 \qquad [1]$$
$$300+0.3077F_{AC}-0.6667F_{AD} = 0 \qquad [2]$$
$$-600-0.9231F_{AC}-0.6667F_{AD}+F = 0 \qquad [3]$$

Solving Eqs. [1], [2] and [3] yields

$F_{AC} = 130$ N $\quad F_{AD} = 510$ N $\quad F = 1060$ N $= 1.06$ kN **Ans**

3-47. Determine the stretch in each of the two springs required to hold the 20-kg crate in the equilibrium position shown. Each spring has an unstretched length of 2 m and a stiffness of $k = 300\ \text{N/m}$.

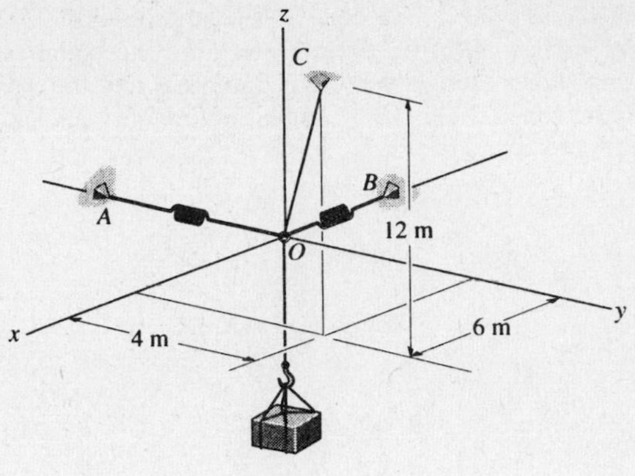

Cartesian Vector Notation :

$$\mathbf{F}_{OC} = F_{OC}\left(\frac{6\mathbf{i}+4\mathbf{j}+12\mathbf{k}}{\sqrt{6^2+4^2+12^2}}\right) = \frac{3}{7}F_{OC}\mathbf{i}+\frac{2}{7}F_{OC}\mathbf{j}+\frac{6}{7}F_{OC}\mathbf{k}$$

$$\mathbf{F}_{OA} = -F_{OA}\mathbf{j} \qquad \mathbf{F}_{OB} = -F_{OB}\mathbf{i}$$

$$\mathbf{F} = \{-196.2\mathbf{k}\}\ \text{N}$$

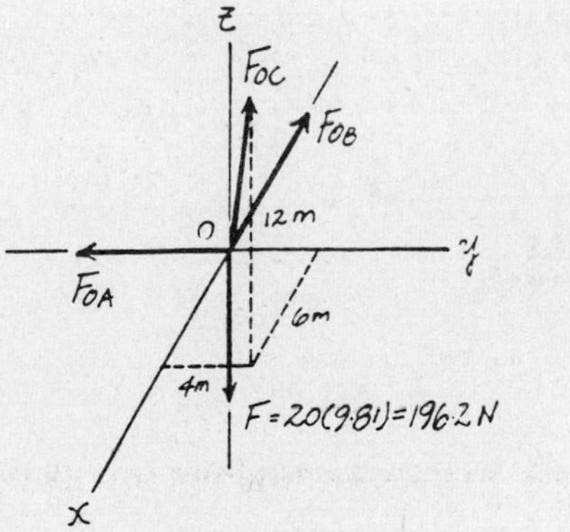

Equations of Equilibrium :

$$\Sigma\mathbf{F} = \mathbf{0}; \qquad \mathbf{F}_{OC}+\mathbf{F}_{OA}+\mathbf{F}_{OB}+\mathbf{F} = \mathbf{0}$$

$$\left(\frac{3}{7}F_{OC}-F_{OB}\right)\mathbf{i}+\left(\frac{2}{7}F_{OC}-F_{OA}\right)\mathbf{j}+\left(\frac{6}{7}F_{OC}-196.2\right)\mathbf{k} = \mathbf{0}$$

Equating **i**, **j** and **k** components, we have

$$\frac{3}{7}F_{OC}-F_{OB} = 0 \qquad [1]$$

$$\frac{2}{7}F_{OC}-F_{OA} = 0 \qquad [2]$$

$$\frac{6}{7}F_{OC}-196.2 = 0 \qquad [3]$$

Solving Eqs.[1], [2] and [3] yields

$$F_{OC} = 228.9\ \text{N} \qquad F_{OB} = 98.1\ \text{N} \qquad F_{OA} = 65.4\ \text{N}$$

Spring Elongation : Using spring formula, Eq.3 – 2, the spring elongation is $s = \dfrac{F}{k}$.

$$s_{OB} = \frac{98.1}{300} = 0.327\ \text{m} = 327\ \text{mm} \qquad \textbf{Ans}$$

$$s_{OA} = \frac{65.4}{300} = 0.218\ \text{m} = 218\ \text{mm} \qquad \textbf{Ans}$$

***3-48.** The shear leg derrick is used to haul the 200-kg net of fish onto the dock. Determine the compressive force along each of the legs AB and CB and the tension in the winch cable DB. Assume the force in each leg acts along its axis.

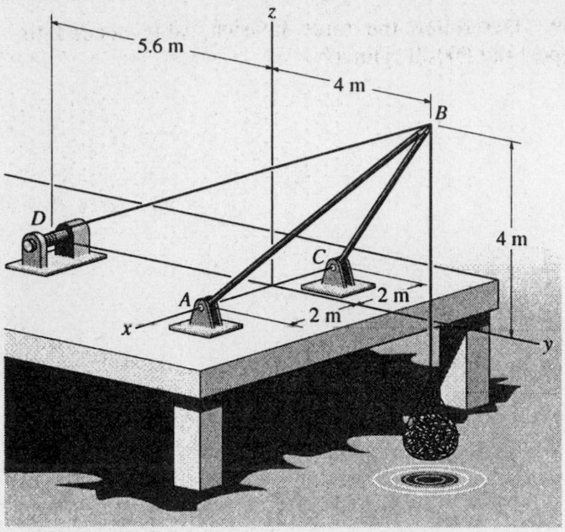

$$\mathbf{F}_{AB} = F_{AB}\left(-\frac{2}{6}\mathbf{i} + \frac{4}{6}\mathbf{j} + \frac{4}{6}\mathbf{k}\right)$$

$$= -0.3333\,F_{AB}\,\mathbf{i} + 0.6667\,F_{AB}\,\mathbf{j} + 0.6667\,F_{AB}\,\mathbf{k}$$

$$\mathbf{F}_{CB} = F_{CB}\left(\frac{2}{6}\mathbf{i} + \frac{4}{6}\mathbf{j} + \frac{4}{6}\mathbf{k}\right)$$

$$= 0.3333\,F_{CB}\,\mathbf{i} + 0.6667\,F_{CB}\,\mathbf{j} + 0.6667\,F_{CB}\,\mathbf{k}$$

$$\mathbf{F}_{BD} = F_{BD}\left(-\frac{9.6}{10.4}\mathbf{j} - \frac{4}{10.4}\mathbf{k}\right)$$

$$= -0.9231\,F_{BD}\,\mathbf{j} - 0.3846\,F_{BD}\,\mathbf{k}$$

$$\mathbf{W} = -1962\,\mathbf{k}$$

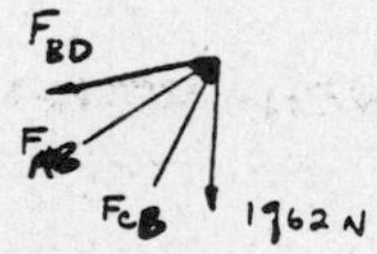

$\Sigma F_x = 0;\quad -0.3333\,F_{AB} + 0.3333\,F_{CB} = 0$

$\Sigma F_y = 0;\quad 0.6667\,F_{AB} + 0.6667\,F_{CB} - 0.9231\,F_{BD} = 0$

$\Sigma F_z = 0;\quad 0.6667\,F_{AB} + 0.6667\,F_{CB} - 0.3846\,F_{BD} - 1962 = 0$

$F_{AB} = 2.52$ kN **Ans**

$F_{CB} = 2.52$ kN **Ans**

$F_{BD} = 3.64$ kN **Ans**

3-49. Determine the force in each cable needed to support the 500-lb cylinder.

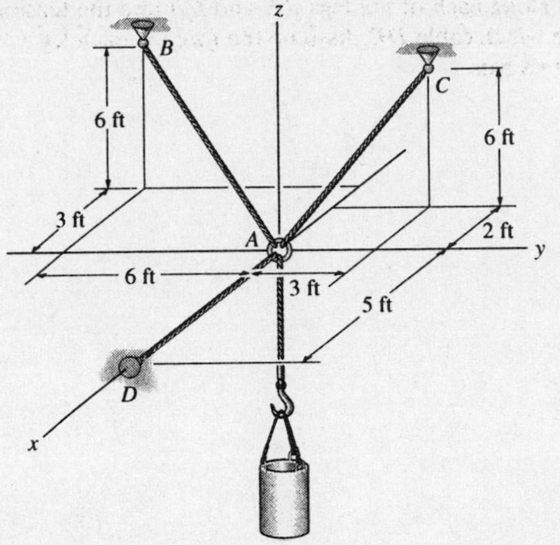

$$\mathbf{F}_{AB} = F_{AB}\left(-\frac{3}{9}\mathbf{i} - \frac{6}{9}\mathbf{j} + \frac{6}{9}\mathbf{k}\right)$$

$$= -0.3333\,F_{AB}\,\mathbf{i} - 0.6667\,F_{AB}\,\mathbf{j} + 0.6667\,F_{AB}\,\mathbf{k}$$

$$\mathbf{F}_{AC} = F_{AC}\left(-\frac{2}{7}\mathbf{i} + \frac{3}{7}\mathbf{j} + \frac{6}{7}\mathbf{k}\right)$$

$$= -0.2857\,F_{AC}\,\mathbf{i} + 0.4286\,F_{AC}\,\mathbf{j} + 0.8571\,F_{AC}\,\mathbf{k}$$

$$\mathbf{F}_{AD} = F_{AD}\,\mathbf{i}$$

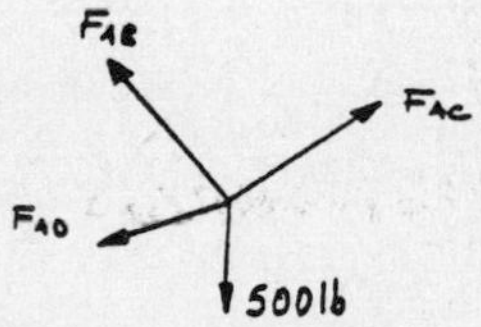

$\Sigma F_x = 0;$ $\quad -0.3333\,F_{AB} - 0.2857\,F_{AC} + F_{AD} = 0$

$\Sigma F_y = 0;$ $\quad -0.6667\,F_{AB} + 0.4286\,F_{AC} = 0$

$\Sigma F_z = 0;$ $\quad 0.6667\,F_{AB} + 0.8571\,F_{AC} - 500 = 0$

$F_{AB} = 250$ lb **Ans**

$F_{AC} = 389$ lb **Ans**

$F_{BD} = 194$ lb **Ans**

3-50. Determine the force in each cable needed to support the 3500-lb platform. Set $d = 2$ ft.

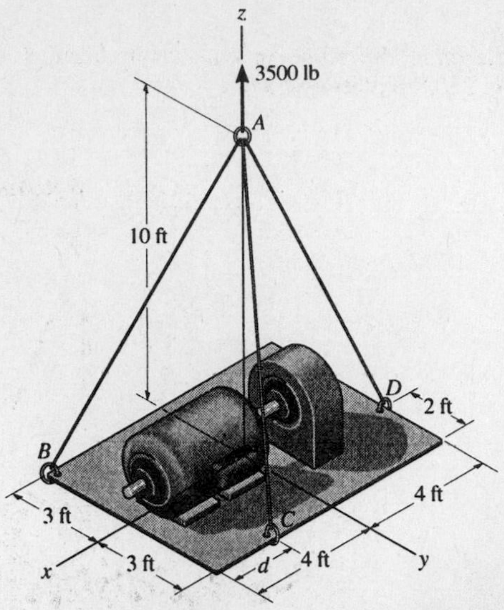

Cartesian Vector Notation :

$$\mathbf{F}_{AB} = F_{AB}\left(\frac{4\mathbf{i} - 3\mathbf{j} - 10\mathbf{k}}{\sqrt{4^2 + (-3)^2 + (-10)^2}}\right) = 0.3578F_{AB}\mathbf{i} - 0.2683F_{AB}\mathbf{j} - 0.8944F_{AB}\mathbf{k}$$

$$\mathbf{F}_{AC} = F_{AC}\left(\frac{2\mathbf{i} + 3\mathbf{j} - 10\mathbf{k}}{\sqrt{2^2 + 3^2 + (-10)^2}}\right) = 0.1881F_{AC}\mathbf{i} + 0.2822F_{AC}\mathbf{j} - 0.9407F_{AC}\mathbf{k}$$

$$\mathbf{F}_{AD} = F_{AD}\left(\frac{-4\mathbf{i} + 1\mathbf{j} - 10\mathbf{k}}{\sqrt{(-4)^2 + 1^2 + (-10)^2}}\right) = -0.3698F_{AD}\mathbf{i} + 0.09245F_{AD}\mathbf{j} - 0.9245F_{AD}\mathbf{k}$$

$$\mathbf{F} = \{3500\mathbf{k}\}\ \text{lb}$$

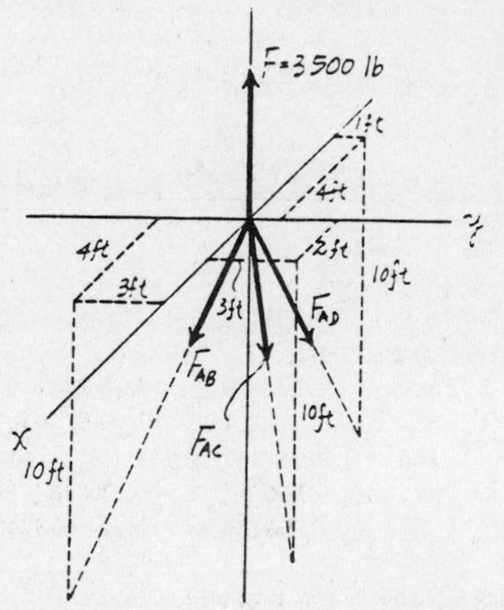

Equations of Equilibrium :

$$\Sigma \mathbf{F} = \mathbf{0}; \qquad \mathbf{F}_{AB} + \mathbf{F}_{AC} + \mathbf{F}_{AD} + \mathbf{F} = \mathbf{0}$$

$$(0.3578F_{AB} + 0.1881F_{AC} - 0.3698F_{AD})\mathbf{i} + (-0.2683F_{AB} + 0.2822F_{AC} + 0.09245F_{AD})\mathbf{j}$$
$$+ (-0.8944F_{AB} - 0.9407F_{AC} - 0.9245F_{AD} + 3500)\mathbf{k} = \mathbf{0}$$

Equating **i**, **j** and **k** components, we have

$$0.3578F_{AB} + 0.1881F_{AC} - 0.3698F_{AD} = 0 \qquad [1]$$
$$-0.2683F_{AB} + 0.2822F_{AC} + 0.09245F_{AD} = 0 \qquad [2]$$
$$-0.8944F_{AB} - 0.9407F_{AC} - 0.9245F_{AD} + 3500 = 0 \qquad [3]$$

Solving Eqs. [1], [2] and [3] yields

$F_{AB} = 1369.59$ lb $= 1.37$ kip $\qquad F_{AC} = 744.11$ lb $= 0.744$ kip $\qquad$ **Ans**

$F_{AD} = 1703.62$ lb $= 1.70$ kip $\qquad$ **Ans**

3-51. Determine the force in each cable needed to support the 3500-lb platform. Set $d = 4$ ft.

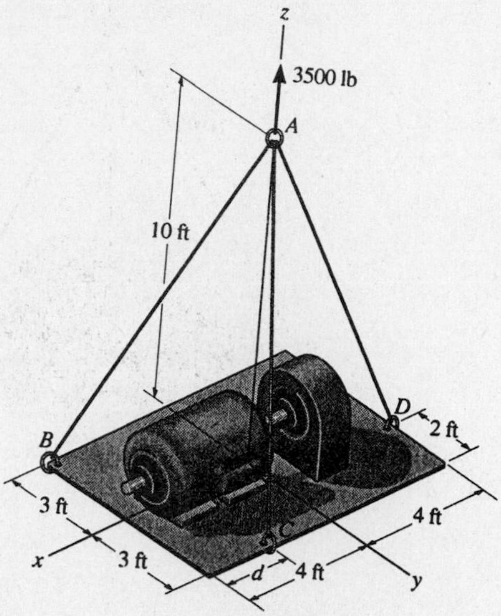

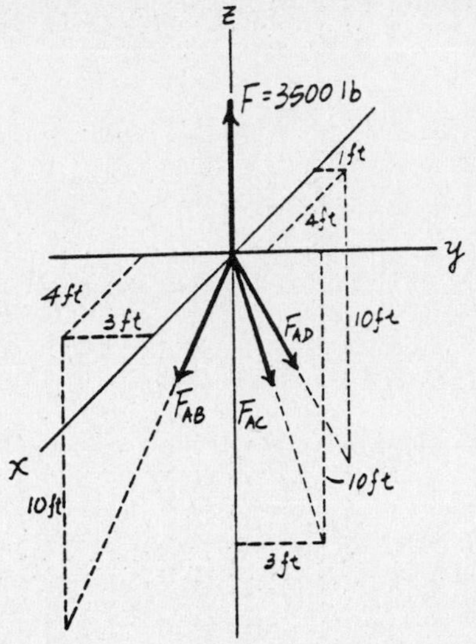

Cartesian Vector Notation :

$$\mathbf{F}_{AB} = F_{AB}\left(\frac{4\mathbf{i} - 3\mathbf{j} - 10\mathbf{k}}{\sqrt{4^2 + (-3)^2 + (-10)^2}}\right) = 0.3578F_{AB}\mathbf{i} - 0.2683F_{AB}\mathbf{j} - 0.8944F_{AB}\mathbf{k}$$

$$\mathbf{F}_{AC} = F_{AC}\left(\frac{3\mathbf{j} - 10\mathbf{k}}{\sqrt{3^2 + (-10)^2}}\right) = 0.2873F_{AC}\mathbf{j} - 0.9578F_{AC}\mathbf{k}$$

$$\mathbf{F}_{AD} = F_{AD}\left(\frac{-4\mathbf{i} + 1\mathbf{j} - 10\mathbf{k}}{\sqrt{(-4)^2 + 1^2 + (-10)^2}}\right) = -0.3698F_{AD}\mathbf{i} + 0.09245F_{AD}\mathbf{j} - 0.9245F_{AD}\mathbf{k}$$

$$\mathbf{F} = \{3500\mathbf{k}\}\ \text{lb}$$

Equations of Equilibrium :

$$\Sigma\mathbf{F} = \mathbf{0}; \qquad \mathbf{F}_{AB} + \mathbf{F}_{AC} + \mathbf{F}_{AD} + \mathbf{F} = \mathbf{0}$$

$$(0.3578F_{AB} - 0.3698F_{AD})\mathbf{i} + (-0.2683F_{AB} + 0.2873F_{AC} + 0.09245F_{AD})\mathbf{j}$$
$$+ (-0.8944F_{AB} - 0.9578F_{AC} - 0.9245F_{AD} + 3500)\mathbf{k} = \mathbf{0}$$

Equating **i**, **j** and **k** components, we have

$$0.3578F_{AB} - 0.3698F_{AD} = 0 \qquad [1]$$
$$-0.2683F_{AB} + 0.2873F_{AC} + 0.09245F_{AD} = 0 \qquad [2]$$
$$-0.8944F_{AB} - 0.9578F_{AC} - 0.9245F_{AD} + 3500 = 0 \qquad [3]$$

Solving Eqs. [1], [2] and [3] yields

$F_{AB} = 1467.42$ lb $= 1.47$ kip $\qquad F_{AC} = 913.53$ lb $= 0.914$ kip $\qquad$ **Ans**

$F_{AD} = 1419.69$ lb $= 1.42$ kip $\qquad$ **Ans**

***3-52.** Determine the force in each of the three cables needed to lift the machine that has a weight of 10 kN.

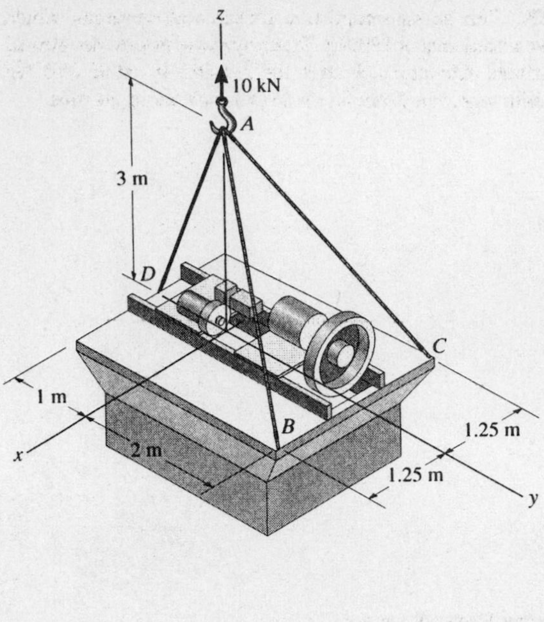

$$\mathbf{F}_{AB} = F_{AB}\left(\frac{1.25\,\mathbf{i} + 2\,\mathbf{j} - 3\,\mathbf{k}}{\sqrt{(1.25)^2 + 2^2 + (-3)^2}}\right)$$

$$= 0.3276\,F_{AB}\,\mathbf{i} + 0.5241\,F_{AB}\,\mathbf{j} - 0.7861\,F_{AB}\,\mathbf{k}$$

$$\mathbf{F}_{AC} = F_{AC}\left(\frac{-1.25\,\mathbf{i} + 2\,\mathbf{j} - 3\,\mathbf{k}}{\sqrt{(-1.25)^2 + 2^2 + (-3)^2}}\right)$$

$$= -0.3276\,F_{AC}\,\mathbf{i} + 0.5241\,F_{AC}\,\mathbf{j} - 0.7861\,F_{AC}\,\mathbf{k}$$

$$\mathbf{F}_{AD} = F_{AD}\left(\frac{-1\mathbf{j} - 3\,\mathbf{k}}{\sqrt{(-1)^2 + (-3)^2}}\right)$$

$$= -0.3162\,F_{AD}\,\mathbf{j} - 0.9487\,F_{AD}\,\mathbf{k}$$

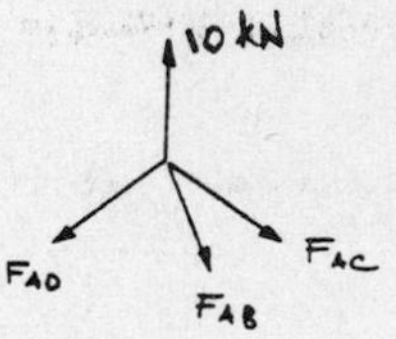

$\Sigma F_x = 0;\quad 0.3276\,F_{AB} - 0.3276\,F_{AC} = 0$

$\Sigma F_y = 0;\quad 0.5241\,F_{AB} + 0.5241\,F_{AC} - 0.3162\,F_{AD} = 0$

$\Sigma F_z = 0;\quad -0.7861\,F_{AB} - 0.7861\,F_{AC} - 0.9487\,F_{AD} + 10 = 0$

$F_{AB} = 2.12$ kN **Ans**

$F_{AC} = 2.12$ kN **Ans**

$F_{AD} = 7.03$ kN **Ans**

3-53. The boom supports a bucket and contents, which have a total mass of 300 kg. Determine the forces developed in struts AD and AE and the tension in cable AB for equilibrium. The force in each strut acts along its axis.

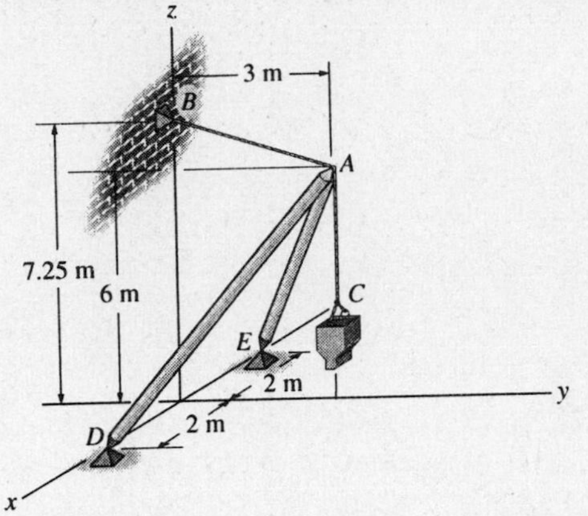

Cartesian Vector Notation :

$$\mathbf{F}_{AB} = F_{AB}\left(\frac{2\mathbf{i} - 1.25\mathbf{j} - 3\mathbf{k}}{\sqrt{2^2 + (-1.25)^2 + (-3)^2}}\right) = 0.5241F_{AB}\mathbf{i} - 0.3276F_{AB}\mathbf{j} - 0.7861F_{AB}\mathbf{k}$$

$$\mathbf{F}_{AC} = F_{AC}\left(\frac{2\mathbf{i} + 1.25\mathbf{j} - 3\mathbf{k}}{\sqrt{2^2 + 1.25^2 + (-3)^2}}\right) = 0.5241F_{AC}\mathbf{i} + 0.3276F_{AC}\mathbf{j} - 0.7861F_{AC}\mathbf{k}$$

$$\mathbf{F}_{AD} = F_{AD}\left(\frac{-1\mathbf{i} - 3\mathbf{k}}{\sqrt{(-1)^2 + (-3)^2}}\right) = -0.3162F_{AD}\mathbf{i} - 0.9487F_{AD}\mathbf{k}$$

$$\mathbf{F} = \{78.48\mathbf{k}\}\ \text{kN}$$

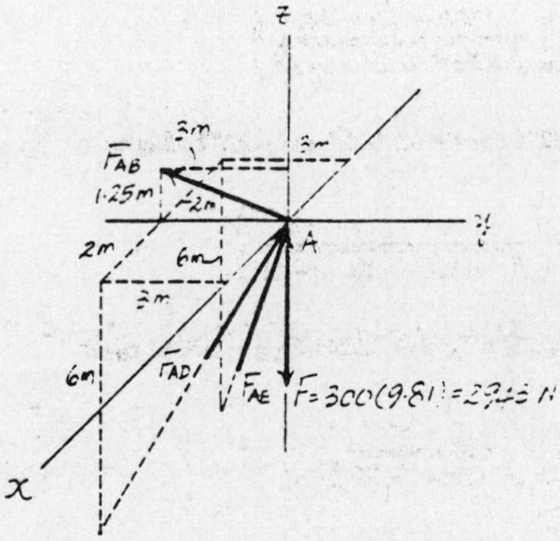

Equations of Equilibrium

$$\Sigma\mathbf{F} = 0; \qquad \mathbf{F}_{AB} + \mathbf{F}_{AC} + \mathbf{F}_{AD} + \mathbf{F} = \mathbf{0}$$

$$(0.5241F_{AB} + 0.5241F_{AC} - 0.3162F_{AD})\mathbf{i} + (-0.3276F_{AB} + 0.3276F_{AC})\mathbf{j}$$
$$+ (-0.7861F_{AB} - 0.7861F_{AC} - 0.9487F_{AD} + 78.48)\mathbf{k} = \mathbf{0}$$

Equating **i**, **j** and **k** components, we have

$$0.5241F_{AB} + 0.5241F_{AC} - 0.3162F_{AD} = 0 \qquad [1]$$
$$-0.3276F_{AB} + 0.3276F_{AC} = 0 \qquad [2]$$
$$-0.7861F_{AB} - 0.7861F_{AC} - 0.9487F_{AD} + 78.48 = 0 \qquad [3]$$

Solving Eqs. [1], [2] and [3] yields

$F_{AB} = F_{AC} = 16.6$ kN $\qquad F_{AD} = 55.2$ kN $\qquad$ **Ans**

3-54. Determine the force in each of the three cables needed to lift the tractor which has a mass of 8 Mg.

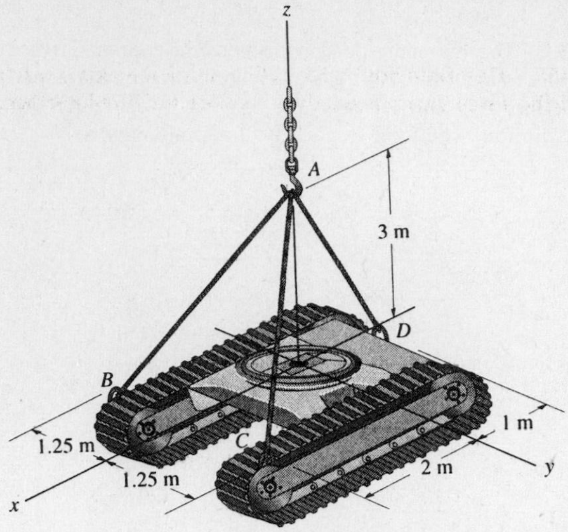

Cartesian Vector Notation :

$$\mathbf{F}_{AB} = F_{AB}\left(\frac{-3\mathbf{j}+1.25\mathbf{k}}{\sqrt{(-3)^2+1.25^2}}\right) = -\frac{12}{13}F_{AB}\mathbf{j}+\frac{5}{13}F_{AB}\mathbf{k}$$

$$\mathbf{F}_{AD} = F_{AD}\left(\frac{-2\mathbf{i}+3\mathbf{j}+6\mathbf{k}}{\sqrt{(-2)^2+3^2+6^2}}\right) = -\frac{2}{7}F_{AD}\mathbf{i}+\frac{3}{7}F_{AD}\mathbf{j}+\frac{6}{7}F_{AD}\mathbf{k}$$

$$\mathbf{F}_{AE} = F_{AE}\left(\frac{2\mathbf{i}+3\mathbf{j}+6\mathbf{k}}{\sqrt{2^2+3^2+6^2}}\right) = \frac{2}{7}F_{AE}\mathbf{i}+\frac{3}{7}F_{AE}\mathbf{j}+\frac{6}{7}F_{AE}\mathbf{k}$$

$$\mathbf{F} = \{-2943\mathbf{k}\}\ \text{N}$$

Equations of Equilibrium :

$$\Sigma\mathbf{F} = \mathbf{0}; \qquad \mathbf{F}_{AB}+\mathbf{F}_{AD}+\mathbf{F}_{AE}+\mathbf{F} = \mathbf{0}$$

$$\left(-\frac{2}{7}F_{AD}+\frac{2}{7}F_{AE}\right)\mathbf{i}+\left(-\frac{12}{13}F_{AB}+\frac{3}{7}F_{AD}+\frac{3}{7}F_{AE}\right)\mathbf{j}+\left(\frac{5}{13}F_{AB}+\frac{6}{7}F_{AD}+\frac{6}{7}F_{AE}-2943\right)\mathbf{k} = \mathbf{0}$$

Equating **i**, **j** and **k** components, we have

$$-\frac{2}{7}F_{AD}+\frac{2}{7}F_{AE} = 0 \qquad [1]$$

$$-\frac{12}{13}F_{AB}+\frac{3}{7}F_{AD}+\frac{3}{7}F_{AE} = 0 \qquad [2]$$

$$\frac{5}{13}F_{AB}+\frac{6}{7}F_{AD}+\frac{6}{7}F_{AE}-2943 = 0 \qquad [3]$$

Solving Eqs.[1], [2] and [3] yields

$$F_{AE} = F_{AD} = 1420.76\ \text{N} = 1.42\ \text{kN} \qquad \textbf{Ans}$$

$$F_{AB} = 1319.28\ \text{N} = 1.32\ \text{kN} \qquad \textbf{Ans}$$

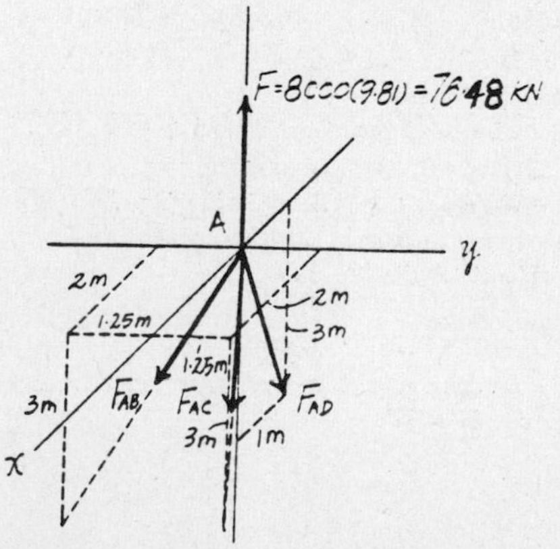

3-55. Determine the force acting along the axis of each of the three struts needed to support the 500-kg block.

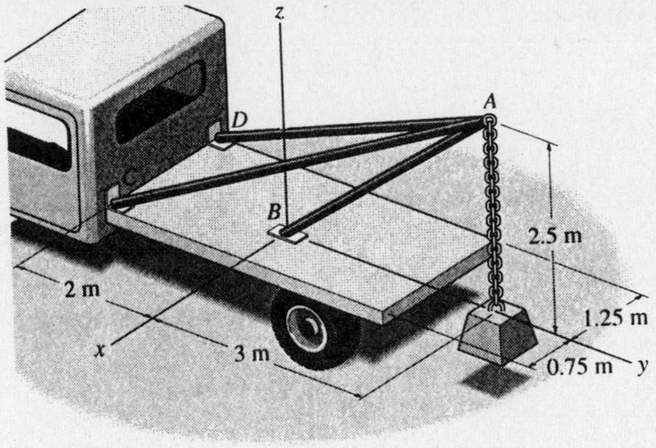

$$\mathbf{F}_B = F_B\left(\frac{3\,\mathbf{j} + 2.5\,\mathbf{k}}{3.905}\right)$$

$$= 0.7682\,F_B\,\mathbf{j} + 0.6402\,F_B\,\mathbf{k}$$

$$\mathbf{F}_C = F_C\left(\frac{0.75\,\mathbf{i} - 5\,\mathbf{j} - 2.5\,\mathbf{k}}{5.640}\right)$$

$$= 0.1330\,F_C\,\mathbf{i} - 0.8865\,F_C\,\mathbf{j} - 0.4432\,F_C\,\mathbf{k}$$

$$\mathbf{F}_D = F_D\left(\frac{-1.25\,\mathbf{i} - 5\,\mathbf{j} - 2.5\,\mathbf{k}}{5.728}\right)$$

$$= -0.2182\,F_D\,\mathbf{i} - 0.8729\,F_D\,\mathbf{j} - 0.4364\,F_D\,\mathbf{k}$$

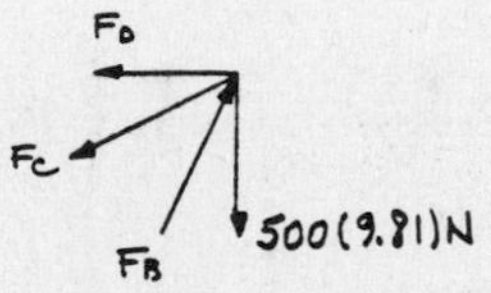

$$\mathbf{W} = -500(9.81)\,\mathbf{k} = -4905\,\mathbf{k}$$

$\Sigma \mathbf{F} = 0;\quad \mathbf{F}_B + \mathbf{F}_C + \mathbf{F}_D + \mathbf{W} = \mathbf{0}$

$\Sigma F_x = 0;\quad 0.1330\,F_C - 0.2182\,F_D = 0$

$\Sigma F_y = 0;\quad 0.7682\,F_B - 0.8865\,F_C - 0.8729\,F_D = 0$

$\Sigma F_z = 0;\quad 0.6402\,F_B - 0.4432\,F_C - 0.4364\,F_D - 4905 = 0$

$F_B = 19.2\text{ kN}$ **Ans**

$F_C = 10.4\text{ kN}$ **Ans**

$F_D = 6.32\text{ kN}$ **Ans**

***3-56.** The 50-kg pot is supported from A by the three cables. Determine the force acting in each cable for equilibrium. Take $d = 2.5$ m.

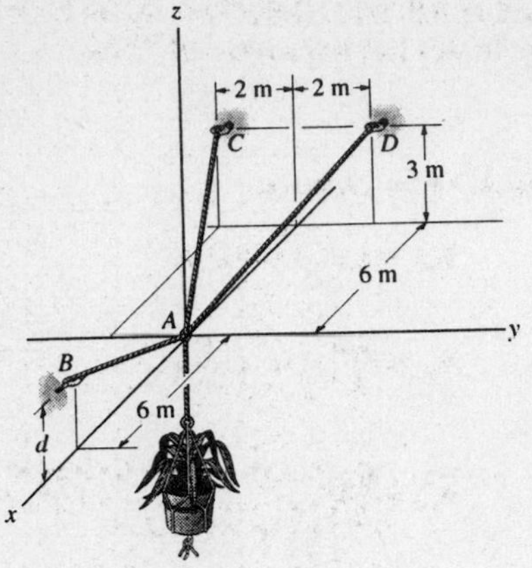

Cartesian Vector Notation :

$$\mathbf{F}_{AB} = F_{AB}\left(\frac{6\mathbf{i}+2.5\mathbf{k}}{\sqrt{6^2+2.5^2}}\right) = \frac{12}{13}F_{AB}\mathbf{i} + \frac{5}{13}F_{AB}\mathbf{k}$$

$$\mathbf{F}_{AC} = F_{AC}\left(\frac{-6\mathbf{i}-2\mathbf{j}+3\mathbf{k}}{\sqrt{(-6)^2+(-2)^2+3^2}}\right) = -\frac{6}{7}F_{AC}\mathbf{i} - \frac{2}{7}F_{AC}\mathbf{j} + \frac{3}{7}F_{AC}\mathbf{k}$$

$$\mathbf{F}_{AD} = F_{AD}\left(\frac{-6\mathbf{i}+2\mathbf{j}+3\mathbf{k}}{\sqrt{(-6)^2+2^2+3^2}}\right) = -\frac{6}{7}F_{AD}\mathbf{i} + \frac{2}{7}F_{AD}\mathbf{j} + \frac{3}{7}F_{AD}\mathbf{k}$$

$$\mathbf{F} = \{-490.5\mathbf{k}\}\ \mathrm{N}$$

Equations of Equilibrium :

$$\Sigma\mathbf{F} = 0; \quad \mathbf{F}_{AB} + \mathbf{F}_{AC} + \mathbf{F}_{AD} + \mathbf{F} = \mathbf{0}$$

$$\left(\frac{12}{13}F_{AB} - \frac{6}{7}F_{AC} - \frac{6}{7}F_{AD}\right)\mathbf{i} + \left(-\frac{2}{7}F_{AC} + \frac{2}{7}F_{AD}\right)\mathbf{j} + \left(\frac{5}{13}F_{AB} + \frac{3}{7}F_{AC} + \frac{3}{7}F_{AD} - 490.5\right)\mathbf{k} = \mathbf{0}$$

Equating **i**, **j** and **k** components, we have

$$\frac{12}{13}F_{AB} - \frac{6}{7}F_{AC} - \frac{6}{7}F_{AD} = 0 \qquad [1]$$

$$-\frac{2}{7}F_{AC} + \frac{2}{7}F_{AD} = 0 \qquad [2]$$

$$\frac{5}{13}F_{AB} + \frac{3}{7}F_{AC} + \frac{3}{7}F_{AD} - 490.5 = 0 \qquad [3]$$

Solving Eqs. [1], [2] and [3] yields

$$F_{AC} = F_{AD} = 312\ \mathrm{N}$$

$$F_{AB} = 580\ \mathrm{N} \qquad \textbf{Ans}$$

3-57. Determine the height d of cable AB so that the force in cables AD and AC is one-half as great as the force in cable AB. What is the force in each cable for this case? The flower pot has a mass of 50 kg.

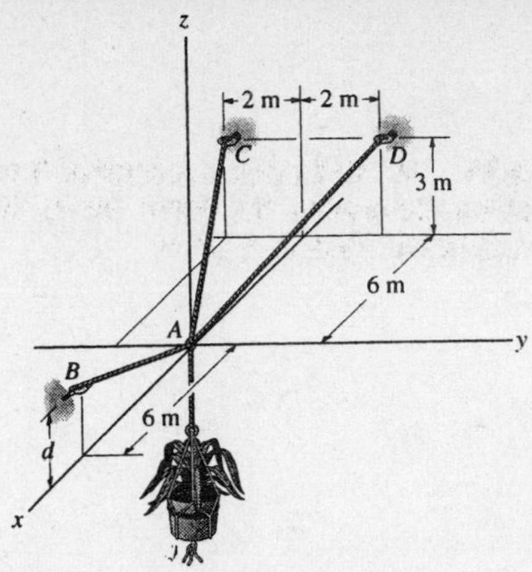

Cartesian Vector Notation :

$$\mathbf{F}_{AB} = (F_{AB})_x\,\mathbf{i} + (F_{AB})_z\,\mathbf{k}$$

$$\mathbf{F}_{AC} = \frac{F_{AB}}{2}\left(\frac{-6\mathbf{i}-2\mathbf{j}+3\mathbf{k}}{\sqrt{(-6)^2+(-2)^2+3^2}}\right) = -\frac{3}{7}F_{AB}\mathbf{i} - \frac{1}{7}F_{AB}\mathbf{j} + \frac{3}{14}F_{AB}\mathbf{k}$$

$$\mathbf{F}_{AD} = \frac{F_{AB}}{2}\left(\frac{-6\mathbf{i}+2\mathbf{j}+3\mathbf{k}}{\sqrt{(-6)^2+2^2+3^2}}\right) = -\frac{3}{7}F_{AB}\mathbf{i} + \frac{1}{7}F_{AB}\mathbf{j} + \frac{3}{14}F_{AB}\mathbf{k}$$

$$\mathbf{F} = \{-490.5\mathbf{k}\}\ \text{N}$$

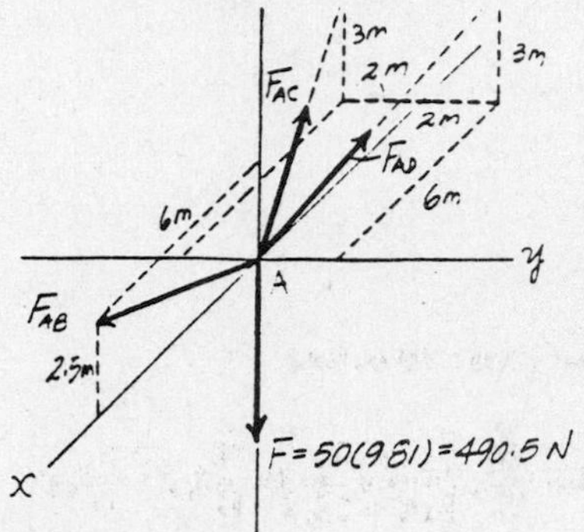

Equations of Equilibrium :

$$\Sigma\mathbf{F} = 0; \qquad \mathbf{F}_{AB} + \mathbf{F}_{AC} + \mathbf{F}_{AD} + \mathbf{F} = \mathbf{0}$$

$$\left((F_{AB})_x - \frac{3}{7}F_{AB} - \frac{3}{7}F_{AB}\right)\mathbf{i} + \left(-\frac{1}{7}F_{AB} + \frac{1}{7}F_{AB}\right)\mathbf{j}$$
$$+\left((F_{AB})_z + \frac{3}{14}F_{AB} + \frac{3}{14}F_{AB} - 490.5\right)\mathbf{k} = \mathbf{0}$$

Equating **i**, **j** and **k** components, we have

$$(F_{AB})_x - \frac{3}{7}F_{AB} - \frac{3}{7}F_{AB} = 0 \qquad (F_{AB})_x = \frac{6}{7}F_{AB} \qquad [1]$$

$$-\frac{1}{7}F_{AB} + \frac{1}{7}F_{AB} = 0 \qquad \textit{(Satisfied!)}$$

$$(F_{AB})_z + \frac{3}{14}F_{AB} + \frac{3}{14}F_{AB} - 490.5 = 0 \qquad (F_{AB})_z = 490.5 - \frac{3}{7}F_{AB} \qquad [2]$$

However, $F_{AB}^2 = (F_{AB})_x^2 + (F_{AB})_z^2$, then substitute Eqs. [1] and [2] into this expression yields

$$F_{AB}^2 = \left(\frac{6}{7}F_{AB}\right)^2 + \left(490.5 - \frac{3}{7}F_{AB}\right)^2$$

Solving for positive root, we have

$$F_{AB} = 519.79\ \text{N} = 520\ \text{N} \qquad \textbf{Ans}$$

Thus,
$$F_{AC} = F_{AD} = \frac{1}{2}(519.79) = 260\ \text{N} \qquad \textbf{Ans}$$

Also,

$$(F_{AB})_x = \frac{6}{7}(519.79) = 445.53\ \text{N}$$

$$(F_{AB})_z = 490.5 - \frac{3}{7}(519.79) = 267.73\ \text{N}$$

then,
$$\theta = \tan^{-1}\left[\frac{(F_{AB})_z}{(F_{AB})_x}\right] = \tan^{-1}\left(\frac{267.73}{445.53}\right) = 31.00^\circ$$

$$d = 6\tan\theta = 6\tan 31.00^\circ = 3.61\ \text{m} \qquad \textbf{Ans}$$

3-58. A force of $F = 100$ lb holds the 400-lb crate in equilibrium. Determine the coordinates $(0, y, z)$ of point A if the tension in cords AC and AB is 700 lb each.

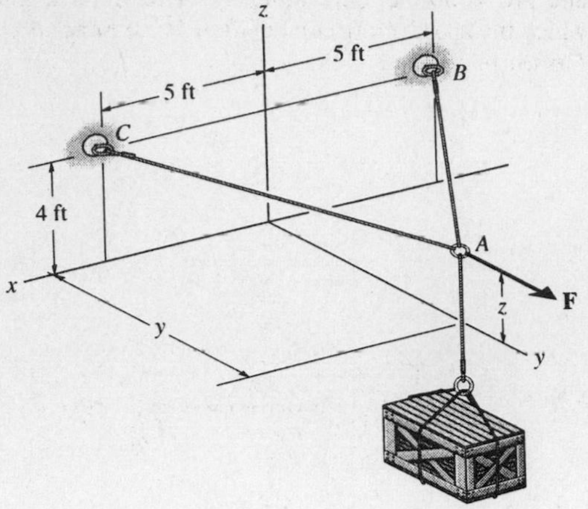

$$\mathbf{F}_{AC} = 700\left(\frac{5\mathbf{i} - y\mathbf{j} + (4-z)\mathbf{k}}{\sqrt{5^2 + (-y)^2 + (4-z)^2}}\right)$$

$$\mathbf{F}_{AB} = 700\left(\frac{-5\mathbf{i} - y\mathbf{j} + (4-z)\mathbf{k}}{\sqrt{(-5)^2 + (-y)^2 + (4-z)^2}}\right)$$

$\mathbf{F} = \{100\,\mathbf{j}\}$ lb $\qquad \mathbf{W} = \{-400\,\mathbf{k}\}$ lb

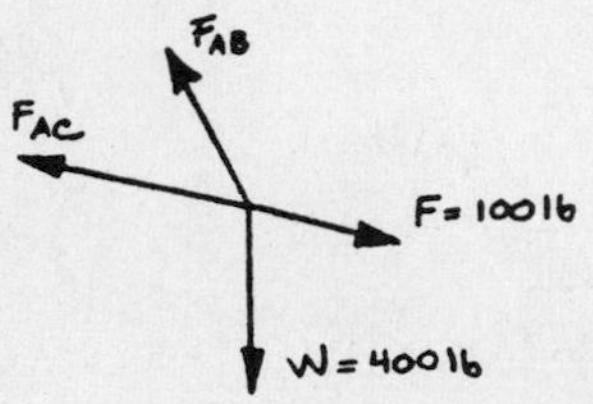

$$\Sigma F_x = 0; \quad \frac{3500}{\sqrt{25 + y^2 + (4-z)^2}} + \frac{-3500}{\sqrt{25 + y^2 + (4-z)^2}} = 0$$

$$\Sigma F_y = 0; \quad \frac{-700y}{\sqrt{25 + y^2 + (4-z)^2}} + \frac{-700y}{\sqrt{25 + y^2 + (4-z)^2}} + 100 = 0 \qquad (1)$$

$$\Sigma F_z = 0; \quad \frac{700(4-z)}{\sqrt{25 + y^2 + (4-z)^2}} + \frac{700(4-z)}{\sqrt{25 + y^2 + (4-z)^2}} - 400 = 0 \qquad (2)$$

$$1400\,y = 100\sqrt{25 + y^2 + (4-z)^2}$$

$$1400(4-z) = 400\sqrt{25 + y^2 + (4-z)^2}$$

Dividing,

$$\frac{y}{4-z} = \frac{1}{4} \qquad 4y = 4 - z$$

Thus,

$$1400\,y = 100\sqrt{25 + y^2 + 16\,y^2}$$

$$196\,y^2 = 25 + 17\,y^2$$

$y = 0.3737$ ft $= 0.374$ ft **Ans**

$4(0.3737) = 4 - z; \quad z = 2.51$ ft **Ans**

3-59. If the maximum allowable tension in cables AB and AC is 500 lb, determine the maximum height z to which the 200-lb crate can be lifted. What horizontal force F must be applied? Take $y = 8$ ft.

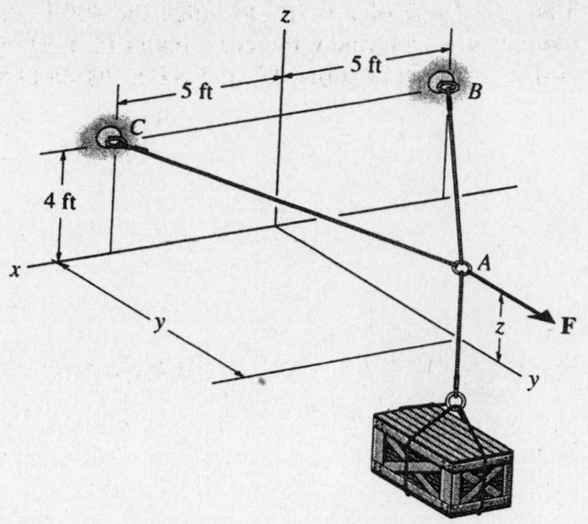

$$\Sigma F_y = 0; \quad -2\left[500\left(\frac{8}{\sqrt{5^2 + 8^2 + (4 - z)^2}}\right)\right] + F = 0 \qquad (1)$$

$$\Sigma F_z = 0; \quad 2\left[500\left(\frac{4 - z}{\sqrt{5^2 + 8^2 + (4 - z)^2}}\right)\right] - 200 = 0 \qquad (2)$$

Dividing Eq. (2) by Eq. (1),

$$\frac{4 - z}{8} = \frac{200}{F}$$

$$(4 - z) = \frac{1600}{F}$$

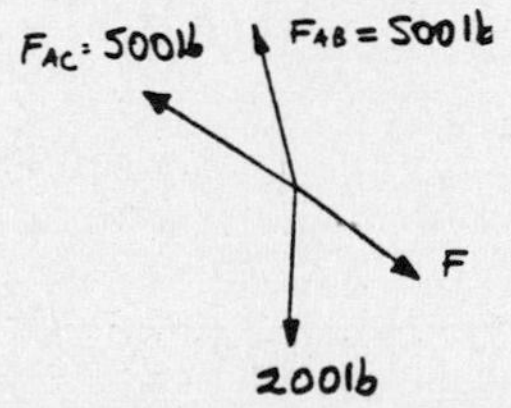

From Eq. (1):

$$\frac{8000}{F} = \sqrt{89 + \left(\frac{1600}{F}\right)^2}$$

$$\left(\frac{8000}{F}\right)^2 = 89 + \left(\frac{1600}{F}\right)^2$$

$F = 831$ lb **Ans**

$z = 2.07$ ft **Ans**

***3-60.** Three cables are used to support a 900-lb ring. Determine the tension in each cable for equilibrium.

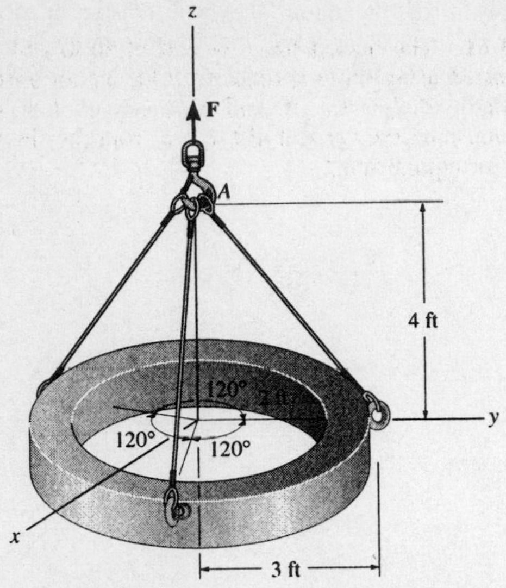

Cartesian Vector Notation :

$$\mathbf{F}_{AB} = F_{AB}\left(\frac{3\mathbf{j}-4\mathbf{k}}{\sqrt{3^2+(-4)^2}}\right) = 0.6F_{AB}\mathbf{j}-0.8F_{AB}\mathbf{k}$$

$$\mathbf{F}_{AC} = F_{AC}\left(\frac{3\cos 30°\mathbf{i}-3\sin 30°\mathbf{j}-4\mathbf{k}}{\sqrt{(3\cos 30°)^2+(-3\sin 30°)^2+(-4)^2}}\right)$$
$$= 0.5196F_{AC}\mathbf{i}-0.3F_{AC}\mathbf{j}-0.8F_{AC}\mathbf{k}$$

$$\mathbf{F}_{AD} = F_{AD}\left(\frac{-3\cos 30°\mathbf{i}-3\sin 30°\mathbf{j}-4\mathbf{k}}{\sqrt{(-3\cos 30°)^2+(-3\sin 30°)^2+(-4)^2}}\right)$$
$$= -0.5196F_{AD}\mathbf{i}-0.3F_{AD}\mathbf{j}-0.8F_{AD}\mathbf{k}$$

$$\mathbf{F} = \{900\mathbf{k}\}\ \text{lb}$$

Equations of Equilibrium :

$$\Sigma\mathbf{F} = 0; \qquad \mathbf{F}_{AB}+\mathbf{F}_{AC}+\mathbf{F}_{AD}+\mathbf{F} = \mathbf{0}$$

$$(0.5196F_{AC}-0.5196F_{AD})\mathbf{i}+(0.6F_{AB}-0.3F_{AC}-0.3F_{AD})\mathbf{j}$$
$$+(-0.8F_{AB}-0.8F_{AC}-0.8F_{AD}+900)\mathbf{k} = \mathbf{0}$$

Equating **i**, **j** and **k** components, we have

$$0.5196F_{AC}-0.5196F_{AD} = 0 \qquad [1$$
$$0.6F_{AB}-0.3F_{AC}-0.3F_{AD} = 0 \qquad [2$$
$$-0.8F_{AB}-0.8F_{AC}-0.8F_{AD}+900 = 0 \qquad [3$$

Solving Eqs.[1], [2] and [3] yields

$$F_{AB} = F_{AC} = F_{AD} = 375\ \text{lb} \qquad \textbf{Ans}$$

This problem also can be easily solved if one realizes that due to symmetry all cables are subjected to a same tensile force, that is $F_{AB} = F_{AC} = F_{AD} = F$. Summing forces along z axis yields

$$\Sigma F_z = 0; \qquad 900-3F\left(\frac{4}{5}\right) = 0 \qquad F = 375\ \text{lb}$$

■3-61. The bucket has a weight of 80 lb and is being hoisted using three springs, each having an unstretched length of $l_0 = 1.5$ ft and stiffness of $k = 50$ lb/ft. Determine the vertical distance d from the rim to point A for equilibrium.

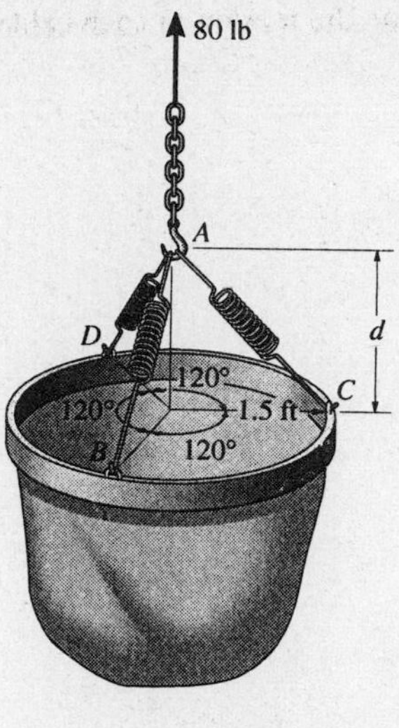

$\Sigma F_z = 0;$ $$80 - \left(\frac{3d}{\sqrt{d^2 + (1.5)^2}}\right) F = 0$$

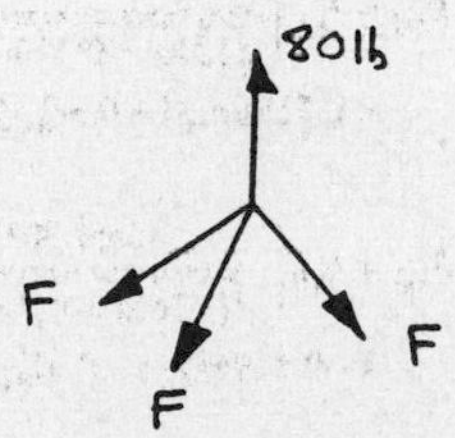

$$80 - \frac{3d}{\sqrt{d^2 + (1.5)^2}}\left[50\left(\sqrt{d^2 + (1.5)^2} - 1.5\right)\right] = 0$$

$$\frac{d}{\sqrt{d^2 + (1.5)^2}}\left(\sqrt{d^2 + (1.5)^2} - 1.5\right) = 0.5333$$

$$d\sqrt{d^2 + (1.5)^2} - 1.5\,d = 0.5333\sqrt{d^2 + (1.5)^2}$$

$$\sqrt{d^2 + (1.5)^2}\,(d - 0.5333) = 1.5\,d$$

$$\left[d^2 + (1.5)^2\right]\left[d^2 - 2\,d\,(0.5333) + (0.5333)^2\right] = (1.5)^2\,d^2$$

$$d^4 - 1.067\,d^3 + 0.284\,d^2 - 2.4\,d + 0.64 = 0$$

$d = 1.64$ ft **Ans**

3-62. A small peg P rests on a spring that is contained inside the smooth pipe. When the spring is compressed so that $s = 0.15$ m, the spring exerts an upward force of 60 N on the peg. Determine the point of attachment $A(x, y, 0)$ of cord PA so that the tension in cords PB and PC equals 30 N and 50 N, respectively.

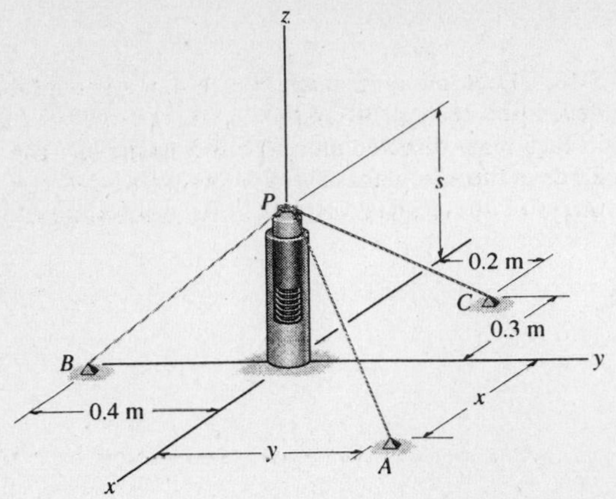

Cartesian Vector Notation :

$$\mathbf{F}_{PA} = (F_{PA})_x\mathbf{i} + (F_{PA})_y\mathbf{j} + (F_{PA})_z\mathbf{k}$$

$$\mathbf{F}_{PB} = 30\left(\frac{-0.4\mathbf{j} - 0.15\mathbf{k}}{\sqrt{(-0.4)^2 + (-0.15)^2}}\right) = \{-28.09\mathbf{j} - 10.53\mathbf{k}\}\ \text{N}$$

$$\mathbf{F}_{PC} = 50\left(\frac{-0.3\mathbf{i} + 0.2\mathbf{j} - 0.15\mathbf{k}}{\sqrt{(-0.3)^2 + 0.2^2 + (-0.15)^2}}\right) = \{-38.41\mathbf{i} + 25.61\mathbf{j} - 19.21\mathbf{k}\}\ \text{N}$$

$$\mathbf{F} = \{60\mathbf{k}\}\ \text{N}$$

Equations of Equilibrium :

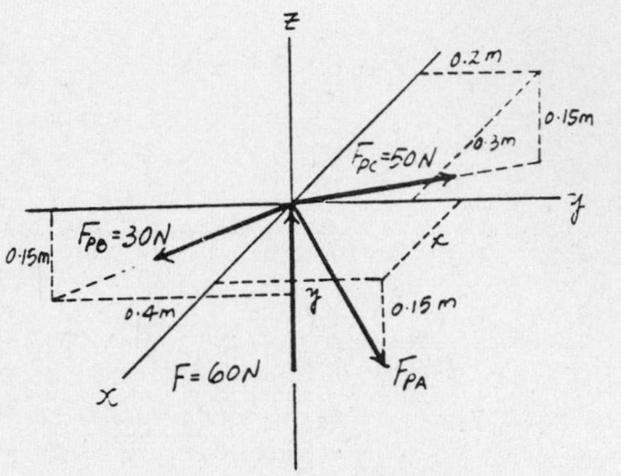

$$\Sigma\mathbf{F} = 0; \qquad \mathbf{F}_{PA} + \mathbf{F}_{PB} + \mathbf{F}_{PC} + \mathbf{F} = \mathbf{0}$$

$$[(F_{PA})_x - 38.41]\mathbf{i} + [(F_{PA})_y - 28.09 + 25.61]\mathbf{j} + [(F_{PA})_z - 10.53 - 19.21 + 60]\mathbf{k} = \mathbf{0}$$

Equating **i**, **j** and **k** components, we have

$$(F_{PA})_x - 38.41 = 0 \qquad (F_{PA})_x = 38.41\ \text{N}$$
$$(F_{PA})_y - 28.09 + 25.61 = 0 \qquad (F_{PA})_y = 2.48\ \text{N}$$
$$(F_{PA})_z - 10.53 - 19.21 + 60 = 0 \qquad (F_{PA})_z = -30.26\ \text{N}$$

The magnitude of $\mathbf{F}_{PA}$ is

$$F_{PA} = \sqrt{(F_{PA})_x^2 + (F_{PA})_y^2 + (F_{PA})_z^2} = \sqrt{38.41^2 + 2.48^2 + (-30.26)^2} = 48.96\ \text{N}$$

The coordinate direction angles are

$$\alpha = \cos^{-1}\left[\frac{(F_{PA})_x}{F_{PA}}\right] = \cos^{-1}\left(\frac{38.41}{48.96}\right) = 38.32°$$

$$\beta = \cos^{-1}\left[\frac{(F_{PA})_y}{F_{PA}}\right] = \cos^{-1}\left(\frac{2.48}{48.96}\right) = 87.09°$$

$$\gamma = \cos^{-1}\left[\frac{(F_{PA})_z}{F_{PA}}\right] = \cos^{-1}\left(\frac{-30.26}{48.96}\right) = 128.17°$$

The wire PA has a length of

$$PA = \frac{(PA)_z}{\cos\gamma} = \frac{-0.15}{\cos 128.17°} = 0.2427\ \text{m}$$

Thus,

$$x = PA\cos\alpha = 0.2427\cos 38.32° = 0.190\ \text{m} \qquad \textbf{Ans}$$
$$y = PA\cos\beta = 0.2427\cos 87.09° = 0.0123\ \text{m} \qquad \textbf{Ans}$$

3-63. Determine the angle θ such that an equal force is developed in legs OB and OC. Assume the force acting in each leg is directed along the axis of the leg. The force **F** lies in the x–y plane. The supports at A, B, C can exert forces in either direction along the attached legs.

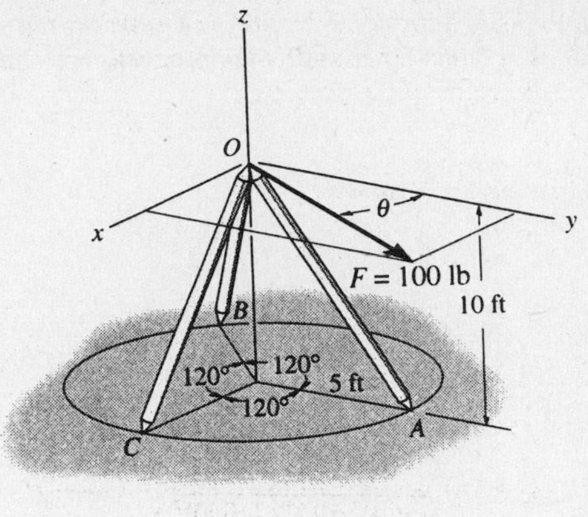

$$\mathbf{F}_{OA} = F_{OA}\left(-\frac{5}{11.180}\mathbf{j} + \frac{10}{11.180}\mathbf{k}\right)$$

$$= F_{OA}\,(-0.4472\,\mathbf{j} + 0.89443\,\mathbf{k})$$

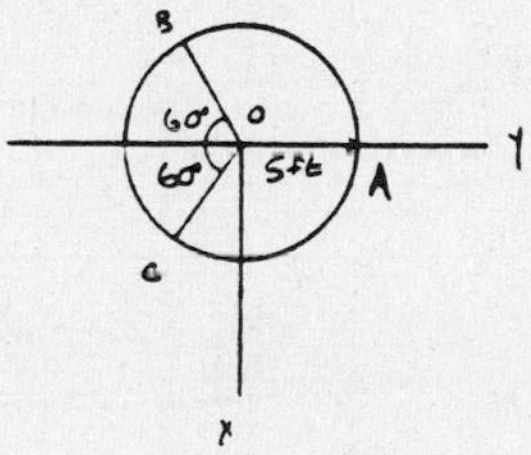

$$\mathbf{F}_{OB} = F_{OB}\left(-\frac{5\sin 60^\circ}{11.18}\mathbf{i} - \frac{5\cos 60^\circ}{11.18}\mathbf{j} - \frac{10}{11.18}\mathbf{k}\right)$$

$$= F_{OB}\,(-\,0.3873\,\mathbf{i} - 0.2236\,\mathbf{j} - 0.8944\,\mathbf{k})$$

$$\mathbf{F}_{OC} = F_{OC}\left(\frac{5\sin 60^\circ}{11.18}\mathbf{i} - \frac{5\cos 60^\circ}{11.18}\mathbf{j} - \frac{10}{11.18}\mathbf{k}\right)$$

$$= F_{OC}\,(\,0.3873\,\mathbf{i} - 0.2236\,\mathbf{j} - 0.8944\,\mathbf{k})$$

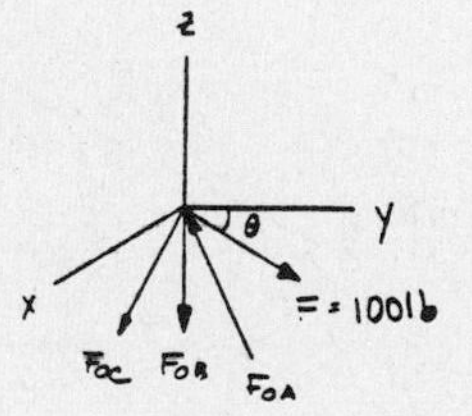

$\mathbf{F} = 100\,(\sin\theta\,\mathbf{i} + \cos\theta\,\mathbf{j})$

$\Sigma F_x = 0;\qquad -\,0.3873\,F_{OB} + 0.3873\,F_{OC} + 100\sin\theta = 0$

If $F_{OC} = F_{OB}$, then $100\sin\theta = 0;\qquad \theta = 0^\circ$ **Ans**

$\Sigma F_y = 0;\qquad -\,0.4472\,F_{OA} - 0.2236\,F_{OB} - 0.2236\,F_{OC} + 100 = 0$

$\Sigma F_z = 0;\qquad 0.8944\,F_{OA} - 0.8944\,F_{OB} - 0.8944\,F_{OC} = 0$

$F_{OA} = 149\ \text{lb}$ **Ans**

$F_{OB} = F_{OC} = 74.5\ \text{lb}$ **Ans**

***3-64.** Three 10-lb spheres and one 15-lb sphere are suspended from the pulley-and-cable system. If the pulleys are frictionless and the centers of all of them lie in the same horizontal plane, determine the sag s for equilibrium of the system.

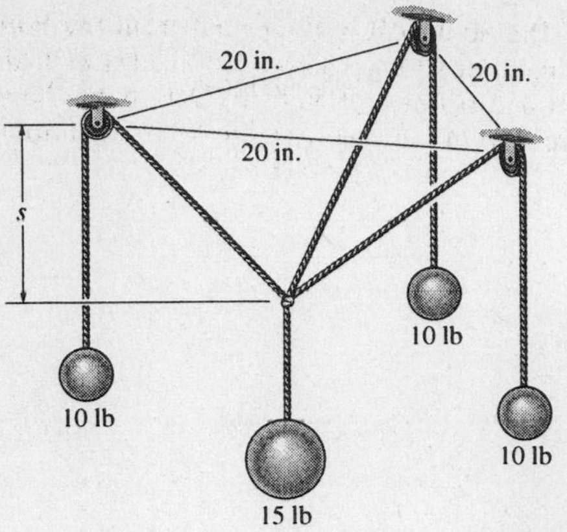

$$\mathbf{F}_1 = 10\left(\frac{11.547\,\mathbf{j}+s\,\mathbf{k}}{\sqrt{11.547^2+s^2}}\right) = \frac{115.47\,\mathbf{j}+10s\,\mathbf{k}}{\sqrt{133.33+s^2}}$$

$$\mathbf{F}_2 = 10\left(\frac{10\,\mathbf{i}-5.773\,\mathbf{j}+s\,\mathbf{k}}{\sqrt{10^2+(-5.773)^2+s^2}}\right) = \frac{100\,\mathbf{i}-57.73\,\mathbf{j}+10s\,\mathbf{k}}{\sqrt{133.33+s^2}}$$

$$\mathbf{F}_3 = 10\left(\frac{-10\,\mathbf{i}-5.773\,\mathbf{j}+s\,\mathbf{k}}{\sqrt{(-10)^2+(-5.773)^2+s^2}}\right) = \frac{-100\,\mathbf{i}-57.73\,\mathbf{j}+10s\,\mathbf{k}}{\sqrt{133.33+s^2}}$$

$\mathbf{F}_4 = \{-15\,\mathbf{k}\}$ lb

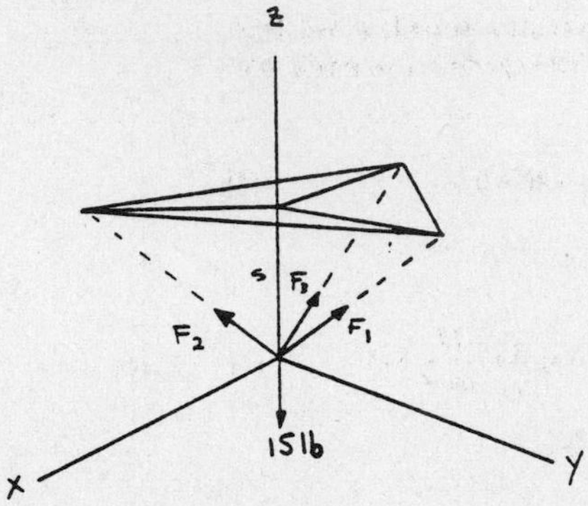

Equilibrium :

$\Sigma F_x = 0;\quad \frac{100}{\sqrt{133.33+s^2}} + \frac{-100}{\sqrt{133.33+s^2}} = 0$ OK

$\Sigma F_y = 0;\quad \frac{115.47}{\sqrt{133.33+s^2}} + \frac{-57.73}{\sqrt{133.33+s^2}} + \frac{-57.73}{\sqrt{133.33+s^2}} = 0$ OK

$\Sigma F_z = 0;\quad \frac{10s}{\sqrt{133.33+s^2}} + \frac{10s}{\sqrt{133.33+s^2}} + \frac{10s}{\sqrt{133.33+s^2}} - 15 = 0$

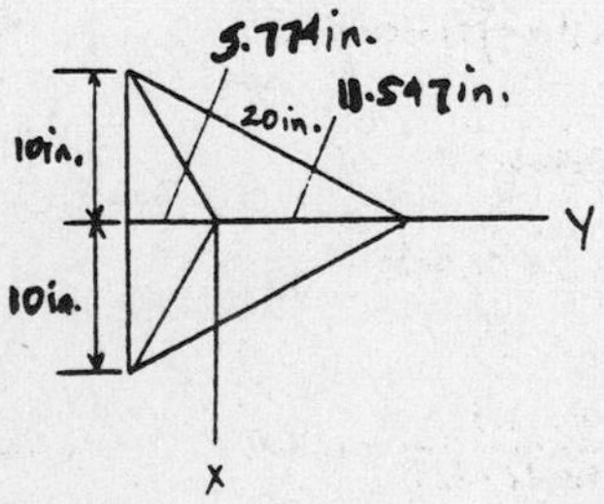

Solving yields :

$s = 6.67$ in. **Ans**

3-65. The 80-lb ball is suspended from the horizontal ring using three springs each having an unstretched length of 1.5 ft and stiffness of 50 lb/ft. Determine the vertical distance h from the ring to point A for equilibrium.

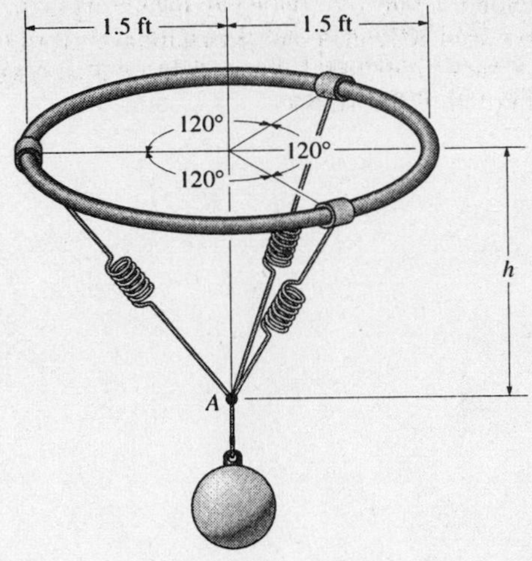

Equation of Equilibrium : This problem also can be easily solved if one realizes that due to symmetry all springs are subjected to a same tensile force of F_{sp}. Summing forces along z axis yields

$$\Sigma F_z = 0; \quad 3F_{sp}\cos\gamma - 80 = 0 \qquad [1]$$

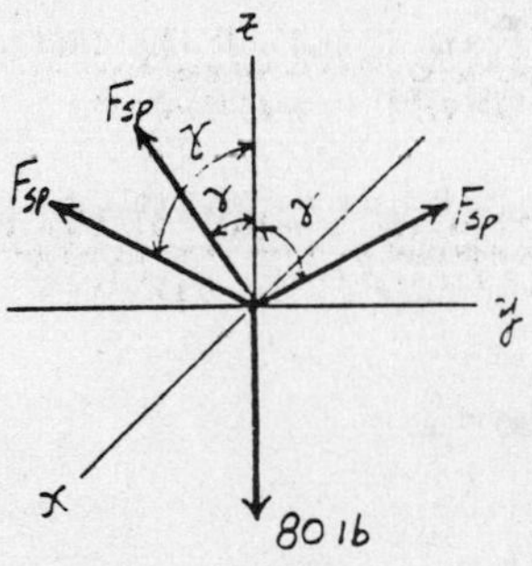

Spring Force : Applying Eq.3 – 2, we have

$$F_{sp} = ks = k(l - l_0) = 50\left(\frac{1.5}{\sin\gamma} - 1.5\right) = \frac{75}{\sin\gamma} - 75 \qquad [2]$$

Substituting Eq.[2] into [1] yields

$$3\left(\frac{75}{\sin\gamma} - 75\right)\cos\gamma - 80 = 0$$

$$\tan\gamma = \frac{45}{16}(1 - \sin\gamma)$$

Solving by trial and error, we have

$$\gamma = 42.4425°$$

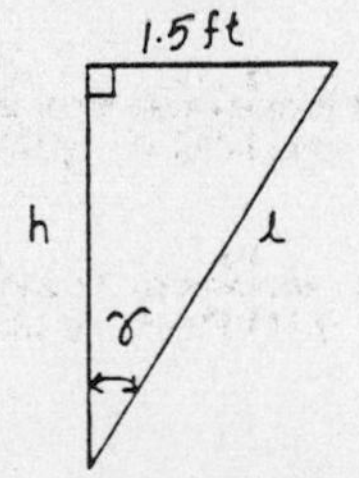

Geometry :

$$h = \frac{1.5}{\tan\gamma} = \frac{1.5}{\tan 42.4425°} = 1.64 \text{ ft} \qquad \textbf{Ans}$$

3-66. The three outer blocks each have a mass of 2 kg, and the central block E has a mass of 3 kg. Determine the sag s for equilibrium of the system.

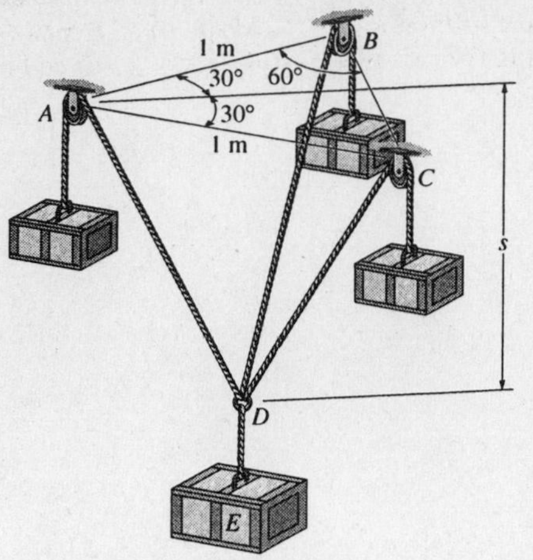

$T_A = T_B = T_C = 2\,(9.81)$

$\Sigma F_z = 0; \quad 3\,(2\,(9.81))\cos\gamma - 3\,(9.81) = 0$

$\cos\gamma = 0.5; \quad \gamma = 60°$

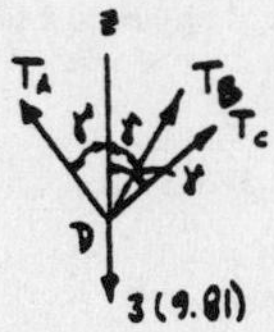

$$d = \frac{0.5}{\cos 30°} = 0.577 \text{ m}$$

$$s = \frac{0.577}{\tan 60°} = 0.333 \text{ m} = 333 \text{ mm} \qquad \textbf{Ans}$$

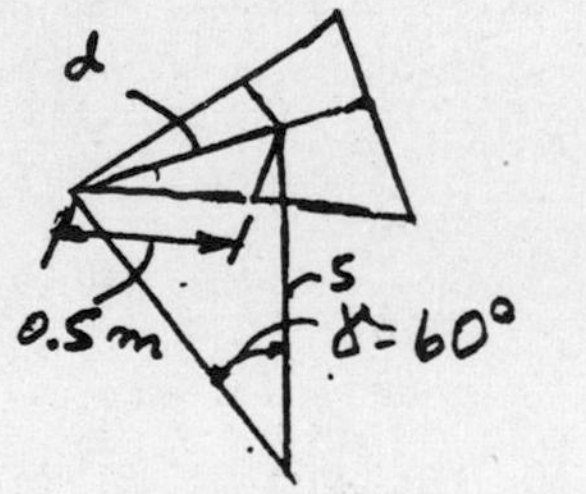

3-67. Determine the tension developed in cables OD and OB and the strut OC, required to support the 50-kg crate. The spring OA has an unstretched length of 0.8 m and a stiffness $k_{OA} = 1.2$ kN/m. The force in the strut acts along the axis of the strut.

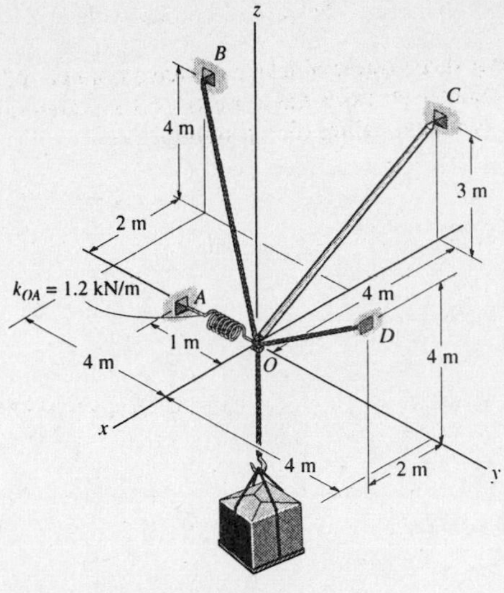

Free Body Diagram : The spring stretches $s = l - l_0 = 1 - 0.8 = 0.2$ m. Hence, the spring force is $F_{sp} = ks = 1.2(0.2) = 0.24$ kN $= 240$ N.

Cartesian Vector Notation :

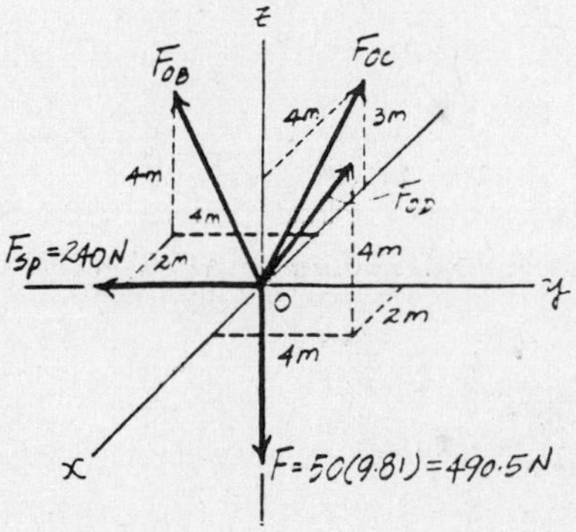

$$\mathbf{F}_{OB} = F_{OB}\left(\frac{-2\mathbf{i} - 4\mathbf{j} + 4\mathbf{k}}{\sqrt{(-2)^2 + (-4)^2 + 4^2}}\right) = -\frac{1}{3}F_{OB}\mathbf{i} - \frac{2}{3}F_{OB}\mathbf{j} + \frac{2}{3}F_{OB}\mathbf{k}$$

$$\mathbf{F}_{OC} = F_{OC}\left(\frac{-4\mathbf{i} + 3\mathbf{k}}{\sqrt{(-4)^2 + 3^2}}\right) = -\frac{4}{5}F_{OC}\mathbf{i} + \frac{3}{5}F_{OC}\mathbf{k}$$

$$\mathbf{F}_{OD} = F_{OD}\left(\frac{2\mathbf{i} + 4\mathbf{j} + 4\mathbf{k}}{\sqrt{2^2 + 4^2 + 4^2}}\right) = \frac{1}{3}F_{OD}\mathbf{i} + \frac{2}{3}F_{OD}\mathbf{j} + \frac{2}{3}F_{OD}\mathbf{k}$$

$$\mathbf{F}_{sp} = \{-240\mathbf{j}\}\text{ N} \qquad \mathbf{F} = \{-490.5\mathbf{k}\}\text{ N}$$

Equations of Equilibrium :

$$\Sigma\mathbf{F} = \mathbf{0}; \qquad \mathbf{F}_{OB} + \mathbf{F}_{OC} + \mathbf{F}_{OD} + \mathbf{F}_{sp} + \mathbf{F} = \mathbf{0}$$

$$\left(-\frac{1}{3}F_{OB} - \frac{4}{5}F_{OC} + \frac{1}{3}F_{OD}\right)\mathbf{i} + \left(-\frac{2}{3}F_{OB} + \frac{2}{3}F_{OD} - 240\right)\mathbf{j} + \left(\frac{2}{3}F_{OB} + \frac{3}{5}F_{OC} + \frac{2}{3}F_{OD} - 490.5\right)\mathbf{k} = \mathbf{0}$$

Equating **i**, **j** and **k** components, we have

$$-\frac{1}{3}F_{OB} - \frac{4}{5}F_{OC} + \frac{1}{3}F_{OD} = 0 \qquad [1]$$

$$-\frac{2}{3}F_{OB} + \frac{2}{3}F_{OD} - 240 = 0 \qquad [2]$$

$$\frac{2}{3}F_{OB} + \frac{3}{5}F_{OC} + \frac{2}{3}F_{OD} - 490.5 = 0 \qquad [3]$$

Solving Eqs. [1], [2] and [3] yields

$F_{OB} = 120$ N $\qquad F_{OC} = 150$ N $\qquad F_{OD} = 480$ N $\qquad$ **Ans**

■*3-68. The motor at B winds up the cord attached to the 65-lb crate with a constant speed. Determine the force in rope CD supporting the pulley and the angle θ for equilibrium. Neglect the size of the pulley at C.

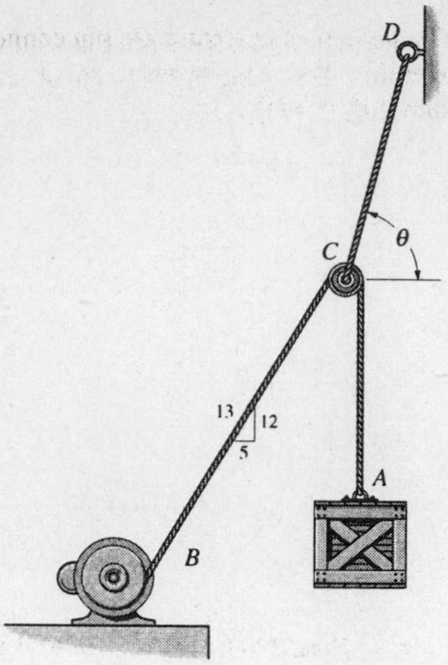

Free Body Diagram : Since the rope passes through a smooth ring, the tension in the rope is the same throughout rope, that is 70 lb.

Cartesian Vector Notation :

$$\mathbf{F}_A = 70\left(\frac{-2\mathbf{i}+3\mathbf{j}-6\mathbf{k}}{\sqrt{(-2)^2+3^2+(-6)^2}}\right) = \{-20.0\mathbf{i}+30.0\mathbf{j}-60.0\mathbf{k}\}\ \text{lb}$$

$$\mathbf{F}_C = \{-70\mathbf{k}\}\ \text{lb}$$

$$\mathbf{F} = F_x\mathbf{i}+F_y\mathbf{j}+F_z\mathbf{k}$$

Equations of Equilibrium :

$$\Sigma\mathbf{F} = 0; \qquad \mathbf{F}_A + \mathbf{F}_C + \mathbf{F} = \mathbf{0}$$

$$(F_x - 20.0)\mathbf{i} + (F_y + 30.0)\mathbf{j} + (F_z - 60 - 70.0)\mathbf{k} = \mathbf{0}$$

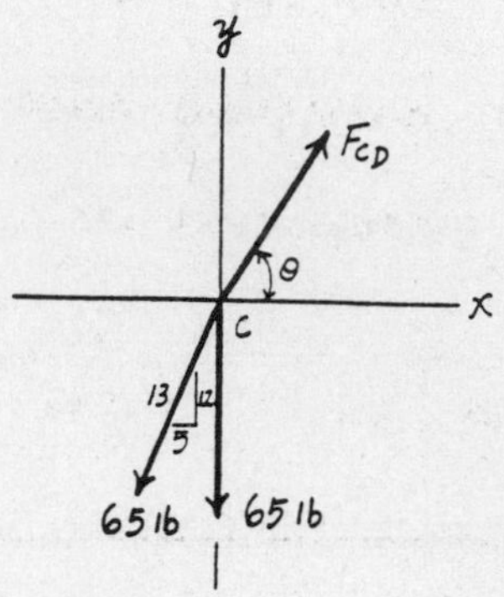

Equating **i**, **j** and **k** components, we have

$$F_x - 20.0 = 0 \qquad F_x = 20.0\ \text{lb}$$
$$F_y + 30.0 = 0 \qquad F_y = -30.0\ \text{lb}$$
$$F_z - 70 - 60.0 = 0 \qquad F_z = 130.0\ \text{lb}$$

Thus, the force **F** is

$$\mathbf{F} = \{20.0\mathbf{i} - 30.0\mathbf{j} + 130\mathbf{k}\}\ \text{lb} \qquad \textbf{Ans}$$

$$F = \sqrt{(20.0)^2+(-30.0)^2+(130)^2} = 134.1\ \text{lb}$$

$$\alpha = \cos^{-1}\frac{20.0}{134.91} = 81.5^\circ \qquad \textbf{Ans}$$

$$\beta = \cos^{-1}\frac{-30}{134.91} = 103^\circ \qquad \textbf{Ans}$$

$$\gamma = \cos^{-1}\frac{130}{134.91} = 15.5^\circ \qquad \textbf{Ans}$$

3-69. The members of a truss are pin connected at joint O. Determine the magnitude of $\mathbf{F}_1$ and its angle θ for equilibrium. Set $F_2 = 6$ kN.

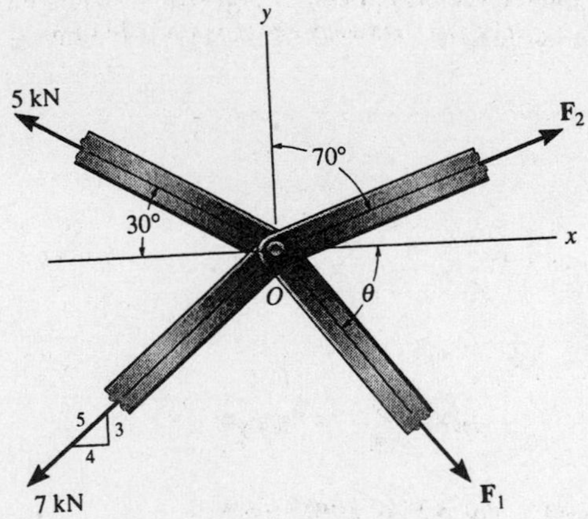

$$\overset{+}{\rightarrow}\Sigma F_x = 0; \qquad 6\sin 70^\circ + F_1\cos\theta - 5\cos 30^\circ - \frac{4}{5}(7) = 0$$

$$F_1\cos\theta = 4.2920$$

$$+\uparrow\Sigma F_y = 0; \qquad 6\cos 70^\circ + 5\sin 30^\circ - F_1\sin\theta - \frac{3}{5}(7) = 0$$

$$F_1\sin\theta = 0.3521$$

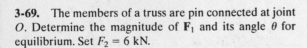

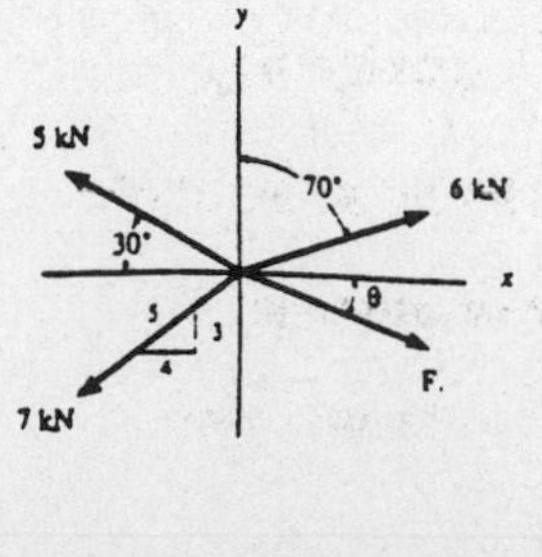

Solving:

$\theta = 4.69^\circ$ **Ans** $\qquad F_1 = 4.31$ kN **Ans**

3-70. The members of a truss are pin connected at joint O. Determine the magnitudes of $\mathbf{F}_1$ and $\mathbf{F}_2$ for equilibrium. Set $\theta = 60°$.

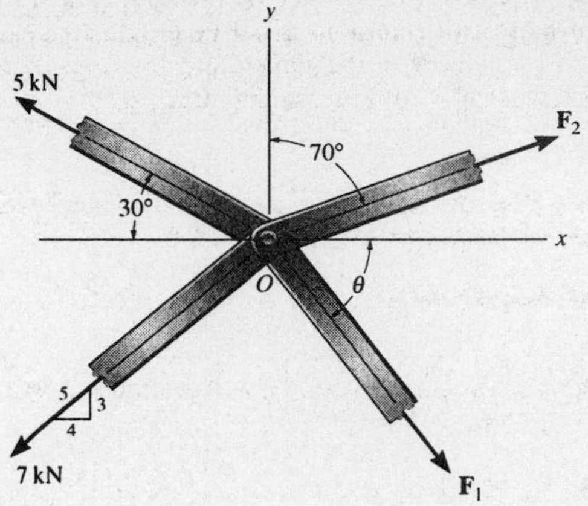

$\overset{+}{\rightarrow} \Sigma F_x = 0;\quad F_2 \sin 70° + F_1 \cos 60° - 5\cos 30° - \frac{4}{5}(7) = 0$

$0.9397F_2 + 0.5F_1 = 9.930$

$+\uparrow \Sigma F_y = 0;\quad F_2 \cos 70° + 5\sin 30° - F_1 \sin 60° - \frac{3}{5}(7) = 0$

$0.3420F_2 - 0.8660F_1 = 1.7$

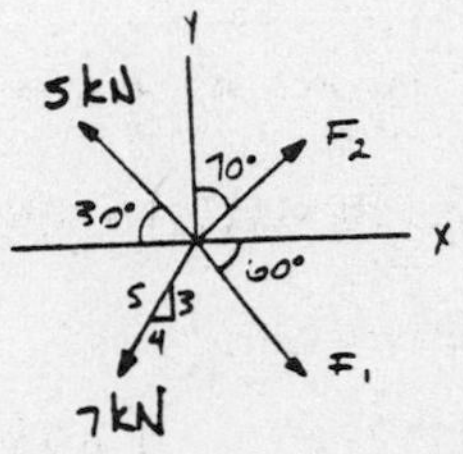

Solving:

$F_2 = 9.60\text{ kN}$ **Ans** $F_1 = 1.83\text{ kN}$ **Ans**

3-71. Two electrically charged pith balls, each having a mass of 0.15 g, are suspended from light threads of equal length. Determine the magnitude of the resultant horizontal force of repulsion, F, acting on each ball if the measured distance between them is $r = 200$ mm.

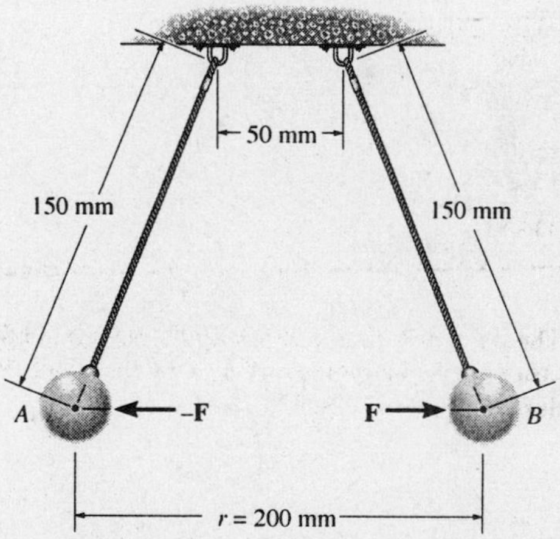

$\cos\theta = \frac{75}{150} \qquad \theta = 60°$

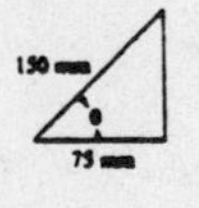

$+\uparrow \Sigma F_y = 0;\quad T\sin 60° - 0.15(10)^{-3}(9.81) = 0$

$T = 1.699(10)^{-3}\text{ N}$

$\overset{+}{\rightarrow} \Sigma F_x = 0;\quad 1.699(10)^{-3}\cos 60° - F = 0$

$F = 0.850(10)^{-3}\text{ N}$

$= 0.850\text{ mN}$ **Ans**

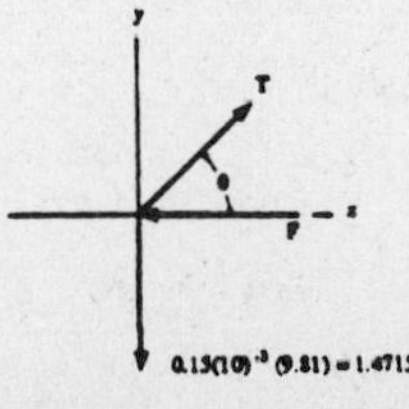

■*3-72. The lamp has a mass of 15 kg and is supported by a pole AO and cables AB and AC. If the force in the pole acts along its axis, determine the forces in AO, AB, and AC for equilibrium.

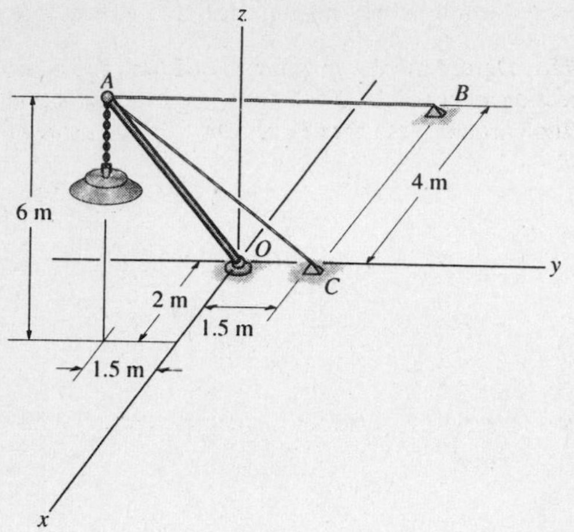

Cartesian Vector Notation :

$$\mathbf{F}_{AB} = F_{AB}\left(\frac{-6\mathbf{i}+3\mathbf{j}-6\mathbf{k}}{\sqrt{(-6)^2+3^2+(-6)^2}}\right) = -\frac{2}{3}F_{AB}\mathbf{i}+\frac{1}{3}F_{AB}\mathbf{j}-\frac{2}{3}F_{AB}\mathbf{k}$$

$$\mathbf{F}_{AC} = F_{AC}\left(\frac{-2\mathbf{i}+3\mathbf{j}-6\mathbf{k}}{\sqrt{(-2)^2+3^2+(-6)^2}}\right) = -\frac{2}{7}F_{AC}\mathbf{i}+\frac{3}{7}F_{AC}\mathbf{j}-\frac{6}{7}F_{AC}\mathbf{k}$$

$$\mathbf{F}_{AO} = F_{AO}\left(\frac{2\mathbf{i}-1.5\mathbf{j}+6\mathbf{k}}{\sqrt{2^2+(-1.5)^2+6^2}}\right) = \frac{4}{13}F_{AO}\mathbf{i}-\frac{3}{13}F_{AO}\mathbf{j}+\frac{12}{13}F_{AO}\mathbf{k}$$

$$\mathbf{F} = \{-147.15\mathbf{k}\}\ \text{N}$$

Equations of Equilibrium :

$$\Sigma\mathbf{F} = 0; \qquad \mathbf{F}_{AB}+\mathbf{F}_{AC}+\mathbf{F}_{AO}+\mathbf{F} = \mathbf{0}$$

$$\left(-\frac{2}{3}F_{AB}-\frac{2}{7}F_{AC}+\frac{4}{13}F_{AO}\right)\mathbf{i}+\left(\frac{1}{3}F_{AB}+\frac{3}{7}F_{AC}-\frac{3}{13}F_{AO}\right)\mathbf{j}$$
$$+\left(-\frac{2}{3}F_{AB}-\frac{6}{7}F_{AC}+\frac{12}{13}F_{AO}-147.15\right)\mathbf{k} = \mathbf{0}$$

Equating **i**, **j** and **k** components, we have

$$-\frac{2}{3}F_{AB}-\frac{2}{7}F_{AC}+\frac{4}{13}F_{AO} = 0 \qquad [1]$$

$$\frac{1}{3}F_{AB}+\frac{3}{7}F_{AC}-\frac{3}{13}F_{AO} = 0 \qquad [2]$$

$$-\frac{2}{3}F_{AB}-\frac{6}{7}F_{AC}+\frac{12}{13}F_{AO}-147.15 = 0 \qquad [3]$$

Solving Eqs. [1], [2] and [3] yields

$F_{AB} = 110$ N $\quad F_{AC} = 85.8$ N $\quad F_{AO} = 319$ N **Ans**

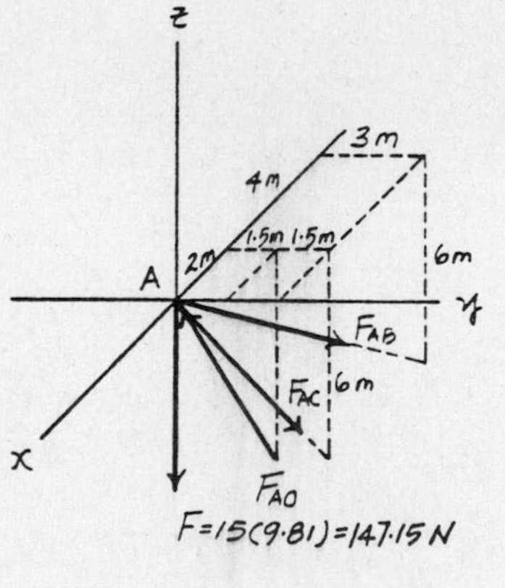

3-73. Determine the magnitude of **P** and the coordinate direction angles of the 200-lb force required for equilibrium of the particle. Note that $\mathbf{F}_3$ acts in the octant shown.

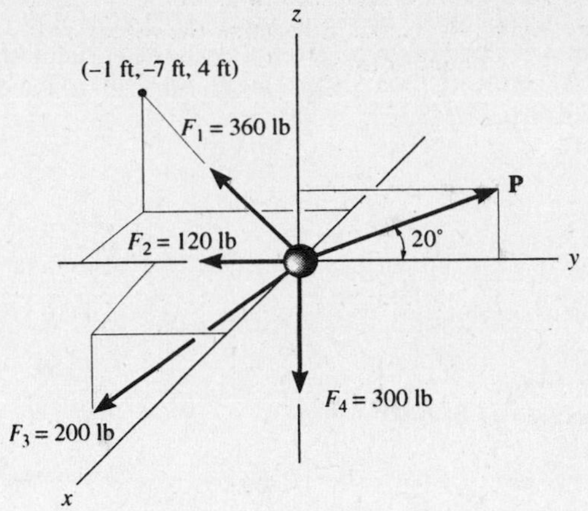

$$\mathbf{F}_1 = 360\left(-\frac{1}{\sqrt{66}}\mathbf{i} - \frac{7}{\sqrt{66}}\mathbf{j} + \frac{4}{\sqrt{66}}\mathbf{k}\right)$$

$$= -44.313\,\mathbf{i} - 310.191\,\mathbf{j} + 177.252\,\mathbf{k}$$

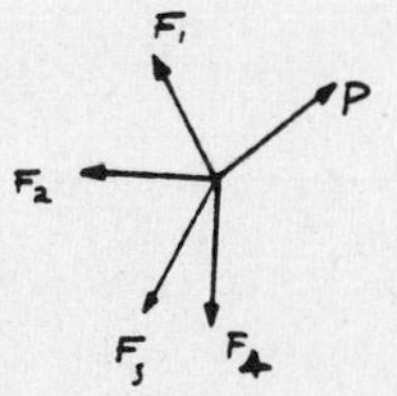

$\mathbf{F}_2 = -120\,\mathbf{j}$

$\mathbf{F}_4 = -300\,\mathbf{k}$

$\mathbf{F}_3 = F_x\,\mathbf{i} + F_y\,\mathbf{j} + F_z\,\mathbf{k}$ (1)

$\mathbf{P} = P\cos 20^\circ\,\mathbf{j} + P\sin 20^\circ\,\mathbf{k}$

$\Sigma F_x = 0;$ $-44.313 + F_x = 0$

$F_x = 44.313$ lb

$\Sigma F_y = 0;$ $-310.191 - 120 + F_y + 0.9397P = 0$

$\Sigma F_z = 0;$ $177.252 - 300 + F_z + 0.3420P = 0$

From Eq. (1), require

$$200 = \sqrt{F_x^2 + F_y^2 + F_z^2}$$

$$(200)^2 = (44.313)^2 + (430.191 - 0.9397P)^2 + (122.748 - 0.3420P)^2$$

$$P^2 - 892.459P + 162\,095 = 0$$

Solving,

$P = 638.65$ lb and $P = 253.81$ lb

Thus, with $P = 638.65$ lb, $F_y = -169.95$ lb.
With $P = 253.81$ lb, $F_y = 191.69$ lb.
In order for F_3 to be within the octant shown, choose

$P = 639$ lb **Ans**

so that

$F_z = -95.672$

Thus, the direction of F_3 is :

$\alpha_3 = \cos^{-1}\left(\frac{44.313}{200}\right) = 77.2^\circ$ **Ans**

$\beta_3 = \cos^{-1}\left(\frac{-169.95}{200}\right) = 148^\circ$ **Ans**

$\gamma_3 = \cos^{-1}\left(\frac{-95.672}{200}\right) = 119^\circ$ **Ans**

3-74. The ring of negligible size is subjected to a vertical force of 200 lb. Determine the required length l of cord AC such that the tension acting in AC is 160 lb. Also, what is the force acting in cord AB? *Hint:* Use the equilibrium condition to determine the required angle θ for attachment, then determine l using trigonometry applied to ΔABC.

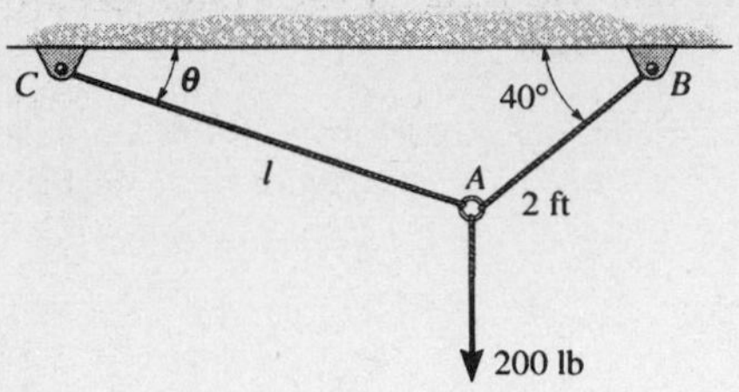

Equations of Equilibrium :

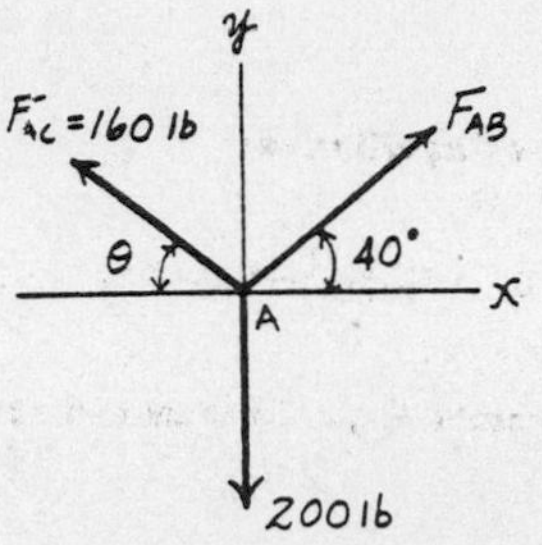

$\xrightarrow{+} \Sigma F_x = 0; \quad F_{AB}\cos 40^\circ - 160\cos\theta = 0$ [1]

$+\uparrow \Sigma F_y = 0; \quad F_{AB}\sin 40^\circ + 160\sin\theta - 200 = 0$ [2]

Solving Eqs. [1] and [2] yields

$\theta = 33.25^\circ$

$F_{AB} = 175$ lb **Ans**

Geometry : Applying law of sines, we have

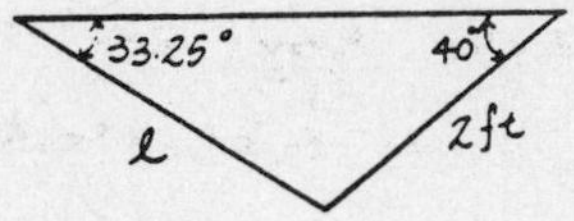

$$\frac{l}{\sin 40^\circ} = \frac{2}{\sin 33.25^\circ}$$

$l = 2.34$ ft **Ans**

3-75. Determine the magnitudes of $\mathbf{F}_1$, $\mathbf{F}_2$, and $\mathbf{F}_3$ for equilibrium of the particle.

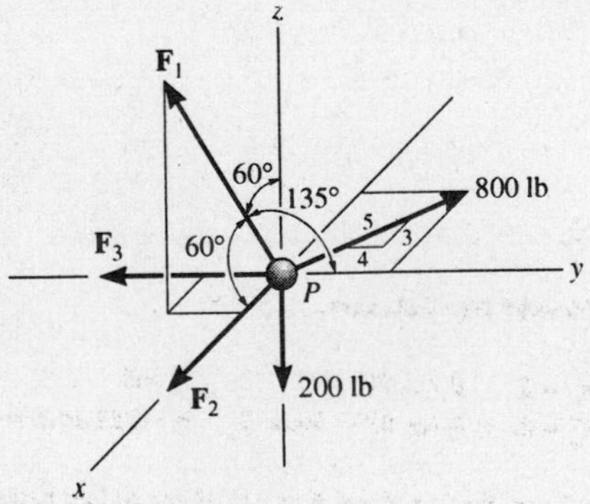

$\Sigma F_x = 0; \quad F_2 + F_1\cos 60^\circ - 800\left(\frac{3}{5}\right) = 0$

$\Sigma F_y = 0; \quad 800\left(\frac{4}{5}\right) + F_1\cos 135^\circ - F_3 = 0$

$\Sigma F_z = 0; \quad F_1\cos 60^\circ - 200 = 0$

$F_1 = 400$ lb **Ans**

$F_2 = 280$ lb **Ans**

$F_3 = 357$ lb **Ans**

***3-76.** Determine the force in each cable needed to support the 500-lb load.

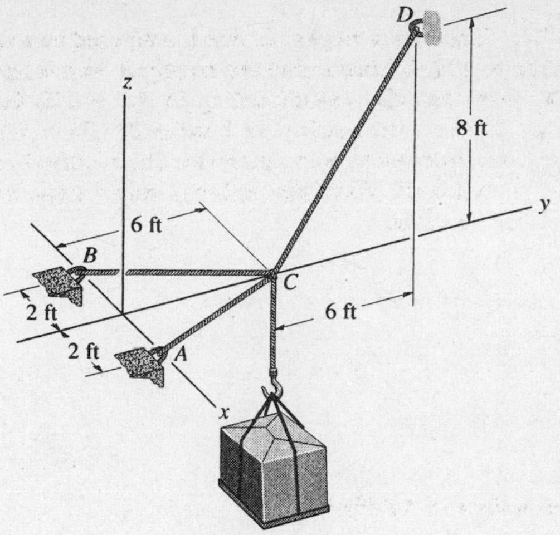

Equation of Equilibrium :

$\Sigma F_z = 0; \quad F_{CD}\left(\frac{4}{5}\right) - 500 = 0 \qquad F_{CD} = 625 \text{ lb}$ **Ans**

Using the results $F_{CD} = 625$ lb and then summing forces along x and y axes we have

$\Sigma F_x = 0; \quad F_{CA}\left(\frac{2}{\sqrt{40}}\right) - F_{CB}\left(\frac{2}{\sqrt{40}}\right) = 0 \qquad F_{CA} = F_{CB} = F$

$\Sigma F_y = 0; \quad 2F\left(\frac{6}{\sqrt{40}}\right) - 625\left(\frac{3}{5}\right) = 0$

$F_{CA} = F_{CB} = F = 198 \text{ lb}$ **Ans**

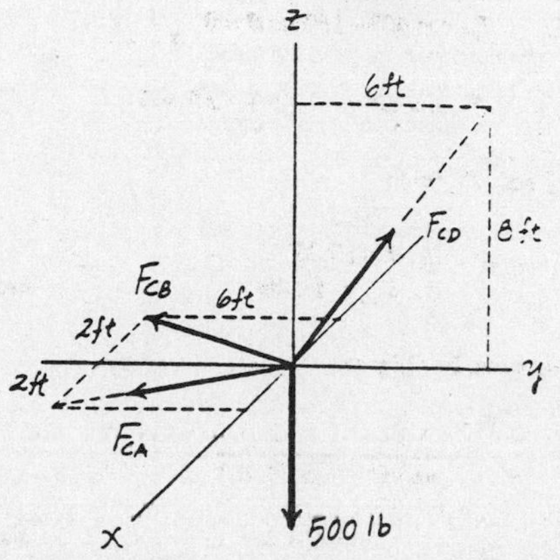

3-77. The joint of a space frame is subjected to four member forces. Member OA lies in the x–y plane and member OB lies in the y–z plane. Determine the forces acting in each of the members required for equilibrium of the joint.

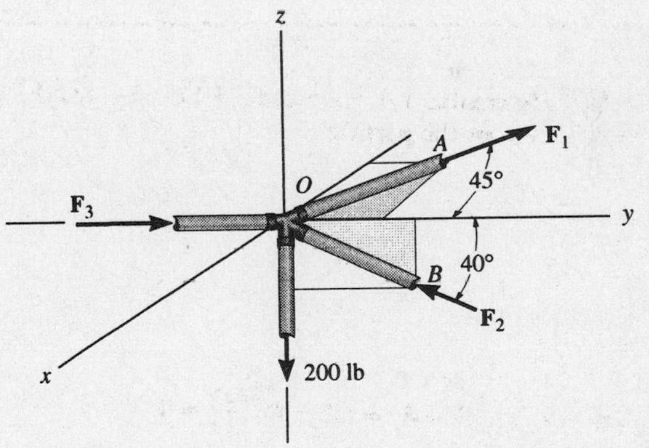

Equation of Equilibrium :

$\Sigma F_x = 0; \quad F_1 \sin 45° = 0 \qquad F_1 = 0$ **Ans**

$\Sigma F_z = 0; \quad F_2 \sin 40° - 200 = 0 \qquad F_2 = 311.14 \text{ lb} = 311 \text{ lb}$ **Ans**

Using the results $F_1 = 0$ and $F_2 = 311.14$ lb and then summing forces along the y axis, we have

$\Sigma F_y = 0; \quad F_3 - 311.14 \cos 40° = 0 \qquad F_3 = 238 \text{ lb}$ **Ans**

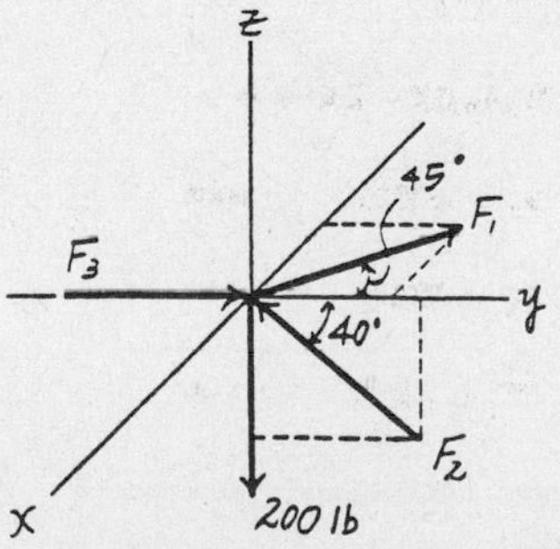

4-1. If **A**, **B**, and **D** are given vectors, prove the distributive law for the vector cross product, i.e., $\mathbf{A} \times (\mathbf{B} + \mathbf{D}) = (\mathbf{A} \times \mathbf{B}) + (\mathbf{A} \times \mathbf{D})$.

Consider the three vectors; with **A** vertical.

Note *obd* is perpendicular to **A**.

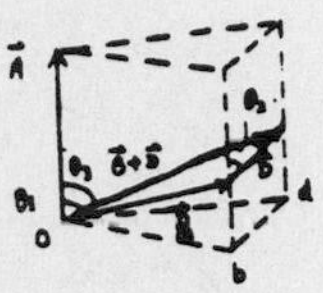

$$od = |\mathbf{A} \times (\mathbf{B} + \mathbf{D})| = |\mathbf{A}|(|\mathbf{B} + \mathbf{D}|) \sin\theta_3$$

$$ob = |\mathbf{A} \times \mathbf{B}| = |\mathbf{A}||\mathbf{B}| \sin\theta_1$$

$$bd = |\mathbf{A} \times \mathbf{D}| = |\mathbf{A}||\mathbf{D}| \sin\theta_2$$

Also, these three cross products all lie in the plane *obd* since they are all perpendicular to **A**. As noted the magnitude of each cross product is proportional to the length of each side of the triangle.

The three vector cross-products also form a closed triangle *o′b′d′* which is similar to triangle *obd*. Thus from the figure,

$$\mathbf{A} \times (\mathbf{B} + \mathbf{D}) = \mathbf{A} \times \mathbf{B} + \mathbf{A} \times \mathbf{D} \qquad \text{(QED)}$$

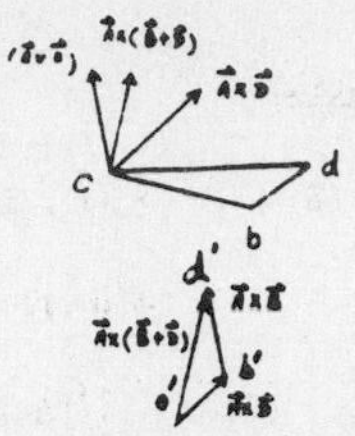

Note also,

$$\mathbf{A} = A_x\mathbf{i} + A_y\mathbf{j} + A_z\mathbf{k}$$

$$\mathbf{B} = B_x\mathbf{i} + B_y\mathbf{j} + B_z\mathbf{k}$$

$$\mathbf{D} = D_x\mathbf{i} + D_y\mathbf{j} + D_z\mathbf{k}$$

$$\mathbf{A} \times (\mathbf{B} + \mathbf{D}) = \begin{vmatrix} \mathbf{i} & \mathbf{j} & \mathbf{k} \\ A_x & A_y & A_z \\ B_x + D_x & B_y + D_y & B_z + D_z \end{vmatrix}$$

$$= [A_y(B_z + D_z) - A_z(B_y + D_y)]\mathbf{i}$$
$$-[A_x(B_z + D_z) - A_z(B_x + D_x)]\mathbf{j}$$
$$+ [A_x(B_y + D_y) - A_y(B_x + D_x)]\mathbf{k}$$
$$= [(A_yB_z - A_zB_y)\mathbf{i} - (A_xB_z - A_zB_x)\mathbf{j} + (A_xB_y - A_yB_x)\mathbf{k}]$$
$$+ [(A_yD_z - A_zD_y)\mathbf{i} - (A_xD_z - A_zD_x)\mathbf{j} + (A_xD_y - A_yD_x)\mathbf{k}]$$

$$= \begin{vmatrix} \mathbf{i} & \mathbf{j} & \mathbf{k} \\ A_x & A_y & A_z \\ B_x & B_y & B_z \end{vmatrix} + \begin{vmatrix} \mathbf{i} & \mathbf{j} & \mathbf{k} \\ A_x & A_y & A_z \\ D_x & D_y & D_z \end{vmatrix}$$

$$= (\mathbf{A} \times \mathbf{B}) + (\mathbf{A} \times \mathbf{D}) \qquad \text{(QED)}$$

4-2. Prove the triple scalar product identity $\mathbf{A} \cdot \mathbf{B} \times \mathbf{C} = \mathbf{A} \times \mathbf{B} \cdot \mathbf{C}$.

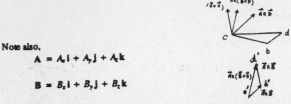

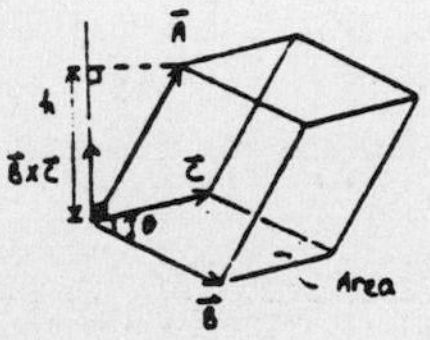

As shown in the figure

$$\text{Area} = B(C \sin\theta) = |\mathbf{B} \times \mathbf{C}|$$

Thus,

Volume of parallelepiped is $|\mathbf{B} \times \mathbf{C}||h|$

But,

$$|h| = |\mathbf{A} \cdot \mathbf{u}_{(\mathbf{B} \times \mathbf{C})}| = \left|\mathbf{A} \cdot \left(\frac{\mathbf{B} \times \mathbf{C}}{|\mathbf{B} \times \mathbf{C}|}\right)\right|$$

Thus,

$$\text{Volume} = |\mathbf{A} \cdot \mathbf{B} \times \mathbf{C}|$$

Since $|\mathbf{A} \times \mathbf{B} \cdot \mathbf{C}|$ represents this same volume then

$$\mathbf{A} \cdot \mathbf{B} \times \mathbf{C} = \mathbf{A} \times \mathbf{B} \cdot \mathbf{C} \qquad \text{(QED)}$$

Also,

$$LHS = \mathbf{A} \cdot \mathbf{B} \times \mathbf{C}$$

$$= (A_x\mathbf{i} + A_y\mathbf{j} + A_z\mathbf{k}) \cdot \begin{vmatrix} \mathbf{i} & \mathbf{j} & \mathbf{k} \\ B_x & B_y & B_z \\ C_x & C_y & C_z \end{vmatrix}$$

$$= A_x(B_yC_z - B_zC_y) - A_y(B_xC_z - B_zC_x) + A_z(B_xC_y - B_yC_x)$$
$$= A_xB_yC_z - A_xB_zC_y - A_yB_xC_z + A_yB_zC_x + A_zB_xC_y - A_zB_yC_x$$

$$RHS = \mathbf{A} \times \mathbf{B} \cdot \mathbf{C}$$

$$= \begin{vmatrix} \mathbf{i} & \mathbf{j} & \mathbf{k} \\ A_x & A_y & A_z \\ B_x & B_y & B_z \end{vmatrix} \cdot (C_x\mathbf{i} + C_y\mathbf{j} + C_z\mathbf{k})$$
$$= C_x(A_yB_z - A_zB_y) - C_y(A_xB_z - A_zB_x) + C_z(A_xB_y - A_yB_x)$$
$$= A_xB_yC_z - A_xB_zC_y - A_yB_xC_z + A_yB_zC_x + A_zB_xC_y - A_zB_yC_x$$

Thus, $LHS = RHS$

$$\mathbf{A} \cdot \mathbf{B} \times \mathbf{C} = \mathbf{A} \times \mathbf{B} \cdot \mathbf{C} \qquad \text{(QED)}$$

4-3. Given the three nonzero vectors **A**, **B**, and **C**, show that if $\mathbf{A}\cdot(\mathbf{B}\times\mathbf{C}) = 0$, the three vectors *must* lie in the same plane.

Consider,

$$|\mathbf{A}\cdot(\mathbf{B}\times\mathbf{C})| = |\mathbf{A}||\mathbf{B}\times\mathbf{C}|\cos\theta$$

$$= (|\mathbf{A}|\cos\theta)|\mathbf{B}\times\mathbf{C}|$$

$$= |h||\mathbf{B}\times\mathbf{C}|$$

$$= BC\,|h|\,\sin\phi$$

= volume of parallelepiped.

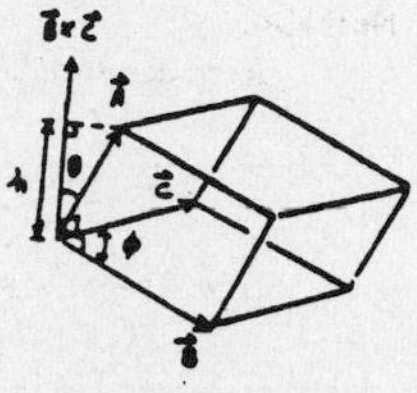

If $\mathbf{A}\cdot(\mathbf{B}\times\mathbf{C}) = 0$, then the volume equals zero, so that **A**, **B**, and **C** are coplanar.

***4-4.** Determine the magnitude and directional sense of the moment of the force at A about point O.

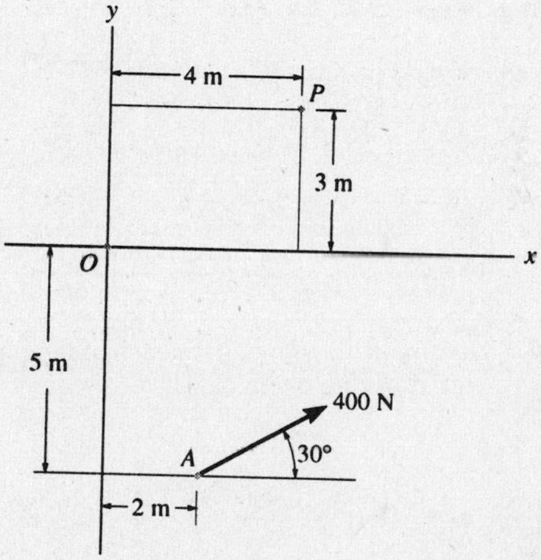

$$\curvearrowleft + M_O = 400\cos 30°(5) + 400\sin 30°(2)$$
$$= 2132 \text{ N}\cdot\text{m}$$
$$= 2.13 \text{ kN}\cdot\text{m} \quad \textit{(Counterclockwise)} \qquad \textbf{Ans}$$

4-5. Determine the magnitude and directional sense of the moment of the force at A about point P.

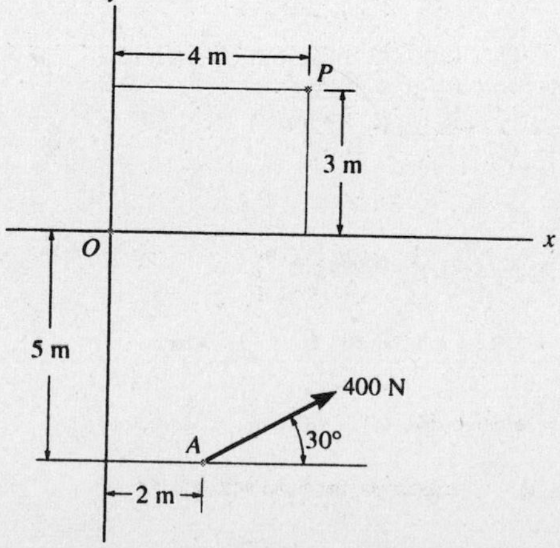

$$\curvearrowleft + M_P = 400\cos 30°(8) - 400\sin 30°(2)$$
$$= 2371 \text{ N}\cdot\text{m}$$
$$= 2.37 \text{ kN}\cdot\text{m} \quad \textit{(Counterclockwise)} \qquad \textbf{Ans}$$

4-6. Determine the magnitude and directional sense of the moment of the force at A about point O.

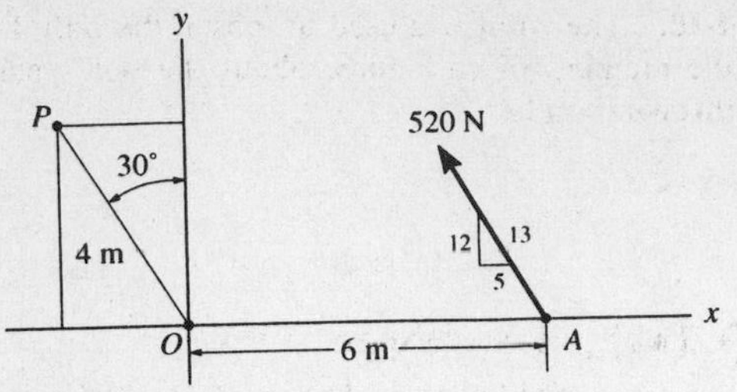

$$\curvearrowleft + \quad M_O = 520\left(\frac{12}{13}\right)(6)$$
$$= 2880 \text{ N}\cdot\text{m} = 2.88 \text{ kN}\cdot\text{m} \quad \textit{(Counterclockwise)} \qquad \textbf{Ans}$$

4-7. Determine the magnitude and directional sense of the moment of the force at A about point P.

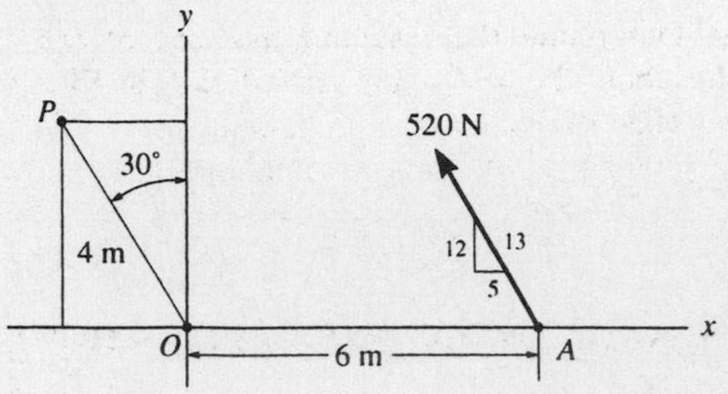

$$\curvearrowleft + \quad M_P = 520\left(\frac{12}{13}\right)(6 + 4\sin 30°) - 520\left(\frac{5}{13}\right)(4\cos 30°)$$
$$= 3147 \text{ N}\cdot\text{m}$$
$$= 3.15 \text{ kN}\cdot\text{m} \quad \textit{(Counterclockwise)} \qquad \textbf{Ans}$$

***4-8.** Determine the moment of each of the three forces about point A on the beam.

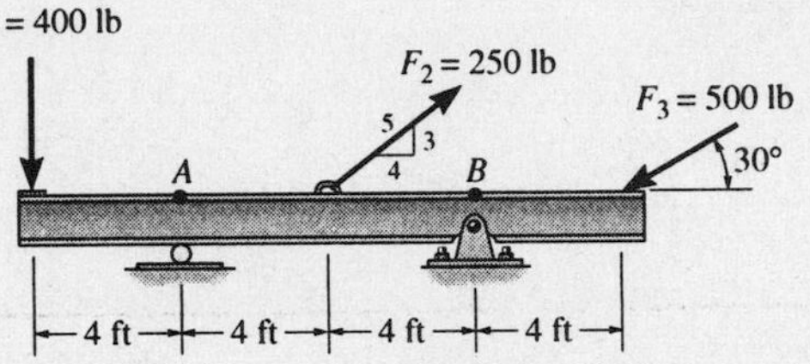

$(M_A)_1 = 400(4) = 1600 \text{ lb}\cdot\text{ft}$ ↻ **Ans**

$(M_A)_2 = 250\left(\frac{3}{5}\right)(4) = 600 \text{ lb}\cdot\text{ft}$ ↺ **Ans**

$(M_A)_3 = 500(\sin 30°)(12) = 3000 \text{ lb}\cdot\text{ft}$ ↻ **Ans**

4-9. Determine the moment of each of the three forces about point B on the beam.

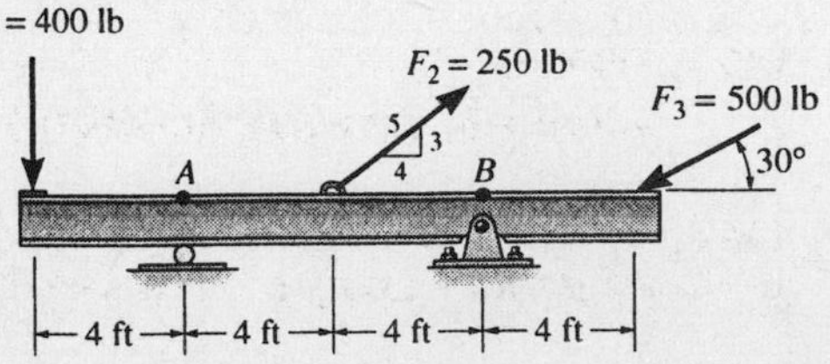

$(M_B)_1 = 400(12) = 4800 \text{ lb}\cdot\text{ft}$ ↻ **Ans**

$(M_B)_2 = 250\left(\frac{3}{5}\right)(4) = 600 \text{ lb}\cdot\text{ft}$ ↻ **Ans**

$(M_B)_3 = 500(\sin 30°)(4) = 1000 \text{ lb}\cdot\text{ft}$ ↻ **Ans**

4-10. The wrench is used to loosen the bolt. Determine the moment of each force about the bolt's axis passing through point O.

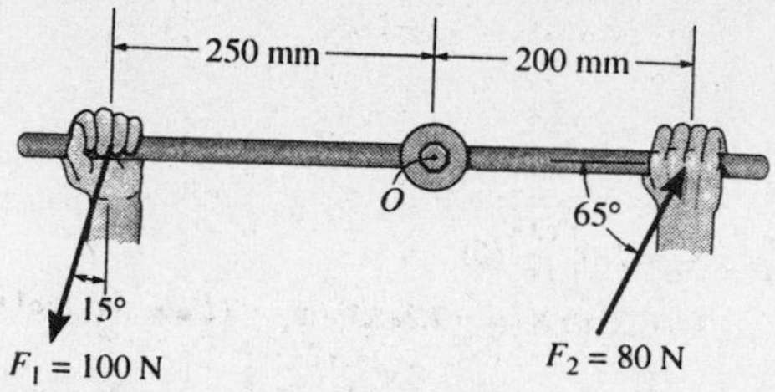

$\curvearrowleft + \; (M_{F_1})_O = 100\cos 15°(0.25)$

$= 24.1 \text{ N}\cdot\text{m}$ ***(Counterclockwise)*** **Ans**

$\curvearrowleft + \; (M_{F_2})_O = 80\sin 65°(0.2)$

$= 14.5 \text{ N}\cdot\text{m}$ ***(Counterclockwise)*** **Ans**

4-11. Determine the resultant moment of the cable weights about the base of the powerline pole. Each cable has a weight of 560 lb.

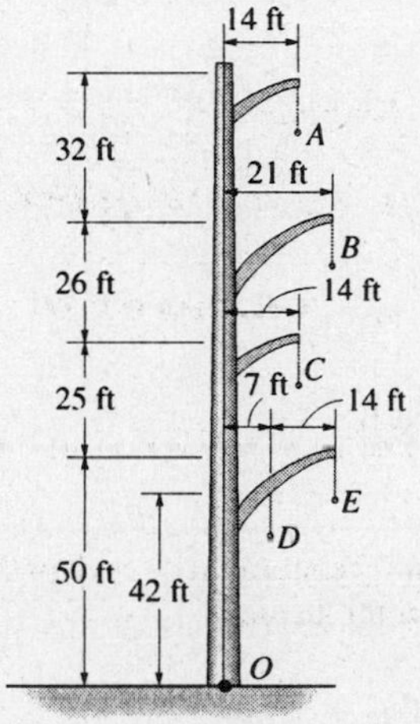

$M_O = 560(14) + 560(21) + 560(14) + 560(7) + 560(21)$

$M_O = 43.1 \text{ kip}\cdot\text{ft}$ ↻ **Ans**

***4-12.** Determine the moment about point A of each of the three forces acting on the beam.

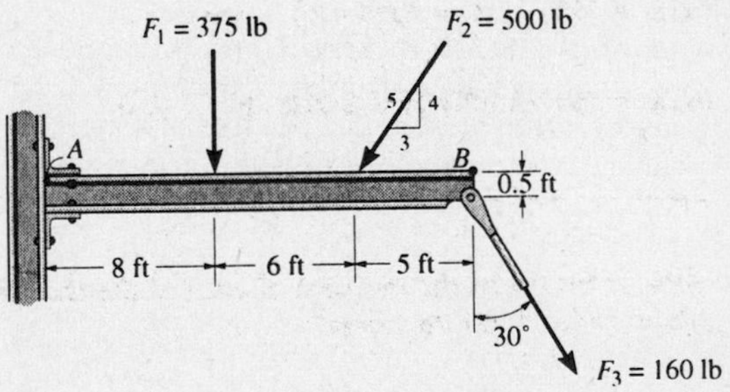

$\curvearrowleft + \; (M_{F_1})_A = -375(8)$

$= -3000 \text{ lb}\cdot\text{ft} = 3.00 \text{ kip}\cdot\text{ft}$ ***(Clockwise)*** **Ans**

$\curvearrowleft + \; (M_{F_2})_A = -500\left(\frac{4}{5}\right)(14)$

$= -5600 \text{ lb}\cdot\text{ft} = 5.60 \text{ kip}\cdot\text{ft}$ ***(Clockwise)*** **Ans**

$\curvearrowleft + \; (M_{F_3})_A = -160(\cos 30°)(19) + 160\sin 30°(0.5)$

$= -2593 \text{ lb}\cdot\text{ft} = 2.59 \text{ kip}\cdot\text{ft}$ ***(Clockwise)*** **Ans**

4-13. Determine the moment about point B of each of the three forces acting on the beam.

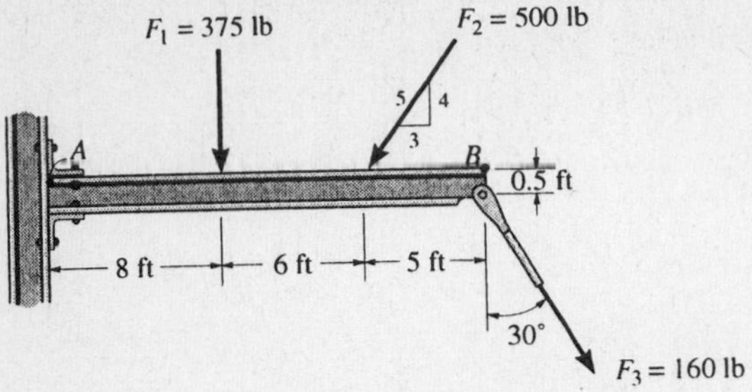

$$\curvearrowleft + \left(M_{F_1}\right)_B = 375(11)$$
$$= 4125 \text{ lb}\cdot\text{ft} = 4.125 \text{ kip}\cdot\text{ft} \quad (\textit{Counterclockwise}) \quad \textbf{Ans}$$

$$\curvearrowleft + \left(M_{F_2}\right)_B = 500\left(\frac{4}{5}\right)(5)\text{-}$$
$$= 2000 \text{ lb}\cdot\text{ft} = 2.00 \text{ kip}\cdot\text{ft} \quad (\textit{Counterclockwise}) \quad \textbf{Ans}$$

$$\curvearrowleft + \left(M_{F_3}\right)_B = 160\sin 30°(0.5) - 160\cos 30°(0)$$
$$= 40.0 \text{ lb}\cdot\text{ft} \quad (\textit{Counterclockwise}) \quad \textbf{Ans}$$

4-14. Two men exert forces of $F = 80$ lb and $P = 50$ lb on the ropes. Determine the moment of each force about A. Which way will the pole rotate, clockwise or counterclockwise?

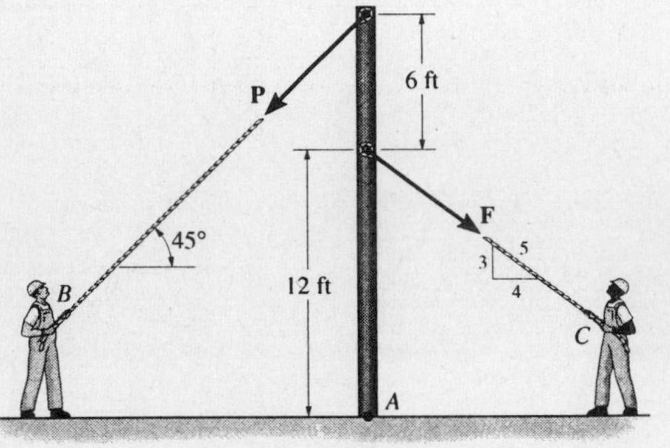

$$\curvearrowright + (M_A)_C = 80\left(\frac{4}{5}\right)(12) = 768 \text{ lb}\cdot\text{ft} \curvearrowright \quad \textbf{Ans}$$

$$\curvearrowleft + (M_A)_B = 50(\cos 45°)(18) = 636 \text{ lb}\cdot\text{ft} \curvearrowleft \quad \textbf{Ans}$$

Since $(M_A)_C > (M_A)_B$

Clockwise **Ans**

4-15. If the man at B exerts a force of $P = 30$ lb on his rope, determine the magnitude of the force **F** the man at C must exert to prevent the pole from tipping, i.e., so the resultant moment about A of both forces is zero.

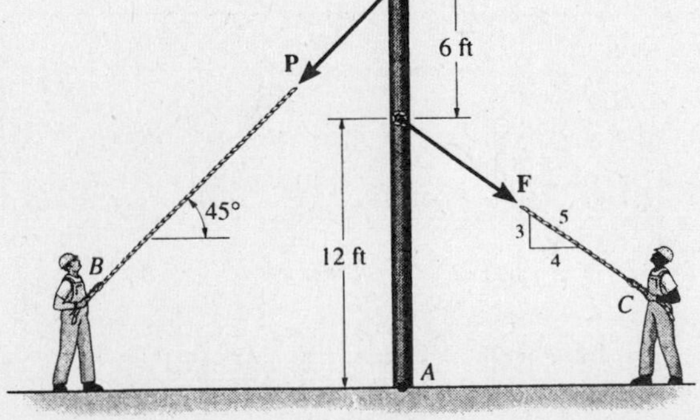

$$\curvearrowleft + \quad 30(\cos 45°)(18) = F\left(\frac{4}{5}\right)(12)$$

$F = 39.8$ lb **Ans**

*4-16. The power pole supports the three lines, each line exerting a vertical force on the pole due to its weight as shown. Determine the resultant moment at the base D due to all of these forces. If it is possible for wind or ice to snap the lines, determine which line(s) when removed create(s) a condition for the greatest moment about the base. What is this resultant moment?

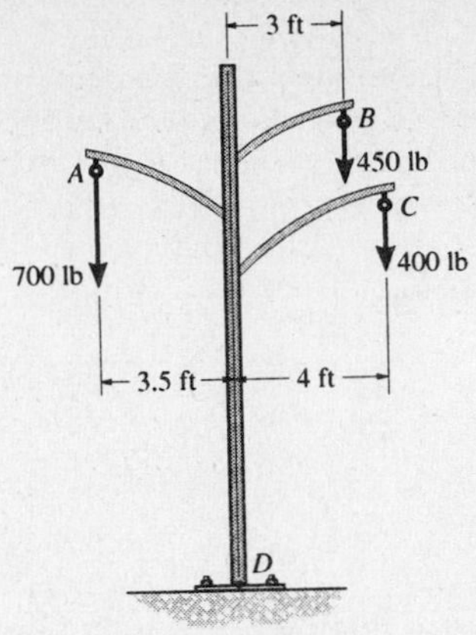

$\curvearrowleft + M_{R_D} = \Sigma Fd;\quad M_{R_D} = 700(3.5) - 450(3) - 400(4)$

$= -500 \text{ lb}\cdot\text{ft} = 500 \text{ lb}\cdot\text{ft}$ **(Clockwise)** **Ans**

When the cable at A is removed it will create the greatest moment at point D. **Ans**

$\curvearrowleft + (M_{R_D})_{max} = \Sigma Fd;$

$(M_{R_D})_{max} = -450(3) - 400(4)$

$= -2950 \text{ lb}\cdot\text{ft} = 2.95 \text{ kip}\cdot\text{ft}$ **(Clockwise)** **Ans**

4-17. A force of 80 N acts on the handle of the paper cutter at A. Determine the moment created by this force about the hinge at O, if $\theta = 60°$. At what angle θ should the force be applied so that the moment it creates about point O is a maximum (clockwise)? What is this maximum moment?

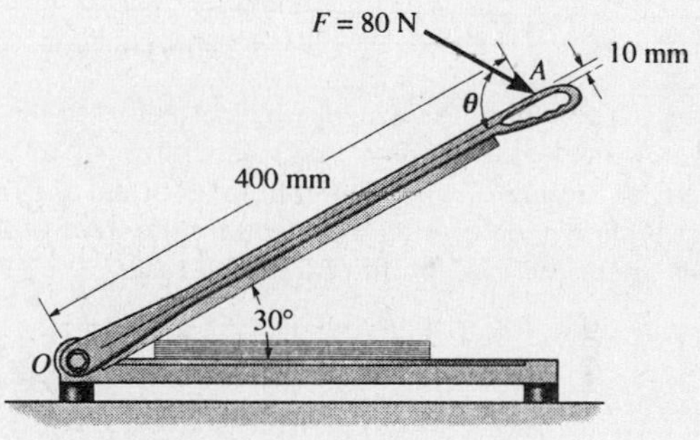

$\curvearrowleft + M_O = \Sigma Fd;\quad M_O = -80\cos\theta(0.01) - 80\sin\theta(0.4)$

$= -(0.800\cos\theta + 32.0\sin\theta) \text{ N}\cdot\text{m}$

$= (0.800\cos\theta + 32.0\sin\theta) \text{ N}\cdot\text{m}$ **(Clockwise)**

At $\theta = 60°$, $\quad M_O = 0.800\cos 60° + 32.0\sin 60°$

$= 28.1 \text{ N}\cdot\text{m}$ **(Clockwise)** **Ans**

In order to produce the maximum and minimum moment about point A, $\dfrac{dM_O}{d\theta} = 0$

$$\frac{dM_O}{d\theta} = 0 = -0.800\sin\theta + 32.0\cos\theta$$

$\theta = 88.568° = 88.6°$ **Ans**

$$\frac{d^2M_A}{d\theta^2} = -0.800\cos\theta - 32.0\sin\theta$$

Since $\left.\dfrac{d^2M_A}{d\theta^2}\right|_{\theta=88.568°} = -0.800\cos 88.568° - 32.0\sin 88.568° = -32.00$ is a negative value, indeed at $\theta = 88.568°$, the 80 N produces a maximum clockwise moment at A. This maximum clockwise moment is

$(M_A)_{max} = 0.800\cos 88.568° + 32.0\sin 88.568°$

$= 32.0 \text{ N}\cdot\text{m}$ **(Clockwise)** **Ans**

■4-18. Determine the moment produced about the support A as a function of the leg angle θ. Plot the results of M (ordinate) versus θ (abscissa) for $0 \leq \theta \leq 180°$. Use M clockwise as positive.

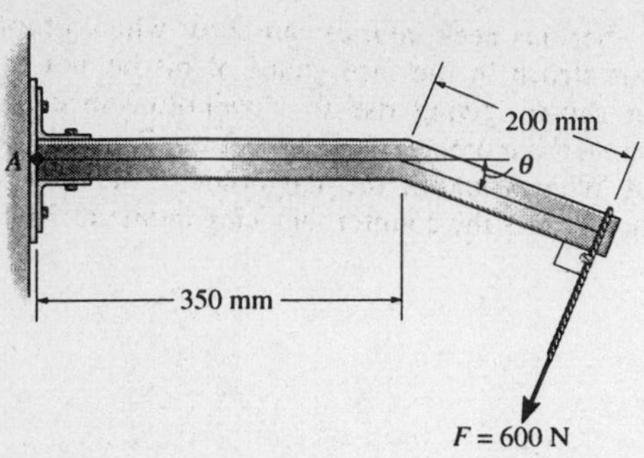

$$\circlearrowleft + M_A = 600\sin\theta(0.2\sin\theta) + 600\cos\theta(0.2\cos\theta + 0.35)$$

$$= 120 + 210\cos\theta$$

$$\frac{dM_A}{d\theta} = -210\sin\theta = 0$$

$\theta = 0°$; $M_{max} = 330\ \text{N}\cdot\text{m}$

$\theta = 180°$; $M_{min} = -90\ \text{N}\cdot\text{m}$

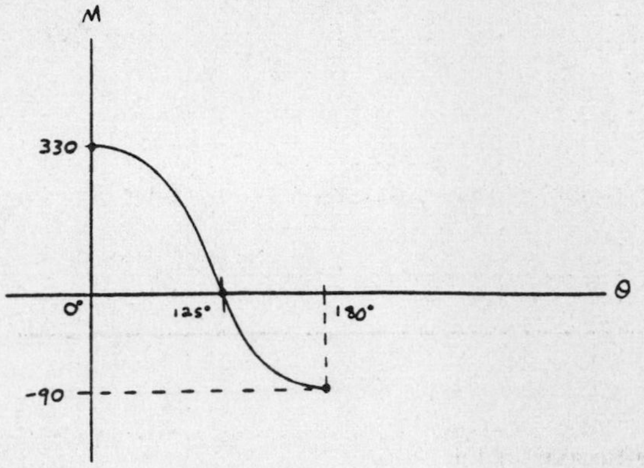

*4-19. The hub of the wheel can be attached to the axle either with negative offset (left) or with positive offset (right). If the tire is subjected to both a normal and radial load as shown, determine the resultant moment of these loads about the axle, point O for both cases.

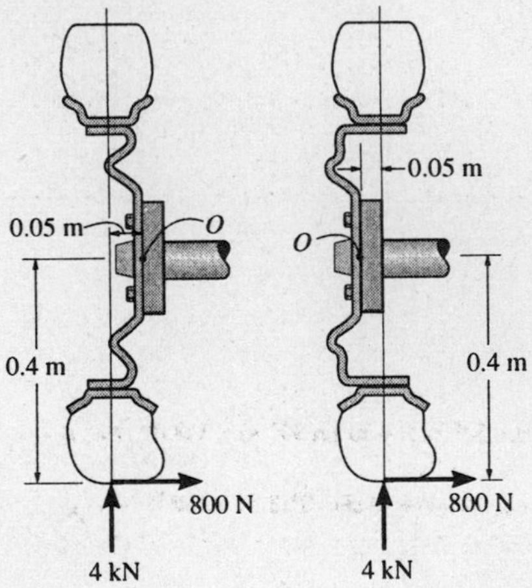

For case 1 with negative offset, we have

$$\circlearrowleft + M_O = 800(0.4) - 4000(0.05)$$
$$= 120\ \text{N}\cdot\text{m} \quad (\textit{Counterclockwise}) \qquad \textbf{Ans}$$

For case 2 with positive offset, we have

$$\circlearrowleft + M_O = 800(0.4) + 4000(0.05)$$
$$= 520\ \text{N}\cdot\text{m} \quad (\textit{Counterclockwise}) \qquad \textbf{Ans}$$

***4-20.** Serious neck injuries can occur when a football player is struck in the face guard of his helmet in the manner shown, giving rise to a guillotine mechanism. Determine the moment of the knee force $P = 50$ lb about point A. What would be the magnitude of the neck force **F** so that it gives the counterbalancing moment about A?

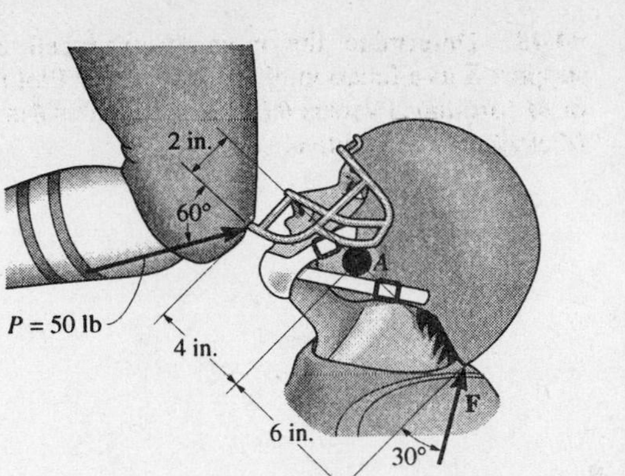

$\circlearrowleft + M_A = 50 \sin 60° (4) - 50 \cos 60° (2) = 123.2 = 123 \text{ lb} \cdot \text{in.} \circlearrowright$ **Ans**

$123.2 = F \cos 30° (6)$

$F = 23.7 \text{ lb}$ **Ans**

4-21. The foot segment is subjected to the pull of the two plantarflexor muscles. Determine the moment of each force about the point of contact A on the ground.

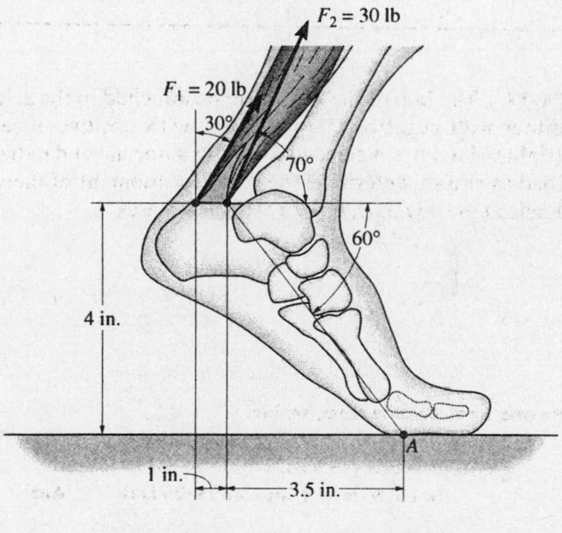

$(M_A)_1 = 20 \cos 30° (4.5) + 20 \sin 30° (4) = 118 \text{ lb} \cdot \text{in.} \circlearrowright$ **Ans**

$(M_A)_2 = 30 \cos 70° (4) + 30 \sin 70° (3.5) = 140 \text{ lb} \cdot \text{in.} \circlearrowright$ **Ans**

4-22. Determine the moment of each of the three forces about point A. Solve the problem first by using each force as a whole, and then by using the principle of moments.

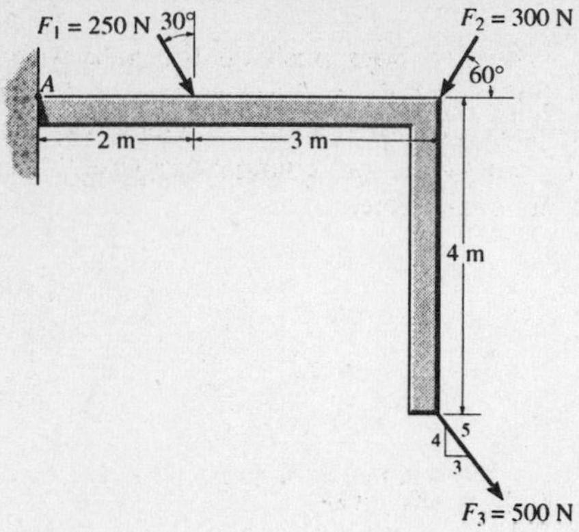

The moment arm measured perpendicular to each force from point A is

$$d_1 = 2\sin 60° = 1.732\text{ m}$$
$$d_2 = 5\sin 60° = 4.330\text{ m}$$
$$d_3 = 2\sin 53.13° = 1.60\text{ m}$$

Using each force where $M_A = Fd$, we have

$$\circlearrowleft+\ (M_{F_1})_A = -250(1.732)$$
$$= -433\text{ N}\cdot\text{m} = 433\text{ N}\cdot\text{m} \quad (\textit{Clockwise}) \quad \textbf{Ans}$$

$$\circlearrowleft+\ (M_{F_2})_A = -300(4.330)$$
$$= -1299\text{ N}\cdot\text{m} = 1.30\text{ kN}\cdot\text{m} \quad (\textit{Clockwise}) \quad \textbf{Ans}$$

$$\circlearrowleft+\ (M_{F_3})_A = -500(1.60)$$
$$= -800\text{ N}\cdot\text{m} = 800\text{ N}\cdot\text{m} \quad (\textit{Clockwise}) \quad \textbf{Ans}$$

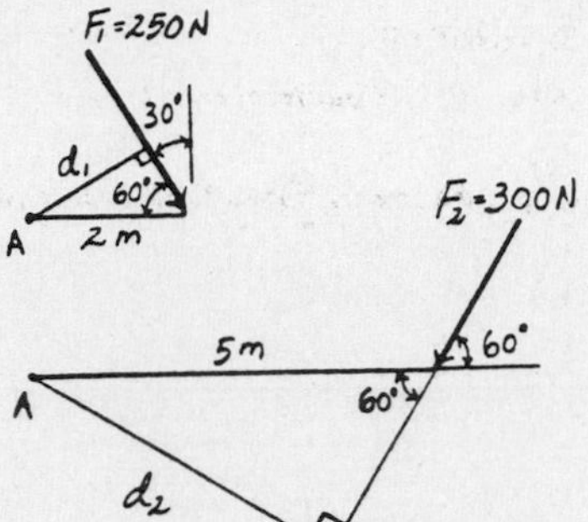

Using principle of moments, we have

$$\circlearrowleft+\ (M_{F_1})_A = -250\cos 30°(2)$$
$$= -433\text{ N}\cdot\text{m} = 433\text{ N}\cdot\text{m} \quad (\textit{Clockwise}) \quad \textbf{Ans}$$

$$\circlearrowleft+\ (M_{F_2})_A = -300\sin 60°(5)$$
$$= -1299\text{ N}\cdot\text{m} = 1.30\text{ kN}\cdot\text{m} \quad (\textit{Clockwise}) \quad \textbf{Ans}$$

$$\circlearrowleft+\ (M_{F_3})_A = 500\left(\frac{3}{5}\right)(4) - 500\left(\frac{4}{5}\right)(5)$$
$$= -800\text{ N}\cdot\text{m} = 800\text{ N}\cdot\text{m} \quad (\textit{Clockwise}) \quad \textbf{Ans}$$

4-23. As part of an acrobatic stunt, a man supports a girl who has a weight of 120 lb and is seated on a chair on top of the pole. If her center of gravity is at G, and if the maximum counterclockwise moment the man can exert on the pole at A is 250 lb·ft, determine the maximum angle of tilt, θ, which will not allow the girl to fall, i.e., so her clockwise moment about A does not exceed 250 lb·ft.

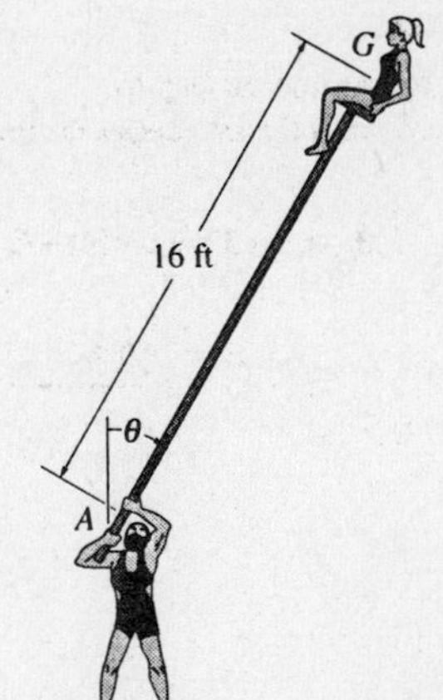

In order to prevent the girl from falling down, the clockwise moment produced by the girl's weight must not exceded 250 lb · ft.

$$M_A = 120(16\sin\theta) \le 250$$
$$\sin\theta \le 0.1302$$

$$\theta = 7.48° \quad \textbf{Ans}$$

4-24. The two boys push on the gate with forces of $F_A = 30$ lb and $F_B = 50$ lb as shown. Determine the moment of each force about C. Which way will the gate rotate, clockwise or counterclockwise? Neglect the thickness of the gate.

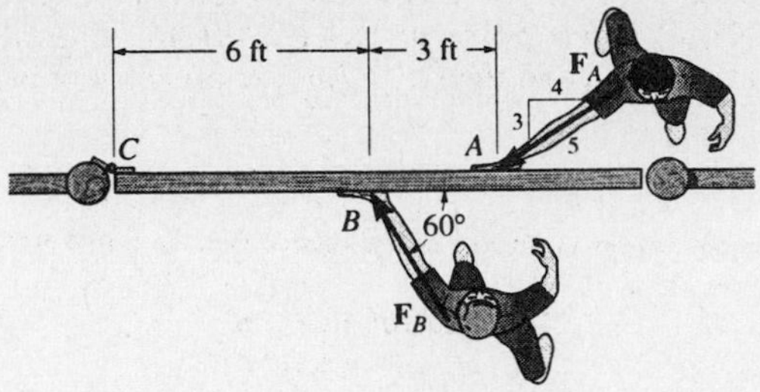

$$\circlearrowleft + \quad (M_{F_A})_C = -30\left(\frac{3}{5}\right)(9)$$

$$= -162 \text{ lb}\cdot\text{ft} = 162 \text{ lb}\cdot\text{ft} \quad \textit{(Clockwise)} \qquad \textbf{Ans}$$

$$\circlearrowleft + \quad (M_{F_B})_C = 50(\sin 60°)(6)$$

$$= 260 \text{ lb}\cdot\text{ft} \quad \textit{(Counterclockwise)} \qquad \textbf{Ans}$$

Since $(M_{F_B})_C > (M_{F_A})_C$, the gate will rotate ***Counterclockwise***. **Ans**

4-25. Two boys push on the gate as shown. If the boy at B exerts a force of $F_B = 30$ lb, determine the magnitude of the force F_A the boy at A must exert in order to prevent the gate from turning. Neglect the thickness of the gate.

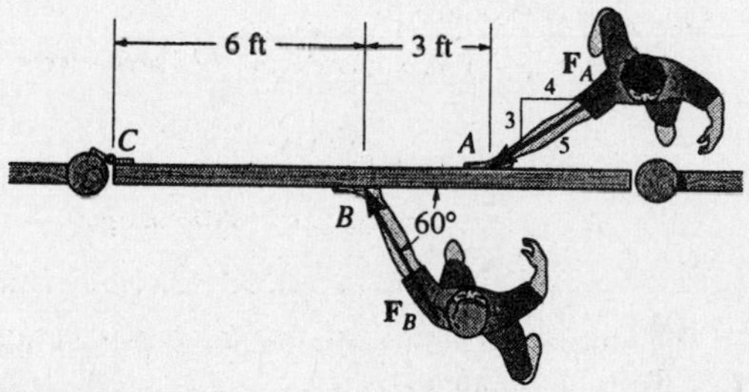

In order to prevent the gate from turning, the resultant moment about point C must be equal to zero.

$$+ M_{R_C} = \Sigma Fd; \qquad M_{R_C} = 0 = 30\sin 60°(6) - F_A\left(\frac{3}{5}\right)(9)$$

$$F_A = 28.9 \text{ lb} \qquad \textbf{Ans}$$

4-26. The tongs are used to grip the ends of the drilling pipe P. Determine the torque (moment) M_P that the applied force $F = 150$ lb exerts on the pipe as a function of θ. Plot this moment M_P versus θ for $0 \le \theta \le 90°$.

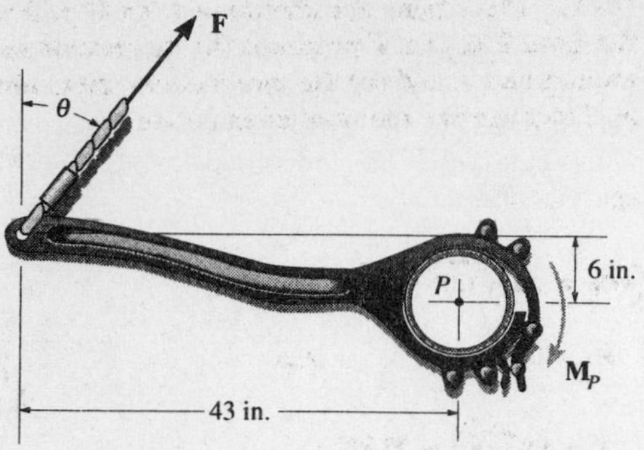

$$M_P = 150\cos\theta(43) + 150\sin\theta(6)$$

$$= (6450\cos\theta + 900\sin\theta)\ \text{lb}\cdot\text{in.}$$

$$= (537.5\cos\theta + 75\sin\theta)\ \text{lb}\cdot\text{ft} \qquad \textbf{Ans}$$

$$\frac{dM_P}{d\theta} = -537.5\sin\theta + 75\cos\theta = 0 \qquad \tan\theta = \frac{75}{537.5} \qquad \theta = 7.943°$$

At $\theta = 7.943°$, M_P is maximum.

$$(M_P)_{max} = 538\cos 7.943° + 75\sin 7.943° = 543\ \text{lb}\cdot\text{ft}$$

Also $(M_P)_{max} = 150\ \text{lb}\left(\left(\frac{43}{12}\right)^2 + \left(\frac{6}{12}\right)^2\right)^{\frac{1}{2}} = 543\ \text{lb}\cdot\text{ft}$

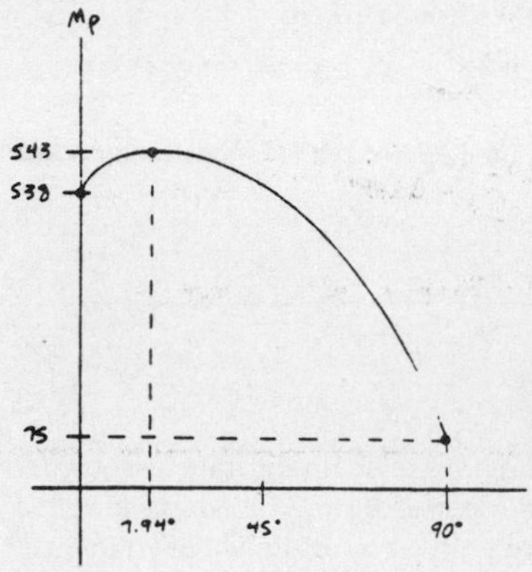

4-27. The tongs are used to grip the ends of the drilling pipe P. If a torque (moment) of $M_P = 800$ lb · ft is needed at P to turn the pipe, determine the cable force **F** that must be applied to the tongs. Set $\theta = 30°$.

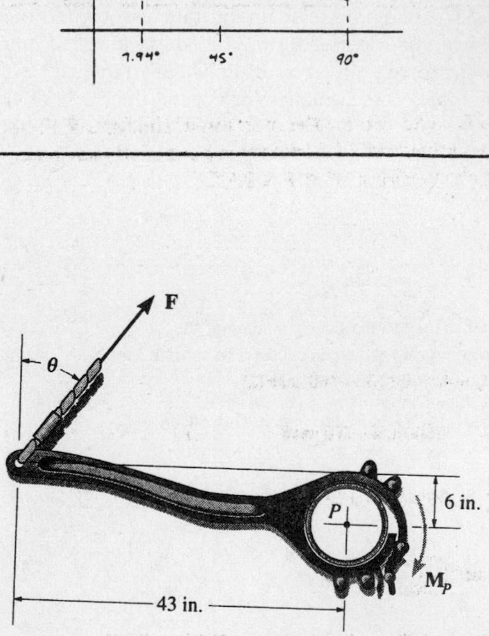

$$M_P = F\cos 30°(43) + F\sin 30°(6) \qquad \text{Set } M_P = 800(12)\ \text{lb}\cdot\text{in.}$$

$$800(12) = F\cos 30°(43) + F\sin 30°(6)$$

$$F = 239\ \text{lb} \qquad \textbf{Ans}$$

***4-28.** Determine the direction θ for $0° \le \theta \le 180°$ of the force **F** so that **F** produces (a) the maximum moment about point A and (b) the minimum moment about point A. Calculate the moment in each case.

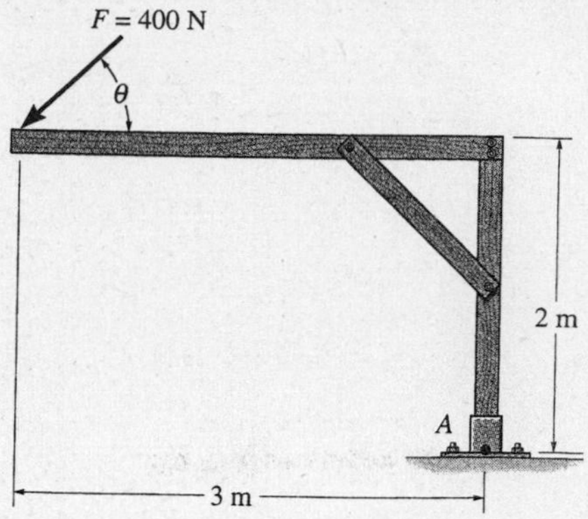

a)

$$\circlearrowleft + M_A = 400\sqrt{(3)^2 + (2)^2} = 1442 \text{ N}\cdot\text{m}$$

$$M_A = 1.44 \text{ kN}\cdot\text{m} \qquad \textbf{Ans}$$

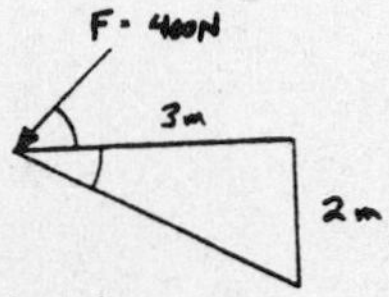

$$\phi = \tan^{-1}\left(\frac{2}{3}\right) = 33.69°$$

$$\theta = 90° - 33.69° = 56.3° \qquad \textbf{Ans}$$

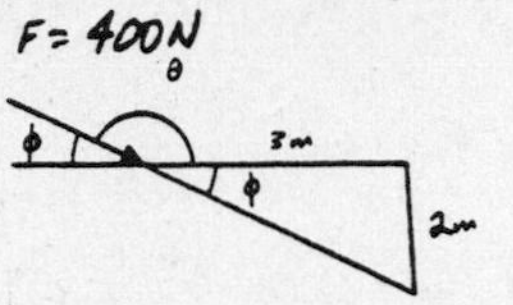

b)

$$\circlearrowleft + M_A = 0 \qquad \textbf{Ans}$$

$$\phi = \tan^{-1}\left(\frac{2}{3}\right) = 33.69°$$

$$\theta = 180° - 33.69° = 146° \qquad \textbf{Ans}$$

4-29. Determine the moment of the force **F** about point A as a function of θ. Plot the results of M (ordinate) versus θ (abscissa) for $0° \le \theta \le 180°$.

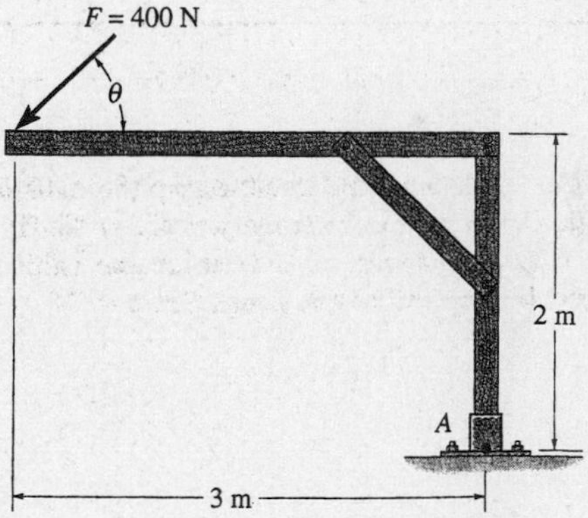

$$\circlearrowleft + M_A = 400\sin\theta(3) + 400\cos\theta(2)$$

$$= 1200\sin\theta + 800\cos\theta \qquad \textbf{Ans}$$

$$\frac{dM_A}{d\theta} = 1200\cos\theta - 800\sin\theta = 0$$

$$\theta = \tan^{-1}\left(\frac{1200}{800}\right) = 56.3°$$

$$(M_A)_{max} = 1200\sin 56.3° + 800\cos 56.3° = 1442 \text{ N}\cdot\text{ m}$$

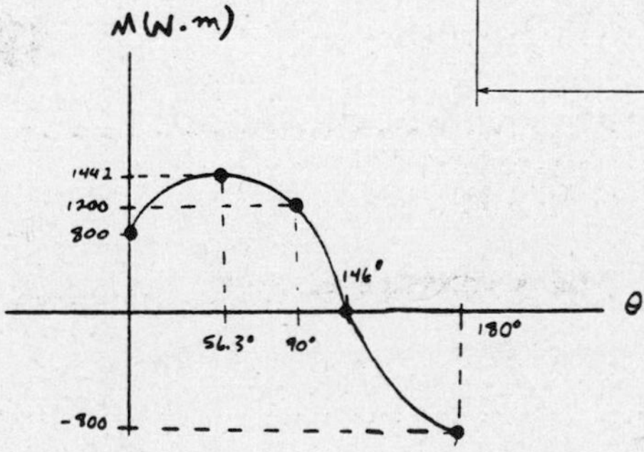

4-30. Determine the maximum and minimum moment produced by the force **F** about point *A*. Specify the angle θ ($0° \le \theta \le 180°$) in each case.

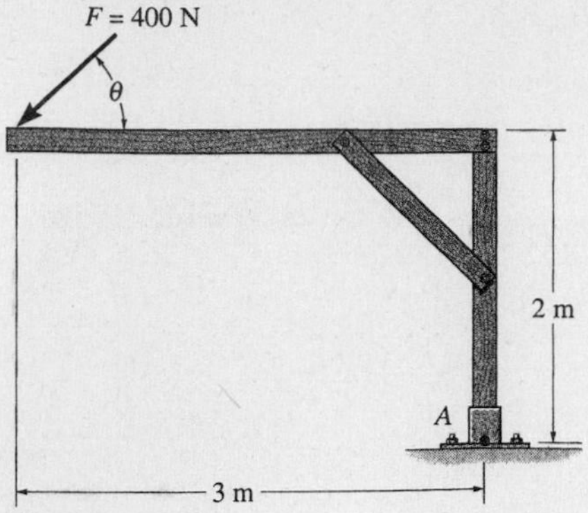

$M_{max} = 400\sqrt{13} = 1.44$ kN·m **Ans**

$\theta_{max} = \tan^{-1}\left(\frac{3}{2}\right) = 56.3°$ **Ans**

$M_{min} = 400(0) = 0$ **Ans**

$\theta_{min} = 90° + 56.3° = 146°$ **Ans**

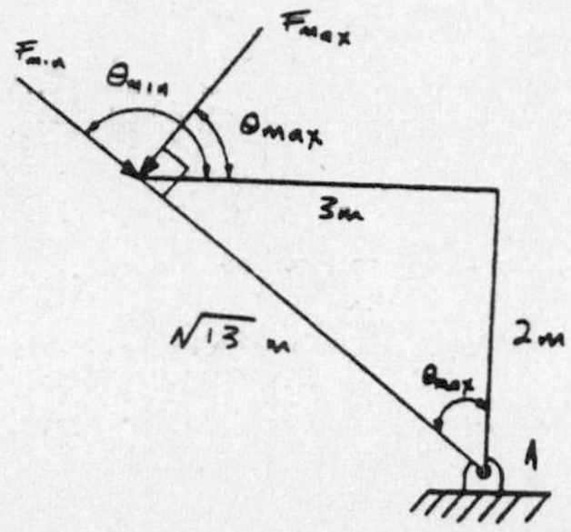

4-31. The total hip replacement is subjected to a force of $F = 120$ N. Determine the moment of this force about the neck at *A* and at the stem *B*.

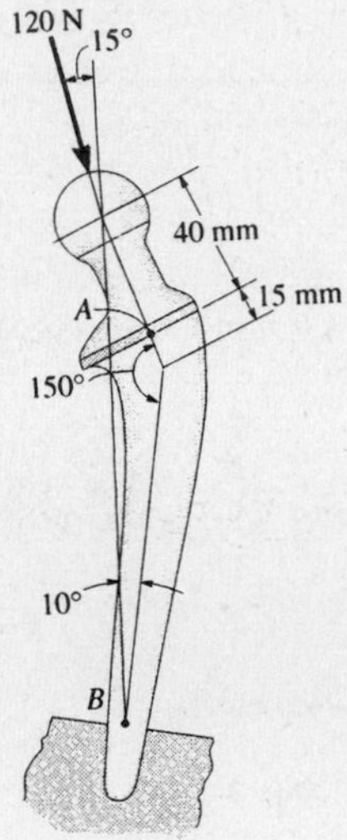

Moment About Point A : The angle between the line of action of the load and the neck axis is $20° - 15° = 5°$.

$\curvearrowleft + \; M_A = 120\sin 5°(0.04)$
$= 0.418$ N·m ***(Counterclockwise)*** **Ans**

Moment About Point B : The dimension l can be determined using the law of sines.

$$\frac{l}{\sin 150°} = \frac{55}{\sin 10°} \qquad l = 158.4 \text{ mm} = 0.1584 \text{ m}$$

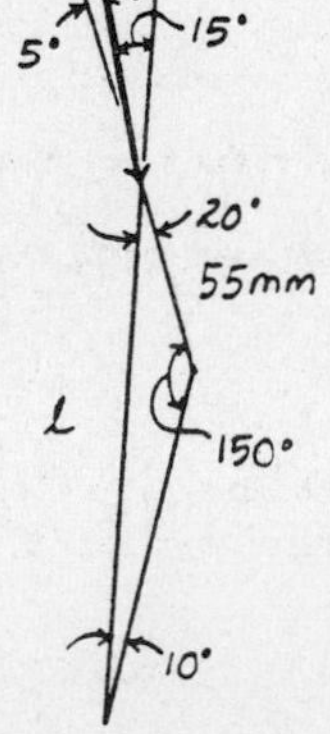

Then,

$+ \; M_B = -120\sin 15°(0.1584)$
$= -4.92$ N·m $= 4.92$ N·m ***(Clockwise)*** **Ans**

***4-32.** The crane can be adjusted for any angle $0° \leq \theta \leq 90°$ and any extension $0 \leq x \leq 5$ m. For a suspended mass of 120 kg, determine the moment developed at A as a function of x and θ. What values of both x and θ develop the maximum possible moment at A? Compute this moment. Neglect the size of the pulley at B.

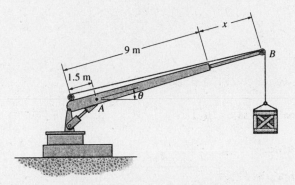

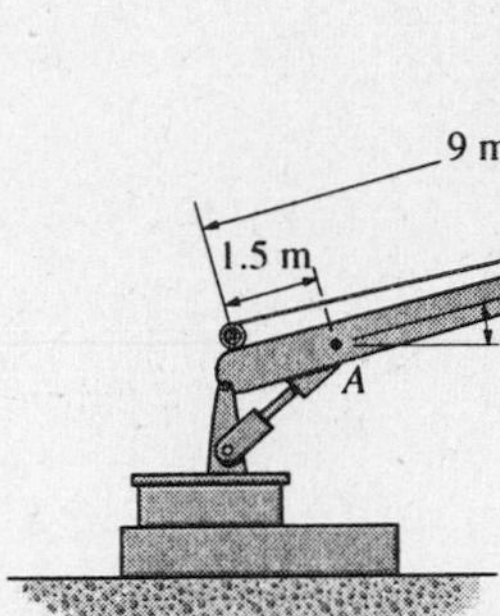

$$\circlearrowleft + \; M_A = -120(9.81)(7.5+x)\cos\theta$$
$$= \{-1177.2\cos\theta(7.5+x)\}\ \text{N}\cdot\text{m}$$
$$= \{1.18\cos\theta(7.5+x)\}\ \text{kN}\cdot\text{m} \quad \textit{(clockwise)} \qquad \textbf{Ans}$$

The maximum moment at A occurs when $\theta = 0°$ and $x = 5$ m. **Ans**

$$\circlearrowleft + \; (M_A)_{max} = \{-1177.2\cos 0°(7.5+5)\}\ \text{N}\cdot\text{m}$$
$$= -14715\ \text{N}\cdot\text{m}$$
$$= 14.7\ \text{kN}\cdot\text{m} \quad \textit{(clockwise)} \qquad \textbf{Ans}$$

4-33. Determine the angle θ at which the 500-N force must act at A so that the moment of this force about point B is equal to zero.

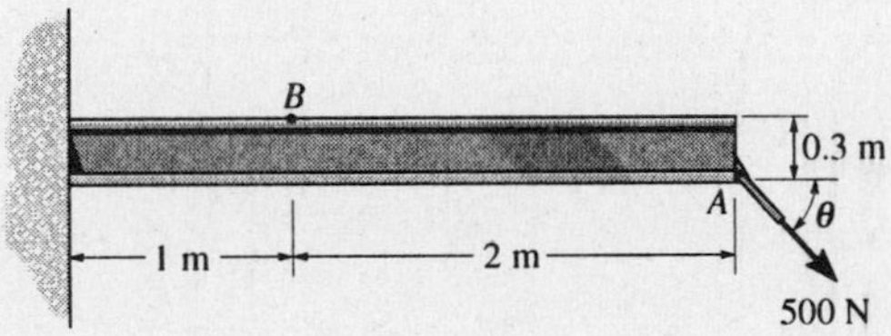

This problem requires that the resultant moment about point B be equal to zero.

$$\circlearrowleft + \; M_{R_B} = \Sigma Fd; \quad M_{R_B} = 0 = 500\cos\theta(0.3) - 500\sin\theta(2)$$

$$\theta = 8.53° \qquad \textbf{Ans}$$

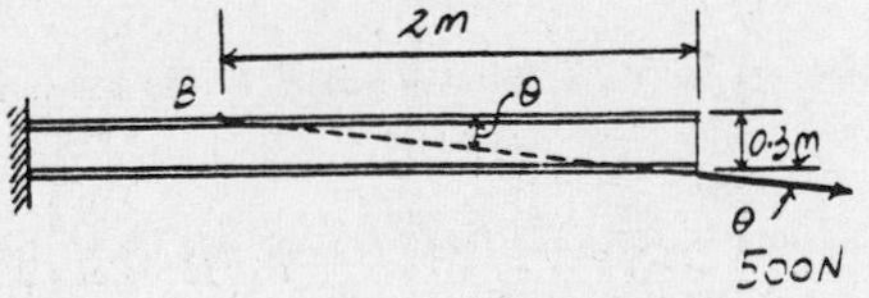

Also note that if the line of action of the 500 N force passes through point B, it produces zero moment about point B. Hence, from the geometry

$$\theta = \tan^{-1}\left(\frac{0.3}{2}\right) = 8.53°$$

4-34. Segments of drill pipe D for an oil well are tightened a prescribed amount by using a set of tongs T, which grip the pipe, and a hydraulic cylinder (not shown) to regulate the force **F** applied to the tongs. This force acts along the cable which passes around the small pulley P. If the cable is originally perpendicular to the tongs as shown, determine the magnitude of force **F** which must be applied so that the moment about the pipe is M = 2000 lb·ft. In order to maintain this same moment what magnitude of **F** is required when the tongs rotate 30° to the dashed position? *Note:* The angle DAP is not 90° in this position.

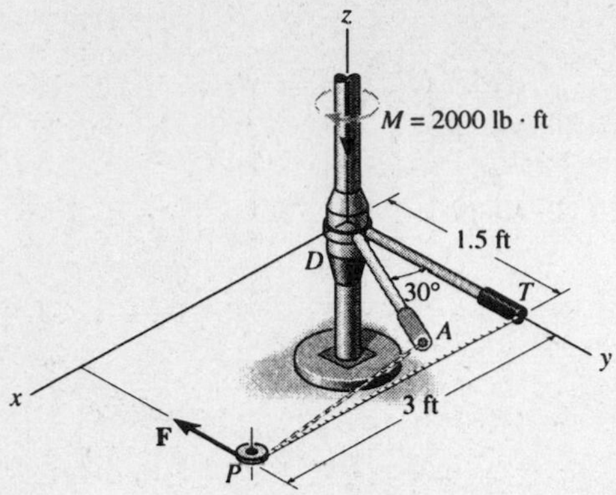

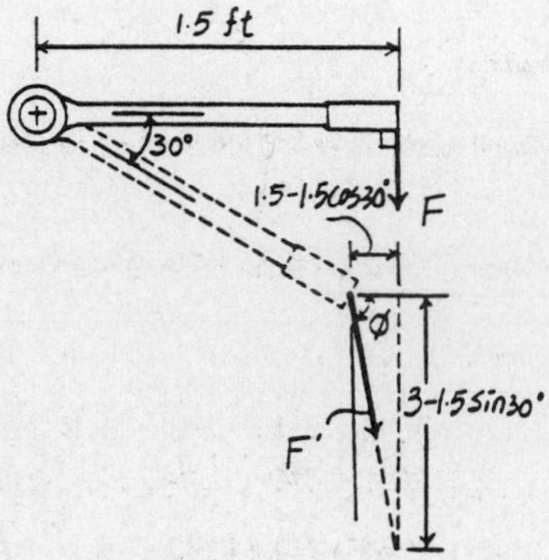

This problem requires that the moment produced by **F** and **F′** about the z axis is 2000 lb · ft.

$$M_z = 2000 = F(1.5)$$
$$F = 1333.3 \text{ lb} = 1.33 \text{ kip} \qquad \textbf{Ans}$$

From the geometry, $\phi = \tan^{-1}\left(\dfrac{3 - 1.5\sin 30°}{1.5 - 1.5\cos 30°}\right) = 84.90°$. Then the angle between the line of action of force **F′** and the tong's axis is $84.90° - 30° = 54.90°$.

$$M_z = 2000 = F'(1.5\sin 54.90°)$$
$$F' = 1629.8 \text{ lb} = 1.63 \text{ kip} \qquad \textbf{Ans}$$

4-35. Determine the moment of the force at A about point O. Express the result as a Cartesian vector.

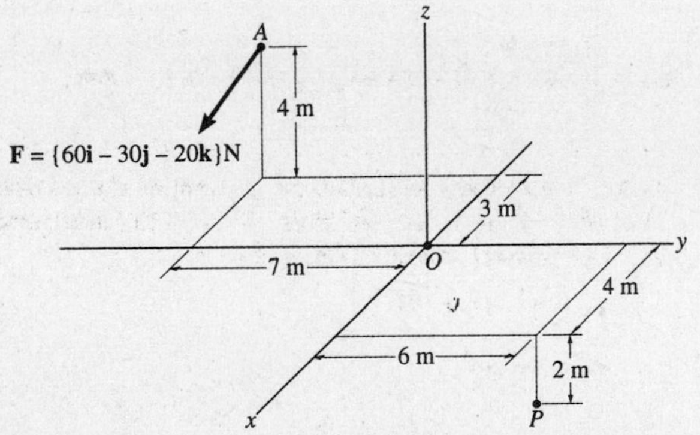

Position Vector :

$$\mathbf{r}_{OA} = \{(-3-0)\mathbf{i} + (-7-0)\mathbf{j} + (4-0)\mathbf{k}\} \text{ m}$$
$$= \{-3\mathbf{i} - 7\mathbf{j} + 4\mathbf{k}\} \text{ m}$$

***Moment of Force* F *About Point O* :** Applying Eq. 4–7, we have

$$\mathbf{M}_O = \mathbf{r}_{OA} \times \mathbf{F}$$
$$= \begin{vmatrix} \mathbf{i} & \mathbf{j} & \mathbf{k} \\ -3 & -7 & 4 \\ 60 & -30 & -20 \end{vmatrix}$$

$$= \{260\mathbf{i} + 180\mathbf{j} + 510\mathbf{k}\} \text{ N} \cdot \text{m} \qquad \textbf{Ans}$$

***4-36.** Determine the moment of the force at A about point P. Express the result as a Cartesian vector.

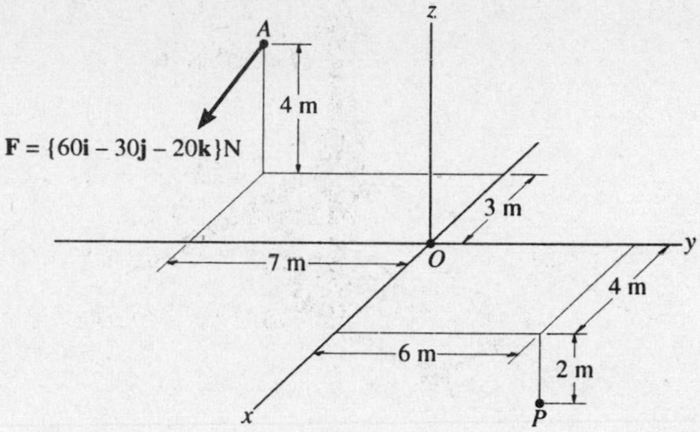

Position Vector :

$$\mathbf{r}_{PA} = \{(-3-4)\mathbf{i}+(-7-6)\mathbf{j}+[4-(-2)]\mathbf{k}\}\ \text{m}$$
$$= \{-7\mathbf{i}-13\mathbf{j}+6\mathbf{k}\}\ \text{m}$$

***Moment of Force* F *About Point O* :** Applying Eq. 4 – 7, we have

$$\mathbf{M}_O = \mathbf{r}_{OA} \times \mathbf{F}$$
$$= \begin{vmatrix} \mathbf{i} & \mathbf{j} & \mathbf{k} \\ -7 & -13 & 6 \\ 60 & -30 & -20 \end{vmatrix}$$
$$= \{440\mathbf{i}+220\mathbf{j}+990\mathbf{k}\}\ \text{N}\cdot\text{m} \qquad \textbf{Ans}$$

4-37. If $a = 3$ in., $b = 6$ in., and $c = 2$ in., determine the moment of **F** about point P.

$$\mathbf{M}_P = \begin{vmatrix} \mathbf{i} & \mathbf{j} & \mathbf{k} \\ 3 & 6 & -2 \\ 3 & 2 & -1 \end{vmatrix} = \{-2\mathbf{i}-3\mathbf{j}-12\mathbf{k}\}\ \text{lb}\cdot\text{in.} \qquad \textbf{Ans}$$

4-38. The applied force **F** creates a moment about point P of $\mathbf{M}_P = \{-1\mathbf{i} - 3\mathbf{j} - 9\mathbf{k}\}$ lb·in. If $a = 3$ in., determine the dimensions b and c of the block.

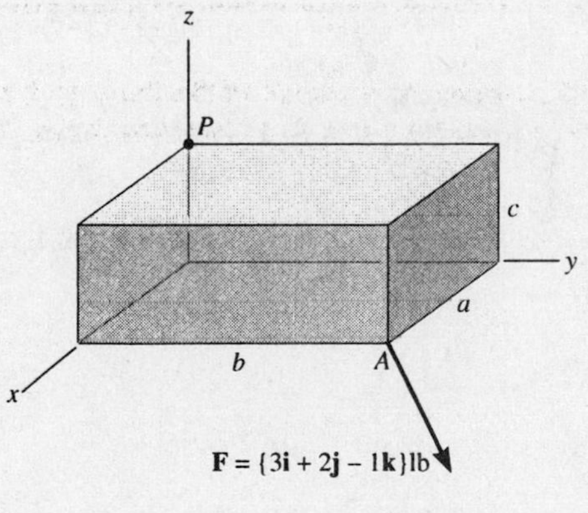

$$\mathbf{r}_{PA} = a\mathbf{i} + b\mathbf{j} - c\mathbf{k}$$

$$\mathbf{M}_P = \mathbf{r}_{PA} \times \mathbf{F}$$

$$-1\mathbf{i} - 3\mathbf{j} - 9\mathbf{k} = \begin{vmatrix} \mathbf{i} & \mathbf{j} & \mathbf{k} \\ 3 & b & -c \\ 3 & 2 & -1 \end{vmatrix}$$

Expand and equate the i, j, and k components,

$$-1 = -b + 2c$$

$$-3 = 3 - 3c$$

$$-9 = 6 - 3b$$

Solving;

$b = 5$ in. **Ans** $\qquad c = 2$ in. **Ans**

4-39. Determine the moment created by the force $\mathbf{F} = \{50\mathbf{i} + 100\mathbf{j} - 50\mathbf{k}\}$ N acting at D, about each of the joints at B and C.

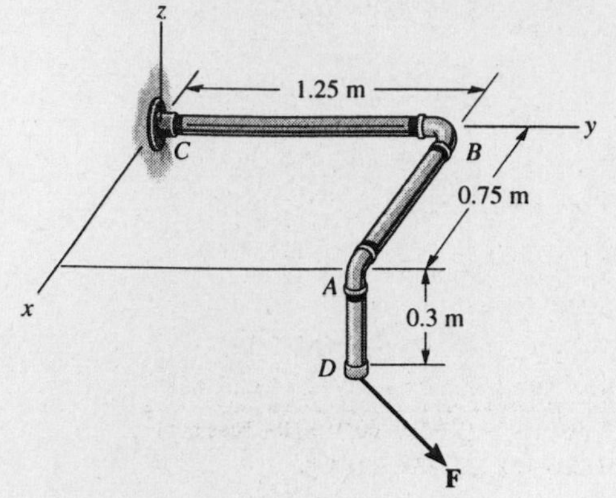

Position Vector :

$$\mathbf{r}_{BD} = \{(0.75-0)\mathbf{i}+(1.25-1.25)\mathbf{j}+(-0.3-0)\mathbf{k}\}\text{ m}$$
$$= \{0.75\mathbf{i}-0.3\mathbf{k}\}\text{ m}$$

$$\mathbf{r}_{CD} = \{(0.75-0)\mathbf{i}+(1.25-0)\mathbf{j}+(-0.3-0)\mathbf{k}\}\text{ m}$$
$$= \{0.75\mathbf{i}+1.25\mathbf{j}-0.3\mathbf{k}\}\text{ m}$$

Moment of Force* F *About Point B and C : Applying Eq. 4–7, we have

$$\mathbf{M}_B = \mathbf{r}_{BD}\times\mathbf{F} = \begin{vmatrix} \mathbf{i} & \mathbf{j} & \mathbf{k} \\ 0.75 & 0 & -0.3 \\ 50 & 100 & -50 \end{vmatrix}$$

$$= \{30.0\mathbf{i}+22.5\mathbf{j}+75.0\mathbf{k}\}\ \text{N}\cdot\text{m} \qquad \textbf{Ans}$$

$$\mathbf{M}_C = \mathbf{r}_{CD}\times\mathbf{F} = \begin{vmatrix} \mathbf{i} & \mathbf{j} & \mathbf{k} \\ 0.75 & 1.25 & -0.3 \\ 50 & 100 & -50 \end{vmatrix}$$

$$= \{-32.5\mathbf{i}+22.5\mathbf{j}+12.5\mathbf{k}\}\ \text{N}\cdot\text{m} \qquad \textbf{Ans}$$

***4-40.** The curved rod has a radius of 5 ft. If a force of 60 lb acts at its end as shown, determine the moment of this force about point C.

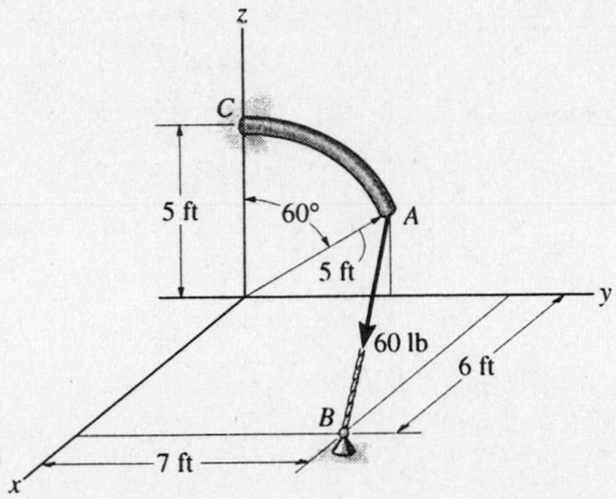

Position Vector and Force Vector :

$$\mathbf{r}_{CA} = \{(5\sin 60° - 0)\mathbf{j} + (5\cos 60° - 5)\mathbf{k}\}\ \text{m}$$
$$= \{4.330\mathbf{j} - 2.50\mathbf{k}\}\ \text{m}$$

$$\mathbf{F}_{AB} = 60\left(\frac{(6-0)\mathbf{i} + (7 - 5\sin 60°)\mathbf{j} + (0 - 5\cos 60°)\mathbf{k}}{\sqrt{(6-0)^2 + (7 - 5\sin 60°)^2 + (0 - 5\cos 60°)^2}}\right)\ \text{lb}$$
$$= \{51.231\mathbf{i} + 22.797\mathbf{j} - 21.346\mathbf{k}\}\ \text{lb}$$

Moment of Force $\mathbf{F}_{AB}$ About Point C : Applying Eq. 4 – 7, we have

$$\mathbf{M}_C = \mathbf{r}_{CA} \times \mathbf{F}_{AB}$$
$$= \begin{vmatrix} \mathbf{i} & \mathbf{j} & \mathbf{k} \\ 0 & 4.330 & -2.50 \\ 51.231 & 22.797 & -21.346 \end{vmatrix}$$

$$= \{-35.4\mathbf{i} - 128\mathbf{j} - 222\mathbf{k}\}\ \text{lb}\cdot\text{ft}$$ **Ans**

4-41. Determine the smallest force F that must be applied to the rope, when held in the direction shown, in order to cause the pole to break at its base O. This requires a moment of $M = 900$ N·m to be developed at O.

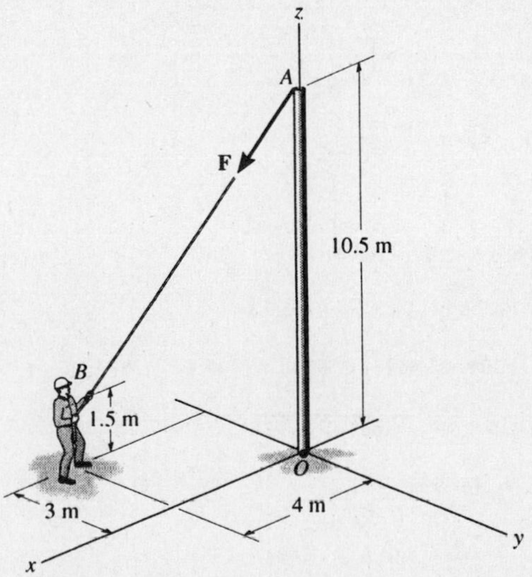

$$\mathbf{F} = F\left(\frac{4\mathbf{i} - 3\mathbf{j} - 9\mathbf{k}}{\sqrt{(4)^2 + (-3)^2 + (-9)^2}}\right)$$

$$\mathbf{F} = F(0.3885\,\mathbf{i} - 0.29139\,\mathbf{j} - 0.87416\,\mathbf{k})$$

$$\mathbf{M}_O = F\begin{vmatrix} \mathbf{i} & \mathbf{j} & \mathbf{k} \\ 0 & 0 & 10.5 \\ 0.3885 & -0.29139 & -0.87416 \end{vmatrix}$$

$$\mathbf{M}_O = (3.05955\,\mathbf{i} + 4.07940\,\mathbf{j})F$$

$$F = \frac{M_O}{\sqrt{(3.05955)^2 + (4.07940)^2}} = \frac{900}{5.09925} = 176\ \text{N}$$ **Ans**

4-42. A force **F** having a magnitude of $F = 100$ N acts along the diagonal of the parallelepiped. Determine the moment of **F** about point A, using $\mathbf{M}_A = \mathbf{r}_B \times \mathbf{F}$ and $\mathbf{M}_A = \mathbf{r}_C \times \mathbf{F}$.

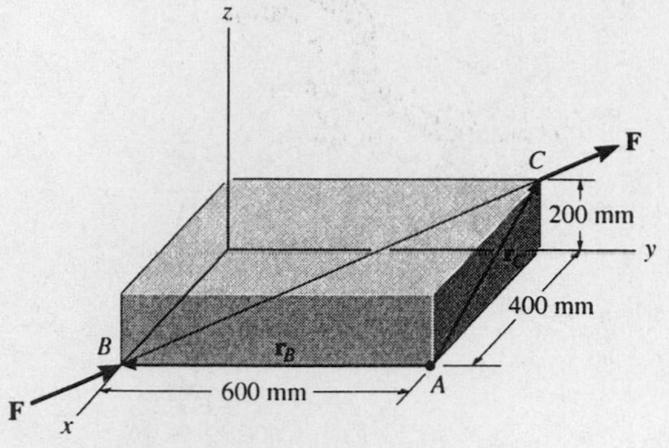

$$\mathbf{F} = 100\left(\frac{-0.4\mathbf{i} + 0.6\mathbf{j} + 0.2\mathbf{k}}{0.7483}\right)$$

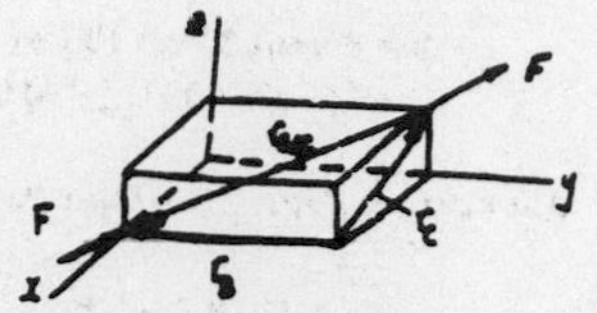

$$\mathbf{F} = \{-53.5\mathbf{i} + 80.2\mathbf{j} + 26.7\mathbf{k}\}\ \text{N}$$

$$\mathbf{M}_A = \mathbf{r}_B \times \mathbf{F} = \begin{vmatrix} \mathbf{i} & \mathbf{j} & \mathbf{k} \\ 0 & -0.6 & 0 \\ -53.5 & 80.2 & 26.7 \end{vmatrix} = \{-16.0\mathbf{i} - 32.1\mathbf{k}\}\ \text{N}\cdot\text{m} \qquad \textbf{Ans}$$

Also,

$$\mathbf{M}_A = \mathbf{r}_C \times \mathbf{F} = \begin{vmatrix} \mathbf{i} & \mathbf{j} & \mathbf{k} \\ -0.4 & 0 & 0.2 \\ -53.5 & 80.2 & 26.7 \end{vmatrix} = \{-16.0\mathbf{i} - 32.1\mathbf{k}\}\ \text{N}\cdot\text{m} \qquad \textbf{Ans}$$

4-43. The 5-m-long boom AB lies in the y–z plane. If the cable exerts a force of $F = 500$ N at B, determine the moment of this force about point A. What is the shortest distance from point A to the cable?

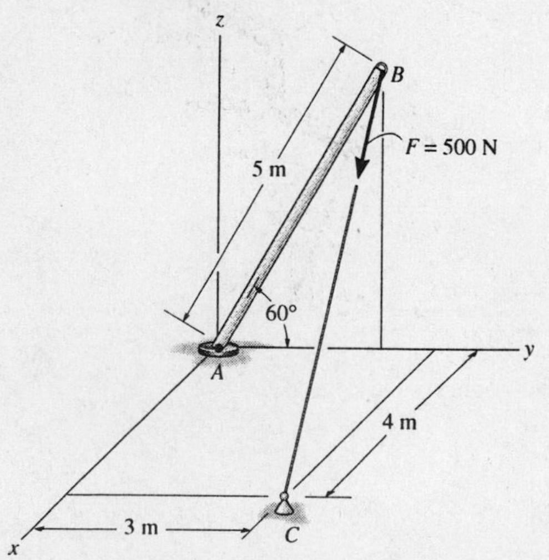

$$\mathbf{F} = 500\left(\frac{4\mathbf{i} + (3 - 5\cos 60°)\mathbf{j} - 5\sin 60°\,\mathbf{k}}{5.92}\right)$$

$$= \{338.1\mathbf{i} + 42.3\mathbf{j} - 366.0\mathbf{k}\}\ \text{N}$$

$$\mathbf{r}_C = \{4\mathbf{i} + 3\mathbf{j}\}\ \text{m}$$

$$\mathbf{M}_A = \begin{vmatrix} \mathbf{i} & \mathbf{j} & \mathbf{k} \\ 4 & 3 & 0 \\ 338.1 & 42.3 & -366.0 \end{vmatrix}$$

$$\mathbf{M}_A = -1097.9\mathbf{i} + 1463.8\mathbf{j} - 845.2\mathbf{k}$$

$$\mathbf{M}_A = \{-1.10\mathbf{i} + 1.46\mathbf{j} - 0.845\mathbf{k}\}\ \text{kN}\cdot\text{m} \qquad \textbf{Ans}$$

$$M_A = \sqrt{(-1097.9)^2 + (1463.8)^2 + (-845.2)^2} = 2015.6\ \text{N}\cdot\text{m}$$

Since $M_A = Fd$ then

$$d = \frac{M_A}{F} = \frac{2015.6}{500} = 4.03\ \text{m} \qquad \textbf{Ans}$$

*4-44.** The pipe assembly is subjected to the 80-N force. Determine the moment of this force about point *A*.

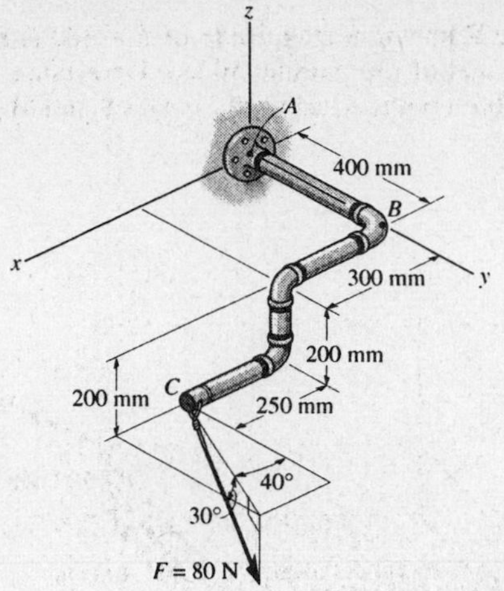

Position Vector And Force Vector :

$$\mathbf{r}_{AC} = \{(0.55-0)\mathbf{i}+(0.4-0)\mathbf{j}+(-0.2-0)\mathbf{k}\}\text{ m}$$
$$= \{0.55\mathbf{i}+0.4\mathbf{j}-0.2\mathbf{k}\}\text{ m}$$

$$\mathbf{F} = 80(\cos 30°\sin 40°\mathbf{i}+\cos 30°\cos 40°\mathbf{j}-\sin 30°\mathbf{k})\text{ N}$$
$$= \{44.53\mathbf{i}+53.07\mathbf{j}-40.0\mathbf{k}\}\text{ N}$$

Moment of Force* F *About Point A : Applying Eq.4 – 7, we have

$$\mathbf{M}_A = \mathbf{r}_{AC}\times\mathbf{F} = \begin{vmatrix} \mathbf{i} & \mathbf{j} & \mathbf{k} \\ 0.55 & 0.4 & -0.2 \\ 44.53 & 53.07 & -40.0 \end{vmatrix}$$

$$= \{-5.39\mathbf{i}+13.1\mathbf{j}+11.4\mathbf{k}\}\text{ N}\cdot\text{m} \qquad \textbf{Ans}$$

4-45. The pipe assembly is subjected to the 80-N force. Determine the moment of this force about point *B*.

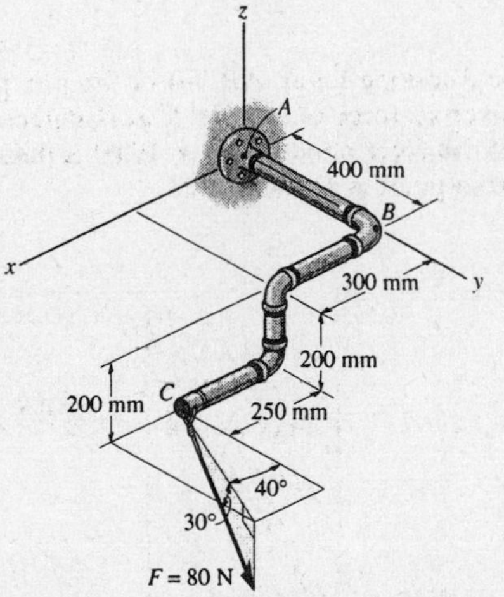

Position Vector And Force Vector :

$$\mathbf{r}_{BC} = \{(0.55-0)\mathbf{i}+(0.4-0.4)\mathbf{j}+(-0.2-0)\mathbf{k}\}\text{ m}$$
$$= \{0.55\mathbf{i}-0.2\mathbf{k}\}\text{ m}$$

$$\mathbf{F} = 80(\cos 30°\sin 40°\mathbf{i}+\cos 30°\cos 40°\mathbf{j}-\sin 30°\mathbf{k})\text{ N}$$
$$= \{44.53\mathbf{i}+53.07\mathbf{j}-40.0\mathbf{k}\}\text{ N}$$

Moment of Force* F *About Point B : Applying Eq.4 – 7, we have

$$\mathbf{M}_B = \mathbf{r}_{BC}\times\mathbf{F} = \begin{vmatrix} \mathbf{i} & \mathbf{j} & \mathbf{k} \\ 0.55 & 0 & -0.2 \\ 44.53 & 53.07 & -40.0 \end{vmatrix}$$

$$= \{10.6\mathbf{i}+13.1\mathbf{j}+29.2\mathbf{k}\}\text{ N}\cdot\text{m} \qquad \textbf{Ans}$$

4-46. Strut AB of the 1-m-diameter hatch door exerts a force of 450 N on point B. Determine the moment of this force about point O.

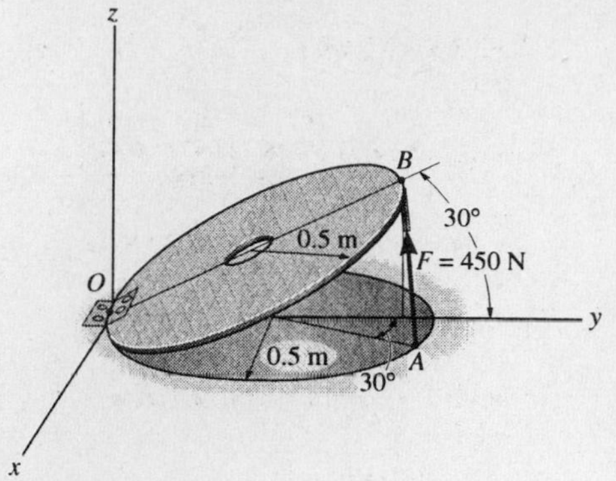

Position Vector And Force Vector :

$$\mathbf{r}_{OB} = \{(0-0)\,\mathbf{i} + (1\cos 30° - 0)\,\mathbf{j} + (1\sin 30° - 0)\,\mathbf{k}\}\ \text{m}$$
$$= \{0.8660\mathbf{j} + 0.5\mathbf{k}\}\ \text{m}$$

$$\mathbf{r}_{OA} = \{(0.5\sin 30° - 0)\,\mathbf{i} + (0.5 + 0.5\cos 30° - 0)\,\mathbf{j} + (0-0)\,\mathbf{k}\}\ \text{m}$$
$$= \{0.250\mathbf{i} + 0.9330\mathbf{j}\}\ \text{m}$$

$$\mathbf{F} = 450\left(\frac{(0-0.5\sin 30°)\,\mathbf{i} + [1\cos 30° - (0.5+0.5\cos 30°)]\,\mathbf{j} + (1\sin 30° - 0)\,\mathbf{k}}{\sqrt{(0-0.5\sin 30°)^2 + [1\cos 30° - (0.5+0.5\cos 30°)]^2 + (1\sin 30° - 0)^2}}\right)\text{N}$$
$$= \{-199.82\mathbf{i} - 53.54\mathbf{j} + 399.63\mathbf{k}\}\ \text{N}$$

Moment of Force* F *About Point O : Applying Eq. 4 − 7, we have

$$\mathbf{M}_O = \mathbf{r}_{OB} \times \mathbf{F}$$
$$= \begin{vmatrix} \mathbf{i} & \mathbf{j} & \mathbf{k} \\ 0 & 0.8660 & 0.5 \\ -199.82 & -53.54 & 399.63 \end{vmatrix}$$

$$= \{373\mathbf{i} - 99.9\mathbf{j} + 173\mathbf{k}\}\ \text{N}\cdot\text{m} \qquad \textbf{Ans}$$

Or

$$\mathbf{M}_O = \mathbf{r}_{OA} \times \mathbf{F}$$
$$= \begin{vmatrix} \mathbf{i} & \mathbf{j} & \mathbf{k} \\ 0.250 & 0.9330 & 0 \\ -199.82 & -53.54 & 399.63 \end{vmatrix}$$

$$= \{373\mathbf{i} - 99.9\mathbf{j} + 173\mathbf{k}\}\ \text{N}\cdot\text{m}$$

4-47. A 20-N horizontal force is applied perpendicular to the handle of the socket wrench. Determine the magnitude and direction of the moment created by this force about point O.

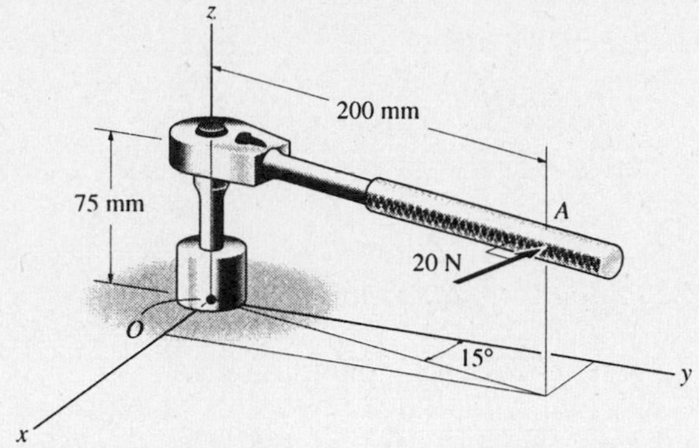

$\mathbf{r}_A = 0.2 \sin 15°\,\mathbf{i} + 0.2 \cos 15°\,\mathbf{j} + 0.075\,\mathbf{k}$

$= 0.05176\,\mathbf{i} + 0.1932\,\mathbf{j} + 0.075\,\mathbf{k}$

$\mathbf{F} = -20 \cos 15°\,\mathbf{i} + 20 \sin 15°\,\mathbf{j}$

$= -19.32\,\mathbf{i} + 5.176\,\mathbf{j}$

$$\mathbf{M}_O = \mathbf{r}_A \times \mathbf{F} = \begin{vmatrix} \mathbf{i} & \mathbf{j} & \mathbf{k} \\ 0.05176 & 0.1932 & 0.075 \\ -19.32 & 5.176 & 0 \end{vmatrix}$$

$= \{-0.3882\,\mathbf{i} - 1.449\,\mathbf{j} + 4.00\,\mathbf{k}\}\ \text{N}\cdot\text{m}$

$M_O = 4.272 = 4.27\ \text{N}\cdot\text{m}$ **Ans**

$\alpha = \cos^{-1}\left(\frac{-0.3882}{4.272}\right) = 95.2°$ **Ans**

$\beta = \cos^{-1}\left(\frac{-1.449}{4.272}\right) = 110°$ **Ans**

$\gamma = \cos^{-1}\left(\frac{4}{4.272}\right) = 20.6°$ **Ans**

***4-48.** A force of $\mathbf{F} = \{6\mathbf{i} - 2\mathbf{j} + 1\mathbf{k}\}$ kN produces a moment of $\mathbf{M}_O = \{4\mathbf{i} + 5\mathbf{j} - 14\mathbf{k}\}$ kN·m about the origin of coordinates, point O. If the force acts at a point having an x coordinate of $x = 1$ m, determine the y and z coordinates.

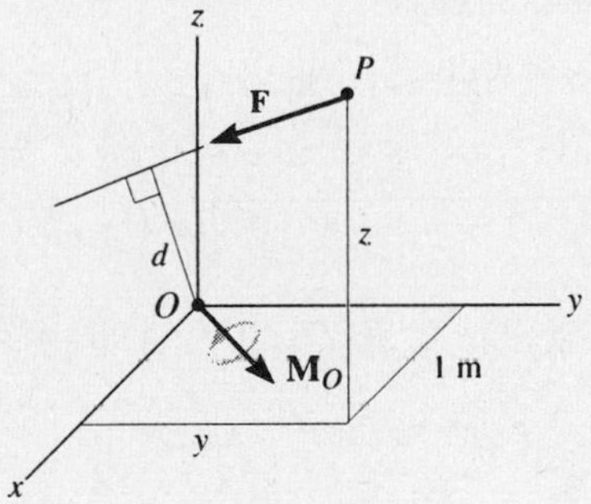

$\mathbf{M}_O = \mathbf{r} \times \mathbf{F}$

$$4\mathbf{i} + 5\mathbf{j} - 14\mathbf{k} = \begin{vmatrix} \mathbf{i} & \mathbf{j} & \mathbf{k} \\ 1 & y & z \\ 6 & -2 & 1 \end{vmatrix}$$

$4 = y + 2z$

$5 = -1 + 6z$

$-14 = -2 - 6y$

$y = 2$ m **Ans**

$z = 1$ m **Ans**

4-49. The force $\mathbf{F} = \{6\mathbf{i} + 8\mathbf{j} + 10\mathbf{k}\}$ N creates a moment about point O of $\mathbf{M}_O = \{-14\mathbf{i} + 8\mathbf{j} + 2\mathbf{k}\}$ N·m. If the force passes through a point having an x coordinate of 1 m, determine the y and z coordinates of the point. Also, realizing that $M_O = Fd$, determine the perpendicular distance d from point O to the line of action of **F**.

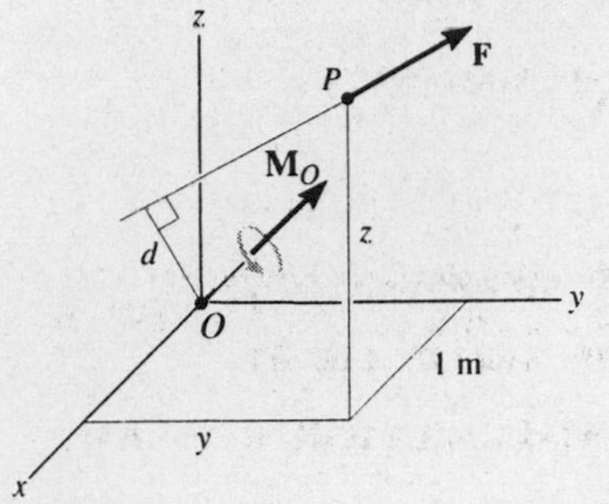

$$-14\mathbf{i} + 8\mathbf{j} + 2\mathbf{k} = \begin{vmatrix} \mathbf{i} & \mathbf{j} & \mathbf{k} \\ 1 & y & z \\ 6 & 8 & 10 \end{vmatrix}$$

$$-14 = 10y - 8z$$

$$8 = -10 + 6z$$

$$2 = 8 - 6y$$

$y = 1$ m **Ans**

$z = 3$ m **Ans**

$$M_O = \sqrt{(-14)^2 + (8)^2 + (2)^2} = 16.25 \text{ N}\cdot\text{m}$$

$$F = \sqrt{(6)^2 + (8)^2 + (10)^2} = 14.14 \text{ N}$$

$$d = \frac{16.25}{14.14} = 1.15 \text{ m}$$ **Ans**

■**4-50.** Using a ring collar the 75-N force can act in the vertical plane at various angles θ. Determine the magnitude of the moment it produces about point A, plot the result of M (ordinate) versus θ (abscissa) for $0° \leq \theta \leq 180°$, and specify the angles that give the maximum and minimum moment.

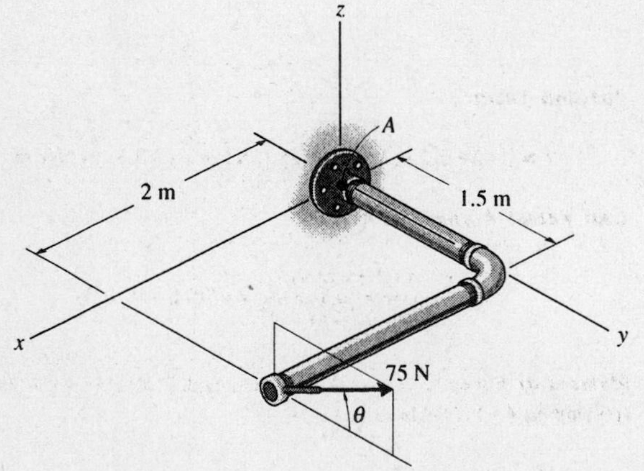

$$\mathbf{M}_A = \begin{vmatrix} \mathbf{i} & \mathbf{j} & \mathbf{k} \\ 2 & 1.5 & 0 \\ 0 & 75\cos\theta & 75\sin\theta \end{vmatrix}$$

$$= 112.5\sin\theta\,\mathbf{i} - 150\sin\theta\,\mathbf{j} + 150\cos\theta\,\mathbf{k}$$

$$M_A = \sqrt{(112.5\sin\theta)^2 + (-150\sin\theta)^2 + (150\cos\theta)^2} = \sqrt{12\,656.25\sin^2\theta + 22\,500}$$

$$\frac{dM_A}{d\theta} = \frac{1}{2}(12\,656.25\sin^2\theta + 22\,500)^{-\frac{1}{2}}(12\,656.25)(2\sin\theta\cos\theta) = 0$$

$\sin\theta\cos\theta = 0;\quad \theta = 0°, 90°, 180°$ **Ans**

$M_{max} = 187.5$ N·m at $\theta = 90°$

$M_{min} = 150$ N·m at $\theta = 0°, 180°$

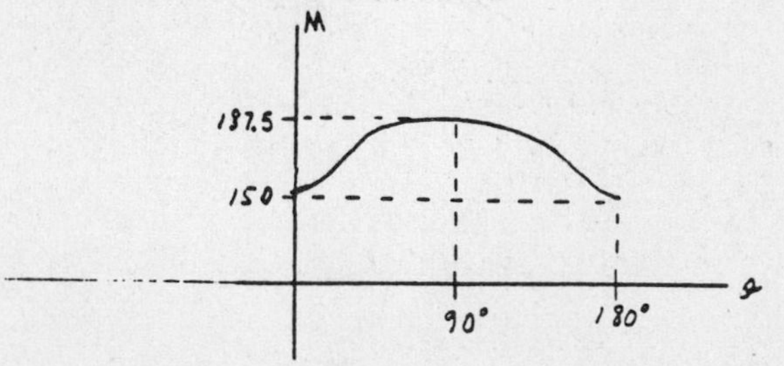

4-51. Determine the moment of the force **F** about the *aa* axis. Express the result as a Cartesian vector.

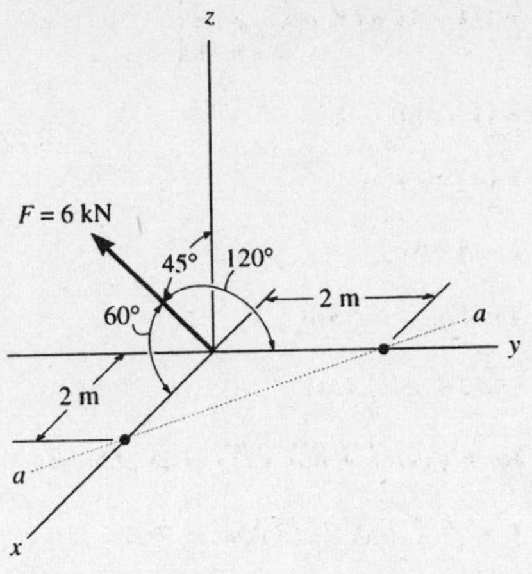

$$\mathbf{u}_{aa} = \frac{1}{\sqrt{2}}\mathbf{i} - \frac{1}{\sqrt{2}}\mathbf{j} = 0.707\,\mathbf{i} - 0.707\,\mathbf{j}$$

$$\mathbf{r} = -2\,\mathbf{i}$$

$$M_{aa} = \begin{vmatrix} 0.707 & -0.707 & 0 \\ -2 & 0 & 0 \\ 6\cos 60° & 6\cos 120° & 6\cos 45° \end{vmatrix} = -6\text{ kN}\cdot\text{m}$$

$$\mathbf{M}_{aa} = -6(\mathbf{u}_{aa}) = \{-4.24\,\mathbf{i} + 4.24\,\mathbf{j}\}\text{ kN}\cdot\text{m} \qquad \textbf{Ans}$$

***4-52.** Determine the moment of the force **F** about the *aa* axis. Express the result as a Cartesian vector.

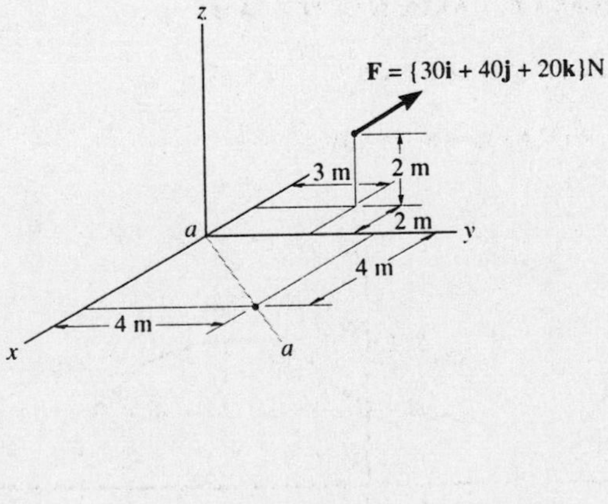

Position Vector :

$$\mathbf{r} = \{(-2-0)\,\mathbf{i} + (3-0)\,\mathbf{j} + (2-0)\,\mathbf{k}\}\text{ m} = \{-2\mathbf{i} + 3\mathbf{j} + 2\mathbf{k}\}\text{ m}$$

Unit Vector Along a − a Axis :

$$\mathbf{u}_{aa} = \frac{(4-0)\,\mathbf{i} + (4-0)\,\mathbf{j}}{\sqrt{(4-0)^2 + (4-0)^2}} = 0.7071\mathbf{i} + 0.7071\mathbf{j}$$

Moment of Force F About a − a Axis : With $\mathbf{F} = \{30\mathbf{i} + 40\mathbf{j} + 20\mathbf{k}\}$ N, applying Eq. 4 − 11, we have

$$M_{aa} = \mathbf{u}_{aa} \cdot (\mathbf{r} \times \mathbf{F})$$

$$= \begin{vmatrix} 0.7071 & 0.7071 & 0 \\ -2 & 3 & 2 \\ 30 & 40 & 20 \end{vmatrix}$$

$$= 0.7071[3(20) - 40(2)] - 0.7071[(-2)(20) - 30(2)] + 0$$

$$= 56.6\text{ N}\cdot\text{m} \qquad \text{Ans}$$

4-53. Determine the resultant moment of the two forces about the *aa* axis. Express the result as a Cartesian vector.

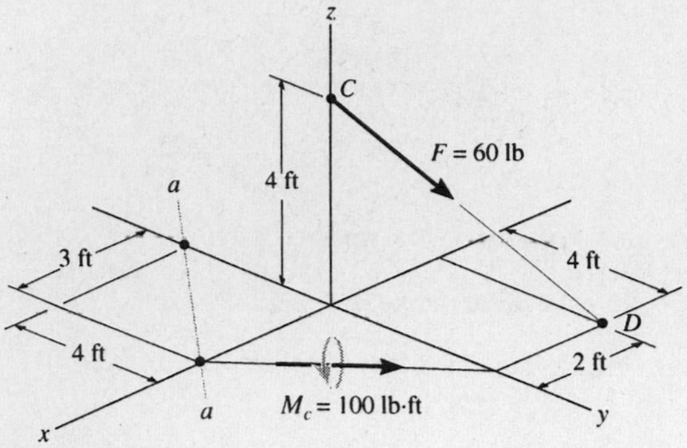

$$\mathbf{F}_{CD} = 60\text{ lb}\left(-\frac{2}{6}\mathbf{i} + \frac{4}{6}\mathbf{j} - \frac{4}{6}\mathbf{k}\right)$$

$$= \{-20\mathbf{i} + 40\mathbf{j} - 40\mathbf{k}\}\text{ lb}$$

$$\mathbf{M}_c = -100\left(\frac{3}{5}\right)\mathbf{i} + 100\left(\frac{4}{5}\right)\mathbf{j}$$

$$= \{-60\mathbf{i} + 80\mathbf{j}\}\text{ lb}\cdot\text{ft}$$

$$M_a = \begin{vmatrix} 0.6 & 0.8 & 0 \\ -3 & 0 & 4 \\ -20 & 40 & -40 \end{vmatrix} + (-60\mathbf{i} + 80\mathbf{j})\cdot(0.6\mathbf{i} + 0.8\mathbf{j})$$

$$= 0.6(-160) - 0.8(200) + 0 - 60(0.6) + 80(0.8)$$

$$= -228\text{ lb}\cdot\text{ ft}$$

$$\mathbf{M}_a = -228(\mathbf{u}_a) = -228(0.6)\mathbf{i} - 228(0.8)\mathbf{j}$$

$$= \{-137\mathbf{i} - 182\mathbf{j}\}\text{ lb}\cdot\text{ft} \qquad \textbf{Ans}$$

4-54. Determine the magnitude of the moment of each of the three forces about the axis AB. Solve the problem (a) using a Cartesian vector approach and (b) using a scalar approach.

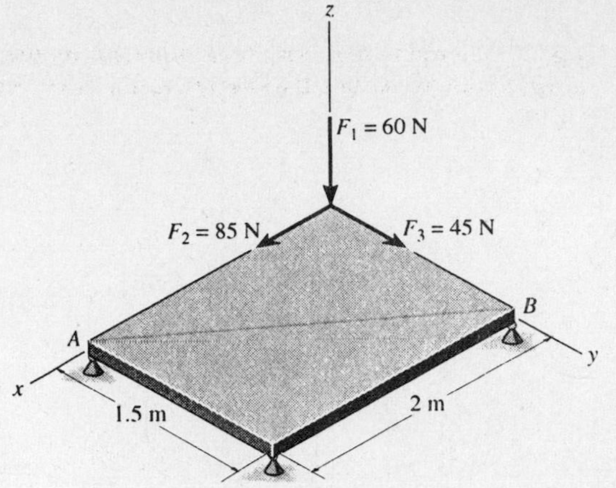

a) *Vector Analysis*

Position Vector and Force Vector :

$$\mathbf{r}_1 = \{-1.5\mathbf{j}\}\text{ m} \qquad \mathbf{r}_2 = \mathbf{r}_3 = 0$$

$$\mathbf{F}_1 = \{-60\mathbf{k}\}\text{ N} \qquad \mathbf{F}_2 = \{85\mathbf{i}\}\text{ N} \qquad \mathbf{F}_3 = \{45\mathbf{j}\}\text{ N}$$

Unit Vector Along AB Axis :

$$\mathbf{u}_{AB} = \frac{(2-0)\mathbf{i} + (0-1.5)\mathbf{j}}{\sqrt{(2-0)^2 + (0-1.5)^2}} = 0.8\mathbf{i} - 0.6\mathbf{j}$$

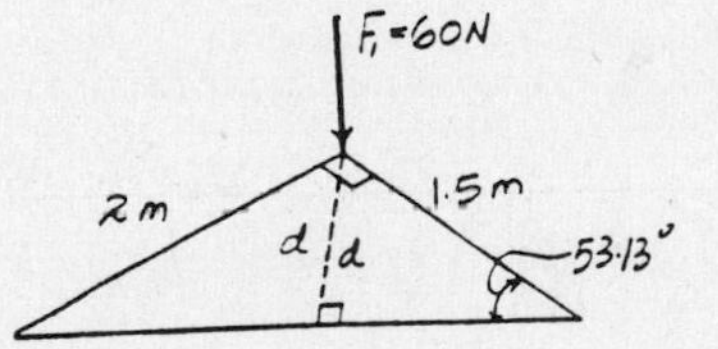

Moment of Each Force About AB Axis : Applying Eq. 4 – 11, we have

$$(M_{AB})_1 = \mathbf{u}_{AB} \cdot (\mathbf{r}_1 \times \mathbf{F}_1)$$

$$= \begin{vmatrix} 0.8 & -0.6 & 0 \\ 0 & -1.5 & 0 \\ 0 & 0 & -60 \end{vmatrix}$$

$$= 0.8[(-1.5)(-60) - 0] - 0 + 0 = 72.0\text{ N}\cdot\text{m} \qquad \textbf{Ans}$$

$$(M_{AB})_2 = \mathbf{u}_{AB} \cdot (\mathbf{r}_2 \times \mathbf{F}_2)$$

$$= \begin{vmatrix} 0.8 & -0.6 & 0 \\ 0 & 0 & 0 \\ 85 & 0 & 0 \end{vmatrix} = 0 \qquad \textbf{Ans}$$

$$(M_{AB})_3 = \mathbf{u}_{AB} \cdot (\mathbf{r}_3 \times \mathbf{F}_3)$$

$$= \begin{vmatrix} 0.8 & -0.6 & 0 \\ 0 & 0 & 0 \\ 0 & 45 & 0 \end{vmatrix} = 0 \qquad \textbf{Ans}$$

b) *Scalar Analysis :* Since moment arm from force $\mathbf{F}_2$ and $\mathbf{F}_3$ is equal to zero, Hence

$$(M_{AB})_2 = (M_{AB})_3 = 0 \qquad \textbf{Ans}$$

Moment arm d from force $\mathbf{F}_1$ to axis AB is $d = 1.5\sin 53.13° = 1.20$ m, Hence

$$(M_{AB})_1 = F_1 d = 60(1.20) = 72.0\text{ N}\cdot\text{m} \qquad \textbf{Ans}$$

4-55. The chain AB exerts a force of 20 lb on the door at B. Determine the magnitude of the moment of this force along the hinged axis x of the door.

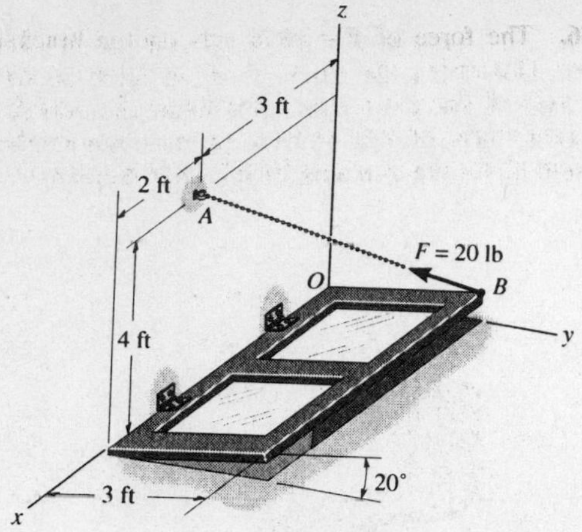

Position Vector and Force Vector :

$$\mathbf{r}_{OA} = \{(3-0)\mathbf{i}+(4-0)\mathbf{k}\}\ \text{ft} = \{3\mathbf{i}+4\mathbf{k}\}\ \text{ft}$$

$$\mathbf{r}_{OB} = \{(0-0)\mathbf{i}+(3\cos 20^\circ-0)\mathbf{j}+(3\sin 20^\circ-0)\mathbf{k}\}\ \text{ft} = \{2.8191\mathbf{j}+1.0261\mathbf{k}\}\ \text{ft}$$

$$\mathbf{F} = 20\left(\frac{(3-0)\mathbf{i}+(0-3\cos 20^\circ)\mathbf{j}+(4-3\sin 20^\circ)\mathbf{k}}{\sqrt{(3-0)^2+(0-3\cos 20^\circ)^2+(4-3\sin 20^\circ)^2}}\right)\text{lb} = \{11.814\mathbf{i}-11.102\mathbf{j}+11.712\mathbf{k}\}\ \text{lb}$$

Moment of Force* F *About x Axis : The unit vector along the x axis is $\mathbf{i}$. Applying Eq. 4 – 11, we have

$$M_x = \mathbf{i}\cdot(\mathbf{r}_{OA}\times\mathbf{F}) = \begin{vmatrix} 1 & 0 & 0 \\ 3 & 0 & 4 \\ 11.814 & -11.102 & 11.712 \end{vmatrix}$$

$$= 1[0(11.712)-(-11.102)(4)]-0+0$$

$$= 44.4\ \text{lb}\cdot\text{ft}$$ **Ans**

Or

$$M_x = \mathbf{i}\cdot(\mathbf{r}_{OB}\times\mathbf{F}) = \begin{vmatrix} 1 & 0 & 0 \\ 0 & 2.8191 & 1.0261 \\ 11.814 & -11.102 & 11.712 \end{vmatrix}$$

$$= 1[2.8191(11.712)-(-11.102)(1.0261)]-0+0$$

$$= 44.4\ \text{lb}\cdot\text{ft}$$

*4-56. The force of $F = 30$ N acts on the bracket as shown. Determine the moment of the force about the a–a axis of the pipe. Also, determine the coordinate direction angles of F in order to produce the maximum moment about the a–a axis. What is this moment?

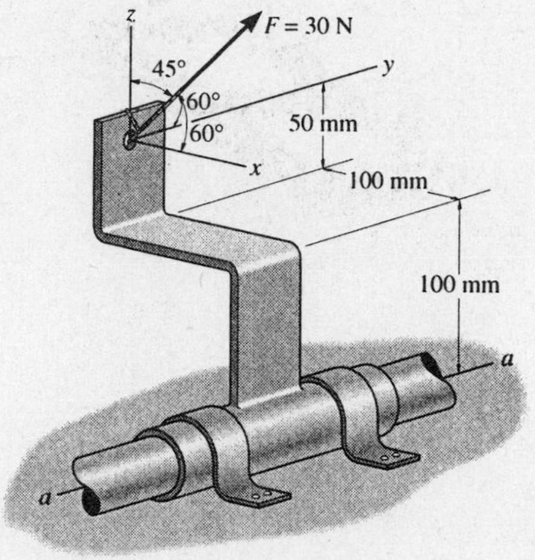

$\mathbf{F} = 30\,(\cos 60°\,\mathbf{i} + \cos 60°\,\mathbf{j} + \cos 45°\,\mathbf{k})$

$= \{15\,\mathbf{i} + 15\,\mathbf{j} + 21.21\,\mathbf{k}\}$ N

$\mathbf{r} = \{-0.1\,\mathbf{i} + 0.15\,\mathbf{k}\}$ m

$\mathbf{u} = \mathbf{j}$

$$M_a = \begin{vmatrix} 0 & 1 & 0 \\ -0.1 & 0 & 0.15 \\ 15 & 15 & 21.21 \end{vmatrix} = 4.37\ \text{N}\cdot\text{m} \quad \textbf{Ans}$$

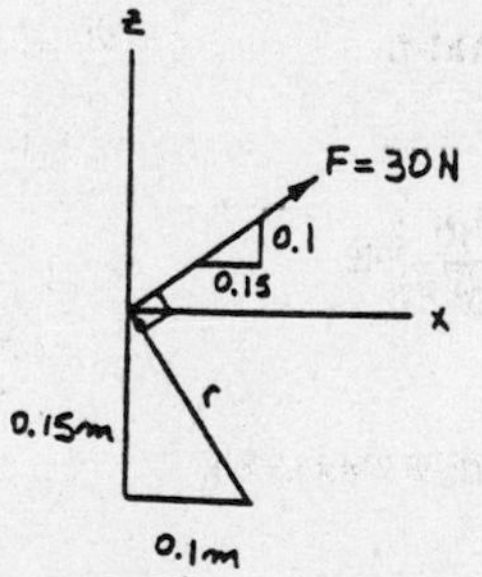

F must be perpendicular to **u** and **r**.

$$\mathbf{u}_F = \frac{0.15}{0.1803}\,\mathbf{i} + \frac{0.1}{0.1803}\,\mathbf{k}$$

$= 0.8321\,\mathbf{i} + 0.5547\,\mathbf{k}$

$\alpha = \cos^{-1} 0.8321 = 33.7°$ **Ans**

$\beta = \cos^{-1} 0 = 90°$ **Ans**

$\gamma = \cos^{-1} 0.5547 = 56.3°$ **Ans**

$M = 30\,(0.1803) = 5.41\ \text{N}\cdot\text{m}$ **Ans**

4-57. The tool is used to shut off gas valves that are difficult to access. If the force **F** is applied to the handle, determine the component of the moment created about the z axis of the valve.

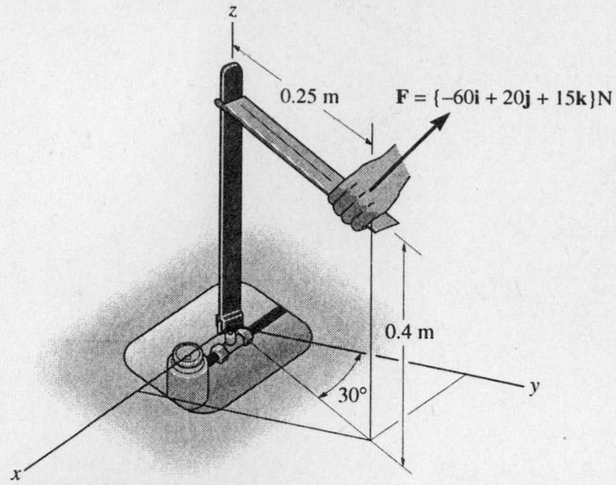

$\mathbf{u} = \mathbf{k}$

$\mathbf{r} = 0.25 \sin 30° \, \mathbf{i} + 0.25 \cos 30° \, \mathbf{j}$

$= 0.125 \, \mathbf{i} + 0.2165 \, \mathbf{j}$

$$M_z = \begin{vmatrix} 0 & 0 & 1 \\ 0.125 & 0.2165 & 0 \\ -60 & 20 & 15 \end{vmatrix} = 15.5 \text{ N} \cdot \text{m} \qquad \textbf{Ans}$$

4-58. The chain AB exerts a force of $F = 20$ lb on the door at B. Determine the moment of this force along the hinged axis x of the door.

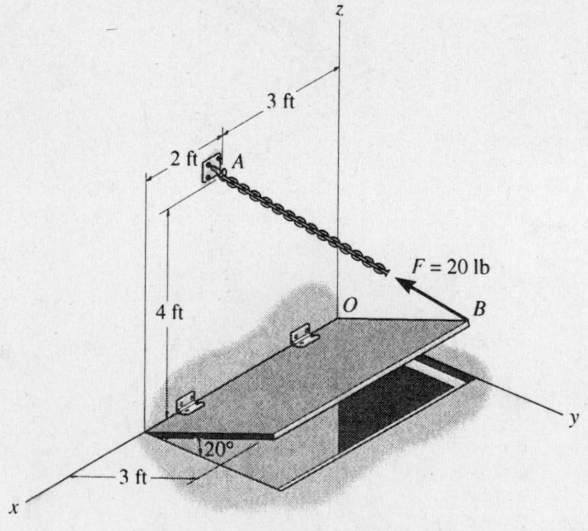

$\mathbf{r}_{BA} = 3\,\mathbf{i} - (3 \cos 20°)\,\mathbf{j} + (4 - 3 \sin 20°)\,\mathbf{k}$

$= 3\,\mathbf{i} - 2.8191\,\mathbf{j} + 2.9739\,\mathbf{k}$

$$\mathbf{F}_{BA} = 20\left(\frac{3}{5.0785}\mathbf{i} - \frac{2.8191}{5.0785}\mathbf{j} + \frac{2.9739}{5.0785}\mathbf{k}\right)$$

$= 11.814\,\mathbf{i} - 11.102\,\mathbf{j} + 11.712\,\mathbf{k}$

$\mathbf{r}_{OA} = 3\,\mathbf{i} + 4\,\mathbf{k}$

$\mathbf{u} = \mathbf{i}$

$$M_x = \begin{vmatrix} 1 & 0 & 0 \\ 3 & 0 & 4 \\ 11.814 & -11.102 & 11.712 \end{vmatrix} = 44.4 \text{ ft} \cdot \text{lb}$$

$\mathbf{M}_x = M_x \, \mathbf{i} = \{44.4\,\mathbf{i}\}$ ft · lb $\qquad$ **Ans**

4-59. Determine the magnitude of the moments of the force **F** about the x, y, and z axes. Solve the problem (a) using a Cartesian vector approach and (b) using a scalar approach.

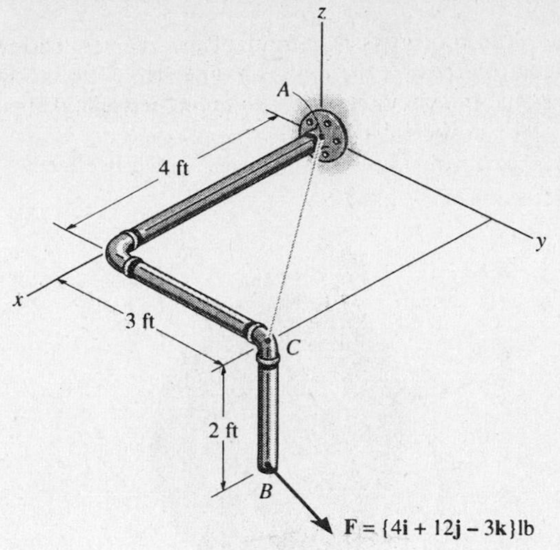

a) *Vector Analysis*

Position Vector :

$$\mathbf{r}_{AB} = \{(4-0)\mathbf{i}+(3-0)\mathbf{j}+(-2-0)\mathbf{k}\}\text{ ft} = \{4\mathbf{i}+3\mathbf{j}-2\mathbf{k}\}\text{ ft}$$

Moment of Force F About x, y and z Axes : The unit vectors along x, y and z axes are **i**, **j** and **k** respectively. Applying Eq.4 − 11, we have

$$M_x = \mathbf{i}\cdot(\mathbf{r}_{AB}\times\mathbf{F}) = \begin{vmatrix} 1 & 0 & 0 \\ 4 & 3 & -2 \\ 4 & 12 & -3 \end{vmatrix}$$

$$= 1[3(-3)-(12)(-2)]-0+0 = 15.0\text{ lb}\cdot\text{ft} \quad \textbf{Ans}$$

$$M_y = \mathbf{j}\cdot(\mathbf{r}_{AB}\times\mathbf{F}) = \begin{vmatrix} 0 & 1 & 0 \\ 4 & 3 & -2 \\ 4 & 12 & -3 \end{vmatrix}$$

$$= 0-1[4(-3)-(4)(-2)]+0 = 4.00\text{ lb}\cdot\text{ft} \quad \textbf{Ans}$$

$$M_z = \mathbf{k}\cdot(\mathbf{r}_{AB}\times\mathbf{F}) = \begin{vmatrix} 0 & 0 & 1 \\ 4 & 3 & -2 \\ 4 & 12 & -3 \end{vmatrix}$$

$$= 0-0+1[4(12)-4(3)] = 36.0\text{ lb}\cdot\text{ft} \quad \textbf{Ans}$$

b) *Scalar Analysis*

$M_x = \Sigma M_x;\quad M_x = 12(2)-3(3) = 15.0\text{ lb}\cdot\text{ft}$ **Ans**

$M_y = \Sigma M_y;\quad M_y = -4(2)+3(4) = 4.00\text{ lb}\cdot\text{ft}$ **Ans**

$M_z = \Sigma M_z;\quad M_z = -4(3)+12(4) = 36.0\text{ lb}\cdot\text{ft}$ **Ans**

***4-60.** Determine the moment of the force **F** about an axis extending between A and C. Express the result as a Cartesian vector.

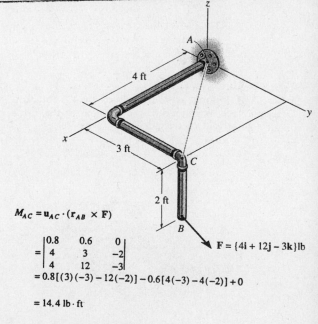

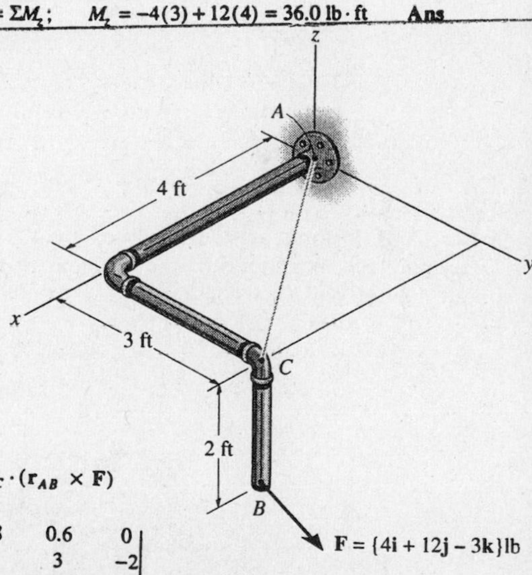

Position Vector :

$$\mathbf{r}_{CB} = \{-2\mathbf{k}\}\text{ ft}$$
$$\mathbf{r}_{AB} = \{(4-0)\mathbf{i}+(3-0)\mathbf{j}+(-2-0)\mathbf{k}\}\text{ ft} = \{4\mathbf{i}+3\mathbf{j}-2\mathbf{k}\}\text{ ft}$$

Unit Vector Along AC Axis :

$$\mathbf{u}_{AC} = \frac{(4-0)\mathbf{i}+(3-0)\mathbf{j}}{\sqrt{(4-0)^2+(3-0)^2}} = 0.8\mathbf{i}+0.6\mathbf{j}$$

Moment of Force F About AC Axis : With $\mathbf{F} = \{4\mathbf{i}+12\mathbf{j}-3\mathbf{k}\}$ lb, applying Eq.4 − 11, we have

$$M_{AC} = \mathbf{u}_{AC}\cdot(\mathbf{r}_{CB}\times\mathbf{F}) = \begin{vmatrix} 0.8 & 0.6 & 0 \\ 0 & 0 & -2 \\ 4 & 12 & -3 \end{vmatrix}$$

$$= 0.8[(0)(-3)-12(-2)]-0.6[0(-3)-4(-2)]+0$$

$$= 14.4\text{ lb}\cdot\text{ft}$$

Or

$$M_{AC} = \mathbf{u}_{AC}\cdot(\mathbf{r}_{AB}\times\mathbf{F}) = \begin{vmatrix} 0.8 & 0.6 & 0 \\ 4 & 3 & -2 \\ 4 & 12 & -3 \end{vmatrix}$$

$$= 0.8[(3)(-3)-12(-2)]-0.6[4(-3)-4(-2)]+0$$

$$= 14.4\text{ lb}\cdot\text{ft}$$

Expressing $\mathbf{M}_{AC}$ as a Cartesian vector yields

$$\mathbf{M}_{AC} = M_{AC}\mathbf{u}_{AC} = 14.4(0.8\mathbf{i}+0.6\mathbf{j}) = \{11.5\mathbf{i}+8.64\mathbf{j}\}\text{ lb}\cdot\text{ft} \quad \textbf{Ans}$$

4-61. The lug and box wrenches are used in combination to remove the lug nut from the wheel hub. If the applied force on the end of the box wrench is $\mathbf{F} = \{4\mathbf{i} - 12\mathbf{j} + 2\mathbf{k}\}$ N, determine the magnitude of the moment of this force about the x axis which is effective in unscrewing the lug nut.

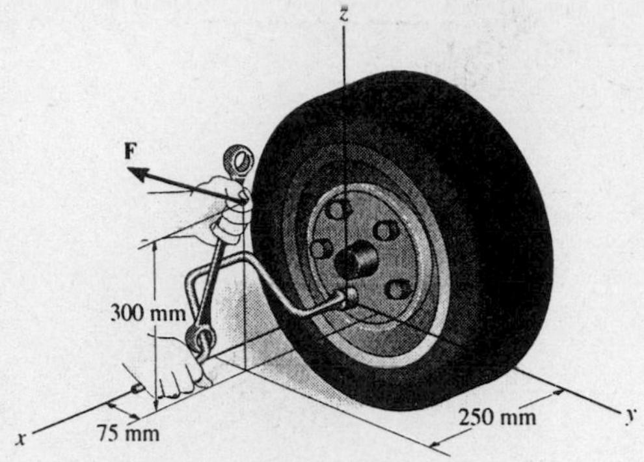

Position Vector and Force Vector:

$$\mathbf{r} = \{(0.075-0)\mathbf{j} + (0.3-0)\mathbf{k}\}\ \text{m} = \{0.075\mathbf{j} + 0.3\mathbf{k}\}\ \text{m}$$

Moment of Force F About x Axis: The unit vector along x axis is $\mathbf{i}$. With $\mathbf{F} = \{4\mathbf{i} - 12\mathbf{j} + 2\mathbf{k}\}$ N, applying Eq. 4-11, we have

$$M_x = \mathbf{i}\cdot(\mathbf{r}\times\mathbf{F})$$

$$= \begin{vmatrix} 1 & 0 & 0 \\ 0 & 0.075 & 0.3 \\ 4 & -12 & 2 \end{vmatrix}$$

$$= 1[0.075(2) - (-12)(0.3)] - 0 + 0$$

$$= 3.75\ \text{N}\cdot\text{m} \qquad \textbf{Ans}$$

4-62. A 70-lb force acts vertically on the "Z" bracket. Determine the magnitude of the moment of this force about the bolt axis (z axis).

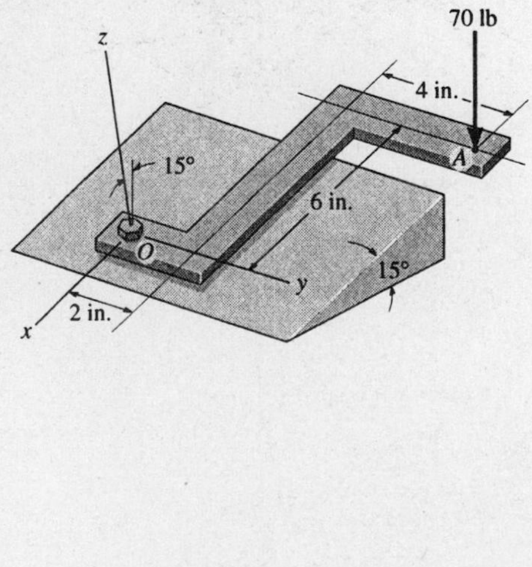

Position Vector And Force Vector:

$$\mathbf{r}_{OA} = \{(-6-0)\mathbf{i} + (6-0)\mathbf{j}\}\ \text{in.} = \{-6\mathbf{i} + 6\mathbf{j}\}\ \text{in.}$$

$$\mathbf{F} = 70(\sin 15^\circ\mathbf{i} - \cos 15^\circ\mathbf{k})\ \text{lb} = \{18.117\mathbf{i} - 67.615\mathbf{k}\}\ \text{lb}$$

Moment of Force F About z Axis: The unit vector along z axis is $\mathbf{k}$. Applying Eq. 4-11, we have

$$M_z = \mathbf{k}\cdot(\mathbf{r}_{OA}\times\mathbf{F})$$

$$= \begin{vmatrix} 0 & 0 & 1 \\ -6 & 6 & 0 \\ 18.117 & 0 & -67.615 \end{vmatrix}$$

$$= 0 - 0 + 1[(-6)(0) - (6)(18.117)]$$

$$= -109\ \text{lb}\cdot\text{in}$$

Negative sign indicates that $\mathbf{M}_z$ is directed toward negative z axis.

$M_z = 109\ \text{lb}\cdot\text{in}$

4-63. Determine the magnitude of the moment that the force **F** exerts about the y axis of the shaft. Solve the problem using a Cartesian vector approach and using a scalar approach.

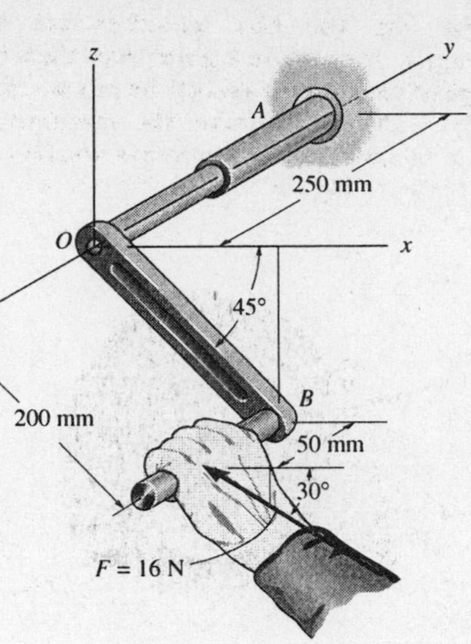

a) *Vector Analysis*

Position Vector and Force Vector :

$$\mathbf{r}_{OB} = \{0.2\cos 45°\mathbf{i} - 0.2\sin 45°\mathbf{k}\}\ \text{m} = \{0.1414\mathbf{i} - 0.1414\mathbf{k}\}\ \text{m}$$

$$\mathbf{F} = 16\{-\cos 30°\mathbf{i} + \sin 30°\mathbf{k}\}\ \text{N} = \{-13.856\mathbf{i} + 8.00\mathbf{k}\}\ \text{N}$$

Moment of Force* F *About y Axis : The unit vector along the y axis is $\mathbf{j}$. Applying Eq. 4 – 11, we have

$$M_y = \mathbf{j}\cdot(\mathbf{r}_{OB} \times \mathbf{F})$$

$$= \begin{vmatrix} 0 & 1 & 0 \\ 0.1414 & 0 & -0.1414 \\ -13.856 & 0 & 8 \end{vmatrix}$$

$$= 0 - 1[0.1414(8) - (-13.856)(-0.1414)] + 0$$

$$= 0.828\ \text{N}\cdot\text{m} \qquad \textbf{Ans}$$

b) *Scalar Analysis*

$$M_y = \Sigma M_y; \quad M_y = 16\cos 30°(0.2\sin 45°) - 16\sin 30°(0.2\cos 45°)$$

$$= 0.828\ \text{N}\cdot\text{m} \qquad \textbf{Ans}$$

***4-64.** The A-frame is being hoisted into an upright position by the vertical force of $F = 80$ lb. Determine the moment of this force about the y' axis passing through points A and B when the frame is in the position shown.

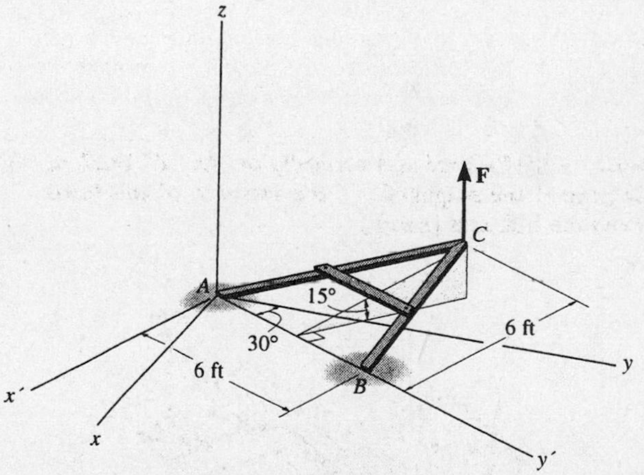

Scalar analysis :

$$M_{y'} = 80\,(6\cos 15°) = 464\ \text{lb}\cdot\text{ft} \qquad \textbf{Ans}$$

Vector analysis :

$$\mathbf{u}_{AB} = \cos 60°\,\mathbf{i} + \cos 30°\,\mathbf{j}$$

Coordinates of point C :

$$x = 3\sin 30° - 6\cos 15°\cos 30° = -3.52\ \text{ft}$$

$$y = 3\cos 30° + 6\cos 15°\sin 30° = 5.50\ \text{ft}$$

$$z = 6\sin 15° = 1.55\ \text{ft}$$

$$\mathbf{r}_{AC} = -3.52\,\mathbf{i} + 5.50\,\mathbf{j} + 1.55\,\mathbf{k}$$

$$\mathbf{F} = 80\,\mathbf{k}$$

$$M_{y'} = \begin{vmatrix} \sin 30° & \cos 30° & 0 \\ -3.52 & 5.50 & 1.55 \\ 0 & 0 & 80 \end{vmatrix}$$

$$M_{y'} = 464\ \text{lb}\cdot\text{ft} \qquad \textbf{Ans}$$

4-65. The A-frame is being hoisted into an upright position by the vertical force of $F = 80$ lb. Determine the moment of this force about the x axis when the frame is in the position shown.

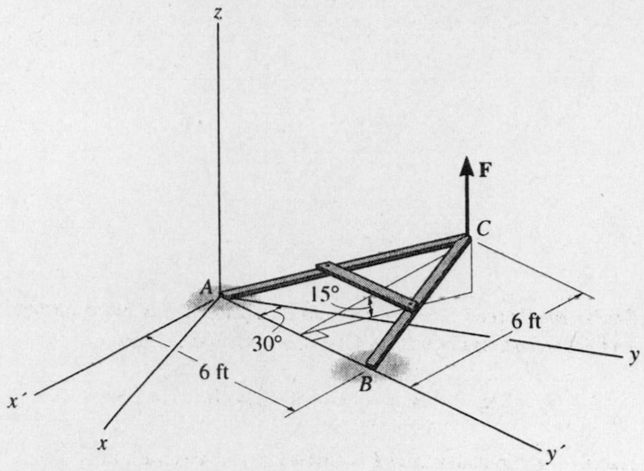

Using x', y', z:

$\mathbf{u}_x = \cos 30° \, \mathbf{i}' + \sin 30° \, \mathbf{j}'$

$\mathbf{r}_{AC} = -6 \cos 15° \, \mathbf{i}' + 3 \, \mathbf{j}' + 6 \sin 15° \, \mathbf{k}$

$\mathbf{F} = 80 \, \mathbf{k}$

$$M_x = \begin{vmatrix} \cos 30° & \sin 30° & 0 \\ -6 \cos 15° & 3 & 6 \sin 15° \\ 0 & 0 & 80 \end{vmatrix} = 207.85 + 231.82 + 0$$

$M_x = 440$ lb · ft **Ans**

Also, using x, y, z.

Coordinates of point C :

$x = 3 \sin 30° - 6 \cos 15° \cos 30° = -3.52$ ft

$y = 3 \cos 30° + 6 \cos 15° \sin 30° = 5.50$ ft

$z = 6 \sin 15° = 1.55$ ft

$\mathbf{r}_{AC} = -3.52 \, \mathbf{i} + 5.50 \, \mathbf{j} + 1.55 \, \mathbf{k}$

$\mathbf{F} = 80 \, \mathbf{k}$

$$M_x = \begin{vmatrix} 1 & 0 & 0 \\ -3.52 & 5.50 & 1.55 \\ 0 & 0 & 80 \end{vmatrix} = 440 \text{ lb} \cdot \text{ft} \quad \textbf{Ans}$$

4-66. The A-frame is being hoisted into an upright position by the vertical force of $F = 80$ lb. Determine the moment of this force about the y axis when the frame is in the position shown.

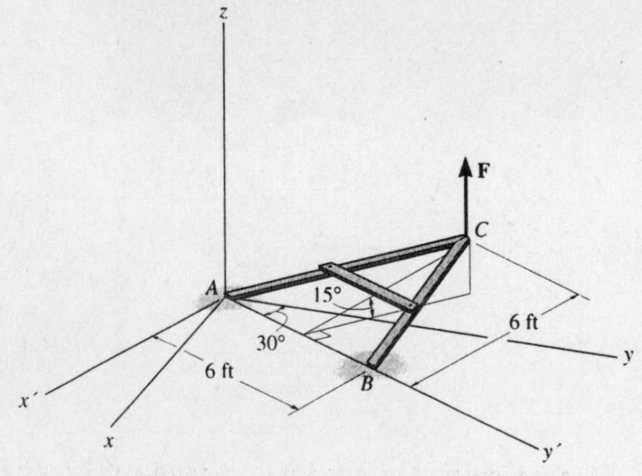

Using x', y', z:

$\mathbf{u}_y = -\sin 30° \, \mathbf{i}' + \cos 30° \, \mathbf{j}'$

$\mathbf{r}_{AC} = -6 \cos 15° \, \mathbf{i}' + 3 \, \mathbf{j}' + 6 \sin 15° \, \mathbf{k}$

$\mathbf{F} = 80 \, \mathbf{k}$

$$M_y = \begin{vmatrix} -\sin 30° & \cos 30° & 0 \\ -6 \cos 15° & 3 & 6 \sin 15° \\ 0 & 0 & 80 \end{vmatrix} = -120 + 401.52 + 0$$

$M_y = 282$ lb · ft **Ans**

Also, using x, y, z:

Coordinates of point C :

$x = 3 \sin 30° - 6 \cos 15° \cos 30° = -3.52$ ft

$y = 3 \cos 30° + 6 \cos 15° \sin 30° = 5.50$ ft

$z = 6 \sin 15° = 1.55$ ft

$\mathbf{r}_{AC} = -3.52 \, \mathbf{i} + 5.50 \, \mathbf{j} + 1.55 \, \mathbf{k}$

$\mathbf{F} = 80 \, \mathbf{k}$

$$M_y = \begin{vmatrix} 0 & 1 & 0 \\ -3.52 & 5.50 & 1.55 \\ 0 & 0 & 80 \end{vmatrix} = 282 \text{ lb} \cdot \text{ft} \quad \textbf{Ans}$$

4-67. A vertical force of $F = 60$ N is applied to the handle of the pipe wrench. Determine the moment that this force exerts along the axis AB (x axis) of the pipe assembly. Both the wrench and pipe assembly ABC lie in the x–y plane. *Suggestion:* Use a scalar analysis.

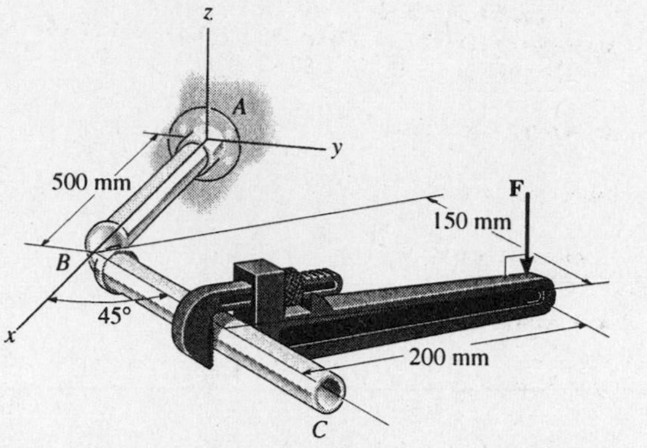

Scalar Analysis **:** From the geometry, the perpendicular distance from x axis to force **F** is $d = 0.15\sin 45° + 0.2\sin 45° = 0.2475$ m.

$$M_x = \Sigma M_x; \qquad M_x = -Fd = -60(0.2475) = -14.8 \text{ N} \cdot \text{m}$$

Negative sign indicates that $\mathbf{M}_x$ is directed toward negative x axis.

$\mathbf{M}_x = 14.8$ N · m **Ans**

***4-68.** Determine the magnitude of the vertical force **F** acting on the handle of the wrench so that this force produces a component of moment along the AB axis (x axis) of the pipe assembly of $(M_A)_x = \{-5\mathbf{i}\}$ N · m. Both the pipe assembly ABC and the wrench lie in the x–y plane. *Suggestion:* Use a scalar analysis.

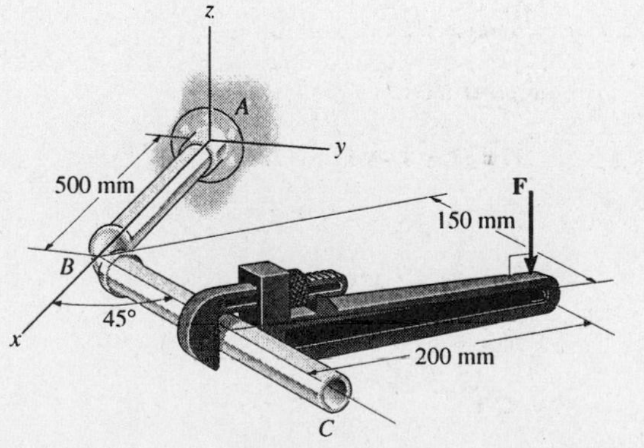

Scalar Analysis **:** From the geometry, the perpendicular distance from x axis to **F** is $d = 0.15\sin 45° + 0.2\sin 45° = 0.2475$ m.

$$M_x = \Sigma M_x; \qquad -5 = -F(0.2475)$$
$$F = 20.2 \text{ N}$$ **Ans**

4-69. Determine the magnitude and sense of the couple moment.

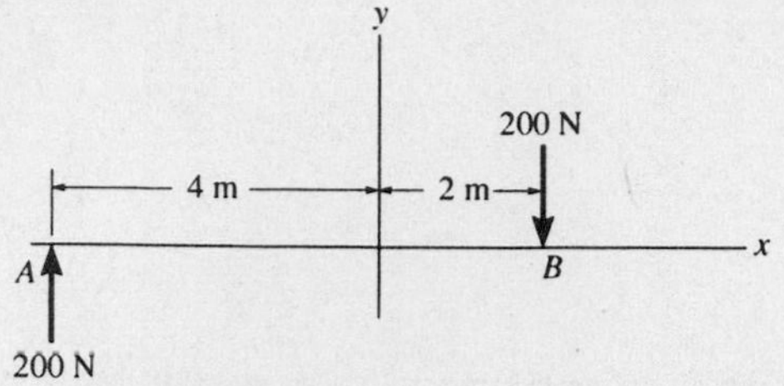

$M_C = Fd = 200(6) = 1200 \text{ N}\cdot\text{m} = 1.20 \text{ kN}\cdot\text{m}$ **Ans**

4-70. Determine the magnitude and sense of the couple moment. Each force has a magnitude of $F = 65$ lb.

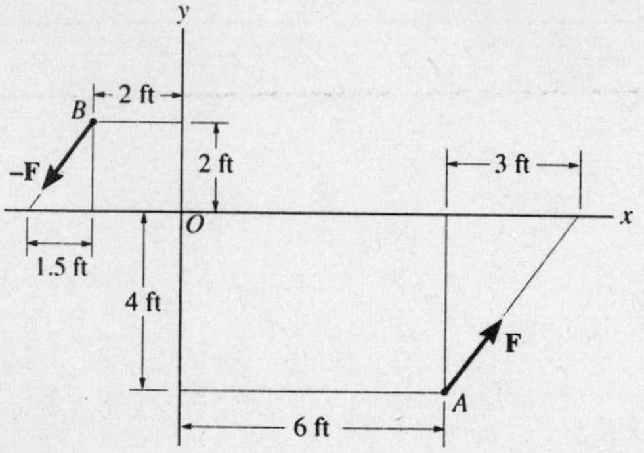

$\circlearrowleft + M_C = \Sigma M_B;\quad M_C = 65\left(\frac{4}{5}\right)(6+2) + 65\left(\frac{3}{5}\right)(4+2)$

$= 650 \text{ lb}\cdot\text{ft}$ ***(Counterclockwise)*** **Ans**

4-71. Determine the magnitude and sense of the couple moment. Each force has a magnitude of $F = 8$ kN.

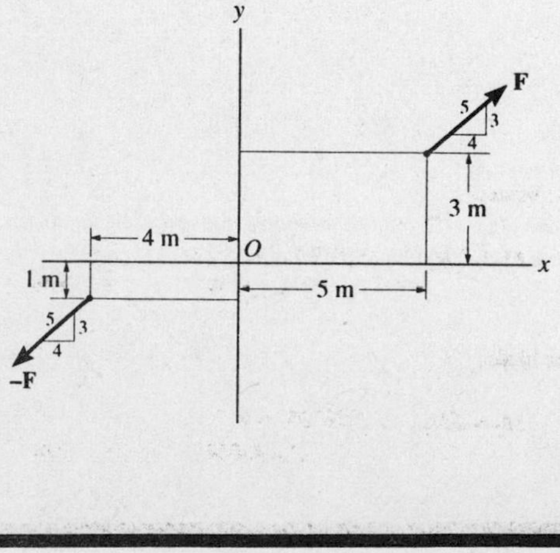

$\circlearrowleft + M_C = \Sigma M_B;\quad M_C = 8\left(\frac{3}{5}\right)(5+4) - 8\left(\frac{4}{5}\right)(3+1)$

$= 17.6 \text{ kN}\cdot\text{m}$ ***(Counterclockwise)*** **Ans**

*4-72. Determine the magnitude and sense of the couple moment.

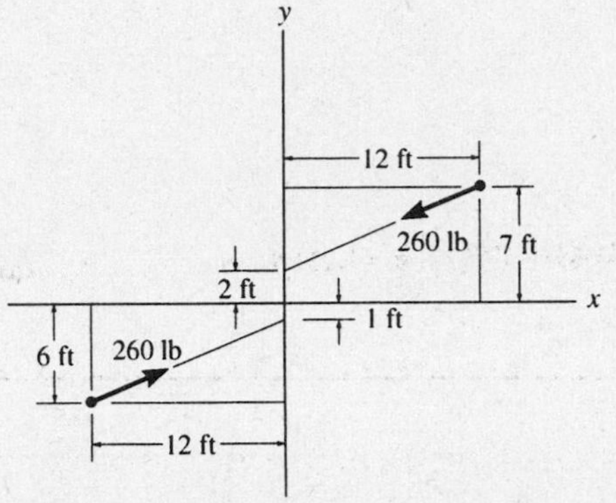

$$\circlearrowleft + M_C = 260\left(\frac{12}{13}\right)(13) - 260\left(\frac{5}{13}\right)(24)$$

$$M_C = 720 \text{ lb}\cdot\text{ft} \circlearrowleft \quad \textbf{Ans}$$

4-73. A twist of 4 N·m is applied to the handle of the screwdriver. Resolve this couple moment into a pair of couple forces **F** exerted on the handle and **P** exerted on the blade.

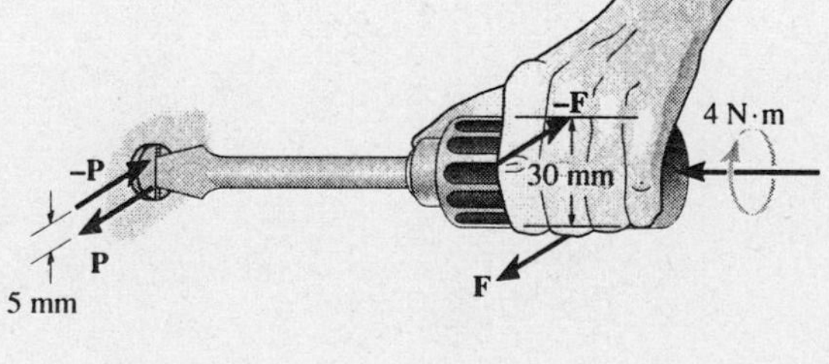

For the handle

$M_C = \Sigma M_x;$ $\quad F(0.03) = 4$

$F = 133$ N **Ans**

For the blade,

$M_C = \Sigma M_x;$ $\quad P(0.005) = 4$

$F = 800$ N **Ans**

4-74. The main beam along the wing of an airplane is swept back at an angle of 25°. From load calculations it is determined that the beam is subjected to couple moments $M_x = 25\,000$ lb·ft and $M_y = 17\,000$ lb·ft. Determine the equivalent couple moments created about the x' and y' axes.

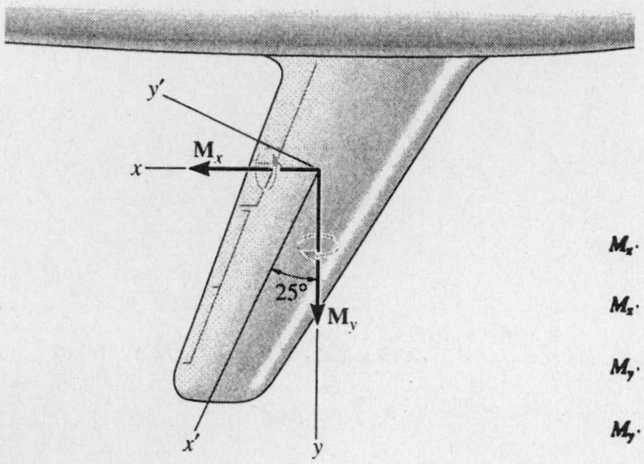

$M_{x'} = 17\,000 \cos 25° + 25\,000 \sin 25°$

$M_{x'} = 25\,973$ lb · ft = 26.0 kip · ft **Ans**

$M_{y'} = 25\,000 \cos 25° - 17\,000 \sin 25°$

$M_{y'} = 15\,473$ lb · ft = 15.5 kip · ft **Ans**

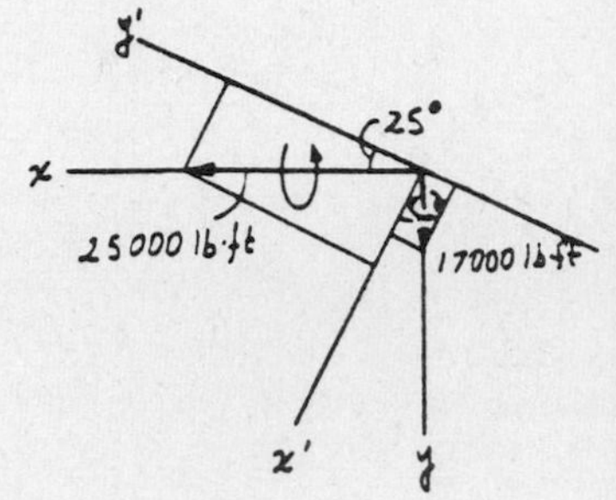

4-75. A device called a rolamite is used in various ways to replace slipping motion with rolling motion. If the belt, which wraps between the rollers, is subjected to a tension of 15 N, determine the reactive forces N of the top and bottom plates on the rollers so that the resultant couple acting on the rollers is equal to zero.

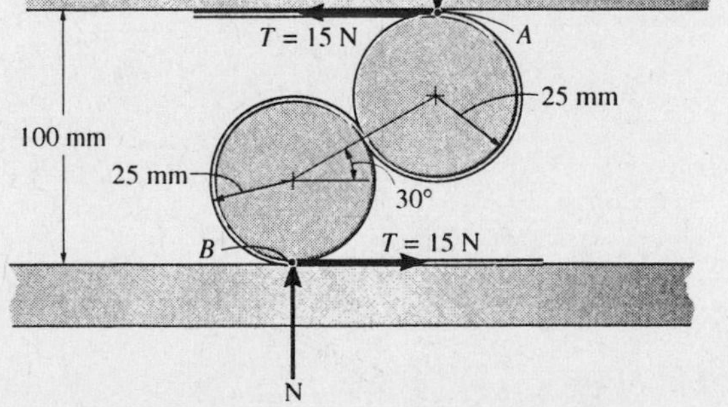

$\curvearrowleft + \Sigma M_A = 0; \quad 15(50 + 50\sin 30°) - N(50\cos 30°) = 0$

$N = 26.0$ N **Ans**

4-76. The caster wheel is subjected to the two couples. Determine the forces **F** that the bearings create on the shaft so that the resultant couple moment on the caster is zero.

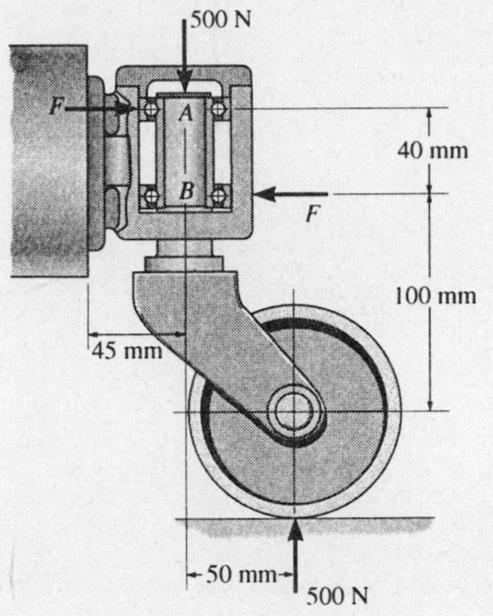

$\circlearrowleft + \Sigma M_A = 0; \quad 500(50) - F(40) = 0$

$F = 625$ N **Ans**

4-77. When the engine of the plane is running, the vertical reaction that the ground exerts on the wheel at A is measured as 650 lb. When the engine is turned off, however, the vertical reactions at A and B are 575 lb each. The difference in readings at A is caused by a couple acting on the propeller when the engine is running. This couple tends to overturn the plane counterclockwise, which is opposite to the propeller's clockwise rotation. Determine the magnitude of this couple and the magnitude of the reaction force exerted at B when the engine is running.

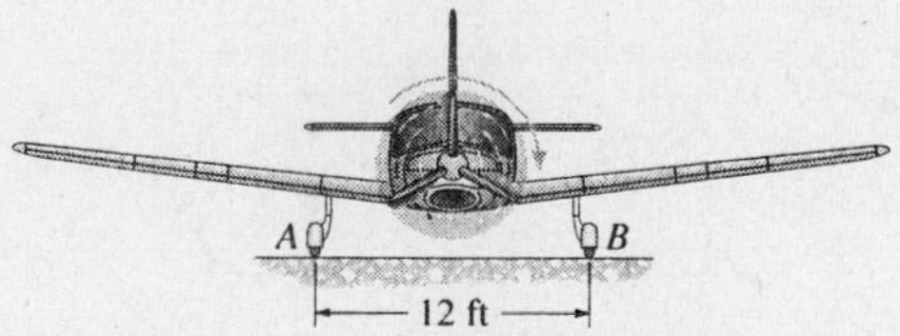

When the engine of the plane is turned on, the resulting couple moment exerts an additional force of $F = 650 - 575 = 75.0$ lb on wheel A and a lesser the reactive force on wheel B of $F = 75.0$ lb as well. Hence,

$M = 75.0(12) = 900$ lb · ft **Ans**

The reactive force at wheel B is

$R_B = 575 - 75.0 = 500$ lb **Ans**

4-78. The crossbar wrench is used to remove a lug nut from the automobile wheel. The mechanic applies a couple to the wrench such that his hands are a constant distance apart. Is it necessary that $a = b$ in order to produce the most effective turning of the nut? Explain. Also, what is the effect of changing the shaft dimension c in this regard? The forces act in the vertical plane.

Couple moment, $M_C = F(a + b)$

The couple moment depends on the total distance between grips, not $a = b$.

No. **Ans**

Changing dimension c has no effect on turning the nut **Ans**

4-79. The cord passing over the two small pegs A and B of the square board is subjected to a tension of 100 N. Determine the required tension P acting on the cord that passes over pegs C and D so that the resultant couple produced by the two couples is 15 N·m acting clockwise. Take $\theta = 15°$.

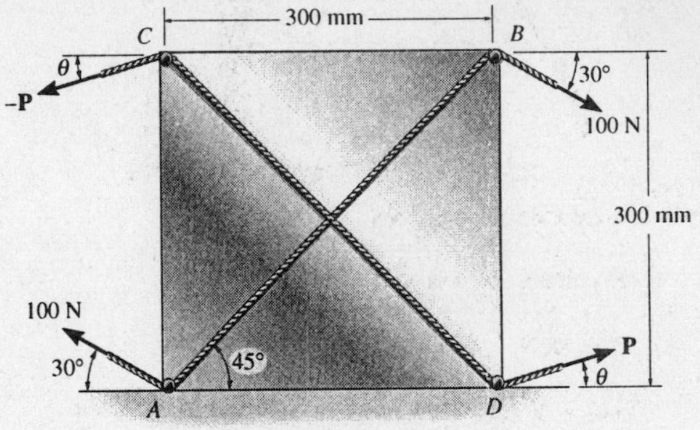

$\curvearrowright + M_R = 100 \cos 30° (0.3) + 100 \sin 30° (0.3) - P \sin 15° (0.3) - P \cos 15° (0.3$

$P = 70.7$ N **Ans**

***4-80.** The cord passing over the two small pegs A and B of the board is subjected to a tension of 100 N. Determine the *minimum* tension P and the orientation θ of the cord passing over pegs C and D, so that the resultant couple moment produced by the two cords is 20 N·m, clockwise.

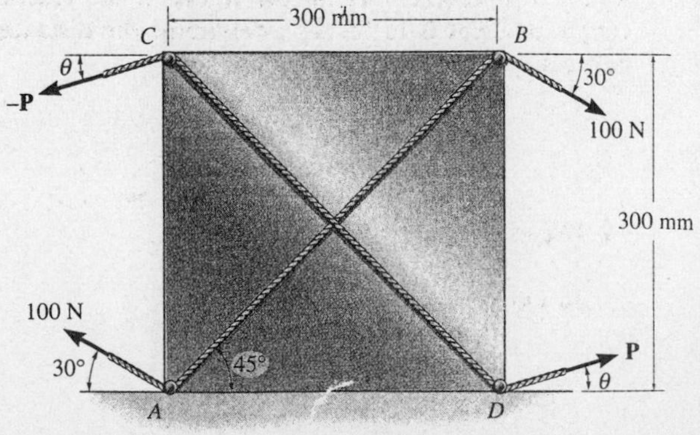

For minimum P require $\theta = 45°$ **Ans**

$$M_R = 100 \cos 30° (0.3) + 100 \sin 30° (0.3) - P\left(\frac{0.3}{\cos 45°}\right) = 20$$

$P = 49.5$ N **Ans**

4-81. The ends of the triangular plate are subjected to three couples. Determine the plate dimension d so that the resultant couple is 350 N·m clockwise.

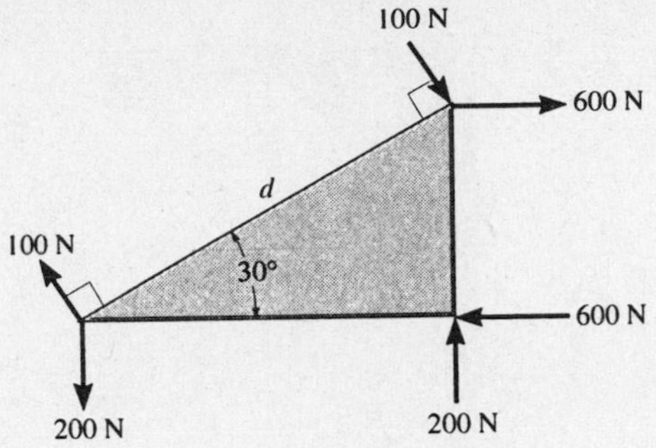

$\curvearrowleft + M_R = \Sigma M_A;\quad -350 = 200(d\cos 30°) - 600(d\sin 30°) - 100d$

$d = 1.54$ m **Ans**

4-82. Two couples act on the beam. If the resultant couple is to be zero, determine the magnitudes of **P** and **F**, and the distance d between A and B.

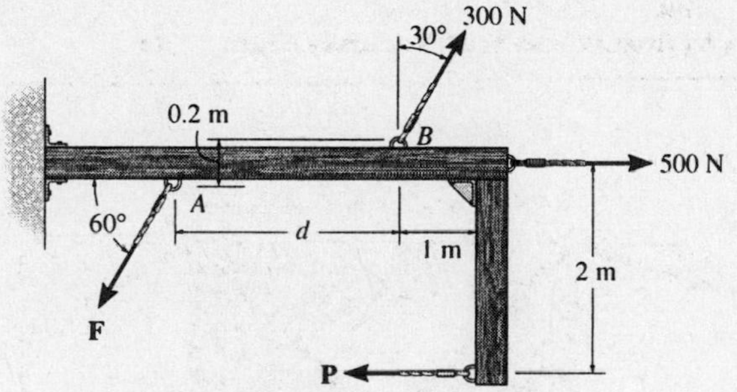

In order to have two couples,

$F = 300$ N **Ans**

$P = 500$ N **Ans**

$\curvearrowleft + M_R = 500(2) - 300\cos 30°(d) + 300\sin 30°(0.2) = 0$

$d = 3.96$ m **Ans**

4-83. Two couples act on the frame. If the resultant couple moment is to be zero, determine the distance d between the 40-lb couple forces.

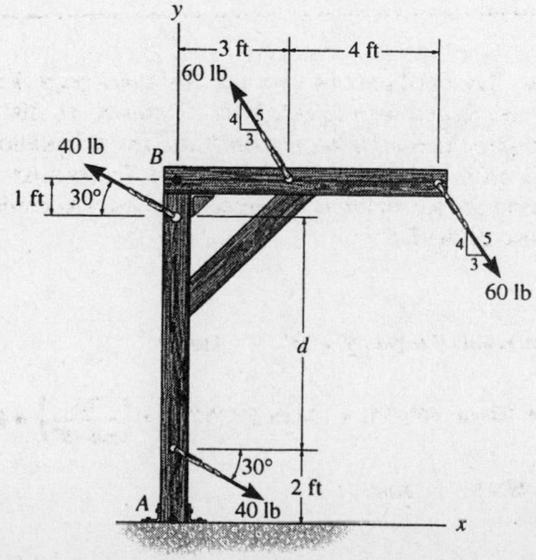

$\curvearrowleft + M_C = 0 = 40\cos 30°(d) - 60\left(\frac{4}{5}\right)(4)$

$d = 5.54$ ft **Ans**

*4-84. Two couples act on the frame. If $d = 4$ ft, determine the resultant couple moment. Compute the result by resolving each force into x and y components and (a) finding the moment of each couple (Eq. 4–13) and (b) summing the moments of all the force components about point A.

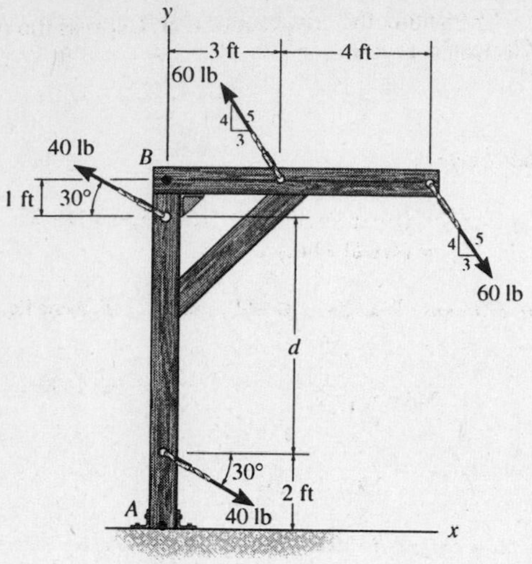

(a)

$$\circlearrowleft +M_C = 40\cos 30°(4) - 60\left(\frac{4}{5}\right)(4) = -53.4\text{ lb}\cdot\text{ft} = 53.4\text{ lb}\cdot\text{ft} \circlearrowright \quad \textbf{Ans}$$

(b)

$$\circlearrowleft +M_C = -40\cos 30°(2) + 40\cos 30°(6) + 60\left(\frac{4}{5}\right)(3) + 60\left(\frac{3}{5}\right)(7) - 60\left(\frac{4}{5}\right)(7) - 60\left(\frac{3}{5}\right)(7)$$

$$= -53.4\text{ lb}\cdot\text{ft} = 53.4\text{ lb}\cdot\text{ft} \circlearrowright \quad \textbf{Ans}$$

4-85. Two couples act on the frame. If $d = 4$ ft, determine the resultant couple moment. Compute the result by resolving each force into x and y components and (a) finding the moment of each couple (Eq. 4–13) and (b) summing the moments of all the force components about point B.

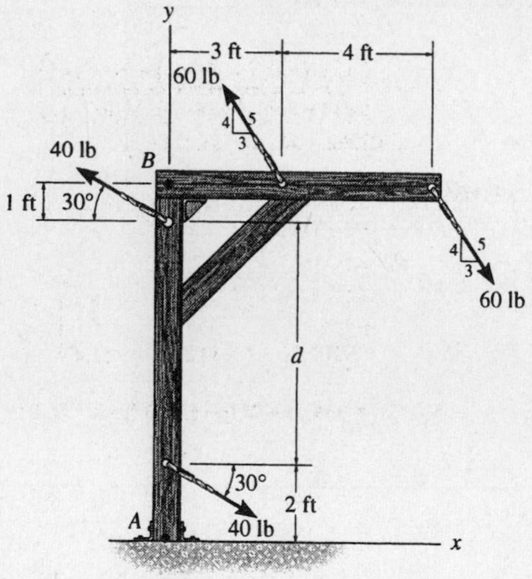

(a)

$$\circlearrowleft +M_C = 40\cos 30°(4) - 60\left(\frac{4}{5}\right)(4) = -53.4\text{ lb}\cdot\text{ft} = 53.4\text{ lb}\cdot\text{ft} \circlearrowright \quad \textbf{Ans}$$

(b)

$$\circlearrowleft +M_C = 40\cos 30°(5) - 40\cos 30°(1) + 60\left(\frac{4}{5}\right)(3) - 60\left(\frac{4}{5}\right)(7)$$

$$= -53.4\text{ lb}\cdot\text{ft} = 53.4\text{ lb}\cdot\text{ft} \circlearrowright \quad \textbf{Ans}$$

4-86. Determine the couple moment. Express the result as a Cartesian vector.

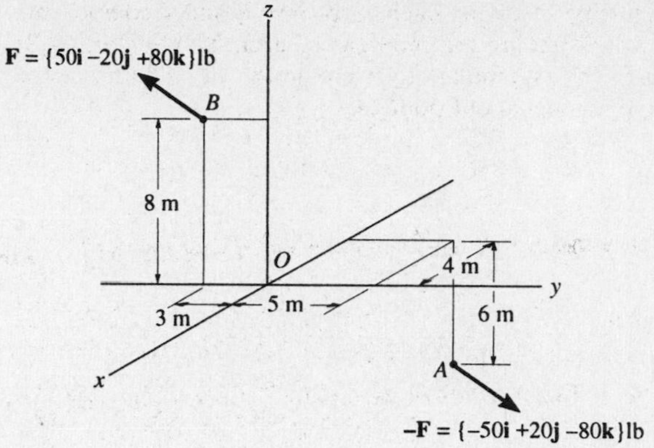

Position Vector :

$$\mathbf{r}_{AB} = \{[0-(-4)]\mathbf{i}+(-3-5)\mathbf{j}+[8-(-6)]\mathbf{k}\}\ \text{ft}$$
$$= \{4\mathbf{i}-8\mathbf{j}+14\mathbf{k}\}\ \text{ft}$$

Couple Moment : With $\mathbf{F} = \{50\mathbf{i}-20\mathbf{j}+80\mathbf{k}\}$ lb, applying Eq. 4 − 15, we have

$$\mathbf{M}_C = \mathbf{r}_{AB}\times\mathbf{F}$$
$$= \begin{vmatrix} \mathbf{i} & \mathbf{j} & \mathbf{k} \\ 4 & -8 & 14 \\ 50 & -20 & 80 \end{vmatrix}$$
$$= \{-360\mathbf{i}+380\mathbf{j}+320\mathbf{k}\}\ \text{lb}\cdot\text{ft} \qquad \textbf{Ans}$$

4-87. Determine the couple moment. Express the result as a Cartesian vector. Each force has a magnitude of $F = 120$ lb.

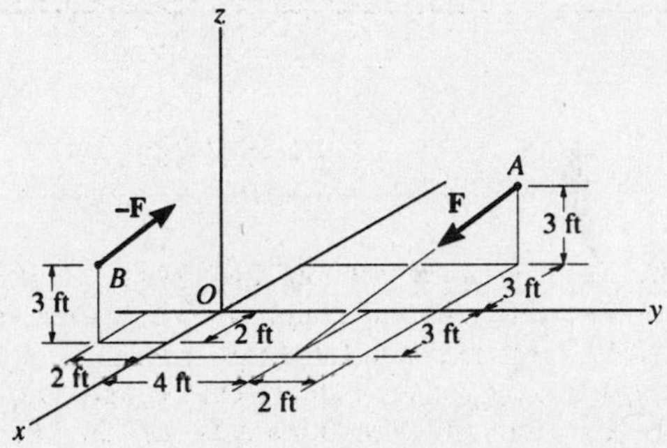

Position Vector and Force Vector :

$$\mathbf{r}_{BA} = \{(-3-2)\mathbf{i}+[6-(-2)]\mathbf{j}+(3-3)\mathbf{k}\}\ \text{ft}$$
$$= \{-5\mathbf{i}+8\mathbf{j}\}\ \text{ft}$$

$$\mathbf{F} = 120\left(\frac{[3-(-3)]\mathbf{i}+(4-6)\mathbf{j}+(0-3)\mathbf{k}}{\sqrt{[3-(-3)]^2+(4-6)^2+(0-3)^2}}\right)$$
$$= \{102.86\mathbf{i}-34.26\mathbf{j}-51.43\mathbf{k}\}\ \text{lb}$$

Couple Moment : Applying Eq. 4 − 15, we have

$$\mathbf{M}_C = \mathbf{r}_{BA}\times\mathbf{F}$$
$$= \begin{vmatrix} \mathbf{i} & \mathbf{j} & \mathbf{k} \\ -5 & 8 & 0 \\ 102.86 & -34.26 & -51.43 \end{vmatrix}$$
$$= \{-411\mathbf{i}-257\mathbf{j}-651\mathbf{k}\}\ \text{lb}\cdot\text{ft} \qquad \textbf{Ans}$$

*4-88. The gear reducer is subjected to the four couple moments. Determine the magnitude of the resultant couple moment and its coordinate direction angles.

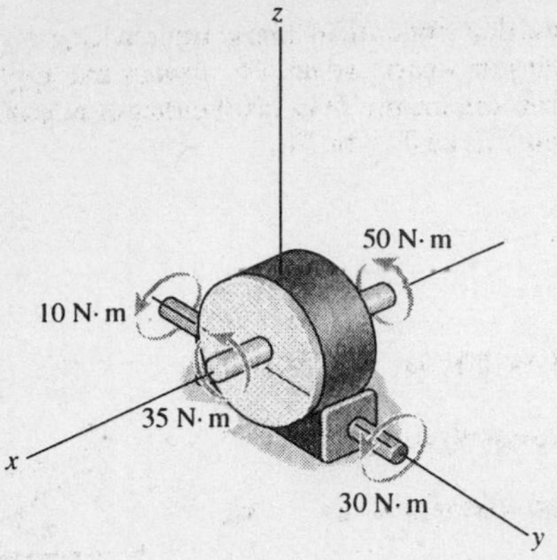

$(M_R)_x = \Sigma M_x; \quad (M_R)_x = 35 + 50 = 85.0 \text{ N}\cdot\text{m}$

$(M_R)_y = \Sigma M_y; \quad (M_R)_y = 30 + 10 = 40.0 \text{ N}\cdot\text{m}$

The magnitude of the resultant couple moment is

$$M_R = \sqrt{(M_R)_x^2 + (M_R)_y^2}$$
$$= \sqrt{85.0^2 + 40.0^2}$$
$$= 93.941 \text{ N}\cdot\text{m} = 93.9 \text{ N}\cdot\text{m} \quad \textbf{Ans}$$

The coordinate direction angles are

$$\alpha = \cos^{-1}\left[\frac{(M_R)_x}{M_R}\right] = \cos^{-1}\left(\frac{85.0}{93.941}\right) = 25.2° \quad \textbf{Ans}$$

$$\beta = \cos^{-1}\left[\frac{(M_R)_y}{M_R}\right] = \cos^{-1}\left(\frac{40.0}{93.941}\right) = 64.8° \quad \textbf{Ans}$$

$$\gamma = \cos^{-1}\left[\frac{(M_R)_z}{M_R}\right] = \cos^{-1}\left(\frac{0}{93.941}\right) = 90.0° \quad \textbf{Ans}$$

4-89. The main beam along the wing of an airplane is swept back at an angle of 25°. From load calculations it is determined that the beam is subjected to couple moments $M_x = 17$ kip·ft and $M_y = 25$ kip·ft. Determine the resultant couple moments created about the x' and y' axes. The axes all lie in the same horizontal plane.

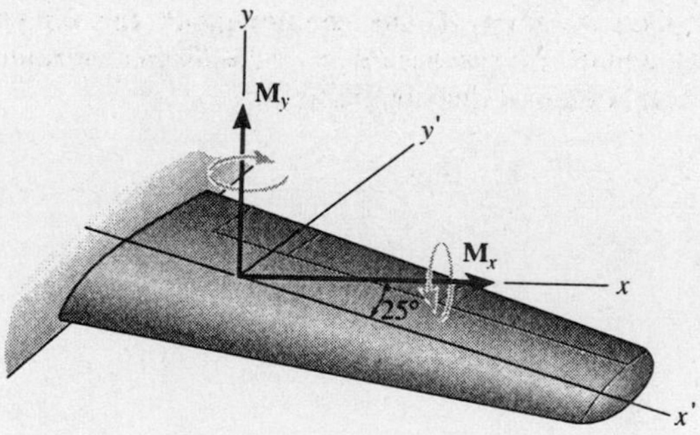

$(M_R)_{x'} = \Sigma M_{x'}; \quad (M_R)_{x'} = 17\cos 25° - 25\sin 25°$

$= 4.84 \text{ kip}\cdot\text{ft} \quad \textbf{Ans}$

$(M_R)_{y'} = \Sigma M_{y'}; \quad (M_R)_{y'} = 17\sin 25° + 25\cos 25°$

$= 29.8 \text{ kip}\cdot\text{ft} \quad \textbf{Ans}$

4-90. Express the moment of the couple acting on the frame in Cartesian vector form. The forces are applied perpendicular to the frame. What is the magnitude of the couple moment? Take $F = 50$ N.

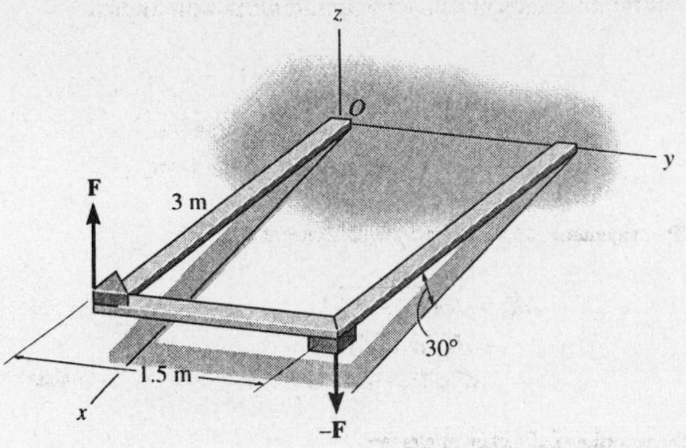

$M_C = 50\,(1.5) = 75\ \text{N}\cdot\text{m}$ **Ans**

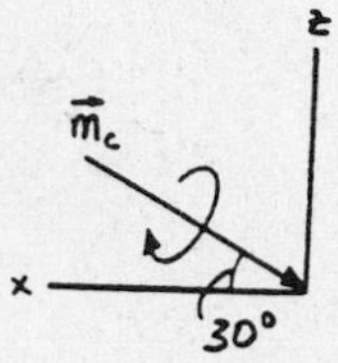

$\mathbf{M}_C = -75\,(\cos 30^\circ\,\mathbf{i} + \cos 60^\circ\,\mathbf{k})$

$= \{-65.0\,\mathbf{i} - 37.5\,\mathbf{k}\}\ \text{N}\cdot\text{m}$ **Ans**

4-91. In order to turn over the frame, a couple moment is applied as shown. If the component of this couple moment along the x axis is $\mathbf{M}_x = \{-20\mathbf{i}\}$ N·m, determine the magnitude F of the couple forces.

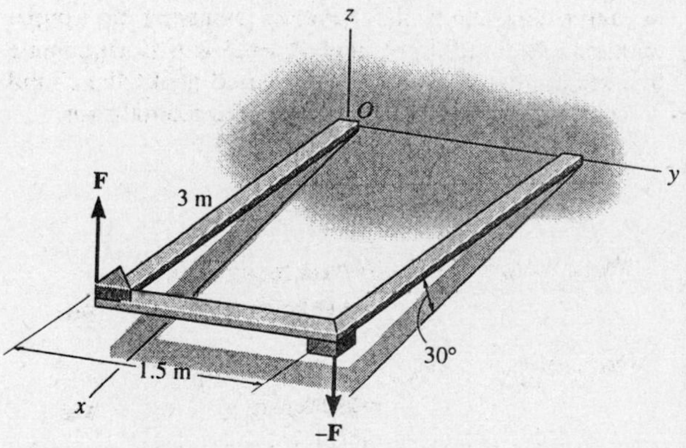

$M_C = F\,(1.5)$

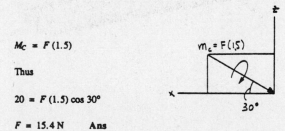

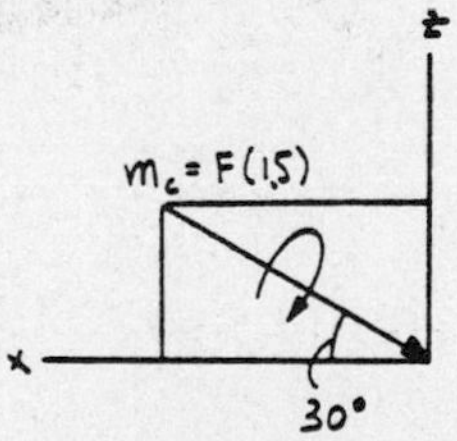

Thus

$20 = F\,(1.5)\cos 30^\circ$

$F = 15.4$ N **Ans**

4-92. The gear reducer is subjected to the couple moments shown. Determine the resultant couple moment and specify its magnitude and coordinate direction angles.

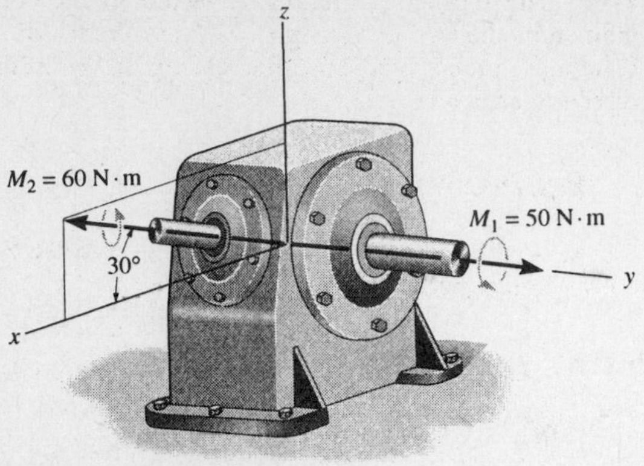

Express Each Couple Moment as a Cartesian Vector :

$$\mathbf{M}_1 = \{50\mathbf{j}\} \text{ N}\cdot\text{m}$$

$$\mathbf{M}_2 = 60(\cos 30°\mathbf{i} + \sin 30°\mathbf{k}) \text{ N}\cdot\text{m} = \{51.96\mathbf{i} + 30.0\mathbf{k}\} \text{ N}\cdot\text{m}$$

Resultant Couple Moment :

$$\mathbf{M}_R = \Sigma\mathbf{M}; \quad \mathbf{M}_R = \mathbf{M}_1 + \mathbf{M}_2 = \{51.96\mathbf{i} + 50.0\mathbf{j} + 30.0\mathbf{k}\} \text{ N}\cdot\text{m}$$

The magnitude of the resultant couple moment is

$$M_R = \sqrt{51.96^2 + 50.0^2 + 30.0^2} = 78.102 \text{ N}\cdot\text{m} = 78.1 \text{ N}\cdot\text{m} \qquad \textbf{Ans}$$

The coordinate direction angles are

$$\alpha = \cos^{-1}\left(\frac{51.96}{78.102}\right) = 48.3° \qquad \textbf{Ans}$$

$$\beta = \cos^{-1}\left(\frac{50.0}{78.102}\right) = 50.2° \qquad \textbf{Ans}$$

$$\gamma = \cos^{-1}\left(\frac{30.0}{78.102}\right) = 67.4° \qquad \textbf{Ans}$$

4-93. The gear reducer is subject to the couple moments shown. Determine the resultant couple moment and specify its magnitude and coordinate direction angles.

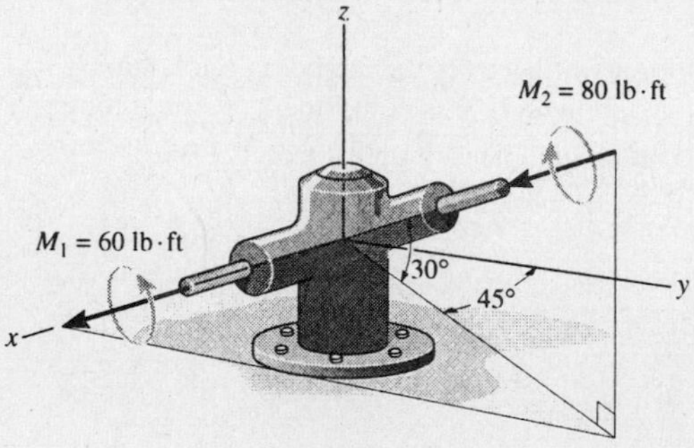

Express Each :

$$\mathbf{M}_1 = \{60\mathbf{i}\} \text{ lb}\cdot\text{ft}$$

$$\mathbf{M}_2 = 80(-\cos 30°\sin 45°\mathbf{i} - \cos 30°\cos 45°\mathbf{j} - \sin 30°\mathbf{k}) \text{ lb}\cdot\text{ft} = \{-48.99\mathbf{i} - 48.99\mathbf{j} - 40.0\mathbf{k}\} \text{ lb}\cdot\text{ft}$$

Resultant Couple Moment :

$$\mathbf{M}_R = \Sigma\mathbf{M}; \quad \mathbf{M}_R = \mathbf{M}_1 + \mathbf{M}_2$$
$$= \{(60 - 48.99)\mathbf{i} - 48.99\mathbf{j} - 40.0\mathbf{k}\} \text{ lb}\cdot\text{ft}$$
$$= \{11.01\mathbf{i} - 48.99\mathbf{j} - 40.0\mathbf{k}\} \text{ lb}\cdot\text{ft}$$
$$= \{11.0\mathbf{i} - 49.0\mathbf{j} - 40.0\mathbf{k}\} \text{ lb}\cdot\text{ft} \qquad \textbf{Ans}$$

The magnitude of the resultant couple moment is

$$M_R = \sqrt{11.01^2 + (-48.99)^2 + (-40.0)^2} = 64.20 \text{ lb}\cdot\text{ft} = 64.2 \text{ lb}\cdot\text{ft} \qquad \textbf{Ans}$$

The coordinate direction angles are

$$\alpha = \cos^{-1}\left(\frac{11.01}{64.20}\right) = 80.1° \qquad \textbf{Ans}$$

$$\beta = \cos^{-1}\left(\frac{-48.99}{64.20}\right) = 140° \qquad \textbf{Ans}$$

$$\gamma = \cos^{-1}\left(\frac{-40.0}{64.20}\right) = 129° \qquad \textbf{Ans}$$

4-94. The meshed gears are subjected to the couple moments shown. Determine the magnitude of the resultant couple moment and specify its coordinate direction angles.

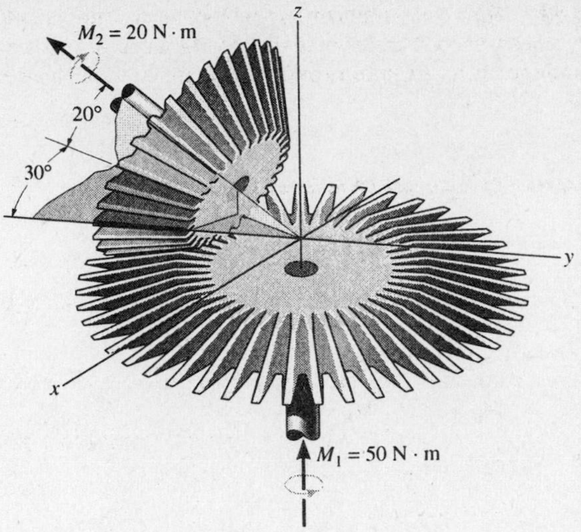

$$\mathbf{M}_1 = \{50\mathbf{k}\}\ \text{N}\cdot\text{m}$$

$$\mathbf{M}_2 = 20(-\cos 20°\sin 30°\mathbf{i} - \cos 20°\cos 30°\mathbf{j} + \sin 20°\mathbf{k})\ \text{N}\cdot\text{m}$$
$$= \{-9.397\mathbf{i} - 16.276\mathbf{j} + 6.840\mathbf{k}\}\ \text{N}\cdot\text{m}$$

Resultant Couple Moment :

$$\mathbf{M}_R = \Sigma\mathbf{M};\quad \mathbf{M}_R = \mathbf{M}_1 + \mathbf{M}_2$$
$$= \{-9.397\mathbf{i} - 16.276\mathbf{j} + (50 + 6.840)\mathbf{k}\}\ \text{N}\cdot\text{m}$$
$$= \{-9.397\mathbf{i} - 16.276\mathbf{j} + 56.840\mathbf{k}\}\ \text{N}\cdot\text{m}$$

The magnitude of the resultant couple moment is

$$M_R = \sqrt{(-9.397)^2 + (-16.276)^2 + 56.840^2}$$
$$= 59.867\ \text{N}\cdot\text{m} = 59.9\ \text{N}\cdot\text{m} \qquad \textbf{Ans}$$

The coordinate direction angles are

$$\alpha = \cos^{-1}\left(\frac{-9.397}{59.867}\right) = 99.0° \qquad \textbf{Ans}$$
$$\beta = \cos^{-1}\left(\frac{-16.276}{59.867}\right) = 106° \qquad \textbf{Ans}$$
$$\gamma = \cos^{-1}\left(\frac{56.840}{59.867}\right) = 18.3° \qquad \textbf{Ans}$$

4-95. Determine the resultant couple moment of the two couples that act on the assembly. Specify its magnitude and coordinate direction angles.

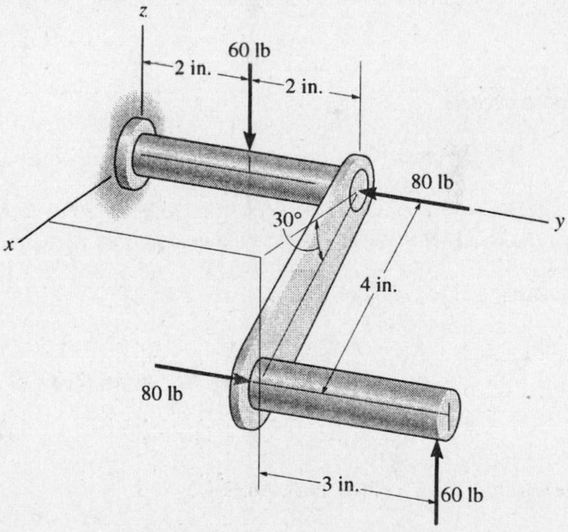

$$\mathbf{M}_R = \begin{vmatrix} \mathbf{i} & \mathbf{j} & \mathbf{k} \\ 4\cos 30° & 5 & -4\sin 30° \\ 0 & 0 & 60 \end{vmatrix} + \begin{vmatrix} \mathbf{i} & \mathbf{j} & \mathbf{k} \\ 4\cos 30° & 0 & -4\sin 30° \\ 0 & 80 & 0 \end{vmatrix}$$

$$= 300\mathbf{i} - 207.85\mathbf{j} + 160\mathbf{i} + 277.13\mathbf{k}$$

$$= \{460\mathbf{i} - 207.85\mathbf{j} + 277.13\mathbf{k}\}\ \text{lb}\cdot\text{in.}$$

$$M_R = \sqrt{(460)^2 + (-207.85)^2 + (277.13)^2} = 575.85 = 576\ \text{lb}\cdot\text{in.} \qquad \textbf{Ans}$$

$$\alpha = \cos^{-1}\left(\frac{460}{575.85}\right) = 37.0° \qquad \textbf{Ans}$$

$$\beta = \cos^{-1}\left(\frac{-207.85}{575.85}\right) = 111° \qquad \textbf{Ans}$$

$$\gamma = \cos^{-1}\left(\frac{277.13}{575.85}\right) = 61.2° \qquad \textbf{Ans}$$

***4-96.** Determine the resultant couple moment of the two couples that act on the pipe assembly. The distance from A to B is d = 400 mm. Express the result as a Cartesian vector.

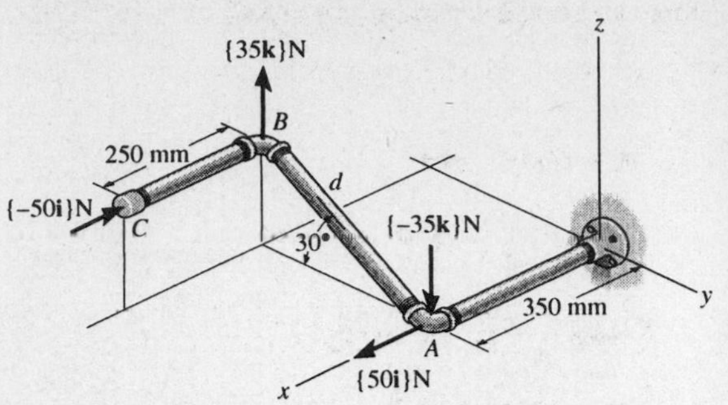

Vector Analysis

Position Vector :

$$\mathbf{r}_{AB} = \{(0.35-0.35)\mathbf{i} + (-0.4\cos 30^\circ - 0)\mathbf{j} + (0.4\sin 30^\circ - 0)\mathbf{k}\}\ \text{m}$$
$$= \{-0.3464\mathbf{j} + 0.20\mathbf{k}\}\ \text{m}$$

Couple Moments : With $\mathbf{F}_1 = \{35\mathbf{k}\}$ N and $\mathbf{F}_2 = \{-50\mathbf{i}\}$ N, applying Eq.4 − 15, we have

$$(\mathbf{M}_C)_1 = \mathbf{r}_{AB} \times \mathbf{F}_1$$
$$= \begin{vmatrix} \mathbf{i} & \mathbf{j} & \mathbf{k} \\ 0 & -0.3464 & 0.20 \\ 0 & 0 & 35 \end{vmatrix} = \{-12.12\mathbf{i}\}\ \text{N}\cdot\text{m}$$

$$(\mathbf{M}_C)_2 = \mathbf{r}_{AB} \times \mathbf{F}_2$$
$$= \begin{vmatrix} \mathbf{i} & \mathbf{j} & \mathbf{k} \\ 0 & -0.3464 & 0.20 \\ -50 & 0 & 0 \end{vmatrix} = \{-10.0\mathbf{j} - 17.32\mathbf{k}\}\ \text{N}\cdot\text{m}$$

Resultant Couple Moment :

$$\mathbf{M}_R = \Sigma\mathbf{M}; \quad \mathbf{M}_R = (\mathbf{M}_C)_1 + (\mathbf{M}_C)_2$$
$$= \{-12.1\mathbf{i} - 10.0\mathbf{j} - 17.3\mathbf{k}\}\ \text{N}\cdot\text{m} \qquad \textbf{Ans}$$

Scalar Analysis : Summing moments about x, y and z axes, we have

$$(M_R)_x = \Sigma M_x; \quad (M_R)_x = -35(0.4\cos 30^\circ) = -12.12\ \text{N}\cdot\text{m}$$
$$(M_R)_y = \Sigma M_y; \quad (M_R)_y = -50(0.4\sin 30^\circ) = -10.0\ \text{N}\cdot\text{m}$$
$$(M_R)_z = \Sigma M_z; \quad (M_R)_z = -50(0.4\cos 30^\circ) = -17.32\ \text{N}\cdot\text{m}$$

Express $\mathbf{M}_R$ as a Cartesian vector, we have

$$\mathbf{M}_R = \{-12.1\mathbf{i} - 10.0\mathbf{j} - 17.3\mathbf{k}\}\ \text{N}\cdot\text{m}$$

4-97. Determine the distance d between A and B so that the resultant couple moment has a magnitude of M_R = 20 N·m.

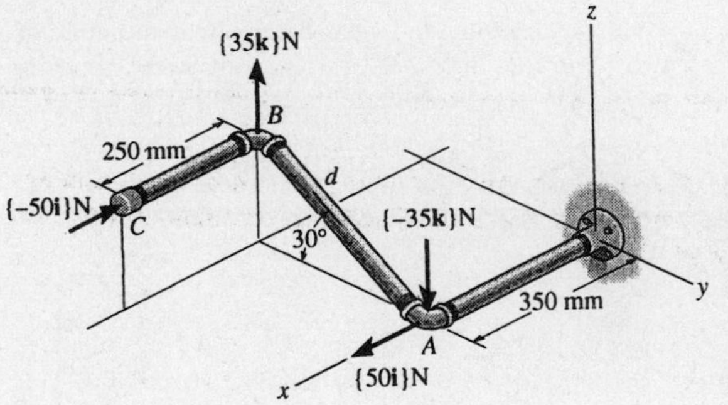

Position Vector :

$$\mathbf{r}_{AB} = \{(0.35-0.35)\mathbf{i} + (-d\cos 30^\circ - 0)\mathbf{j} + (d\sin 30^\circ - 0)\mathbf{k}\}\ \text{m}$$
$$= \{-0.8660d\ \mathbf{j} + 0.50d\ \mathbf{k}\}\ \text{m}$$

Couple Moments : With $\mathbf{F}_1 = \{35\mathbf{k}\}$ N and $\mathbf{F}_2 = \{-50\mathbf{i}\}$ N, applying Eq.4 − 15, we have

$$(\mathbf{M}_C)_1 = \mathbf{r}_{AB} \times \mathbf{F}_1$$
$$= \begin{vmatrix} \mathbf{i} & \mathbf{j} & \mathbf{k} \\ 0 & -0.8660d & 0.50d \\ 0 & 0 & 35 \end{vmatrix} = \{-30.31d\ \mathbf{i}\}\ \text{N}\cdot\text{m}$$

$$(\mathbf{M}_C)_2 = \mathbf{r}_{AB} \times \mathbf{F}_2$$
$$= \begin{vmatrix} \mathbf{i} & \mathbf{j} & \mathbf{k} \\ 0 & -0.8660d & 0.50d \\ -50 & 0 & 0 \end{vmatrix} = \{-25.0d\ \mathbf{j} - 43.30d\ \mathbf{k}\}\ \text{N}\cdot\text{m}$$

Resultant Couple Moment :

$$\mathbf{M}_R = \Sigma\mathbf{M}; \quad \mathbf{M}_R = (\mathbf{M}_C)_1 + (\mathbf{M}_C)_2$$
$$= \{-30.31d\ \mathbf{i} - 25.0d\ \mathbf{j} - 43.30d\ \mathbf{k}\}\ \text{N}\cdot\text{m}$$

The magnitude of $\mathbf{M}_R$ is 20 N · m thus

$$20 = \sqrt{(-30.31d)^2 + (-25.0d)^2 + (43.30d)^2}$$

$$d = 0.3421\ \text{m} = 342\ \text{mm} \qquad \textbf{Ans}$$

4-98. Replace the force at A by an equivalent resultant force and couple moment at point O.

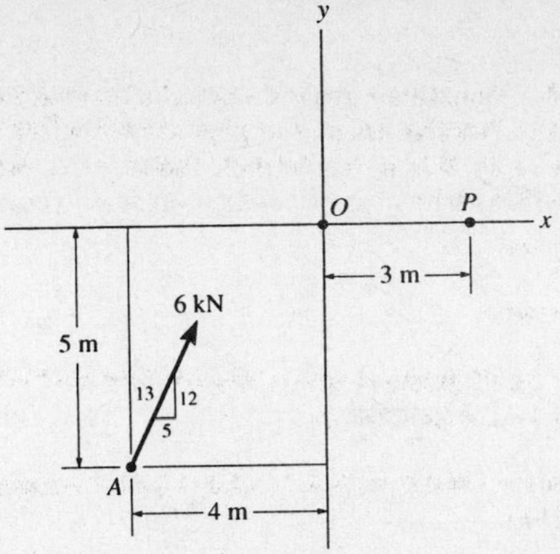

$F_R = 6\text{ kN}$ **Ans**

$\theta = \tan^{-1}\left(\frac{12}{5}\right) = 67.4°$ **Ans**

$\curvearrowleft + M_{RO} = 6\left(\frac{12}{13}\right)(4) - 6\left(\frac{5}{13}\right)(5)$

$M_{RO} = 10.6\text{ kN}\cdot\text{m}$ **Ans**

4-99. Replace the force at A by an equivalent resultant force and couple moment at point P.

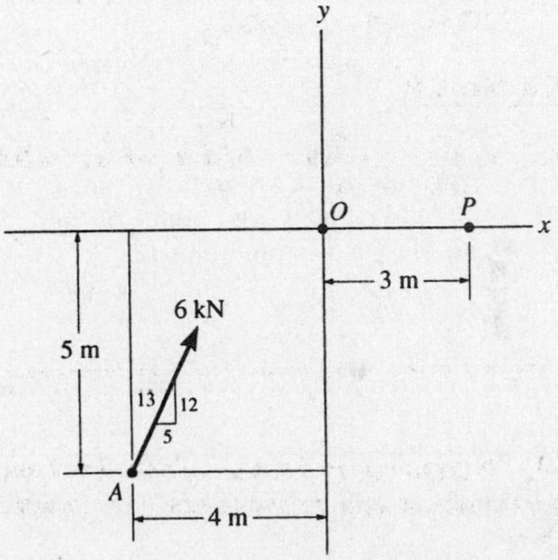

$F_R = 6\text{ kN}$ **Ans**

$\theta = \tan^{-1}\left(\frac{12}{5}\right) = 67.4°$ **Ans**

$\curvearrowleft + M_{RP} = 6\left(\frac{12}{13}\right)(7) - 6\left(\frac{5}{13}\right)(5)$

$M_{RP} = 27.2\text{ kN}\cdot\text{m}$ **Ans**

4-100. Replace the force and couple moment system by an equivalent force and couple moment acting at point O.

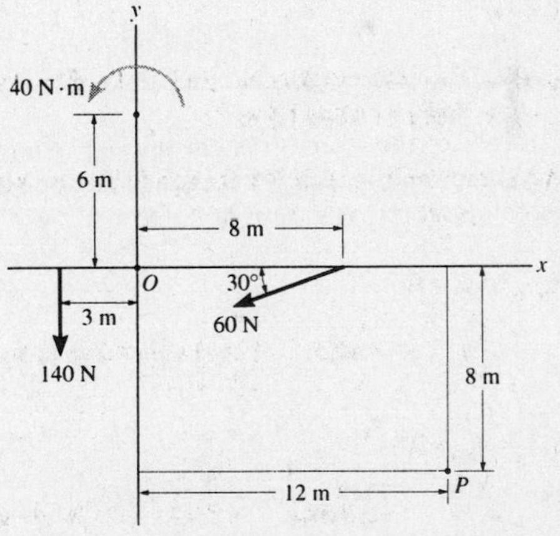

$\xrightarrow{+} F_{R_x} = \Sigma F_x;\quad F_{R_x} = -60\cos 30° = -51.96\text{ N} = 51.96\text{ N} \leftarrow$

$+\uparrow F_{R_y} = \Sigma F_y;\quad F_{R_y} = -60\sin 30° - 140$
$= -170.0\text{ N} = 170.0\text{ N}\downarrow$

Thus,

$F_R = \sqrt{F_{R_x}^2 + F_{R_y}^2} = \sqrt{51.96^2 + 170.0^2} = 178\text{ N}$ **Ans**

and

$\theta = \tan^{-1}\left(\frac{F_{R_y}}{F_{R_x}}\right) = \tan^{-1}\left(\frac{170.0}{51.96}\right) = 73.0°$ **Ans**

$\curvearrowleft + M_{R_O} = \Sigma M_O;\quad M_{R_O} = -60\sin 30°(8) + 40 + 140(3)$
$= 220\text{ N}\cdot\text{m}$ ***(Counterclockwise)*** **Ans**

4-101. Replace the force and couple moment system by an equivalent force and couple moment acting at point P.

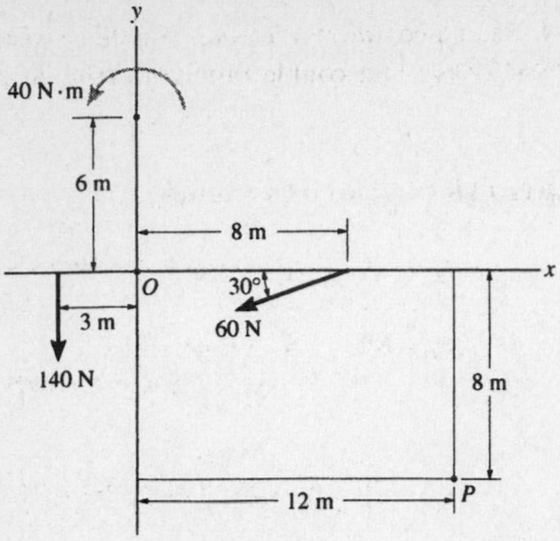

$\xrightarrow{+} F_{R_x} = \Sigma F_x;\quad F_{R_x} = -60\cos 30° = -51.96\text{ N} = 51.96\text{ N} \leftarrow$

$+\uparrow F_{R_y} = \Sigma F_y;\quad F_{R_y} = -60\sin 30° - 140$

$= -170.0\text{ N} = 170.0\text{ N} \downarrow$

Thus,

$$F_R = \sqrt{F_{R_x}^2 + F_{R_y}^2} = \sqrt{51.96^2 + 170.0^2} = 178\text{ N} \qquad \textbf{Ans}$$

and

$$\theta = \tan^{-1}\left(\frac{F_{R_y}}{F_{R_x}}\right) = \tan^{-1}\left(\frac{170.0}{51.96}\right) = 73.0° \qquad \textbf{Ans}$$

$\curvearrowleft + M_{R_P} = \Sigma M_P;\quad M_{R_P} = 60\sin 30°(12-8) + 60\cos 30°(8)$

$+40 + 140(3+12)$

$= 2676\text{ N}\cdot\text{m}$

$= 2.68\text{ kN}\cdot\text{m}$ ***(Counterclockwise)*** **Ans**

4-102. Replace the force system by an equivalent resultant force and specify its point of application, measured along the y axis from point O.

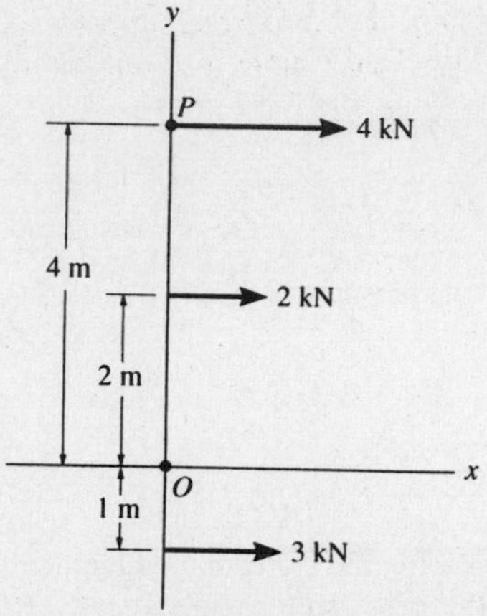

$\xrightarrow{+} F_{Rx} = \Sigma F_x;\quad F_{Rx} = 4 + 2 + 3 = 9\text{ kN} \rightarrow$ **Ans**

$\curvearrowleft +M_O = \Sigma M_O;\quad 9(d) = 4(4) + 2(2) - 3(1)$

$d = 1.89\text{ m}$ (up) **Ans**

4-103. Replace the force system by an equivalent resultant force and specify its point of application, measured along the y axis from point B.

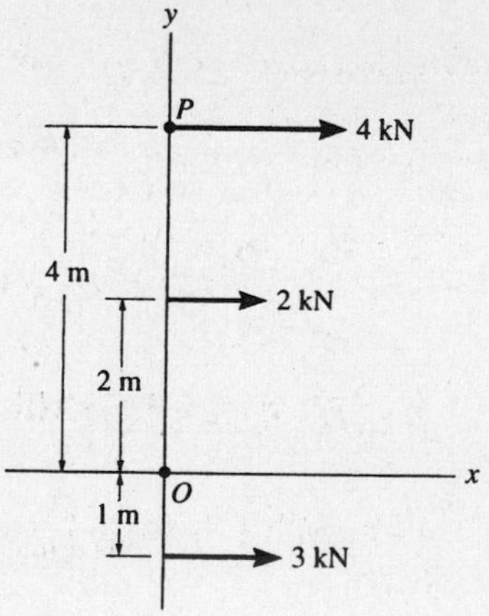

$\xrightarrow{+} F_{Rx} = \Sigma F_x;\quad F_{Rx} = 4 + 2 + 3 = 9\text{ kN}$ **Ans**

$\curvearrowleft +M_{RP} = \Sigma M_P;\quad 9(d) = 0(4) + 2(2) + 5(3)$

$d = 2.11\text{ m}$ (down) **Ans**

***4-104.** Replace the force and couple system by an equivalent force and couple moment acting at point *O*.

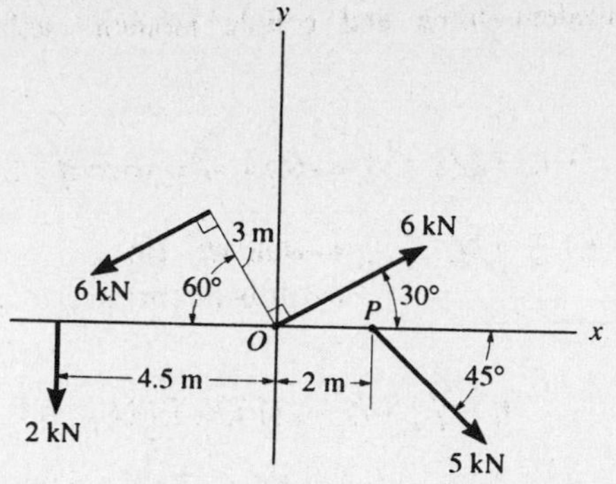

Note that the 6 kN pair of forces form a couple.

$\xrightarrow{+} F_{R_x} = \Sigma F_x;\quad F_{R_x} = 5\cos 45° = 3.536 \text{ kN} \rightarrow$

$+\uparrow F_{R_y} = \Sigma F_y;\quad F_{R_y} = -5\sin 45° - 2$

$= -5.536 \text{ kN} = 5.536 \text{ kN} \downarrow$

Thus,

$$F_R = \sqrt{F_{R_x}^2 + F_{R_y}^2} = \sqrt{3.536^2 + 5.536^2} = 6.57 \text{ kN} \qquad \textbf{Ans}$$

and

$$\theta = \tan^{-1}\left(\frac{F_{R_y}}{F_{R_x}}\right) = \tan^{-1}\left(\frac{5.536}{3.536}\right) = 57.4° \qquad \textbf{Ans}$$

$\curvearrowleft + M_{R_O} = \Sigma M_O;\quad M_{R_O} = 6(3) + 2(4.5) - 5\sin 45°(2)$

$= 19.9 \text{ kN}\cdot\text{m}$ **(Counterclockwise) Ans**

4-105. Replace the force and couple system by an equivalent force and couple moment acting at point *P*.

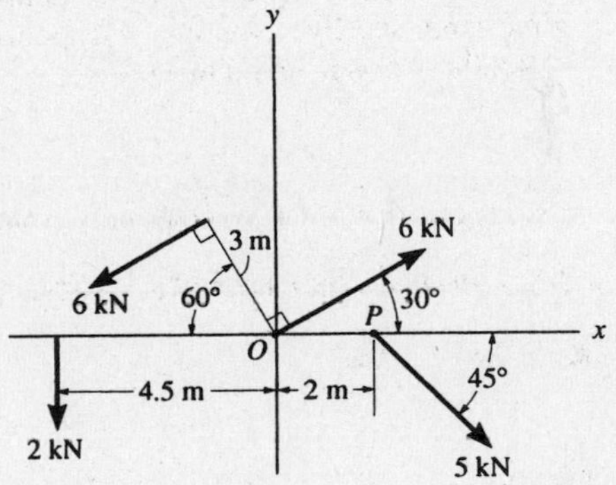

Note that the 6 kN pair of forces form a couple.

$\xrightarrow{+} F_{R_x} = \Sigma F_x;\quad F_{R_x} = 5\cos 45° = 3.536 \text{ kN} \rightarrow$

$+\uparrow F_{R_y} = \Sigma F_y;\quad F_{R_y} = -5\sin 45° - 2$

$= -5.536 \text{ kN} = 5.536 \text{ kN} \downarrow$

Thus,

$$F_R = \sqrt{F_{R_x}^2 + F_{R_y}^2} = \sqrt{3.536^2 + 5.536^2} = 6.57 \text{ kN} \qquad \textbf{Ans}$$

and

$$\theta = \tan^{-1}\left(\frac{F_{R_y}}{F_{R_x}}\right) = \tan^{-1}\left(\frac{5.536}{3.536}\right) = 57.4° \qquad \textbf{Ans}$$

$\curvearrowleft + M_{R_P} = \Sigma M_P;\quad M_{R_P} = 6(3) + 2(4.5 + 2) - 5(0)$

$= 31.0 \text{ kN}\cdot\text{m}$ **(Counterclockwise) Ans**

4-106. Replace the force system by an equivalent resultant force and specify its coordinate point of application $(x, 0)$ on the x axis.

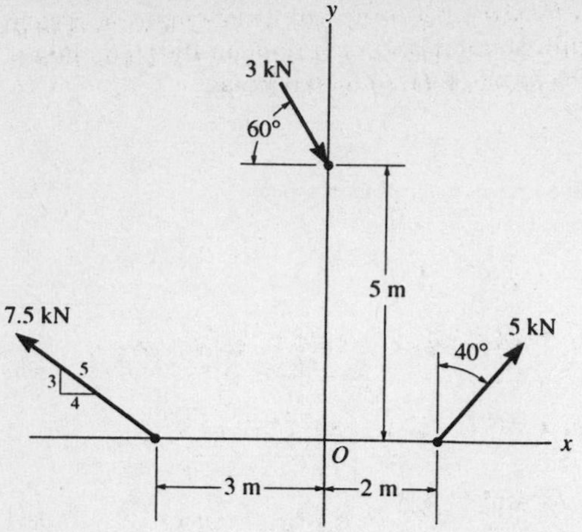

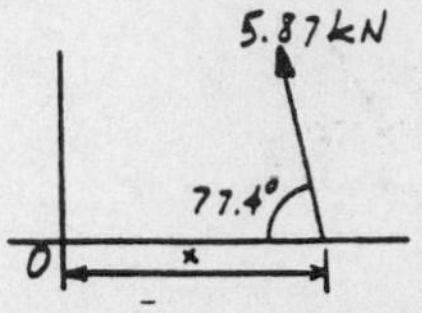

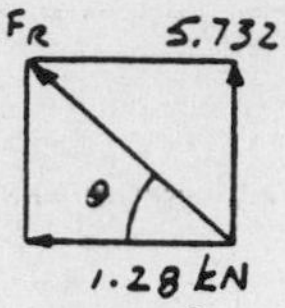

$$\xrightarrow{+} F_{Rx} = \Sigma F_x; \quad F_{Rx} = 3\cos 60° + 5\sin 40° - 7.5\left(\frac{4}{5}\right) = -1.286 \text{ kN}$$

$$+\uparrow F_{Ry} = \Sigma F_y; \quad F_{Ry} = -3\sin 60° + 7.5\left(\frac{3}{5}\right) + 5\cos 40° = 5.732 \text{ kN}$$

$$F_R = \sqrt{(-1.286)^2 + (5.732)^2} = 5.87 \text{ kN} \quad \textbf{Ans}$$

$$\theta = \tan^{-1}\left(\frac{5.732}{1.286}\right) = 77.4° \quad \textbf{Ans}$$

$$\circlearrowleft + M_{RO} = \Sigma M_O; \quad -5.87\sin 77.4°\,(x) = 7.5\left(\frac{3}{5}\right)(3) + 3\cos 60°\,(5) - 5\cos 40°\,(2)$$

$$x = -2.33 \text{ m} \quad \textbf{Ans}$$

4-107. Replace the force system by an equivalent resultant force and specify its coordinate point of application $(0, y)$ on the y axis.

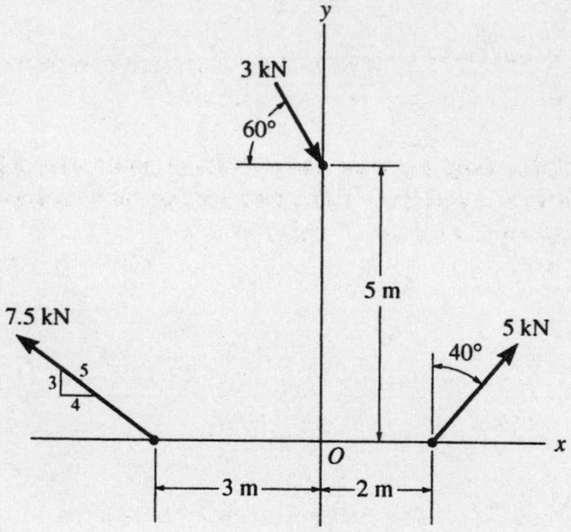

$$\xrightarrow{+} F_{Rx} = \Sigma F_x; \quad F_{Rx} = 3\cos 60° + 5\sin 40° - 7.5\left(\frac{4}{5}\right) = -1.286 \text{ kN}$$

$$+\uparrow F_{Ry} = \Sigma F_y; \quad F_{Ry} = -3\sin 60° + 7.5\left(\frac{3}{5}\right) + 5\cos 40° = 5.732 \text{ kN}$$

$$F_R = \sqrt{(-1.286)^2 + (5.732)^2} = 5.87 \text{ kN} \quad \textbf{Ans}$$

$$\theta = \tan^{-1}\left(\frac{5.732}{1.286}\right) = 77.4° \quad \textbf{Ans}$$

$$\circlearrowleft + M_{RO} = \Sigma M_O; \quad -5.87\cos 77.4°\,(y) = 7.5\left(\frac{3}{5}\right)(3) + 3\cos 60°\,(5) - 5\cos 40°\,(2)$$

$$y = -10.4 \text{ m} \quad \textbf{Ans}$$

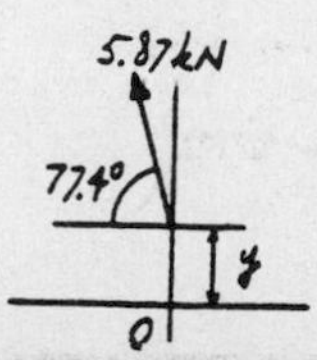

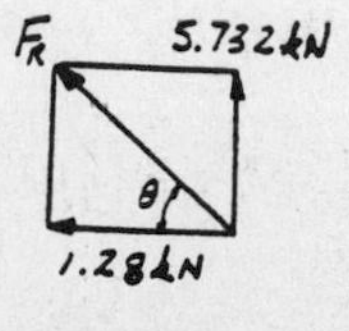

***4-108.** Replace the force and couple-moment system by an equivalent resultant force and specify its coordinate point of application $(x, 0)$ on the x axis.

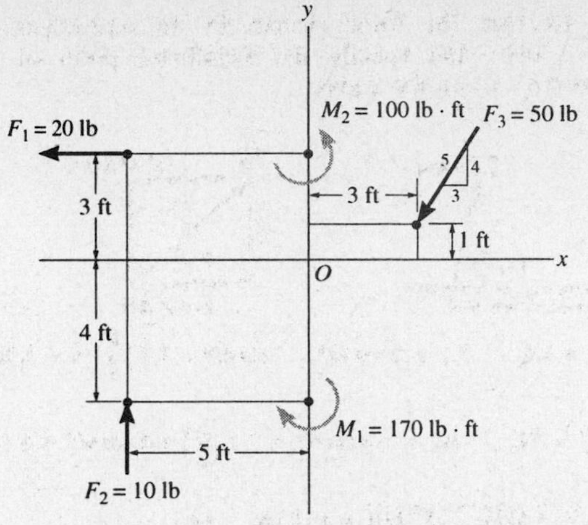

$\xrightarrow{+} F_{Rx} = \Sigma F_x; \quad F_{Rx} = -50\left(\frac{3}{5}\right) - 20 = -50$ lb

$+\uparrow F_{Ry} = \Sigma F_y; \quad F_{Ry} = -50\left(\frac{4}{5}\right) + 10 = -30$ lb

$F_R = \sqrt{(-50)^2 + (-30)^2} = 58.3$ lb **Ans**

$\theta = \tan^{-1}\left(\frac{30}{50}\right) = 31.0°$ **Ans**

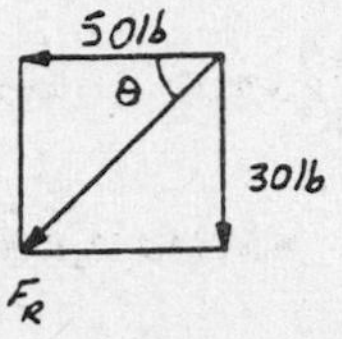

$\circlearrowleft + M_{RO} = \Sigma M_O; \quad -30(x) = -50\left(\frac{4}{5}\right)(3) + 50\left(\frac{3}{5}\right)(1) + 20(3) + 100 - 170 - 10(5)$

$x = 5.00$ ft **Ans**

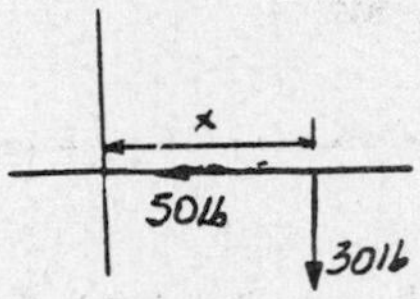

4-109. Replace the force and couple-moment system by an equivalent resultant force and specify its coordinate point of application $(0, y)$ on the y axis.

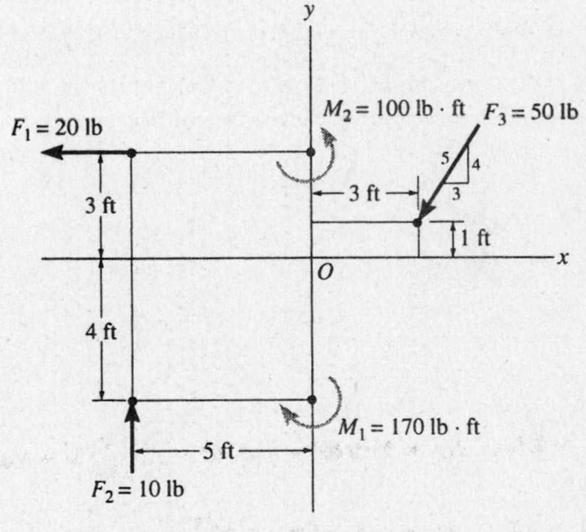

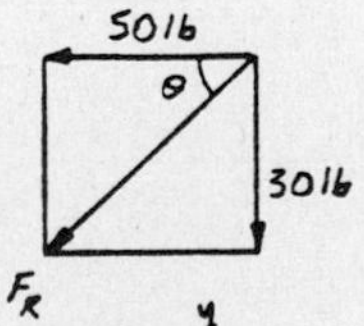

$\xrightarrow{+} F_{Rx} = \Sigma F_x; \quad F_{Rx} = -50\left(\frac{3}{5}\right) - 20 = -50$ lb

$+\uparrow F_{Ry} = \Sigma F_y; \quad F_{Ry} = -50\left(\frac{4}{5}\right) + 10 = -30$ lb

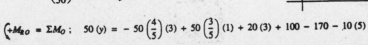

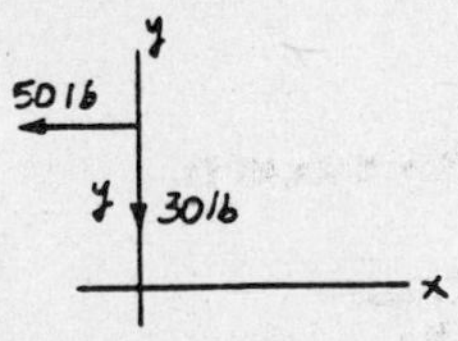

$F_R = \sqrt{(-50)^2 + (-30)^2} = 58.3$ lb **Ans**

$\theta = \tan^{-1}\left(\frac{30}{50}\right) = 31.0°$ **Ans**

$\circlearrowleft + M_{RO} = \Sigma M_O; \quad 50(y) = -50\left(\frac{4}{5}\right)(3) + 50\left(\frac{3}{5}\right)(1) + 20(3) + 100 - 170 - 10(5)$

$y = -3.00$ ft **Ans**

4-110. Replace the force system acting on the beam by an equivalent force and couple moment at point *A*.

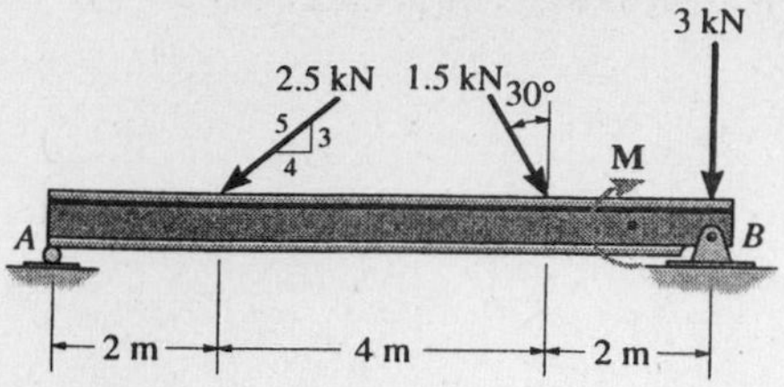

$\overset{+}{\rightarrow} F_{R_x} = \Sigma F_x;\quad F_{R_x} = 1.5\sin 30° - 2.5\left(\frac{4}{5}\right)$

$= -1.25 \text{ kN} = 1.25 \text{ kN} \leftarrow$

$+\uparrow F_{R_y} = \Sigma F_y;\quad F_{R_y} = -1.5\cos 30° - 2.5\left(\frac{3}{5}\right) - 3$

$= -5.799 \text{ kN} = 5.799 \text{ kN} \downarrow$

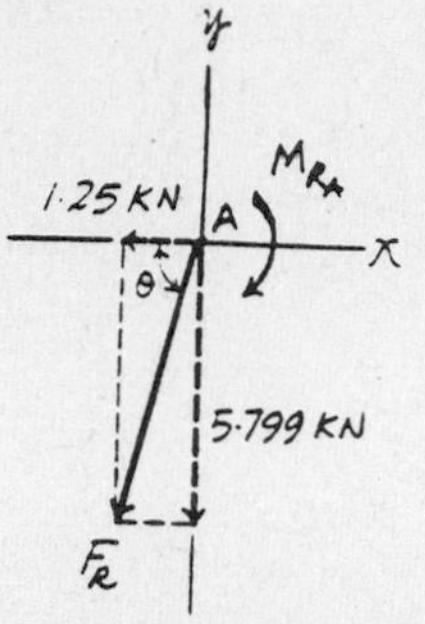

Thus,

$F_R = \sqrt{F_{R_x}^2 + F_{R_y}^2} = \sqrt{1.25^2 + 5.799^2} = 5.93 \text{ kN}$ **Ans**

and

$\theta = \tan^{-1}\left(\frac{F_{R_y}}{F_{R_x}}\right) = \tan^{-1}\left(\frac{5.799}{1.25}\right) = 77.8°$ **Ans**

$\circlearrowleft + M_{R_A} = \Sigma M_A;\quad M_{R_A} = -2.5\left(\frac{3}{5}\right)(2) - 1.5\cos 30°(6) - 3(8)$

$= -34.8 \text{ kN}\cdot\text{m} = 34.8 \text{ kN}\cdot\text{m}$ ***(Clockwise)*** **Ans**

4-111. Replace the force system acting on the beam by an equivalent force and couple moment at point *B*.

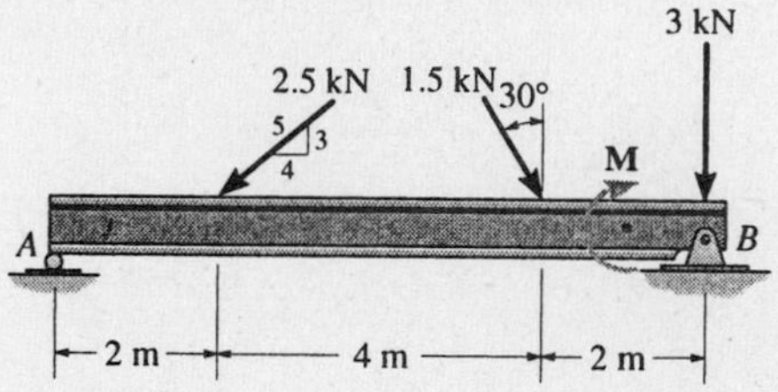

$\overset{+}{\rightarrow} F_{R_x} = \Sigma F_x;\quad F_{R_x} = 1.5\sin 30° - 2.5\left(\frac{4}{5}\right)$

$= -1.25 \text{ kN} = 1.25 \text{ kN} \leftarrow$

$+\uparrow F_{R_y} = \Sigma F_y;\quad F_{R_y} = -1.5\cos 30° - 2.5\left(\frac{3}{5}\right) - 3$

$= -5.799 \text{ kN} = 5.799 \text{ kN} \downarrow$

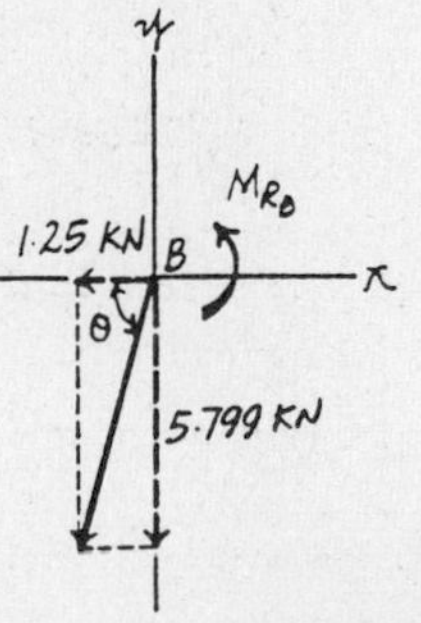

Thus,

$F_R = \sqrt{F_{R_x}^2 + F_{R_y}^2} = \sqrt{1.25^2 + 5.799^2} = 5.93 \text{ kN}$ **Ans**

and

$\theta = \tan^{-1}\left(\frac{F_{R_y}}{F_{R_x}}\right) = \tan^{-1}\left(\frac{5.799}{1.25}\right) = 77.8°$ **Ans**

$\circlearrowleft + M_{R_B} = \Sigma M_B;\quad M_{R_B} = 1.5\cos 30°(2) + 2.5\left(\frac{3}{5}\right)(6)$

$= 11.6 \text{ kN}\cdot\text{m}$ ***(Counterclockwise)*** **Ans**

*4-112.** Replace the two forces by an equivalent resultant force and couple moment at point O. Set $F = 20$ lb.

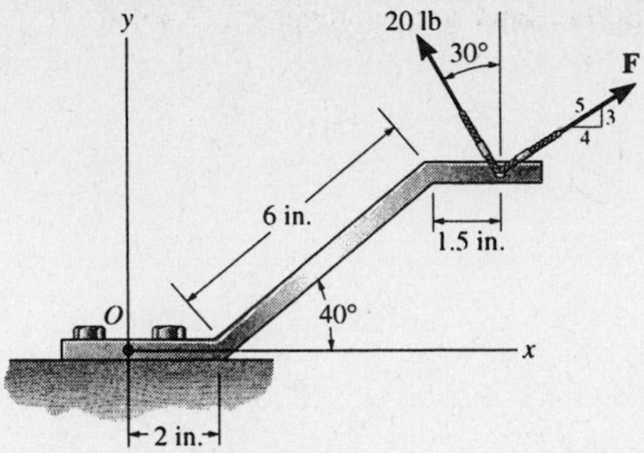

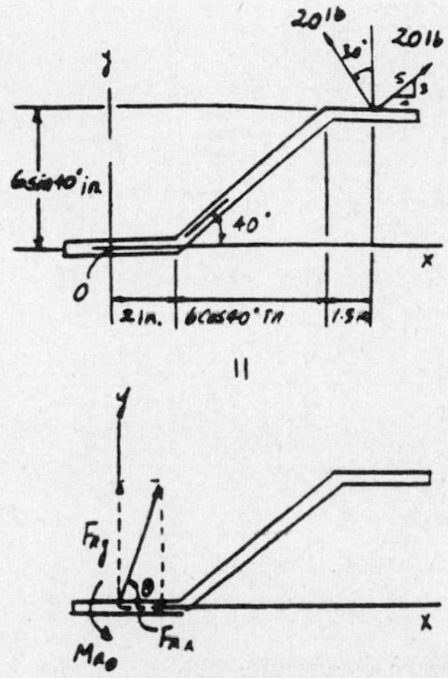

$\xrightarrow{+} F_{Rx} = \Sigma F_x;\quad F_{Rx} = \frac{4}{5}(20) - 20 \sin 30° = 6 \text{ lb}$

$+\uparrow F_{Ry} = \Sigma F_y;\quad F_{Ry} = 20 \cos 30° + \frac{3}{5}(20) = 29.32 \text{ lb}$

$F_R = \sqrt{F_{Rx}^2 + F_{Ry}^2} = \sqrt{6^2 + (29.32)^2} = 29.9 \text{ lb}$ **Ans**

$\theta = \tan^{-1}\frac{F_{Ry}}{F_{Rx}} = \tan^{-1}\left(\frac{29.32}{6}\right) = 78.4°$ **Ans**

$\curvearrowleft + M_{R_O} = \Sigma M_O;\quad M_{R_O} = 20 \sin 30°(6 \sin 40°) + 20 \cos 30°(3.5 + 6 \cos 40°)$

$- \frac{4}{5}(20)(6 \sin 40°) + \frac{3}{5}(20)(3.5 + 6 \cos 40°)$

$= 214 \text{ lb} \cdot \text{in.}$ ↺ **Ans**

4-113. Replace the two forces by an equivalent resultant force and couple moment at point O. Set $F = 15$ lb.

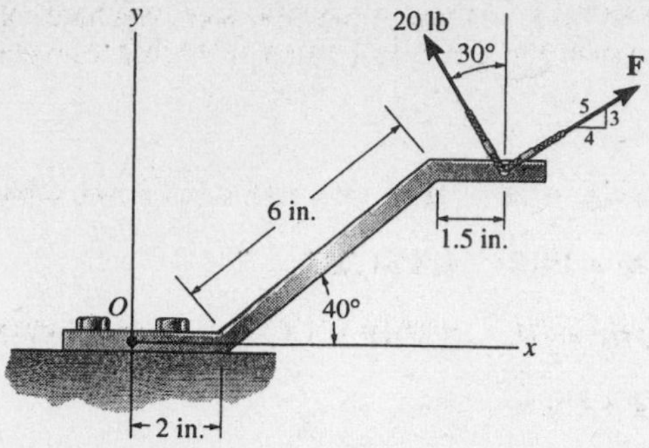

$\xrightarrow{+} F_{Rx} = \Sigma F_x; \quad F_{Rx} = \frac{4}{5}(15) - 20 \sin 30° = 2$ lb

$+\uparrow F_{Ry} = \Sigma F_y; \quad F_{Ry} = 20 \cos 30° + \frac{3}{5}(15) = 26.32$ lb

$F_R = \sqrt{F_{Rx}^2 + F_{Ry}^2} = \sqrt{2^2 + 26.32^2} = 26.4$ lb **Ans**

$\theta = \tan^{-1}\frac{F_{Ry}}{F_{Rx}} = \tan^{-1}\left(\frac{26.32}{2}\right) = 85.7°$ **Ans**

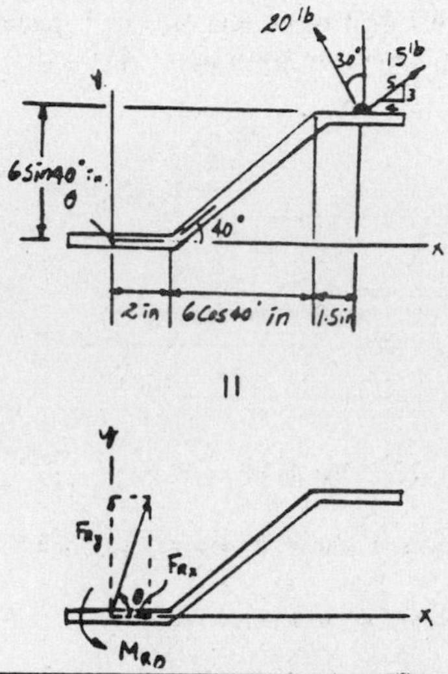

$\circlearrowleft + M_{R_O} = \Sigma M_O; \quad M_{R_O} = 20 \sin 30°(6 \sin 40°) + 20 \cos 30°(3.5 + 6 \cos 40°)$

$- \frac{4}{5}(15)(6 \sin 40°) + \frac{3}{5}(15)(3.5 + 6 \cos 40°)$

$= 205$ lb · in. **Ans**

4-114. The tires of a truck exert the forces shown on the deck of the bridge. Replace this system of forces by an equivalent resultant force and specify its location measured from point A.

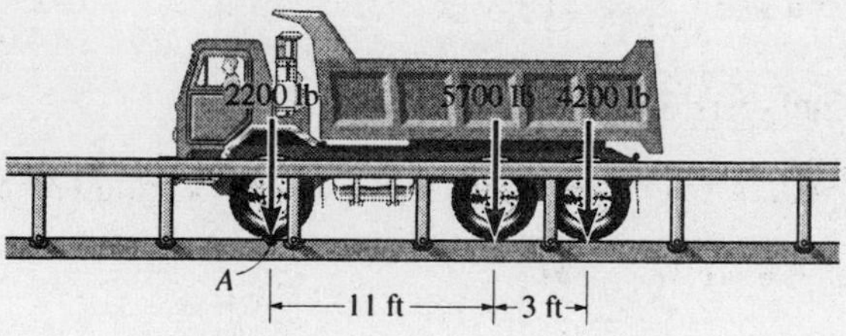

$+\downarrow F_R = \Sigma F_z; \quad F_R = 5700 + 4200 + 2200 = 12\,100$ lb $= 12.1$ kip **Ans**

$\circlearrowleft + M_A = \Sigma M_A; \quad 12\,100(d) = 5700(11) + 4200(14)$

$d = 10.0$ ft **Ans**

4-115. The system of parallel forces acts on the top of the *Warren truss.* Determine the equivalent resultant force of the system and specify its location measured from point A.

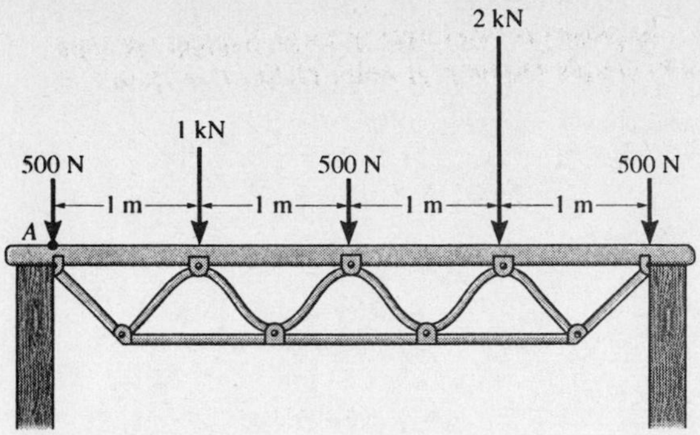

$+\downarrow F_R = \Sigma F;\quad F_R = 500 + 1000 + 500 + 2000 + 500$

$F_R = 4500\text{ N} = 4.50\text{ kN}$ **Ans**

$\circlearrowleft + M_R = \Sigma M_A;\quad 4500\,(d) = 1000(1) + 500\,(2) + 2000\,(3) + 500\,(4)$

$d = 2.22\text{ m}$ **Ans**

***4-116.** The system of four forces acts on the roof truss. Determine the equivalent resultant force and specify its location along AB, measured from point A.

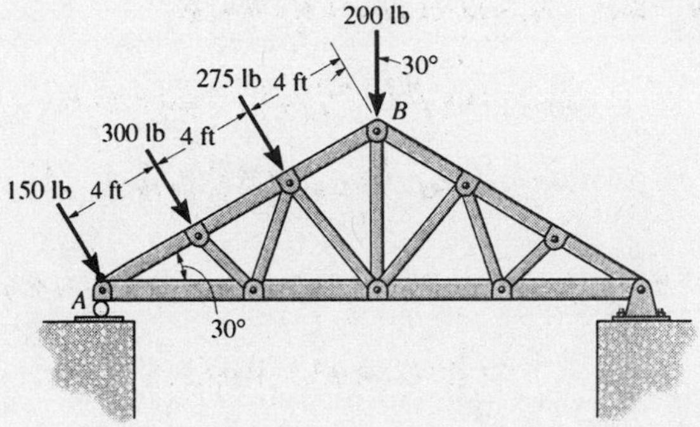

$\swarrow + F_{Rx} = \Sigma F_x;\quad F_{Rx} = 200 \sin 30° = 100\text{ lb}$

$\searrow + F_{Ry} = \Sigma F_y;\quad F_{Ry} = 150 + 300 + 275 + 200 \cos 30° = 898.2\text{ lb}$

$F_R = \sqrt{(100)^2 + (898.2)^2} = 904\text{ lb}$ **Ans**

$\theta = \tan^{-1}\left(\dfrac{100}{898.2}\right) = 6.35°$

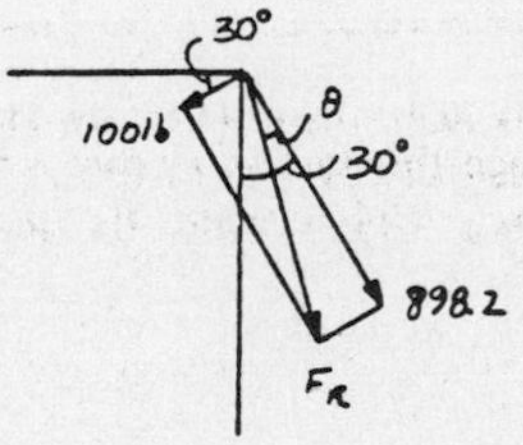

$30° - 6.35° = 23.6°$ **Ans**

$\circlearrowleft + M_{RA} = \Sigma M_A;\quad 898.2\,(d) = 4\,(300) + 8\,(275) + 12 \cos 30°\,(200)$

$d = 6.10\text{ ft}$ **Ans**

4-117. Determine the magnitudes of $\mathbf{F}_1$ and $\mathbf{F}_2$ and the direction of $\mathbf{F}_1$ so that the loading creates a zero resultant force and couple moment on the wheel.

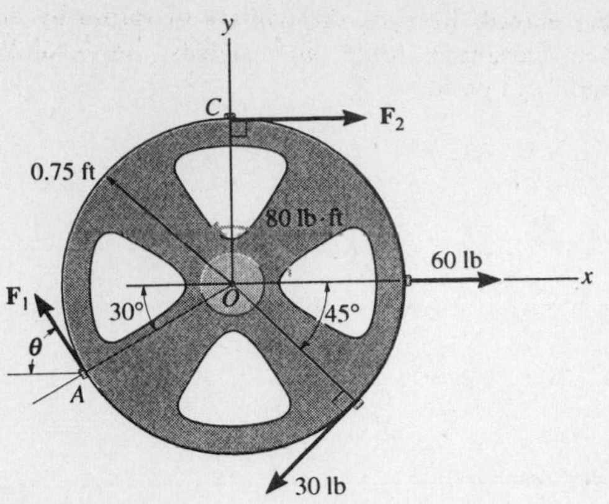

Force Summation :

$$\xrightarrow{+} 0 = \Sigma F_x; \quad 0 = F_2 + 60 - F_1 \cos\theta - 30\cos 45°$$

$$F_2 - F_1 \cos\theta = -38.79 \quad [1]$$

$$+\uparrow 0 = \Sigma F_y; \quad 0 = F_1 \sin\theta - 30\sin 45°$$

$$F_1 \sin\theta = 21.21 \quad [2]$$

Moment Summation :

$$\curvearrowleft + \; 0 = \Sigma M_O; \quad 0 = 80 - F_2(0.75) - 30(0.75) - F_1 \sin\theta(0.75\cos 30°) - F_1\cos\theta(0.75\sin 30°)$$

$$0.6495F_1\cos\theta + 0.375F_1\sin\theta + 0.75F_2 = 57.5 \quad [3]$$

Solving Eqs.[1], [2] and [3] yields

$F_2 = 25.9$ lb $\quad \theta = 18.1°$ $\quad F_1 = 68.1$ lb **Ans**

4-118. The weights of the various components of the truck are shown. Replace this system of forces by an equivalent resultant force and couple moment acting at point *A*.

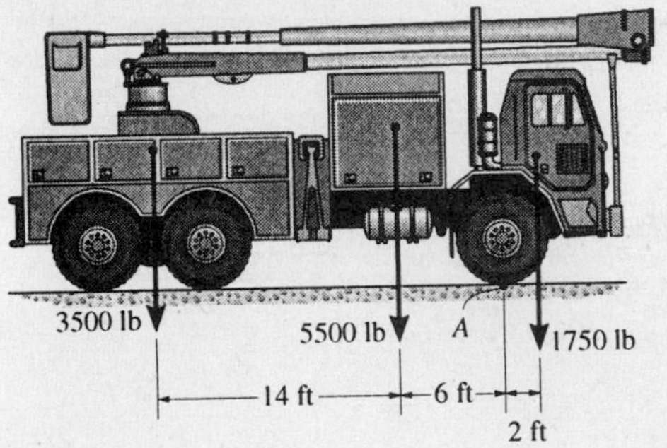

$$+\uparrow F_R = \Sigma F_y; \quad F_R = -1750 - 5500 - 3500$$

$$= -10750 \text{ lb} = 10.75 \text{ kip} \downarrow \quad \textbf{Ans}$$

$$\curvearrowleft + \; M_{R_A} = \Sigma M_A; \quad M_{R_A} = 3500(20) + 5500(6) - 1750(2)$$

$$= 99500 \text{ lb}\cdot\text{ft}$$

$$= 99.5 \text{ kip}\cdot\text{ft} \; (\textit{Counterclockwise}) \quad \textbf{Ans}$$

4-119. The weights of the various components of the truck are shown. Replace this system of forces by an equivalent resultant force and specify its location measured from point A.

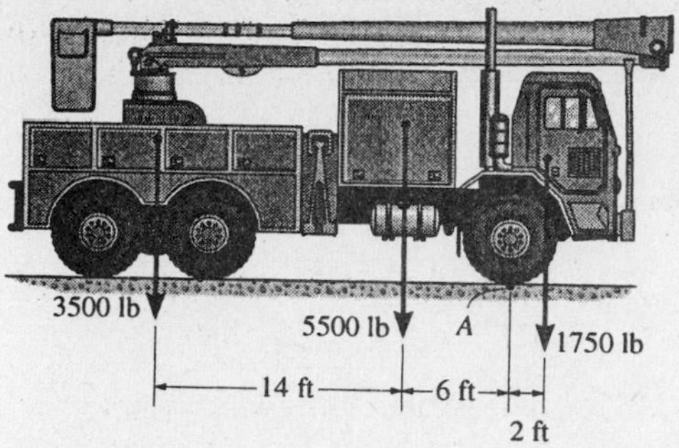

Equivalent Force :

$+\uparrow F_R = \Sigma F_y;\quad F_R = -1750 - 5500 - 3500$

$= -10750 \text{ lb} = 10.75 \text{ kip} \downarrow$ **Ans**

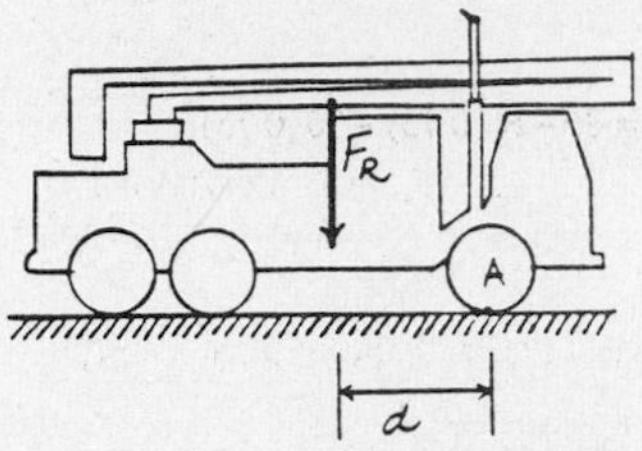

Location of Resultant Force From Point A :

$\circlearrowleft + M_{R_A} = \Sigma M_A;\quad 10750(d) = 3500(20) + 5500(6) - 1750(2)$

$d = 9.26 \text{ ft}$ **Ans**

***4-120.** Replace the force and couple system acting on the frame by an equivalent resultant force and specify where the resultant's line of action intersects member AB, measured from A.

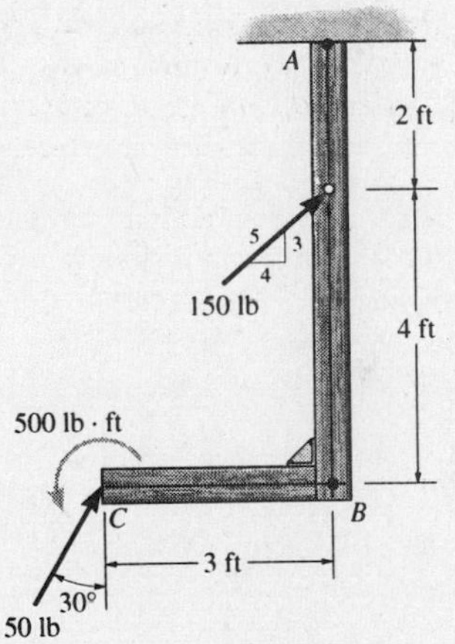

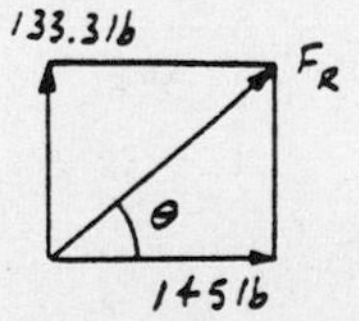

$\xrightarrow{+} F_{Rx} = \Sigma F_x;\quad F_{Rx} = 150\left(\frac{4}{5}\right) + 50 \sin 30° = 145 \text{ lb}$

$+\uparrow F_{Ry} = \Sigma F_y;\quad F_{Ry} = 50 \cos 30° + 150\left(\frac{3}{5}\right) = 133.3 \text{ lb}$

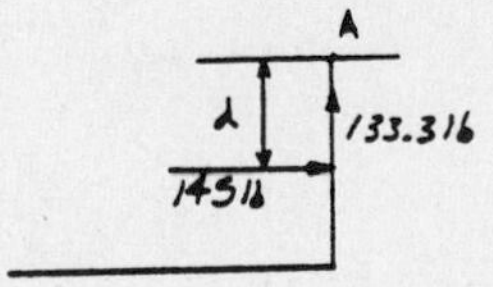

$F_R = \sqrt{(145)^2 + (133.3)^2} = 197 \text{ lb}$ **Ans**

$\theta = \tan^{-1}\left(\frac{133.3}{145}\right) = 42.6°$ **Ans**

$\circlearrowleft + M_{RA} = \Sigma M_A;\quad 145\,(d) = 150\left(\frac{4}{5}\right)(2) - 50 \cos 30°\,(3) + 50 \sin 30°\,(6) + 500$

$d = 5.24 \text{ ft}$ **Ans**

4-121. Replace the force and couple system acting on the frame by an equivalent resultant force and specify where the resultant's line of action intersects member BC, measured from B.

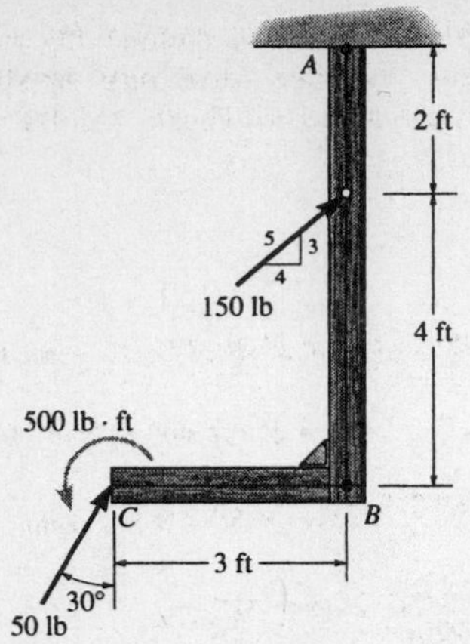

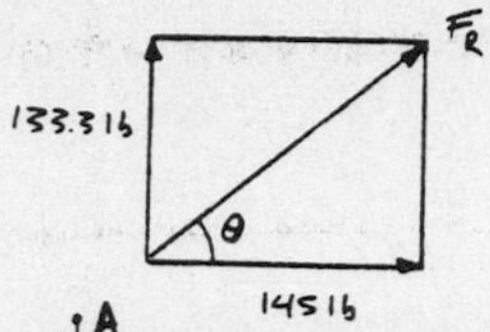

$\xrightarrow{+} F_{Rx} = \Sigma F_x;\quad F_{Rx} = 150\left(\frac{4}{5}\right) + 50\sin 30° = 145 \text{ lb}$

$+\uparrow F_{Ry} = \Sigma F_y;\quad F_{Ry} = 50\cos 30° + 150\left(\frac{3}{5}\right) = 133.3 \text{ lb}$

$F_R = \sqrt{(145)^2 + (133.3)^2} = 197 \text{ lb}$ **Ans**

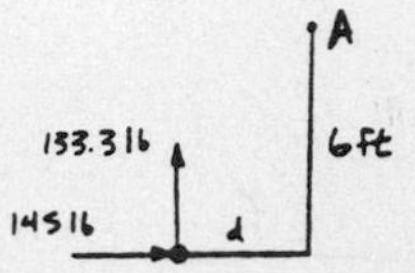

$\theta = \tan^{-1}\left(\frac{133.3}{145}\right) = 42.6°$ ∠ **Ans**

$\curvearrowleft + M_{RA} = \Sigma M_A;\quad 145(6) - 133.3(d) = 150\left(\frac{4}{5}\right)(2) - 50\cos 30°(3) + 50\sin 30°(6) + 500$

$d = 0.824 \text{ ft}$ **Ans**

4-122. Replace the force system acting on the frame by an equivalent resultant force and specify where the resultant's line of action intersects member AB, measured from point A.

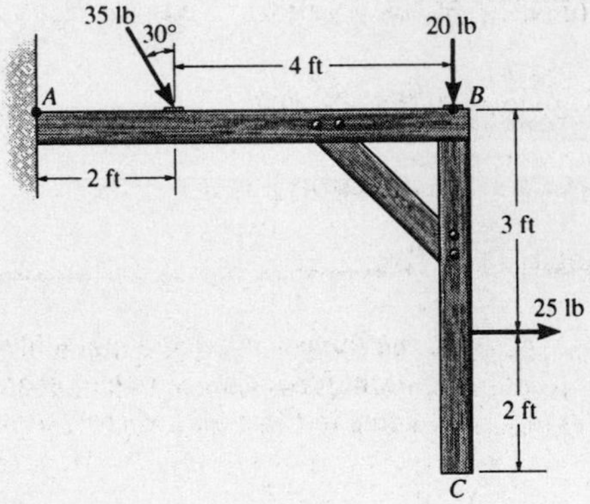

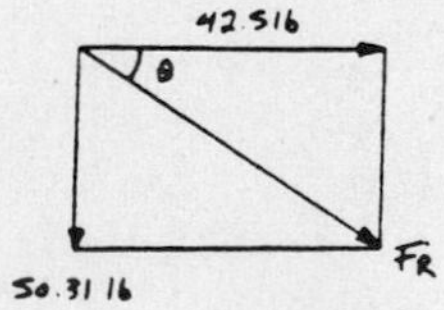

$\xrightarrow{+} F_{Rx} = \Sigma F_x;\quad F_{Rx} = 35\sin 30° + 25 = 42.5 \text{ lb}$

$+\downarrow F_{Ry} = \Sigma F_y;\quad F_{Ry} = 35\cos 30° + 20 = 50.31 \text{ lb}$

$F_R = \sqrt{(42.5)^2 + (50.31)^2} = 65.9 \text{ lb}$ **Ans**

$\theta = \tan^{-1}\left(\frac{50.31}{42.5}\right) = 49.8°$ **Ans**

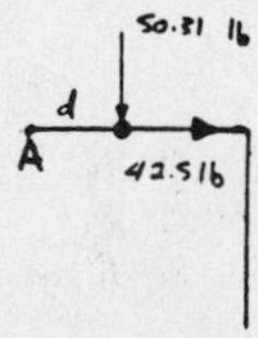

$\curvearrowright + M_{RA} = \Sigma M_A;\quad 50.31(d) = 35\cos 30°(2) + 20(6) - 25(3)$

$d = 2.10 \text{ ft}$ **Ans**

4-123. Replace the force system acting on the frame by an equivalent resultant force and specify where the resultant's line of action intersects member BC, measured from point B.

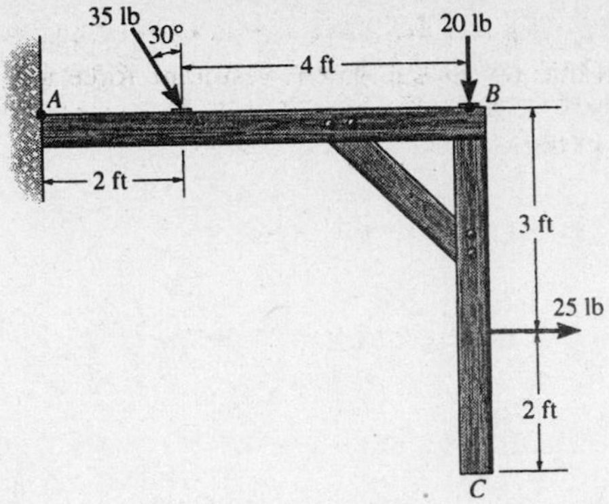

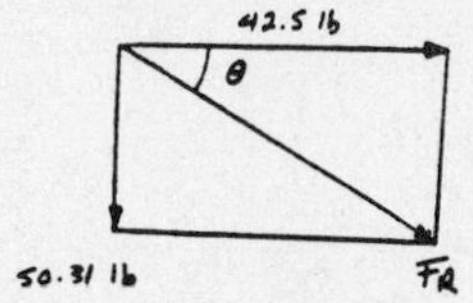

$\xrightarrow{+} F_{Rx} = \Sigma F_x;\quad F_{Rx} = 35 \sin 30° + 25 = 42.5 \text{ lb}$

$+\downarrow F_{Ry} = \Sigma F_y;\quad F_{Ry} = 35 \cos 30° + 20 = 50.31 \text{ lb}$

$F_R = \sqrt{(42.5)^2 + (50.31)^2} = 65.9 \text{ lb}$ **Ans**

$\theta = \tan^{-1}\left(\dfrac{50.31}{42.5}\right) = 49.8°$ **Ans**

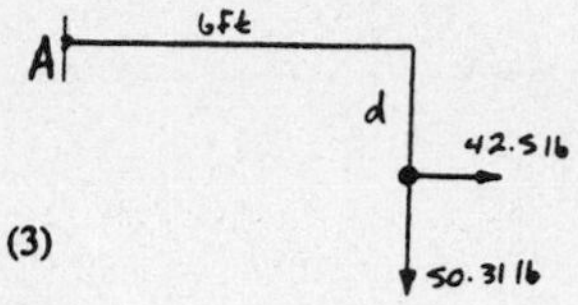

$\circlearrowleft +M_{RA} = \Sigma M_A;\quad 50.31\,(6) - 42.5\,(d) = 35 \cos 30°\,(2) + 20\,(6) - 25\,(3)$

$d = 4.62 \text{ ft}$ **Ans**

***4-124.** Replace the force system acting on the frame by an equivalent resultant force and couple moment acting at point A.

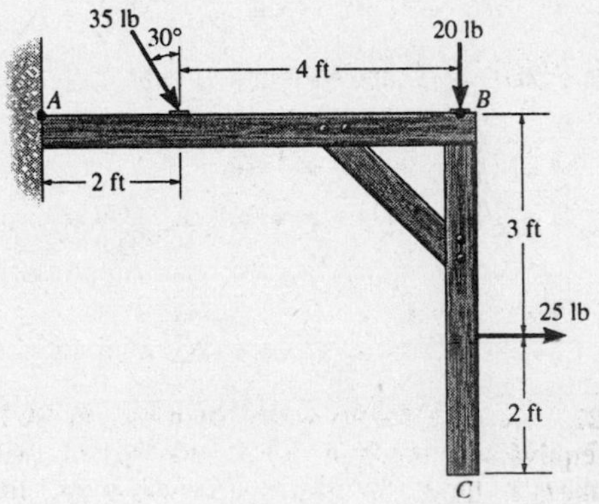

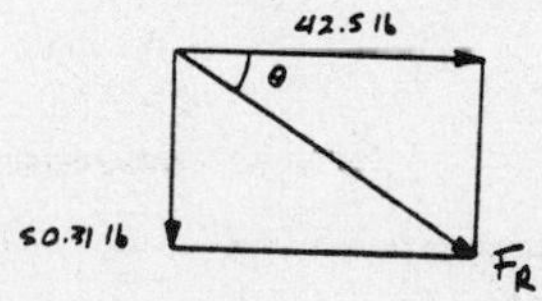

$\xrightarrow{+} F_{Rx} = \Sigma F_x;\quad F_{Rx} = 35 \sin 30° + 25 = 42.5 \text{ lb}$

$+\downarrow F_{Ry} = \Sigma F_y;\quad F_{Ry} = 35 \cos 30° + 20 = 50.31 \text{ lb}$

$F_R = \sqrt{(42.5)^2 + (50.31)^2} = 65.9 \text{ lb}$ **Ans**

$\theta = \tan^{-1}\left(\dfrac{50.31}{42.5}\right) = 49.8°$ **Ans**

$\circlearrowleft +M_{RA} = \Sigma M_A;\quad M_{RA} = 35\cos 30°(2) + 20(6) - 25(3)$

$M_{RA} = 106 \text{ lb}\cdot\text{ft}$ **Ans**

4-125. Replace the force and couple-moment system by an equivalent resultant force and couple moment at point O. Express the results in Cartesian vector form.

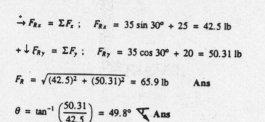

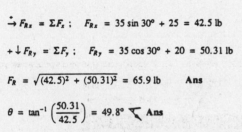

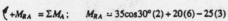

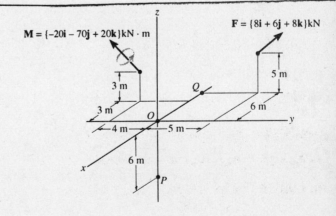

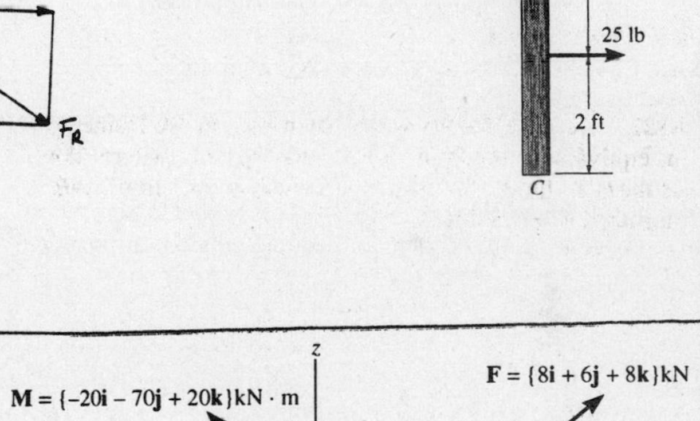

$\mathbf{F}_R = \Sigma \mathbf{F};\quad \mathbf{F}_R = \{8\mathbf{i} + 6\mathbf{j} + 8\mathbf{k}\} \text{ kN}$ **Ans**

$$\mathbf{M}_{RO} = \Sigma \mathbf{M}_O;\quad \mathbf{M}_{RO} = -20\mathbf{i} - 70\mathbf{j} + 20\mathbf{k} + \begin{vmatrix} \mathbf{i} & \mathbf{j} & \mathbf{k} \\ -6 & 5 & 5 \\ 8 & 6 & 8 \end{vmatrix}$$

$= \{-10\mathbf{i} + 18\mathbf{j} - 56\mathbf{k}\} \text{ kN}\cdot\text{m}$ **Ans**

4-126. Replace the force and couple-moment system by an equivalent resultant force and couple moment at point *P*. Express the results in Cartesian vector form.

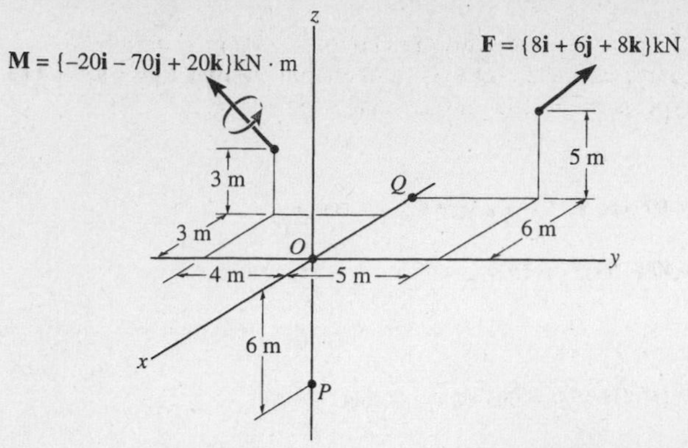

$\mathbf{F}_R = \{8\mathbf{i} + 6\mathbf{j} + 8\mathbf{k}\}$ kN **Ans**

$$\mathbf{M}_{RP} = \Sigma\mathbf{M}_P = -20\mathbf{i} - 70\mathbf{j} + 20\mathbf{k} + \begin{vmatrix} \mathbf{i} & \mathbf{j} & \mathbf{k} \\ -6 & 5 & 11 \\ 8 & 6 & 8 \end{vmatrix}$$

$$= \{-46\mathbf{i} + 66\mathbf{j} - 56\mathbf{k}\}\ \text{kN}\cdot\text{m} \quad \textbf{Ans}$$

4-127. Replace the force and couple-moment system by an equivalent resultant force and couple moment at point *Q*. Express the results in Cartesian vector form.

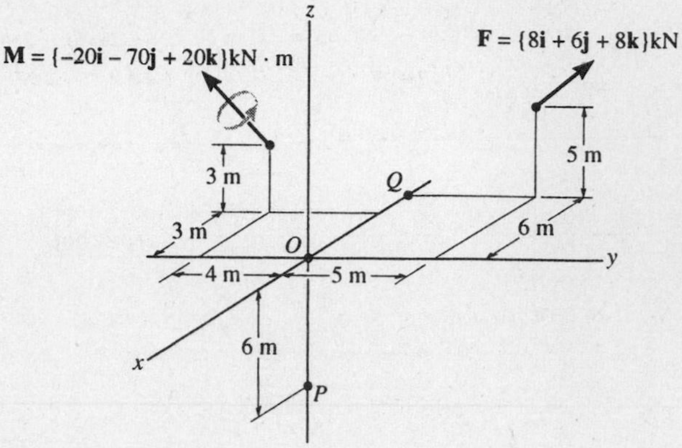

$\mathbf{F}_R = \{8\mathbf{i} + 6\mathbf{j} + 8\mathbf{k}\}$ kN **Ans**

$$\mathbf{M}_{RQ} = -20\mathbf{i} - 70\mathbf{j} + 20\mathbf{k} + \begin{vmatrix} \mathbf{i} & \mathbf{j} & \mathbf{k} \\ 0 & 5 & 5 \\ 8 & 6 & 8 \end{vmatrix}$$

$$= \{-10\mathbf{i} - 30\mathbf{j} - 20\mathbf{k}\}\ \text{kN}\cdot\text{m} \quad \textbf{Ans}$$

***4-128.** Replace the force and couple-moment system by an equivalent resultant force and couple moment at point *O*. Express the results in Cartesian vector form.

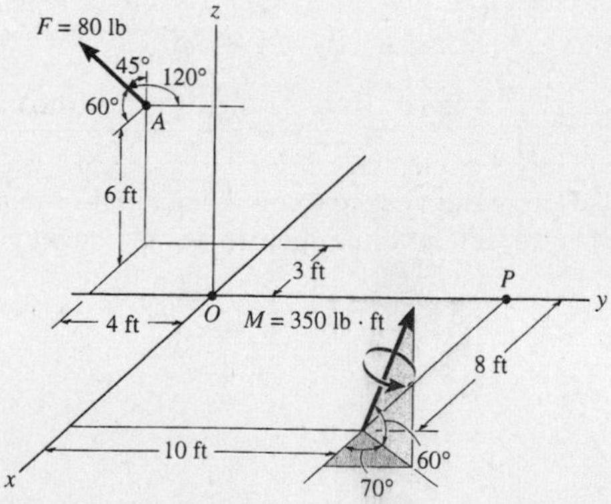

$\mathbf{F}_R = 80\{\cos 60°\,\mathbf{i} + \cos 120°\,\mathbf{j} + \cos 45°\,\mathbf{k}\}$

$= 40\mathbf{i} - 40\mathbf{j} + 56.57\mathbf{k}$

$= \{40\mathbf{i} - 40\mathbf{j} + 56.6\mathbf{k}\}$ lb **Ans**

$$\mathbf{M}_{RO} = \mathbf{r}_{OA} \times \mathbf{F} + \mathbf{M} = \begin{vmatrix} \mathbf{i} & \mathbf{j} & \mathbf{k} \\ -3 & -4 & 6 \\ 40 & -40 & 56.57 \end{vmatrix}$$

$$+ 350\{\cos 60° \cos 70°\,\mathbf{i} + \cos 60° \sin 70°\,\mathbf{j} + \sin 60°\,\mathbf{k}\}$$

$$= \{73.6\mathbf{i} + 574\mathbf{j} + 583\mathbf{k}\}\ \text{lb}\cdot\text{ft} \quad \textbf{Ans}$$

4-129. Replace the force and couple-moment system by an equivalent resultant force and couple moment at point P. Express the results in Cartesian vector form.

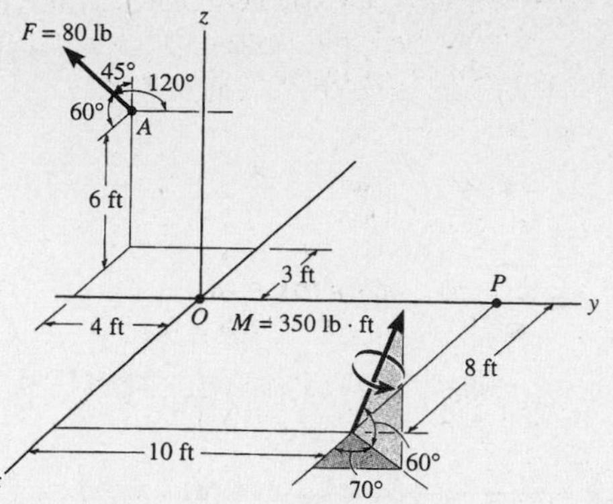

$$\mathbf{F}_R = 80\{\cos 60°\,\mathbf{i} + \cos 120°\,\mathbf{j} + \cos 45°\,\mathbf{k}\}$$

$$= 40\,\mathbf{i} - 40\,\mathbf{j} + 56.57\,\mathbf{k}$$

$$\mathbf{F}_R = \{40\,\mathbf{i} - 40\,\mathbf{j} + 56.6\,\mathbf{k}\}\text{ lb} \qquad \textbf{Ans}$$

$$\mathbf{M}_{RP} = \mathbf{r}_{PA} \times \mathbf{F} + \mathbf{M} = \begin{vmatrix} \mathbf{i} & \mathbf{j} & \mathbf{k} \\ -3 & -14 & 6 \\ 40 & -40 & 56.57 \end{vmatrix}$$

$$+ 350\{\cos 60° \cos 70°\,\mathbf{i} + \cos 60° \sin 70°\,\mathbf{j} + \sin 60°\,\mathbf{k}\}$$

$$= \{-492\,\mathbf{i} + 574\,\mathbf{j} + 983\,\mathbf{k}\}\text{ lb}\cdot\text{ft} \qquad \textbf{Ans}$$

4-130. Replace the force system by an equivalent force and couple moment at point A.

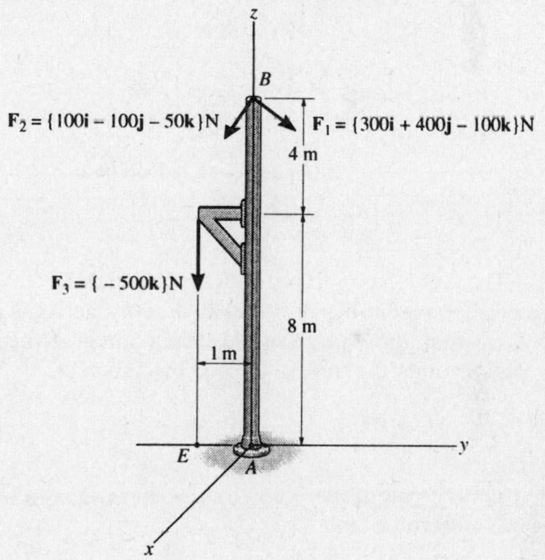

$$\mathbf{F}_R = \Sigma\mathbf{F}; \quad \mathbf{F}_R = \mathbf{F}_1 + \mathbf{F}_2 + \mathbf{F}_3$$
$$= (300 + 100)\,\mathbf{i} + (400 - 100)\,\mathbf{j} + (-100 - 50 - 500)\,\mathbf{k}$$
$$= \{400\mathbf{i} + 300\mathbf{j} - 650\mathbf{k}\}\text{ N} \qquad \textbf{Ans}$$

The position vectors are $\mathbf{r}_{AB} = \{12\mathbf{k}\}$ m and $\mathbf{r}_{AE} = \{-1\mathbf{j}\}$ m.

$$\mathbf{M}_{R_A} = \Sigma\mathbf{M}_A; \quad \mathbf{M}_{R_A} = \mathbf{r}_{AB} \times \mathbf{F}_1 + \mathbf{r}_{AB} \times \mathbf{F}_2 + \mathbf{r}_{AE} \times \mathbf{F}_3$$

$$= \begin{vmatrix} \mathbf{i} & \mathbf{j} & \mathbf{k} \\ 0 & 0 & 12 \\ 300 & 400 & -100 \end{vmatrix} + \begin{vmatrix} \mathbf{i} & \mathbf{j} & \mathbf{k} \\ 0 & 0 & 12 \\ 100 & -100 & -50 \end{vmatrix}$$

$$+ \begin{vmatrix} \mathbf{i} & \mathbf{j} & \mathbf{k} \\ 0 & -1 & 0 \\ 0 & 0 & -500 \end{vmatrix}$$

$$= \{-3100\mathbf{i} + 4800\mathbf{j}\}\text{ N}\cdot\text{m} \qquad \textbf{Ans}$$

4-131. The slab is to be hoisted using the three slings shown. Replace the system of forces acting on slings by an equivalent force and couple moment at point O. The force $\mathbf{F}_1$, is vertical.

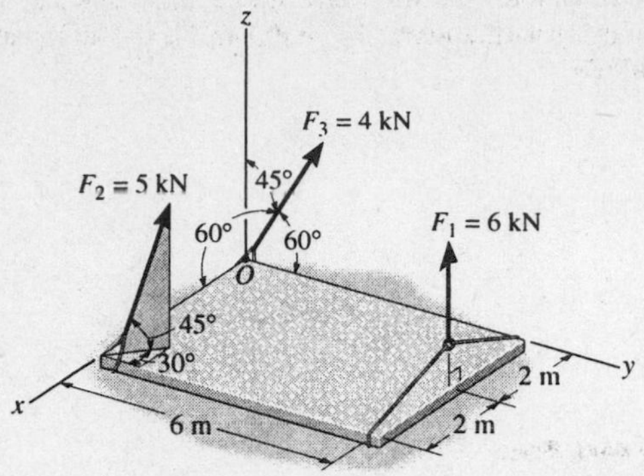

Force Vectors :

$$\mathbf{F}_1 = \{6.00\mathbf{k}\} \text{ kN}$$

$$\mathbf{F}_2 = 5(-\cos 45°\sin 30°\mathbf{i} + \cos 45°\cos 30°\mathbf{j} + \sin 45°\mathbf{k})$$
$$= \{-1.768\mathbf{i} + 3.062\mathbf{j} + 3.536\mathbf{k}\} \text{ kN}$$

$$\mathbf{F}_3 = 4(\cos 60°\mathbf{i} + \cos 60°\mathbf{j} + \cos 45°\mathbf{k})$$
$$= \{2.00\mathbf{i} + 2.00\mathbf{j} + 2.828\mathbf{k}\} \text{ kN}$$

Equivalent Force and Couple Moment At Point O :

$$\mathbf{F}_R = \Sigma\mathbf{F}; \quad \mathbf{F}_R = \mathbf{F}_1 + \mathbf{F}_2 + \mathbf{F}_3$$
$$= (-1.768 + 2.00)\,\mathbf{i} + (3.062 + 2.00)\,\mathbf{j} + (6.00 + 3.536 + 2.828)\,\mathbf{k}$$

$$= \{0.232\mathbf{i} + 5.06\mathbf{j} + 12.4\mathbf{k}\} \text{ kN} \qquad \textbf{Ans}$$

The position vectors are $\mathbf{r}_1 = \{2\mathbf{i} + 6\mathbf{j}\}$ m and $\mathbf{r}_2 = \{4\mathbf{i}\}$ m.

$$\mathbf{M}_{R_O} = \Sigma\mathbf{M}_O; \quad \mathbf{M}_{R_O} = \mathbf{r}_1 \times \mathbf{F}_1 + \mathbf{r}_2 \times \mathbf{F}_2$$
$$= \begin{vmatrix} \mathbf{i} & \mathbf{j} & \mathbf{k} \\ 2 & 6 & 0 \\ 0 & 0 & 6.00 \end{vmatrix} + \begin{vmatrix} \mathbf{i} & \mathbf{j} & \mathbf{k} \\ 4 & 0 & 0 \\ -1.768 & 3.062 & 3.536 \end{vmatrix}$$

$$= \{36.0\mathbf{i} - 26.1\mathbf{j} + 12.2\mathbf{k}\} \text{ kN}\cdot\text{m} \qquad \textbf{Ans}$$

***4-132.** The tube supports the four parallel forces. Determine the magnitudes of forces $\mathbf{F}_C$ and $\mathbf{F}_D$ acting at C and D so that the equivalent resultant force of the system acts through the midpoint O of the tube.

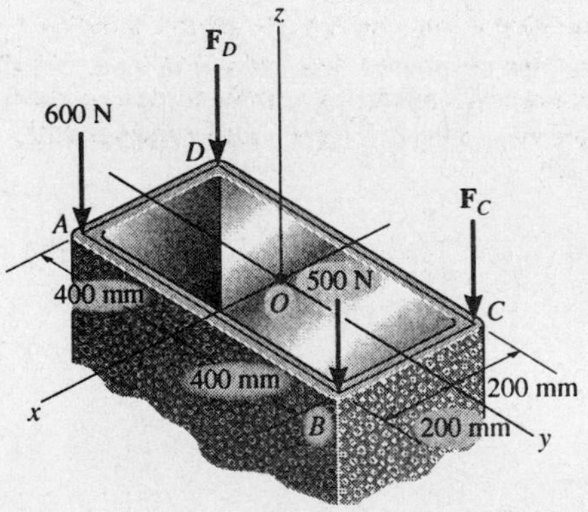

Since the resultant force passes through point O, the resultant moment components about x and y axes are both zero.

$$\Sigma M_x = 0; \quad F_D(0.4) + 600(0.4) - F_C(0.4) - 500(0.4) = 0$$

$$F_C - F_D = 100 \qquad (1)$$

$$\Sigma M_y = 0; \quad 500(0.2) + 600(0.2) - F_C(0.2) - F_D(0.2) = 0$$

$$F_C + F_D = 1100 \qquad (2)$$

Solving Eqs. (1) and (2) yields :

$$F_C = 600 \text{ N} \qquad F_D = 500 \text{ N} \qquad \textbf{Ans}$$

4-133. Three parallel bolting forces act on the circular plate. Determine the resultant force, and specify its location (x, z) on the plate. $F_A = 200$ lb, $F_B = 100$ lb, and $F_C = 400$ lb.

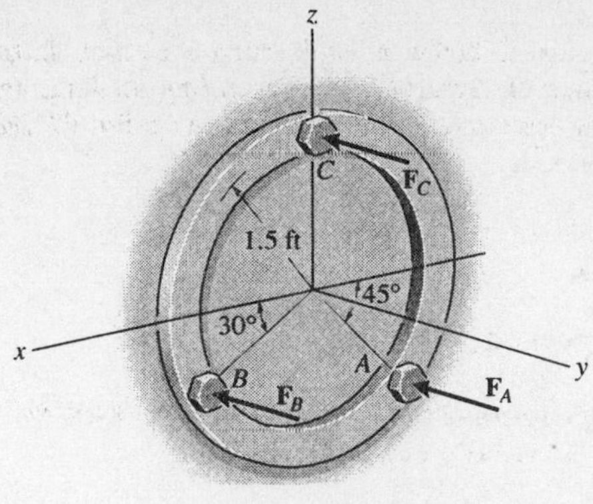

Equivalent Force :

$$F_R = \Sigma F_y; \qquad -F_R = -400 - 200 - 100$$

$$F_R = 700 \text{ lb} \qquad \textbf{Ans}$$

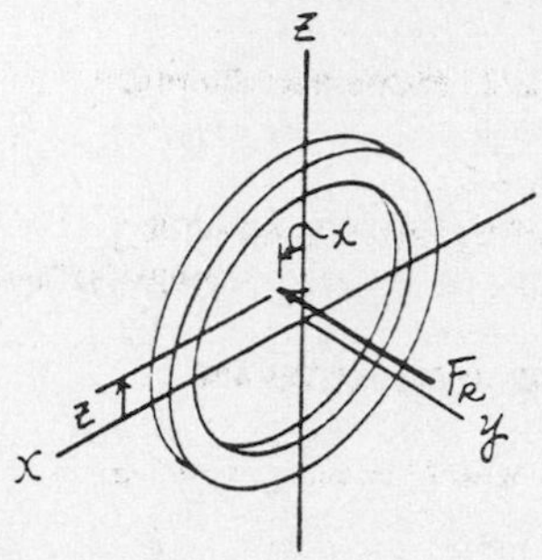

Location of Resultant Force :

$$M_{R_x} = \Sigma M_x; \qquad 700(z) = 400(1.5) - 200(1.5\sin 45°) - 100(1.5\sin 30°)$$

$$z = 0.447 \text{ ft} \qquad \textbf{Ans}$$

$$M_{R_z} = \Sigma M_z; \qquad -700(x) = 200(1.5\cos 45°) - 100(1.5\cos 30°)$$

$$x = -0.117 \text{ ft} \qquad \textbf{Ans}$$

4-134. The three parallel bolting forces act on the circulate plate. If the force at A has a magnitude of $F_A = 200$ lb, determine the magnitudes of $\mathbf{F}_B$ and $\mathbf{F}_C$ so that the resultant force $\mathbf{F}_R$ of the system has a line of action that coincides with the y axis. *Hint:* This requires $\Sigma M_x = 0$ and $\Sigma M_z = 0$.

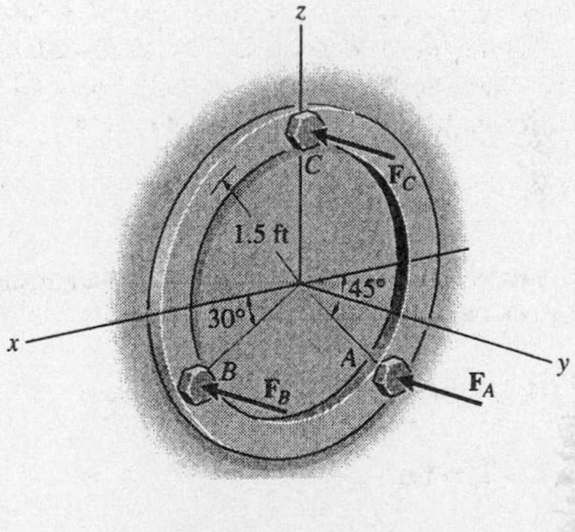

Since $\mathbf{F}_R$ coincides with y axis, $M_{R_z} = M_{R_x} = 0$.

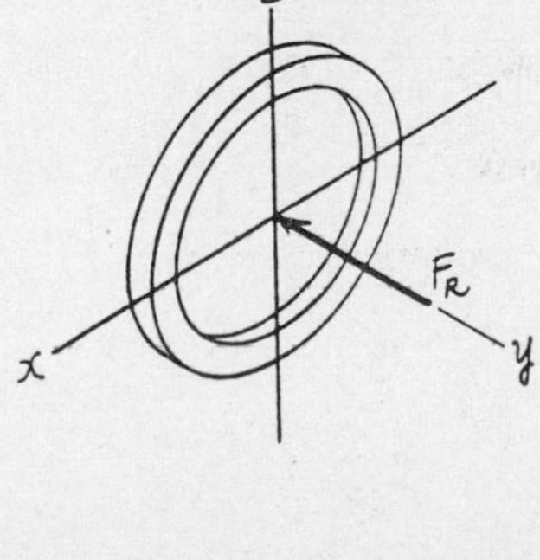

$$M_{R_z} = \Sigma M_z; \qquad 0 = 200(1.5\cos 45°) - F_B(1.5\cos 30°)$$

$$F_B = 163.30 \text{ lb} = 163 \text{ lb} \qquad \textbf{Ans}$$

Using the result $F_B = 163.30$ lb,

$$M_{R_x} = \Sigma M_x; \qquad 0 = F_C(1.5) - 200(1.5\sin 45°) - 163.30(1.5\sin 30°)$$

$$F_C = 223 \text{ lb} \qquad \textbf{Ans}$$

***4-135.** Replace the two wrenches and the force, acting on the pipe assembly, by an equivalent resultant force and couple moment at point O.

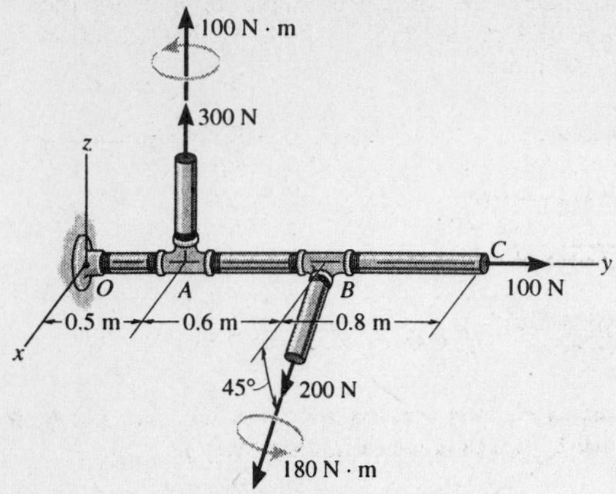

Force And Moment Vectors :

$\mathbf{F}_1 = \{300\mathbf{k}\}$ N $\qquad \mathbf{F}_3 = \{100\mathbf{j}\}$ N

$\mathbf{F}_2 = 200\{\cos 45°\mathbf{i} - \sin 45°\mathbf{k}\}$ N
$= \{141.42\mathbf{i} - 141.42\mathbf{k}\}$ N

$\mathbf{M}_1 = \{100\mathbf{k}\}$ N · m

$\mathbf{M}_2 = 180\{\cos 45°\mathbf{i} - \sin 45°\mathbf{k}\}$ N · m
$= \{127.28\mathbf{i} - 127.28\mathbf{k}\}$ N · m

Equivalent Force and Couple Moment At Point O :

$\mathbf{F}_R = \Sigma\mathbf{F};\quad \mathbf{F}_R = \mathbf{F}_1 + \mathbf{F}_2 + \mathbf{F}_3$
$= 141.42\mathbf{i} + 100.0\mathbf{j} + (300 - 141.42)\mathbf{k}$

$= \{141\mathbf{i} + 100\mathbf{j} + 159\mathbf{k}\}$ N **Ans**

The position vectors are $\mathbf{r}_1 = \{0.5\mathbf{j}\}$ m and $\mathbf{r}_2 = \{1.1\mathbf{j}\}$ m.

$$\mathbf{M}_{R_O} = \Sigma\mathbf{M}_O;\quad \mathbf{M}_{R_O} = \mathbf{r}_1 \times \mathbf{F}_1 + \mathbf{r}_2 \times \mathbf{F}_2 + \mathbf{M}_1 + \mathbf{M}_2$$

$$= \begin{vmatrix} \mathbf{i} & \mathbf{j} & \mathbf{k} \\ 0 & 0.5 & 0 \\ 0 & 0 & 300 \end{vmatrix} + \begin{vmatrix} \mathbf{i} & \mathbf{j} & \mathbf{k} \\ 0 & 1.1 & 0 \\ 141.42 & 0 & -141.42 \end{vmatrix}$$

$$+ 100\mathbf{k} + 127.28\mathbf{i} - 127.28\mathbf{k}$$

$= \{122\mathbf{i} - 183\mathbf{k}\}$ N · m **Ans**

***4-136.** Replace the force and couple-moment system acting on the plate by a single resultant force. Specify the coordinates $(x, y, 0)$ through which the line of action of the resultant passes.

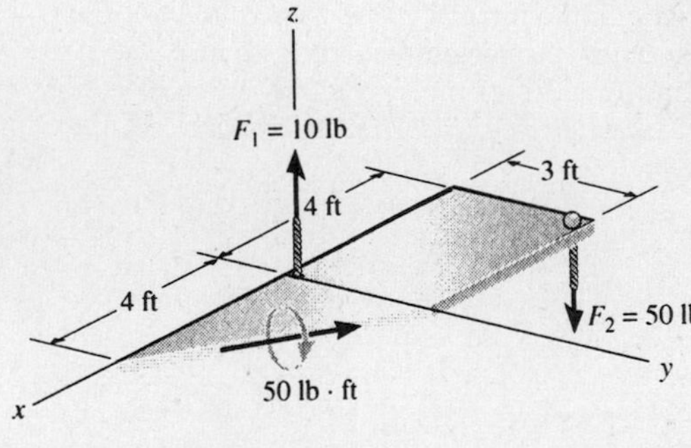

$F_R = \Sigma F;\quad F_R = 10 - 50 = -40 \text{ lb} = 40 \text{ lb} \downarrow$ **Ans**

$M_{Rx} = \Sigma M_x;\quad -40(y) = -50\left(\frac{4}{5}\right) - 50(3)$

$y = 4.75$ ft **Ans**

$M_{Ry} = \Sigma M_y;\quad 40(x) = 50\left(\frac{3}{5}\right) - 50(4)$

$x = -4.25$ ft **Ans**

4-137. Replace the three forces acting on the plate by a wrench. Specify the force and couple moment for the wrench and the point $P(x, y)$ where its line of action intersects the plate.

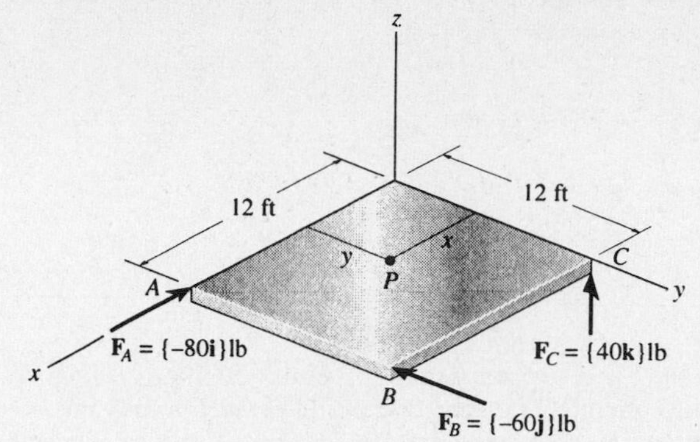

Resultant force vector :

$$\mathbf{F}_R = \{-80\,\mathbf{i} - 60\,\mathbf{j} + 40\,\mathbf{k}\}\text{ lb}$$

$$F_R = \sqrt{(-80)^2 + (-60)^2 + 40^2} = 107.7\text{ lb} = 108\text{ lb} \qquad \textbf{Ans}$$

$$\mathbf{u}_{F_R} = \frac{-80\,\mathbf{i} - 60\,\mathbf{j} + 40\,\mathbf{k}}{107.7} = -0.7428\,\mathbf{i} - 0.5571\,\mathbf{j} + 0.3714\,\mathbf{k}$$

The line of action of $\mathbf{M}_R$ of the wrench is parallel to the line of action of $\mathbf{F}_R$; also assume that both $\mathbf{M}_R$ and $\mathbf{F}_R$ have the same sense. Therefore

$$\mathbf{u}_{M_R} = -0.7428\,\mathbf{i} - 0.5571\,\mathbf{j} + 0.3714\,\mathbf{k}$$

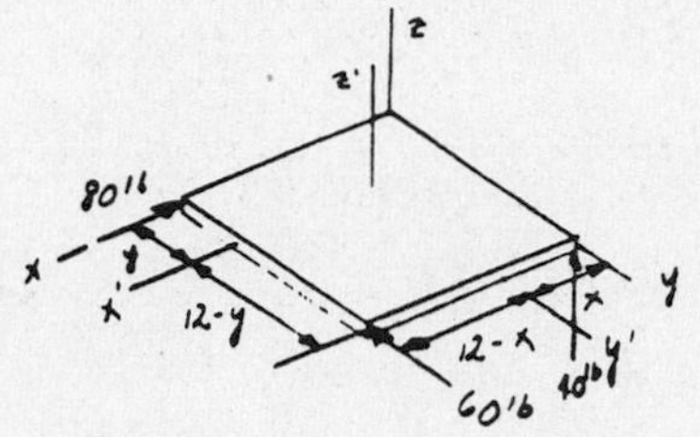

$(M_R)_{x'} = \Sigma M_{x'};\qquad -0.7428 M_R = 40(12 - y) \qquad (1)$

$(M_R)_{y'} = \Sigma M_{y'};\qquad -0.5571 M_R = 40x \qquad (2)$

$(M_R)_{z'} = \Sigma M_{z'};\qquad 0.3714 M_R = -60(12 - x) - 80y \qquad (3)$

Solving Eq. (1), (2), and (3) yields :

$M_R = -624\text{ lb}\cdot\text{ft} \qquad x = 8.69\text{ ft} \qquad y = 0.414\text{ ft} \qquad$ **Ans**

Negative sign indicates that $\mathbf{M}_R$ has a sense which is opposite to that of $\mathbf{F}_R$.

4-138. Replace the three forces acting on the plate by a wrench. Specify the magnitude of the force and couple moment for the wrench and the point $P(y, z)$ where its line of action intersects the plate.

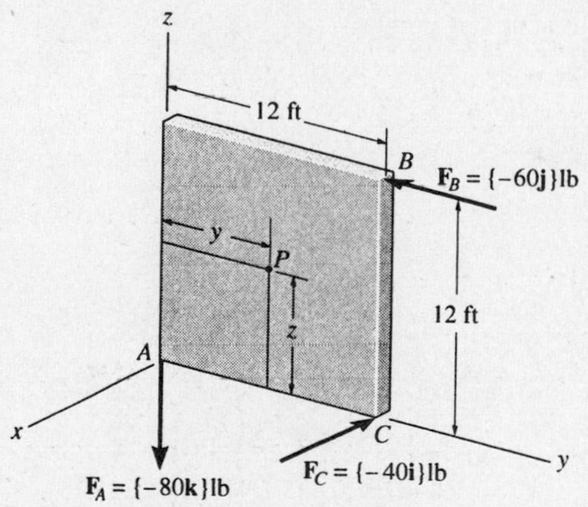

Resultant Force Vector :

$$\mathbf{F}_R = \{-40\mathbf{i} - 60\mathbf{j} - 80\mathbf{k}\}\text{ lb}$$

$$F_R = \sqrt{(-40)^2 + (-60)^2 + (-80)^2} = 107.70\text{ lb} = 108\text{ lb} \qquad \textbf{Ans}$$

$$\mathbf{u}_{F_R} = \frac{-40\mathbf{i} - 60\mathbf{j} - 80\mathbf{k}}{107.70} = -0.3714\mathbf{i} - 0.5571\mathbf{j} - 0.7428\mathbf{k}$$

Resultant Moment: The line of action of $\mathbf{M}_R$ of the wrench is parallel to the line of action of $\mathbf{F}_R$. Assume that both $\mathbf{M}_R$ and $\mathbf{F}_R$ have the same sense . Therefore, $\mathbf{u}_{M_R} = -0.3714\mathbf{i} - 0.5571\mathbf{j} - 0.7428\mathbf{k}$.

$(M_R)_{x'} = \Sigma M_{x'};\qquad -0.3714 M_R = 60(12 - z) + 80y \qquad [1]$

$(M_R)_{y'} = \Sigma M_{y'};\qquad -0.5571 M_R = 40z \qquad [2]$

$(M_R)_{z'} = \Sigma M_{z'};\qquad -0.7428 M_R = 40(12 - y) \qquad [3]$

Solving Eqs.[1], [2], and [3] yields :

$M_R = -624\text{ lb}\cdot\text{ft} \qquad z = 8.69\text{ ft} \qquad y = 0.414\text{ ft} \qquad$ **Ans**

The negative sign indicates that the line of action for $\mathbf{M}_R$ is directed in the opposite sense to that of $\mathbf{F}_R$.

4-139. Replace the distributed loading by an equivalent resultant force and specify its location on the beam, measured from the pin at A.

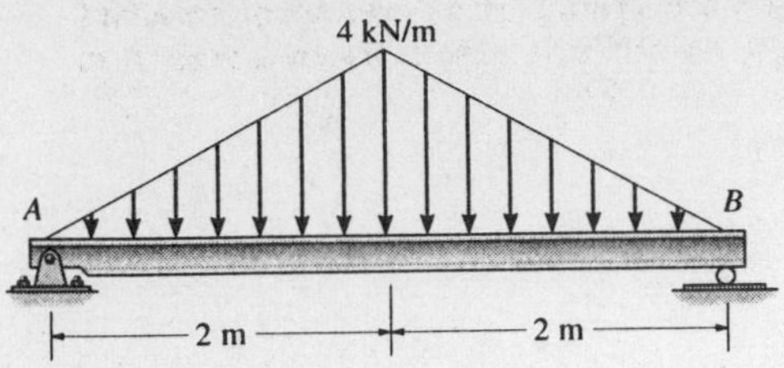

$$F_R = \frac{1}{2}(4)(4) = 8 \text{ kN} \qquad \textbf{Ans}$$

Centroid is at

$$x = 2 \text{ m} \qquad \textbf{Ans}$$

***4-140.** The masonry support creates the loading distribution acting on the end of the beam. Simplify this load to a single resultant force and specify its location measured from point O.

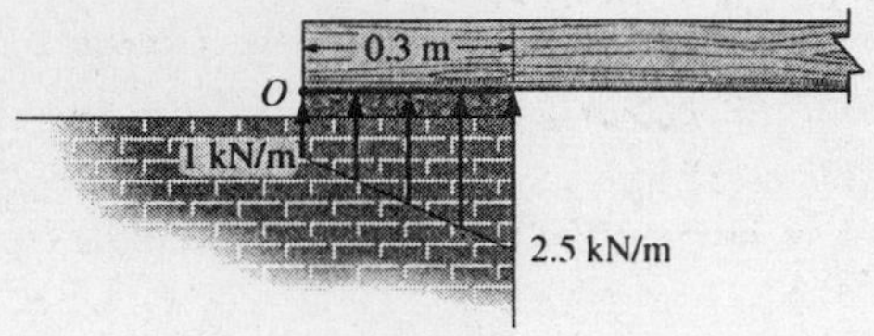

Equivalent Resultant Force :

$$+\uparrow F_R = \Sigma F_y; \qquad F_R = 0.300 + 0.225 = 0.525 \text{ kN} \uparrow \qquad \textbf{Ans}$$

Location of Equivalent Resultant Force :

$$\curvearrowleft + (M_R)_O = \Sigma M_O; \qquad 0.525(d) = 0.300(0.15) + 0.225(0.2)$$

$$d = 0.171 \text{ m} \qquad \textbf{Ans}$$

4-141. Replace the loading by an equivalent force and couple moment acting at point O.

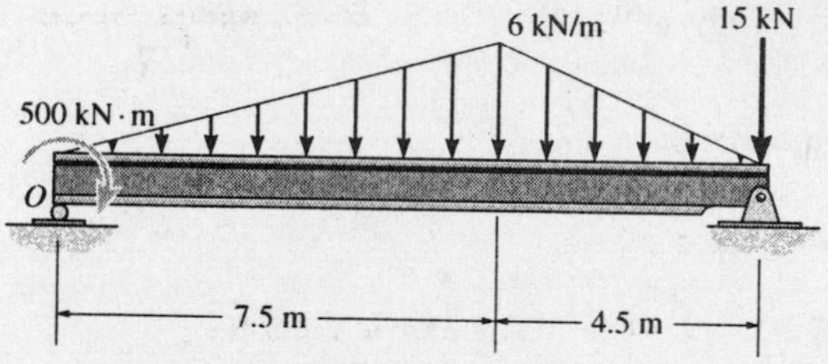

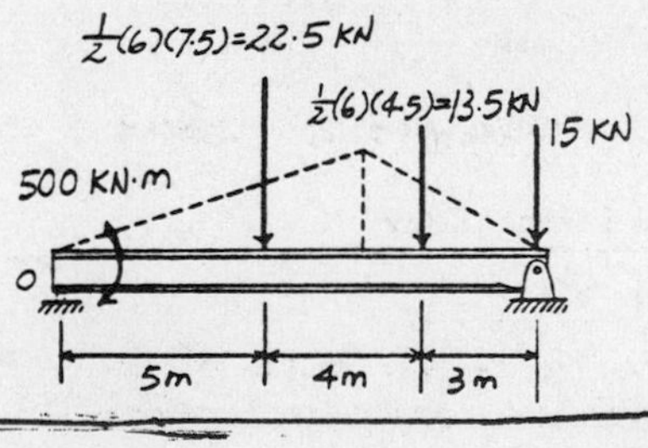

$$+\uparrow F_R = \Sigma F_y; \qquad F_R = -22.5 - 13.5 - 15.0$$

$$= -51.0 \text{ kN} = 51.0 \text{ kN} \downarrow \qquad \textbf{Ans}$$

$$\curvearrowleft + M_{R_O} = \Sigma M_O; \qquad M_{R_O} = -500 - 22.5(5) - 13.5(9) - 15(12)$$

$$= -914 \text{ kN} \cdot \text{m}$$

$$= 914 \text{ kN} \cdot \text{m} \ \textit{(Clockwise)} \qquad \textbf{Ans}$$

4-142. Replace the loading by a single resultant force, and specify the location of the force on the beam measured from point O.

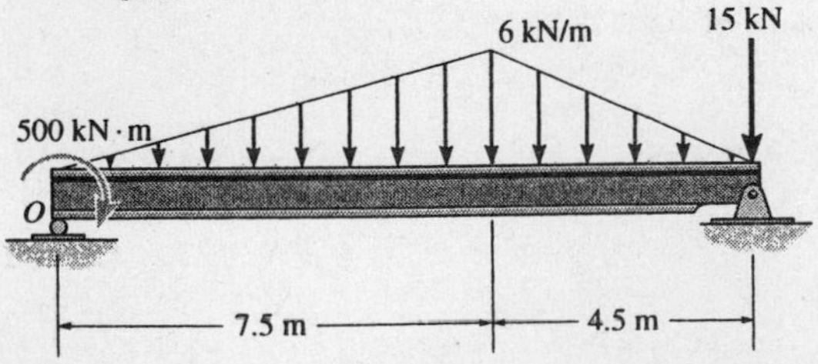

Equivalent Resultant Force :

$$+\uparrow F_R = \Sigma F_y; \qquad -F_R = -22.5 - 13.5 - 15$$

$$F_R = 51.0 \text{ kN} \downarrow \qquad \textbf{Ans}$$

Location of Equivalent Resultant Force :

$$\curvearrowleft + (M_R)_O = \Sigma M_O; \qquad -51.0(d) = -500 - 22.5(5) - 13.5(9) - 15(12)$$

$$d = 17.9 \text{ m} \qquad \textbf{Ans}$$

4-143. Replace the loading by an equivalent resultant force and specify its location on the beam, measured from point O.

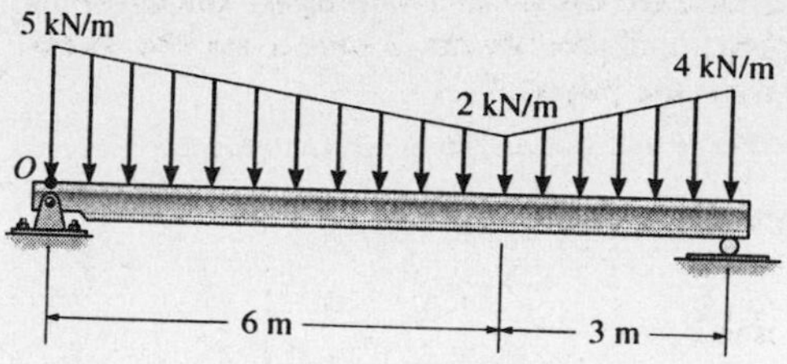

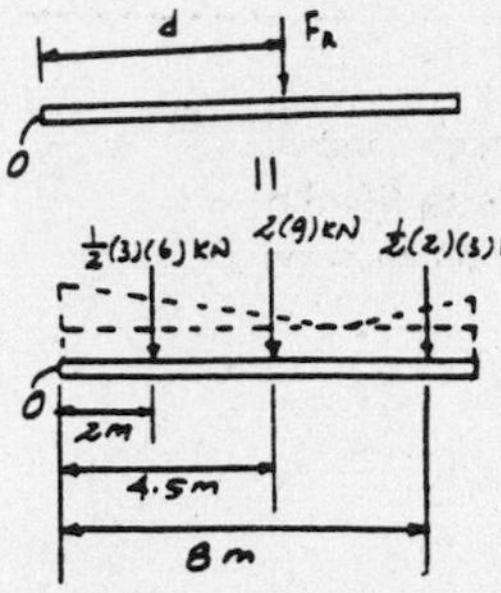

$+\downarrow F_R = \Sigma F_y; \quad F_R = \frac{1}{2}(3)(6) + 2(9) + \frac{1}{2}(2)(3)$

$= 30 \text{ kN} \downarrow$ **Ans**

$\curvearrowleft + M_{R_O} = \Sigma M_O; \quad -30d = -\frac{1}{2}(3)(6)(2) - 2(9)(4.5) - \frac{1}{2}(2)(3)(8)$

$d = 4.10 \text{ m}$ **Ans**

***4-144.** Replace the loading by an equivalent resultant force and specify its location on the beam, measured from point B.

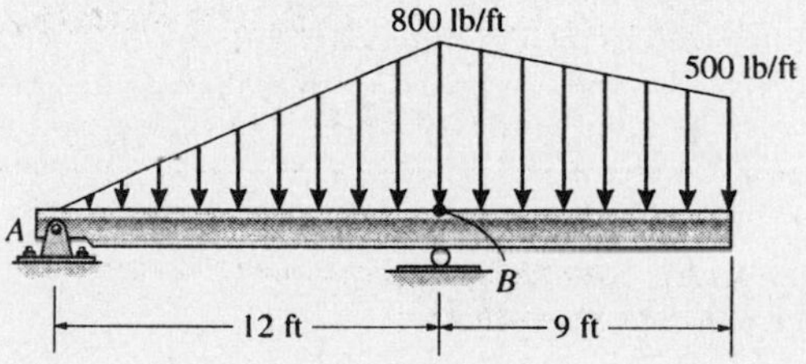

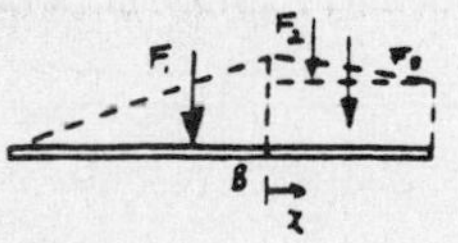

$F_1 = \frac{1}{2}(800)(12) = 4800 \text{ lb}$

$F_2 = \frac{1}{2}(300)(9) = 1350 \text{ lb}$

$F_3 = 500(9) = 4500 \text{ lb}$

$+\downarrow F_R = \Sigma F_y; \quad F_R = 4800 + 1350 + 4500 = 10\,650 \text{ lb}$

$F_R = 10.7 \text{ kip} \downarrow$ **Ans**

$\curvearrowleft + M_{RB} = \Sigma M_B; \quad 10\,650\, d = -4800(4) + 1350(3) + 4500(4.5)$

$d = 0.479 \text{ ft}$ **Ans**

4-145. Replace the loading on the beam by an equivalent resultant force and specify its location, measured from point A.

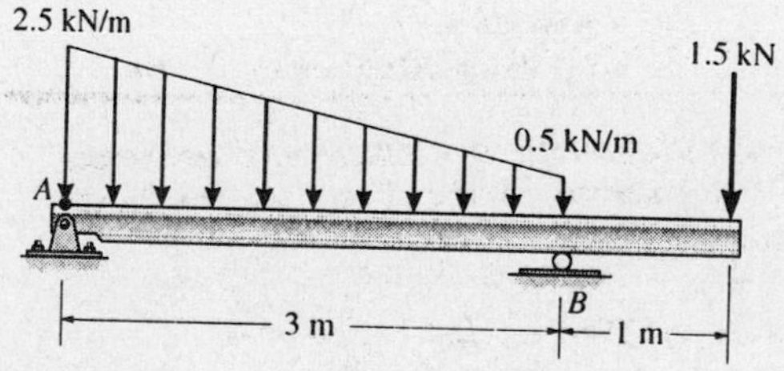

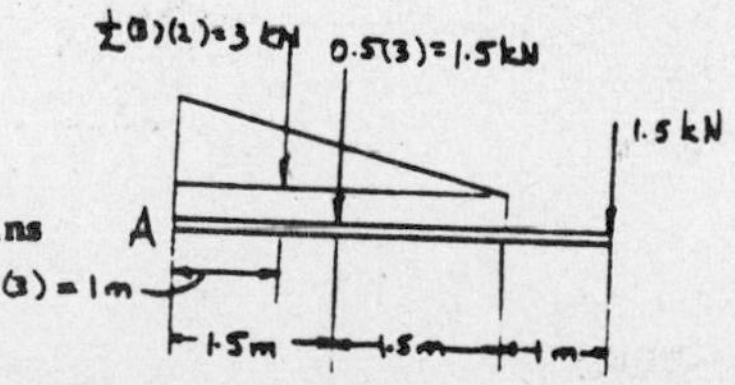

$+\downarrow F_R = \Sigma F; \quad F_R = 3 + 1.5 + 1.5 = 6 \text{ kN} \downarrow$ **Ans**

$\curvearrowleft + M_{RA} = \Sigma M_A; \quad 6(d) = 3(1) + 1.5(1.5) + 1.5(4)$

$d = 1.875 = 1.88 \text{ m}$ **Ans**

4-146. Replace the loading by an equivalent force and couple moment acting at point O.

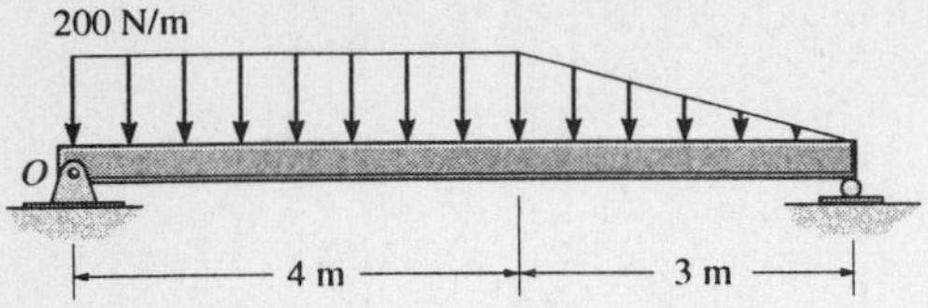

Equivalent Force and Couple Moment At Point O :

$$+\uparrow F_R = \Sigma F_y; \quad F_R = -800 - 300$$
$$= -1100 \text{ N} = 1.10 \text{ kN} \downarrow \qquad \textbf{Ans}$$

$$+ M_{R_O} = \Sigma M_O; \quad M_{R_O} = -800(2) - 300(5)$$
$$= -3100 \text{ N}\cdot\text{m}$$
$$= 3.10 \text{ kN}\cdot\text{m} \ (\textit{Clockwise}) \qquad \textbf{Ans}$$

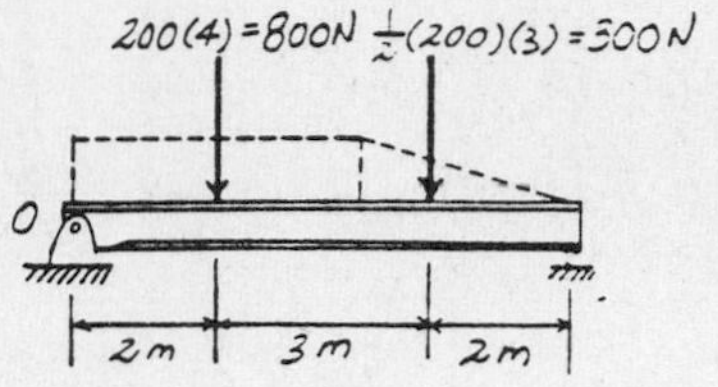

***4-147.** The bricks on top of the beam and the supports at the bottom create the distributed loading shown in the second figure. Determine the required intensity w and dimension d of the right support so that the resultant force and couple moment about point A of the system are both zero.

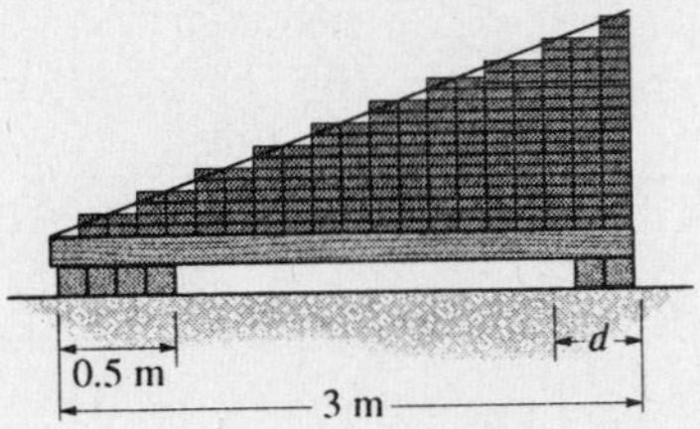

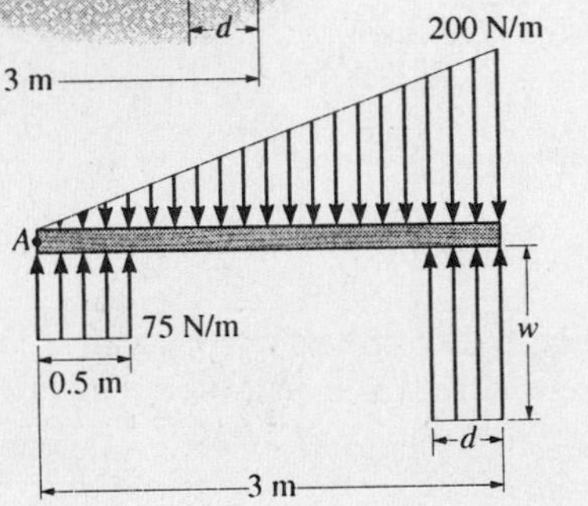

Require $F_R = 0$.

$$+\uparrow F_R = \Sigma F_y; \quad 0 = wd + 37.5 - 300$$
$$wd = 262.5 \qquad [1]$$

Require $M_{R_A} = 0$.

$$\curvearrowleft + M_{R_A} = \Sigma M_A; \quad 0 = 37.5(0.25) + wd\left(3 - \frac{d}{2}\right) - 300(2)$$
$$3wd - \frac{wd^2}{2} = 590.625 \qquad [2]$$

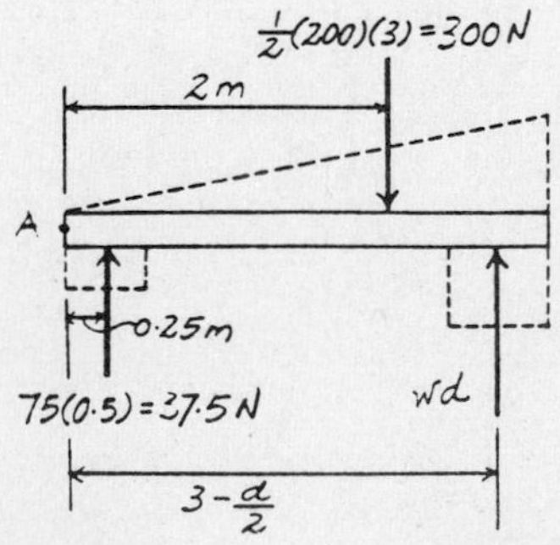

Solving Eqs. [1] and [2] yields

$$d = 1.50 \text{ m} \qquad w = 175 \text{ N/m} \qquad \textbf{Ans}$$

***4-148.** Replace the distributed loading by an equivalent resultant force and couple moment at point A.

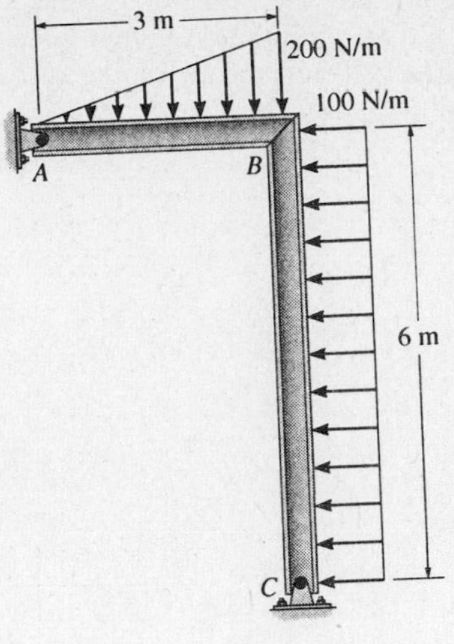

$\overset{+}{\leftarrow} F_{Rx} = \Sigma F_x;\quad F_{Rx} = 100\,(6) = 600\text{ N}$

$+\downarrow F_{Ry} = \Sigma F_y;\quad F_{Ry} = \frac{1}{2}(200)\,(3) = 300\text{ N}$

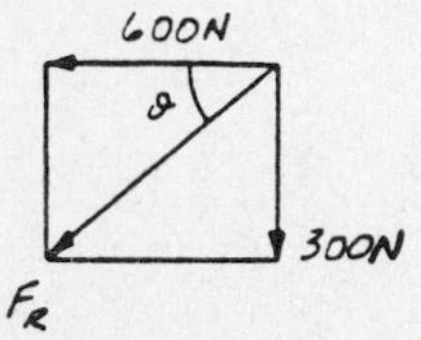

$F_R = \sqrt{(600)^2 + (300)^2} = 671\text{ N}$ **Ans**

$\theta = \tan^{-1}\left(\frac{300}{600}\right) = 26.6°$ **Ans**

$\curvearrowleft + M_{RA} = \Sigma M_A;\quad M_{RA} = 300\,(2) + 600\,(3) = 2400\text{ N}\cdot\text{m} = 2.40\text{ kN}\cdot\text{m}$ **Ans**

4-149. Replace the distributed loading by an equivalent resultant force and specify where the resultant's line of action intersects member BC, measured from point C.

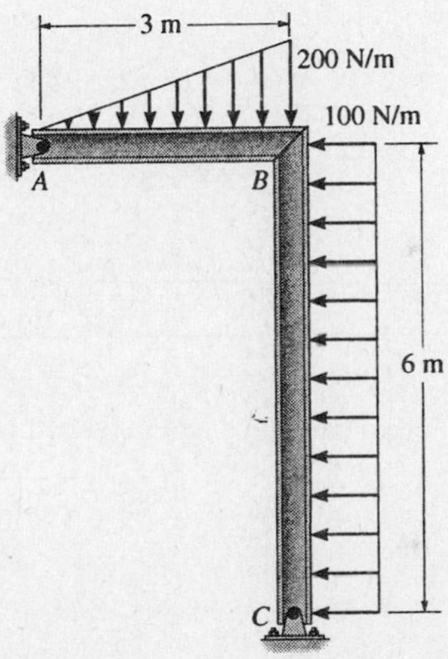

$\overset{+}{\leftarrow} F_{Rx} = \Sigma F_x;\quad F_{Rx} = 100\,(6) = 600\text{ N}$

$+\downarrow F_{Ry} = \Sigma F_y;\quad F_{Ry} = \frac{1}{2}(200)\,(3) = 300\text{ N}$

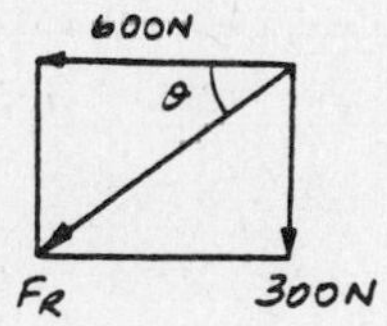

$F_R = \sqrt{(600)^2 + (300)^2} = 671\text{ N}$ **Ans**

$\theta = \tan^{-1}\left(\frac{300}{600}\right) = 26.6°$ **Ans**

$\curvearrowleft + M_{RC} = \Sigma M_C;\quad 600\,d = 600\,(3) + 300\,(1)$

$d = 3.50\text{ m}$ **Ans**

4-150. The beam is subjected to the distributed loading. Determine the length b of the uniform load and its position a on the beam such that the resultant force and couple moment acting on the beam are zero.

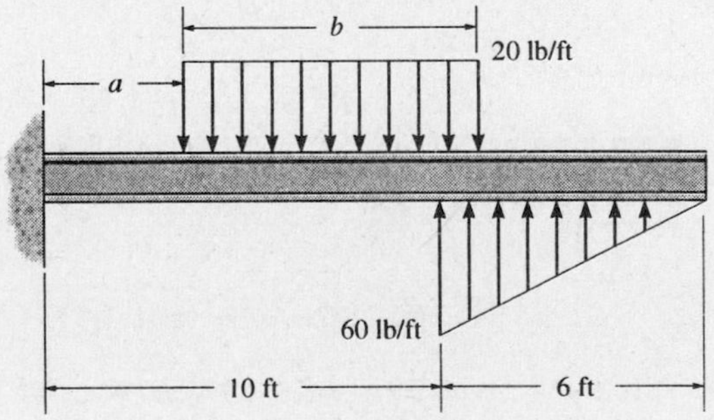

Require $F_R = 0$.

$+\uparrow F_R = \Sigma F_y;\quad 0 = 180 - 20b$

$b = 9.00\text{ ft}$ **Ans**

Require $M_{R_A} = 0$. Using the result $b = 9.00$ ft, we have

$\curvearrowleft + M_{R_A} = \Sigma M_A;\quad 0 = 180(12) - 20(9.00)\left(a + \frac{9.00}{2}\right)$

$a = 7.50\text{ ft}$ **Ans**

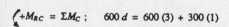

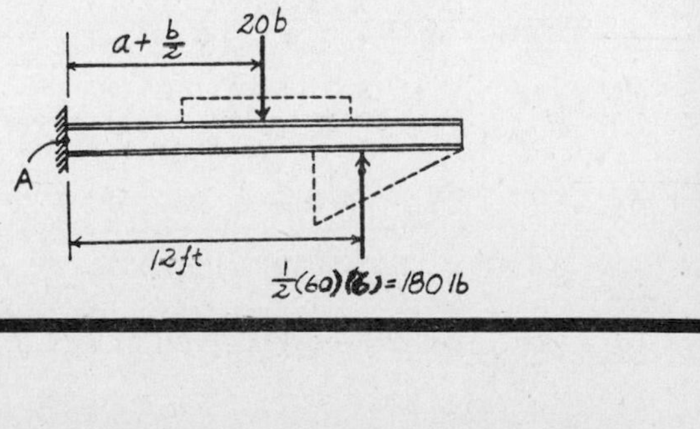

4-151. Determine the intensities w_1 and w_2 of the distributed loading acting on the bottom of the slab so that this loading has an equivalent resultant force that is equal but opposite to the resultant of the distributed loading acting on the top of the plate.

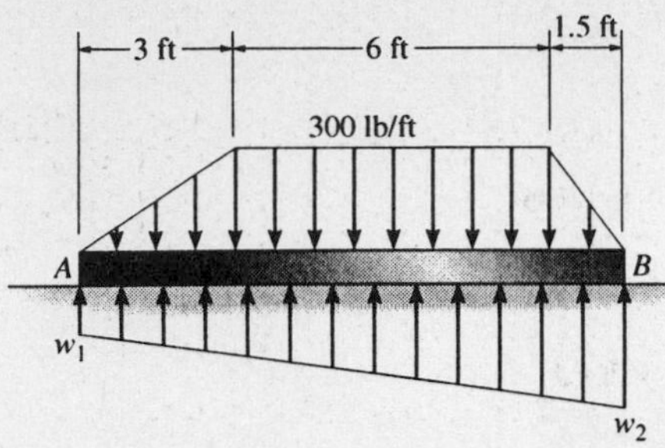

$+\uparrow F_R = \Sigma F;\quad 0 = w_1(10.5) + \frac{1}{2}(w_2 - w_1)(10.5) - \frac{1}{2}(300)(3) - 300(6) - \frac{1}{2}(300)(1.5)$

$w_1 + w_2 = 471.429 \qquad (1)$

$\circlearrowleft + M_{RA} = \Sigma M_A;\quad 0 = w_1(10.5)(5.25) + \frac{1}{2}(w_2 - w_1)(10.5)(7) - \frac{1}{2}(300)(3)(2)$

$- 300(6)(6) - \frac{1}{2}(300)(1.5)(9.5)$

$w_1 + 2w_2 = 753.061 \qquad (2)$

Solving Eqs. (1) and (2),

$w_1 = 190 \text{ lb/ft}$ **Ans**

$w_2 = 282 \text{ lb/ft}$ **Ans**

***4-152.** Replace the loading by an equivalent resultant force and couple moment at point A.

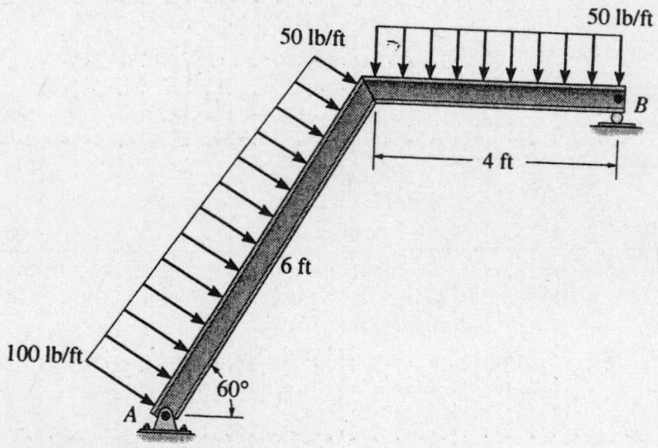

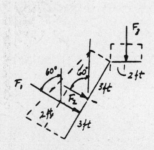

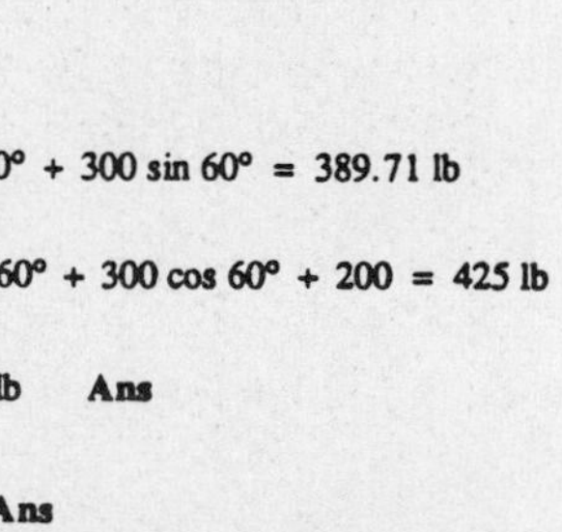

$F_1 = \frac{1}{2}(6)(50) = 150 \text{ lb}$

$F_2 = (6)(50) = 300 \text{ lb}$

$F_3 = (4)(50) = 200 \text{ lb}$

$\xrightarrow{+} F_{Rx} = \Sigma F_x;\quad F_{Rx} = 150\sin 60^\circ + 300\sin 60^\circ = 389.71 \text{ lb}$

$+\downarrow F_{Ry} = \Sigma F_y;\quad F_{Ry} = 150\cos 60^\circ + 300\cos 60^\circ + 200 = 425 \text{ lb}$

$F_R = \sqrt{(389.71)^2 + (425)^2} = 577 \text{ lb}$ **Ans**

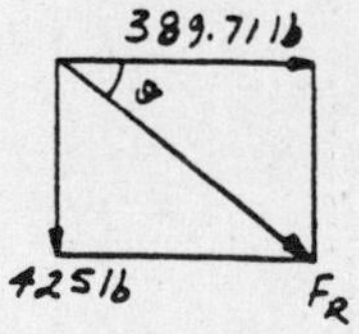

$\theta = \tan^{-1}\left(\frac{425}{389.71}\right) = 47.5^\circ$ **Ans**

$\circlearrowright + M_{RA} = \Sigma M_A;\quad M_{RA} = 150(2) + 300(3) + 200(6\cos 60^\circ + 2)$

$= 2200 \text{ lb}\cdot\text{ft} = 2.20 \text{ kip}\cdot\text{ft}$ **Ans**

4-153. Replace the loading by an equivalent resultant force and couple moment acting at point *B*.

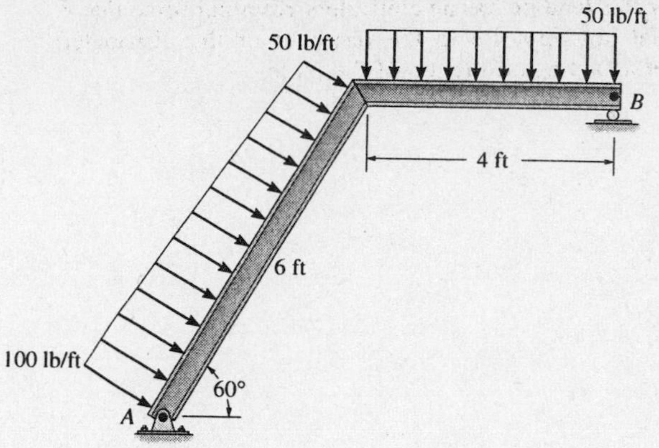

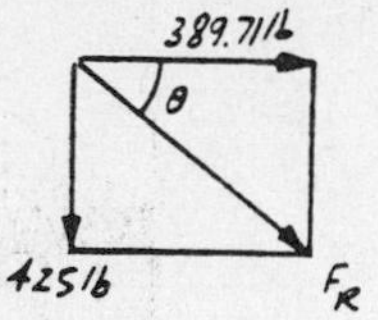

$F_1 = \frac{1}{2}(6)(50) = 150$ lb

$F_2 = (6)(50) = 300$ lb

$F_3 = (4)(50) = 200$ lb

$\xrightarrow{+} F_{Rx} = \Sigma F_x;\quad F_{Rx} = 150 \sin 60° + 300 \sin 60° = 389.71$ lb

$+\downarrow F_{Ry} = \Sigma F_y;\quad F_{Ry} = 150 \cos 60° + 300 \cos 60° + 200 = 425$ lb

$F_R = \sqrt{(389.71)^2 + (425)^2} = 577$ lb **Ans**

$\theta = \tan^{-1}\left(\frac{425}{389.71}\right) = 47.5°$ **Ans**

$\circlearrowleft + M_{RB} = \Sigma M_B;\quad M_{RB} = 150 \cos 60° (4 \cos 60° + 4) + 150 \sin 60° (4 \sin 60°)$

$+ 300 \cos 60° (3 \cos 60° + 4) + 300 \sin 60° (3 \sin 60°) + 200(2)$

$M_{RB} = 2800$ lb · ft $= 2.80$ kip · ft **Ans**

4-154. The wind pressure acting on a triangular sign is uniform. Replace this loading by an equivalent resultant force and couple moment at point *O*.

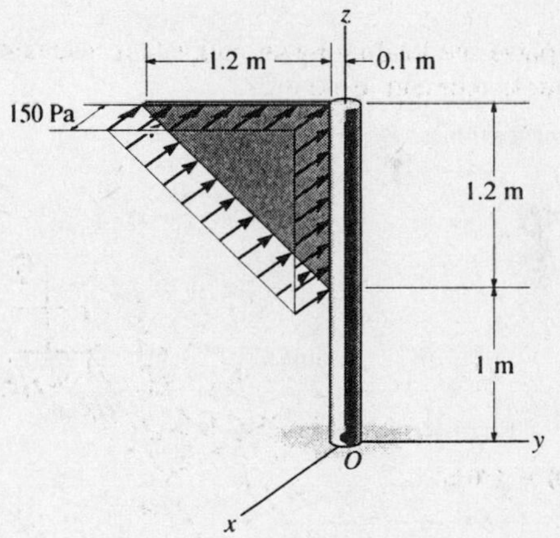

$F_R = \frac{1}{2}(1.2)(1.2)(150)$

$\mathbf{F}_R = \{-108\,\mathbf{i}\}$ N **Ans**

$\mathbf{M}_{RO} = -\left(1 + \frac{2}{3}(1.2)\right)(108)\,\mathbf{j} - \left(0.1 + \frac{1}{3}(1.2)\right)(108)\,\mathbf{k}$

$\mathbf{M}_{RO} = \{-194\,\mathbf{j} - 54\,\mathbf{k}\}$ N · m **Ans**

4-155. Wet concrete exerts a pressure distribution along the wall of the form. Determine the resultant force of this distribution and specify the height h where the bracing strut should be placed so that it lies through the line of action of the resultant force. The wall has a width of 5 m.

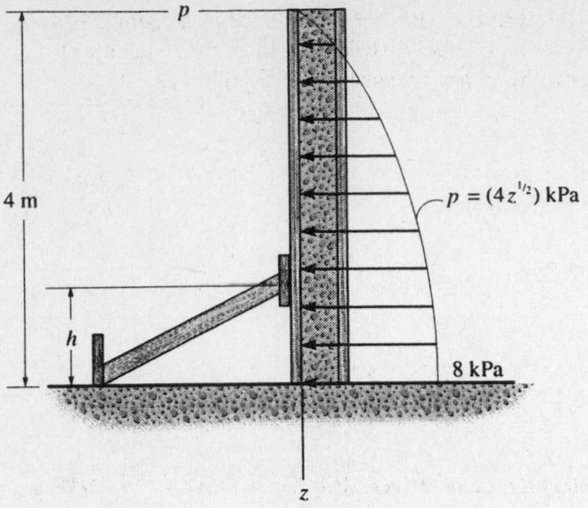

Equivalent Resultant Force :

$$\overset{+}{\rightarrow} F_R = \Sigma F_x; \quad -F_R = -\int_A dA = -\int_0^z w\,dz$$

$$F_R = \int_0^{4\text{m}} \left(20z^{\frac{1}{2}}\right)\left(10^3\right) dz$$

$$= 106.67\left(10^3\right) \text{ N} = 107 \text{ kN} \leftarrow \qquad \textbf{Ans}$$

Location of Equivalent Resultant Force :

$$\bar{z} = \frac{\int_A z\,dA}{\int_A dA} = \frac{\int_0^z zw\,dz}{\int_0^z w\,dz}$$

$$= \frac{\int_0^{4\text{m}} z\left[\left(20z^{\frac{1}{2}}\right)\left(10^3\right)\right] dz}{\int_0^{4\text{m}} \left(20z^{\frac{1}{2}}\right)\left(10^3\right) dz}$$

$$= \frac{\int_0^{4\text{m}} \left[\left(20z^{\frac{3}{2}}\right)\left(10^3\right)\right] dz}{\int_0^{4\text{m}} \left(20z^{\frac{1}{2}}\right)\left(10^3\right) dz}$$

$$= 2.40 \text{ m}$$

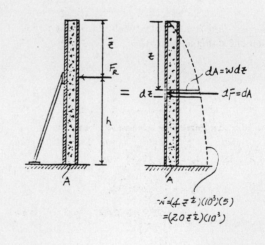

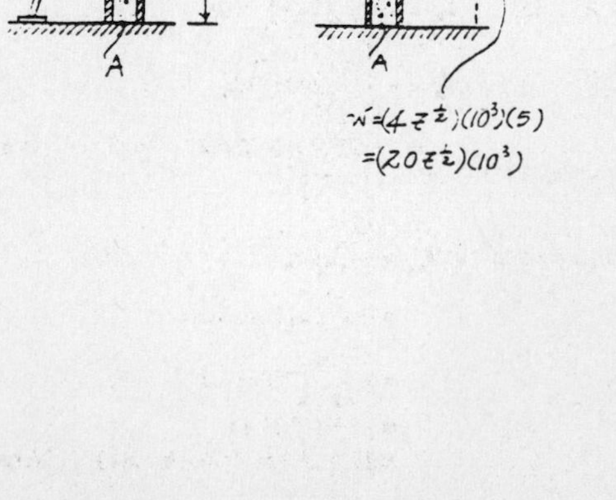

Thus, $\quad h = 4 - \bar{z} = 4 - 2.40 = 1.60 \text{ m} \qquad$ **Ans**

***4-156.** Determine the magnitude of the equivalent resultant force of the distributed load and specify its location on the beam measured from point A.

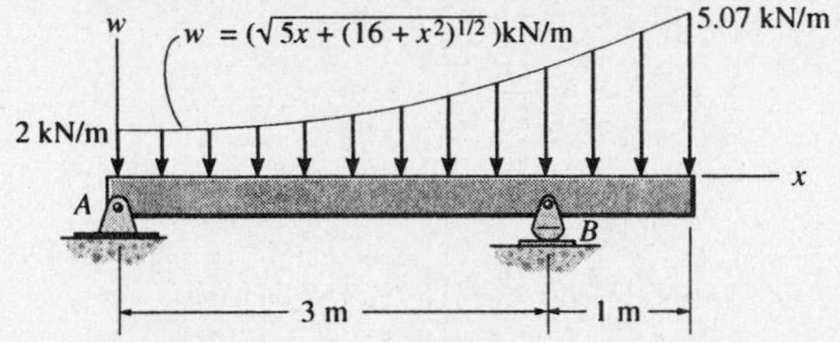

Equivalent Resultant Force : Use Simpson's rule to evaluate the intergal.

$$+\uparrow F_R = \Sigma F_y; \quad -F_R = -\int_A dA = -\int_0^x w\,dx$$

$$F_R = \int_0^{4\,\text{m}} \left[\sqrt{5x + (16 + x^2)^{\frac{1}{2}}}\right] dx$$

$$= 14.885 \text{ kN} = 14.9 \text{ kN} \downarrow \qquad \textbf{Ans}$$

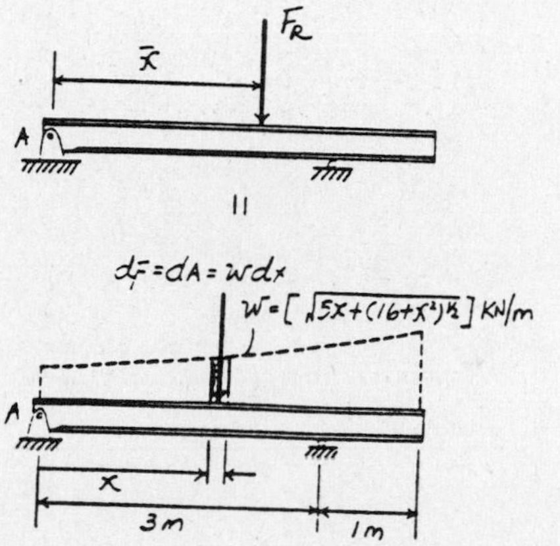

Location of Equivalent Resultant Force : Use Simpson's rule to evaluate the intergal.

$$\bar{x} = \frac{\int_A x\,dA}{\int_A dA} = \frac{\int_0^x xw\,dx}{\int_0^x w\,dx}$$

$$= \frac{\int_0^{4\,\text{m}} x\left[\sqrt{5x + (16 + x^2)^{\frac{1}{2}}}\right] dx}{\int_0^{4\,\text{m}} \left[\sqrt{5x + (16 + x^2)^{\frac{1}{2}}}\right] dx}$$

$$= \frac{33.735}{14.885} = 2.27 \text{ m} \qquad \textbf{Ans}$$

4-157. Replace the loading by an equivalent force and couple moment acting at point O.

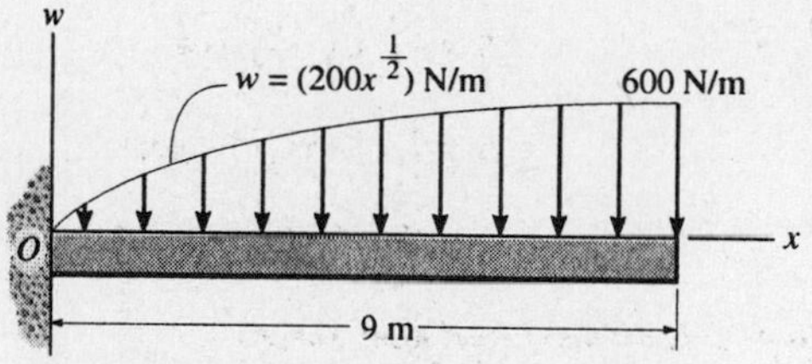

Equivalent Resultant Force And Moment At Point O :

$$+\uparrow F_R = \Sigma F_y; \quad F_R = -\int_A dA = -\int_0^x w\,dx$$

$$F_R = -\int_0^{9\,\text{m}} \left(200x^{\frac{1}{2}}\right) dx$$

$$= -3600 \text{ N} = 3.60 \text{ kN} \downarrow \qquad \textbf{Ans}$$

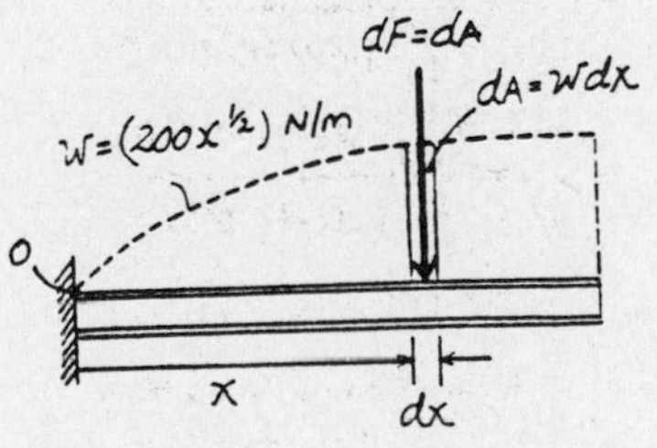

$$\curvearrowleft + M_{R_O} = \Sigma M_O; \quad M_{R_O} = -\int_0^x xw\,dx$$

$$= -\int_0^{9\,\text{m}} x\left(200x^{\frac{1}{2}}\right) dx$$

$$= -\int_0^{9\,\text{m}} \left(200x^{\frac{3}{2}}\right) dx$$

$$= -19\,440 \text{ N}\cdot\text{m}$$

$$= 19.4 \text{ kN}\cdot\text{m} \ (\textit{Clockwise}) \qquad \textbf{Ans}$$

***4-158.** The lifting force along the wing of a jet aircraft consists of a uniform distribution along AB, and a semiparabolic distribution along BC with origin at B. Replace this loading by a single resultant force and specify its location measured from point A.

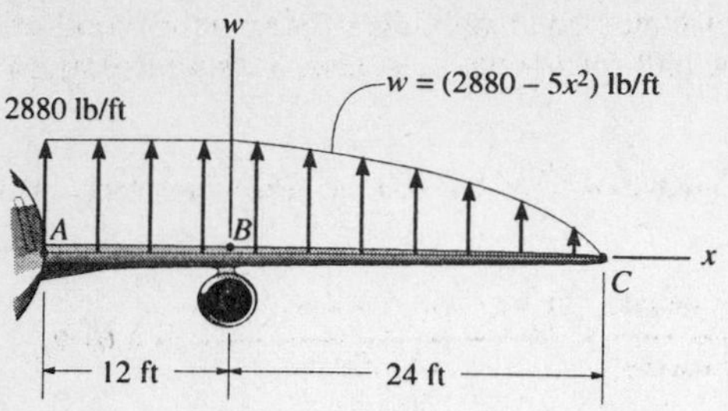

Equivalent Resultant Force :

$$+\uparrow F_R = \Sigma F_y; \quad F_R = 34560 + \int_0^x w\,dx$$

$$F_R = 34560 + \int_0^{24\text{ft}} \left(2880 - 5x^2\right) dx$$

$$= 80640 \text{ lb} = 80.6 \text{ kip} \uparrow$$ **Ans**

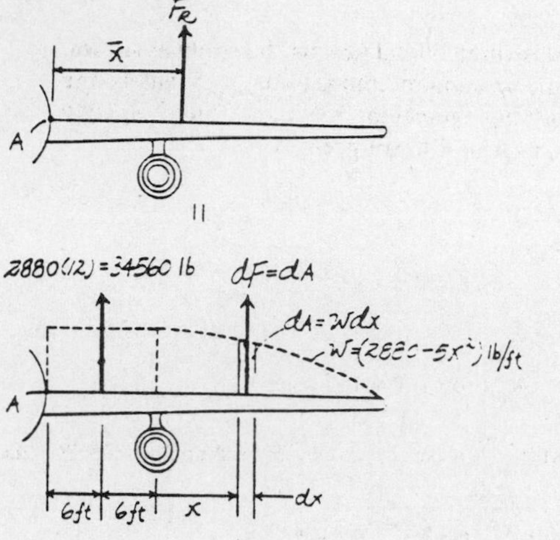

Location of Equivalent Resultant Force :

$$\curvearrowleft + M_{R_A} = \Sigma M_A;$$

$$80640\bar{x} = 34560(6) + \int_0^x (x+12)\,w\,dx$$

$$80640\bar{x} = 207360 + \int_0^{24\text{ft}} (x+12)\left(2880 - 5x^2\right) dx$$

$$80640\bar{x} = 207360 + \int_0^{24\text{ft}} \left(-5x^3 - 60x^2 + 2880x + 34560\right) dx$$

$$\bar{x} = 14.6 \text{ ft}$$ **Ans**

4-159. Determine the magnitude of the equivalent resultant force of the distributed load and specify its location on the beam measured from point A.

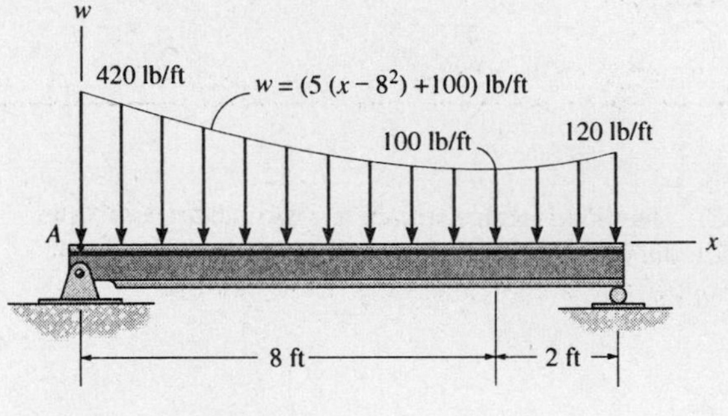

Equivalent Resultant Force :

$$+\uparrow F_R = \Sigma F_y; \quad -F_R = -\int_A dA = -\int_0^x w\,dx$$

$$F_R = \int_0^{10\text{ft}} \left[5(x-8)^2 + 100\right] dx$$

$$= 1866.67 \text{ lb} = 1.87 \text{ kip} \downarrow$$ **Ans**

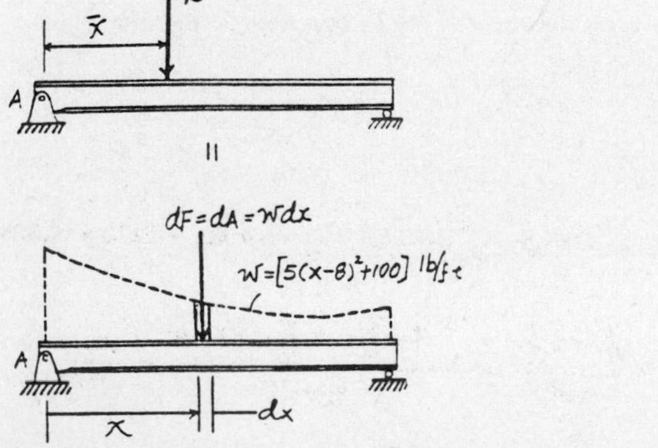

Location of Equivalent Resultant Force :

$$\bar{x} = \frac{\int_A x\,dA}{\int_A dA} = \frac{\int_0^x x w\,dx}{\int_0^x w\,dx}$$

$$= \frac{\int_0^{10\text{ft}} x\left[5(x-8)^2 + 100\right] dx}{\int_0^{10\text{ft}} \left[5(x-8)^2 + 100\right] dx}$$

$$= \frac{\int_0^{10\text{ft}} \left(5x^3 - 80x^2 + 420x\right) dx}{\int_0^{10\text{ft}} \left[5(x-8)^2 + 100\right] dx}$$

$$= 3.66 \text{ ft}$$ **Ans**

***4-160.** The distributed load acts on the beam as shown. Determine the magnitude of the equivalent resultant force and specify where it acts, measured from point A.

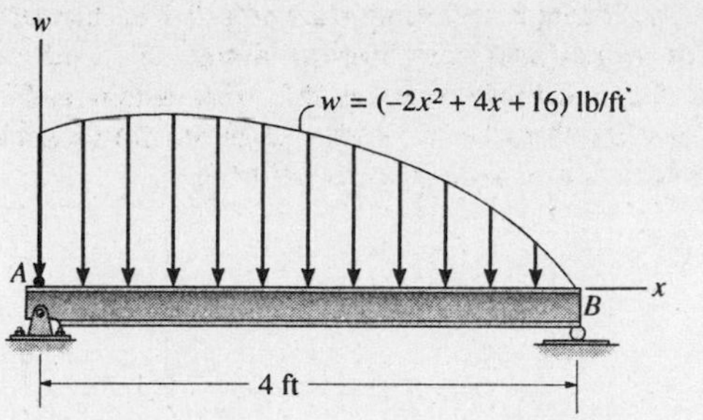

$$F_R = \int w(x)\,dx = \int_0^4 (-2x^2 + 4x + 16)\,dx = 53.333 = 53.3 \text{ lb} \quad \textbf{Ans}$$

$$\bar{x} = \frac{\int x\,w(x)\,dx}{\int w(x)\,dx} = \frac{\int_0^4 x(-2x^2 + 4x + 16)\,dx}{53.333} = 1.60 \text{ ft} \quad \textbf{Ans}$$

4-161. The distributed load acts on the beam as shown. Determine the maximum intensity w_{max}. What is the magnitude of the equivalent resultant force? Specify where it acts, measured from point B.

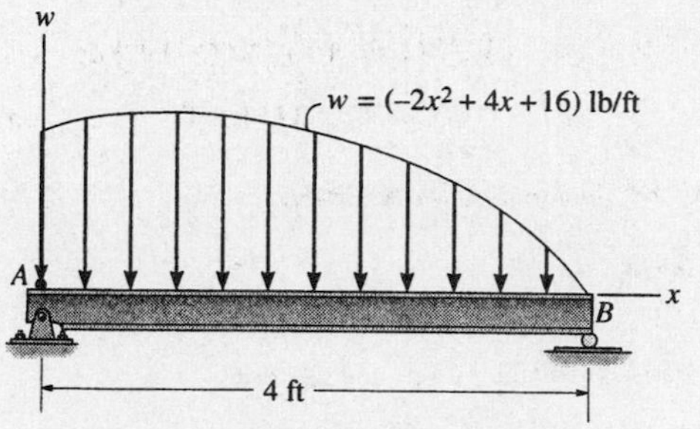

$$\frac{dw}{dx} = -4x + 4 = 0$$

$$x = 1$$

$$w_{max} = -2(1)^2 + 4(1) + 16 = 18 \text{ lb/ft} \quad \textbf{Ans}$$

$$F_R = \int w(x)\,dx = \int_0^4 (-2x^2 + 4x + 16)\,dx = 53.333 = 53.3 \text{ lb} \quad \textbf{Ans}$$

$$\bar{x} = \frac{\int x\,w(x)\,dx}{\int w(x)\,dx} = \frac{\int_0^4 x(-2x^2 + 4x + 16)\,dx}{53.333} = 1.60 \text{ ft}$$

So that from B,

$$x' = 4 - 1.60 = 2.40 \text{ ft} \quad \textbf{Ans}$$

4-162. The distributed load acts on the beam as shown. Determine the magnitude of the equivalent resultant force and specify its location, measured from point A.

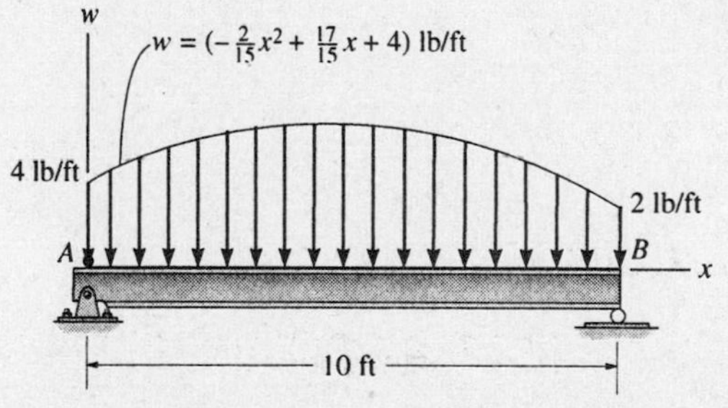

$$F_R = \int w(x)\,dx = \int_0^{10} \left(-\frac{2}{15}x^2 + \frac{17}{15}x + 4\right)dx = 52.22 = 52.2 \text{ lb} \quad \textbf{Ans}$$

$$\bar{x} = \frac{\int x\,w(x)\,dx}{\int w(x)\,dx} = \frac{\int_0^{10} x\left(-\frac{2}{15}x^2 + \frac{17}{15}x + 4\right)dx}{52.22} = \frac{244.44}{52.22}$$

$$\bar{x} = 4.68 \text{ ft} \quad \textbf{Ans}$$

4-163. The beam is subjected to the parabolic loading. Determine an equivalent force and couple system at point A.

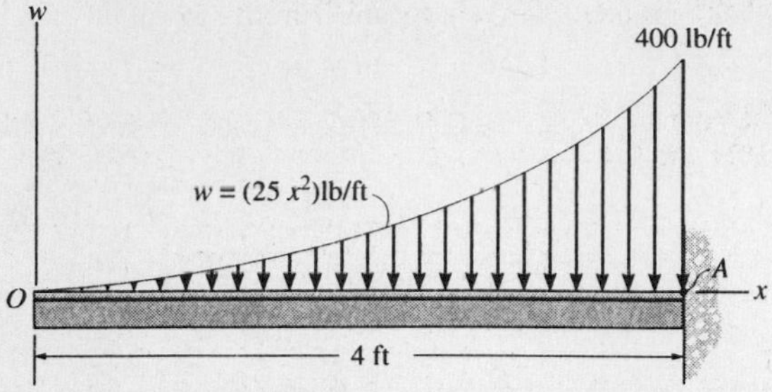

$+\uparrow F_R = \Sigma F_y;\quad F_R = -\int_A dA = -\int_0^x w\,dx$

$F_R = -\int_0^{4\text{ft}} (25x^2)\,dx$

$= -533.33 \text{ lb} = 533 \text{ lb} \downarrow$ **Ans**

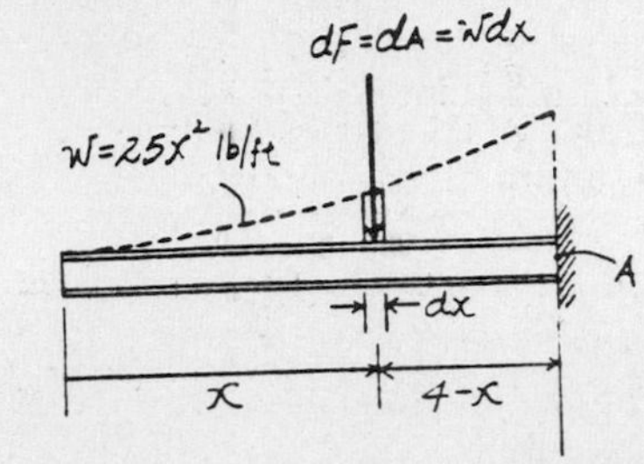

$\circlearrowleft + M_{R_A} = \Sigma M_A;\quad M_{R_A} = \int_0^x (4-x)\,w\,dx$

$= \int_0^{4\text{ft}} (4-x)(25x^2)\,dx$

$= \int_0^{4\text{ft}} (25x^3 - 100x^2)\,dx$

$= 533 \text{ lb}\cdot\text{ft}$ (***Counterclockwise***) **Ans**

*4-164. Two couples act on the frame. If the resultant couple moment is to be zero, determine the distance d between the 100-lb couple forces.

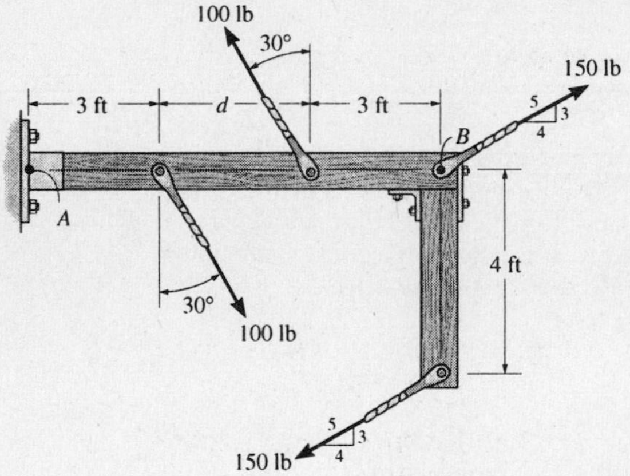

$\circlearrowleft + M_R = 0 = \Sigma M;\quad 0 = 100\cos 30°(d) - \frac{4}{5}(150)(4)$

$d = 5.54 \text{ ft}$ **Ans**

4-165. Determine the coordinate direction angles α, β, γ of **F**, which is applied to the end A of the pipe assembly, so that the moment of **F** about O is zero.

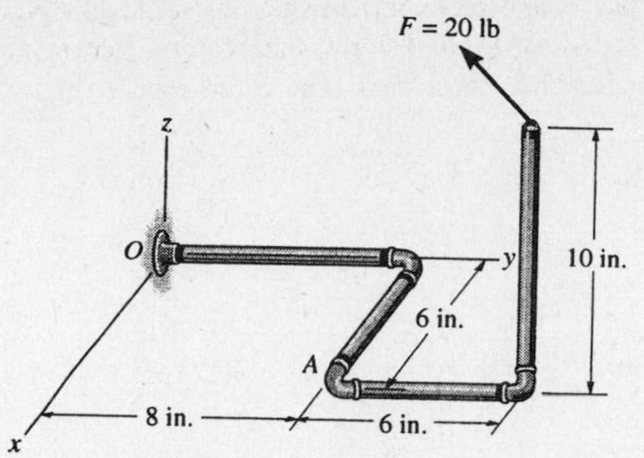

Require $\mathbf{M}_O = \mathbf{0}$. This happens when force **F** is directed along line OA either from point O to A or from point A to O. The unit vectors $\mathbf{u}_{OA}$ and $\mathbf{u}_{AO}$ are

$$\mathbf{u}_{OA} = \frac{(6-0)\mathbf{i}+(14-0)\mathbf{j}+(10-0)\mathbf{k}}{\sqrt{(6-0)^2+(14-0)^2+(10-0)^2}}$$
$$= 0.3293\mathbf{i} + 0.7683\mathbf{j} + 0.5488\mathbf{k}$$

Thus,

$\alpha = \cos^{-1} 0.3293 = 70.8°$ **Ans**

$\beta = \cos^{-1} 0.7683 = 39.8°$ **Ans**

$\gamma = \cos^{-1} 0.5488 = 56.7°$ **Ans**

$$\mathbf{u}_{AO} = \frac{(0-6)\mathbf{i}+(0-14)\mathbf{j}+(0-10)\mathbf{k}}{\sqrt{(0-6)^2+(0-14)^2+(0-10)^2}}$$
$$= -0.3293\mathbf{i} - 0.7683\mathbf{j} - 0.5488\mathbf{k}$$

Thus,

$\alpha = \cos^{-1}(-0.3293) = 109°$ **Ans**

$\beta = \cos^{-1}(-0.7683) = 140°$ **Ans**

$\gamma = \cos^{-1}(-0.5488) = 123°$ **Ans**

4-166. Determine the moment of the force **F** about point O. The force has coordinate direction angles of $\alpha = 60°$, $\beta = 120°$, $\gamma = 45°$. Express the result as a Cartesian vector.

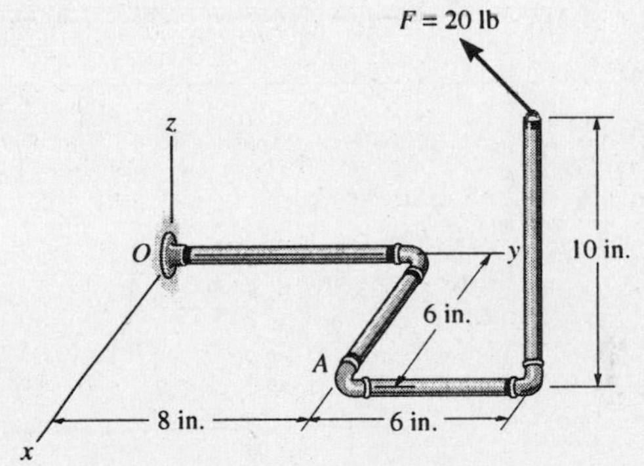

Position Vector And Force Vectors :

$$\mathbf{r}_{OA} = \{(6-0)\mathbf{i}+(14-0)\mathbf{j}+(10-0)\mathbf{k}\}\ \text{in.}$$
$$= \{6\mathbf{i}+14\mathbf{j}+10\mathbf{k}\}\ \text{in.}$$

$$\mathbf{F} = 20(\cos 60°\mathbf{i} + \cos 120°\mathbf{j} + \cos 45°\mathbf{k})\ \text{lb}$$
$$= \{10.0\mathbf{i} - 10.0\mathbf{j} + 14.142\mathbf{k}\}\ \text{lb}$$

Moment of Force* F *About Point O : Applying Eq. 4−7, we have

$$\mathbf{M}_O = \mathbf{r}_{OA} \times \mathbf{F}$$
$$= \begin{vmatrix} \mathbf{i} & \mathbf{j} & \mathbf{k} \\ 6 & 14 & 10 \\ 10.0 & -10.0 & 14.142 \end{vmatrix}$$

$= \{298\mathbf{i} + 15.1\mathbf{j} - 200\mathbf{k}\}\ \text{lb}\cdot\text{in}$ **Ans**

4-167. The Snorkel boom lift is extended into the position shown. If the worker weighs 160 lb, determine the moment of this force about the connection at A.

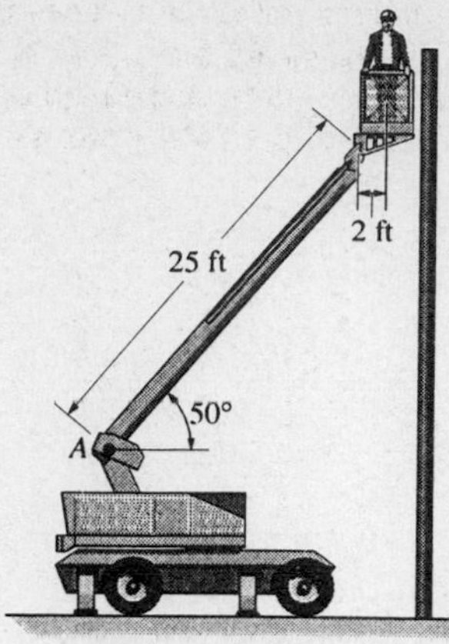

$$M_A = 160\,(2 + 25\cos 50^\circ) = 2891 \text{ lb}\cdot\text{ft} = 2.89 \text{ kip}\cdot\text{ft} \curvearrowright \quad \textbf{Ans}$$

***4-168.** Determine the moment of the force $\mathbf{F}_C$ about the door hinge at A. Express the result as a Cartesian vector.

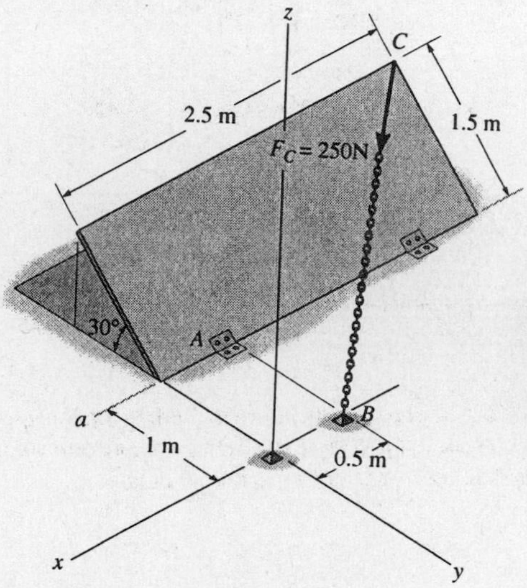

Position Vector And Force Vector :

$$\mathbf{r}_{AB} = \{[-0.5-(-0.5)]\mathbf{i}+[0-(-1)]\mathbf{j}+(0-0)\mathbf{k}\}\text{ m} = \{1\mathbf{j}\}\text{ m}$$

$$\mathbf{F}_C = 250\left(\frac{[-0.5-(-2.5)]\mathbf{i}+\{0-[-(1+1.5\cos 30^\circ)]\}\mathbf{j}+(0-1.5\sin 30^\circ)\mathbf{k}}{\sqrt{[-0.5-(-2.5)]^2+\{0-[-(1+1.5\cos 30^\circ)]\}^2+(0-1.5\sin 30^\circ)^2}}\right)\text{N}$$

$$= \{159.33\mathbf{i}+183.15\mathbf{j}-59.75\mathbf{k}\}\text{ N}$$

Moment of Force $\mathbf{F}_C$ About Point A : Applying Eq. 4 − 7, we have

$$\mathbf{M}_A = \mathbf{r}_{OA}\times\mathbf{F} = \begin{vmatrix} \mathbf{i} & \mathbf{j} & \mathbf{k} \\ 0 & 1 & 0 \\ 159.33 & 183.15 & -59.75 \end{vmatrix}$$

$$= \{-59.7\mathbf{i}-159\mathbf{k}\}\text{ N}\cdot\text{m} \quad \textbf{Ans}$$

4-169. Determine the magnitude of the moment of the force $\mathbf{F}_C$ about the hinged axis aa of the door.

Position Vector And Force Vectors :

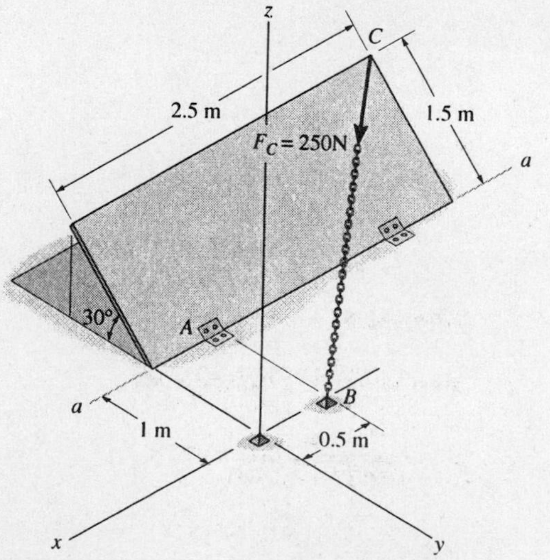

$$\mathbf{r}_{AB} = \{[-0.5-(-0.5)]\mathbf{i}+[0-(-1)]\mathbf{j}+(0-0)\mathbf{k}\}\text{ m} = \{1\mathbf{j}\}\text{ m}$$

$$\mathbf{F}_C = 250\left(\frac{[-0.5-(-2.5)]\mathbf{i}+\{0-[-(1+1.5\cos 30^\circ)]\}\mathbf{j}+(0-1.5\sin 30^\circ)\mathbf{k}}{\sqrt{[-0.5-(-2.5)]^2+\{0-[-(1+1.5\cos 30^\circ)]\}^2+(0-1.5\sin 30^\circ)^2}}\right)\text{N}$$

$$= \{159.33\mathbf{i}+183.15\mathbf{j}-59.75\mathbf{k}\}\text{ N}$$

Moment of Force $\mathbf{F}_C$ About a - aAxis : The unit vector along the $a-a$ axis is $\mathbf{i}$. Applying Eq. 4 − 11, we have

$$M_{a-a} = \mathbf{i}\cdot(\mathbf{r}_{AB}\times\mathbf{F}_C) = \begin{vmatrix} 1 & 0 & 0 \\ 0 & 1 & 0 \\ 159.33 & 183.15 & -59.75 \end{vmatrix}$$

$$= 1[1(-59.75)-(183.15)(0)]-0+0$$
$$= -59.7\text{ N}\cdot\text{m}$$

The negative sign indicates that $\mathbf{M}_{a-a}$ is directed toward negative x axis.

$\mathbf{M}_{a-a} = 59.7\text{ N}\cdot\text{m}$ **Ans**

4-170. Express the moment of the couple acting on the pipe assembly in Cartesian vector form. Solve the problem (a) using Eq. 4–13 and (b) summing the moment of each force about point O. Take $\mathbf{F} = \{25\mathbf{k}\}$ N.

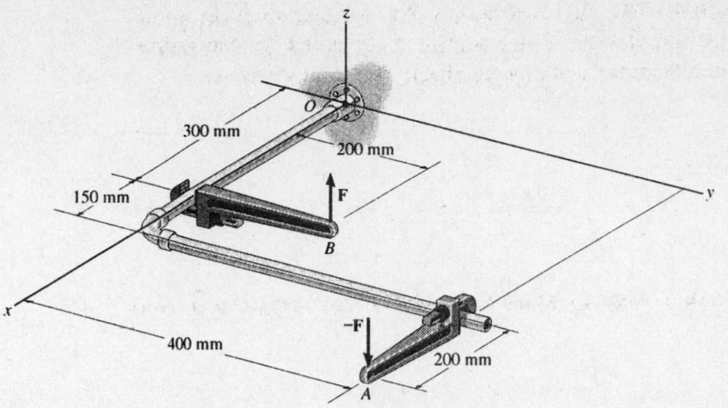

a) $\mathbf{M}_C = \mathbf{r}_{AB} \times (25\,\mathbf{k})$

$$= \begin{vmatrix} \mathbf{i} & \mathbf{j} & \mathbf{k} \\ -0.35 & -0.2 & 0 \\ 0 & 0 & 25 \end{vmatrix}$$

$\mathbf{M}_C = \{-5\,\mathbf{i} + 8.75\,\mathbf{j}\}$ N·m **Ans**

(b) $\mathbf{M}_C = \mathbf{r}_{OB} \times (25\,\mathbf{k}) + \mathbf{r}_{OA} \times (-25\,\mathbf{k})$

$$= \begin{vmatrix} \mathbf{i} & \mathbf{j} & \mathbf{k} \\ 0.3 & 0.2 & 0 \\ 0 & 0 & 25 \end{vmatrix} + \begin{vmatrix} \mathbf{i} & \mathbf{j} & \mathbf{k} \\ 0.65 & 0.4 & 0 \\ 0 & 0 & -25 \end{vmatrix}$$

$\mathbf{M}_C = (5 - 10)\,\mathbf{i} + (-7.5 + 16.25)\,\mathbf{j}$

$\mathbf{M}_C = \{-5\,\mathbf{i} + 8.75\,\mathbf{j}\}$ N·m **Ans**

4-171. If the couple moment acting on the pipe has a magnitude of 400 N·m, determine the magnitude F of the vertical force applied to each wrench.

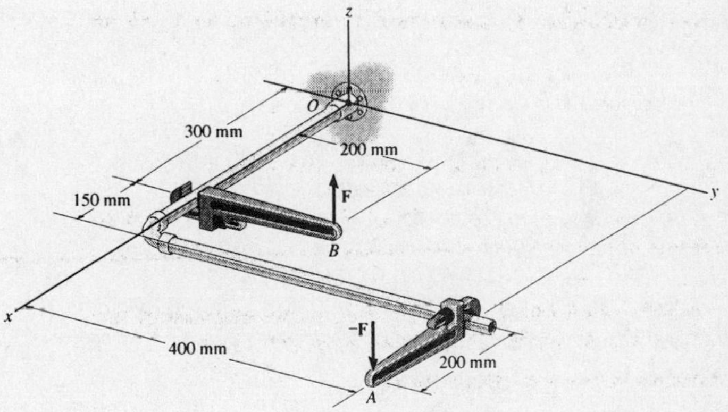

$\mathbf{M}_C = \mathbf{r}_{AB} \times (F\,\mathbf{k})$

$$= \begin{vmatrix} \mathbf{i} & \mathbf{j} & \mathbf{k} \\ -0.35 & -0.2 & 0 \\ 0 & 0 & F \end{vmatrix}$$

$\mathbf{M}_C = \{-0.2F\,\mathbf{i} + 0.35F\,\mathbf{j}\}$ N·m

$M_C = \sqrt{(-0.2F)^2 + (0.35F)^2} = 400$

$$F = \frac{400}{\sqrt{(-0.2)^2 + (0.35)^2}} = 992 \text{ N}$$

***4-172.** Replace the force at A by an equivalent resultant force and couple moment at point P. Express the results in Cartesian vector form.

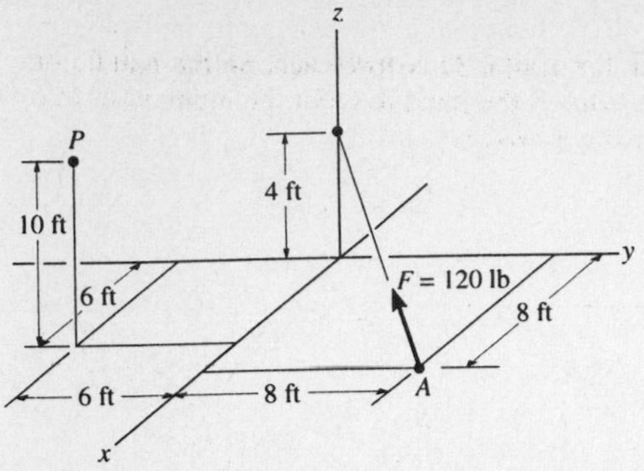

$$\mathbf{F}_R = 120\left(\frac{-8\mathbf{i} - 8\mathbf{j} + 4\mathbf{k}}{\sqrt{(-8)^2 + (-8)^2 + 4^2}}\right) = \{-80\mathbf{i} - 80\mathbf{j} + 40\mathbf{k}\}\text{ lb} \qquad \textbf{Ans}$$

$$\mathbf{M}_{RP} = \Sigma\mathbf{M}_P = \begin{vmatrix} \mathbf{i} & \mathbf{j} & \mathbf{k} \\ 2 & 14 & -10 \\ -80 & -80 & 40 \end{vmatrix}$$

$$= \{-240\mathbf{i} + 720\mathbf{j} + 960\mathbf{k}\}\text{ lb}\cdot\text{ft} \qquad \textbf{Ans}$$

***4-173.** The horizontal 30-N force acts on the handle of the wrench. Determine the moment of this force about point O. Specify the coordinate direction angles α, β, γ of the moment axis.

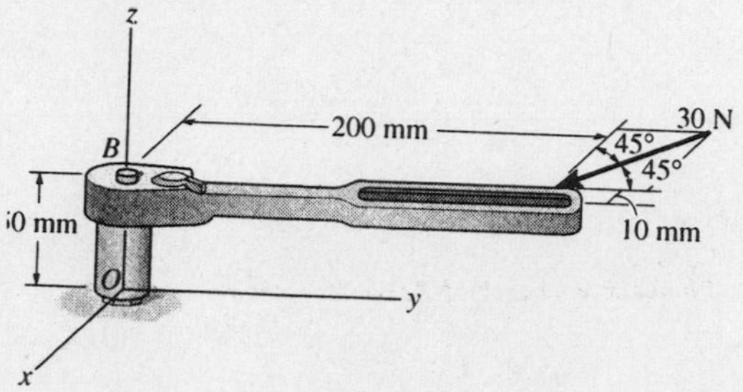

Position Vector And Force Vectors :

$$\mathbf{r}_{OA} = \{(-0.01-0)\mathbf{i} + (0.2-0)\mathbf{j} + (0.05-0)\mathbf{k}\}\text{ m}$$
$$= \{-0.01\mathbf{i} + 0.2\mathbf{j} + 0.05\mathbf{k}\}\text{ m}$$

$$\mathbf{F} = 30(\sin 45°\mathbf{i} - \cos 45°\mathbf{j})\text{ N}$$
$$= \{21.213\mathbf{i} - 21.213\mathbf{j}\}\text{ N}$$

Moment of Force* F *About Point O : Applying Eq. 4 – 7, we have

$$\mathbf{M}_O = \mathbf{r}_{OA} \times \mathbf{F}$$
$$= \begin{vmatrix} \mathbf{i} & \mathbf{j} & \mathbf{k} \\ -0.01 & 0.2 & 0.05 \\ 21.213 & -21.213 & 0 \end{vmatrix}$$

$$= \{1.061\mathbf{i} + 1.061\mathbf{j} - 4.031\mathbf{k}\}\text{ N}\cdot\text{m}$$
$$= \{1.06\mathbf{i} + 1.06\mathbf{j} - 4.03\mathbf{k}\}\text{ N}\cdot\text{m} \qquad \textbf{Ans}$$

The magnitude of $\mathbf{M}_O$ is

$$M_O = \sqrt{1.061^2 + 1.061^2 + (-4.031)^2} = 4.301\text{ N}\cdot\text{m}$$

The coordinate direction angles for $\mathbf{M}_O$ are

$$\alpha = \cos^{-1}\left(\frac{1.061}{4.301}\right) = 75.7° \qquad \textbf{Ans}$$

$$\beta = \cos^{-1}\left(\frac{1.061}{4.301}\right) = 75.7° \qquad \textbf{Ans}$$

$$\gamma = \cos^{-1}\left(\frac{-4.031}{4.301}\right) = 160° \qquad \textbf{Ans}$$

4-174. The horizontal 30-N force acts on the handle of the wrench. What is the magnitude of the moment of this force about the z axis?

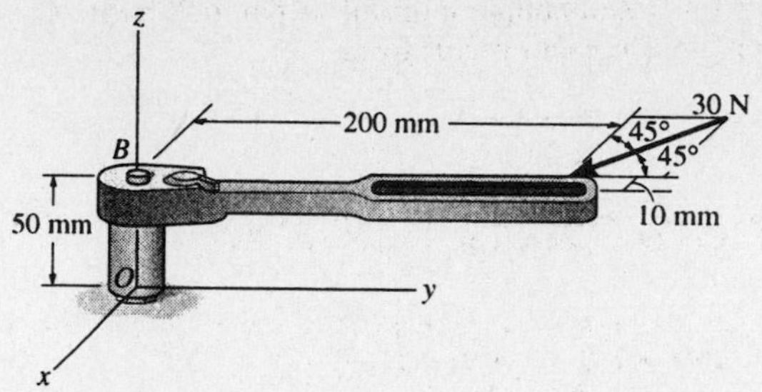

Position Vector And Force Vectors :

$$\mathbf{r}_{BA} = \{-0.01\mathbf{i} + 0.2\mathbf{j}\}\ \text{m}$$
$$\mathbf{r}_{OA} = \{(-0.01-0)\mathbf{i} + (0.2-0)\mathbf{j} + (0.05-0)\mathbf{k}\}\ \text{m}$$
$$= \{-0.01\mathbf{i} + 0.2\mathbf{j} + 0.05\mathbf{k}\}\ \text{m}$$

$$\mathbf{F} = 30(\sin 45°\mathbf{i} - \cos 45°\mathbf{j})\ \text{N}$$
$$= \{21.213\mathbf{i} - 21.213\mathbf{j}\}\ \text{N}$$

Moment of Force* F *About z Axis : The unit vector along the z axis is **k**. Applying Eq. 4 − 11, we have

$$M_z = \mathbf{k} \cdot (\mathbf{r}_{BA} \times \mathbf{F})$$
$$= \begin{vmatrix} 0 & 0 & 1 \\ -0.01 & 0.2 & 0 \\ 21.213 & -21.213 & 0 \end{vmatrix}$$

$$= 0 - 0 + 1[(-0.01)(-21.213) - 21.213(0.2)]$$
$$= -4.03\ \text{N}\cdot\text{m} \qquad \textbf{Ans}$$

Or

$$M_z = \mathbf{k} \cdot (\mathbf{r}_{BA} \times \mathbf{F})$$
$$= \begin{vmatrix} 0 & 0 & 1 \\ -0.01 & 0.2 & 0.05 \\ 21.213 & -21.213 & 0 \end{vmatrix}$$

$$= 0 - 0 + 1[(-0.01)(-21.213) - 21.213(0.2)]$$
$$= -4.03\ \text{N}\cdot\text{m} \qquad \textbf{Ans}$$

The negative sign indicates that $\mathbf{M}_z$ is directed along the negative z axis.

5-1. Draw the free-body diagram of the 50-kg paper roll which has a center of mass at G and rests on the smooth blade of the paper hauler. Explain the significance of each force acting on the diagram. (See Fig. 5–7*b*.)

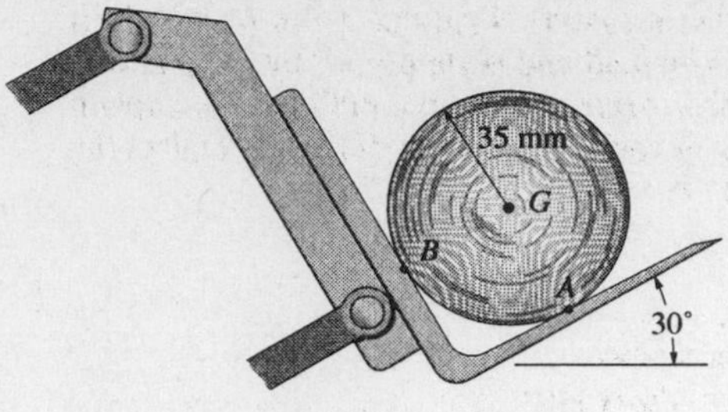

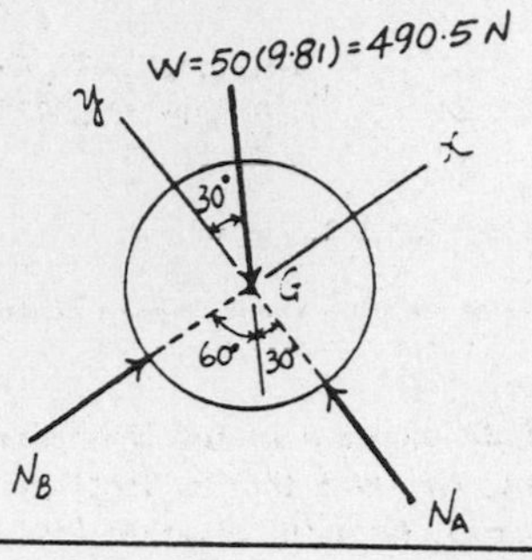

The Significance of Each Force :

W is the effect of gravity (weight) on the paper roll.

N_A and N_B are the smooth blade reactions on the paper roll.

5-2. Draw the free-body diagram of member AB, which is supported by a roller at A and a pin at B. Explain the significance of each force on the diagram. (See Fig. 5–7*b*.)

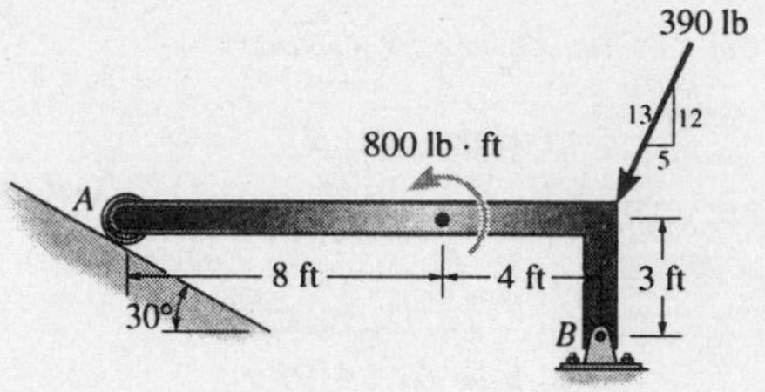

N_A force of plane on roller.

B_x, B_y force of pin on member.

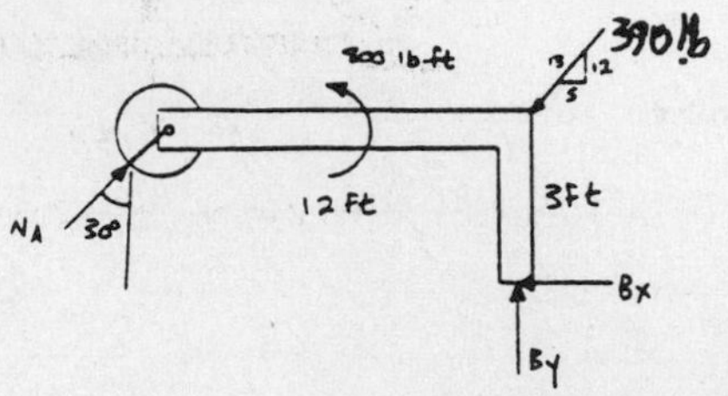

5-3. Draw the free-body diagram of the dumpster D of the truck, which has a weight of 5000 lb and a center of gravity at G. It is supported by a pin at A and a pin-connected hydraulic cylinder BC (short link) Explain the significance of each force on the diagram. (See Fig. 5–7*b*.)

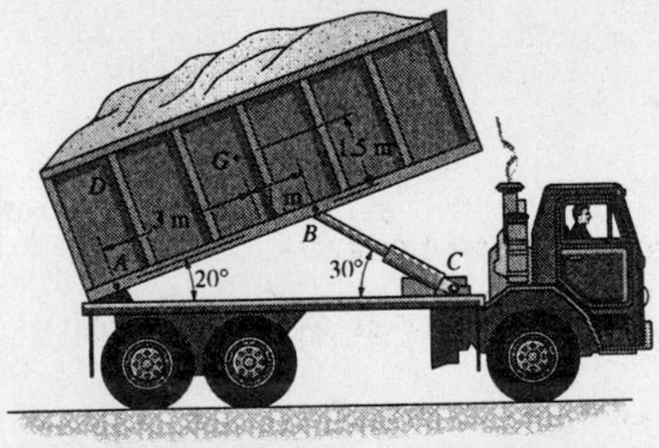

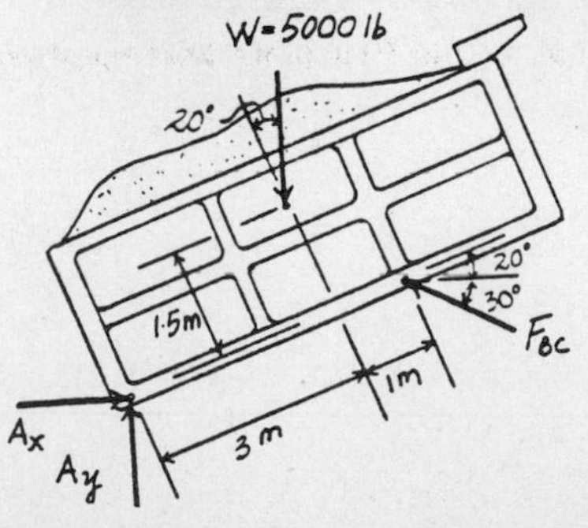

The Significance of Each Force :

W is the effect of gravity (weight) on the dumpster.

A_y and A_x are the pin A reactions on the dumpster.

F_{BC} is the hydraulic cylinder BC reaction on the dumpster.

*5-4. Draw the free-body diagram of the beam which supports the 80-kg load and is supported by the pin at A and a cable which wraps around the pulley at D. Explain the significance of each force on the diagram. Neglect the thickness of the beam. (See Fig. 5–7b.)

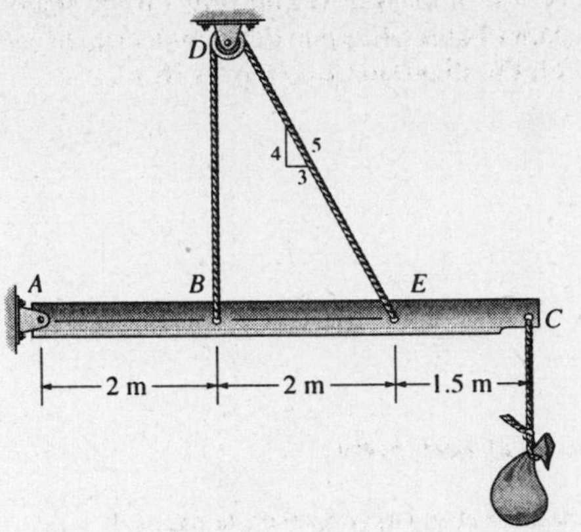

T force of cable on beam.

A_x, A_y force of pin on beam.

80(9.81)N force of cable on beam.

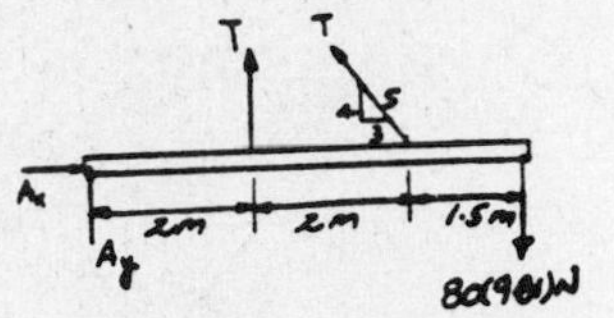

5-5. Draw the free-body diagram of the truss that is supported by the cable AB and pin C. Explain the significance of each force acting on the diagram. (See Fig. 5–7b.)

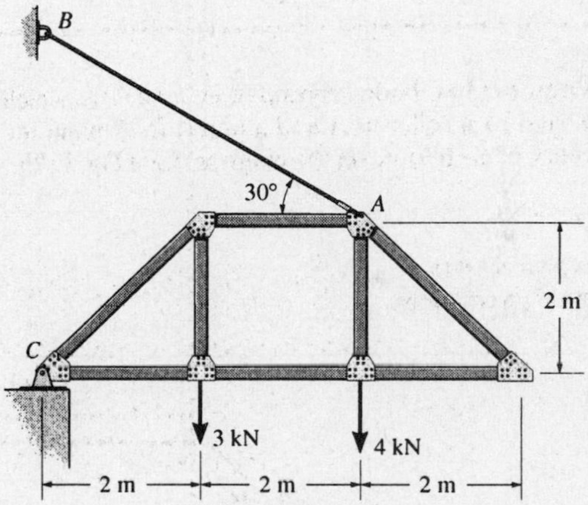

The Significance of Each Force :

C_y and C_x are the pin C reactions on the truss.

T_{AB} is the cable AB tension on the truss.

3 kN and 4 kN force are the effect of external applied forces on the truss.

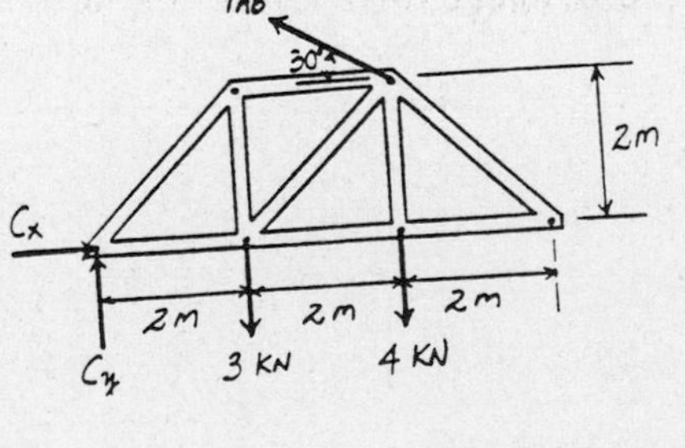

5-6. Draw the free-body diagram of the crane boom AB which has a weight of 650 lb and center of gravity at G. The boom is supported by a pin at A and cable BC. The load of 1250 lb is suspended from a cable attached at B. Explain the significance of each force acting on the diagram. (See Fig. 5–7*b*.)

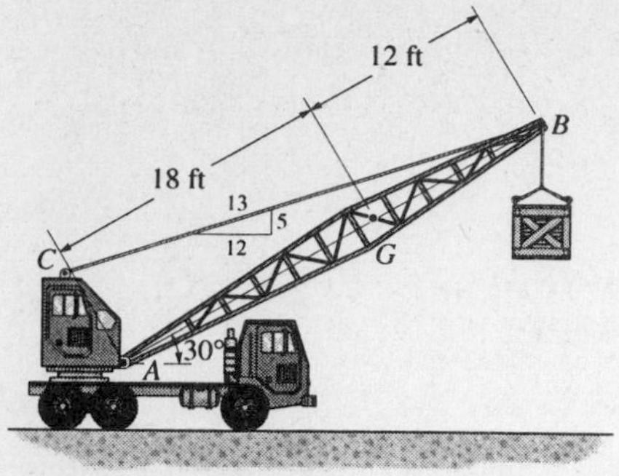

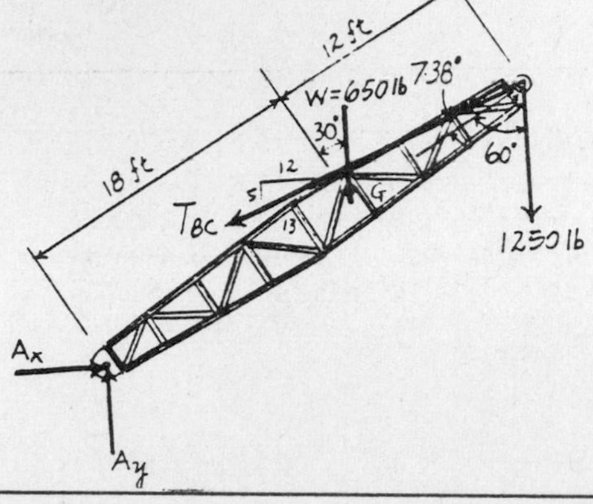

The Significance of Each Force :

W is the effect of gravity (weight) on the boom.

A_y and A_x are the pin A reactions on the boom.

T_{BC} is the cable BC force reactions on the boom.

1250 lb force is the suspended load reaction on the boom.

5-7. Draw the free-body diagram of the "spanner wrench" subjected to the 20-lb force. The support at A can be considered a pin, and the surface of contact at B is smooth. Explain the significance of each force on the diagram. (See Fig. 5–7*b*.)

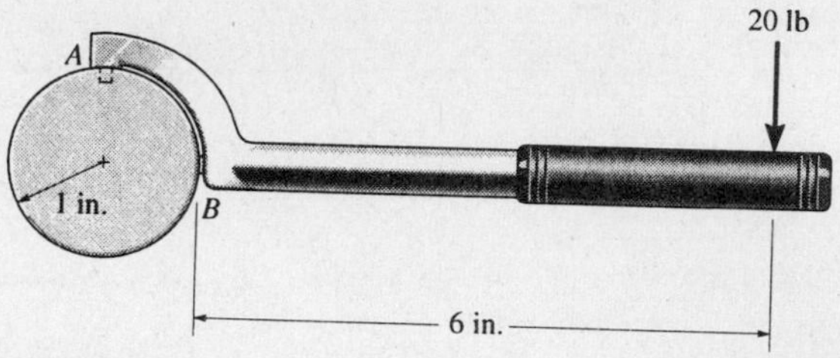

A_x, A_y, N_B force of cylinder on wrench.

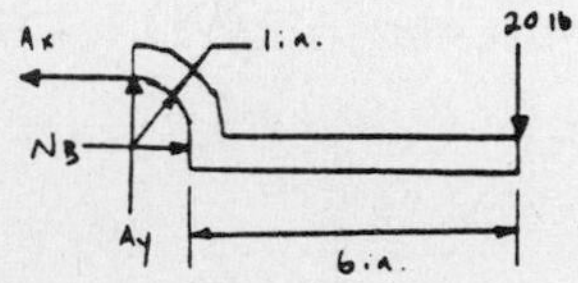

***5-8.** Draw the free-body diagram of member ABC which is supported by a smooth collar at A, roller at B, and short link CD. Explain the significance of each force acting on the diagram. (See Fig. 5–7*b*.)

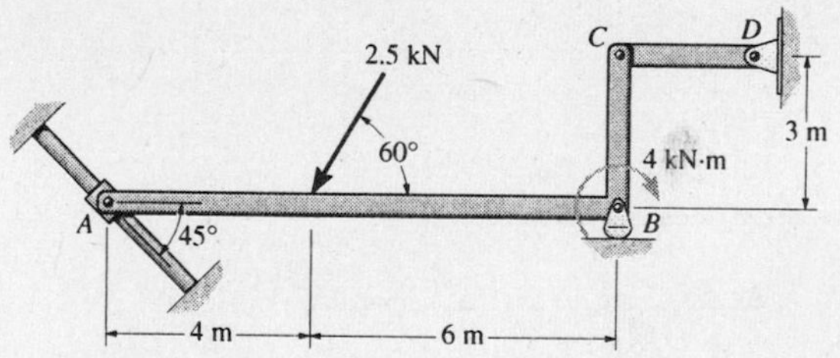

The Significance of Each Force :

N_A is the smooth collar reaction on member ABC.

N_B is the roller support B reaction on member ABC.

F_{CD} is the short link reaction on member ABC.

2.5 kN is the effect of external applied force on member ABC.

4 kN · m is the effect of external applied couple moment on member ABC.

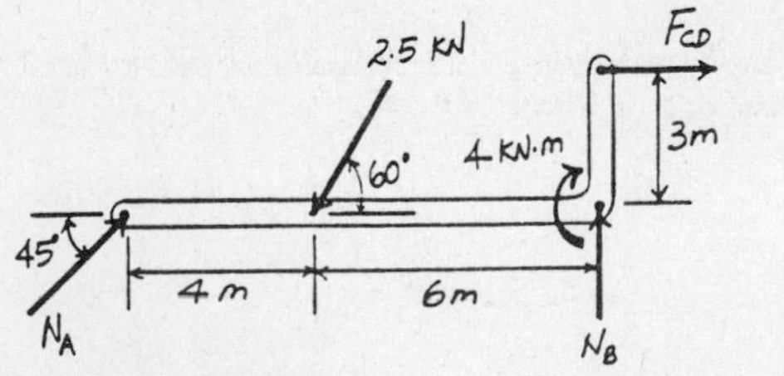

5-9. Draw the free-body diagram of the bar, which has smooth points of contact at A, B, and C. Explain the significance of each force on the diagram. (See Fig. 5–7*b*.)

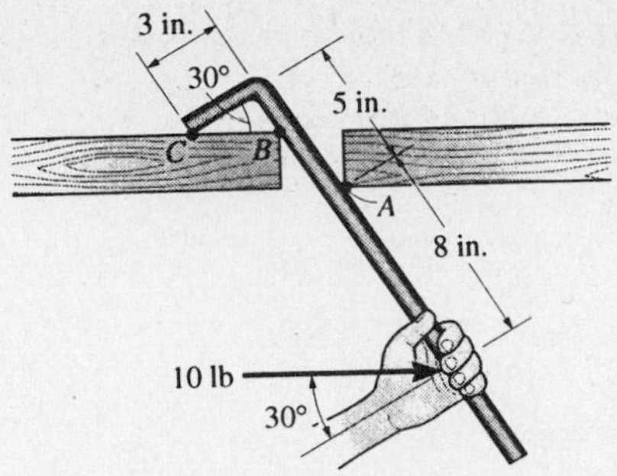

N_A, N_B, N_C force of wood on bar.
10 lb force of hand on bar.

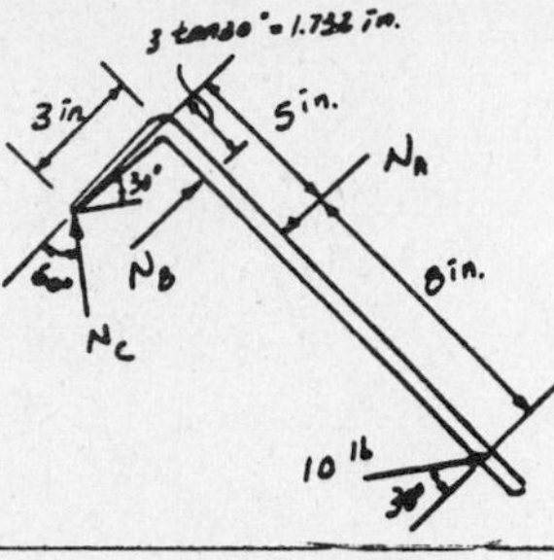

5-10. Draw the free-body diagram of the winch, which consists of a drum of radius 4 in. It is pin-connected at its center C, and at its outer rim is a ratchet gear having a mean radius of 6 in. The pawl AB serves as a two-force member (short link) and prevents the drum from rotating. Explain the significance of each force on the diagram. (See Fig. 5–7*b*.)

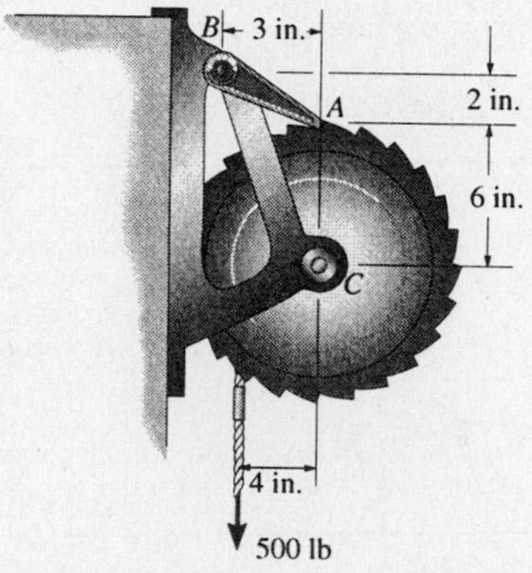

C_x, C_y force of pin on drum.
F_{AB} force of pawl on drum gear.
500 lb force of cable on drum.

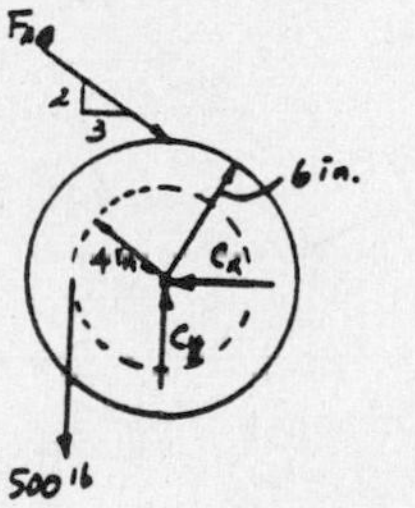

5-11. Determine the reactions at the supports in Prob. 5–1.

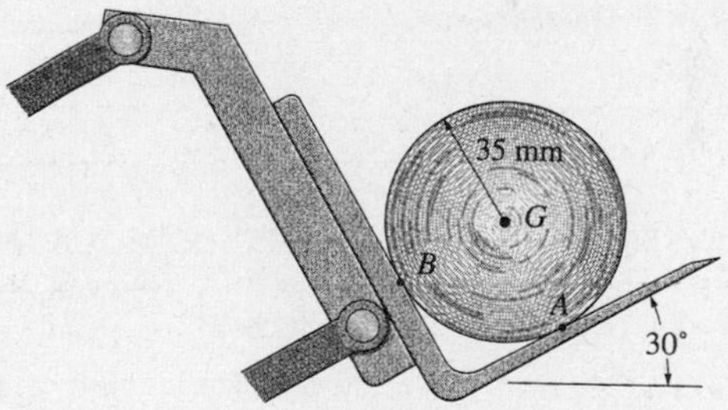

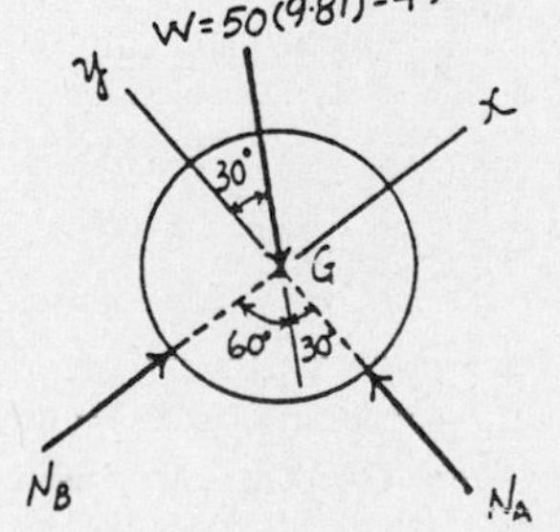

Equations of Equilibrium : By setting up the x and y axes in the manner shown, one can obtain the direct solution for N_A and N_B.

$\nearrow + \Sigma F_x = 0;\quad N_B - 490.5\sin 30° = 0 \quad N_B = 245\text{ N}$ **Ans**

$\nwarrow + \Sigma F_y = 0;\quad N_A - 490.5\cos 30° = 0 \quad N_A = 425\text{ N}$ **Ans**

***5-12.** Determine the tension in the cord and the reactions at support A of the beam in Prob. 5–4.

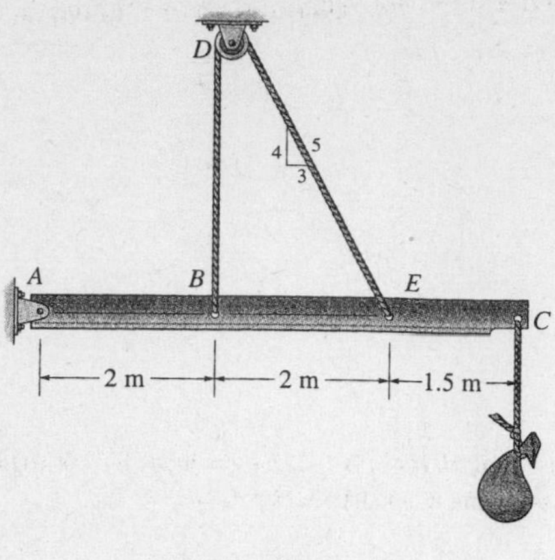

$\circlearrowleft + \Sigma M_A = 0; \quad T(2) + T\left(\frac{4}{5}\right)(4) - 80(9.81)(5.5) = 0$

$T = 830.1 \text{ N} = 830 \text{ N}$ **Ans**

$\xrightarrow{+} \Sigma F_x = 0; \quad A_x - 830.1\left(\frac{3}{5}\right) = 0$

$A_x = 498 \text{ N}$ **Ans**

$+\uparrow \Sigma F_y = 0; \quad -A_y + 830.1 + 830.1\left(\frac{4}{5}\right) - 80(9.81) = 0$

$A_y = 709 \text{ N}$ **Ans**

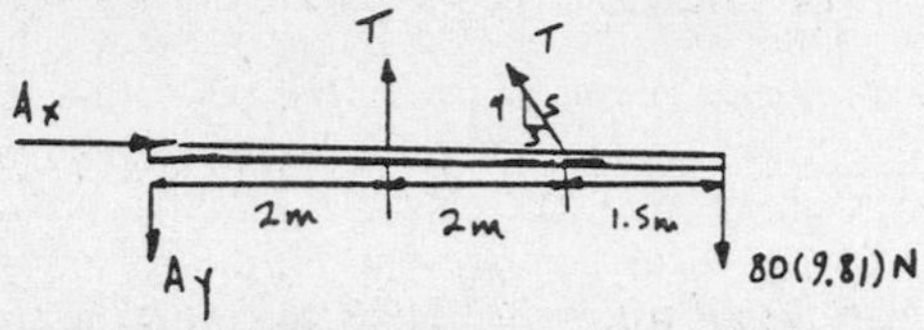

5-13. Determine the reactions at the supports for the truss in Prob. 5–5.

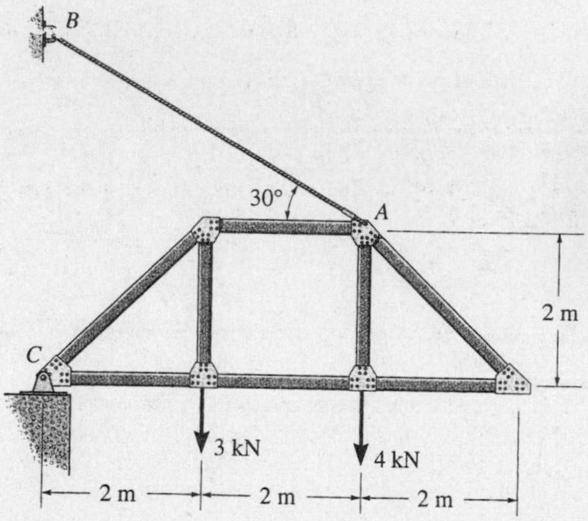

Equations of Equilibrium : The tension in the cable can be obtained directly by summing moments about point C.

$\circlearrowleft + \Sigma M_C = 0; \quad T_{AB}\cos 30°(2) + T_{AB}\sin 30°(4) - 3(2) - 4(4) = 0$

$T_{AB} = 5.89 \text{ kN}$ **Ans**

$\xrightarrow{+} \Sigma F_x = 0; \quad C_x - 5.89\cos 30° = 0$

$C_x = 5.11 \text{ kN}$ **Ans**

$+\uparrow \Sigma F_y = 0; \quad C_y + 5.89\sin 30° - 3 - 4 = 0$

$C_y = 4.05 \text{ kN}$ **Ans**

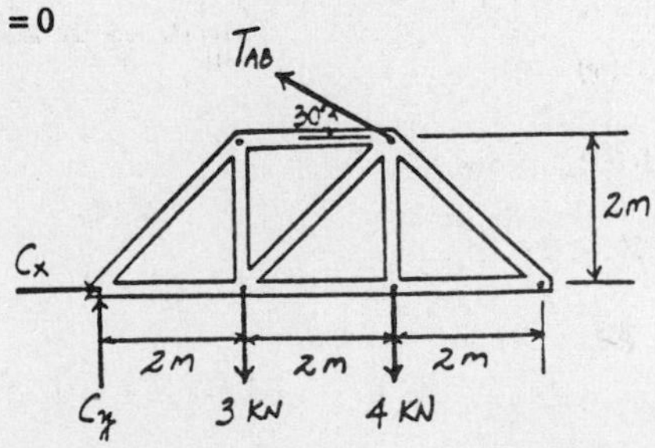

5-14. Determine the reactions on the boom in Prob. 5–6.

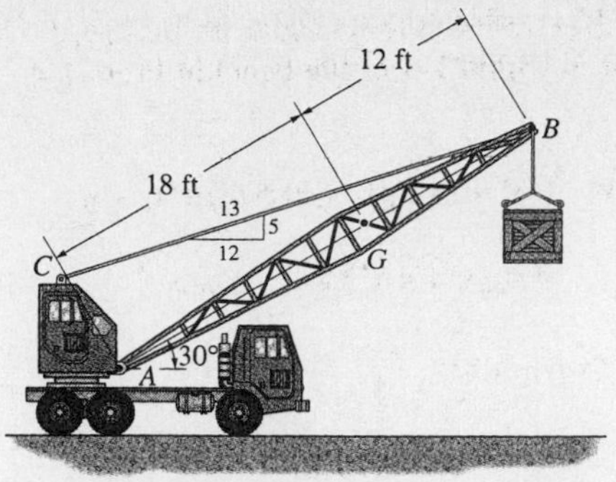

Equations of Equilibrium : The force in cable BC can be obtained directly by summing moments about point A.

$\circlearrowleft + \Sigma M_A = 0;\quad T_{BC}\sin 7.380°(30) - 650\cos 30°(18) - 1250\sin 60°(30) = 0$

$T_{BC} = 11056.9 \text{ lb} = 11.1 \text{ kip}$ **Ans**

$\xrightarrow{+} \Sigma F_x = 0;\quad A_x - 11056.9\left(\frac{12}{13}\right) = 0$

$A_x = 10206.4 \text{ lb} = 10.2 \text{ kip}$ **Ans**

$+\uparrow \Sigma F_y = 0;\quad A_y - 650 - 1250 - 11056.9\left(\frac{5}{13}\right) = 0$

$A_y = 6152.7 \text{ lb} = 6.15 \text{ kip}$ **Ans**

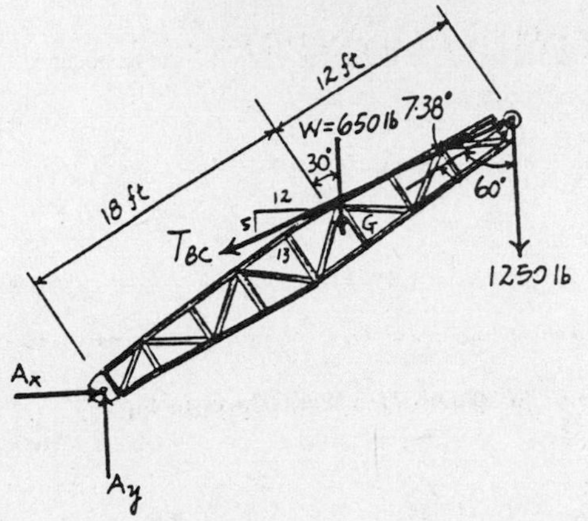

5-15. Determine the reactions on the spanner wrench in Prob. 5–7.

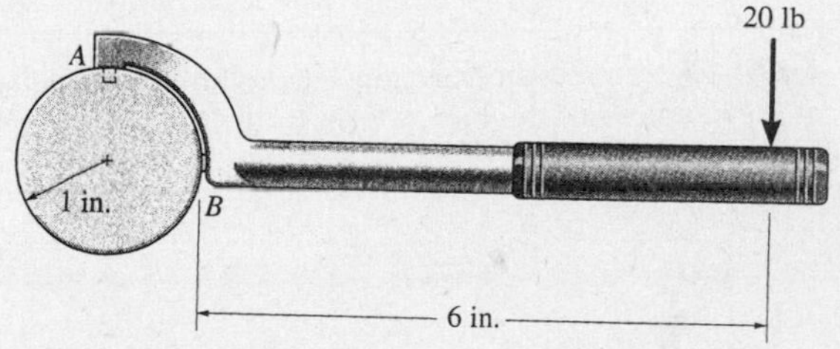

$\circlearrowleft + \Sigma M_A = 0;\quad N_B(1) - 20(7) = 0$

$N_B = 140 \text{ lb}$ **Ans**

$\xrightarrow{+} \Sigma F_x = 0;\quad -A_x + 140 = 0$

$A_x = 140 \text{ lb}$ **Ans**

$+\uparrow \Sigma F_y = 0;\quad A_y - 20 = 0$

$A_y = 20 \text{ lb}$ **Ans**

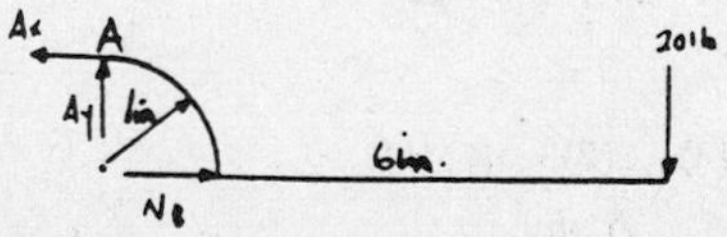

***5-16.** Determine the reactions on the member *A, B, C* in Prob. 5–8.

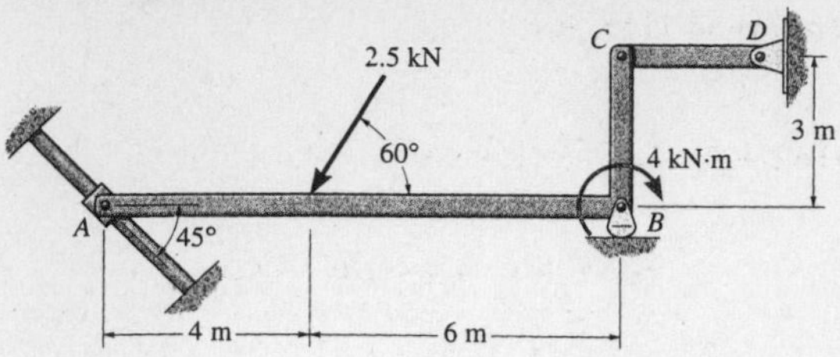

Equations of Equilibrium : The normal reaction N_A can be obtained directly by summing moments about point *C*.

$\circlearrowleft + \Sigma M_C = 0;\quad 2.5\sin 60°(6) - 2.5\cos 60°(3) - 4 + N_A\cos 45°(3) - N_A\sin 45°(10) = 0$

$N_A = 1.059\ \text{kN} = 1.06\ \text{kN}$ **Ans**

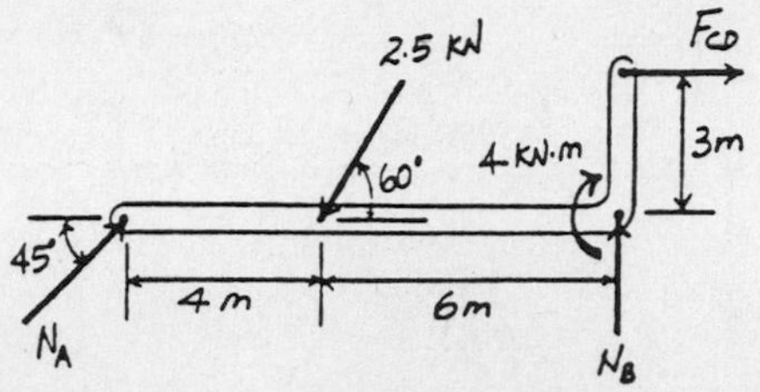

$\overset{+}{\rightarrow} \Sigma F_x = 0;\quad 1.059\cos 45° - 2.5\cos 60° + F_{CD} = 0$

$F_{CD} = 0.501\ \text{kN}$ **Ans**

$+\uparrow \Sigma F_y = 0;\quad N_B + 1.059\sin 45° - 2.5\sin 60° = 0$

$N_B = 1.42\ \text{kN}$ **Ans**

5-17. Determine the reactions at the points of contact at *A*, *B*, and *C* of the bar in Prob. 5–9.

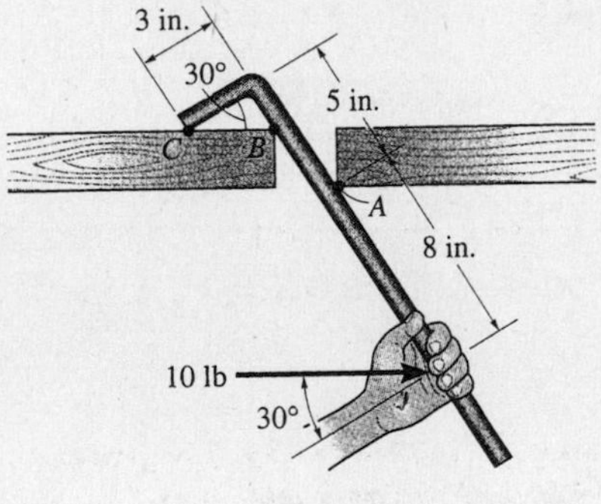

$+\nwarrow \Sigma F_x = 0;\quad N_C\sin 60° - 10\sin 30° = 0$

$N_C = 5.77\ \text{lb}$ **Ans**

$\circlearrowleft + \Sigma M_B = 0;\quad 10\cos 30°(13 - 1.732) - N_A(5 - 1.732) - 5.77(3.464) = 0$

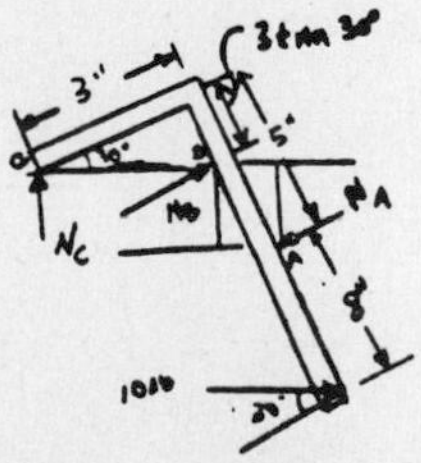

$N_A = 23.7\ \text{lb}$ **Ans**

$+\nearrow \Sigma F_y = 0;\quad N_B + 5.77\cos 60° + 10\cos 30° - 23.7 = 0$

$N_B = 12.2\ \text{lb}$ **Ans**

5-18. Determine the reactions at A and at the pin C of the winch in Prob. 5–10.

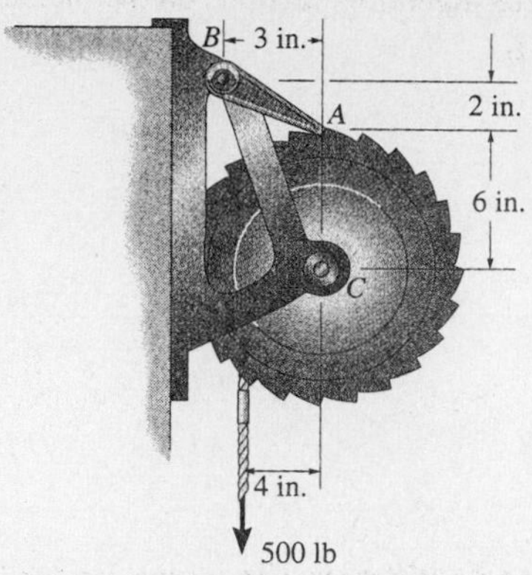

$$\circlearrowleft + \Sigma M_C = 0;\quad F_{AB}\left(\frac{3}{\sqrt{13}}\right)6 - 500(4) = 0$$

$$F_{AB} = 400.6\text{ lb} = 401\text{ lb}\qquad \textbf{Ans}$$

$$\xrightarrow{+} \Sigma F_x = 0;\quad -C_x + 400.6\left(\frac{3}{\sqrt{13}}\right) = 0$$

$$C_x = 333\text{ lb}\qquad \textbf{Ans}$$

$$+\uparrow \Sigma F_y = 0;\quad -500 + C_y - 400.6\left(\frac{2}{\sqrt{13}}\right) = 0$$

$$C_y = 722\text{ lb}\qquad \textbf{Ans}$$

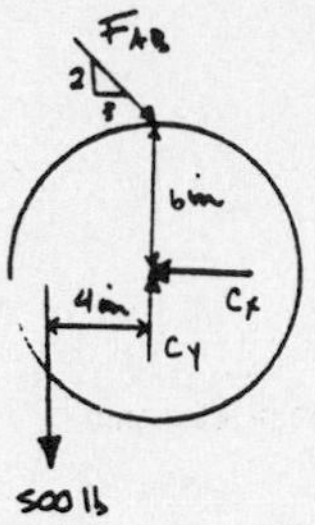

5-19. Determine the reactions at the supports.

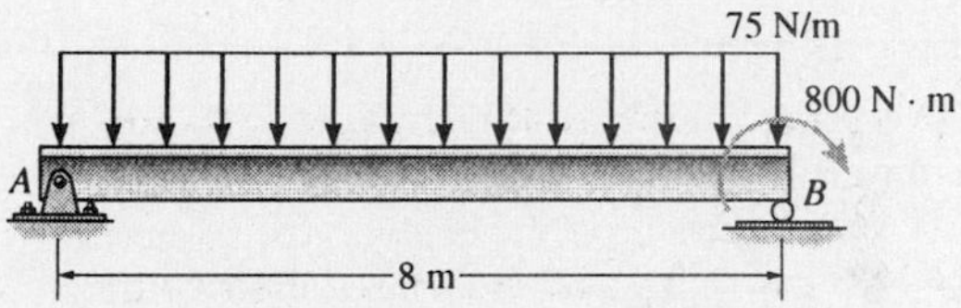

$$\circlearrowleft + \Sigma M_A = 0;\quad 600(4) + 800 - (8)B_y = 0$$

$$B_y = 400\text{ N}\qquad \textbf{Ans}$$

$$\xrightarrow{+} \Sigma F_x = 0;\quad A_x = 0\qquad \textbf{Ans}$$

$$+\uparrow \Sigma F_y = 0;\quad A_y - 600 + 400 = 0$$

$$A_y = 200\text{ N}\qquad \textbf{Ans}$$

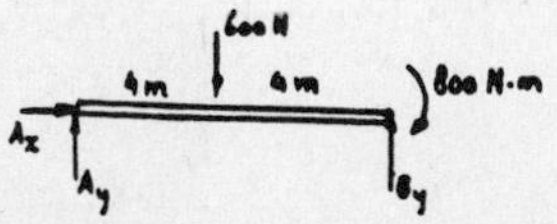

***5-20.** Determine the reactions at the roller A and pin B.

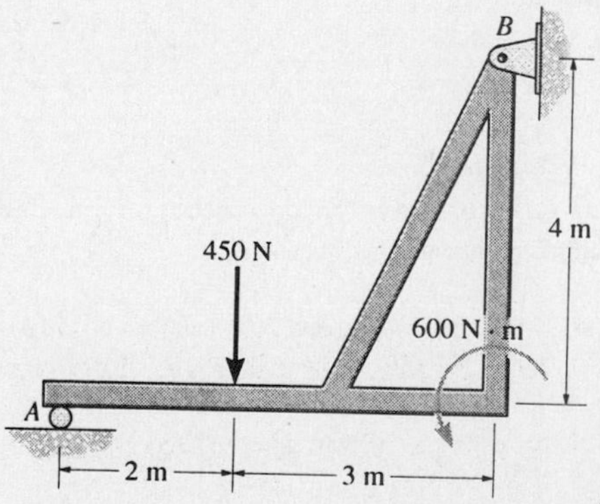

Equations of Equilibrium : The vertical reaction A_y can be obtained directly by summing moments about point B.

$$\circlearrowleft + \Sigma M_B = 0;\quad 450(3) + 600 - A_y(5) = 0$$

$$A_y = 390\text{ N}\qquad \textbf{Ans}$$

$$\xrightarrow{+} \Sigma F_x = 0;\quad B_x = 0\qquad \textbf{Ans}$$

$$+\uparrow \Sigma F_y = 0;\quad B_y + 390 - 450 = 0$$

$$B_y = 60.0\text{ N}\qquad \textbf{Ans}$$

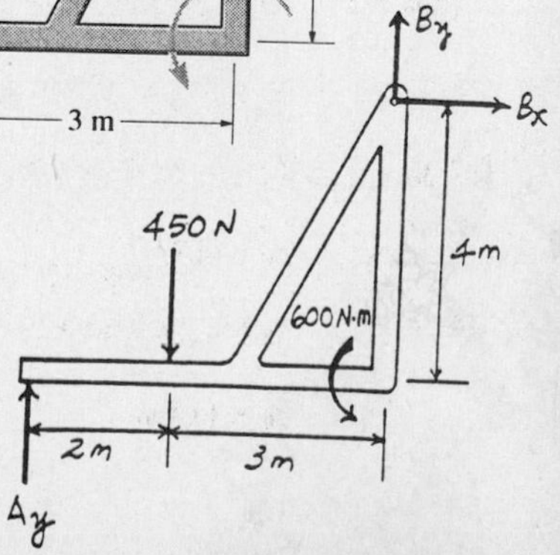

5-21. Determine the reactions at the supports.

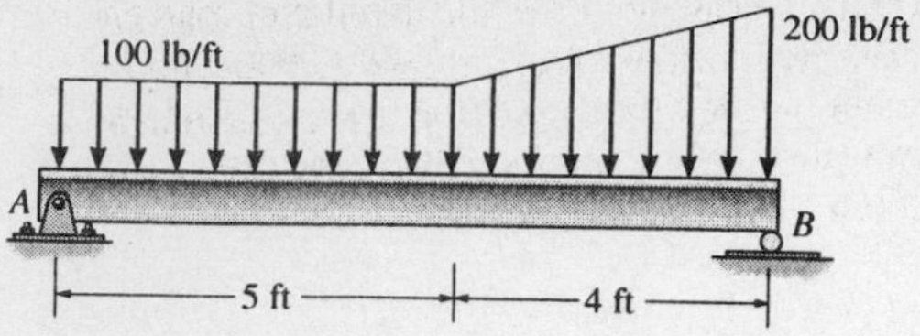

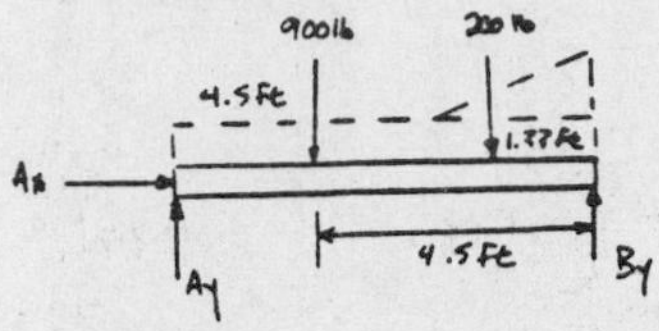

$\xrightarrow{+} \Sigma F_x = 0; \quad A_x = 0$ **Ans**

$\circlearrowleft + \Sigma M_B = 0; \quad 900\,(4.5) + 200\,(1.333) - A_y\,(9) = 0$

$A_y = 480 \text{ lb}$ **Ans**

$+\uparrow \Sigma F_y = 0; \quad 480 - 1100 + B_y = 0$

$B_y = 620 \text{ lb}$ **Ans**

5-22. As an airplane's brakes are applied, the nose wheel exerts two forces on the end of the landing gear as shown. Determine the horizontal and vertical components of reaction at the pin C and the force in strut AB.

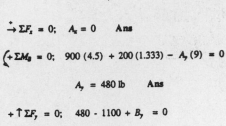

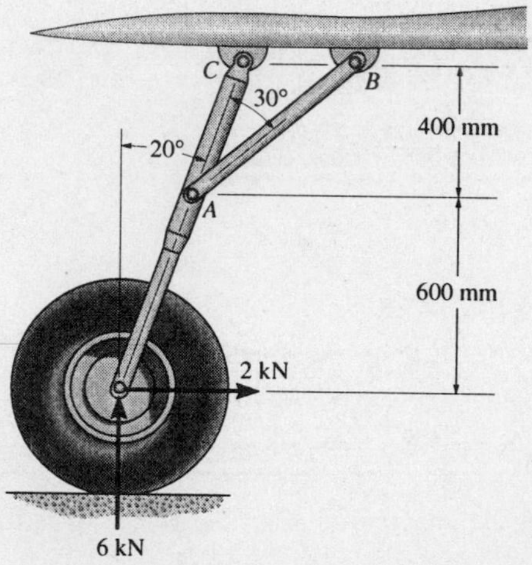

Equations of Equilibrium : The force in strut AB can be obtained directly by summing moments about point C.

$$\circlearrowleft + \Sigma M_C = 0; \quad 2(1) - 6(1\tan 20°) + F_{AB}\sin 50°(0.4) - F_{AB}\cos 50°(0.4\tan 20°) = 0$$

$F_{AB} = 0.8637 \text{ kN} = 0.864 \text{ kN}$ **Ans**

Using the result $F_{AB} = 0.8637$ kN and sum forces along x and y axes, we have,

$+\uparrow \Sigma F_y = 0; \quad 6 + 0.8637\cos 50° - C_y = 0$

$C_y = 6.56 \text{ kN}$ **Ans**

$\xrightarrow{+} \Sigma F_x = 0; \quad 0.8637\sin 50° + 2 - C_x = 0$

$C_x = 2.66 \text{ kN}$ **Ans**

5-23. The train car has a weight of 24 000 lb and a center of gravity at G. It is suspended from its front and rear on the track by six tires located at A, B, and C. Determine the normal reactions on these tires if the track is assumed to be a smooth surface and an equal portion of the load is carried at both the front and rear.

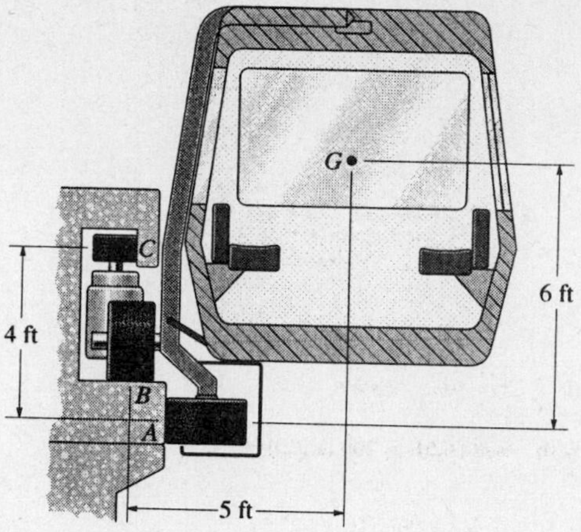

$\circlearrowleft + \Sigma M_O = 0; \quad (2\,N_C)(4) - 24\,000(5) = 0$

$N_C = 15\,000 \text{ lb} = 15 \text{ kip}$ **Ans**

$\xrightarrow{+} \Sigma F_x = 0; \quad 2\,N_A - 2(15) = 0$

$N_A = 15 \text{ kip}$ **Ans**

$+\uparrow \Sigma F_y = 0; \quad 2\,N_B - 24\,000 = 0$

$N_B = 12 \text{ kip}$ **Ans**

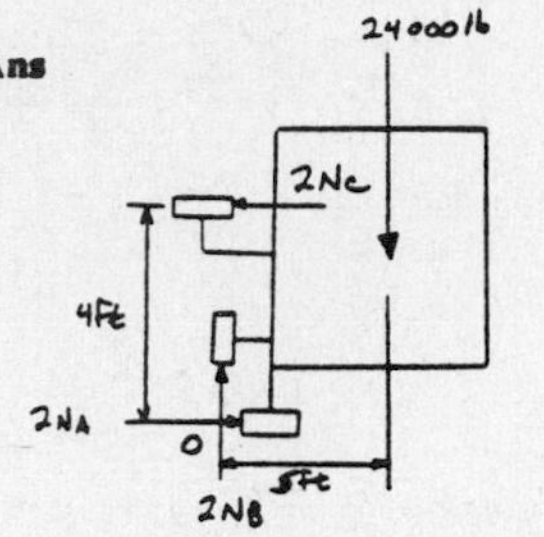

***5-24.** Determine the magnitude of force at the pin A and in the cable BC needed to support the 500-lb load. Neglect the weight of the boom AB.

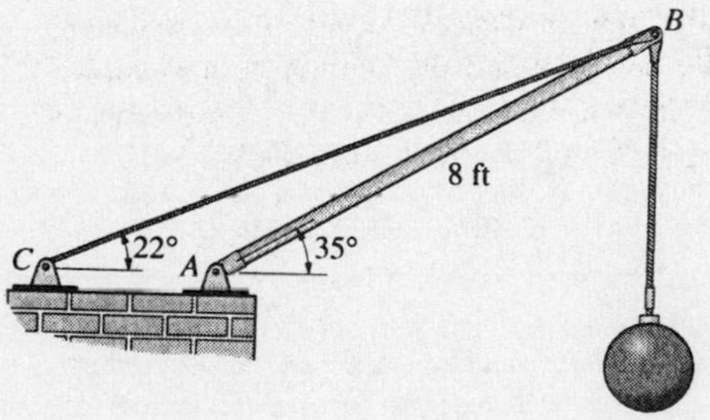

Equations of Equilibrium : The force in cable BC can be obtained directly by summing moments about point A.

$\circlearrowleft + \Sigma M_A = 0; \quad F_{BC} \sin 13°(8) - 500\cos 35°(8) = 0$

$F_{BC} = 1820.7 \text{ lb} = 1.82 \text{ kip}$ **Ans**

$\nearrow + \Sigma F_x = 0; \quad A_x - 1820.7\cos 13° - 500\sin 35° = 0$

$A_x = 2060.9 \text{ lb}$

$\nwarrow + \Sigma F_y = 0; \quad A_y + 1820.7\sin 13° - 500\cos 35° = 0$

$A_y = 0$

Thus, $F_A = A_x = 2060.9 \text{ lb} = 2.06 \text{ kip}$ **Ans**

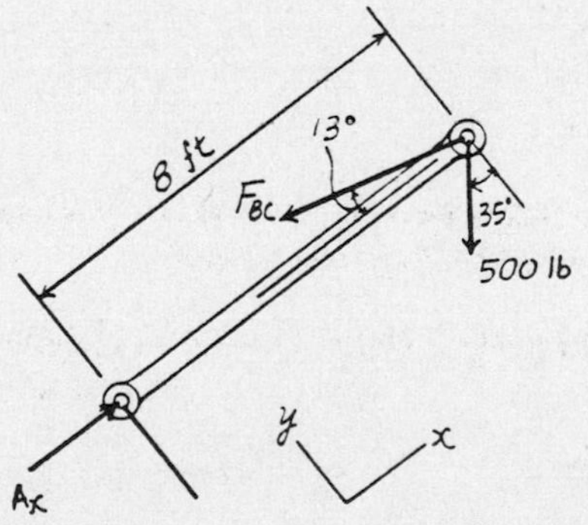

5-25. Compare the force exerted on the toe and heel of a 120-lb woman when she is wearing regular shoes and stiletto heels. Assume all her weight is placed on one foot and the reactions occur at points A and B as shown.

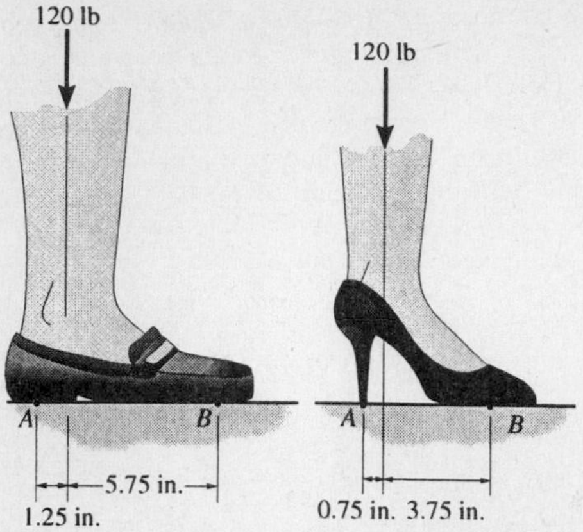

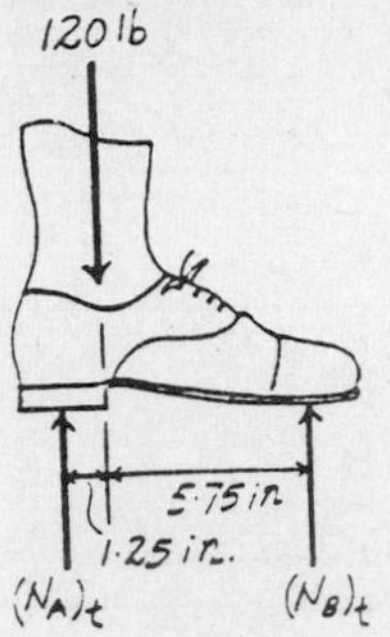

Equations of Equilibrium : Regular shoe, we have

$$\circlearrowleft + \Sigma M_B = 0; \qquad 120(5.75) - (N_A)_r(7) = 0$$

$$(N_A)_r = 98.6 \text{ lb} \qquad \textbf{Ans}$$

Stiletto heal shoe,

$$\circlearrowleft + \Sigma M_B = 0; \qquad 120(3.75) - (N_A)_s(4.5) = 0$$

$$(N_A)_s = 100 \text{ lb} \qquad \textbf{Ans}$$

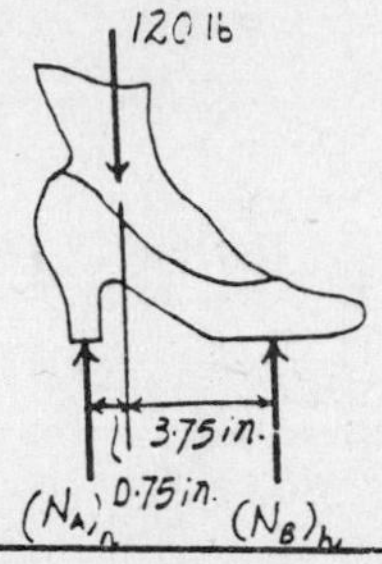

The heal of the stiletto shoe is subjected to a **greater** force than that of the heel of the regular shoe. Actually the force per area (stress) under the stilletto heel will be much greater than that of the regular shoe. It is this stress that can cause damage to soft flooring.

5-26. Determine the reactions at the pins A and B. The spring has an unstretched length of 80 mm.

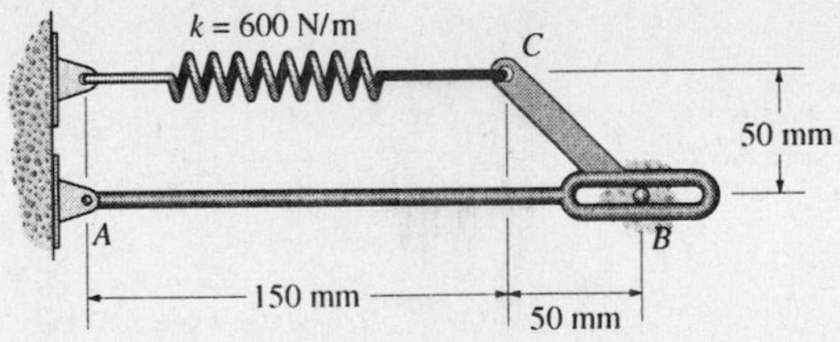

Spring Force : The spring stretches $x = 0.15 - 0.08 = 0.07$ m. Applying the spring formula, we have

$$F_{sp} = kx = 600(0.07) = 42.0 \text{ N}$$

Equations of Equilibrium : The normal reaction N_B can be obtained directly by summing moments about point A.

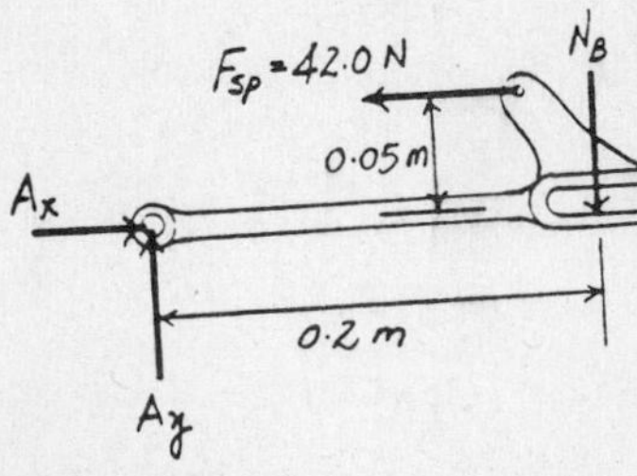

$$\circlearrowleft + \Sigma M_A = 0; \qquad 42.0(0.05) - N_B(0.2) = 0$$

$$N_B = 10.5 \text{ N} \qquad \textbf{Ans}$$

$$\xrightarrow{+} \Sigma F_x = 0; \qquad A_x - 42.0 = 0 \qquad A_x = 42.0 \text{ N} \qquad \textbf{Ans}$$

$$+\uparrow \Sigma F_y = 0; \qquad A_y - 10.5 = 0 \qquad A_y = 10.5 \text{ N} \qquad \textbf{Ans}$$

5-27. Determine the reactions at the supports.

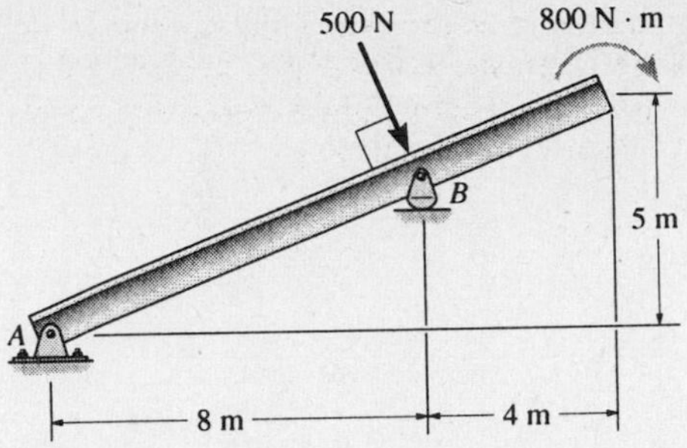

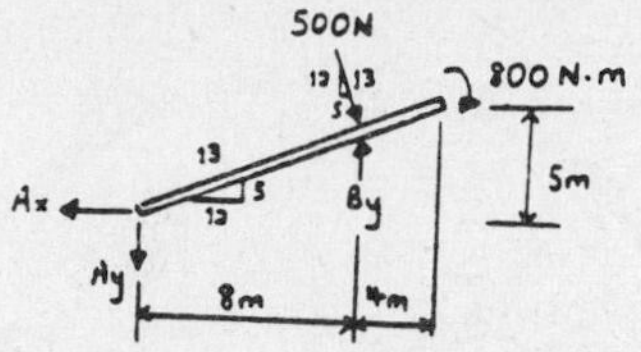

$$\curvearrowleft +\Sigma M_A = 0; \quad -500(8)\left(\frac{13}{12}\right) - 800 + B_y(8) = 0$$

$$B_y = 641.67 \text{ N} = 642 \text{ N} \quad \textbf{Ans}$$

$$+\uparrow \Sigma F_y = 0; \quad -A_y + 641.67 - 500\left(\frac{12}{13}\right) = 0$$

$$A_y = 180 \text{ N} \quad \textbf{Ans}$$

$$\xrightarrow{+} \Sigma F_x = 0; \quad -A_x + 500\left(\frac{5}{13}\right) = 0$$

$$A_x = 192 \text{ N} \quad \textbf{Ans}$$

***5-28.** Determine the tension in the cable and the horizontal and vertical components of reaction of the pin A. The pulley at D is frictionless and the cylinder weighs 80 lb.

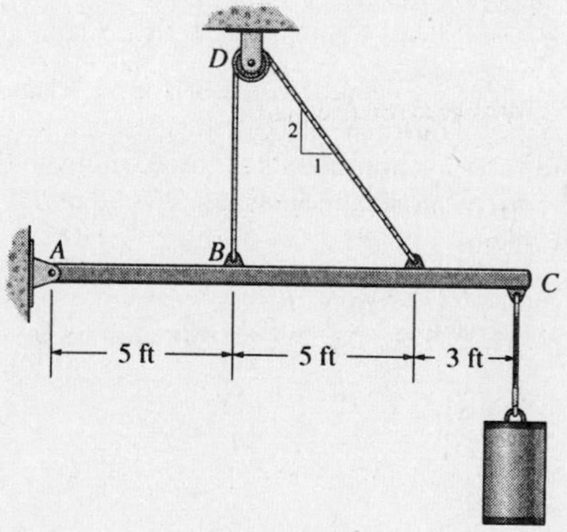

Equations of Equilibrium : The tension force developed in the cable is the same throughout the whole cable. The force in the cable can be obtained directly by summing moments about point A.

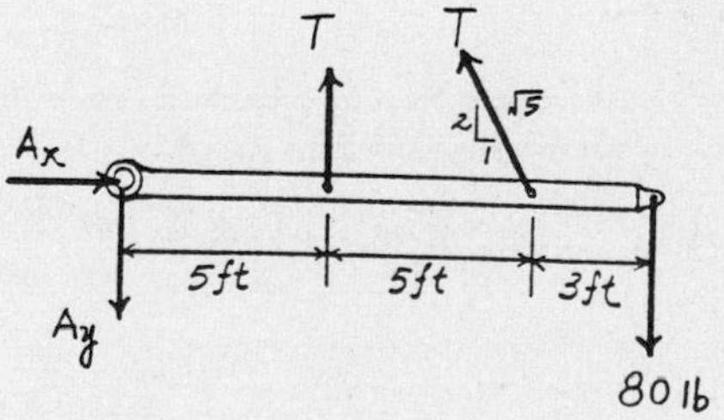

$$\curvearrowleft + \Sigma M_A = 0; \quad T(5) + T\left(\frac{2}{\sqrt{5}}\right)(10) - 80(13) = 0$$

$$T = 74.583 \text{ lb} = 74.6 \text{ lb} \quad \textbf{Ans}$$

$$\xrightarrow{+} \Sigma F_x = 0; \quad A_x - 74.583\left(\frac{1}{\sqrt{5}}\right) = 0$$

$$B_x = 33.4 \text{ lb} \quad \textbf{Ans}$$

$$+\uparrow \Sigma F_y = 0; \quad 74.583 + 74.583\left(\frac{2}{\sqrt{5}}\right) - 80 - B_y = 0$$

$$B_y = 61.3 \text{ lb} \quad \textbf{Ans}$$

5-29. Determine the horizontal and vertical components of force at the pin A and the reaction at the rocker B of the curved beam.

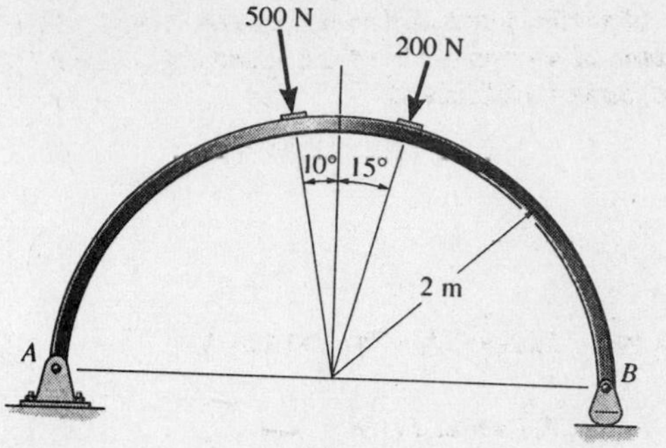

$\curvearrowleft + \Sigma M_A = 0;\quad N_B\,(4) - 200\cos 15°\,(2) - 500\cos 10°\,(2) = 0$

$N_B = 342.79 = 343 \text{ N}$ **Ans**

$+\uparrow \Sigma F_y = 0;\quad A_y - 500\cos 10° - 200\cos 15° + 342.79 = 0$

$A_y = 342.8 = 343 \text{ N}$ **Ans**

$\xrightarrow{+} \Sigma F_x = 0;\quad -A_x + 500\sin 10° - 200\sin 15° = 0$

$A_x = 35.1 \text{ N}$ **Ans**

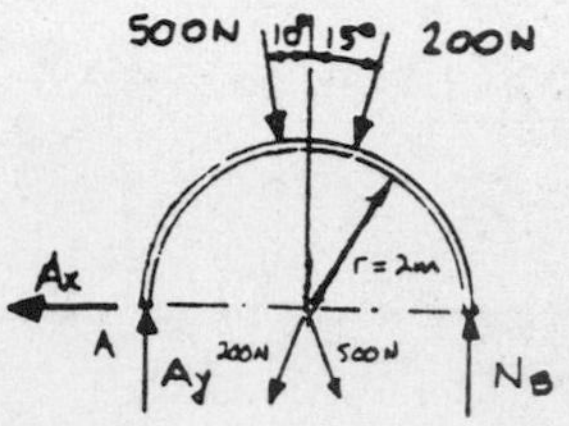

5-30. The cutter is subjected to a horizontal force of 580 lb and a normal force of 350 lb. Determine the horizontal and vertical components of force acting on the pin A and the force along the hydraulic cylinder BC (a two-force member).

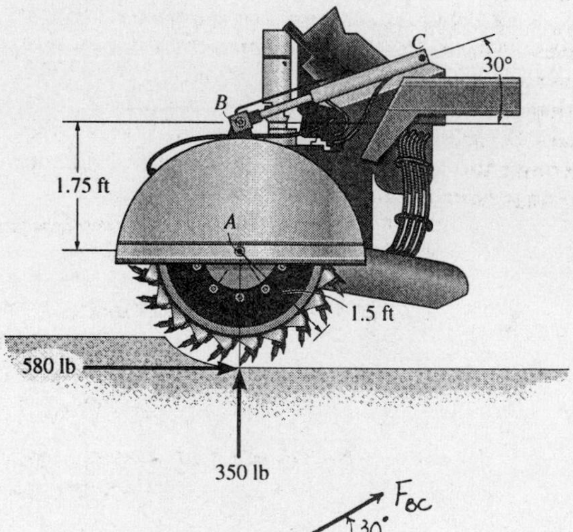

Equations of Equilibrium : The force in hydraulic cylinder BC can be obtained directly by summing moments about point A.

$\curvearrowleft + \Sigma M_A = 0;\quad 580(1.5) - F_{BC}\cos 30°(1.75) = 0$

$F_{BC} = 574.05 \text{ lb} = 574 \text{ lb}$ **Ans**

$\xrightarrow{+} \Sigma F_x = 0;\quad 574.05\cos 30° + 580 - A_x = 0$

$A_x = 1077 \text{ lb} = 1.08 \text{ kip}$ **Ans**

$+\uparrow \Sigma F_y = 0;\quad 574.05\sin 30° + 350 - A_y = 0$

$A_y = 637 \text{ lb}$ **Ans**

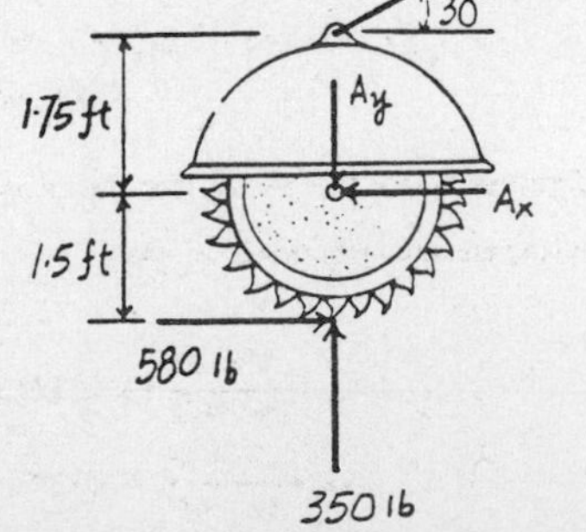

5-31. The mass of 700 kg is suspended from a trolley which moves along the crane rail from $d = 1.7$ m to $d = 3.5$ m. Determine the force along the pin-connected knee strut BC (short link) and the magnitude of force at pin A as a function of position d. Plot these results of F_{BC} and F_A (ordinate) versus d (abscissa).

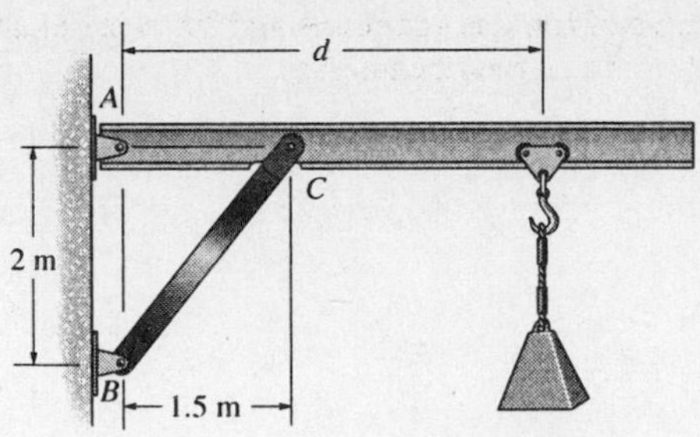

$\circlearrowleft + \Sigma M_A = 0; \quad F_{BC}\left(\frac{4}{5}\right)(1.5) - 700(9.81)(d) = 0$

$F_{BC} = 5722.5d$ **Ans**

$\xrightarrow{+} \Sigma F_x = 0; \quad -A_x + (5722.5d)\left(\frac{3}{5}\right) = 0$

$A_x = 3433.5d$

$+\uparrow \Sigma F_y = 0; \quad -A_y + (5722.5d)\left(\frac{4}{5}\right) - 700(9.81) = 0$

$A_y = 4578d - 6867$

$F_A = \sqrt{(3433.5d)^2 + (4578d - 6867)^2}$ **Ans**

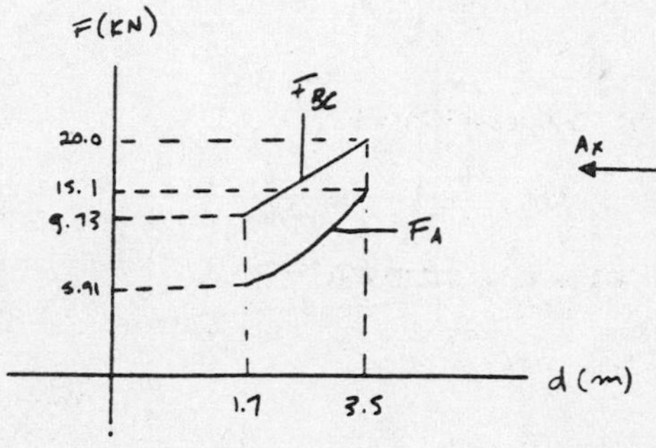

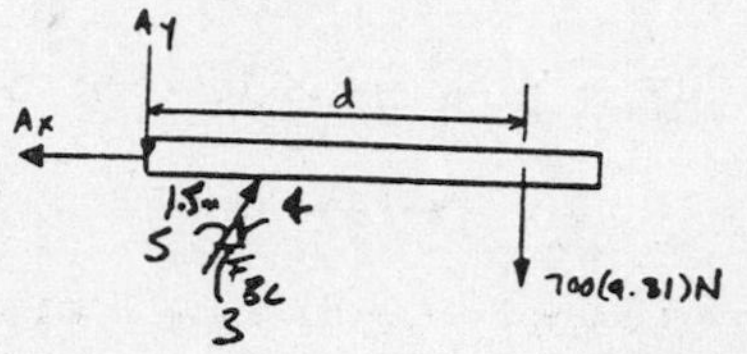

***5-32.** The sports car has a mass of 1.5 Mg and mass center at G. If the front two springs each have a stiffness of $k_A = 58$ kN/m and the rear two springs each have a stiffness of $k_B = 65$ kN/m, determine their compression when the car is parked on the 30° incline. Also, what friction force $\mathbf{F}_B$ must be applied to each of the rear wheels to hold the car in equilibrium? *Hint:* First determine the normal force at A and B, then determine the compression in the springs.

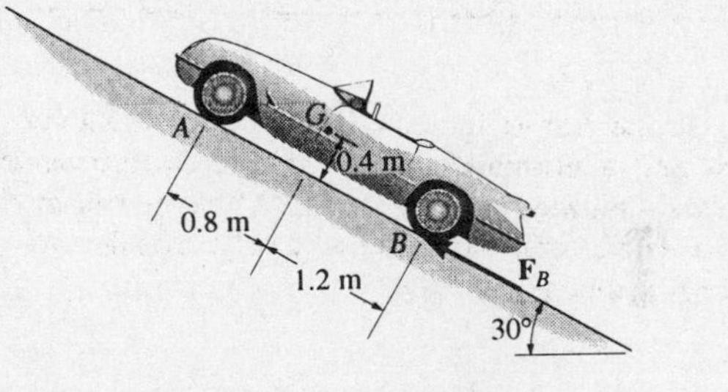

Equations of Equilibrium : The normal reaction N_A can be obtained directly by summing moments about point B.

$$\circlearrowleft + \Sigma M_B = 0; \quad 14\,715\cos 30°(1.2) - 14\,715\sin 30°(0.4) - 2N_A(2) = 0$$

$$N_A = 3087.32 \text{ N}$$

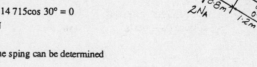

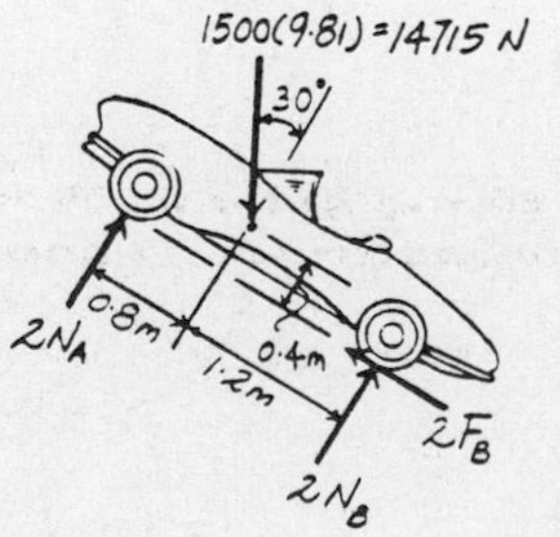

$\nwarrow + \Sigma F_{x'} = 0; \quad 2F_B - 14\,715\sin 30° = 0$

$F_B = 3678.75 \text{ N} = 3.68 \text{ kN}$ **Ans**

$\nearrow + \Sigma F_{y'} = 0; \quad 2N_B + 2(3087.32) - 14\,715\cos 30° = 0$

$N_B = 3284.46 \text{ N}$

Spring Force Formula : The compression of the sping can be determined using the spring formula $x = \frac{F_{sp}}{k}$.

$x_A = \frac{3087.32}{58(10^3)} = 0.05323 \text{ m} = 53.2 \text{ mm}$ **Ans**

$x_B = \frac{3284.46}{65(10^3)} = 0.05053 \text{ m} = 50.5 \text{ mm}$ **Ans**

5-33. The framework is supported by the member AB which rests on the smooth floor. When loaded, the pressure distribution on AB is linear as shown. Determine the smallest length d of member AB so that it will prevent the frame from tipping over. What is the intensity w for this case?

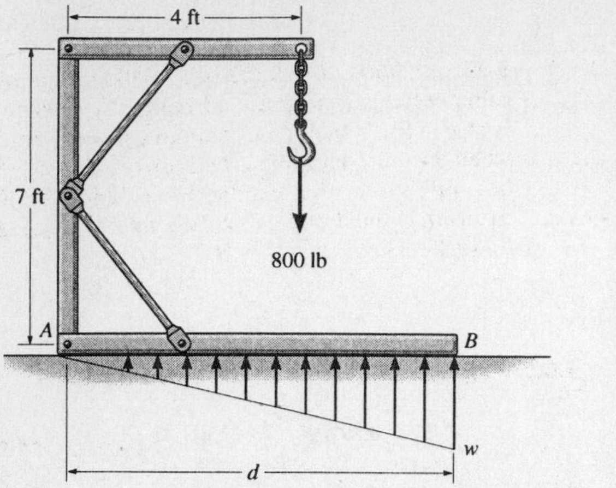

$+\uparrow \Sigma F_y = 0; \quad F_P - 800 = 0$

$F_P = 800 \text{ lb}$

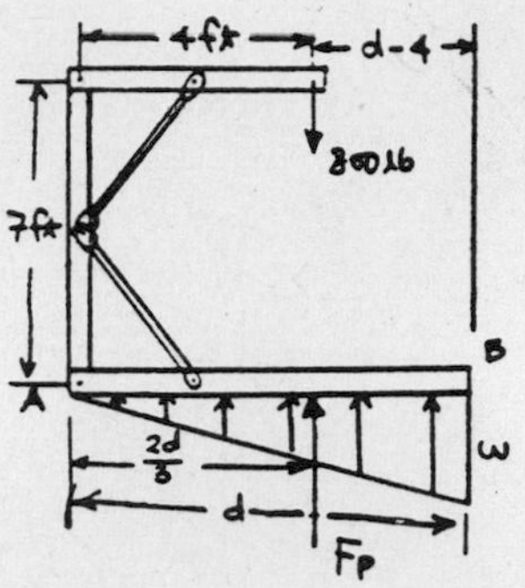

When tipping;

$\curvearrowleft + \Sigma M_B = 0; \quad -800\left(\frac{d}{3}\right) + 800(d-4) = 0$

$d = 6 \text{ ft}$ **Ans**

$F_P = \frac{1}{2}wd = \frac{1}{2}(w)(6) = 800$

$w = 267 \text{ lb/ft}$ **Ans**

5-34. The jib crane is pin-connected at A and supported by a smooth collar at B. Determine the roller placement x of the 5000-lb load so that it gives the maximum and minimum reactions at the supports. Calculate these reactions in each case. Neglect the weight of the crane. Require 4 ft $\leq x \leq$ 10 ft.

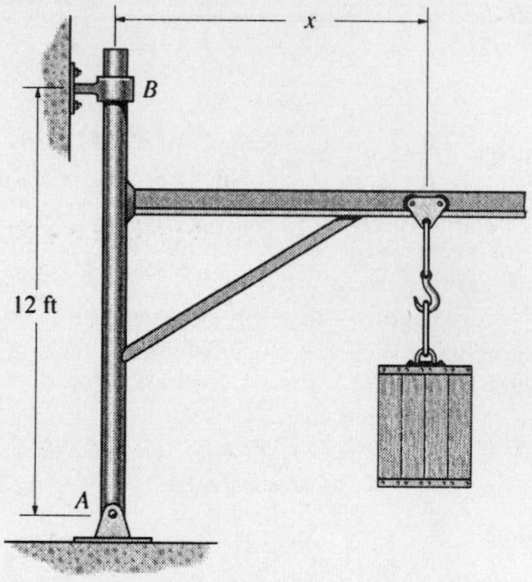

Equations of Equilibrium :

$\curvearrowleft + \Sigma M_A = 0; \quad N_B(12) - 5x = 0 \quad N_B = 0.4167x$ [1]

$+\uparrow \Sigma F_y = 0; \quad A_y - 5 = 0 \quad A_y = 5.00 \text{ kip}$ [2]

$\overset{+}{\rightarrow} \Sigma F_x = 0; \quad A_x - 0.4167x = 0 \quad A_x = 0.4167x$ [3]

By observation, the **maximum support reactions** occur when

$x = 10 \text{ ft}$ **Ans**

With $x = 10$ ft, from Eqs. [1], [2] and [3], the **maximum support reactions** are

$A_x = N_B = 4.17 \text{ kip} \quad A_y = 5.00 \text{ kip}$ **Ans**

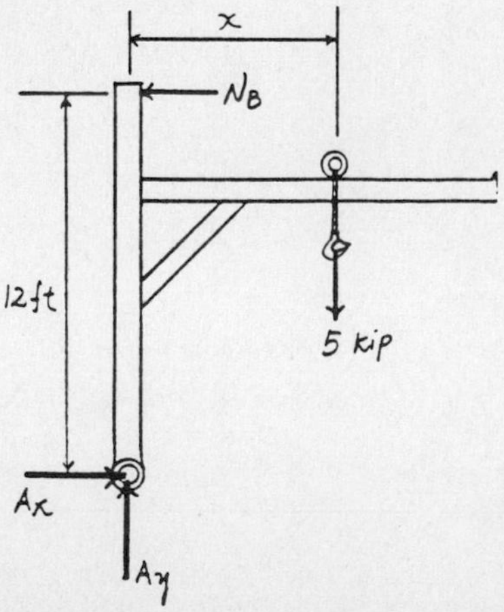

By observation, the **minimum support reactions** occur when

$x = 4 \text{ ft}$ **Ans**

With $x = 4$ ft, from Eqs. [1], [2] and [3], the **minimum support reactions** are

$A_x = N_B = 1.67 \text{ kip} \quad A_y = 5.00 \text{ kip}$ **Ans**

5-35. A horizontal force of $F = 300$ lb is applied to the cable connected to the load binder at B when the lever is at $\theta = 0°$. If this force increases linearly to $F = 650$ lb when $\theta = 60°$, determine the horizontal force P that must be applied to the handle as a function of θ. Also, determine the force T applied to the cable at A. Plot these forces for $0° \leq \theta \leq 60°$.

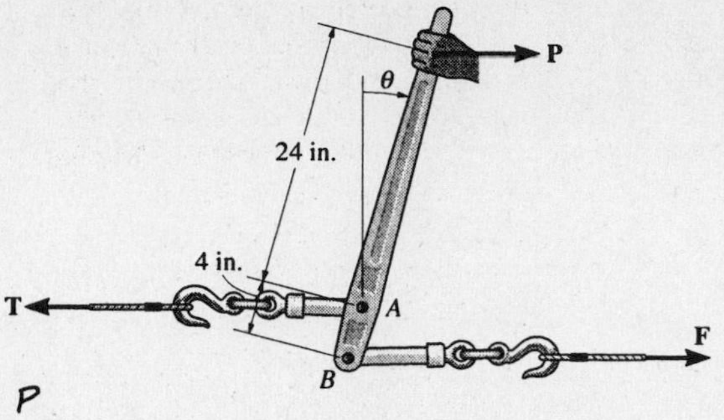

$\circlearrowleft + \Sigma M_A = 0;\quad -P(24\cos\theta) + F(4\cos\theta) = 0$

$P = 0.1667\,F$

When $\theta = 0°$, $F = 300$ lb

When $\theta = 60°$, $F = 650$ lb

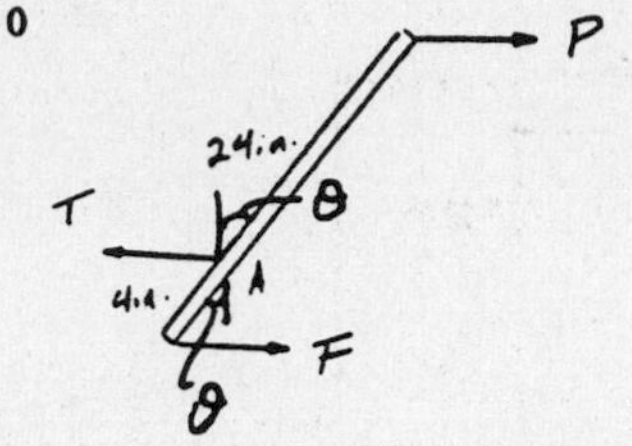

$$F = \frac{650 - 300}{60 - 0}(\theta) + 300$$

$F = 5.833\,\theta + 300$

$P = 0.1667\,(5.833\,\theta + 300)$

$P = 0.972\,\theta + 50$ **Ans**

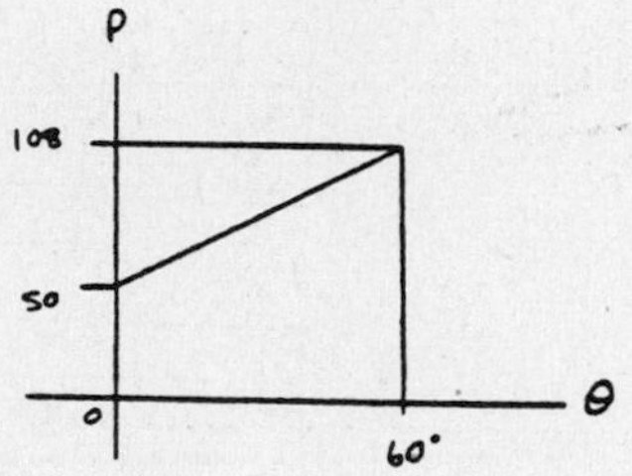

$\overset{+}{\rightarrow} \Sigma F_x = 0;\quad -T + P + F = 0$

$T = P + F = 0.972\,\theta + 50 + 5.833\,\theta + 300$

$= 6.81\,\theta + 350$ **Ans**

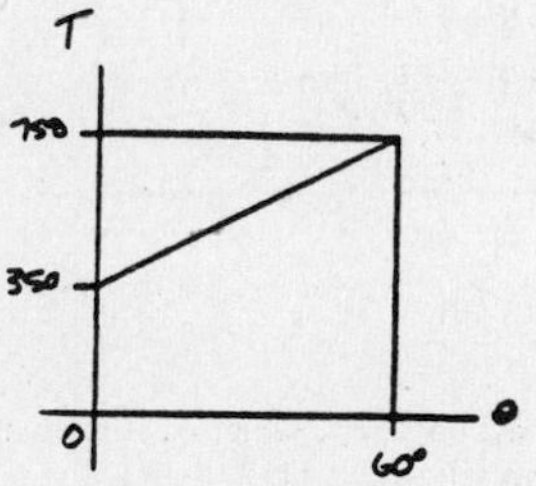

*5-36. The pad footing is used to support the load of 12 000 lb. Determine the intensities w_1 and w_2 of the distributed loading acting on the base of the footing for the equilibrium.

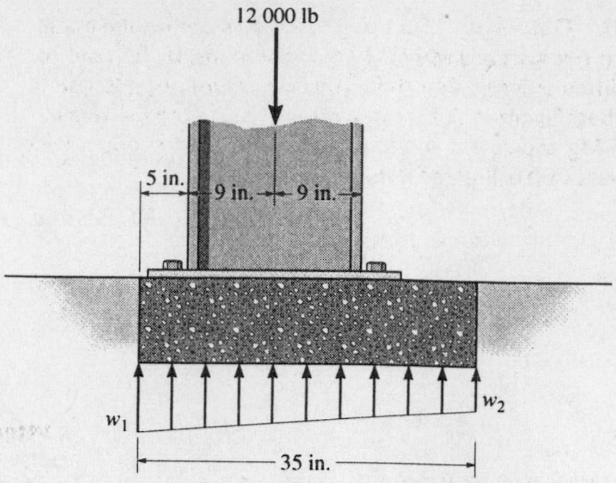

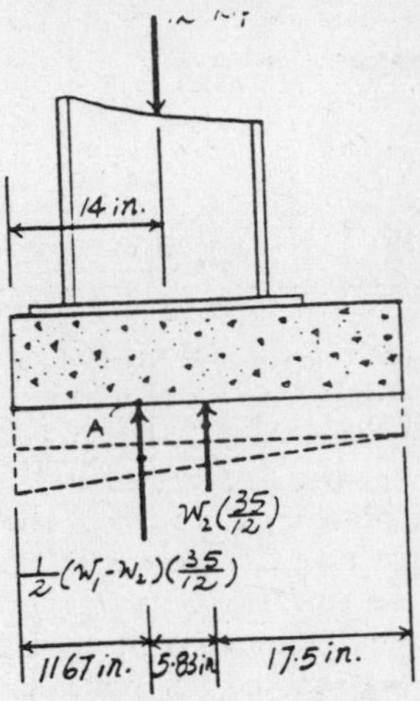

Equations of Equilibrium : The load intensity w_2 can be determined directly by summing moments about point A.

$$\curvearrowleft + \Sigma M_A = 0; \quad w_2\left(\frac{35}{12}\right)(17.5-11.67)-12(14-11.67)=0$$

$$w_2 = 1.646 \text{ kip/ft} = 1.65 \text{ kip/ft} \qquad \textbf{Ans}$$

$$+\uparrow \Sigma F_y = 0; \quad \frac{1}{2}(w_1-1.646)\left(\frac{35}{12}\right)+2.743\left(\frac{35}{12}\right)-12=0$$

$$w_1 = 6.58 \text{ kip/ft} \qquad \textbf{Ans}$$

5-37. The bulk head AD is subjected to both water and soil-backfill pressures. Assuming AD is "pinned" to the ground at A, determine the horizontal and vertical reactions there and also the required tension in the ground anchor BC necessary for equilibrium. The bulk head has a mass of 800 kg.

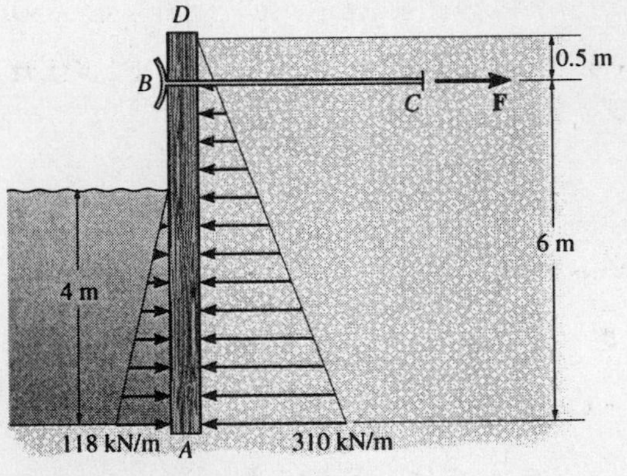

Equations of Equilibrium : The force in ground anchor BC can be obtained directly by summing moments about point A.

$$\curvearrowleft + \Sigma M_A = 0; \quad 1007.5(2.167)-236(1.333)-F(6)=0$$

$$F = 311.375 \text{ kN} = 311 \text{ kN} \qquad \textbf{Ans}$$

$$\xrightarrow{+} \Sigma F_x = 0; \quad A_x + 311.375 + 236 - 1007.5 = 0$$

$$A_x = 460 \text{ kN} \qquad \textbf{Ans}$$

$$+\uparrow \Sigma F_y = 0; \quad A_y - 7.848 = 0 \quad A_y = 7.85 \text{ kN} \qquad \textbf{Ans}$$

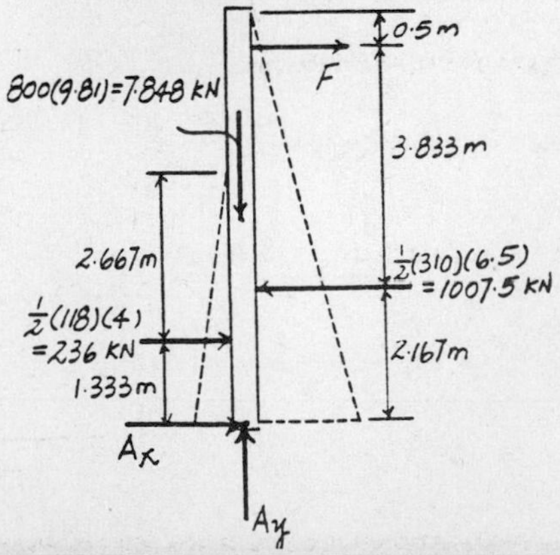

5-38. Outriggers A and B are used to stabilize the crane from overturning when lifting large loads. If the load to be lifted is 3 Mg, determine the *maximum* boom angle θ so that the crane does not overturn. The crane has a mass of 5 Mg and center of mass at G_C, whereas the boom has a mass of 0.6 Mg and center of mass at G_B.

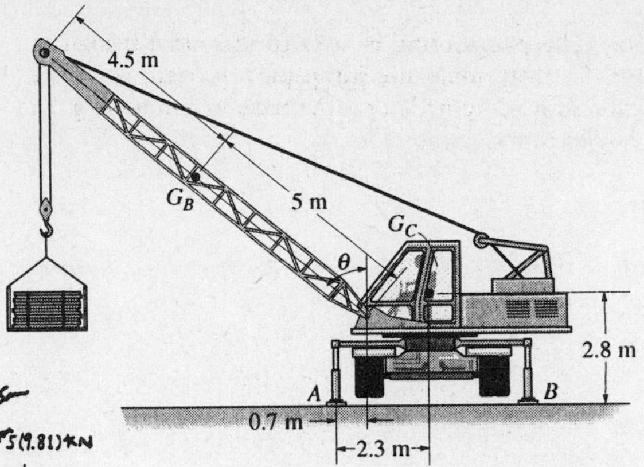

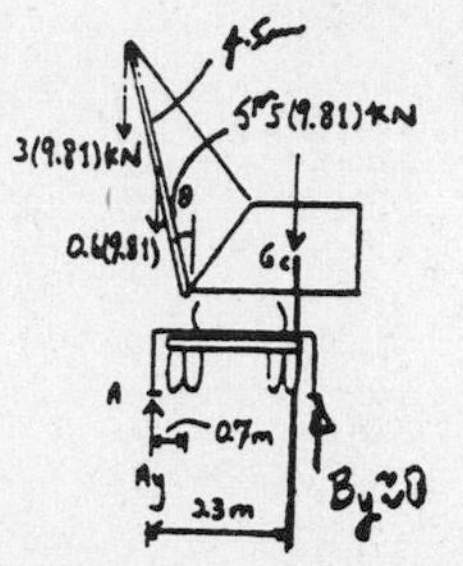

$$\circlearrowleft + \Sigma M_A = 0; \quad -5\,(9.81)\,(2.3) + 3\,(9.81)\,(9.5 \sin\theta - 0.7)$$

$$+\, 0.6\,(9.81)\,(5 \sin\theta - 0.7) = 0$$

$$\theta = 26.4° \qquad \textbf{Ans}$$

5-39. The mobile crane is symmetrically supported by two outriggers at A and two at B in order to relieve the suspension of the truck upon which it rests and to provide greater stability. If the crane and truck have a mass of 18 Mg and center of mass at G_1, and the boom has a mass of 1.8 Mg and a center of mass at G_2, determine the vertical reactions at each of the four outriggers as a function of the boom angle θ when the boom is supporting a load having a mass of 1.2 Mg. Plot the results measured from $\theta = 0°$ to the critical angle where tipping starts to occur.

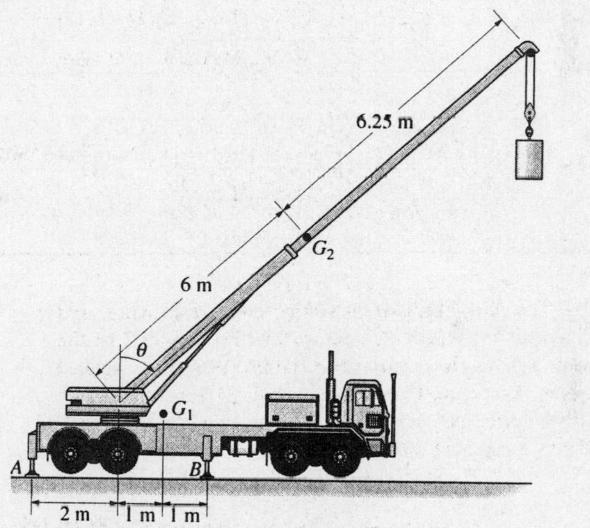

$$+\Sigma M_B = 0; \quad -N_A\,(4) + 18\,(10^3)\,(9.81)\,(1) + 1.8\,(10^3)\,(9.81)\,(2 - 6 \sin\theta)$$

$$+\, 1.2\,(10^3)\,(9.81)\,(2 - 12.25 \sin\theta) = 0$$

$$N_A = 58\,860 - 62\,539 \sin\theta$$

Tipping occurs when $N_A = 0$, or

$$\theta = 70.3° \qquad \textbf{Ans}$$

$$+\uparrow \Sigma F_y = 0; \quad N_B + 58\,860 - 62\,539 \sin\theta - (18 + 1.8 + 1.2)\,(10^3)\,(9.81) = 0$$

$$N_B = 147\,150 + 62\,539 \sin\theta$$

Since there are two outriggers on each side of the crane,

$$N_A' = \frac{N_A}{2} = (29.4 - 31.3 \sin\theta)\ \text{kN} \qquad \textbf{Ans}$$

$$N_B' = \frac{N_B}{2} = (73.6 + 31.3 \sin\theta)\ \text{kN} \qquad \textbf{Ans}$$

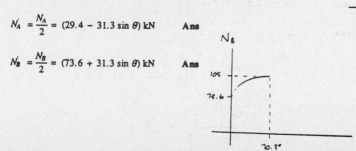

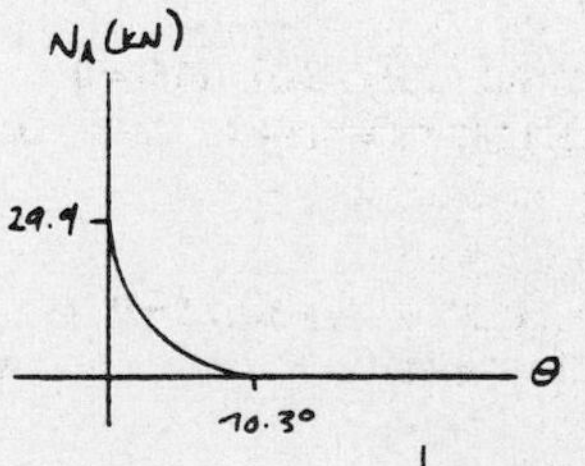

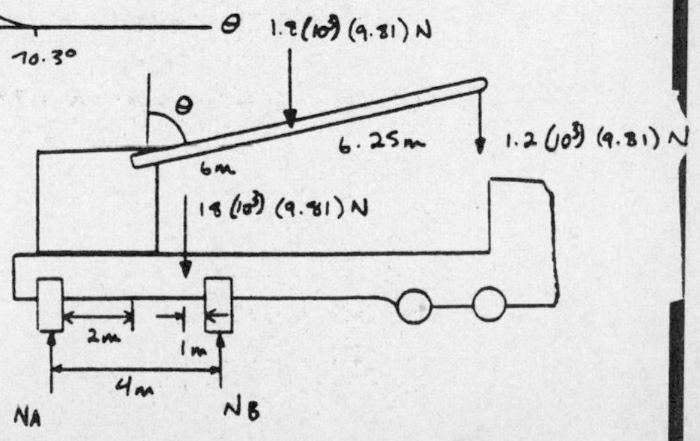

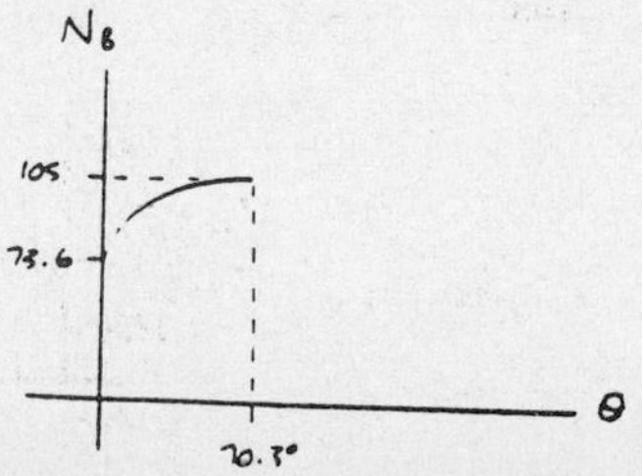

***5-40.** The beam is subjected to the two concentrated loads as shown. Assuming that the foundation exerts a linearly varying load distribution on its bottom, determine the load intensities w_1 and w_2 for equilibrium (a) in terms of the parameters shown; (b) set $P = 500$ lb, $L = 12$ ft.

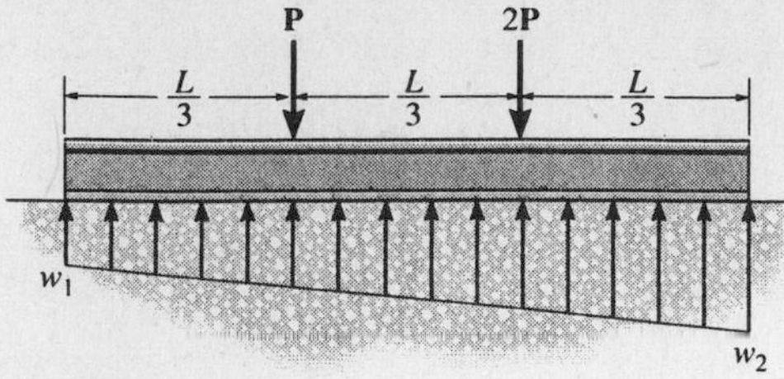

Equations of Equilibrium : The load intensity w_1 can be determined directly by summing moments about point A.

$$\curvearrowleft + \Sigma M_A = 0; \quad P\left(\frac{L}{3}\right) - w_1 L\left(\frac{L}{6}\right) = 0$$

$$w_1 = \frac{2P}{L} \qquad \textbf{Ans}$$

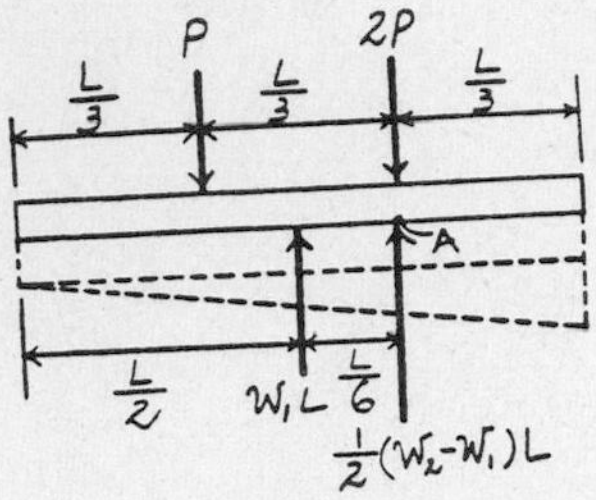

$$+\uparrow \Sigma F_y = 0; \quad \frac{1}{2}\left(w_2 - \frac{2P}{L}\right)L + \frac{2P}{L}(L) - 3P = 0$$

$$w_2 = \frac{4P}{L} \qquad \textbf{Ans}$$

If $P = 500$ lb and $L = 12$ft,

$$w_1 = \frac{2(500)}{12} = 83.3 \text{ lb/ft} \qquad \textbf{Ans}$$

$$w_2 = \frac{4(500)}{12} = 167 \text{ lb/ft} \qquad \textbf{Ans}$$

5-41. The cantilever footing is used to support a wall near its edge A so that it causes a uniform soil pressure under the footing. Determine the uniform distribution loads, w_A and w_B, measured in lb/ft at pads A and B, necessary to support the wall forces of 8 000 lb and 20 000 lb.

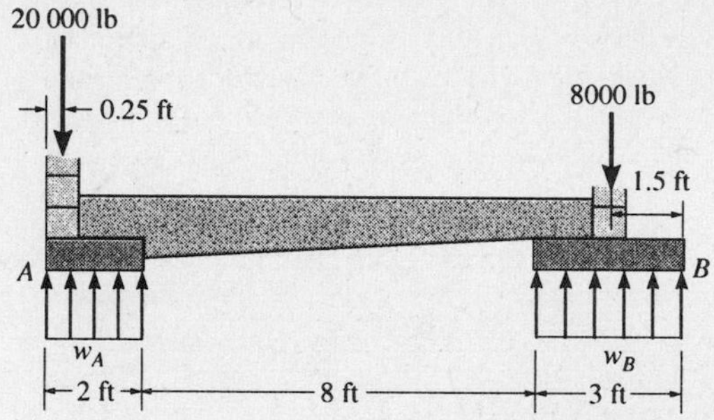

$$\curvearrowleft + \Sigma M_{A'} = 0; \quad -8000(10.5) + w_B(3)(10.5) + 20\,000(0.75) = 0$$

$$w_B = 2190.5 \text{ lb/ft} = 2.19 \text{ kip/ft} \qquad \textbf{Ans}$$

$$+\uparrow \Sigma F_y = 0; \quad 2190.5(3) - 28\,000 + w_A(2) = 0$$

$$w_A = 10.7 \text{ kip/ft} \qquad \textbf{Ans}$$

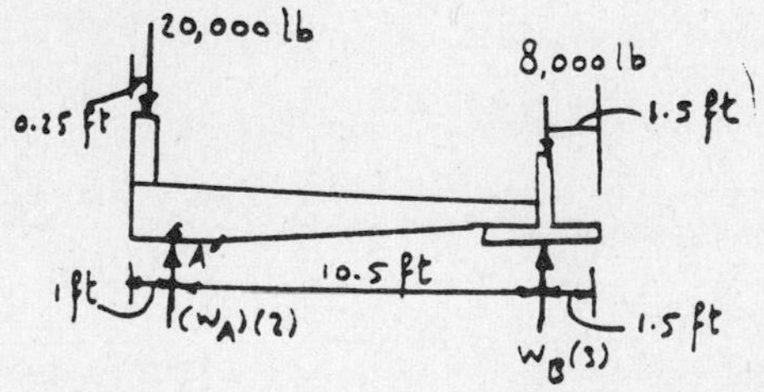

5-42. A cantilever beam, having an extended length of 3 m, is subjected to a vertical force of 500 N. Assuming that the wall resists this load with linearly varying distributed loads over the 0.15-m length of the beam portion inside the wall, determine the intensities w_1 and w_2 for equilibrium.

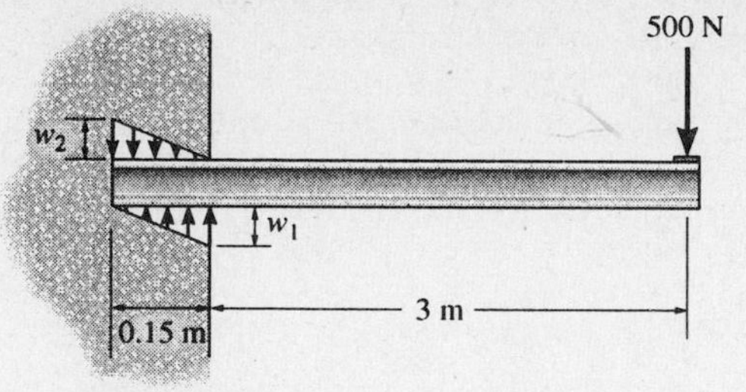

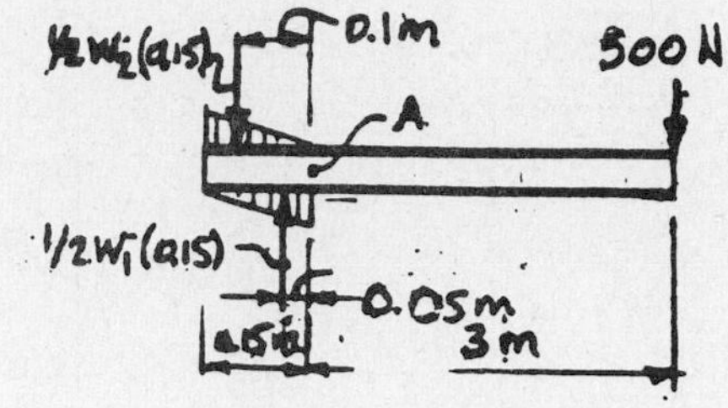

$$+\uparrow\Sigma F_y = 0;\quad \frac{1}{2}(w_1)(0.15) - \frac{1}{2}(w_2)(0.15) - 500 = 0$$

$$\circlearrowleft+\Sigma M_A = 0;\quad -(500)\,3 - \frac{1}{2}(w_1)(0.15)(0.05) + \frac{1}{2}(w_2)(0.15)(0.1) = 0$$

These equations become

$$w_1 - w_2 = 6666.7$$

$$2\,w_2 - w_1 = 400\,000$$

Solving,

$w_1 = 413$ kN/m **Ans**

$w_2 = 407$ kN/m **Ans**

5-43. The wooden plank resting between the buildings deflects slightly when it supports the 50-kg boy. This deflection causes a triangular distribution of load at its ends, having maximum intensities of w_A and w_B. Determine w_A and w_B, each measured in N/m, when the boy is standing 3 m from one end as shown. Neglect the mass of the plank.

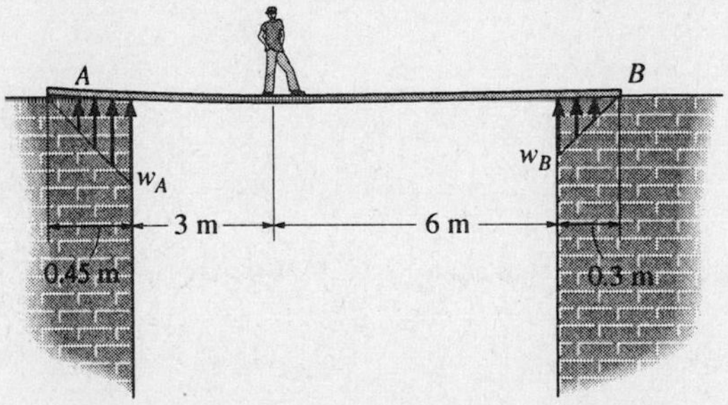

$$\circlearrowleft+\Sigma M_A = 0;\quad -490.5\,(3.15) + \frac{1}{2}\,w_B\,(0.3)(9.25) = 0$$

$w_B = 1113.6$ N/m $= 1.11$ kN/m **Ans**

$$+\uparrow\Sigma F_y = 0;\quad \frac{1}{2}\,w_A\,(0.45) + \frac{1}{2}\,(1113.6)(0.3) - 490.5 = 0$$

$w_A = 1437.6$ N/m $= 1.44$ kN/m **Ans**

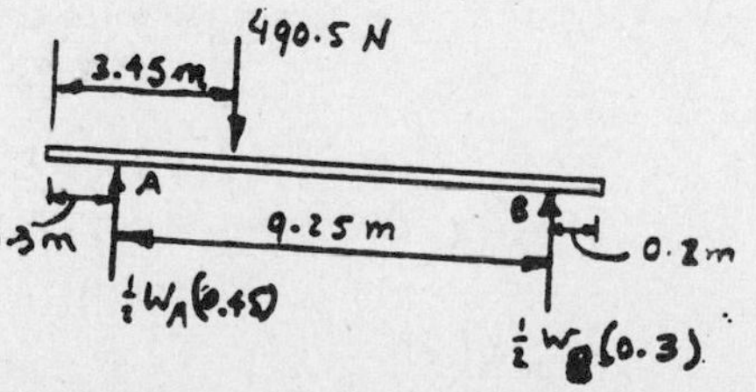

***5-44.** The dimensions of a jib crane, which is manufactured by the Basick Co., are given in the figure. If the crane has a mass of 800 kg and a center of mass at G, and the maximum rated force at its end is $F = 15$ kN, determine the reactions at its bearings. The bearing at A is a journal bearing and supports only a horizontal force, whereas the bearing at B is a thrust bearing that supports both horizontal and vertical components.

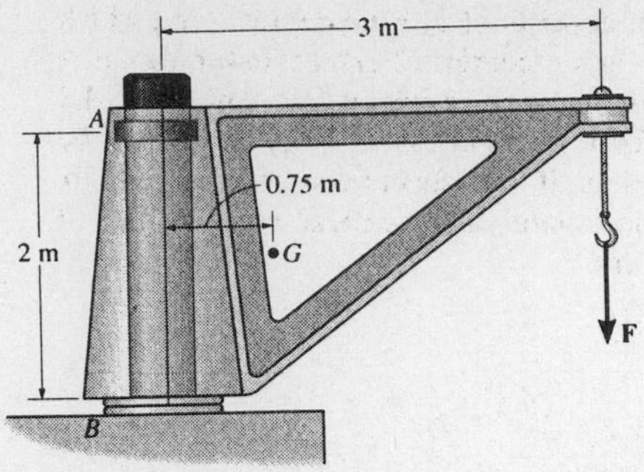

$\circlearrowleft + \Sigma M_B = 0;\quad A_x(2) - 800(9.81)(0.75) - 15\,000(3) = 0$

$A_x = 25.4$ kN **Ans**

$+\uparrow \Sigma F_y = 0;\quad B_y - 800(9.81) - 15\,000 = 0$

$B_y = 22.8$ kN **Ans**

$\xrightarrow{+} \Sigma F_x = 0;\quad B_x - 25.4 = 0$

$B_x = 25.4$ kN **Ans**

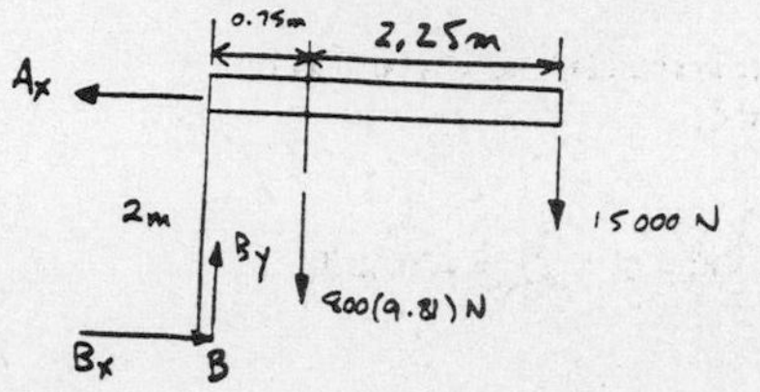

5-45. The dimensions of a jib crane, which is manufactured by the Basick Co., are given in the figure. The crane has a mass of 800 kg and a center of mass at G. The bearing at A is a journal bearing and can support a horizontal force, whereas the bearing at B is a thrust bearing that supports both horizontal and vertical components. Determine the maximum load F that can be suspended from its end if the selected bearings at A and B can sustain a maximum resultant load of 24 kN and 34 kN, respectively.

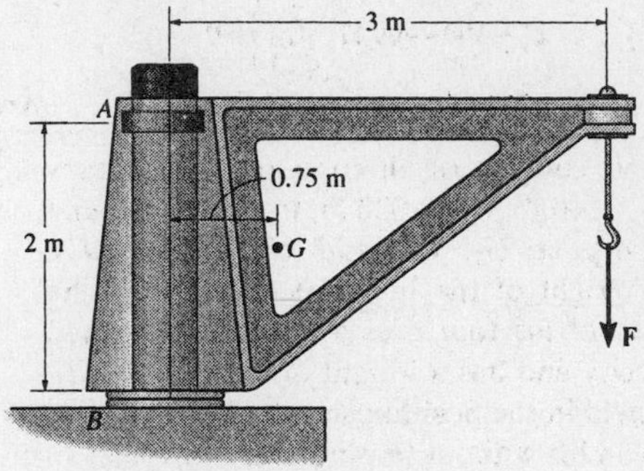

$\circlearrowleft + \Sigma M_B = 0;\quad A_x(2) - 800(9.81)(0.75) - F(3) = 0$

$+\uparrow \Sigma F_y = 0;\quad B_y - 800(9.81) - F = 0$

$\xrightarrow{+} \Sigma F_x = 0;\quad B_x - A_x = 0$

Assume $A_x = 24\,000$ N ,

Solving,

$B_x = 24$ kN

$B_y = 21.9$ kN

$F = 14.0$ kN **Ans**

$F_B = \sqrt{(24)^2 + (21.9)^2} = 32.5 \text{ kN} < 34 \text{ kN}$ OK

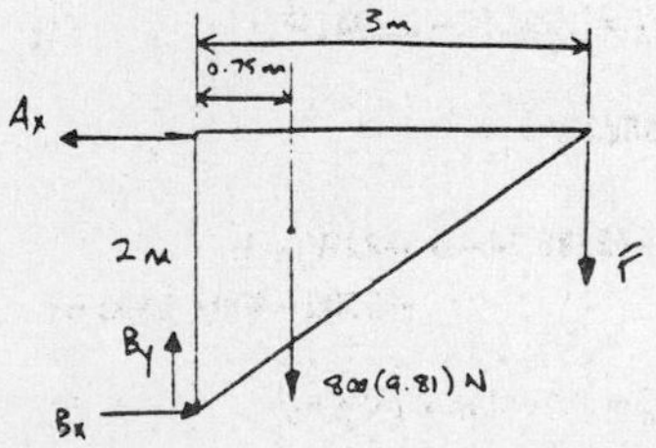

5-46. The winch consists of a drum radius 4 in., which is pin-connected at its center C. At its outer rim is a ratchet gear having a mean radius of 6 in. The pawl AB serves as a two-force member (short link) and holds the drum from rotating. If the suspended load is 500 lb, determine the horizontal and vertical components of reaction at the pin C.

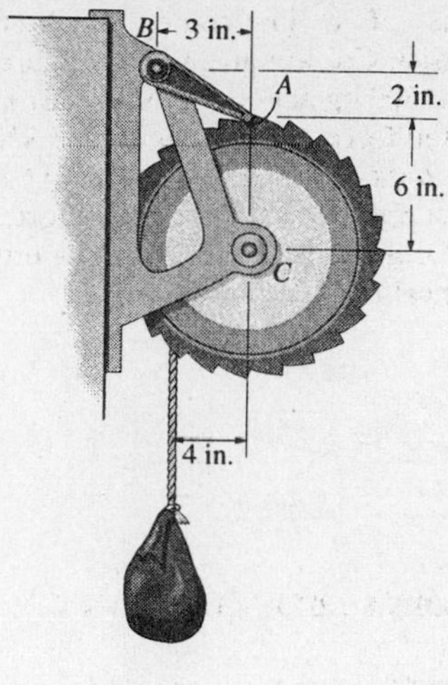

Equations of Equilibrium : The force in short link AB can be obtained directly by summing moments about point C.

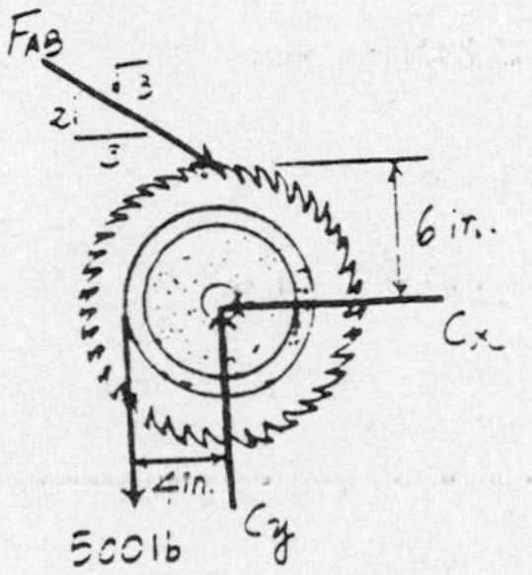

$$\circlearrowleft + \Sigma M_C = 0; \quad 500(4) - F_{AB}\left(\frac{3}{\sqrt{13}}\right)(6) = 0 \quad F_{AB} = 400.62 \text{ lb}$$

$$\xrightarrow{+} \Sigma F_x = 0; \quad 400.62\left(\frac{3}{\sqrt{13}}\right) - C_x = 0$$

$$C_x = 333 \text{ lb} \qquad \textbf{Ans}$$

$$+\uparrow \Sigma F_y = 0; \quad C_y - 500 - 400.62\left(\frac{2}{\sqrt{13}}\right) = 0$$

$$C_y = 722 \text{ lb} \qquad \textbf{Ans}$$

5-47. The crane consists of three parts, which have weights of $W_1 = 3500$ lb, $W_2 = 900$ lb, $W_3 = 1500$ lb and centers of gravity at G_1, G_2, and G_3, respectively. Neglecting the weight of the boom, determine (a) the reactions on each of the four tires if the load is hoisted at constant velocity and has a weight of 800 lb, and (b), with the boom held in the position shown, the maximum load the crane can lift without tipping over.

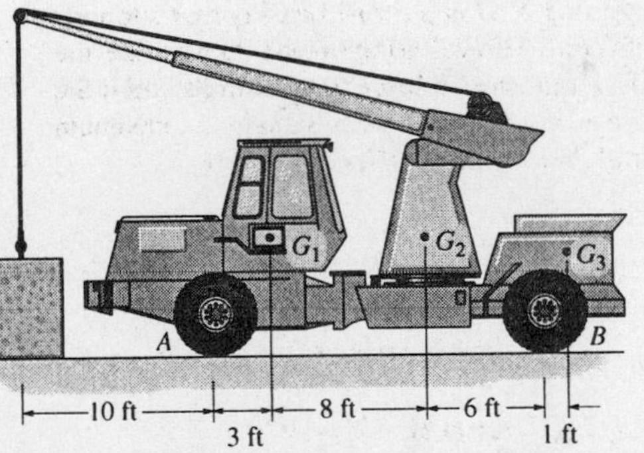

Equations of Equilibrium : The normal reaction N_B can be obtained directly by summing moments about point A.

$$\circlearrowleft + \Sigma M_A = 0; \quad 2N_B(17) + W(10) - 3500(3) - 900(11) - 1500(18) = 0$$

$$N_B = 1394.12 - 0.2941W \qquad [1]$$

Using the result $N_B = 2788.24 - 0.5882W$,

$$+\uparrow \Sigma F_y = 0; \quad 2N_A + (2788.24 - 0.5882W) - W - 3500 - 900 - 1500 = 0$$

$$N_A = 0.7941W + 1555.88 \qquad [2]$$

a) Set $W = 800$ lb and substitute into Eqs. [1] and [2] yields

$$N_A = 0.7941(800) + 1555.88 = 2191.18 \text{ lb} = 2.19 \text{ kip} \qquad \textbf{Ans}$$

$$N_B = 1394.12 - 0.2941(800) = 1158.82 \text{ lb} = 1.16 \text{ kip} \qquad \textbf{Ans}$$

b) When the crane is about to tip over, the normal reaction on $N_E = 0$. From Eq. [1],

$$N_B = 0 = 1394.12 - 0.2941W$$

$$W = 4740 \text{ lb} = 4.74 \text{ kip} \qquad \textbf{Ans}$$

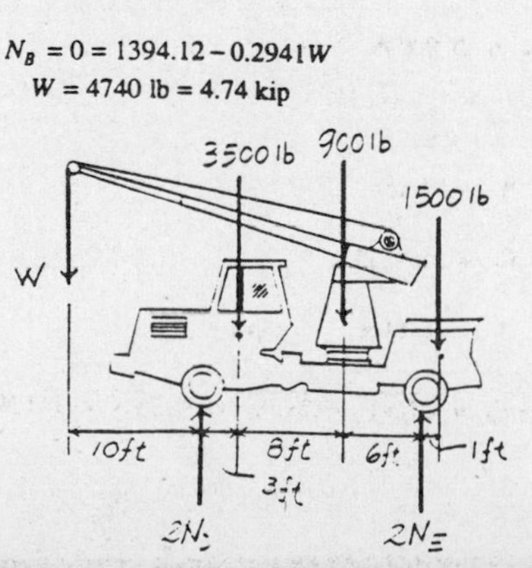

***5-48.** The winch cable on a tow truck is subjected to a force of $T = 6$ kN when the cable is directed at $\theta = 60°$. Determine the magnitudes of the total brake frictional force **F** for the rear set of wheels B and the total normal forces at *both* front wheels A and both rear wheels B for equilibrium. The truck has a total mass of 4 Mg and mass center at G.

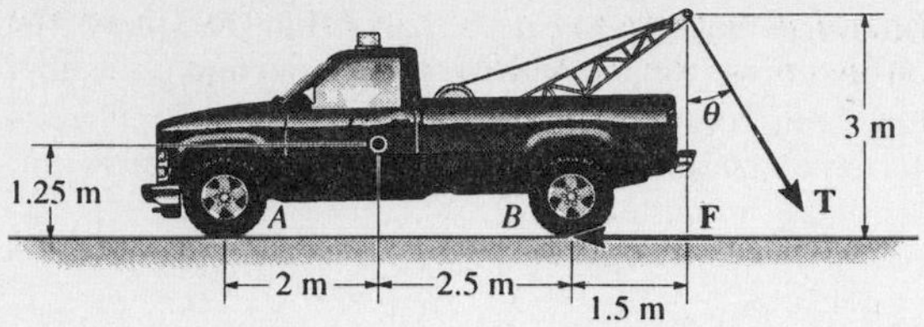

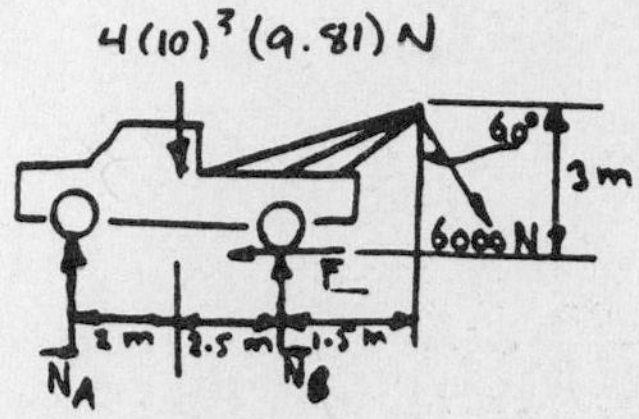

$\xrightarrow{+} \Sigma F_x = 0; \quad 6000 \sin 60° - F = 0$

$F = 5196 \text{ N} = 5.20 \text{ kN}$ **Ans**

$\circlearrowleft + \Sigma M_B = 0; \quad -N_A\,(4.5) + 4(10^3)(9.81)\,(2.5) - 6000 \sin 60°\,(3) - 6000 \cos 60°\,(1.5) = 0$

$N_A = 17\,336 \text{ N} = 17.3 \text{ kN}$ **Ans**

$+\uparrow \Sigma F_y = 0; \quad 17\,336 - 4(10^3)(9.81) - 6000 \cos 60° + N_B = 0$

$N_B = 24\,904 \text{ N} = 24.9 \text{ kN}$ **Ans**

5-49. Determine the minimum cable force T and critical angle θ which will cause the tow truck in Prob. 5–48 to start tipping, i.e., for the normal reaction at A to be zero. Assume that the truck is braked and will not slip at B.

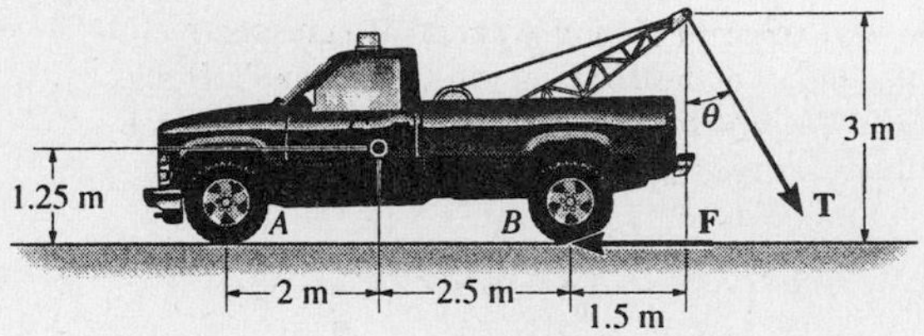

$\circlearrowleft + \Sigma M_B = 0; \quad 4(10^3)(9.81)(2.5) - T \sin\theta\,(3) - T \cos\theta\,(1.5) = 0$

$$T = \frac{65\,400}{(\cos\theta + 2\sin\theta)}$$

$$\frac{dT}{d\theta} = \frac{-65\,400(-\sin\theta + 2\cos\theta)}{(\cos\theta + 2\sin\theta)^2} = 0$$

$-\sin\theta + 2\cos\theta = 0$

$\theta = \tan^{-1} 2 = 63.43° = 63.4°$ **Ans**

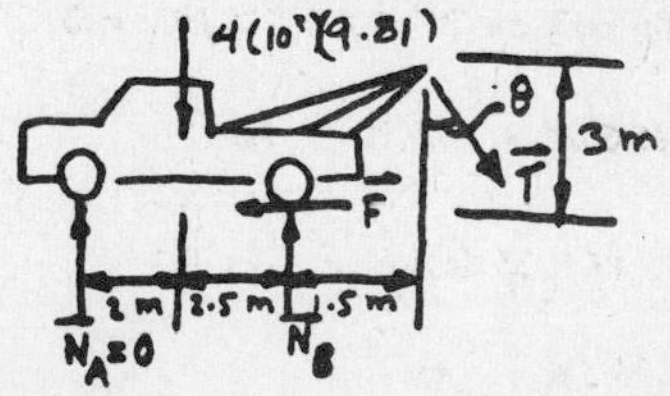

$$T = \frac{65\,400}{(\cos 63.43° + 2\sin 63.43°)} = 29.2 \text{ kN}$$ **Ans**

5-50. Three uniform books, each having a weight W and length a, are stacked as shown. Determine the maximum distance d that the top book can extend out from the bottom one so the stack does not topple over.

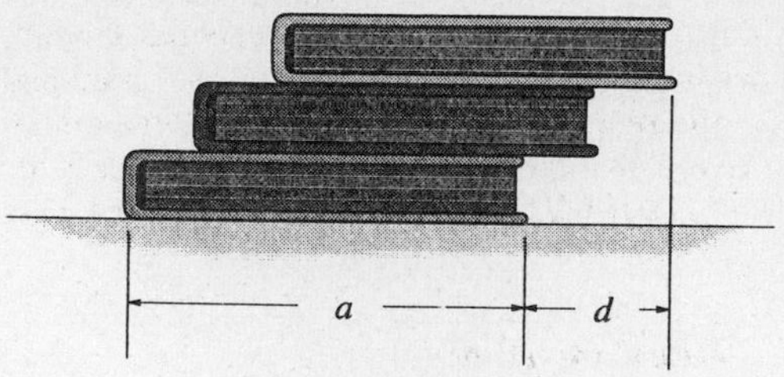

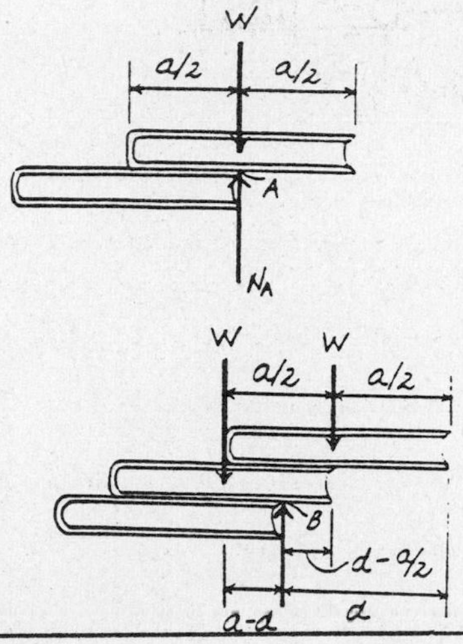

Equilibrium : For top two books, the upper book will topple when the center of gravity of this book is to the right of point A. Therefore, the maximum distance from the right edge of this book to point A is $a/2$.

Equation of Equilibrium : For the entire three books, the top two books will topple about point B.

$$+\Sigma M_B = 0; \qquad W(a-d) - W\left(d - \frac{a}{2}\right) = 0$$

$$d = \frac{3a}{4} \qquad \textbf{Ans}$$

5-51. The operation of the fuel pump for an automobile depends on the reciprocating action of the rocker arm ABC, which is pinned at B and is spring loaded at A and D. When the smooth cam C is in the position shown, determine the horizontal and vertical components of force at the pin and the force along the spring DF for equilibrium. The vertical force acting on the rocker arm at A is $F_A = 60$ N, and at C it is $F_C = 125$ N.

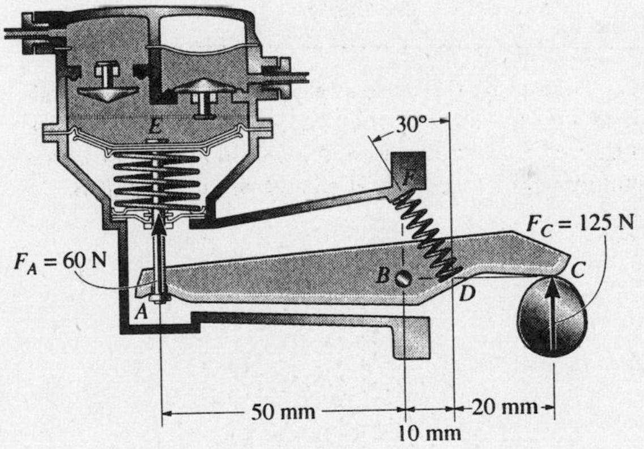

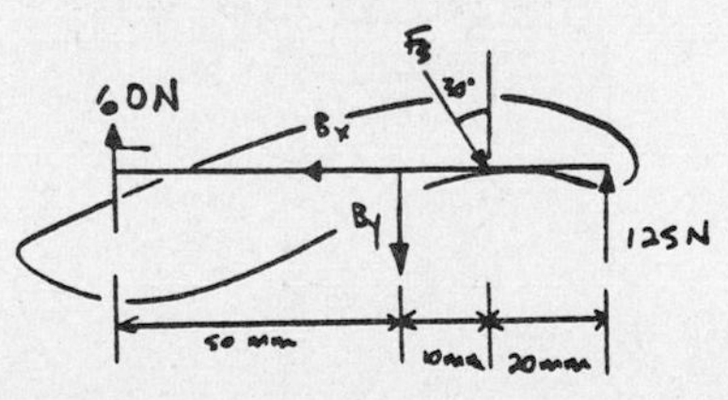

$$\curvearrowleft + \Sigma M_B = 0; \quad -60(50) - F_s \cos 30° (10) + 125(30) = 0$$

$$F_s = 86.6025 = 86.6 \text{ N} \qquad \textbf{Ans}$$

$$\xrightarrow{+} \Sigma F_x = 0; \quad -B_x + 86.6025 \sin 30° = 0$$

$$B_x = 43.3 \text{ N} \qquad \textbf{Ans}$$

$$+\uparrow \Sigma F_y = 0; \quad 60 - B_y - 86.6025 \cos 30° + 125 = 0$$

$$B_y = 110 \text{ N} \qquad \textbf{Ans}$$

*5-52. Determine the angle θ at which the link ABC is held in equilibrium if member BD moves 2 in. to the right. The springs are originally unstretched when $\theta = 0°$. Each spring has the stiffness shown. The springs remain horizontal since they are attached to roller guides.

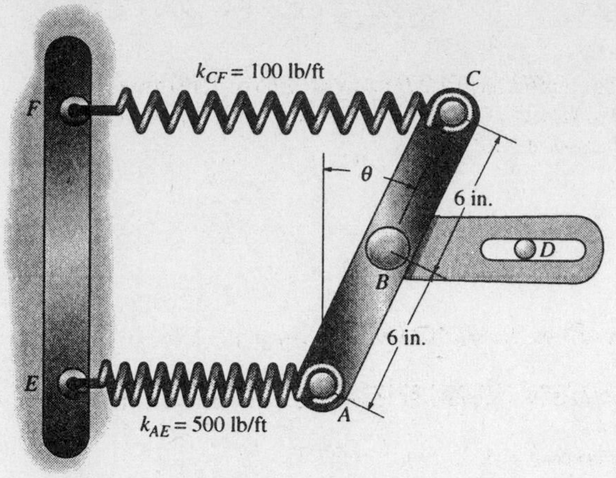

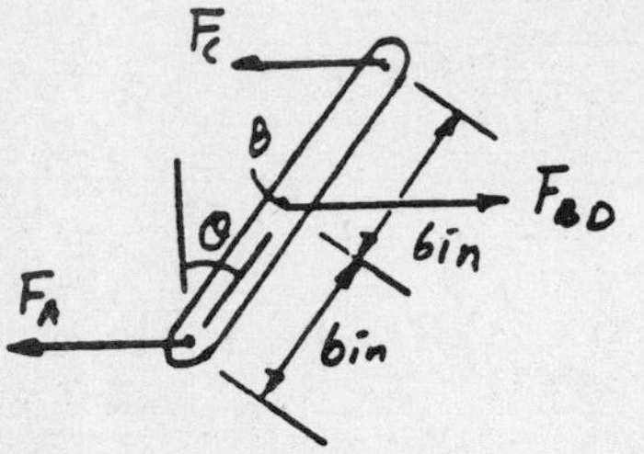

$\curvearrowleft + \Sigma M_B = 0; \quad F_C(6\cos\theta) - F_A(6\cos\theta) = 0 \quad F_C = F_A = F$

$x_C = \dfrac{F}{\left(\frac{100}{12}\right)} = 0.12F$ and $x_A = \dfrac{F}{\left(\frac{500}{12}\right)} = 0.024F$

Using similar triangles

$\dfrac{0.096F}{12} = \dfrac{2 - 0.024F}{6} \qquad F = 27.77$ lb

$\sin\theta = \dfrac{0.096(27.77)}{12} = 0.2222$

$\theta = 12.8°$ **Ans**

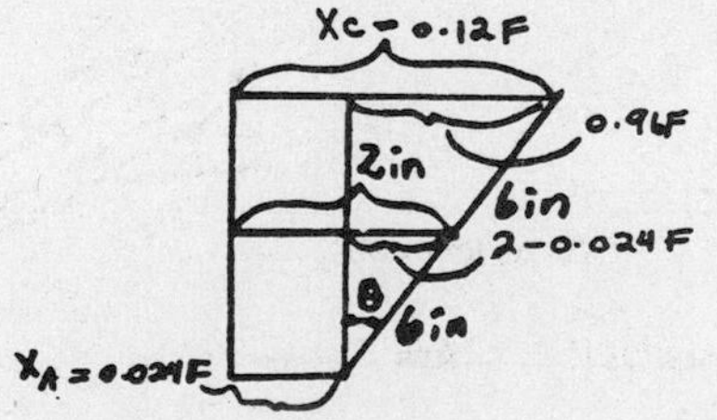

5-53. The uniform rod AB has a weight of 15 lb and the spring is unstretched when $\theta = 0°$. If $\theta = 30°$, determine the stiffness k of the spring.

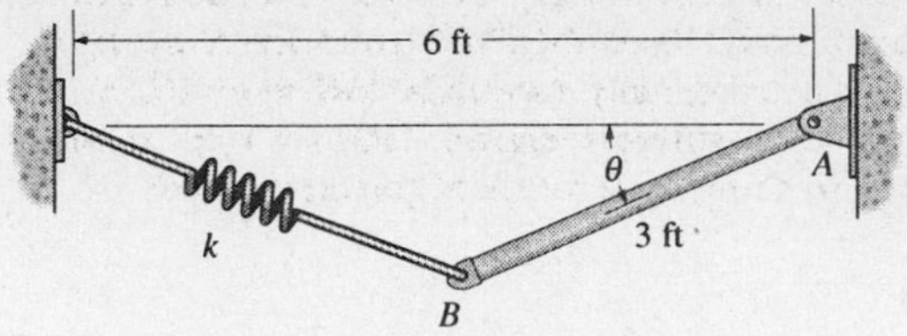

Geometry **:** From triangle $\overline{CDE}$, the cosine law gives

$$l = \sqrt{2.536^2 + 1.732^2 - 2(2.536)(1.732)\cos 120°} = 3.718 \text{ ft}$$

Using the sine law,

$$\frac{\sin\alpha}{2.536} = \frac{\sin 120°}{3.718} \qquad \alpha = 36.21°$$

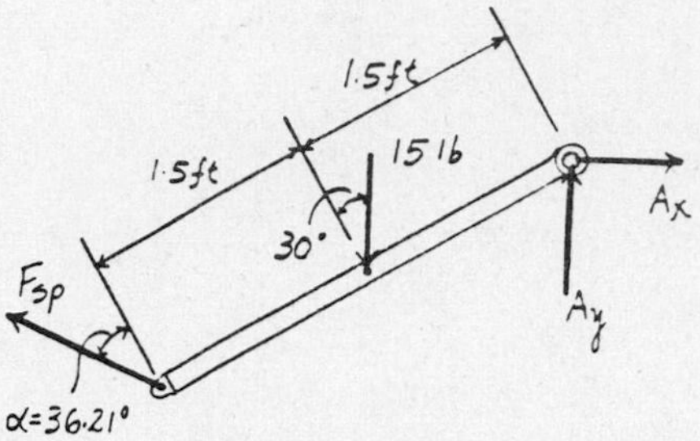

Equations of Equilibrium **:** The force in the spring can be obtained directly by summing moments about point A.

$$\curvearrowleft + \Sigma M_A = 0; \qquad 15\cos 30°(1.5) - F_{sp}\cos 36.21°(3) = 0$$

$$F_{sp} = 8.050 \text{ lb}$$

Spring Force Formula **:** The spring stretches $x = 3.718 - 3 = 0.718$ ft.

$$k = \frac{F_{sp}}{x} = \frac{8.050}{0.718} = 11.2 \text{ lb/ft} \qquad \textbf{Ans}$$

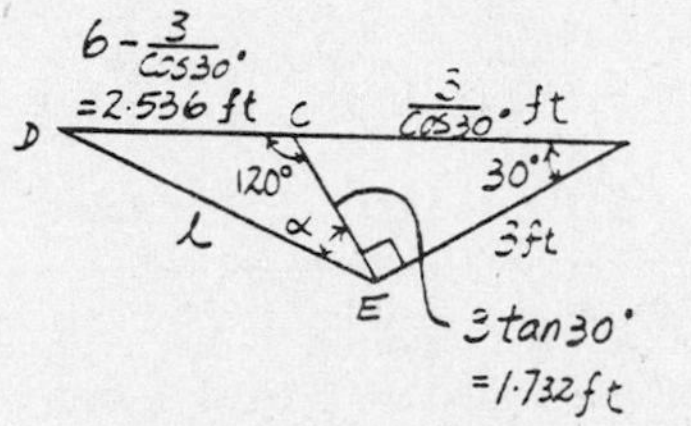

5-54. The relay regulates voltage and current. Determine the force in the spring CD, which has a stiffness of $k = 120$ N/m, so that it will allow the armature to make contact at A in figure (a) with a vertical force of 0.4 N. Also, determine the force in the spring when the coil is energized and attracts the armature to E, figure (b), thereby breaking contact at A.

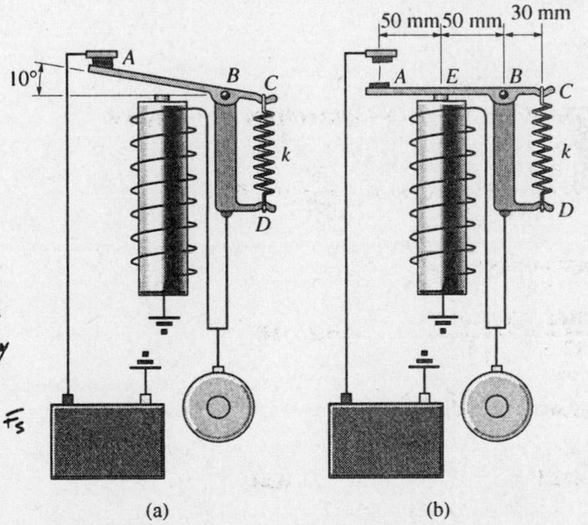

(a) (b)

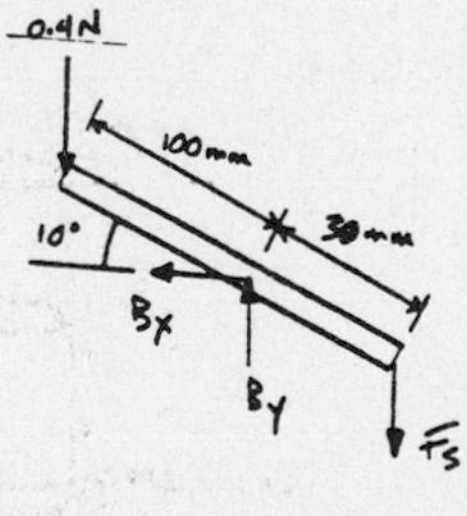

From Fig. (*a*) :

$$\curvearrowleft + \Sigma M_B = 0; \quad 0.4\,(100\cos 10°) - F_s\,(30\cos 10°) = 0$$

$$F_s = 1.333 \text{ N} = 1.33 \text{ N} \qquad \textbf{Ans}$$

$$F_s = kx; \quad 1.333 = 120x$$

$$x = 0.01111 \text{ m} = 11.11 \text{ mm}$$

From Fig (*b*), energizing the coil requires the spring to be stretched an additional amount

$$\Delta x = 30\sin 10° = 5.209 \text{ mm}.$$

Thus

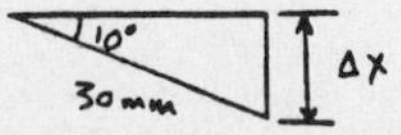

$$x' = 11.11 + 5.209 = 16.32 \text{ mm}$$

$$F_s = 120\,(0.01632) = 1.96 \text{ N} \qquad \textbf{Ans}$$

***5-55.** The horizontal beam is supported by springs at its ends. Each spring has a stiffness of $k = 5$ kN/m and is originally unstretched so that the beam is in the horizontal position. Determine the angle of tilt of the beam if a load of 800 N is applied at point C as shown.

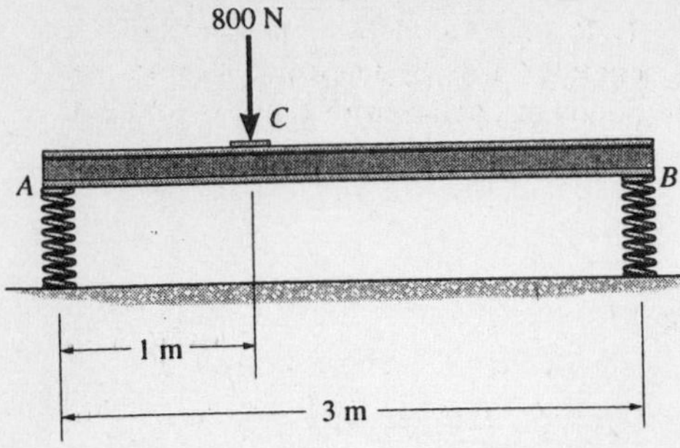

Equations of Equilibrium : The spring force at A and B can be obtained directly by summing moments about points B and A, respectively.

$$\circlearrowleft + \Sigma M_B = 0; \quad 800(2) - F_A(3) = 0 \quad F_A = 533.33 \text{ N}$$

$$\circlearrowleft + \Sigma M_A = 0; \quad F_B(3) - 800(1) = 0 \quad F_B = 266.67 \text{ N}$$

Spring Formula : Applying $\Delta = \frac{F}{k}$, we have

$$\Delta_A = \frac{533.33}{5(10^3)} = 0.1067 \text{ m}$$
$$\Delta_B = \frac{266.67}{5(10^3)} = 0.05333 \text{ m}$$

Geometry : The angle of tilt α is

$$\alpha = \tan^{-1}\left(\frac{0.05333}{3}\right) = 1.02^\circ \qquad \textbf{Ans}$$

***5-56.** The horizontal beam is supported by springs at its ends. If the stiffness of the spring at A is $k_A = 5$kN/m, determine the required stiffness of the spring at B so that if the beam is loaded with the 800 N it remains in the horizontal position. The springs are originally constructed so that the beam is in the horizontal position when it is unloaded.

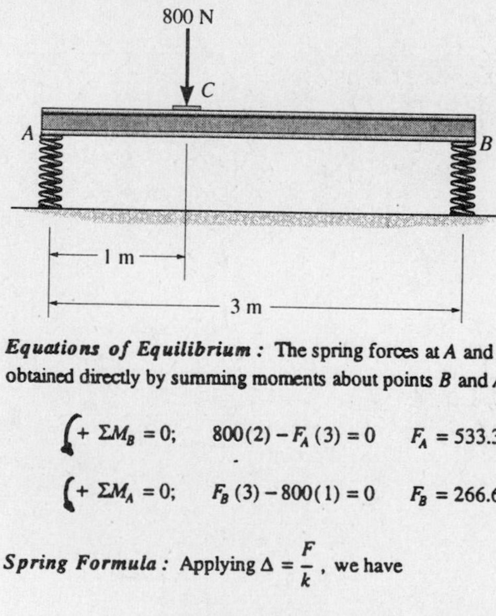

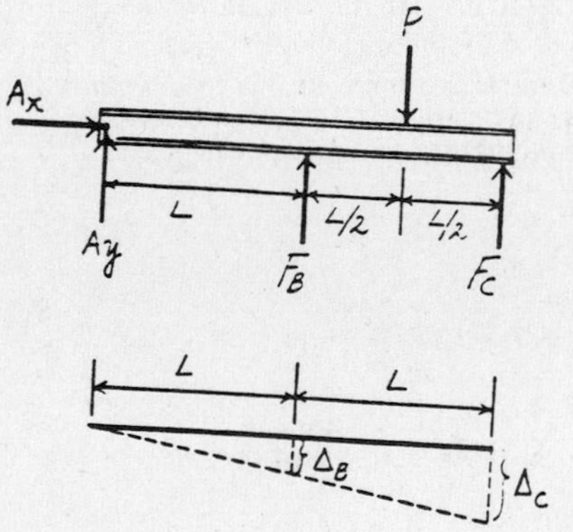

Equations of Equilibrium : The spring forces at A and B can be obtained directly by summing moments about points B and A respectively.

$$\circlearrowleft + \Sigma M_B = 0; \quad 800(2) - F_A(3) = 0 \quad F_A = 533.33 \text{ N}$$

$$\circlearrowleft + \Sigma M_A = 0; \quad F_B(3) - 800(1) = 0 \quad F_B = 266.67 \text{ N}$$

Spring Formula : Applying $\Delta = \frac{F}{k}$, we have

$$\Delta_A = \frac{533.33}{5(10^3)} = 0.1067 \text{ m} \qquad \Delta_B = \frac{266.67}{k_B}$$

Geometry : Requires, $\Delta_B = \Delta_A$. Then

$$\frac{266.67}{k_B} = 0.1067$$
$$k_B = 2500 \text{ N/m} = 2.50 \text{ kN/m} \qquad \textbf{Ans}$$

5-57. The disks D and E have a weight of 200 lb and 100 lb, respectively. If a horizontal force of $P = 200$ lb is applied to the center of disk E, determine the normal reactions at the points of contact with the ground at A, B, and C.

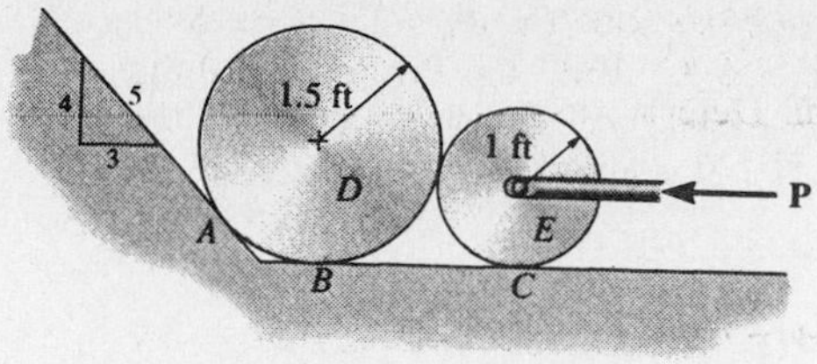

For disk E:

$\xrightarrow{+} \Sigma F_x = 0; \quad -P + N'\left(\frac{\sqrt{24}}{5}\right) = 0$

$+\uparrow \Sigma F_y = 0; \quad N_C - 100 - N'\left(\frac{1}{5}\right) = 0$

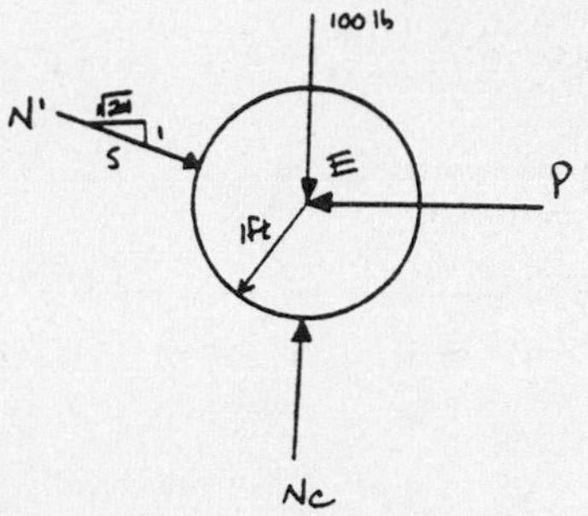

For disk D:

$\xrightarrow{+} \Sigma F_x = 0; \quad N_A\left(\frac{4}{5}\right) - N'\left(\frac{\sqrt{24}}{5}\right) = 0$

$+\uparrow \Sigma F_y = 0; \quad N_A\left(\frac{3}{5}\right) + N_B - 200 + N'\left(\frac{1}{5}\right) = 0$

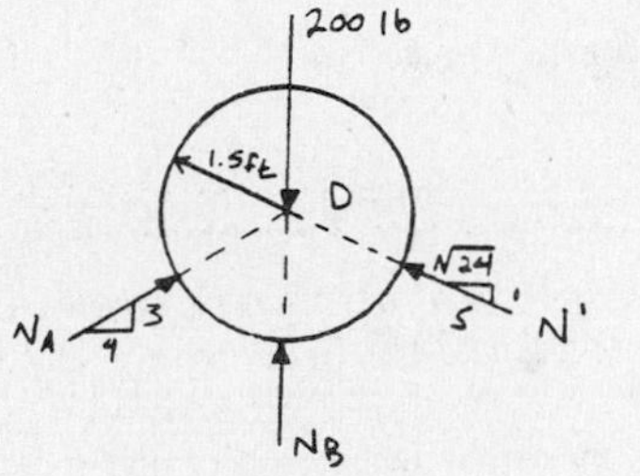

Set $P = 200$ lb and solve:

$N' = 204.12$ lb

$N_A = 250$ lb **Ans**

$N_B = 9.18$ lb **Ans**

$N_C = 141$ lb **Ans**

5-58. The disks D and E have a weight of 200 lb and 100 lb, respectively. Determine the maximum horizontal force P that can be applied to the center of disk E without causing the disk D to move up the incline.

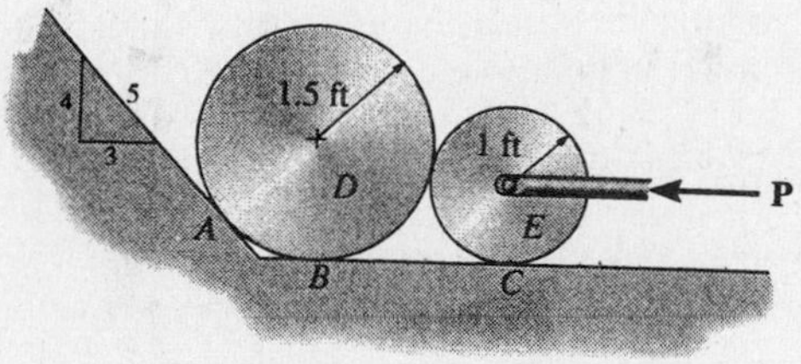

For disk E:

$\xrightarrow{+} \Sigma F_x = 0; \quad -P + N'\left(\frac{\sqrt{24}}{5}\right) = 0$

$+\uparrow \Sigma F_y = 0; \quad N_C - 100 - N'\left(\frac{1}{5}\right) = 0$

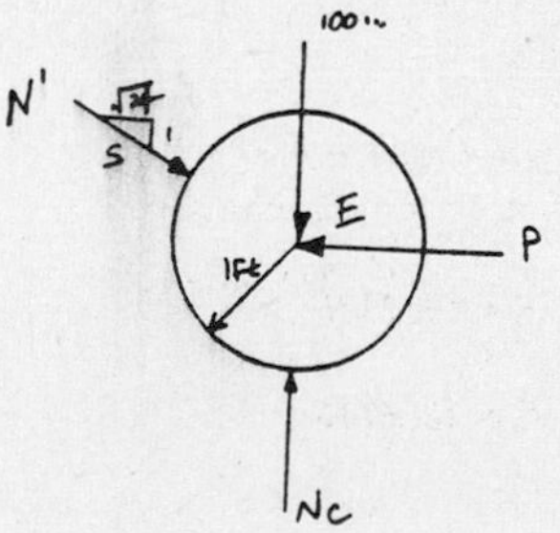

For disk D:

$\xrightarrow{+} \Sigma F_x = 0; \quad N_A\left(\frac{4}{5}\right) - N'\left(\frac{\sqrt{24}}{5}\right) = 0$

$+\uparrow \Sigma F_y = 0; \quad N_A\left(\frac{3}{5}\right) + N_B - 200 + N'\left(\frac{1}{5}\right) = 0$

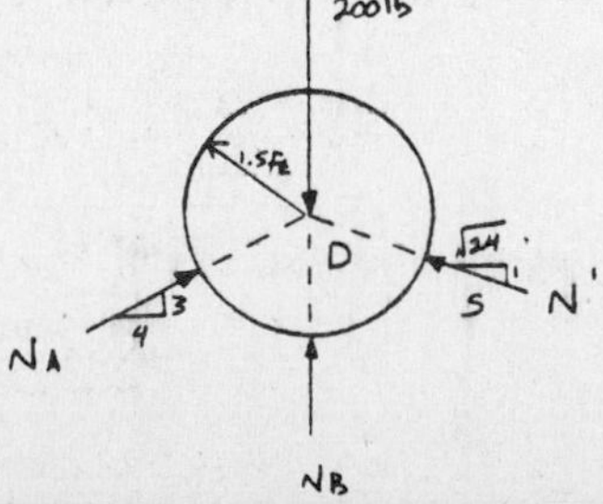

Require $N_B = 0$ for P_{max}. Solving,

$P_{max} = 210$ lb **Ans**

$N_A = 262$ lb **Ans**

$N_C = 143$ lb **Ans**

5-59. A man stands out at the end of the diving board, which is supported by two springs A and B, each having a stiffness of $k = 15$ kN/m. In the position shown the board is horizontal. If the man has a mass of 40 kg, determine the angle of tilt which the board makes with the horizontal after he jumps off. Neglect the weight of the board and assume it is rigid.

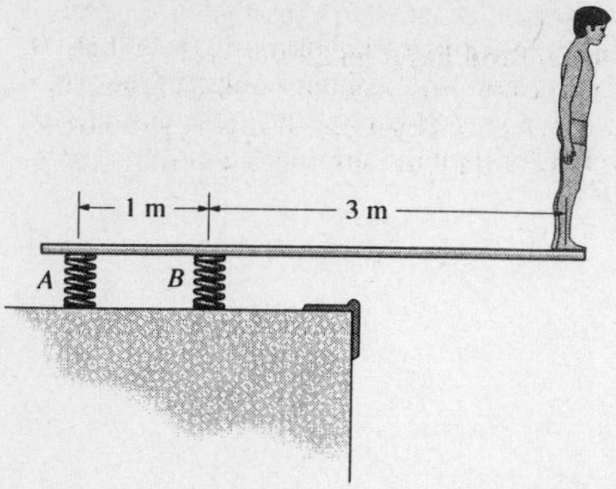

Equations of Equilibrium : The spring force at A and B can be obtained directly by summing moments about points B and A, respectively.

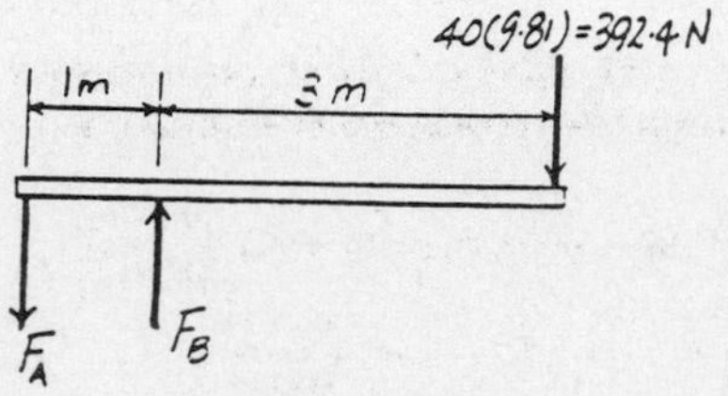

$$\curvearrowleft + \Sigma M_B = 0; \quad F_A(1) - 392.4(3) = 0 \quad F_A = 1177.2\text{ N}$$

$$\curvearrowleft + \Sigma M_A = 0; \quad F_B(1) - 392.4(4) = 0 \quad F_B = 1569.6\text{ N}$$

Spring Formula : Applying $\Delta = \frac{F}{k}$, we have

$$\Delta_A = \frac{1177.2}{15(10^3)} = 0.07848\text{ m} \qquad \Delta_B = \frac{1569.6}{15(10^3)} = 0.10464\text{ m}$$

Geometry : The angle of tilt α is

$$\alpha = \tan^{-1}\left(\frac{0.10464 + 0.07848}{1}\right) = 10.4° \qquad \textbf{Ans}$$

***5-60.** The uniform beam has a weight W and length l and is supported by a pin at A and a cable BC. Determine the horizontal and vertical components of reaction at A and the tension in the cable necessary to hold the beam in the position shown.

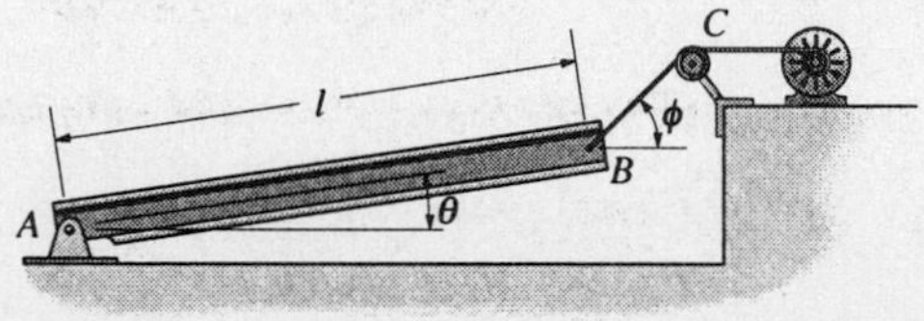

Equations of Equilibrium : The tension the cable can be obtained directly by summing moments about point A.

$$\curvearrowleft + \Sigma M_A = 0; \quad T\sin(\phi - \theta)\,l - W\cos\theta\left(\frac{l}{2}\right) = 0$$

$$T = \frac{W\cos\theta}{2\sin(\phi - \theta)} \qquad \textbf{Ans}$$

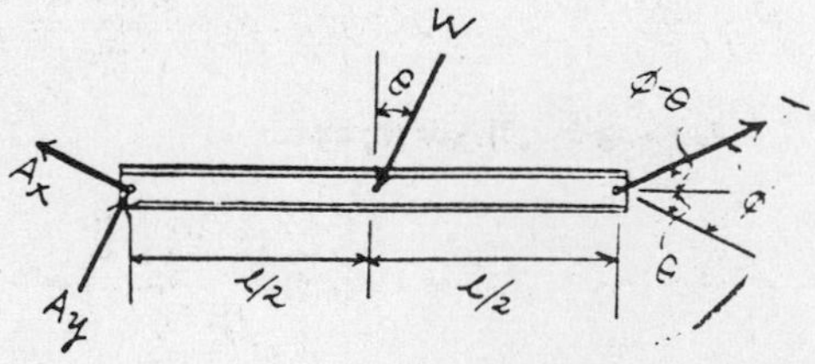

Using the result $T = \dfrac{W\cos\theta}{2\sin(\phi - \theta)}$

$$\xrightarrow{+} \Sigma F_x = 0; \quad \left(\frac{W\cos\theta}{2\sin(\phi - \theta)}\right)\cos\phi - A_x = 0$$

$$A_x = \frac{W\cos\phi\cos\theta}{2\sin(\phi - \theta)} \qquad \textbf{Ans}$$

$$+\uparrow \Sigma F_y = 0; \quad A_y + \left(\frac{W\cos\theta}{2\sin(\phi - \theta)}\right)\sin\phi - W = 0$$

$$A_y = \frac{W(\sin\phi\cos\theta - 2\cos\phi\sin\theta)}{2\sin(\phi - \theta)} \qquad \textbf{Ans}$$

5-61. The uniform rod has a length l and weight W. It is supported at one end A by a smooth wall and the other end by a cord of length s which is attached to the wall as shown. Show that for equilibrium it is required that $h = [(s^2 - l^2)/3]^{1/2}$.

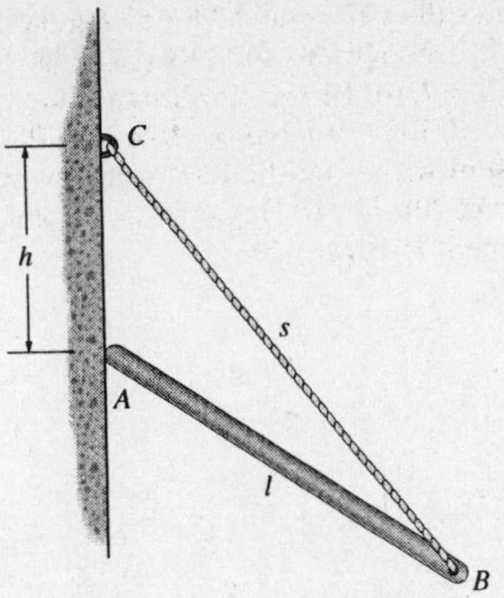

Equations of Equilibrium : The tension in the cable can be obtained directly by summing moments about point A.

$$\circlearrowleft + \Sigma M_A = 0; \quad T\sin\phi\,(l) - W\sin\theta\left(\frac{l}{2}\right) = 0$$

$$T = \frac{W\sin\theta}{2\sin\phi}$$

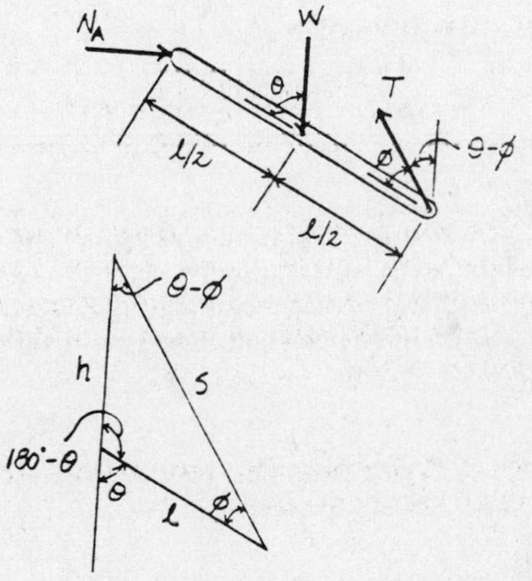

Using the result $T = \dfrac{W\sin\theta}{2\sin\phi}$,

$$+\uparrow \Sigma F_y = 0; \quad \frac{W\sin\theta}{2\sin\phi}\cos(\theta-\phi) - W = 0$$

$$\sin\theta\cos(\theta-\phi) - 2\sin\phi = 0 \qquad [1]$$

Geometry : Applying the sine law with $\sin(180° - \theta) = \sin\theta$, we have

$$\frac{\sin\phi}{h} = \frac{\sin\theta}{s} \qquad \sin\phi = \frac{h}{s}\sin\theta \qquad [2]$$

Substituting Eq.[2] into [1] yields

$$\cos(\theta-\phi) = \frac{2h}{s} \qquad [3]$$

Using the cosine law,

$$l^2 = h^2 + s^2 - 2hs\cos(\theta-\phi)$$

$$\cos(\theta-\phi) = \frac{h^2+s^2-l^2}{2hs} \qquad [4]$$

Equating Eqs.[3] and [4] yields

$$\frac{2h}{s} = \frac{h^2+s^2-l^2}{2hs}$$

$$h = \sqrt{\frac{s^2-l^2}{3}} \qquad (Q.E.D)$$

5-62. The thin rod of length l is supported by the smooth tube. Determine the distance a needed for equilibrium if the applied load is **P**.

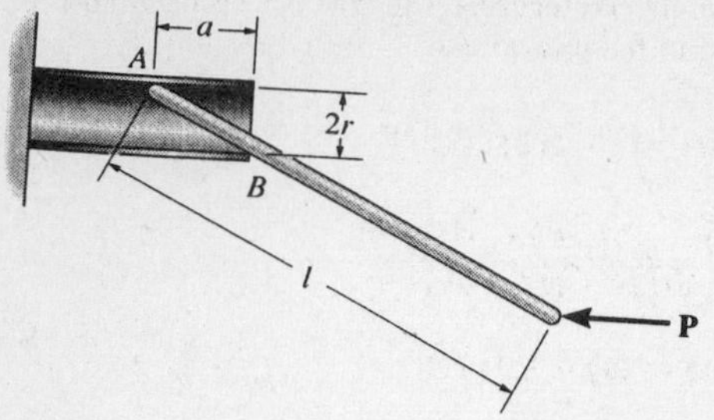

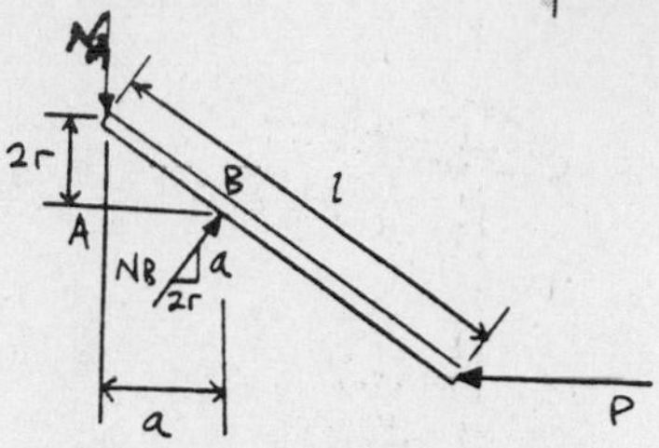

$\xrightarrow{+} \Sigma F_x = 0; \quad \frac{2r}{\sqrt{4r^2 + a^2}} N_B - P = 0$

$\curvearrowleft + \Sigma M_A = 0; \quad -P\left(\frac{2r}{\sqrt{4r^2 + a^2}}\right)l + N_B\sqrt{4r^2 + a^2} = 0$

$$\frac{4r^2 l}{4r^2 + a^2} - \sqrt{4r^2 + a^2} = 0$$

$$4r^2 l = (4r^2 + a^2)^{\frac{3}{2}}$$

$$(4r^2 l)^{\frac{2}{3}} = 4r^2 + a^2$$

$$a = \sqrt{(4r^2 l)^{\frac{2}{3}} - 4r^2} \quad \textbf{Ans}$$

5-63. The uniform load has a mass of 600 kg and is lifted using a uniform 30-kg strongback beam and four wire ropes as shown. Determine the tension in each segment of rope and the force that must be applied to the sling at A.

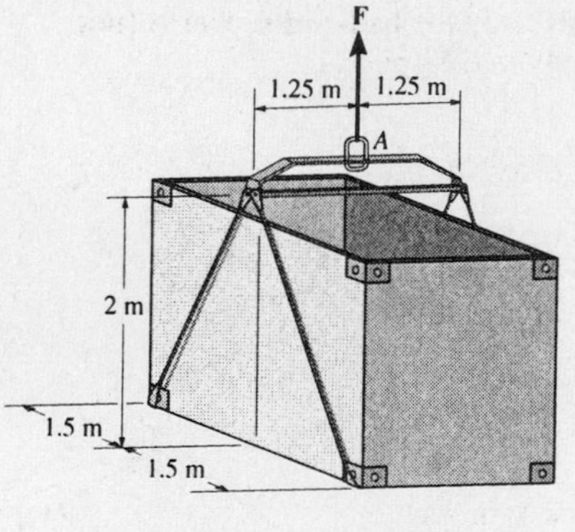

Prob. 5-64

Equations of Equilibrium : Due to symmetry, all wires are subjected to the same tension. This condition statisfies moment equilibrium about the x and y axes and force equilibrium along y axis.

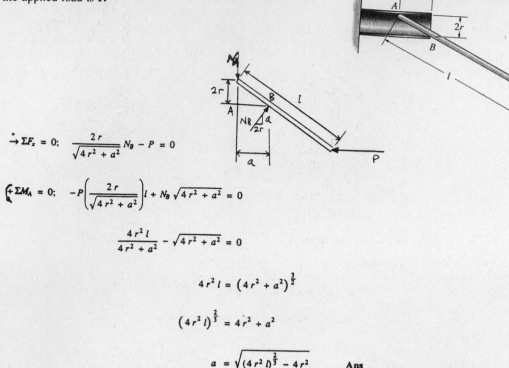

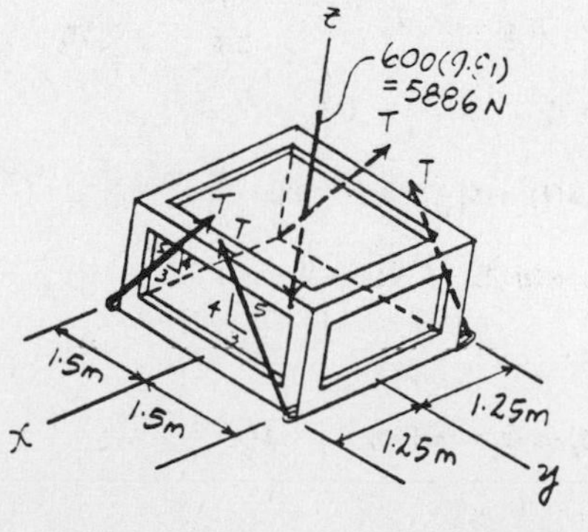

$\Sigma F_z = 0; \quad 4T\left(\frac{4}{5}\right) - 5886 = 0$

$T = 1839.375 \text{ N} = 1.84 \text{ kN}$ **Ans**

The force **F** applied to the sling A must support the weight of the load and strongback beam. Hence

$\Sigma F_z = 0; \quad F - 600(9.81) - 30(9.81) = 0$

$F = 6180.3 \text{ N} = 6.18 \text{ kN}$ **Ans**

***5-64.** The cable of the tower crane is subjected to a force of 840 N. Determine the x, y, z components of reaction at the fixed base A.

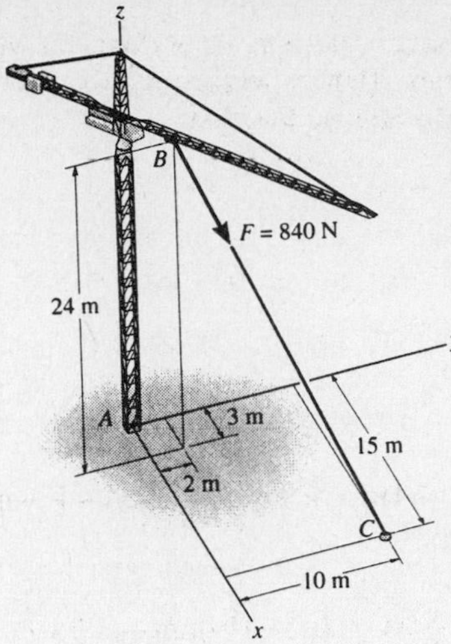

$\mathbf{r}_{BC} = \{12\mathbf{i} + 8\mathbf{j} - 24\mathbf{k}\}$ m

$$\mathbf{F} = 840\left[\frac{12\mathbf{i} + 8\mathbf{j} - 24\mathbf{k}}{\sqrt{(12)^2 + (8)^2 + (-24)^2}}\right]$$

$= \{360\mathbf{i} + 240\mathbf{j} - 720\mathbf{k}\}$ N

$\mathbf{F}_A = A_x\,\mathbf{i} + A_y\,\mathbf{j} + A_z\,\mathbf{k}$

Thus

$\Sigma\mathbf{F} = 0;\quad \mathbf{F} + \mathbf{F}_A = 0$

$A_x = -360$ N **Ans**

$A_y = -240$ N **Ans**

$A_z = 720$ N **Ans**

$\Sigma\mathbf{M} = 0;\quad \mathbf{M}_A + \mathbf{r}_{AC} \times \mathbf{F} = 0$

$$\mathbf{M}_A + \begin{vmatrix} \mathbf{i} & \mathbf{j} & \mathbf{k} \\ 15 & 10 & 0 \\ 360 & 240 & -720 \end{vmatrix} = 0$$

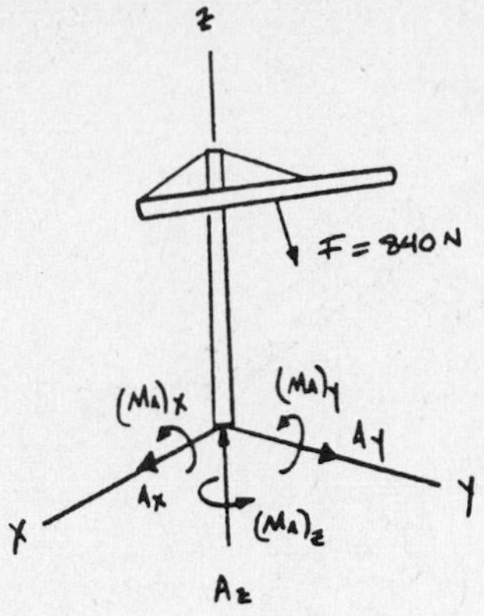

$\mathbf{M}_A - 7200\mathbf{i} + 10\,800\mathbf{j} = 0$

Thus

$M_{Ax} = 7.20$ kN·m **Ans**

$M_{Ay} = -10.8$ kN·m **Ans**

$M_{Az} = 0$ **Ans**

5-65. Determine the x, y, z components of reaction at the ball supports B and C and the ball-and-socket A (not shown) for the uniformly loaded plate.

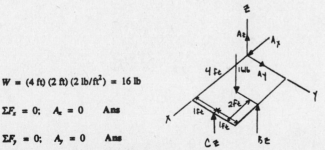

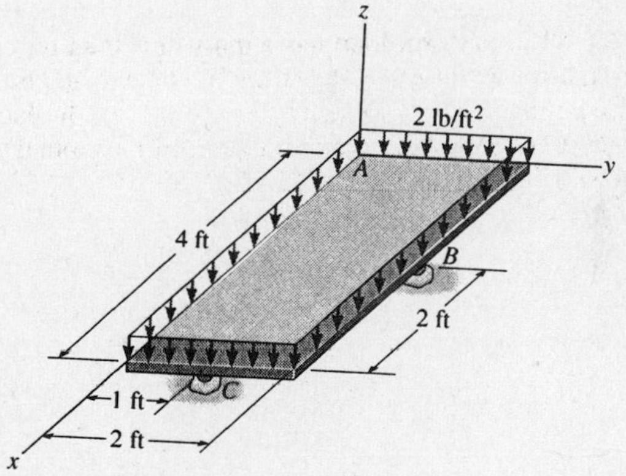

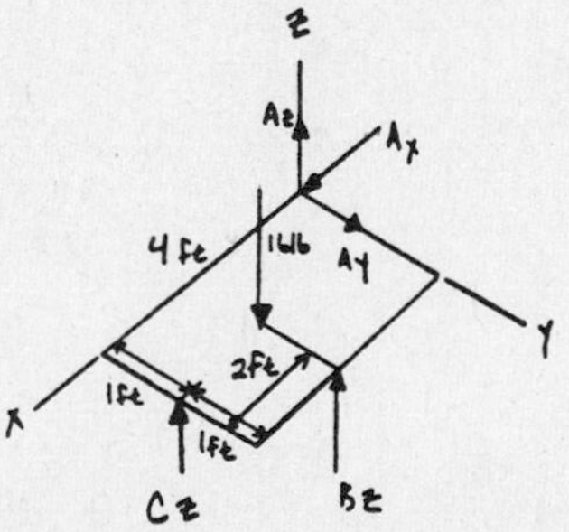

$W = (4\text{ ft})(2\text{ ft})(2\text{ lb/ft}^2) = 16$ lb

$\Sigma F_x = 0;\quad A_x = 0$ **Ans**

$\Sigma F_y = 0;\quad A_y = 0$ **Ans**

$\Sigma F_z = 0;\quad A_z + B_z + C_z - 16 = 0$ (1)

$\Sigma M_x = 0;\quad 2B_z - 16(1) + C_z(1) = 0$ (2)

$\Sigma M_y = 0;\quad -B_z(2) + 16(2) - C_z(4) = 0$ (3)

Solving Eqs. (1) – (3):

$A_z = B_z = C_z = 5.33$ lb **Ans**

5-66. Determine the x, y, z components of reaction acting on the ball-and-socket at A, the reaction at the roller B, and the tension in the cord CD required for equilibrium of the plate.

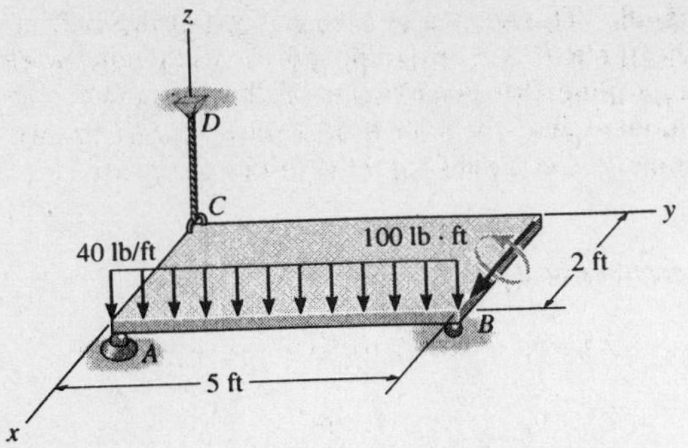

$\Sigma M_x = 0;\quad 100 + B_z(5) - 200(2.5) = 0;\quad B_z = 80\text{ lb}$ **Ans**

$\Sigma M_y = 0;\quad 200(2) - A_z(2) - 80(2) = 0;\quad A_z = 120\text{ lb}$ **Ans**

$\Sigma F_z = 0;\quad 80 + 120 - 200 + T_{CD} = 0;\quad T_{CD} = 0$ **Ans**

$\Sigma F_x = 0;\quad A_x = 0$ **Ans**

$\Sigma F_y = 0;\quad A_y = 0$ **Ans**

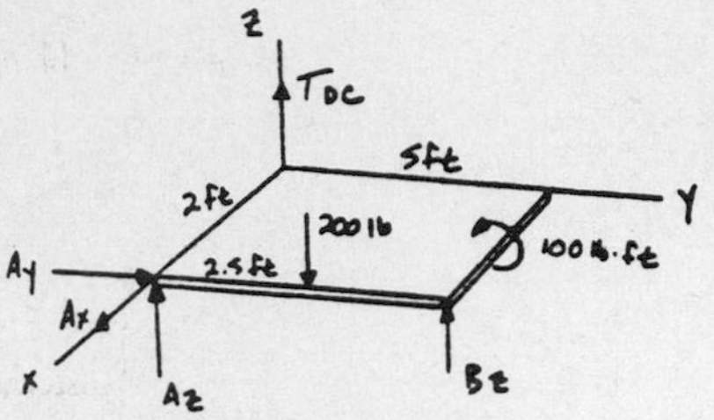

5-67. Determine the components of reaction acting at the ball-and-socket A, roller B, and cord CD.

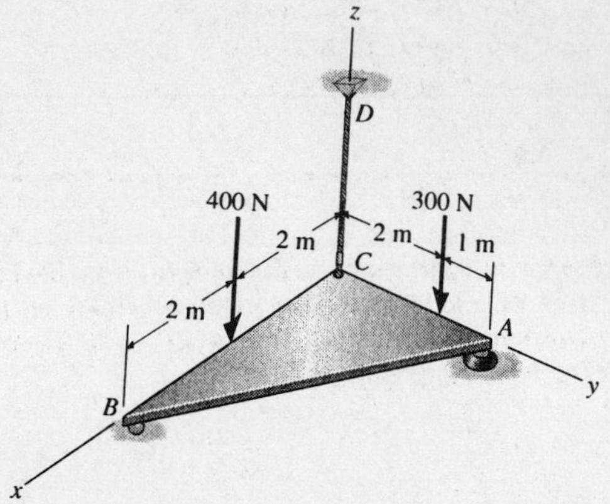

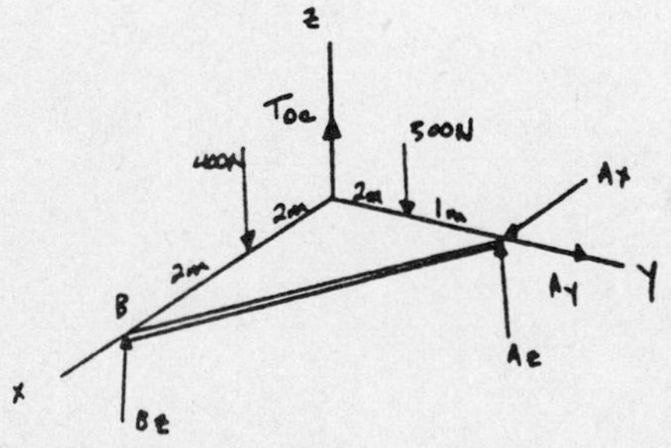

$\Sigma F_x = 0;\quad A_x = 0$ **Ans**

$\Sigma F_y = 0;\quad A_y = 0$ **Ans**

$\Sigma M_x = 0;\quad -300(2) + A_z(3) = 0;\quad A_z = 200\text{ N}$ **Ans**

$\Sigma M_y = 0;\quad 400(2) - B_z(4) = 0;\quad B_z = 200\text{ N}$ **Ans**

$\Sigma F_z = 0;\quad 200 + 200 + T_{CD} - 700 = 0;\quad T_{CD} = 300\text{ N}$ **Ans**

***5-68.** The wrench is used to tighten the bolt at A. If the force $F = 6$ lb is applied to the handle as shown, determine the magnitudes of the resultant force and moment that the bolt head exerts on the wrench. The force $\mathbf{F}$ is in a plane parallel to the x–z plane.

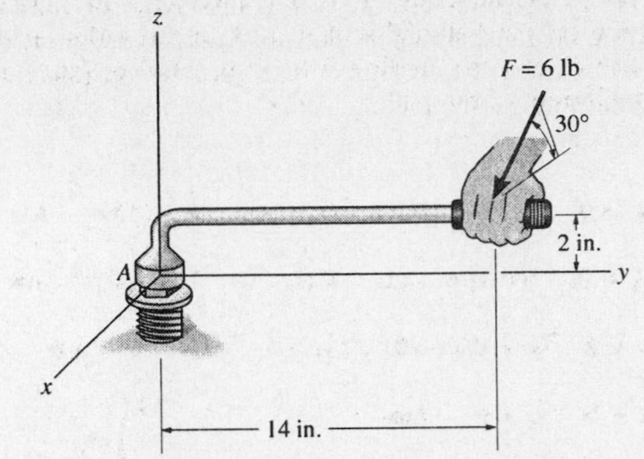

Equations of Equilibrium :

$\Sigma F_x = 0; \quad 6\cos 30° - A_x = 0 \quad A_x = 5.196 \text{ lb}$

$\Sigma F_y = 0; \quad A_y = 0$

$\Sigma F_z = 0; \quad A_z - 6\sin 30° = 0 \quad A_z = 3.00 \text{ lb}$

$\Sigma M_x = 0; \quad (M_A)_x - 6\sin 30°(14) = 0 \quad (M_A)_x = 42.0 \text{ lb}\cdot\text{in}$

$\Sigma M_y = 0; \quad 6\cos 30°(2) - (M_A)_y = 0 \quad (M_A)_y = 10.39 \text{ lb}\cdot\text{in}$

$\Sigma M_z = 0; \quad (M_A)_z - 6\cos 30°(14) = 0 \quad (M_A)_z = 72.75 \text{ lb}\cdot\text{in}$

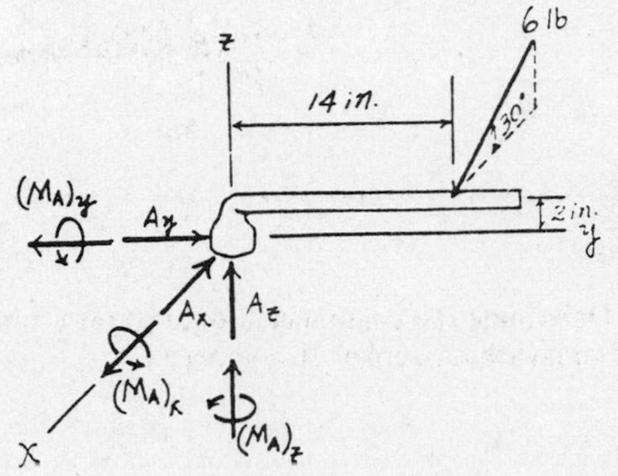

The magnitude of force and moment reactions are

$F_A = \sqrt{A_x^2 + A_z^2} = \sqrt{5.196^2 + 3.00^2} = 6.00 \text{ lb}$ **Ans**

$$M_A = \sqrt{(M_A)_x^2 + (M_A)_y^2 + (M_A)_z^2}$$
$$= \sqrt{42.0^2 + 10.39^2 + 72.75^2}$$
$$= 84.64 \text{ lb}\cdot\text{in} = 7.05 \text{ lb}\cdot\text{ft}$$ **Ans**

5-69. The cart supports the uniform crate having a mass of 85 kg. Determine the vertical reactions on the three casters at A, B, and C. The casater at B is not shown. Neglect the mass of the cart.

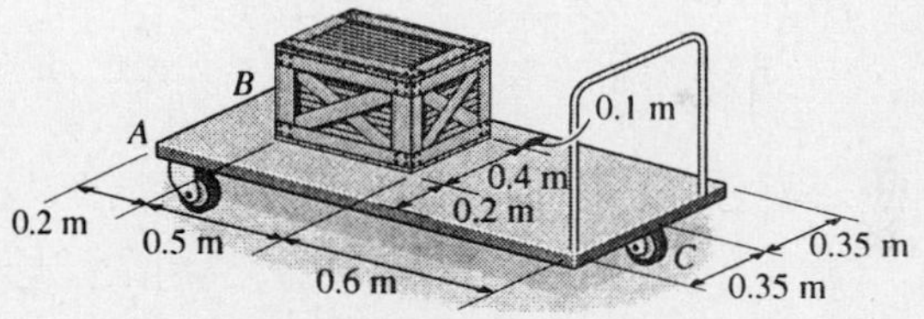

5-72

Equations of Equilibrium : The normal reaction N_C can be obtained directly by summing moments about x axis.

$\Sigma M_x = 0; \quad N_C(1.3) - 833.85(0.45) = 0$
$N_C = 288.64 \text{ N} = 289 \text{ N}$ **Ans**

$\Sigma M_y = 0; \quad 833.85(0.3) - 288.64(0.35) - N_A(0.7) = 0$
$N_A = 213.04 \text{ N} = 213 \text{ N}$ **Ans**

$\Sigma F_z = 0; \quad N_B + 288.64 + 213.04 - 833.85 = 0$
$N_B = 332 \text{ N}$ **Ans**

5-70. The circular plate has a weight W and center of gravity at its center. If it is supported by three vertical cords tied to its edge, determine the largest distance d from the center to where any vertical force **P** can be applied so as not to cause the force in any one of the cables to become zero.

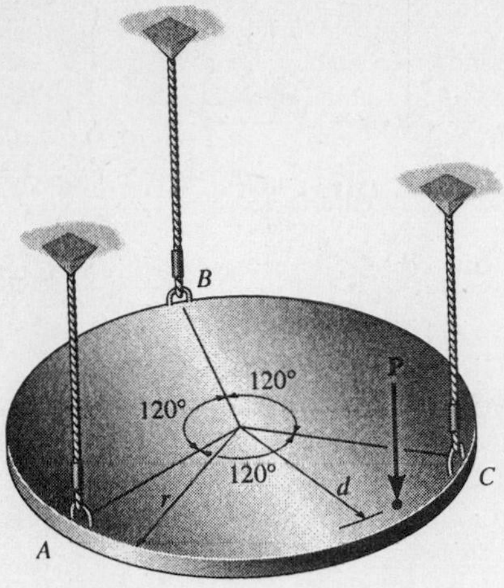

Assume $T_A = T_B = 0$

$\Sigma M_{a-a} = 0;\quad T_C(r + r\cos 60°) - W(r\cos 60°) - P(d + r\cos 60°) = 0$

$\Sigma F_z = 0;\quad T_C - W - P = 0$

Eliminating T_C we get

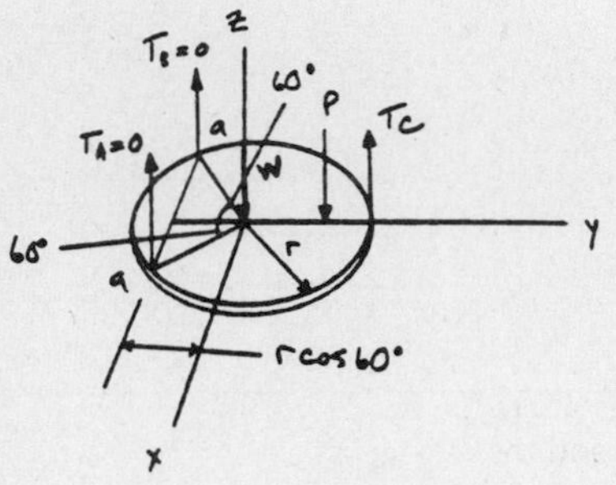

$$Wr + Pr - Pd = 0$$

$$d = r\left(1 + \frac{W}{P}\right) \qquad (1)$$

Assume $T_C = 0$

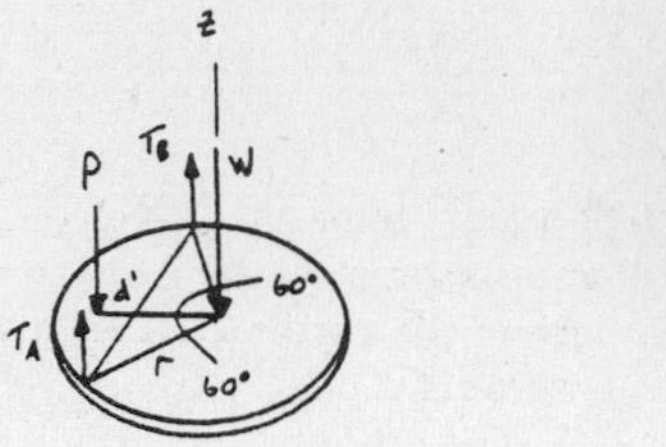

$\Sigma M_{a-a} = 0;\quad W(r\cos 60°) - P(d') = 0$

$$d' = \frac{Wr}{2P}$$

Thus

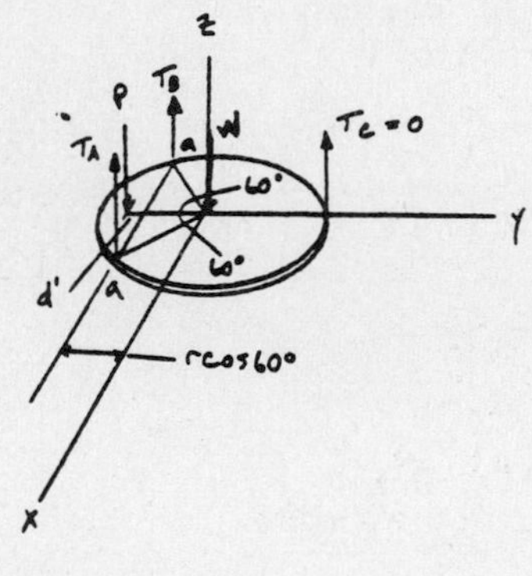

$$d = r\cos 60° + \frac{Wr}{2P}$$

$$d = \frac{r}{2}\left(1 + \frac{W}{P}\right) \qquad \textbf{Ans}$$

This value for d satisfies Eq. (1). i.e., $d < r\left(1 + \frac{W}{P}\right)$

5-71. Solve Prob. 5–70 if the plate's weight W is neglected.

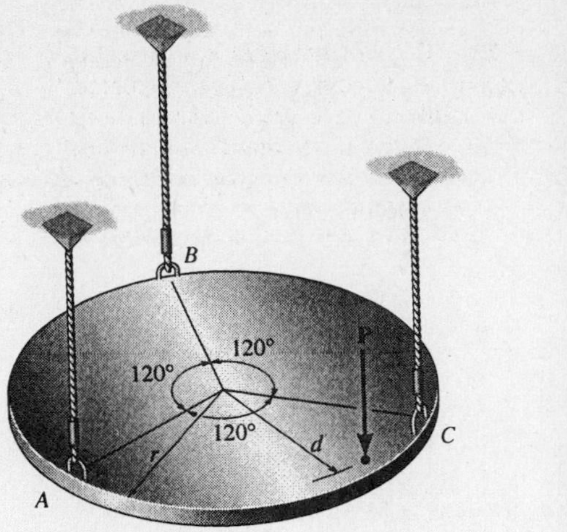

Assume $T_A = T_B = 0$

$\Sigma M_{a-a} = 0;\quad T_C(r + r\cos 60°) - P(d + r\cos 60°) = 0$

$\Sigma F_z = 0;\quad T_C - P = 0$

$d = r$

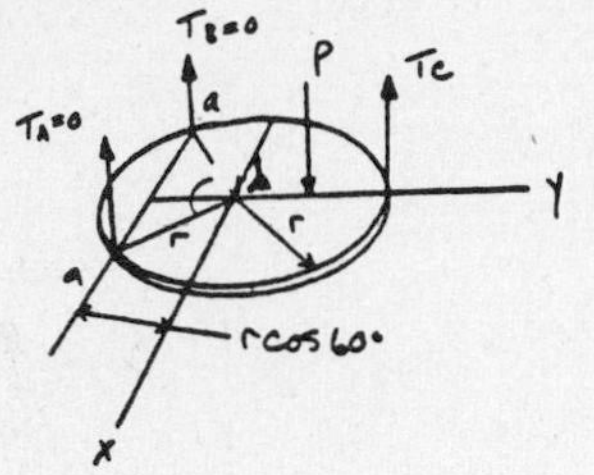

Assume $T_C = 0$:

$\Sigma M_{a-a} = 0;\quad P(d') = 0$

$d' = 0$

Thus,

$d = r\cos 60° + 0$

$d = \frac{r}{2}$ **Ans**

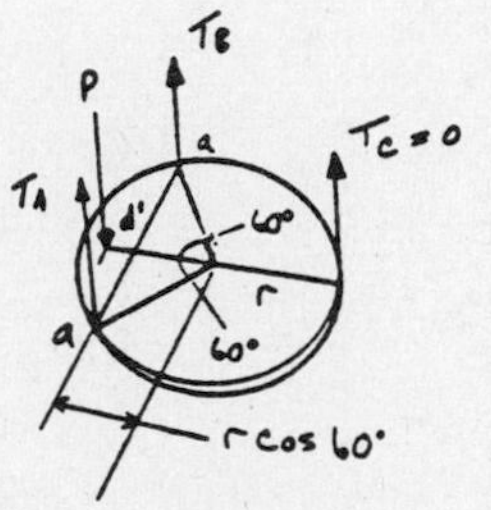

***5-72.** Determine the force components acting on the ball-and-socket at A, the reaction at the roller B and the tension on the cord CD needed for equilibrium of the quarter circular plate.

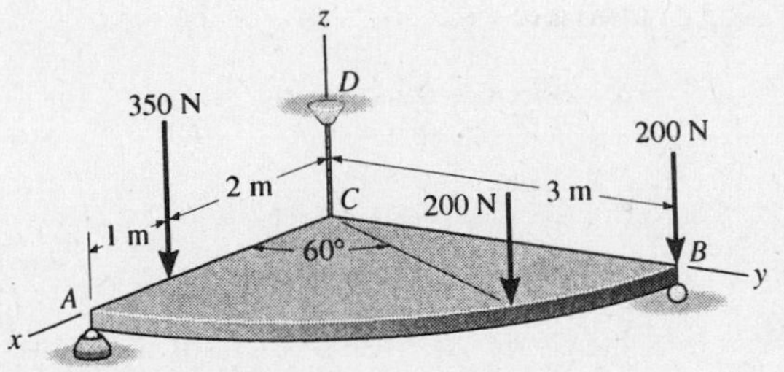

Equations of Equilibrium : The normal reaction N_B and A_z can be obtained directly by summing moments about the x and y axes respectively.

$\Sigma M_x = 0;\quad N_B(3) - 200(3) - 200(3\sin 60°) = 0$

$N_B = 373.21\text{ N} = 373\text{ N}$ **Ans**

$\Sigma M_y = 0;\quad 350(2) + 200(3\cos 60°) - A_z(3) = 0$

$A_z = 333.33\text{ N} = 333\text{ N}$ **Ans**

$\Sigma F_z = 0;\quad T_{CD} + 373.21 + 333.33 - 350 - 200 - 200 = 0$

$T_{CD} = 43.5\text{ N}$ **Ans**

$\Sigma F_x = 0;\quad A_x = 0$ **Ans**

$\Sigma F_y = 0;\quad A_y = 0$ **Ans**

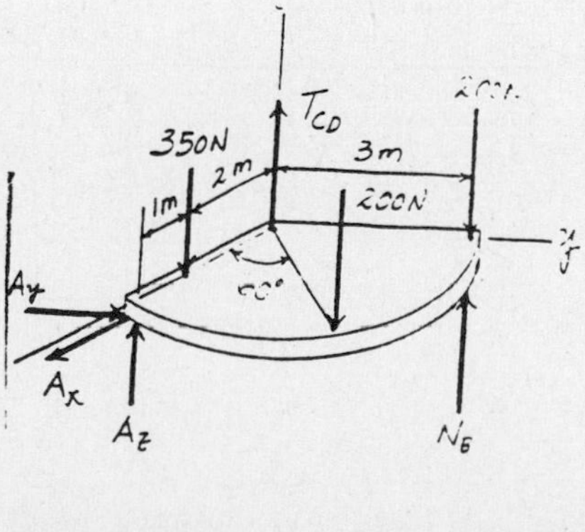

5-73. A uniform square table having a weight W and sides a is supported by three vertical legs. Determine the smallest vertical force **P** that can be applied to its top that will cause it to tip over.

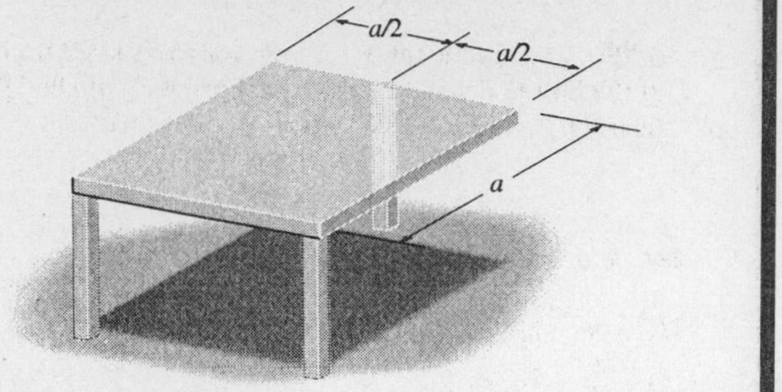

Place the legs as shown since this provides the largest triangle that can be inscribed on the table so that the perpendicular distance from each axis AB, BC, or AC to the center of the table is as large as possible.

$$\theta = \tan^{-1}\left(\frac{\frac{a}{2}}{a}\right) = 26.565°$$

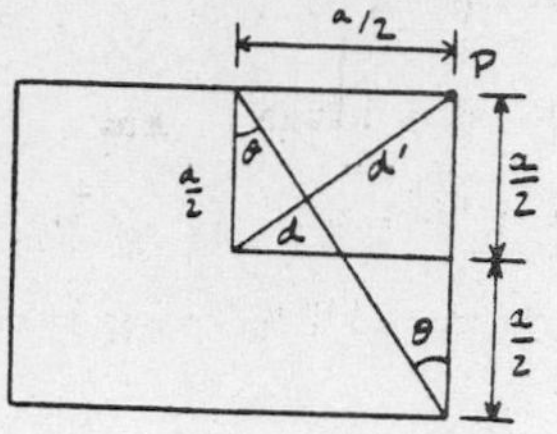

$$d = \left(\frac{a}{2}\right)\sin 26.565° = 0.2236\,a < \frac{a}{2}$$

$$d' = a\sin 26.565° = 0.4472\,a$$

For P_{min}, put P at the corner as shown.

$\Sigma M_{BC} = 0;\quad W(0.2236\,a) - P(0.4472\,a) = 0$

$P = 0.5\,W$ **Ans**

5-74. The pole for a power line is subjected to the two cable forces of 60 lb, each force lying in a plane parallel to the x–y plane. If the tension in the guy wire AB is 80 lb, determine the x, y, z components of reaction at the fixed base of the pole, O.

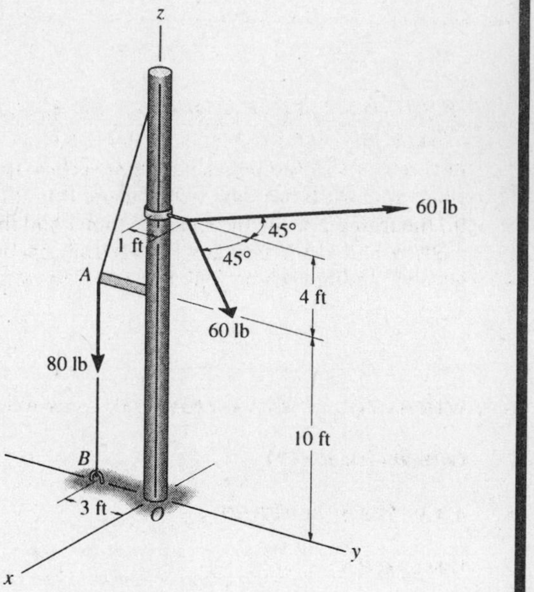

Equations of Equilibrium :

$\Sigma F_x = 0;\quad O_x + 60\sin 45° - 60\sin 45° = 0$

$O_x = 0$ **Ans**

$\Sigma F_y = 0;\quad O_y + 60\cos 45° + 60\cos 45° = 0$

$O_y = -84.9\text{ lb}$ **Ans**

$\Sigma F_z = 0;\quad O_z - 80 = 0 \quad O_z = 80.0\text{ lb}$ **Ans**

$\Sigma M_x = 0;\quad (M_O)_x + 80(3) - 2[60\cos 45°(14)] = 0$

$(M_O)_x = 948\text{ lb}\cdot\text{ft}$ **Ans**

$\Sigma M_y = 0;\quad (M_O)_y + 60\sin 45°(14) - 60\sin 45°(14) = 0$

$(M_O)_y = 0$ **Ans**

$\Sigma M_z = 0;\quad (M_O)_y + 60\sin 45°(1) - 60\sin 45°(1) = 0$

$(M_O)_z = 0$ **Ans**

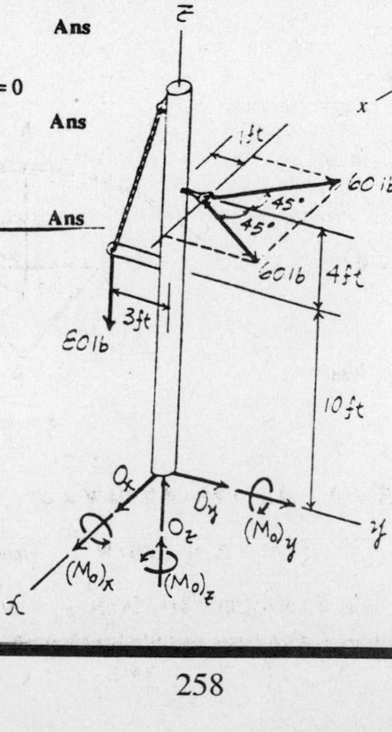

5-75. Determine the x, y, z components of reaction acting at the ball-and-socket joint A and properly aligned journal bearing B. Member DC acts as a short link.

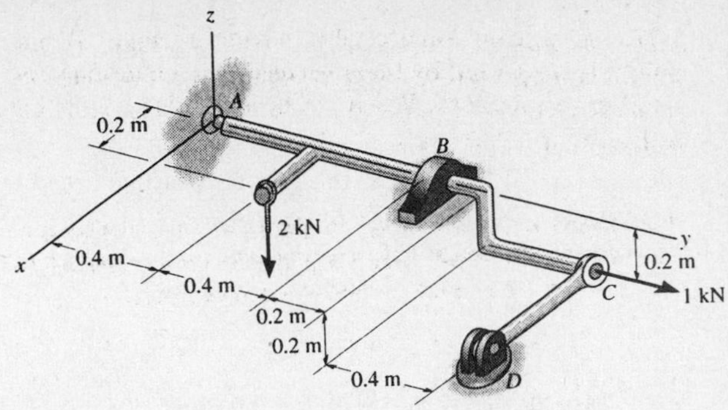

$\Sigma M_y = 0; \quad -F_{CD}(0.2) + 2(0.2) = 0; \quad F_{CD} = 2 \text{ kN}$ **Ans**

$\Sigma F_y = 0; \quad A_y + 1 = 0; \quad A_y = -1 \text{ kN}$ **Ans**

$\Sigma M_z = 0; \quad -B_x(0.8) - 2(1.4) = 0; \quad B_x = -3.50 \text{ kN}$ **Ans**

$\Sigma F_x = 0; \quad A_x - 3.50 + 2 = 0; \quad A_x = 1.50 \text{ kN}$ **Ans**

$\Sigma M_x = 0; \quad -2(0.4) + B_z(0.8) + 1(0.2) = 0; \quad B_z = 0.750 \text{ kN}$ **Ans**

$\Sigma F_z = 0; \quad A_z + 0.750 - 2 = 0; \quad A_z = 1.25 \text{ kN}$ **Ans**

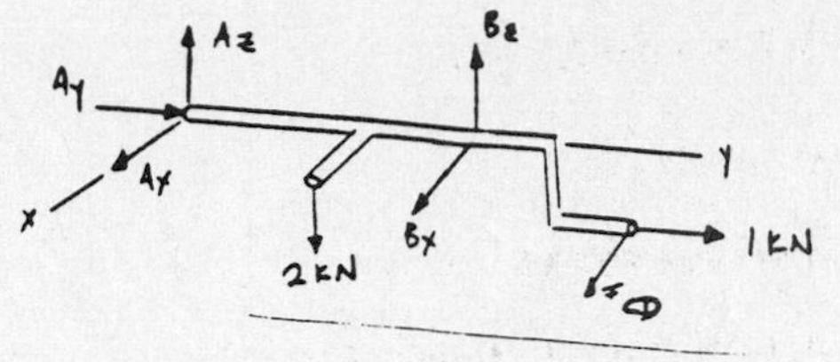

***5-76.** The 50-kg glass tabletop rests on the centrally located equilateral triangular frame which is supported by three legs. Determine the smallest vertical force P that, when applied to the glass, would cause it to lift or topple off the frame. Specify the force location r and the smallest angle θ, and also determine the vertical reactions of the legs on the floor when tipping is about to occur.

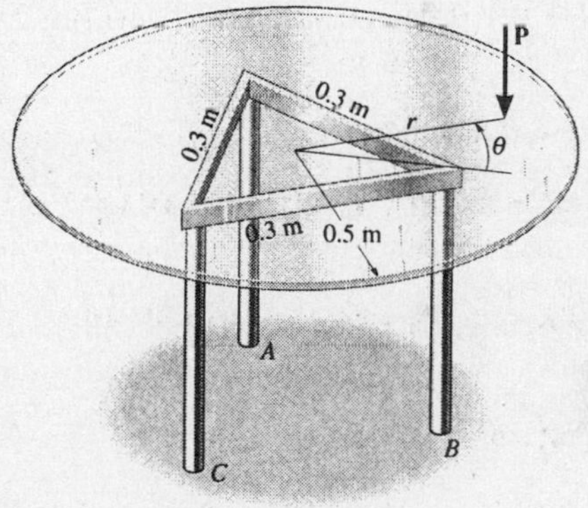

Rotation should occur about the AB axis since this axis is closest to the center of the table (W).

$d = 0.15 \tan 30° = 0.0866 \text{ m}$

Hence, put P at

$r = 0.5 \text{ m}$ **Ans**

$\theta = 60°$ **Ans**

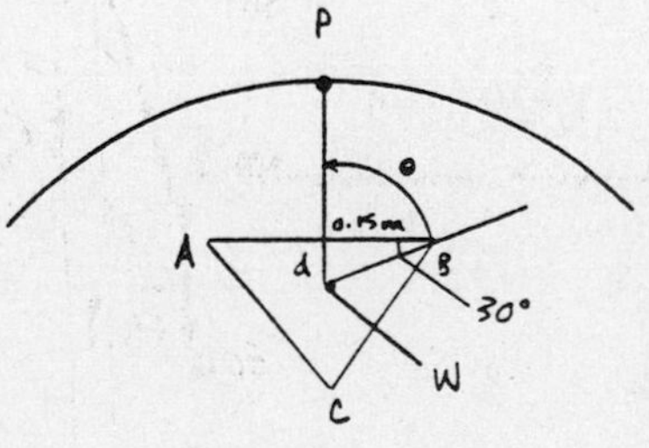

$\Sigma M_{AB} = 0; \quad W(0.0866) - P(0.5 - 0.15 \tan 30°) = 0$

$P = 0.20948\,W$

$= 0.20948(50)(9.81) = 103 \text{ N}$ **Ans**

This would require

$C_z = 0$ **Ans**

$\Sigma M_{a\text{-}a} = 0; \quad A_z(0.15) - B_z(0.15) = 0$

$A_z = B_z$

$\Sigma F_z = 0; \quad 2A_z - W - 0.20948\,W = 0$

$A_z = B_z = 0.6047\,W$ **Ans**

$A_z = B_z = 0.6047(50)(9.81) = 297 \text{ N}$ **Ans**

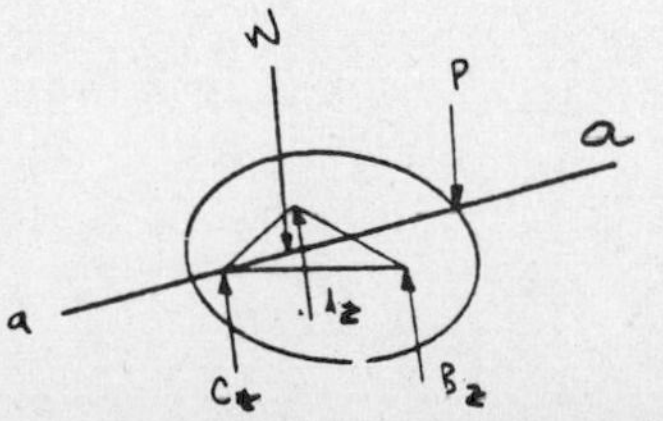

5-77. Both pulleys are fixed to the shaft and as the shaft turns with constant angular velocity, the power of pulley A is transmitted to pulley B. Determine the horizontal tension $\mathbf{T}$ in the belt on pulley B and the x, y, z components of reaction at the journal bearing C and thrust bearing D if $\theta = 0°$. The bearings are in proper alignment and exert only force reactions on the shaft.

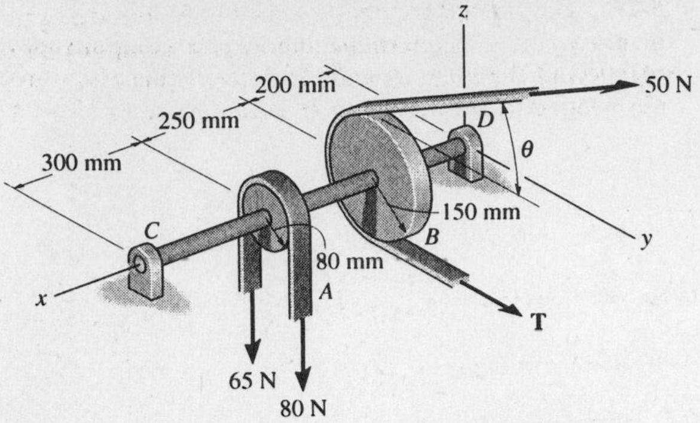

Equations of Equilibrium :

$\Sigma M_x = 0;\quad 65(0.08) - 80(0.08) + T(0.15) - 50(0.15) = 0$

$T = 58.0\ \text{N}$ **Ans**

$\Sigma M_y = 0;\quad (65 + 80)(0.45) - C_z(0.75) = 0$

$C_z = 87.0\ \text{N}$ **Ans**

$\Sigma M_z = 0;\quad (50 + 58.0)(0.2) - C_y(0.75) = 0$

$C_y = 28.8\ \text{N}$ **Ans**

$\Sigma F_x = 0;\quad D_x = 0$ **Ans**

$\Sigma F_y = 0;\quad D_y + 28.8 - 50 - 58.0 = 0$

$D_y = 79.2\ \text{N}$ **Ans**

$\Sigma F_z = 0;\quad D_z + 87.0 - 80 - 65 = 0$

$D_z = 58.0\ \text{N}$ **Ans**

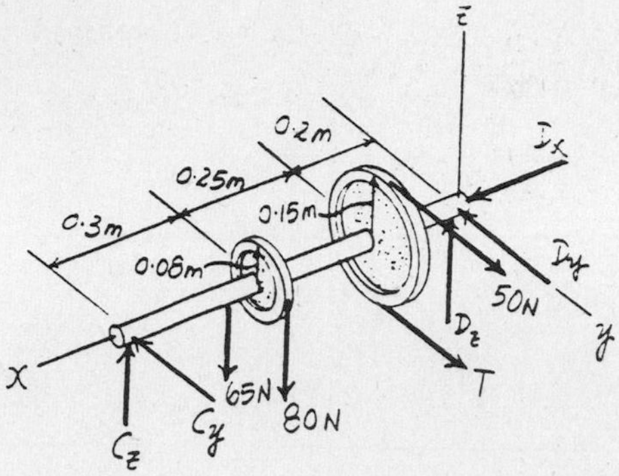

5-78. Both pulleys are fixed to the shaft and as the shaft turns with constant angular velocity, the power of pulley A is transmitted to pulley B. Determine the horizontal tension $\mathbf{T}$ in the belt on pulley B and the x, y, z components of reaction at the journal bearing C and thrust bearing D if $\theta = 45°$. The bearings are in proper alignment and exert only force reactions on the shaft.

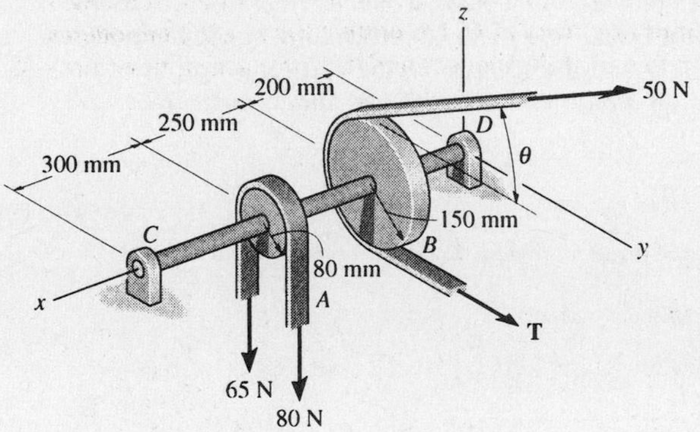

Equations of Equilibrium :

$\Sigma M_x = 0;\quad 65(0.08) - 80(0.08) + T(0.15) - 50(0.15) = 0$

$T = 58.0\ \text{N}$ **Ans**

$\Sigma M_y = 0;\quad (65 + 80)(0.45) - 50\sin 45°(0.2) - C_z(0.75) = 0$

$C_z = 77.57\ \text{N} = 77.6\ \text{N}$ **Ans**

$\Sigma M_z = 0;\quad 58.0(0.2) + 50\cos 45°(0.2) - C_y(0.75) = 0$

$C_y = 24.89\ \text{N} = 24.9\ \text{N}$ **Ans**

$\Sigma F_x = 0;\quad D_x = 0$ **Ans**

$\Sigma F_y = 0;\quad D_y + 24.89 - 50\cos 45° - 58.0 = 0$

$D_y = 68.5\ \text{N}$ **Ans**

$\Sigma F_z = 0;\quad D_z + 77.57 + 50\sin 45° - 80 - 65 = 0$

$D_z = 32.1\ \text{N}$ **Ans**

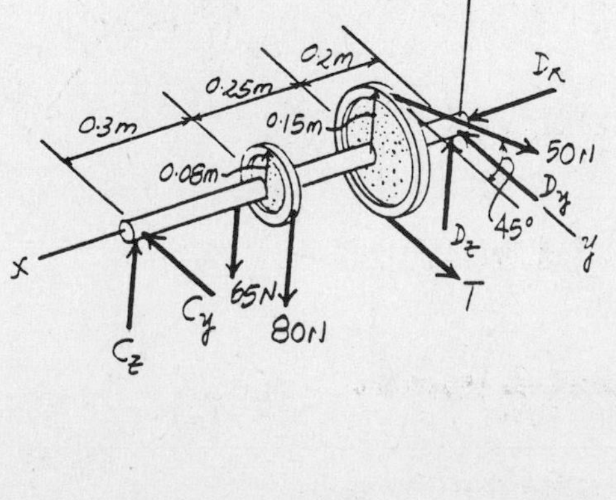

5-79. The circular door has a weight of 55 lb and a center of gravity at G. Determine the x, y, z components of reaction at the hinge A and the force acting along strut CB needed to hold the door in equilibrium. Set $\theta = 45°$.

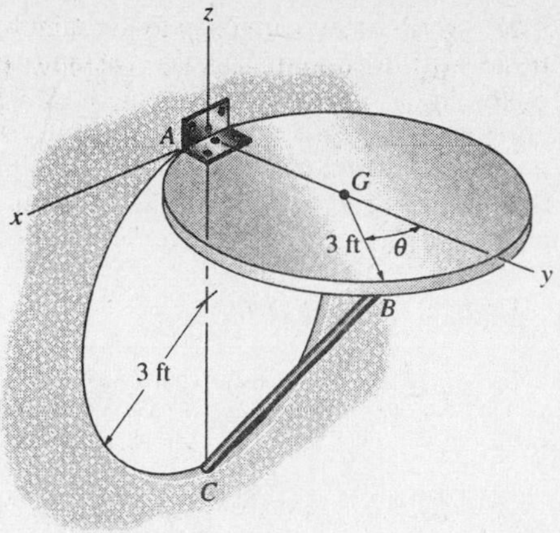

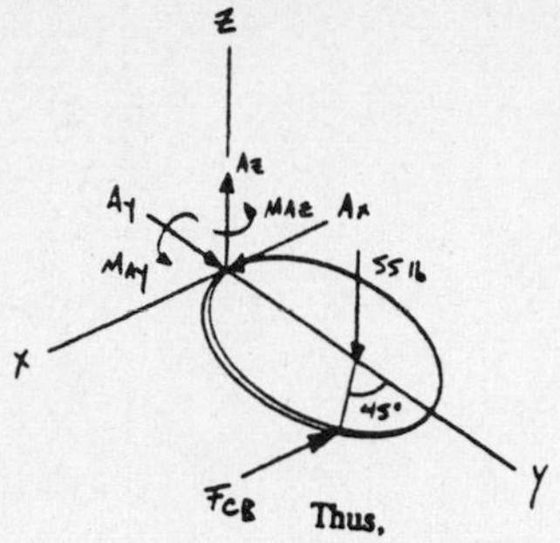

$$\mathbf{r}_{CB} = 3\sin 45°\,\mathbf{i} + (3 + 3\cos 45°)\,\mathbf{j} + 6\,\mathbf{k}$$

$$= \{2.121\,\mathbf{i} + 5.121\,\mathbf{j} + 6\,\mathbf{k}\}\text{ ft}$$

$$r_{CB} = \sqrt{(2.121)^2 + (5.121)^2 + (6)^2} = 8.169$$

$\Sigma F_x = 0;\quad A_x + \left(\dfrac{2.121}{8.169}\right)F_{CB} = 0$

$\Sigma F_y = 0;\quad A_y + \left(\dfrac{5.121}{8.169}\right)F_{CB} = 0$

$\Sigma F_z = 0;\quad A_z - 55 + \left(\dfrac{6}{8.169}\right)F_{CB} = 0$

$\Sigma M_x = 0;\quad -55(3) + \left(\dfrac{6}{8.169}\right)F_{CB}\,(3 + 3\cos 45°) = 0$

$F_{CB} = 43.9$ lb **Ans**

Thus,

$A_x = -11.4$ lb **Ans**

$A_y = -27.5$ lb **Ans**

$A_z = 22.8$ lb **Ans**

$\Sigma M_y = 0;\quad M_{Ay} - \left(\dfrac{6}{8.169}\right)(43.9)(3\sin 45°) = 0;\quad M_{Ay} = 68.3\text{ lb}\cdot\text{ft}$ **Ans**

$\Sigma M_z = 0;\quad M_{Az} - \left(\dfrac{2.121}{8.169}\right)(43.9)(3 + 3\cos 45°) + \left(\dfrac{5.121}{8.169}\right)(43.9)(3\sin 45°) = 0$

$M_{Az} = 0$ **Ans**

***5-80.** The circular door has a weight of 55 lb and a center of gravity at G. Determine the x, y, z components of reaction at the hinge A and the force acting along strut CB needed to hold the door in equilibrium. Set $\theta = 90°$.

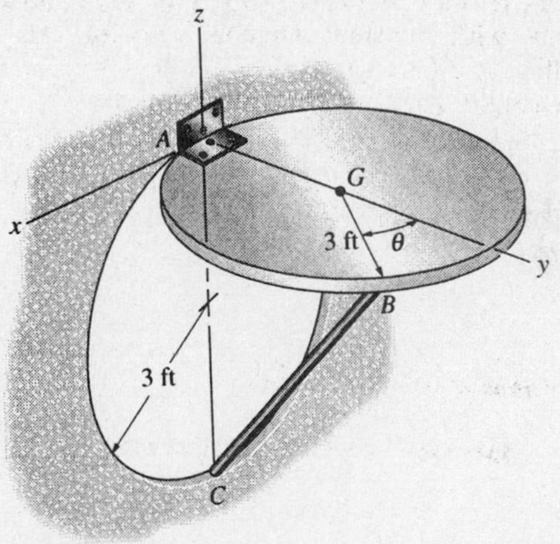

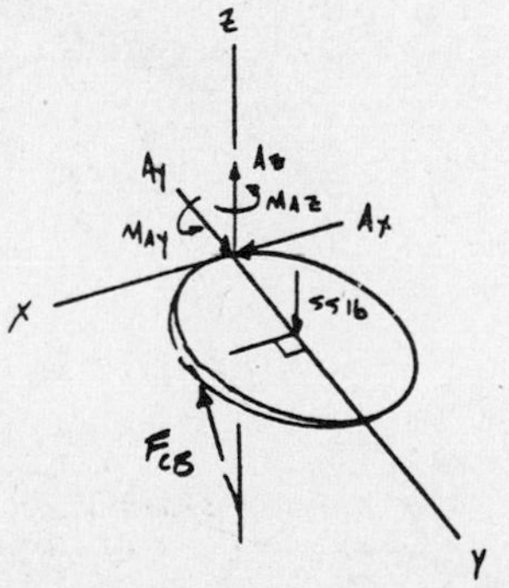

$$\mathbf{r}_{CB} = \{3\,\mathbf{i} + 3\,\mathbf{j} + 6\,\mathbf{k}\}\text{ ft}$$

$$r_{CB} = \sqrt{(3)^2 + (3)^2 + (6)^2} = \sqrt{54}$$

$\Sigma F_x = 0;\quad A_x + \left(\dfrac{3}{\sqrt{54}}\right)F_{CB} = 0$

$\Sigma F_y = 0;\quad A_y + \left(\dfrac{3}{\sqrt{54}}\right)F_{CB} = 0$

$\Sigma F_z = 0;\quad A_z - 55 + \left(\dfrac{6}{\sqrt{54}}\right)F_{CB} = 0$

$\Sigma M_x = 0;\quad -55(3) + \left(\dfrac{6}{\sqrt{54}}\right)F_{CB}(3) = 0$

$F_{CB} = 67.36 = 67.4$ lb **Ans**

Thus,

$A_x = -27.5$ lb **Ans**

$A_y = -27.5$ lb **Ans**

$A_z = 0$ **Ans**

$\Sigma M_y = 0;\quad M_{Ay} - \left(\dfrac{6}{\sqrt{54}}\right)(67.36)(3) = 0;\quad M_{Ay} = 165\text{ lb}\cdot\text{ft}$ **Ans**

$\Sigma M_z = 0;\quad M_{Az} - \left(\dfrac{3}{\sqrt{54}}\right)(67.36)(3) + \left(\dfrac{3}{\sqrt{54}}\right)(67.36)(3) = 0$

$M_{Az} = 0$ **Ans**

5-81. The windlass supports the 50-kg mass. Determine the horizontal force **P** needed to hold the handle in the position shown, and the x, y, z components of reaction at the ball-and-socket joint A and the smooth bearing B. The bearing at B is in proper alignment and exerts only a force reaction on the windlass.

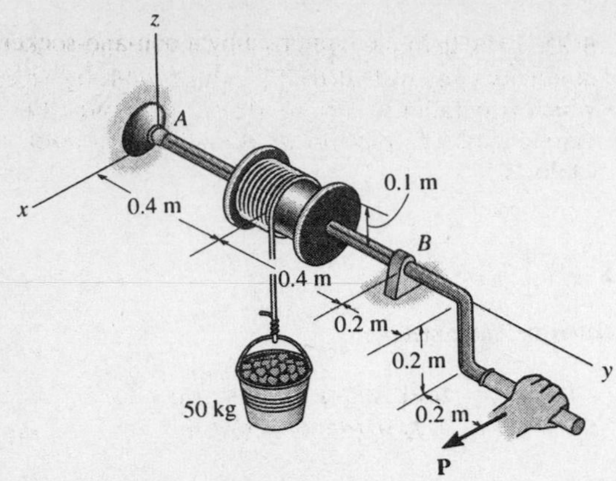

Equations of Equilibrium :

$\Sigma M_x = 0;\quad B_z(0.8) - 490.5(0.4) = 0$

$B_z = 245.25\text{ N} = 245\text{ N}$ **Ans**

$\Sigma M_y = 0;\quad 490.5(0.1) - P(0.2) = 0$

$P = 245.25\text{ N} = 245\text{ N}$ **Ans**

$\Sigma M_z = 0;\quad B_x(0.8) - 245.25(1.2) = 0$

$B_x = 367.875\text{ N} = 368\text{ N}$ **Ans**

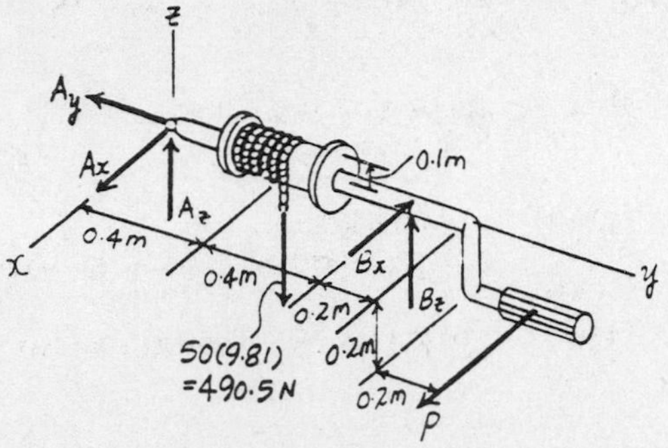

$\Sigma F_x = 0;\quad A_x + 245.25 - 367.875 = 0$

$A_x = 123\text{ N}$ **Ans**

$\Sigma F_y = 0;\quad A_y = 0$ **Ans**

$\Sigma F_z = 0;\quad A_z + 245.25 - 490.5 = 0$

$A_z = 245\text{ N}$ **Ans**

5-82. The shaft assembly is supported by two smooth journal bearings A and B and a short link DC. If a couple moment is applied to the shaft as shown, determine the components of force reaction at the bearings and the force in the link. The link lies in a plane parallel to the y–z plane and the bearings are properly aligned on the shaft.

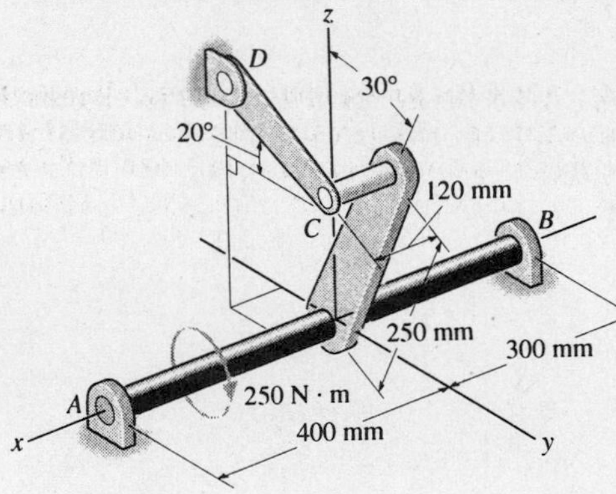

$\Sigma M_x = 0;\quad -250 + F_{CD}\cos 20°(0.25\cos 30°) + F_{CD}\sin 20°(0.25\sin 30°) = 0$

$F_{CD} = 1015.43\text{ N} = 1.02\text{ kN}$ **Ans**

$\Sigma(M_B)_y = 0;\quad -A_z(0.7) - 1015.43\sin 20°(0.42) = 0$

$A_z = -208.38 = -208\text{ N}$ **Ans**

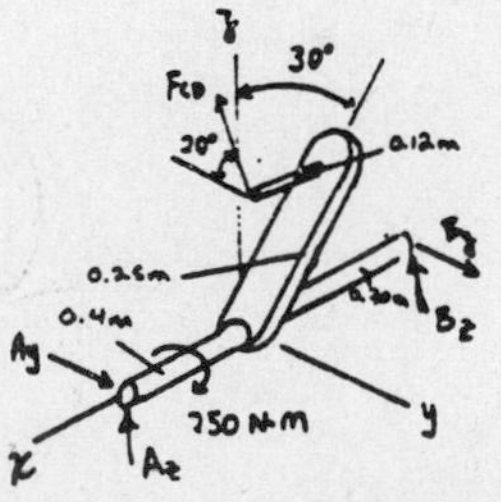

$\Sigma F_z = 0;\quad -208.38 + 1015.43\sin 20° + B_z = 0$

$B_z = -139\text{ N}$ **Ans**

$\Sigma(M_B)_z = 0;\quad A_y(0.7) - 1015.43\cos 20°(0.42) = 0$

$A_y = 572.51 = 573\text{ N}$ **Ans**

$\Sigma F_y = 0;\quad 572.51 - 1015.43\cos 20° + B_y = 0$

$B_y = 382\text{ N}$ **Ans**

5-83. The boom is supported by a ball-and-socket joint at A and a guy wire at B. If the 5-kN loads lie in a plane which is parallel to the x–y plane, determine the x, y, z components of reaction at A and the tension in the cable at B.

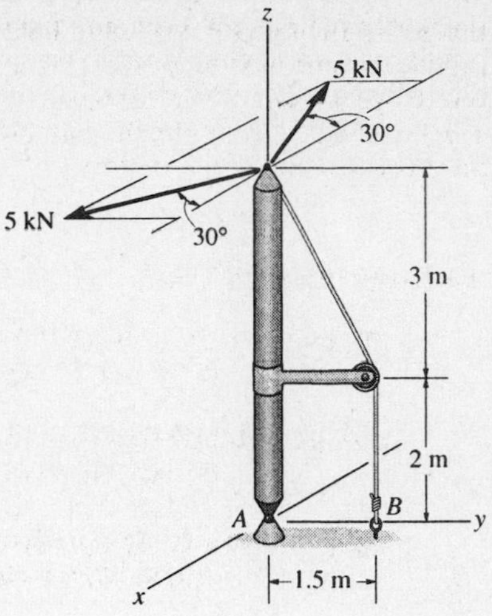

Equations of Equilibrium :

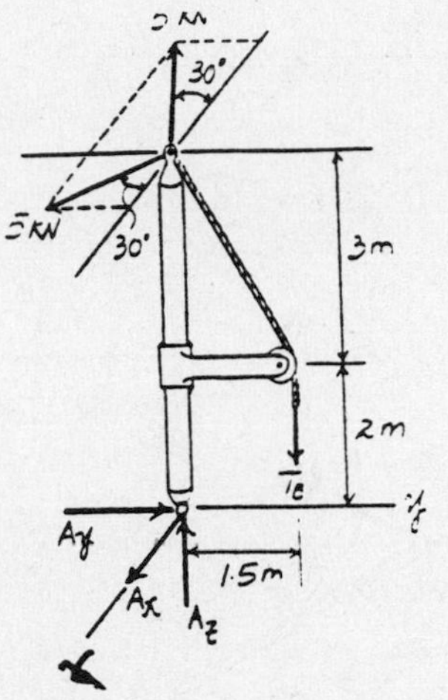

$\Sigma M_x = 0;\quad 2[5\sin 30°(5)] - T_B(1.5) = 0$

$T_B = 16.67\text{ kN} = 16.7\text{ kN}$ **Ans**

$\Sigma M_y = 0;\quad 5\cos 30°(5) - 5\cos 30°(5) = 0$ ***(Statisfied!)***

$\Sigma F_x = 0;\quad A_x + 5\cos 30° - 5\cos 30° = 0$

$A_x = 0$ **Ans**

$\Sigma F_y = 0;\quad A_y - 2(5\sin 30°) = 0$

$A_y = 5.00\text{ kN}$ **Ans**

$\Sigma F_z = 0;\quad A_z - 16.67 = 0 \quad A_z = 16.7\text{ kN}$ **Ans**

***5-84.** A ball has a mass of $m = 2.5$ kg. If it rests on the surface of the smooth arc, determine the normal force per unit length along the ring of contact C which the support exerts on the ball. Set $r_1 = 75$ mm and $r_2 = 100$ mm.

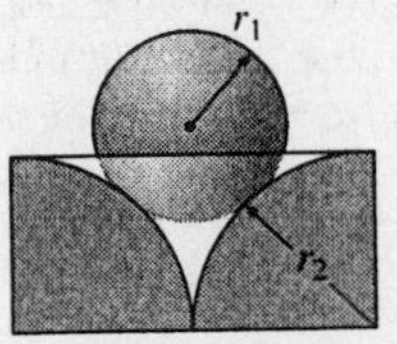

Side view

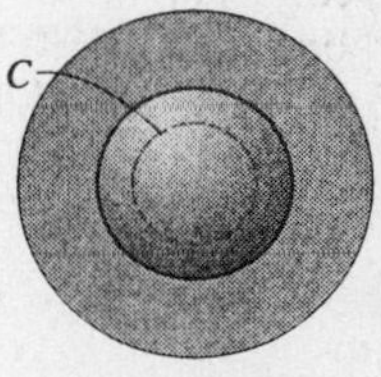

Top view

Geometry :

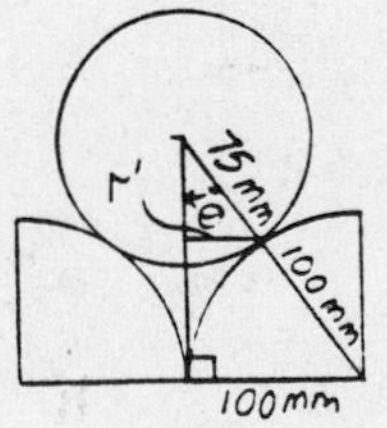

$$\theta = \sin^{-1}\left(\frac{100}{175}\right) = 34.85°$$

$$r' = 75\sin 34.85° = 42.86\text{ mm}$$

Equations of Equilibrium :

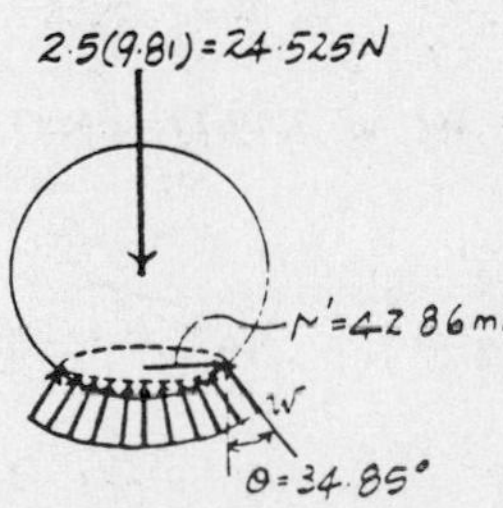

$\Sigma F_z = 0;\quad w[2\pi(0.04286)]\cos 34.85° - 24.525 = 0$

$w = 111\text{ N/m}$ **Ans**

Note : Others equilibrium requirements are statisfied due to symmetry.

5-85. Rod AB is supported by a ball-and-socket joint at A and a cable at B. Determine the x, y, z components of reaction at these supports if the rod is subjected to a 50-lb vertical force as shown.

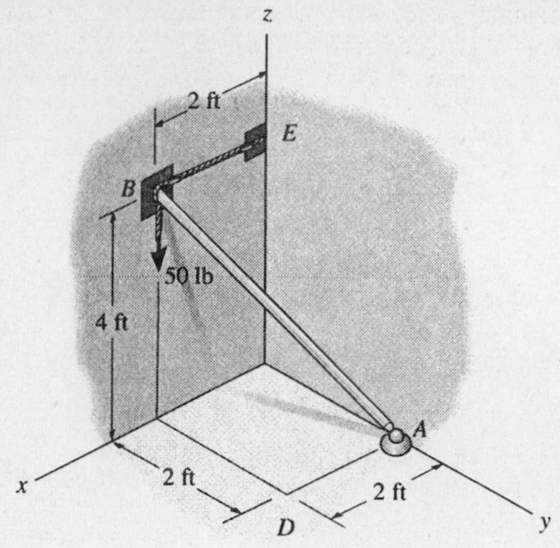

$\Sigma F_x = 0;\quad -T_B + A_x = 0$

$\Sigma F_y = 0;\quad A_y + B_y = 0$

$\Sigma F_z = 0;\quad -50 + A_z = 0$

$\Sigma M_{Ax} = 0;\quad 50(2) - B_y(4) = 0$

$\Sigma M_{Ay} = 0;\quad 50(2) - T_B(4) = 0$

$\Sigma M_{Az} = 0;\quad B_y(2) - T_B(2) = 0$

Solving,

$T_B = 25\text{ lb}$ **Ans**

$A_x = 25\text{ lb}$ **Ans**

$A_y = -25\text{ lb}$ **Ans**

$A_z = 50\text{ lb}$ **Ans**

$B_y = 25\text{ lb}$ **Ans**

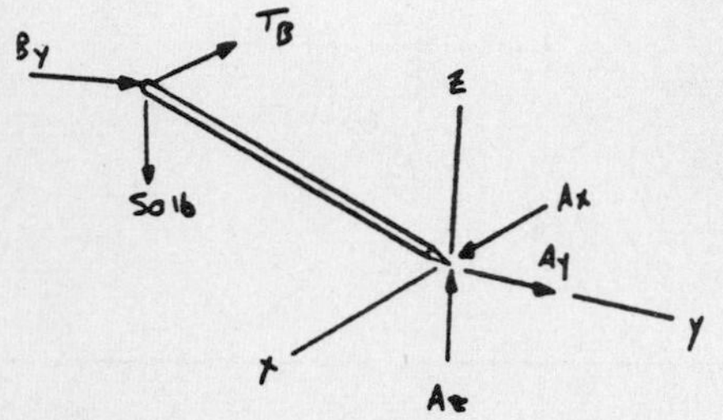

5-86. A vertical force of 50 lb acts on the crankshaft. Determine the horizontal equilibrium force **P** that must be applied to the handle and the x, y, z components of reaction at the journal bearing A and thrust bearing B. The bearings are properly aligned and exert only force reactions on the shaft.

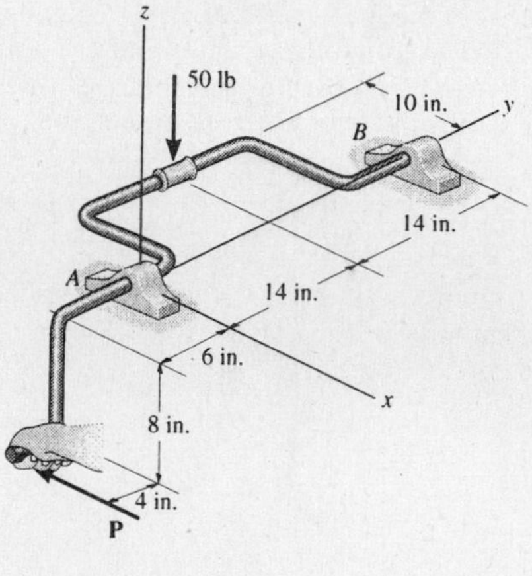

Equations of Equilibrium :

$\Sigma M_x = 0;\quad B_z(28) - 50(14) = 0\quad B_z = 25.0\text{ lb}$ **Ans**

$\Sigma M_y = 0;\quad P(8) - 50(10) = 0\quad P = 62.5\text{ lb}$ **Ans**

$\Sigma M_z = 0;\quad B_x(28) - 62.5(10) = 0$
$B_x = 22.32\text{ lb} = 22.3\text{ lb}$ **Ans**

$\Sigma F_x = 0;\quad 62.5 + 22.32 - A_x = 0\quad A_x = 84.8\text{ lb}$ **Ans**

$\Sigma F_y = 0;\quad B_y = 0$ **Ans**

$\Sigma F_z = 0;\quad A_z + 25.0 - 50 = 0\quad A_z = 25.0\text{ lb}$ **Ans**

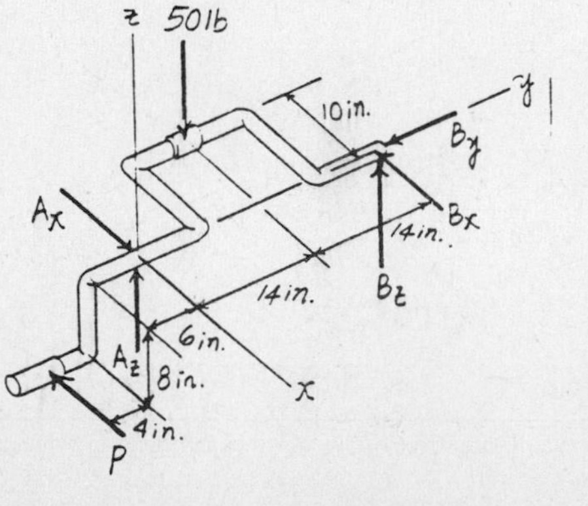

5-87. Member AB is supported at B by a cable and at A by a smooth fixed *square* rod which fits loosely through the square hole of the collar. If $\mathbf{F} = \{20\mathbf{i} - 40\mathbf{j} - 75\mathbf{k}\}$ lb, determine the x, y, z components of reaction at A and the tension in the cable.

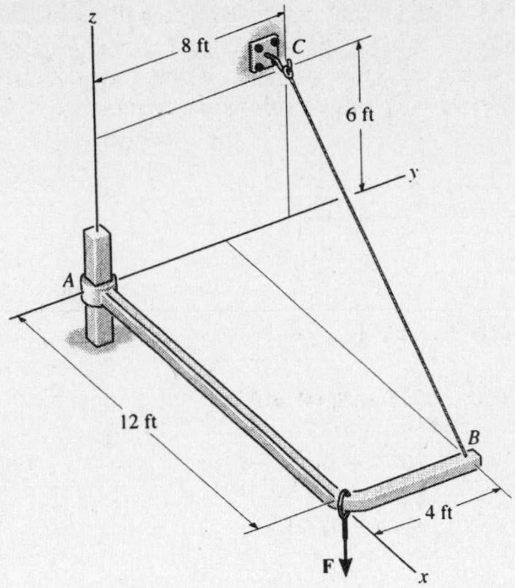

$$\mathbf{F}_{BC} = -\frac{12}{14}F_{BC}\mathbf{i} + \frac{4}{14}F_{BC}\mathbf{j} + \frac{6}{14}F_{BC}\mathbf{k}$$

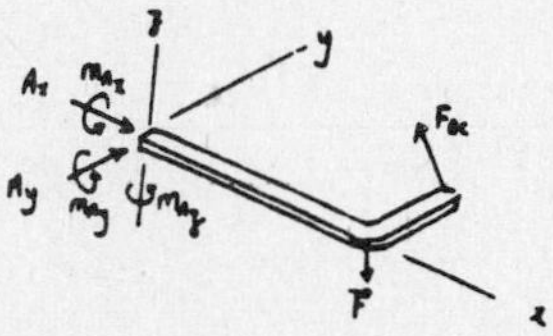

$\Sigma F_x = 0;\quad A_x + 20 - \frac{12}{14}F_{BC} = 0$

$\Sigma F_y = 0;\quad A_y - 40 + \frac{4}{14}F_{BC} = 0$

$\Sigma F_z = 0;\quad -75 + \frac{6}{14}F_{BC} = 0$

$F_{BC} = 175$ lb **Ans**

$A_x = 130$ lb **Ans**

$A_y = -10$ lb **Ans**

$\Sigma M_x = 0;\quad \frac{6}{14}(175)(4) + M_{Ax} = 0$

$M_{Ax} = -300$ lb·ft **Ans**

$\Sigma M_y = 0;\quad 75(12) - \frac{6}{14}(175)(12) + M_{Ay} = 0$

$M_{Ay} = 0$ **Ans**

$\Sigma M_z = 0;\quad -40(12) + \frac{12}{14}(175)(4) + \frac{4}{14}(175)(12) + M_{Az} = 0$

$M_{Az} = -720$ lb·ft **Ans**

***5-88.** Member AB is supported at B by a cable and at A by a smooth fixed *square* rod which fits loosely through the square hole of the collar. Determine the tension in cable BC if the force $\mathbf{F} = \{-45\mathbf{k}\}$ lb.

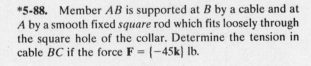

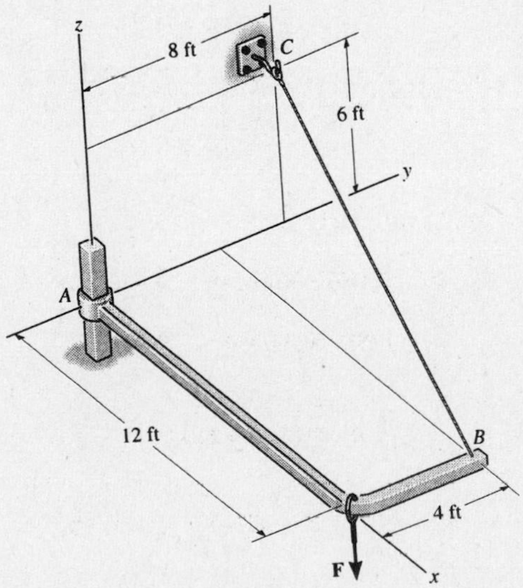

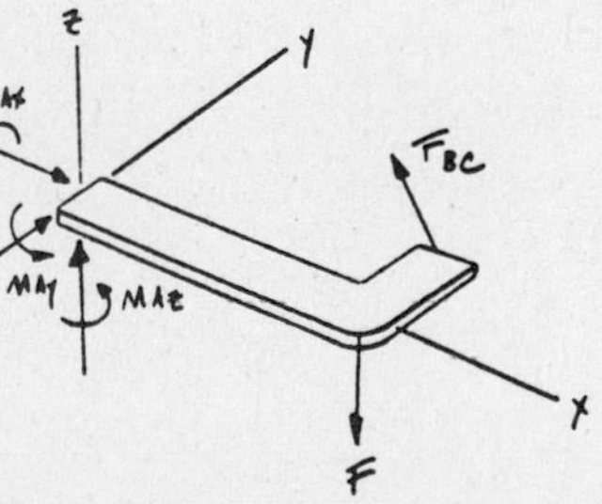

$$\mathbf{F}_{BC} = -\frac{12}{14}F_{BC}\mathbf{i} + \frac{4}{14}F_{BC}\mathbf{j} + \frac{6}{14}F_{BC}\mathbf{k}$$

$\Sigma F_z = 0;\quad \frac{6}{14}F_{BC} - 45 = 0$

$F_{BC} = 105$ lb **Ans**

5-89. Determine the force acting along the short links at joints A, B, D, and F of the space truss.

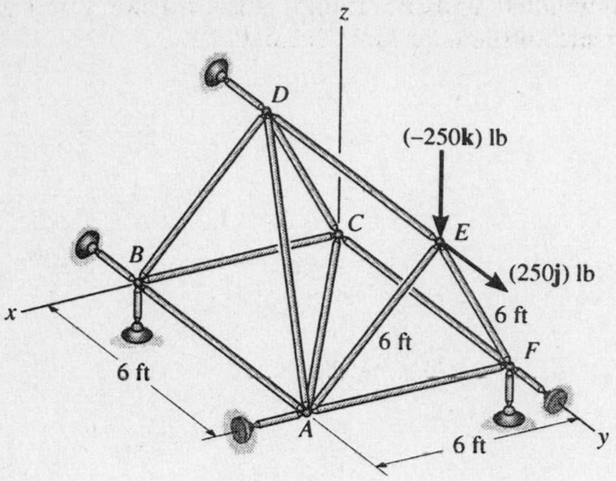

Equations of Equilibrium :

$\Sigma F_x = 0;\quad F_A = 0$ **Ans**

$\Sigma M_y = 0;\quad 250(3) - (F_B)_z(6) = 0 \quad (F_B)_z = 125 \text{ lb}$ **Ans**

$\Sigma F_z = 0;\quad (F_F)_z + 125 - 250 = 0 \quad (F_F)_z = 125 \text{ lb}$ **Ans**

$\Sigma M_x = 0;\quad F_D(5.196) + 125(6) - 250(6) - 250(5.196) = 0$

$F_D = 394.34 \text{ lb} = 394 \text{ lb}$ **Ans**

$\Sigma M_z = 0;\quad (F_B)_y(6) - 394.34(3) + 250(3) = 0$

$(F_B)_y = 72.17 \text{ lb} = 72.2 \text{ lb}$ **Ans**

$\Sigma F_y = 0;\quad (F_F)_y + 72.17 - 394.34 + 250 = 0$

$(F_F)_y = 72.2 \text{ lb}$ **Ans**

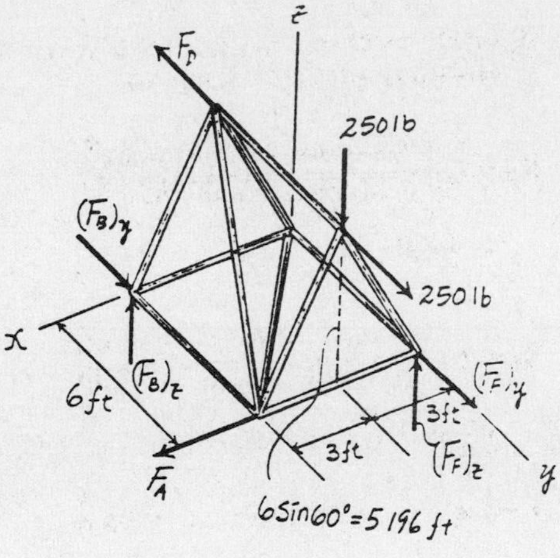

5-90. The pole is subjected to the two forces shown. Determine the components of reaction at A assuming it to be a ball-and-socket joint. Also, compute the tension in each of the guy wires, BC and ED.

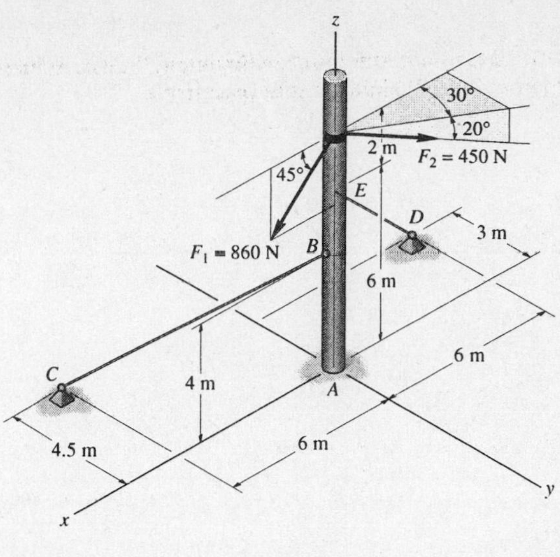

Force Vector and Position Vectors :

$$\mathbf{F}_A = A_x\mathbf{i} + A_y\mathbf{j} + A_z\mathbf{k}$$

$$\mathbf{F}_1 = 860\{\cos 45°\mathbf{i} - \sin 45°\mathbf{k}\}\ \text{N} = \{608.11\mathbf{i} - 608.11\mathbf{k}\}\ \text{N}$$

$$\mathbf{F}_2 = 450\{-\cos 20°\cos 30°\mathbf{i} + \cos 20°\sin 30°\mathbf{k} - \sin 20°\mathbf{k}\}\ \text{N}$$
$$= \{-366.21\mathbf{i} + 211.43\mathbf{j} - 153.91\mathbf{k}\}\ \text{N}$$

$$\mathbf{F}_{ED} = F_{ED}\left[\frac{(-6-0)\mathbf{i} + (-3-0)\mathbf{j} + (0-6)\mathbf{k}}{\sqrt{(-6-0)^2 + (-3-0)^2 + (0-6)^2}}\right]$$
$$= -\frac{2}{3}F_{ED}\mathbf{i} - \frac{1}{3}F_{ED}\mathbf{j} - \frac{2}{3}F_{ED}\mathbf{k}$$

$$\mathbf{F}_{BC} = F_{BC}\left[\frac{(6-0)\mathbf{i} + (-4.5-0)\mathbf{j} + (0-4)\mathbf{k}}{\sqrt{(6-0)^2 + (-4.5-0)^2 + (0-4)^2}}\right]$$
$$= \frac{12}{17}F_{BC}\mathbf{i} - \frac{9}{17}F_{BC}\mathbf{j} - \frac{8}{17}F_{BC}\mathbf{k}$$

$\mathbf{r}_1 = \{4\mathbf{k}\}$ m $\mathbf{r}_2 = \{8\mathbf{k}\}$ m $\mathbf{r}_3 = \{6\mathbf{k}\}$ m

Equations of Equilibrium : Force equilibrium requires

$$\Sigma\mathbf{F} = 0; \quad \mathbf{F}_A + \mathbf{F}_1 + \mathbf{F}_2 + \mathbf{F}_{ED} + \mathbf{F}_{BC} = \mathbf{0}$$

$$\left(A_x + 608.11 - 366.21 - \frac{2}{3}F_{ED} + \frac{12}{17}F_{BC}\right)\mathbf{i} + \left(A_y + 211.43 - \frac{1}{3}F_{ED} - \frac{9}{17}F_{BC}\right)\mathbf{j} + \left(A_z - 608.11 - 153.91 - \frac{2}{3}F_{ED} - \frac{8}{17}F_{BC}\right)\mathbf{k} = \mathbf{0}$$

Equating **i**, **j** and **k** components, we have

$$\Sigma F_x = 0; \quad A_x + 608.11 - 366.21 - \frac{2}{3}F_{ED} + \frac{12}{17}F_{BC} = 0 \qquad [1]$$

$$\Sigma F_y = 0; \quad A_y + 211.43 - \frac{1}{3}F_{ED} - \frac{9}{17}F_{BC} = 0 \qquad [2]$$

$$\Sigma F_z = 0; \quad A_z - 608.11 - 153.91 - \frac{2}{3}F_{ED} - \frac{8}{17}F_{BC} = 0 \qquad [3]$$

Moment equilibrium requires

$$\Sigma\mathbf{M}_A = \mathbf{0}; \quad \mathbf{r}_1 \times \mathbf{F}_{BC} + \mathbf{r}_2 \times (\mathbf{F}_1 + \mathbf{F}_2) + \mathbf{r}_3 \times \mathbf{F}_{ED} = \mathbf{0}$$

$$4\mathbf{k} \times \left(\frac{12}{17}F_{BC}\mathbf{i} - \frac{9}{17}F_{BC}\mathbf{j} - \frac{8}{17}F_{BC}\mathbf{k}\right) + 8\mathbf{k} \times (241.90\mathbf{i} + 211.43\mathbf{j} - 762.02\mathbf{k}) + 6\mathbf{k} \times \left(-\frac{2}{3}F_{ED}\mathbf{i} - \frac{1}{3}F_{ED}\mathbf{j} - \frac{2}{3}F_{ED}\mathbf{k}\right) = \mathbf{0}$$

Equating **i**, **j** and **k** components, we have

$$\Sigma M_x = 0; \quad \frac{36}{17}F_{BC} + 2F_{ED} - 1691.45 = 0 \qquad [4]$$

$$\Sigma M_y = 0; \quad \frac{48}{17}F_{BC} - 4F_{ED} + 1935.22 = 0 \qquad [5]$$

Solving Eqs. [4] and [5] yields

$F_{BC} = 205.09\ \text{N} = 205\ \text{N}$ $F_{ED} = 628.57\ \text{N} = 629\ \text{N}$ **Ans**

Substituting the results into Eqs. [1], [2] and [3] yields

$A_x = 32.4\ \text{N}$ $A_y = 107\ \text{N}$ $A_z = 1277.58\ \text{N} = 1.28\ \text{kN}$ **Ans**

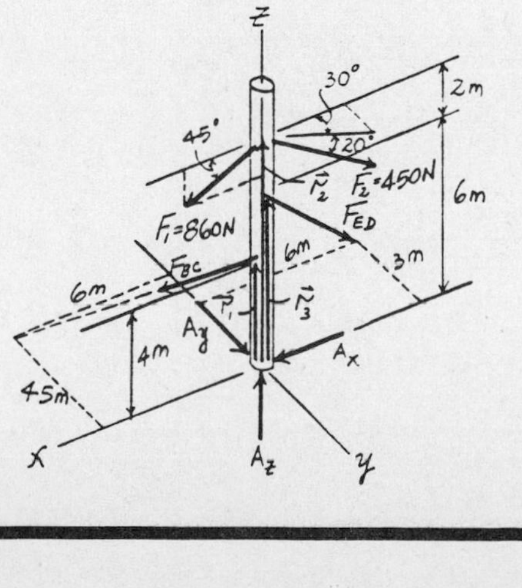

5-91. The forked rod is supported by a collar at A, a thrust bearing at B, and a cable CD. Determine the tension within cable CD and the x, y, z components of reaction at supports A and B due to the loading shown. The supports at A and B are in proper alignment and exert only force reactions on the rod.

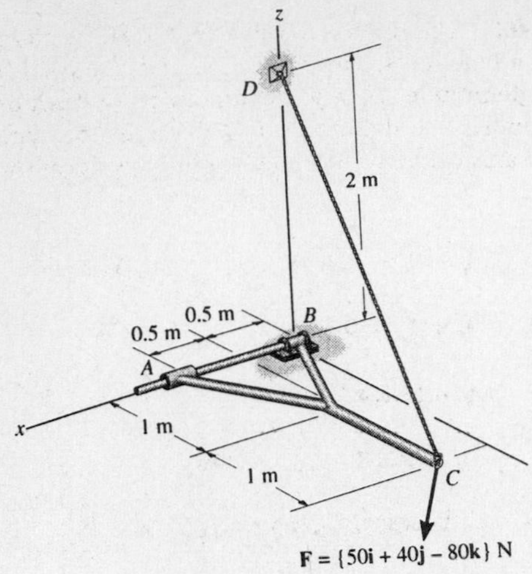

Force Vector and Position Vectors :

$$\mathbf{F}_A = A_y\mathbf{j} + A_z\mathbf{k} \qquad \mathbf{F}_B = B_x\mathbf{i} + B_y\mathbf{j} + B_z\mathbf{k} \qquad \mathbf{F} = \{50\mathbf{i} + 40\mathbf{j} - 80\mathbf{k}\}\ \text{N}$$

$$\mathbf{F}_{CD} = F_{CD}\left[\frac{(0-0.5)\mathbf{i} + (0-2)\mathbf{j} + (2-0)\mathbf{k}}{\sqrt{(0-0.5)^2 + (0-2)^2 + (2-0)^2}}\right]$$
$$= -0.1741F_{CD}\mathbf{i} - 0.6963F_{CD}\mathbf{j} + 0.6963F_{CD}\mathbf{k}$$

$$\mathbf{r}_1 = \{0.5\mathbf{i} + 2\mathbf{j}\}\ \text{m} \qquad \mathbf{r}_2 = \{1\mathbf{i}\}\ \text{m}$$

Equations of Equilibrium : Force equilibrium requires

$$\Sigma\mathbf{F} = \mathbf{0}; \qquad \mathbf{F}_A + \mathbf{F}_B + \mathbf{F} + \mathbf{F}_{CD} = \mathbf{0}$$

$$(B_x + 50 - 0.1741F_{CD})\mathbf{i} + (A_y + B_y + 40 - 0.6963F_{CD})\mathbf{j} + (A_z + B_z - 80 + 0.6963F_{CD})\mathbf{k} = \mathbf{0}$$

Equating **i**, **j** and **k** components, we have

$$\Sigma F_x = 0; \qquad B_x + 50 - 0.1741F_{CD} = 0 \qquad [1]$$
$$\Sigma F_y = 0; \qquad A_y + B_y + 40 - 0.6963F_{CD} = 0 \qquad [2]$$
$$\Sigma F_z = 0; \qquad A_z + B_z - 80 + 0.6963F_{CD} = 0 \qquad [3]$$

Moment equilibrium requires

$$\Sigma\mathbf{M}_B = \mathbf{0}; \qquad \mathbf{r}_1 \times (\mathbf{F} + \mathbf{F}_{CD}) + \mathbf{r}_2 \times \mathbf{F}_A = \mathbf{0}$$

$$(0.5\mathbf{i} + 2\mathbf{j}) \times [(50 - 0.1741F_{CD})\mathbf{i} + (40 - 0.6963F_{CD})\mathbf{j} + (0.6963F_{CD} - 80)\mathbf{k}] + 1\mathbf{i} \times (A_y\mathbf{j} + A_z\mathbf{k}) = \mathbf{0}$$

Equating **i**, **j** and **k** components, we have

$$\Sigma M_x = 0; \qquad 1.3926F_{CD} - 160 = 0 \qquad [4]$$
$$\Sigma M_y = 0; \qquad -(0.3482F_{CD} - 40) - A_z = 0 \qquad [5]$$
$$\Sigma M_z = 0; \qquad A_y - 80.0 = 0 \qquad [6]$$

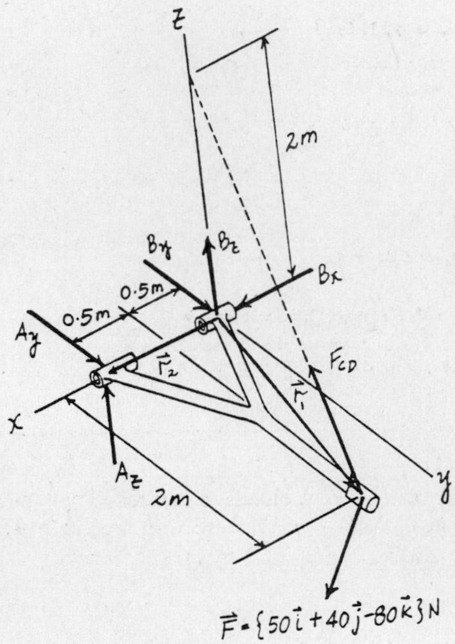

Solving Eqs. [1], [2], [3], [4], [5] and [6] yields

$F_{CD} = 115$ N $\quad A_y = 80.0$ N $\quad A_z = 0$ **Ans**

$B_x = -30.0$ N $\quad B_y = -40.0$ N $\quad B_z = 0$ **Ans**

Negative signs indicate that the reaction components act in the opposite sense to those shown on FBD.

***5-92.** The rod has a weight of 6 lb/ft. If it is supported by a ball-and-socket joint at C and a journal bearing at D, determine the x, y, z components of reaction at these supports and the moment M that must be applied along the axis of the rod to hold it in the position shown.

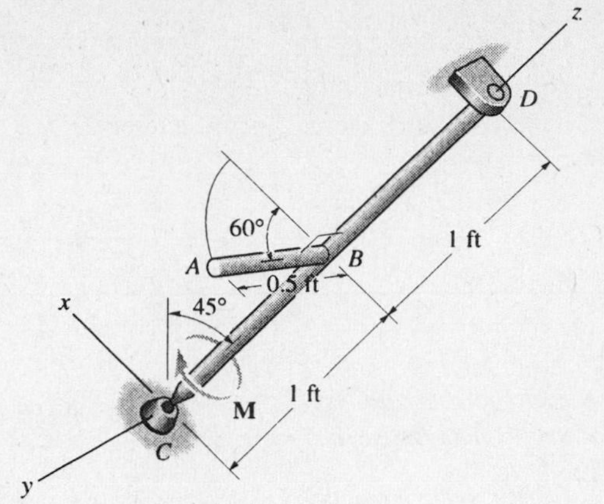

$\Sigma F_x = 0;\quad A_x + D_x - 15\sin 45° = 0 \qquad (1)$

$\Sigma F_y = 0;\quad A_y + D_y = 0 \qquad (2)$

$\Sigma F_z = 0;\quad A_z - 15\cos 45° = 0$

$A_z = 10.6 \text{ lb}$ **Ans**

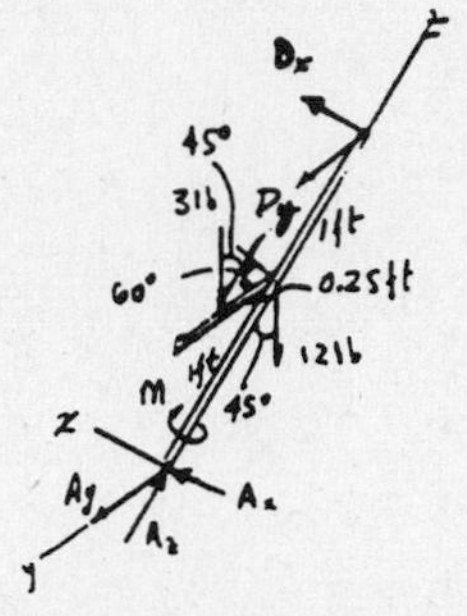

$\Sigma M_x = 0;\quad -3\cos 45°(0.25\sin 60°) - D_y(2) = 0$

$D_y = -0.230 \text{ lb}$ **Ans**

From Eq. (2);

$A_y = 0.230 \text{ lb}$ **Ans**

$\Sigma M_y = 0;\quad -(12\sin 45°)(1) - (3\sin 45°)(1) + (3\cos 45°)(0.25\cos 60°) + D_x(2) = 0$

$D_x = 5.17 \text{ lb}$ **Ans**

From Eq. (1);

$A_x = 5.44 \text{ lb}$ **Ans**

$\Sigma M_z = 0;\quad -M + (3\sin 45°)(0.25\sin 60°) = 0$

$M = 0.459 \text{ lb}\cdot\text{ft}$ **Ans**

5-93. Determine the horizontal and vertical components of reaction at the pin A and the force in the cable BC. Neglect the thickness of the members.

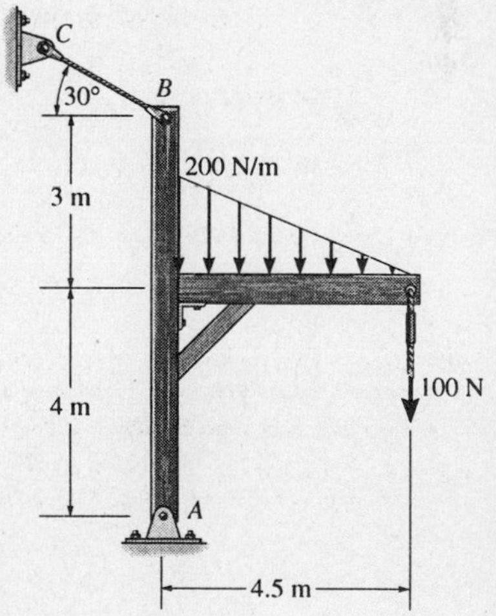

$\circlearrowleft + \Sigma M_A = 0;\quad F_{BC}\cos 30°(7) - 450(1.5) - 100(4.5) = 0$

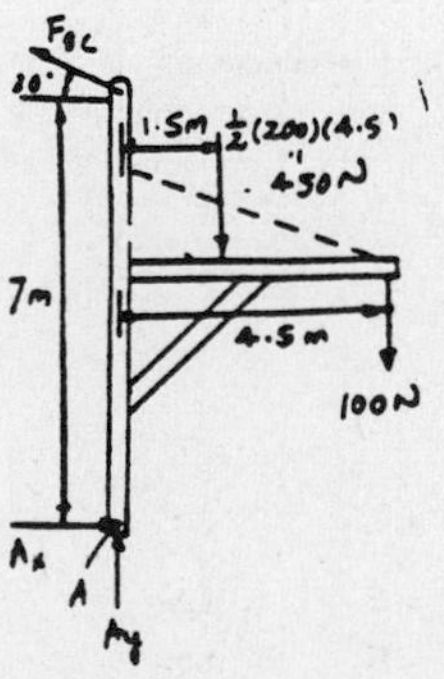

$F_{BC} = 185.58 \text{ N} = 186 \text{ N}$ **Ans**

$\xrightarrow{+} \Sigma F_x = 0;\quad A_x - 185.58\cos 30° = 0 \qquad A_x = 161 \text{ N}$ **Ans**

$+\uparrow \Sigma F_y = 0;\quad A_y + 185.58\sin 30° - 450 - 100 = 0$

$A_y = 457 \text{ N}$ **Ans**

5-94. Determine the horizontal and vertical components of reaction at the pin A and the reaction at the roller B required to support the truss. Set $F = 600$ N.

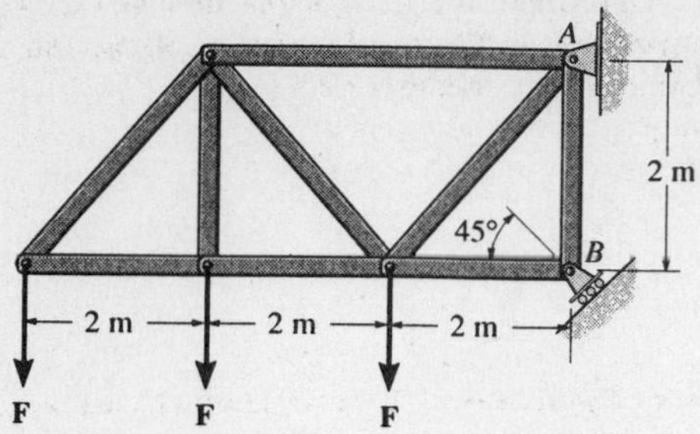

Equations of Equilibrium : The normal reaction N_B can be obtained directly by summing moments about point A.

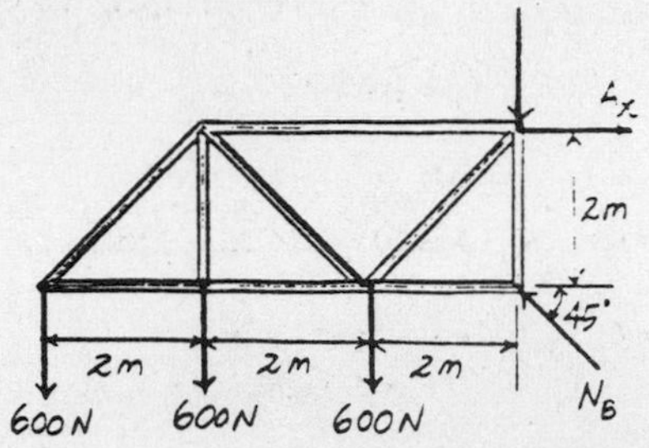

$$\curvearrowleft + \Sigma M_A = 0; \quad 600(6) + 600(4) + 600(2) - N_B \cos 45°(2) = 0$$

$$N_B = 5091.17 \text{ N} = 5.09 \text{ kN} \quad \textbf{Ans}$$

$$\overset{+}{\rightarrow} \Sigma F_x = 0; \quad A_x - 5091.17\cos 45° = 0$$

$$A_x = 3600 \text{ N} = 3.60 \text{ kN} \quad \textbf{Ans}$$

$$+\uparrow \Sigma F_y = 0; \quad 5091.17\sin 45° - 3(600) - A_y = 0$$

$$A_y = 1800 \text{ N} = 1.80 \text{ kN} \quad \textbf{Ans}$$

5-95. If the roller at B can sustain a maximum load of 3 kN, determine the largest magnitude of each of the three forces **F** that can be supported by the truss.

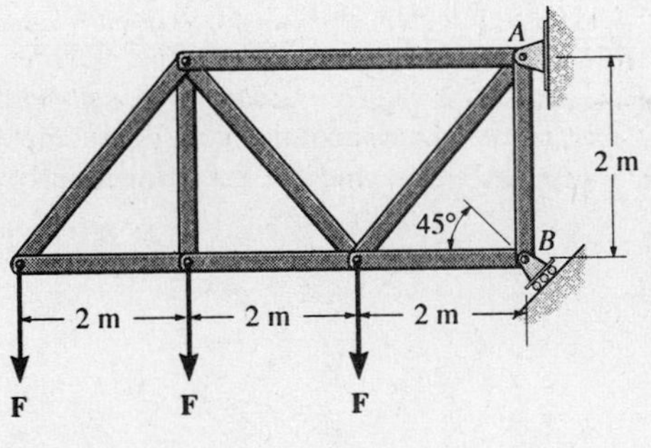

Equations of Equilibrium : The unknowns A_x and A_y can be eliminated by summing moments about point A.

$$\curvearrowleft + \Sigma M_A = 0; \quad F(6) + F(4) + F(2) - 3\cos 45°(2) = 0$$

$$F = 0.3536 \text{ kN} = 354\text{N} \quad \textbf{Ans}$$

*5-96. Determine the normal reaction at the roller A and horizontal and vertical components at pin B for equilibrium of the member.

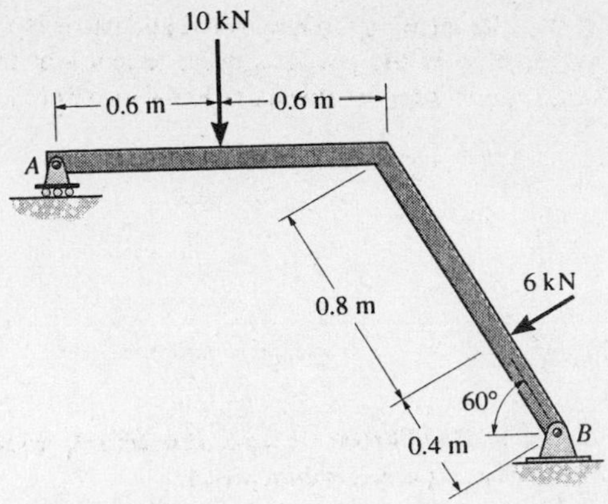

Equations of Equilibrium : The normal reaction N_A can be obtained directly by summing moments about point B.

$$\circlearrowleft + \Sigma M_A = 0; \quad 10(0.6+1.2\cos 60°)+6(0.4) - N_A(1.2+1.2\cos 60°) = 0$$

$$N_A = 8.00 \text{ kN} \qquad \textbf{Ans}$$

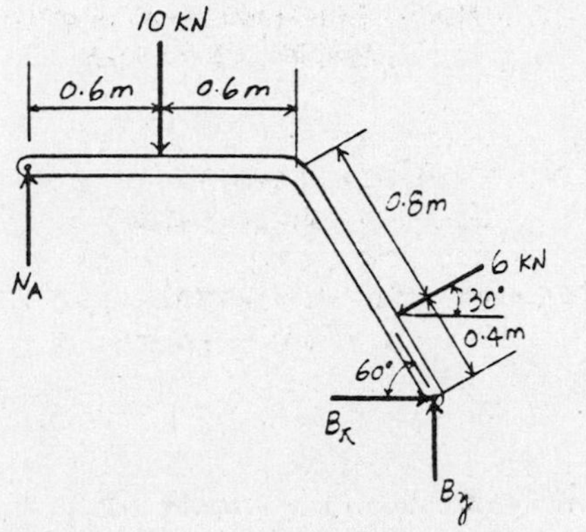

$$\xrightarrow{+} \Sigma F_x = 0; \quad B_x - 6\cos 30° = 0 \quad B_x = 5.20 \text{ kN} \qquad \textbf{Ans}$$

$$+\uparrow \Sigma F_y = 0; \quad B_y + 8.00 - 6\sin 30° - 10 = 0$$

$$B_y = 5.00 \text{ kN} \qquad \textbf{Ans}$$

5-97. The symmetrical shelf is subjected to a uniform load of 4 kPa. Support is provided by a bolt (or pin) located at each end A and A' and by the symmetrical brace arms, which bear against the smooth wall on both sides at B and B'. Determine the force resisted by each bolt at the wall and the normal force at B for equilibrium.

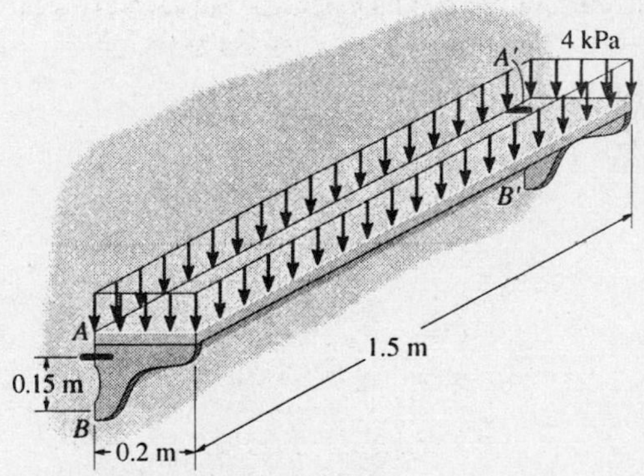

Equations of Equilibrium : Each shelf s post at its end supports half of the applied load, ie, $4000(0.2)(0.75) = 600$ N. The normal reaction N_B can be obtained directly by summing moments about point A.

$$\circlearrowleft + \Sigma M_A = 0; \quad N_B(0.15) - 600(0.1) = 0 \quad N_B = 400 \text{ N} \qquad \textbf{Ans}$$

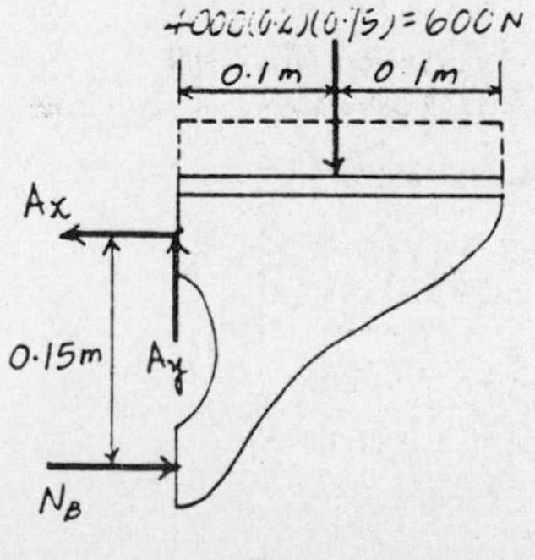

$$\xrightarrow{+} \Sigma F_x = 0; \quad 400 - A_x = 0 \quad A_x = 400\text{N}$$

$$+\uparrow \Sigma F_y = 0; \quad A_y - 600 = 0 \quad A_y = 600 \text{ N}$$

The force resisted by the bolt at A is

$$F_A = \sqrt{A_x^2 + A_y^2} = \sqrt{400^2 + 600^2} = 721 \text{ N} \qquad \textbf{Ans}$$

5-98. Determine the reactions at the supports A and B of the frame.

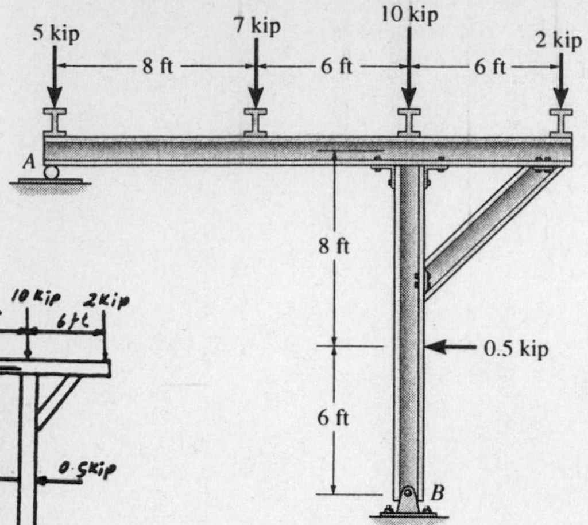

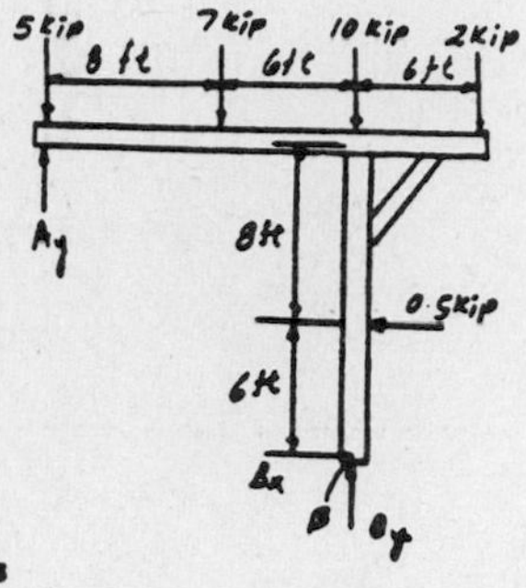

$\circlearrowleft + \Sigma M_B = 0;\quad 5(14) + 7(6) + 0.5(6) - 2(6) - A_y(14) = 0$

$A_y = 7.357 \text{ kip} = 7.36 \text{ kip}$ **Ans**

$\xrightarrow{+} \Sigma F_x = 0;\quad B_x - 0.5 = 0 \qquad B_x = 0.5 \text{ kip}$ **Ans**

$+\uparrow \Sigma F_y = 0;\quad B_y + 7.357 - 5 - 7 - 10 - 2 = 0$

$B_y = 16.6 \text{ kip}$ **Ans**

5-99. A skeletal diagram of the lower leg is shown in the lower figure. Here it can be noted that this portion of the leg is lifted by the quadriceps muscle attached to the hip at A and to the patella bone at B. This bone slides freely over cartilage at the knee joint. The quadriceps is further extended and attached to the tibia at C. Using the mechanical system shown in the upper figure to model the lower leg, determine the tension T in the quadriceps at C and the magnitude of the resultant force at the femur (pin), D, in order to hold the lower leg in the position shown. The lower leg has a mass of 3.2 kg and a mass center at G_1; the foot has a mass of 1.6 kg and a mass center at G_2.

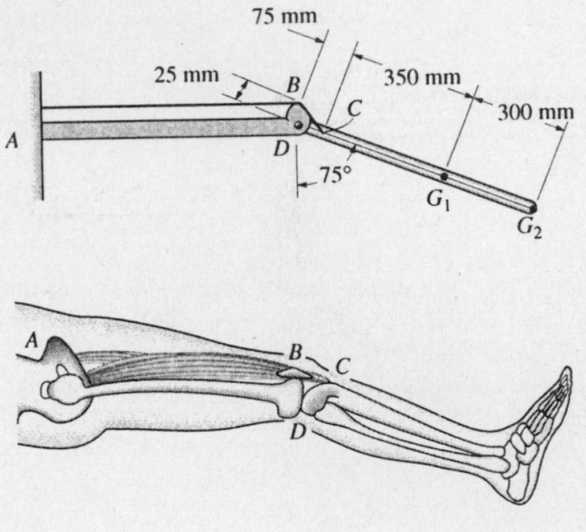

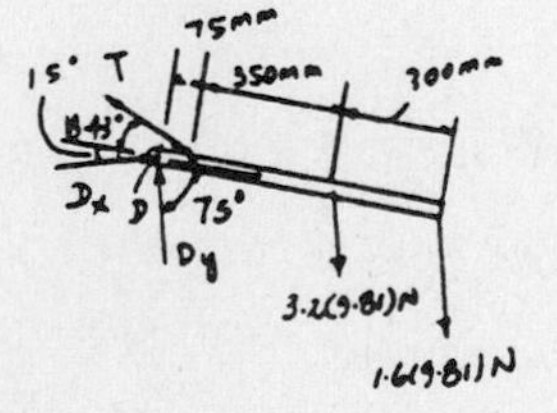

$\circlearrowleft + \Sigma M_D = 0;\quad T \sin 18.43°(75) - 3.2(9.81)(425 \sin 75°)$

$- 1.6(9.81)(725 \sin 75°) = 0$

$T = 1006.82 \text{ N} = 1.01 \text{ kN}$ **Ans**

$+\uparrow \Sigma F_y = 0;\quad D_y + 1006.82 \sin 33.43° - 3.2(9.81) - 1.6(9.81) = 0$

$D_y = -507.66 \text{ N}$

$\xrightarrow{+} \Sigma F_x = 0;\quad D_x - 1006.82 \cos 33.43° = 0$

$D_x = 840.20 \text{ N}$

$F_D = \sqrt{D_x^2 + D_y^2} = \sqrt{(-507.66)^2 + 840.20^2} = 982 \text{ N}$ **Ans**

***5-100.** Determine the reactions at the supports A and B for equilibrium of the beam.

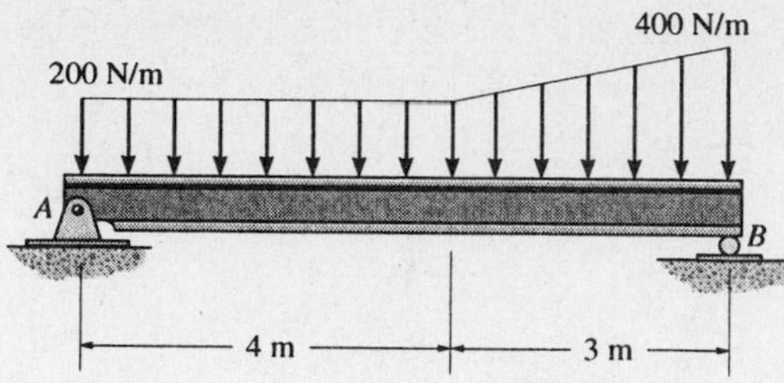

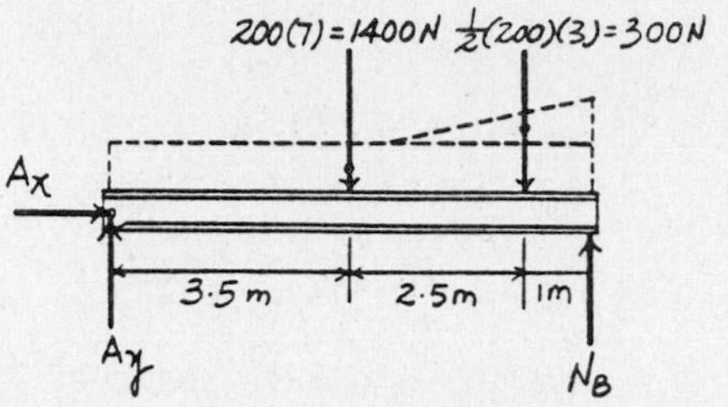

Equations of Equilibrium : The normal reaction N_B can be obtained directly by summing moments about point A.

$+\Sigma M_A = 0;\quad N_B(7) - 1400(3.5) - 300(6) = 0$

$N_B = 957.14\text{ N} = 957\text{ N}$ **Ans**

$+\uparrow \Sigma F_y = 0$

$\xrightarrow{+} \Sigma F_x = 0;\quad A_x = 0$ **Ans**

5-101. The uniform concrete slab has a weight of 5500 lb. Determine the tension in each of the three parallel supporting cables when the slab is held in the horizontal plane as shown.

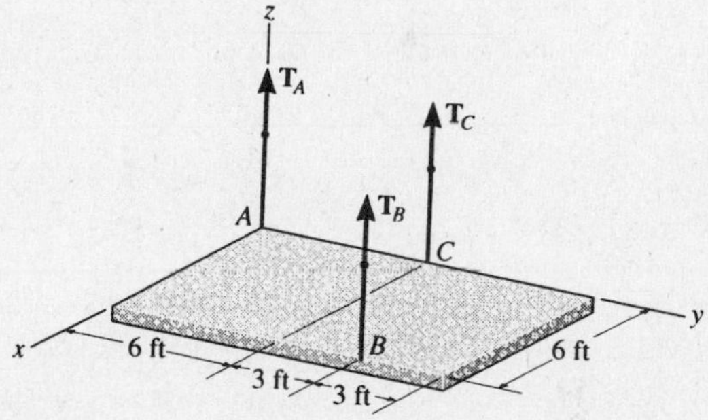

Equations of Equilibrium : The cable tension T_B can be obtained directly by summing moments about the y axis.

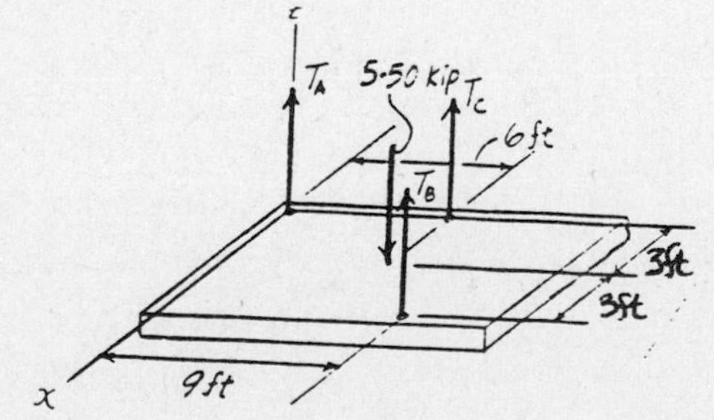

$\Sigma M_y = 0;\quad 5.50(3) - T_B(6) = 0\quad T_B = 2.75\text{ kip}$ **Ans**

$\Sigma M_x = 0;\quad T_C(6) + 2.75(9) - 5.50(6) = 0$

$T_C = 1.375\text{ kip}$ **Ans**

$\Sigma F_z = 0;\quad T_A + 2.75 + 1.375 - 5.50 = 0$

$T_A = 1.375\text{ kip}$ **Ans**

5-102. Determine the x, y, z components of reaction at the fixed wall A. The 150-N force is parallel to the z axis and the 200-N force is parallel to the y axis.

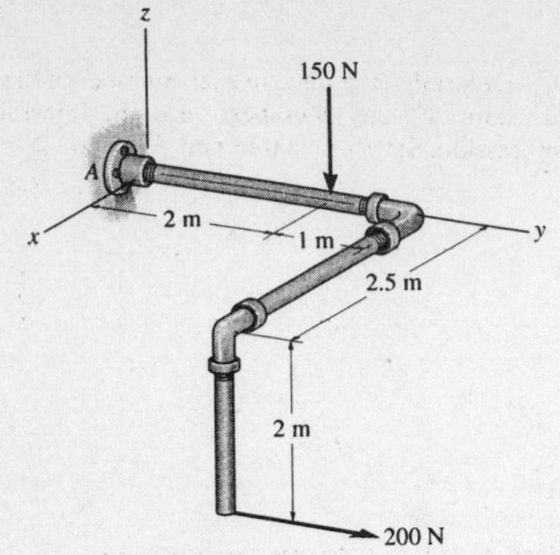

Equations of Equilibrium :

$\Sigma F_x = 0;\qquad A_x = 0$ **Ans**

$\Sigma F_y = 0;\qquad A_y + 200 = 0 \qquad A_y = -200\text{ N}$ **Ans**

$\Sigma F_z = 0;\qquad A_z - 150 = 0 \qquad A_z = 150\text{ N}$ **Ans**

$\Sigma M_x = 0;\qquad (M_A)_x + 200(2) - 150(2) = 0$
$(M_A)_x = -100\text{ N}\cdot\text{m}$ **Ans**

$\Sigma M_y = 0;\qquad (M_A)_y = 0$ **Ans**

$\Sigma M_z = 0;\qquad (M_A)_z + 200(2.5) = 0$
$(M_A)_z = -500\text{ N}\cdot\text{m}$ **Ans**

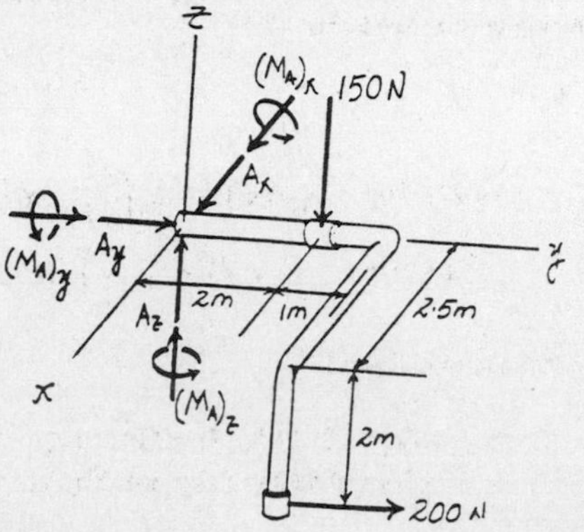

The negative signs indicate that the direction of the reaction components are in the opposite sense of those shown on FBD.

5-103. The horizontal beam is supported by springs at its ends. If the stiffness of the spring at A is $k_A = 5$ kN/m, determine the required stiffness of the spring at B so that if the beam is loaded with the 800-N force, it remains in the horizontal position both before and after loading.

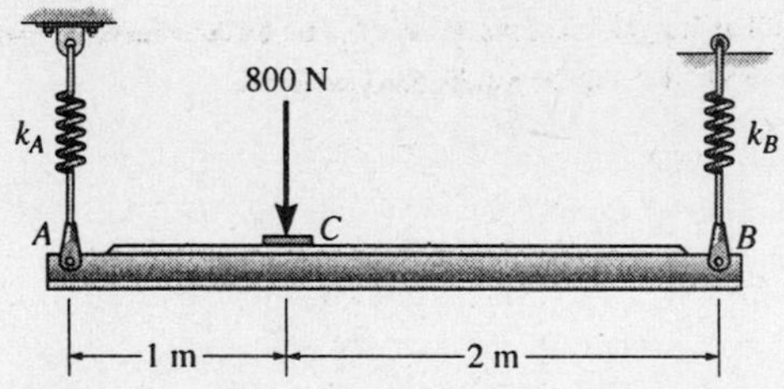

Equilibrium :

$\circlearrowleft + \Sigma M_A = 0;\qquad F_B(3) - 800(1) = 0 \qquad F_B = 266.67\text{ N}$

$\circlearrowleft + \Sigma M_B = 0;\qquad 800(2) - F_A(3) = 0 \qquad F_A = 533.33\text{ N}$

Spring force formula : $\quad x = \dfrac{F}{k}$

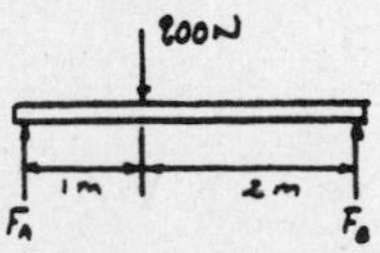

$x_A = x_B$

$$\frac{533.33}{5000} = \frac{266.67}{k_B}$$

$k_B = 2500\text{ N/m} = 2.50\text{ kN/m}$ **Ans**

6-1. Determine the force in each member of the truss and state if the members are in tension or compression. Set $P_1 = 800$ lb and $P_2 = 400$ lb.

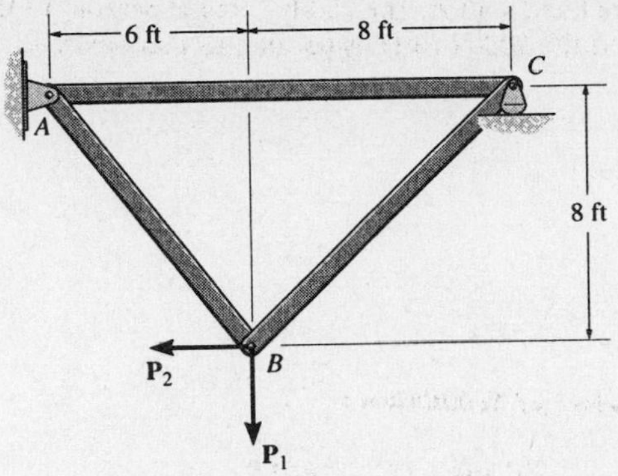

Method of Joints **: In this case, the support reactions are not required for determining the member forces.**

Joint *B*

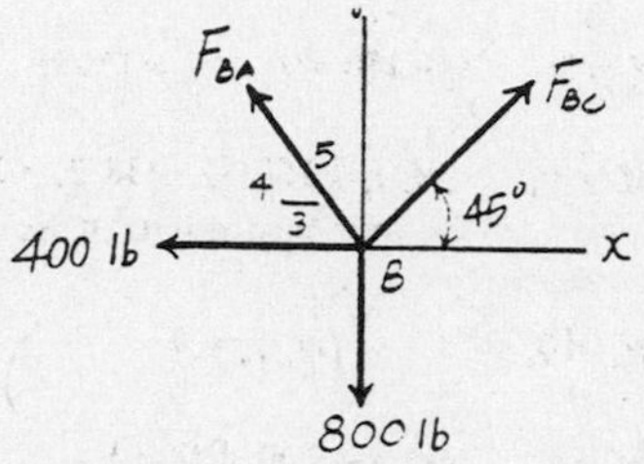

$$\xrightarrow{+} \Sigma F_x = 0; \quad F_{BC}\cos 45° - F_{BA}\left(\frac{3}{5}\right) - 400 = 0 \qquad [1]$$

$$+\uparrow \Sigma F_y = 0; \quad F_{BC}\sin 45° + F_{BA}\left(\frac{4}{5}\right) - 800 = 0 \qquad [2]$$

Solving Eqs. [1] and [2] yields

$$F_{BA} = 285.71 \text{ lb (T)} = 286 \text{ lb (T)} \qquad \textbf{Ans}$$
$$F_{BC} = 808.12 \text{ lb (T)} = 808 \text{ lb (T)} \qquad \textbf{Ans}$$

Joint *C*

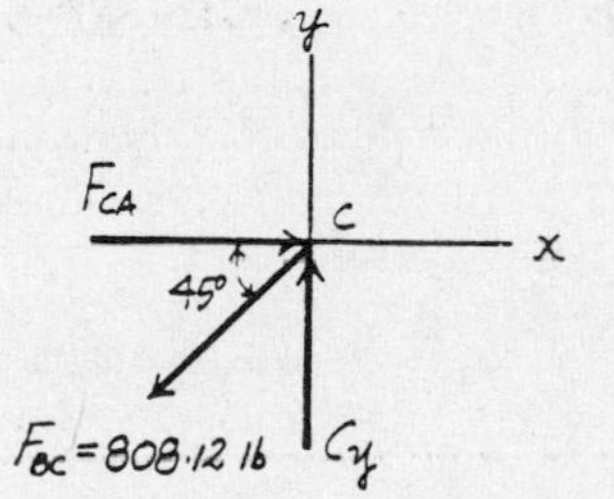

$$\xrightarrow{+} \Sigma F_x = 0; \quad F_{CA} - 808.12\cos 45° = 0$$
$$F_{CA} = 571 \text{ lb (C)} \qquad \textbf{Ans}$$

$$+\uparrow \Sigma F_y = 0; \quad C_y - 808.12\cos 45° = 0$$
$$C_y = 571.43 \text{ lb}$$

Note : The support reactions A_x and A_y can be determined by analyzing Joint *A* using the results obtained above.

6-2. Determine the force on each member of the truss and state if the members are in tension or compression. Set $P_1 = 500$ lb and $P_2 = 100$ lb.

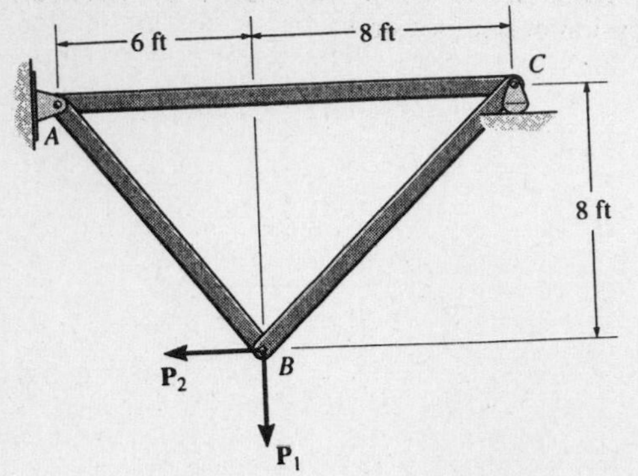

Method of Joints : In this case, the support reactions are not required for determining the member forces.

Joint *B*

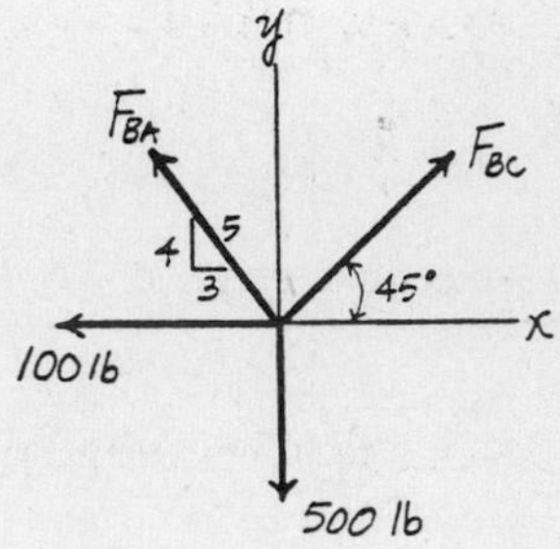

$$\xrightarrow{+}\Sigma F_x = 0;\quad F_{BC}\cos 45^\circ - F_{BA}\left(\frac{3}{5}\right) - 100 = 0 \qquad [1]$$

$$+\uparrow\Sigma F_y = 0;\quad F_{BC}\sin 45^\circ + F_{BA}\left(\frac{4}{5}\right) - 500 = 0 \qquad [2]$$

Solving Eqs.[1] and [2] yields

$$F_{BA} = 285.71 \text{ lb (T)} = 286 \text{ lb (T)} \qquad \textbf{Ans}$$
$$F_{BC} = 383.86 \text{ lb (T)} = 384 \text{ lb (T)} \qquad \textbf{Ans}$$

Joint *C*

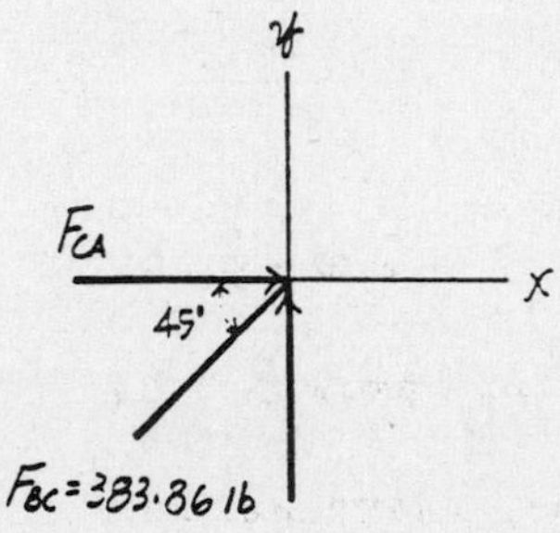

$$\xrightarrow{+}\Sigma F_x = 0;\quad F_{CA} - 383.86\cos 45^\circ = 0$$
$$F_{CA} = 271 \text{ lb (C)} \qquad \textbf{Ans}$$

$$+\uparrow\Sigma F_y = 0;\quad C_y - 383.86\cos 45^\circ = 0$$
$$C_y = 271.43 \text{ lb}$$

Note : The support reactions A_x and A_y can be determined by analyzing Joint *A* using the results obtained above.

6-3. Determine the force in each member of the truss in terms of the load P and state if the members are in tension or compression.

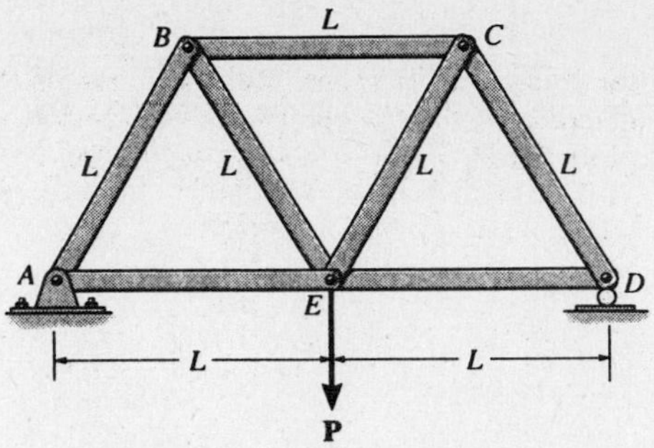

Entire truss :

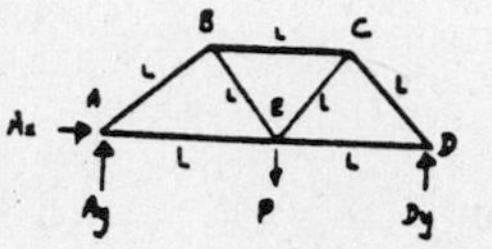

$\circlearrowleft + \Sigma M_A = 0; \quad -P(L) + D_y(2L) = 0$

$D_y = \frac{P}{2}$

$+\uparrow \Sigma F_y = 0; \quad \frac{P}{2} - P + A_y = 0$

$A_y = \frac{P}{2}$

$\xrightarrow{+} \Sigma F_x = 0; \quad A_x = 0$

Joint D :

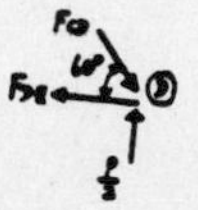

$+\uparrow \Sigma F_y = 0; \quad -F_{CD} \sin 60° + \frac{P}{2} = 0$

$F_{CD} = 0.577\,P\,(C)$ **Ans**

$\overset{+}{\leftarrow} \Sigma F_x = 0; \quad F_{DE} - 0.577P \cos 60° = 0$

$F_{DE} = 0.289\,P\,(T)$ **Ans**

Joint C :

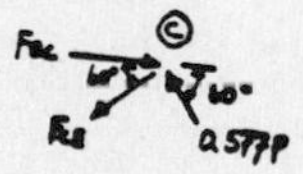

$+\uparrow \Sigma F_y = 0; \quad 0.577\,P \sin 60° - F_{CE} \sin 60° = 0$

$F_{CE} = 0.577\,P\,(T)$ **Ans**

$\xrightarrow{+} \Sigma F_x = 0; \quad F_{BC} - 0.577\,P \cos 60° - 0.577\,P \cos 60° = 0$

$F_{BC} = 0.577\,P\,(C)$ **Ans**

Due to symmetry :

$F_{BE} = F_{CE} = 0.577\,P\,(T)$ **Ans**

$F_{AB} = F_{CD} = 0.577\,P\,(C)$ **Ans**

$F_{AE} = F_{DE} = 0.289\,P\,(T)$ **Ans**

*6-4. Each member of the truss is uniform and has a weight W. Remove the external force **P** and determine the approximate force in each member due to the weight of the truss. State if the members are in tension or compression. Solve the problem by *assuming* the weight of each member can be represented as a vertical force, half of which is applied at each end of the member.

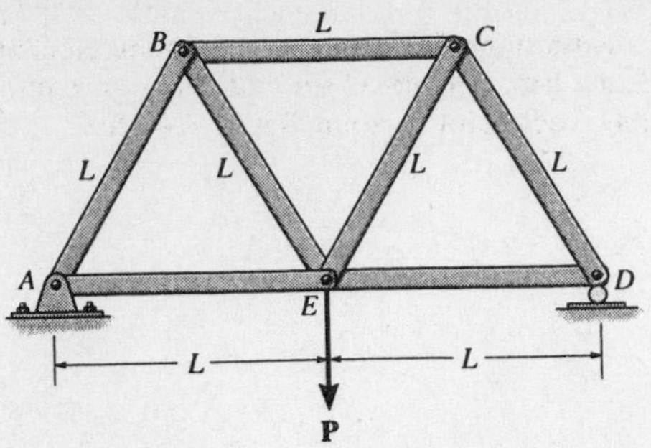

Entire truss :

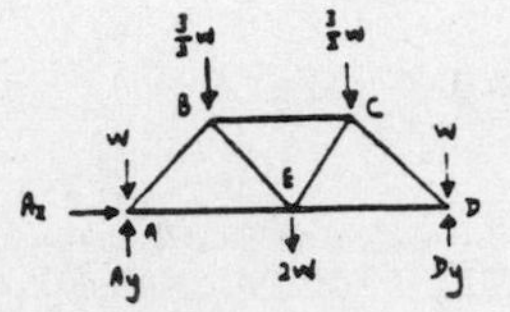

$$\circlearrowleft + \Sigma M_A = 0; \quad -\frac{3}{2}W\left(\frac{L}{2}\right) - 2W(L) - \frac{3}{2}W\left(\frac{3}{2}L\right) - W(2L) + D_y(2L) = 0$$

$$D_y = \frac{7}{2}W$$

Joint D :

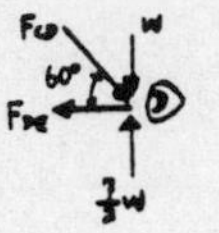

$$+\uparrow \Sigma F_y = 0; \quad \frac{7}{2}W - W - F_{CD}\sin 60^\circ = 0$$

$F_{CD} = 2.887W = 2.89\ W\ (C)$ **Ans**

$$\xrightarrow{+} \Sigma F_x = 0; \quad 2.887W\cos 60^\circ - F_{DE} = 0$$

$F_{DE} = 1.44\ W\ (T)$ **Ans**

Joint C :

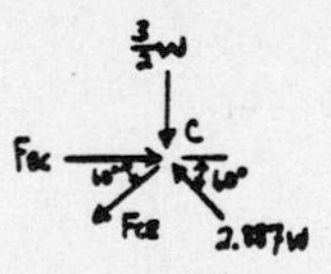

$$+\uparrow \Sigma F_y = 0; \quad 2.887W\sin 60^\circ - \frac{3}{2}W - F_{CE}\sin 60^\circ = 0$$

$F_{CE} = 1.1547W = 1.15\ W\ (T)$ **Ans**

$$\xrightarrow{+} \Sigma F_x = 0; \quad F_{BC} - 1.1547W\cos 60^\circ - 2.887W\cos 60^\circ = 0$$

$F_{BC} = 2.02\ W\ (C)$ **Ans**

Due to symmetry :

$F_{BE} = F_{CE} = 1.15\ W\ (T)$ **Ans**

$F_{AB} = F_{CD} = 2.89\ W\ (C)$ **Ans**

$F_{AE} = F_{DE} = 1.44\ W\ (T)$ **Ans**

6-5. Determine the force in each member of the truss and state if the members are in tension or compression. Assume each joint as a pin. Set $P = 4$ kN.

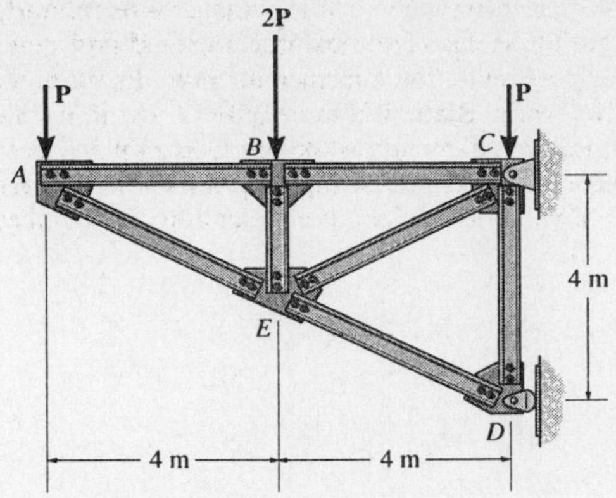

Method of Joints : In this case, the support reactions are not required for determining the member forces.

Joint *A*

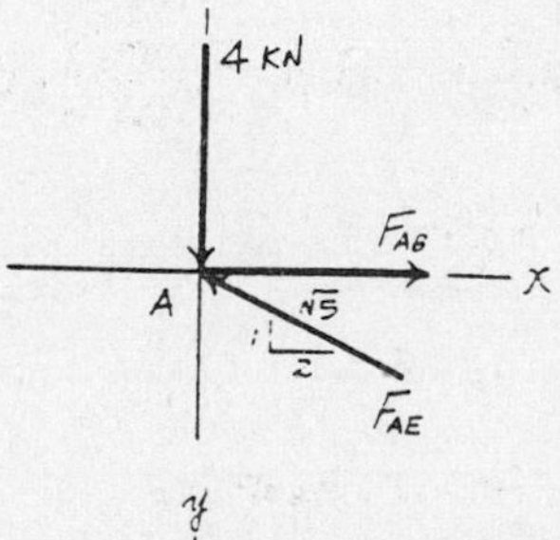

$$+\uparrow \Sigma F_y = 0; \quad F_{AE}\left(\frac{1}{\sqrt{5}}\right) - 4 = 0$$

$$F_{AE} = 8.944 \text{ kN (C)} = 8.94 \text{ kN (C)} \quad \textbf{Ans}$$

$$\overset{+}{\rightarrow} \Sigma F_x = 0; \quad F_{AB} - 8.944\left(\frac{2}{\sqrt{5}}\right) = 0$$

$$F_{AB} = 8.00 \text{ kN (T)} \quad \textbf{Ans}$$

Joint *B*

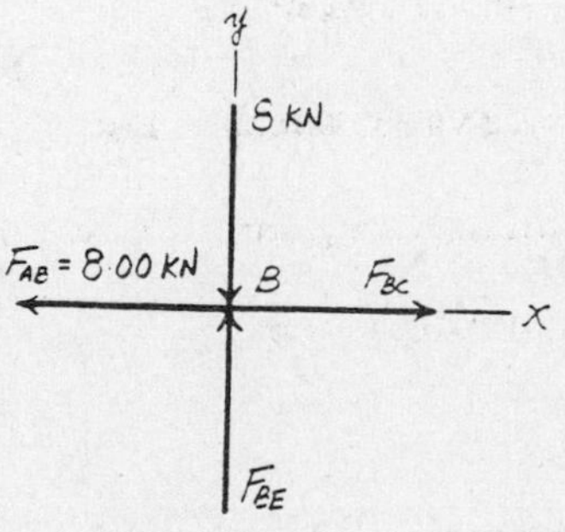

$$\overset{+}{\rightarrow} \Sigma F_x = 0; \quad F_{BC} - 8.00 = 0 \quad F_{BC} = 8.00 \text{ kN (T)} \quad \textbf{Ans}$$

$$+\uparrow \Sigma F_y = 0; \quad F_{BE} - 8 = 0 \quad F_{BE} = 8.00 \text{ kN (C)} \quad \textbf{Ans}$$

Joint *E*

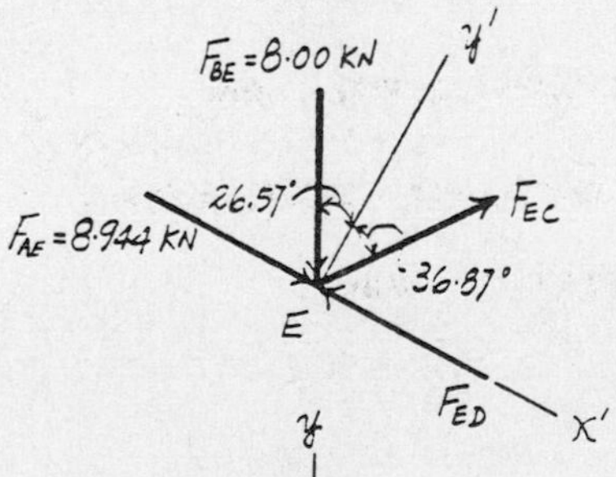

$$+ \Sigma F_{y'} = 0; \quad F_{EC}\cos 36.87° - 8.00\cos 26.57° = 0$$

$$F_{EC} = 8.944 \text{ kN (T)} = 8.94 \text{ kN (T)} \quad \textbf{Ans}$$

$$+ \Sigma F_{x'} = 0; \quad 8.944 + 8.00\sin 26.57° + 8.944\sin 36.87° - F_{ED} = 0$$

$$F_{ED} = 17.89 \text{ kN (C)} = 17.9 \text{ kN (C)} \quad \textbf{Ans}$$

Joint *D*

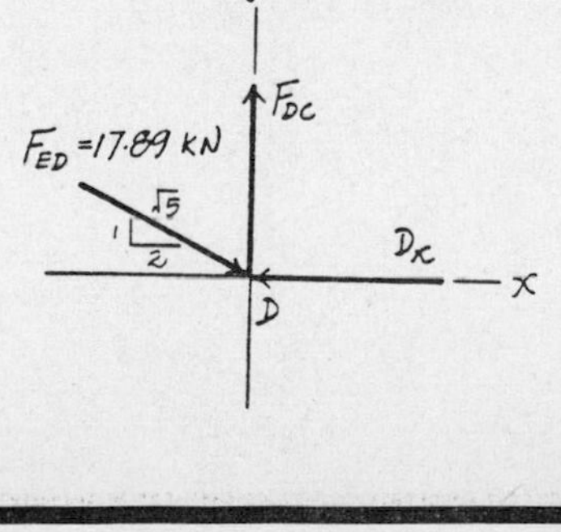

$$+\uparrow \Sigma F_y = 0; \quad F_{DC} - 17.89\left(\frac{1}{\sqrt{5}}\right) = 0 \quad F_{DC} = 8.00 \text{ kN (T)} \quad \textbf{Ans}$$

$$\overset{+}{\rightarrow} \Sigma F_x = 0; \quad D_x - 17.89\left(\frac{2}{\sqrt{5}}\right) = 0 \quad D_x = 16.0 \text{ kN}$$

Note : The support reactions C_x and C_y can be determined by analysing Joint *C* using the results obtained above.

6-6. Assume that each member of the truss is made of steel having a mass per length of 4 kg/m. Set $P = 0$, determine the force in each member, and indicate if the members are in tension or compression. Neglect the weight of the gusset plates and assume each joint is a pin. Solve the problem by assuming the weight of each member can be represented as a vertical force, half of which is applied at the end of each member.

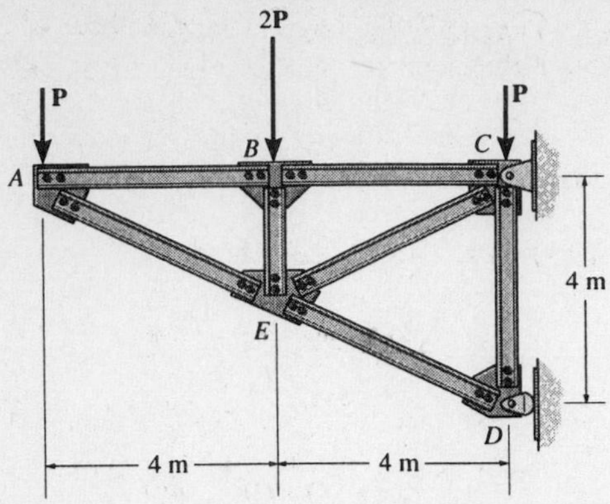

Joint Forces :

$$F_A = 4(9.81)\left(2+\frac{\sqrt{20}}{2}\right) = 166.22\text{ N}$$

$$F_B = 4(9.81)(2+2+1) = 196.2\text{ N}$$

$$F_E = 4(9.81)\left[1+3\left(\frac{\sqrt{20}}{2}\right)\right] = 302.47\text{ N}$$

$$F_D = 4(9.81)\left(2+\frac{\sqrt{20}}{2}\right) = 166.22\text{ N}$$

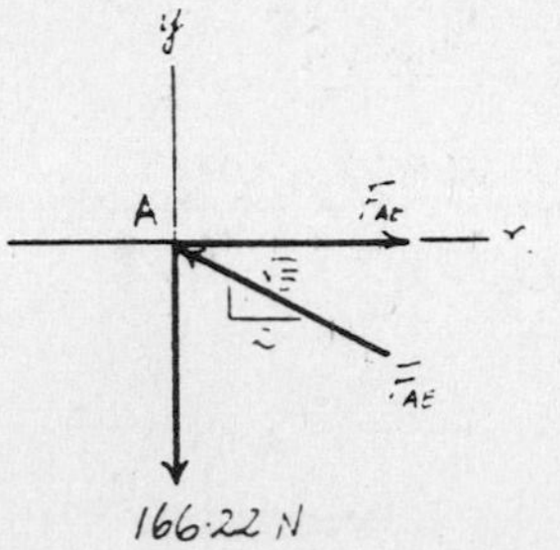

Method of Joints : In this case, the support reactions are not required for determining the member forces.

Joint *A*

$+\uparrow \Sigma F_y = 0;\quad F_{AE}\left(\frac{1}{\sqrt{5}}\right) - 166.22 = 0$

$F_{AE} = 371.69\text{ N (C)} = 372\text{ N (C)}$ **Ans**

$\overset{+}{\rightarrow} \Sigma F_x = 0;\quad F_{AB} - 371.69\left(\frac{2}{\sqrt{5}}\right) = 0$

$F_{AB} = 332.45\text{ N (T)} = 332\text{ N (T)}$ **Ans**

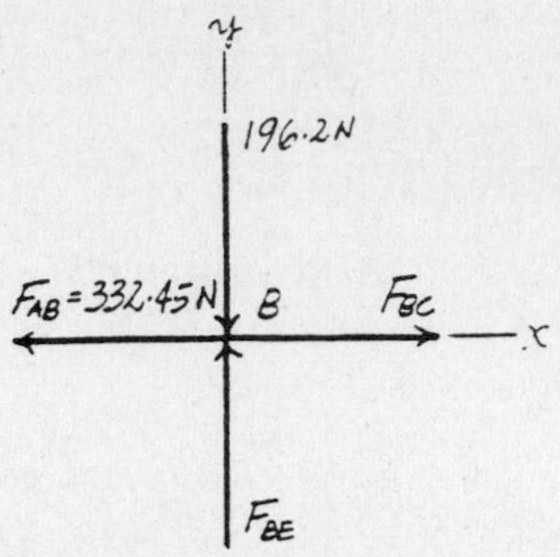

Joint *B*

$\overset{+}{\rightarrow} \Sigma F_x = 0;\quad F_{BC} - 332.45 = 0 \quad F_{BC} = 332\text{ N (T)}$ **Ans**

$+\uparrow \Sigma F_y = 0;\quad F_{BE} - 196.2 = 0$

$F_{BE} = 196.2\text{ N (C)} = 196\text{ N (C)}$ **Ans**

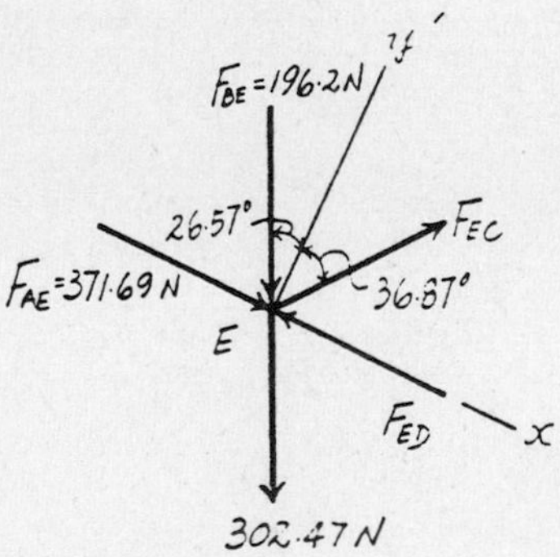

Joint *E*

$\nearrow + \Sigma F_{y'} = 0;\quad F_{EC}\cos 36.87° - (196.2+302.47)\cos 26.57° = 0$

$F_{EC} = 557.53\text{ N (T)} = 558\text{ N (T)}$ **Ans**

$\searrow + \Sigma F_{x'} = 0;\quad 371.69 + (196.2+302.47)\sin 26.57° + 557.53\sin 36.87° - F_{ED} = 0$

$F_{ED} = 929.22\text{ N (C)} = 929\text{ N (C)}$ **Ans**

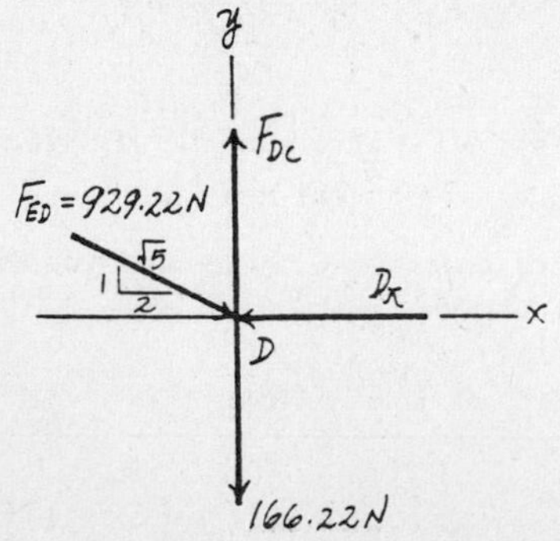

6-7. Determine the force in each member of the truss. State if the members are in tension or compression.

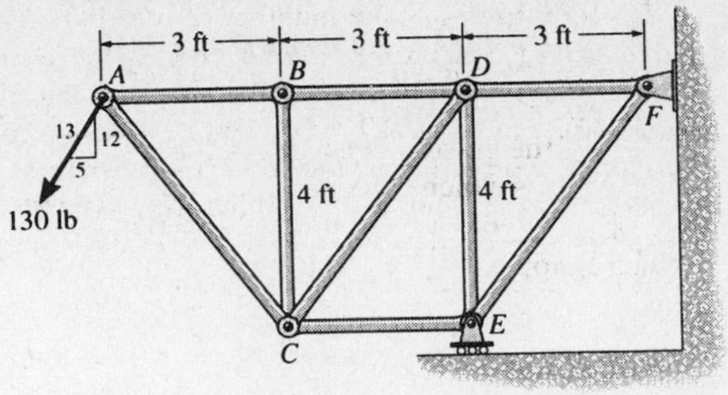

Joint *A*:

$+\uparrow \Sigma F_y = 0;\quad \frac{4}{5}(F_{AC}) - \frac{12}{13}(130) = 0$

$F_{AC} = 150 \text{ lb (C)}$ **Ans**

$\xrightarrow{+} \Sigma F_x = 0;\quad F_{AB} - \frac{3}{5}(150) - \frac{5}{13}(130) = 0$

$F_{AB} = 140 \text{ lb (T)}$ **Ans**

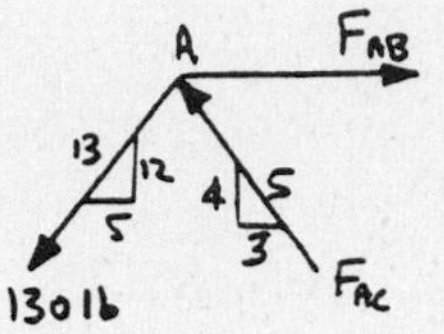

Joint *B*:

$\xrightarrow{+} \Sigma F_x = 0;\quad F_{BD} - 140 = 0$

$F_{BD} = 140 \text{ lb (T)}$ **Ans**

$+\uparrow \Sigma F_y = 0;\quad F_{BC} = 0$ **Ans**

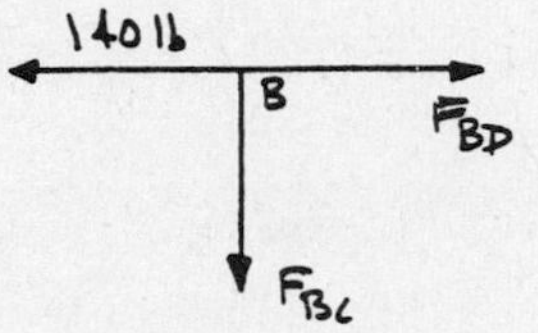

Joint *C*:

$+\uparrow \Sigma F_y = 0;\quad \left(\frac{4}{5}\right) F_{CD} - \left(\frac{4}{5}\right) 150 = 0$

$F_{CD} = 150 \text{ lb (T)}$ **Ans**

$\xrightarrow{+} \Sigma F_x = 0;\quad - F_{CE} + \frac{3}{5}(150) + \frac{3}{5}(150) = 0$

$F_{CE} = 180 \text{ lb (C)}$ **Ans**

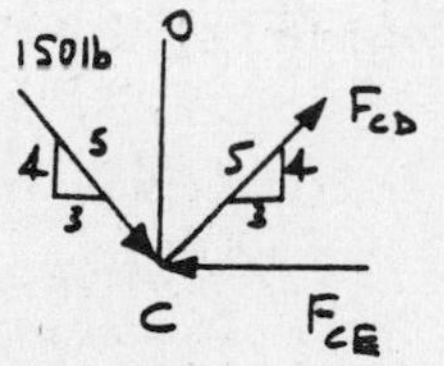

Joint *D*:

$+\uparrow \Sigma F_y = 0;\quad F_{DE} - \frac{4}{5}(150) = 0$

$F_{DE} = 120 \text{ lb (C)}$ **Ans**

$\xrightarrow{+} \Sigma F_x = 0;\quad F_{DF} - 140 - \frac{3}{5}(150) = 0$

$F_{DF} = 230 \text{ lb (T)}$ **Ans**

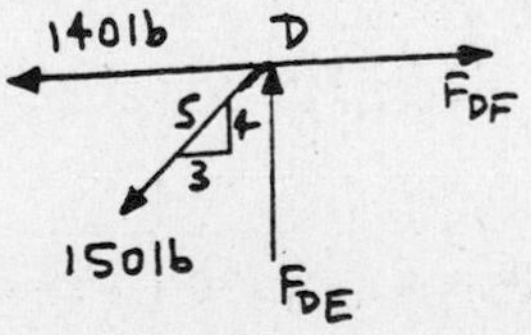

Joint *E*:

$\xrightarrow{+} \Sigma F_x = 0;\quad 180 - \frac{3}{5}(F_{EF}) = 0$

$F_{EF} = 300 \text{ lb (C)}$ **Ans**

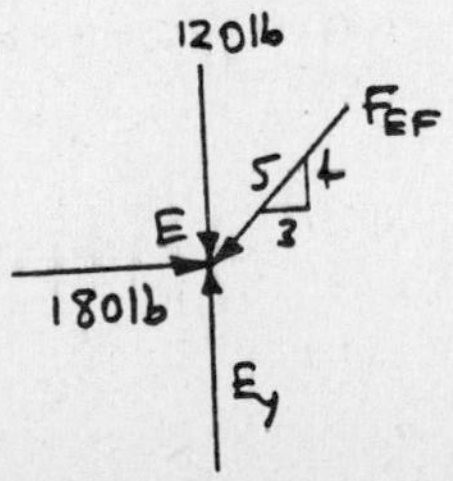

*6-8. Determine the force in each member of the truss and state if the members are in tension or compression. Set $P_1 = 2$ kN and $P_2 = 1.5$ kN.

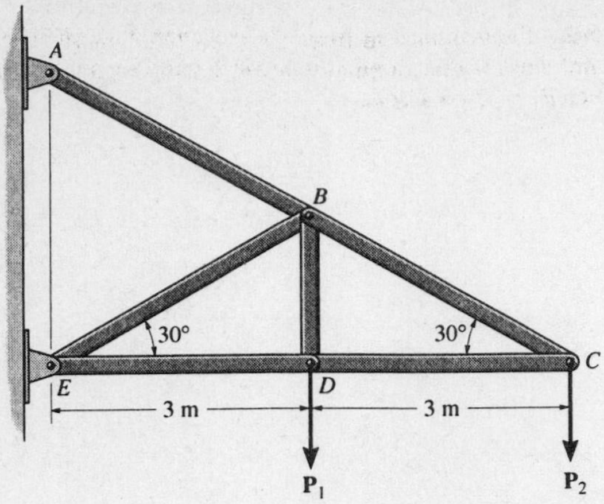

Method of Joints : In this case, the support reactions are not required for determining the member forces.

Joint *C*

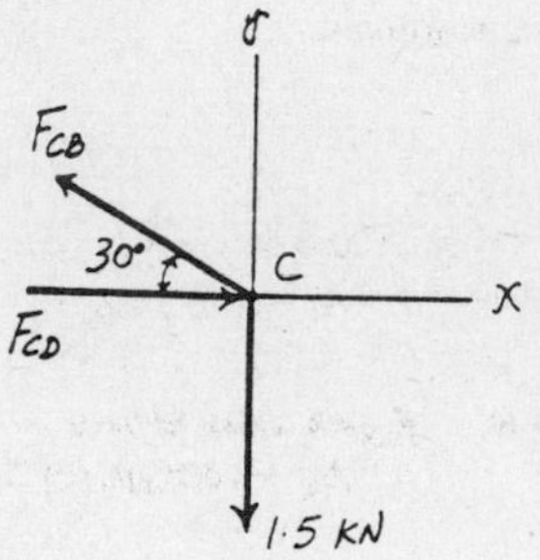

$+\uparrow\Sigma F_y = 0;\quad F_{CB}\sin 30° - 1.5 = 0$

$F_{CB} = 3.00\text{ kN (T)}$ **Ans**

$\xrightarrow{+}\Sigma F_x = 0;\quad F_{CD} - 3.00\cos 30° = 0$

$F_{CD} = 2.598\text{ kN (C)} = 2.60\text{ kN (C)}$ **Ans**

Joint *D*

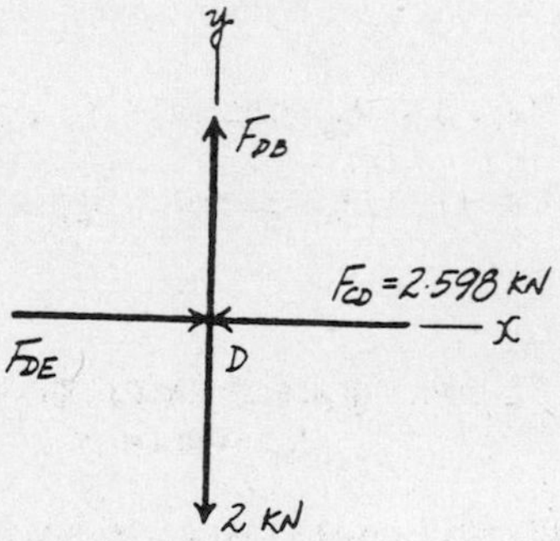

$\xrightarrow{+}\Sigma F_x = 0;\quad F_{DE} - 2.598 = 0 \quad F_{DE} = 2.60\text{ kN (C)}$ **Ans**

$+\uparrow\Sigma F_y = 0;\quad F_{DB} - 2 = 0 \quad F_{DB} = 2.00\text{ kN (T)}$ **Ans**

Joint *B*

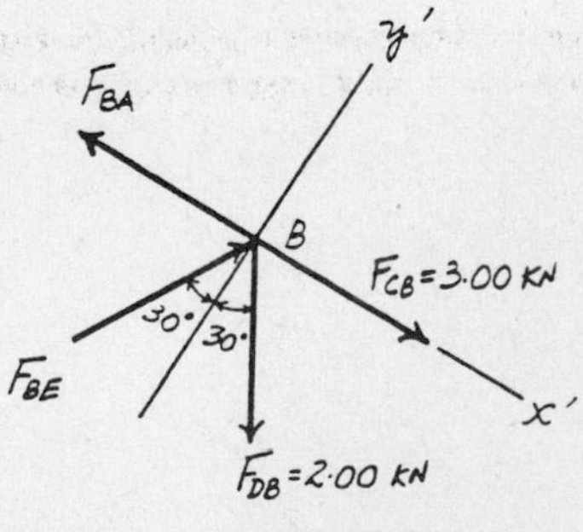

$+\ \Sigma F_{y'} = 0;\quad F_{BE}\cos 30° - 2.00\cos 30° = 0$

$F_{BE} = 2.00\text{ kN (C)}$ **Ans**

$+\Sigma F_{x'} = 0;\quad (2.00 + 2.00)\sin 30° + 3.00 - F_{BA} = 0$

$F_{BA} = 5.00\text{ kN (T)}$ **Ans**

Note : The support reactions at support *A* and *E* can be determined by analyzing Joints *A* and *E* respectively using the results obtained above.

6-9. Determine the force in each member of the truss and state if the members are in tension or compression. Set $P_1 = P_2 = 4$ kN.

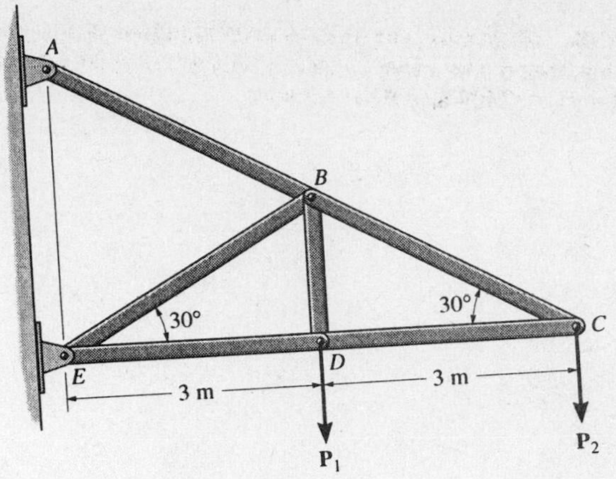

Method of Joints **:** In this case, the support reactions are not required for determining the member forces.

Joint *C*

$+\uparrow \Sigma F_y = 0;\quad F_{CB} \sin 30° - 4 = 0$

$F_{CB} = 8.00 \text{ kN (T)}$ **Ans**

$\overset{+}{\rightarrow} \Sigma F_x = 0;\quad F_{CD} - 8.00 \cos 30° = 0$

$F_{CD} = 6.928 \text{ kN (C)} = 6.93 \text{ kN (C)}$ **Ans**

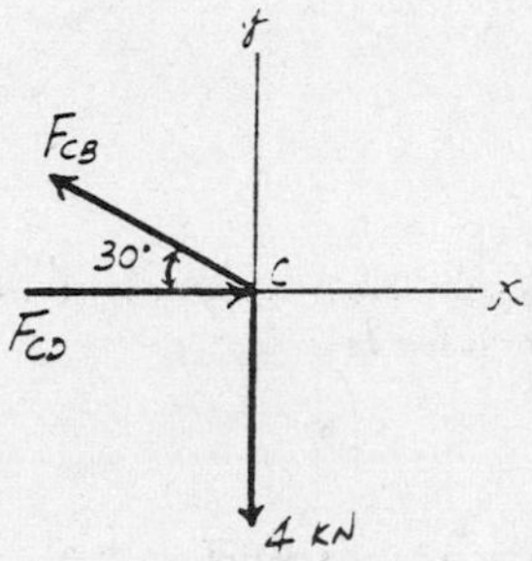

Joint *D*

$\overset{+}{\rightarrow} \Sigma F_x = 0;\quad F_{DE} - 6.928 = 0 \quad F_{DE} = 6.93 \text{ kN (C)}$ **Ans**

$+\uparrow \Sigma F_y = 0;\quad F_{DB} - 4 = 0 \quad F_{DB} = 4.00 \text{ kN (T)}$ **Ans**

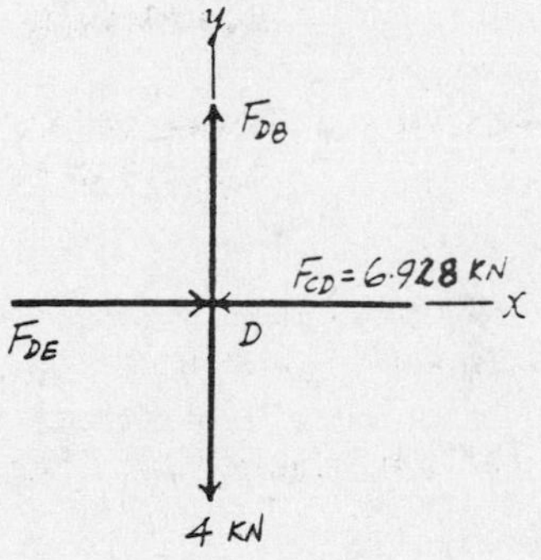

Joint *B*

$\nearrow + \Sigma F_{y'} = 0;\quad F_{BE} \cos 30° - 4.00 \cos 30° = 0$

$F_{BE} = 4.00 \text{ kN (C)}$ **Ans**

$\searrow + \Sigma F_{x'} = 0;\quad (4.00 + 4.00) \sin 30° + 8.00 - F_{BA} = 0$

$F_{BA} = 12.0 \text{ kN (T)}$ **Ans**

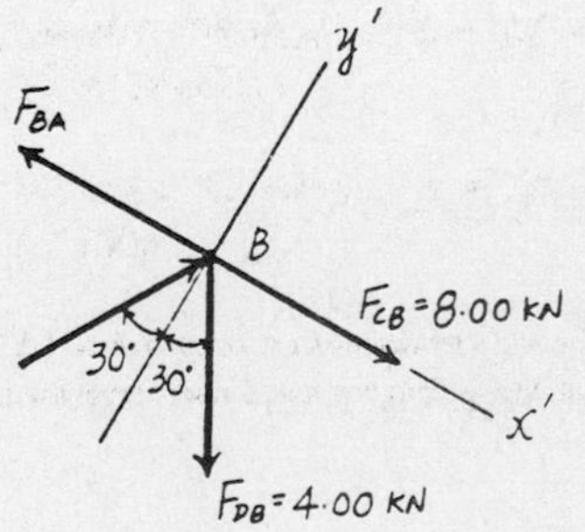

Note : The support reactions at support *A* and *E* can be determined by analyzing Joints *A* and *E* respectively using the results obtained above.

6-10. Determine the force in each member of the truss and state if the members are in tension or compression. Set $P_1 = 800$ lb, $P_2 = 0$.

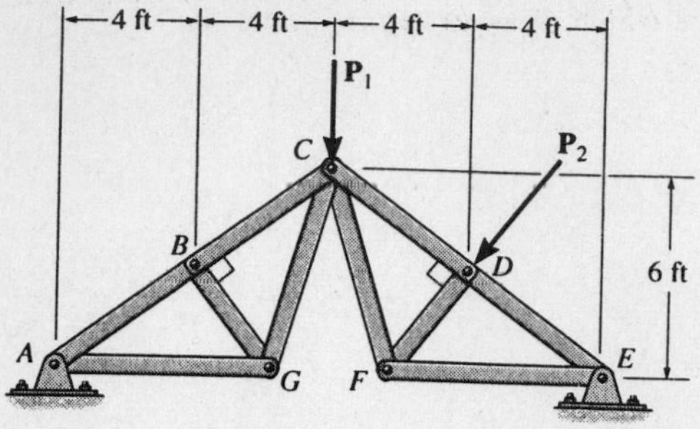

Joint B:

$\searrow^{+}\Sigma F_y = 0;\quad F_{BG} = 0$ **Ans**

$+\swarrow\Sigma F_x = 0;\quad F_{BA} = F_{BC}$

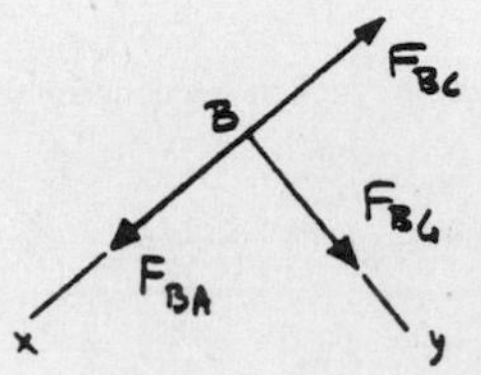

Joint G:

$+\uparrow\Sigma F_y = 0;\quad F_{CG}\sin\theta = 0$

$F_{CG} = 0$ **Ans**

$\overset{+}{\rightarrow}\Sigma F_x = 0;\quad F_{AG} = 0$ **Ans**

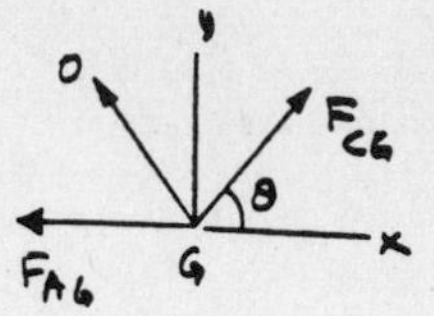

Joint C:

$\overset{+}{\rightarrow}\Sigma F_x = 0;\quad \frac{4}{5}F_{BC} - \frac{4}{5}F_{CD} = 0$

$+\uparrow\Sigma F_y = 0;\quad \frac{3}{5}(F_{BC}) + \frac{3}{5}(F_{CD}) - 800 = 0$

$F_{BC} = F_{CD} = 667$ lb (C) **Ans**

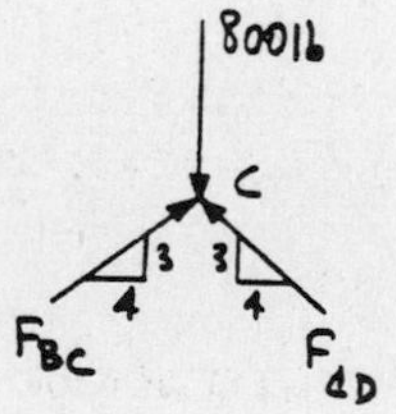

Due to symmetry:

$F_{DF} = F_{BG} = 0$ **Ans**

$F_{CF} = F_{CG} = 0$ **Ans**

$F_{EF} = F_{AG} = 0$ **Ans**

$F_{AB} = F_{DE} = 667$ lb (C) **Ans**

$F_{BC} = F_{CD} = 667$ lb (C) **Ans**

6-11. Determine the force in each member of the truss and state if the members are in tension or compression. Set $P_1 = 600$ lb, $P_2 = 400$ lb.

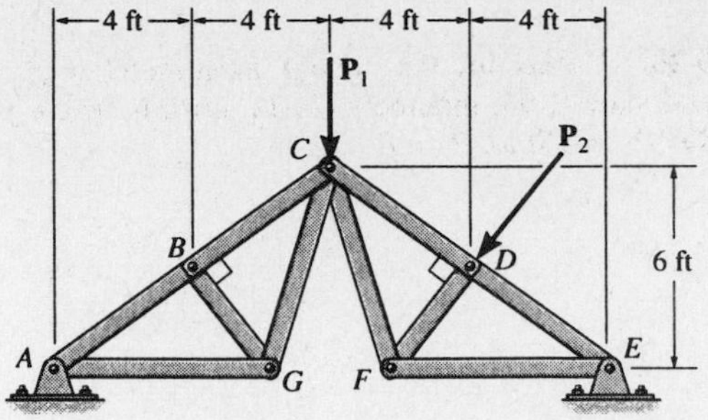

Joint *B* :

$+\searrow \Sigma F_y = 0;\quad F_{BG} = 0$ **Ans**

$+\swarrow \Sigma F_x = 0;\quad F_{BC} = F_{BA}$

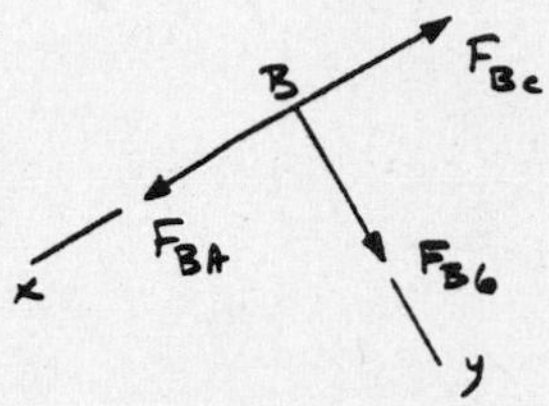

Joint *G* :

$+\uparrow \Sigma F_y = 0;\quad F_{GC}\sin\theta = 0$

$F_{GC} = 0$ **Ans**

$\xrightarrow{+} \Sigma F_x = 0;\quad F_{GA} = 0$ **Ans**

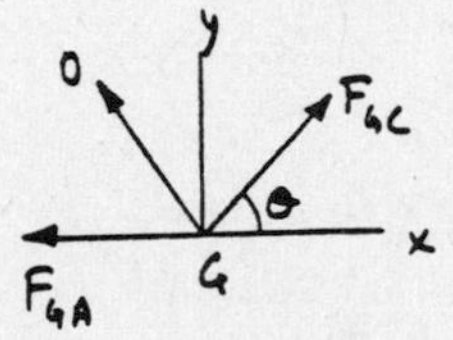

Joint *D* :

$+\searrow \Sigma F_x = 0;\quad F_{DE} - F_{DC} = 0$

$F_{DE} = F_{DC}$

$+\nearrow \Sigma F_y = 0;\quad F_{DF} - 400 = 0$

$F_{DF} = 400 \text{ lb (C)}$ **Ans**

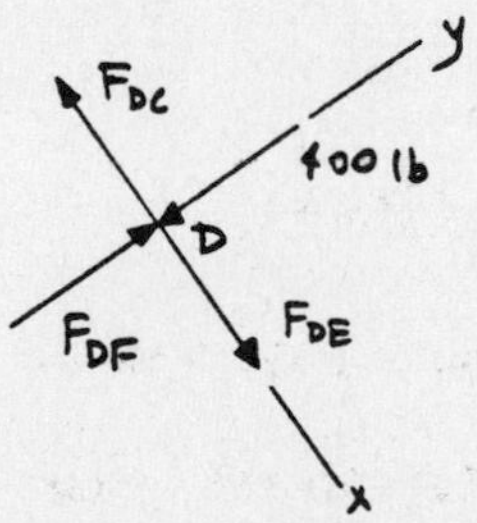

Joint *F* :

$+\searrow \Sigma F_x = 0;\quad F_{FE}\sin 53.13^\circ - F_{FC}\sin 53.13^\circ = 0$

$F_{FE} = F_{FC}$

$+\nearrow \Sigma F_y = 0;\quad 2F\cos 53.13^\circ - 400 = 0$

$F_{FC} = F_{FE} = 333.33 = 333 \text{ lb (T)}$ **Ans**

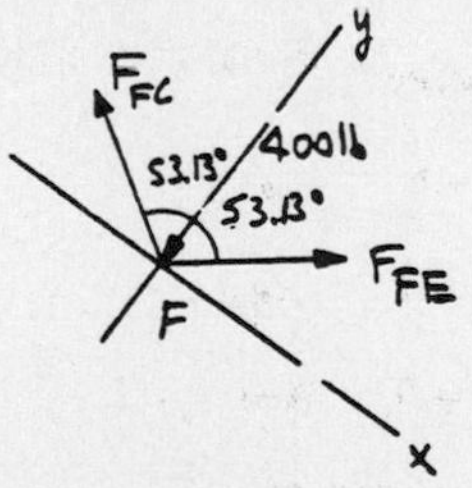

Joint *C* :

$\xrightarrow{+} \Sigma F_x = 0;\quad F_{BC}\cos 36.87^\circ - F_{DC}\cos 36.87^\circ + 333.33\cos 73.74^\circ = 0$

$+\uparrow \Sigma F_y = 0;\quad F_{BC}\sin 36.87^\circ + F_{DC}\sin 36.87^\circ - 600 - 333.33\sin 73.74^\circ = 0$

$F_{BC} = F_{BA} = 708 \text{ lb (C)}$ **Ans**

$F_{DC} = F_{DE} = 825 \text{ lb (C)}$ **Ans**

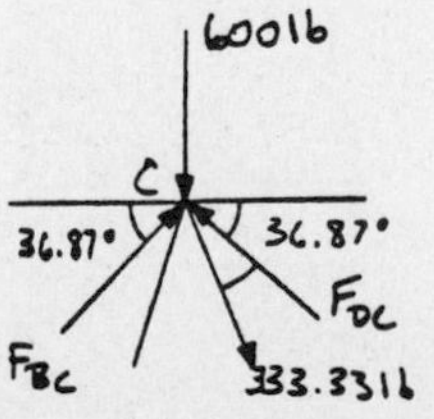

***6-12.** Determine the force in each member of the truss and state if the members are in tension or compression. Set $P_1 = 240$ lb, $P_2 = 100$ lb.

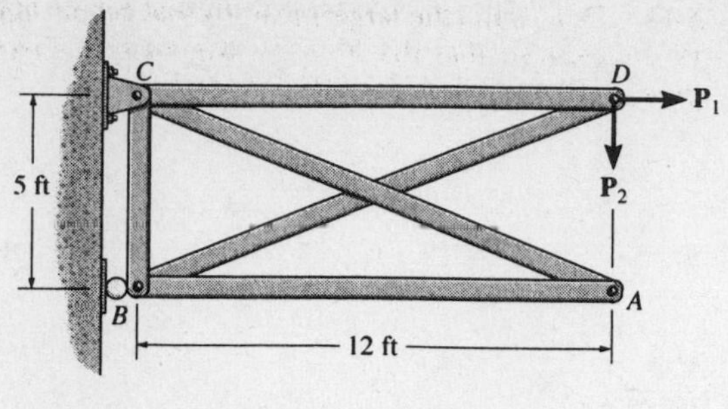

Joint D:

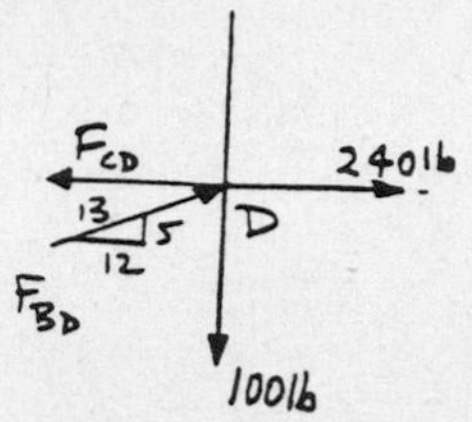

$+\uparrow \Sigma F_y = 0;\quad F_{BD}\left(\frac{5}{13}\right) - 100 = 0$

$F_{BD} = 260$ lb (C) **Ans**

$\xrightarrow{+} \Sigma F_x = 0;\quad 240 - F_{CD} + 260\left(\frac{12}{13}\right) = 0$

$F_{CD} = 480$ lb (T) **Ans**

Joint A:

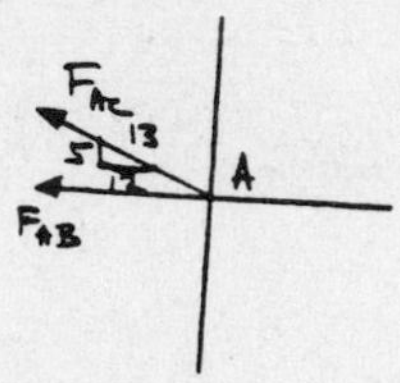

$+\uparrow \Sigma F_y = 0;\quad F_{AC} = 0$ **Ans**

$\xrightarrow{+} \Sigma F_x = 0;\quad F_{AB} = 0$ **Ans**

Joint B:

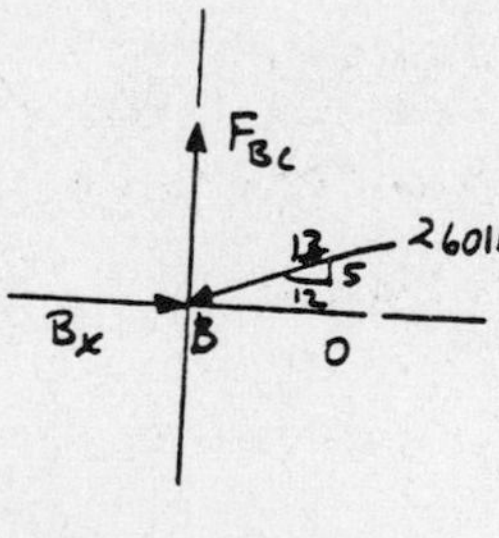

$+\uparrow \Sigma F_y = 0;\quad F_{BC} - 260\left(\frac{5}{13}\right) = 0$

$F_{BC} = 100$ lb (T) **Ans**

6-13. Determine the largest load P_2 that can be applied to the truss so that the force in any member does not exceed 500 lb (T) or 350 lb (C). Take $P_1 = 0$.

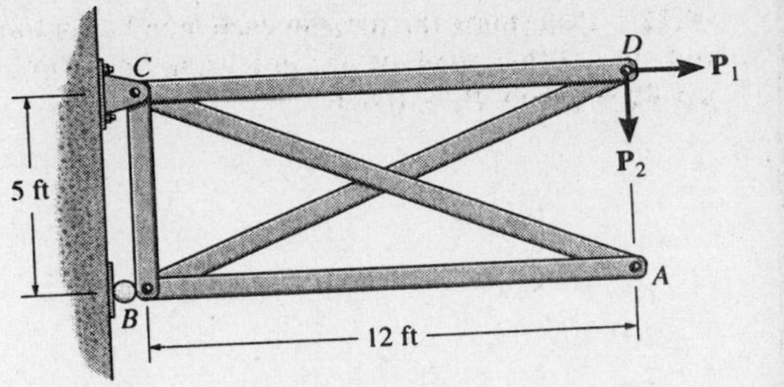

Joint A:

$+\uparrow\Sigma F_y = 0;\quad F_{AC}\sin\theta = 0$

$F_{AC} = 0$

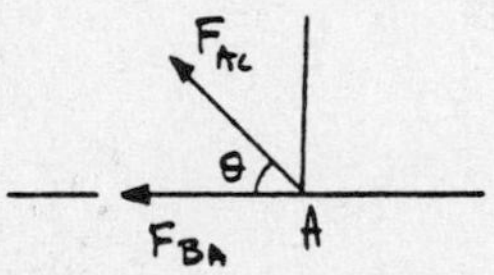

$\xrightarrow{+}\Sigma F_x = 0;\quad F_{AB} = 0$

Joint D:

$+\uparrow\Sigma F_y = 0;\quad -P_2 + F_{DB}\sin 22.62^\circ = 0$

$F_{DB} = 2.60\,P_2$ (C)

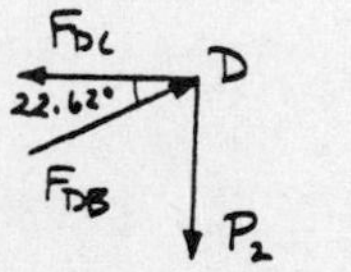

$\xrightarrow{+}\Sigma F_x = 0;\quad 2.60\,P_2\cos 22.62^\circ - F_{DC} = 0$

$F_{DC} = 2.40\,P_2$ (T)

Joint B:

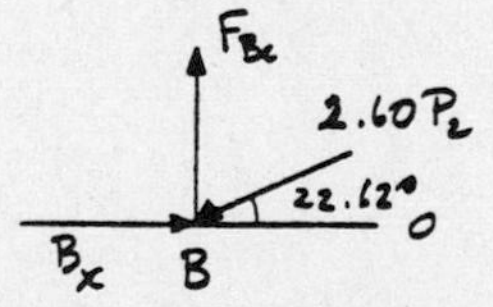

$+\uparrow\Sigma F_y = 0;\quad F_{BC} - 2.60\,P_2\sin 22.62^\circ = 0$

$F_{BC} = P_2$ (T)

Maximum tension member is DC:

$500 = 2.40\,P_2$

$P_2 = 208$ lb

Maximum compression member is DB:

$350 = 2.60\,P_2$

$P_2 = 135$ lb

Thus member DB reaches the critical value first.

$P_2 = 135$ lb **Ans**

6-14. Determine the force in each member of the truss and state if the members are in tension or compression. The load has a mass of 40 kg.

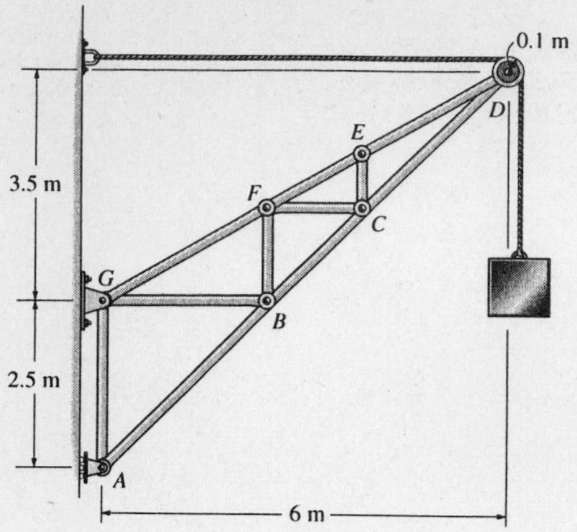

Joint D :

$$\xrightarrow{+} \Sigma F_x = 0; \quad F_{DC}\left(\frac{1}{\sqrt{2}}\right) - 392.4 - F_{DE}\left(\frac{12}{\sqrt{193}}\right) = 0$$

$$+\uparrow \Sigma F_y = 0; \quad F_{DC}\left(\frac{1}{\sqrt{2}}\right) - F_{DE}\left(\frac{7}{\sqrt{193}}\right) - 392.4 = 0$$

Solving,

$F_{DE} = 0$ **Ans**

$F_{DC} = 555$ N (C) **Ans**

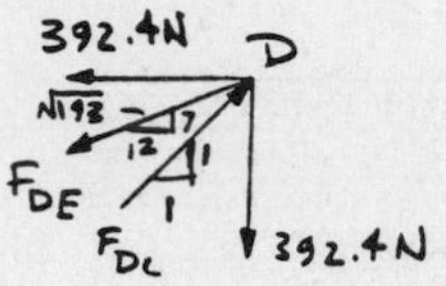

Joint E :

$+\searrow \Sigma F_y = 0; \quad F_{EC} = 0$ **Ans**

$+\nearrow \Sigma F_x = 0; \quad F_{EF} = 0$ **Ans**

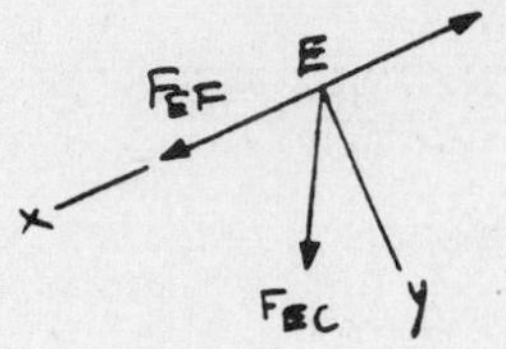

Joint C :

$+\searrow \Sigma F_y = 0; \quad F_{CF} = 0$ **Ans**

$+\nearrow \Sigma F_x = 0; \quad -555 + F_{CB} = 0$

$F_{CB} = 555$ N (C) **Ans**

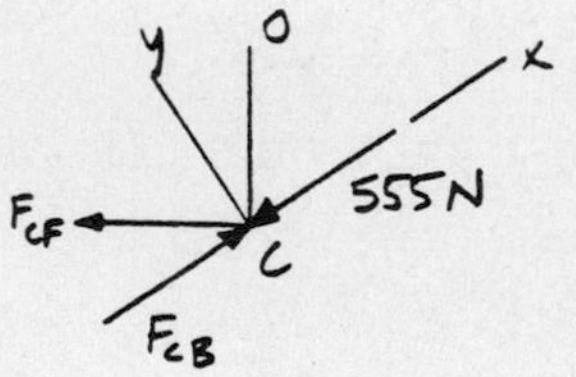

Joint F :

$+\searrow \Sigma F_y = 0; \quad F_{FB} = 0$ **Ans**

$+\nearrow \Sigma F_x = 0; \quad F_{FG} = 0$ **Ans**

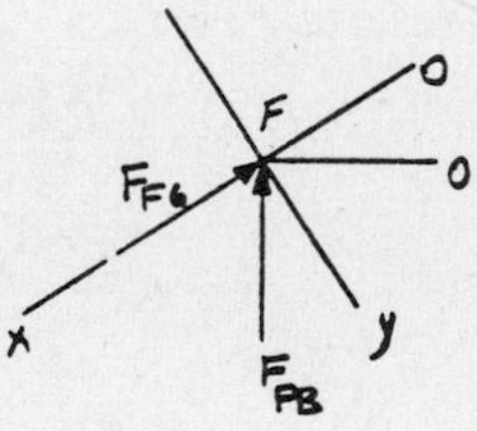

Joint B :

$+\nwarrow \Sigma F_y = 0; \quad F_{BG} = 0$ **Ans**

$+\nearrow \Sigma F_x = 0; \quad F_{BA} = 555$ N (C) **Ans**

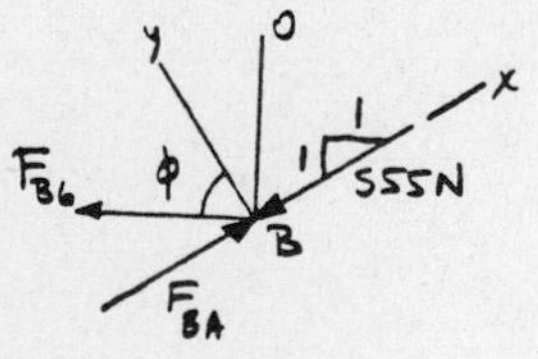

Joint A :

$$+\uparrow \Sigma F_y = 0; \quad F_{GA} - 555\left(\frac{1}{\sqrt{2}}\right) = 0$$

$F_{GA} = 392$ N (T) **Ans**

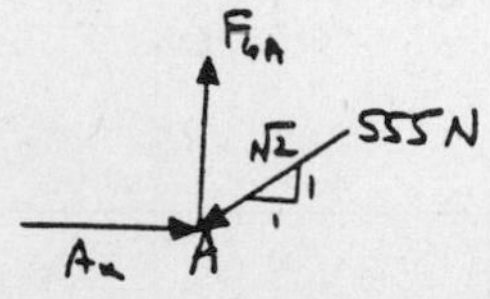

6-15. Determine the largest mass m of the suspended block so that the force in any member does not exceed 30 kN (T) or 25 kN (C).

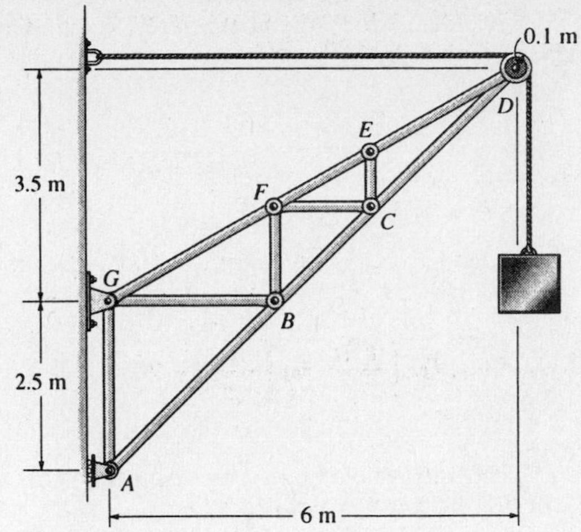

Inspection of joints E, C, F, and B indicates that EC, CF, FB, and BG are all zero - force members.

Joint D:

$\xrightarrow{+} \Sigma F_x = 0; \quad F_{DC} \sin 45° + F_{DE} \cos 30.25° - W = 0$

$+\uparrow \Sigma F_y = 0; \quad F_{DC} \cos 45° + F_{DE} \sin 30.25° - W = 0$

$F_{DC} = 1.414\ W\ (C)$

$F_{DE} = 0$

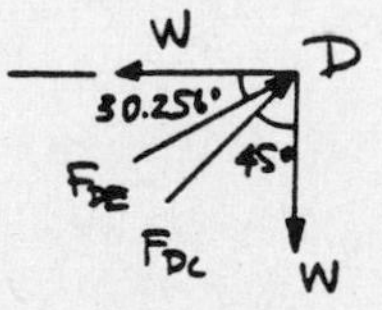

Joint A:

$+\uparrow \Sigma F_y = 0; \quad F_{AG} - 1.414\ W \sin 45° = 0$

$F_{AG} = W\ (T)$

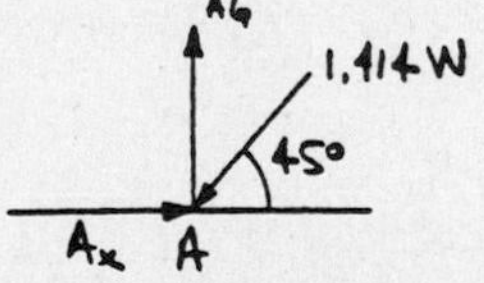

For compression of members DC, BC, and AB,

$25\ \text{kN} = 1.414\ W$

$W = 17.678\ \text{kN}$

For tension of member AG,

$W = 30\ \text{kN}$

Thus the critical value is compression.

$$m = \frac{17.678\ (10^3)\ \text{N}}{9.81} = 1.80\ \text{Mg} \quad \text{Ans}$$

***6-16.** Determine the force in each member of the truss. State whether the members are in tension or compression. Set $P = 8$ kN.

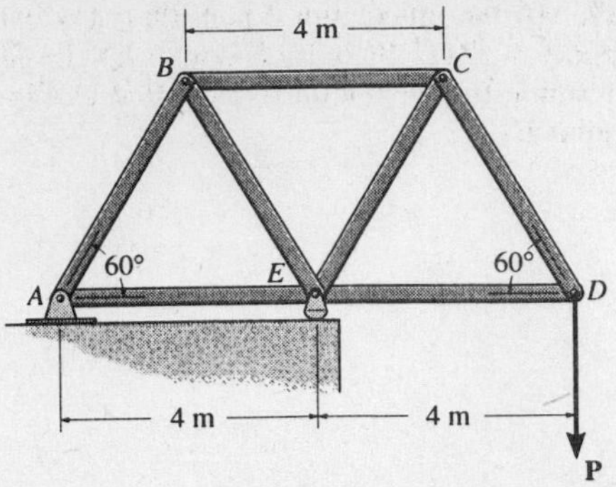

Method of Joints : In this case, the support reactions are not required for determining the member forces.

Joint D

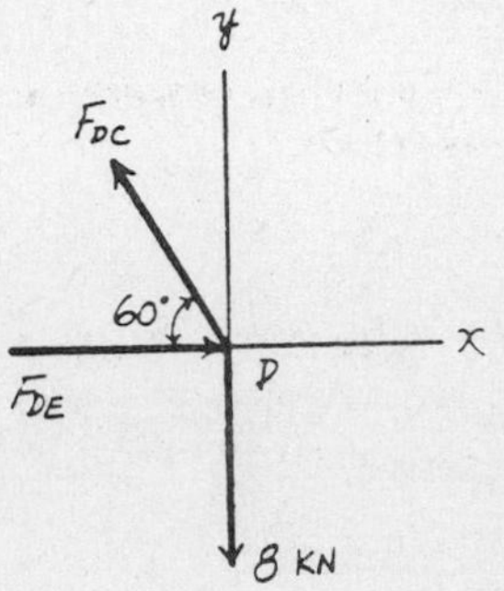

$+\uparrow \Sigma F_y = 0;\quad F_{DC} \sin 60° - 8 = 0$

$F_{DC} = 9.238 \text{ kN (T)} = 9.24 \text{ kN (T)}$ **Ans**

$\overset{+}{\rightarrow} \Sigma F_x = 0;\quad F_{DE} - 9.238 \cos 60° = 0$

$F_{DE} = 4.619 \text{ kN (C)} = 4.62 \text{ kN (C)}$ **Ans**

Joint C

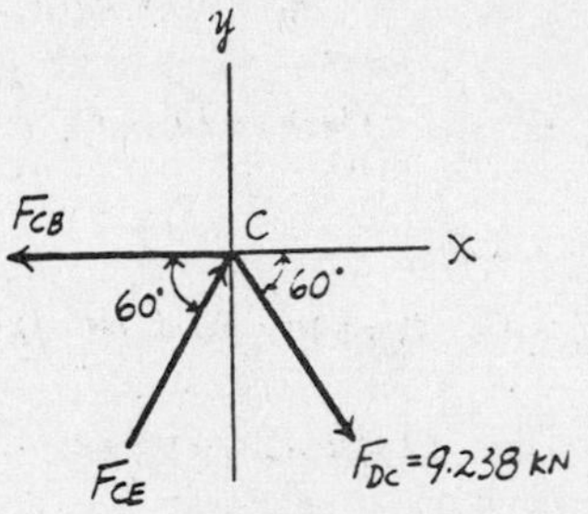

$+\uparrow \Sigma F_y = 0;\quad F_{CE} \sin 60° - 9.238 \sin 60° = 0$

$F_{CE} = 9.238 \text{ kN (C)} = 9.24 \text{ kN (C)}$ **Ans**

$\overset{+}{\rightarrow} \Sigma F_x = 0;\quad 2(9.238 \cos 60°) - F_{CB} = 0$

$F_{CB} = 9.238 \text{ kN (T)} = 9.24 \text{ kN (T)}$ **Ans**

Joint B

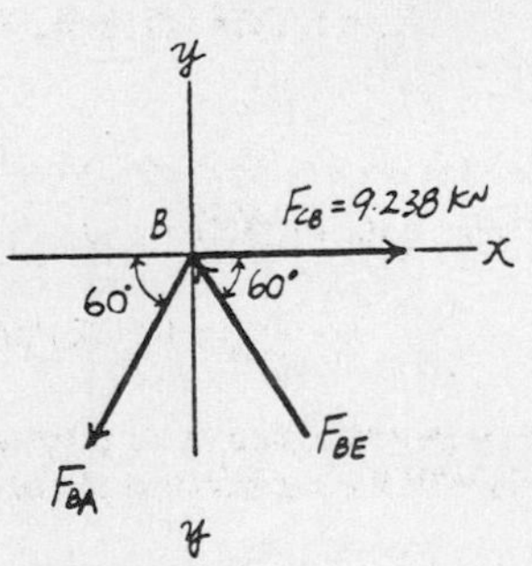

$+\uparrow \Sigma F_y = 0;\quad F_{BE} \sin 60° - F_{BA} \sin 60° = 0$

$F_{BE} = F_{BA} = F$

$\overset{+}{\rightarrow} \Sigma F_x = 0;\quad 9.238 - 2F \cos 60° = 0$

$F = 9.238 \text{ kN}$

Thus, $F_{BE} = 9.24 \text{ kN (C)} \quad F_{BA} = 9.24 \text{ kN (T)}$ **Ans**

Joint E

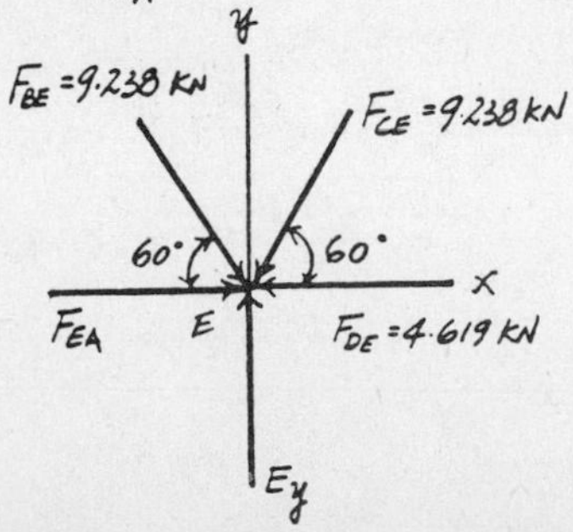

$+\uparrow \Sigma F_y = 0;\quad E_y - 2(9.238 \sin 60°) = 0 \quad E_y = 16.0 \text{ kN}$

$\overset{+}{\rightarrow} \Sigma F_x = 0;\quad F_{EA} + 9.238 \cos 60° - 9.238 \cos 60° + 4.619 = 0$

$F_{EA} = 4.62 \text{ kN (C)}$ **Ans**

Note : The support reactions A_x and A_y can be determined by analysing Joint A using the results obtained above.

6-17. If the maximum force that any member can support is 8 kN in tension and 6 kN in compression, determine the maximum force P that can be supported at joint D.

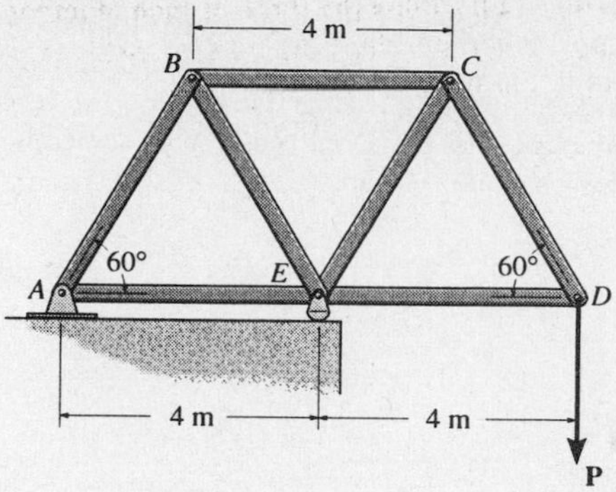

Method of Joints : In this case, the support reactions are not required for determining the member forces.

Joint D

$+\uparrow \Sigma F_y = 0;\quad F_{DC}\sin 60° - P = 0 \quad F_{DC} = 1.1547P$ (T)

$\xrightarrow{+} \Sigma F_x = 0;\quad F_{DE} - 1.1547P\cos 60° = 0 \quad F_{DE} = 0.57735P$ (C)

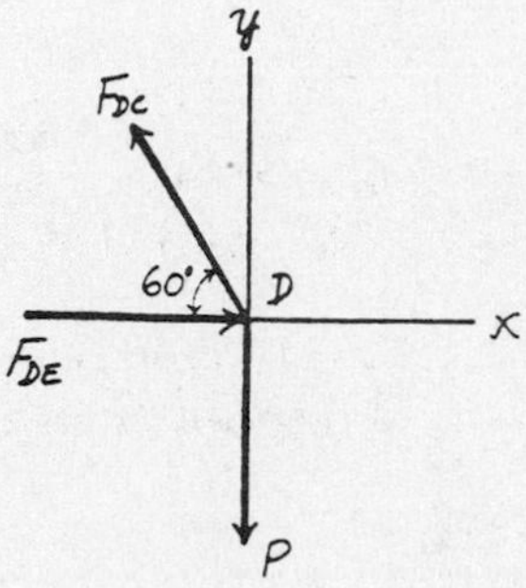

Joint C

$+\uparrow \Sigma F_y = 0;\quad F_{CE}\sin 60° - 1.1547P\sin 60° = 0$

$F_{CE} = 1.1547P$ (C)

$\xrightarrow{+} \Sigma F_x = 0;\quad 2(1.1547P\cos 60°) - F_{CB} = 0 \quad F_{CB} = 1.1547P$ (T)

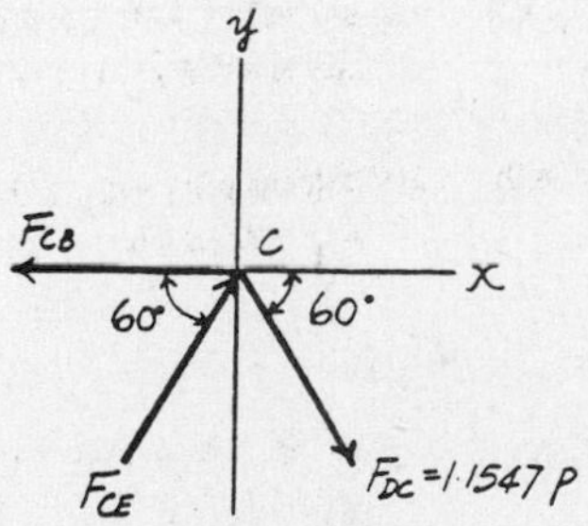

Joint B

$+\uparrow \Sigma F_y = 0;\quad F_{BE}\sin 60° - F_{BA}\sin 60° = 0 \quad F_{BE} = F_{BA} = F$

$\xrightarrow{+} \Sigma F_x = 0;\quad 1.1547P - 2F\cos 60° = 0 \quad F = 1.1547P$

Thus, $\quad F_{BE} = 1.1547P$ (C) $\quad F_{BA} = 1.1547P$ (T)

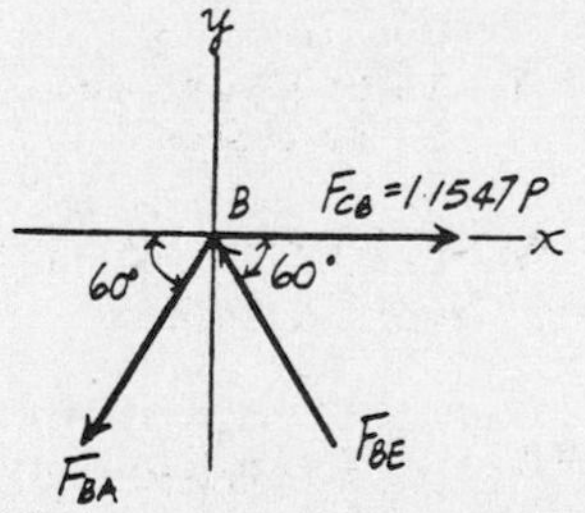

Joint E

$\xrightarrow{+} \Sigma F_x = 0;\quad F_{EA} + 1.1547P\cos 60° - 1.1547P\cos 60° + 0.57735P = 0$

$F_{EA} = 0.57735P$ (C)

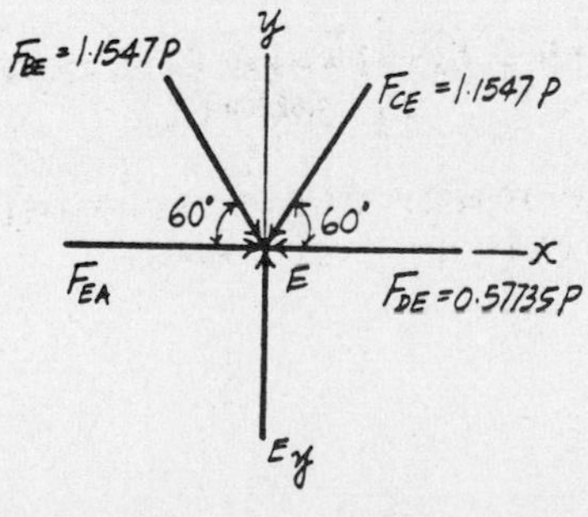

From the above analysis, the maximum compression and tension in the truss member is $1.1547P$. For this case, compression controls which requires

$$1.1547P = 6$$
$$P = 5.20 \text{ kN} \qquad \textbf{Ans}$$

6-18. A sign is subjected to a wind loading that exerts horizontal forces of 300 lb on joints B and C of one of the side supporting trusses. Determine the force in each member of the truss and state if the members are in tension or compression.

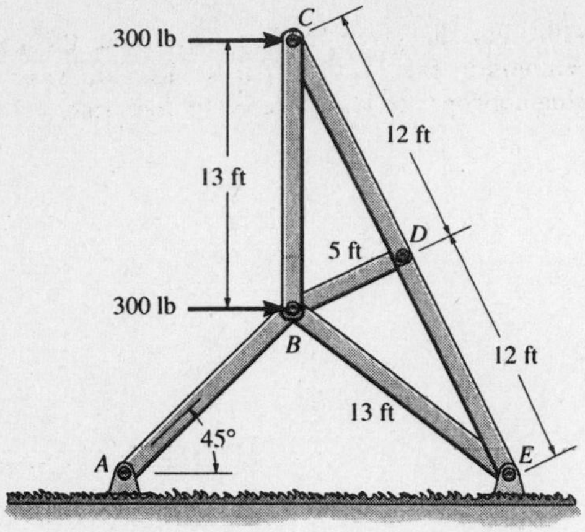

Joint C:

$\xrightarrow{+} \Sigma F_x = 0; \quad 300 - F_{CD} \sin 22.62° = 0$

$F_{CD} = 780 \text{ lb (C)}$ **Ans**

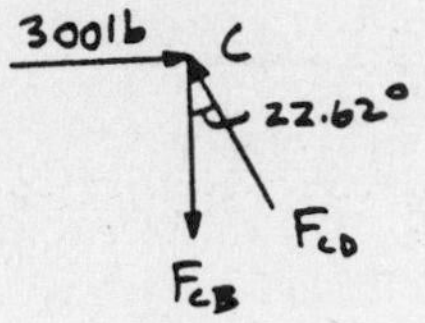

$+\uparrow \Sigma F_y = 0; \quad -F_{CB} + 780 \cos 22.62° = 0$

$F_{CB} = 720 \text{ lb (T)}$ **Ans**

Joint D:

$+\swarrow \Sigma F_x = 0; \quad F_{DB} = 0$ **Ans**

$+\searrow \Sigma F_y = 0; \quad 780 - F_{DE} = 0$

$F_{DE} = 780 \text{ lb (C)}$ **Ans**

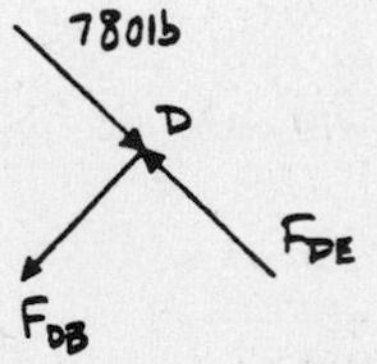

Joint B:

$\xrightarrow{+} \Sigma F_x = 0; \quad 300 - F_{BA} \cos 45° + F_{BE} \sin 45.24° = 0$

$+\uparrow \Sigma F_y = 0; \quad 720 - F_{BA} \sin 45° - F_{BE} \cos 45.24° = 0$

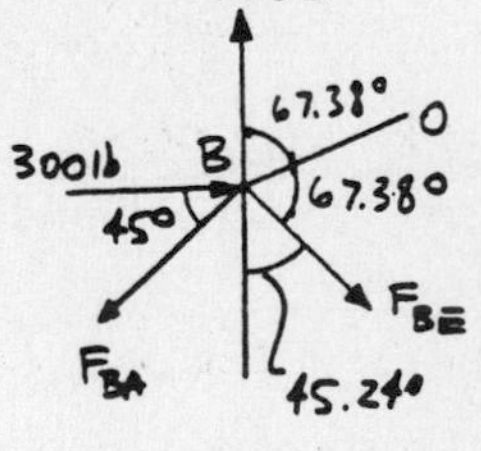

$F_{BE} = 297 \text{ lb (T)}$ **Ans**

$F_{BA} = 722 \text{ lb (T)}$ **Ans**

6-19. For the given loading, determine the zero-force members in the *Pratt roof truss*. Explain your answers using appropriate joint free-body diagrams.

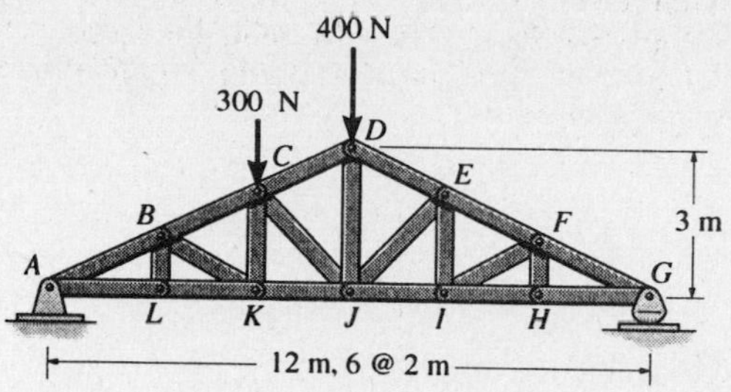

Method of Joints :

Joint *L*

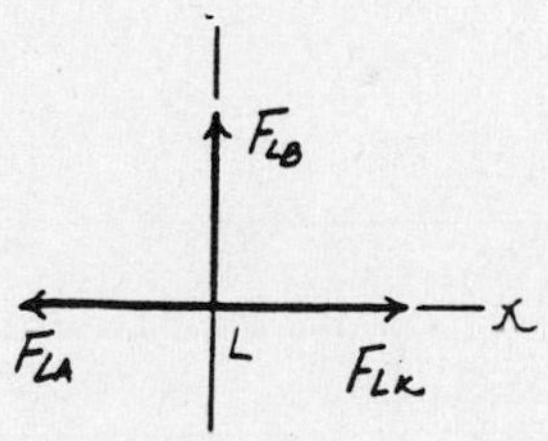

$+\uparrow \Sigma F_y = 0;$ $\qquad F_{LB} = 0$

Joint *B*

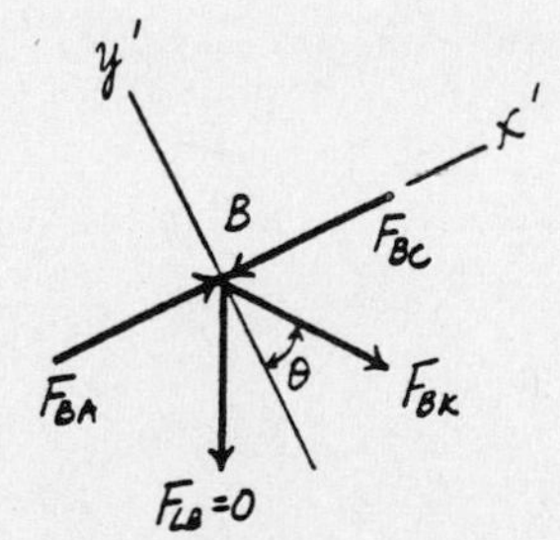

$+\Sigma F_{y'} = 0;$ $\qquad F_{BK}\cos\theta = 0 \qquad F_{BK} = 0$

Joint *K*

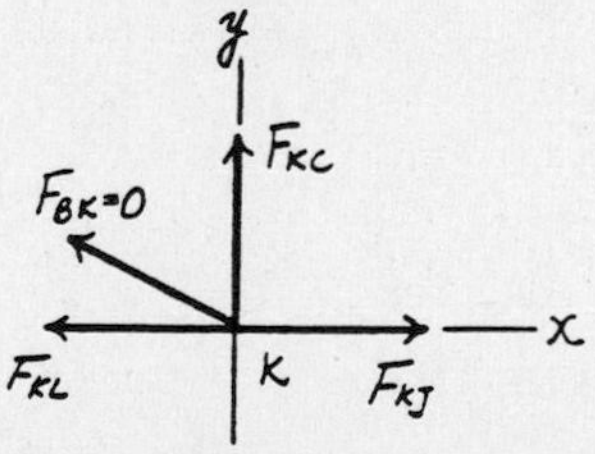

$+\uparrow \Sigma F_y = 0;$ $\qquad F_{KC} = 0$

Joint *H*

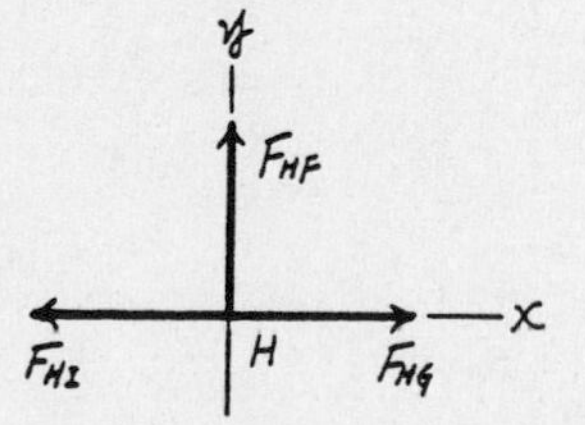

$+\uparrow \Sigma F_y = 0;$ $\qquad F_{HF} = 0$

Joint *F*

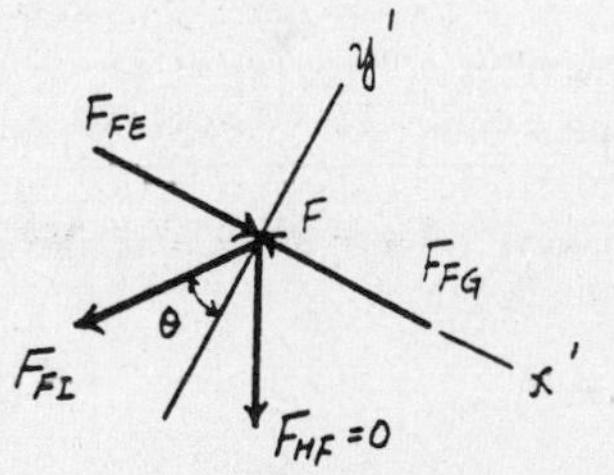

$+\Sigma F_{y'} = 0;$ $\qquad F_{FI}\cos\theta = 0 \qquad F_{FI} = 0$

Joint *I*

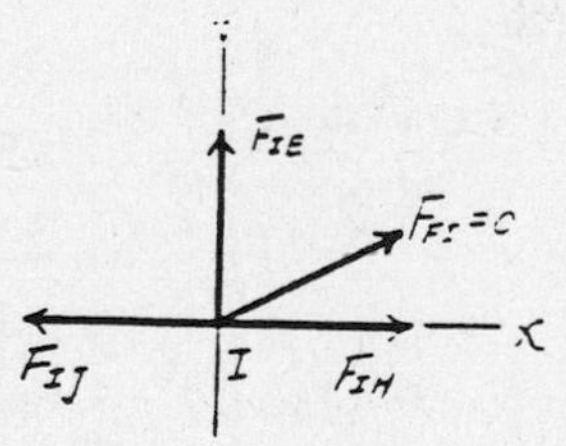

$+\uparrow \Sigma F_y = 0;$ $\qquad F_{IE} = 0$

Joint *E*

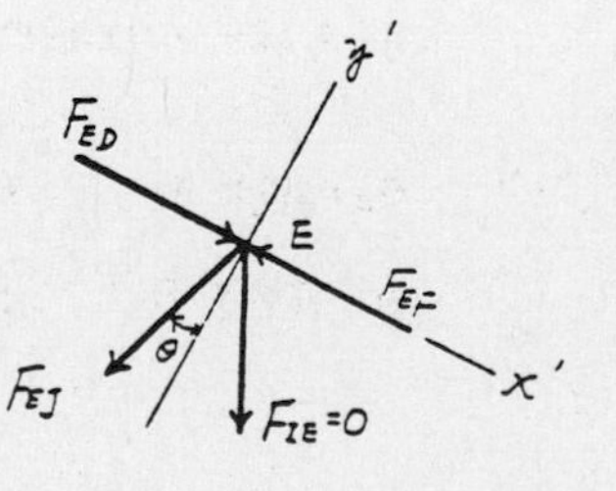

$+\Sigma F_{y'} = 0;$ $\qquad F_{EJ}\cos\theta = 0 \qquad F_{EJ} = 0$

Hence, members ***LB, BK, KC, HF, FI, IE*** and ***EJ*** are zero force member.

***6-20.** Determine the force in each member of the truss in terms of the load P and state if the members are in tension or compression.

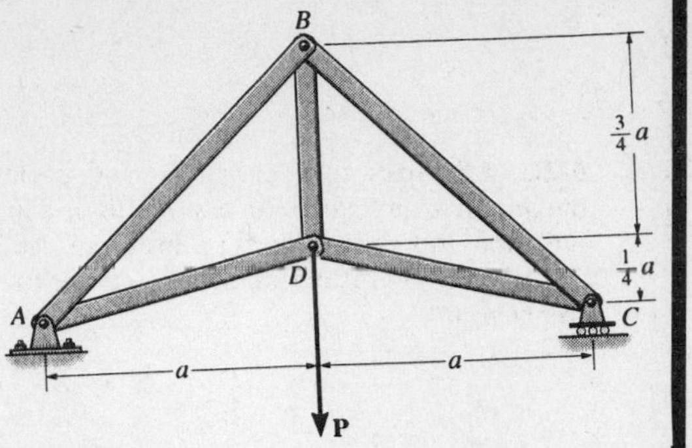

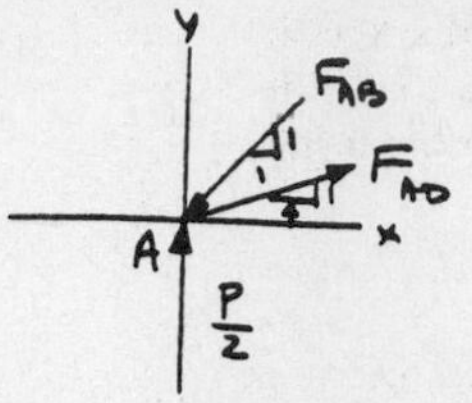

Joint A:

$\xrightarrow{+}\Sigma F_x = 0;\quad \frac{4}{\sqrt{17}}(F_{AD}) - \frac{1}{\sqrt{2}}F_{AB} = 0$

$+\uparrow\Sigma F_y = 0;\quad \frac{P}{2} - \frac{1}{\sqrt{2}}(F_{AB}) + \frac{1}{\sqrt{17}}(F_{AD}) = 0$

$F_{CD} = F_{AD} = 0.687\,P$ (T) **Ans**

$F_{CB} = F_{AB} = 0.943\,P$ (C) **Ans**

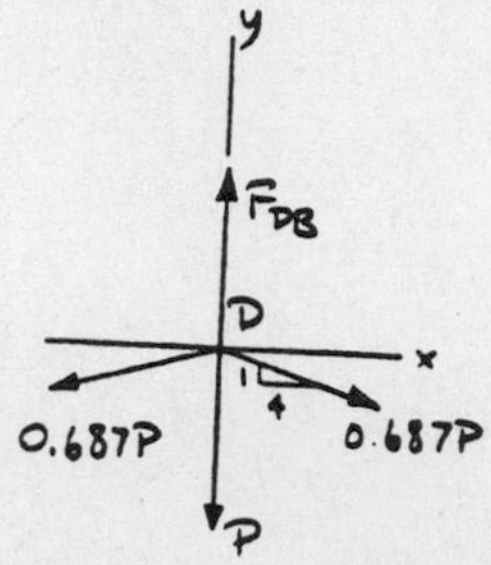

Joint D:

$+\uparrow\Sigma F_y = 0;\quad F_{DB} - 0.687\,P\left(\frac{1}{\sqrt{17}}\right) - \frac{1}{\sqrt{17}}(0.687\,P) - P = 0$

$F_{DB} = 1.33\,P$ (T) **Ans**

6-21. Members AB and BC can each support a maximum compressive force of 800 lb, and members AD, DC, and BD can support a maximum tensile force of 1500 lb. If $a = 10$ ft, determine the greatest load P the truss can support.

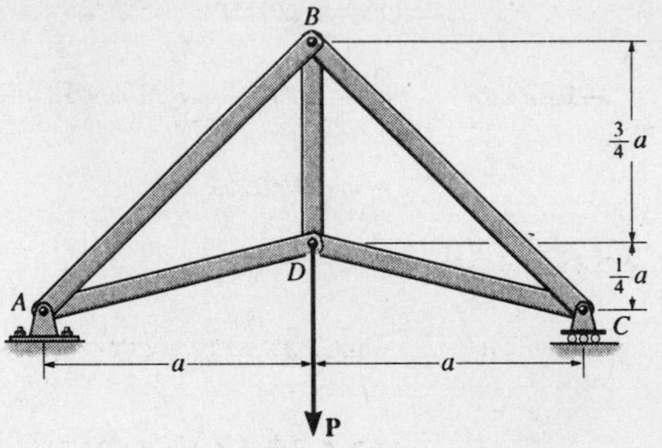

1) Assume $F_{AB} = 800$ lb (C)

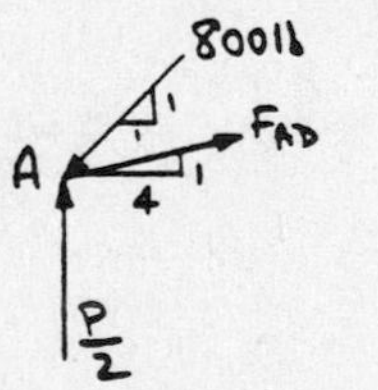

Joint A:

$\xrightarrow{+}\Sigma F_x = 0;\quad -800\left(\frac{1}{\sqrt{2}}\right) + F_{AD}\left(\frac{4}{\sqrt{17}}\right) = 0$

$F_{AD} = 583.0952$ lb $<$ 1500 lb OK

$+\uparrow\Sigma F_y = 0;\quad \frac{P}{2} - \frac{1}{\sqrt{2}}(800) + \frac{1}{\sqrt{17}}(583.0952) = 0$

$P = 848.5297$ lb

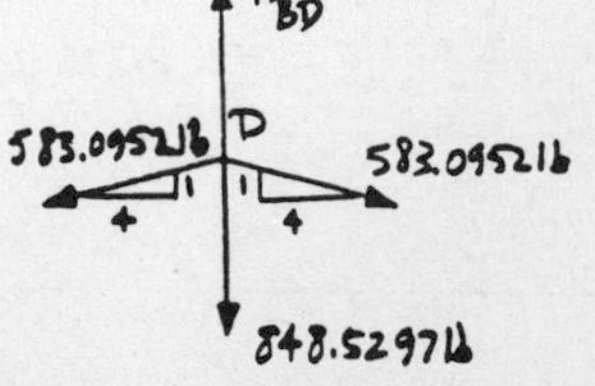

Joint D:

$+\uparrow\Sigma F_y = 0;\quad -848.5297 - 583.0952(2)\left(\frac{1}{\sqrt{17}}\right) + F_{DB} = 0$

$F_{BD} = 1131.3724$ lb $<$ 1500 lb OK

Thus, $P_{max} = 849$ lb **Ans**

6-22. Members AB and BC can each support a maximum compressive force of 800 lb, and members AD, DC, and BD can support a maximum tensile force of 2000 lb. If $a = 6$ ft, determine the greatest load P the truss can support.

1) Assume $F_{AB} = 800$ lb (C)

Joint A:

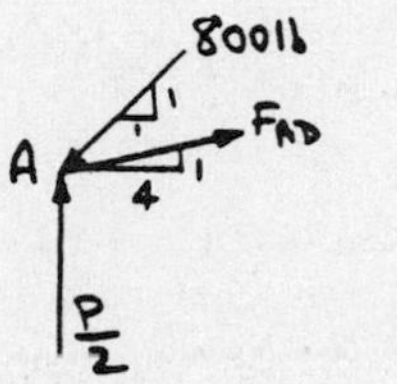

$\xrightarrow{+}\Sigma F_x = 0;$ $\quad -800\left(\frac{1}{\sqrt{2}}\right) + F_{AD}\left(\frac{4}{\sqrt{17}}\right) = 0$

$F_{AD} = 583.0952 \text{ lb} < 1500 \text{ lb}$ OK

$+\uparrow\Sigma F_y = 0;$ $\quad \frac{P}{2} - \frac{1}{\sqrt{2}}(800) + \frac{1}{\sqrt{17}}(583.0952) = 0$

$P = 848.5297$ lb

Joint D:

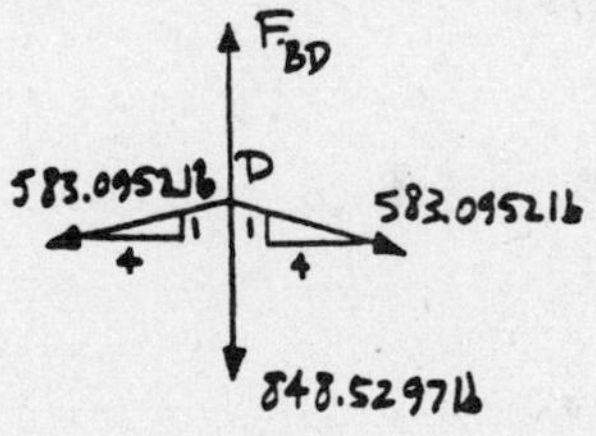

$+\uparrow\Sigma F_y = 0;$ $\quad -848.5297 - 583.0952(2)\left(\frac{1}{\sqrt{17}}\right) + F_{DB} = 0$

$F_{BD} = 1131.3724 \text{ lb} < 1500 \text{ lb}$ OK

Thus, $\quad P_{max} = 849$ lb **Ans**

6-23. Determine the force in each member of the truss and state if the members are in tension or compression.

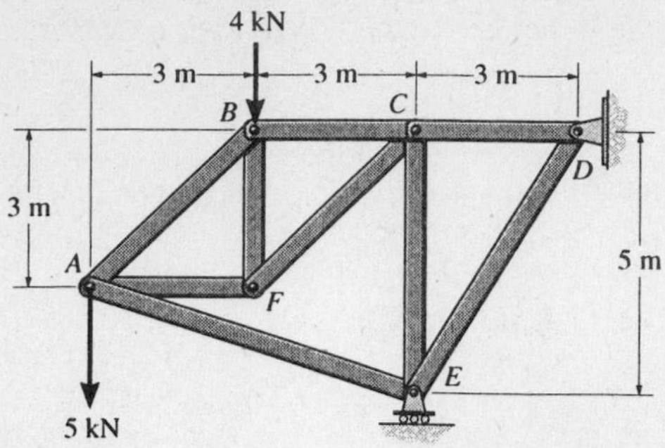

Support Reactions :

$+\Sigma M_D = 0;\quad 4(6) + 5(9) - E_y(3) = 0 \qquad E_y = 23.0\text{ kN}$

$+\uparrow \Sigma F_y = 0;\quad 23.0 - 4 - 5 - D_y = 0 \qquad D_y = 14.0\text{ kN}$

$\overset{+}{\rightarrow} \Sigma F_x = 0 \qquad D_x = 0$

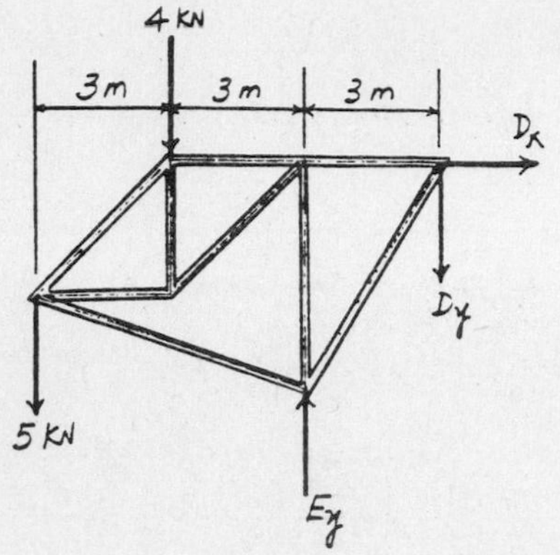

Method of Joints :

Joint D

$+\uparrow \Sigma F_y = 0;\quad F_{DE}\left(\frac{5}{\sqrt{34}}\right) - 14.0 = 0$

$F_{DE} = 16.33\text{ kN (C)} = 16.3\text{ kN (C)}$ **Ans**

$\overset{+}{\rightarrow} \Sigma F_x = 0;\quad 16.33\left(\frac{3}{\sqrt{34}}\right) - F_{DC} = 0$

$F_{DC} = 8.40\text{ kN (T)}$ **Ans**

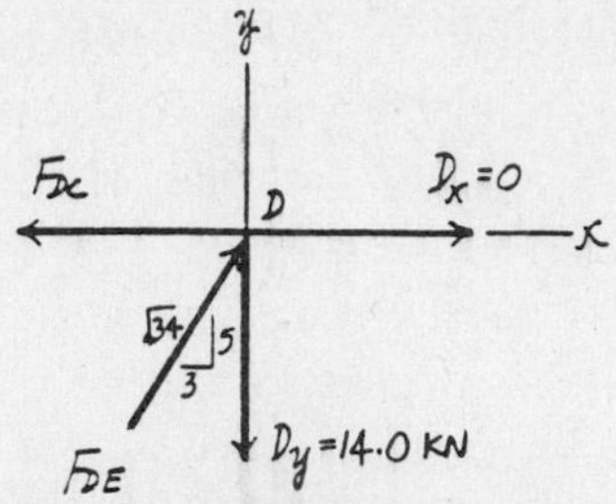

Joint E

$\overset{+}{\rightarrow} \Sigma F_x = 0;\quad F_{EA}\left(\frac{3}{\sqrt{10}}\right) - 16.33\left(\frac{3}{\sqrt{34}}\right) = 0$

$F_{EA} = 8.854\text{ kN (C)} = 8.85\text{ kN (C)}$ **Ans**

$+\uparrow \Sigma F_y = 0;\quad 23.0 - 16.33\left(\frac{5}{\sqrt{34}}\right) - 8.854\left(\frac{1}{\sqrt{10}}\right) - F_{EC} = 0$

$F_{EC} = 6.20\text{ kN (C)}$ **Ans**

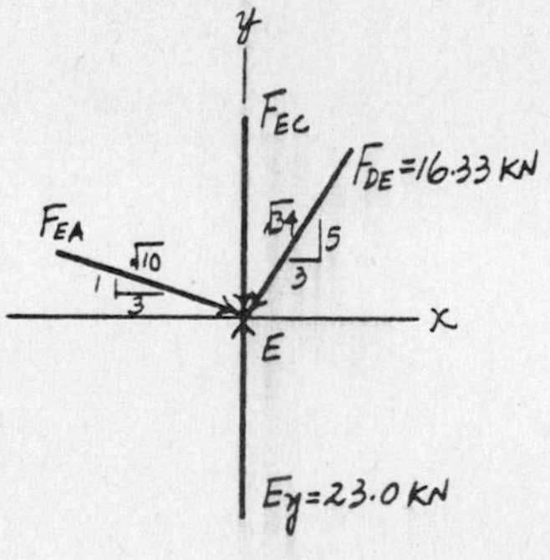

Joint C

$+\uparrow \Sigma F_y = 0;\quad 6.20 - F_{CF}\sin 45° = 0$

$F_{CF} = 8.768\text{ kN (T)} = 8.77\text{ kN (T)}$ **Ans**

$\overset{+}{\rightarrow} \Sigma F_x = 0;\quad 8.40 - 8.768\cos 45° - F_{CB} = 0$

$F_{CB} = 2.20\text{ kN (T)}$ **Ans**

Joint B

$\overset{+}{\rightarrow} \Sigma F_x = 0;\quad 2.20 - F_{BA}\cos 45° = 0$

$F_{BA} = 3.111\text{ kN (T)} = 3.11\text{ kN (T)}$ **Ans**

$+\uparrow \Sigma F_y = 0;\quad F_{BF} - 4 - 3.111\sin 45° = 0$

$F_{BF} = 6.20\text{ kN (C)}$ **Ans**

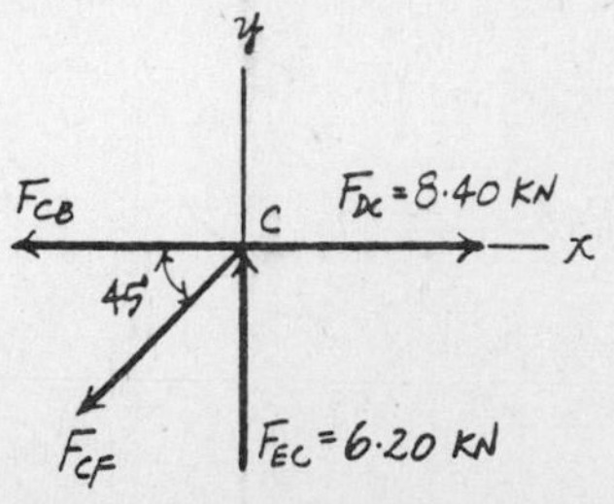

Joint F

$+\uparrow \Sigma F_y = 0;\quad 8.768\sin 45° - 6.20 = 0$ ***(Check!)***

$\overset{+}{\rightarrow} \Sigma F_x = 0;\quad 8.768\cos 45° - F_{FA} = 0$

$F_{FA} = 6.20\text{ kN (T)}$ **Ans**

***6-24.** Determine the force in each member of the truss and state if the members are in tension or compression.

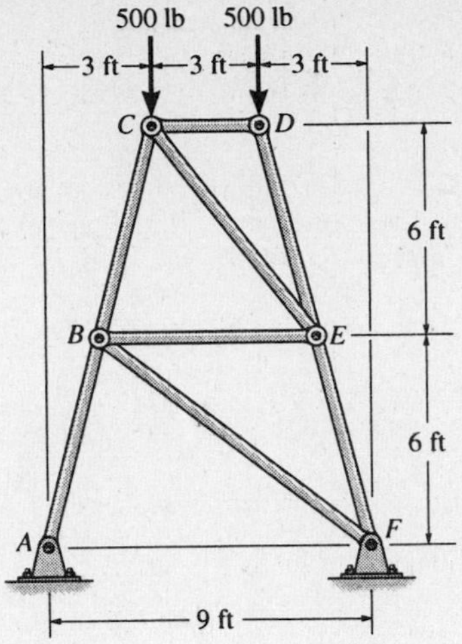

Joint D :

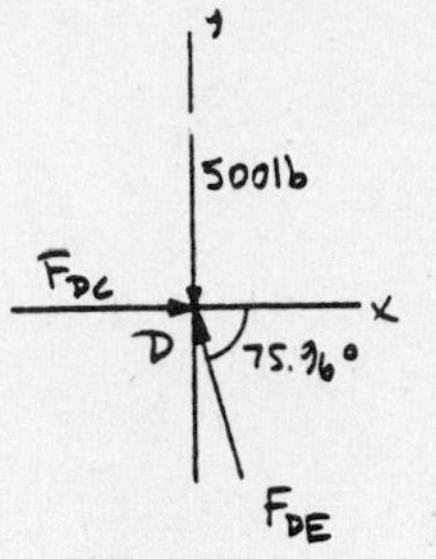

$+\uparrow\Sigma F_y = 0;\quad F_{DE}\sin 75.96° - 500 = 0$

$F_{DE} = 515.39\text{ lb} = 515\text{ lb (C)}$ **Ans**

$\xrightarrow{+}\Sigma F_x = 0;\quad F_{CD} - 515.39\cos 75.96° = 0 \quad F_{CD} = 125\text{ lb (C)}$ **Ans**

Joint C :

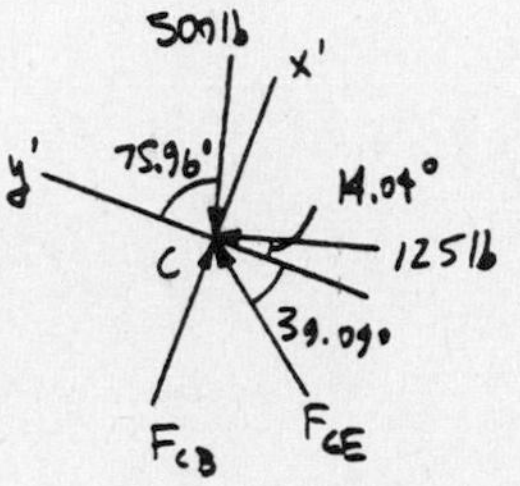

$+\nwarrow\Sigma F_{y'} = 0;\quad F_{CE}\cos 39.09° + 125\cos 14.04° - 500\cos 75.96° = 0$

$F_{CE} = 0$ **Ans**

$+\nearrow\Sigma F_{x'} = 0;\quad F_{CB} - 500\sin 75.96° - 125\sin 14.04° = 0$

$F_{CB} = 515.39\text{ lb} = 515\text{ lb (C)}$ **Ans**

Joint E :

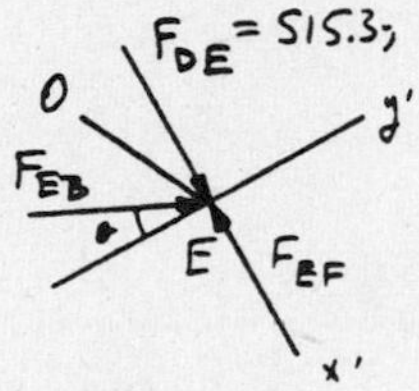

$+\nearrow\Sigma F_{y'} = 0;\quad F_{EB}\cos\theta = 0 \quad F_{EB} = 0$ **Ans**

$+\searrow\Sigma F_{x'} = 0;\quad 515.39 - F_{EF} = 0 \quad F_{EF} = 515\text{ lb (C)}$ **Ans**

Joint B :

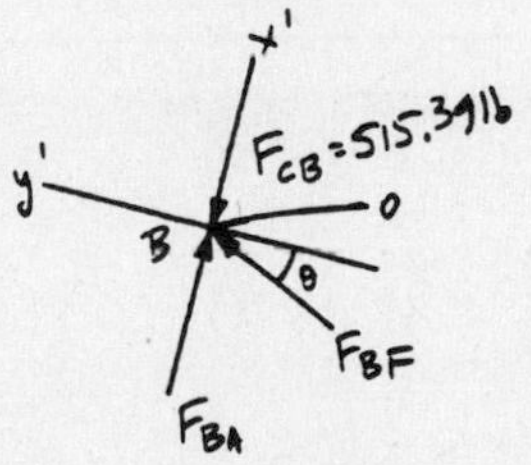

$+\nwarrow\Sigma F_{y'} = 0;\quad F_{BF}\cos\theta = 0 \quad F_{BF} = 0$ **Ans**

$+\nearrow\Sigma F_{x'} = 0;\quad F_{BA} - 515.39 = 0 \quad F_{BA} = 515\text{ lb (C)}$ **Ans**

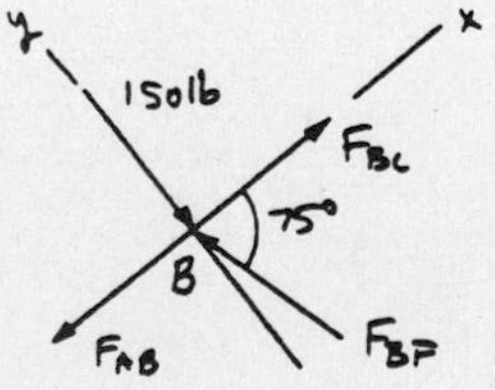

Joint B :

$+\nwarrow\Sigma F_y = 0;\quad F_{BF}\sin 75° - 150 = 0$

$F_{BF} = 155\text{ lb (C)}$ **Ans**

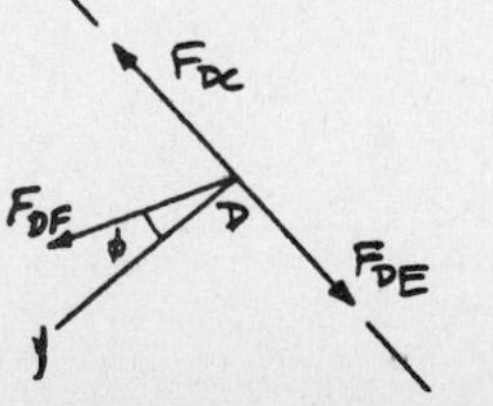

Joint D :

$+\swarrow\Sigma F_y = 0;\quad F_{DF} = 0$ **Ans**

6-25. Determine the force in members BF and FD of the truss and state if the members are in tension or compression. Set $P_1 = 200$ lb, $P_2 = 150$ lb.

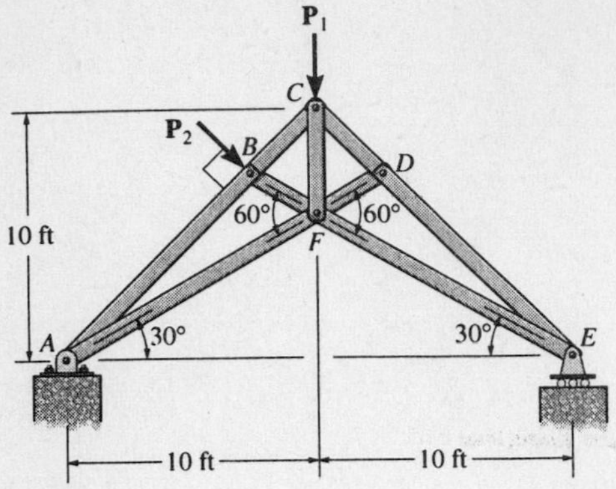

Joint B :

$+\nwarrow \Sigma F_y = 0;\quad F_{BF} \sin 75° - 150 = 0$

$F_{BF} = 155 \text{ lb (C)}$ **Ans**

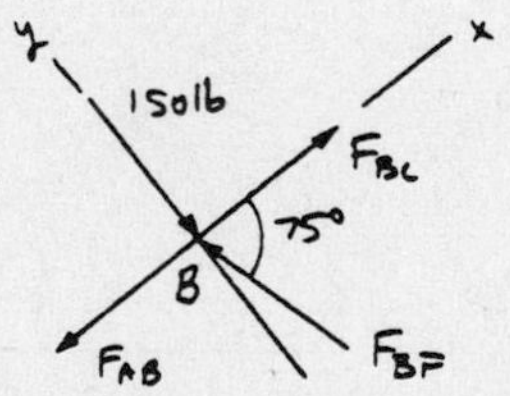

Joint D :

$+\swarrow \Sigma F_y = 0;\quad F_{DF} = 0$ **Ans**

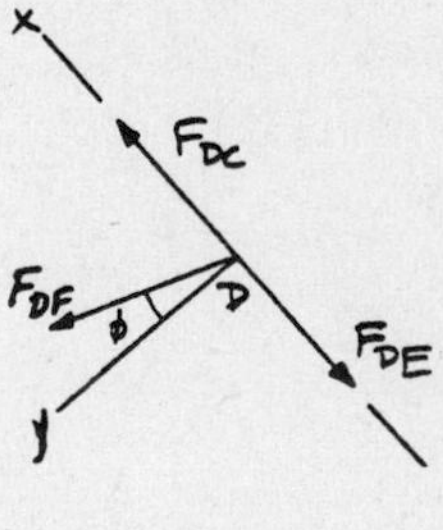

6-27. Determine the force in each member of the truss in terms of the load P, and indicate whether the members are in tension or compression.

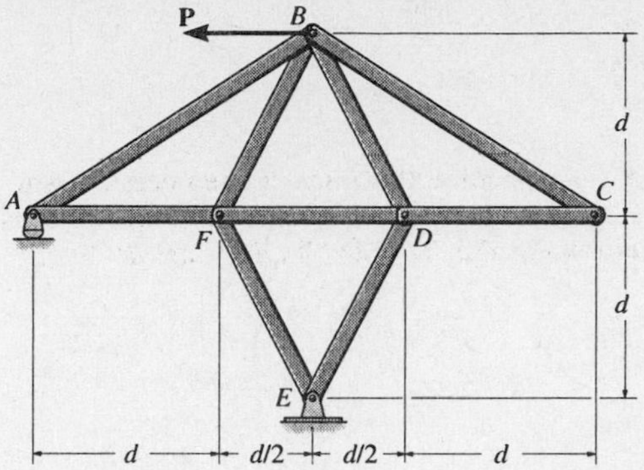

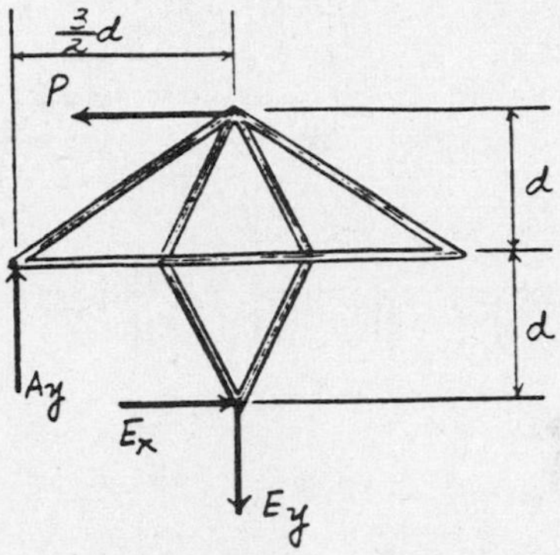

Support Reactions :

$$\circlearrowleft + \Sigma M_E = 0; \quad P(2d) - A_y\left(\frac{3}{2}d\right) = 0 \quad A_y = \frac{4}{3}P$$

$$+\uparrow \Sigma F_y = 0; \quad \frac{4}{3}P - E_y = 0 \quad E_y = \frac{4}{3}P$$

$$\xrightarrow{+} \Sigma F_x = 0 \quad E_x - P = 0 \quad E_x = P$$

Method of Joints : By inspection of joint C, members CB and CD are zero force member. Hence

$$F_{CB} = F_{CD} = 0 \qquad \textbf{Ans}$$

Joint A

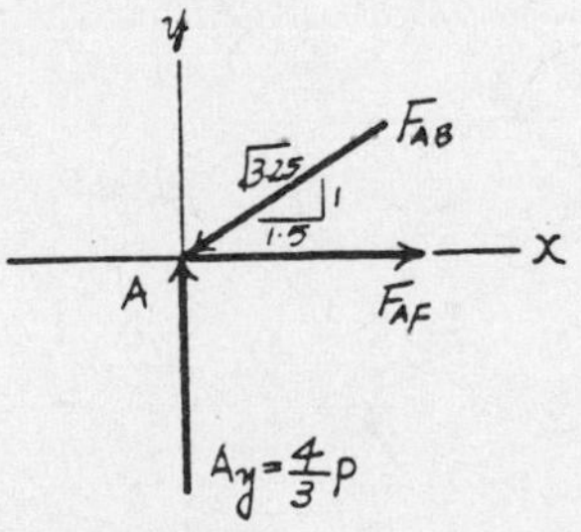

$$+\uparrow \Sigma F_y = 0; \quad F_{AB}\left(\frac{1}{\sqrt{3.25}}\right) - \frac{4}{3}P = 0$$

$$F_{AB} = 2.404P \text{ (C)} = 2.40P \text{ (C)} \qquad \textbf{Ans}$$

$$\xrightarrow{+} \Sigma F_x = 0; \quad F_{AF} - 2.404P\left(\frac{1.5}{\sqrt{3.25}}\right) = 0$$

$$F_{AF} = 2.00P \text{ (T)} \qquad \textbf{Ans}$$

Joint B

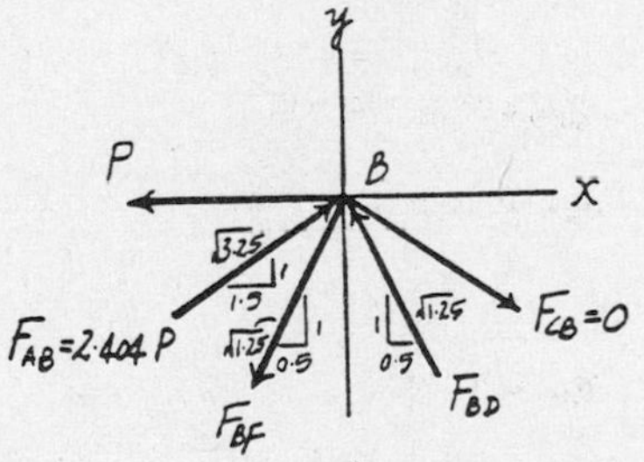

$$\xrightarrow{+} \Sigma F_x = 0; \quad 2.404P\left(\frac{1.5}{\sqrt{3.25}}\right) - P - F_{BF}\left(\frac{0.5}{\sqrt{1.25}}\right) - F_{BD}\left(\frac{0.5}{\sqrt{1.25}}\right) = 0$$

$$1.00P - 0.4472F_{BF} - 0.4472F_{BD} = 0 \qquad [1]$$

$$+\uparrow \Sigma F_y = 0; \quad 2.404P\left(\frac{1}{\sqrt{3.25}}\right) + F_{BD}\left(\frac{1}{\sqrt{1.25}}\right) - F_{BF}\left(\frac{1}{\sqrt{1.25}}\right) = 0$$

$$1.333P + 0.8944F_{BD} - 0.8944F_{BF} = 0 \qquad [2]$$

Solving Eqs. [1] and [2] yield,

$$F_{BF} = 1.863P\text{(T)} = 1.86P\text{(T)} \qquad \textbf{Ans}$$

$$F_{BD} = 0.3727P\text{(C)} = 0.373P\text{(C)} \qquad \textbf{Ans}$$

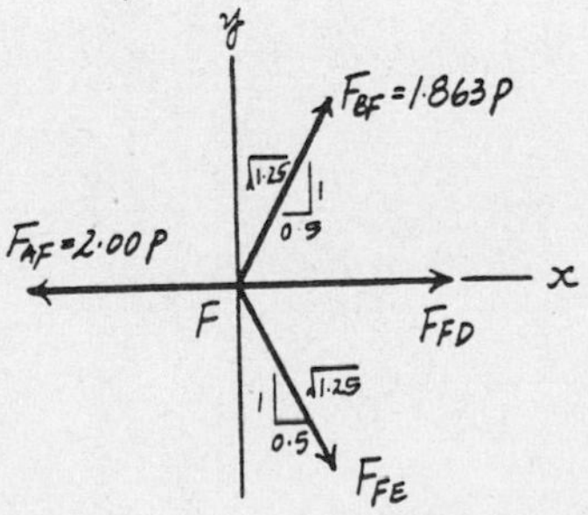

Joint *F*

$$+\uparrow \Sigma F_y = 0; \quad 1.863P\left(\frac{1}{\sqrt{1.25}}\right) - F_{FE}\left(\frac{1}{\sqrt{1.25}}\right) = 0$$

$$F_{FE} = 1.863P(\text{T}) = 1.86P(\text{T}) \qquad \textbf{Ans}$$

$$\overset{+}{\rightarrow} \Sigma F_x = 0; \quad F_{FD} + 2\left[1.863P\left(\frac{0.5}{\sqrt{1.25}}\right)\right] - 2.00P = 0$$

$$F_{FD} = 0.3333P(\text{T}) = 0.333P\ (\text{T}) \qquad \textbf{Ans}$$

Joint *D*

$$+\uparrow \Sigma F_y = 0; \quad F_{DE}\left(\frac{1}{\sqrt{1.25}}\right) - 0.3727P\left(\frac{1}{\sqrt{1.25}}\right) = 0$$

$$F_{DE} = 0.3727P\ (\text{C}) = 0.373P\ (\text{C}) \qquad \textbf{Ans}$$

$$\overset{+}{\rightarrow} \Sigma F_y = 0; \quad 2\left[0.3727P\left(\frac{0.5}{\sqrt{1.25}}\right)\right] - 0.3333P = 0\ (\textbf{\textit{Check!}})$$

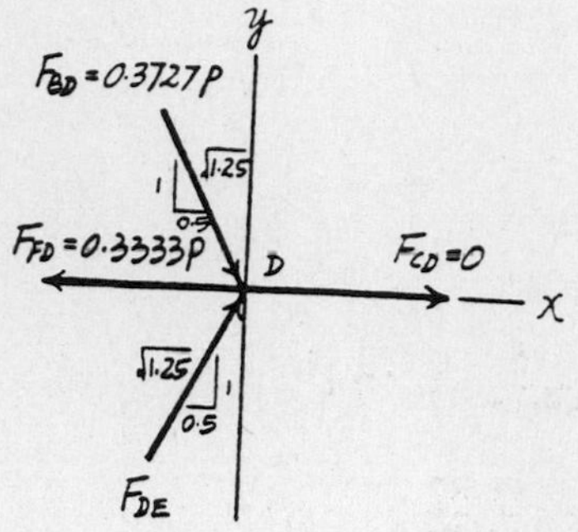

6-26. Determine the force in each member of the truss and state if the members are in tension or compression. Set $P_1 = 800$ lb, $P_2 = 600$ lb.

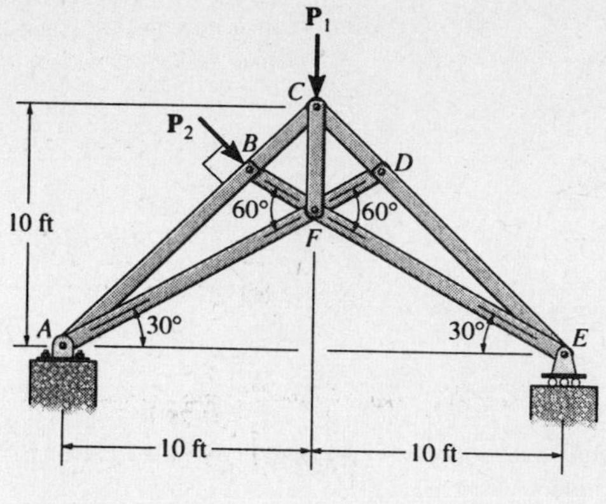

$$AF = \frac{10}{\cos 30^\circ} = 11.547 \text{ ft}$$

$$\frac{AB}{\sin 60^\circ} = \frac{11.547}{\sin 105^\circ}$$

$$AB = 10.3528 \text{ ft}$$

$\xrightarrow{+} \Sigma F_x = 0; \quad 600 \sin 45^\circ - A_x = 0$

$A_x = 424.264$ lb

$\curvearrowleft + \Sigma M_A = 0; \quad E_y(20) - 800(10) - 600(10.3528) = 0$

$E_y = 710.583$ lb

$+\uparrow \Sigma F_y = 0; \quad A_y + 710.583 - 800 - 600 \cos 45^\circ = 0$

$A_y = 513.681$ lb

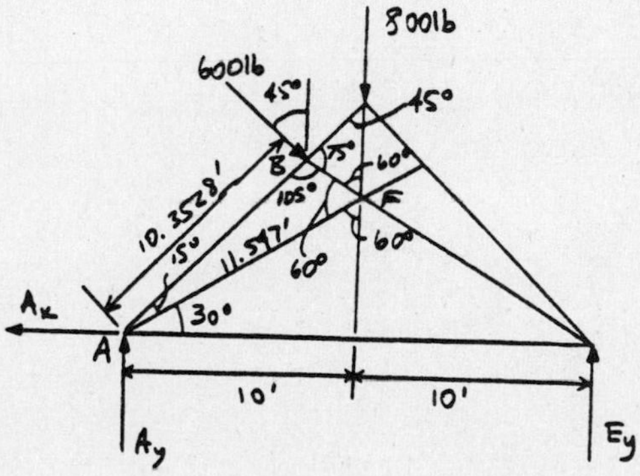

Joint E:

$\xrightarrow{+} \Sigma F_x = 0; \quad -F_{EF} \cos 30^\circ + F_{ED} \cos 45^\circ = 0$

$+\uparrow \Sigma F_y = 0; \quad 710.583 - F_{ED} \sin 45^\circ + F_{EF} \sin 30^\circ = 0$

$F_{ED} = 2377.66 \text{ lb} = 2.38 \text{ kip (C)}$ **Ans**

$F_{EF} = 1941.35 \text{ lb} = 1.94 \text{ kip (T)}$ **Ans**

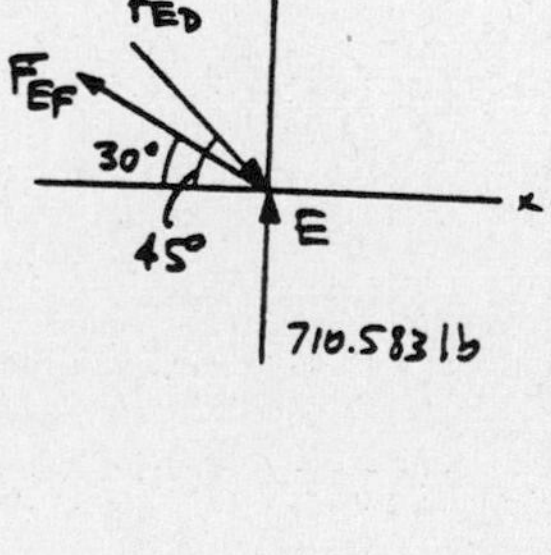

Joint D:

$+\swarrow \Sigma F_y = 0; \quad F_{DF} \sin \theta = 0$

$F_{DF} = 0$ **Ans**

$+\nwarrow \Sigma F_x = 0; \quad 2.38 - F_{DC} = 0$

$F_{DC} = 2.38 \text{ kip (C)}$ **Ans**

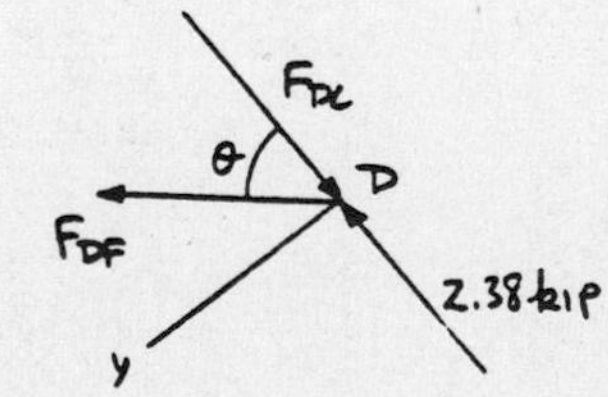

*6-28. If the maximum force that any member can support is 4 kN in tension and 3 kN in compression, determine the maximum force P that can be supported at point B. Take $d = 1$m.

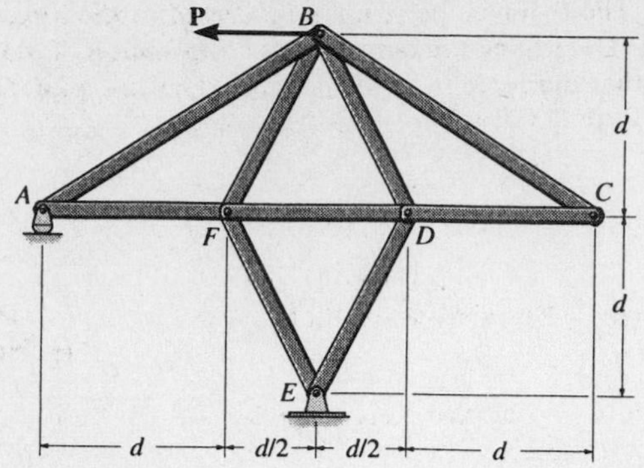

Support Reactions :

$$\circlearrowleft + \Sigma M_E = 0; \quad P(2d) - A_y\left(\frac{3}{2}d\right) = 0 \quad A_y = \frac{4}{3}P$$

$$+\uparrow \Sigma F_y = 0; \quad \frac{4}{3}P - E_y = 0 \quad E_y = \frac{4}{3}P$$

$$\xrightarrow{+} \Sigma F_x = 0 \quad E_x - P = 0 \quad E_x = P$$

Method of Joints : By inspection of joint C, members CB and CD are zero force member. Hence

$$F_{CB} = F_{CD} = 0$$

Joint *A*

$$+\uparrow \Sigma F_y = 0; \quad F_{AB}\left(\frac{1}{\sqrt{3.25}}\right) - \frac{4}{3}P = 0 \quad F_{AB} = 2.404P \text{ (C)}$$

$$\xrightarrow{+} \Sigma F_x = 0; \quad F_{AF} - 2.404P\left(\frac{1.5}{\sqrt{3.25}}\right) = 0 \quad F_{AF} = 2.00P \text{ (T)}$$

Joint *B*

$$\xrightarrow{+} \Sigma F_x = 0; \quad 2.404P\left(\frac{1.5}{\sqrt{3.25}}\right) - P - F_{BF}\left(\frac{0.5}{\sqrt{1.25}}\right) - F_{BD}\left(\frac{0.5}{\sqrt{1.25}}\right) = 0$$

$$1.00P - 0.4472F_{BF} - 0.4472F_{BD} = 0 \qquad [1]$$

$$+\uparrow \Sigma F_y = 0; \quad 2.404P\left(\frac{1}{\sqrt{3.25}}\right) + F_{BD}\left(\frac{1}{\sqrt{1.25}}\right) - F_{BF}\left(\frac{1}{\sqrt{1.25}}\right) = 0$$

$$1.333P + 0.8944F_{BD} - 0.8944F_{BF} = 0 \qquad [2]$$

Solving Eqs.[1] and [2] yield,

$$F_{BF} = 1.863P\text{(T)} \quad F_{BD} = 0.3727P\text{(C)}$$

Joint *F*

$$+\uparrow \Sigma F_y = 0; \quad 1.863P\left(\frac{1}{\sqrt{1.25}}\right) - F_{FE}\left(\frac{1}{\sqrt{1.25}}\right) = 0$$

$$F_{FE} = 1.863P\text{(T)}$$

$$\xrightarrow{+} \Sigma F_x = 0; \quad F_{FD} + 2\left[1.863P\left(\frac{0.5}{\sqrt{1.25}}\right)\right] - 2.00P = 0$$

$$F_{FD} = 0.3333P\text{(T)}$$

Joint *D*

$$+\uparrow \Sigma F_y = 0; \quad F_{DE}\left(\frac{1}{\sqrt{1.25}}\right) - 0.3727P\left(\frac{1}{\sqrt{1.25}}\right) = 0$$

$$F_{DE} = 0.3727P \text{ (C)}$$

$$\xrightarrow{+} \Sigma F_y = 0; \quad 2\left[0.3727P\left(\frac{0.5}{\sqrt{1.25}}\right)\right] - 0.3333P = 0 \text{ (\textit{Check!})}$$

From the above analysis, the maximum compression and tension in the truss members are $2.404P$ and $2.00P$, respectively. For this case, compression controls which requires

$$2.404P = 3$$
$$P = 1.25 \text{ kN}$$

■6-29. The two-member truss is subjected to the force of 300 lb. Determine the range of θ for application of the load so that the force in either member does not exceed 400 lb (T) or 200 lb (C).

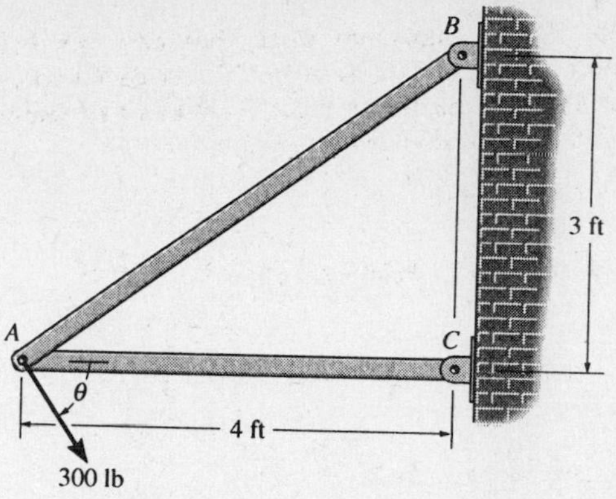

Joint A:

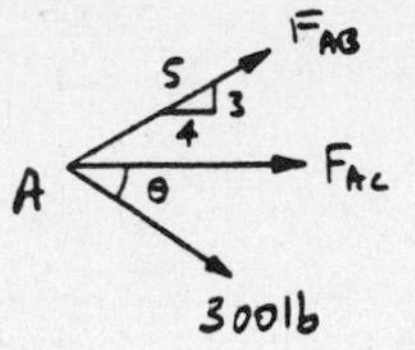

$\xrightarrow{+} \Sigma F_x = 0; \quad 300 \cos\theta + F_{AC} + F_{AB}\left(\frac{4}{5}\right) = 0$

$+\uparrow \Sigma F_y = 0; \quad -300 \sin\theta + F_{AB}\left(\frac{3}{5}\right) = 0$

Thus,

$F_{AB} = 500 \sin\theta$

$F_{AC} = -300\cos\theta - 400\sin\theta$

For AB require:

$-200 \le 500\sin\theta \le 400$

$-2 \le 5\sin\theta \le 4 \qquad (1)$

For AC require:

$-200 \le -300\cos\theta - 400\sin\theta \le 400$

$-4 \le 3\cos\theta + 4\sin\theta \le 2 \qquad (2)$

Solving Eqs. (1) and (2) simultaneously,

$127° \le \theta \le 196°$ **Ans**

$336° \le \theta \le 347°$ **Ans**

A possible hand solution:

$\theta_2 = \theta_1 + \tan^{-1}\left(\frac{3}{4}\right) = \theta_1 + 36.870$

Then

$F_{AB} = 500\sin\theta_1$

$F_{AC} = -300\cos(\theta_2 - 36.870°) - 400\sin(\theta_2 - 36.870°)$

$= -300[\cos\theta_2\cos 36.870° + \sin\theta_2 \sin 36.870°]$

$-400[\sin\theta_2\cos 36.870° - \cos\theta_2\sin 36.870°]$

$= -240\cos\theta_2 - 180\sin\theta_2 - 320\sin\theta_2 + 240\cos\theta_2$

$= -500\sin\theta_2$

Thus, we require

$-2 \le 5\sin\theta_1 \le 4 \quad \text{or} \quad -0.4 \le \sin\theta_1 \le 0.8 \qquad (1)$

$-4 \le 5\sin\theta_2 \le 2 \quad \text{or} \quad -0.8 \le \sin\theta_2 \le 0.4 \qquad (2)$

The range of values for Eqs. (1) and (2) are shown in the figures:

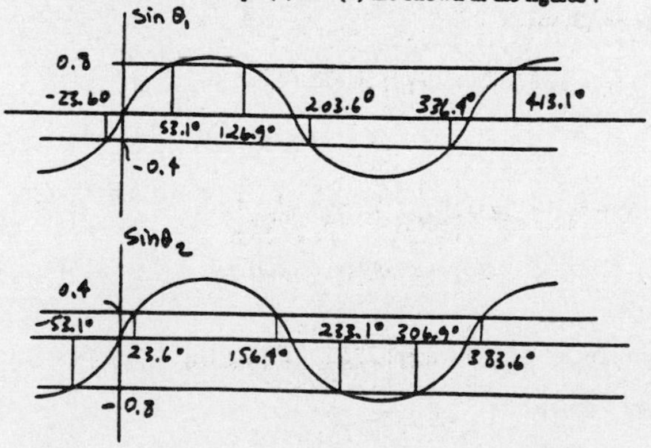

Since $\theta_1 = \theta_2 - 36.870°$, the range of acceptable values for $\theta = \theta_1$ is

$127° \le \theta \le 196°$ **Ans**

$336° \le \theta \le 347°$ **Ans**

6-30. Determine the force in members BC, HC, and HG of the bridge truss, and indicate whether the members are in tension or compression.

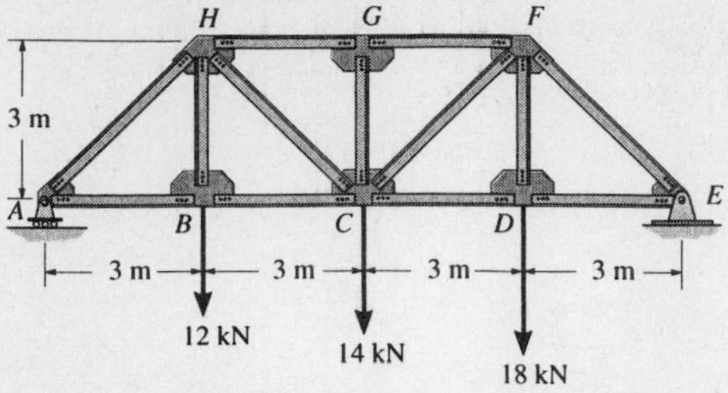

Support Reactions :

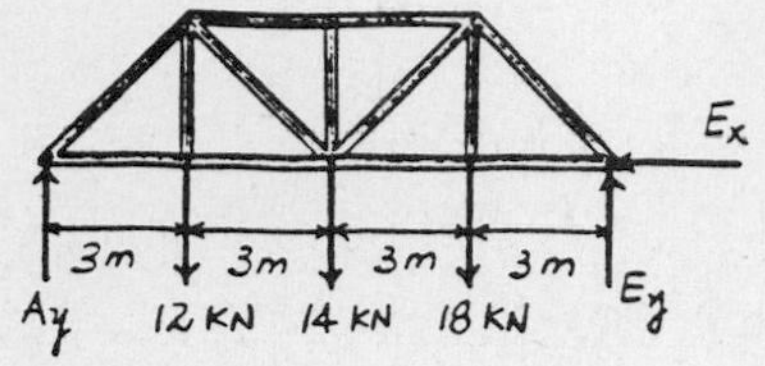

$\circlearrowleft + \Sigma M_E = 0; \quad 18(3) + 14(6) + 12(9) - A_y(12) = 0 \qquad A_y = 20.5 \text{ kN}$

Method of Sections :

$\circlearrowleft + \Sigma M_C = 0; \quad F_{HG}(3) + 12(3) - 20.5(6) = 0$

$F_{HG} = 29.0 \text{ kN (C)}$ **Ans**

$\circlearrowleft + \Sigma M_H = 0; \quad F_{BC}(3) - 20.5(3) = 0$

$F_{BC} = 20.5 \text{ kN (T)}$ **Ans**

$+\uparrow \Sigma F_y = 0; \quad 20.5 - 12 - F_{HC}\sin 45° = 0$

$F_{HC} = 12.0 \text{ kN (T)}$ **Ans**

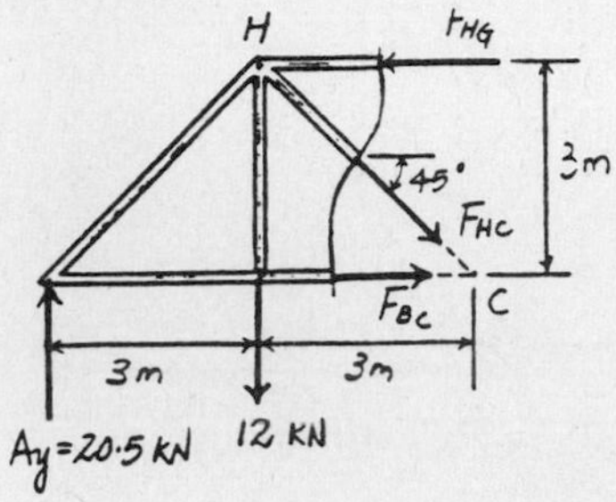

6-31. Determine the force in members GF, CF, and CD of the bridge truss, and indicate whether the members are in tension or compression.

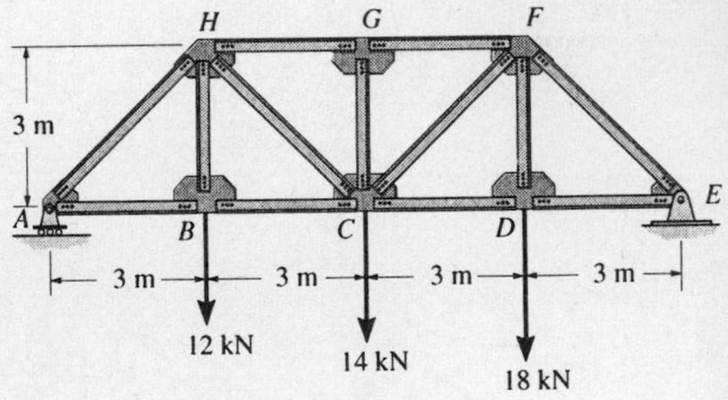

Support Reactions :

$\circlearrowleft + \Sigma M_A = 0; \quad E_y(12) - 18(9) - 14(6) - 12(3) = 0 \qquad E_y = 23.5 \text{ kN}$

$\overset{+}{\rightarrow} \Sigma F_x = 0; \quad E_x = 0$

Method of Sections :

$\circlearrowleft + \Sigma M_C = 0; \quad 23.5(6) - 18(3) - F_{GF}(3) = 0$

$F_{GF} = 29.0 \text{ kN (C)}$ **Ans**

$\circlearrowleft + \Sigma M_F = 0; \quad 23.5(3) - F_{CD}(3) = 0$

$F_{CD} = 23.5 \text{ kN (T)}$ **Ans**

$+\uparrow \Sigma F_y = 0; \quad 23.5 - 18 - F_{CF}\sin 45° = 0$

$F_{CF} = 7.78 \text{ kN (T)}$ **Ans**

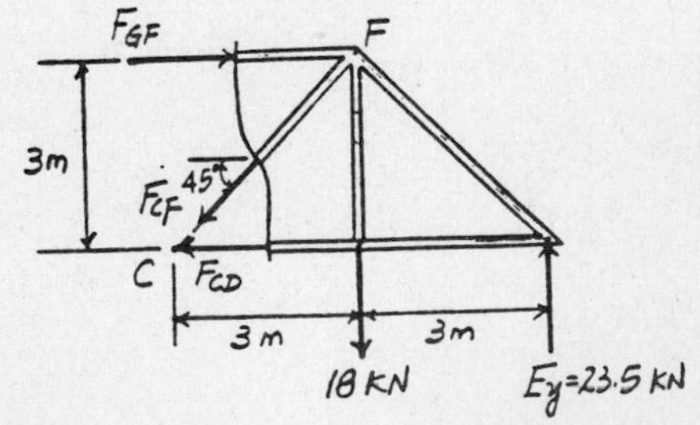

***6-32.** Determine the force in members *DE*, *DF*, and *GF* of the cantilevered truss and state if the members are in tension or compression.

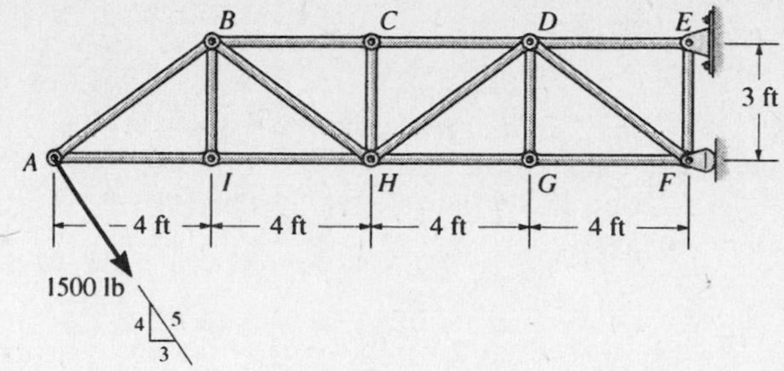

$+\uparrow\Sigma F_y = 0;\quad \frac{3}{5}F_{DF} - \frac{4}{5}(1500) = 0$

$F_{DF} = 2000 \text{ lb} = 2.0 \text{ kip (C)}$ **Ans**

$\circlearrowleft +\Sigma M_D = 0;\quad \frac{4}{5}(1500)(12) + \frac{3}{5}(1500)(3) - F_{GF}(3) = 0$

$F_{GF} = 5700 \text{ lb} = 5.70 \text{ kip (C)}$ **Ans**

$\circlearrowleft +\Sigma M_F = 0;\quad \frac{4}{5}(1500)(16) - F_{DE}(3) = 0$

$F_{DE} = 6400 \text{ lb} = 6.40 \text{ kip (T)}$ **Ans**

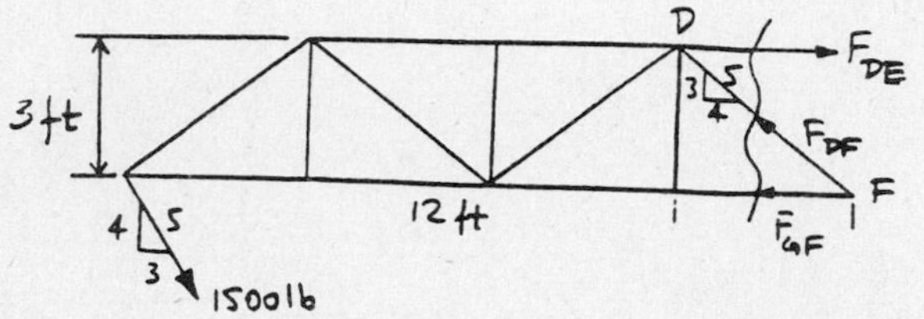

6-33. The internal drag truss for the wing of a light airplane is subjected to the forces shown. Determine the force in members *BC*, *BH*, and *HC*, and state if the members are in tension or compression.

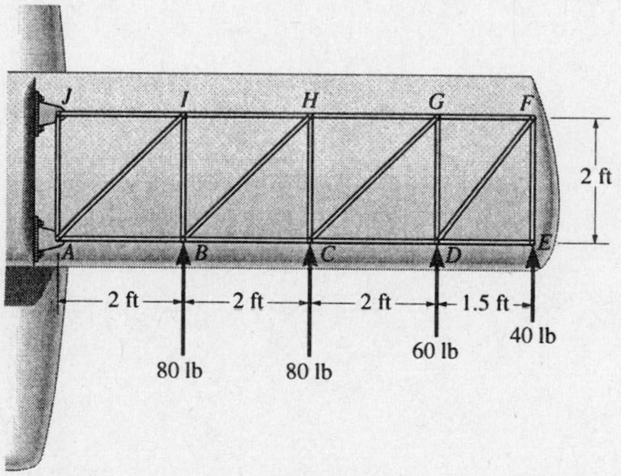

$+\uparrow\Sigma F_y = 0;\quad 180 - F_{BH}\sin 45° = 0$

$F_{BH} = 255 \text{ lb (T)}$ **Ans**

$\circlearrowleft +\Sigma M_H = 0;\quad -F_{BC}(2) + 60(2) + 40(3.5) = 0$

$F_{BC} = 130 \text{ lb (T)}$ **Ans**

Section 2 :

$+\uparrow\Sigma F_y = 0;\quad 80 + 60 + 40 - F_{HC} = 0$

$F_{HC} = 180 \text{ lb (C)}$ **Ans**

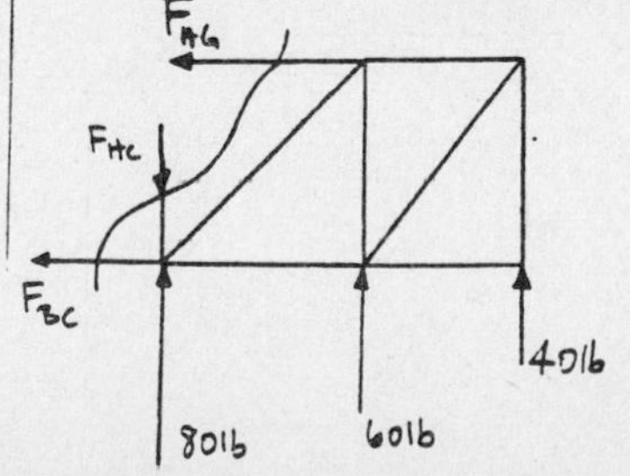

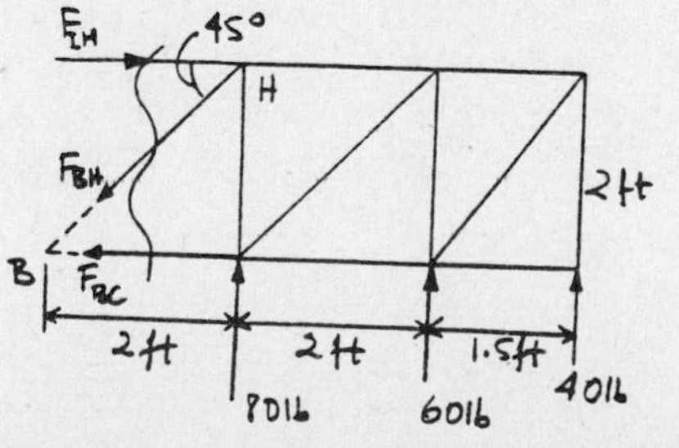

6-34. The *Howe bridge truss* is subjected to the loading shown. Determine the force in members *HD*, *CD*, and *GD*, and state if the members are in tension or compression.

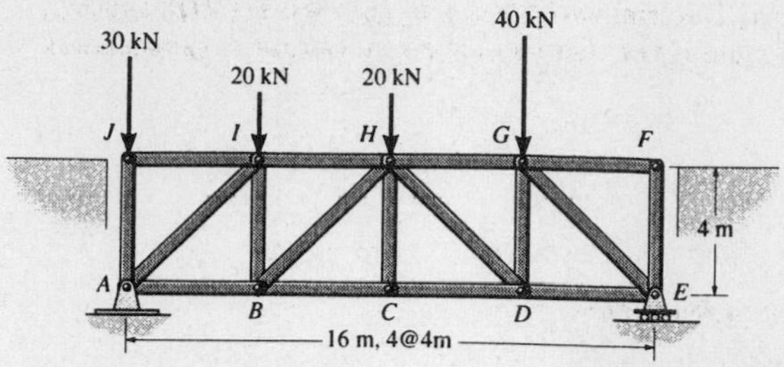

Support Reactions :

$$\circlearrowleft + \Sigma M_A = 0; \quad E_y(16) - 40(12) - 20(8) - 20(4) = 0$$

$$E_y = 45.0 \text{ kN}$$

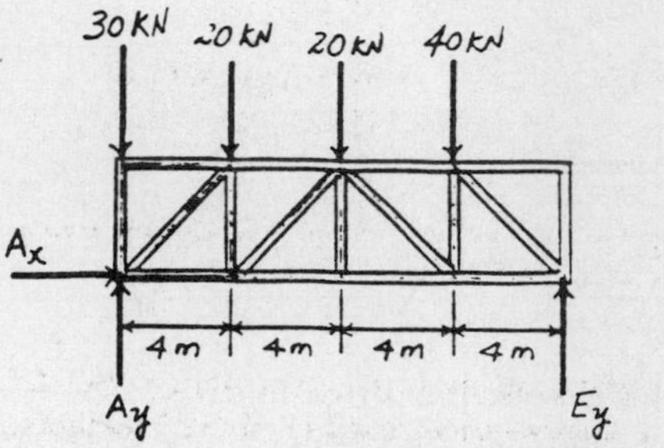

Method of Sections :

$$\circlearrowleft + \Sigma M_H = 0; \quad 45.0(8) - 40(4) - F_{CD}(4) = 0$$

$$F_{CD} = 50.0 \text{ kN (T)} \qquad \textbf{Ans}$$

$$+\uparrow \Sigma F_y = 0; \quad 45.0 - 40 - F_{HD} \sin 45^\circ = 0$$

$$F_{HD} = 7.071 \text{ kN (C)} = 7.07 \text{ kN (C)} \qquad \textbf{Ans}$$

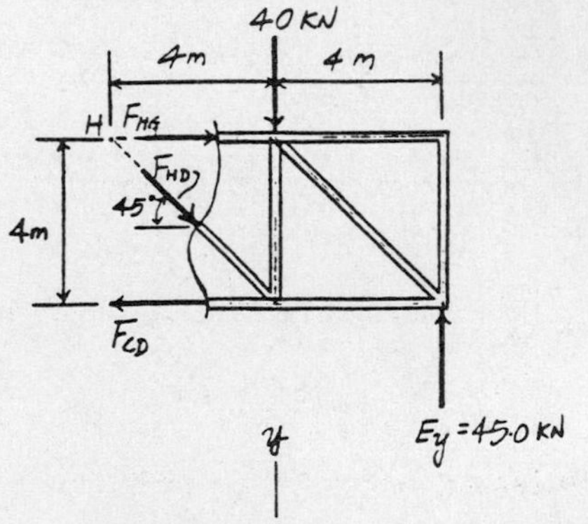

Method of Joints : Analysing joint *D*, we have

$$+\uparrow \Sigma F_y = 0; \quad F_{GD} - 7.071 \sin 45^\circ = 0$$

$$F_{GD} = 5.00 \text{ kN (T)} \qquad \textbf{Ans}$$

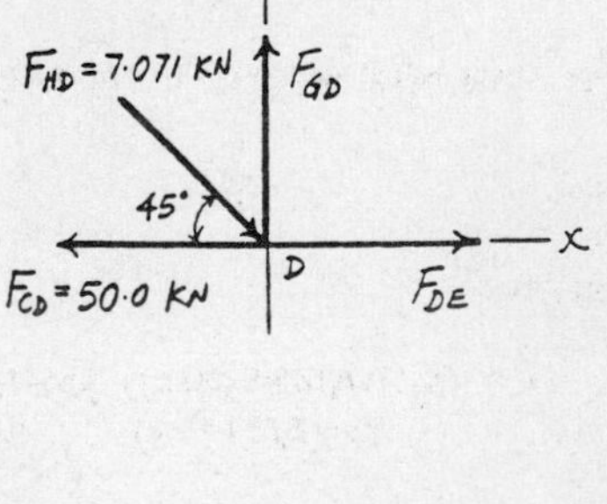

6-35. The *Howe bridge truss* is subjected to the loading shown. Determine the force in members *HI*, *HB*, and *BC*, and state if the members are in tension or compression.

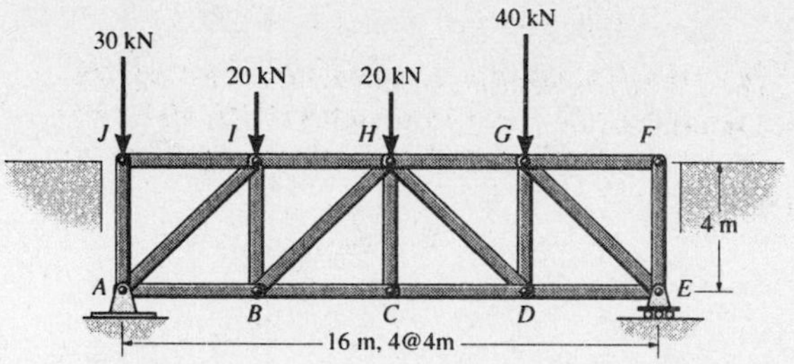

Support Reactions :

$\circlearrowleft + \Sigma M_E = 0;\quad 30(16) + 20(12) + 20(8) + 40(4) - A_y(16) = 0$

$A_y = 65.0 \text{ kN}$

$\xrightarrow{+} \Sigma F_x = 0;\quad A_x = 0$

Method of Sections :

$\circlearrowleft + \Sigma M_H = 0;\quad F_{BC}(4) + 20(4) + 30(8) - 65.0(8) = 0$

$F_{BC} = 50.0 \text{ kN (T)}$ **Ans**

$\circlearrowleft + \Sigma M_B = 0;\quad F_{HI}(4) + 30(4) - 65.0(4) = 0$

$F_{HI} = 35.0 \text{ kN (C)}$ **Ans**

$+\uparrow \Sigma F_y = 0;\quad 65.0 - 30 - 20 - F_{HB} \sin 45° = 0$

$F_{HB} = 21.2 \text{ kN (C)}$ **Ans**

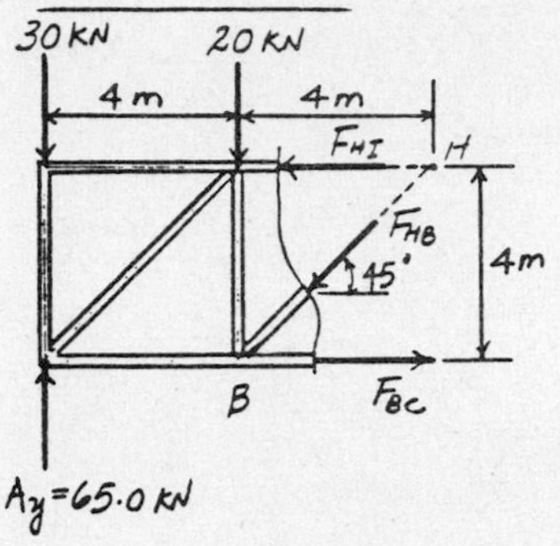

***6-36.** Determine the force in members *BC*, *CG*, and *GF* of the *Warren truss*. Indicate if the members are in tension or compression.

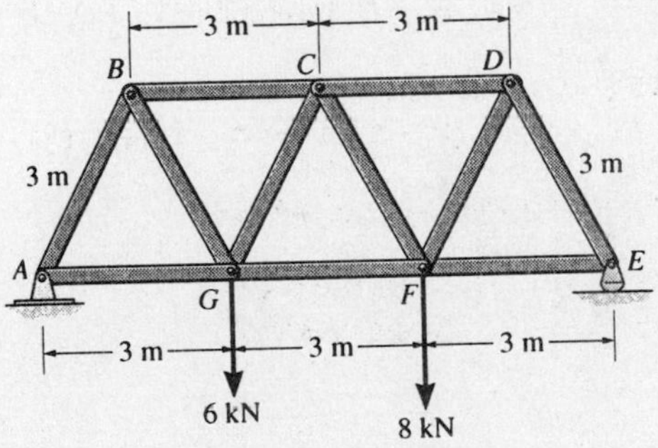

Support Reactions :

$+\Sigma M_E = 0;\quad 6(6) + 8(3) - A_y(9) = 0 \quad A_y = 6.667 \text{ kN}$

$\xrightarrow{+} \Sigma F_x = 0;\quad A_x = 0$

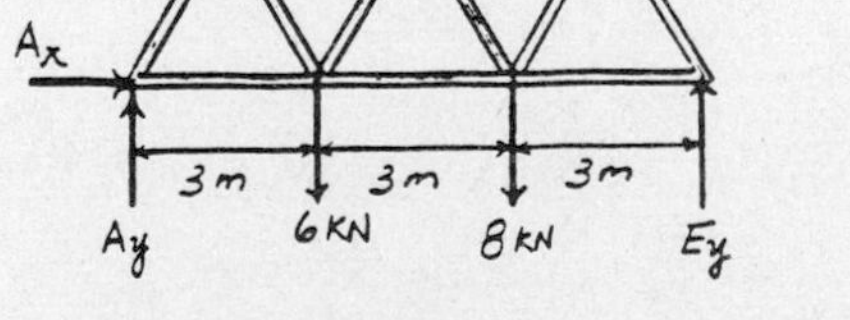

Method of Sections :

$\circlearrowleft + \Sigma M_C = 0;\quad F_{GF}(3\sin 60°) + 6(1.5) - 6.667(4.5) = 0$

$F_{GF} = 8.08 \text{ kN (T)}$ **Ans**

$\circlearrowleft + \Sigma M_G = 0;\quad F_{BC}(3\sin 60°) - 6.667(3) = 0$

$F_{BC} = 7.70 \text{ kN (C)}$ **Ans**

$+\uparrow \Sigma F_y = 0;\quad 6.667 - 6 - F_{CG}\sin 60° = 0$

$F_{CG} = 0.770 \text{ kN (C)}$ **Ans**

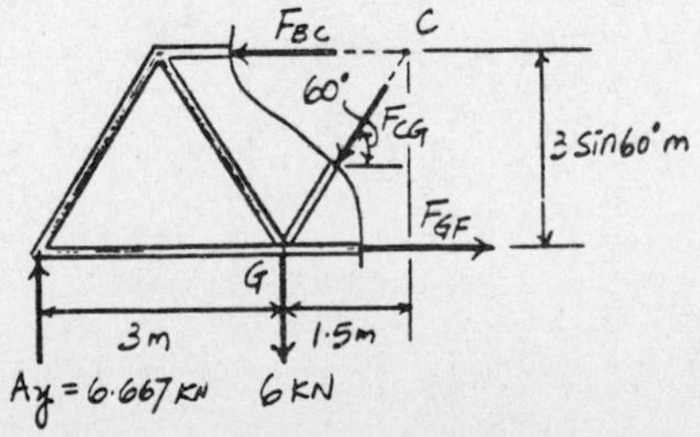

6-37. Determine the force in members *CD*, *CF*, and *FG* of the *Warren truss*. Indicate if the members are in tension or compression.

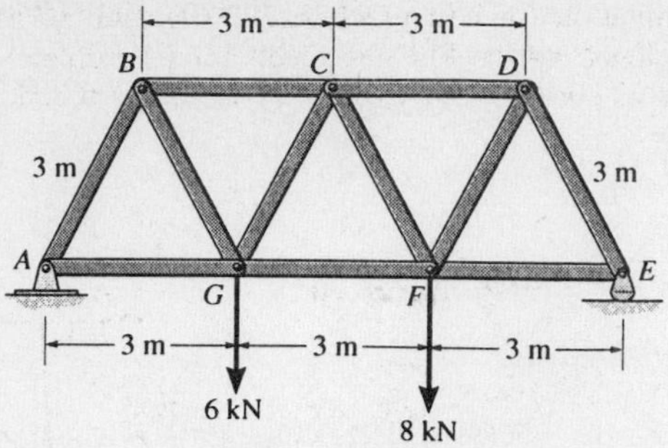

Support Reactions :

$\circlearrowleft + \Sigma M_A = 0;\quad E_y(9) - 8(6) - 6(3) = 0 \quad E_y = 7.333 \text{ kN}$

Method of Sections :

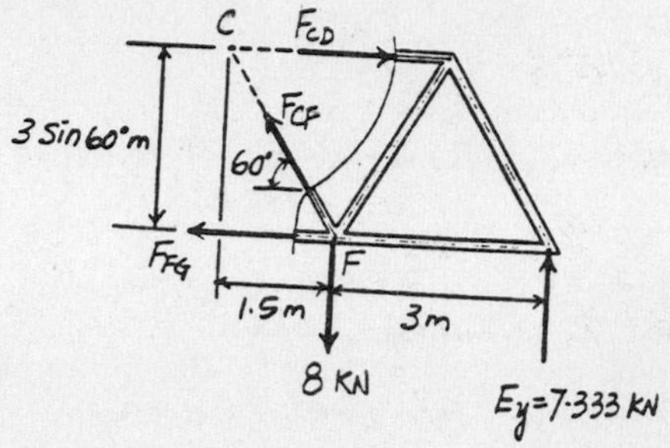

$\circlearrowleft + \Sigma M_C = 0;\quad 7.333(4.5) - 8(1.5) - F_{FG}(3\sin 60°) = 0$

$F_{FG} = 8.08 \text{ kN (T)}$ **Ans**

$\circlearrowleft + \Sigma M_G = 0;\quad 7.333(3) - F_{CD}(3\sin 60°) = 0$

$F_{CD} = 8.47 \text{ kN (C)}$ **Ans**

$+\uparrow \Sigma F_y = 0;\quad F_{CF}\sin 60° + 7.333 - 8 = 0$

$F_{CF} = 0.770 \text{ kN (T)}$ **Ans**

6-38. Determine the force in members *BC*, *CG*, and *GF* of the truss and state if the members are in tension or compression.

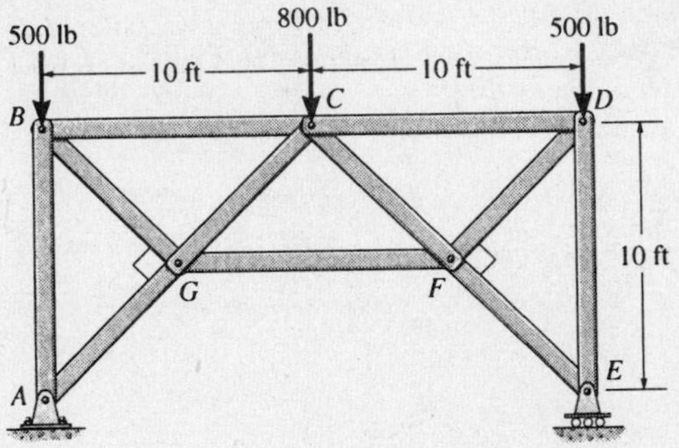

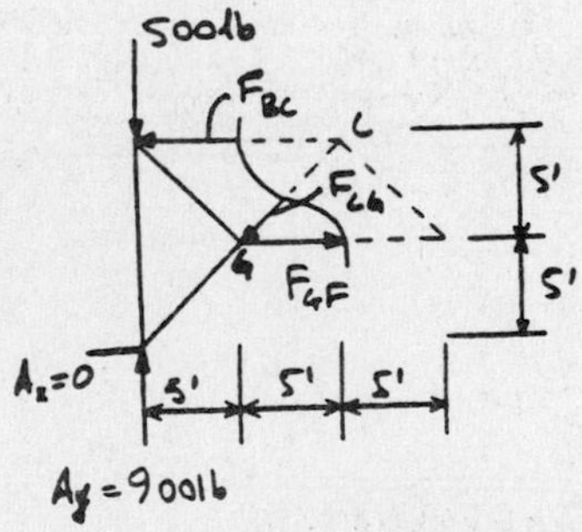

$\circlearrowleft + \Sigma M_C = 0;\quad -900(10) + 500(10) + F_{GF}(5) = 0$

$F_{GF} = 800 \text{ lb (T)}$ **Ans**

$\circlearrowleft + \Sigma M_G = 0;\quad -900(5) + 500(5) + F_{BC}(5) = 0$

$F_{BC} = 400 \text{ lb (C)}$ **Ans**

$+\uparrow \Sigma F_y = 0;\quad 900 - 500 - \frac{1}{\sqrt{2}} F_{CG} = 0$

$F_{CG} = 566 \text{ lb (C)}$ **Ans**

■6-39. The truss supports the vertical load of 600 N. Determine the force in members BC, BG, and HG as the dimension L varies. Plot the results of F (ordinate with tension as positive) versus L (abscissa) for $0 \le L \le 3$ m.

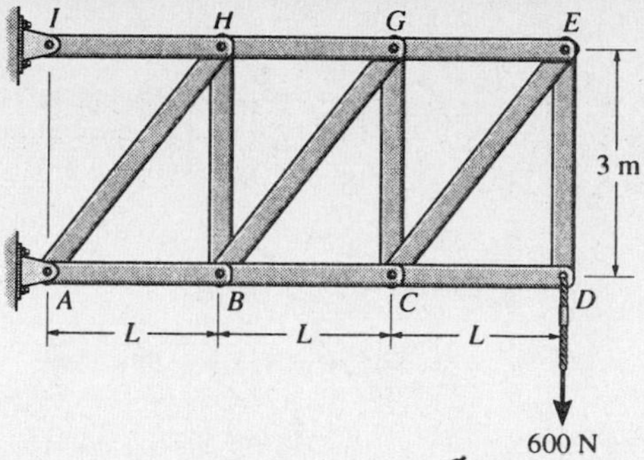

$+\uparrow \Sigma F_y = 0; \quad -600 - F_{BG}\sin\theta = 0$

$F_{BG} = -\dfrac{600}{\sin\theta}$

$\sin\theta = \dfrac{3}{\sqrt{L^2+9}}$

$F_{BG} = -200\sqrt{L^2+9}$

$\curvearrowleft + \Sigma M_G = 0; \quad -F_{BC}(3) - 600(L) = 0$

$F_{BC} = -200L$

$\curvearrowleft + \Sigma M_B = 0; \quad F_{HG}(3) - 600(2L) = 0$

$F_{HG} = 400L$

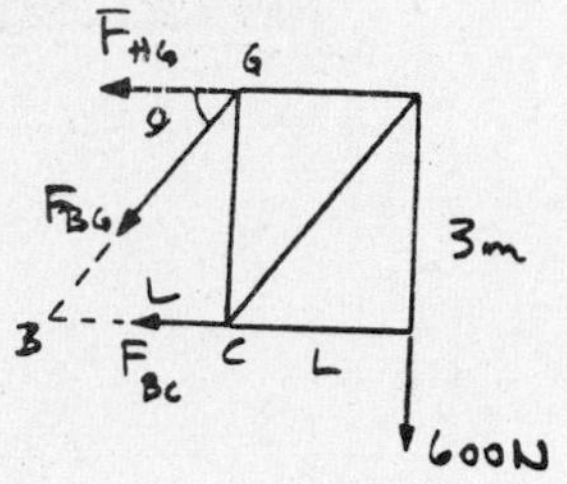

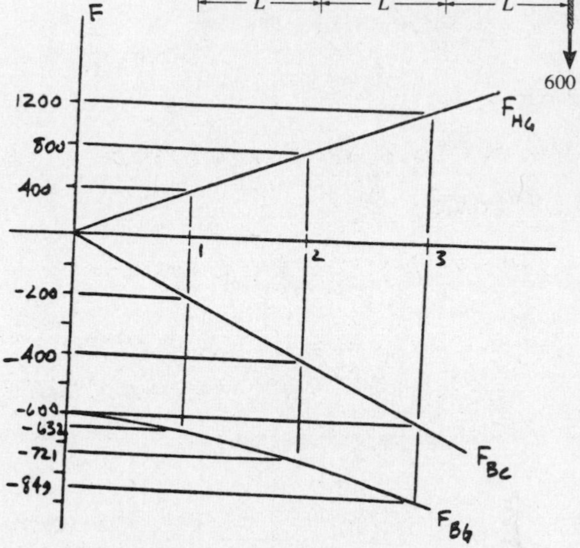

*6-40. The *Howe roof truss* supports the vertical loading shown. Determine the force in members KJ, CD, and KD, and state if the members are in tension or compression.

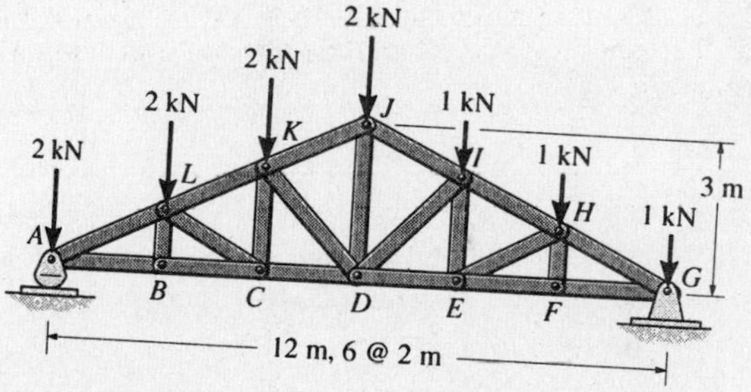

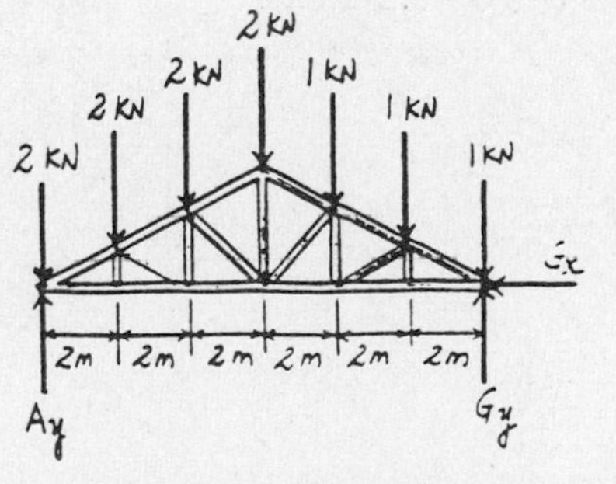

Support Reactions :

$+\Sigma M_G = 0; \quad 2(12) + 2(10) + 2(8) + 2(6) + 1(4) + 1(2) - A_y(12) = 0$

$A_y = 6.50$ kN

Method of Sections :

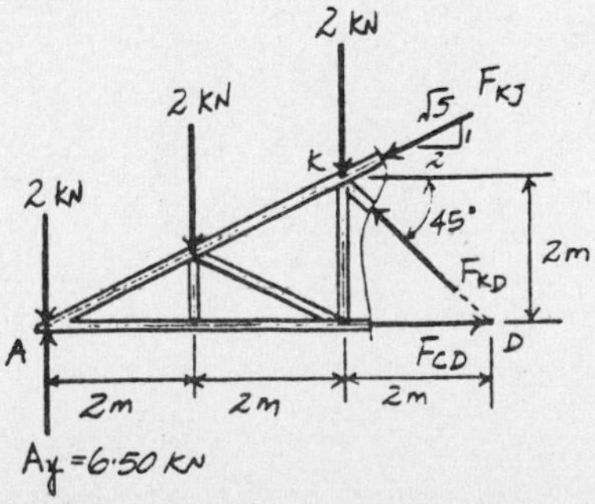

$\curvearrowleft + \Sigma M_A = 0; \quad F_{KD}\sin 45°(4) + F_{KD}\cos 45°(2) - 2(2) - 2(4) = 0$

$F_{KD} = 2.83$ kN (C) **Ans**

$\curvearrowleft + \Sigma M_K = 0; \quad F_{CD}(2) + 2(2) + 2(4) - 6.50(4) = 0$

$F_{CD} = 7.00$ kN (T) **Ans**

$\curvearrowleft + \Sigma M_D = 0; \quad F_{KJ}\left(\dfrac{2}{\sqrt{5}}\right)(2) + F_{KJ}\left(\dfrac{1}{\sqrt{5}}\right)(2) + 2(2) + 2(4) + 2(6) - 6.50(6) = 0$

$F_{KJ} = 5.59$ kN (C) **Ans**

6-41. The *Howe roof truss* supports the vertical loading shown. Determine the force in members *JI* and *JD*, and state if the members are in tension or compression.

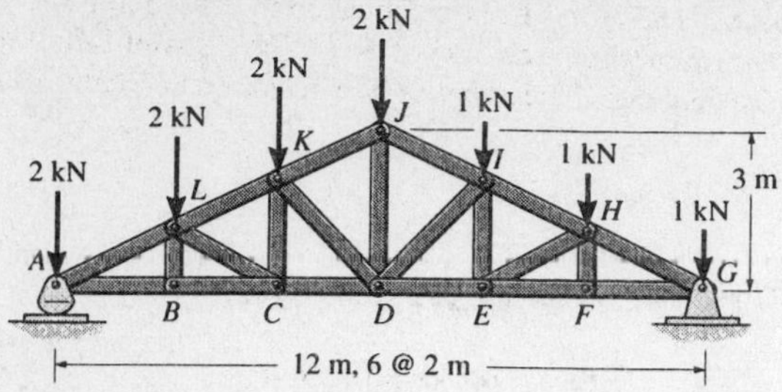

Support Reactions :

$$\circlearrowleft + \Sigma M_A = 0; \quad G_y(12) - 1(12) - 1(10) - 1(8) - 2(6) - 2(4) - 2(2) = 0$$

$$G_y = 4.50 \text{ kN}$$

$$\xrightarrow{+} \Sigma F_x = 0; \quad G_x = 0$$

Method of Sections :

$$\circlearrowleft + \Sigma M_D = 0; \quad 4.50(6) - 1(2) - 1(4) - 1(6) - F_{JI}\left(\frac{2}{\sqrt{5}}\right)(2) - F_{JI}\left(\frac{1}{\sqrt{5}}\right)(2) = 0$$

$$F_{JI} = 5.590 \text{ kN (C)} = 5.59 \text{ kN (C)} \qquad \textbf{Ans}$$

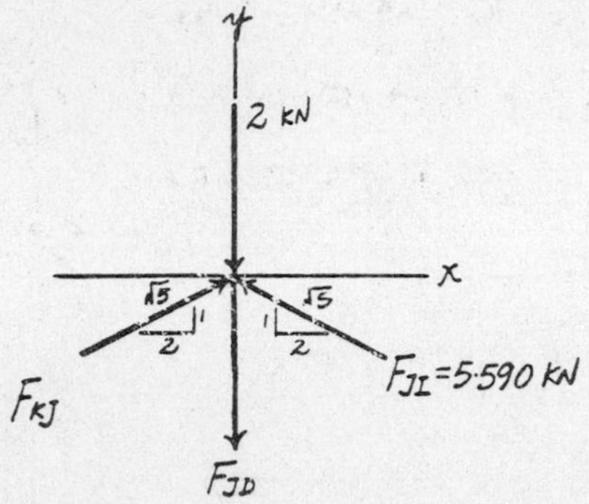

Method of Joints : Analyzing Joint *J*, we have

$$\xrightarrow{+} \Sigma F_x = 0; \quad F_{KJ}\left(\frac{2}{\sqrt{5}}\right) - 5.590\left(\frac{2}{\sqrt{5}}\right) = 0 \qquad F_{KJ} = 5.590 \text{ kN (C)}$$

$$+\uparrow \Sigma F_y = 0; \quad 2\left[5.590\left(\frac{1}{\sqrt{5}}\right)\right] - 2 - F_{JD} = 0$$

$$F_{JD} = 3.00 \text{ kN (T)} \qquad \textbf{Ans}$$

6-42. The *Howe truss* is subjected to the loading shown. Determine the force in members *GF*, *CD*, and *GC*, and state if the members are in tension or compression.

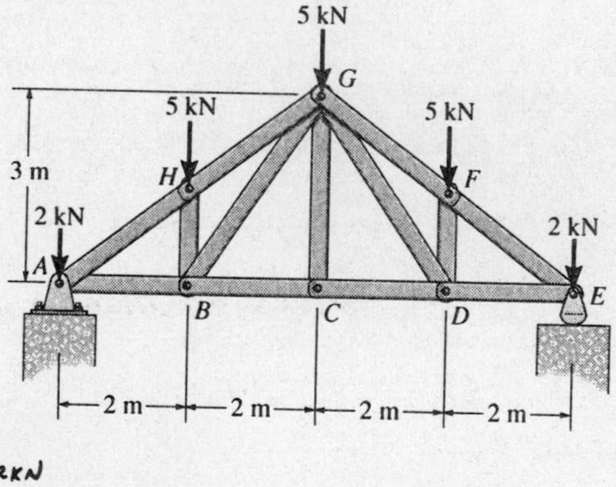

$$\circlearrowleft + \Sigma M_A = 0; \quad E_y(8) - 2(8) - 5(6) - 5(4) - 5(2) = 0 \qquad E_y = 9.5 \text{ kN}$$

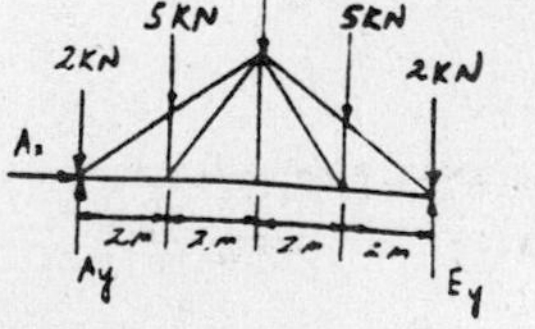

$$\circlearrowleft + \Sigma M_D = 0; \quad -\frac{4}{5}F_{GF}(1.5) - 2(2) + 9.5(2) = 0$$

$$F_{GF} = 12.5 \text{ kN (C)} \qquad \textbf{Ans}$$

$$\circlearrowleft + \Sigma M_G = 0; \quad 9.5(4) - 2(4) - 5(2) - F_{CD}(3) = 0$$

$$F_{CD} = 6.67 \text{ kN (T)} \qquad \textbf{Ans}$$

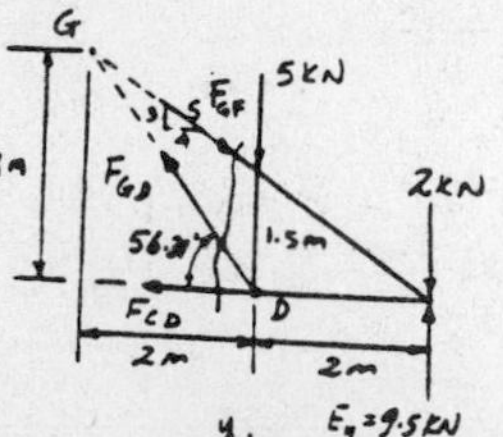

Joint C :

$$+\uparrow \Sigma F_y = 0; \quad F_{GC} = 0 \qquad \textbf{Ans}$$

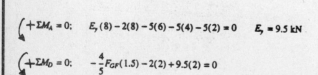

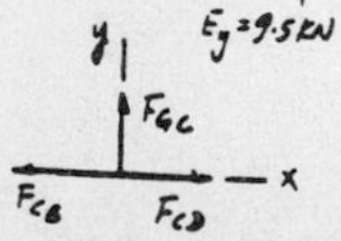

6-43. The *Howe truss* is subjected to the loading shown. Determine the force in members GH, BC, and BG of the truss and state if the members are in tension or compression.

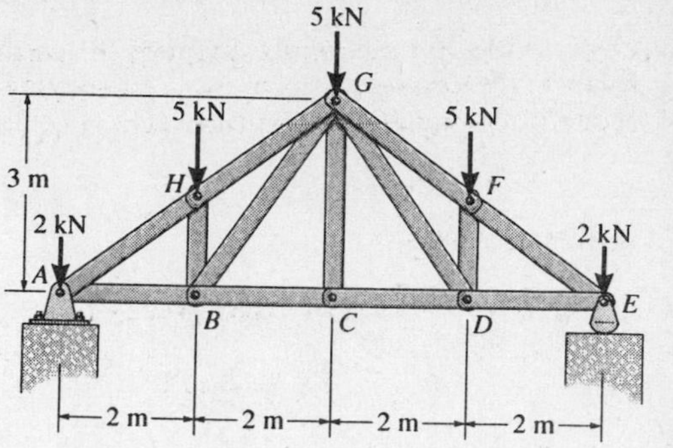

$\circlearrowleft + \Sigma M_B = 0; \quad -7.5\,(2) + F_{GH} \sin 36.87°\,(2) = 0$

$F_{GH} = 12.5 \text{ kN (C)}$ **Ans**

$\circlearrowleft + \Sigma M_A = 0; \quad -5\,(2) + F_{BG} \sin 56.31°\,(2) = 0$

$F_{BG} = 6.01 \text{ kN (T)}$ **Ans**

$\circlearrowleft + \Sigma M_H = 0; \quad -7.5\,(4) + 5\,(2) + F_{BC}\,(3) = 0$

$F_{BC} = 6.67 \text{ kN (T)}$ **Ans**

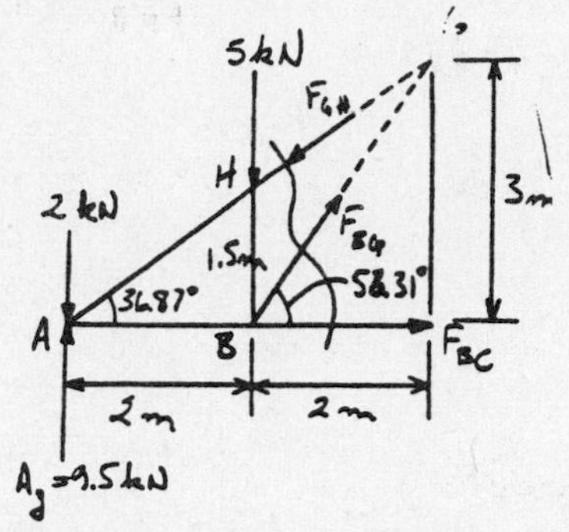

***6-44.** Determine the force in members GF, FB, and BC of the *Fink truss* and state if the members are in tension or compression.

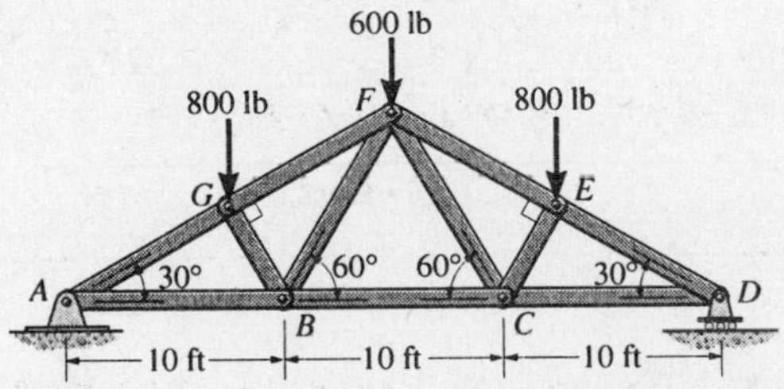

Support Reactions : Due to symmetry, $D_y = A_y$.

$+\uparrow \Sigma F_y = 0; \quad 2A_y - 800 - 600 - 800 = 0 \quad A_y = 1100 \text{ lb}$

$\overset{+}{\rightarrow} \Sigma F_x = 0; \quad A_x = 0$

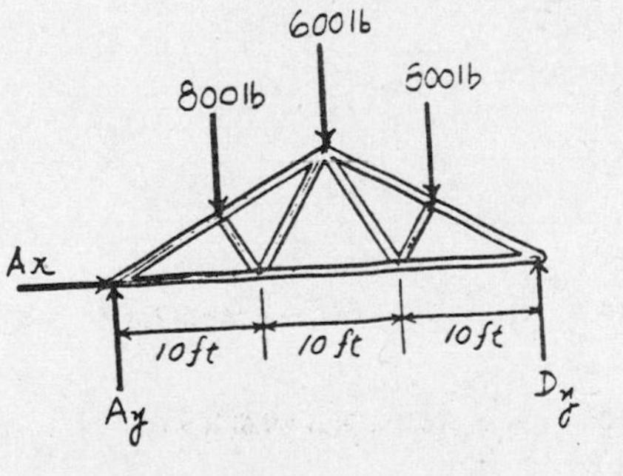

Method of Sections :

$\circlearrowleft + \Sigma M_B = 0; \quad F_{GF} \sin 30°(10) + 800(10 - 10\cos^2 30°) - 1100(10) = 0$

$F_{GF} = 1800 \text{ lb (C)} = 1.80 \text{ kip (C)}$ **Ans**

$\circlearrowleft + \Sigma M_A = 0; \quad F_{FB} \sin 60°(10) - 800(10\cos^2 30°) = 0$

$F_{FB} = 692.82 \text{ lb (T)} = 693 \text{ lb (T)}$ **Ans**

$\circlearrowleft + \Sigma M_F = 0; \quad F_{BC}(15\tan 30°) + 800(15 - 10\cos^2 30°) - 1100(15) = 0$

$F_{BC} = 1212.43 \text{ lb (T)} = 1.21 \text{ kip (T)}$ **Ans**

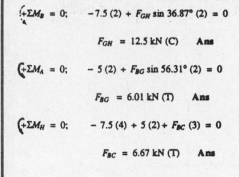

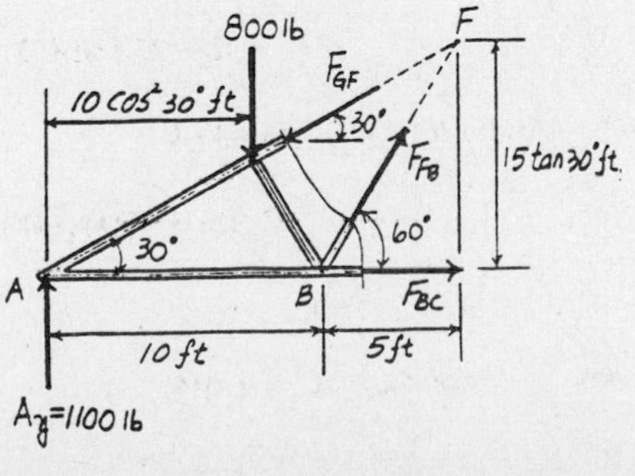

6-45. Determine the force in members GF, GD, and CD of the truss and state if the members are in tension or compression.

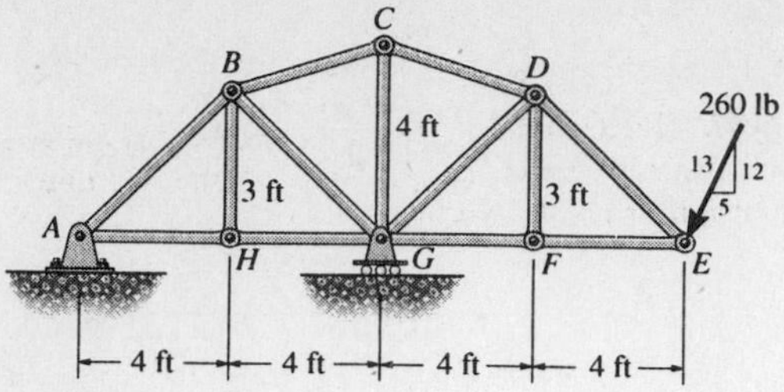

$\curvearrowleft + \Sigma M_O = 0; \quad \left(\frac{12}{13}\right) 260\,(8) - F_{GD} \sin 36.87^\circ\,(16) = 0$

$F_{GD} = 200 \text{ lb (C)}$ **Ans**

$\curvearrowleft + \Sigma M_D = 0; \quad F_{GF}\,(3) - \left(\frac{12}{13}\right)(260)\,(4) - \left(\frac{5}{13}\right)(260)\,(3) = 0$

$F_{GF} = 420 \text{ lb (C)}$ **Ans**

$\curvearrowleft + \Sigma M_G = 0; \quad F_{CD} \cos 14.04^\circ\,(4) - \left(\frac{12}{13}\right)(260)\,(8) = 0$

$F_{CD} = 495 \text{ lb (T)}$ **Ans**

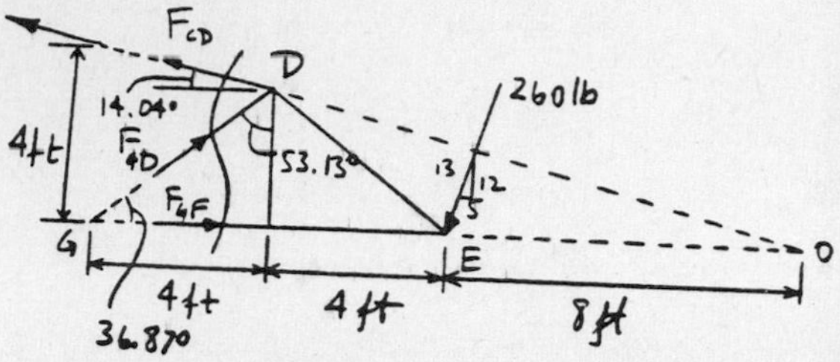

6-46. Determine the force in members BG, BC, and HG of the truss and state if the members are in tension or compression.

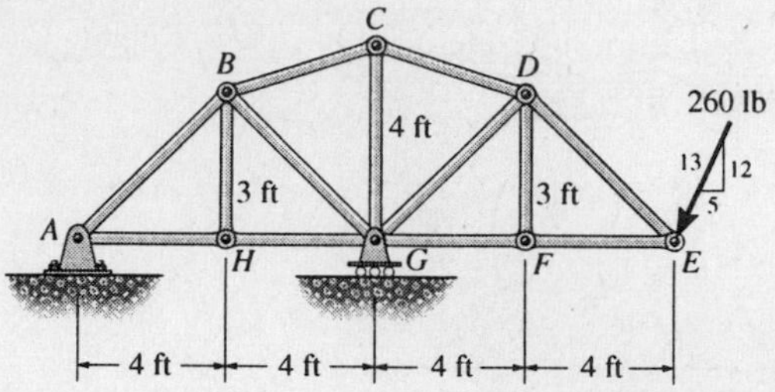

Entire truss :

$\curvearrowleft + \Sigma M_G = 0; \quad A_y\,(8) - \left(\frac{12}{13}\right)(260)\,(8) = 0$

$A_y = 240 \text{ lb}$

$\xrightarrow{+} \Sigma F_x = 0; \quad A_x - \left(\frac{5}{13}\right)(260) = 0$

$A_x = 100 \text{ lb}$

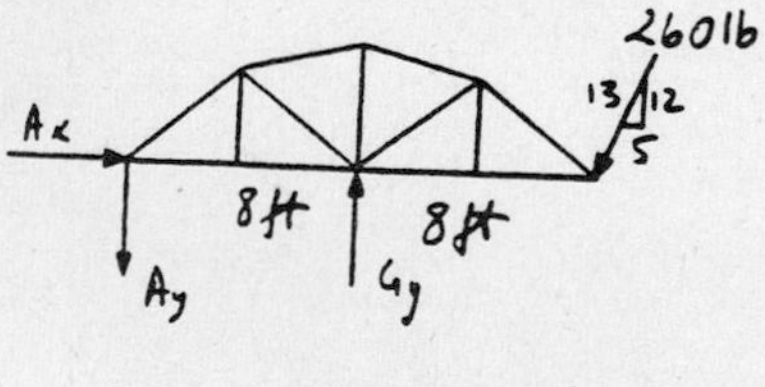

Section :

$\curvearrowleft + \Sigma M_G = 0; \quad 240\,(8) - F_{BC} \cos 14.04^\circ\,(4) = 0$

$F_{BC} = 495 \text{ lb (T)}$ **Ans**

$\curvearrowleft + \Sigma M_B = 0; \quad 240\,(4) + 100\,(3) - F_{HG}\,(3) = 0$

$F_{HG} = 420 \text{ lb (C)}$ **Ans**

$\curvearrowleft + \Sigma M_O = 0; \quad -240\,(8) + F_{BG} \sin 36.87^\circ\,(16) = 0$

$F_{BG} = 200 \text{ lb (C)}$ **Ans**

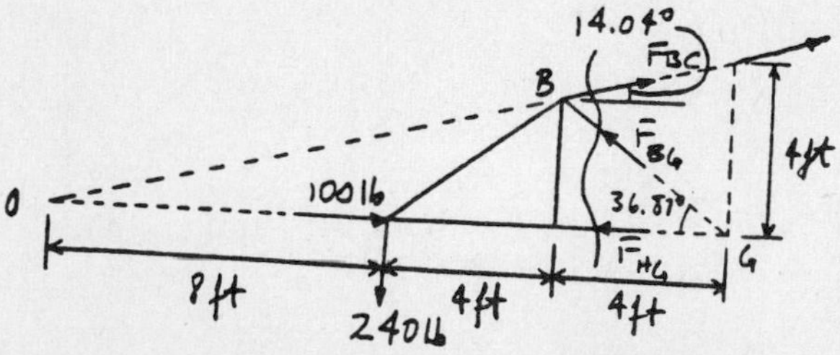

6-47. Determine the force in members *GF*, *CF*, and *CD* of the roof truss and indicate if the members are in tension or compression.

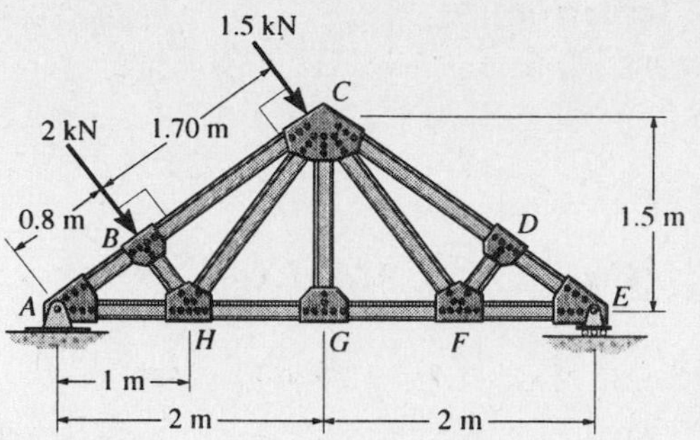

$\circlearrowleft + \Sigma M_A = 0;\quad E_y(4) - 2(0.8) - 1.5(2.50) = 0 \quad E_y = 1.3375 \text{ kN}$

Method of Sections :

$\circlearrowleft + \Sigma M_C = 0;\quad 1.3375(2) - F_{GF}(1.5) = 0$

$F_{GF} = 1.78 \text{ kN (T)}$ **Ans**

$\circlearrowleft + \Sigma M_F = 0;\quad 1.3375(1) - F_{CD}\left(\frac{3}{5}\right)(1) = 0$

$F_{CD} = 2.23 \text{ kN (C)}$ **Ans**

$\circlearrowleft + \Sigma M_E = 0;\quad F_{CF}\left(\frac{1.5}{\sqrt{3.25}}\right)(1) = 0 \quad F_{CF} = 0$ **Ans**

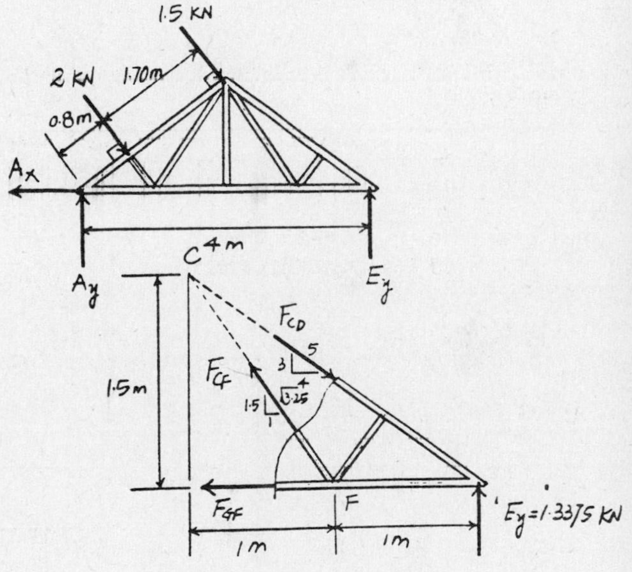

*6-48. Determine the force in members BG, HG, and BC of the truss and state if the members are in tension or compression.

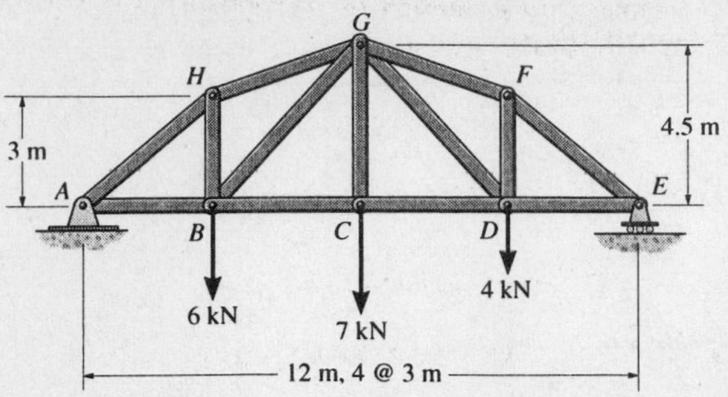

$\curvearrowleft + \Sigma M_E = 0;\quad 6(9) + 7(6) + 4(3) - A_y(12) = 0 \quad A_y = 9.00 \text{ kN}$

$\xrightarrow{+} \Sigma F_x = 0;\quad A_x = 0$

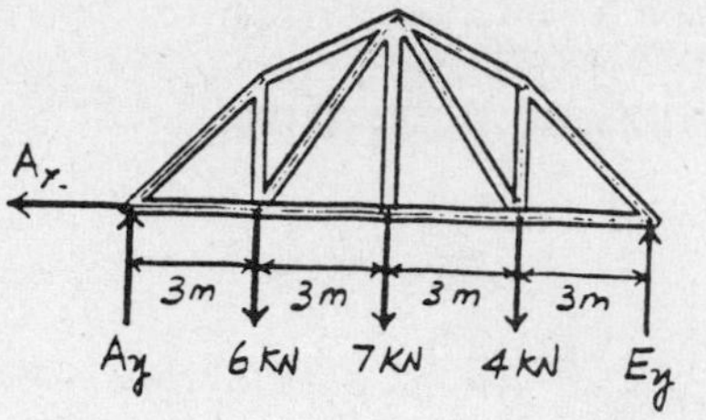

Method of Sections :

$\curvearrowleft + \Sigma M_G = 0;\quad F_{BC}(4.5) + 6(3) - 9(6) = 0$

$F_{BC} = 8.00 \text{ kN (T)}$ **Ans**

$\curvearrowleft + \Sigma M_B = 0;\quad F_{HG}\left(\frac{1}{\sqrt{5}}\right)(6) - 9(3) = 0$

$F_{HG} = 10.1 \text{ kN (C)}$ **Ans**

$\curvearrowleft + \Sigma M_O = 0;\quad F_{BG}\left(\frac{1.5}{\sqrt{3.25}}\right)(6) + 9(3) - 6(6) = 0$

$F_{BG} = 1.80 \text{ kN (T)}$ **Ans**

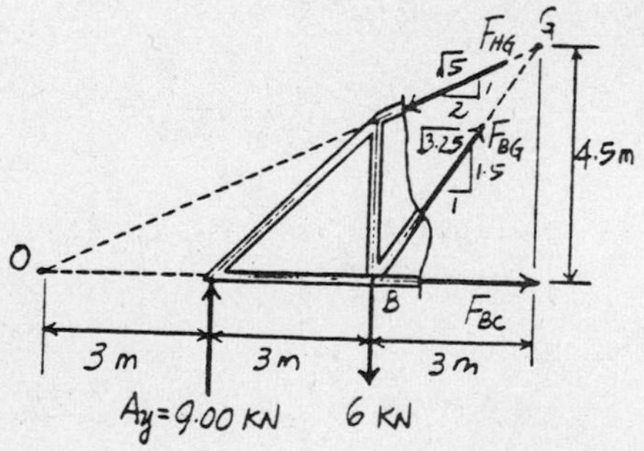

6-49. The tower truss is subjected to the loads shown. Determine the force in *BC*, *BF*, and *FG*, and state if the members are in tension or compression. The left side, *ABCD*, stands vertical.

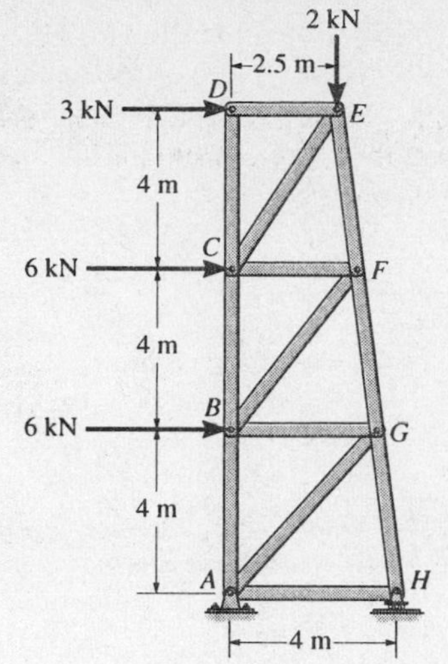

$\circlearrowleft + \Sigma M_B = 0; \quad -3(8) - 6(4) - 2(2.5) + F_{FG}\left(\frac{8}{\sqrt{65}}\right)(3.5) = 0$

$F_{FG} = 15.26 \text{ kN} = 15.3 \text{ kN (C)}$ **Ans**

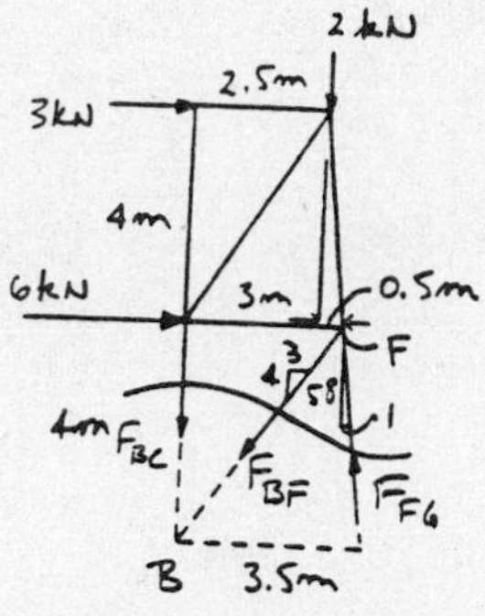

$\circlearrowleft + \Sigma M_F = 0; \quad -3(4) + 2(0.5) + F_{BC}(3) = 0$

$F_{BC} = 3.67 \text{ kN (T)}$ **Ans**

$\overset{+}{\rightarrow} \Sigma F_x = 0; \quad 3 + 6 - 15.26\left(\frac{1}{\sqrt{65}}\right) - \left(\frac{3}{5}\right)F_{BF} = 0$

$F_{BF} = 11.8 \text{ kN (T)}$ **Ans**

6-50. The tower truss is subjected to the loads shown. Determine the force in members *BG* and *CF*, and state if the members are in tension or compression. The left side *ABCD* stands vertical.

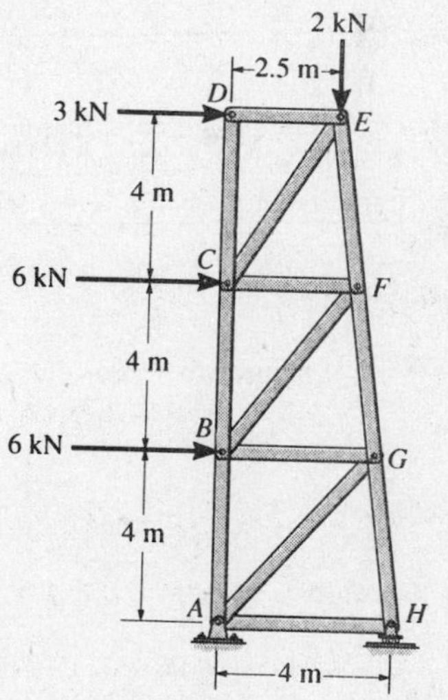

Section 1 :

$\circlearrowleft + \Sigma M_B = 0; \quad -2(2.5) - 3(8) - 6(4) + \frac{8}{\sqrt{65}} F_{GF}(3.5) = 0$

$F_{GF} = 15.26 \text{ kN (C)}$

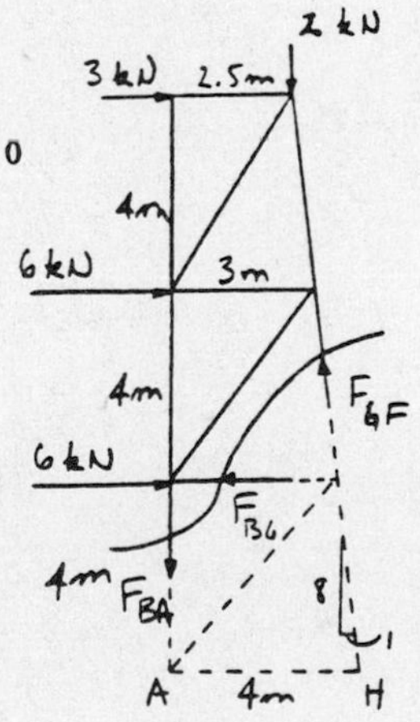

$\overset{+}{\rightarrow} \Sigma F_x = 0; \quad 3 + 6 + 6 - F_{BG} - \frac{1}{\sqrt{65}}(15.26) = 0$

$F_{BG} = 13.1 \text{ kN (C)}$ **Ans**

Section 2 :

$\circlearrowleft + \Sigma M_C = 0; \quad -2(2.5) - 3(4) + \frac{8}{\sqrt{65}} F_{EF}(3) = 0$

$F_{EF} = 5.71 \text{ kN (C)}$

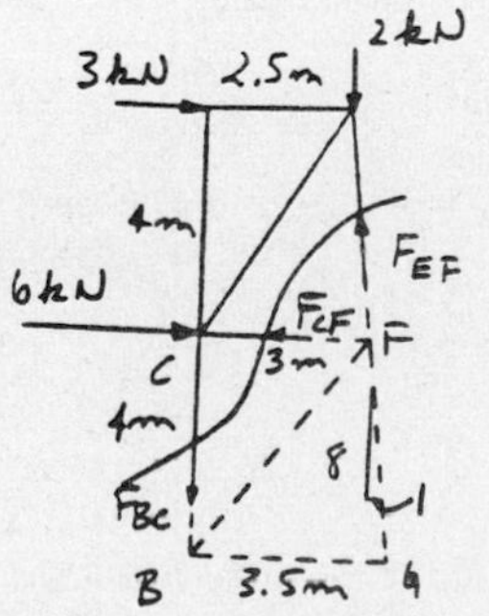

$\overset{+}{\rightarrow} \Sigma F_x = 0; \quad 3 + 6 - F_{CF} - \frac{1}{\sqrt{65}}(5.71) = 0$

$F_{CF} = 8.29 \text{ kN (C)}$ **Ans**

***6-51.** Determine the force in members *CD* and *CM* of the *Baltimore bridge truss* and state if the members are in tension or compression. Also, indicate all zero-force members.

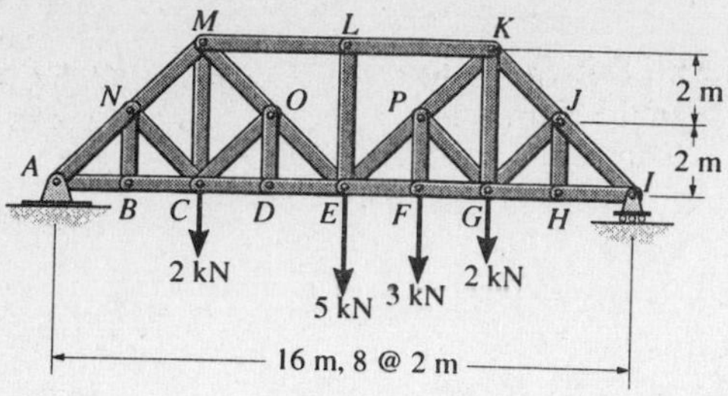

Support Reactions :

$$\curvearrowleft + \Sigma M_I = 0; \quad 2(12) + 5(8) + 3(6) + 2(4) - A_y(16) = 0$$
$$A_y = 5.625 \text{ kN}$$

$$\overset{+}{\rightarrow} \Sigma F_x = 0; \quad A_x = 0$$

Method of Joints : By inspection, members ***BN, NC, DO, OC, HJ LE*** and ***JG*** are zero force member. **Ans**

Method of Sections :

$$\curvearrowleft + \Sigma M_M = 0; \quad F_{CD}(4) - 5.625(4) = 0$$
$$F_{CD} = 5.625 \text{ kN (T)} \quad \textbf{Ans}$$

$$\curvearrowleft + \Sigma M_A = 0; \quad F_{CM}(4) - 2(4) = 0$$
$$F_{CM} = 2.00 \text{ kN (T)} \quad \textbf{Ans}$$

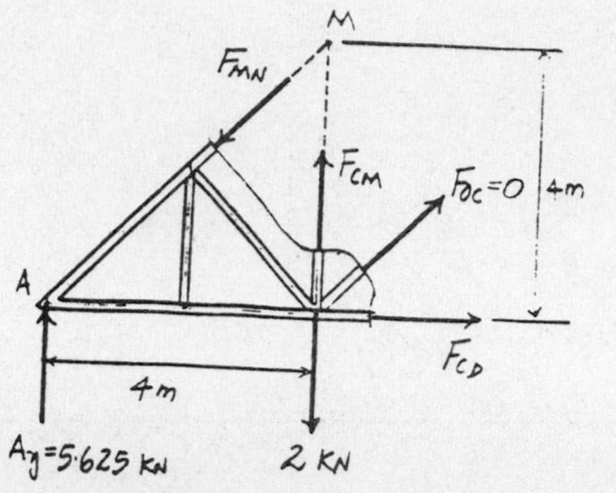

***6-52.** Determine the force in members *EF*, *EP*, and *LK* of the *Baltimore bridge truss* and state if the members are in tension or compression. Also, indicate all zero-force members.

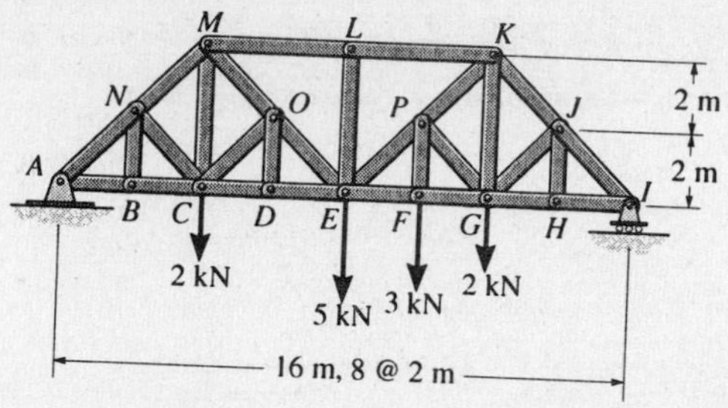

Support Reactions :

$$\curvearrowleft + \Sigma M_A = 0; \quad I_y(16) - 2(12) - 3(10) - 5(8) - 2(4) = 0$$
$$I_y = 6.375 \text{ kN}$$

Method of Joints : By inspection, members ***BN, NC, DO, OC, HJ LE*** and ***JG*** are zero force member. **Ans**

Method of Sections :

$$\curvearrowleft + \Sigma M_K = 0; \quad 3(2) + 6.375(4) - F_{EF}(4) = 0$$
$$F_{EF} = 7.875 \text{ kN (T)} \quad \textbf{Ans}$$

$$\curvearrowleft + \Sigma M_E = 0; \quad 6.375(8) - 2(4) - 3(2) - F_{LK}(4) = 0$$
$$F_{LK} = 9.25 \text{ kN (C)} \quad \textbf{Ans}$$

$$+\uparrow \Sigma F_y = 0; \quad 6.375 - 3 - 2 - F_{ED}\sin 45° = 0$$
$$F_{EP} = 1.94 \text{ kN (T)} \quad \textbf{Ans}$$

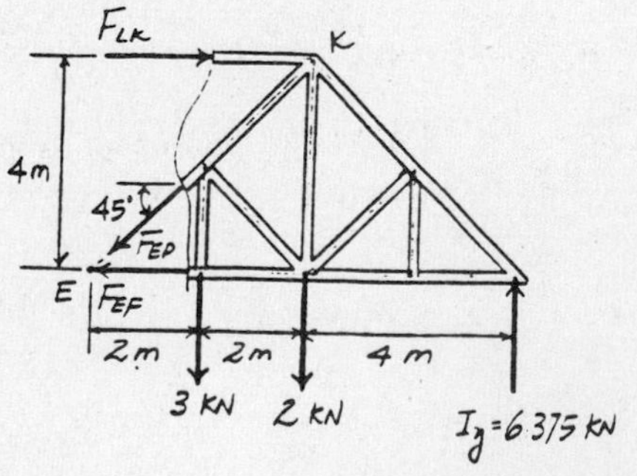

6-53. Determine the force in members *KJ*, *NJ*, *ND*, and *CD* of the *K truss*. Indicate if the members are in tension or compression. *Hint:* Use sections *aa* and *bb*.

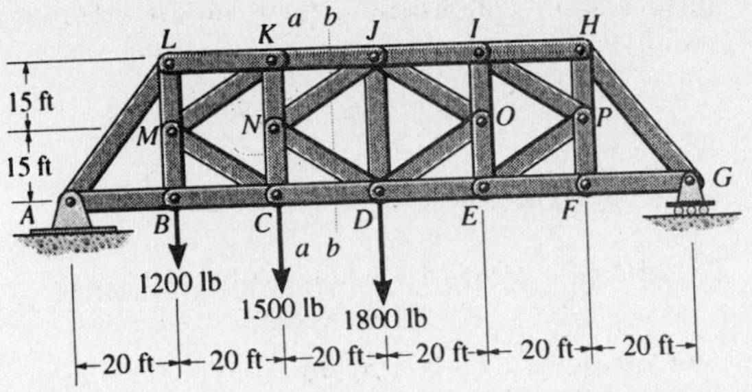

Support Reactions :

$\circlearrowleft + \Sigma M_G = 0;\quad 1.20(100) + 1.50(80) + 1.80(60) - A_y(120) = 0$

$A_y = 2.90$ kip

$\xrightarrow{+} \Sigma F_x = 0;\quad A_x = 0$

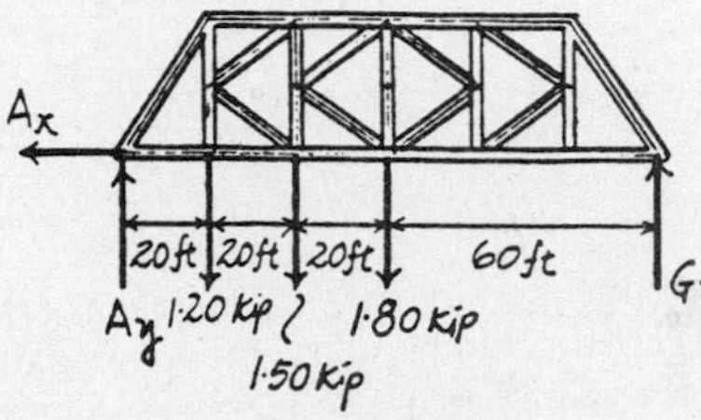

Method of Sections : From section $a-a$, F_{KJ} and F_{CD} can be obtained directly by summing moment about points C and K respectively.

$\circlearrowleft + \Sigma M_C = 0;\quad F_{KJ}(30) + 1.20(20) - 2.90(40) = 0$

$F_{KJ} = 3.067$ kip (C) = 3.07 kip (C) **Ans**

$\circlearrowleft + \Sigma M_K = 0;\quad F_{CD}(30) + 1.20(20) - 2.90(40) = 0$

$F_{CD} = 3.067$ kip (T) = 3.07 kip (T) **Ans**

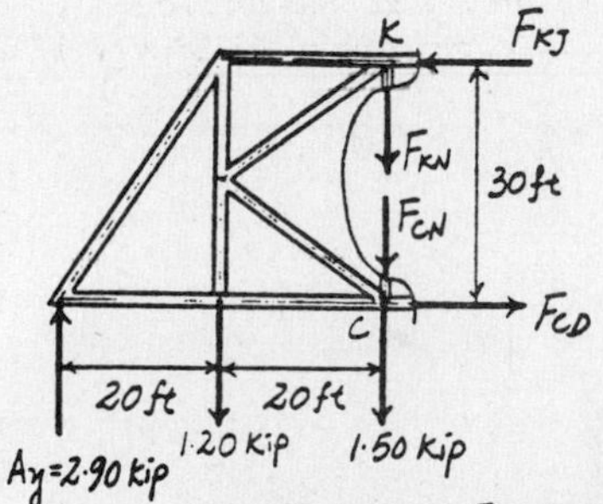

From sec $b-b$, summing forces along x and y axes yields

$\xrightarrow{+} \Sigma F_x = 0;\quad F_{ND}\left(\frac{4}{5}\right) - F_{NJ}\left(\frac{4}{5}\right) + 3.067 - 3.067 = 0$

$F_{ND} = F_{NJ}$ [1]

$+\uparrow \Sigma F_y = 0;\quad 2.90 - 1.20 - 1.50 - F_{ND}\left(\frac{3}{5}\right) - F_{NJ}\left(\frac{3}{5}\right) = 0$

$F_{ND} + F_{NJ} = 0.3333$ [2]

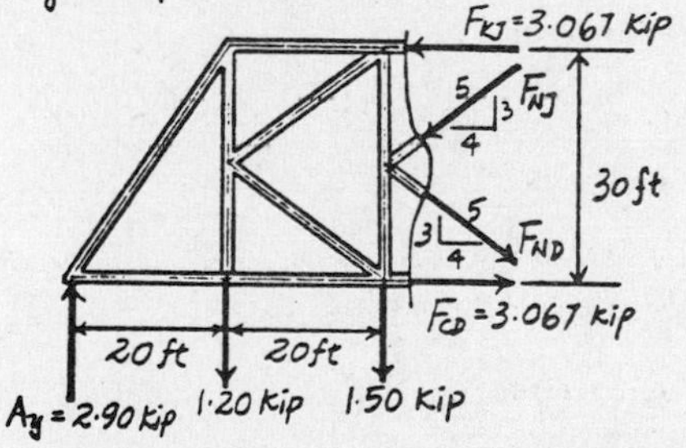

Solving Eqs. [1] and [2] yields

$F_{ND} = 0.167$ kip (T) $\quad F_{NJ} = 0.167$ kip (C) **Ans**

6-54. Determine the force in members JI and DE of the K *truss*. Indicate if the members are in tension or compression.

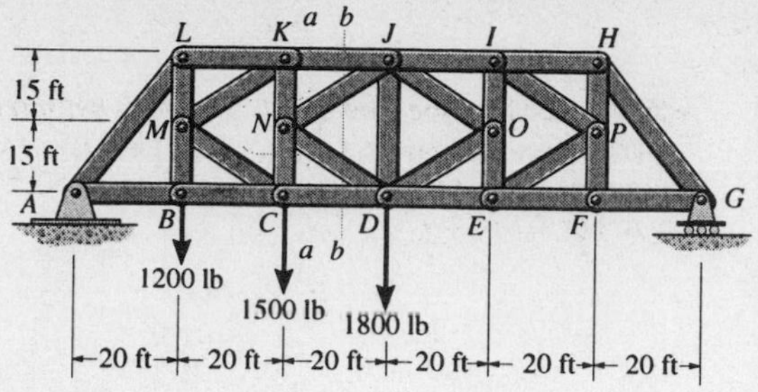

Support Reactions :

$\curvearrowleft + \Sigma M_A = 0; \quad G_y(120) - 1.80(60) - 1.50(40) - 1.20(20) = 0$

$G_y = 1.60 \text{ kip}$

Method of Sections :

$\curvearrowleft + \Sigma M_E = 0; \quad 1.60(40) - F_{JI}(30) = 0$

$F_{JI} = 2.13 \text{ kip (C)}$ **Ans**

$\curvearrowleft + \Sigma M_I = 0; \quad 1.60(40) - F_{DE}(30) = 0$

$F_{DE} = 2.13 \text{ kip (T)}$ **Ans**

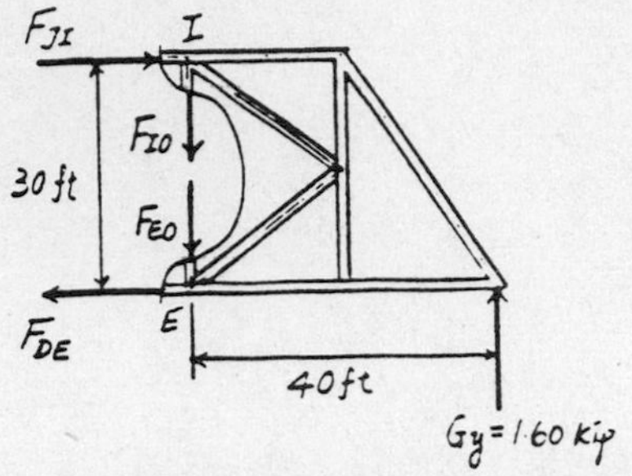

6-55. Determine the force in each member of the three-member space truss that supports the loading of 1000 lb and state if the members are in tension or compression.

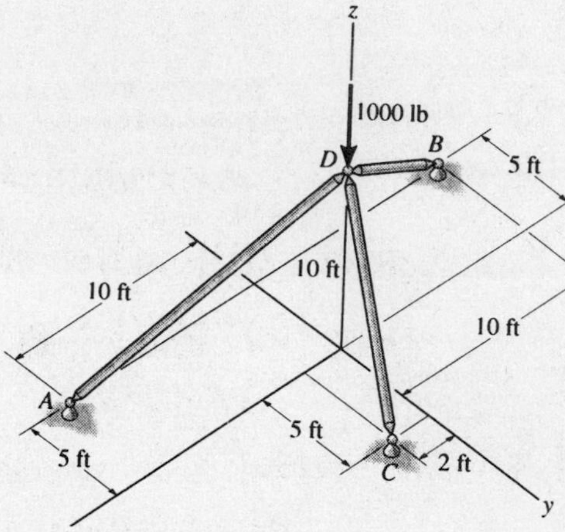

Joint D :

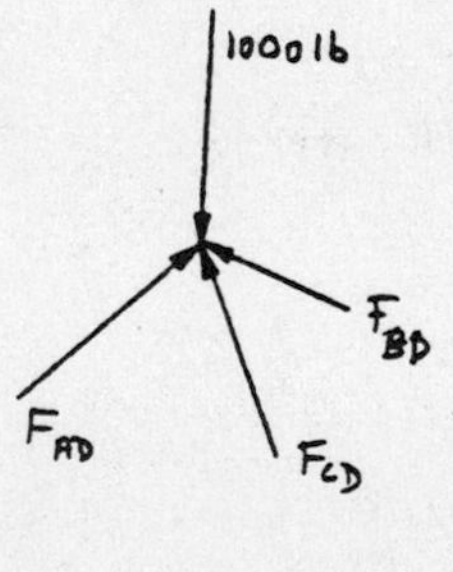

$$\mathbf{F}_{AD} = F_{AD}\left(-\frac{10}{15}\mathbf{i} + \frac{5}{15}\mathbf{j} + \frac{10}{15}\mathbf{k}\right)$$

$$\mathbf{F}_{CD} = F_{CD}\left(-\frac{2}{11.358}\mathbf{i} - \frac{5}{11.358}\mathbf{j} + \frac{10}{11.358}\mathbf{k}\right)$$

$$\mathbf{F}_{BD} = F_{BD}\left(\frac{10}{15}\mathbf{i} + \frac{5}{15}\mathbf{j} + \frac{10}{15}\mathbf{k}\right)$$

$$\mathbf{P} = -1000\,\mathbf{k}$$

$$\Sigma F_x = 0; \quad F_{AD}\left(-\frac{10}{15}\right) + F_{CD}\left(-\frac{2}{11.358}\right) + F_{BD}\left(\frac{10}{15}\right) = 0$$

$$\Sigma F_y = 0; \quad F_{AD}\left(\frac{5}{15}\right) + F_{CD}\left(-\frac{5}{11.358}\right) + F_{BD}\left(\frac{5}{15}\right) = 0$$

$$\Sigma F_z = 0; \quad F_{AD}\left(\frac{10}{15}\right) + F_{CD}\left(\frac{10}{11.358}\right) + F_{BD}\left(\frac{10}{15}\right) - 1000 = 0$$

Solving,

$F_{AD} = 300 \text{ lb (C)}$ **Ans**

$F_{BD} = 450 \text{ lb (C)}$ **Ans**

$F_{CD} = 568 \text{ lb (C)}$ **Ans**

*6-56. Determine the force in each member of the space truss and state if the members are in tension or compression. *Hint:* The support reaction at *E* acts along member *EB*. Why?

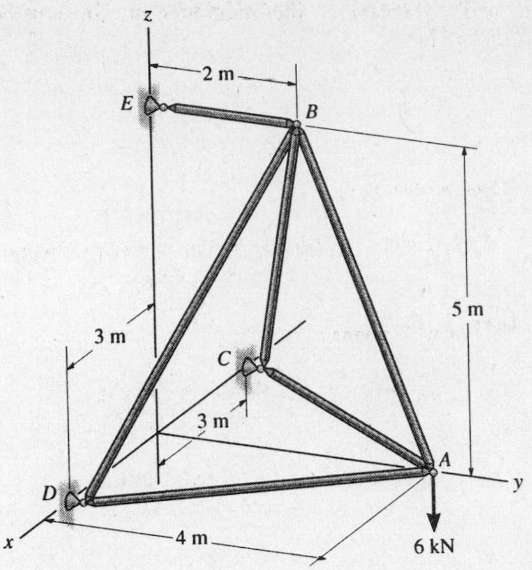

Method of Joints **:** In this case, the support reactions are not required for determining the member forces.

Joint *A*

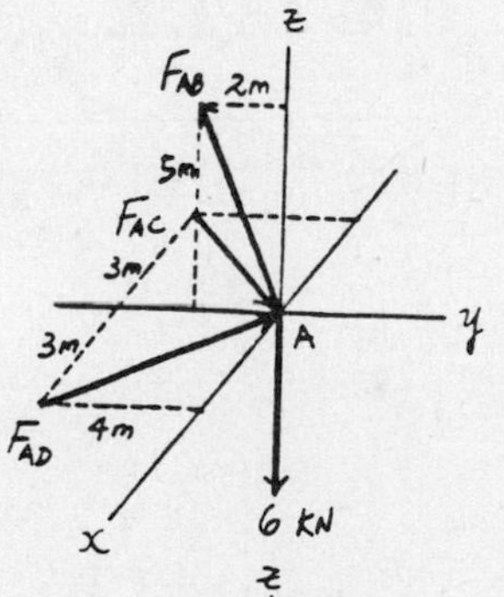

$$\Sigma F_z = 0; \quad F_{AB}\left(\frac{5}{\sqrt{29}}\right) - 6 = 0$$

$$F_{AB} = 6.462 \text{ kN (T)} = 6.46 \text{ kN (T)} \qquad \textbf{Ans}$$

$$\Sigma F_x = 0; \quad F_{AC}\left(\frac{3}{5}\right) - F_{AD}\left(\frac{3}{5}\right) = 0 \quad F_{AC} = F_{AD} \qquad [1]$$

$$\Sigma F_y = 0; \quad F_{AC}\left(\frac{4}{5}\right) + F_{AD}\left(\frac{4}{5}\right) - 6.462\left(\frac{2}{\sqrt{29}}\right) = 0$$

$$F_{AC} + F_{AD} = 3.00 \qquad [2]$$

Solving Eqs.[1] and [2] yields

$$F_{AC} = F_{AD} = 1.50 \text{ kN (C)} \qquad \textbf{Ans}$$

Joint *B*

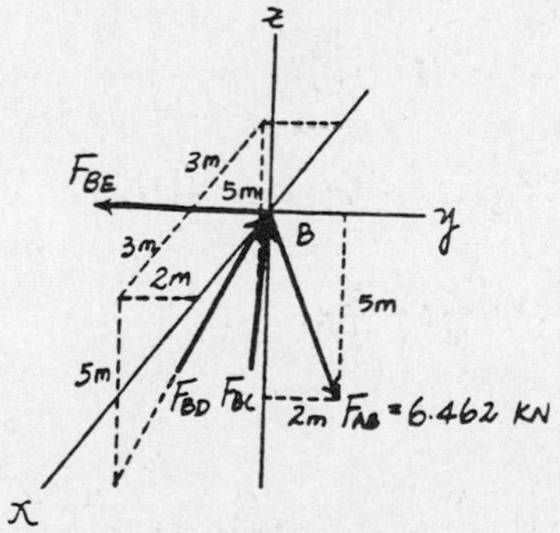

$$\Sigma F_x = 0; \quad F_{BC}\left(\frac{3}{\sqrt{38}}\right) - F_{BD}\left(\frac{3}{\sqrt{38}}\right) = 0 \quad F_{BC} = F_{BD} \qquad [1]$$

$$\Sigma F_z = 0; \quad F_{BC}\left(\frac{5}{\sqrt{38}}\right) + F_{BD}\left(\frac{5}{\sqrt{38}}\right) - 6.462\left(\frac{5}{\sqrt{29}}\right) = 0$$

$$F_{BC} + F_{BD} = 7.397 \qquad [2]$$

Solving Eqs.[1] and [2] yields

$$F_{BC} = F_{BD} = 3.699 \text{ kN (C)} = 3.70 \text{ kN (C)} \qquad \textbf{Ans}$$

$$\Sigma F_y = 0; \quad 2\left[3.699\left(\frac{2}{\sqrt{38}}\right)\right] + 6.462\left(\frac{2}{\sqrt{29}}\right) - F_{BE} = 0$$

$$F_{BE} = 4.80 \text{ kN (T)} \qquad \textbf{Ans}$$

Note : The support reactions at supports *C* and *D* can be determined by analyzing joints *C* and *D*, respectively using the results obtained above.

6-58. Determine the force in each member of the space truss and state if the members are in tension or compression. The truss is supported by ball-and-socket joints at A, B, and E. Set $\mathbf{F} = \{800\mathbf{j}\}$ N. *Hint:* The support reaction at E acts along member EC. Why?

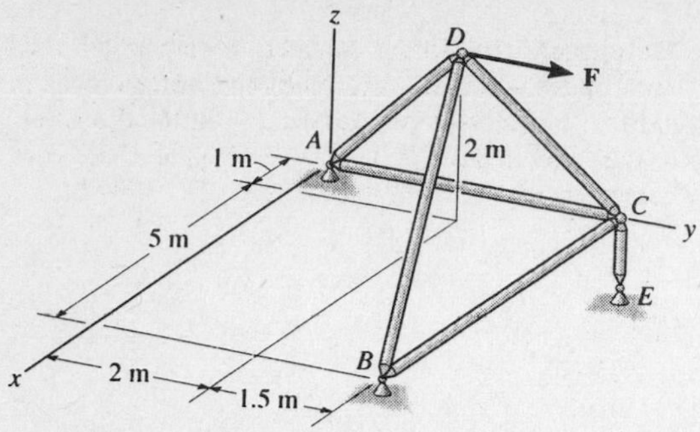

Joint D :

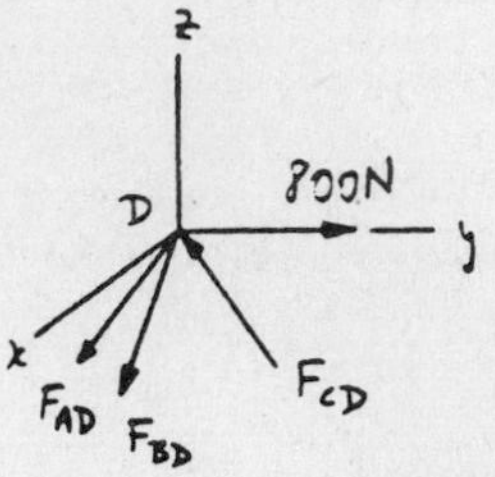

$\Sigma F_x = 0;\quad -\frac{1}{3}F_{AD} + \frac{5}{\sqrt{31.25}}F_{BD} + \frac{1}{\sqrt{7.25}}F_{CD} = 0$

$\Sigma F_y = 0;\quad -\frac{2}{3}F_{AD} + \frac{1.5}{\sqrt{31.25}}F_{BD} - \frac{1.5}{\sqrt{7.25}}F_{CD} + 800 = 0$

$\Sigma F_z = 0;\quad -\frac{2}{3}F_{AD} - \frac{2}{\sqrt{31.25}}F_{BD} + \frac{2}{\sqrt{7.25}}F_{CD} = 0$

$F_{AD} = 686$ N (T) **Ans**

$F_{BD} = 0$ **Ans**

$F_{CD} = 615.4 = 615$ N (C) **Ans**

Joint C :

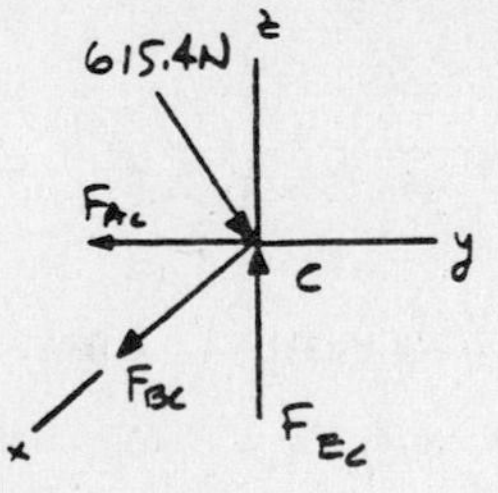

$\Sigma F_x = 0;\quad F_{BC} - \frac{1}{\sqrt{7.25}}(615.4) = 0$

$F_{BC} = 229$ N (T) **Ans**

$\Sigma F_y = 0;\quad \frac{1.5}{\sqrt{7.25}}(615.4) - F_{AC} = 0$

$F_{AC} = 343$ N (T) **Ans**

$\Sigma F_z = 0;\quad F_{EC} - \frac{2}{\sqrt{7.25}}(615.4) = 0$

$F_{EC} = 457$ N (C) **Ans**

6-59. Determine the force in each member of the space truss and state if the members are in tension or compression. The truss is supported by ball-and-socket joints at A, B, and E. Set $\mathbf{F} = \{-200\mathbf{i} + 400\mathbf{j}\}$ N. *Hint:* The support reaction at E acts along member EC. Why?

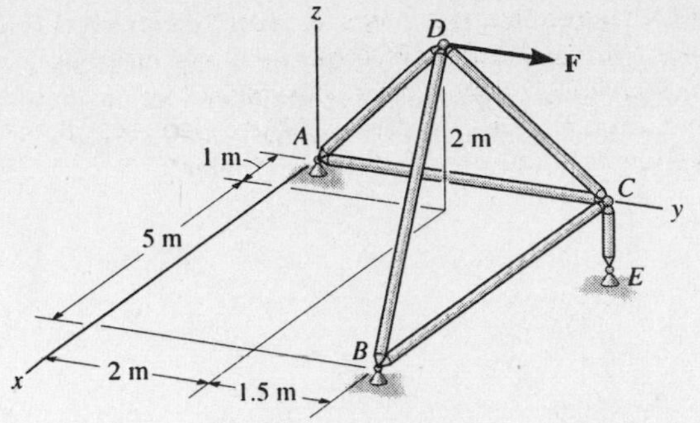

Joint D:

$\Sigma F_x = 0;\quad -\frac{1}{3}F_{AD} + \frac{5}{\sqrt{31.25}}F_{BD} + \frac{1}{\sqrt{7.25}}F_{CD} - 200 = 0$

$\Sigma F_y = 0;\quad -\frac{2}{3}F_{AD} + \frac{1.5}{\sqrt{31.25}}F_{BD} - \frac{1.5}{\sqrt{7.25}}F_{CD} + 400 = 0$

$\Sigma F_z = 0;\quad -\frac{2}{3}F_{AD} - \frac{2}{\sqrt{31.25}}F_{BD} + \frac{2}{\sqrt{7.25}}F_{CD} = 0$

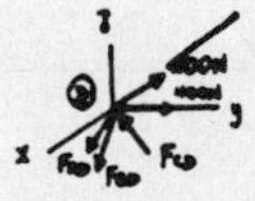

$F_{AD} = 343$ N (T) **Ans**

$F_{BD} = 186$ N (T) **Ans**

$F_{CD} = 397.5 = 397$ N (C) **Ans**

Joint C:

$\Sigma F_x = 0;\quad F_{BC} - \frac{1}{\sqrt{7.25}}(397.5) = 0$

$F_{BC} = 148$ N (T) **Ans**

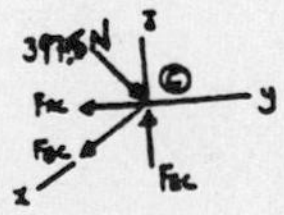

$\Sigma F_y = 0;\quad \frac{1.5}{\sqrt{7.25}}(397.5) - F_{AC} = 0$

$F_{AC} = 221$ N (T) **Ans**

$\Sigma F_z = 0;\quad F_{EC} - \frac{2}{\sqrt{7.25}}(397.5) = 0$

$F_{EC} = 295$ N (C) **Ans**

*6-60. Determine the force in each member of the space truss and state if the members are in tension or compression. The crate has a mass of 50 kg.

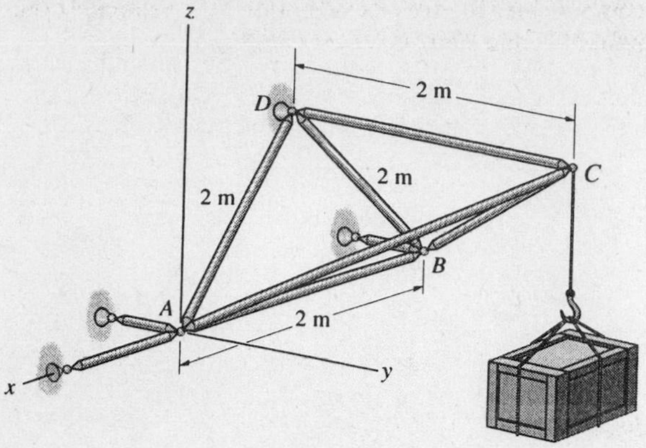

Method of Joints **:** In this case, the support reactions are not required for determining the member forces.

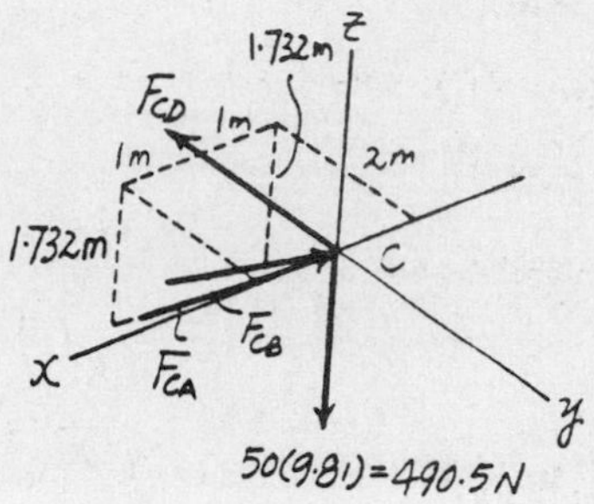

Joint C

$$\Sigma F_x = 0; \quad F_{CB}\left(\frac{1}{\sqrt{8}}\right) - F_{CA}\left(\frac{1}{\sqrt{8}}\right) = 0 \qquad F_{CB} = F_{CA} \qquad [1]$$

$$\Sigma F_z = 0; \quad F_{CB}\left(\frac{1.732}{\sqrt{8}}\right) + F_{CA}\left(\frac{1.732}{\sqrt{8}}\right) - 490.5 = 0 \qquad [2]$$

Solving Eqs. [1] and [2] yields

$$F_{CA} = F_{CB} = 400.49 \text{ N (C)} = 400 \text{ N (C)} \qquad \textbf{Ans}$$

$$\Sigma F_y = 0; \quad 2\left[400.49\left(\frac{2}{\sqrt{8}}\right)\right] - F_{CD} = 0$$

$$F_{CD} = 566.38 \text{ N (T)} = 566 \text{ N (T)} \qquad \textbf{Ans}$$

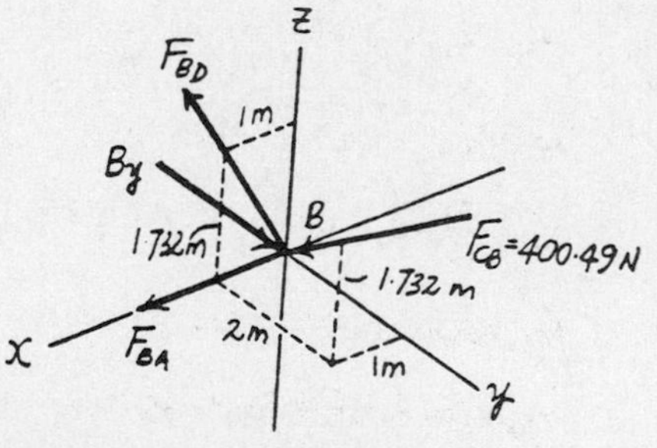

Joint B

$$\Sigma F_z = 0 \quad F_{BD}\left(\frac{1.732}{2}\right) - 400.49\left(\frac{1.732}{\sqrt{8}}\right) = 0$$

$$F_{BD} = 283.19 \text{ N (T)} = 283 \text{ N (T)} \qquad \textbf{Ans}$$

$$\Sigma F_x = 0; \quad F_{BA} + 283.19\left(\frac{1}{2}\right) - 400.49\left(\frac{1}{\sqrt{8}}\right) = 0$$

$$F_{BA} = 0 \qquad \textbf{Ans}$$

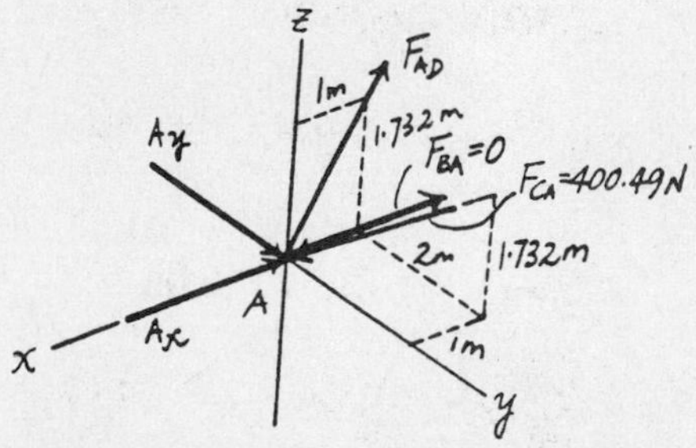

Joint A

$$\Sigma F_z = 0 \quad F_{AD}\left(\frac{1.732}{2}\right) - 400.49\left(\frac{1.732}{\sqrt{8}}\right) = 0$$

$$F_{AD} = 283.19 \text{ N (T)} = 283 \text{ N (T)} \qquad \textbf{Ans}$$

6-61. Determine the force in each member of the space truss and state if the members are in tension or compression. The truss is supported by a ball-and-socket joint at A and short links at B and C.

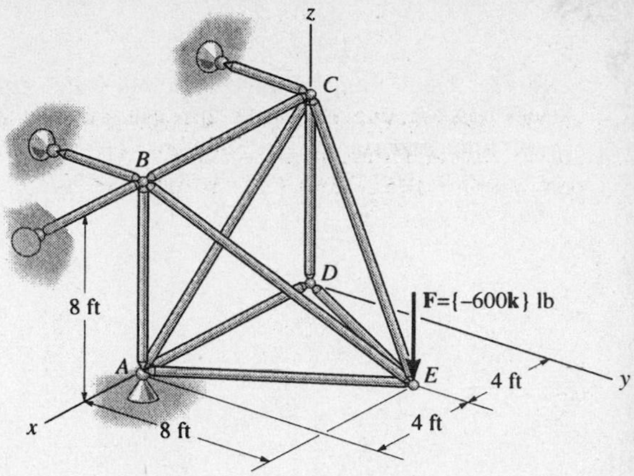

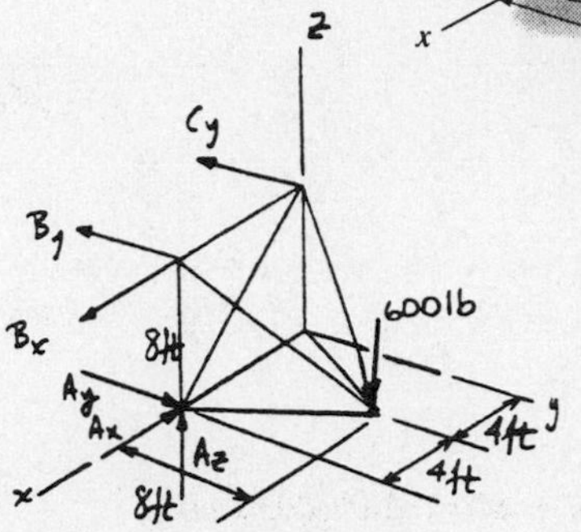

$\Sigma(M_{AB})_x = 0;\quad C_y = 0$

$\Sigma M_x = 0;\quad B_y(8) - 600(8) = 0$

$B_y = 600 \text{ lb}$

$\Sigma F_y = 0;\quad A_y = 600 \text{ lb}$

$\Sigma F_z = 0;\quad A_z = 600 \text{ lb}$

$\Sigma M_y = 0;\quad 600(4) - 600(8) + B_x(8) = 0$

$B_x = 300 \text{ lb}$

$\Sigma F_x = 0;\quad A_x = 300 \text{ lb}$

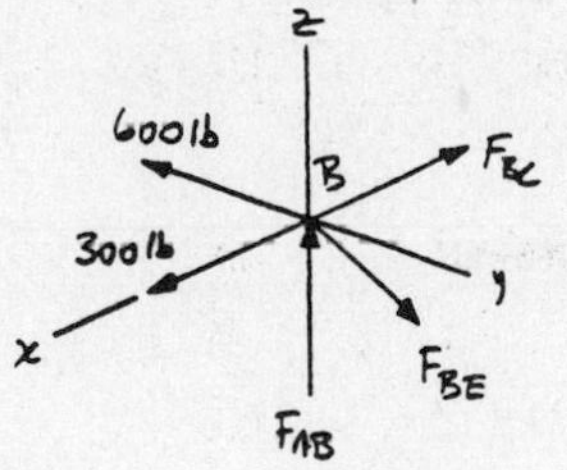

Joint B :

$\Sigma F_y = 0;\quad \frac{8}{12}F_{BE} - 600 = 0$

$F_{BE} = 900 \text{ lb (T)}$ **Ans**

$\Sigma F_x = 0;\quad 300 - F_{BC} - \frac{4}{12}(900) = 0$

$F_{BC} = 0$ **Ans**

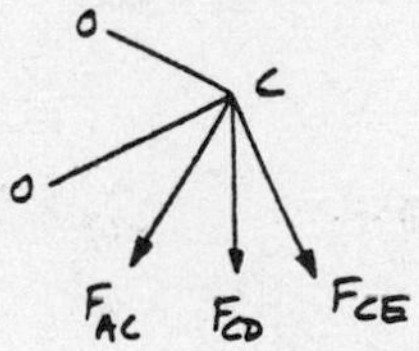

$\Sigma F_z = 0;\quad F_{AB} - \frac{8}{12}(900) = 0$

$F_{AB} = 600 \text{ lb (C)}$ **Ans**

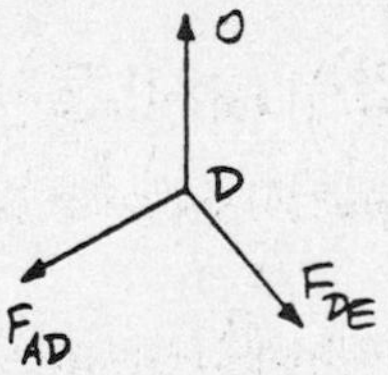

Joints C and D :

$F_{DE} = F_{CD} = F_{AD} = F_{CE} = F_{AC} = 0$ **Ans**

Joint E :

$\Sigma F_x = 0;\quad \frac{4}{12}(900) - \frac{4}{\sqrt{80}}F_{AE} = 0$

$F_{AE} = 670.8 = 671 \text{ lb (C)}$ **Ans**

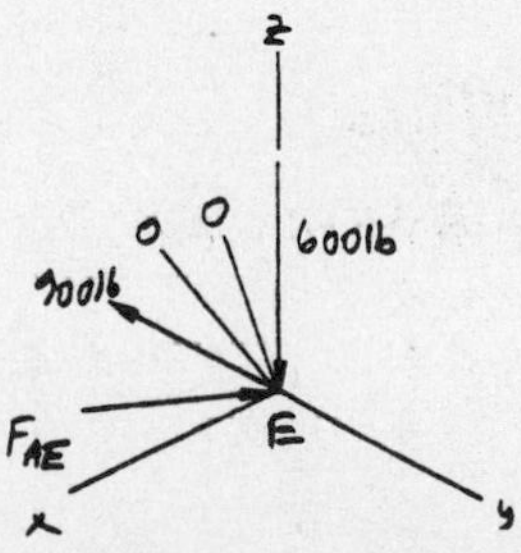

$\Sigma F_z = 0;\quad \frac{8}{12}(900) - 600 = 0$ Check!

$\Sigma F_y = 0;\quad \frac{8}{\sqrt{80}}(670.8) - \frac{8}{12}(900) = 0$ Check!

6-62. Determine the force in members BE, DF, and BC of the space truss and state if the members are in tension or compression.

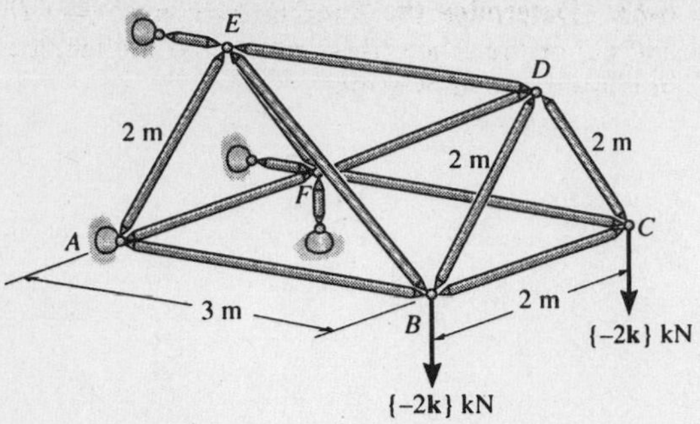

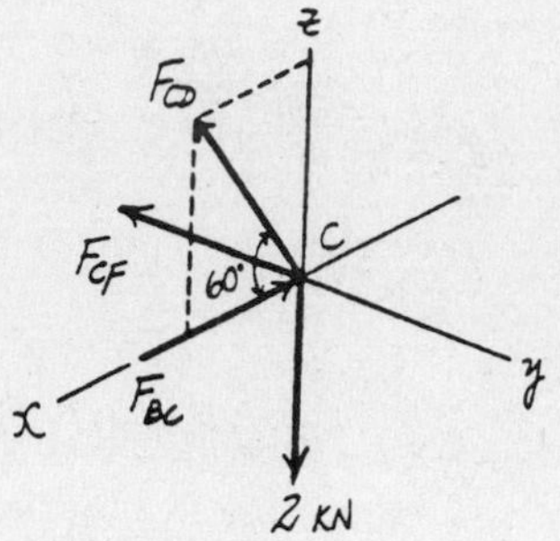

Method of Joints : In this case, the support reactions are not required for determining the member forces.

Joint C

$\Sigma F_z = 0;\quad F_{CD}\sin 60° - 2 = 0 \qquad F_{CD} = 2.309 \text{ kN (T)}$

$\Sigma F_x = 0;\quad 2.309\cos 60° - F_{BC} = 0$

$F_{BC} = 1.154 \text{ kN (C)} = 1.15 \text{ kN (C)}$ **Ans**

Joint D Since F_{CD}, F_{DE} and F_{DE} lie within the same plane and F_{DB} is out of this plane, then $F_{DB} = 0$.

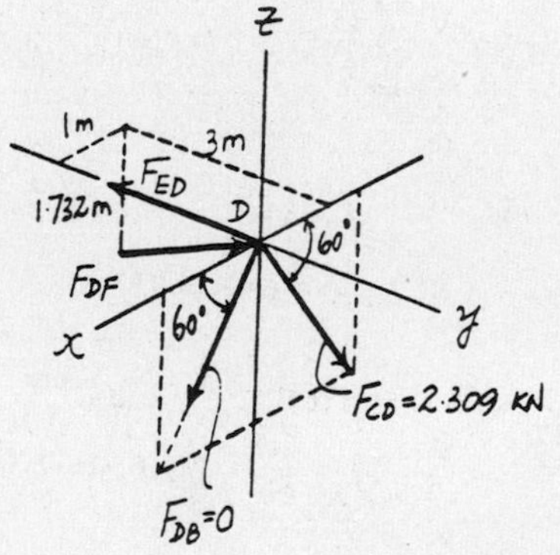

$\Sigma F_x = 0;\quad F_{DF}\left(\frac{1}{\sqrt{13}}\right) - 2.309\cos 60° = 0$

$F_{DF} = 4.16 \text{ kN (C)}$ **Ans**

Joint B

$\Sigma F_z = 0;\quad F_{BE}\left(\frac{1.732}{\sqrt{13}}\right) - 2 = 0$

$F_{BE} = 4.16 \text{ kN (T)}$ **Ans**

6-63. Determine the force in members *AB, CD, ED,* and *CF* of the space truss and state if the members are in tension or compression.

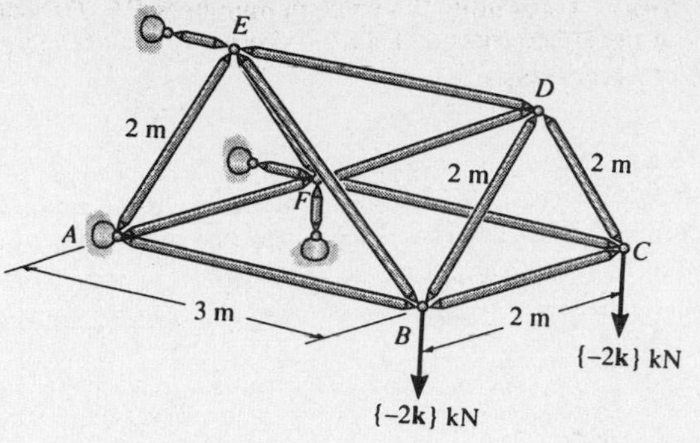

Method of Joints : In this case, the support reactions are not required for determining the member forces.

Joint *C* Since F_{CD}, F_{BC} and 2 kN force lie within the same plane and F_{CF} is out of this plane, then

$$F_{CF} = 0 \qquad \textbf{Ans}$$

$\Sigma F_z = 0;\quad F_{CD}\sin 60° - 2 = 0$

$$F_{CD} = 2.309 \text{ kN (T)} = 2.31 \text{ kN (T)} \qquad \textbf{Ans}$$

$\Sigma F_x = 0;\quad 2.309\cos 60° - F_{BC} = 0 \qquad F_{BC} = 1.154 \text{ kN (C)}$

Joint *D* Since F_{CD}, F_{DE} and F_{DE} lie within the same plane and F_{DB} is out of this plane, then $F_{DB} = 0$.

$\Sigma F_x = 0;\quad F_{DF}\left(\dfrac{1}{\sqrt{13}}\right) - 2.309\cos 60° = 0$

$$F_{DF} = 4.163 \text{ kN (C)}$$

$\Sigma F_y = 0;\quad 4.163\left(\dfrac{3}{\sqrt{13}}\right) - F_{ED} = 0$

$$F_{ED} = 3.46 \text{ kN (T)} \qquad \textbf{Ans}$$

Joint *B*

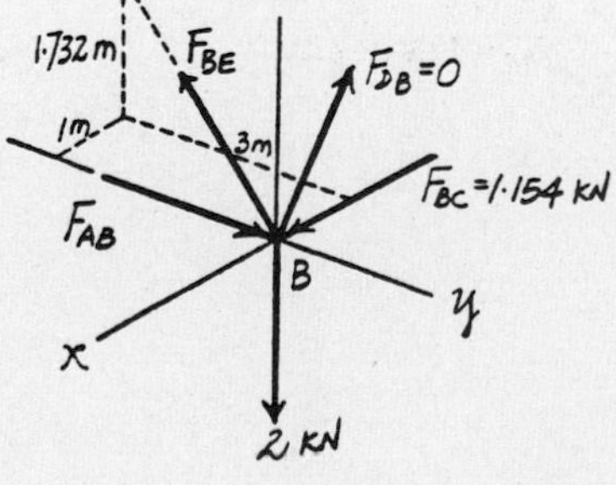

$\Sigma F_z = 0;\quad F_{BE}\left(\dfrac{1.732}{\sqrt{13}}\right) - 2 = 0 \qquad F_{BE} = 4.163 \text{ kN (T)}$

$\Sigma F_y = 0;\quad F_{AB} - 4.163\left(\dfrac{3}{\sqrt{13}}\right) = 0$

$$F_{AB} = 3.46 \text{ kN (C)} \qquad \textbf{Ans}$$

*6-64. Determine the force in members FE and ED of the space truss and state if the members are in tension or compression. The truss is supported by a ball-and-socket joint at C and short links at A and B.

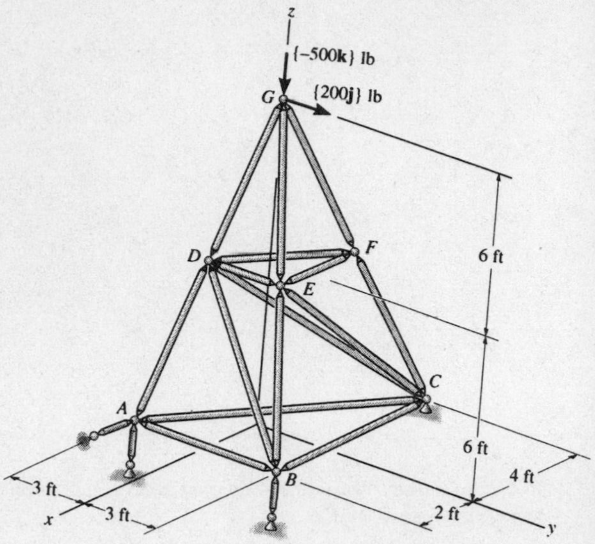

Joint F : F_{FG}, F_{FD}, and F_{FC} are lying in the same plane and x' axis is normal to that plane. Thus

$\Sigma F_{x'} = 0;$ $F_{FE} \cos\theta = 0$ $F_{FE} = 0$ **Ans**

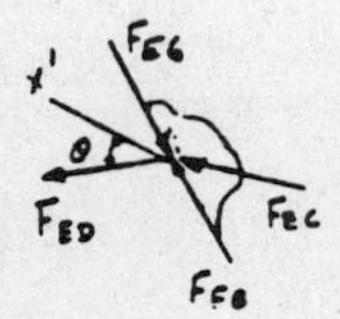

Joint E : F_{EG}, F_{EC}, and F_{EB} are lying in the same plane and x' axis is normal to that plane. Thus

$\Sigma F_{x'} = 0;$ $F_{ED} \cos\theta = 0$ $F_{ED} = 0$ **Ans**

6-65. Determine the force in members *GD*, *GE*, and *FD* of the space truss and state if the members are in tension or compression.

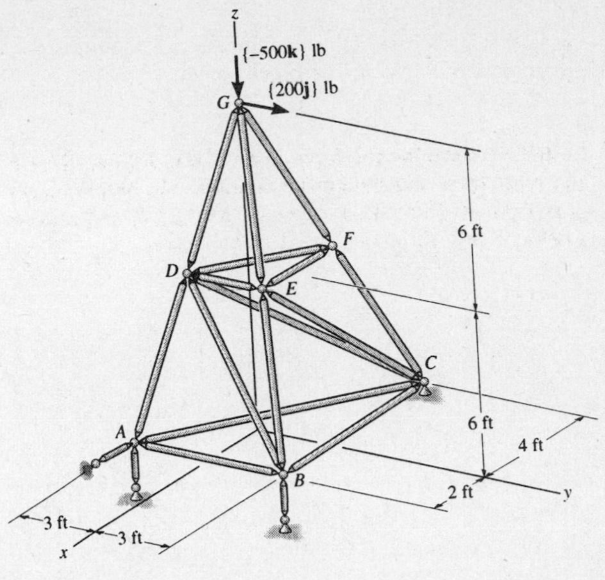

Joint G:

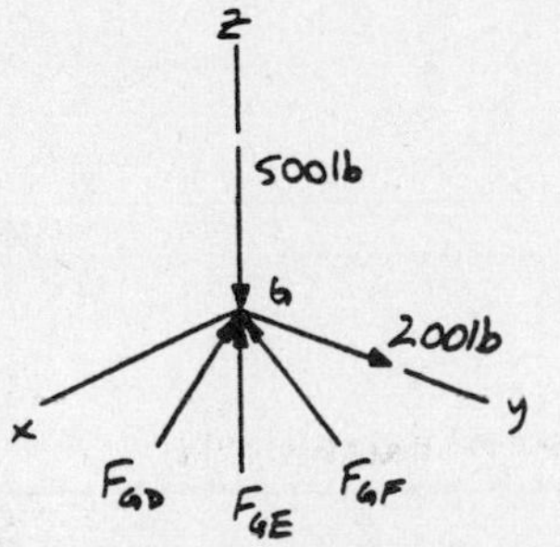

$$\mathbf{F}_{GD} = F_{GD}\left(-\frac{2}{12.53}\mathbf{i} + \frac{3}{12.53}\mathbf{j} + \frac{12}{12.53}\mathbf{k}\right)$$

$$\mathbf{F}_{GF} = F_{GF}\left(\frac{4}{13}\mathbf{i} - \frac{3}{13}\mathbf{j} + \frac{12}{13}\mathbf{k}\right)$$

$$\mathbf{F}_{GE} = F_{GE}\left(-\frac{2}{12.53}\mathbf{i} - \frac{3}{12.53}\mathbf{j} + \frac{12}{12.53}\mathbf{k}\right)$$

$$\Sigma F_x = 0; \quad -F_{GD}\left(\frac{2}{12.53}\right) + F_{GF}\left(\frac{4}{13}\right) - F_{GE}\left(\frac{2}{12.53}\right) = 0$$

$$\Sigma F_y = 0; \quad F_{GD}\left(\frac{3}{12.53}\right) - F_{GF}\left(\frac{3}{13}\right) - F_{GE}\left(\frac{3}{12.53}\right) + 200 = 0$$

$$\Sigma F_z = 0; \quad F_{GD}\left(\frac{12}{12.53}\right) + F_{GF}\left(\frac{12}{13}\right) + F_{GE}\left(\frac{12}{12.53}\right) - 500 = 0$$

Solving,

$F_{GD} = -157 \text{ lb} = 157 \text{ lb (T)}$ **Ans**

$F_{GF} = 181 \text{ lb (C)}$

$F_{GE} = 505 \text{ lb (C)}$ **Ans**

Joint F:

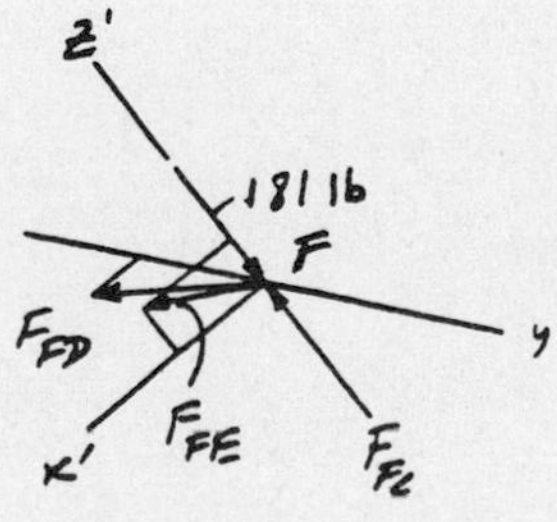

Orient the x', y', z' axes as shown.

$\Sigma F_{y'} = 0; \quad F_{FD} = 0$ **Ans**

6-66. In each case, determine the force **P** required to maintain equilibrium. The block weighs 100 lb.

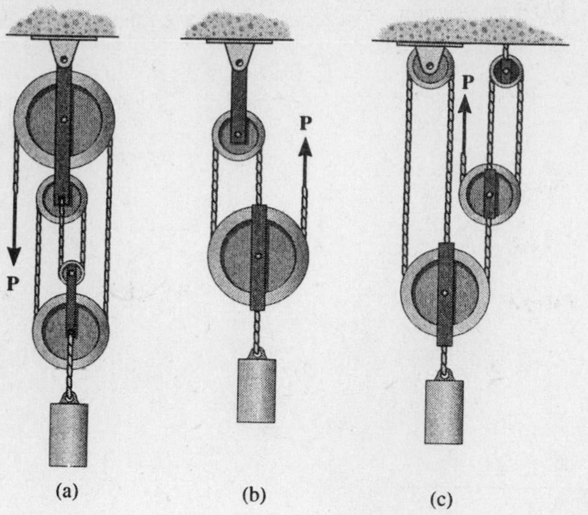

Equations of Equilibrium :

a) $+\uparrow \Sigma F_y = 0;\quad 4P - 100 = 0$

$P = 25.0 \text{ lb}$ **Ans**

b) $+\uparrow \Sigma F_y = 0;\quad 3P - 100 = 0$

$P = 33.3 \text{ lb}$ **Ans**

c) $+\uparrow \Sigma F_y = 0;\quad 3P' - 100 = 0$

$P' = 33.33 \text{ lb}$

$+\uparrow \Sigma F_y = 0;\quad 3P - 33.33 = 0$

$P = 11.1 \text{ lb}$ **Ans**

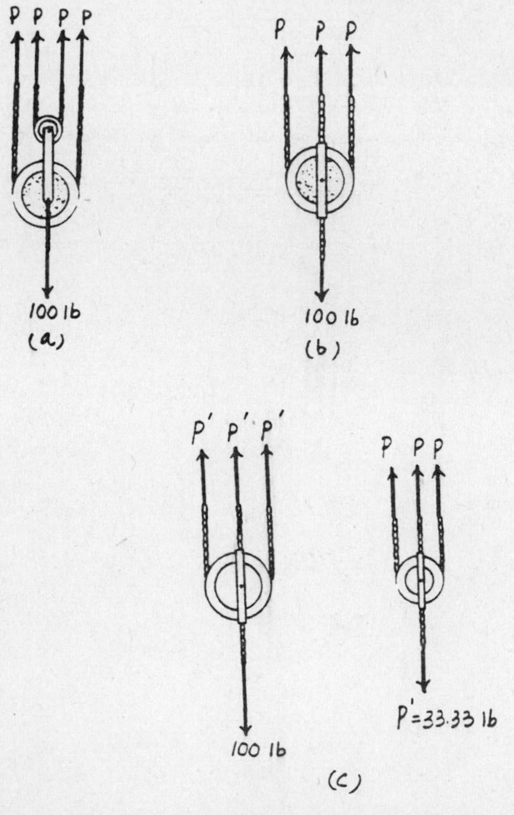

6-67. Determine the force **P** needed to hold the 20-lb block in equilibrium.

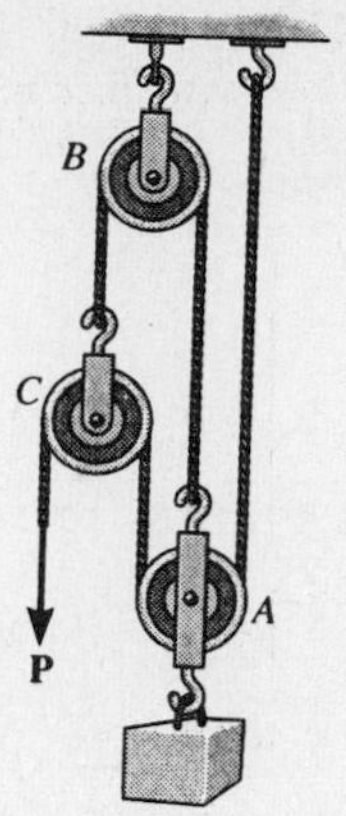

Pulley C:

$+\uparrow\Sigma F_y = 0;\quad T - 2P = 0$

Pulley A:

$+\uparrow\Sigma F_y = 0;\quad 2P + T - 20 = 0$

$P = 5\text{ lb}$ **Ans**

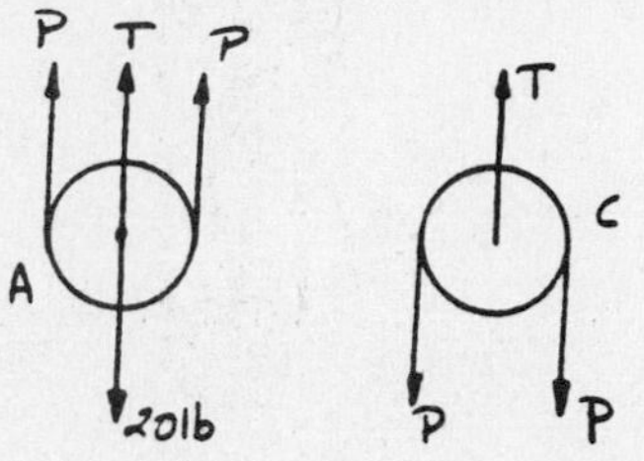

***6-68.** Determine the force **P** needed to support the 100-lb weight. Each pulley has a weight of 10 lb. Also, what are the cord reactions at A and B?

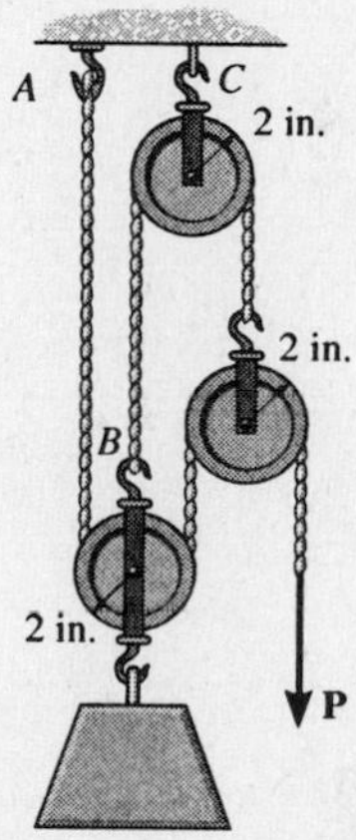

Equations of Equilibrium : From FBD (a),

$+\uparrow\Sigma F_y = 0;\quad P' - 2P - 10 = 0$ [1]

From FBD (b),

$+\uparrow\Sigma F_y = 0;\quad 2P + P' - 100 - 10 = 0$ [2]

Solving Eqs. [1] and [2] yields,

$P = 25.0\text{ lb}$ **Ans**
$P' = 60.0\text{ lb}$

The cord reactions at A and B are

$F_A = P = 25.0\text{ lb}\quad F_B = P' = 60.0\text{ lb}$ **Ans**

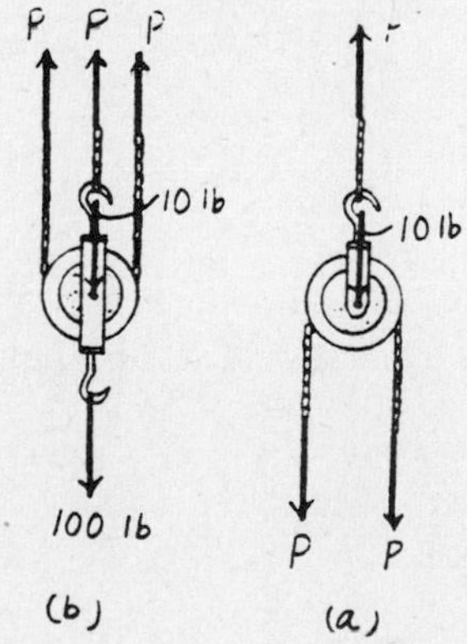

6-69. The cable and pulleys are used to lift the 600-lb stone. Determine the force that must be exerted on the cable at A and the magnitude of the resultant force the pulley at C must exert on pin B when the cables are in the position shown.

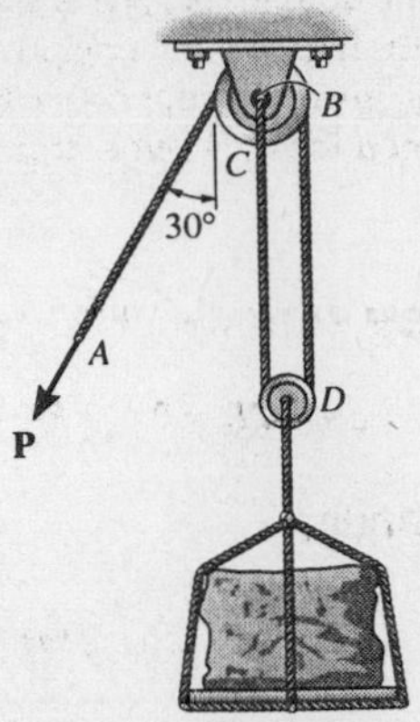

Pulley D :

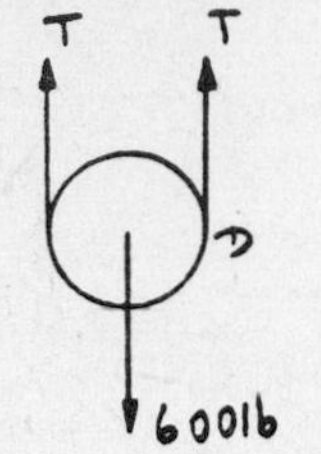

$+\uparrow \Sigma F_y = 0; \quad 2T - 600 = 0$

$T = 300 \text{ lb}$ **Ans**

Pulley B :

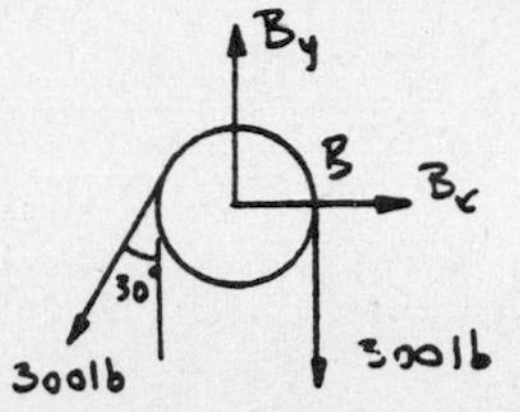

$\xrightarrow{+} \Sigma F_x = 0; \quad B_x - 300 \sin 30° = 0$

$B_x = 150 \text{ lb}$

$+\uparrow \Sigma F_y = 0; \quad B_y - 300 - 300 \cos 30° = 0$

$B_y = 559.8 \text{ lb}$

$F_B = \sqrt{(150)^2 + (559.8)^2} = 580 \text{ lb}$ **Ans**

6-70. The principles of a *differential chain block* are indicated schematically in the figure. Determine the magnitude of force **P** needed to support the 800-N force. Also, find the distance x where the cable must be attached to bar AB so the bar remains horizontal. All pulleys have a radius of 60 mm.

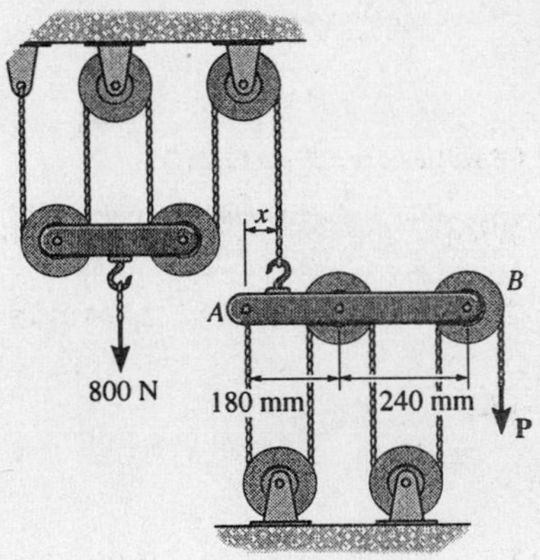

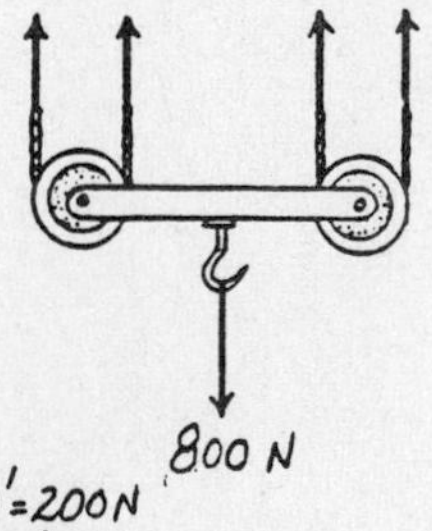

(a)

Equations of Equilibrium : From FBD(a),

$+\uparrow \Sigma F_y = 0; \quad 4P' - 800 = 0 \quad P' = 200 \text{ N}$

From FBD(b),

$+\uparrow \Sigma F_y = 0; \quad 200 - 5P = 0 \quad P = 40.0 \text{ N}$ **Ans**

$\circlearrowleft + \Sigma M_A = 0; \quad 200(x) - 40.0(120) - 40.0(240) - 40.0(360) - 40.0(480) = 0$

$x = 240 \text{ mm}$ **Ans**

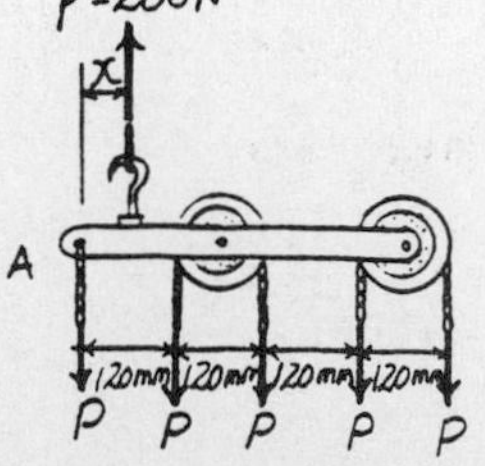

(b)

6-71. The double tree AB is used to support the loadings applied to each of the single trees. Determine the total load that must be supported by the chain EG and its placement d for the double tree AB to remain horizontal.

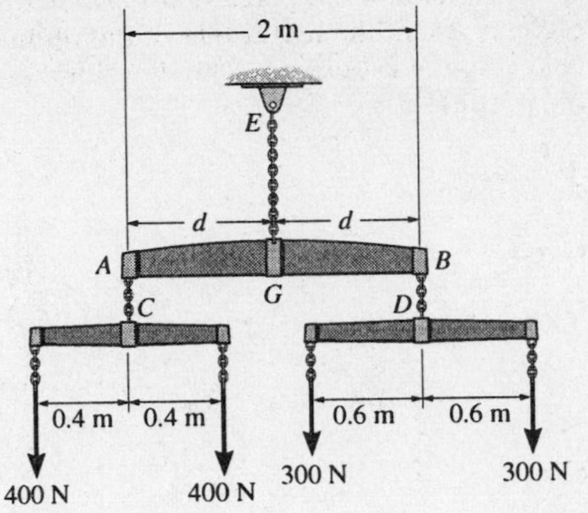

Equations of Equilibrium : From FBD(a),

$+\uparrow \Sigma F_y = 0; \quad F_{AC} - 400 - 400 = 0 \quad F_{AC} = 800 \text{ N}$

From FBD(b),

$+\uparrow \Sigma F_y = 0; \quad F_{BD} - 300 - 300 = 0 \quad F_{BD} = 600 \text{ N}$

From FBD(c),

$+\uparrow \Sigma F_y = 0; \quad F_{EG} - 800 - 600 = 0$

$F_{EG} = 1400 \text{ N} = 1.40 \text{ kN}$ **Ans**

$\circlearrowleft + \Sigma M_G = 0; \quad 800(d) - 600(2 - d) = 0$

$d = 0.857 \text{ m}$ **Ans**

***6-72.** The compound beam is fixed at A and supported by a rocker at B and C. There are hinges (pins) at D and E. Determine the reactions at the supports.

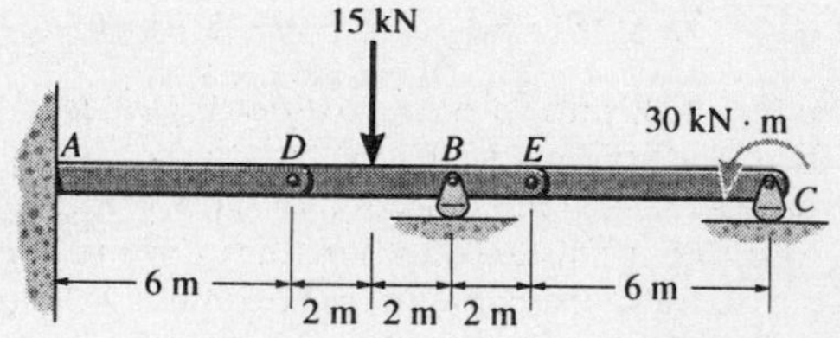

Equations of Equilibrium : From FBD(a),

$\circlearrowleft + \Sigma M_E = 0; \quad 30 - C_y(6) = 0 \quad C_y = 5.00 \text{ kN}$ **Ans**

$+\uparrow \Sigma F_y = 0; \quad E_y - 5.00 = 0 \quad E_y = 5.00 \text{ kN}$

$\xrightarrow{+} \Sigma F_x = 0; \quad E_x = 0$

From FBD(b),

$\circlearrowleft + \Sigma M_D = 0; \quad B_y(4) - 15(2) - 5.00(6) = 0$

$B_y = 15.0 \text{ kN}$ **Ans**

$+\uparrow \Sigma F_y = 0; \quad D_y + 15.0 - 15 - 5.00 = 0$

$D_y = 5.00 \text{ kN}$

$\xrightarrow{+} \Sigma F_x = 0; \quad D_x = 0$

From FBD(c),

$\circlearrowleft + \Sigma M_A = 0; \quad M_A - 5.00(6) = 0$

$M_A = 30.0 \text{ kN} \cdot \text{m}$ **Ans**

$+\uparrow \Sigma F_y = 0; \quad A_y - 5.00 = 0 \quad A_y = 5.00 \text{ kN}$ **Ans**

$\xrightarrow{+} \Sigma F_x = 0; \quad A_x = 0$ **Ans**

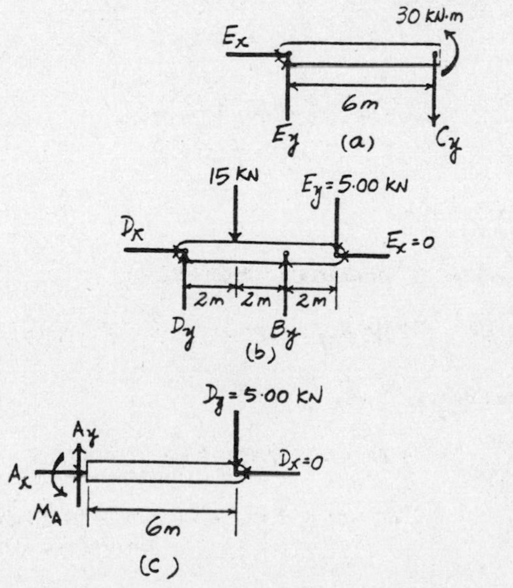

6-73. The compound beam is pin-supported at C and supported by a roller at A and B. There is a hinge (pin) at D. Determine the reactions at the supports. Neglect the thickness of the beam.

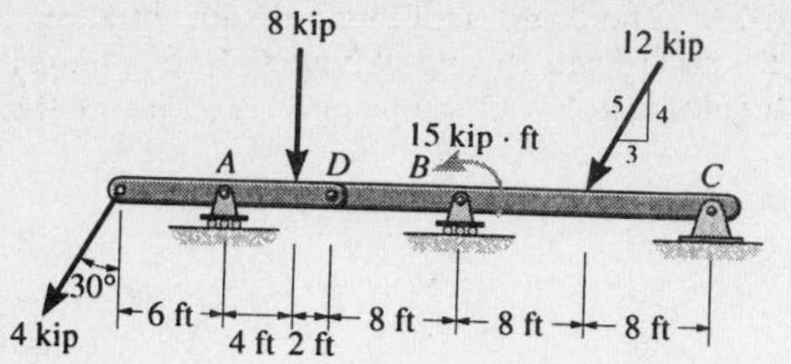

Equations of Equilibrium : From FBD(a),

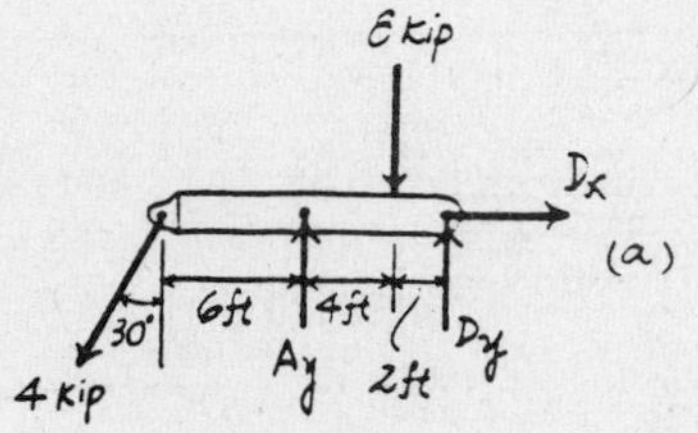

$\curvearrowleft + \Sigma M_D = 0;\quad 4\cos 30°(12) + 8(2) - A_y(6) = 0$

$A_y = 9.595 \text{ kip} = 9.59 \text{ kip}$ **Ans**

$+\uparrow \Sigma F_y = 0;\quad D_y + 9.595 - 4\cos 30° - 8 = 0$

$D_y = 1.869 \text{ kip}$

$\overset{+}{\rightarrow} \Sigma F_x = 0;\quad D_x - 4\sin 30° = 0 \qquad D_x = 2.00 \text{ kip}$

From FBD(b),

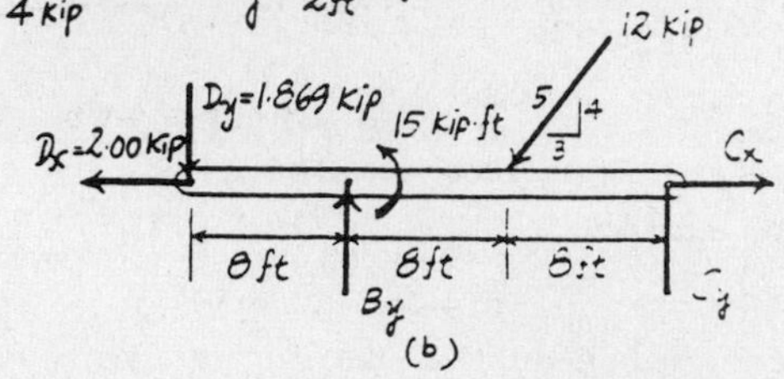

$\curvearrowleft + \Sigma M_C = 0;\quad 1.869(24) + 15 + 12\left(\frac{4}{5}\right)(8) - B_y(16) = 0$

$B_y = 8.541 \text{ kip} = 8.54 \text{ kip}$ **Ans**

$+\uparrow \Sigma F_y = 0;\quad C_y + 8.541 - 1.869 - 12\left(\frac{4}{5}\right) = 0$

$C_y = 2.93 \text{ kip}$ **Ans**

$\overset{+}{\rightarrow} \Sigma F_x = 0;\quad C_x - 2.00 - 12\left(\frac{3}{5}\right) = 0$

$C_x = 9.20 \text{ kip}$ **Ans**

6-74. The compound beam is supported by a rocker at *B* and is fixed to the wall at *A*. If it is hinged (pinned) together at *C*, determine the reactions at the supports.

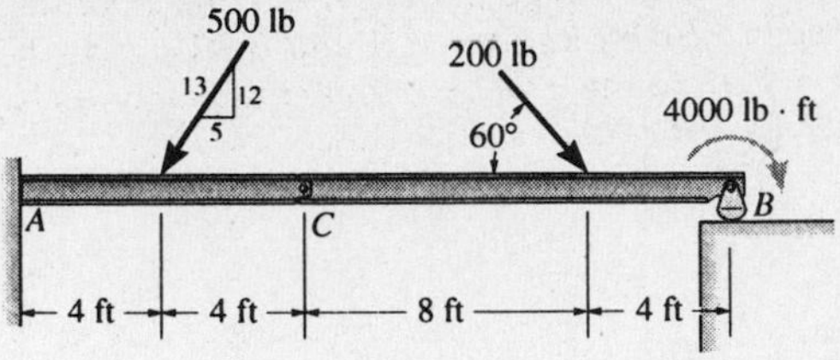

Member *CB* :

$\overset{+}{\rightarrow} \Sigma F_x = 0;\quad -C_x + 200\cos 60° = 0$

$C_x = 100 \text{ lb}$

$\circlearrowleft + \Sigma M_C = 0;\quad -200\sin 60°(8) + B_y(12) - 4000 = 0$

$B_y = 448.8 \text{ lb} = 449 \text{ lb}$ **Ans**

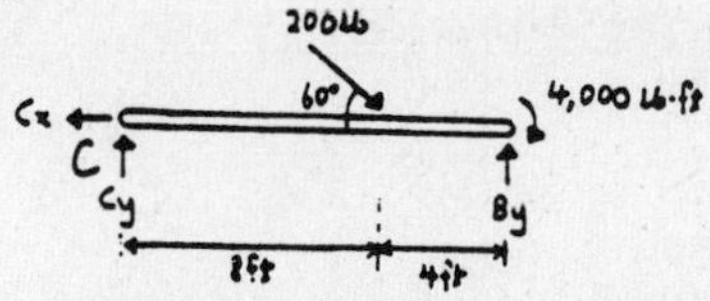

$+\uparrow \Sigma F_y = 0;\quad C_y - 200\sin 60° + 448.8 = 0$

$C_y = -275.6 \text{ lb}$

Member *AC* :

$\overset{+}{\rightarrow} \Sigma F_x = 0;\quad A_x - 500\left(\frac{5}{13}\right) + 100 = 0$

$A_x = 92.3 \text{ lb}$ **Ans**

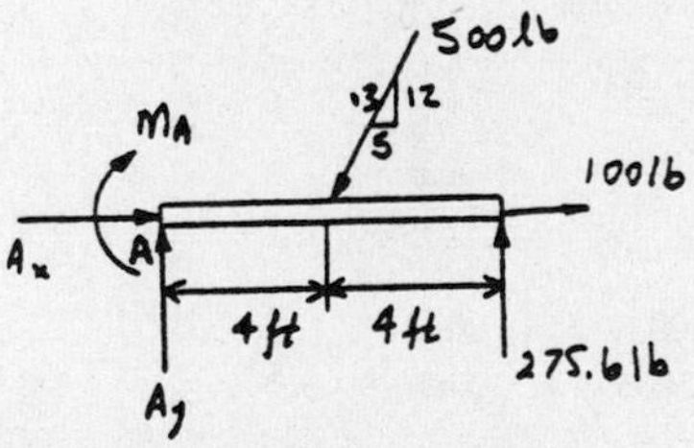

$+\uparrow \Sigma F_y = 0;\quad A_y - 500\left(\frac{12}{13}\right) + 275.6 = 0$

$A_y = 186 \text{ lb}$ **Ans**

$\circlearrowleft + \Sigma M_A = 0;\quad -M_A - 500\left(\frac{12}{13}\right)(4) + 275.6(8) = 0$

$M_A = 359 \text{ lb}\cdot\text{ft}$ **Ans**

6-75. Determine the horizontal and vertical components force at pins A and C of the two-member frame.

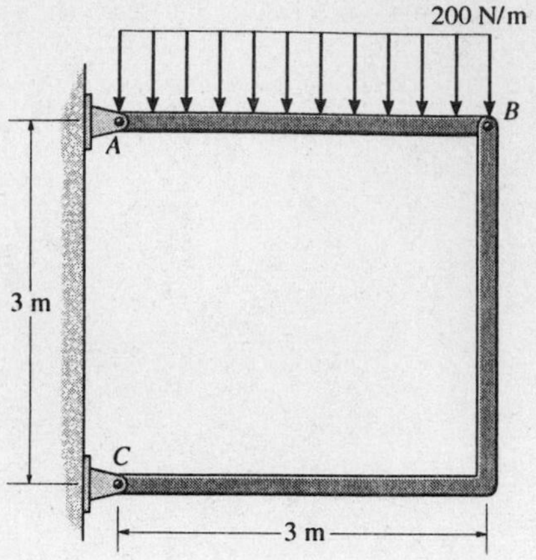

Free Body Diagram : The solution for this problem will be simplified if one realizes that member BC is a two force member.

Equations of Equilibrium :

$$\circlearrowleft + \Sigma M_A = 0; \quad F_{BC}\cos 45°(3) - 600(1.5) = 0$$
$$F_{BC} = 424.26 \text{ N}$$

$$+\uparrow \Sigma F_y = 0; \quad A_y + 424.26\cos 45° - 600 = 0$$
$$A_y = 300 \text{ N} \qquad \textbf{Ans}$$

$$\overset{+}{\rightarrow} \Sigma F_x = 0; \quad 424.26\sin 45° - A_x = 0$$
$$A_x = 300 \text{ N} \qquad \textbf{Ans}$$

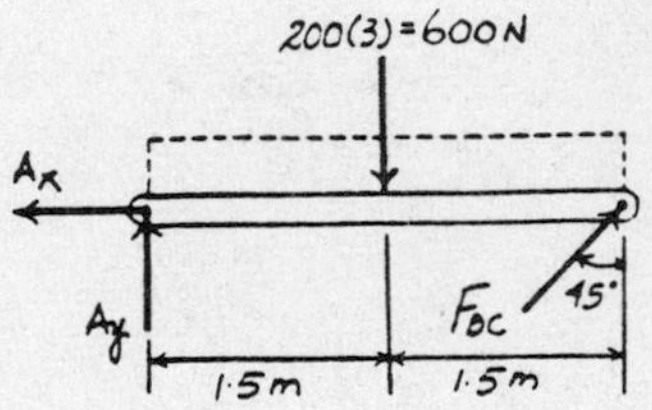

For pin C,

$$C_x = F_{BC}\sin 45° = 424.26\sin 45° = 300 \text{ N} \qquad \textbf{Ans}$$
$$C_y = F_{BC}\cos 45° = 424.26\cos 45° = 300 \text{ N} \qquad \textbf{Ans}$$

*6-76. The compound beam is fixed supported at A and supported by rockers at B and C. If there are hinges (pins) at D and E, determine the reactions at the supports A, B, and C.

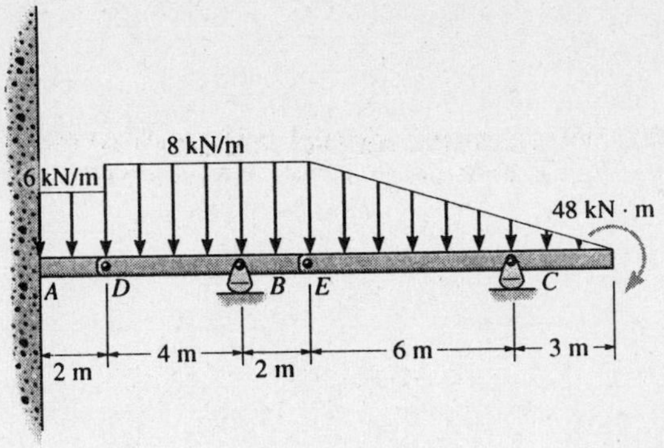

Member EC:

$\xrightarrow{+} \Sigma F_x = 0; \quad E_x = 0$

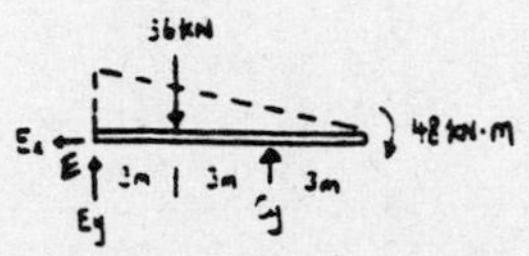

$\curvearrowleft + \Sigma M_E = 0; \quad -36(3) + C_y(6) - 48 = 0$

$C_y = 26\text{ kN}$ **Ans**

$+\uparrow \Sigma F_y = 0; \quad E_y - 36 + 26 = 0$

$E_y = 10\text{ kN}$

Member DE:

$\xrightarrow{+} \Sigma F_x = 0; \quad D_x = 0$

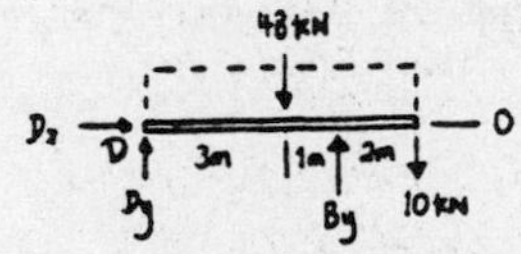

$\curvearrowleft + \Sigma M_D = 0; \quad B_y(4) - 48(3) - 10(6) = 0$

$B_y = 51\text{ kN}$ **Ans**

$+\uparrow \Sigma F_y = 0; \quad D_y - 48 + 51 - 10 = 0$

$D_y = 7\text{ kN}$

Member AD:

$\xrightarrow{+} \Sigma F_x = 0; \quad A_x = 0$ **Ans**

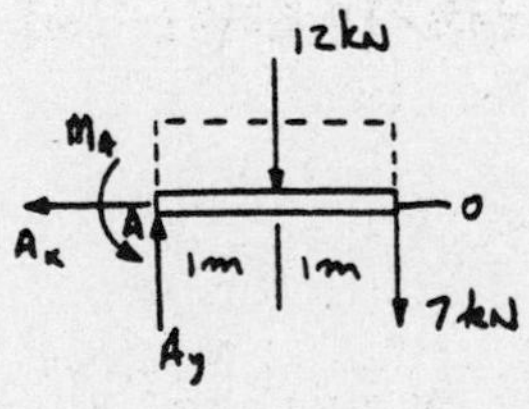

$+\uparrow \Sigma F_y = 0; \quad A_y - 7 - 12 = 0$

$A_y = 19\text{ kN}$ **Ans**

$\curvearrowleft + \Sigma M_A = 0; \quad M_A - 12(1) - 7(2) = 0$

$M_A = 26\text{ kN}\cdot\text{m}$ **Ans**

6-77. Determine the horizontal and vertical components of force at pins A, B, and C, and the reactions to the fixed support D of the three-member frame.

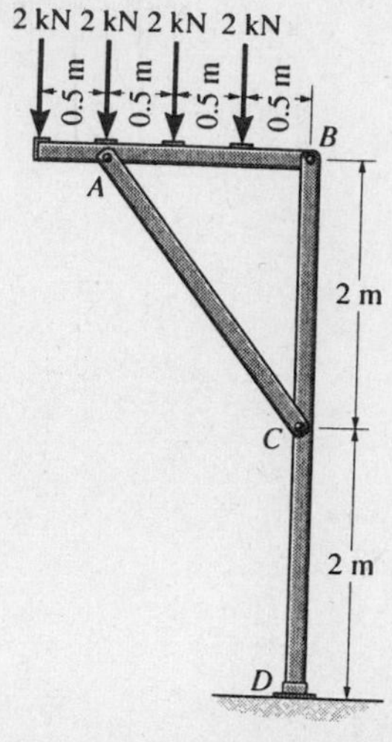

Free Body Diagram : The solution for this problem will be simplified if one realizes that member AC is a two force member.

Equations of Equilibrium : For FBD(a),

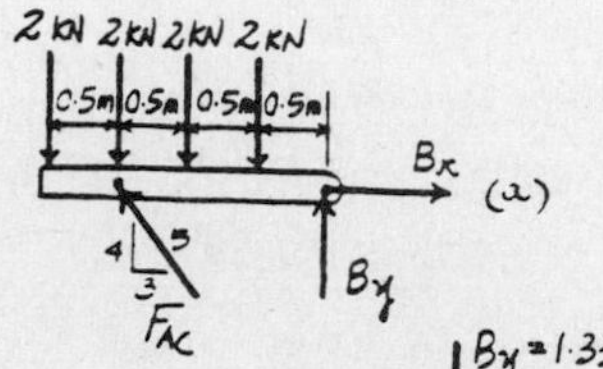

$$\circlearrowleft + \Sigma M_B = 0; \quad 2(0.5) + 2(1) + 2(1.5) + 2(2) - F_{AC}\left(\frac{4}{5}\right)(1.5) = 0$$

$$F_{AC} = 8.333 \text{ kN}$$

$$+\uparrow \Sigma F_y = 0; \quad B_y + 8.333\left(\frac{4}{5}\right) - 2 - 2 - 2 - 2 = 0$$

$$B_y = 1.333 \text{ kN} = 1.33 \text{ kN} \qquad \textbf{Ans}$$

$$\overset{+}{\rightarrow} \Sigma F_x = 0; \quad B_x - 8.333\left(\frac{3}{5}\right) = 0$$

$$B_x = 5.00 \text{ kN} \qquad \textbf{Ans}$$

For pin A and C,

$$A_x = C_x = F_{AC}\left(\frac{3}{5}\right) = 8.333\left(\frac{3}{5}\right) = 5.00 \text{ kN} \qquad \textbf{Ans}$$

$$A_y = C_y = F_{AC}\left(\frac{4}{5}\right) = 8.333\left(\frac{4}{5}\right) = 6.67 \text{ kN} \qquad \textbf{Ans}$$

From FBD (b),

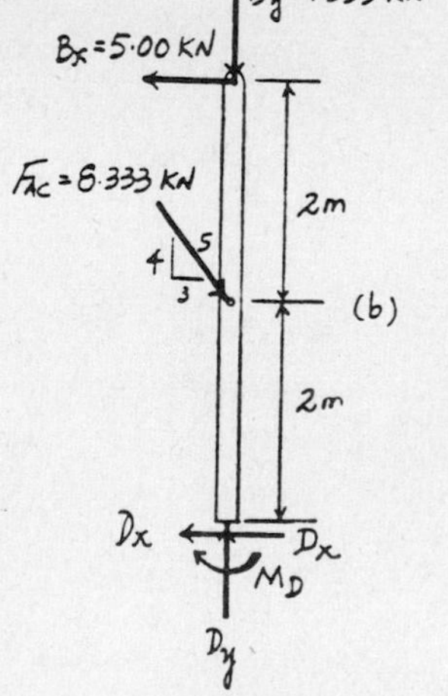

$$\circlearrowleft + \Sigma M_D = 0; \quad 5.00(4) - 8.333\left(\frac{3}{5}\right)(2) - M_D = 0$$

$$M_D = 10.0 \text{ kN} \cdot \text{m} \qquad \textbf{Ans}$$

$$+\uparrow \Sigma F_y = 0; \quad D_y - 1.333 - 8.333\left(\frac{4}{5}\right) = 0$$

$$D_y = 8.00 \text{ kN} \qquad \textbf{Ans}$$

$$\overset{+}{\rightarrow} \Sigma F_x = 0; \quad 8.333\left(\frac{3}{5}\right) - 5.00 - D_x = 0$$

$$D_x = 0 \qquad \textbf{Ans}$$

6-78. The bridge frame consists of three segments which can be considered pinned at A, D, and E, rocker supported at C and F, and roller supported at B. Determine the horizontal and vertical components of reaction at all these supports due to the loading shown.

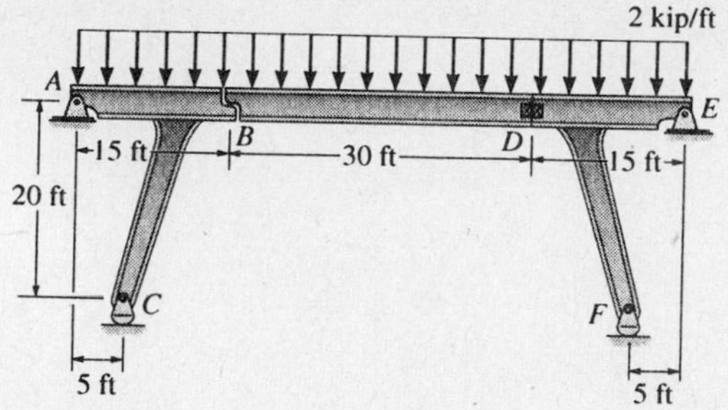

For segment BD :

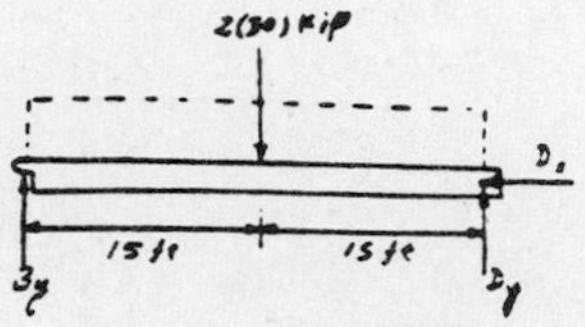

$\circlearrowleft +\Sigma M_D = 0;\quad 2(30)(15) - B_y(30) = 0 \quad B_y = 30\text{ kip}$ **Ans**

$\xrightarrow{+} \Sigma F_x = 0;\quad D_x = 0$ **Ans**

$+\uparrow \Sigma F_y = 0;\quad D_y + 30 - 2(30) = 0 \quad D_y = 30\text{ kip}$ **Ans**

For segment ABC :

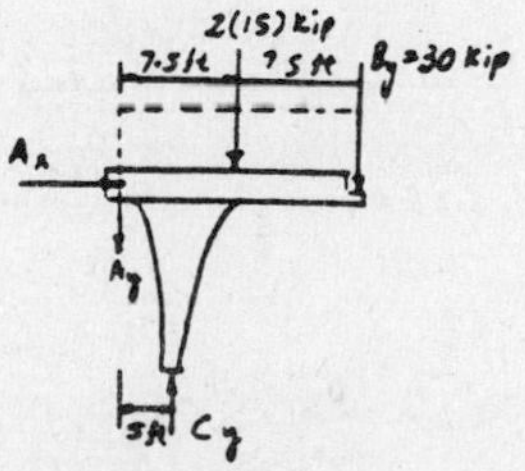

$\circlearrowleft +\Sigma M_A = 0;\quad C_y(5) - 2(15)(7.5) - 30(15) = 0 \quad C_y = 135\text{ kip}$ **Ans**

$\xrightarrow{+} \Sigma F_x = 0;\quad A_x = 0$ **Ans**

$+\uparrow \Sigma F_y = 0;\quad -A_y + 135 - 2(15) - 30 = 0 \quad A_y = 75\text{ kip}$ **Ans**

For segment DEF :

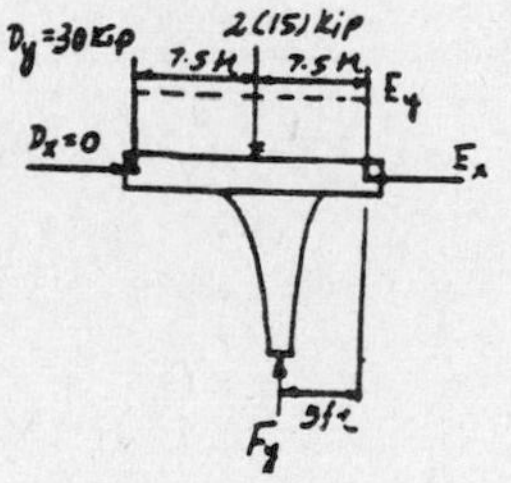

$\circlearrowleft +\Sigma M_E = 0;\quad -F_y(5) + 2(15)(7.5) + 30(15) = 0 \quad F_y = 135\text{ kip}$ **Ans**

$\xrightarrow{+} \Sigma F_x = 0;\quad E_x = 0$ **Ans**

$+\uparrow \Sigma F_y = 0;\quad -E_y + 135 - 2(15) - 30 = 0 \quad E_y = 75\text{ kip}$ **Ans**

6-79. Determine the horizontal and vertical components of force that pins A and C exert on the two-member arch.

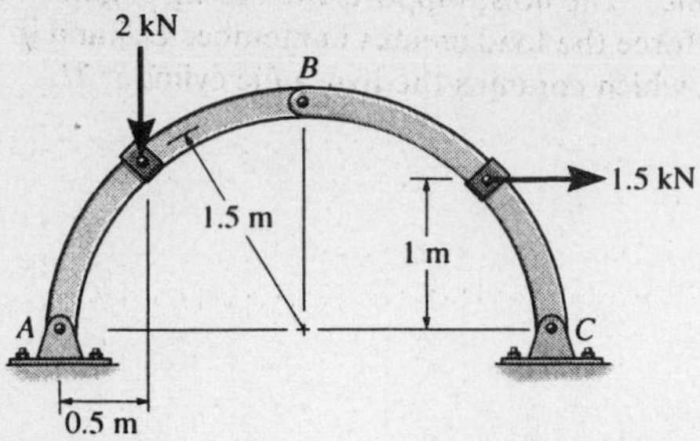

Member AB :

$\circlearrowleft +\Sigma M_A = 0;\quad -2(0.5) + B_y(1.5) - B_x(1.5) = 0$

Member BC :

$\circlearrowleft +\Sigma M_C = 0;\quad B_y(1.5) + B_x(1.5) - 1.5(1) = 0$

Solving :

$B_y = 0.8333\text{ kN} = 833\text{ N}$

$B_x = 0.1667\text{ kN} = 167\text{ N}$

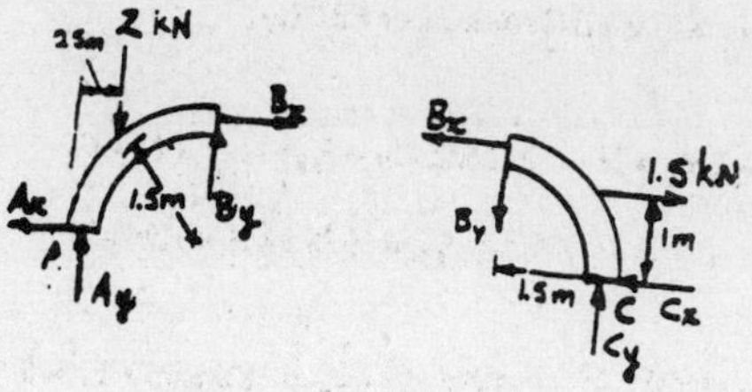

Member AB :

$\xrightarrow{+} \Sigma F_x = 0;\quad -A_x + 167 = 0$

$A_x = 167\text{ N}$ **Ans**

$+\uparrow \Sigma F_y = 0;\quad A_y - 2000 + 833 = 0$

$A_y = 1.17\text{ kN}$ **Ans**

Member BC :

$\xrightarrow{+} \Sigma F_x = 0;\quad -C_x + 1500 - 167 = 0$

$C_x = 1.33\text{ kN}$ **Ans**

$+\uparrow \Sigma F_y = 0;\quad C_y - 833 = 0$

$C_y = 833\text{ N}$ **Ans**

*6-80. The hoist supports the 125-kg engine. Determine the force the load creates in member DB and in member FB, which contains the hydraulic cylinder H.

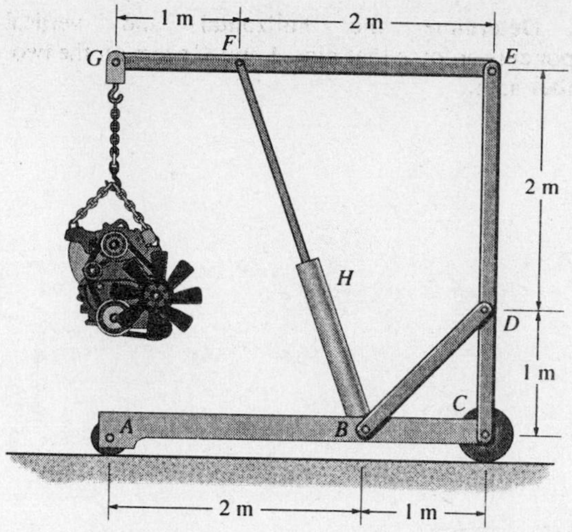

Free Body Diagram : The solution for this problem will be simplified if one realizes that members FB and DB are two force members.

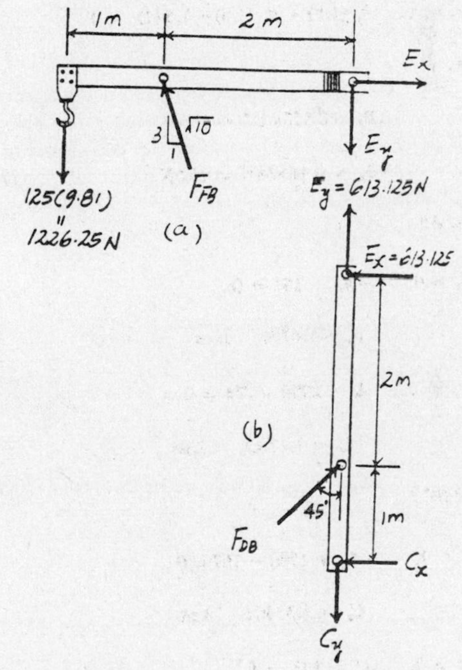

***Equations of Equilibrium* :** For FBD(a),

$$\circlearrowleft + \Sigma M_E = 0; \quad 1226.25(3) - F_{FB}\left(\frac{3}{\sqrt{10}}\right)(2) = 0$$

$$F_{FB} = 1938.87 \text{ N} = 1.94 \text{ kN} \qquad \textbf{Ans}$$

$$+\uparrow \Sigma F_y = 0; \quad 1938.87\left(\frac{3}{\sqrt{10}}\right) - 1226.25 - E_y = 0$$

$$E_y = 613.125\text{N}$$

$$\overset{+}{\rightarrow} \Sigma F_x = 0; \quad E_x - 1938.87\left(\frac{1}{\sqrt{10}}\right) = 0$$

$$E_x = 613.125 \text{ N}$$

From FBD (b),

$$\circlearrowleft + \Sigma M_C = 0; \quad 613.125(3) - F_{BD}\sin 45°(1) = 0$$

$$F_{BD} = 2601.27 \text{ N} = 2.60 \text{ kN} \qquad \textbf{Ans}$$

6-81. The clamping hooks are used to lift the uniform smooth 500-kg plate. Determine the resultant compressive force that the hook exerts on the plate at A and B, and the pin reaction at C.

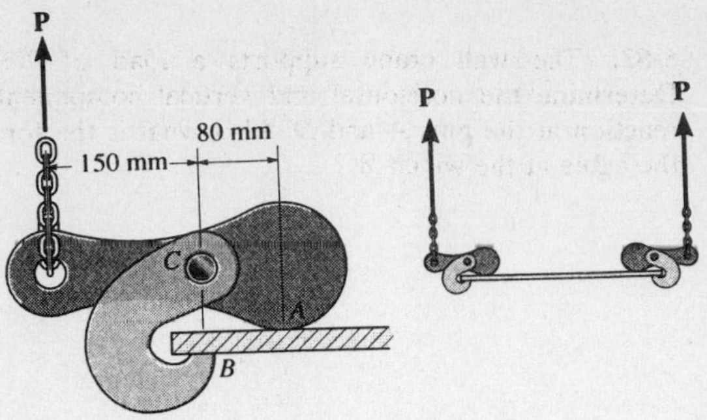

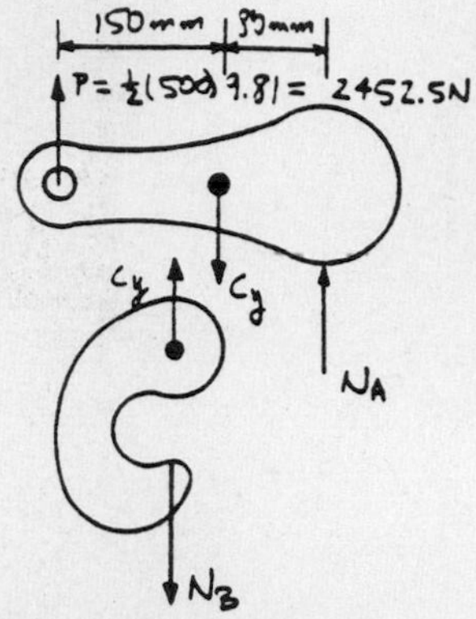

$\curvearrowleft + \Sigma M_C = 0;\quad N_A(80) - 2452.5(150) = 0$

$N_A = 4598.4 \text{ N} \doteq 4.60 \text{ kN}$ **Ans**

$+\uparrow \Sigma F_y = 0;\quad 2452.5 + 4598.4 - C_y = 0$

$C_y = 7050.9 \text{ N} = 7.05 \text{ kN}$ **Ans**

CB is a two-force member.

$N_B = C_y = 7.05 \text{ kN}$ **Ans**

6-82. The front of the car is to be lifted using a smooth, rigid 10-ft long board. The car has a weight of 3500 lb and a center of gravity at G. Determine the position x of the fulcrum so that an applied force of 100 lb at E will lift the front wheels of the car.

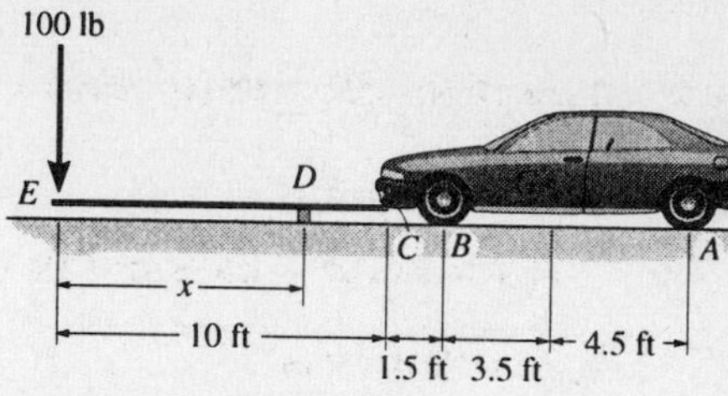

Free Body Diagram : When the front wheels are lifted, the normal reaction $N_B = 0$.

Equations of Equilibrium : From FBD (a),

$\curvearrowleft + \Sigma M_A = 0;\quad 3500(4.5) - F_C(9.5) = 0 \qquad F_C = 1657.89 \text{ lb}$

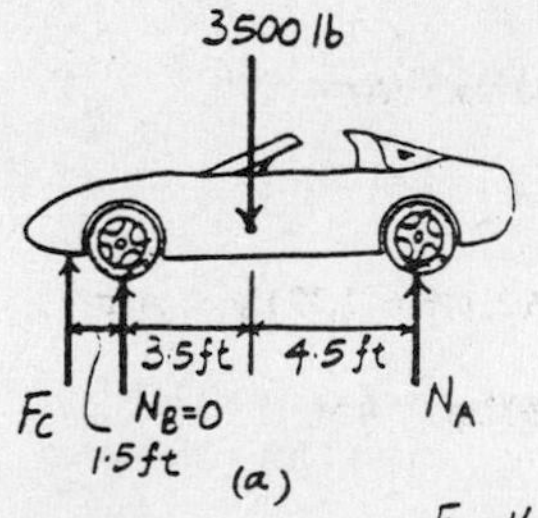

From FBD (b),

$\curvearrowleft + \Sigma M_D = 0;\quad 100(x) - 1657.89(10 - x) = 0$

$x = 9.43 \text{ ft}$ **Ans**

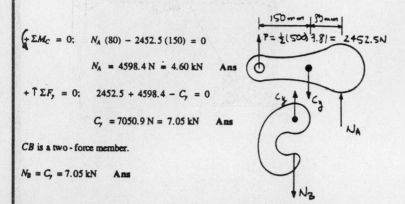

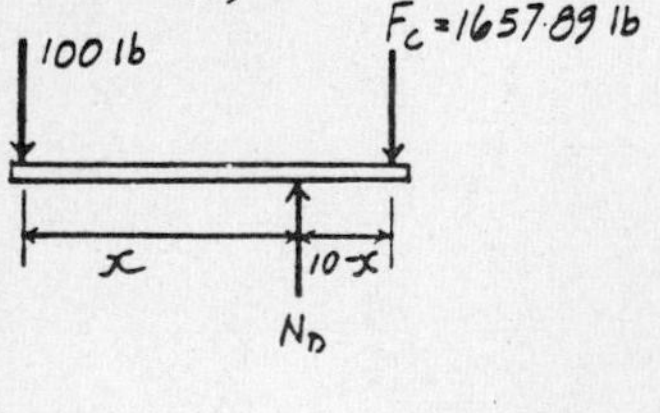

6-83. The wall crane supports a load of 700 lb. Determine the horizontal and vertical components of reaction at the pins A and D. Also, what is the force in the cable at the winch W?

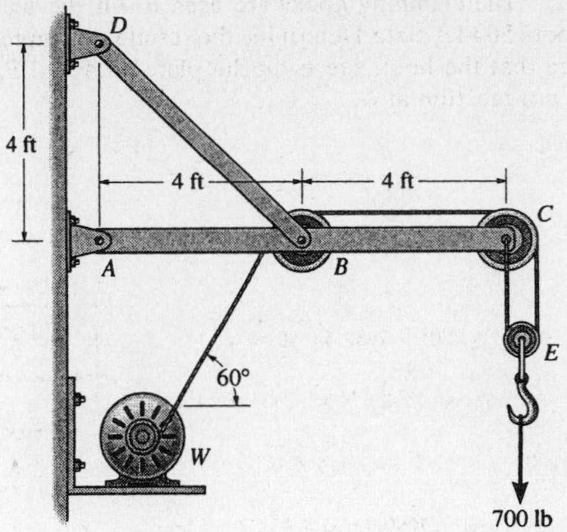

Pulley E:

$+\uparrow \Sigma F_y = 0;\quad 2T - 700 = 0$

$T = 350\text{ lb}$ **Ans**

Member ABC:

$\circlearrowleft + \Sigma M_A = 0;\quad T_{BD} \sin 45° (4) - 350 \sin 60° (4) - 700 (8) = 0$

$T_{BD} = 2409\text{ lb}$

$+\uparrow \Sigma F_y = 0;\quad -A_y + 2409 \sin 45° - 350 \sin 60° - 700 = 0$

$A_y = 700\text{ lb}$ **Ans**

$\xrightarrow{+} \Sigma F_x = 0;\quad A_x - 2409 \cos 45° - 350 \cos 60° + 350 - 350 = 0$

$A_x = 1.88\text{ kip}$ **Ans**

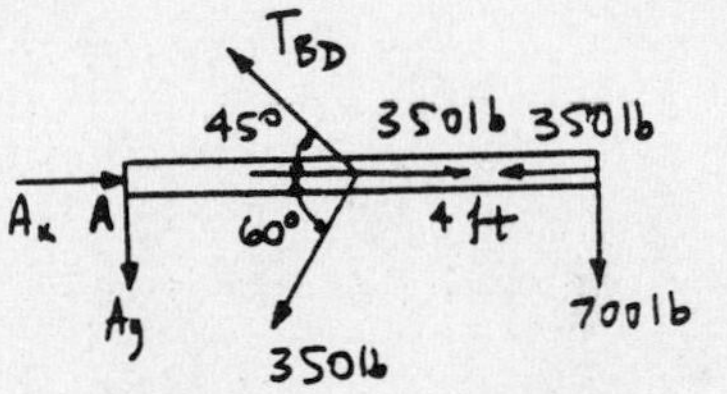

At D:

$D_x = 2409 \cos 45° = 1703.1\text{ lb} = 1.70\text{ kip}$ **Ans**

$D_y = 2409 \sin 45° = 1.70\text{ kip}$ **Ans**

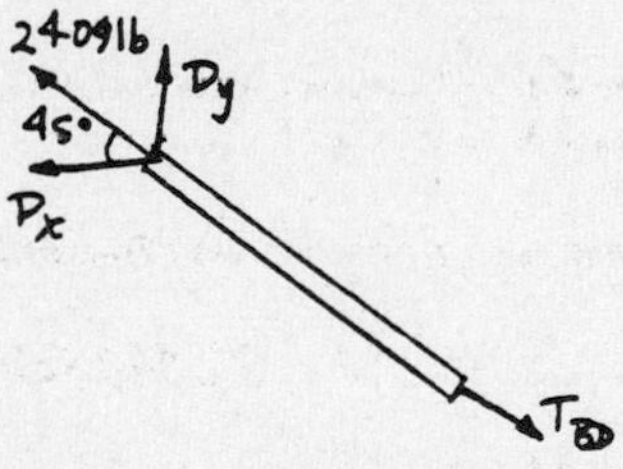

***6-84.** The wall crane supports a load of 700 lb. Determine the horizontal and vertical components of reaction at the pins *A* and *D*. Also, what is the force in the cable at the winch *W*? The jib *ABC* has a weight of 100 lb and member *BD* has a weight of 40 lb. Each member is uniform and has a center of gravity at its center.

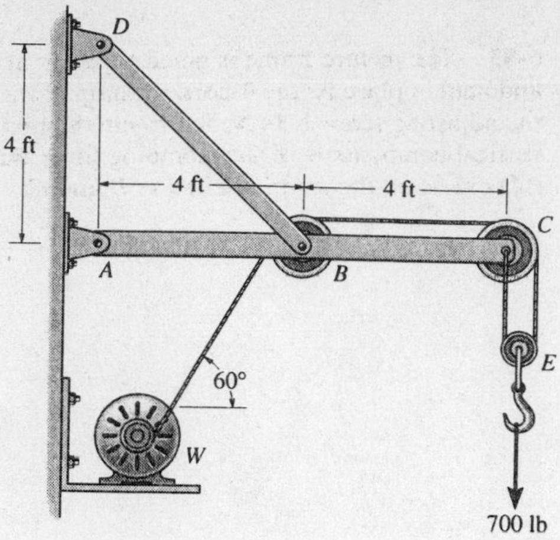

Pulley E :

$+\uparrow \Sigma F_y = 0;\qquad 2T - 700 = 0$

$T = 350$ lb **Ans**

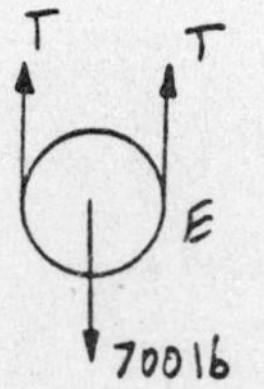

Member ABC :

$\circlearrowleft + \Sigma M_A = 0;\qquad B_y(4) - 700(8) - 100(4) - 350\sin 60^\circ(4) = 0$

$B_y = 1803.1$ lb

$+\uparrow \Sigma F_y = 0;\qquad -A_y - 350\sin 60^\circ - 100 - 700 + 1803.1 = 0$

$A_y = 700$ lb **Ans**

$\xrightarrow{+} \Sigma F_x = 0;\qquad A_x - 350\cos 60^\circ - B_x + 350 - 350 = 0$

$A_x = B_x + 175 \qquad (1)$

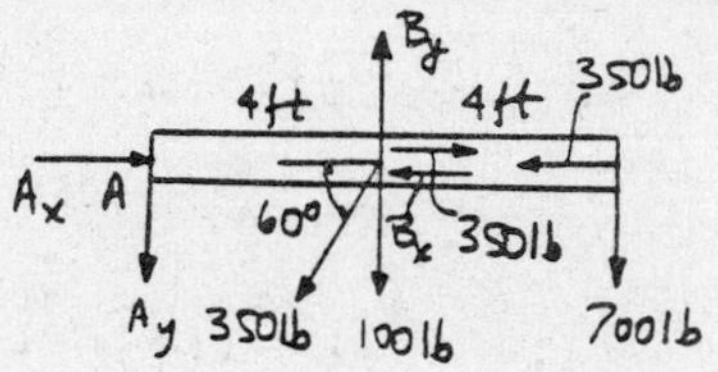

Member DB :

$\circlearrowleft + \Sigma M_D = 0;\qquad -40(2) - 1803.1(4) + B_x(4) = 0$

$B_x = 1823.1$ lb

$\xrightarrow{+} \Sigma F_x = 0;\qquad -D_x + 1823.1 = 0$

$D_x = 1.82$ kip **Ans**

$+\uparrow \Sigma F_y = 0;\qquad D_y - 40 - 1803.1 = 0$

$D_y = 1843.1 = 1.84$ kip **Ans**

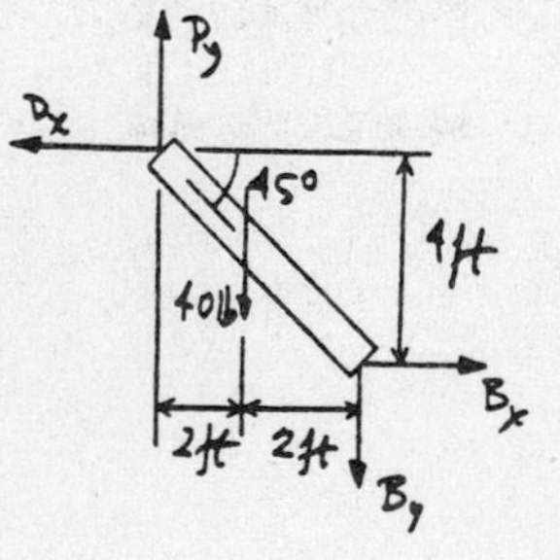

From Eq. (1)

$A_x = 2.00$ kip **Ans**

6-85. The picture frame is glued together at its corners and held in place by the 4-corner clamp. If the tension in the adjusting screw is 14 N, determine the horizontal and vertical components of the clamping force that member *AD* exerts on the smooth joints at *B* and *C*.

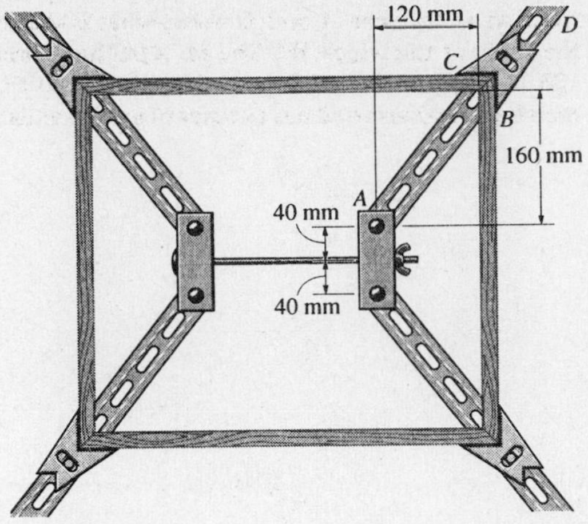

$+\uparrow\Sigma F_y = 0;\quad T\left(\frac{4}{5}\right) - T'\left(\frac{4}{5}\right) = 0$

$T = T'$

$\xrightarrow{+}\Sigma F_x = 0;\quad 2T\left(\frac{3}{5}\right) - 14 = 0$

$T = 11.67\text{ N}$

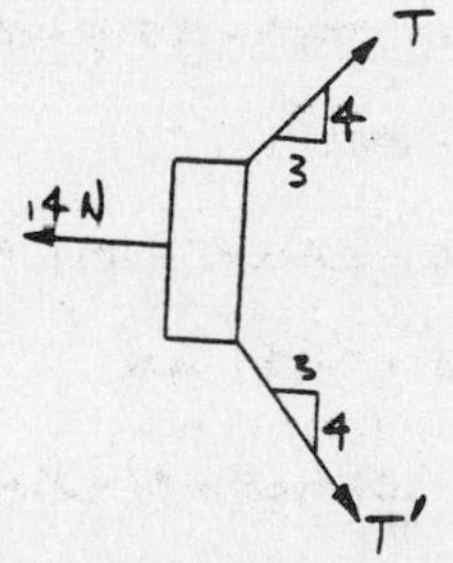

$\xrightarrow{+}\Sigma F_x = 0;\quad N_B - 11.67\left(\frac{3}{5}\right) = 0$

$N_B = 7\text{ N}$ **Ans**

$+\uparrow\Sigma F_y = 0;\quad N_C - 11.67\left(\frac{4}{5}\right) = 0$

$N_C = 9.33\text{ N}$ **Ans**

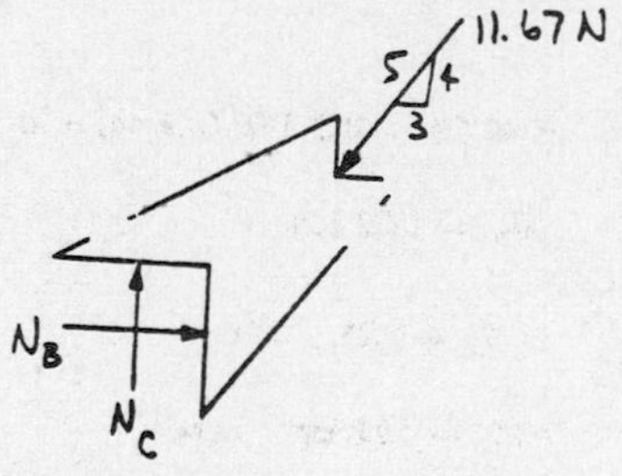

6-86. The engine hoist is used to support the 200-kg engine. Determine the force acting in the hydraulic cylinder AB, the horizontal and vertical components of force at the pin C, and the reactions at the fixed support D.

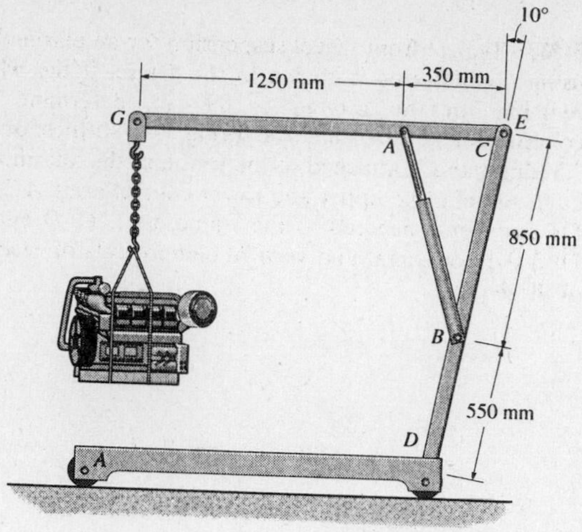

Free Body Diagram : The solution for this problem will be simplified if one realizes that member AB is a two force member. From the geometry,

$$l_{AB} = \sqrt{350^2 + 850^2 - 2(350)(850)\cos 80^\circ} = 861.21 \text{ mm}$$

$$\frac{\sin\theta}{850} = \frac{\sin 80^\circ}{861.21} \qquad \theta = 76.41^\circ$$

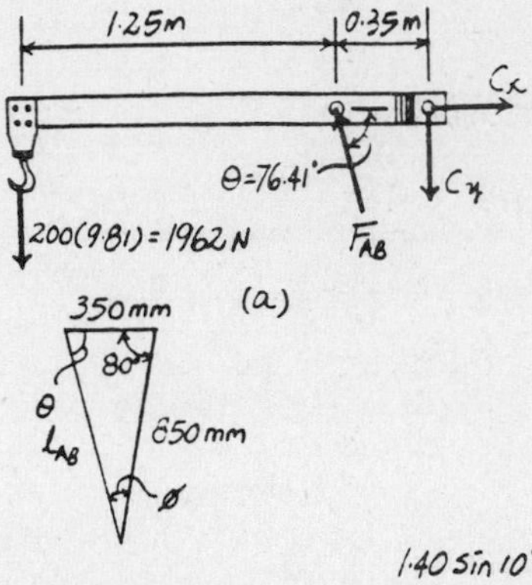

Equations of Equilibrium : From FBD (a),

$\circlearrowleft + \Sigma M_C = 0;\quad 1962(1.60) - F_{AB}\sin 76.41^\circ(0.35) = 0$

$F_{AB} = 9227.60 \text{ N} = 9.23 \text{ kN}$ **Ans**

$\overset{+}{\rightarrow} \Sigma F_x = 0;\quad C_x - 9227.60\cos 76.41^\circ = 0$

$C_x = 2168.65 \text{ N} = 2.17 \text{ kN}$ **Ans**

$+\uparrow \Sigma F_y = 0;\quad 9227.60\sin 76.41^\circ - 1962 - C_y = 0$

$C_y = 7007.14 \text{ N} = 7.01 \text{ kN}$ **Ans**

From FBD (b),

$\overset{+}{\rightarrow} \Sigma F_x = 0;\quad D_x = 0$ **Ans**

$+\uparrow \Sigma F_y = 0;\quad D_y - 1962 = 0$

$D_y = 1962 \text{ N} = 1.96 \text{ kN}$ **Ans**

$+\Sigma M_D = 0;\quad 1962(1.60 - 1.40\sin 10^\circ) - M_D = 0$

$M_D = 2662.22 \text{ N}\cdot\text{m} = 2.66 \text{ kN}\cdot\text{m}$ **Ans**

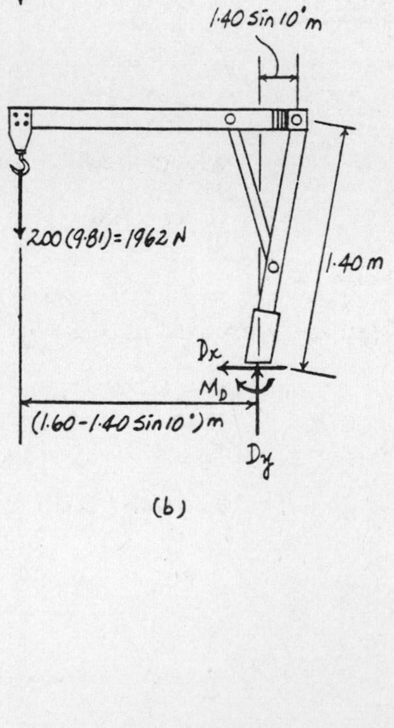

6-87. Typical front wheel suspension for an automobile using a coil spring is shown in the figure. If the wheel reaction on the ground is 800 lb, determine the compression of the spring. The spring has a stiffness of k = 3.5 kip/ft and is attached to the frame of the automobile at B. Assume the upper and lower control arms AC and DE are pin connected to the frame at A, C, D and E. Find the horizontal and vertical components of reaction at these pins.

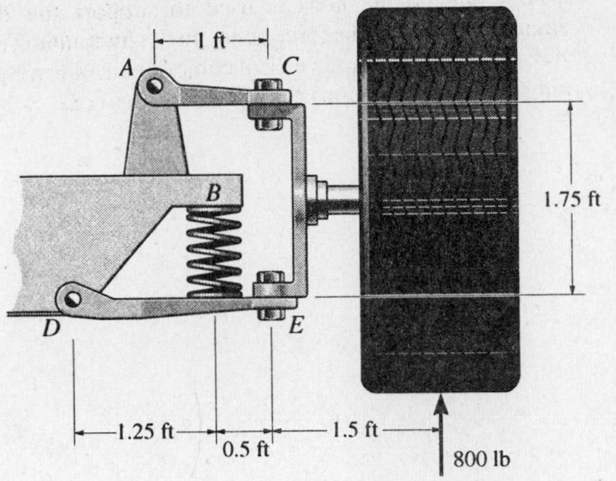

AC is a two - force member.

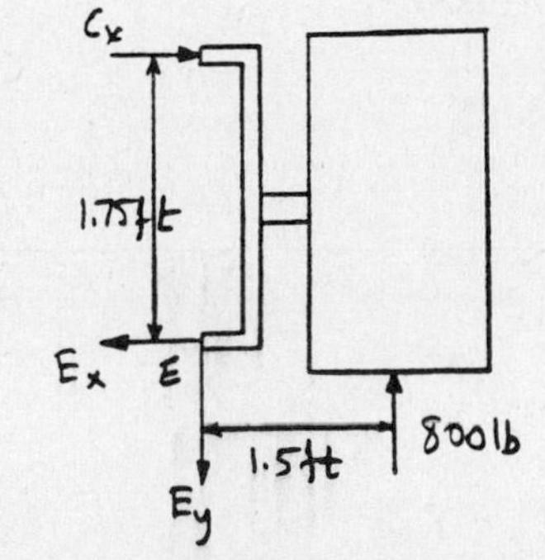

$+\uparrow \Sigma F_y = 0;\quad 800 - E_y = 0$

$E_y = 800$ lb

$\circlearrowleft + \Sigma M_E = 0;\quad -C_x\,(1.75) + 800\,(1.5) = 0$

$C_x = 685.71$ lb

$\overset{+}{\rightarrow} \Sigma F_x = 0;\quad -E_x + 685.71 = 0$

$E_x = 685.71$ lb

Thus,

$A_x = C_x = 686$ lb **Ans**

$A_y = 0$ **Ans**

Member DE :

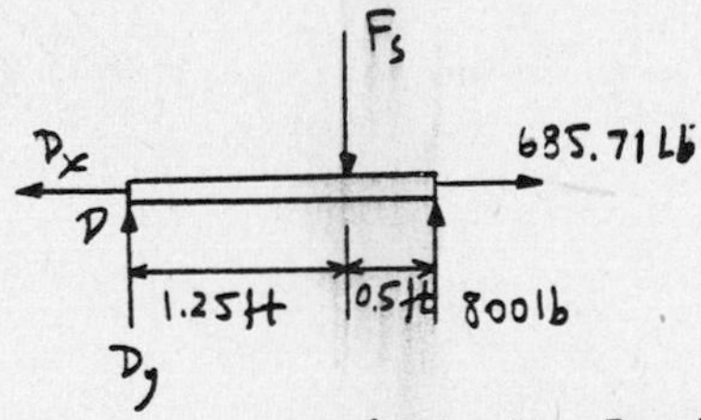

$\circlearrowleft + \Sigma M_D = 0;\quad 800\,(1.75) - F_s\,(1.25) = 0$

$F_s = 1120$ lb

$\overset{+}{\rightarrow} \Sigma F_x = 0;\quad -D_x + 685.71 = 0$

$D_x = 686$ lb **Ans**

$+\uparrow \Sigma F_y = 0;\quad D_y - 1120 + 800 = 0$

$D_y = 320$ lb **Ans**

$F_s = kx;\quad 1120 = 3500\,x$

$x = 0.320$ ft $= 3.84$ in. **Ans**

***6-88.** The pipe cutter is clamped around the pipe P. If the wheel at A exerts a normal force of $F_A = 80$ N on the pipe, determine the normal forces of wheels B and C on the pipe. Also compute the pin reaction on the wheel at C. The three wheels each have a radius of 7 mm and the pipe has an outer radius of 10 mm.

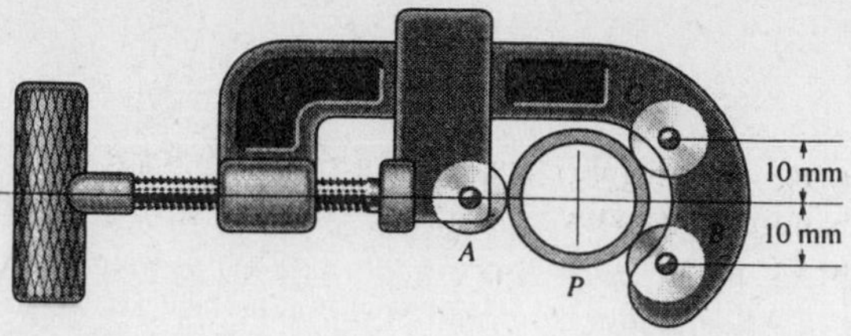

$$\theta = \sin^{-1}\left(\frac{10}{19}\right) = 36.03°$$

Equations of Equilibrium:

$$+\uparrow \Sigma F_y = 0; \quad N_B \sin 36.03° - N_C \sin 36.03° = 0$$

$$N_B = N_C$$

$$\xrightarrow{+} \Sigma F_x = 0; \quad 80 - N_C \cos 36.03° - N_C \cos 36.03° = 0$$

$$N_B = N_C = 49.5 \text{ N} \qquad \textbf{Ans}$$

6-89. The two-member structure is connected at C by a pin, which is fixed to BDE and passes through the smooth slot in member AC. Determine the horizontal and vertical components of reaction at the supports.

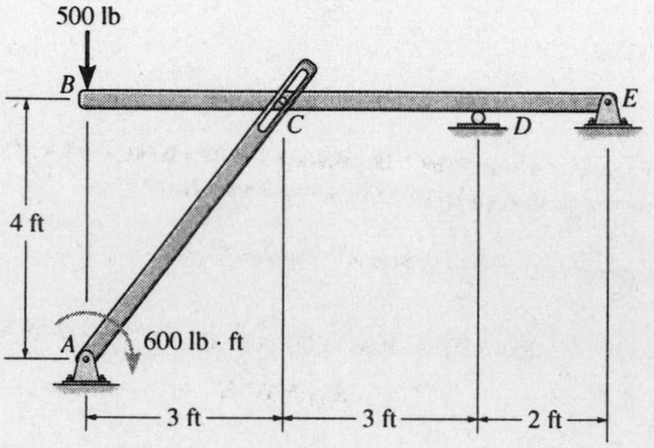

Member AC:

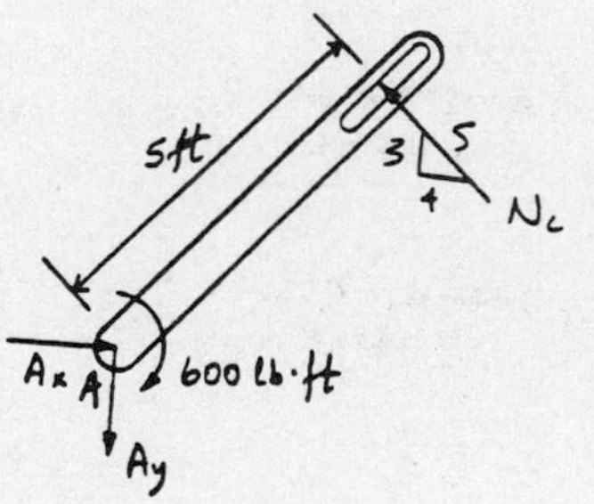

$$\circlearrowleft + \Sigma M_A = 0; \quad N_C(5) - 600 = 0$$

$$N_C = 120 \text{ lb}$$

$$\xrightarrow{+} \Sigma F_x = 0; \quad A_x - 120\left(\frac{4}{5}\right) = 0$$

$$A_x = 96 \text{ lb} \qquad \textbf{Ans}$$

$$+\uparrow \Sigma F_y = 0; \quad -A_y + 120\left(\frac{3}{5}\right) = 0$$

$$A_y = 72 \text{ lb} \qquad \textbf{Ans}$$

Member BDE:

$$\circlearrowleft + \Sigma M_E = 0; \quad 500(8) + 120\left(\frac{3}{5}\right)(5) - D_y(2) = 0$$

$$D_y = 2180 \text{ lb} = 2.18 \text{ kip} \qquad \textbf{Ans}$$

$$\xrightarrow{+} \Sigma F_x = 0; \quad -E_x + 120\left(\frac{4}{5}\right) = 0$$

$$E_x = 96 \text{ lb} \qquad \textbf{Ans}$$

$$+\uparrow \Sigma F_y = 0; \quad -500 - 120\left(\frac{3}{5}\right) + 2180 - E_y = 0$$

$$E_y = 1608 \text{ lb} = 1.61 \text{ kip} \qquad \textbf{Ans}$$

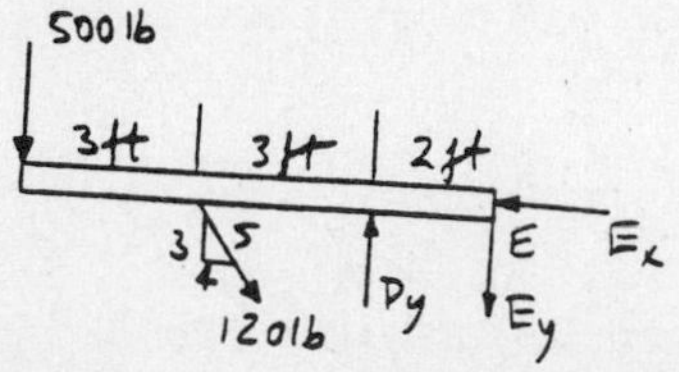

6-90. The toggle clamp is subjected to a force **F** at the handle. Determine the vertical clamping force acting at E.

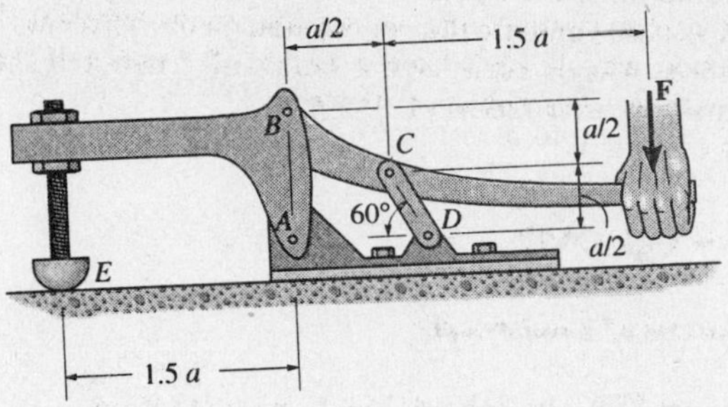

Free Body Diagram : The solution for this problem will be simplified if one realizes that member CD is a two force member.

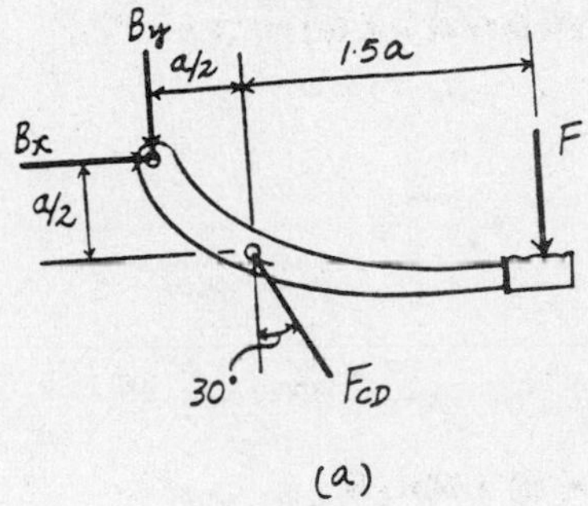

Equations of Equilibrium : From FBD (a),

$$\curvearrowleft + \Sigma M_B = 0; \quad F_{CD}\cos 30°\left(\frac{a}{2}\right) - F_{CD}\sin 30°\left(\frac{a}{2}\right) - F(2a) = 0$$
$$F_{CD} = 10.93F$$

$$+\uparrow \Sigma F_y = 0; \quad 10.93F\cos 30° - F - B_y = 0$$
$$B_y = 8.464F$$

$$\xrightarrow{+} \Sigma F_x = 0; \quad B_x - 10.93\sin 30° = 0$$
$$B_x = 5.464F$$

From (b),

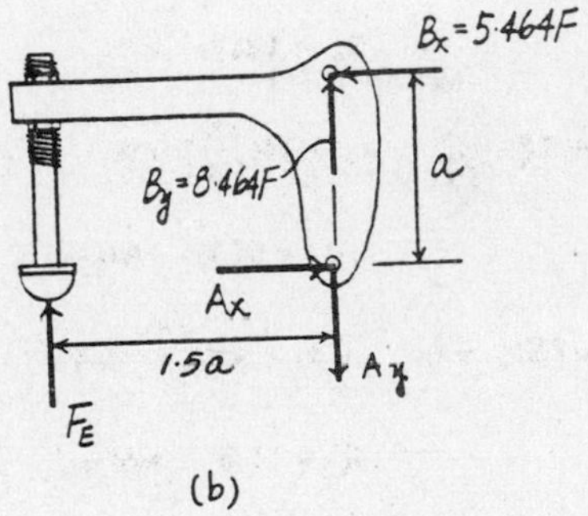

$$\curvearrowleft + \Sigma M_A = 0; \quad 5.464F(a) - F_E(1.5a) = 0$$
$$F_E = 3.64F \qquad \textbf{Ans}$$

6-91. Determine the reactions at the supports. The pin, attached to member BCD, passes through a smooth slot in member AB.

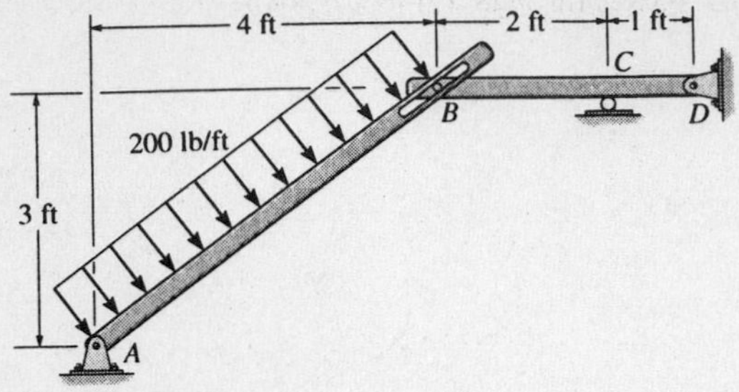

Member AB :

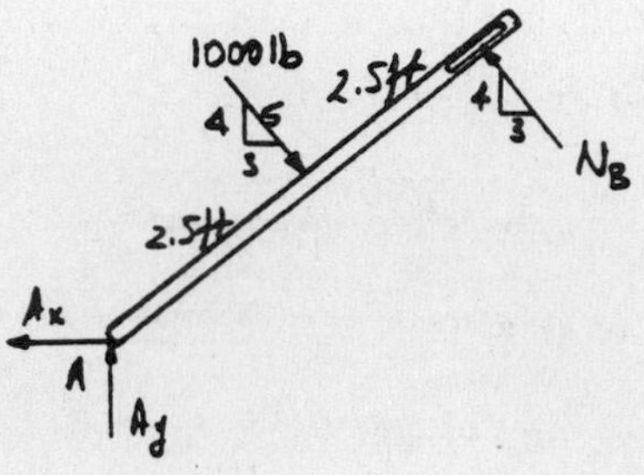

$\curvearrowleft +\Sigma M_A = 0;\quad N_B(5) - 1000(2.5) = 0$

$N_B = 500 \text{ lb}$

$\xrightarrow{+} \Sigma F_x = 0;\quad -A_x + \frac{3}{5}(1000) - \frac{3}{5}(500) = 0$

$A_x = 300 \text{ lb}$ **Ans**

$+\uparrow \Sigma F_y = 0;\quad A_y - \frac{4}{5}(1000) + \frac{4}{5}(500) = 0$

$A_y = 400 \text{ lb}$ **Ans**

Member BCD :

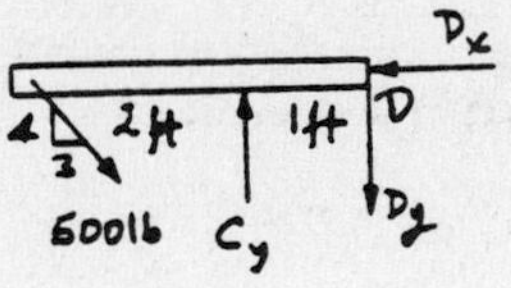

$\curvearrowleft +\Sigma M_D = 0;\quad 500\left(\frac{4}{5}\right)(3) - C_y(1) = 0$

$C_y = 1200 \text{ lb}$ **Ans**

$\xrightarrow{+} \Sigma F_x = 0;\quad -D_x + 500\left(\frac{3}{5}\right) = 0$

$D_x = 300 \text{ lb}$ **Ans**

$+\uparrow \Sigma F_y = 0;\quad -500\left(\frac{4}{5}\right) + 1200 - D_y = 0$

$D_y = 800 \text{ lb}$ **Ans**

***6-92.** Determine the reactions at the fixed support E and the smooth support A. The pin, attached to member BD, passes through a smooth slot at D.

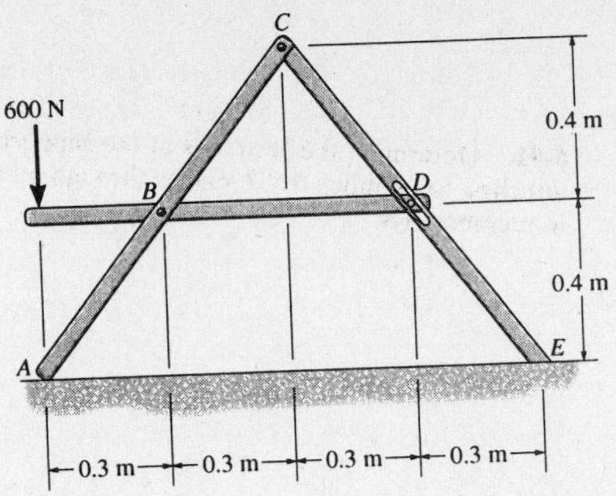

Member BD :

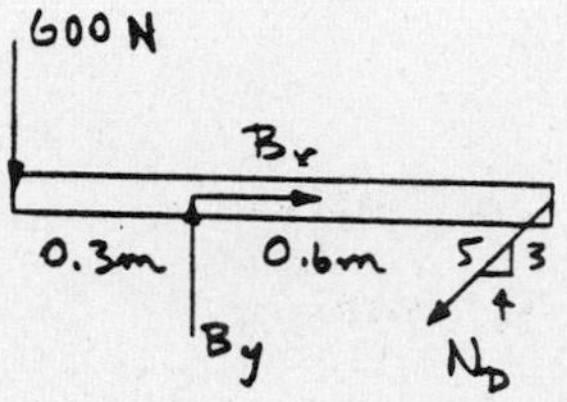

$\circlearrowleft + \Sigma M_B = 0;\quad 600\,(0.3) - N_D\left(\frac{3}{5}\right)(0.6) = 0$

$N_D = 500\text{ N}$

$\xrightarrow{+} \Sigma F_x = 0;\quad B_x - \frac{4}{5}(500) = 0$

$B_x = 400\text{ N}$

$+\uparrow \Sigma F_y = 0;\quad -600 + B_y - \frac{3}{5}(500) = 0$

$B_y = 900\text{ N}$

Member ABC :

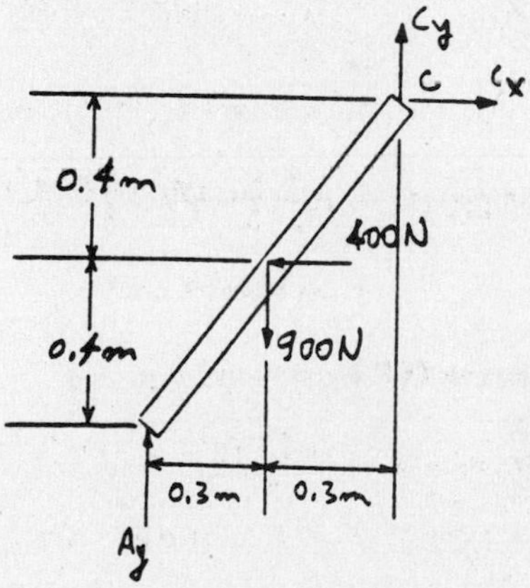

$\circlearrowleft + \Sigma M_C = 0;\quad 900\,(0.3) - 400\,(0.4) - A_y\,(0.6) = 0$

$A_y = 183.33 = 183\text{ N}$ **Ans**

$\xrightarrow{+} \Sigma F_x = 0;\quad -400 + C_x = 0$

$C_x = 400\text{ N}$

$+\uparrow \Sigma F_y = 0;\quad 183.33 - 900 + C_y = 0$

$C_y = 716.67\text{ N}$

Member CDE :

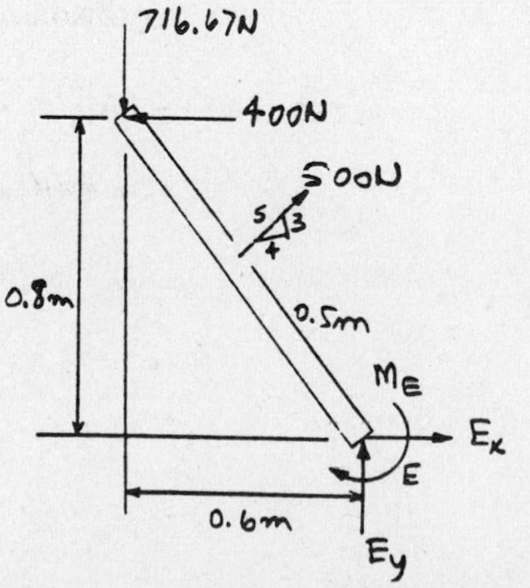

$\xrightarrow{+} \Sigma F_x = 0;\quad -400 + 500\left(\frac{4}{5}\right) + E_x = 0$

$E_x = 0$ **Ans**

$+\uparrow \Sigma F_y = 0;\quad -716.67 + 500\left(\frac{3}{5}\right) + E_y = 0$

$E_y = 417\text{ N}$ **Ans**

$\circlearrowleft + \Sigma M_E = 0;\quad -M_E - 500\,(0.5) + 400\,(0.8) + 716.67\,(0.6) = 0$

$M_E = 500\text{ N}\cdot\text{m}$ **Ans**

6-93. Determine the horizontal and vertical components of reaction at A and B. The pin at C is fixed to member AE and fits through a smooth slot in member BD.

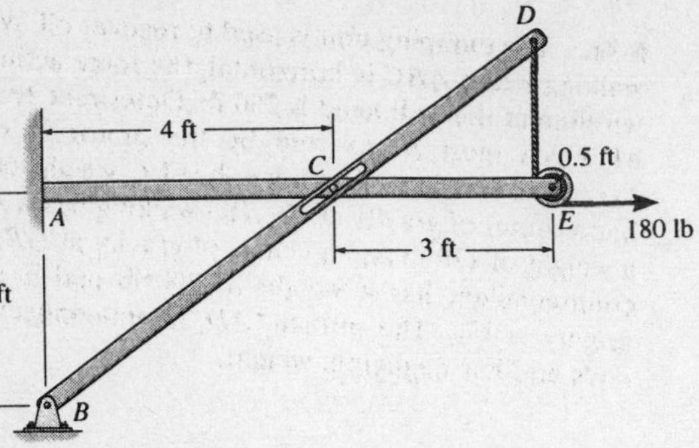

Member BCD:

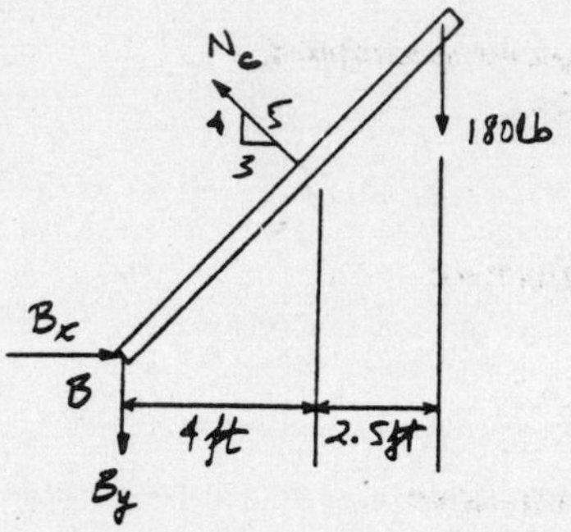

$\curvearrowleft +\Sigma M_B = 0; \quad -180(6.5) + N_C(5) = 0$

$N_C = 234 \text{ lb}$

$\xrightarrow{+} \Sigma F_x = 0; \quad B_x - \frac{3}{5}(234) = 0$

$B_x = 140 \text{ lb}$ **Ans**

$+\uparrow \Sigma F_y = 0; \quad \frac{4}{5}(234) - 180 - B_y = 0$

$B_y = 7.20 \text{ lb}$ **Ans**

Member ACE:

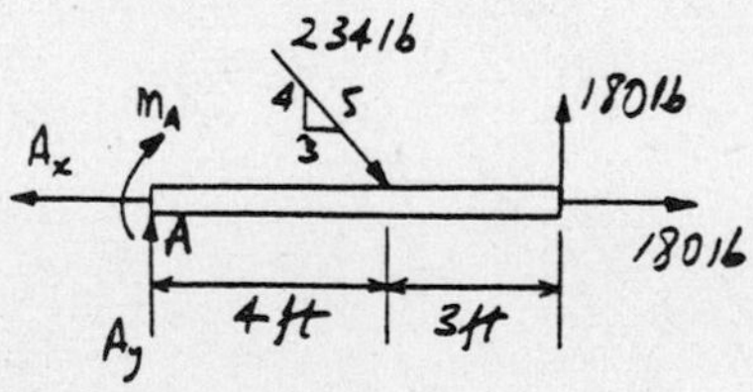

$+\uparrow \Sigma F_y = 0; \quad A_y - \frac{4}{5}(234) + 180 = 0$

$A_y = 7.20 \text{ lb}$ **Ans**

$\xrightarrow{+} \Sigma F_x = 0; \quad 180 + \frac{3}{5}(234) - A_x = 0$

$A_x = 320 \text{ lb}$ **Ans**

$\curvearrowleft +\Sigma M_A = 0; \quad -\frac{4}{5}(234)(4) + 180(7) - M_A = 0$

$M_A = 511 \text{ lb} \cdot \text{ft}$ **Ans**

6-94. The pumping unit is used to recover oil. When the walking beam ABC is horizontal, the force acting in the wireline at the well head is 250 lb. Determine the torque **M** which must be exerted by the motor in order to overcome this load. The horse-head C weighs 60 lb and has a center of gravity at G_C. The walking beam ABC has a weight of 130 lb and a center of gravity at GB, and the counterweight has a weight of 200 lb and a center of gravity at G_W. The pitman, AD, is pin-connected at its ends and has negligible weight.

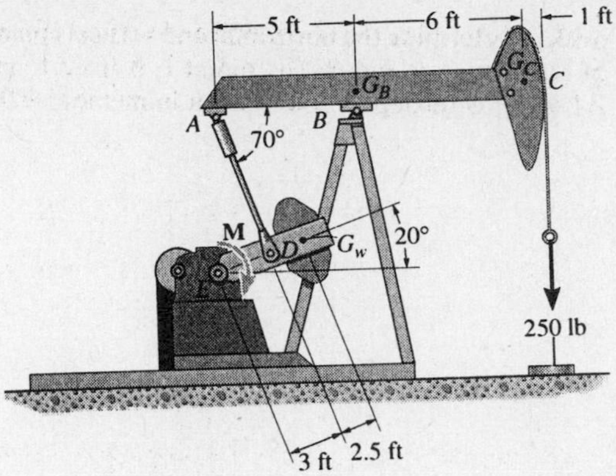

Free Body Diagram : The solution for this problem will be simplified if one realizes that the pitman AD is a two force member.

Equations of Equilibrium : From FBD (a),

$\curvearrowleft + \Sigma M_B = 0;\quad F_{AD}\sin 70°(5) - 60(6) - 250(7) = 0$

$F_{AD} = 449.08 \text{ lb}$

From (b),

$\curvearrowleft + \Sigma M_E = 0;\quad 449.08(3) - 200\cos 20°(5.5) - M = 0$

$M = 314 \text{ lb}\cdot\text{ft}$ **Ans**

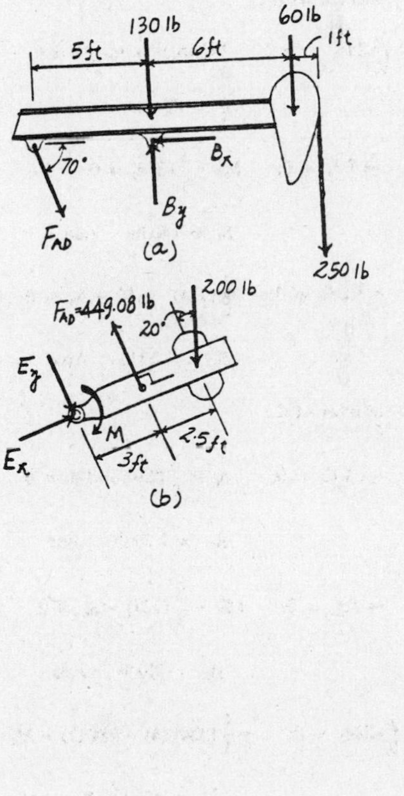

6-95. Using a series of levers is more effective than using a single lever. For example, the 8000-lb truck is balanced on a scale using either (a) three levers or (b) one lever as shown. In case (a) determine the force **P** required for equilibrium of the truck, and in case (b), using the same force **P**, determine the length l of the single lever necessary for balancing the truck.

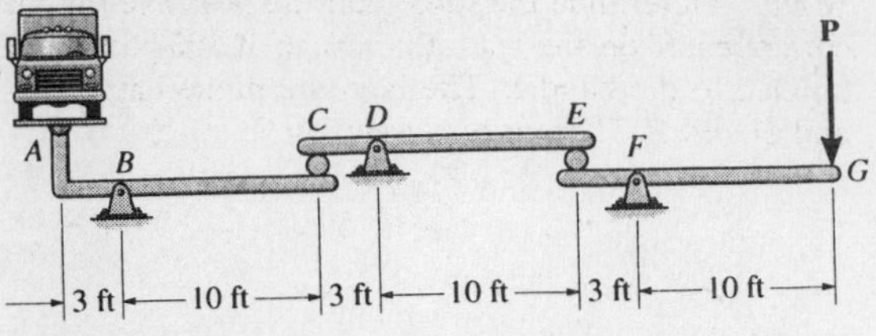

(a)

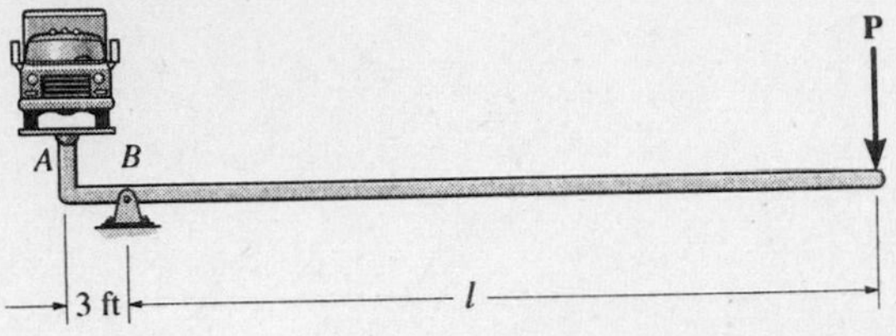

(b)

Case (a) :

Member ABC :

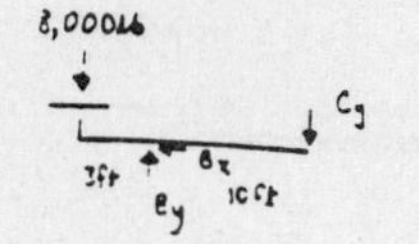

$\curvearrowleft + \Sigma M_B = 0;\qquad -C_y\,(10) + 8000\,(3) = 0$

$C_y = 2400$ lb

Member CDE :

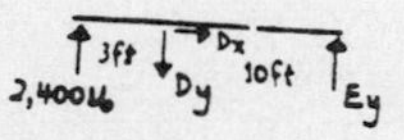

$\curvearrowleft + \Sigma M_D = 0;\qquad -2400\,(3) + E_y\,(10) = 0$

$E_y = 720$ lb

Member EFG :

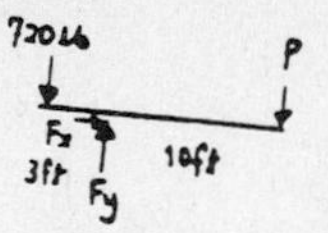

$\curvearrowleft + \Sigma M_F = 0;\qquad -P\,(10) + 720\,(3) = 0$

$P = 216$ lb **Ans**

Case (b) :

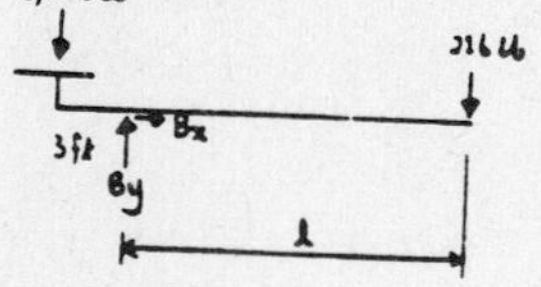

$\curvearrowleft + \Sigma M_B = 0;\qquad -216\,(l) + 8000\,(3) = 0$

$l = 111$ ft **Ans**

*6-96. Determine the force that the jaws J of the metal cutters exert on the smooth cable C if 100-N forces are applied to the handles. The jaws are pinned at E and A, and D and B. There is also a pin at F.

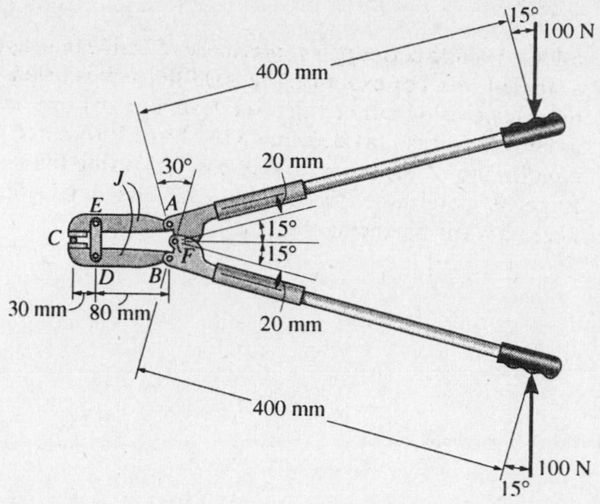

Free Body Diagram : The solution for this problem will be simplified if one realizes that member ED is a two force member.

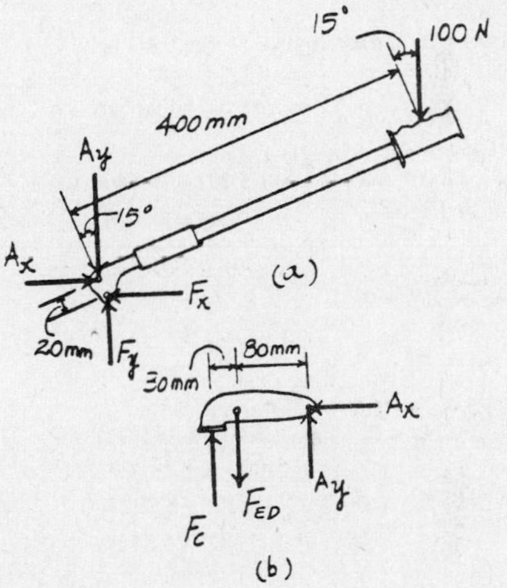

Equations of Equilibrium : From FBD (b),

$\xrightarrow{+} \Sigma F_x = 0; \qquad A_x = 0$

From (a),

$\circlearrowleft + \Sigma M_F = 0; \qquad A_y \sin 15°(20) + 100\sin 15°(20) - 100\cos 15°(400) = 0$

$A_y = 7364.10 \text{ N}$

From FBD (b),

$\circlearrowleft + \Sigma M_E = 0; \qquad 7364.10(80) - F_C(30) = 0$

$F_C = 19637.60 \text{ N} = 19.6 \text{ kN}$ **Ans**

6-97. The compound arrangement of the pan scale is shown. If the mass on the pan is 4 kg, determine the horizontal and vertical components at pins A, B, and C and the distance x of the 25-g mass to keep the scale in balance.

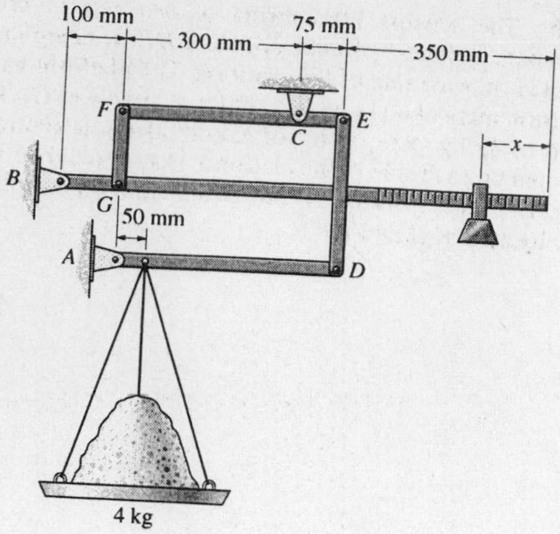

Free Body Diagram : The solution for this problem will be simplified if one realizes that members *DE* and *FG* are two force members.

Equations of Equilibrium : From FBD (a).

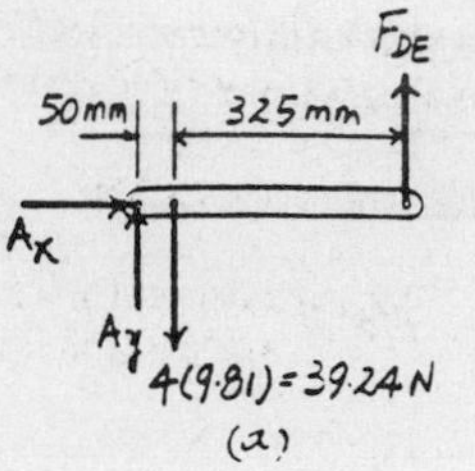

$\circlearrowleft + \Sigma M_A = 0;\quad F_{DE}(375) - 39.24(50) = 0 \quad F_{DE} = 5.232\text{ N}$

$+\uparrow \Sigma F_y = 0;\quad A_y + 5.232 - 39.24 = 0$

$A_y = 34.0\text{ N}$ **Ans**

$\overset{+}{\rightarrow} \Sigma F_x = 0;\quad A_x = 0$ **Ans**

From (b).

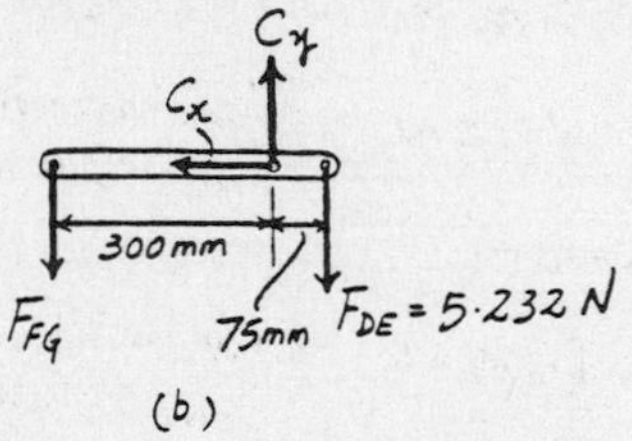

$\circlearrowleft + \Sigma M_C = 0;\quad F_{FG}(300) - 5.232(75) = 0 \quad F_{FG} = 1.308\text{ N}$

$+\uparrow \Sigma F_y = 0;\quad C_y - 1.308 - 5.232 = 0$

$C_y = 6.54\text{ N}$ **Ans**

$\overset{+}{\rightarrow} \Sigma F_x = 0;\quad C_x = 0$ **Ans**

From (c).

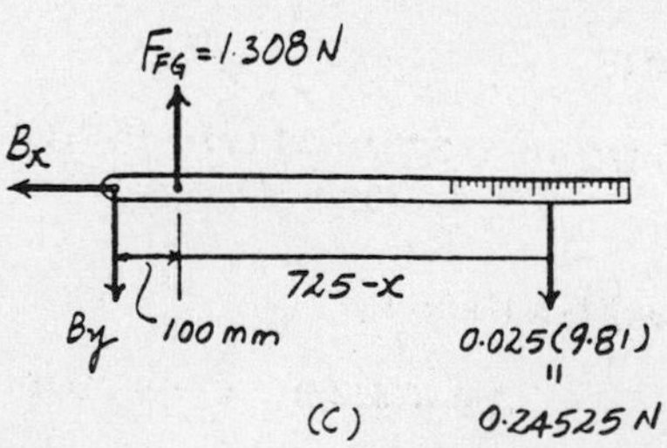

$\circlearrowleft + \Sigma M_B = 0;\quad 1.308(100) - 0.24525(825 - x) = 0$

$x = 292\text{ mm}$ **Ans**

$+\uparrow \Sigma F_y = 0;\quad 1.308 - 0.24525 - B_y = 0$

$B_y = 1.06\text{ N}$ **Ans**

$\overset{+}{\rightarrow} \Sigma F_x = 0;\quad B_x = 0$ **Ans**

6-98. The scissors lift consists of *two* sets of cross members and *two* hydraulic cylinders, DE, symmetrically located on *each side* of the platform. The platform has a uniform mass of 60 kg, with a center of gravity at G_1. The load of 85 kg, with center of gravity at G_2, is centrally located on each side of the platform. Determine the force in each of the hydraulic cylinders for equilibrium. Rollers are located at B and D.

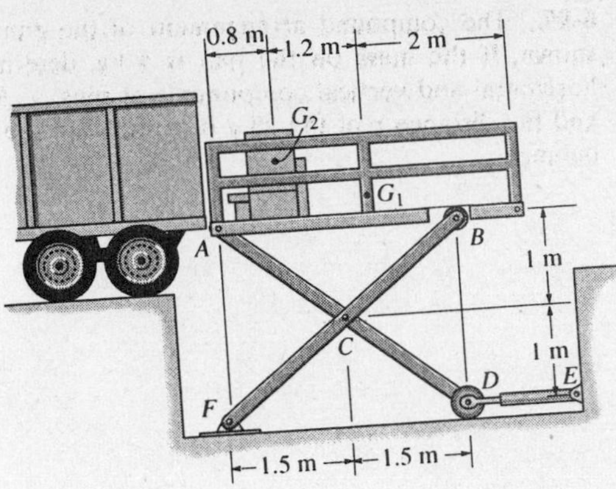

Free Body Diagram : The solution for this problem will be simplified if one realizes that the hydraulic cyclinder DE is a two force member.

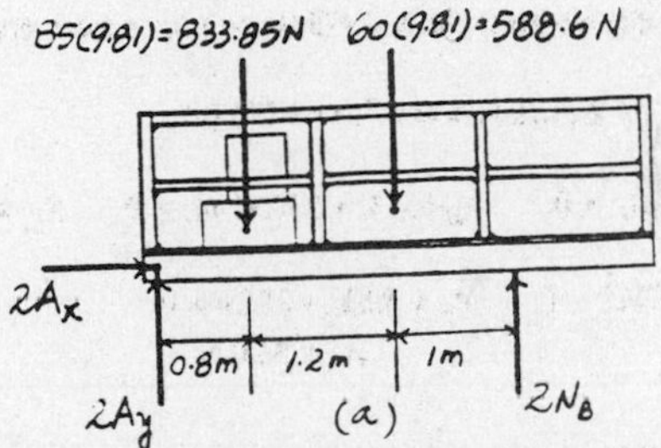

Equations of Equilibrium : From FBD (a),

$$\curvearrowleft + \Sigma M_A = 0; \quad 2N_B(3) - 833.85(0.8) - 588.6(2) = 0$$
$$2N_B = 614.76 \text{ N}$$

$$\xrightarrow{+} \Sigma F_x = 0; \quad A_x = 0$$

$$+\uparrow \Sigma F_y = 0; \quad 2A_y + 614.76 - 833.85 - 588.6 = 0$$
$$2A_y = 807.69 \text{ N}$$

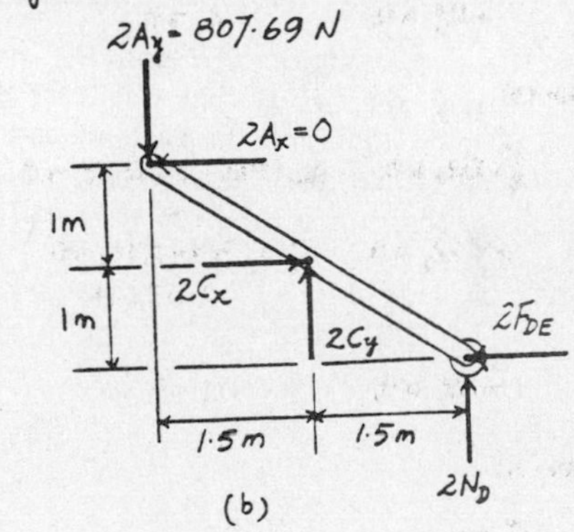

From FBD (b),

$$\curvearrowleft + \Sigma M_D = 0; \quad 807.69(3) - 2C_y(1.5) - 2C_x(1) = 0$$
$$2C_x + 3C_y = 2423.07 \qquad [1]$$

From FBD (c),

$$\curvearrowleft + \Sigma M_F = 0; \quad 2C_x(1) - 2C_y(1.5) - 614.76(3) = 0$$
$$2C_x - 3C_y = 1844.28 \qquad [2]$$

Solving Eqs.[1] and [2] yields

$$C_x = 1066.84 \text{ N} \qquad C_y = 96.465 \text{ N}$$

From FBD (b),

$$\xrightarrow{+} \Sigma F_x = 0; \quad 2(1066.84) - 2F_{DE} = 0$$
$$F_{DE} = 1066.84 \text{ N} = 1.07 \text{ kN} \qquad \textbf{Ans}$$

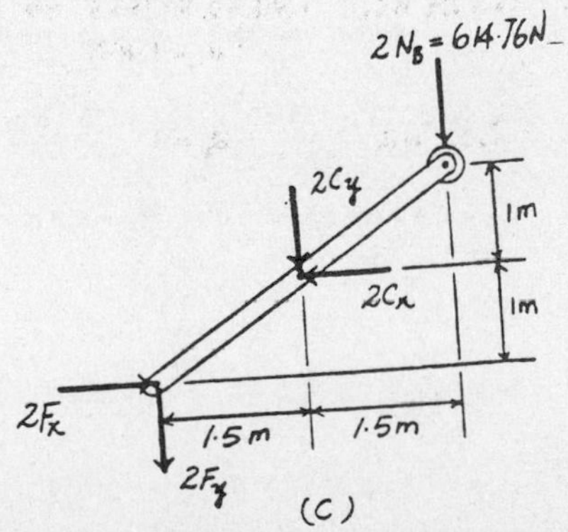

6-99. Determine the horizontal and vertical components of force that the pins at A, B, and C exert on the frame. The cylinder has a mass of 80 kg.

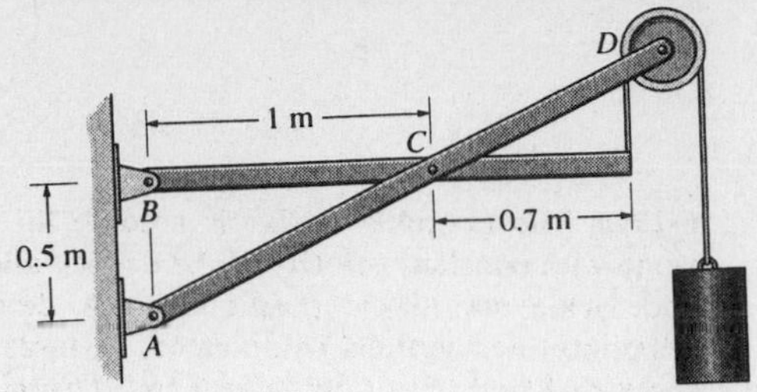

Equations of Equilibrium : From FBD (b),

$\circlearrowleft + \Sigma M_B = 0;\quad 784.8(1.7) - C_y(1) = 0$

$C_y = 1334.16\ \text{N} = 1.33\ \text{kN}$ **Ans**

$+\uparrow \Sigma F_y = 0;\quad B_y + 784.8 - 1334.16 = 0$

$B_y = 549\ \text{N}$ **Ans**

$\xrightarrow{+} \Sigma F_x = 0;\quad C_x - B_x = 0$ [1]

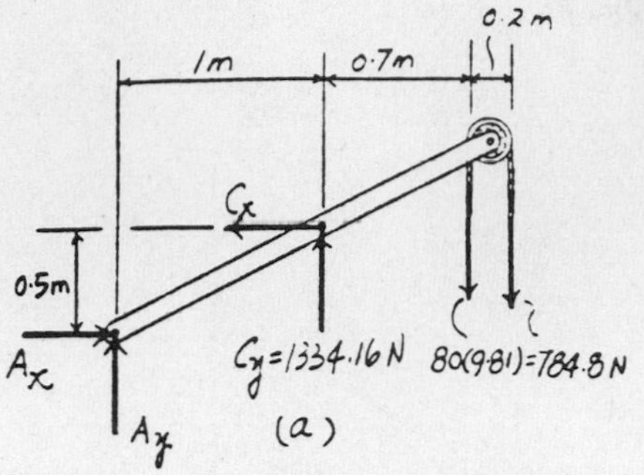

From FBD (a),

$\circlearrowleft + \Sigma M_A = 0;\quad C_x(0.5) + 1334.16(1) - 784.8(1.7) - 784.8(1.9) =$

$C_x = 2982.24\ \text{N} = 2.98\ \text{kN}$ **Ans**

$+\uparrow \Sigma F_y = 0;\quad A_y + 1334.16 - 784.8 - 784.8 = 0$

$A_y = 235\ \text{N}$ **Ans**

$\xrightarrow{+} \Sigma F_x = 0;\quad A_x - 2982.24 = 0$

$A_x = 2982.24\ \text{N} = 2.98\ \text{kN}$ **Ans**

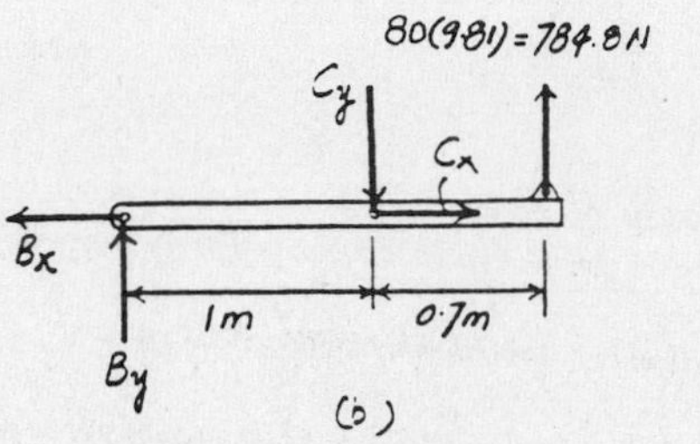

Substitute $C_x = 2982.24$ N into Eq.[1] yields,

$B_x = 2982.24\ \text{N} = 2.98\ \text{kN}$ **Ans**

***6-100.** The two insulators AB and BC are used to support the powerline P. If the weight of the line is 450 N, determine the force in each insulator if they are pin connected at their ends. Also, what are the components of reaction at the fixed support D?

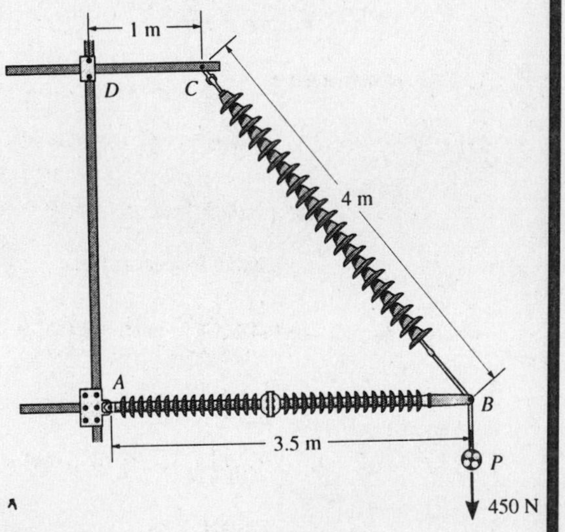

Equilibrium of joint B : Since members AB and BC are two- force members, we can use the method of joints to analyze the member forces.

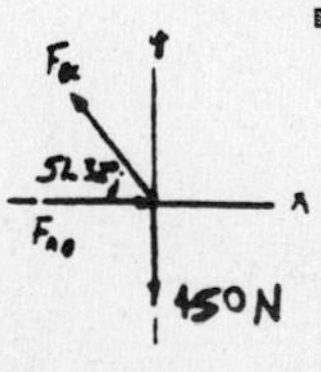

$+\uparrow \Sigma F_y = 0;\quad F_{BC} \sin 51.32° - 450 = 0 \quad F_{BC} = 576.4\ \text{N} = 576\ \text{N}$ **Ans**

$\xrightarrow{+} \Sigma F_x = 0;\quad F_{AB} - 576.4 \cos 51.32° = 0 \quad F_{AB} = 360\ \text{N}$ **Ans**

Components of reaction at D:

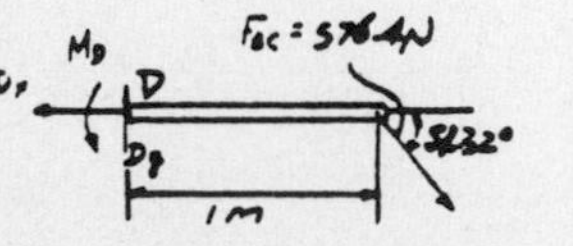

$\xrightarrow{+} \Sigma F_x = 0;\quad 576.4 \cos 51.32° - D_x = 0 \quad D_x = 360\ \text{N}$ **Ans**

$+\uparrow \Sigma F_y = 0;\quad D_y - 576.4 \sin 51.32° = 0 \quad D_y = 450\ \text{N}$ **Ans**

$\circlearrowleft + \Sigma M_D = 0;\quad M_D - 576.4 \sin 51.32°(1) = 0 \quad M_D = 450\ \text{N}\cdot\text{m}$ **Ans**

6-101. The gin-pole derrick is used to lift the 300-kg stone with constant velocity. If the derrick and the block and tackle are in the position shown, determine the horizontal and vertical components of force at the pin support A and the orientation θ and tension in the guy cable BC.

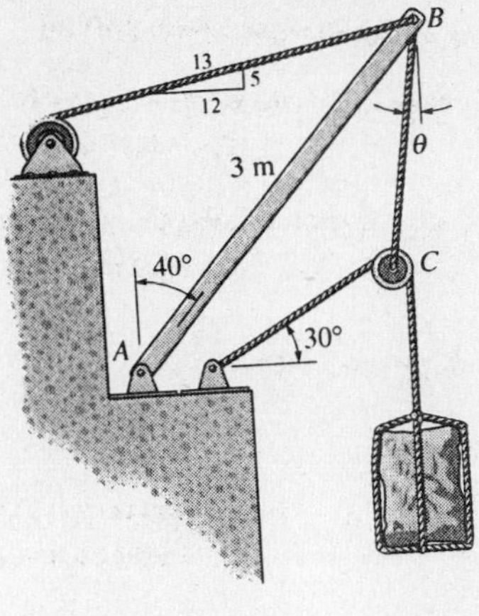

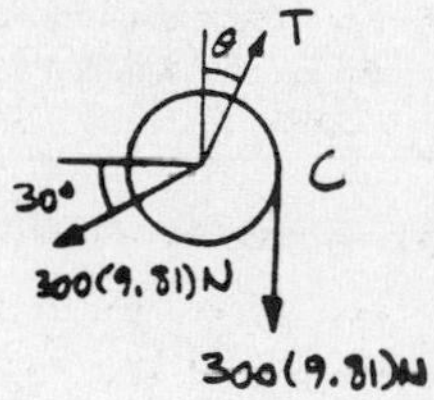

$\xrightarrow{+} \Sigma F_x = 0;\quad -300(9.81)\cos 30° + T\sin\theta = 0$

$+\uparrow \Sigma F_y = 0;\quad -300(9.81) - 300(9.81)\sin 30° + T\cos\theta = 0$

$T = 5097.4\text{ N} = 5.10\text{ kN}$ **Ans**

$\theta = 30°$ **Ans**

AB is a two-force member.

$\circlearrowleft + \Sigma M_A = 0;\quad R\left(\frac{12}{13}\right)(3\cos 40°) - R\left(\frac{5}{13}\right)(3\sin 40°)$

$+ 5097.4\sin 30°(3\cos 40°) - 5097.4\cos 30°(3\sin 40°) = 0$

$R = 1924.7\text{ N} = 1.92\text{ kN}$

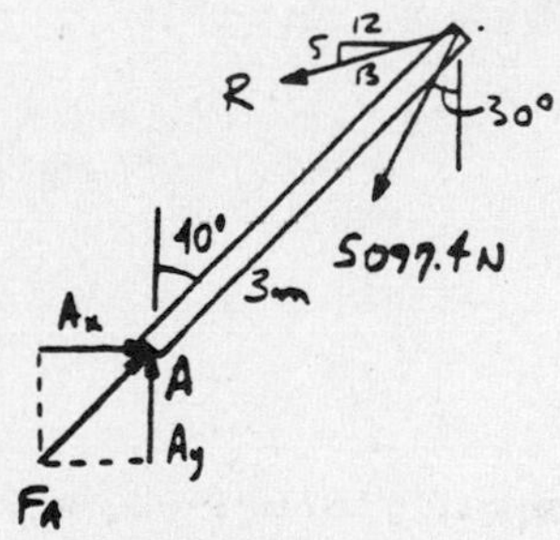

$\xrightarrow{+} \Sigma F_x = 0;\quad A_x - 1924.7\left(\frac{12}{13}\right) - 5097.4\sin 30° = 0$

$A_x = 4.33\text{ kN}$ **Ans**

$+\uparrow \Sigma F_y = 0;\quad A_y - 1924.7\left(\frac{5}{13}\right) - 5097.4\cos 30° = 0$

$A_y = 5.15\text{ kN}$ **Ans**

6-102. The bucket of the backhoe and its contents have a weight of 1200 lb and a center of gravity at G. Determine the forces of the hydraulic cylinder AB and in links AC and AD in order to hold the load in the position shown. The bucket is pinned at E.

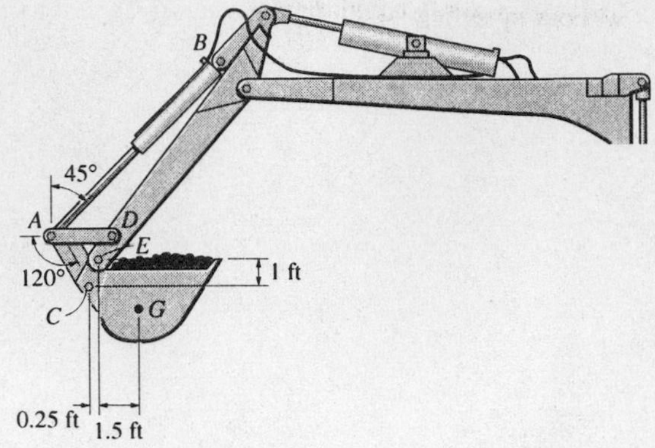

Free Body Diagram : The solution for this problem will be simplified if one realizes that the hydraulic cylinder AB, links AD and AC are two force members.

Equations of Equilibrium : From FBD (a),

$$\circlearrowleft + \Sigma M_E = 0; \quad F_{AC}\cos 60°(1) + F_{AC}\sin 60°(0.25) - 1200(1.5) = 0$$

$$F_{AC} = 2512.19 \text{ lb} = 2.51 \text{ kip} \qquad \textbf{Ans}$$

Using method of joint [FBD (b)],

$$+\uparrow \Sigma F_y = 0; \quad 2512.19\sin 60° - F_{AB}\cos 45° = 0$$

$$F_{AB} = 3076.79 \text{ lb} = 3.08 \text{ kip} \qquad \textbf{Ans}$$

$$\overset{+}{\rightarrow} \Sigma F_x = 0; \quad F_{AD} - 3076.79\sin 45° - 2512.19\cos 60° = 0$$

$$F_{AD} = 3431.72 \text{ lb} = 3.43 \text{ kip} \qquad \textbf{Ans}$$

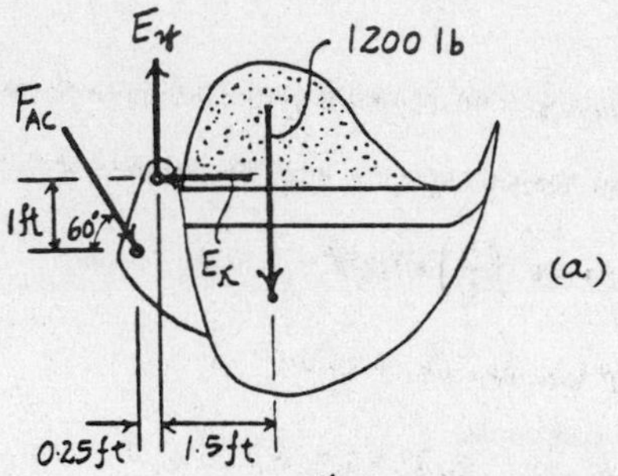

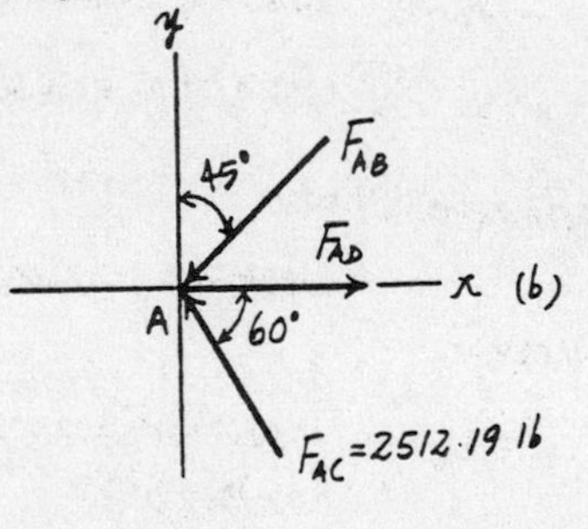

6-103. Two smooth tubes A and B, each having the same weight, W, are suspended from a common point O by means of equal-length cords. A third tube, C, is placed between A and B. Determine the greatest weight of C without upsetting equilibrium.

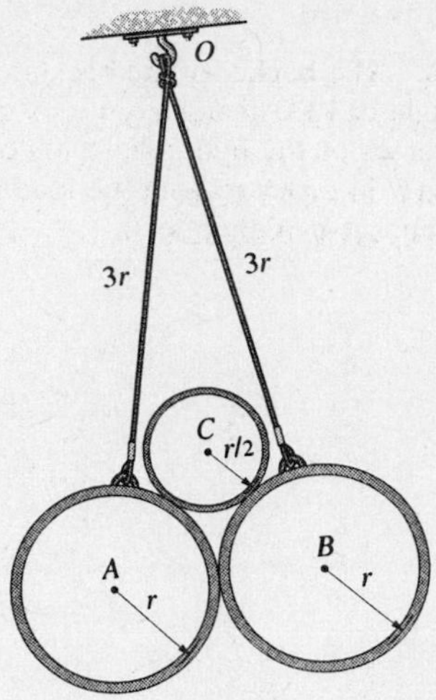

Free Body Diagram : When the equilibrium is about to be upset, the reaction at B must be zero ($N_B = 0$). From the geometry, $\phi = \cos^{-1}\left(\frac{r}{\frac{3}{2}r}\right) = 48.19°$ and $\theta = \cos^{-1}\left(\frac{r}{4r}\right) = 75.52°$.

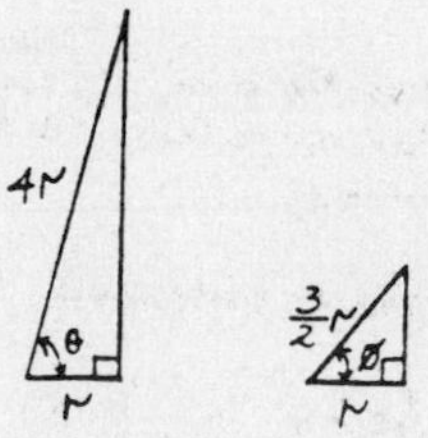

Equations of Equilibrium : From FBD (a),

$$\xrightarrow{+} \Sigma F_x = 0; \quad T\cos 75.52° - N_C\cos 48.19° = 0 \qquad [1]$$

$$+\uparrow \Sigma F_y = 0; \quad T\sin 75.52° - N_C\sin 48.19° - W = 0 \qquad [2]$$

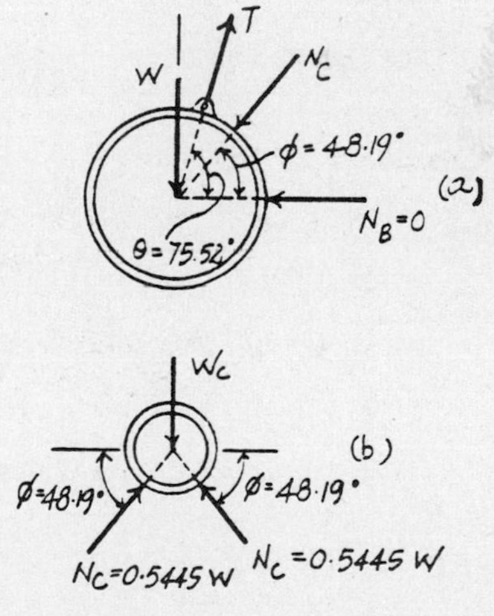

Solving Eq.[1] and [2] yields,

$$T = 1.452W \qquad N_C = 0.5445W$$

From FBD (b),

$$+\uparrow \Sigma F_y = 0; \quad 2(0.5445W\sin 48.19°) - W_C = 0$$

$$W_C = 0.812W \qquad \textbf{Ans}$$

***6-104.** The double link grip is used to lift the beam. If the beam weighs 4 kN, determine the horizontal and vertical components of force acting on the pin at A and the horizontal and vertical components of force that the flange of the beam exerts on the jaw at B.

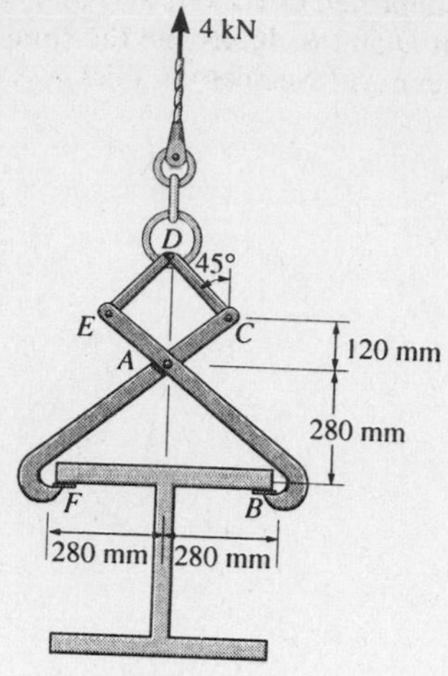

Prob. 6–104

Free Body Diagram : The solution for this problem will be simplified if one realizes that members ED and CD are two force members.

Equations of Equilibrium : Using method of joint [FBD (a)],

$+\uparrow \Sigma F_y = 0; \quad 4 - 2F\sin 45^\circ = 0 \quad F = 2.828 \text{ kN}$

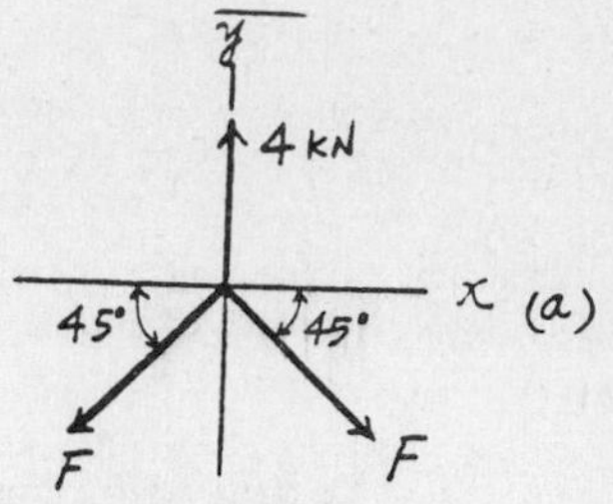

From FBD (b),

$+\uparrow \Sigma F_y = 0; \quad 2B_y - 4 = 0 \quad B_y = 2.00 \text{ kN}$ **Ans**

From FBD (c),

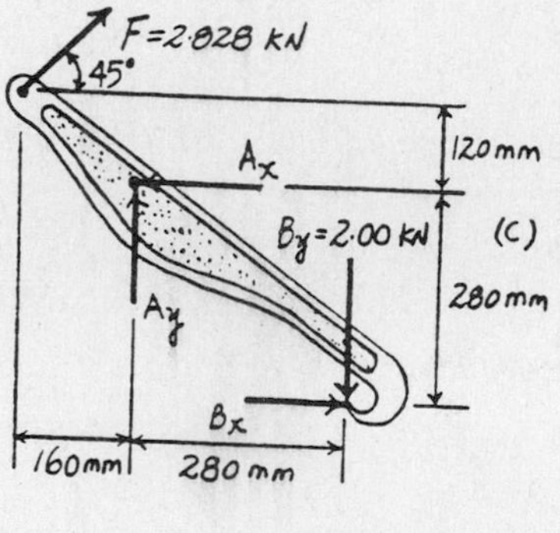

$\curvearrowleft + \Sigma M_A = 0; \quad B_x(280) - 2.00(280) - 2.828\cos 45^\circ(120)$
$\qquad - 2.828\sin 45^\circ(160) = 0$
$B_x = 4.00 \text{ kN}$ **Ans**

$+\uparrow \Sigma F_y = 0; \quad A_y + 2.828\sin 45^\circ - 2.00 = 0$
$A_y = 0$ **Ans**

$\xrightarrow{+} \Sigma F_x = 0; \quad 4.00 + 2.828\cos 45^\circ - A_x = 0$
$A_x = 6.00 \text{ kN}$ **Ans**

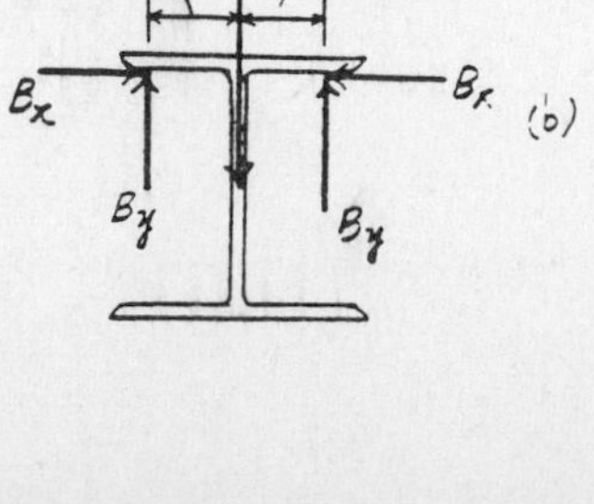

6-105. The compound beam is fixed supported at C and supported by rockers at A and B. If there are hinges (pins) at D and E, determine the components of reaction at the supports. Neglect the thickness of the beam.

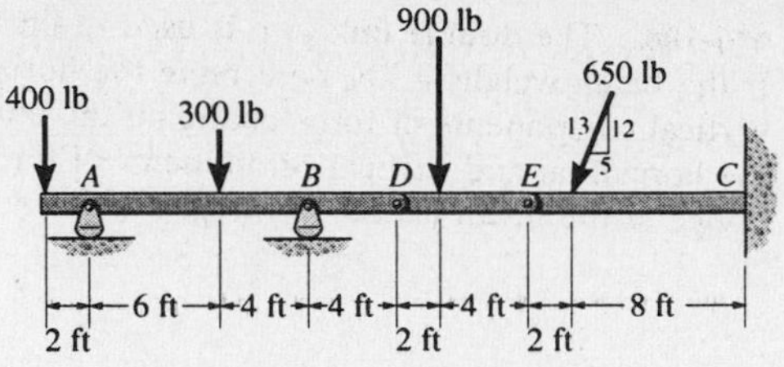

Equations of Equilibrium **:** From FBD (a),

$\circlearrowleft + \Sigma M_D = 0; \quad E_y(6) - 900(2) = 0 \quad E_y = 300 \text{ lb}$

$+\uparrow \Sigma F_y = 0; \quad D_y + 300 - 900 = 0 \quad D_y = 600 \text{ lb}$

$\xrightarrow{+} \Sigma F_x = 0; \quad D_x - E_x = 0 \quad\quad [1]$

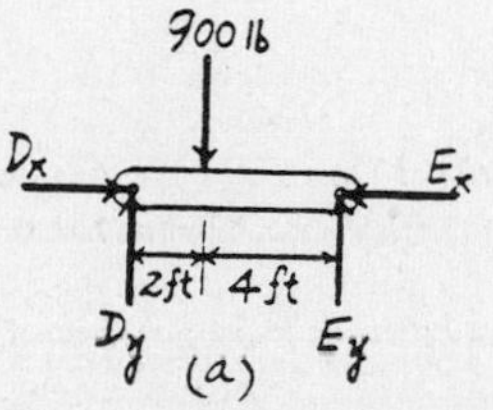

From FBD (b),

$\circlearrowleft + \Sigma M_A = 0; \quad B_y(10) + 400(2) - 300(6) - 600(14) = 0$

$B_y = 940 \text{ lb}$ **Ans**

$+\uparrow \Sigma F_y = 0; \quad A_y + 940 - 400 - 300 - 600 = 0$

$A_y = 360 \text{ lb}$ **Ans**

$\xrightarrow{+} \Sigma F_x = 0; \quad D_x = 0$

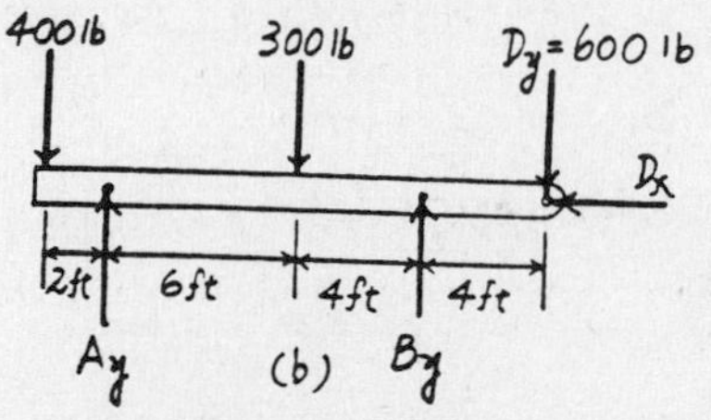

Substitute $D_x = 0$ into Eq. [1] yields $E_x = 0$

From FBD (c),

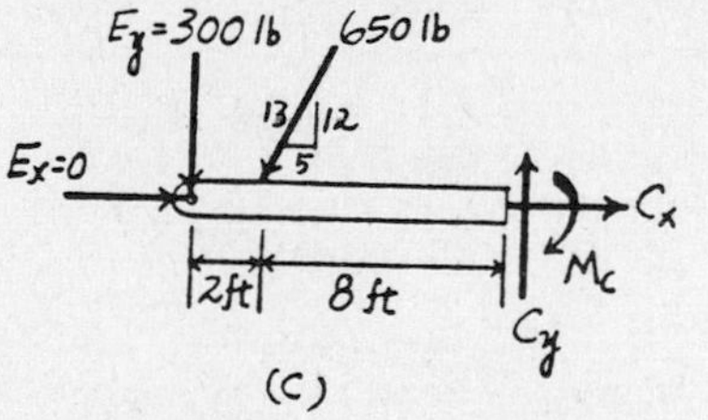

$\circlearrowleft + \Sigma M_C = 0; \quad 300(10) + 650\left(\frac{12}{13}\right)(8) - M_C = 0$

$M_C = 7800 \text{ lb} \cdot \text{ft} = 7.80 \text{ kip} \cdot \text{ft}$ **Ans**

$+\uparrow \Sigma F_y = 0; \quad C_y - 300 - 650\left(\frac{12}{13}\right) = 0 \quad C_y = 900 \text{ lb}$ **Ans**

$\xrightarrow{+} \Sigma F_x = 0; \quad C_x - 650\left(\frac{5}{13}\right) = 0 \quad C_x = 250 \text{ lb}$ **Ans**

6-106. The two disks each have a mass of 20 kg and are attached at their centers by an elastic cord that has a stiffness of $k = 2$ kN/m. Determine the stretch of the cord when the system is in equilibrium, and the angle θ of the cord.

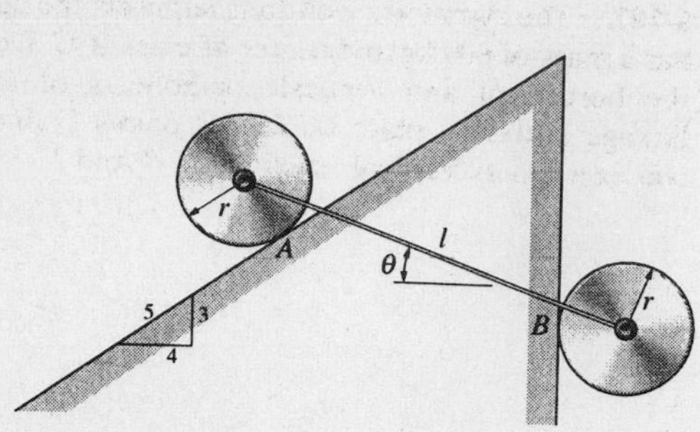

Entire system :

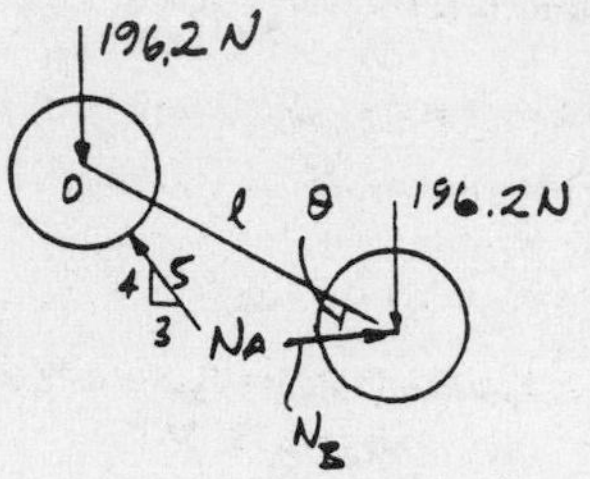

$\xrightarrow{+} \Sigma F_x = 0; \quad N_B - N_A\left(\frac{3}{5}\right) = 0$

$+\uparrow \Sigma F_y = 0; \quad N_A\left(\frac{4}{5}\right) - 2\,(196.2) = 0$

$\circlearrowleft + \Sigma M_O = 0; \quad N_B\,(l \sin\theta) - 196.2\, l \cos\theta = 0$

Solving,

$N_A = 490.5$ N

$N_B = 294.3$ N

$\theta = 33.69° = 33.7°$ **Ans**

Disk *B* :

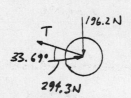

$\xrightarrow{+} \Sigma F_x = 0; \quad -T\cos 33.69° + 294.3 = 0$

$T = 353.70$ N

$F_s = kx; \quad 353.70 = 2000\,x$

$x = 0.177$ m $= 177$ mm **Ans**

6-107. The symmetric coil tong supports the coil which has a mass of 800 kg and center of mass at G. Determine the horizontal and vertical components of force the linkage exerts on plate $DEIJH$ at points D and E. The coil exerts only vertical reactions at K and L.

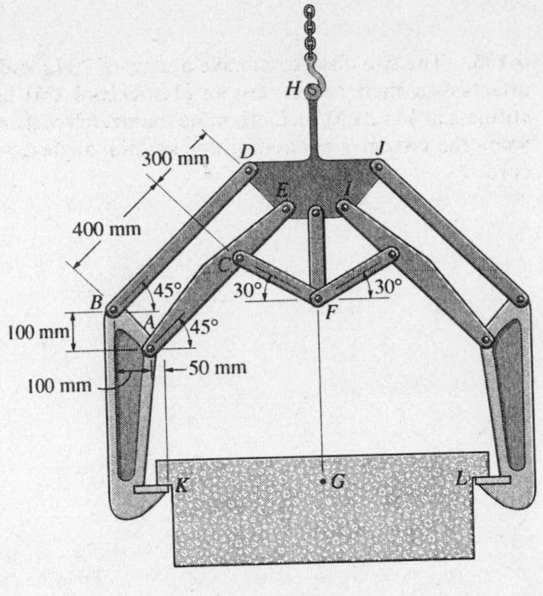

Free Body Diagram : The solution for this problem will be simplified if one realizes that links BD and CF are the two force members.

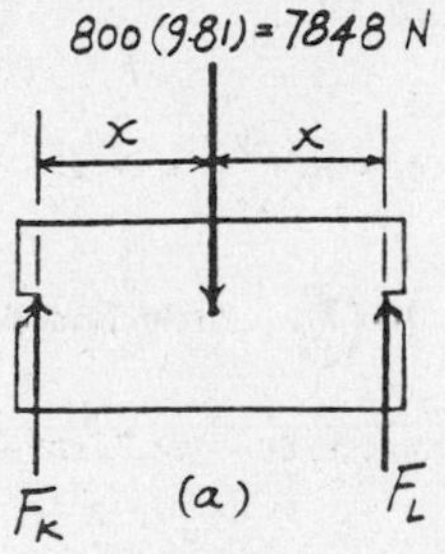

Equations of Equilibrium : From FBD (a),

$$\circlearrowleft + \Sigma M_L = 0; \quad 7848(x) - F_K(2x) = 0 \quad F_K = 3924 \text{ N}$$

From FBD (b),

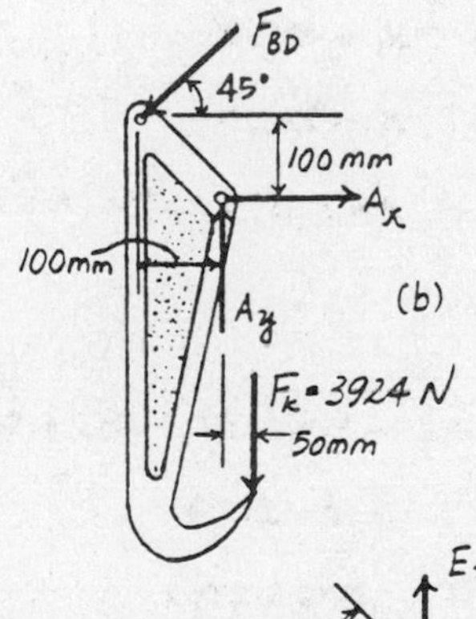

$$\circlearrowleft + \Sigma M_A = 0; \quad F_{BD}\cos 45°(100) + F_{BD}\sin 45°(100) - 3924(50) = 0$$

$$F_{BD} = 1387.34 \text{ N}$$

$$\xrightarrow{+} \Sigma F_x = 0; \quad A_x - 1387.34\cos 45° = 0 \quad A_x = 981 \text{ N}$$

$$+\uparrow \Sigma F_y = 0; \quad A_y - 3924 - 1387.34\sin 45° = 0$$

$$A_y = 4905 \text{ N}$$

From FBD (b),

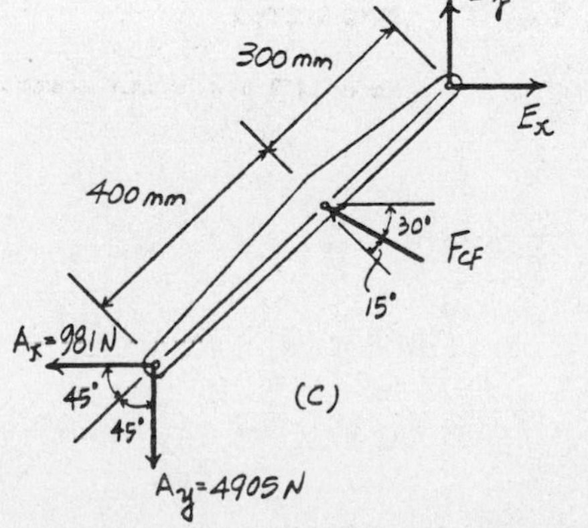

$$\circlearrowleft + \Sigma M_E = 0; \quad 4905\sin 45°(700) - 981\sin 45°(700)$$

$$- F_{CF}\cos 15°(300) = 0$$

$$F_{CF} = 6702.66 \text{ N}$$

$$\xrightarrow{+} \Sigma F_x = 0; \quad E_x - 981 - 6702.66\cos 30° = 0$$

$$E_x = 6785.67 \text{ N} = 6.79 \text{ kN} \qquad \textbf{Ans}$$

$$+\uparrow \Sigma F_y = 0; \quad E_y + 6702.66\sin 30° - 4905 = 0$$

$$E_y = 1553.67 \text{ N} = 1.55 \text{ kN} \qquad \textbf{Ans}$$

At point D,

$$D_x = F_{BD}\cos 45° = 1387.34\cos 45° = 981 \text{ N} \qquad \textbf{Ans}$$

$$D_y = F_{BD}\sin 45° = 1387.34\sin 45° = 981 \text{ N} \qquad \textbf{Ans}$$

***6-108.** If a force of 10 lb is applied to the grip of the clamp, determine the compressive force F that the wood block exerts on the clamp.

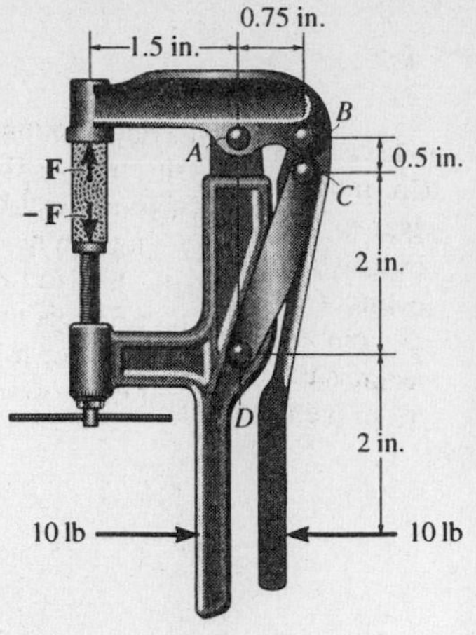

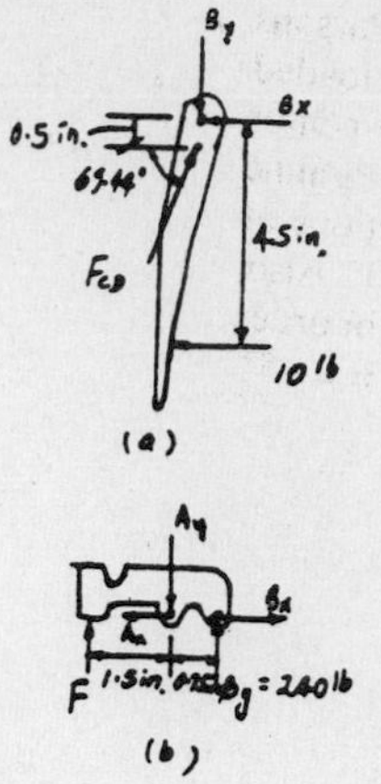

From FBD (a)

$\circlearrowleft + \Sigma M_B = 0;\quad F_{CD} \cos 69.44°(0.5) - 10(4.5) = 0 \quad F_{CD} = 256.32 \text{ lb}$

$+\uparrow \Sigma F_y = 0;\quad 256.32 \sin 69.44° - B_y = 0 \quad B_y = 240 \text{ lb}$

From FBD (b)

$\circlearrowleft + \Sigma M_A = 0;\quad 240(0.75) - F(1.5) = 0 \quad F = 120 \text{ lb}$ **Ans**

6-109. If each of the three uniform links of the mechanism has a length L and weight W, determine the angle θ for equilibrium. The spring, which always remains vertical, is unstretched when $\theta = 0°$.

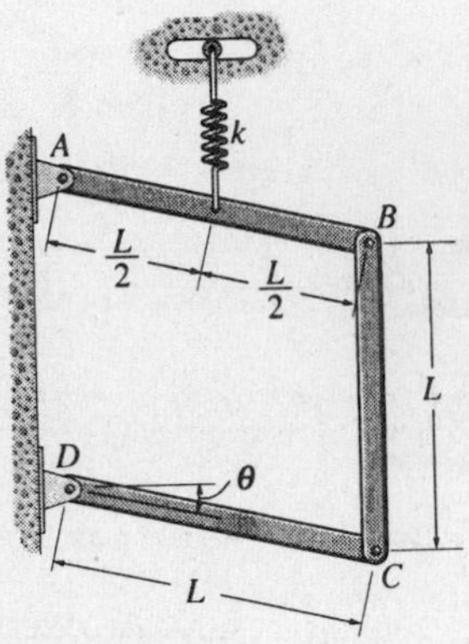

Free Body Diagram : The spring stretches $x = \frac{L}{2}\sin\theta$. Then, the spring force is $F_{sp} = kx = \frac{kL}{2}\sin\theta$.

Equations of Equilibrium : From FBD (b),

$\circlearrowleft + \Sigma M_B = 0;\quad C_x = 0$

$\xrightarrow{+} \Sigma F_x = 0;\quad B_x = 0$

$+\uparrow \Sigma F_y = 0;\quad B_y - C_y - W = 0 \quad [1]$

From FBD (a),

$\circlearrowleft + \Sigma M_D = 0;\quad C_y (L\cos\theta) - W\left(\frac{L}{2}\cos\theta\right) = 0$

$$C_y = \frac{W}{2}$$

Substitute $C_y = \frac{W}{2}$ into Eq.[1], we have $B_y = \frac{3W}{2}$. From FBD (c),

$$\circlearrowleft + \Sigma M_A = 0;\quad \frac{kL}{2}\sin\theta\left(\frac{L}{2}\cos\theta\right) - W\left(\frac{L}{2}\cos\theta\right) - \frac{3W}{2}(L\cos\theta) = 0$$

$$\theta = \sin^{-1}\left(\frac{8W}{kL}\right)$$ **Ans**

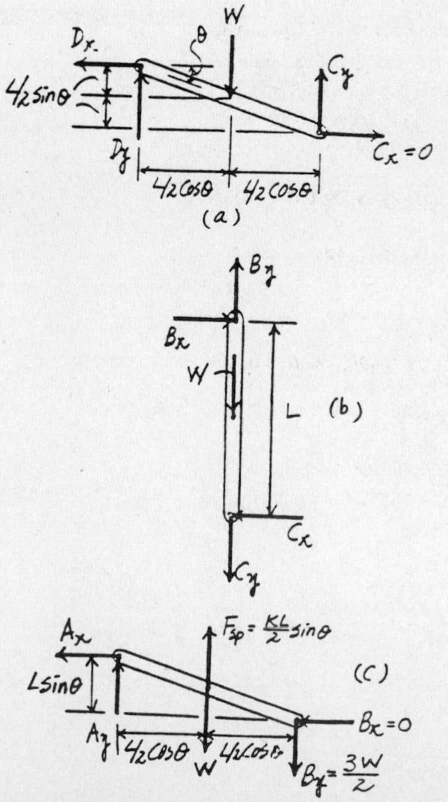

6-110. The carrier boom is manufactured by the Parsons Co. and is used to lift, transport, and dispense fully loaded drums. The drum has a weight of 800 lb, and the center of gravity is at G. Determine the force in the hydraulic cylinder BC and the horizontal and vertical reactions at the pin A when the boom is in the position $\theta = 30°$. Also, what is the smallest distance d to the outer wheels in order to prevent tipping of the boom for any angle $0° \leq \theta \leq 45°$.

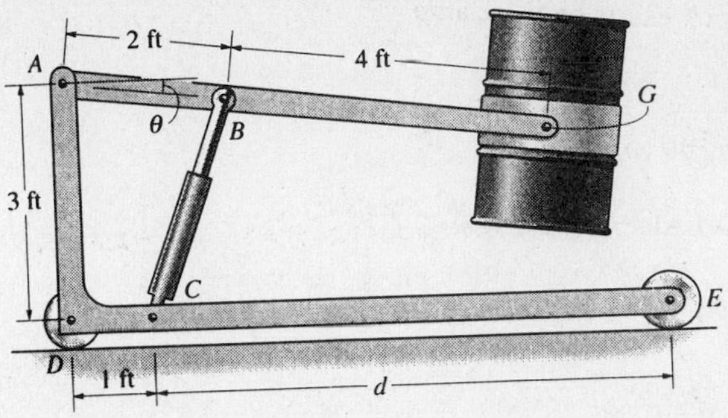

$$\phi = \tan^{-1}\left(\frac{0.73205}{2}\right) = 20.104°$$

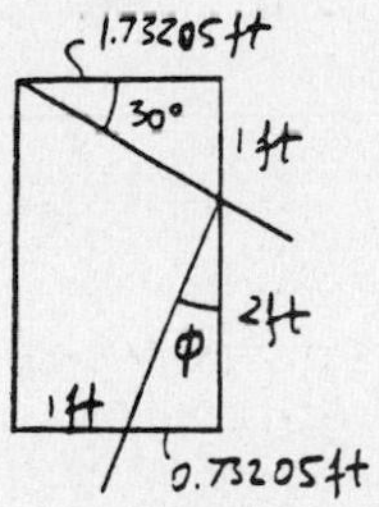

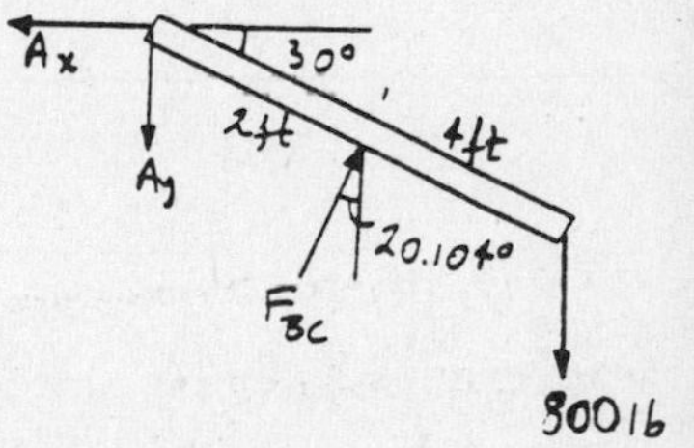

$\circlearrowleft + \Sigma M_A = 0;\quad -800\,(6\cos 30°) + F_{BC}\cos 20.104°\,(1.73205)$

$+ F_{BC}\sin 20.104°\,(1) = 0$

$F_{BC} = 2109.85\text{ lb} = 2.11\text{ kip}$ **Ans**

$\xrightarrow{+} \Sigma F_x = 0;\quad -A_x + 2109.85\sin 20.104° = 0$

$A_x = 725\text{ lb}$ **Ans**

$+\uparrow \Sigma F_y = 0;\quad -A_y + 2109.85\cos 20.104° - 800 = 0$

$A_y = 1.18\text{ kip}$ **Ans**

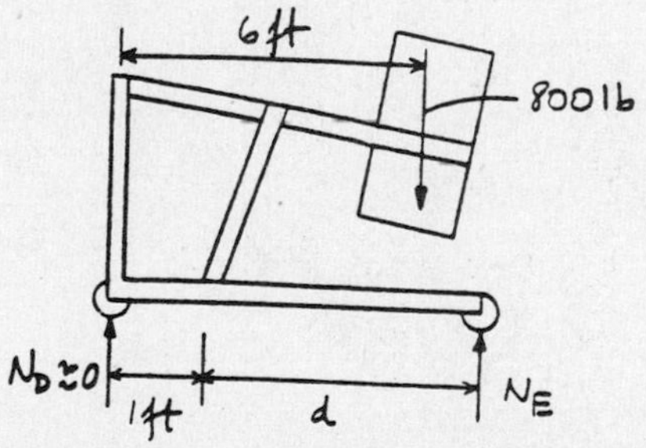

For tipping, require $\theta = 0°$:

$\circlearrowleft + \Sigma M_E = 0;\quad -N_D\,(d+1) + (800)\,(5-d) = 0$

$N_D = 0$, thus $d = 5$ ft **Ans**

6-111. The three pin-connected members shown in the *top view* support a downward force of 60 lb at G. If only vertical forces are supported at the connections B, C, E and pad supports A, D, F, determine the reactions at each pad.

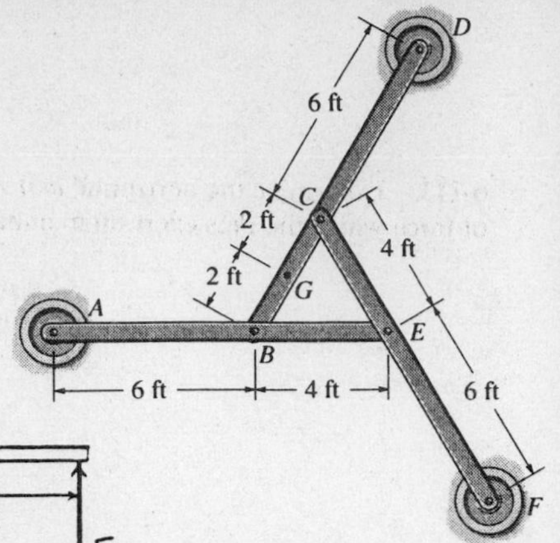

Equations of Equilibrium : From FBD (a),

$\circlearrowleft + \Sigma M_D = 0; \quad 60(8) + F_C(6) - F_B(10) = 0$ [1]

$+\uparrow \Sigma F_y = 0; \quad F_B + F_D - F_C - 60 = 0$ [2]

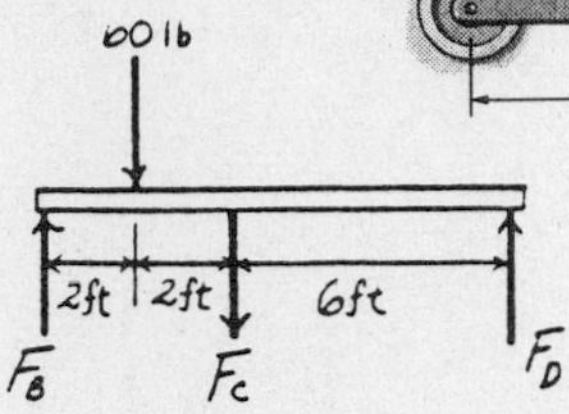

(a)

From FBD (b),

$\circlearrowleft + \Sigma M_F = 0; \quad F_E(6) - F_C(10) = 0$ [3]

$+\uparrow \Sigma F_y = 0; \quad F_C + F_F - F_E = 0$ [4]

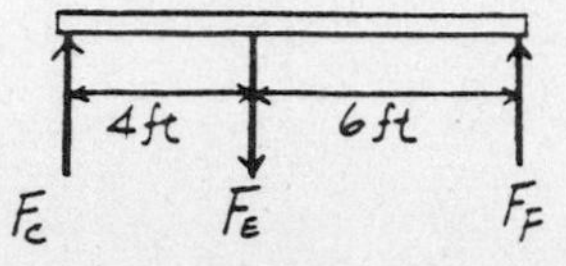

(b)

From FBD (c),

$\circlearrowleft + \Sigma M_A = 0; \quad F_E(10) - F_B(6) = 0$ [5]

$+\uparrow \Sigma F_y = 0; \quad F_A + F_E - F_B = 0$ [6]

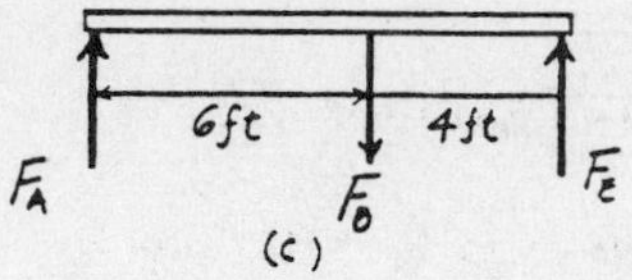

(c)

Solving Eqs. [1], [2], [3], [4], [5] and [6] yields,

$F_E = 36.73$ lb $\quad F_C = 22.04$ lb $\quad F_B = 61.22$ lb

$F_D = 20.8$ lb $\quad F_F = 14.7$ lb $\quad F_A = 24.5$ lb **Ans**

***6-112.** Determine the horizontal and vertical components of reaction at pins A, B, and C of the two-member arch.

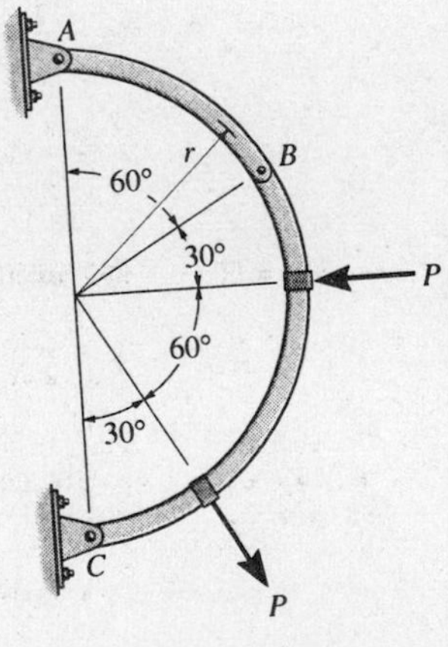

Member *CB* :

$\circlearrowleft + \Sigma M_C = 0; \quad -P \sin 30° (r) + P\,r - F_{AB} \cos 30°(r + r \sin 30°)$

$- F_{AB} \sin 30° (r \cos 30°) = 0$

$F_{AB} = 0.2887\,P$

Thus,

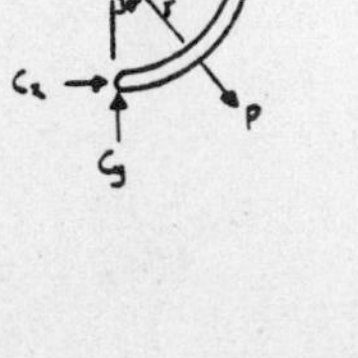

$A_x = B_x = 0.2887\,P \cos 30° = 0.25\,P$ **Ans**

$A_y = B_y = 0.2887\,P \sin 30° = 0.144\,P$ **Ans**

$\xrightarrow{+} \Sigma F_x = 0; \quad 0.2887\,P \cos 30° - P + P \sin 30° + C_x = 0$

$C_x = 0.25\,P$ **Ans**

$+\uparrow \Sigma F_y = 0; \quad C_y - P \cos 30° - 0.2887\,P \sin 30° = 0$

$C_y = 1.01\,P$ **Ans**

6-113. Determine the horizontal and vertical components of force which the pins exert on member AB of the frame.

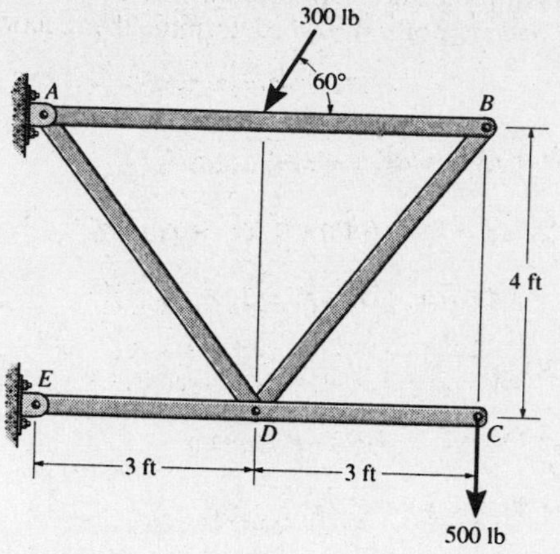

Member AB :

$\circlearrowleft + \Sigma M_A = 0; \quad -300 \sin 60° (3) + \frac{4}{5} F_{BD} (6) = 0$

$F_{BD} = 162.4 \text{ lb}$

Thus,

$B_x = \frac{3}{5}(162.4) = 97.4 \text{ lb}$ **Ans**

$B_y = \frac{4}{5}(162.4) = 130 \text{ lb}$ **Ans**

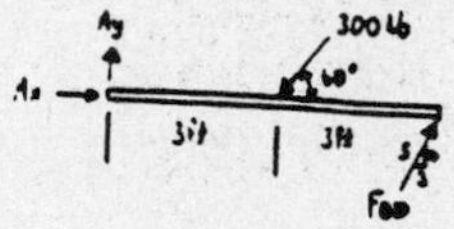

$\xrightarrow{+} \Sigma F_x = 0; \quad -300 \cos 60° + \frac{3}{5}(162.4) + A_x = 0$

$A_x = 52.6 \text{ lb}$ **Ans**

$+\uparrow \Sigma F_y = 0; \quad A_y - 300 \sin 60° + \frac{4}{5}(162.4) = 0$

$A_y = 130 \text{ lb}$ **Ans**

6-114. Determine the horizontal and vertical components of force which the pins exert on member *EDC* of the frame.

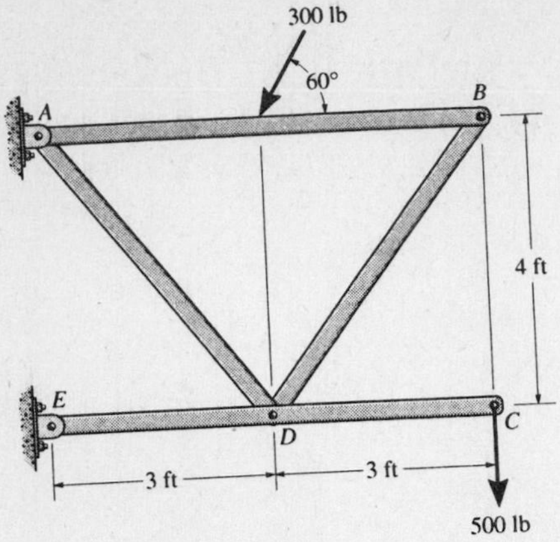

Member *AB* :

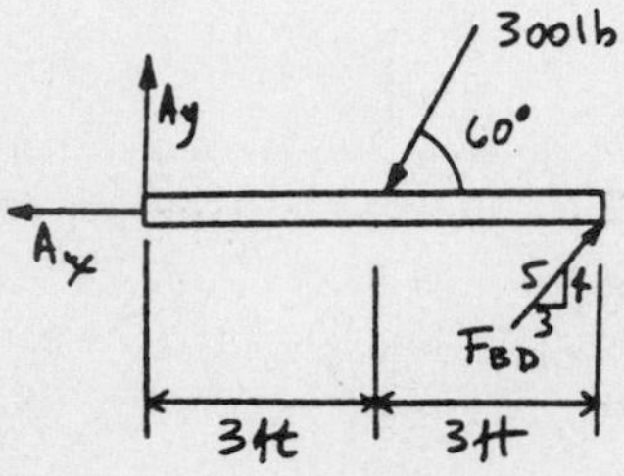

$\curvearrowleft + \Sigma M_A = 0; \quad -300 \sin 60° (3) + \frac{4}{5} F_{BD} (6) = 0$

$F_{BD} = 162.4 \text{ lb}$

Member *EDC* :

$\curvearrowleft + \Sigma M_E = 0; \quad -500 (6) - \frac{4}{5} (162.4) (3) + \frac{4}{5} F_{AD} (3) = 0$

$F_{AD} = 1412.4 \text{ lb}$

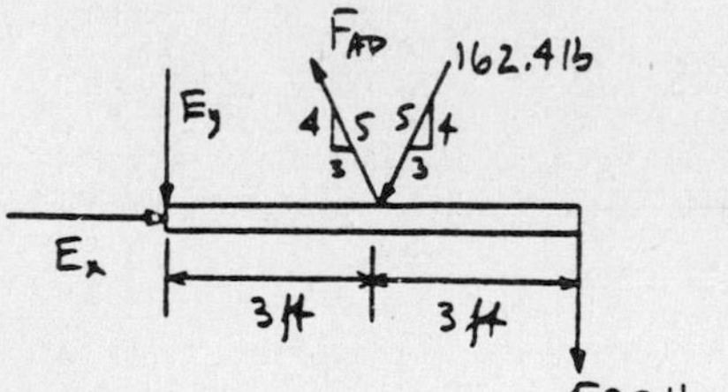

$\xrightarrow{+} \Sigma F_x = 0; \quad E_x - 162.4\left(\frac{3}{5}\right) - 1412.4\left(\frac{3}{5}\right) = 0$

$E_x = 945 \text{ lb}$ **Ans**

$+\uparrow \Sigma F_y = 0; \quad -E_y + 1412.4\left(\frac{4}{5}\right) - 162.4\left(\frac{4}{5}\right) - 500 = 0$

$E_y = 500 \text{ lb}$ **Ans**

Pin *D* :

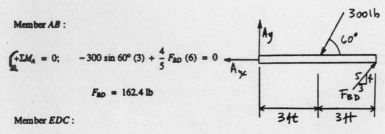

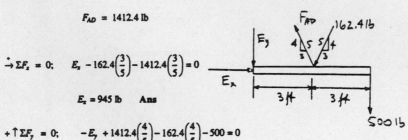

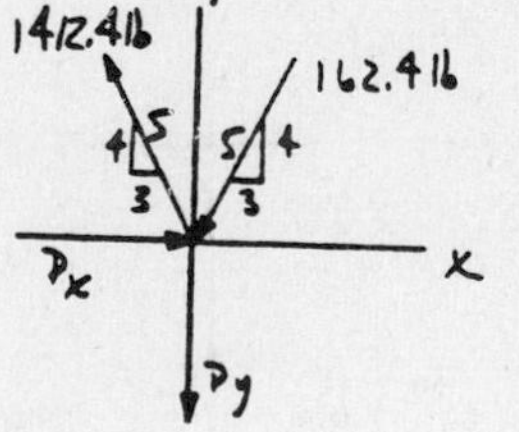

$\xrightarrow{+} \Sigma F_x = 0; \quad D_x - \frac{3}{5} (162.4) - \frac{3}{5} (1412.4) = 0$

$D_x = 945 \text{ lb}$ **Ans**

$+\uparrow \Sigma F_y = 0; \quad -D_y - \frac{4}{5} (162.4) + \frac{4}{5} (1412.4) = 0$

$D_y = 1000 \text{ lb}$ **Ans**

6-115. The piston C moves vertically between the two smooth walls. If the spring has a stiffness of $k = 15$ lb/in., and is unstretched when $\theta = 0°$, determine the couple **M** that must be applied to AB to hold the mechanism in equilibrium when $\theta = 30°$.

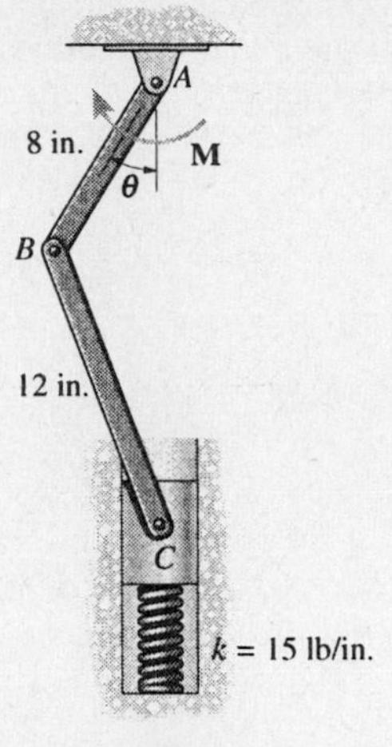

Geometry :

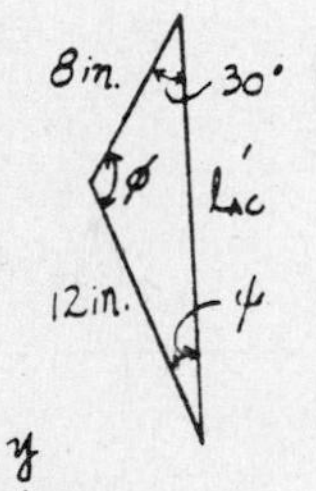

$$\frac{\sin\psi}{8} = \frac{\sin 30°}{12} \qquad \psi = 19.47°$$

$$\phi = 180° - 30° - 19.47 = 130.53°$$

$$\frac{l'_{AC}}{\sin 130.53°} = \frac{12}{\sin 30°} \qquad l'_{AC} = 18.242 \text{ in.}$$

Free Body Diagram : The solution for this problem will be simplified if one realizes that member CB is a two force member. Since the spring stretches $x = l_{AC} - l'_{AC} = 20 - 18.242 = 1.758$ in. the spring force is $F_{sp} = kx = 15(1.758) = 26.37$ lb.

Equations of Equilibrium : Using the method of joints [FBD (a)],

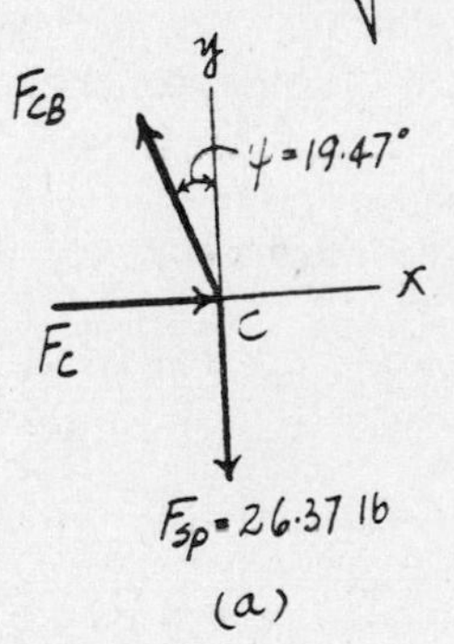

$$+\uparrow \Sigma F_y = 0; \qquad F_{CB}\cos 19.47° - 26.37 = 0$$

$$F_{CB} = 27.97 \text{ lb}$$

From FBD (b),

$$+\Sigma M_A = 0; \qquad 27.97\cos 40.53°(8) - M = 0$$

$$M = 170.08 \text{ lb}\cdot\text{in} = 14.2 \text{ lb}\cdot\text{ft} \qquad \textbf{Ans}$$

***6-116.** The two-member frame supports the loading shown. Determine the force of the roller at B on member AC and the horizontal and vertical components of force which the pin at C exerts on member CB and the pin at A exerts on member AC. The roller does not contact member CB.

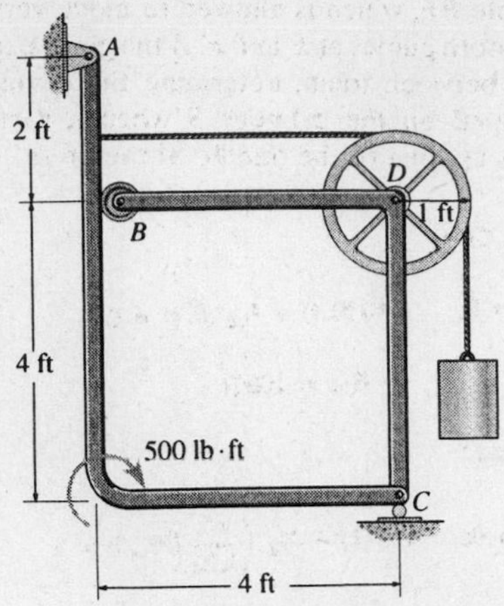

Equations of Equilibrium : From FBD (a),

$\circlearrowleft + \Sigma M_A = 0;\quad N_C(4) - 200(5) - 500 = 0 \quad N_C = 375 \text{ lb}$

$\xrightarrow{+} F_x = 0;\quad A_x = 0$ **Ans**

$+\uparrow \Sigma F_y = 0;\quad 375 - 200 - A_y = 0 \quad A_y = 175 \text{ lb}$ **Ans**

From FBD (b),

$\circlearrowleft + \Sigma M_C = 0;\quad 200(5) - 200(1) - B_x(4) = 0$

$B_x = 200 \text{ lb}$ **Ans**

$\xrightarrow{+} F_x = 0;\quad 200 - 200 - C_x = 0 \quad C_x = 0$ **Ans**

$+\uparrow \Sigma F_y = 0;\quad C_y - 200 = 0 \quad C_y = 200 \text{ lb}$ **Ans**

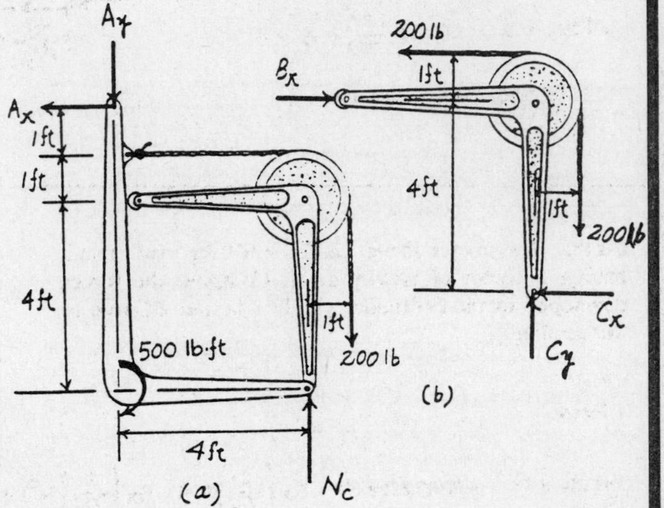

6-117. The handle of the sector press is fixed to gear G, which in turn is in mesh with the sector gear C. Note that AB is pinned at its ends to gear C and the underside of the table EF, which is allowed to move vertically due to the smooth guides at E and F. If the gears exert tangential forces between them, determine the compressive force developed on the cylinder S when a vertical force of 40 N is applied to the handle of the press.

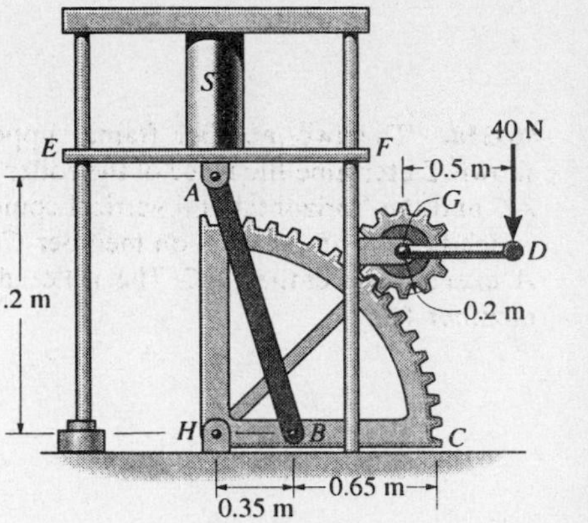

Member GD :

$$\circlearrowleft + \Sigma M_G = 0; \quad -40\,(0.5) + F_{CG}\,(0.2) = 0$$

$$F_{CG} = 100 \text{ N}$$

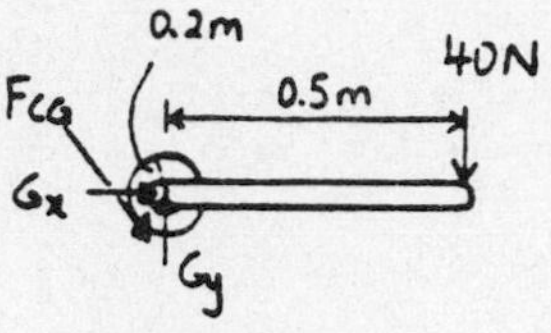

Sector gear :

$$\circlearrowleft + \Sigma M_H = 0; \quad 100\,(1) - F_{AB}\left(\frac{1.2}{1.25}\right)(0.35) = 0$$

$$F_{AB} = 297.62 \text{ N}$$

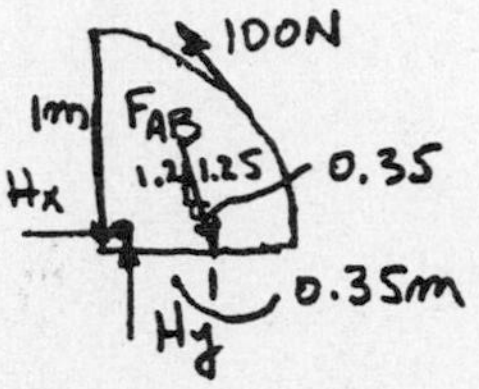

Table :

$$+\uparrow \Sigma F_y = 0; \quad 297.62\left(\frac{1.2}{1.25}\right) - F_S = 0$$

$$F_S = 286 \text{ N} \quad \textbf{Ans}$$

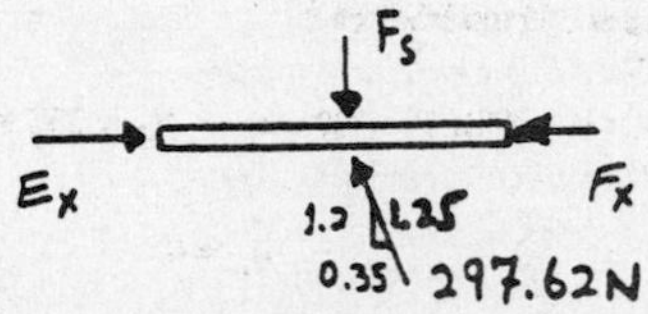

6-118. The tractor shovel carries a 500-kg load of soil, having a center of gravity at G. Compute the forces developed in the hydraulic cylinders IJ and BC due to this loading.

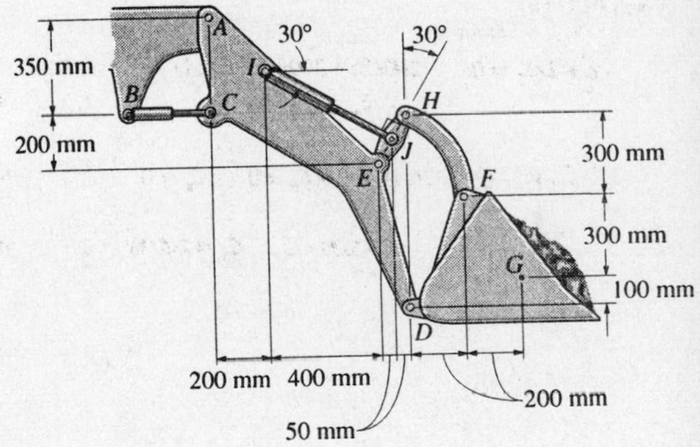

Shovel :

$$\circlearrowleft + \Sigma M_D = 0; \quad -500(9.81)\,(0.4) + F_{FH}\left(\frac{2}{\sqrt{13}}\right)(0.4) + F_{FH}\left(\frac{3}{\sqrt{13}}\right)(0.2) = 0$$

$$F_{FH} = 5052.92 \text{ N}$$

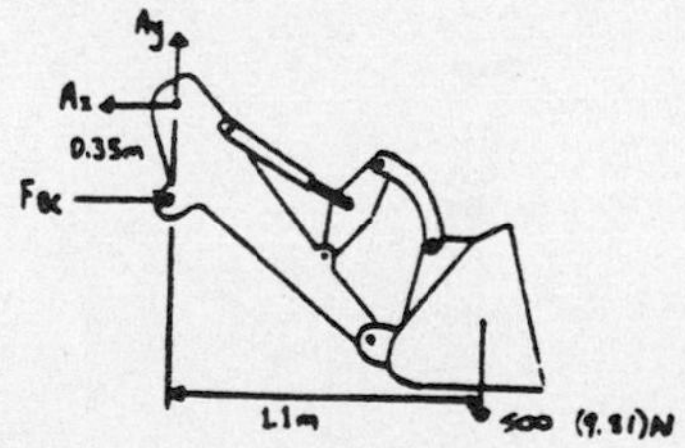

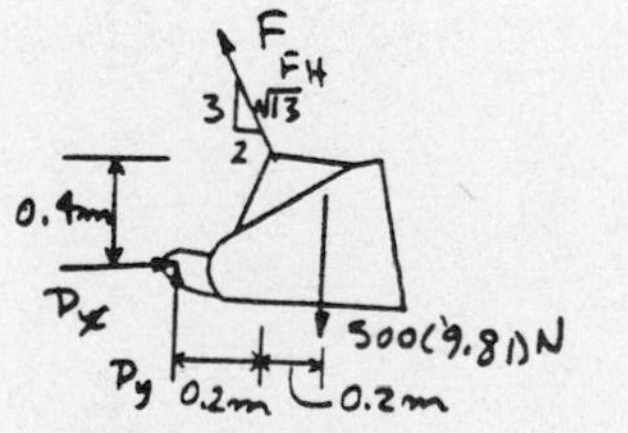

Member EH :

$$\circlearrowleft + \Sigma M_E = 0; \quad F_{IJ}\left(\frac{0.05}{\sin 30^\circ}\right) - 5052.92\left(\frac{3}{\sqrt{13}}\right)(0.1)$$

$$- 5052.92\left(\frac{2}{\sqrt{13}}\right)\left(\frac{0.1}{\tan 30^\circ}\right) = 0$$

$$F_{IJ} = 9059 \text{ N} = 9.06 \text{ kN (T)} \quad \textbf{Ans}$$

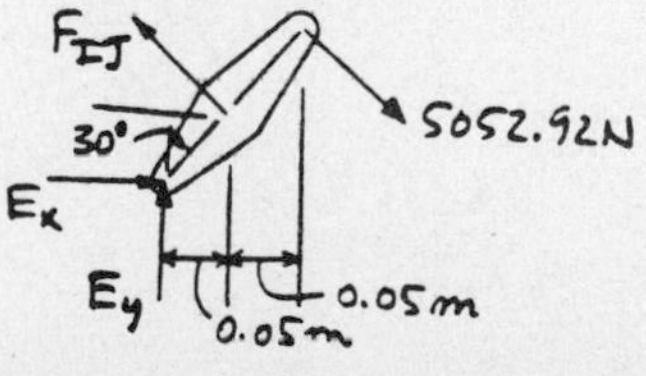

Assembly :

$$\circlearrowleft + \Sigma M_A = 0; \quad -500(9.81)\,(1.1) + F_{BC}\,(0.35) = 0$$

$$F_{BC} = 15\,415.7 \text{ N} = 15.4 \text{ kN (C)} \quad \textbf{Ans}$$

6-119. The frame supports the 80-lb weight. Determine the horizontal and vertical components of force which the pins exert on member *ABCD*. Note that the pin at *C* is attached to member *ABCD* and passes through the smooth slot in member *ECF*.

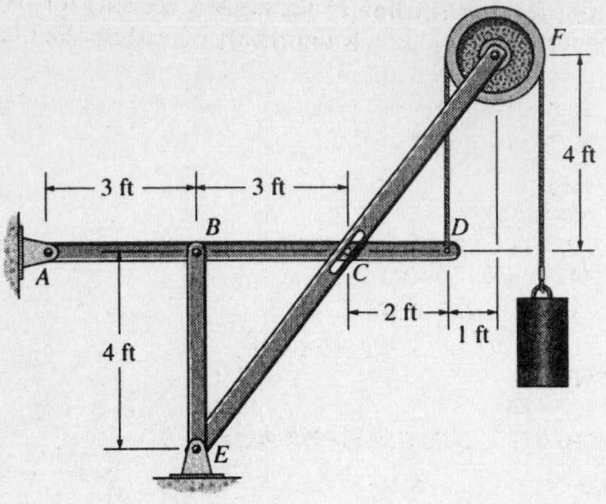

Free Body Diagram : The solution for this problem will be simplified if one realizes that member *BE* is a two force member.

Equations of Equilibrium : From FBD (a),

$\curvearrowleft + \Sigma M_E = 0; \quad F_C(5) - 80(5) - 80(7) = 0 \quad F_C = 192 \text{ lb}$

From FBD (b),

$\curvearrowleft + \Sigma M_A = 0; \quad F_{BE}(3) + 80(8) - 192\left(\frac{3}{5}\right)(6) = 0$

$F_{BE} = 17.07 \text{ lb}$

$\xrightarrow{+} \Sigma F_x = 0; \quad 192\left(\frac{4}{5}\right) - A_x = 0 \quad A_x = 154 \text{ lb}$ **Ans**

$+\uparrow \Sigma F_y = 0; \quad A_y + 17.07 + 80 - 192\left(\frac{3}{5}\right) = 0$

$A_y = 18.1 \text{ lb}$ **Ans**

For pins *B* and *C*,

$B_x = 0 \quad B_y = F_{BE} = 17.1 \text{ lb}$ **Ans**

$C_x = F_C\left(\frac{4}{5}\right) = 192\left(\frac{4}{5}\right) = 154 \text{ lb}$ **Ans**

$C_y = F_C\left(\frac{3}{5}\right) = 192\left(\frac{3}{5}\right) = 115 \text{ lb}$ **Ans**

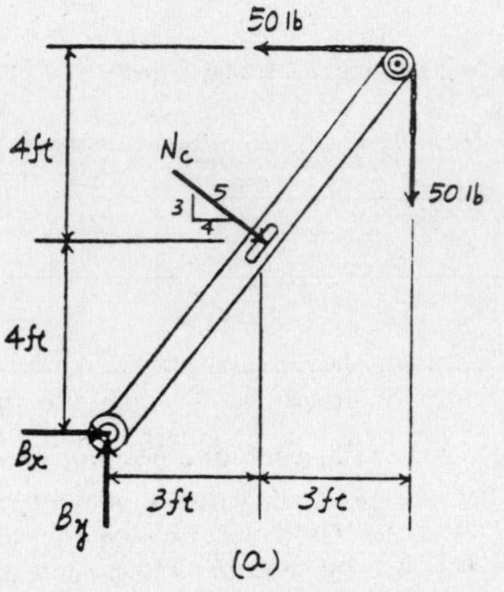

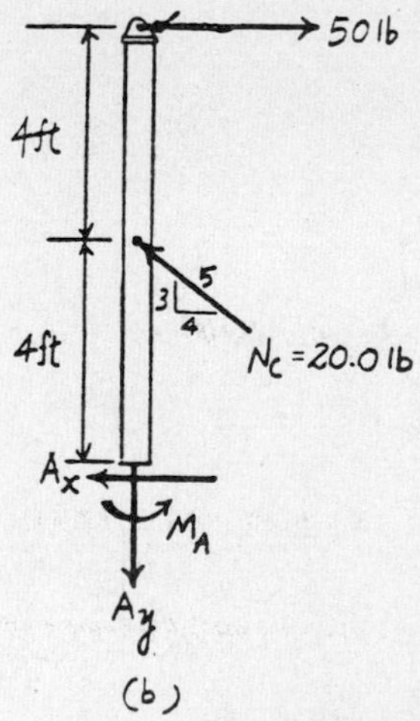

■*6-120. The scissors hoist is operated by applying a force P to the roller support C using a hydraulic cylinder. Determine the force P as a function of position θ and plot the results P (ordinate) versus θ (abscissa) for $0° \leq \theta \leq 90°$. The 400-kg load is uniformly placed on the platform.

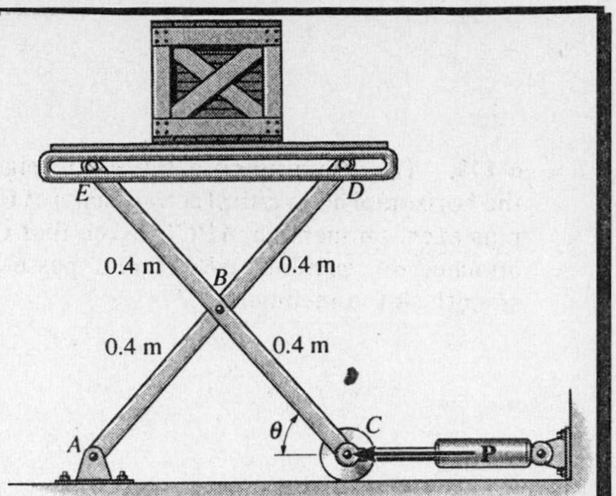

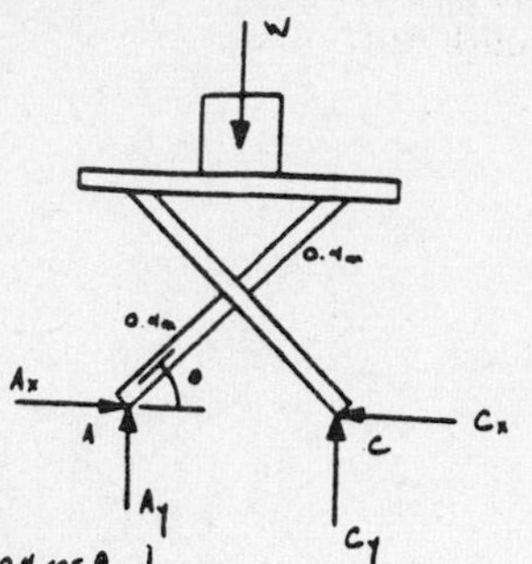

System :

$\circlearrowleft + \Sigma M_A = 0; \quad C_y(0.8\cos\theta) - W(0.4\cos\theta) = 0$

$C_y = 0.5W$

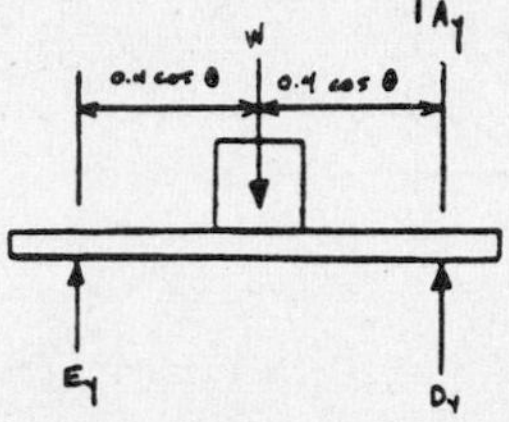

Platform :

$\circlearrowleft + \Sigma M_E = 0; \quad D_y(0.8\cos\theta) - W(0.4\cos\theta) = 0$

$D_y = 0.5W$

$+\uparrow \Sigma F_y = 0; \quad E_y + 0.5W - W = 0$

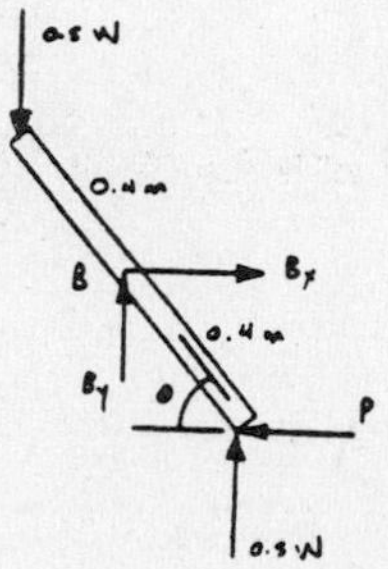

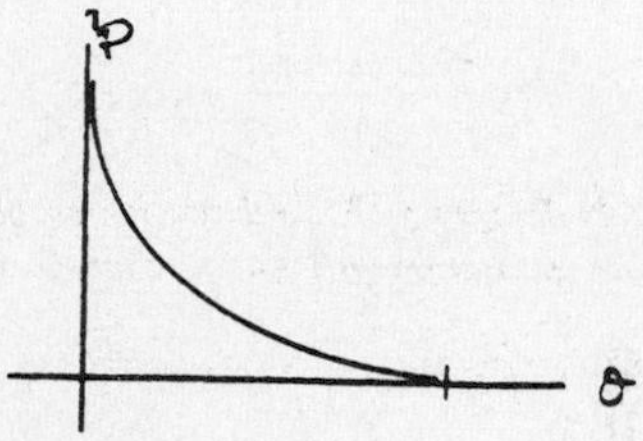

Member EBC :

$\circlearrowleft + \Sigma M_B = 0; \quad 0.5W(0.4\cos\theta) + 0.5W(0.4\cos\theta) - P(0.4\sin\theta) = 0$

$P = W\cot\theta$

Set $W = 400(9.81) = 3924$ N

$P = 3924\cot\theta$

6-121. The lever mechanism for a machine press serves as a toggle which develops a large force at E when a small force is applied at the handle H. To show that this is the case, determine the force at E if someone applies a vertical force of 80 N at H. The smooth head at D is able to slide freely downward. All members are pin connected.

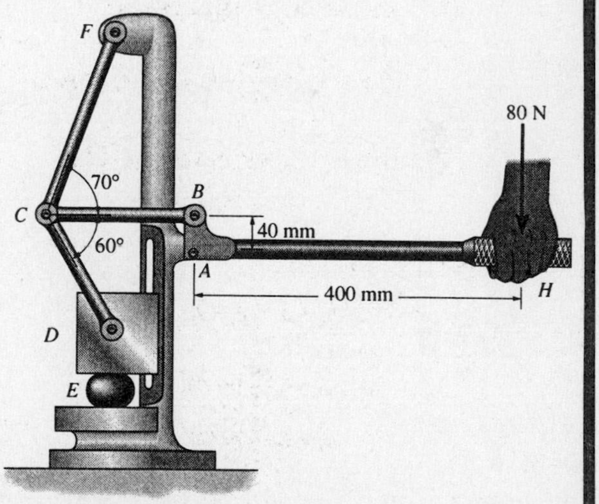

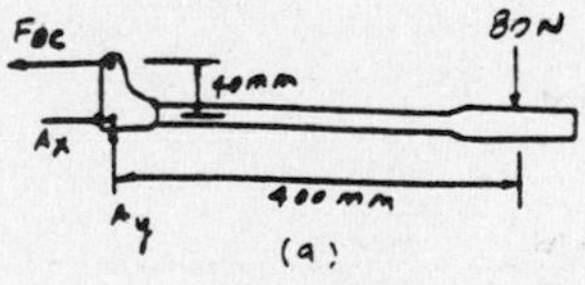

From FBD (a)

$\circlearrowleft + \Sigma M_A = 0; \quad F_{BC}(40) - 80(400) = 0 \qquad F_{BC} = 800$ N

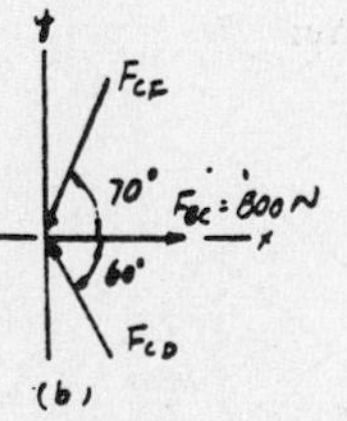

From FBD (b)

$+\uparrow \Sigma F_y = 0; \quad F_{CD}\sin 60° - F_{CF}\sin 70° = 0 \qquad (1)$

$\xrightarrow{+} \Sigma F_x = 0; \quad 800 - F_{CF}\cos 70° - F_{CD}\cos 60° = 0 \qquad (2)$

Solving Eqs. (1) and (2) yields :

$F_{CF} = 904.41$ N $\qquad F_{CD} = 981.35$ N

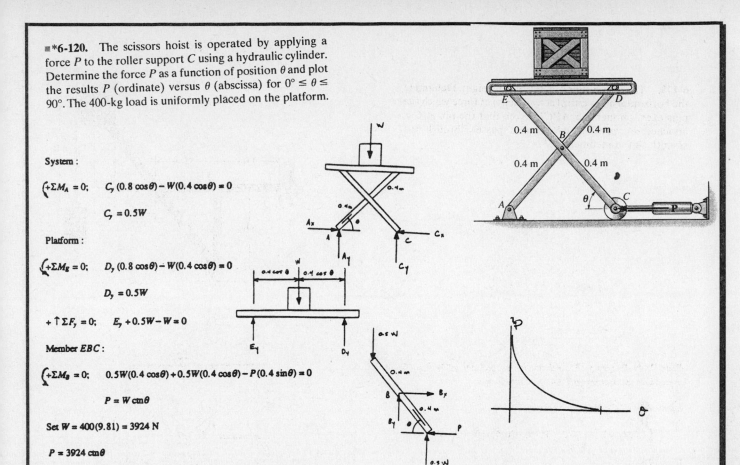

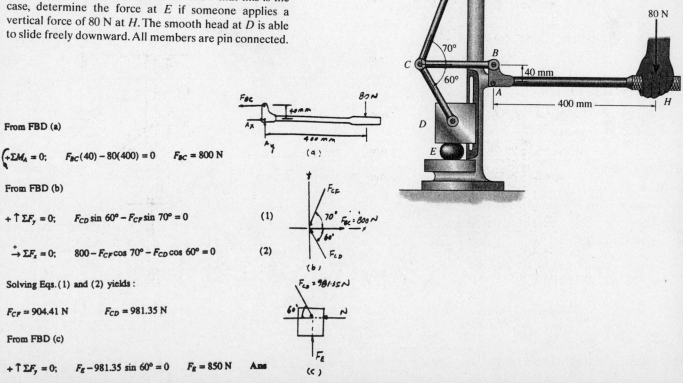

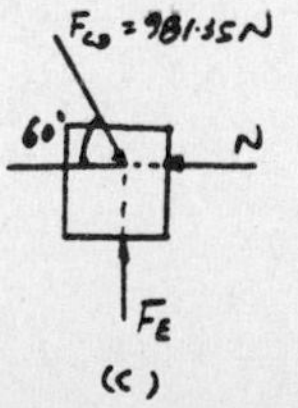

From FBD (c)

$+\uparrow \Sigma F_y = 0; \quad F_E - 981.35\sin 60° = 0 \qquad F_E = 850$ N **Ans**

6-122. Determine the couple moment **M** that must be applied to member DC for equilibrium of the quick-return mechanism. Express the result in terms of the angles ϕ and θ, dimension L, and the applied vertical load P. The block at C is confined to slide within the slot of member AB.

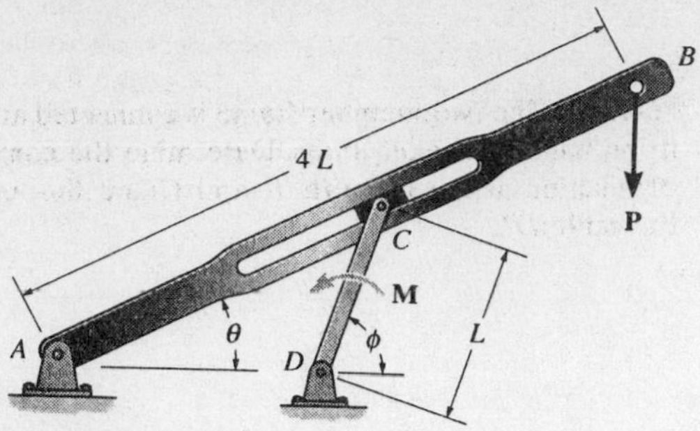

$$\frac{x}{4L} = \frac{L\sin\phi}{4L\sin\theta} \qquad x = \frac{L\sin\phi}{\sin\theta}$$

From FBD (a)

$$\curvearrowleft +\Sigma M_A = 0; \quad N_C\left(\frac{L\sin\phi}{\sin\theta}\right) - P(4L\cos\theta) = 0 \qquad N_C = \frac{4P\cos\theta\sin\theta}{\sin\phi}$$

From FBD (b)

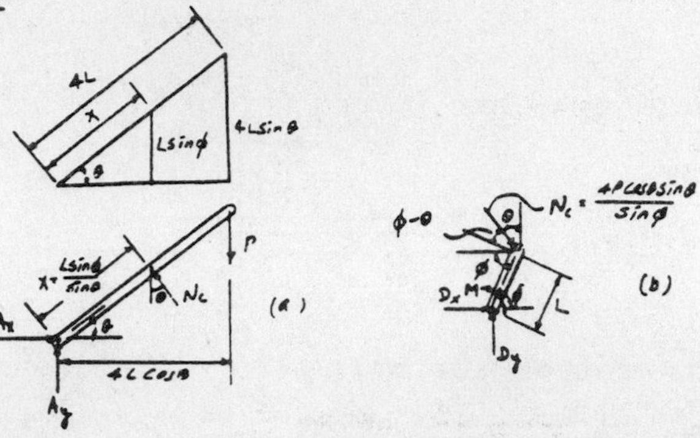

$$\curvearrowleft +\Sigma M_D = 0; \quad M - \frac{4P\cos\theta\sin\theta}{\sin\phi}[\cos(\phi-\theta)]L = 0$$

$$M = \frac{4PL\cos\theta\sin\theta}{\sin\phi}[\cos(\phi-\theta)]$$

$$= \frac{2PL\sin 2\theta}{\sin\phi}[\cos(\phi-\theta)] \qquad \textbf{Ans}$$

6-123. Determine the couple moment **M** that must be applied to member DC for equilibrium of the quick-return mechanism. Express the result in terms of the angles ϕ and θ, dimension L, and the applied horizontal load P. The block at C is confined to slide within the slot of member AB.

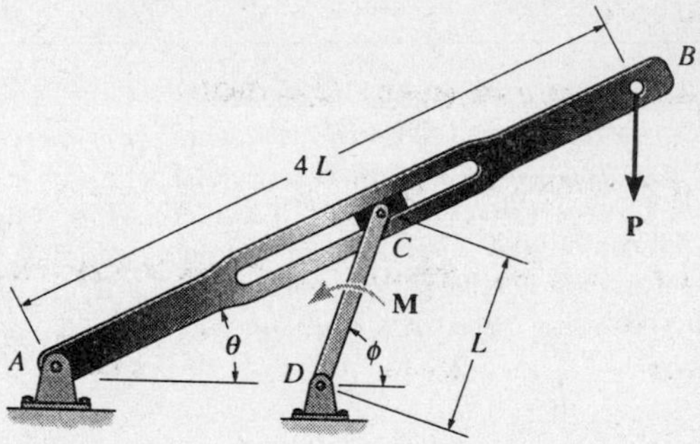

$$\frac{x}{4L} = \frac{L\sin\phi}{4L\sin\theta} \qquad x = \frac{L\sin\phi}{\sin\theta}$$

From FBD (a)

$$\curvearrowleft +\Sigma M_A = 0; \quad N_C\left(\frac{L\sin\phi}{\sin\theta}\right) - P(4L\sin\theta) = 0 \qquad N_C = \frac{4P\sin^2\theta}{\sin\phi}$$

From FBD (b)

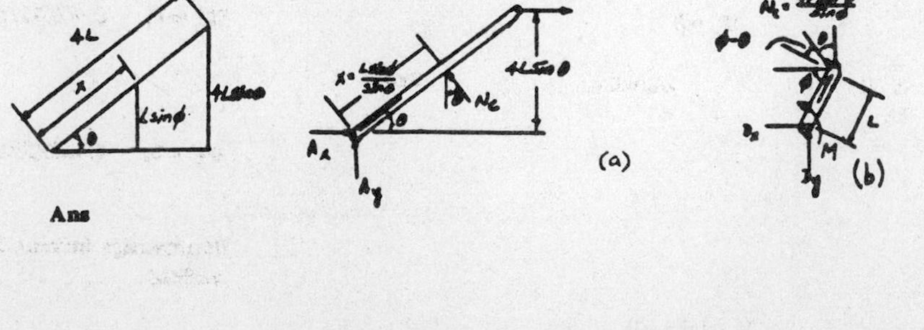

$$\curvearrowleft +\Sigma M_D = 0; \quad M - \frac{4P\sin^2\theta}{\sin\phi}[\cos(\phi-\theta)]L = 0$$

$$M = \frac{4PL\sin^2\theta}{\sin\phi}[\cos(\phi-\theta)] \qquad \textbf{Ans}$$

*6-124.** The two-member frame is connected at its ends using ball-and-socket joints. Determine the components of reaction at the supports A and C and the tension in the cable DE.

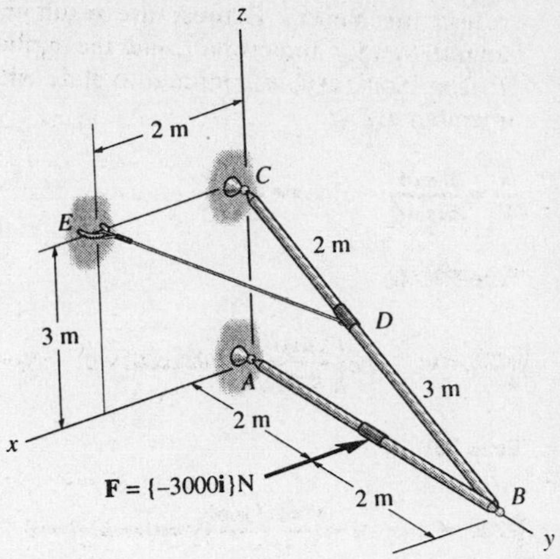

$\frac{4-y}{3} = \frac{4}{5}$; $y = 1.6\text{m}$ $\frac{z}{(4-1.6)} = \frac{3}{4}$; $z = 1.8\text{m}$

$$\mathbf{F}_{DE} = F_{DE}\left(\frac{2\mathbf{i} - 1.6\mathbf{j} + (3-1.8)\mathbf{k}}{\sqrt{2^2 + (-1.6)^2 + 1.2^2}}\right) = 0.7071F_{DE}\mathbf{i} - 0.5657F_{DE}\mathbf{j} + 0.4243F_{DE}\mathbf{k}$$

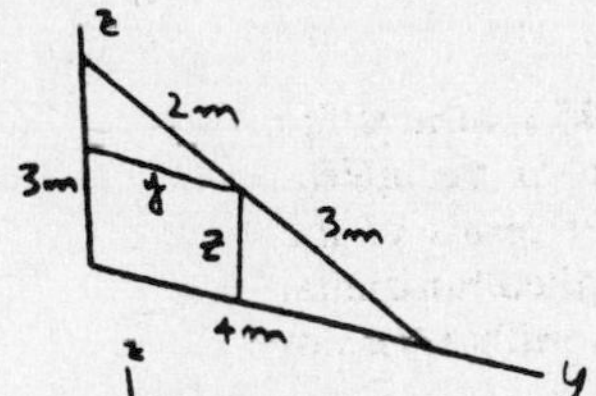

From FBD (a)

$\Sigma M_x = 0;$ $3000(2) - B_z(4) = 0$ $B_z = 1500\text{ N}$

$\Sigma M_z = 0;$ $-B_x(4) = 0$ $B_x = 0$

$\Sigma F_z = 0;$ $A_z + 1500 - 3000 = 0$ $A_z = 1500\text{ N} = 1.5\text{ kN}$ **Ans**

$\Sigma F_x = 0;$ $A_x = 0$ **Ans**

$\Sigma F_y = 0;$ $A_y - B_y = 0$ (1)

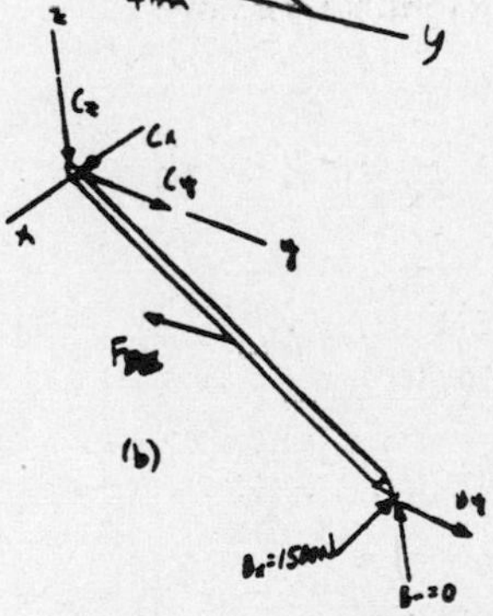

(b)

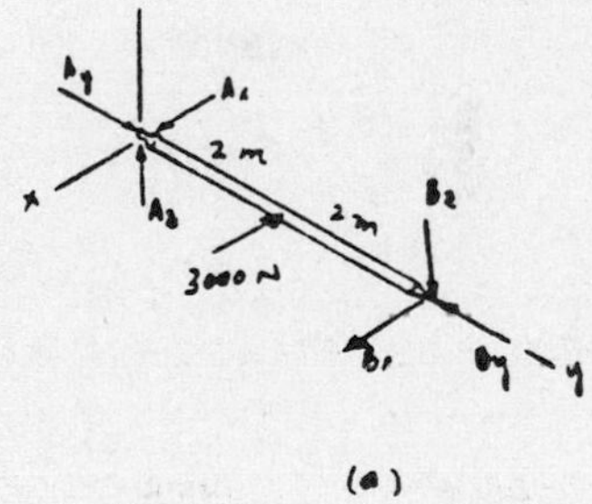

(a)

From FBD (b)

$\Sigma M_z = 0;$ $1500(4) - 0.7071F_{DE}(1.6) = 0$

$F_{DE} = 5303.3\text{ N} = 5.30\text{ kN}$ **Ans**

$\Sigma M_x = 0;$ $B_y(3) - 0.5657(5303.3)(3-1.8) + 0.4243(5303.3)(1.6) = 0$

$B_y = 0$

From Eq. (1) $A_y = 0$ **Ans**

$\Sigma F_x = 0;$ $C_x + 0.7071(5303.3) - 1500 = 0$

$C_x = -2250\text{ N} = -2.25\text{ kN}$ **Ans**

$\Sigma F_y = 0;$ $C_y - 0.5657(5303.3) = 0$

$C_y = 3000\text{ N} = 3.0\text{ kN}$ **Ans**

$\Sigma F_z = 0;$ $0.4243(5303.3) - C_z = 0$ $C_z = 2250\text{ N} = 2.25\text{ kN}$ **Ans**

Negative sign indicates C_x acts in the opposite sense of that shown on the FBD.

6-125. The Spider Power Drive Co. manufactures the symmetrical tripod, which permits access through a hatched opening in a silo, digester, or similar structure. If a suspended load has a weight of 700 lb, determine the force in each of the cables AB, BC, and CA, and the force in legs AD, BE, and CF, when the load is descending at a constant velocity. The legs rest on a smooth surface at A, B, and C.

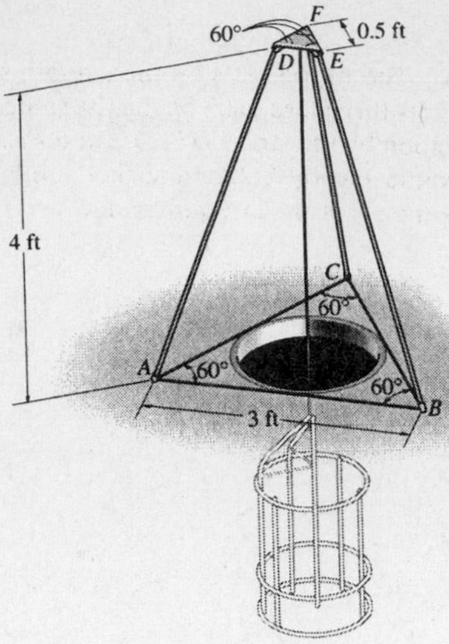

Each leg is a two - force member.

$$\theta = \tan^{-1}\left(\frac{4}{1.4434}\right) = 70.158°$$

Top plate :

$\Sigma F_z = 0;\quad 3\,F \sin 70.158° - 700 = 0$

$F = 248.06 = 248 \text{ lb}$ **Ans**

Bottom of leg :

$\Sigma F_x = 0;\quad 2\,T \cos 30° - 248.06 \cos 70.158° = 0$

$T = 48.6 \text{ lb}$ **Ans**

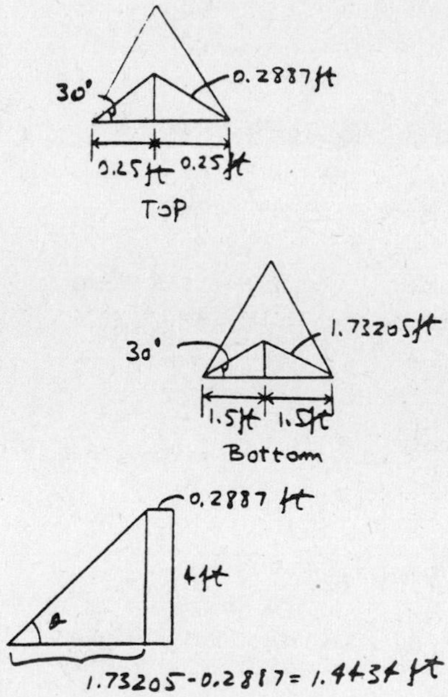

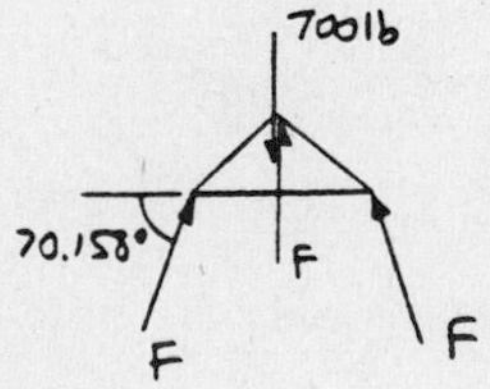

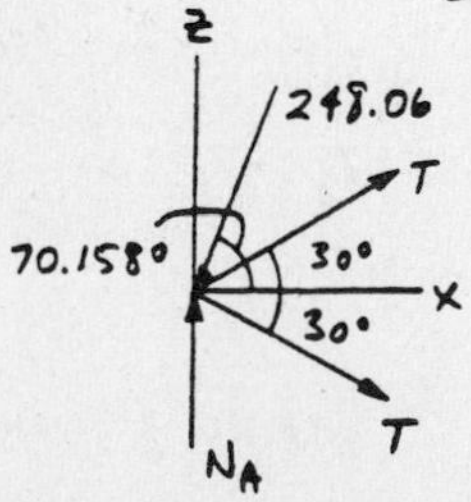

6-126. The tripod rests on the smooth surface at A, B, and C. Its three legs, each havng the same length, are held in position by the struts DE, DF, and FE. If the members are connected by ball-and-socket joints, determine the force in each strut for equilibrium.

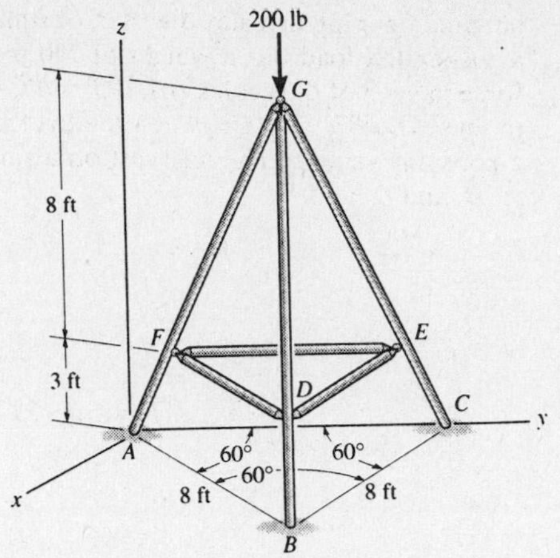

Due to the symmetry of geometry and loading $A_z = B_z = C_z = F_z$ and $F_{DE} = F_{DF} = F_{EF} = F$.

Equilibrium for entire frame :

$\Sigma F_z = 0;\quad 3F_z - 200 = 0 \quad F_z = 66.67\ \text{lb}$

Equilibrium of member AFG : The distance $AG' = (4/\cos 30°) = 4.619$ ft.

$\Sigma M_{z'} = 0;\quad 2(F\cos 30°)(8) - 66.67(4.619) = 0 \quad F = 22.2\ \text{lb}$

$F_{DF} = F_{FE} = F_{DE} = 22.2\ \text{lb}$ **Ans**

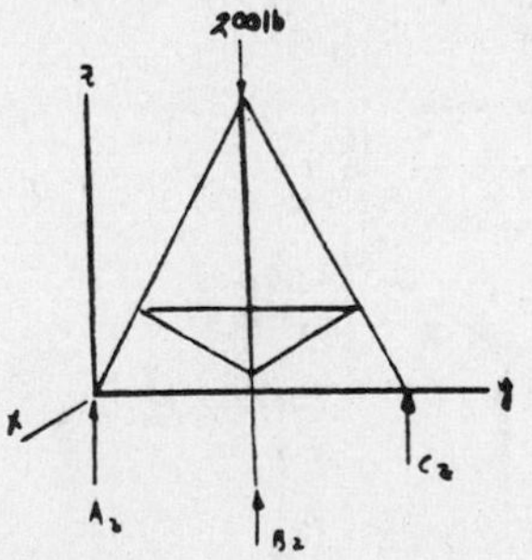

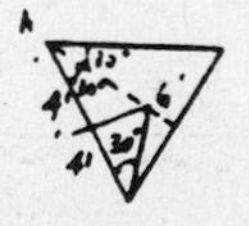

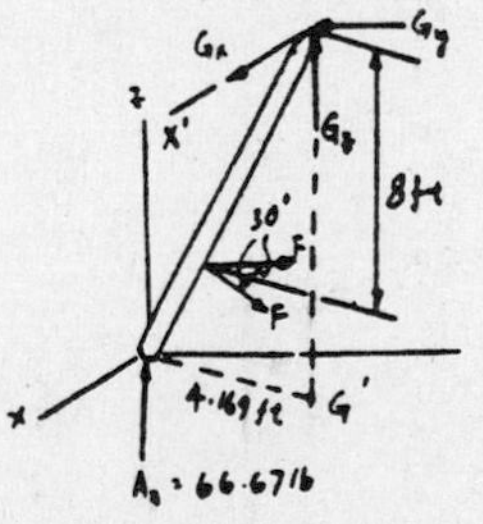

6-127. The structure is subjected to the loadings shown. Member AD is supported by a cable AB and roller at C and fits through a smooth circular hole at D. Member ED is supported by a roller at D and a pole that fits in a smooth snug circular hole at E. Determine the x, y, z components of reaction at E and the tension in cable AB.

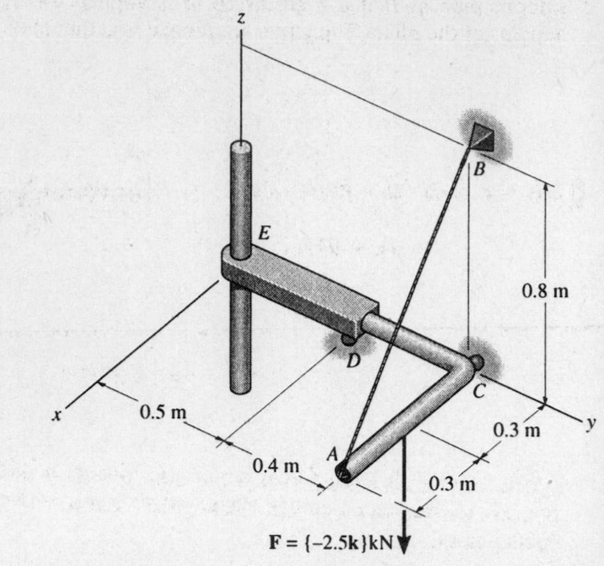

From FBD (a)

$\Sigma M_y = 0;$ $\quad M_{By} = 0$

$\Sigma M_x = 0;$ $\quad -M_{Bx} + 800 = 0 \qquad M_{Bx} = 800\ \text{N}\cdot\text{m}$

$\Sigma M_z = 0;$ $\quad B_y(3) - B_x(2) = 0 \qquad (1)$

$\Sigma F_z = 0;$ $\quad A_z = 0 \qquad$ **Ans**

$\Sigma F_x = 0;$ $\quad -A_x + B_x = 0 \qquad (2)$

$\Sigma F_y = 0;$ $\quad -A_y + B_y = 0 \qquad (3)$

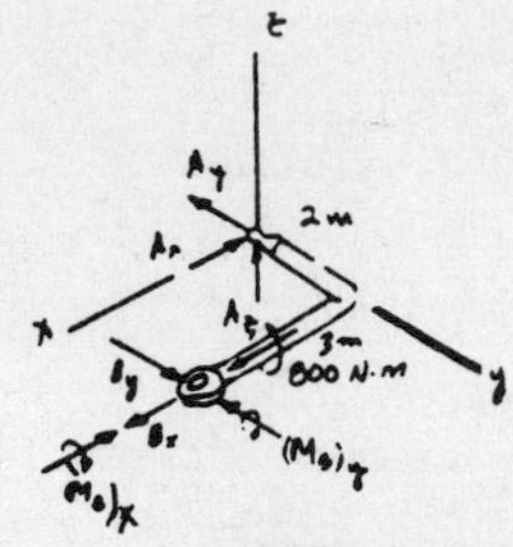

(a)

From FBD (b)

$\Sigma M_z = 0;$ $\quad B_y(1.5) + 800 - 250\cos 45°(5.5) = 0 \qquad B_y = 114.85\ \text{N}$

From Eq. (1) $\quad 114.85(3) - B_x(2) = 0 \qquad B_x = 172.27\ \text{N}$

From Eq. (2) $\quad A_x = 172\ \text{N} \qquad$ **Ans**

From Eq. (3) $\quad A_y = 115\ \text{N} \qquad$ **Ans**

$\Sigma F_x = 0;$ $\quad C_x + 250\cos 60° - 172.27 = 0 \qquad C_x = 47.3\ \text{N} \qquad$ **Ans**

$\Sigma F_y = 0;$ $\quad 250\cos 45° - 114.85 - C_y = 0 \qquad C_y = 61.9\ \text{N} \qquad$ **Ans**

$\Sigma F_z = 0;$ $\quad 250\cos 60° - C_z = 0 \qquad C_z = 125\ \text{N} \qquad$ **Ans**

$\Sigma M_y = 0;$ $\quad M_{Cy} - 172.27(1.5) + 250\cos 60°(5.5) = 0$

$M_{Cy} = -429\ \text{N}\cdot\text{m} \qquad$ **Ans**

$\Sigma M_z = 0;$ $\quad M_{Cz} = 0 \qquad$ **Ans**

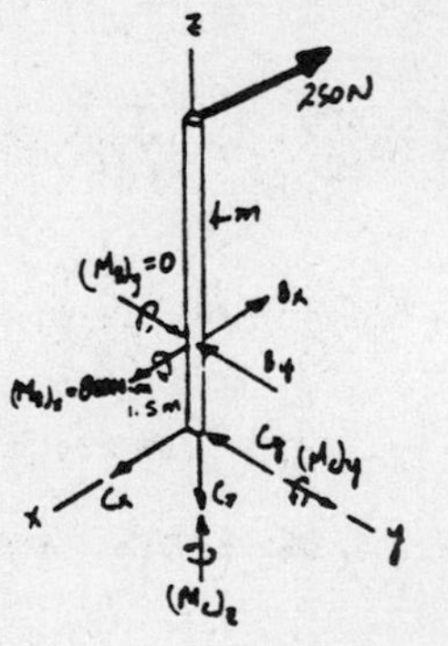

(b)

Negative sign indicates that M_{Cy} acts in the opposite sense to that shown on FBD.

*6-128. Determine the clamping force exerted on the smooth pipe at B if a force of 20 lb is applied to the handles of the pliers. The pliers are pinned together at A.

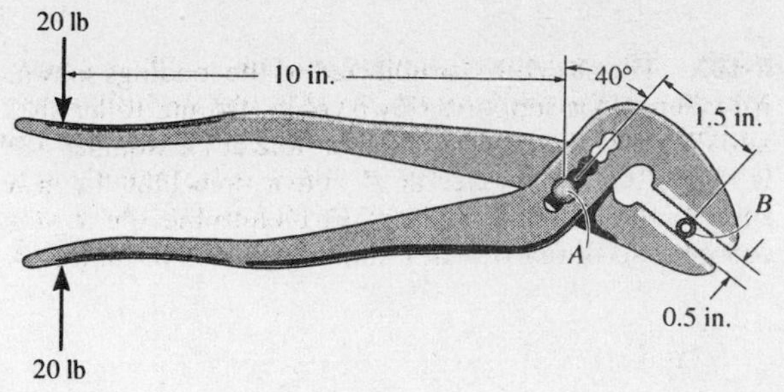

$\circlearrowleft + \Sigma M_A = 0;\quad 20\,(10) - 1.5\,(F_B) = 0$

$F_B = 133$ lb **Ans**

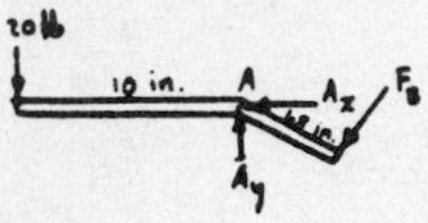

6-129. Determine the forces which the pins at A and B exert on the two-member frame which supports the 100-kg crate.

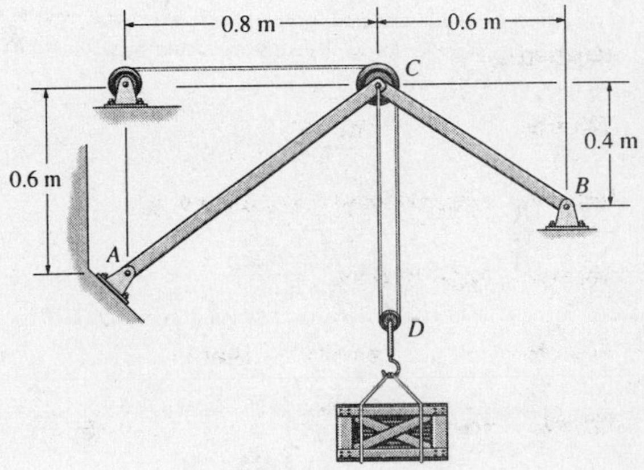

AC and BC are two-force members.

Pin C:

$\xrightarrow{+} \Sigma F_x = 0;\quad F_{AC}\left(\frac{4}{5}\right) - F_{BC}\left(\frac{3}{\sqrt{13}}\right) - 50(9.81) = 0$

$+\uparrow \Sigma F_y = 0;\quad F_{AC}\left(\frac{3}{5}\right) + F_{BC}\left(\frac{2}{\sqrt{13}}\right) - 100(9.81) = 0$

$F_{AC} = 1154\text{ N} = 1.15\text{ kN}$ **Ans**

$F_{BC} = 520\text{ N}$ **Ans**

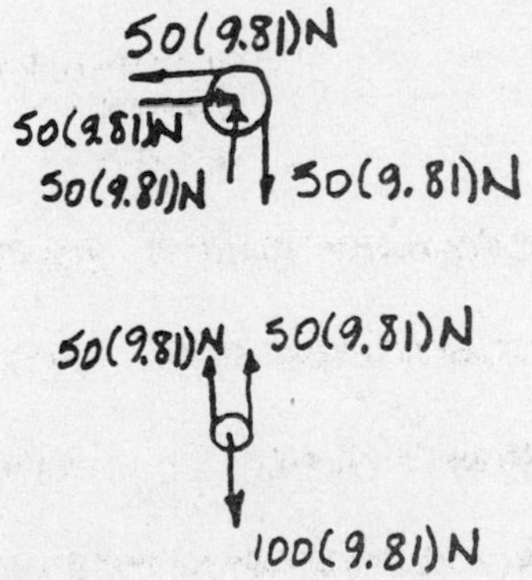

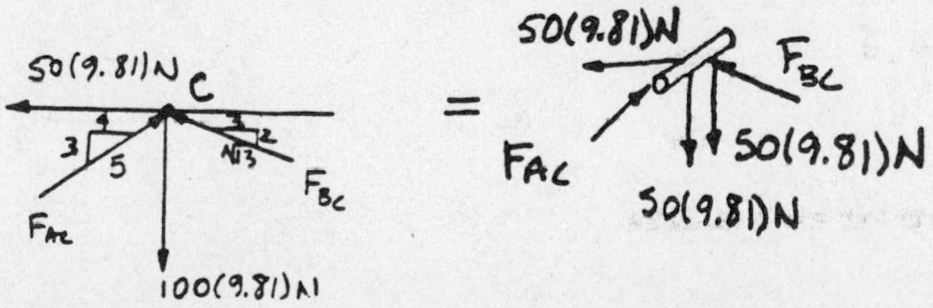

6-130. Determine the force in each member of the truss and state if the members are in tension or compression.

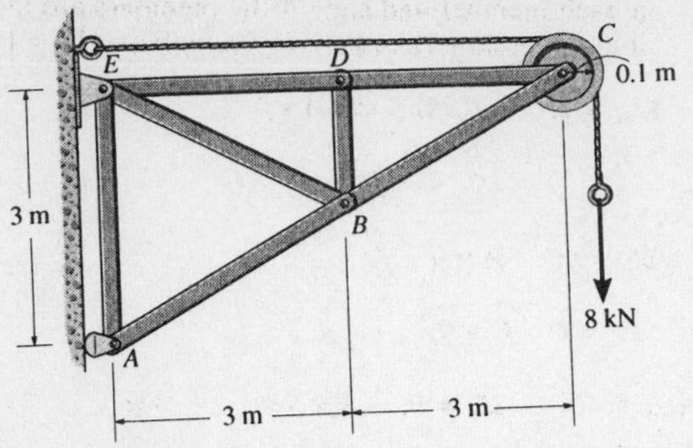

Method of Joint : In this case, support reactions are not required for determining the member forces. By inspection, members *DB* and *BE* are zero force members. Hence

$$F_{DB} = F_{BE} = 0 \qquad \textbf{Ans}$$

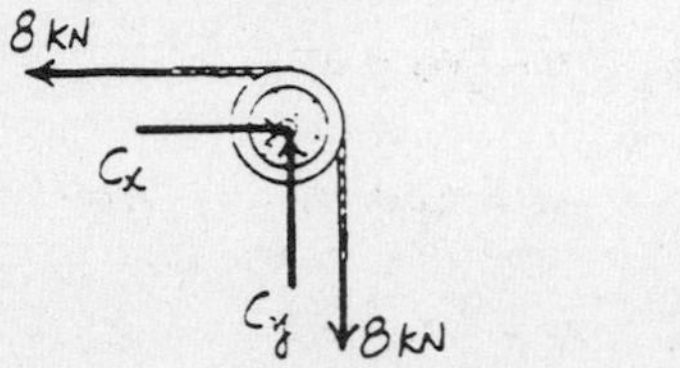

Joint C

$+\uparrow \Sigma F_y = 0; \quad F_{CB}\left(\frac{1}{\sqrt{5}}\right) - 8 = 0$

$F_{CB} = 17.89 \text{ kN (C)} = 17.9 \text{ kN(C)} \qquad$ **Ans**

$\overset{+}{\rightarrow} \Sigma F_x = 0; \quad 17.89\left(\frac{2}{\sqrt{5}}\right) - 8 - F_{CD} = 0$

$F_{CD} = 8.00 \text{ kN (T)} \qquad$ **Ans**

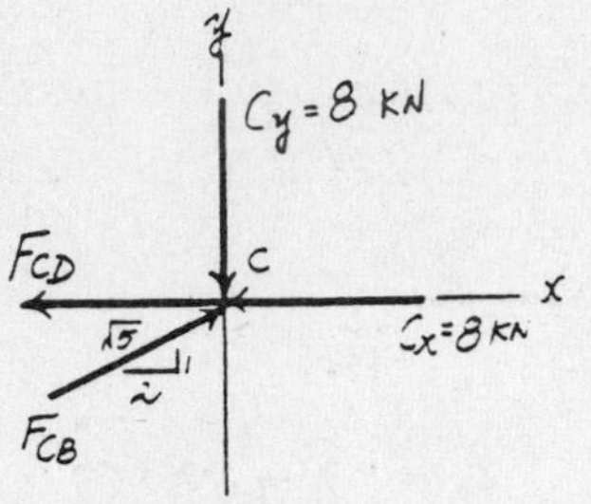

Joint D

$\overset{+}{\rightarrow} \Sigma F_x = 0; \quad 8.00 - F_{DE} = 0 \quad F_{DE} = 8.00 \text{ kN (T)} \qquad$ **Ans**

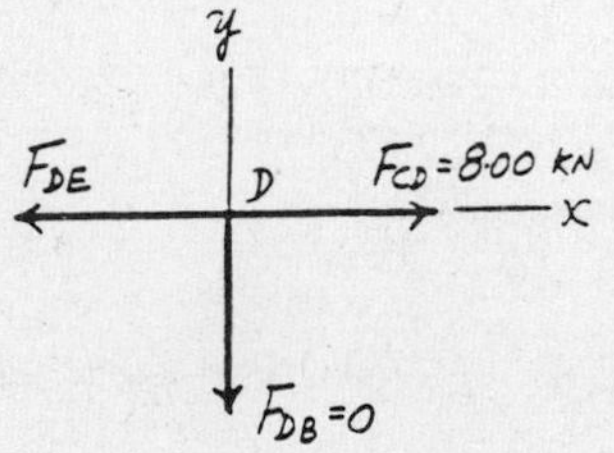

Joint B

$+ \; \Sigma F_{x'} = 0; \quad F_{BA} - 17.89 = 0$

$F_{BA} = 17.89 \text{ kN (C)} = 17.9 \text{ kN(C)} \qquad$ **Ans**

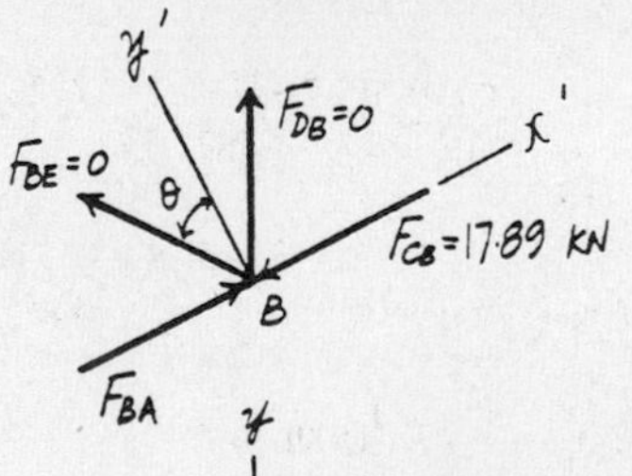

Joint A

$+\uparrow \Sigma F_y = 0; \quad F_{AE} - 17.89\left(\frac{1}{\sqrt{5}}\right) = 0$

$F_{AE} = 8.00 \text{ kN (T)} \qquad$ **Ans**

$\overset{+}{\rightarrow} \Sigma F_x = 0; \quad A_x - 17.89\left(\frac{2}{\sqrt{5}}\right) = 0 \quad A_x = 16.0 \text{ kN}$

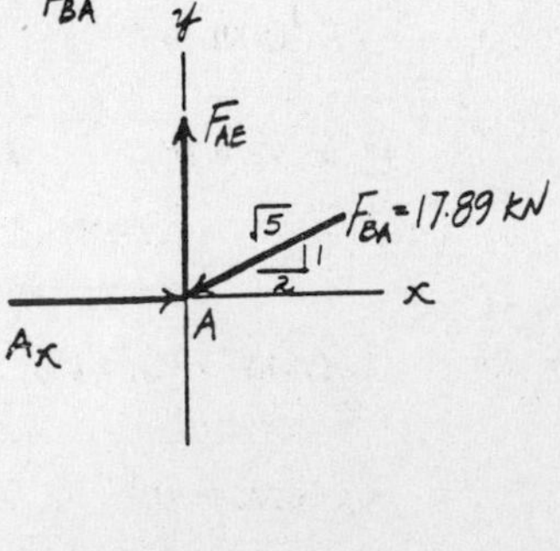

Note : The support reactions E_x and E_y can be determined by analyzing Joint *E* using the results obtained above.

6-131. The space truss is supported by a ball-and-socket joint at D and short links at C and E. Determine the force in each member and state if the members are in tension or compression. Take $\mathbf{F}_1 = \{-500\mathbf{k}\}$ lb and $\mathbf{F}_2 = \{400\mathbf{j}\}$ lb.

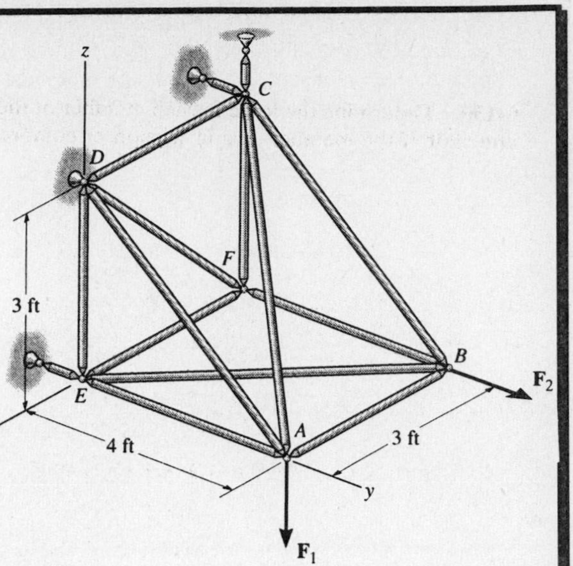

$\Sigma M_z = 0;\quad -C_y(3) - 400(3) = 0$

$C_y = -400$ lb

$\Sigma F_x = 0;\quad D_x = 0$

$\Sigma M_y = 0;\quad C_z = 0$

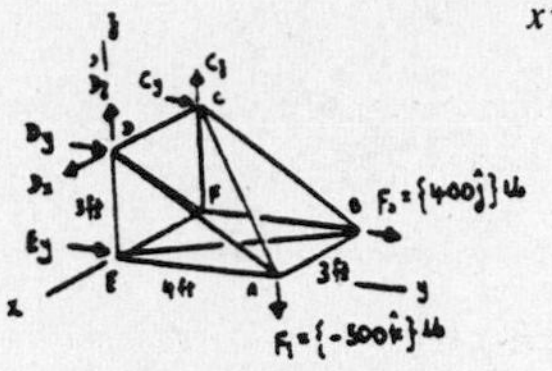

Joint F: $\quad \Sigma F_y = 0;\quad F_{BF} = 0$ **Ans**

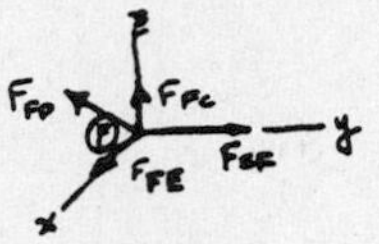

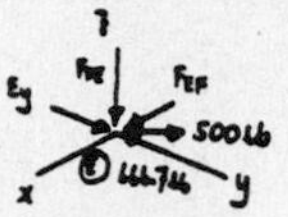

Joint B:

$\Sigma F_z = 0;\quad F_{BC} = 0$ **Ans**

$\Sigma F_y = 0;\quad 400 - \frac{4}{5}F_{BE} = 0$

$F_{BE} = 500$ lb (T) **Ans**

$\Sigma F_x = 0;\quad F_{AB} - \frac{3}{5}(500) = 0$

$F_{AB} = 300$ lb (C) **Ans**

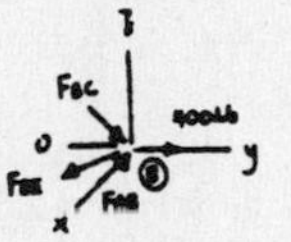

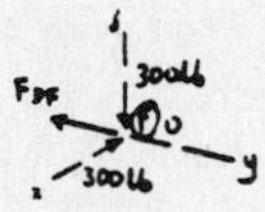

Joint A:

$\Sigma F_x = 0;\quad 300 - \frac{3}{\sqrt{34}}F_{AC} = 0$

$F_{AC} = 583.1 = 583$ lb (T) **Ans**

$\Sigma F_z = 0;\quad \frac{3}{\sqrt{34}}(583.1) - 500 + \frac{3}{5}F_{AD} = 0$

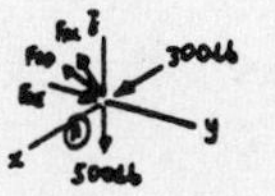

$F_{AD} = 333$ lb (T) **Ans**

$\Sigma F_y = 0;\quad F_{AE} - \frac{4}{5}(333.3) - \frac{4}{\sqrt{34}}(583.1) = 0$

$F_{AE} = 667$ lb (C) **Ans**

Joint E:

$\Sigma F_z = 0;\quad F_{DE} = 0$ **Ans**

$\Sigma F_x = 0;\quad F_{EF} - \frac{3}{5}(500) = 0$

$F_{EF} = 300$ lb (C) **Ans**

Joint C:

$\Sigma F_x = 0;\quad \frac{3}{\sqrt{34}}(583.1) - F_{CD} = 0$

$F_{CD} = 300$ lb (C) **Ans**

$\Sigma F_z = 0;\quad F_{CF} - \frac{3}{\sqrt{34}}(583.1) = 0$

$F_{CF} = 300$ lb (C) **Ans**

$\Sigma F_y = 0;\quad \frac{4}{\sqrt{34}}(583.1) - 400 = 0$ **Check!**

Joint F:

$\Sigma F_x = 0;\quad \frac{3}{\sqrt{18}}F_{DF} - 300 = 0$

$F_{DF} = 424$ lb (T) **Ans**

$\Sigma F_z = 0;\quad \frac{3}{\sqrt{18}}(424.3) - 300 = 0$ **Check!**

***6-132.** The space truss is supported by a ball-and-socket joint at D and short links at C and E. Determine the force in each member and state if the members are in tension or compression. Take $\mathbf{F}_1 = \{200\mathbf{i} + 300\mathbf{j} - 500\mathbf{k}\}$ lb and $\mathbf{F}_2 = \{400\mathbf{j}\}$ lb.

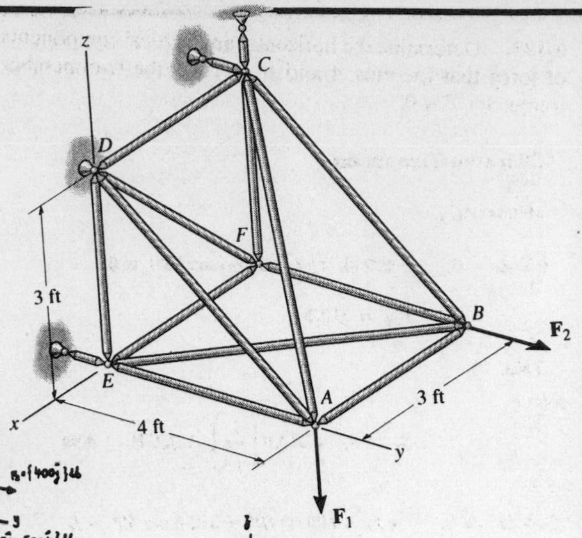

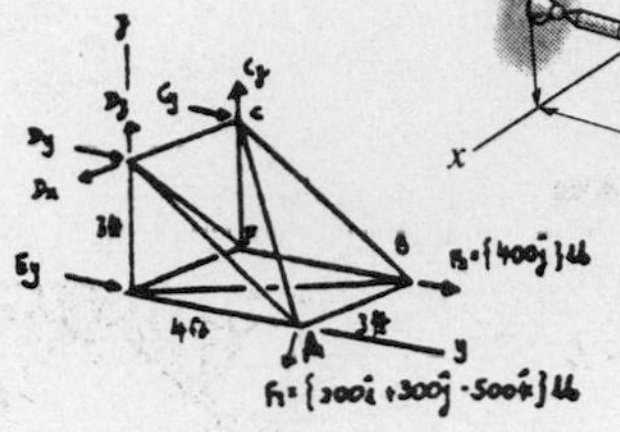

$\Sigma F_x = 0;\quad D_x + 200 = 0$

$D_x = -200$ lb

$\Sigma M_z = 0;\quad -C_y(3) - 400(3) - 200(4) = 0$

$C_y = -666.7$ lb

$\Sigma M_y = 0;\quad C_z(3) - 200(3) = 0$

$C_z = 200$ lb

Joint F:

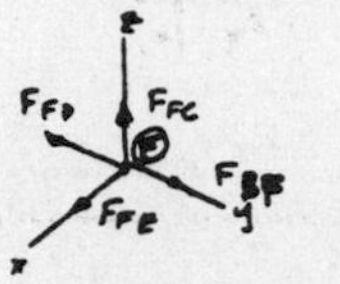

$\Sigma F_y = 0;\quad F_{BF} = 0$ **Ans**

Joint B:

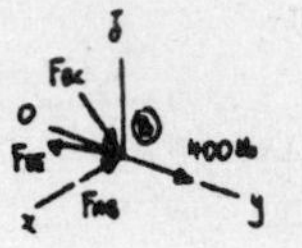

$\Sigma F_z = 0;\quad F_{BC} = 0$ **Ans**

$\Sigma F_y = 0;\quad 400 - \frac{4}{5}F_{BE} = 0$

$F_{BE} = 500$ lb (T) **Ans**

$\Sigma F_x = 0;\quad F_{AB} - \frac{3}{5}(500) = 0$

$F_{AB} = 300$ lb (C) **Ans**

Joint A:

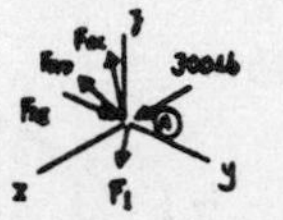

$\Sigma F_x = 0;\quad 300 + 200 - \frac{3}{\sqrt{34}}F_{AC} = 0$

$F_{AC} = 971.8 = 972$ lb (T) **Ans**

$\Sigma F_z = 0;\quad \frac{3}{\sqrt{34}}(971.8) - 500 + \frac{3}{5}F_{AD} = 0$

$F_{AD} = 0$ **Ans**

$\Sigma F_y = 0;\quad F_{AE} + 300 - \frac{4}{\sqrt{34}}(971.8) = 0$

$F_{AE} = 367$ lb (C) **Ans**

Joint E:

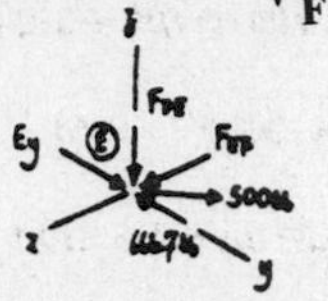

$\Sigma F_z = 0;\quad F_{DE} = 0$ **Ans**

$\Sigma F_x = 0;\quad F_{EF} - \frac{3}{5}(500) = 0$

$F_{EF} = 300$ lb (C) **Ans**

Joint C:

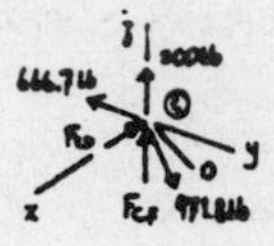

$\Sigma F_x = 0;\quad \frac{3}{\sqrt{34}}(971.8) - F_{CD} = 0$

$F_{CD} = 500$ lb (C) **Ans**

$\Sigma F_z = 0;\quad F_{CF} - \frac{3}{\sqrt{34}}(971.8) + 200 = 0$

$F_{CF} = 300$ lb (C) **Ans**

$\Sigma F_y = 0;\quad \frac{4}{\sqrt{34}}(971.8) - 666.7 = 0$ **Check!**

Joint F:

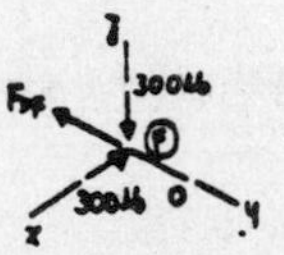

$\Sigma F_x = 0;\quad \frac{3}{\sqrt{18}}F_{DF} - 300 = 0$

$F_{DF} = 424$ lb (T) **Ans**

6-133. Determine the horizontal and vertical components of force that the pins A and B exert on the two-member frame. Set $F = 0$.

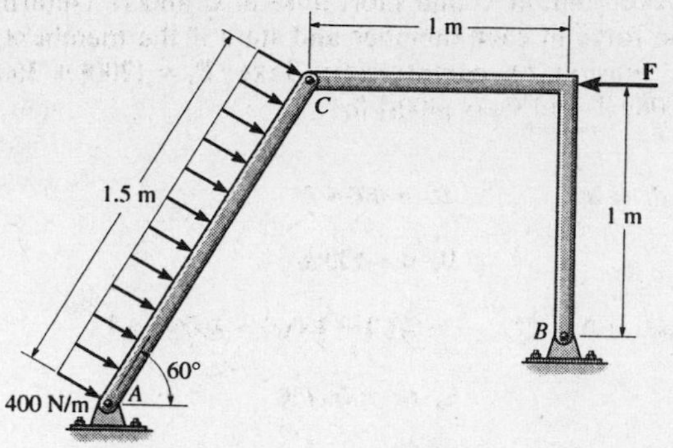

CB is a two - force member.

Member *AC* :

$\circlearrowleft + \Sigma M_A = 0; \quad -600\,(0.75) + 1.5\,(F_{CB} \sin 75°) = 0$

$F_{CB} = 310.6$

Thus,

$B_x = B_y = 310.6\left(\frac{1}{\sqrt{2}}\right) = 220 \text{ N} \quad \text{Ans}$

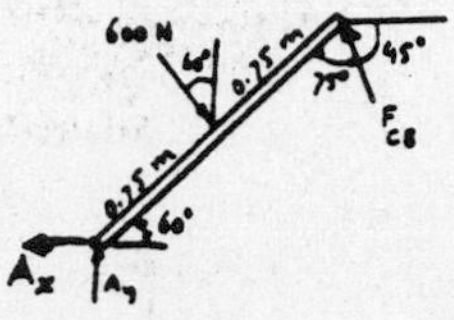

$\xrightarrow{+} \Sigma F_x = 0; \quad -A_x + 600 \sin 60° - 310.6 \cos 45° = 0$

$A_x = 300 \text{ N} \quad \text{Ans}$

$+\uparrow \Sigma F_y = 0; \quad A_y - 600 \cos 60° + 310.6 \sin 45° = 0$

$A_y = 80.4 \text{ N} \quad \text{Ans}$

6-134. Determine the horizontal and vertical components of force that pins A and B exert on the two-member frame. Set $F = 500$ N.

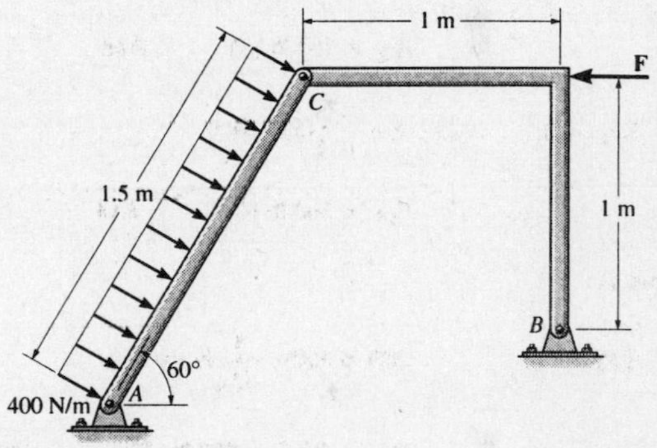

Member *AC* :

$\circlearrowleft + \Sigma M_A = 0; \quad -600\,(0.75) - C_y\,(1.5 \cos 60°) + C_x\,(1.5 \sin 60°) = 0$

Member *CB* :

$\circlearrowleft + \Sigma M_B = 0; \quad -C_x\,(1) - C_y\,(1) + 500\,(1) = 0$

Solving,

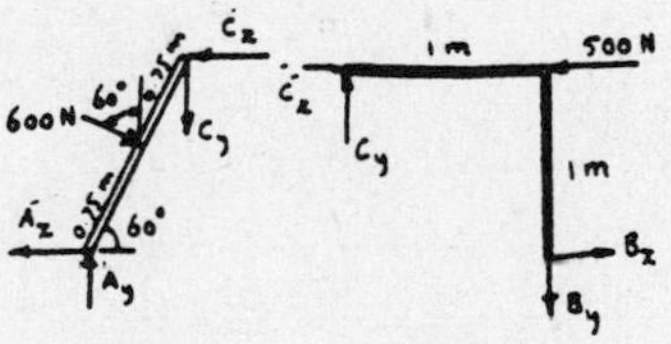

$C_x = 402.6 \text{ N}$

$C_y = 97.4 \text{ N}$

Member *AC* :

$\xrightarrow{+} \Sigma F_x = 0; \quad -A_x + 600 \sin 60° - 402.6 = 0$

$A_x = 117 \text{ N} \quad \text{Ans}$

$+\uparrow \Sigma F_y = 0; \quad A_y - 600 \cos 60° - 97.4 = 0$

$A_y = 397 \text{ N} \quad \text{Ans}$

Member *CB* :

$\xrightarrow{+} \Sigma F_x = 0; \quad 402.6 - 500 + B_x = 0$

$B_x = 97.4 \text{ N} \quad \text{Ans}$

$+\uparrow \Sigma F_y = 0; \quad -B_y + 97.4 = 0$

$B_y = 97.4 \text{ N} \quad \text{Ans}$

6-135. The two-bar mechanism consists of a lever arm AB and smooth link CD, which has a fixed collar at its end C and a roller at the other end D. Determine the force $\mathbf{P}$ needed to hold the lever in the position θ. The spring has a stiffness k and unstretched length $2L$. The roller contacts either the top or bottom portion of the horizontal guide.

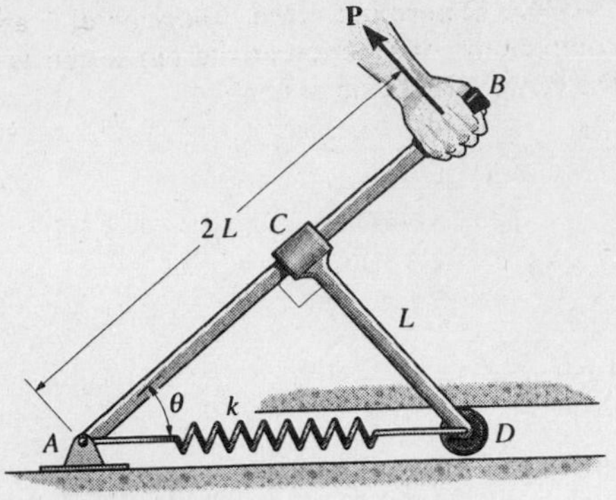

Free Body Diagram **:** The spring compresses $x = 2L - \frac{L}{\sin\theta}$. Then, the spring force developed is $F_{sp} = kx = kL\left(2 - \frac{1}{\sin\theta}\right)$.

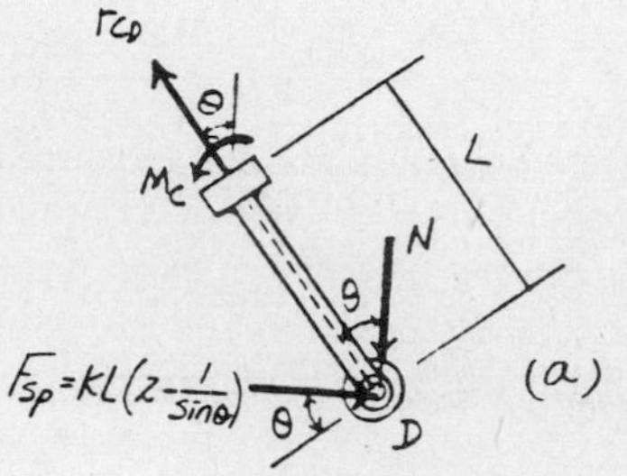

Equations of Equilibrium **:** From FBD (a),

$$\overset{+}{\rightarrow}\Sigma F_x = 0; \quad kL\left(2 - \frac{1}{\sin\theta}\right) - F_{CD}\sin\theta = 0$$

$$F_{CD} = \frac{kL}{\sin\theta}\left(2 - \frac{1}{\sin\theta}\right)$$

$$+\Sigma M_D = 0; \quad M_C = 0$$

From FBD (b),

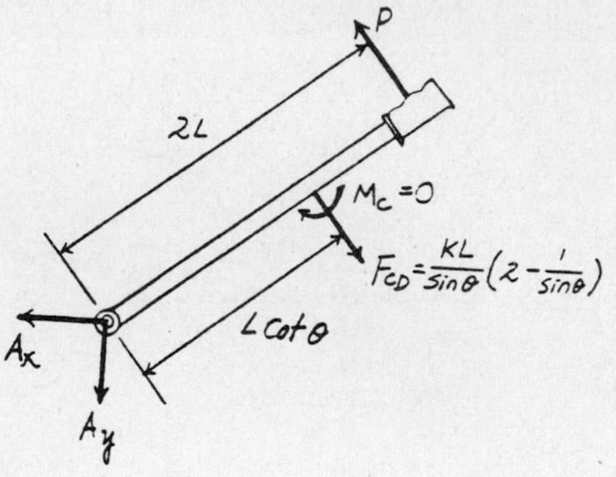

$$+\Sigma M_A = 0; \quad P(2L) - \frac{kL}{\sin\theta}\left(2 - \frac{1}{\sin\theta}\right)(L\cot\theta) = 0$$

$$P = \frac{kL}{2\tan\theta\sin\theta}(2 - \csc\theta) \quad \textbf{Ans}$$

*6-136. Determine the horizontal and vertical components of reaction at the pin supports A and E of the compound beam assembly.

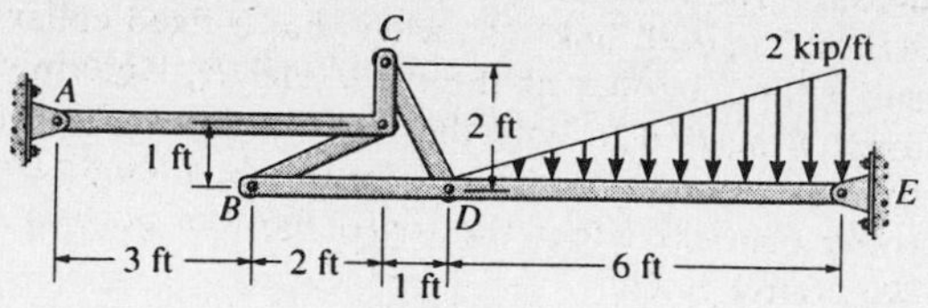

Member BDE :

$$\curvearrowleft + \Sigma M_E = 0; \quad 6(2) + T\left(\frac{2}{\sqrt{5}}\right)(6) - R\left(\frac{1}{\sqrt{5}}\right)(9) = 0$$

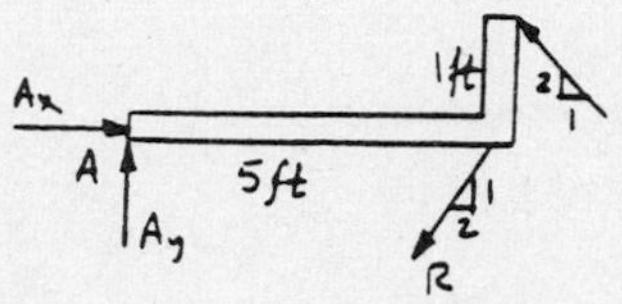

Member AC :

$$\curvearrowleft + \Sigma M_A = 0; \quad T\left(\frac{1}{\sqrt{5}}\right)(1) + T\left(\frac{2}{\sqrt{5}}\right)(5) - R\left(\frac{1}{\sqrt{5}}\right)(5) = 0$$

Solving,

$$T = 3.440 \text{ kip}, \quad R = 7.568 \text{ kip}$$

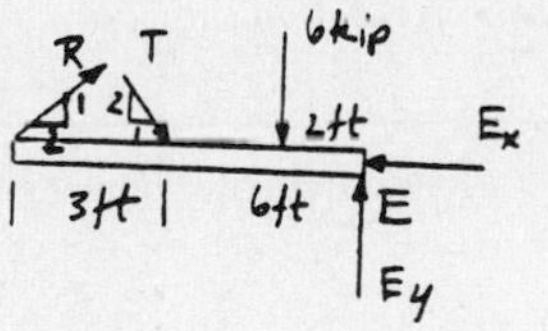

Member AC :

$$\xrightarrow{+} \Sigma F_x = 0; \quad A_x - 7.568\left(\frac{2}{\sqrt{5}}\right) - 3.440\left(\frac{1}{\sqrt{5}}\right) = 0$$

$$A_x = 8.31 \text{ kip} \quad \textbf{Ans}$$

$$+\uparrow \Sigma F_y = 0; \quad A_y - 7.568\left(\frac{1}{\sqrt{5}}\right) + 3.440\left(\frac{2}{\sqrt{5}}\right) = 0$$

$$A_y = 0.308 \text{ kip} \quad \textbf{Ans}$$

Member BDE :

$$\xrightarrow{+} \Sigma F_x = 0; \quad 7.568\left(\frac{2}{\sqrt{5}}\right) + 3.440\left(\frac{1}{\sqrt{5}}\right) - E_x = 0$$

$$E_x = 8.31 \text{ kip} \quad \textbf{Ans}$$

$$+\uparrow \Sigma F_y = 0; \quad 7.568\left(\frac{1}{\sqrt{5}}\right) - 3.440\left(\frac{2}{\sqrt{5}}\right) - 6 + E_y = 0$$

$$E_y = 5.69 \text{ kip} \quad \textbf{Ans}$$

6-137. Determine the force in members AB, AD, and AC of the space truss and state if the members are in tension or compression.

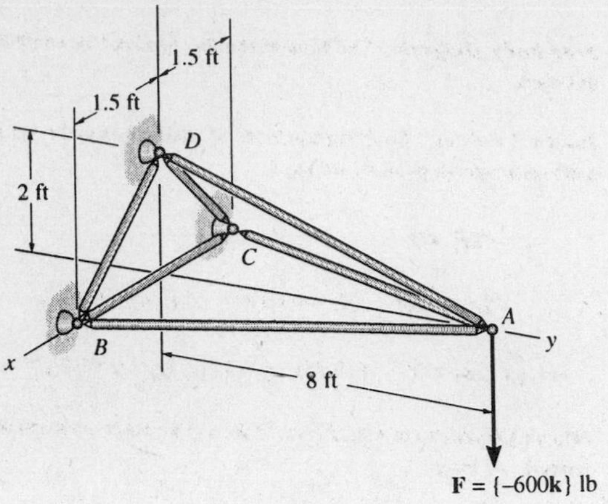

Method of Joints : **In this case the support reactions are not required for determining the member forces.**

Joint ***A***

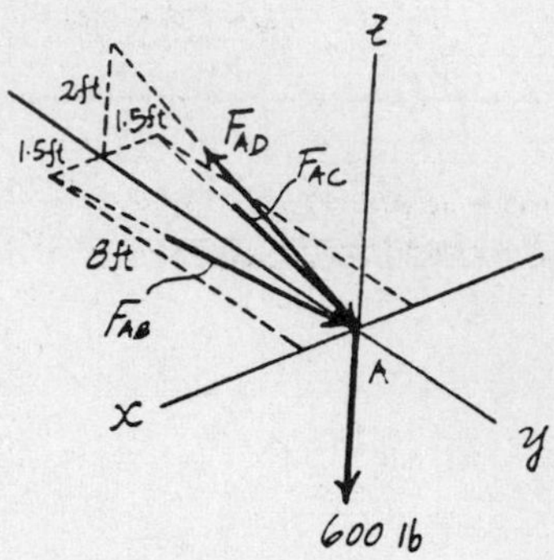

$$\Sigma F_z = 0; \quad F_{AD}\left(\frac{2}{\sqrt{68}}\right) - 600 = 0$$

$$F_{AD} = 2473.86 \text{ lb (T)} = 2.47 \text{ kip (T)} \qquad \textbf{Ans}$$

$$\Sigma F_x = 0; \quad F_{AC}\left(\frac{1.5}{\sqrt{66.25}}\right) - F_{AB}\left(\frac{1.5}{\sqrt{66.25}}\right) = 0$$

$$F_{AC} = F_{AB} \qquad [1]$$

$$\Sigma F_y = 0; \quad F_{AC}\left(\frac{8}{\sqrt{66.25}}\right) + F_{AB}\left(\frac{8}{\sqrt{66.25}}\right) - 2473.86\left(\frac{8}{\sqrt{68}}\right) = 0$$

$$0.9829F_{AC} + 0.9829F_{AB} = 2400 \qquad [2]$$

Solving Eqs. [1] and [2] yields

$$F_{AC} = F_{AB} = 1220.91 \text{ lb (C)} = 1.22 \text{ kip (C)} \qquad \textbf{Ans}$$

7-1. The column is fixed to the floor and is subjected to the loads shown. Determine the internal normal force, shear force, and moment at points A and B.

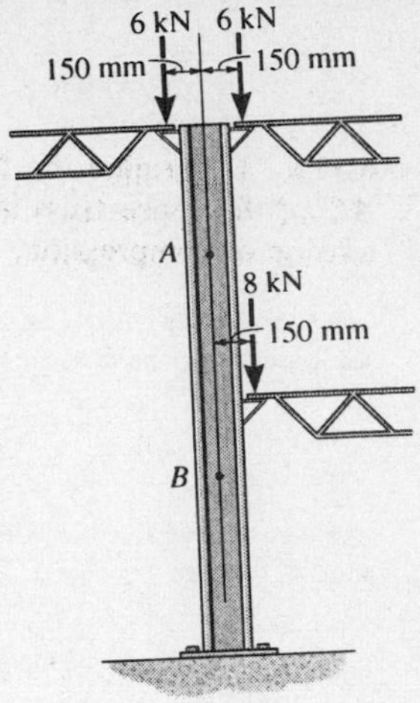

Free body Diagram : The support reaction need not be computed in this case.

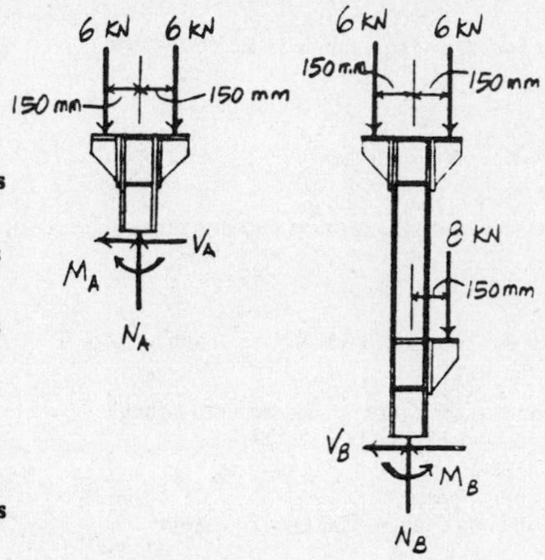

Internal Forces : Applying equations of equilibrium to the top segment sectioned through point A, we have

$\overset{+}{\rightarrow} \Sigma F_x = 0; \quad V_A = 0$ **Ans**

$+\uparrow \Sigma F_y = 0; \quad N_A - 6 - 6 = 0 \quad N_A = 12.0\ \text{kN}$ **Ans**

$\circlearrowleft + \Sigma M_A = 0; \quad 6(0.15) - 6(0.15) - M_A = 0 \quad M_A = 0$ **Ans**

Applying equations of equilibrium to the top segment sectioned through point B, we have

$\overset{+}{\rightarrow} \Sigma F_x = 0; \quad V_B = 0$ **Ans**

$+\uparrow \Sigma F_y = 0; \quad N_B - 6 - 6 - 8 = 0 \quad N_B = 20.0\ \text{kN}$ **Ans**

$+\Sigma M_B = 0; \quad 6(0.15) - 6(0.15) - 8(0.15) + M_B = 0$

$M_B = 1.20\ \text{kN}\cdot\text{m}$ **Ans**

7-2. The rod is subjected to the forces shown. Determine the internal normal force at points A, B, and C.

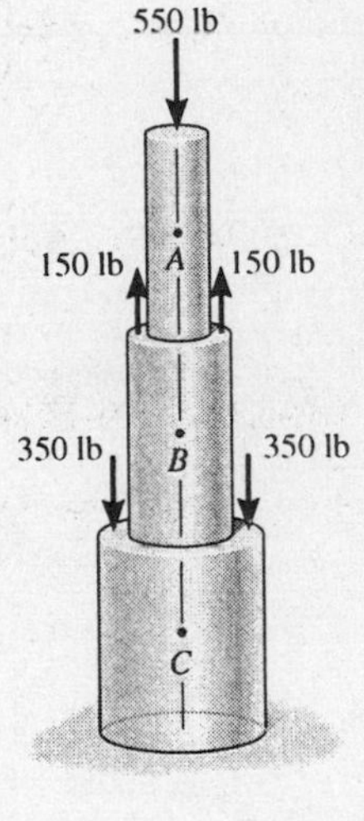

Free body Diagram : The support reaction need not be computed in this case.

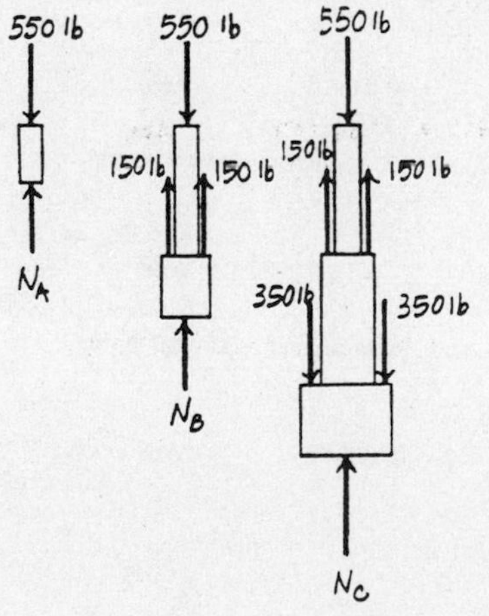

Internal Forces : Applying equations of equilibrium to the top segment sectioned through point A, we have

$+\uparrow \Sigma F_y = 0; \quad N_A - 550 = 0 \quad N_A = 550\ \text{lb}$ **Ans**

Applying equations of equilibrium to the top segment sectioned through point B, we have

$+\uparrow \Sigma F_y = 0; \quad N_B - 550 + 150 + 150 = 0$

$N_B = 250\ \text{lb}$ **Ans**

Applying equations of equilibrium to the top segment sectioned through point C, we have

$+\uparrow \Sigma F_y = 0; \quad N_C - 550 + 150 + 150 - 350 - 350 = 0$

$N_C = 950\ \text{lb}$ **Ans**

7-3. The forces act on the shaft shown. Determine the internal normal force at points A, B, and C.

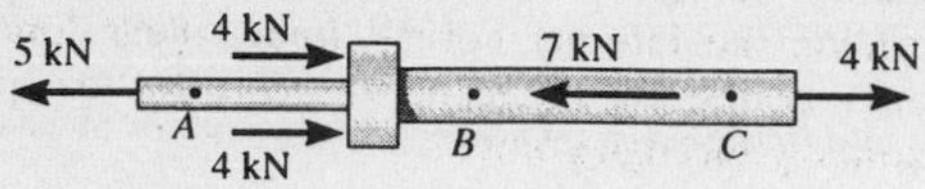

Internal Forces : Applying the equation of equilibrium to the left segment sectioned through point A, we have

$\xrightarrow{+} \Sigma F_x = 0;\quad N_A - 5 = 0\quad N_A = 5.00\text{ kN}$ **Ans**

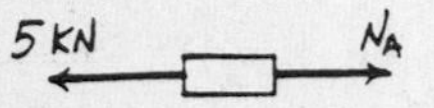

Applying the equation of equilibrium to the right segment sectioned through point B, we have

$\xrightarrow{+} \Sigma F_x = 0;\quad 4 - N_C = 0\quad N_C = 4.00\text{ kN}$ **Ans**

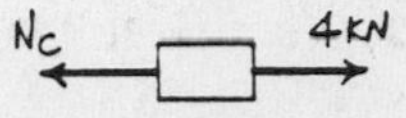

Applying the equation of equilibrium to the right segment sectioned through point C, we have

$\xrightarrow{+} \Sigma F_x = 0;\quad N_B + 4 - 7 = 0\quad N_B = 3.00\text{ kN}$ **Ans**

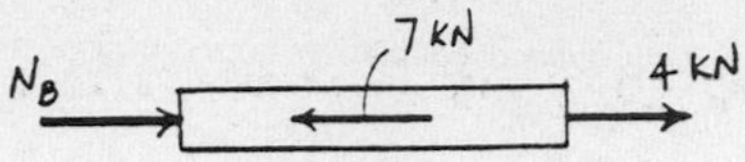

***7-4.** The shaft is supported by the two smooth bearings A and B. The four pulleys attached to the shaft are used to transmit power to adjacent machinery. If the torques applied to the pulleys are as shown, determine the internal torques at points C, D, and E.

Internal Forces : Applying the equation of equilibrium to the left segment sectioned through point C, we have

$\Sigma M_x = 0;\quad 40 - T_C = 0\quad T_C = 40.0\text{ lb}\cdot\text{ft}$ **Ans**

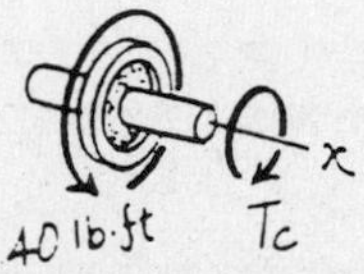

Applying the equation of equilibrium to the left segment sectioned through point D, we have

$\Sigma M_x = 0;\quad 40 + 15 - T_D = 0\quad T_D = 55.0\text{ lb}\cdot\text{ft}$ **Ans**

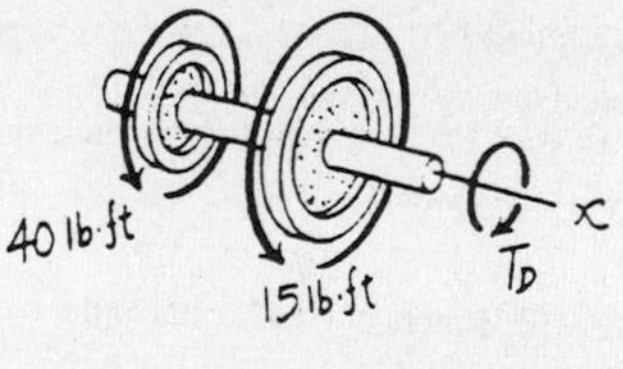

Applying the equation of equilibrium to the right segment sectioned through point E, we have

$\Sigma M_x = 0;\quad 10 - T_E = 0\quad T_E = 10.0\text{ lb}\cdot\text{ft}$ **Ans**

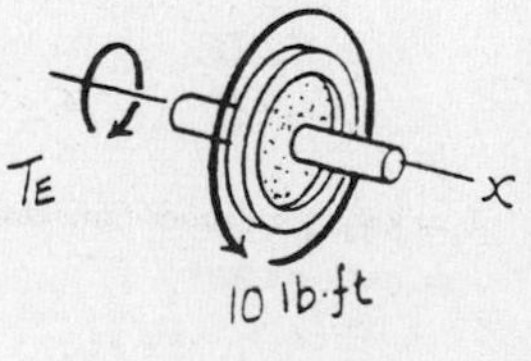

7-5. Two beams are attached to the column such that structural connections transmit the loads shown. Determine the internal normal force, shear force, and moment acting in the column at a section passing horizontally through point A.

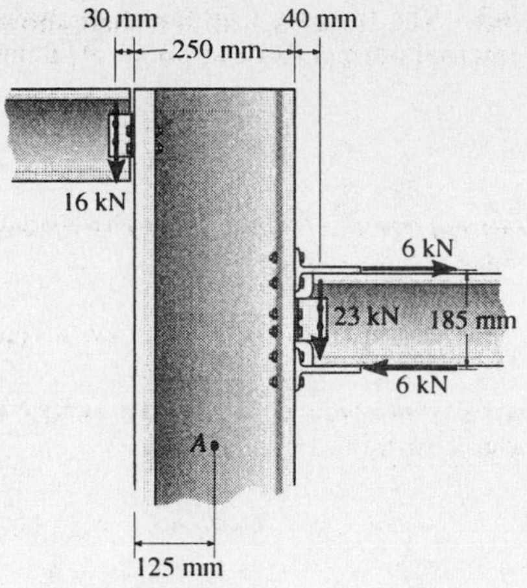

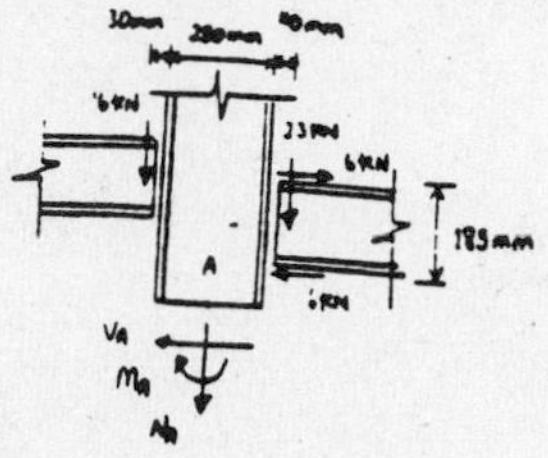

$\xrightarrow{+} \Sigma F_x = 0; \quad 6 - 6 - V_A = 0$

$V_A = 0$ **Ans**

$+\uparrow \Sigma F_y = 0; \quad -N_A - 16 - 23 = 0$

$N_A = -39 \text{ kN}$ **Ans**

$\curvearrowleft + \Sigma M_A = 0; \quad -M_A + 16(0.155) - 23(0.165) - 6(0.185) = 0$

$M_A = -2.42 \text{ kN}\cdot\text{m}$ **Ans**

7-6. Determine the internal normal force and shear force, and the bending moment in the beam at points C and D. Assume the support at B is a roller. Point C is located just to the right of the 8-kip load.

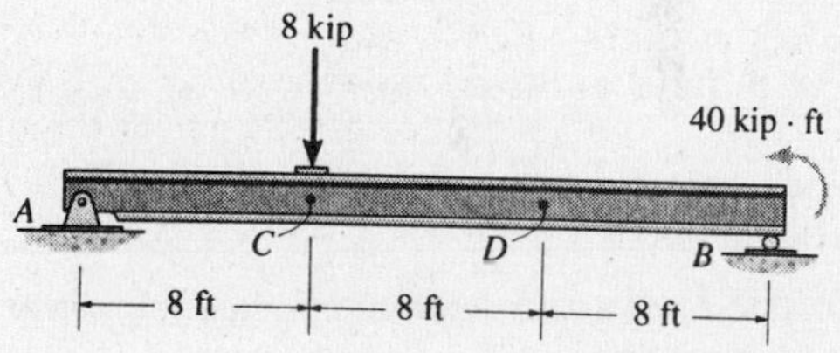

Support Reactions : FBD (a).

$\curvearrowleft + \Sigma M_A = 0; \quad B_y(24) + 40 - 8(8) = 0 \quad B_y = 1.00 \text{ kip}$

$+\uparrow \Sigma F_y = 0; \quad A_y + 1.00 - 8 = 0 \quad A_y = 7.00 \text{ kip}$

$\xrightarrow{+} \Sigma F_x = 0 \quad A_x = 0$

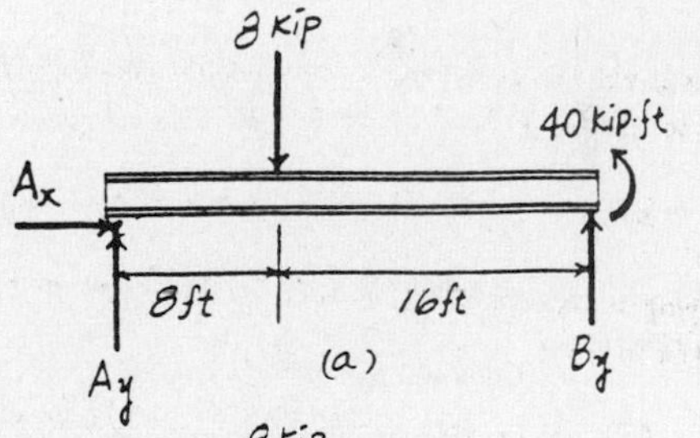

Internal Forces : Applying the equations of equilibrium to segment AC [FBD (b)], we have

$\xrightarrow{+} \Sigma F_x = 0; \quad N_C = 0$ **Ans**

$+\uparrow \Sigma F_y = 0; \quad 7.00 - 8 - V_C = 0 \quad V_C = -1.00 \text{ kip}$ **Ans**

$\curvearrowleft + \Sigma M_C = 0; \quad M_C - 7.00(8) = 0 \quad M_C = 56.0 \text{ kip}\cdot\text{ft}$ **Ans**

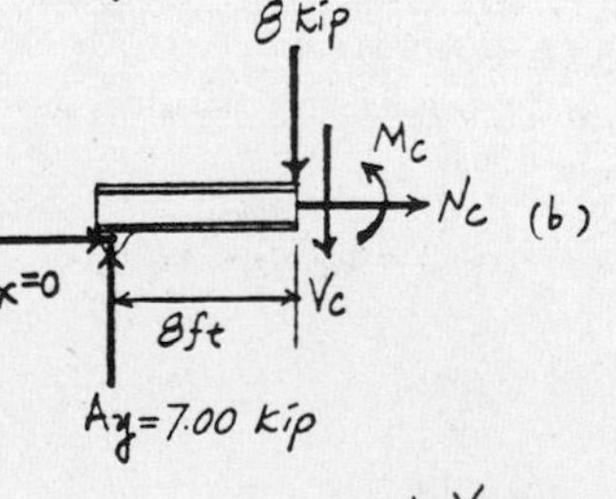

Applying the equations of equilibrium to segment BD [FBD (c)], we have

$\xrightarrow{+} \Sigma F_x = 0; \quad N_D = 0$ **Ans**

$+\uparrow \Sigma F_y = 0; \quad V_D + 1.00 = 0 \quad V_D = -1.00 \text{ kip}$ **Ans**

$\curvearrowleft + \Sigma M_D = 0; \quad 1.00(8) + 40 - M_D = 0$

$M_D = 48.0 \text{ kip}\cdot\text{ft}$ **Ans**

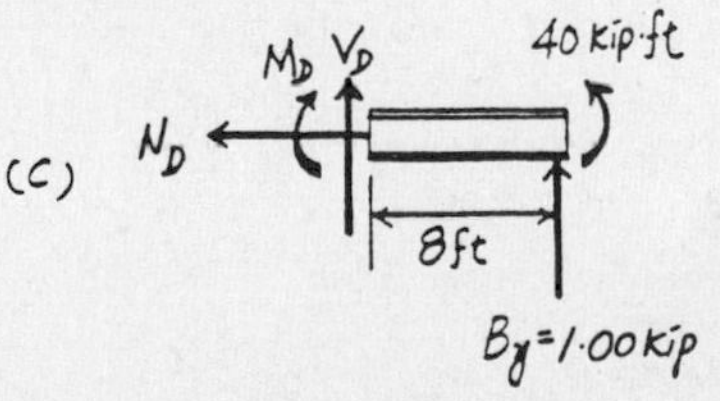

7-7. Determine the shear force and moment at points C and D.

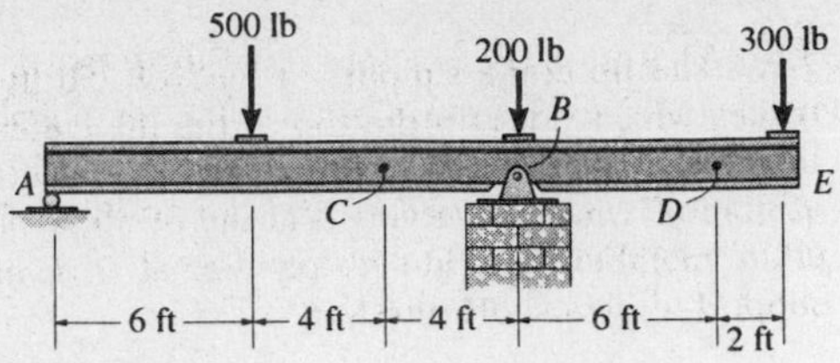

Support Reactions : FBD (a).

$$\curvearrowleft + \Sigma M_B = 0; \quad 500(8) - 300(8) - A_y(14) = 0$$
$$A_y = 114.29 \text{ lb}$$

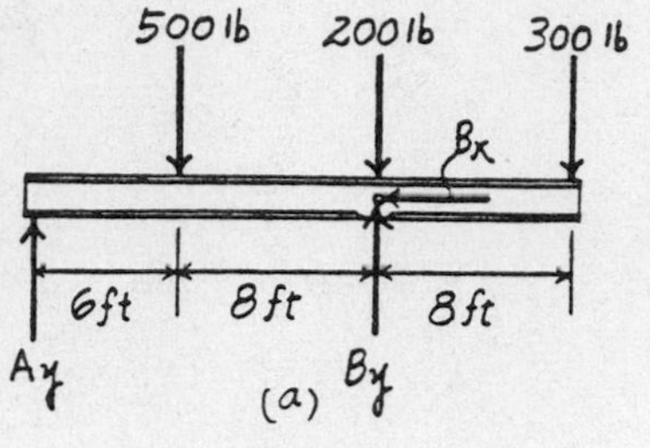

Internal Forces : Applying the equations of equilibrium to segment AC [FBD (b)], we have

$$\xrightarrow{+} \Sigma F_x = 0; \quad N_C = 0 \qquad \textbf{Ans}$$

$$+\uparrow \Sigma F_y = 0; \quad 114.29 - 500 - V_C = 0 \quad V_C = -386 \text{ lb} \qquad \textbf{Ans}$$

$$\curvearrowleft + \Sigma M_C = 0; \quad M_C + 500(4) - 114.29(10) = 0$$
$$M_C = -857 \text{ lb} \cdot \text{ft} \qquad \textbf{Ans}$$

Applying the equations of equilibrium to segment ED [FBD (c)] , we have

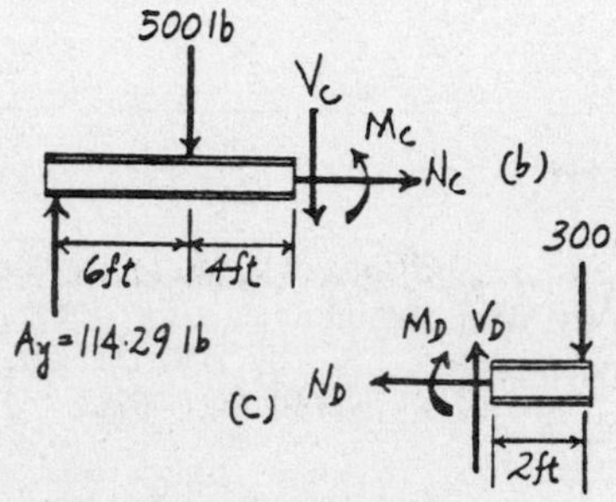

$$\xrightarrow{+} \Sigma F_x = 0; \quad N_D = 0 \qquad \textbf{Ans}$$

$$+\uparrow \Sigma F_y = 0; \quad V_D - 300 = 0 \quad V_D = 300 \text{ lb} \qquad \textbf{Ans}$$

$$\curvearrowleft + \Sigma M_D = 0; \quad -M_D - 300(2) = 0 \quad M_D = -600 \text{ lb} \cdot \text{ft} \qquad \textbf{Ans}$$

***7-8.** Determine the internal normal force, shear force, and moment at point C.

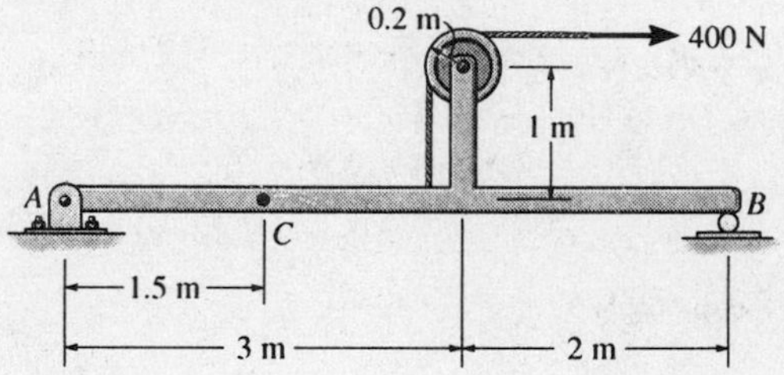

Beam :

$$\xrightarrow{+} \Sigma F_x = 0; \quad -A_x + 400 = 0$$
$$A_x = 400 \text{ N}$$

$$+\Sigma M_B = 0; \quad A_y(5) - 400(1.2) = 0$$
$$A_y = 96 \text{ N}$$

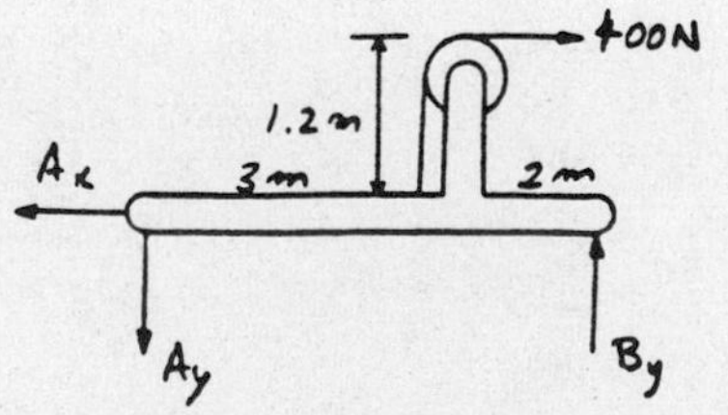

Segment AC :

$$\xrightarrow{+} \Sigma F_x = 0; \quad N_C - 400 = 0$$
$$N_C = 400 \text{ N} \qquad \textbf{Ans}$$

$$+\uparrow \Sigma F_y = 0; \quad -96 - V_C = 0$$
$$V_C = -96 \text{ N} \qquad \textbf{Ans}$$

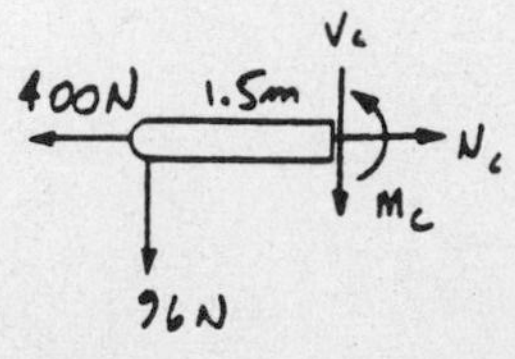

$$\curvearrowleft + \Sigma M_C = 0; \quad M_C + 96(1.5) = 0$$
$$M_C = -144 \text{ N} \cdot \text{m} \qquad \textbf{Ans}$$

7-9. The jib crane supports a load of 750 lb from the trolley which rides on the top of the jib. Determine the internal normal force, shear force, and moment in the jib at point C when the trolley is at the position shown. The crane members are pinned together at B, E and F and supported by a short link BH.

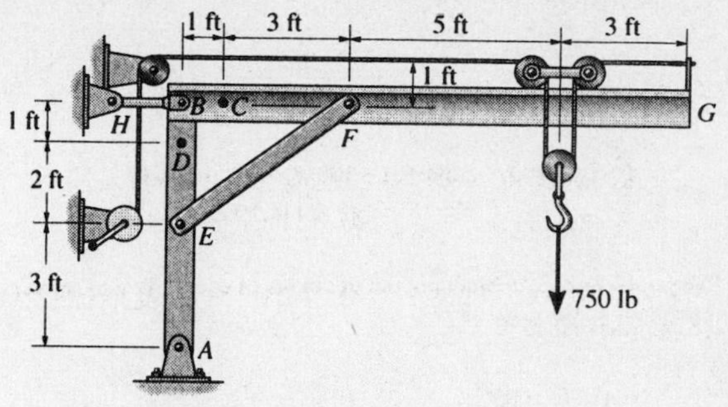

Member BFG:

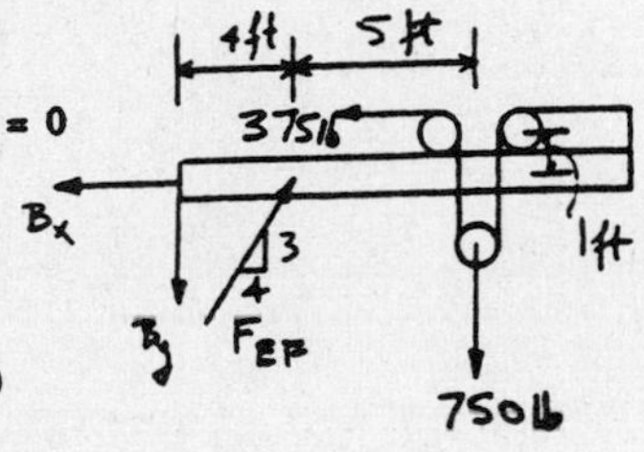

$\curvearrowleft + \Sigma M_B = 0; \quad F_{EF}\left(\frac{3}{5}\right)(4) - 750(9) + 375(1) = 0$

$F_{EF} = 2656.25 \text{ lb}$

$\xrightarrow{+} \Sigma F_x = 0; \quad -B_x + 2656.25\left(\frac{4}{5}\right) - 375 = 0$

$B_x = 1750 \text{ lb}$

$+\uparrow \Sigma F_y = 0; \quad -B_y + 2656.25\left(\frac{3}{5}\right) - 750 = 0$

$B_y = 843.75 \text{ lb}$

Segment BC:

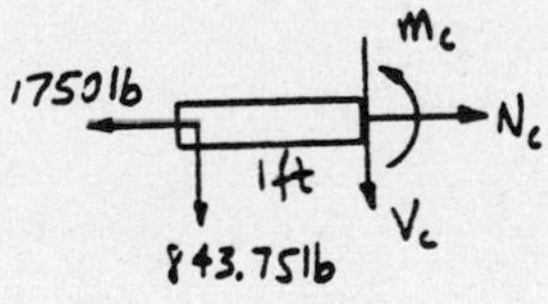

$\xrightarrow{+} \Sigma F_x = 0; \quad N_C - 1750 = 0$

$N_C = 1.75 \text{ kip}$ **Ans**

$+\uparrow \Sigma F_y = 0; \quad -843.75 - V_C = 0$

$V_C = -844 \text{ lb}$ **Ans**

$\curvearrowleft + \Sigma M_C = 0; \quad M_C + 843.75(1) = 0$

$M_C = -844 \text{ lb} \cdot \text{ft}$ **Ans**

7-10. The jib crane supports a load of 750 lb from the trolley which rides on the top of the jib. Determine the internal normal force, shear force, and moment in the column at point D when the trolley is at the position shown. The crane members are pinned together at B, E and F and supported by a short link BH.

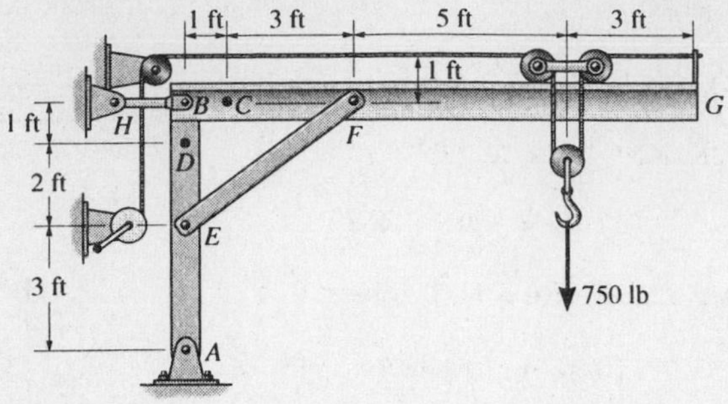

Member BFG:

$$\curvearrowleft + \Sigma M_B = 0; \quad F_{EF}\left(\frac{3}{5}\right)(4) - 750(9) + 375(1) = 0$$

$$F_{EF} = 2656.25 \text{ lb}$$

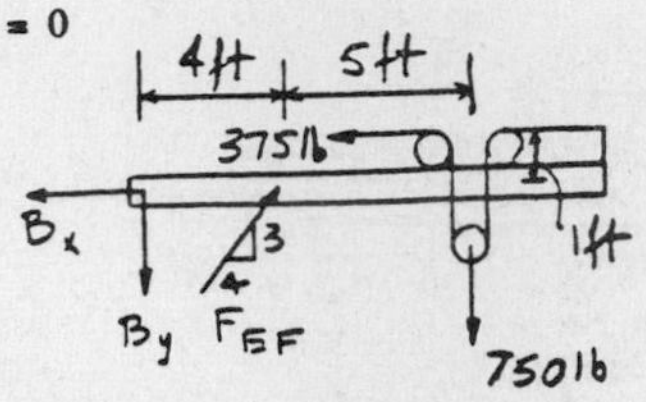

Entire Crane:

$$\curvearrowleft + \Sigma M_A = 0; \quad T_B(6) - 750(9) + 375(7) = 0$$

$$T_B = 687.5 \text{ lb}$$

$$\xrightarrow{+} \Sigma F_x = 0; \quad A_x - 687.5 - 375 = 0$$

$$A_x = 1062.5 \text{ lb}$$

$$+\uparrow \Sigma F_y = 0; \quad A_y - 750 = 0$$

$$A_y = 750 \text{ lb}$$

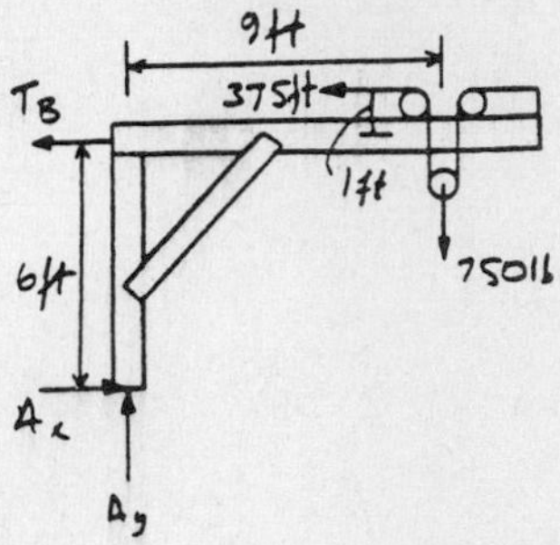

Segment AED:

$$+\uparrow \Sigma F_y = 0; \quad N_D + 750 - 2656.25\left(\frac{3}{5}\right) = 0$$

$$N_D = 844 \text{ lb} \qquad \textbf{Ans}$$

$$\xrightarrow{+} \Sigma F_x = 0; \quad 1062.5 - 2656.25\left(\frac{4}{5}\right) + V_D = 0$$

$$V_D = 1.06 \text{ kip} \qquad \textbf{Ans}$$

$$\curvearrowleft + \Sigma M_D = 0; \quad -M_D - 2656.25\left(\frac{4}{5}\right)(2) + 1062.5(5) = 0$$

$$M_D = 1.06 \text{ kip}\cdot\text{ft} \qquad \textbf{Ans}$$

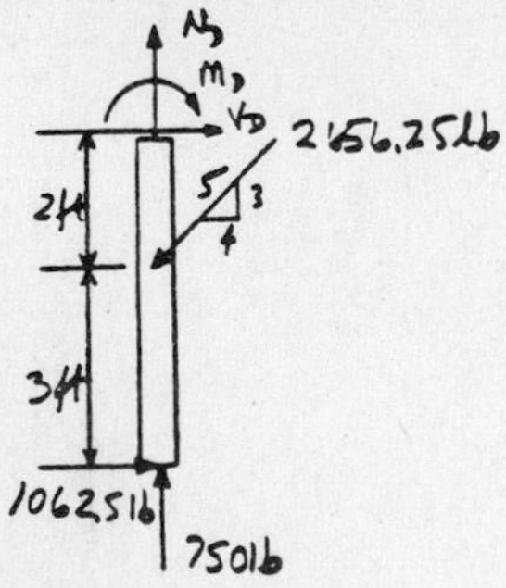

7-11. Determine the internal normal force, shear force, and moment at points E and D of the compound beam.

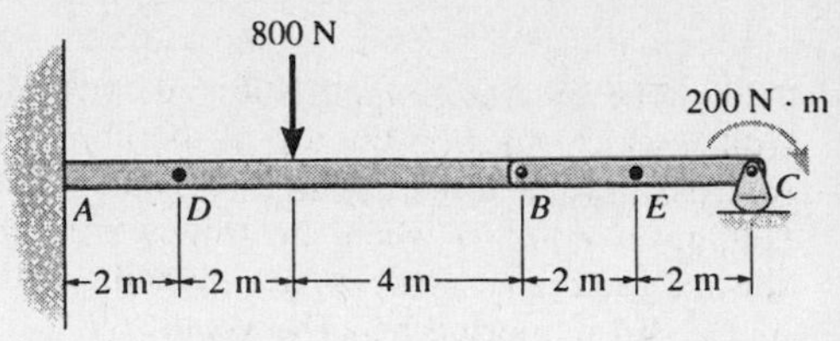

Segment EC:

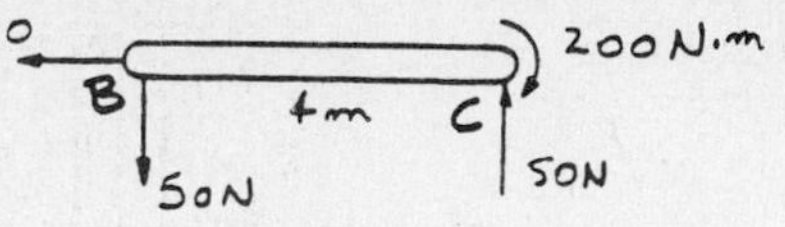

$\xrightarrow{+} \Sigma F_x = 0;\quad N_E = 0$ **Ans**

$+\uparrow \Sigma F_y = 0;\quad V_E + 50 = 0$

$V_E = -50\text{ N}$ **Ans**

$\curvearrowleft + \Sigma M_E = 0;\quad -200 + 50(2) - M_E = 0$

$M_E = -100\text{ N}\cdot\text{m}$ **Ans**

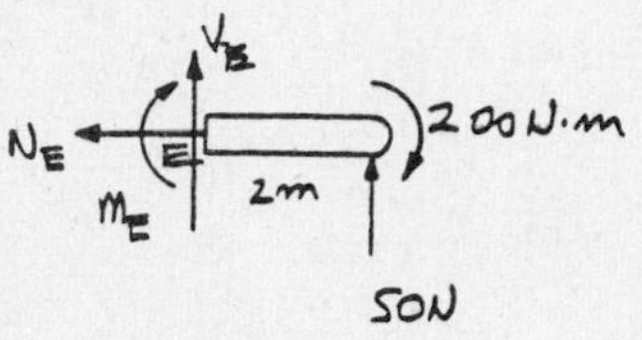

Segment DB:

$\xrightarrow{+} \Sigma F_x = 0;\quad N_D = 0$ **Ans**

$+\uparrow \Sigma F_y = 0;\quad V_D - 800 + 50 = 0$

$V_D = 750\text{ N}$ **Ans**

$\curvearrowleft + \Sigma M_D = 0;\quad -800(2) + 6(50) - M_D = 0$

$M_D = -1300\text{ N}\cdot\text{m} = -1.30\text{ kN}\cdot\text{m}$ **Ans**

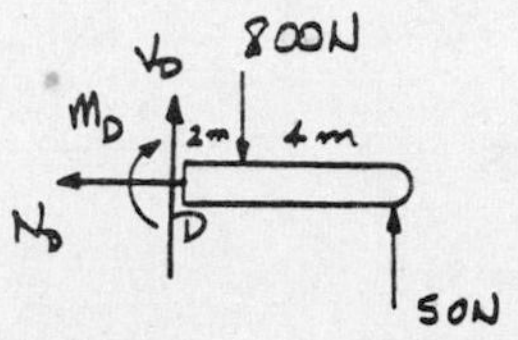

***7-12.** Determine the internal normal force, shear force, and moment in the beam at points C and D. Point D is just to the right of the 5-kip load.

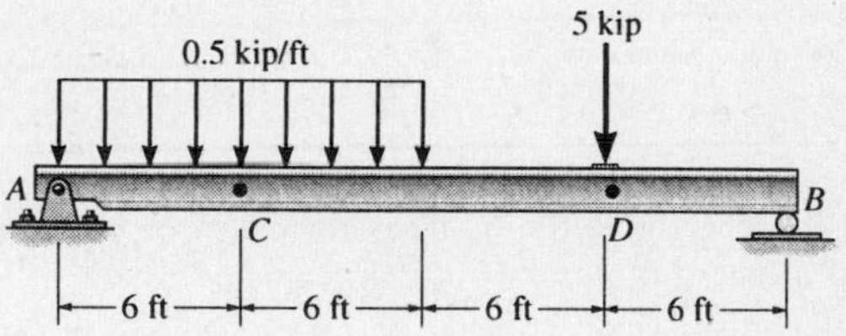

Entire beam:

$\curvearrowleft + \Sigma M_B = 0;\quad 5(6) + 6(18) - A_y(24) = 0$

$A_y = 5.75\text{ kip}$

$\xrightarrow{+} \Sigma F_x = 0;\quad A_x = 0$

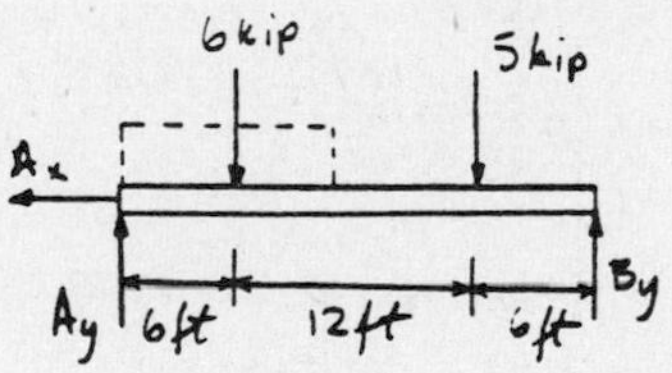

Segment AC:

$\xrightarrow{+} \Sigma F_x = 0;\quad N_C = 0$ **Ans**

$+\uparrow \Sigma F_y = 0;\quad 5.75 - 3 - V_C = 0$

$V_C = 2.75\text{ kip}$ **Ans**

$\curvearrowleft + \Sigma M_C = 0;\quad M_C + 3(3) - 5.75(6) = 0$

$M_C = 25.5\text{ kip}\cdot\text{ft}$ **Ans**

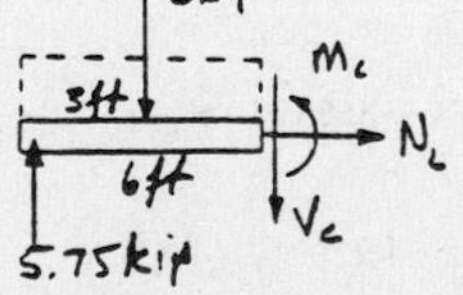

Segment AD:

$\xrightarrow{+} \Sigma F_x = 0;\quad N_D = 0$ **Ans**

$+\uparrow \Sigma F_y = 0;\quad 5.75 - 6 - 5 - V_D = 0$

$V_D = -5.25\text{ kip}$ **Ans**

$\curvearrowleft + \Sigma M_D = 0;\quad M_D + 6(12) - 5.75(18) = 0$

$M_D = 31.5\text{ kip}\cdot\text{ft}$ **Ans**

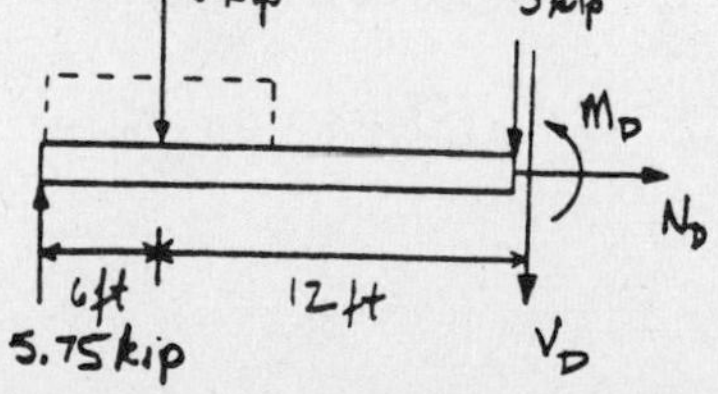

7-13. Determine the internal normal force, shear force, and moment acting at point C and at point D, which is located just to the right of the roller support at B.

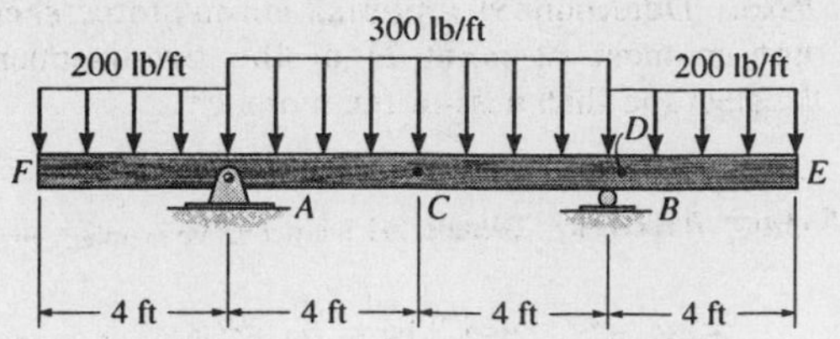

Support Reactions : From FBD (a),

$$\curvearrowleft + \Sigma M_A = 0; \quad B_y(8) + 800(2) - 2400(4) - 800(10) = 0$$
$$B_y = 2000 \text{ lb}$$

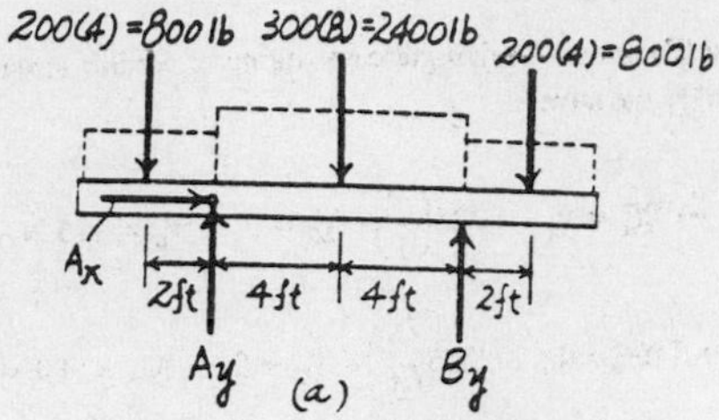

Internal Forces : Applying the equations of equilibrium to segment ED [FBD (b)], we have

$$\xrightarrow{+} \Sigma F_x = 0; \qquad N_D = 0 \qquad \textbf{Ans}$$

$$+\uparrow \Sigma F_y = 0; \quad V_D - 800 = 0 \quad V_D = 800 \text{ lb} \qquad \textbf{Ans}$$

$$\curvearrowleft + \Sigma M_D = 0; \quad -M_D - 800(2) = 0$$
$$M_D = -1600 \text{ lb}\cdot\text{ft} = -1.60 \text{ kip}\cdot\text{ft} \qquad \textbf{Ans}$$

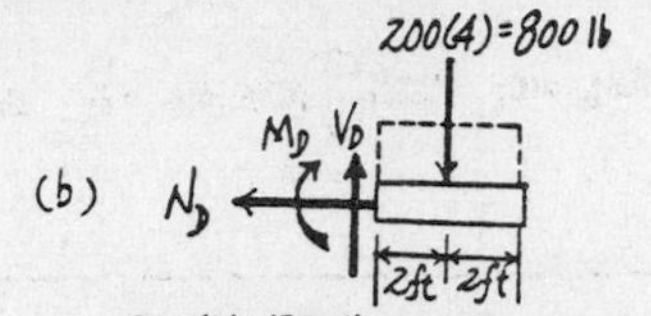

Applying the equations of equilibrium to segment EC [FBD (c)], we have

$$\xrightarrow{+} \Sigma F_x = 0; \qquad N_C = 0 \qquad \textbf{Ans}$$

$$+\uparrow \Sigma F_y = 0; \quad V_C + 2000 - 1200 - 800 = 0 \quad V_C = 0 \qquad \textbf{Ans}$$

$$\curvearrowleft + \Sigma M_C = 0; \quad 2000(4) - 1200(2) - 800(6) - M_C = 0$$
$$M_C = 800 \text{ lb}\cdot\text{ft} \qquad \textbf{Ans}$$

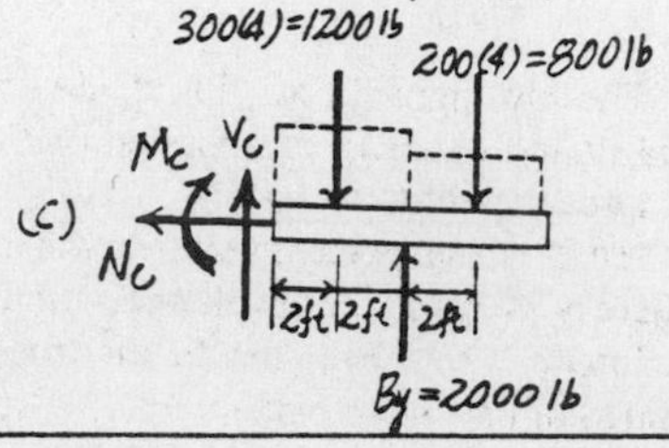

7-14. Determine the internal normal force, shear force, and moment at point D of the beam.

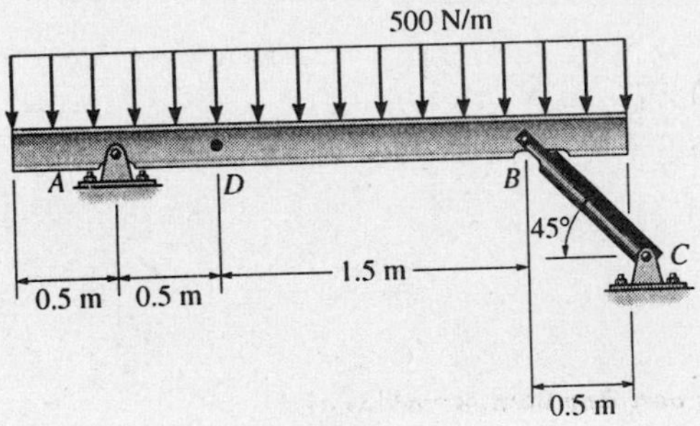

Support reactions :

$$\curvearrowleft + \Sigma M_A = 0; \quad F_{BC} \sin 45°(2) - 500(3)(1) = 0 \quad F_{BC} = 1060.7 \text{ N}$$

$$\xrightarrow{+} \Sigma F_x = 0; \quad A_x - 1060.7 \cos 45° = 0 \quad A_x = 750 \text{ N}$$

$$+\uparrow \Sigma F_y = 0; \quad A_y + 1060.7 \sin 45° - 500(3) = 0 \quad A_y = 750 \text{ N}$$

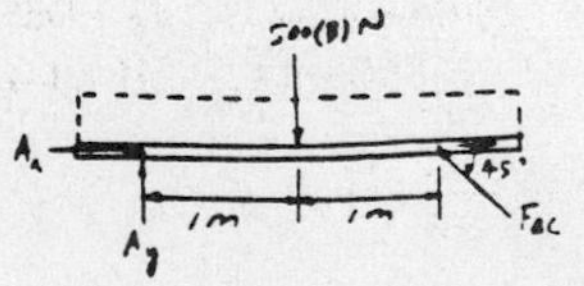

For segment AD :

$$\xrightarrow{+} \Sigma F_x = 0; \quad N_D + 750 = 0 \quad N_D = -750 \text{ N} \qquad \textbf{Ans}$$

$$+\uparrow \Sigma F_y = 0; \quad -V_D - 500(1) + 750 = 0 \quad V_D = 250 \text{ N} \qquad \textbf{Ans}$$

$$\curvearrowleft + \Sigma M_D = 0; \quad M_D + 500(1)(0.5) - 750(0.5) = 0 \quad M_D = 125 \text{ N}\cdot\text{m} \qquad \textbf{Ans}$$

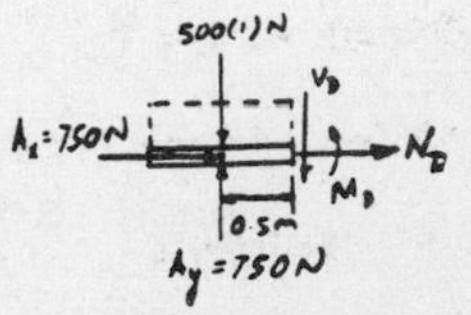

7-15. Determine the internal normal force, shear force, and moment at point D of the two-member frame. Neglect the thickness of the member.

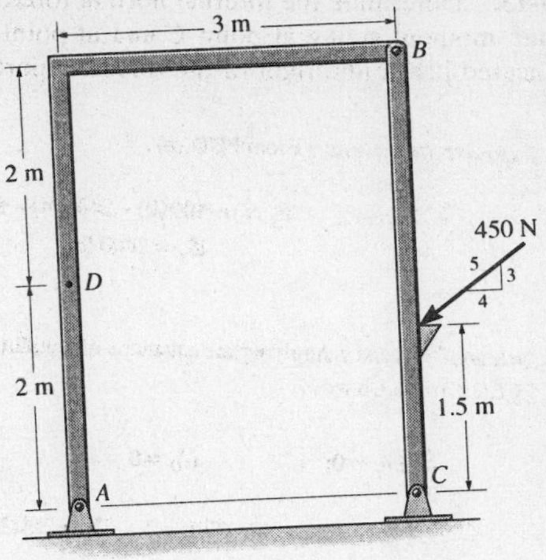

Support Reactions : Member AB is a two force member. From FBD (a),

$$+\Sigma M_C = 0; \quad 450\left(\frac{4}{5}\right)(1.5) - F_{AB}\left(\frac{3}{5}\right)(4) = 0 \quad F_{AB} = 225 \text{ N}$$

Internal Forces : Applying the equations of equilibrium to segment AD [FBD (b)], we have

$$\xrightarrow{+} \Sigma F_x = 0; \quad 225\left(\frac{3}{5}\right) - V_D = 0 \quad V_D = 135 \text{ N} \qquad \textbf{Ans}$$

$$+\uparrow \Sigma F_y = 0; \quad 225\left(\frac{4}{5}\right) - N_D = 0 \quad N_D = 180 \text{ N} \qquad \textbf{Ans}$$

$$\circlearrowleft + \Sigma M_E = 0; \quad 225\left(\frac{3}{5}\right)(2) - M_D = 0 \quad M_D = 270 \text{ N}\cdot\text{m} \qquad \textbf{Ans}$$

7-16. The strongback or lifting beam is used for materials handling. If the suspended load has a weight of 2 kN and a center of gravity of G, determine the placement d of the padeyes on the top of the beam so that there is no moment developed within the length AB of the beam. The lifting bridle has two legs that are positioned at 45°, as shown.

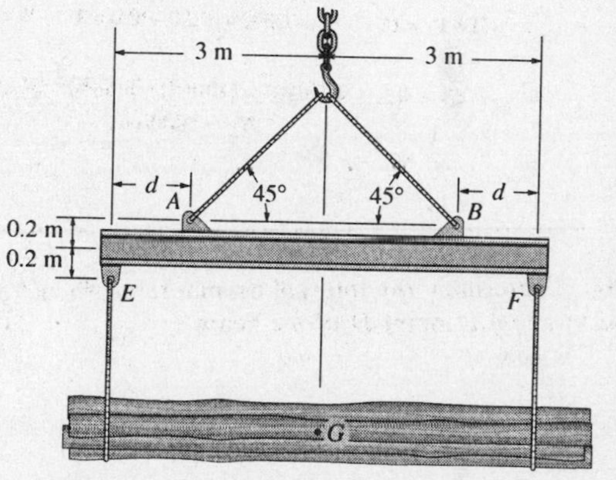

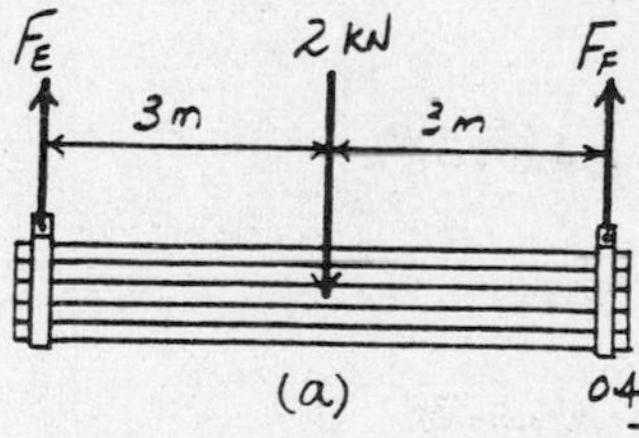

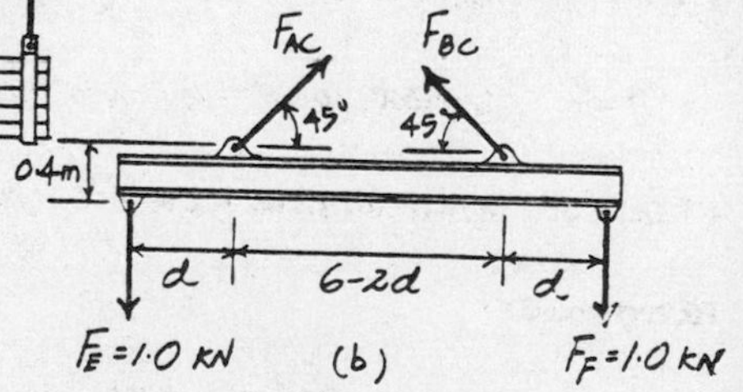

Support Reactions : From FBD (a),

$$\circlearrowleft + \Sigma M_E = 0; \quad F_F(6) - 2(3) = 0 \quad F_E = 1.00 \text{ kN}$$

$$+\uparrow \Sigma F_y = 0; \quad F_F + 1.00 - 2 = 0 \quad F_F = 1.00 \text{ kN}$$

From FBD (b),

$$\xrightarrow{+} \Sigma F_x = 0; \quad F_{AC}\cos 45° - F_{BC}\cos 45° = 0 \quad F_{AC} = F_{BC} = F$$

$$+\uparrow \Sigma F_y = 0; \quad 2F\sin 45° - 1.00 - 1.00 = 0$$

$$F_{AC} = F_{BC} = F = 1.414 \text{ kN}$$

Internal Forces : This problem requires $M_H = 0$. Summing moments about point H of segment EH [FBD (c)], we have

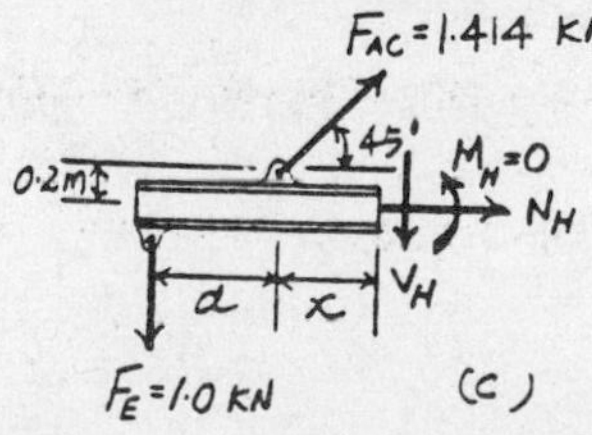

$$\circlearrowleft + \Sigma M_H = 0; \quad 1.00(d+x) - 1.414\sin 45°(x) - 1.414\cos 45°(0.2) = 0$$

$$d = 0.200 \text{ m} \qquad \textbf{Ans}$$

7-17. Determine the internal normal force, shear force, and moment at point D of the two-member frame.

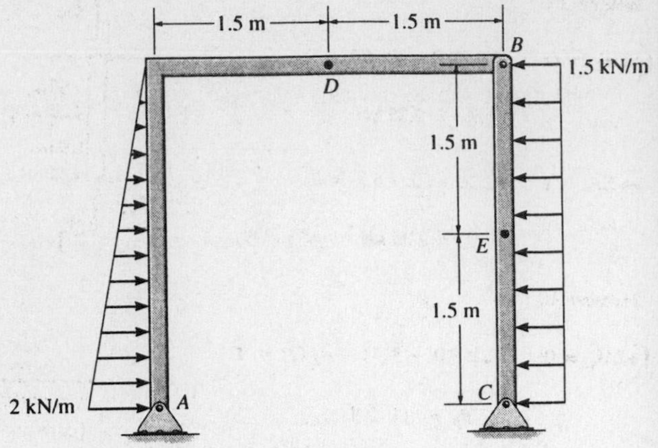

Member BC :

$\curvearrowleft + \Sigma M_C = 0;\quad 4.5\,(1.5) - B_x\,(3) = 0$

$B_x = 2.25\text{ kN}$

$\xrightarrow{+} \Sigma F_x = 0;\quad 2.25 + C_x - 4.5 = 0$

$C_x = 2.25\text{ kN}$

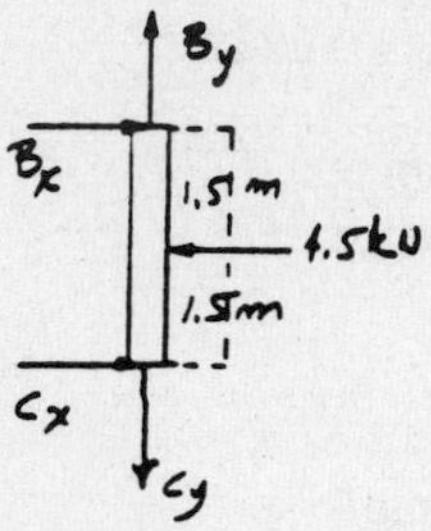

Member AB :

$\curvearrowleft + \Sigma M_A = 0;\quad 2.25\,(3) - 3\,(1) - B_y\,(3) = 0$

$B_y = 1.25\text{ kN}$

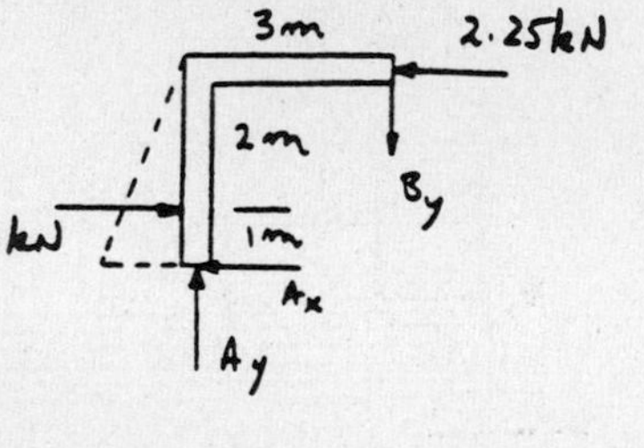

Segment DB :

$\xrightarrow{+} \Sigma F_x = 0;\quad -N_D - 2.25 = 0$

$N_D = -2.25\text{ kN}$ **Ans**

$+\uparrow \Sigma F_y = 0;\quad V_D - 1.25 = 0$

$V_D = 1.25\text{ kN}$ **Ans**

$\curvearrowleft + \Sigma M_D = 0;\quad -M_D - 1.25\,(1.5) = 0$

$M_D = -1.88\text{ kN}\cdot\text{m}$ **Ans**

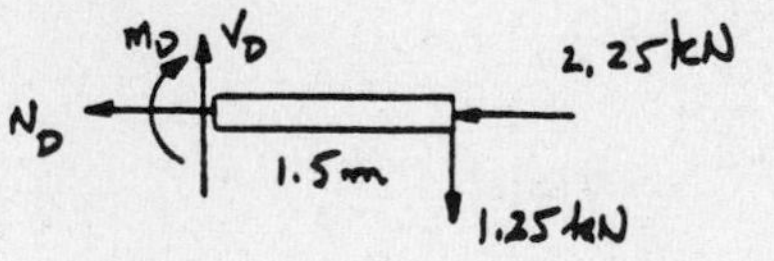

7-18. Determine the internal normal force, shear force, and moment at point E.

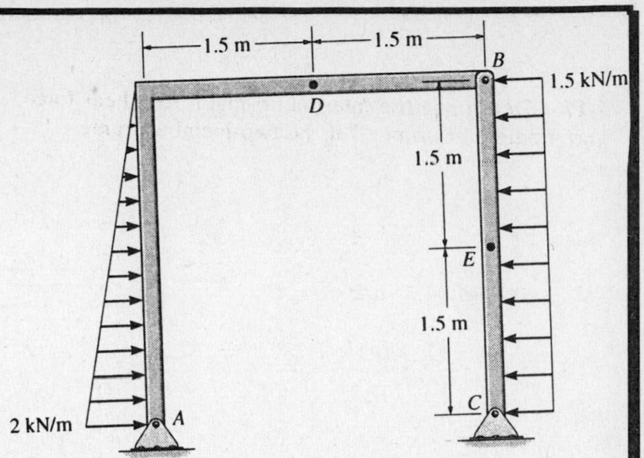

Member BC:

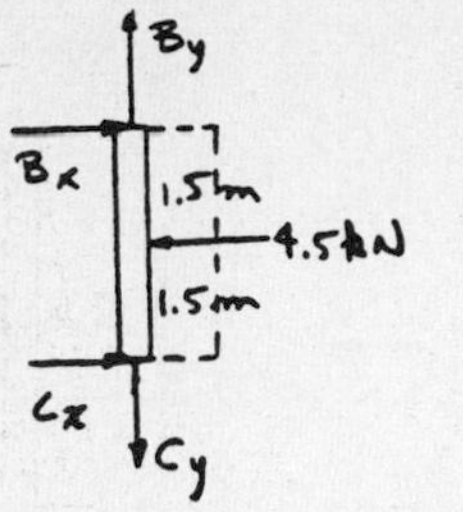

$\curvearrowleft + \Sigma M_C = 0; \quad 4.5\,(1.5) - B_x\,(3) = 0$

$B_x = 2.25 \text{ kN}$

$\xrightarrow{+} \Sigma F_x = 0; \quad 2.25 + C_x - 4.5 = 0$

$C_x = 2.25 \text{ kN}$

Member AB:

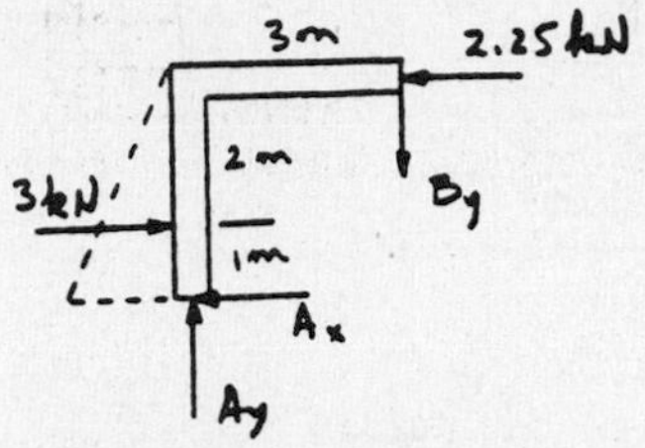

$\curvearrowleft + \Sigma M_A = 0; \quad 2.25\,(3) - 3\,(1) - B_y\,(3) = 0$

$B_y = 1.25 \text{ kN}$

Segment BE:

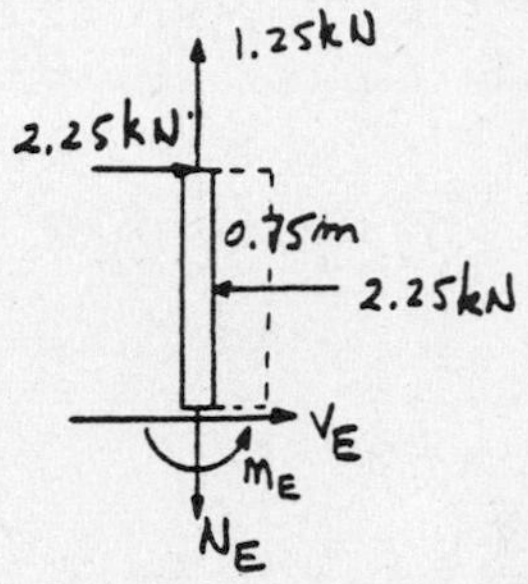

$+\uparrow \Sigma F_y = 0; \quad 1.25 - N_E = 0$

$N_E = 1.25 \text{ kN}$ **Ans**

$\xrightarrow{+} \Sigma F_x = 0; \quad V_E + 2.25 - 2.25 = 0$

$V_E = 0$ **Ans**

$+\Sigma M_E = 0; \quad M_E - 2.25\,(0.75) = 0$

$M_E = 1.6875 \text{ kN} \cdot \text{m} = 1.69 \text{ kN} \cdot \text{m}$ **Ans**

7-19. Determine the internal normal force, shear force, and moment at point D of the two-member frame.

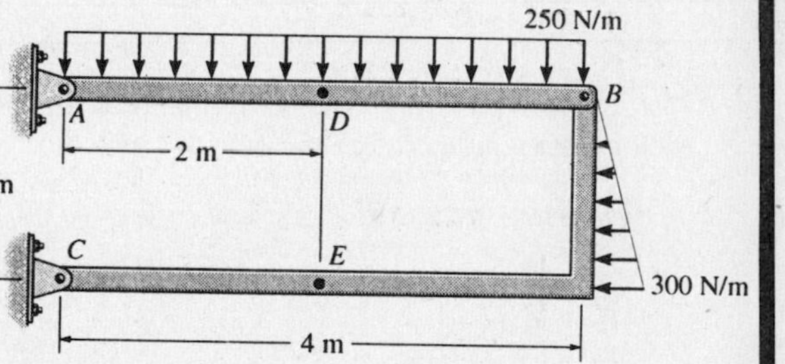

Member AB:

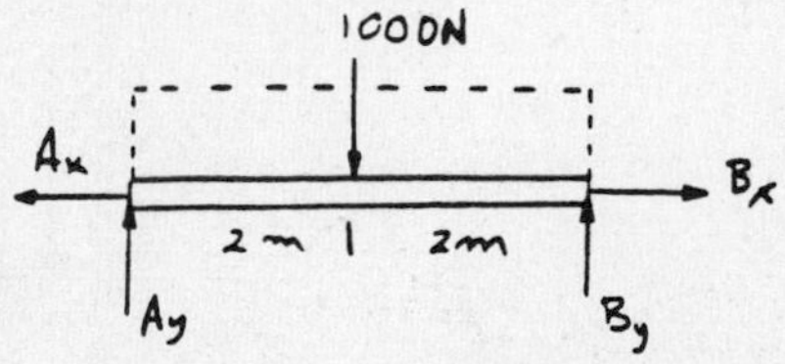

$\curvearrowleft + \Sigma M_A = 0; \quad B_y\,(4) - 1000\,(2) = 0$

$B_y = 500 \text{ N}$

Member BC:

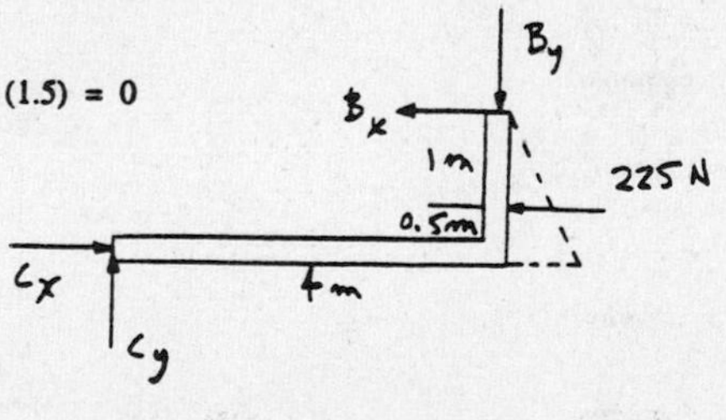

$\curvearrowleft + \Sigma M_C = 0; \quad -500\,(4) + 225\,(0.5) + B_x\,(1.5) = 0$

$B_x = 1258.33 \text{ N}$

Segment DB:

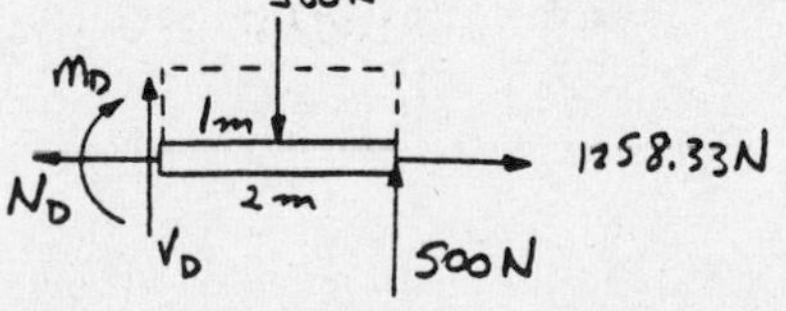

$\xrightarrow{+} \Sigma F_x = 0; \quad -N_D + 1258.33 = 0$

$N_D = 1.26 \text{ kN}$ **Ans**

$+\uparrow \Sigma F_y = 0; \quad V_D - 500 + 500 = 0$

$V_D = 0$ **Ans**

$\curvearrowleft + \Sigma M_D = 0; \quad -M_D + 500\,(1) = 0$

$M_D = 500 \text{ N} \cdot \text{m}$ **Ans**

***7-20.** Determine the internal normal force, shear force, and moment at point E of the two-member frame.

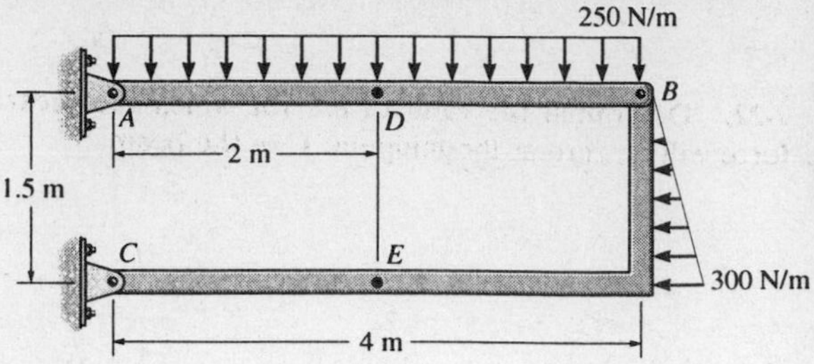

Member AB :

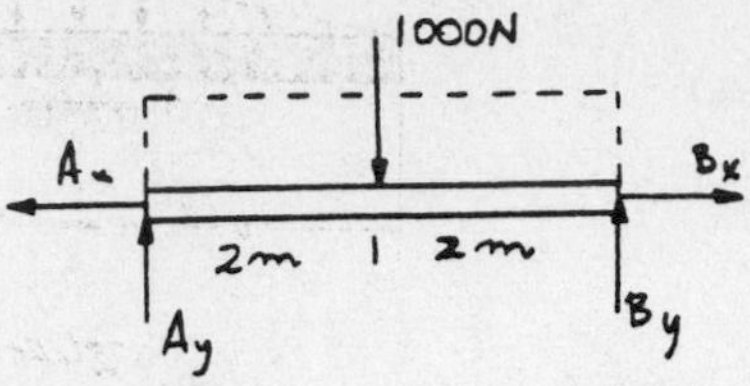

$\circlearrowleft + \Sigma M_A = 0; \quad B_y(4) - 1000(2) = 0$

$B_y = 500 \text{ N}$

Member BC :

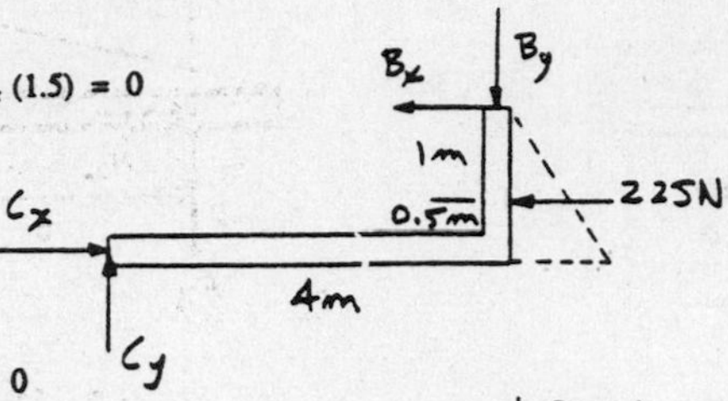

$\circlearrowleft + \Sigma M_C = 0; \quad -500(4) + 225(0.5) + B_x(1.5) = 0$

$B_x = 1258.33 \text{ N}$

Segment EB :

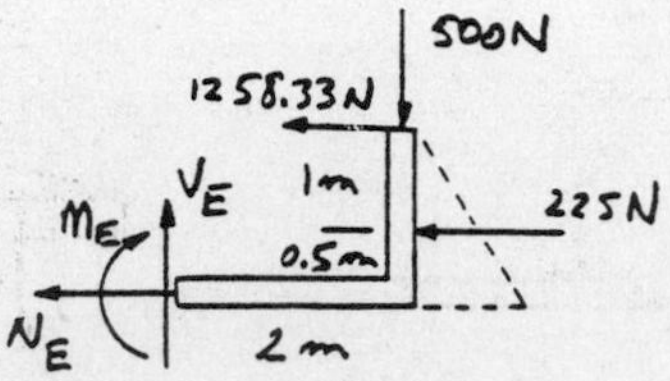

$\xrightarrow{+} \Sigma F_x = 0; \quad -N_E - 1258.33 - 225 = 0$

$N_E = -1.48 \text{ kN}$ **Ans**

$+\uparrow \Sigma F_y = 0; \quad V_E - 500 = 0$

$V_E = 500 \text{ N}$ **Ans**

$\circlearrowleft + \Sigma M_E = 0; \quad -M_E + 225(0.5) + 1258.33(1.5) - 500(2) = 0$

$M_E = 1000 \text{ N} \cdot \text{m}$ **Ans**

7-21. Determine the internal normal force, shear force, and bending moment in the beam at point B.

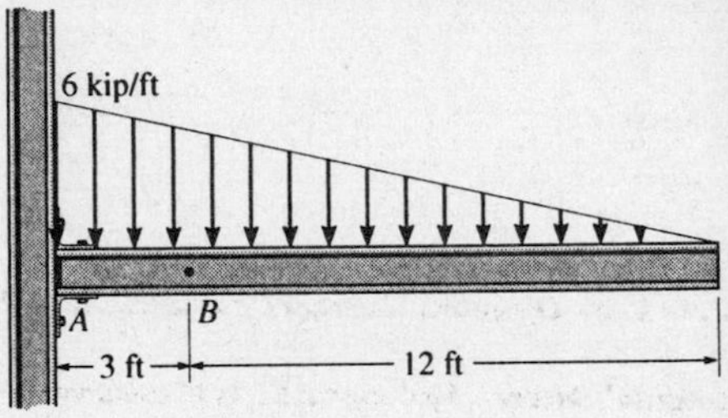

Free body Diagram : The support reactions at A need not be computed.

Internal Forces : Applying the equations of equilibrium to segment CB, we have

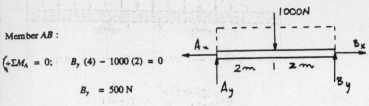

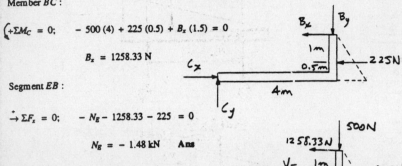

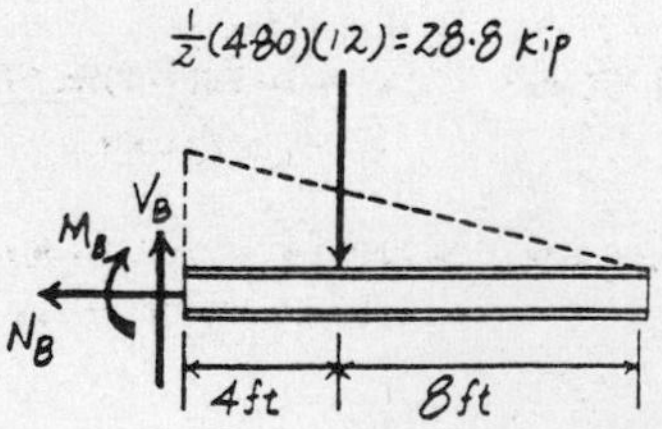

$\xrightarrow{+} \Sigma F_x = 0; \quad N_B = 0$ **Ans**

$+\uparrow \Sigma F_y = 0; \quad V_B - 28.8 = 0 \quad V_B = 28.8 \text{ kip}$ **Ans**

$\circlearrowleft + \Sigma M_B = 0; \quad -28.8(4) - M_B = 0$

$M_B = -115 \text{ kip} \cdot \text{ft}$ **Ans**

7-22. Determine the ratio of a/b for which the shear force will be zero at the midpoint C of the beam.

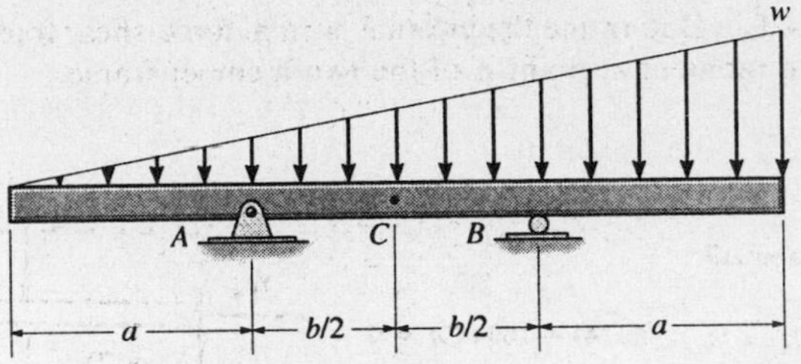

Support Reactions : . From FBD (a),

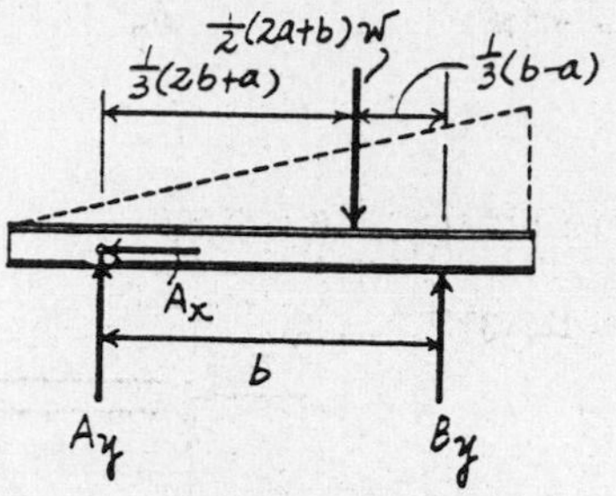

$$\curvearrowleft + \Sigma M_B = 0; \quad \frac{1}{2}(2a+b)\,w\left[\frac{1}{3}(b-a)\right] - A_y\,(b) = 0$$

$$A_y = \frac{w}{6b}(2a+b)(b-a)$$

Internal Forces : This problem requires $V_C = 0$. Summing forces vertically [FBD (b)], we have

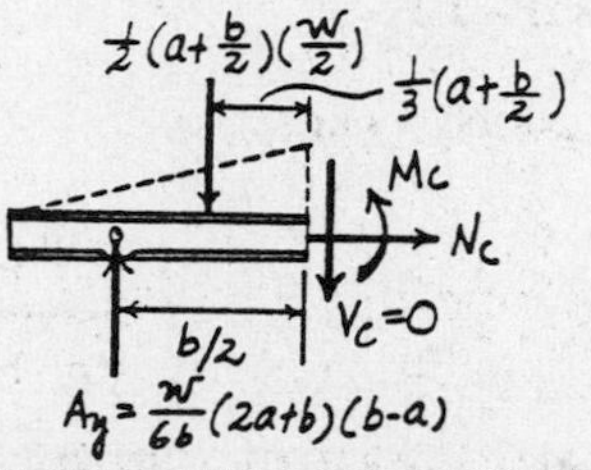

$$+\uparrow \Sigma F_y = 0; \quad \frac{w}{6b}(2a+b)(b-a) - \frac{1}{2}\left(a+\frac{b}{2}\right)\left(\frac{w}{2}\right) = 0$$

$$\frac{w}{6b}(2a+b)(b-a) = \frac{w}{8}(2a+b)$$

$$\frac{a}{b} = \frac{1}{4} \qquad \textbf{Ans}$$

7-23. Determine the internal normal force, shear force, and bending moment at point C.

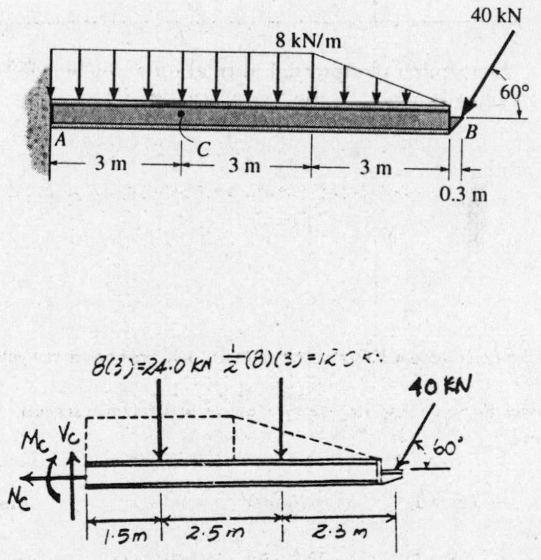

Free body Diagram : The support reactions at A need not be computed.

Internal Forces : Applying equations of equilibrium to segment BC, we have

$$\xrightarrow{+} \Sigma F_x = 0; \quad 40\cos 60^\circ - N_C = 0 \quad N_C = 20.0\ \text{kN} \qquad \textbf{Ans}$$

$$+\uparrow \Sigma F_y = 0; \quad V_C - 24.0 - 12.0 - 40\sin 60^\circ = 0$$

$$V_C = 70.6\ \text{kN} \qquad \textbf{Ans}$$

$$\curvearrowleft + \Sigma M_C = 0; \quad -24.0(1.5) - 12.0(4) - 40\sin 60^\circ(6.3) - M_C = 0$$

$$M_C = -302\ \text{kN}\cdot\text{m} \qquad \textbf{Ans}$$

*7-24. The jack AB is used to straighten the bent beam DE using the arrangement shown. If the axial compressive force in the jack is 5000 lb, determine the internal moment developed at point C of the top beam. Neglect the weight of the beams.

Segment :

$\curvearrowleft + \Sigma M_C = 0; \quad M_C + 2500\,(10) = 0$

$M_C = -25.0 \text{ kip} \cdot \text{ft}$ **Ans**

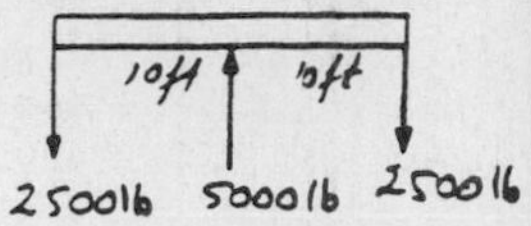

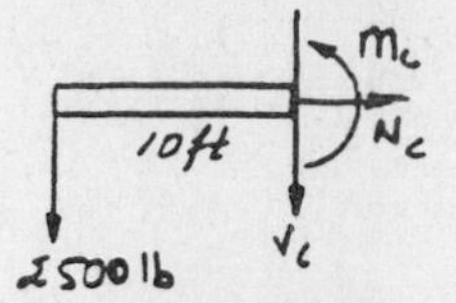

7-25. Solve Prob. 7-24 assuming that each beam has a uniform weight of 150 lb/ft.

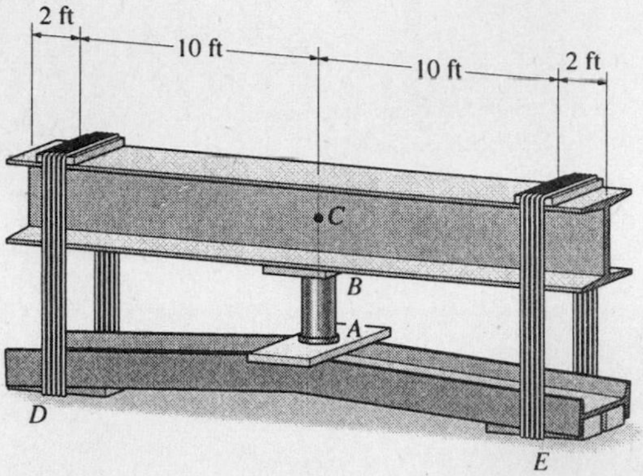

Beam :

$+\uparrow \Sigma F_y = 0; \quad 5000 - 3600 - 2R = 0$

$R = 700 \text{ lb}$

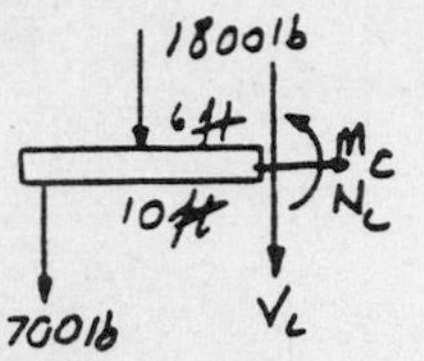

Segment :

$\curvearrowleft + \Sigma M_C = 0; \quad M_C + 700\,(10) + 1800\,(6) = 0$

$M_C = -17.8 \text{ kip} \cdot \text{ft}$ **Ans**

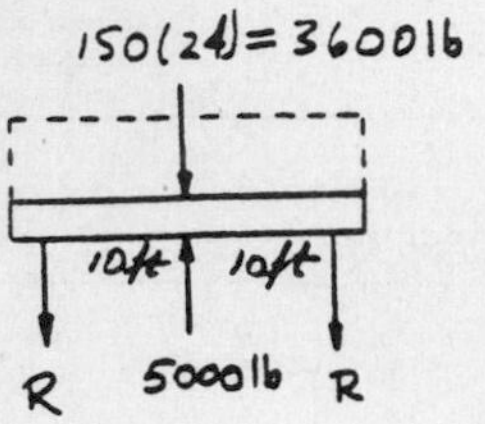

7-26. Determine the internal normal force, shear force, and moment at point C of the beam.

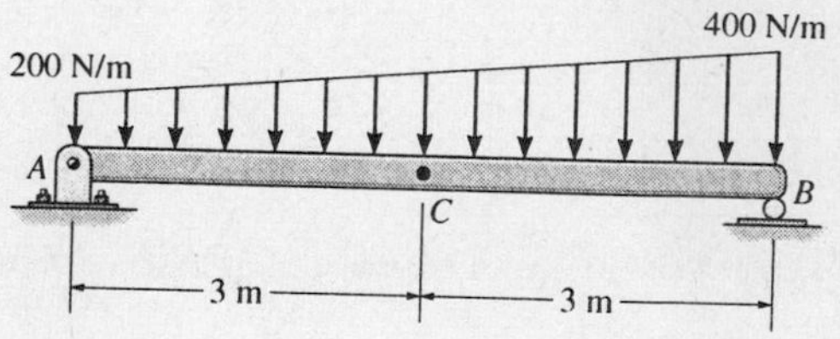

Beam :

$\curvearrowleft + \Sigma M_B = 0; \quad 600\,(2) + 1200\,(3) - A_y\,(6) = 0$

$A_y = 800 \text{ N}$

$\xrightarrow{+} \Sigma F_x = 0; \quad A_x = 0$

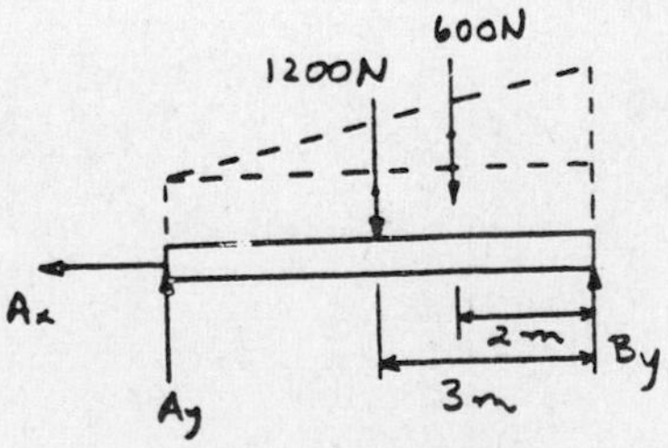

Segment AC :

$\xrightarrow{+} \Sigma F_x = 0; \quad N_C = 0$ **Ans**

$+\uparrow \Sigma F_y = 0; \quad 800 - 600 - 150 - V_C = 0$

$V_C = 50 \text{ N}$ **Ans**

$\curvearrowleft + \Sigma M_C = 0; \quad -800\,(3) + 600\,(1.5) + 150\,(1) + M_C = 0$

$M_C = 1350 \text{ N} \cdot \text{m} = 1.35 \text{ kN} \cdot \text{m}$ **Ans**

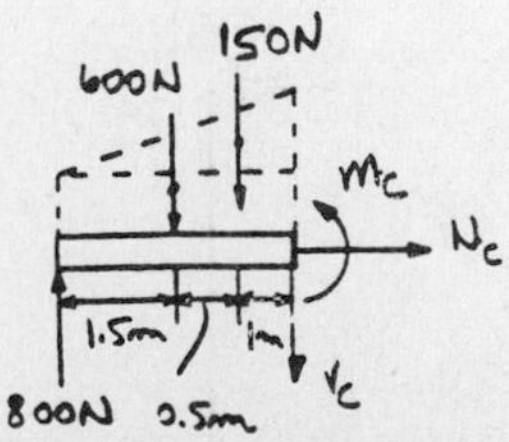

7-27. Determine the distance a between the supports in terms of the shaft's length L so that the bending moment in the *symmetric* shaft is zero at the shaft's center. The intensity of the distributed load at the center of the shaft is w_0. The supports are journal bearings.

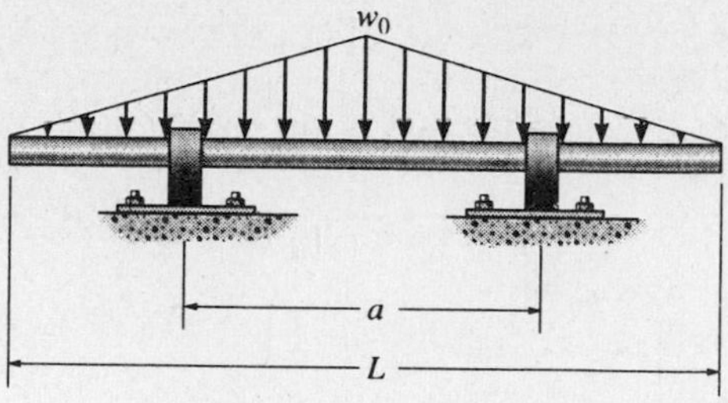

Support reactions : FBD(a)

Moments Function :

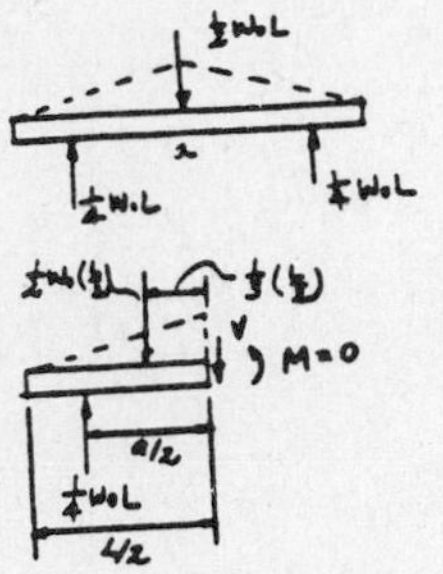

$\circlearrowleft + \Sigma M = 0; \quad 0+\frac{1}{2}(w_0)\left(\frac{L}{2}\right)\left(\frac{1}{3}\right)\left(\frac{L}{2}\right)-\frac{1}{4}w_0 L\left(\frac{a}{2}\right)=0$

$a = \frac{L}{3}$ **Ans**

***7-28.** Determine the distance a between the bearings in terms of the shaft's length L so that the moment in the *symmetric* shaft is zero at its center.

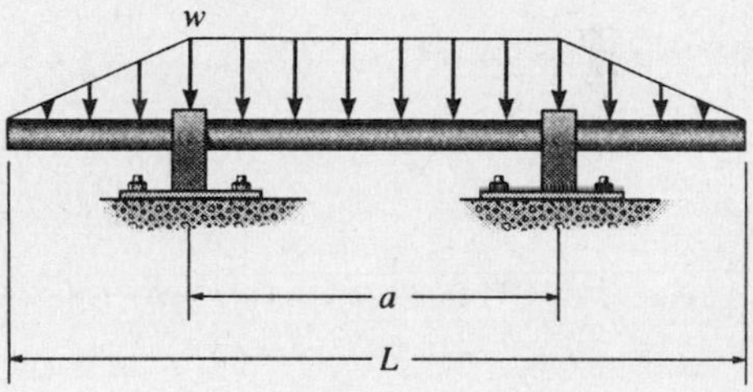

Due to symmetry, $\quad A_y = B_y$

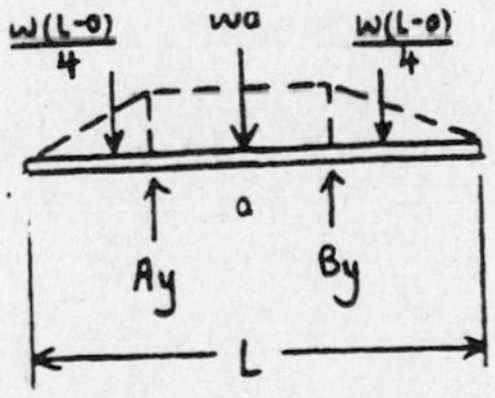

$+\uparrow \Sigma F_y = 0; \quad A_y + B_y - \frac{w(L-a)}{4} - wa - \frac{w(L-a)}{4} = 0$

$A_y = B_y = \frac{w}{4}(L+a)$

$\circlearrowleft + \Sigma M = 0; \quad -M - \frac{wa}{2}\left(\frac{a}{4}\right) - \frac{w(L-a)}{4}\left(\frac{a}{2}+\frac{L}{6}-\frac{a}{6}\right) + \frac{w}{4}(L+a)\left(\frac{a}{2}\right) = 0$

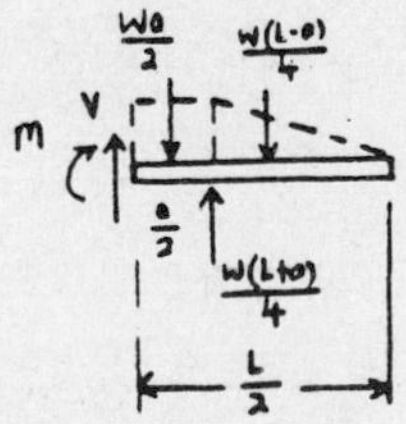

Since $M = 0$;

$3a^2 + (L-a)(L+2a) - 3a(L+a) = 0$

$2a^2 + 2aL - L^2 = 0$

$a = 0.366\,L$ **Ans**

7-29. Determine the internal normal force, shear force, and the moment at points C and D.

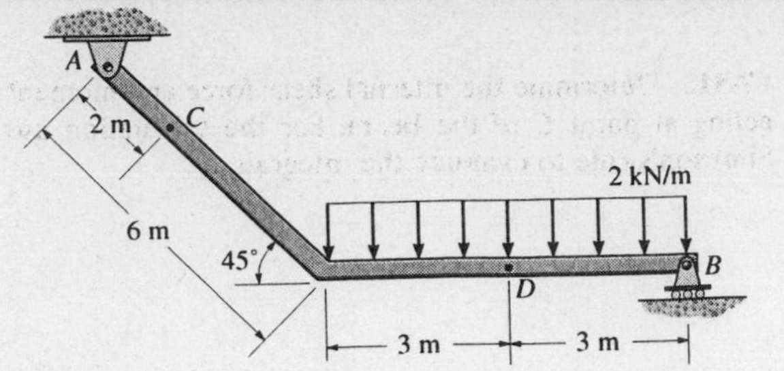

Support Reactions : FBD (a).

$$\circlearrowleft + \Sigma M_A = 0; \quad B_y\,(6 + 6\cos 45°) - 12.0(3 + 6\cos 45°) = 0$$
$$B_y = 8.485 \text{ kN}$$
$$+\uparrow \Sigma F_y = 0; \quad A_y + 8.485 - 12.0 = 0 \quad A_y = 3.515 \text{ kN}$$
$$\xrightarrow{+} \Sigma F_x = 0 \quad A_x = 0$$

Internal Forces : Applying the equations of equilibrium to segment AC [FBD (b)], we have

$$\nearrow + \Sigma F_{x'} = 0; \quad 3.515\cos 45° - V_C = 0 \quad V_C = 2.49 \text{ kN} \quad \textbf{Ans}$$

$$\nwarrow + \Sigma F_{y'} = 0; \quad 3.515\sin 45° - N_C = 0 \quad N_C = 2.49 \text{ kN} \quad \textbf{Ans}$$

$$\circlearrowleft + \Sigma M_C = 0; \quad M_C - 3.515\cos 45°(2) = 0$$
$$M_C = 4.97 \text{ kN}\cdot\text{m} \quad \textbf{Ans}$$

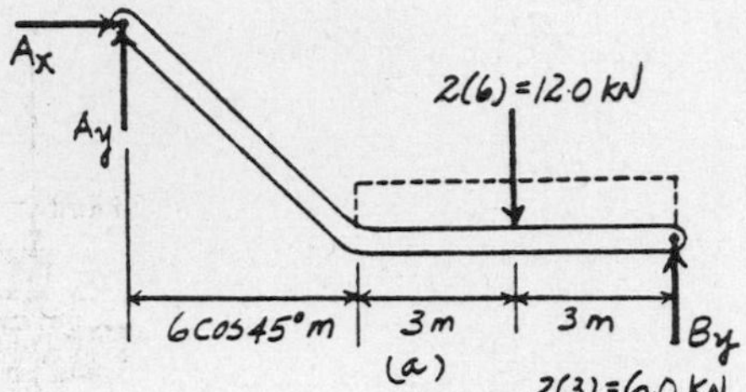

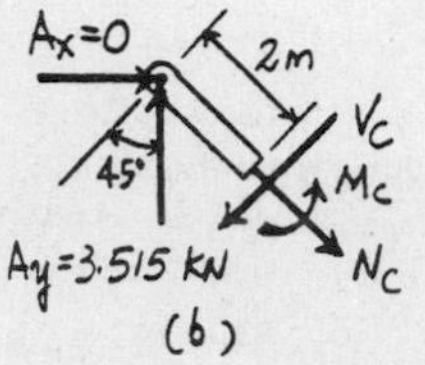

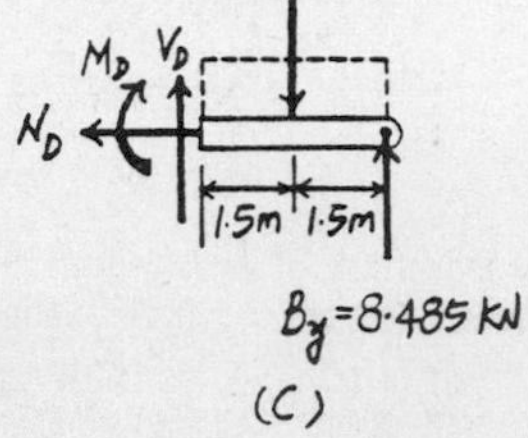

Applying the equations of equilibrium to segment BD [FBD (c)], we have

$$\xrightarrow{+} \Sigma F_x = 0; \quad N_D = 0 \quad \textbf{Ans}$$

$$+\uparrow \Sigma F_y = 0; \quad V_D + 8.485 - 6.00 = 0 \quad V_D = -2.49 \text{ kN} \quad \textbf{Ans}$$

$$\circlearrowleft + \Sigma M_D = 0; \quad 8.485(3) - 6(1.5) - M_D = 0$$
$$M_D = 16.5 \text{ kN}\cdot\text{m} \quad \textbf{Ans}$$

7-30. The pliers are used to grip the tube. If a force of 20 lb is applied to the handles, determine the internal shear force and moment at point C. Assume the jaws of the pliers exert only normal forces on the tube.

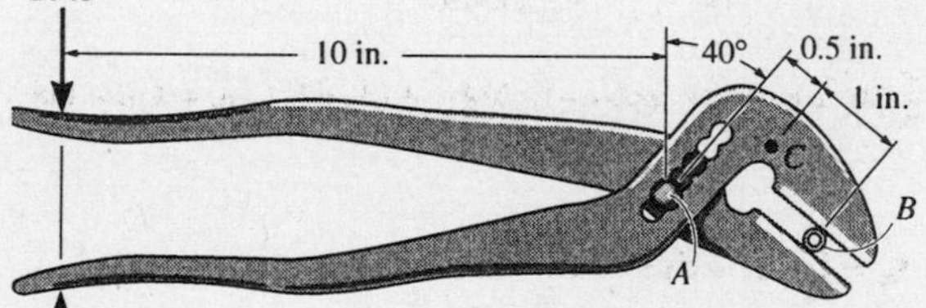

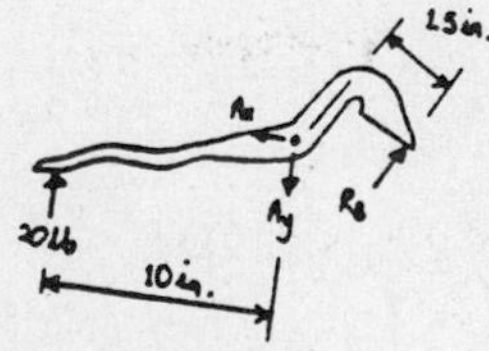

$$+\Sigma M_A = 0; \quad -20\,(10) + R_B\,(1.5) = 0$$

$$R_B = 133.3 \text{ lb}$$

Segment BC :

$$+\nearrow \Sigma F_y = 0; \quad V_C + 133.3 = 0$$

$$V_C = -133 \text{ lb} \quad \textbf{Ans}$$

$$\circlearrowleft + \Sigma M_C = 0; \quad -M_C + 133.3\,(1) = 0$$

$$M_C = 133 \text{ lb}\cdot\text{in.} \quad \textbf{Ans}$$

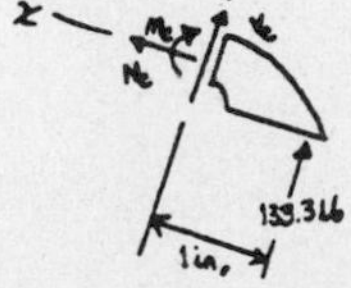

■**7-31.** Determine the internal shear force and moment acting at point C of the beam. For the calculation use Simpson's rule to evaluate the integrals.

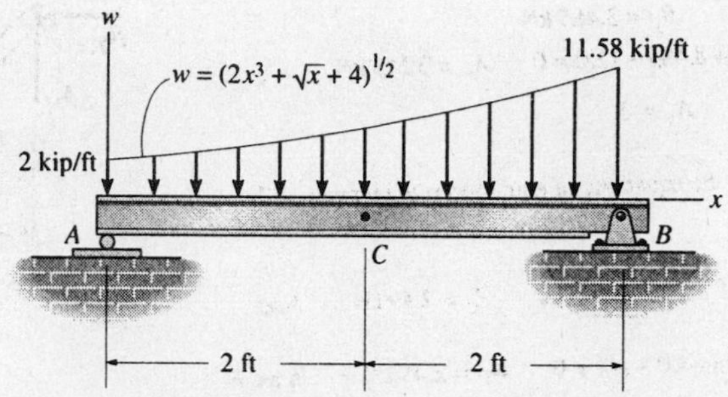

$$F_R = \int_0^4 \left(2x^3 + \sqrt{x} + 4\right)^{\frac{1}{2}} dx = 21.4899 \text{ kip}$$

$$\bar{x} = \frac{\int_0^4 x\left(2x^3 + \sqrt{x} + 4\right)^{\frac{1}{2}} dx}{F_R} = \frac{56.0634}{21.4899} = 2.6088 \text{ ft}$$

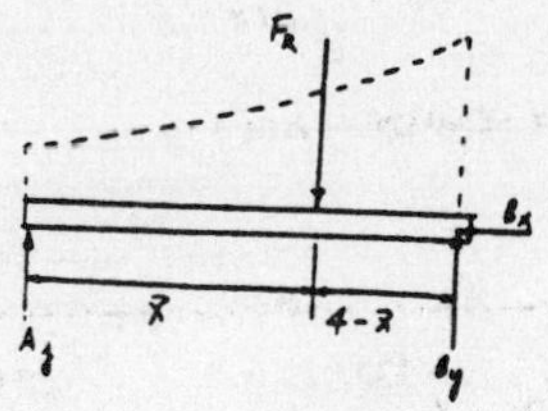

$\curvearrowleft + \Sigma M_B = 0;\quad 21.4899(4 - 2.6088) - A_y(4) = 0 \qquad A_y = 7.4740 \text{ kip}$

$$F_{R_1} = \int_0^2 \left(2x^3 + \sqrt{x} + 4\right)^{\frac{1}{2}} dx = 5.7862 \text{ kip}$$

$$\bar{x}_1 = \frac{\int_0^2 x\left(2x^3 + \sqrt{x} + 4\right)^{\frac{1}{2}} dx}{F_{R_1}} = \frac{6.6255}{5.7862} = 1.1451 \text{ ft}$$

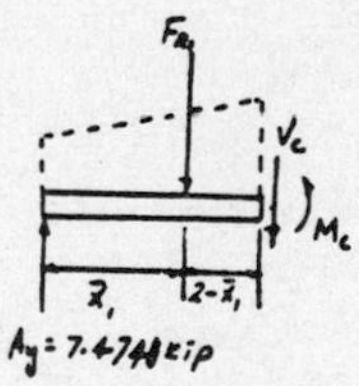

$+\uparrow \Sigma F_y = 0;\quad 7.4740 - 5.7862 - V_C = 0$

$V_C = 1.69 \text{ kip}$ **Ans**

$\curvearrowleft + \Sigma M_C = 0;\quad M_C + 5.7862(2 - 1.1451) - 7.4740(2) = 0$

$M_C = 10.0 \text{ kip} \cdot \text{ft}$ **Ans**

***7-32.** Determine the internal normal force, shear force, and moment acting at point C. The cooling unit has a total weight of 225 kg and a center of gravity at G.

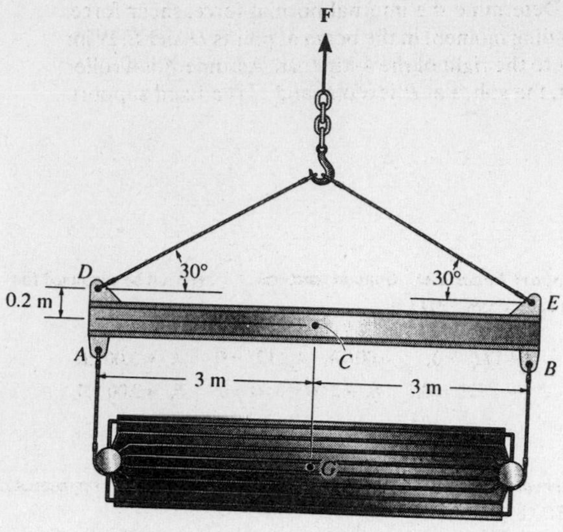

From FBD (a)

$\circlearrowleft + \Sigma M_A = 0;\quad T_B(6) - 225(9.81)(3) = 0 \qquad T_B = 1103.625\ \text{N}$

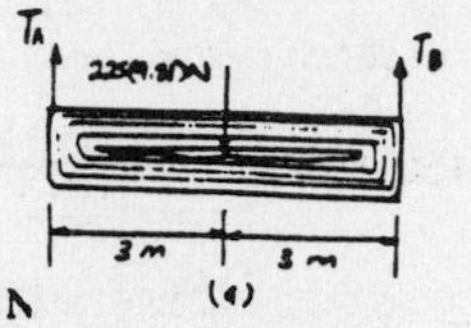

From FBD (b)

$\circlearrowleft + \Sigma M_D = 0;\quad T_E \sin 30°(6) - 1103.625(6) = 0 \qquad T_E = 2207.25\ \text{N}$

From FBD (c)

$\xrightarrow{+} \Sigma F_x = 0;\quad -N_C - 2207.25 \cos 30° = 0 \qquad N_C = -1.91\ \text{kN}$ **Ans**

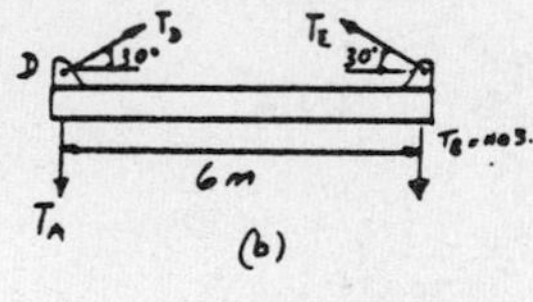

$+\uparrow \Sigma F_y = 0;\quad V_C + 2207.25 \sin 30° - 1103.625 = 0 \qquad V_C = 0$ **Ans**

$\circlearrowleft + \Sigma M_C = 0;\quad 2207.25 \cos 30°(0.2) + 2207.25 \sin 30°(3) - 1103.625(3) - M_C = 0$

$M_C = 382\ \text{N} \cdot \text{m}$ **Ans**

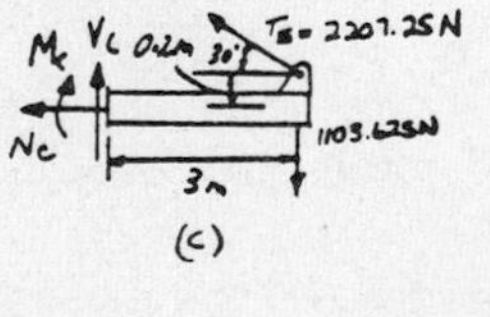

7-33. Determine the internal normal force, shear force, and bending moment in the beam at points D and E. Point E is just to the right of the 4-kip load. Assume A is a roller support, the splice at B is a pin, and C is a fixed support.

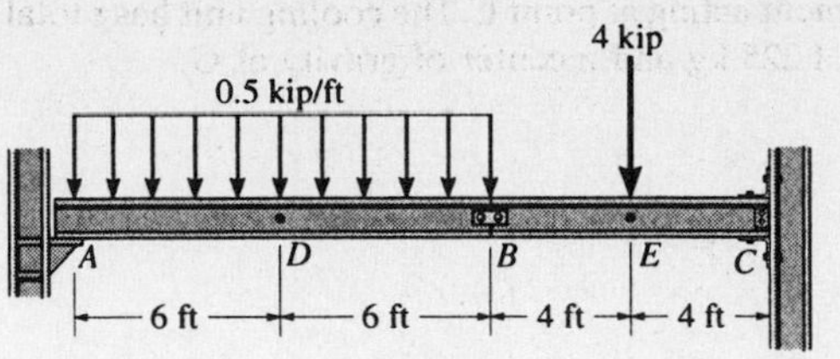

Support Reactions : Support reactions at C need not be computed for this case. From FBD (a),

$\circlearrowleft + \Sigma M_B = 0;\quad 6.00(6) - A_y(12) = 0\quad A_y = 3.00\text{ kN}$

$+\uparrow \Sigma F_y = 0;\quad B_y + 3.00 - 6.00 = 0\quad B_y = 3.00\text{ kN}$

$\xrightarrow{+} \Sigma F_x = 0\quad B_x = 0$

Internal Forces : Applying the equations of equilibrium to segment AD [FBD (b)], we have

$\xrightarrow{+} \Sigma F_x = 0;\quad N_D = 0$ **Ans**

$+\uparrow \Sigma F_y = 0;\quad 3.00 - 3.00 - V_D = 0\quad V_D = 0$ **Ans**

$\circlearrowleft + \Sigma M_D = 0;\quad M_D - 3.00(3) = 0\quad M_D = 9.00\text{ kN}\cdot\text{m}$ **Ans**

Applying the equations of equilibrium to segment BE [FBD (c)], we have

$\xrightarrow{+} \Sigma F_x = 0;\quad N_E = 0$ **Ans**

$+\uparrow \Sigma F_y = 0;\quad -3.00 - 4 - V_E = 0\quad V_E = -7.00\text{ kN}$ **Ans**

$\circlearrowleft + \Sigma M_E = 0;\quad M_E + 3.00(4) = 0\quad M_E = -12.0\text{ kN}\cdot\text{m}$ **Ans**

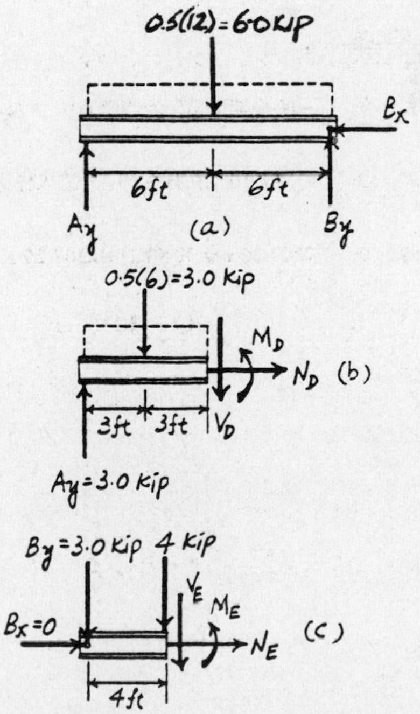

7-34. Determine the internal normal force, shear force, and bending moment at points E and F of the frame.

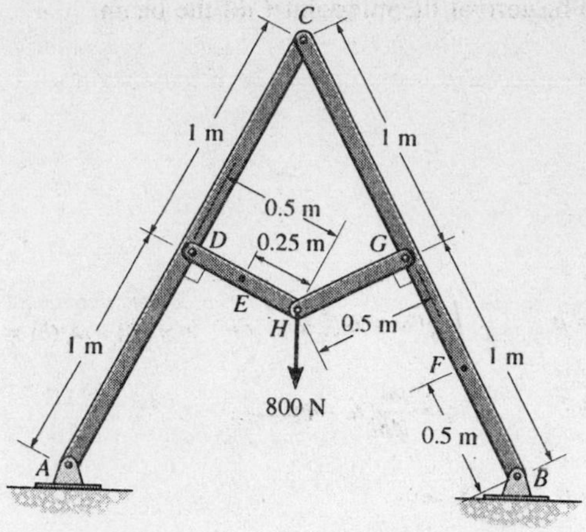

Support Reactions : Members HD and HG are two force members. Using method of joint [FBD (a)], we have

$$\xrightarrow{+} \Sigma F_x = 0 \qquad F_{HG}\cos 26.57° - F_{HD}\cos 26.57° = 0$$

$$F_{HD} = F_{HG} = F$$

$$+\uparrow \Sigma F_y = 0; \qquad 2F\sin 26.57° - 800 = 0$$

$$F_{HD} = F_{HG} = F = 894.43 \text{ N}$$

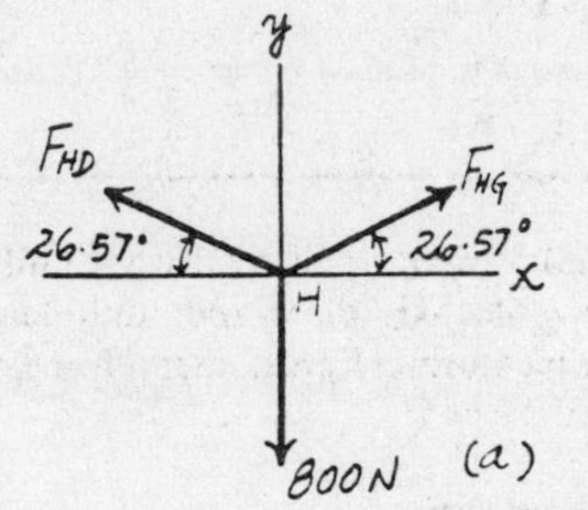

From FBD (b),

$$\curvearrowleft + \Sigma M_A = 0; \qquad C_x(2\cos 26.57°) + C_y(2\sin 26.57°) - 894.43(1) = 0 \quad [1]$$

From FBD (c),

$$\curvearrowleft + \Sigma M_A = 0; \qquad 894.43(1) - C_x(2\cos 26.57°) + C_y(2\sin 26.57°) = 0 \quad [2]$$

Solving Eqs.[2] and [2] yields,

$$C_y = 0 \qquad C_x = 500 \text{ N}$$

Internal Forces : Applying the equations of equilibrium to segment DE [FBD (d)], we have

$$+ \ \Sigma F_{x'} = 0; \qquad V_E = 0 \qquad \textbf{Ans}$$

$$+\Sigma F_{y'} = 0; \qquad 894.43 - N_E = 0 \qquad N_E = 894 \text{ N} \qquad \textbf{Ans}$$

$$\curvearrowleft + \Sigma M_E = 0; \qquad M_E = 0 \qquad \textbf{Ans}$$

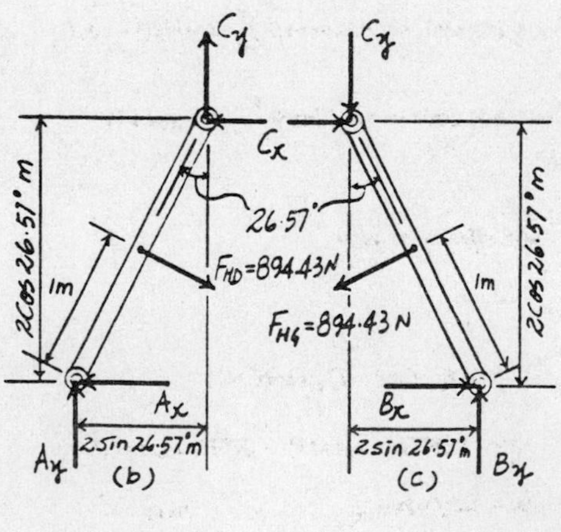

Applying the equations of equilibrium to segment CF[FBD (e)] , we have

$$+ \ \Sigma F_{x'} = 0; \qquad V_F + 500\cos 26.57° - 894.43 = 0$$

$$V_F = 447 \text{ N} \qquad \textbf{Ans}$$

$$+\Sigma F_{y'} = 0; \qquad N_F - 500\sin 26.57° = 0 \qquad N_F = 224 \text{ N} \qquad \textbf{Ans}$$

$$\curvearrowleft + \Sigma M_F = 0; \qquad M_F + 894.43(0.5) - 500\cos 26.57°(1.5) = 0$$

$$M_F = 224 \text{ N}\cdot\text{m} \qquad \textbf{Ans}$$

7-35. Determine the ratio of a/b for which the shear force will be zero at the midpoint C of the beam.

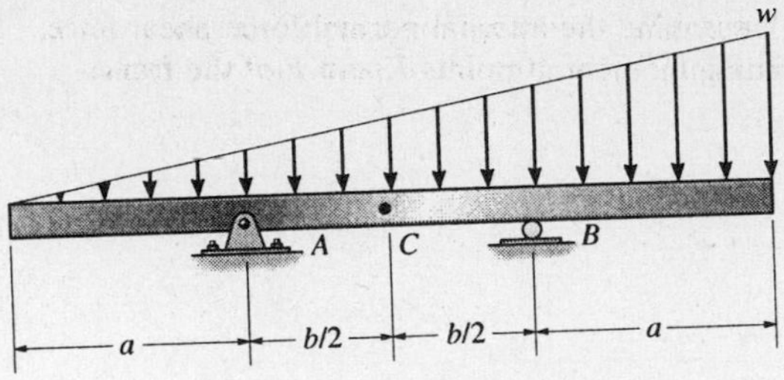

$\curvearrowleft + \Sigma M_B = 0;\quad -\frac{w}{2}(2a+b)[\frac{2}{3}(2a+b) - (a+b)] + A_y(b) = 0$

$A_y = \frac{w}{6b}(2a+b)(a-b)$

$\xrightarrow{+} \Sigma F_x = 0;\quad A_x = 0$

$+\uparrow \Sigma F_y = 0;\quad -\frac{w}{6b}(2a+b)(a-b) - \frac{w}{4}(a+\frac{b}{2}) - V_C = 0$

Since $V_C = 0$,

$-\frac{1}{6b}(2a+b)(a-b) = \frac{1}{4}(2a+b)(\frac{1}{2})$

$-\frac{1}{6b}(a-b) = \frac{1}{8}$

$-a+b = \frac{3}{4}b$

$\frac{a}{b} = \frac{1}{4}$ **Ans**

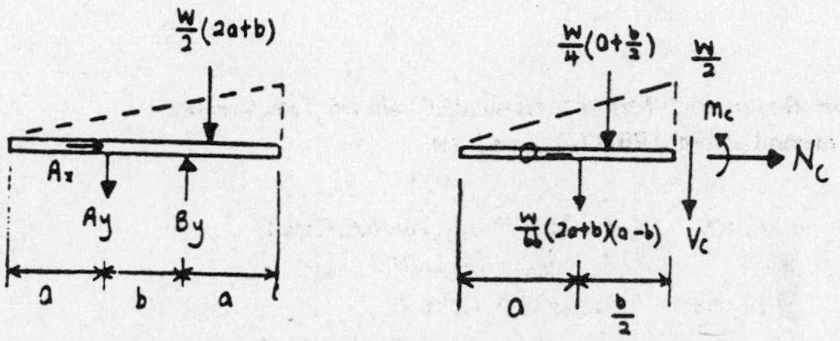

***7-36.** The semicircular arch is subjected to a uniform distributed load along its axis of w_0 per unit length. Determine the internal normal force, shear force, and moment in the arch at $\theta = 45°$.

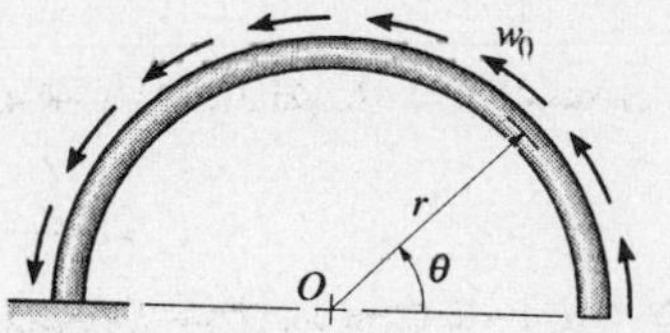

Resultants of distributed load:

$F_{Rx} = \int_0^\theta w_0(r\,d\theta)\sin\theta = r w_0(-\cos\theta)\Big|_0^\theta = r w_0(1-\cos\theta)$

$F_{Ry} = \int_0^\theta w_0(r\,d\theta)\cos\theta = r w_0(\sin\theta)\Big|_0^\theta = r w_0(\sin\theta)$

$M_{R_O} = \int_0^\theta w_0(r\,d\theta)\,r = r^2 w_0 \theta$

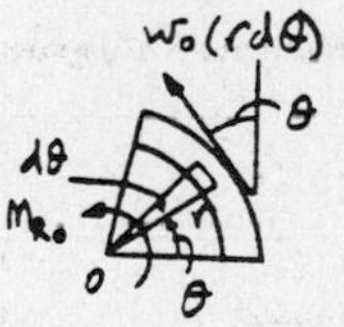

At $\theta = 45°$

$+\swarrow \Sigma F_x = 0;\quad -V + F_{Rx}\cos\theta - F_{Ry}\sin\theta = 0$

$V = 0.2929 r w_0 \cos 45° - 0.707 r w_0 \sin 45°$

$V = -0.293\, r w_0$ **Ans**

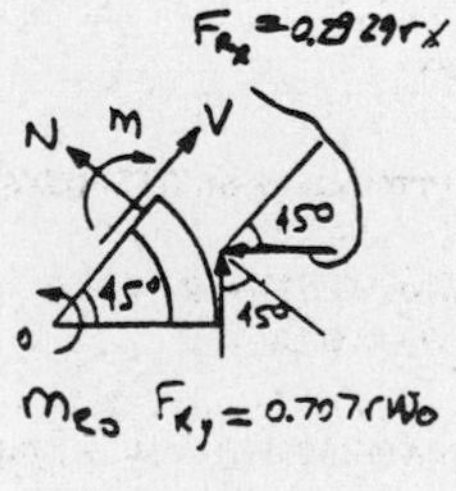

$+\nwarrow \Sigma F_y = 0;\quad N + F_{Ry}\cos\theta + F_{Rx}\sin\theta = 0$

$N = -0.707 r w_0 \sin 45° - 0.2929 r w_0 \cos 45°$

$N = -0.707\, r w_0$ **Ans**

$\curvearrowleft + \Sigma M_O = 0;\quad -M + r^2 w_0\left(\frac{\pi}{4}\right) + (-0.707\, r w_0)(r) = 0$

$M = -0.0783\, r^2 w_0$ **Ans**

7-37. Solve Prob. 7-36 for $\theta = 120°$.

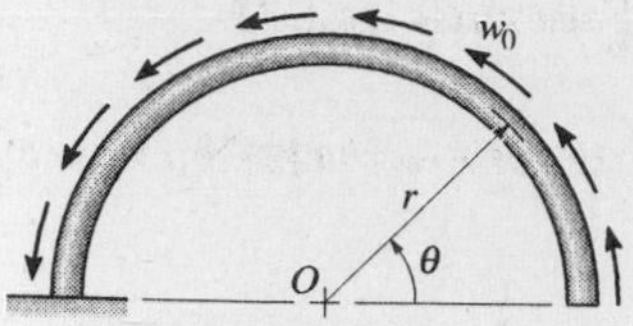

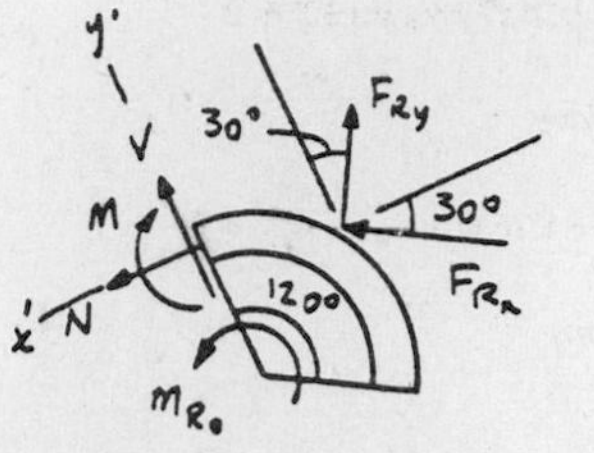

Resultants of distributed load:

$$F_{Rx} = \int_0^{\theta} w_0 (r\,d\theta)\sin\theta = r\,w_0(-\cos\theta)\Big|_0^{\theta} = r\,w_0(1-\cos\theta)$$

$$F_{Ry} = \int_0^{\theta} w_0 (r\,d\theta)\cos\theta = r\,w_0(\sin\theta)\Big|_0^{\theta} = r\,w_0(\sin\theta)$$

$$M_{Ro} = \int_0^{\theta} w_0 (r\,d\theta)\,r = r^2 w_0 \theta$$

At $\theta = 120°$,

$F_{Rx} = r\,w_0(1-\cos 120°) = 1.5\,r\,w_0$

$F_{Ry} = r\,w_0 \sin 120° = 0.86603\,r\,w_0$

$+\swarrow \Sigma F_{x'} = 0;\quad N + 1.5\,r\,w_0\cos 30° - 0.86603\,r\,w_0 \sin 30° = 0$

$N = -0.866\,r\,w_0$ **Ans**

$+\nwarrow \Sigma F_{y'} = 0;\quad V + 1.5\,r\,w_0\sin 30° + 0.86603\,r\,w_0\cos 30° = 0$

$V = -1.5\,r w_0$ **Ans**

$\circlearrowleft + \Sigma M_O = 0;\quad -M + r^2 w_0(\pi)\left(\frac{120°}{180°}\right) + (-0.866\,r\,w_0)r = 0$

$M = 1.23\,r^2 w_0$ **Ans**

7-38. The distributed loading $w = w_0 \sin\theta$, measured per unit length, acts on the curved rod. Determine the internal normal force, shear force, and moment in the rod at $\theta = 45°$.

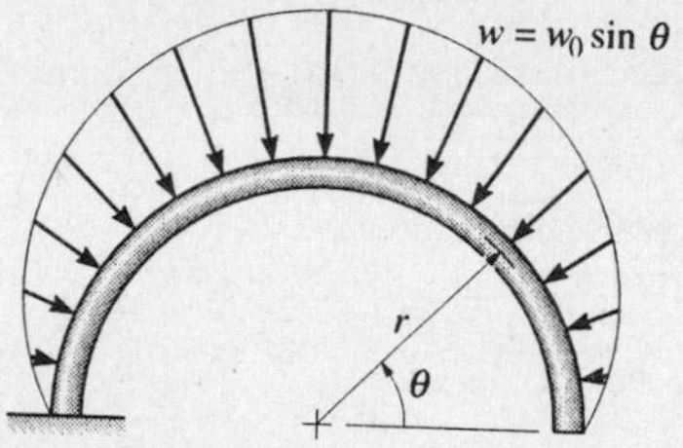

$w = w_0 \sin\theta$

Resultants of distributed loading:

$$F_{Rx} = \int_0^{\theta} w_0 \sin\theta (r\,d\theta)\cos\theta = r\,w_0\int_0^{\theta}\sin\theta\cos\theta\,d\theta = \frac{1}{2} r\,w_0 \sin^2\theta$$

$$F_{Ry} = \int_0^{\theta} w_0 \sin\theta (r\,d\theta)\sin\theta = r\,w_0\int_0^{\theta}\sin^2\theta\,d\theta = r\,w_0\left[\frac{1}{2}\theta - \frac{1}{4}\sin 2\theta\right]$$

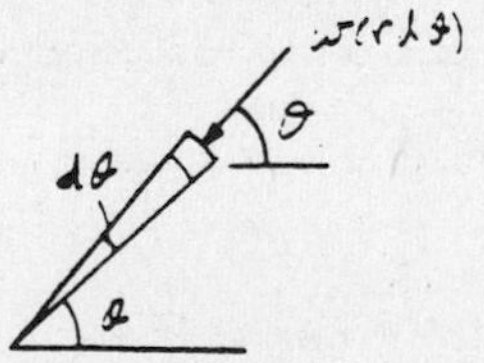

$\swarrow + \Sigma F_x = 0;\quad -V + F_{Rx}\cos 45° + F_{Ry}\sin 45° = 0$

$$V = \left(\frac{1}{2} r\,w_0 \sin^2 45°\right)\cos 45° + r\,w_0\left(\frac{1}{2}\frac{\pi}{4} - \frac{1}{4}\sin 90°\right)\sin 45°$$

$V = 0.278\,w_0 r$ **Ans**

$\nwarrow + \Sigma F_y = 0;\quad -N - F_{Ry}\cos 45° + F_{Rx}\sin 45° = 0$

$$N = -r\,w_0\left[\frac{1}{2}\left(\frac{\pi}{4}\right) - \frac{1}{4}\sin 90°\right]\cos 45° + \left(\frac{1}{2} r\,w_0 \sin^2 45°\right)\sin 45°$$

$N = 0.0759\,w_0 r$ **Ans**

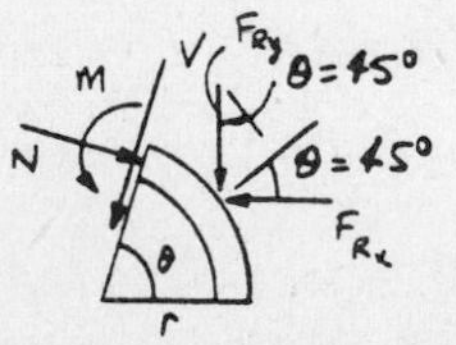

$\circlearrowleft + \Sigma M_O = 0;\quad M - (0.0759 r\,w_0)(r) = 0$

$M = 0.0759\,w_0 r^2$ **Ans**

7-39. Solve Prob. 7-38 for $\theta = 120°$.

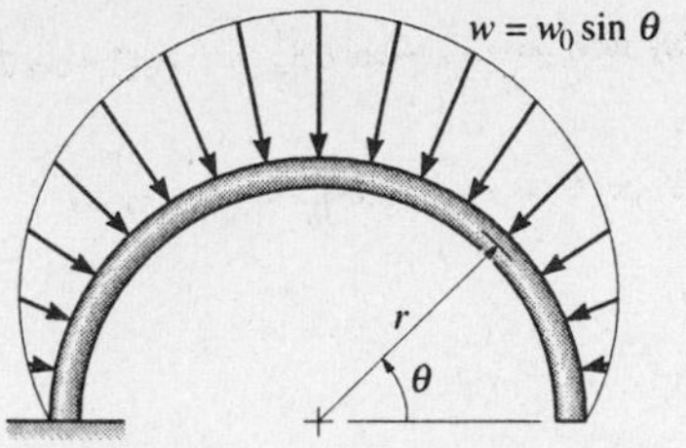

Resultants of distributed load :

$$F_{Rx} = \int_0^\theta w_0 \sin\theta (r\, d\theta) \cos\theta = r\, w_0 \int_0^\theta \sin\theta \cos\theta = \tfrac{1}{2} r w_0 \sin^2\theta$$

$$F_{Ry} = \int_0^\theta w_0 \sin\theta (r\, d\theta) \sin\theta = r w_0 \int_0^\theta \sin^2\theta\, d\theta = r w_0 \left[\tfrac{1}{2}\theta\ \tfrac{1}{4}\sin 2\theta\right] r\, w_0 (\sin\theta)\Big|_0^\theta = r\, w_0 (\sin\theta)$$

$$F_{Rx} = \tfrac{1}{2} r\, w_0 \sin^2 120° = 0.375\, r\, w_0$$

$$F_{Ry} = r\, w_0 \left[\tfrac{1}{2}(\pi)\left(\frac{120°}{180°}\right) - \tfrac{1}{4}\sin 240°\right] = 1.2637\, r\, w_0$$

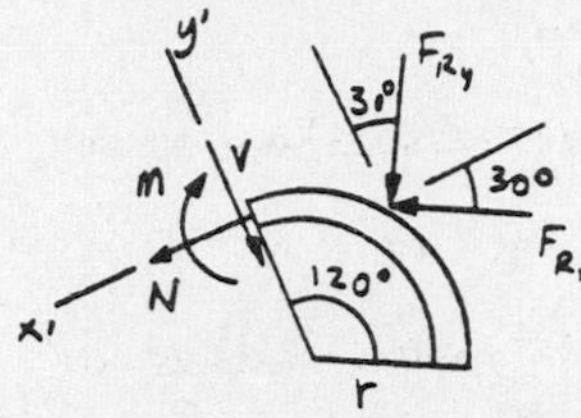

$+\swarrow \Sigma F_{x'} = 0;$ $\quad N + 0.375\, r\, w_0 \cos 30° + 1.2637\, r\, w_0 \sin 30° = 0$

$N = -0.957\, r\, w_0$ **Ans**

$+\nwarrow \Sigma F_{y'} = 0;$ $\quad -V + 0.375\, r\, w_0 \sin 30° - 1.2637\, r\, w_0 \cos 30° = 0$

$V = -0.907\, r w_0$ **Ans**

$\circlearrowleft + \Sigma M_O = 0;$ $\quad -M - 0.957\, r\, w_0\, (r) = 0$

$M = -0.957\, r^2 w_0$ **Ans**

***7-40.** Determine the x, y, z components of force and moment at point C in the pipe assembly. Neglect the weight of the pipe. The load acting at (0, 3.5 ft, 3 ft)is $\mathbf{F}_1 = \{-24\mathbf{i} - 10\mathbf{k}\}$ lb and $\mathbf{M} = \{-30\mathbf{k}\}$ lb · ft and at point (0, 3.5 ft, 0) $\mathbf{F}_2 = \{-80\mathbf{i}\}$ lb.

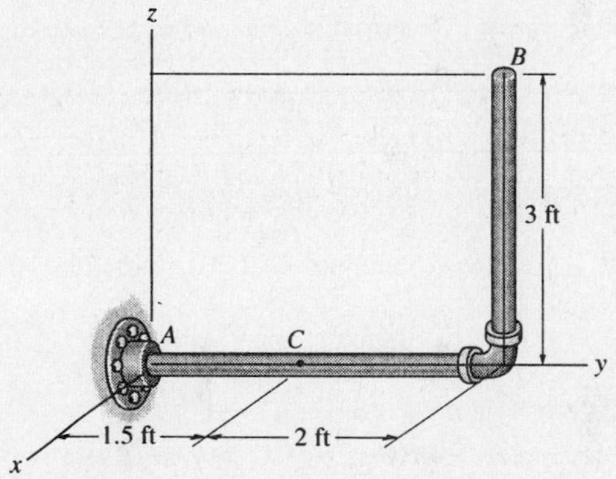

Free body Diagram : The support reactions need not be computed.

Internal Forces : Applying the equations of equilibrium to segment BC, we have

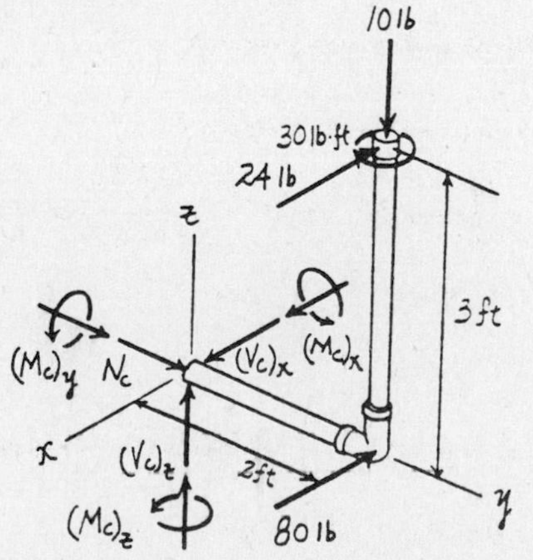

$\Sigma F_x = 0;$ $\quad (V_C)_x - 24 - 80 = 0 \quad (V_C)_x = 104$ lb **Ans**

$\Sigma F_y = 0;$ $\quad N_C = 0$ **Ans**

$\Sigma F_z = 0;$ $\quad (V_C)_z - 10 = 0 \quad (V_C)_z = 10.0$ lb **Ans**

$\Sigma M_x = 0;$ $\quad (M_C)_x - 10(2) = 0 \quad (M_C)_x = 20.0$ lb · ft **Ans**

$\Sigma M_y = 0;$ $\quad (M_C)_y - 24(3) = 0 \quad (M_C)_y = 72.0$ lb · ft **Ans**

$\Sigma M_z = 0;$ $\quad (M_C)_z + 24(2) + 80(2) - 30 = 0$

$(M_C)_z = -178$ lb · ft **Ans**

7-41. Determine the x, y, z components of force and moment at point C in the pipe assembly. Neglect the weight of the pipe. Take $\mathbf{F}_1 = \{350\mathbf{i} - 400\mathbf{j}\}$ lb and $\mathbf{F}_2 = \{-300\mathbf{j} + 150\mathbf{k}\}$ lb.

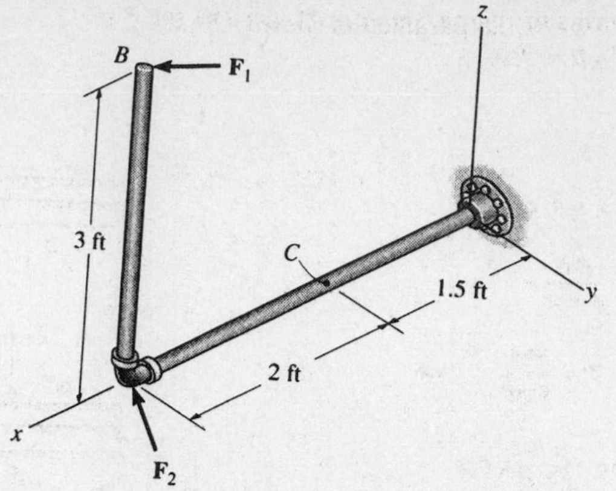

Free body Diagram : The support reactions need not be computed.

Internal Forces : Applying the equations of equilibrium to segment BC, we have

$\Sigma F_x = 0;\quad N_C + 350 = 0 \quad N_C = -350 \text{ lb}$ **Ans**

$\Sigma F_y = 0;\quad (V_C)_y - 400 - 300 = 0 \quad (V_C)_y = 700 \text{ lb}$ **Ans**

$\Sigma F_z = 0;\quad (V_C)_z + 150 = 0 \quad (V_C)_z = -150 \text{ lb}$ **Ans**

$\Sigma M_x = 0;\quad (M_C)_x + 400(3) = 0$

$(M_C)_x = -1200 \text{ lb}\cdot\text{ft} = -1.20 \text{ kip}\cdot\text{ft}$ **Ans**

$\Sigma M_y = 0;\quad (M_C)_y + 350(3) - 150(2) = 0$

$(M_C)_y = -750 \text{ lb}\cdot\text{ft}$ **Ans**

$\Sigma M_z = 0;\quad (M_C)_z - 300(2) - 400(2) = 0$

$(M_C)_z = 1400 \text{ lb}\cdot\text{ft} = 1.40 \text{ kip}\cdot\text{ft}$ **Ans**

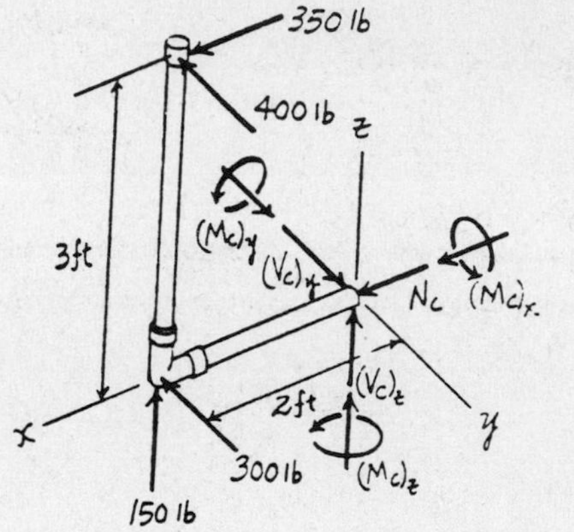

7-42. Draw the shear and moment diagrams for the beam (a) in terms of the parameters shown; (b) set $P = 600$ lb, $a = 5$ ft, $b = 7$ ft.

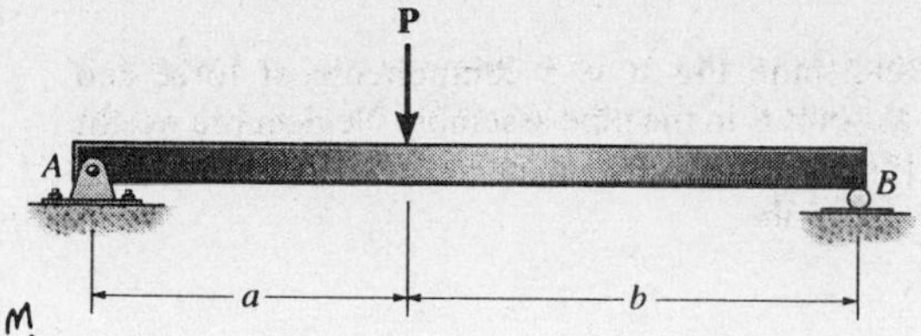

(a) For $0 \le x < a$

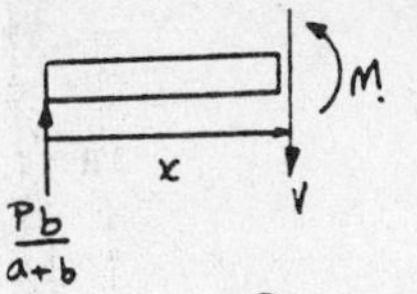

$+\uparrow \Sigma F_y = 0; \quad \frac{Pb}{a+b} - V = 0$

$V = \frac{Pb}{a+b}$ **Ans**

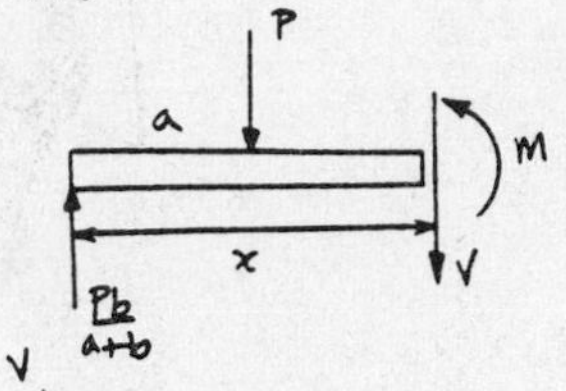

$\circlearrowleft + \Sigma M = 0; \quad M - \frac{Pb}{a+b}x = 0$

$M = \frac{Pb}{a+b}x$ **Ans**

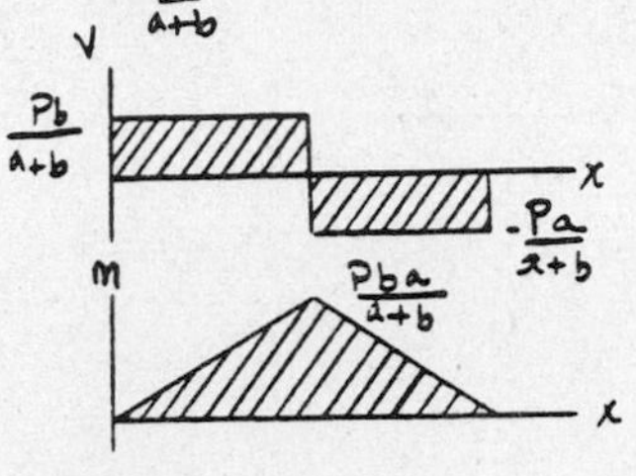

For $a < x \le (a+b)$

$+\uparrow \Sigma F_y = 0; \quad \frac{Pb}{a+b} - P - V = 0$

$V = -\frac{Pa}{a+b}$ **Ans**

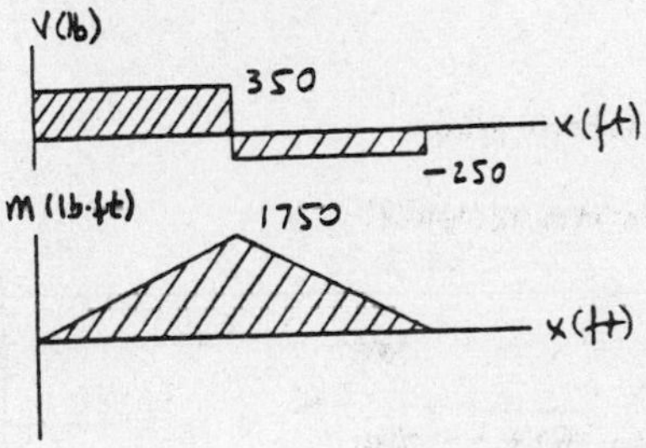

$\circlearrowleft + \Sigma M = 0; \quad -\frac{Pb}{a+b}x + P(x-a) + M = 0$

$M = Pa - \frac{Pa}{a+b}x$ **Ans**

(b) For $P = 600$ lb, $a = 5$ ft, $b = 7$ ft

7-43. Draw the shear and moment diagrams for the cantilevered beam.

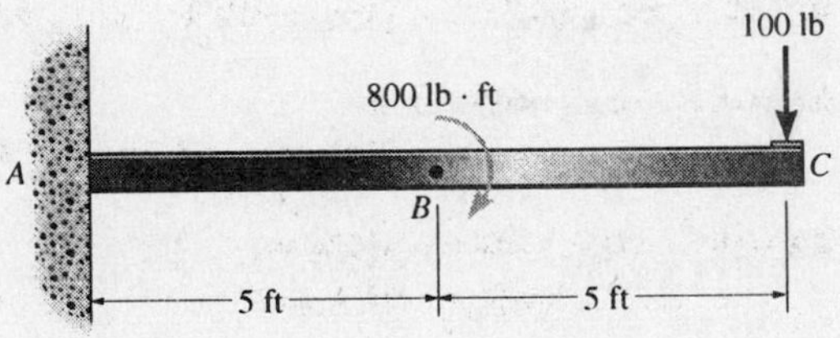

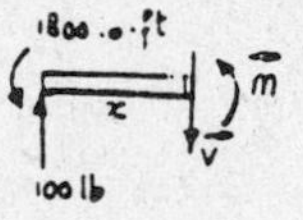

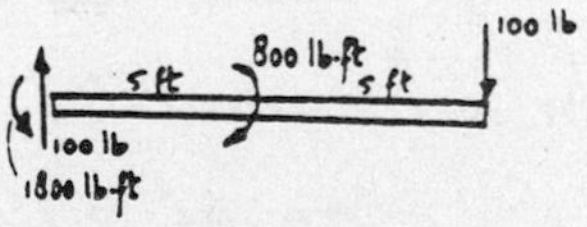

For $0 \le x < 5$ ft:

$+\uparrow \Sigma F_y = 0; \quad 100 - V = 0; \quad V = 100$ **Ans**

$\circlearrowleft + \Sigma M = 0; \quad M - 100x + 1800 = 0; \quad M = 100x - 1800$ **Ans**

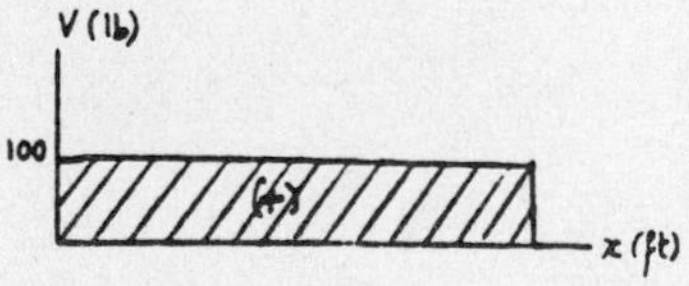

For $5 < x \le 10$ ft:

$+\uparrow \Sigma F_y = 0; \quad 100 - V = 0; \quad V = 100$ **Ans**

$\circlearrowleft + \Sigma M = 0; \quad M - 100x + 1000 = 0; \quad M = 100x - 1000$ **Ans**

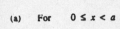

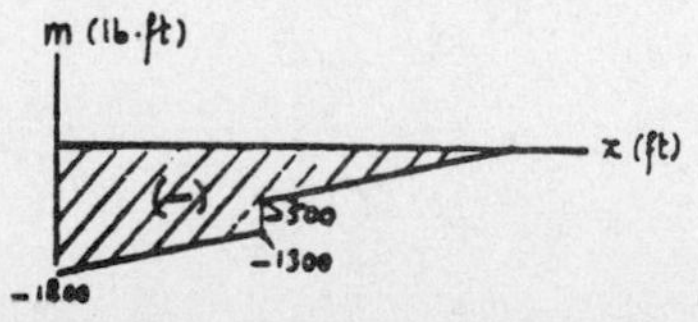

*7-44.** The suspender bar supports the 600-lb engine. Draw the shear and moment diagrams for the bar.

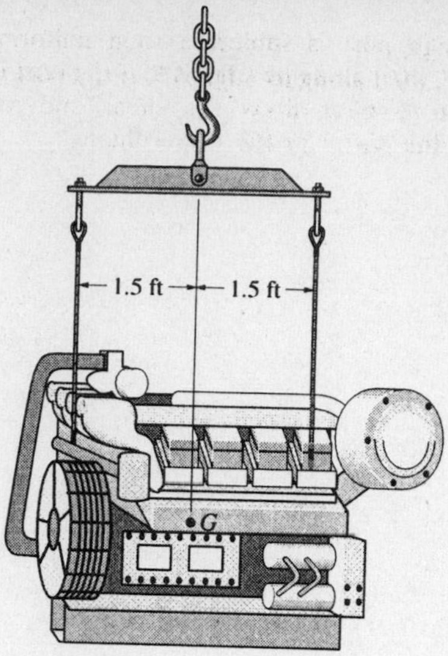

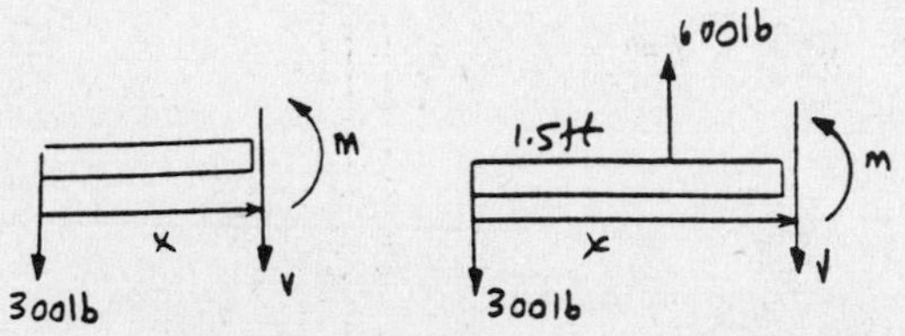

For $0 \leq x < 1.5$ ft:

$+\uparrow \Sigma F_y = 0;\quad -300 - V = 0$

$V = -300$ **Ans**

$\circlearrowleft + \Sigma M = 0;\quad M + 300x = 0$

$M = -300x$ **Ans**

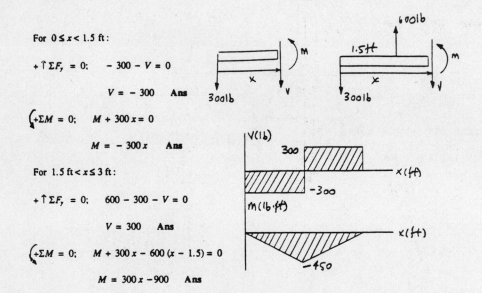

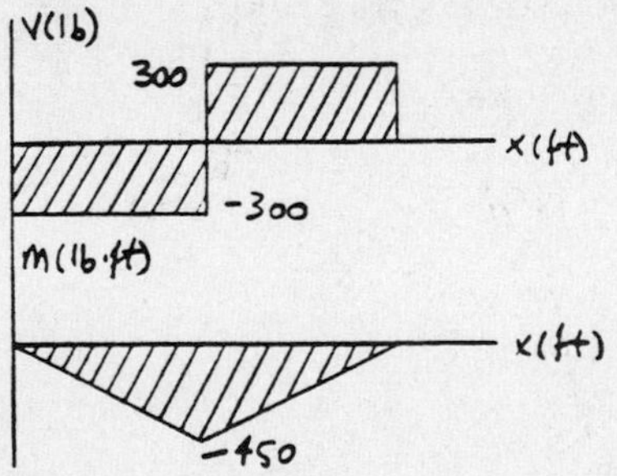

For $1.5 \text{ ft} < x \leq 3$ ft:

$+\uparrow \Sigma F_y = 0;\quad 600 - 300 - V = 0$

$V = 300$ **Ans**

$\circlearrowleft + \Sigma M = 0;\quad M + 300x - 600(x - 1.5) = 0$

$M = 300x - 900$ **Ans**

7-45. The sign post is subjected to a uniform wind loading of 300 lb/ft along its edge AB. If the post is fixed connected at its base, draw the shear and moment diagrams for the post. Use the y coordinate.

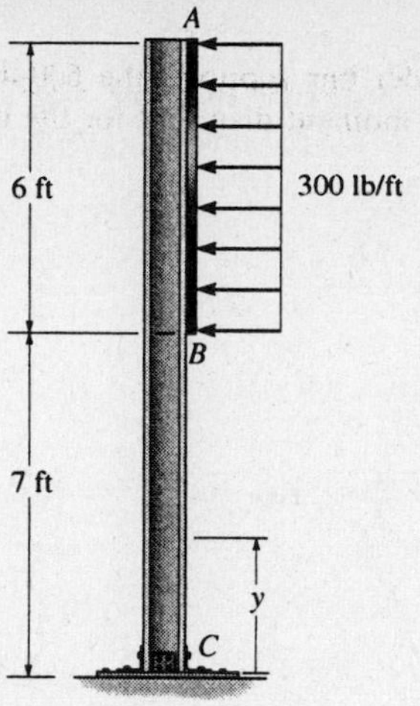

For $0 \le y < 7$ ft:

$\xrightarrow{+} \Sigma F_x = 0;\quad V + 1800 = 0$

$V = -1800$ lb **Ans**

$\curvearrowleft + \Sigma M = 0;\quad M - 18\,000 + 1800y = 0$

$M = 18\,000 - 1800y$ **Ans**

For $7 \text{ ft} < y \le 13$ ft:

$\xrightarrow{+} \Sigma F_x = 0;\quad 1800 - 900 + V = 0$

$V = -900$ lb **Ans**

$\curvearrowleft + \Sigma M = 0;\quad M - 18\,000 + 1800y - 900(y - 7) = 0$

$M = 11\,700 - 900y$ **Ans**

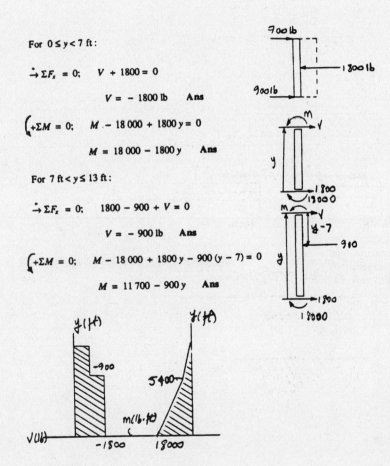

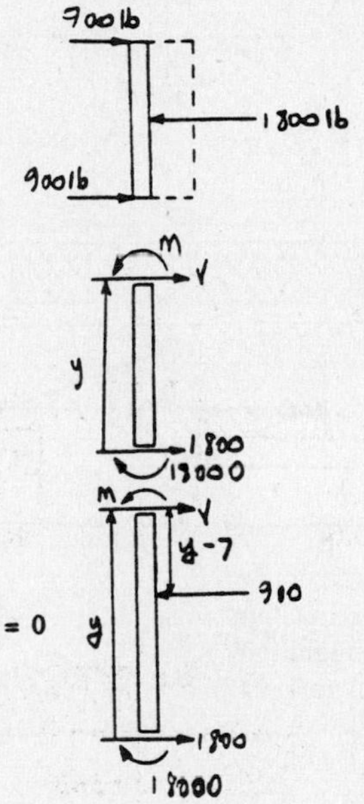

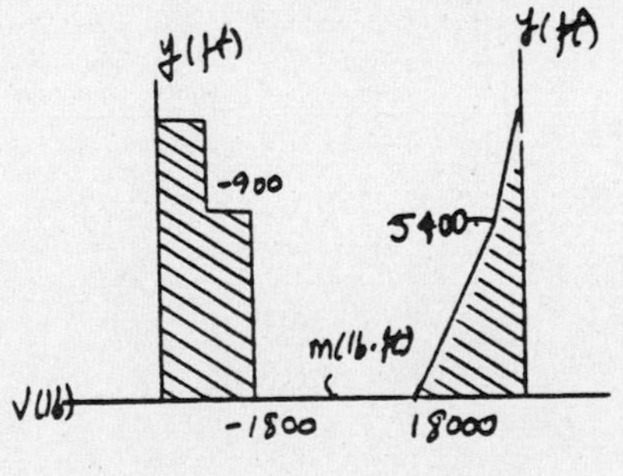

7-46. Draw the shear and moment diagrams for the beam (a) in terms of the parameters shown; (b) set $M_0 = 500$ N·m, $L = 8$ m.

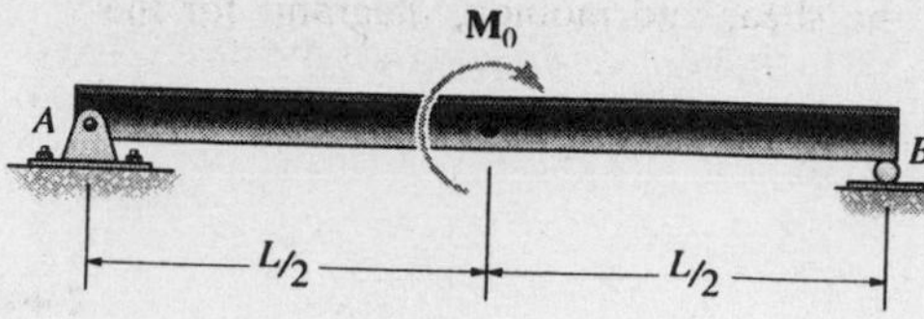

(a) $\quad 0 \le x < \frac{L}{2}$

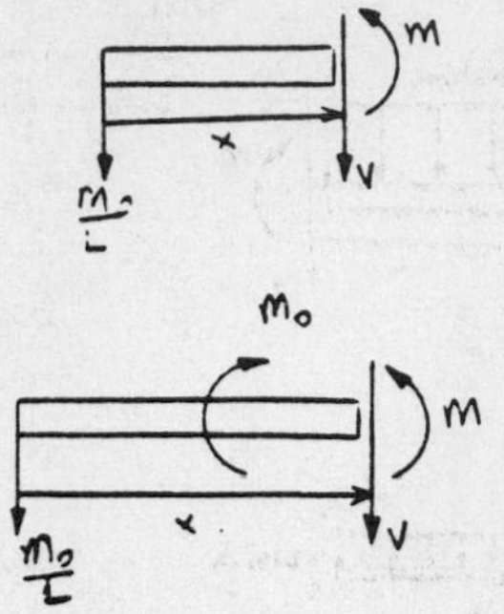

$+\uparrow\Sigma F_y = 0; \quad -\frac{M_0}{L} - V = 0$

$V = -\frac{M_0}{L}$ **Ans**

$\circlearrowleft + \Sigma M = 0; \quad M + \frac{M_0}{L}x = 0$

$M = -\frac{M_0}{L}x$ **Ans**

$\frac{L}{2} < x \le L$

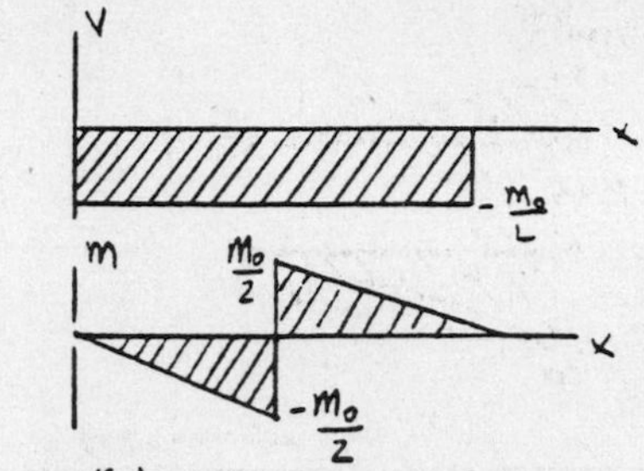

$+\uparrow\Sigma F_y = 0; \quad -\frac{M_0}{L} - V = 0$

$V = -\frac{M_0}{L}$ **Ans**

$\circlearrowleft + \Sigma M = 0; \quad M + \frac{M_0}{L}x - M_0 = 0$

$M = M_0\left(1 - \frac{x}{L}\right)$ **Ans**

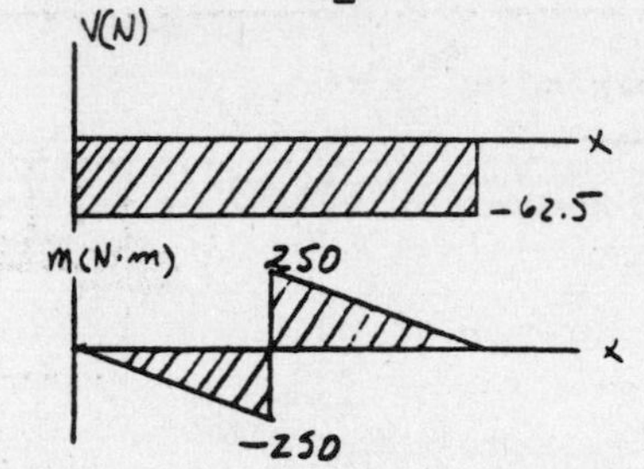

(b) When $M_0 = 500$ N · m, and $L = 8$ m

7-47. If $L = 9$ m, the beam will fail when the maximum shear force is $V_{max} = 5$ kN or the maximum bending moment is $M_{max} = 22$ kN·m. Determine the magnitude M_0 of the largest couple moment the beam will support.

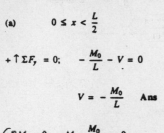

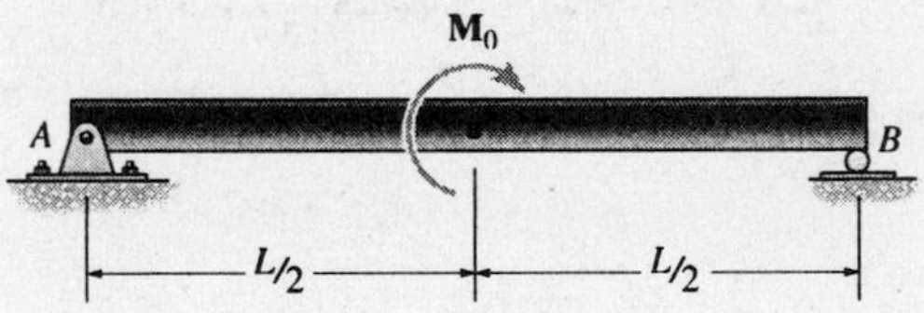

See solution to part (a) of Prob. 7-46

$V_{max} = \frac{M_0}{L}; \quad 5 = \frac{M_0}{9}; \quad M_0 = 45$ kN · m

$M_{max} = \frac{M_0}{2}; \quad 22 = \frac{M_0}{2}; \quad M_0 = 44$ kN · m

Thus,

$M_0 = 44$ kN · m **Ans**

***7-48.** Draw the shear and moment diagrams for the beam.

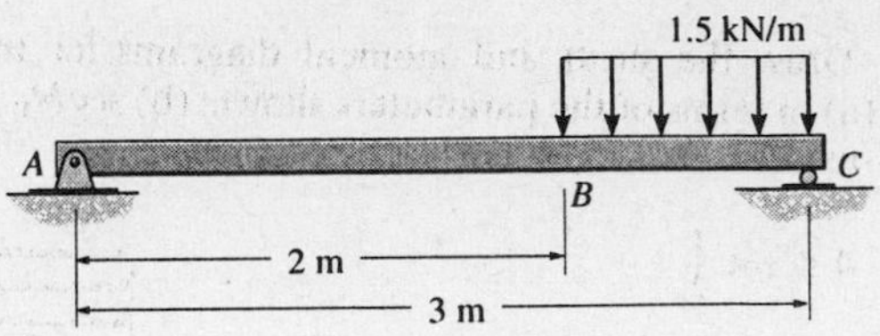

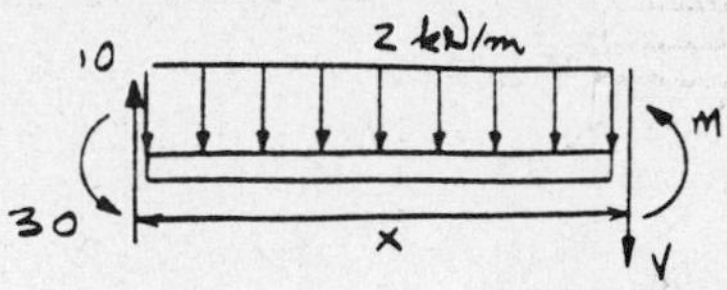

$+\uparrow\Sigma F_y = 0; \quad -V + 10 - 2x = 0$

$V = 10 - 2x$

$\curvearrowleft + \Sigma M = 0; \quad M + 30 - 10x + 2x\left(\frac{x}{2}\right) = 0$

$M = 10x - x^2 - 30$

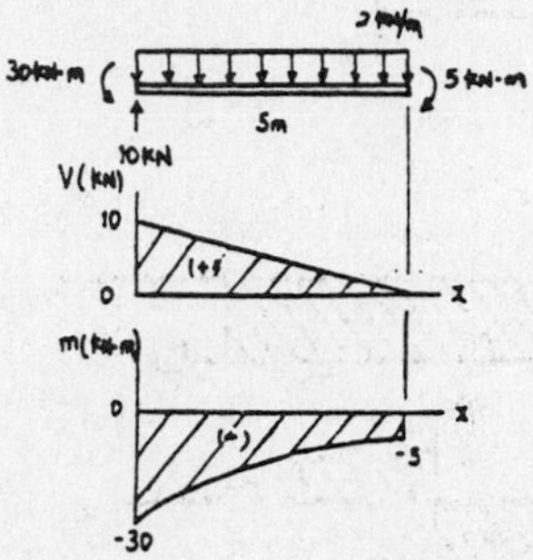

7-49. Draw the shear and bending-moment diagrams for the beam.

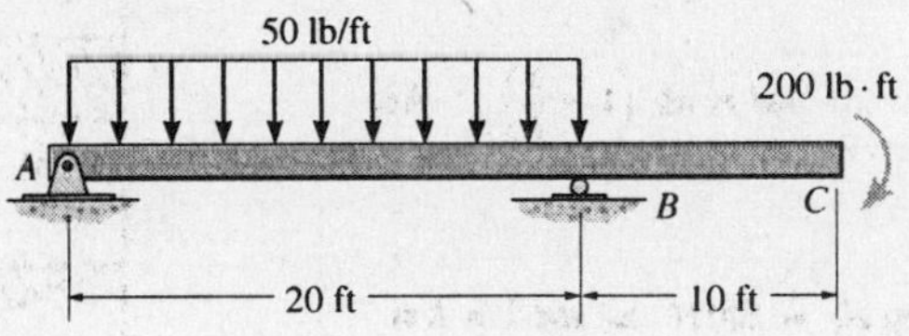

$+\uparrow\Sigma F_y = 0; \quad 28 - 3x - V = 0$

$V = 28 - 3x$

$\curvearrowleft + \Sigma M = 0; \quad 114 - 28x + 3x\left(\frac{x}{2}\right) + M = 0$

$M = 28x - 1.5x^2 - 114$

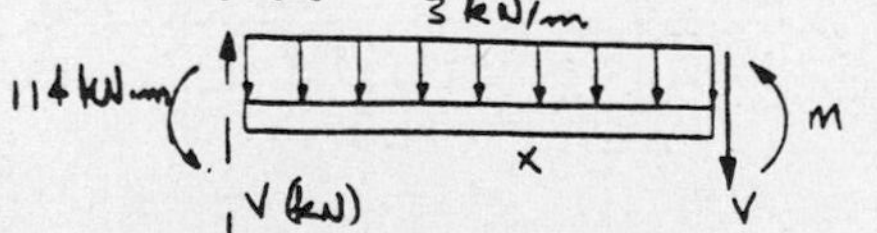

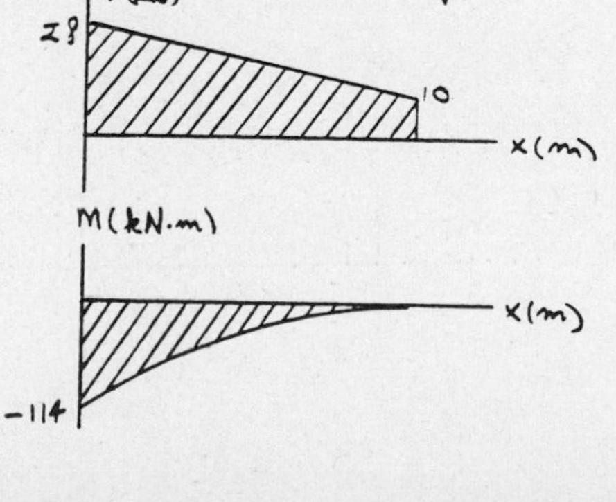

7-50. Draw the shear and moment diagrams for the beam.

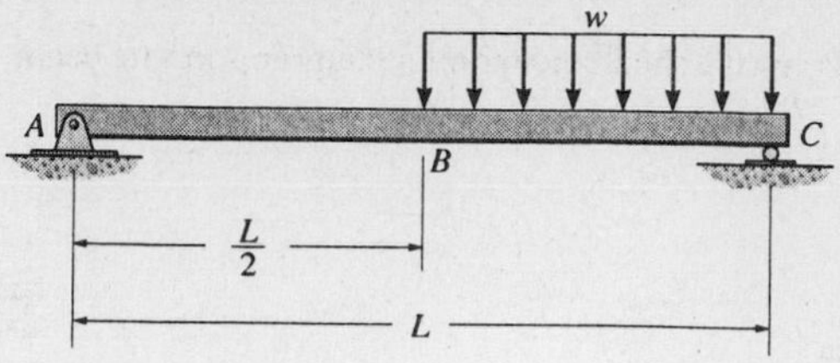

Support Reactions : From FBD (a),

$$\circlearrowleft + \Sigma M_A = 0; \quad C_y(L) - \frac{wL}{2}\left(\frac{3L}{4}\right) = 0 \quad C_y = \frac{3wL}{8}$$

$$+\uparrow \Sigma F_y = 0; \quad A_y + \frac{3wL}{8} - \frac{wL}{2} = 0 \quad A_y = \frac{wL}{8}$$

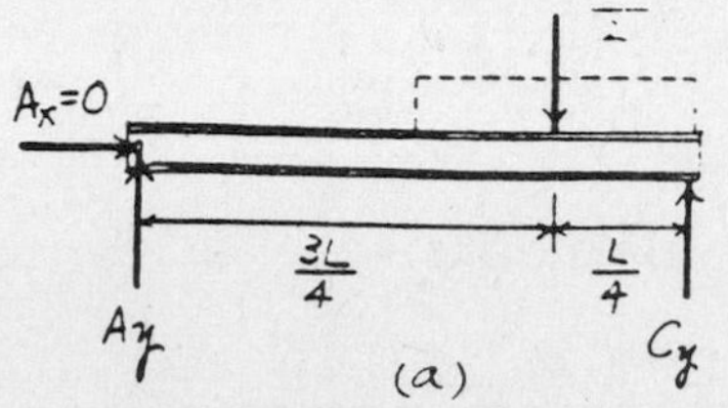

Shear and Moment Functions : For $0 \le x < \frac{L}{2}$ [FBD (b)],

$$+\uparrow \Sigma F_y = 0; \quad \frac{wL}{8} - V = 0 \quad V = \frac{wL}{8} \quad \textbf{Ans}$$

$$\circlearrowleft + \Sigma M = 0; \quad M - \frac{wL}{8}(x) = 0 \quad M = \frac{wL}{8}x \quad \textbf{Ans}$$

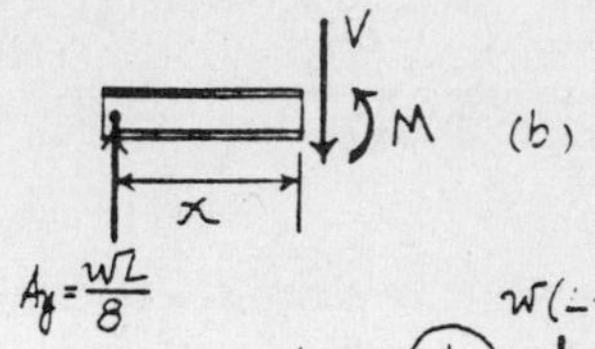

For $\frac{L}{2} < x \le L$ [FBD (c)],

$$+\uparrow \Sigma F_y = 0; \quad V + \frac{3wL}{8} - w(L-x) = 0$$

$$V = \frac{w}{8}(5L - 8x) \quad \textbf{Ans}$$

$$\circlearrowleft + \Sigma M = 0; \quad \frac{3wL}{8}(L-x) - w(L-x)\left(\frac{L-x}{2}\right) - M = 0$$

$$M = \frac{w}{8}\left(-L^2 + 5Lx - 4x^2\right) \quad \textbf{Ans}$$

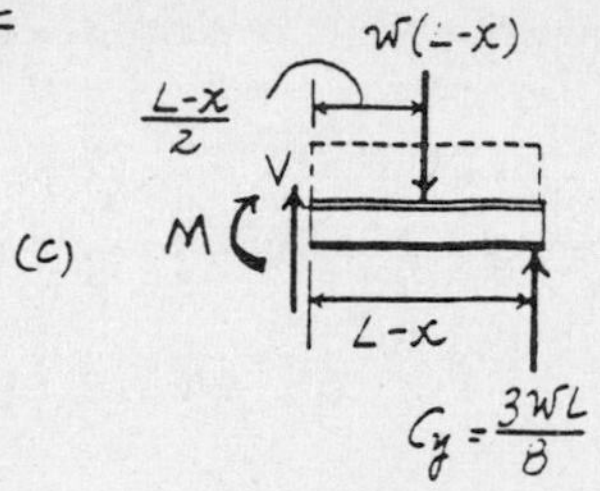

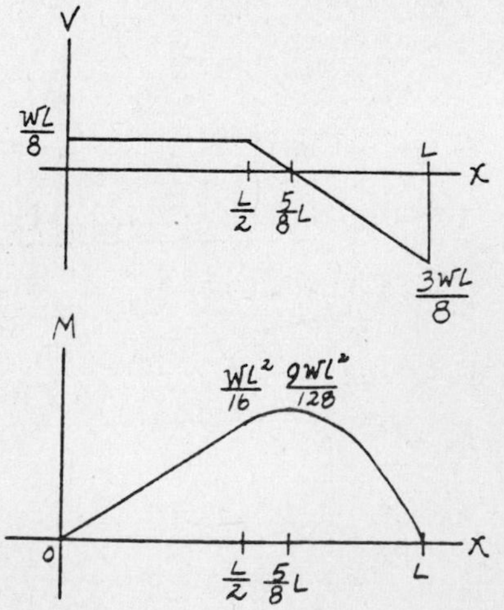

7-51. Draw the shear and moment diagrams for the beam.

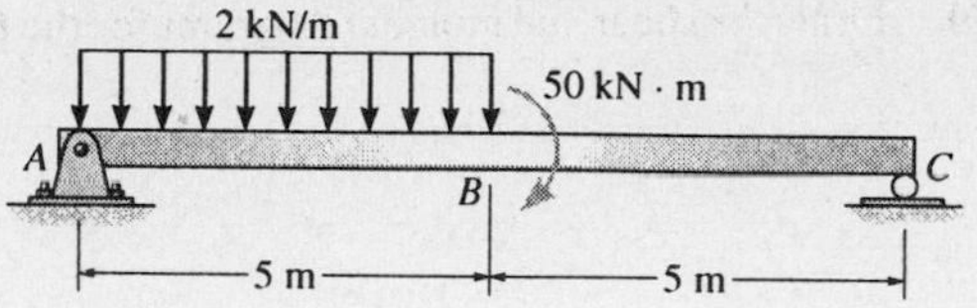

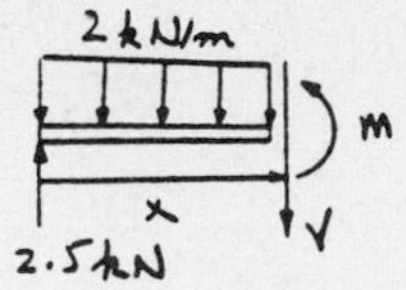

$0 \leq x < 5\text{ m}:$

$+\uparrow \Sigma F_y = 0; \quad 2.5 - 2x - V = 0$

$V = 2.5 - 2x$

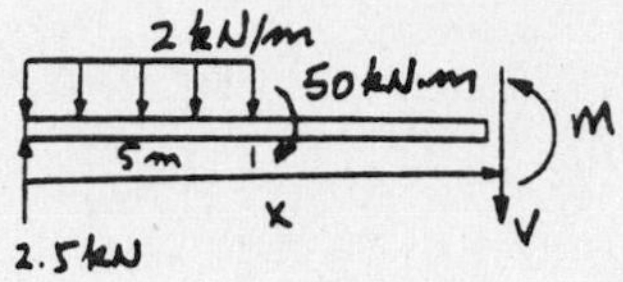

$\curvearrowleft + \Sigma M = 0; \quad M + 2x\left(\frac{1}{2}x\right) - 2.5x = 0$

$M = 2.5x - x^2$

$5\text{ m} < x < 10\text{ m}:$

$+\uparrow \Sigma F_y = 0; \quad 2.5 - 10 - V = 0$

$V = -7.5$

$\curvearrowleft + \Sigma M = 0; \quad M + 10(x - 2.5) - 2.5x - 50 = 0$

$M = -7.5x + 75$

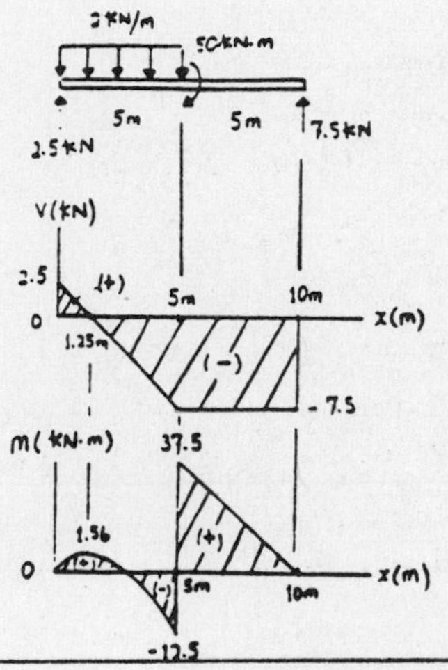

***7-52.** Draw the shear and moment diagrams for the beam.

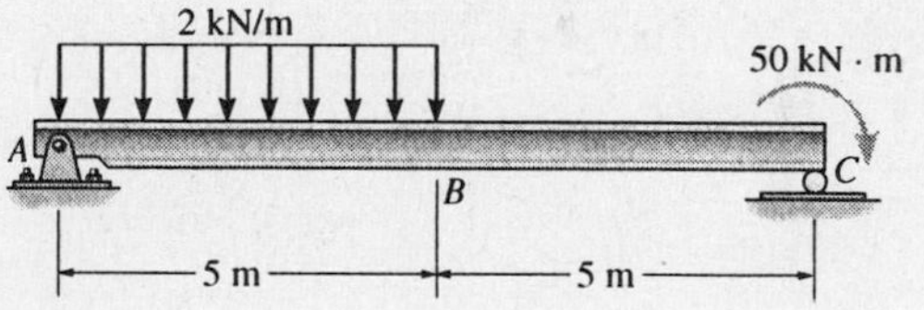

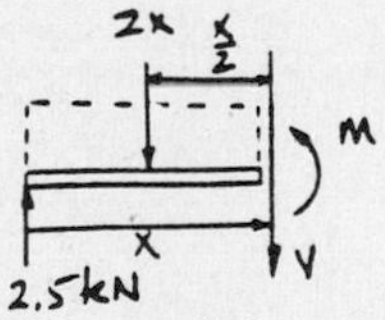

$0 \leq x < 5\text{ m}:$

$+\uparrow \Sigma F_y = 0; \quad 2.5 - 2x - V = 0$

$V = 2.5 - 2x$

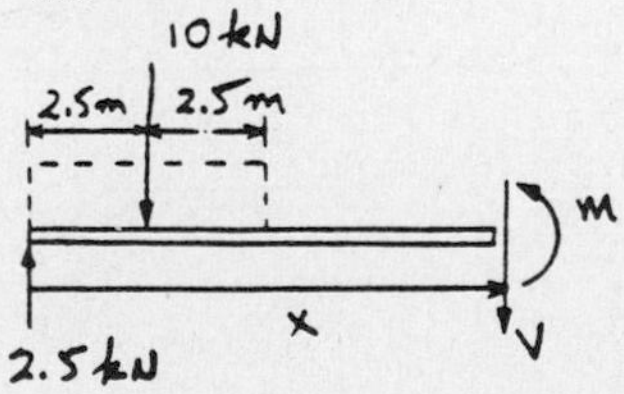

$\curvearrowleft + \Sigma M = 0; \quad M + 2x\left(\frac{1}{2}x\right) - 2.5x = 0$

$M = 2.5x - x^2$

$5\text{ m} < x \leq 10\text{ m}:$

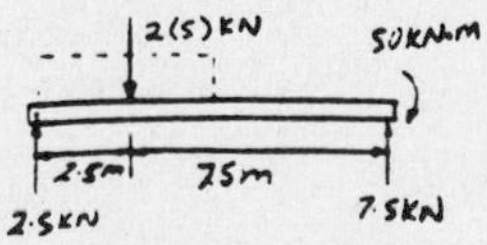

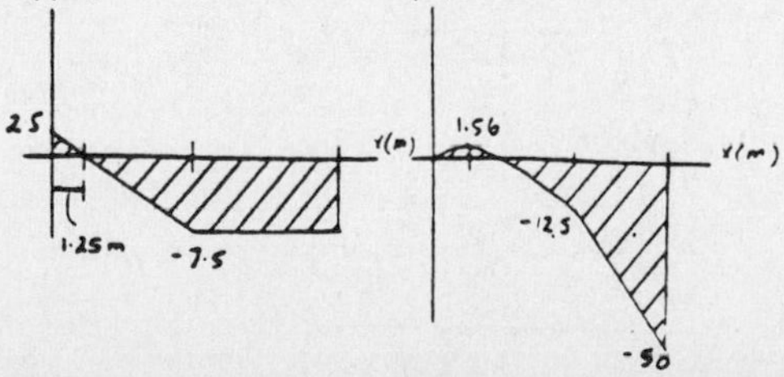

$+\uparrow \Sigma F_y = 0; \quad 2.5 - 10 - V = 0$

$V = -7.5$

$\curvearrowleft + \Sigma M = 0; \quad M + 10(x - 2.5) - 2.5x = 0$

$M = -7.5x + 25$

7-53. Draw the shear and bending-moment diagrams for each of the two segments of the compound beam.

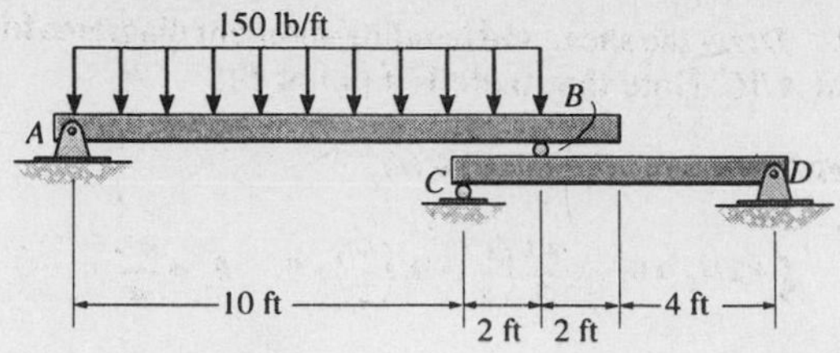

Support Reactions : **From FBD (a).**

$\curvearrowleft + \Sigma M_A = 0;\quad B_y(12) - 2100(7) = 0 \quad B_y = 1225 \text{ lb}$

$+\uparrow \Sigma F_y = 0;\quad A_y + 1225 - 2100 = 0 \quad A_y = 875 \text{ lb}$

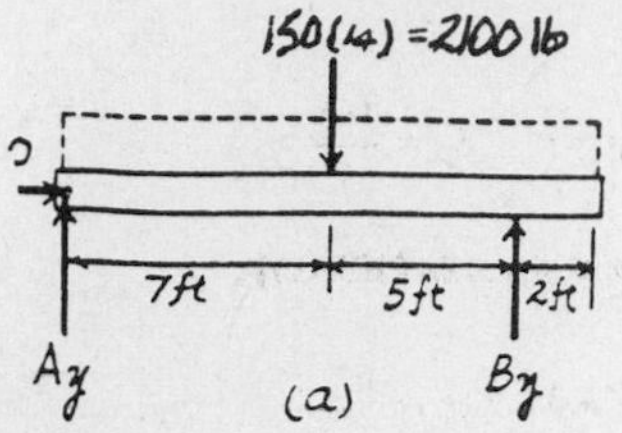

From FBD (b).

$\curvearrowleft + \Sigma M_D = 0;\quad 1225(6) - C_y(8) = 0 \quad C_y = 918.75 \text{ lb}$

$+\uparrow \Sigma F_y = 0;\quad D_y + 918.75 - 1225 = 0 \quad D_y = 306.25 \text{ lb}$

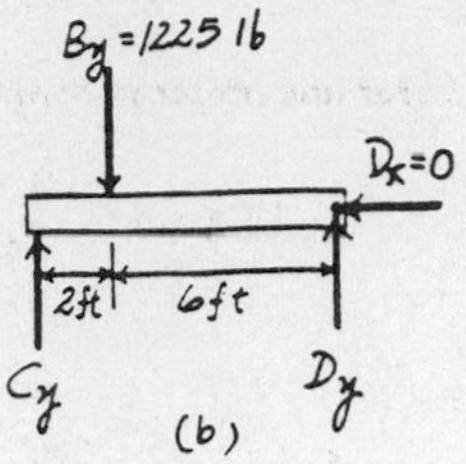

Shear and Moment Functions : *Member AB.*

For $0 \le x < 12$ ft [FBD (c)].

$+\uparrow \Sigma F_y = 0;\quad 875 - 150x - V = 0$

$V = \{875 - 150x\} \text{ lb}$ **Ans**

$\curvearrowleft + \Sigma M = 0;\quad M + 150x\left(\frac{x}{2}\right) - 875x = 0$

$M = \{875x - 75.0x^2\} \text{ lb}\cdot\text{ft}$ **Ans**

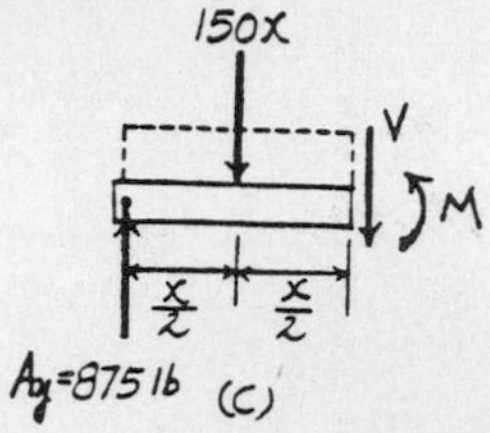

For $12 \text{ ft} < x \le 14$ ft [FBD (d)].

$+\uparrow \Sigma F_y = 0;\quad V - 150(14 - x) = 0$

$V = \{2100 - 150x\} \text{ lb}$ **Ans**

$\curvearrowleft + \Sigma M = 0;\quad -150(14 - x)\left(\frac{14 - x}{2}\right) - M = 0$

$M = \{-75.0x^2 + 2100x - 14700\} \text{ lb}\cdot\text{ft}$ **Ans**

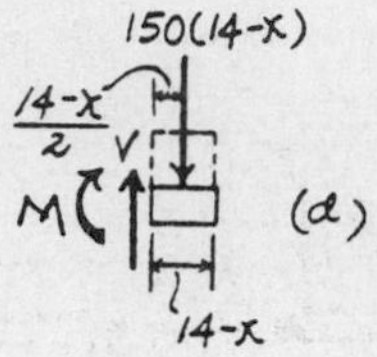

For member *CBD*, $0 \le x < 2$ ft [FBD (e)].

$+\uparrow \Sigma F_y = 0;\quad 918.75 - V = 0 \quad V = 919 \text{ lb}$ **Ans**

$\curvearrowleft + \Sigma M = 0;\quad 918.75x - M = 0 \quad M = \{919x\} \text{ lb}\cdot\text{ft}$ **Ans**

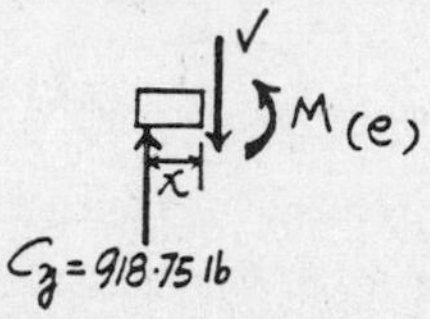

For $2 \text{ ft} < x \le 8$ ft [FBD (f)].

$+\uparrow \Sigma F_y = 0;\quad V + 306.25 = 0 \quad V = 306 \text{ lb}$ **Ans**

$+\Sigma M = 0;\quad 306.25(8 - x) - M = 0$

$M = \{2450 - 306x\} \text{ lb}\cdot\text{ft}$ **Ans**

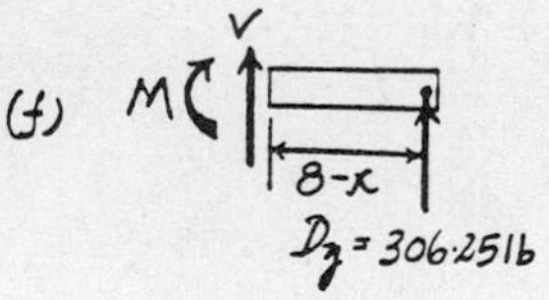

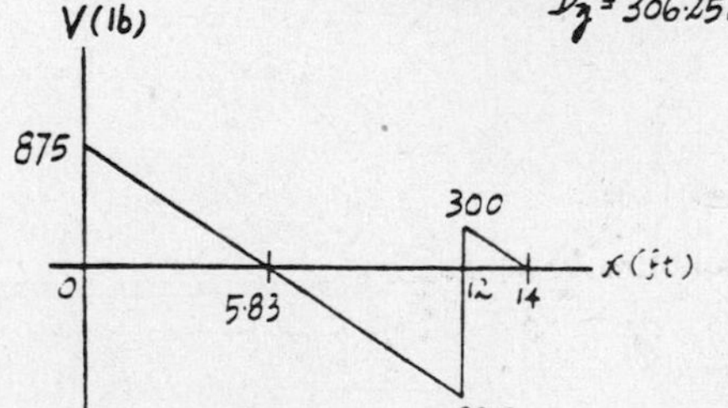

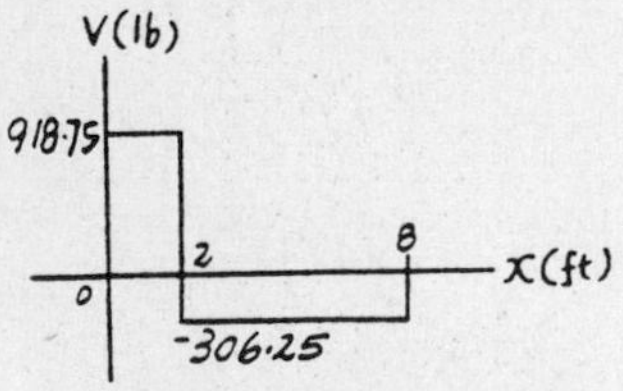

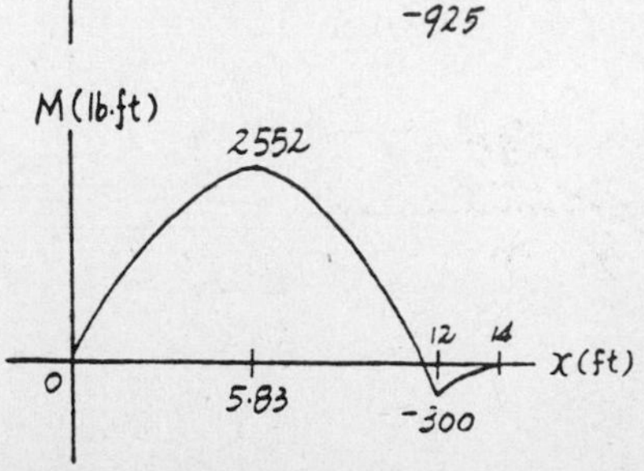

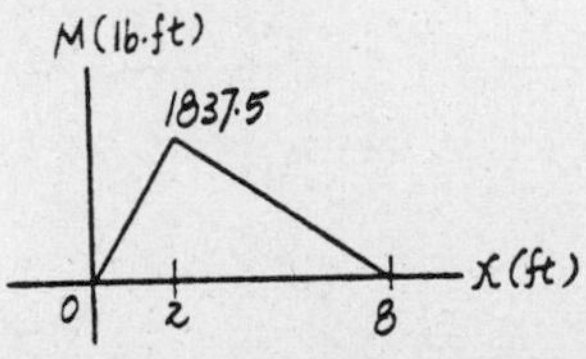

7-54. Draw the shear and bending-moment diagrams for beam ABC. Note that there is a pin at B.

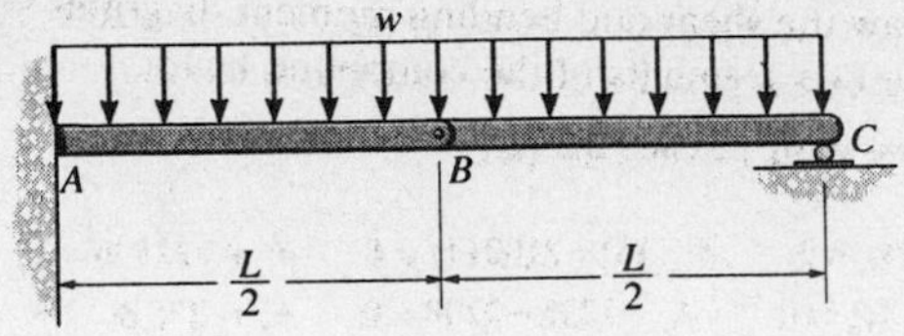

Support Reactions : From FBD (a),

$$\circlearrowleft + \Sigma M_C = 0; \quad \frac{wL}{2}\left(\frac{L}{4}\right) - B_y\left(\frac{L}{2}\right) = 0 \qquad B_y = \frac{wL}{4}$$

From FBD (b),

$$+\uparrow \Sigma F_y = 0; \quad A_y - \frac{wL}{2} - \frac{wL}{4} = 0 \qquad A_y = \frac{3wL}{4}$$

Shear and Moment Functions : For $0 \le x \le L$[FBD (c)],

$$+\uparrow \Sigma F_y = 0; \quad \frac{3wL}{4} - wx - V = 0$$

$$V = \frac{w}{4}(3L - 4x) \qquad \textbf{Ans}$$

$$\circlearrowleft + \Sigma M = 0; \quad \frac{3wL}{4}(x) - wx\left(\frac{x}{2}\right) - \frac{wL^2}{4} - M = 0$$

$$M = \frac{w}{4}\left(3Lx - 2x^2 - L^2\right) \qquad \textbf{Ans}$$

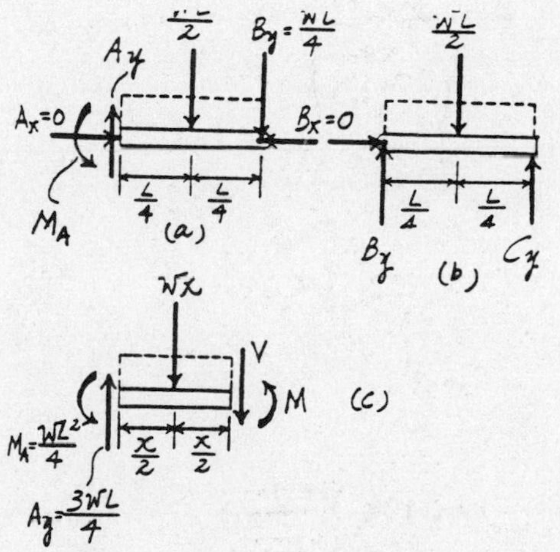

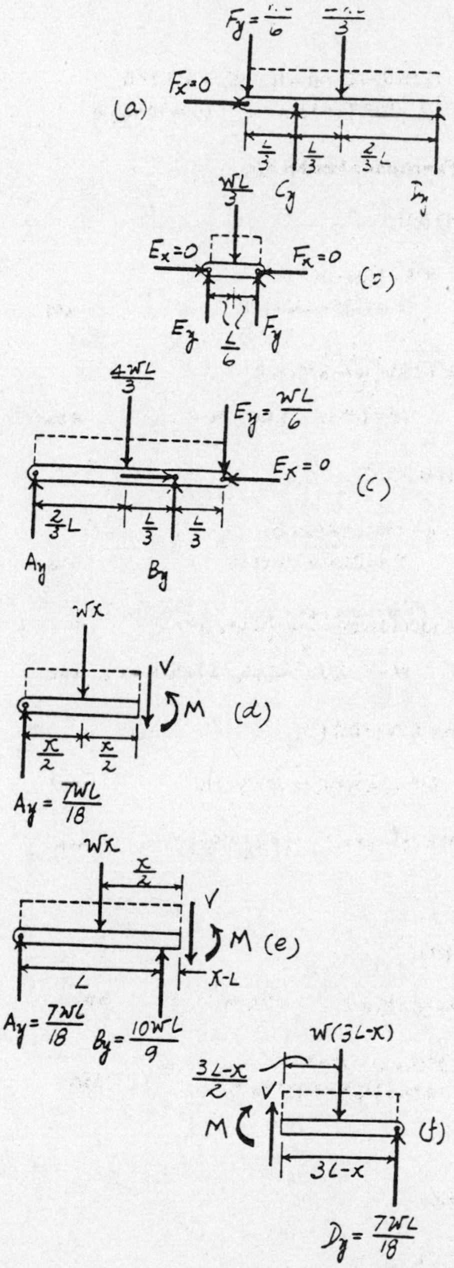

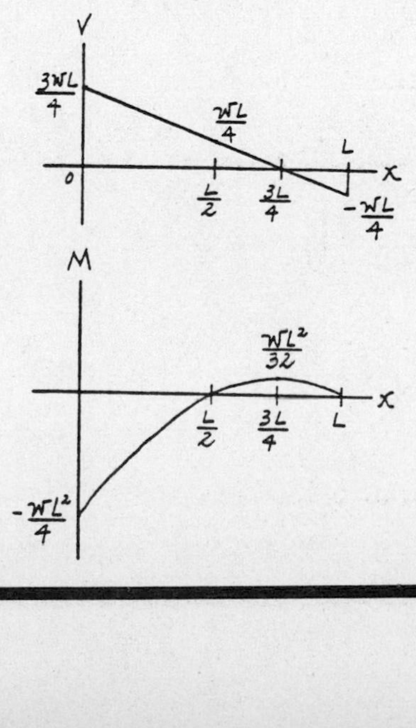

7-55. Draw the shear and moment diagrams for the compound beam. The beam is pin-connected at E and F.

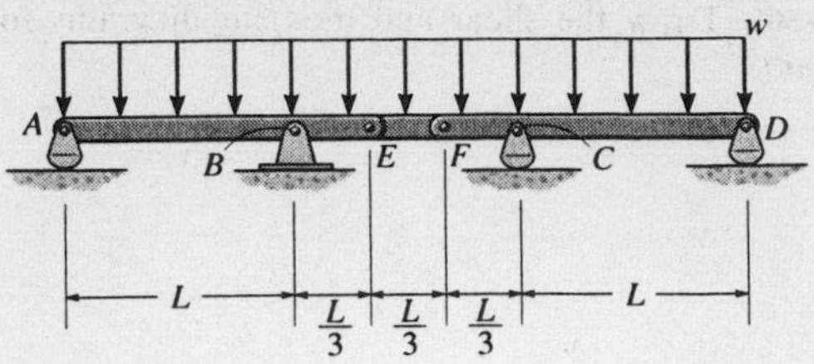

Support Reactions : From FBD (b),

$$\curvearrowleft + \Sigma M_E = 0; \quad F_y\left(\frac{L}{3}\right) - \frac{wL}{3}\left(\frac{L}{6}\right) = 0 \qquad F_y = \frac{wL}{6}$$

$$+\uparrow \Sigma F_y = 0; \quad E_y + \frac{wL}{6} - \frac{wL}{3} = 0 \qquad E_y = \frac{wL}{6}$$

From FBD (a),

$$\curvearrowleft + \Sigma M_C = 0; \quad D_y(L) + \frac{wL}{6}\left(\frac{L}{3}\right) - \frac{4wL}{3}\left(\frac{L}{3}\right) = 0 \qquad D_y = \frac{7wL}{18}$$

From FBD (c),

$$\curvearrowleft + \Sigma M_B = 0; \quad \frac{4wL}{3}\left(\frac{L}{3}\right) - \frac{wL}{6}\left(\frac{L}{3}\right) - A_y(L) = 0 \qquad A_y = \frac{7wL}{18}$$

$$+\uparrow \Sigma F_y = 0; \quad B_y + \frac{7wL}{18} - \frac{4wL}{3} - \frac{wL}{6} = 0 \qquad B_y = \frac{10wL}{9}$$

Shear and Moment Functions : For $0 \le x < L$ [FBD (d)],

$$+\uparrow \Sigma F_y = 0; \quad \frac{7wL}{18} - wx - V = 0$$

$$V = \frac{w}{18}(7L - 18x) \qquad \textbf{Ans}$$

$$\curvearrowleft + \Sigma M = 0; \quad M + wx\left(\frac{x}{2}\right) - \frac{7wL}{18}x = 0$$

$$M = \frac{w}{18}\left(7Lx - 9x^2\right) \qquad \textbf{Ans}$$

For $L \le x < 2L$ [FBD (e)],

$$+\uparrow \Sigma F_y = 0; \quad \frac{7wL}{18} + \frac{10wL}{9} - wx - V = 0$$

$$V = \frac{w}{2}(3L - 2x) \qquad \textbf{Ans}$$

$$\curvearrowleft + \Sigma M = 0; \quad M + wx\left(\frac{x}{2}\right) - \frac{7wL}{18}x - \frac{10wL}{9}(x - L) = 0$$

$$M = \frac{w}{18}\left(27Lx - 20L^2 - 9x^2\right) \qquad \textbf{Ans}$$

For $2L < x \le 3L$ [FBD (f)],

$$+\uparrow \Sigma F_y = 0; \quad V + \frac{7wL}{18} - w(3L - x) = 0$$

$$V = \frac{w}{18}(47L - 18x) \qquad \textbf{Ans}$$

$$\curvearrowleft + \Sigma M = 0; \quad \frac{7wL}{18}(3L - x) - w(3L - x)\left(\frac{3L - x}{2}\right) - M = 0$$

$$M = \frac{w}{18}\left(47Lx - 9x^2 - 60L^2\right) \qquad \textbf{Ans}$$

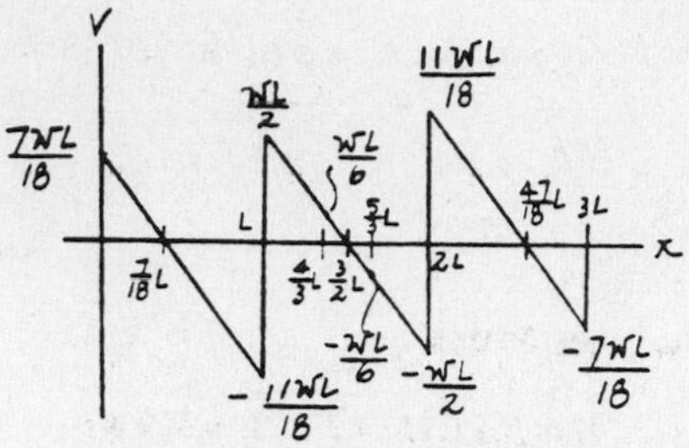

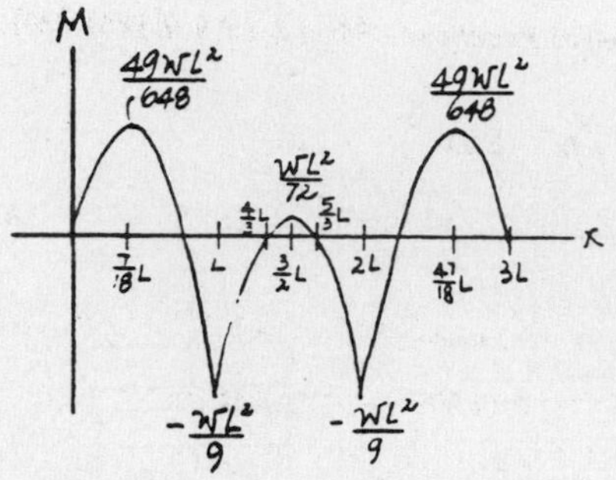

*7-56. Draw the shear and moment diagrams for the beam.

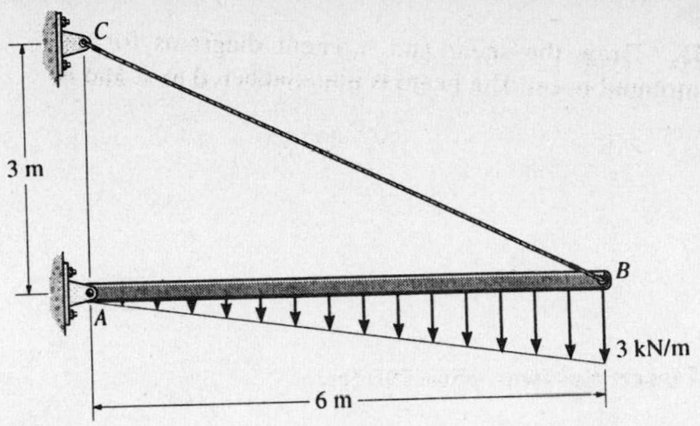

Support Reactions : From FBD (a).

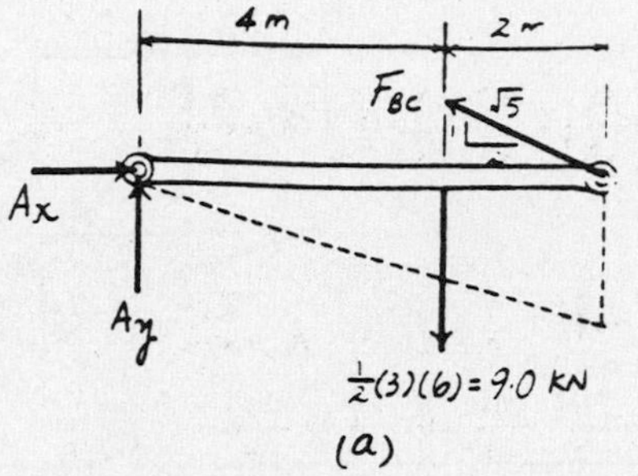

$\curvearrowleft + \Sigma M_B = 0;\quad 9.00(2) - A_y(6) = 0 \quad A_y = 3.00 \text{ kN}$

Shear and Moment Functions : For $0 \le x \le 6$ m [FBD (b)].

$+\uparrow \Sigma F_y = 0;\quad 3.00 - \frac{x^2}{4} - V = 0$

$$V = \left\{3.00 - \frac{x^2}{4}\right\} \text{ kN} \qquad \textbf{Ans}$$

The maximum moment occurs when $V = 0$, then

$$0 = 3.00 - \frac{x^2}{4} \qquad x = 3.464 \text{ m}$$

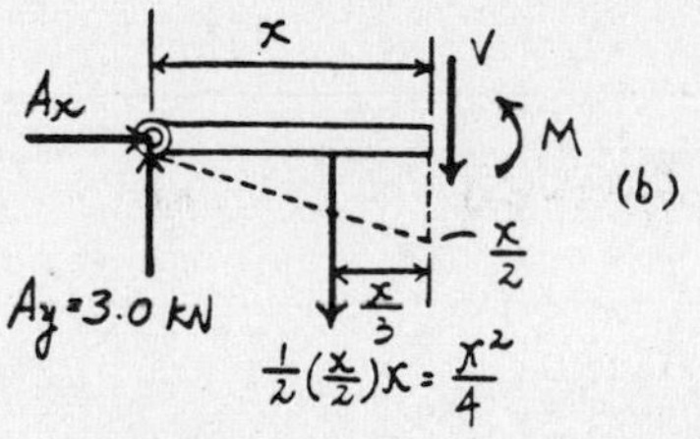

$\curvearrowleft + \Sigma M = 0;\quad M + \left(\frac{x^2}{4}\right)\left(\frac{x}{3}\right) - 3.00x = 0$

$$M = \left\{3.00x - \frac{x^3}{12}\right\} \text{ kN}\cdot\text{m} \qquad \textbf{Ans}$$

Thus,

$$M_{max} = 3.00(3.464) - \frac{3.464^3}{12} = 6.93 \text{ kN}\cdot\text{m}$$

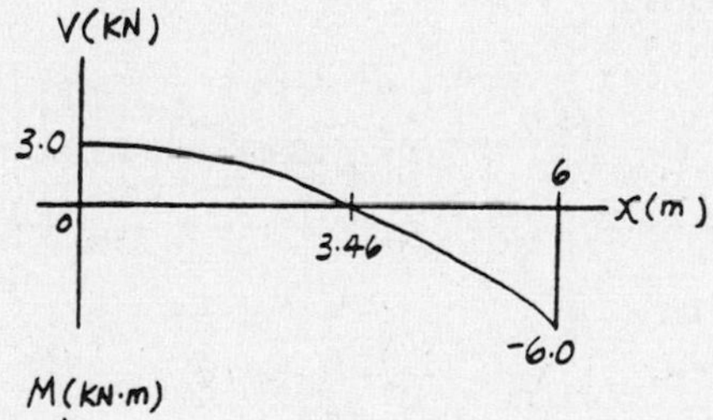

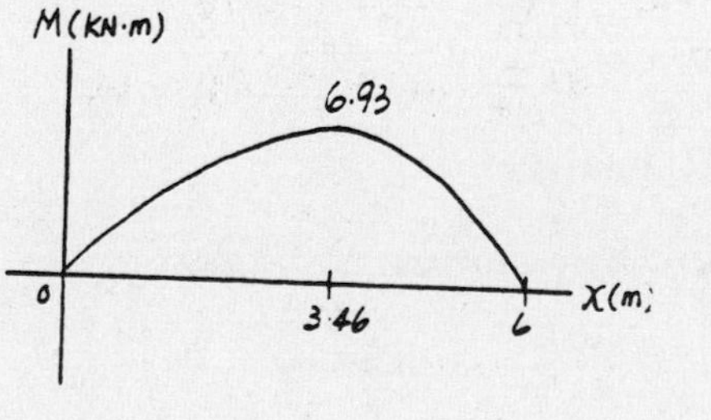

7-57. If $L = 6$ ft, the beam will fail when the maximum moment is $M_{max} = 200$ lb·ft. Determine the largest intensity w of the distributed load the beam will support.

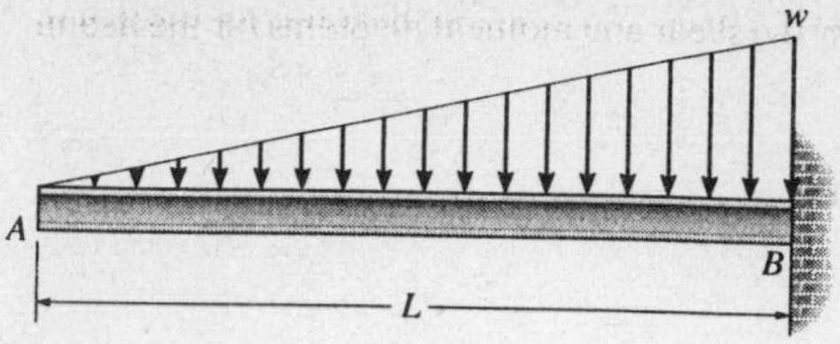

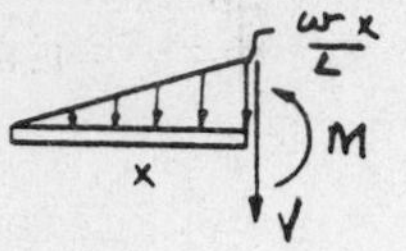

$+\uparrow\Sigma F_y = 0; \quad -V - \frac{1}{2}x\left(\frac{wx}{L}\right) = 0$

$V = -\left(\frac{1}{2}\right)\frac{wx^2}{L}$

$\curvearrowleft+\Sigma M = 0; \quad M + \left(\frac{x}{2}\right)\left(\frac{wx}{L}\right)\left(\frac{1}{3}x\right) = 0$

$M = -\frac{1}{6}\left(\frac{wx^3}{L}\right)$

$M_{max} = -\frac{1}{6}wL^2$

$200 = \frac{1}{6}w(6)^2$

$w = 33.3$ lb/ft **Ans**

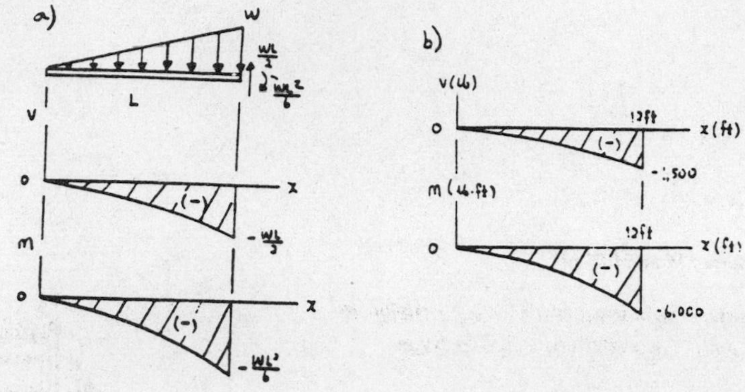

7-58. Draw the shear and moment diagrams for the beam.

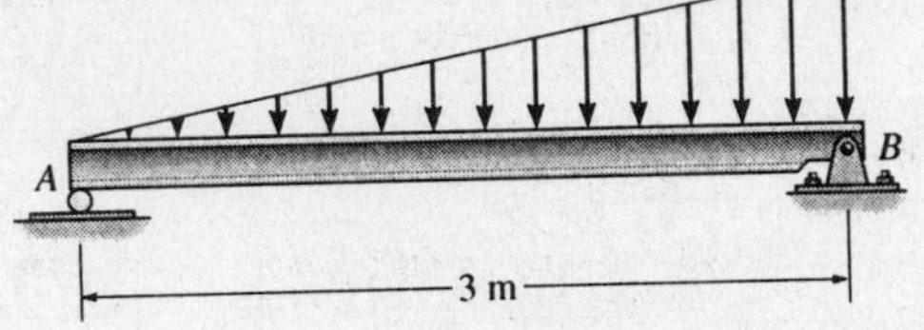

$+\uparrow\Sigma F_y = 0; \quad 0.75 - \frac{1}{2}x(0.5x) - V = 0$

$V = 0.75 - 0.25x^2$

$V = 0 = 0.75 - 0.25x^2$

$x = 1.732$ m

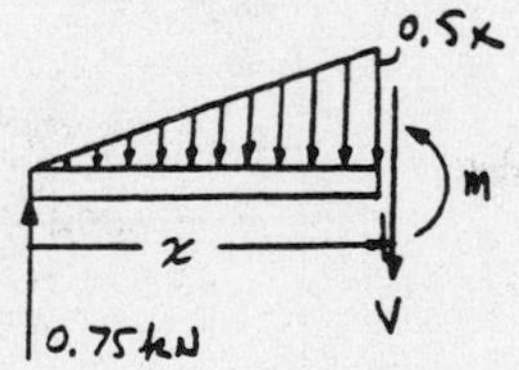

$\curvearrowleft+\Sigma M = 0; \quad M + \left(\frac{1}{2}\right)(0.5x)(x)\left(\frac{1}{3}x\right) - 0.75x = 0$

$M = 0.75x - 0.08333x^3$

$M_{max} = 0.75(1.732) - 0.08333(1.732)^3 = 0.866$

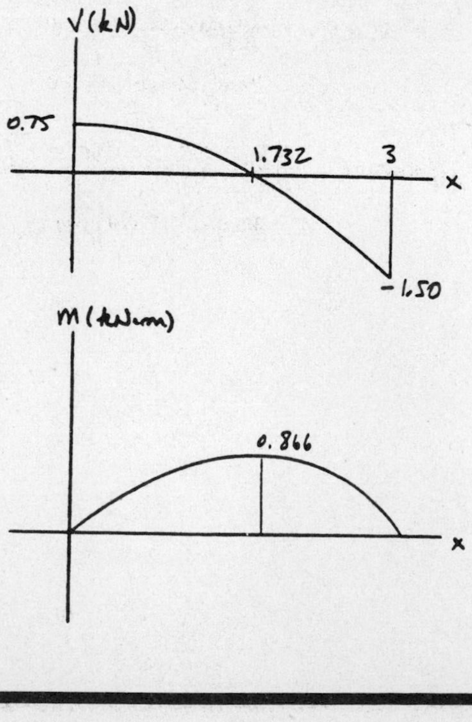

7-59. Draw the shear and moment diagrams for the beam.

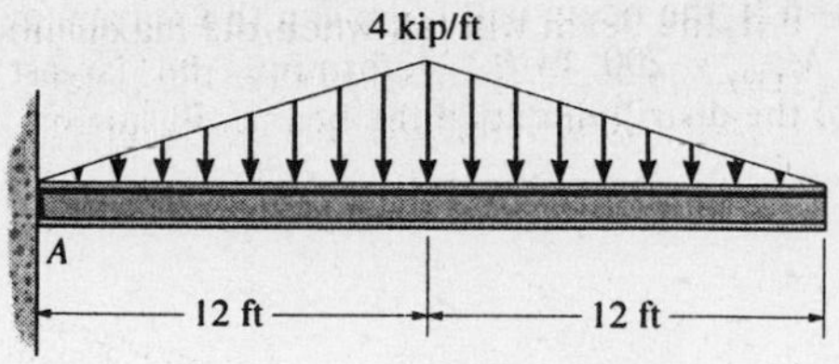

Support Reactions : From FBD (a),

$\circlearrowleft + \Sigma M_A = 0; \quad M_A - 48.0(12) = 0 \quad M_A = 576 \text{ kip}\cdot\text{ft}$

$+\uparrow \Sigma F_y = 0; \quad A_y - 48.0 = 0 \quad A_y = 48.0 \text{ kip}$

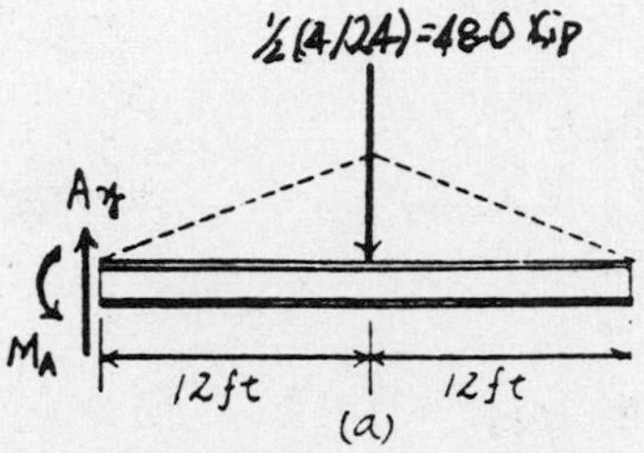

Shear and Moment Functions : For $0 \le x < 12$ ft [FBD (b)],

$+\uparrow \Sigma F_y = 0; \quad 48.0 - \frac{x^2}{6} - V = 0$

$$V = \left\{48.0 - \frac{x^2}{6}\right\} \text{ kip} \qquad \textbf{Ans}$$

$\circlearrowleft + \Sigma M = 0; \quad M + \frac{x^2}{6}\left(\frac{x}{3}\right) + 576 - 48.0x = 0$

$$M = \left\{48.0x - \frac{x^3}{18} - 576\right\} \text{ kip}\cdot\text{ft} \qquad \textbf{Ans}$$

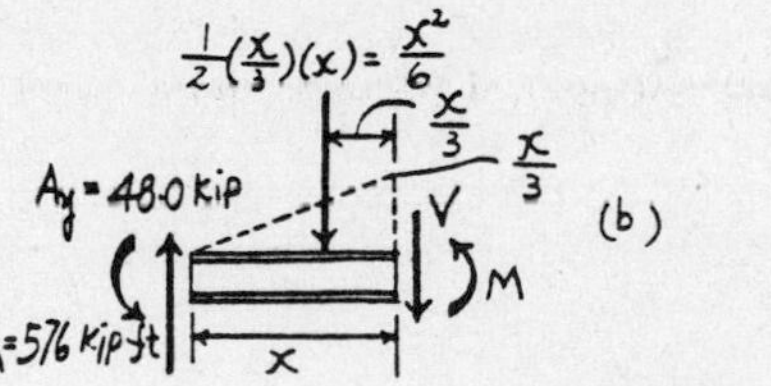

For $12 \text{ ft} < x \le 24$ ft [FBD (c)],

$+\uparrow \Sigma F_y = 0; \quad V - \frac{1}{2}\left[\frac{1}{3}(24-x)\right](24-x) = 0$

$$V = \left\{\frac{1}{6}(24-x)^2\right\} \text{ kip} \qquad \textbf{Ans}$$

$\circlearrowleft + \Sigma M = 0; \quad -\frac{1}{2}\left[\frac{1}{3}(24-x)\right](24-x)\left(\frac{24-x}{3}\right) - M = 0$

$$M = \left\{-\frac{1}{18}(24-x)^3\right\} \text{ kip}\cdot\text{ft} \qquad \textbf{Ans}$$

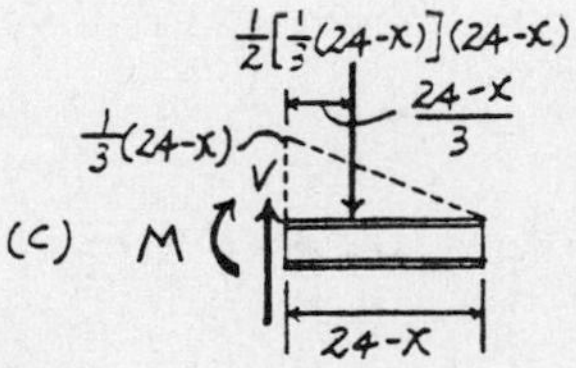

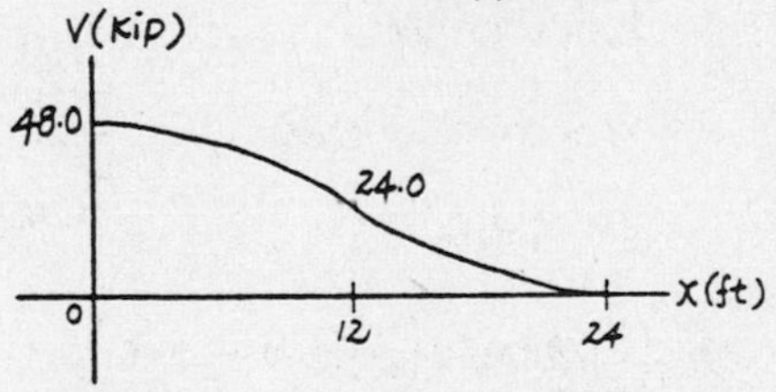

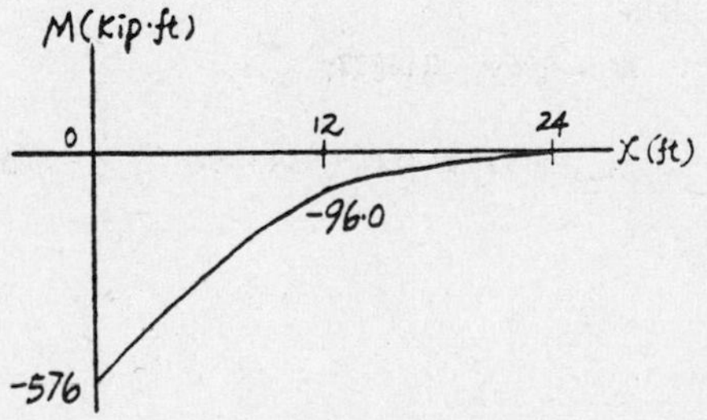

***7-60.** Draw the shear and bending-moment diagrams for the beam.

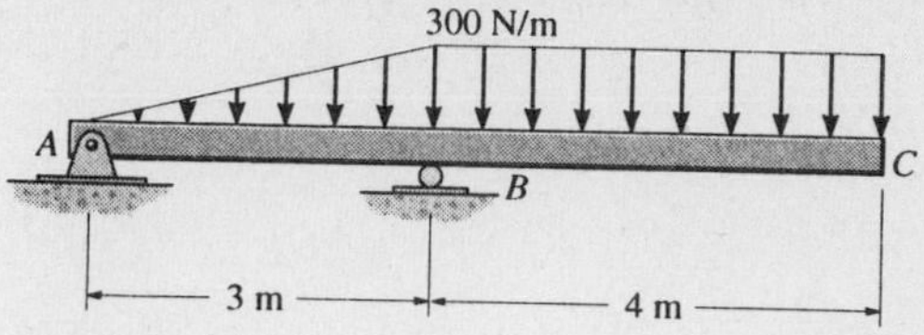

Support Reactions : From FBD (a),

$\curvearrowleft + \Sigma M_B = 0; \quad A_y(3) + 450(1) - 1200(2) = 0 \qquad A_y = 650 \text{ N}$

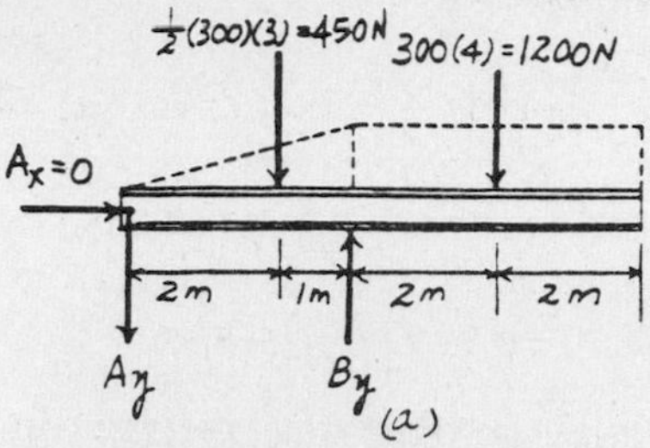

Shear and Moment Functions : For $0 \le x < 3$ m [FBD (b)],

$+\uparrow \Sigma F_y = 0; \quad -650 - 50.0x^2 - V = 0$

$V = \{-650 - 50.0x^2\}$ N **Ans**

$\curvearrowleft + \Sigma M = 0; \quad M + \left(50.0x^2\right)\left(\frac{x}{3}\right) + 650x = 0$

$M = \{-650x - 16.7x^3\}$ N·m **Ans**

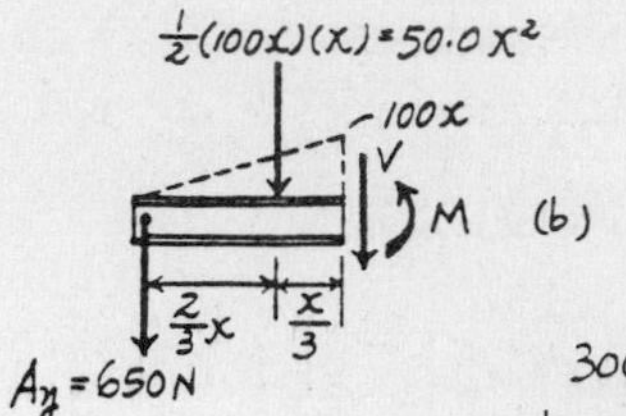

For 3 m $< x \le 7$ m [FBD (c)],

$+\uparrow \Sigma F_y = 0; \quad V - 300(7 - x) = 0$

$V = \{2100 - 300x\}$ N **Ans**

$\curvearrowleft + \Sigma M = 0; \quad -300(7 - x)\left(\frac{7 - x}{2}\right) - M = 0$

$M = \{-150(7 - x)^2\}$ N·m **Ans**

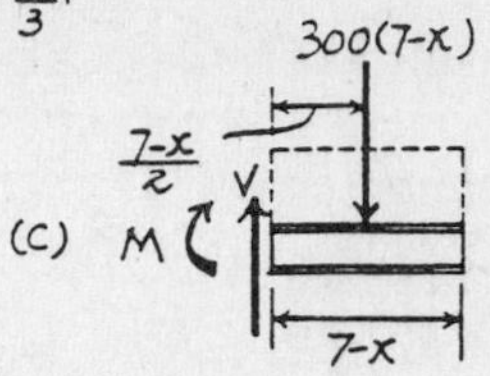

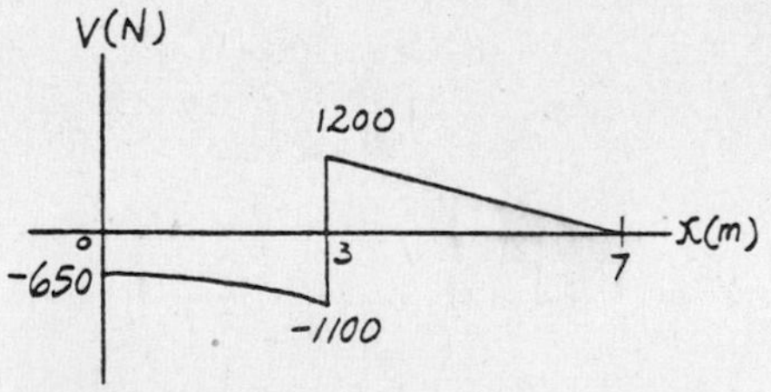

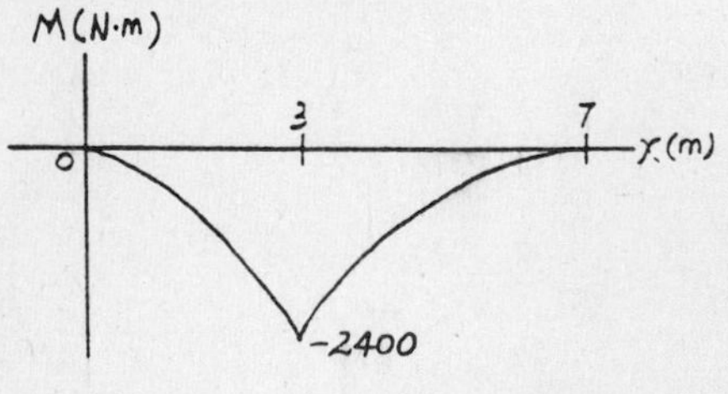

7-61. Draw the shear and moment diagrams for the beam.

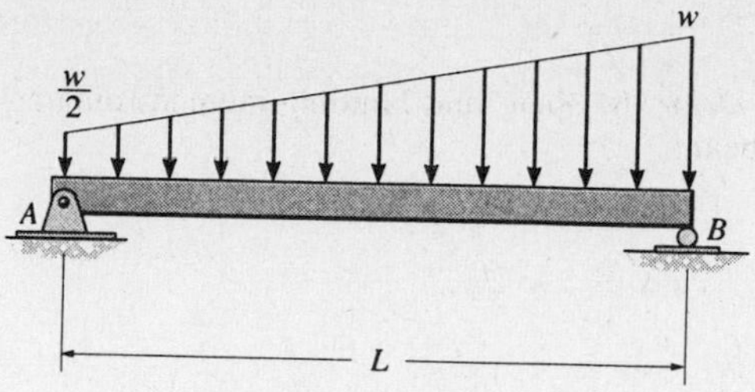

Support Reactions : From FBD (a),

$$\curvearrowleft + \Sigma M_B = 0; \quad \frac{wL}{4}\left(\frac{L}{3}\right) + \frac{wL}{2}\left(\frac{L}{2}\right) - A_y(L) = 0 \quad A_y = \frac{wL}{3}$$

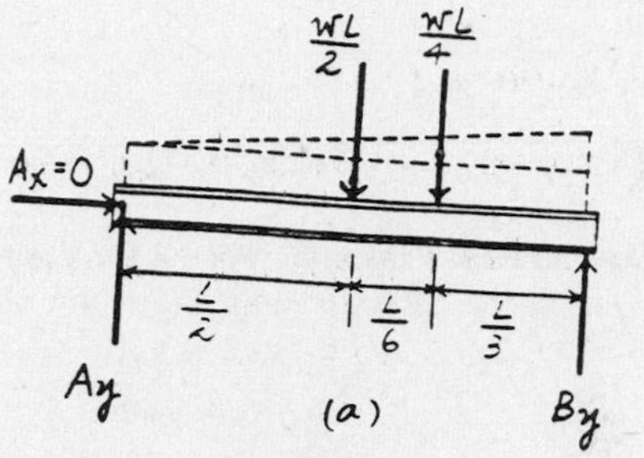

Shear and Moment Functions : For $0 \le x \le L$ [FBD (b)],

$$+\uparrow \Sigma F_y = 0; \quad \frac{wL}{3} - \frac{w}{2}x - \frac{1}{2}\left(\frac{w}{2L}x\right)x - V = 0$$

$$V = \frac{w}{12L}\left(4L^2 - 6Lx - 3x^2\right) \qquad \textbf{Ans}$$

The maximum moment occurs when $V = 0$, then

$$0 = 4L^2 - 6Lx - 3x^2 \qquad x = 0.5275L$$

$$\curvearrowleft + \Sigma M = 0; \quad M + \frac{1}{2}\left(\frac{w}{2L}x\right)x\left(\frac{x}{3}\right) + \frac{wx}{2}\left(\frac{x}{2}\right) - \frac{wL}{3}(x) = 0$$

$$M = \frac{w}{12L}\left(4L^2x - 3Lx^2 - x^3\right) \qquad \textbf{Ans}$$

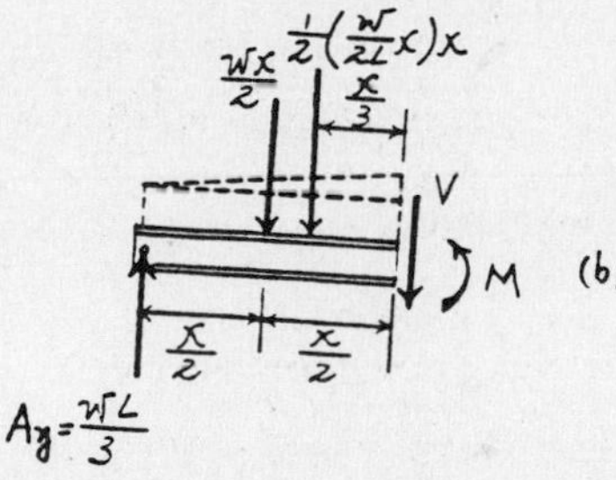

Thus,

$$M_{max} = \frac{w}{12L}\left[4L^2(0.5275L) - 3L(0.5275L)^2 - (0.5275L)^3\right]$$

$$= 0.0940wL^2$$

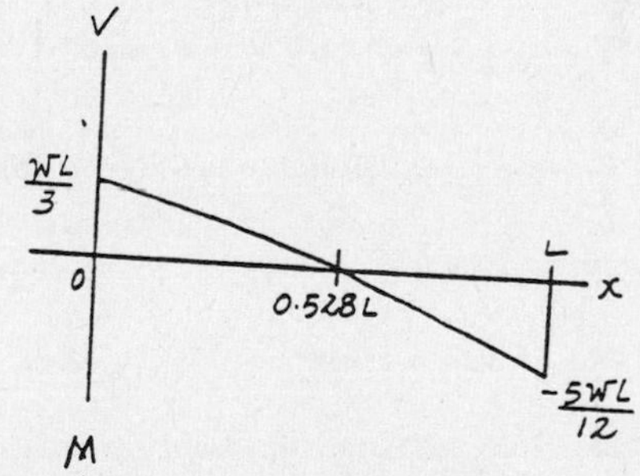

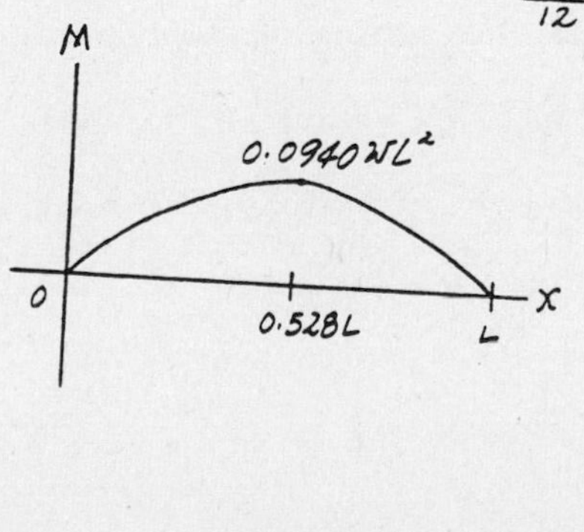

7-62. Determine the internal normal force, shear force, and moment in the curved rod as a function of θ.

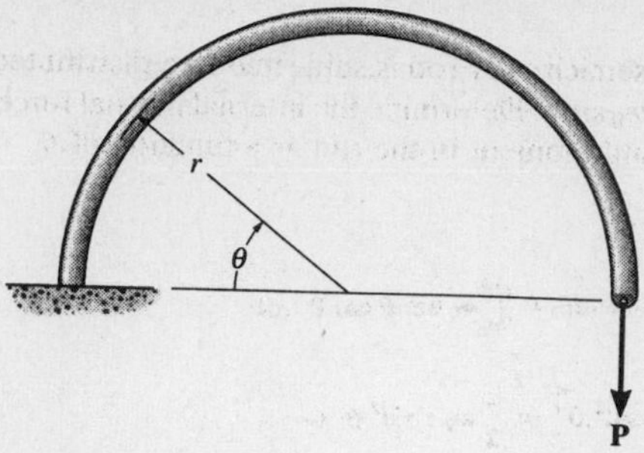

$+\nearrow \Sigma F_x = 0; \quad N + P\cos\theta = 0$

$N = -P\cos\theta$ **Ans**

$+\nwarrow \Sigma F_y = 0; \quad -V + P\sin\theta = 0$

$V = P\sin\theta$ **Ans**

$\curvearrowleft + \Sigma M_O = 0; \quad 2Pr - Pr - (-P\cos\theta)r + M = 0$

$M = -Pr(1 + \cos\theta)$ **Ans**

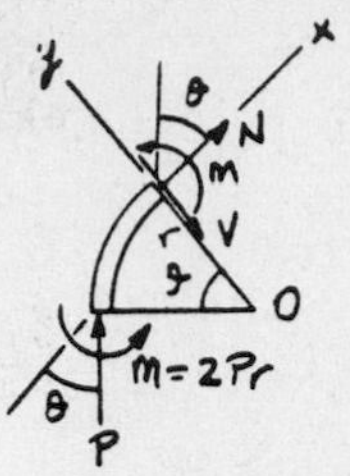

7-63. Determine the internal normal force, shear force, and moment in the curved rod as a function of θ.

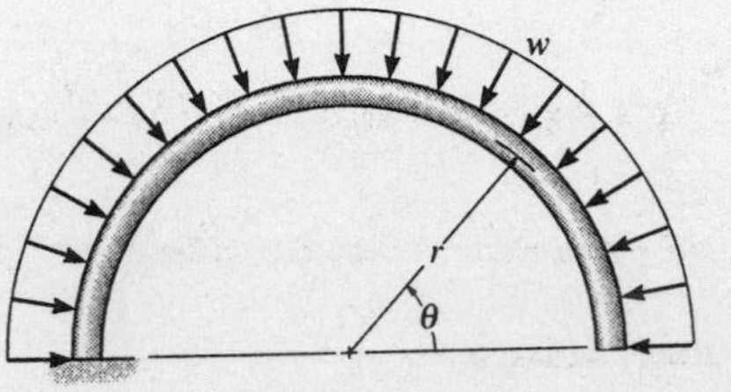

$\xrightarrow{+} F_{Rx} = -\int_0^\theta w(r\,d\theta)\cos\theta = -wr\sin\theta$

$+\uparrow F_{Ry} = -\int_0^\theta w(r\,d\theta)\sin\theta = -wr(1 - \cos\theta)$

$+\nearrow \Sigma F_x = 0; \quad V - (wr\sin\theta)\cos\theta - rw(1 - \cos\theta)\sin\theta = 0$

$V = wr\sin\theta$ **Ans**

$+\nwarrow \Sigma F_y = 0; \quad N + (wr\sin\theta)\sin\theta - rw(1 - \cos\theta)\cos\theta = 0$

$N = wr(\cos\theta - 1)$ **Ans**

$\curvearrowleft + \Sigma M_O = 0; \quad wr(\cos\theta - 1)r - M = 0$

$M = wr^2(\cos\theta - 1)$ **Ans**

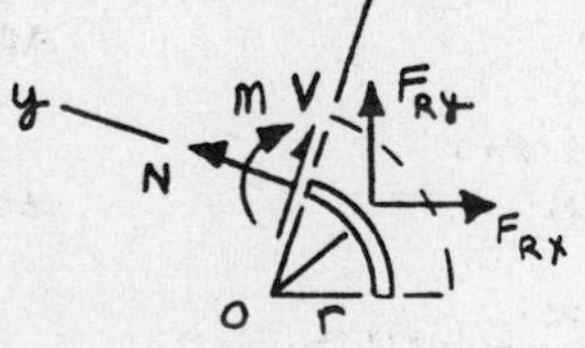

***7-64.** The semicircular rod is subjected to a distributed loading $w = w_0 \sin\theta$. Determine the internal normal force, shear force, and moment in the rod as a function of θ.

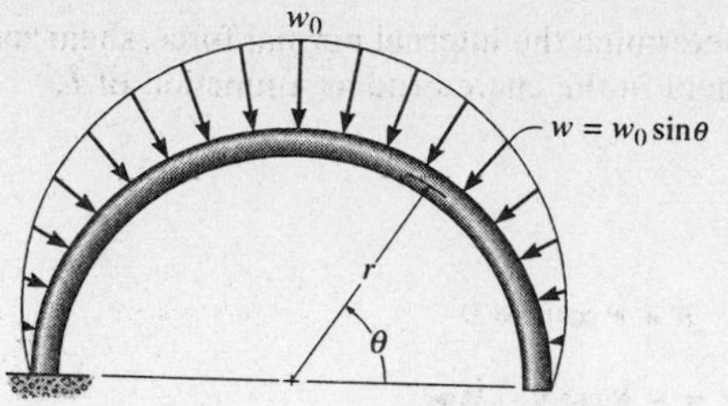

$$F_{Rx} = \int_0^{\theta} w \cos\theta \, r\, d\theta = \int_0^{\theta} w_0 \sin\theta \cos\theta \, r\, d\theta$$

$$= w_0\, r\left[\frac{1}{2}\sin^2\theta\right]_0^{\theta} = \frac{1}{2} w_0\, r \sin^2\theta \leftarrow$$

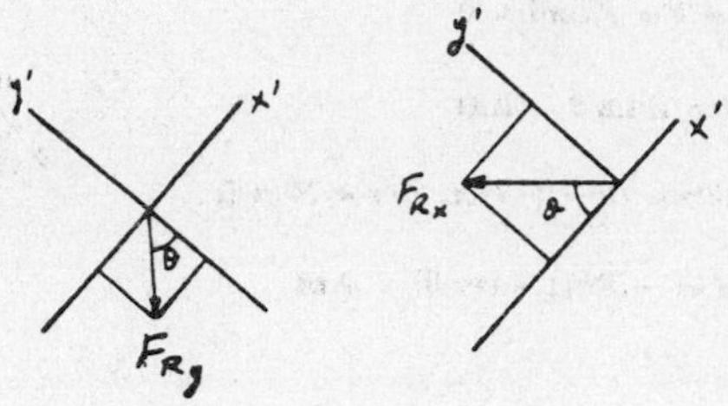

$$F_{Ry} = \int_0^{\theta} w \sin\theta \, r\, d\theta = \int_0^{\theta} w_0 \sin^2\theta \, r\, d\theta = w_0\, r\left[\frac{1}{2}\theta - \frac{1}{4}\sin 2\theta\right]_0^{\theta}$$

$$= w_0\, r\left(\frac{1}{2}\theta - \frac{1}{4}\sin 2\theta\right) \downarrow$$

$+\nearrow\Sigma F_{x'} = 0;\quad V - \frac{1}{2} w_0\, r \sin^2\theta\,(\cos\theta) - w_0\, r\left(\frac{1}{2}\theta - \frac{1}{2}(\sin\theta\cos\theta)\right)\sin\theta = 0$

$$V = \frac{1}{2} w_0\, r\,\theta \sin\theta \qquad \textbf{Ans}$$

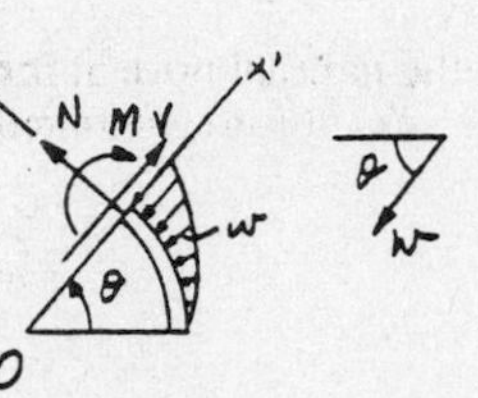

$+\nwarrow\Sigma F_{y'} = 0;\quad N + \frac{1}{2} w_0\, r \sin^2\theta\,(\sin\theta) - w_0\, r\left(\frac{1}{2}\theta - \frac{1}{2}(\sin\theta\cos\theta)\right)\cos\theta = 0$

$$N = \frac{1}{2} w_0\, r\,(\sin\theta - \theta\cos\theta) \qquad \textbf{Ans}$$

$\circlearrowleft +\Sigma M_O = 0;\quad N(r) - M = 0$

$$M = \frac{1}{2} w_0\, r^2\,(\sin\theta - \theta\cos\theta) \qquad \textbf{Ans}$$

7-65. Express the internal shear and moment components acting in the rod as a function of y, where $0 \leq y \leq 4$ ft.

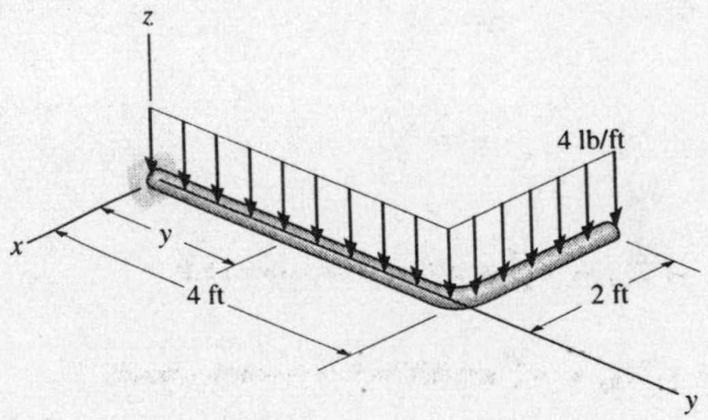

Shear and Moment Functions :

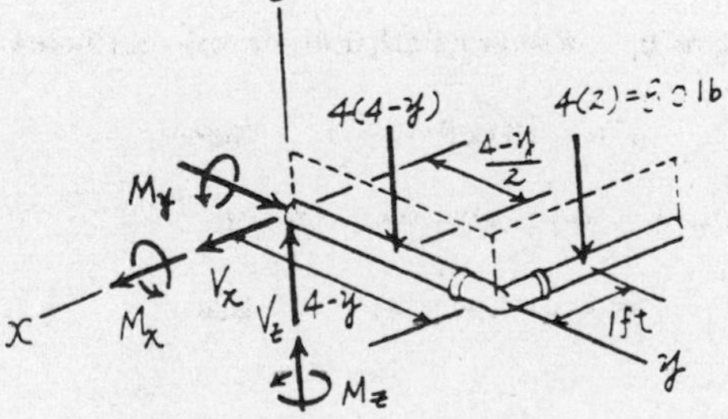

$\Sigma F_x = 0;\qquad V_x = 0 \qquad$ **Ans**

$\Sigma F_z = 0;\qquad V_z - 4(4-y) - 8.00 = 0$

$V_z = \{24.0 - 4y\}$ lb $\qquad$ **Ans**

$\Sigma M_x = 0;\qquad M_x - 4(4-y)\left(\frac{4-y}{2}\right) - 8.00(4-y) = 0$

$M_x = \{2y^2 - 24y + 64.0\}$ lb·ft $\qquad$ **Ans**

$\Sigma M_y = 0;\qquad M_y - 8.00(1) = 0 \qquad M_y = 8.00$ lb·ft. $\qquad$ **Ans**

$\Sigma M_z = 0;\qquad M_z = 0 \qquad$ **Ans**

7-66. Draw the shear and moment diagrams for the beam.

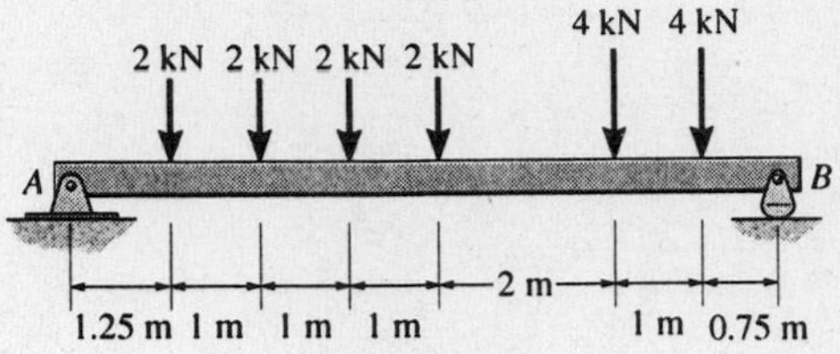

Support Reactions :

$$\circlearrowleft + \Sigma M_A = 0; \quad B_y(8) - 4(7.25) - 4(6.25) - 2(4.25) - 2(3.25) - 2(2.25) - 2(1.25) = 0$$

$$B_y = 9.50 \text{ kN}$$

$$+\uparrow \Sigma F_y = 0; \quad A_y + 9.50 - 2 - 2 - 2 - 2 - 4 - 4 = 0$$

$$A_y = 6.50 \text{ kN}$$

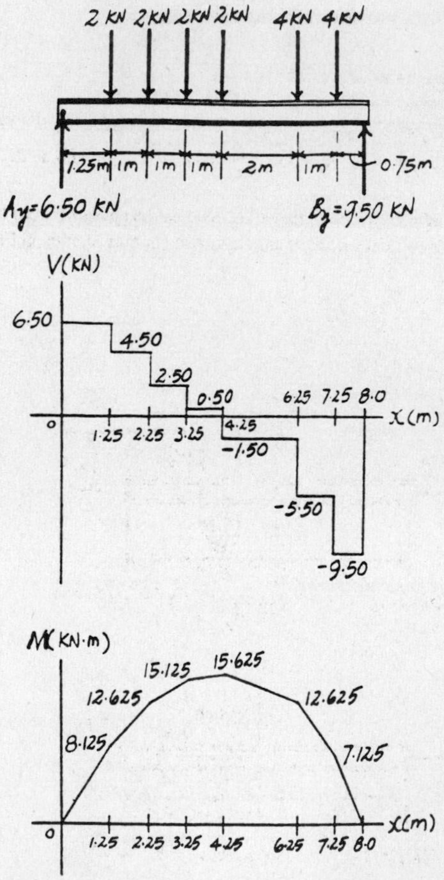

7-67. Draw the shear and moment diagrams for the beam $ABCDE$. All pulleys have a radius of 1 ft. Neglect the weight of the beam and pulley arrangement. The load weighs 500 lb.

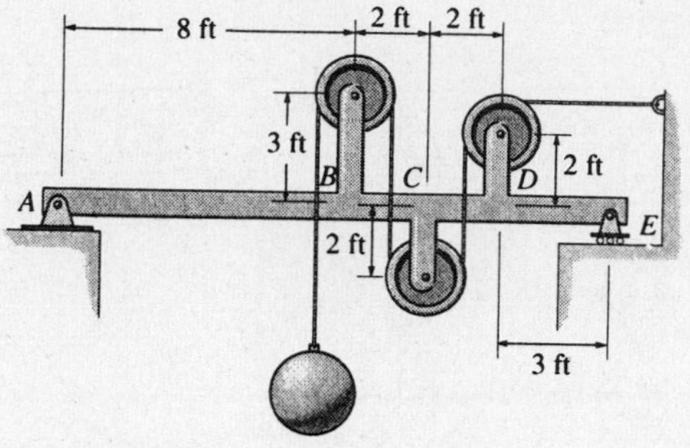

Support Reactions : From FBD (a).

$\circlearrowleft + \Sigma M_A = 0;\quad E_y(15) - 500(7) - 500(3) = 0 \quad E_y = 333.33 \text{ lb}$

$+\uparrow \Sigma F_y = 0;\quad A_y + 333.33 - 500 = 0 \quad A_y = 166.67 \text{ lb}$

Shear and Moment Diagrams : The load on the pulley at D can be replaced by equivalent force and couple moment at D as shown on FBD (b).

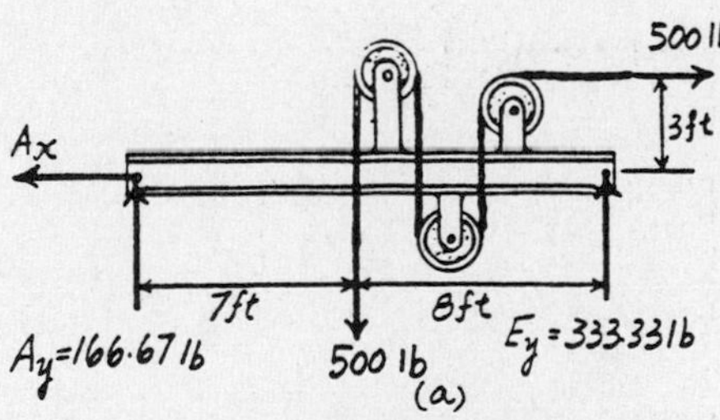

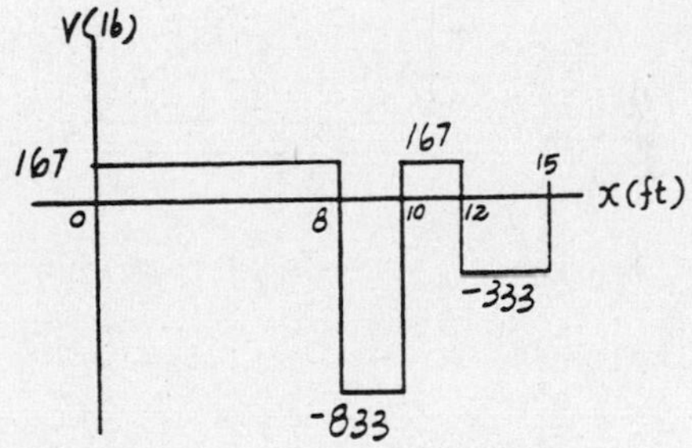

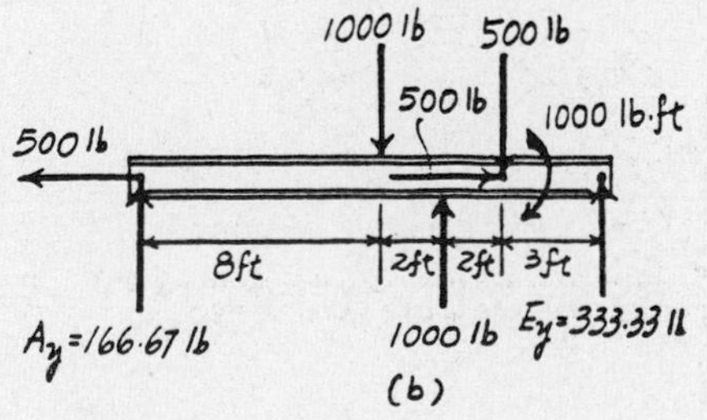

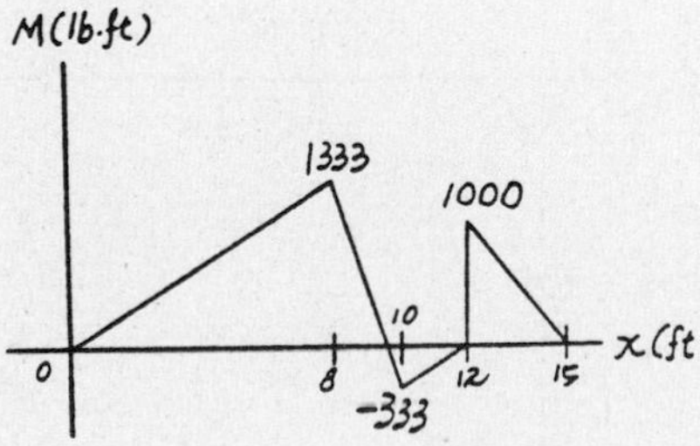

***7-68.** Draw the shear and moment diagrams for the beam.

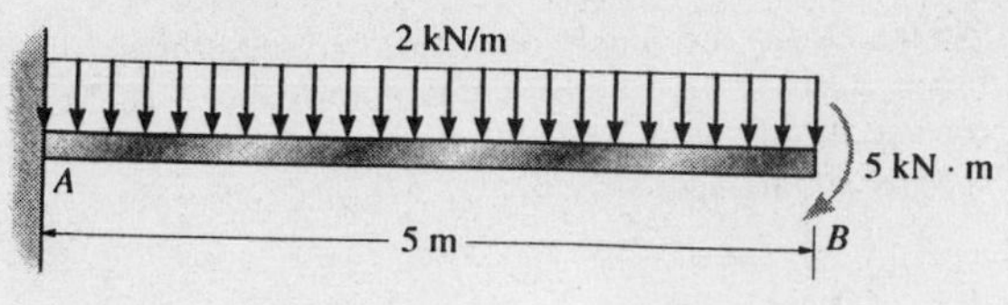

$+\uparrow \Sigma F_y = 0; \quad -V + 10 - 2x = 0$

$V = 10 - 2x$

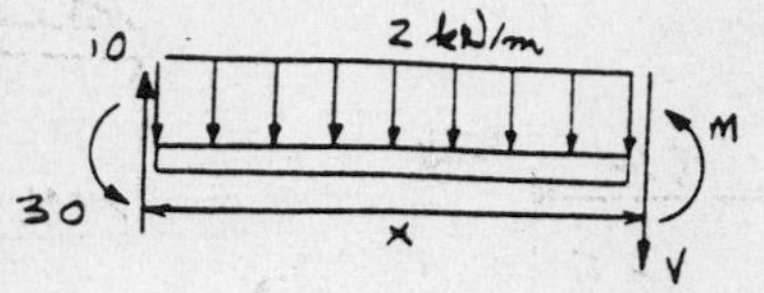

$\curvearrowleft + \Sigma M = 0; \quad M + 30 - 10x + 2x\left(\frac{x}{2}\right) = 0$

$M = 10x - x^2 - 30$

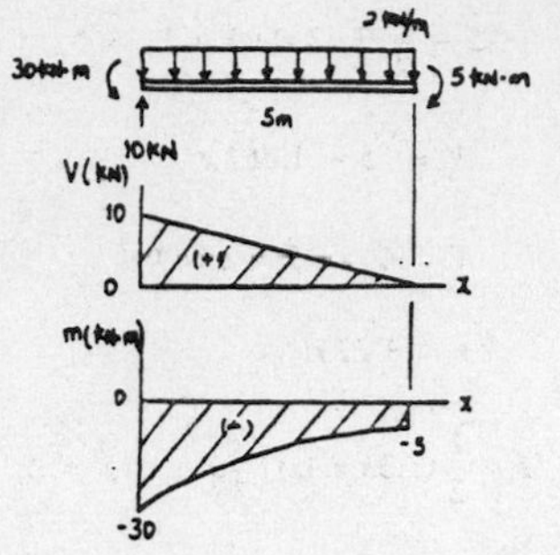

7-69. Draw the shear and moment diagrams for the beam.

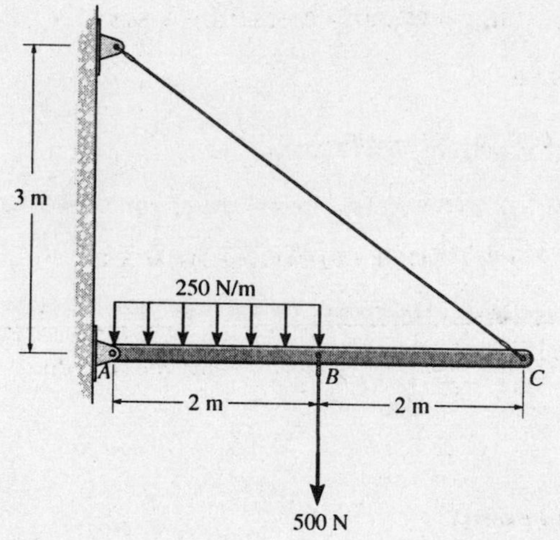

Support Reactions :

$\curvearrowleft + \Sigma M_A = 0; \quad F_C\left(\frac{3}{5}\right)(4) - 500(2) - 500(1) = 0 \qquad F_C = 625 \text{ N}$

$+\uparrow \Sigma F_y = 0; \quad A_y + 625\left(\frac{3}{5}\right) - 500 - 500 = 0 \qquad A_y = 625 \text{ N}$

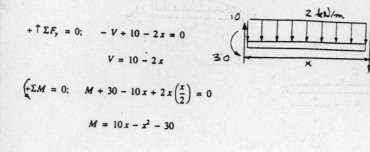

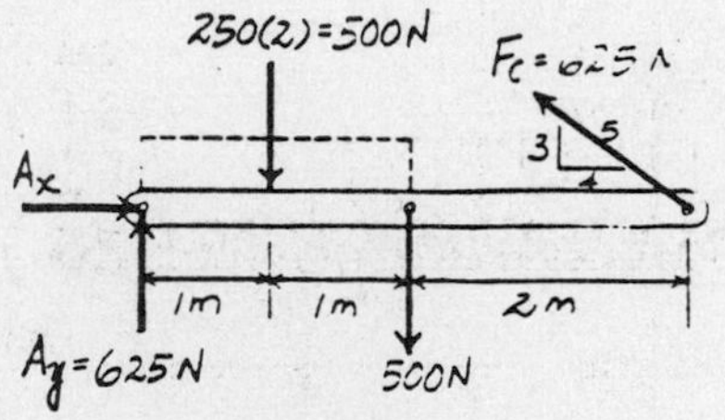

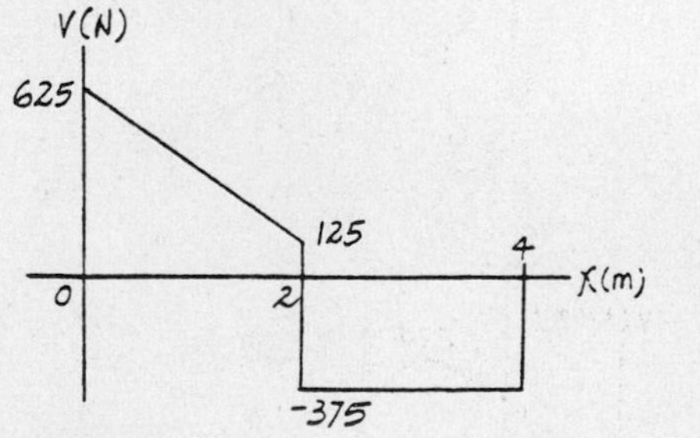

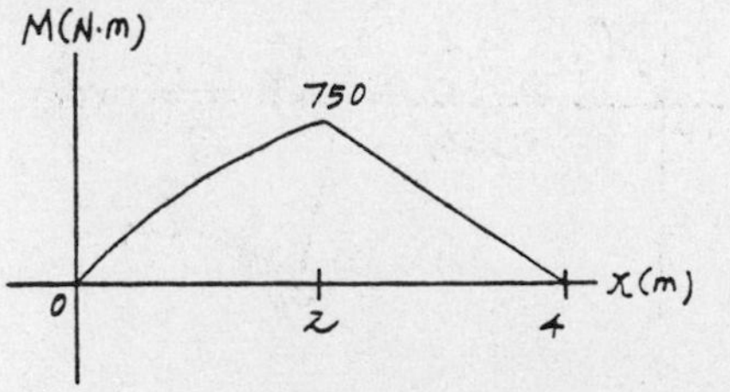

7-70. Draw the shear and moment diagrams for the beam.

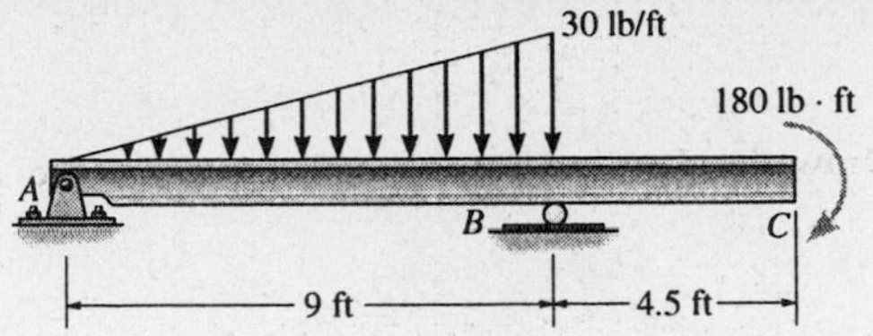

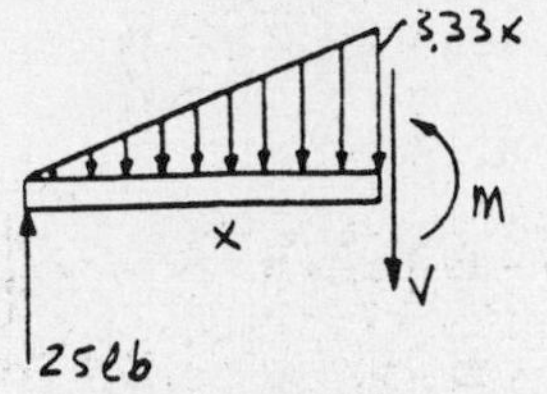

$0 \le x < 9$ ft :

$+\uparrow \Sigma F_y = 0; \quad 25 - \frac{1}{2}(3.33\,x)(x) - V = 0$

$V = 25 - 1.667\,x^2$

$V = 0 = 25 - 1.667\,x^2$

$x = 3.87$ ft

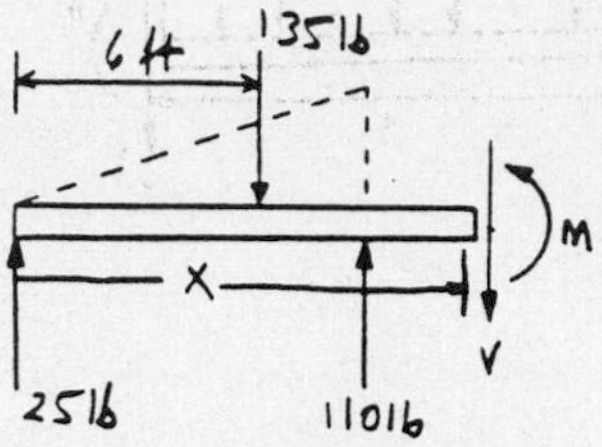

$\circlearrowleft + \Sigma M = 0; \quad M + \frac{1}{2}(3.33\,x)(x)\left(\frac{x}{3}\right) - 25\,x = 0$

$M = 25\,x - 0.5556\,x^3$

$M_{max} = 25\,(3.87) - 0.5556\,(3.87)^3 = 64.5$ lb · ft

9 ft $< x < 13.5$ ft :

$+\uparrow \Sigma F_y = 0; \quad 25 - 135 + 110 - V = 0$

$V = 0$

$\circlearrowleft + \Sigma M = 0; \quad -25\,x + 135\,(x - 6) - 110\,(x - 9) + M = 0$

$M = -180$

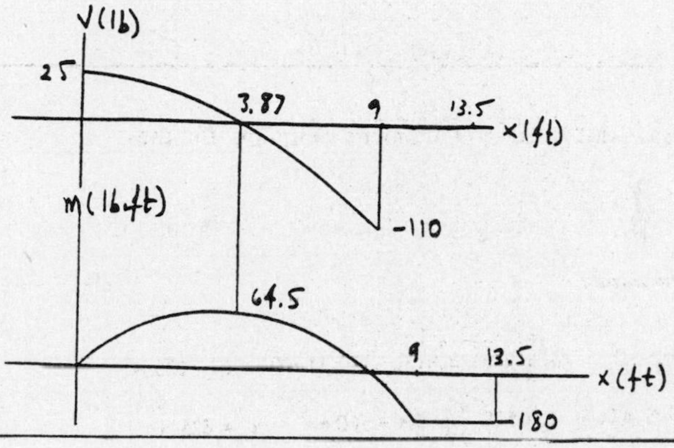

7-71. Draw the shear and moment diagrams for the beam.

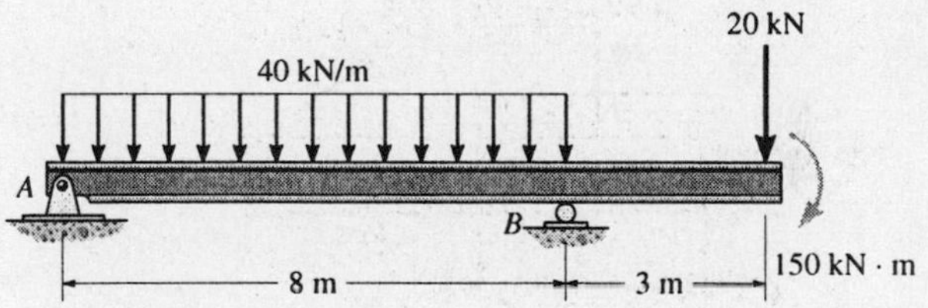

Support Reactions :

$\circlearrowleft + \Sigma M_A = 0; \quad B_y(8) - 320(4) - 20(11) - 150 = 0$

$B_y = 206.25$ kN

$+\uparrow \Sigma F_y = 0; \quad A_y + 206.25 - 320 - 20 = 0 \quad A_y = 133.75$ kN

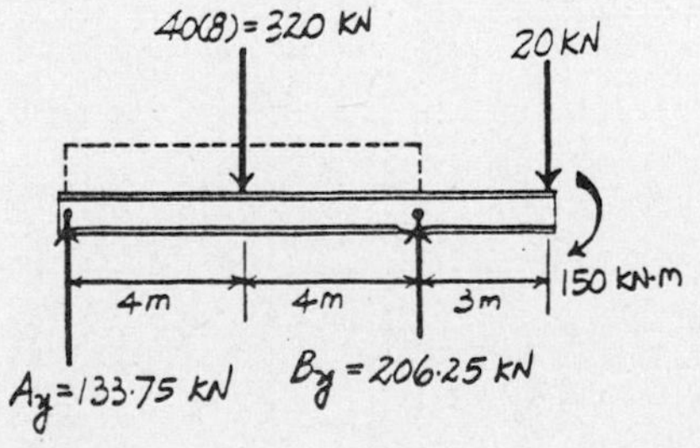

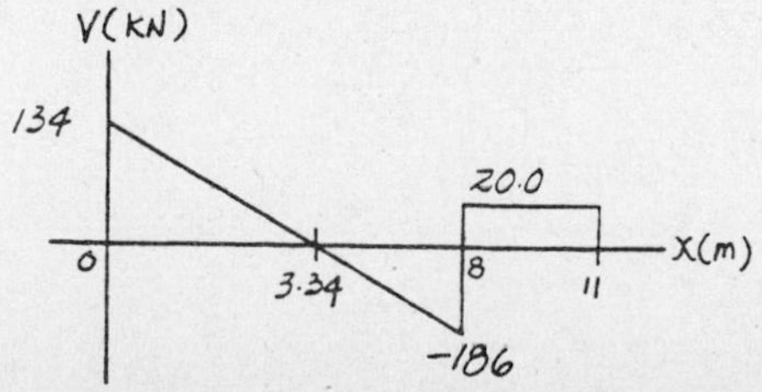

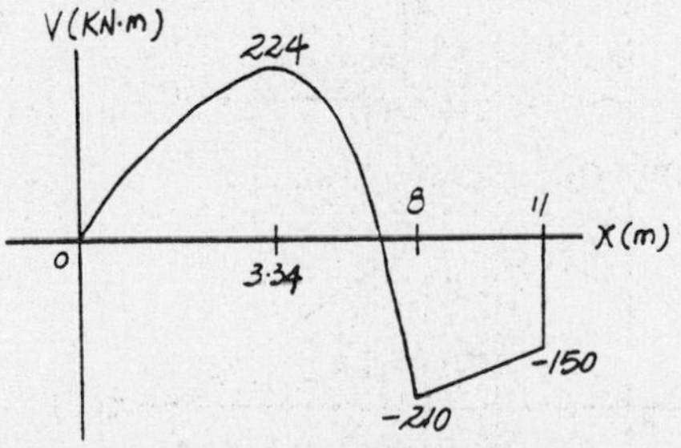

*7-72. Draw the shear and moment diagrams for the beam.

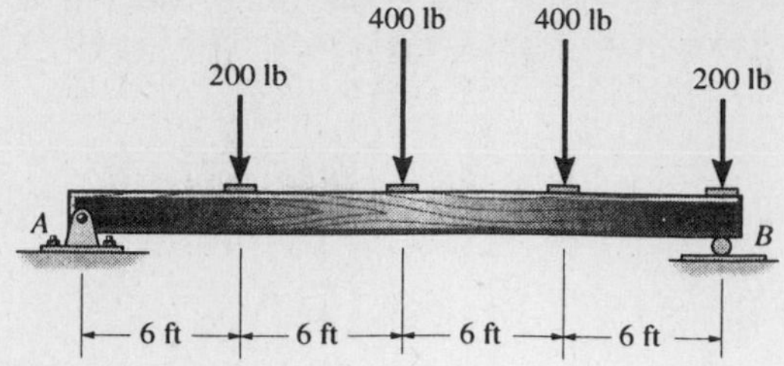

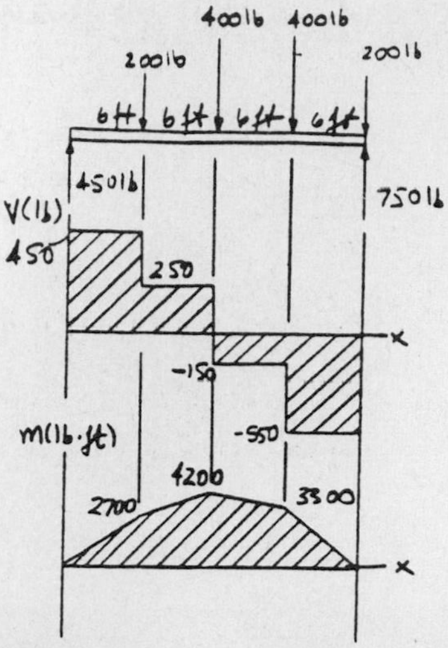

7-73. Draw the shear and moment diagrams for the beam.

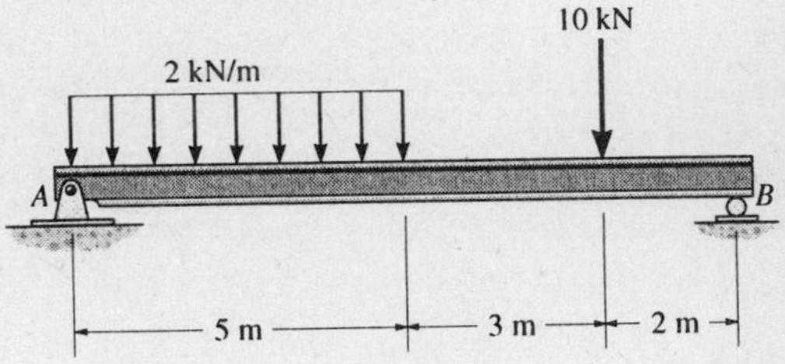

Support Reactions :

$\curvearrowleft + \Sigma M_A = 0;\quad B_y(10) - 10.0(2.5) - 10(8) = 0\quad B_y = 10.5\text{ kN}$

$+\uparrow \Sigma F_y = 0;\quad A_y + 10.5 - 10.0 - 10 = 0\quad A_y = 9.50\text{ kN}$

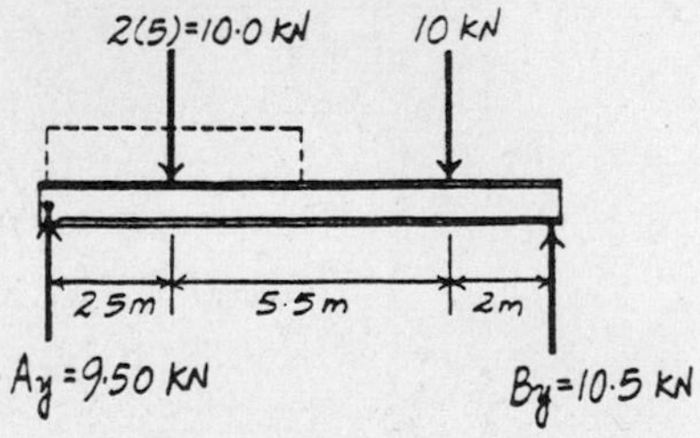

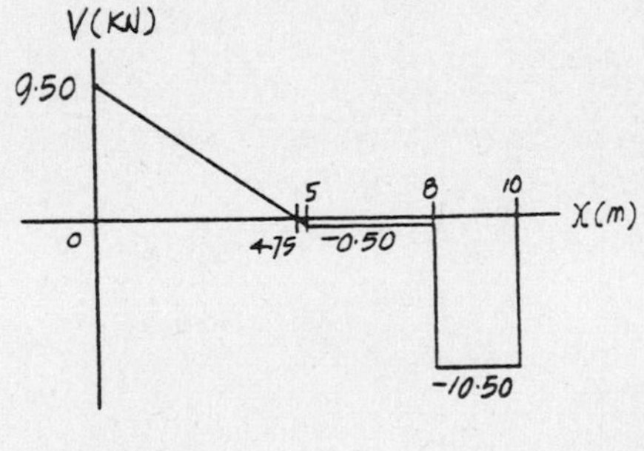

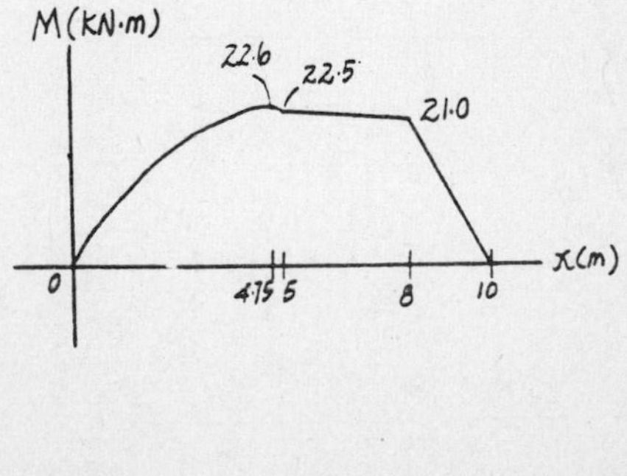

7-74. Draw the shear and moment diagrams for the lathe shaft if it is subjected to the loads shown. The bearing at A is a journal bearing, and B is a thrust bearing.

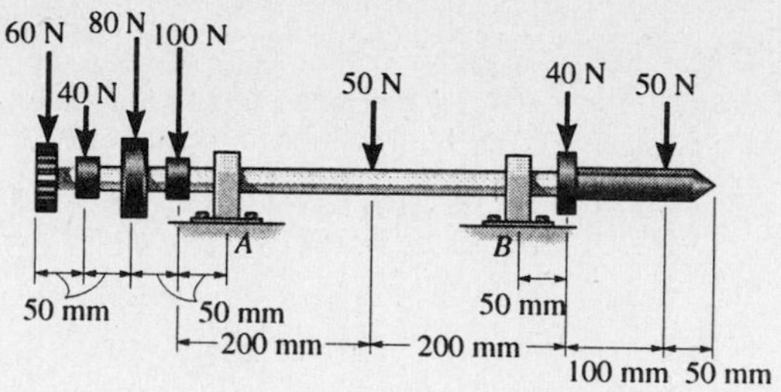

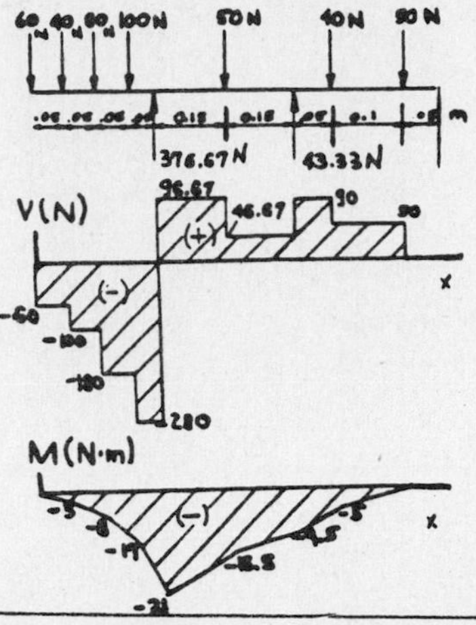

7-75. Draw the shear and moment diagrams for the boom AB of the jib crane. The boom has a mass of 20 kg/m and the trolley supports a force of 600 N in the position shown. Neglect the size of the trolley.

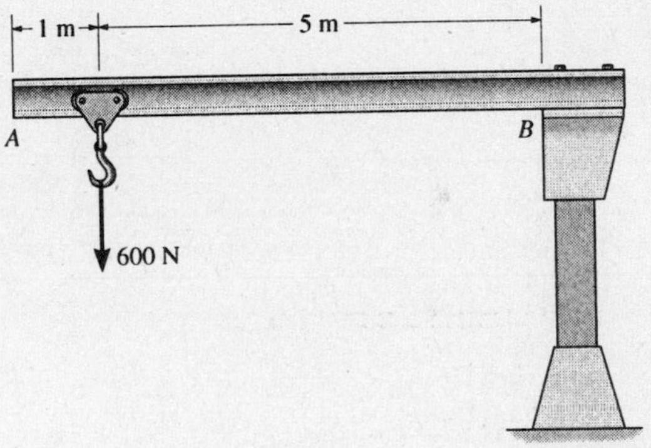

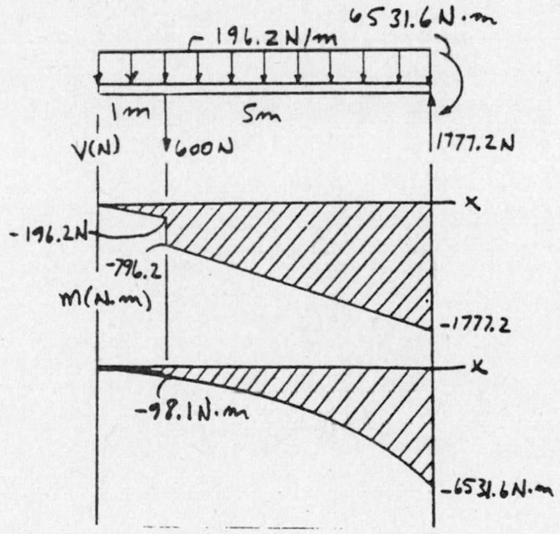

***7-76.** Draw the shear and moment diagrams for the shaft. The support at A is a thrust bearing and at B it is a journal bearing.

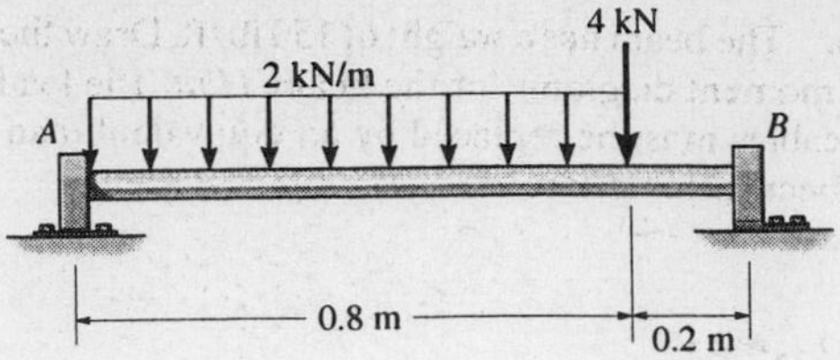

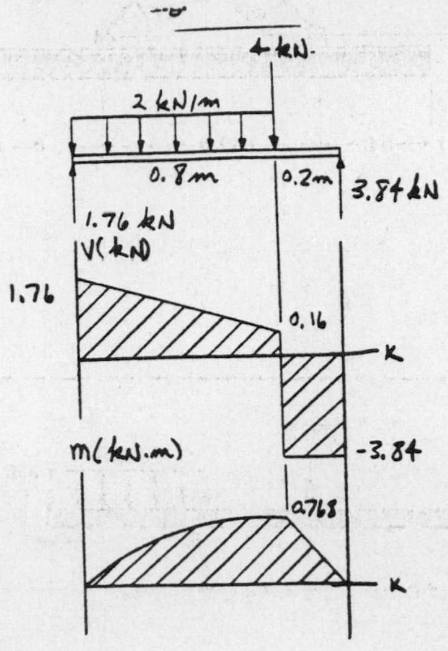

7-77. Draw the shear and moment diagrams for the beam.

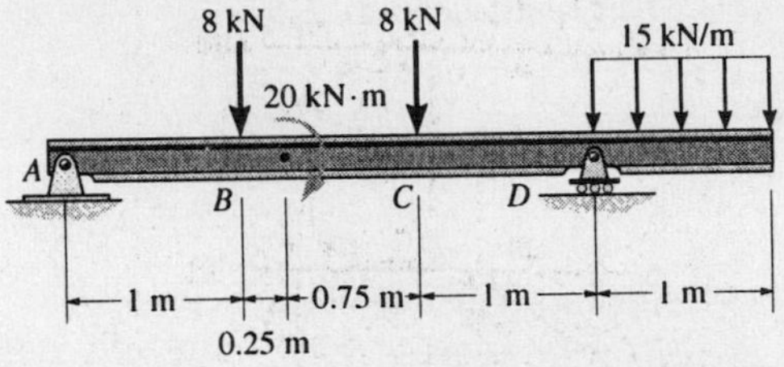

Support Reactions :

$\curvearrowleft + \Sigma M_A = 0;\quad D_y(3) - 8(1) - 8(2) - 15.0(3.5) - 20 = 0$

$D_y = 32.167 \text{ kN}$

$+\uparrow \Sigma F_y = 0;\quad 32.167 - 8 - 8 - 15.0 - A_y = 0$

$A_y = 1.167 \text{ kN}$

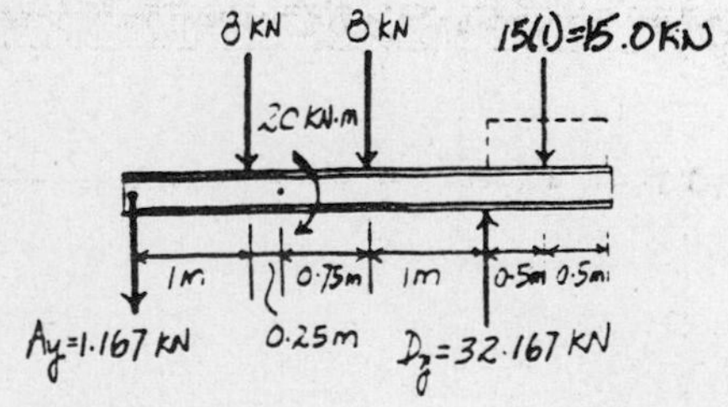

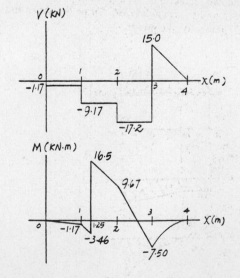

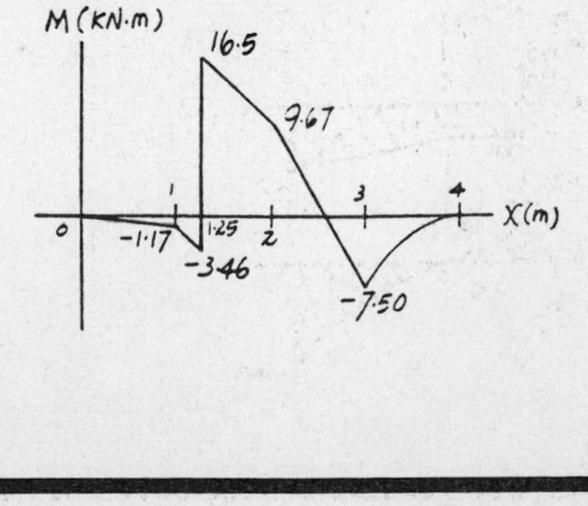

7-78. The beam has a weight of 150 lb/ft. Draw the shear and moment diagrams for the beam. *Hint:* The loading of the cables must be replaced by an equivalent load along the beam's centerline.

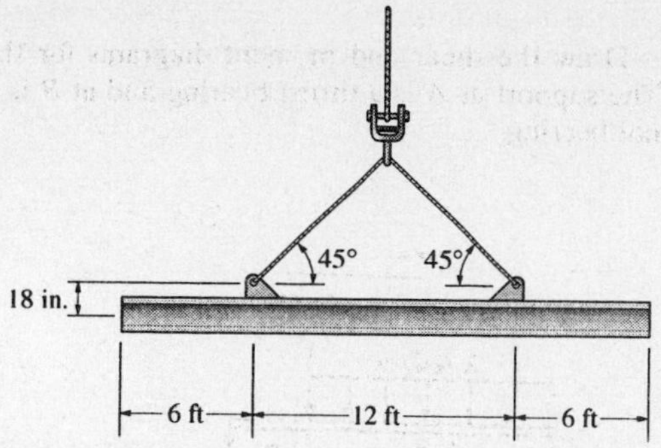

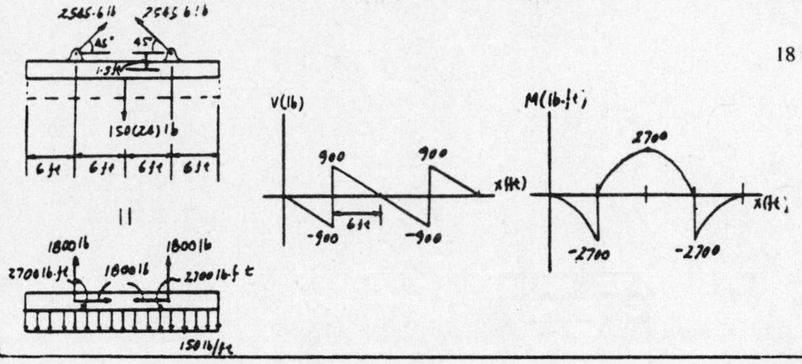

7-79. The beam consists of two segments pin connected at *B*. Draw the shear and moment diagrams for the beam.

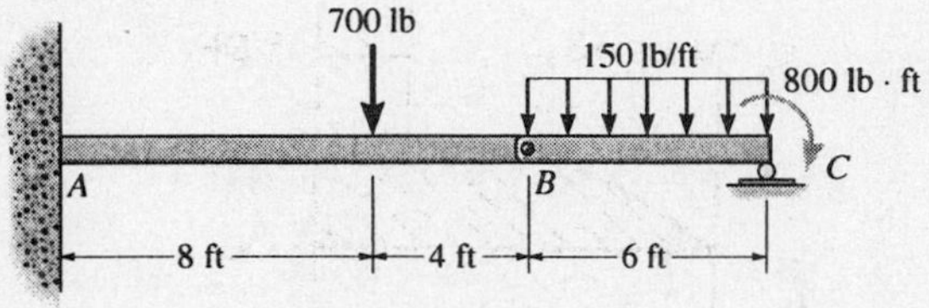

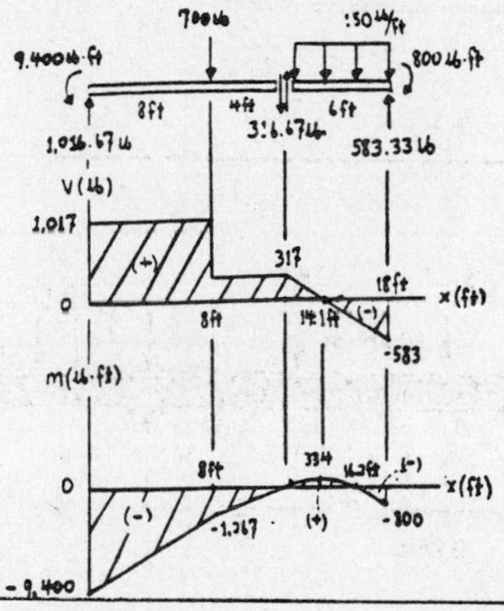

***7-80.** The two segments of the girder are pin connected together by a short vertical link *BC*. Draw the shear and moment diagrams for the girder.

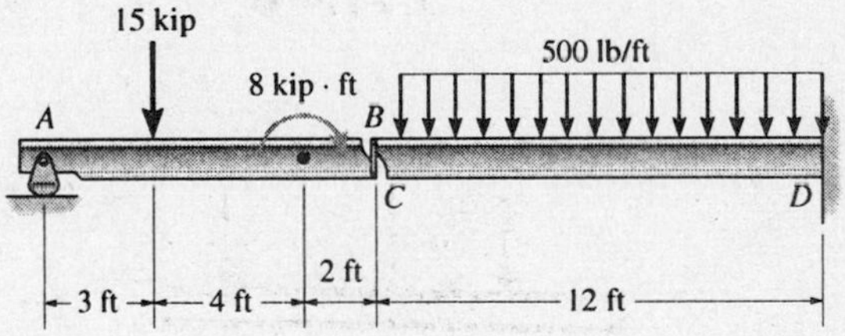

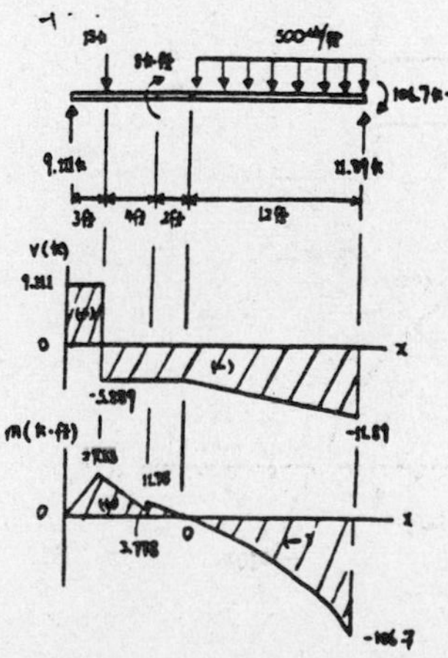

7-81. The beam consists of two segments pin-connected at B. Draw the shear and moment diagrams for the beam.

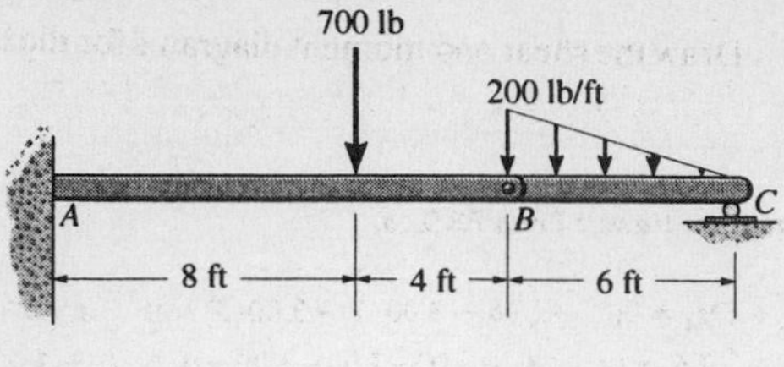

Support Reactions : From FBD (a),

$$+\Sigma M_B = 0; \quad C_y(6) - 0.600(2) = 0 \quad C_y = 0.200 \text{ kip}$$

$$+\uparrow \Sigma F_y = 0; \quad B_y + 0.200 - 0.600 = 0 \quad B_y = 0.400 \text{ kip}$$

From FBD (b),

$$\curvearrowleft + \Sigma M_A = 0; \quad M_A - 0.700(8) - 0.400(12) = 0$$

$$M_A = 10.4 \text{ kip} \cdot \text{ft}$$

$$+\uparrow \Sigma F_y = 0; \quad A_y - 0.700 - 0.400 = 0 \quad A_y = 1.10 \text{ kip}$$

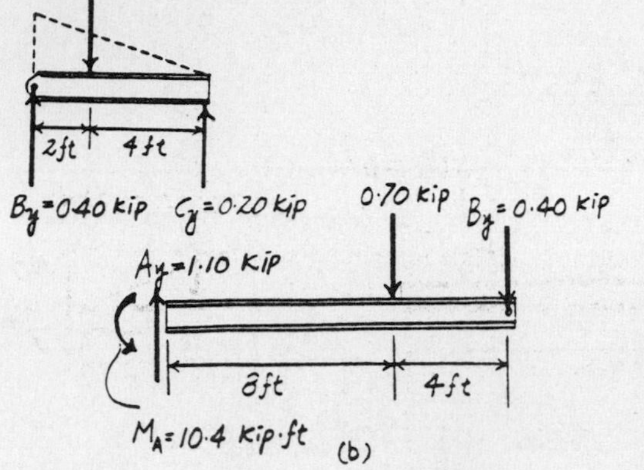

Shear and Moment Diagrams : The peak value of the moment for segment BC can be evaluated using the method of sections. The maximum moment occurs when $V = 0$. From FBD (c)

$$+\uparrow \Sigma F_y = 0; \quad 0.200 - \frac{1}{2}\left(\frac{x}{30}\right)x = 0 \quad x = 2\sqrt{3} \text{ ft}$$

$$\curvearrowleft + \Sigma M = 0; \quad 0.200x - \frac{1}{2}\left(\frac{x}{30}\right)x\left(\frac{x}{3}\right) - M = 0$$

$$M = 0.200x - \frac{x^3}{180}$$

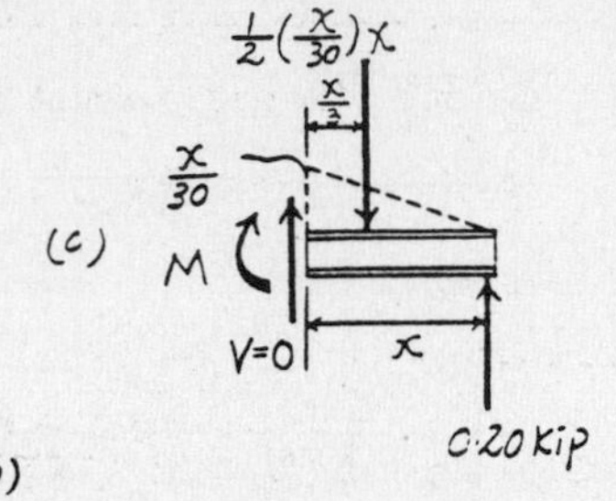

Thus,

$$(M_{max})_{BC} = 0.200\left(2\sqrt{3}\right) - \frac{\left(2\sqrt{3}\right)^3}{180} = 0.462 \text{ kip} \cdot \text{ft}$$

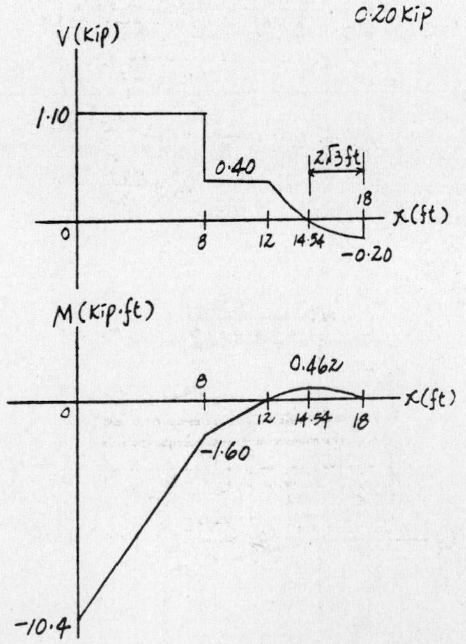

7-82. Draw the shear and moment diagrams for the beam.

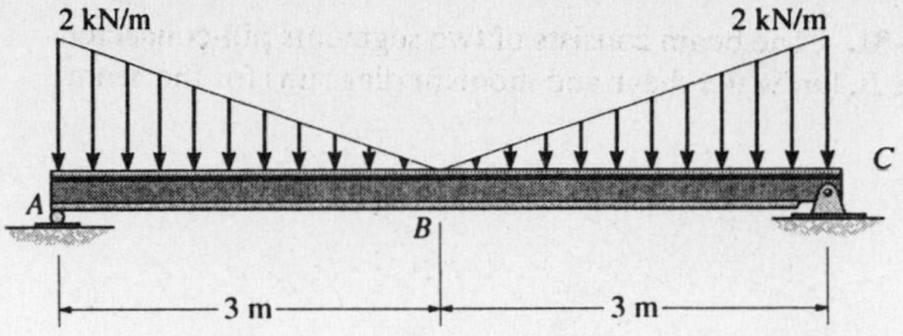

Support Reactions : From FBD (a),

$$\circlearrowleft + \Sigma M_A = 0; \quad C_y(6) - 3.00(1) - 3.00(5) = 0 \quad C_y = 3.00 \text{ kN}$$

$$+\uparrow \Sigma F_y = 0; \quad A_y + 3.00 - 3.00 - 3.00 = 0 \quad A_y = 3.00 \text{ kN}$$

Shear and Moment Diagrams : The peak value of the moment diagram can be evaluated using the method of sections. The maximum moment occurs at the midspan ($x = 3$ m) where $V = 0$. From FBD (b),

$$\circlearrowleft + \Sigma M = 0; \quad M - 3.00(1) = 0 \quad M = 3.00 \text{ kN} \cdot \text{m}$$

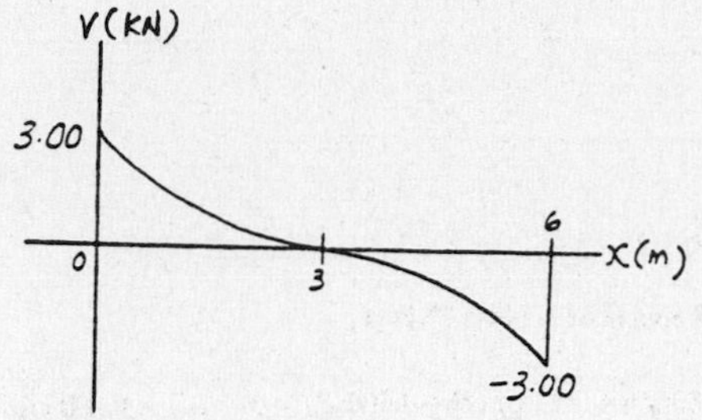

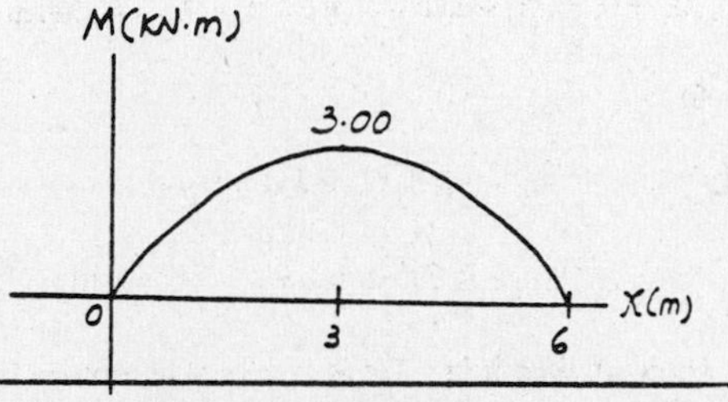

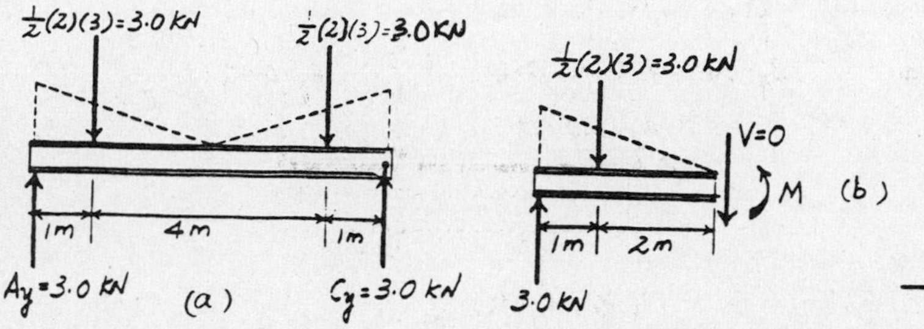

7-83. Draw the shear and moment diagrams for the beam.

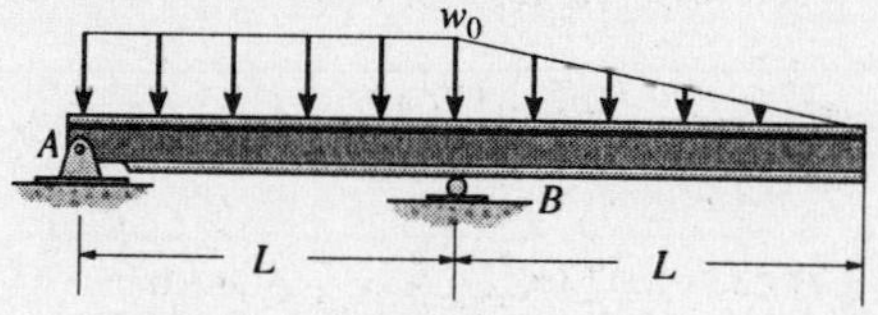

Support Reactions :

$$\circlearrowleft + \Sigma M_A = 0; \quad B_y(L) - w_0 L\left(\frac{L}{2}\right) - \frac{w_0 L}{2}\left(\frac{4L}{3}\right) = 0$$

$$B_y = \frac{7w_0 L}{6}$$

$$+\uparrow \Sigma F_y = 0; \quad A_y + \frac{7w_0 L}{6} - w_0 L - \frac{w_0 L}{2} = 0$$

$$A_y = \frac{w_0 L}{3}$$

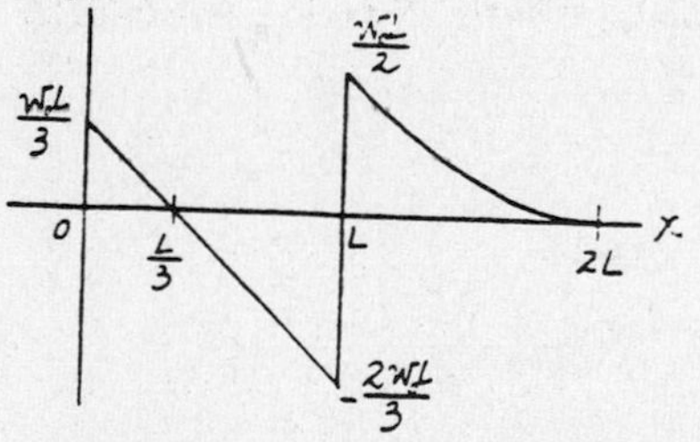

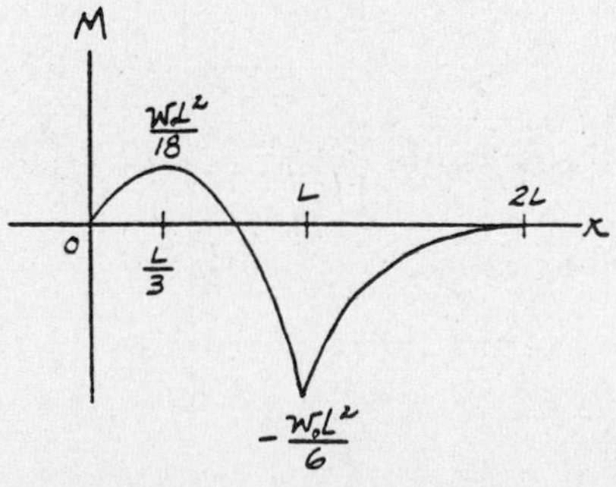

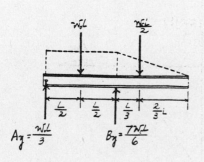

***7-84.** Draw the shear and moment diagrams for the beam.

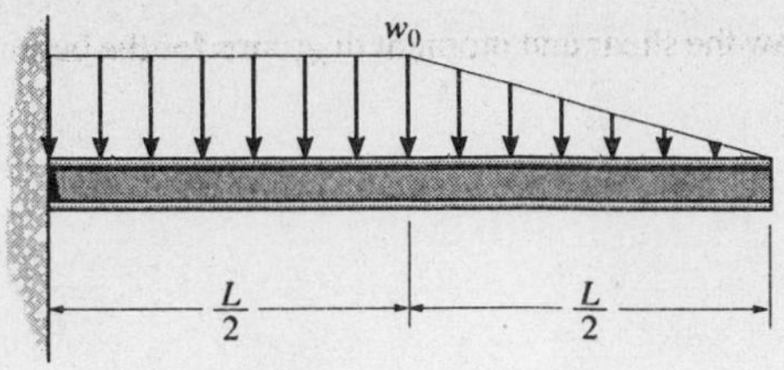

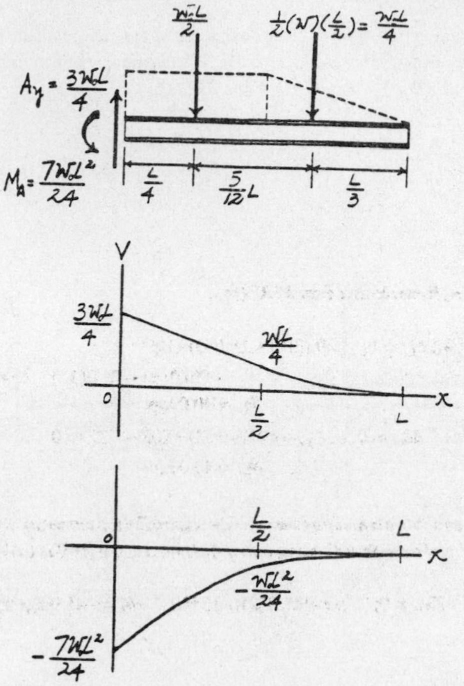

Support Reactions :

$$\curvearrowleft + \Sigma M_A = 0; \quad M_A - \frac{w_0 L}{2}\left(\frac{L}{4}\right) - \frac{w_0 L}{4}\left(\frac{2L}{3}\right) = 0$$

$$M_A = \frac{7w_0 L^2}{24}$$

$$+\uparrow \Sigma F_y = 0; \quad A_y - \frac{w_0 L}{2} - \frac{w_0 L}{4} = 0 \quad A_y = \frac{3w_0 L}{4}$$

7-85. Draw the shear and moment diagrams for the beam.

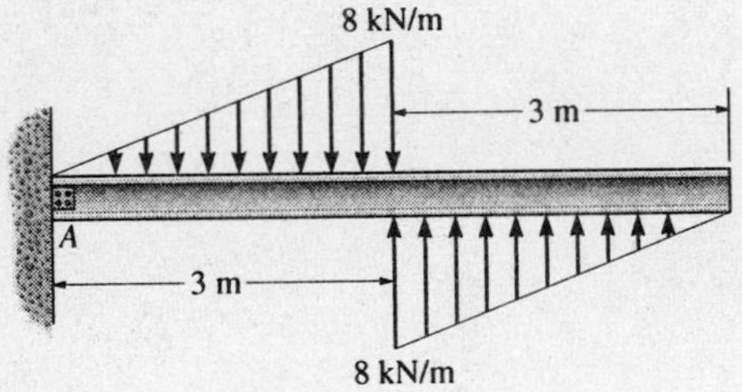

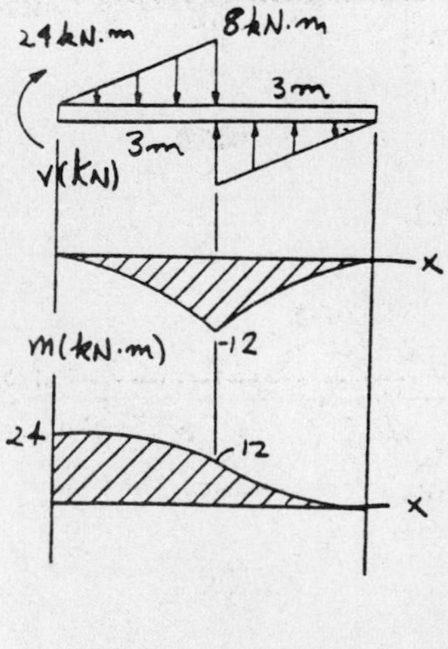

7-86. Draw the shear and moment diagrams for the beam.

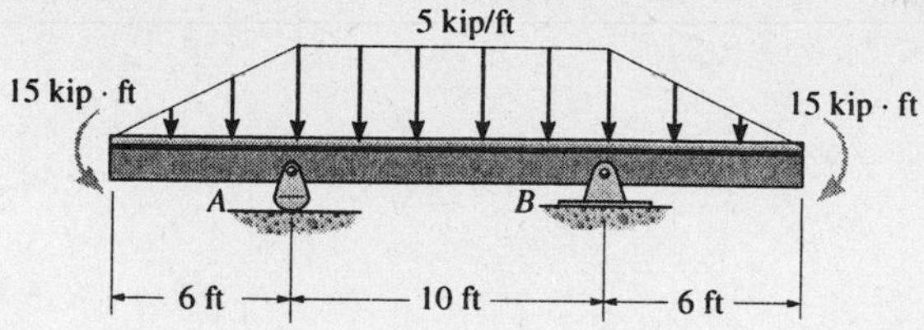

Support Reactions : From FBD (a),

$$\circlearrowleft + \Sigma M_A = 0; \quad B_y(10) + 15.0(2) + 15 - 50.0(5) - 15.0(12) - 15 = 0$$

$$B_y = 40.0 \text{ kip}$$

$$+\uparrow \Sigma F_y = 0; \quad A_y + 40.0 - 15.0 - 50.0 - 15.0 = 0$$

$$A_y = 40.0 \text{ kip}$$

Shear and Moment Diagrams : The value of the moment at supports A and B can be evaluated using the method of sections [FBD (c)].

$$+\Sigma M = 0; \quad M + 15.0(2) + 15 = 0 \quad M = -45.0 \text{ kip} \cdot \text{ft}$$

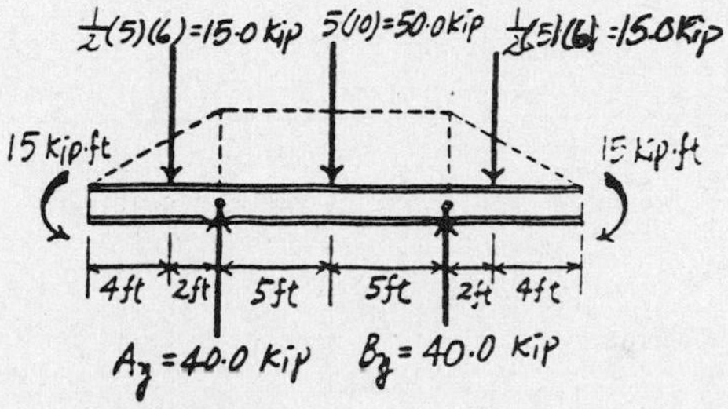

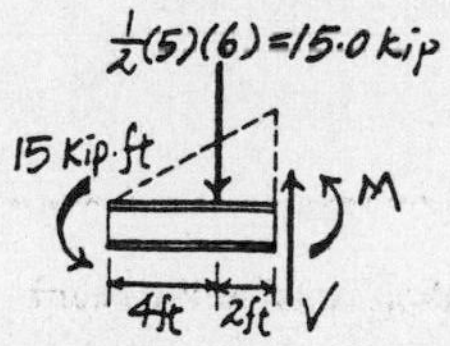

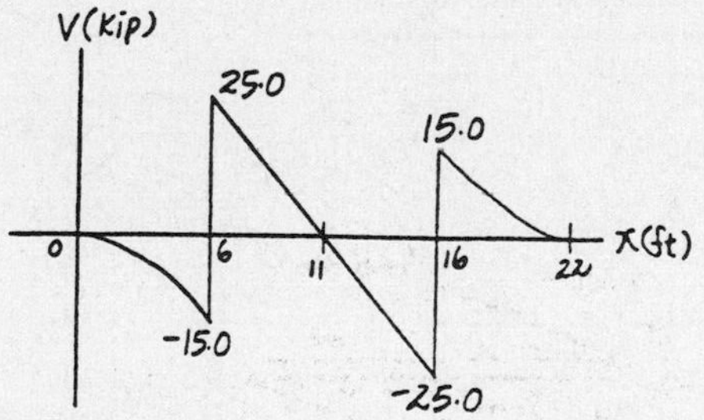

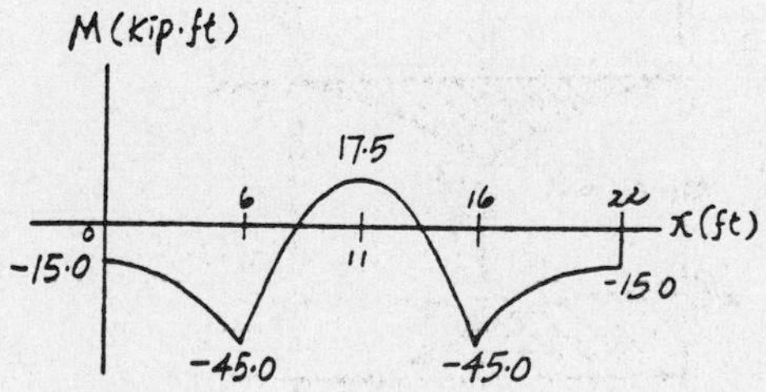

7-87. Draw the shear and moment diagrams for the shaft. The supports at A and B are journal bearings.

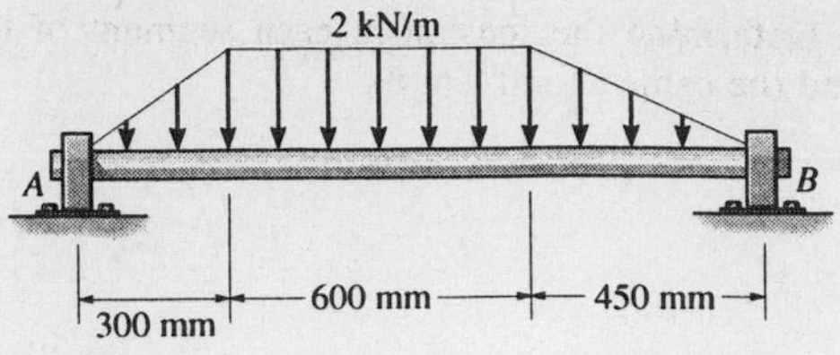

$+\uparrow\Sigma F_y = 0;\quad 1022.2 - \frac{1}{2}(2000)(0.3) - V_{0.3} = 0$

$V_{0.3} = 722\text{ N}$

$\circlearrowleft + \Sigma M = 0;\quad M_{0.3} + \frac{1}{2}(2000)(0.3)(0.1) - 1022.2(0.3) = 0$

$M_{0.3} = 277\text{ N}\cdot\text{m}$

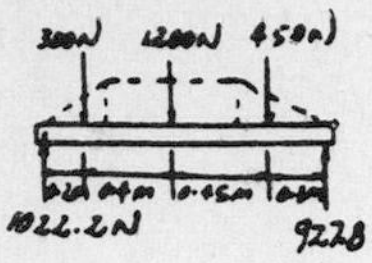

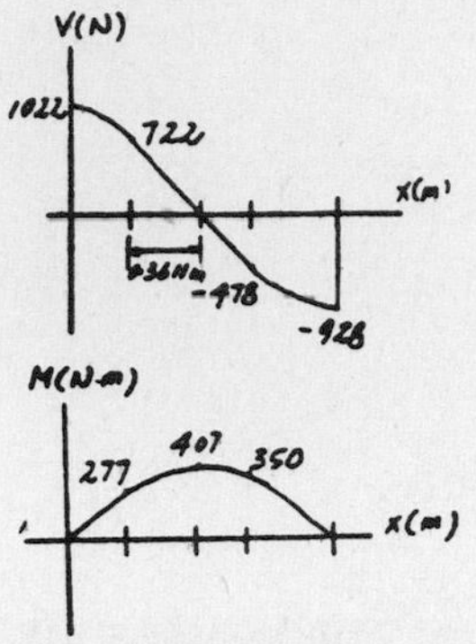

***7-88.** Draw the shear and moment diagrams for the beam.

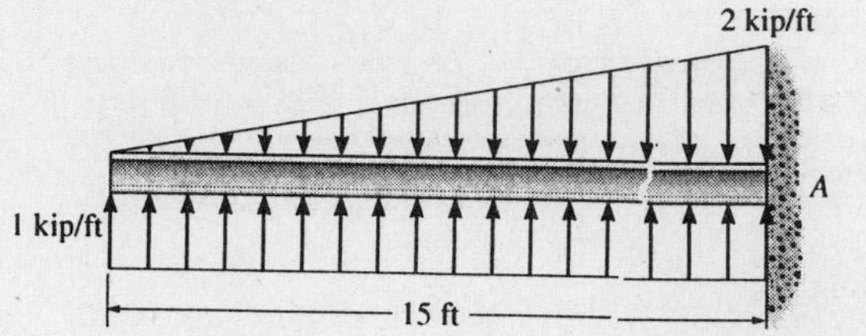

Support Reactions :

$\circlearrowleft + \Sigma M_A = 0;\quad B_y(12) + 2 - 2(8) - 4(10) = 0 \quad B_y = 4.50\text{ kip}$

$+\uparrow\Sigma F_y = 0;\quad A_y + 4.50 - 2 - 4 = 0 \quad A_y = 1.50\text{ kip}$

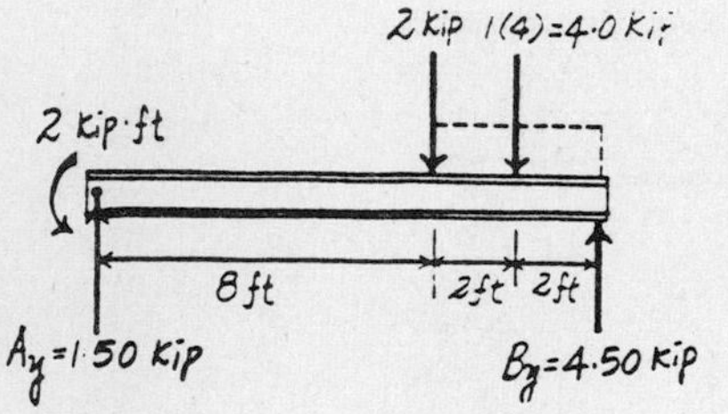

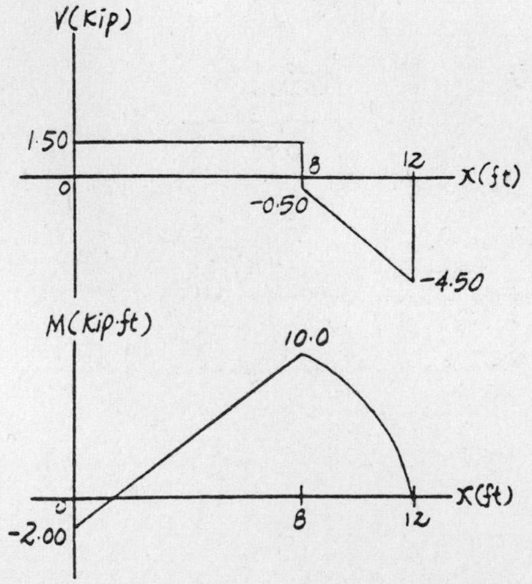

***7-89.** Determine the tension in each segment of the cable and the cable's total length.

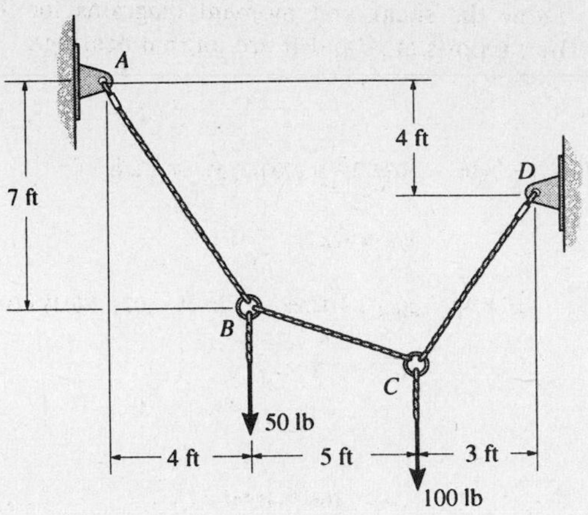

Equations of Equilibrium : Applying method of joints, we have

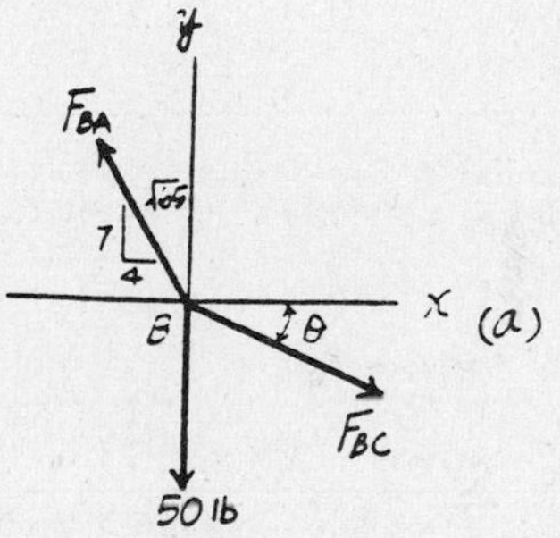

Joint *B*

$$\overset{+}{\rightarrow}\Sigma F_x = 0; \quad F_{BC}\cos\theta - F_{BA}\left(\frac{4}{\sqrt{65}}\right) = 0 \qquad [1]$$

$$+\uparrow\Sigma F_y = 0; \quad F_{BA}\left(\frac{7}{\sqrt{65}}\right) - F_{BC}\sin\theta - 50 = 0 \qquad [2]$$

Joint *C*

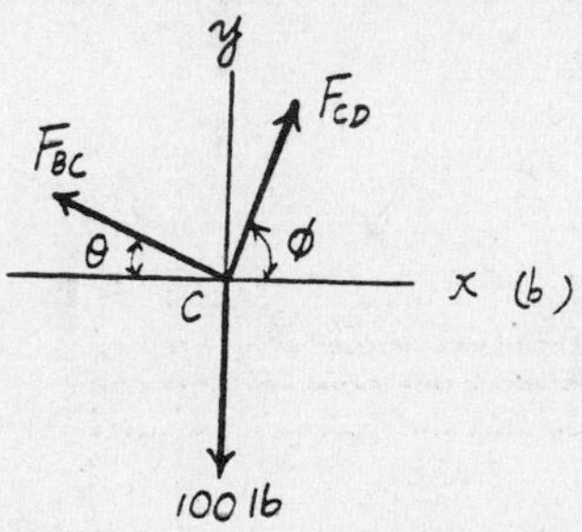

$$\overset{+}{\rightarrow}\Sigma F_x = 0; \quad F_{CD}\cos\phi - F_{BC}\cos\theta = 0 \qquad [3]$$

$$+\uparrow\Sigma F_y = 0; \quad F_{BC}\sin\theta + F_{CD}\sin\phi - 100 = 0 \qquad [4]$$

Geometry :

$$\sin\theta = \frac{y}{\sqrt{y^2+25}} \qquad \cos\theta = \frac{5}{\sqrt{y^2+25}}$$

$$\sin\phi = \frac{3+y}{\sqrt{y^2+6y+18}} \qquad \cos\phi = \frac{3}{\sqrt{y^2+6y+18}}$$

Substitute the above results into Eqs. [1], [2], [3] and [4] and solve. We have

$F_{BC} = 46.7$ lb $\quad F_{BA} = 83.0$ lb $\quad F_{CD} = 88.1$ lb **Ans**

$y = 2.679$ ft

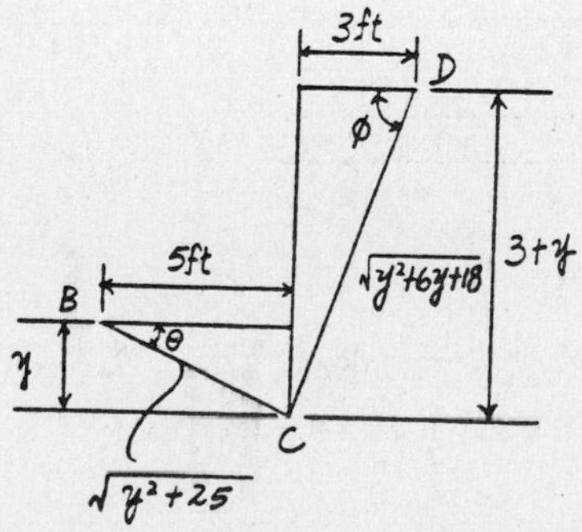

The total length of the cable is

$$l = \sqrt{7^2+4^2} + \sqrt{5^2+2.679^2} + \sqrt{3^2+(2.679+3)^2}$$
$$= 20.2 \text{ ft} \qquad \textbf{Ans}$$

7-90. Determine the tension in each segment of the cable and the cable's total length.

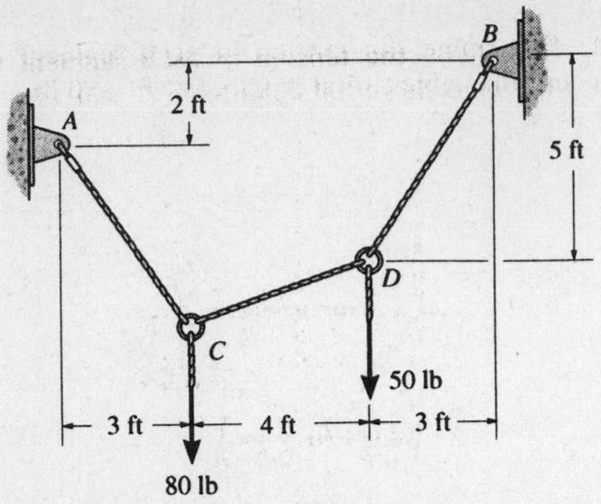

Equations of Equilibrium : Applying method of joints, we have

Joint *D*

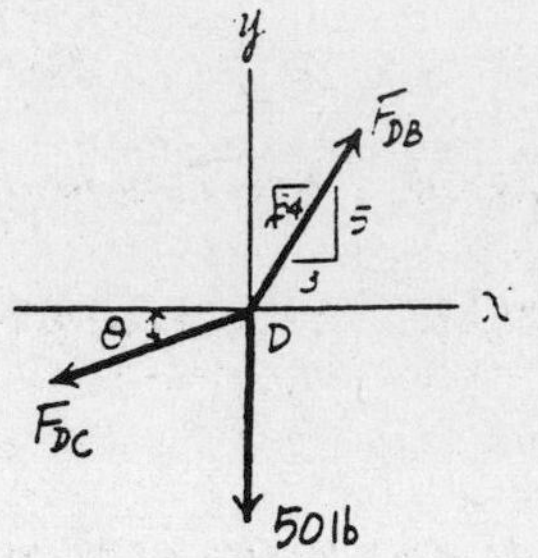

$$\xrightarrow{+} \Sigma F_x = 0; \quad F_{DB}\left(\frac{3}{\sqrt{34}}\right) - F_{DC}\cos\theta = 0 \qquad [1]$$

$$+\uparrow \Sigma F_y = 0; \quad F_{DB}\left(\frac{5}{\sqrt{34}}\right) - F_{DC}\sin\theta - 50 = 0 \qquad [2]$$

Joint *C*

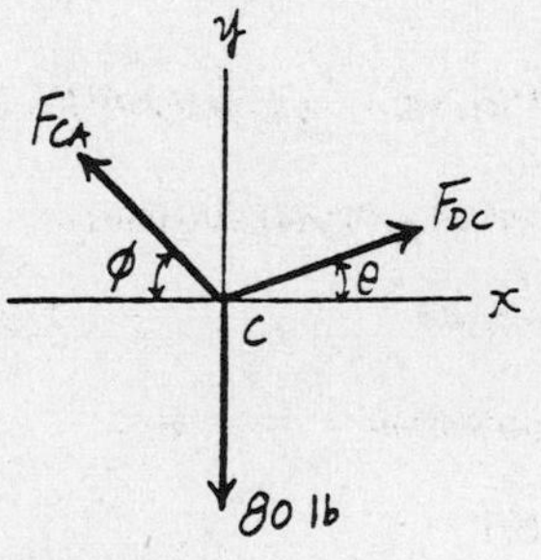

$$\xrightarrow{+} \Sigma F_x = 0; \quad F_{DC}\cos\theta - F_{CA}\cos\phi = 0 \qquad [3]$$

$$+\uparrow \Sigma F_y = 0; \quad F_{DC}\sin\theta + F_{CA}\sin\phi - 80 = 0 \qquad [4]$$

Geometry :

$$\sin\theta = \frac{y}{\sqrt{y^2+16}} \qquad \cos\theta = \frac{4}{\sqrt{y^2+16}}$$

$$\sin\phi = \frac{y+3}{\sqrt{y^2+6y+18}} \qquad \cos\phi = \frac{3}{\sqrt{y^2+6y+18}}$$

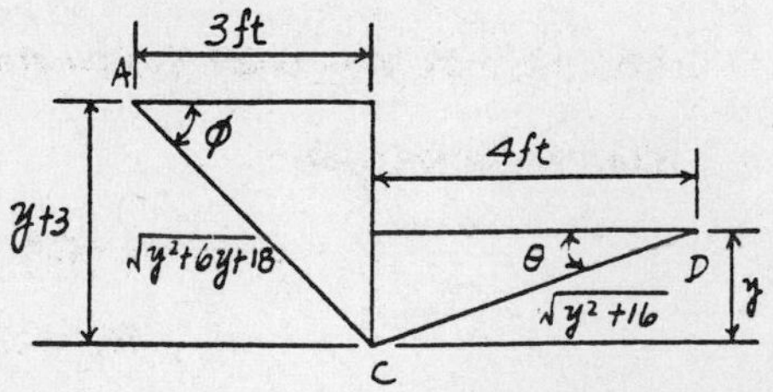

Substitute the above results into Eqs. [1], [2], [3] and [4] and solve. We have

$F_{DC} = 43.7$ lb $\quad F_{DB} = 78.2$ lb $\quad F_{CA} = 74.7$ lb **Ans**

$y = 1.695$ ft

The total length of the cable is

$$l = \sqrt{5^2+3^2} + \sqrt{4^2+1.695^2} + \sqrt{3^2+(1.695+3)^2}$$
$$= 15.7 \text{ ft}$$ **Ans**

7-91. Determine the tension in each segment of the cable and the cable's total length. Set $P = 80$ lb.

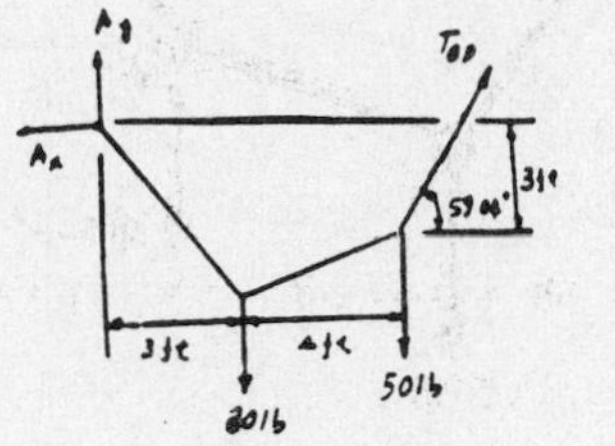

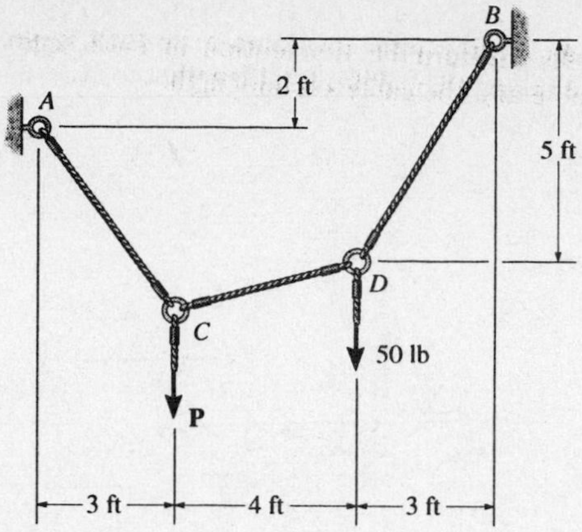

From FBD (a)

$\circlearrowleft + \Sigma M_A = 0;\quad T_{BD}\cos 59.04°(3) + T_{BD}\sin 59.04°(7) - 50(7) - 80(3) = 0$

$T_{BD} = 78.188\text{ lb} = 78.2\text{ lb}$ **Ans**

$\overset{+}{\rightarrow} \Sigma F_x = 0;\quad 78.188\cos 59.04° - A_x = 0 \quad A_x = 40.227\text{ lb}$

$+\uparrow \Sigma F_y = 0;\quad A_y + 78.188\sin 59.04° - 80 - 50 = 0 \quad A_y = 62.955\text{ lb}$

Joint A :

$\overset{+}{\rightarrow} \Sigma F_x = 0;\quad T_{AC}\cos\phi - 40.227 = 0$ (1)

$+\uparrow \Sigma F_y = 0;\quad -T_{AC}\sin\phi + 62.955 = 0$ (2)

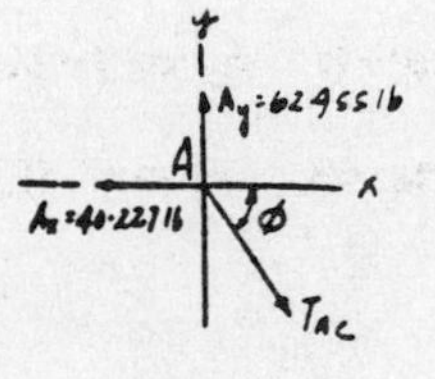

Solving Eqs. (1) and (2) yields :

$\phi = 57.42°$

$T_{AC} = 74.7\text{ lb}$ **Ans**

Joint D :

$\overset{+}{\rightarrow} \Sigma F_x = 0;\quad 78.188\cos 59.04° - T_{CD}\cos\theta = 0$ (3)

$+\uparrow \Sigma F_y = 0;\quad 78.188\sin 59.04° - T_{CD}\sin\theta - 50 = 0$ (4)

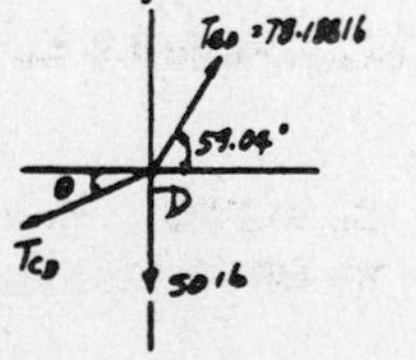

Solving Eqs. (3) and (4) yields :

$\theta = 22.96°$

$T_{CD} = 43.7\text{ lb}$ **Ans**

Total length of the cable : $l_T = \frac{5}{\sin 59.04°} + \frac{4}{\cos 22.96°} + \frac{3}{\cos 57.42°} = 15.7\text{ ft}$ **Ans**

***7-92.** If each cable segment can support a maximum tension of 75 lb, determine the largest load P that can be applied.

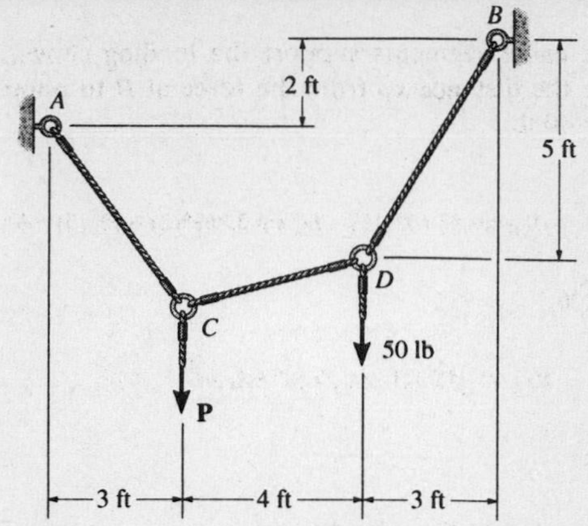

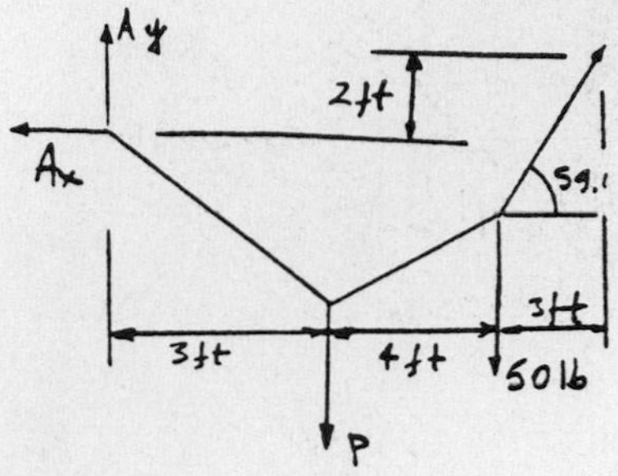

$\circlearrowleft + \Sigma M_A = 0;\quad -T_{BD}(\cos 59.04°)\,2 + T_{BD}(\sin 59.04°)(10) - 50(7) - P(3) = 0$

$T_{BD} = 0.39756\,P + 46.383$

$\xrightarrow{+} \Sigma F_x = 0;\quad -A_x + T_{BD}\cos 59.04° = 0$

$+\uparrow \Sigma F_y = 0;\quad A_y - P - 50 + T_{BD}\sin 59.04° = 0$

Assume maximum tension is in cable BD.

$T_{BD} = 75 \text{ lb}$

$P = 71.98 \text{ lb}$

$A_x = 38.59 \text{ lb}$

$A_y = 57.670 \text{ lb}$

Pin A:

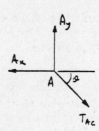

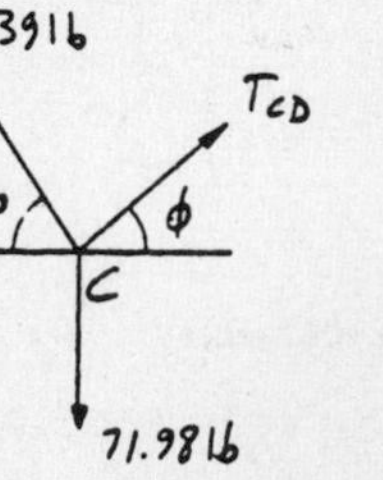

$T_{AC} = \sqrt{(38.59)^2 + (57.670)^2} = 69.39 \text{ lb} < 75 \text{ lb}$ OK

$\theta = \tan^{-1}\left(\dfrac{57.670}{38.59}\right) = 56.21°$

Joint C:

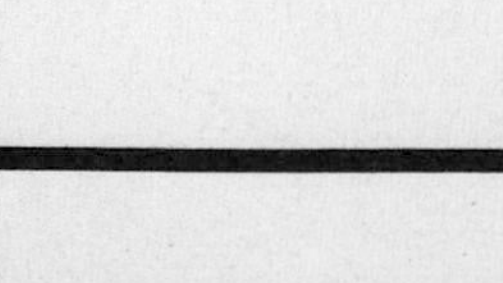

$\xrightarrow{+} \Sigma F_x = 0;\quad T_{CD}\cos\phi - 69.39\cos 56.21° = 0$

$+\uparrow \Sigma F_y = 0;\quad T_{CD}\sin\phi + 69.39\sin 56.21° - 71.98 = 0$

$T_{CD} = 41.2 \text{ lb} < 75 \text{ lb}$ OK

$\phi = 20.3°$

Thus, $P = 72.0 \text{ lb}$ **Ans**

7-93. The cable segments support the loading shown. Determine the distance x_B from the force at B to point A. Set $P = 40$ lb.

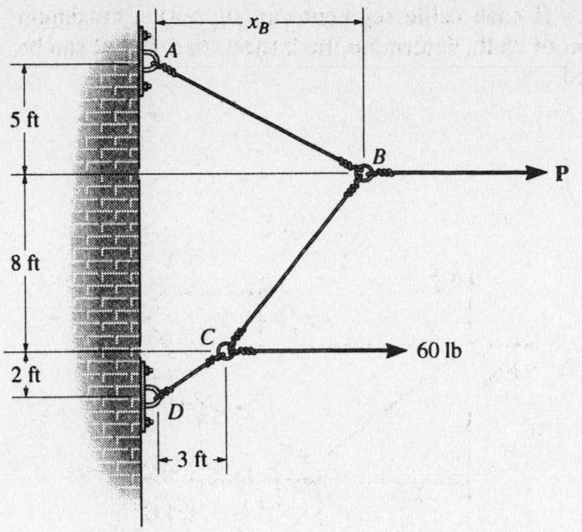

$\circlearrowleft + \Sigma M_A = 0; \quad -T_{CD}\cos 33.69°(13) - T_{CD}\sin 33.69°(3) + 60(13) + 40(5) = 0$

$T_{CD} = 78.521$ lb

$\xrightarrow{+} \Sigma F_x = 0; \quad 40 + 60 - 78.521\cos 33.69° - A_x = 0$

$A_x = 34.667$ lb

$+\uparrow \Sigma F_y = 0; \quad A_y - 78.521\sin 33.69° = 0$

$A_y = 43.555$ lb

Joint A :

$\xrightarrow{+} \Sigma F_x = 0; \quad T_{AB}\cos\theta - 34.667 = 0 \qquad (1)$

$+\uparrow \Sigma F_y = 0; \quad 43.555 - T_{AB}\sin\theta = 0 \qquad (2)$

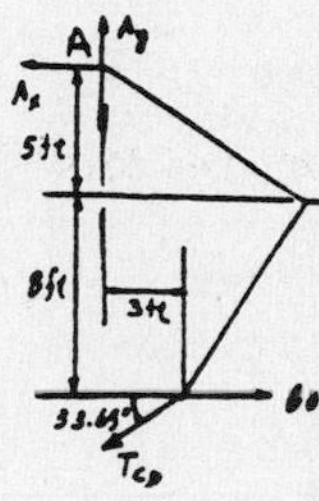

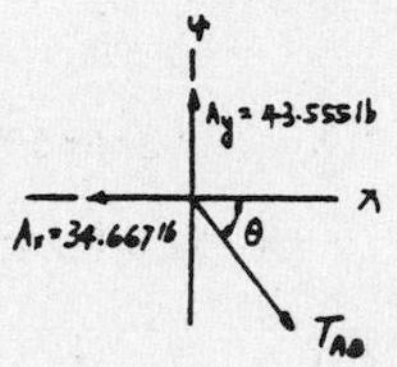

Solving Eqs. (1) and (2) yields :

$\theta = 51.48°$

$T_{AB} = 55.67$ lb

$$x_B = \frac{5}{\tan 51.48°} = 3.98 \text{ ft} \qquad \textbf{Ans}$$

7-94. The cable segments support the loading shown. Determine the magnitude of the horizontal force **P** so that $x_B = 6$ ft.

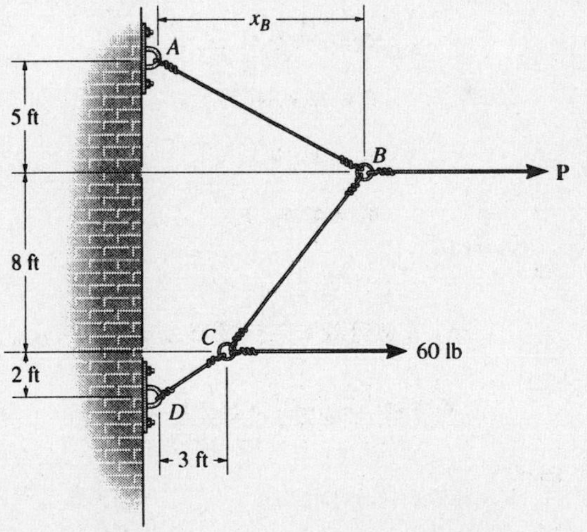

$\circlearrowleft + \Sigma M_D = 0; \quad T_{AB}\cos 39.81°(10) + T_{AB}\sin 39.81°(6) - 60(2) - P(10) = 0$

$11.523 T_{AB} - 10P = 120 \qquad (1)$

Joint B :

$+\nwarrow \Sigma F_{y'} = 0; \quad T_{AB}\cos 19.25° - P\sin 69.44° = 0 \qquad (2)$

Solving Eqs. (1) and (2) yields :

$P = 84.0$ lb $\qquad$ **Ans**

$T_{AB} = 83.32$ lb

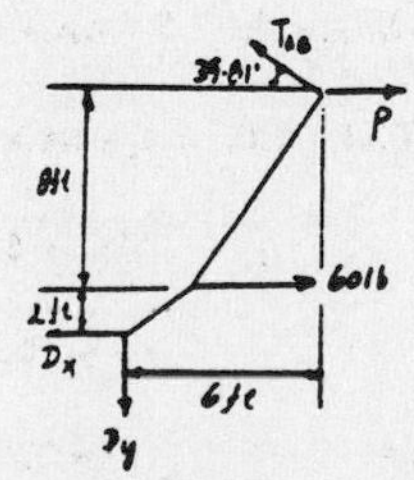

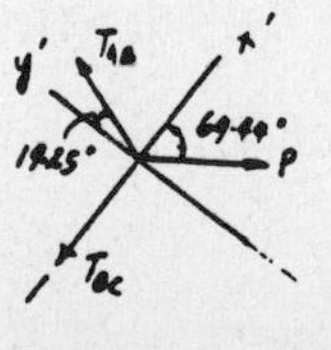

7-95. Determine the force **P** needed to hold the cable in the position shown, i.e., so segment CD remains horizontal. Also, compute the sag y_D and the maximum tension in the cable.

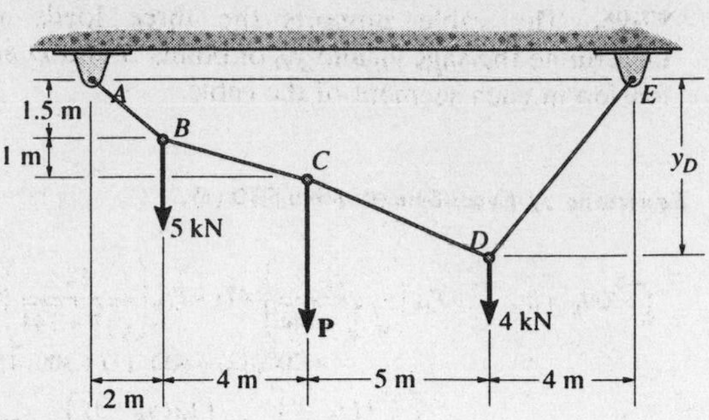

Method of Joints :

Joint *B*

$\xrightarrow{+} \Sigma F_x = 0; \quad F_{BC}\left(\frac{4}{\sqrt{17}}\right) - F_{AB}\left(\frac{2}{2.5}\right) = 0 \qquad [1]$

$+\uparrow \Sigma F_y = 0; \quad F_{AB}\left(\frac{1.5}{2.5}\right) - F_{BC}\left(\frac{1}{\sqrt{17}}\right) - 5 = 0 \qquad [2]$

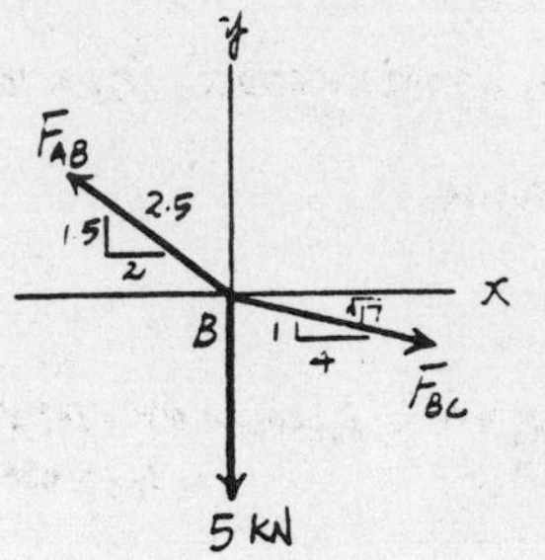

Solving Eqs. [1] and [2] yields

$$F_{BC} = 10.31 \text{ kN} \qquad F_{AB} = 12.5 \text{ kN}$$

Joint *C*

$\xrightarrow{+} \Sigma F_x = 0; \quad F_{CD} - 10.31\left(\frac{4}{\sqrt{17}}\right) = 0 \qquad F_{CD} = 10.0 \text{ kN}$

$+\uparrow \Sigma F_y = 0; \quad 10.31\left(\frac{1}{\sqrt{17}}\right) - P = 0 \qquad P = 2.50 \text{ kN} \qquad$ **Ans**

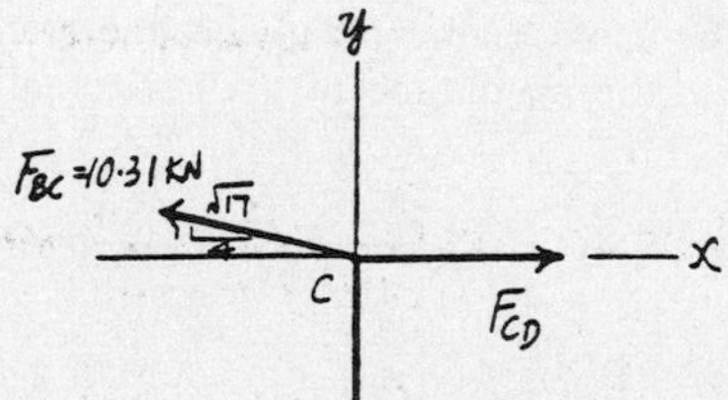

Joint *D*

$\xrightarrow{+} \Sigma F_x = 0; \quad F_{DE}\left(\frac{4}{\sqrt{y_D^2 + 16}}\right) - 10 = 0 \qquad [1]$

$+\uparrow \Sigma F_y = 0; \quad F_{DE}\left(\frac{y_D}{\sqrt{y_D^2 + 16}}\right) - 4 = 0 \qquad [2]$

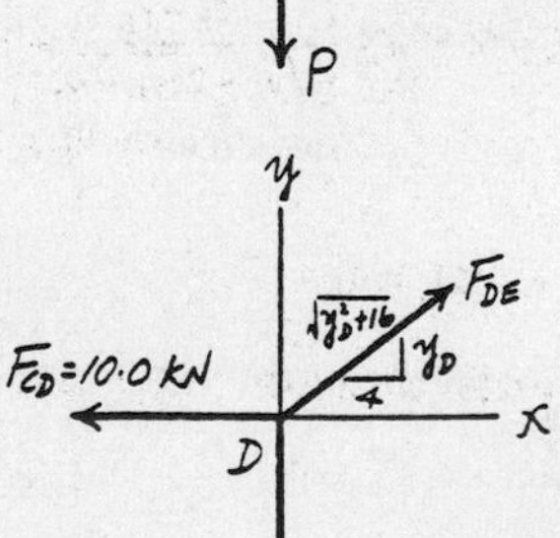

Solving Eqs. [1] and [2] yields

$$y_D = 1.60 \text{ m} \qquad \textbf{Ans}$$
$$F_{DE} = 10.77 \text{ kN}$$

Thus, the maximum tension in the cable is

$$F_{max} = F_{AB} = 12.5 \text{ kN} \qquad \textbf{Ans}$$

***7-96.** The cable supports the three loads shown. Determine the sags y_B and y_D of points B and D and the tension in each segment of the cable.

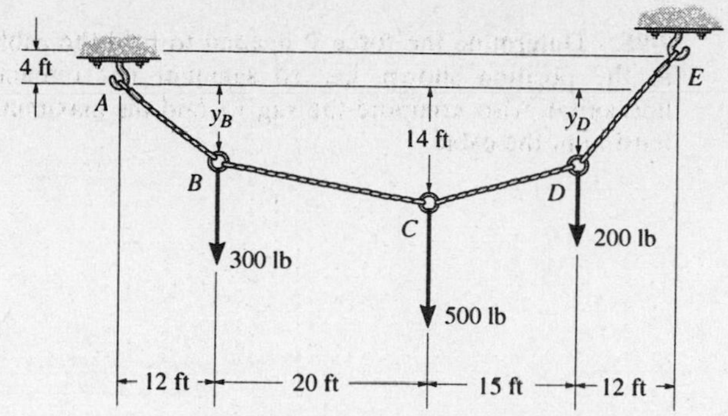

Equations of Equilibrium : From FBD (a),

$$\curvearrowleft + \Sigma M_E = 0; \quad -F_{AB}\left(\frac{y_B}{\sqrt{y_B^2+144}}\right)(47) - F_{AB}\left(\frac{12}{\sqrt{y_B^2+144}}\right)(y_B+4)$$
$$+200(12)+500(27)+300(47)=0$$

$$F_{AB}\left(\frac{47y_B}{\sqrt{y_B^2+144}}\right)+F_{AB}\left(\frac{12(y_B+4)}{\sqrt{y_B^2+144}}\right)=30000 \quad [1]$$

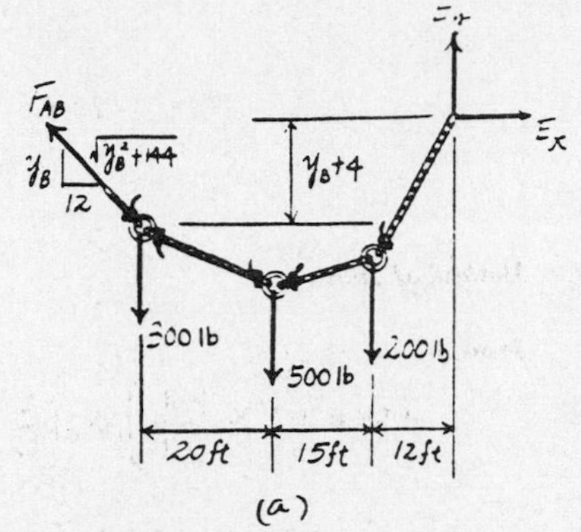

From FBD (b),

$$\curvearrowleft + \Sigma M_C = 0; \quad -F_{AB}\left(\frac{y_B}{\sqrt{y_B^2+144}}\right)(20) + F_{AB}\left(\frac{12}{\sqrt{y_B^2+144}}\right)(14-y_B)$$
$$+300(20)=0$$

$$F_{AB}\left(\frac{20y_B}{\sqrt{y_B^2+144}}\right)-F_{AB}\left(\frac{12(14-y_B)}{\sqrt{y_B^2+144}}\right)=6000 \quad [2]$$

Solving Eqs. [1] and [2] yields

$y_B = 8.792 \text{ ft} = 8.79 \text{ ft} \qquad F_{AB} = 787.47 \text{ lb} = 787 \text{ lb}$ **Ans**

Method of Joints :

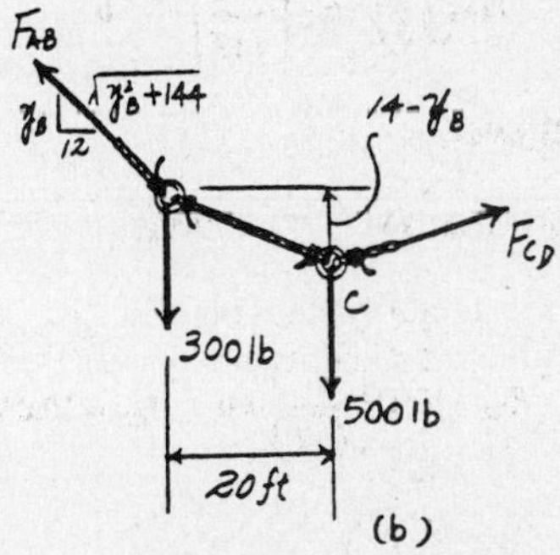

Joint B

$$\xrightarrow{+} \Sigma F_x = 0; \quad F_{BC}\cos 14.60° - 787.47\cos 36.23° = 0$$
$$F_{BC} = 656.40 \text{ lb} = 656 \text{ lb} \quad \textbf{Ans}$$

$$+\uparrow \Sigma F_y = 0; \quad 787.47\sin 36.23°$$
$$-656.40\sin 14.60° - 300 = 0 \ (\textit{Checks!})$$

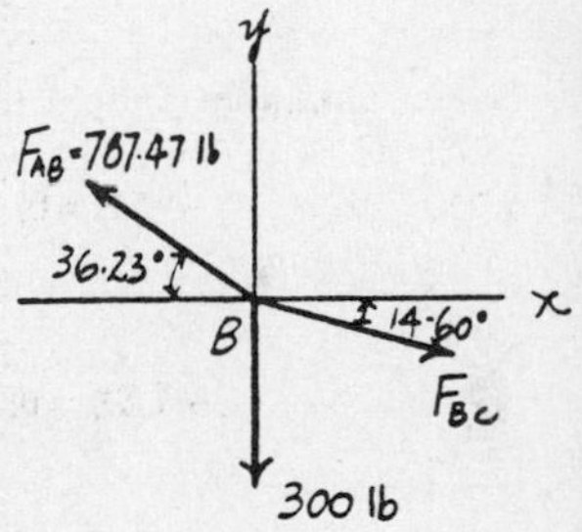

Joint C

$$\xrightarrow{+} \Sigma F_x = 0; \quad F_{CD}\left(\frac{15}{\sqrt{y_D^2-28y_D+421}}\right)-656.40\cos 14.60° = 0 \quad [3]$$

$$+\uparrow \Sigma F_y = 0; \quad F_{CD}\left(\frac{14-y_D}{\sqrt{y_D^2-28y_D+421}}\right)$$
$$+656.40\sin 14.60° - 500 = 0 \quad [4]$$

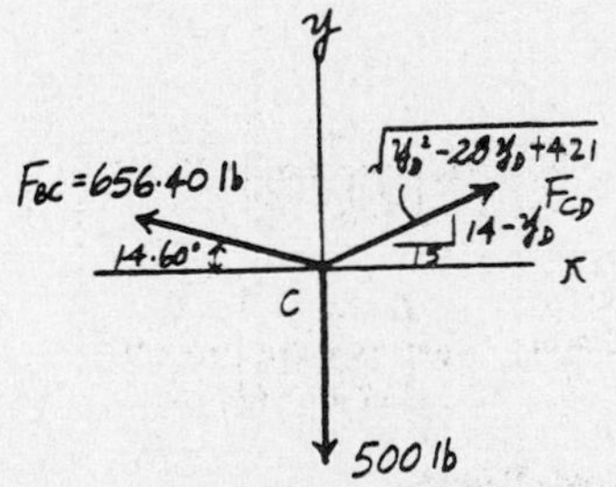

Solving Eqs. [1] and [2] yields

$y_D = 6.099 \text{ ft} = 6.10 \text{ ft} \qquad F_{CD} = 717.95 \text{ lb} = 718 \text{ lb}$ **Ans**

Joint B

$$\xrightarrow{+} \Sigma F_x = 0; \quad F_{DE}\cos 40.08° - 717.95\cos 27.78° = 0$$
$$F_{DE} = 830.24 \text{ lb} = 830 \text{ lb} \quad \textbf{Ans}$$

$$+\uparrow \Sigma F_y = 0; \quad 830.24\sin 40.08°$$
$$-717.95\sin 27.78° - 200 = 0 \ (\textit{Checks!})$$

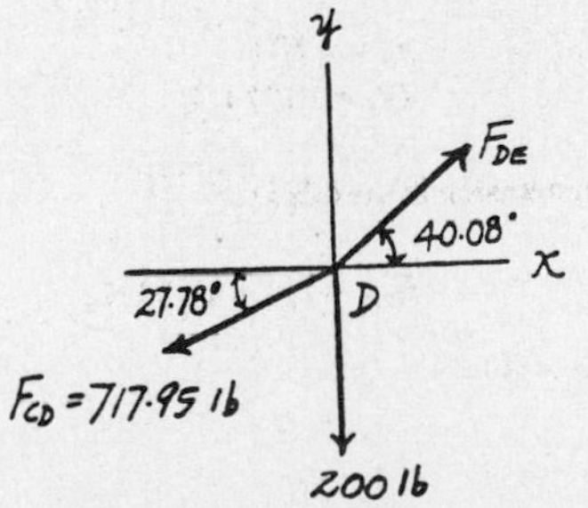

7-97. Determine the maximum uniform loading w, measured in lb/ft, that the cable can support if it is capable of sustaining a maximum tension of 3000 lb before it will break.

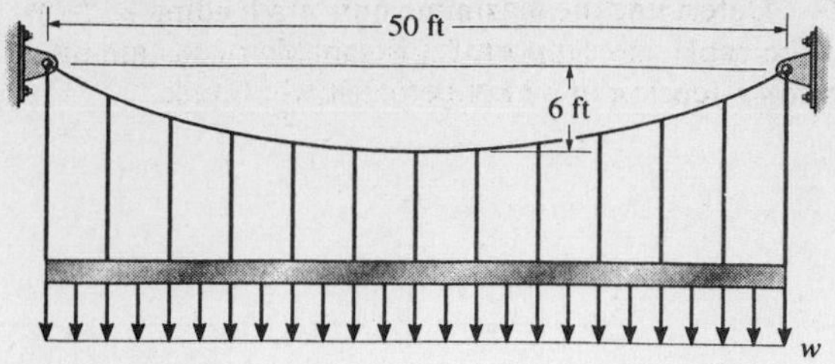

$$y = \frac{1}{F_H}\int\left(\int w\,dx\right)dx$$

At $x = 0$, $\frac{dy}{dx} = 0$

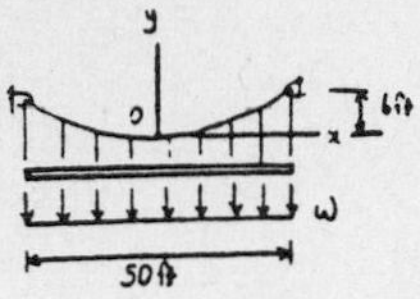

At $x = 0$, $y = 0$

$$C_1 = C_2 = 0$$

$$y = \frac{w}{2F_H}x^2$$

At $x = 25$ ft, $y = 6$ ft $\quad F_H = 52.08\,w$

$$\left.\frac{dy}{dx}\right|_{max} = \tan\theta_{max} = \left.\frac{w}{F_H}x\right|_{x=25\text{ ft}}$$

$$\theta_{max} = \tan^{-1}(0.48) = 25.64°$$

$$T_{max} = \frac{F_H}{\cos\theta_{max}} = 3000$$

$$F_H = 2705 \text{ lb}$$

$w = 51.9$ lb/ft **Ans**

7-98. The cable is subjected to a uniform loading of w = 250 lb/ft. Determine the maximum and minimum tension in the cable.

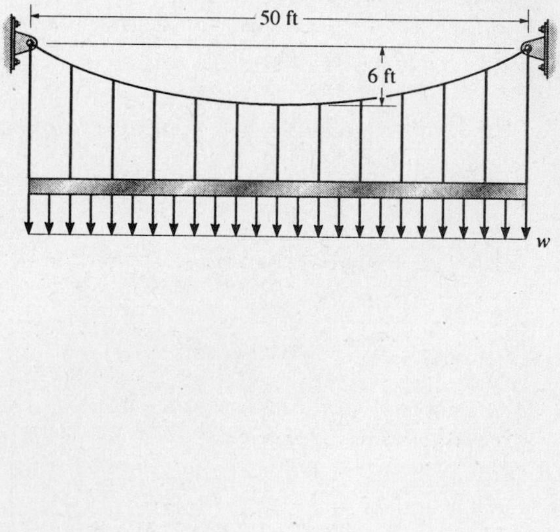

From Example 7 - 14;

$$F_H = \frac{w_0 L^2}{8h} = \frac{250\,(50)^2}{8\,(6)} = 13\,021 \text{ lb}$$

$$\theta_{max} = \tan^{-1}\left(\frac{w_0 L}{2F_H}\right) = \tan^{-1}\left(\frac{250\,(50)}{2\,(13\,021)}\right) = 25.64°$$

$$T_{max} = \frac{F_H}{\cos\theta_{max}} = \frac{13\,021}{\cos 25.64°} = 14.4 \text{ kip}$$ **Ans**

The minimum tension occurs at $\theta = 0°$.

$T_{min} = F_H = 13.0$ kip **Ans**

7-99. Determine the maximum uniform loading w_o N/m that the cable can support if it is capable of sustaining a maximum tension of 60 kN before it will break.

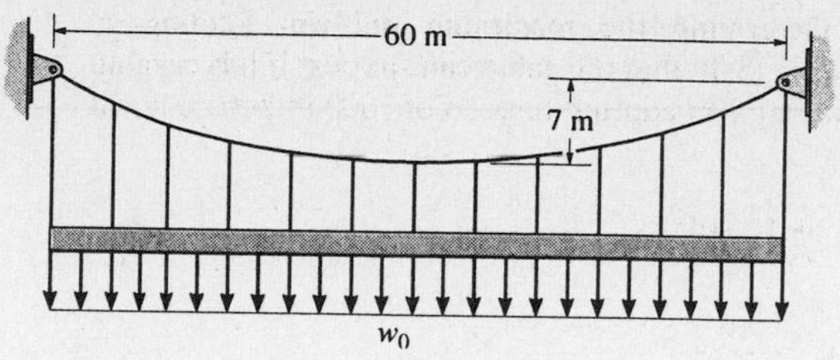

The Equation of The Cable :

$$y = \frac{1}{F_H}\int\left(\int w(x)\,dx\right)dx$$

$$= \frac{1}{F_H}\left(\frac{w_0}{2}x^2 + C_1x + C_2\right) \qquad [1]$$

$$\frac{dy}{dx} = \frac{1}{F_H}(w_0x + C_1) \qquad [2]$$

Boundary Conditions :

$y = 0$ at $x = 0$, then from Eq.[1] $\quad 0 = \frac{1}{F_H}(C_2) \quad C_2 = 0$

$\frac{dy}{dx} = 0$ at $x = 0$, then from Eq.[2] $\quad 0 = \frac{1}{F_H}(C_1) \quad C_1 = 0$

Thus,

$$y = \frac{w_0}{2F_H}x^2 \qquad [3]$$

$$\frac{dy}{dx} = \frac{w_0}{F_H}x \qquad [4]$$

$y = 7$ m at $x = 30$ m, then from Eq.[3] $\quad 7 = \frac{w_0}{2F_H}(30^2) \quad F_H = \frac{450}{7}w_0$

$\theta = \theta_{max}$ at $x = 30$ m and the maximum tension occurs when $\theta = \theta_{max}$. From Eq.[4]

$$\tan\theta_{max} = \left.\frac{dy}{dx}\right|_{x=30\text{ m}} = \frac{w_0}{\frac{450}{7}w_0}x = 0.01556(30) = 0.4667$$

$$\theta_{max} = 25.02^\circ$$

The maximum tension in the cable is

$$T_{max} = \frac{F_H}{\cos\theta_{max}}$$

$$60 = \frac{\frac{450}{7}w_0}{\cos 25.02^\circ}$$

$w_0 = 0.846$ kN/m **Ans**

*7-100. The cable supports the uniform load of $w_0 = 600$ lb/ft. Determine the tension in the cable at each support A and B.

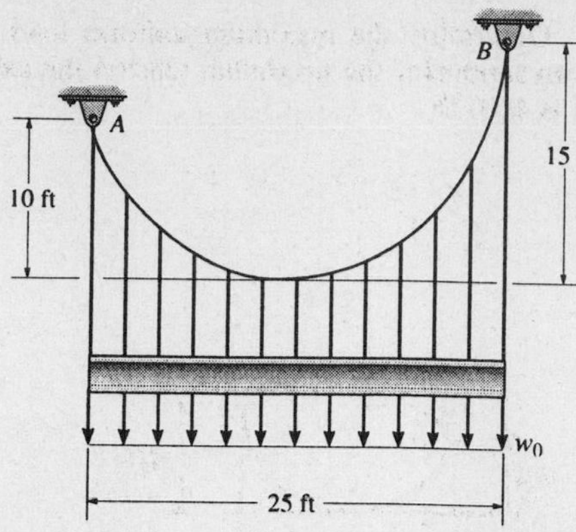

Use the equations of Example 7 - 14.

$$y = \frac{w_0}{2\,F_H}x^2$$

$$15 = \frac{600}{2\,F_H}x^2$$

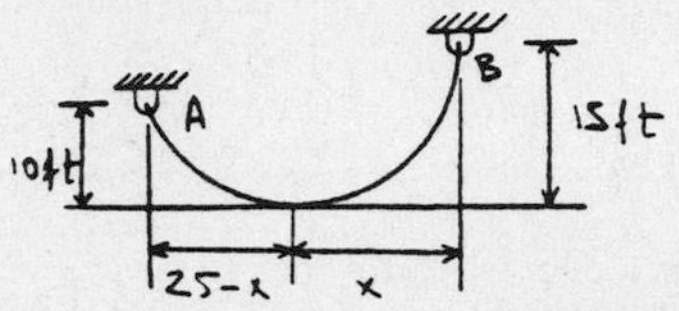

$$10 = \frac{600}{2\,F_H}(25-x)^2$$

$$\frac{600}{2\,(15)}x^2 = \frac{600}{2\,(10)}(25-x)^2$$

$$x^2 = 1.5\,(625 - 50x + x^2)$$

$$0.5x^2 - 75x + 937.50 = 0$$

Choose root < 25 ft.

$$x = 13.76 \text{ ft}$$

$$F_H = \frac{w_0}{2\,y}x^2 = \frac{600}{2\,(15)}(13.76)^2 = 3788 \text{ lb}$$

At B :

$$y = \frac{w_0}{2\,F_H}x^2 = \frac{600}{2\,(3788)}x^2$$

$$\frac{dy}{dx} = \tan\theta_B = 0.15838\,x\Big|_{x=13.76} = 2.180$$

$$\theta_B = 65.36^\circ$$

$$T_B = \frac{F_H}{\cos\theta_B} = \frac{3788}{\cos 65.36^\circ} = 9085 \text{ lb} = 9.09 \text{ kip} \qquad \textbf{Ans}$$

At A

$$y = \frac{w_0}{2\,F_H}x^2 = \frac{600}{2\,(3788)}x^2$$

$$\frac{dy}{dx} = \tan\theta_A = 0.15838\,x\Big|_{x=(25-13.76)} = 1.780$$

$$\theta_A = 60.67^\circ$$

$$T_A = \frac{F_H}{\cos\theta_A} = \frac{3788}{\cos 60.67^\circ} = 7733 \text{ lb} = 7.73 \text{ kip} \qquad \textbf{Ans}$$

7-101. Determine the maximum uniform load w_0 the cable can support if the maximum tension the cable can sustain is 4000 lb.

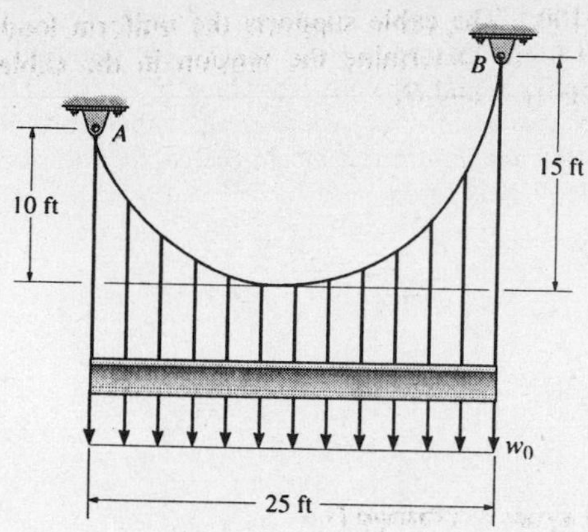

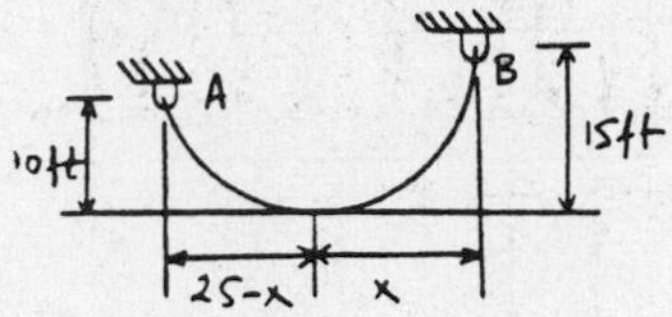

Use the equations of Example 7 - 14.

$$y = \frac{w_0}{2F_H}x^2$$

$$15 = \frac{w_0}{2F_H}x^2$$

$$10 = \frac{w_0}{2F_H}(25-x)^2$$

$$\frac{x^2}{15} = \frac{1}{10}(25-x)^2$$

$$x^2 = 1.5(625 - 50x + x^2)$$

$$0.5x^2 - 75x + 937.50 = 0$$

Choose root < 25 ft.

$$x = 13.76 \text{ ft}$$

$$F_H = \frac{w_0}{2y}x^2 = \frac{w_0}{2(15)}(13.76)^2 = 6.31378\,w_0$$

Maximum tension occurs at *B* since the slope *y* of the cable is greatest there.

$$y = \frac{w_0}{2F_H}x^2$$

$$\left.\frac{dy}{dx}\right|_{x=13.76\text{ ft}} = \tan\theta_{max} = \frac{w_0 x}{F_H} = \frac{w_0(13.76)}{6.31378\,w_0}$$

$$\theta_{max} = 65.36°$$

$$T_{max} = \frac{F_H}{\cos\theta_{max}}$$

$$4000 = \frac{6.31378\,w_0}{\cos 65.36°} \qquad w_0 = 264 \text{ lb/ft} \qquad \textbf{Ans}$$

7-102. The cable is subjected to the parabolic loading $w = 200(1 - (x/50)^2)$ lb/ft, where x is in ft. Determine the equation $y = f(x)$ which defines the cable shape AB, and the maximum tension in the cable. The slope of the cable at A is zero.

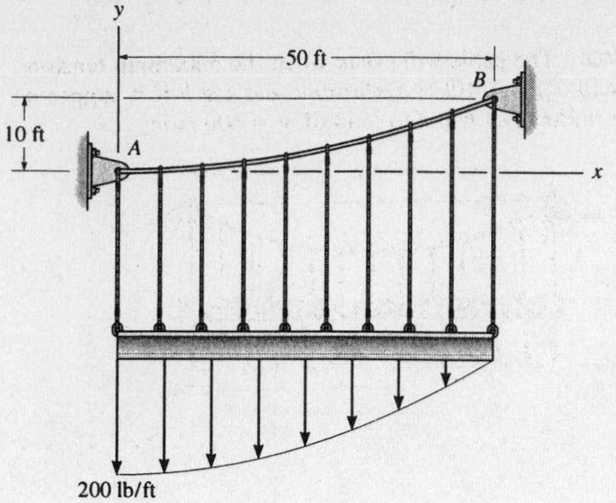

$$y = \frac{1}{F_H}\int\left(\int w(x)\,dx\right)dx$$

$$y = \frac{1}{F_H}\int\left(\int 200\left(1 - \left(\frac{x}{50}\right)^2\right)dx\right)dx$$

$$y = \frac{1}{F_H}\int\left(200\left(x - \frac{x^3}{3\,(50)^2}\right) + C_1\right)dx$$

$$y = \frac{1}{F_H}\left(100x^2 - \frac{x^4}{150} + C_1 x + C_2\right)$$

$$\frac{dy}{dx} = \frac{200\,x}{F_H} - \frac{x^3}{37.5\,F_H} + \frac{C_1}{F_H}$$

At $x = 0$, $\frac{dy}{dx} = 0$, $\quad C_1 = 0$

At $x = 0$, $y = 0$, $\quad C_2 = 0$

$$y = \frac{1}{F_H}\left(100\,x^2 - \frac{x^4}{150}\right)$$

At $x = 50$ ft, $y = 10$ ft, $\quad F_H = 20\,833$ lb

$$y = \frac{1}{20\,833}\left[100\,x^2 - \frac{x^4}{150}\right] \text{ ft} \qquad \textbf{Ans}$$

$$\frac{dy}{dx} = \frac{1}{20\,833}\left[200\,x - \frac{x^3}{37.5}\right]_{x=50} = \tan\theta_{max}$$

$$\theta_{max} = 17.74°$$

$$T_{max} = \frac{F_H}{\cos\theta_{max}} = \frac{20\,833}{\cos 17.74°} = 21\,874 \text{ lb}$$

$T_{max} = 21.9$ kip $\qquad$ **Ans**

7-103. The cable will break when the maximum tension reachs T_{max} = 10kN. Determine the sag h if it supports the uniform distributed load of w = 600 N/m.

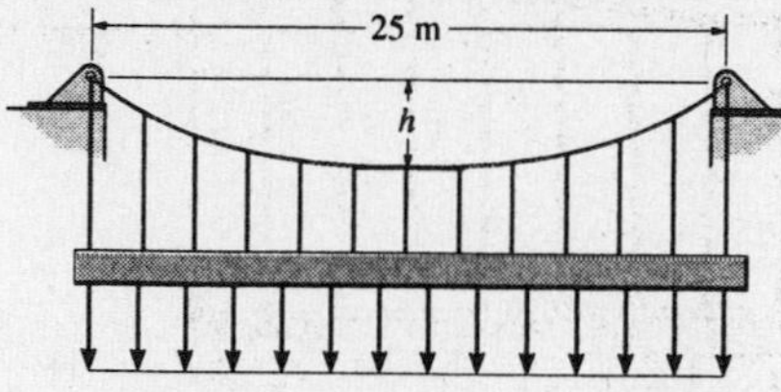

The Equation of The Cable :

$$y = \frac{1}{F_H}\int\left(\int w(x)\,dx\right)dx$$

$$= \frac{1}{F_H}\left(\frac{w_0}{2}x^2 + C_1x + C_2\right) \qquad [1]$$

$$\frac{dy}{dx} = \frac{1}{F_H}(w_0x + C_1) \qquad [2]$$

Boundary Conditions :

$y = 0$ at $x = 0$, then from Eq.[1] $\quad 0 = \frac{1}{F_H}(C_2) \quad C_2 = 0$

$\frac{dy}{dx} = 0$ at $x = 0$, then from Eq.[2] $\quad 0 = \frac{1}{F_H}(C_1) \quad C_1 = 0$

Thus,

$$y = \frac{w_0}{2F_H}x^2 \qquad [3]$$

$$\frac{dy}{dx} = \frac{w_0}{F_H}x \qquad [4]$$

$y = h$ at $x = 12.5$ m, then from Eq.[3] $\quad h = \frac{w_0}{2F_H}(12.5^2) \quad F_H = \frac{78.125}{h}w_0$

$\theta = \theta_{max}$ at $x = 12.5$ m and the maximum tension occurs when $\theta = \theta_{max}$. From Eq.[4]

$$\tan\theta_{max} = \left.\frac{dy}{dx}\right|_{x=12.5\text{ m}} = \frac{w_0}{\frac{78.125}{h}w_0}x = 0.0128h(12.5) = 0.160h$$

Thus,

$$\cos\theta_{max} = \frac{1}{\sqrt{0.0256h^2 + 1}}$$

The maximum tension in the cable is

$$T_{max} = \frac{F_H}{\cos\theta_{max}}$$

$$10 = \frac{\frac{78.125}{h}(0.6)}{\frac{1}{\sqrt{0.0256h^2+1}}}$$

$h = 7.09$ m **Ans**

***7-104.** Determine the maximum tension developed in the cable if it is subjected to a uniform load of 600 N/m.

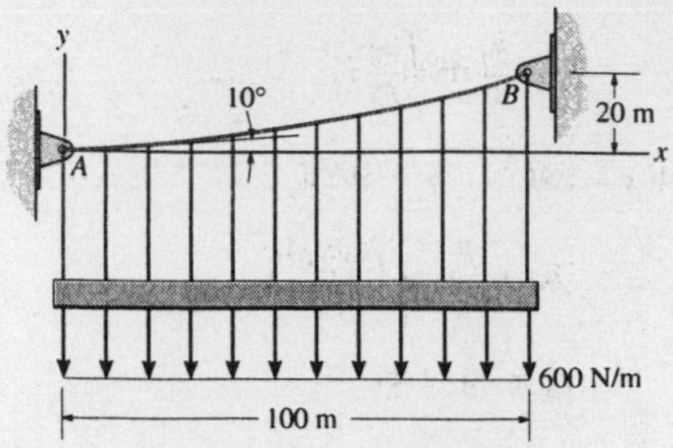

The Equation of The Cable :

$$y = \frac{1}{F_H}\int\left(\int w(x)\,dx\right)dx$$

$$= \frac{1}{F_H}\left(\frac{w_0}{2}x^2 + C_1x + C_2\right) \qquad [1]$$

$$\frac{dy}{dx} = \frac{1}{F_H}(w_0x + C_1) \qquad [2]$$

Boundary Conditions :

$y = 0$ at $x = 0$, then from Eq.[1] $\quad 0 = \frac{1}{F_H}(C_2) \quad C_2 = 0$

$\frac{dy}{dx} = \tan 10°$ at $x = 0$, then from Eq.[2] $\quad \tan 10° = \frac{1}{F_H}(C_1) \quad C_1 = F_H \tan 10°$

Thus,

$$y = \frac{w_0}{2F_H}x^2 + \tan 10° x \qquad [3]$$

$y = 20$ m at $x = 100$ m, then from Eq.[3]

$$20 = \frac{600}{2F_H}(100^2) + \tan 10°(100) \qquad F_H = 1\,267\,265.47 \text{ N}$$

and

$$\frac{dy}{dx} = \frac{w_0}{F_H}x + \tan 10°$$

$$= \frac{600}{1\,267\,265.47}x + \tan 10°$$

$$= 0.4735(10^{-3})\,x + \tan 10°$$

$\theta = \theta_{max}$ at $x = 100$ m and the maximum tension occurs when $\theta = \theta_{max}$.

$$\tan\theta_{max} = \left.\frac{dy}{dx}\right|_{x=100\text{ m}} = 0.4735(10^{-3})(100) + \tan 10°$$

$$\theta_{max} = 12.61°$$

The maximum tension in the cable is

$$T_{max} = \frac{F_H}{\cos\theta_{max}} = \frac{1\,267\,265.47}{\cos 12.61°} = 1\,298\,579.00 \text{ N} = 1.30 \text{ MN} \qquad \textbf{Ans}$$

■7-105. A cable has a weight of 3 lb/ft and is supported at points that are 500 ft apart and at the same elevation. If it has a length of 600 ft, determine the sag.

$w_0 = 3$ lb/ft

From Example 7 – 15,

$$s = \frac{F_H}{w_0}\sinh\left(\frac{w_0}{F_H}x\right)$$

At $x = 250$ ft, $s = 300$ ft

$$300 = \frac{F_H}{3}\sinh\left(\frac{3(250)}{F_H}\right)$$

$$F_H = 704.3 \text{ lb}$$

$$y = \frac{F_H}{w_0}\left[\cosh\frac{w_0}{F_H}x - 1\right]$$

$$h = \frac{704.3}{3}\left[\cosh\left(\frac{3(250)}{704.3}\right) - 1\right]$$

$h = 146$ ft **Ans**

7-106. Show that the deflection curve of the cable discussed in Example 7–15 reduces to Eq. (4) in Example 7–14 when the *hyperbolic cosine function* is expanded in terms of a series and only the first two terms are retained. (The answer indicates that the *catenary* may be replaced by a *parabola* in the analysis of problems in which the sag is small. In this case, the cable weight is assumed to be uniformly distributed along the horizontal.)

$$\cosh x = 1 + \frac{x^2}{2!} + \ldots$$

Substituting into

$$y = \frac{F_H}{w_0}\left[\cosh\left(\frac{w_0}{F_H}x\right) - 1\right]$$

$$= \frac{F_H}{w_0}\left[1 + \frac{w_0^2x^2}{2F_H^2} + \ldots - 1\right]$$

$$\equiv \frac{w_0x^2}{2F_H}$$

Using Eq. (3) in Example 7 – 14,

$$F_H = \frac{w_0L^2}{8h}$$

We get $y = \frac{4h}{L^2}x^2$ **QED**

7-107. A uniform cord is suspended between two points having the same elevation. Determine the sag-to-span ratio so that the maximum tension in the cord equals the cord's total weight.

From Example 7 – 15.

$$s = \frac{F_H}{w_0}\sinh\left(\frac{w_0}{F_H}x\right)$$

$$y = \frac{F_H}{w_0}\left[\cosh\left(\frac{w_0}{F_H}x\right) - 1\right]$$

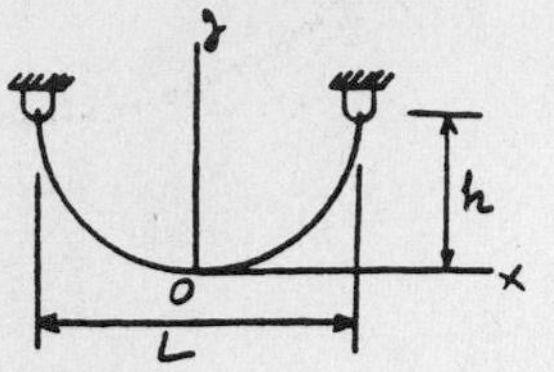

At $x = \frac{L}{2}$,

$$\left.\frac{dy}{dx}\right|_{max} = \tan\theta_{max} = \sinh\left(\frac{w_0 L}{2F_H}\right)$$

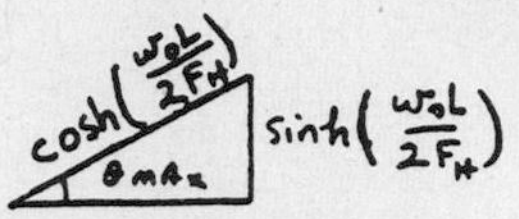

$$\cos\theta_{max} = \frac{1}{\cosh\left(\frac{w_0 L}{2F_H}\right)}$$

$$T_{max} = \frac{F_H}{\cos\theta_{max}}$$

$$w_0(2s) = F_H\cosh\left(\frac{w_0 L}{2F_H}\right)$$

$$2F_H\sinh\left(\frac{w_0 L}{2F_H}\right) = F_H\cosh\left(\frac{w_0 L}{2F_H}\right)$$

$$\tanh\left(\frac{w_0 L}{2F_H}\right) = \frac{1}{2}$$

$$\frac{w_0 L}{2F_H} = \tanh^{-1}(0.5) = 0.5493$$

when $x = \frac{L}{2}$, $\quad y = h$

$$h = \frac{F_H}{w_0}\left[\cosh\left(\frac{w_0}{F_H}x\right) - 1\right]$$

$$h = \frac{F_H}{w_0}\left\{\frac{1}{\sqrt{1-\tanh^2\left(\frac{w_0 L}{2F_H}\right)}} - 1\right\} = 0.1547\left(\frac{F_H}{w_0}\right)$$

$$\frac{0.1547\,L}{2h} = 0.5493$$

$$\frac{h}{L} = 0.141 \qquad \textbf{Ans}$$

■*7-108. A cable has a weight of 2 lb/ft. If it can span 100 ft and has a sag of 12 ft, determine the length of the cable. The ends of the cable are supported from the same elevation.

From Eq. (5) of Example 7 - 15 :

$$h = \frac{F_H}{w_0}\left[\cosh\left(\frac{w_0 L}{2F_H}\right) - 1\right]$$

$$12 = \frac{F_H}{2}\left[\cosh\left(\frac{2(100)}{2F_H}\right) - 1\right]$$

$$24 = F_H\left[\cosh\left(\frac{100}{F_H}\right) - 1\right]$$

$$F_H = 212.2 \text{ lb}$$

From Eq. (3) of Example 7 - 15 :

$$s = \frac{F_H}{w_0}\sinh\left(\frac{w_0}{F_H}x\right)$$

$$\frac{l}{2} = \frac{212.2}{2}\sinh\left(\frac{2(50)}{212.2}\right)$$

$$l = 104 \text{ ft} \qquad \textbf{Ans}$$

7-109. The chain has a weight of 3 lb/ft. Determine the tension at points A, B, and C necessary for equilibrium.

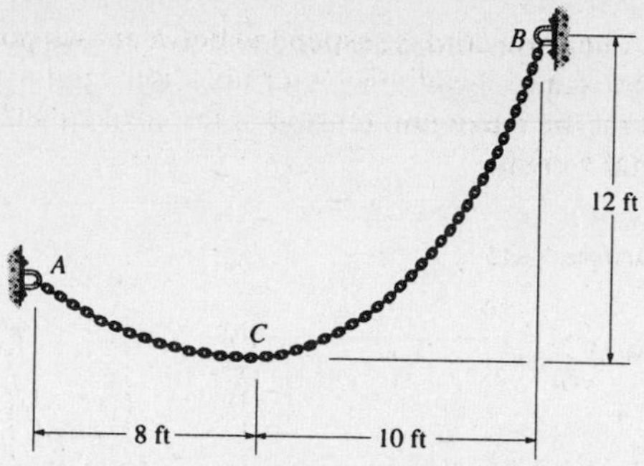

$$x = \int \frac{ds}{\left\{1 + \frac{1}{F_H^2}\left(\int w_0\, ds\right)^2\right\}^{\frac{1}{2}}}$$

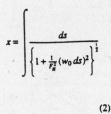

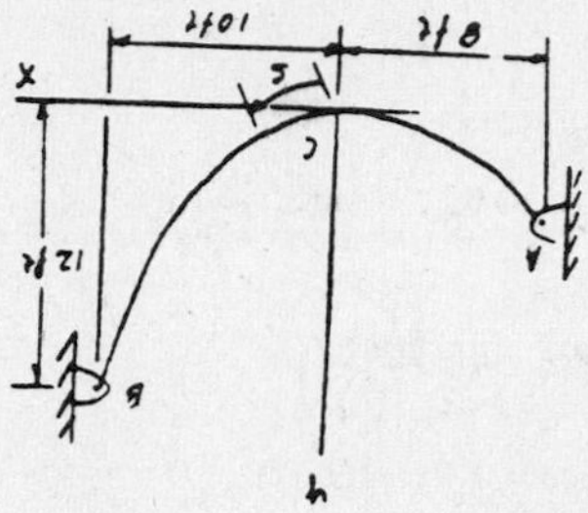

Performing the integration yields :

$$x = \frac{F_H}{3}\left\{\sinh^{-1}\left[\frac{1}{F_H}(3s + C_1)\right] + C_2\right\}$$

From Eq. 7-14

$$\frac{dy}{dx} = \frac{1}{F_H}\int w_0\, ds$$

$$\frac{dy}{dx} = \frac{1}{F_H}(3s + C_1)$$

At $s = 0$; $\frac{dy}{dx} = 0$ hence $C_1 = 0$

$$\frac{dy}{dx} = \tan\theta = \frac{3s}{F_H} \qquad (2)$$

Applying boundary conditions at $x = 0$; $s = 0$ to Eq.(1) and using the result $C_1 = 0$ yields $C_2 = 0$. Hence

$$s = \frac{F_H}{3}\sinh\left(\frac{3}{F_H}x\right) \qquad (3)$$

Substituting Eq.(3) into (2) yields :

$$\frac{dy}{dx} = \sinh\left(\frac{3x}{F_H}\right) \qquad (4)$$

Performing the integration

$$y = \frac{F_H}{3}\cosh\left(\frac{3}{F_H}x\right) + C_3 \qquad (5)$$

Applying boundary conditions at $x = 0$; $y = 0$ yields $C_3 = -\frac{F_H}{3}$. Therefore

$$y = \frac{F_H}{3}\left[\cosh\left(\frac{3}{F_H}x\right) - 1\right]$$

At $x = 10$ ft; $y = 12$ ft. $\quad 12 = \frac{F_H}{3}\left[\cosh\left(\frac{3}{F_H}(10)\right) - 1\right]$

By trial and error $\quad F_H = 16.40$ lb

At point A $\quad x = -8$ ft $\quad$ From Eq.(4)

$$\tan\theta_A = \frac{dy}{dx} = \sinh\left(\frac{3(-8)}{16.40}\right) \qquad \theta_A = -63.94°$$

$$T_A = \frac{F_H}{\cos\theta_A} = \frac{16.40}{\cos(-63.94°)} = 37.3 \text{ lb} \qquad \textbf{Ans}$$

At point B $\quad x = 10$ ft $\quad$ From Eq.(4)

$$\tan\theta_B = \frac{dy}{dx} = \sinh\left(\frac{3(10)}{16.40}\right) \qquad \theta_B = 71.76°$$

$$T_B = \frac{F_H}{\cos\theta_B} = \frac{16.40}{\cos 71.76°} = 52.4 \text{ lb} \qquad \textbf{Ans}$$

At point C, $\quad \frac{dy}{dx} = \tan\theta_C = 0 \qquad \theta_C = 0°$

$$T_C = \frac{F_H}{\cos\theta_C} = \frac{16.40}{\cos 0°} = 16.4 \text{ lb} \qquad \textbf{Ans}$$

7-110. The cable weighs 6 lb/ft and is 150 ft in length. Determine the sag h so that the cable spans 100 ft. Find the minimum tension in the cable.

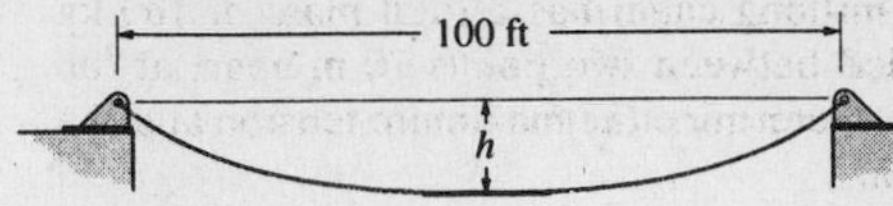

Deflection Curve of The Cable :

$$x = \int \frac{ds}{\left[1+\left(1/F_H^2\right)\left(\int w_0\,ds\right)^2\right]^{\frac{1}{2}}} \qquad \text{where } w_0 = 6 \text{ lb/ft}$$

Performing the integration yields

$$x = \frac{F_H}{6}\left\{\sinh^{-1}\left[\frac{1}{F_H}(6s+C_1)\right]+C_2\right\} \qquad [1]$$

From Eq. 7 – 14

$$\frac{dy}{dx} = \frac{1}{F_H}\int w_0\,ds = \frac{1}{F_H}(6s+C_1) \qquad [2]$$

Boundary Conditions :

$\frac{dy}{dx} = 0$ at $s = 0$. From Eq.[2] $\quad 0 = \frac{1}{F_H}(0+C_1) \qquad C_1 = 0$

Then, Eq.[2] becomes

$$\frac{dy}{dx} = \tan\theta = \frac{6s}{F_H} \qquad [3]$$

$s = 0$ at $x = 0$ and use the result $C_1 = 0$. From Eq.[1]

$$x = \frac{F_H}{6}\left\{\sinh^{-1}\left[\frac{1}{F_H}(0+0)\right]+C_2\right\} \qquad C_2 = 0$$

Rearranging Eq.[1], we have

$$s = \frac{F_H}{6}\sinh\left(\frac{6}{F_H}x\right) \qquad [4]$$

Substituting Eq.[4] into [3] yields

$$\frac{dy}{dx} = \sinh\left(\frac{6}{F_H}x\right)$$

Performing the integration

$$y = \frac{F_H}{6}\cosh\left(\frac{6}{F_H}x\right)+C_3 \qquad [5]$$

$y = 0$ at $x = 0$. From Eq.[5] $\quad 0 = \frac{F_H}{6}\cosh 0 + C_3$, thus, $C_3 = -\frac{F_H}{6}$

Then, Eq.[5] becomes

$$y = \frac{F_H}{6}\left[\cosh\left(\frac{6}{F_H}x\right)-1\right] \qquad [6]$$

$s = 75$ ft at $x = 50$ ft. From Eq.[4]

$$75 = \frac{F_H}{6}\sinh\left[\frac{6}{F_H}(50)\right]$$

By trial and error $\qquad F_H = 184.9419$ lb

$y = h$ at $x = 50$ ft. From Eq.[6]

$$h = \frac{184.9419}{6}\left\{\cosh\left[\frac{6}{184.9419}(50)\right]-1\right\} = 50.3 \text{ ft} \qquad \textbf{Ans}$$

The maximum tension occurs at $\theta = \theta_{min} = 0°$. Thus,

$$T_{min} = \frac{F_H}{\cos\theta_{min}} = \frac{184.9419}{\cos 0°} = 185 \text{ lb} \qquad \textbf{Ans}$$

■7-111. A 40-m-long chain has a total mass of 100 kg and is suspended between two points 10 m apart at the same elevation. Determine the maximum tension and the sag in the chain.

$$w_0 = \frac{100\,(9.81)}{40} = 24.525\ \text{N/m}$$

From Eq. (3) of Example 7 - 15 :

$$s = \frac{F_H}{w_0}\sinh\left(\frac{w_0\,x}{F_H}\right)$$

$$\frac{40}{2} = \frac{F_H}{24.525}\sinh\left(\frac{24.525}{F_H}\left(\frac{10}{2}\right)\right)$$

$$490.5 = F_H \sinh\left(\frac{122.625}{F_H}\right)$$

Solving,

$$F_H = 37.57\ \text{N}$$

From Eq. (5) of Example 7 - 15 :

$$h = \frac{F_H}{w_0}\left[\cosh\left(\frac{w_0\,L}{2\,F_H}\right) - 1\right]$$

$$= \frac{37.57}{24.525}\left[\cosh\left(\frac{24.525\,(10)}{2\,(37.57)}\right) - 1\right]$$

$h = 18.5$ m **Ans**

$$\tan\theta_{max} = \frac{w_0\,s}{F_H} = \frac{24.525\left(\frac{40}{2}\right)}{37.57}$$

$$\theta_{max} = 85.6^\circ$$

$$T_{max} = \frac{F_H}{\cos\theta_{max}} = \frac{37.57}{\cos 85.6^\circ} = 492\ \text{N}$$ **Ans**

*7-112. The uniform beam weighs 500 lb and is held in the horizontal position by means of cable AB, which has a weight of 5 lb/ft. If the slope of the cable at A is 30°, determine the length of the cable.

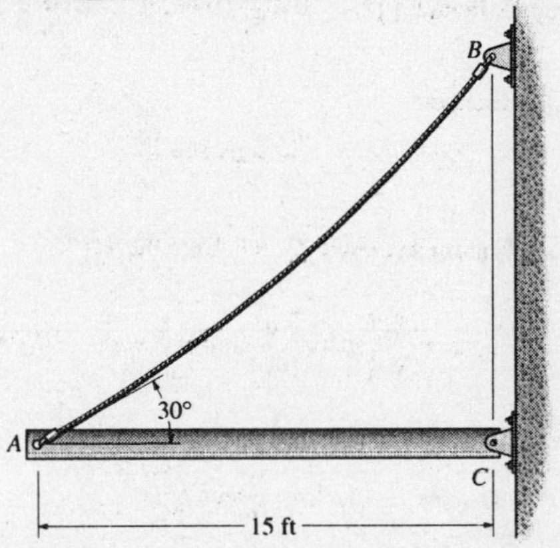

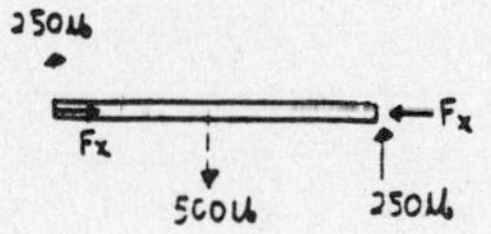

$$T = \frac{250}{\sin 30^\circ} = 500\ \text{lb}$$

$$F_H = 500\cos 30^\circ = 433.0\ \text{lb}$$

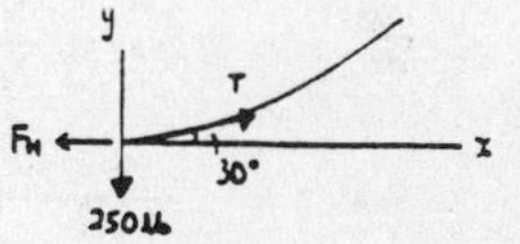

From Example 7 - 15,

$$\frac{dy}{dx} = \frac{1}{F_H}(w_0 s + C_1)$$

At $s = 0$, $\frac{dy}{dx} = \tan 30^\circ = 0.577$

$$\therefore\ C_1 = 433.0\,(0.577) = 250$$

$$x = \frac{F_H}{w_0}\left\{\sinh^{-1}\left[\frac{1}{F_H}(w_0 s + C_1)\right] + C_2\right\}$$

$$= \frac{433.0}{5}\left\{\sinh^{-1}\left[\frac{1}{433.0}(5s + 250)\right] + C_2\right\}$$

$s = 0$ at $x = 0$, $C_2 = -0.5493$

Thus,

$$x = 86.6\left\{\sinh^{-1}\left[\frac{1}{433.0}(5s + 250)\right] - 0.5493\right\}$$

When $x = 15$ ft,

$s = 18.2$ ft **Ans**

■7-113. A 50-ft cable is suspended between two points a distance of 15 ft apart and at the same elevation. If the minimum tension in the cable is 200 lb, determine the total weight of the cable and the maximum tension developed in the cable.

$T_{min} = F_H = 200$ lb

From Example 7 – 15 :

$$s = \frac{F_H}{w_0} \sinh\left(\frac{w_0\, x}{F_H}\right)$$

$$\frac{50}{2} = \frac{200}{w_0} \sinh\left(\frac{w_0}{200}\left(\frac{15}{2}\right)\right)$$

Solving,

$w_0 = 79.9$ lb/ft

Total weight $= w_0\, l = 79.9\,(50) = 4.00$ kip **Ans**

$$\left.\frac{dy}{dx}\right|_{max} = \tan\theta_{max} = \frac{w_0\, s}{F_H}$$

$$\theta_{max} = \tan^{-1}\left[\frac{79.9\,(25)}{200}\right] = 84.3°$$

Then,

$$T_{max} = \frac{F_H}{\cos\theta_{max}} = \frac{200}{\cos 84.3°} = 2.01 \text{ kip}$$ **Ans**

7-114. The man picks up the 52-ft chain and holds it just high enough so it is completely off the ground. The chain has points of attachment A and B that are 50 ft apart. If the chain has a weight of 3 lb/ft, and the man weighs 150 lb, determine the force he exerts on the ground. Also, how high h must he lift the chain? *Hint*: The slopes at A and B are zero.

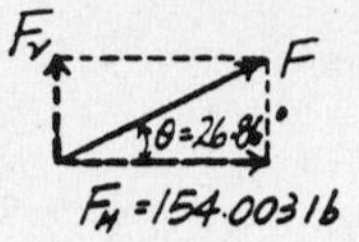

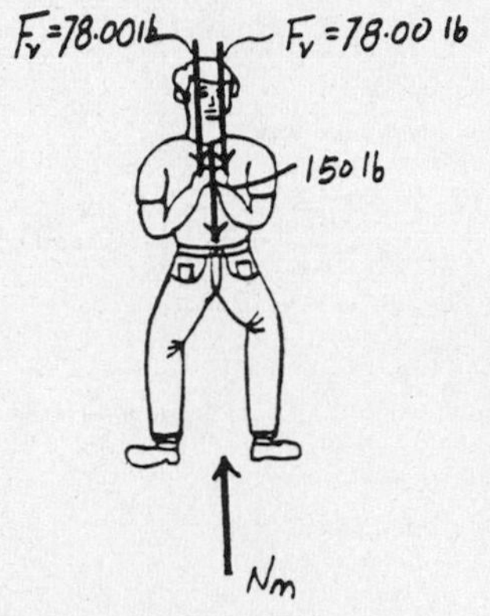

Deflection Curve of The Cable :

$$x = \int \frac{ds}{\left[1+(1/F_H^2)\left(\int w_0\,ds\right)^2\right]^{\frac{1}{2}}} \quad \text{where } w_0 = 3 \text{ lb/ft}$$

Performing the integration yields

$$x = \frac{F_H}{3}\left\{\sinh^{-1}\left[\frac{1}{F_H}(3s+C_1)\right]+C_2\right\} \qquad [1]$$

From Eq. 7 − 14

$$\frac{dy}{dx} = \frac{1}{F_H}\int w_0\,ds = \frac{1}{F_H}(3s+C_1) \qquad [2]$$

Boundary Conditions :

$\frac{dy}{dx} = 0$ at $s = 0$. From Eq. [2] $\quad 0 = \frac{1}{F_H}(0+C_1) \qquad C_1 = 0$

Then, Eq. [2] becomes

$$\frac{dy}{dx} = \tan\theta = \frac{3s}{F_H} \qquad [3]$$

$s = 0$ at $x = 0$ and use the result $C_1 = 0$. From Eq. [1]

$$x = \frac{F_H}{3}\left\{\sinh^{-1}\left[\frac{1}{F_H}(0+0)\right]+C_2\right\} \qquad C_2 = 0$$

Rearranging Eq. [1], we have

$$s = \frac{F_H}{3}\sinh\left(\frac{3}{F_H}x\right) \qquad [4]$$

Substituting Eq. [4] into [3] yields

$$\frac{dy}{dx} = \sinh\left(\frac{3}{F_H}x\right)$$

Performing the integration

$$y = \frac{F_H}{3}\cosh\left(\frac{3}{F_H}x\right)+C_3 \qquad [5]$$

$y = 0$ at $x = 0$. From Eq. [5] $\quad 0 = \frac{F_H}{3}\cosh 0 + C_3$, thus, $C_3 = -\frac{F_H}{3}$

Then, Eq. [5] becomes

$$y = \frac{F_H}{3}\left[\cosh\left(\frac{3}{F_H}x\right)-1\right] \qquad [6]$$

$s = 26$ ft at $x = 25$ ft. From Eq. [4]

$$26 = \frac{F_H}{3}\sinh\left[\frac{3}{F_H}(25)\right]$$

By trial and error $\qquad F_H = 154.003$ lb

$y = h$ at $x = 25$ ft. From Eq. [6]

$$h = \frac{154.003}{3}\left\{\cosh\left[\frac{3}{154.003}(25)\right]-1\right\} = 6.21 \text{ ft} \qquad \textbf{Ans}$$

From Eq. [3]

$$\left.\frac{dy}{dx}\right|_{s=26\text{ft}} = \tan\theta = \frac{3(26)}{154.003} = 0.5065 \qquad \theta = 26.86^\circ$$

The vertical force F_V that each chain exerts on the man is

$$F_V = F_H \tan\theta = 154.003 \tan 26.86^\circ = 78.00 \text{ lb}$$

Equation of Equilibrium : By considering the equilibrium of the man,

$$+\uparrow \Sigma F_y = 0; \quad N_m - 150 - 2(78.00) = 0 \qquad N_m = 306 \text{ lb} \qquad \textbf{Ans}$$

7-115. The balloon is held in place using a 400-ft cord that weighs 0.8 lb/ft and makes a 60° angle with the horizontal. If the tension in the cord at point A is 150 lb, determine the length of the cord, l, that is lying on the ground and the height h. *Hint:* Establish the coordinate system at B as shown.

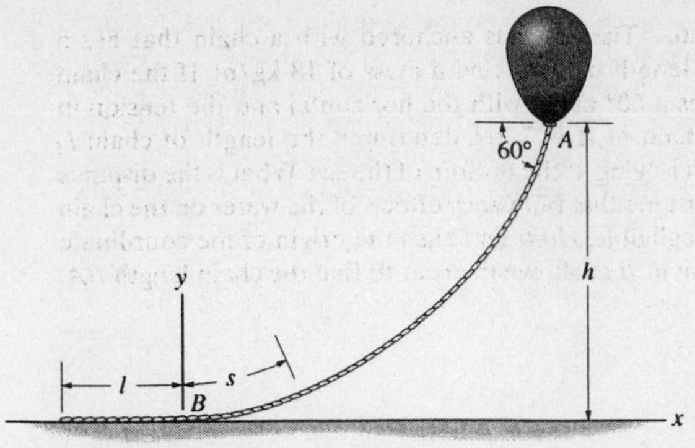

Deflection Curve of The Cable :

$$x = \int \frac{ds}{\left[1+(1/F_H^2)\left(\int w_0 ds\right)^2\right]^{\frac{1}{2}}} \qquad \text{where } w_0 = 0.8 \text{ lb/ft}$$

Performing the integration yields

$$x = \frac{F_H}{0.8}\left\{\sinh^{-1}\left[\frac{1}{F_H}(0.8s + C_1)\right] + C_2\right\} \qquad [1]$$

From Eq. 7 – 14

$$\frac{dy}{dx} = \frac{1}{F_H}\int w_0 ds = \frac{1}{F_H}(0.8s + C_1) \qquad [2]$$

Boundary Conditions :

$\frac{dy}{dx} = 0$ at $s = 0$. From Eq.[2] $\quad 0 = \frac{1}{F_H}(0 + C_1) \quad C_1 = 0$

Then, Eq.[2] becomes

$$\frac{dy}{dx} = \tan\theta = \frac{0.8s}{F_H} \qquad [3]$$

$s = 0$ at $x = 0$ and use the result $C_1 = 0$. From Eq.[1]

$$x = \frac{F_H}{3}\left\{\sinh^{-1}\left[\frac{1}{F_H}(0+0)\right] + C_2\right\} \qquad C_2 = 0$$

Rearranging Eq.[1], we have

$$s = \frac{F_H}{0.8}\sinh\left(\frac{0.8}{F_H}x\right) \qquad [4]$$

Substituting Eq.[4] into [3] yields

$$\frac{dy}{dx} = \sinh\left(\frac{0.8}{F_H}x\right)$$

Performing the integration

$$y = \frac{F_H}{0.8}\cosh\left(\frac{0.8}{F_H}x\right) + C_3 \qquad [5]$$

$y = 0$ at $x = 0$. From Eq.[5] $\quad 0 = \frac{F_H}{0.8}\cosh 0 + C_3$, thus, $C_3 = -\frac{F_H}{0.8}$

Then, Eq.[5] becomes

$$y = \frac{F_H}{0.8}\left[\cosh\left(\frac{0.8}{F_H}x\right) - 1\right] \qquad [6]$$

The tension developed at the end of the cord is $T = 150$ lb and $\theta = 60°$. Thus

$$T = \frac{F_H}{\cos\theta} \qquad 150 = \frac{F_H}{\cos 60°} \qquad F_H = 75.0 \text{ lb}$$

From Eq.[3]

$$\frac{dy}{dx} = \tan 60° = \frac{0.8s}{75} \qquad s = 162.38 \text{ ft}$$

Thus, $\quad l = 400 - 162.38 = 238$ ft **Ans**

Substituting $s = 162.38$ ft into Eq.[4],

$$162.38 = \frac{75}{0.8}\sinh\left(\frac{0.8}{75}x\right)$$

$$x = 123.46 \text{ ft}$$

$y = h$ at $x = 123.46$ ft. From Eq.[6]

$$h = \frac{75.0}{0.8}\left[\cosh\left[\frac{0.8}{75.0}(123.46)\right] - 1\right] = 93.75 \text{ ft} \qquad \textbf{Ans}$$

***7-116.** The yacht is anchored with a chain that has a total length of 40 m and a mass of 18 kg/m. If the chain makes a 60° angle with the horizontal and the tension in the chain at A is 7 kN, determine the length of chain l_d which is lying at the bottom of the sea. What is the distance d? Assume that buoyancy effects of the water on the chain are negligible. *Hint:* Establish the origin of the coordinate system at B as shown in order to find the chain length BA.

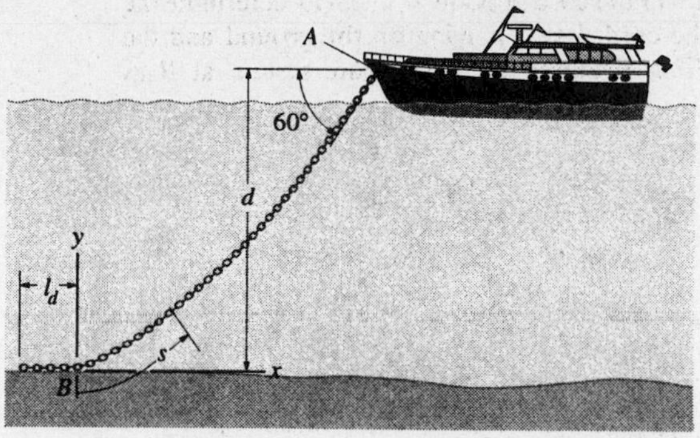

Component of force at A is

$$F_H = T\cos\theta = 7000\cos 60^\circ = 3500\ \text{N}$$

From Eq. (1) of Example 7-15,

$$x = \frac{3500}{18\,(9.81)}\left(\sinh^{-1}\left[\frac{1}{3500}(18)(9.81)\,s + C_1\right] + C_2\right)$$

Since $\frac{dy}{dx} = 0,\ s = 0,$ then

$$\frac{dy}{dx} = \frac{1}{F_H}(w_0\,s + C_1);\quad C_1 = 0$$

Also $x = 0,\ s = 0,$ so that $C_2 = 0$ and the above equation becomes

$$x = 19.82\left(\sinh^{-1}\left(\frac{s}{19.82}\right)\right) \quad (1)$$

or,

$$s = 19.82\left(\sinh\left(\frac{x}{19.82}\right)\right) \quad (2)$$

From Example 7-15

$$\frac{dy}{dx} = \frac{w_0\,s}{F_H} = \frac{18\,(9.81)}{3500}s = \frac{s}{19.82} \quad (3)$$

Substituting Eq. (2) into Eq. (3),

$$\frac{dy}{dx} = \sinh\left(\frac{x}{19.82}\right)$$

Integrating,

$$y = 19.82\cosh\left(\frac{x}{19.82}\right) + C_3$$

Since $x = 0,\ y = 0,$ then $C_3 = -19.82$

Thus,

$$y = 19.82\left(\cosh\left(\frac{x}{19.82}\right) - 1\right) \quad (4)$$

Slope of the cable at point A is

$$\frac{dy}{dx} = \tan 60^\circ = 1.732$$

Using Eq. (3),

$$s_{AB} = 19.82\,(1.732) = 34.33\ \text{m}$$

Length of chain on the ground is thus

$$l_d = 40 - 34.33 = 5.67\ \text{m} \qquad \textbf{Ans}$$

From Eq. (1), with $s = 34.33$ m

$$x = 19.82\left(\sinh^{-1}\left(\frac{34.33}{19.82}\right)\right) = 26.10\ \text{m}$$

Using Eq. (4),

$$y = 19.82\left(\cosh\left(\frac{26.10}{19.82}\right) - 1\right)$$

$$d = y = 19.83\ \text{m} \qquad \textbf{Ans}$$

7-117. A 100-lb cable is attached between two points at a distance 50 ft apart having equal elevations. If the maximum tension developed in the cable is 75 lb, determine the length of the cable and the sag.

From Example 7 - 15,

$$T_{max} = \frac{F_H}{\cos\theta_{max}} = 75 \text{ lb}$$

$$\cos\theta_{max} = \frac{F_H}{75}$$

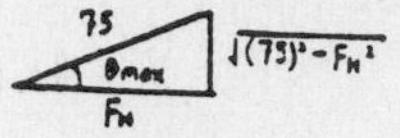

For $\frac{1}{2}$ of cable,

$$w_0 = \frac{\frac{100}{2}}{s} = \frac{50}{s}$$

$$\tan\theta_{max} = \frac{w_0\, s}{F_H} = \frac{\sqrt{(75)^2 - F_H^2}}{F_H} = \frac{50}{F_H}$$

Thus,

$$\sqrt{(75)^2 - F_H^2} = 50; \qquad F_H = 55.9 \text{ lb}$$

$$s = \frac{F_H}{w_0}\sinh\left(\frac{w_0}{F_H}x\right) = \frac{55.9}{\left(\frac{50}{s}\right)}\sinh\left\{\left(\frac{50}{s\,(55.9)}\right)\left(\frac{50}{2}\right)\right\}$$

$$s = 27.8 \text{ ft}$$

$$w_0 = \frac{50}{27.8} = 1.80 \text{ lb/ft}$$

Total length $= 2s = 55.6$ ft **Ans**

$$h = \frac{F_H}{w_0}\left[\cosh\left(\frac{w_0 L}{2F_H}\right) - 1\right] = \frac{55.9}{1.80}\left[\cosh\left(\frac{1.80\,(50)}{2\,(55.9)}\right) - 1\right]$$

$= 10.6$ ft **Ans**

7-118. Draw the shear and moment diagrams for beam *CD*.

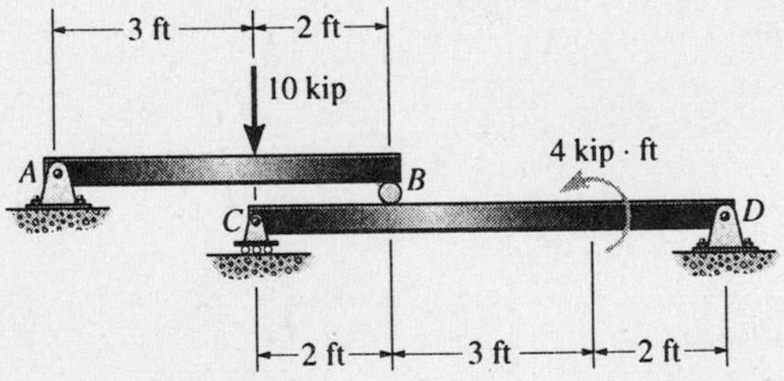

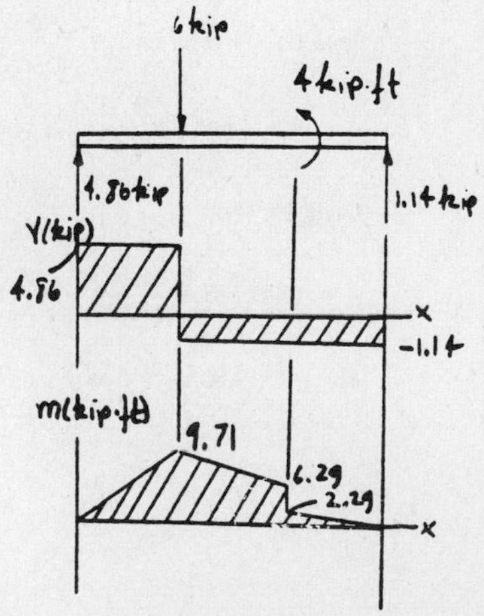

7-119. Determine the normal force, shear force, and moment at points B and C of the beam.

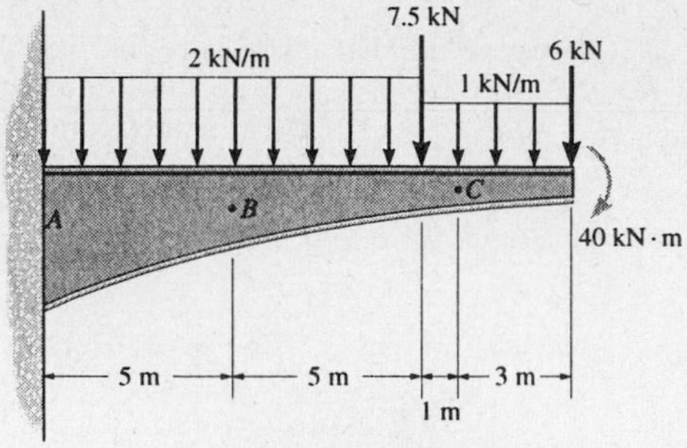

Free body Diagram : The Support reactions need not be computed for this case.

Internal Forces : Applying the equations of equilibrium to segment DC [FBD (a)], we have

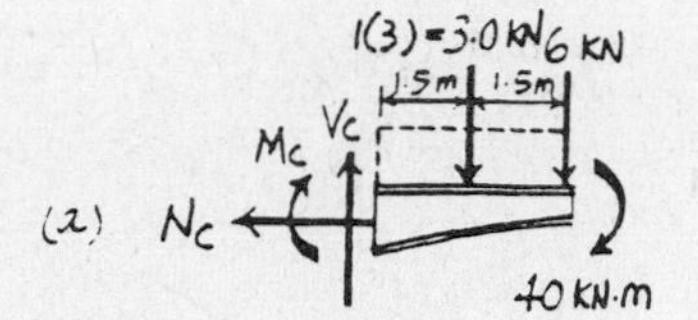

$\xrightarrow{+} \Sigma F_x = 0; \quad N_C = 0$ **Ans**

$+\uparrow \Sigma F_y = 0; \quad V_C - 3.00 - 6 = 0 \quad V_C = 9.00 \text{ kN}$ **Ans**

$\circlearrowleft + \Sigma M_C = 0; \quad -M_C - 3.00(1.5) - 6(3) - 40 = 0$

$M_C = -62.5 \text{ kN} \cdot \text{m}$ **Ans**

Applying the equations of equilibrium to segment DB [FBD (b)], we have

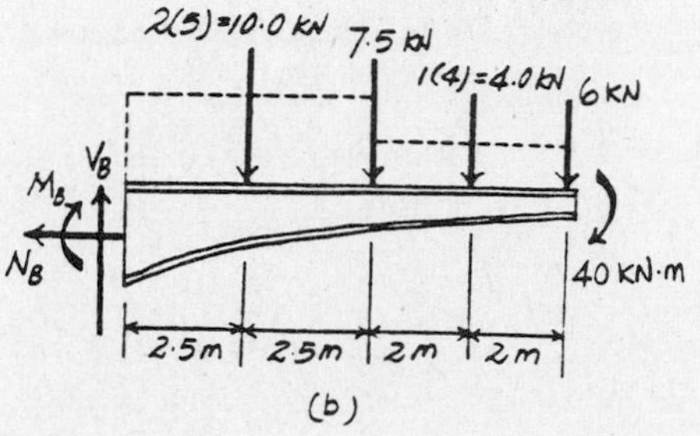

$\xrightarrow{+} \Sigma F_x = 0; \quad N_B = 0$ **Ans**

$+\uparrow \Sigma F_y = 0; \quad V_B - 10.0 - 7.5 - 4.00 - 6 = 0$

$V_D = 27.5 \text{ kN}$ **Ans**

$\circlearrowleft + \Sigma M_B = 0; \quad -M_B - 10.0(2.5) - 7.5(5)$

$-4.00(7) - 6(9) - 40 = 0$

$M_B = -184.5 \text{ kN} \cdot \text{m}$ **Ans**

***7-120.** Determine the internal normal force, shear force and moment at points D and E of the frame.

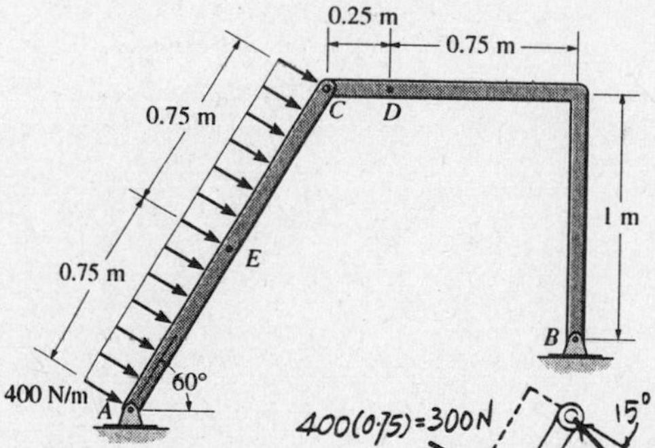

Support Reactions : Member BC is a two force member. From FBD (a),

$\circlearrowleft + \Sigma M_B = 0; \quad F_{BC} \cos 15°(1.5) - 600(0.75) = 0$

$F_{BC} = 310.58 \text{ N}$

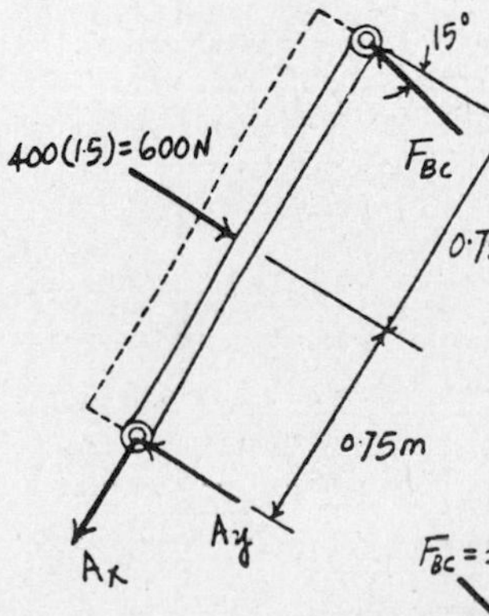

Internal Forces : Applying the equations of equilibrium to segment CE [FBD (b)], we have

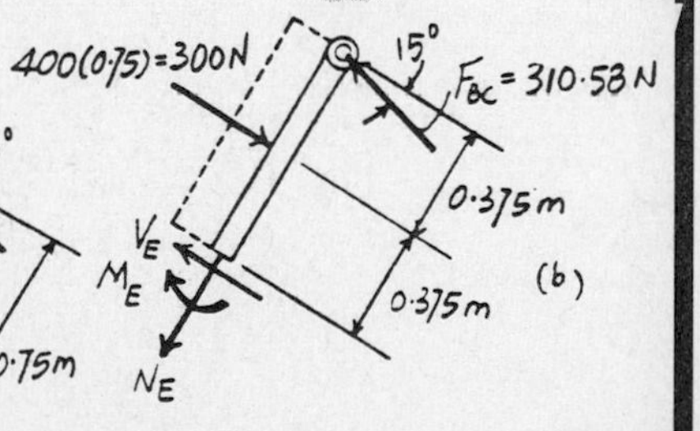

$\nearrow + \Sigma F_{x'} = 0; \quad 310.58 \sin 15° - N_E = 0 \quad N_E = 80.4 \text{ N}$ **Ans**

$\nwarrow + \Sigma F_{y'} = 0; \quad V_E + 310.58 \cos 15° - 300 = 0 \quad V_E = 0$ **Ans**

$\circlearrowleft + \Sigma M_E = 0; \quad 310.58 \cos 15°(0.75) - 300(0.375) - M_E = 0$

$M_E = 112.5 \text{ N} \cdot \text{m}$ **Ans**

Applying the equations of equilibrium to segment CD[FBD (c)], we have

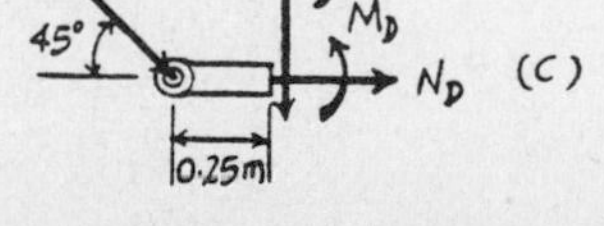

$\xrightarrow{+} \Sigma F_x = 0; \quad N_D + 310.58 \cos 45° = 0 \quad N_D = -220 \text{ N}$ **Ans**

$+\uparrow \Sigma F_y = 0; \quad -310.58 \sin 45° - V_D = 0 \quad V_D = -220 \text{ N}$ **Ans**

$\circlearrowleft + \Sigma M_D = 0; \quad M_D + 310.58 \sin 45°(0.25) = 0$

$M_D = -54.9 \text{ N} \cdot \text{m}$ **Ans**

7-121. Determine the distance a between the supports in terms of the beam's length L so that the moment in the *symmetric* beam is zero at the beam's center.

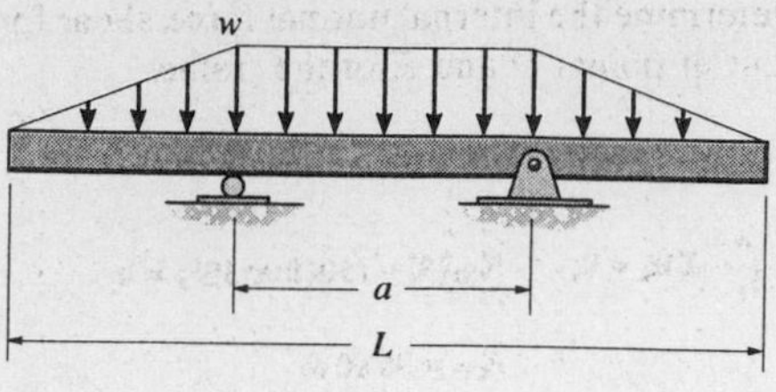

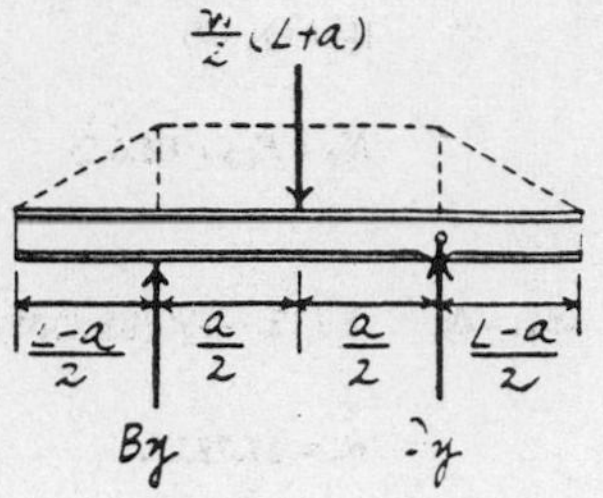

Support Reactions : . From FBD (a),

$$\circlearrowleft + \Sigma M_C = 0; \quad \frac{w}{2}(L+a)\left(\frac{a}{2}\right) - B_y(a) = 0 \quad B_y = \frac{w}{4}(L+a)$$

Free body Diagram : The FBD for segment AC sectioned through point C is drawn.

Internal Forces : This problem requires $M_C = 0$. Summing moments about point C[FBD (b)], we have

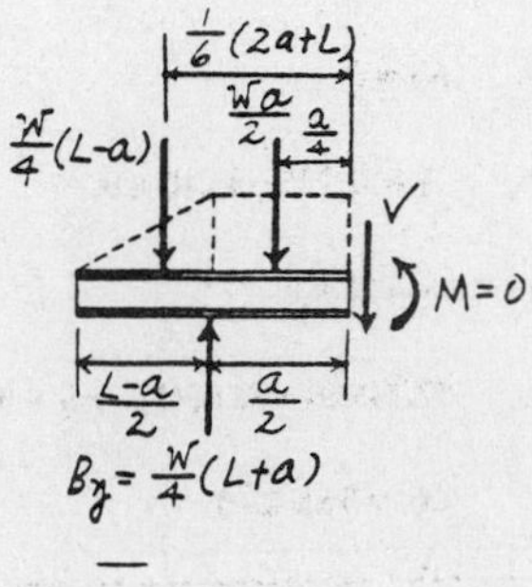

$$\circlearrowleft + \Sigma M_C = 0; \quad \frac{wa}{2}\left(\frac{a}{4}\right) + \frac{w}{4}(L-a)\left[\frac{1}{6}(2a+L)\right] - \frac{w}{4}(L+a)\left(\frac{a}{2}\right) = 0$$

$$2a^2 + 2aL - L^2 = 0$$

$$a = 0.366L \qquad \textbf{Ans}$$

7-122. Determine the internal normal force, shear force, and moment at points D and E of the frame.

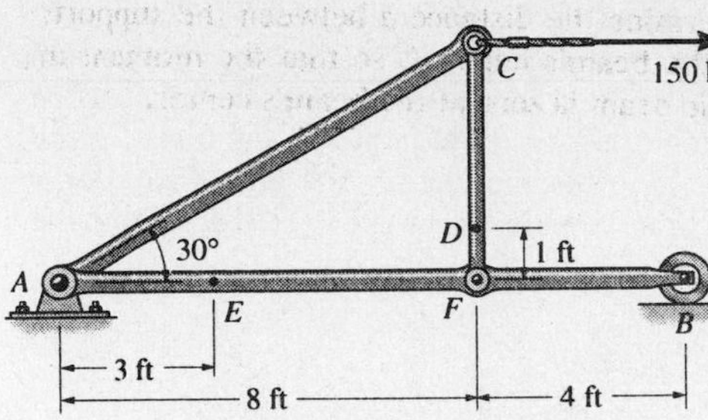

$\curvearrowleft + \Sigma M_A = 0;\quad F_{CD}(8) - 150(8\tan 30°) = 0$

$F_{CD} = 86.60$ lb

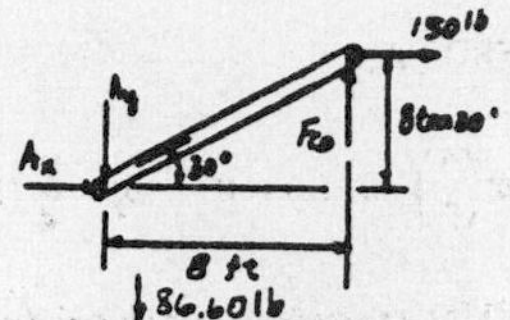

Since member CF is a two-force member

$V_D = M_D = 0$ Ans

$N_D = F_{CD} = 86.6$ lb Ans

$\curvearrowleft + \Sigma M_A = 0;\quad B_y(12) - 150(8\tan 30°) = 0$

$B_y = 57.735$ lb

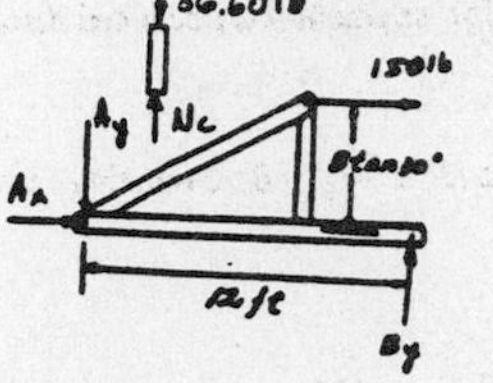

$\overset{+}{\rightarrow} \Sigma F_x = 0;\quad N_E = 0$ Ans

$+\uparrow \Sigma F_y = 0;\quad V_E + 57.735 - 86.60 = 0$

$V_E = 28.9$ lb Ans

$\curvearrowleft + \Sigma M_E = 0;\quad 57.735(9) - 86.60(5) - M_E = 0$

$M_E = 86.6$ lb·ft Ans

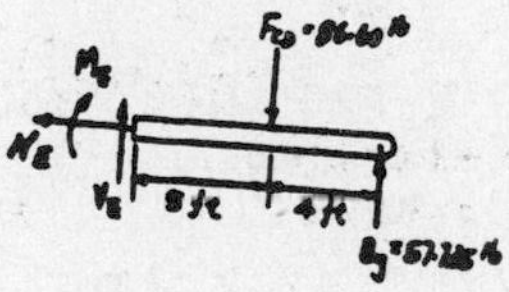

7-123. Draw the shear and moment diagrams for the beam ABC.

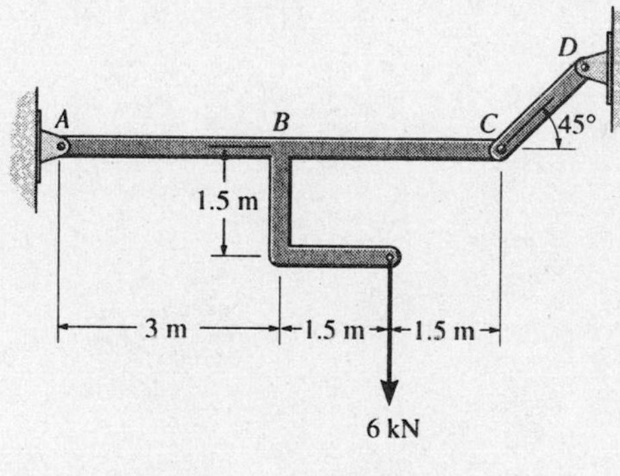

Support Reactions : The 6 kN load can be replacde by an equivalent force and couple moment at B as shown on FBD (a).

$\curvearrowleft + \Sigma M_A = 0;\quad F_{CD}\sin 45°(6) - 6(3) - 9.00 = 0 \quad F_{CD} = 6.364$ kN

$+\uparrow \Sigma F_y = 0;\quad A_y + 6.364\sin 45° - 6 = 0 \quad A_y = 1.50$ kN

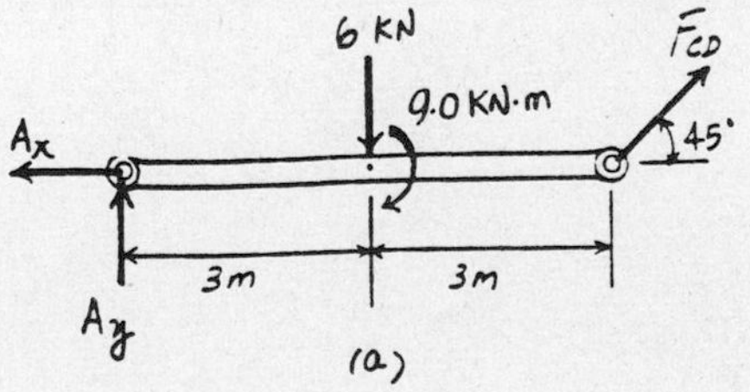

Shear and Moment Functions : For $0 \le x < 3$ m [FBD (b)],

$+\uparrow \Sigma F_y = 0;\quad 1.50 - V = 0 \quad V = 1.50$ kN Ans

$\curvearrowleft + \Sigma M = 0;\quad M - 1.50x = 0 \quad M = \{1.50x\}$ kN·m Ans

For $3\text{ m} < x \le 6$ m [FBD (c)],

$+\uparrow \Sigma F_y = 0;\quad V + 6.364\sin °45 = 0 \quad V = -4.50$ kN Ans

$\curvearrowleft + \Sigma M = 0;\quad 6.364\sin 45°(6 - x) - M = 0$

$M = \{27.0 - 4.50x\}$ kN·m Ans

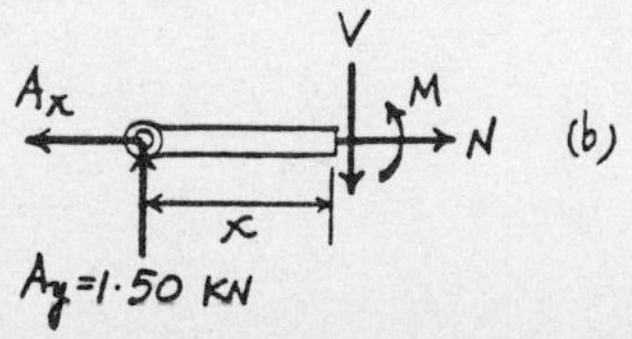

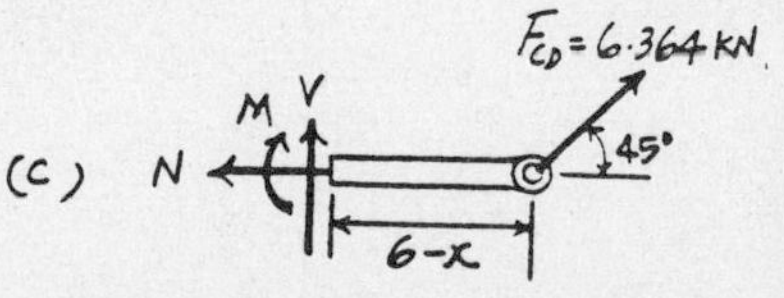

*7-124. The traveling crane consists of a 5-m-long beam having a uniform mass of 20 kg/m. The chain hoist and its supported load exert a force of 8 kN on the beam when $x = 2$ m. Draw the shear and moment diagrams for the beam. The guide wheels at the ends A and B exert only vertical reactions on the beam. Neglect the size of the trolley at C.

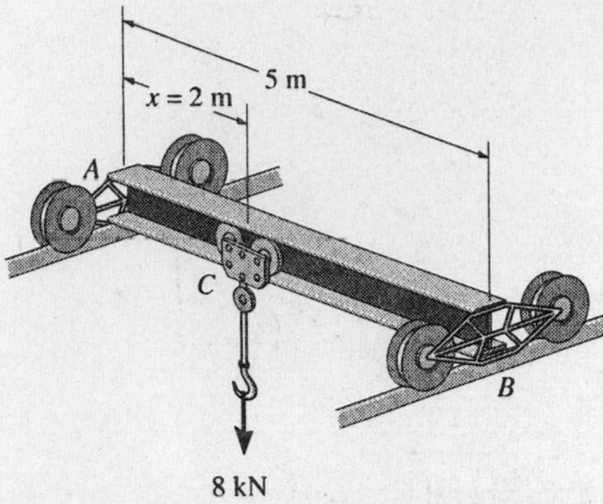

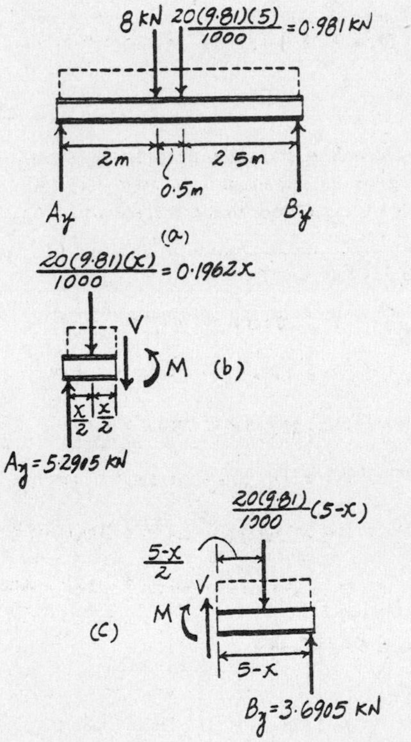

Support Reactions : From FBD (a),

$\curvearrowleft + \Sigma M_A = 0;\quad B_y(5) - 8(2) - 0.981(2.5) = 0 \qquad B_y = 3.6905\text{ kN}$

$+\uparrow \Sigma F_y = 0;\quad A_y + 3.6905 - 8 - 0.981 = 0 \qquad A_y = 5.2905\text{ kN}$

Shear and Moment Functions : For $0 \le x < 2$ m [FBD (b)],

$+\uparrow \Sigma F_y = 0;\quad 5.2905 - 0.1962x - V = 0$

$V = \{5.29 - 0.196x\}\text{ kN}$ **Ans**

$\curvearrowleft + \Sigma M = 0;\quad M + 0.1962x\left(\frac{x}{2}\right) - 5.2905x = 0$

$M = \{5.29x - 0.0981x^2\}\text{ kN}\cdot\text{m}$ **Ans**

For $2\text{ m} < x \le 5$ m [FBD (c)],

$+\uparrow \Sigma F_y = 0;\quad V + 3.6905 - \frac{20(9.81)}{1000}(5-x) = 0$

$V = \{-0.196x - 2.71\}\text{ kN}$ **Ans**

$\curvearrowleft + \Sigma M = 0;\quad 3.6905(5-x) - \frac{20(9.81)}{1000}(5-x)\left(\frac{5-x}{2}\right) - M = 0$

$M = \{16.0 - 2.71x - 0.0981x^2\}\text{ kN}\cdot\text{m}$ **Ans**

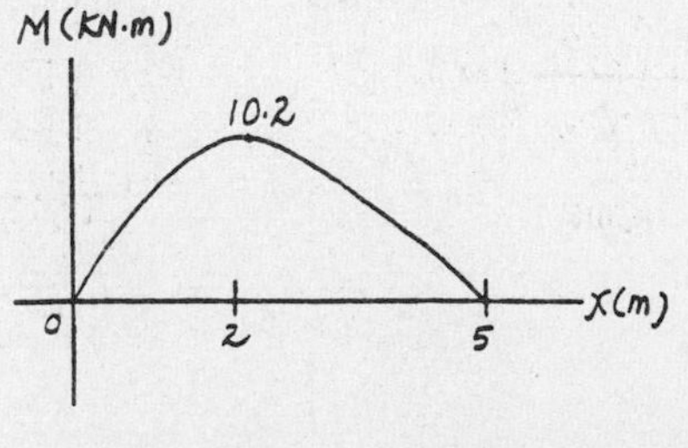

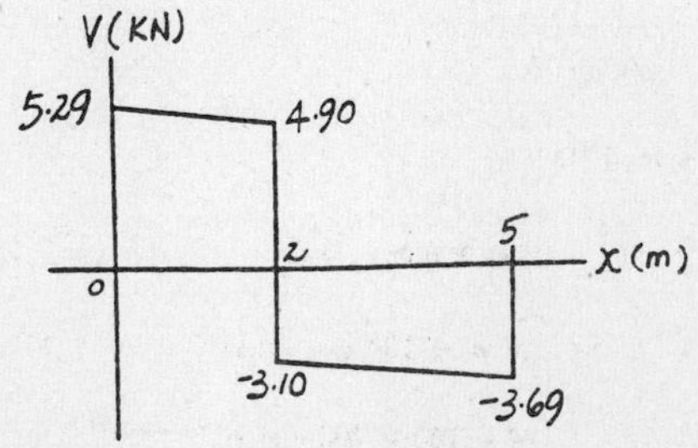

7-125. A 200-lb cable is attached between two points that are 75 ft apart and at the same elevation. If the maximum tension developed in the cable is 120 lb, determine the length of the cable and the sag.

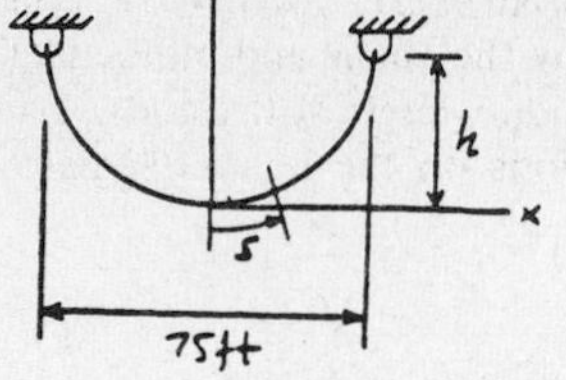

$$s = \frac{F_H}{w_0}\sinh\left(\frac{w_0}{F_H}x\right)$$

$$y = \frac{F_H}{w_0}\left[\cosh\left(\frac{w_0}{F_H}x\right) - 1\right]$$

At $x = 37.5$ ft,

$$s = \frac{F_H}{\frac{200}{2s}}\sinh\left(\frac{\frac{200}{2s}}{F_H}(37.5)\right)$$

$$100 = F_H \sinh\left(\frac{3\,750}{sF_H}\right) \qquad (1)$$

$$\frac{dy}{dx} = \tan\theta = \frac{w_0 s}{F_H}$$

$$\cos\theta = \frac{F_H}{\sqrt{F_H^2 + w_0^2 s^2}}$$

At $x = 37.5$ ft, $\quad T_{max} = 120$ lb

$$\cos\theta = \frac{F_H}{120} = \frac{F_H}{\sqrt{F_H^2 + 100^2}}$$

$$F_H = 66.33 \text{ lb}$$

From Eq. (1)

$$\sinh^{-1}\left(\frac{100}{F_H}\right) = \frac{3\,750}{sF_H}$$

$$s = 47.15 \text{ ft}$$

$$L = 2s = 94.3 \text{ ft} \qquad \textbf{Ans}$$

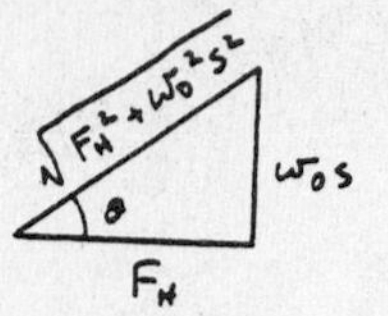

At $x = 37.5$ ft,

$$h = \frac{F_H}{w_0}\left[\cosh\left(\frac{w_0}{F_H}x\right) - 1\right]$$

$$h = \frac{66.33}{\frac{200}{94.3}}\left[\cosh\left(\frac{\frac{200}{94.3}}{66.33}(37.5)\right) - 1\right] = 25.3 \text{ ft} \qquad \textbf{Ans}$$

7-126. Determine the internal normal force, shear force, and the moment as a function of $0° \le \theta \le 180°$ and $0 \le y \le 2$ ft for the member loaded as shown.

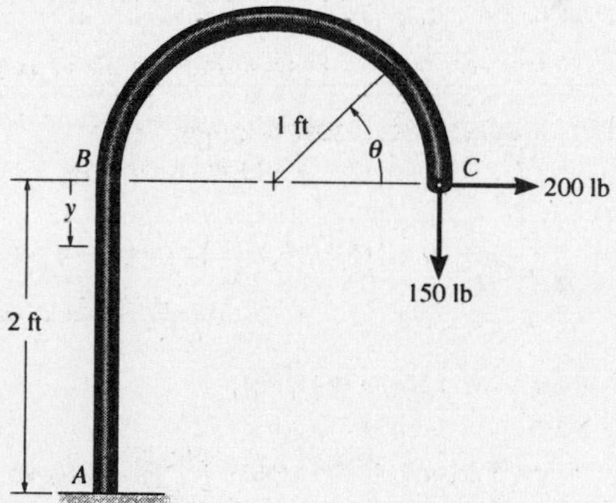

For $0° \le \theta \le 180°$:

$+\nearrow\Sigma F_x = 0;\quad V + 200\cos\theta - 150\sin\theta = 0$

$V = 150\sin\theta - 200\cos\theta \qquad$ **Ans**

$+\nwarrow\Sigma F_y = 0;\quad N - 200\sin\theta - 150\cos\theta = 0$

$N = 150\cos\theta + 200\sin\theta \qquad$ **Ans**

$\circlearrowleft+\Sigma M = 0;\quad -M - 150(1)(1 - \cos\theta) + 200(1)\sin\theta = 0$

$M = 150\cos\theta + 200\sin\theta - 150 \qquad$ **Ans**

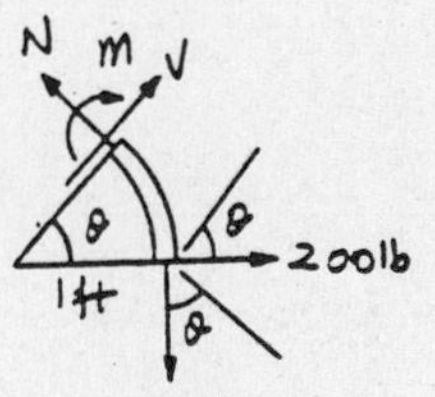

At section B, $\theta = 180°$, thus

$V_B = 200$ lb

$N_B = -150$ lb

$M_B = -300$ lb · ft

For $0 \le y \le 2$ ft :

$\xrightarrow{+}\Sigma F_x = 0;\quad V = 200$ lb $\qquad$ **Ans**

$+\uparrow\Sigma F_y = 0;\quad N = -150$ lb $\qquad$ **Ans**

$\circlearrowleft+\Sigma M = 0;\quad -M - 300 - 200y = 0$

$M = -300 - 200y \qquad$ **Ans**

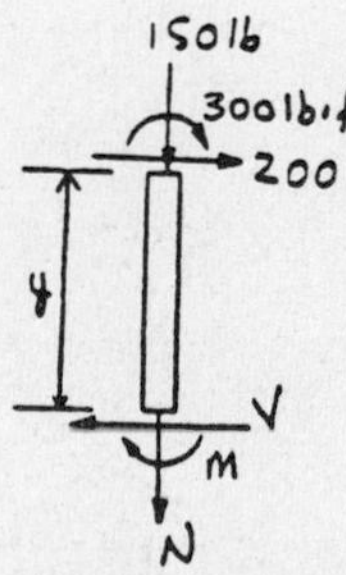

8-1. The mine car and its contents have a total mass of 6 Mg and a center of gravity at G. If the coefficient of static friction between the wheels and the tracks is $\mu_s = 0.4$ when the wheels are locked, find the normal force acting on the front wheels at B and the rear wheels at A when (a) only the brakes at A are locked, and (b) the brakes at both A and B are locked. In either case, does the car move?

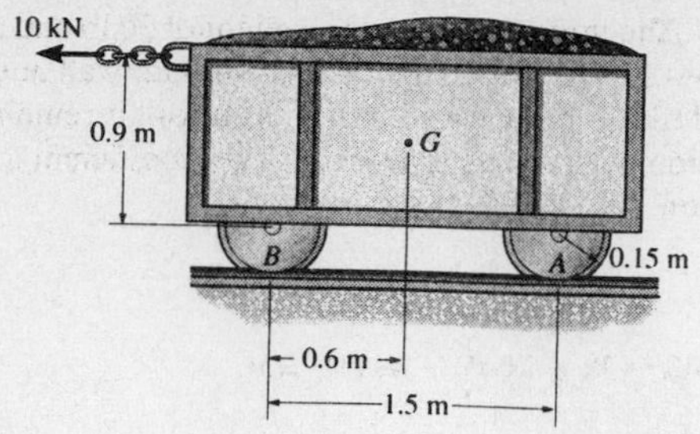

Equations of Equilibrium : The normal reactions acting on the wheels at (A and B) are independent as to whether the wheels are locked or not. Hence, The normal reactions acting on the wheels are the same for both cases.

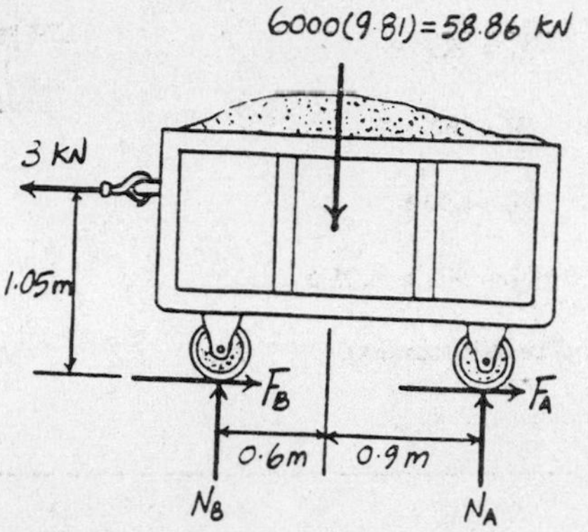

$\curvearrowleft + \Sigma M_B = 0; \quad N_A(1.5) + 10(1.05) - 58.86(0.6) = 0$

$N_A = 16.544 \text{ kN} = 16.5 \text{ kN}$ **Ans**

$+\uparrow \Sigma F_y = 0; \quad N_B + 16.544 - 58.86 = 0$

$N_B = 42.316 \text{ kN} = 42.3 \text{ kN}$ **Ans**

Friction : When the wheels at A are locked, $(F_A)_{max} = \mu_s N_A = 0.4(16.544) = 6.6176$ kN. Since $(F_A)_{max} < 10$ kN, the wheels at A will slip and the wheels at B will roll. Thus, **the mine car moves.** **Ans**

When both wheels at A and B are locked, then $(F_A)_{max} = \mu_s N_A = 0.4(16.544) = 6.6176$ kN and $(F_B)_{max} = \mu_s N_B = 0.4(42.316) = 16.9264$ kN. Since $(F_A)_{max} + (F_B)_{max} = 23.544 \text{ kN} > 10$ kN, the wheels do not slip. Thus, **the mine car does not move.** **Ans**

8-2. If the horizontal force $P = 140$ lb, determine the normal and frictional forces acting on the 300-lb pipe. Take $\mu_s = 0.3$, $\mu_k = 0.2$.

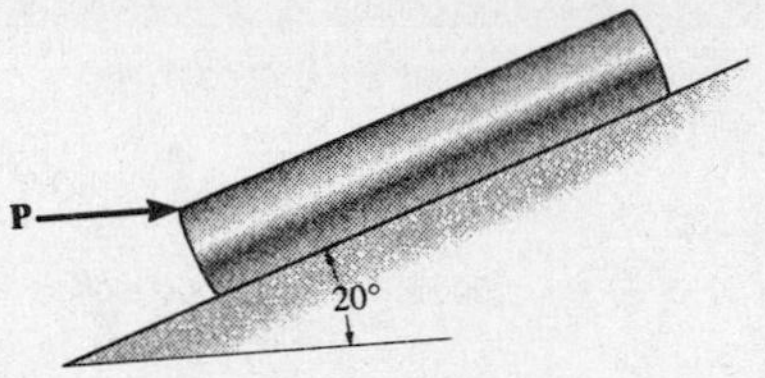

Assume no slipping :

$+\nearrow \Sigma F_x = 0; \quad 140\cos 20° - 300\sin 20° - F_C = 0$

$F_C = 28.95$ lb

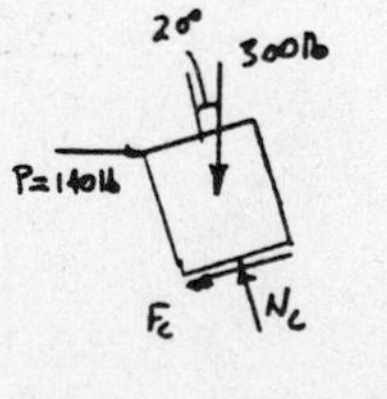

$+\nwarrow \Sigma F_y = 0; \quad N_C - 300\cos 20° - 140\sin 20° = 0$

$N_C = 329.79$ lb

$(F_C)_{max} = \mu_s N_C; \quad (F_C)_{max} = 0.3(329.79) = 98.9 \text{ lb} > 28.95 \text{ lb}$ **(O.K!)**

$F_C = 29.0$ lb **Ans**

$N_C = 330$ lb **Ans**

8-3. The uniform pole has a weight of 30 lb and a length of 26 ft. If it is placed against the smooth wall and on the rough floor in the position $d = 10$ ft, will it remain in this position when it is released? The coefficient of static friction is $\mu_s = 0.3$.

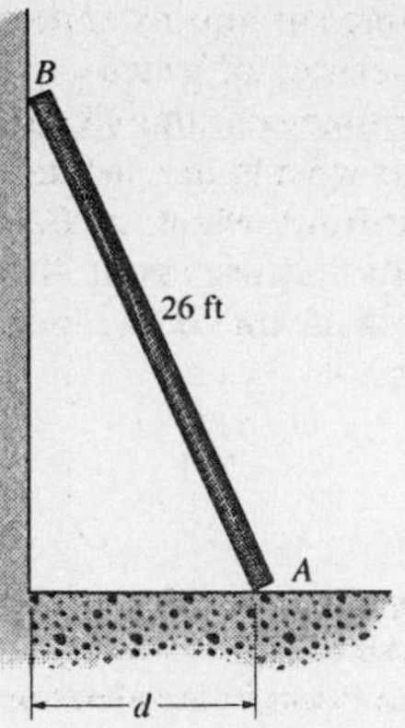

$\circlearrowleft + \Sigma M_A = 0; \quad 30\,(5) - N_B\,(24) = 0$

$N_B = 6.25$ lb

$\xrightarrow{+} \Sigma F_x = 0; \quad 6.25 - F_A = 0$

$F_A = 6.25$ lb

$+\uparrow \Sigma F_y = 0; \quad N_A - 30 = 0$

$N_A = 30$ lb

$(F_A)_{max} = 0.3\,(30) = 9 \text{ lb} > 6.25$ lb

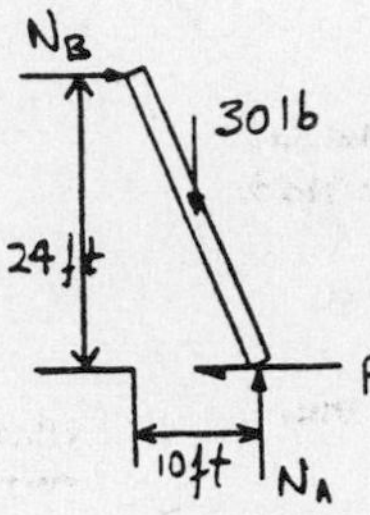

Yes, the pole will remain stationary. **Ans**

***8-4.** The uniform pole has a weight of 30 lb and a length of 26 ft. Determine the maximum distance d it can be placed from the smooth wall and not slip. The coefficient of static friction between the floor and the pole is $\mu_s = 0.3$.

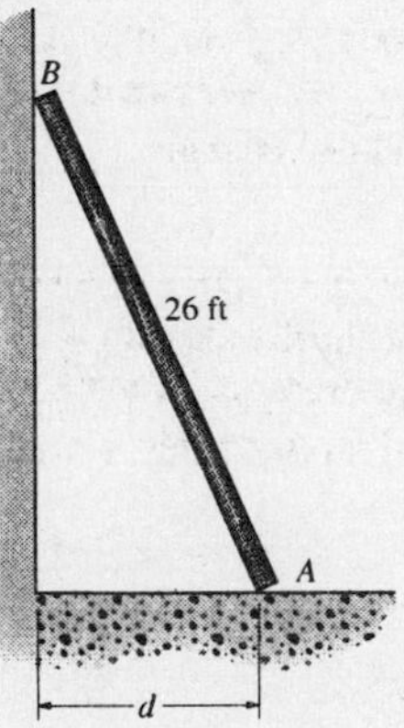

$+\uparrow \Sigma F_y = 0; \quad N_A - 30 = 0$

$N_A = 30$ lb

$F_A = (F_A)_{max} = 0.3\,(30) = 9$ lb

$\xrightarrow{+} \Sigma F_x = 0; \quad N_B - 9 = 0$

$N_B = 9$ lb

$\circlearrowleft + \Sigma M_A = 0; \quad 30\,(13 \cos\theta) - 9\,(26 \sin\theta) = 0$

$\theta = 59.04°$

$d = 26 \cos 59.04° = 13.4$ ft **Ans**

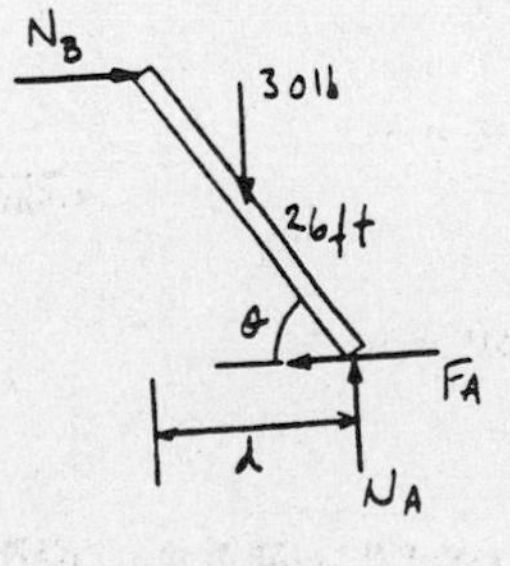

8-5. The uniform 20-lb ladder rests on the rough floor for which the coefficient of static friction is $\mu_s = 0.8$ and against the smooth wall at B. Determine the horizontal force P the man must exert on the ladder in order to cause it to move.

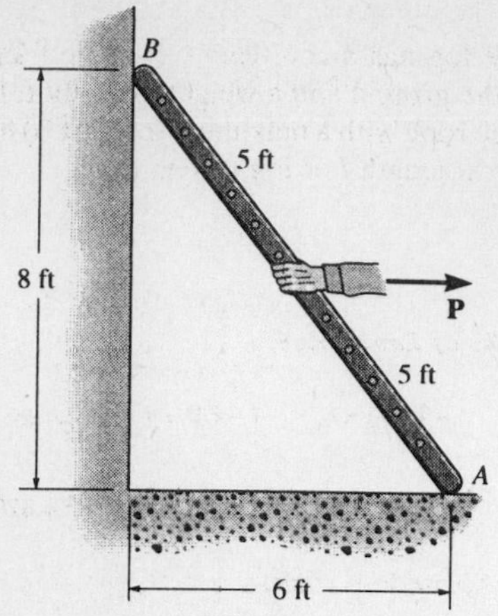

Assume that the ladder tips about A:

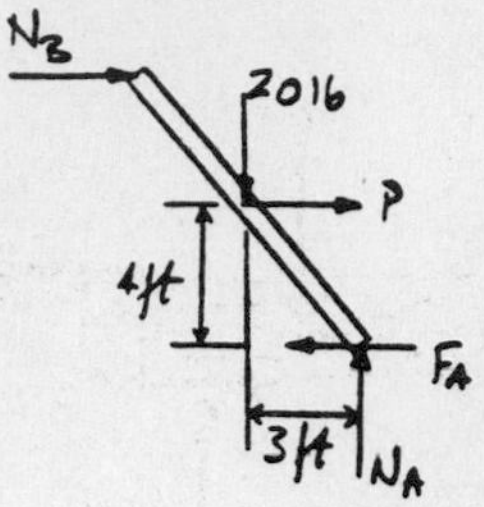

$N_B = 0;$

$\xrightarrow{+} \Sigma F_x = 0; \quad P - F_A = 0$

$+\uparrow \Sigma F_y = 0; \quad -20 + N_A = 0$

$N_A = 20 \text{ lb}$

$\circlearrowleft + \Sigma M_A = 0; \quad 20(3) - P(4) = 0$

$P = 15 \text{ lb}$

Thus

$F_A = 15 \text{ lb}$

$(F_A)_{max} = 0.8(20) = 16 \text{ lb} > 15 \text{ lb}$ OK

Ladder tips as assumed.

$P = 15 \text{ lb}$ **Ans**

8-6. The uniform 20-lb ladder rests on the rough floor for which the coefficient of static friction is $\mu_s = 0.4$ and against the smooth wall at B. Determine the horizontal force P the man must exert on the ladder in order to cause it to move.

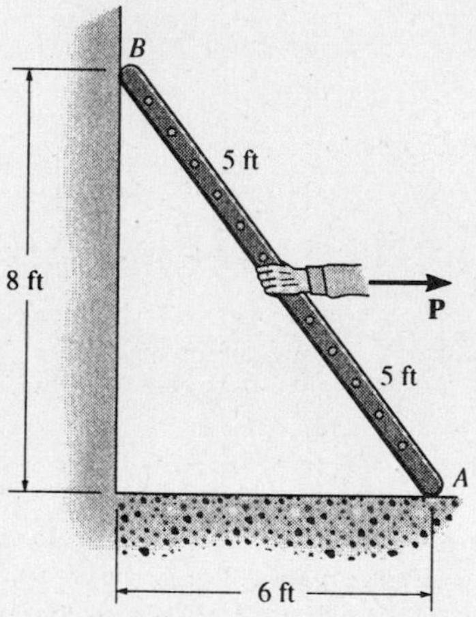

Assume that the ladder slips at A:

$F_A = 0.4 N_A$

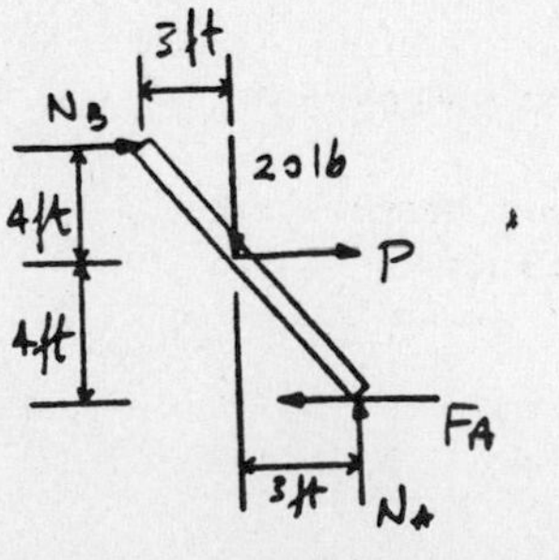

$+\uparrow \Sigma F_y = 0; \quad N_A - 20 = 0$

$N_A = 20 \text{ lb}$

$F_A = 0.4(20) = 8 \text{ lb}$

$\circlearrowleft + \Sigma M_B = 0; \quad P(4) - 20(3) + 20(6) - 8(8) = 0$

$P = 1 \text{ lb}$ **Ans**

$\xrightarrow{+} \Sigma F_x = 0; \quad N_B + 1 - 8 = 0$

$N_B = 7 \text{ lb} > 0$ OK

The ladder will remain in contact with the wall.

8-7. The log has a coefficient of static friction of $\mu_s = 0.3$ with the ground and a weight of 40 lb/ft. If a man can pull on the rope with a maximum force of 80 lb, determine the greatest length l of log he can drag.

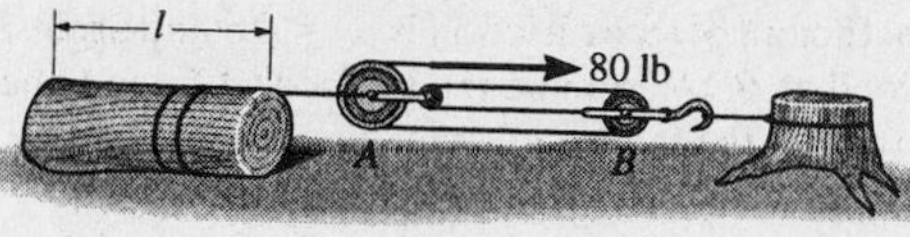

Equations of Equilibrium :

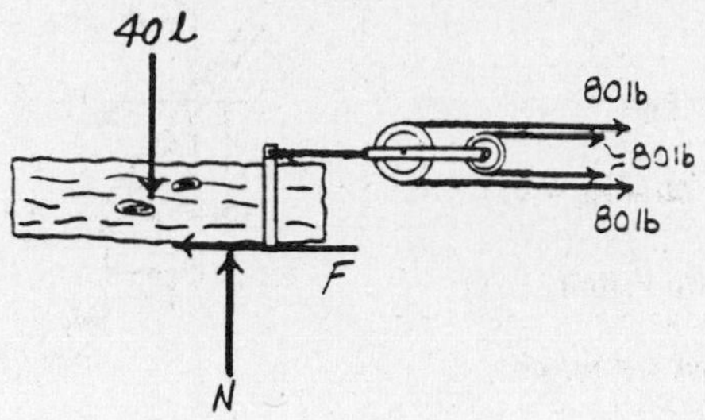

$+\uparrow \Sigma F_y = 0;\quad N - 40l = 0 \quad N = 40l$

$\xrightarrow{+} \Sigma F_x = 0;\quad 4(80) - F = 0 \quad F = 320 \text{ lb}$

Friction : Since the log slides,

$F = (F)_{max} = \mu_s N$

$320 = 0.3(40l)$

$l = 26.7 \text{ ft}$ **Ans**

***8-8.** The roll of paper of weight W rest between the two supports at A and B. If the coefficient of static friction at these points is $\mu_s = 0.3$, determine the horizontal force P needed to cause motion.

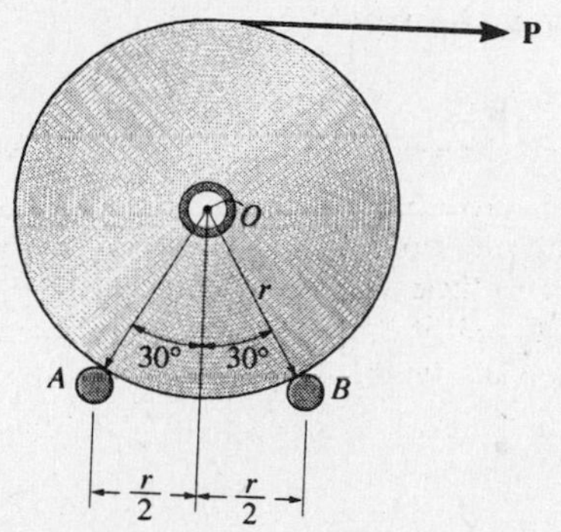

Equations of Equilibrium :

$+\uparrow \Sigma F_y = 0;\quad N_B \cos 30° + N_A \cos 30° + F_B \sin 30° - F_A \sin 30° - W = 0 \quad [1]$

$\xrightarrow{+} \Sigma F_x = 0;\quad P + N_A \sin 30° + F_A \cos 30° - N_B \sin 30° + F_B \cos 30° = 0 \quad [2]$

$\curvearrowleft + \Sigma M_O = 0;\quad F_A(r) + F_B(r) - Pr = 0 \quad [3]$

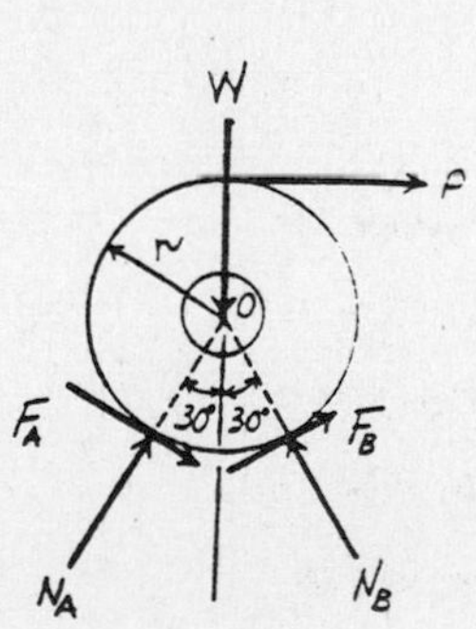

Friction : There are two possible cases of motion. The paper roll slips at points A and B and rotates about point O. Then $F_A = \mu_s N_A = 0.3N_A$ and $F_B = \mu_s N_B = 0.3N_B$. Substituting these value into Eqs [1], [2] and [3] and solving, we have

$N_A = -0.05784W$ (*No Good!*) $\quad N_B = 1.025W \quad P = 0.2901W$

Since a negative value of N_A was obtained, the above assumption is incorrect. Hence, the paper roll will roll over point B. When this happens, $N_A = 0$ thus $F_A = 0$. Substituting these values into Eqs [1], [2] and [3] and solving, we have

$P = 0.268W$ **Ans**

$F_B = 0.2679W \quad N_B = 1.00W$

Since $F_B < (F_B)_{max} = \mu_s N_B = 0.3(1.00W) = 0.300W$, the paper roll will not slip at B but rather it rolls over at B.

8-9. Gravel is stored in a conical pile at a materials yard. If the height of the pile is $h = 10$ m and the coefficient of static friction between the gravel particles is $\mu_s = 0.4$, determine the approximate diameter d of the pile. For the calculation, neglect the "irregularities" of the particles, and first determine the angle θ of the pile by considering one of the particles to be represented by a *block* resting on an inclined plane of angle θ, where $\mu_s = 0.4$.

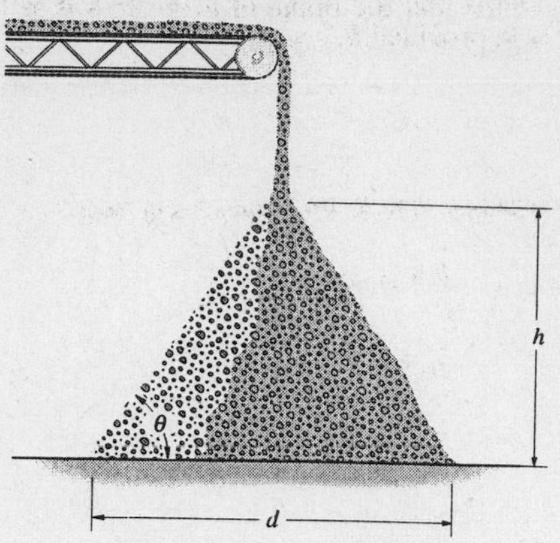

$$+\nearrow \Sigma F_x = 0; \quad 0.4N - W\sin\theta = 0$$

$$+\nwarrow \Sigma F_y = 0; \quad N - W\cos\theta = 0$$

Solving,

$$\theta = \tan^{-1}(0.4) = 21.8^\circ$$

$$10 = \left(\frac{d}{2}\right)\tan 21.8^\circ$$

$$d = 50 \text{ m} \quad \textbf{Ans}$$

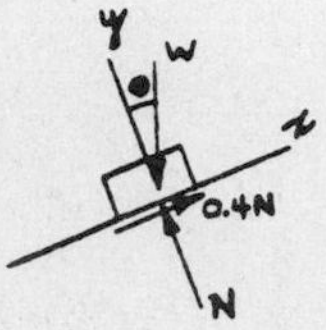

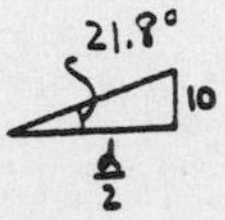

8-10. The block brake is used to stop the wheel from rotating when the wheel is subjected to a couple moment $\mathbf{M}_O$. If the coefficient of static friction between the wheel and the block is μ_s, determine the smallest force P that should be applied.

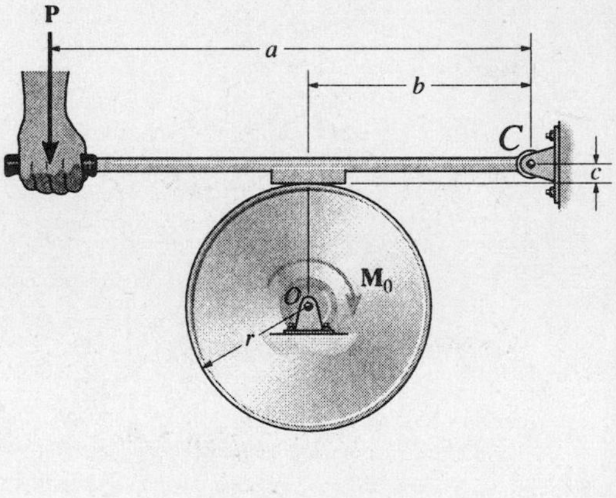

$$\circlearrowleft + \Sigma M_C = 0; \quad Pa - Nb + \mu_s Nc = 0$$

$$N = \frac{Pa}{(b - \mu_s c)}$$

$$\circlearrowleft + \Sigma M_O = 0; \quad \mu_s Nr - M_O = 0$$

$$\mu_s P\left(\frac{a}{b - \mu_s c}\right)r = M_O$$

$$P = \frac{M_O}{\mu_s ra}(b - \mu_s c) \quad \textbf{Ans}$$

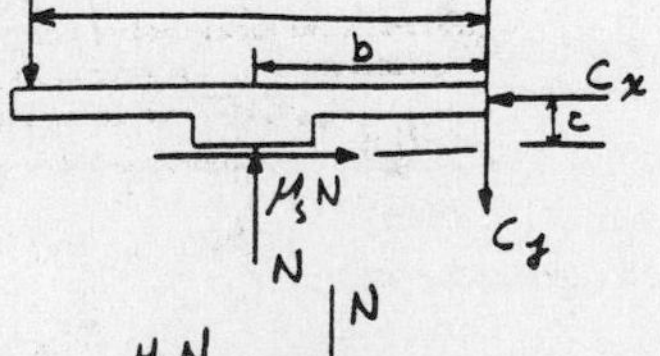

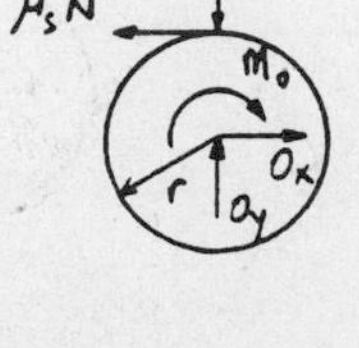

8-11. Show that the brake in Prob. 8-10 is self locking, i.e., $P \leq 0$, provided $b/c \leq \mu_s$.

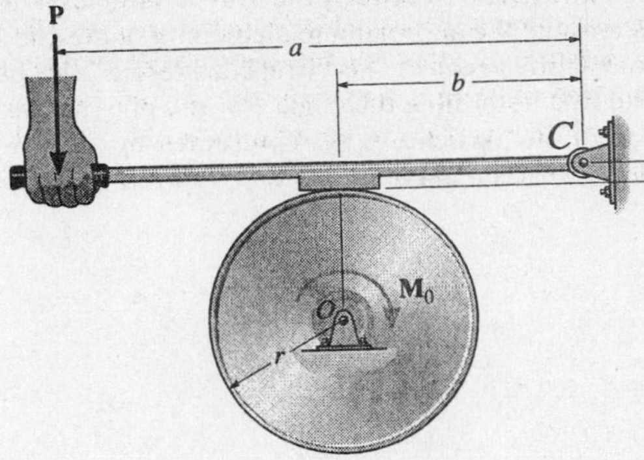

See solution to Prob. 8 - 10. Require $P \leq 0$. Then

$$b \leq \mu_s c$$

$$\mu_s \geq \frac{b}{c} \quad \textbf{Ans}$$

***8-12.** Solve Prob. 8-10 if the couple moment $\mathbf{M}_O$ is applied counterclockwise.

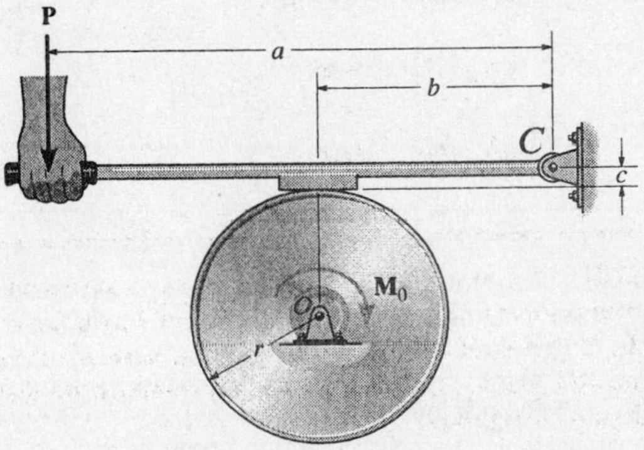

$\circlearrowleft + \Sigma M_C = 0; \quad Pa - Nb - \mu_s Nc = 0$

$$N = \frac{Pa}{(b + \mu_s c)}$$

$\circlearrowleft + \Sigma M_O = 0; \quad \mu_s Nr - M_O = 0$

$$\mu_s P\left(\frac{a}{b + \mu_s c}\right)r = M_O$$

$$P = \frac{M_O}{\mu_s ra}(b + \mu_s c) \quad \textbf{Ans}$$

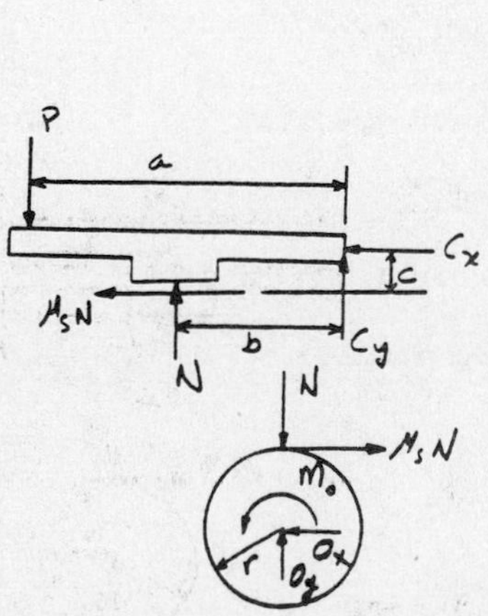

8-13. The coefficients of static and kinetic friction between the drum and brake bar are $\mu_s = 0.4$ and $\mu_k = 0.3$, respectively. If $M = 50$ N · m and $P = 85$ N determine the horizontal and vertical components of reaction at the pin O. Neglect the weight and thickness of the brake. The drum has a mass of 25 kg.

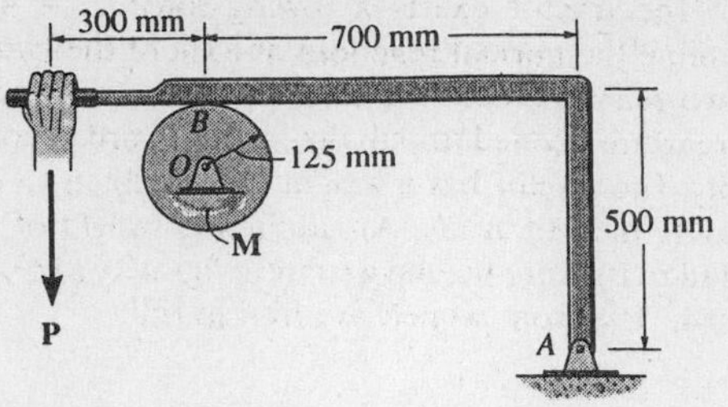

Equations of Equilibrium : From FBD (b),

$$\circlearrowleft + \Sigma M_O = 0 \qquad 50 - F_B(0.125) = 0 \qquad F_B = 400 \text{ N}$$

From FBD (a),

$$\circlearrowleft + \Sigma M_A = 0; \qquad 85(1.00) + 400(0.5) - N_B(0.7) = 0$$
$$N_B = 407.14 \text{ N}$$

Friction : Since $F_B > (F_B)_{max} = \mu_s N_B = 0.4(407.14) = 162.86$ N, the drum slips at point B and rotates. Therefore, the coefficient of kinetic friction should be used. Thus, $F_B = \mu_k N_B = 0.3N_B$.

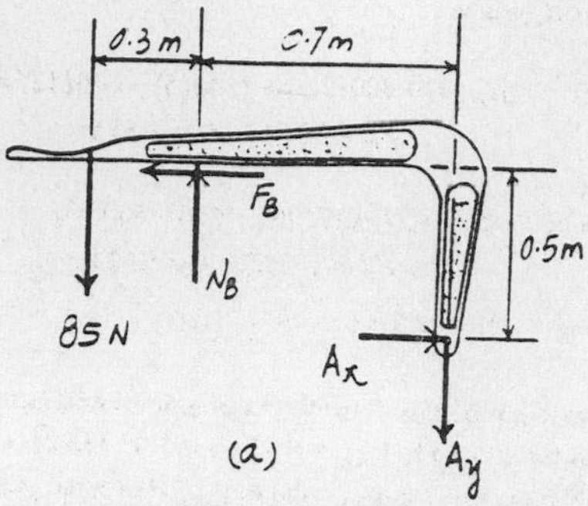

Equations of Equilibrium : From FBD (b),

$$\circlearrowleft + \Sigma M_A = 0; \qquad 85(1.00) + 0.3N_B(0.5) - N_B(0.7) = 0$$
$$N_B = 154.54 \text{ N}$$

From FBD (a),

$$+\uparrow \Sigma F_y = 0; \qquad O_y - 245.25 - 154.54 = 0 \qquad O_y = 400 \text{ N} \qquad \textbf{Ans}$$

$$\xrightarrow{+} \Sigma F_x = 0; \qquad 0.3(154.54) - O_x = 0 \qquad O_x = 46.4 \text{ N} \qquad \textbf{Ans}$$

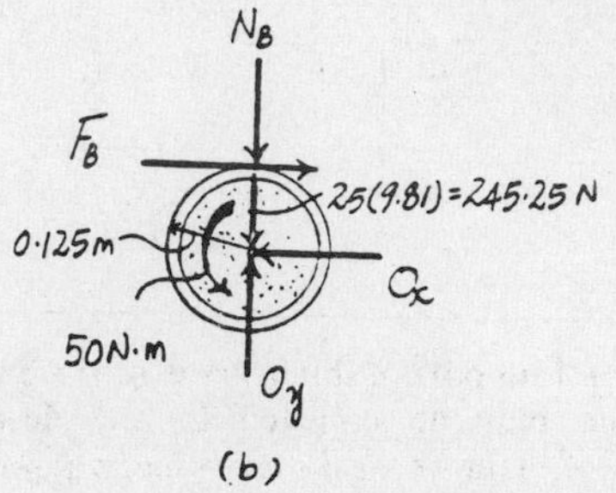

8-14. The coefficient of static friction between the drum and brake bar is $\mu_s = 0.4$. If the moment $M = 35$ N · m, determine the smallest force P that can be applied to the brake bar in order to prevent the drum from rotating. Also determine the horizontal and vertical components of reaction at pin O. Neglect the weight and thickness of the brake. The drum has a mass of 25 kg.

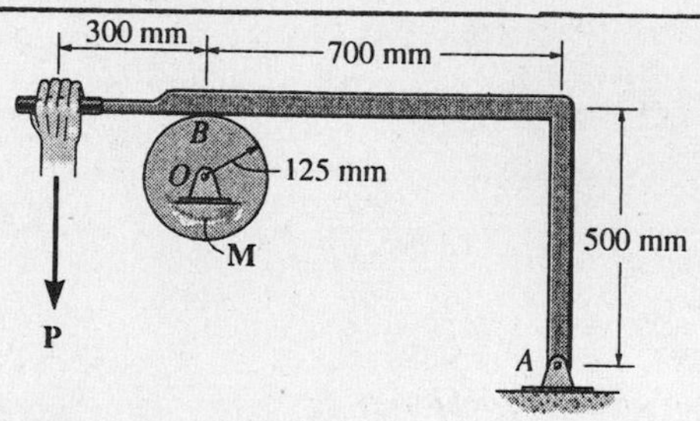

Equations of Equilibrium : From FBD (b),

$$\circlearrowleft + \Sigma M_O = 0 \qquad 35 - F_B(0.125) = 0 \qquad F_B = 280 \text{ N}$$

From FBD (a),

$$\circlearrowleft + \Sigma M_A = 0; \qquad P(1.00) + 280(0.5) - N_B(0.7) = 0$$

Friction : When the drum is on the verge of rotating,

$$F_B = \mu_s N_B$$
$$280 = 0.4N_B$$
$$N_B = 700 \text{ N}$$

Substituting $N_B = 700$ N into Eq. [1] yields

$$P = 350 \text{ N} \qquad \textbf{Ans}$$

Equations of Equilibrium : From FBD (b),

$$+\uparrow \Sigma F_y = 0; \qquad O_y - 245.25 - 700 = 0 \qquad O_y = 945 \text{ N} \qquad \textbf{Ans}$$

$$\xrightarrow{+} \Sigma F_x = 0; \qquad 280 - O_x = 0 \qquad O_x = 280 \text{ N} \qquad \textbf{Ans}$$

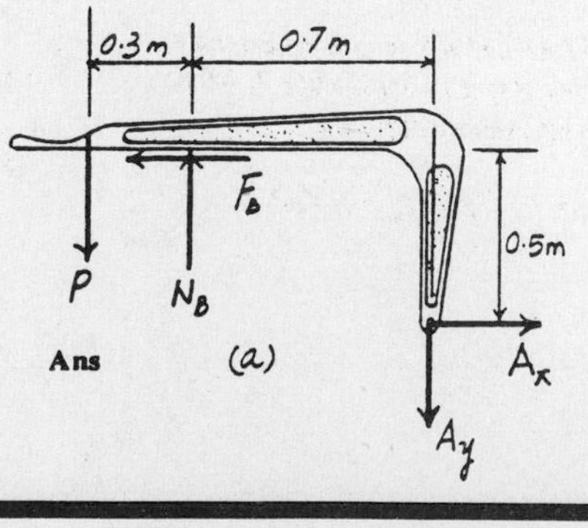

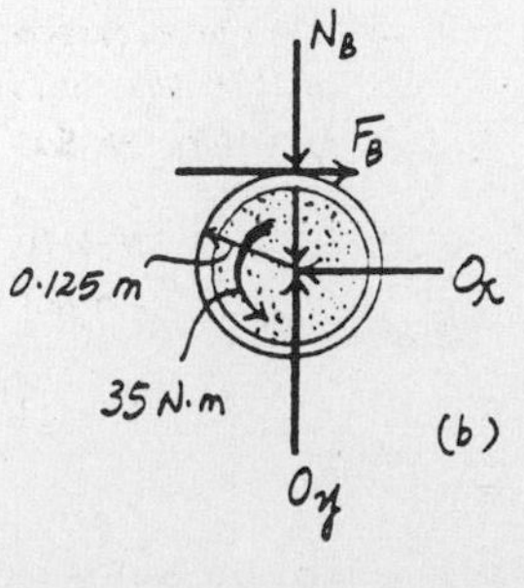

8-15. The tractor exerts a towing force $T = 400$ lb. Determine the normal reactions at each of the two front and two rear tires and the tractive frictional force **F** on each rear tire needed to pull the load forward at constant velocity. The tractor has a weight of 7500 lb and a center of gravity located at G_T. An additional weight of 600 lb is added to its front having a center of gravity at G_A. Take $\mu_s = 0.4$. The front wheels are free to roll.

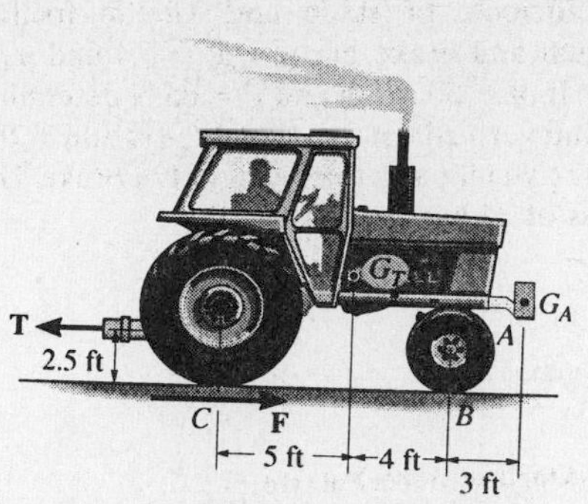

Equations of Equilibrium :

$$\circlearrowleft + \Sigma M_C = 0 \qquad 2N_B(9) + 400(2.5) - 7500(5) - 600(12) = 0$$

$$N_B = 2427.78 \text{ lb} = 2.43 \text{ kip} \qquad \textbf{Ans}$$

$$+\uparrow \Sigma F_y = 0; \qquad 2N_C + 2(2427.78) - 7500 - 600 = 0$$

$$N_C = 1622.22 \text{ lb} = 1.62 \text{ kip} \qquad \textbf{Ans}$$

$$\overset{+}{\rightarrow} \Sigma F_x = 0; \qquad 2F - 400 = 0 \qquad F = 200 \text{ lb} \qquad \textbf{Ans}$$

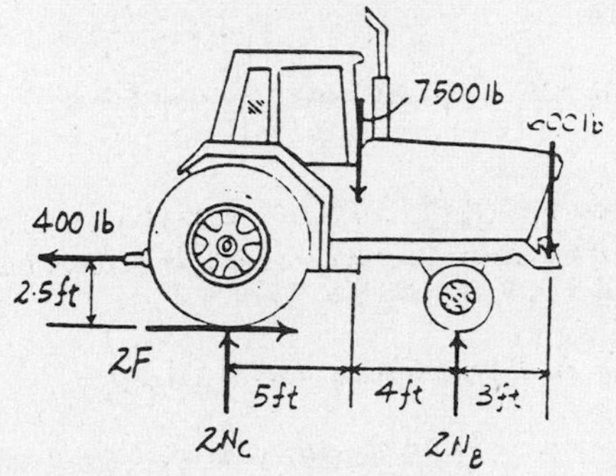

Friction : The maximum friction force that can be developed between each of the rear tires and the ground is $F_{max} = \mu_s N_C = 0.4(1622.22) = 648.89$ lb. Since $F_{max} > F = 200$ lb, the rear tires will not slip. Hence the tractor is capable of towing the 400 lb load.

***8-16.** The left-end support of the beam acts as a collar so that the beam may be adjusted to any desired elevation. Contact with the vertical shaft is made at points A and B. If $\mu_s = 0.6$, determine the smallest distance x a load P may be placed on the beam without causing it to slip. Neglect the weight of the beam.

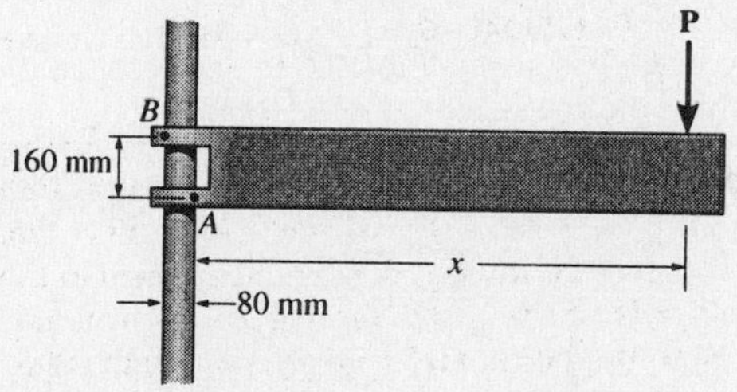

Equations of Equilibrium :

$$\overset{+}{\rightarrow} \Sigma F_x = 0; \qquad N_A - N_B = 0 \qquad N_A = N_B \qquad [1]$$

$$+\uparrow \Sigma F_y = 0; \qquad F_A + F_B - P = 0 \qquad [2]$$

$$\circlearrowleft + \Sigma M_B = 0; \qquad F_A(80) + N_A(160) - p(x + 80) = 0 \qquad [3]$$

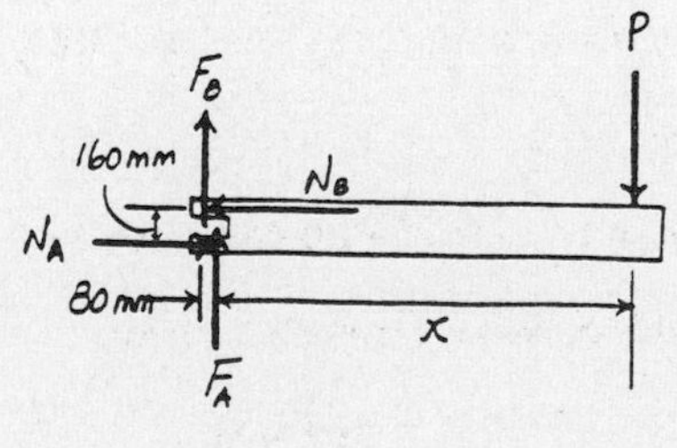

Friction : When the beam is on the verge of sliding along the collar, $F_A = \mu_s N_A = 0.6N_A$ and $F_B = \mu_s N_B = 0.6N_B$. Substituting $F_A = 0.6N_A$ and $F_B = 0.6N_B$ into Eqs. [2] and [3] and solving yields

$$N_A = N_B = 0.8333P \qquad F_A = F_B = 0.500P$$

$$x = 93.3 \text{ mm} \qquad \textbf{Ans}$$

8-17. The drum has a weight of 100 lb and rests on the floor for which the coefficient of static friction is $\mu_s = 0.6$. If $a = 2$ ft and $b = 3$ ft, determine the smallest magnitude of the force **P** that will cause impending motion of the drum.

Assume that the drum tips :

$x = 1$ ft

$\circlearrowleft + \Sigma M_O = 0;\quad 100(1) + P\left(\frac{3}{5}\right)(2) - P\left(\frac{4}{5}\right)(3) = 0$

$P = 83.3$ lb

$\xrightarrow{+} \Sigma F_x = 0;\quad -F + 83.3\left(\frac{4}{5}\right) = 0$

$F = 66.7$ lb

$+\uparrow \Sigma F_y = 0;\quad N - 100 - 83.3\left(\frac{3}{5}\right) = 0$

$N = 150$ lb

$F_{max} = 0.6(150) = 90 \text{ lb} > 66.7$ OK

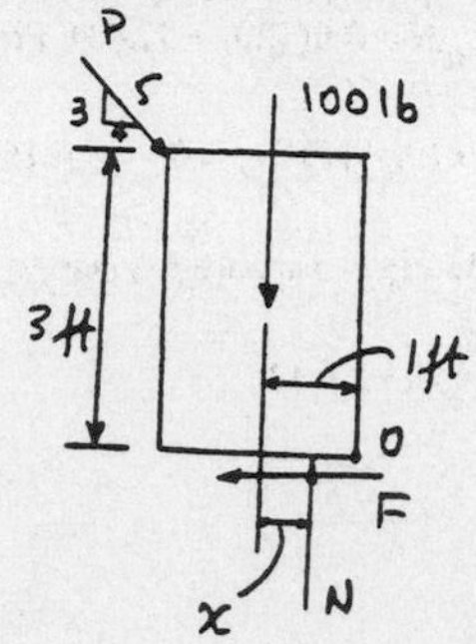

Drum tips as assumed.

$P = 83.3$ lb **Ans**

8-18. The drum has a weight of 100 lb and rests on the floor for which the coefficient of static friction is $\mu_s = 0.5$. If $a = 3$ ft and $b = 4$ ft, determine the smallest magnitude of the force **P** that will cause impending motion of the drum.

Assume that the drum slips :

$F = 0.5N$

$\xrightarrow{+} \Sigma F_x = 0;\quad -0.5N + P\left(\frac{4}{5}\right) = 0$

$+\uparrow \Sigma F_y = 0;\quad -P\left(\frac{3}{5}\right) - 100 + N = 0$

$P = 100$ lb

$N = 160$ lb

$\circlearrowleft + \Sigma M_O = 0;\quad 160(x) + 100\left(\frac{3}{5}\right)(1.5) - 100\left(\frac{4}{5}\right)(4) = 0$

$x = 1.44 \text{ ft} < 1.5 \text{ ft}$ OK

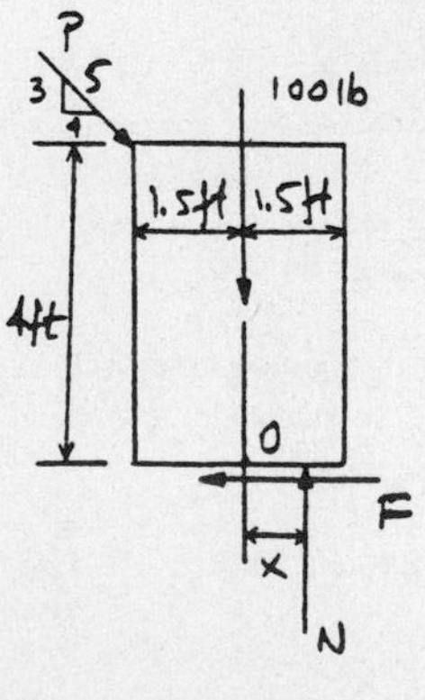

Drum slips as assumed.

$P = 100$ lb **Ans**

8-19. A man attempts to support a stack of books horizontally by applying a compressive force of $F = 120$ N to the ends of the stack with his hands. If each book has a mass of 0.95 kg, determine the greatest number of books that can be supported in the stack. The coefficient of static friction between the man's hands and a book is $(\mu_s)_h = 0.6$ and between any two books is $(\mu_s)_b = 0.4$.

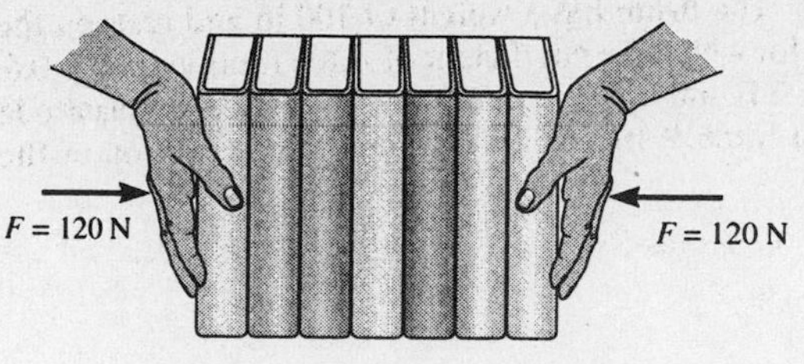

Equations of Equilibrium and Friction : Let n' be the number of books that are on the verge of sliding together between the two books at the edge. Thus, $F_b = (\mu_s)_b N = 0.4(120) = 48.0$ N. From FBD (a),

$$+\uparrow \Sigma F_y = 0; \quad 2(48.0) - n'(0.95)(9.81) = 0 \quad n' = 10.30$$

Let n be the number of books are on the verge of sliding together in the stack between the hands. Thus, $F_h = (\mu_s)_h N = 0.6(120) = 72.0$ N. From FBD (b),

$$+\uparrow \Sigma F_y = 0; \quad 2(72.0) - n(0.95)(9.81) = 0 \quad n = 15.45$$

Thus, the maximum number of books can be supported in stack is

$$n = 10 + 2 = 12 \qquad \textbf{Ans}$$

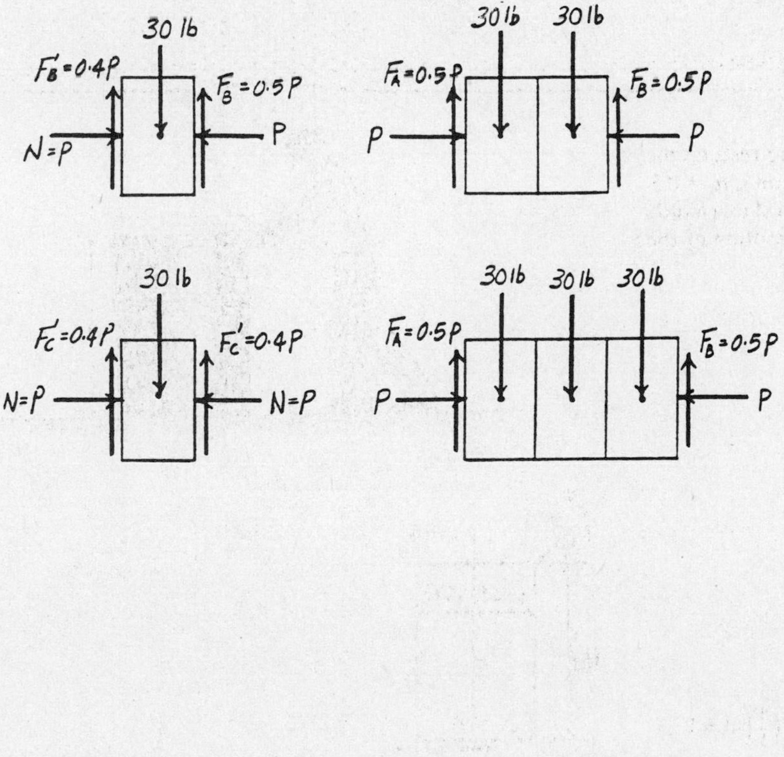

*8-20. The paper towel dispenser carries two rolls of paper. The one in use is called the stub roll A and the other is the fresh roll B. They weigh 2 lb and 5 lb, respectively. If the coefficient of static friction at the points of contact C and D are $(\mu_s)_C = 0.2$ and $(\mu_s)_D = 0.5$, determine the initial vertical force P that must be applied to the paper on the stub roll in order to pull down a sheet. The stub roll is pinned in the center, whereas the fresh roll is not. Neglect friction at the pin.

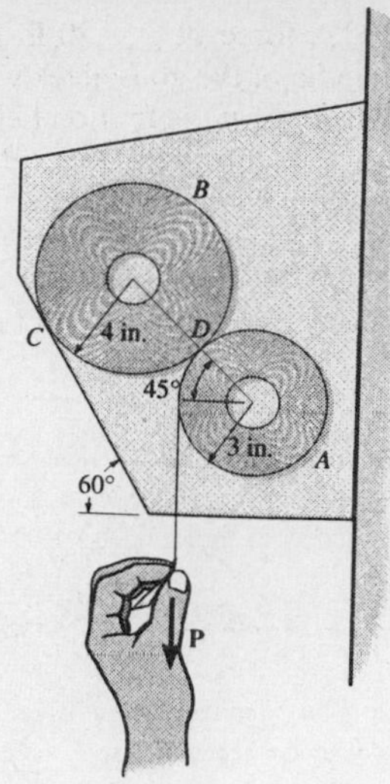

Equations of Equilibrium : From FBD (a),

$$\curvearrowleft + \Sigma M_E = 0; \quad P(3) - F_D(3) = 0 \qquad [1]$$

From FBD (b),

$$\curvearrowleft + \Sigma M_F = 0; \quad F_C(4) - F_D(4) = 0 \qquad [2]$$

$$+\uparrow \Sigma F_y = 0; \quad N_C \sin 30° + N_D \sin 45° - F_C \sin 60° - F_D \sin 45° - 5 = 0 \qquad [3]$$

$$\xrightarrow{+} \Sigma F_x = 0; \quad N_C \cos 30° + F_C \cos 60° - N_D \cos 45° - F_D \cos 45° = 0 \qquad [4]$$

Friction : Assume slipping occurs at point C. Hence, $F_C = \mu_{s\,C} N_C = 0.2N_C$. Substituting this value into Eqs. [1], [2], [3] and [4] and solving we have

$N_D = 5.773$ lb $\quad N_C = 4.951$ lb $\quad F_D = 0.9901$ lb

$P = 0.990$ lb **Ans**

Since $F_D < (F_D)_{max} = (\mu_s)_D N_D = 0.5(5.773) = 2.887$ lb, then slipping does not occur at point D. Therefore, the above assumption is correct.

8-21. Determine the force P that must be applied perpendicular to the handle of the gooseneck wrecking bar in order to develop a normal force of 130 lb at A. The coefficient of static friction between the bar and the wood is $\mu_s = 0.5$. Assume the surface at C is smooth.

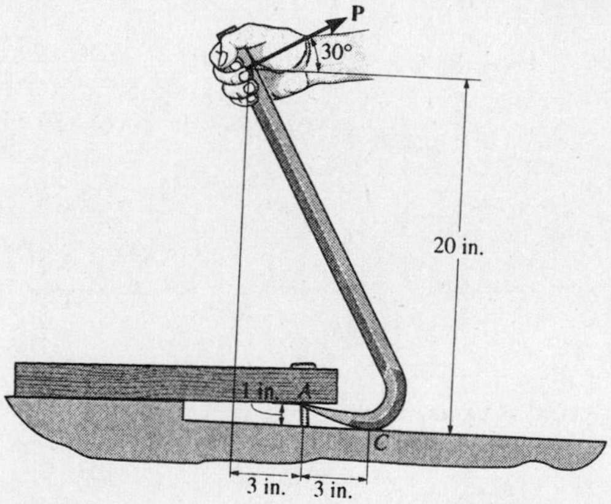

$$\xrightarrow{+} \Sigma F_x = 0; \quad P \cos 30° - F_A = 0$$

$$F_A = 0.8660\,P$$

$$\curvearrowleft + \Sigma M_C = 0; \quad 0.8660\,P\,(1) + 130\,(3) - P \cos 30°\,(20) - P \sin 30°\,(6) = 0$$

$P = 20.0$ lb **Ans**

$F_A = 17.4$ lb

$F_{max} = 0.5\,(130) = 65$ lb > 17.4 lb

The bar will not slip.

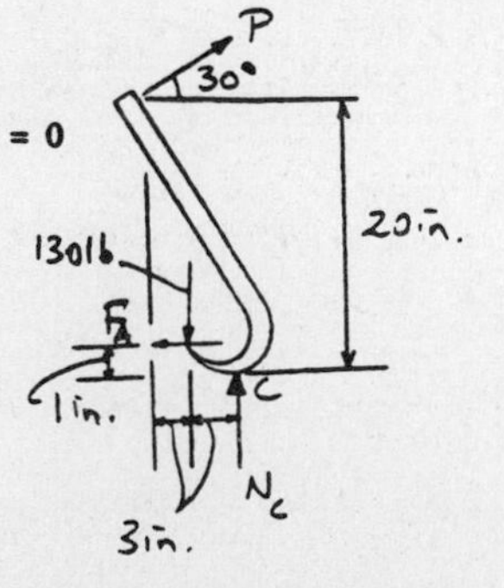

8-22. A force of $P = 20$ lb is applied perpendicular to the handle of the gooseneck wrecking bar as shown. If the coefficient of static friction between the bar and the wood is $\mu_s = 0.5$, determine the normal force of the tines at A on the upper board. Assume the surface at C is smooth.

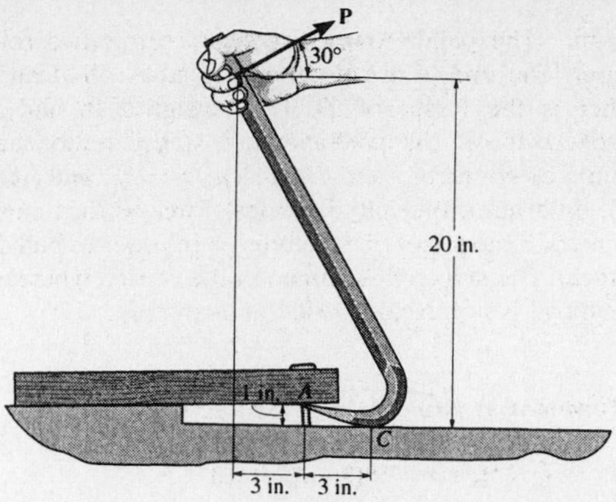

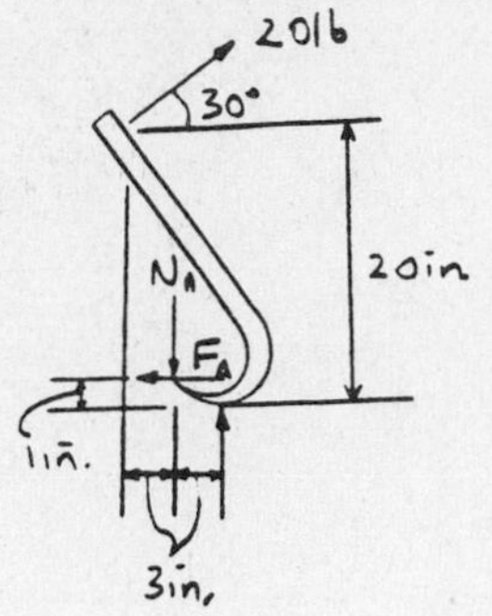

$\xrightarrow{+} \Sigma F_x = 0;\quad 20 \cos 30° - F_A = 0$

$F_A = 17.32$ lb

$\curvearrowleft + \Sigma M_C = 0;\quad N_A(3) + 17.32(1) - 20 \cos 30°(20) - 20 \sin 30°(6) = 0$

$N_A = 129.7 \text{ lb} = 130 \text{ lb}$ **Ans**

$F_{max} = 0.5(129.7) = 64.8 \text{ lb} > 17.32 \text{ lb}$

The bar will not slip.

8-23. The rod has a weight W and rests against the floor and wall for which the coefficients of static friction are μ_A and μ_B, respectively. Determine the smallest value of θ for which the rod will not move.

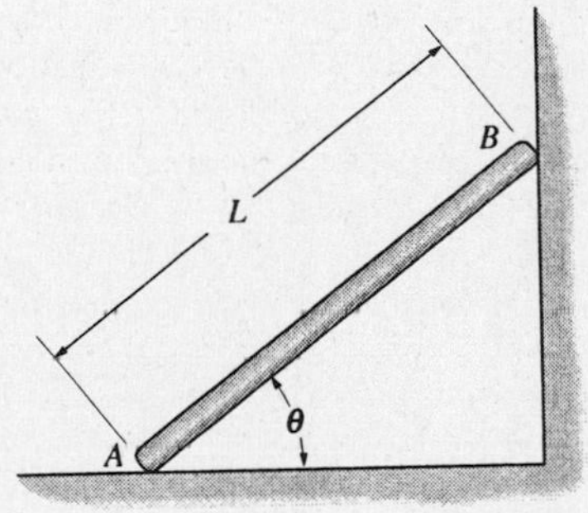

Equations of Equilibrium :

$\xrightarrow{+} \Sigma F_x = 0;\quad F_A - N_B = 0 \qquad [1]$

$+\uparrow \Sigma F_y = 0 \quad N_A + F_B - W = 0 \qquad [2]$

$\curvearrowleft + \Sigma M_A = 0;\quad N_B(L \sin\theta) + F_B(\cos\theta) - W\cos\theta\left(\frac{L}{2}\right) = 0 \qquad [3]$

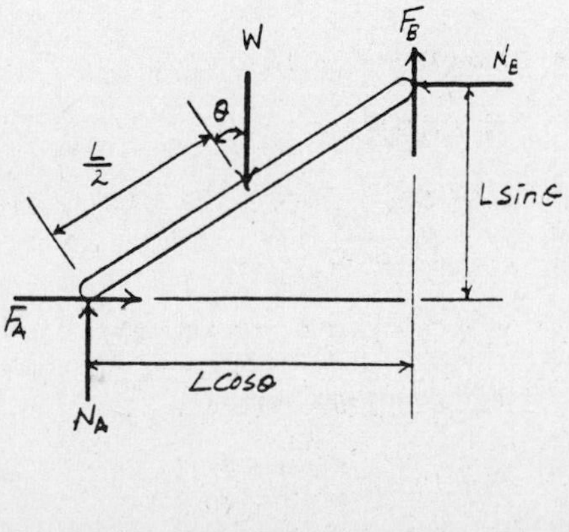

Friction : If the rod is on the verge of moving, slipping will have to occur at points A and B. Hence, $F_A = \mu_A N_A$ and $F_B = \mu_B N_B$. Substituting these values into Eqs. [1], [2] and [3] and solving we have

$$N_A = \frac{W}{1 + \mu_A \mu_B} \qquad N_B = \frac{\mu_A W}{1 + \mu_A \mu_B}$$

$$\theta = \tan^{-1}\left(\frac{1 - \mu_A \mu_B}{2\mu_A}\right)$$ **Ans**

***8-24.** The 5-kg cylinder is suspended from two equal-length cords. The end of each cord is attached to a ring of negligible mass, which passes along a horizontal shaft. If the coefficient of static friction between each ring and the shaft is $\mu_s = 0.5$, determine the greatest distance d by which the rings can be separated and still support the cylinder.

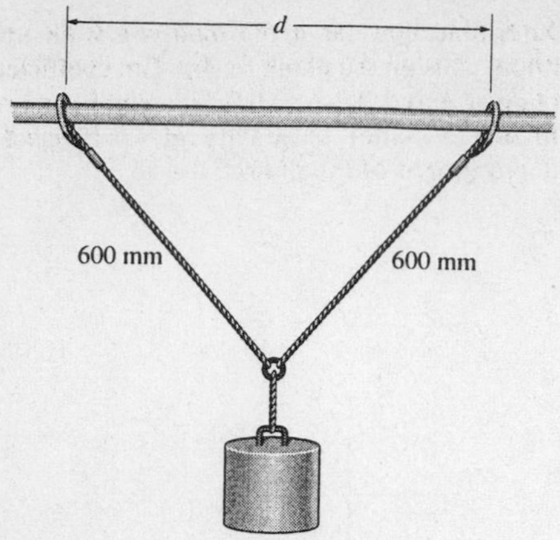

Friction : When the ring is on the verge to sliding along the rod, slipping will have to occur. Hence, $F = \mu N = 0.5N$. From the force diagram (T is the tension developed by the cord)

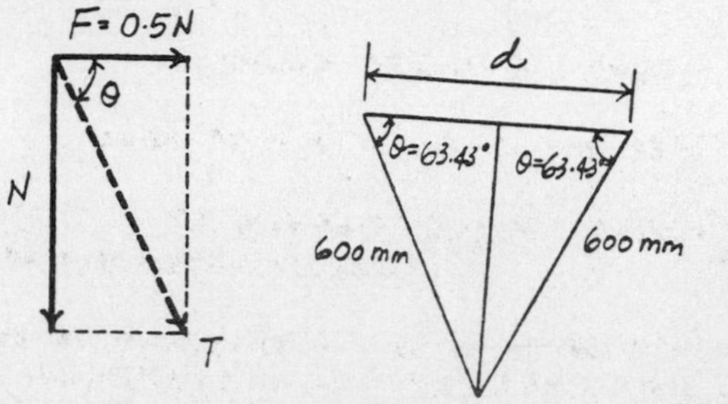

$$\tan\theta = \frac{N}{0.5N} = 2 \qquad \theta = 63.43°$$

Geometry :

$$d = 2(600\cos 63.43°) = 537 \text{ mm} \qquad \textbf{Ans}$$

8-25. The 200-mm uniform rod has a weight W and is placed in a glass as shown. If the smallest angle at which it can lean against the glass without slipping is $\theta = 60°$, determine the coefficient static friction between the glass and rod. Neglect the thickness of the rod.

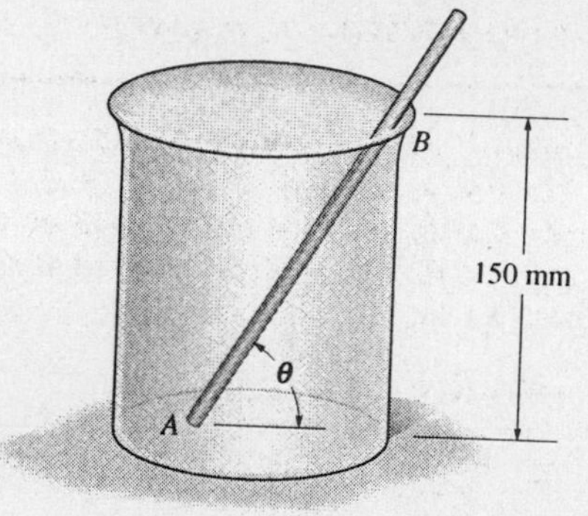

Equations of Equilibrium :

$$\overset{+}{\rightarrow}\Sigma F_x = 0; \qquad F_A + F_B\cos 60° - N_B\cos 30° = 0 \qquad [1]$$

$$+\uparrow\Sigma F_y = 0 \qquad N_A + F_B\sin 60° + N_B\sin 30° - W = 0 \qquad [2]$$

$$\curvearrowleft+\Sigma M_A = 0; \qquad N_B\left(\frac{150}{\sin 60°}\right) - W\cos 60°(100) = 0 \qquad [3]$$

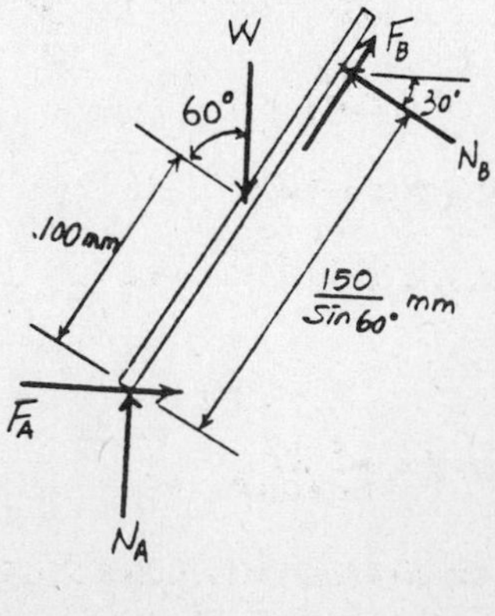

Friction : If the rod is on the verge to move, slipping would have to occur at point A and B. Hence, $F_A = \mu_s N_A$ and $F_B = \mu_s N_B$. Substituting these values into Eqs.[1], [2] and [3] and solving, we have

$$\mu = 0.268 \qquad \textbf{Ans}$$

$$N_B = 0.2887W \qquad N_A = 0.7887W$$

8-26. Determine how far d the man can walk up the plank without causing the plank to slip. The coefficient of static friction at A and B is $\mu_s = 0.3$. The man has a weight of 200 lb and a center of gravity at G. Neglect the thickness and weight of the plank.

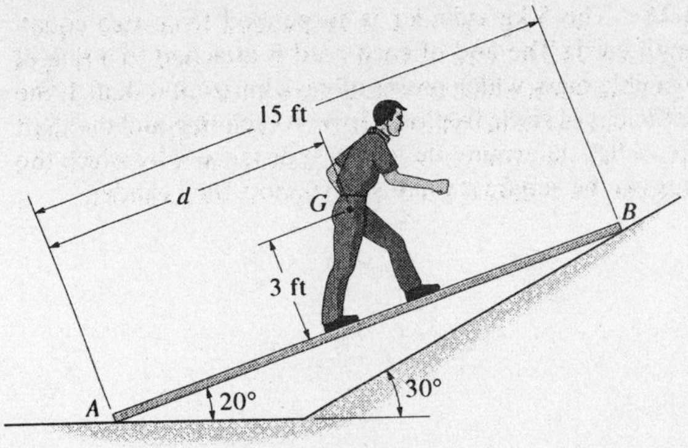

Equations of Equilibrium :

$$\xrightarrow{+} \Sigma F_x = 0; \quad F_A + F_B \cos 30° - N_B \cos 60° = 0 \qquad [1]$$

$$+\uparrow \Sigma F_y = 0; \quad N_A + F_B \sin 30° + N_B \sin 60° - 200 = 0 \qquad [2]$$

$$+\Sigma M_A = 0; \quad N_B \cos 10°(15) + F_B \sin 10°(15) + 200\sin 20°(3) - 200\cos 20°(d) = 0 \qquad [3]$$

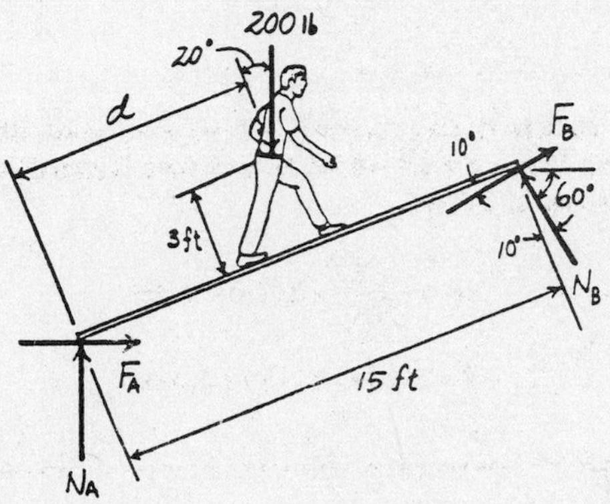

Friction : If the plank is on the verge of moving, slipping would have to occur at point A and B. Hence, $F_A = \mu N_A = 0.3N_A$ and $F_B = \mu N_B = 0.3N_B$. Substituting these values into Eqs. [1], [2] and [3] and solving, we have

$$d = 10.2 \text{ ft} \qquad \textbf{Ans}$$

$$N_B = 110.09 \text{ lb} \qquad N_A = 88.14 \text{ lb}$$

■8-27. The uniform pole has a weight W and is lowered slowly from a vertical position $\theta = 90°$ toward the horizontal using a cable AB. If the coefficient of static friction is $\mu_s = 0.3$ at C, determine the angle θ at which the pole will start to slip.

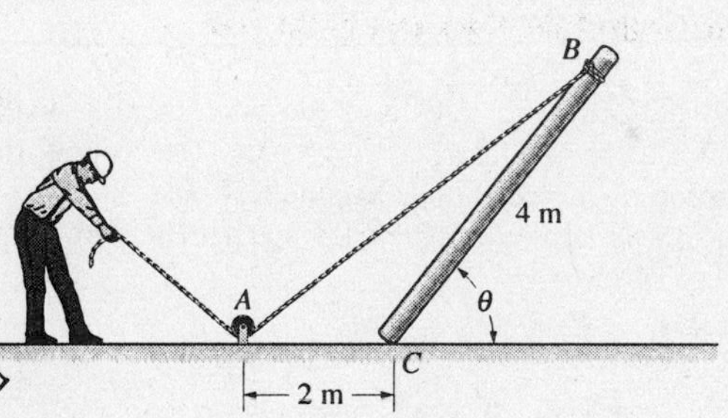

$$+\Sigma M_C = 0; \quad -W(2)\cos\theta + T\sin\phi\,(2) = 0$$

$$T = \frac{W\cos\theta}{\sin\phi}$$

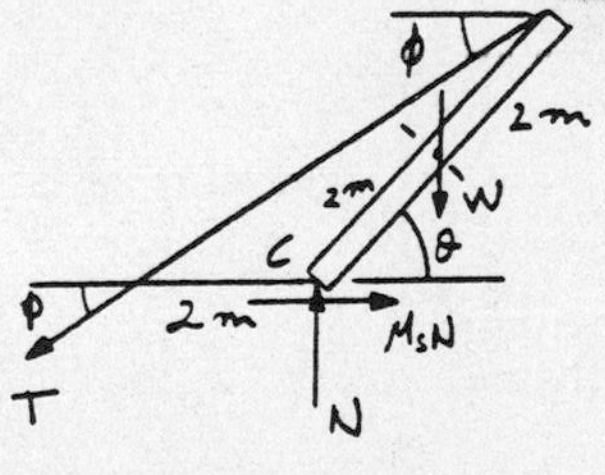

$$\xrightarrow{+} \Sigma F_x = 0; \quad \mu_s N - T\cos\phi = 0$$

$$\mu_s N = \frac{W\cos\theta}{\tan\phi}$$

$$+\uparrow \Sigma F_y = 0; \quad N - W - T\sin\phi = 0$$

$$N = W(1 + \cos\theta)$$

$$\mu_s (1 + \cos\theta)\tan\phi = \cos\theta$$

From geometry

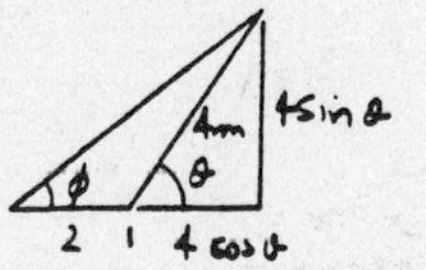

$$\tan\phi = \frac{4\sin\theta}{2 + 4\cos\theta}$$

$$4\mu_s \sin\theta(1 + \cos\theta) = \cos\theta(2 + 4\cos\theta)$$

Set $\mu_s = 0.3$, solving for θ,

$$\theta = 65.2° \qquad \textbf{Ans}$$

***8-28.** A 35-kg disk rests on an inclined surface for which $\mu_s = 0.2$. Determine the maximum vertical force **P** that may be applied to link AB without causing the disk to slip at C.

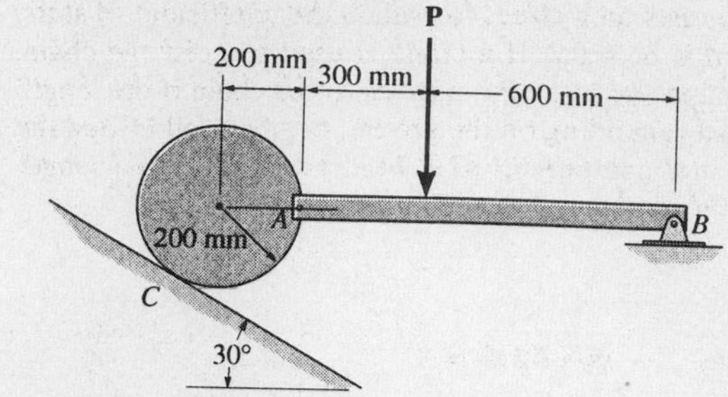

Equations of Equilibrium : From FBD (a),

$$\curvearrowleft + \Sigma M_B = 0; \quad P(600) - A_y(900) = 0 \quad A_y = 0.6667P$$

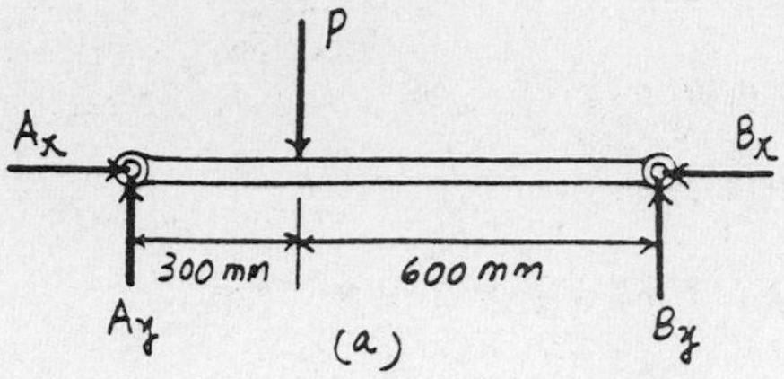

From FBD (b),

$$+\uparrow \Sigma F_y = 0 \quad N_C \sin 60° - F_C \sin 30° - 0.6667P - 343.35 = 0 \qquad [1]$$

$$\curvearrowleft + \Sigma M_O = 0; \quad F_C(200) - 0.6667P(200) = 0 \qquad [2]$$

Friction : If the disk is on the verge of moving, slipping would have to occur at point C. Hence, $F_C = \mu_s N_C = 0.2N_C$. Substituting this value into Eqs.[1] and [2] and solving, we have

$$P = 182 \text{ N} \qquad \textbf{Ans}$$
$$N_C = 606.60 \text{ N}$$

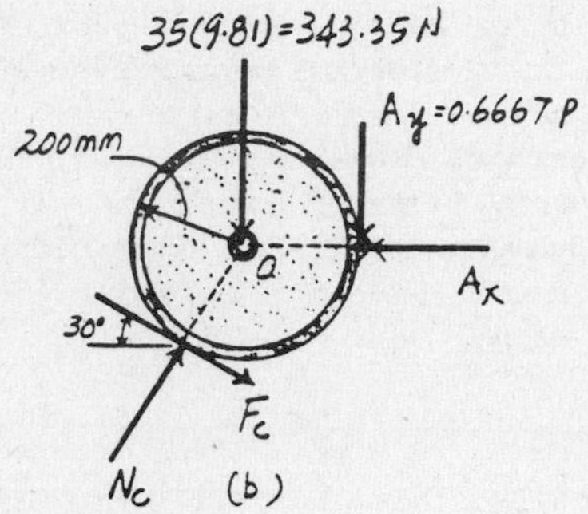

8-29. The crate has a W and the coefficient of static friction at the surface is $\mu_s = 0.3$. Determine the orientation of the cord and the smallest possible force **P** that has to be applied to the cord so that the crate is on the verge of moving.

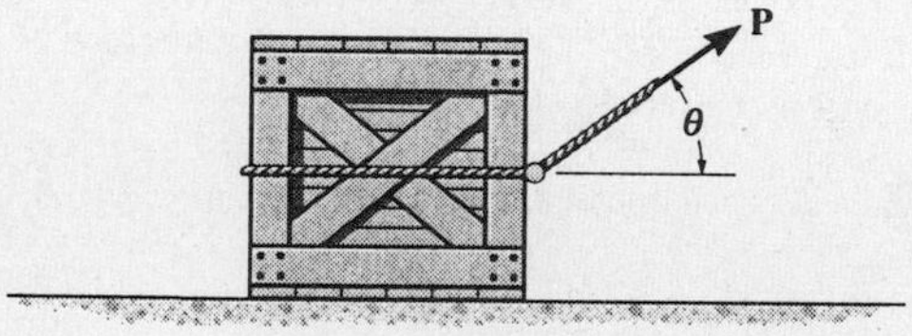

Equations of Equilibrium :

$$+\uparrow \Sigma F_y = 0; \quad N + P\sin\theta - W = 0 \qquad [1]$$

$$\xrightarrow{+} \Sigma F_x = 0; \quad P\cos\theta - F = 0 \qquad [2]$$

Friction : If the crate is on the verge of moving, slipping will have to occur. Hence, $F = \mu_s N = 0.3N$. Substituting this value into Eqs.[1] and [2] and solving, we have

$$P = \frac{0.3W}{\cos\theta + 0.3\sin\theta} \qquad N = \frac{W\cos\theta}{\cos\theta + 0.3\sin\theta}$$

In order to obtain the minimum P, $\frac{dP}{d\theta} = 0$.

$$\frac{dP}{d\theta} = 0.3W\left[\frac{\sin\theta - 0.3\cos\theta}{(\cos\theta + 0.3\sin\theta)^2}\right] = 0$$
$$\sin\theta - 0.3\cos\theta = 0$$
$$\theta = 16.70° = 16.7° \qquad \textbf{Ans}$$

$$\frac{d^2P}{d\theta^2} = 0.3W\left[\frac{(\cos\theta + 0.3\sin\theta)^2 + 2(\sin\theta - 0.3\cos\theta)^2}{(\cos\theta + 0.3\sin\theta)^3}\right]$$

At $\theta = 16.70°$, $\frac{d^2P}{d\theta^2} = 0.2873W > 0$. Thus, $\theta = 16.70°$ will result in a minimun P.

$$P = \frac{0.3W}{\cos 16.70° + 0.3\sin 16.70°} = 0.287W \qquad \textbf{Ans}$$

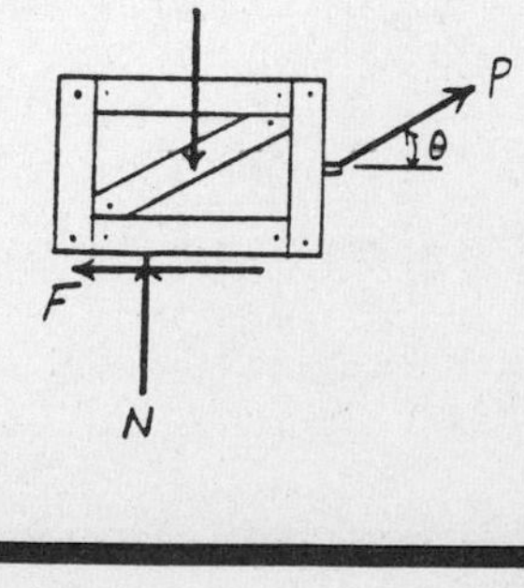

8-30. A chain having a length of 20 ft and weight of 8 lb/ft rests on a street for which the coefficient of static friction is $\mu_s = 0.2$. If a crane is used to hoist the chain, determine the force P it applies to the chain if the length of chain remaining on the ground begins to slip when the horizontal component of P becomes 10 lb. What length of chain remains on the ground?

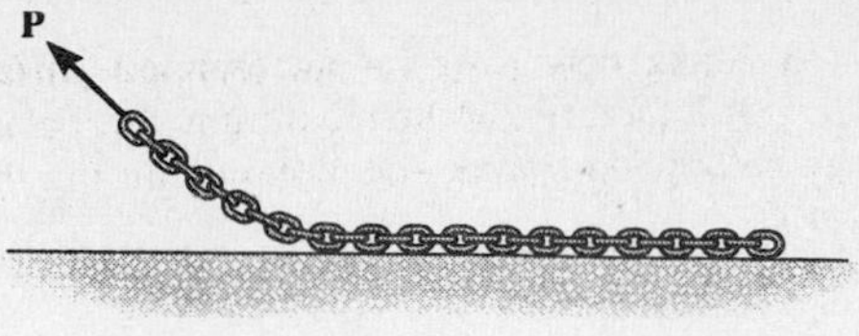

$\xrightarrow{+} \Sigma F_x = 0;\quad -10 + 0.2N_C = 0$

$N_C = 50 \text{ lb}$

$+\uparrow \Sigma F_y = 0;\quad P_y - 160 + 50 = 0$

$P_y = 110 \text{ lb}$

$P = \sqrt{(10)^2 + (110)^2} = 110 \text{ lb}$ **Ans**

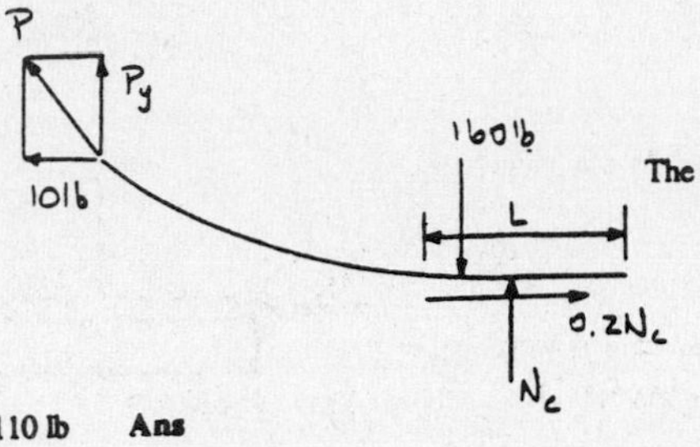

The length on the ground is supported by $N_C = 50$ lb, thus

$L = \frac{50}{8} = 6.25 \text{ ft}$ **Ans**

8-31. The friction pawl is pinned at A and rests against the wheel at B. It allows freedom of movement when the wheel is rotating counterclockwise about C. Clockwise rotation is prevented due to friction of the pawl which tends to bind the wheel. If $(\mu_s)_B = 0.6$, determine the design angle θ which will prevent clockwise motion for any value of applied moment M. *Hint:* Neglect the weight of the pawl so that it becomes a two-force member.

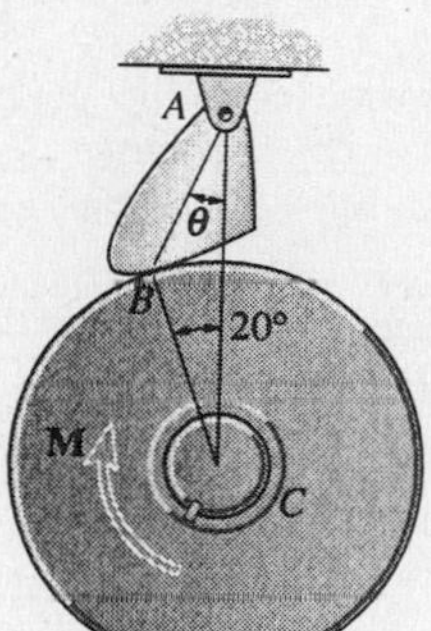

Friction : When the wheel is on the verge of rotating, slipping would have to occur . Hence, $F_B = \mu N_B = 0.6N_B$. From the force diagram (F_{AB} is the force developed in the two force member AB)

$$\tan(20° + \theta) = \frac{0.6N_B}{N_B} = 0.6$$

$\theta = 11.0°$ **Ans**

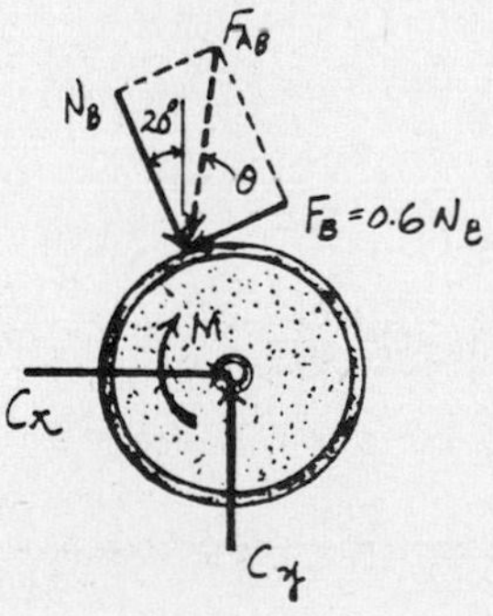

***8-32.** The semicylinder of mass m and radius r lies on the rough inclined plane for which $\phi = 10°$ and the coefficient of static friction is $\mu_s = 0.3$. Determine if the semicylinder slides down the plane, and if not, find the angle of tip θ of its base AB.

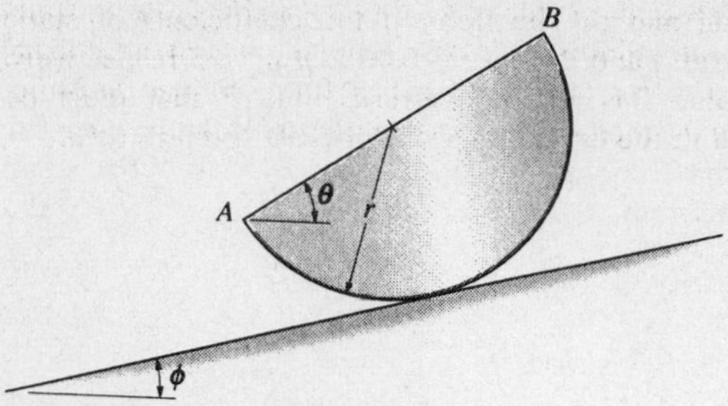

Equations of Equilibrium :

$$\curvearrowleft + \Sigma M_O = 0; \quad F(r) - 9.81m\sin\theta\left(\frac{4r}{3\pi}\right) = 0 \qquad [1]$$

$$\overset{+}{\rightarrow} \Sigma F_x = 0; \quad F\cos 10° - N\sin 10° = 0 \qquad [2]$$

$$+\uparrow \Sigma F_y = 0 \quad F\sin 10° + N\cos 10° - 9.81m = 0 \qquad [3]$$

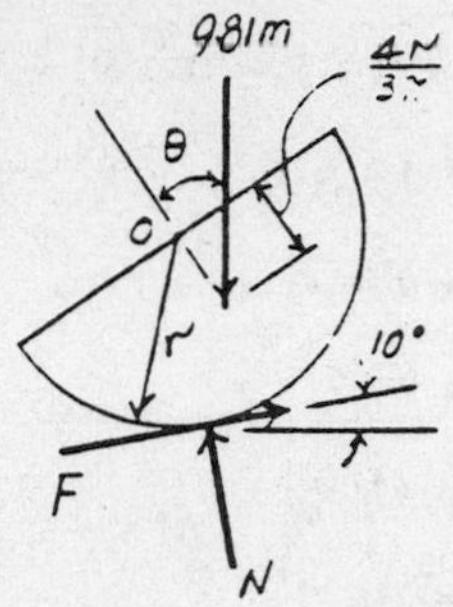

Solving Eqs. [1], [2] and [3] yields

$$N = 9.661m \qquad F = 1.703m$$
$$\theta = 24.2° \qquad \textbf{Ans}$$

Friction : The maximum friction force that can be developed between the semicylinder and the inclined plane is $(F)_{max} = \mu N = 0.3(9.661m) = 2.898m$. Since $F_{max} > F = 1.703m$, **the semicylinder will not slide down the plane.** **Ans**

8-33. The semicylinder of mass m and radius r lies on the rough inclined plane. If the inclination $\phi = 15°$, determine the smallest coefficient of static friction which will prevent the semicylinder from slipping.

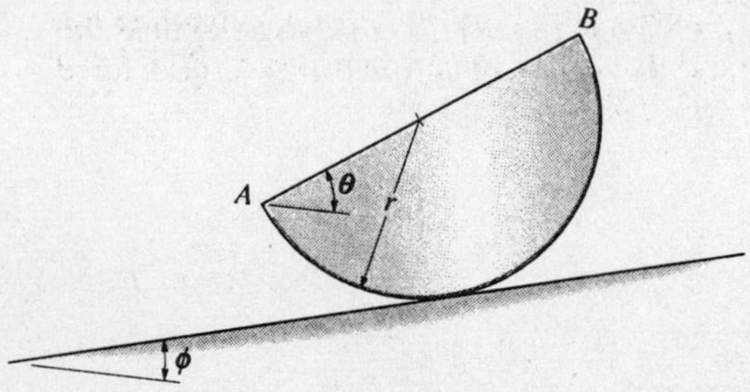

Equations of Equilibrium :

$$\nearrow + \Sigma F_{x'} = 0; \quad F - 9.81m\sin 15° = 0 \qquad F = 2.539m$$

$$\nwarrow + \Sigma F_{y'} = 0; \quad N - 9.81m\cos 15° = 0 \qquad N = 9.476m$$

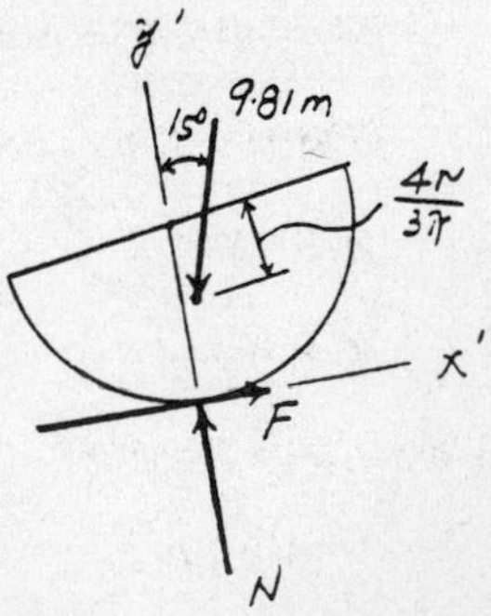

Friction : If the semicylinder is on the verge of moving, slipping would have to occur. Hence,

$$F = \mu_s N$$
$$2.539m = \mu_s (9.476m)$$

$$\mu_s = 0.268 \qquad \textbf{Ans}$$

8-34. The spool has a mass of 200 kg and rests against the wall and on the floor. If the coefficients of static friction at A and B are $\mu_A = 0.4$ and $\mu_B = 0.5$, respectively, determine the smallest vertical force P that must be applied to the cable that will cause the spool to turn.

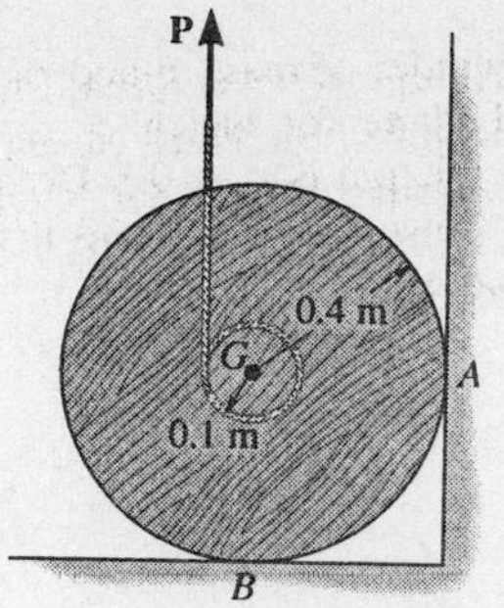

$\xrightarrow{+}\Sigma F_x = 0;$ $F_B - N_A = 0$

$+\uparrow \Sigma F_y = 0;$ $N_B + F_A + P - 200(9.81) = 0$

$\circlearrowleft + \Sigma M_O = 0;$ $F_A(0.4) + F_B(0.4) - P(0.1) = 0$

$F = \mu N;$ $F_A = 0.4 N_A$

$F_B = 0.5 N_B$

$N_B = 490.5 \text{ N}$

$N_A = 245.3 \text{ N}$

$P = 1.37 \text{ kN}$ **Ans**

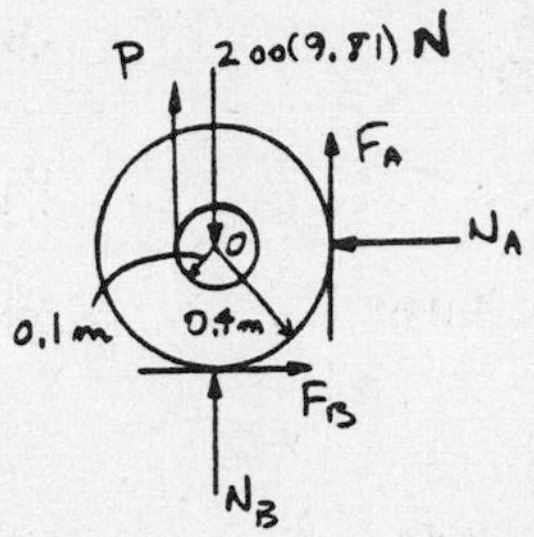

8-35. The spool has a mass of 200 kg and rests against the wall and on the floor. If the coefficient of static friction at B is $\mu_B = 0.3$ and the wall is smooth, determine the friction force developed at B when the vertical force applied to the cable is $P = 800$ N.

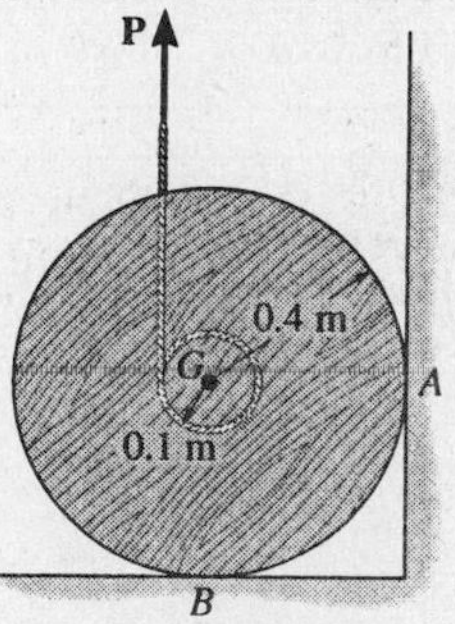

$\xrightarrow{+}\Sigma F_x = 0;$ $F_B - N_A = 0$

$+\uparrow \Sigma F_y = 0;$ $800 - 200(9.81) + N_B = 0$

$\circlearrowleft + \Sigma M_O = 0;$ $-800(0.1) + F_B(0.4) = 0$

$F_B = 200 \text{ N}$

$N_B = 1162 \text{ N}$

$(F_B)_{max} = 0.3(1162) = 348.6 \text{ N} > 200 \text{ N}$

Thus, $F_B = 200 \text{ N}$ **Ans**

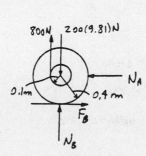

***8-36.** The 80-lb boy stands on the beam and pulls on the cord with a force large enough to just cause him to slip. If $(\mu_s)_D = 0.4$ between his shoes and the beam, determine the reactions at A and B. The beam is uniform and has a weight of 100 lb. Neglect the size of the pulleys and the thickness of the beam.

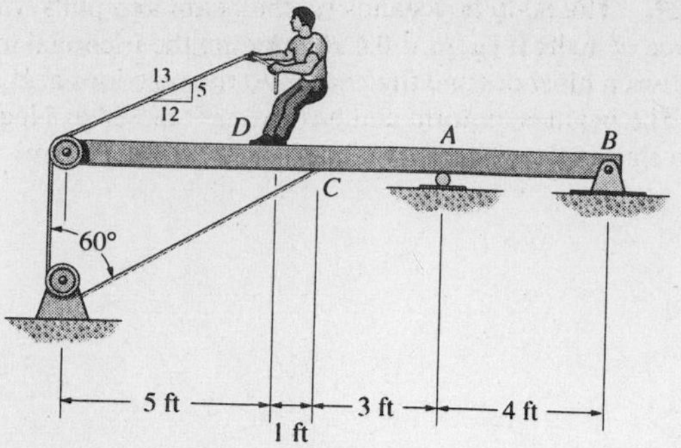

Equations of Equilibrium and Friction : When the boy is on the verge to slipping, then $F_D = (\mu_s)_D N_D = 0.4N_D$. From FBD (a),

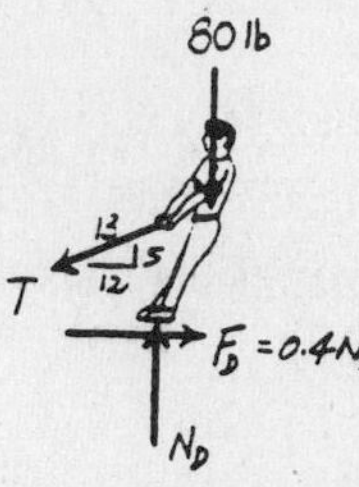

(a)

$$+\uparrow \Sigma F_y = 0; \quad N_D - T\left(\frac{5}{13}\right) - 80 = 0 \qquad [1]$$

$$\xrightarrow{+} \Sigma F_x = 0; \quad 0.4N_D - T\left(\frac{12}{13}\right) = 0 \qquad [2]$$

Solving Eqs. [1] and [2] yields

$$T = 41.6 \text{ lb} \qquad N_D = 96.0 \text{ lb}$$

Hence, $F_D = 0.4(96.0) = 38.4$ lb. From FBD (b),

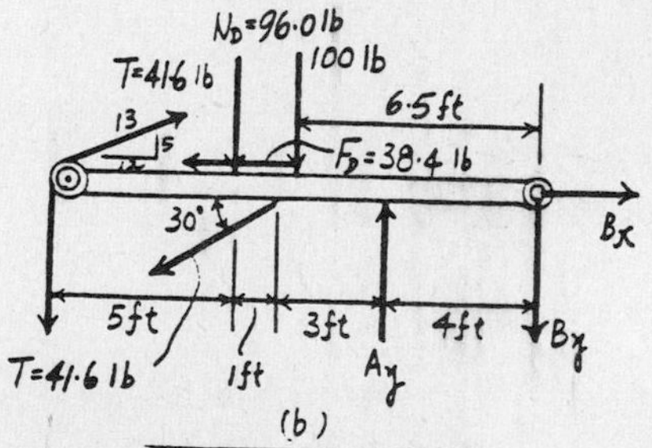

(b)

$$\curvearrowleft + \Sigma M_B = 0; \quad 100(6.5) + 96.0(8) - 41.6\left(\frac{5}{13}\right)(13)$$
$$+ 41.6(13) + 41.6\sin 30°(7) - A_y(4) = 0$$
$$A_y = 474.1 \text{ lb} = 474 \text{ lb} \qquad \textbf{Ans}$$

$$\xrightarrow{+} \Sigma F_x = 0; \quad B_x + 41.6\left(\frac{12}{13}\right) - 38.4 - 41.6\cos 30° = 0$$
$$B_x = 36.0 \text{ lb} \qquad \textbf{Ans}$$

$$+\uparrow \Sigma F_x = 0; \quad 474.1 + 41.6\left(\frac{5}{13}\right) - 41.6$$
$$-41.6\sin 30° - 96.0 - 100 - B_y = 0$$
$$B_y = 231.7 \text{ lb} = 232 \text{ lb} \qquad \textbf{Ans}$$

8-37. The 80-lb boy stands on the beam and pulls with a force of 40 lb. If $(\mu_s)_D = 0.4$, determine the frictional force between his shoes and the beam and the reactions at A and B. The beam is uniform and has a weight of 100 lb. Neglect the size of the pulleys and the thickness of the beam.

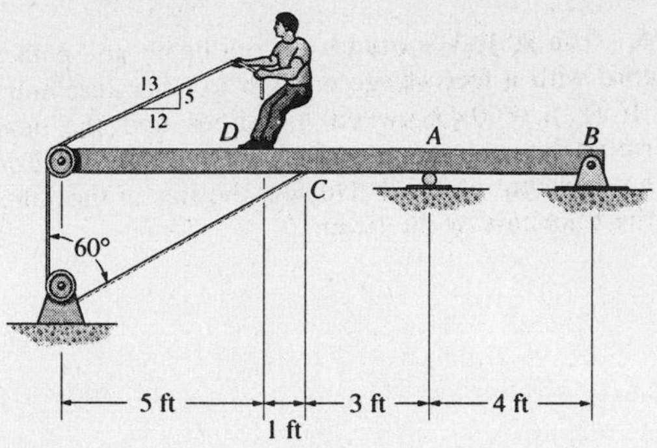

***Equations of Equilibrium and Friction*:** From FBD (a).

$+\uparrow \Sigma F_y = 0;\quad N_D - 40\left(\frac{5}{13}\right) - 80 = 0 \quad N_D = 95.38 \text{ lb}$

$\xrightarrow{+} \Sigma F_x = 0;\quad F_D - 40\left(\frac{12}{13}\right) = 0 \quad F_D = 36.92 \text{ lb}$

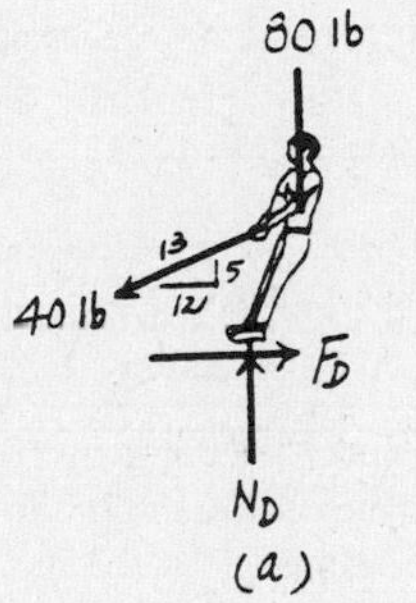

Since $(F_D)_{max} = (\mu_s)N_D = 0.4(95.38) = 38.15 \text{ lb} > F_D$, then the boy does not slip. Therefore, the friction force developed is

$F_D = 36.92 \text{ lb} = 36.9 \text{ lb}$ **Ans**

From FBD (b).

$\circlearrowleft + \Sigma M_B = 0;\quad 100(6.5) + 95.38(8) - 40\left(\frac{5}{13}\right)(13)$
$+ 40(13) + 40\sin 30°(7) - A_y(4) = 0$
$A_y = 468.27 \text{ lb} = 468 \text{ lb}$ **Ans**

$\xrightarrow{+} \Sigma F_x = 0;\quad B_x + 40\left(\frac{12}{13}\right) - 36.92 - 40\cos 30° = 0$
$B_x = 34.64 \text{ lb} = 34.6 \text{ lb}$ **Ans**

$+\uparrow \Sigma F_x = 0;\quad 468.27 + 40\left(\frac{5}{13}\right) - 40$
$- 40\sin 30° - 95.38 - 100 - B_y = 0$
$B_y = 228.27 \text{ lb} = 228 \text{ lb}$ **Ans**

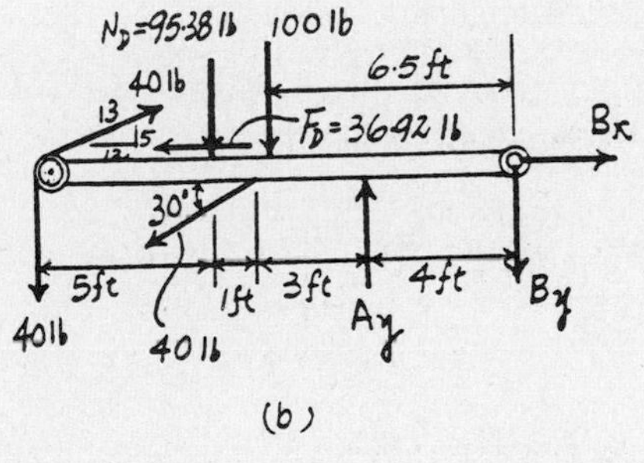

8-38. Two blocks A and B have a weight of 10 lb and 6 lb, respectively. They are resting on the incline for which the coefficients of static friction are $\mu_A = 0.15$ and $\mu_B = 0.25$. Determine the incline angle θ for which both blocks begin to slide. Also find the required stretch or compression in the connecting spring for this to occur. The spring has a stiffness of $k = 2$ lb/ft.

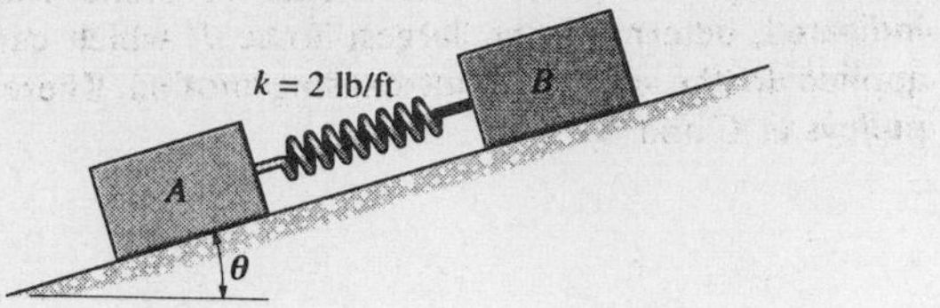

Equations of Equilibrium : Using the spring force formula, $F_{sp} = kx = 2x$. From FBD (a),

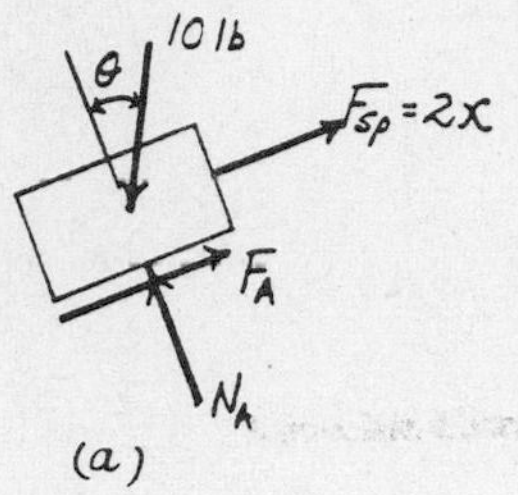

$$+\nearrow \Sigma F_{x'} = 0; \quad 2x + F_A - 10\sin\theta = 0 \qquad [1]$$

$$+\nwarrow \Sigma F_{y'} = 0; \quad N_A - 10\cos\theta = 0 \qquad [2]$$

From FBD (b),

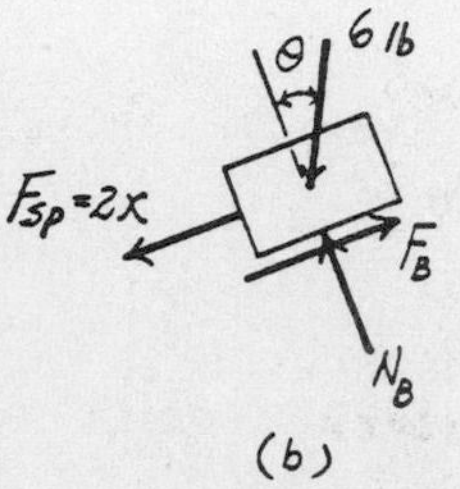

$$+\nearrow \Sigma F_{x'} = 0; \quad F_B - 2x - 6\sin\theta = 0 \qquad [3]$$

$$+\nwarrow \Sigma F_{y'} = 0; \quad N_B - 6\cos\theta = 0 \qquad [4]$$

Friction : If block A and B are on the verge to move, slipping would have to occur at point A and B. Hence, $F_A = \mu_{sA} N_A = 0.15 N_A$ and $F_B = \mu_{sB} N_B = 0.25 N_B$. Substituting these values into Eqs.[1], [2], [3] and [4] and solving, we have

$$\theta = 10.6^\circ \qquad x = 0.184 \text{ ft} \qquad \textbf{Ans}$$

$$N_A = 9.829 \text{ lb} \qquad N_B = 5.897 \text{ lb}$$

8-39. Two blocks A and B have a weight of 10 lb and 6 lb, respectively. They are resting on the incline for which the coefficients of static friction are $\mu_A = 0.15$ and $\mu_B = 0.25$. Determine the angle θ which will cause motion of one of the blocks. What is the friction force under each of the blocks when this occurs? The spring has a stiffness of $k = 2$ lb/ft and is originally unstretched.

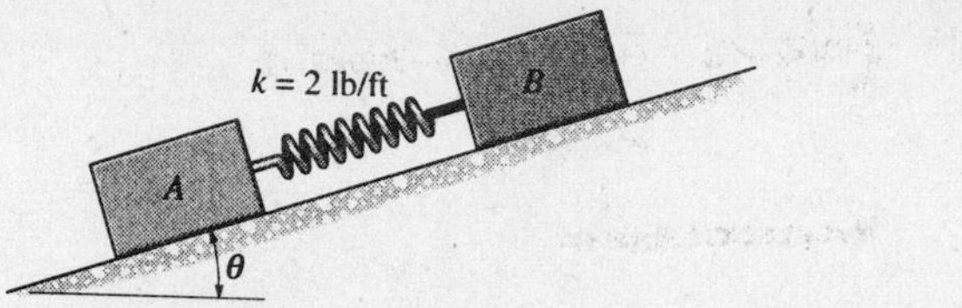

Equations of Equilibrium : Since Block A and B is either not moving or on the verge of moving, the spring force $F_{sp} = 0$. From FBD (a),

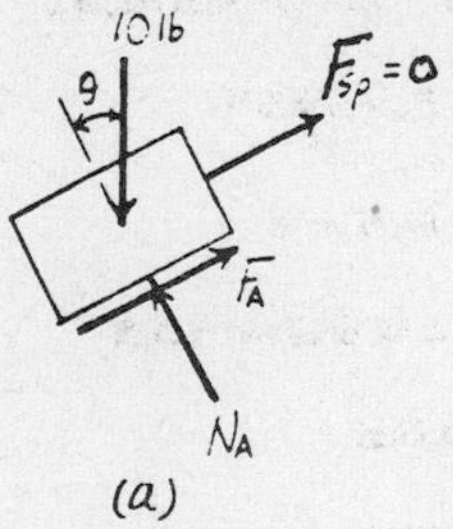

$$+\nearrow \Sigma F_{x'} = 0; \quad F_A - 10\sin\theta = 0 \qquad [1]$$

$$+\nwarrow \Sigma F_{y'} = 0; \quad N_A - 10\cos\theta = 0 \qquad [2]$$

From FBD (b),

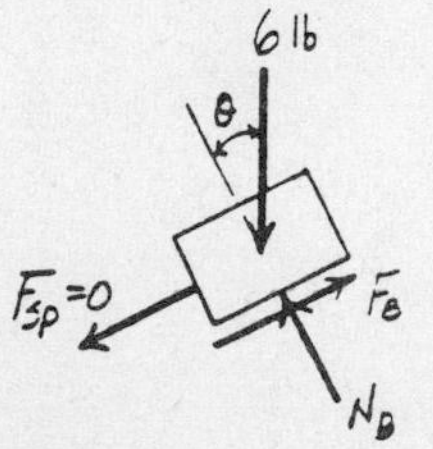

$$+\nearrow \Sigma F_{x'} = 0; \quad F_B - 6\sin\theta = 0 \qquad [3]$$

$$+\nwarrow \Sigma F_{y'} = 0; \quad N_B - 6\cos\theta = 0 \qquad [4]$$

Friction : Assuming block A is on the verge of slipping, then

$$F_A = \mu_{sA} N_A = 0.15 N_A \qquad [5]$$

Solving Eqs.[1], [2], [3], [4] and [5] yields

$$\theta = 8.531^\circ \qquad N_A = 9.889 \text{ lb} \qquad F_A = 1.483 \text{ lb}$$

$$F_B = 0.8900 \text{ lb} \qquad N_B = 5.934 \text{ lb}$$

Since $(F_B)_{max} = \mu_{sB} N_B = 0.25(5.934) = 1.483 \text{ lb} > F_B$, block B does not slip. Therefore, the above assumption is correct. Thus

$$\theta = 8.53^\circ \qquad F_A = 1.48 \text{ lb} \qquad F_B = 0.890 \text{ lb} \qquad \textbf{Ans}$$

***8-40.** Blocks A and B have a mass of 7 kg and 10 kg, respectively. Using the coefficients of static friction indicated, determine the largest force P which can be applied to the cord without causing motion. There are pulleys at C and D.

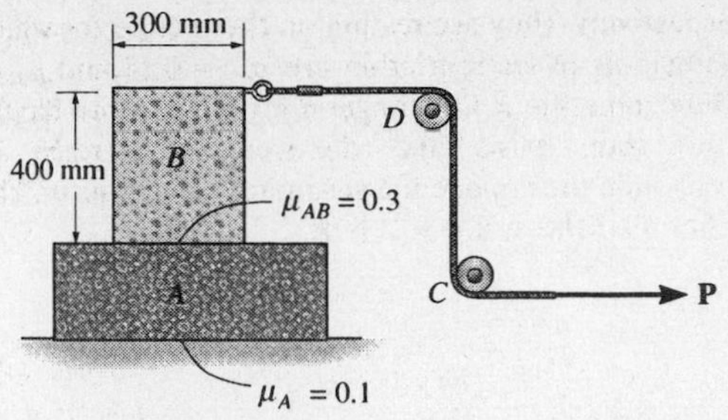

Assume block B slides on A.

$F_B = 0.3N_B$

$+\uparrow \Sigma F_y = 0;\quad N_B - 10(9.81) = 0$

$N_B = 98.1\text{ N}$

$\xrightarrow{+} \Sigma F_x = 0;\quad P - 0.3N_B = 0$

$P = 0.3(98.1) = 29.4\text{ N}$

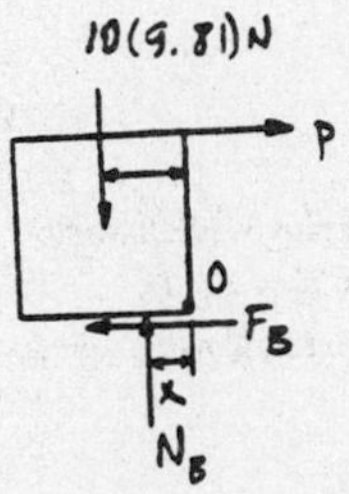

Assume block B tips on A.

$x = 0$

$\curvearrowleft + \Sigma M_O = 0;\quad 10(9.81)(0.15) - P(0.4) = 0$

$P = 36.8\text{ N}$

Assume block A slides.

$F_A = 0.1N_A$

$+\uparrow \Sigma F_y = 0;\quad N_A - 7(9.81) - 10(9.81) = 0$

$N_A = 166.8\text{ N}$

$\xrightarrow{+} \Sigma F_x = 0;\quad P - 0.1N_A = 0$

$P = 0.1(166.8) = 16.7\text{ N}$

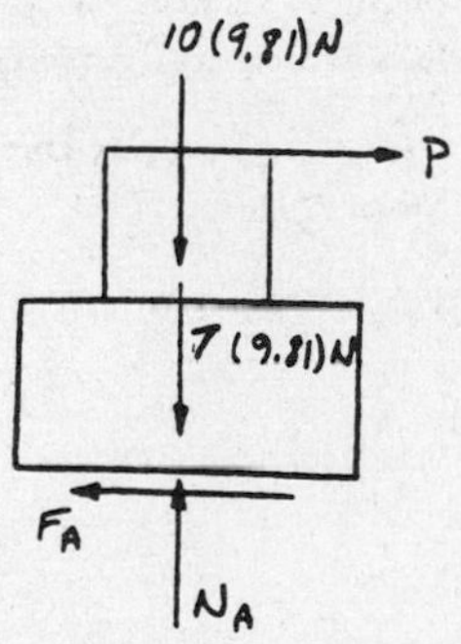

The smallest P is therefore

$P = 16.7\text{ N}$ **Ans**

8-41. The three bars have a weight of $W_A = 20$ lb, $W_B = 40$ lb, and $W_C = 60$ lb, respectively. If the coefficients of static friction at the surfaces of contact are as shown, determine the smallest horizontal force P needed to move block A.

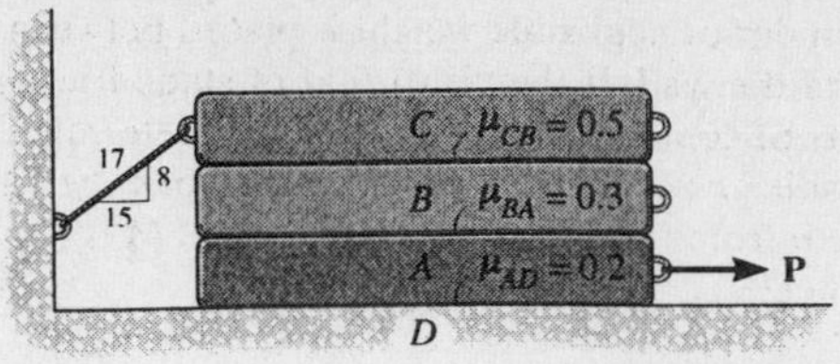

Equations of Equilibrium and Friction : If blocks *A* and *B* move together, then slipping will have to occur at the contact surfaces *CB* and *AD*. Hence, $F_{CB} = \mu_{s\,CB} N_{CB} = 0.5N_{CB}$ and $F_{AD} = \mu_{s\,AD} N_{AD} = 0.2N_{AD}$. From FBD (a)

$$+\uparrow \Sigma F_y = 0; \quad N_{CB} - T\left(\frac{8}{17}\right) - 60 = 0 \qquad [1]$$

$$\xrightarrow{+} \Sigma F_x = 0; \quad 0.5N_{CB} - T\left(\frac{15}{17}\right) = 0 \qquad [2]$$

and FBD (b)

$$+\uparrow \Sigma F_y = 0; \quad N_{AD} - N_{CB} - 60 = 0 \qquad [3]$$

$$\xrightarrow{+} \Sigma F_x = 0; \quad P - 0.5N_{CB} - 0.2N_{AD} = 0 \qquad [4]$$

Solving Eqs. [1], [2], [3] and [4] yields

$T = 46.36$ lb $\quad N_{CB} = 81.82$ lb $\quad N_{AD} = 141.82$ lb
$P = 69.27$ lb

If blocks *A* move only, then slipping will have to occur at contact surfaces *BA* and *AD*. Hence, $F_{BA} = \mu_{s\,BA} N_{BA} = 0.3N_{BA}$ and $F_{AD} = \mu_{s\,AD} N_{AD} = 0.2N_{AD}$. From FBD (c)

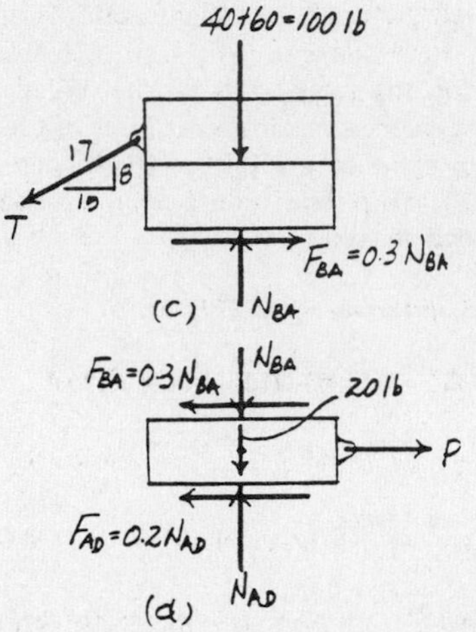

$$+\uparrow \Sigma F_y = 0; \quad N_{BA} - T\left(\frac{8}{17}\right) - 100 = 0 \qquad [5]$$

$$\xrightarrow{+} \Sigma F_x = 0; \quad 0.3N_{BA} - T\left(\frac{15}{17}\right) = 0 \qquad [6]$$

and FBD (d)

$$+\uparrow \Sigma F_y = 0; \quad N_{AD} - N_{BA} - 20 = 0 \qquad [7]$$

$$\xrightarrow{+} \Sigma F_x = 0; \quad P - 0.3N_{BA} - 0.2N_{AD} = 0 \qquad [8]$$

Solving Eqs. [5], [6], [7] and [8] yields

$T = 40.48$ lb $\quad N_{BA} = 119.05$ lb $\quad N_{AD} = 139.05$ lb
$P = 63.52$ lb $= 63.5$ lb (***Control!***) **Ans**

8-42. To prevent clockwise rotation of the wheel A, a small cylinder of negligible weight is placed between the wheel and the wall. If the coefficient of static friction at the points of contact B and C is $\mu_s = 0.4$, determine the largest radius r of the cylinder which can lock the wheel and keep it from rotating when any moment $\mathbf{M}$ is applied to the wheel.

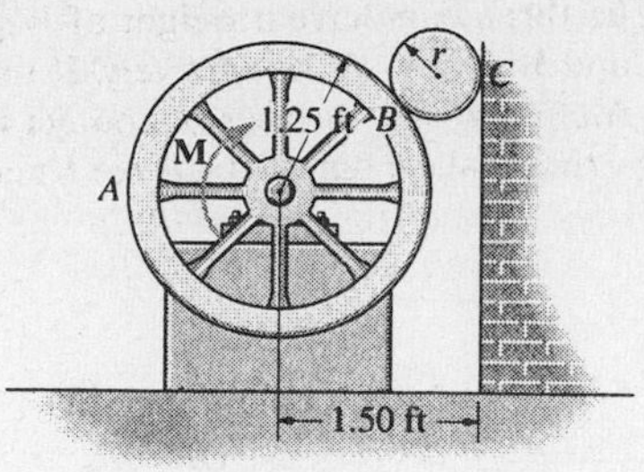

$\circlearrowleft + \Sigma M_O = 0;\quad N_C = N_B = N'$

$+\uparrow \Sigma F_y = 0;\quad 2N'\sin\theta - 2(0.4N'\cos\theta) = 0$

$$\theta = \tan^{-1}(0.4) = 21.8^\circ$$

$$\cos[2(21.8^\circ)] = \frac{1.5 - r}{1.25 + r}$$

$$0.905 + 0.724r = 1.5 - r$$

$$r = 0.345 \text{ ft} \qquad \textbf{Ans}$$

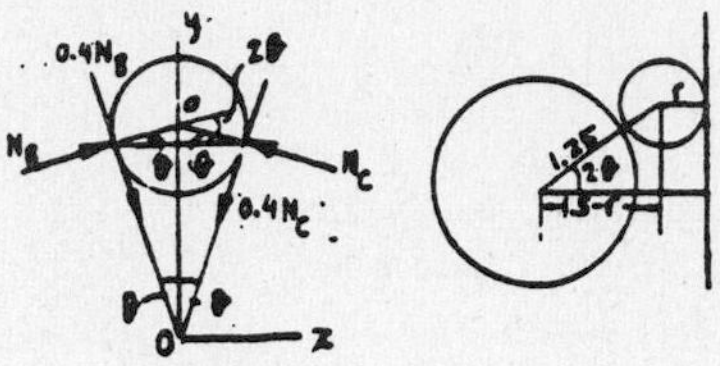

8-43. The refrigerator has a weight of 180 lb and rests on a tile floor for which $\mu_s = 0.25$. If the man pushes horizontally on the refrigerator in the direction shown, determine the smallest magnitude of force needed to move it. Also, if the man has a weight of 150 lb, determine the smallest coefficient of friction between his shoes and the floor so that he does not slip.

Equations of Equilibrium : From FBD (a),

$+\uparrow \Sigma F_y = 0;\quad N - 180 = 0 \quad N = 180 \text{ lb}$

$\xrightarrow{+} \Sigma F_x = 0;\quad P - F = 0 \qquad [1]$

$\circlearrowleft + \Sigma M_A = 0;\quad 180(x) - P(4) = 0 \qquad [2]$

Friction : Assuming the refrigerator is on the verge of slipping, then $F = \mu N = 0.25(180) = 45$ lb. Substituting this value into Eqs. [1], and [2] and solving yields

$$P = 45.0 \text{ lb} \qquad x = 1.00 \text{ ft}$$

Since $x < 1.5$ ft, the refrigerator does not tip. Therefore, the above assumption is correct. Thus

$$P = 45.0 \text{ lb} \qquad \textbf{Ans}$$

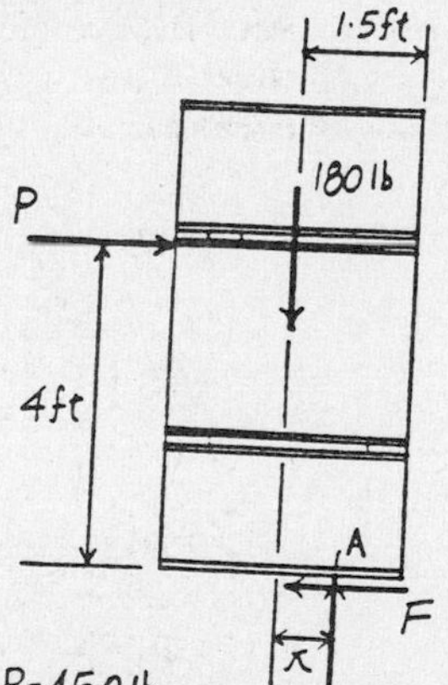

From FBD (b),

$+\uparrow \Sigma F_y = 0;\quad N_m - 150 = 0 \quad N_m = 150 \text{ lb}$

$\xrightarrow{+} \Sigma F_x = 0;\quad F_m - 45.0 = 0 \quad F_m = 45.0 \text{ lb}$

When the man is on the verge of slipping, then

$$F_m = \mu_s' N_m$$
$$45.0 = \mu_s'(150)$$
$$\mu_s' = 0.300 \qquad \textbf{Ans}$$

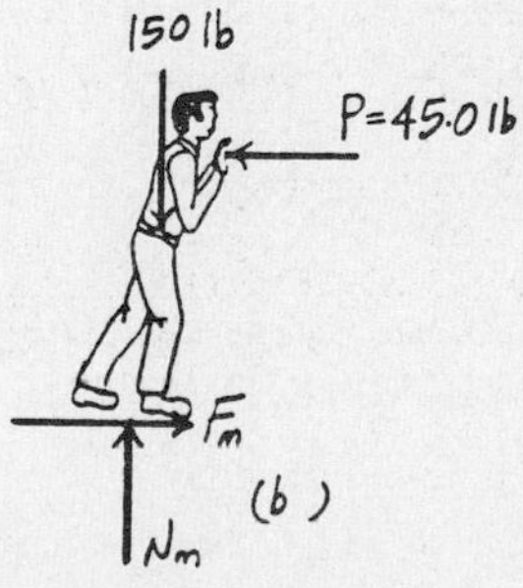

***8-44.** The refrigerator has a weight of 180 lb and rests on a tile floor for which $\mu_s = 0.25$. Also, the man has a weight of 150 lb and the coefficient of static friction between the floor and his shoes is $\mu_s = 0.6$. If he pushes horizontally on the refrigerator, determine if he can move it. If so does the refrigerator slip or tip?

Equations of Equilibrium : From FBD (a),

$$+\uparrow \Sigma F_y = 0; \quad N - 180 = 0 \quad N = 180 \text{ lb}$$

$$\xrightarrow{+} \Sigma F_x = 0; \quad P - F = 0 \qquad [1]$$

$$\circlearrowleft + \Sigma M_A = 0; \quad 180(x) - P(4) = 0 \qquad [2]$$

Friction : Assuming the refrigerator is on the verge of slipping, then $F = \mu N = 0.25(180) = 45$ lb. Substituting this value into Eqs. [1], and [2] and solving yields

$$P = 45.0 \text{ lb} \quad x = 1.00 \text{ ft}$$

Since $x < 1.5$ ft, the refrigerator does not tip. Therefore, the above assumption is correct. Thus, **the refrigerator slips.** **Ans**

From FBD (b),

$$+\uparrow \Sigma F_y = 0; \quad N_m - 150 = 0 \quad N_m = 150 \text{ lb}$$

$$\xrightarrow{+} \Sigma F_x = 0; \quad F_m - 45.0 = 0 \quad F_m = 45.0 \text{ lb}$$

Since $(F_m)_{max} = \mu_s' N_m = 0.6(150) = 90.0 \text{ lb} > F_m$, then the man does not slip. Thus, **The man is capable of moving the refrigerator.** **Ans**

8-45. Determine the minimum force P needed to push the two 75-kg cylinders up the incline. The force acts parallel to the plane and the coefficients of static friction of the contacting surfaces are $\mu_A = 0.3$, $\mu_B = 0.25$, and $\mu_C = 0.4$. Each cylinder has a radius of 150 mm.

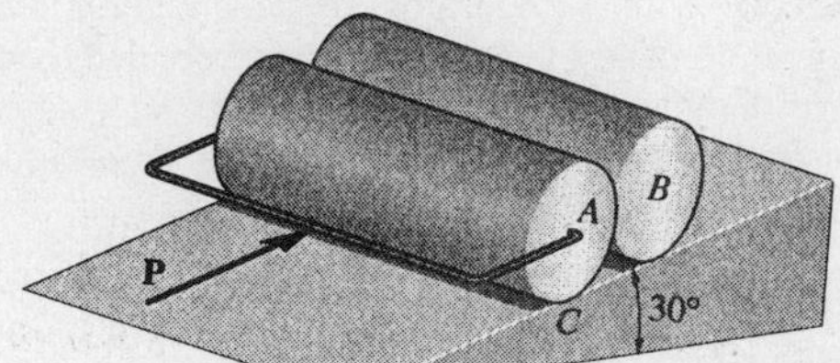

Equations of Equilibrium : From FBD (a),

$$\nearrow + \Sigma F_{x'} = 0; \quad P - N_A - F_C - 735.75\sin 30^\circ = 0 \qquad [1]$$

$$\nwarrow + \Sigma F_{y'} = 0; \quad N_C + F_A - 735.75\cos 30^\circ = 0 \qquad [2]$$

$$\circlearrowleft + \Sigma M_O = 0; \quad F_A(r) - F_C(r) = 0 \qquad [3]$$

From FBD (b),

$$\nearrow + \Sigma F_{x'} = 0; \quad N_A - F_B - 735.75\sin 30^\circ = 0 \qquad [4]$$

$$\nwarrow + \Sigma F_{y'} = 0; \quad N_B - F_A - 735.75\cos 30^\circ = 0 \qquad [5]$$

$$\circlearrowleft + \Sigma M_O = 0; \quad F_A(r) - F_B(r) = 0 \qquad [6]$$

Friction : Assuming slipping occur at point A, then $F_A = \mu_{s_A} N_A = 0.3 N_A$. Substituting this value into Eqs. [1], [2], [3], [4], [5] and [6] and solving, we have

$$N_A = 525.54 \text{ N} \quad N_B = 794.84 \text{ N}$$
$$N_C = 479.52 \quad F_C = F_B = 157.66 \text{ N}$$

$$P = 1051.07 \text{ N} = 1.05 \text{ kN}$$ **Ans**

Since $(F_C)_{max} = \mu_{s_C} N_C = 0.4(479.52) = 191.81 \text{ N} > F_C$ and $(F_B)_{max} = \mu_{s_B} N_B = 0.25(794.84) = 198.71 \text{ N} > F_B$, slipping do not occur at points C and B. Therefore the above assumption is correct.

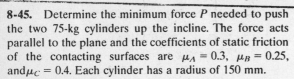

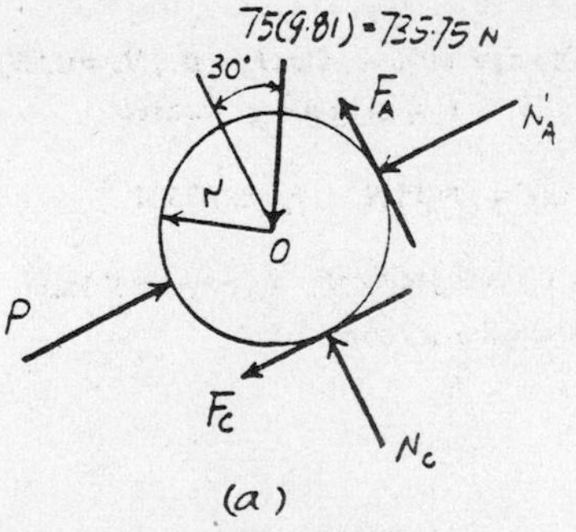

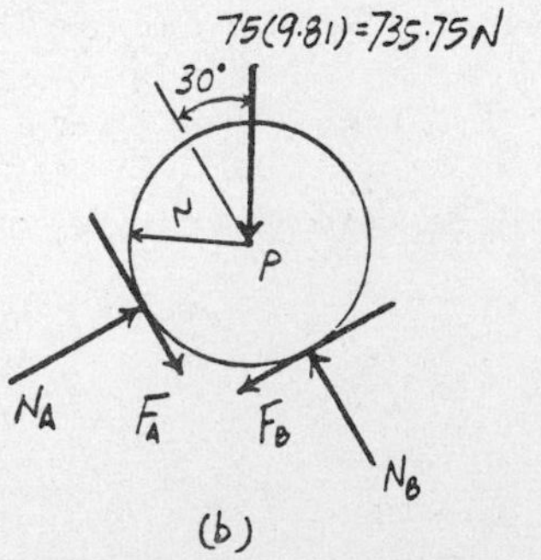

8-46. Each of the cylinders has a mass of 50 kg. If the coefficients of static friction at the points of contact are $\mu_A = 0.5, \mu_B = 0.5, \mu_C = 0.5$, and $\mu_D = 0.6$, determine the couple moment M needed to rotate cylinder E.

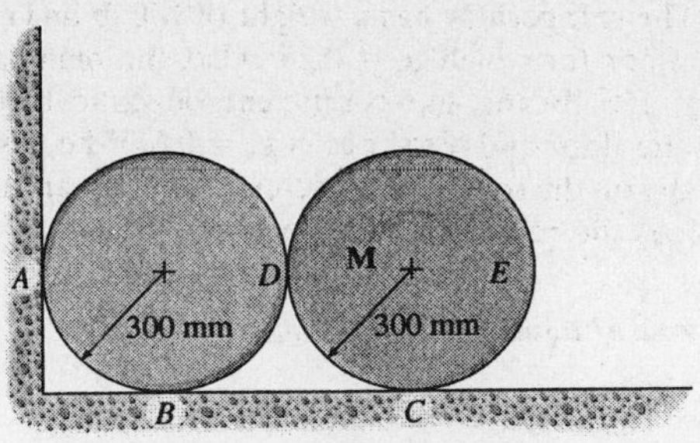

Equations of Equilibrium : From FBD (a),

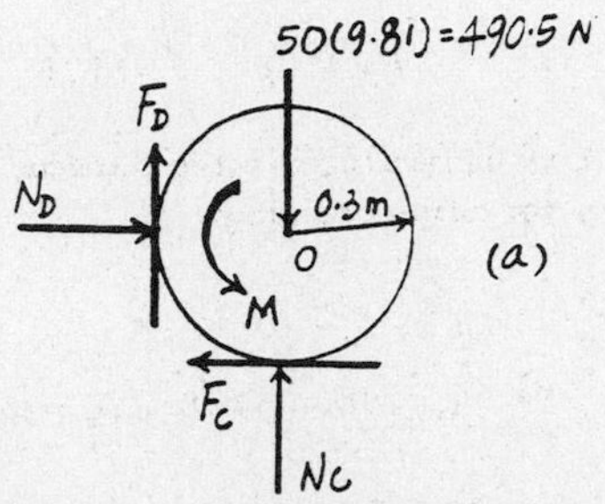

$$\xrightarrow{+} \Sigma F_x = 0; \quad N_D - F_C = 0 \qquad [1]$$

$$+\uparrow \Sigma F_y = 0 \quad N_C + F_D - 490.5 = 0 \qquad [2]$$

$$\curvearrowleft + \Sigma M_O = 0; \quad M - F_C(0.3) - F_D(0.3) = 0 \qquad [3]$$

From FBD (b),

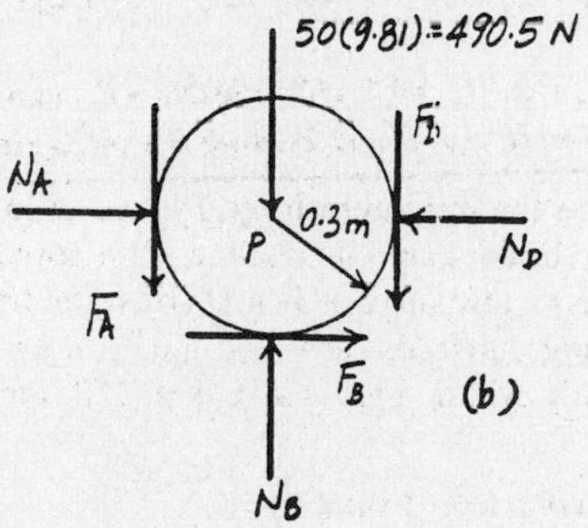

$$\xrightarrow{+} \Sigma F_x = 0; \quad N_A + F_B - N_D = 0 \qquad [4]$$

$$+\uparrow \Sigma F_y = 0 \quad N_B - F_A - F_D - 490.5 = 0 \qquad [5]$$

$$\curvearrowleft + \Sigma M_P = 0; \quad F_A(0.3) + F_B(0.3) - F_D(0.3) = 0 \qquad [6]$$

Friction : Assuming cylinder E slips at points C and D and cylinder F does not move, then $F_C = \mu_{s\,C} N_C = 0.5N_C$ and $F_D = \mu_{s\,D} N_D = 0.6N_D$. Substituting these values into Eqs. [1], [2] and [3] and solving, we have

$$N_C = 377.31 \text{ N} \quad N_D = 188.65 \text{ N}$$
$$M = 90.55 \text{ N}\cdot\text{m} = 90.6 \text{ N}\cdot\text{m} \qquad \textbf{Ans}$$

If cylinder F is on the verge of slipping at point A, then $F_A = \mu_{s\,A} N_A = 0.5N_A$. Substitute this value into Eqs. [4], [5] and [6] and solving, we have

$$N_A = 150.92 \text{ N} \quad N_B = 679.15 \text{ N} \quad F_B = 37.73 \text{ N}$$

Since $(F_B)_{max} = \mu_{s\,B} N_B = 0.5(679.15) = 339.58 \text{ N} > F_B$, cylinder F does not move. Therefore the above assumption is correct.

8-47. The tractor has a weight of 8000 lb and center of gravity at G. Determine if it can push the 550-lb log up the incline. The coefficient of static friction between the log and the ground is $\mu_s = 0.5$, and between the rear wheels of the tractor and the ground $\mu'_s = 0.8$. The front wheels are free to roll. Assume the engine can develop enough torque to cause the rear wheels to slip.

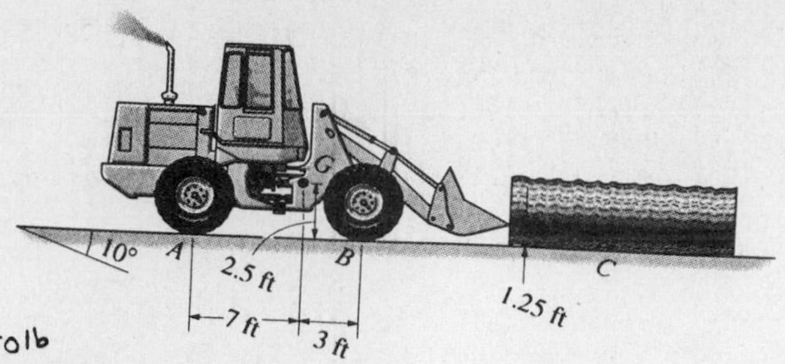

Log :

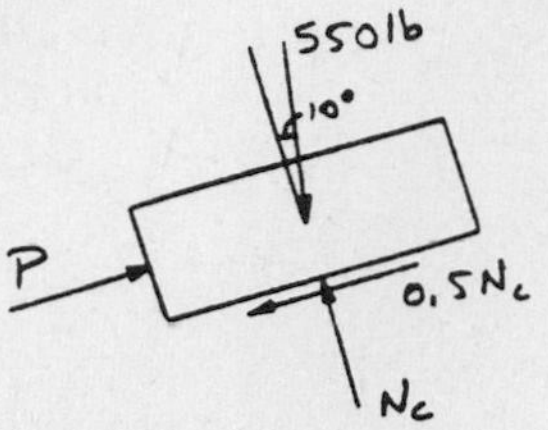

$+\nwarrow \Sigma F_y = 0; \quad N_C - 550 \cos 10° = 0$

$N_C = 541.6 \text{ lb}$

$+\nearrow \Sigma F_x = 0; \quad -0.5(541.6) - 550 \sin 10° + P = 0$

$P = 366.3 \text{ lb}$

Tractor :

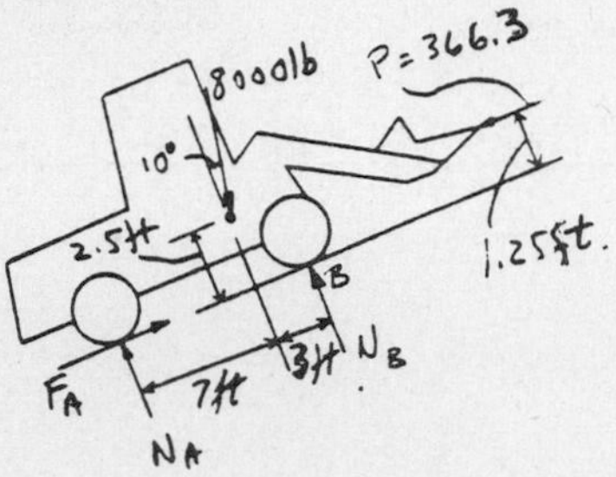

$\curvearrowleft + \Sigma M_B = 0; \quad 366.3(1.25) + 8000(\cos 10°)(3) + 8000(\sin 10°)(2.5) - N_A(10) = 0$

$N_A = 2757 \text{ lb}$

$+\nearrow \Sigma F_x = 0; \quad F_A - 8000 \sin 10° - 366.3 = 0$

$F_A = 1756 \text{ lb}$

$(F_A)_{max} = 0.8(2757) = 2205 \text{ lb} > 1756 \text{ lb}$

Tractor can move log. **Ans**

***8-48.** The tractor has a weight of 8000 lb and center of gravity at G. Determine the greatest weight of the log that can be pushed up the incline. The coefficient of static friction between the log and the ground is $\mu_s = 0.5$, and between the rear wheels of the tractor and the ground $\mu'_s = 0.7$. The front wheels are free to roll. Assume the engine can develop enough torque to cause the rear wheels to slip.

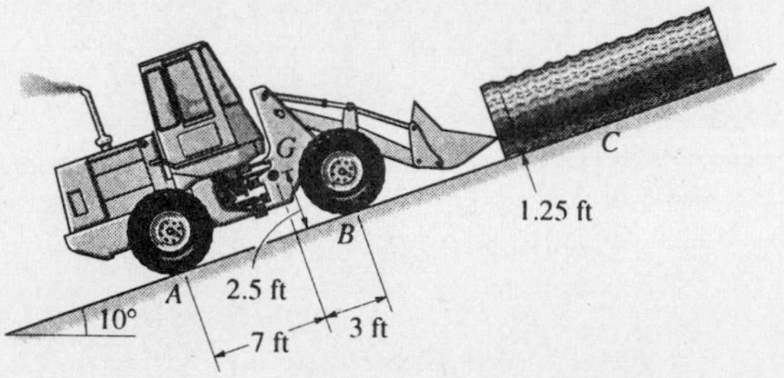

Tractor :

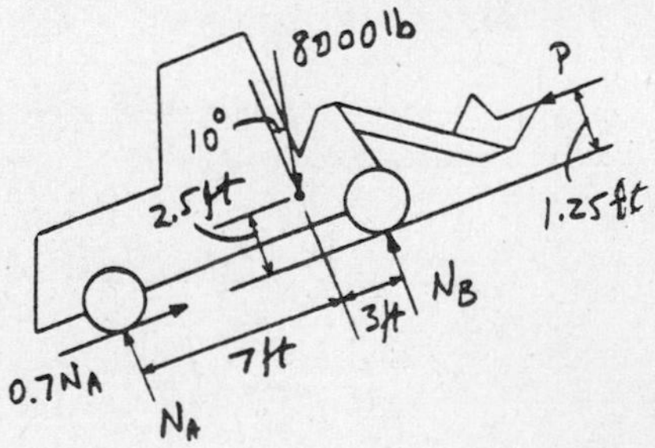

$\curvearrowleft + \Sigma M_B = 0; \quad 8000(\cos 10°)(3) + 8000(\sin 10°)(2.5) + P(1.25) - N_A(10) = 0$

$N_A - P(0.125) = 2710.8$

$+\nearrow \Sigma F_x = 0; \quad 0.7 N_A - 8000 \sin 10° - P = 0$

$0.7 N_A - P = 1389.2$

$N_A = 2780 \text{ lb}$

$P = 557.15 \text{ lb}$

Log :

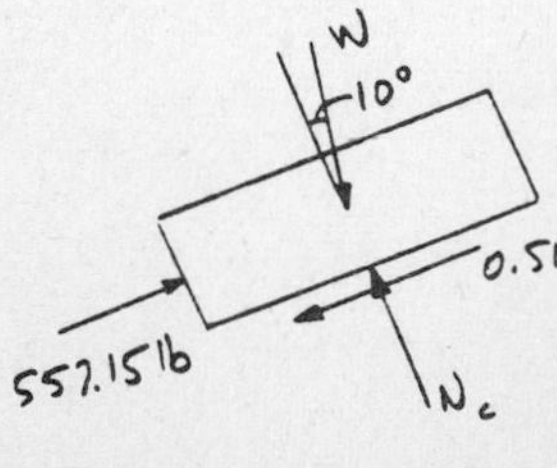

$+\nwarrow \Sigma F_y = 0; \quad N_C - W \cos 10° = 0$

$+\nearrow \Sigma F_x = 0; \quad 557.15 - W \sin 10° - 0.5 N_C = 0$

$N_C = 824 \text{ lb}$

$W = 836 \text{ lb}$ **Ans**

8-49. The passengers sitting in the front of the Jeep have a combined weight of 375 lb and center of gravity at G_1, whereas the combined weight of the ones sitting in the back is 280 lb with center of gravity at G_2. The curb (or empty) weight of the Jeep is 3000 lb with center of gravity at G. Determine the maximum load that can be towed at constant velocity if the vehicle is equipped with four-wheel drive. The coefficient of static friction between the tires and the ground is $\mu_s = 0.4$, and between the load and the ground $\mu'_s = 0.3$. Assume the engine can develop enough torque to cause the wheels to slip.

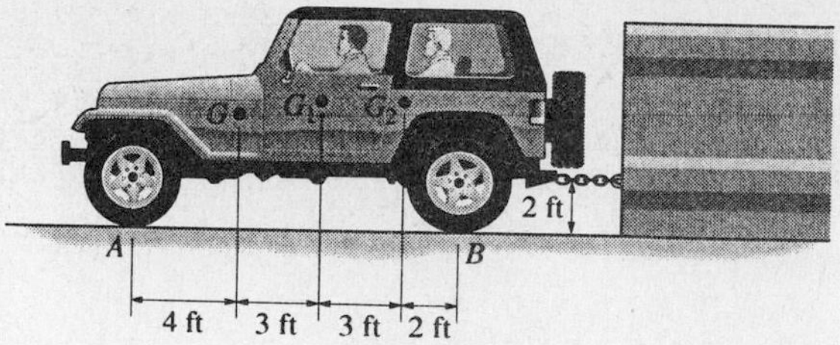

Jeep :

$+\uparrow \Sigma F_y = 0;\quad N_A + N_B - 3000 - 375 - 280 = 0$

$N_A + N_B = 3655$

$\overset{+}{\leftarrow} \Sigma F_x = 0;\quad 0.4\,(N_A + N_B) - P = 0$

$P = 0.4\,(3655) = 1462 \text{ lb}$

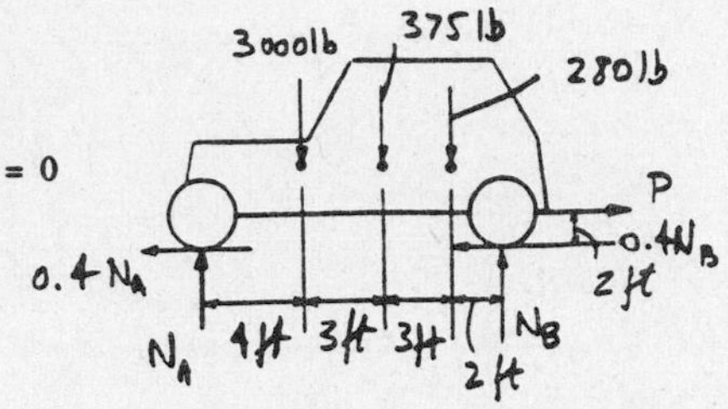

Crate :

$+\uparrow \Sigma F_y = 0;\quad N_C - W = 0$

$\overset{+}{\leftarrow} \Sigma F_x = 0;\quad 1462 - 0.3\,N_C = 0$

$W = 4873 \text{ lb} = 4.87 \text{ kip}$ **Ans**

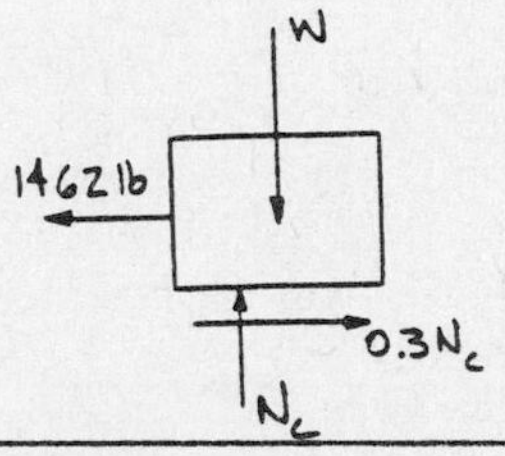

8-50. The passengers sitting in the front of the Jeep have a combined weight of 375 lb and center of gravity at G_1, whereas the combined weight of the ones sitting in the back is 280 lb with center of gravity at G_2. The curb (or empty) weight of the Jeep is 3000 lb with center of gravity at G. Determine the maximum load that can be towed at constant velocity if the vehicle is equipped with (a) front-wheel drive, where the rear wheels are free to roll, (b) rear-wheel drive, where the front wheels are free to roll. The coefficient of static friction between the tires and the ground is $\mu_s = 0.4$, and between the load and the ground $\mu'_s = 0.3$.

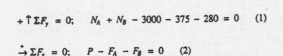

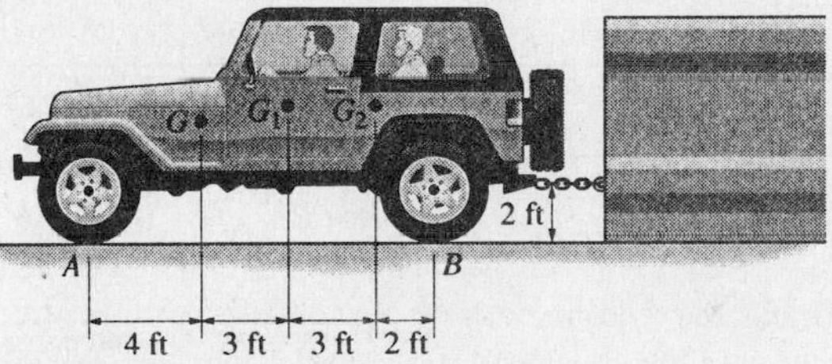

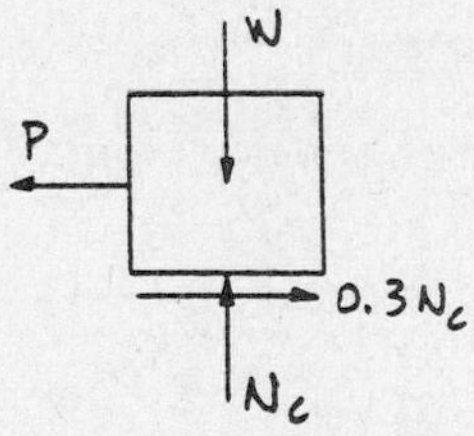

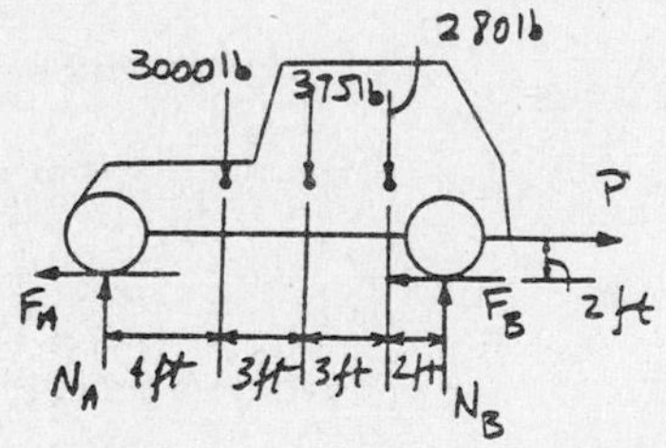

$+\uparrow \Sigma F_y = 0;\quad N_A + N_B - 3000 - 375 - 280 = 0 \quad (1)$

$\overset{+}{\rightarrow} \Sigma F_x = 0;\quad P - F_A - F_B = 0 \quad (2)$

$\curvearrowleft+ \Sigma M_A = 0;\quad N_B\,(12) - P\,(2) - 3000\,(4) - 375\,(7) - 280\,(10) = 0 \quad (3)$

Crate :

$\overset{+}{\rightarrow} \Sigma F_x = 0;\quad -P + 0.3\,N_C = 0$

$+\uparrow \Sigma F_y = 0;\quad N_C - W = 0$

$P = 0.3\,W \quad (4)$

(a) Front - wheel drive :

Set $F_B = 0$, $F_A = 0.4\,N_A$

Solving Eqs. (1) – (4) :

$N_A = 2065.2 \text{ lb}$

$N_B = 1589.8 \text{ lb}$

$P = 826 \text{ lb}$

$W = 2753.6 \text{ lb} = 2.75 \text{ kip}$ **Ans**

(b) Rear - wheel drive :

Set $F_A = 0$, $F_B = 0.4\,N_B$

Solving Eqs. (1) – (4) :

$N_A = 2099.2 \text{ lb}$

$N_B = 1555.8 \text{ lb}$

$P = 622 \text{ lb}$

$W = 2074.4 \text{ lb} = 2.07 \text{ kip}$ **Ans**

8-51. The beam AB has a negligible mass and thickness and is subjected to a force of 200 N. It is supported at one end by a pin and at the other end by a spool having a mass of 40 kg. If a cable is wrapped around the inner core of the spool, determine the minimum cable force P needed to move the spool. The coefficients of static friction at B and D are $\mu_B = 0.4$ and $\mu_D = 0.2$, respectively.

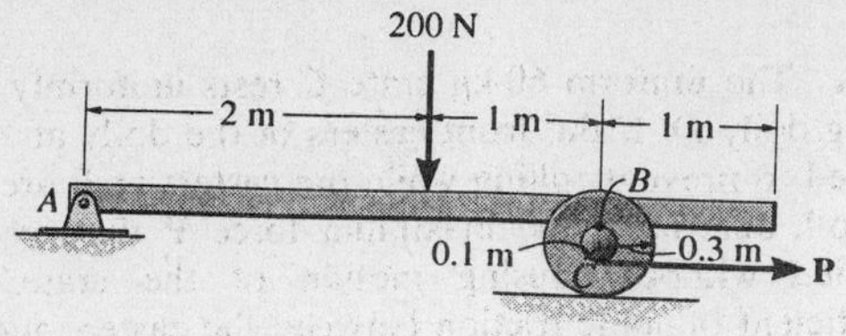

Equations of Equilibrium : From FBD (a),

$\circlearrowleft + \Sigma M_A = 0; \quad N_B(3) - 200(2) = 0 \quad N_B = 133.33 \text{ N}$

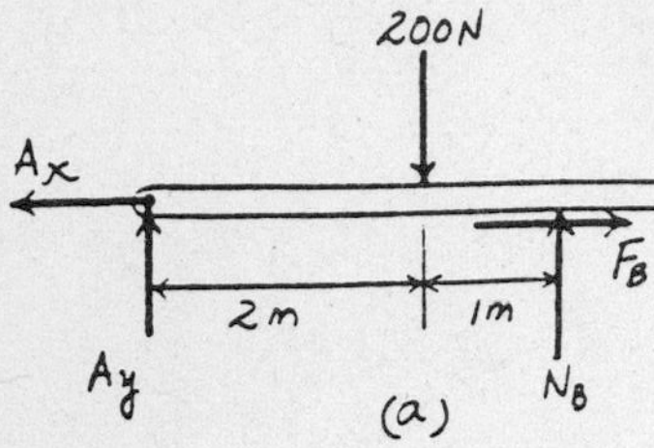

From FBD (b),

$+\uparrow \Sigma F_y = 0 \quad N_D - 133.33 - 392.4 = 0 \quad N_D = 525.73 \text{ N}$

$\xrightarrow{+} \Sigma F_x = 0; \quad P - F_B - F_D = 0 \qquad [1]$

$\circlearrowleft + \Sigma M_D = 0; \quad F_B(0.4) - P(0.2) = 0 \qquad [2]$

Friction : Assuming the spool slips at point B, then $F_B = \mu_{s\,B} N_B = 0.4(133.33) = 53.33$ N. Substituting this value into Eqs. [1] and [2] and solving, we have

$$F_D = 53.33 \text{ N}$$
$$P = 106.67 \text{ N} = 107 \text{ N} \qquad \textbf{Ans}$$

Since $(F_D)_{max} = \mu_{s\,D} N_D = 0.2(525.73) = 105.15 \text{ N} > F_B$, the spool does not slip at point D. Therefore the above assumption is correct.

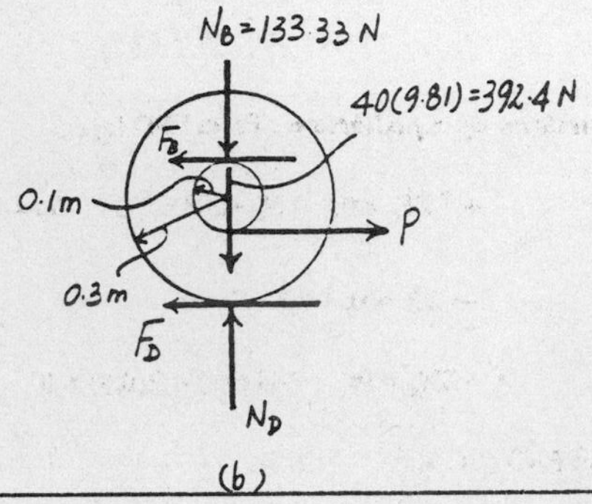

***8-52.** The beam AB has a negligible mass and thickness and is subjected to a triangular distributed loading. It is supported at one end by a pin and at the other by a post having a mass of 50 kg and negligible thickness. Determine the minimum force P needed to move the post. The coefficients of static friction at B and C are $\mu_B = 0.4$ and $\mu_C = 0.2$, respectively.

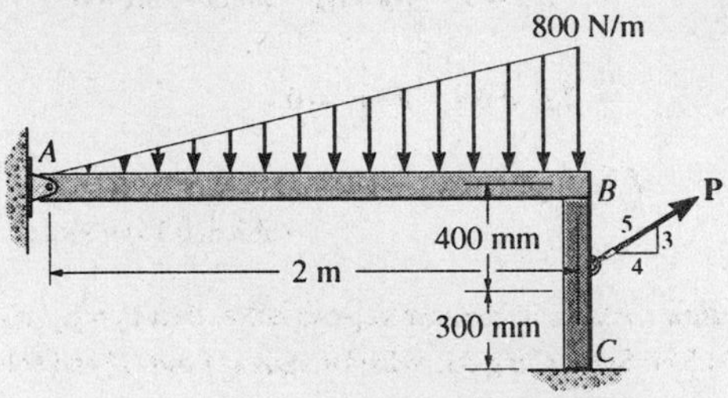

Equations of Equilibrium : From FBD (a),

$\circlearrowleft + \Sigma M_A = 0; \quad N_B(2) - 800(1.3333) = 0 \quad N_B = 533.33 \text{ N}$

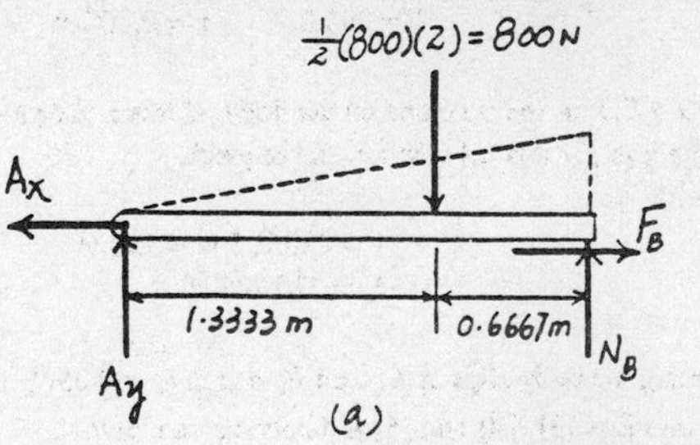

From FBD (b),

$+\uparrow \Sigma F_y = 0 \quad N_C + P\left(\frac{3}{5}\right) - 490.5 - 533.33 = 0 \qquad [1]$

$\xrightarrow{+} \Sigma F_x = 0; \quad P\left(\frac{4}{5}\right) - F_B - F_C = 0 \qquad [2]$

$\circlearrowleft + \Sigma M_B = 0; \quad P\left(\frac{4}{5}\right)(0.4) - F_C(0.7) = 0 \qquad [3]$

Friction : Assuming the post slips at point C, then $F_C = \mu_{s\,C} N_C = 0.2 N_C$. Substituting this value into Eqs. [1], [2] and [3] and solving, we have

$$N_C = 810.96 \text{ N} \qquad F_B = 121.64 \text{ N}$$
$$P = 354.79 \text{ N} = 355 \text{ N} \qquad \textbf{Ans}$$

Since $(F_B)_{max} = \mu_{s\,B} N_B = 0.4(533.33) = 213.33 \text{ N} > F_B$, the post does not slip at point B. Therefore the above assumption is correct.

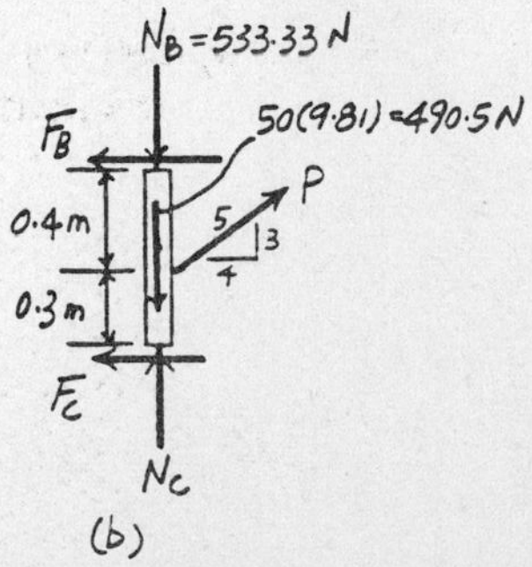

8-53. The uniform 60-kg crate C rests uniformly on a 10-kg dolly D. If the front casters of the dolly at A are locked to prevent rolling while the casters at B are free to roll, determine the maximum force $\mathbf{P}$ that may be applied without causing motion of the crate. The coefficient of static friction between the casters and the floor is $\mu_f = 0.35$ and between the dolly and the crate, $\mu_d = 0.5$.

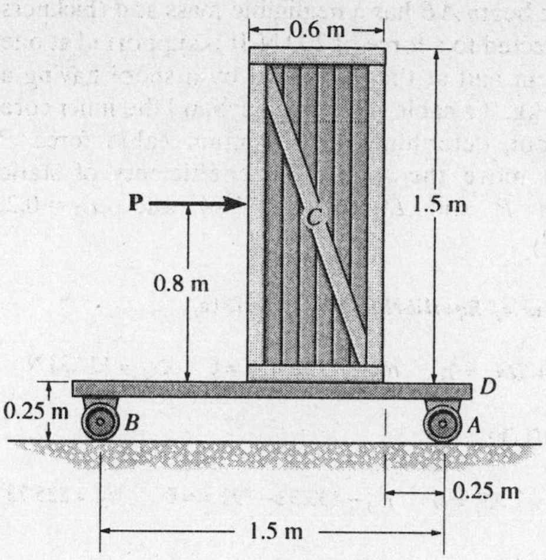

Equations of Equilibrium : From FBD (a),

$+\uparrow \Sigma F_y = 0; \quad N_d - 588.6 = 0 \quad N_d = 588.6 \text{ N}$

$\overset{+}{\rightarrow} \Sigma F_x = 0; \quad P - F_d = 0 \qquad [1]$

$\circlearrowleft + \Sigma M_A = 0; \quad 588.6(x) - P(0.8) = 0 \qquad [2]$

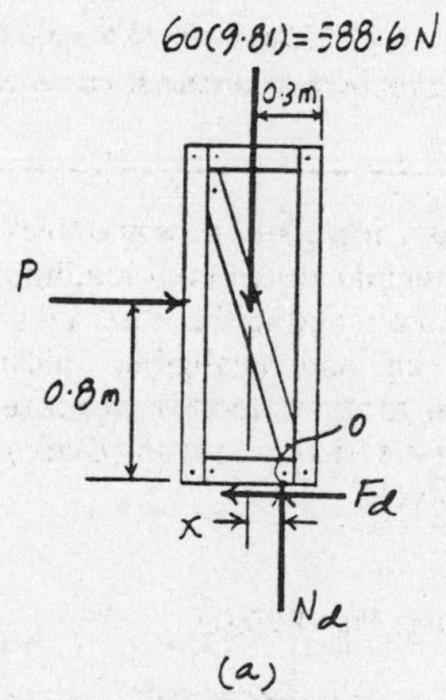

From FBD (b),

$+\uparrow \Sigma F_y = 0 \quad N_B + N_A - 588.6 - 98.1 = 0 \qquad [3]$

$\overset{+}{\rightarrow} \Sigma F_x = 0; \quad P - F_A = 0 \qquad [4]$

$\circlearrowleft + \Sigma M_B = 0; \quad N_A(1.5) - P(1.05) - 588.6(0.75) - 98.1(0.75) = 0 \qquad [5]$

Friction : Assuming the crate slips on dolly, then $F_d = \mu_{s_d} N_d = 0.5(588.6) = 294.3$ N. Substituting this value into Eqs.[1] and [2] and solving, we have

$$P = 294.3 \text{ N} \qquad x = 0.400 \text{ m}$$

Since $x > 0.3$ m, the crate tips on the dolly. If this is the case $x = 0.3$ m. Solving Eqs.[1] and [2] with $x = 0.3$ m yields

$$P = 220.725 \text{ N} = 221 \text{ N}$$
$$F_d = 220.725 \text{ N}$$

Assuming the dolly slips at A, then $F_A = \mu_{s_f} N_A = 0.35 N_A$. Substituting this value into Eqs.[3], [4] and [5] and solving, we have

$$N_A = 454.77 \text{ N} \qquad N_B = 231.93 \text{ N}$$
$$P = 159.17 \text{ N} = 159 \text{ N } (\textit{Control!}) \qquad \textbf{Ans}$$

8-54. Two blocks A and B, each having a mass of 6 kg, are connected by the linkage shown. If the coefficients of static friction at the contacting surfaces are $\mu_A = 0.2$ and $\mu_B = 0.8$, determine the largest vertical force P that may be applied to pin C without causing the blocks to slip. Neglect the weight of the links.

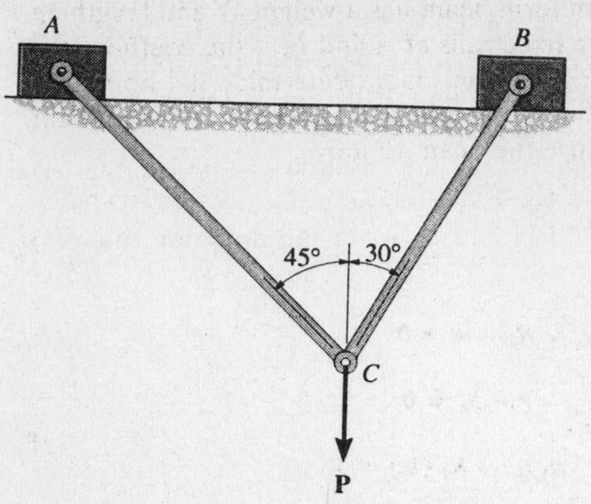

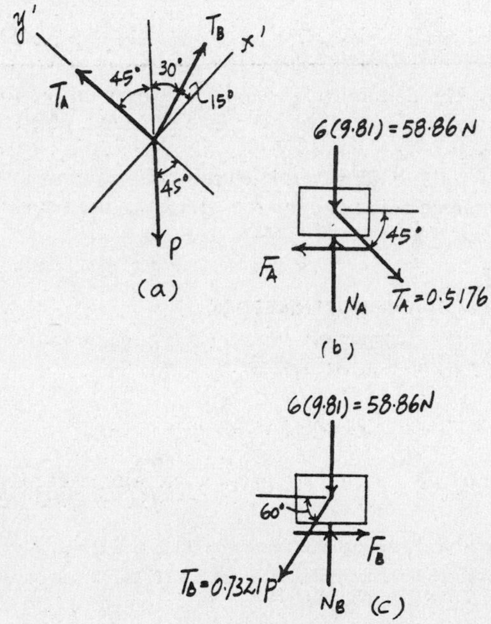

Equations of Equilibrium : From FBD (a),

$+ \ \Sigma F_{x'} = 0; \quad T_B \cos 15° - P\sin 45° = 0 \quad T_B = 0.7321P$

$+\Sigma F_{y'} = 0; \quad T_A + 0.7321P\sin 15° - P\cos 45° = 0 \quad T_A = 0.5176P$

From FBD (b),

$+\uparrow \Sigma F_y = 0; \quad N_A - 0.5176P\sin 45° - 58.86 = 0 \qquad [1]$

$\overset{+}{\rightarrow} \Sigma F_x = 0; \quad 0.5176P\cos 45° - F_A = 0 \qquad [2]$

From FBD (c),

$+\uparrow \Sigma F_y = 0; \quad N_B - 0.7321P\sin 60° - 58.86 = 0 \qquad [3]$

$\overset{+}{\rightarrow} \Sigma F_x = 0; \quad F_B - 0.7321P\cos 60° = 0 \qquad [4]$

Friction : Assuming block A slips, then $F_A = \mu_{s A} N_A = 0.2N_A$. Substituting this value into Eqs. [1], [2], [3] and [4] and solving, we have

$P = 40.20 \text{ N} = 40.2 \text{ N}$ **Ans**

$N_A = 73.575 \text{ N} \quad N_B = 84.35 \text{ N} \quad F_B = 14.715 \text{ N}$ Since $(F_B)_{max} = \mu_{s B} N_B = 0.8(84.35) = 67.48 \text{ N} > F_B$, block B does not slip. Therefore, the above assumption is correct.

8-55. The uniform beam has a weight W and length $4a$. It rests on the fixed rails at A and B. If the coefficient of static friction at the rails is μ_s, determine the horizontal force P, applied perpendicular to the face of the beam, which will cause the beam to move.

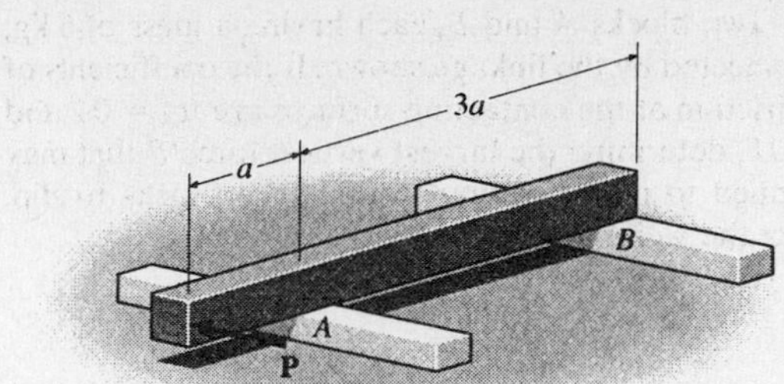

$$N_A = \frac{2W}{3}$$

$$\Sigma F_z = 0; \quad N_A + N_B - W = 0 \qquad N_B = \frac{W}{3}$$

$$\Sigma F_x = 0; \quad F_A - P - F_B = 0$$

$$F_A = \frac{2\mu_s W}{3}$$

$$\Sigma M_x = 0; \quad -N_A(a) + N_B(2a) = 0$$

$$\Sigma M_z = 0; \quad F_B(2a) + F_A(a) - P(2a) = 0 \qquad F_B = \frac{\mu_s W}{6}$$

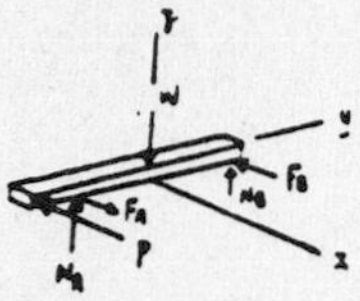

Assume slipping occurs at A; $F_A = \mu_s N_A$, then

$$P = \frac{\mu_s W}{2} \quad \textbf{Ans}$$

$$(F_B)_{max} = \mu_s N_B = \frac{\mu_s W}{3} > \frac{\mu_s W}{6} \quad \text{OK}$$

***8-56.** The uniform 6-kg slender rod rests on the top center of the 3-kg block. If the coefficients of static friction at the points of contact are $\mu_A = 0.4$, $\mu_B = 0.6$, and $\mu_C = 0.3$, determine the largest couple moment M which can be applied to the rod without causing motion of the rod.

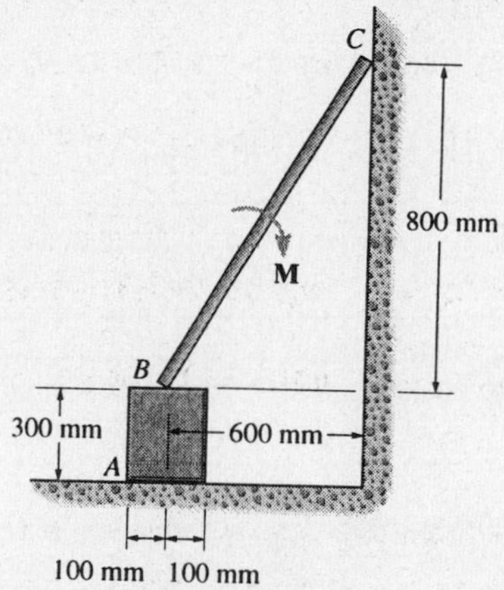

Equations of Equilibrium : From FBD (a),

$$\xrightarrow{+} \Sigma F_x = 0; \quad F_B - N_C = 0 \qquad [1]$$

$$+\uparrow \Sigma F_y = 0; \quad N_B + F_C - 58.86 = 0 \qquad [2]$$

$$+\Sigma M_B = 0; \quad F_C(0.6) + N_C(0.8) - M - 58.86(0.3) = 0 \qquad [3]$$

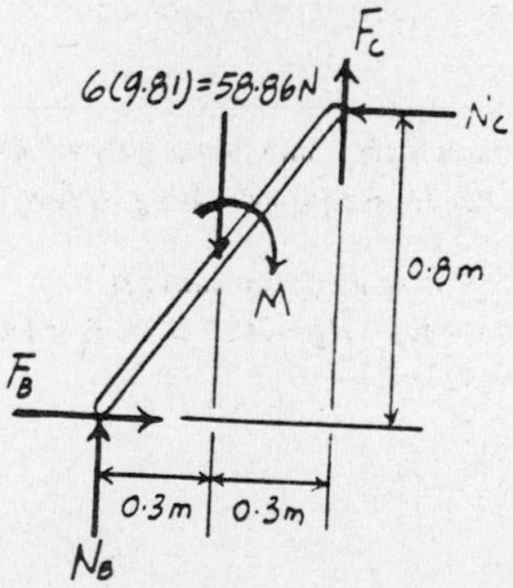

(a)

From FBD (b),

$$+\uparrow \Sigma F_y = 0; \quad N_A - N_B - 29.43 = 0 \qquad [4]$$

$$\xrightarrow{+} \Sigma F_x = 0; \quad F_A - F_B = 0 \qquad [5]$$

$$+\Sigma M_O = 0; \quad F_B(0.3) - N_B(x) - 29.43(x) = 0 \qquad [6]$$

Friction : Assume slipping occurs at point C and the block tips, then $F_C = \mu_{s\,C} N_C = 0.3N_C$ and $x = 0.1$ m. Substituting these values into Eqs.[1], [2], [3], [4], [5] and [6] and solving, we have

$$M = 8.561\ \text{N}\cdot\text{m} = 8.56\ \text{N}\cdot\text{m} \quad \textbf{Ans}$$

$$N_B = 50.83\ \text{N} \qquad N_A = 80.26\ \text{N} \qquad F_A = F_B = N_C = 26.75\ \text{N}$$

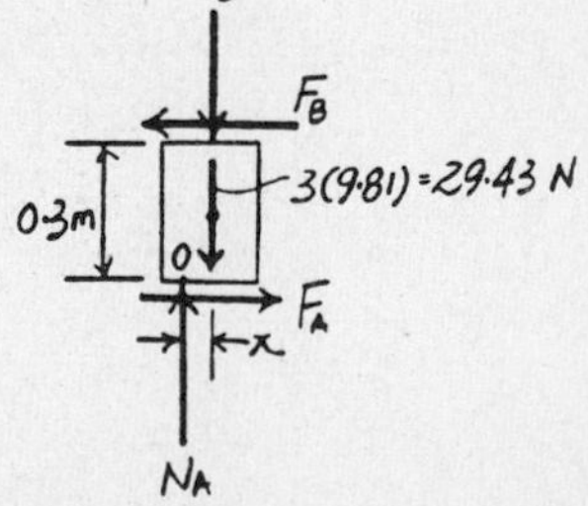

(b)

Since $(F_A)_{max} = \mu_{s\,A} N_A = 0.4(80.26) = 32.11\ \text{N} > F_A$, the block does not slip. Also, $(F_B)_{max} = \mu_{s\,B} N_B = 0.6(50.83) = 30.50\ \text{N} > F_B$, then slipping does not occur at point B. Therefore, the above assumption is correct.

8-57. Block C has a mass of 50 kg and is confined between two walls by smooth rollers. If the block rests on top of the 40-kg spool, determine the minimum cable force P needed to move the spool. The cable is wrapped around the spool's inner core. The coefficients of static friction at A and B are $\mu_A = 0.3$ and $\mu_B = 0.6$.

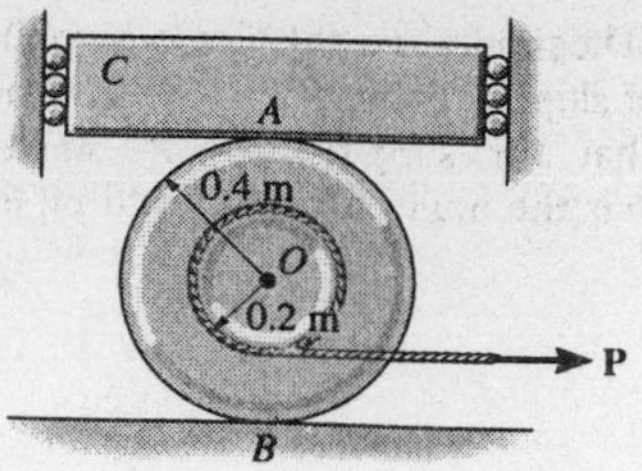

$+\uparrow \Sigma F_y = 0;\quad N_B - 40(9.81) - 50(9.81) = 0$

$N_B = 882.9 \text{ N}$

$\circlearrowleft + \Sigma M_O = 0;\quad F_A(0.4) - F_B(0.4) + P(0.2) = 0$

$\overset{+}{\rightarrow} \Sigma F_x = 0;\quad -F_A + P - F_B = 0$

Assume spool slips at A, then

$F_A = 0.3(50)(9.81) = 147.2 \text{ N}$

Solving,

$F_B = 441.4 \text{ N}$

$P = 589 \text{ N}$ **Ans**

$N_B = 882.9 \text{ N}$

Since $(F_B)_{max} = 0.6(882.9) = 529.7 \text{ N} > 441.4 \text{ N}$ OK

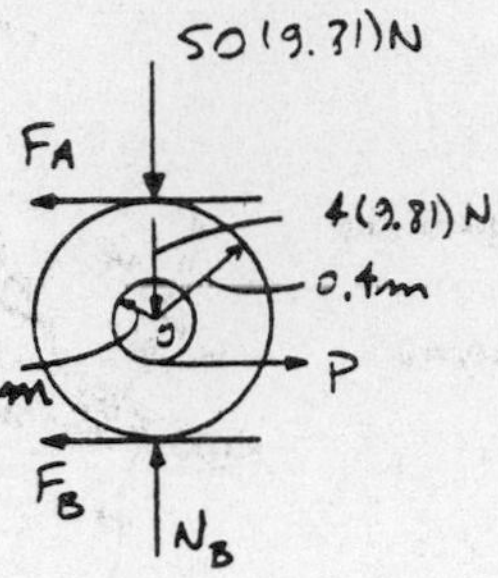

8-58. Block C has a mass of 50 kg and is confined between two walls by smooth rollers. If the block rests on top of the 40-kg spool, determine the required coefficients of static friction at A and B so that the spool slips at A and B when the magnitude of the applied force is increased to $P = 300$ N.

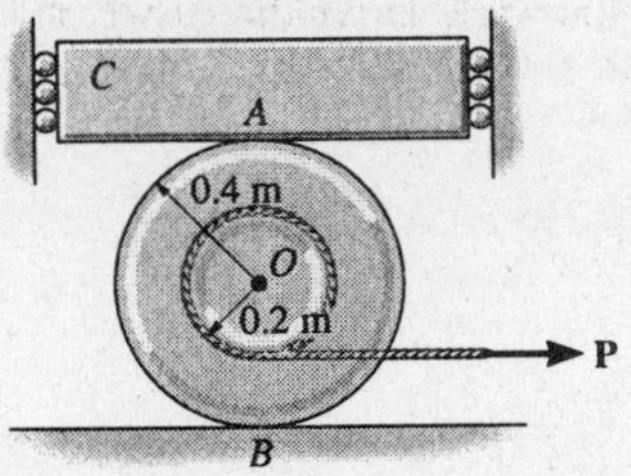

$\overset{+}{\rightarrow} \Sigma F_x = 0;\quad 300 - F_A - F_B = 0$

$\circlearrowleft + \Sigma M_B = 0;\quad F_A(0.8) - 300(0.2) = 0$

$F_A = 75 \text{ N}$

$F_B = 225 \text{ N}$

$\mu_A = \dfrac{F_A}{N_A} = \dfrac{75}{50(9.81)} = 0.153$ **Ans**

$\mu_B = \dfrac{F_B}{N_B} = \dfrac{225}{90(9.81)} = 0.255$ **Ans**

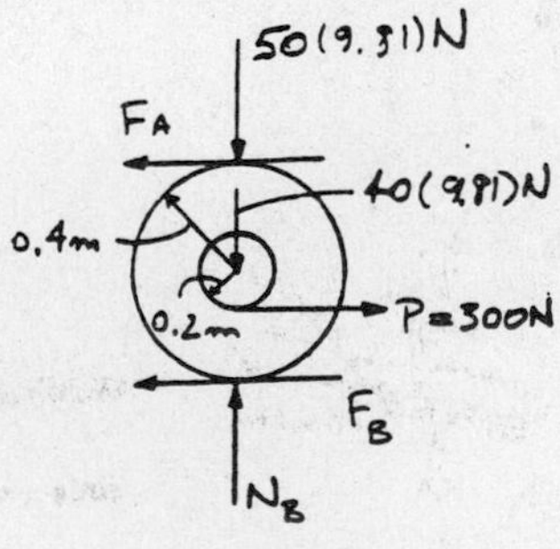

8-59. The pipe of weight W is to be pulled up the inclined plane of slope α using a force **P**. If **P** acts at an angle ϕ, show that for slipping $P = W \sin(\alpha + \theta)/\cos(\phi - \theta)$, where θ is the angle of static friction; $\theta = \tan^{-1} \mu_s$.

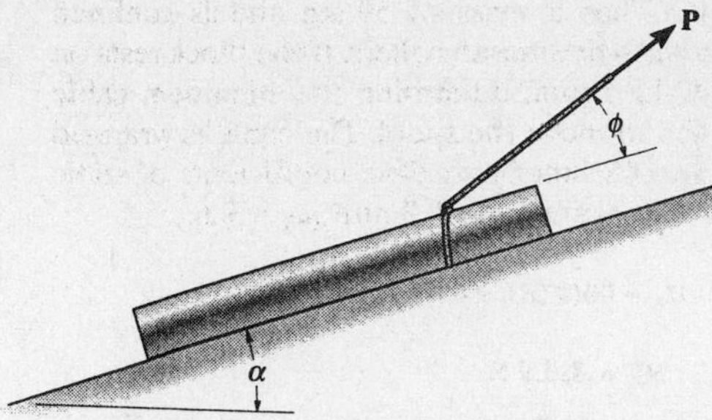

$+\nwarrow \Sigma F_{y'} = 0; \quad N + P\sin\phi - W\cos\alpha = 0 \quad N = W\cos\alpha - P\sin\phi$

$+\nearrow \Sigma F_{x'} = 0; \quad P\cos\phi - W\sin\alpha - \tan\theta(W\cos\alpha - P\sin\phi) = 0$

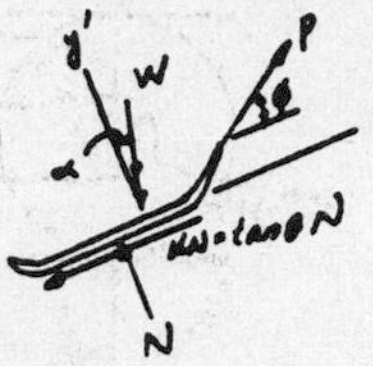

$$P = \frac{W(\sin\alpha + \tan\theta\cos\alpha)}{\cos\phi + \tan\theta\sin\phi}$$

$$= \frac{W(\cos\theta\sin\alpha + \sin\theta\cos\alpha)}{\cos\phi\cos\theta + \sin\phi\sin\theta} = \frac{W\sin(\alpha+\theta)}{\cos(\phi-\theta)} \quad \text{Q.E.D.}$$

***8-60.** Determine the angle ϕ at which the applied force **P** should act on the pipe so that the magnitude of **P** is as small as possible for pulling the pipe up the incline. What is the corresponding value of P? The pipe weighs W and the slope α is known. Express the answer in terms of the angle of kinetic friction, $\theta = \tan^{-1} \mu_k$.

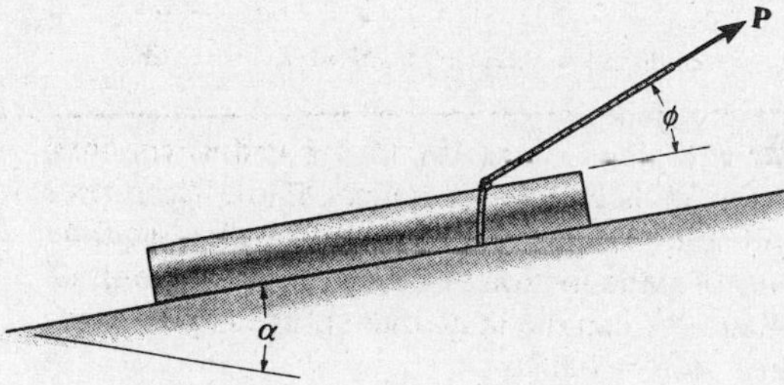

$\nwarrow \Sigma F_{y'} = 0; \quad N + P\sin\phi - W\cos\alpha = 0 \quad N = W\cos\alpha - P\sin\phi$

$\nearrow \Sigma F_{x'} = 0; \quad P\cos\phi - W\sin\alpha - \tan\theta(W\cos\alpha - P\sin\phi) = 0$

$$P = \frac{W(\sin\alpha + \tan\theta\cos\alpha)}{\cos\phi + \tan\theta\sin\phi}$$

$$= \frac{W(\cos\theta\sin\alpha + \sin\theta\cos\alpha)}{\cos\phi\cos\theta + \sin\phi\sin\theta}$$

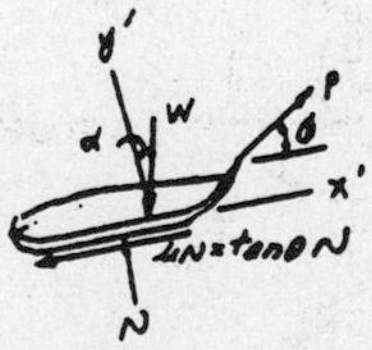

$$= \frac{W\sin(\alpha+\theta)}{\cos(\phi-\theta)}$$

$$\frac{dP}{d\phi} = \frac{W\sin(\alpha+\theta)\sin(\phi-\theta)}{\cos^2(\phi-\theta)} = 0$$

$W\sin(\alpha+\theta)\sin(\phi-\theta) = 0 \quad W\sin(\alpha+\theta) \neq 0$

$\sin(\phi-\theta) = 0 \quad \phi - \theta = 0 \quad \phi = \theta$ **Ans**

$P = \frac{W\sin(\alpha+\theta)}{\cos(\theta-\theta)} = W\sin(\alpha+\theta)$ **Ans**

8-61. The disk has a weight W and lies on a plane which has a coefficient of static friction μ. Determine the maximum height h to which the plane can be lifted without causing the disk to slip.

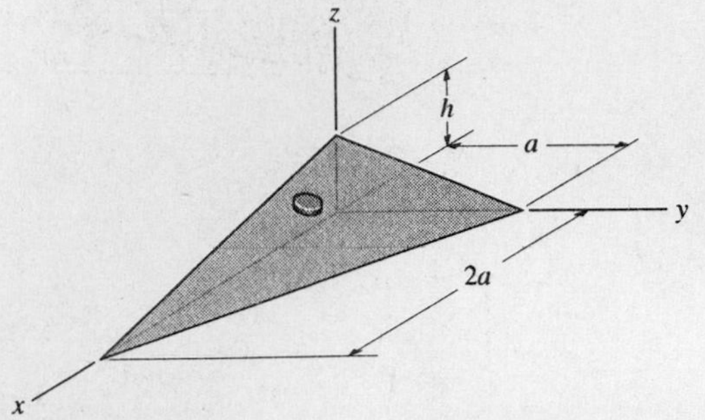

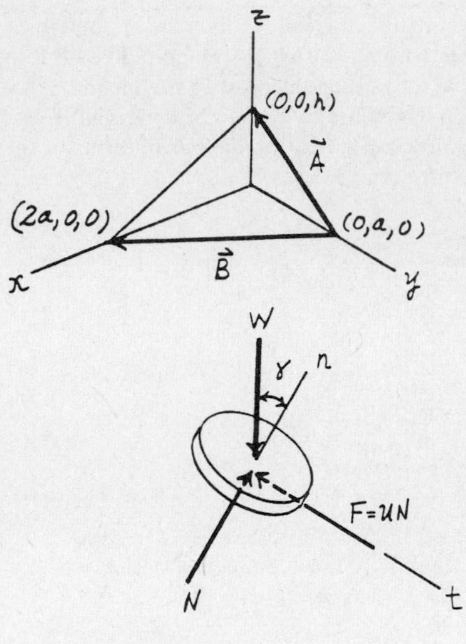

Unit Vector : The unit vector perpendicular to the inclined plane can be determined using cross product.

$$\mathbf{A} = (0-0)\mathbf{i} + (0-a)\mathbf{j} + (h-0)\mathbf{k} = -a\mathbf{j} + h\mathbf{k}$$
$$\mathbf{B} = (2a-0)\mathbf{i} + (0-a)\mathbf{j} + (0-0)\mathbf{k} = 2a\mathbf{i} - a\mathbf{j}$$

Then

$$\mathbf{N} = \mathbf{A}\times\mathbf{B} = \begin{vmatrix} \mathbf{i} & \mathbf{j} & \mathbf{k} \\ 0 & -a & h \\ 2a & -a & 0 \end{vmatrix} = ah\mathbf{i} + 2ah\mathbf{j} + 2a^2\mathbf{k}$$

$$\mathbf{n} = \frac{\mathbf{N}}{N} = \frac{ah\mathbf{i} + 2ah\mathbf{j} + 2a^2\mathbf{k}}{a\sqrt{5h^2+4a^2}}$$

Thus

$$\cos\gamma = \frac{2a}{\sqrt{5h^2+4a^2}} \qquad \text{hence} \qquad \sin\gamma = \frac{\sqrt{5}h}{\sqrt{5h^2+4a^2}}$$

Equations of Equilibrium and Friction : When the disk is on the verge of sliding down the plane, $F = \mu N$.

$$\Sigma F_n = 0; \quad N - W\cos\gamma = 0 \quad N = W\cos\gamma \qquad [1]$$

$$\Sigma F_t = 0; \quad W\sin\gamma - \mu N = 0 \quad N = \frac{W\sin\gamma}{\mu} \qquad [2]$$

Divide Eq. [2] by [1] yields

$$\frac{\sin\gamma}{\mu\cos\gamma} = 1$$

$$\frac{\frac{\sqrt{5}h}{\sqrt{5h^2+4a^2}}}{\mu\left(\frac{2a}{\sqrt{5h^2+4a^2}}\right)} = 1$$

$$h = \frac{2}{\sqrt{5}}a\mu \qquad \textbf{Ans}$$

8-62. Determine the minimum applied force **P** required to move wedge A to the right. The spring is compressed a distance of 175 mm. Neglect the weight of A and B. The coefficient of static friction for all contacting surfaces is $\mu_s = 0.35$. Neglect friction at the rollers.

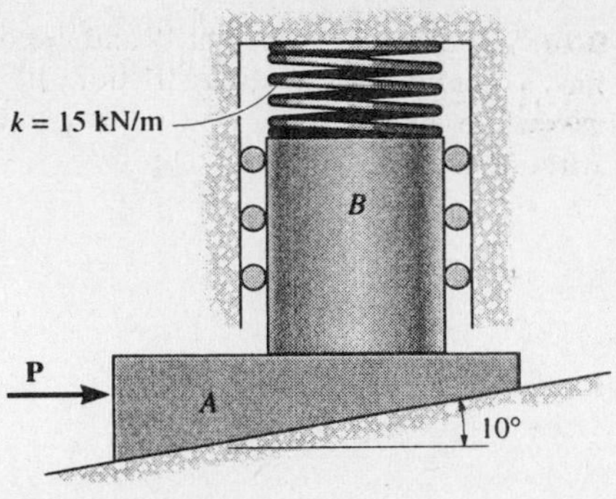

Equations of Equilibrium and Friction : Using the spring formula, $F_{sp} = kx = 15(0.175) = 2.625$ kN. If the wedge is on the verge of moving to the right, then slipping will have to occur at both contact surfaces. Thus, $F_A = \mu_s N_A = 0.35N_A$ and $F_B = \mu_s N_B = 0.35N_B$. From FBD (a),

$$+\uparrow \Sigma F_y = 0; \quad N_B - 2.625 = 0 \quad N_B = 2.625 \text{ kN}$$

From FBD (b),

$$+\uparrow \Sigma F_y = 0; \quad N_A \cos 10° - 0.35N_A \sin 10° - 2.625 = 0$$

$$N_A = 2.841 \text{ kN}$$

$$\xrightarrow{+} \Sigma F_x = 0; \quad P - 0.35(2.625) - 0.35(2.841)\cos 10° - 2.841 \sin 10° = 0$$

$$P = 2.39 \text{ kN} \qquad \textbf{Ans}$$

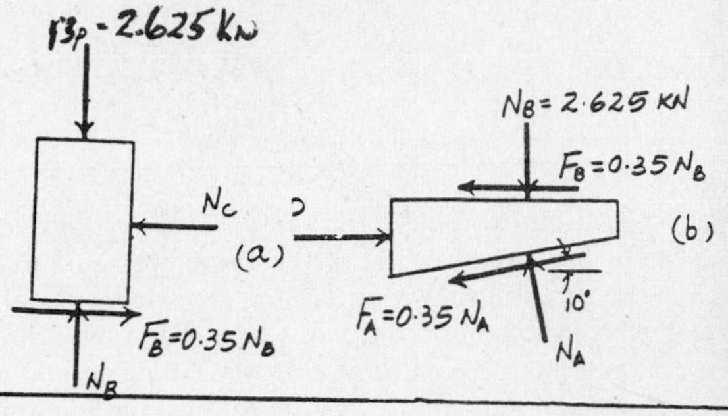

8-63. Determine the largest weight of the wedge that can be placed between the 8-lb cylinder and the wall without upsetting equilibrium. The coefficient of static friction at A and C is $\mu_s = 0.5$ and at B, $\mu'_s = 0.6$.

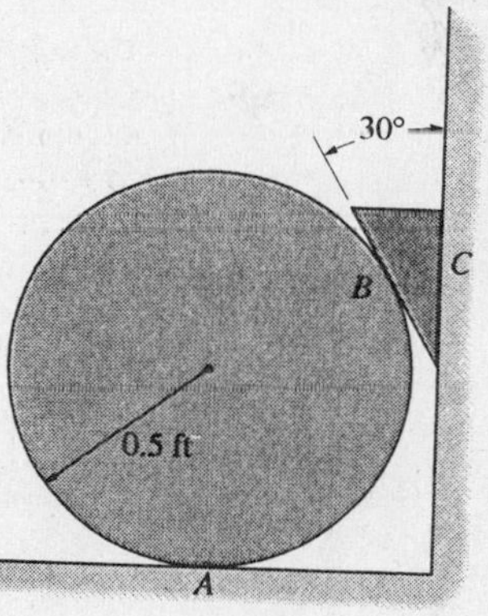

Equations of Equilibrium : From FBD (a),

$$\xrightarrow{+} \Sigma F_x = 0; \quad N_B \cos 30° - F_B \cos 60° - N_C = 0 \qquad [1]$$

$$+\uparrow \Sigma F_y = 0; \quad N_B \sin 30° + F_B \sin 60° + F_C - W = 0 \qquad [2]$$

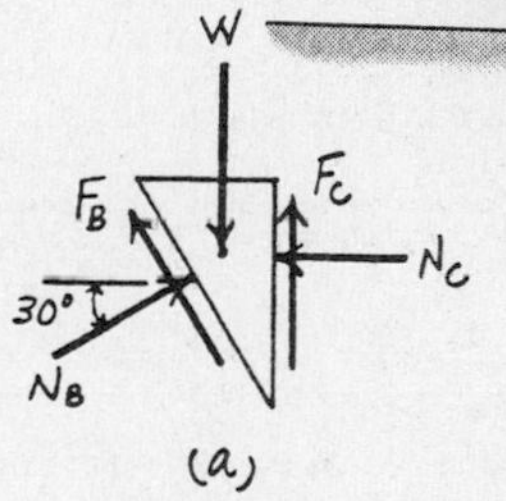

From FBD (b),

$$+\uparrow \Sigma F_y = 0; \quad N_A - N_B \sin 30° - F_B \sin 60° - 8 = 0 \qquad [3]$$

$$\xrightarrow{+} \Sigma F_x = 0; \quad F_A + F_B \cos 60° - N_B \cos 30° = 0 \qquad [4]$$

$$\circlearrowleft + \Sigma M_O = 0; \quad F_A(0.5) - F_B(0.5) = 0 \qquad [5]$$

Friction : Assume slipping occurs at points C and A, then $F_C = \mu_s N_C = 0.5N_C$ and $F_A = \mu_s N_A = 0.5N_A$. Substituting these values into Eqs. [1], [2], [3], [4], and [5] and solving, we have

$$W = 66.64 \text{ lb} = 66.6 \text{ lb} \qquad \textbf{Ans}$$

$$N_B = 51.71 \text{ lb} \quad N_A = 59.71 \text{ lb} \quad F_B = N_C = 29.86 \text{ lb}$$

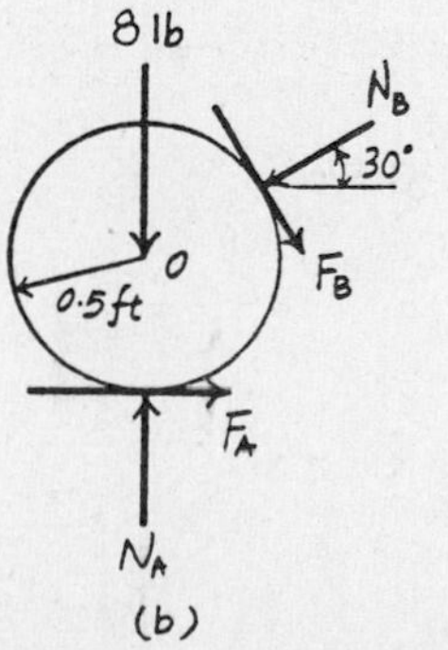

Since $(F_B)_{max} = \mu'_s N_B = 0.6(51.71) = 31.03 \text{ lb} > F_B$, slipping does not occur at point B. Therefore, the above assumption is correct.

***8-64.** The wedge has a negligible weight and a coefficient of static friction $\mu_s = 0.35$ with all contacting surfaces. Determine the angle θ so that it is "self-locking." This requires no slipping for any magnitude of the force **P** applied to the joint.

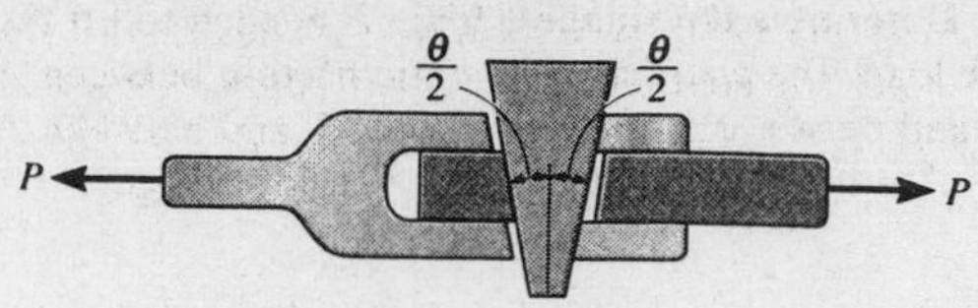

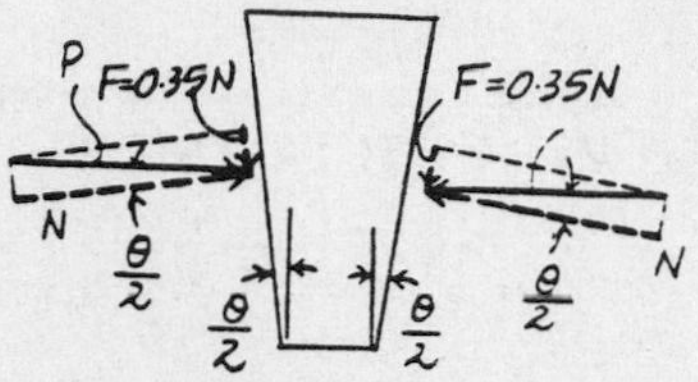

Friction : When the wedge is on the verge of slipping, then $F = \mu N = 0.35N$. From the force diagram (P is the 'locking' force.),

$$\tan\frac{\theta}{2} = \frac{0.35N}{N} = 0.35$$

$$\theta = 38.6°$$ **Ans**

8-65. The two blocks used in a measuring device have negligible weight. If the spring is compressed 5 in. when in the position shown, determine the smallest axial force P which the adjustment screw must exert on B in order to start the movement of B downward. The end of the screw is *smooth* and the coefficient of static friction at all other points of contact is $\mu_s = 0.3$.

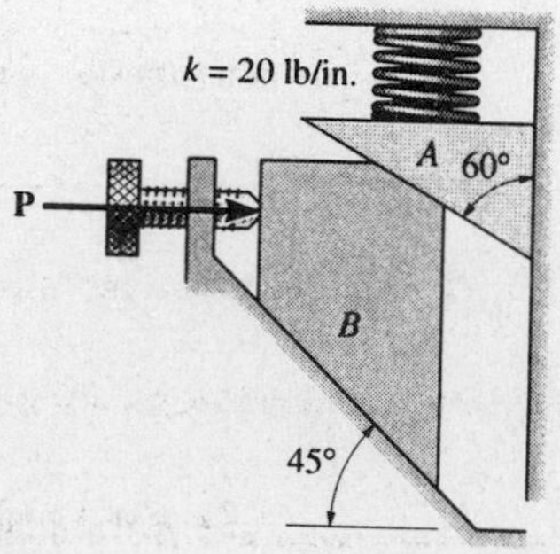

Note that when block B moves downward, block A will also come downward.

Block A :

$\xrightarrow{+} \Sigma F_x = 0;\quad N' \cos 60° + 0.3\,N' \sin 60° - N_A = 0$

$+\uparrow \Sigma F_y = 0;\quad 0.3\,N_A - 0.3\,N' \cos 60° + N' \sin 60° - 100 = 0$

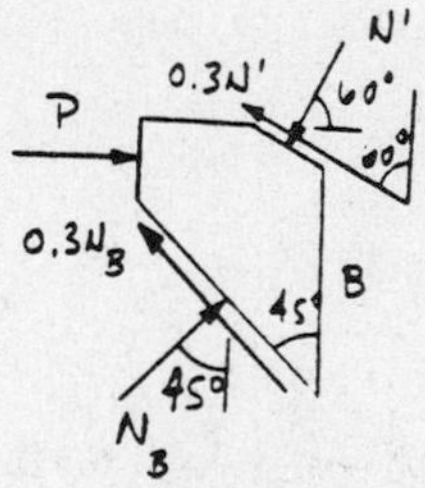

Block B :

$\xrightarrow{+} \Sigma F_x = 0;\quad N_B \sin 45° - 0.3\,N_B \sin 45° + P - 0.3\,N' \sin 60° - N' \cos 60° = 0$

$+\uparrow \Sigma F_y = 0;\quad N_B \cos 45° + 0.3\,N_B \cos 45° + 0.3\,N' \cos 60° - N' \sin 60° = 0$

Solving,

$N' = 105.9$ lb

$N_B = 82.5$ lb

$N_A = 80.5$ lb

$P = 39.6$ lb **Ans**

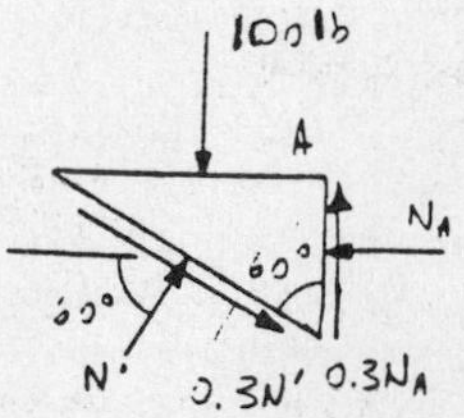

8-66. Determine the smallest force P needed to lift the 3000-lb load. The coefficient of static friction between A and C and between B and D is $\mu_s = 0.3$, and between A and B $\mu'_s = 0.4$. Neglect the weight of each wedge.

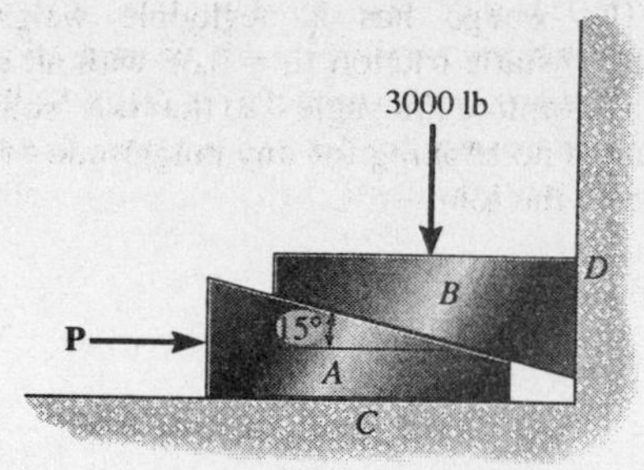

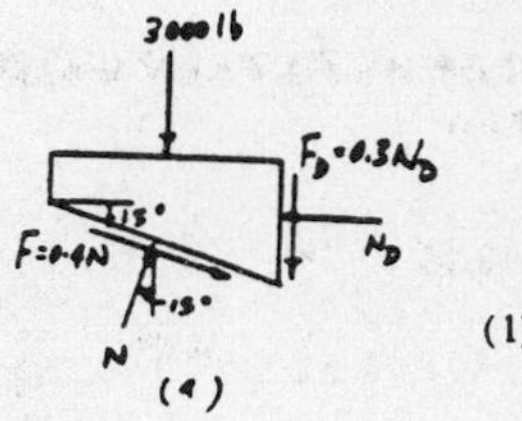

From FBD (a):

$$\xrightarrow{+} \Sigma F_x = 0; \quad 0.4N\cos 15° + N\sin 15° - N_D = 0 \quad (1)$$

$$+\uparrow \Sigma F_y = 0; \quad N\cos 15° - 0.4N\sin 15° - 0.3N_D - 3000 = 0 \quad (2)$$

Solving Eqs. (1) and (2) yields:

$$N = 4485.4 \text{ lb} \qquad N_D = 2893.9 \text{ lb}$$

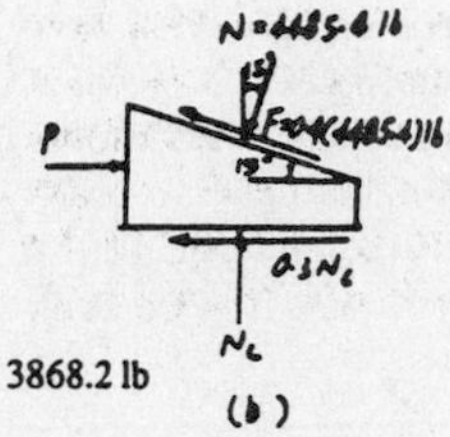

From FBD (b):

$$+\uparrow \Sigma F_y = 0; \quad N_C + 0.4(4485.4)\sin 15° - 4485.4\cos 15° = 0 \qquad N_C = 3868.2 \text{ lb}$$

$$\xrightarrow{+} \Sigma F_x = 0; \quad P - 0.3(3868.2) - 4485.4\sin 15° - 1794.1\cos 15° = 0$$

$$P = 4054 \text{ lb} = 4.05 \text{ kip} \qquad \textbf{Ans}$$

8-67. Determine the reversed horizontal force $-\mathbf{P}$ needed to pull out wedge A. The coefficient of static friction between A and C and between B and D is $\mu_s = 0.2$, and between A and B $\mu'_s = 0.1$. Neglect the weight of each wedge.

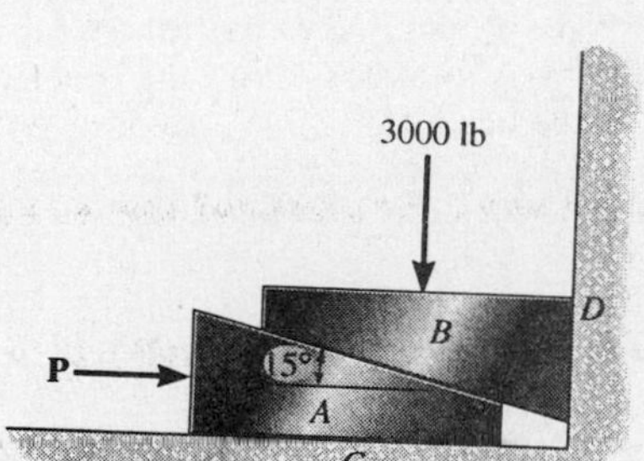

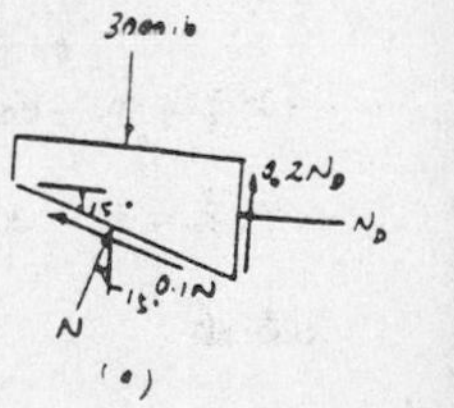

From FBD (a):

$$\xrightarrow{+} \Sigma F_x = 0; \quad N\sin 15° - 0.1N\cos 15° - N_D = 0 \quad (1)$$

$$+\uparrow \Sigma F_y = 0; \quad N\cos 15° + 0.1N\sin 15° + 0.2N_D - 3000 = 0 \quad (2)$$

Solving Eqs. (1) and (2) yields:

$$N = 2929.0 \text{ lb} \qquad N_D = 475.2 \text{ lb}$$

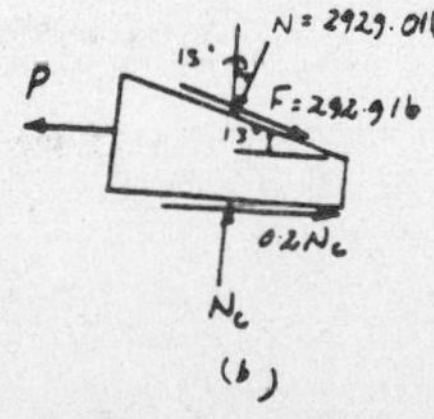

From FBD (b):

$$+\uparrow \Sigma F_y = 0; \quad N_C - 292.9\sin 15° - 2929.0\cos 15° = 0 \qquad N_C = 2905.0 \text{ lb}$$

$$\xrightarrow{+} \Sigma F_x = 0; \quad 0.2(2905.0) + 292.9\cos 15° - 2929.0\sin 15° - P = 0$$

$$P = 106 \text{ lb} \qquad \textbf{Ans}$$

***8-68.** The wedge is used to level the member. Determine the horizontal force **P** that must be applied to move the wedge to the right. The coefficient of static friction between the wedge and the two surfaces of contact is $\mu_s = 0.25$. Neglect the size and weight of the wedge.

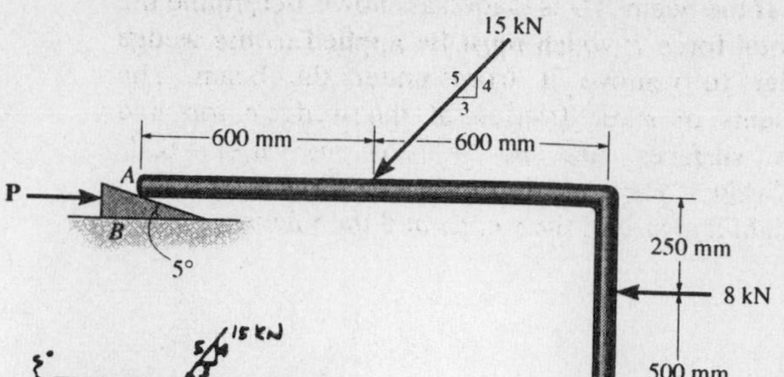

From FBD (a)

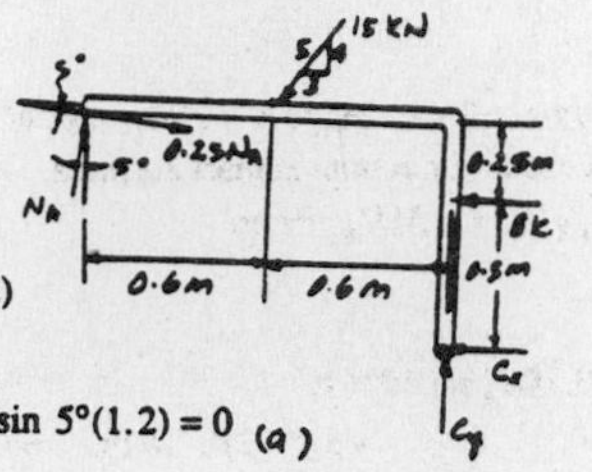

$$\curvearrowleft + \Sigma M_C = 0; \quad \frac{4}{5}(15)(0.6) + \frac{3}{5}(15)(0.75) + 8(0.5) - N_A \cos 5°(1.2)$$

$$-N_A \sin 5°(0.75) - 0.25 N_A \cos 5°(0.75) + 0.25 N_A \sin 5°(1.2) = 0$$

$$N_A = 12.628 \text{ kN}$$

From FBD (b)

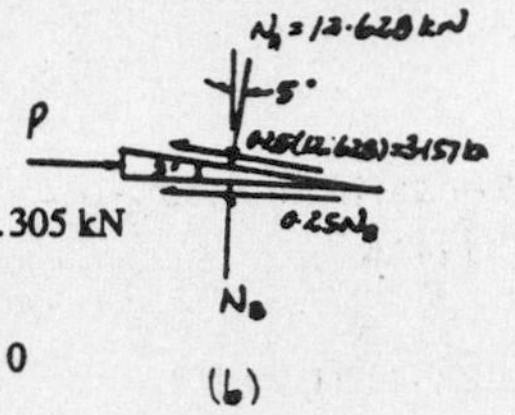

$$+\uparrow \Sigma F_y = 0; \quad N_B + 3.157 \sin 5° - 12.628 \cos 5° = 0 \quad N_B = 12.305 \text{ kN}$$

$$\xrightarrow{+} \Sigma F_x = 0; \quad P - 0.25(12.305) - 3.157 \cos 5° - 12.628 \sin 5° = 0$$

$$P = 7.32 \text{ kN}$$ **Ans**

8-69. The beam is adjusted to the horizontal position by means of a wedge located at its right support. If the coefficient of static friction between the wedge and the two surfaces of contact is $\mu_s = 0.25$, determine the horizontal force **P** required to push the wedge forward. Neglect the weight and size of the wedge and the thickness of the beam.

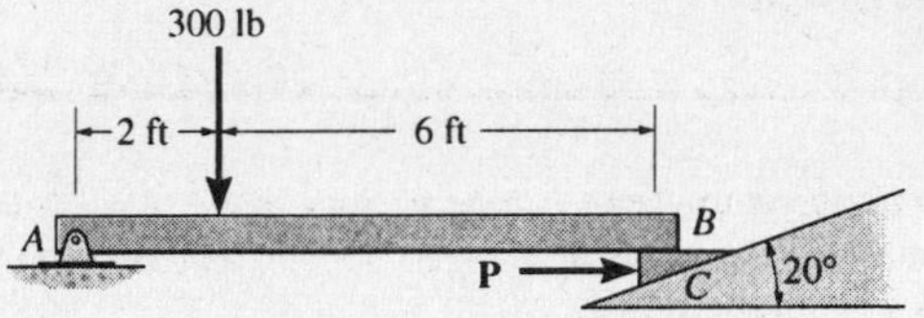

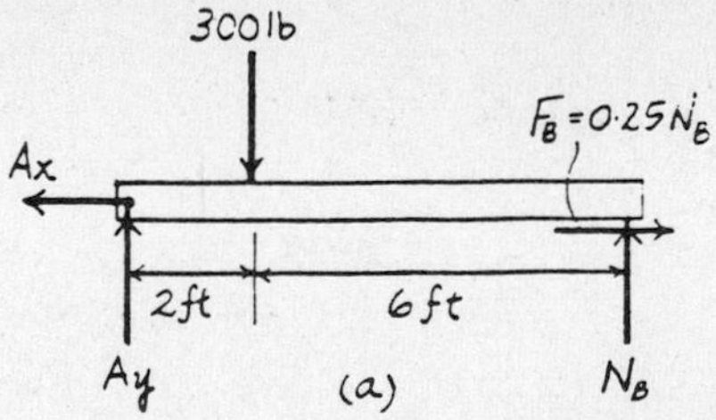

Equations of Equilibrium and Friction : If the wedge is on the verge of moving to the right, then slipping will have to occur at both contact surfaces. Thus, $F_B = \mu_s N_B = 0.25 N_A$ and $F_C = \mu_s N_C = 0.25 N_C$. From FBD (a),

$$\curvearrowleft + \Sigma M_A = 0; \quad N_B(8) - 300(2) = 0 \quad N_B = 75.0 \text{ lb}$$

From FBD (b),

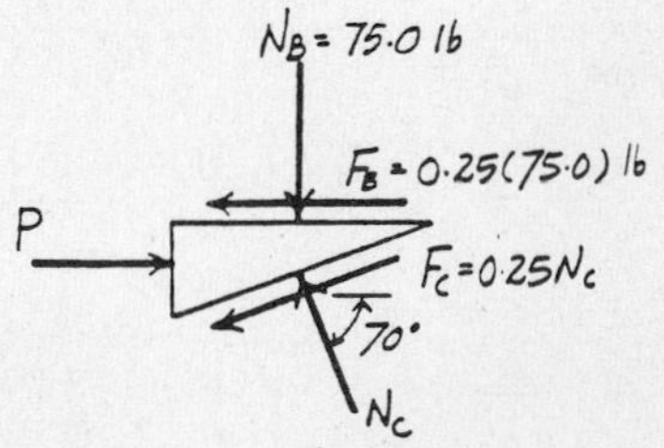

$$+\uparrow \Sigma F_y = 0; \quad N_C \sin 70° - 0.25 N_C \sin 20° - 75.0 = 0$$

$$N_C = 87.80 \text{ lb}$$

$$\xrightarrow{+} \Sigma F_x = 0; \quad P - 0.25(75.0) - 0.25(87.80)\cos 20° - 87.80 \cos 70° = 0$$

$$P = 69.4 \text{ lb}$$ **Ans**

8-70. If the beam AD is loaded as shown, determine the horizontal force P which must be applied to the wedge in order to remove it from under the beam. The coefficients of static friction at the wedge's top and bottom surfaces are $\mu_{CA} = 0.25$ and $\mu_{CB} = 0.35$, respectively. If $P = 0$, is the wedge self-locking? Neglect the weight and size of the wedge and the thickness of the beam.

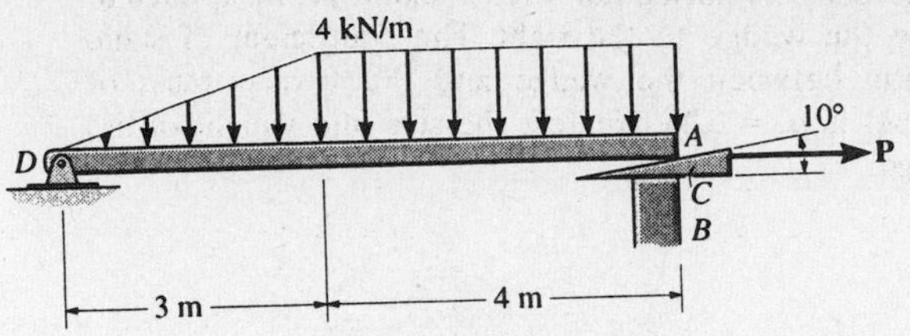

Equations of Equilibrium and Friction : If the wedge is on the verge of moving to the right, then slipping will have to occur at both contact surfaces. Thus, $F_A = \mu_{s_A} N_A = 0.25N_A$ and $F_B = \mu_{s_B} N_B = 0.35N_B$. From FBD (a),

$$\circlearrowleft + \Sigma M_D = 0; \quad N_A \cos 10°(7) + 0.25N_A \sin 10°(7) - 6.00(2) - 16.0(5) = 0$$

$$N_A = 12.78 \text{ kN}$$

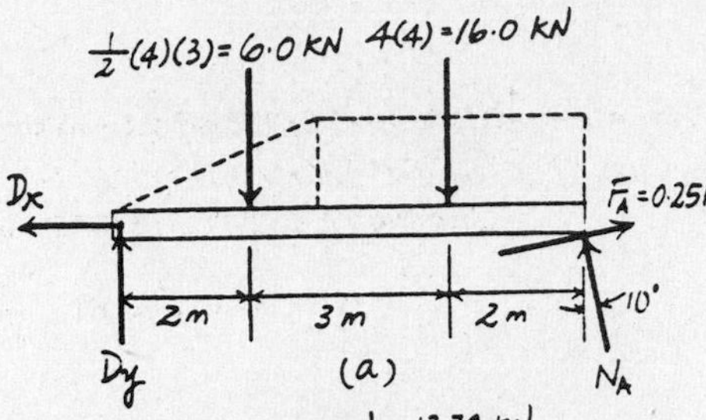

From FBD (b),

$$+\uparrow \Sigma F_y = 0; \quad N_B - 12.78\sin 80° - 0.25(12.78)\sin 10° = 0$$

$$N_B = 13.14 \text{ kN}$$

$$\xrightarrow{+} \Sigma F_x = 0; \quad P + 12.78\cos 80° - 0.25(12.78)\cos 10° - 0.35(13.14) = 0$$

$$P = 5.53 \text{ kN} \qquad \textbf{Ans}$$

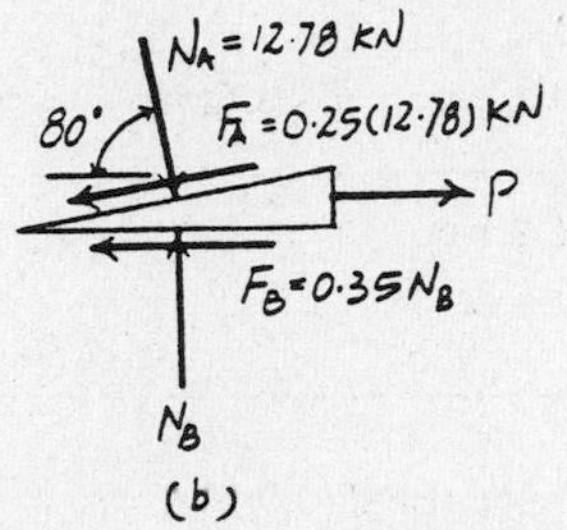

Since a force $P(> 0)$ is required to pull out the wedge, **the wedge will be self-locking when** $P = 0$. **Ans**

8-71. Prove that the lead l must be less than $2\pi r \mu_s$ for the jack screw shown in Fig. 8-16 to be "self-locking."

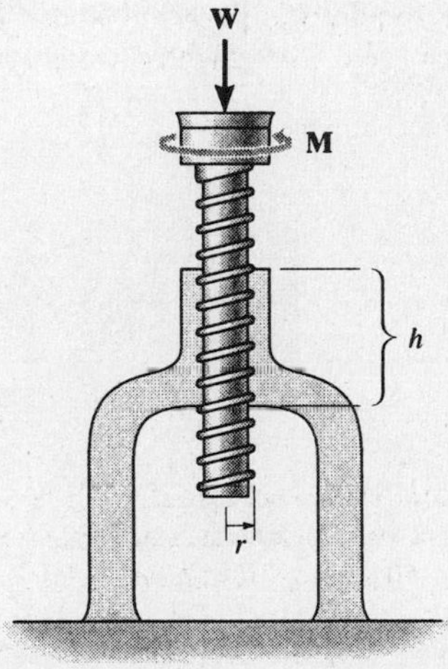

For self-locking, $\phi_s > \theta_p$ or $\tan \phi_s > \tan \theta_p$;

$$\mu_s > \frac{l}{2\pi r}; \quad l < 2\pi r \mu_s \quad \text{Q.E.D.}$$

***8-72.** The square-threaded bolt is used to join two plates together. If the bolt has a mean diameter of d = 20 mm and a lead of l = 3 mm, determine the smallest torque M required to loosen the bolt if the tension in the bolt is T = 40 kN. The coefficient of static friction between the threads and the bolt is μ_s = 0.15.

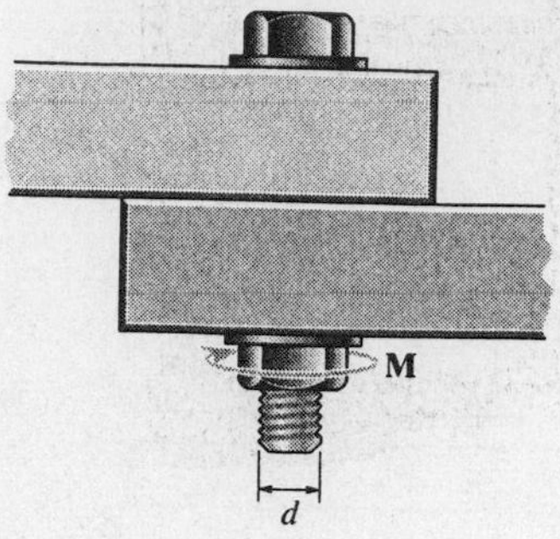

$\phi = \tan^{-1} 0.15 = 8.531°$

$\theta = \tan^{-1} \frac{3}{2\pi(10)} = 2.734°$

$M = r\,W \tan(\phi - \theta) = (0.01)(40\,000) \tan(8.531° - 2.734°)$

$M = 40.6\ \text{N} \cdot \text{m}$ **Ans**

8-73. The square-threaded screw has a mean diameter of 20 mm and a lead of 4 mm. If the weight of the plate A is 5 lb, determine the smallest coefficient of static friction between the screw and the plate so that the plate does not travel down the screw when the plate is suspended as shown.

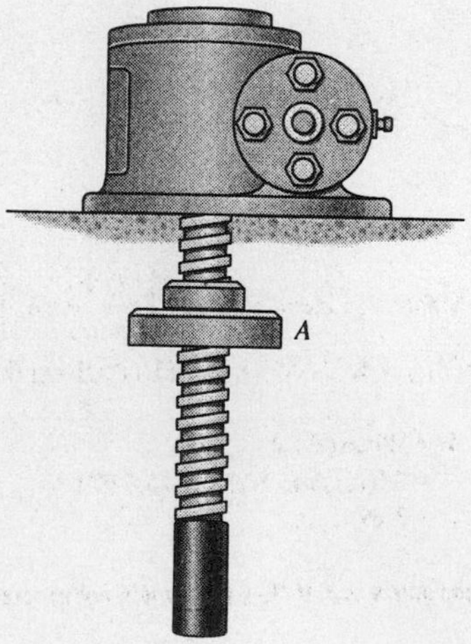

Frictional Forces on Screw : This requires a "self - locking" screw where $\phi_s \geq \theta$. Here, $\theta = \tan^{-1}\left(\frac{l}{2\pi r}\right) = \tan^{-1}\left[\frac{4}{2\pi(10)}\right] = 3.643°$.

$\phi_s = \tan^{-1}\mu_s$

$\mu_s = \tan\phi_s$ where $\phi_s = \theta = 3.643°$

$= 0.0637$ **Ans**

8-74. The square threaded screw of the clamp has a mean diameter of 14 mm and a lead of 6 mm. If $\mu_s = 0.2$ for the threads, and the torque applied to the handle is 1.5 N · m, determine the compressive force **F** on the block.

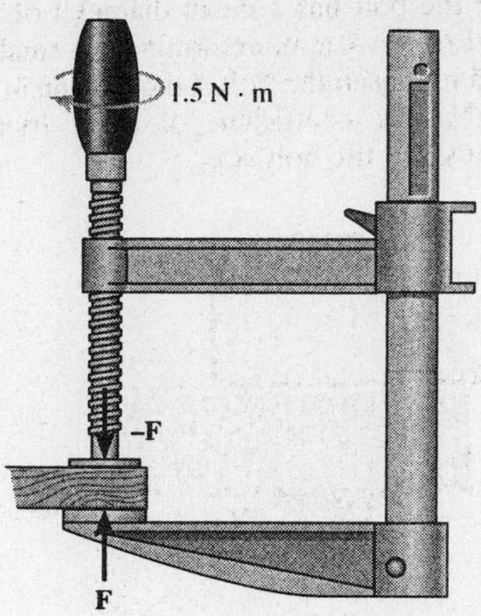

Frictional Forces on Screw : Here, $\theta = \tan^{-1}\left(\frac{l}{2\pi r}\right) = \tan^{-1}\left[\frac{6}{2\pi(7)}\right] = 7.768°$, $W = F$ and $\phi_s = \tan^{-1}\mu_s = \tan^{-1}(0.2) = 11.310°$. Applying Eq. 8 – 3, we have

$$M = Wr\tan(\theta + \phi)$$
$$1.5 = F(0.007)\tan(7.768° + 11.310°)$$
$$F = 620 \text{ N} \qquad \textbf{Ans}$$

Note : Since $\phi_s > \theta$, the screw is self-locking. It will not unscrew even if the moment is removed.

8-75. The device is used to pull the battery cable terminal C from the post of a battery. If the required pulling force is 85 lb, determine the torque **M** that must be applied to the handle on the screw to tighten it. The screw has square threads, a mean diameter of 0.2 in., a lead of 0.08 in., and the coefficient of static friction is $\mu_s = 0.5$.

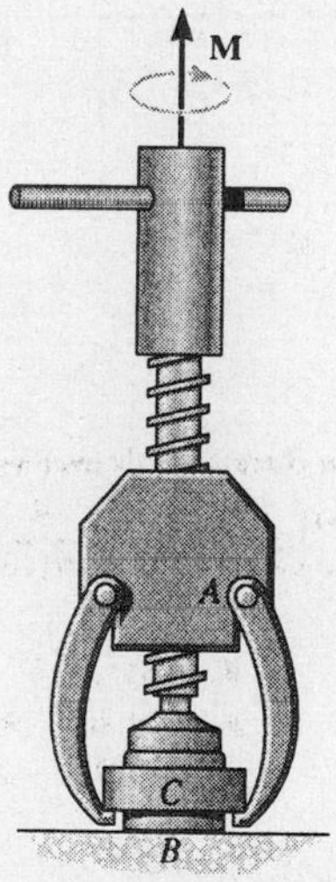

Frictional Forces on Screw : Here, $\theta = \tan^{-1}\left(\frac{l}{2\pi r}\right) = \tan^{-1}\left[\frac{0.08}{2\pi(0.1)}\right] = 7.256°$, $W = 85$ lb and $\phi_s = \tan^{-1}\mu_s = \tan^{-1}(0.5) = 26.565°$. Applying Eq. 8 – 3, we have

$$M = Wr\tan(\theta + \phi)$$
$$= 85(0.1)\tan(7.256° + 26.565°)$$
$$= 5.69 \text{ lb} \cdot \text{in} \qquad \textbf{Ans}$$

Note : Since $\phi_s > \theta$, the screw is self-locking. It will not unscrew even if the moment is removed.

8-76. The automobile jack is subjected to a vertical load of $F = 8$ kN. If a square-threaded screw, having a lead of 5 mm and a mean diameter of 10 mm, is used in the jack, determine the force that must be applied perpendicular to the handle to (a) raise the load, and (b) lower the load; $\mu_s = 0.2$. The supporting plate exerts only vertical forces at A and B, and each cross link has a total length of 200 mm.

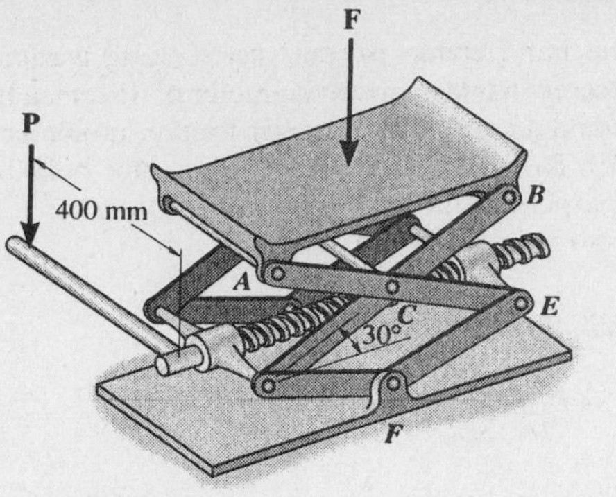

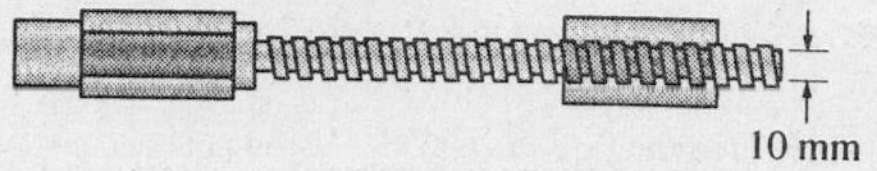

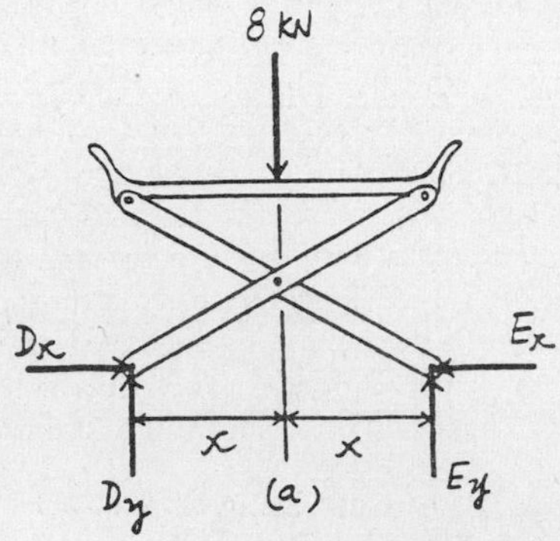

Equations of Equilibrium : From FBD (a),

$$\curvearrowleft + \Sigma M_E = 0; \quad 8(x) - D_y(2x) = 0 \quad D_y = 4.00 \text{ kN}$$

From FBD (b),

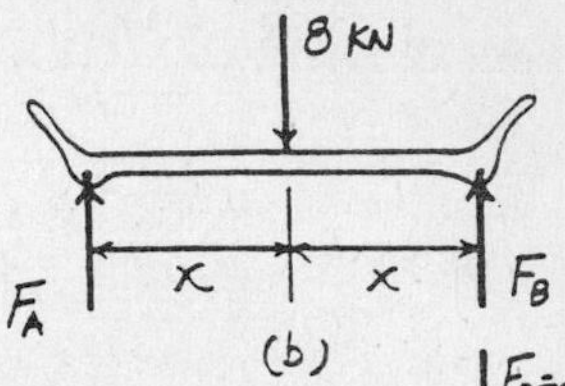

$$\curvearrowleft + \Sigma M_A = 0; \quad F_B(2x) - 8(x) = 0 \quad F_B = 4.00 \text{ kN}$$

From FBD (c),

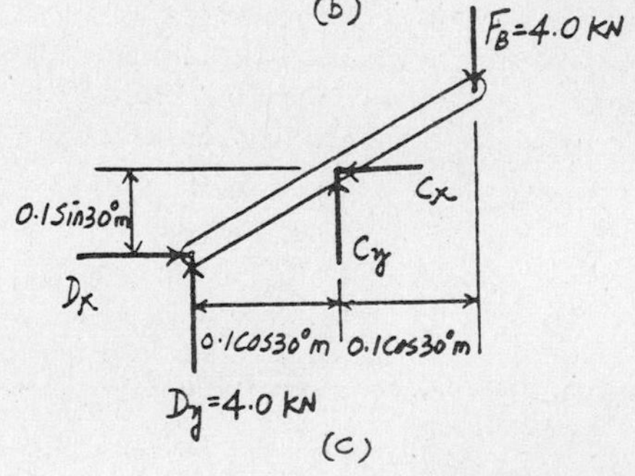

$$\curvearrowleft + \Sigma M_C = 0; \quad D_x(0.1\sin 30°) - 4.00(0.2\cos 30°) = 0$$
$$D_x = 13.86 \text{ kN}$$

Member DF is a two force member. Analysing the forces that act on pin D[FBD (d)], we have

$$+\uparrow \Sigma F_y = 0; \quad F_{DF}\sin 30° - 4.00 = 0 \quad F_{DF} = 8.00 \text{ kN}$$

$$\xrightarrow{+} \Sigma F_x = 0; \quad P' - 13.86 - 8.00\cos 30° = 0 \quad P' = 20.78 \text{ kN}$$

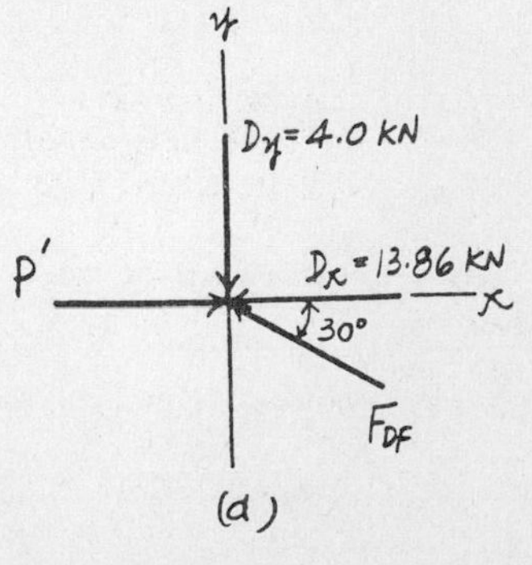

Frictional Forces on Screw : Here, $\theta = \tan^{-1}\left(\frac{l}{2\pi r}\right) = \tan^{-1}\left[\frac{5}{2\pi(5)}\right] = 9.043°$, $W = P' = 20.78$ kN, $M = 0.4P$ and $\phi_s = \tan^{-1}\mu_s = \tan^{-1}(0.2) = 11.310°$. Applying Eq. 8-3 if the jack is **raising the load**, we have

$$M = Wr\tan(\theta + \phi)$$
$$0.4P = 20.78(0.005)\tan(9.043° + 11.310°)$$
$$P = 0.09638 \text{ kN} = 96.4 \text{ N} \qquad \textbf{Ans}$$

Applying Eq. 8-5 if the jack is **lowering the load**, we have

$$M'' = Wr\tan(\phi - \theta)$$
$$0.4P = 20.78(0.005)\tan(11.310° - 9.043°)$$
$$P = 0.01028 \text{ kN} = 10.3 \text{ N} \qquad \textbf{Ans}$$

Note : Since $\phi_s > \theta$, the screw is self-locking. It will not unscrew even if force **P** is removed.

8-77. The hand clamp is constructed using a square-threaded screw having a mean diameter of 36 mm, a lead of 4 mm, and a coefficient of static friction at the screw of $\mu_s = 0.3$. To tighten the screw, a force of $F = 20$ N is applied perpendicular to the handle. Determine the clamping force in the board AB.

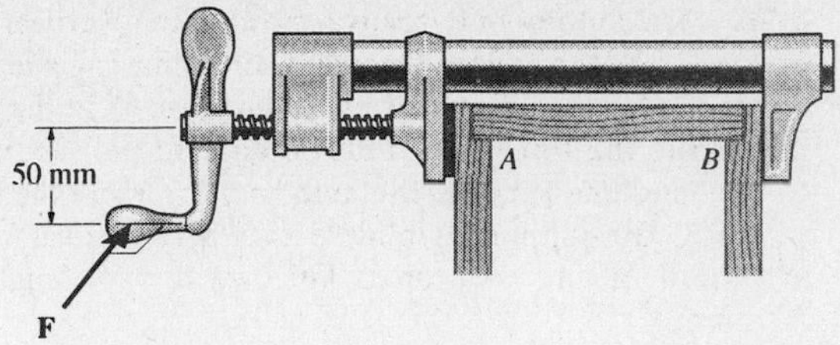

$$\phi = \tan^{-1}(0.3) = 16.70°$$

$$\theta = \tan^{-1}\left(\frac{4}{2\pi(18)}\right) = 2.026°$$

$$M = Wr\tan(\phi + \theta)$$

$$20\,(0.05) = F_{AB}\,(0.018)\tan(16.70° + 2.026°)$$

$F_{AB} = 164$ N **Ans**

8-78. The hand clamp is constructed using a square-threaded screw having a mean diameter of 36 mm, a lead of 4 mm, and a coefficient of static friction at the screw of $\mu_s = 0.3$. If the clamping force in the board AB is 300 N, determine the reversed force $-\mathbf{F}$ that must be applied perpendicular to the handle in order to loosen the screw.

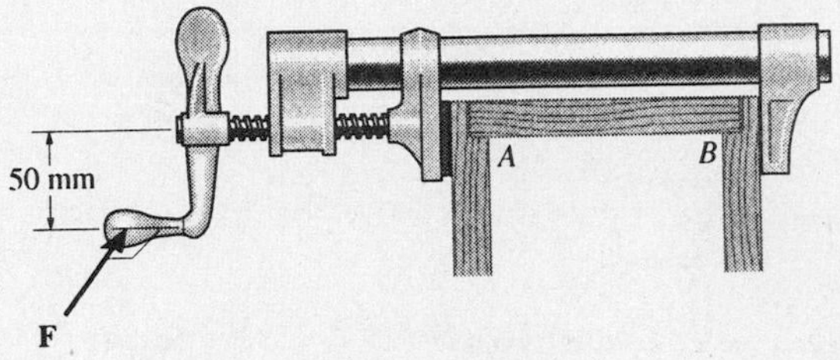

$$\phi = \tan^{-1}(0.3) = 16.70°$$

$$\theta = \tan^{-1}\left(\frac{4}{2\pi(18)}\right) = 2.026°$$

$$F\,(0.05) = 300\,(0.018)\tan(16.70° - 2.026°)$$

$F = 28.3$ N **Ans**

8-79. The shaft has a square-threaded screw with a lead of 8 mm and a mean radius of 15 mm. If it is in contact with a plate gear having a mean radius of 30 mm, determine the resisting torque **M** on the plate gear which can be overcome if a torque of 7 N · m is applied to the shaft. The coefficient of static friction at the screw is $\mu_B = 0.2$. Neglect friction of the bearings located at A and B.

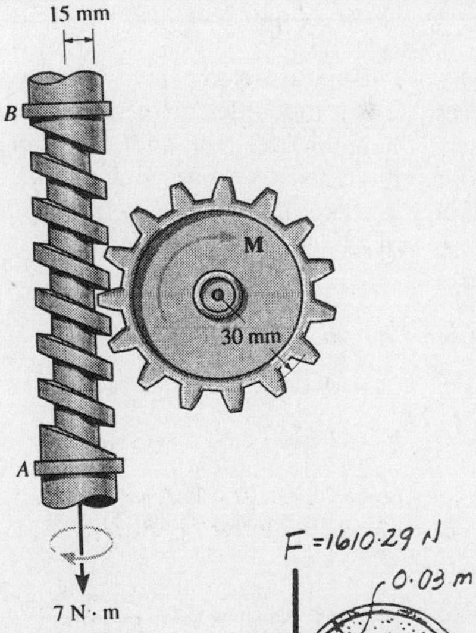

Frictional Forces on Screw : Here, $\theta = \tan^{-1}\left(\frac{l}{2\pi r}\right) = \tan^{-1}\left[\frac{8}{2\pi(15)}\right] = 4.852°$, $W = F$, $M = 7$ N · m and $\phi_s = \tan^{-1}\mu_s = \tan^{-1}(0.2) = 11.310°$. Applying Eq. 8 – 3, we have

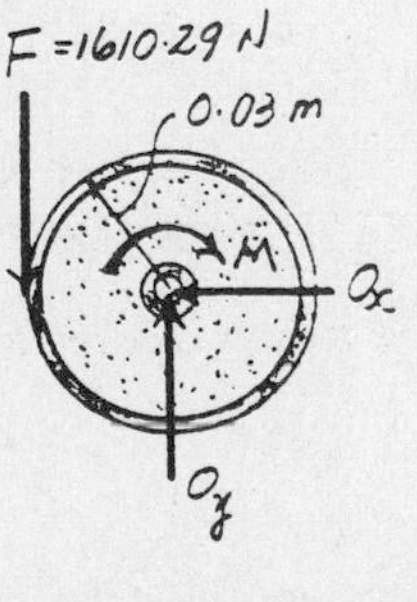

$$M = Wr\tan(\theta + \phi)$$
$$7 = F(0.015)\tan(4.852° + 11.310°)$$
$$F = 1610.29 \text{ N}$$

Note : Since $\phi_s > \theta$, the screw is self - locking. It will not unscrew even if force **F** is removed.

Equations of Equilibrium :

$$+\Sigma M_O = 0; \quad 1610.29(0.03) - M = 0$$
$$M = 48.3 \text{ N} \cdot \text{m}$$ **Ans**

***8-80.** The braking mechanism consists of two pinned arms and a square-threaded screw with left and right-hand threads. Thus when turned, the screw draws the two arms together. If the lead of the screw is 4 mm, the mean diameter 12 mm, and the coefficient of static friction is $\mu_s = 0.35$, determine the tension in the screw when a torque of 5 N · m is applied to tighten the screw. If the coefficient of static friction between the brake pads A and B and the circular shaft is $\mu'_s = 0.5$, determine the maximum torque M the brake can resist.

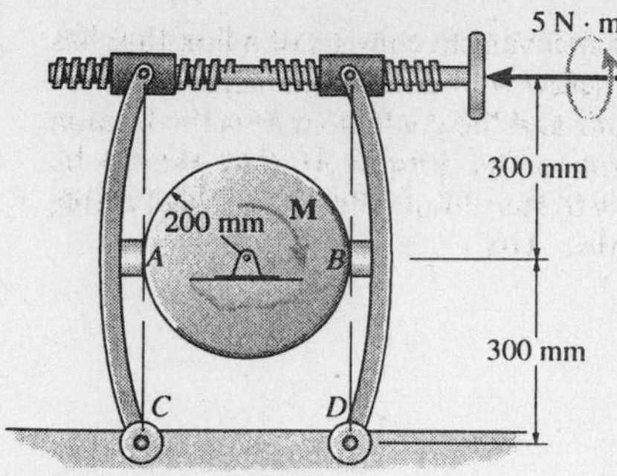

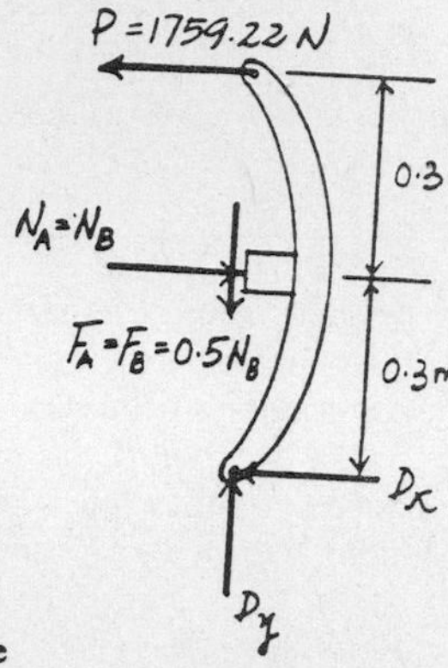

Frictional Forces on Screw : Here, $\theta = \tan^{-1}\left(\frac{l}{2\pi r}\right) = \tan^{-1}\left[\frac{4}{2\pi(6)}\right] = 6.057°$, $M = 5$ N · m and $\phi_s = \tan^{-1}\mu_s = \tan^{-1}(0.35) = 19.290°$. Since friction at two screws must be overcome, then, $W = 2P$. Applying Eq. 8 – 3, we have

$$M = Wr\tan(\theta + \phi)$$
$$5 = 2P(0.006)\tan(6.057° + 19.290°)$$
$$P = 879.61 \text{ N} = 880 \text{ N}$$ **Ans**

Note : Since $\phi_s > \theta$, the screw is self-locking. It will not unscrew even if moment M is removed.

Equations of Equilibrium and Friction : Since the shaft is on the verge to rotate about point O, then, $F_A = \mu_s' N_A = 0.5N_A$ and $F_B = \mu_s' N_B = 0.5N_B$. From FBD (a),

$\circlearrowleft + \Sigma M_D = 0;$ $\quad 879.61(0.6) - N_B(0.3) = 0 \qquad N_B = 1759.22$ N

From FBD (b),

$\circlearrowleft + \Sigma M_O = 0;$ $\quad 2[0.5(1759.22)](0.2) - M = 0 \qquad M = 352$ N · m **Ans**

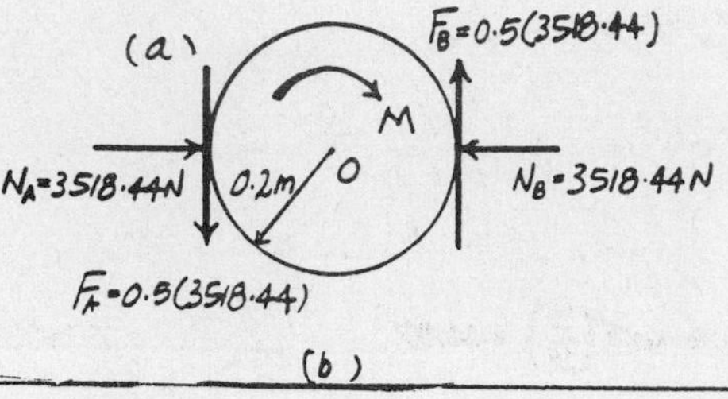

8-81. The fixture clamp consist of a square-threaded screw having a coefficient of static friction of $\mu_s = 0.3$, mean diameter of 3 mm, and a lead of 1 mm. The five points indicated are pin connections. Determine the clamping force at the smooth blocks D and E when a torque of $M = 0.08$ N · m is applied to the handle of the screw.

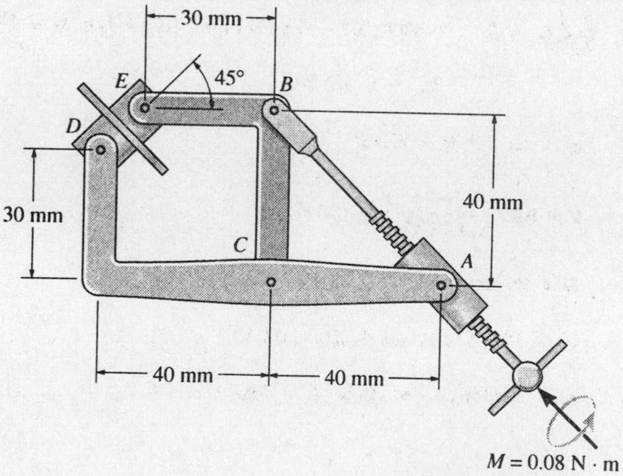

Frictional Forces on Screw : Here, $\theta = \tan^{-1}\left(\frac{l}{2\pi r}\right) = \tan^{-1}\left[\frac{1}{2\pi(1.5)}\right] = 6.057°$, $W = P$, $M = 0.08$ N · m and $\phi_s = \tan^{-1}\mu_s = \tan^{-1}(0.3) = 16.699°$. Applying Eq. 8 – 3, we have

$$M = Wr\tan(\theta + \phi)$$
$$0.08 = P(0.0015)\tan(6.057° + 16.699°)$$
$$P = 127.15 \text{ N}$$

Note : Since $\phi_s > \theta$, the screw is self-locking. It will not unscrew even if moment M is removed.

Equation of Equilibrium :

$\circlearrowleft + \Sigma M_C = 0;$ $\quad 127.15\cos 45°(40) - F_E\cos 45°(40) - F_E\sin 45°(30) = 0$

$F_E = 72.65 \text{ N} = 72.7 \text{ N}$ **Ans**

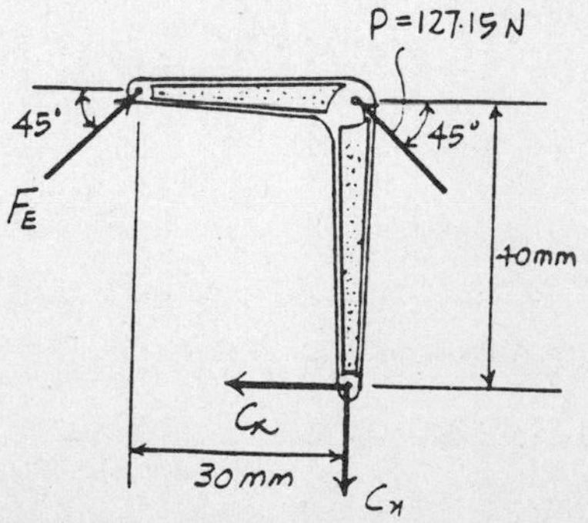

The equilibrium of clamped block requires that

$F_D = F_E = 72.7$ N **Ans**

8-82. The jacking mechanism consists of a link that has a square-threaded screw with a mean diameter of 0.5 in. and a lead of 0.20 in., and the coefficient of static friction is $\mu_s = 0.4$. Determine the torque M that should be applied to the screw to start lifting the 6000-lb load acting at the end of member ABC.

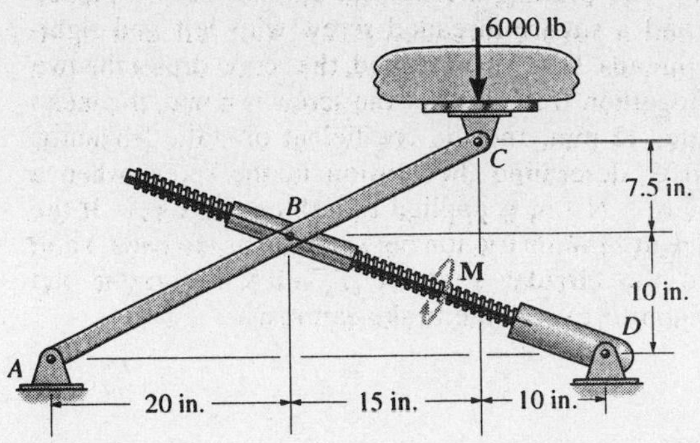

$$\alpha = \tan^{-1}\left(\frac{10}{25}\right) = 21.80°$$

$$\circlearrowleft + \Sigma M_A = 0; \qquad -6000\,(35) + F_{BD} \cos 21.80°\,(10) + F_{BD} \sin 21.80°\,(20) = 0$$

$$F_{BD} = 12\,565 \text{ lb}$$

$$\phi_s = \tan^{-1}(0.4) = 21.80°$$

$$\theta = \tan^{-1}\left(\frac{0.2}{2\pi\,(0.25)}\right) = 7.256°$$

$$M = Wr \tan(\theta + \phi)$$

$$M = 12\,565\,(0.25) \tan(7.256° + 21.80°)$$

$$M = 1745 \text{ lb}\cdot\text{in.} = 145 \text{ lb}\cdot\text{ft} \qquad \textbf{Ans}$$

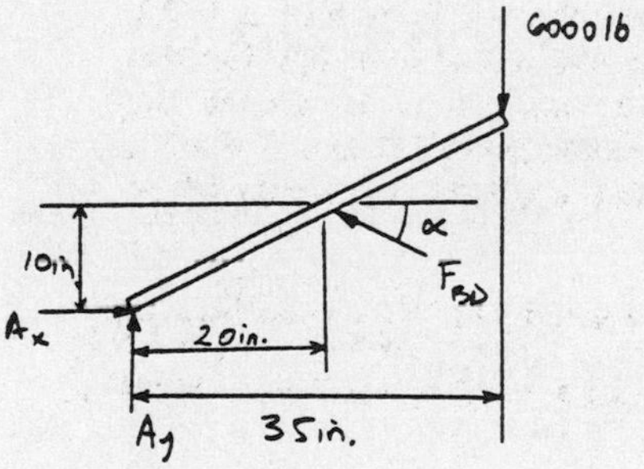

8-83. A turnbuckle, similar to that shown in Fig. 8-18, is used to tension member AB of the truss. The coefficient of the static friction between the square threaded screws and the turnbuckle is $\mu_s = 0.5$. The screws have a mean radius of 6 mm and a lead of 3 mm. If a torque of $M = 10\ \text{N}\cdot\text{m}$ is applied to the turnbuckle, to draw the screws closer together, determine the force in each member of the truss. No external forces act on the truss.

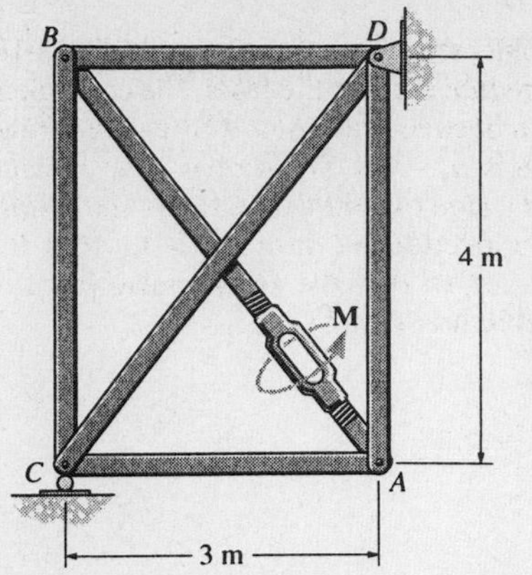

Frictional Forces on Screw : Here, $\theta = \tan^{-1}\left(\dfrac{l}{2\pi r}\right) = \tan^{-1}\left[\dfrac{3}{2\pi(6)}\right]$ $= 4.550°$, $M = 5\ \text{N}\cdot\text{m}$ and $\phi_s = \tan^{-1}\mu_s = \tan^{-1}(0.5) = 26.565°$. Since friction at two screws must be overcome, then, $W = 2F_{AB}$. Applying Eq. 8 – 3, we have

$$M = Wr\tan(\theta + \phi)$$
$$10 = 2F_{AB}\,(0.006)\tan(4.550° + 26.565°)$$
$$F_{AB} = 1380.62\ \text{N (T)} = 1.38\ \text{kN} \qquad \textbf{Ans}$$

Note : Since $\phi_s > \theta$, the screw is self - locking. It will not unscrew even if moment **M** is removed.

Method of Joints :

Joint B

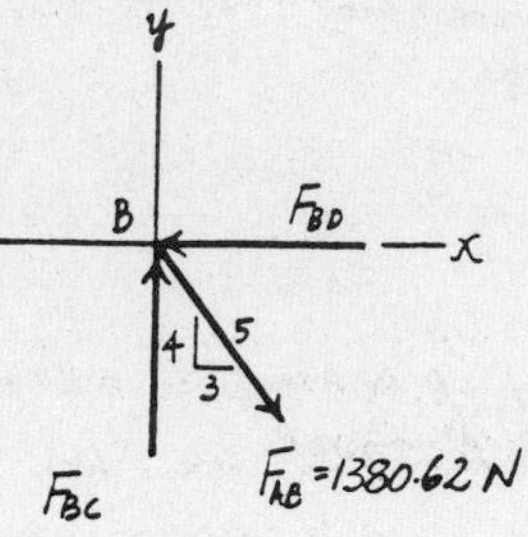

$\overset{+}{\rightarrow}\Sigma F_x = 0;\quad 1380.62\left(\dfrac{3}{5}\right) - F_{BD} = 0$

$F_{BD} = 828.37\ \text{N (C)} = 828\ \text{N (C)}$ **Ans**

$+\uparrow\Sigma F_y = 0;\quad F_{BC} - 1380.62\left(\dfrac{4}{5}\right) = 0$

$F_{BC} = 1104.50\ \text{N (C)} = 1.10\ \text{kN (C)}$ **Ans**

Joint A

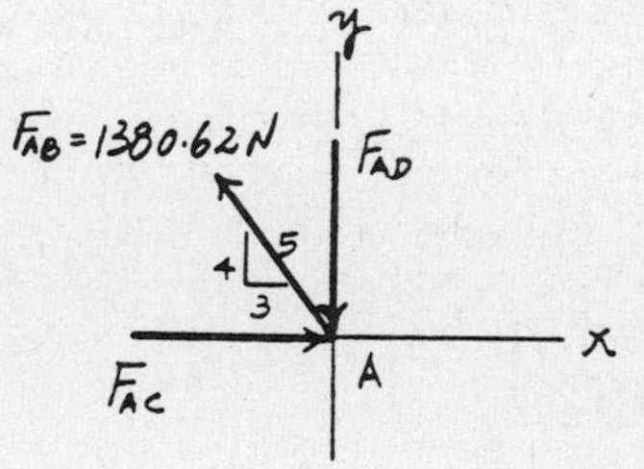

$\overset{+}{\rightarrow}\Sigma F_x = 0;\quad F_{AC} - 1380.62\left(\dfrac{3}{5}\right) = 0$

$F_{AC} = 828.37\ \text{N (C)} = 828\ \text{N (C)}$ **Ans**

$+\uparrow\Sigma F_y = 0;\quad 1380.62\left(\dfrac{4}{5}\right) - F_{AD} = 0$

$F_{AD} = 1104.50\ \text{N (C)} = 1.10\ \text{kN (C)}$ **Ans**

Joint C

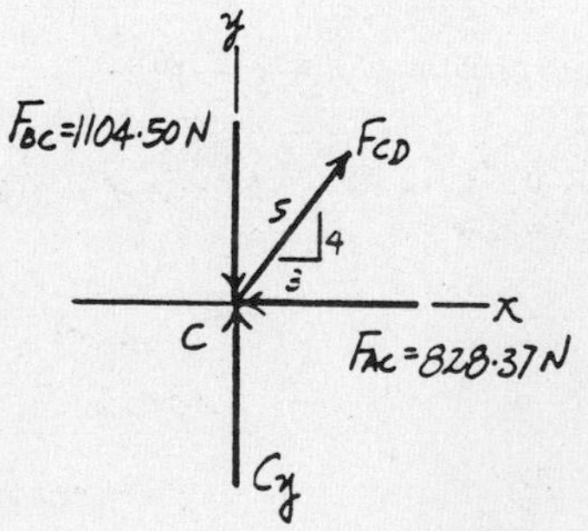

$\overset{+}{\rightarrow}\Sigma F_x = 0;\quad F_{CD}\left(\dfrac{3}{5}\right) - 828.37 = 0$

$F_{CD} = 1380.62\ \text{N (T)} = 1.38\ \text{kN (T)}$ **Ans**

$+\uparrow\Sigma F_y = 0;\quad C_y + 1380.62\left(\dfrac{4}{5}\right) - 1104.50 = 0$

$C_y = 0$ (***No external applied load. check!***)

***8-84.** A turnbuckle, similar to that shown in Fig. 8-18, is used to tension member AB of the truss. The coefficient of the static friction between the square-threaded screws and the turnbuckle is $\mu_s = 0.5$. The screws have a mean radius of 6 mm and a lead of 3 mm. Determine the torque M which must be applied to the turnbuckle to draw the screws closer together, so that the compressive force of 500 N is developed in member BC.

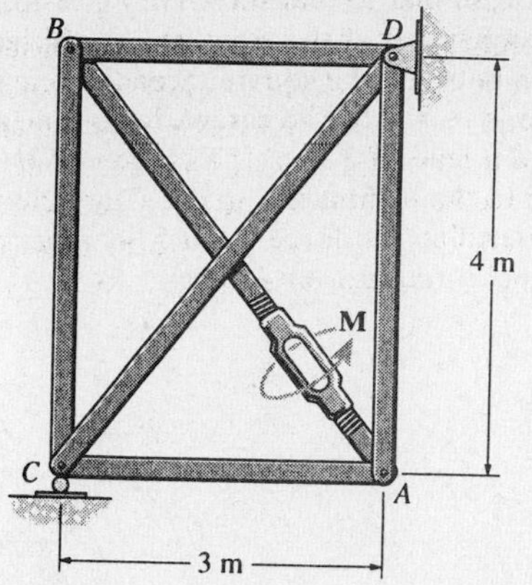

Method of Joints :

Joint B

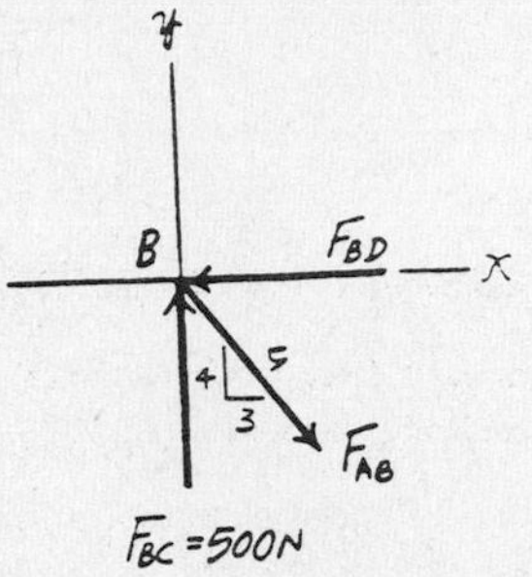

$$+\uparrow \Sigma F_y = 0; \quad 500 - F_{AB}\left(\frac{4}{5}\right) = 0 \quad F_{AB} = 625 \text{ N (C)}$$

Frictional Forces on Screws : Here, $\theta = \tan^{-1}\left(\frac{l}{2\pi r}\right) = \tan^{-1}\left[\frac{3}{2\pi(6)}\right] = 4.550°$, $M = 5$ N·m and $\phi_s = \tan^{-1}\mu_s = \tan^{-1}(0.5) = 26.565°$. Since friction at two screws must be overcome, then, $W = 2F_{AB} = 2(625) = 1250$ N. Applying Eq. 8 – 3, we have

$$M = Wr\tan(\theta + \phi)$$
$$= 1250(0.006)\tan(4.550° + 26.565°)$$
$$= 4.53 \text{ N} \cdot \text{m} \qquad \textbf{Ans}$$

Note : Since $\phi_s > \theta$, the screw is self-locking. It will not unscrew even if moment M is removed.

8-85. A "hawser" is wrapped around a fixed "capstan" to secure a ship for docking. If the tension in the rope, caused by the ship, is 1500 lb, determine the least number of complete turns the rope must be rapped around the capstan in order to prevent slipping of the rope. The greatest horizontal force that a longshoreman can exert on the rope is 50 lb. The coefficient of static friction is $\mu_s = 0.3$.

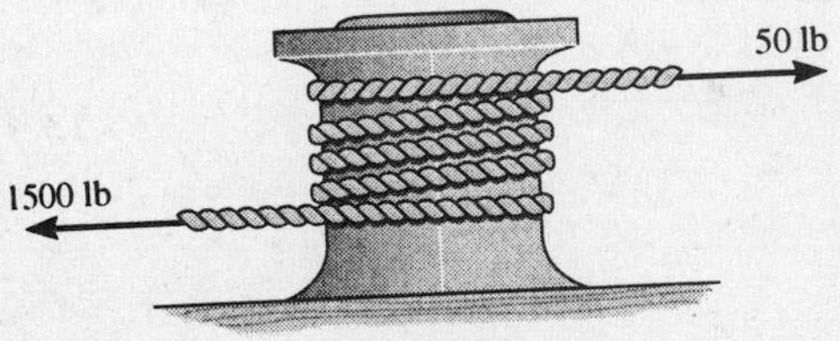

Frictional Force on Flat Belt : Here, $T_1 = 50$ lb and $T_2 = 1500$ lb. Applying Eq. 8 – 6, we have

$$T_2 = T_1 e^{\mu\beta}$$
$$1500 = 50e^{0.3\beta}$$
$$\beta = 11.337 \text{ rad}$$

The least number of turns of the rope required is $\frac{11.337}{2\pi} = 1.80$ turns. Thus

Use $\quad n = 2$ turns $\qquad$ **Ans**

8-86. If the force T_1 is applied to the rope at A, determine the force T_2 at B needed to pull the rope over the two fixed drums having the angles of contact and the coefficients of static friction shown.

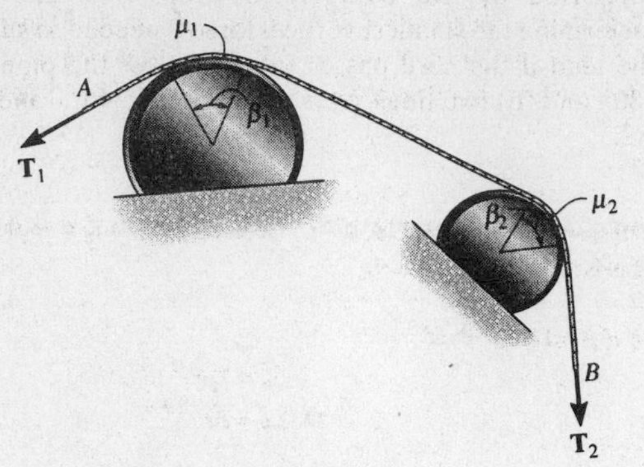

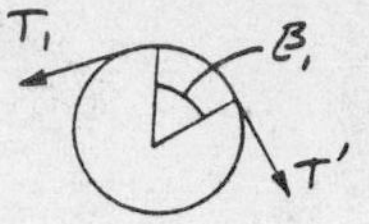

$T' = T_1 e^{\mu_1 \beta_1}$

$T_2 = T' e^{\mu_2 \beta_2}$

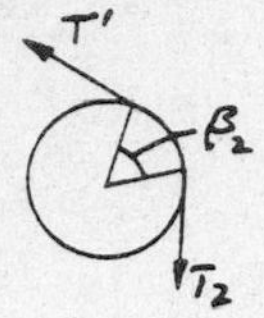

Thus,

$T_2 = T_1 e^{\mu_1 \beta_1} e^{\mu_2 \beta_2}$

or

$T_2 = T_1 e^{(\mu_1 \beta_1 + \mu_2 \beta_2)}$ **Ans**

8-87. Determine the maximum and the minimum values of weight W which may be applied without causing the 50-lb block to slip. The coefficient of static friction between the block and the plane is $\mu_s = 0.2$, and between the rope and the drum D $\mu'_s = 0.3$.

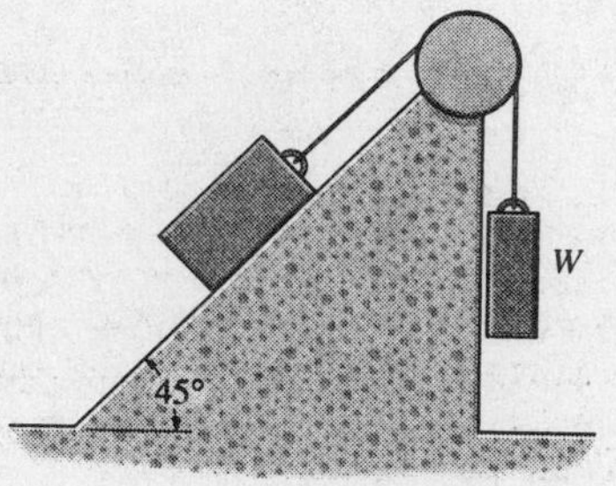

Equations of Equilibrium and Friction : Since the block is on the verge of sliding up or down the plane, then, $F = \mu_s N = 0.2N$. If the block is on the verge of sliding up the plane [FBD (a)],

$\nwarrow + \Sigma F_{y'} = 0; \quad N - 50\cos 45° = 0 \quad N = 35.36 \text{ lb}$

$\nearrow + \Sigma F_{x'} = 0; \quad T_1 - 0.2(35.36) - 50\sin 45° = 0 \quad T_1 = 42.43 \text{ lb}$

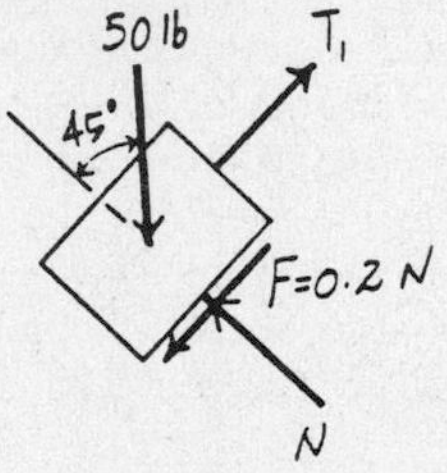

(a)

If the block is on the verge of sliding down the plane[FBD (b)],

$\nwarrow + \Sigma F_{y'} = 0; \quad N - 50\cos 45° = 0 \quad N = 35.36 \text{ lb}$

$\nearrow + \Sigma F_{x'} = 0; \quad T_2 + 0.2(35.36) - 50\sin 45° = 0 \quad T_2 = 28.28 \text{ lb}$

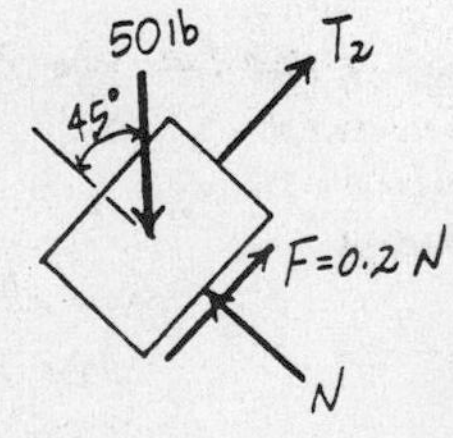

(b)

Frictional Force on Flat Belt : Here, $\beta = 45° + 90° = 135° = \dfrac{3\pi}{4}$ rad.

If the block is on the verge of sliding up the plane, $T_1 = 42.43$ lb and $T_2 = W$.

$$T_2 = T_1 e^{\mu\beta}$$
$$W = 42.43 e^{0.3\left(\frac{3\pi}{4}\right)}$$
$$= 86.02 \text{ lb} = 86.0 \text{ lb} \qquad \textbf{Ans}$$

If the block is on the verge of sliding down the plane, $T_1 = W$ and $T_2 = 28.28$ lb.

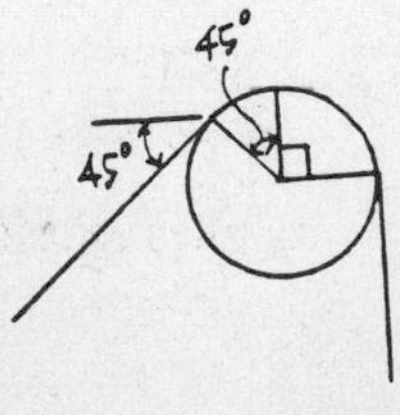

$$T_2 = T_1 e^{\mu\beta}$$
$$28.28 = W e^{0.3\left(\frac{3\pi}{4}\right)}$$

$$W = 13.95 \text{ lb} = 13.9 \text{ lb} \qquad \textbf{Ans}$$

***8-88.** A cylinder having a mass of 250 kg is to be supported by the cord which wraps over the pipe. Determine the smallest vertical force **F** needed to support the load if the cord passes (a) once over the pipe, $\beta = 180°$, and (b) two times over the pipe, $\beta = 540°$. Take $\mu_s = 0.2$.

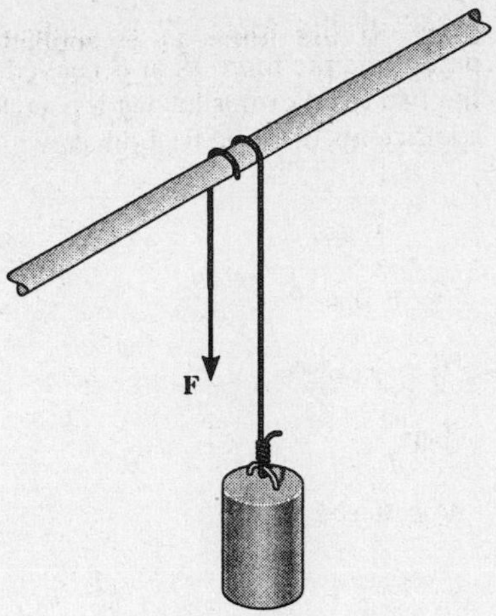

Frictional Force on Flat Belt : Here, $T_1 = F$ and $T_2 = 250(9.81) = 2452.5$ N. Applying Eq. 8 – 6, we have

a) If $\beta = 180° = \pi$ rad

$$T_2 = T_1 e^{\mu\beta}$$
$$2452.5 = Fe^{0.2\pi}$$

$$F = 1308.38 \text{ N} = 1.31 \text{ kN} \qquad \textbf{Ans}$$

b) If $\beta = 540° = 3\pi$ rad

$$T_2 = T_1 e^{\mu\beta}$$
$$2452.5 = Fe^{0.2(3\pi)}$$

$$F = 372.38 \text{ N} = 372 \text{ N} \qquad \textbf{Ans}$$

8-89. A cylinder having a mass of 250 kg is to be supported by the cord which wraps over the pipe. Determine the largest vertical force **F** that can be applied to the cord without moving the cylinder. The cord passes (a) once over the pipe, $\beta = 180°$, and (b) two times over the pipe, $\beta = 540°$. Take $\mu_s = 0.2$.

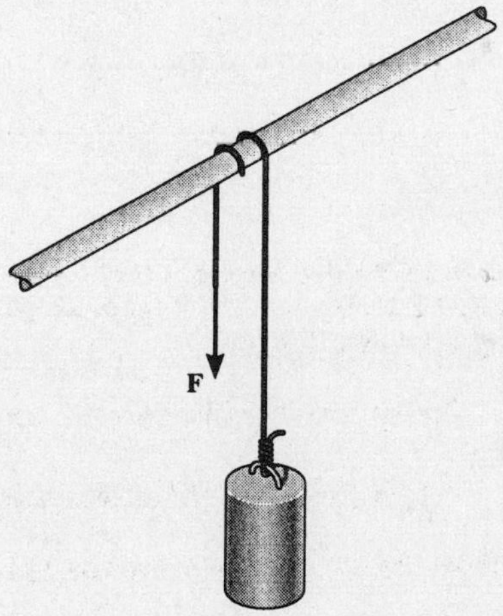

Frictional Force on Flat Belt : Here, $T_1 = 250(9.81) = 2452.5$ N and $T_2 = F$. Applying Eq. 8 – 6, we have

a) If $\beta = 180° = \pi$ rad

$$T_2 = T_1 e^{\mu\beta}$$
$$F = 2452.5e^{0.2\pi}$$

$$F = 4597.10 \text{ N} = 4.60 \text{ kN} \qquad \textbf{Ans}$$

b) If $\beta = 540° = 3\pi$ rad

$$T_2 = T_1 e^{\mu\beta}$$
$$F = 2452.5e^{0.2(3\pi)}$$

$$F = 15152.32 \text{ N} = 16.2 \text{ kN} \qquad \textbf{Ans}$$

***8-90.** The boat has a weight of 500 lb and is held in position off the side of a ship by the spars at A and B. A man having a weight of 130 lb gets in the boat, wraps a rope around an overhead boom at C, and ties it to the end of the boat as shown. If the boat is disconnected from the spars, determine the *minimum number* of *half turns* the rope must make around the boom so that the boat can be safely lowered into the water at constant velocity. Also, what is the normal force between the boat and the man? The coefficient of kinetic friction between the rope and the boom is $\mu_s = 0.15$. *Hint*: The problem requires that the normal force between the man's feet and the boat be as small as possible.

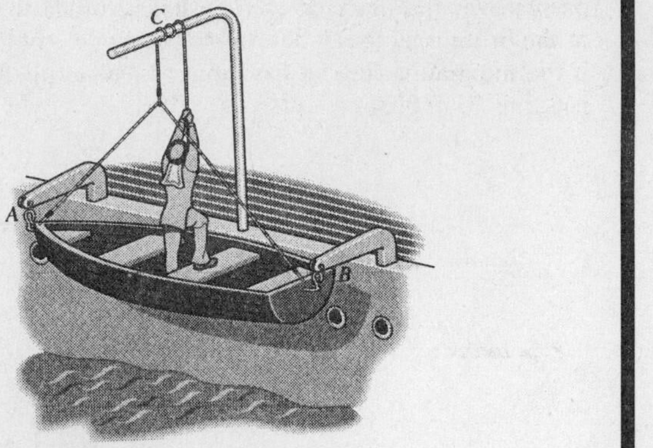

Frictional Force on Flat Belt : If the normal force between the man and the boat is equal to zero, then, $T_1 = 130$ lb and $T_2 = 500$ lb. Applying Eq. 8–6, we have

$$T_2 = T_1 e^{\mu\beta}$$

$$500 = 130e^{0.15\beta}$$

$$\beta = 8.980 \text{ rad}$$

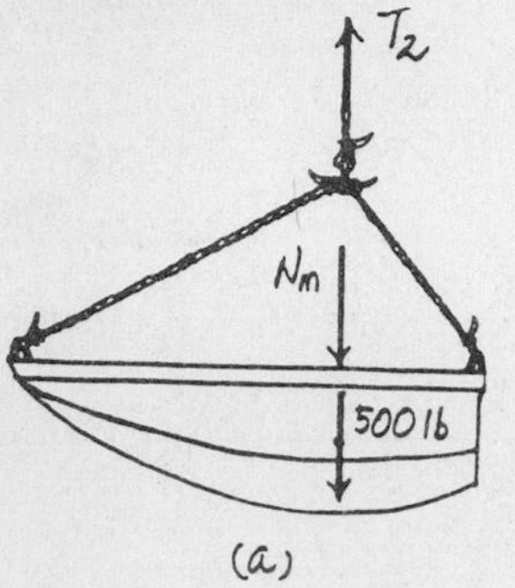

The least number of half turns of the rope required is $\dfrac{8.980}{\pi} = 2.86$ turns. Thus

Use $n = 3$ half turns **Ans**

Equations of Equilibrium : From FBD (a),

$$+\uparrow \Sigma F_y = 0; \quad T_2 - N_m - 500 = 0 \quad T_2 = N_m + 500$$

From FBD (b),

$$+\uparrow \Sigma F_y = 0; \quad T_1 + N_m - 130 = 0 \quad T_1 = 130 - N_m$$

Frictional Force on Flat Belts : Here, $\beta = 3\pi$ rad. Applying Eq. 8–6, we have

$$T_2 = T_1 e^{\mu\beta}$$

$$N_m + 500 = (130 - N_m)e^{0.15(3\pi)}$$

$$N_m = 6.74 \text{ lb} \quad \textbf{Ans}$$

8-91. The 50-lb cylinder is attached to a cord which passes over the drum. If the coefficient of static friction at the drum is $\mu_s = 0.3$, determine the maximum vertical force **P** that can be applied to the roller when $\theta = 30°$ without causing the cylinder to move.

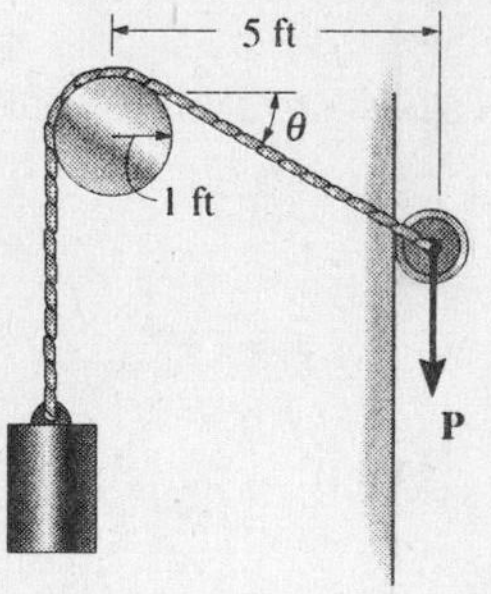

$$T_2 = T_1 e^{\mu\beta}$$

$$T_2 = 50e^{0.3(\frac{\pi}{2}+\frac{\pi}{6})}$$

$$T_2 = 93.723 \text{ lb}$$

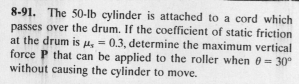

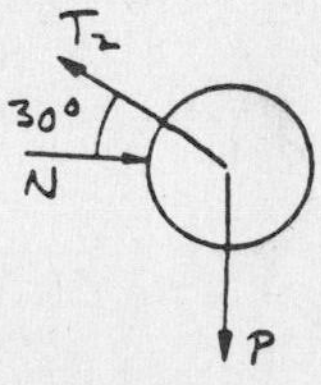

$$+\uparrow \Sigma F_y = 0; \quad T_2 \sin 30° - P = 0$$

$$P = 93.723 \sin 30° = 46.9 \text{ lb} \quad \textbf{Ans}$$

***8-92.** The 50-lb cylinder is attached to a cord which passes over the drum. If the coefficient of static friction at the drum is $\mu_s = 0.3$, determine the angle θ of the cord if the maximum vertical load that can be applied to the roller is $P = 100$ lb.

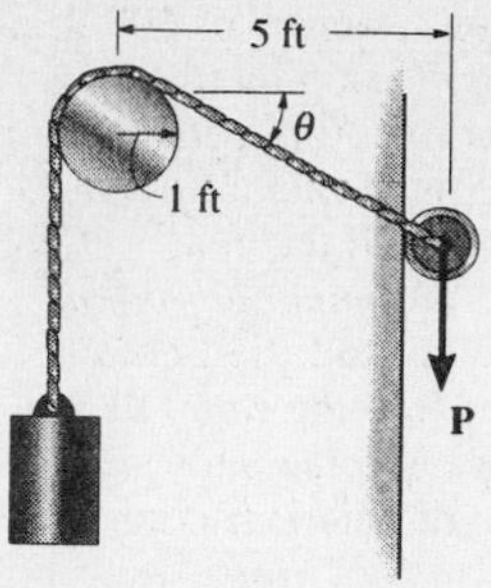

Rope friction :

$$T_2 = T_1 e^{\mu\beta} \quad \text{where} \quad T_1 = 50 \text{ lb}, \ \beta = \frac{\pi}{2} + \theta$$

$$T_2 = 50e^{0.3(\pi/2+\theta)} \qquad (1)$$

From FBD (a)

$$+\uparrow \Sigma F_y = 0; \quad T_2 \sin\theta - 100 = 0 \qquad (2)$$

Substituting Eq. (1) into (2) yields :

$$50e^{0.3(\pi/2+\theta)} \sin\theta = 100$$

$$50e^{0.3(\pi/2)} e^{0.3\theta} \sin\theta = 100$$

$$e^{0.3\theta} \sin\theta = 1.2485$$

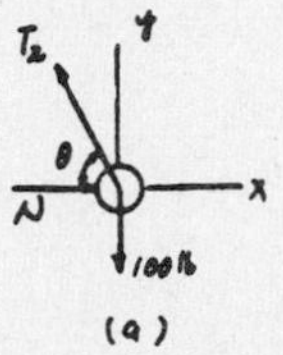

By trial and error $\qquad \theta = 1.1089 \text{ rad} = 63.5°$ $\qquad$ **Ans**

8-93. The 100-lb boy at A is suspended from the cable that passes over the quarter circular cliff rock. Determine if it is possible for the 185-lb woman to hoist him up; and if this is possible, what force must she exert on the cable? The coefficient of static friction between the cable and the rock is $\mu_s = 0.2$, and between the shoes of the woman and the ground $\mu'_s = 0.8$.

$$\beta = \frac{\pi}{2}$$

$$T_2 = T_1 e^{\mu\beta} = 100\, e^{0.2\frac{\pi}{2}} = 136.9 \text{ lb}$$

$$+\uparrow \Sigma F_y = 0; \quad N - 185 = 0$$

$$N = 185 \text{ lb}$$

$$\xrightarrow{+} \Sigma F_x = 0; \quad 136.9 - F = 0$$

$$F = 136.9 \text{ lb}$$

$$F_{max} = 0.8\,(185) = 148 \text{ lb} > 136.9 \text{ lb}$$

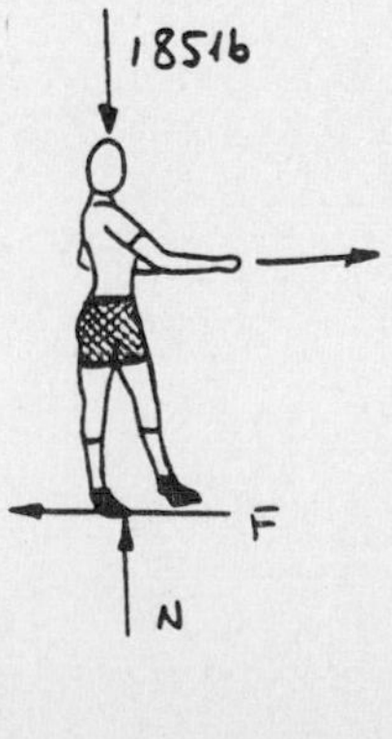

Yes, just barely. $\quad$ **Ans**

8-94. The 100-lb boy at A is suspended from the cable that passes over the quarter circular cliff rock. What force must the woman at A exert on the cable in order to let the boy descend at constant velocity? The coefficient of static friction between the cable and the rock is $\mu_s = 0.4$, and the coefficient of kinetic friction is $\mu_k = 0.35$.

$$\beta = \frac{\pi}{2}$$

$$T_2 = T_1\, e^{\mu\beta}; \qquad 100 = T_1\, e^{0.35\,\frac{\pi}{2}}$$

$$T_1 = 57.7\ \text{lb} \qquad \textbf{Ans}$$

8-95. Show that the frictional relationship between the belt tensions, the coefficient of friction μ, and the angular contacts α and β for the V-belt is $T_2 = T_1 e^{\mu\beta/\sin(\alpha/2)}$.

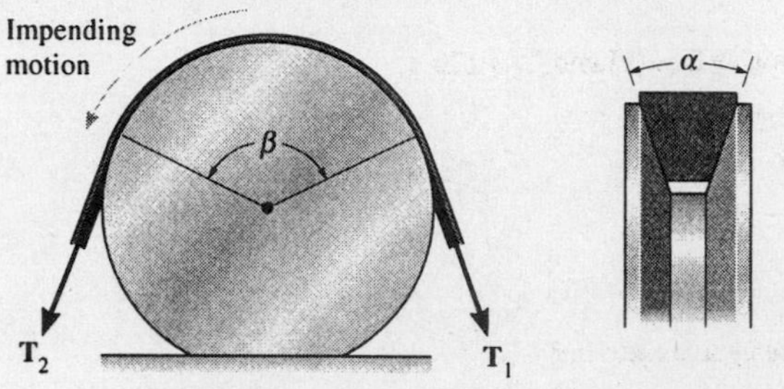

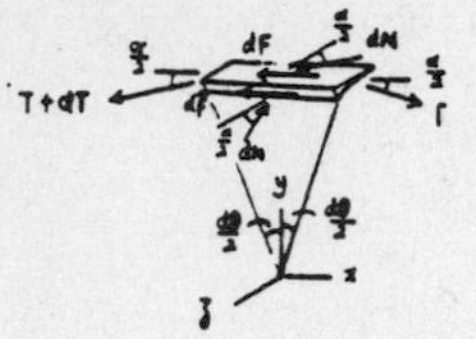

F.B.D of a section of the belt is shown.
Proceeding in the general manner :

$$\Sigma F_x = 0; \qquad -(T+dT)\cos\frac{d\theta}{2} + T\cos\frac{d\theta}{2} + 2\,dF = 0$$

$$\Sigma F_y = 0; \qquad -(T+dT)\sin\frac{d\theta}{2} - T\sin\frac{d\theta}{2} + 2\,dN\sin\frac{\alpha}{2} = 0$$

Replace $\sin\frac{d\theta}{2}$ by $\frac{d\theta}{2}$,

$\cos\frac{d\theta}{2}$ by 1,

$dF = \mu\, dN$

Using this and $(dT)(d\theta) \rightarrow 0$, the above relations become

$$dT = 2\mu\, dN$$

$$T\,d\theta = 2\left(dN\sin\frac{\alpha}{2}\right)$$

Combine $\qquad \frac{dT}{T} = \mu\frac{d\theta}{\sin\frac{\alpha}{2}}$

Integrate from $\theta = 0,\ T = T_1$
to $\theta = \beta,\ T = T_2$

we get,

$$T_2 = T_1\, e^{\left(\frac{\mu\beta}{\sin\frac{\alpha}{2}}\right)} \qquad \textbf{Q.E.D}$$

***8-96.** The smooth beam is being hoisted using a rope which is wrapped around the beam and passes through a ring at A as shown. If the end of the rope is subjected to a tension $\mathbf{T}$ and the coefficient of static friction between the rope and ring is $\mu_s = 0.3$, determine the angle of θ for equilibrium.

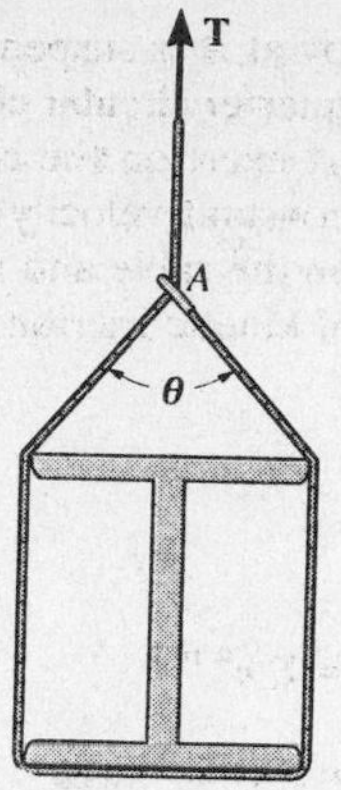

Equation of Equilibrium :

$$+\uparrow \Sigma F_z = 0; \quad T - 2T'\cos\frac{\theta}{2} = 0 \quad T = 2T'\cos\frac{\theta}{2} \quad [1]$$

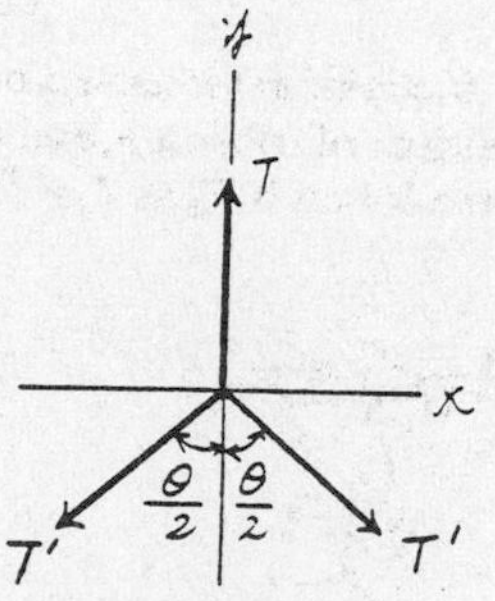

Frictional Force on Flat Belt : Here, $\beta = \frac{\theta}{2}$, $T_2 = T$ and $T_1 = T'$. Applying Eq. 8 – 6 $T_2 = T_1 e^{\mu\beta}$, we have

$$T = T'e^{0.3(\theta/2)} = T'e^{0.15\theta} \quad [2]$$

Substituting Eqs. [1] into [2] yields

$$2T'\cos\frac{\theta}{2} = T'e^{0.15\theta}$$

$$e^{0.15\theta} = 2\cos\frac{\theta}{2}$$

Solving by trial and error

$$\theta = 1.73104 \text{ rad} = 99.2° \qquad \textbf{Ans}$$

8-97. The 20-kg motor has a center of gravity at G and is pin-connected at C to maintain a tension in the drive belt. Determine the smallest counterclockwise twist or torque $\mathbf{M}$ that must be supplied by the motor to turn the disk B if wheel A locks and causes the belt to slip over the disk. No slipping occurs at A. The coefficient of static friction between the belt and the disk is $\mu_s = 0.3$.

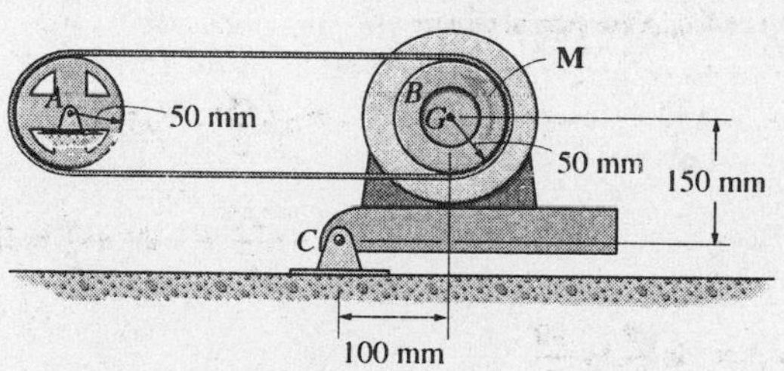

Equations of Equilibrium : From FBD (a),

$$\curvearrowleft + \Sigma M_C = 0; \quad T_2(100) + T_1(200) - 196.2(100) = 0 \quad [1]$$

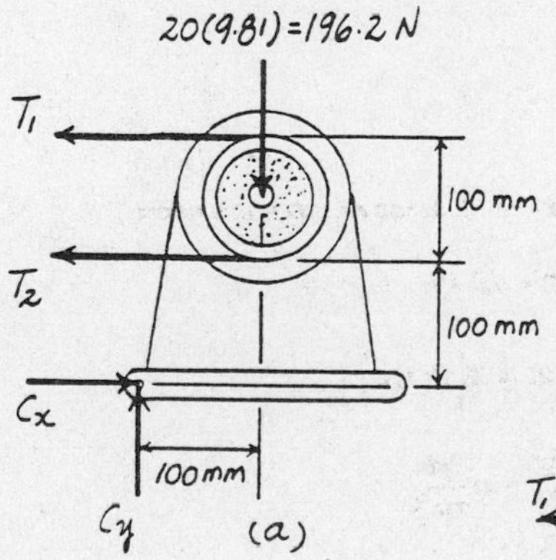

From FBD (b),

$$\curvearrowleft + \Sigma M_O = 0; \quad M + T_1(0.05) - T_2(0.05) = 0 \quad [2]$$

Frictional Force on Flat Belt : Here, $\beta = 180° = \pi$ rad. Applying Eq. 8 – 6, $T_2 = T_1 e^{\mu\beta}$, we have

$$T_2 = T_1 e^{0.3\pi} = 2.566 T_1 \quad [3]$$

Solving Eqs. [1], [2] and [3] yields

$$M = 3.37 \text{ N} \cdot \text{m} \qquad \textbf{Ans}$$

$$T_1 = 42.97 \text{ N} \quad T_2 = 110.27 \text{ N}$$

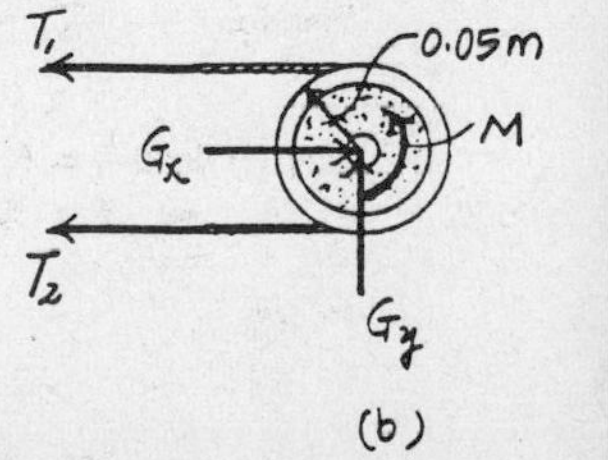

8-98. A cable is attached to the 50-lb plate B, passes over a fixed peg at C, and is attached to the block at A. Using the coefficients of static friction shown, determine the smallest weight of block A.

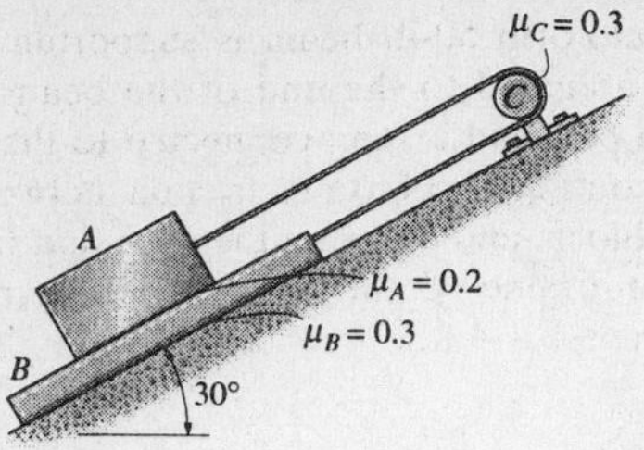

Block A:

$+\nearrow \Sigma F_x = 0; \quad T_1 - 0.2N_A - W_A \sin 30° = 0 \quad (1)$

$+\nwarrow \Sigma F_y = 0; \quad N_A - W_A \cos 30° = 0 \quad (2)$

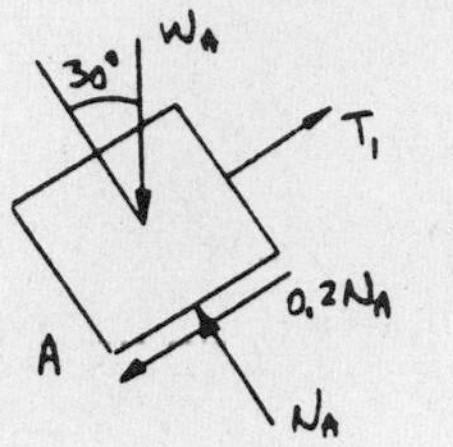

Plate B:

$+\nearrow \Sigma F_x = 0; \quad T_2 - 50 \sin 30° + 0.3N_B + 0.2N_A = 0 \quad (3)$

$+\nwarrow \Sigma F_y = 0; \quad N_B - N_A - 50 \cos 30° = 0 \quad (4)$

Peg C:

$T_2 = T_1 e^{\mu\beta}; \quad T_2 = T_1 e^{0.3\pi} \quad (5)$

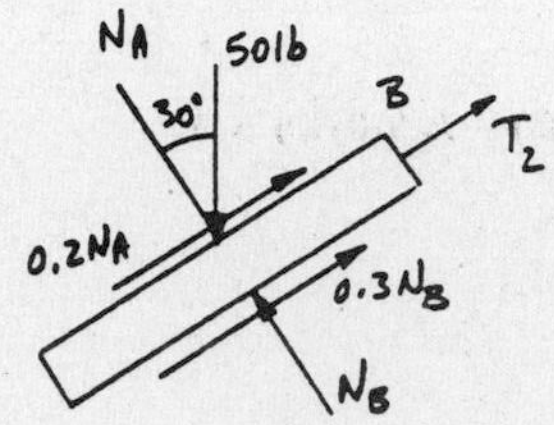

Solving Eqs. (1)–(5),

$T_1 = 3.74$ lb; $\quad T_2 = 9.60$ lb; $\quad N_A = 4.81$ lb; $\quad N_B = 48.1$ lb;

$W_A = 5.56$ lb **Ans**

8-99. The cylinder weighs 10 lb and is held in equilibrium by the belt and wall. If slipping does not occur at the wall, determine the minimum vertical force P which must be applied to the belt for equilibrium. The coefficient of static friction between the belt and the cylinder is $\mu_s = 0.25$.

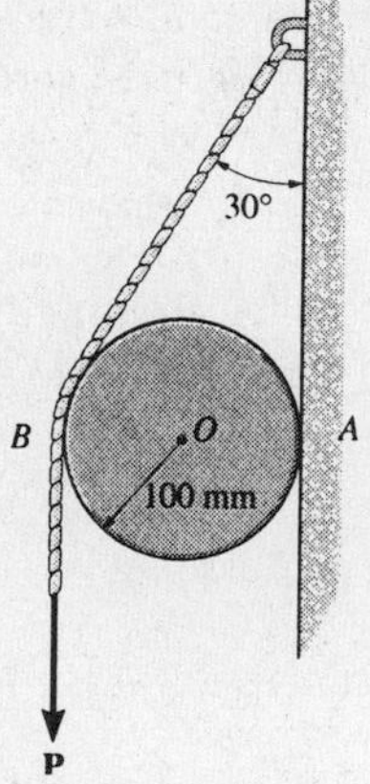

Equations of Equilibrium :

$$\circlearrowleft + \Sigma M_A = 0; \quad P(0.2) + 10(0.1) - T_2 \cos 30°(0.1 + 0.1\cos 30°) - T_2 \sin 30°(0.1 \sin 30°) = 0 \quad [1]$$

Frictional Force on Flat Belt : Here, $\beta = 30° = \frac{\pi}{6}$ rad and $T_1 = P$.

Applying Eq. 8–6, $T_2 = T_1 e^{\mu\beta}$, we have

$$T_2 = Pe^{0.25(\pi/6)} = 1.140P \quad [2]$$

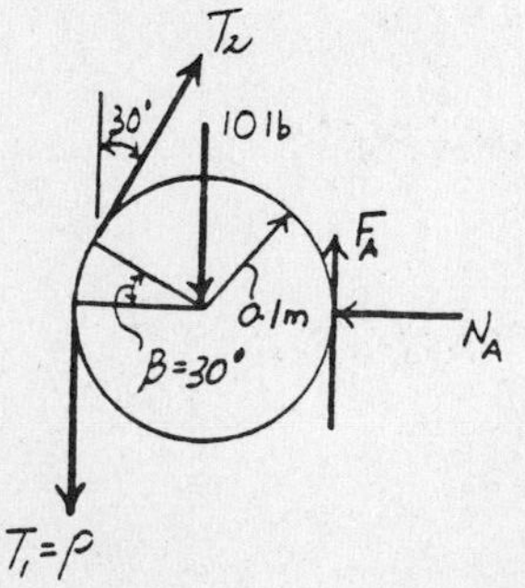

Solving Eqs. [1] and [2] yields

$P = 78.7$ lb **Ans**

$T_2 = 89.76$ lb

***8-100.** The uniform 50-lb beam is supported by the rope which is attached to the end of the beam, wraps over the rough peg, and is then connected to the 100-lb block. If the coefficient of static friction between the beam and the block, and between the rope and the peg, is $\mu_s = 0.4$, determine if the system will remain in equilibrium when $d = 4$ ft.

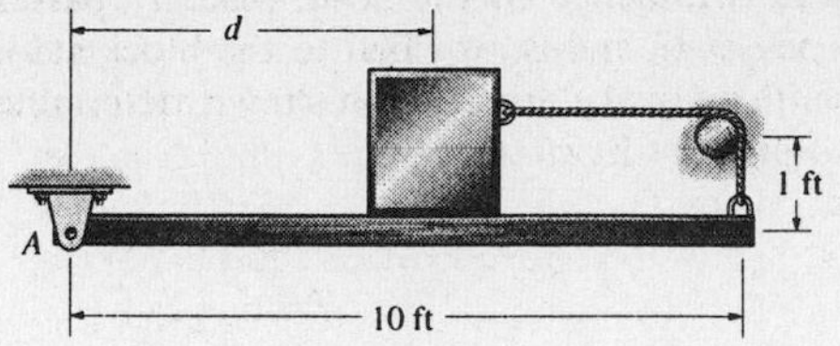

Block :

$+\uparrow \Sigma F_y = 0;\quad N_1 - 100 = 0$

$N_1 = 100 \text{ lb}$

$\xrightarrow{+} \Sigma F_x = 0;\quad T_1 - 0.4(100) = 0$

$T_1 = 40 \text{ lb}$

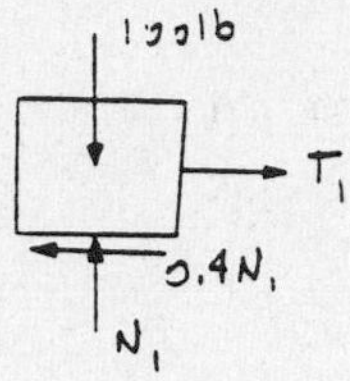

$T_2 = T_1 e^{\mu\beta};\quad T_2 = 40e^{0.4\left(\frac{\pi}{2}\right)} = 74.978 \text{ lb}$

System :

$\circlearrowleft + \Sigma M_A = 0;\quad -100(d) - 40(1) - 50(5) + 74.978(10) = 0$

$d = 4.60 \text{ ft}$

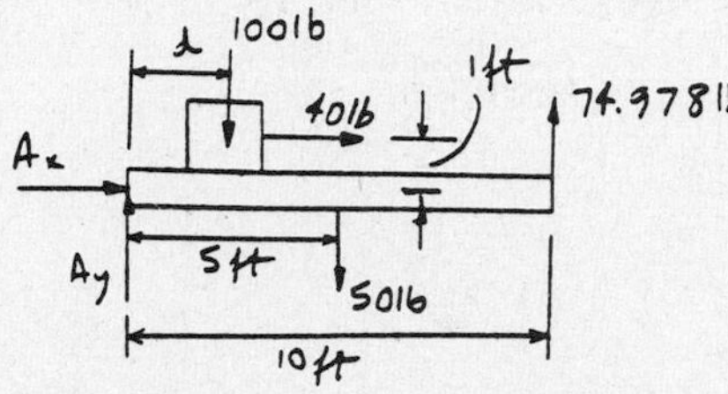

Since $d = 4$ ft < 4.60 ft
Yes, the beam will remain in equilibrium. **Ans**

■8-101. Two 8-kg blocks are attached to a cord that passes over two fixed drums. If $\mu_s = 0.3$ at the drums, determine the equilibrium angle θ the cord makes with the horizontal when a vertical force $P = 200$ N is applied to the cord to pull it downward.

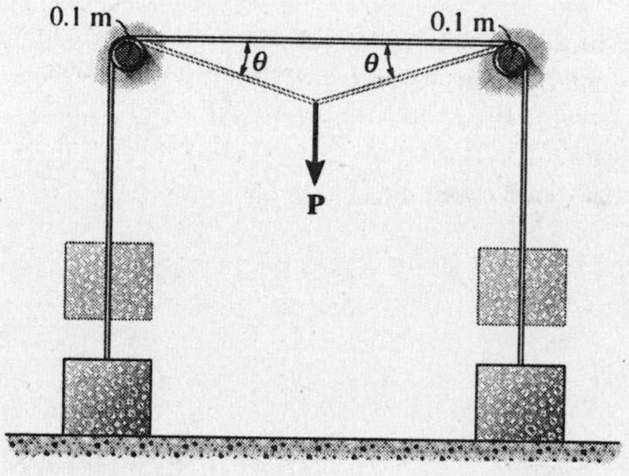

$+\uparrow \Sigma F_y = 0;\quad 2T_2 \sin\theta = 200$

$T_2 \sin\theta = 100$

$T_2 = T_1 e^{\mu\beta};\quad T_2 = 8(9.81)e^{0.3\left(\frac{\pi}{2} + \theta\right)}$

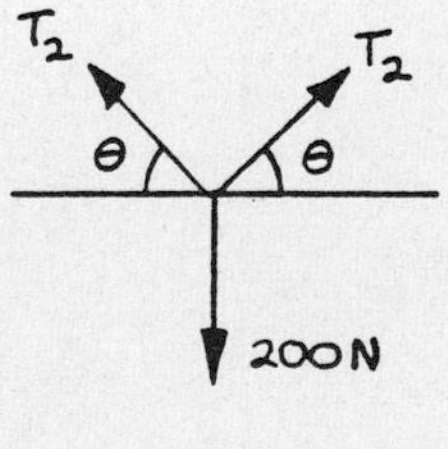

Thus,

$$\frac{100}{\sin\theta} = (8)(9.81)\left(e^{0.3\left(\frac{\pi}{2}\right)}\right)\left(e^{0.3\theta}\right)$$

$0.795 = \sin\theta\left(e^{0.3\theta}\right)$

Solving,

$\theta = 0.701 \text{ rad.} = 40.1°$ **Ans**

8-102. A conveyer belt is used to transfer granular material and the frictional resistance on the top of the belt is $F = 500$ N. Determine the smallest stretch of the spring attached to the moveable axle of the idle pulley B so that the belt does not slip at the drive pulley A when the torque **M** is applied. What minimum torque **M** is required to keep the belt moving? The coefficient of static friction between the belt and the wheel at A is $\mu_s = 0.2$.

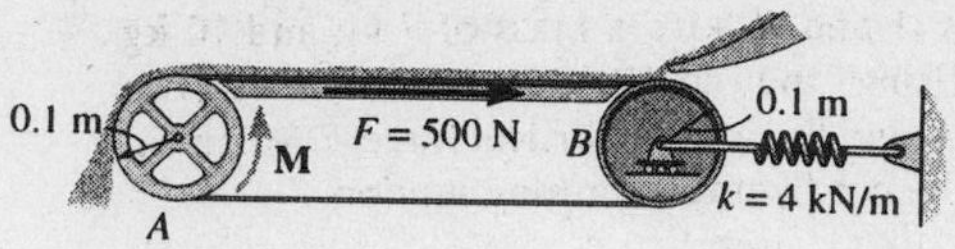

Frictional Force on Flat Belt : Here, $\beta = 180° = \pi$ rad and $T_2 = 500 + T$ and $T_1 = T$. Applying Eq. 8-6, , we have

$$T_2 = T_1 e^{\mu\beta}$$
$$500 + T = Te^{0.2\pi}$$
$$T = 571.78 \text{ N}$$

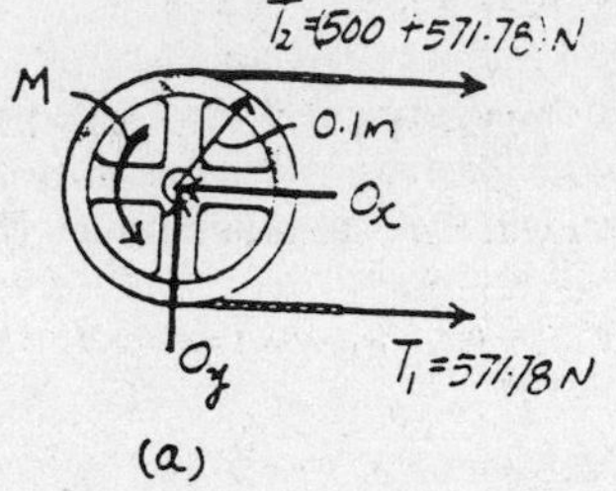

Equations of Equilibrium : From FBD (a),

$$\curvearrowleft + \Sigma M_O = 0; \quad M + 571.78(0.1) - (500 + 578.1)(0.1) = 0$$
$$M = 50.0 \text{ N}\cdot\text{m} \quad \textbf{Ans}$$

From FBD (b),

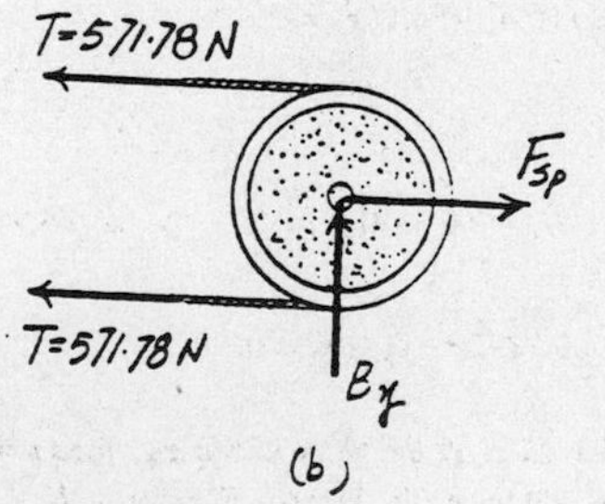

$$\overset{+}{\rightarrow} \Sigma F_x = 0; \quad F_{sp} - 2(578.71) = 0 \quad F_{sp} = 1143.57 \text{ N}$$

Thus, the spring stretch is

$$x = \frac{F_{sp}}{k} = \frac{1143.57}{4000} = 0.2859 \text{ m} = 286 \text{ mm} \quad \textbf{Ans}$$

8-103. Blocks A and B have a mass of 7 kg and 10 kg, respectively. Using the coefficients of static friction indicated, determine the largest vertical force P which can be applied to the cord without causing motion.

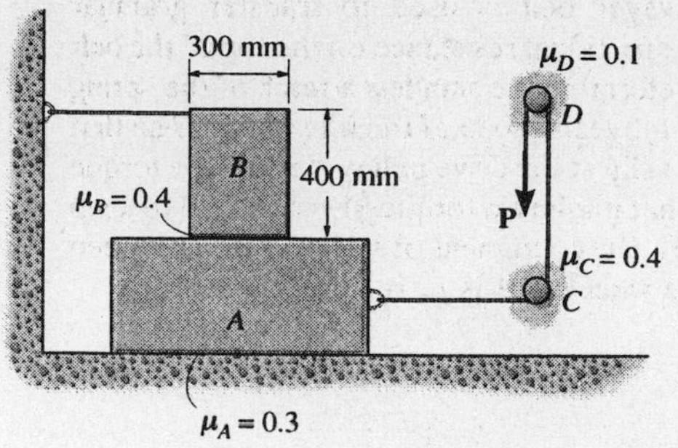

Frictional Forces on Flat Belts : When the cord pass over peg D, $\beta = 180° = \pi$ rad and $T_2 = P$. Applying Eq. 8 – 6, $T_2 = T_1 e^{\mu\beta}$, we have

$$P = T_1 e^{0.1\pi} \qquad T_1 = 0.7304P$$

When the cord pass over peg C, $\beta = 90° = \dfrac{\pi}{2}$ rad and $T_2{}' = T_1 = 0.7304P$. Applying Eq. 8 – 6, $T_2{}' = T_1{}' e^{\mu\beta}$, we have

$$0.7304P = T_1{}' e^{0.4(\pi/2)} \qquad T_1{}' = 0.3897P$$

Equations of Equilibrium : From FBD (b),

$$+\uparrow \Sigma F_y = 0; \quad N_B - 98.1 = 0 \quad N_B = 98.1 \text{ N}$$

$$\overset{+}{\rightarrow} \Sigma F_x = 0; \quad F_B - T = 0 \qquad [1]$$

$$\circlearrowleft + \Sigma M_O = 0; \quad T(0.4) - 98.1(x) = 0 \qquad [2]$$

From FBD (b),

$$+\uparrow \Sigma F_y = 0; \quad N_A - 98.1 - 68.67 = 0 \quad N_A = 166.77 \text{ N}$$

$$\overset{+}{\rightarrow} \Sigma F_x = 0; \quad 0.3897P - F_B - F_A = 0 \qquad [3]$$

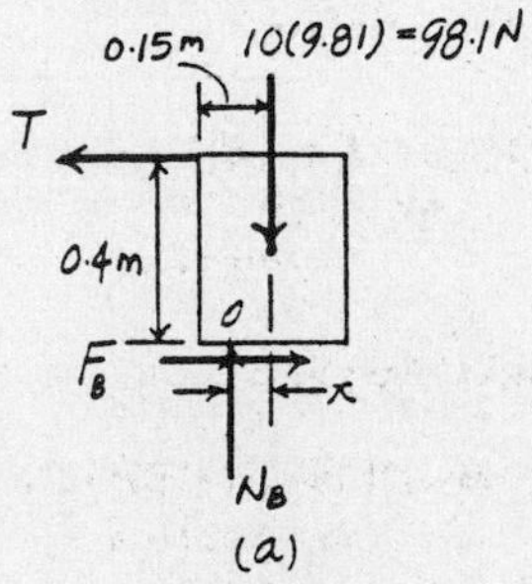

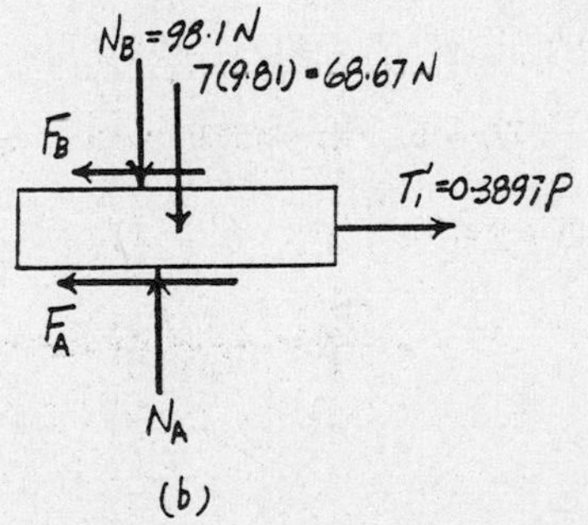

Friction : Assuming the block B is on the verge of tipping, then $x = 0.15$ m. Al for motion to occur, block A will have slip. Hence, $F_A = (\mu_s)_A N_A = 0.3(166.77) = 50.031$ N. Substituting these values into Eqs.[1], [2] and [3] and solving yields

$$P = 222.81 \text{ N} = 223 \text{ N} \qquad \textbf{Ans}$$

$$F_B = T = 36.79 \text{ N}$$

Since $(F_B)_{max} = (\mu_s)_B N_B = 0.4(98.1) = 39.24 \text{ N} > F_B$, block B does not slip but tips. Therefore, the above assumption is correct.

***8-104.** Block A has a weight of 100 lb and rests on a surface for which $\mu_s = 0.25$. If the coefficient of static friction between the cord and the fixed peg at C is $\mu_s = 0.3$, determine the greatest weight of the suspended cylinder B without causing motion.

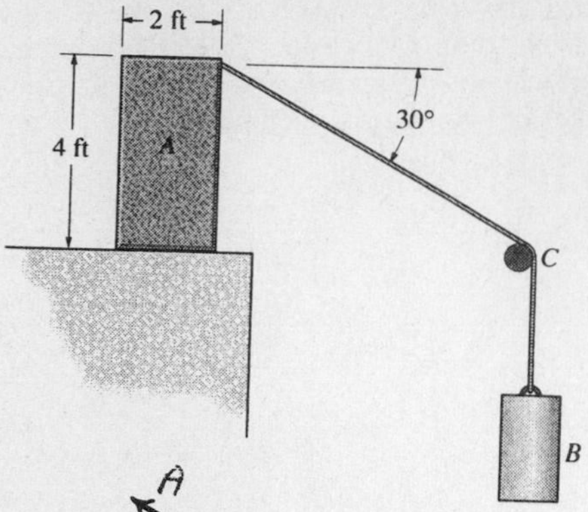

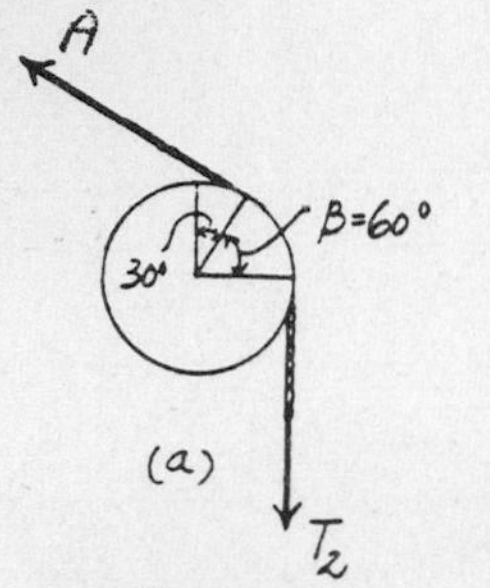

Frictional Force on Flat Belt : Here, $\beta = 60° = \dfrac{\pi}{3}$ rad and $T_2 = W$.

Applying Eq. 8 – 6, $T_2 = T_1 e^{\mu\beta}$, we have

$$W = T_1 e^{0.3(\pi/3)} \qquad T_1 = 0.7304W$$

Equations of Equilibrium : From FBD (b),

$$+\uparrow \Sigma F_y = 0; \qquad N - 0.7304W\sin 30° - 100 = 0 \qquad [1]$$

$$\xrightarrow{+} \Sigma F_x = 0; \qquad 0.7304W\cos 30° - F = 0 \qquad [2]$$

$$\circlearrowleft + \Sigma M_A = 0; \qquad 100(x) - 0.7304W\cos 30°(4) - 0.7304W\sin 30°(1 - x) = 0 \qquad [3]$$

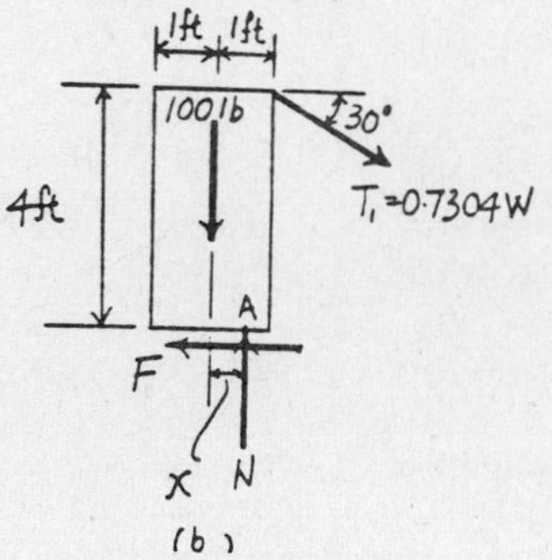

Friction : Assuming the block is on the verge of tipping, then $x = 1$ ft. Substituting this value into Eqs.[1], [2] and [3] and solving yields

$$W = 39.5 \text{ lb} \qquad \textbf{Ans}$$

$$F = 25.0 \text{ lb} \qquad N = 114.43 \text{ lb}$$

Since $F_{max} = \mu_s N = 0.25(114.43) = 28.61$ lb $> F$, the block does not slip but tips. Therefore, the above assumption is correct.

8-105. Block A has a mass of 50 kg and rests on surface B for which $\mu_s = 0.25$. If the coefficient of static friction between the cord and the fixed peg at C is $\mu'_s = 0.3$, determine the greatest mass of the suspended cylinder D without causing motion.

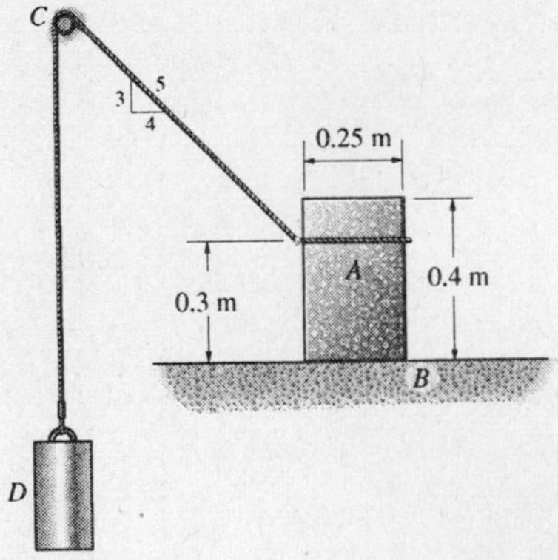

Block A :

Assume block A slips and does not tip.

$$+\uparrow \Sigma F_y = 0; \quad N_B + \frac{3}{5}T - 50(9.81) = 0$$

$$\xrightarrow{+} \Sigma F_x = 0; \quad 0.25 N_B - \frac{4}{5}T = 0$$

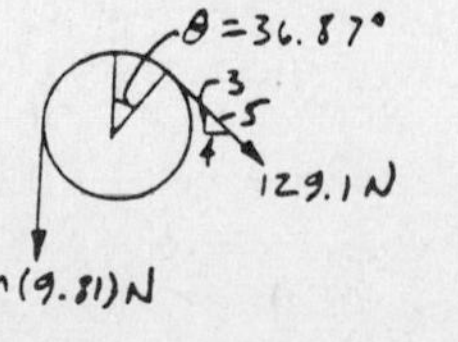

$$N_B = 413.1 \text{ N}$$

$$T = 129.1 \text{ N}$$

$$\circlearrowleft + \Sigma M_B = 0; \quad -50(9.81)x + \frac{4}{5}(129.1)(0.3) - \frac{3}{5}(129.1)(0.125 - x) = 0$$

$$x = 0.0516 \text{ m} < 0.125 \text{ m} \qquad \text{OK}$$

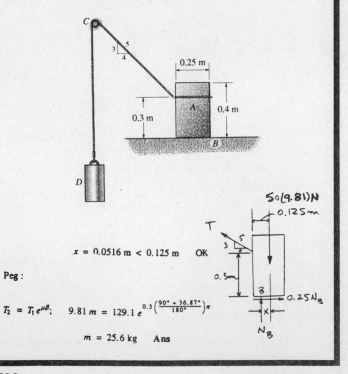

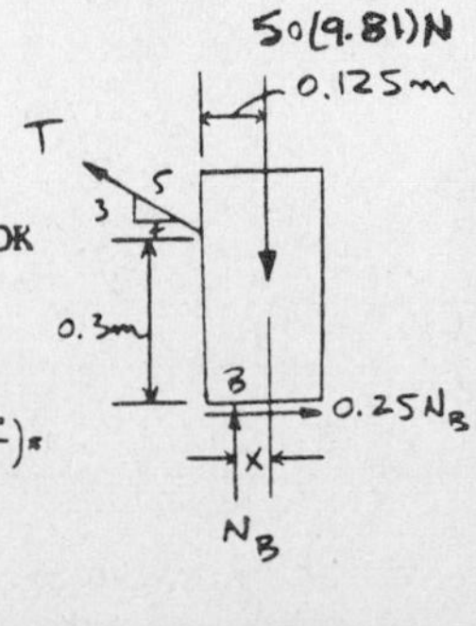

Peg :

$$T_2 = T_1 e^{\mu\beta}; \qquad 9.81\,m = 129.1\,e^{0.3\left(\frac{90° + 36.87°}{180°}\right)\pi}$$

$$m = 25.6 \text{ kg} \qquad \textbf{Ans}$$

8-106. Block A has a mass of 50 kg and rests on surface B for which $\mu_s = 0.25$. If the mass of the suspended cylinder D is 4 kg, determine the frictional force acting on A and check if tipping occurs. The coefficient of static friction between the cord and the fixed peg at C is $\mu'_s = 0.3$.

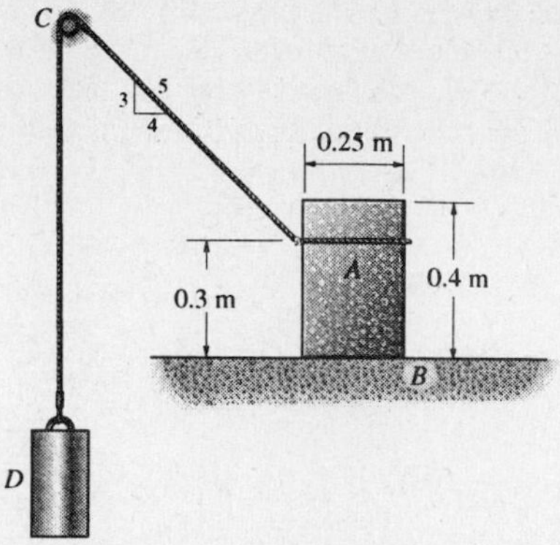

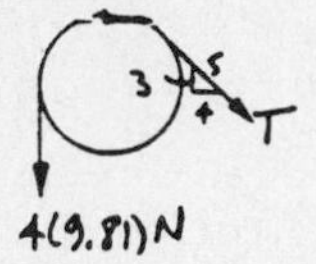

$T_2 = T_1 e^{\mu\beta}$; $\quad 4(9.81) = T e^{0.3\left(\frac{90+36.87}{180}\right)\pi}$

$T = 20.19$ N

Block A:

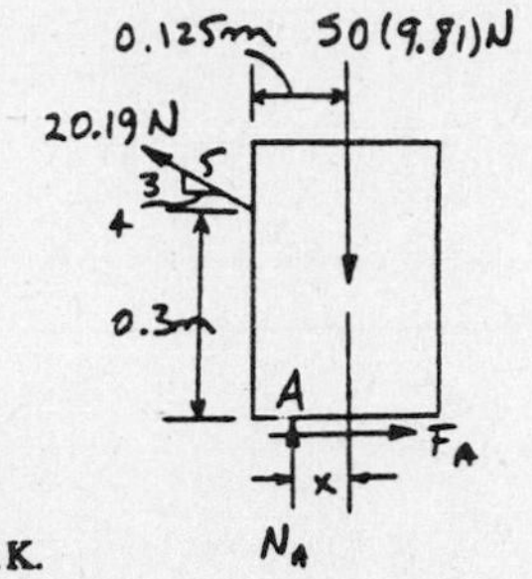

$\xrightarrow{+} \Sigma F_x = 0;\quad F_A - \frac{4}{5}(20.19) = 0$

$F_A = 16.2$ N **Ans**

$+\uparrow \Sigma F_y = 0;\quad N_A - 50(9.18) + \frac{3}{5}(20.19) = 0$

$N_A = 478.4$ N

$(F_A)_{max} = 0.25(478.4) = 119.6 \text{ N} > 16.16 \text{ N}$ O.K.

Block does not slip.

$\curvearrowleft +\Sigma M_B = 0;\quad -50(9.81)x + \frac{4}{5}(20.19)(0.3) - \frac{3}{5}(20.19)(0.125 - x) = 0$

$x = 0.00697 \text{ m} < 0.125 \text{ m}$ O.K.

No tipping occurs. **Ans**

8-107. The collar bearing uniformly supports an axial force of $P = 500$ lb. If the coefficient of static friction is $\mu_s = 0.3$, determine the torque M required to overcome friction.

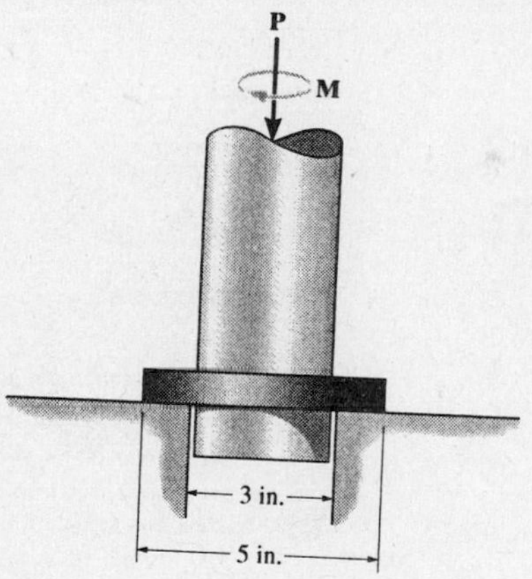

Bearing Friction : Applying Eq. 8–7 with $R_2 = 1.5$ in., $R_1 = 1$ in., $\mu_s = 0.3$ and $P = 500$ lb, we have

$$M = \frac{2}{3}\mu_s P\left(\frac{R_2^3 - R_1^3}{R_2^2 - R_1^2}\right)$$

$$= \frac{2}{3}(0.3)(500)\left(\frac{1.5^3 - 1^3}{1.5^2 - 1^2}\right)$$

$$= 190 \text{ lb}\cdot\text{in} = 15.8 \text{ lb}\cdot\text{ft}$$ **Ans**

***8-108.** The collar bearing uniformly supports an axial force of $P = 500$ lb. If a torque of $M = 3$ lb · ft is applied to the shaft and causes it to rotate at constant velocity, determine the coefficient of kinetic friction at the surface of contact.

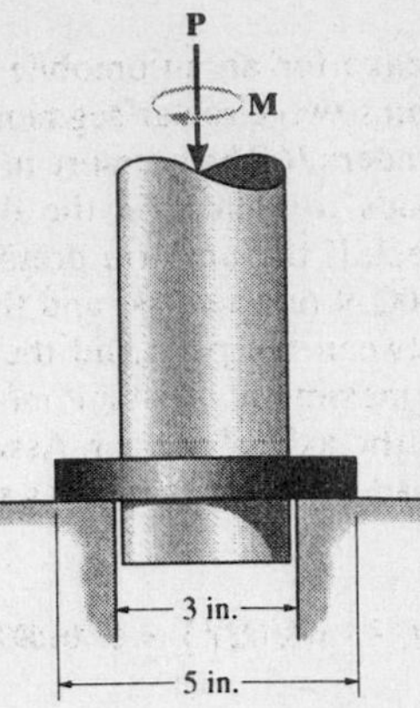

Bearing Friction : Applying Eq. 8–7 with $R_2 = 1.5$ in., $R_1 = 1$ in., $M = 3(12) = 36$ lb · in and $P = 500$ lb, we have

$$M = \frac{2}{3}\mu_k P\left(\frac{R_2^3 - R_1^3}{R_2^2 - R_1^2}\right)$$

$$36 = \frac{2}{3}(\mu_k)(500)\left(\frac{1.5^3 - 1^3}{1.5^2 - 1^2}\right)$$

$$\mu_k = 0.0568 \qquad \textbf{Ans}$$

8-109. The *disk clutch* is used in standard transmissions of automobiles. If four springs are used to force the two plates A and B together, determine the force in each spring required to transmit a moment of $M = 600$ lb · ft across the plates. The coefficient of static friction between A and B is $\mu_s = 0.3$.

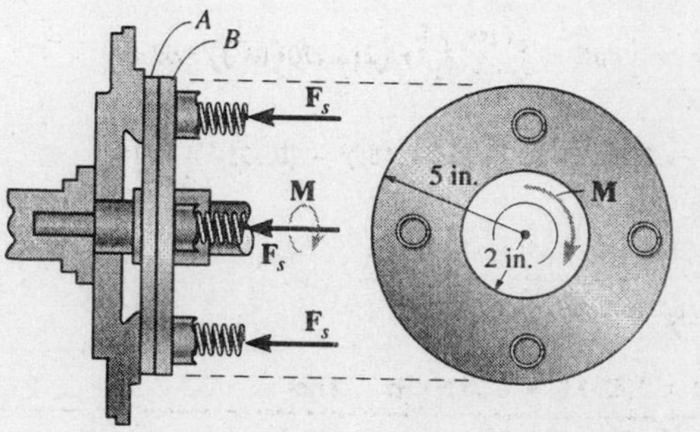

Bearing Friction : Applying Eq. 8–7 with $R_2 = 5$ in., $R_1 = 2$ in., $M = 600(12) = 7200$ lb · in, $\mu_s = 0.3$ and $P = 4F_{sp}$, we have

$$M = \frac{2}{3}\mu_s P\left(\frac{R_2^3 - R_1^3}{R_2^2 - R_1^2}\right)$$

$$7200 = \frac{2}{3}(0.3)(4F_{sp})\left(\frac{5^3 - 2^3}{5^2 - 2^2}\right)$$

$$F_{sp} = 1615.38 \text{ lb} = 1.62 \text{ kip} \qquad \textbf{Ans}$$

8-110. The disk brake for an automobile consists of a caliper C that contains two circular segment brake pads P and hydraulic cylinders H. The pressure in the cylinders forces the brake pads to clamp on the disk, which is attached to the wheel. If the uniform pressure develops a normal force of 600 N on the disk, and the coefficient of static friction between the pads and the disk is $\mu_s = 0.4$, determine the maximum resistant moment **M** the brakes create about the axle of the car. Assume the area of contact of each pad with the drum is as shown.

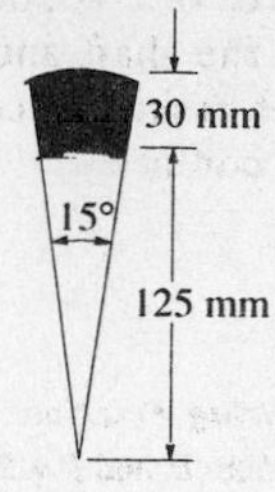

$$A = \frac{15°}{360°}\left(\pi(0.155)^2 - \pi(0.125)^2\right) = 0.0010996 \text{ m}^2$$

$$p = \frac{P}{A} = \frac{600}{0.0010996} = 545.674\left(10^3\right) \text{ Pa}$$

$$dF = \mu_s\, p\, dA = 0.4\,(545.674)\left(10^3\right)dA = 218.270\,(10^3)\,dA$$

$$M' = \int r\,dF = \int_{0.125}^{0.155}\int_0^{\frac{\pi}{12}} r\left(218.270\left(10^3\right)\right) r\,d\theta\,dr$$

$$= 218.270\left(10^3\right)\left(\frac{1}{3}\right)\left((0.155)^3 - (0.125)^3\right)\left(\frac{\pi}{12}\right)$$

$$= 33.73 \text{ N}\cdot\text{m}$$

Since there are two pads,

$M = 2(33.73) = 67.5 \text{ N}\cdot\text{m}$ **Ans**

8-111. The disk brake for an automobile consists of a caliper C that contains two circular segment brake pads P and hydraulic cylinders H. The pressure in the cylinders forces the brake pads to clamp on the disk, which is attached to the wheel. If the maximum normal force of the tire on the ground is 6.5 kN and the radius of the tire is 0.30 m, determine the minimum uniform pressure that must be developed within the cylinders in order to cause the tire to skid on the pavement. The coefficient of static friction between the pads and the disk is $\mu_s = 0.4$, and between the tires and the road $\mu'_s = 0.3$. Assume the area of contact of each pad with the drum is as shown.

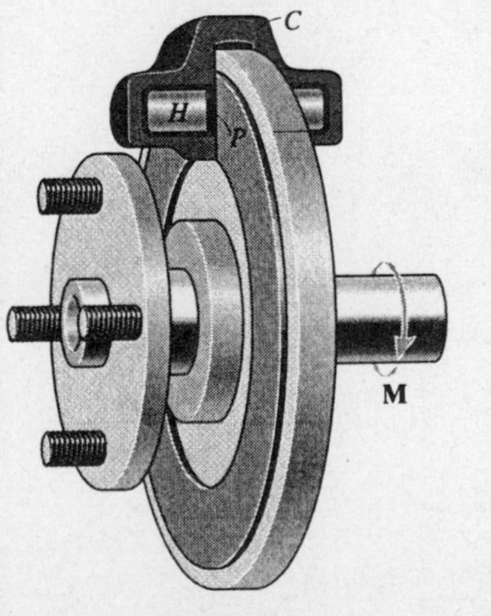

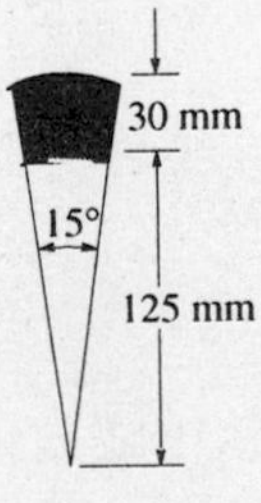

$$A = \frac{15°}{360°}\left(\pi(0.155)^2 - \pi(0.125)^2\right) = 0.0010996 \text{ m}^2$$

$$\theta = 15° = \frac{\pi}{12}$$

$$dF = \mu_s\,dN = \mu_s\,p\,dA = 0.4\,p\,dA$$

$$M = \int r\,dF = \int_{0.125}^{0.155}\int_0^{\frac{\pi}{12}} r\,(0.4\,p)\,r\,d\theta\,dr$$

$$= 0.4\,p\left(\frac{1}{3}\right)\left((0.155)^3 - (0.125)^3\right)\left(\frac{\pi}{12}\right)$$

$$= 61.81\,(10^{-6})p$$

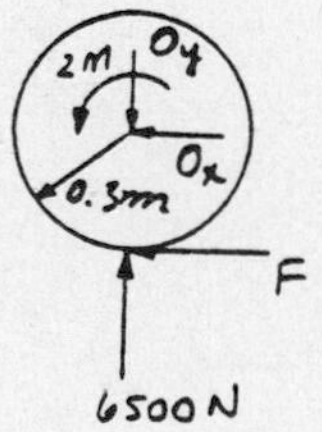

$F = 0.3\,(6500) = 1950 \text{ N}$

$\circlearrowleft + \Sigma M_O = 0;\quad 2M - 1950\,(0.3) = 0$

$M = 292.5 \text{ N}\cdot\text{m}$

Thus,

$292.5 = 61.81\,(10^{-6})p$

$p = 4.73 \text{ MPa}$ **Ans**

***8-112.** If the coefficient of static friction at the cone clutch is μ_s, determine the smallest force P that should be applied to the handle in order to transmit the torque **M**.

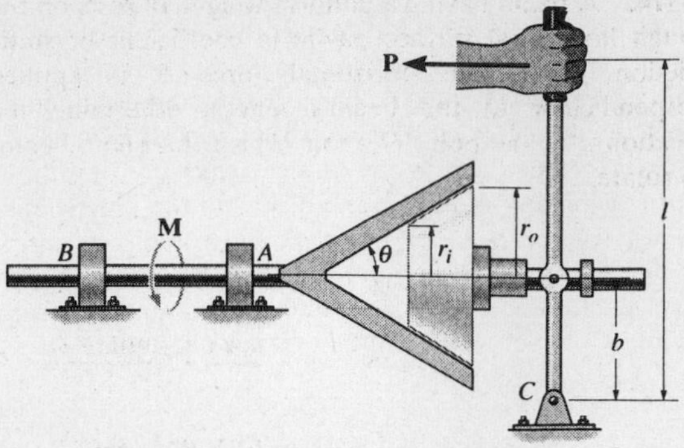

$$dA = 2\pi r\left(\frac{dr}{\sin\theta}\right)$$

Since $dN = p\,dA$, then

$$\Sigma F_x = 0;\quad P' = \int dN \sin\theta = \int_{r_i}^{r_o} (\sin\theta)p(2\pi r)\left(\frac{dr}{\sin\theta}\right)$$

$$= \frac{2\pi p}{2}\int_{r_i}^{r_o} r\,dr$$

$$= \pi p\,(r_o^2 - r_i^2)$$

$$p = \frac{P'}{\pi\,(r_o^2 - r_i^2)}$$

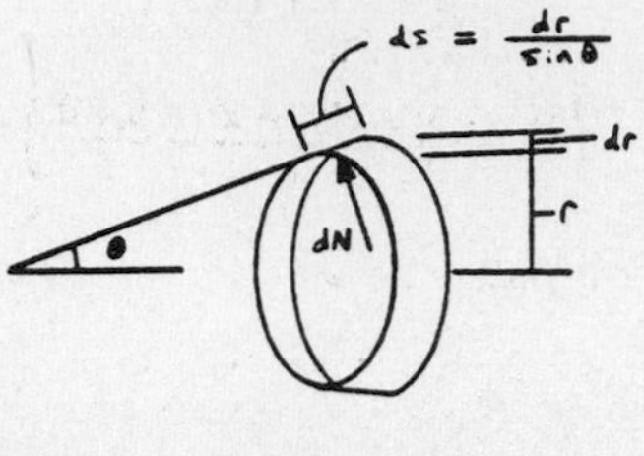

$$\Sigma M = 0;\quad M = \int r\,dF = \int r\mu_s\,dN = \int_{r_i}^{r_o} 2\pi r\,\mu_s\,p\left(\frac{r\,dr}{\sin\theta}\right)$$

$$= \frac{2}{3}\frac{\mu_s\,p\,\pi\,(r_o^3 - r_i^3)}{\sin\theta}$$

$$= \frac{2}{3}\frac{\mu_s\,P'}{\sin\theta}\frac{(r_o^3 - r_i^3)}{(r_o^2 - r_i^2)}$$

$$+\Sigma M_C = 0;\quad P\,l - P'b = 0$$

$$P' = P\left(\frac{l}{b}\right)$$

Thus

$$P = \frac{3Mb\sin\theta(r_o^2 - r_i^2)}{2\mu_s l(r_o^3 - r_i^3)}\qquad \textbf{Ans}$$

8-113. A tube has a total weight of 200 lb, length l = 8 ft, and radius = 0.75 ft. If it rests in sand for which the coefficient of static friction it is μ_s = 0.23, determine the torque **M** needed to turn it. Assume that the pressure distribution along the length of the tube is defined by $p = p_0 \sin\theta$. For the solution it is necessary to determine p_0, the peak pressure, in terms of the weight and tube dimensions.

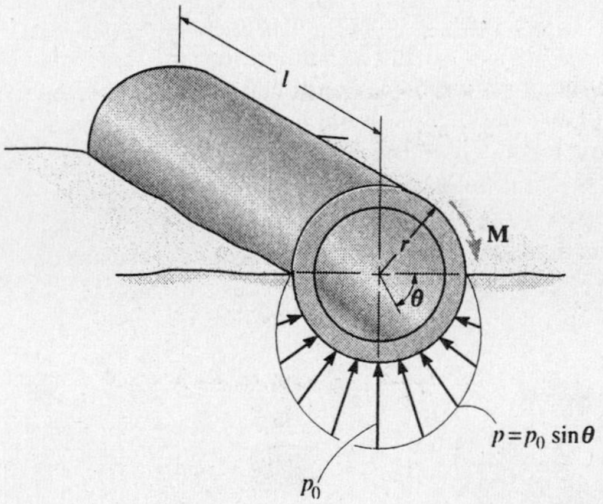

Equations of Equilibrium and Friction : Here, $dN = plrd\theta = p_0 lr\sin\theta d\theta$. Since the tube is on the verge of slipping, $dF = \mu_s dN = p_0\mu_s lr\sin\theta d\theta$.

$$+\uparrow\Sigma F_y = 0;\quad 2\int_0^{\frac{\pi}{2}} dN\sin\theta - W = 0$$

$$2\int_0^{\frac{\pi}{2}} p_0 lr\sin^2\theta\,d\theta = W$$

$$P_0 lr\int_0^{\frac{\pi}{2}}(1-\cos 2\theta)\,d\theta = W$$

$$p_0 lr\left(\frac{\pi}{2}\right) = W$$

$$p_0 = \frac{2W}{\pi lr}\qquad [1]$$

$$\curvearrowleft+\Sigma M_O = 0;\quad 2\int_0^{\frac{\pi}{2}} dF(r) - M = 0$$

$$M = 2\int_0^{\frac{\pi}{2}} p_0\mu_s lr^2\sin\theta\,d\theta = 2p_0\mu_s lr^2\qquad [2]$$

Substituting Eq.[1] into [2] yields

$$M = \frac{4W\mu_s r}{\pi}$$

However, W = 200 lb, μ_s = 0.23 and r = 0.75 ft, then

$$M = \frac{4(200)(0.23)(0.75)}{\pi} = 43.9\ \text{lb}\cdot\text{ft}\qquad \textbf{Ans}$$

8-114. A beam having a uniform weight W rests on the rough horizontal surface having a coefficient of static friction μ_s. If the horizontal force $\mathbf{P}$ is applied perpendicular to the beam's length, determine the location d of the point O about which the beam begins to rotate.

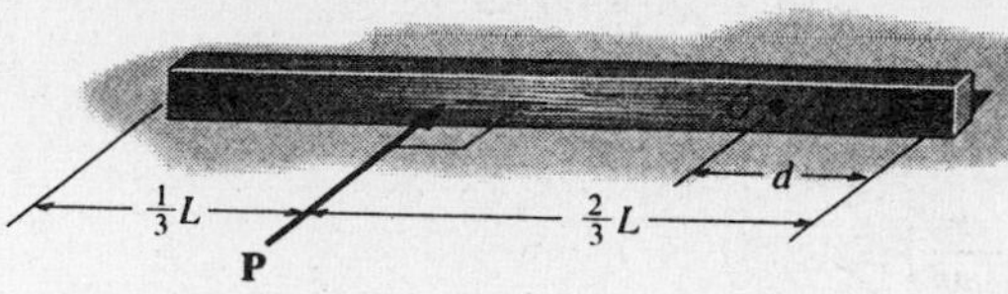

$$w = \frac{\mu_s N}{L}$$

$$\Sigma F_z = 0; \quad N = W$$

$$\Sigma F_x = 0; \quad P + \frac{\mu_s N d}{L} - \frac{\mu_s N(L-d)}{L} = 0$$

$$\Sigma M_{Oz} = 0; \quad \frac{\mu_s N(L-d)^2}{2L} + \frac{\mu_s N d^2}{2L} - P\left(\frac{2L}{3} - d\right) = 0$$

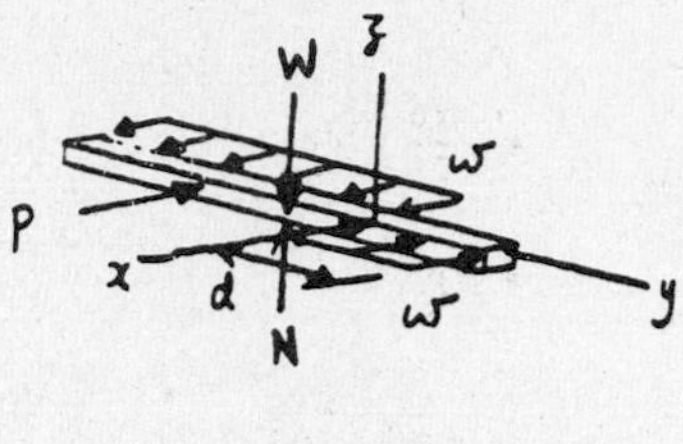

$$\frac{\mu_s W(L-d)^2}{2L} + \frac{\mu_s W d^2}{2L} - \left(\frac{2L}{3} - d\right)\left(\frac{\mu_s W(L-d)}{L} - \frac{\mu_s W d}{L}\right) = 0$$

$$3(L-d)^2 + 3d^2 - 2(2L - 3d)(L - 2d) = 0$$

$$6d^2 - 8Ld + L^2 = 0$$

Choose the root $< L$.

$$d = 0.140\,L \qquad \textbf{Ans}$$

8-115. Because of wearing at the edges, the pivot bearing is subjected to a conical pressure distribution at its surface of contact. Determine the torque M required to overcome friction and turn the shaft, which supports an axial force $\mathbf{P}$. The coefficient of static friction is μ_s. For the solution, it is necessary to determine the peak pressure p_0 in terms of P and the bearing radius R.

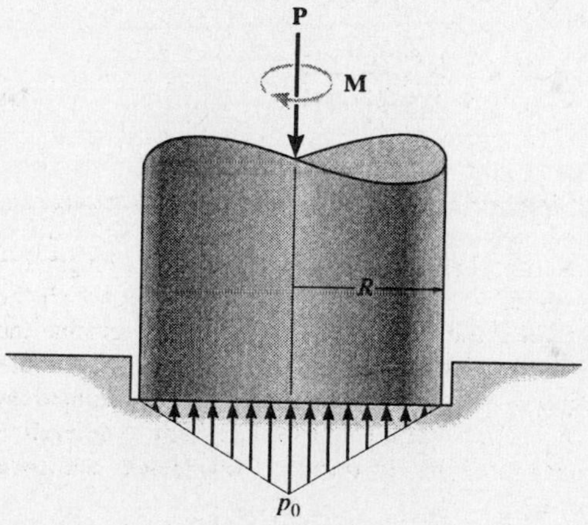

Equations of Equilibrium and Bearing Friction : Using similar triangles, $\frac{p}{R-r} = \frac{p_0}{R}$, $p = \frac{p_0}{R}(R-r)$. Also, $dA = 2\pi r dr$, $dN = p dA$ and $dF = \mu_s dN = \mu_s p dA$.

$$+\uparrow \Sigma F_y = 0; \qquad \int p dA - P = 0$$

$$\int \frac{p_0}{R}(R-r)(2\pi r dr) - P = 0$$

$$\frac{2\pi p_0}{R}\int_0^R r(R-r)\,dr - P = 0$$

$$p_0 = \frac{3P}{\pi R^2} \qquad [1]$$

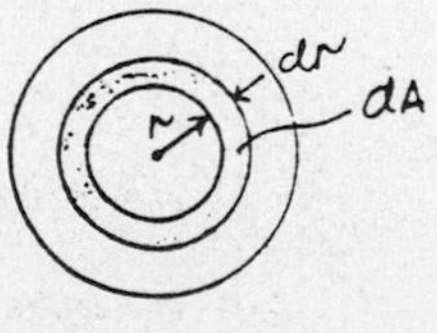

$$\curvearrowleft + \Sigma M_z = 0; \qquad \int (\mu_s p dA) r - M = 0$$

$$\int_0^R \frac{\mu_s p_0}{R}(R-r)(2\pi r dr)\,r - M = 0$$

$$\frac{2\pi \mu_s p_0}{R}\int_0^R r^2(R-r)\,dr - M = 0$$

$$M = \frac{\pi \mu_s R^3 p_0}{6} \qquad [2]$$

Substituting Eq. [1] into [2] yields

$$M = \frac{\pi \mu_s R^3}{6}\left(\frac{3P}{\pi R^2}\right) = \frac{\mu_s P R}{2} \qquad \textbf{Ans}$$

***8-116.** The pivot bearing is subjected to a parabolic pressure distribution at its surface of contact. If the coefficient of static friction is μ_s, determine the torque **M** required to overcome friction and turn the shaft if it supports an axial force **P**.

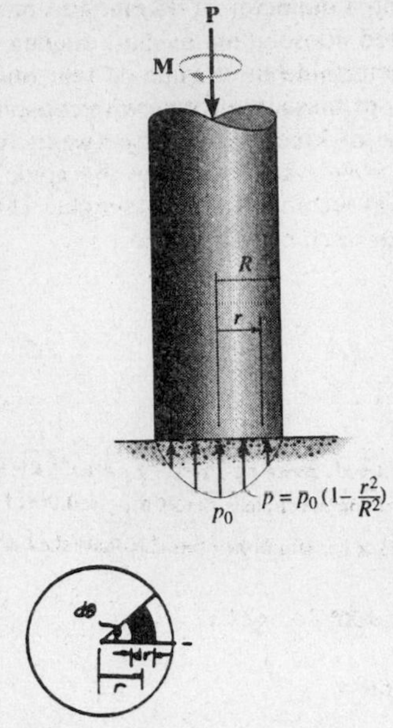

The differential area $dA = (rd\theta)(dr)$

$$P = \int p\,dA = \int p_0\left(1-\frac{r^2}{R^2}\right)(rd\theta)(dr) = p_0\int_0^{2\pi} d\theta\int_0^R r\left(1-\frac{r^2}{R^2}\right)dr$$

$$P = \frac{\pi R^2 p_0}{2} \qquad p_0 = \frac{2P}{\pi R^2}$$

$$dN = p\,dA = \frac{2P}{\pi R^2}\left(1-\frac{r^2}{R^2}\right)(rd\theta)(dr)$$

$$M = \int r\,dF = \int \mu_s r\,dN = \frac{2\mu_s P}{\pi R^2}\int_0^{2\pi} d\theta\int_0^R r^2\left(1-\frac{r^2}{R^2}\right)dr$$

$$= \frac{8}{15}\mu_s PR \qquad \textbf{Ans}$$

8-117. A 200-mm diameter post is driven 3 m into sand for which $\mu_s = 0.3$. If the normal pressure acting *completely around the post* varies linearly with depth as shown, determine the frictional torque **M** that must be overcome to rotate the post.

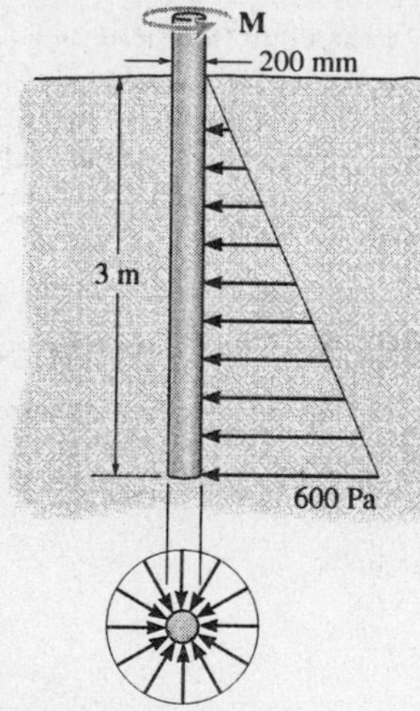

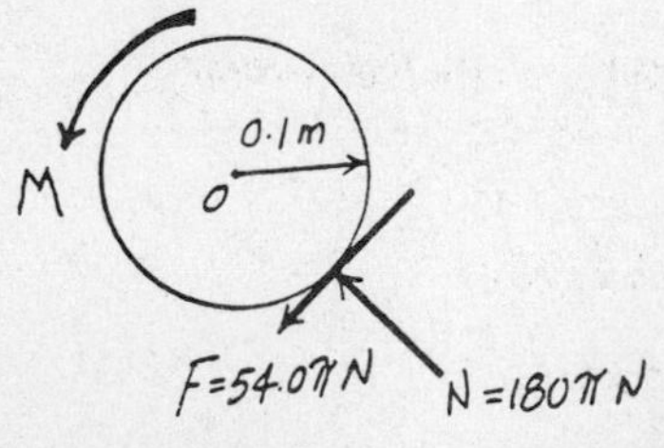

Equations of Equilibrium and Friction : The resultant normal force on the post is $N = \frac{1}{2}(600+0)(3)(\pi)(0.2) = 180\pi$ N. Since the post is on the verge of rotating, $F = \mu_s N = 0.3(180\pi) = 54.0\pi$ N.

$$\circlearrowleft +\Sigma M_O = 0; \qquad M - 54.0\pi(0.1) = 0$$
$$M = 17.0\ \text{N}\cdot\text{m} \qquad \textbf{Ans}$$

8-118. A pulley having a diameter of 80 mm and mass of 1.25 kg is supported loosely on a shaft having a diameter of 20 mm. Determine the torque M that must be applied to the pulley to cause it to rotate with constant motion. The coefficient of kinetic friction between the shaft and pulley is $\mu_k = 0.4$. Also calculate the angle θ which the normal force at the point of contact makes with the horizontal. The shaft itself cannot rotate.

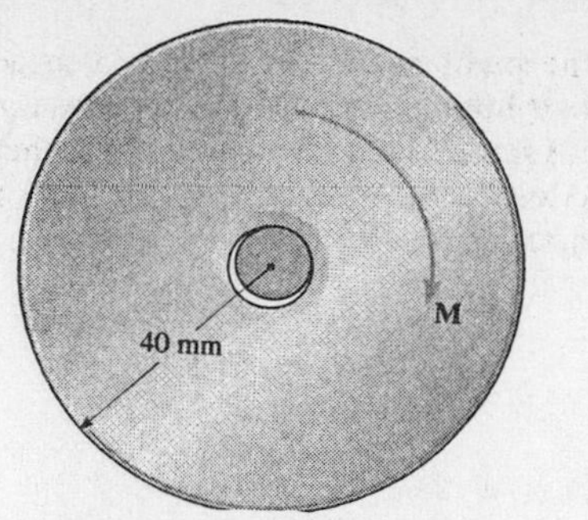

Frictional Force on Journal Bearing : Here, $\phi_k = \tan^{-1}\mu_k = \tan^{-1}0.4 = 21.80°$. Then the radius of friction circle is $r_f = r\sin\phi_k = 0.01\sin 21.80° = 3.714(10^{-3})$ m. The angle for which the normal force makes with horizontal is

$$\theta = 90° - \phi_k = 68.2° \qquad \textbf{Ans}$$

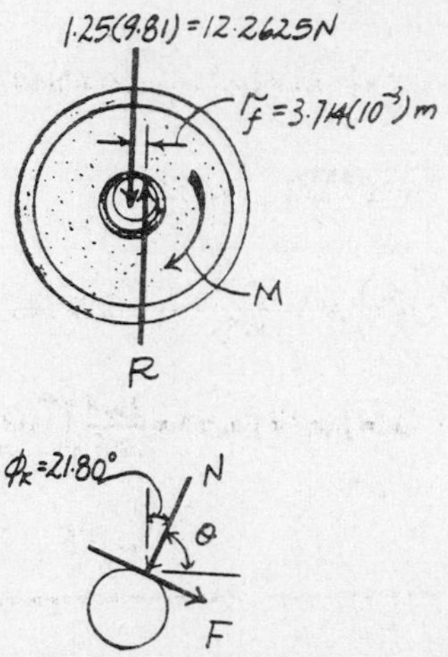

Equations of Equilibrium :

$+\uparrow \Sigma F_y = 0;\quad R - 12.2625 = 0 \quad R = 12.2625$ N

$\circlearrowleft + \Sigma M_O = 0;\quad 12.2625(3.714)(10^{-3}) - M = 0$

$$M = 0.0455 \text{ N}\cdot\text{m} \qquad \textbf{Ans}$$

8-119. The axle of the pulley fits loosely in a 50-mm-diameter pinhole. If $\mu_k = 0.30$, determine the minimum tension T required to turn the pulley clockwise at constant velocity if the block weighs 80 N. Neglect the weight of the pulley and assume that the cord does not slip on the pulley.

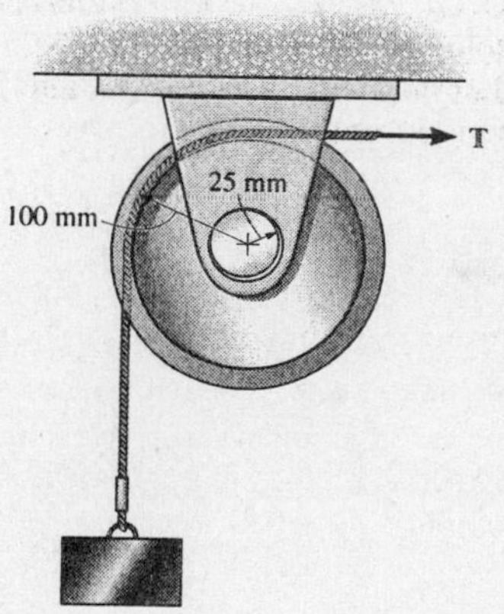

$\phi_k = \tan^{-1}(0.3) = 16.70°$

$r_f = r\sin\phi_k = 25\sin 16.70° = 7.184$ mm

Reaction on pulley is represented by R. Summing moments about the center of the pulley, O,

$\circlearrowleft + \Sigma M_O = 0;\quad 80(100) - T(100) + R(7.184) = 0$

$+\uparrow \Sigma F_y = 0;\quad R_y = 80$

$\xrightarrow{+} \Sigma F_x = 0;\quad R_x = T$

$$R = \sqrt{(80)^2 + T^2}$$

$$80(100) - T(100) + 7.184\sqrt{(80)^2 + T^2} = 0$$

$$51.61\left[(80)^2 + T^2\right] = \left[100(T - 80)\right]^2$$

Solving,

$$T = 88.6 \text{ N} \qquad \textbf{Ans}$$

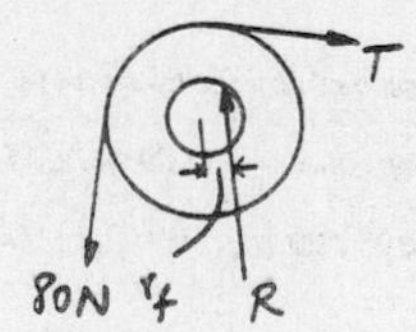

Also, by the approximate method

$r_f = 25(0.3) = 7.50$ mm

Then,

$\circlearrowleft + \Sigma M_O = 0;\quad 80(100) - T(100) + R(7.5) = 0$

So that Eq. (1) becomes

$$80(100) - T(100) + (7.5)\sqrt{(80)^2 + T^2} = 0$$

$$56.25\left[(80)^2 + T^2\right] = \left[100(T - 80)\right]^2$$

Solving,

$$T = 89.0 \text{ N} \qquad \textbf{Ans} \qquad \text{(approx.)}$$

***8-120.** The axle of the pulley fits loosely in a 50-mm-diameter pinhole. If $\mu_k = 0.30$, determine the minimum tension T required to turn the pulley counterclockwise at constant velocity if the block weighs 60 N. Neglect the weight of the pulley and assume that the cord does not slip on the pulley.

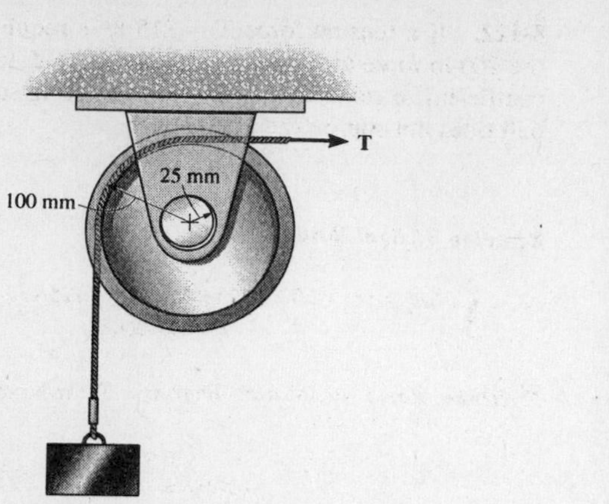

$\phi_k = \tan^{-1}(0.30) = 16.70°$

$r_f = r\sin\phi_k = 25\sin 16.70° = 7.184\text{ mm}$

Using the approximate method

$r_f \approx 25\,(0.3) = 7.50\text{ mm}$

Reaction on pulley is represented by R. Summing moments about the center of the pulley, point O.

$$\circlearrowleft + \Sigma M_O = 0; \quad 60\,(100) - T\,(100) - R\,(7.50) = 0$$

$$+\uparrow \Sigma F_y = 0; \quad R_y = 60$$

$$\xrightarrow{+} \Sigma F_x = 0; \quad R_x = T$$

$$R = \sqrt{(60)^2 + T^2}$$

$$60\,(100) - T\,(100) = 7.5\sqrt{(60)^2 + T^2}$$

$$177.78\,(60 - T)^2 = (60)^2 + T^2$$

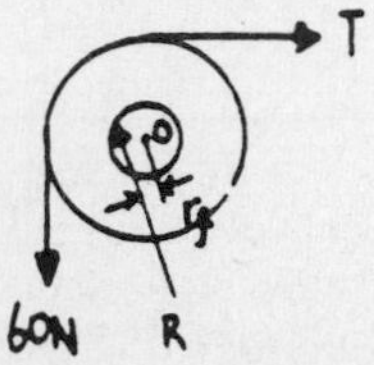

Solving,

$T = 53.9\text{ N}$ **Ans** (Approx.)

Using the more exact value of $r_f = 7.184\text{ mm}$

$T = 54.2\text{ N}$ **Ans**

8-121. Determine the tension **T** in the belt needed to overcome the tension of 200 lb created on the other side. Also, what are the normal and frictional components of force developed on the collar bushing? The coefficient of static friction is $\mu_s = 0.21$.

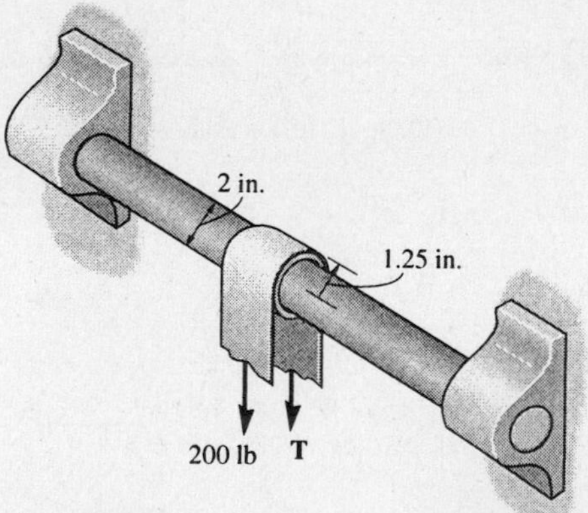

Frictional Force on Journal Bearing : Here, $\phi_s = \tan^{-1}\mu_s = \tan^{-1}0.21 = 11.86°$. Then the radius of friction circle is

$$r_f = r\sin\phi_k = 1\sin 11.86° = 0.2055\text{ in.}$$

Equations of Equilibrium :

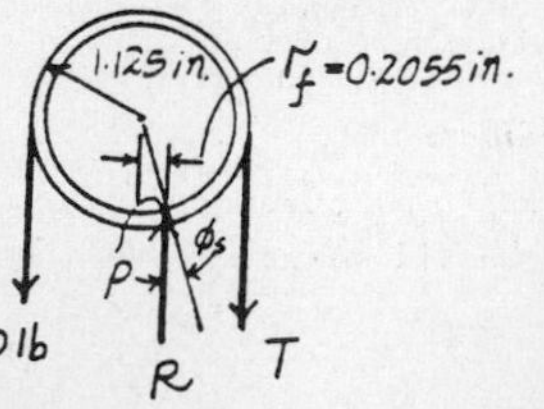

$$\circlearrowleft + \Sigma M_P = 0; \quad 200(1.125 + 0.2055) - T(1.125 - 0.2055) = 0$$
$$T = 289.41\text{ lb} = 289\text{ lb} \quad \textbf{Ans}$$

$$+\uparrow F_y = 0; \quad R - 200 - 289.4 = 0 \quad R = 489.41\text{ lb}$$

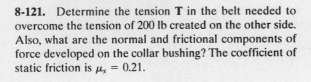

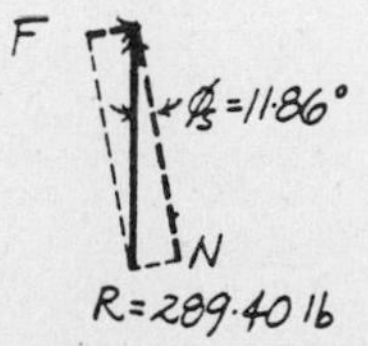

Thus, the normal and friction force are

$$N = R\cos\phi_s = 489.41\cos 11.86° = 479\text{ lb} \quad \textbf{Ans}$$
$$F = R\sin\phi_s = 489.41\sin 11.86° = 101\text{ lb} \quad \textbf{Ans}$$

8-122. If a tension force $T = 215$ lb is required to pull the 200-lb force around the collar bushing, determine the coefficient of static friction at the contacting surface. The belt does not slip on the collar.

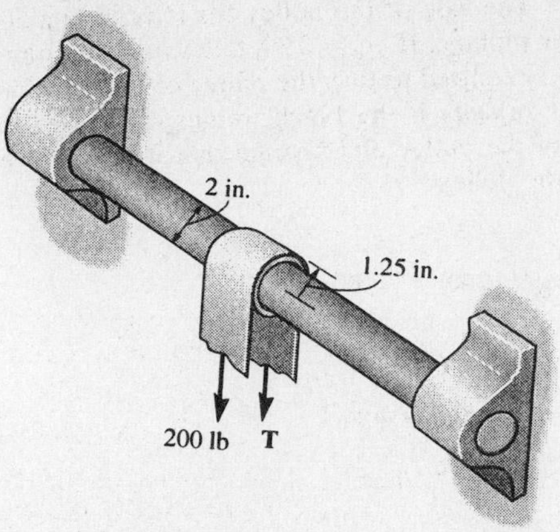

Equation of Equilibrium :

$$\curvearrowleft + \Sigma M_P = 0; \quad 200(1.125 + r_f) - 215(1.125 - r_f) = 0$$
$$r_f = 0.04066 \text{ in.}$$

Frictional Force on Journal Bearing : The radius of friction circle is

$$r_f = r\sin\phi_k$$
$$0.04066 = 1\sin\phi_k$$
$$\phi_k = 2.330°$$

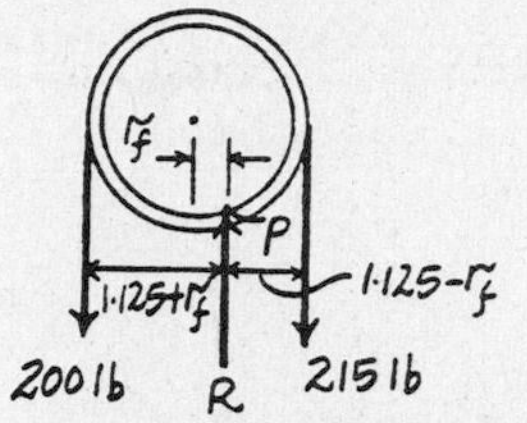

and the coefficient of static friction is

$$\mu_s = \tan\phi_s = \tan 2.330° = 0.0407 \qquad \textbf{Ans}$$

8-123. A disk having an outer diameter of 120 mm fits loosely over a fixed shaft having a diameter of 30 mm. If the coefficient of static friction between the disk and the shaft is $\mu_s = 0.15$ and the disk has a mass of 50 kg, determine the smallest vertical force **F** acting on the rim which must be applied to the disk to cause it to slip over the shaft.

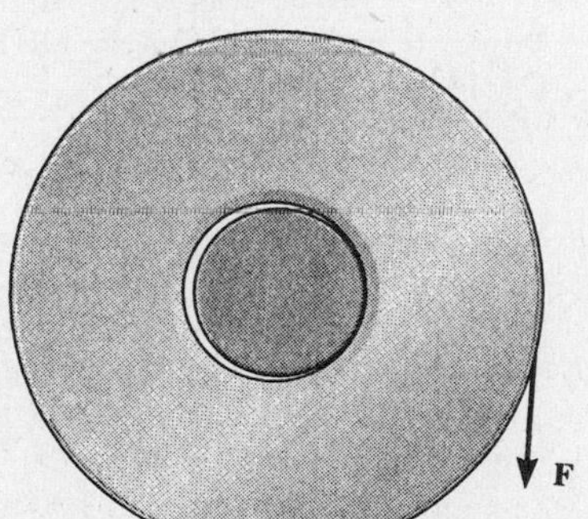

Frictional Force on Journal Bearing : Here, $\phi_s = \tan^{-1}\mu_s = \tan^{-1}0.15 = 8.531°$. Then the radius of friction circle is

$$r_f = r\sin\phi_s = 0.015\sin 8.531° = 2.225\left(10^{-3}\right) \text{ m}$$

Equation of Equilibrium :

$$\curvearrowleft + \Sigma M_P = 0; \quad 490.5(2.225)\left(10^{-3}\right) - F\left[0.06 - (2.225)\left(10^{-3}\right)\right] = 0$$
$$F = 18.9 \text{ N} \qquad \textbf{Ans}$$

***8-124.** The trailer has a total weight of 850 lb and center of gravity at G which is directly over its axle. If the axle has a diameter of 1 in., the radius of the wheel is $r = 1.5$ ft, and the coefficient of kinetic friction at the bearing is $\mu_k = 0.08$, determine the horizontal force P needed to pull the trailer.

$\xrightarrow{+} \Sigma F_x = 0; \quad R \sin\phi = P$

$+\uparrow \Sigma F_y = 0; \quad R\cos\phi = 850$

Thus,

$P = 850 \tan\phi$

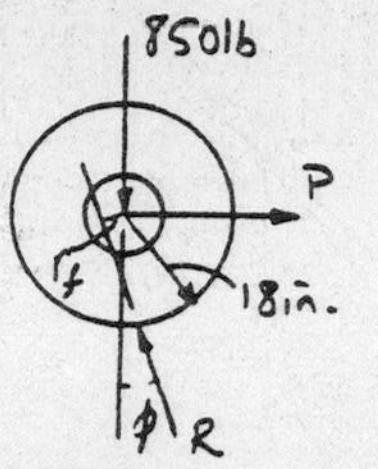

$\phi_k = \tan^{-1}(0.08) = 4.574°$

$r_f = r\sin\phi_k = 0.5 \sin 4.574° = 0.03987$ in.

$\phi = \sin^{-1}\left(\frac{r_f}{18}\right) = \sin^{-1}\left(\frac{0.03987}{18}\right) = 0.1269°$

Thus,

$P = 850 \tan 0.1269° = 1.88$ lb **Ans**

Note that this is equivalent to an overall coefficient of kinetic friction μ_k

$\mu_k = \frac{1.88}{850} = 0.00222$

Obviously, it is eaiser to pull the load on the trailer than push it.
If the approximate value of $r_f = r\mu_k = 0.5\,(0.08) = 0.04$ in. is used, then

$P = 1.89$ lb **Ans** (approx.)

8-125. The bell crank is used to control the elevator of a light airplane. If a maximum force of 50 N is required for operation of the elevator, determine the operating force P necessary to cause the crank to rotate counterclockwise. The coefficient of static friction at the 20-mm-diameter journal bearing is $\mu_s = 0.3$.

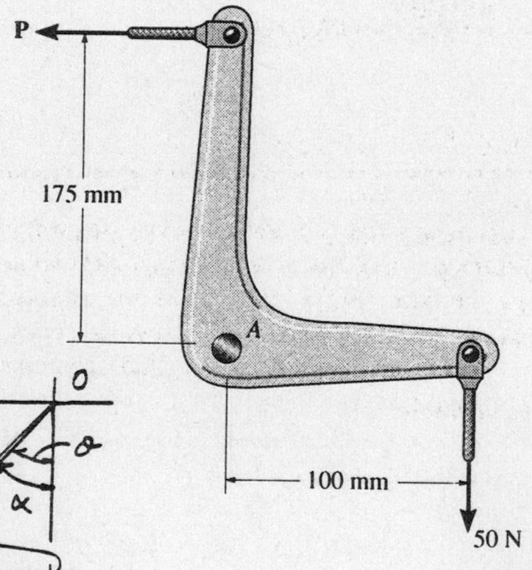

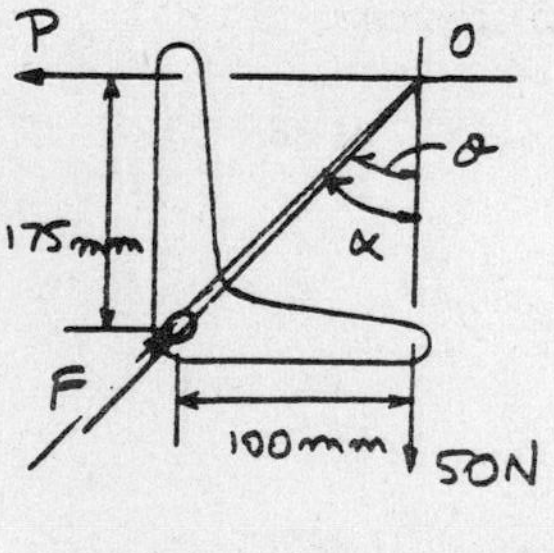

$r_f = r\mu_s = 10\,(0.3) = 3$ mm

$\theta = \tan^{-1}\left(\frac{100}{175}\right) = 29.745°$

$\cos\alpha = \cos\theta$

$\circlearrowleft + \Sigma M_{O'} = 0; \quad P\,(175) - 50\left(100 + \frac{3}{\cos 29.745°}\right) = 0$

$P = 29.6$ N **Ans**

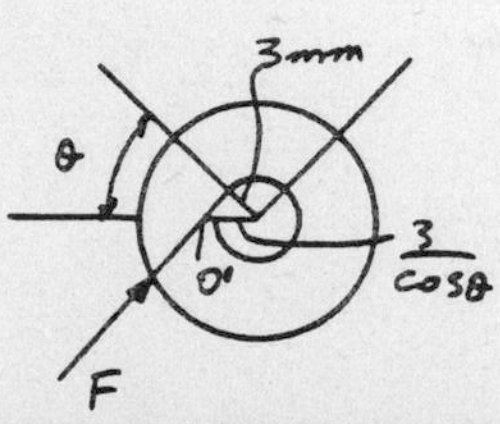

8-126. The bell crank is used to control the elevator of a light airplane. If a maximum force of 50 N is required for operation of the elevator, determine the operating force P necessary to cause the crank to rotate clockwise. The coefficient of static friction at the 20-mm-diameter journal bearing is $\mu_s = 0.3$.

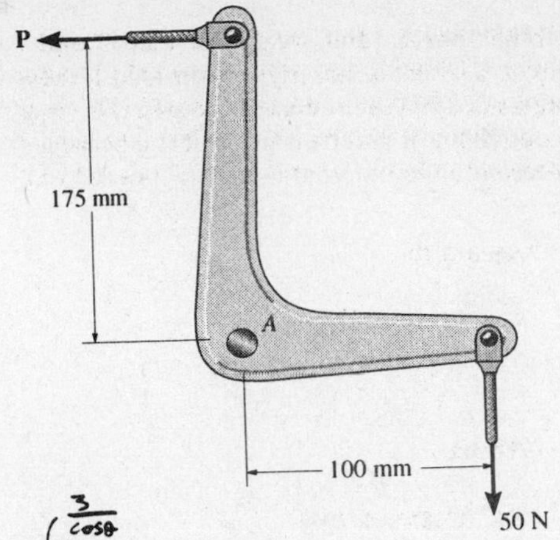

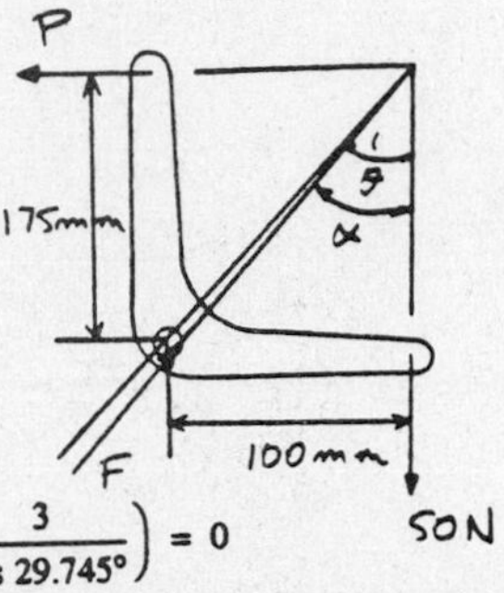

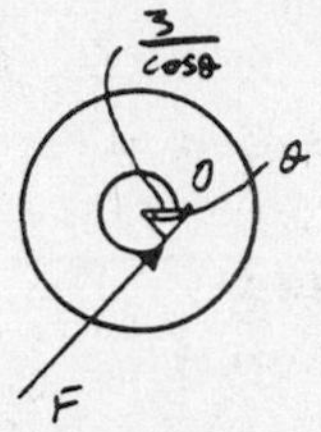

$r_f = r\mu_s = 10\,(0.3) = 3\text{ mm}$

$\theta = \tan^{-1}\left(\frac{100}{175}\right) = 29.745°$

$\cos\alpha = \cos\theta$

$\curvearrowleft +\Sigma M_O = 0;\quad P\,(175) - 50\left(100 - \frac{3}{\cos 29.745°}\right) = 0$

$P = 27.6\text{ N}$ **Ans**

8-127. The connecting rod is attached to the piston by a 0.75-in.-diameter pin at B and to the crank shaft by a 2-in.-diameter bearing A. If the piston is moving downwards, and the coefficient of static friction at these points is $\mu_s = 0.2$, determine the radius of the friction circle at each connection.

$(r_f)_A = r_A\mu_s = 0.2\text{ in.}$ **Ans**

$(r_f)_B = r_B\mu_s = \frac{0.75(0.2)}{2} = 0.075\text{ in.}$ **Ans**

***8-128.** The connecting rod is attached to the piston by a 20-mm-diameter pin at B and to the crank shaft by a 50-mm-diameter bearing A. If the piston is moving upwards, and the coefficient of static friction at these points is $\mu_s = 0.3$, determine the radius of the friction circle at each connection.

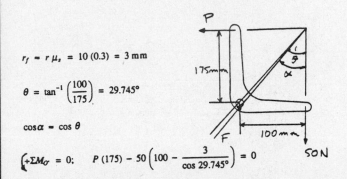

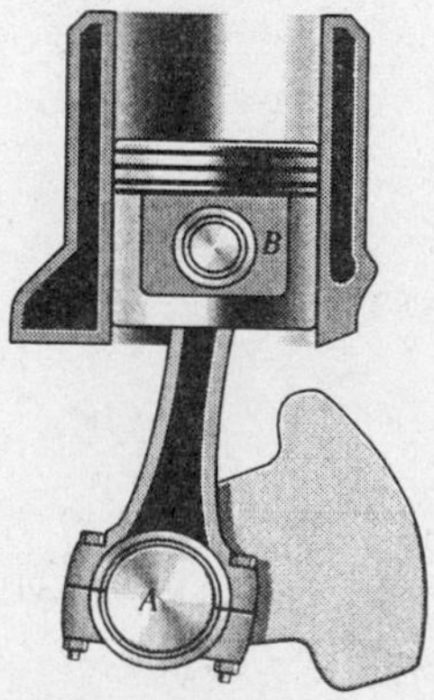

$(r_f)_A = r_A\mu_s = 25\,(0.3) = 7.50\text{ mm}$ **Ans**

$(r_f)_B = r_B\mu_s = 10\,(0.3) = 3\text{ mm}$ **Ans**

8-129. The vehicle has a weight of 2600 lb and center of gravity at G. Determine the horizontal force **P** that must be applied to overcome the rolling resistance of the wheels. The coefficient of rolling resistance is 0.5 in. The tires have a diameter of 2.75 ft.

Equations of Equilibrium :

$$\circlearrowleft + \Sigma M_A = 0; \quad N_B(7) + P(2.5) - 2600(2) = 0$$

$$N_B = \frac{5200 - 2.5P}{7}$$

$$\circlearrowleft + \Sigma M_B = 0; \quad P(2.5) + 2600(5) - N_A(7) = 0$$

$$N_A = \frac{13000 + 2.5P}{7}$$

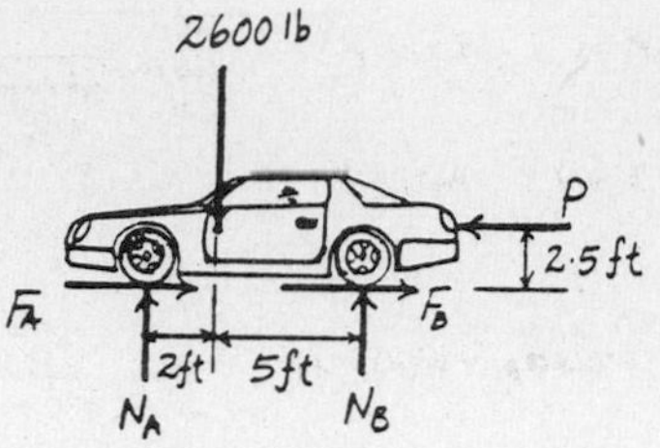

Rolling Resistance : Here, $W = N_A + N_B = \frac{5200 - 2.5P}{7} + \frac{13000 + 2.5P}{7}$ $= 2600$ lb, $a = 0.5$ in. and $r = \left(\frac{2.75}{2}\right)(12) = 16.5$ in.. Applying Eq. 8 – 11, we have

$$P = \frac{Wa}{r}$$

$$= \frac{2600(0.5)}{16.5}$$

$$= 78.8 \text{ lb} \qquad \textbf{Ans}$$

8-130. The handcart has wheels with a diameter of 6 in. If a crate having a weight of 1500 lb is placed on the cart, determine the force P that must be applied to the handle to overcome the rolling resistance. The coefficient of rolling resistance is 0.04 in. Neglect the weight of the cart.

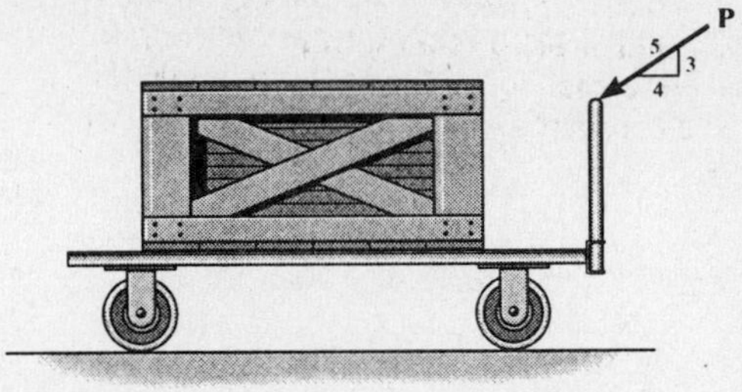

$$+\uparrow \Sigma F_y = 0; \quad N - 1500 - P\left(\frac{3}{5}\right) = 0$$

$$P = \frac{Wa}{r}; \quad \frac{4}{5}P = \frac{\left[1500 + P\left(\frac{3}{5}\right)\right](0.04)}{3}$$

$$2.4P = 60 + 0.024P$$

$$P = 25.3 \text{ lb} \qquad \textbf{Ans}$$

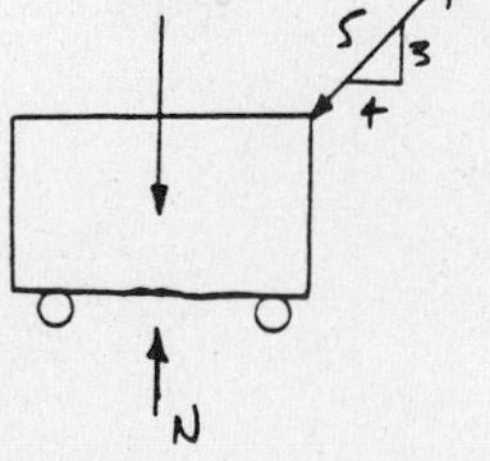

8-131. The cylinder is subjected to a load that has a weight W. If the coefficients of rolling resistance for the cylinder's top and bottom surfaces are a_A and a_B, respectively, show that a force having a magnitude of $P = [W(a_A + a_B)]/2r$ is required to move the load and thereby roll the cylinder forward. Neglect the weight of the cylinder.

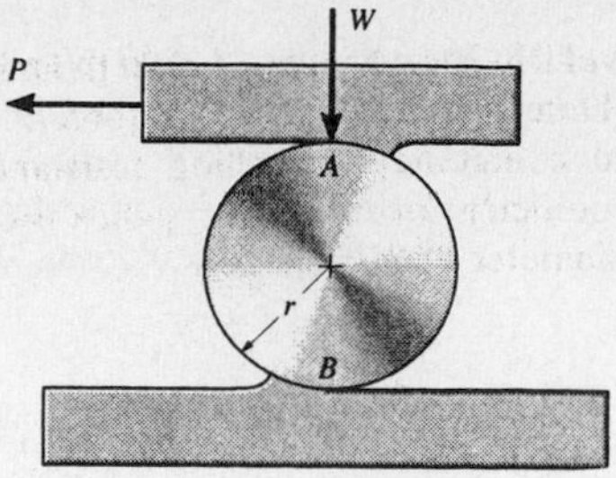

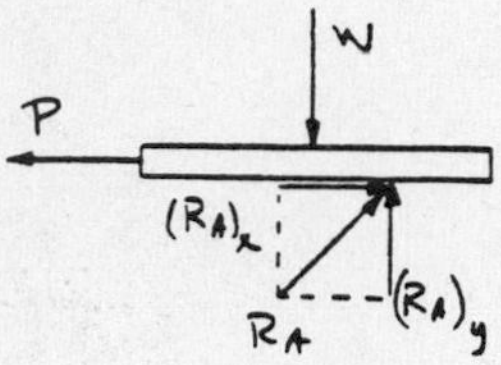

$\xrightarrow{+} \Sigma F_x = 0;\quad (R_A)_x - P = 0 \quad (R_A)_x = P$

$+\uparrow \Sigma F_y = 0;\quad (R_A)_y - W = 0 \quad (R_A)_y = W$

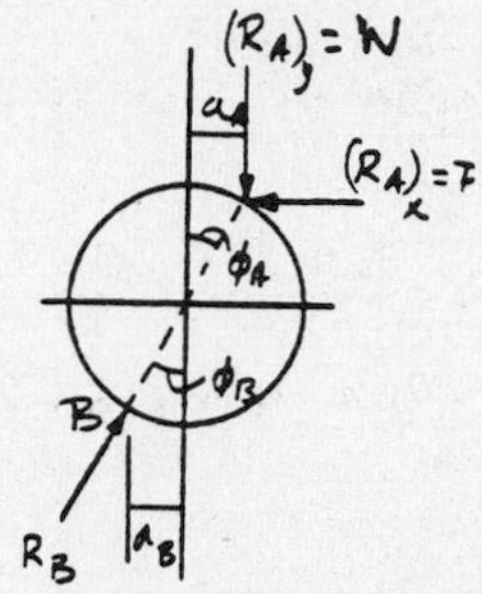

$\circlearrowleft + \Sigma M_B = 0;\quad P(r\cos\phi_A + r\cos\phi_B) - W(a_A + a_B) = 0 \qquad (1)$

Since ϕ_A and ϕ_B are very small, $\cos\phi_A \approx \cos\phi_B \approx 1$. Hence, from Eq. (1)

$$P = \frac{W(a_A + a_B)}{2r} \qquad \text{(QED)}$$

***8-132.** A large crate having a mass of 200 kg is moved along the floor using a series of 150-mm-diameter rollers for which the coefficient of rolling resistance is 3 mm at the ground and 7 mm at the bottom surface of the crate. Determine the horizontal force **P** needed to push the crate forward at a constant speed. *Hint:* Use the result of Prob. 8-131.

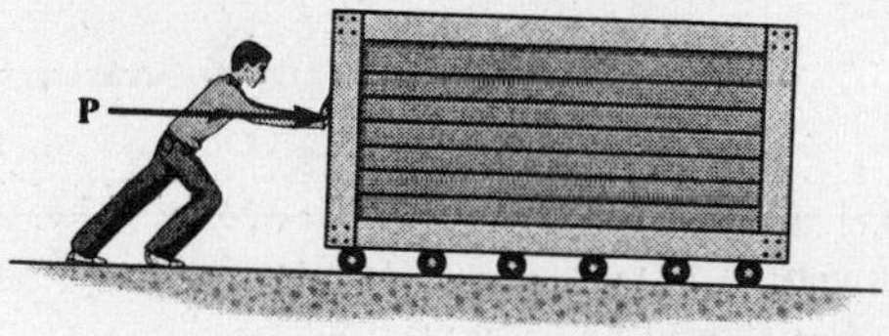

Rolling Resistance : Applying the result obtained in Prob. 8 – 131.

$P = \dfrac{W(a_A + a_B)}{2r}$, with $a_A = 7$ mm, $a_B = 3$ mm, $W = 200(9.81) = 1962$ N, and $r = 75$ mm, we have

$$P = \frac{1962(7+3)}{2(75)} = 130.8 \text{ N} = 131 \text{ N} \qquad \textbf{Ans}$$

8-133. The lawn roller weighs 300 lb. If the rod BA is held at an angle of 30° from the horizontal and the coefficient of rolling resistance for the roller is 2 in., determine the force **F** needed to push the roller at constant speed. Neglect friction developed at the axle and assume that the resultant force acting on the handle is applied along BA.

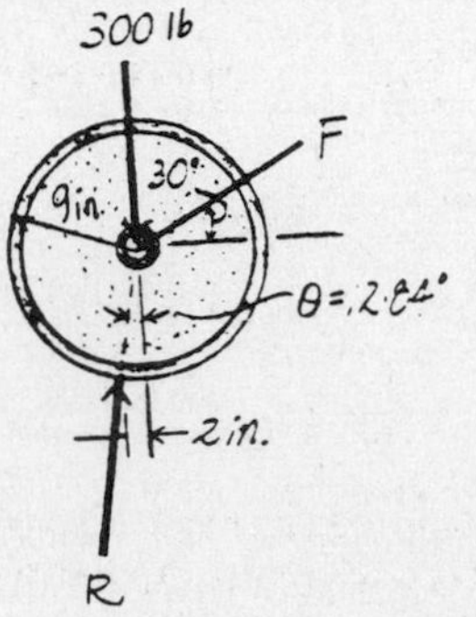

Rolling Resistance : The angle $\theta = \sin^{-1}\frac{2}{9} = 12.84°$. From the eqilibrium of the lawn roller, we have

$$\overset{+}{\rightarrow} \Sigma F_x = 0; \quad R\sin 12.84° - F\cos 30° = 0 \quad [1]$$

$$+\uparrow \Sigma F_y = 0; \quad R\cos 12.84° - 300 - F\sin 30° = 0 \quad [2]$$

Solving Eq. [1] and [2]

$$F = 90.9 \text{ lb} \quad \textbf{Ans}$$

$$R = 354.31 \text{ lb}$$

8-134. Determine the smallest horizontal force P that must be exerted on the 200-lb block to move it forward. The rollers each weigh 50 lb, and the coefficient of rolling resistance at the top and bottom surfaces is $a = 0.2$ in.

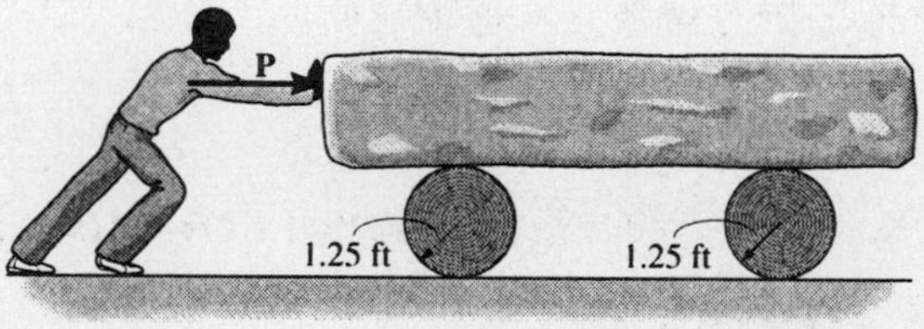

In general :

$$\circlearrowleft + \Sigma M_B = 0; \quad P\,(r\cos\phi_A + r\cos\phi_B) - W_1\,(a_A + a_B) - W_2\,a_B = 0$$

Since ϕ_A and ϕ_B are very small, $\cos\phi_A \approx \cos\phi_B \approx 1$. Hence,

$$P\,(2r) = W_1\,(a_A + a_B) + W_2\,a_B$$

$$P = \frac{W_1\,(a_A + a_B) + W_2\,a_B}{2r}$$

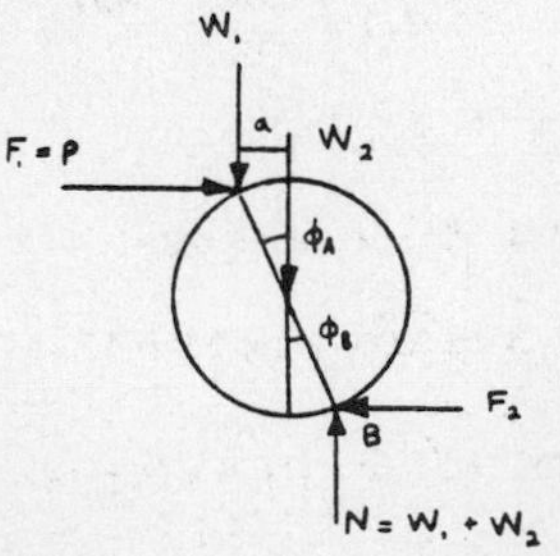

Thus, for the problem,

$$P = \left(\frac{200\,(0.2 + 0.2) + 2\,(50)\,(0.2)}{2\,(1.25)}\right)$$

$$P = 40 \text{ lb} \quad \textbf{Ans}$$

8-135. A single force **P** is applied to the handle of the drawer. If friction is neglected at the bottom side and the coefficient of static friction along the sides is $\mu_s = 0.4$, determine the largest spacing s between the symmetrically placed handles so that the drawer does not bind at the corners A and B when the force **P** is applied to one of the handles.

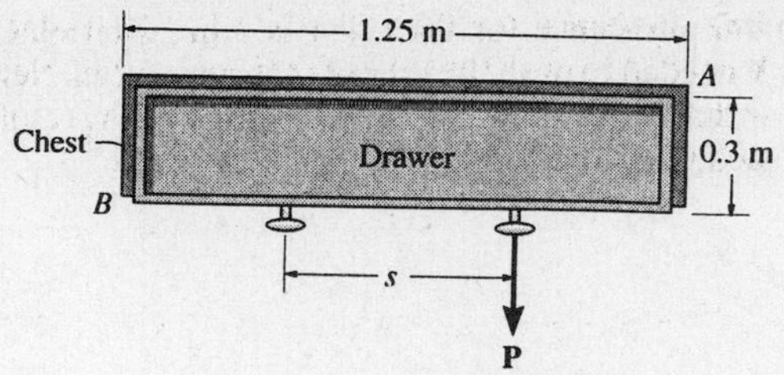

Equations of Equilibrium and Friction : If the drawer does not bind at corners A and B, slipping would have to occur at points A and B. Hence, $F_A = \mu N_A = 0.4N_A$ and $F_B = \mu N_B = 0.4N_B$.

$$\xrightarrow{+} \Sigma F_x = 0; \quad N_B - N_A = 0 \quad N_A = N_B = N$$

$$+\uparrow \Sigma F_y = 0; \quad 0.4N + 0.4N - P = 0 \quad P = 0.8N$$

$$\circlearrowleft + \Sigma M_B = 0; \quad N(0.3) + 0.4N(1.25) - 0.8N\left(\frac{s+1.25}{2}\right) = 0$$

$$N\left[0.3 + 0.5 - 0.8\left(\frac{s+1.25}{2}\right)\right] = 0$$

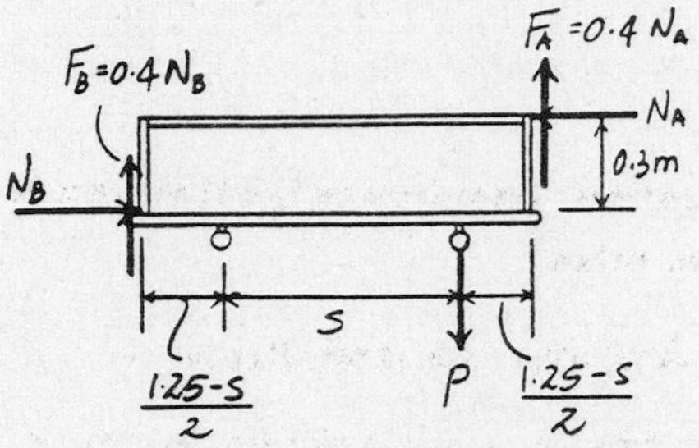

Since $N \neq 0$, then

$$0.3 + 0.5 - 0.8\left(\frac{s+1.25}{2}\right) = 0$$

$$s = 0.750 \text{ m} \qquad \textbf{Ans}$$

***8-136.** The semicircular hoop of weight W and center of gravity at G is suspended by the small peg at A. A horizontal force P is slowly applied at B. If the hoop begins to slip at A when $\theta = 30°$, determine the coefficient of static friction between the hoop and the peg.

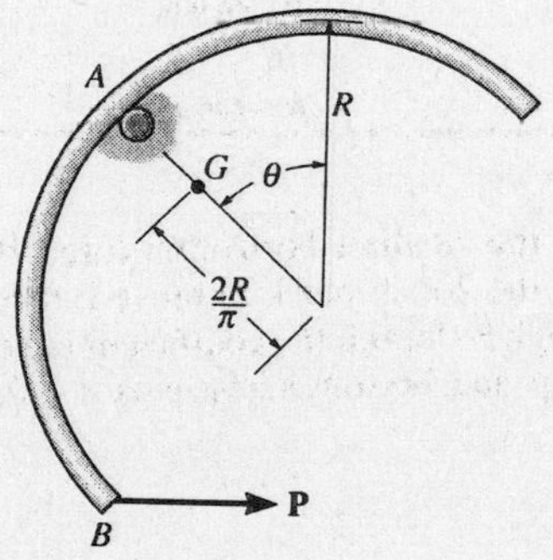

$$\xrightarrow{+} \Sigma F_x = 0; \quad P + F_A \cos 30° - N_A \sin 30° = 0$$

$$+\uparrow \Sigma F_y = 0; \quad F_A \sin 30° + N_A \cos 30° - W = 0$$

$$\circlearrowleft + \Sigma M_A = 0; \quad -W \sin 30° \left(R - \frac{2R}{\pi}\right) + P \sin 30° (R) + P \cos 30° (R) = 0$$

$$P = 0.1330\, W$$

$$0.1330\,(F_A \sin 30° + N_A \cos 30°) + F_A \cos 30° - N_A \sin 30° = 0$$

$$F_A\,(0.9325) - N_A\,(0.3848) = 0$$

$$\mu_A = \frac{F_A}{N_A} = \frac{0.3848}{0.9325} = 0.413 \qquad \textbf{Ans}$$

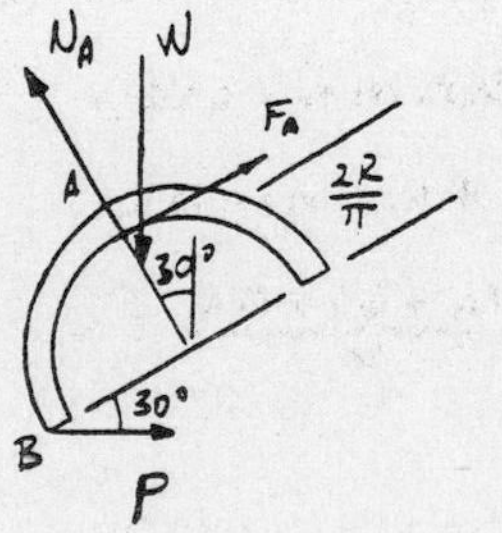

Also,

$$+\nwarrow \Sigma F_x = 0; \quad N_A - W \cos 30° - P \sin 30° = 0$$

$$+\nearrow \Sigma F_y = 0; \quad \mu_A N_A - W \sin 30° + P \cos 30° = 0$$

$$\circlearrowleft + \Sigma M_A = 0; \quad -W \sin 30° (R) \left(1 - \frac{2}{\pi}\right) + P \cos 30° (R) + P \sin 30° (R) = 0$$

$$P = 0.133\, W$$

$$\mu_A = 0.413 \qquad \textbf{Ans}$$

8-137. The truck has a mass of 1.25 Mg and a center of mass at G. Determine the greatest load it can pull if (a) the truck has rear-wheel drive while the front wheels are free to roll, and (b) the truck has four-wheel drive. The coefficient of static friction between the wheels and the ground is $\mu_s = 0.5$, and between the crate and the ground, it is $\mu'_s = 0.4$.

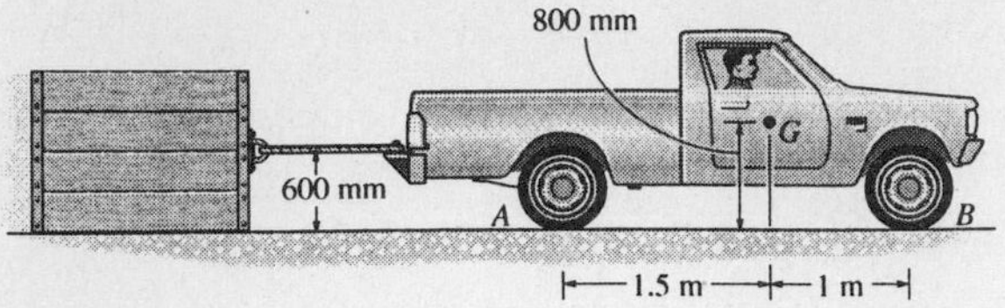

a) The truck with rear wheel drive.

Equations of Equilibrium and Friction : It is required that the rear wheels of the truck slip. Hence $F_A = \mu_s N_A = 0.5N_A$. From FBD (a),

$$\curvearrowleft + \Sigma M_B = 0; \quad 1.25(10^3)(9.81)(1) + T(0.6) - N_A(2.5) = 0 \quad [1]$$

$$\xrightarrow{+} \Sigma F_x = 0; \quad 0.5N_A - T = 0 \quad [2]$$

Solving Eqs. [1] and [2] yields

$$N_A = 5573.86 \text{ N} \qquad T = 2786.93 \text{ N}$$

Since the crate moves, $F_C = \mu_s' N_C = 0.4N_C$. From FBD (c),

$$+\uparrow \Sigma F_y = 0; \quad N_C - W = 0 \quad N_C = W$$

$$\xrightarrow{+} \Sigma F_x = 0; \quad 2786.93 - 0.4W = 0$$

$$W = 6967.33 \text{ N} = 6.97 \text{ kN} \qquad \textbf{Ans}$$

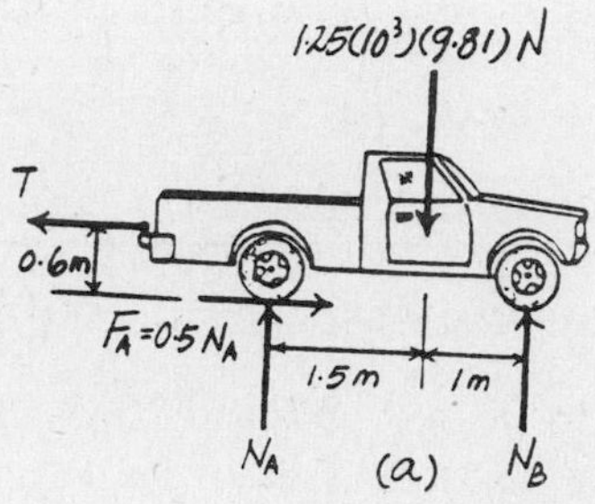

b) The truck with four wheel drive.

Equations of Equilibrium and Friction : It is required that the rear wheel and front wheels of the truck slip. Hence $F_A = \mu_s N_A = 0.5N_A$ and $F_B = \mu_s N_B = 0.5N_B$. From FBD (b),

$$\curvearrowleft + \Sigma M_B = 0; \quad 1.25(10^3)(9.81)(1) + T(0.6) - N_A(2.5) = 0 \quad [3]$$

$$\curvearrowleft + \Sigma M_A = 0; \quad N_B(2.5) + T(0.6) - 1.25(10^3)(9.81)(1.5) = 0 \quad [4]$$

$$\xrightarrow{+} \Sigma F_x = 0; \quad 0.5N_A + 0.5N_B - T = 0 \quad [5]$$

Solving Eqs. [3], [4] and [5] yields

$$N_A = 6376.5 \text{ N} \qquad N_B = 5886.0 \text{ N} \qquad T = 6131.25 \text{ N}$$

Since the crate moves, $F_C = \mu_s' N_C = 0.4N_C$. From FBD (c),

$$+\uparrow \Sigma F_y = 0; \quad N_C - W = 0 \quad N_C = W$$

$$\xrightarrow{+} \Sigma F_x = 0; \quad 6131.25 - 0.4W = 0$$

$$W = 15328.125 \text{ N} = 15.3 \text{ kN} \qquad \textbf{Ans}$$

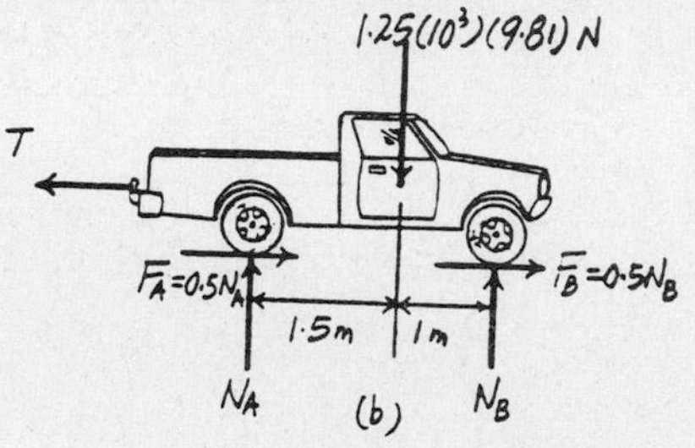

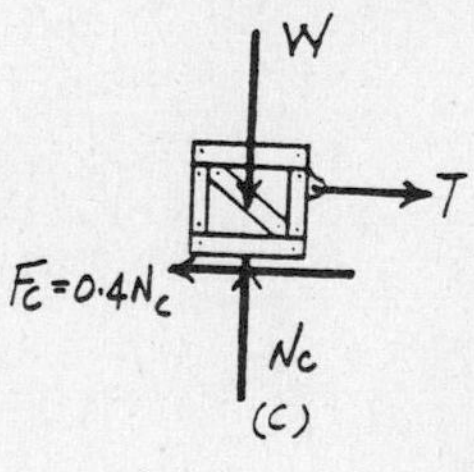

8-138. Solve Prob. 8-137 if the truck and crate are traveling up a 10° incline.

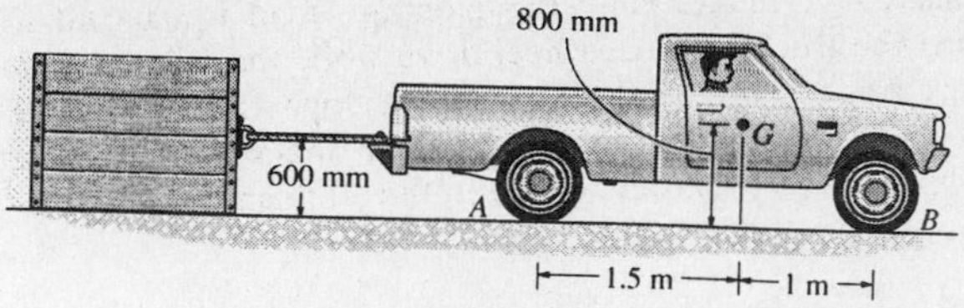

a) The truck with rear wheel drive.

Equations of Equilibrium and Friction : It is required that the rear wheel of the truck slip hence $F_A = \mu_s N_A = 0.5N_A$. From FBD (a),

$$\circlearrowleft + \Sigma M_B = 0; \quad 1.25(10^3)(9.81)\cos 10°(1) + 1.25(10^3)(9.81)\sin 10°(0.8) + T(0.6) - N_A(2.5) = 0 \quad [1]$$

$$+ \Sigma F_{x'} = 0; \quad 0.5N_A - 1.25(10^3)(9.81)\sin 10° - T = 0 \quad [2]$$

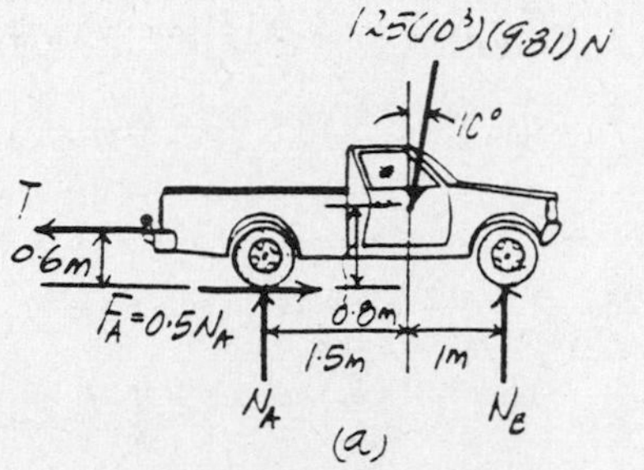

Solving Eqs. [1] and [2] yields

$$N_A = 5682.76 \text{ N} \qquad T = 712.02 \text{ N}$$

Since the crate moves, $F_C = \mu_s' N_C = 0.4N_C$. From FBD (c),

$$+\Sigma F_{y'} = 0; \quad N_C - W\cos 10° = 0 \qquad N_C = 0.9848W$$

$$\xrightarrow{+} \Sigma F_x = 0; \quad 712.02 - W\sin 10° - 0.4(0.9848W) = 0$$

$$W = 1254.50 \text{ N} = 1.25 \text{ kN} \qquad \textbf{Ans}$$

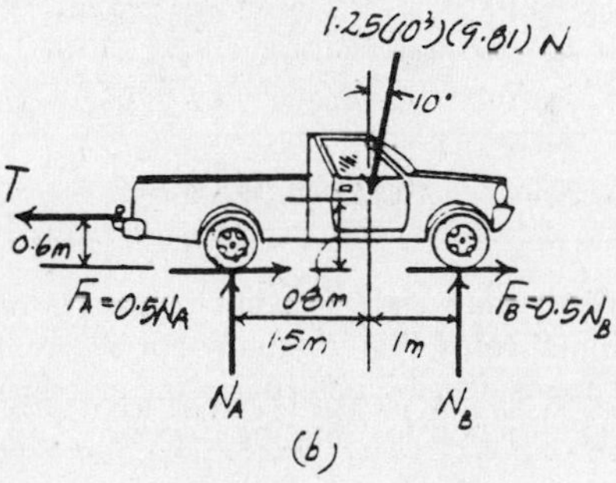

b) The truck with four wheel drive.

Equations of Equilibrium and Friction : It is required that the rear wheels of the truck slip hence $F_A = \mu_s N_A = 0.5N_A$. From FBD (a),

$$\circlearrowleft + \Sigma M_B = 0; \quad 1.25(10^3)(9.81)\cos 10°(1) + 1.25(10^3)(9.81)\sin 10°(0.8) + T(0.6) - N_A(2.5) = 0 \quad [3]$$

$$\circlearrowleft + \Sigma M_A = 0; \quad -1.25(10^3)(9.81)\cos 10°(1.5) + 1.25(10^3)(9.81)\sin 10°(0.8) + T(0.6) + N_B(2.5) = 0 \quad [4]$$

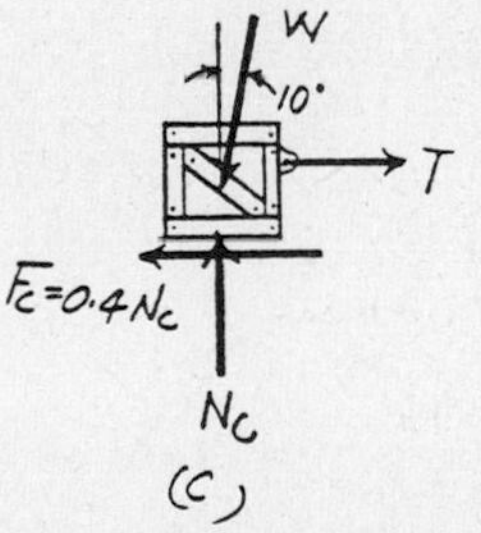

$$+ \Sigma F_{x'} = 0; \quad 0.5N_A + 0.5N_B - 1.25(10^3)(9.81)\sin 10° - T = 0 \quad [5]$$

Solving Eqs. [3], [4] and [5] yields

$$N_A = 6449.98 \text{ N} \qquad N_B = 5626.23 \text{ N} \qquad T = 3908.74 \text{ N}$$

Since the crate moves, $F_C = \mu_s' N_C = 0.4N_C$. From FBD (c),

$$+\Sigma F_{y'} = 0; \quad N_C - W\cos 10° = 0 \qquad N_C = 0.9848W$$

$$\xrightarrow{+} \Sigma F_x = 0; \quad 3908.74 - W\sin 10° - 0.4(0.9848W) = 0$$

$$W = 6886.79 \text{ N} = 6.89 \text{ kN} \qquad \textbf{Ans}$$

8-139. If block A has a mass of 1.5 kg, determine the largest mass of block B without causing motion of the system. The coefficient of static friction between the blocks and inclined planes is $\mu_s = 0.2$.

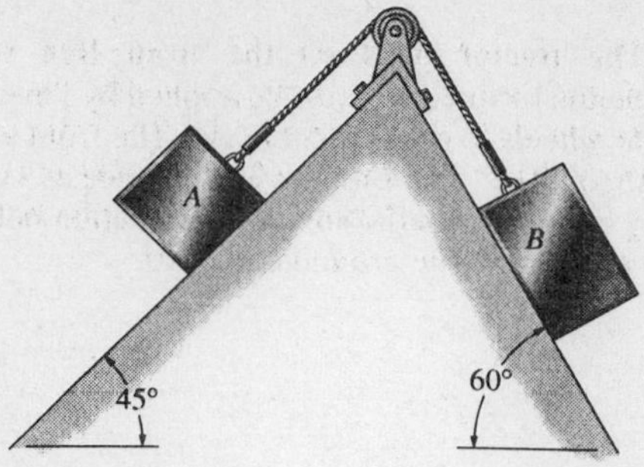

By inspection, B will tend to move down the plane.

Block A:

$+\nearrow \Sigma F_x = 0; \quad T - 0.2N_A - 1.5(9.81)\sin 45° = 0$

$+\nwarrow \Sigma F_y = 0; \quad N_A - 1.5(9.81)\cos 45° = 0$

Block B:

$+\nwarrow \Sigma F_x = 0; \quad T + 0.2N_B - 9.81(m_B)\sin 60° = 0$

$+\nearrow \Sigma F_y = 0; \quad N_B - 9.81(m_B)\cos 60° = 0$

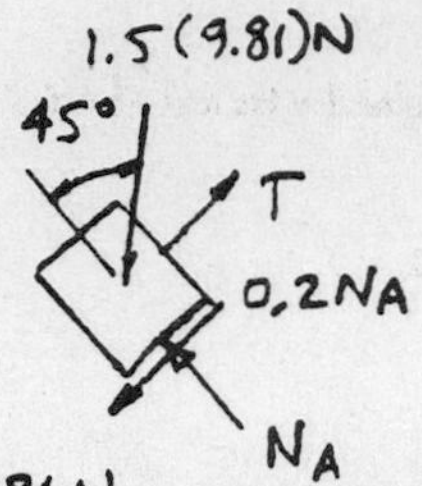

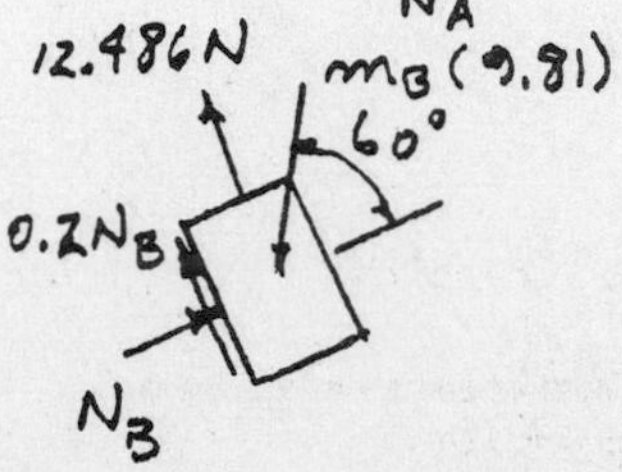

Solving,

$N_A = 10.4$ N; $\quad N_B = 8.15$ N; $\quad T = 12.5$ N;

$m_B = 1.66$ kg **Ans**

***8-140.** The cone has a weight W and center of gravity at G. If a horizontal force **P** is gradually applied to the string attached to its vertex, determine the maximum coefficient of static friction for slipping to occur.

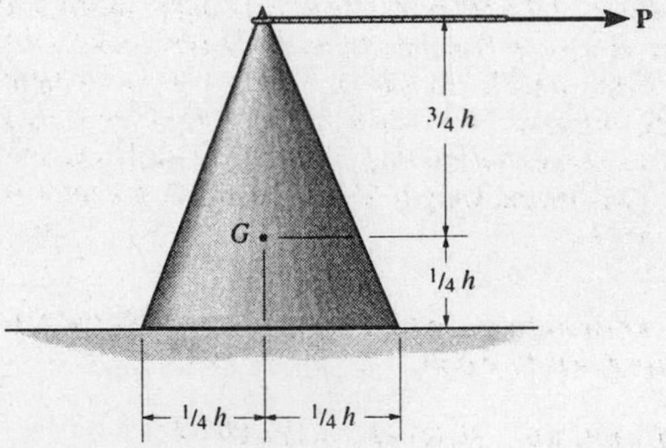

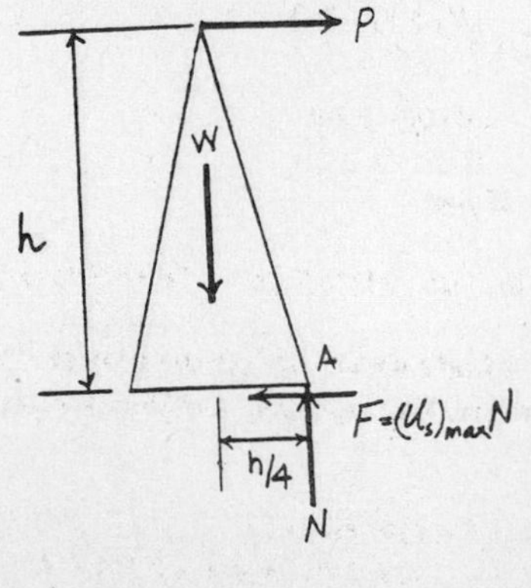

Equations of Equilibrium : In this case, it is required that the cone slips and about to tip about point A. Hence, $F = (\mu_s)_{max} N$.

$\circlearrowleft + \Sigma M_A = 0; \quad W\left(\frac{h}{4}\right) - P(h) = 0 \qquad P = \frac{W}{4}$

$+\uparrow \Sigma F_y = 0; \quad N - W = 0 \qquad N = W$

$\xrightarrow{+} \Sigma F_x = 0; \quad \frac{W}{4} - (\mu_s)_{max} W = 0$

$(\mu_s)_{max} = 0.250$ **Ans**

8-141. The tractor pulls on the fixed tree stump. Determine the torque that must be applied by the engine to the rear wheels to cause them to slip. The front wheels are free to roll. The tractor weighs 3500 lb and has a center of gravity at G. The coefficient of static friction between the rear wheels and the ground is $\mu_s = 0.5$.

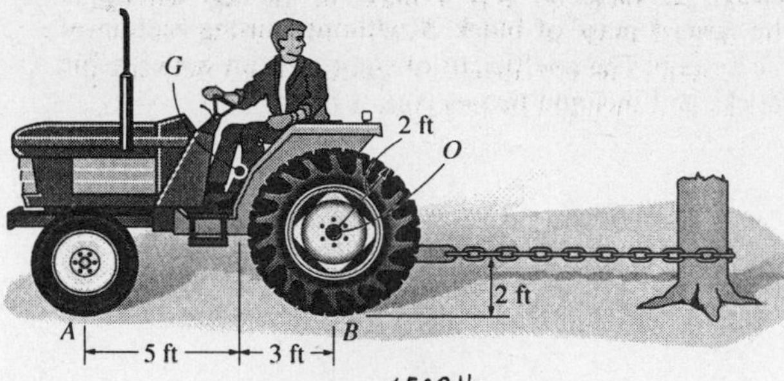

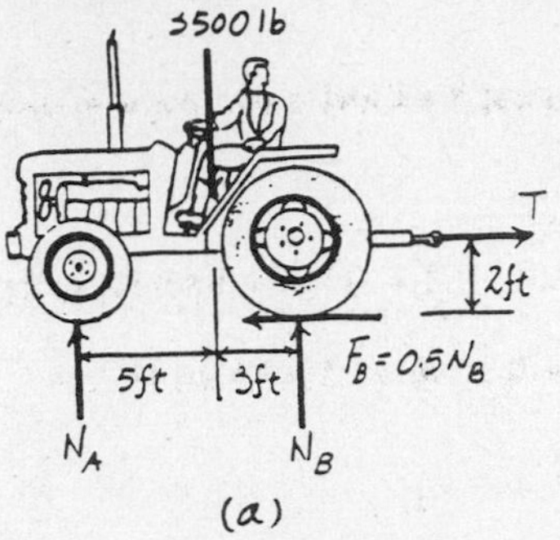

Equations of Equilibrium and Friction : Assume that the rear wheels B slip. Hence $F_B = \mu_s N_B = 0.5N_B$.

$$\circlearrowleft + \Sigma M_A = 0 \qquad N_B(8) - T(2) - 3500(5) = 0 \qquad [1]$$

$$+\uparrow \Sigma F_y = 0; \qquad N_B + N_A - 3500 = 0 \qquad [2]$$

$$\xrightarrow{+} \Sigma F_x = 0; \qquad T - 0.5N_B = 0 \qquad [3]$$

Solving Eqs. [1], [2] and [3] yields

$$N_A = 1000 \text{ lb} \qquad N_B = 2500 \text{ lb} \qquad T = 1250 \text{ lb}$$

Since $N_A > 0$, the front wheels do not lift up. Therefore the rear wheels slip as assumed. Thus, $F_B = 0.5(2500) = 1250$ lb. From FBD (b),

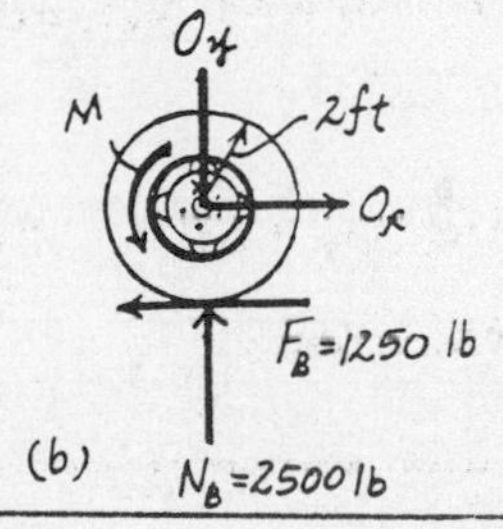

$$\circlearrowleft + \Sigma M_O = 0, \qquad M - 1250(2) = 0$$

$$M = 2500 \text{ lb}\cdot\text{ft} = 2.50 \text{ kip}\cdot\text{ft} \qquad \textbf{Ans}$$

8-142. The tractor pulls on the fixed tree stump. If the coefficient of static friction between the rear wheels and the ground is $\mu_s = 0.6$, determine if the rear wheels slip or the front wheels lift off the ground as the engine provides torque to the rear wheels. What is the torque needed to cause the motion? The front wheels are free to roll. The tractor weighs 2500 lb and has a center of gravity at G.

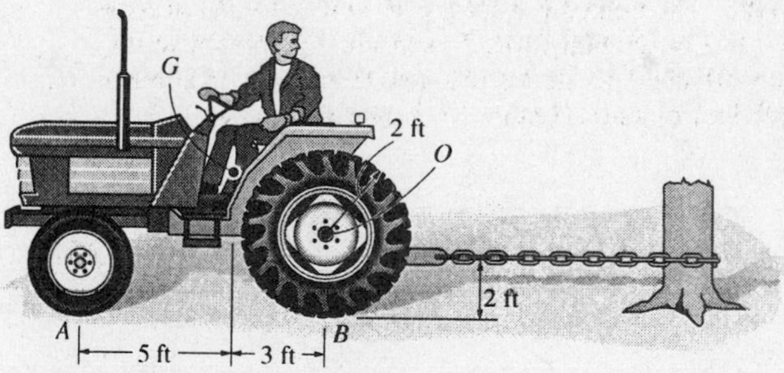

Equations of Equilibrium and Friction : Assume that the rear wheels B slip. Hence $F_B = \mu_s N_B = 0.6N_B$.

$$\circlearrowleft + \Sigma M_A = 0 \qquad N_B(8) - T(2) - 2500(5) = 0 \qquad [1]$$

$$+\uparrow \Sigma F_y = 0; \qquad N_B + N_A - 2500 = 0 \qquad [2]$$

$$\xrightarrow{+} \Sigma F_x = 0; \qquad T - 0.6N_B = 0 \qquad [3]$$

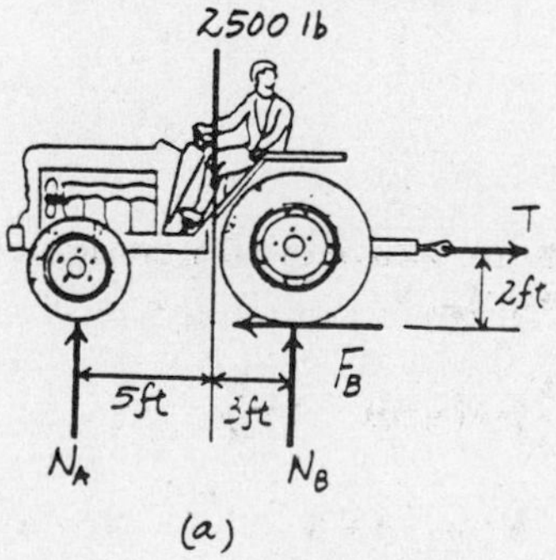

Solving Eqs. [1], [2] and [3] yields

$$N_A = 661.76 \text{ lb} \qquad N_B = 1838.24 \text{ lb} \qquad T = 1102.94 \text{ lb}$$

Since $N_A > 0$, **the front wheels do not lift off the ground.** Therefore the rear wheels slip as assumed. Thus, $F_B = 0.6(1838.24) = 1102.94$ lb. From FBD (b),

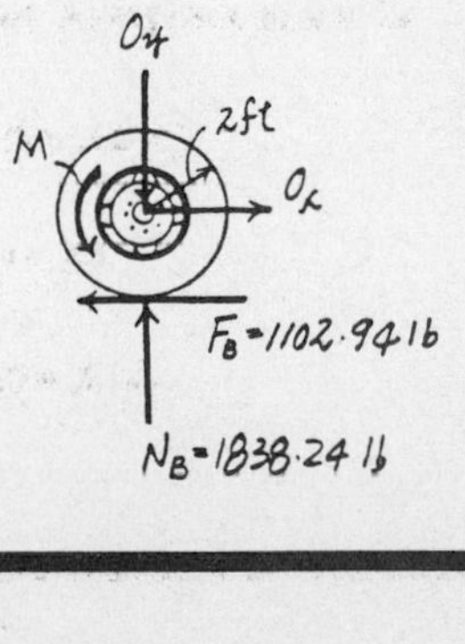

$$+\Sigma M_O = 0, \qquad M - 1102.94(2) = 0$$

$$M = 2205.88 \text{ lb}\cdot\text{ft} = 2.21 \text{ kip}\cdot\text{ft} \qquad \textbf{Ans}$$

9-1. Determine the distance $\bar{x}$ to the center of mass of the homogeneous rod bent into the shape shown. If the rod has a mass per unit length of 0.5 kg/m, determine the reactions at the fixed support O.

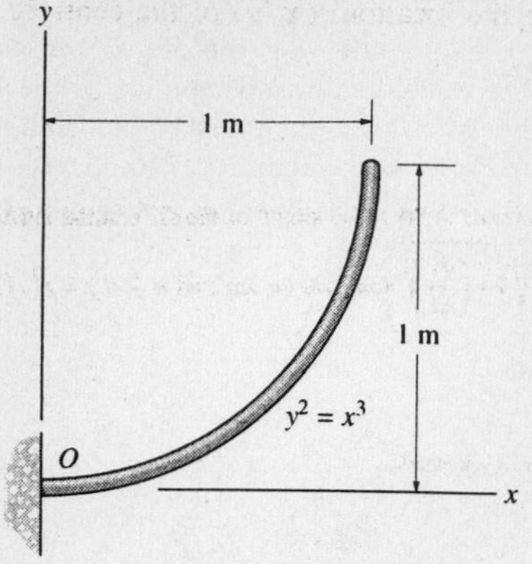

Length and Moment Arm : The length of the differential element is $dL = \sqrt{dx^2 + dy^2} = \left(\sqrt{1+\left(\frac{dy}{dx}\right)^2}\right)dx$ and its centroid is $\tilde{x} = x$. Here, $\frac{dy}{dx} = \frac{3}{2}x^{\frac{1}{2}}$.

Performing the integration, we have

$$L = \int dL = \int_0^{1\text{ m}} \left(\sqrt{1+\frac{9}{4}x}\right)dx = \frac{8}{27}\left(1+\frac{9}{4}x\right)^{\frac{3}{2}}\Bigg|_0^{1\text{ m}} = 1.4397\text{ m}$$

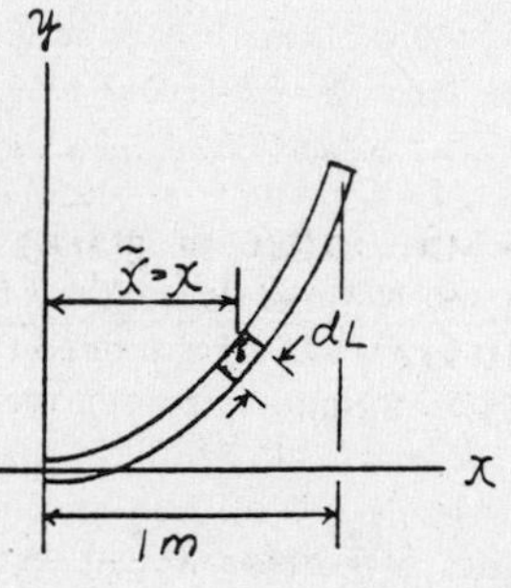

$$\int_L \tilde{x}\,dL = \int_0^{1\text{ m}} x\sqrt{1+\frac{9}{4}x}\,dx$$

$$= \left[\frac{8}{27}x\left(1+\frac{9}{4}x\right)^{\frac{3}{2}} - \frac{64}{1215}\left(1+\frac{9}{4}x\right)^{\frac{5}{2}}\right]\Bigg|_0^{1\text{ m}}$$

$$= 0.7857$$

Centroid : Applying Eq. 9 − 7 , we have

$$\bar{x} = \frac{\int_L \tilde{x}\,dL}{\int_L dL} = \frac{0.7857}{1.4397} = 0.5457\text{ m} = 0.546\text{ m} \qquad \textbf{Ans}$$

Equations of Equilibrium :

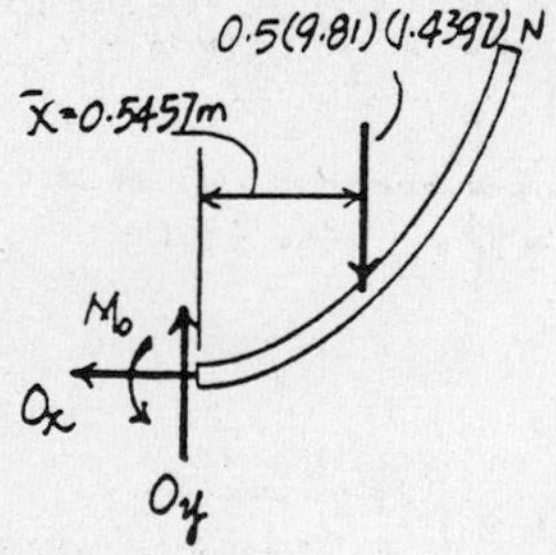

$\xrightarrow{+} \Sigma F_x = 0;\qquad O_x = 0$ **Ans**

$+\uparrow \Sigma F_y = 0;\qquad O_y - 0.5(9.81)(1.4397) = 0$

$O_y = 7.06\text{ N}$ **Ans**

$\circlearrowleft + \Sigma M_O = 0;\qquad M_O - 0.5(9.81)(1.4397)(0.5457) = 0$

$M_O = 3.85\text{ N}\cdot\text{m}$ **Ans**

9-2. Determine the location $(\bar{x}, \bar{y})$ of the centroid of the wire.

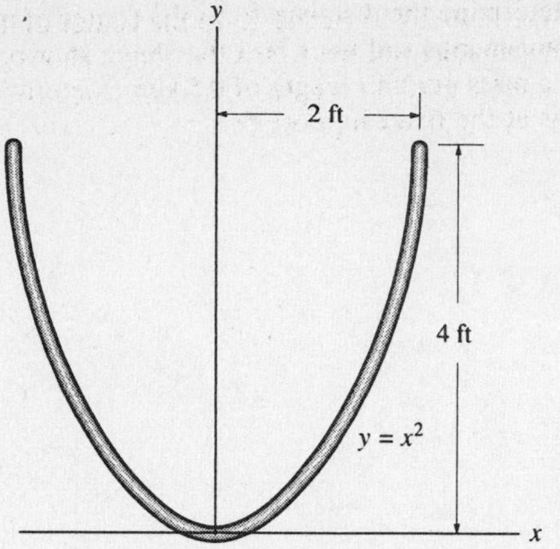

Length and Moment Arm : The length of the differential element is $dL = \sqrt{dx^2 + dy^2} = \left(\sqrt{1 + \left(\frac{dy}{dx}\right)^2}\right) dx$ and its centroid is $\tilde{y} = y = x^2$. Here, $\frac{dy}{dx} = 2x$.

Centroid : Due to symmetry

$$\bar{x} = 0 \qquad \textbf{Ans}$$

Applying Eq. 9–7 and performing the integration, we have

$$\bar{y} = \frac{\int_L \tilde{y}\,dL}{\int_L dL} = \frac{\int_{-2\text{ft}}^{2\text{ft}} x^2\sqrt{1+4x^2}\,dx}{\int_{-2\text{ft}}^{2\text{ft}} \sqrt{1+4x^2}\,dx}$$

$$= \frac{16.9423}{9.2936} = 1.82 \text{ ft} \qquad \textbf{Ans}$$

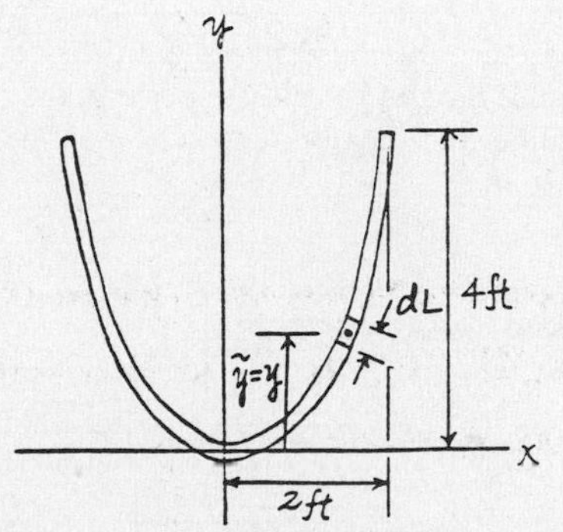

9-3. Locate the center of gravity $(\bar{x}, \bar{y})$ of the homogeneous rod. What is its weight if it has a mass per unit length of 3 kg/m? Solve the problem by evaluating the integrals using Simpson's rule.

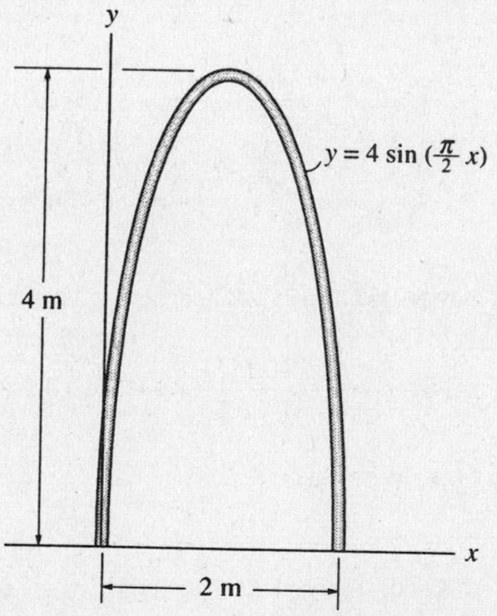

$$y = 4 \sin\left(\frac{\pi}{2} x\right); \qquad \frac{dy}{dx} = 2\pi \cos\left(\frac{\pi}{2} x\right)$$

$$dL = \left[\sqrt{1 + \left(\frac{dy}{dx}\right)^2}\right] dx = \left[\sqrt{1 + \left(2\pi \cos\left(\frac{\pi}{2} x\right)\right)^2}\right] dx$$

$$L = \int_0^2 \sqrt{1 + \left(2\pi \cos\left(\frac{\pi}{2} x\right)\right)^2}\, dx = 8.377 \text{ m}$$

$$\tilde{y} = y$$

$$\int_L \tilde{y}\, dL = \int_0^2 4 \sin\left(\frac{\pi}{2} x\right) \sqrt{1 + \left(2\pi \cos\left(\frac{\pi}{2} x\right)\right)^2}\, dx = 17.23 \text{ m}^2$$

Thus,

$$W = 8.377\,(3)\,(9.81) = 247 \text{ N} \qquad \textbf{Ans}$$

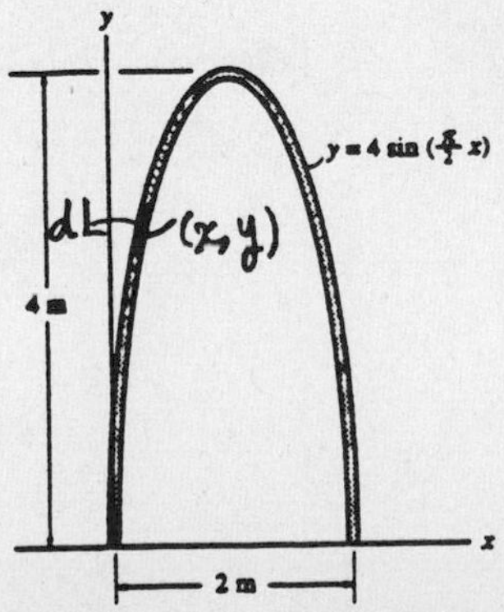

Due to symmetry,

$$\bar{x} = 1 \text{ m} \qquad \textbf{Ans}$$

$$\bar{y} = \frac{\int_L \tilde{y}\, dL}{\int_L dL} = \frac{17.23}{8.377} = 2.06 \text{ m} \qquad \textbf{Ans}$$

***9-4.** Locate the centroid $\bar{x}$ of the circular rod. Express the answer in terms of the radius r and semiarc angle α.

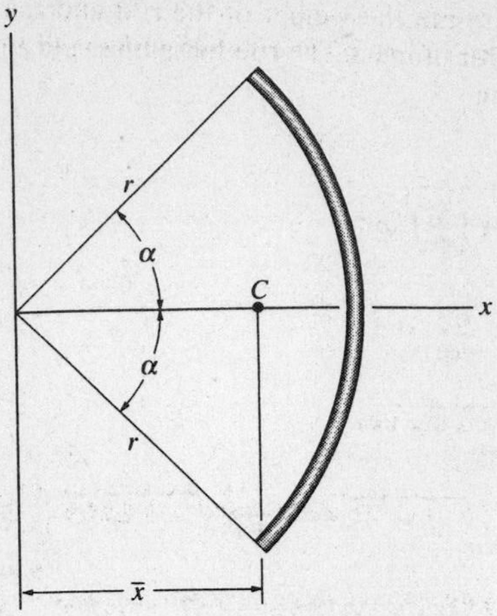

$L = 2r\alpha$

$\tilde{x} = r\cos\theta$

$\int \tilde{x}\, dL = \int_{-\alpha}^{\alpha} r\cos\theta\, r d\theta$

$= 2r^2 \sin\alpha$

$\bar{x} = \dfrac{2r^2\sin\alpha}{2r\alpha} = \dfrac{r\sin\alpha}{\alpha}$ **Ans**

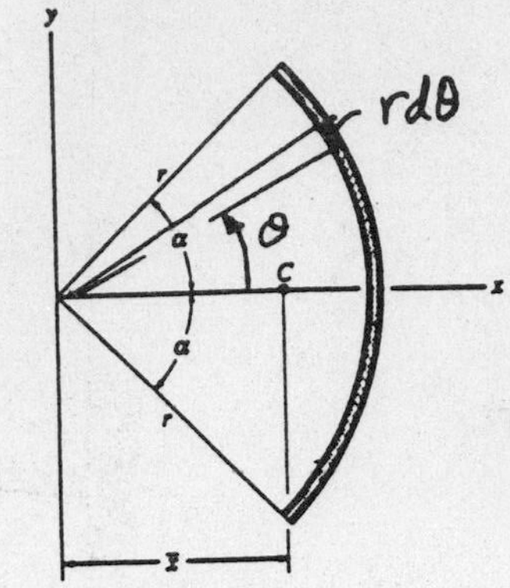

9-5. Determine the distance $\bar{x}$ to the center of mass of the rod. If the rod has a mass per unit length of 0.5 kg/m, determine the components of reaction at the fixed support O.

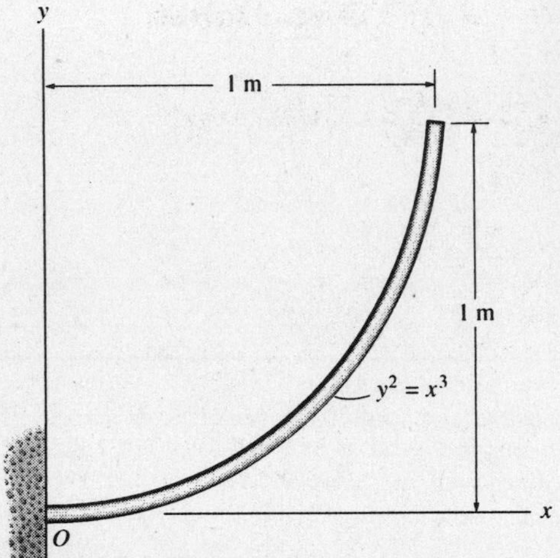

The differential element :

$$dL = \sqrt{(dx)^2 + (dy)^2} = \left(\sqrt{1 + \left(\frac{dy}{dx}\right)^2}\right)dx \qquad \text{Since } y = x^{\frac{3}{2}} \text{ then } \frac{dy}{dx} = \frac{3}{2}x^{\frac{1}{2}}$$

$$dL = \left(\sqrt{1 + \tfrac{9}{4}x}\right)dx$$

Centroid : $\tilde{x} = x$

$$\int_L \tilde{x}\, dL = \int_0^1 x\left(\sqrt{1 + \tfrac{9}{4}x}\right)dx = 0.7856 \text{ m}^2$$

$$L = \int_L dL = \int_0^1 \left(\sqrt{1 + \tfrac{9}{4}x}\right)dx = 1.4397 \text{ m}$$

$$\bar{x} = \frac{\int_L \tilde{x}\, dL}{\int_L dL} = \frac{0.7856}{1.4397} = 0.5457 \text{ m} = 0.546 \text{ m} \qquad \textbf{Ans}$$

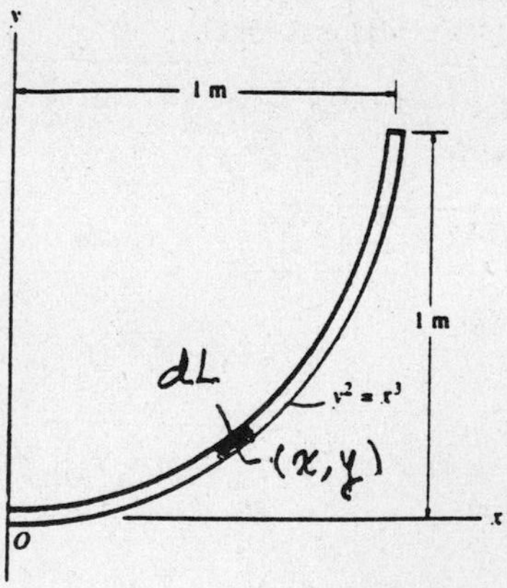

Equilibrium :

$\xrightarrow{+} \Sigma F_x = 0;$ $\quad O_x = 0$ **Ans**

$+\uparrow \Sigma F_y = 0;$ $\quad O_y - 1.4397(0.5)(9.81) = 0 \quad O_y = 7.06 \text{ N}$ **Ans**

$\circlearrowleft + \Sigma M_O = 0;$ $\quad M_O - 1.4397(0.5)(9.81)(0.5457) = 0$

$M_O = 3.85 \text{ N}\cdot\text{m}$ **Ans**

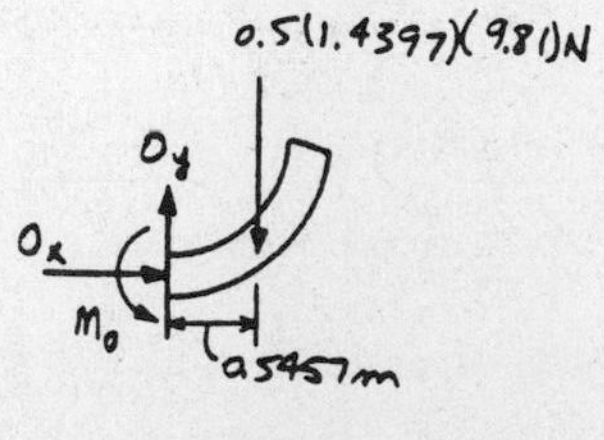

9-6. Determine the weight of the rod and the distance $\bar{y}$ to its center of mass. The rod has a mass per unit length of 0.5 kg/m.

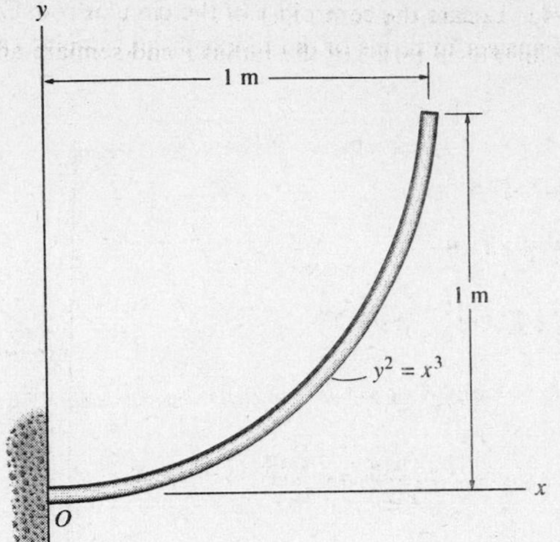

$$dL = \sqrt{1 + \left(\frac{dy}{dx}\right)^2}\, dx$$

$$y = x^{\frac{3}{2}}; \quad \frac{dy}{dx} = 1.5\, x^{\frac{1}{2}}$$

$$dL = \sqrt{1 + 2.25x}\, dx$$

$$\int_L dL = \int_0^1 \sqrt{1 + 2.25x}\, dx = \frac{2}{6.75}\sqrt{(1 + 2.25x)^3}\Big|_0^1 = 1.4397 \text{ m}$$

$W = 0.5\,(9.81)\,L = 0.5\,(9.81)\,(1.4397) = 7.06 \text{ N}$ **Ans**

$$\tilde{y} = y = x^{\frac{3}{2}}$$

$$\int_L \tilde{y}\, dL = \int_0^1 x^{\frac{3}{2}} \sqrt{1 + 2.25x}\, dx = 0.64285 \text{ m}^2$$

$\bar{y} = \dfrac{\int_L \tilde{y}\, dL}{\int_L dL} = \dfrac{0.64285}{1.4397} = 0.447 \text{ m}$ **Ans**

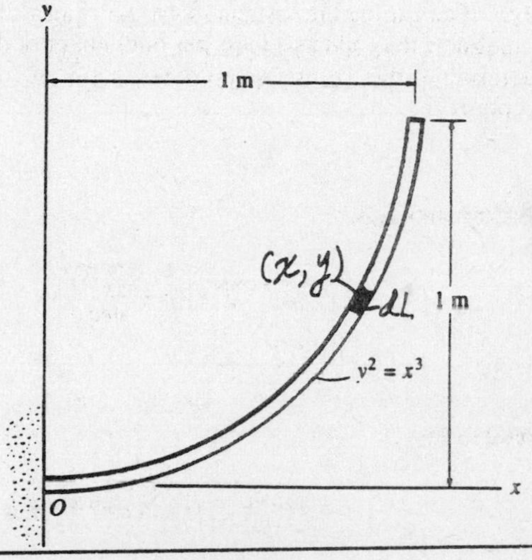

9-7. Locate the center of gravity of the thin homogeneous cylindrical shell.

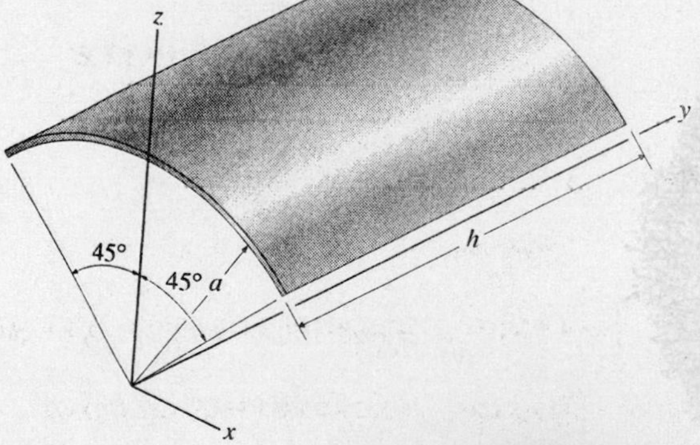

Due to symmetry,

$x = 0$ **Ans**

$y = \dfrac{h}{2}$ **Ans**

$dL = a\, d\theta$

$\tilde{z} = a \sin\theta$

$\bar{z} = \dfrac{\int_L \tilde{z}\, dL}{\int_L dL} = \dfrac{\int_{\frac{\pi}{4}}^{\frac{3\pi}{4}} a \sin\theta\, (a\, d\theta)}{\int_{\frac{\pi}{4}}^{\frac{3\pi}{4}} (a\, d\theta)} = 0.900\, a$ **Ans**

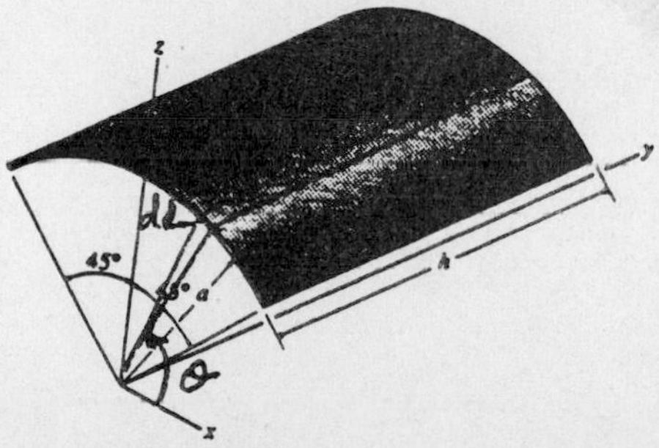

***9-8.** Locate the centroid $(\bar{x}, \bar{y})$ of the shaded area.

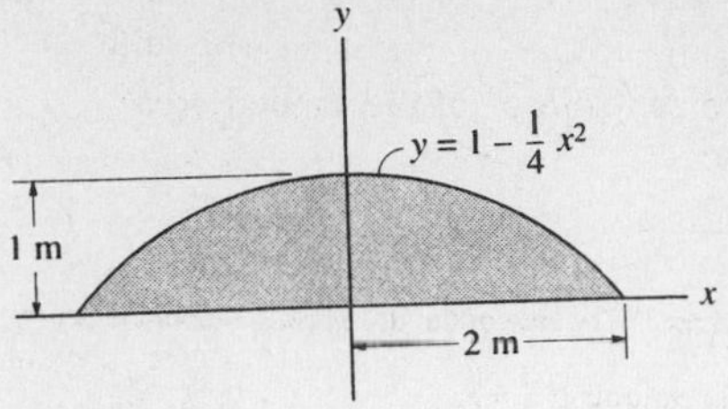

Area and Moment Arm : The area of the differential element is $dA = ydx$ $= \left(1 - \frac{1}{4}x^2\right)dx$ and its centroid is $\tilde{y} = \frac{y}{2} = \frac{1}{2}\left(1 - \frac{1}{4}x^2\right)$.

Centroid : Due to symmetry

$$\bar{x} = 0 \qquad \textbf{Ans}$$

Applying Eq. 9 – 6 and performing the integration, we have

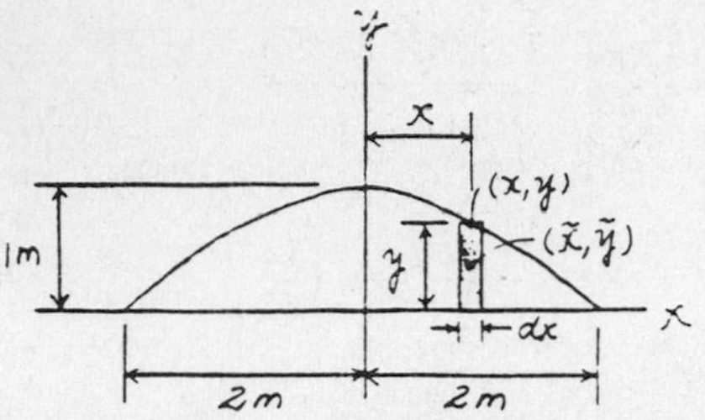

$$\bar{y} = \frac{\int_A \tilde{y}dA}{\int_A dA} = \frac{\int_{-2\text{m}}^{2\text{m}} \frac{1}{2}\left(1 - \frac{1}{4}x^2\right)\left(1 - \frac{1}{4}x^2\right)dx}{\int_{-2\text{m}}^{2\text{m}} \left(1 - \frac{1}{4}x^2\right)dx}$$

$$= \frac{\left(\frac{x}{2} - \frac{x^3}{12} + \frac{x^5}{160}\right)\Big|_{-2\text{m}}^{2\text{m}}}{\left(x - \frac{x^3}{12}\right)\Big|_{-2\text{m}}^{2\text{m}}} = \frac{2}{5}\text{ m} \qquad \textbf{Ans}$$

9-9. Locate the centroid $(\bar{x}, \bar{y})$ of the shaded area.

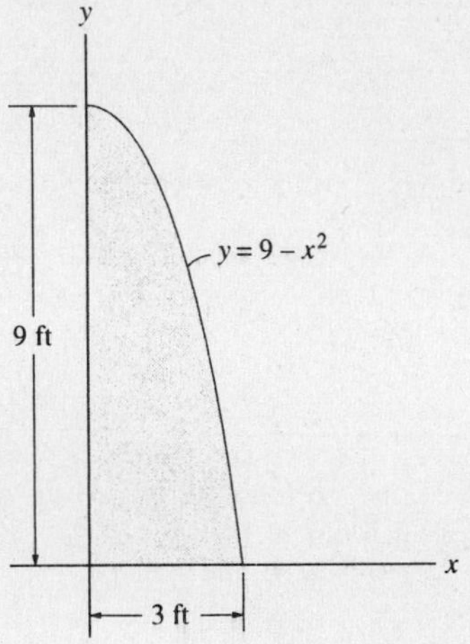

$$dA = y\,dx = (9 - x^2)dx$$

$$\tilde{x} = x$$

$$\tilde{y} = \frac{y}{2} = \frac{1}{2}(9 - x^2)dx$$

$$\bar{x} = \frac{\int_A \tilde{x}\,dA}{\int_A dA} = \frac{\int_0^3 x(9 - x^2)\,dx}{\int_0^3 (9 - x^2)\,dx} = 1.13\text{ ft} \qquad \textbf{Ans}$$

$$\bar{y} = \frac{\int_A \tilde{y}\,dA}{\int_A dA} = \frac{\frac{1}{2}\int_0^3 (9 - x^2)^2\,dx}{\int_0^3 (9 - x^2)\,dx} = 3.60\text{ ft} \qquad \textbf{Ans}$$

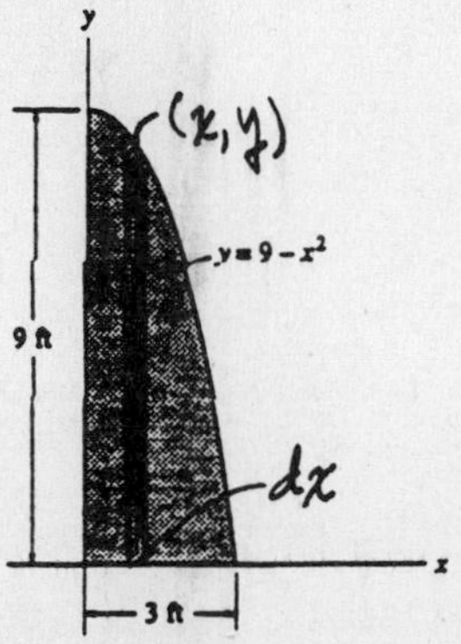

9-10. Locate the centroid $\bar{x}$ of the shaded area.

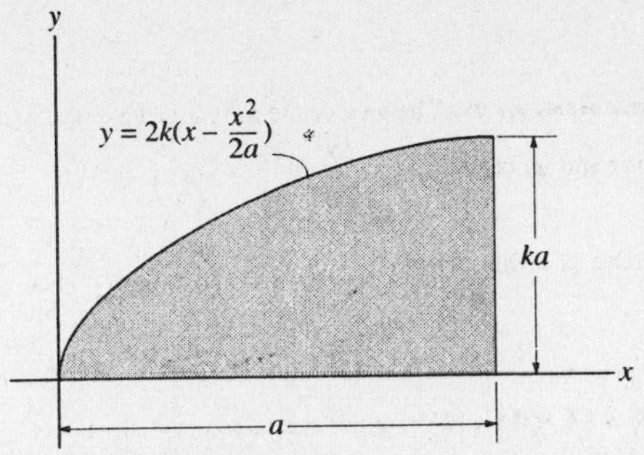

Area and Moment Arm : The area of the differential element is $dA = y dx$ $= 2k\left(x - \frac{x^2}{2a}\right)dx$ and its centroid is $\tilde{x} = x$.

Centroid : Applying Eq. 9 – 6 and performing the integration, we have

$$\bar{x} = \frac{\int_A \tilde{x}\,dA}{\int_A dA} = \frac{\int_0^a x\left[2k\left(x - \frac{x^2}{2a}\right)dx\right]}{\int_0^a 2k\left(x - \frac{x^2}{2a}\right)dx}$$

$$= \frac{2k\left(\frac{x^3}{3} - \frac{x^4}{8a}\right)\Big|_0^a}{2k\left(\frac{x^2}{2} - \frac{x^3}{6a}\right)\Big|_0^a} = \frac{5a}{8} \qquad \textbf{Ans}$$

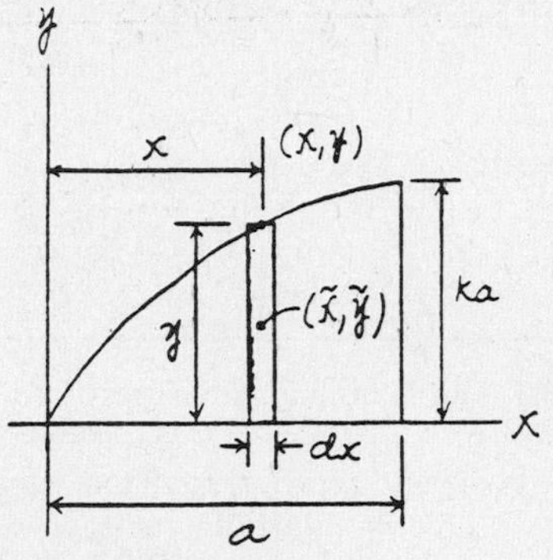

9-11. Locate the centroid $\bar{x}$ of the shaded area.

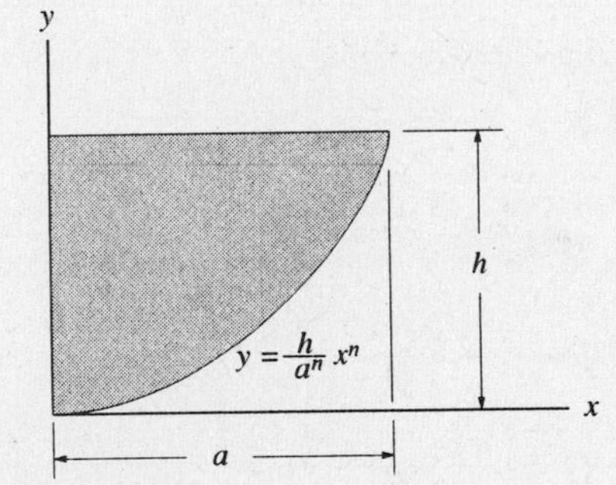

Area and Moment Arm : The area of the differential element is $dA = (h - y)dx$ $= h\left(1 - \frac{x^n}{a^n}\right)dx$ and its centroid is $\tilde{x} = x$.

Centroid : Applying Eq. 9 – 6 and performing the integration, we have

$$\bar{x} = \frac{\int_A \tilde{x}\,dA}{\int_A dA} = \frac{\int_0^a x\left[h\left(1 - \frac{x^n}{a^n}\right)dx\right]}{\int_0^a h\left(1 - \frac{x^n}{a^n}\right)dx}$$

$$= \frac{h\left(\frac{x^2}{2} - \frac{x^{n+2}}{(n+2)a^n}\right)\Big|_0^a}{h\left(x - \frac{x^{n+1}}{(n+1)a^n}\right)\Big|_0^a}$$

$$= \frac{n+1}{2(n+2)}a \qquad \textbf{Ans}$$

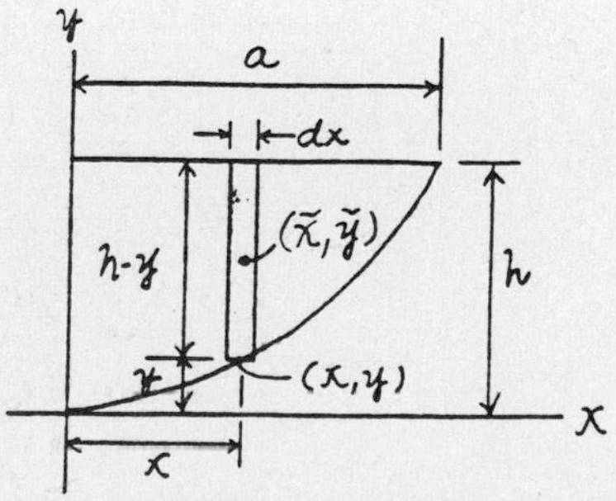

***9-12.** Locate the centroid $(\bar{x}, \bar{y})$ of the semielliptical area.

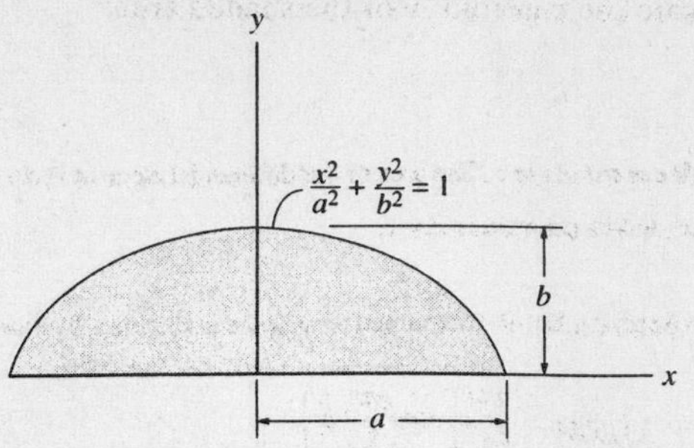

Due to symmetry,

$\bar{x} = 0$ **Ans**

$dA = 2x\,dy$

$\tilde{y} = y$

$$\int_A dA = \int_0^b \frac{2a}{b}(b^2 - y^2)^{\frac{1}{2}}\,dy = \frac{a}{b}\left[y\sqrt{b^2 - y^2} + b^2\sin^{-1}\frac{y}{b}\right]_0^b = \frac{\pi}{2}ab$$

$$\int_A \tilde{y}\,dA = \int_0^b \frac{2a}{b}(y)(b^2 - y^2)^{\frac{1}{2}}\,dy = -\frac{2a}{3b}\sqrt{(b^2 - y^2)^3}\Big|_0^b = \frac{2}{3}ab^2$$

$$\bar{y} = \frac{\int_A \tilde{y}\,dA}{\int_A dA} = \frac{\frac{2}{3}ab^2}{\frac{\pi}{2}ab} = \frac{4b}{3\pi} \quad \textbf{Ans}$$

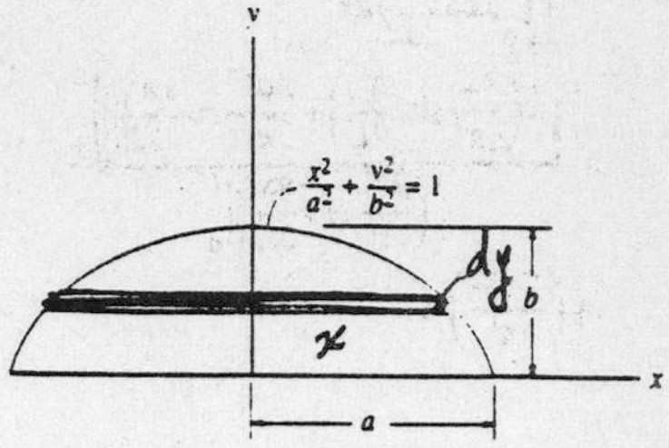

9-13. The plate has a thickness of 0.25 ft and a specific weight of $\gamma = 180\ \text{lb/ft}^3$. Determine the location of its center of gravity. Also, find the tension in each of the cords used to support it.

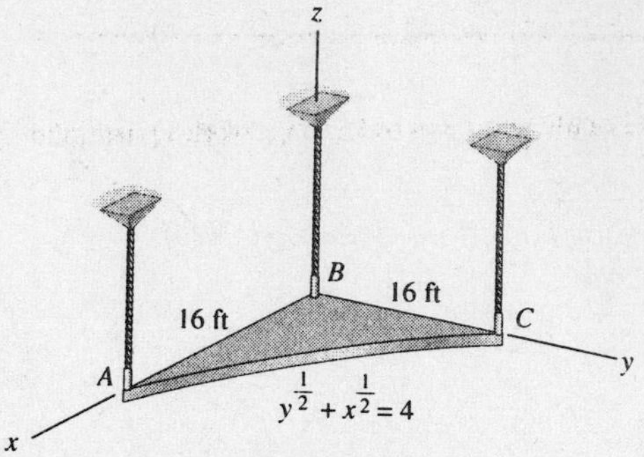

Area and Moment Arm : Here, $y = x - 8x^{\frac{1}{2}} + 16$. The area of the differential element is $dA = y\,dx = \left(x - 8x^{\frac{1}{2}} + 16\right)dx$ and its centroid is $\tilde{x} = x$ and $\tilde{y} = \frac{1}{2}\left(x - 8x^{\frac{1}{2}} + 16\right)$. Evaluating the integrals, we have

$$A = \int_A dA = \int_0^{16\text{ft}} \left(x - 8x^{\frac{1}{2}} + 16\right)dx = \left(\frac{1}{2}x^2 - \frac{16}{3}x^{\frac{3}{2}} + 16x\right)\Big|_0^{16\text{ft}} = 42.67\ \text{ft}^2$$

$$\int_A \tilde{x}\,dA = \int_0^{16\text{ft}} x\left[\left(x - 8x^{\frac{1}{2}} + 16\right)dx\right] = \left(\frac{1}{3}x^3 - \frac{16}{5}x^{\frac{5}{2}} + 8x^2\right)\Big|_0^{16\text{ft}} = 136.53\ \text{ft}^3$$

$$\int_A \tilde{y}\,dA = \int_0^{16\text{ft}} \frac{1}{2}\left(x - 8x^{\frac{1}{2}} + 16\right)\left[\left(x - 8x^{\frac{1}{2}} + 16\right)dx\right] = \frac{1}{2}\left(\frac{1}{3}x^3 - \frac{32}{5}x^{\frac{5}{2}} + 48x^2 - \frac{512}{3}x^{\frac{3}{2}} + 256x\right)\Big|_0^{16\text{ft}} = 136.53\ \text{ft}^3$$

Centroid : Applying Eq. 9 – 6 , we have

$$\bar{x} = \frac{\int_A \tilde{x}\,dA}{\int_A dA} = \frac{136.53}{42.67} = 3.20\ \text{ft} \quad \textbf{Ans}$$

$$\bar{y} = \frac{\int_A \tilde{y}\,dA}{\int_A dA} = \frac{136.53}{42.67} = 3.20\ \text{ft} \quad \textbf{Ans}$$

Equations of Equilibrium : The weight of the plate is $W = 42.67(0.25)(180) = 1920\ \text{lb}$.

$\Sigma M_x = 0;\quad 1920(3.20) - T_A(16) = 0 \quad T_A = 384\ \text{lb}$ **Ans**

$\Sigma M_y = 0;\quad T_C(16) - 1920(3.20) = 0 \quad T_C = 384\ \text{lb}$ **Ans**

$\Sigma F_z = 0;\quad T_B + 384 + 384 - 1920 = 0$

$T_B = 1152\ \text{lb} = 1.15\ \text{kip}$ **Ans**

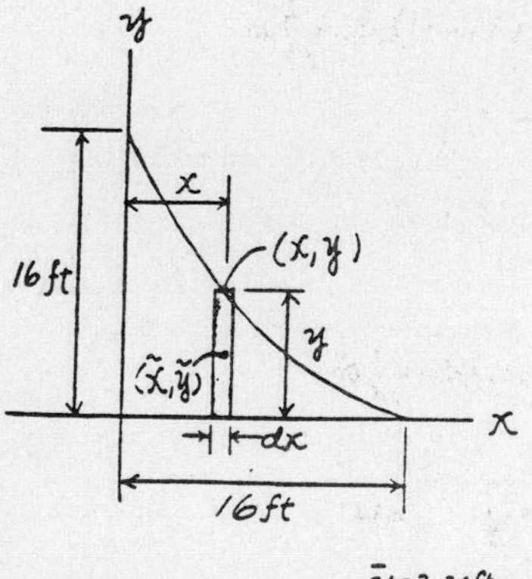

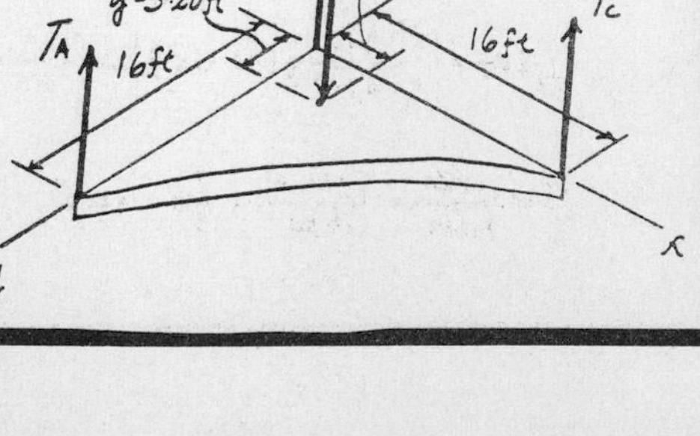

9-14. Locate the centroid $\bar{x}$ of the shaded area.

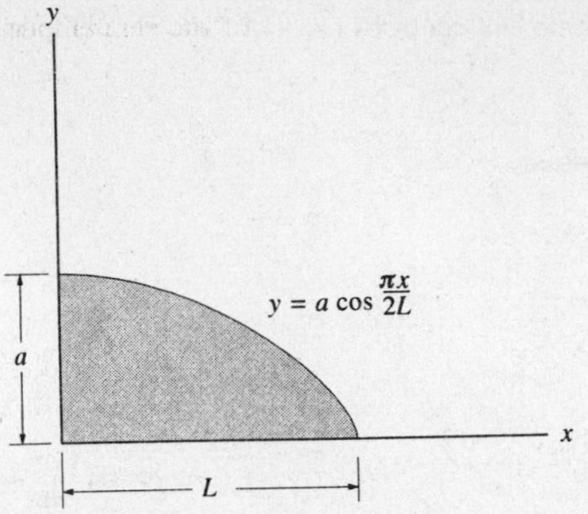

Area and Moment Arm : The area of the differential element is $dA = ydx = a\cos\frac{\pi x}{2L}dx$ and its centroid is $\tilde{x} = x$.

Centroid : Applying Eq. 9 – 6 and performing the integration, we have

$$\bar{x} = \frac{\int_A \tilde{x}\,dA}{\int_A dA} = \frac{\int_0^L x\left[a\cos\frac{\pi x}{2L}dx\right]}{\int_0^L a\cos\frac{\pi x}{2L}dx}$$

$$= \frac{\left[x\left(\frac{2aL}{\pi}\sin\frac{\pi x}{2L}\right)+\frac{4aL^2}{\pi^2}\cos\frac{\pi x}{2L}\right]_0^L}{\left(\frac{2aL}{\pi}\sin\frac{\pi x}{2L}\right)\Big|_0^L}$$

$$= \left(\frac{\pi-2}{\pi}\right)L \qquad \textbf{Ans}$$

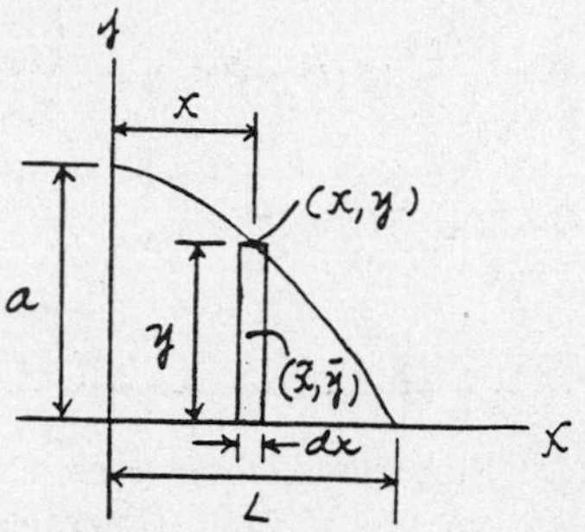

9-15. Locate the centroid $(\bar{x}, \bar{y})$ of the parabolic area.

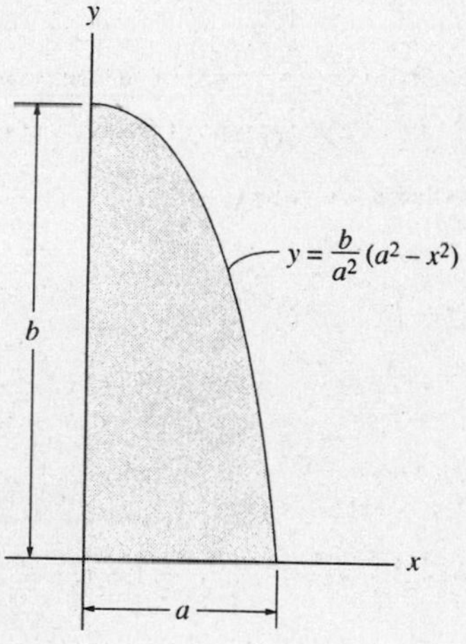

$$\int_A dA = \int_0^a y\,dx = \int_0^a \frac{b}{a^2}(a^2 - x^2)\,dx = \frac{2}{3}ba$$

$$\tilde{x} = x$$

$$\tilde{y} = \frac{y}{2} = \frac{1}{2}\left(\frac{b}{a^2}\right)(a^2 - x^2)$$

$$\int_A \tilde{x}\,dA = \int_0^a \frac{b}{a^2}(xa^2 - x^3)\,dx = \frac{1}{4}ba^2$$

$$\bar{x} = \frac{\int_A \tilde{x}\,dA}{\int_A dA} = \frac{\frac{1}{4}ba^2}{\frac{2}{3}ba} = \frac{3}{8}a \qquad \textbf{Ans}$$

$$\int_A \tilde{y}\,dA = \int_0^a \frac{1}{2}\left(\frac{b^2}{a^4}\right)(a^2 - x^2)^2\,dx = \frac{4}{15}(b^2a)$$

$$\bar{y} = \frac{\int_A \tilde{y}\,dA}{\int_A dA} = \frac{\frac{4}{15}(b^2a)}{\frac{2}{3}ba} = \frac{2}{5}b \qquad \textbf{Ans}$$

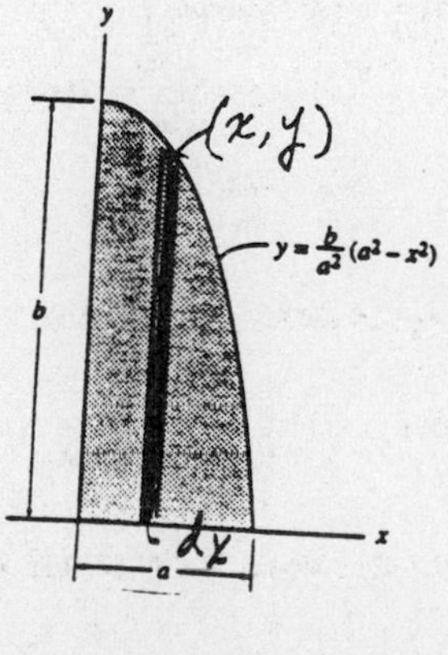

***9-16.** Locate the centroid $\bar{x}$ of the shaded area.

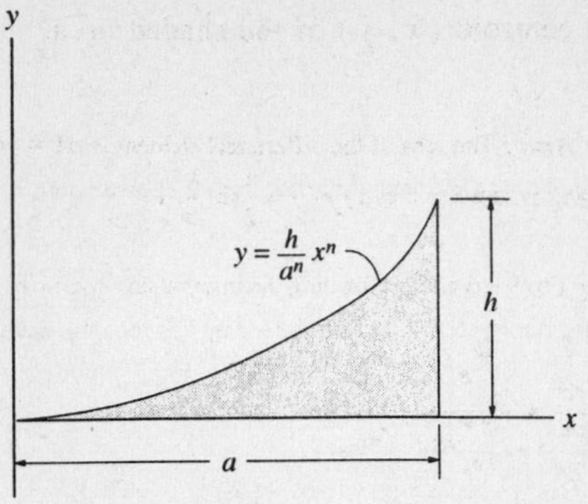

$dA = y\,dx$

$\tilde{x} = x$

$$\bar{x} = \frac{\int_A \tilde{x}\,dA}{\int_A dA} = \frac{\int_0^a \frac{h}{a^n} x^{n+1}\,dx}{\int_0^a \frac{h}{a^n} x^n\,dx} = \frac{\frac{h(a^{n+2})}{a^n(n+2)}}{\frac{h(a^{n+1})}{a^n(n+1)}} = \frac{n+1}{n+2}a$$

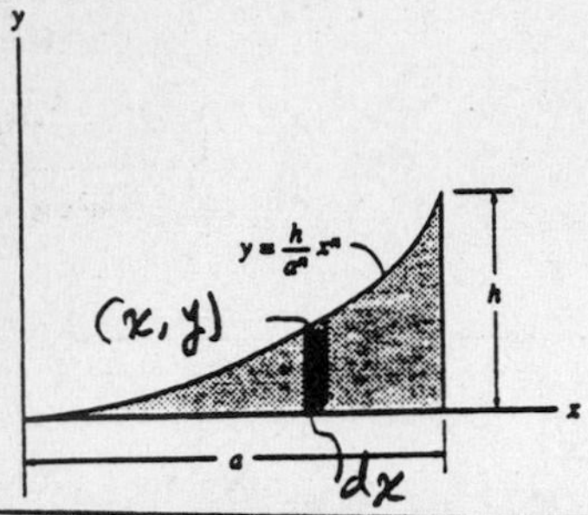

9-17. Locate the centroid $\bar{y}$ of the shaded area.

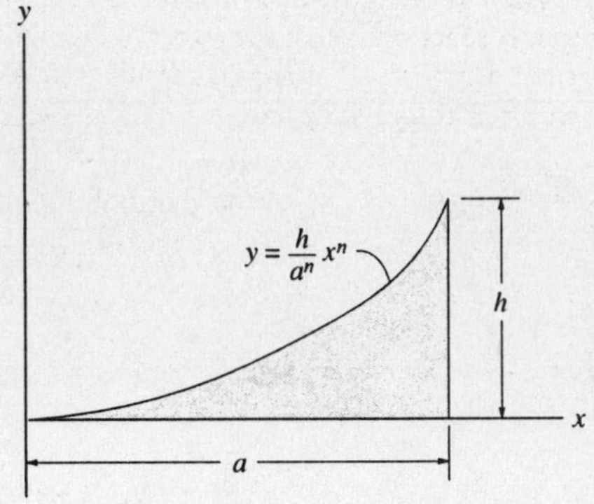

$dA = y\,dx$

$\tilde{y} = \frac{y}{2}$

$$\bar{y} = \frac{\int_A \tilde{y}\,dA}{\int_A dA} = \frac{\frac{1}{2}\int_0^a \frac{h^2}{a^{2n}} x^{2n}\,dx}{\int_0^a \frac{h}{a^n} x^n\,dx} = \frac{\frac{h^2(a^{2n+1})}{2a^{2n}(2n+1)}}{\frac{h(a^{n+1})}{a^n(n+1)}} = \frac{n+1}{2(2n+1)}h \qquad \textbf{Ans}$$

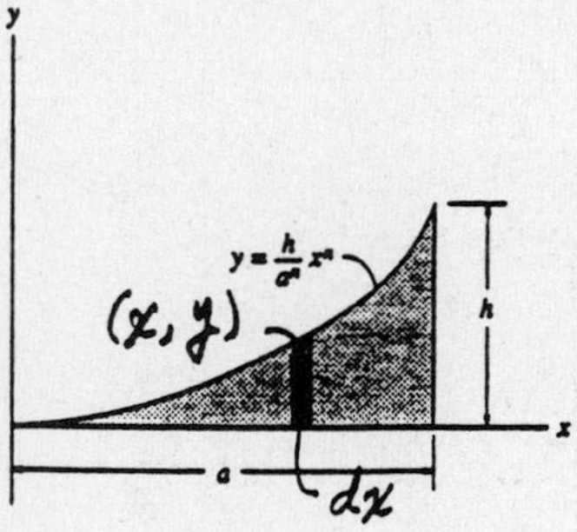

9-18. Locate the centroid $(\bar{x}, \bar{y})$ of the shaded area.

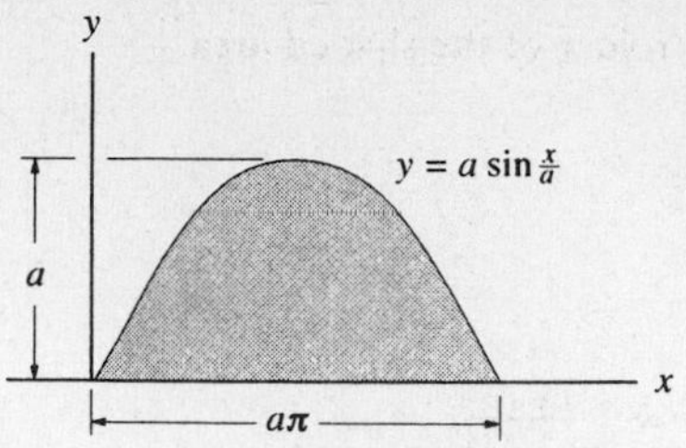

Area and Moment Arm : The area of the differential element is $dA = y\,dx = a\sin\frac{x}{a}dx$ and its centroid are $\tilde{x} = x$ and $\tilde{y} = \frac{y}{2} = \frac{a}{2}\sin\frac{x}{a}$.

Centroid : Applying Eq. 9 – 6 and performing the integration, we have

$$\bar{x} = \frac{\int_A \tilde{x}\,dA}{\int_A dA} = \frac{\int_0^{\pi a} x\left(a\sin\frac{x}{a}dx\right)}{\int_0^{\pi a} a\sin\frac{x}{a}dx}$$

$$= \frac{\left[a^3\sin\frac{x}{a} - x\left(a^2\cos\frac{x}{a}\right)\right]_0^{\pi a}}{\left(-a^2\cos\frac{x}{a}\right)\Big|_0^{\pi a}}$$

$$= \frac{\pi}{2}a \qquad \textbf{Ans}$$

$$\bar{y} = \frac{\int_A \tilde{y}\,dA}{\int_A dA} = \frac{\int_0^{\pi a} \frac{a}{2}\sin\frac{x}{a}\left(a\sin\frac{x}{a}dx\right)}{\int_0^{\pi a} a\sin\frac{x}{a}dx}$$

$$= \frac{\left[\frac{1}{4}a^2\left(x - \frac{1}{2}a\sin\frac{2x}{a}\right)\right]_0^{\pi a}}{\left(-a^2\cos\frac{x}{a}\right)\Big|_0^{\pi a}} = \frac{\pi}{8}a \qquad \textbf{Ans}$$

9-19. The steel plate is 0.3 m thick and has a density of 7850 kg/m³. Determine the location of its center of gravity. Also determine the horizontal and vertical reactions at the pin and the reaction at the roller support. Assume the support reactions act at the edges of the plate. *Hint:* The normal force at *B* is perpendicular to the tangent at *B*, which is found from $\tan\theta = dy/dx$.

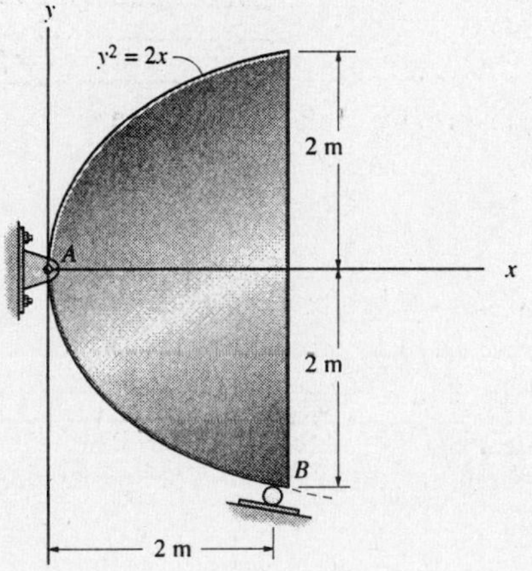

$dA = 2y\,dx$

$\tilde{x} = x$

$\tilde{y} = 0$

$$\int_A dA = \int_0^2 2\sqrt{2x}\,dx = \frac{4\sqrt{2}}{3}x^{\frac{3}{2}}\Big|_0^2 = 5.333\text{ m}^2$$

$$\int_A \tilde{x}\,dA = \int_0^2 2\sqrt{2x}\,x\,dx = \frac{4\sqrt{2}}{5}x^{\frac{5}{2}}\Big|_0^2 = 6.40\text{ m}^3$$

$$\bar{x} = \frac{\int_A \tilde{x}\,dA}{\int_A dA} = \frac{6.40}{5.333} = 1.20\text{ m} \qquad \textbf{Ans}$$

$\bar{y} = 0$ **Ans** (by symmetry)

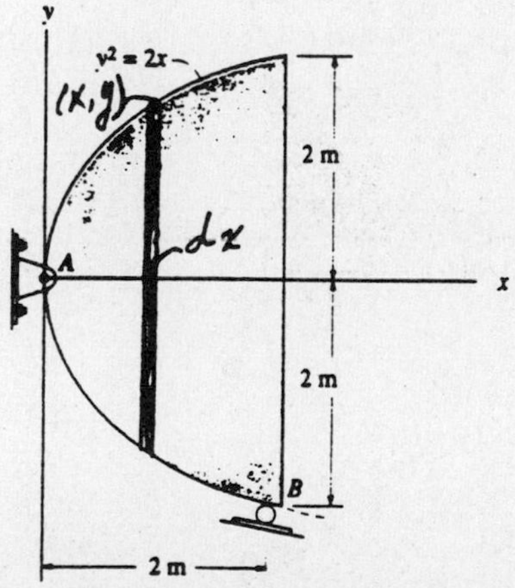

$y^2 = 2x$

$2y\,dy = 2\,dx$

$$\tan\theta = \frac{dy}{dx}\Big|_{(2,-2)} = -0.5$$

$\theta = \tan^{-1}(-0.5) = -26.57°$

$W = 7850(0.3)(5.333)(9.81) = 123.2\text{ kN}$

$\circlearrowleft + \Sigma M_A = 0;\quad -123.2\,(1.2) + N_B(\cos 26.57°)(2) + N_B(\sin 26.57°)(2) = 0$

$N_B = 55.10 = 55.1\text{ kN}$ **Ans**

$\xrightarrow{+} \Sigma F_x = 0;\quad -A_x + 55.10\sin 26.57° = 0$

$A_x = 24.6\text{ kN}$ **Ans**

$+\uparrow \Sigma F_y = 0;\quad A_y - 123.2 + 55.10\cos 26.57° = 0$

$A_y = 73.9\text{ kN}$ **Ans**

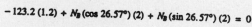

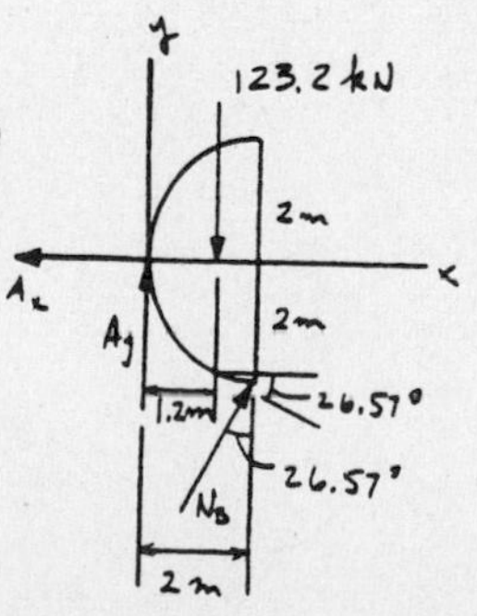

■ *9-20. Locate the centroid $\bar{x}$ of the shaded area. Solve the problem by evaluating the integrals using Simpson's rule.

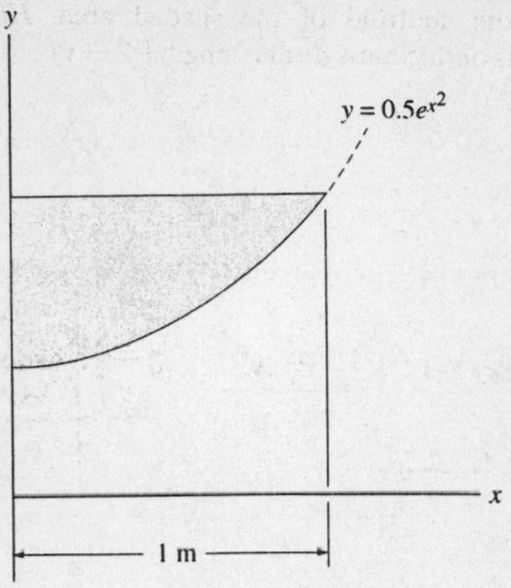

At $x = 1$ m

$$y = 0.5e^{1^2} = 1.359 \text{ m}$$

$$\int_A dA = \int_0^1 (1.359 - y)\,dx = \int_0^1 \left(1.359 - 0.5\,e^{x^2}\right) dx = 0.6278 \text{ m}^2$$

$$\tilde{x} = x$$

$$\int_A \tilde{x}\,dA = \int_0^1 x\left(1.359 - 0.5\,e^{x^2}\right) dx$$

$$= 0.25 \text{ m}^3$$

$$\bar{x} = \frac{\int_A \tilde{x}\,dA}{\int_A dA} = \frac{0.25}{0.6278} = 0.398 \text{ m} \quad \textbf{Ans}$$

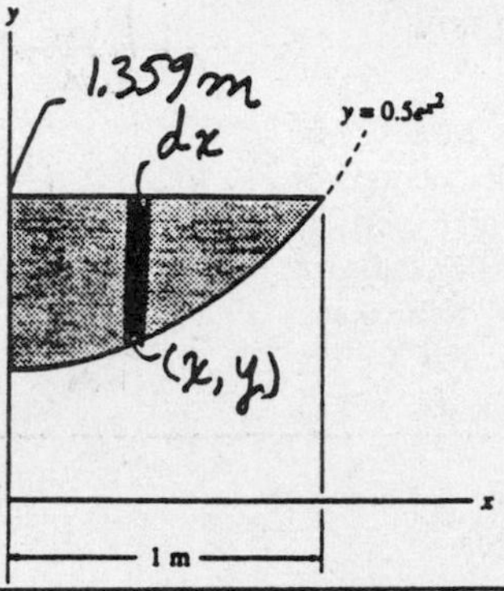

■ 9-21. Locate the centroid $\bar{y}$ of the shaded area. Solve the problem by evaluating the integrals using Simpson's rule.

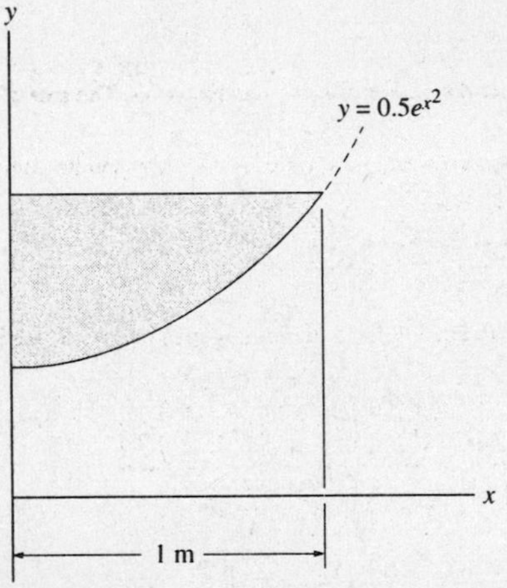

$$\int_A dA = \int_0^1 (1.359 - y)\,dx = \int_0^1 \left(1.359 - 0.5\,e^{x^2}\right) dx = 0.6278 \text{ m}^2$$

$$\tilde{y} = \frac{1.359 + y}{2}$$

$$\int_A \tilde{y}\,dA = \int_0^1 \left(\frac{1.359 + 0.5\,e^{x^2}}{2}\right)\left(1.359 - 0.5\,e^{x^2}\right) dx$$

$$= \frac{1}{2}\int_0^1 \left(1.847 - 0.25\,e^{2x^2}\right) dx = 0.6278 \text{ m}^3$$

$$\bar{y} = \frac{\int_A \tilde{y}\,dA}{\int_A dA} = \frac{0.6278}{0.6278} = 1.00 \text{ m} \quad \textbf{Ans}$$

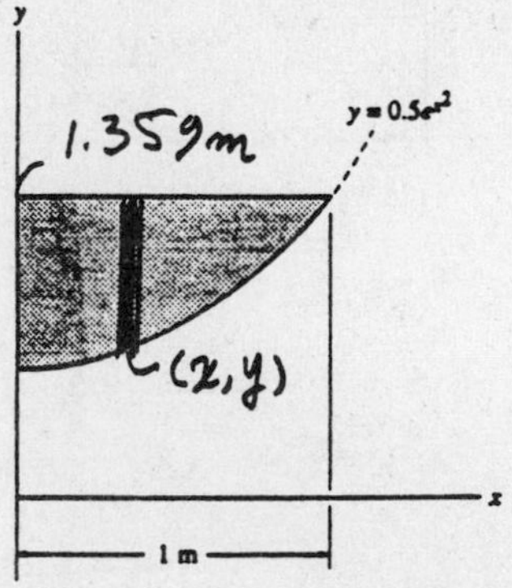

9-22. Locate the centroid of the shaded area. *Hint:* Choose elements of thickness dy and length $[(2 - y) - y^2]$.

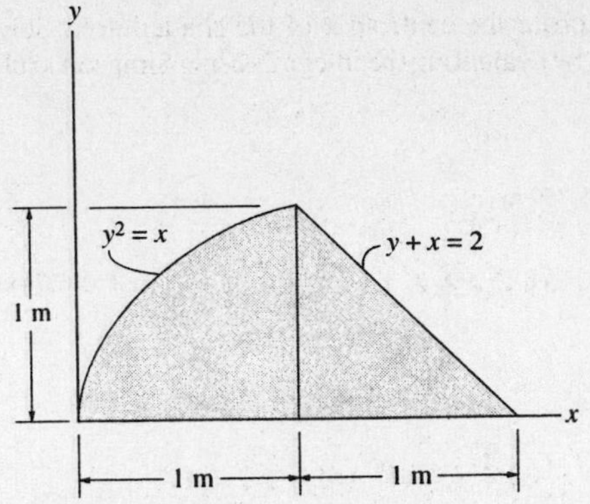

$x_1 = y^2$

$x_2 = 2 - y$

$dA = (x_2 - x_1)\,dy = (2 - y - y^2)\,dy$

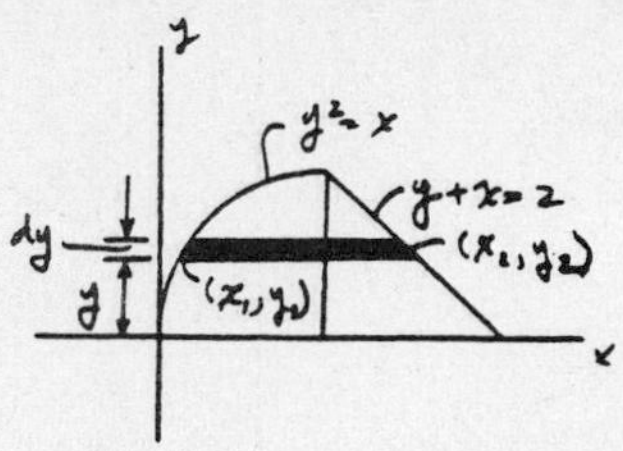

$\tilde{x} = \dfrac{x_2 + x_1}{2} = \dfrac{2 - y + y^2}{2}$

$\tilde{y} = y$

$$\int_A dA = \int_0^1 (2 - y - y^2)\,dy = \left[2y - \frac{y^2}{2} - \frac{y^3}{3}\right]_0^1 = 1.167\ \text{m}^2$$

$$\int_A \tilde{x}\,dA = \int_0^1 \frac{1}{2}(2 - y + y^2)(2 - y - y^2)\,dy$$

$$= \frac{1}{2}\left[4y - 2y^2 + \frac{y^3}{3} - \frac{y^5}{5}\right]_0^1 = 1.067\ \text{m}^3$$

$$\bar{x} = \frac{\int_A \tilde{x}\,dA}{\int_A dA} = \frac{1.067}{1.167} = 0.914\ \text{m} \qquad \textbf{Ans}$$

$$\int_A \tilde{y}\,dA = \int_0^1 y(2 - y - y^2)\,dy = \left[y^2 - \frac{y^3}{3} - \frac{y^4}{4}\right]_0^1 = 0.4167\ \text{m}^3$$

$$\bar{y} = \frac{\int_A \tilde{y}\,dA}{\int_A dA} = \frac{0.4167}{1.167} = 0.357\ \text{m} \qquad \textbf{Ans}$$

9-23. Locate the centroid $\bar{x}$ of the shaded area.

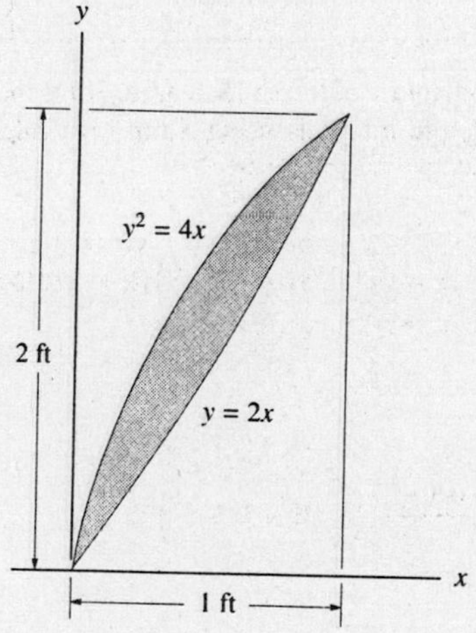

Area and Moment Arm : Here, $x_1 = \dfrac{y}{2}$ and $x_2 = \dfrac{y^2}{4}$. The area of the differential element is $dA = (x_1 - x_2)\,dy = \left(\dfrac{y}{2} - \dfrac{y^2}{4}\right)dy$ and its centroid is $\tilde{x} = x_2 + \dfrac{x_1 - x_2}{2} = \dfrac{1}{2}(x_1 + x_2) = \dfrac{1}{2}\left(\dfrac{y}{2} + \dfrac{y^2}{4}\right)$.

Centroid : Applying Eq. 9 – 6 and performing the integration, we have

$$\bar{x} = \frac{\int_A \tilde{x}\,dA}{\int_A dA} = \frac{\int_0^{2\text{ft}} \frac{1}{2}\left(\frac{y}{2} + \frac{y^2}{4}\right)\left[\left(\frac{y}{2} - \frac{y^2}{4}\right)dy\right]}{\int_0^{2\text{ft}} \left(\frac{y}{2} - \frac{y^2}{4}\right)dy}$$

$$= \frac{\left[\frac{1}{2}\left(\frac{1}{12}y^3 - \frac{1}{80}y^5\right)\right]_0^{2\text{ft}}}{\left(\frac{1}{4}y^2 - \frac{1}{12}y^3\right)\Big|_0^{2\text{ft}}} = \frac{2}{5}\ \text{ft} = 0.4\ \text{ft} \qquad \textbf{Ans}$$

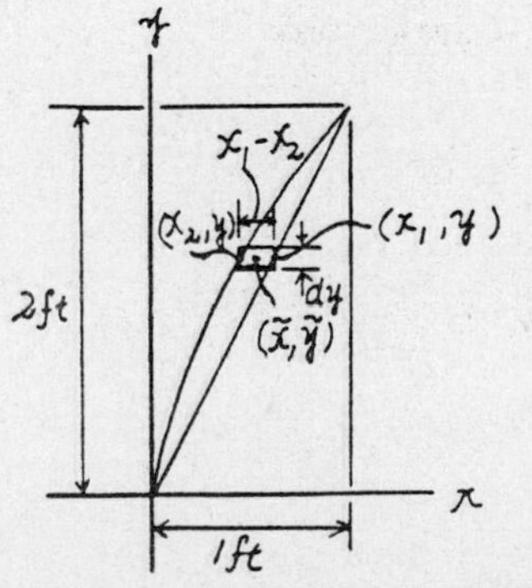

***9-24.** Locate the centroid $\bar{y}$ of the shaded area.

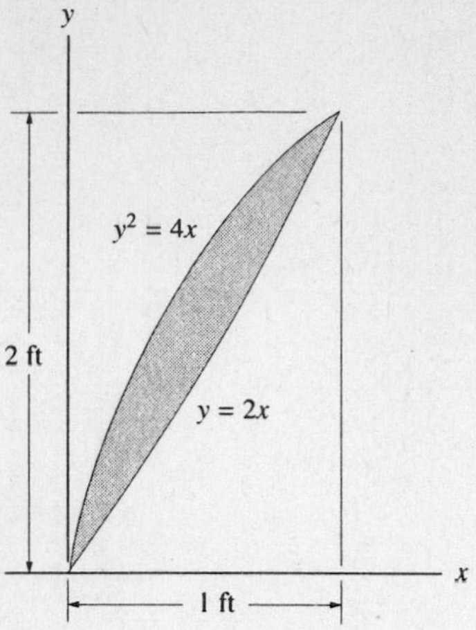

Area and Moment Arm : Here, $x_1 = \dfrac{y}{2}$ and $x_2 = \dfrac{y^2}{4}$. The area of the differential element is $dA = (x_1 - x_2)\,dy = \left(\dfrac{y}{2} - \dfrac{y^2}{4}\right)dy$ and its centroid is $\tilde{y} = y$.

Centroid : Applying Eq. 9 – 6 and performing the integration, we have

$$\bar{y} = \frac{\int_A \tilde{x}\,dA}{\int_A dA} = \frac{\int_0^{2\text{ft}} y\left[\left(\dfrac{y}{2} - \dfrac{y^2}{4}\right)dy\right]}{\int_0^{2\text{ft}} \left(\dfrac{y}{2} - \dfrac{y^2}{4}\right)dy}$$

$$= \frac{\left(\dfrac{1}{6}y^3 - \dfrac{1}{16}y^4\right)\Big|_0^{2\text{ft}}}{\left(\dfrac{1}{4}y^2 - \dfrac{1}{12}y^3\right)\Big|_0^{2\text{ft}}} = 1 \text{ ft} \qquad \textbf{Ans}$$

9-25. Locate the centroid $\bar{x}$ of the shaded area.

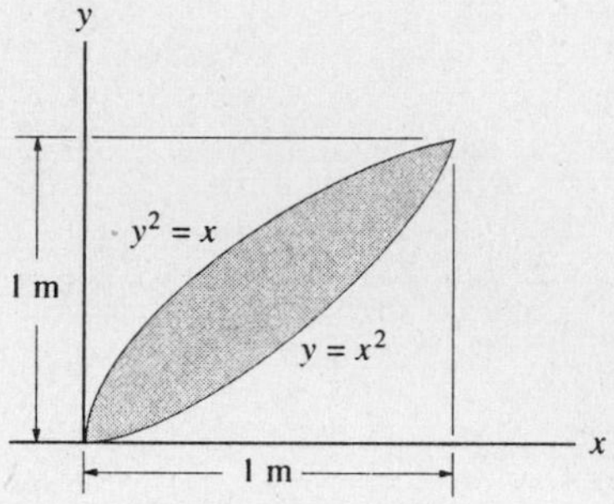

Area and Moment Arm : Here, $y_1 = x^{\frac{1}{2}}$ and $y_2 = x^2$. The area of the differential element is $dA = (y_1 - y_2)\,dx = \left(x^{\frac{1}{2}} - x^2\right)dx$ and its centroid is $\tilde{x} = x$.

Centroid : Applying Eq. 9 – 6 and performing the integration, we have

$$\bar{x} = \frac{\int_A \tilde{x}\,dA}{\int_A dA} = \frac{\int_0^{1\text{m}} x\left[\left(x^{\frac{1}{2}} - x^2\right)dx\right]}{\int_0^{1\text{m}} \left(x^{\frac{1}{2}} - x^2\right)dx}$$

$$= \frac{\left(\dfrac{2}{5}x^{\frac{5}{2}} - \dfrac{1}{4}x^4\right)\Big|_0^{1\text{m}}}{\left(\dfrac{2}{3}x^{\frac{3}{2}} - \dfrac{1}{3}x^3\right)\Big|_0^{1\text{m}}} = \frac{9}{20} \text{ m} = 0.45 \text{ m} \qquad \textbf{Ans}$$

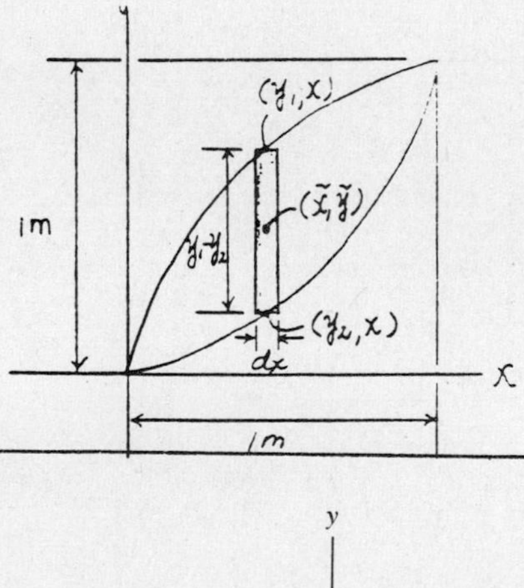

9-26. Locate the centroid $\bar{y}$ of the shaded area.

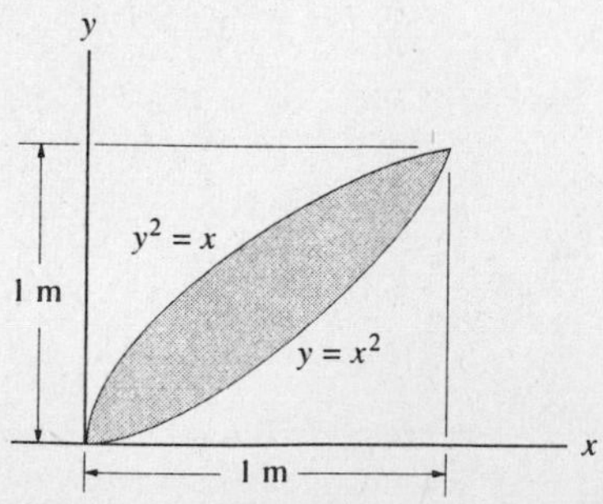

Area and Moment Arm : Here, $y_1 = x^{\frac{1}{2}}$ and $y_2 = x^2$. The area of the differential element is $dA = (y_1 - y_2)\,dx = \left(x^{\frac{1}{2}} - x^2\right)dx$ and its centroid is $\tilde{y} = y_2 + \dfrac{y_1 - y_2}{2} = \dfrac{1}{2}(y_1 + y_2) = \dfrac{1}{2}\left(x^{\frac{1}{2}} + x^2\right)$.

Centroid : Applying Eq. 9 – 6 and performing the integration, we have

$$\bar{y} = \frac{\int_A \tilde{y}\,dA}{\int_A dA} = \frac{\int_0^{1\text{m}} \frac{1}{2}\left(x^{\frac{1}{2}} + x^2\right)\left[\left(x^{\frac{1}{2}} - x^2\right)dx\right]}{\int_0^{1\text{m}} \left(x^{\frac{1}{2}} - x^2\right)dx}$$

$$= \frac{\dfrac{1}{2}\left(\dfrac{1}{2}x^2 - \dfrac{1}{5}x^5\right)\Big|_0^{1\text{m}}}{\left(\frac{2}{3}x^{\frac{3}{2}} - \frac{1}{3}x^3\right)\Big|_0^{1\text{m}}} = \frac{9}{20} \text{ m} = 0.45 \text{ m} \qquad \textbf{Ans}$$

9-27. Locate the centroid $\bar{x}$ of the shaded area.

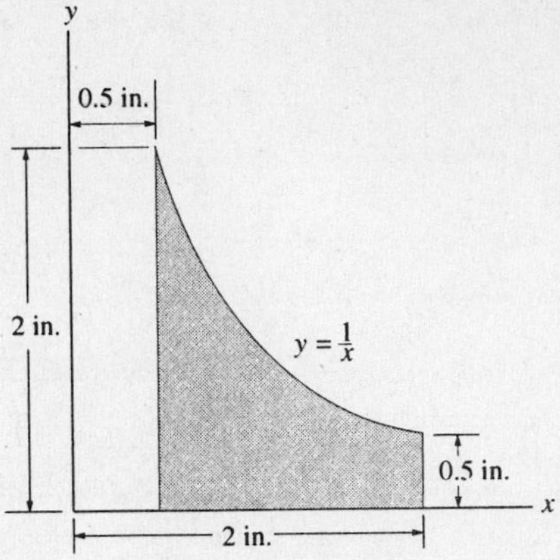

Area and Moment Arm : The area of the differential element is $dA = ydx = \frac{1}{x}dx$ and its centroid is $\tilde{x} = x$.

Centroid : Applying Eq. 9 – 6 and performing the integration, we have

$$\bar{x} = \frac{\int_A \tilde{x}dA}{\int_A dA} = \frac{\int_{0.5\text{in}}^{2\text{in}} x\left(\frac{1}{x}dx\right)}{\int_{0.5\text{in}}^{2\text{in}} \frac{1}{x}dx} = \frac{x\Big|_{0.5\text{in}}^{2\text{in}}}{\ln x\Big|_{0.5\text{in}}^{2\text{in}}} = 1.08 \text{ in.} \qquad \textbf{Ans}$$

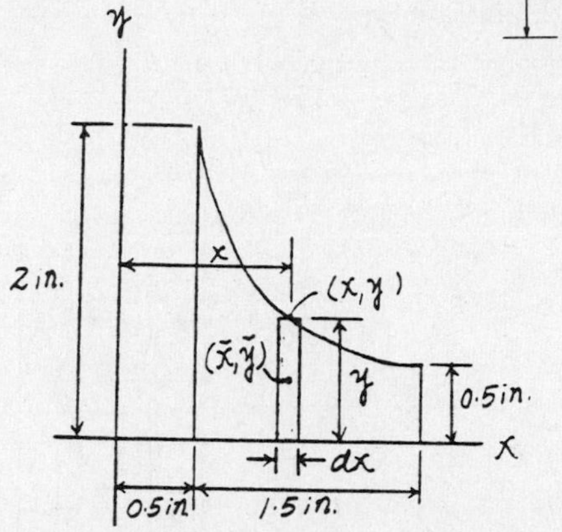

***9-28.** Locate the centroid $\bar{y}$ of the shaded area.

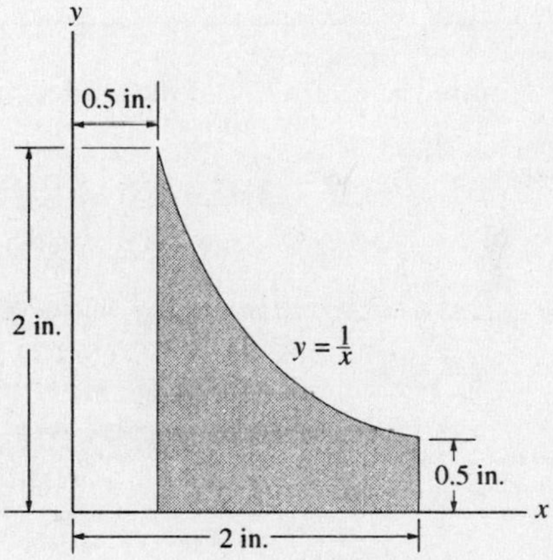

Area and Moment Arm : The area of the differential element is $dA = ydx = \frac{1}{x}dx$ and its centroid is $\tilde{y} = \frac{y}{2} = \frac{1}{2x}$.

Centroid : Applying Eq. 9 – 6 and performing the integration, we have

$$\bar{y} = \frac{\int_A \tilde{y}dA}{\int_A dA} = \frac{\int_{0.5\text{in}}^{2\text{in}} \frac{1}{2x}\left(\frac{1}{x}dx\right)}{\int_{0.5\text{in}}^{2\text{in}} \frac{1}{x}dx} = \frac{-\frac{1}{2x}\Big|_{0.5\text{in}}^{2\text{in}}}{\ln x\Big|_{0.5\text{in}}^{2\text{in}}} = 0.541 \text{ in} \qquad \textbf{Ans}$$

9-29. Locate the centroid $\bar{x}$ of the shaded area.

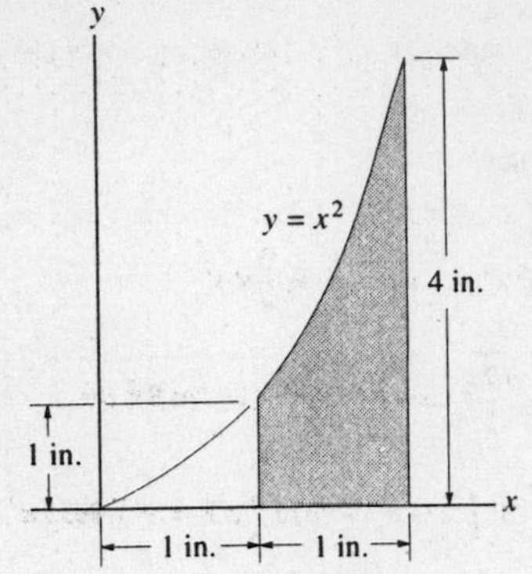

Area and Moment Arm : The area of the differential element is $dA = ydx = x^2dx$ and its centroid is $\tilde{x} = x$.

Centroid : Applying Eq. 9 – 6 and performing the integration, we have

$$\bar{x} = \frac{\int_A \tilde{x}dA}{\int_A dA} = \frac{\int_{1\text{in}}^{2\text{in}} x(x^2dx)}{\int_{1\text{in}}^{2\text{in}} x^2dx} = \frac{\left.\frac{x^4}{4}\right|_{1\text{in}}^{2\text{in}}}{\left.\frac{x^3}{3}\right|_{1\text{in}}^{2\text{in}}} = 1.61 \text{ in} \qquad \textbf{Ans}$$

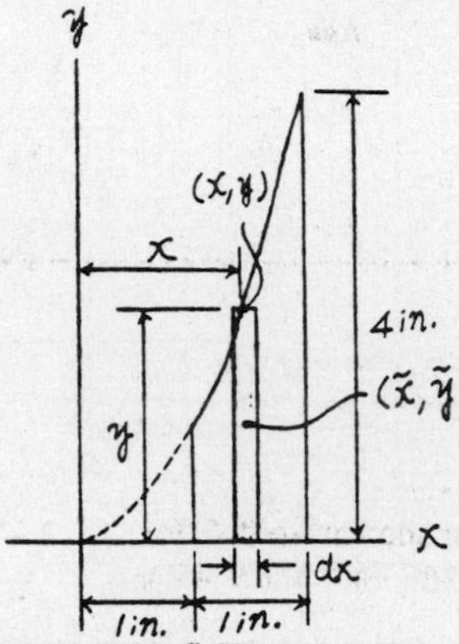

9-30. Locate the centroid $\bar{y}$ of the shaded area.

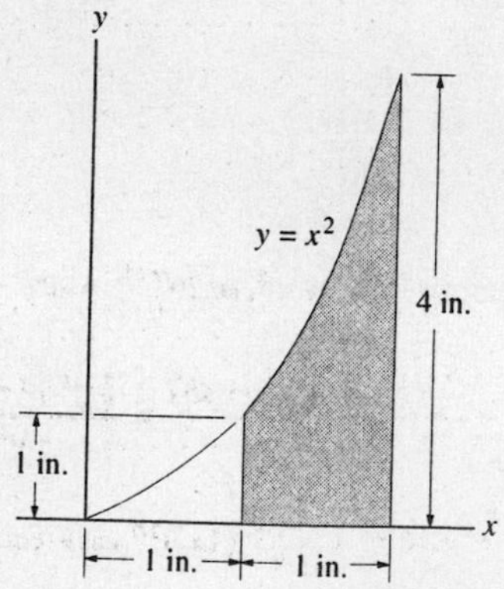

Area and Moment Arm : The area of the differential element is $dA = ydx = x^2dx$ and its centroid is $\tilde{y} = \frac{y}{2} = \frac{1}{2}x^2$.

Centroid : Applying Eq. 9 – 6 and performing the integration, we have

$$\bar{y} = \frac{\int_A \tilde{y}dA}{\int_A dA} = \frac{\int_{1\text{in.}}^{2\text{in.}} \frac{1}{2}x^2(x^2dx)}{\int_{1\text{in.}}^{2\text{in.}} x^2dx} = \frac{\left.\frac{x^5}{10}\right|_{1\text{in.}}^{2\text{in.}}}{\left.\frac{x^3}{3}\right|_{1\text{in.}}^{2\text{in.}}} = 1.33 \text{ in.} \qquad \textbf{Ans}$$

9-31. Determine the location $\bar{x}$ to the centroid C of the upper portion of the cardioid, $r = a(1 - \cos\theta)$.

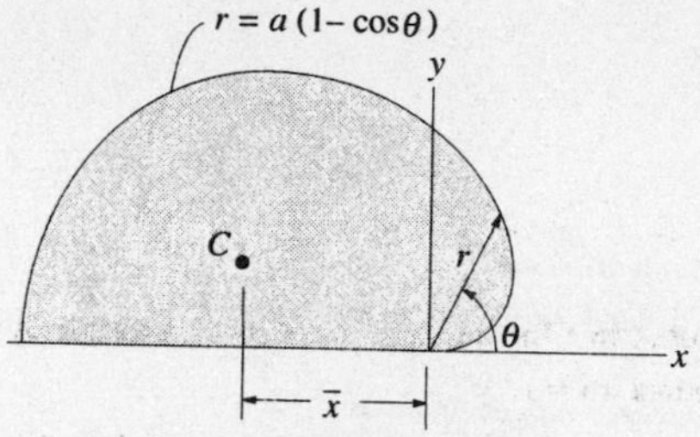

$$dA = \frac{1}{2} r^2\, d\theta$$

$$A = \int_0^{\pi} \frac{1}{2}(a^2)(1-\cos\theta)^2 d\theta = \frac{3}{4}\pi a^2$$

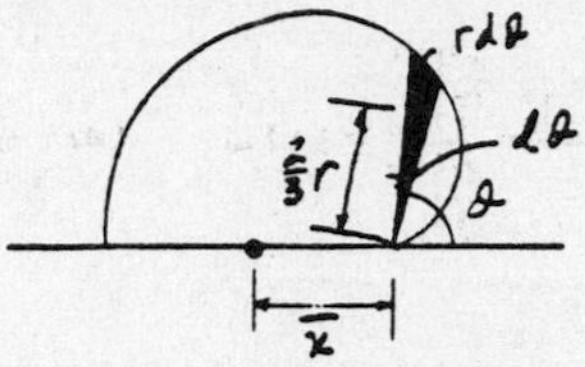

$$\int_A \tilde{x}\, dA = \int_0^{\pi}\left(\frac{2}{3} r \cos\theta\right)\left(\frac{1}{2}\right)(a^2)(1-\cos\theta)^2\, d\theta$$

$$= \frac{2}{6} a^3 \int_0^{\pi} \cos\theta(1-\cos\theta)^3\, d\theta = -1.9635\, a^3$$

$$\bar{x} = \frac{\int_A \tilde{x}\, dA}{\int_A dA} = \frac{-1.9635\, a^3}{\frac{3}{4}\pi a^2} = -0.833\, a \qquad \textbf{Ans}$$

***9-32.** Determine the location $\bar{r}$ of the centroid C for the loop of the lemniscate, $r^2 = 2a^2 \cos 2\theta$, $(-45° \le \theta \le 45°)$.

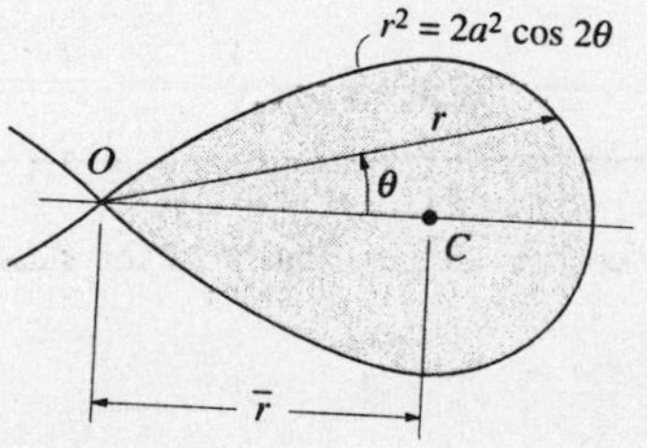

$$dA = \frac{1}{2}(r)\, r\, d\theta = \frac{1}{2} r^2\, d\theta$$

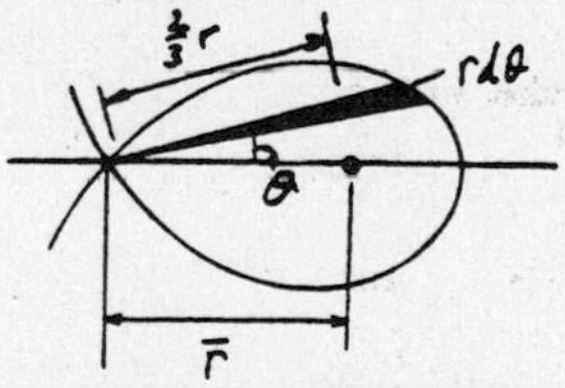

$$A = 2\int_0^{45°} \frac{1}{2}(2a^2 \cos 2\theta)\, d\theta = a^2\left[\sin 2\theta\right]_0^{45°} = a^2$$

$$\bar{x} = \frac{\int_A \tilde{x}\, dA}{\int_A dA} = \frac{2\int_0^{45°}\left(\frac{2}{3} r\cos\theta\right)\left(\frac{1}{2} r^2\, d\theta\right)}{a^2} = \frac{\frac{2}{3}\int_0^{45°} r^3 \cos\theta\, d\theta}{a^2}$$

$$\int_A \tilde{x}\, dA = \frac{2}{3}\int_0^{45°} r^3 \cos\theta\, d\theta = \frac{2}{3}\int_0^{45°} (2a^2)^{3/2} \cos\theta\, (\cos 2\theta)^{3/2}\, d\theta = 0.7854\, a^3$$

$$\bar{x} = \frac{0.7854\, a^3}{a^2} = 0.785\, a \qquad \textbf{Ans}$$

9-33. Locate the center of gravity of the volume generated by revolving the shaded area about the z axis. The material is homogeneous.

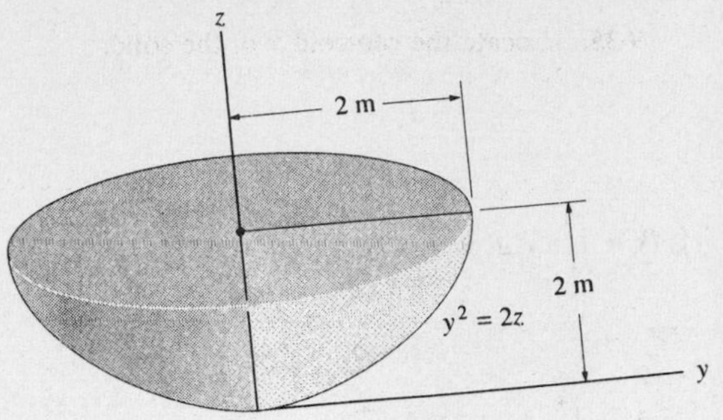

Volume and Moment Arm : The volume of the thin disk differential element is $dV = \pi y^2 dz = \pi(2z)\,dz = 2\pi z dz$ and its centroid $\tilde{z} = z$.

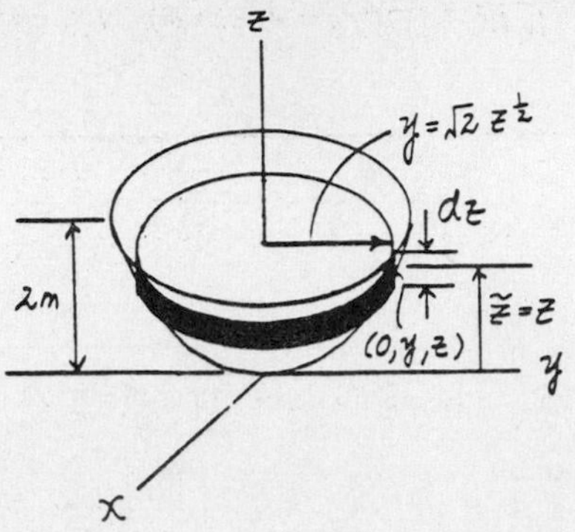

Centroid : Due to symmetry about z axis

$$\bar{x} = \bar{y} = 0 \qquad \textbf{Ans}$$

Applying Eq. 9 – 5 and performing the integration, we have

$$\bar{z} = \frac{\int_V \tilde{z}\,dV}{\int_V dV} = \frac{\int_0^{2\text{m}} z(2\pi z dz)}{\int_0^{2\text{m}} 2\pi z dz} = \frac{2\pi\left(\frac{z^3}{3}\right)\Big|_0^{2\text{m}}}{2\pi\left(\frac{z^2}{2}\right)\Big|_0^{2\text{m}}} = \frac{4}{3}\text{ m} \qquad \textbf{Ans}$$

9-34. Locate the centroid $\bar{z}$ of the hemisphere.

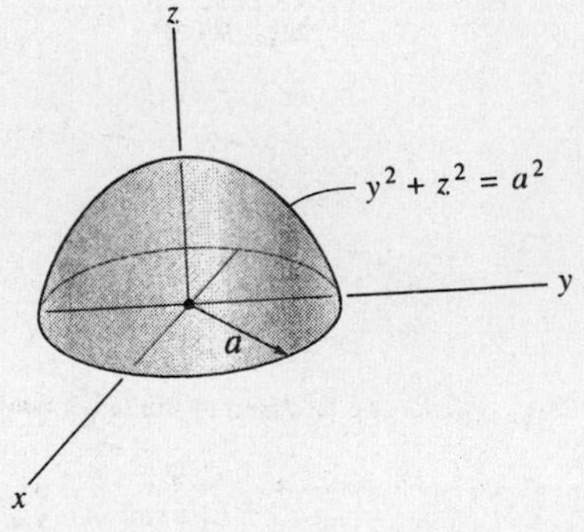

Volume and Moment Arm : The volume of the thin disk differential element is $dV = \pi y^2 dz = \pi\left(a^2 - z^2\right) dz$ and its centroid $\tilde{z} = z$.

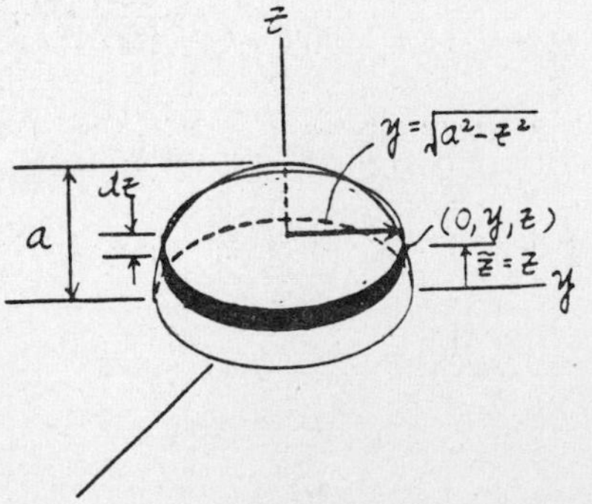

Centroid : Applying Eq. 9 – 5 and performing the integration, we have

$$\bar{z} = \frac{\int_V \tilde{z}\,dV}{\int_V dV} = \frac{\int_0^a z\left[\pi(a^2 - z^2)\,dz\right]}{\int_0^a \pi(a^2 - z^2)\,dz}$$

$$= \frac{\pi\left(\frac{a^2 z^2}{2} - \frac{z^4}{4}\right)\Big|_0^a}{\pi\left(a^2 z - \frac{z^3}{3}\right)\Big|_0^a} = \frac{3}{8}a \qquad \textbf{Ans}$$

9-35. Locate the centroid $\bar{x}$ of the solid.

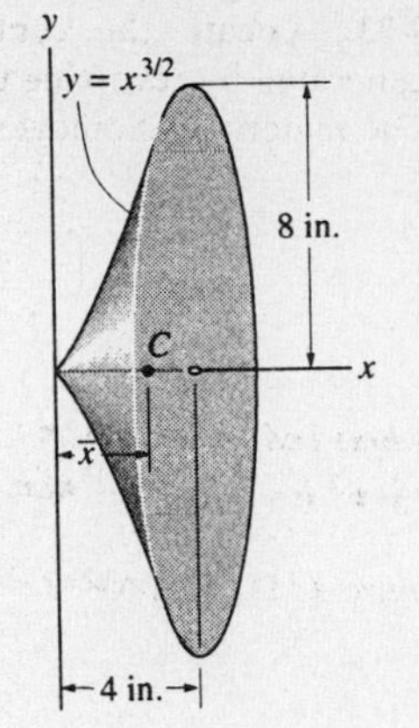

$$\int_V dV = \int_0^4 \pi y^2\,dx = \int_0^4 \pi\,(x^3\,dx) = \pi\frac{1}{4}x^4\Big|_0^4 = 64\pi\ \text{in}^3$$

$\tilde{x} = x$

$$\int_V \tilde{x}\,dV = \int_0^4 x\,(\pi y^2\,dx) = \int_0^4 \pi x^4 dx = \pi\left(\frac{1}{5}x^5\right)\Big|_0^4 = 204.8\pi\ \text{in}^4$$

$$\bar{x} = \frac{\int_V \tilde{x}\,dV}{\int_V dV} = \frac{204.8\,\pi}{64\,\pi} = 3.20\ \text{in.}\qquad \textbf{Ans}$$

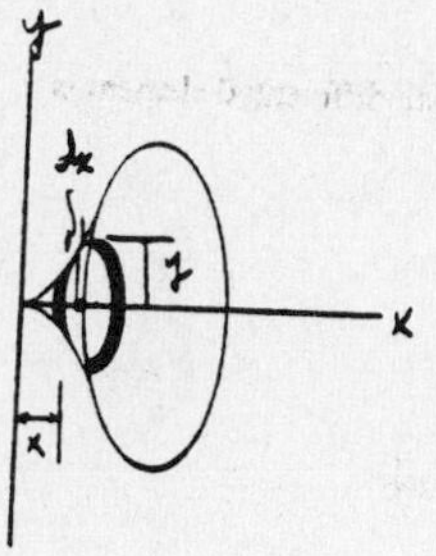

***9-36.** Locate the centroid $\bar{z}$ of the solid.

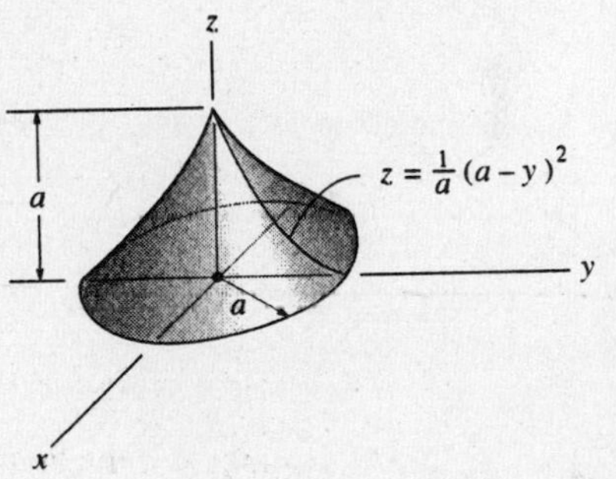

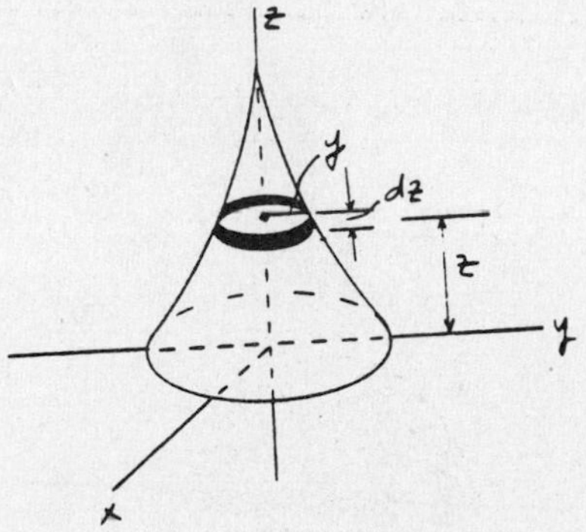

The volume of the differential thin- disk element $dV = \pi y^2 dz = \pi\left(a - \sqrt{az}\right)^2 dz$

$dV = \pi\left(a^2 + az - 2a^{\frac{3}{2}}z^{\frac{1}{2}}\right)dz$ and $\tilde{z} = z$.

$$\bar{z} = \frac{\int_V \tilde{z}\,dV}{\int_V dV} = \frac{\int_0^a z\left[\pi\left(a^2 + az - 2a^{\frac{3}{2}}z^{\frac{1}{2}}\right)dz\right]}{\int_0^a \pi\left(a^2 + az - 2a^{\frac{3}{2}}z^{\frac{1}{2}}\right)dz} = \frac{1}{5}a \qquad \textbf{Ans}$$

9-37. Locate the centroid $\bar{y}$ of the bell-shaped volume formed by revolving the shaded area about the y axis.

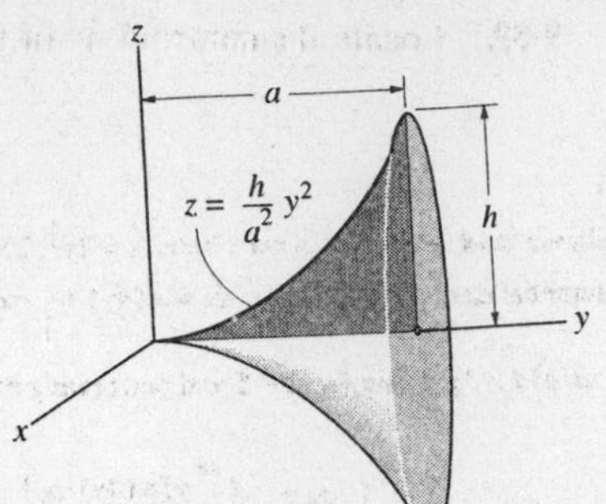

$$\int_V dV = \int_0^a \pi z^2\, dy = \pi \int_0^a \left(\frac{h^2}{a^4}\right) y^4\, dy = \frac{\pi a h^2}{5}$$

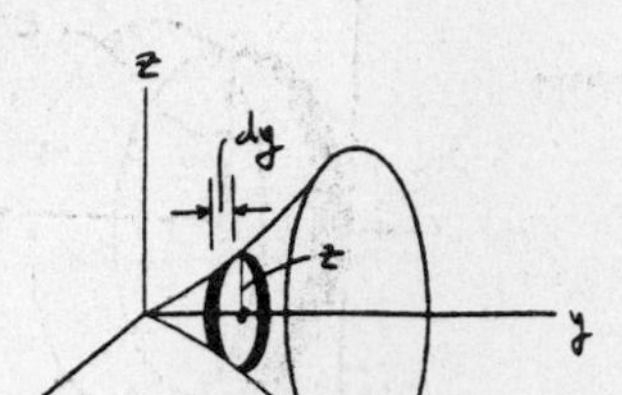

$$\tilde{y} = y$$

$$\int_V \tilde{y}\, dV = \int_0^a y\,(\pi z^2\, dy) = \pi \int_0^a \left(\frac{h^2}{a^4}\right) y^5\, dy = \frac{\pi a^2 h^2}{6}$$

$$\bar{y} = \frac{\int_V \tilde{y}\, dV}{\int_V dV} = \frac{\frac{\pi a^2 h^2}{6}}{\frac{\pi a h^2}{5}} = \frac{5}{6} a \quad \textbf{Ans}$$

9-38. Locate the centroid $\bar{z}$ of the right-elliptical cone.

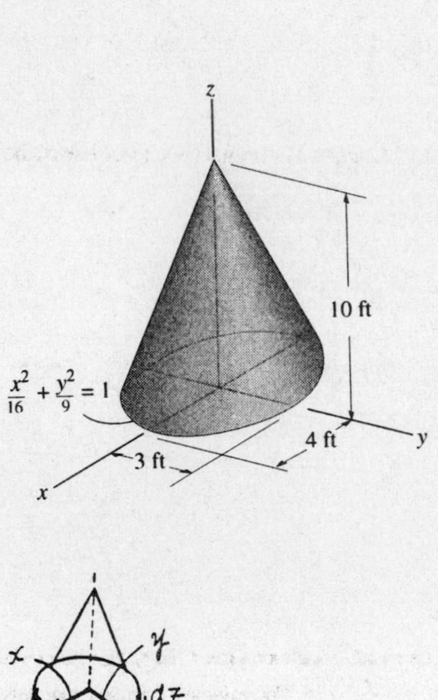

Volume and Moment Arm : From the geometry, $\frac{x}{10-z} = \frac{4}{10}$, $x = 0.4(10-z)$ and $\frac{y}{10-z} = \frac{3}{10}$, $y = 0.3(10-z)$. The volume of the thin disk differential element is $dV = \pi xy\,dz = \pi[0.4(10-z)][0.3(10-z)]\,dz = 0.12\pi(z^2 - 20z + 100)\,dz$ and its centroid $\tilde{z} = z$.

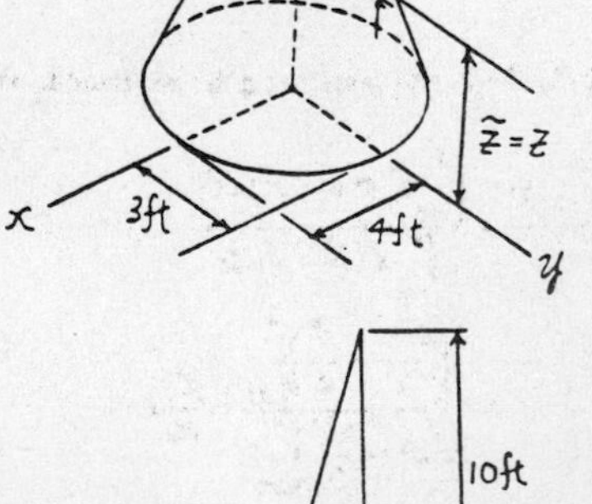

Centroid : Applying Eq. 9 – 5 and performing the integration, we have

$$\bar{z} = \frac{\int_V \tilde{z}\, dV}{\int_V dV} = \frac{\int_0^{10\text{ft}} z[0.12\pi(z^2 - 20z + 100)\,dz]}{\int_0^{10\text{ft}} 0.12\pi(z^2 - 20z + 100)\,dz}$$

$$= \frac{0.12\pi\left(\frac{z^4}{4} - \frac{20z^3}{3} + 50z^2\right)\Big|_0^{10\text{ft}}}{0.12\pi\left(\frac{z^3}{3} - 10z^2 + 100z\right)\Big|_0^{10\text{ft}}} = 2.50\text{ ft} \quad \textbf{Ans}$$

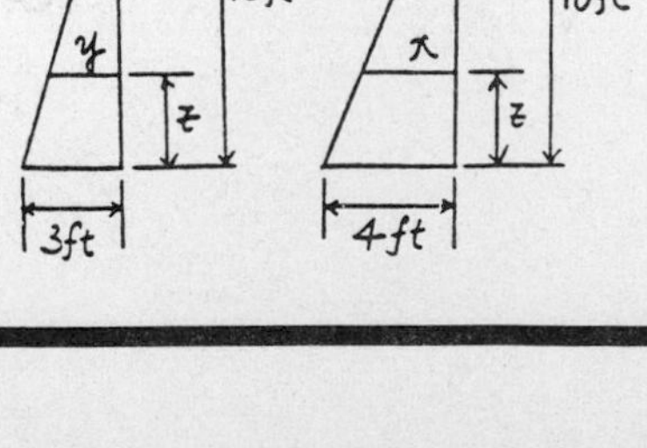

9-39. Locate the centroid $\bar{y}$ of the paraboloid.

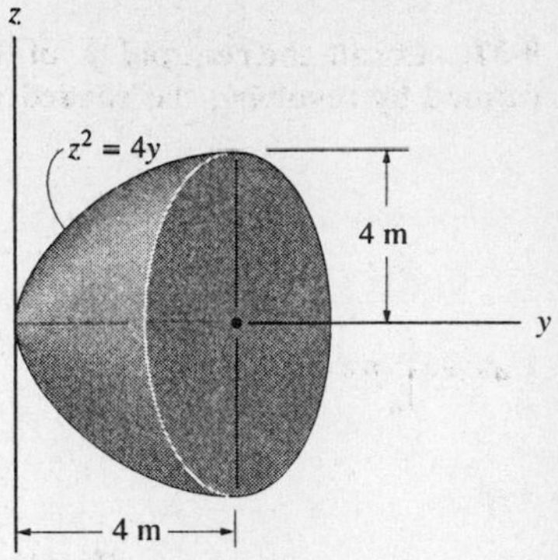

Volume and Moment Arm : here, $z = 2y^{\frac{1}{2}}$. The volume of the thin disk differential element is $dV = \pi z^2 dy = \pi(4y)\,dy$ and its centroid $\tilde{y} = y$.

Centroid : Applying Eq. 9 – 5 and performing the integration, we have

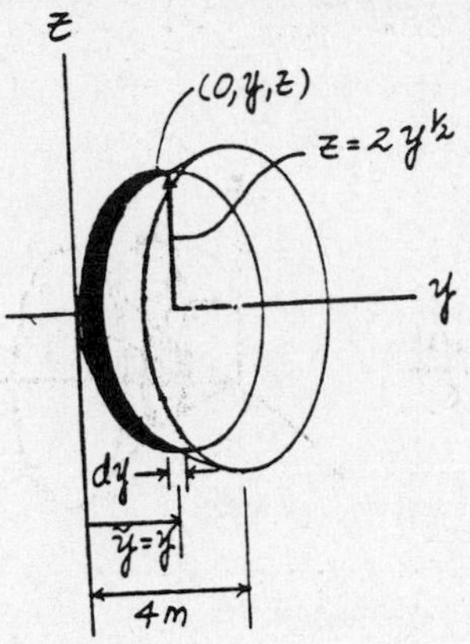

$$\bar{y} = \frac{\int_V \tilde{y}\,dV}{\int_V dV} = \frac{\int_0^{4\text{m}} y[\pi(4y)\,dy]}{\int_0^{4\text{m}} \pi(4y)\,dy}$$

$$= \frac{4\pi\left(\frac{y^3}{3}\right)\Big|_0^{4\text{m}}}{4\pi\left(\frac{y^2}{2}\right)\Big|_0^{4\text{m}}} = 2.67 \text{ m} \qquad \textbf{Ans}$$

***9-40.** Locate the centroid $\bar{z}$ of the spherical segment.

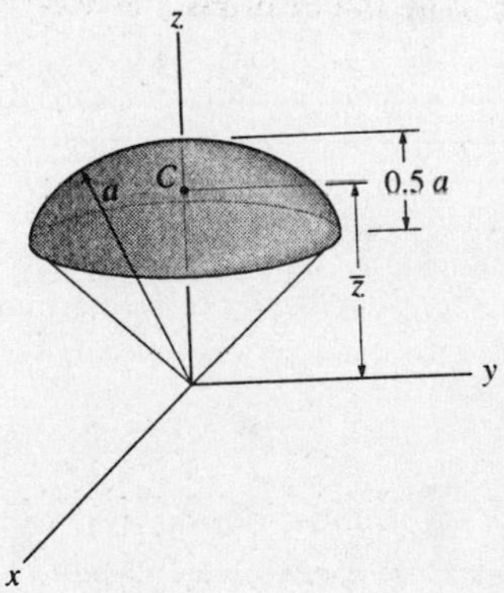

Volume and Moment Arm : Here, the equation of the circle is $z^2 + y^2 = a^2$. Then, $y = \sqrt{a^2 - z^2}$. The volume of the thin disk differential element is $dV = \pi y^2 dz = \pi\left(a^2 - z^2\right) dz$ and its centroid $\tilde{z} = z$.

Centroid : Applying Eq. 9 – 5 and performing the integration, we have

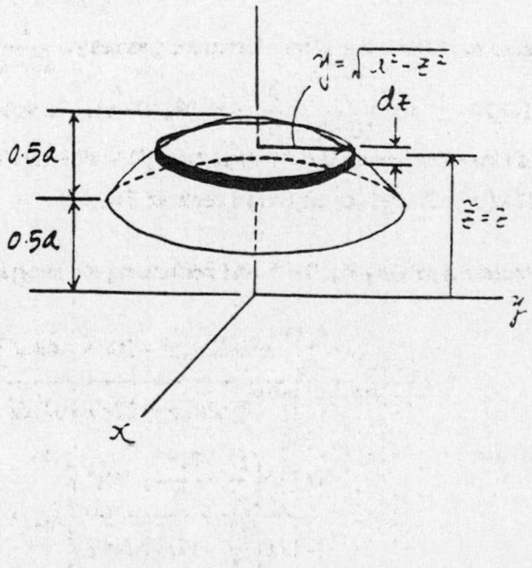

$$\bar{z} = \frac{\int_V \tilde{z}\,dV}{\int_V dV} = \frac{\int_{a/2}^{a} z[\pi(a^2 - z^2)\,dz]}{\int_{a/2}^{a} \pi(a^2 - z^2)\,dz}$$

$$= \frac{\pi\left(\frac{a^2 z^2}{2} - \frac{z^4}{4}\right)\Big|_{a/2}^{a}}{\pi\left(a^2 z - \frac{z^3}{3}\right)\Big|_{a/2}^{a}} = \frac{27}{40}a \qquad \textbf{Ans}$$

9-41. Locate the centroid $\bar{z}$ of the frustum of the right-circular cone.

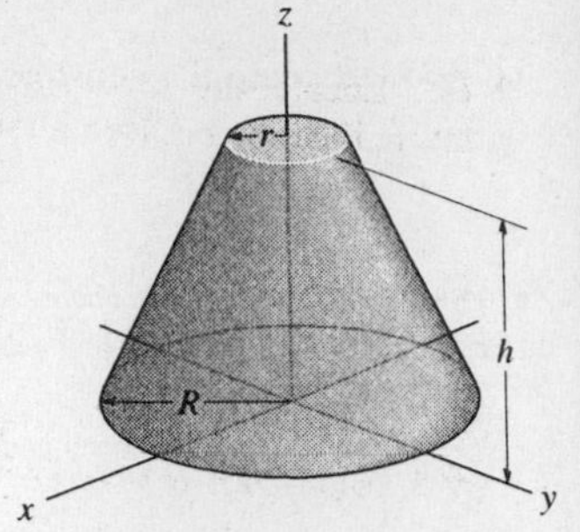

Volume and Moment Arm : From the geometry, $\frac{y-r}{R-r}=\frac{h-z}{h}$, $y=\frac{(r-R)z+Rh}{h}$. The volume of the thin disk differential element is

$$dV=\pi y^2 dz=\pi\left[\left(\frac{(r-R)z+Rh}{h}\right)^2\right]dz$$

$$=\frac{\pi}{h^2}\left[(r-R)^2z^2+2Rh(r-R)z+R^2h^2\right]dz$$

and its centroid $\tilde{z}=z$.

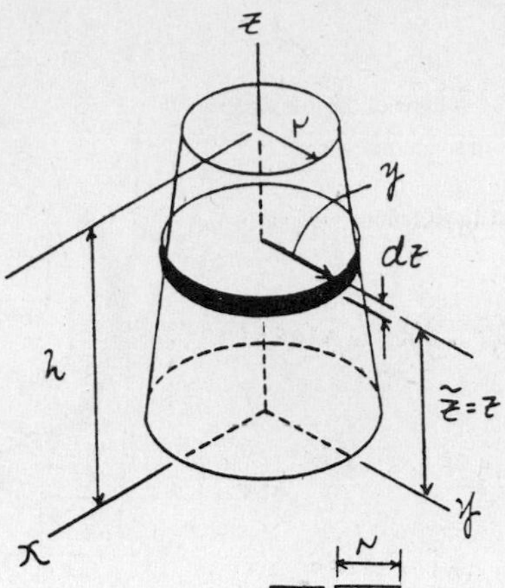

Centroid : Applying Eq. 9 – 5 and performing the integration, we hav

$$\bar{z}=\frac{\int_V \tilde{z}\,dV}{\int_V dV}=\frac{\int_0^h z\left\{\frac{\pi}{h^2}\left[(r-R)^2z^2+2Rh(r-R)z+R^2h^2\right]dz\right\}}{\int_0^h \frac{\pi}{h^2}\left[(r-R)^2z^2+2Rh(r-R)z+R^2h^2\right]dz}$$

$$=\frac{\frac{\pi}{h^2}\left[(r-R)^2\left(\frac{z^4}{4}\right)+2Rh(r-R)\left(\frac{z^3}{3}\right)+R^2h^2\left(\frac{z^2}{2}\right)\right]\Big|_0^h}{\frac{\pi}{h^2}\left[(r-R)^2\left(\frac{z^3}{3}\right)+2Rh(r-R)\left(\frac{z^2}{2}\right)+R^2h^2(z)\right]\Big|_0^h}$$

$$=\frac{R^2+3r^2+2rR}{4(R^2+r^2+rR)}h \qquad \textbf{Ans}$$

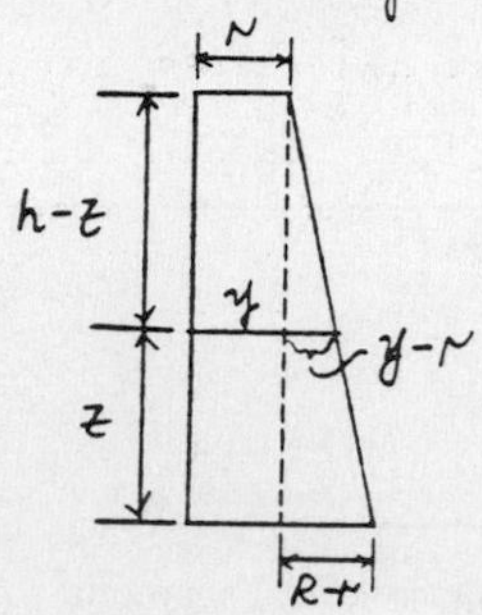

9-42. The hemisphere of radius r is made from a stack of very thin plates such that the density varies with height $\rho=kz$, where k is a constant. Determine its mass and the distance $\bar{z}$ to the center of mass G.

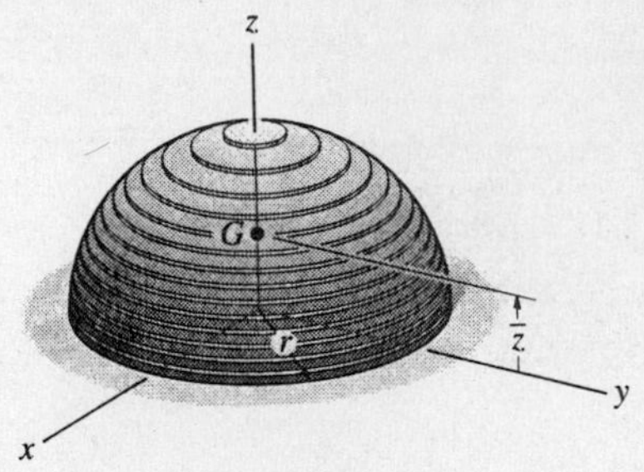

Mass and Moment Arm : The density of the material is $\rho=kz$. The mass of the thin disk differential element is $dm=\rho dV=\rho\pi y^2 dz=kz\left[\pi\left(r^2-z^2\right)dz\right]$ and its centroid $\tilde{z}=z$. Evaluating the integrals, we have

$$m=\int_m dm=\int_0^r kz\left[\pi\left(r^2-z^2\right)dz\right]$$

$$=\pi k\left(\frac{r^2z^2}{2}-\frac{z^4}{4}\right)\Big|_0^r=\frac{\pi kr^4}{4} \qquad \textbf{Ans}$$

$$\int_m \tilde{z}\,dm=\int_0^r z\left\{kz\left[\pi\left(r^2-z^2\right)dz\right]\right\}$$

$$=\pi k\left(\frac{r^2z^3}{3}-\frac{z^5}{5}\right)\Big|_0^r=\frac{2\pi kr^5}{15}$$

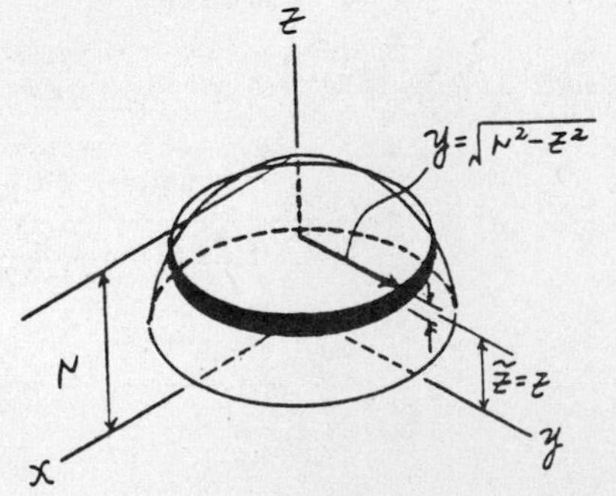

Centroid : Applying Eq. 9 – 4, we have

$$\bar{z}=\frac{\int_m \tilde{z}\,dm}{\int_m dm}=\frac{2\pi kr^5/15}{\pi kr^4/4}=\frac{8}{15}r \qquad \textbf{Ans}$$

9-43. Locate the centroid of the volume formed by rotating the shaded area about the aa axis.

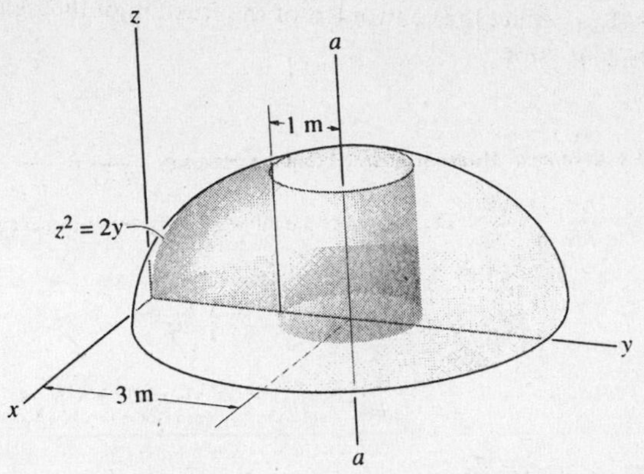

$$\tilde{z} = \frac{z}{2} = \frac{1}{2}\sqrt{2}\sqrt{y}$$

$$dV = 2\pi(3-y)(z)\,dy = 2\sqrt{2}\,\pi\left(3y^{\frac{1}{2}} - y^{\frac{3}{2}}\right)dy$$

$$V = 2\sqrt{2}\,\pi\int_0^2\left(3y^{\frac{1}{2}} - y^{\frac{3}{2}}\right)dy = 2\sqrt{2}\,\pi\left[2y^{\frac{3}{2}} - \frac{2}{5}y^{\frac{5}{2}}\right]_0^2 = 30.16\ \text{m}^3$$

$$\tilde{z}\,dV = \frac{1}{2}\sqrt{2}\sqrt{y}\,(2\pi)(3-y)\left(\sqrt{2}\sqrt{y}\right)dy = 2\pi\left(3y - y^2\right)dy$$

$$\int_V \tilde{z}\,dV = 2\pi\int_0^2\left(3y - y^2\right)dy = 2\pi\left[\frac{3}{2}y^2 - \frac{1}{3}y^3\right]_0^2 = 20.94\ \text{m}^4$$

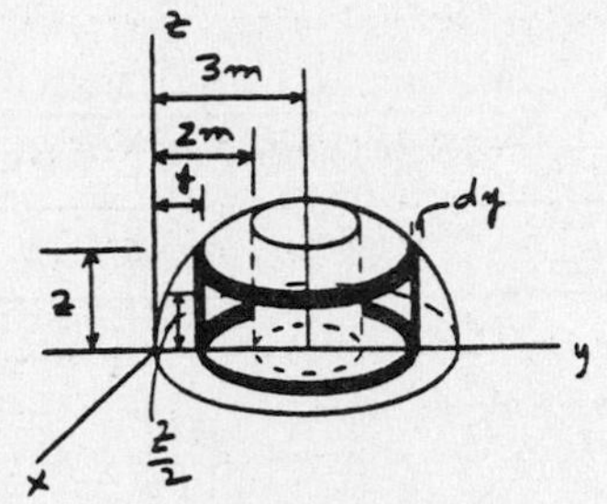

$$\bar{z} = \frac{\int_V \tilde{z}\,dV}{\int_V dV} = \frac{20.94}{30.16} = 0.694\ \text{m} \qquad \textbf{Ans}$$

Due to symmetry:

$\bar{y} = 3$ m **Ans**

$\bar{x} = 0$ **Ans**

***9-44.** Locate the center of gravity G of the five particles with respect to the origin O.

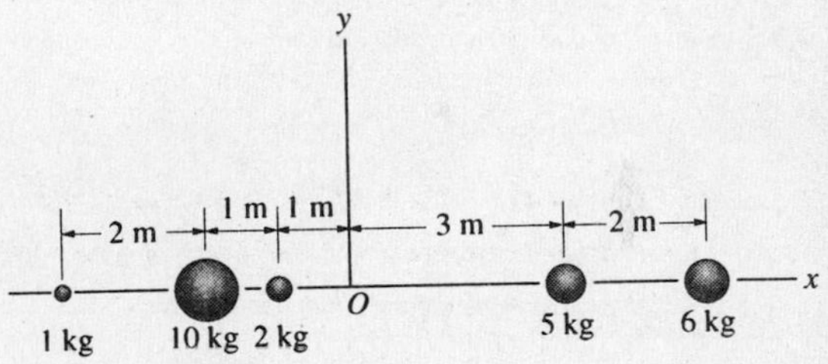

Center of Gravity **:** The weight of the particles are $W_1 = 5g$, $W_2 = 6g$, $W_3 = 2g$, $W_4 = 10g$ and $W_5 = 1g$ and their respective centers of gravity are $\tilde{x}_1 = 3$ m, $\tilde{x}_2 = 5$ m, $\tilde{x}_3 = -1$ m, $\tilde{x}_4 = -2$ m and $\tilde{x}_5 = -4$ m. Applying Eq. 9 – 8, we have

$$\bar{x} = \frac{\Sigma\tilde{x}W}{\Sigma W} = \frac{3(5g) + 5(6g) + (-1)(2g) + (-2)(10g) + (-4)(1g)}{5g + 6g + 2g + 10g + 1g}$$

$$= 0.792\ \text{m} \qquad \textbf{Ans}$$

9-45. Locate the center of mass $(\bar{x}, \bar{y})$ of the four particles.

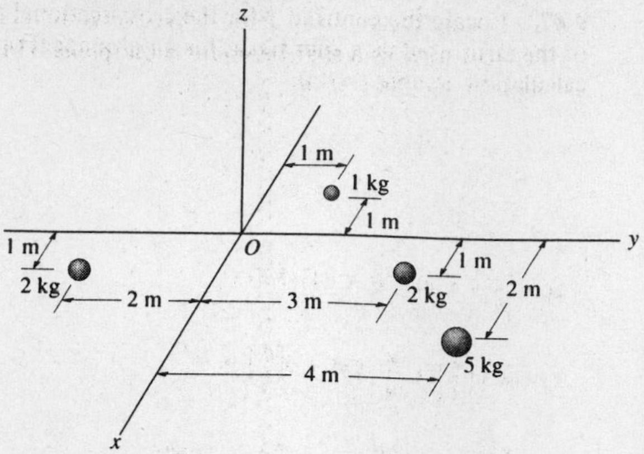

Center of Gravity : The weight of the particles are $W_1 = 2$ kg, $W_2 = 5$ kg, $W_3 = 2$ kg and $W_4 = 1$ kg. Their respective centers of mass are $\bar{x}_1 = 1$ m and $\bar{y}_1 = 3$ m, $\bar{x}_2 = 2$ m and $\bar{y}_2 = 4$ m, $\bar{x}_3 = 1$ m and $\bar{y}_3 = -2$ m and $\bar{x}_4 = -1$ m and $\bar{y}_4 = 1$ m. Applying Eq. 9−8, we have

$$\bar{x} = \frac{\Sigma \bar{x} W}{\Sigma W} = \frac{1(2) + 2(5) + 1(2) + (-1)(1)}{2 + 5 + 2 + 1}$$

$$= 1.30 \text{ m} \qquad \textbf{Ans}$$

$$\bar{y} = \frac{\Sigma \bar{y} W}{\Sigma W} = \frac{3(2) + 4(5) + (-2)(2) + 1(1)}{2 + 5 + 2 + 1}$$

$$= 2.30 \text{ m} \qquad \textbf{Ans}$$

9-46. Locate the centroid $(\bar{x}, \bar{y})$ of the uniform wire bent in the shape shown.

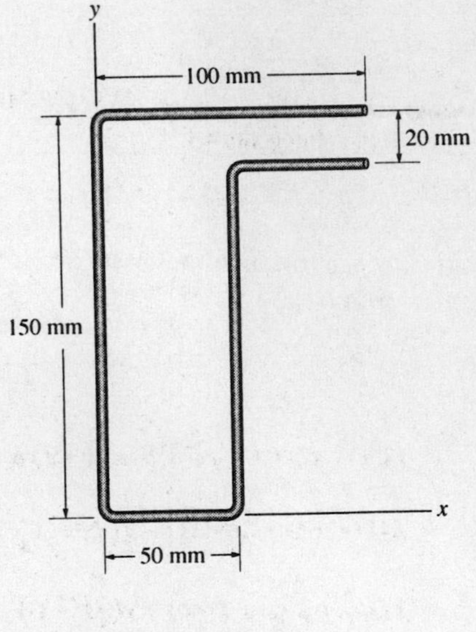

Centroid : The length of each segment and its respective centroid are tabulated below.

Segment	L(mm)	$\bar{x}$(mm)	$\bar{y}$(mm)	$\bar{x}L$(mm²)	$\bar{y}L$(mm²)
1	150	0	75	0	11250
2	50	25	0	1250	0
3	130	50	65	6500	8450
4	100	50	150	5000	15000
5	50	75	130	3750	6500
Σ	480			16500	41200

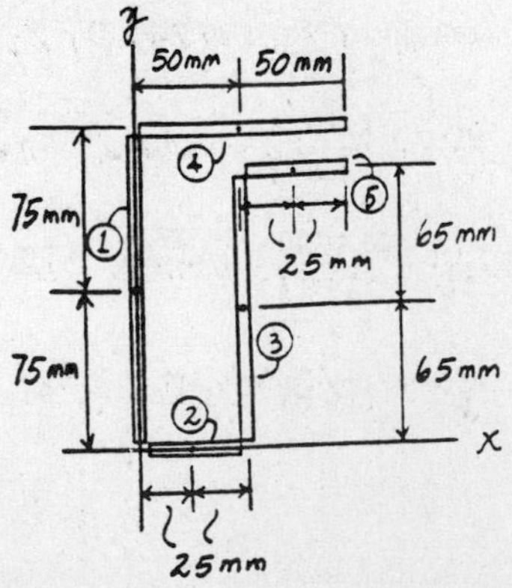

Thus,

$$\bar{x} = \frac{\Sigma \bar{x} L}{\Sigma L} = \frac{16500}{480} = 34.375 \text{ mm} = 34.4 \text{ mm} \qquad \textbf{Ans}$$

$$\bar{y} = \frac{\Sigma \bar{y} L}{\Sigma L} = \frac{41200}{480} = 85.83 \text{ mm} = 85.8 \text{ mm} \qquad \textbf{Ans}$$

9-47. Locate the centroid $\bar{x}$ for the cross-sectional area of the strut used as a spar beam for an airplane. For the calculation assume $t \ll a$.

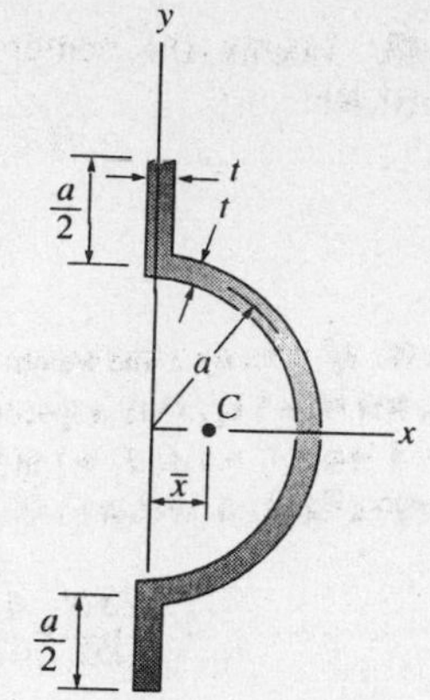

$$\Sigma L = \frac{a}{2} + \pi(a) + \frac{a}{2} = a(1+\pi)$$

$$\Sigma \tilde{x} L = 0\left(\frac{a}{2}\right) + \frac{2a}{\pi}(\pi a) + 0\left(\frac{a}{2}\right) = 2a^2$$

$$\bar{x} = \frac{\Sigma \tilde{x} L}{\Sigma L} = \frac{2a^2}{a(1+\pi)} = \frac{2a}{1+\pi} \quad \textbf{Ans}$$

***9-48.** Locate the centroid $(\bar{x}, \bar{y}, \bar{z})$ of the wire which is bent in the shape shown.

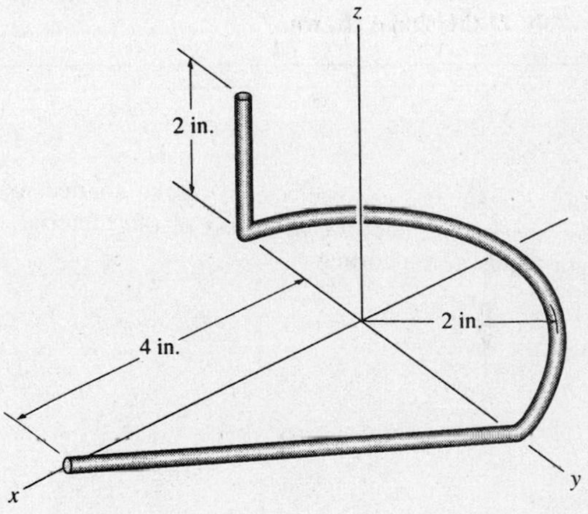

$$\Sigma L = 2 + \pi(2) + \sqrt{4^2 + 2^2} = 12.7553 \text{ in.}$$

$$\Sigma \tilde{x} L = 0(2) - \frac{2(2)}{\pi}(\pi 2) + 2\left(\sqrt{4^2 + 2^2}\right) = 0.94427 \text{ in}^2$$

$$\Sigma \tilde{y} L = (-2)(2) - 0(\pi 2) + 1\left(\sqrt{4^2 + 2^2}\right) = 0.47214 \text{ in}^2$$

$$\Sigma \tilde{z} L = 1(2) - 0(\pi 2) + 0\left(\sqrt{4^2 + 2^2}\right) = 2 \text{ in}^2$$

$$\bar{x} = \frac{\Sigma \tilde{x} L}{\Sigma L} = \frac{0.94427}{12.7553} = 0.0740 \text{ in.} \quad \textbf{Ans}$$

$$\bar{y} = \frac{\Sigma \tilde{y} L}{\Sigma L} = \frac{0.47214}{12.7553} = 0.0370 \text{ in.} \quad \textbf{Ans}$$

$$\bar{z} = \frac{\Sigma \tilde{z} L}{\Sigma L} = \frac{2}{12.7553} = 0.157 \text{ in.} \quad \textbf{Ans}$$

9-49. Locate the centroid for the cold-formed metal strut having the cross section show. Neglect the thickness of the material and slight bends at the corners.

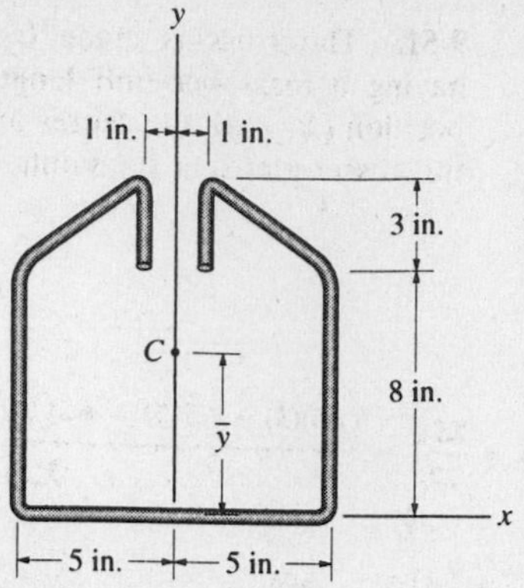

Centroid : The length of each segment and its respective centroid are tabulated below.

Segment	L (in.)	$\tilde{y}$ (in.)	$\tilde{y}L$ (in²)
1	3	9.5	28.5
2	5	9.5	47.5
3	8	4	32.0
4	10	0	0
5	8	4	32.0
6	5	9.5	47.5
7	3	9.5	28.5
Σ	42.0		216.0

Due to symmetry about y axis, $\bar{x} = 0$ **Ans**

$$\bar{y} = \frac{\Sigma \tilde{y}L}{\Sigma L} = \frac{216.0}{42.0} = 5.143 \text{ in.} = 5.14 \text{ in.}$$ **Ans**

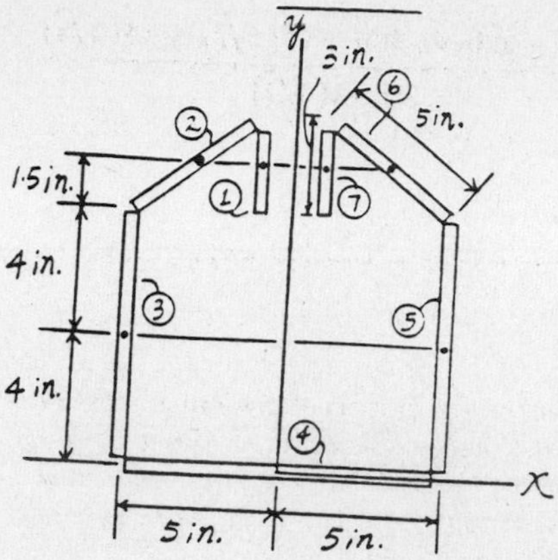

9-50. Locate the centroid $(\bar{x}, \bar{y})$ of the shaded metal cross section. Neglect the thickness of the material and slight bends at the corners.

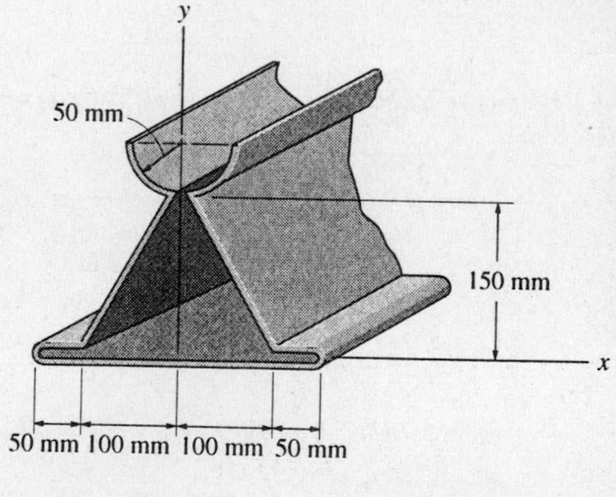

Centroid : The length of each segment and its respective centroid are tabulated below.

Segment	L (mm)	$\tilde{y}$ (mm)	$\tilde{y}L$ (mm²)
1	50π	168.17	26415.93
2	180.28	75	13520.82
3	400	0	0
4	180.28	75	13520.82
Σ	917.63		53457.56

Due to symmetry about y axis, $\bar{x} = 0$ **Ans**

$$\bar{y} = \frac{\Sigma \tilde{y}L}{\Sigma L} = \frac{53457.56}{917.63} = 58.26 \text{ mm} = 58.3 \text{ mm}$$ **Ans**

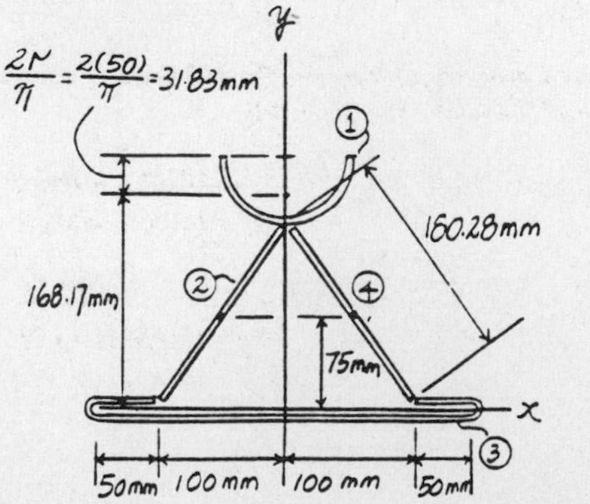

9-51. The truss is made from seven members, each having a mass per unit length of 6 kg/m. Locate the position $(\bar{x}, \bar{y})$ of the center of mass. Neglect the mass of the gusset plates at the joints.

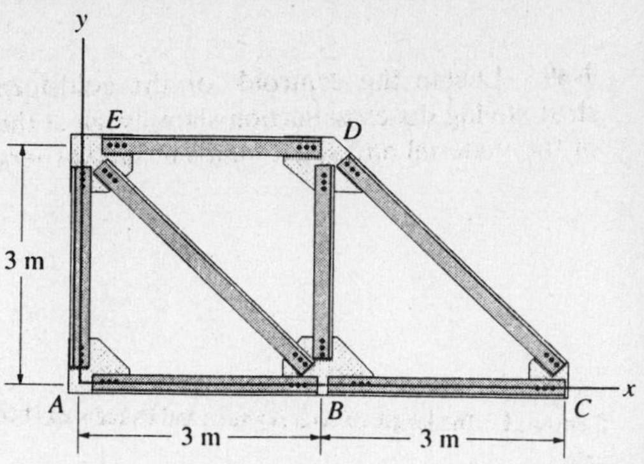

$$\bar{x} = \frac{\Sigma \tilde{x} L}{\Sigma L} = \frac{(1.5)(3) + 4.5(3) + 4.5(3\sqrt{2}) + 1.5(3) + 3(3) + 1.5(3\sqrt{2})}{5(3) + 2(3\sqrt{2})}$$

$= 2.43$ m **Ans**

$$\bar{y} = \frac{\Sigma \tilde{y} L}{\Sigma L} = \frac{(1.5)(3) + 3(3) + 1.5(3) + 1.5(3\sqrt{2}) + 1.5(3\sqrt{2})}{5(3) + 2(3\sqrt{2})}$$

$= 1.31$ m **Ans**

***9-52.** Each of the three members of the frame has a mass per unit length of 6 kg/m. Locate the position $(\bar{x}, \bar{y})$ of the center of gravity. Neglect the size of the pins at the joints and the thickness of the members. Also, calculate the reactions at the pin A and roller E.

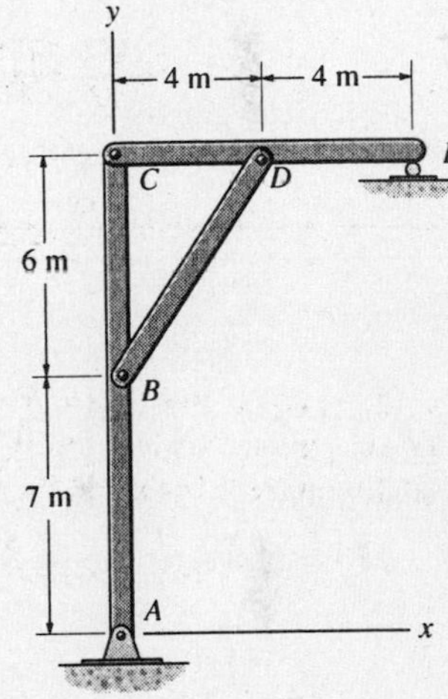

Centroid : The length of each segment and its respective centroid are tabulated below.

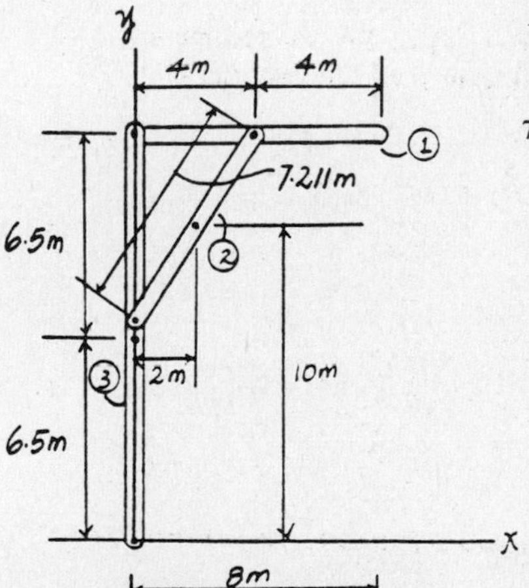

Segment	L(m)	$\tilde{x}$(m)	$\tilde{y}$(m)	$\tilde{x}L$(m²)	$\tilde{y}L$(m²)
1	8	4	13	32.0	104.0
2	7.211	2	10	14.42	72.11
3	13	0	6.5	0	84.5
Σ	28.211			46.42	260.61

Thus,

$$\bar{x} = \frac{\Sigma \tilde{x} L}{\Sigma L} = \frac{46.42}{28.211} = 1.646 \text{ m} = 1.65 \text{ m} \qquad \textbf{Ans}$$

$$\bar{y} = \frac{\Sigma \tilde{y} L}{\Sigma L} = \frac{260.61}{28.211} = 9.238 \text{ m} = 9.24 \text{ m} \qquad \textbf{Ans}$$

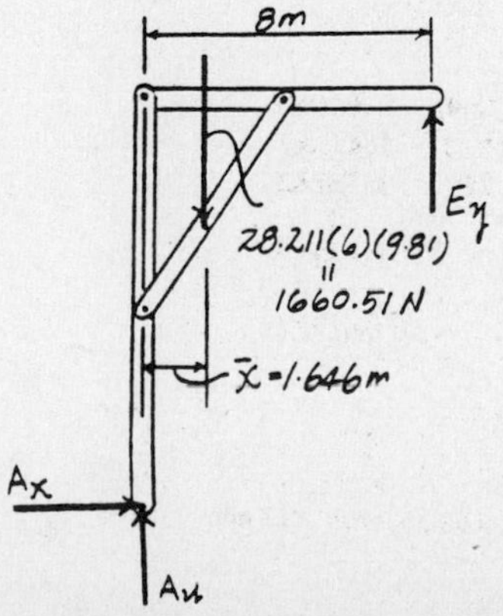

Equations of Equilibrium : The total weight of the frame is $W = 28.211(6)(9.81) = 1660.51$ N.

$+\Sigma M_A = 0; \quad E_y(8) - 1660.51(1.646) = 0$

$E_y = 341.55 \text{ N} = 342 \text{ N}$ **Ans**

$+\uparrow \Sigma F_y = 0; \quad A_y + 341.55 - 1660.51 = 0$

$A_y = 1318.95 \text{ N} = 1.32 \text{ kN}$ **Ans**

$\xrightarrow{+} \Sigma F_x = 0; \quad A_x = 0$ **Ans**

9-53. Determine the location $\bar{y}$ of the centroid of the beam's cross-sectional area. Neglect the size of the corner welds at A and B for the calculation.

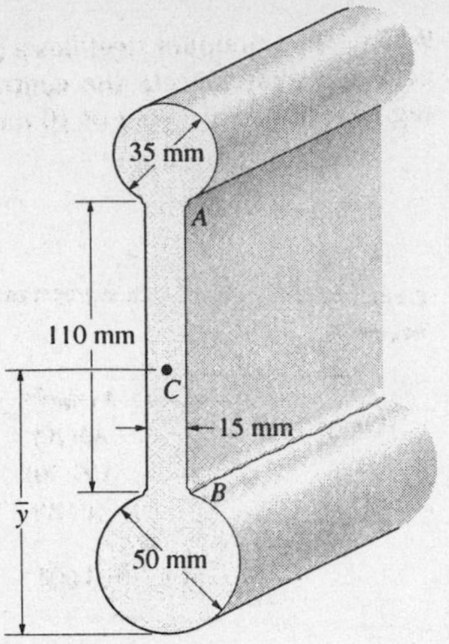

$$\Sigma \tilde{y} A = \pi(25)^2(25) + 15(110)(50 + 55) + \pi\left(\frac{35}{2}\right)^2\left(50 + 110 + \frac{35}{2}\right) = 393\ 112\ \text{mm}^3$$

$$\Sigma A = \pi(25)^2 + 15(110) + \pi\left(\frac{35}{2}\right)^2 = 4575.6\ \text{mm}^2$$

$$\bar{y} = \frac{\Sigma \tilde{y} A}{\Sigma A} = \frac{393\ 112}{4575.6} = 85.9\ \text{mm} \qquad \textbf{Ans}$$

9-54. The gravity wall is made of concrete. Determine the location $(\bar{x}, \bar{y})$ of the center of gravity G for the wall.

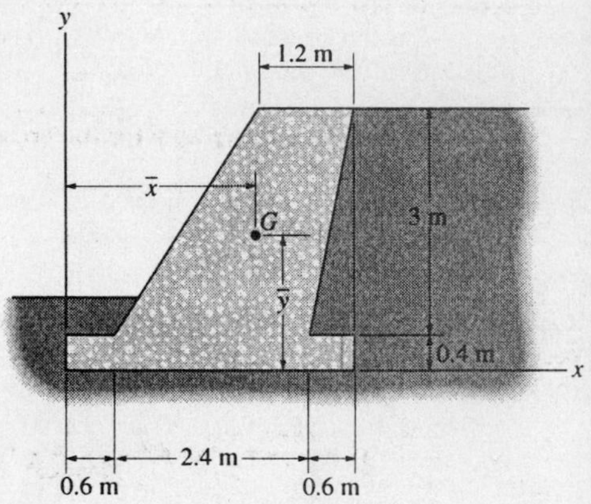

$$\Sigma \tilde{x} A = 1.8(3.6)(0.4) + 2.1(3)(3) - 3.4\left(\frac{1}{2}\right)(3)(0.6) - 1.2\left(\frac{1}{2}\right)(1.8)(3)$$

$$= 15.192\ \text{m}^3$$

$$\Sigma \tilde{y} A = 0.2(3.6)(0.4) + 1.9(3)(3) - 1.4\left(\frac{1}{2}\right)(3)(0.6) - 2.4\left(\frac{1}{2}\right)(1.8)(3)$$

$$= 9.648\ \text{m}^3$$

$$\Sigma A = 3.6(0.4) + 3(3) - \frac{1}{2}(3)(0.6) - \frac{1}{2}(1.8)(3)$$

$$= 6.84\ \text{m}^2$$

$$\bar{x} = \frac{\Sigma \tilde{x} A}{\Sigma A} = \frac{15.192}{6.84} = 2.22\ \text{m} \qquad \textbf{Ans}$$

$$\bar{y} = \frac{\Sigma \tilde{y} A}{\Sigma A} = \frac{9.648}{6.84} = 1.41\ \text{m} \qquad \textbf{Ans}$$

9-55. An aluminum strut has a cross section referred to as a deep hat. Locate the centroid $\bar{y}$ of its area. Each segment has a thickness of 10 mm.

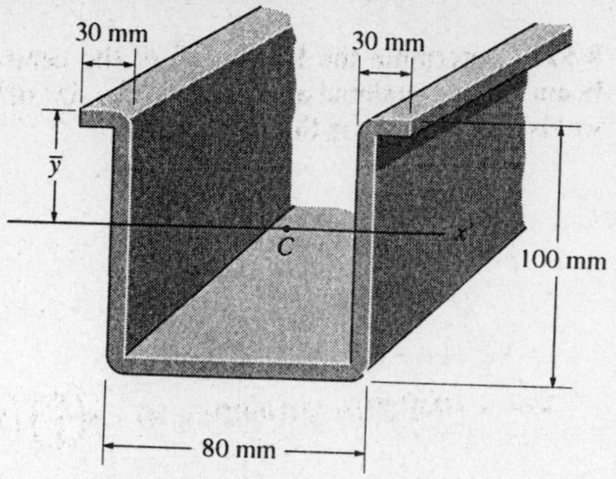

Centroid : The area of each segment and its respective centroid are tabulated below.

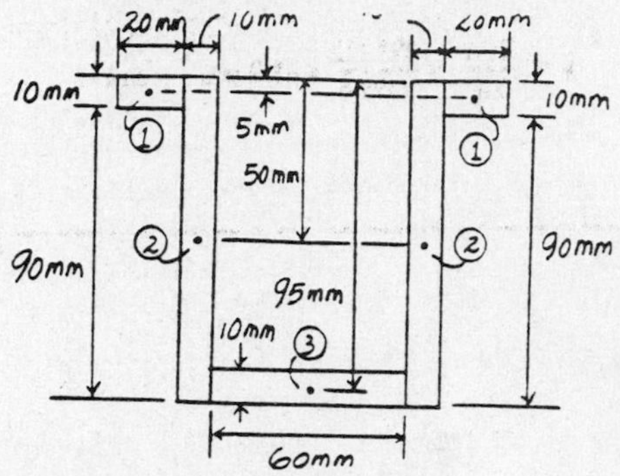

Segment	$A\,(\text{mm}^2)$	$\tilde{y}\,(\text{mm})$	$\tilde{y}A\,(\text{mm}^3)$
1	40(10)	5	2 000
2	100(20)	50	100 000
3	60(10)	95	57 000
Σ	3 000		159 000

Thus,

$$\bar{y} = \frac{\Sigma \tilde{y}A}{\Sigma A} = \frac{159\,000}{3\,000} = 53.0 \text{ mm} \qquad \textbf{Ans}$$

***9-56.** Locate the centroid $\bar{y}$ for the cross-sectional area of the angle.

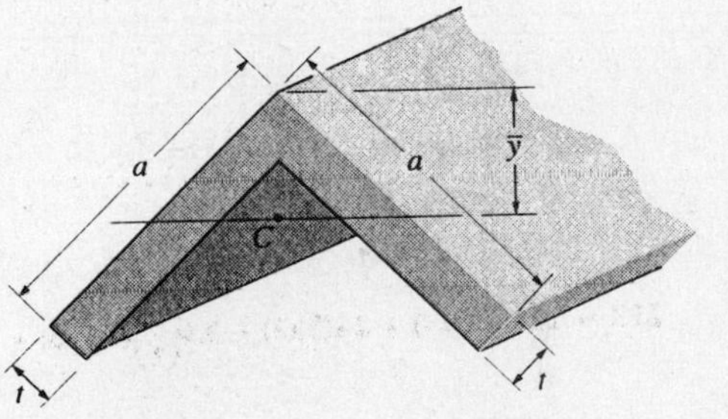

Centroid : The area and the centroid for segments 1 and 2 are

$$A_1 = t(a-t)$$

$$\tilde{y}_1 = \left(\frac{a-t}{2} + \frac{t}{2}\right)\cos 45° + \frac{t}{2\cos 45°} = \frac{\sqrt{2}}{4}(a+2t)$$

$$A_2 = at$$

$$\tilde{y}_2 = \left(\frac{a}{2} - \frac{t}{2}\right)\cos 45° + \frac{t}{2\cos 45°} = \frac{\sqrt{2}}{4}(a+t)$$

Listed in a tabular form, we have

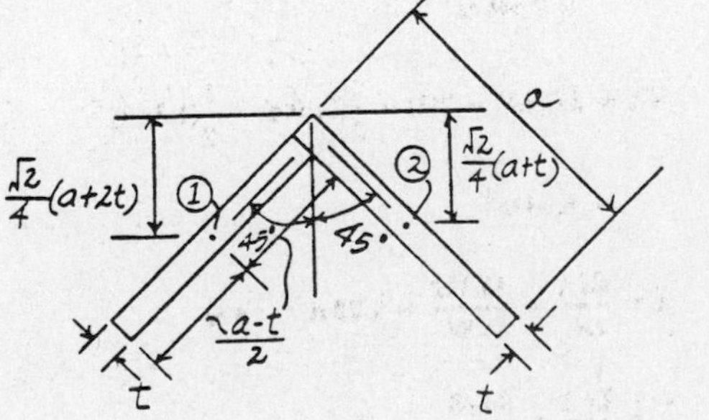

Segment	A	$\tilde{y}$	$\tilde{y}A$
1	$t(a-t)$	$\frac{\sqrt{2}}{4}(a+2t)$	$\frac{\sqrt{2}t}{4}(a^2+at-2t^2)$
2	at	$\frac{\sqrt{2}}{4}(a+t)$	$\frac{\sqrt{2}t}{4}(a^2+at)$
Σ	$t(2a-t)$		$\frac{\sqrt{2}t}{2}(a^2+at-t^2)$

Thus,

$$\bar{y} = \frac{\Sigma \tilde{y}A}{\Sigma A} = \frac{\frac{\sqrt{2}t}{2}(a^2+at-t^2)}{t(2a-t)}$$

$$= \frac{\sqrt{2}(a^2+at-t^2)}{2(2a-t)} \qquad \textbf{Ans}$$

9-57. Divide the plate into parts, and using the grid for measurement, determine approximately the location $(\bar{x}, \bar{y})$ of the centroid of the plate.

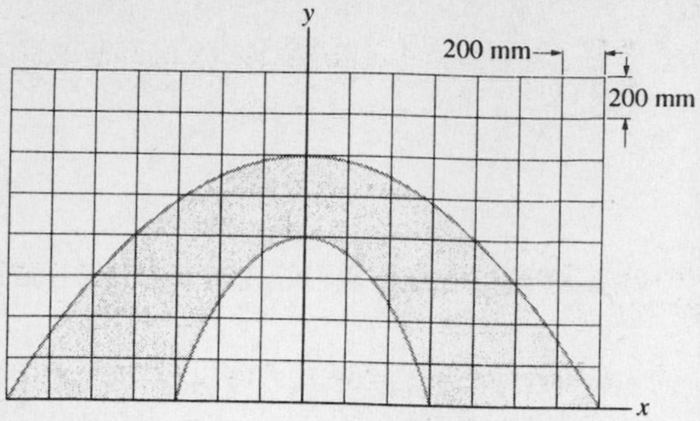

Due to symmetry,

$\bar{x} = 0$ **Ans**

Divide half the area into 8 segments as shown.

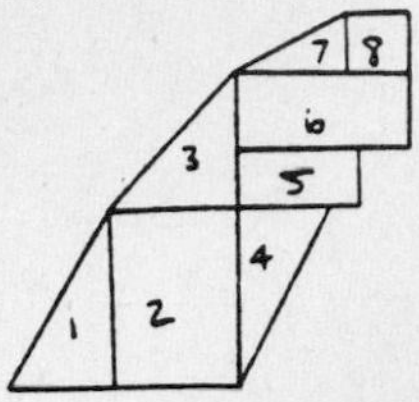

	A (Approx. 10^4)	$\bar{y}$ (Approx. 10^2)	$\bar{y}A$ (10^6)
1)	$\frac{1}{2}(6)(4)$	2	24
2)	4(6)	3	72
3)	$\frac{1}{2}(4)(4)$	7.32	58.56
4)	$\frac{1}{2}(3)(6)$	4	36
5)	8	7	56
6)	6(2)	9	108
7)	$\frac{1}{2}(4)(2)$	10.66	42.64
8)	(2)(2)	11	44

$$\bar{y} = \frac{\Sigma \bar{y}A}{\Sigma A} = \frac{441.2(10^6)}{81(10^4)} = 544 \text{ mm} \quad \textbf{Ans}$$

A simpler solution consists of dividing the area into two parabolas.
For parabola :

$$\Sigma \bar{y}A = \frac{2}{5}(1200)\left(\frac{4}{3}\right)(2800)(1200) - \frac{2}{5}(800)\left(\frac{4}{3}\right)(1200)(800)$$

$$\Sigma A = \frac{4}{3}(2800)(1200) - \frac{4}{3}(1200)(800)$$

$$\bar{y} = \frac{\Sigma \bar{y}A}{\Sigma A} = 544 \text{ mm} \quad \textbf{Ans}$$

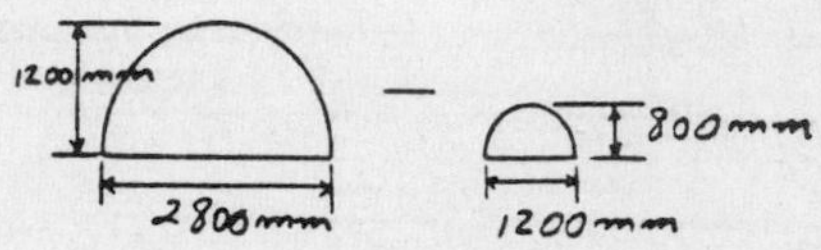

9-58. Locate the distance $\bar{y}$ to the centroid of the member's cross-sectional area.

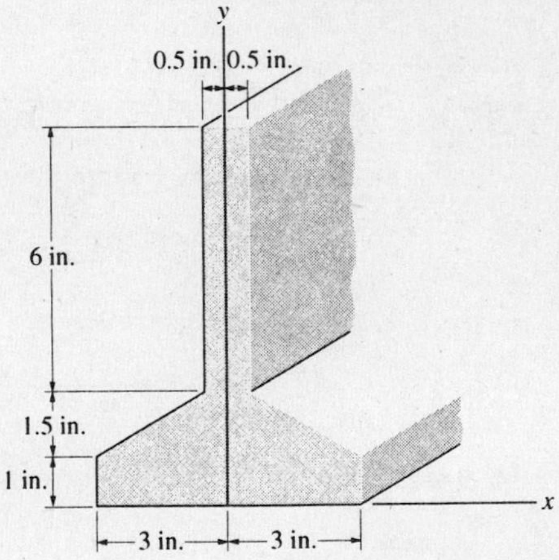

$$\Sigma \bar{y}A = 0.5(6)(1) + 2(1.5)\left(\frac{1}{2}\right)(2.5)(1.5) + 4.75(7.5)(1)$$

$$= 44.25 \text{ in}^3$$

$$\Sigma A = 6(1) + (2)\left(\frac{1}{2}\right)(2.5)(1.5) + 7.5(1)$$

$$= 17.25 \text{ in}^2$$

$$\bar{y} = \frac{\Sigma \bar{y}A}{\Sigma A} = \frac{44.25}{17.25} = 2.57 \text{ in.} \quad \textbf{Ans}$$

9-59. Locate the centroid $(\bar{x}, \bar{y})$ for the angle's cross-sectional area.

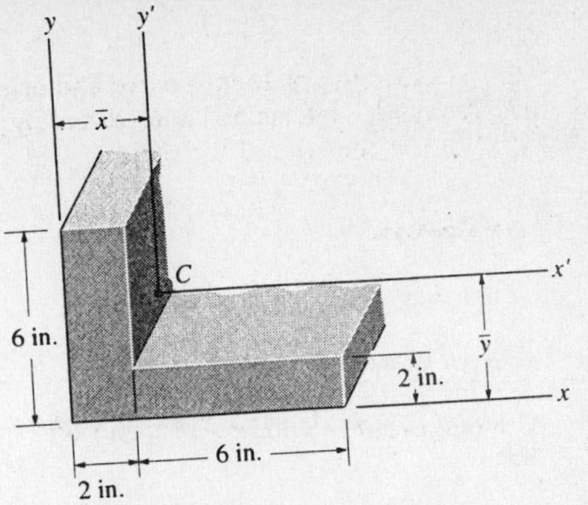

Centroid : The area of each segment and its respective centroid are tabulated below.

Segment	$A\,(\text{in}^2)$	$\tilde{x}\,(\text{in.})$	$\tilde{y}\,(\text{in.})$	$\tilde{x}A\,(\text{in}^3)$	$\tilde{y}A\,(\text{in}^3)$
1	6(2)	1	3	12.0	36.0
2	6(2)	5	1	60.0	12.0
Σ	24.0			72.0	48.0

Thus,

$$\bar{x} = \frac{\Sigma\tilde{x}A}{\Sigma A} = \frac{72.0}{24.0} = 3.00 \text{ in.} \qquad \textbf{Ans}$$

$$\bar{y} = \frac{\Sigma\tilde{y}A}{\Sigma A} = \frac{48.0}{24.0} = 2.00 \text{ in.} \qquad \textbf{Ans}$$

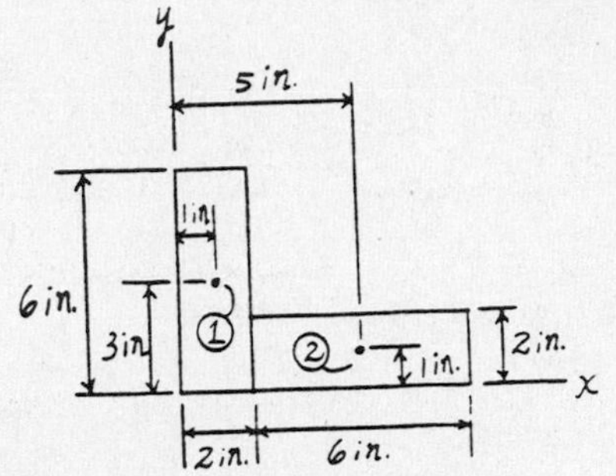

***9-60.** The *rectangular horn antenna* is used for receiving microwaves. Determine the location $\bar{x}$ of its center of gravity G. The horn is made of plates having a constant thickness and density and is open at each end.

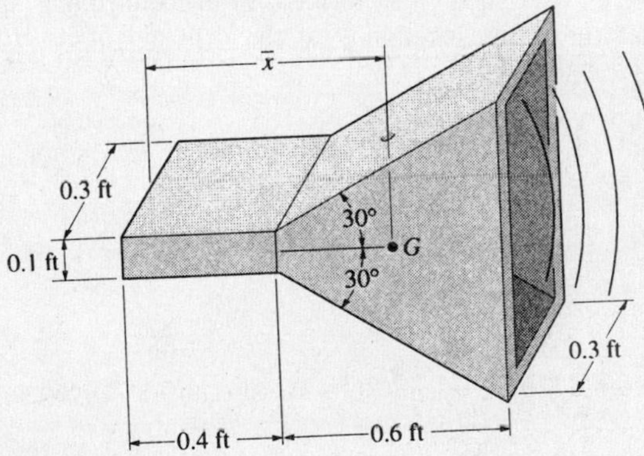

$$\Sigma\tilde{x}A = 2(0.2)(0.3)(0.4) + 2(0.2)(0.1)(0.4) + 2(0.7)(0.1)(0.6)$$

$$+ 4\left(0.4 + \frac{2}{3}(0.6)\right)\left(\frac{1}{2}\right)(0.6)(0.6\tan 30^\circ) + 2(0.4 + 0.3)(0.3)\left(\frac{0.6}{\cos 30^\circ}\right)$$

$$= 0.7715 \text{ ft}^3$$

$$\Sigma A = 2(0.3)(0.4) + 2(0.1)(0.4) + 2(0.1)(0.6) + 4\left(\frac{1}{2}\right)(0.6)(0.6\tan 30^\circ) + 2(0.3)\left(\frac{0.6}{\cos 30^\circ}\right)$$

$$= 1.2714 \text{ ft}^2$$

$$\bar{x} = \frac{\Sigma\tilde{x}A}{\Sigma A} = \frac{0.7715}{1.2714} = 0.607 \text{ ft} \qquad \textbf{Ans}$$

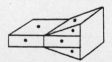

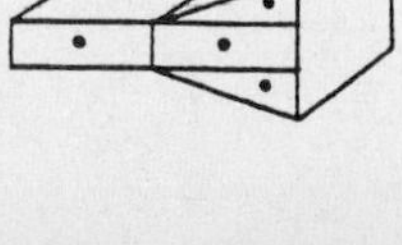

9-61. Locate the centroid $\bar{y}$ of the cross-sectional area of the beam.

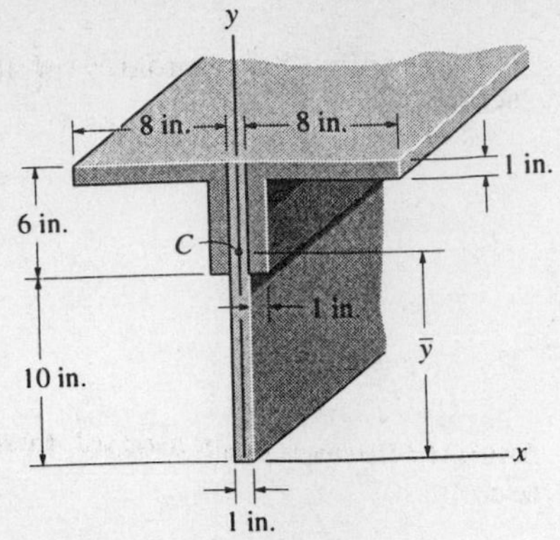

Centroid **:** The area of each segment and its respective centroid are tabulated below.

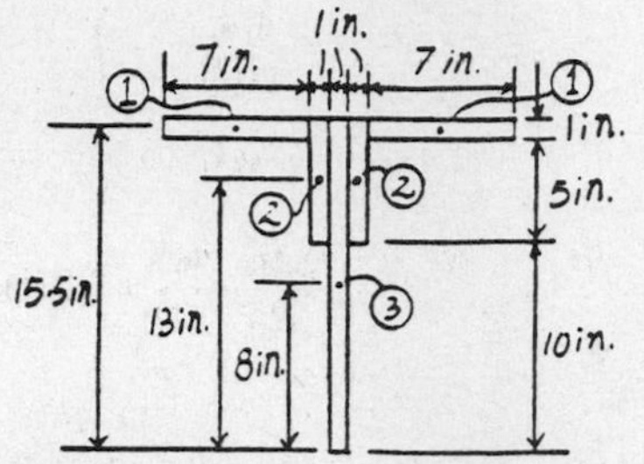

Segment	$A\,(\text{in}^2)$	$\bar{y}\,(\text{in.})$	$\bar{y}A\,(\text{in}^3)$
1	14(1)	15.5	217.0
2	6(2)	13	156.0
3	16(1)	8	128.0
Σ	42.0		501.0

Thus,

$$\bar{y} = \frac{\Sigma \bar{y}A}{\Sigma A} = \frac{501.0}{42.0} = 11.93 \text{ in.} = 11.9 \text{ in.} \qquad \textbf{Ans}$$

9-62. The strut was formed in a cold-rolling mill. Determine the location $\bar{y}$ of the centroid of its cross-sectional area.

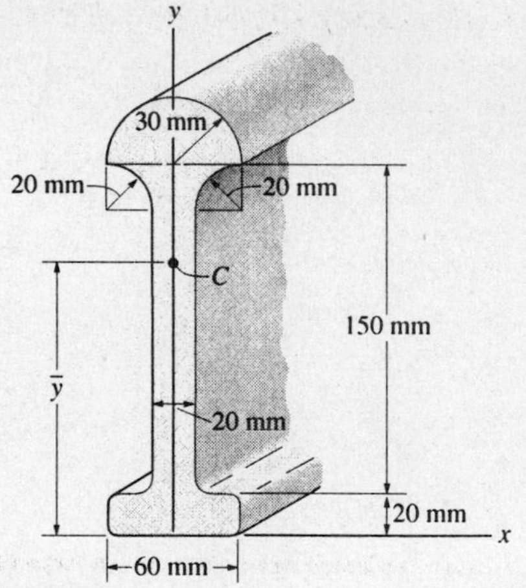

$$\Sigma \bar{y}A = \left[170 + \frac{4(30)}{3\pi}\right]\left(\frac{\pi}{2}\right)(30)^2 + 85(60)(170) - 85(2)[20(130)]$$

$$-\left[150 + \frac{4(20)}{3\pi}\right](2)\left[\frac{\pi}{4}(20)^2\right] = 583.8(10^3)\ \text{mm}^3$$

$$\Sigma A = \frac{\pi}{2}(30)^2 + 60(170) - 2[20(130)] - 2\left[\frac{\pi}{4}(20)^2\right]$$

$$= 5.785(10^3)\ \text{mm}^2$$

$$\bar{y} = \frac{583.8(10^3)}{5.785(10^3)} = 101\ \text{mm} \qquad \textbf{Ans}$$

9-63. Locate the centroid $\bar{y}$ of the channel's cross-sectional area.

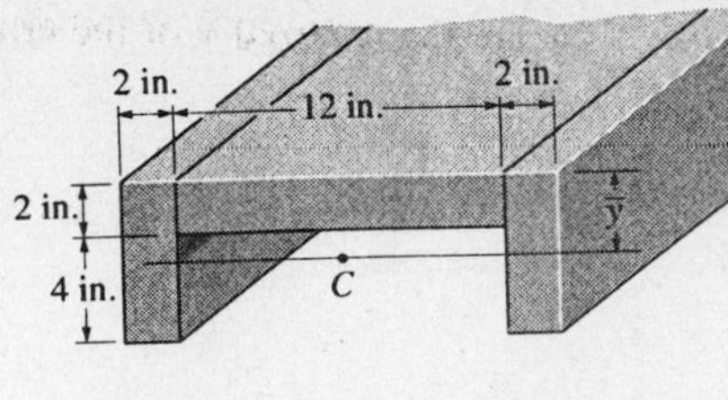

Centroid : The area of each segment and its respective centroid are tabulated below.

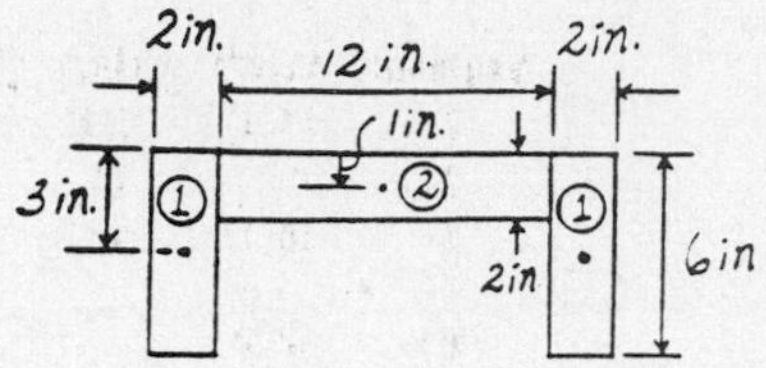

Segment	A (in^2)	$\tilde{y}$ (in.)	$\tilde{y}A$ (in^3)
1	6(4)	3	72.0
2	12(2)	1	24.0
Σ	48.0		96.0

Thus,

$$\bar{y} = \frac{\Sigma\tilde{y}A}{\Sigma A} = \frac{96.0}{48.0} = 2.00 \text{ in.} \quad \textbf{Ans}$$

***9-64.** Locate the centroid $\bar{y}$ of the cross-sectional area of the beam constructed from a channel and a plate. Assume all corners are square and neglect the size of the weld at A.

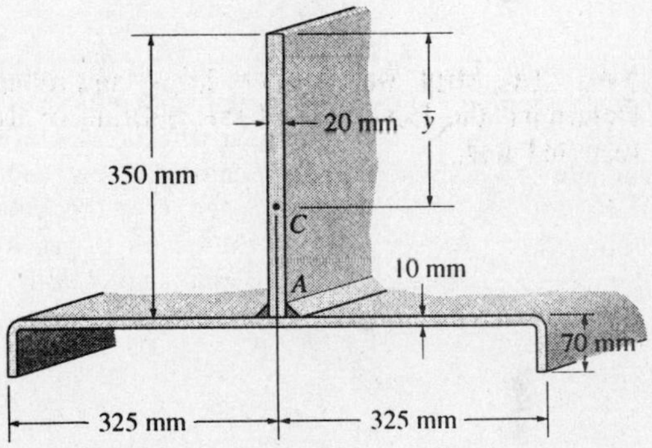

Centroid : The area of each segment and its respective centroid are tabulated below.

Segment	A (mm^2)	$\tilde{y}$ (mm)	$\tilde{y}A$ (mm^3)
1	350(20)	175	1 225 000
2	630(10)	355	2 236 500
3	70(20)	385	539 000
Σ	14 700		4 000 500

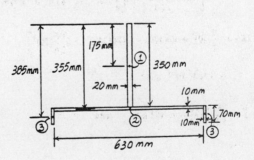

Thus,

$$\bar{y} = \frac{\Sigma\tilde{y}A}{\Sigma A} = \frac{4\,000\,500}{14\,700} = 272.14 \text{ mm} = 272 \text{ mm} \quad \textbf{Ans}$$

9-65. Locate the centroid $(\bar{x}, \bar{y})$ of the member's cross-sectional area.

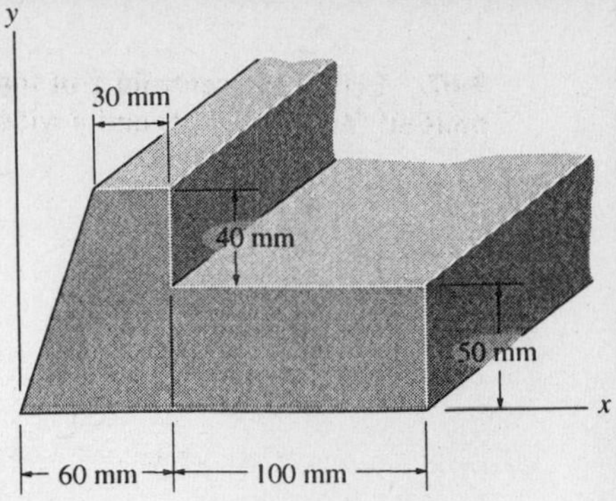

Centroid **:** The area of each segment and its respective centroid are tabulated below.

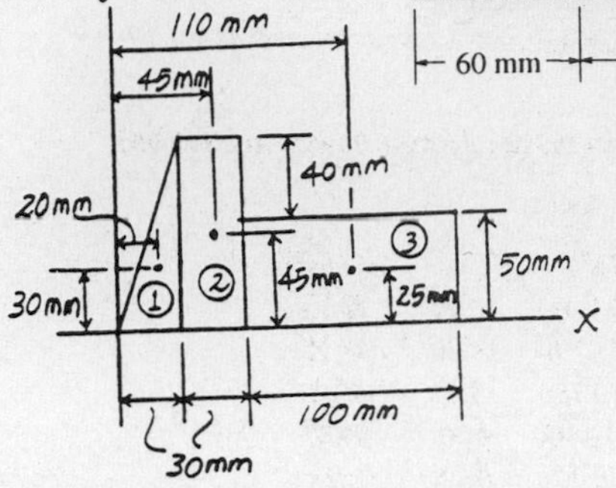

Segment	$A\ (\text{mm}^2)$	$\tilde{x}\ (\text{mm})$	$\tilde{y}\ (\text{mm})$	$\tilde{x}A\ (\text{mm}^3)$	$\tilde{y}A\ (\text{mm}^3)$
1	$\frac{1}{2}(30)(90)$	20	30	27 000	40 500
2	30(90)	45	45	121 500	121 500
3	100(50)	110	25	550 000	125 000
Σ	9 050			698 500	287 000

Thus,

$$\bar{x} = \frac{\Sigma\tilde{x}A}{\Sigma A} = \frac{698\ 500}{9\ 050} = 77.18 \text{ mm} = 77.2 \text{ mm} \qquad \textbf{Ans}$$

$$\bar{y} = \frac{\Sigma\tilde{y}A}{\Sigma A} = \frac{287\ 000}{9\ 050} = 31.71 \text{ mm} = 31.7 \text{ mm} \qquad \textbf{Ans}$$

9-66. The car rests on four scales and in this position the scale readings of both the front and rear tires are shown by F_A and F_B. When the rear wheels are elevated to a height of 3 ft above the front scales, the new readings of the front wheels are also recorded. Use this data to compute the location $\bar{x}$ and $\bar{y}$ to the center of gravity G of the car. The tires each have a diameter of 1.98 ft.

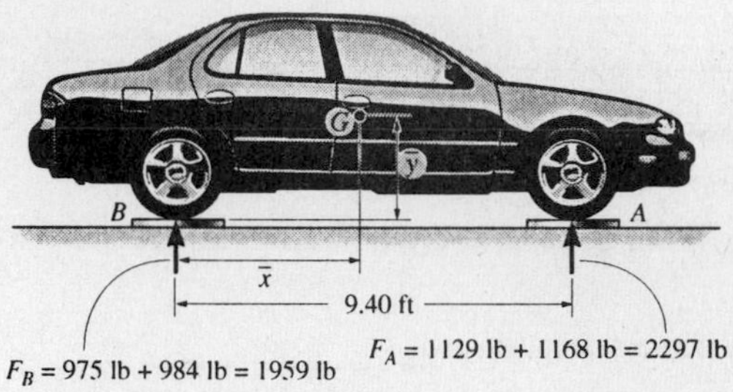

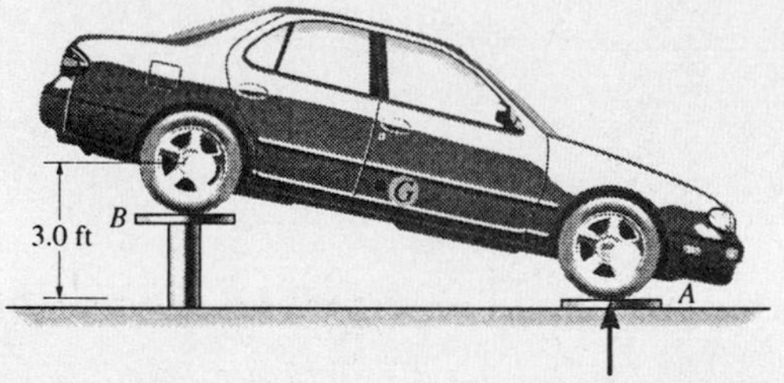

In horizontal position

$W = 1959 + 2297 = 4256$ lb

$\curvearrowleft +\Sigma M_O = 0; \quad 2297(9.40) - 4256\,\bar{x} = 0$

$\bar{x} = 5.0733 = 5.07$ ft **Ans**

$\theta = \sin^{-1}\left(\frac{3 - 0.990}{9.40}\right) = 12.347°$

$+\Sigma M_B = 0; \quad 2576(9.40 \cos 12.347°) - 4256 \cos 12.347°(5.0733)$

$- 4256 \sin 12.347°\,\bar{y}' = 0$

$\bar{y}' = 2.85$ ft

$\bar{y} = 2.815 + 0.990 = 3.80$ ft **Ans**

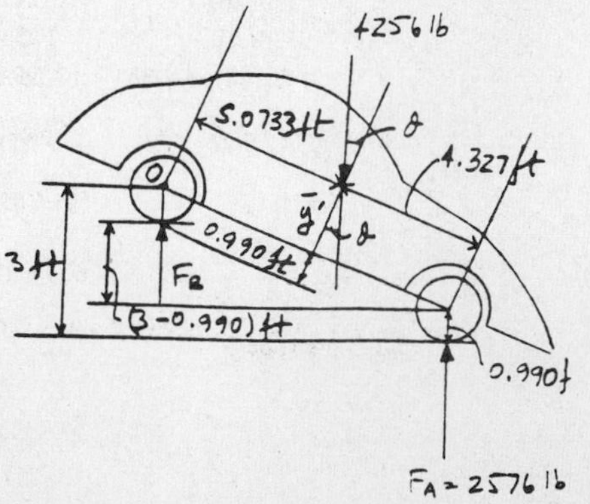

9-67. Locate the centroid $\bar{y}$ of the beam's cross-section built up from a channel and a wide-flange beam.

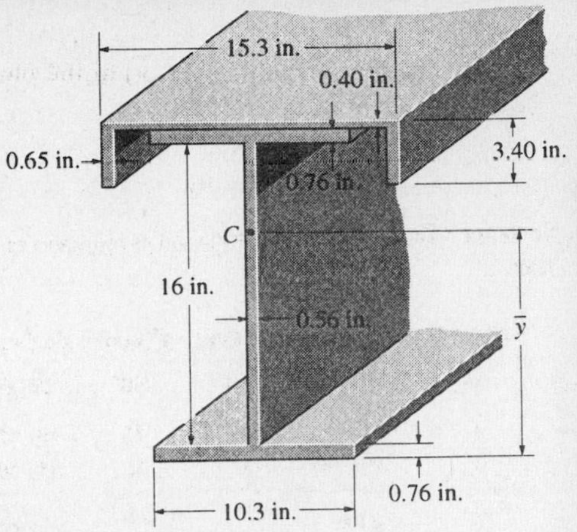

Centroid **:** The area of each segment and its respective centroid are tabulated below.

Segment	A (in^2)	$\tilde{y}$ (in.)	$\tilde{y}A$ (in^3)
1	14.0(0.4)	16.20	90.72
2	3.40(1.30)	14.70	64.97
3	10.3(0.76)	15.62	122.27
4	14.48(0.56)	8.00	64.87
5	10.3(0.76)	0.38	2.97
Σ	33.78		345.81

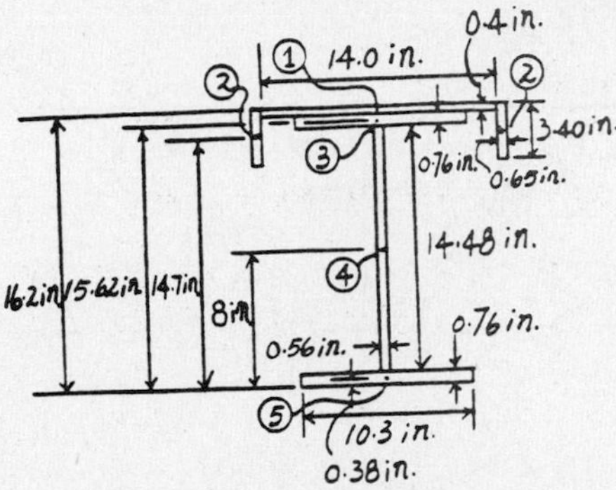

Thus,

$$\bar{y} = \frac{\Sigma\tilde{y}A}{\Sigma A} = \frac{345.81}{33.78} = 10.24 \text{ in.} = 10.2 \text{ in.} \qquad \textbf{Ans}$$

***9-68.** Locate the centroid $\bar{y}$ of the bulb-tee cross section.

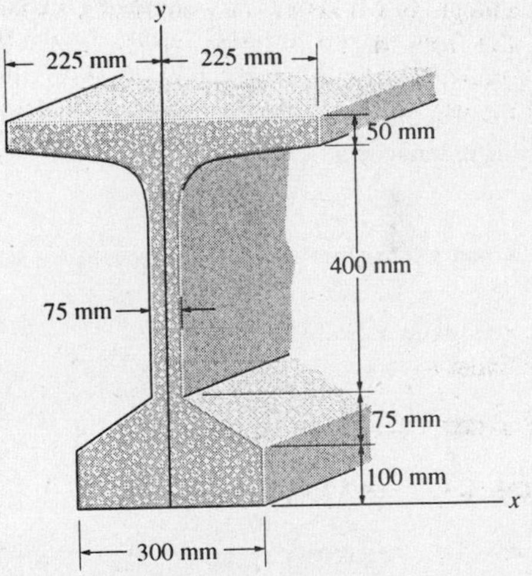

Centroid **:** The area of each segment and its respective centroid are tabulated below.

Segment	A (mm^2)	$\tilde{y}$ (mm)	$\tilde{y}A$ (mm^3)
1	450(50)	600	13 500 000
2	475(75)	337.5	12 023 437.5
3	$\frac{1}{2}(225)(75)$	125	1 054 687.5
4	300(100)	50	1 500 000
Σ	96 562.5		28 078 125

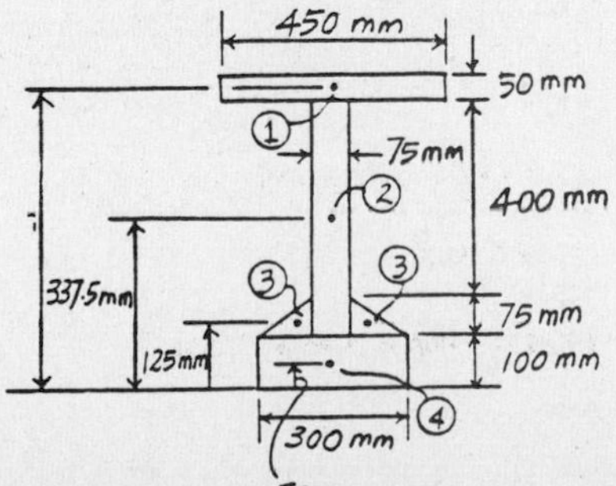

Thus,

$$\bar{y} = \frac{\Sigma\tilde{y}A}{\Sigma A} = \frac{28\ 078\ 125}{96\ 562.5} = 290.78 \text{ mm} = 291 \text{ mm} \qquad \textbf{Ans}$$

9-69. Uniform blocks having a length L and mass m are stacked one on top of the other, with each block overhanging the other by a distance d, as shown. If the blocks are glued together, so that they will not topple over, determine the location $\bar{x}$ of the center of mass of a pile of n blocks.

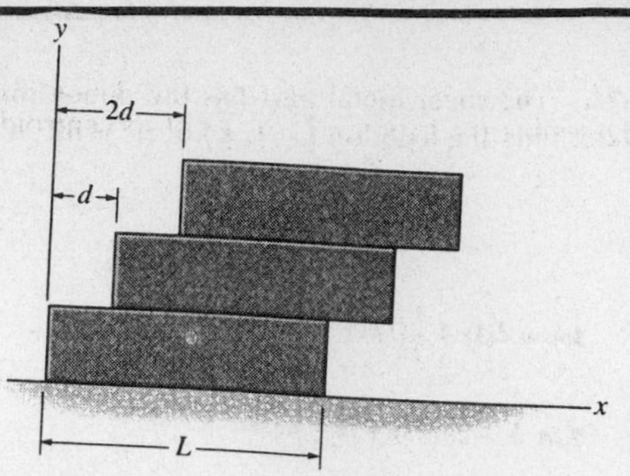

$n = 1$: $\quad \bar{x} = \frac{L}{2} = \frac{L}{2} + 0\left(\frac{d}{2}\right)$

$n = 2$: $\quad \bar{x} = \dfrac{\frac{L}{2}(W) + \left(\frac{L}{2} + d\right)W}{2W}$

$$= \frac{L}{4} + \frac{L}{4} + \frac{d}{2} = \frac{L}{2} + (1)\frac{d}{2}$$

$n = 3$: $\quad \bar{x} = \dfrac{\frac{L}{2}(W) + \left(\frac{L}{2} + d\right)W + \left(\frac{L}{2} + 2d\right)W}{3W}$

$$= \frac{L}{6} + \frac{L}{6} + \frac{d}{3} + \frac{L}{6} + \frac{2}{3}d = \frac{L}{2} + 2\left(\frac{d}{2}\right)$$

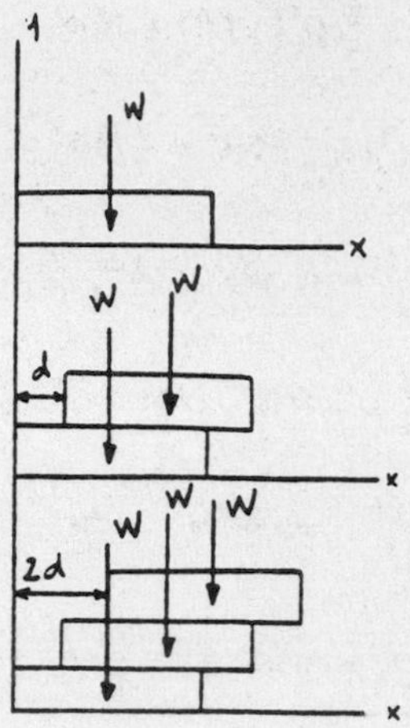

In general :

$$\bar{x} = \frac{L}{2} + (n-1)\left(\frac{d}{2}\right) = \frac{L + (n-1)d}{2} \qquad \textbf{Ans}$$

9-70. Uniform blocks having a length L and mass m are stacked one on top of the other, with each block overhanging the other by a distance d, as shown. Show that the maximum number of blocks which can be stacked in this manner is $n < L/d$.

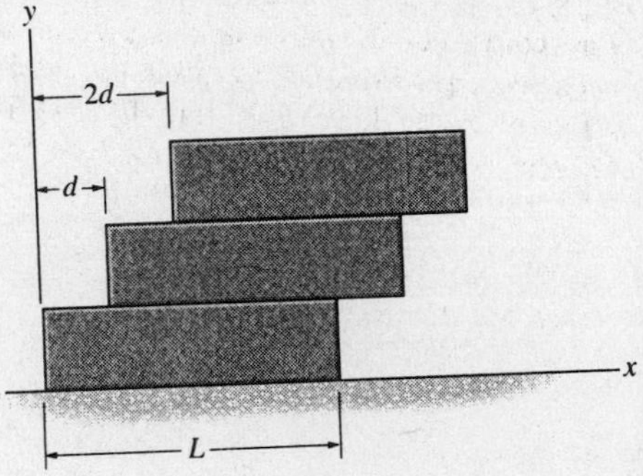

Bottom block will not tip over. Stack above bottom will tip if center of mass is beyond $\bar{x} > L$.

Also, blocks cannot be stacked if $d > \frac{L}{2}$.

$n = 2$: $\quad \bar{x} = \frac{L}{2} + d = \frac{L}{2} + 2\left(\frac{d}{2}\right)$

$n = 3$: $\quad \bar{x} = \dfrac{\left(d + \frac{L}{2}\right)W + \left(2d + \frac{L}{2}\right)W}{2W} = \frac{L}{2} + 3\left(\frac{d}{2}\right)$

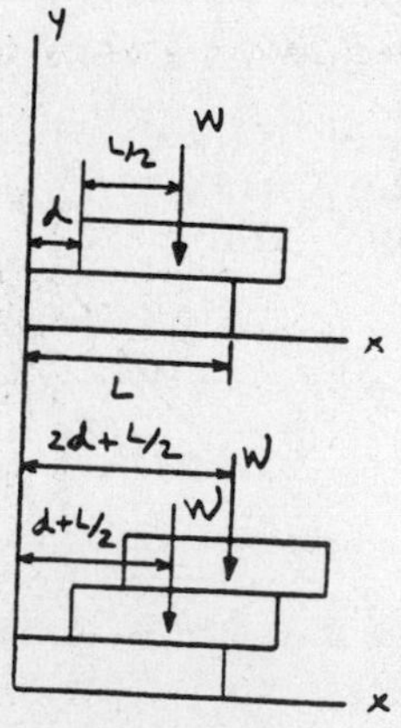

In general :

$$\bar{x} = \frac{L}{2} + n\left(\frac{d}{2}\right)$$

For stable stack :

$$\bar{x} = \frac{L}{2} + n\left(\frac{d}{2}\right) \le L$$

$$n \le \frac{L}{d} \qquad \textbf{Ans}$$

9-71. The sheet metal part has the dimensions shown. Determine the location $(\bar{x}, \bar{y}, \bar{z})$ of its centroid.

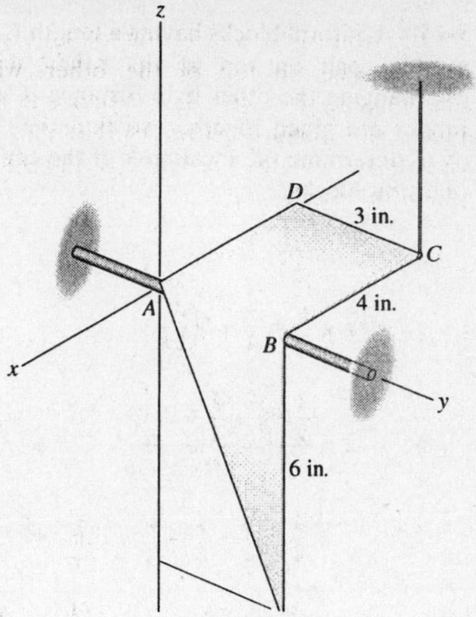

$$\Sigma A = 4(3) + \frac{1}{2}(3)(6) = 21 \text{ in}^2$$

$$\Sigma \tilde{x}A = -2(4)(3) + 0\left(\frac{1}{2}\right)(3)(6) = -24 \text{ in}^3$$

$$\Sigma \tilde{y}A = 1.5(4)(3) + \frac{2}{3}(3)\left(\frac{1}{2}\right)(3)(6) = 36 \text{ in}^3$$

$$\Sigma \tilde{z}A = 0(4)(3) - \frac{1}{3}(6)\left(\frac{1}{2}\right)(3)(6) = -18 \text{ in}^3$$

$$\bar{x} = \frac{\Sigma \tilde{x}A}{\Sigma A} = \frac{-24}{21} = -1.14 \text{ in.} \quad \textbf{Ans}$$

$$\bar{y} = \frac{\Sigma \tilde{y}A}{\Sigma A} = \frac{36}{21} = 1.71 \text{ in.} \quad \textbf{Ans}$$

$$\bar{z} = \frac{\Sigma \tilde{z}A}{\Sigma A} = \frac{-18}{21} = -0.857 \text{ in.} \quad \textbf{Ans}$$

***9-72.** The sheet metal part has a weight per unit area of 2 lb/ft^2 and is supported by the smooth rod and at C. If the cord is cut, the part will rotate about the y axis until it reaches equilibrium. Determine the equilibrium angle of tilt, measured downward from the negative x axis, that AD makes with the $-x$ axis.

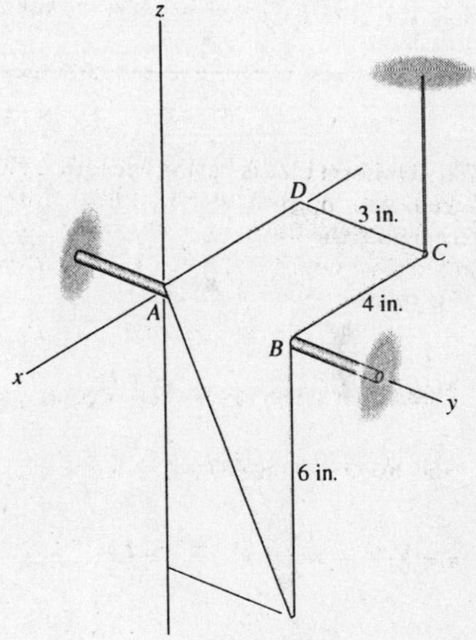

Since the material is homogeneous, the center of gravity coincides with the centroid.

See solution to Prob. 9-71.

$$\theta = \tan^{-1}\left(\frac{1.14}{0.857}\right) = 53.1° \quad \textbf{Ans}$$

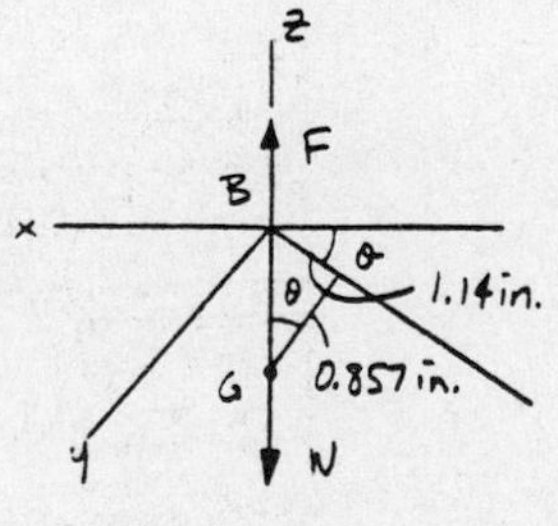

9-73. Locate the center of gravity $(\bar{x}, \bar{z})$ of the sheet-metal bracket if the material is homogeneous and has a constant thickness. If the bracket is resting on the horizontal x-y plane shown, determine the maximum angle of tilt θ which it can have before it falls over, i.e., begins to rotate about the y axis.

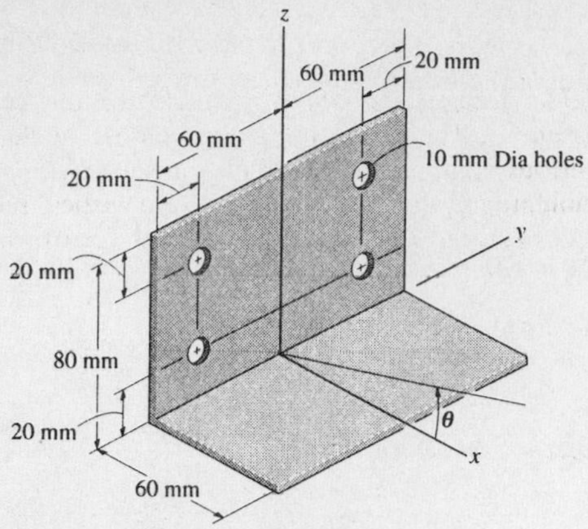

Centroid **:** The area of each segment and its respective centroid are tabulated below.

Segment	$A\,(\text{mm}^2)$	$\tilde{x}\,(\text{mm})$	$\tilde{z}\,(\text{mm})$	$\tilde{x}A\,(\text{mm}^3)$	$\tilde{z}A\,(\text{mm}^3)$
1	120(80)	0	40	0	384 000
2	120(60)	30	0	216 000	0
3	$-2\left[\frac{\pi}{4}(10^2)\right]$	0	60	0	−9424.78
4	$-2\left[\frac{\pi}{4}(10^2)\right]$	0	20	0	−3141.59
Σ	16 485.84			216 000	371 433.63

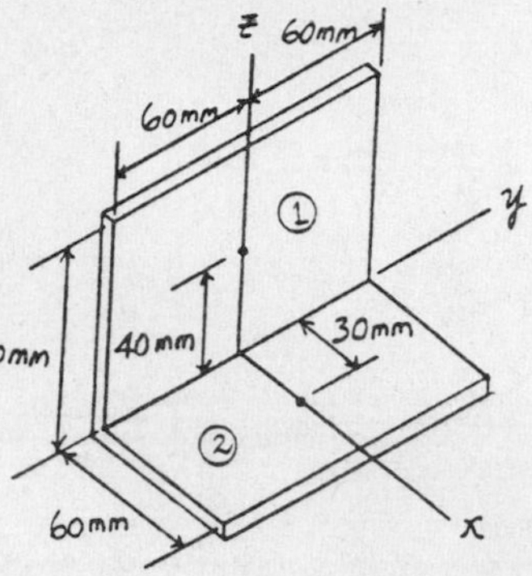

Thus,

$$\bar{x} = \frac{\Sigma\tilde{x}A}{\Sigma A} = \frac{216\,000}{16\,485.84} = 13.10 \text{ mm} = 13.1 \text{ mm} \qquad \textbf{Ans}$$

$$\bar{z} = \frac{\Sigma\tilde{z}A}{\Sigma A} = \frac{371\,433.63}{16\,485.84} = 22.53 \text{ mm} = 22.5 \text{ mm} \qquad \textbf{Ans}$$

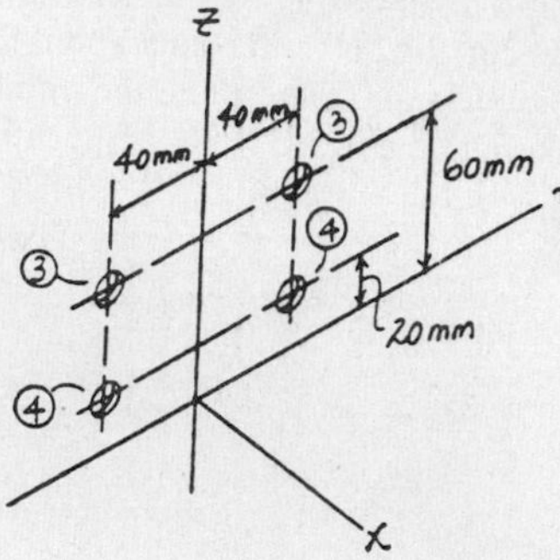

Equilibrium **:** In order for the bracket not to rotate about y axis, the weight of the bracket must coincide with the reaction. From the FBD,

$$\theta = \tan^{-1}\frac{13.10}{22.53} = 30.2° \qquad \textbf{Ans}$$

9-74. Locate the center of mass for the compressor assembly. The locations of the centers of mass of the various components and their masses are indicated and tabulated in the figure. What are the vertical reactions at blocks A and B needed to support the platform?

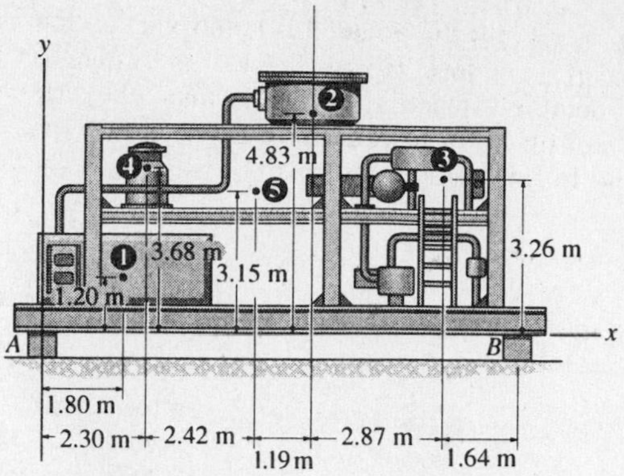

1	Instrument panel	230 kg
2	Filter system	183 kg
3	Piping assembly	120 kg
4	Liquid storage	85 kg
5	Structural framework	468 kg

Centroid **:** The mass of each component of the compressor and its respective centroid are tabulated below.

Component	m (kg)	$\tilde{x}$ (m)	$\tilde{y}$ (m)	$\tilde{x}m$ (kg · m)	$\tilde{y}m$ (kg · m)
1	230	1.80	1.20	414.00	276.00
2	183	5.91	4.83	1081.53	883.89
3	120	8.78	3.26	1053.60	391.20
4	85	2.30	3.68	195.50	312.80
5	468	4.72	3.15	2208.96	1474.20
Σ	1086			4953.59	3338.09

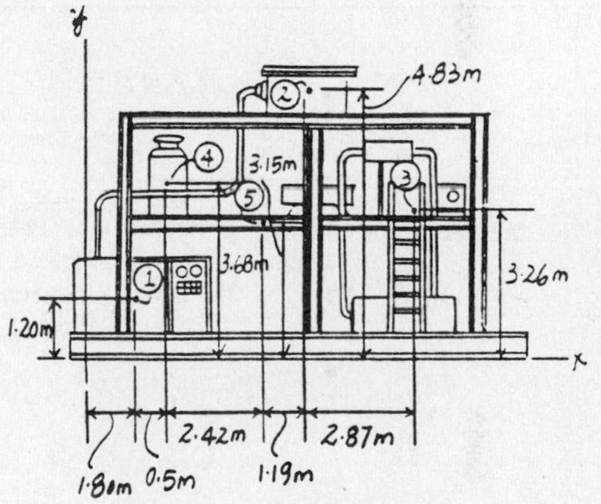

Thus,

$$\bar{x} = \frac{\Sigma \tilde{x}m}{\Sigma m} = \frac{4953.59}{1086} = 4.561 \text{ m} = 4.56 \text{ m} \quad \textbf{Ans}$$

$$\bar{y} = \frac{\Sigma \tilde{y}m}{\Sigma m} = \frac{3338.09}{1086} = 3.074 \text{ m} = 3.07 \text{ m} \quad \textbf{Ans}$$

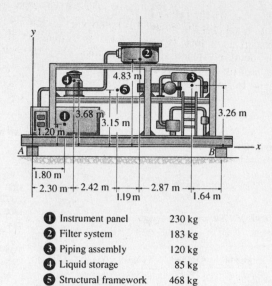

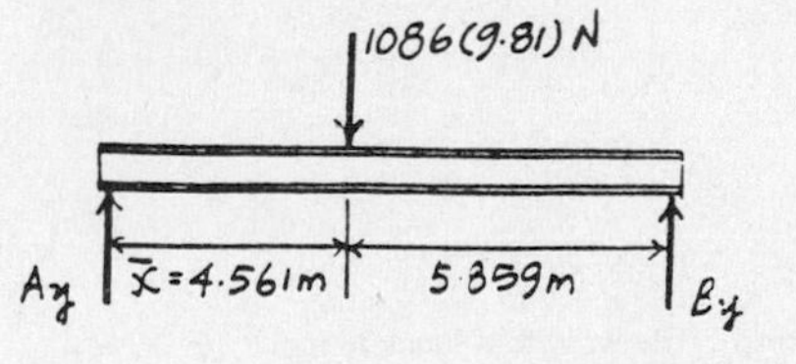

Equations of Equilibrium :

$$+\Sigma M_A = 0; \quad B_y(10.42) - 1086(9.81)(4.561) = 0$$

$$B_y = 4663.60 \text{ N} = 4.66 \text{ kN} \quad \textbf{Ans}$$

$$+\uparrow \Sigma F_y = 0; \quad A_y + 4663.60 - 1086(9.81) = 0$$

$$A_y = 5990.06 \text{ N} = 5.99 \text{ kN} \quad \textbf{Ans}$$

9-75. Major floor loadings in a shop are caused by the weights of the objects shown. Each force acts through its respective center of gravity G. Locate the center of gravity $(\bar{x}, \bar{y})$ of all these components.

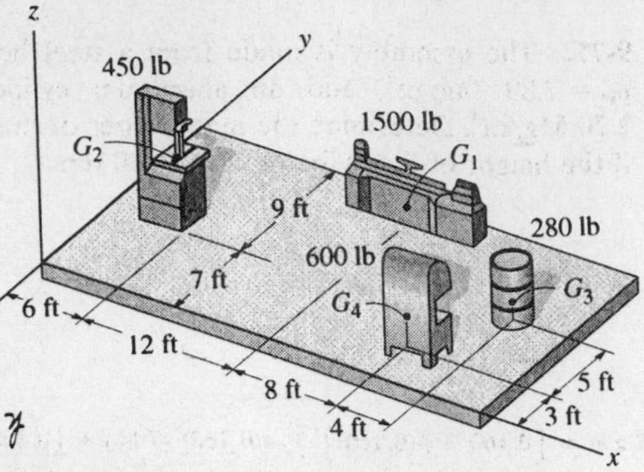

Centroid **:** The floor loadings on the floor and its respective centroid are tabulated below.

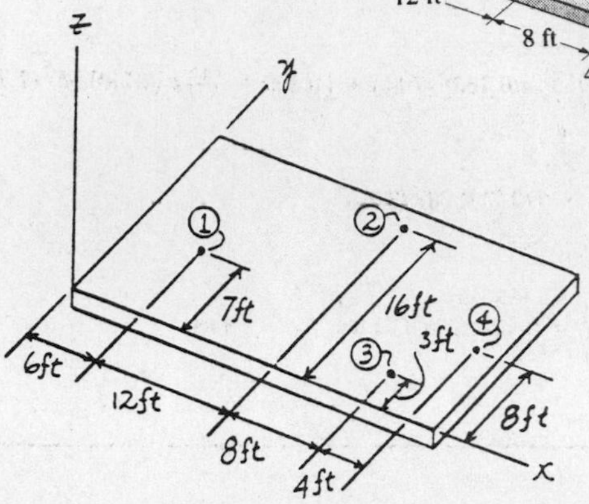

Loading	W (lb)	$\bar{x}$ (ft)	$\bar{y}$ (ft)	$\bar{x}W$ (lb·ft)	$\bar{y}W$ (lb·ft)
1	450	6	7	2700	3150
2	1500	18	16	27000	24000
3	600	26	3	15600	1800
4	280	30	8	8400	2240
Σ	2830			53700	31190

Thus,

$$\bar{x} = \frac{\Sigma \bar{x}W}{\Sigma W} = \frac{53700}{2830} = 18.98 \text{ ft} = 19.0 \text{ ft} \qquad \textbf{Ans}$$

$$\bar{y} = \frac{\Sigma \bar{y}W}{\Sigma W} = \frac{31190}{2830} = 11.02 \text{ ft} = 11.0 \text{ ft} \qquad \textbf{Ans}$$

***9-76.** Locate the center of gravity of the two-block assembly. The specific weights of the materials A and B are $\gamma_A = 150 \text{ lb/ft}^3$ and $\gamma_B = 400 \text{ lb/ft}^3$, respectively.

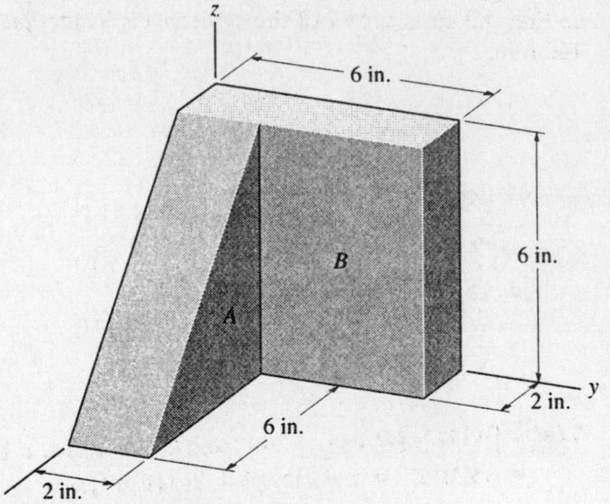

Centroid **:** The weight of block A and B are $W_A = \frac{1}{2}\left(\frac{6}{12}\right)\left(\frac{6}{12}\right)\left(\frac{2}{12}\right)(150) = 3.125$ lb and $W_B = \left(\frac{6}{12}\right)\left(\frac{6}{12}\right)\left(\frac{2}{12}\right)(400) = 16.67$ lb. The weight of each block and its respective centroid are tabulated below.

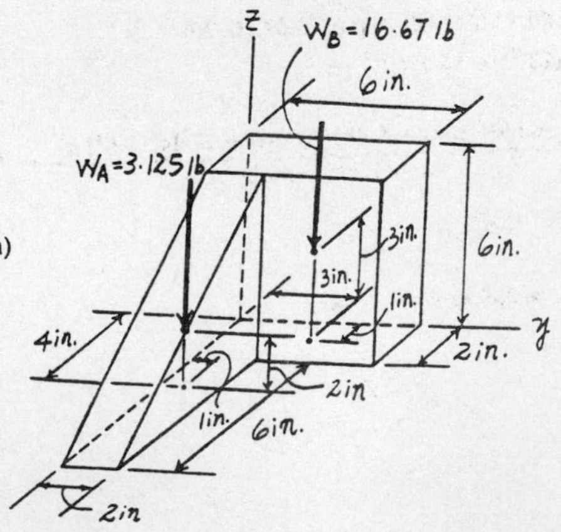

Block	W (lb)	$\bar{x}$ (in.)	$\bar{y}$ (in.)	$\bar{z}$ (in.)	$\bar{x}W$ (lb·in)	$\bar{y}W$ (lb·in)	$\bar{z}W$ (lb·in)
A	3.125	4	1	2	12.5	3.125	6.25
B	16.667	1	3	3	16.667	50.0	50.0
Σ	19.792				29.167	53.125	56.25

Thus,

$$\bar{x} = \frac{\Sigma \bar{x}W}{\Sigma W} = \frac{29.167}{19.792} = 1.474 \text{ in.} = 1.47 \text{ in.} \qquad \textbf{Ans}$$

$$\bar{y} = \frac{\Sigma \bar{y}W}{\Sigma W} = \frac{53.125}{19.792} = 2.684 \text{ in.} = 2.68 \text{ in.} \qquad \textbf{Ans}$$

$$\bar{z} = \frac{\Sigma \bar{z}W}{\Sigma W} = \frac{56.25}{19.792} = 2.842 \text{ in.} = 2.84 \text{ in.} \qquad \textbf{Ans}$$

9-77. The assembly is made from a steel hemisphere, $\rho_{st} = 7.80\ \text{Mg/m}^3$, and an aluminum cylinder, $\rho_{al} = 2.70\ \text{Mg/m}^3$. Determine the mass center of the assembly if the height of the cylinder is $h = 200$ mm.

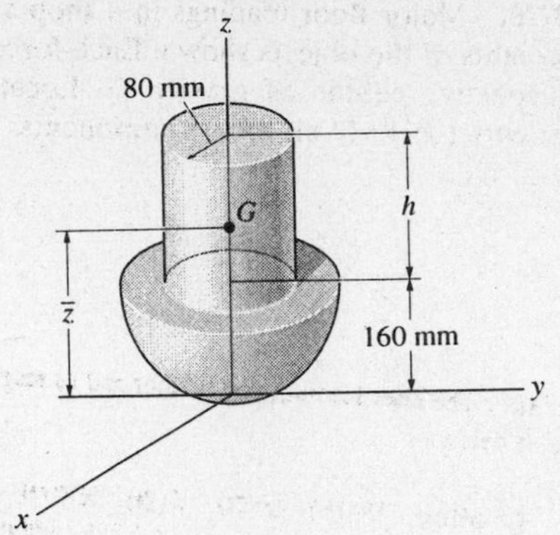

$$\Sigma \tilde{z} m = \left[0.160 - \tfrac{3}{8}(0.160)\right]\left(\tfrac{2}{3}\right)\pi(0.160)^3(7.80) + \left(0.160 + \tfrac{0.2}{2}\right)\pi(0.2)(0.08)^2(2.70)$$
$$= 9.51425(10^{-3})\ \text{Mg}\cdot\text{m}$$

$$\Sigma m = \left(\tfrac{2}{3}\right)\pi(0.160)^3(7.80) + \pi(0.2)(0.08)^2(2.70)$$
$$= 77.7706(10^{-3})\ \text{Mg}$$

$$\bar{z} = \frac{\Sigma \tilde{z} m}{\Sigma m} = \frac{9.51425(10^{-3})}{77.7706(10^{-3})} = 0.122\ \text{m} = 122\ \text{mm}$$ **Ans**

9-78. The assembly is made from a steel hemisphere, $\rho_{st} = 7.80\ \text{Mg/m}^3$, and an aluminum cylinder, $\rho_{al} = 2.70\ \text{Mg/m}^3$. Determine the height h of the cylinder so that the mass center of the assembly is located at $\bar{z} = 160$ mm.

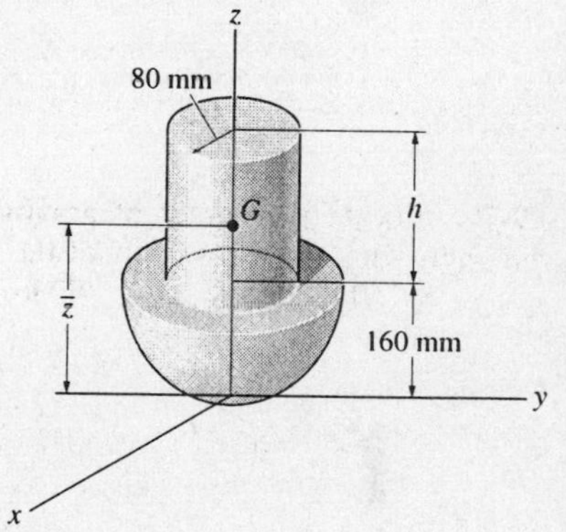

$$\Sigma \tilde{z} m = \left[0.160 - \tfrac{3}{8}(0.160)\right]\left(\tfrac{2}{3}\right)\pi(0.160)^3(7.80) + \left(0.160 + \tfrac{h}{2}\right)\pi(h)(0.08)^2(2.70)$$
$$= 6.691(10^{-3}) + 8.686(10^{-3})\,h + 27.143(10^{-3})\,h^2$$

$$\Sigma m = \left(\tfrac{2}{3}\right)\pi(0.160)^3(7.80) + \pi(h)(0.08)^2(2.70)$$
$$= 66.91(10^{-3}) + 54.29(10^{-3})\,h$$

$$\bar{z} = \frac{\Sigma \tilde{z} m}{\Sigma m} = \frac{6.691(10^{-3}) + 8.686(10^{-3})\,h + 27.143(10^{-3})\,h^2}{66.91(10^{-3}) + 54.29(10^{-3})\,h} = 0.160$$

Solving

$h = 0.385\ \text{m} = 385\ \text{mm}$ **Ans**

9-79. Locate the centroid $\bar{z}$ of the top made from a hemisphere and a cone.

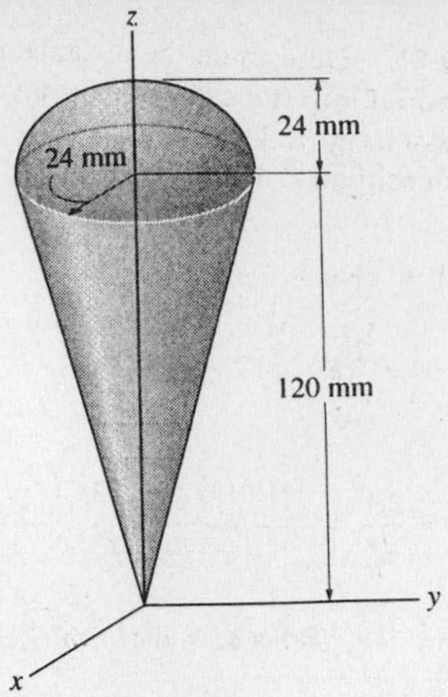

Centroid : The volume of each segment and its respective centroid are tabulated below.

Segment	$V\,(\text{mm}^3)$	$\bar{z}\,(\text{mm})$	$\bar{z}V\,(\text{mm}^4)$
1	$\frac{2}{3}\pi(24^3)$	129	$1.188864\pi(10^6)$
2	$\frac{1}{3}\pi(24^2)(120)$	90	$2.0736\pi(10^6)$
Σ	$32.256\pi(10^3)$		$3.262464\pi(10^6)$

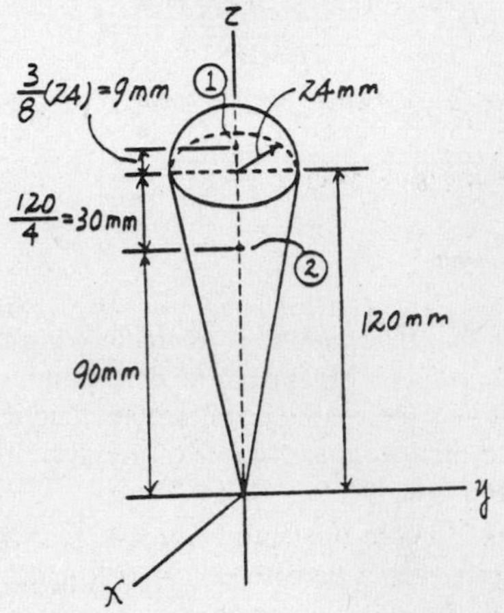

Thus,

$$\bar{z} = \frac{\Sigma \bar{z}V}{\Sigma V} = \frac{3.262464\pi(10^6)}{32.256\pi(10^3)} = 101.14 \text{ mm} = 101 \text{ mm} \quad \textbf{Ans}$$

***9-80.** Determine the distance $\bar{x}$ to the centroid of the solid which consists of a cylinder with a hole of length $h = 50$ mm bored into its base.

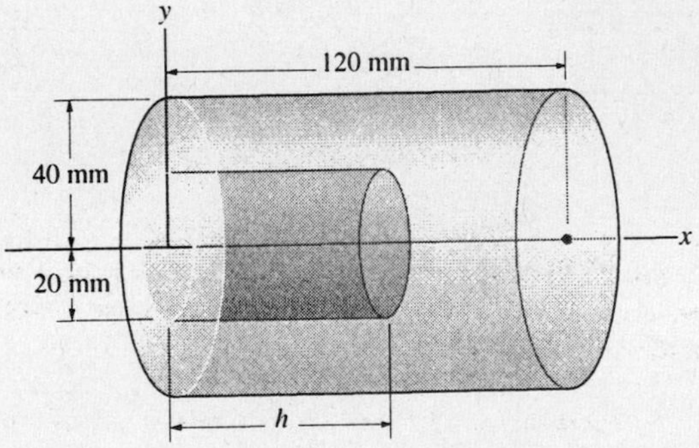

$$\Sigma V = \pi(40)^2(120) - \pi(20)^2(50) = 172\left(10^3\right)\pi \text{ mm}^3$$

$$\Sigma \tilde{x}V = 60(\pi)(40)^2(120) - 25(\pi)(20)^2(50) = 11.02\left(10^6\right)\pi \text{ mm}^4$$

$$\bar{x} = \frac{\Sigma \tilde{x}V}{\Sigma V} = \frac{11.02(10^6)\pi}{172(10^3)\pi} = 64.1 \text{ mm} \quad \textbf{Ans}$$

9-81. Determine the distance h to which a hole must be bored into the cylinder so that the center of mass of the assembly is located at $\bar{x} = 64$ mm. The material has a density of 8 Mg/m^3.

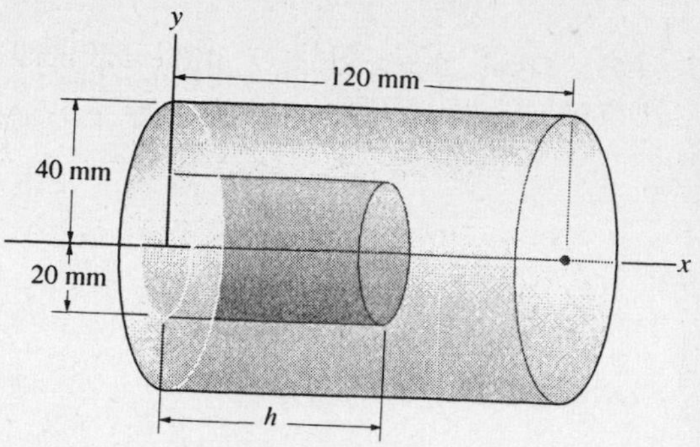

$$\Sigma V = \pi r_2^2 d - \pi r_1^2 h$$

$$\Sigma \tilde{x} V = \frac{d}{2}(\pi)(r_2^2)\,d - \frac{h}{2}(\pi)(r_1^2)\,h$$

$$\bar{x} = \frac{\Sigma \tilde{x} V}{\Sigma V} = \frac{\frac{d^2}{2}(\pi)(r_2^2) - \frac{h^2}{2}(\pi)(r_1^2)}{\pi r_2^2 d - \pi r_1^2 h}$$

$$2\bar{x}\,(r_2^2 d) - 2\bar{x}(r_1^2 h) = d^2 r_2^2 - h^2 r_1^2$$

$$h^2 - 2\bar{x}h + d\,(2\bar{x} - d)\left(\frac{r_2}{r_1}\right)^2 = 0$$

Set $\bar{x} = 64$ mm, $r_2 = 40$ mm, $r_1 = 20$ mm, $d = 120$ mm

$$h^2 - 128h + 3840 = 0$$

Solving,

$h = 80$ mm **Ans** or $h = 48$ mm **Ans**

9-82. Locate the center of mass $\bar{z}$ of the assembly. The material has a density of $\rho = 3$ Mg/m^3. There is a hole bored through the center.

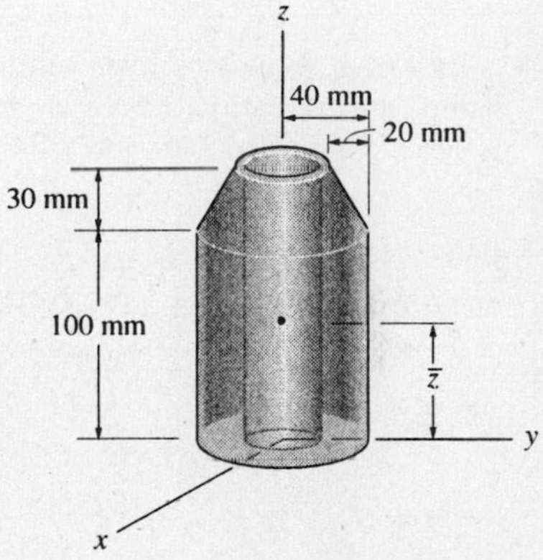

Centroid : Since the density is the same for the whole material, the centroid of the volume coincide with centriod of the mass. The volume of each segment and its respective centroid are tabulated below.

Segment	$V\,(\text{mm}^3)$	$\tilde{z}\,(\text{mm})$	$\tilde{z}V\,(\text{mm}^4)$
1	$\frac{1}{3}\pi(40^2)(60)$	115	$3.68\pi(10^6)$
2	$\pi(40^2)(100)$	50	$8.00\pi(10^6)$
3	$-\frac{1}{3}\pi(20^2)(30)$	137.5	$-0.550\pi(10^6)$
4	$-\pi(15^2)(130)$	65	$-1.90125\pi(10^6)$
Σ	$158.75\pi(10^3)$		$9.22875\pi(10^6)$

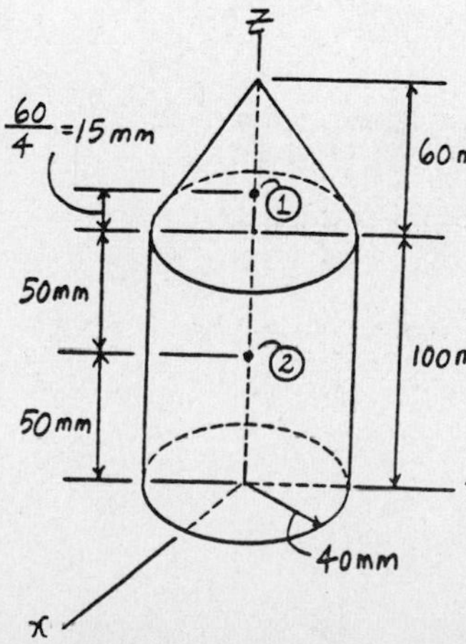

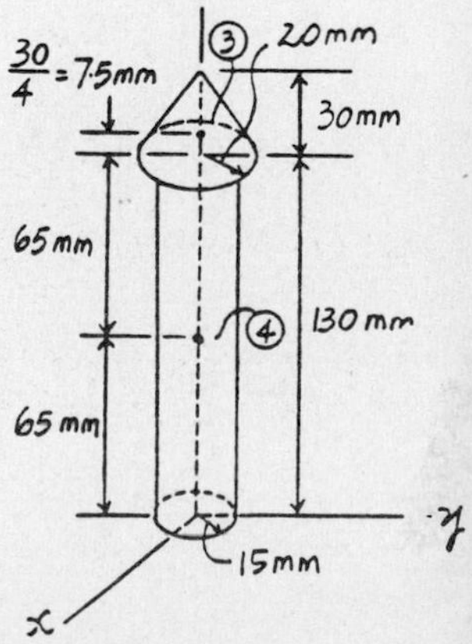

Thus,

$$\bar{z} = \frac{\Sigma \tilde{z} V}{\Sigma V} = \frac{9.22875\pi(10^6)}{158.75\pi(10^3)} = 58.13 \text{ mm} = 58.1 \text{ mm} \quad \textbf{Ans}$$

9-83. A hole having a radius r is to be drilled in the center of the homogeneous block. Determine the depth h of the hole so that the center of gravity G is as low as possible.

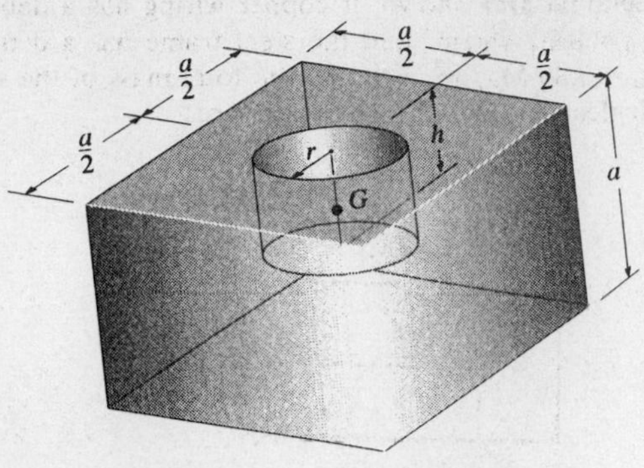

$$\Sigma V = a^3 - \pi r^2 h$$

$$\Sigma \tilde{z} V = \left(\tfrac{a}{2}\right) a^3 - \left(\tfrac{h}{2}\right)\left[\pi r^2 h\right] = \tfrac{1}{2}\left(a^4 - \pi r^2 h^2\right)$$

$$\bar{z} = \frac{\Sigma \tilde{z} V}{\Sigma V} = \frac{\frac{1}{2}(a^4 - \pi r^2 h^2)}{a^3 - \pi r^2 h} = \frac{a^4 - \pi r^2 h^2}{2(a^3 - \pi r^2 h)}$$

$$\frac{d\bar{z}}{dh} = \frac{1}{2}\left[\frac{(a^3 - \pi r^2 h)(-2\pi r^2 h) - (a^4 - \pi r^2 h^2)(-\pi r^2)}{(a^3 - \pi r^2 h)^2}\right] = 0$$

$$\pi r^2 h^2 - 2a^3 h + a^4 = 0$$

Solving for the smaller root,

$$h = \frac{2a^3 - \sqrt{(2a^3)^2 - 4(\pi r^2) a^4}}{2(\pi r^2)}$$

$$= \frac{a^3 - a^2\sqrt{a^2 - \pi r^2}}{\pi r^2} \quad \textbf{Ans}$$

***9-84.** The process tank is used to store liquids during manufacturing. Estimate both the volume of the tank and its surface area. The tank has a flat top.

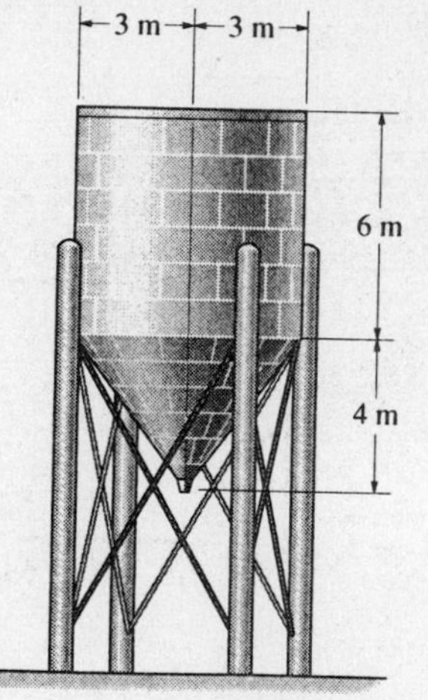

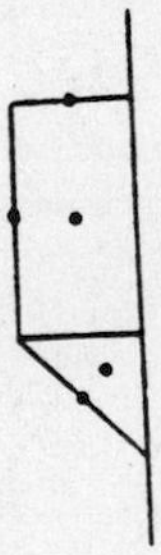

$$V = \Sigma \theta \bar{r} A = 2\pi\left[1\left(\frac{1}{2}\right)(3)(4) + 1.5(3)(6)\right] = 207 \text{ m}^3 \quad \textbf{Ans}$$

$$A = \Sigma \theta \bar{r} L = 2\pi[1.5(5) + 3(6) + 1.5(3)] = 188 \text{ m}^2 \quad \textbf{Ans}$$

9-85. The starter for an electric motor has the cross-sectional area shown. If copper wiring has a density of $\rho_{cu} = 8.90\ \text{Mg/m}^3$ and the steel frame has a density of $\rho_{st} = 7.80\ \text{Mg/m}^3$, estimate the total mass of the starter. Neglect the size of the copper wire.

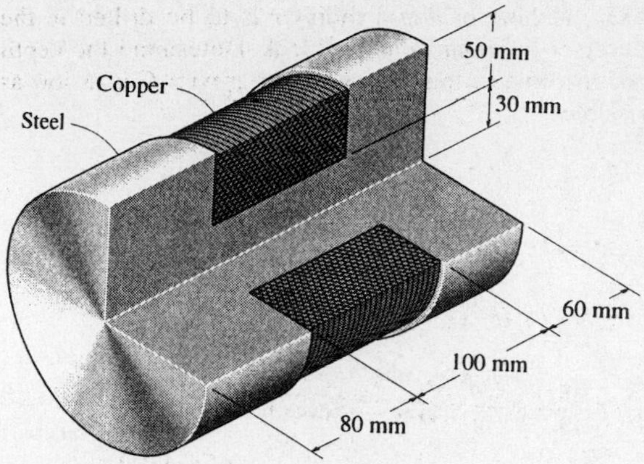

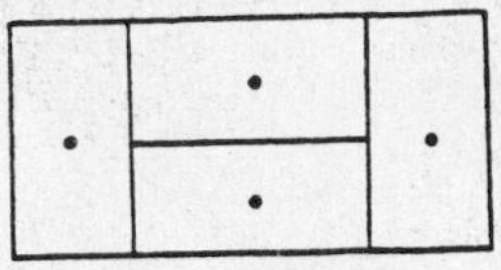

$$V_{st} = \Sigma\theta\bar{r}A = 2\pi[80(80)(40) + 60(80)(40) + 15(100)(30)]$$

$$= 986(10^3)\pi\ \text{mm}^3$$

$$V_{cu} = \theta\bar{r}A = 2\pi[55(100)(50)] = 550(10^3)\pi\ \text{mm}^3$$

$$m = \Sigma\rho V = \left[7.80(986\pi) + 8.90(550\pi)\right]\left(\frac{10^3}{10^9}\right) = 0.0395\ \text{Mg} = 39.5\ \text{kg} \qquad \textbf{Ans}$$

9-86. Determine the surface area and the volume of the ring formed by rotating the square about the vertical axis.

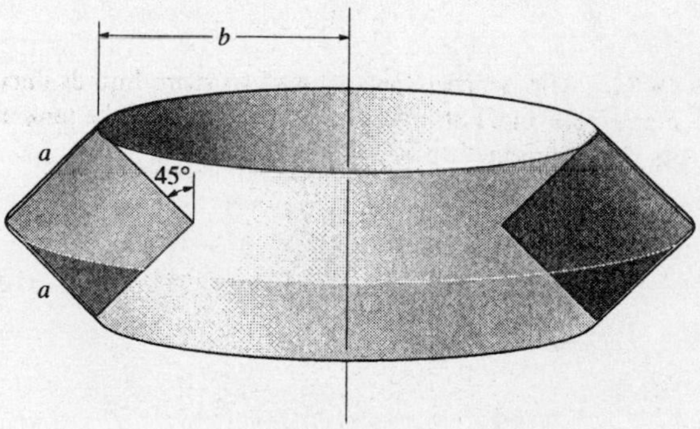

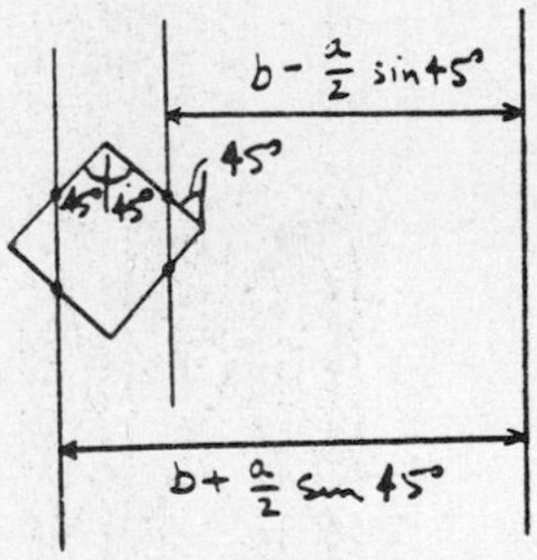

$$A = \Sigma\theta\bar{r}L = 2\left[2\pi\left(b - \frac{a}{2}\sin 45°\right)(a)\right] + 2\left[2\pi\left(b + \frac{a}{2}\sin 45°\right)(a)\right]$$

$$= 4\pi\left[ba - \frac{a^2}{2}\sin 45° + ba + \frac{a^2}{2}\sin 45°\right]$$

$$= 8\pi ba \qquad \textbf{Ans}$$

$$V = \Sigma\theta\bar{r}A = 2\pi(b)(a)^2 = 2\pi ba^2 \qquad \textbf{Ans}$$

9-87. A steel wheel has a diameter of 840 mm and a cross section as shown in the figure. Determine the total mass of the wheel if $\rho = 5\ \text{Mg/m}^3$.

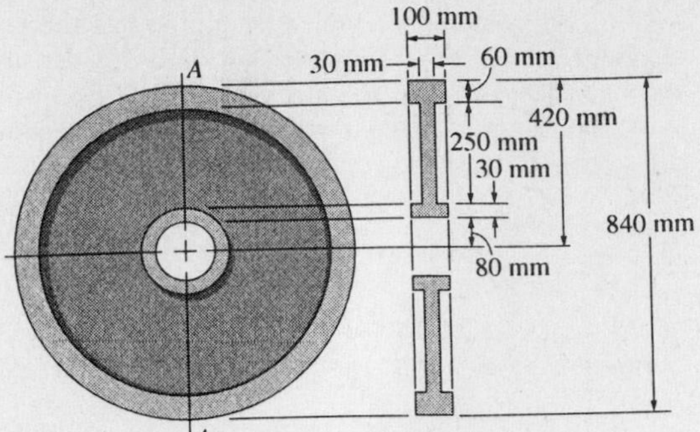

Volume **:** Applying the theorem of Pappus and Guldinus, Eq. 9–12, with $\theta = 2\pi$, $\bar{r}_1 = 0.095$ m, $\bar{r}_2 = 0.235$ m, $\bar{r}_3 = 0.39$ m, $A_1 = 0.1(0.03) = 0.003\ \text{m}^2$, $A_2 = 0.25(0.03) = 0.0075\ \text{m}^2$ and $A_3 = (0.1)(0.06) = 0.006\ \text{m}^2$, we have

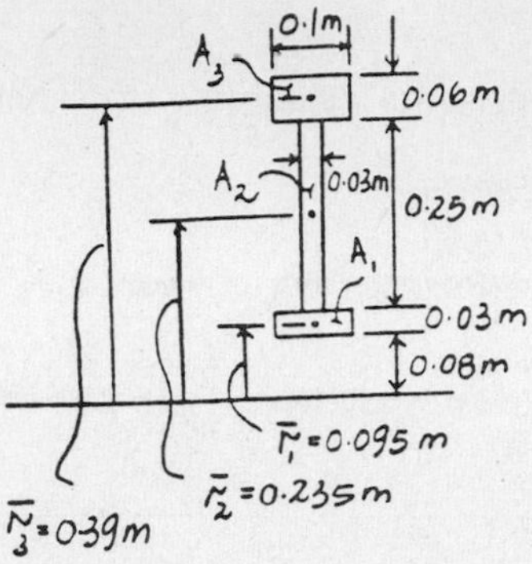

$$V = \theta\Sigma\bar{r}A = 2\pi[0.095(0.003) + 0.235(0.0075) + 0.39(0.006)]$$
$$= 8.775\pi\left(10^{-3}\right)\ \text{m}^3$$

The mass of the wheel is

$$m = \rho V = 5\left(10^3\right)\left[8.775\left(10^{-3}\right)\pi\right]$$
$$= 138\ \text{kg} \qquad \textbf{Ans}$$

***9-88.** The hopper is filled to its top with coal. Determine the volume of coal if the voids (air space) are 35 percent of the volume of the hopper.

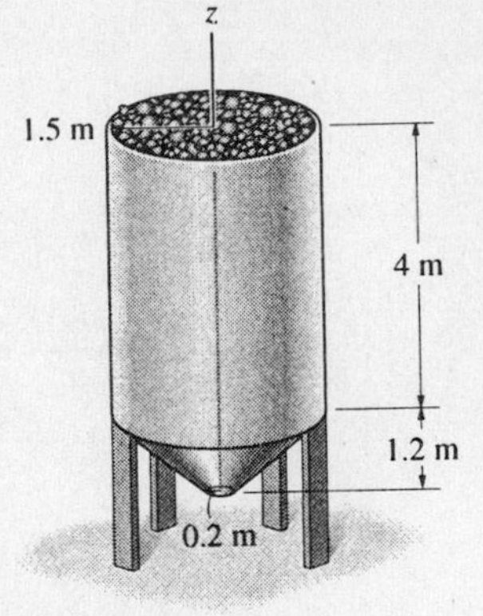

Volume **:** The volume of the hopper can be obtained by applying the theorem of Pappus and Guldinus, Eq. 9–12, with $\theta = 2\pi$, $\bar{r}_1 = 0.75$ m, $\bar{r}_2 = 0.6333$ m, $\bar{r}_3 = 0.1$ m, $A_1 = 1.5(4) = 6.00\ \text{m}^2$, $A_2 = \frac{1}{2}(1.3)(1.2) = 0.780\ \text{m}^2$ and $A_3 = (0.2)(1.2) = 0.240\ \text{m}^2$.

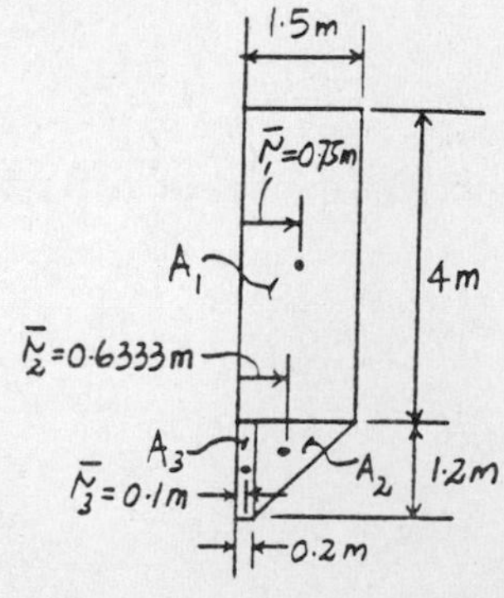

$$V_h = \theta\Sigma\bar{r}A = 2\pi[0.75(6.00) + 0.6333(0.780) + 0.1(0.240)]$$
$$= 10.036\pi\ \text{m}^3$$

The volume of the coal is

$$V_c = 0.65V_h = 0.65(10.036\pi) = 20.5\ \text{m}^3 \qquad \textbf{Ans}$$

9-89. The heat exchanger radiates thermal energy at the rate of 2500 kJ/h for each square meter of its surface area. Determine how many joules (J) are radiated within a 5-hour period.

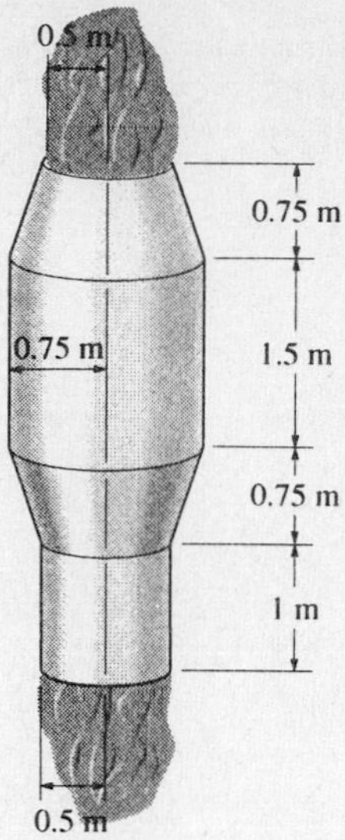

$$A = \Sigma\theta\bar{r}L = (2\pi)\left[2\left(\frac{0.75+0.5}{2}\right)\sqrt{(0.75)^2+(0.25)^2} + (0.75)(1.5) + (0.5)(1)\right]$$

$$= 16.419\ \text{m}^2$$

$$Q = 2500\left(10^3\right)\left(\frac{J}{h\cdot m^2}\right)\left(16.416\ \text{m}^2\right)(5\ \text{h}) = 205\ \text{MJ} \qquad \textbf{Ans}$$

9-90. A circular V-belt has an inner radius of 600 mm and the cross-sectional area shown. Determine the volume of material required to make the belt.

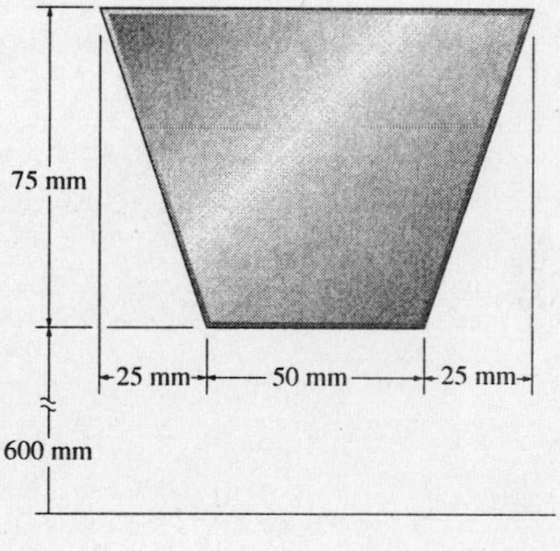

$$V = \Sigma\theta\bar{y}A = 2\pi\left[2(650)\left(\frac{1}{2}\right)(25)(75) + (637.5)(75)(50)\right]$$

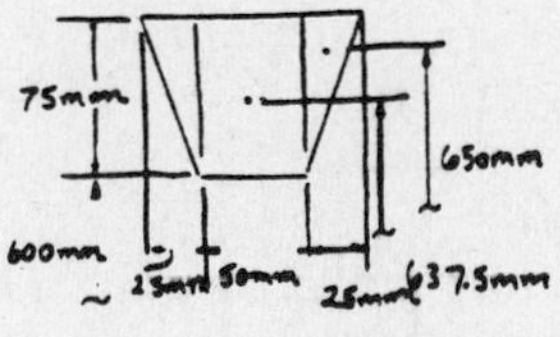

$$= 22.7\left(10^6\right)\ \text{mm}^3 \qquad \textbf{Ans}$$

9-91. The tank is fabricated from a hemisphere and cylindrical shell. Determine the vertical reactions that each of the four symmetrically placed legs exerts on the floor if the tank contains water which is 12 ft deep in the tank. The specific gravity of water is 62.4 lb/ft^3. Neglect the weight of the tank.

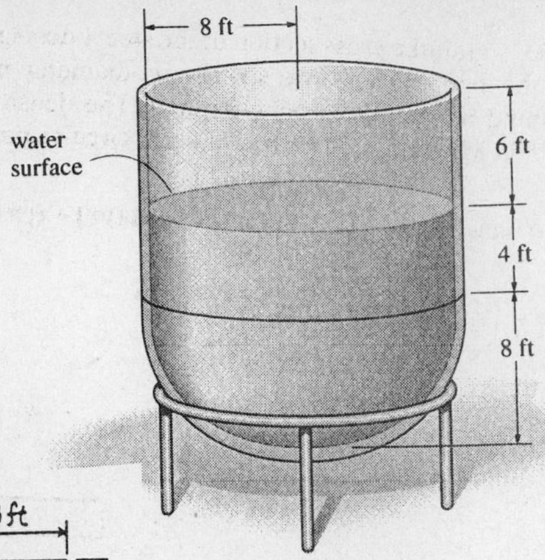

Volume : The volume of the water can be obtained by applying the theorem of Pappus and Guldinus, Eq. 9 – 12, with $\theta = 2\pi$, $\bar{r}_1 = 4$ ft, $\bar{r}_2 = 3.395$ ft, $A_1 = 8(4) = 32.0$ ft^2 and $A_2 = \frac{1}{4}\pi(8^2) = 50.27$ ft^2.

$$V = \theta\Sigma\bar{r}A = 2\pi[4(32.0) + 3.395(50.27)] = 1876.58 \text{ ft}^3$$

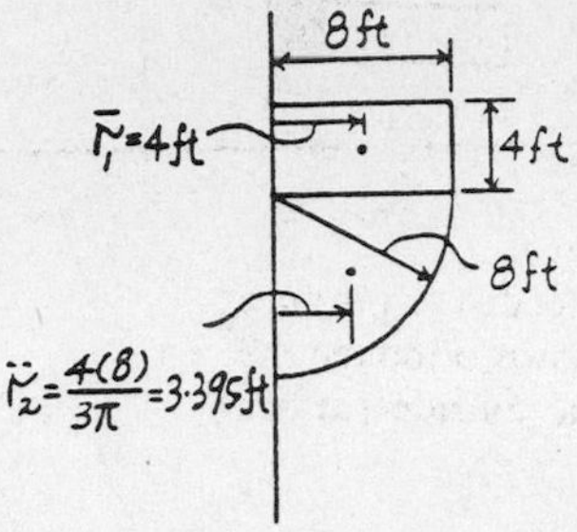

The weight of the water is

$$W = \gamma_w V = 62.4(1876.58) = 117098.47 \text{ lb}$$

Thus, the reaction of each leg on the floor is

$$R = \frac{W}{4} = \frac{117098.47}{4} = 29274.62 \text{ lb} = 29.3 \text{ kip} \qquad \textbf{Ans}$$

***9-92.** Determine the approximate amount of paint needed to cover the outside surface of the tank. Assume that a gallon of paint covers 400 ft^2.

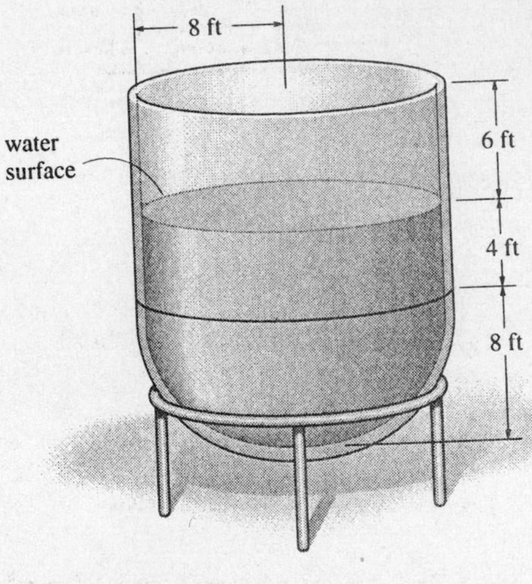

Surface Area : Applying the theorem of Pappus and Guldinus, Eq. 9 – 11, with $\theta = 2\pi$, $L_1 = 10$ ft, $L_2 = \frac{\pi(8)}{2} = 4\pi$ ft, $\bar{r}_1 = 8$ ft and $\bar{r}_2 = \frac{16}{\pi}$ ft, we have

$$A = \theta\Sigma\bar{r}L = 2\pi\left[8(10) + \frac{16}{\pi}(4\pi)\right] = 288\pi \text{ ft}^2$$

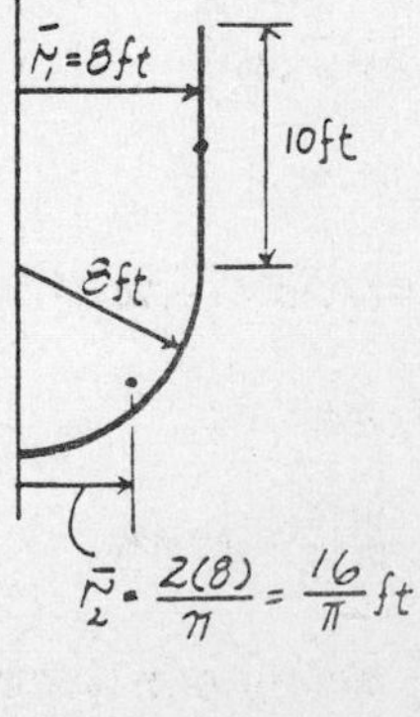

Thus,

$$\text{The required amount paint} = \frac{288\pi}{400} = 2.26 \text{ gallon} \qquad \textbf{Ans}$$

9-93. Half the cross section of the steel housing is shown in the figure. There are six 10-mm-diameter bolt holes around its rim. Determine its mass. The density of steel is 7.85 Mg/m³. The housing is a full circular part.

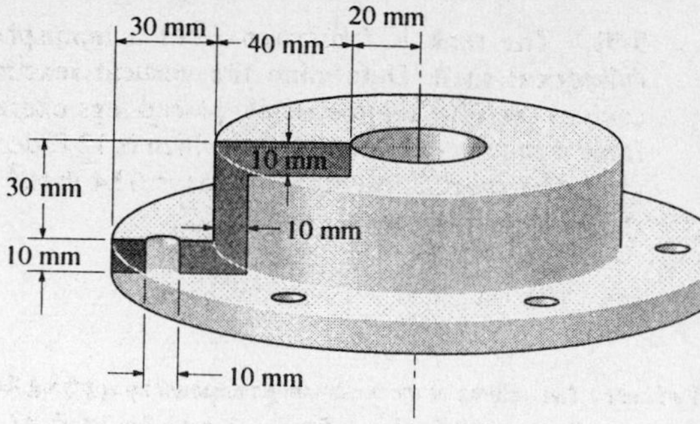

$$V = 2\pi[\,(40)(40)(10) + (55)(30)(10) + (75)(30)(10)] - 6\left[\pi(5)^2(10)\right] = 340.9(10^3)\ \text{mm}^3$$

$$m = \rho V = \left(7850\ \frac{\text{kg}}{\text{m}^3}\right)(340.9)(10^3)(10^{-9})\ \text{m}^3$$

$= 2.68$ kg **Ans**

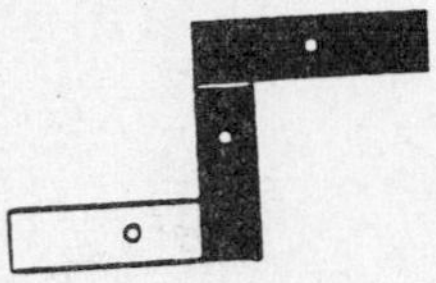

9-94. Determine the volume of steel needed to produce the tapered part. The cross section is shown, although the part is 360° around. Also, compute the outside surface area of the part, excluding its ends.

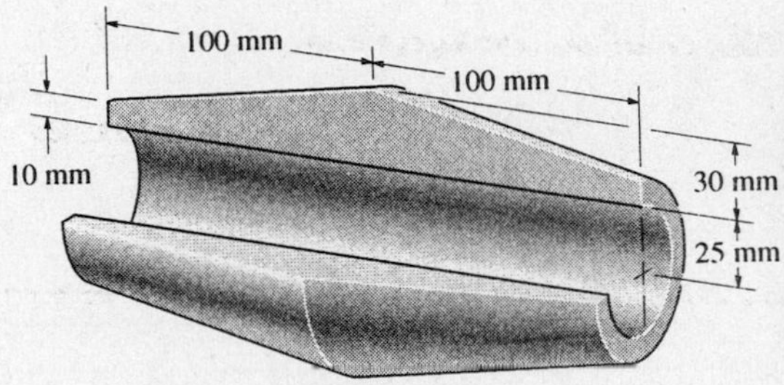

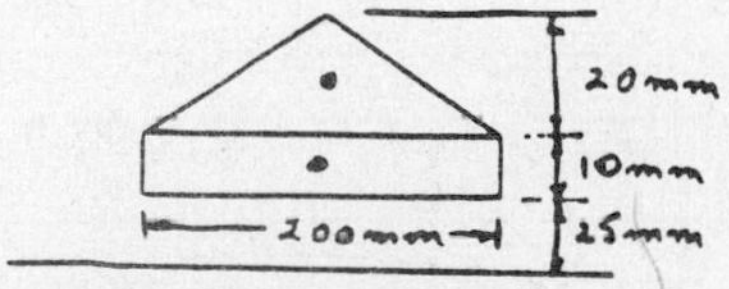

$\Sigma A = 200(10) + \frac{1}{2}(200)(20)$

$= 4000\ \text{mm}^2$

$\Sigma \bar{y}A = 30(200)(10) + 41.67\left(\frac{1}{2}\right)(200)(20)$

$= 143.3(10^3)\ \text{mm}^3$

$$\bar{y} = \frac{\Sigma \bar{y}A}{\Sigma A} = \frac{143.3(10^3)}{4000} = 35.83\ \text{mm}$$

$V = \theta \bar{r} A = 2\pi(35.83)(4000) = 901(10^3)\ \text{mm}^3$ **Ans**

$\Sigma L = 2\sqrt{(100)^2 + (20)^2}$

$= 204.0$ mm

$\Sigma \bar{y}L = (45)\,2\sqrt{(100)^2 + (20)^2}$

$= 9178\ \text{mm}^2$

$$\bar{y} = \frac{\Sigma \bar{y}L}{\Sigma L} = \frac{9178}{204.0} = 45\ \text{mm}$$

$A_s = \theta \bar{r} L = 2\pi(45)(204.0) = 57.7(10^3)\ \text{mm}^2$ **Ans**

9-95. Determine the outside surface area of the storage tank.

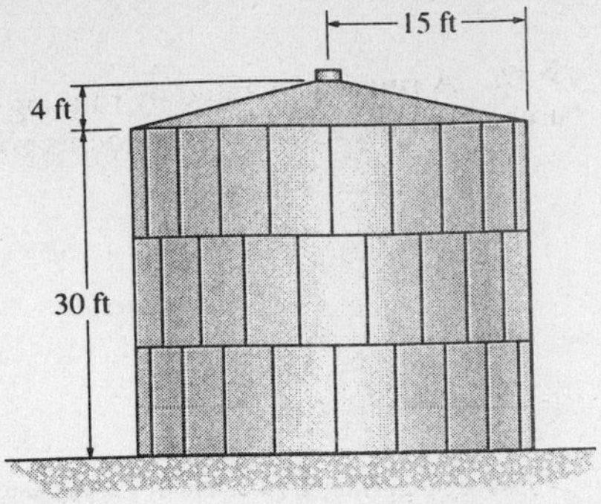

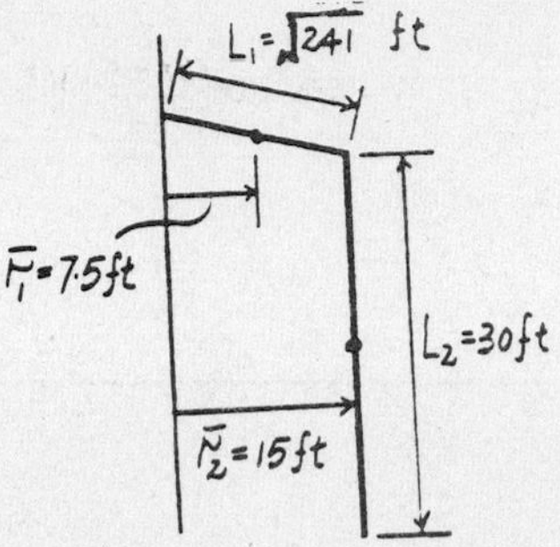

Surface Area : Applying the theorem of Pappus and Guldinus, Eq. 9 – 11, with $\theta = 2\pi$, $L_1 = \sqrt{15^2 + 4^2} = \sqrt{241}$ ft, $L_2 = 30$ ft, $\bar{r}_1 = 7.5$ ft and $\bar{r}_2 = 15$ ft, we have

$$A = \theta \Sigma \bar{r} L = 2\pi\left[7.5\left(\sqrt{241}\right) + 15(30)\right] = 3.56\left(10^3\right)\ \text{ft}^2 \quad \textbf{Ans}$$

***9-96.** Determine the volume of the storage tank.

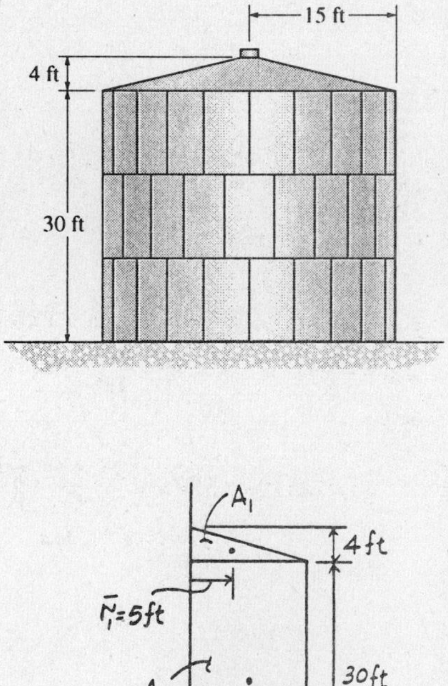

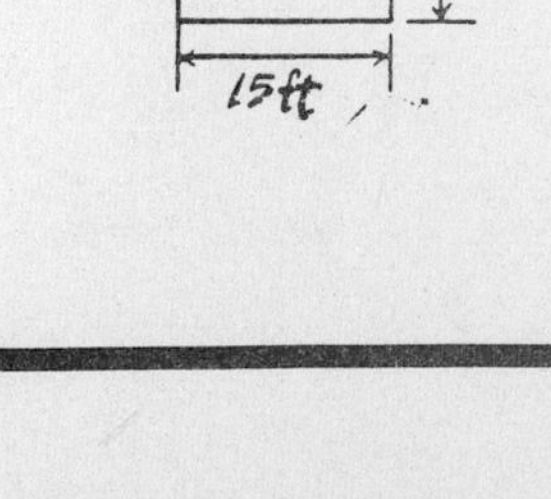

Volume : Applying the theorem of Pappus and Guldinus, Eq. 9 – 12, with $\theta = 2\pi$, $\bar{r}_1 = 5$ ft, $\bar{r}_2 = 7.5$ ft, $A_1 = \frac{1}{2}(15)(4) = 30.0\ \text{ft}^2$ and $A_2 = 30(15) = 450\ \text{ft}^2$, we have

$$V = \theta \Sigma \bar{r} A = 2\pi[5(30.0) + 7.5(450)] = 22.1\left(10^3\right)\ \text{ft}^3 \quad \textbf{Ans}$$

9-97. A ring is generated by rotating the quartercircular area about the x axis. Determine its volume.

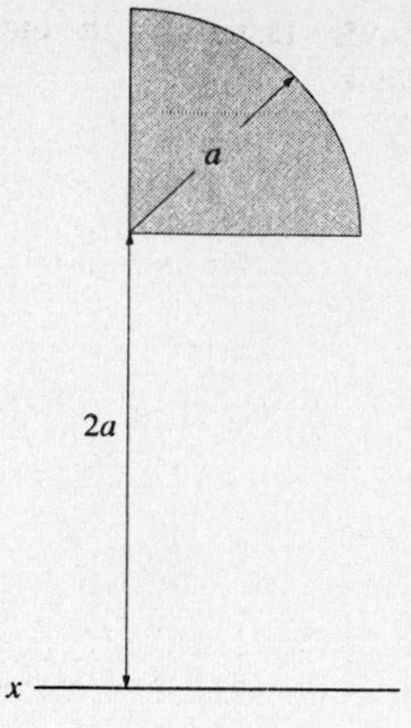

Volume : Applying the theorem of Pappus and Guldinus, Eq. 9 – 10, with $\theta = 2\pi$, $\bar{r} = 2a + \frac{4a}{3\pi} = \frac{6\pi + 4}{3\pi}a$ and $A = \frac{\pi}{4}a^2$, we have

$$V = \theta \bar{r} A = 2\pi\left(\frac{6\pi+4}{3\pi}a\right)\left(\frac{\pi}{4}a^2\right) = \frac{\pi(6\pi+4)}{6}a^3 \qquad \textbf{Ans}$$

9-98. A ring is generated by rotating the quartercircular area about the x axis. Determine its surface area.

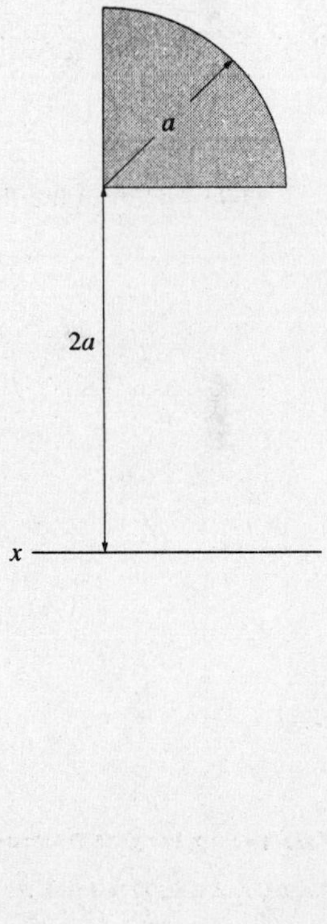

Surface Area : Applying the theorem of Pappus and Guldinus, Eq.9 – 11, with $\theta = 2\pi$, $L_1 = L_3 = a$, $L_2 = \frac{\pi a}{2}$, $\bar{r}_1 = 2a$, $\bar{r}_2 = \frac{2(\pi+1)}{\pi}a$ and $\bar{r}_3 = \frac{5}{2}a$, we have

$$A = \theta \Sigma \bar{r} L = 2\pi\left[2a(a) + \left(\frac{2(\pi+1)}{\pi}a\right)\left(\frac{\pi a}{2}\right) + \frac{5}{2}a\,(a)\right]$$

$$= \pi(2\pi + 11)a^2 \qquad \textbf{Ans}$$

■**9-99.** The circular footing A having a diameter of 7 ft is used to anchor the circular leg B of an electrical transmission tower and thereby prevent the tower from overturning due to the wind. When computing the vertical uplifting strength T of the anchor, it is generally assumed that the weight of the soil within an inverted frustum of a cone with sides sloping outward at 30° with the vertical will resist the upward force of **T**. If the soil has a specific weight of 90 lb/ft^3 and the footing and leg are made of concrete having a specific weight of 150 lb/ft^3, determine the approximate depth h to which it must be buried in order to resist a force of $T = 25$ kip on the leg of the tower.

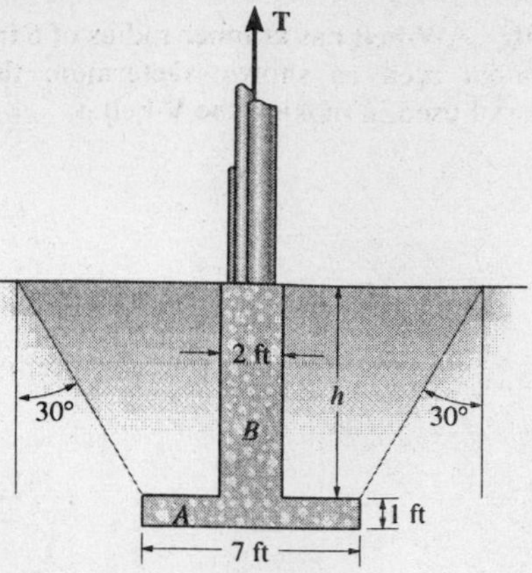

$$V_{soil} = \Sigma\theta\bar{r}A = 2\pi\left[(2.25)(h)(2.5) + \left(3.5 + \tfrac{h}{3}\tan 30°\right)\left(\tfrac{1}{2}\right)(h)(h\tan 30°)\right]$$

$$= 35.343h + 6.3483h^2 + 0.3491h^3$$

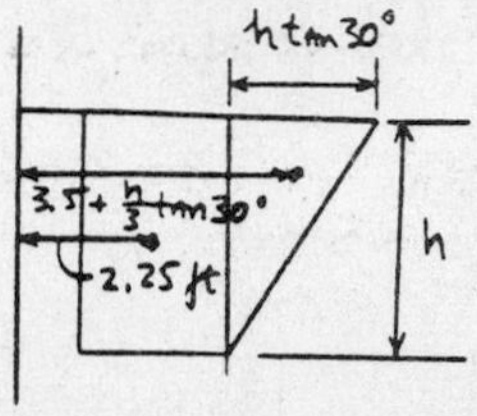

$$V_{conc} = \Sigma\theta\bar{r}A = 2\pi\left[1.75(3.5)(1) + 0.5(1)(h)\right]$$

$$= 38.485 + 3.1416h$$

$$25\,000 = \Sigma\rho V$$

$$25\,000 = 150(38.485 + 3.1416h) + 90\left(35.343h + 6.3483h^2 + 0.3491h^3\right)$$

$$-19\,227 + 3652.1015h + 571.347h^2 + 31.4159h^3 = 0$$

$$h^3 + 18.185h^2 + 116.239h - 611.986 = 0$$

Choosing the real root :

$h = 3.28$ ft **Ans**

***9-100.** Using integration, determine the area and the centroidal distance $\bar{y}$ of the shaded area. Then, using the second theorem of Pappus–Guldinus, determine the volume of a paraboloid formed by revolving the area about the x axis.

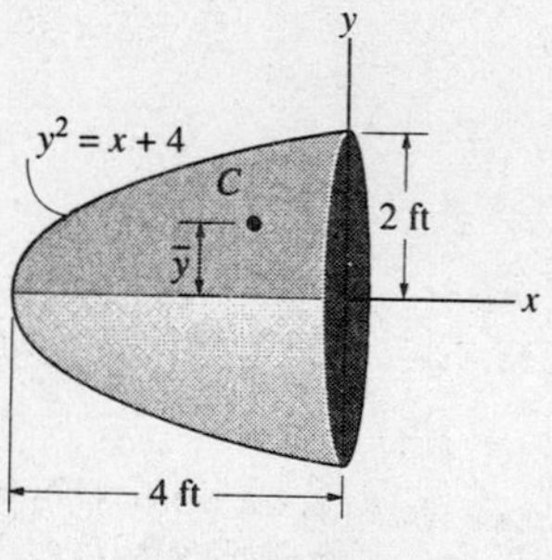

$dA = -x\,dy$

$\tilde{y} = y$

$A = \int_0^2 -x\,dy = -\int_0^2 (y^2 - 4)\,dy = 5.33\text{ ft}^2$ **Ans**

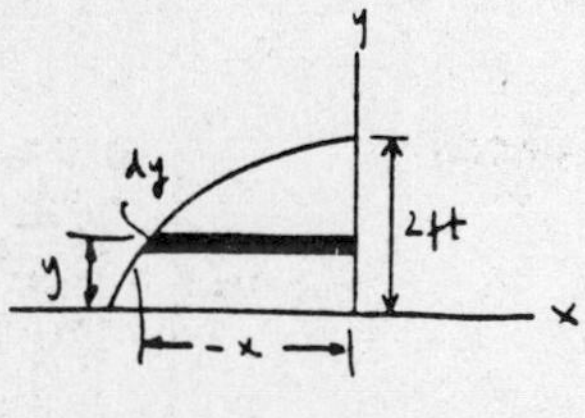

$\bar{y} = \dfrac{\int_A \tilde{y}\,dA}{\int_A dA} = \dfrac{-\int_0^2 (y)(y^2 - 4)\,dy}{5.33} = 0.750\text{ ft}$ **Ans**

$V = 2\pi\bar{y}A = 2\pi(0.75)(5.33)$

$V = 25.1\text{ ft}^3$ **Ans**

9-101. A V-belt has as inner radius of 6 in., and a cross-sectional area as shown. Determine the volume of material used in making the V-belt.

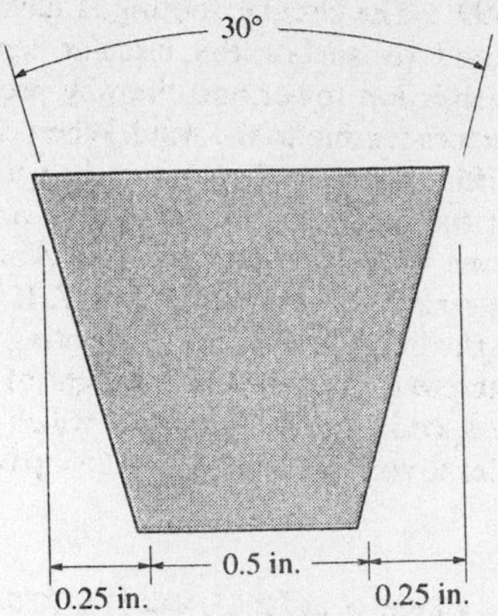

Volume : Applying the theorem of Pappus and Guldinus, Eq. 9 – 12, with $\theta = 2\pi$, $\bar{r}_1 = 6.4665$ in., $\bar{r}_2 = 6.6220$ in., $A_1 = 0.5(0.9330) = 0.4665$ in^2 and $A_2 = \frac{1}{2}(0.5)(0.9330) = 0.2333$ in^2, we have

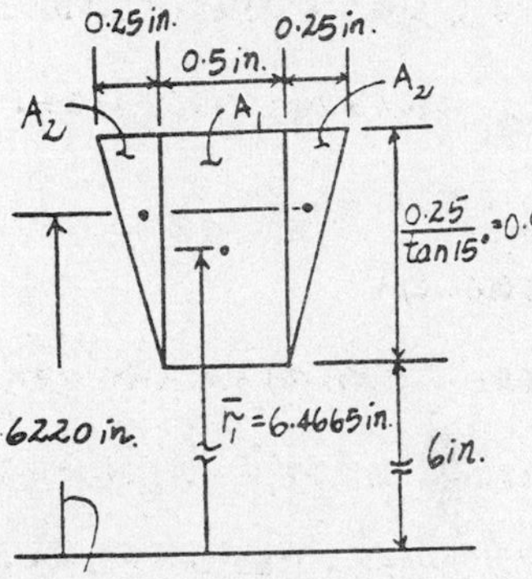

$$V = \theta\Sigma\bar{r}A = 2\pi[6.4665(0.4665) + 6.6220(0.2333)]$$
$$= 28.7 \text{ in}^3 \qquad \textbf{Ans}$$

9-102. The full circular aluminum housing is used in an automotive brake system. The cross section is shown in the figure. Determine its weight if aluminum has a specific weight of 169 lb/ft^3.

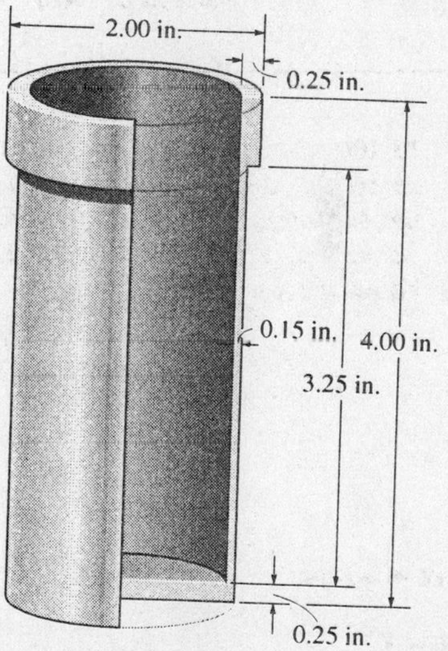

Volume : Applying the theorem of Pappus and Guldinus, Eq. 9 – 12, with $\theta = 2\pi$, $\bar{r}_1 = 0.875$ in., $\bar{r}_2 = 0.825$ in., $\bar{r}_3 = 0.45$ in., $A_1 = 0.25(0.5) = 0.125$ in^2, $A_2 = 0.15(3.25) = 0.4875$ in^2 and $A_3 = 0.25(0.9) = 0.225$ in^2, we have

$$V = \theta\Sigma\bar{r}A = 2\pi[0.875(0.125) + 0.825(0.4875) + 0.45(0.225)]$$
$$= 3.850 \text{ in}^3$$

The weight of the housing is

$$W = \gamma V = 169\left(\frac{3.850}{12^3}\right) = 0.377 \text{ lb} \qquad \textbf{Ans}$$

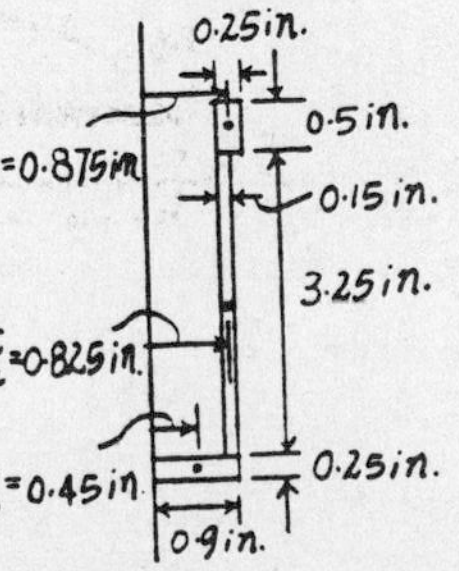

9-103. Determine the height h to which liquid should be poured into the conical cup so that it contacts half the surface area on the inside of the cup.

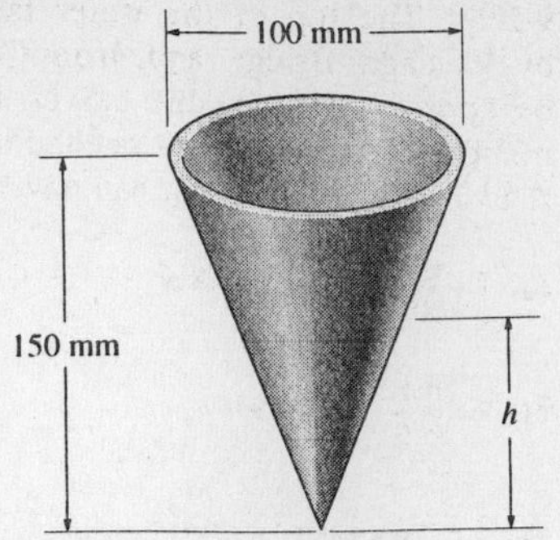

Surface Area : This problem requires that $\frac{1}{2}A_1 = A_2$. Applying the theorem of Pappus and Guldinus, Eq.9–9, with $\theta = 2\pi$, $L_1 = \sqrt{50^2 + 150^2} = 158.11$ mm, $L_2 = \sqrt{h^2 + \left(\frac{h}{3}\right)^2} = \frac{\sqrt{10}}{3}h$, $\bar{r}_1 = 25$ mm and $\bar{r}_2 = \frac{h}{6}$, we have

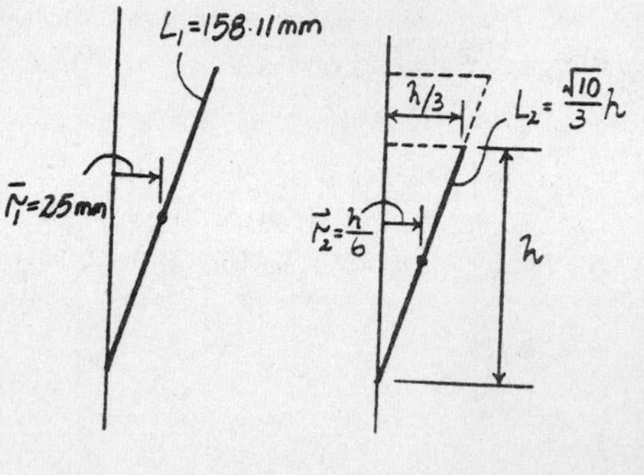

$$\frac{1}{2}(\theta\bar{r}_1 L_1) = \theta\bar{r}_2 L_2$$

$$\frac{1}{2}[2\pi(25)(158.11)] = 2\pi\left(\frac{h}{6}\right)\left(\frac{\sqrt{10}}{3}h\right)$$

$$h = 106 \text{ mm} \qquad \textbf{Ans}$$

***9-104.** Determine the surface area of the roof of the structure if it is formed by rotating the parabola about the y axis.

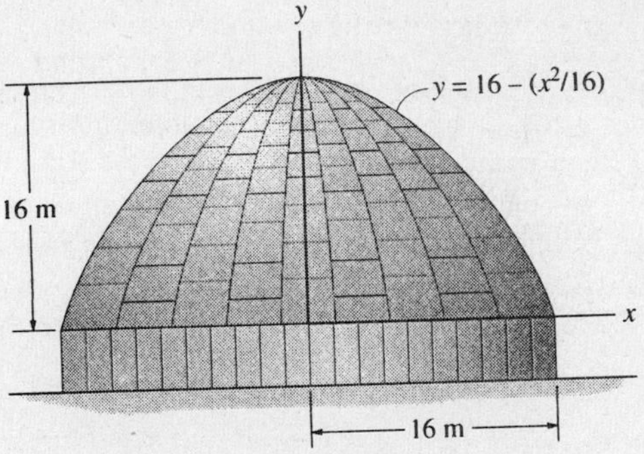

Centroid : The length of the differential element is $dL = \sqrt{dx^2 + dy^2} = \left(\sqrt{1 + \left(\frac{dy}{dx}\right)^2}\right)dx$ and its centroid is $\tilde{x} = x$. Here, $\frac{dy}{dx} = -\frac{x}{8}$. Evaluating the integrals, we have

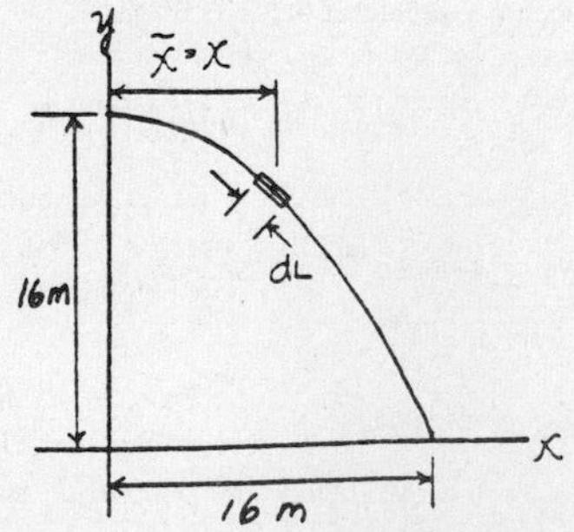

$$L = \int dL = \int_0^{16\text{m}} \left(\sqrt{1 + \frac{x^2}{64}}\right)dx = 23.663 \text{ m}$$

$$\int_L \tilde{x}\,dL = \int_0^{16\text{m}} x\left(\sqrt{1 + \frac{x^2}{64}}\right)dx = 217.181 \text{ m}^2$$

Applying Eq. 9–7, we have

$$\bar{x} = \frac{\int_L \tilde{x}\,dL}{\int_L dL} = \frac{217.181}{23.663} = 9.178 \text{ m}$$

Surface Area : Applying the theorem of Pappus and Guldinus, Eq.9–9, with $\theta = 2\pi$, $L = 23.663$ m, $\bar{r} = \bar{x} = 9.178$, we have

$$A = \theta\bar{r}L = 2\pi(9.178)(23.663) = 1365 \text{ m}^2 \qquad \textbf{Ans}$$

9-105. The top of the water tank was manufactured by Chicago Bridge and Iron Co. and its shape can be approximated by the curves shown. Determine the number of liters of paint needed to coat its surface from A to B if a liter of paint can cover 12 m^2.

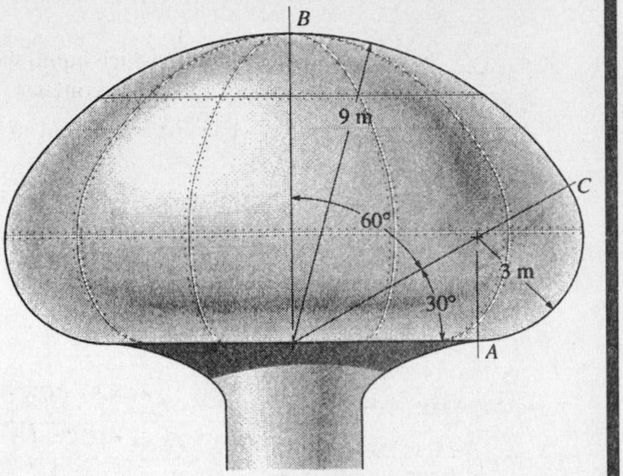

$$L_{BC} = \frac{60°}{180°}(\pi)(9) = 9.4248 \text{ m}$$

$$\bar{r}_{BC} = \frac{9 \sin 30°}{\frac{\pi}{6}} = 8.5944 \text{ m}$$

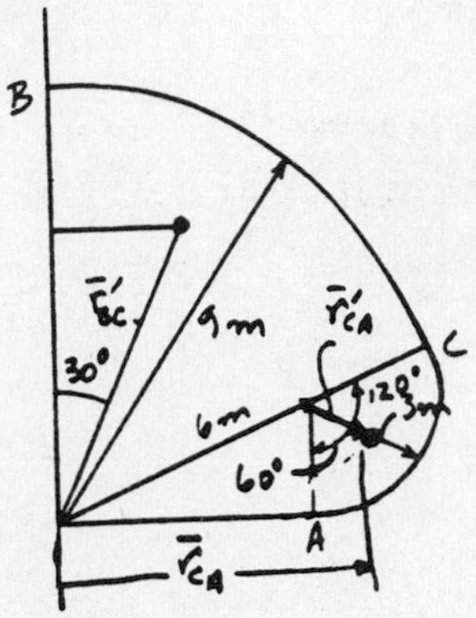

$$\bar{r}_{BC} = 8.5943 \sin 30° = 4.2972 \text{ m}$$

$$L_{AC} = \frac{120°}{180°}(\pi)(3) = 6.2832 \text{ m}$$

$$\bar{r}'_{CA} = \frac{3(\sin 60°)}{\frac{\pi}{3}} = 2.4810 \text{ m}$$

$$\bar{r}_{CA} = 6 \cos 30° + 2.4810 \sin 60° = 7.3447 \text{ m}$$

$$A = \Sigma\theta\bar{r}L = 2\pi\left[4.2972(9.4248) + 7.3447(6.2832)\right]$$

$$A = 544 \text{ m}^2$$

$$n = \frac{544 \text{ m}^2}{12 \text{ m}^2/\text{liter}} = 45.4 \text{ liters} \qquad \textbf{Ans}$$

9-106. The tank is 1.25 m wide on each side and 4 m high. If it is filled to a depth of 1 m with water and 3 m with oil, determine the resultant force created by both of these fluids along side AB of the tank and its location measured from the top of the tank. $\rho_o = 0.90$ Mg/m^3 and $\rho_w = 1.0$ Mg/m^3.

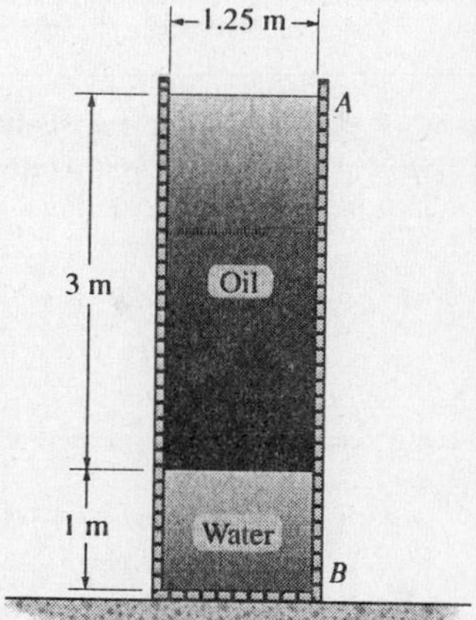

***Fluid Pressure*:** The fluid pressure at points C and B are

$$p_C = \rho_{oil} g z_{AC} = 0.9(10^3)(9.81)(3) = 26\,487 \text{ N/m}^2 = 26.49 \text{ kN/m}^2$$

$$p_B = p_C + \rho_w g z_{CB} = 26\,487 + 1.0(10^3)(9.81)(1)$$

$$= 36\,297 \text{ N/m}^2 = 36.30 \text{ kN/m}^2$$

Thus,

$$w_C = 26.49(1.25) = 33.11 \text{ kN/m}$$

$$w_B = 36.30(1.25) = 45.37 \text{ kN/m}$$

***Resultant Force and its Location*:**

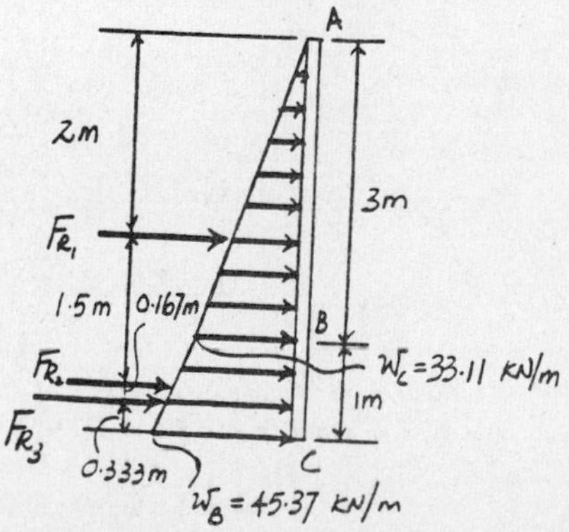

$$F_{R_1} = \frac{1}{2}(33.11)(3) = 49.66 \text{ kN}$$

$$F_{R_2} = 33.11(1) = 33.11 \text{ kN}$$

$$F_{R_3} = \frac{1}{2}(45.37 - 33.11)(1) = 6.13 \text{ kN}$$

The resultant force is

$$F_R = F_{R_1} + F_{R_2} + F_{R_3}$$

$$= 49.66 + 33.11 + 6.13$$

$$= 88.90 \text{ kN} = 88.9 \text{ kN} \qquad \textbf{Ans}$$

The location of the resultant force is

$$\bar{z} = \frac{\Sigma \bar{z} F_{R_i}}{\Sigma F_{R_i}} = \frac{2(49.66) + 3.5(33.11) + 3.667(6.13)}{88.90}$$

$$= 2.67 \text{ m} \qquad \textbf{Ans}$$

9-107. The factor of safety for tipping of the concrete dam is defined as the ratio of the stabilizing moment about O due to the dam's weight divided by the overturning moment about O due to the water pressure. Determine this factor if the concrete has a specific weight of $\gamma_{conc} = 150\ \text{lb/ft}^3$ and for water $\gamma_w = 62.4\ \text{lb/ft}^3$.

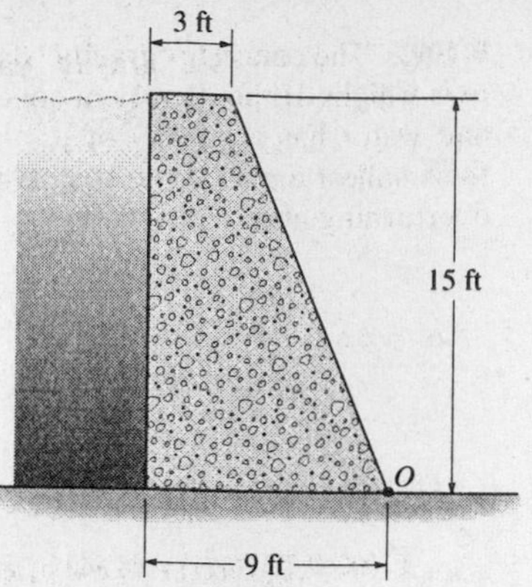

For a 1 - ft thick section :

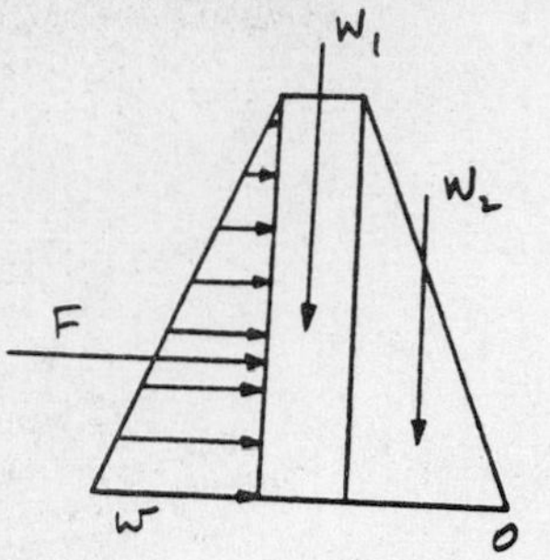

$$w = 62.4(15)(1) = 936\ \text{lb/ft}$$

$$F = \frac{1}{2}(936)(15) = 7020\ \text{lb}$$

$$W_1 = 150(1)(3)(15) = 6750\ \text{lb}$$

$$W_2 = 150\left(\frac{1}{2}\right)(6)(15)(1) = 6750\ \text{lb}$$

Moment to overturn :

$$M_O = 7020\left(\frac{1}{3}(15)\right) = 35\ 100\ \text{lb}\cdot\text{ft}$$

Moment to stabilize :

$$M_S = (6750)(6 + 1.5) + 6750\left(\frac{2}{3}(6)\right) = 77\ 625\ \text{lb}\cdot\text{ft}$$

$$\text{F.S.} = \frac{M_S}{M_O} = \frac{77\ 625}{35\ 100} = 2.21 \qquad \textbf{Ans}$$

***9-108.** When the tide water A subsides, the tide gate automatically swings open to drain the marsh B. For the condition of high tide shown, determine the horizontal reactions developed at the hinge C and stop block D. The length of the gate is 6 m and its height is 4 m. $\rho_w = 1.0\ \text{Mg/m}^3$.

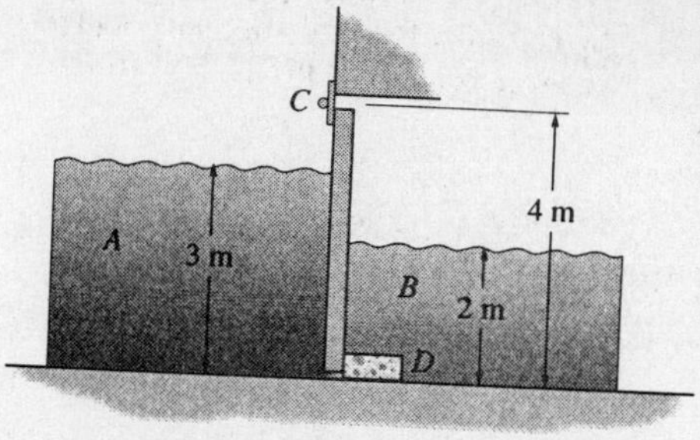

Fluid Pressure : The fluid pressure at points D and E can be determined using Eq. 9 – 15, $p = \rho g z$.

$$p_D = 1.0(10^3)(9.81)(2) = 19\ 620\ \text{N/m}^2 = 19.62\ \text{kN/m}^2$$

$$p_E = 1.0(10^3)(9.81)(3) = 29\ 430\ \text{N/m}^2 = 29.43\ \text{kN/m}^2$$

Thus,

$$w_D = 19.62(6) = 117.72\ \text{kN/m}$$

$$w_E = 29.43(6) = 176.58\ \text{kN/m}$$

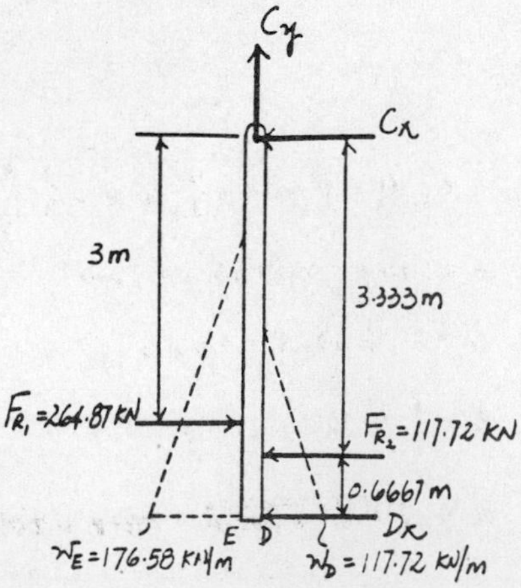

Resultant Forces :

$$F_{R_1} = \frac{1}{2}(176.58)(3) = 264.87\ \text{kN}$$

$$F_{R_2} = \frac{1}{2}(117.72)(2) = 117.72\ \text{kN}$$

Equations of Equilibrium :

$$+\Sigma M_C = 0; \quad 264.87(3) - 117.72(3.333) - D_x(4) = 0$$

$$D_x = 100.55\ \text{kN} = 101\ \text{kN} \qquad \textbf{Ans}$$

$$\xrightarrow{+} \Sigma F_x = 0; \quad 264.87 - 117.72 - 100.55 - C_x = 0$$

$$C_x = 46.6\ \text{kN} \qquad \textbf{Ans}$$

9-109. The concrete "gravity" dam is held in place by its own weight. If the density of concrete is $\rho_c = 2.5\ \text{Mg/m}^3$, and water has a density of $\rho_w = 1.0\ \text{Mg/m}^3$, determine the smallest dimension d that will prevent the dam from overturning about its end A.

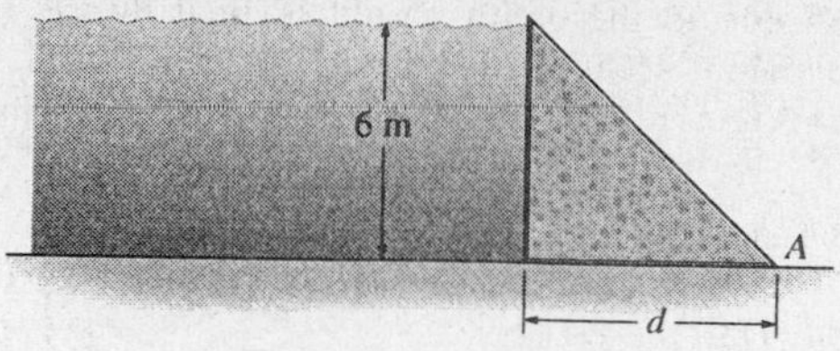

Consider a 1 – m width of dam.

$w = 1000(9.81)(6)(1) = 58\,860\ \text{N/m}$

$F = \frac{1}{2}(58\,860)(6)(1) = 176\,580\ \text{N}$

$W = \frac{1}{2}(d)(6)(1)(2500)(9.81) = 73\,575d\ \text{N}$

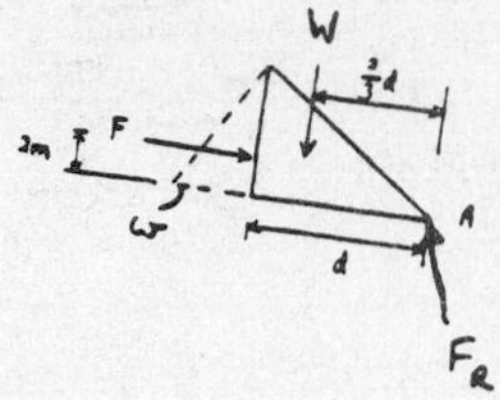

$\curvearrowleft + \Sigma M_A = 0; \quad -176\,580(2) + 73\,575d\left(\frac{2}{3}d\right) = 0$

$d = 2.68\ \text{m}$ **Ans**

9-110. Determine the magnitude of the resultant hydrostatic force acting per meter of length on the seawall. $\gamma_w = 62.4\ \text{lb/ft}^3$.

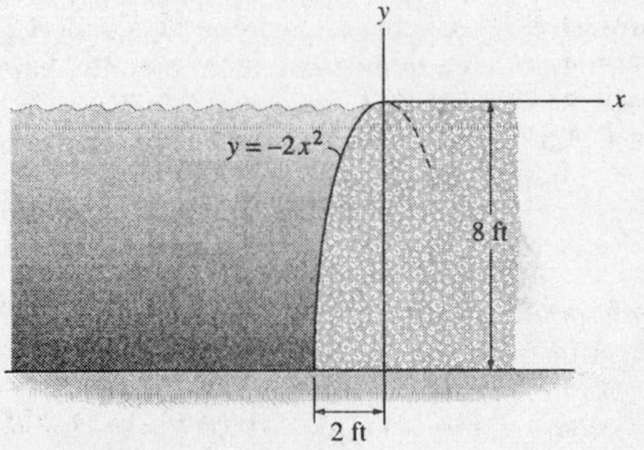

$A = \int_A dA = \int_{-2}^{0} -y\,dx = \int_{-2}^{0} 2x^2\,dx = \frac{2}{3}x^3\Big|_{-2}^{0} = 5.333\ \text{ft}^2$

$w = b\gamma h = 1(62.4)(8) = 499.2\ \text{lb/ft}$

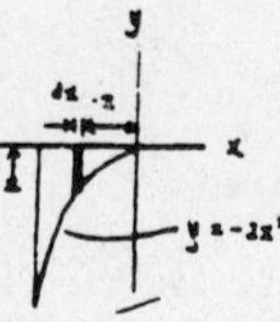

$F_y = 5.333(1)(62.4) = 332.8\ \text{lb}$

$F_x = \frac{1}{2}(499.2)(8) = 1997\ \text{lb}$

$F_R = \sqrt{(332.8)^2 + (1997)^2} = 2024\ \text{lb} = 2.02\ \text{kip}$ **Ans**

9-111. The symmetric concrete "gravity" dam is held in place by its own weight. If the density of concrete is $\rho_c = 2.5\ \text{Mg/m}^3$, and water has a density of $\rho_w = 1.0\ \text{Mg/m}^3$, determine the smallest distance d at its base that will prevent the dam from overturning about its end A. The dam has a width of 8 m.

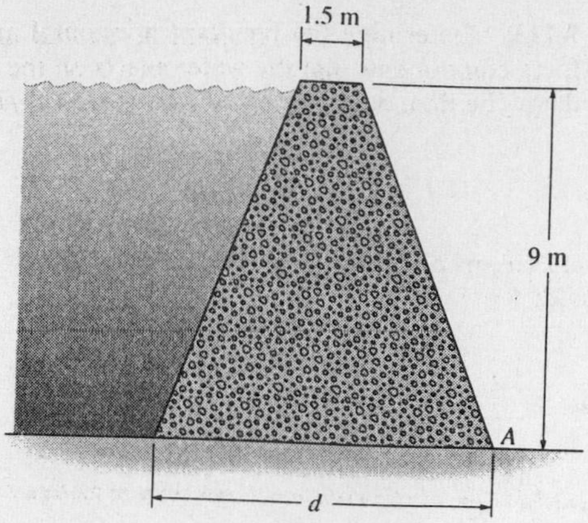

$$w = b\rho_w g h = 8(1000)(9.81)(9) = 706.32(10^3)\ \text{N/m}$$

$$F_h = \tfrac{1}{2}\left[706.32(10^3)\right](9) = 3178.44(10)^3\ \text{N}$$

$$F_v = 1000(9.81)(\tfrac{1}{2})(\tfrac{d-1.5}{2})(9)(8) = (176.58d - 264.87)(10^3)$$

$$W = 2.5(10^3)(9.81)\left[\tfrac{1}{2}(d+1.5)(9)(8)\right] = (882.9d + 1324.35)(10^3)$$

$$x_1 = d - \tfrac{1}{3}(\tfrac{d-1.5}{2}) = \tfrac{5}{6}d + 0.25$$

$$x_2 = \tfrac{d}{2}$$

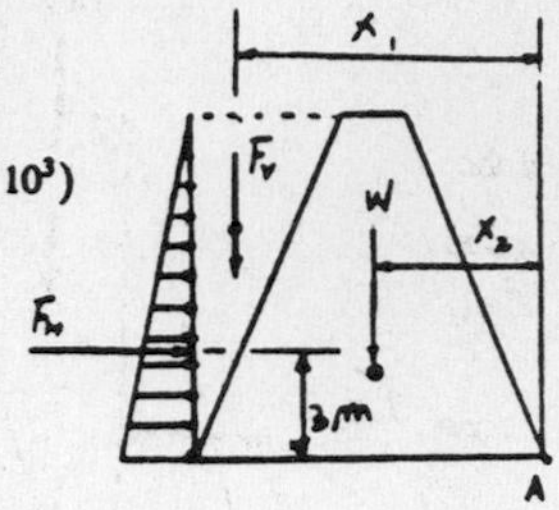

$\circlearrowleft + \Sigma M_A = 0;\quad (176.58d - 264.87)(10^3)(\tfrac{5}{6}d + 0.25)$

$+ (882.9d + 1324.35)(10^3)(\tfrac{d}{2}) - 3178.44(10^3)(3) = 0$

$$588.6d^2 + 485.595d - 9601.54 = 0$$

$$d = 3.65\ \text{m}$$

***9-112.** The tank is used to store a liquid having a specific weight of 80 lb/ft³. If it is filled to the top, determine the magnitude of force the liquid exerts on each of its two sides $ABDC$ and $BDFE$.

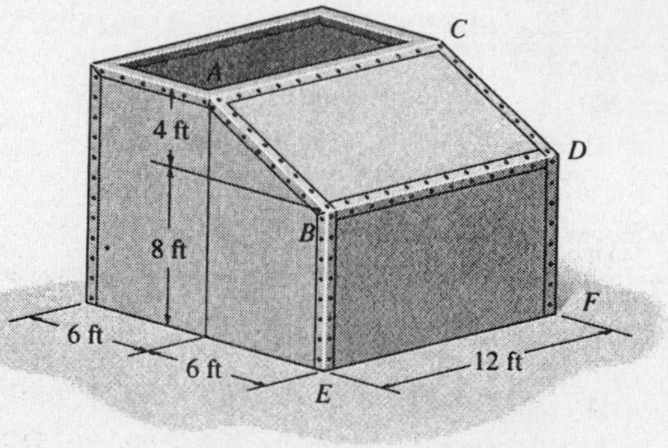

Fluid Pressure : The fluid pressure at points B and E can be determined using Eq. 9 − 15, $p = \gamma z$.

$$p_B = 80(4) = 320\ \text{lb/ft}^2 \qquad p_E = 80(12) = 960\ \text{lb/ft}^2$$

Thus,

$$w_B = 320(12) = 3840\ \text{lb/ft} \qquad w_E = 960(12) = 11520\ \text{lb/ft}$$

Resultant Forces **:** The resultant force acts on suface $ABCD$ is

$$F_{R_1} = \frac{1}{2}(3840)\left(\sqrt{52}\right) = 13\,845.31\ \text{lb} = 13.8\ \text{kip} \qquad \textbf{Ans}$$

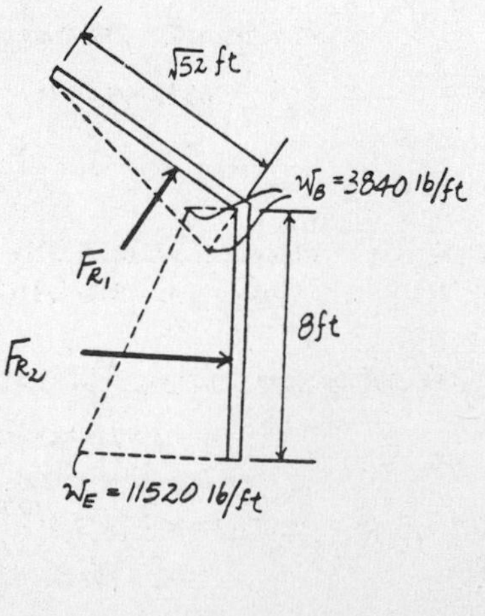

and acts on surface $BDFE$ is

$$F_{R_2} = \frac{1}{2}(3840 + 11520)(8) = 61\,440\ \text{lb} = 61.4\ \text{kip} \qquad \textbf{Ans}$$

9-113. Determine the resultant horizontal and vertical force components that the water exerts on the side of the dam. The dam is 25 ft long and $\gamma_w = 62.4\ \text{lb/ft}^3$.

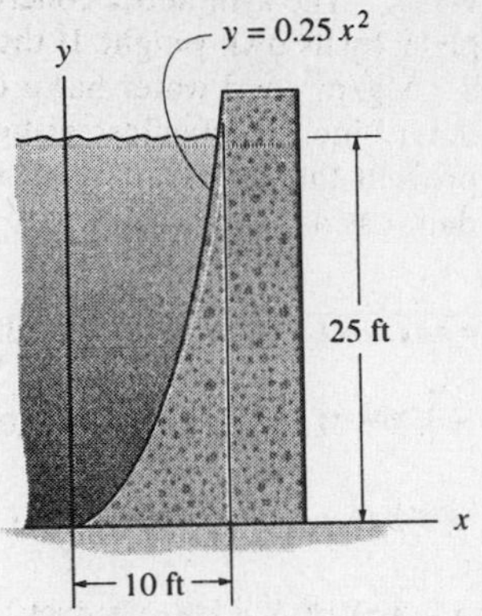

Fluid Pressure : The fluid pressure at the toe of the dam can be determined using Eq. 9 – 15, $p = \gamma z$.

$$p = 62.4(25) = 1560\ \text{lb/ft}^2 = 1.56\ \text{kip/ft}^2$$

Thus,

$$w = 1.56(25) = 39.0\ \text{kip/ft}$$

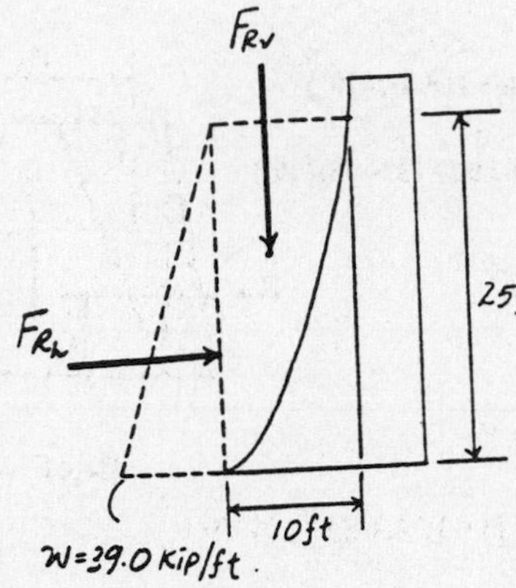

Resultant Force : From the inside back cover of the text, the area of the semiparabolic area is $A = \frac{2}{3}ab = \frac{2}{3}(10)(25) = 166.67\ \text{ft}^2$. Then, the vertical component of the resultant force is

$$F_{R_v} = \gamma V = 62.4[166.67(25)] = 260\ 000\ \text{lb} = 260\ \text{kip} \qquad \textbf{Ans}$$

and the horizontal component of the resultant force is

$$F_{R_h} = \frac{1}{2}(39.0)(25) = 487.5\ \text{kip} \qquad \textbf{Ans}$$

9-114. The gate AB is 8 m wide. Determine the horizontal and vertical components of force acting on the pin at B and the vertical reaction at the smooth support A. $\rho_w = 1.0\ \text{Mg/m}^3$.

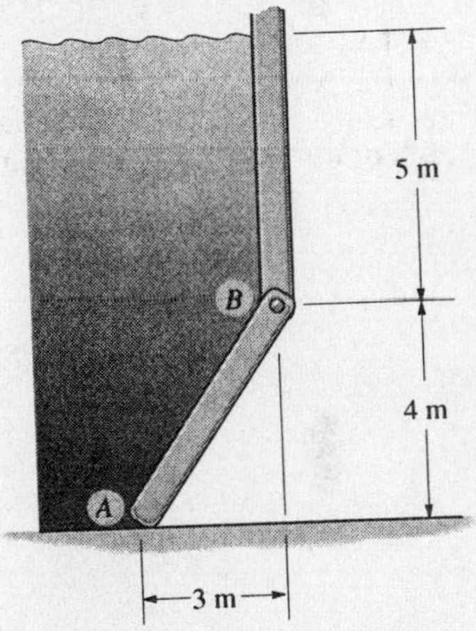

Fluid Pressure : The fluid pressure at points A and B can be determined using Eq. 9 – 15, $p = \rho g z$.

$$p_A = 1.0(10^3)(9.81)(9) = 88\ 290\ \text{N/m}^2 = 88.29\ \text{kN/m}^2$$

$$p_B = 1.0(10^3)(9.81)(5) = 49\ 050\ \text{N/m}^2 = 49.05\ \text{kN/m}^2$$

Thus,

$$w_A = 88.29(8) = 706.32\ \text{kN/m}$$

$$w_B = 49.05(8) = 392.40\ \text{kN/m}$$

Resultant Forces :

$$F_{R_1} = 392.4(5) = 1962.0\ \text{kN}$$

$$F_{R_2} = \frac{1}{2}(706.32 - 392.4)(5) = 784.8\ \text{kN}$$

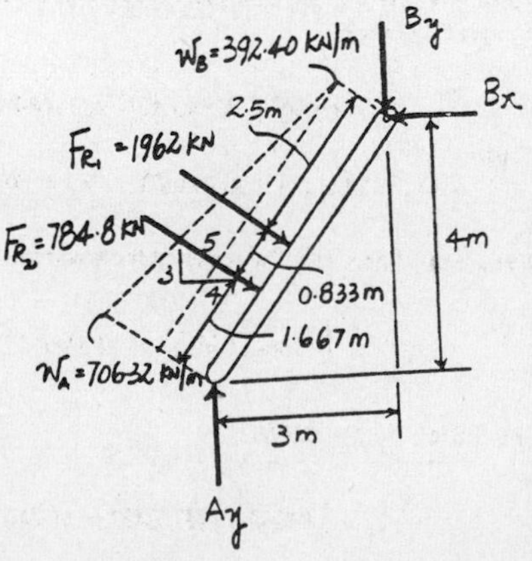

Equations of Equilibrium :

$$+\Sigma M_B = 0; \quad 1962.0(2.5) + 784.8(3.333) - A_y(3) = 0$$

$$A_y = 2507\ \text{kN} = 2.51\ \text{MN} \qquad \textbf{Ans}$$

$$\xrightarrow{+} \Sigma F_x = 0; \quad 784.8\left(\frac{4}{5}\right) - 1962\left(\frac{4}{5}\right) - B_x = 0$$

$$B_x = 2197\ \text{kN} = 2.20\ \text{MN} \qquad \textbf{Ans}$$

$$+\uparrow \Sigma F_y = 0; \quad 2507 - 784.8\left(\frac{3}{5}\right) - 1962\left(\frac{3}{5}\right) - B_y = 0$$

$$B_y = 859\ \text{kN} \qquad \textbf{Ans}$$

9-115. The 3-ft-wide rectangular gate is pinned at its center C. Determine the torque M that must be applied to its central shaft in order to open the gate. $\gamma_w = 62.4 \text{ lb/ft}^3$.

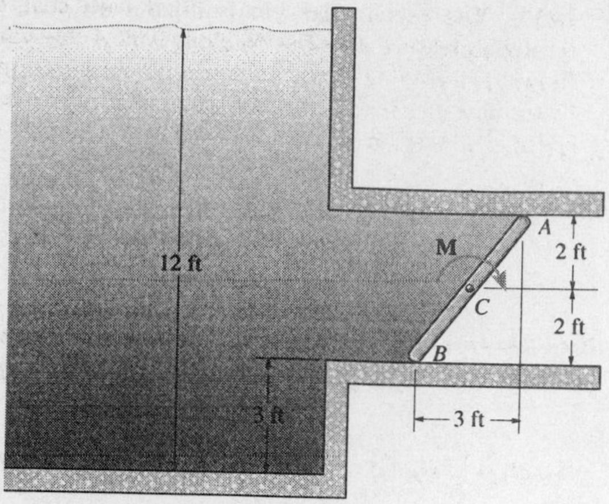

$w_1 = 62.4(5)(3) = 936 \text{ lb/ft}$

$w_2 = 62.4(4)(3) = 748.8 \text{ lb/ft}$

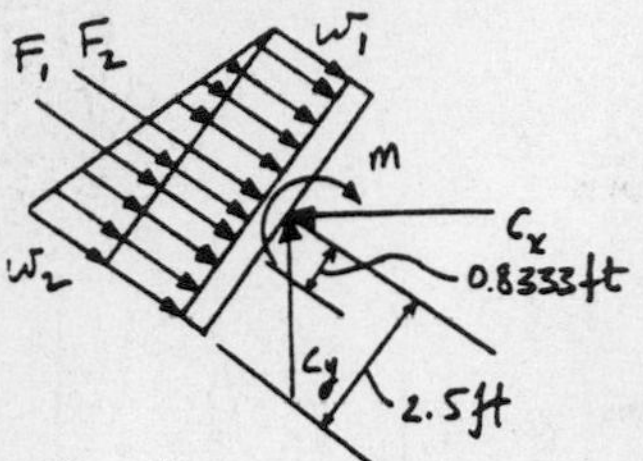

$\curvearrowleft + \Sigma M_C = 0; \quad F_1(0.8333) - M = 0$

$F_1 = \frac{1}{2}(748.8)(5) = 1872 \text{ lb}$

$M = 0.8333(1872) = 1560 \text{ lb}\cdot\text{ft} = 1.56 \text{ kip}\cdot\text{ft}$ **Ans**

***9-116.** Determine the magnitude of the resultant force acting on the gate ABC due to hydrostatic pressure. The gate has a width of 1.5 m. $\rho_w = 1.0 \text{ Mg/m}^3$.

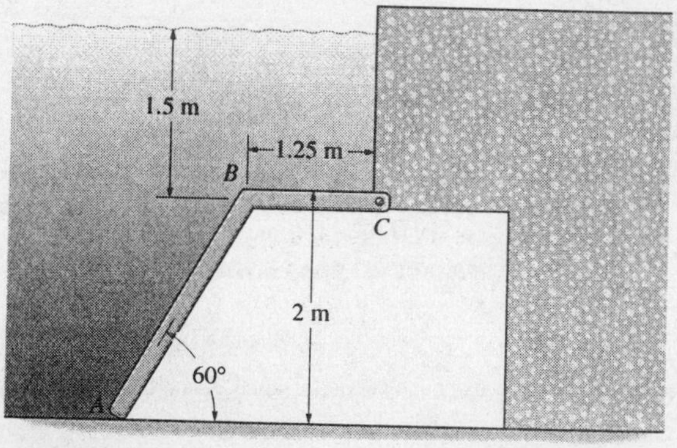

$w_1 = 1000(9.81)(1.5)(1.5) = 22.072 \text{ kN/m}$

$w_2 = 1000(9.81)(2)(1.5) = 29.43 \text{ kN/m}$

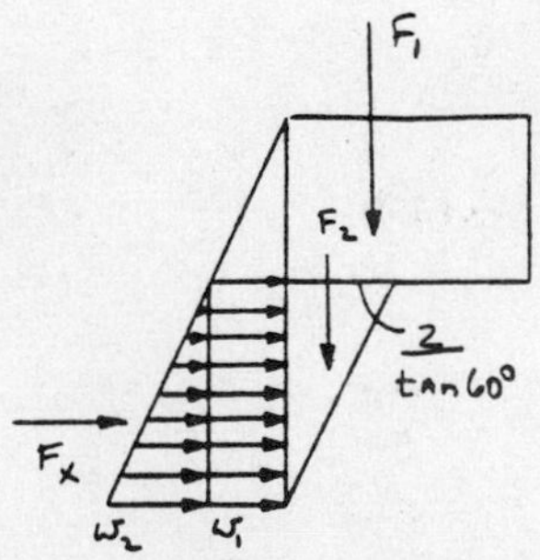

$F_x = \frac{1}{2}(29.43)(2) + (22.0725)(2) = 73.58 \text{ kN}$

$F_1 = \left[(22.072)\left(1.25 + \frac{2}{\tan 60°}\right)\right] = 53.078 \text{ kN}$

$F_2 = \frac{1}{2}(1.5)(2)\left(\frac{2}{\tan 60°}\right)(1000)(9.81) = 16.99 \text{ kN}$

$F_y = F_1 + F_2 = 70.069 \text{ kN}$

$F = \sqrt{F_x^2 + F_y^2} = \sqrt{(73.58)^2 + (70.069)^2} = 102 \text{ kN}$ **Ans**

9-117. The rectangular bin is filled with coal, which creates a pressure distribution along wall A that varies as shown, i.e., $p = 4z^3$ lb/ft^2, where z is measured in feet. Determine the resultant force created by the coal, and specify its location measured from the top surface of the coal.

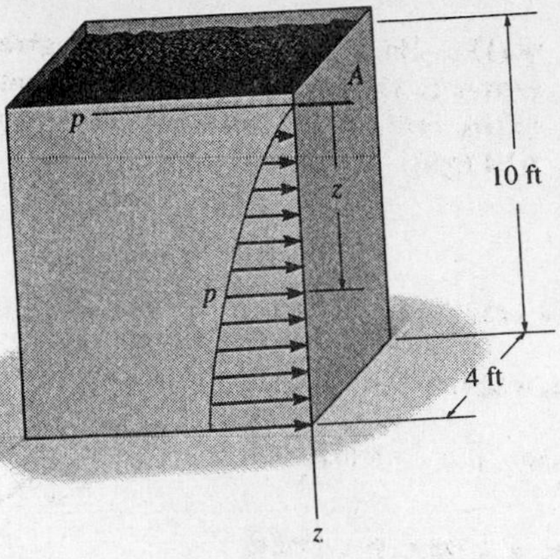

Resultant Force and Its Location : The voume of the differential element is $dV = dF_R = 4p\,dz = 4(4z^3)\,dz = 16z^3 dz$ and its centroid is at $\tilde{z} = z$.

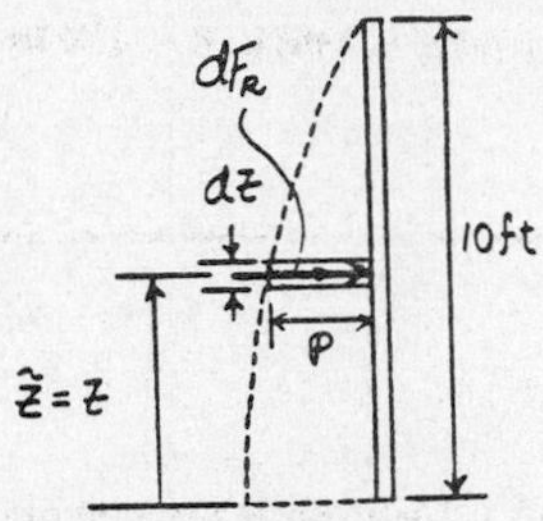

$$F_R = \int_{F_R} dF_R = \int_0^{10\,\text{ft}} 16z^3\,dz = 4z^4\Big|_0^{10\,\text{ft}} = 40\,000 \text{ lb} = 40.0 \text{ kip} \qquad \textbf{Ans}$$

$$\int_{F_R} \tilde{y}\,dF_R = \int_0^{10\,\text{ft}} z\left(16z^3\,dz\right) = \frac{16}{5}z^5\Big|_0^{10\,\text{ft}} = 320\,000 \text{ lb}\cdot\text{ft}$$

$$\bar{z} = \frac{\int_{F_R} \tilde{z}\,dF_R}{\int_{F_R} dF_R} = \frac{320\,000}{40\,000} = 8.00 \text{ ft} \qquad \textbf{Ans}$$

9-118. The semicircular drainage pipe is filled with water. Determine the resultant horizontal and vertical force components that the water exerts on the side AB of the pipe per foot of pipe length; $\gamma_w = 62.4$ lb/ft^3.

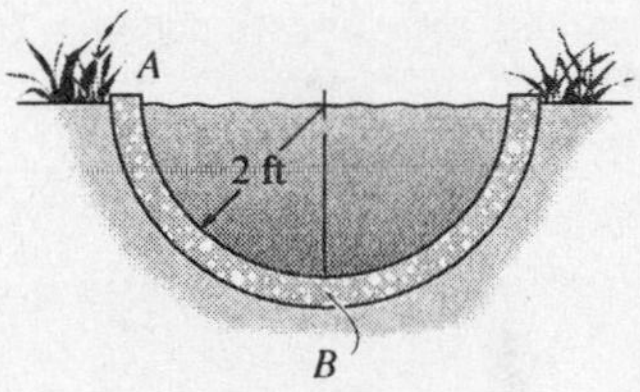

Fluid Pressure : The fluid pressure at the bottom of the drain can be determined using Eq. 9 – 15, $p = \gamma z$.

$$p = 62.4(2) = 124.8 \text{ lb/ft}^2$$

Thus,

$$w = 124.8(1) = 124.8 \text{ lb/ft}$$

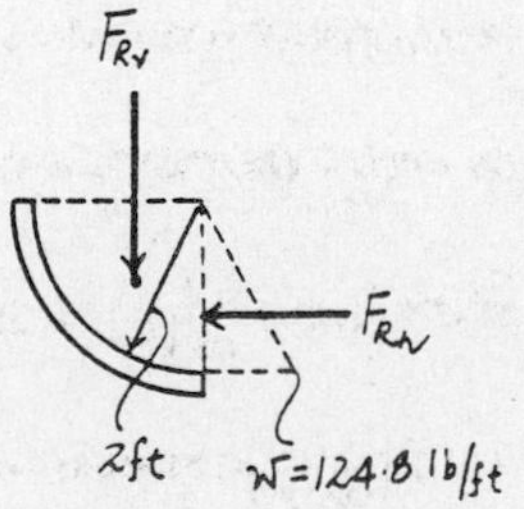

Resultant Forces : The area of the quarter circle is $A = \frac{1}{4}\pi r^2 = \frac{1}{4}\pi\left(2^2\right) = \pi$ ft^2. Then, the vertical component of the resultant force is

$$F_{R_v} = \gamma V = 62.4[\pi(1)] = 196 \text{ lb} \qquad \textbf{Ans}$$

and the horizontal component of the resultant force is

$$F_{R_h} = \frac{1}{2}(124.8)(2) = 125 \text{ lb} \qquad \textbf{Ans}$$

9-119. The pressure loading on the plate is described by the function $p = 10[6/(x+1) + 8]$ lb/ft^2. Determine the magnitude of the resultant force and the coordinates $(\bar{x}, \bar{y})$ of the point where the line of action of the force intersects the plate.

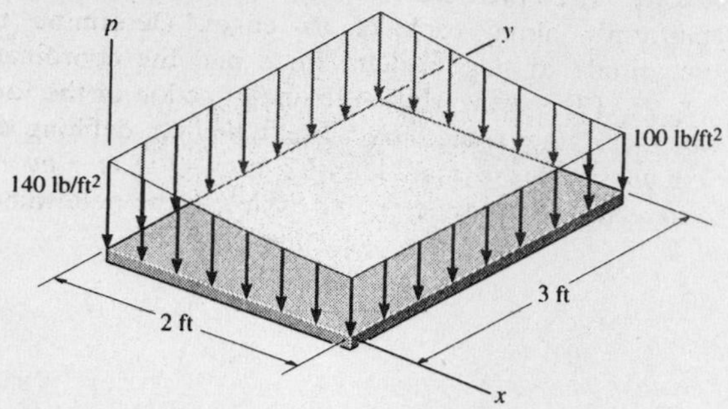

$$p = 10\left[\frac{6}{(x+1)} + 8\right]$$

$$F_R = \int_A p\,dA = \int_0^2 10\left[\frac{6}{(x+1)} + 8\right]3\,dx$$

$$F_R = 30[6\ln(x+1) + 8x]|_0^2 = 677.75 \text{ lb} = 678 \text{ lb} \quad \textbf{Ans}$$

$$\int_A \tilde{x}p\,dA = \int_0^2 x(10)\left[\frac{6}{(x+1)} + 8\right]3\,dx = 30\left[6(x - \ln(1+x)) + 4x^2\right]_0^2 = 642.250$$

$$\bar{x} = \frac{\int_A \tilde{x}p\,dA}{\int_A p\,dA} = \frac{642.250}{677.75} = 0.948 \text{ ft} \quad \textbf{Ans}$$

$\bar{y} = 1.50$ ft (by symmetry) **Ans**

***9-120.** The rectangular plate is subjected to a distributed load over its *entire surface*. If the load is defined by the expression $p = p_o \sin(\pi x/a)$, where p_o represents the pressure acting at the center of the plate, determine the magnitude and location of the resultant force acting on the plate.

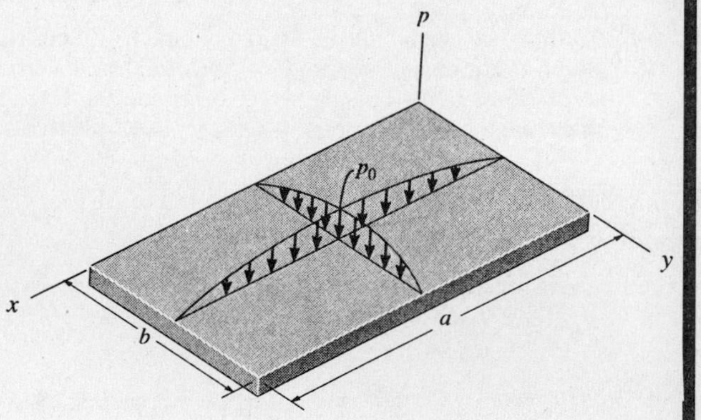

Resultant Force and its Location : The volume of the differential element is

$$dV = dF_R = p\,dx\,dy = p_0\left(\sin\frac{\pi x}{a}dx\right)\left(\sin\frac{\pi y}{b}dy\right).$$

$$F_R = \int_{F_R} dF_R = p_0\int_0^a\left(\sin\frac{\pi x}{a}dx\right)\int_0^b\left(\sin\frac{\pi y}{b}dy\right)$$

$$= p_0\left[\left(-\frac{a}{\pi}\cos\frac{\pi x}{a}\right)\Big|_0^a\left(-\frac{b}{\pi}\cos\frac{\pi x}{b}\right)\Big|_0^b\right]$$

$$= \frac{4ab}{\pi^2}p_0 \quad \textbf{Ans}$$

Since the loading is symmetric, the location of the resultant force is at the center of the plate. Hence,

$$\bar{x} = \frac{a}{2} \quad \bar{y} = \frac{b}{2} \quad \textbf{Ans}$$

9-121. The pressure loading on the plate varies uniformly along each of its edges. Determine the magnitude of the resultant force and the coordinates $(\bar{x}, \bar{y})$ of the point where the line of action of the force intersects the plate. *Hint:* The equation defining the boundary of the load has the form $p = ax + by + c$, where the constants a, b, and c have to be determined.

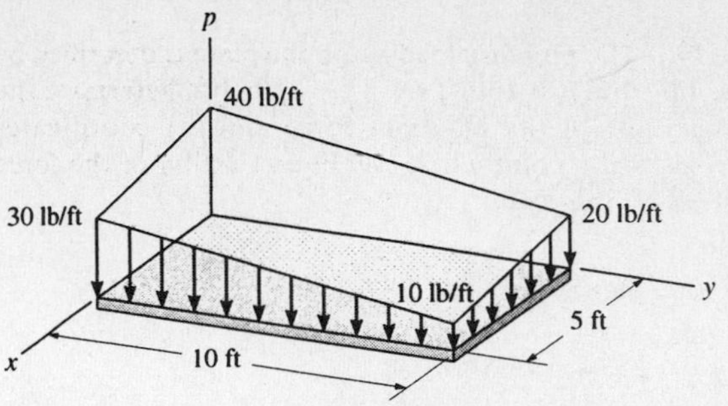

$p = ax + by + c$

At $x = 0,\ y = 0,\quad p = 40$

$40 = 0 + 0 + c;\quad c = 40$

At $x = 5,\ y = 0,\quad p = 30$

$30 = a(5) + 0 + 40;\quad a = -2$

At $x = 0,\ y = 10,\quad p = 20$

$20 = 0 + b(10) + 40;\quad b = -2$

Thus,

$p = -2x - 2y + 40$

$$F_R = \int_A p(x,y)\,dA = \int_0^5\int_0^{10}(-2x - 2y + 40)\,dy\,dx$$

$$= -2\left(\tfrac{1}{2}(5)^2\right)(10) - 2\left(\tfrac{1}{2}(10)^2\right)5 + 40(5)(10)$$

$$= 1250\text{ lb}\qquad \textbf{Ans}$$

$$\int_A x\,p(x,y)\,dA = \int_0^5\int_0^{10}(-2x^2 - 2yx + 40x)\,dy\,dx$$

$$= -2\left(\tfrac{1}{3}(5)^3\right)(10) - 2\left(\tfrac{1}{2}(10)^2\right)\left(\tfrac{1}{2}(5)^2\right) + 40\left(\tfrac{1}{2}(5)^2\right)(10)$$

$$= 2916.67\text{ lb}\cdot\text{ft}$$

$$\bar{x} = \frac{\int_A x\,p(x,y)\,dA}{\int_A p(x,y)\,dA} = \frac{2916.67}{1250} = 2.33\text{ ft}\qquad \textbf{Ans}$$

$$\int_A y\,p(x,y)\,dA = \int_0^5\int_0^{10}(-2xy - 2y^2 + 40y)\,dy\,dx$$

$$= -2\left(\tfrac{1}{2}(5)^2\right)\left(\tfrac{1}{2}(10)^2\right) - 2\left(\tfrac{1}{3}(10)^3\right)(5) + 40(5)\left(\tfrac{1}{2}(10)^2\right)$$

$$= 5416.67\text{ lb}\cdot\text{ft}$$

$$\bar{y} = \frac{\int_A y\,p(x,y)\,dA}{\int_A p(x,y)\,dA} = \frac{5416.67}{1250} = 4.33\text{ ft}\qquad \textbf{Ans}$$

9-122. The drum is filled to the top ($y = 1.5$ ft) with oil having a density of $\rho_o = 55\ \text{lb/ft}^3$. Determine the resultant force of the oil pressure acting on the flat end plate A of the drum and specify its location measured from the top of the drum.

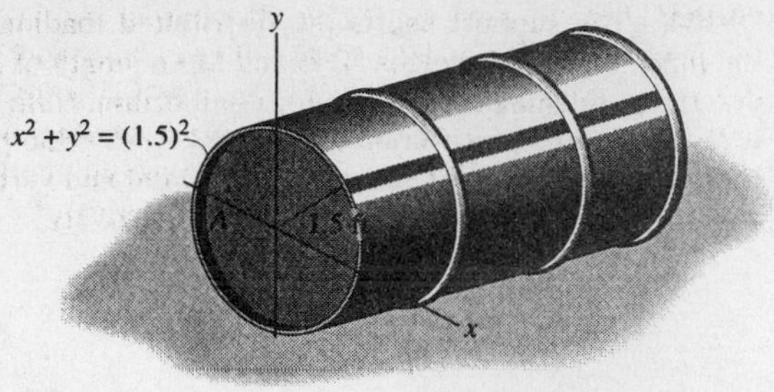

$$dF = dV = p\,dA$$

$$= 55(1.5 - y)(2x\,dy)$$

$$F = V = \int_V dV = \int_{-1.5}^{1.5} 55(2)(1.5 - y)\sqrt{(1.5)^2 - y^2}\,dy = 583.2\ \text{lb}$$

$$= 583\ \text{lb} \qquad \textbf{Ans}$$

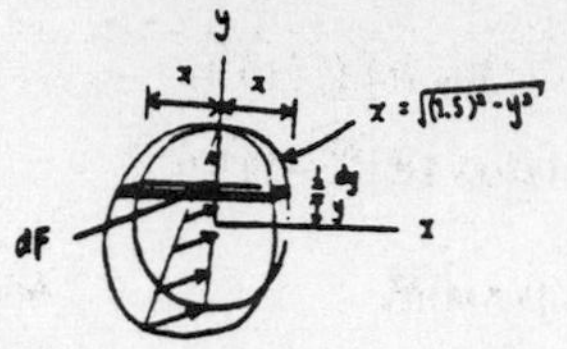

$$\int \tilde{y}\,dV = \int_{-1.5}^{1.5} 55(2)(1.5 - y)\,y\sqrt{(1.5)^2 - y^2}\,dy$$

$$= -218.7\ \text{lb}\cdot\text{ft}$$

$$\bar{y} = \frac{\int \tilde{y}\,dV}{\int_V dV} = \frac{-218.8}{583.2} = -0.375\ \text{ft}$$

Measured from the top $= 1.5 + 0.375 = 1.88$ ft **Ans**

9-123. The curved rod is subjected to the distributed loading shown. Determine the reaction of the fixed support O.

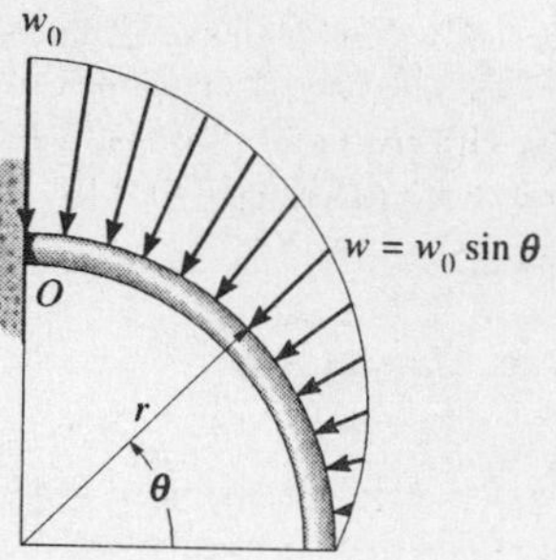

Equilibrium : The area of the differential element is $dA = dF_R = w\,(r d\theta) = w_0 \sin\theta (r d\theta) = w_0 r \sin\theta\,d\theta$. The horizontal component of this differential force is $(dF_R)_x = dF_R \cos\theta = w_0 r \sin\theta \cos\theta\,d\theta$ and the vertical component of this differential force is $(dF_R)_y = dF_R \sin\theta = w_0 r \sin^2\theta\,d\theta$.

$$\xrightarrow{+} \Sigma F_x = 0; \quad O_x - \int_0^{\frac{\pi}{2}} w_0 r \sin\theta\cos\theta\,d\theta = 0$$

$$O_x = \frac{w_0 r}{2}\int_0^{\frac{\pi}{2}} \sin 2\theta\,d\theta = \frac{w_0 r}{2} \qquad \textbf{Ans}$$

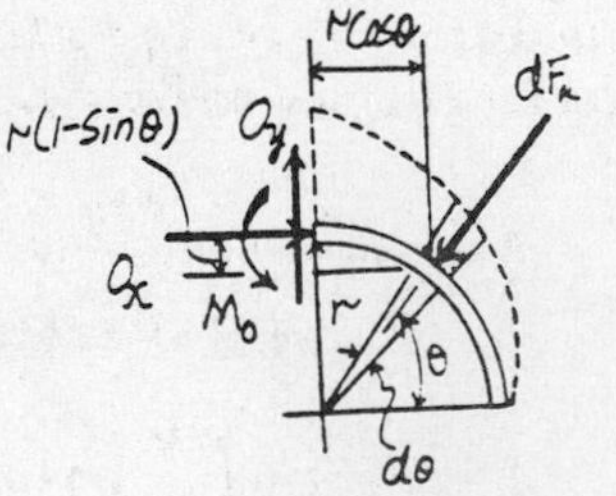

$$+\uparrow \Sigma F_y = 0; \quad O_y - \int_0^{\frac{\pi}{2}} w_0 r \sin^2\theta\,d\theta = 0$$

$$O_y = \frac{w_0 r}{2}\int_0^{\frac{\pi}{2}} (1 - \cos 2\theta)\,d\theta = \frac{\pi w_0 r}{4} \qquad \textbf{Ans}$$

$$+\Sigma M_O = 0; \quad M_O - \int_0^{\frac{\pi}{2}} w_0 r \sin^2\theta\,d\theta (r\cos\theta)$$

$$- \int_0^{\frac{\pi}{2}} w_0 r \sin\theta\cos\theta\,d\theta [r(1 - \sin\theta)] = 0$$

$$M_O = \int_0^{\frac{\pi}{2}} w_0 r^2 \sin\theta\cos\theta\,d\theta$$

$$= \frac{w_0 r^2}{2}\int_0^{\frac{\pi}{2}} \sin 2\theta\,d\theta = \frac{w_0 r^2}{2} \qquad \textbf{Ans}$$

***9-124.** The support exerts the distributed loading on the pipe. If the pipe weighs 50 lb and has a length of 3 ft, determine the magnitude of p_0 for equilibrium. *Hint:* The force acting on the differential segment $r\,d\theta$ of the pipe is $dF = p(3\text{ ft})\,r\,d\theta$. This force has horizontal and vertical components of $dF \sin\theta$ and $dF\cos\theta$, respectively.

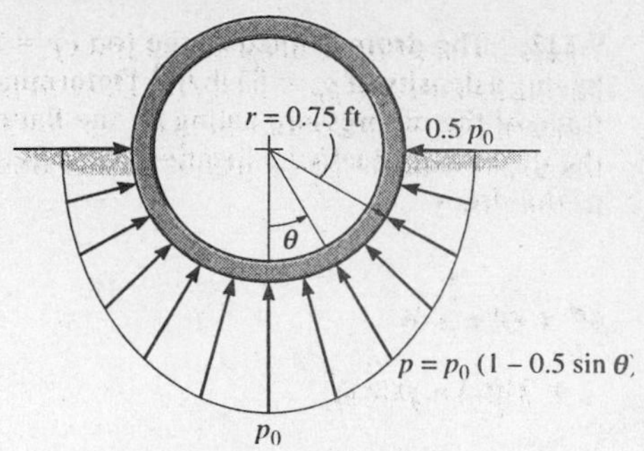

Equilibrium : The voume of the differential element $dV = dF_R = pl(rd\theta)$ $= p_0(1-0.5\sin\theta)(3)(0.75d\theta) = 2.25p_0(1-0.5\sin\theta)\,d\theta$. The vertical component of this differential force $(dF_R)_y = dF_R\cos\theta = 2.25p_0(\cos\theta - 0.5\sin\theta\cos\theta)\,d\theta$ $= 2.25p_0(\cos\theta - 0.25\sin 2\theta)\,d\theta$.

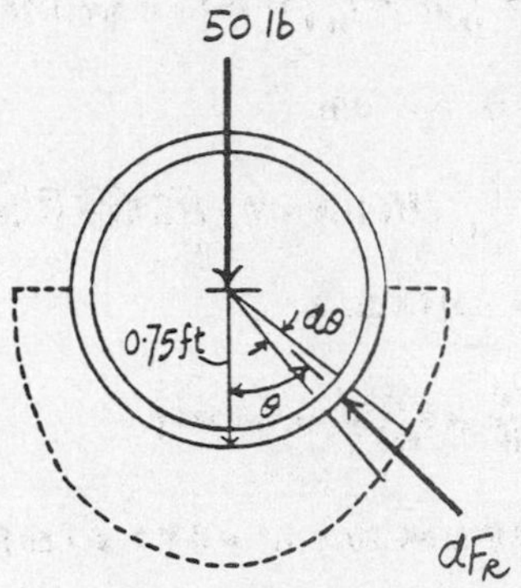

$$+\uparrow \Sigma F_y = 0;\qquad 2\int_0^{90^\circ} 2.25p_0(\cos\theta - 0.25\sin 2\theta)\,d\theta - 50 = 0$$

$$4.50p_0(\sin\theta + 0.125\cos 2\theta)\Big|_0^{90^\circ} - 50 = 0$$

$$p_0 = 14.8\text{ lb/ft}^2 \qquad \textbf{Ans}$$

9-125. The tank is filled with a liquid which has a density of 900 kg/m³. Determine the resultant force that it exerts on the elliptical end plate, and the location of the center of pressure, measured from the x axis.

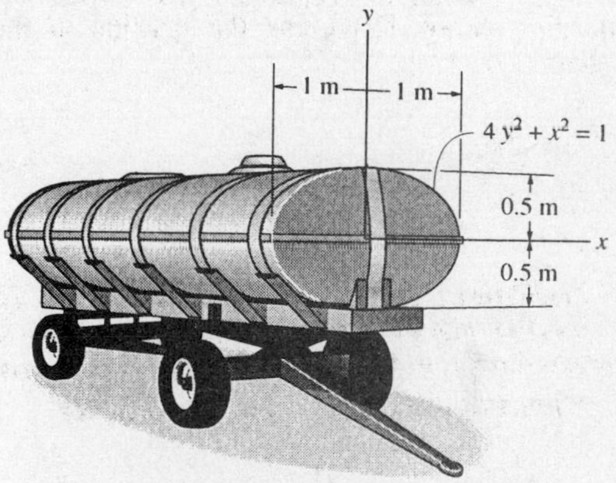

Fluid Pressure : The fluid pressure at an arbitrary point along y axis can be determined using Eq. 9 − 15, $p = \gamma(0.5 - y) = 900(9.81)(0.5-y)$ $= 8829(0.5-y)$.

Resultant Force and its Location : Here, $x = \sqrt{1-4y^2}$. The volume of the differential element is $dV = dF_R = p(2xdy) = 8829(0.5-y)\left[2\sqrt{1-4y^2}\right]dy$. Evaluating the integrals using Simpson's rule, we have

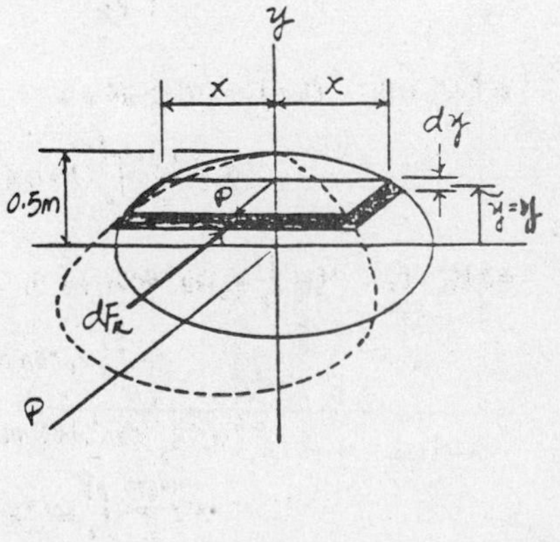

$$F_R = \int_{F_R} dF_R = 17658\int_{-0.5\text{m}}^{0.5\text{m}} (0.5-y)\left(\sqrt{1-4y^2}\right)dy$$

$$= 6934.2\text{ N} = 6.93\text{ kN} \qquad \textbf{Ans}$$

$$\int_{F_R} \tilde{y}\,dF_R = 17658\int_{-0.5\text{m}}^{0.5\text{m}} y(0.5-y)\left(\sqrt{1-4y^2}\right)dy$$

$$= -866.7\text{ N}\cdot\text{m}$$

$$\bar{y} = \frac{\int_{F_R}\tilde{y}\,dF_R}{\int_{F_R} dF_R} = \frac{-866.7}{6934.2} = -0.125\text{ m} \qquad \textbf{Ans}$$

9-126. Locate the centroid $\bar{x}$ of the shaded area.

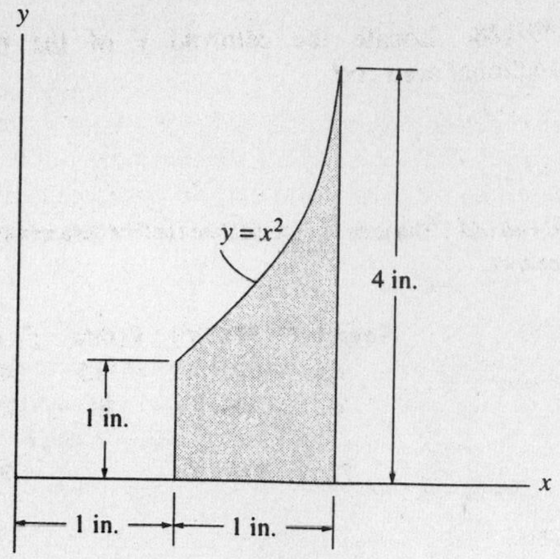

$dA = y\,dx = x^2\,dx$

$\tilde{x} = x$

$$\bar{x} = \frac{\int_A \tilde{x}\,dA}{\int_A dA} = \frac{\int_1^2 x^3\,dx}{\int_1^2 x^2\,dx} = 1.61 \text{ in.} \quad \textbf{Ans}$$

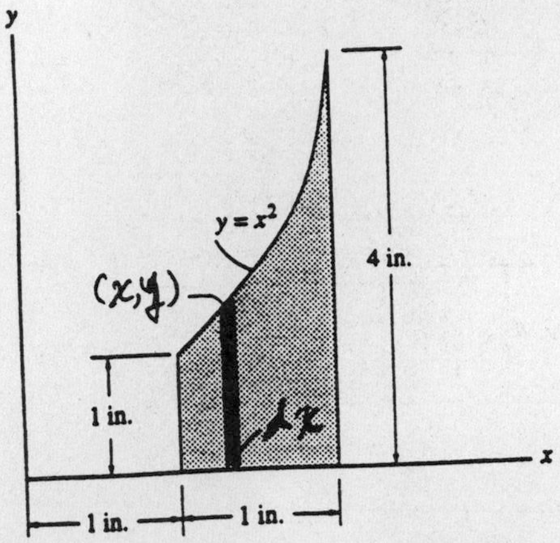

9-127. Locate the centroid $\bar{y}$ of the shaded area.

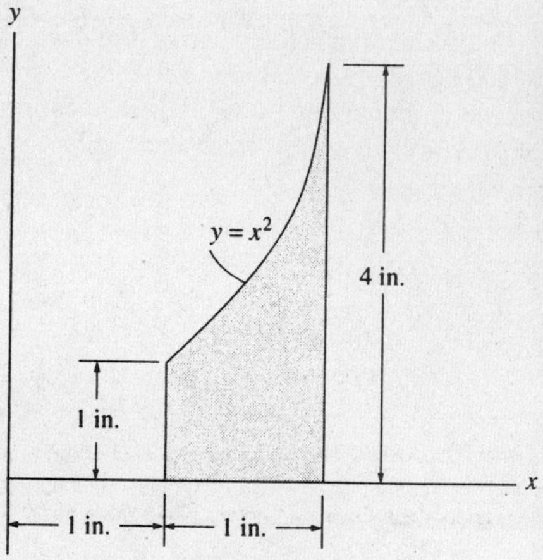

$dA = y\,dx = x^2\,dx$

$\tilde{y} = \frac{y}{2} = \frac{x^2}{2}$

$$\bar{y} = \frac{\int_A \tilde{y}\,dA}{\int_A dA} = \frac{\frac{1}{2}\int_1^2 x^4\,dx}{\int_1^2 x^2\,dx} = \frac{\frac{1}{10}\left[(2)^5-(1)^5\right]}{\frac{1}{3}\left[(2)^3-(1)^3\right]} = 1.33 \text{ in.} \quad \textbf{Ans}$$

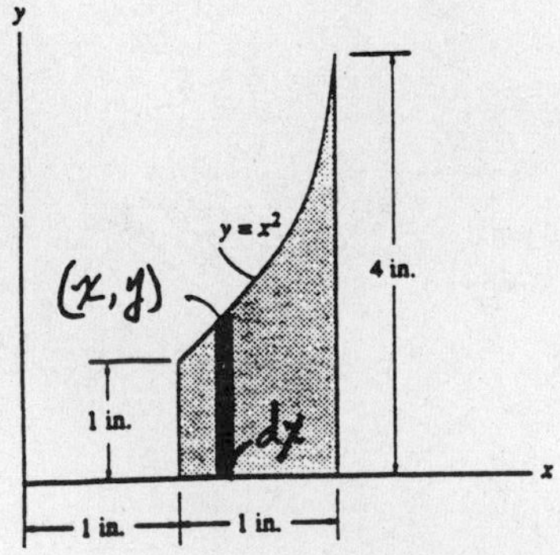

***9-128.** Locate the centroid $\bar{y}$ of the beam's cross-sectional area rod.

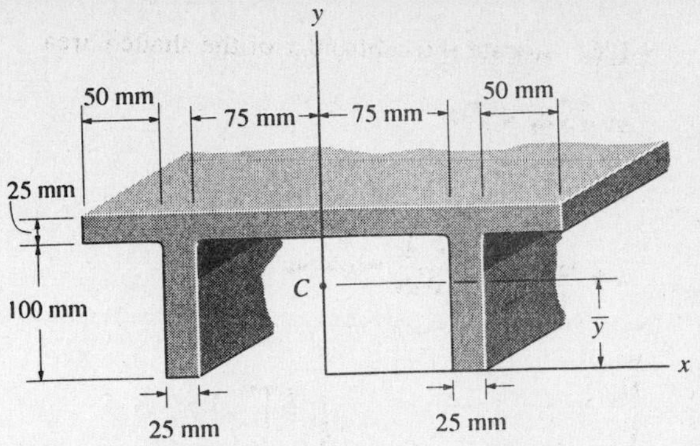

Centroid : The area of each segment and its respective centroid are tabulated below.

Segment	$A\,(\text{mm}^2)$	$\tilde{y}\,(\text{mm})$	$\tilde{y}A\,(\text{mm}^3)$
1	300(25)	112.5	843 750
2	100(50)	50	250 000
Σ	12 500		1 093 750

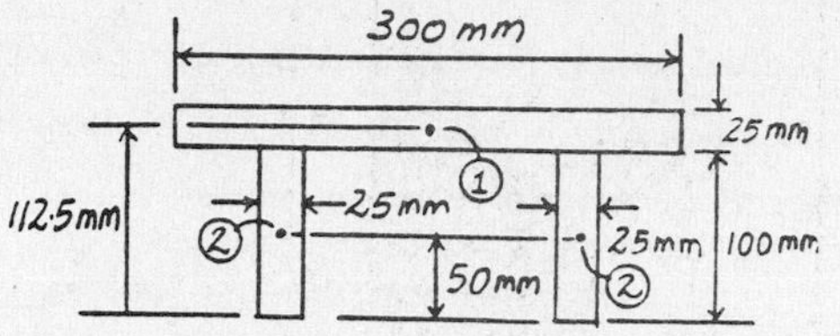

Thus,

$$\bar{y} = \frac{\Sigma \tilde{y}A}{\Sigma A} = \frac{1\,093\,750}{12\,500} = 87.5\ \text{mm} \qquad \textbf{Ans}$$

9-129. Locate the centroid of the solid.

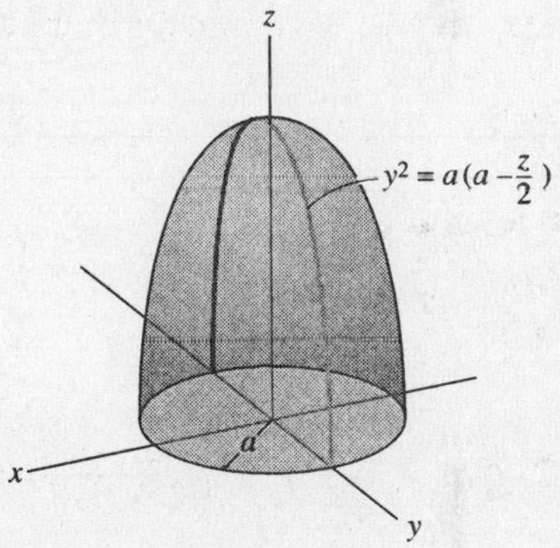

Volume and Moment Arm : The volume of the thin disk differential element is $dV = \pi y^2 dz = \pi\left[a\left(a - \frac{z}{2}\right)\right]dz = \pi a\left(a - \frac{z}{2}\right)dz$ and its centroid is at $\tilde{z} = z$.

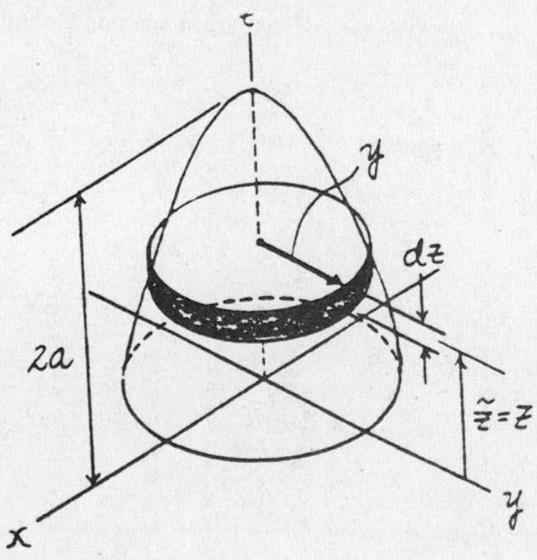

Centroid : Due to symmetry about the z axis

$$\bar{x} = \bar{y} = 0 \qquad \textbf{Ans}$$

Applying Eq. 9–5 and performing the integration, we have

$$\bar{z} = \frac{\int_V \tilde{z}\,dV}{\int_V dV} = \frac{\int_0^{2a} z\left[\pi a\left(a - \frac{z}{2}\right)dz\right]}{\int_0^{2a} \pi a\left(a - \frac{z}{2}\right)dz}$$

$$= \frac{\pi a\left(\frac{az^2}{2} - \frac{z^3}{6}\right)\Big|_0^{2a}}{\pi a\left(az - \frac{z^2}{4}\right)\Big|_0^{2a}} = \frac{2}{3}a \qquad \textbf{Ans}$$

9-130. Determine the magnitude of the resultant hydrostatic force acting per foot of length on the sea wall; $\gamma_w = 62.4\ \text{lb/ft}^3$.

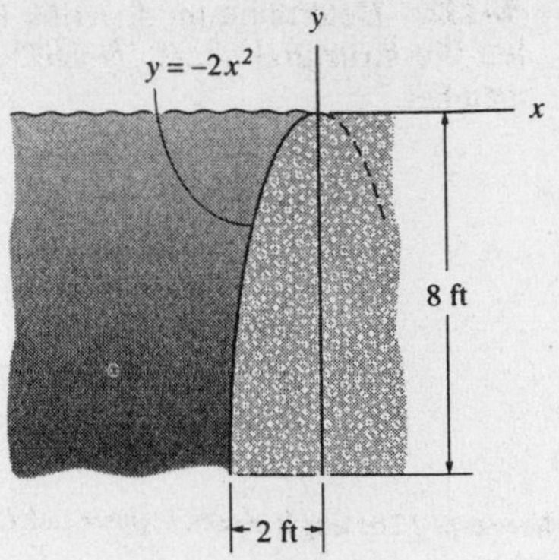

Fluid Pressure : The fluid pressure at the toe of the dam can be determined using Eq. 9 – 15, $p = \gamma z$.

$$p = 62.4(8) = 499.2\ \text{lb/ft}^2$$

Thus,

$$w = 499.2(1) = 499.2\ \text{lb/ft}$$

Resultant Forces : From the inside back cover of the text, the exparabolic area is $A = \frac{1}{3}ab = \frac{1}{3}(8)(2) = 5.333\ \text{ft}^2$. Then, the vertical and horizontal components of the resultant force are

$$F_{R_v} = \gamma V = 62.4[5.333(1)] = 332.8\ \text{lb}$$

$$F_{R_h} = \frac{1}{2}(499.2)(8) = 1996.8\ \text{lb}$$

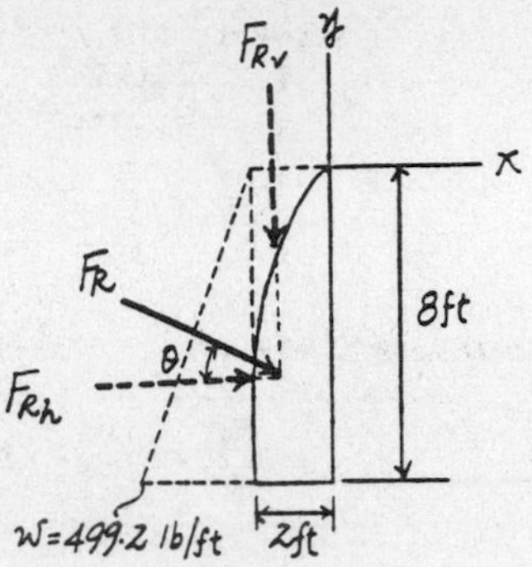

The resultant force and is

$$F_R = \sqrt{F_{R_v}^2 + F_{R_h}^2} = \sqrt{332.8^2 + 1996.8^2}$$

$$= 2024.34\ \text{lb} = 2.02\ \text{kip} \qquad \textbf{Ans}$$

9-131. Locate the centroid $(\bar{x}, \bar{y})$ of the shaded area.

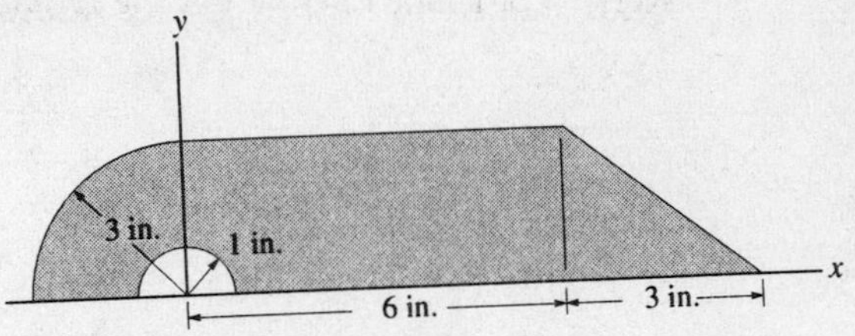

Centroid : The area of each segment and its respective centroid are tabulated below.

Segment	A (in²)	$\tilde{x}$ (in.)	$\tilde{y}$ (in.)	$\tilde{x}A$ (in³)	$\tilde{y}A$ (in³)
1	$\frac{1}{2}(3)(3)$	7	1	31.5	4.50
2	$6(3)$	3	1.5	54.0	27.0
3	$\frac{\pi}{4}(3^2)$	$-\frac{4}{\pi}$	$\frac{4}{\pi}$	−9.00	9.00
4	$-\frac{\pi}{2}(1^2)$	0	$\frac{4}{3\pi}$	0	−0.667
Σ	27.998			76.50	39.833

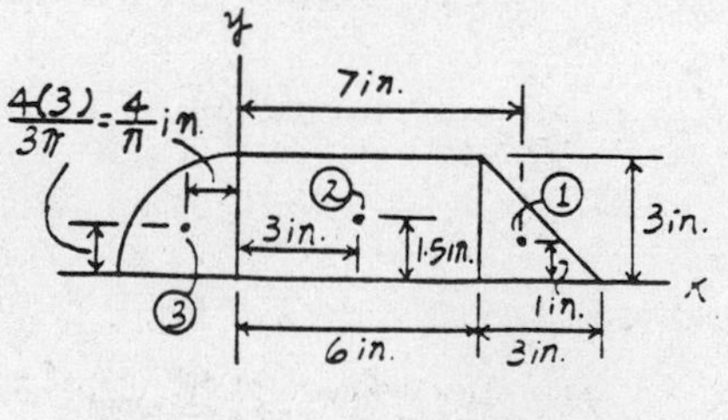

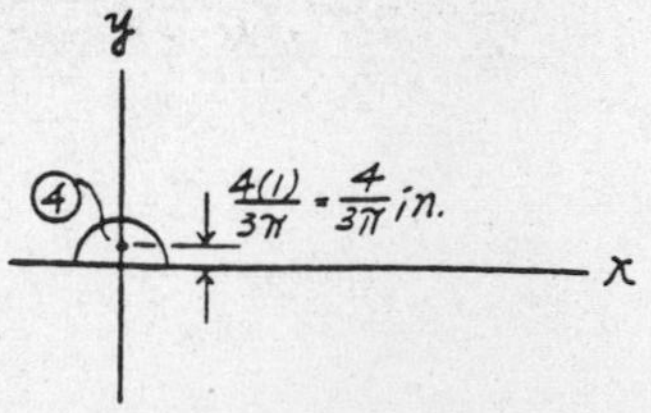

Thus,

$$\bar{x} = \frac{\Sigma\tilde{x}A}{\Sigma A} = \frac{76.50}{27.998} = 2.73\ \text{in.} \qquad \textbf{Ans}$$

$$\bar{y} = \frac{\Sigma\tilde{y}A}{\Sigma A} = \frac{39.833}{27.998} = 1.42\ \text{in.} \qquad \textbf{Ans}$$

***9-132.** Determine the location $(\bar{x}, \bar{y})$ of the centroid for the structural shape. Neglect the thickness of the member.

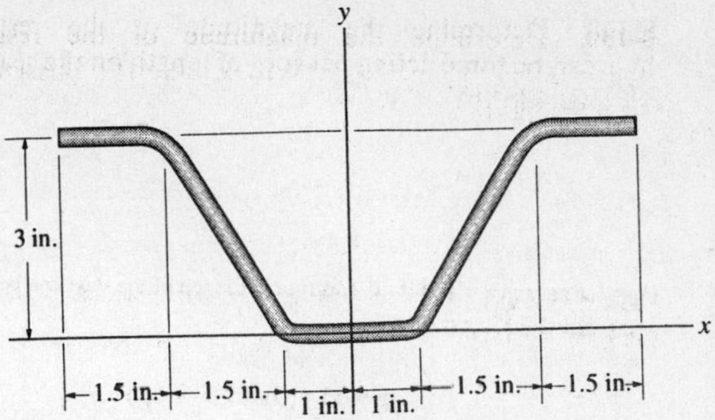

Centroid **:** The length of each segment and its respective centroid are tabulated below.

Segment	L(in.)	$\tilde{y}$(in.)	$\tilde{y}L$(in^2)
1	2(1.5)	3	9.00
2	2(3.354)	1.5	10.06
3	2	0	0
Σ	11.71		19.06

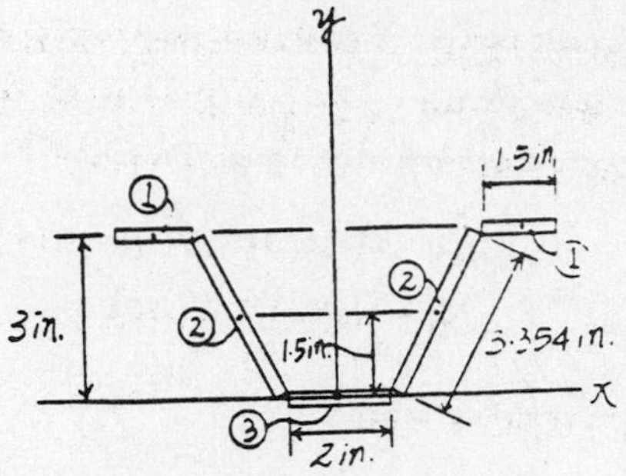

Due to symmetry about y axis, $\bar{x} = 0$ **Ans**

$$\bar{y} = \frac{\Sigma \tilde{y} L}{\Sigma L} = \frac{19.06}{11.71} = 1.628 \text{ in.} = 1.63 \text{ in.}$$ **Ans**

9-133. Locate the centroid $\bar{y}$ of the shaded area.

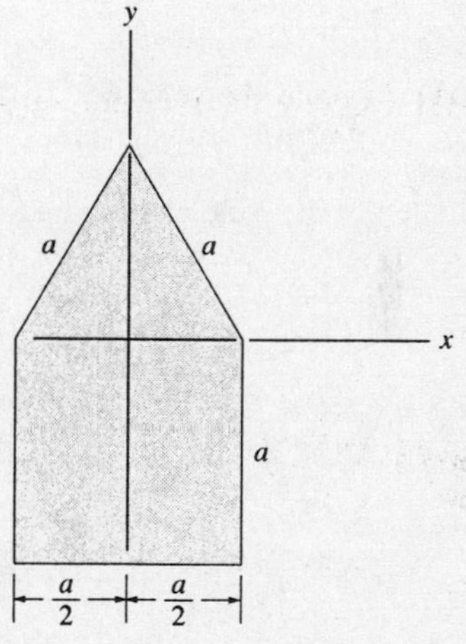

$$\bar{y} = \frac{\Sigma \tilde{y} A}{\Sigma A} = \frac{\frac{a}{3}\cos 30^\circ\left[\frac{1}{2}(a)(a\cos 30^\circ)\right] - \frac{a}{2}[a(a)]}{\frac{1}{2}(a)(a\cos 30^\circ) + [a(a)]} = -0.262a$$

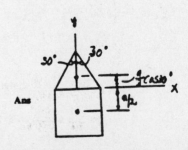

Ans

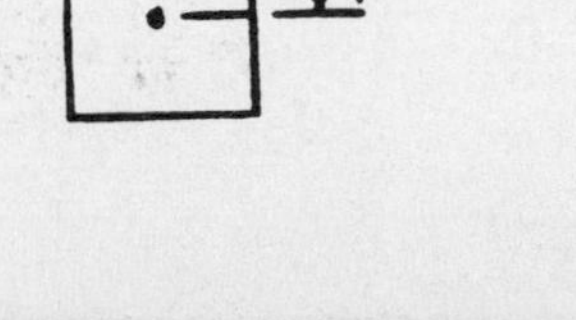

9-134. The load over the plate varies linearly along the sides of the plate such that $p = \frac{2}{3}[x(4 - y)]$ kPa. Determine the resultant force and its position $(\bar{x}, \bar{y})$ on the plate.

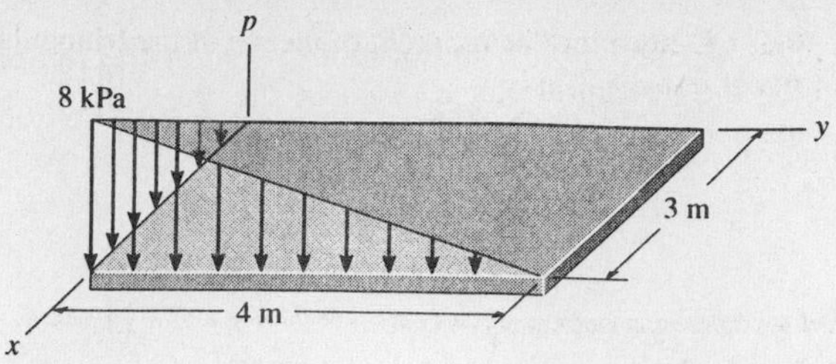

Resultant Force and its Location : The volume of the differential element is $dV = dF_R = p\,dx\,dy = \frac{2}{3}(x\,dx)[(4-y)\,dy]$ and its centroid are $\tilde{x} = x$ and $\tilde{y} = y$.

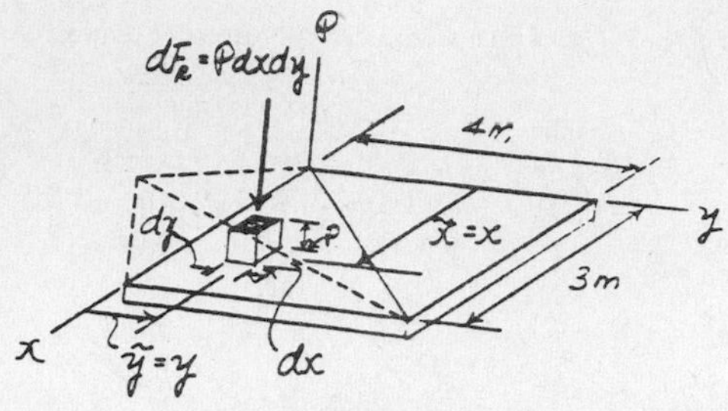

$$F_R = \int_{F_R} dF_R = \int_0^{3\text{m}} \frac{2}{3}(x\,dx)\int_0^{4\text{m}}(4-y)\,dy$$
$$= \frac{2}{3}\left[\left(\frac{x^2}{2}\right)\Big|_0^{3\text{m}}\left(4y - \frac{y^2}{2}\right)\Big|_0^{4\text{m}}\right] = 24.0\text{ kN} \qquad \textbf{Ans}$$

$$\int_{F_R} \tilde{x}\,dF_R = \int_0^{3\text{m}} \frac{2}{3}(x^2\,dx)\int_0^{4\text{m}}(4-y)\,dy$$
$$= \frac{2}{3}\left[\left(\frac{x^3}{3}\right)\Big|_0^{3\text{m}}\left(4y - \frac{y^2}{2}\right)\Big|_0^{4\text{m}}\right] = 48.0\text{ kN}\cdot\text{m}$$

$$\int_{F_R} \tilde{y}\,dF_R = \int_0^{3\text{m}} \frac{2}{3}(x\,dx)\int_0^{4\text{m}} y(4-y)\,dy$$
$$= \frac{2}{3}\left[\left(\frac{x^2}{2}\right)\Big|_0^{3\text{m}}\left(2y^2 - \frac{y^3}{3}\right)\Big|_0^{4\text{m}}\right] = 32.0\text{ kN}\cdot\text{m}$$

$$\bar{x} = \frac{\int_{F_R}\tilde{x}\,dF_R}{\int_{F_R} dF_R} = \frac{48.0}{24.0} = 2.00\text{ m} \qquad \textbf{Ans}$$

$$\bar{y} = \frac{\int_{F_R}\tilde{y}\,dF_R}{\int_{F_R} dF_R} = \frac{32.0}{24.0} = 1.33\text{ m} \qquad \textbf{Ans}$$

9-135. The pressure loading on the plate is described by the function $p = \{-240/(x + 1) + 340\}$ Pa. Determine the magnitude of the resultant force and coordinates of the point where the line of action of the force intersects the plate.

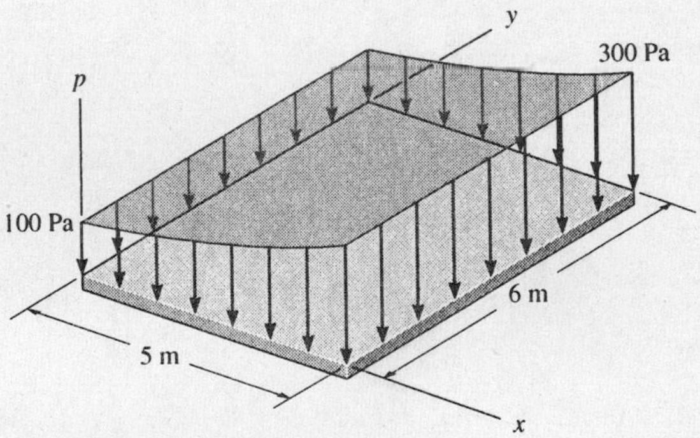

Resultant Force and its Location : The volume of the differential element is $dV = dF_R = 6p\,dx = 6\left(-\frac{240}{x+1} + 340\right)dx$ and its centroid is $\tilde{x} = x$.

$$F_R = \int_{F_R} dF_R = \int_0^{5\text{m}} 6\left(-\frac{240}{x+1} + 340\right)dx$$
$$= 6[-240\ln(x+1) + 340x]\big|_0^{5\text{m}}$$
$$= 7619.87\text{ N} = 7.62\text{ kN} \qquad \textbf{Ans}$$

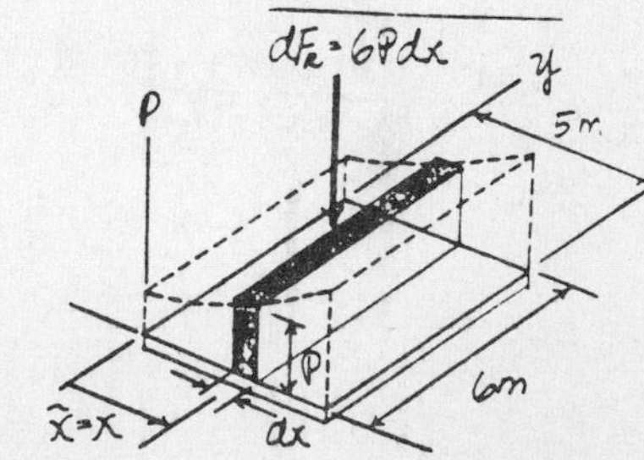

$$\int_{F_R} \tilde{x}\,dF_R = \int_0^{5\text{m}} 6x\left(-\frac{240}{x+1} + 340\right)$$
$$= \left[-1440[x - \ln(x+1)] + 1020x^2\right]\Big|_0^{5\text{m}}$$
$$= 20880.13\text{ N}\cdot\text{m}$$

$$\bar{x} = \frac{\int_{F_R}\tilde{x}\,dF_R}{\int_{F_R} dF_R} = \frac{20880.13}{7619.87} = 2.74\text{ m} \qquad \textbf{Ans}$$

Due to symmetry,

$$\bar{y} = 3.00\text{ m} \qquad \textbf{Ans}$$

10-1. Determine the moment of inertia of the triangular area about the x axis.

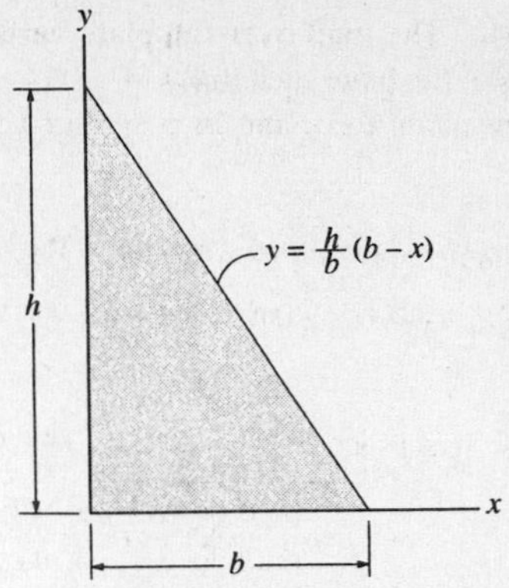

Area of the differential element (shaded) $dA = x\,dy$ where $x = b - \frac{b}{h}y$, hence, $dA = x\,dy = \left(b - \frac{b}{h}y\right)dy$.

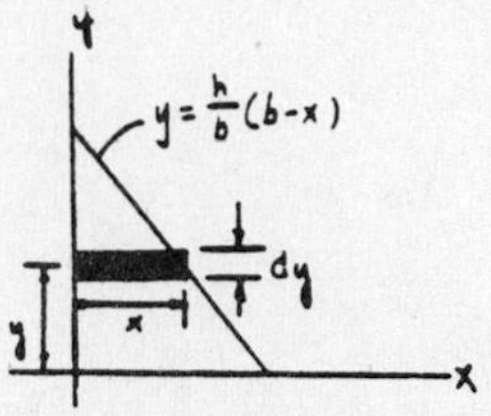

$$I_x = \int_A y^2\,dA = \int_0^h y^2\left(b - \frac{b}{h}y\right)dy$$

$$= \int_0^h \left(by^2 - \frac{b}{h}y^3\right)dy$$

$$= \frac{b}{3}y^3 - \frac{b}{4h}y^4\Big|_0^h$$

$$= \frac{1}{12}bh^3 \qquad \textbf{Ans}$$

10-2. Determine the moment of inertia of the triangular area about the y axis.

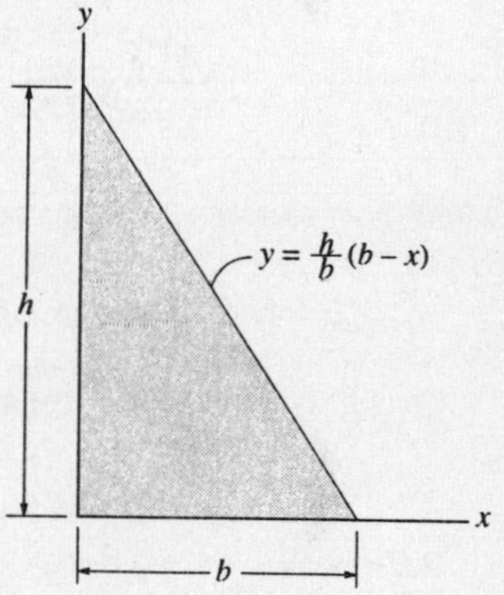

Area of the differential element (shaded) $dA = y\,dx$ where $y = h - \frac{h}{b}x$, hence, $dA = y\,dx = \left(h - \frac{h}{b}x\right)dx$.

$$I_y = \int_A x^2\,dA = \int_0^b x^2\left(h - \frac{h}{b}x\right)dx$$

$$= \int_0^b \left(hx^2 - \frac{h}{b}x^3\right)dx$$

$$= \frac{h}{3}x^3 - \frac{h}{4b}x^4\Big|_0^b$$

$$= \frac{1}{12}hb^3 \qquad \textbf{Ans}$$

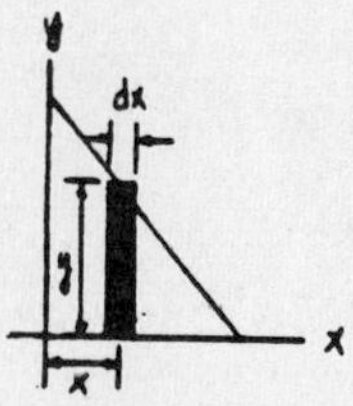

10-3. Determine the moment of inertia of the area about the x axis. Solve the problem in two ways, using rectangular differential elements: (a) having a thickness dx and (b) having a thickness of dy.

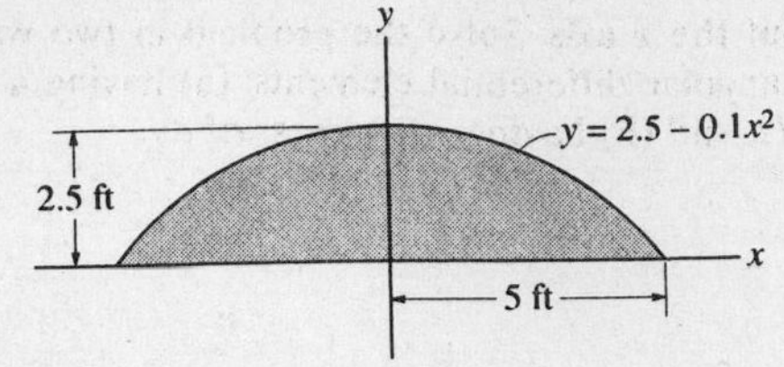

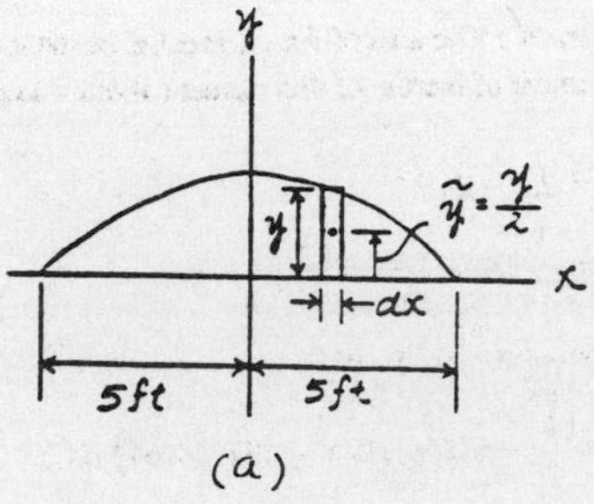

a) ***Differential Element :*** The area of the differential element parallel to y axis is $dA = ydx$. The moment of inertia of this element about x axis is

$$dI_x = d\bar{I}_{x'} + dA\tilde{y}^2$$
$$= \frac{1}{12}(dx)y^3 + ydx\left(\frac{y}{2}\right)^2$$
$$= \frac{1}{3}\left(2.5 - 0.1x^2\right)^3 dx$$
$$= \frac{1}{3}\left(-0.001x^6 + 0.075x^4 - 1.875x^2 + 15.625\right) dx$$

Moment of Inertia : Performing the integration, we have

$$I_x = \int dI_x = \frac{1}{3}\int_{-5\text{ft}}^{5\text{ft}} \left(-0.001x^6 + 0.075x^4 - 1.875x^2 + 15.625\right) dx$$
$$= \frac{1}{3}\left(-\frac{0.001}{7}x^7 + \frac{0.075}{5}x^5 - \frac{1.875}{3}x^3 + 15.625x\right)\Bigg|_{-5\text{ft}}^{5\text{ft}}$$
$$= 23.8\ \text{ft}^4$$

Ans

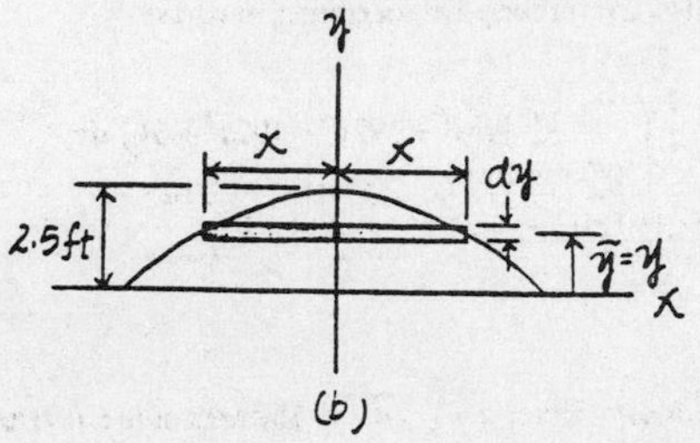

b) ***Differential Element :*** Here, $x = \sqrt{25 - 10y}$. The area of the differential element parallel to x axisis $dA = 2xdy = 2\sqrt{25 - 10y}dy$.

Moment of Inertia : Applying Eq. 10 − 1 and performing the integration, we have

$$I_x = \int_A y^2 dA$$
$$= 2\int_0^{2.5\text{ft}} y^2\sqrt{25 - 10y}dy$$
$$= 2\left[-\frac{y^2}{15}(25 - 10y)^{\frac{3}{2}} - \frac{2y}{375}(25 - 10y)^{\frac{5}{2}} - \frac{2}{13125}(25 - 10y)^{\frac{7}{2}}\right]\Bigg|_0^{2.5\text{ft}}$$
$$= 23.8\ \text{ft}^4$$

Ans

***10-4.** Determine the moment of inertia of the area about the x axis. Solve the problem in two ways, using rectangular differential elements: (a) having a thickness of dx, and (b) having a thickness of dy.

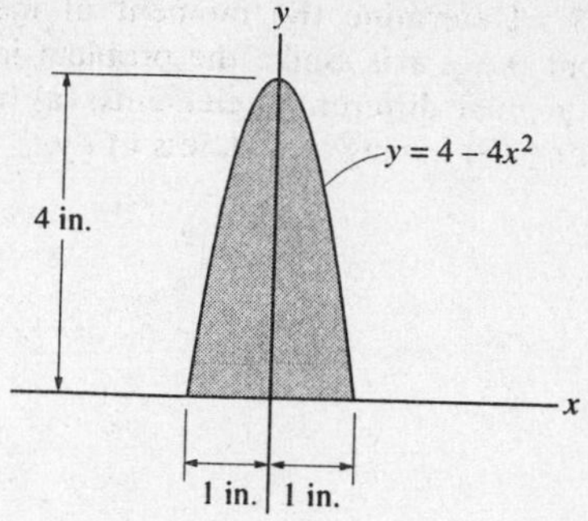

a)***Differential Element :*** The area of the differential element parallel to y axis is $dA = y dx$. The moment of inertia of this element about x axis is

$$
\begin{aligned}
dI_x &= d\bar{I}_{x'} + dA\,\tilde{y}^2 \\
&= \frac{1}{12}(dx)\,y^3 + y\,dx\left(\frac{y}{2}\right)^2 \\
&= \frac{1}{3}\left(4-4x^2\right)^3 dx \\
&= \frac{1}{3}\left(-64x^6+192x^4-192x^2+64\right) dx
\end{aligned}
$$

Moment of Inertia : Performing the integration, we have

$$
\begin{aligned}
I_x = \int dI_x &= \frac{1}{3}\int_{-1\text{in.}}^{1\text{in.}} \frac{1}{3}\left(-64x^6+192x^4-192x^2+64\right) dx \\
&= \frac{1}{3}\left(-\frac{64}{7}x^7+\frac{192}{5}x^5-\frac{192}{3}x^3+64x\right)\Bigg|_{-1\text{in.}}^{1\text{in.}} \\
&= 19.5\ \text{in}^4
\end{aligned}
$$

Ans

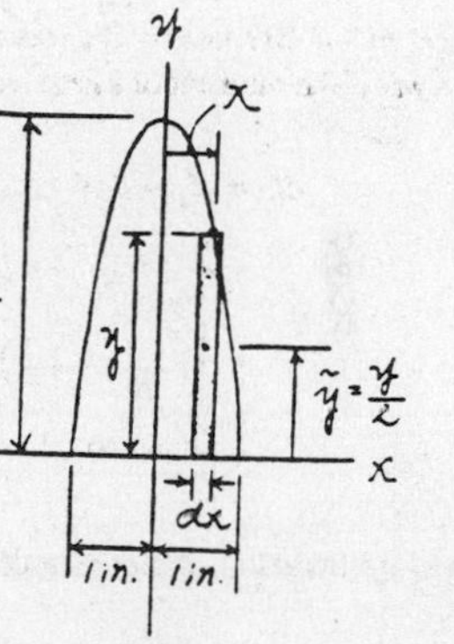

(a)

b)***Differential Element :*** Here, $x = \frac{1}{2}\sqrt{4-y}$. The area of the differential element parallel to x axis is $dA = 2x\,dy = \sqrt{4-y}\,dy$.

Moment of Inertia : Applying Eq. 10 − 1 and performing the integration, we have

$$
\begin{aligned}
I_x &= \int_A y^2 dA \\
&= \int_0^{4\text{in.}} y^2\sqrt{4-y}\,dy \\
&= \left[-\frac{2y^2}{3}(4-y)^{\frac{3}{2}}-\frac{8y}{15}(4-y)^{\frac{5}{2}}-\frac{16}{105}(4-y)^{\frac{7}{2}}\right]_0^{4\text{in.}} \\
&= 19.5\ \text{in}^4
\end{aligned}
$$

Ans

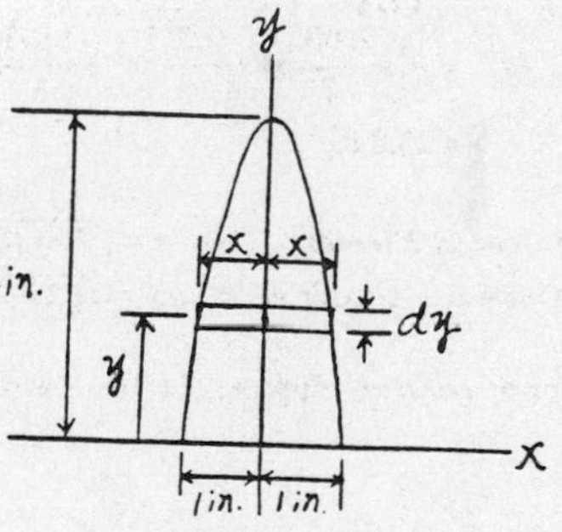

(b)

10-5. Determine the moment of inertia of the area about the y axis. Solve the problem in two ways, using rectangular differential elements : (a) having a thickness of dx, and (b) having a thickness of dy.

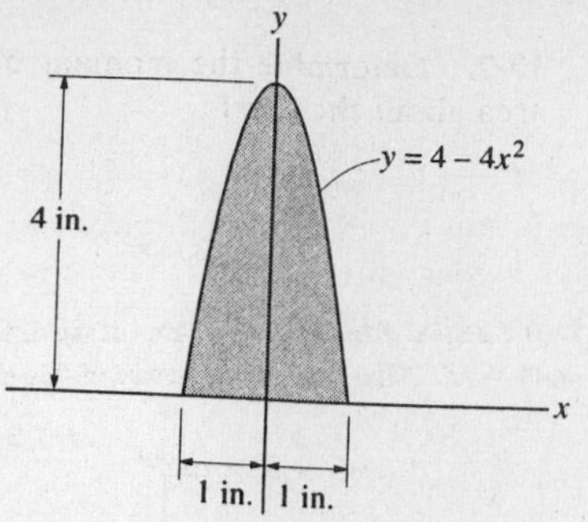

a)***Differential Element :*** The area of the differential element parallel to yaxis is $dA = ydx = (4-4x^2)\,dx$.

Moment of Inertia : Applying Eq. 10 − 1 and performing the integration, we have

$$I_y = \int_A x^2 dA = \int_{-1\text{in.}}^{1\text{in.}} x^2(4-4x^2)\,dx$$
$$= \left[\frac{4}{3}x^3 - \frac{4}{5}x^5\right]\Big|_{-1\text{in.}}^{1\text{in.}}$$
$$= 1.07\ \text{in}^4$$

Ans

b)***Differential Element :*** Here, $x = \frac{1}{2}\sqrt{4-y}$. The moment of inertia of the differential element about y axis is

$$dI_y = \frac{1}{12}(dy)(2x^3) = \frac{2}{3}x^3 dy = \frac{1}{12}(4-y)^{\frac{3}{2}}dy$$

Moment of Inertia : Performing the integration, we have

$$I_y = \int dI_y = \frac{1}{12}\int_0^{4\text{in.}} (4-y)^{\frac{3}{2}}dy$$
$$= \frac{1}{12}\left[-\frac{2}{5}(4-y)^{\frac{5}{2}}\right]\Big|_0^{4\text{in.}}$$
$$= 1.07\ \text{in}^4$$

Ans

10-6. Determine the radius of gyration of the shaded area about the y axis.

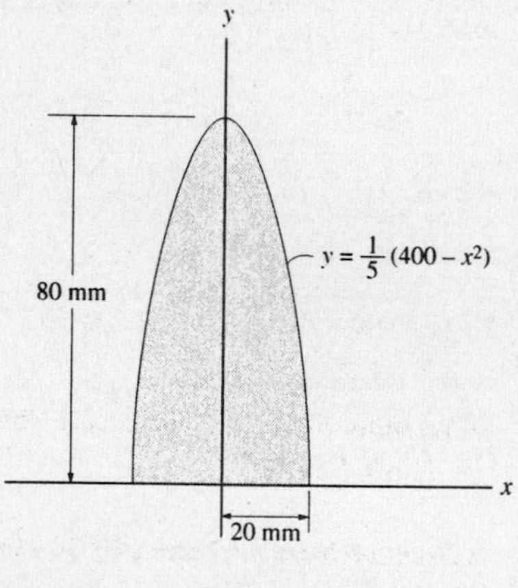

Area of the differential element (shaded) $dA = ydx$ where $y = \frac{1}{5}(400-x^2)$, hence,
$dA = ydx = \frac{1}{5}(400-x^2)\,dx$.

Area :

$$A = \int_A dA = \frac{1}{5}\int_{-20}^{20}(400-x^2)\,dx$$
$$= \left[\frac{1}{5}\left(400x - \frac{1}{3}x^3\right)\right]\Big|_{-20}^{20}$$
$$= 2133.33\ \text{mm}^2$$

Moment of inertia about y axis :

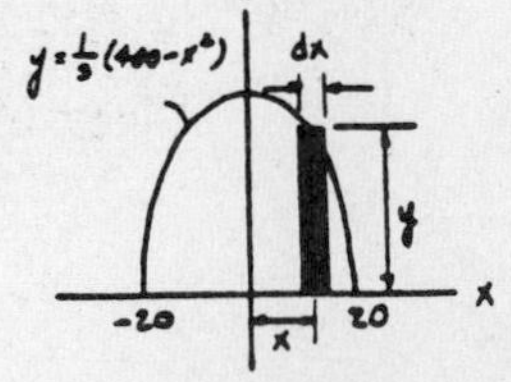

$$I_y = \int_A x^2 dA = \frac{1}{5}\int_{-20}^{20} x^2(400-x^2)\,dx$$
$$= \frac{1}{5}\int_{-20}^{20}(400x^2 - x^4)\,dx$$
$$= \left[\frac{1}{5}\left(\frac{400}{3}x^3 - \frac{1}{5}x^5\right)\right]\Big|_{-20}^{20}$$
$$= 170.66(10)^3\ \text{mm}^4$$

Radius of gyration about y axis :

$$k_y = \sqrt{\frac{I_y}{A}} = \sqrt{\frac{170.66(10)^3}{2133.33}} = 8.94\ \text{mm}$$

Ans

10-7. Determine the moment of inertia of the shaded area about the x axis.

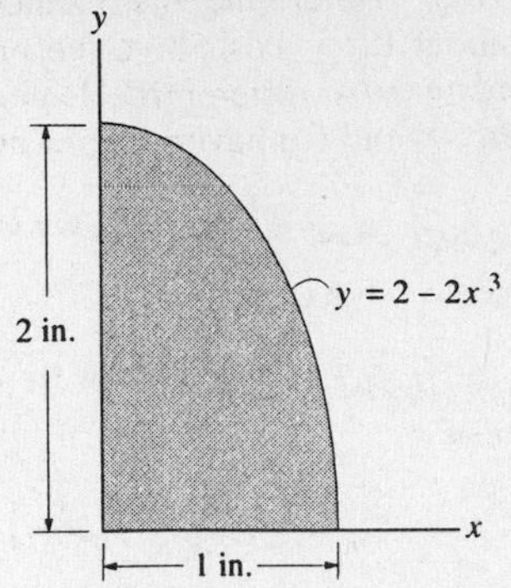

Differential Element : The area of the differential element parallel to y axis is $dA = ydx$. The moment of inertia of this element about x axis is

$$dI_x = d\bar{I}_{x'} + dA\tilde{y}^2$$
$$= \frac{1}{12}(dx)y^3 + ydx\left(\frac{y}{2}\right)^2$$
$$= \frac{1}{3}\left(2-2x^3\right)^3 dx$$
$$= \frac{1}{3}\left(-8x^9 + 24x^6 - 24x^3 + 8\right) dx$$

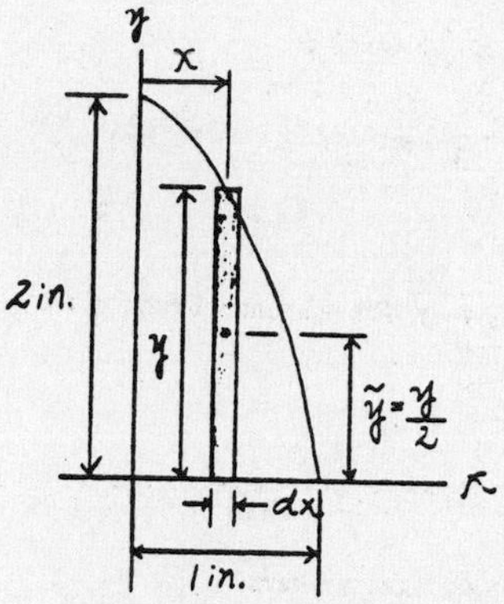

Moment of Inertia : Performing the integration, we have

$$I_x = \int dI_x = \frac{1}{3}\int_0^{1\text{in.}} \left(-8x^9 + 24x^6 - 24x^3 + 8\right) dx$$
$$= \frac{1}{3}\left(-\frac{4}{5}x^{10} + \frac{24}{7}x^7 - 6x^4 + 8x\right)\Big|_0^{1\text{in.}}$$
$$= 1.54 \text{ in}^4$$

Ans

***10-8.** Determine the moment of inertia of the shaded area about the y axis.

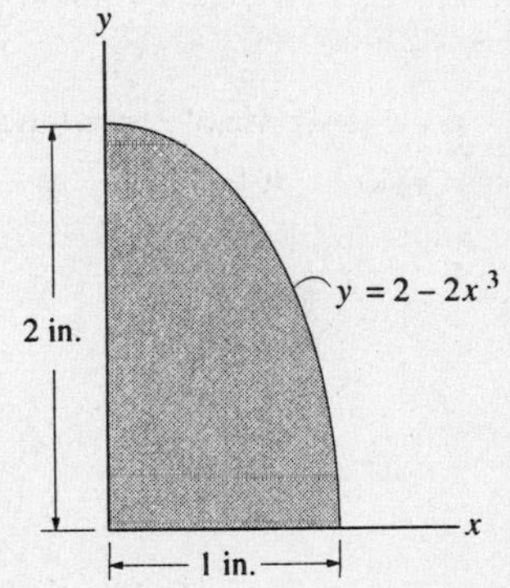

Differential Element : The area of the differential element parallel to yaxis is $dA = ydx = \left(2-2x^3\right) dx$.

Moment of Inertia : Applying Eq. 10 − 1and performing the integration, we have

$$I_y = \int_A x^2 dA = \int_0^{1\text{in.}} x^2\left(2-2x^3\right) dx$$
$$= \left[\frac{2}{3}x^3 - \frac{1}{3}x^6\right]\Big|_0^{1\text{in.}}$$
$$= 0.333 \text{ in}^4$$

Ans

10-9. Determine the moment of inertia of the shaded area about the x axis.

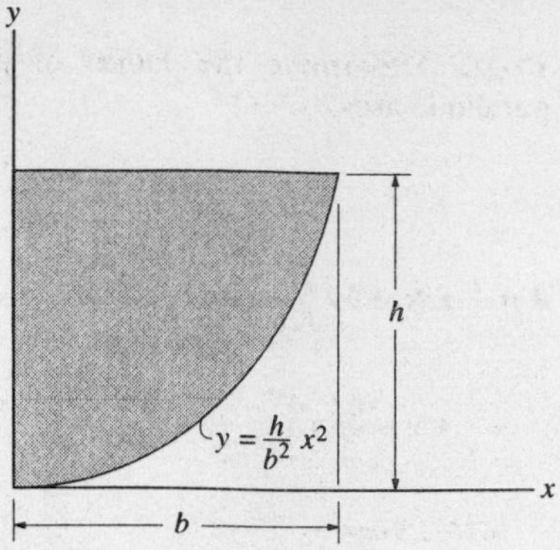

Differential Element : Here, $x = \frac{b}{\sqrt{h}}y^{\frac{1}{2}}$. The area of the differential element parallel to xaxis is $dA = xdy = \left(\frac{b}{\sqrt{h}}y^{\frac{1}{2}}\right)dy$.

Moment of Inertia : Applying Eq. 10 – 1 and performing the integration, we have

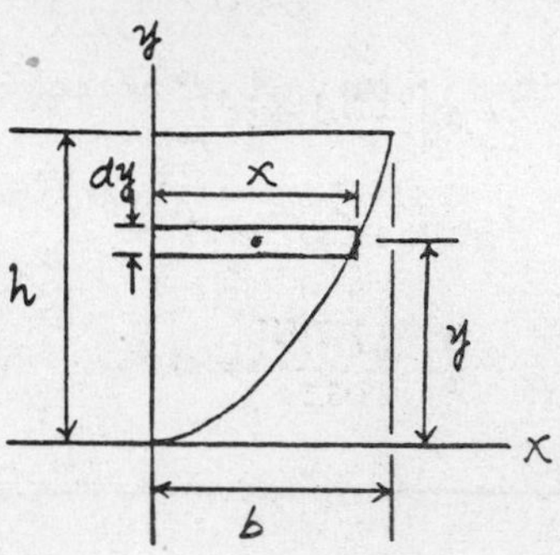

$$I_x = \int_A y^2 dA = \int_0^h y^2\left(\frac{b}{\sqrt{h}}y^{\frac{1}{2}}\right)dy$$
$$= \frac{b}{\sqrt{h}}\left(\frac{2}{7}y^{\frac{7}{2}}\right)\Bigg|_0^h$$
$$= \frac{2}{7}bh^3 \qquad \textbf{Ans}$$

10-10. Determine the moment of inertia of the shaded area about the y axis.

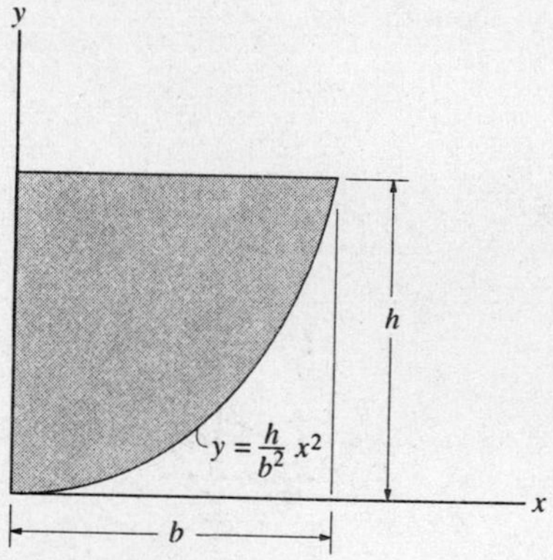

Differential Element : The area of the differential element parallel to yaxis is $dA = (h-y)\,dx = \left(h - \frac{h}{b^2}x^2\right)dx$.

Moment of Inertia : Applying Eq. 10 – 1 and performing the integration, we have

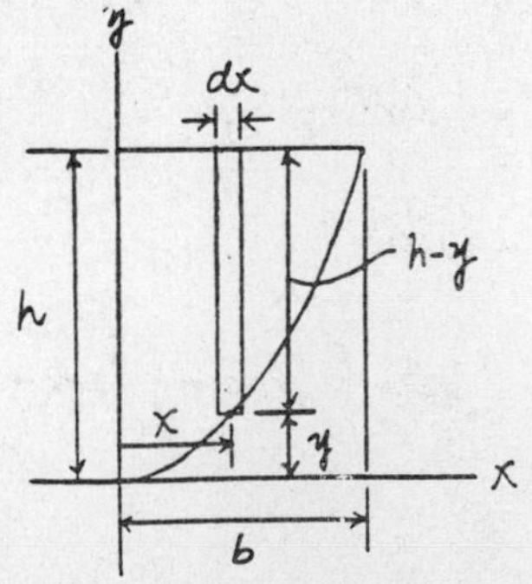

$$I_y = \int_A x^2 dA = \int_0^b x^2\left(h - \frac{h}{b^2}x^2\right)dx$$
$$= \left(\frac{h}{3}x^3 - \frac{h}{5b^2}x^5\right)\Bigg|_0^b$$
$$= \frac{2}{15}hb^3 \qquad \textbf{Ans}$$

10-11. Determine the radius of gyration k_y of the parabolic area.

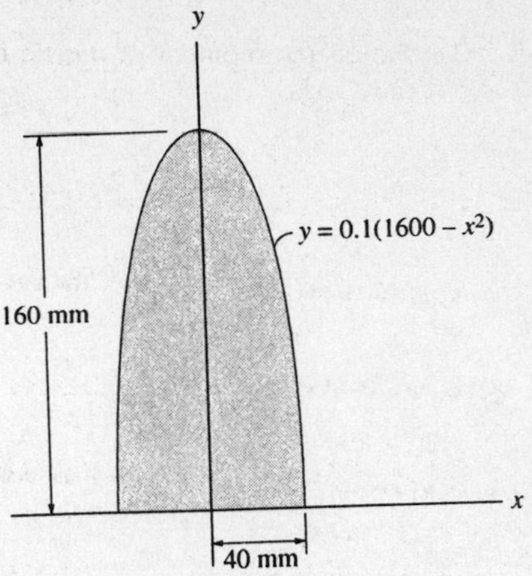

$$A = \int_A y\,dx = 0.1\int_{-40}^{40} (1600 - x^2)\,dx$$

$$= \left[160x - \frac{0.1}{3}x^3\right]_{-40}^{40}$$

$$= 8533.3\ \text{mm}^2$$

$$I_y = \int_A x^2\,dA = 0.1\int_{-40}^{40} (1600x^2 - x^4)\,dx$$

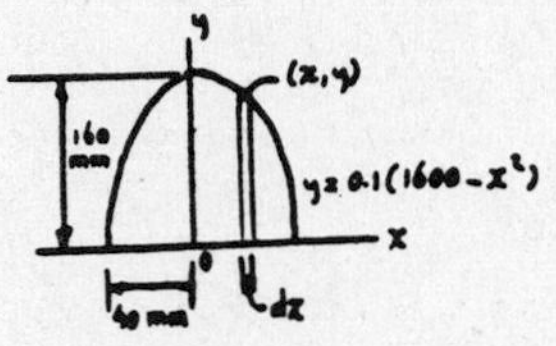

$$= 0.1\left[\frac{1600}{3}x^3 - \frac{1}{5}x^5\right]_{-40}^{40}$$

$$= 2730.67(10^3)\ \text{mm}^4$$

$$k_y = \sqrt{\frac{2730.67(10^3)}{8533.3}} = 17.9\ \text{mm} \quad \textbf{Ans}$$

***10-12.** Determine the moment of inertia of the shaded area about the x axis.

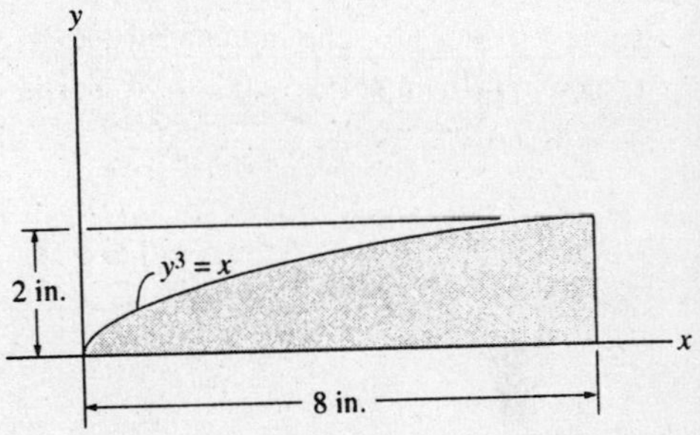

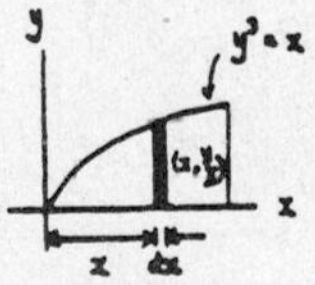

$$dI_x = dI_{\bar{x}} + dA\,\bar{y}^2$$

$$= \frac{1}{12}dx\,y^3 + y\,dx\left(\frac{y}{2}\right)^2$$

$$= \frac{1}{3}y^3\,dx$$

$$I_x = \int_A dI_x = \int_0^8 \frac{1}{3}y^3\,dx = \int_0^8 \frac{1}{3}x\,dx = \left.\frac{x^2}{6}\right]_0^8 = 10.7\ \text{in}^4 \quad \textbf{Ans}$$

10-13. Determine the moment of inertia of the shaded area about the y axis.

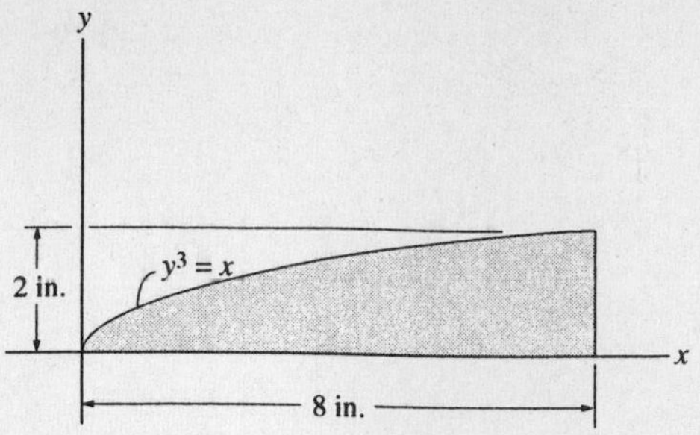

$$dI_y = dI_{\bar{y}} + dA\,\bar{x}^2$$

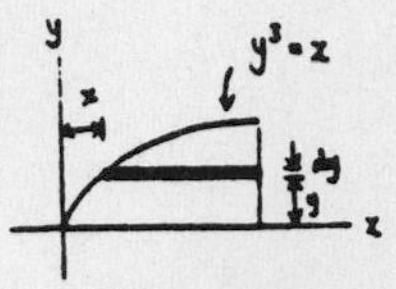

$$= \frac{1}{12}dy\,(8 - y^3)^3 + (8 - y^3)\,dy\left(y^3 + \frac{1}{2}(8 - y^3)\right)^2$$

$$= \left[\frac{1}{12}(8 - y^3)^3 + (8 - y^3)\left(\frac{1}{4}\right)(y^3 + 8)^2\right]dy$$

$$I_y = \int_A dI_y = \int_0^8\left[\frac{1}{12}(8 - y^3)^3 + (8 - y^3)\left(\frac{1}{4}\right)(y^3 + 8)^2\right]dy = 307\ \text{in}^4 \qquad \textbf{Ans}$$

Also,

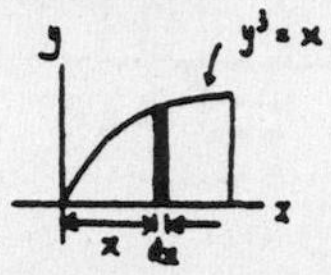

$$I_y = \int_A x^2\,dA = \int_A x^2\,y\,dx = \int_0^8 x^{\frac{7}{3}}\,dx = \frac{3}{10}x^{\frac{10}{3}}\Big]_0^8 = 307\ \text{in}^4 \qquad \textbf{Ans}$$

10-14. Determine the moment of inertia of the shaded area about the x axis.

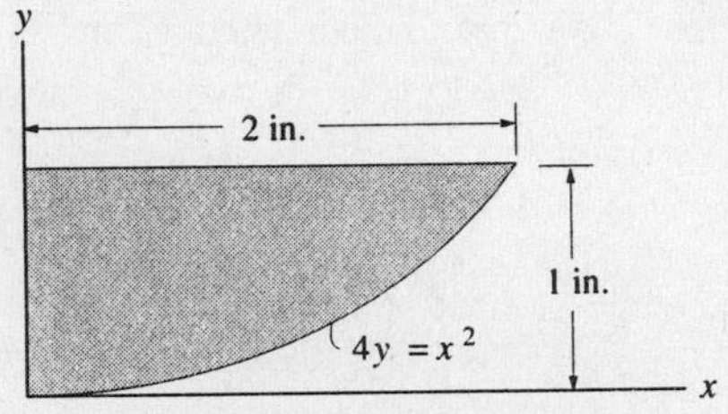

Differential Element : Here, $x = 2y^{\frac{1}{2}}$. The area of the differential element parallel to x axis is $dA = x\,dy = \left(2y^{\frac{1}{2}}\right)dy$.

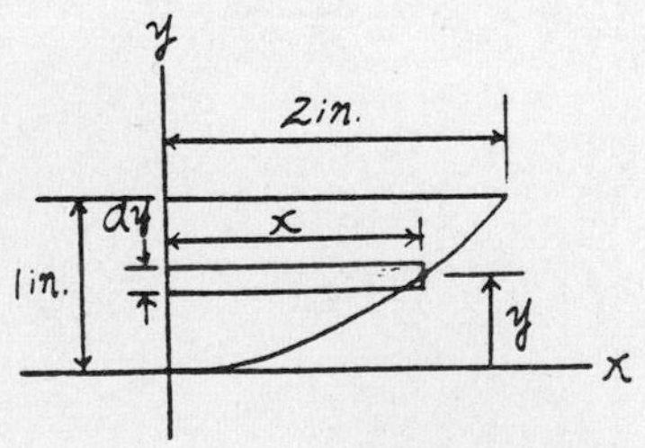

Moment of Inertia : Applying Eq. 10 – 1 and performing the integration, we have

$$I_x = \int_A y^2\,dA = \int_0^{1\,\text{in.}} y^2\left(2y^{\frac{1}{2}}\right)dy$$

$$= \left(\frac{4}{7}y^{\frac{7}{2}}\right)\Big|_0^{1\,\text{in.}}$$

$$= 0.571\ \text{in}^4 \qquad \textbf{Ans}$$

10-15. Determine the moment of inertia of the shaded area about the y axis.

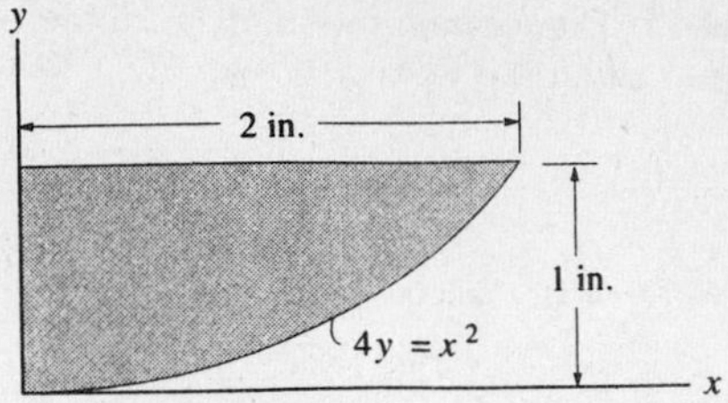

Differential Element : The area of the differential element parallel to yaxis is $dA = (1-y)\,dx = \left(1-\frac{1}{4}x^2\right)dx$.

Moment of Inertia : Applying Eq. 10 – 1 and performing the integration, we have

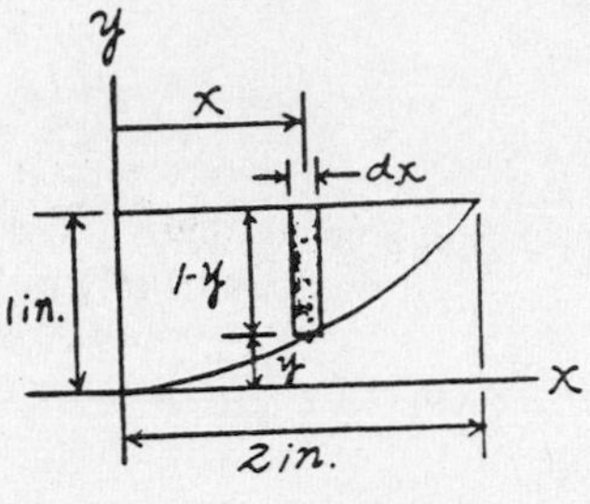

$$I_y = \int_A x^2 dA = \int_0^{2\text{in.}} x^2\left(1-\frac{1}{4}x^2\right)dx$$
$$= \left(\frac{1}{3}x^3 - \frac{1}{20}x^5\right)\Big|_0^{2\text{in.}}$$
$$= 1.07 \text{ in}^4 \qquad \textbf{Ans}$$

***10-16.** Determine the moment of inertia of the shaded area about the x axis.

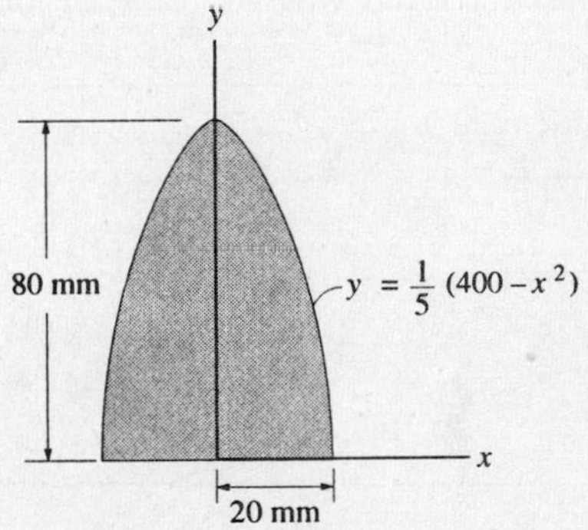

Differential Element : The area of the differential element parallel to y axis is $dA = ydx$. The moment of inertia of this element about x axis is

$$dI_x = d\bar{I}_{x'} + dA\tilde{y}^2$$
$$= \frac{1}{12}(dx)y^3 + ydx\left(\frac{y}{2}\right)^2$$
$$= \frac{1}{3}\left[\frac{1}{5}\left(400-x^2\right)\right]^3 dx$$
$$= \frac{1}{375}\left[-x^6 + 1200x^4 - 480\left(10^3\right)x^2 + 64\left(10^6\right)\right]dx$$

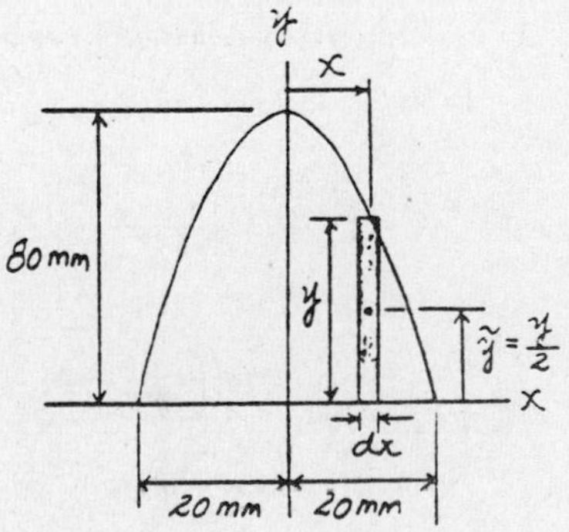

Moment of Inertia : Performing the integration, we have

$$I_x = \int dI_x = \frac{1}{375}\int_{-20\text{mm}}^{20\text{mm}}\left[-x^6 + 1200x^4 - 480\left(10^3\right)x^2 + 64\left(10^6\right)\right]dx$$
$$= \frac{1}{375}\left[-\frac{1}{7}x^7 + 240x^5 - 160\left(10^3\right)x^3 + 64\left(10^6\right)x\right]\Big|_{-20\text{mm}}^{20\text{mm}}$$
$$= 3.12\left(10^6\right)\text{ mm}^4 \qquad \textbf{Ans}$$

10-17. Determine the moment of inertia of the shaded area about the y axis.

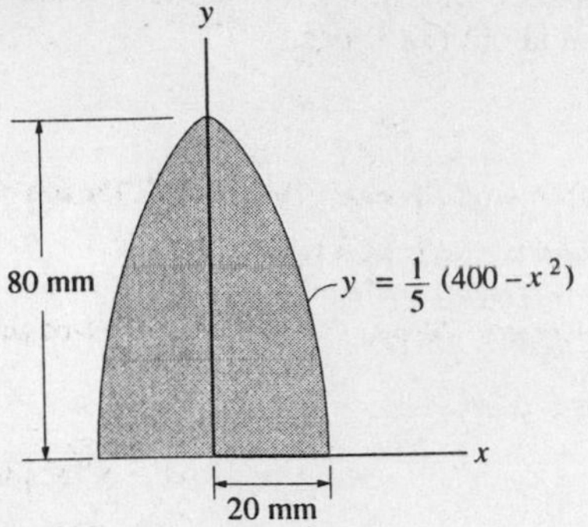

Differential Element : The area of the element parallel to yaxis is

$$dA = y\,dx = \frac{1}{5}\left(400 - x^2\right) dx\,.$$

Moment of Inertia : Applying Eq. 10–1and performing the integration, we have

$$I_y = \int_A x^2 dA = \int_{-20\text{mm}}^{20\text{mm}} x^2\left[\frac{1}{5}\left(400 - x^2\right) dx\right]$$

$$= \left(\frac{400}{3}x^3 - \frac{1}{5}x^5\right)\Bigg|_{-20\text{mm}}^{20\text{mm}}$$

$$= 171\left(10^3\right)\ \text{mm}^4$$ **Ans**

10-18. Determine the moment of inertia of the shaded area about the x axis.

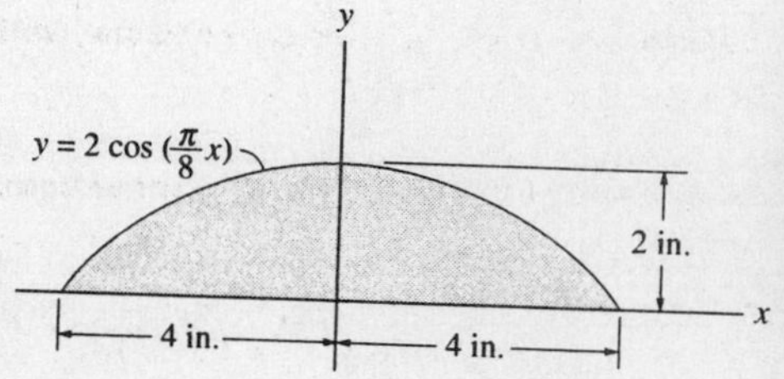

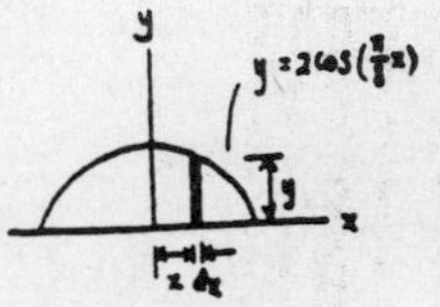

$$dI_x = dI_{\bar{x}} + dA\,\bar{y}^2$$

$$= \frac{1}{12}dx\,y^3 + y\,dx\left(\frac{y}{2}\right)^2 = \frac{1}{3}y^3\,dx$$

$$I_x = \int_A dI_x = \int_{-4}^{4}\frac{8}{3}\cos^3\left(\frac{\pi}{8}x\right)dx$$

$$= \frac{8}{3}\left[\frac{\sin\left(\frac{\pi}{8}x\right)}{\frac{\pi}{8}} - \frac{\sin^3\left(\frac{\pi}{8}x\right)}{\frac{3\pi}{8}}\right]_{-4}^{4} = \frac{256}{9\pi} = 9.05\ \text{in}^4$$ **Ans**

10-19. Determine the moment of inertia of the shaded area about the y axis.

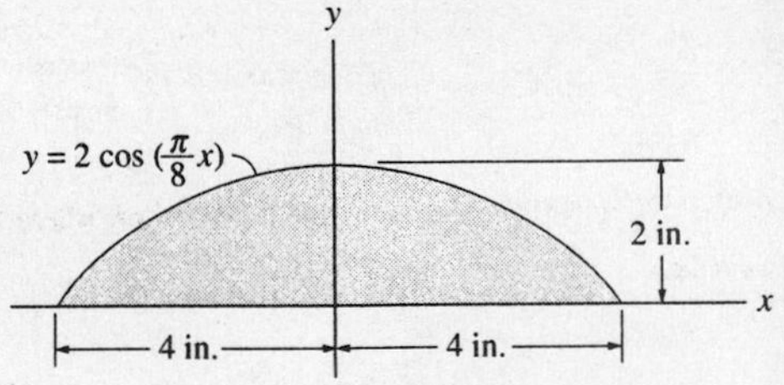

$$I_y = \int_A x^2 dA = \int_{-4}^{4} x^2\,2\cos\left(\frac{\pi}{8}x\right)dx$$

$$= 2\left[\frac{x^2\sin\left(\frac{\pi}{8}x\right)}{\frac{\pi}{8}} + \frac{2x\cos\left(\frac{\pi}{8}x\right)}{\left(\frac{\pi}{8}\right)^2} - \frac{2\sin\left(\frac{\pi}{8}x\right)}{\left(\frac{\pi}{8}\right)^3}\right]_{-4}^{4}$$

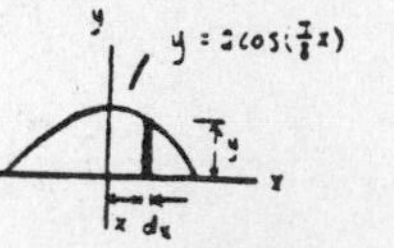

$$= 4\left(\frac{128}{\pi} - \frac{1024}{\pi^3}\right) = 30.9\ \text{in}^4$$ **Ans**

***10-20.** Determine the moment of inertia of the shaded area about the x axis.

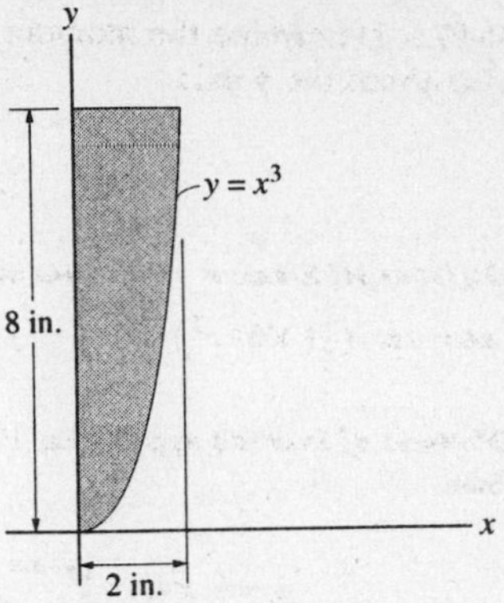

Differential Element : Here, $x = y^{\frac{1}{3}}$. The area of the differential element parallel to $x$axis is $dA = xdy = y^{\frac{1}{3}}dy$.

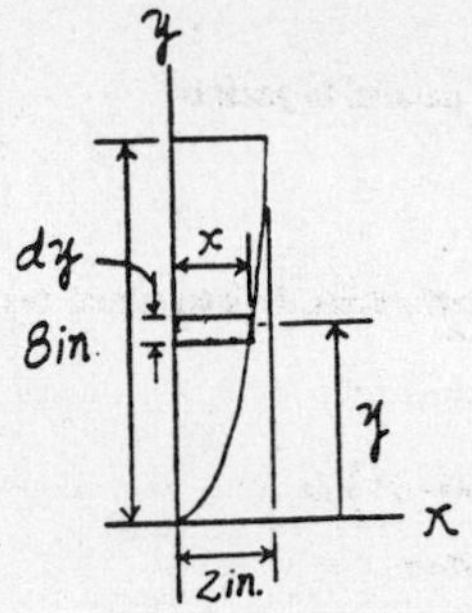

Moment of Inertia : Applying Eq. 10 − 1and performing the integration, we have

$$I_x = \int_A y^2 dA = \int_0^{8\text{in.}} y^2\left(y^{\frac{1}{3}}\right)dy$$

$$= \left[\frac{3}{10}y^{\frac{10}{3}}\right]_0^{8\text{in.}}$$

$$= 307\ \text{in}^4$$ **Ans**

10-21. Determine the moment of inertia of the shaded area about the y axis.

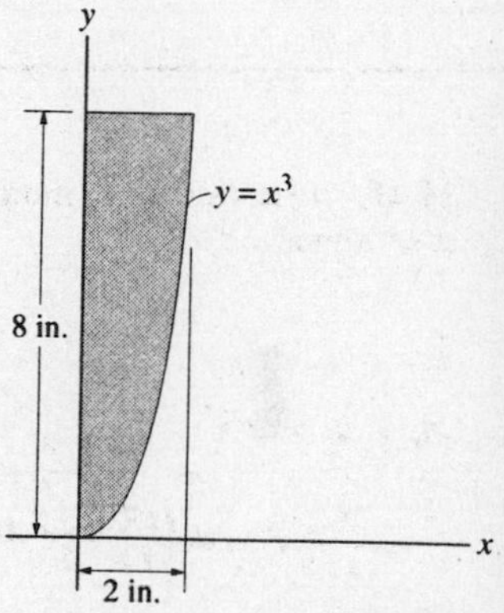

Differential Element : The area of the differential element parallel to $y$axis is $dA = (8-y)\,dx = \left(8-x^3\right)dx$.

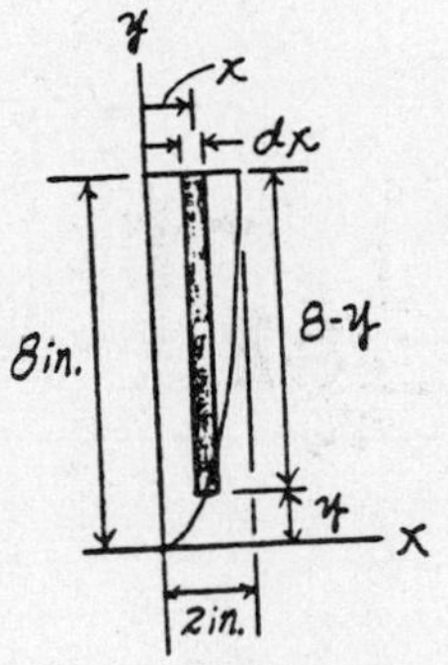

Moment of Inertia : Applying Eq. 10 − 1 and performing the integration, we have

$$I_y = \int_A x^2 dA = \int_0^{2\text{in.}} x^2\left(8-x^3\right)dx$$

$$= \left(\frac{8}{3}x^3 - \frac{1}{6}x^6\right)\Big|_0^{2\text{in.}}$$

$$= 10.7\ \text{in}^4$$ **Ans**

10-22. Determine the moment of inertia of the shaded area about the x axis.

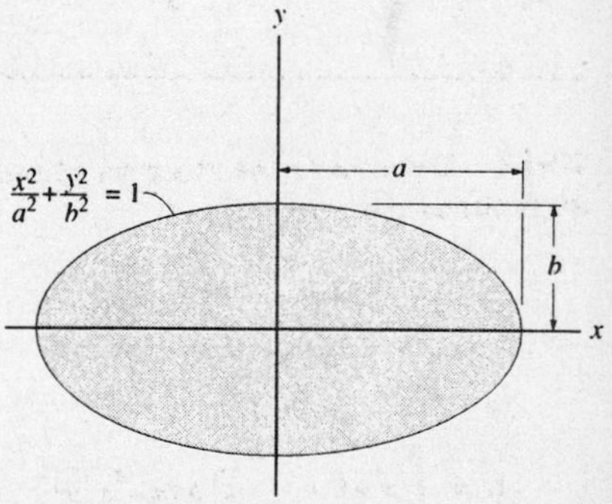

Area of the differential element (shaded) $dA = 2xdy$ where $x = \frac{a}{b}(b^2-y^2)^{\frac{1}{2}}$, hence, $dA = 2xdy = \frac{2a}{b}(b^2-y^2)^{\frac{1}{2}}dy$.

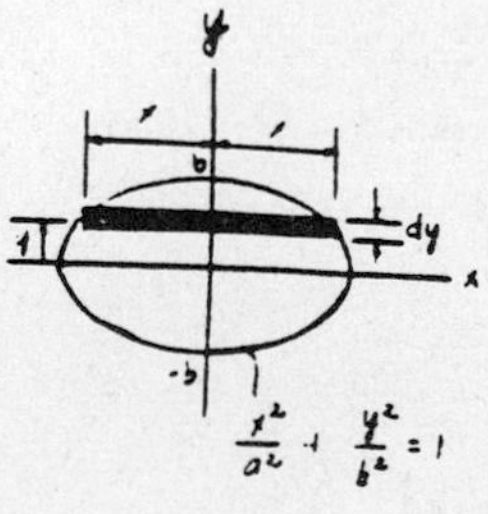

$$I_x = \int_A y^2 dA = \int_{-b}^{b} y^2\left(\frac{2a}{b}(b^2-y^2)^{\frac{1}{2}}\right)dy$$

$$= \frac{2a}{b}\int_{-b}^{b} y^2(b^2-y^2)^{\frac{1}{2}}dy$$

$$= \frac{2a}{b}\left[-\frac{y}{4}\sqrt{(b^2-y^2)^3}+\frac{b^2}{8}\left(y\sqrt{b^2-y^2}\right)+b^2\sin^{-1}\frac{y}{b}\right]_{-b}^{b}$$

$$= \frac{\pi a b^3}{4}$$ **Ans**

■10-23. Determine the moment of inertia of the shaded area about the y axis. Use Simpson's rule to evaluate the integral.

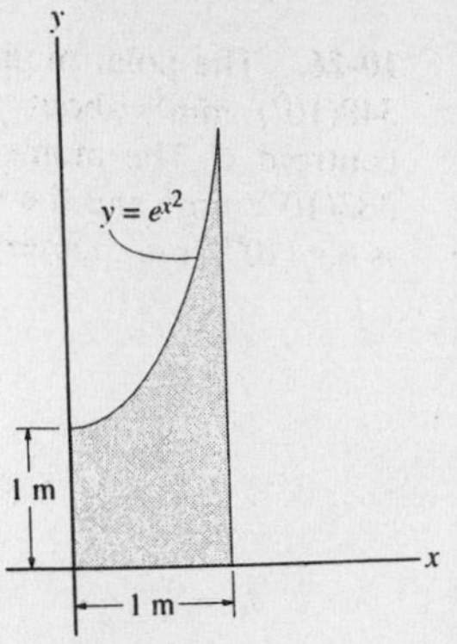

Area of the differential element (shaded) $dA = ydx$ where $y = e^{x^2}$, hence, $dA = ydx = e^{x^2}dx$.

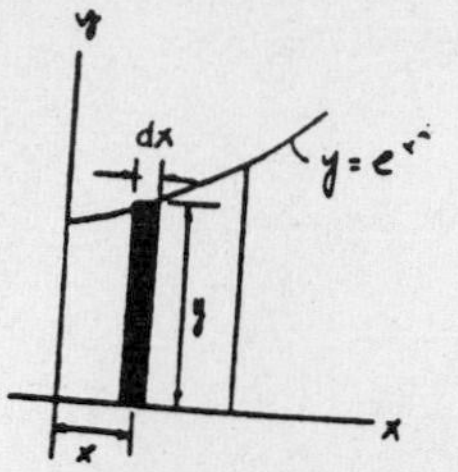

$$I_y = \int_A x^2 dA = \int_0^1 x^2\left(e^{x^2}\right)dx$$

Use Simpson's rule to evaluate the integral : (to 500 intervals)

$I_y = 0.628 \text{ m}^4$ **Ans**

■*10-24. Determine the moment of inertia of the shaded area about the x axis. Use Simpson's rule to evaluate the integral.

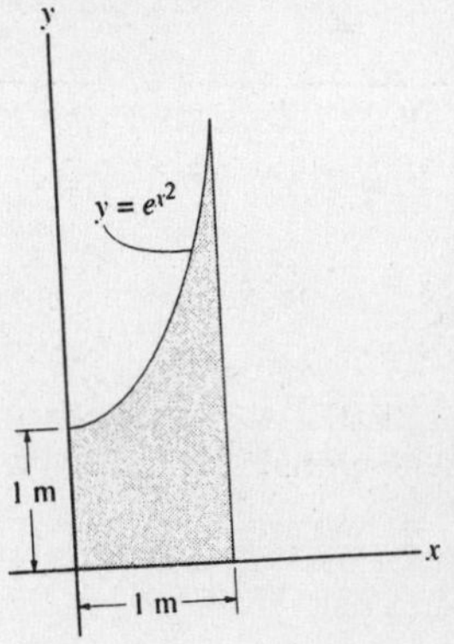

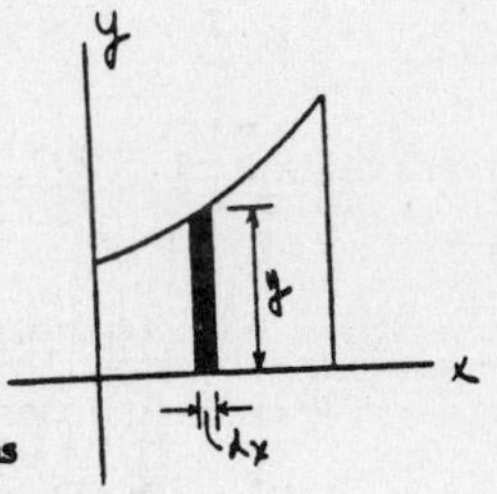

$dI_x = d\bar{I}_x + dA\,\bar{y}^2$

$$= \frac{1}{12}dx\,y^3 + y\,dx\left(\frac{y}{2}\right)^2 = \frac{1}{3}y^3\,dx$$

$I_x = \frac{1}{3}\int_0^1 y^3\,dx = \frac{1}{3}\int_0^1\left(e^{x^2}\right)^3 dx = 1.41 \text{ m}^4$ **Ans**

10-25. The polar moment of inertia of the area is $\bar{J}_C = 23 \text{ in}^4$ about the z axis passing through the centroid C. If the moment of inertia about the y axis is 5 in^4, and the moment of inertia about the x axis is 40 in^4, determine the area A.

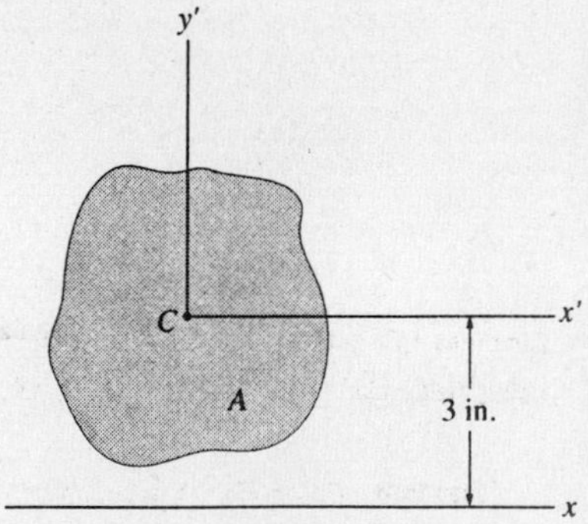

Moment of Inertia : The polar of moment inertia $J_C = \bar{I}_{x'} + \bar{I}_y$. Then, $\bar{I}_{x'} = J_C - I_y = 23 - 5 = 18.0 \text{ in}^4$. Applying the parallel – axis theorem, Eq. 10–3, we have

$$I_x = \bar{I}_{x'} + Ad_y^2$$
$$40 = 18.0 + A(3^2)$$
$$A = 2.44 \text{ in}^2$$ **Ans**

10-26. The polar moment of inertia of the area is $\bar{J}_C = 548(10^6)\ \text{mm}^4$, about the z' axis passing through the centroid C. The moment of inertia about the y' axis is $383(10^6)\ \text{mm}^4$, and the moment of inertia about the x axis is $856(10^6)\ \text{mm}^4$. Determine the area A.

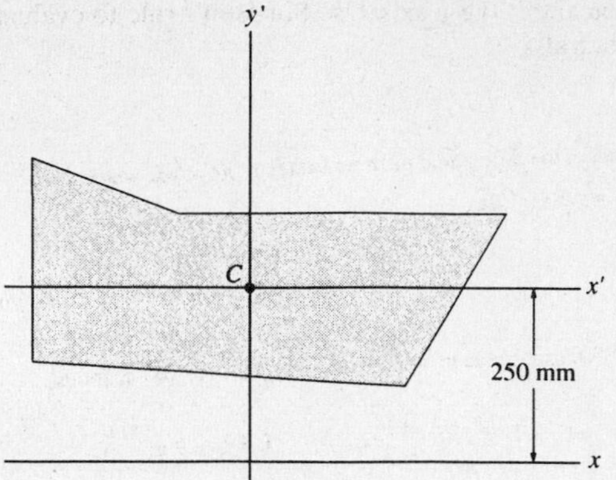

$$I_{x'} = \bar{I}_{x'} + Ad^2 = 856(10^6) - A(250)^2$$

$$\bar{J}_C = \bar{I}_{x'} + \bar{I}_{y'}$$

$$548(10^6) = 856(10^6) - A(250)^2 + 383(10^6)$$

$$A = 11.1(10^3)\ \text{mm}^2 \qquad \textbf{Ans}$$

10-27. Determine the moment of inertia $I_{x'}$ of the section. The origin of coordinates is at the centroid C.

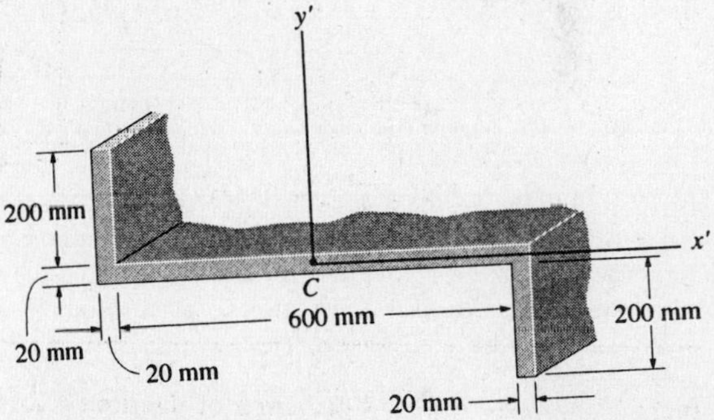

Moment of Inertia : The moment of inertia about the x' axis for each segment can be determined using the parallel – axis theorem $I_{x'} = \bar{I}_{x'} + Ad_y^2$.

Segment	A_i (mm²)	$(d_y)_i$ (mm)	$(\bar{I}_{x'})_i$ (mm⁴)	$(Ad_y^2)_i$ (mm⁴)	$(I_{x'})_i$ (mm⁴)
1	200(20)	110	$\frac{1}{12}(20)(200^3)$	$48.4(10^6)$	$61.733(10^6)$
2	640(20)	0	$\frac{1}{12}(640)(20^3)$	0	$0.427(10^6)$
3	200(20)	110	$\frac{1}{12}(20)(200^3)$	$48.4(10^6)$	$61.733(10^6)$

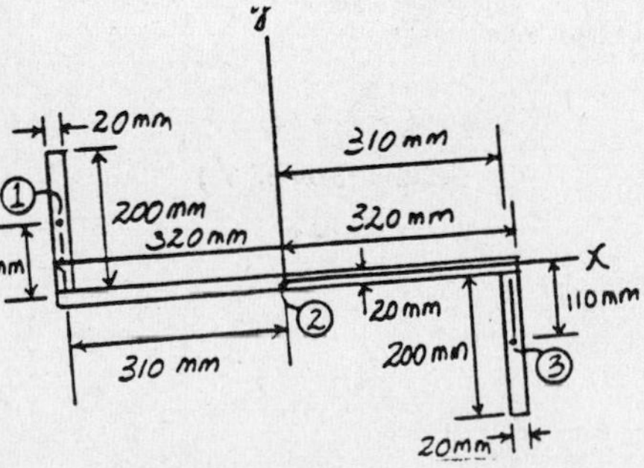

Thus,

$$I_{x'} = \Sigma(I_{x'})_i = 123.89(10^6)\ \text{mm}^4 = 124(10^6)\ \text{mm}^4 \qquad \textbf{Ans}$$

***10-28.** Determine the moment of inertia $I_{y'}$ of the section. The origin of coordinates is at the centroid C.

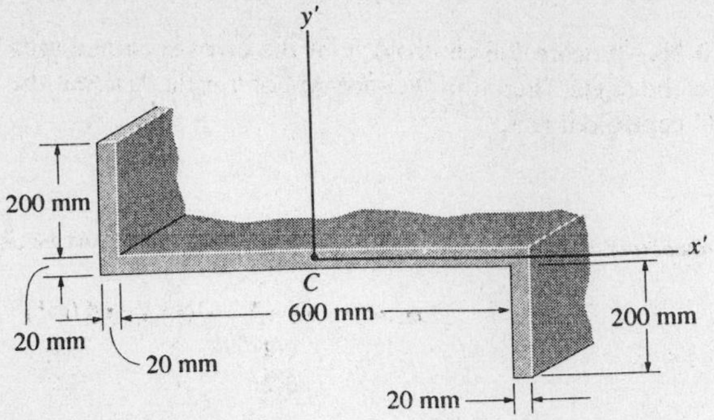

Moment of Inertia : The moment of inertia about the y' axis for each segment can be determined using the parallel – axis theorem $I_{y'} = \bar{I}_{y'} + Ad_x^2$.

Segment	A_i (mm²)	$(d_x)_i$ (mm)	$(\bar{I}_{y'})_i$ (mm⁴)	$(Ad_x^2)_i$ (mm⁴)	$(I_{y'})_i$ (mm⁴)
1	200(20)	310	$\frac{1}{12}(200)(20^3)$	421.6(10⁶)	384.53(10⁶)
2	640(20)	0	$\frac{1}{12}(20)(640^3)$	0	436.91(10⁶)
3	200(20)	310	$\frac{1}{12}(200)(20^3)$	384.4(10⁶)	384.53(10⁶)

Thus,

$$I_{y'} = \Sigma(I_{y'})_i = 1.206(10^9)\ \text{mm}^4 = 1.21(10^9)\ \text{mm}^4 \qquad \textbf{Ans}$$

10-29. Determine the moment of inertia of the beam's cross-sectional area with respect to the x' centroidal axis. Neglect the size of all the rivet heads, R, for the calculation. Handbook values for the area, moment of inertia, and location of the centroid C of one of the angles are listed in the figure.

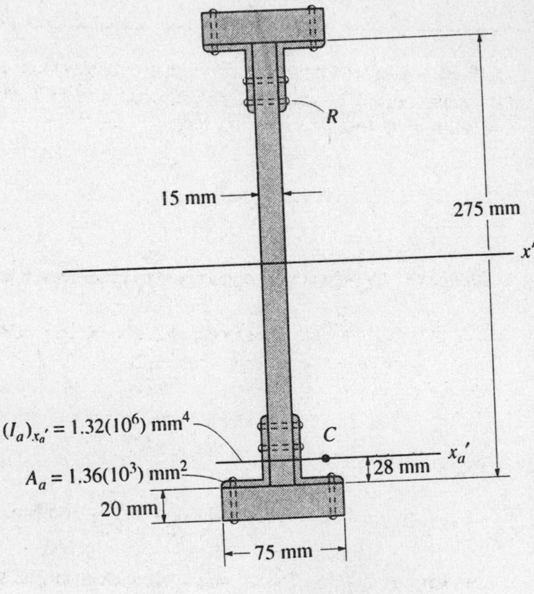

$$\bar{I}_{x'} = \frac{1}{12}(15)(275)^3 + 4\left[1.32(10^6) + 1.36(10^3)\left(\frac{275}{2} - 28\right)^2\right]$$

$$+ 2\left[\frac{1}{12}(75)(20)^3 + (75)(20)\left(\frac{275}{2} + 10\right)^2\right] = 162(10^6)\ \text{mm}^4 \qquad \textbf{Ans}$$

10-30. Locate the centroid $\bar{y}$ of the cross-sectional area for the angle. Then find the moment of inertia $\bar{I}_{x'}$ about the x' centroidal axis.

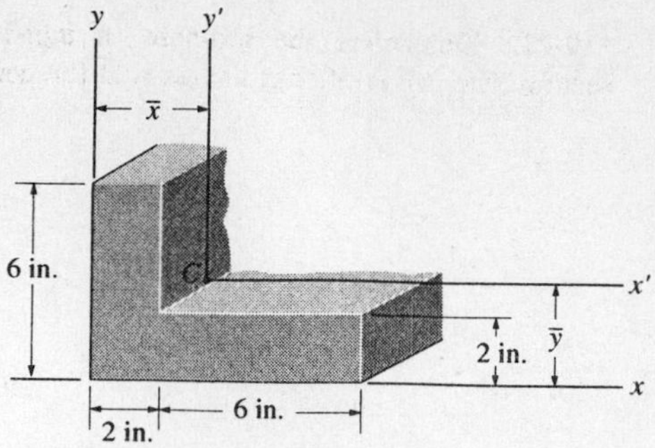

Centroid : The area of each segment and its respective centroid are tabulated below.

Segment	A (in²)	$\tilde{y}$ (in.)	$\tilde{y}A$ (in³)
1	6(2)	3	36.0
2	6(2)	1	12.0
Σ	24.0		48.0

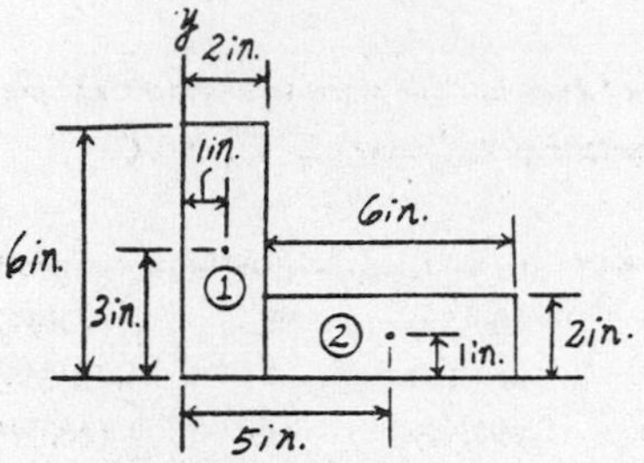

Thus,

$$\bar{y} = \frac{\Sigma\tilde{y}A}{\Sigma A} = \frac{48.0}{24.0} = 2.00 \text{ in.} \qquad \textbf{Ans}$$

Moment of Inertia : The moment of inertia about the x'axis for each segment can be determined using the parallel – axis theorem $I_{x'} = \bar{I}_{x'} + Ad_y^2$.

Segment	A_i (in²)	$(d_y)_i$ (in.)	$(\bar{I}_{x'})_i$ (in⁴)	$(Ad_y^2)_i$ (in⁴)	$(I_{x'})_i$ (in⁴)
1	2(6)	1	$\frac{1}{12}(2)(6^3)$	12.0	48.0
2	6(2)	1	$\frac{1}{12}(6)(2^3)$	12.0	16.0

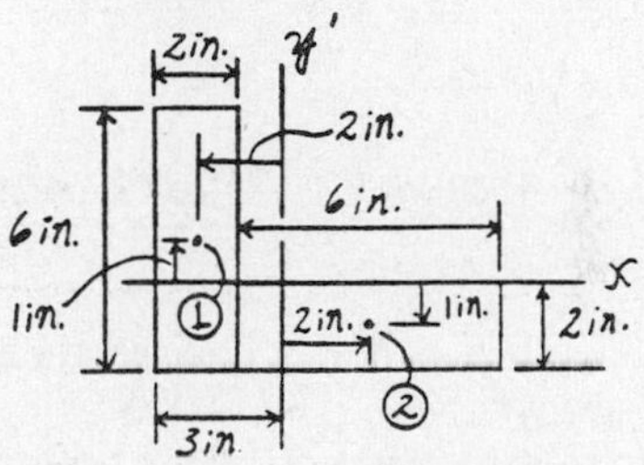

Thus,

$$I_{x'} = \Sigma(I_{x'})_i = 64.0 \text{ in}^4 \qquad \textbf{Ans}$$

10-31. Locate the centroid $\bar{x}$ of the cross-sectional area for the angle. Then find the moment of inertia $\bar{I}_{\bar{y}}$ about the y' centroidal axis.

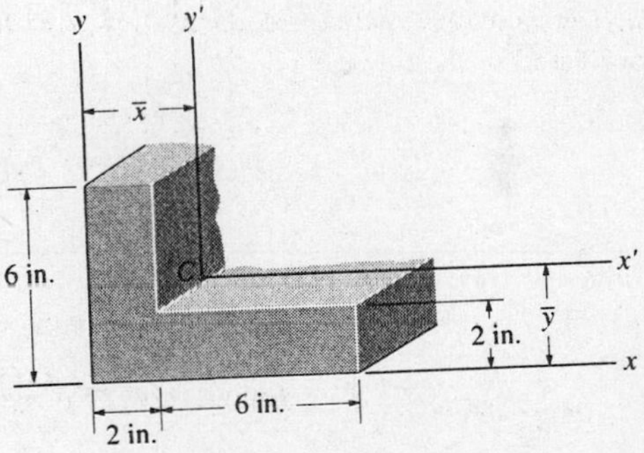

Centroid : The area of each segment and its respective centroid are tabulated below.

Segment	A (in²)	$\tilde{x}$ (in.)	$\tilde{x}A$ (in³)
1	6(2)	1	12.0
2	6(2)	5	60.0
Σ	24.0		72.0

Thus,

$$\bar{x} = \frac{\Sigma\tilde{x}A}{\Sigma A} = \frac{72.0}{24.0} = 3.00 \text{ in.} \qquad \textbf{Ans}$$

Moment of Inertia : The moment of inertia about the y'axis for each segmentcan be determined using the parallel – axis theorem $I_{y'} = \bar{I}_{y'} + Ad_x^2$.

Segment	A_i (in²)	$(d_x)_i$ (in.)	$(\bar{I}_{y'})_i$ (in⁴)	$(Ad_x^2)_i$ (in⁴)	$(I_{y'})_i$ (in⁴)
1	6(2)	2	$\frac{1}{12}(6)(2^3)$	48.0	52.0
2	2(6)	2	$\frac{1}{12}(2)(6^3)$	48.0	84.0

Thus,

$$I_{y'} = \Sigma(I_{y'})_i = 136 \text{ in}^4 \qquad \textbf{Ans}$$

*10-32. Determine the distance $\bar{x}$ to the centroid of the beam's cross-sectional area: then find the moment of inertia about the y' axis.

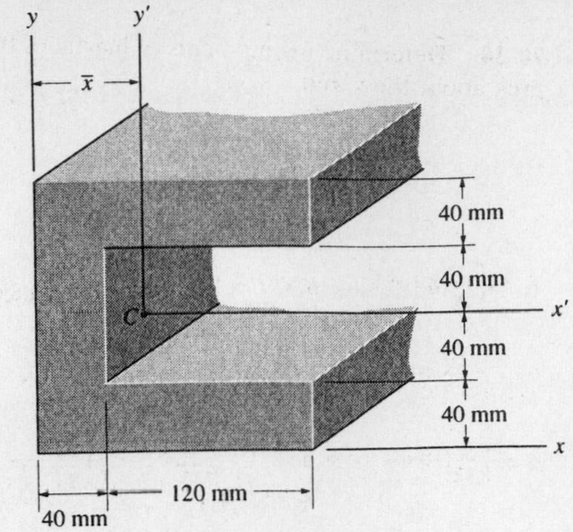

Centroid : The area of each segment and its respective centroid are tabulated below.

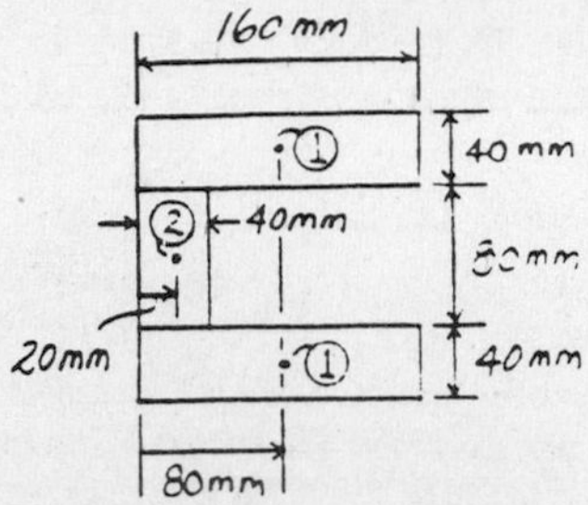

Segment	$A\,(\text{mm}^2)$	$\tilde{x}\,(\text{mm})$	$\tilde{x}A\,(\text{mm}^3)$
1	160(80)	80	$1.024(10^6)$
2	40(80)	20	$64.0(10^3)$
Σ	$16.0(10^3)$		$1.088(10^6)$

Thus,

$$\bar{x} = \frac{\Sigma \tilde{x}A}{\Sigma A} = \frac{1.088(10^6)}{16.0(10^3)} = 68.0 \text{ mm} \quad \textbf{Ans}$$

Moment of Inertia : The moment of inertia about the y' axis for each segment can be determined using the parallel – axis theorem $I_{y'} = \bar{I}_{y'} + Ad_x^2$.

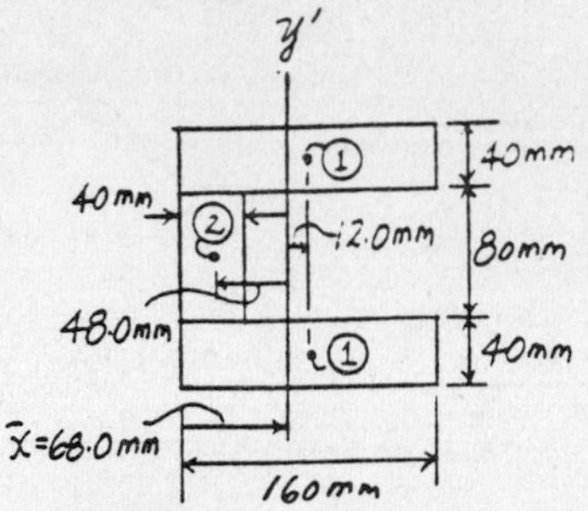

Segment	$A_i\,(\text{mm}^2)$	$(d_x)_i\,(\text{mm})$	$(\bar{I}_{y'})_i\,(\text{mm}^4)$	$(Ad_x^2)_i\,(\text{mm}^4)$	$(I_{y'})_i\,(\text{mm}^4)$
1	80(160)	12.0	$\frac{1}{12}(80)(160^3)$	$1.8432(10^6)$	$29.150(10^6)$
2	80(40)	48.0	$\frac{1}{12}(80)(40^3)$	$7.3728(10^6)$	$7.799(10^6)$

Thus,

$$I_{y'} = \Sigma(I_{y'})_i = 36.949(10^6)\text{ mm}^4 = 36.9(10^6)\text{ mm}^4 \quad \textbf{Ans}$$

10-33. Determine the moment of inertia of the beam's cross-sectional area about the x' axis.

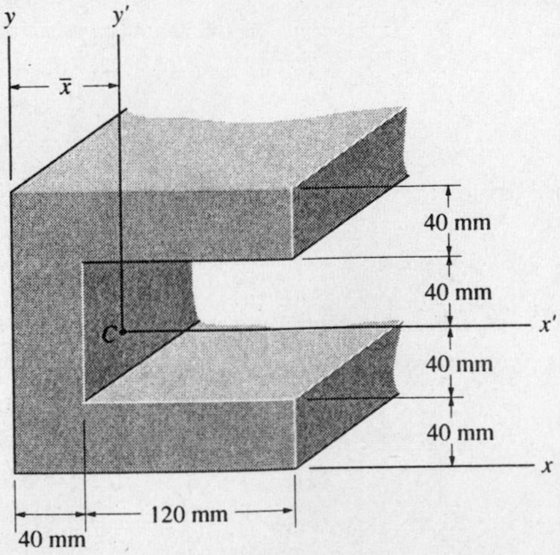

Moment of Inertia : The moment inertia for the rectangle about itscentroidal axis can be determined using the formula, $I_{x'} = \frac{1}{12}bh^3$, given on the inside back cover of the textbook.

$$I_{x'} = \frac{1}{12}(160)(160^3) - \frac{1}{12}(120)(80^3) = 49.5(10^6)\text{ mm}^4 \quad \textbf{Ans}$$

10-34. Determine the moments of inertia of the shaded area about the x and y axes.

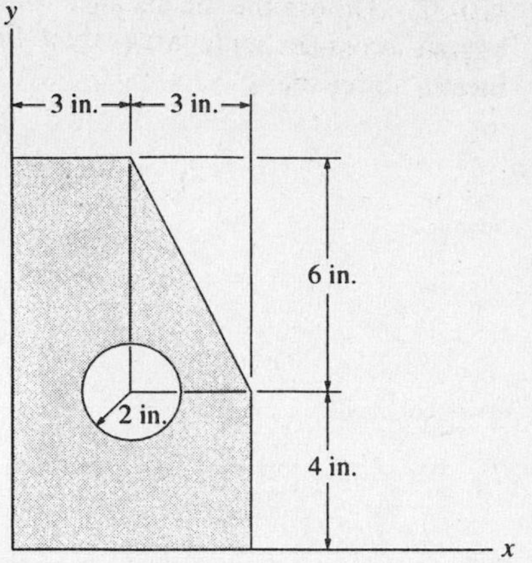

$$I_x = \left[\frac{1}{12}(6)(10)^3 + 6(10)(5)^2\right] - \left[\frac{1}{36}(3)(6)^2 + \left(\frac{1}{2}\right)(3)(6)(8)^2\right]$$

$$-\left[\frac{1}{4}\pi(2)^4 + \pi(2)^2(4)^2\right] = 1.21\left(10^3\right)\text{ in}^4 \quad \textbf{Ans}$$

$$I_y = \left[\frac{1}{12}(10)(6)^3 + 6(10)(3)^2\right] - \left[\frac{1}{36}(6)(3)^2 + \left(\frac{1}{2}\right)(6)(3)(5)^2\right]$$

$$-\left[\frac{1}{4}\pi(2)^4 + \pi(2)^2(3)^2\right] = 368\text{ in}^4 \quad \textbf{Ans}$$

10-35. Determine the moment of inertia of the beam's cross-sectional area about the x' axis. Neglect the size of the corner welds at A and B for the calculation, $\bar{y}$ = 154.4 mm.

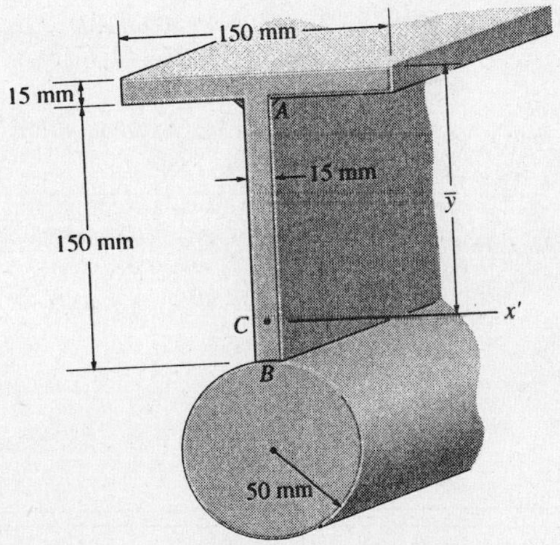

Moment of Inertia : The moment of inertia about the x' axis for each segment can be determined using the parallel – axis theorem $I_{x'} = \bar{I}_{x'} + Ad_y^2$.

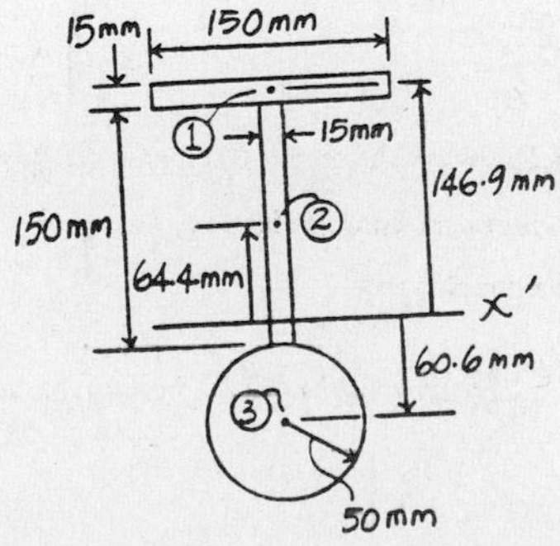

Segment	A_i (mm²)	$(d_y)_i$ (mm)	$(\bar{I}_{x'})_i$ (mm⁴)	$(Ad_y^2)_i$ (mm⁴)	$(I_{x'})_i$ (mm⁴)
1	150(15)	146.9	$\frac{1}{12}(150)(15^3)$	$48.554(10^6)$	$48.596(10^6)$
2	15(150)	64.4	$\frac{1}{12}(15)(150^3)$	$9.332(10^6)$	$13.550(10^6)$
3	$\pi(50^2)$	60.6	$\frac{\pi}{4}(50^4)$	$28.843(10^6)$	$33.751(10^6)$

Thus,

$$I_{x'} = \Sigma(I_{x'})_i = 95.898\left(10^6\right)\text{ mm}^4 = 95.9\left(10^6\right)\text{ mm}^4 \quad \textbf{Ans}$$

*10-36. Determine the distance $\bar{y}$ to the centroid of the beam's cross-sectional area; then find the moment of inertia about the x' axis.

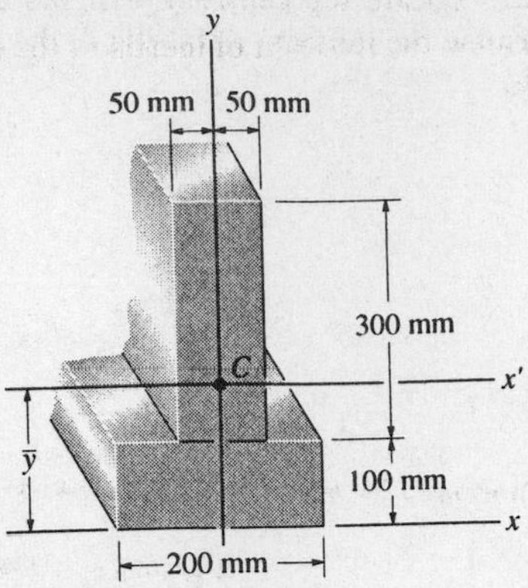

Centroid :

$$\bar{y} = \frac{\Sigma \tilde{y}A}{\Sigma A} = \frac{50(100)(200) + 250(100)(300)}{100(200) + 100(300)} = 170 \text{ mm} \quad \textbf{Ans}$$

Moment of inertia :

$$I_{x'} = \frac{1}{12}(200)(100)^3 + 200(100)(170-50)^2$$

$$+ \frac{1}{12}(100)(300)^3 + 100(300)(250-170)^2$$

$$= 722(10)^6 \text{ mm}^4 \quad \textbf{Ans}$$

10-37. Determine the moment of inertia of the beam's cross-sectional area about the x axis.

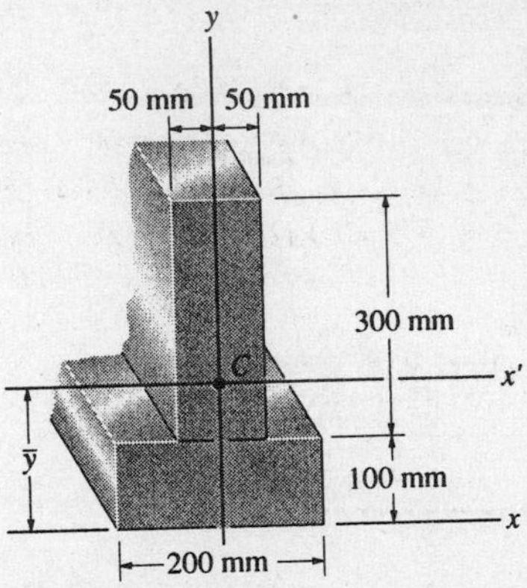

$$I_x = \left[\frac{1}{12}(0.2)(0.1)^3 + (0.2)(0.1)(0.05)^2\right]$$

$$+ \left[\frac{1}{12}(0.1)(0.3)^3 + (0.1)(0.3)(0.25)^2\right] = 2.17(10^{-3}) \text{ m}^4 \quad \textbf{Ans}$$

10-38. Determine the moment of inertia of the beam's cross-sectional area about the y axis.

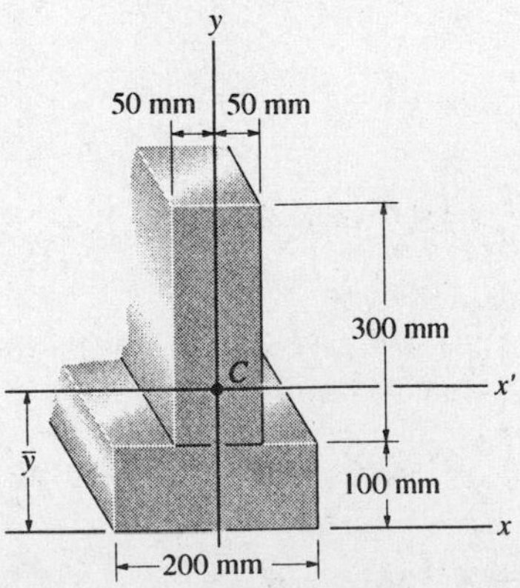

$$I_y = \frac{1}{12}(100)(200)^3 + \frac{1}{12}(300)(100)^3 = 91.7(10)^6 \text{ mm}^4 \quad \textbf{Ans}$$

10-39. Locate the centroid $\bar{y}$ of the cross section and determine the moment of inertia of the section about the x axis.

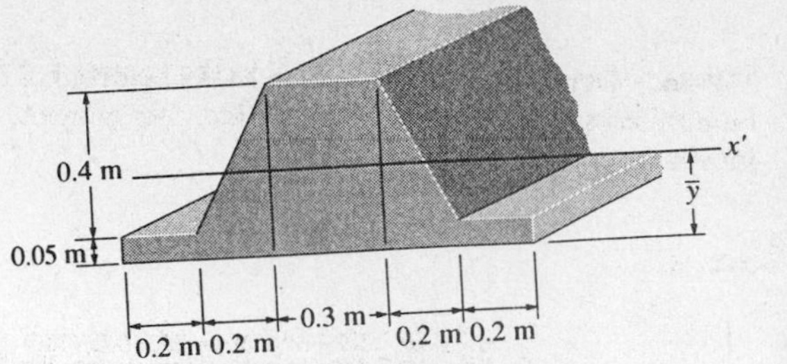

Centroid **:** The area of each segment and its respective centroid are tabulated below.

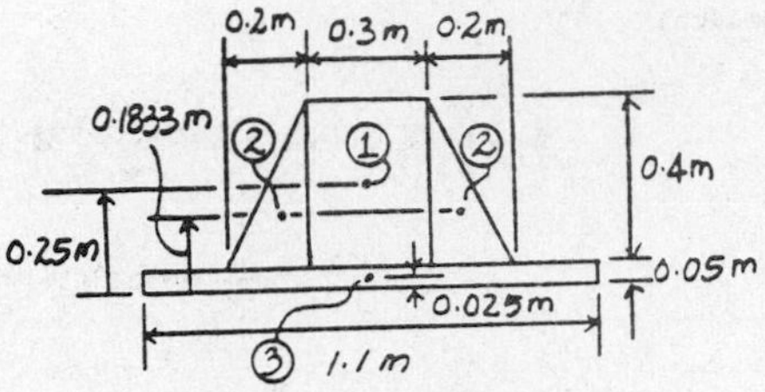

Segment	$A\,(\mathrm{m}^2)$	$\bar{y}\,(\mathrm{m})$	$\bar{y}A\,(\mathrm{m}^3)$
1	$0.3(0.4)$	0.25	0.03
2	$\frac{1}{2}(0.4)(0.4)$	0.1833	0.014667
3	$1.1(0.05)$	0.025	0.001375
Σ	0.255		0.046042

Thus,

$$\bar{y} = \frac{\Sigma \bar{y}A}{\Sigma A} = \frac{0.046042}{0.255} = 0.1806\ \mathrm{m} = 0.181\ \mathrm{m} \qquad \textbf{Ans}$$

Moment of Inertia **:** The moment of inertia about the x' axis for each segment can be determined using the parallel – axis theorem $I_{x'} = \bar{I}_{x'} + Ad_y^2$.

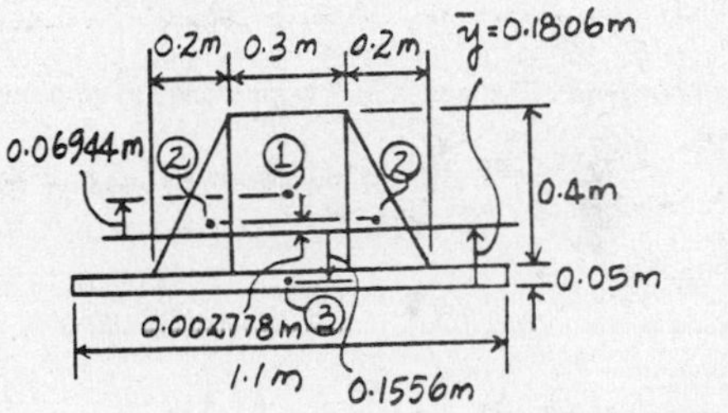

Segment	$A_i\,(\mathrm{m}^2)$	$(d_y)_i\,(\mathrm{m})$	$(\bar{I}_{x'})_i\,(\mathrm{m}^4)$	$(Ad_y^2)_i\,(\mathrm{m}^4)$	$(I_{x'})_i\,(\mathrm{m}^4)$
1	$0.3(0.4)$	0.06944	$\frac{1}{12}(0.3)(0.4^3)$	$0.5787(10^{-3})$	$2.1787(10^{-3})$
2	$\frac{1}{2}(0.4)(0.4)$	0.002778	$\frac{1}{36}(0.4)(0.4^3)$	$0.6173(10^{-6})$	$0.7117(10^{-3})$
3	$1.1(0.05)$	0.1556	$\frac{1}{12}(1.1)(0.05^3)$	$1.3309(10^{-3})$	$1.3423(10^{-3})$

Thus,

$$I_{x'} = \Sigma(I_{x'})_i = 4.233(10^{-3})\ \mathrm{m}^4 = 4.23(10^{-3})\ \mathrm{m}^4 \qquad \textbf{Ans}$$

***10-40.** The composite beam consists of a wide-flange beam and a cover plate welded together as shown. Determine the moment of inertia of the cross-sectional area with respect to the x' centroidal axis. $\bar{y} = 77.8$ mm.

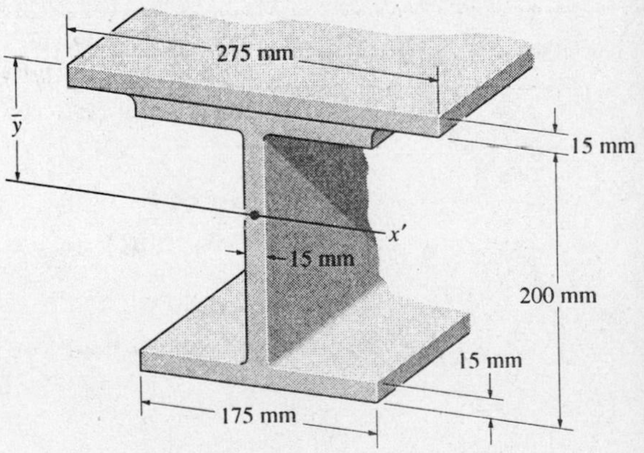

$$I_x = \left[\frac{1}{12}(275)(15)^3 + 275(15)(77.8-7.5)^2\right] + \left[\frac{1}{12}(175)(15)^3 + 175(15)(77.8-15-7.5)^2\right]$$

$$+ \left[\frac{1}{12}(15)(200-30)^3 + 15(200-30)\left(15+15+\frac{200-30}{2}-77.8\right)^2\right]$$

$$+ \left[\frac{1}{12}(175)(15)^3 + 175(15)\left(215-\frac{15}{2}-77.8\right)^2\right]$$

$$= 82.4(10^6)\ \mathrm{mm}^4 \qquad \textbf{Ans}$$

10-41. Determine the distance $\bar{y}$ to the centroid for the beam's cross-sectional area; then determine the moment of inertia about the x' axis.

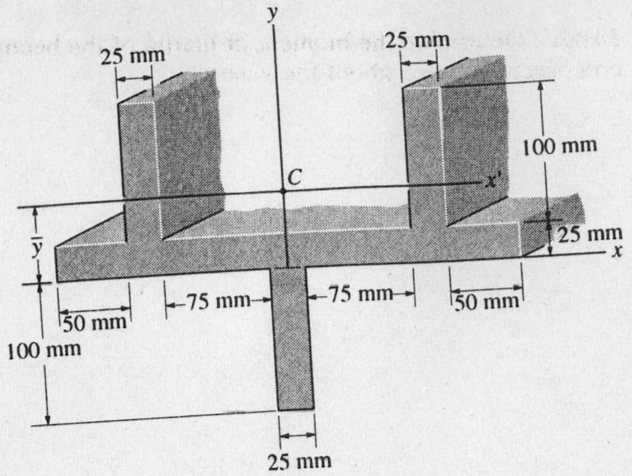

Centroid : The area of each segment and its respective centroid are tabulated below.

Segment	$A\,(\text{mm}^2)$	$\tilde{y}\,(\text{mm})$	$\tilde{y}A\,(\text{mm}^3)$
1	50(100)	75	$375(10^3)$
2	325(25)	12.5	$101.5625(10^3)$
3	25(100)	−50	$-125(10^3)$
Σ	$15.625(10^3)$		$351.5625(10^3)$

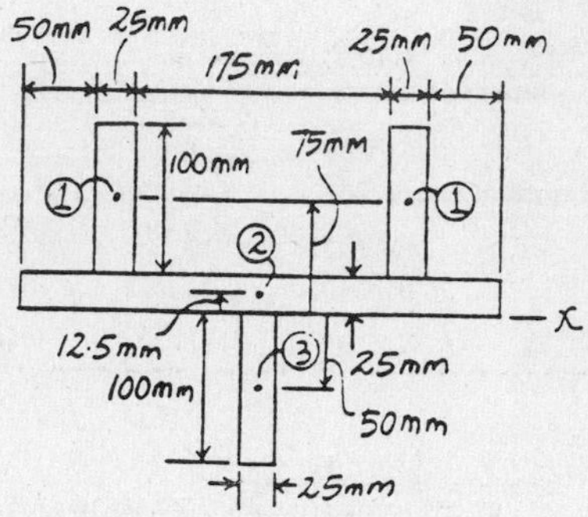

Thus,

$$\bar{y} = \frac{\Sigma\tilde{y}A}{\Sigma A} = \frac{351.5625(10^3)}{15.625(10^3)} = 22.5 \text{ mm} \qquad \textbf{Ans}$$

Moment of Inertia : The moment of inertia about the x' axis for each segment can be determined using the parallel − axis theorem $I_{x'} = \bar{I}_{x'} + Ad_y^2$.

Segment	$A_i\,(\text{mm}^2)$	$(d_y)_i\,(\text{mm})$	$(\bar{I}_{x'})_i\,(\text{mm}^4)$	$(Ad_y^2)_i\,(\text{mm}^4)$	$(I_{x'})_i\,(\text{mm}^4)$
1	50(100)	52.5	$\frac{1}{12}(50)(100^3)$	$13.781(10^6)$	$17.948(10^6)$
2	325(25)	10	$\frac{1}{12}(325)(25^3)$	$0.8125(10^6)$	$1.236(10^6)$
3	25(100)	72.5	$\frac{1}{12}(25)(100^3)$	$13.141(10^6)$	$15.224(10^6)$

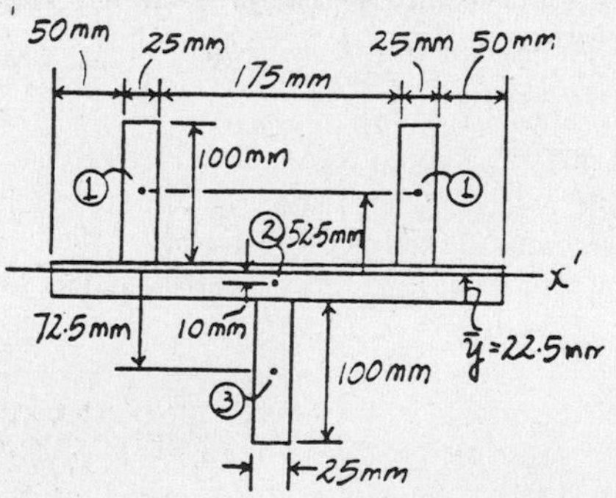

Thus,

$$I_{x'} = \Sigma(I_{x'})_i = 34.41\left(10^6\right) \text{ mm}^4 = 34.4\left(10^6\right) \text{ mm}^4 \qquad \textbf{Ans}$$

10-42. Determine the moment of inertia of the beam's cross-sectional area about the y axis.

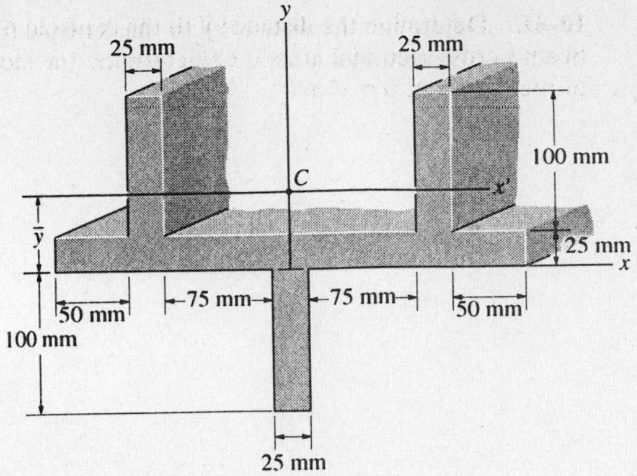

Moment of Inertia : The moment of inertia about the y' axis for each segment can be determined usin the parallel – axis theorem $I_{y'} = \bar{I}_{y'} + Ad_x^2$.

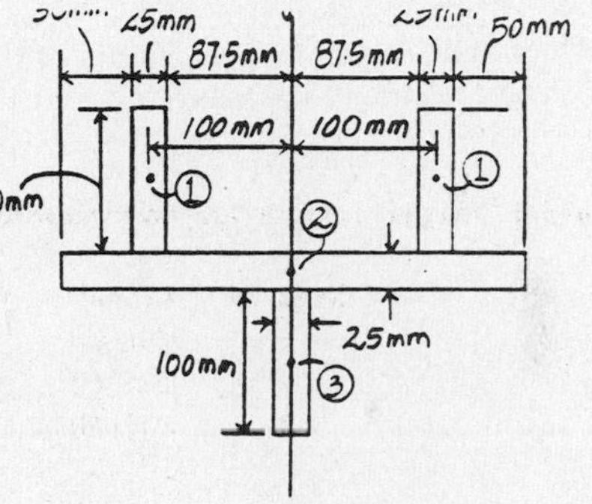

Segment	A_i (mm²)	$(d_x)_i$ (mm)	$(\bar{I}_{y'})_i$ (mm⁴)	$(Ad_x^2)_i$ (mm⁴)	$(I_{y'})_i$ (mm⁴)
1	2[100(25)]	100	$\frac{1}{12}(100)(25^3)$	$50.0(10^6)$	$50.130(10^6)$
2	25(325)	0	$\frac{1}{12}(25)(325^3)$	0	$71.519(10^6)$
3	100(25)	0	$\frac{1}{12}(100)(25^3)$	0	$0.130(10^6)$

Thus,

$$I_{y'} = \Sigma(I_{y'})_i = 121.78(10^6)\ \text{mm}^4 = 122(10^6)\ \text{mm}^4 \quad \textbf{Ans}$$

10-43. Determine the distance $\bar{y}$ to the centroid of the beam's cross-sectional area; then find the moment of inertia about the x' axis.

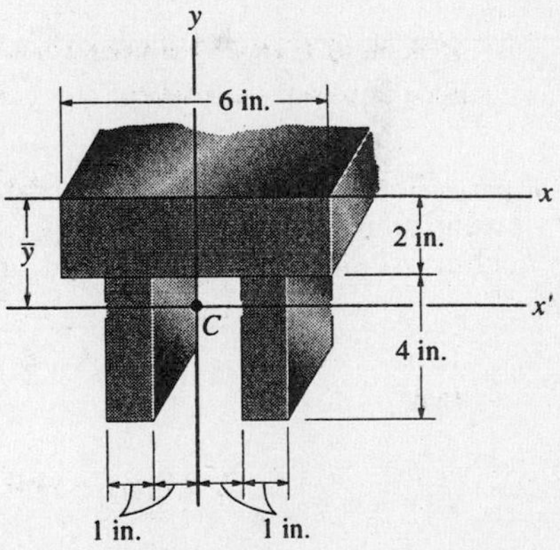

Centroid :

$$\bar{y} = \frac{\Sigma \tilde{y}A}{\Sigma A} = \frac{1(6)(2) + 2[4(4)(1)]}{6(2) + 2[4(1)]} = 2.20 \text{ in.} \quad \textbf{Ans}$$

Moment inertia :

$$I_{x'} = \frac{1}{12}(6)(2)^3 + 6(2)(2.20-1)^2 + 2\left[\frac{1}{12}(1)(4)^3 + 1(4)(4-2.20)^2\right]$$

$$= 57.9 \text{ in}^4 \quad \textbf{Ans}$$

*10-44.** Determine the moment of inertia of the beam's cross-sectional area about the x axis.

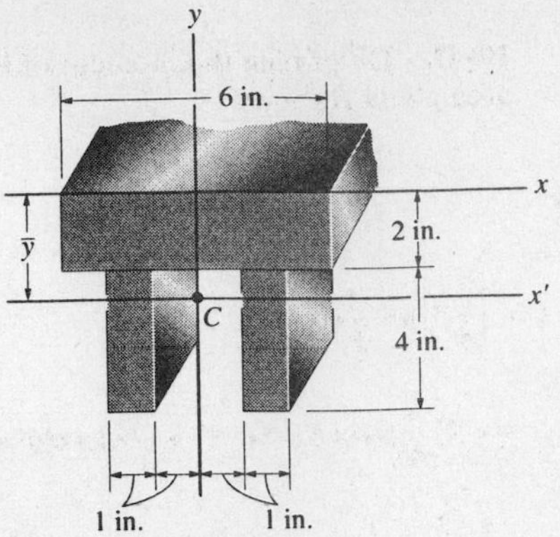

$$I_x = \left[\frac{1}{12}(6)(2)^3 + (6)(2)(1)^2\right] + 2\left[\frac{1}{12}(1)(4)^3 + (4)(1)(4)^2\right]$$

$$= 155\text{ in.}^4 \quad \textbf{Ans}$$

10-45. Determine the moment of inertia of the beam's cross-sectional area about the y axis.

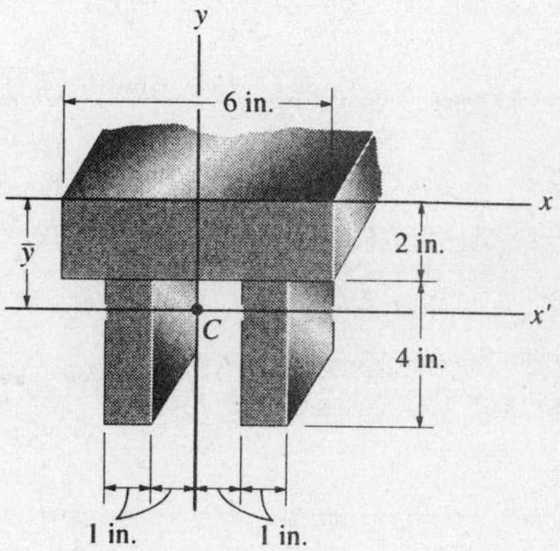

$$I_y = \frac{1}{12}(2)(6)^3 + 2\left[\frac{1}{12}(4)(1)^3 + 1(4)(1.5)^2\right] = 54.7\text{ in}^4 \quad \textbf{Ans}$$

10-46. Compute the polar radius of gyration, k_O, for the pipe and show that for small thickness, $t = r_2 - r_1$, k_O is equal to the mean radius r_m of the pipe.

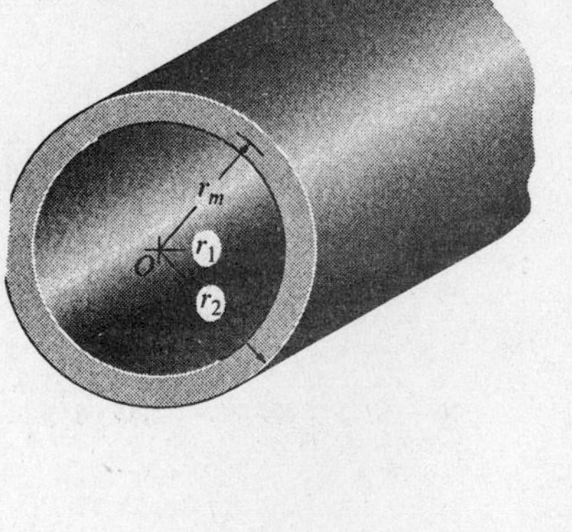

$$J_O = I_x + I_y = \frac{1}{2}\pi r^4 = \frac{1}{2}\pi r_2^4 - \frac{1}{2}\pi r_1^4 = \frac{1}{2}\pi\left(r_2^4 - r_1^4\right)$$

$$k_O = \sqrt{\frac{J_O}{A}} = \sqrt{\frac{\frac{1}{2}\pi\left(r_2^4 - r_1^4\right)}{\pi\left(r_2^2 - r_1^2\right)}} = \sqrt{\frac{\left(r_2^2 - r_1^2\right)\left(r_2^2 + r_1^2\right)}{2\left(r_2^2 - r_1^2\right)}}$$

$$k_O = \sqrt{\frac{1}{2}\left(r_2^2 + r_1^2\right)} \quad \textbf{Ans}$$

For $r_1 = r_2 = r_m$ we have,

$$k_O = \sqrt{\frac{1}{2}\left(r_m^2 + r_m^2\right)} = r_m \quad \textbf{Q.E.D.}$$

10-47. Determine the moment of inertia of the shaded area about the x axis.

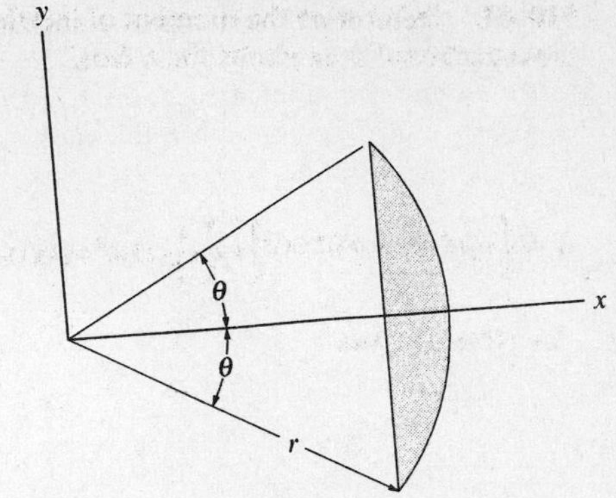

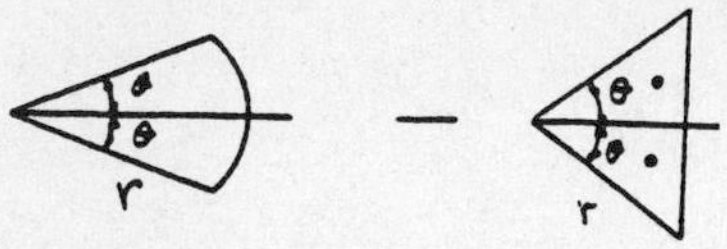

$$I_x = \left[\frac{1}{4}r^4\left(\theta - \frac{1}{2}\sin 2\theta\right)\right]$$

$$- 2\left[\frac{1}{36}(r\cos\theta)(r\sin\theta)^3 + \frac{1}{2}(r\cos\theta)(r\sin\theta)\left(\frac{1}{3}r\sin\theta\right)^2\right]$$

$$= \frac{1}{4}r^4\left(\theta - \frac{1}{2}\sin 2\theta\right) - \frac{1}{18}r^4\cos\theta\sin^3\theta - \frac{1}{9}r^4\cos\theta\sin^3\theta$$

$$= \frac{r^4}{24}(6\theta - 3\sin 2\theta - 4\cos\theta\sin^3\theta) \quad \textbf{Ans}$$

***10-48.** Determine the moment of inertia of the shaded area about the y axis.

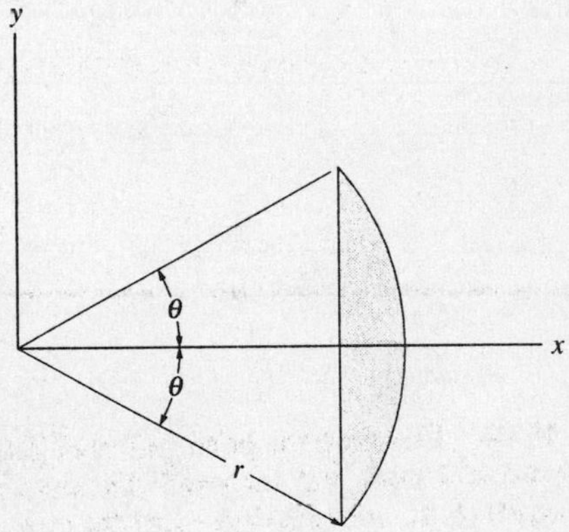

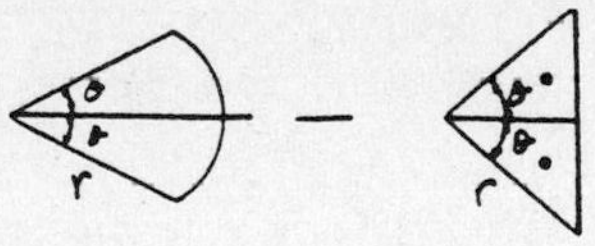

$$I_y = \left[\frac{1}{4}r^4\left(\theta + \frac{1}{2}\sin 2\theta\right)\right]$$

$$- \left[\frac{1}{36}(2r\sin\theta)(r\cos\theta)^3 + \frac{1}{2}(2r\sin\theta)(r\cos\theta)\left(\frac{2}{3}r\cos\theta\right)^2\right]$$

$$= \frac{1}{4}r^4\left(\theta + \frac{1}{2}\sin 2\theta\right) - \left[\frac{1}{18}r^4\sin\theta\cos^3\theta + r^3\sin\theta\cos^3\theta\right]$$

$$= \frac{r^4}{4}\left(\theta + \frac{1}{2}\sin 2\theta - 2\sin\theta\cos^3\theta\right) \quad \textbf{Ans}$$

10-49. An aluminum strut has a cross section referred to as a deep hat. Determine the location $\bar{y}$ of the centroid of its area and the moment of inertia of the area about the x' axis. Each segment has a thickness of 10 mm.

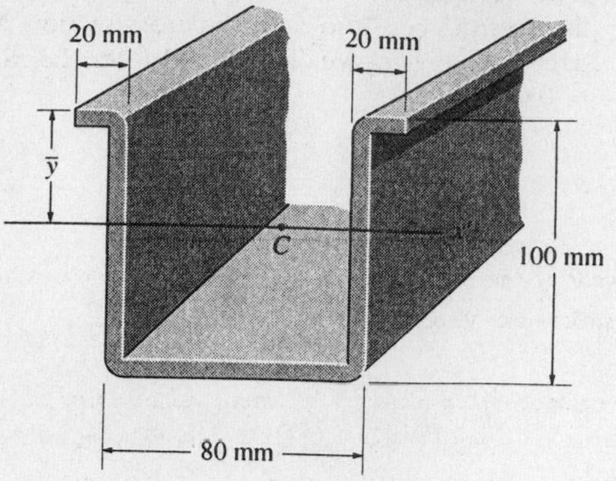

Centroid **:** The area of each segment and its respective centroid are tabulated below.

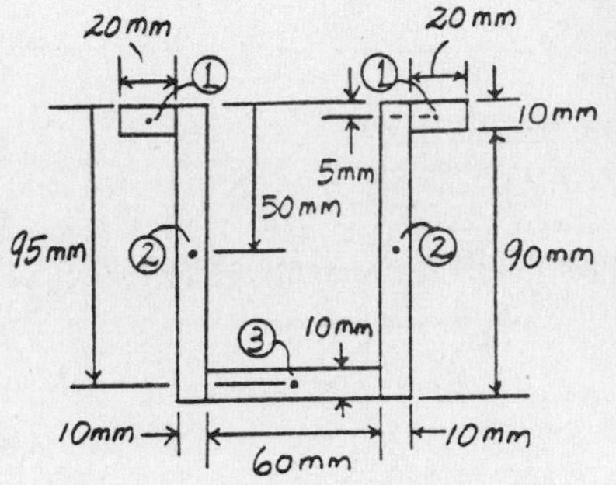

Segment	$A\,(\text{mm}^2)$	$\bar{y}\,(\text{mm})$	$\bar{y}A\,(\text{mm}^3)$
1	40(10)	5	$2.00(10^3)$
2	20(100)	50	$100.0(10^3)$
3	60(10)	95	$57.0(10^3)$
Σ	$3.00(10^3)$		$159.0(10^3)$

Thus,

$$\bar{y} = \frac{\Sigma \bar{y}A}{\Sigma A} = \frac{159.0(10^3)}{3.00(10^3)} = 53.0\text{ mm} \qquad \textbf{Ans}$$

Moment of Inertia **:** The moment of inertia about the x' axis for each segment can be determined usin the parallel – axis theorem $I_{x'} = \bar{I}_{x'} + Ad_y^2$.

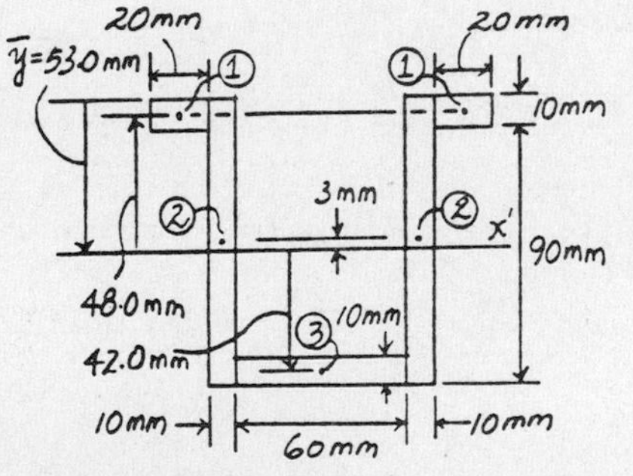

Segment	$A_i\,(\text{mm}^2)$	$(d_y)_i\,(\text{mm})$	$(\bar{I}_{x'})_i\,(\text{mm}^4)$	$(Ad_y^2)_i\,(\text{mm}^4)$	$(I_{x'})_i\,(\text{mm}^4)$
1	40(10)	48.0	$\frac{1}{12}(40)(10^3)$	$0.9216(10^6)$	$0.9249(10^6)$
2	20(100)	3.00	$\frac{1}{12}(20)(100^3)$	$0.018(10^6)$	$1.6847(10^6)$
3	60(10)	42.0	$\frac{1}{12}(60)(10^3)$	$1.0584(10^6)$	$1.0634(10^6)$

Thus,

$$I_{x'} = \Sigma(I_{x'})_i = 3.673\left(10^6\right)\text{ mm}^4 = 3.67\left(10^6\right)\text{ mm}^4 \qquad \textbf{Ans}$$

10-50. Determine the moment of inertia of the beam's cross-sectional area with respect to the x' axis passing through the centroid C of the cross section. Neglect the size of the corner welds at A and B for the calculation, $\bar{y} = 104.3$ mm.

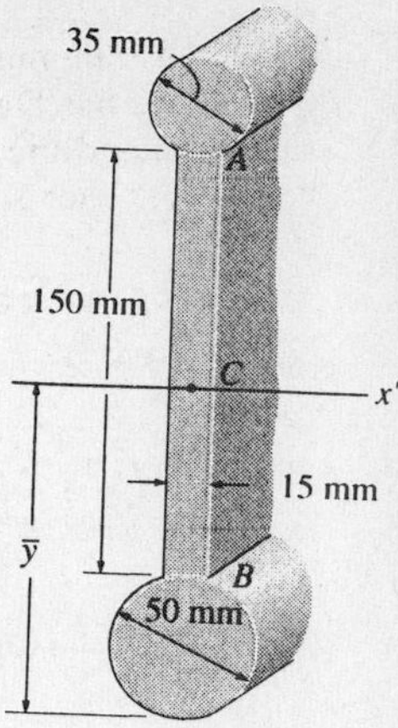

Moment of Inertia : The moment of inertia about the x' axis for each segment can be determined usin the parallel – axis theorem $I_{x'} = \bar{I}_{x'} + Ad_y^2$.

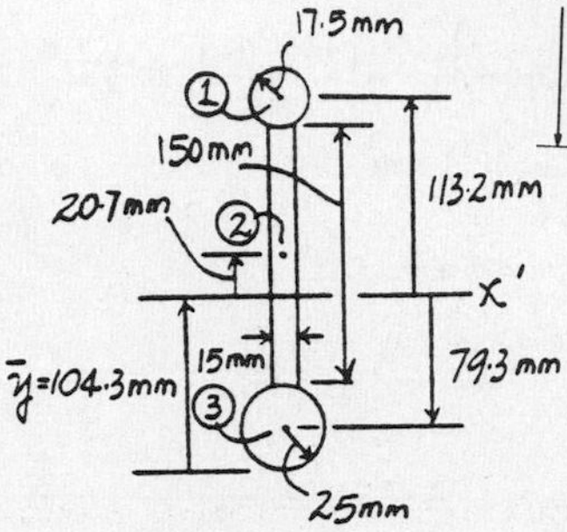

Segment	A_i (mm²)	$(d_y)_i$ (mm)	$(\bar{I}_{x'})_i$ (mm⁴)	$(Ad_y^2)_i$ (mm⁴)	$(I_{x'})_i$ (mm⁴)
1	$\pi(17.5^2)$	113.2	$\frac{\pi}{4}(17.5^4)$	$12.329(10^6)$	$12.402(10^6)$
2	$15(150)$	20.7	$\frac{1}{12}(15)(150^3)$	$0.964(10^6)$	$5.183(10^6)$
3	$\pi(25^2)$	79.3	$\frac{\pi}{4}(25^4)$	$12.347(10^6)$	$12.654(10^6)$

Thus,

$$I_{x'} = \Sigma(I_{x'})_i = 30.24(10^6)\ \text{mm}^4 = 30.2(10^6)\ \text{mm}^4 \qquad \textbf{Ans}$$

10-51. Determine the location $\bar{y}$ of the centroid of the channel's cross-sectional area and then calculate the moment of inertia of the area about this axis.

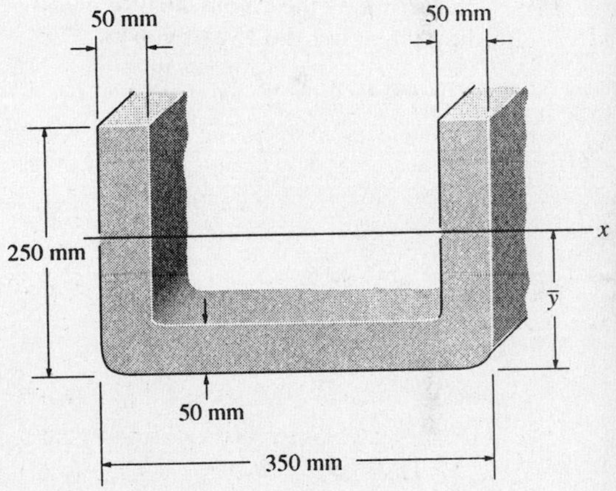

Centroid : The area of each segment and its respective centroid are tabulated below.

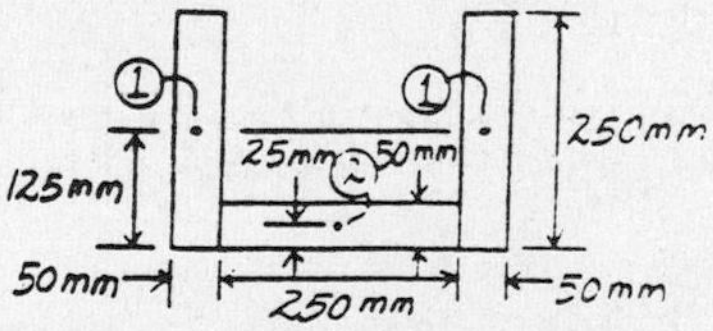

Segment	A (mm²)	$\tilde{y}$ (mm)	$\tilde{y}A$ (mm³)
1	100(250)	125	$3.125(10^6)$
2	250(50)	25	$0.3125(10^6)$
Σ	$37.5(10^3)$		$3.4375(10^6)$

Thus,

$$\bar{y} = \frac{\Sigma\tilde{y}A}{\Sigma A} = \frac{3.4375(10^6)}{37.5(10^3)} = 91.67\ \text{mm} = 91.7\ \text{mm} \qquad \textbf{Ans}$$

Moment of Inertia : The moment of inertia about the x' axis for each segment can be determined using the parallel – axis theorem $I_{x'} = \bar{I}_{x'} + Ad_y^2$.

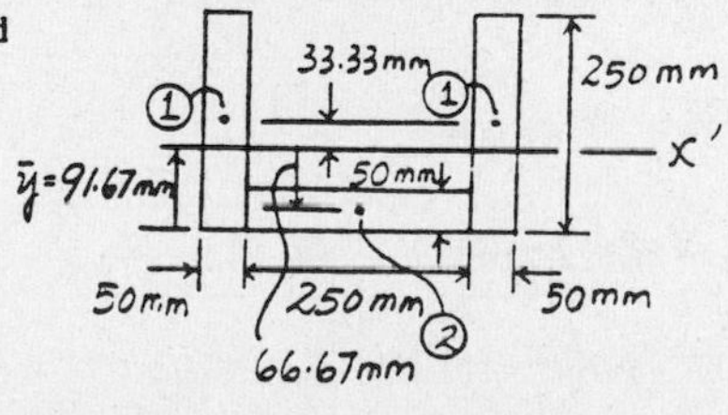

Segment	A_i (mm²)	$(d_y)_i$ (mm)	$(\bar{I}_{x'})_i$ (mm⁴)	$(Ad_y^2)_i$ (mm⁴)	$(I_{x'})_i$ (mm⁴)
1	100(250)	33.33	$\frac{1}{12}(100)(250^3)$	$27.778(10^6)$	$157.99(10^6)$
2	250(50)	66.67	$\frac{1}{12}(250)(50^3)$	$55.556(10^6)$	$58.16(10^6)$

Thus,

$$I_{x'} = \Sigma(I_{x'})_i = 216.15(10^6)\ \text{mm}^4 = 216(10^6)\ \text{mm}^4 \qquad \textbf{Ans}$$

***10-52.** Determine the polar moment of inertia of the shaded area about the origin of coordinates C, located at the centroid.

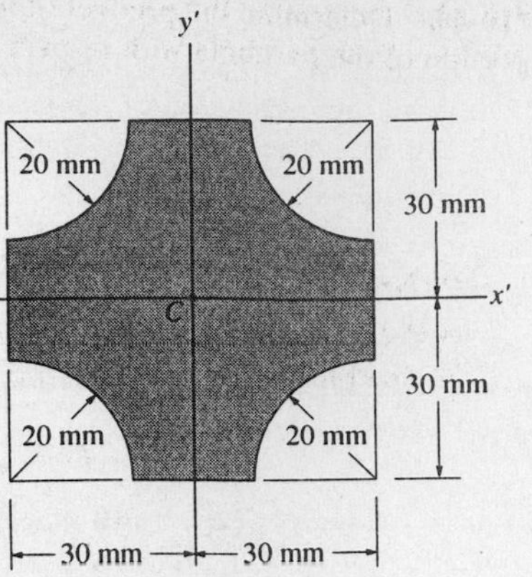

Moment of inertia : The moment inertia for the rectangle and quarter circular area about their centroidal axis can be determined using the formula, $I_{x'} = \frac{1}{12}bh^3$ and $I_{x'} = \frac{\pi}{16}r^4 - \frac{\pi}{4}r^2\left(\frac{4r}{3\pi}\right)^2 = \frac{9\pi^2 - 64}{144\pi}r^4$ respectively, given on the inside back cover of the textbook.

$$I_{y'} = I_{x'} = \frac{1}{12}(60)(60^3) - 4\left[\left(\frac{9\pi^2 - 64}{144\pi}\right)(20^4) + \frac{\pi}{4}(20^2)(21.512^2)\right]$$
$$= 463.36(10^3)\ \text{mm}^4$$

The polar moment of inertia about C is

$$J_C = I_{x'} + I_{y'} = 927(10^3)\ \text{mm}^4 \qquad \textbf{Ans}$$

10-53. Determine the moments of inertia of the composite area about the x' and y axes.

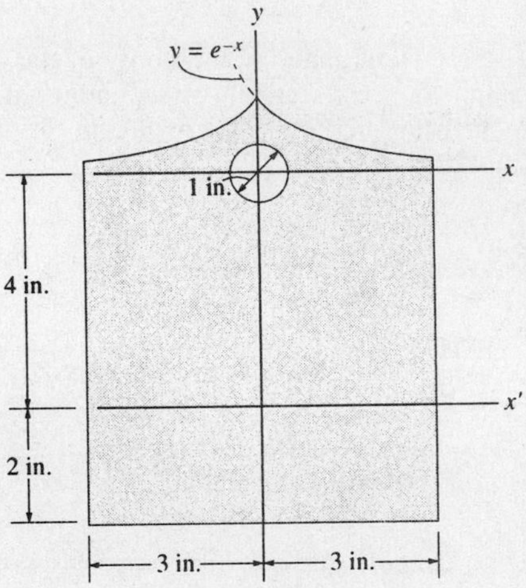

$$I_{x'} = 2\int_0^3\left[\frac{1}{12}(dx)(4+y)^3 + (4+y)dx\left(\frac{4+y}{2}\right)^2\right] + \frac{1}{12}(6)(2)^3 + 6(2)(1)^2$$

$$-\left[\frac{1}{4}\pi(0.5)^4 + \pi(0.5)^2(4)^2\right]$$

$$= 2\int_{-3}^3 \frac{1}{3}(4+e^{-x})^3\,dx + 3.3845 = 2(81.31) + 3.3845$$

$$= 166\ \text{in}^4 \qquad \textbf{Ans}$$

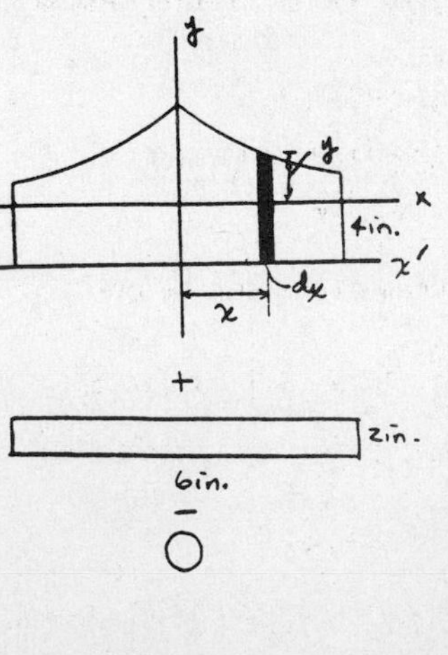

$$I_y = 2\int_0^3 x^2e^{-x}dx + \frac{1}{12}(6)(6)^3 - \frac{1}{4}\pi(0.5)^4$$

$$= 2.307 + 107.95 = 110\ \text{in}^4 \qquad \textbf{Ans}$$

***10-54.** Determine the product of inertia of the shaded portion of the parabola with respect to the x and y axes.

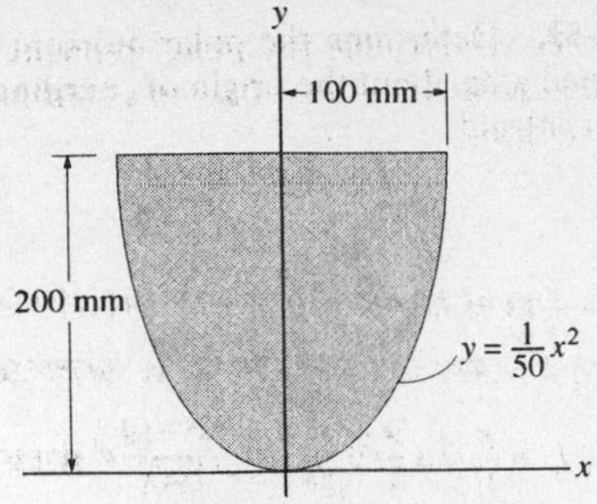

Differential Element : Here, $x = \sqrt{50}y^{\frac{1}{2}}$. The area of the differential element parallel to the x axis is $dA = 2xdy = 2\sqrt{50}y^{\frac{1}{2}}dy$. The coordinates of the centroid for this element are $\tilde{x} = 0$, $\tilde{y} = y$. Then the product of inertia for this element is

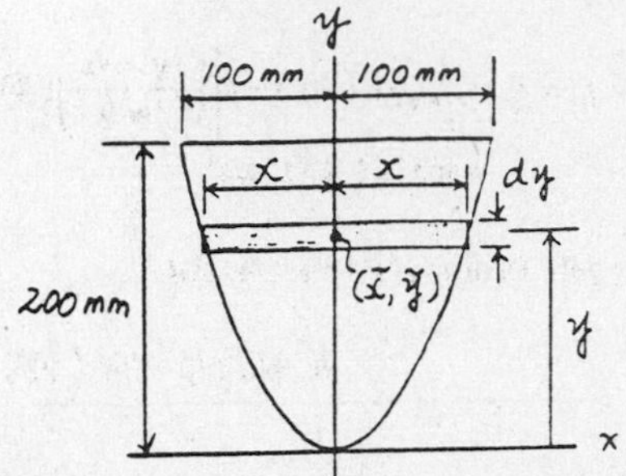

$$dI_{xy} = d\bar{I}_{x'y'} + dA\tilde{x}\tilde{y}$$
$$= 0 + \left(2\sqrt{50}y^{\frac{1}{2}}dy\right)(0)(y)$$
$$= 0$$

Product of Inertia : Performing the integration, we have

$$I_{xy} = \int dI_{xy} = 0$$ **Ans**

Note : By inspection, $I_{xy} = 0$ since the shaded area is symmetrical about the y axis.

10-55. Determine the product of inertia of the shaded area with respect to the x and y axes.

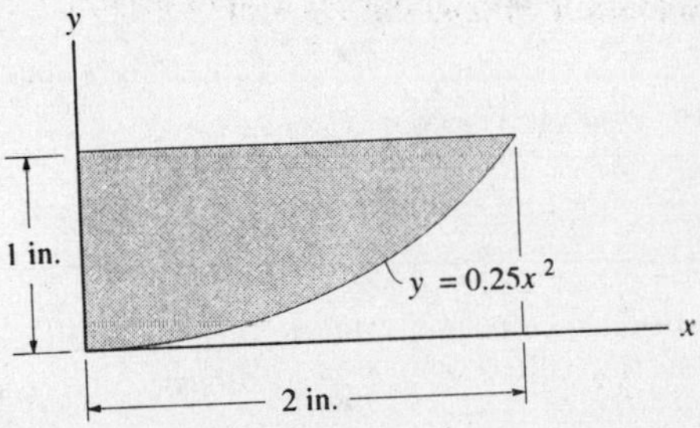

Differential Element : Here, $x = 2y^{\frac{1}{2}}$. The area of the differential element parallel to the x axis is $dA = xdy = 2y^{\frac{1}{2}}dy$. The coordinates of the centroid for this element are $\tilde{x} = \frac{x}{2} = y^{\frac{1}{2}}$, $\tilde{y} = y$. Then the product of inertia for this element is

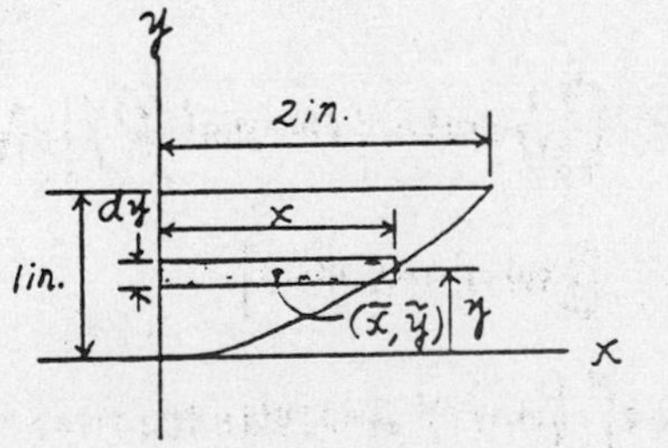

$$dI_{xy} = d\bar{I}_{x'y'} + dA\tilde{x}\tilde{y}$$
$$= 0 + \left(2y^{\frac{1}{2}}dy\right)\left(y^{\frac{1}{2}}\right)(y)$$
$$= 2y^2dy$$

Product of Inertia : Performing the integration, we have

$$I_{xy} = \int dI_{xy} = \int_0^{1\,\text{in.}} 2y^2dy = \frac{2}{3}y^3\Big|_0^{1\,\text{in.}} = 0.667\ \text{in}^4$$ **Ans**

***10-56.** Determine the product of inertia of the shaded area of the ellipse with respect to the x and y axes.

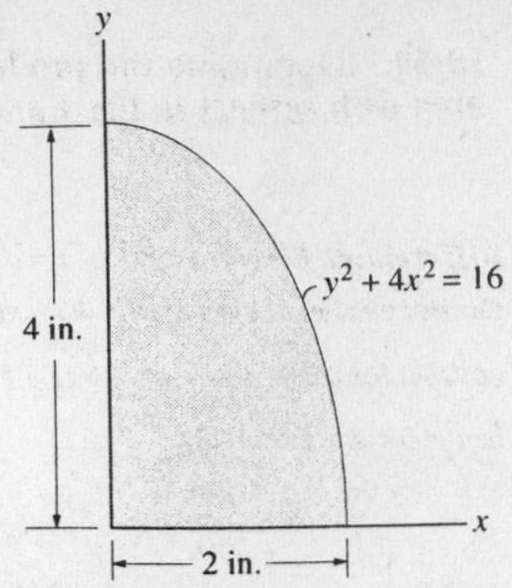

$$dI_{xy} = d\bar{I}_{x'y'} + dA\tilde{x}\tilde{y}$$

$$= 0 + y\,dx(x)\left(\frac{y}{2}\right) = \frac{1}{2}y^2 x\,dx \qquad \text{Where } y^2 = 16 - 4x^2$$

$$= (8x - 2x^3)\,dx$$

Integrating

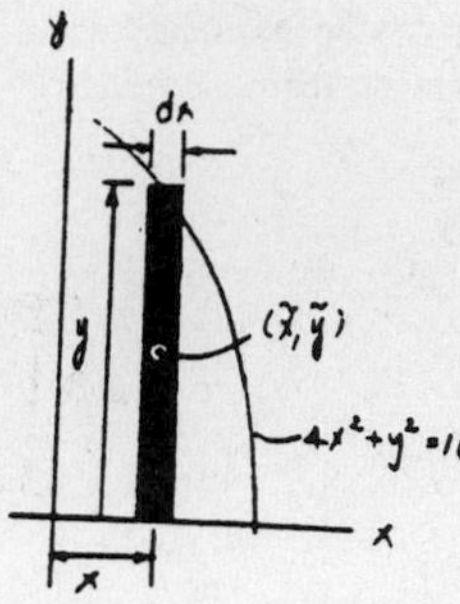

$$\int dI_{xy} = I_{xy} = \int_0^2 (8x - 2x^3)\,dx$$

$$= \left[4x^2 - \frac{1}{2}x^4\right]_0^2$$

$$= 8 \text{ in}^4 \qquad \textbf{Ans}$$

10-57. Determine the product of inertia of the parabolic area with respect to the x and y axes.

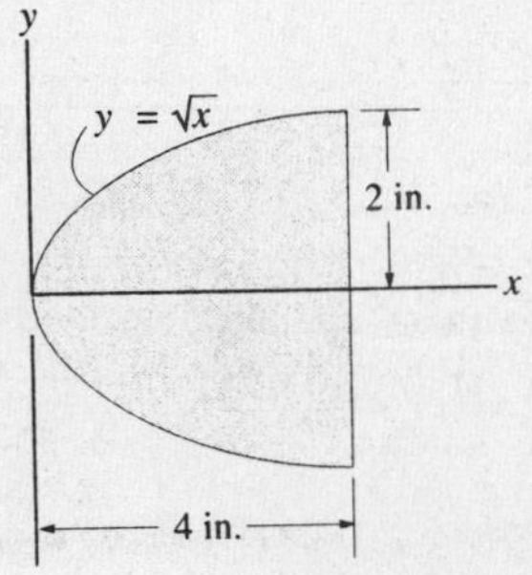

The shaded area is symmetric about the x axis, hence $I_{xy} = 0$ **Ans**

10-58. Determine the product of inertia of the shaded section of the ellipse with respect to the x and y axes.

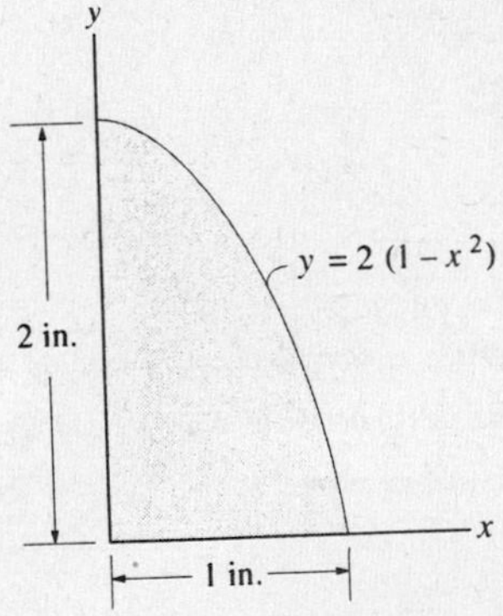

The product of inertia of the element (shaded) is

$$dI_{xy} = d\bar{I}_{x'y'} + dA\tilde{x}\tilde{y}$$

$$= 0 + y\,dx(x)\left(\frac{y}{2}\right) = \tfrac{1}{2}y^2 x\,dx \qquad \text{where } y^2 = 4(1 - x^2)^2$$

$$= 2(x + x^5 - 2x^3)\,dx$$

Integrating

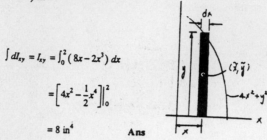

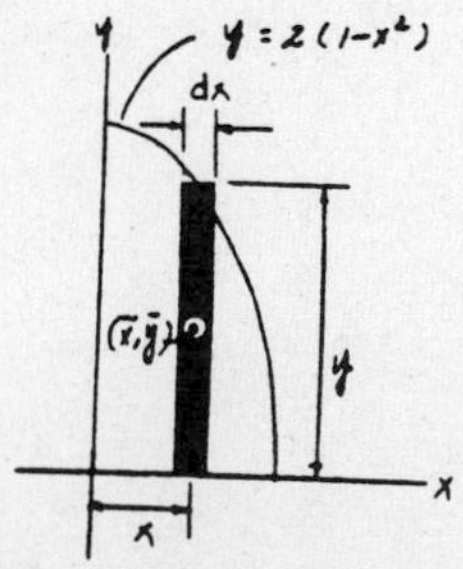

$$\int dI_{xy} = I_{xy} = 2\int_0^1 (x + x^5 - 2x^3)\,dx$$

$$= \left[2\left(\frac{1}{2}x^2 + \frac{1}{6}x^6 - \frac{1}{2}x^4\right)\right]_0^1$$

$$= 0.333 \text{ in}^4 \qquad \textbf{Ans}$$

10-59. Determine the product of inertia of the shaded area with respect to the x and y axes.

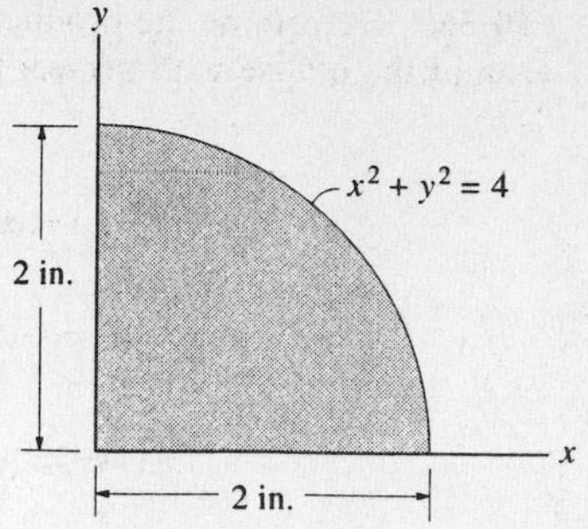

Differential Element : Here, $y = \sqrt{4-x^2}$. The area of the differential element parallel to the y axis is $dA = ydx = \sqrt{4-x^2}dx$. The coordinates of the centroid for this element are $\tilde{x} = x$, $\tilde{y} = \frac{y}{2} = \frac{1}{2}\sqrt{4-x^2}$. Then the product of inertia for this element is

$$dI_{xy} = d\bar{I}_{x'y'} + dA\tilde{x}\tilde{y}$$
$$= 0 + \left(\sqrt{4-x^2}dx\right)(x)\left(\frac{1}{2}\sqrt{4-x^2}\right)$$
$$= \frac{1}{2}\left(4x - x^3\right)dx$$

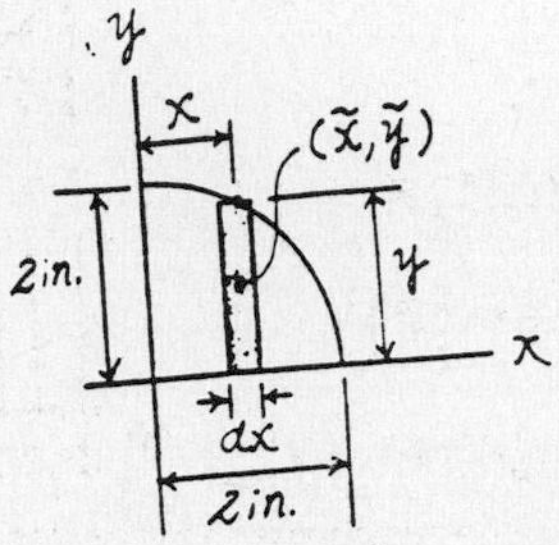

Product of Inertia : Performing the integration, we have

$$I_{xy} = \int dI_{xy} = \frac{1}{2}\int_0^{2\text{ in.}} \left(4x - x^3\right)dx$$
$$= \frac{1}{2}\left(2x^2 - \frac{x^4}{4}\right)\Big|_0^{2\text{ in.}} = 2.00\text{ in}^4 \quad \textbf{Ans}$$

***10-60.** Determine the product of inertia of the parabolic area with respect to the x and y axes.

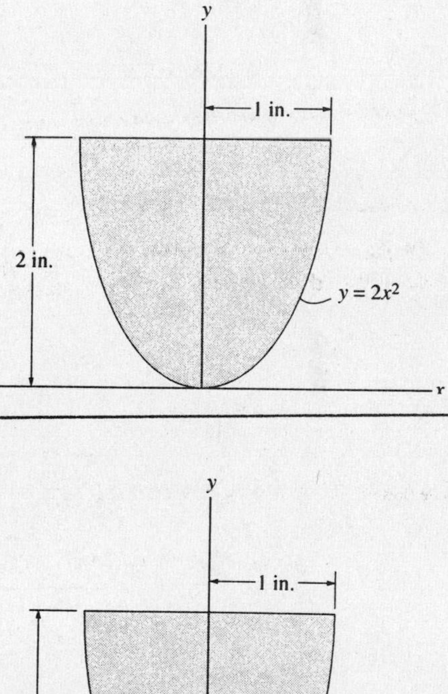

Due to symmetry about y axis

$I_{xy} = 0$ **Ans**

10-61. Determine the product of inertia I_{xy} of the right half of the parabolic area in Prob. 10-60, bounded by the lines $y = 2$ in. and $x = 0$.

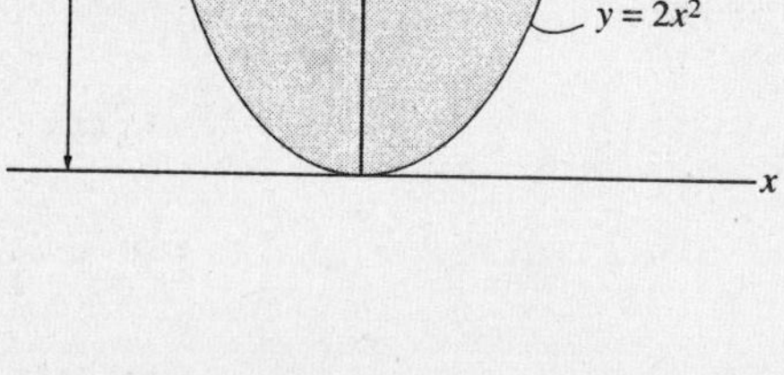

$\tilde{x} = \frac{x}{2}$

$\tilde{y} = y$

$dA = x\,dy$

$$I_{xy} = \int_A \tilde{x}\tilde{y}\,dA = \int_A \left(\frac{x}{2}\right)(y)(x\,dy)$$

$$= \int_0^2 \frac{1}{2}\left(\frac{1}{2}y^2\right)dy = \frac{1}{12}y^3\Big]_0^2 = 0.667\text{ in}^4 \quad \textbf{Ans}$$

*10-62. Determine the product of inertia of the shaded area with respect to the x and y axes.

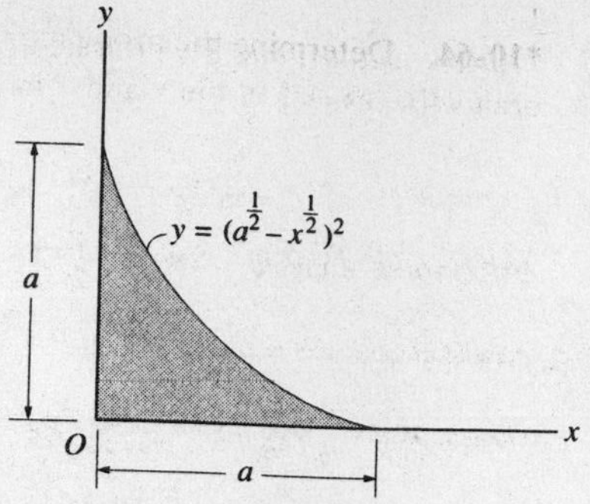

Differential Element : The area of the differential element parallel to the y axis is $dA = ydx = \left(a^{\frac{1}{2}} - x^{\frac{1}{2}}\right)^2 dx$. The coordinates of the centroid for this element are $\tilde{x} = x$, $\tilde{y} = \frac{y}{2} = \frac{1}{2}\left(a^{\frac{1}{2}} - x^{\frac{1}{2}}\right)^2$. Then the product of inertia for this element is

$$
\begin{aligned}
dI_{xy} &= d\bar{I}_{x'y'} + dA\tilde{x}\tilde{y} \\
&= 0 + \left[\left(a^{\frac{1}{2}} - x^{\frac{1}{2}}\right)^2 dx\right](x)\left[\frac{1}{2}\left(a^{\frac{1}{2}} - x^{\frac{1}{2}}\right)^2\right] \\
&= \frac{1}{2}\left(x^3 + a^2x + 6ax^2 - 4a^{\frac{3}{2}}x^{\frac{3}{2}} - 4a^{\frac{1}{2}}x^{\frac{5}{2}}\right)dx
\end{aligned}
$$

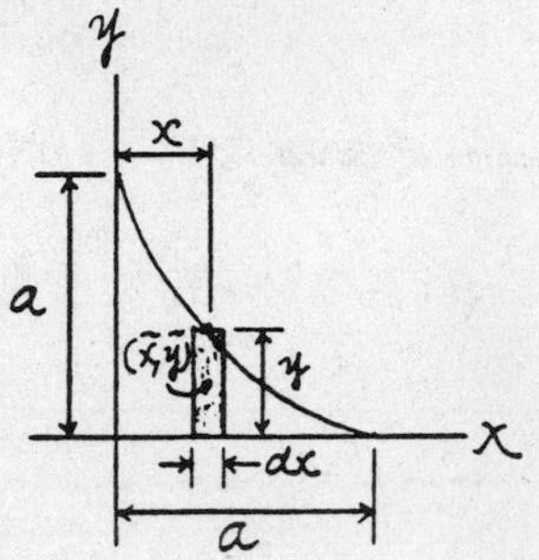

Product of Inertia : Performing the integration, we have

$$
\begin{aligned}
I_{xy} = \int dI_{xy} &= \frac{1}{2}\int_0^a \left(x^3 + a^2x + 6ax^2 - 4a^{\frac{3}{2}}x^{\frac{3}{2}} - 4a^{\frac{1}{2}}x^{\frac{5}{2}}\right)dx \\
&= \frac{1}{2}\left(\frac{x^4}{4} + \frac{a^2}{2}x^2 + 2ax^3 - \frac{8}{5}a^{\frac{3}{2}}x^{\frac{5}{2}} - \frac{8}{7}a^{\frac{1}{2}}x^{\frac{7}{2}}\right)\Bigg|_0^a \\
&= \frac{a^4}{280}
\end{aligned}
$$

Ans

10-63. Determine the product of inertia of the shaded area with respect to the x and y axes.

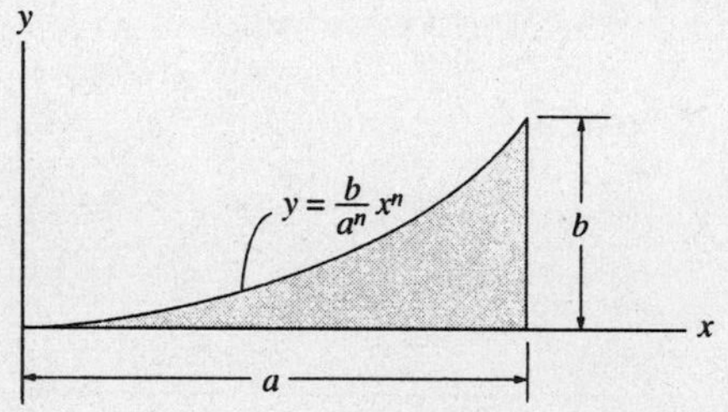

$$dI_{xy} = d\bar{I}_{xy} + \tilde{x}\tilde{y}\,dA$$

$$I_{xy} = 0 + \int_0^a (x)\left(\frac{y}{2}\right)(y\,dx) = \frac{1}{2}\int_0^a \left(\frac{b^2}{a^{2n}}\right)x^{2n+1}dx$$

$$= \left(\frac{b^2}{2a^{2n}}\right)\left(\frac{1}{2n+2}\right)x^{2n+2}\Big|_0^a = \frac{b^2a^{2n+2}}{4(n+1)\,a^{2n}}$$

$$= \frac{a^2b^2}{4(n+1)}$$

Ans

***10-64.** Determine the product of inertia of the shaded area with respect to the x and y axes.

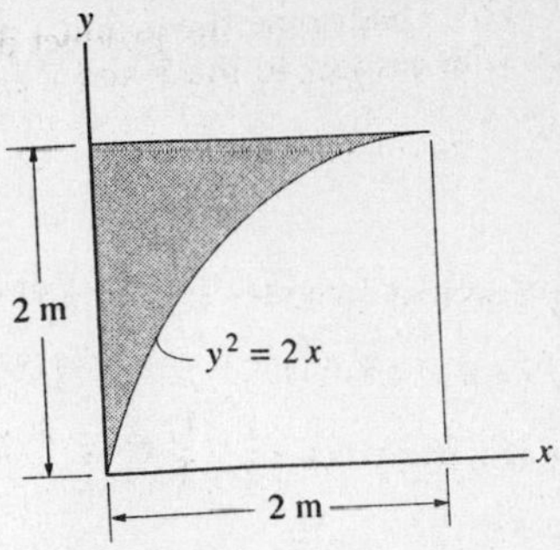

Differential Element : Here, $x = \frac{y^2}{2}$. The area of the differential element parallel to the x axis is $dA = xdy = \frac{y^2}{2}dy$. The coordinates of the centroid for this element are $\tilde{x} = \frac{x}{2} = \frac{y^2}{4}$, $\tilde{y} = y$. Then the product of inertia for this element is

$$dI_{xy} = d\bar{I}_{x'y'} + dA\tilde{x}\tilde{y}$$
$$= 0 + \left(\frac{y^2}{2}dy\right)\left(\frac{y^2}{4}\right)(y)$$
$$= \frac{1}{8}y^5 dy$$

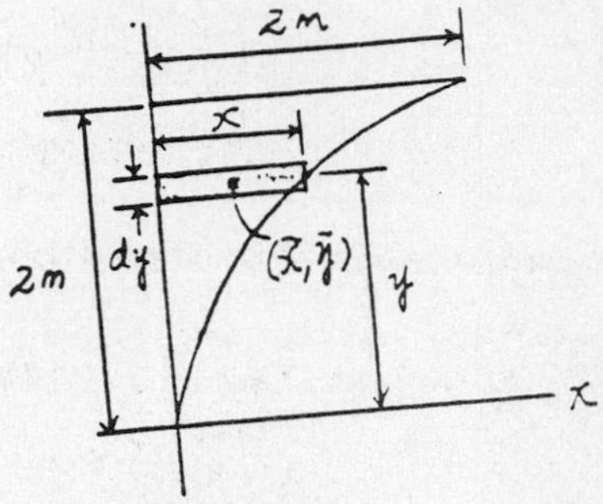

Product of Inertia : Performing the integration, we have

$$I_{xy} = \int dI_{xy} = \frac{1}{8}\int_0^{2m} y^5 dy = \frac{1}{48}y^6\Big|_0^{2m} = 1.33 \text{ m}^4$$ **Ans**

10-65. Determine the product of inertia of the quarter circular area with respect to the x and y axes. Then use the parallel-axis theorem to determine the product of inertia about the centroidal x' and y' axes.

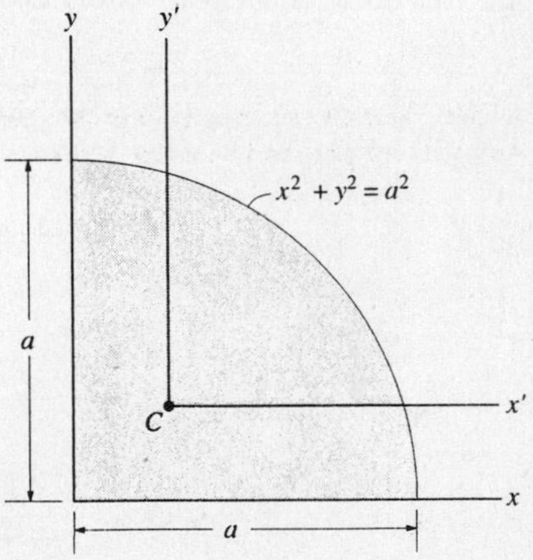

$\tilde{x} = x$

$\tilde{y} = \frac{1}{2}y$

$dA = y\,dx$

$$I_{xy} = \int_0^a \frac{y}{2}(x)(y)\,dx = \frac{1}{2}\int_0^a x(a^2 - x^2)dx$$

$$= \frac{1}{2}\left[\frac{a^2x^2}{2} - \frac{x^4}{4}\right]_0^a = \frac{1}{8}a^4$$ **Ans**

$$I_{xy} = \bar{I}_{x'y'} + \bar{x}\bar{y}A$$

$$\frac{1}{8}a^4 = \bar{I}_{x'y'} + \left(\frac{4a}{3\pi}\right)\left(\frac{4a}{3\pi}\right)\left(\frac{\pi a^2}{4}\right)$$

$$\bar{I}_{x'y'} = -0.0165\,a^4$$ **Ans**

10-66. Determine the product of inertia of the thin strip of area with respect to the x and y axes. The strip is oriented at an angle θ from the x axis. Assume that $t \ll l$.

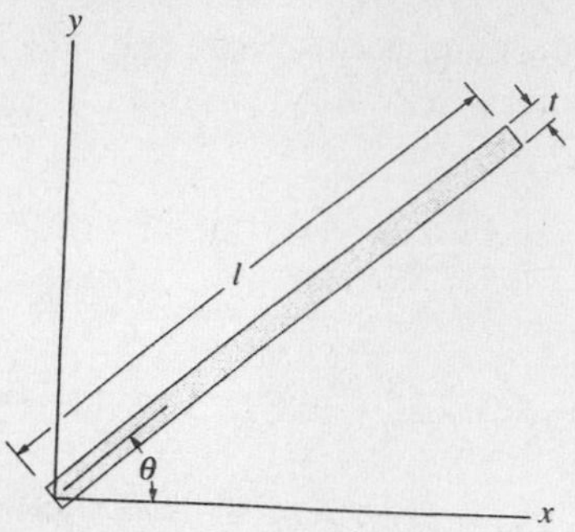

$$I_{xy} = \int_A xy\,dA = \int_0^l (s\cos\theta)(s\sin\theta)\,t\,ds = \sin\theta\cos\theta\,t\int_0^l s^2\,ds$$

$$= \frac{1}{6}l^3 t\sin 2\theta \qquad \textbf{Ans}$$

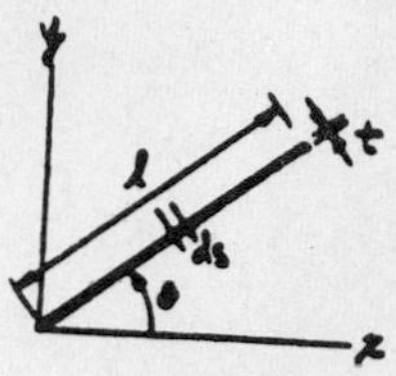

10-67. Determine the product of inertia of the beam's cross-sectional area with respect to the x and y axes that have their origin located at the centroid C.

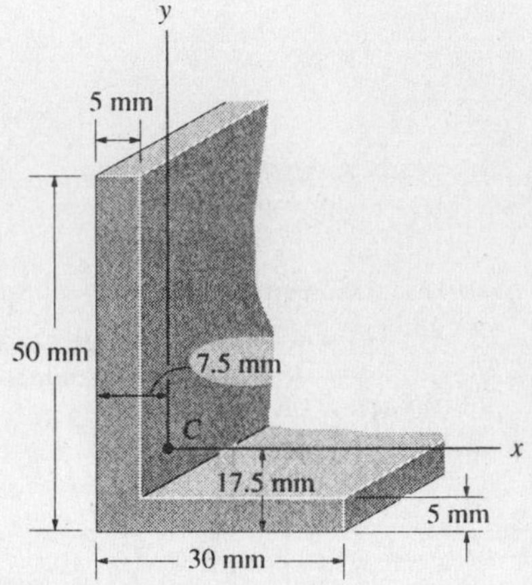

Product of Inertia : The area for each segment, its centroid and product of inertia with respect to x and y axes are tabulated below.

Segment	A_i (mm²)	$(d_x)_i$ (mm)	$(d_y)_i$ (mm)	$(I_{xy})_i$ (mm⁴)
1	50(5)	−5	7.5	−9.375(10³)
2	25(5)	10	−15	−18.75(10³)

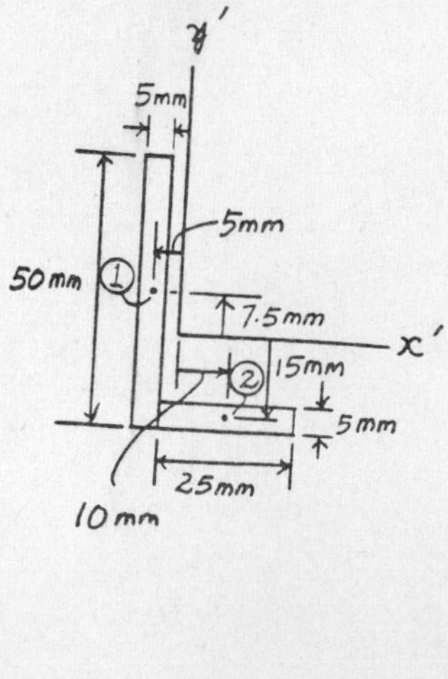

Thus,

$$I_{xy} = \Sigma(I_{xy})_i = -28.125(10^3)\text{ mm}^4 = -28.1(10^3)\text{ mm}^4 \qquad \textbf{Ans}$$

***10-68.** Determine the product of inertia of the cross-sectional area of the channel with respect to the x' and y' axes. $\bar{x} = 33.9$ mm, $\bar{y} = 150$ mm.

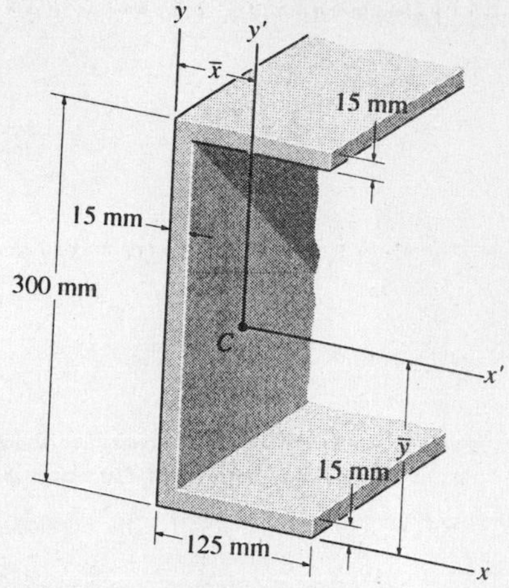

$$I_{x'y'} = \Sigma \bar{I}_{x'y'} + dx\,dy\,A = \left[0 + (-26.4)(0)(300)(15)\right] + \left[0 + (36.1)(-142.5)(110)(15)\right]$$

$$+ \left[0 + (36.1)(142.5)(110)(15)\right]$$

$I_{x'y'} = 0$ **Ans**

Note : Since the $\bar{x}$ axis in an axis of symmetry, $I_{x'y'} = 0$.

10-69. Determine the product of inertia of the cross-sectional area with respect to the x and y axes that have their origin located at the centroid C.

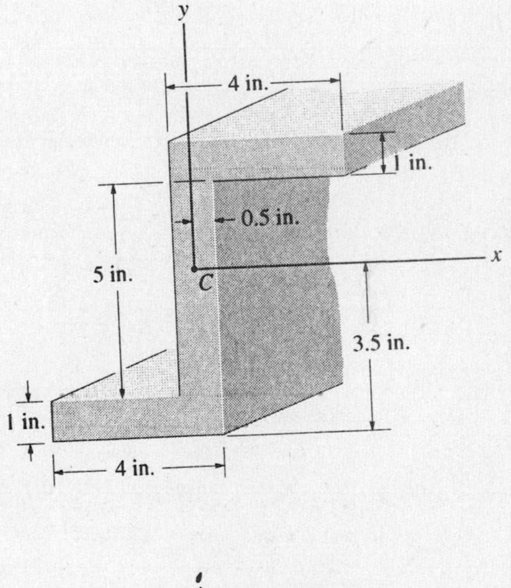

Product of Inertia : The area for each segment, its centroid and product of inertia with respect to x and y axes are tabulated below.

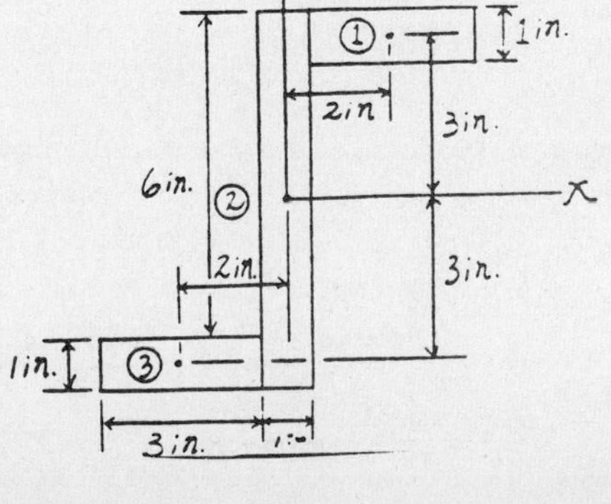

Segment	A_i (in²)	$(d_x)_i$ (in.)	$(d_y)_i$ (in.)	$(I_{xy})_i$ (in⁴)
1	3(1)	2	3	18.0
2	7(1)	0	0	0
3	3(1)	−2	−3	18.0

Thus,

$$I_{xy} = \Sigma\left(I_{xy}\right)_i = 36.0 \text{ in}^4 \qquad \textbf{Ans}$$

10-70. Determine the product of inertia of the parallelogram with respect to the x and y axes.

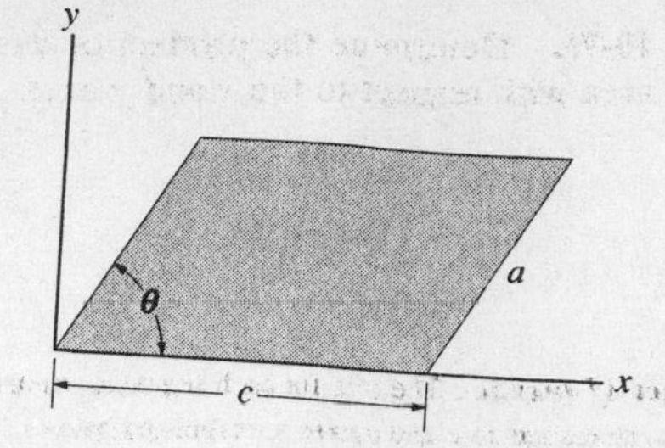

Product of Inertia of the Triangle : The product of inertia with respect to x and y axes can be determined by integration. The area of the differential element parallel to y axis is $dA = y\,dx = \left(h + \frac{h}{b}x\right)dx$ [Fig. (a)] . The coordinates of the centroid for this element are $\tilde{x} = -x$, $\tilde{y} = \frac{y}{2} = \frac{1}{2}\left(h + \frac{h}{b}x\right)$. Then the product of inertia for this element is

$$dI_{xy} = d\bar{I}_{x'y'} + dA\,\tilde{x}\tilde{y}$$

$$= 0 + \left[\left(h + \frac{h}{b}x\right)dx\right](-x)\left[\frac{1}{2}\left(h + \frac{h}{b}x\right)\right]$$

$$= -\frac{1}{2}\left(h^2x + \frac{h^2}{b^2}x^3 + \frac{2h^2}{b}x^2\right)dx$$

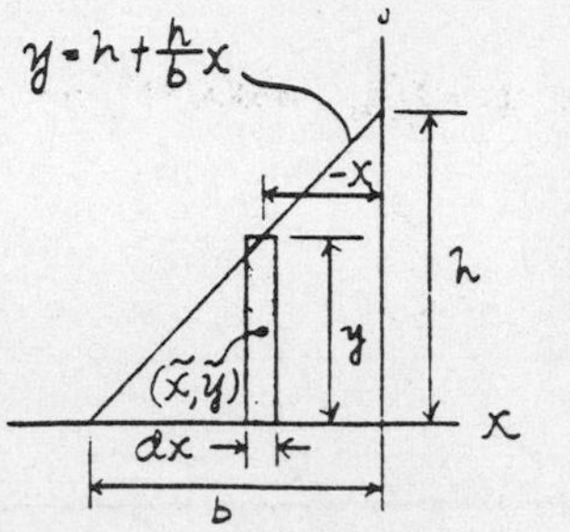

(a)

Performing the integration, we have

$$I_{xy} = \int dI_{xy} = -\frac{1}{2}\int_{-b}^{0}\left(h^2x + \frac{h^2}{b^2}x^3 + \frac{2h^2}{b}x^2\right)dx = -\frac{b^2h^2}{24}$$

The product of inertia with respect to centroidal axes, x' and y', can be determined by applying Eq. 10−8 [Fig. (b) or (c)].

$$I_{xy} = \bar{I}_{x'y'} + A d_x d_y$$

$$-\frac{b^2h^2}{24} = \bar{I}_{x'y'} + \frac{1}{2}bh\left(-\frac{b}{3}\right)\left(\frac{h}{3}\right)$$

$$\bar{I}_{x'y'} = \frac{b^2h^2}{72}$$

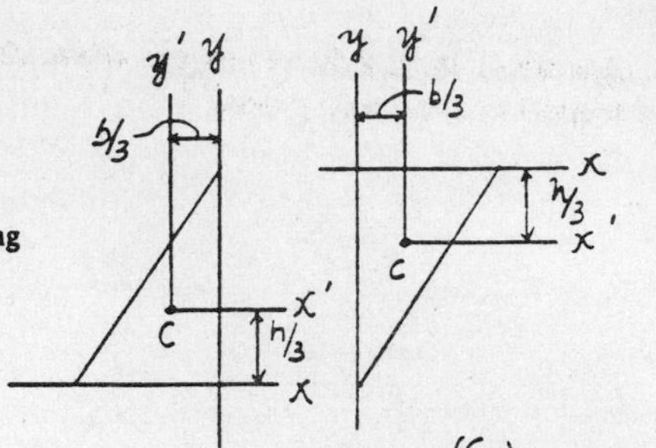

(b) (c)

Here, $b = a\cos\theta$ and $h = a\sin\theta$. Then, $\bar{I}_{x'y'} = \dfrac{a^2b^2\sin^2\theta\cos^2\theta}{72}$.

Product of inertia of the parallelogram [Fig. (d)] with respect to centroidal x' and y' axes, is

$$\bar{I}_{x'y'} = 2\left[\frac{a^4\cos^2\theta\sin^2\theta}{72} + \frac{1}{2}(a\sin\theta)(a\cos\theta)\left(\frac{3c - a\cos\theta}{6}\right)\left(\frac{a\sin\theta}{6}\right)\right]$$

$$= \frac{a^3c\sin^2\theta\cos\theta}{12}$$

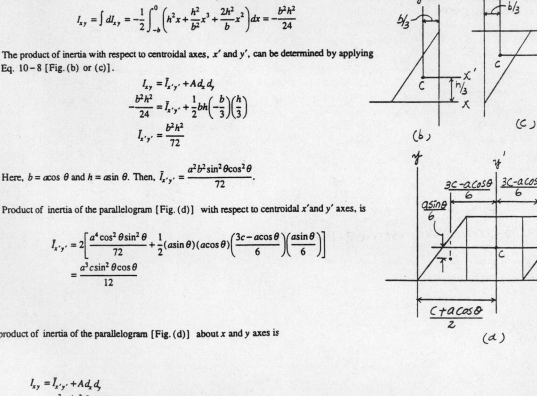

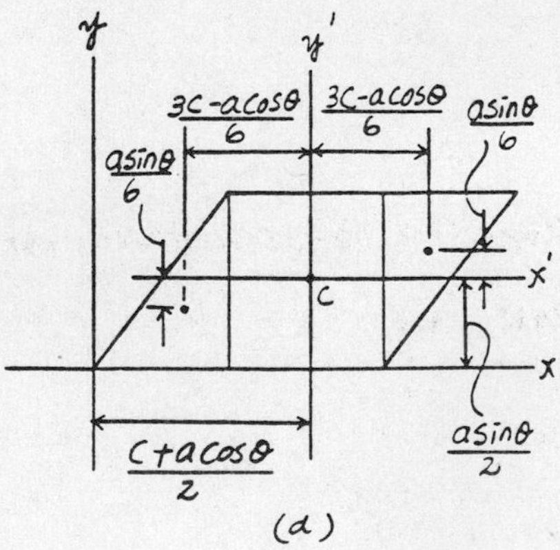

(d)

The product of inertia of the parallelogram [Fig. (d)] about x and y axes is

$$I_{xy} = \bar{I}_{x'y'} + A d_x d_y$$

$$= \frac{a^3c\sin^2\theta\cos\theta}{12} + (a\sin\theta)(c)\left(\frac{c + a\cos\theta}{2}\right)\left(\frac{a\sin\theta}{2}\right)$$

$$= \frac{a^2c\sin^2\theta}{12}(4a\cos\theta + 3c) \qquad \textbf{Ans}$$

10-71. Determine the product of inertia of the shaded area with respect to the x and y axes.

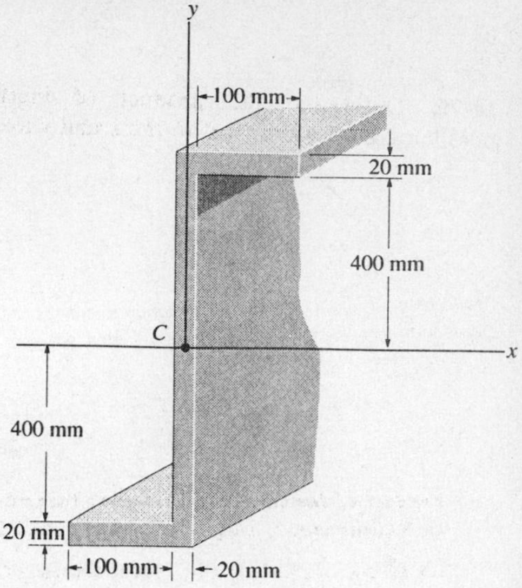

Product of Inertia : The area for each segment, its centroid and product of inertia with respect to x and y axes are tabulated below.

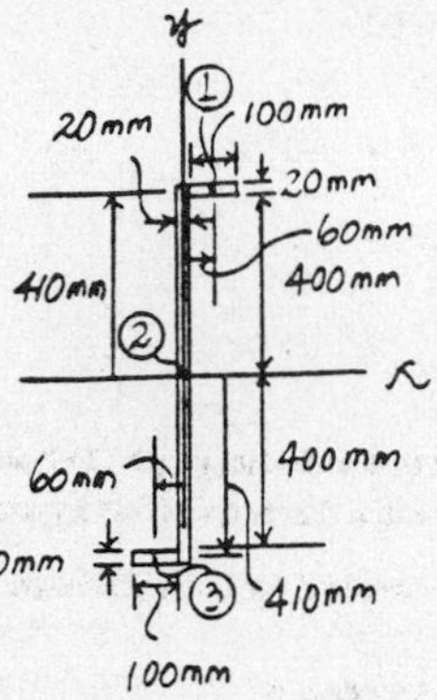

Segment	A_i (mm²)	$(d_x)_i$ (mm)	$(d_y)_i$ (mm)	$(I_{xy})_i$ (mm⁴)
1	100(20)	60	410	$49.2(10^6)$
2	840(20)	0	0	0
3	100(20)	−60	−410	$49.2(10^6)$

Thus,

$$I_{xy} = \Sigma(I_{xy})_i = 98.4(10^6)\ \text{mm}^4 \qquad \textbf{Ans}$$

***10-72.** Determine the product of inertia of the shaded area with respect to the x and y axes.

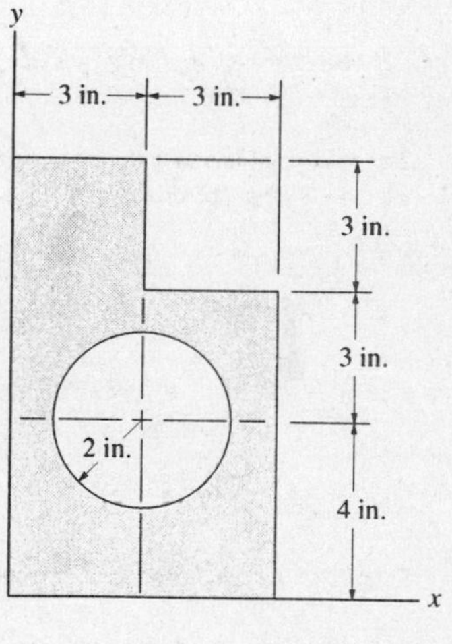

$$I_{xy} = \Sigma(\bar{I}_{x'y'} + \bar{x}\bar{y}A) = [0 + 3(5)(6)(10)] - [0 + 4.5(8.5)(3)(3)] - [0 + (3)(4)(\pi)(2)^2]$$

$$= 405\ \text{in}^4 \qquad \textbf{Ans}$$

10-73. Determine the product of inertia of the Z-section with respect to the x and y axes that have their origin located at the centroid C.

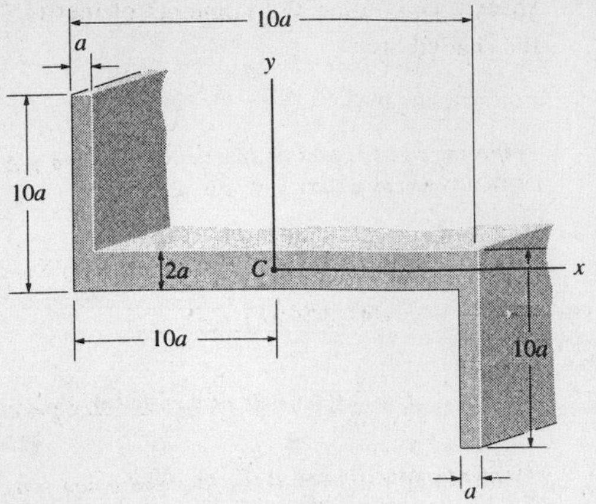

Product of Inertia : The area for each segment, its centroid and product of inertia with respect to x and y axes are tabulated below.

Segment	A_i	$(d_x)_i$	$(d_y)_i$	$(I_{xy})_i$
1	$8a(a)$	$-9.5a$	$5a$	$-380a^4$
2	$8a(a)$	$9.5a$	$-5a$	$-380a^4$

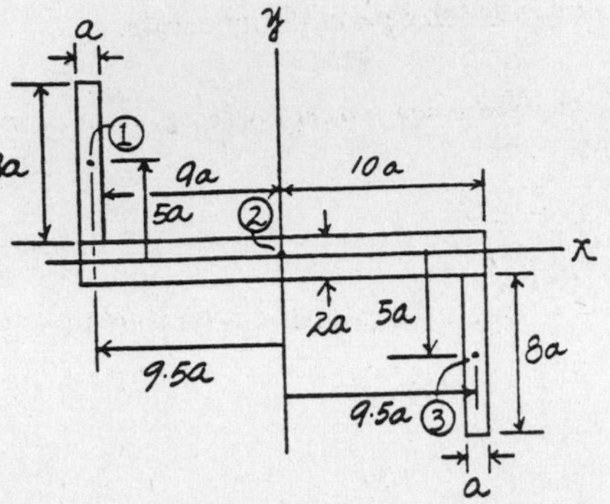

Thus,

$$I_{xy} = \Sigma(I_{xy})_i = -760a^4$$ **Ans**

10-74. Determine the moments of inertia I_u and I_v and the product of inertia I_{uv} for the semicircular area.

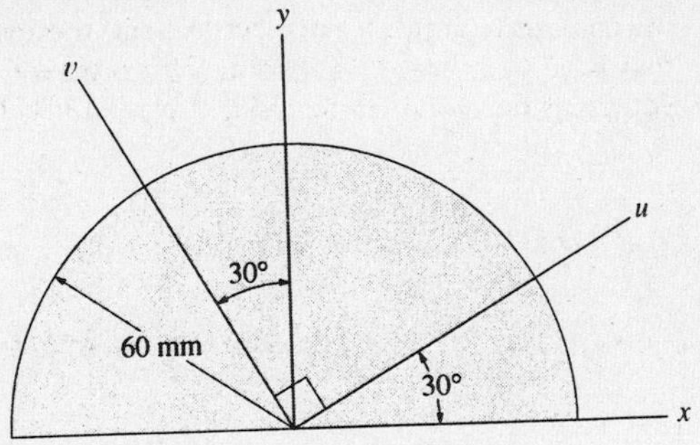

$$I_x = I_y = \frac{1}{8}\pi(60)^4 = 5\,089\,380.1 \text{ mm}^4$$

$$I_{xy} = 0 \quad \text{(due to symmetry)}$$

$$I_u = \frac{I_x + I_y}{2} + \frac{I_x - I_y}{2}\cos 2\theta - I_{xy}\sin 2\theta$$

$$I_u = \frac{5\,089\,380.1 + 5\,089\,380.1}{2} = 5.09(10^6)\text{mm}^4$$ **Ans**

$$I_v = \frac{I_x + I_y}{2} - \frac{I_x - I_y}{2}\cos 2\theta + I_{xy}\sin 2\theta$$

$$I_v = 5\,089\,380.1 - 0 + 0$$

$$I_v = 5.09(10^6)\text{mm}^4$$ **Ans**

$$I_{uv} = \frac{I_x - I_y}{2}\sin 2\theta + I_{xy}\cos 2\theta$$

$$I_{uv} = 0 + 0 = 0$$ **Ans**

10-75. Determine the moments of inertia I_u and I_v of the shaded area.

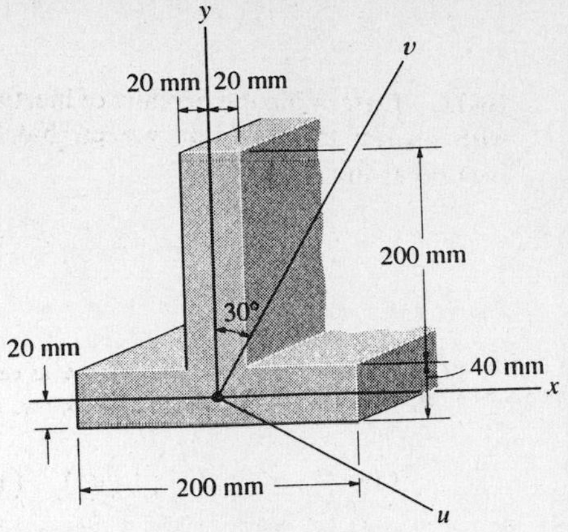

Moment and Product of Inertia about x and y Axes : Since the shaded area is symmetrical about the y axis, $I_{xy} = 0$.

$$I_x = \frac{1}{12}(40)(200^3) + 40(200)(120^2) + \frac{1}{12}(200)(40^3) = 142.93(10^6)\ \text{mm}^4$$

$$I_y = \frac{1}{12}(200)(40^3) + \frac{1}{12}(40)(200^3) = 27.73(10^6)\ \text{mm}^4$$

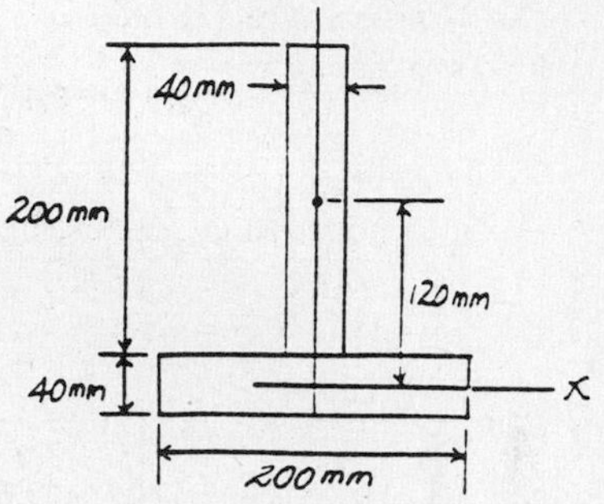

Moment of Inertia about the Inclined u and v Axes : Applying Eq. 10–9 with $\theta = -30°$, we have

$$I_u = \frac{I_x + I_y}{2} + \frac{I_x - I_y}{2}\cos 2\theta - I_{xy}\sin 2\theta$$

$$= \left(\frac{142.93 + 27.73}{2} + \frac{142.93 - 27.73}{2}\cos(-60°) - 0[\sin(-60°)]\right)(10^6)$$

$$= 114(10^6)\ \text{mm}^4 \qquad \textbf{Ans}$$

$$I_v = \frac{I_x + I_y}{2} - \frac{I_x - I_y}{2}\cos 2\theta + I_{xy}\sin 2\theta$$

$$= \left(\frac{142.93 + 27.73}{2} - \frac{142.93 - 27.73}{2}\cos(-60°) - 0[\sin(-60°)]\right)(10^6)$$

$$= 56.5(10^6)\ \text{mm}^4 \qquad \textbf{Ans}$$

***10-76.** Determine the principal moments of inertia of the composite area with respect to a set of principal axes that have their origin located at the centroid C. Use the equations developed in Sec. 10.7. $I_{xy} = -15.84(10^6)\ \text{mm}^4$.

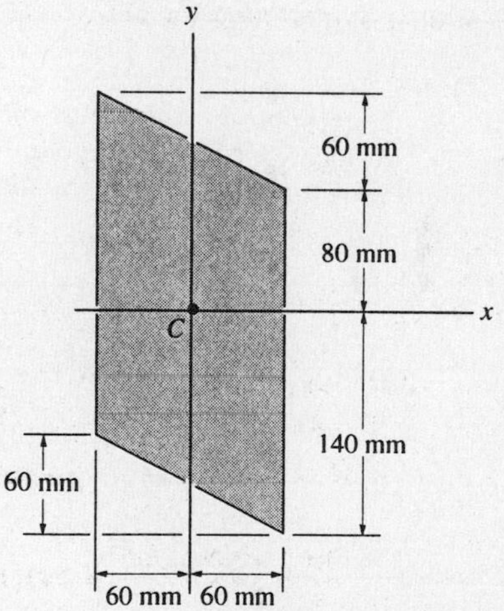

$$I_{xy} = -15.84(10^6)\text{mm}^4$$

$$I_x = \left[\frac{1}{12}(120)(160)^3\right] + \left[\frac{1}{36}(120)(60)^3 + \frac{1}{2}(120)(60)(100)^2\right]$$

$$+ \left[\frac{1}{36}(120)(60)^3 + \frac{1}{2}(120)(60)(-100)^2\right] = 114.4(10^6)\text{mm}^4$$

$$I_y = \left[\frac{1}{12}(160)(120)^3\right] + \left[\frac{1}{36}(60)(120)^3 + \frac{1}{2}(60)(120)(20)^2\right]$$

$$+ \left[\frac{1}{36}(60)(120)^3 + \frac{1}{2}(60)(120)(-20)^2\right] = 31.68(10^6)\text{mm}^4$$

$$\tan 2\theta = \frac{-2I_{xy}}{I_x - I_y} - \frac{-2(15.84)(10^6)}{114.4(10^6) - 31.68(10^6)}$$

$$\theta = 10.5° \qquad \textbf{Ans}$$

$$I_{\substack{max\\min}} = \frac{I_x + I_y}{2} \pm \sqrt{\left(\frac{I_x - I_y}{2}\right)^2 + I_{xy}^2}$$

$$= \frac{114.4(10^6) + 31.68(10^6)}{2} \pm \sqrt{\left(\frac{114.4(10^6) - 31.68(10^6)}{2}\right)^2 + (-15.84(10^6))^2}$$

$$I_{max} = 117(10^6)\text{mm}^4 \qquad \textbf{Ans}$$

$$I_{min} = 28.8(10^6)\text{mm}^4 \qquad \textbf{Ans}$$

***10-77.** Determine the moments of inertia of the shaded area with respect to the u and v axes.

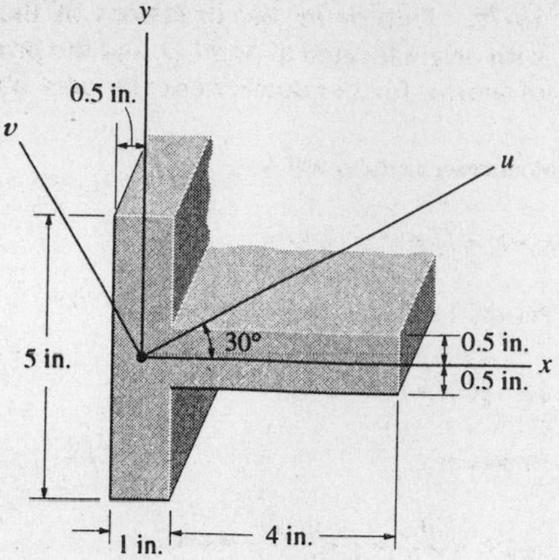

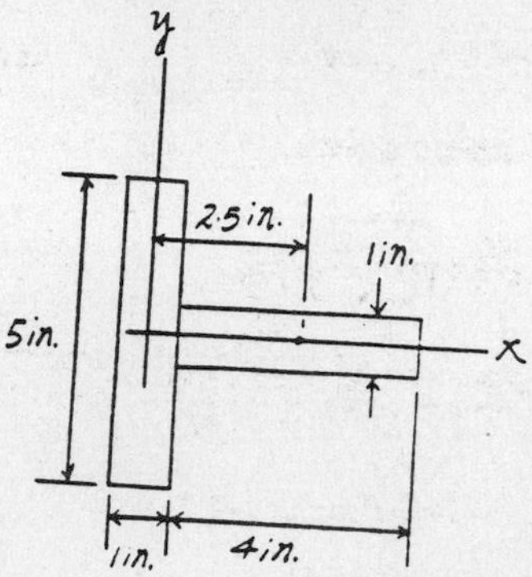

Moment and Product of Inertia about x and y Axes : Since the shaded area is symmetrical about the x axis, $I_{xy} = 0$.

$$I_x = \frac{1}{12}(1)(5^3) + \frac{1}{12}(4)(1^3) = 10.75 \text{ in}^4$$

$$I_y = \frac{1}{12}(1)(4^3) + 1(4)(2.5^2) + \frac{1}{12}(5)(1^3) = 30.75 \text{ in}^4$$

Moment of Inertia about the Inclined u and v Axes : Applying Eq. 10−9 with $\theta = 30°$, we have

$$I_u = \frac{I_x + I_y}{2} + \frac{I_x - I_y}{2}\cos 2\theta - I_{xy}\sin 2\theta$$
$$= \frac{10.75 + 30.75}{2} + \frac{10.75 - 30.75}{2}\cos 60° - 0(\sin 60°)$$
$$= 15.75 \text{ in}^4$$ **Ans**

$$I_v = \frac{I_x + I_y}{2} - \frac{I_x - I_y}{2}\cos 2\theta + I_{xy}\sin 2\theta$$
$$= \frac{10.75 + 30.75}{2} - \frac{10.75 - 30.75}{2}\cos 60° + 0(\sin 60°)$$
$$= 25.75 \text{ in}^4$$ **Ans**

10-78. Determine the directions of the principal axes with origin located at point O, and the principal moments of inertia for the rectangular area about these axes.

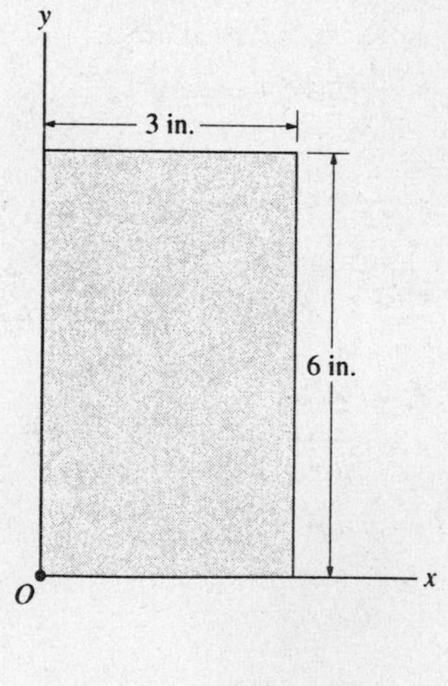

$$I_x = \frac{1}{12}(3)(6)^3 + (3)(6)(3)^2 = 216 \text{ in}^4$$

$$I_y = \frac{1}{12}(6)(3)^3 + (3)(6)(1.5)^2 = 54 \text{ in}^4$$

$$I_{xy} = \bar{x}\bar{y}A = (1.5)(3)(3)(6) = 81 \text{ in}^4$$

$$\tan 2\theta = \frac{-2\,I_{xy}}{I_x - I_y} = \frac{-2(81)}{216 - 54} = -1$$

$\theta = -22.5°$ **Ans**

$$I_{\substack{max\\min}} = \frac{I_x + I_y}{2} \pm \sqrt{\left(\frac{I_x - I_y}{2}\right)^2 + I_{xy}^2} = \frac{216 + 54}{2} \pm \sqrt{\left(\frac{216 - 54}{2}\right)^2 + (81)^2}$$

$I_{max} = 250 \text{ in}^4$ **Ans**

$I_{min} = 20.4 \text{ in}^4$ **Ans**

10-79. Determine the directions of the principal axes with origin located at point O, and the principal moments of inertia for the quarter-circular area about these axes.

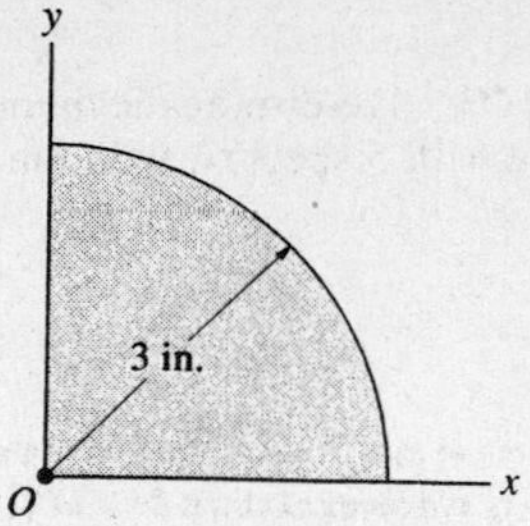

Moments of inertia I_x and I_y :

$$I_x = I_y = \frac{1}{16}\pi(3)^4 = 15.90 \text{ in}^4$$

Product of inertial I_{xy} : From Prob. 10-65

$$I_{xy} = \frac{1}{8}(3)^4 = 10.125 \text{ in}^4$$

Orientation:

$$\tan 2\theta_p = \frac{-I_{xy}}{\frac{I_x - I_y}{2}} = \frac{-10.125}{\frac{15.90-15.90}{2}} = -\infty$$

$2\theta_p = -90°$ $\theta_p = -45°$ **Ans**

Principal moments of inertia :

$$I_{\substack{max\\min}} = \frac{I_x + I_y}{2} \pm \sqrt{\left(\frac{I_x - I_y}{2}\right)^2 + I_{xy}^2}$$

$$= \frac{15.90 + 15.90}{2} \pm \sqrt{\left(\frac{15.90 - 15.90}{2}\right)^2 + 10.125^2}$$

$I_{max} = 26.0 \text{ in}^4$ $I_{min} = 5.78 \text{ in}^4$ **Ans**

***10-80.** Determine the directions of the principal axes with origin located at point O, and the principal moments of inertia of the area about these axes.

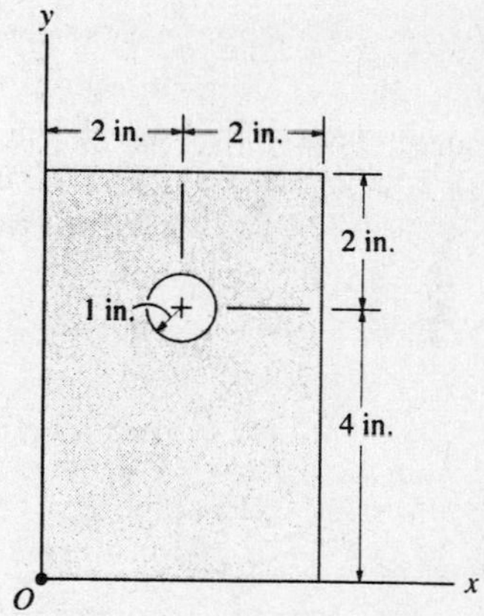

$$I_x = \left[\frac{1}{12}(4)(6)^3 + (4)(6)(3)^2\right] - \left[\frac{1}{4}\pi(1)^4 + \pi(1)^2(4)^2\right] = 236.95 \text{ in}^4$$

$$I_y = \left[\frac{1}{12}(6)(4)^3 + (4)(6)(2)^2\right] - \left[\frac{1}{4}\pi(1)^4 + \pi(1)^2(2)^2\right] = 114.65 \text{ in}^4$$

$$I_{xy} = [0 + (4)(6)(2)(3)] - [0 + \pi(1)(2)(4)] = 118.87 \text{ in}^4$$

$$\tan 2\theta_p = \frac{-I_{xy}}{\frac{I_x - I_y}{2}} = \frac{-118.87}{\frac{(236.95 - 114.65)}{2}}$$

$\theta_p = -31.388°;$ $58.612°$

Thus,

$\theta_{p_1} = -31.4°;$ $\theta_{p_2} = 58.6°$ **Ans**

$$I_{\substack{max\\min}} = \frac{I_x + I_y}{2} \pm \sqrt{\left(\frac{I_x - I_y}{2}\right)^2 + I_{xy}^2}$$

$$= \frac{236.95 + 114.65}{2} \pm \sqrt{\left(\frac{236.95 - 114.65}{2}\right)^2 + (118.87)^2}$$

$I_{max} = 309 \text{ in}^4$ **Ans**

$I_{min} = 42.1 \text{ in}^4$ **Ans**

10-81. Determine the directions of the principal axes with origin located at point O, and the principal moments of inertia of the area about these axes.

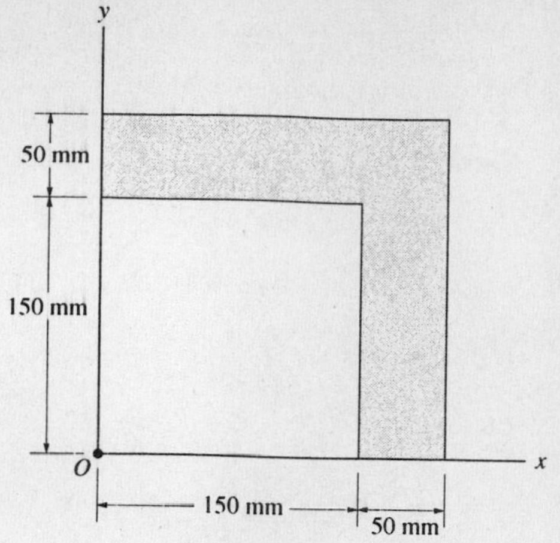

$$I_x = I_y = \left[\frac{1}{12}(0.2)(0.2)^3 + (0.2)(0.2)(0.1)^2\right]$$

$$- \left[\frac{1}{12}(0.15)(0.15)^3 + (0.15)(0.15)(0.075)^2\right] = 364.583(10^{-6})\ \text{m}^4$$

$$I_{xy} = \left[0 + (0.1)(0.1)(0.2)(0.2)\right] - [0 + (0.075)(0.075)(0.15)(0.15)] = 273.4375(10^{-6})\text{m}^4$$

$$\tan 2\theta_p = \frac{-I_{xy}}{\frac{I_x - I_y}{2}} = -\frac{273.4375(10^{-6})}{\frac{(364.583 - 364.583)(10^{-6})}{2}}$$

Thus,

$\theta_{p_1} = -45°; \quad \theta_{p_2} = 45°$ **Ans**

$$I_{\substack{max \\ min}} = \frac{I_x + I_y}{2} \pm \sqrt{\left(\frac{I_x - I_y}{2}\right)^2 + I_{xy}^2}$$

$$= (364.583 \pm 273.4375)(10^{-6})$$

$I_{max} = 638(10^{-6})\ \text{m}^4$ **Ans**

$I_{min} = 91.1(10^{-6})\ \text{m}^4$ **Ans**

10-82. Use the results of Probs. 10-9, 10-10, and 10-59, and determine the directions of the principal axes with origin located at point O, and the principal moments of inertia for the parabolic area about these axes.

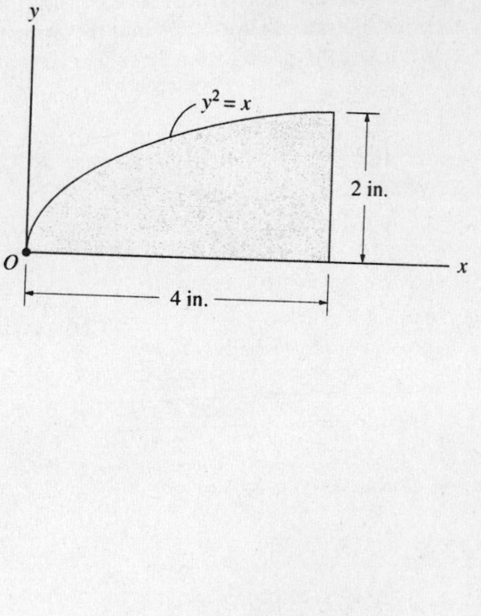

$I_x = 4.267\ \text{in}^4$

$I_y = 36.5714\ \text{in}^4$

$I_{xy} = 10.6667\ \text{in}^4$

$$\tan 2\theta_p = \frac{-I_{xy}}{\frac{I_x - I_y}{2}} = \frac{-10.6667}{\frac{(4.267 - 36.5714)}{2}}$$

$\theta_p = 16.7°, \quad -73.3°$

Thus,

$\theta_{p_1} = -73.3° \quad \theta_{p_2} = 16.7°$ **Ans**

$$I_{\substack{max \\ min}} = \frac{I_x + I_y}{2} \pm \sqrt{\left(\frac{I_x - I_y}{2}\right)^2 + I_{xy}^2}$$

$$= \frac{4.267 + 36.5714}{2} \pm \sqrt{\left(\frac{4.267 - 36.5714}{2}\right)^2 + (10.6667)^2}$$

$I_{max} = 39.8\ \text{in}^4$ **Ans**

$I_{min} = 1.06\ \text{in}^4$ **Ans**

10-83. Determine the moments of inertia and the product of inertia for the rectangular area with respect to the u and v axes passing through the centroid C.

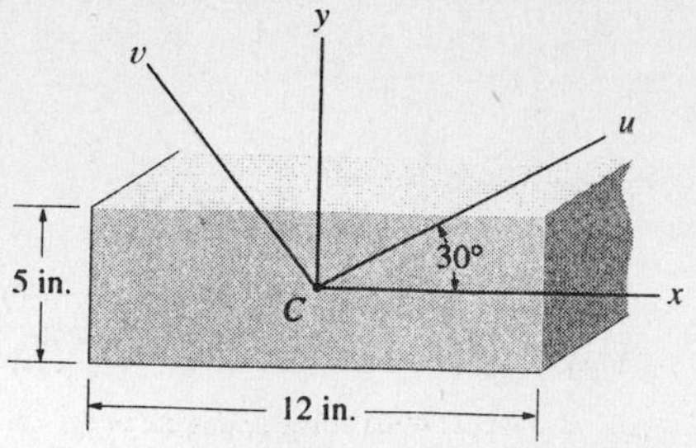

Moment and Product of Inertia about x and y Axes : Since the rectangular area is symmetrical about the x and y axes, $I_{xy} = 0$.

$$I_x = \frac{1}{12}(12)(5^3) = 125 \text{ in}^4 \qquad I_y = \frac{1}{12}(5)(12^3) = 720 \text{ in}^4$$

Moment and Product of Inertia about the Inclined u and v Axes : Applying Eq. 10–9 with $\theta = 30°$, we have

$$I_u = \frac{I_x + I_y}{2} + \frac{I_x - I_y}{2}\cos 2\theta - I_{xy}\sin 2\theta$$
$$= \frac{125+720}{2} + \frac{125-720}{2}\cos 60° - 0(\sin 60°)$$
$$= 274 \text{ in}^4 \qquad \textbf{Ans}$$

$$I_v = \frac{I_x + I_y}{2} - \frac{I_x - I_y}{2}\cos 2\theta + I_{xy}\sin 2\theta$$
$$= \frac{125+720}{2} - \frac{125-720}{2}\cos 60° + 0(\sin 60°)$$
$$= 571 \text{ in}^4 \qquad \textbf{Ans}$$

$$I_{uv} = \frac{I_x - I_y}{2}\sin 2\theta + I_{xy}\cos 2\theta$$
$$= \frac{125-720}{2}\sin 60° + 0(\cos 60°)$$
$$= -258 \text{ in}^4$$

***10-84.** Determine the moments of inertia I_u and I_v of the shaded area.

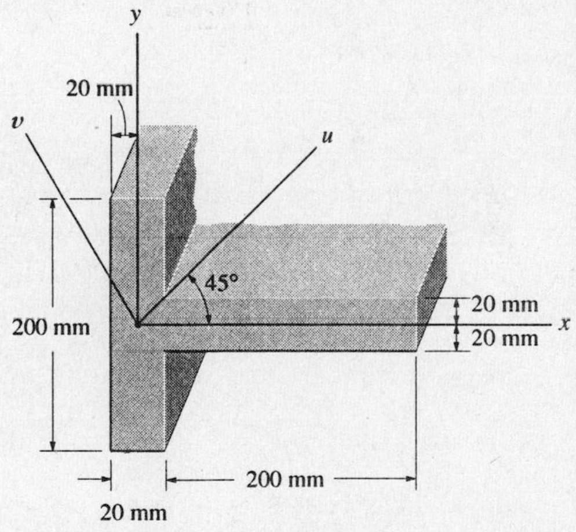

Moment and Product of Inertia about x and y Axes : Since the shaded area is symmetrical about the x axis, $I_{xy} = 0$.

$$I_x = \frac{1}{12}(200)(40^3) + \frac{1}{12}(40)(200^3) = 27.73(10^6) \text{ mm}^4$$

$$I_y = \frac{1}{12}(40)(200^3) + 40(200)(120^2) + \frac{1}{12}(200)(40^3)$$
$$= 142.93(10^6) \text{ mm}^4$$

Moment of Inertia about the Inclined u and v Axes : Applying Eq. 10–9 with $\theta = 45°$, we have

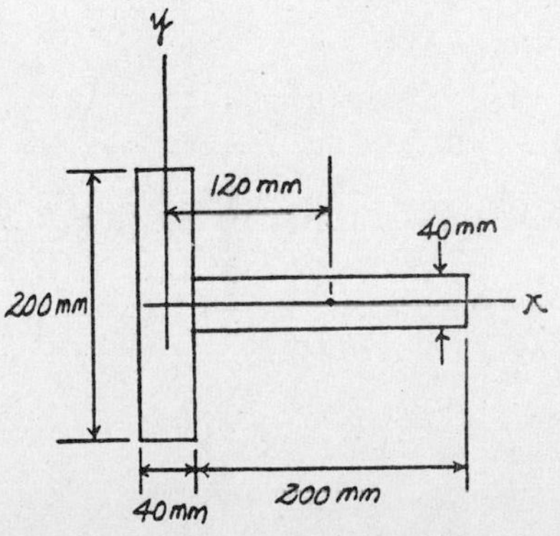

$$I_u = \frac{I_x + I_y}{2} + \frac{I_x - I_y}{2}\cos 2\theta - I_{xy}\sin 2\theta$$
$$= \left(\frac{27.73+142.93}{2} + \frac{27.73-142.93}{2}\cos 90° - 0(\sin 90°)\right)(10^6)$$
$$= 85.3(10^6) \text{ mm}^4 \qquad \textbf{Ans}$$

$$I_v = \frac{I_x + I_y}{2} - \frac{I_x - I_y}{2}\cos 2\theta + I_{xy}\sin 2\theta$$
$$= \left(\frac{27.73+142.93}{2} - \frac{27.73-142.93}{2}\cos 90° - 0(\sin 90°)\right)(10^6)$$
$$= 85.3(10^6) \text{ mm}^4 \qquad \textbf{Ans}$$

10-85. Solve Prob. 10-78 using Mohr's circle.

See solution to Prob. 10-78.

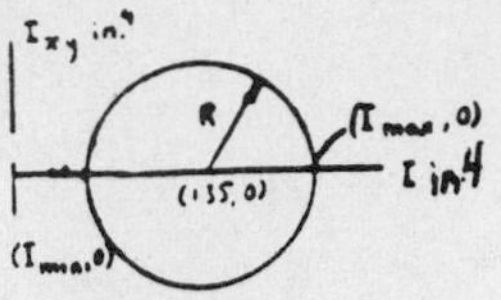

$I_x = 216 \text{ in}^4$

$I_y = 54 \text{ in}^4$

$I_{xy} = 81 \text{ in}^4$

Center of circle : $\dfrac{I_x + I_y}{2} = 135$

$R = \sqrt{(216 - 135)^2 + (81)^2} = 114.55$

$I_{max} = 135 + 114.55 = 250 \text{ in}^4$ **Ans**

$I_{min} = 135 - 114.55 = 20.4 \text{ in}^4$ **Ans**

10-86. Solve Prob. 10-79 using Mohr's circle.

Moments of inertia I_x and I_y :

$I_x = I_y = \frac{1}{16}\pi(3)^4 = 15.90 \text{ in}^4$

Product of inertia I_{xy} : From Prob. 10-79

$I_{xy} = \frac{1}{8}(3)^4 = 10.125 \text{ in}^4$

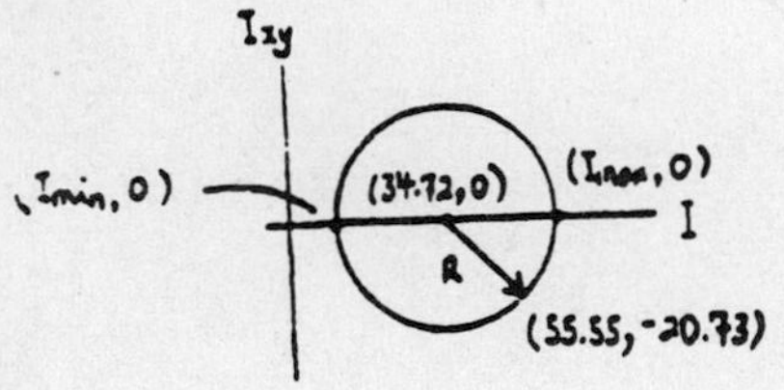

Mohr's circle:

$OA = 10.125$

$I_{max} = 15.90 + 10.125 = 26.0 \text{ in}^4$ **Ans**

$I_{min} = 15.90 - 10.125 = 5.78 \text{ in}^4$ **Ans**

$2\theta = -90°$ $\theta = -45°$ **Ans**

10-87. Solve Prob. 10-81 using Mohr's circle.

See solution to Prob. 10-81.

$I_x = I_y = 364.58(10^{-6})\text{m}^4$.

$I_{xy} = 273.4375(10^{-6})\text{m}^4$

$\frac{I_x + I_y}{2} = 364.58(10^{-6})\text{m}^4$

$R = 273.4375(10^{-6})\text{m}^4$

$I_{max} = (364.58 + 273.4375)(10^{-6}) = 638(10^{-6})\text{m}^4$ **Ans**

$I_{min} = (364.58 - 273.4375)(10^{-6}) = 91.1(10^{-6})\text{m}^4$ **Ans**

$\theta_{p_1} = \frac{90°}{2} = -45°$ **Ans**

$\theta_{p_2} = -\frac{90°}{2} = 45°$ **Ans**

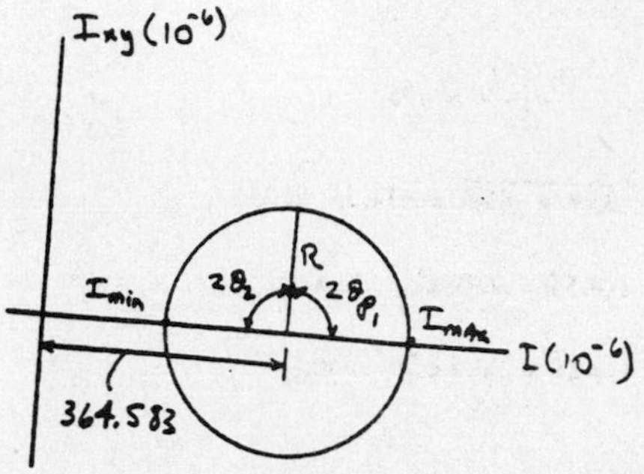

***10-88.** Solve Prob. 10-80 using Mohr's circle.

See solution to Prob. 10-80.

$I_x = 236.95 \text{ in}^4$

$I_y = 114.65 \text{ in}^4$

$I_{xy} = 118.87 \text{ in}^4$

$\frac{I_x + I_y}{2} = \frac{236.95 + 114.65}{2} = 175.8 \text{ in}^4$

$R = \sqrt{(236.95 - 175.8)^2 + (118.87)^2} = 133.68 \text{ in}^4$

$I_{max} = (175.8 + 133.68) = 309 \text{ in}^4$ **Ans**

$I_{min} = (175.8 - 133.68) = 42.1 \text{ in}^4$ **Ans**

$2\theta_{p_1} = \tan^{-1}\left(\frac{118.87}{(236.95 - 175.8)}\right) = 62.78°$

$\theta_{p_1} = -31.4°$ **Ans**

$\theta_{p_2} = 90° - 31.4° = 58.6°$ **Ans**

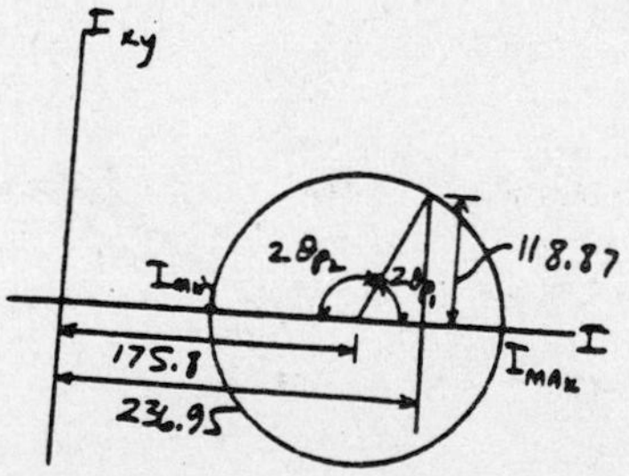

10-89. Solve Prob. 10-82 using Mohr's circle.

See solution to Prob 10-82.

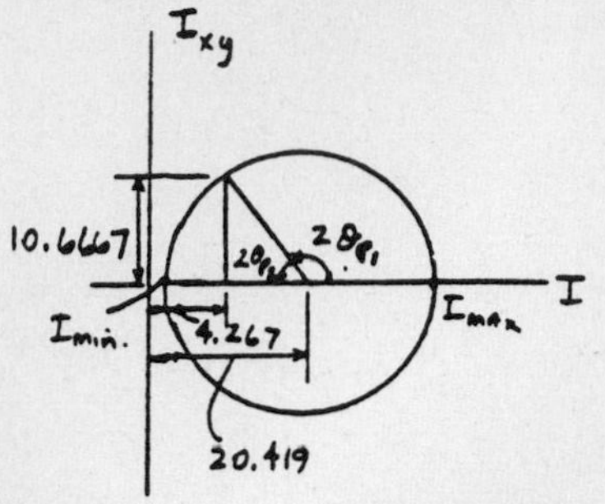

$I_x = 4.267\ \text{in}^4$

$I_y = 36.5714\ \text{in}^4$

$I_{xy} = 10.6667\ \text{in}^4$

$$\frac{I_x + I_y}{2} = \frac{4.267 + 36.5714}{2} = 20.419$$

$$R = \sqrt{(20.419 - 4.267)^2 + (10.6667)^2} = 19.356$$

$I_{max} = (20.419 + 19.356) = 39.8\ \text{in}^4$ **Ans**

$I_{min} = (20.419 - 19.356) = 1.06\ \text{in}^4$ **Ans**

$$2\theta_{p_1} = \tan^{-1}\left(\frac{10.6667}{(20.419 - 4.267)}\right)$$

$\theta_{p_2} = 16.7°$ **Ans**

$\theta_{p_1} = -73.3°$ **Ans**

***10-90.** Determine the moment of inertia I_y for the slender rod. The rod's density ρ and cross-sectional area A are constant. Express the result in terms of the rod's total mass m.

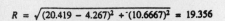

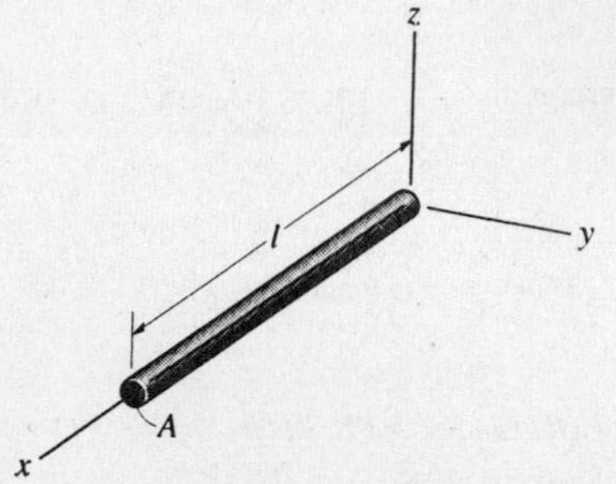

$$I_y = \int_M x^2\, dm$$

$$= \int_0^l x^2 (\rho A\, dx)$$

$$= \frac{1}{3}\rho A l^3$$

$$m = \rho A l$$

Thus,

$$I_y = \frac{1}{3} m l^2 \qquad \textbf{Ans}$$

10-91. Determine the moment of inertia of the thin ring about the z axis. The ring has a mass m.

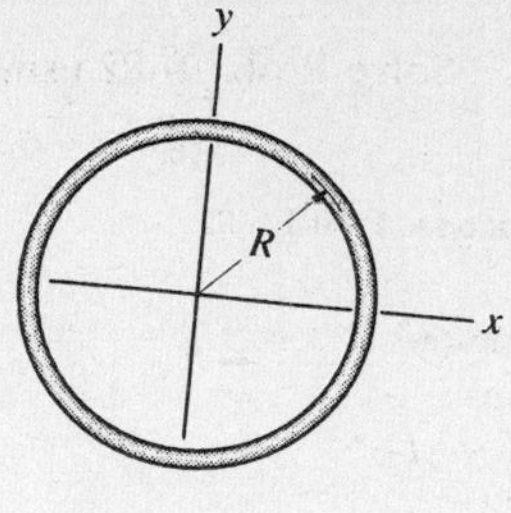

$$I_z = \int_0^{2\pi} \rho A (R\, d\theta) R^2 = 2\pi \rho A R^3$$

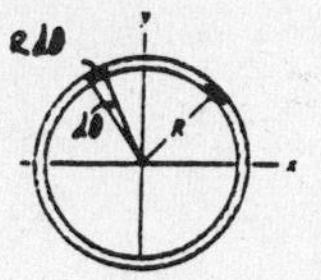

$$m = \int_0^{2\pi} \rho A R\, d\theta = 2\pi \rho A R$$

Thus,

$$I_z = m R^2$$ **Ans**

***10-92.** The right circular cone is formed by revolving the shaded area around the x axis. Determine the moment of inertia I_x and express the result in terms of the total mass m of the cone. The cone has a constant density ρ.

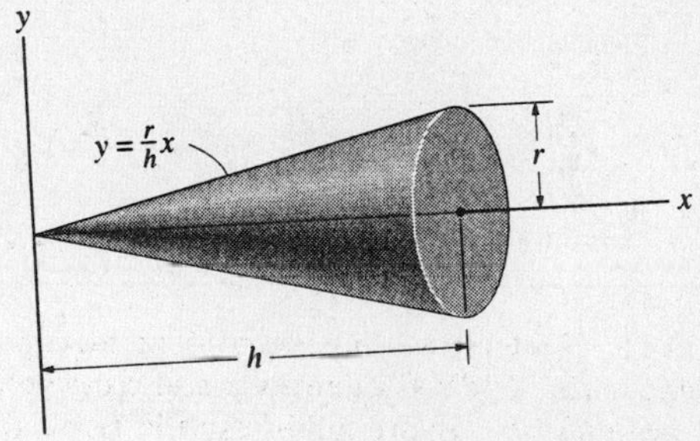

Differential Disk Element : The mass of the differential disk element is $dm = \rho dV = \rho\pi y^2 dx = \rho\pi\left(\frac{r^2}{h^2}x^2\right)dx$. The mass moment of inertia of this element is $dI_x = \frac{1}{2}dm y^2 = \frac{1}{2}\left[\rho\pi\left(\frac{r^2}{h^2}x^2\right)dx\right]\left(\frac{r^2}{h^2}x^2\right) = \frac{\rho\pi r^4}{2h^4}x^4 dx$.

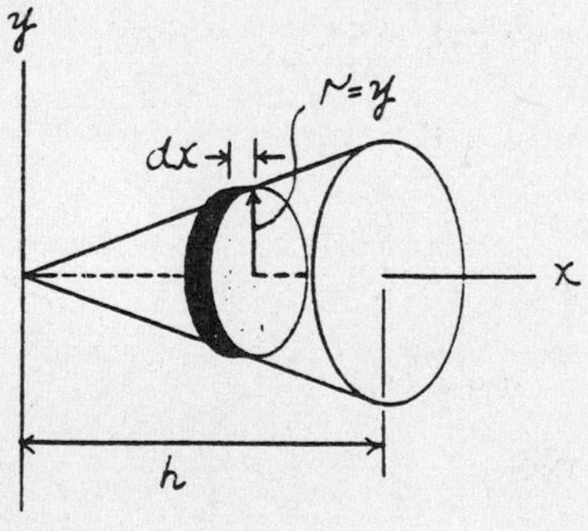

Total Mass : Performing the integration, we have

$$m = \int_m dm = \int_0^h \rho\pi\left(\frac{r^2}{h^2}x^2\right)dx = \frac{\rho\pi r^2}{h^2}\left(\frac{x^3}{3}\right)\Bigg|_0^h = \frac{1}{3}\rho\pi r^2 h$$

Mass Moment of Inertia : Performing the integration, we have

$$I_x = \int dI_x = \int_0^h \frac{\rho\pi r^4}{2h^4}x^4 dx = \frac{\rho\pi r^4}{2h^4}\left(\frac{x^5}{5}\right)\Bigg|_0^h = \frac{1}{10}\rho\pi r^4 h$$

The mass moment of inertia expressed in terms of the total mass is

$$I_x = \frac{3}{10}\left(\frac{1}{3}\rho\pi r^2 h\right)r^2 = \frac{3}{10}mr^2$$ **Ans**

10-93. The solid is formed by revolving the shaded are around the x axis. Determine the radius of gyration k_x. The density of the material is $\rho = 5\ \text{Mg/m}^3$.

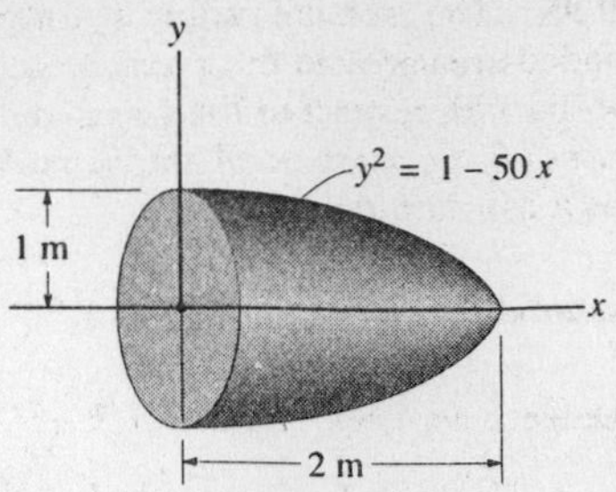

Differential Disk Element : The mass of the differential disk element is $dm = \rho dV = \rho\pi y^2 dx = \rho\pi(1-0.5x)\,dx$. The mass moment of inertia of this element is $dI_x = \frac{1}{2}dmy^2 = \frac{1}{2}[\rho\pi(1-0.5x)\,dx](1-0.5x) = \frac{\rho\pi}{2}(0.25x^2 - x + 1)\,dx$.

Total Mass : Performing the integration, we have

$$m = \int_m dm = \int_0^{2\text{m}} \rho\pi(1-0.5x)\,dx = \rho\pi\left(x - \frac{0.5x^2}{2}\right)\Bigg|_0^{2\text{m}} = \rho\pi$$

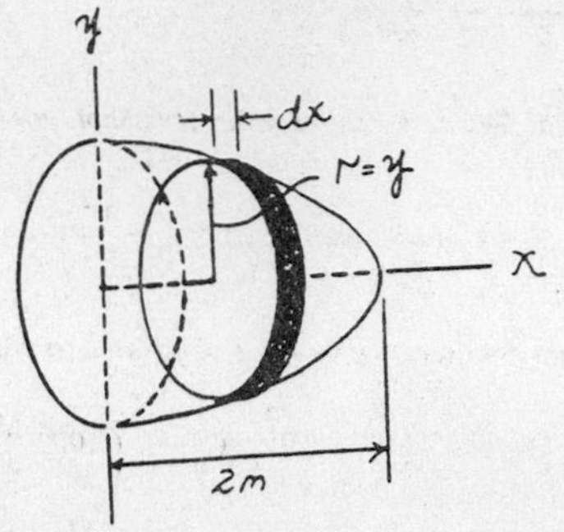

Mass Moment of Inertia : Performing the integration, we have

$$I_x = \int dI_x = \int_0^{2\text{m}} \frac{\rho\pi}{2}(0.25x^2 - x + 1)\,dx$$
$$= \frac{\rho\pi}{2}\left(\frac{0.25x^3}{3} - \frac{x^2}{2} + x\right)\Bigg|_0^{2\text{m}}$$
$$= 0.3333\rho\pi$$

The radius of gyration is

$$k_x = \sqrt{\frac{I_x}{m}} = \sqrt{\frac{0.3333\rho\pi}{\rho\pi}} = 0.577\ \text{m} \qquad \textbf{Ans}$$

10-94. The paraboloid is formed by revolving the shaded area around the x axis. Determine the radius of gyration k_x. The density of the material is $\rho = 5\ \text{Mg/m}^3$.

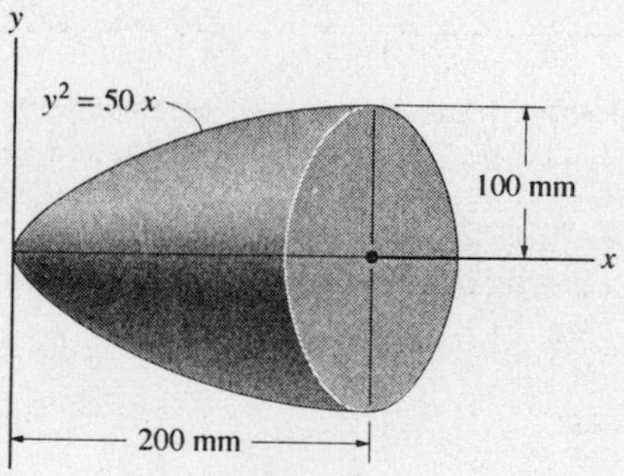

Differential Disk Element : The mass of the differential disk element is $dm = \rho dV = \rho\pi y^2 dx = \rho\pi(50x)\,dx$. The mass moment of inertia of this element is $dI_x = \frac{1}{2}dmy^2 = \frac{1}{2}[\rho\pi(50x)\,dx](50x) = \frac{\rho\pi}{2}(2500x^2)\,dx$.

Total Mass : Performing the integration, we have

$$m = \int_m dm = \int_0^{200\text{mm}} \rho\pi(50x)\,dx = \rho\pi(25x^2)\Big|_0^{200\text{mm}} = 1(10^6)\rho\pi$$

Mass Moment of Inertia : Performing the integration, we have

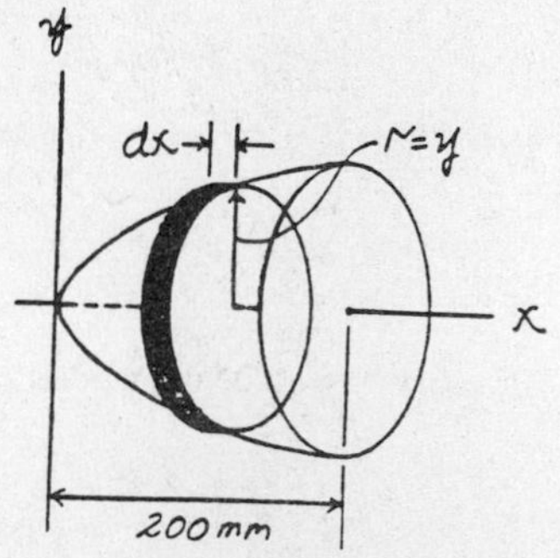

$$I_x = \int dI_x = \int_0^{200\text{mm}} \frac{\rho\pi}{2}(2500x^2)\,dx$$
$$= \frac{\rho\pi}{2}\left(\frac{2500x^3}{3}\right)\Bigg|_0^{200\text{mm}}$$
$$= 3.333(10^9)\rho\pi$$

The radius of gyration is

$$k_x = \sqrt{\frac{I_x}{m}} = \sqrt{\frac{3.333(10^9)\rho\pi}{1(10^6)\rho\pi}} = 57.7\ \text{mm} \qquad \textbf{Ans}$$

10-95. The semiellipsoid is formed by rotating the shaded area around the x axis. Determine the moment of inertia with respect to the x axis and express the result in terms of the mass m of the semiellipsoid. The material has a constant density ρ.

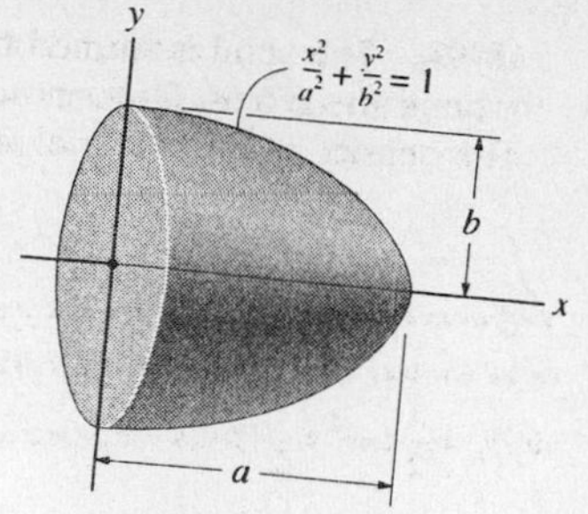

Differential Disk Element : Here, $y^2 = b^2\left(1-\frac{x^2}{a^2}\right)$. The mass of the differential disk element is $dm = \rho dV = \rho\pi y^2 dx = \rho\pi b^2\left(1-\frac{x^2}{a^2}\right)dx$. The mass moment of inertia of this element is $dI_x = \frac{1}{2}dmy^2 = \frac{1}{2}\left[\rho\pi b^2\left(1-\frac{x^2}{a^2}\right)dx\right]\left[b^2\left(1-\frac{x^2}{a^2}\right)\right]$

$$= \frac{\rho\pi b^4}{2}\left(\frac{x^4}{a^4}-\frac{2x^2}{a^2}+1\right)dx.$$

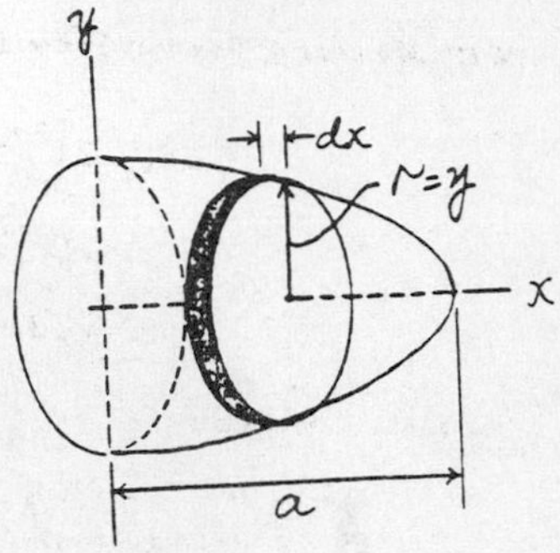

Total Mass : Performing the integration, we have

$$m = \int_m dm = \int_0^a \rho\pi b^2\left(1-\frac{x^2}{a^2}\right)dx = \rho\pi b^2\left(x-\frac{x^3}{3a^2}\right)\Bigg|_0^a = \frac{2}{3}\rho\pi ab^2$$

Mass Moment of Inertia : Performing the integration, we have

$$I_x = \int dI_x = \int_0^a \frac{\rho\pi b^4}{2}\left(\frac{x^4}{a^4}-\frac{2x^2}{a^2}+1\right)dx$$

$$= \frac{\rho\pi b^4}{2}\left(\frac{x^5}{5a^4}-\frac{2x^3}{3a^2}+x\right)\Bigg|_0^a$$

$$= \frac{4}{15}\rho\pi ab^4$$

The mass moment of inertia expressed in terms of the total mass is

$$I_x = \frac{2}{5}\left(\frac{2}{3}\rho\pi ab^2\right)b^2 = \frac{2}{5}mb^2 \qquad \textbf{Ans}$$

***10-96.** The paraboloid is formed by revolving the shaded area around the x axis. Determine the moment of inertia with respect to the x axis and express the result in terms of the mass m of the paraboloid. The material has a constant density ρ.

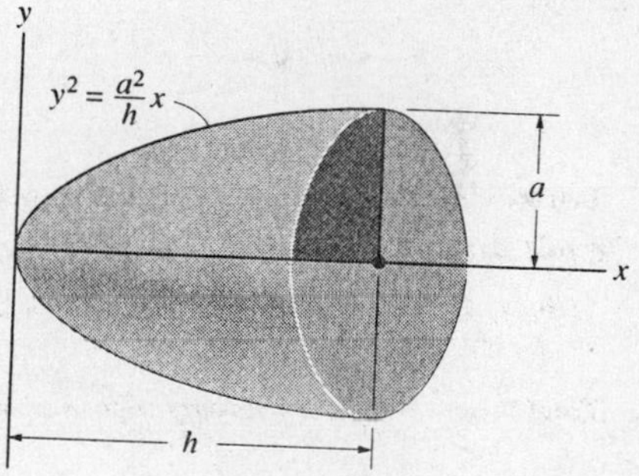

$$dm = \rho\, dV = \rho\,(\pi y^2\, dx)$$

$$dI_x = \frac{1}{2}dm\, y^2 = \frac{1}{2}\rho\,\pi\, y^4\, dx$$

$$I_x = \int_0^h \frac{1}{2}\rho\,\pi\left(\frac{a^4}{h^2}\right)x^2\, dx$$

$$= \frac{1}{6}\pi\,\rho a^4\, h$$

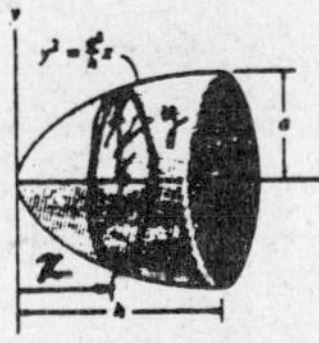

$$m = \int_0^h \frac{1}{2}\rho\,\pi\left(\frac{a^2}{h}\right)x\, dx$$

$$= \frac{1}{2}\rho\,\pi\, a^2\, h$$

$$k_x = \sqrt{\frac{I_x}{m}} = \frac{a}{\sqrt{3}} \qquad \textbf{Ans}$$

10-97. The hemisphere is formed by rotating the shaded area about the y axis. Determine the moment of inertia I_y and express the result in terms of the total mass m of the hemisphere. The material has a constant density ρ.

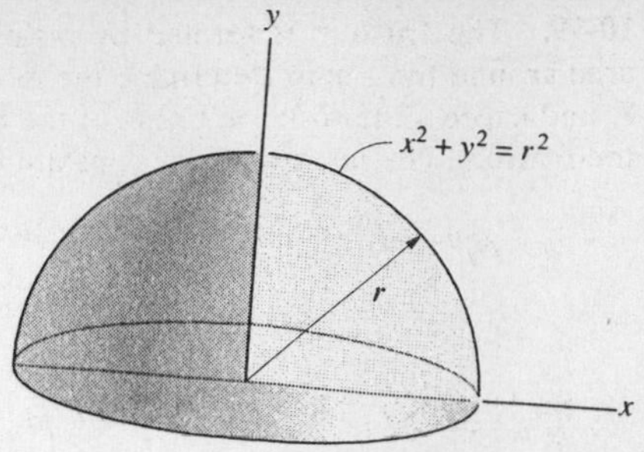

$$m = \int_V \rho\, dV = \rho \int_0^r \pi x^2\, dy = \rho\pi \int_0^r (r^2 - y^2)\, dy$$

$$= \rho\pi\left[r^2 y - \frac{1}{3}y^3\right]_0^r = \frac{2}{3}\rho\pi r^3$$

$$I_y = \int_m \frac{1}{2}(dm)\, x^2 = \frac{\rho}{2}\int_0^r \pi x^4\, dy = \frac{\rho\pi}{2}\int_0^r (r^2 - y^2)^2 dy$$

$$= \frac{\rho\pi}{2}\left[r^4 y - \frac{2}{3}r^2 y^3 + \frac{y^5}{5}\right]_0^r = \frac{4\rho\pi}{15}r^4$$

Thus,

$$I_y = \frac{2}{5}m r^2 \qquad \textbf{Ans}$$

10-98. Determine the moment of inertia of the homogenous triangular prism with respect to the y axis. Express the result in terms of the mass m of the prism. *Hint*: For integration, use thin plate elements parallel to the x-y plane having a thickness of dz.

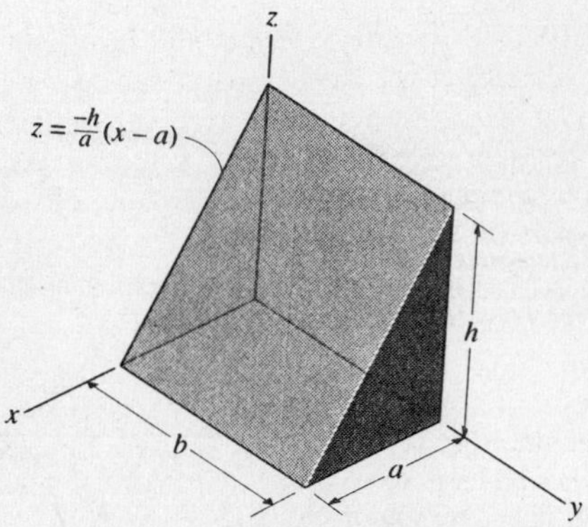

Differential Thin Plate Element : Here, $x = a\left(1 - \frac{z}{h}\right)$. The mass of the differential thin plate element is $dm = \rho dV = \rho bx dz = \rho ab\left(1 - \frac{z}{h}\right)dz$. The mass moment of inertia of this element about y axis is

$$dI_y = dI_G + dmr^2$$
$$= \frac{1}{12}dmx^2 + dm\left(\frac{x^2}{4} + z^2\right)$$
$$= \frac{1}{3}x^2 dm + z^2 dm$$
$$= \left[\frac{a^2}{3}\left(1 - \frac{z}{h}\right)^2 + z^2\right]\left[\rho ab\left(1 - \frac{z}{h}\right)dz\right]$$
$$= \frac{\rho ab}{3}\left(a^2 + \frac{3a^2}{h^2}z^2 - \frac{3a^2}{h}z - \frac{a^2}{h^3}z^3 + 3z^2 - \frac{3z^3}{h}\right)dz$$

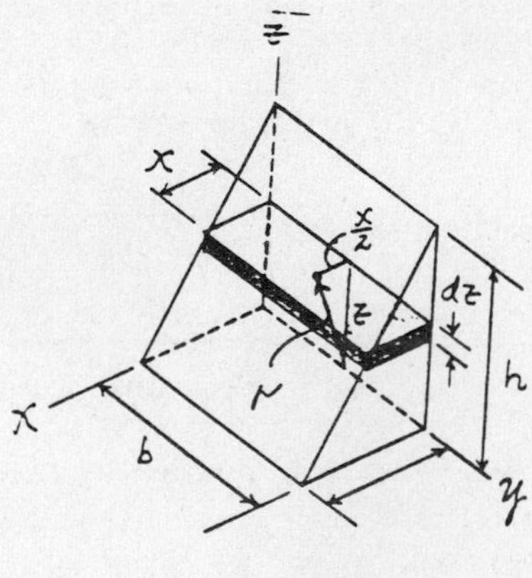

Total Mass : Performing the integration, we have

$$m = \int_m dm = \int_0^h \rho ab\left(1 - \frac{z}{h}\right)dz = \rho\pi b\left(z - \frac{z^2}{2h}\right)\Bigg|_0^h = \frac{1}{2}\rho abh$$

Mass Moment of Inertia : Performing the integration, we have

$$I_y = \int dI_y = \int_0^h \frac{\rho ab}{3}\left(a^2 + \frac{3a^2}{h^2}z^2 - \frac{3a^2}{h}z - \frac{a^2}{h^3}z^3 + 3z^2 - \frac{3z^3}{h}\right)dz$$
$$= \frac{\rho ab}{3}\left(a^2 z + \frac{a^2}{h^2}z^3 - \frac{3a^2}{2h}z^2 - \frac{a^2}{4h^3}z^4 + z^3 - \frac{3z^4}{4h}\right)\Bigg|_0^h$$
$$= \frac{\rho abh}{12}(a^2 + h^2)$$

The mass moment of inertia expressed in terms of the total mass is

$$I_y = \frac{1}{6}\left(\frac{\rho abh}{2}\right)(a^2 + h^2) = \frac{m}{6}(a^2 + h^2) \qquad \textbf{Ans}$$

10-99. The frustum is formed by rotating the shaded area around the x axis. Determine the moment of inertia I_x and express the result in terms of the total mass m of the frustum. The material has a constant density ρ.

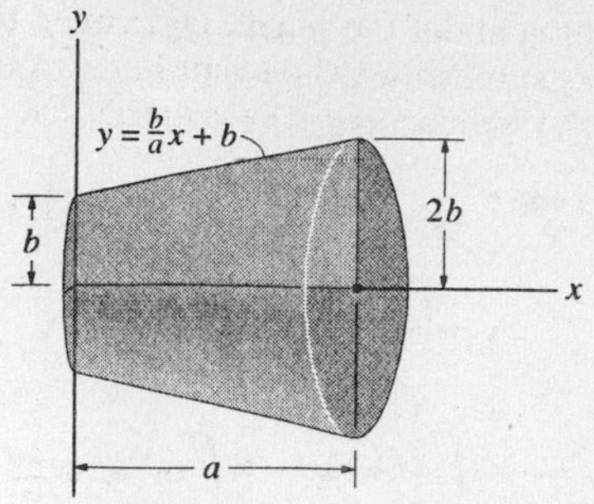

$$dm = \rho dV = \rho \pi y^2 dx = \rho \pi \left(\frac{b^2}{a^2}x^2 + \frac{2b^2}{a}x + b^2\right) dx$$

$$dI_x = \frac{1}{2} dm y^2 = \frac{1}{2} \rho \pi y^4 dx$$

$$dI_x = \frac{1}{2}\rho \pi \left(\frac{b^4}{a^4}x^4 + \frac{4b^4}{a^3}x^3 + \frac{6b^4}{a^2}x^2 + \frac{4b^4}{a}x + b^4\right) dx$$

$$I_x = \int dI_x = \frac{1}{2}\rho \pi \int_0^a \left(\frac{b^4}{a^4}x^4 + \frac{4b^4}{a^3}x^3 + \frac{6b^4}{a^2}x^2 + \frac{4b^4}{a}x + b^4\right) dx$$

$$= \frac{31}{10}\rho \pi a b^4$$

$$m = \int_m dm = \rho \pi \int_0^a \left(\frac{b^2}{a^2}x^2 + \frac{2b^2}{a}x + b^2\right) dx = \frac{7}{3}\rho \pi a b^2$$

$$I_x = \frac{93}{70} m b^2$$ **Ans**

***10-100.** Determine the moment of inertia of the wire triangle about an axis perpendicular to the page and passing through point O. Also, locate the mass center G and determine the moment of inertia about an axis perpendicular to the page and passing through point G. The wire has a mass of 0.3 kg/m. Neglect the size of the ring at O.

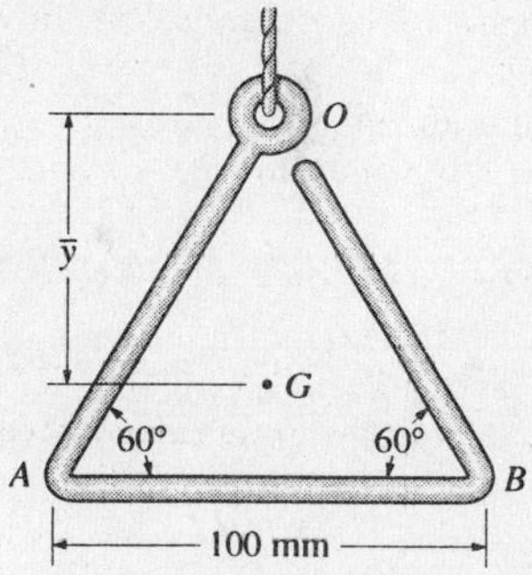

Mass Moment of Inertia About an Axis Through Point O : The mass for each wire segment is $m_i = 0.3(0.1) = 0.03$ kg. The mass moment of inertia of each segment about an axis passing through the center of mass can be determined using $(I_G)_i = \frac{1}{12}ml^2$. Applying Eq. 10 – 16, we have

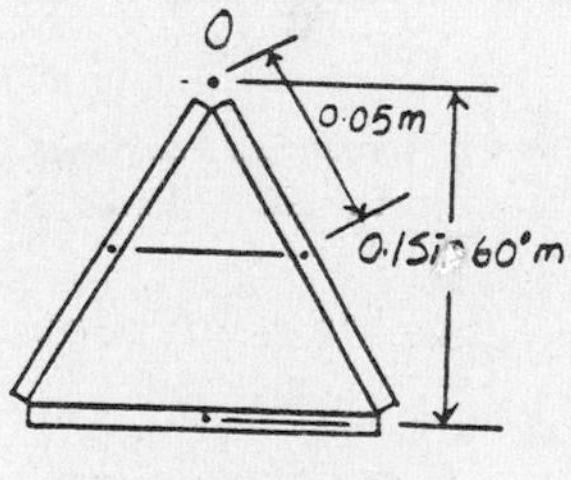

$$I_O = \Sigma (I_G)_i + m_i d_i^2$$
$$= 2\left[\frac{1}{12}(0.03)(0.1^2) + 0.03(0.05^2)\right]$$
$$+ \frac{1}{12}(0.03)(0.1^2) + 0.03(0.1\sin 60°)^2$$
$$= 0.450(10^{-3}) \text{ kg}\cdot\text{m}^2$$ **Ans**

Location of Centroid :

$$\bar{y} = \frac{\Sigma \bar{y} m}{\Sigma m} = \frac{2[0.05\sin 60°(0.03)] + 0.1\sin 60°(0.03)}{3(0.03)}$$
$$= 0.05774 \text{ m} = 57.7 \text{ mm}$$ **Ans**

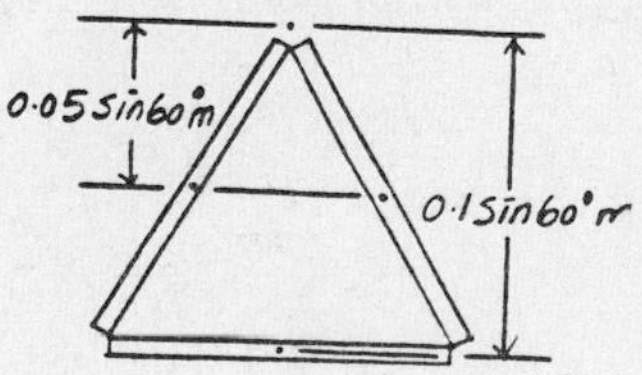

Mass Moment of Inertia About an Axis Through Point G : Using the result $I_O = 0.450(10^{-3})$ kg · m² and $d = \bar{y} = 0.05774$ m and applying Eq. 10 – 16, we have

$$I_O = I_G + md^2$$
$$0.450(10^{-3}) = I_G + 3(0.03)(0.05774^2)$$

$$I_G = 0.150(10^{-3}) \text{ kg}\cdot\text{m}^2$$ **Ans**

10-101. The slender rods have a weight of 3 lb/ft. Determine the moment of inertia of the assembly about an axis perpendicular to the page and passing through point A.

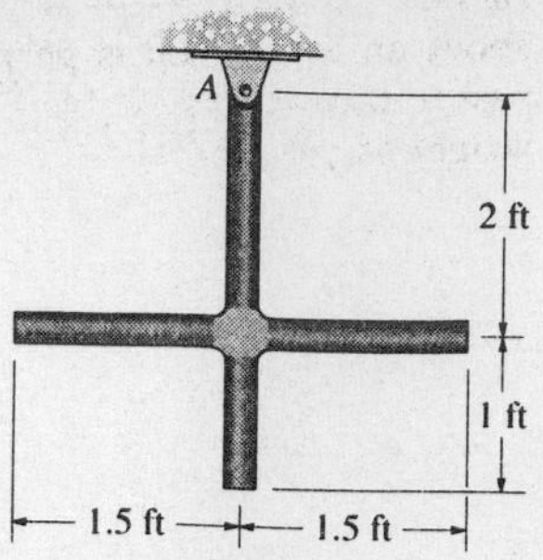

Mass Moment of Inertia About an Axis Through Point A : The mass for each rod segment is $m_i = \dfrac{3(3)}{32.2} = 0.2795$ slug. The mass moment of inertia of each wire about an axis passing through the center of mass can be determine using $(I_G)_i = \dfrac{1}{12}ml^2$. Applying Eq. 10 – 16, we have

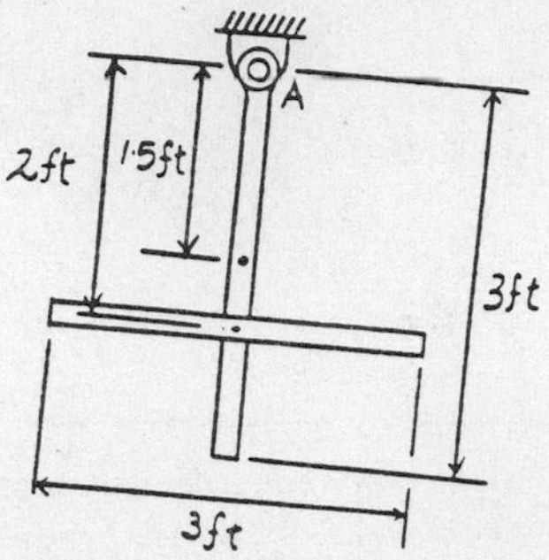

$$I_O = \Sigma(I_G)_i + m_i d_i^2$$

$$= \frac{1}{12}(0.2795)(3^2) + 0.2795(1.5^2)$$

$$+ \frac{1}{12}(0.2795)(3^2) + 0.2795(2^2)$$

$$= 2.17 \text{ slug} \cdot \text{ft}^2 \qquad \textbf{Ans}$$

10-102. Determine the moment of inertia of the wheel about an axis which is perpendicular to the page and passes through the center of mass G. The material has a specific weight of $\gamma = 90$ lb/ft^3.

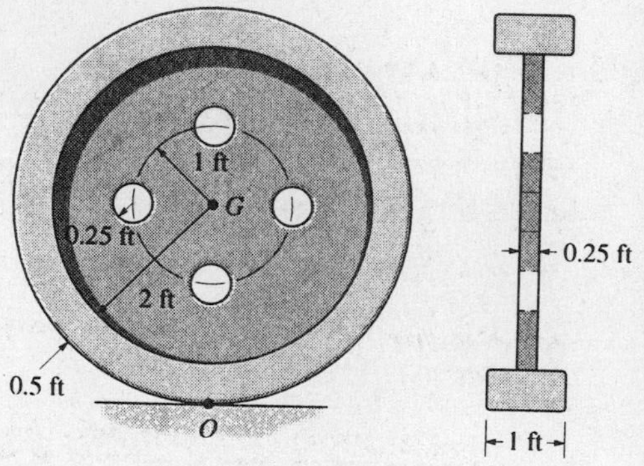

Mass Moment of Inertia About an Axis Through Point G : The mass moment of inertia of each disk about an axis passing through the center of mass can be determine using $(I_G)_i = \dfrac{1}{2}mr^2$. Applying Eq. 10 – 16, we have

$$I_G = \Sigma(I_G)_i + m_i d_i^2$$

$$= \frac{1}{2}\left[\frac{\pi(2.5^2)(1)(90)}{32.2}\right](2.5^2) - \frac{1}{2}\left[\frac{\pi(2^2)(0.75)(90)}{32.2}\right](2^2)$$

$$-4\left\{\frac{1}{2}\left[\frac{\pi(0.25^2)(0.25)(90)}{32.2}\right](0.25^2) + \left[\frac{\pi(0.25^2)(0.25)(90)}{32.2}\right](1^2)\right\}$$

$$= 118 \text{ slug} \cdot \text{ft}^2 \qquad \textbf{Ans}$$

10-103. Determine the moment of inertia of the wheel about an axis which is perpendicular to the page and passes through point O. The material has a specific weight of $\gamma = 90\ \text{lb/ft}^3$.

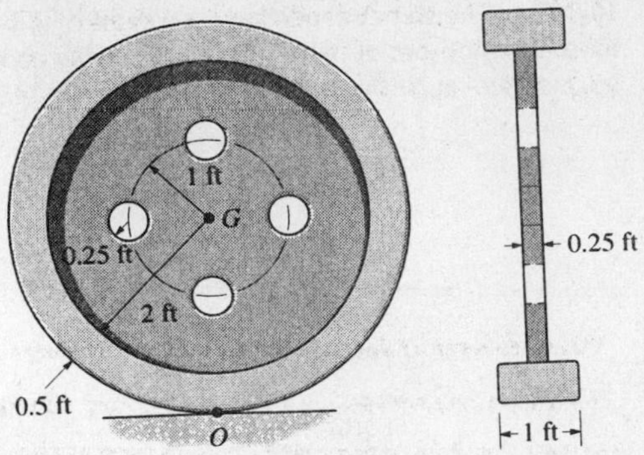

Mass Moment of Inertia About an Axis Through Point G : The mass moment of inertia of each disk about an axis passing through the center of mass can be determine using $(I_G)_i = \frac{1}{2}mr^2$. Applying Eq. 10 – 16, we have

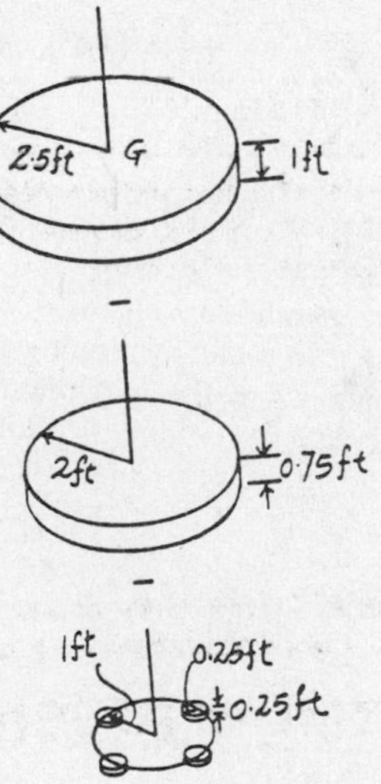

$$I_G = \Sigma(I_G)_i + m_i d_i^2$$
$$= \frac{1}{2}\left[\frac{\pi(2.5^2)(1)(90)}{32.2}\right](2.5^2) - \frac{1}{2}\left[\frac{\pi(2^2)(0.75)(90)}{32.2}\right](2^2)$$
$$-4\left\{\frac{1}{2}\left[\frac{\pi(0.25^2)(0.25)(90)}{32.2}\right](0.25^2) + \left[\frac{\pi(0.25^2)(0.25)(90)}{32.2}\right](1^2)\right\}$$
$$= 118.25\ \text{slug}\cdot\text{ft}^2$$

Mass Moment of Inertia About an Axis Through Point O : The mass of the wheel is

$$m = \frac{\pi(2.5^2)(1)(90)}{32.2} - \frac{\pi(2^2)(0.75)(90)}{32.2} - 4\left[\frac{\pi(0.25^2)(0.25)(90)}{32.2}\right]$$
$$= 27.989\ \text{slug}$$

Using the result $I_G = 118.25\ \text{slug}\cdot\text{ft}^2$ and applying Eq. 10 – 16, we have

$$I_O = I_G + md^2$$
$$= 118.25 + 27.989(2.5^2)$$
$$= 293\ \text{slug}\cdot\text{ft}^2 \qquad \textbf{Ans}$$

***10-104.** The pendulum consists of a disk having a mass of 6 kg and slender rods AB and DC which have a mass of 2 kg/m. Determine the length L of DC so that the center of the mass is at the bearing O. What is the moment of inertia of the assembly about an axis perpendicular to the page and passing through point O?

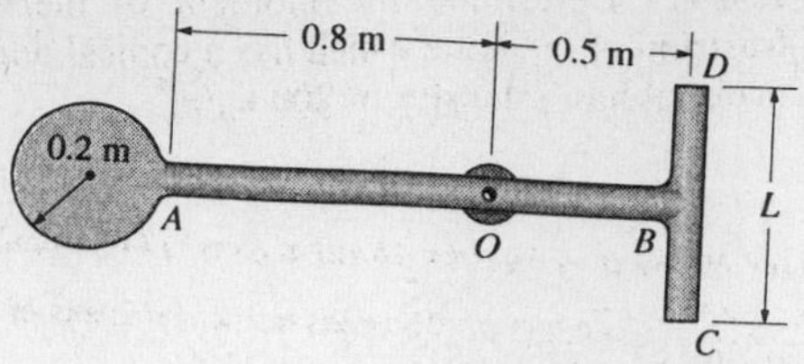

Location of Centroid : This problem requires $\bar{x} = 0.5$ m.

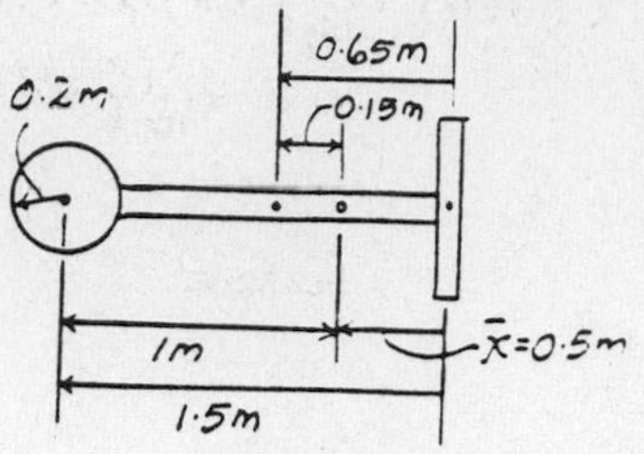

$$\bar{x} = \frac{\Sigma \tilde{x} m}{\Sigma m}$$

$$0.5 = \frac{1.5(6) + 0.65[1.3(2)] + 0[L(2)]}{6 + 1.3(2) + L(2)}$$

$$L = 6.39 \text{ m} \qquad \textbf{Ans}$$

Mass Moment of Inertia About an Axis Through Point O : The mass moment of inertia of each rod segment and disk about an axis passing through the center of mass can be determine using $(I_G)_i = \frac{1}{12}ml^2$ and $(I_G)_i = \frac{1}{2}mr^2$. Applying Eq. 10 – 16, we have

$$I_O = \Sigma(I_G)_i + m_i d_i^2$$

$$= \frac{1}{12}[1.3(2)](1.3^2) + [1.3(2)](0.15^2)$$

$$+ \frac{1}{12}[6.39(2)](6.39^2) + [6.39(2)](0.5^2)$$

$$+ \frac{1}{2}(6)(0.2^2) + 6(1^2)$$

$$= 53.2 \text{ kg} \cdot \text{m}^2 \qquad \textbf{Ans}$$

10-105. The pendulum consists of the 3-kg slender rod and the 5-kg thin plate. Determine the location $\bar{y}$ of the center of mass G of the pendulum; then calculate the moment of inertia of the pendulum about an axis perpendicular to the page and passing through G.

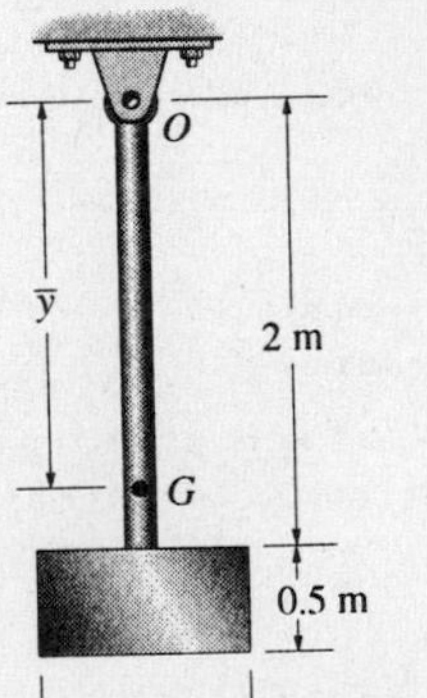

$$\bar{y} = \frac{\Sigma \tilde{y} m}{\Sigma m} = \frac{1(3) + 2.25(5)}{3 + 5} = 1.781 \text{ m} = 1.78 \text{ m} \qquad \textbf{Ans}$$

$$I_G = \Sigma \bar{I}_{G'} + md^2$$

$$= \frac{1}{12}(3)(2)^2 + 3(1.781 - 1)^2 + \frac{1}{12}(5)(0.5^2 + 1^2) + 5(2.25 - 1.781)^2$$

$$= 4.45 \text{ kg} \cdot \text{m}^2 \qquad \textbf{Ans}$$

10-106. Determine the moment of inertia I_z of the frustrum of the cone which has a conical depression. The material has a density of 200 kg/m³.

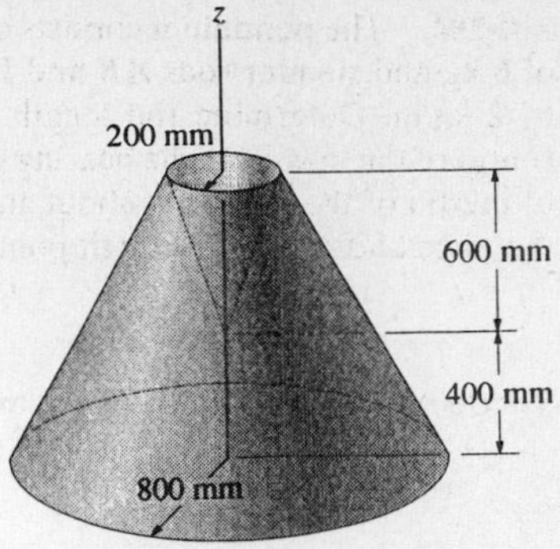

Mass Moment of Inertia About z Axis : From similar triangles, $\frac{z}{0.2} = \frac{z+1}{0.8}$, $z = 0.333$ m . The mass moment of inertia of each cone about z axis can be determine using $I_z = \frac{3}{10}mr^2$.

$$I_z = \Sigma(I_z)_i = \frac{3}{10}\left[\frac{\pi}{3}(0.8^2)(1.333)(200)\right](0.8^2)$$
$$-\frac{3}{10}\left[\frac{\pi}{3}(0.2^2)(0.333)(200)\right](0.2^2)$$
$$-\frac{3}{10}\left[\frac{\pi}{3}(0.2^2)(0.6)(200)\right](0.2^2)$$

$= 34.2 \text{ kg}\cdot\text{m}^2$ **Ans**

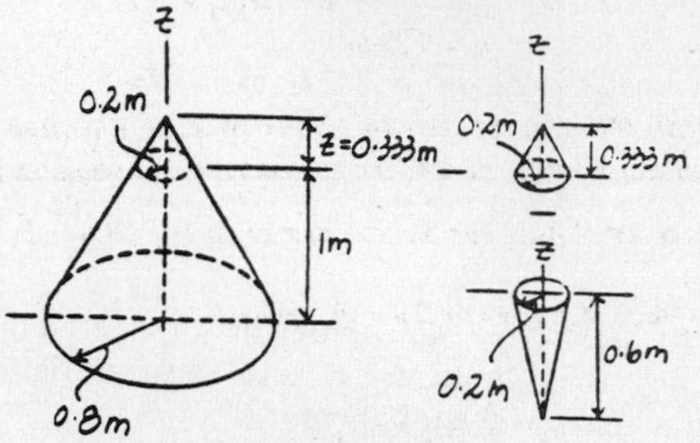

10-107. The slender rods have a weight of 3 lb/ft. Determine the moment of inertia of the assembly about an axis perpendicular to the page and passing through point A

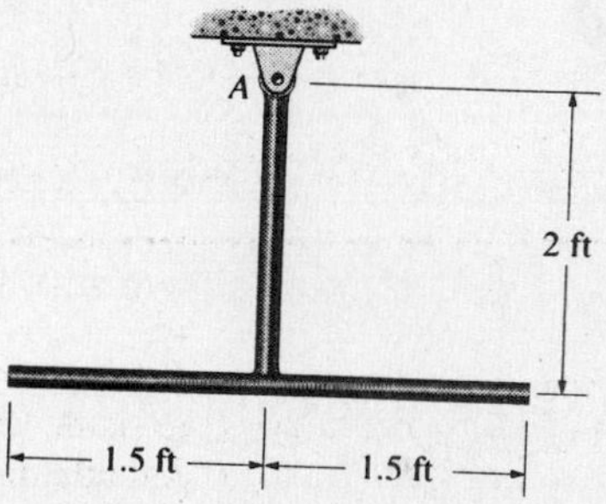

$$I_A = \frac{1}{3}\left[\frac{3(2)}{32.2}\right](2)^2 + \frac{1}{12}\left[\frac{3(3)}{32.2}\right](3)^2 + \left[\frac{3(3)}{32.2}\right](2)^2 = 1.58 \text{ slug}\cdot\text{ft}^2$$ **Ans**

***10-108.** The pendulum consists of a plate having a weight of 12 lb and a slender rod having a weight of 4 lb. Determine the radius of gyration of the pendulum about an axis perpendicular to the page and passing through point O

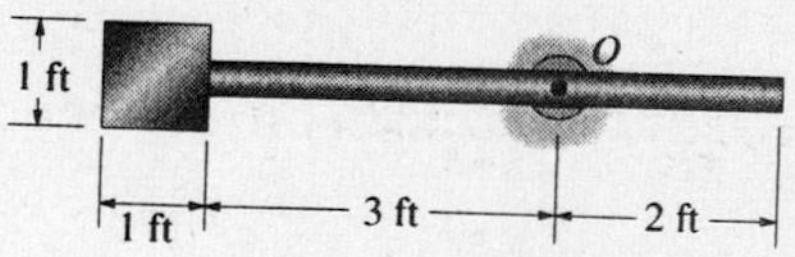

$$I_O = \Sigma I_G + md^2$$
$$= \frac{1}{12}\left(\frac{4}{32.2}\right)(5)^2 + \left(\frac{4}{32.2}\right)(0.5)^2 + \frac{1}{12}\left(\frac{12}{32.2}\right)(1^2+1^2) + \left(\frac{12}{32.2}\right)(3.5)^2$$
$$= 4.917 \text{ slug}\cdot\text{ft}^2$$
$$m = \left(\frac{4}{32.2}\right) + \left(\frac{12}{32.2}\right) = 0.4969 \text{ slug}$$
$$k_O = \sqrt{\frac{I_O}{m}} = \sqrt{\frac{4.917}{0.4969}} = 3.15 \text{ ft}$$ **Ans**

10-109. Determine the moment of inertia of the overhung crank about the x axis. The material is steel having a density of $\rho = 7.85\ \text{Mg/m}^3$.

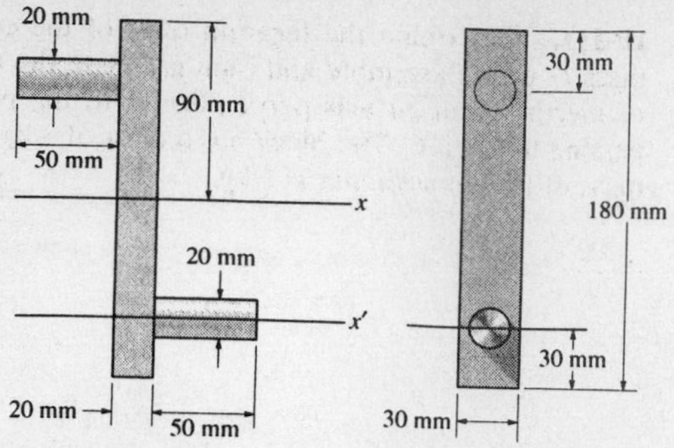

$$m_c = 7.85(10^3)\left((0.05)\pi(0.01)^2\right) = 0.1233\ \text{kg}$$

$$m_p = 7.85(10^3)\left((0.03)(0.180)(0.02)\right) = 0.8478\ \text{kg}$$

$$I_x = 2\left[\frac{1}{2}(0.1233)(0.02)^2 + (0.1233)(0.06)^2\right]$$

$$+\left[\frac{1}{12}(0.8478)\left((0.03)^2 + (0.180)^2\right)\right]$$

$$= 0.00329\ \text{kg}\cdot\text{m}^2 = 3.29\ \text{g}\cdot\text{m}^2 \quad \textbf{Ans}$$

10-110. Determine the moment of inertia of the overhung crank about the x' axis. The material is steel having a density of $\rho = 7.85\ \text{Mg/m}^3$.

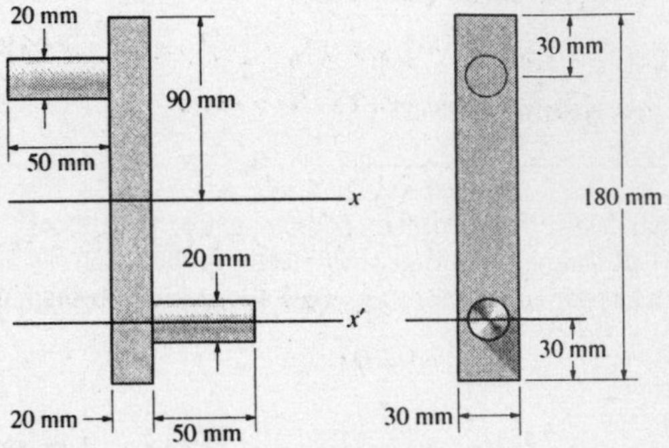

$$m_c = 7.85(10^3)\left((0.05)\pi(0.01)^2\right) = 0.1233\ \text{kg}$$

$$m_p = 7.85(10^3)\left((0.03)(0.180)(0.02)\right) = 0.8478\ \text{kg}$$

$$I_{x'} = \left[\frac{1}{2}(0.1233)(0.02)^2\right] + \left[\frac{1}{2}(0.1233)(0.02)^2 + (0.1233)(0.120)^2\right]$$

$$+\left[\frac{1}{12}(0.8478)\left((0.03)^2 + (0.180)^2\right) + (0.8478)(0.06)^2\right]$$

$$= 0.00723\ \text{kg}\cdot\text{m}^2 = 7.23\ \text{g}\cdot\text{m}^2 \quad \textbf{Ans}$$

10-111. Determine the location of $\bar{y}$ of the center of mass G of the assembly and then calculate the moment of inertia about an axis perpendicular to the page and passing through G. The block has a mass of 3 kg and the mass of the semicylinder is 5 kg.

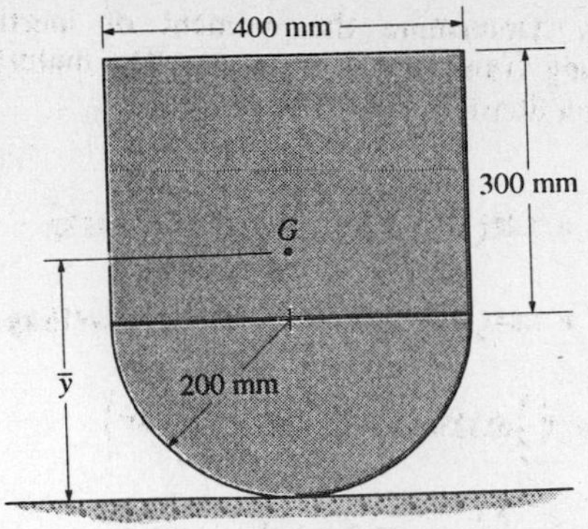

Location of Centroid :

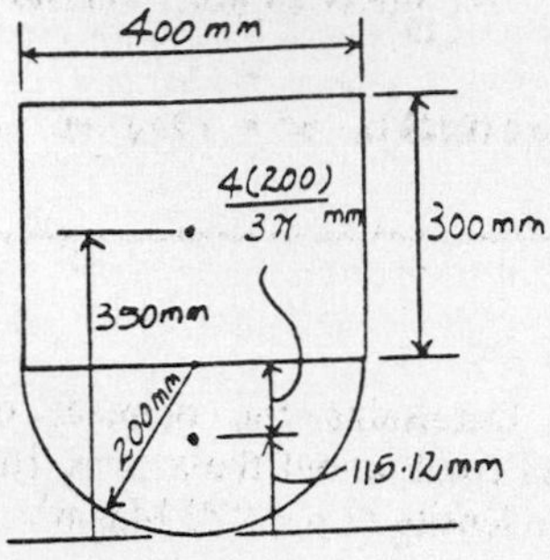

$$\bar{y} = \frac{\Sigma \tilde{y} m}{\Sigma m} = \frac{350(3) + 115.12(5)}{3+5} = 203.20 \text{ mm} = 203 \text{ mm} \qquad \textbf{Ans}$$

Mass Moment of Inertia About an Axis Through Point G : The mass moment of inertia of a rectangular block and a semicylinder about an axis passing through the center of mass perpendicular to the page can be determine using

$$(I_z)_G = \frac{1}{12}m\left(a^2 + b^2\right) \text{ and } (I_z)_G = \frac{1}{2}mr^2 - m\left(\frac{4r}{3\pi}\right)^2 = 0.3199mr^2$$

respectively. Applying Eq. 10 – 16, we have

$$I_G = \Sigma (I_z)_{G_i} + m_i d_i^2$$

$$= \left[\frac{1}{12}(3)\left(0.3^2 + 0.4^2\right) + 3\left(0.1468^2\right)\right]$$

$$+ \left[0.3199(5)\left(0.2^2\right) + 5\left(0.08808^2\right)\right]$$

$$= 0.230 \text{ kg} \cdot \text{m}^2 \qquad \textbf{Ans}$$

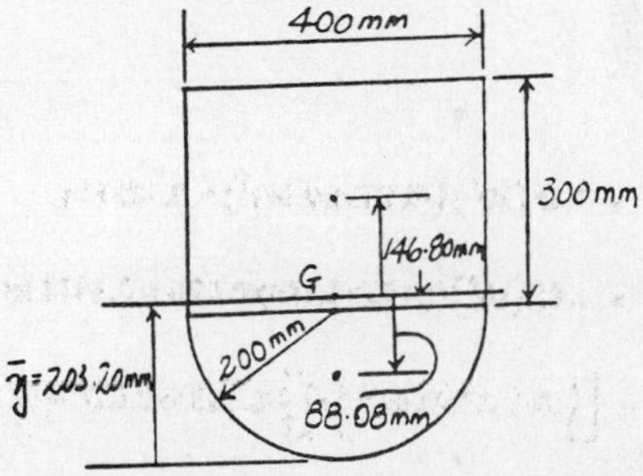

***10-112.** Determine the moment of inertia of the centei crank about the x axis. The material is steel having a specific weight of $\gamma_{st} = 490 \text{ lb/ft}^3$.

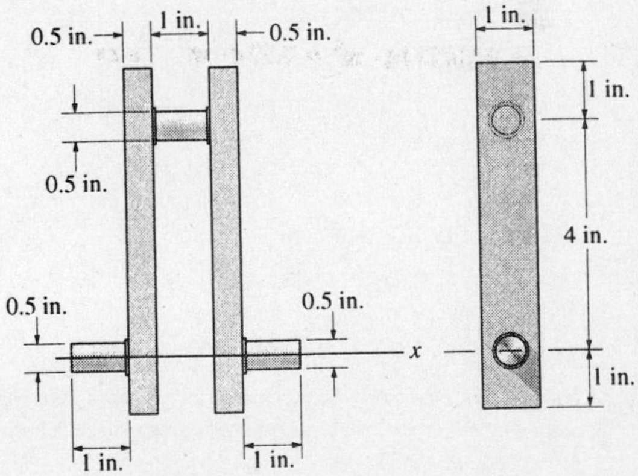

$$m_s = \frac{490}{32.2}\left(\frac{\pi(0.25)^2(1)}{(12)^3}\right) = 0.0017291 \text{ slug}$$

$$m_p = \frac{490}{32.2}\left(\frac{(6)(1)(0.5)}{(12)^3}\right) = 0.02642 \text{ slug}$$

$$I_x = 2\left[\frac{1}{12}(0.02642)\left((1)^2 + (6)^2\right) + (0.02642)(2)^2\right] + 2\left[\frac{1}{2}(0.0017291)(0.25)^2\right]$$

$$+ \left[\frac{1}{2}(0.0017291)(0.25)^2 + (0.0017291)(4)^2\right]$$

$$= 0.402 \text{ slug} \cdot \text{ft}^2 \qquad \textbf{Ans}$$

10-113. Determine the moment of inertia of the beam's cross-sectional area about the x axis which passes through the centroid C.

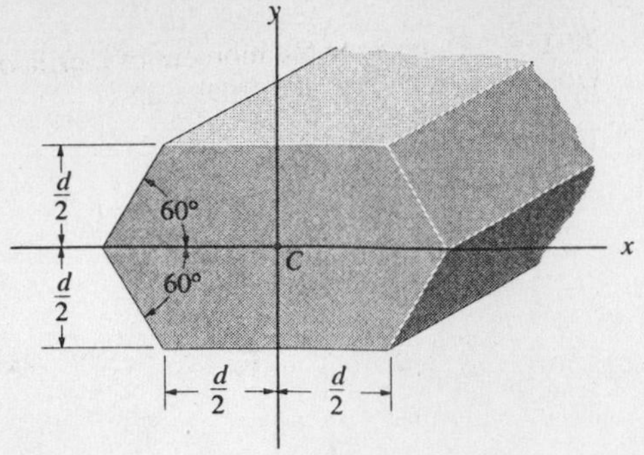

Moment of Inertia : The moment of inertia about the x axis for the composite beam's cross section can be determined using the parallel – axis theorem $I_x = \Sigma\left(\bar{I}_x + Ad_y^2\right)_i$.

$$I_x = \left[\frac{1}{12}(d)\left(d^3\right) + 0\right] + 4\left[\frac{1}{36}(0.2887d)\left(\frac{d}{2}\right)^3 + \frac{1}{2}(0.2887d)\left(\frac{d}{2}\right)\left(\frac{d}{6}\right)^2\right]$$

$$= 0.0954d^4 \qquad \textbf{Ans}$$

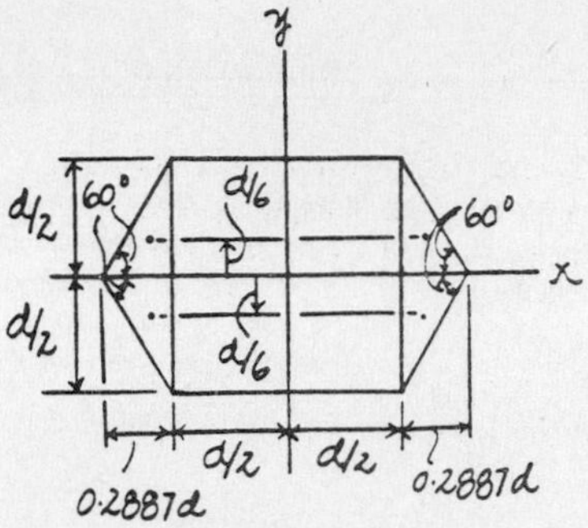

10-114. Determine the moment of inertia of the beam's cross-sectional area about the y axis which passes through the centroid C.

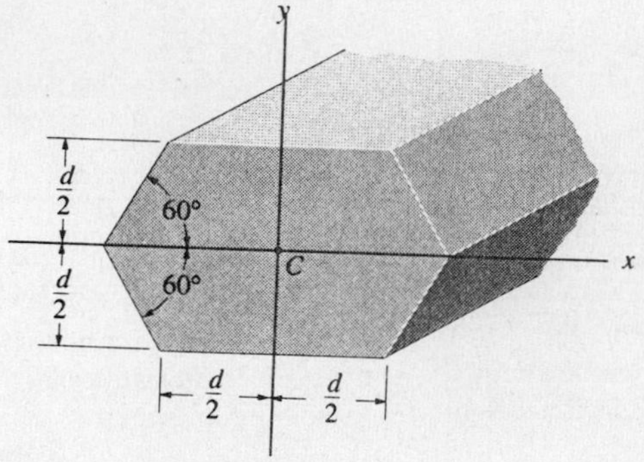

Moment of Inertia : The moment of inertia about y axis for the composite beam's cross section can be determined using the parallel – axis theorem $I_y = \Sigma\left(\bar{I}_y + Ad_x^2\right)_i$.

$$I_y = \left[\frac{1}{12}(d)\left(d^3\right) + 0\right] + 2\left[\frac{1}{36}(d)(0.2887d)^3 + \frac{1}{2}(d)(0.2887d)(0.5962d)^2\right]$$

$$= 0.187d^4 \qquad \textbf{Ans}$$

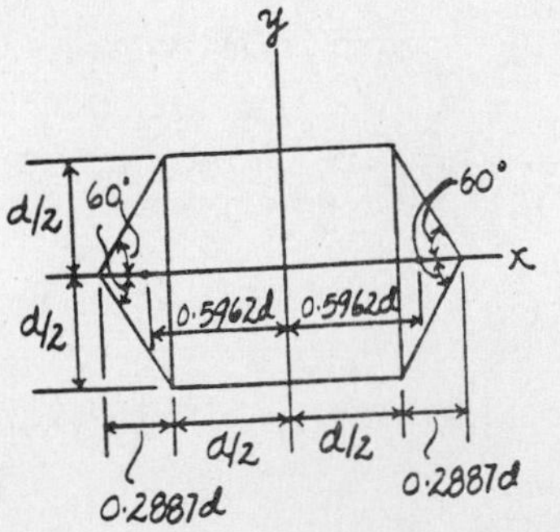

10-115. Determine the moment of inertia of the beam's cross-sectional area about the x axis.

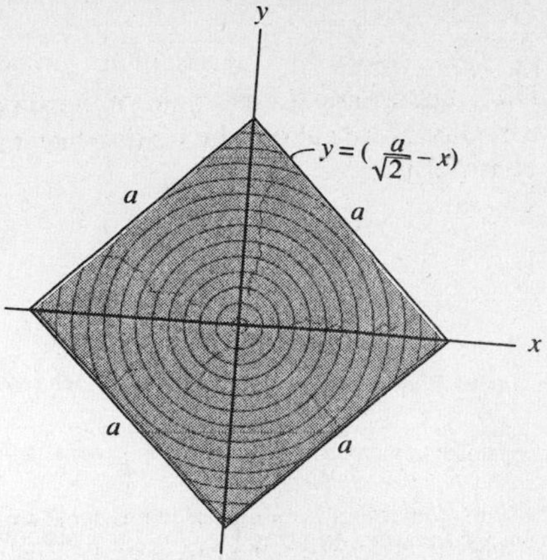

$$I_x = 2\left(\frac{bh^3}{12}\right) = 2\left(\frac{\sqrt{2}\,a\left(\frac{a}{\sqrt{2}}\right)^3}{12}\right) = \frac{1}{12}a^4 \quad \textbf{Ans}$$

***10-116.** Determine the moment of inertia of the beam's cross-sectional area with respect to the x' axis passing through the centroid C.

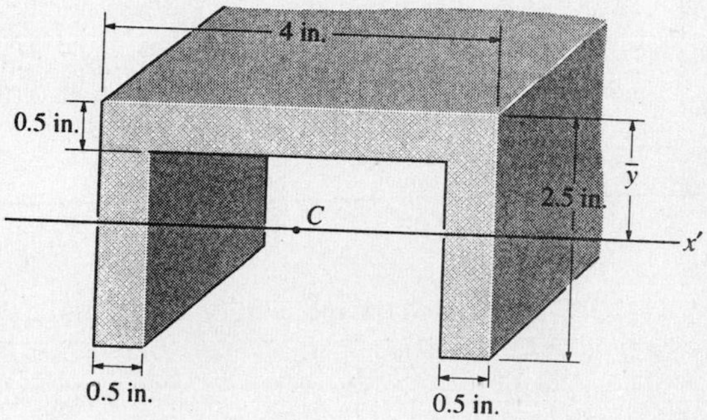

$$\bar{y} = \frac{\Sigma \tilde{y} A}{\Sigma A} = \frac{0.25(0.5)(4) + 2[1.5(2)(0.5)]}{0.5(4) + 2(2)(0.5)} = 0.875 \text{ in.}$$

$$I_{x'} = \frac{1}{12}(4)(0.5)^3 + 4(0.5)(0.875 - 0.25)^2 + 2\left[\frac{1}{12}(0.5)(2)^3 + (0.5)(2)(1.5 - 0.875)^2\right]$$

$$= 2.27 \text{ in}^4 \quad \textbf{Ans}$$

10-117. Determine the product of inertia for the angle's cross-sectional area with respect to the x' and y' axes having their origin located at the centroid C. Assume all corners to be square.

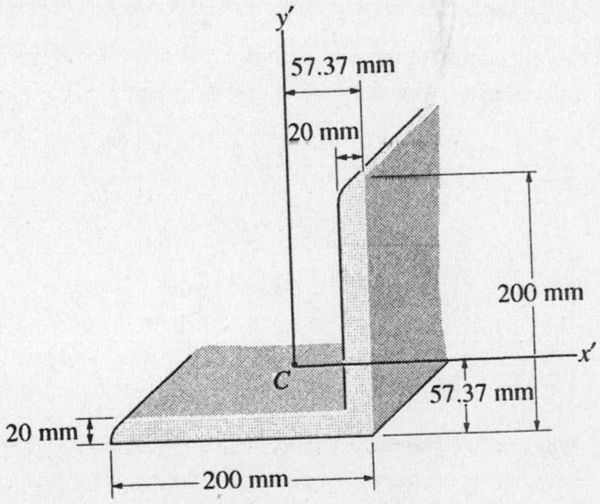

$$I_{xy} = \Sigma \tilde{x} \tilde{y} A$$

$$= \left(\frac{180}{2} + 20 - 57.37\right)(57.37 - 10)(180)(20) + (-(57.37 - 10))(-(100 - 57.37))(200)(20)$$

$$= 17.1(10)^6 \text{ mm}^4 \quad \textbf{Ans}$$

***10-118.** Determine the moment of inertia of the shaded area about the y axis.

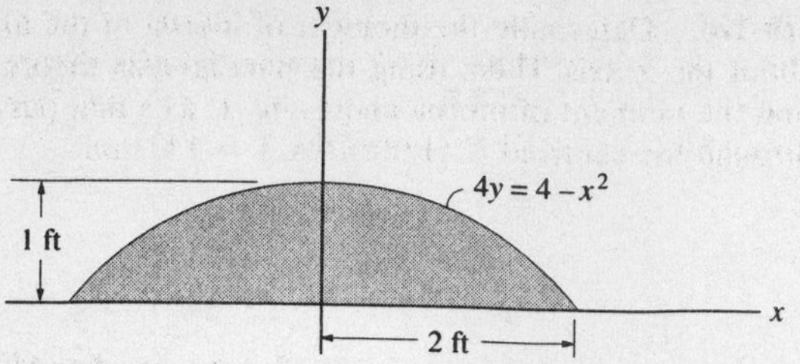

Differential Element : Here, $y = \frac{1}{4}(4-x^2)$. The area of the differential element parallel to the y axis is $dA = y\,dx = \frac{1}{4}(4-x^2)\,dx$.

Moment of Inertia : Applying Eq. 10 − 1 and performing the integration, we have

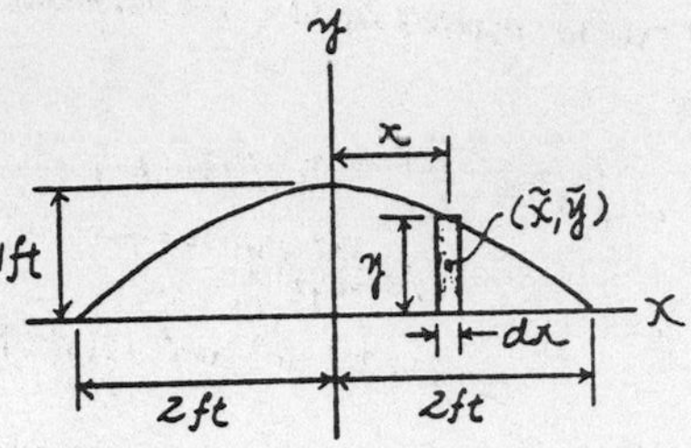

$$I_y = \int_A x^2 dA = \frac{1}{4}\int_{-2\text{ft}}^{2\text{ft}} x^2(4-x^2)\,dx$$
$$= \frac{1}{4}\left[\frac{4}{3}x^3 - \frac{1}{5}x^5\right]_{-2\text{ft}}^{2\text{ft}}$$
$$= 2.13\ \text{ft}^4 \qquad \textbf{Ans}$$

10-119. Determine the moment of inertia of the shaded area about the x axis.

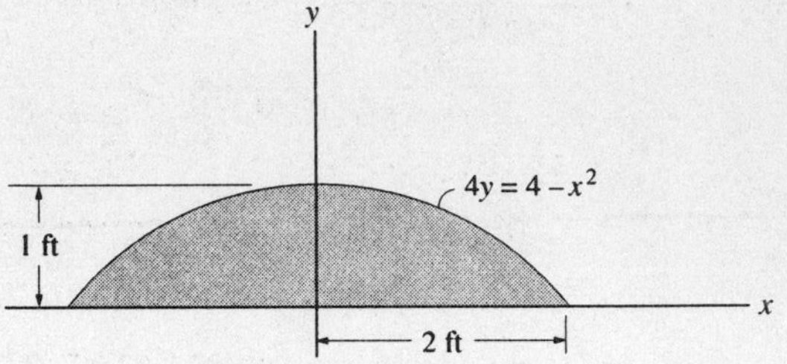

Differential Element : Here, $y = \frac{1}{4}(4-x^2)$. The area of the differential element parallel to the y axis is $dA = y\,dx$. The moment of inertia of this differential element about the x axis is

$$dI_x = d\bar{I}_{x'} + dA\,\tilde{y}^2$$
$$= \frac{1}{12}(dx)y^3 + y\,dx\left(\frac{y}{2}\right)^2$$
$$= \frac{1}{3}\left[\frac{1}{4}(4-x^2)\right]^3 dx$$
$$= \frac{1}{192}(-x^6 + 12x^4 - 48x^2 + 64)\,dx$$

Moment of inertia : Performing the integration, we have

$$I_x = \int dI_x = \frac{1}{192}\int_{-2\text{ft}}^{2\text{ft}} (-x^6 + 12x^4 - 48x^2 + 64)\,dx$$
$$= \frac{1}{192}\left(-\frac{1}{7}x^7 + \frac{12}{5}x^5 - 16x^3 + 64x\right)\Bigg|_{-2\text{ft}}^{2\text{ft}}$$
$$= 0.610\ \text{ft}^4 \qquad \textbf{Ans}$$

***10-120.** Determine the moment of inertia of the area about the x axis. Then, using the parallel-axis theorem, find the moment of inertia about the x' axis that passes through the centroid C of the area. $\bar{y} = 120$ mm.

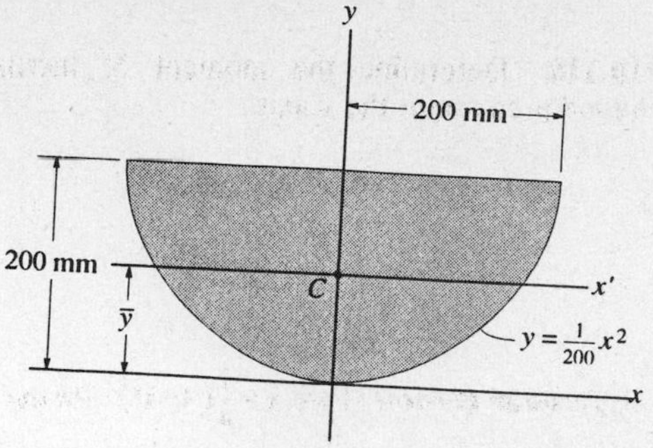

Differential Element **:** Here, $x = \sqrt{200}y^{\frac{1}{2}}$. The area of the differential element parallel to the x axis is $dA = 2x dy = 2\sqrt{200}y^{\frac{1}{2}}dy$.

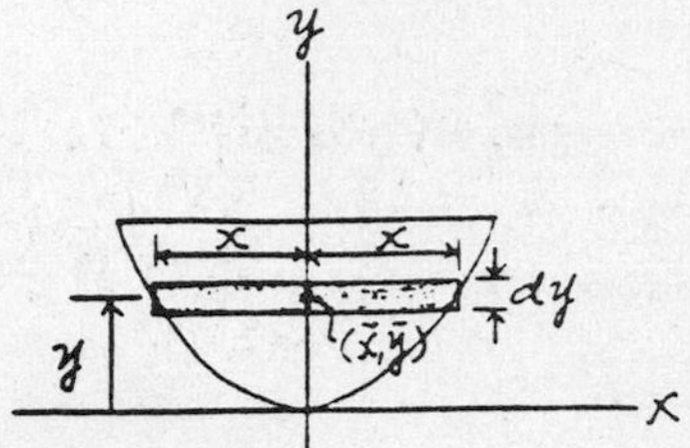

Moment of Inertia **:** Applying Eq. 10 – 1 and performing the integration, we have

$$I_x = \int_A y^2 dA = \int_0^{200\text{mm}} y^2\left(2\sqrt{200}y^{\frac{1}{2}}dy\right)$$
$$= 2\sqrt{200}\left(\frac{2}{7}y^{\frac{7}{2}}\right)\Big|_0^{200\text{mm}}$$
$$= 914.29(10^6)\ \text{mm}^4 = 914(10^6)\ \text{mm}^4 \qquad \textbf{Ans}$$

The moment of inertia about the x' axis can be determined using the parallel – axis theorem. The area is $A = \int_A dA = \int_0^{200\text{mm}} 2\sqrt{200}y^{\frac{1}{2}}dy = 53.33(10^3)\ \text{mm}^2$

$$I_x = \bar{I}_{x'} + Ad_y^2$$
$$914.29(10^6) = \bar{I}_{x'} + 53.33(10^3)(120^2)$$
$$\bar{I}_{x'} = 146(10^6)\ \text{mm}^4 \qquad \textbf{Ans}$$

10-121. The pendulum consists of the slender rod OA, which has a mass of 3 kg/m. The thin plate has a mass of 12 kg/m². Determine the distance $\bar{y}$ to the center of mass G of the pendulum; then calculate the moment of inertia of the pendulum about an axis perpendicular to the page and passing through G.

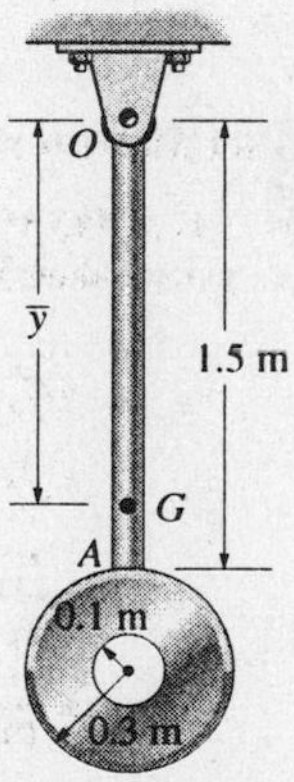

$$\bar{y} = \frac{\Sigma\tilde{y}A}{\Sigma A} = \frac{0.75[1.5(3)] + 1.8[\pi(0.3)^2(12)] - 1.8[\pi(0.1)^2(12)]}{1.5(3) + \pi(0.3)^2(12) - \pi(0.1)^2(12)}$$

$$= 1.1713\ \text{m} = 1.17\ \text{m} \qquad \textbf{Ans}$$

$$I_O = \frac{1}{12}[1.5(3)](1.5)^2 + [1.5(3)](1.1713 - 0.75)^2 + \frac{1}{2}[\pi(0.3)^2(12)](0.3)^2 + [\pi(0.3)^2(12)](1.8 - 1.1713)^2$$
$$-\frac{1}{2}[\pi(0.1)^2(12)](0.1)^2 - [\pi(0.1)^2(12)](1.8 - 1.1713)^2 = 2.99\ \text{kg}\cdot\text{m}^2 \qquad \textbf{Ans}$$

10-122. Determine the product of inertia of the shaded area with respect to the x and y axes.

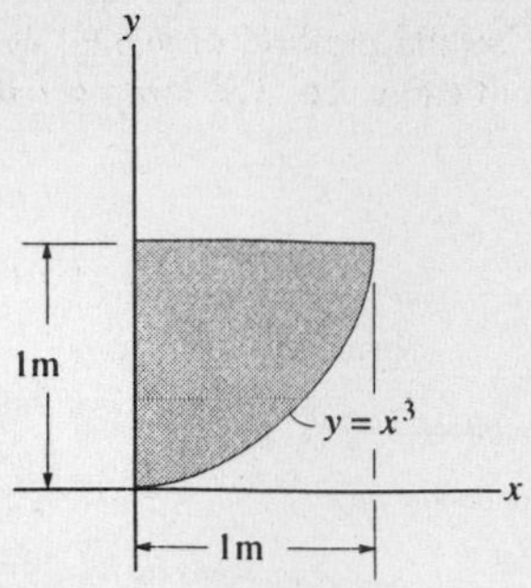

Differential Element : Here, $x = y^{\frac{1}{3}}$. The area of the differential element parallel to the x axis is $dA = xdy = y^{\frac{1}{3}}dy$. The coordinates of the centroid for this element are $\tilde{x} = \frac{x}{2} = \frac{1}{2}y^{\frac{1}{3}}$, $\tilde{y} = y$. Then the product of inertia for this element is

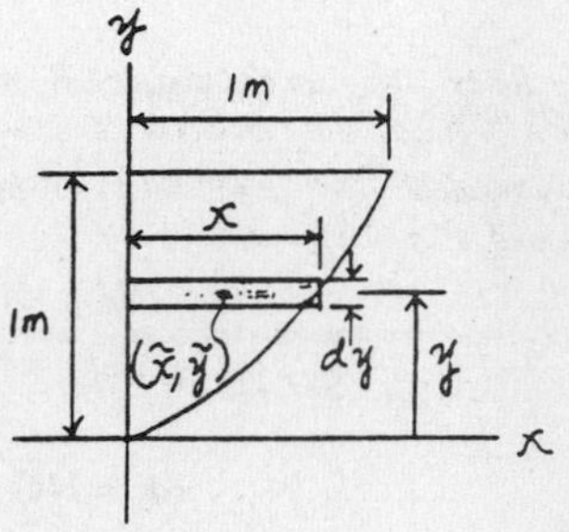

$$dI_{xy} = d\bar{I}_{x'y'} + dA\tilde{x}\tilde{y}$$
$$= 0 + \left(y^{\frac{1}{3}}dy\right)\left(\frac{1}{2}y^{\frac{1}{3}}\right)(y)$$
$$= \frac{1}{2}y^{\frac{5}{3}}dy$$

Product of Inertia : Performing the integration, we have

$$I_{xy} = \int dI_{xy} = \int_0^{1\,\text{m}} \frac{1}{2}y^{\frac{5}{3}}dy = \frac{3}{16}y^{\frac{8}{3}}\Big|_0^{1\,\text{m}} = 0.1875\ \text{m}^4 \qquad \textbf{Ans}$$

11-1. Use the method of virtual work to determine the tensions in cable AC. The lamp weighs 10 lb.

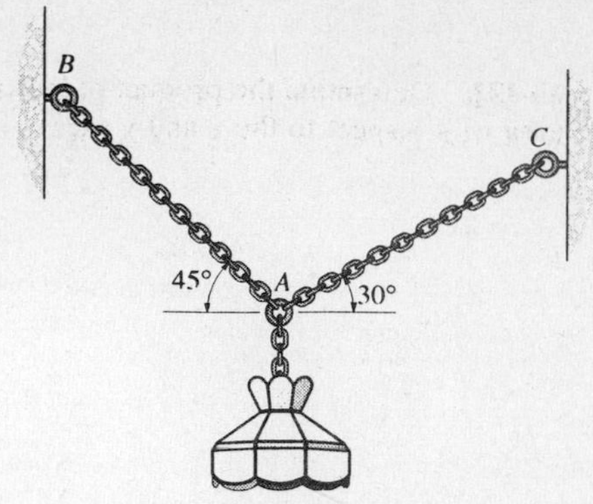

Free Body Diagram : The tension in cable AC can be determined by releasing cable AC. The system has only one degree of freedom defined by the independent coordinate θ. When θ undergoes a positive displacement $\delta\theta$, only $\mathbf{F}_{AC}$ and the weight of lamp (10 lb force) do work.

Virtual Displacements : Force $\mathbf{F}_{AC}$ and 10 lb force are located from the fixed point B using position coordinates y_A and x_A.

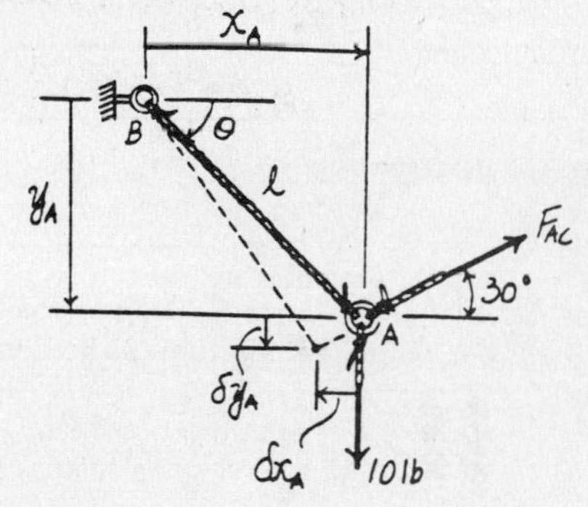

$$x_A = l\cos\theta \qquad \delta x_A = -l\sin\theta\,\delta\theta \qquad [1]$$

$$y_A = l\sin\theta \qquad \delta y_A = l\cos\theta\,\delta\theta \qquad [2]$$

Virtual - Work Equation : When y_A and x_A undergo positive virtual displacements δy_A and δx_A, the 10 lb force and horizontal component of $\mathbf{F}_{AC}$, $F_{AC}\cos 30°$ do positive work while the vertical component of $\mathbf{F}_{AC}$, $F_{AC}\sin 30°$ does negative work.

$$\delta U = 0; \qquad 10\delta y_A - F_{AC}\sin 30°\,\delta y_A + F_{AC}\cos 30°\,\delta x_A = 0 \qquad [3]$$

Substituting Eqs. [1] and [2] into [3] yields

$$(10\cos\theta - 0.5F_{AC}\cos\theta - 0.8660F_{AC}\sin\theta)\,l\delta\theta = 0$$

Since $l\delta\theta \neq 0$, then

$$F_{AC} = \frac{10\cos\theta}{0.5\cos\theta + 0.8660\sin\theta}$$

At the equilibrium position $\theta = 45°$,

$$F_{AC} = \frac{10\cos 45°}{0.5\cos 45° + 0.8660\sin 45°} = 7.32\text{ lb} \qquad \textbf{Ans}$$

11-2. The uniform rod OA has a weight of 10 lb. When the rod is in vertical position, $\theta = 0°$, the spring is unstretched. Determine the angle θ for equilibrium if the end of the spring wraps around the periphery of the disk as the disk turns.

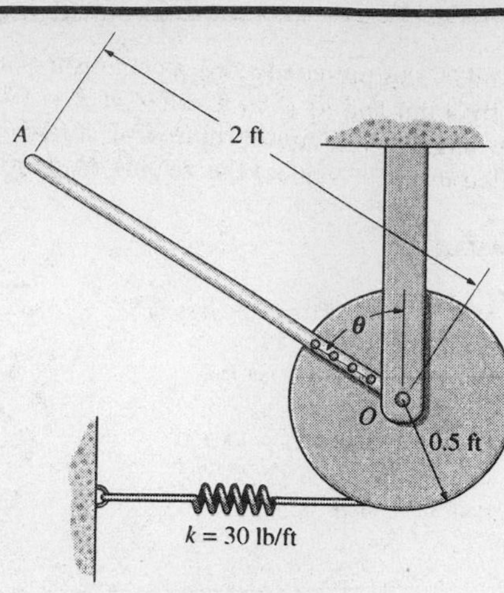

Free Body Diagram : The system has only one degree of freedom defined by the independent coordinate θ. When θ undergoes a positive displacement $\delta\theta$, only the spring force and the weight of rod (10 lb force) do work.

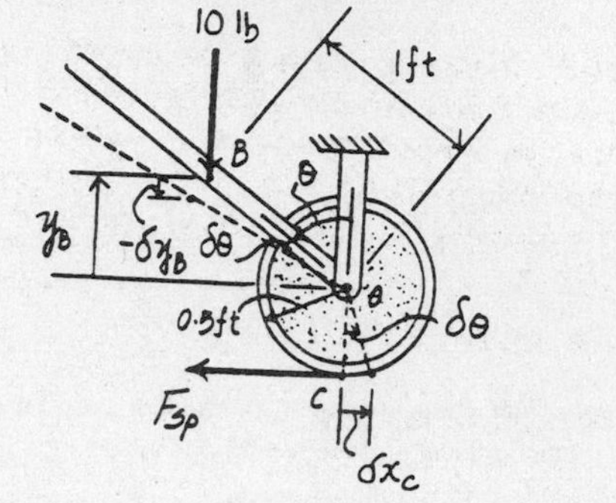

Virtual Displacements : The 10 lb force is located from the fixed point B using the position coordinate y_B, and the virtual displacement of point C is δx_C.

$$y_B = 1\cos\theta \qquad \delta y_B = -\sin\theta\delta\theta \qquad [1]$$

$$\delta x_C = 0.5\delta\theta \qquad [2]$$

Virtual - Work Equation : When points B and C undergo positive virtual displacements δy_B and δx_C, the 10 lb force and the spring force F_{sp}, do positive work.

$$\delta U = 0; \qquad 10\delta y_B + F_{sp}\delta x_C = 0 \qquad [3]$$

Substituting Eqs. [1] and [2] into [3] yields

$$\left(-10\sin\theta + 0.5F_{sp}\right)\delta\theta = 0 \qquad [4]$$

However, from the spring formula, $F_{sp} = kx = 30(0.5\theta) = 15\theta$. Substituting this value into Eq. [4] yields

$$(-10\sin\theta + 7.5\theta)\delta\theta = 0$$

Since $\delta\theta \neq 0$, then

$$-10\sin\theta + 7.5\theta = 0$$

Solving by trial and error

$$\theta = 0° \quad \text{and} \quad \theta = 73.1° \qquad \textbf{Ans}$$

11-3. Determine the force **F** acting on the cord which is required to maintain equilibrium of the horizontal 10-kg bar AB. *Hint*: Express the total *constant vertical length l* of the cord in terms of position coordinates s_1 and s_2. The derivative of this equation yields a relationship between δ_1 and δ_2.

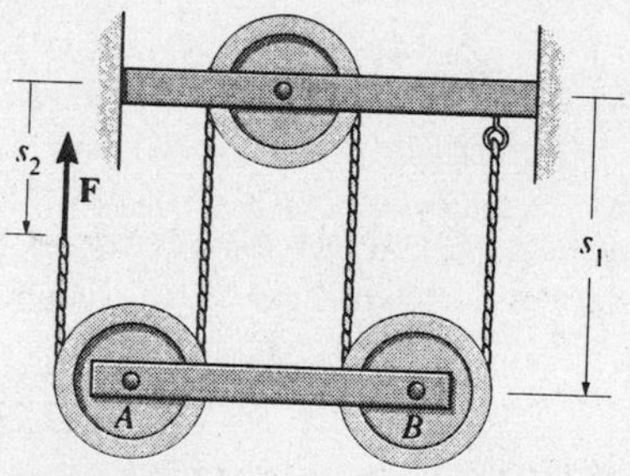

Free - Body Diagram : Only force **F** and the weight of link AB (98.1 N) do work.

Virtual Displacements : Force **F** and the weight of link AB (98.1 N) are located from the top of the fixed link using position coordinates s_2 and s_1. Since the cord has a constant lenght, l, then

$$4s_1 - s_2 = l \qquad 4\delta s_1 - \delta s_2 = 0 \qquad [1]$$

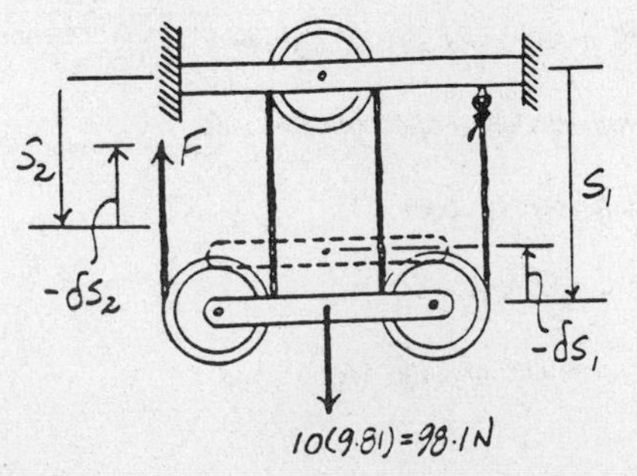

Virtual - Work Equation : When s_1 and s_2 undergo positive virtual displacements δs_1 and δs_2, the weight of link AB (98.1 N) and force **F** do positive work and negative work, respectively.

$$\delta U = 0; \qquad 98.1(-\delta s_1) - F(-\delta s_2) = 0 \qquad [2]$$

Substituting into Eq. [2] into [1] yields

$$(-98.1 + 4F)\delta s_1 = 0$$

Since $\delta s_1 \neq 0$, then

$$-98.1 + 4F = 0$$

$$W = 24.5 \text{ N} \qquad \textbf{Ans}$$

*11-4. The pin-connected mechanism is constrained at A by a pin and at B by a roller. If $P = 10$ lb, determine the angle θ for equilibrium. The spring is unstretched when $\theta = 45°$. Neglect the weight of the members.

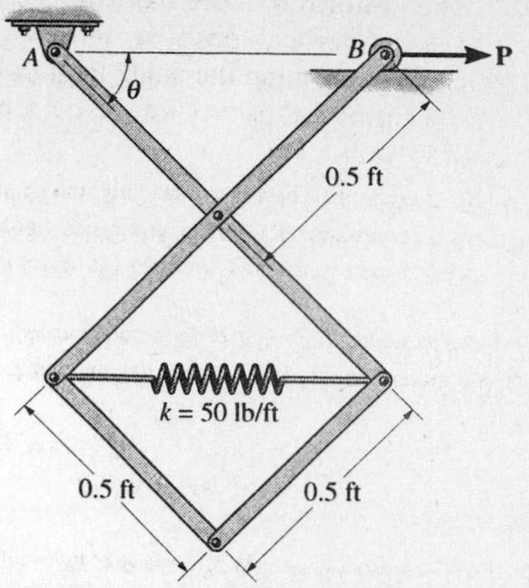

$x = l\cos\theta$

$F_s = ks;\quad F = 50(l\cos\theta - l\cos 45°)$

$\delta U = 0;\quad -F\,\delta x + P\,\delta x = 0$

$-50(l\cos\theta - l\cos 45°) + 10 = 0$

$\theta = 24.9°$ **Ans**

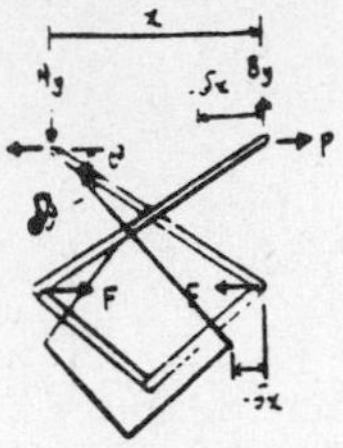

11-5. The pin-connected mechanism is constrained by a pin at A and a roller at B. Determine the force P that must be applied to the roller to hold the mechanism in equilibrium when $\theta = 30°$. The spring is unstretched when $\theta = 45°$. Neglect the weight of the members.

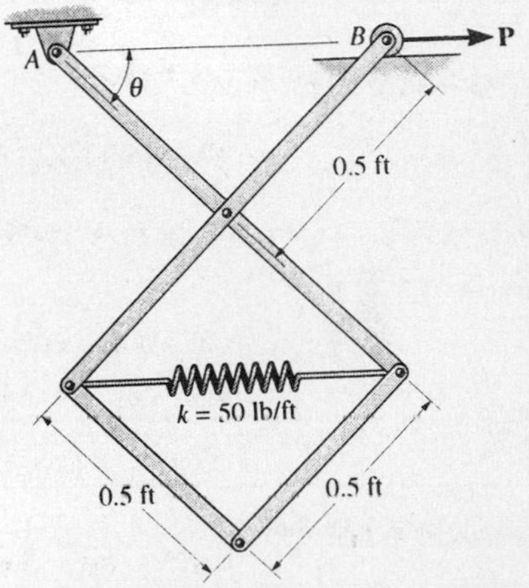

$x = l\cos\theta$

$\delta U = 0;\quad P\,\delta x - F_s\,\delta x = 0$

$P = F_s$

When $\theta = 45°$, $x = l\cos 45° = 0.7071$ ft

When $\theta = 30°$, $x = l\cos 30° = 0.86602$ ft

$F_s = ks;\quad F_s = 50(0.86602 - 0.7071) = 7.95$ lb

$P = 7.95$ lb **Ans**

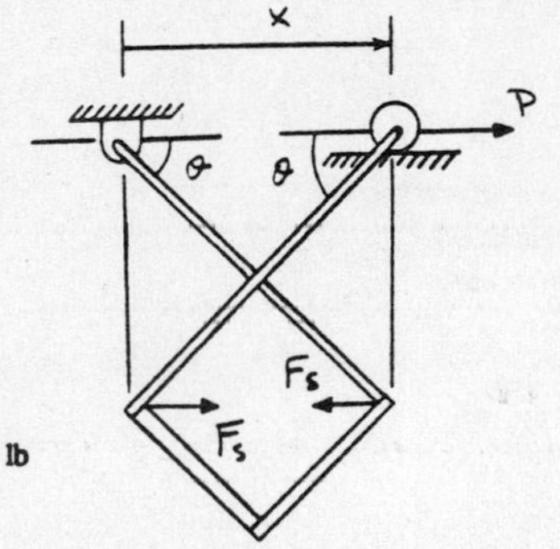

11-6. If the spring has a stiffness k and an unstretched length l_0, determine the load P when the mechanism is in the position shown. Neglect the weight of the members.

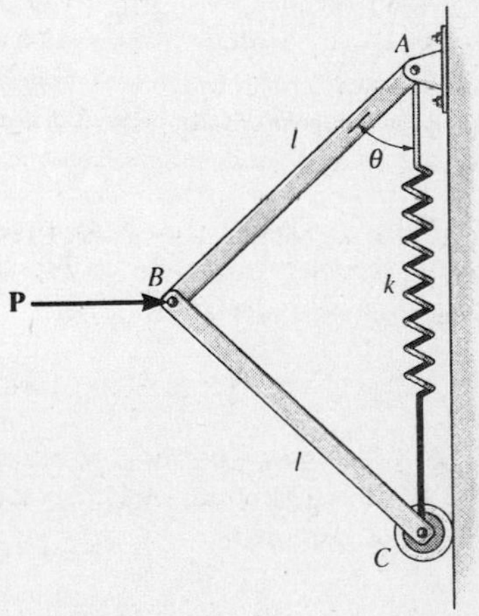

$y = 2l\cos\theta,\quad \delta y = -2l\sin\theta\,\delta\theta$

$x = l\sin\theta,\quad \delta x = l\cos\theta\,\delta\theta$

$\delta U = 0;\quad -P\,\delta x - F_s\,\delta y = 0$

$-P(l\cos\theta\,\delta\theta) + F_s(2l\sin\theta\,\delta\theta) = 0$

$-P\cos\theta + 2F_s\sin\theta = 0$

$F_s = k(2l\cos\theta - l_0)$

$P = 2k\tan\theta\,(2l\cos\theta - l_0)$ **Ans**

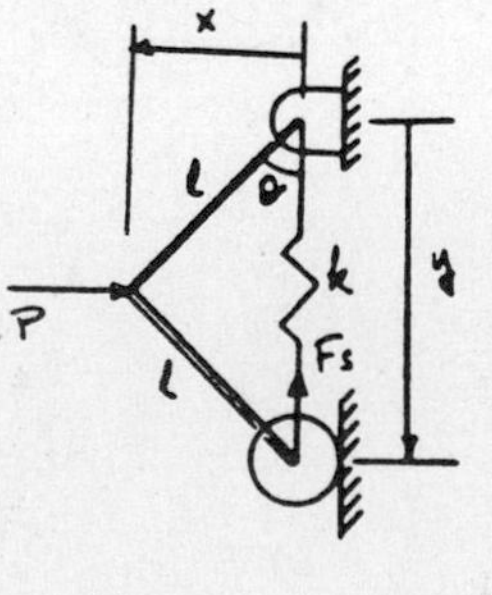

11-7. Solve Prob. 11-6 if the force **P** is applied vertically downward at B.

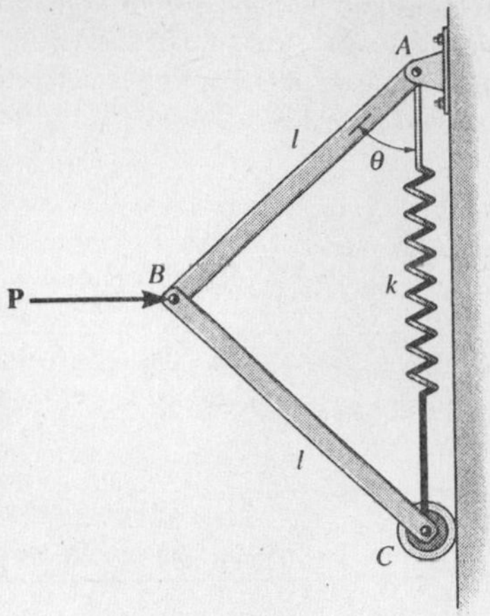

$y_1 = l\cos\theta, \qquad \delta y_1 = -l\sin\theta\,\delta\theta$

$y_2 = 2l\cos\theta, \qquad \delta y_2 = -2l\sin\theta\,\delta\theta$

$\delta U = 0; \qquad P\,\delta y_1 - F_s\,\delta y_2 = 0$

$P(-l\sin\theta)\,\delta\theta - F_s(-2l\sin\theta)\,\delta\theta = 0$

$P = 2F_s$

$F_s = kx; \qquad F_s = k(2l\cos\theta - l_0)$

$P = 2k(2l\cos\theta - l_0)$ **Ans**

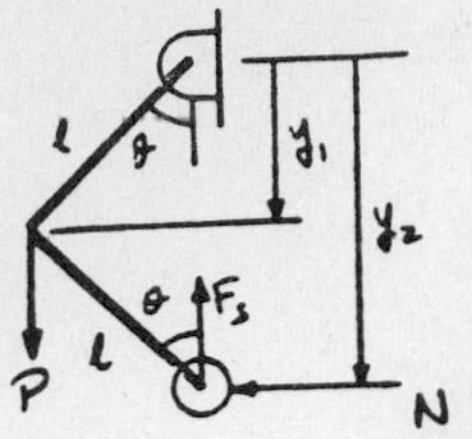

***11-8.** Determine the force developed in the spring required to keep the 10 lb uniform rod AB in equilibrium when $\theta = 35°$.

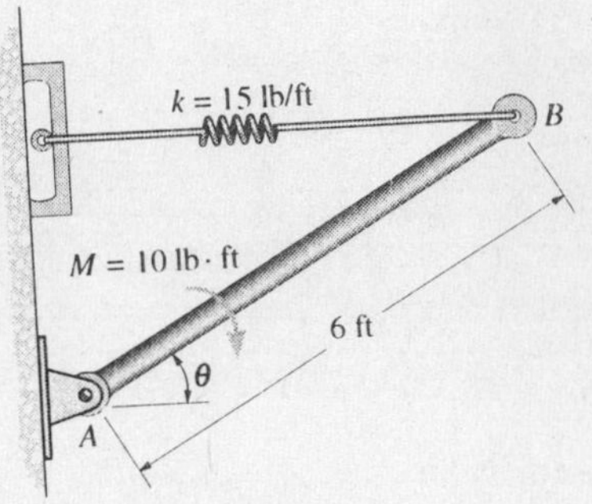

Free - Body Diagram : The system has only one degree of freedom defined by the independent coordinate θ. When θ undergoes a positive displacement $\delta\theta$, only the spring force F_{sp}, the weight of the rod (10 lb) and the 10 lb · ft couple moment do work.

Virtual Displacements : The spring force F_{sp} and the weight of the rod (10 lb) are located from the fixed point A using position coordinates x_B and x_C, respectively.

$$x_B = 6\cos\theta \qquad \delta x_B = -6\sin\theta\,\delta\theta \qquad [1]$$

$$y_C = 3\sin\theta \qquad \delta y_C = 3\cos\theta\,\delta\theta \qquad [2]$$

Virtual - Work Equation : When points B and C undergo positive virtual displacements δx_B and δy_C, the spring force F_{sp} and the weight of the rod (10 lb) do negative work. The 10 lb · ft couple moment does negative work when rod AB undergoes a positive virtual rotation $\delta\theta$.

$$\delta U = 0; \qquad -F_{sp}\,\delta x_B - 10\delta y_C - 10\delta\theta = 0 \qquad [3]$$

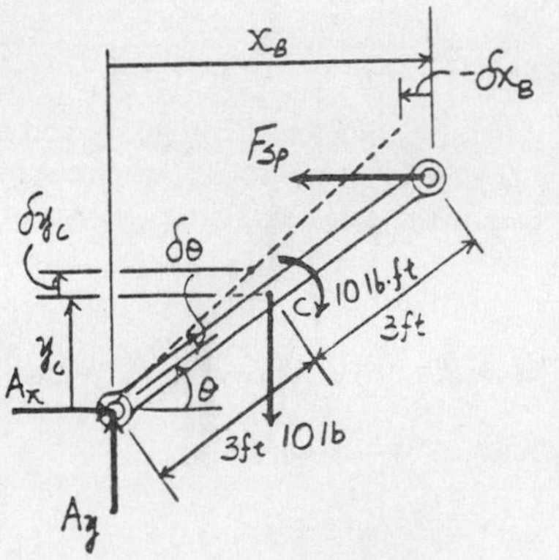

Substituting Eqs. [1] and [2] into [3] yields

$$\left(6F_{sp}\sin\theta - 30\cos\theta - 10\right)\delta\theta = 0 \qquad [4]$$

Since $\delta\theta \neq 0$, then

$$6F_{sp}\sin\theta - 30\cos\theta - 10 = 0$$

$$F_{sp} = \frac{30\cos\theta + 10}{6\sin\theta}$$

At the equilibrium position, $\theta = 35°$. Then

$$F_{sp} = \frac{30\cos 35° + 10}{6\sin 35°} = 10.0 \text{ lb}$$ **Ans**

11-9. Determine the angles θ for equilibrium of the 4-lb disk using using the principle of the virtual work. Neglect the weight of the rod. The spring is unstretched when $\theta = 0°$ and always remains in the vertical position due to the roller guide.

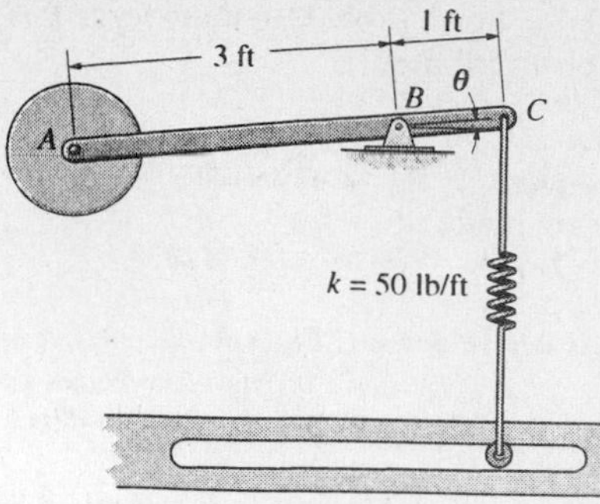

Free Body Diagram **:** The system has only one degree of freedom defined by the independent coordinate θ. When θ undergoes a positive displacement $\delta\theta$, only the spring force F_{sp} and the weight of the disk (4 lb) do work.

Virtual Displacements **:** The spring force F_{sp} and the weight of the disk (4 lb) are located from the fixed point B using position coordinates y_C and y_A, respectively.

$$y_C = 1\sin\theta \qquad \delta y_C = \cos\theta\delta\theta \qquad [1]$$

$$y_A = 3\sin\theta \qquad \delta y_A = 3\cos\theta\delta\theta \qquad [2]$$

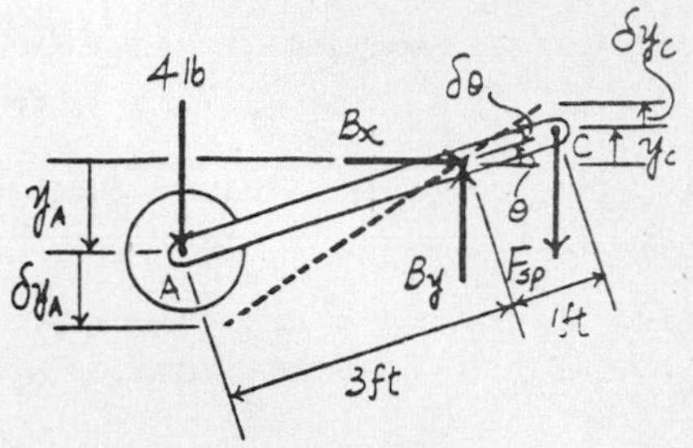

Virtual - Work Equation **:** When points C and A undergo positive virtual displacements δy_C and δy_A, the spring force F_{sp} does negative work while the weight of the disk (4 lb) do positive work.

$$\delta U = 0; \qquad 4\delta y_A - F_{sp}\delta y_C = 0 \qquad [3]$$

Substituting Eqs. [1] and [2] into [3] yields

$$\left(12 - F_{sp}\right)\cos\theta\delta\theta = 0 \qquad [4]$$

However, from the spring formula, $F_{sp} = kx = 50(1\sin\theta) = 50\sin\theta$. Substituting this value into Eq. [4] yields

$$(12 - 50\sin\theta)\cos\theta\delta\theta = 0$$

Since $\delta\theta \neq 0$, then

$$12 - 50\sin\theta = 0 \qquad \theta = 13.9° \qquad \textbf{Ans}$$

$$\cos\theta = 0 \qquad \theta = 90° \qquad \textbf{Ans}$$

11-10. The mechanism consists of the four pin-connected bars and three springs, each having a stiffness k and an unstretched length l_0. Determine the horizontal forces P that must be applied to the pins in order to hold the mechanism in the horizontal position for equilibrium.

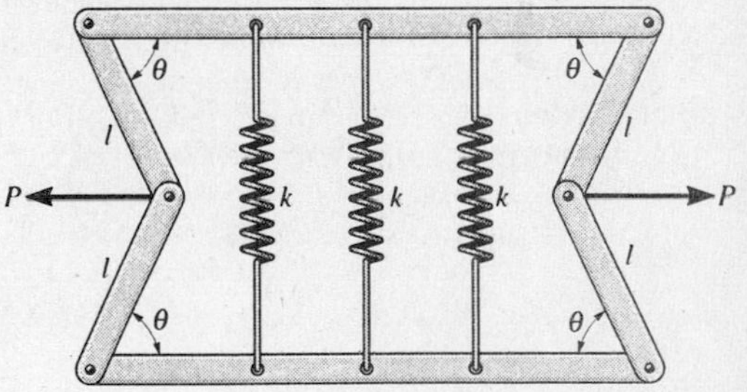

$x = l\cos\theta, \qquad \delta x = -l\sin\theta\,\delta\theta$

$y = 2l\sin\theta, \qquad \delta y = 2l\cos\theta\,\delta\theta$

$\delta U = 0; \qquad -2P\,\delta x - 3F_s\,\delta y = 0$

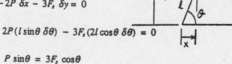

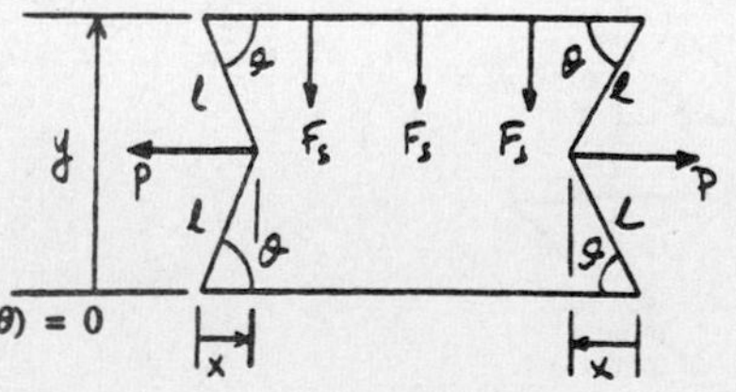

$2P(l\sin\theta\,\delta\theta) - 3F_s(2l\cos\theta\,\delta\theta) = 0$

$P\sin\theta = 3F_s\cos\theta$

Since $F_s = k(2l\sin\theta - l_0)$, then

$P = 3k\,\text{ctn}\,\theta\,(2l\sin\theta - l_0) \qquad$ **Ans**

11-11. When $\theta = 20°$, the 50-lb uniform block compresses the two vertical springs 4 in. If the uniform links AB and CD each weigh 10 lb, determine the magnitude of the applied couple moments **M** needed to maintain equilibrium when $\theta = 20°$.

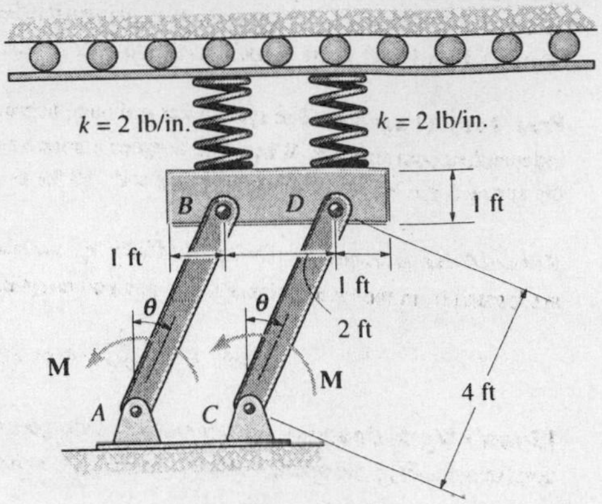

Free Body Diagram : The system has only one degree of freedom defined by the independent coordinate θ. When θ undergoes a positive displacement $\delta\theta$, only the weight of the rod W and force **P** do work.

Virtual Displacements : The weight of the rod W and force **P** are located from the fixed points A and B using position coordinates y_C and x_A, respectively

$$y_C = \frac{l}{2}\sin\theta \qquad \delta y_C = \frac{l}{2}\cos\theta\,\delta\theta \qquad [1]$$

$$x_A = l\cos\theta \qquad \delta x_A = -l\sin\theta\,\delta\theta \qquad [2]$$

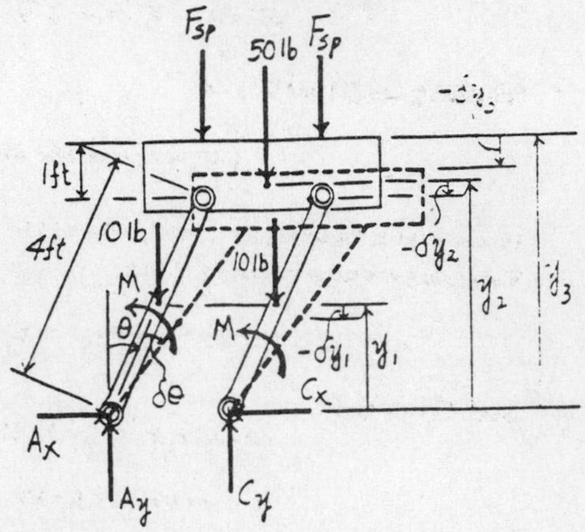

Virtual - Work Equation : When points C and A undergo positive virtual displacements δy_C and δx_A, the weight of the rod W and force **F** do negative work.

$$\delta U = 0; \qquad -W\delta y_C - P\delta y_A = 0 \qquad [3]$$

Substituting Eqs. [1] and [2] into [3] yields

$$\left(Pl\sin\theta - \frac{Wl}{2}\cos\theta\right)\delta\theta = 0$$

Since $\delta\theta \neq 0$, then

$$Pl\sin\theta - \frac{Wl}{2}\cos\theta = 0$$

$$P = \frac{W}{2}\cot\theta \qquad \textbf{Ans}$$

***11-12.** The truck is weighed on the highway inspection scale. If a known mass m is placed a distance s from the fulcrum B of the scale, determine the mass of the truck m_t if its center of gravity is located at a distance d from point C. When the scale is empty, the weight of the lever ABC balances the scale CDE.

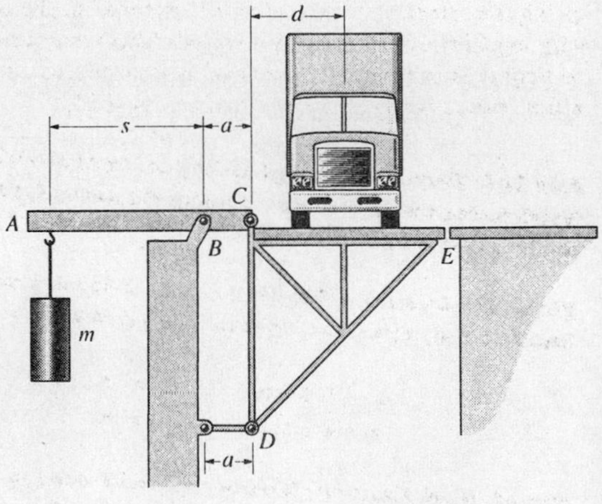

$$\delta U = 0; \qquad (W)(s\,\delta\theta) - W_t a\,\delta\theta = 0$$

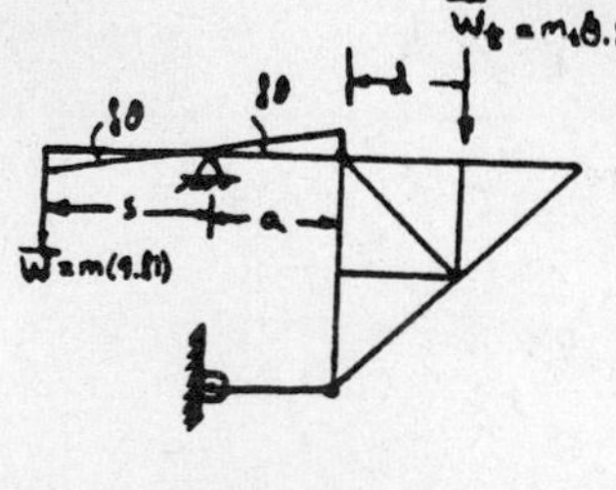

$$(Ws - W_t a)\delta\theta = 0$$

$$W_t = W\left(\frac{s}{a}\right)$$

or,

$$m_t = m\left(\frac{s}{a}\right) \qquad \textbf{Ans}$$

11-13. The thin rod of weight W rest against the smooth wall and floor. Determine the magnitude of force $\mathbf{P}$ needed to hold it in equilibrium for a given angle θ.

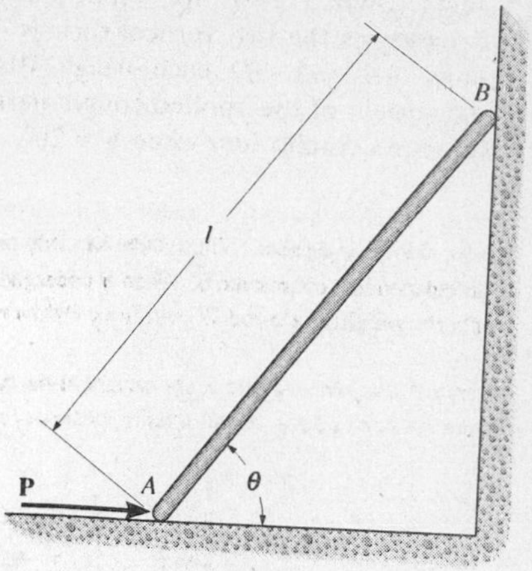

Free Body Diagram : The system has only one degree of freedom defined by the independent coordinate θ. When θ undergoes a positive displacement $\delta\theta$, only the spring force F_{sp} and the weight of the rod (10 lb) do work.

Virtual Displacements : The spring force, F_{sp} and the weight of rod (10 lb) are located from the fixed point A using position coordinate y_C.

$$y_C = 4\sin\theta \qquad \delta y_C = 4\cos\theta\,\delta\theta \qquad [1]$$

Virtual - Work Equation : When point C undergoes positive virtual displacement δy_C, the spring force F_{sp} do positive work while the weight of rod (10 lb) does negative work.

$$\delta U = 0; \qquad F_{sp}\,\delta y_C - 10\delta y_C = 0 \qquad [2]$$

Substituting Eqs. [1] into [2] yields

$$\left(4F_{sp} - 40\right)\cos\theta\,\delta\theta = 0 \qquad [4]$$

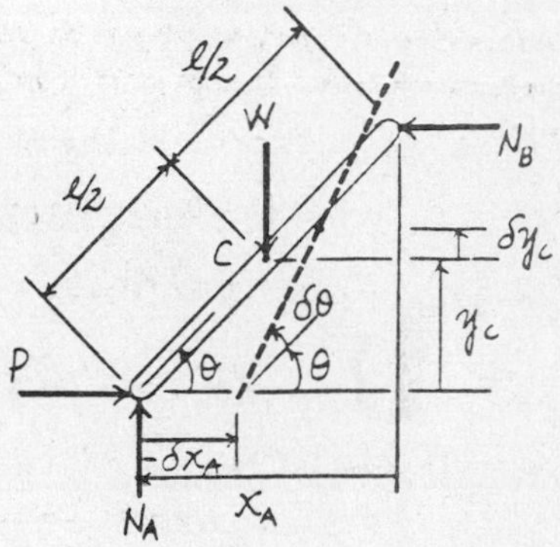

However, from the spring formula, $F_{sp} = kx = 5(4 - 4\sin\theta) = 20(1 - \sin\theta)$. Substituting this value into Eq. [4] yields

$$(40 - 80\sin\theta)\cos\theta\,\delta\theta = 0$$

Since $\delta\theta \neq 0$, then

$$40 - 80\sin\theta = 0 \qquad \theta = 30.0^\circ \qquad \textbf{Ans}$$

$$\cos\theta = 0 \qquad \theta = 90^\circ \qquad \textbf{Ans}$$

11-14. The uniform bar AB weighs 10 lb. If the attached spring is unstretched when $\theta = 90^\circ$, determine the angle θ for equilibrium. Note the spring always remains in the vertical position since the top end is attached to a roller which moves freely along the horizontal guide.

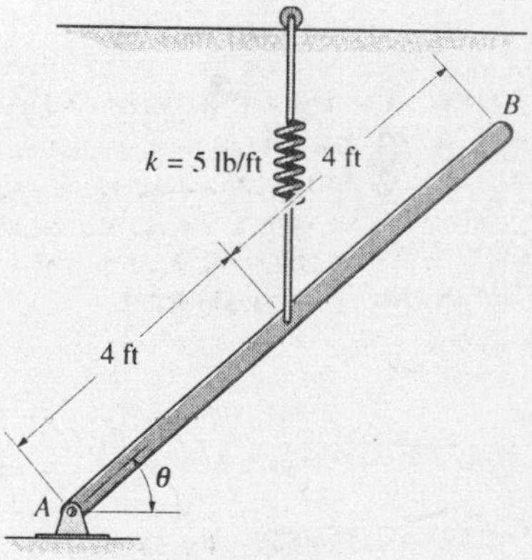

Free Body Diagram : The system has only one degree of freedom defined by the independent coordinate θ. When θ undergoes a positive displacement $\delta\theta$, only the 5 lb force and 2 lb force do work.

Virtual Displacements : The 5 lb force and 2 lb force are located from the fixed point A using position coordinates x_C and y_B, respectively.

$$x_C = 3(0.5\sin\theta) \qquad \delta x_C = 1.5\cos\theta\,\delta\theta \qquad [1]$$

$$y_B = 2(0.5\cos\theta) \qquad \delta y_B = -\sin\theta\,\delta\theta \qquad [2]$$

Virtual - Work Equation : When points C and B undergo positive virtual displacement δx_C and δy_B, the 5 lb force and 2 lb force do positive work.

$$\delta U = 0; \qquad 5\delta x_C + 2\delta y_B = 0 \qquad [3]$$

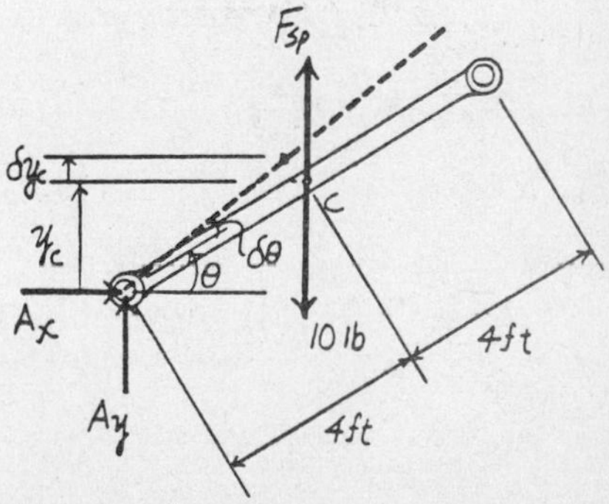

Substituting Eqs. [1] and [2] into [3] yields

$$(7.5\cos\theta - 2\sin\theta)\,\delta\theta = 0$$

Since $\delta\theta \neq 0$, then

$$7.5\cos\theta - 2\sin\theta = 0$$
$$\theta = 75.1^\circ \qquad \textbf{Ans}$$

11-15. The spring has an unstretched length of 0.3 m. Determine the angle θ for equilibrium if the uniform links each have a mass of 5 kg.

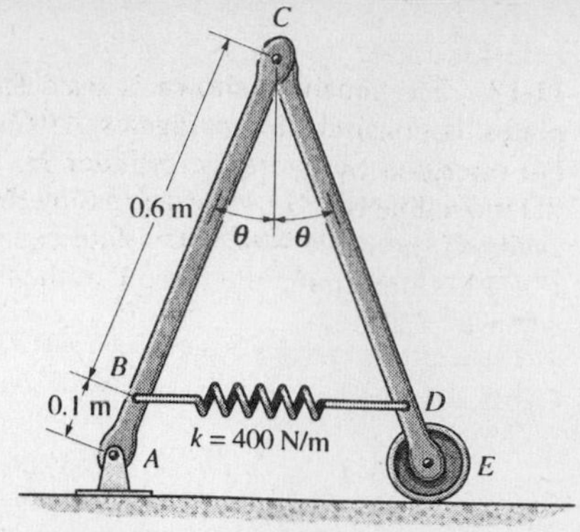

Free Body Diagram : The system has only one degree of freedom defined by the independent coordinate θ. When θ undergoes a positive displacement $\delta\theta$, only the spring force **F** and **P** do work.

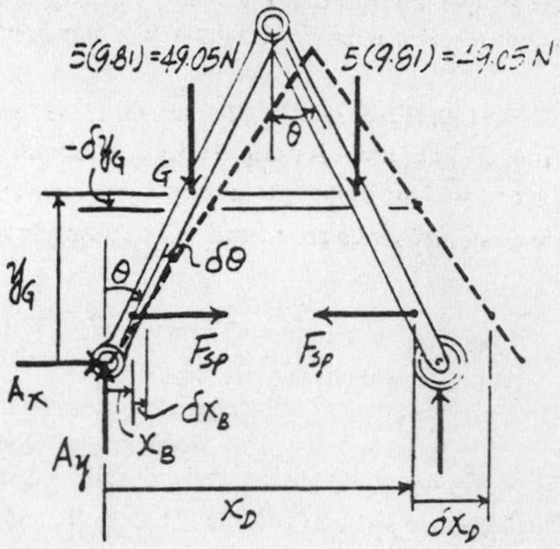

Virtual Displacements : The force **F** acting on joints E and B and force **P** are located from the fixed points D and A using position coordinates y_E and y_B, respectively. The location for force **P** is measured from the fixed point A using position coordinate x_G.

$$y_E = 0.2\sin\theta \qquad \delta y_E = 0.2\cos\theta\,\delta\theta \qquad [1]$$

$$y_B = 0.2\sin\theta \qquad \delta y_B = 0.2\cos\theta\,\delta\theta \qquad [2]$$

$$x_G = 2(0.2\cos\theta) + l \qquad \delta x_G = -0.4\sin\theta\,\delta\theta \qquad [3]$$

Virtual - Work Equation : When points E, B and G undergo positive virtual displacements δy_E, δy_B and δx_G, force **F** and **P** do negative work.

$$\delta U = 0; \qquad -F\delta y_E - F\delta y_B - P\delta x_G = 0 \qquad [4]$$

Substituting Eqs. [1], [2] and [3] into [4] yields

$$(0.4P\sin\theta - 0.4F\cos\theta)\,\delta\theta = 0$$

Since $\delta\theta \neq 0$, then

$$0.4P\sin\theta - 0.4F\cos\theta = 0 \qquad F = P\tan\theta$$

At equilibrium position $\theta = 30°$ set $P = 8$ kN, we have

$$M = 8\tan 30° = 4.62\text{ kN} \qquad \textbf{Ans}$$

***11-16.** The dumpster has a weight W and a center of gravity at G. Determine the force in the hydraulic cylinder needed to hold it in the general position θ.

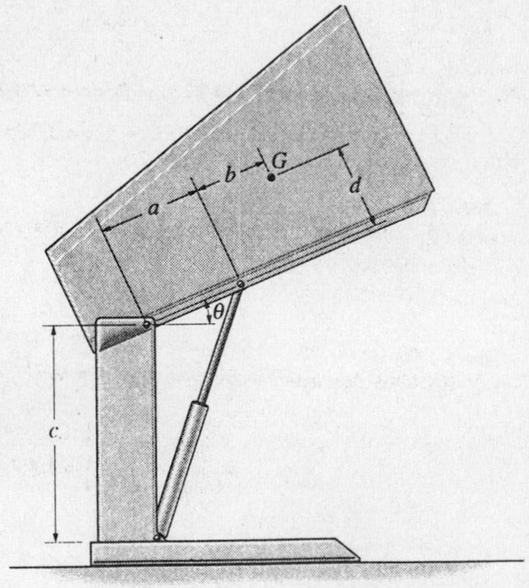

$$s = \sqrt{a^2 + c^2 - 2ac\cos(\theta + 90°)}$$

$$= \sqrt{a^2 + c^2 + 2ac\sin\theta}$$

$$\delta s = \left(a^2 + c^2 + 2ac\sin\theta\right)^{-\frac{1}{2}} ac\cos\theta\,\delta\theta$$

$$y = (a+b)\sin\theta$$

$$\delta y = (a+b)\cos\theta\,\delta\theta$$

$$\delta U = 0; \qquad F\delta s - W\delta y = 0$$

$$F\left(a^2 + c^2 + 2ac\sin\theta\right)^{-\frac{1}{2}} ac\cos\theta\,\delta\theta - W(a+b)\cos\theta\,\delta\theta = 0$$

$$F = \left(\frac{W(a+b)}{ac}\right)\sqrt{a^2 + c^2 + 2ac\sin\theta} \qquad \textbf{Ans}$$

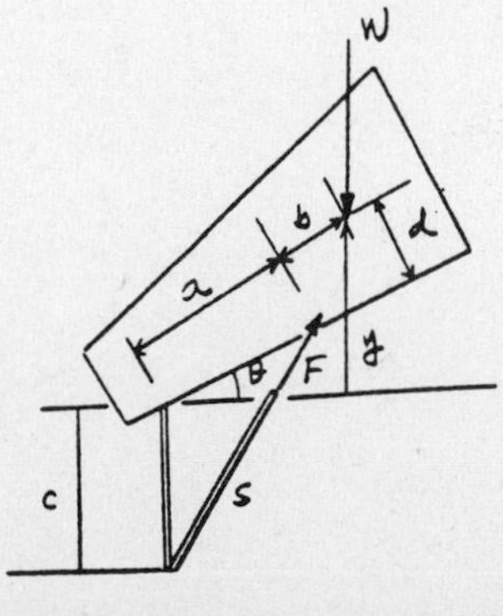

11-17. The machine shown is used for forming metal plates. It consists of two toggles ABC and DEF, which are operated by hydraulic cylinder H. The toggles push the moveable bar G forward, pressing the plate p into the cavity. If the force which the plate exerts on the head is $P = 8$ kN, determine the force **F** in the hydraulic cylinder when $\theta = 30°$.

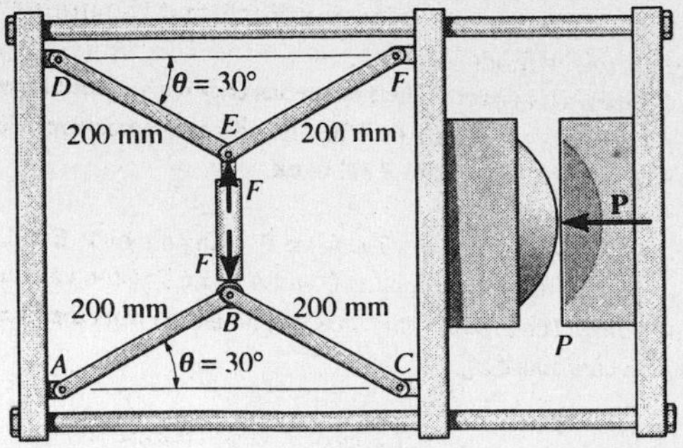

Free Body Diagram : The system has only one degree of freedom defined by the independent coordinate θ. When θ undergoes a positive displacement $\delta\theta$, only the spring force F_{sp} and the weight of the vent plate (15 lb force) do work.

Virtual Displacements : The weight of the vent plate (15 lb force) is located from the fixed point B using the position coordinate y_G. The horizontal and vertical position of the spring force F_{sp} are measured from the fixed point B using the position coordinates x_A and y_A, respectively.

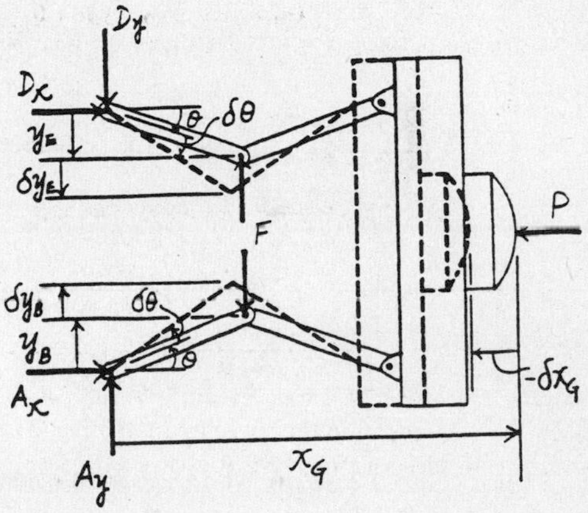

$$y_G = 0.5\cos\theta \qquad \delta y_G = -0.5\sin\theta\delta\theta \qquad [1]$$
$$y_A = 1\cos\theta \qquad \delta y_A = -\sin\theta\delta\theta \qquad [2]$$
$$x_A = 1\sin\theta \qquad \delta x_A = \cos\theta\delta\theta \qquad [3]$$

Virtual - Work Equation : When y_G, y_A and x_A undergo positive virtual displacements δy_G, δy_A and δx_A, the weight of the vent plate (15 lb force), horizontal component of F_{sp}, $F_{sp}\cos\phi$ and vertical component of F_{sp}, $F_{sp}\sin\phi$ do negative work.

$$\delta U = 0; \qquad -F_{sp}\cos\phi\,\delta x_A - F_{sp}\sin\phi\,\delta y_A - 15\delta y_G = 0 \qquad [4]$$

Substituting Eqs. [1], [2] and [3] into [4] yields

$$\left(-F_{sp}\cos\theta\cos\phi + F_{sp}\sin\theta\sin\phi + 7.5\sin\theta\right)\delta\theta = 0$$
$$\left(-F_{sp}\cos(\theta+\phi) + 7.5\sin\theta\right)\delta\theta = 0$$

Since $\delta\theta \neq 0$, then

$$-F_{sp}\cos(\theta+\phi) + 7.5\sin\theta = 0$$
$$F_{sp} = \frac{7.5\sin\theta}{\cos(\theta+\phi)}$$

At equilibrium position $\theta = 30°$, the angle $\phi = \tan^{-1}\left(\dfrac{1\cos 30°}{4 + 1\sin 30°}\right) = 10.89°$.

$$F_{sp} = \frac{7.5\sin 30°}{\cos(30° + 10.89°)} = 4.961 \text{ lb}$$

Spring Formula : From the geometry, the spring stretches
$x = \sqrt{4^2 + 1^2 - 2(4)(1)\cos 120°} - \sqrt{4^2 + 1^2} = 0.4595$ ft.

$$F_{sp} = kx$$
$$4.961 = k(0.4595)$$
$$k = 10.8 \text{ lb/ft} \qquad \textbf{Ans}$$

11-18. The vent plate is supported at B by a pin. If it weighs 15 lb and has a center of gravity at G, determine the stiffness k of the spring so that the plate remains in equilibrium at $\theta = 30°$. The spring is unstretched when $\theta = 0°$.

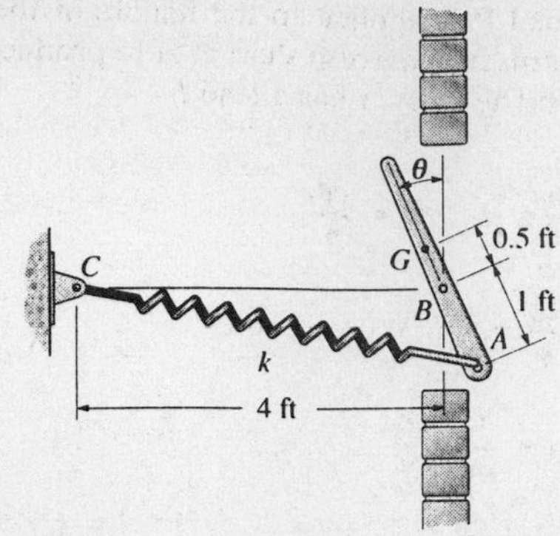

Free Body Diagram : The system has only one degree of freedom defined by the independent coordinate θ. When θ undergoes a positive displacement $\delta\theta$, only the weight of the block W does work.

Virtual Displacements : The weight of the block W is located from the fixed point D using the position coordinate y_A. From the geometry, $a = 200\sin\theta$ $= 300\sin\phi$. Then $\sin\phi = \frac{2}{3}\sin\theta$ and $\cos\phi = \frac{1}{3}\sqrt{9-4\sin^2\theta}$.

$$y_A = 800\cos\phi - 300\cos\phi - 200\cos\theta$$
$$= 500\cos\phi - 200\cos\theta$$
$$= \frac{500}{3}\sqrt{9-4\sin^2\theta} - 200\cos\theta$$

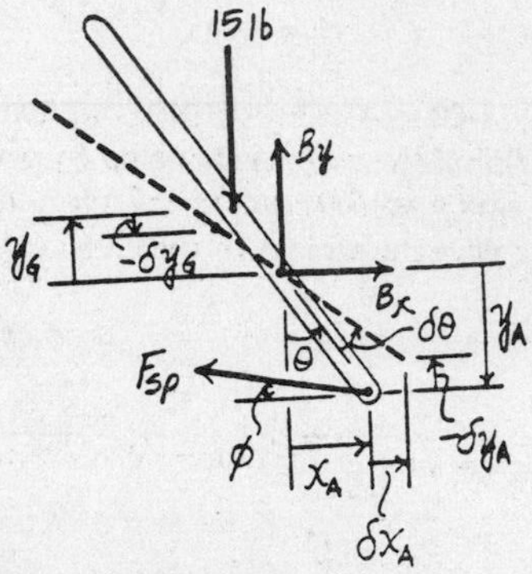

$$\delta y_A = \frac{500}{3}\left[\frac{1}{2}\left(9-4\sin^2\theta\right)^{-\frac{1}{2}}(-8\sin\theta\cos\theta\,\delta\theta)\right] - 200(-\sin\theta)\,\delta\theta$$

$$= \left(-\frac{2000\sin\theta\cos\theta}{3\sqrt{9-4\sin^2\theta}} + 200\sin\theta\right)\delta\theta \qquad [1]$$

Virtual - Work Equation : When points A undergoes a positive virtual displacement δy_A, W does positive work.

$$\delta U = 0; \qquad W\delta y_A = 0 \qquad [2]$$

Substituting Eq. [1] into [2] yields

$$\left(-\frac{2000\cos\theta}{3\sqrt{9-4\sin^2\theta}} + 200\right)\sin\theta W\delta\theta = 0$$

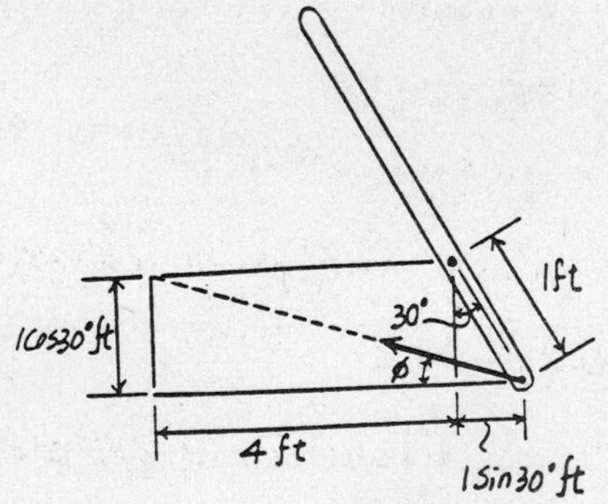

Since $W\delta\theta \neq 0$, then

$$\sin\theta = 0 \qquad \theta = 0° \qquad \textbf{Ans}$$

$$-\frac{2000\cos\theta}{3\sqrt{9-4\sin^2\theta}} + 200 = 0$$
$$4\cos^2\theta + 1.44\sin^2\theta = 3.24$$

$$\theta = 33.0° \qquad \textbf{Ans}$$

11-19. Determine the compression developed at C if a load $\mathbf{P}$ is applied to the handle of the press. It takes n turns of the worm shaft at A to produce one turn of gear B. The screw s has a lead l.

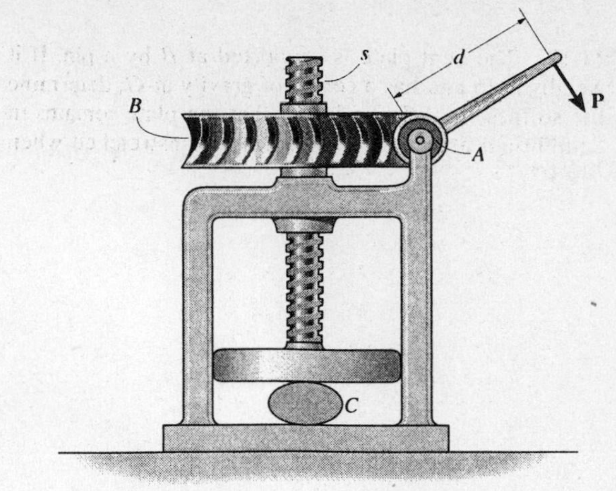

$$\frac{n}{\theta} = \frac{1}{\phi}, \quad d\phi = \frac{d\theta}{n}$$

$$\frac{2\pi}{\phi} = \frac{l}{y}$$

$$y = \frac{l}{2\pi}\phi$$

$$\delta y = \frac{l}{2\pi}\delta\phi = \frac{l}{2\pi n}\delta\theta$$

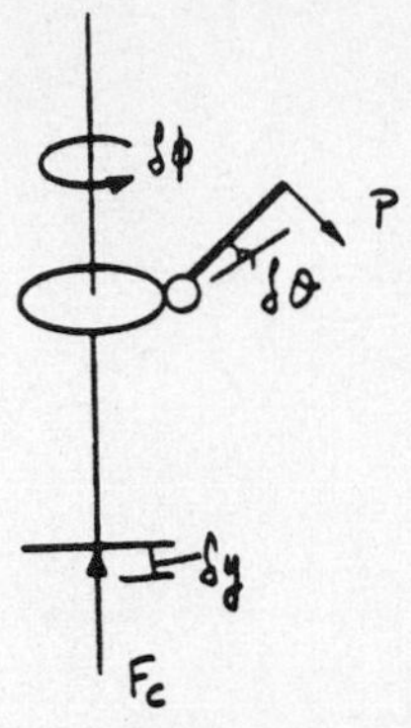

$\delta U = 0;\quad -F_C\,\delta y + Pd\,\delta\theta = 0$

$$\left(F_C\frac{ln}{2\pi} + Pd\right)\delta\theta = 0$$

$$F_C = \frac{2\pi nd}{l}P \quad \textbf{Ans}$$

***11-20.** A 3-lb weight is attached to the end of rod ABC. If the rod is supported by a smooth slider block at C and rod BD, determine the angle θ for equilibrium. Neglect the weight of the rods and the slider.

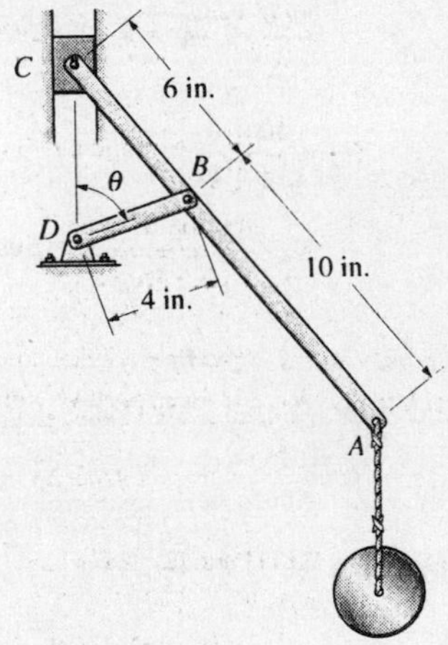

$$x = \sqrt{(6)^2 - (4\sin\theta)^2} = \sqrt{36 - 16\sin^2\theta}$$

$$\frac{6}{x} = \frac{16}{(x + 4\cos\theta) + y}$$

$$x + 4\cos\theta + y = 2.667x$$

$$y = -4\cos\theta + 1.667\sqrt{36 - 16\sin^2\theta}$$

$$\delta y = 4\sin\theta\,\delta\theta + 1.667\left(\frac{1}{2}\right)(36 - 16\sin^2\theta)^{-\frac{1}{2}}(-32\sin\theta\cos\theta)\delta\theta$$

$\delta U = 0;\quad W\,\delta y = 0$

$$W\left[4 - 0.8333(36 - 16\sin^2\theta)^{-\frac{1}{2}}(32\cos\theta)\right]\sin\theta\,\delta\theta = 0$$

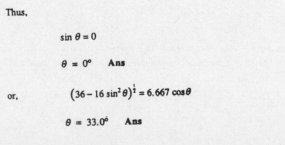

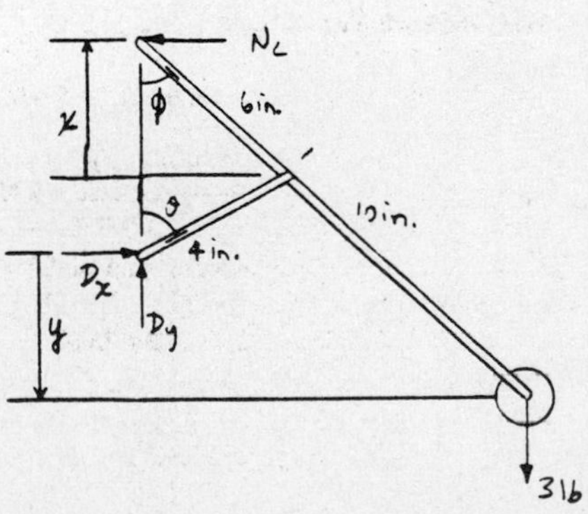

Thus,

$\sin\theta = 0$

$\theta = 0°$ **Ans**

or, $(36 - 16\sin^2\theta)^{\frac{1}{2}} = 6.667\cos\theta$

$\theta = 33.0°$ **Ans**

11-21. The piston C moves vertically between the two smooth walls. If the spring has a stiffness of $k = 1.5$ kN/m and is unstretched when $\theta = 0°$, determine the couple $\mathbf{M}$ that must be applied to link AB to hold the mechanism in equilibrium; $\theta = 30°$.

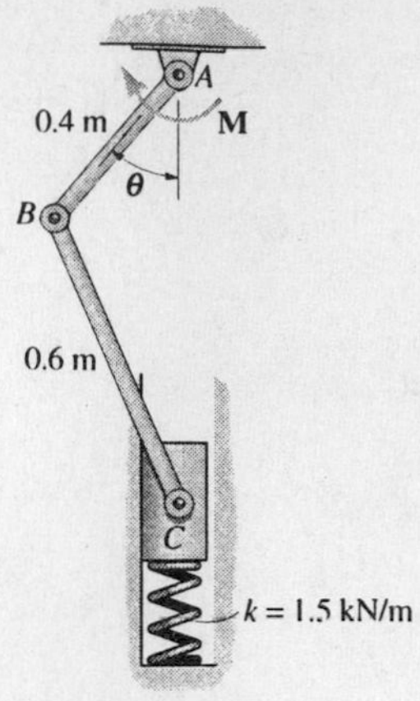

Free Body Diagram : The system has only one degree of freedom defined by the independent coordinate θ. When θ undergoes a positive displacement $\delta\theta$, only the spring force F_{sp} and couple moment $\mathbf{M}$ do work.

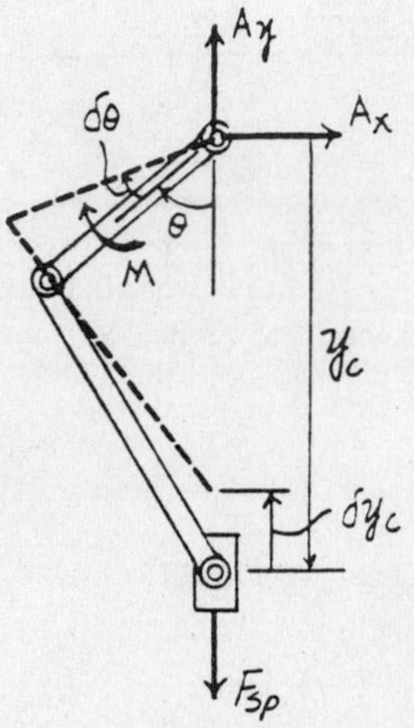

Virtual Displacements : The spring force F_{sp} is located from the fixed point A using the position coordinate y_C. Using the law of cosines

$$0.6^2 = y_C^2 + 0.4^2 - 2(y_C)(0.4)\cos\theta \qquad [1]$$

Differentiating the above expression, we have

$$0 = 2y_C\,\delta y_C - 0.8\,\delta y_C\cos\theta + 0.8y_C\sin\theta\,\delta\theta$$

$$\delta y_C = \frac{0.8y_C\sin\theta}{0.8\cos\theta - 2y_C}\,\delta\theta \qquad [2]$$

Virtual - Work Equation : When point C undergoes a positive virtual displacement δy_C, the spring force F_{sp} does positive work. The couple moment $\mathbf{M}$ does positive work when link AB undergoes a positive virtual rotation $\delta\theta$.

$$\delta U = 0; \qquad F_{sp}\,\delta y_C + M\delta\theta = 0 \qquad [3]$$

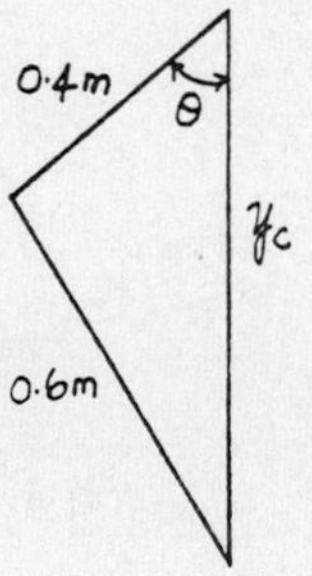

Substituting Eq. [1] into [2] yields

$$\left(\frac{0.8y_C\sin\theta}{0.8\cos\theta - 2y_C}F_{sp} + M\right)\delta\theta = 0$$

Since $\delta\theta \neq 0$, then

$$\frac{0.8y_C\sin\theta}{0.8\cos\theta - 2y_C}F_{sp} + M = 0$$

$$M = -\frac{0.8y_C\sin\theta}{0.8\cos\theta - 2y_C}F_{sp} \qquad [4]$$

At the equilibrium position, $\theta = 30°$. Substituting into Eq. [1],

$$0.6^2 = y_C^2 + 0.4^2 - 2(y_C)(0.4)\cos 30°$$

$$y_C = 0.9121 \text{ m}$$

The spring stretches $x = 1 - 0.9121 = 0.08790$ m. Then the spring force is $F_{sp} = kx = 1500(0.08790) = 131.86$ N. Substituting the above results into Eq. [4], we have

$$M = -\left[\frac{0.8(0.9121)\sin 30°}{0.8\cos 30° - 2(0.9121)}\right]131.86 = 42.5 \text{ N}\cdot\text{m} \qquad \textbf{Ans}$$

11-22. The crankshaft is subjected to a torque of $M = 50$ lb · ft. Determine the vertical compressive force **F** applied to the piston for equilibrium when $\theta = 60°$.

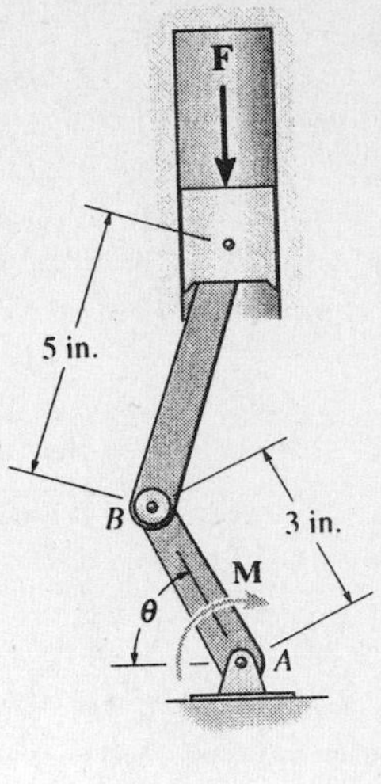

Free Body Diagram : The system has only one degree of freedom defined by the independent coordinate θ. When θ undergoes a positive displacement $\delta\theta$, only the force F and couple moment M do work.

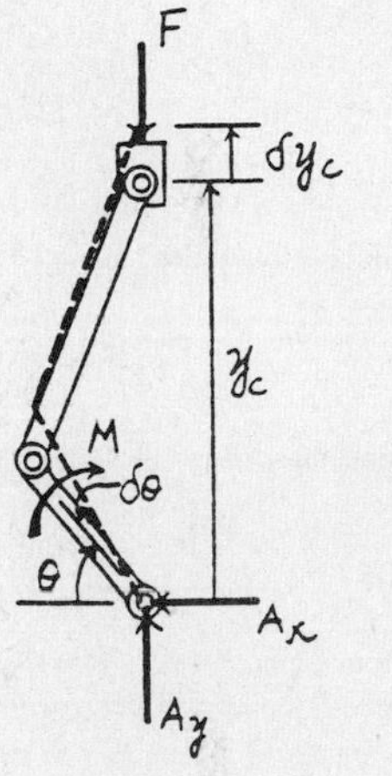

Virtual Displacements : Force F is located from the fixed point A using the positional coordinate y_C. Using the law of cosines.

$$5^2 = y_C^2 + 3^2 - 2(y_C)(3)\cos(90° - \theta) \qquad [1]$$

However, $\cos(90° - \theta) = \sin\theta$. Then Eq.[1] becomes $25 = y_C^2 + 9 - 6y_C\sin\theta$. Differentiating this expression, we have

$$0 = 2y_C\delta y_C - 6\delta y_C\sin\theta - 6y_C\cos\theta\delta\theta$$

$$\delta y_C = \frac{6y_C\cos\theta}{2y_C - 6\sin\theta}\delta\theta \qquad [2]$$

Virtual - Work Equation : When point C undergoes a positive virtual displacement δy_C, force F does negative work. The couple moment M does positive work when link AB undergoes a positive virtual rotation $\delta\theta$.

$$\delta U = 0; \qquad -F\delta y_C + M\delta\theta = 0 \qquad [3]$$

Substituting Eq.[2] into [3] yields

$$\left(-\frac{6y_C\cos\theta}{2y_C - 6\sin\theta}F + M\right)\delta\theta = 0$$

Since $\delta\theta \neq 0$, then

$$-\frac{6y_C\cos\theta}{2y_C - 6\sin\theta}F + M = 0$$

$$F = \frac{2y_C - 6\sin\theta}{6y_C\cos\theta}M \qquad [4]$$

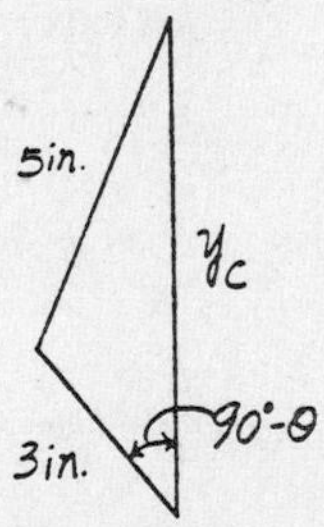

At the equilibrium position, $\theta = 60°$. Substituting into Eq.[1], we have

$$5^2 = y_C^2 + 3^2 - 2(y_C)(3)\cos 30°$$

$$y_C = 7.368 \text{ in.}$$

Substituting the above results into Eq. [4] and setting $M = 50$ lb · ft, we have

$$F = \left[\frac{2(7.368) - 6\sin 60°}{6(7.368)\cos 60°}\right]50 = 21.6 \text{ lb} \qquad \textbf{Ans}$$

11-23. The assembly is used for exercise. It consist of four pin-connected bars, each of length L, and a spring of stiffness k and unstretched length a ($<2L$). If horizontal forces **P** and $-$**P** are applied to the handles so that θ is slowly decreased, determine the angle θ at which the magnitude of **P** becomes a maximum.

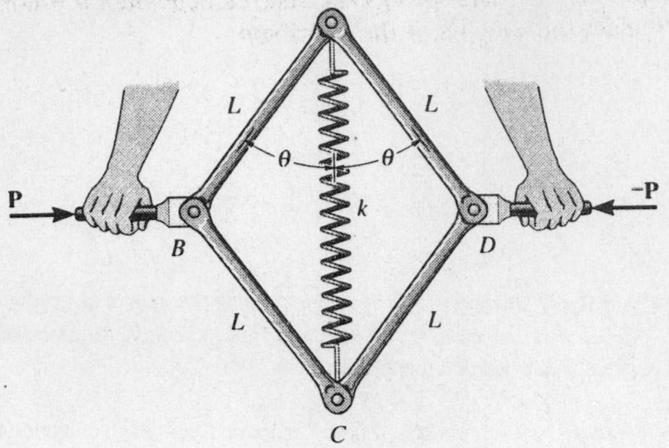

Free Body Diagram : The system has only one degree of freedom defined by the independent coordinate θ. When θ undergoes a positive displacement $\delta\theta$, the spring force F_{sp} and force **P** do work.

Virtual Displacements : The spring force F_{sp} and force **P** are located from the fixed point D and A using position coordinates y and x, respectively.

$$y = L\cos\theta \qquad \delta y = -L\sin\theta\,\delta\theta \qquad [1]$$
$$x = L\sin\theta \qquad \delta x = L\cos\theta\,\delta\theta \qquad [2]$$

Virtual - Work Equation : When points A, C, B and D undergo positive virtual displacement δy and δx, the spring force F_{sp} and force **P** do negative work.

$$\delta U = 0; \qquad -2F_{sp}\,\delta y - 2P\delta x = 0 \qquad [3]$$

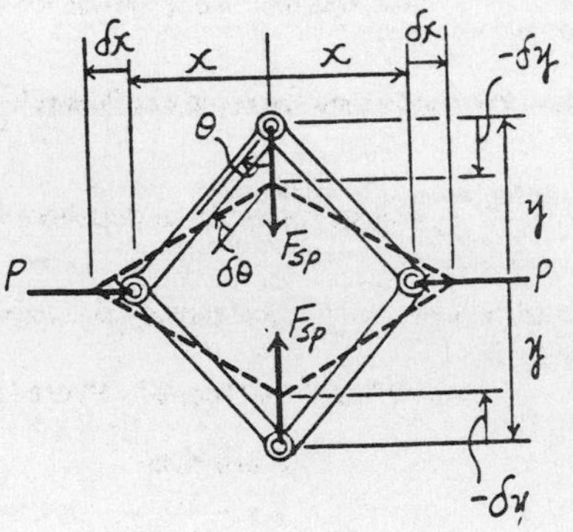

Substituting Eqs. [1] and [2] into [3] yields

$$\left(2F_{sp}\sin\theta - 2P\cos\theta\right)L\delta\theta = 0 \qquad [4]$$

From the geometry, the spring stretches $x = 2L\cos\theta - a$. Then, the spring force $F_{sp} = kx = k(2L\cos\theta - a) = 2kL\cos\theta - ka$. Substituting this value into Eq. [4] yields

$$(4kL\sin\theta\cos\theta - 2ka\sin\theta - 2P\cos\theta)\,L\delta\theta = 0$$

Since $L\delta\theta \neq 0$, then

$$4kL\sin\theta\cos\theta - 2ka\sin\theta - 2P\cos\theta = 0$$
$$P = k(2L\sin\theta - a\tan\theta)$$

In order to obtain maximum P, $\dfrac{dP}{d\theta} = 0$.

$$\frac{dP}{d\theta} = k\left(2L\cos\theta - a\sec^2\theta\right) = 0$$

$$\theta = \cos^{-1}\left(\frac{a}{2L}\right)^{\frac{1}{3}} \qquad \textbf{Ans}$$

***11-24.** Determine the weight W of the crate if the angle $\theta = 45^\circ$. The springs are unstretched when $\theta = 60^\circ$. Neglect the weights of the members.

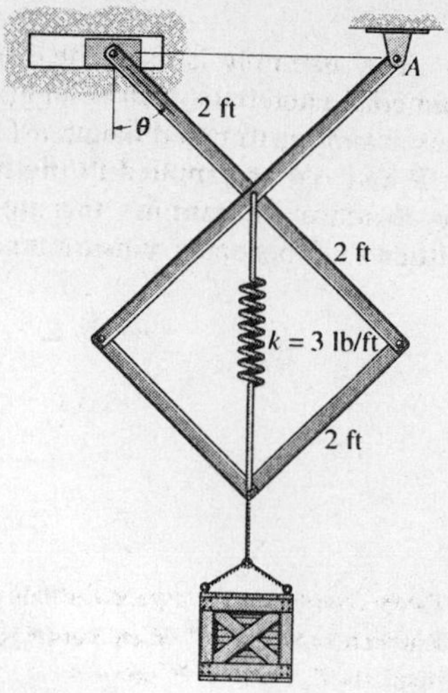

Potential Function : The datum is established at point A. Since the center of gravity of the crate is below the datum, its potential energy is negative. Here, $y = (4\sin\theta + 2\sin\theta) = 6\sin\theta$ ft and the spring stretches $x = 2(2\sin\theta - 2\sin 30^\circ) = (4\sin\theta - 2)$ ft.

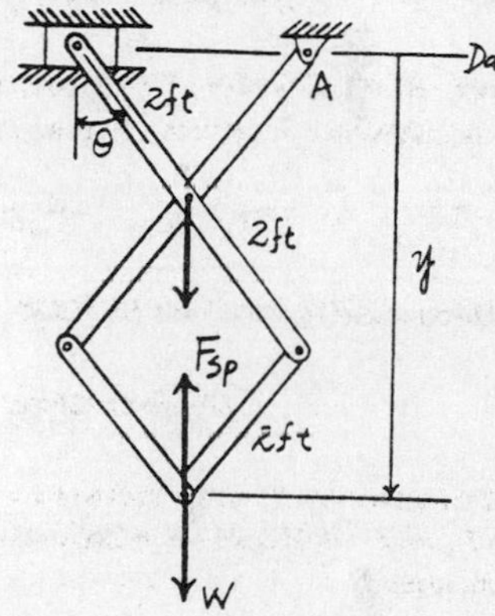

$$\begin{aligned} V &= V_e + V_g \\ &= \frac{1}{2}kx^2 - Wy \\ &= \frac{1}{2}(3)(4\sin\theta - 2)^2 - W(6\sin\theta) \\ &= 24\sin^2\theta - 24\sin\theta - 6W\sin\theta + 6 \end{aligned}$$

Equilibrium Position : The system is in equilibrium if $\frac{dV}{d\theta} = 0$.

$$\frac{dV}{d\theta} = 48\sin\theta\cos\theta + 24\cos\theta + 6W\cos\theta = 0 \qquad [1]$$

At equilibrium position, $\theta = 45^\circ$. Substituting this value into Eq. [1], we have

$$48\sin 45^\circ\cos 45^\circ + 24\cos 45^\circ - 6W\cos 45^\circ = 0$$

$$W = 1.66 \text{ lb} \qquad \textbf{Ans}$$

11-25. The loading arm is used to transfer oil from a ship to land. When the device is in use, the oil flows through the nozzle at C and exits at D as shown by the arrows. If each of the arms AB and BC has a total mass m and they are pin connected at A, B, and I, determine the mass of blocks J and F that will keep the system in balance for any angles θ and ϕ. J is attached to the extended portion of arm AB and has a center of gravity at G_1, whereas F has a center of gravity at G_2 and is attached to a link that is pin connected at A and E. Neglect the weight of links AEH, EI, and the extended portions IB of BC and KA of AB. Assume the weight of AB and BC acts through their centers.

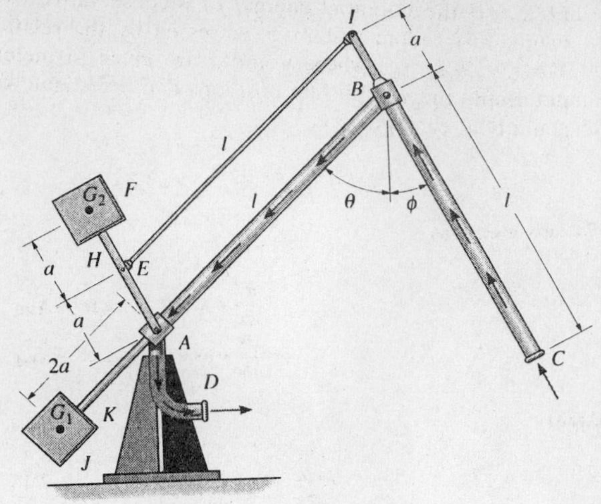

$y_1 = 2a\cos\phi;\quad y_3 = 2a\cos\theta$

$y_2 = \frac{l}{2}\cos\theta;\quad y_4 = l\cos\theta - \frac{l}{2}\cos\phi$

Displacement $\delta\theta$ only :

$\frac{\partial y_1}{\partial\theta} = 0;\quad \frac{\partial y_3}{\partial\theta} = -2a\sin\theta$

$\frac{\partial y_2}{\delta\theta} = -\frac{l}{2}\sin\theta;\quad \frac{\partial y_4}{\partial\theta} = -l\sin\theta$

$\delta U = 0;\quad W_J\,\delta y_3 - W_F\,\delta y_1 - W\,\delta y_2 - W\,\delta y_4 = 0$

$$W_J(-2a\sin\theta\,\delta\theta) - 0 - W\left(-\frac{l}{2}\sin\theta\,\delta\theta\right) - W(-l\sin\theta\,\delta\theta) = 0$$

$$\left[-W_J(2a) + W\left(\frac{3}{2}l\right)\right]\sin\theta\,\delta\theta = 0$$

$$W_J = W\left(\frac{3l}{4a}\right) = \frac{3mgl}{4a} \qquad \textbf{Ans}$$

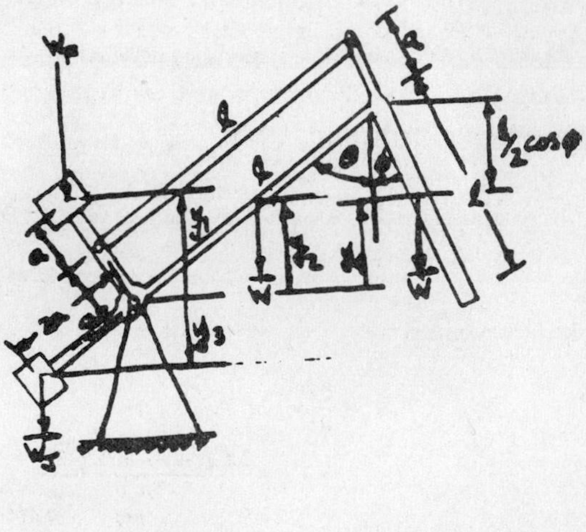

Displacement $\delta\phi$ (only) :

$\frac{\partial y_1}{\partial\phi} = -2a\sin\phi$

$\frac{\partial y_2}{\partial\phi} = \frac{\partial y_3}{\partial\phi} = 0$

$\frac{\partial y_4}{\partial\phi} = \frac{l}{2}\sin\phi$

$\delta U = 0;\quad W_J\,\delta y_3 - W_F\,\delta y_1 - W\,\delta y_2 - W\,\delta y_4 = 0$

$$0 - W_F(-2a\sin\phi\,\delta\phi) - 0 - W\left(\frac{l}{2}\right)\sin\phi\,\delta\phi = 0$$

$$\left[W_F(2a) - W\left(\frac{l}{2}\right)\right]\sin\phi\,\delta\phi = 0$$

$$W_F = W\left(\frac{l}{4a}\right) = \frac{mgl}{4a} \qquad \textbf{Ans}$$

11-26. If the potential energy for a conservative two-degree-of-freedom system is expressed by the relation $V = (3y^2 + 2x^2)$ J, where y and x are given in meters, determine the equilibrium positions and investigate the stability at each position.

$$V = 3y^2 + 2x^2$$

Equilibrium Position :

$$\frac{\partial V}{\partial x} = 4x = 0 \qquad x = 0 \qquad \textbf{Ans}$$

$$\frac{\partial V}{\partial y} = 6y = 0 \qquad y = 0 \qquad \textbf{Ans}$$

Stability :

$$\left.\frac{\partial^2 V}{\partial x^2}\right|_{(0,0)} = 4 \qquad \left.\frac{\partial^2 V}{\partial y^2}\right|_{(0,0)} = 6 \qquad \left.\frac{\partial^2 V}{\partial x \partial y}\right|_{(0,0)} = 0$$

$$\left.\left[\left(\frac{\partial^2 V}{\partial x \partial y}\right)^2 - \left(\frac{\partial^2 V}{\partial x^2}\right)\left(\frac{\partial^2 V}{\partial y^2}\right)\right]\right|_{(0,0)} = \left[0^2 - (4)(6)\right] = -24 < 0$$

$$\left.\left(\frac{\partial^2 V}{\partial x^2} + \frac{\partial^2 V}{\partial y^2}\right)\right|_{(0,0)} = (4+6) = 10 > 0$$

Stable at (0, 0) **Ans**

11-27. If the potential energy for a conservative one-of-freedom system is expressed by the relation $V = (4x^3 - x^2 - 3x + 10)$ ft·lb, where x is given in feet, determine the equilibrium positions and investigate the stability at each position.

$$V = 4x^3 - x^2 - 3x + 10$$

Equilibrium Position :

$$\frac{dV}{dx} = 12x^2 - 2x - 3 = 0$$

$$x = \frac{2 \pm \sqrt{(-2)^2 - 4(12)(-3)}}{24}$$

$x = 0.590$ ft and -0.424 ft **Ans**

Stability :

$$\frac{d^2V}{dx^2} = 24x - 2$$

At $x = 0.590$ ft $\quad \frac{d^2V}{dx^2} = 24(0.590) - 2 = 12.2 > 0$ **stable** **Ans**

At $x = -0.424$ ft $\quad \frac{d^2V}{dx^2} = 24(-0.424) - 2 = -12.2 < 0$ **unstable** **Ans**

*11-28. If the potential energy for a conservative one-degree-of-freedom system is expressed by the relation $V = (24 \sin\theta + 10\cos 2\theta)$ ft·lb, $0° \le \theta \le 180°$, determine the equilibrium positions and investigate the stability at each position.

$$V = 24\sin\theta + 10\cos 2\theta$$

Equilibrium Position :

$$\frac{dV}{d\theta} = 24\cos\theta - 20\sin 2\theta = 0$$

$$24\cos\theta - 40\sin\theta\cos\theta = 0$$

$$\cos\theta(24 - 40\sin\theta) = 0$$

$\cos\theta = 0 \qquad \theta = 90°$ **Ans**

$24 - 40\sin\theta = 0 \qquad \theta = 36.9°$ **Ans**

Stability :

$$\frac{d^2V}{d\theta^2} = -40\cos 2\theta - 24\sin\theta$$

At $\theta = 90°$ $\quad \frac{d^2V}{d\theta^2} = -40\cos 180° - 24\sin 90° = 16 > 0$ **stable** **Ans**

At $\theta = 36.9°$ $\quad \frac{d^2V}{d\theta^2} = -40\cos 73.7° - 24\sin 36.9° = -25.6 < 0$ **unstable** **Ans**

11-29. If the potential energy for a conservative two-degree-of-freedom system is expressed by the relation $V = (6y^2 + 2x^2)$ J, where x and y are given in meters, determine the equilibrium position and investigate the stability at this position.

$$V = 6y^2 + 2x^2$$

Equilibrium Position :

$\frac{\partial V}{\partial x} = 4x = 0 \qquad x = 0$ **Ans**

$\frac{\partial V}{\partial y} = 12y = 0 \qquad y = 0$ **Ans**

Stability :

$$\left.\frac{\partial^2 V}{\partial x^2}\right|_{(0,0)} = 4 \qquad \left.\frac{\partial^2 V}{\partial y^2}\right|_{(0,0)} = 12 \qquad \left.\frac{\partial^2 V}{\partial x \partial y}\right|_{(0,0)} = 0$$

$$\left[\left(\frac{\partial^2 V}{\partial x \partial y}\right)^2 - \left(\frac{\partial^2 V}{\partial x^2}\right)\left(\frac{\partial^2 V}{\partial y^2}\right)\right] = \left[0^2 - (4)(12)\right] = -48 < 0$$

$$\left(\frac{\partial^2 V}{\partial x^2} + \frac{\partial^2 V}{\partial y^2}\right) = (4 + 12) = 16 > 0$$

Stable at (0, 0) **Ans**

11-30. The spring of the scale has an unstretched length of a. Determine the angle θ for equilibrium when a weight W is supported on the platform. Neglect the weight of the members. What value W would be required to keep the scale in neutral equilibrium when $\theta = 0°$?

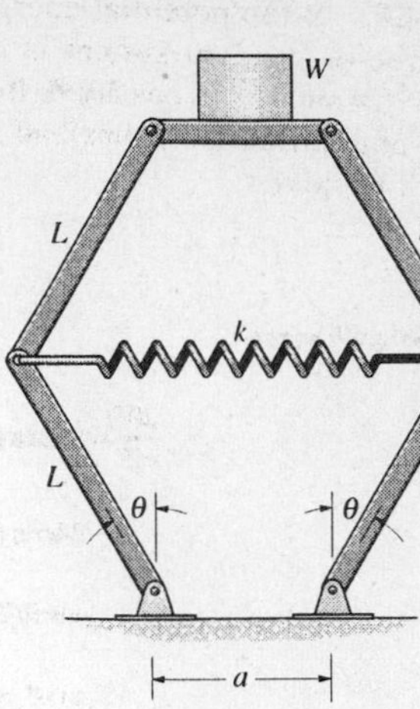

Potential Function : **The datum is established at point A. Since the weight W is above the datum, its potential energy is positive. From the geometry, the spring stretches $x = 2L\sin\theta$ and $y = 2L\cos\theta$.**

$$V = V_e + V_g$$
$$= \frac{1}{2}kx^2 + Wy$$
$$= \frac{1}{2}(k)(2L\sin\theta)^2 + W(2L\cos\theta)$$
$$= 2kL^2\sin^2\theta + 2WL\cos\theta$$

Equilibrium Position : The system is in equilibrium if $\frac{dV}{d\theta} = 0.$

$$\frac{dV}{d\theta} = 4kL^2\sin\theta\cos\theta - 2WL\sin\theta = 0$$
$$\frac{dV}{d\theta} = 2kL^2\sin 2\theta - 2WL\sin\theta = 0$$

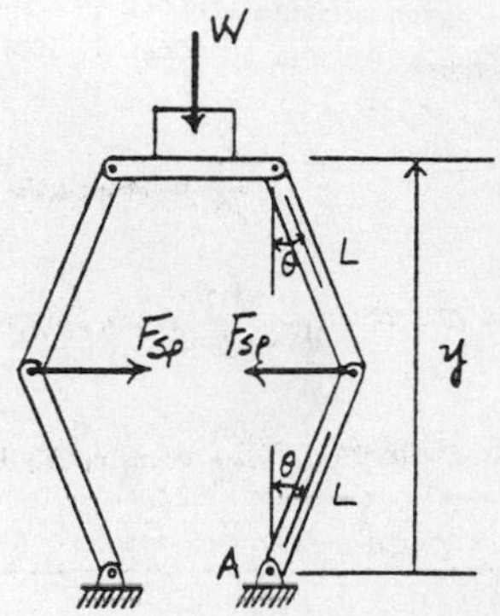

Solving,

$$\theta = 0° \quad \text{or} \quad \theta = \cos^{-1}\left(\frac{W}{2KL}\right)$$ **Ans**

Stability : To have neutral equilibrium at $\theta = 0°$, $\left.\frac{d^2V}{d\theta^2}\right|_{\theta=0°} = 0.$

$$\frac{d^2V}{d\theta^2} = 4kL^2\cos 2\theta - 2WL\cos\theta$$
$$\left.\frac{d^2V}{d\theta^2}\right|_{\theta=0°} = 4kL^2\cos 0° - 2WL\cos 0° = 0$$

$$W = 2kL$$ **Ans**

11-31. Determine the equilibrium position s for the 5-lb block and investigate the stability at this position. The spring is unstretched when $s = 2$ in. and the inclined plane is smooth.

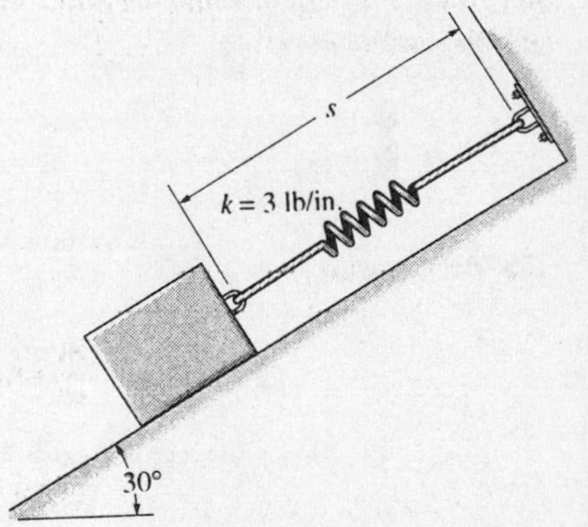

Datum at unstreched position of the spring.

$$V = V_e + V_g$$

$$= \frac{1}{2}(3)(s-2)^2 - 5y$$

$$y = (s-2)\sin 30°$$

$$V = \frac{1}{2}(3)(s-2)^2 - 5(s-2)(0.5)$$

$$= 1.5(s-2)^2 - 2.5(s-2)$$

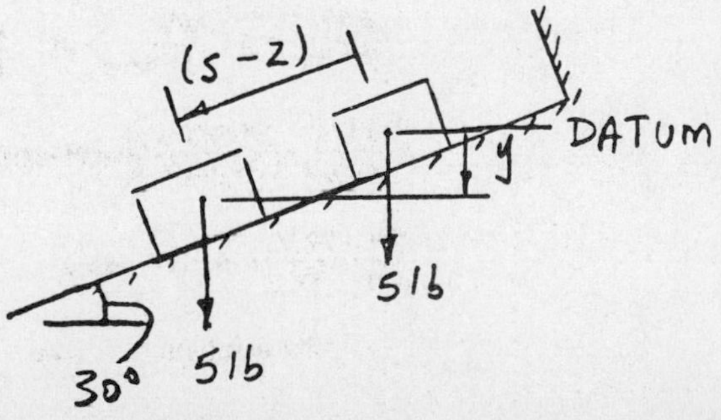

Equilibrium :

$$\frac{dV}{ds} = 3(s-2) - 2.5 = 0$$

$s = 2.83$ in. **Ans**

Stability :

$$\frac{d^2V}{ds^2} = 3 > 0$$ **stable** **Ans**

*11-32. The two bars each have a weight of 8 lb. Determine the angle θ for the equilibrium and investigate the stability at the equilibrium position. The spring has an unstretched length of 1 ft.

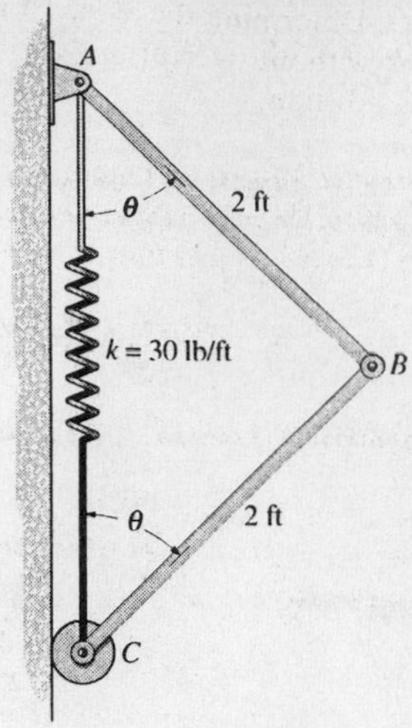

Potential Function : The datum is established at point A. Since the center of gravity of the bars are below the datum, their potential energy is negative. Here, $y_1 = 1\cos\theta$ ft, $y_2 = 2\cos\theta + 1\cos\theta = 3\cos\theta$ ft and the spring stretches $x = 2(2\cos\theta) - 1 = (4\cos\theta - 1)$ ft.

$$V = V_e + V_g$$
$$= \frac{1}{2}kx^2 - \Sigma Wy$$
$$= \frac{1}{2}(30)(4\cos\theta - 1)^2 - 8(1\cos\theta) - 8(3\cos\theta)$$
$$= 240\cos^2\theta - 152\cos\theta + 15$$

Equilibrium Position : The system is in equilibrium if $\frac{dV}{d\theta} = 0$.

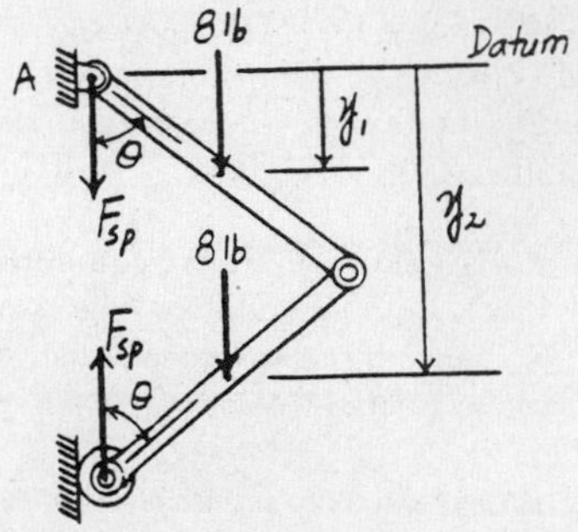

$$\frac{dV}{d\theta} = -480\sin\theta\cos\theta + 152\sin\theta = 0$$
$$\frac{dV}{d\theta} = -240\sin 2\theta + 152\sin\theta = 0$$

Solving,

$$\theta = 0^\circ \quad \text{or} \quad \theta = 71.54^\circ = 71.5^\circ \qquad \textbf{Ans}$$

Stability :

$$\frac{d^2V}{d\theta^2} = -480\cos 2\theta + 152\cos\theta$$

$$\left.\frac{d^2V}{d\theta^2}\right|_{\theta=0^\circ} = -480\cos 0^\circ + 152\cos 0^\circ = -328 < 0$$

Thus, the system is in **unstable equilibrium** at $\theta = 0^\circ$ **Ans**

$$\left.\frac{d^2V}{d\theta^2}\right|_{\theta=71.54^\circ} = -480\cos 143^\circ + 152\cos 71.54^\circ = 431.87 > 0$$

Thus, the system is in **stable equilibrium** at $\theta = 71.54^\circ$ **Ans**

11-33. The truck has a mass of 20 Mg and a mass center at G. Determine the steepest grade θ along which it can park without overturning and investigate the stability in this position.

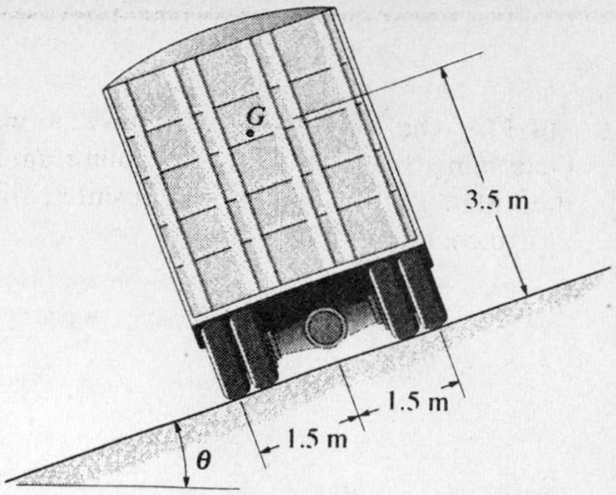

Potential Function : The datum is established at point A. Since the center of gravity for the truck is above the datum, its potential energy is positive. Here, $y = (1.5\sin\theta + 3.5\cos\theta)$ m.

$$V = V_g = Wy = W(1.5\sin\theta + 3.5\cos\theta)$$

Equilibrium Position : The system is in equilibrium if $\dfrac{dV}{d\theta} = 0$

$$\frac{dV}{d\theta} = W(1.5\cos\theta - 3.5\sin\theta) = 0$$

Since $W \neq 0$,

$$1.5\cos\theta - 3.5\sin\theta = 0$$

$$\theta = 23.20° = 23.2° \qquad \textbf{Ans}$$

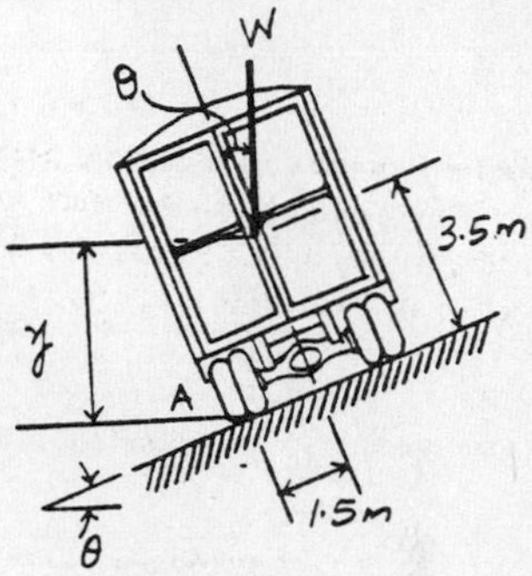

Stability :

$$\frac{d^2V}{d\theta^2} = W(-1.5\sin\theta - 3.5\cos\theta)$$

$$\left.\frac{d^2V}{d\theta^2}\right|_{\theta=23.20°} = W(-1.5\sin 23.20° - 3.5\cos 23.20°) = -3.81W < 0$$

Thus, the truck is in **unstable equilibrium** at $\theta = 23.2°$ **Ans**

11-34. The uniform rod OA weighs 20 lb, and when the rod is in the vertical position, the spring is unstretched. Determine the position θ for equilibrium. Investigate the stability at the equilibrium position.

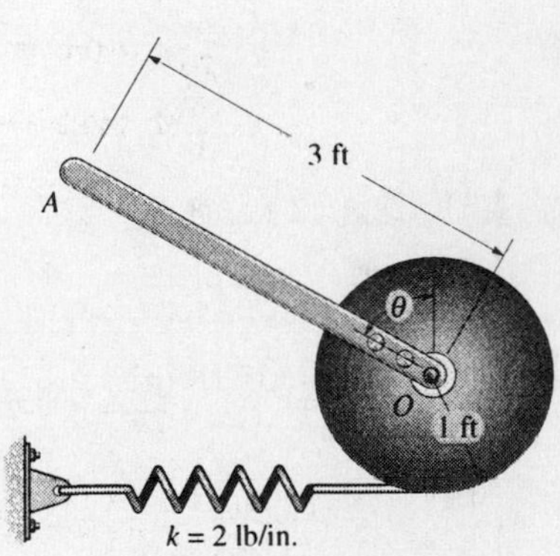

Potential Function : The spring stretches $s = 12(\theta)$ in., where θ is in radians.

$$V = V_e + V_g = \frac{1}{2}(2)(12\theta)^2 + 20\left[1.5(12)\cos\theta\right]$$

$$= 144\theta^2 + 360\cos\theta$$

Equilibrium Position : $\dfrac{dV}{d\theta} = 0$

$$\frac{dV}{d\theta} = 288\theta - 360\sin\theta = 0$$

$$\theta = 1.1311 \text{ rad} = 64.8° \qquad \textbf{Ans}$$

$$\theta = 0° \qquad \textbf{Ans}$$

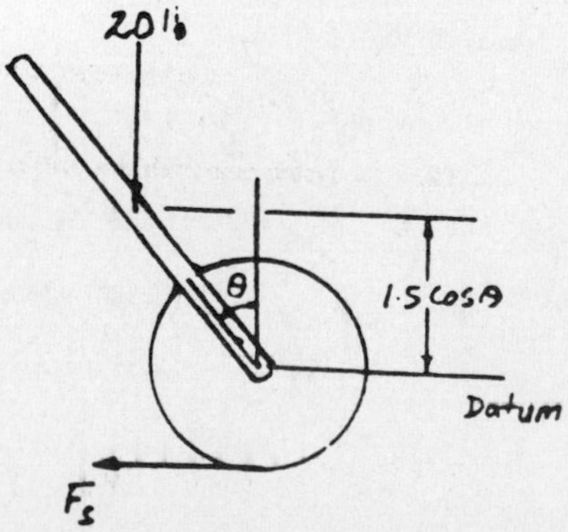

Stability :

$$\frac{d^2V}{d\theta^2} = 288 - 360\cos\theta$$

At $\theta = 64.8°$, $\dfrac{d^2V}{d\theta^2} = 288 - 360\cos 64.8° = 135 > 0$ **stable** **Ans**

At $\theta = 0°$, $\dfrac{d^2V}{d\theta^2} = 288 - 360\cos 0° = -72 < 0$ **unstable** **Ans**

11-35. The cylinder is made of two materials such that it has a mass of m and a center of gravity at point G. Show that when G lies above the centroid C of the cylinder, the equilibrium is unstable.

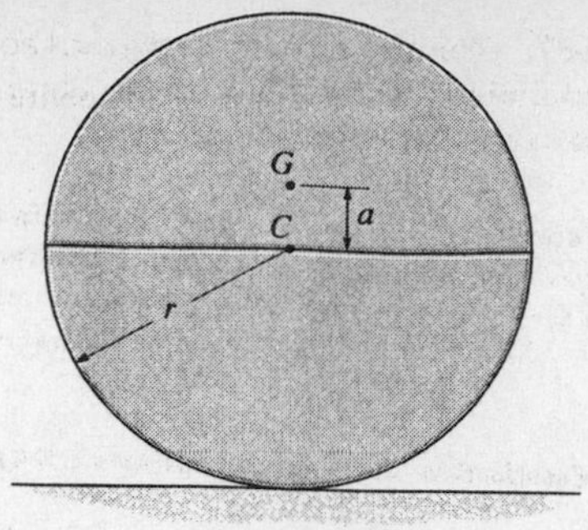

Potential Function : The datum is established at point A. Since the center of gravity of the cylinder is above the datum, its potential energy is positive. Here, $y = r + d\cos\theta$.

$$V = V_g = Wy = mg(r + d\cos\theta)$$

Equilibrium Position : The system is in equilibrium if $\dfrac{dV}{d\theta} = 0$.

$$\frac{dV}{d\theta} = -mgd\sin\theta = 0$$

$$\sin\theta = 0 \qquad \theta = 0°.$$

Stability :

$$\frac{d^2V}{d\theta^2} = -mgd\cos\theta$$

$$\left.\frac{d^2V}{d\theta^2}\right|_{\theta=0°} = -mgd\cos 0° = -mgd < 0$$

Thus, the cylinder is in **unstable equilibrium** at $\theta = 0°$ (*Q. E. D.*)

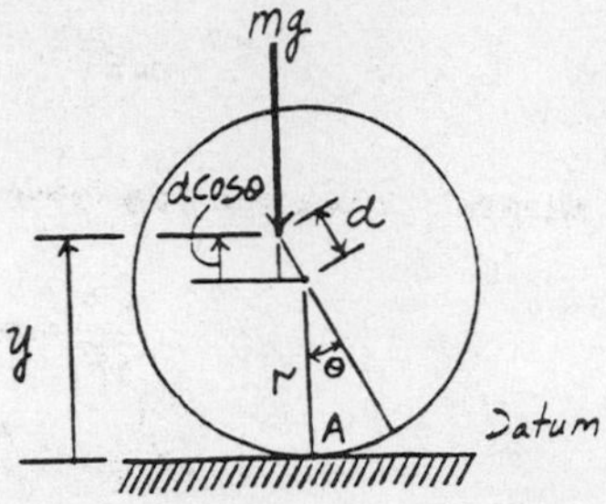

***11-36.** Determine the angle θ for equilibrium of the 10-lb weight. The spring is unstretched when $\theta = 0°$. Investigate the stability at the equilibrium position. Neglect the weight of the link.

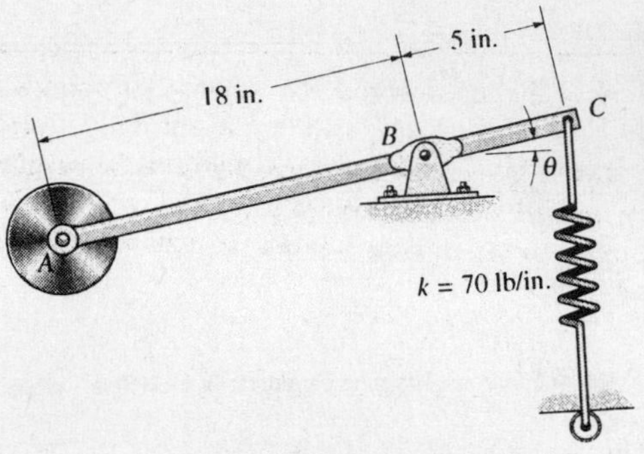

The spring stretches $s = 5\sin\theta$

$$V = V_e + V_g = \frac{1}{2}(70)(5\sin\theta)^2 - 10(18\sin\theta)$$

$$= 875\sin^2\theta - 180\sin\theta$$

$$\frac{dV}{d\theta} = 0$$

$$\frac{dV}{d\theta} = 1750\sin\theta\cos\theta - 180\cos\theta = 0$$

$\cos\theta(1750\sin\theta - 180) = 0$

$\cos\theta = 0 \qquad \theta = 90°$ **Ans**

$1750\sin\theta - 180 = 0 \qquad \theta = 5.90°$ **Ans**

$$\frac{d^2V}{d\theta^2} = 1750\cos 2\theta + 180\sin\theta$$

At $\theta = 90°$, $\dfrac{d^2V}{d\theta^2} = 1750\cos 180° + 180\sin 90° = -1570 < 0$ **(unstable)**

At $\theta = 5.90°$, $\dfrac{d^2V}{d\theta^2} = 1750\cos 11.8° + 180\sin 5.90° = 1732 > 0$ **(stable)**

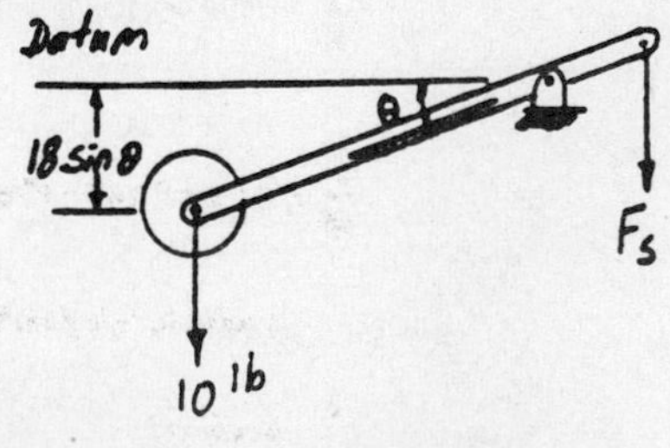

11-37. The cap has a hemispherical bottom and a mass m. Determine the position h of the center of mass G so that the cup is in neutral equilibrium.

Potential Function : The datum is established at point A. Since the center of gravity of the cup is above the datum, its potential energy is positive. Here, $y = r - h\cos\theta$.

$$V = V_g = Wy = mg(r - h\cos\theta)$$

Equilibrium Position : The system is in equilibrium if $\frac{dV}{d\theta} = 0$.

$$\frac{dV}{d\theta} = mgh\sin\theta = 0$$

$$\sin\theta = 0 \qquad \theta = 0°.$$

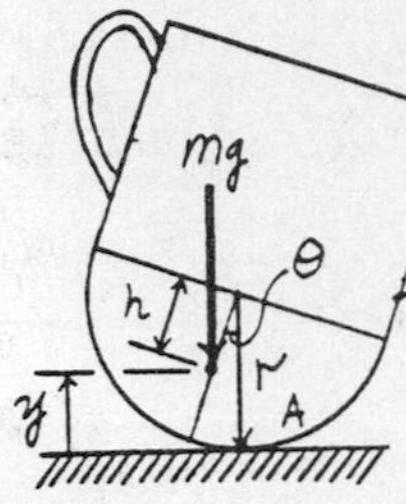

Stability : To have neutral equilibrium at $\theta = 0°$, $\left.\frac{d^2V}{d\theta^2}\right|_{\theta=0°} = 0$.

$$\frac{d^2V}{d\theta^2} = mgh\cos\theta$$

$$\left.\frac{d^2V}{d\theta^2}\right|_{\theta=0°} = mgh\cos 0° = 0$$

$$h = 0 \qquad \textbf{Ans}$$

Note : Stable Equilibrium occurs if $h > 0\left(\left.\frac{d^2V}{d\theta^2}\right|_{\theta=0°} = mgh\cos 0° > 0\right)$.

11-38. If each of the three links of the mechanism has a weight W, determine the angle θ for equilibrium. The spring, which always remains vertical, is unstretched when $\theta = 0°$.

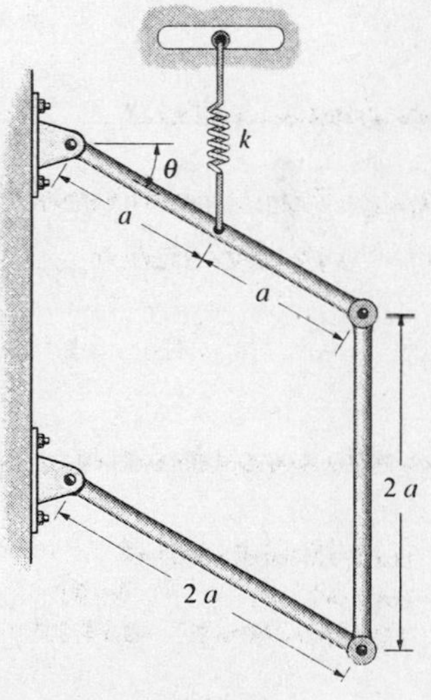

The spring stretches $s = a\sin\theta$

$$V = V_e + V_g = \frac{1}{2}k(a\sin\theta)^2 - W(a\sin\theta) - W(2a\sin\theta + a) - W(a\sin\theta + 2a)$$

$$= \frac{1}{2}ka^2\sin^2\theta - 4Wa\sin\theta - 3Wa$$

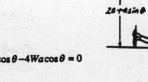

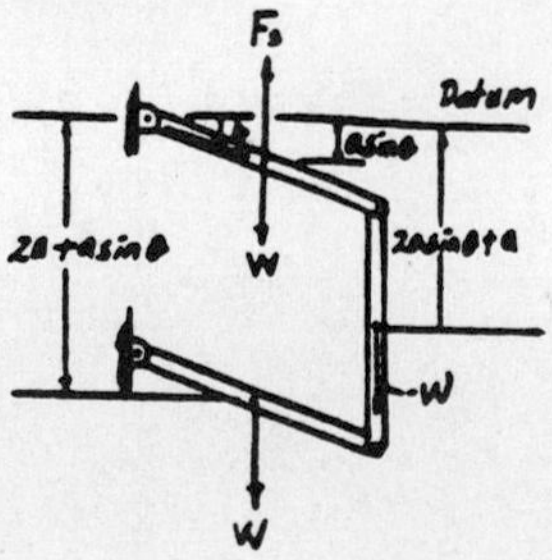

$$\frac{dV}{d\theta} = 0$$

$$\frac{dV}{d\theta} = ka^2\sin\theta\cos\theta - 4Wa\cos\theta = 0$$

$$\cos\theta\,(ka^2\sin\theta - 4Wa) = 0$$

$$\cos\theta = 0 \qquad \theta = 90° \qquad \textbf{Ans}$$

$$\sin\theta = \frac{4W}{ka} \qquad \theta = \sin^{-1}\left(\frac{4W}{ka}\right) \qquad \textbf{Ans}$$

11-39. If the uniform rod OA has a mass of 12 kg, determine the mass m that will hold the rod in equilibrium when $\theta = 30^\circ$. Point C is coincident with B when OA is horizontal. Neglect the size of the pulley at B.

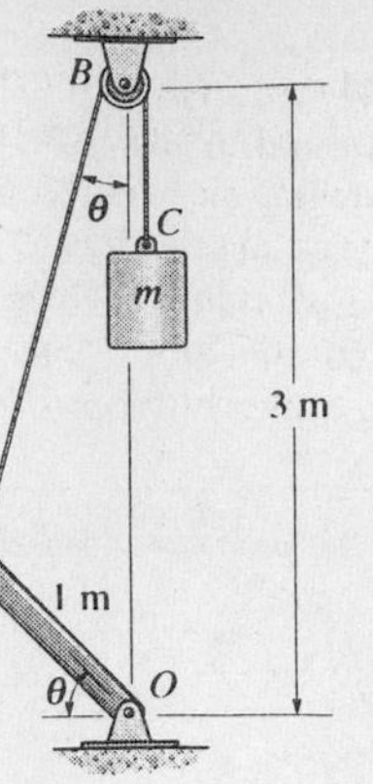

Geometry **:** Using the law of cosines,

$$l_{A'B} = \sqrt{1^2+3^2-2(1)(3)\cos(90^\circ-\theta)} = \sqrt{10-6\sin\theta}$$

$$l_{AB} = \sqrt{1^2+3^2} = \sqrt{10}\text{ m}$$

$$l = l_{AB} - l_{A'B} = \sqrt{10}-\sqrt{10-6\sin\theta}$$

Potential Function **:** The datum is established at point O. Since the center of gravity of the rod and the block are above the datum, their potential energy is positive.

Here, $y_1 = 3 - l = \left[3-\left(\sqrt{10}-\sqrt{10-6\sin\theta}\right)\right]$ m and $y_2 = 0.5\sin\theta$ m.

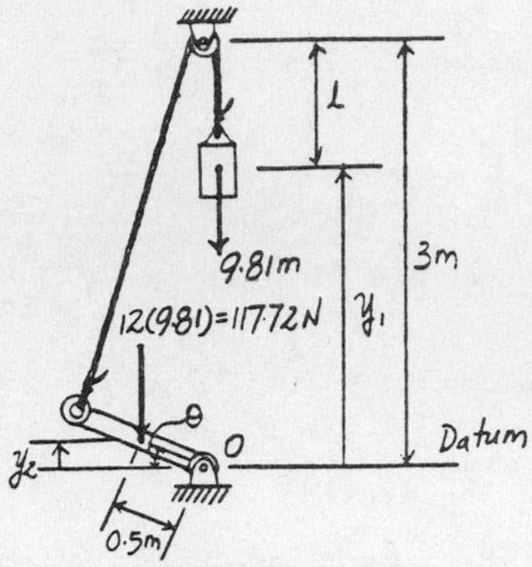

$$V = V_g = W_1y_1 + W_2y_2$$
$$= 9.81m\left[3-\left(\sqrt{10}-\sqrt{10-6\sin\theta}\right)\right]+117.72(0.5\sin\theta)$$
$$= 29.43m - 9.81m\left(\sqrt{10}-\sqrt{10-6\sin\theta}\right)+58.86\sin\theta$$

Equilibrium Position **:** The system is in equilibrium if $\left.\dfrac{dV}{d\theta}\right|_{\theta=30^\circ} = 0.$

$$\frac{dV}{d\theta} = -9.81m\left[-\frac{1}{2}(10-6\sin\theta)^{-\frac{1}{2}}(-6\cos\theta)\right]+58.86\cos\theta$$
$$= -\frac{29.43m\cos\theta}{\sqrt{10-6\sin\theta}}+58.86\cos\theta$$

At $\theta = 30^\circ$,

$$\left.\frac{dV}{d\theta}\right|_{\theta=30^\circ} = -\frac{29.43m\cos 30^\circ}{\sqrt{10-6\sin 30^\circ}}+58.86\cos 30^\circ = 0$$

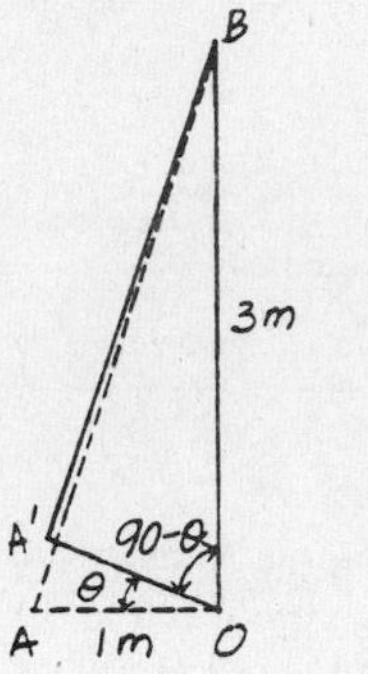

$$m = 5.29\text{ kg} \qquad \textbf{Ans}$$

***11-40.** The bent rod has a weight of 5 lb/ft. A pivot of negligible size is attached at its center A and the rod is balanced as shown. Determine the length L of its vertical segments so that it remains in neutral equilibrium. Neglect the thickness of the rod.

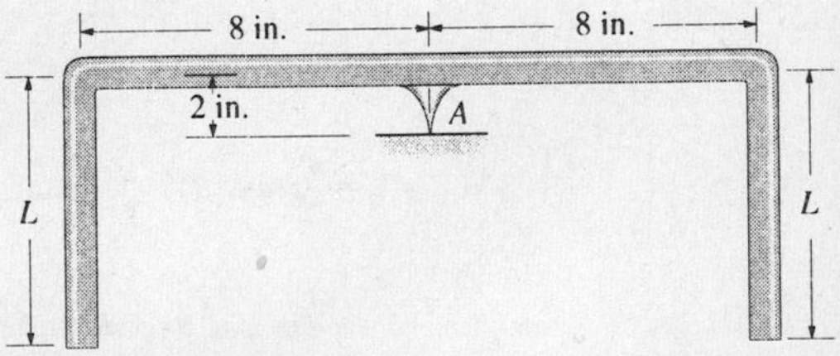

To remain in neutral equilibrium, the center of gravity must be located at A.

$$\bar{y} = \frac{\Sigma \tilde{y}W}{\Sigma W}$$

$$0 = \frac{2\left(\frac{16}{12}\right)(5)-\left(\frac{L}{2}-2\right)\left(\frac{2L}{12}\right)(5)}{\left(\frac{16}{12}\right)(5)+\left(\frac{2L}{12}\right)(5)}$$

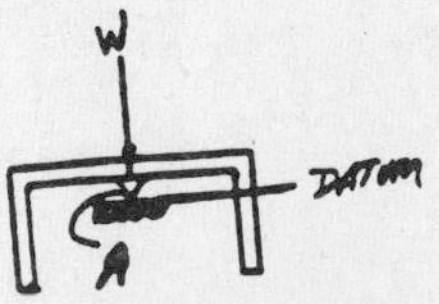

$$0 = 5L^2-20L-160$$

$$L = \frac{20\pm\sqrt{(-20)^2-4(5)(-160)}}{10}$$

Take the positive root

$$L = 8\text{ in.} \qquad \textbf{Ans}$$

11-41. The uniform link AB has a mass of 3 kg and is pin connected at both of its ends. The rod BD, having negligible weight, passes through a swivel block at C. If the spring has a stiffness of $k = 100$ N/m and is unstretched when $\theta = 0°$, determine the angle θ for equilibrium and investigate the stability at the equilibrium position. Neglect the size of the swivel block.

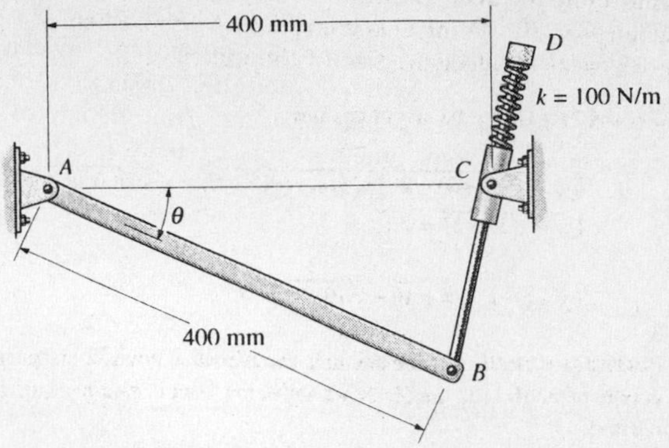

$$s = \sqrt{(0.4)^2 + (0.4)^2 - 2(0.4)^2\cos\theta}$$

$$= (0.4)\sqrt{2(1-\cos\theta)}$$

$$V = V_g + V_e$$

$$= -(0.2)(\sin\theta)3(9.81) + \frac{1}{2}(100)\left[(0.4)^2(2)(1-\cos\theta)\right]$$

$$\frac{dV}{d\theta} = -(5.886)\cos\theta + 16(\sin\theta) = 0 \quad (1)$$

$\theta = 20.2°$ **Ans**

$$\frac{d^2V}{d\theta^2} = 5.886\sin\theta + (16)\cos\theta = 17.0 > 0$$ **stable** **Ans**

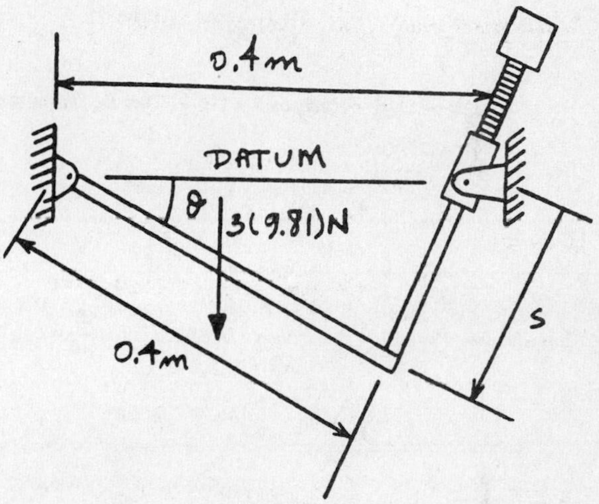

11-42. A homogeneous block rests on top of the cylindrical surface. Derive the relationship between the radius of the cylinder, r, and the dimension of the block, b, for stable equilibrium. *Hint*: Establish the potential energy function for a small angle θ, i.e., approximate $\sin\theta \approx \sigma$, and $\cos\theta \approx 1 - \theta^2/2$.

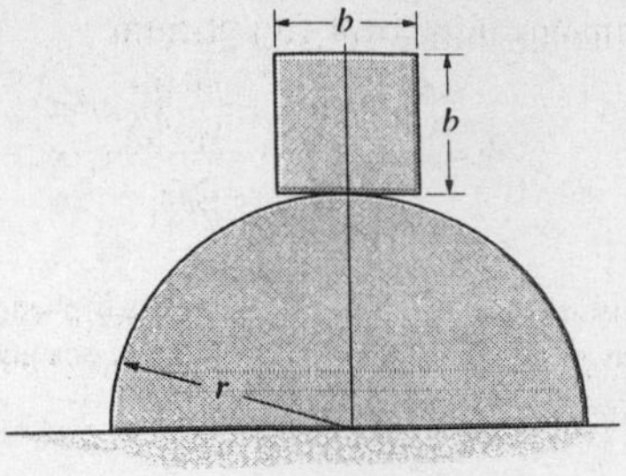

Potential Function : The datum is established at point O. Since the center of gravity for the block is above the datum, its potential energy is positive. Here, $y = \left(r + \frac{b}{2}\right)\cos\theta + r\theta\sin\theta$.

$$V = W_y = W\left[\left(r + \frac{b}{2}\right)\cos\theta + r\theta\sin\theta\right] \qquad [1]$$

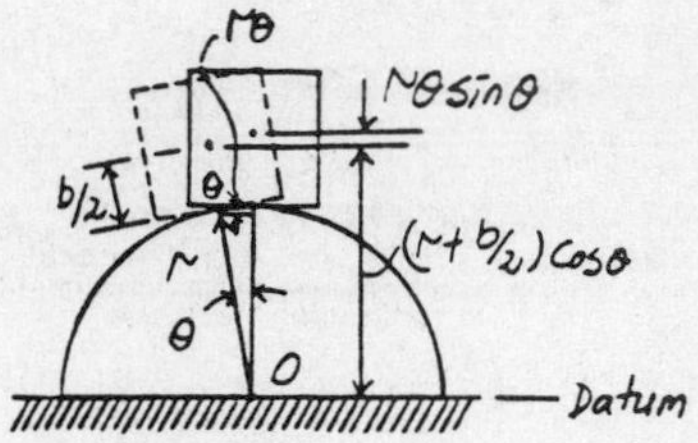

For small angle θ, $\sin\theta = \theta$ and $\cos\theta = 1 - \frac{\theta^2}{2}$. Then Eq. [1] becomes

$$V = W\left[\left(r + \frac{b}{2}\right)\left(1 - \frac{\theta^2}{2}\right) + r\theta^2\right]$$

$$= W\left(\frac{r\theta^2}{2} - \frac{b\theta^2}{4} + r + \frac{b}{2}\right)$$

Equilibrium Position : The system is in equilibrium if $\frac{dV}{d\theta} = 0$

$$\frac{dV}{d\theta} = W\left(r - \frac{b}{2}\right)\theta = 0 \qquad \theta = 0°$$

Stability : To have stable equilibrium, $\left.\frac{d^2V}{d\theta^2}\right|_{\theta=0°} > 0.$

$$\left.\frac{d^2V}{d\theta^2}\right|_{\theta=0°} = W\left(r - \frac{b}{2}\right) > 0$$

$$\left(r - \frac{b}{2}\right) > 0$$

$$b < 2r \qquad \textbf{Ans}$$

11-43. The homogeneous cone has a conical cavity cut into it as shown. Determine the depth of d of the cavity in terms of h so that the cone balances on the pivot and remains in neutral equilibrium.

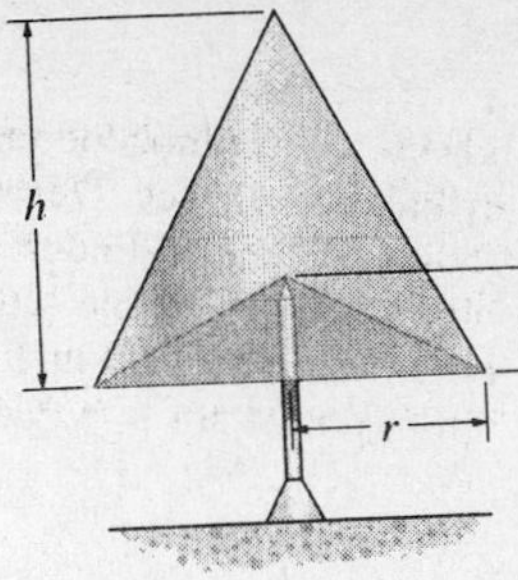

$$\bar{y} = \frac{\left(\frac{h}{4}\right)\left(\frac{1}{3}\pi r^2 h\right) - \left(\frac{d}{4}\right)\left(\frac{1}{3}\pi r^2 d\right)}{\frac{1}{3}\pi r^2 h - \frac{1}{3}\pi r^2 d} = \frac{h^2 - d^2}{4(h-d)} = \frac{1}{4}(h+d) \qquad [1]$$

Potential Function : The datum is established at point A. Since the center of gravity of the cone is above the datum, its potential energy is positive. Here,

$y = (\bar{y} - d)\cos\theta = \left[\frac{1}{4}(h+d) - d\right]\cos\theta = \frac{1}{4}(h - 3d)\cos\theta.$

$$V = W\left[\frac{1}{4}(h-3d)\cos\theta\right]\cos\theta = \frac{W(h-3d)}{4}\cos\theta$$

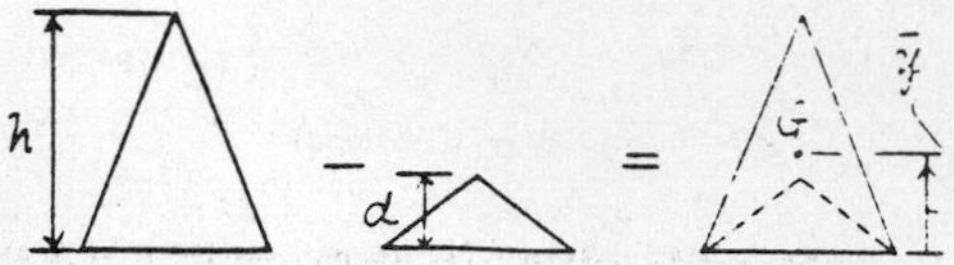

Equilibrium Position : The system is in equilibrium if $\frac{dV}{d\theta} = 0$

$$\frac{dV}{d\theta} = -\frac{W(h-3d)}{4}\sin\theta = 0$$

$$\theta = 0 \qquad \theta = 0^\circ$$

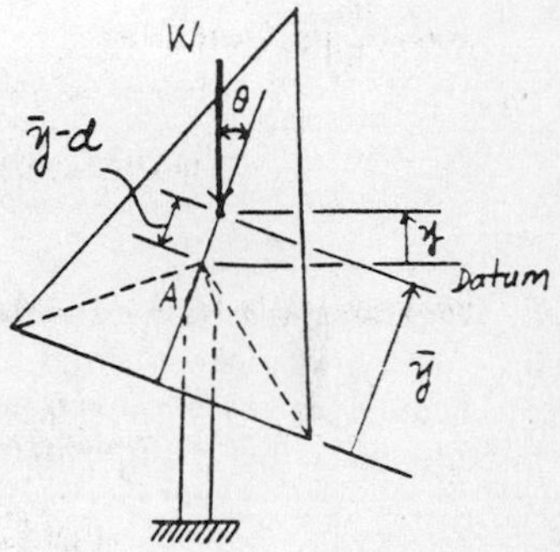

Stability : To have neutral equilibrium at $\theta = 0^\circ$, $\left.\frac{d^2V}{d\theta^2}\right|_{\theta=0^\circ} = 0.$

$$\frac{d^2V}{d\theta^2} = -\frac{W(h-3d)}{4}\cos\theta$$

$$\left.\frac{d^2V}{d\theta^2}\right|_{\theta=0^\circ} = -\frac{W(h-3d)}{4}\cos 0^\circ = 0$$

$$-\frac{W(h-3d)}{4} = 0$$

$$d = \frac{h}{3} \qquad \textbf{Ans}$$

Note : By substituting $d = \frac{h}{3}$ into Eq.[1], one realizes that the fulcrum must be at the center of gravity for neutral equilibrium.

***11-44.** The assembly shown consists of a semicylinder and a rectangular block. If the block weighs 8 lb and the semicylinder weighs 2 lb, investigate the stability when the assembly is resting in the equilibrium position. Set $h = 4$ in.

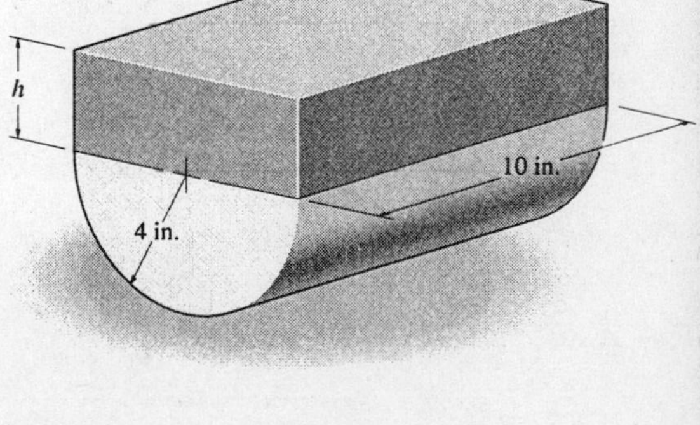

$d = \frac{4(4)}{3\pi} = 1.698$ in.

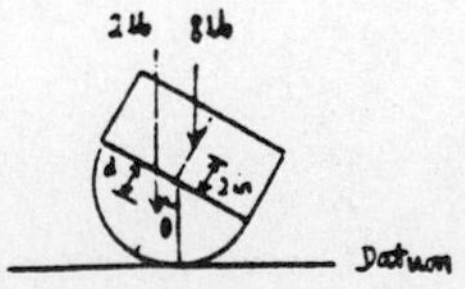

$V = V_g = 2(4 - 1.698\cos\theta) + 8(4 + 2\cos\theta)$

$\frac{dV}{d\theta} = 3.395\sin\theta - 16\sin\theta = 0$

$\sin\theta = 0$

$\theta = 0^\circ$ (equilibrium position)

$\frac{d^2V}{d\theta^2} = 3.395\cos\theta - 16\cos\theta$

At $\theta = 0^\circ$, $\frac{d^2V}{d\theta^2} = -12.6 < 0$ Unstable **Ans**

11-45. The 2-lb semicylinder supports the block which has a specific weight of $\gamma = 80\ \text{lb/ft}^3$. Determine the height h of the block which will produce neutral equilibrium in the position shown.

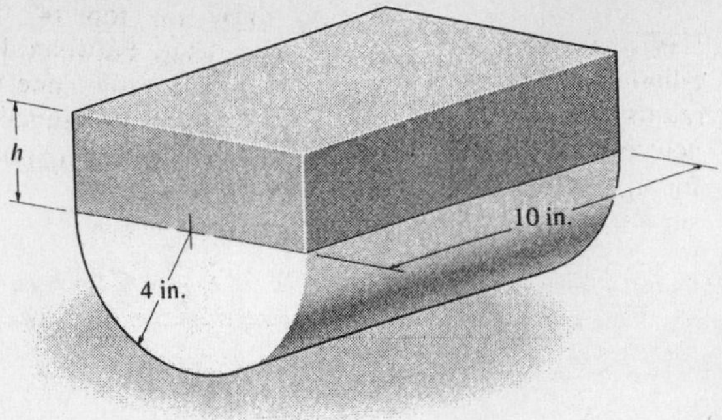

$$d = \frac{4(4)}{3\pi} = 1.698 \text{ in.}$$

$$V = V_g = 2(4 - 1.698\cos\theta) + \left[80\left(\frac{1}{12^3}\right)h(8)(10)\right]\left(4 + \frac{h}{2}\cos\theta\right)$$

$$\frac{dV}{d\theta} = 3.395\sin\theta - 1.852\,h^2\sin\theta = 0$$

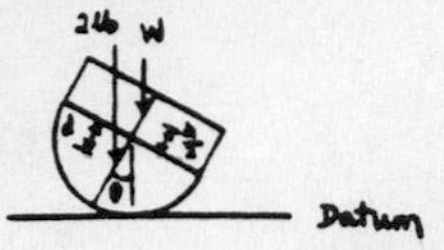

$$\sin\theta = 0$$

$$\theta = 0^\circ \quad \text{(equilibrium position)}$$

$$\frac{d^2V}{d\theta^2} = 3.395\cos\theta - 1.852\,h^2\cos\theta = 0$$

$$h = \sqrt{\frac{3.395}{1.852}} = 1.35 \text{ in.} \qquad \textbf{Ans}$$

11-46. The assembly shown consists of a semicircular cylinder and a triangular prism. If the prism weighs 8 lb and the cylinder weighs 2 lb, investigate the stability when the assembly is resting in the equilibrium position.

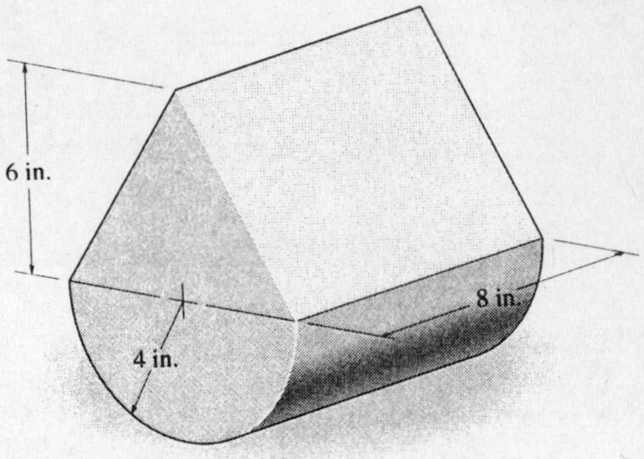

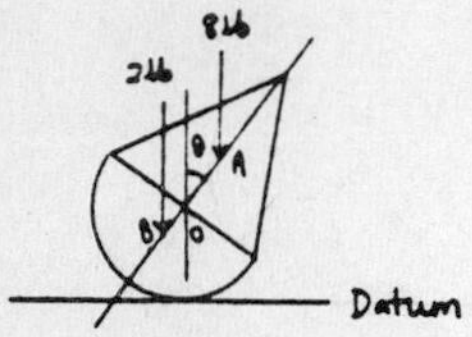

$$OB = \frac{4(4)}{3\pi} = 1.70 \text{ in.}$$

$$OA = \frac{1}{3}(6) = 2 \text{ in.}$$

$$V = V_g = 8(4 + 2\cos\theta) + 2(4 - 1.70\cos\theta)$$

$$V = 40 + 12.6\cos\theta$$

$$\frac{dV}{d\theta} = -12.6\sin\theta = 0$$

$$\theta = 0^\circ \quad \textbf{Ans} \quad \text{(for equilibrium)}$$

$$\frac{d^2V}{d\theta^2} = -12.6\cos\theta$$

At $\theta = 0^\circ$,

$$\frac{d^2V}{d\theta^2} = -12.6 < 0 \quad \textbf{unstable} \quad \textbf{Ans}$$

11-47. A homogeneous cone rests on top of the cylindrical surface. Derive a relationship between the radius r of the cylinder and the height h of the cone for neutral equilibrium. *Hint:* Establish the potential function for a *small* angle θ of tilt of the cone, i.e., approximate $\sin\theta \approx 0$ and $\cos\theta \approx 1 - \theta^2/2$.

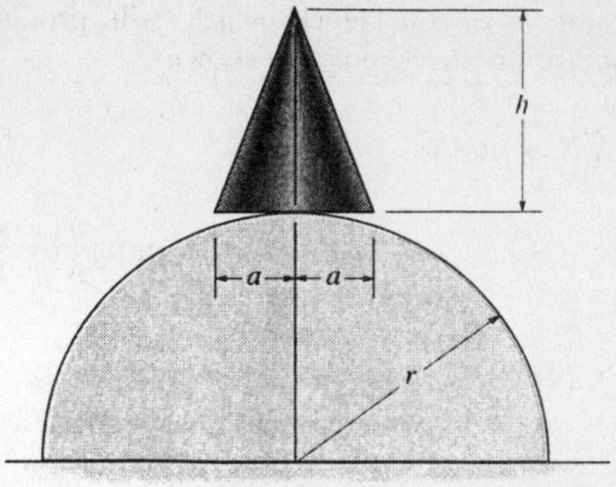

$$V = V_g = \left[\left(r + \frac{h}{4}\right)\cos\theta + r\theta\sin\theta\right]W$$

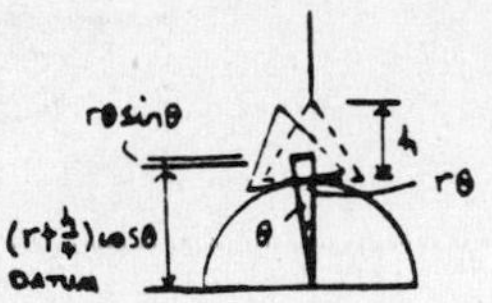

For small θ,

$$\sin\theta = \theta$$

$$\cos\theta = 1 - \frac{\theta^2}{2}$$

$$V = \left[\left(r + \frac{h}{4}\right)\left(1 - \frac{\theta^2}{2}\right) + r\theta^2\right]W$$

$$\frac{dV}{d\theta} = \left[-\left(r + \frac{h}{4}\right)\theta + 2r\theta\right]W = 0$$

$$\theta = 0^\circ \quad \textbf{Ans}$$

For neutral equilibrium :

$$\frac{d^2V}{d\theta^2} = r - \frac{h}{4} = 0$$

$$r = \frac{h}{4} \quad \textbf{Ans}$$

*11-48. The punch press consists of the ram R, connecting rod AB, and a flywheel. If a torque of $M = 50\ \text{N}\cdot\text{m}$ is applied to the flywheel, determine the force $\mathbf{F}$ applied at the ram to hold the rod in the position $\theta = 60°$.

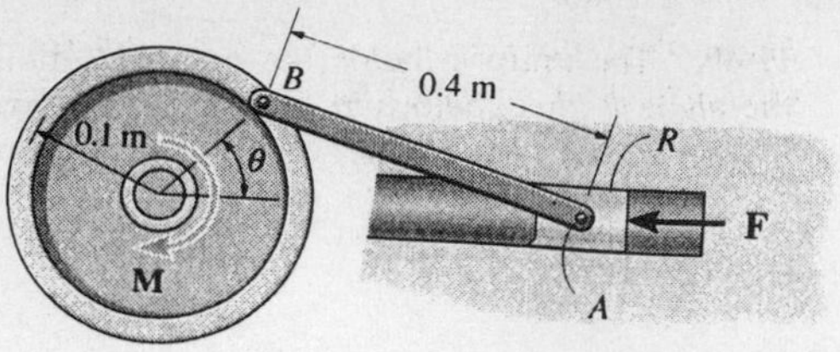

Free Body Diagram : The system has only one degree of freedom defined by the independent coordinate θ. When θ undergoes a positive displacement $\delta\theta$, only force **F** and 50 N · m couple moment do work.

Virtual Displacements : The force **F** is located from the fixed point A using the position coordinate x_A. Using the law of cosines,

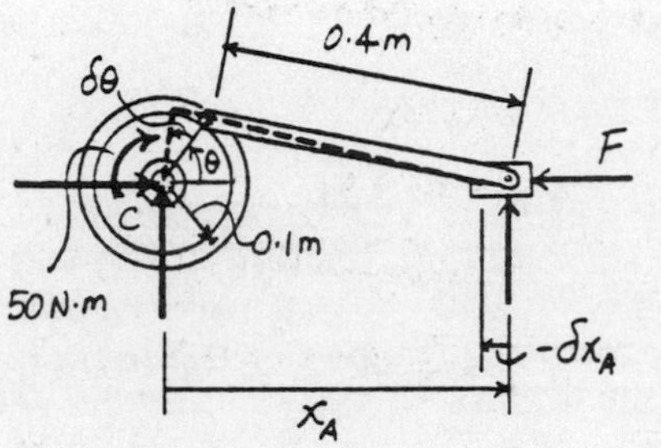

$$0.4^2 = x_A^2 + 0.1^2 - 2(x_A)(0.1)\cos\theta \qquad [1]$$

Differentiating the above expression, we have

$$0 = 2x_A\,\delta x_A - 0.2\delta x_A\cos\theta + 0.2x_A\sin\theta\,\delta\theta$$

$$\delta x_A = \frac{0.2x_A\sin\theta}{0.2\cos\theta - 2x_A}\delta\theta \qquad [2]$$

Virtual - Work Equation : When point A undergoes positive virtual displacement δx_A, force **F** does negative work. The 50 N · m couple moment does negative work when the flywheel undergoes a positive virtual rotation $\delta\theta$.

$$\delta U = 0; \qquad -F\delta x_A - 50\delta\theta = 0 \qquad [3]$$

Substituting Eq. [2] into [3] yields

$$\left(-\frac{0.2x_A\sin\theta}{0.2\cos\theta - 2x_A}F - 50\right)\delta\theta = 0$$

Since $\delta\theta \neq 0$, then

$$-\frac{0.2x_A\sin\theta}{0.2\cos\theta - 2x_A}F - 50 = 0$$

$$F = -\frac{50(0.2\cos\theta - 2x_A)}{0.2x_A\sin\theta} \qquad [4]$$

At the equilibrium position, $\theta = 60°$. Substituting into Eq. [1], we have

$$0.4^2 = x_A^2 + 0.1^2 - 2(x_A)(0.1)\cos 60°$$

$$x_A = 0.4405\ \text{m}$$

Substituting the above results into Eq. [4], we have

$$F = -\frac{50[0.2\cos 60° - 2(0.4405)]}{0.2(0.4405)\sin 60°} = 512\ \text{N} \qquad \textbf{Ans}$$

11-49. The uniform beam has a weight W. Determine the angle θ for equilibrium. The spring is uncompressed when $\theta = 90°$. Neglect the weight of the rollers.

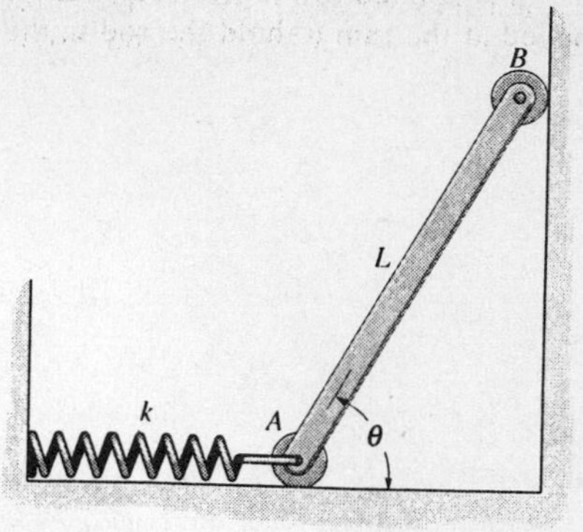

Potential Function : The datum is established at point A. Since the center of gravity of the beam is above the datum, its potential energy is positive. Here, $y = \frac{L}{2}\sin\theta$ and the spring compreeses $x = L\cos\theta$.

$$V = V_e + V_g$$
$$= \frac{1}{2}kx^2 + Wy$$
$$= \frac{1}{2}(k)(L\cos\theta)^2 + W\left(\frac{L}{2}\sin\theta\right)$$
$$= \frac{kL^2}{2}\cos^2\theta + \frac{WL}{2}\sin\theta$$

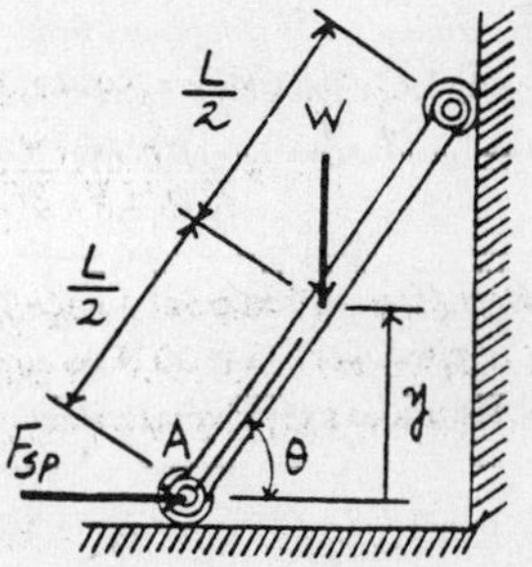

Equilibrium Position : The system is in equilibrium if $\frac{dV}{d\theta} = 0$.

$$\frac{dV}{d\theta} = -kL^2\sin\theta\cos\theta + \frac{WL}{2}\cos\theta = 0$$
$$\cos\theta\left(-kL^2\sin\theta + \frac{WL}{2}\right) = 0$$

Solving,

$$\theta = 90° \quad \text{or} \quad \sin^{-1}\left(\frac{W}{2kL}\right)$$ **Ans**

11-50. The uniform links AB and BC each weigh 2 lb and the cylinder weighs 20 lb. Determine the horizontal force $\mathbf{P}$ required to hold the mechanism in the position when $\theta = 45°$. The spring has an unstretched length of 6 in.

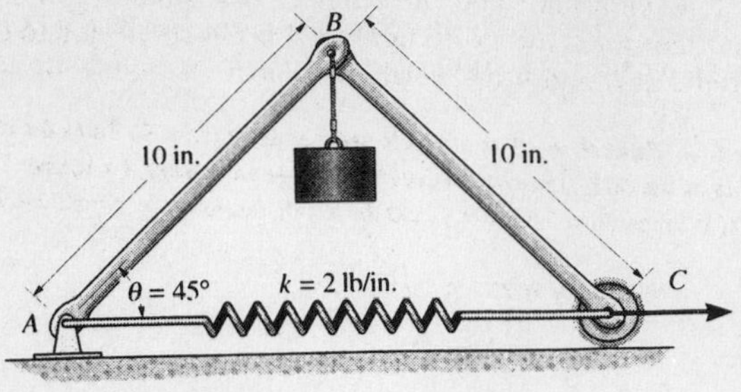

Free Body Diagram **:** The system has only one degree of freedom defined by the independent coordinate θ. When θ undergoes a positive displacement $\delta\theta$, only the spring force F_{sp}, the weight of links (2 lb), 20 lb force and force **P** do work.

Virtual Displacements **:** The positions of points B, D and C are measured from the fixed point A using position coordinates y_B, y_D and x_C respectively.

$$y_B = 10\sin\theta \qquad \delta y_B = 10\cos\theta\delta\theta \qquad [1]$$
$$y_D = 5\sin\theta \qquad \delta y_D = 5\cos\theta\delta\theta \qquad [2]$$
$$x_C = 2(10\cos\theta) \qquad \delta x_C = -20\sin\theta\delta\theta \qquad [3]$$

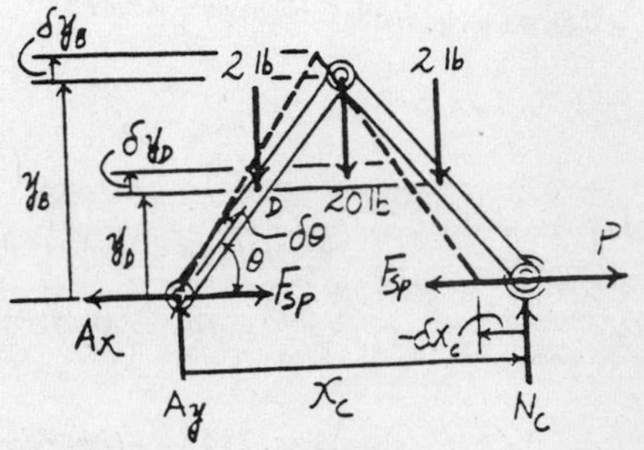

Virtual - Work Equation **:** When points B, D and C undergo positive virtual displacements δy_B, δy_D and δx_C, spring force F_{sp} that acts at point C, the weight of links (2 lb) and 20 lb force do negative work while force **P** does positive work.

$$\delta U = 0; \qquad -F_{sp}\delta x_C - 2(2\delta y_D) - 20\delta y_B + P\delta x_C = 0 \qquad [4]$$

Substituting Eqs. [1], [2] and [3] into [4] yields

$$\left(20F_{sp}\sin\theta - 20P\sin\theta - 220\cos\theta\right)\delta\theta = 0 \qquad [5]$$

However, from the spring formula, $F_{sp} = kx = 2[2(10\cos\theta) - 6] = 40\cos\theta - 12$. Substituting this value into Eq. [5] yields

$$(800\sin\theta\cos\theta - 240\sin\theta - 220\cos\theta - 20P\sin\theta)\delta\theta = 0$$

Since $\delta\theta \neq 0$, then

$$800\sin\theta\cos\theta - 240\sin\theta - 220\cos\theta - 20P\sin\theta = 0$$
$$P = 40\cos\theta - 11\cot\theta - 12$$

At the equilibrium position, $\theta = 45°$. Then

$$P = 40\cos 45° - 11\cot 45° - 12 = 5.28\text{ lb} \qquad \textbf{Ans}$$

11-51. The spring attached to the mechanism has an unstretched length when $\theta = 90°$. Determine the position θ for equilibrium and investigate the stability of the mechanism at this position. Disk A is pin-connected to the frame at B and has a weight of 20 lb.

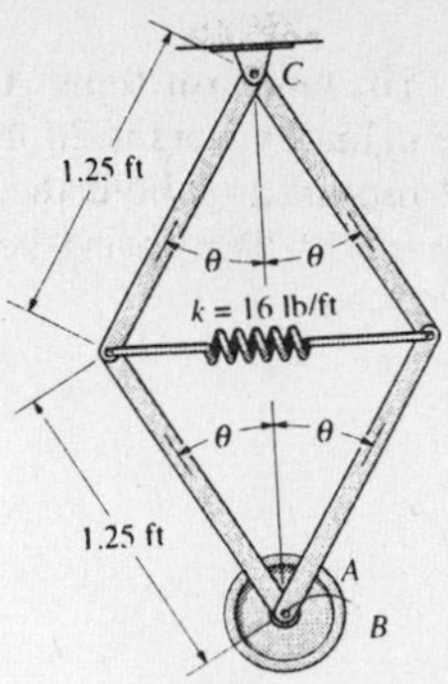

Potential Function : The datum is established at point C. Since the center of gravity of the disk is below the datum, its potential energy is negative. Here, $y = 2(1.25\cos\theta) = 2.5\cos\theta$ ft and the spring compresses $x = (2.5 - 2.5\sin\theta)$ ft.

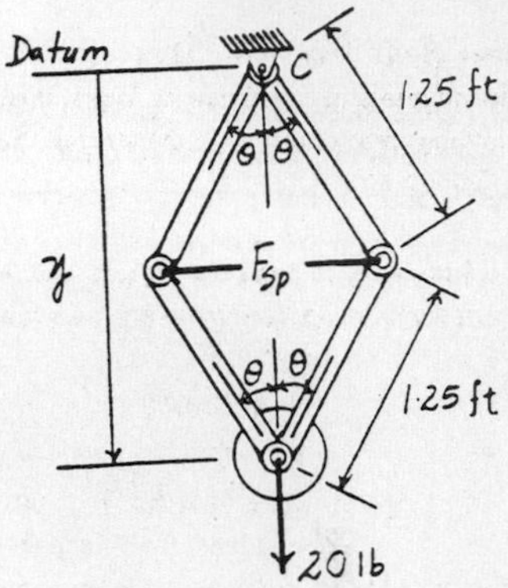

$$V = V_e + V_g$$
$$= \frac{1}{2}kx^2 - Wy$$
$$= \frac{1}{2}(16)(2.5 - 2.5\sin\theta)^2 - 20(2.5\cos\theta)$$
$$= 50\sin^2\theta - 100\sin\theta - 50\cos\theta + 50$$

Equilibrium Position : The system is in equilibrium if $\frac{dV}{d\theta} = 0$.

$$\frac{dV}{d\theta} = 100\sin\theta\cos\theta - 100\cos\theta + 50\sin\theta = 0$$
$$\frac{dV}{d\theta} = 50\sin 2\theta - 100\cos\theta + 50\sin\theta = 0$$

Solving by trial and error,

$$\theta = 37.77° = 37.8° \qquad \textbf{Ans}$$

Stability :

$$\frac{d^2V}{d\theta^2} = 100\cos 2\theta + 100\sin\theta + 50\cos\theta$$

$$\left.\frac{d^2V}{d\theta^2}\right|_{\theta=37.77°} = 100\cos 75.54° + 100\sin 37.77° + 50\cos 37.77°$$
$$= 125.7 > 0$$

Thus, the system is in **stable equilibrium** at $\theta = 37.8°$ **Ans**

***11-52.** Determine the force P that must be applied to the cord wrapped around the drum at C which is necessary to lift the bucket having a mass m. Note that as the bucket is lifted, the pulley rolls on a cord that winds up on shaft B and unwinds from shaft A.

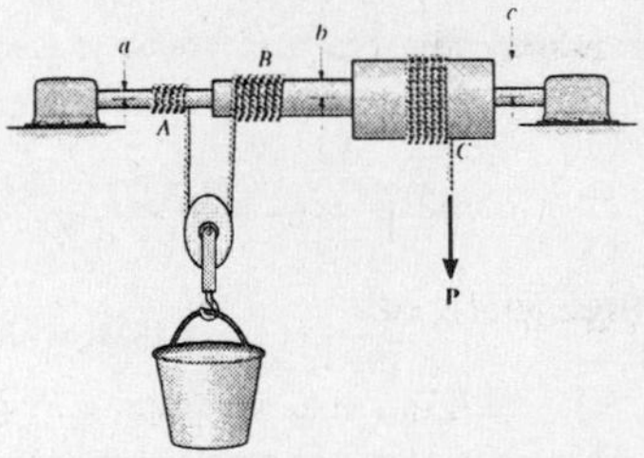

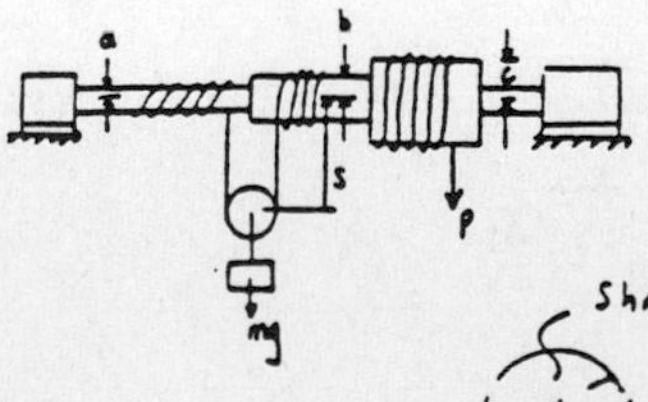

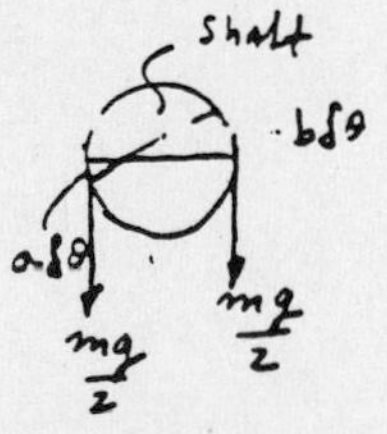

As shaft rotates $\delta\theta$

$$\delta U = 0; \quad P(c)\,\delta\theta - \frac{mg}{2}(b\,\delta\theta) + \frac{mg}{2}(a\,\delta\theta) = 0$$

$$P = \left(\frac{b-a}{2c}\right)mg \qquad \textbf{Ans}$$

11-53. The uniform beam AB weighs 100 lb. If both springs DE and BC are unstretched when $\theta = 90°$, determine the angle θ for equilibrium using the principle of potential energy. Investigate the stability at the equilibrium position. Both springs always act in the horizontal position because of the roller guides at C and E.

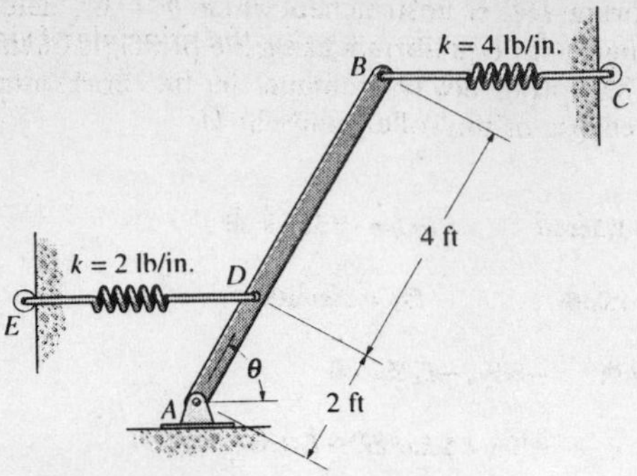

Potential Function : The datum is established at point A. Since the center of gravity of the beam is above the datum, its potential energy is positive. Here, $y = (3\sin\theta)$ ft, the spring at D stretches $x_D = (2\cos\theta)$ ft and the spring at B compreeses $x = (6\cos\theta)$ ft.

$$V = V_e + V_g$$
$$= \Sigma\frac{1}{2}kx^2 + Wy$$
$$= \frac{1}{2}(24)(2\cos\theta)^2 + \frac{1}{2}(48)(6\cos\theta)^2 + 100(3\sin\theta)$$
$$= 912\cos^2\theta + 300\sin\theta$$

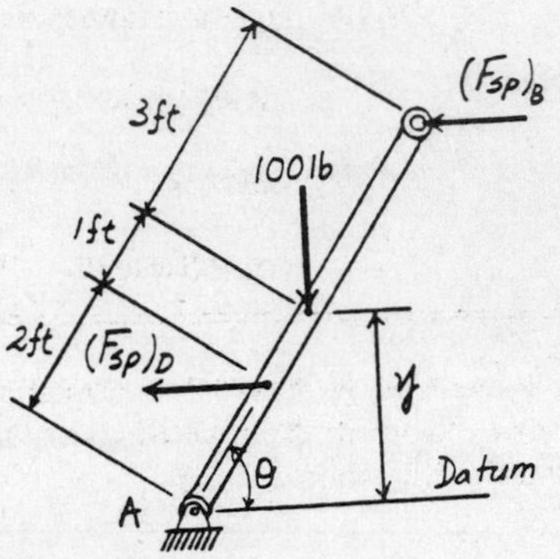

Equilibrium Position : The system is in equilibrium if $\dfrac{dV}{d\theta} = 0$.

$$\frac{dV}{d\theta} = -1824\sin\theta\cos\theta + 300\cos\theta = 0$$
$$\frac{dV}{d\theta} = -912\sin 2\theta + 300\cos\theta = 0$$

Solving,

$$\theta = 90° \quad \text{or} \quad \theta = 9.467° = 9.47°$$ **Ans**

Stability :

$$\frac{d^2V}{d\theta^2} = -1824\cos 2\theta - 300\sin\theta$$

$$\left.\frac{d^2V}{d\theta^2}\right|_{\theta=90°} = -1824\cos 180° - 300\sin 90° = 1524 > 0$$

Thus, the system is in **stable equilibrium** at $\theta = 90°$ **Ans**

$$\left.\frac{d^2V}{d\theta^2}\right|_{\theta=9.467°} = -1824\cos 18.933° - 300\sin 9.467° = -1774.7 < 0$$

Thus, the system is in **unstable equilibrium** at $\theta = 9.47°$ **Ans**

11-54. The uniform rod AB has a weight of 10 lb. If the spring DC is unstretched when $\theta = 0°$, determine the angle θ for equilibrium using the principle of virtual work. The spring always remains in the horizontal position because of the roller guide at D.

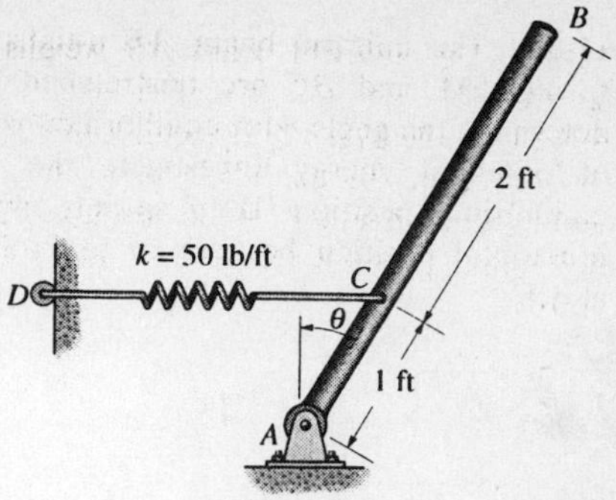

$y_w = 1.5\cos\theta \qquad \delta y_w = -1.5\sin\theta\,\delta\theta$

$x_F = 1\sin\theta \qquad \delta x_F = \cos\theta\,\delta\theta$

$\delta U = 0; \qquad -W\delta y_w - F_s\,\delta x_F = 0$

$$-10(-1.5\sin\theta\,\delta\theta) - F_s(\cos\theta\,\delta\theta) = 0$$

$$\delta\theta(15\sin\theta - F_s\cos\theta) = 0$$

Since $\delta\theta \neq 0$

$$15\sin\theta - F_s\cos\theta = 0$$

$F_s = kx \qquad$ where $\quad x = 1\sin\theta$

$F_s = 50(\sin\theta) = 50\sin\theta$

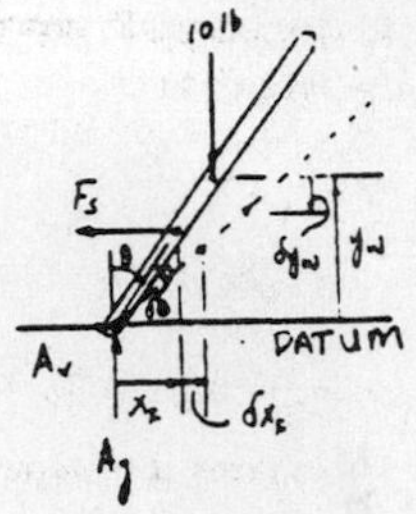

Substituting Eq. (2) into (1) yields :

$$15\sin\theta - (50\sin\theta)\cos\theta = 0$$

$$\sin\theta(15 - 50\cos\theta) = 0$$

$\sin\theta = 0 \qquad \theta = 0° \qquad$ **Ans**

$15 - 50\cos\theta = 0 \qquad \theta = 72.5° \qquad$ **Ans**

11-55. Solve Prob. 11-54 using the principle of potential energy. Investigate the stability of the rod when it is in the equilibrium position.

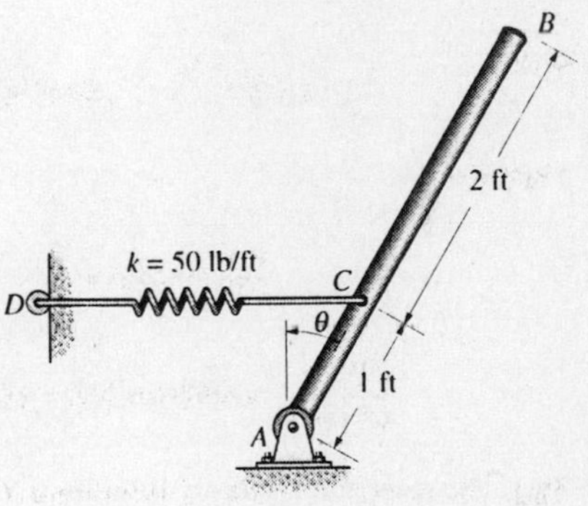

$$V = V_e + V_g = \frac{1}{2}(50)(\sin\theta)^2 + 10(1.5\cos\theta)$$

$$= 25\sin^2\theta + 15\cos\theta$$

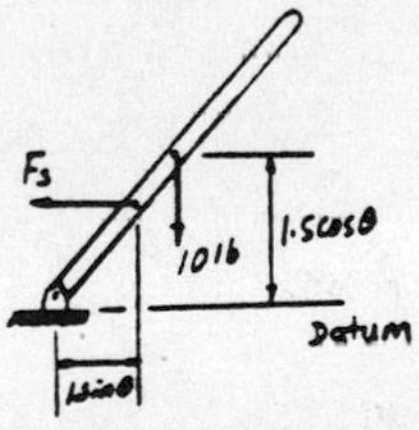

$\frac{dV}{d\theta} = 0$

$\frac{dV}{d\theta} = 50\sin\theta\cos\theta - 15\sin\theta = 0$

$$\sin\theta(50\cos\theta - 15) = 0$$

$\sin\theta = 0 \qquad \theta = 0° \qquad$ **Ans**

$50\cos\theta - 15 = 0 \qquad \theta = 72.5° \qquad$ **Ans**

$$\frac{d^2V}{d\theta^2} = 50\cos 2\theta - 15\cos\theta$$

At $\theta = 0°$, $\quad \frac{d^2V}{d\theta^2} = 50\cos 0° - 15\cos 0° = 35 > 0 \quad$ **stable** $\quad$ **Ans**

At $\theta = 72.5°$, $\quad \frac{d^2V}{d\theta^2} = 50\cos 145° - 15\cos 72.5° = -45.5 < 0 \quad$ **unstable** $\quad$ **Ans**